Peterson's Scholarships, Grants & Prizes

2007

THOMSON

PETERSON'S

Australia • Canada • Mexico • Singapore • Spain • United Kingdom • United States

About Thomson Peterson's

Thomson Peterson's (www.petersons.com) is a leading provider of education information and advice, with books and online resources focusing on education search, test preparation, and financial aid. Its Web site offers searchable databases and interactive tools for contacting educational institutions, online practice tests and instruction, and planning tools for securing financial aid. Thomson Peterson's serves 110 million education consumers annually.

For more information, contact Thomson Peterson's, 2000 Lenox Drive, Lawrenceville, NJ 08648; 800-338-3282; or find us on the World Wide Web at www.petersons.com/about.

Editor: Linda Seghers; Production Editor: L. A. Wagner; Copy Editor: Jill C. Schwartz; Research Project Manager: Jennifer Fishberg; Research Associate: Helen L. Hannan; Programmer: Alex Lin; Manufacturing Manager: Ivona Skibicki; Composition Manager: Gary Rozmierski

ISBN 13: 978-0-7689-2314-8
ISBN 10: 0-7689-2314-X

Printed in the United States of America

10 9 8 7 6 5 4 3 2 1   08 07 06

Eleventh Edition

OTHER RECOMMENDED TITLES

Peterson's College Money Handbook
Peterson's Sports Scholarships & College Athletic Programs

Contents

Contents

A Note from the Peterson's Editors

Billions of dollars are given to students and their families every year to help pay for college. Last year, private donors gave more than $7.3 billion in financial aid to help undergraduate students pay for college. Yet, to the average person, the task of finding financial aid awards in this huge network of scholarships, grants, and prizes appears to be nearly impossible.

For more than thirty-five years, Thomson Peterson's has given students and parents the most comprehensive, up-to-date information on how to get their fair share of the financial aid pie. *Peterson's Scholarships, Grants & Prizes* was created to help students and their families pinpoint those specific private financial aid programs that best match students' backgrounds, interests, talents, or abilities.

In *Peterson's Scholarships, Grants & Prizes,* you will find more than 4,000 scholarship/grant programs and prize sources that provide financial awards to undergraduates in the 2006–07 academic year. Foundations, fraternal and ethnic organizations, community service clubs, churches and religious groups, philanthropies, companies and industry groups, labor unions and public employees' associations, veterans' groups, and trusts and bequests are all possible sources.

For those seeking to enter college, *Peterson's Scholarships, Grants & Prizes* includes information needed to make financing a college education as seamless as possible.

Features include:

- More than 1.6 million awards, totaling more than $7 billion

- Up-to-date eligibility requirements, award amounts, and application deadlines

- Proven tips to identify and avoid scholarship scams

- Information about online financial aid resources

The **How to Find an Award That's Right for You** section paints a complete picture of the financial aid landscape, discusses the connection between honors students and scholarship eligibility, provides important tips on how to avoid scholarship scams, and offers insight into how to make scholarship management organizations work for you.

Also found in **How to Find an Award That's Right for You** is the "How To Use This Guide" article, which describes the more than 4,000 awards included in the guide, along with information on how to search for an award in one of ten categories.

If you would like to compare awards quickly, refer to the **Quick-Reference Chart.** Here you can search through "Scholarships, Grants & Prizes At-a-Glance" and select awards by highest dollar amount.

In the **Profiles of Scholarships, Grants & Prizes** section you'll find updated award programs, along with information about the award sponsor. The profile section is divided into three categories: *Academic Fields/Career Goals, Nonacademic/Noncareer Criteria,* and *Miscellaneous Criteria.* Each profile provides all of the need-to-know information about available scholarships, grants, and prizes.

Finally, the back of the book features thirteen **Indexes** listing scholarships, grants, and prizes based on award name; sponsor; academic fields/career goals; civic, professional, social, or union affiliation; corporate affiliation; employment experience; impairment; military service; nationality or ethnic heritage; religious affiliation; residence; location of study; and talent.

Thomson Peterson's publishes a full line of resources to help guide you and your family through the college admission process. Peterson's publications can be found at your local bookstore, library, and high school guidance office, and you can access us online at www.petersons. com.

We welcome any comments or suggestions you may have about this publication and invite you to complete our online survey at www.petersons.com/booksurvey.

A Note from the Peterson's Editors

Or you can fill out the survey at the back of this book, tear it out, and mail it to us at:

Publishing Department
Thomson Peterson's
2000 Lenox Drive
Lawrenceville, NJ 08648

Your feedback will help us to provide personalized solutions for your educational advancement.

Be sure to take full advantage of the many real opportunities that have been opened up to students and their families by the many organizations, foundations, and businesses that can help you with the burden of college expenses.

The editors at Thomson Peterson's wish you the best of luck in your scholarship search efforts!

How to Find an Award That's Right for You

A Strategy for Finding Awards

Private scholarships and awards can be characterized by unpredictable, sometimes seemingly bizarre, criteria. Before you begin your award search, write a personal profile of yourself that will help establish as many criteria as possible that might form a basis for your scholarship award. Here is a basic checklist of what you should consider:

1. **What are your career goals?** Be both narrow and broad in your designations. If, for example, you have a career aim to be a TV news reporter, you will find many awards specific to this field in the *TV/Radio Broadcasting* section. However, collegiate broadcasting courses can be offered in departments or schools of communication. So, be sure to also consider *Communications* as a relevant section for your search. Consider *Journalism,* too, for the same reasons. Then look under some more broadly inclusive but possibly relevant areas, such as *Trade/Technical Specialties.* Or check a related but different field, such as *Performing Arts.* Finally, look under marginally related basic academic fields, such as *Humanities, Social Sciences, or Political Science.* We make every attempt to provide the best cross-reference aids, but the nuances of specific awards can be difficult to capture with even the most flexible cross-referencing systems. So you will need to be broadly associative in your thinking in order to get the most out of this wealth of information.

   If you have no clear career goal, browsing through the huge variety of academic/career awards may well spark new interest in a career path. Be open to imagining yourself filling different career roles that you previously may not have considered.

2. **In what academic fields might you major?** Your educational experiences to this point or your sense about your personal talents or interests may have given you a good idea of what academic discipline you wish to pursue. Again, use both broad and narrow focuses in designing your search and look at related subject fields. For example, if you want to major in history, there is a *History* section. Also, be sure to check out *Social Sciences* and *Humanities* and, maybe, *Area/Ethnic Studies. Education,* for example, could have the perfect scholarship for a future historian.

3. **In which jobs, industries, or occupations have your parents or other members of your immediate family been employed? What employment experiences might you have?** Individual companies, employee organizations, trade unions, government agencies, and industry associations frequently set up scholarships for workers or children or other relatives of workers from specific companies or industries. These awards might require that you study to stay in the same career field, but most are offered regardless of the field of study you wish to undertake. Also, if one of your parents worked as a public service employee, especially as a firefighter or police officer, and most especially if he or she was killed or disabled in the line of duty, there are many relevant awards available.

4. **Do you have any hobbies or special interests? Have you ever been an officer or leader of a group? Do you possess special skills or talents? Have you won any competitions? Are you a good writer?** From bowling to clarinet playing, from caddying to ham radio operating, from winning a beauty contest to simply "being interested in leadership," there are a host of special interests that can win awards for you from groups that wish to promote and/or reward these pursuits.

5. **Where do you live? Where have you lived? Where will you go to college?** Residence criteria are among

the most common qualifications for scholarship aid. Local clubs and companies provide millions of dollars in scholarship aid to students who live in a particular state, province, region, or section of a state. This means that your residential identity puts you at the head of the line for these grants. State of residence can—depending on the sponsor's criteria—include the place of your official residence, the place you attend college, the place you were born, or any place you have lived for more than a year.

6. **What is your family's ethnic heritage?** Hundreds of scholarships have been endowed for students who can claim a particular nationality or racial or ethnic descent. Partial ethnic descent frequently qualifies, so don't be put off if you do not think of your identity as fully tagged as a specific "ethnic" entity. There are awards for Colonial American, English, Welsh, Scottish, European, and other backgrounds that students may not consider to be especially "ethnic." There is even one for descendants of signers of the Declaration of Independence, whatever ethnicity that might have turned out to be some ten generations later.

7. **Do you have a physical disability?** There are many awards given to individuals with physical disabilities. Of course, commonly recognized impairments of mobility, sight, communication, and hearing are recognized, but, also, learning disabilities and chronic diseases, such as asthma and epilepsy, are criteria for some awards.

8. **Do you currently or have you ever served in a branch of the armed forces? Or, did one of your parents serve? In a war? Was one of your parents lost or disabled in the armed forces?** There are hundreds of awards that use one of these qualifications. There are even awards for descendants of Confederate soldiers.

9. **Do you belong to a civic association, union, or religious organization? Do your parents?** Hundreds of clubs and religious groups provide scholarship assistance to members or children of members.

10. **Are you male or female?**

11. **What is your age?**

12. **Do you qualify for need-based aid?**

13. **Did you graduate in the upper half, upper third, or upper quarter of your class?**

14. **Do you plan to attend a two-year college, a four-year college, or a trade/technical school?**

15. **In what academic year will you be entering?**

Be expansive when considering your possible qualifications. Although some awards may be small, you may qualify for more than one award, and these can add up to significant amounts in the end.

Scholarship Management Organizations

Richard Woodland
Director of Financial Aid, Rutgers University, Camden

The search for private scholarships can be confusing and frustrating for parents and students. Many families feel they just don't know how to go about the process, so they either hire a private scholarship search company or simply give up. The success rate of many scholarship search firms is not good, and college financial aid professionals always warn parents to be skeptical of exaggerated claims.

The process also confuses many donors. A corporation may want to help its employees or the children of its employees or may want to offer a national scholarship program to its customers or the general public. Unfortunately, the corporation may not want to devote valuable administrative time managing a scholarship program. Similarly, there are many donors who want to target their funds to a particular group of students but simply do not know how.

Stepping in to help are scholarship management organizations. Although many have been around for a long time, the majority of the general public knows very little about them. The reason for this is that scholarship management organizations often do not administer scholarship funds directly to students. Rather, they serve as a clearinghouse for their member donor organizations. Today, savvy parents and students can go online to find these organizations and the scholarship programs they administer.

Two of the largest scholarship management programs are the National Merit Scholarship Corporation™ and Scholarship America™ (formerly Citizen's Scholarship Foundation of America). The National Merit Scholarship Corporation sponsors a competitive scholarship program that seeks to identify and reward the top students in the nation. High school students who meet published entry/participation requirements enter these competitions by taking the Preliminary SAT/National Merit Scholarship Qualifying Test (PSAT/NMSQT®), usually as juniors. A particular year's test is the entry vehicle to a specific annual competition. For example, the 2006 PSAT/NMSQT was the qualifying test for entry into competitions for scholarships to be awarded in 2008. For more information, visit http://www.nationalmerit.org.

Another major player is Scholarship America™, which has distributed more than $1 billion dollars to more than one million students over the past forty-five years, making it the nation's largest private-sector scholarship and educational support organization. By involving communities, corporations, organizations, and individuals in the support of students through its three major programs, Dollars for Scholars®, Scholarship Management Services™, and ScholarShop®, Scholarship America distributed more than $159 million in 2005. Whether it is working with national leaders in response to the September 11th tragedy through the Families of Freedom Scholarship Fund, or with corporations such as Target, Kohl's Department Stores, and Tylenol (McNeil Consumer and Specialty Pharmaceuticals), Scholarship America is an important organization that helps thousands of students every year. For more information, go to www.scholarshipamerica.org.

In addition to the National Merit Scholarship Fund and Scholarship America, there are other organizations that raise funds and administer scholarships for specific groups of students. Some of these organizations include:

- American Indian College Fund
  www.collegefund.org
- Hispanic Scholarship Fund Institute **www.hsfi.org**
- United Negro College Fund **www.uncf.org**
- Organization of Chinese Americans
  www.ocanatl.org

Scholarship Management Organizations

- Future Farmers of America **www.ffa.org**
- Gates Millennium Scholarship Fund **www.gmsp.org**

These are just a few of the many scholarship sources available on the Web. In addition to using scholarship search engines, think broadly about yourself, your background, your interests, your family connections (work, religious, fraternal organizations), and your future career plans. Then spend some time browsing the Web. We hope that some of the sources mentioned here will help. Remember, the key is to start early (junior year in high school is best) and be persistent.

Scholarship Scams: What They Are and What to Watch Out For

Several hundred thousand students seek and find scholarships every year. Most students' families require some outside help to pay for tuition costs. Although most of this outside help, in the form of grants, scholarships, low-interest loans, and work-study programs, comes either from the state and federal government or the colleges themselves, scholarships from private sources are an extremely important component of this network. An award from a private source can tilt the scales with respect to a student's ability to attend a specific college during a particular year. Unfortunately, for prospective scholarship seekers, the private aid sector is virtually without patterns or rules. It has, over many years, become a combination of individual programs, each with its own award criteria, timetables, application procedures, and decision-making processes. Considerable effort is required to understand and effectively benefit from private scholarships. One of the principal reasons that *Peterson's Scholarships, Grants & Prizes* has been developed is to facilitate this task of grabbing the applicable prize from this complex web of scholarships.

Regrettably, the combination of an urgency to locate money, limited time, and this complex and bewildering system has created opportunities for fraud. It has been estimated that for every 10 students who receive a legitimate scholarship, one is victimized by a fraudulent scheme or scam that poses as a legitimate foundation, scholarship sponsor, or scholarship search service. Every year, an estimated 350,000 families are cheated in various scholarship scams, totalling more than $5 million.

These fraudulent businesses advertise in campus newspapers, distribute flyers, mail letters and postcards, provide toll-free phone numbers, and have Web sites. The most obvious frauds operate as scholarship search services or scholarship clearinghouses. Another segment sets up as a scholarship sponsor, pockets the money from the fees that are paid by thousands of hopeful scholarship seekers, and returns little, if anything, in proportion to the amount it collects. A few of these scams inflict great harm by gaining access to individuals' credit or checking accounts with the intent to extort funds.

A typical mode of operation is for a fraudulent firm to send out a huge mailing to college and high school students, claiming that the company has either a scholarship or a scholarship list for the students. These companies often provide toll-free numbers. When recipients call, they are told by high-pressure telemarketers that the company has unclaimed scholarships and that for fees ranging from $10 to $400 the callers get back at least $1000 in scholarship money or the fee will be refunded. Customers who pay, if they receive anything at all, are mailed a list of sources of financial aid that are no better than, and are in many cases inferior to, what can be found in *Peterson's Scholarships, Grants & Prizes* or any of the other major scholarship guides available in bookstores and libraries or on the Web. The "lucky" recipients have to apply on their own for the scholarships. Many of the programs are contests, loans, or work-study programs rather than gift aid. Some are no longer in existence, have expired deadlines, or set eligibility requirements that students cannot meet. Customers who seek refunds have to demonstrate that they have applied in writing to each source on the list and received a rejection letter from each of them. Frequently, even when customers can provide this almost-impossible-to-obtain proof, refunds are not given. In the worst cases, the companies ask for consumers' checking account or credit card numbers and take funds without authorization.

Scholarship Scams: What They Are and What to Watch Out For

The Federal Trade Commission (FTC) warns students and their parents to be wary of fraudulent search services that promise to do all the work for you.

"Bogus scholarship search services are just a variation of the 'you have won' prize-promotion scam, targeted to a particular audience—students and parents who are anxious about paying for college," said Jodie Bernstein, former director of the FTC's Bureau of Consumer Protection. "They guarantee students and their families free scholarship money . . . all they have to do to claim it is pay an up-front fee."

There are legitimate scholarship search services. However, a scholarship search service cannot truthfully guarantee that a student will receive a scholarship, and students almost always will fare as well or better by doing their own homework using a reliable scholarship information source, such as *Peterson's Scholarships, Grants & Prizes*, than by wasting money and more importantly time with a search service that promises a scholarship.

The FTC warns scholarship seekers to be alert for these seven warning signs of a scam:

1. "This scholarship is guaranteed or your money back."

No service can guarantee that it will get you a grant or scholarship. Refund guarantees often have impossible conditions attached. Review a service's refund policies in writing before you pay a fee. Typically, fraudulent scholarship search services require that applicants show rejection letters from each of the sponsors on the list they provide. If a sponsor no longer exists, if it really does not provide scholarships, or if it has a rolling application deadline, letters of rejection are almost impossible to obtain.

2. "The scholarship service will do all the work."

Unfortunately, nobody else can fill out the personal information forms, write the essays, and supply the references that many scholarships may require.

3. "The scholarship will cost some money."

Be wary of any charges related to scholarship information services or individual scholarship applications, especially in significant amounts. Some legitimate scholarship sponsors charge fees to defray their processing expenses. True scholarship sponsors, however, should distribute money, not make it from application fees. Before you send money to apply for a scholarship, investigate the sponsor.

4. "You can't get this information anywhere else."

In addition to Peterson's, scholarship directories from other publishers are available in any large bookstore, public library, or high school guidance office. Additional information on private scholarship programs can be found at www.petersons.com/finaid.

5. "You are a finalist"—in a contest you never entered, or "You have been selected by a national foundation to receive a scholarship."

Most legitimate scholarship programs almost never seek out particular applicants. Most scholarship sponsors will only contact you in response to an inquiry. Most lack the budget and mandate to do anything more than this. If you think that there is any real possibility that you may have been selected to receive a scholarship, before you send any money investigate to make sure the sponsor or program is legitimate.

6. "The scholarship service needs your credit card or checking account number in advance."

Never provide your credit card or bank account number over the telephone to the representative of an organization that you do not know. A legitimate need-based scholarship program will not ask for your checking account number. Get information in writing first. **Note:** An unscrupulous operation does not need your signature on a check. It schemes to set up situations that allow it to drain a victim's account with unauthorized withdrawals.

7. "You are invited to a free seminar (or interview) with a trained financial aid consultant who will unlock the secrets of how to make yourself eligible for more financial aid."

Sometimes these consultants offer some good tips on preparing for college, but often they are trying to get you to sign up for a long-term contract for services you don't need. Often these "consultants" are trying to sell you other financial products, such as annuities, life insurance, or other financial services that have little to do with financial aid. By doing your own research with books from Thomson Peterson's or other respected organizations, using the Web, and working with your high school guidance office and the college financial aid office, you will get all the help you need to ensure you have done a thorough job of preparing for the financing of your college education.

In addition to the FTC's seven signs, here are some other points to keep in mind when considering a scholarship program:

- Fraudulent scholarship operations often use official-sounding names containing words such as federal, national, administration, division, federation, and foundation. Their names often are a slight variation of the name of a legitimate government or private organization. Do not be fooled by a name that seems reputable or official, an official-looking seal, or a Washington, D.C., address.

- If you win a scholarship, you will receive official written notification by mail, not over the telephone. If the sponsor calls to inform you, it will follow up with a letter in the mail. If a request for money is made over the phone, the operation is probably fraudulent.

- Be wary if an organization's address is a post office box number or a residential address. If a bona fide scholarship program uses a post office box number, it usually will include a street address and telephone number on its stationery.

- Beware of telephone numbers with a 900 area code. These may charge you a fee of several dollars a minute for a call that could be a long recording that provides only a list of addresses or names.

- A dishonest operation may put pressure on an applicant by claiming that awards are on a first-come, first-served basis. Some scholarship programs give preference to early applicants. However, if you are told, especially over the telephone, that you must respond quickly, but you will not hear about the results for several months, there may be a problem.

- Be wary of endorsements. Fraudulent operations claim endorsements by groups with names similar to well-known private or government organizations. The Better Business Bureau (BBB) and other government agencies do not endorse businesses.

If an organization requires that you pay something for a scholarship and you have never heard of it before and cannot verify that it is a legitimate operation, the best advice is to pay nothing. If you have already paid money to such an organization and find reason to doubt its legitimacy, call your bank to stop payment on your check, if possible, or call your credit card company and tell it that you think you were the victim of consumer fraud.

To find out how to recognize, report, and stop a scholarship scam, contact:

The Federal Trade Commission
600 Pennsylvania Avenue, N.W.
Washington, D.C. 20580
Web site: www.ftc.gov

The National Fraud Information Center can be contacted by phone at 800-876-7060 (toll-free) or online at www.fraud.org. The Better Business Bureau (BBB) maintains files of businesses about which it has received complaints. You should call both your local BBB office and the BBB office where the organization in question is located; each local BBB has different records. Call 703-276-0100 to get the telephone number of your local BBB or log on to www.bbb.org for a directory of local BBBs and downloadable BBB complaint forms. The national address is:

The Council of Better Business Bureaus
4200 Wilson Boulevard, Suite 800
Arlington, VA 22203-1838

There are many wonderful scholarships available to qualified students who spend the time and effort to locate and apply for them. However, we advise you to exercise caution in using scholarship search services and, when you must pay money, always use careful judgment when considering a scholarship program's sponsor.

Honors Students and Scholarships

Dr. Gary M. Bell
Dean, University Honors College, Texas Tech University

Let's begin with some really good news: Students who are considering an honors program are also the very people most likely to be eligible for scholarship assistance. Funding a college education is an important, difficult, and even educational part of being a student. Let's face it, college is expensive! Scholarships provide part of the solution for how to finance your undergraduate career. Honors students are precisely the ones who colleges recruit most eagerly. Good high school students add to the prestige of an institution, and schools typically advertise your decision to attend their institution. Thus, there is an excellent chance that the school of your choice may provide scholarship assistance in order to encourage your enrollment and to enhance their bragging rights.

Another way to view the next four (or more) years you will spend earning your college baccalaureate degree is to think of learning as your primary employment. It is therefore helpful to think of a scholarship as part of the salary for undertaking your job of learning. From this perspective, you then have the right, again as a potential honors student, to seek the best pay, or scholarship, possible. One of your first inquiries as you examine a potential college setting is about the type of assistance they might provide given your interests, academic record, and personal history. Talk to a financial aid officer or a scholarship coordinator at the school. At most schools, these are special officers—people specifically employed to assist you in your quest for financial assistance. Virtually all schools also have brochures or publications that list scholarship opportunities at their institution. Get this literature and read it carefully.

In your search for monetary assistance, visit either your local bookstore or your local public library where there are usually books that have several hundred scholarships listed in different categories. These types of books can be economically purchased, and they can also typically be found in the reference section of libraries. The Internet is similarly a useful tool to obtain additional information. Lastly, high school counselors often have keen insight into resources available at colleges, especially the schools in your area. These people are the key point of contact between institutions of higher education and you, the high school graduate. In general, it is not a particularly good practice to use a private company that promises, frequently for a considerable fee, a list of scholarships for which you might be eligible. Such lists are often very broad, and more importantly, you can secure the same results by using available high school, university, and published information.

What do we mean be the word "scholarship" anyway? In the very broadest sense, scholarships consist of outright grants of monetary assistance to eligible students to help them attend college. The money is of course to be applied to tuition or the cost of living while in school. Scholarships do not need to be repaid. They do often carry stringent criteria for maintaining them, such as the achievement of a certain grade point average, the carrying of a given number of class hours, matriculation in a specific program, or membership in a designated group. Scholarships at many schools may be combined with college work-study programs—where some work is also required. Also be sensitive to the fact that many scholarships can be bundled, that is, put together with other scholarships so that collectively they can provide you with a truly attractive financial aid package. Equally important, scholarships can also be bundled with low-interest loan programs to make the school of your choice financially accessible.

Scholarships generally fall into three major categories. These are need-based scholarships, predicated on your or your family's income; merit-based scholarships, based on your academic and sometimes extracurricular achievements; and association-based scholarships, which are dependent on as many different associations as you can imagine (for instance, your home county, your identification with a particular group, or the company for which a parent may work). The range of reasons for which scholarships are given is almost infinite.

Many schools accommodate students who have financial need. Probably the most widespread of the grant programs are the U.S. government-sponsored Federal Pell Grants and the Federal Supplemental Educational Opportunity Grants, which you might want to explore with the financial aid counselor. Also inquire about state-sponsored grant programs.

Merit-based scholarships can come from a variety of sources—from the university as a whole, individual de-partments or colleges within the university, or special donors who want to assist worthy students. This fact should be remembered as you meet with financial aid officers, because they know that different opportunities may be available for you as a petroleum engineering, agriculture, accounting, pre–veterinary, or performing arts major. Merit-based scholarships are typically designed to reward the highest performers on such precollege mea-sures as standardized tests (the SAT or ACT Assessment) and achievement in high school grades. Since repeated performance on standardized tests often leads to higher scores, it may be financially advantageous for you to take these college admissions tests several times. Practice truly does help and may pay dividends.

Frequently, schools have endowed scholarships (scholarships based on a fund, the principal of which can never be used) given by alumni or others with a particular interest in supporting honors students. Thus, your acceptance to an honors program can carry with it not only enhanced educational benefits, but also substantial monetary assistance. A warning needs to be interjected here, however. If you are joining an honors program only for the financial advantage, you are joining for the wrong reason. Honors education is about broadening your educational experiences, opening an array of academic opportunities, and challenging you to be better than you think you can be. If money is your only incentive in becoming associated with honors, you probably need to look elsewhere for financial assistance.

Inquire quite specifically into each of these three categories of scholarships. The association-based schol-arships can sometimes be particularly helpful and quite surprising. Employers of parents, people from specific geographical locations, or organizations (churches, civic groups, special interest clubs, and even family name associations) may have assistance for college students that few know about or even bother to use. Campus scholarship literature is the primary key to unlocking the mysteries of association-based financial assistance (and the other two categories as well), but personal interviews with financial officers are also crucial.

There are several issues to which you must attend as you seek scholarship assistance. Probably the most important is to determine deadlines that apply to a scholarship for which you may be eligible. It always wise to begin your search early, so that your eligibility is not nullified by having applied too late. Most scholarship opportunities require an application form, and it is time well spent to make sure the application is neat, grammatically correct, and logical. Correct spelling is essential. Have someone proofread your application (these are not bad guidelines to follow with your honors application as well if the honors program of your choice requires an application). Keep in mind that if applica-tions require essays, fewer students typically take the time to complete these essays, giving those students who are willing to write a better chance of winning that particular scholarship. Always be accurate about yourself in these applications, but at the same time, provide the most positive self-portrayal to enhance your chances of being considered. Be sensitive to the fact that most merit-based and association-based scholarships are awarded competitively.

Finally, as soon as your plans become firm, do let the people who offer you assistance know your decision about whether or not you will accept their offer. Too many students simply assume that a scholarship offer means automatic acceptance. This is not the case! In almost all instances, you must send a letter of acknowledgement and acceptance. Nationally, virtually all schools have agreed that students must make up their minds about scholar-ship (and sometimes school) acceptance no later than May 1. But earlier deadlines may apply.

How do you make the choice of which school to attend? There are many elements to consider, such as reputation, programs offered, courses provided, and the school's success in placing graduates. Visit the prospec-tive school and see if the student profile, the campus amenities, and the atmosphere of the campus fit your needs and aspirations. But above most other factors, it is imperative that you pay attention to cost. Where can you realistically afford to go without incurring the very large debts that could plague you after graduation? In the end, you must choose the college or university that seems best for you and that fits your and your family's budget. Scholarships should play a very big role in your decision-making matrix.

As you undoubtedly know, tuition at private schools is typically higher than tuition at state colleges and universities. Scholarships can narrow this gap. Many private institutions have a great deal of money to spend on scholarship assistance, so you may well find that going to a private college will cost no more than attending a state school. You should note one caution, however. A substantial scholarship from a private school may still leave you with a very large annual bill to cover the difference between the scholarship amount and the actual cost of tuition, fees, and living expenses. When you evaluate a scholarship, therefore, do so by comparing your final projected costs as you consider the expense of which school to attend. Another factor to consider is the length of time for which the school extends scholarship support. Be cautious about the school that promises substantial assistance for the first year-in order to get you there-but then provides little or nothing in the second through the fourth or later years.

The most attractive and meaningful scholarships are offered for four to five years.

Incidentally, the scholarship search should never be abandoned once you are enrolled at the school of your choice. There are often a number of opportunities for the enrolled student, especially as you prove your ability and interest in a given field. Also, honors students have been particularly successful in national scholarship competitions, such as the Rhodes, Fulbright, Goldwater, Truman, and Udall. Finally, your earned scholarship may well be applied to study-abroad or the National Collegiate Honors Council (NCHC) Honors Semester programs, so begin to consider early in your college career the benefits that an off-campus experience can bestow upon you.

When considering college funding, low-interest or even interest-free, government-provided educational loans can be available to you, depending on your personal circumstances. Many states also have similar loan provisions available for their citizens. Loans are to be sought only after scholarship possibilities are exhausted, but in the last analysis, your education is probably the best investment you will ever make. Thus, borrowing for your college expenses is both a justifiable and sometimes necessary element in securing that most precious and most enduring of all personal assets, a sound educational background.

Searching for Scholarships, Grants & Prizes Online

Today's students need all the help they can get when looking for ways to pay for their college education. Skyrocketing tuition costs, state budget cuts, and diminished personal savings have combined to make financing a college education perhaps the number one concern for parents. College sticker shock is driving many families away from college. No wonder. The "purchasing power" of all aid programs from federal, state, and institutional sources has declined over the past two decades. State education budgets have been slashed. In 2005–06, tuition and fees increased 7.1% at four-year public institutions and 5.9% at four-year private colleges. And it's not only lower-income families who are affected. Some fear they make *too much* money to qualify for financial aid. Regardless of their situation, most families struggle to make sense of the college financial aid process and to decide which aid package is the right one for them.

Despite the confusion, students and parents can and should continue to research as many sources as they can to find the money they need. The Internet can be a great source of information. There are many worthwhile sites that are ready to help you search and apply for your fair share of awards, including Thomson Peterson's comprehensive financial aid site at www.petersons.com/finaid.

THOMSON PETERSON'S "PAY FOR SCHOOL"

Thomson Peterson's "Pay for School" financial aid Web site at www.petersons.com/finaid provides families with a wealth of information on college funding for every step of their college admission process.

Expert Advice

By logging on to www.petersons.com/finaid you gain access to comprehensive articles that describe the ins and outs of federal and state funding; tips for filing the FAFSA and the CSS/PROFILE®; step-by-step advice on what you should be doing junior and senior year of high school; and an audio clip of an interview with a real live financial aid expert. Links to state programs and agencies help you connect directly to those resources. The "Advice Center" lets you access articles on specific topics, such as advice on 529 Plans, loans and payment plans, scholarship scams, the military, and international students. There is also a section called "Financial Aid This Month," which contains the latest-breaking news on government programs and other college funding topics.

Scholarship Search

Thomson Peterson's free **Scholarship Search** connects you to more than 1.6 million scholarships, grants, and prizes totaling more than $7 billion and lets you do an individualized search for awards that match your financial and educational needs. In just three easy steps you can register; complete a customized profile indicating your scholastic and personal background, intended major, work experience, and a host of other criteria; and access a list of scholarships that match your needs. Each scholarship is described in detail, including

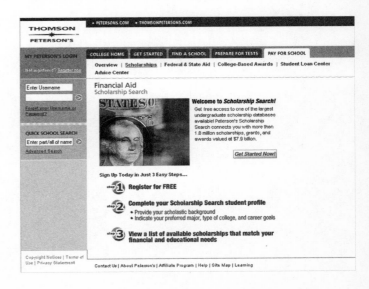

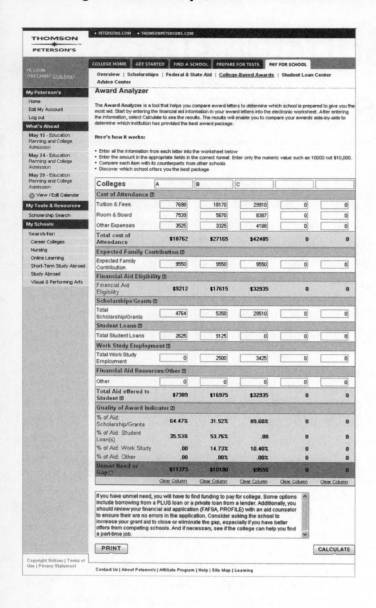

eligibility and application requirements and contact information with links to its e-mail address and Web site. Finding money for college couldn't be easier!

Interactive Tools

When it's time to get to the nuts and bolts of your college financial planning, Peterson's has the tools to help. You can access a calculator to find your Estimated Family Contribution (EFC) as well as a College Financial Planning calculator that lets you figure out your own personal savings plan. After you have received award letters the colleges you've applied to, you can use the **Award Analyzer**, which helps you compare award letters to determine which school is prepared to give you the most aid. You simply enter the information from each award letter you received, press the Calculate button, and you discover which school has offered you the best package.

Searching and applying for financial aid is a complicated process. The resources and tools available to you on www.petersons.com/finaid can help you get your fair share of the financial aid pie. So, what are you waiting for? Log on! Free money for college may be just a mouse click away.

How to Use This Guide

The more than 4,000 award programs described in this book are organized into ten broad categories that represent the major factors used to determine eligibility for scholarships, awards, and prizes. To build a basic list of awards available to you, look under the broad category or categories that fit your particular academic goals, skills, personal characteristics, or background. The ten categories are:

- Academic Fields/Career Goals
- Civic, Professional, Social, or Union Affiliation
- Corporate Affiliation
- Employment Experience
- Impairment
- Military Service
- Nationality or Ethnic Heritage
- Religious Affiliation
- Residence/Location of Study
- Talent

The *Academic Fields/Career Goals* category is subdivided into 117 individual subject areas that are organized alphabetically by the award sponsor. The *Military Service* category is subdivided alphabetically by branch of service. All other categories are simply organized A to Z by the name of the award sponsor.

Full descriptive profiles appear in only one location in the book. Cross-references to the name and page number of the full descriptive profile are made from other locations under the other relevant categories for the award. The full description appears in the first relevant location in the book; cross-references at later locations. You will always be referred toward the front of the book.

Your major field of study and career goal have central importance in college planning. As a result, we have combined these into a single category and have given this category precedence over the others. The *Academic Fields/Career Goals* section appears first in the book. If an academic major or career area is a criterion for a scholarship, the description of this award will appear in this section.

Within the *Academic Fields/Career Goals* section, cross-references are made only from and to other academic fields or career areas. Cross-references are not provided to this section from the other ten categories. You will be able to locate relevant awards from nonacademic or noncareer criteria through the indexes in the back of this book.

For example, the full descriptive profile of a scholarship for any type of engineering student who resides in Ohio, Pennsylvania, or West Virginia might appear under *Aviation/Aerospace,* which happens to be the alphabetically first engineering category heading in the *Academic Fields/Career Goals* section. Cross-references to this first listing may occur from any other relevant engineering or technological academic field subject areas, such as *Chemical Engineering, Civil Engineering, Electrical Engineering/Electronics, Engineering-Related Technologies, Engineering/Technology, Mechanical Engineering,* or *Nuclear Science.* There would not be a cross-reference from the *Residence* category. However, the name of the award will appear in the *Residence* index under Ohio, Pennsylvania, and West Virginia. You will always want to check the indexes relevant to your search to get the most out of the guide's listings.

Within the major category sections, descriptive profiles are organized alphabetically by the name of the sponsoring organization. If more than one award from the same organization appears in a particular section, the awards are listed alphabetically under the sponsor name, which appears only once, by the name of the first award.

HOW THE PROFILES ARE ORGANIZED

Here are the elements of a full profile:

Name of Sponsoring Organization

These appear alphabetically under the appropriate category. In most instances acronyms are given as full names. However, occasionally a sponsor will refer to itself by an acronym. Thus, we present the sponsor's name as an acronym.

World Wide Web Address

Award Name

Brief Textual Description of the Award

Academic/Career Areas (only in the Academic Fields/ Career Goals section of the book)

This is a list of all academic or career subject terms that are assigned to this award.

Award

Is it a scholarship? A prize for winning a competition? A forgivable loan? An internship?

For what type and for what years of college can it be used? Is it renewable or is it for only one year?

Eligibility Requirements

Application Requirements

What do you need to supply in order to be considered? What are the deadlines?

Contact

If provided by the sponsor, this element includes the name, mailing address, telephone and fax numbers, and e-mail address of the person to contact for information about a specific award.

USING THE INDEXES

The alphabetical indexes in the back of the book are designed to aid your search. Two indexes are name indexes. One lists scholarships alphabetically by academic fields and career goals. The other nine indexes supply access by eligibility criteria. The criteria indexes give you the page number of the descriptions of relevant awards regardless of the part of the book in which they appear.

These are the indexes:

Award Name
Sponsor
Academic Fields/Career Goals
  [117 subject areas, from Accounting to Women's Studies]

Civic, Professional, Social, or Union Affiliation
Corporate Affiliation
Employment Experience
Impairment
Military Service
Nationality or Ethnic Heritage
Religious Affiliation
Residence
Location of Study
Talent

In general, when using the indexes, writing down the names and page numbers of the awards that you are interested in is an effective technique.

DATA COLLECTION PROCEDURES

Thomson Peterson's takes its responsibility as a provider of trustworthy information to its readers very seriously. The data on the award programs in this guide were collected by a third-party data provider between February and April 2006 through an online survey, Internet research, and/or phone interviews with the sponsoring organizations. In addition, Peterson's research staff makes every effort to verify unusual figures and resolve discrepancies. Nonetheless, errors and omissions are possible in a data collection endeavor of this scope. Also, facts and figures, such as number and amount of awards, can suddenly change or awards can be discontinued by a sponsoring organization. Therefore, readers should check with the specific sponsoring agency responsible for administering these awards prior to the time of application to verify all pertinent information.

CRITERIA FOR INCLUSION IN THIS BOOK

The programs listed in this book have the primary characteristics of legitimate scholarships: verifiable sponsor addresses and telephone numbers, appropriate descriptive materials, and fees that, if required, are not exorbitant. Thomson Peterson's assumes that these fees are used to defray administrative expenses and are not major sources of income.

Quick-Reference Chart

Scholarships, Grants & Prizes At-a-Glance

This chart lists award programs that indicate that their largest award provides $2000 or more. The awards are ranked in descending order on the basis of the dollar amount of the largest award. Because the award criteria in the "Academic/Career Areas and Eligibility Requirements" column may represent only some of the criteria or limitations that affect eligibility for the award, you should refer to the full description in the award profiles to ascertain all relevant details.

Award Name	Page Number	Highest Dollar Amount	Lowest Dollar Amount	Number of Awards	Academic/Career Areas and Eligibility Requirements
National Health Service Corps Scholarship Program	325	$135,000	$67,500	200–300	Health and Medical Sciences, Nursing.
Intel Science Talent Search	777	$100,000	$ 1000	40	Talent: designated field specified by sponsor.
Careers Through Culinary Arts Program Cooking Competition for Scholarships	200	$ 78,000	$ 1000	88–95	Culinary Arts; State: Arizona, California, District of Columbia, Illinois, Massachusetts, New York, Pennsylvania, Virginia.
DeVry University First Scholar Award	806	$ 64,000	$32,000	1	Must be in high school.
Elks Most Valuable Student Contest	810	$ 60,000	$ 4000	500	Must be in high school.
Micron Science and Technology Scholars Program	165	$ 55,000	$16,500	10–13	Chemical Engineering, Computer Science/Data Processing, Electrical Engineering/Electronics, Engineering-Related Technologies, Engineering/Technology, Materials Science, Engineering, and Metallurgy, Mechanical Engineering, Physical Sciences and Math, Science, Technology, and Society; State: Colorado, Idaho, Texas, Utah, Virginia; Talent: leadership.
DeVry University Regional First Scholar Awards	688	$ 53,370	$21,280	10	Studying in Arizona, California, Colorado, Florida, Georgia, Illinois, New York, Pennsylvania, Texas.
Intel International Science and Engineering Fair	777	$ 50,000	$ 500		Talent: designated field specified by sponsor.
Miss America Organization Competition Scholarships	771	$ 50,000	$ 1000	69	Talent: beauty pageant.
Padgett Business Services Foundation Scholarship Program	833	$ 50,000	$ 500	65–75	Must be in high school.
Young Epidemiology Scholars Competition	291	$ 50,000	$ 1000		Environmental Health, Public Health.
Young Epidemiology Scholars Competition	332	$ 50,000	$15,000	120	Health and Medical Sciences.
Sponsor-crowned International Student Scholarship	606	$ 41,232	$24,744	82	Limited to Asian/Pacific Islander students.
Gates Millennium Scholars Program	605	$ 40,000	$ 500	150	Limited to American Indian/Alaska Native students.
Ron Brown Scholar Program	608	$ 40,000	$10,000	10–20	Talent: leadership. Limited to Black (non-Hispanic) students.
DeVry Skills USA Scholarships	806	$ 32,000	$ 9000	18	

Award Name	Page Number	Highest Dollar Amount	Lowest Dollar Amount	Number of Awards	Academic/Career Areas and Eligibility Requirements
Beinecke Scholarship for Graduate Study	109	$30,000	$ 2000	18–22	Arts, Humanities, Social Sciences.
Best Teen Chef Culinary Scholarship Competition	200	$30,000	$ 2000	10–18	Culinary Arts.
Gina Bachauer International Artists Piano Competition Award	439	$30,000	$ 600	6	Performing Arts; Talent: music/singing.
Kentucky Police Corps Scholarship	821	$30,000	$ 7500	10	
Minnesota Police Corps Scholarship	825	$30,000	$ 7500	10	
South Carolina Police Corps Scholarship	841	$30,000	$ 7500	20	
University and Community College System of Nevada NASA Space Grant and Fellowship Program	125	$30,000	$ 2500	1–20	Aviation/Aerospace, Chemical Engineering, Computer Science/Data Processing, Electrical Engineering/Electronics, Engineering/Technology, Meteorology/Atmospheric Science, Physical Sciences and Math; State: Nevada; Studying in Nevada.
Voice of Democracy Program	851	$30,000	$ 1000	59	Must be in high school.
W. Eugene Smith Grant in Humanistic Photography	780	$30,000	$ 2500	varies	Talent: photography/photogrammetry/filmmaking.
AAA High School Travel Challenge	784	$25,000	$ 500	8	Must be in high school.
Best Buy Scholarships	794	$25,000	$ 1000	60	
CAPPS Scholarship Program	669	$25,000	$ 1000	200–250	State: California; Studying in California.
Discover Card Tribute Award Scholarship Program	787	$25,000	$ 2500	310	Must be in high school.
Lilly Endowment Community Scholarship, Tippecanoe County	696	$25,000	$ 6250	6	State: Indiana; Studying in Indiana.
National Poster Design Contest	315	$25,000	$ 2000	10	Graphics/Graphic Arts/Printing.
Primary Care Resource Initiative for Missouri Loan Program	210	$25,000	$ 3000	varies	Dental Health/Services, Health and Medical Sciences, Nursing; State: Missouri; Studying in Missouri.
Sons of Italy National Leadership Grants Competition General Scholarships	634	$25,000	$ 4000	10–13	Nationality: Italian.
Target All-Around Scholarship Program	844	$25,000	$ 1000	650	
Queen Elisabeth Competition	775	$24,125	$ 1206	varies	Talent: music, music/singing.
College Assistance Migrant Program at St. Edward's University	540	$23,000	$ 500	40	Employment Experience: agriculture.
Tuition Exchange Scholarships	551	$20,800	$10,000	3400–4000	Employment Experience: designated career field.
American Legion Samsung Scholarship	583	$20,000	$ 1000	98	Military Service: General.
CIRI Foundation Special Excellence Scholarship	799	$20,000	$18,000	varies	
Coca-Cola Scholars Program	766	$20,000	$ 4000	250	Talent: leadership.
Discovery Channel Young Scientist Challenge	776	$20,000	$ 500	40	Talent: designated field specified by sponsor.
Duke Energy Scholars Program	530	$20,000	$ 1000	20	Corporate Affiliation.

Award Name	Page Number	Highest Dollar Amount	Lowest Dollar Amount	Number of Awards	Academic/Career Areas and Eligibility Requirements
Four-Year and Three-Year Advance Designees Scholarship	573	$20,000	$ 5000	700–3000	Military Service: Army, Army National Guard.
Fulbright Program	222	$20,000	$ 1000	80–100	Education; Employment Experience: teaching.
George and Mary Newton Scholarship	847	$20,000	$ 500	5	
Glaxo Smith Kline Opportunities Scholarship	751	$20,000	$ 5000	1–5	State: North Carolina; Studying in North Carolina.
Jonathan R. Lax Scholarship Fund	795	$20,000	$ 5000	8–10	
Kermit B. Nash, Jr. Academic Scholarship	839	$20,000	$ 5000	1	Must be in high school.
Marc A. Klein Playwright Award	438	$20,000	$ 1000	1–4	Performing Arts.
National Art Honor Society Scholarship	109	$20,000	$ 2000	5	Arts.
National Security Education Program David L. Boren Undergraduate Scholarships	817	$20,000	$ 2500	150–200	
Paul and Helen Trussel Science and Technology Scholarship	93	$20,000	$ 5000	1	Applied Sciences, Biology, Chemical Engineering, Computer Science/Data Processing, Earth Science, Geography, Meteorology/Atmospheric Science, Natural Resources, Natural Sciences, Nuclear Science, Physical Sciences and Math, Science, Technology, and Society; State: British Columbia; Studying in Alberta, British Columbia.
Rural Health Student Loan Program	210	$20,000	$ 5000		Dental Health/Services, Health and Medical Sciences; Employment Experience: designated career field; State: Nebraska; Studying in Nebraska.
Samsung American Legion Scholarship	585	$20,000	$ 5000	98	Military Service: General.
Scholastic Art and Writing Awards-Art Section	108	$20,000	$ 100	600	Arts, Literature/English/Writing; Talent: art.
SME Family Scholarship	275	$20,000	$ 5000	3	Engineering/Technology.
Washington Crossing Foundation Scholarship	780	$20,000	$ 1000	5–10	Talent: designated field specified by sponsor.
William Kapell International Piano Competition and Festival	438	$20,000	$ 1000	12	Performing Arts; Talent: music.
Maryland Association of Private Colleges and Career Schools Scholarship	150	$19,950	$ 500	50	Business/Consumer Services, Computer Science/Data Processing, Dental Health/Services, Engineering/Technology, Food Science/Nutrition, Home Economics, TV/Radio Broadcasting, Trade/Technical Specialties; State: Maryland; Studying in Maryland.
Rotary Foundation Cultural Ambassadorial Scholarship	312	$19,000	$12,000	150–250	Foreign Language; Talent: leadership.
American Legion National Headquarters National High School Oratorical Contest	760	$18,000	$ 1500	54	Talent: public speaking.
Girl Scout Gold Award Scholarship- High School Graduate	806	$18,000	$ 2000		
Sharon Christa McAuliffe Teacher Education-Critical Shortage Grant Program	230	$17,000	$ 200	137	Education; State: Maryland; Studying in Maryland.

Award Name	Page Number	Highest Dollar Amount	Lowest Dollar Amount	Number of Awards	Academic/Career Areas and Eligibility Requirements
Army ROTC Historically Black Colleges and Universities Program	573	$16,000	$ 5000	180–250	Military Service: Army, Army National Guard.
Army ROTC Two-Year, Three-Year and Four-Year Scholarships for Active Duty Army Enlisted Personnel	573	$16,000	$ 5000	150–350	Military Service: Army, Army National Guard.
Two- and Three-Year Campus-Based Scholarships	573	$16,000	$ 5000	250–1500	Military Service: Army, Army National Guard.
Two-Year Reserve Forces Duty Scholarships	576	$16,000	$ 5000	140–300	Military Service: Army National Guard.
Air Force ROTC College Scholarship	567	$15,000	$ 9000	2000–4000	Military Service: Air Force.
Armenian Relief Society Undergraduate Scholarship	606	$15,000	$13,000	varies	Nationality: Armenian.
First in Family Scholarship	702	$15,000	$12,500	10	State: Alabama; Studying in Alabama.
Illinois Department of Public Health Center for Rural Health Allied Health Care Professional Scholarship Program	327	$15,000	$ 7500	20	Health and Medical Sciences; State: Illinois.
Jesse Brown Memorial Youth Scholarship Program	541	$15,000	$ 5000	12	Employment Experience: helping handicapped.
McFarland Charitable Nursing Scholarship	423	$15,000	$ 1000	3–5	Nursing.
National Beta Club Scholarship	505	$15,000	$ 1000	208	Civic Affiliation: National Beta Club.
National Beta Scholarship	851	$15,000	$ 1000	210	
National FFA College and Vocational/Technical School Scholarship Program	828	$15,000	$ 1000	1700	
Police Corps Incentive Scholarship	817	$15,000	$ 3750	20	
Texas 4-H Opportunity Scholarship	749	$15,000	$ 1500	150	State: Texas; Studying in Texas.
Utah Police Corps Scholarship Program	374	$15,000	$ 7500	30	Law Enforcement/Police Administration.
Arkansas Health Education Grant Program (ARHEG)	86	$14,600	$ 5000	258–288	Animal/Veterinary Sciences, Dental Health/Services, Health and Medical Sciences; State: Arkansas.
Guaranteed Access Grant-Maryland	712	$13,800	$ 400	1000	State: Maryland; Studying in Maryland.
Dutch Education: Learning at Top Level Abroad Scholarship	830	$13,603	$ 2764	300	
DeVry Dean's Scholarships	687	$13,500	$ 1500	varies	Studying in Alberta, Arizona, California, Colorado, Florida, Georgia, Illinois, Missouri, New Jersey, New York, Ohio, Pennsylvania, Texas, Virginia, Washington.
Elizabeth Greenshields Award/Grant	110	$12,500	$10,000	40–60	Arts; Talent: art.
Amarillo Area Foundation Scholarships	53	$12,000	$ 400	varies	Accounting, Agriculture, Education, Nursing; State: Texas.
California Masonic Foundation Scholarship Awards	670	$12,000	$ 1000		State: California.
Central Valley Nursing Scholarship	424	$12,000	$ 8000	90–140	Nursing; State: California; Studying in California.
Fond du Lac Scholarship Program	811	$12,000	$ 500	75–100	

Award Name	Page Number	Highest Dollar Amount	Lowest Dollar Amount	Number of Awards	Academic/Career Areas and Eligibility Requirements
Kenneth Jernigan Scholarship	546	$12,000	$10,000	1	Employment Experience: community service; Disability: Visually Impaired.
Math and Science Scholarship Program for Alabama Teachers	135	$12,000	$ 2000		Biology, Earth Science, Meteorology/ Atmospheric Science, Natural Sciences, Physical Sciences and Math; Studying in Alabama.
California Junior Miss Scholarship Program	670	$11,500	$ 500	25	State: California; Talent: leadership.
Competitive Cal Grant B	671	$11,259	$ 700	22,500	State: California; Studying in California.
Entitlement Cal Grant B	671	$11,259	$ 700	varies	State: California; Studying in California.
Cisco Scholarship-High School Graduates	260	$10,800	$ 1200		Engineering-Related Technologies, Engineering/ Technology, Health Information Management/Technology.
Tupperware U.S., Inc. Scholarship	528	$10,500	$ 1000	varies	Corporate Affiliation.
A Legacy of Hope Scholarships for Survivors of Childhood Cancer	748	$10,000	$ 1000	1–6	State: Arizona, California, Colorado, Montana.
American Legion National Headquarters Eagle Scout of the Year	490	$10,000	$ 2500	4	Civic Affiliation: American Legion or Auxiliary, Boy Scouts; Employment Experience: community service.
America's National Teenager Scholarship Program	829	$10,000	$ 500	250–1510	
Angelus Awards Student Film Festival	762	$10,000	$ 1500	5–7	Talent: photography/photogrammetry/filmmaking.
AQHF Telephony Scholarship for Senior Veterinary Students	86	$10,000	$ 5000	1	Animal/Veterinary Sciences; Civic Affiliation: American Quarter Horse Association.
Arts Recognition and Talent Search (ARTS)	113	$10,000	$ 100	varies	Arts, Filmmaking/Video, Literature/English/ Writing, Performing Arts, Photojournalism/Photography.
CIRI Foundation Excellence Annual Scholarships	799	$10,000	$ 9000	varies	
CMP Group Scholarship Fund	709	$10,000	$ 1000	3	State: Maine.
CollegeNET Scholarship	802	$10,000	$ 1000	1–3	
DC Tuition Assistance Grant Program	689	$10,000	$ 2500	7000	State: District of Columbia.
Executive Women International Scholarship Program	768	$10,000	$ 1000	75–100	Talent: designated field specified by sponsor.
Federation of American Consumers and Travelers Graduating High School Senior Scholarship	499	$10,000	$ 2500	2	Civic Affiliation: Federation of American Consumers and Travelers.
Film and Fiction Scholarship	111	$10,000	$ 3000	varies	Arts, Filmmaking/Video, Literature/English/Writing.
Fisher Broadcasting, Inc., Scholarship for Minorities	181	$10,000	$ 1000	2–4	Communications, Engineering/Technology, Journalism, Photojournalism/Photography, TV/Radio Broadcasting. Limited to ethnic minority students.
Fountainhead College Scholarship Essay Contest	765	$10,000	$ 50	251	Talent: writing.
Future Culinarian of America Scholarship	201	$10,000	$ 3000		Culinary Arts.
Girls Going Places Scholarship Program	815	$10,000	$ 1000	15	Must be in high school.
Governor's Scholars-Arkansas	666	$10,000	$ 4000	75–250	State: Arkansas; Studying in Arkansas.

Scholarships, Grants & Prizes At-a-Glance

Award Name	Page Number	Highest Dollar Amount	Lowest Dollar Amount	Number of Awards	Academic/Career Areas and Eligibility Requirements
GUIDEPOSTS Young Writer's Contest	384	$10,000	$ 250	20	Literature/English/Writing.
Harness Tracks of America Scholarship	543	$10,000	$7500	6	Employment Experience: harness racing.
Health Professions Education Scholarship Program	208	$10,000	$5000	10–15	Dental Health/Services, Health and Medical Sciences, Nursing; State: California; Studying in California.
Hellenic Times Scholarship Fund	614	$10,000	$ 500	30–40	Nationality: Greek.
HSF-ALPFA Scholarships	55	$10,000	$1250	varies	Accounting, Business/Consumer Services; Nationality: Hispanic. Limited to Hispanic students.
Illinois Police Corps Scholarship	373	$10,000	$7500	10	Law Enforcement/Police Administration.
Individuals/Teams Balance Bar Grants	765	$10,000	$ 500	4	Talent: athletics/sports.
James R. Hoffa Memorial Scholarship Fund	818	$10,000	$1000	100	Must be in high school.
John Lennon Scholarship Program	401	$10,000	$5000	3	Music.
Junior Girls Scholarship Program	504	$10,000	$5000	2	Civic Affiliation: Veterans of Foreign Wars or Auxiliary; Talent: leadership.
Kappa Alpha Theta Foundation Merit Based Scholarship Program	502	$10,000	$1000	120–150	Civic Affiliation: Greek Organization.
Lazof Family Foundation Scholarship	565	$10,000	$2500		Disability: Physically Disabled.
Lee-Jackson Educational Foundation Scholarship Competition	704	$10,000	$1000	27	State: Virginia; Talent: writing.
Les Dames d'Escoffier Scholarship	203	$10,000	$2500	3	Culinary Arts, Food Science/Nutrition.
Mas Family Scholarships	146	$10,000	$1000	10–15	Business/Consumer Services, Chemical Engineering, Communications, Economics, Electrical Engineering/Electronics, Engineering-Related Technologies, Engineering/Technology, Journalism, Mechanical Engineering, Political Science; Nationality: Latin American/Caribbean; Talent: leadership.
Medicus Student Exchange	635	$10,000	$2000	1–5	Nationality: Swiss; Talent: foreign language.
Miller Electric International World Skills Competition Scholarship	254	$10,000	$1000	1	Engineering/Technology, Trade/Technical Specialties.
NAAS-USA Awards	826	$10,000	$ 200	10–14	Must be in high school.
National Association of Black Journalists and Newhouse Foundation Scholarship	364	$10,000	$5000	2	Journalism; Talent: writing. Limited to Black (non-Hispanic) students.
National Aviation Explorer Scholarships	121	$10,000	$3000	5	Aviation/Aerospace.
National Italian American Foundation Category I Scholarship	625	$10,000	$2500	varies	Nationality: Italian.
National Italian American Foundation Category II Scholarship	106	$10,000	$2500	varies	Area/Ethnic Studies; Talent: Italian language.
National Peace Essay Contest	438	$10,000	$1000	50	Peace and Conflict Studies.
NCTA Help Santa Find the Perfect Real Christmas Tree	826	$10,000	$5000	3	

Award Name	Page Number	Highest Dollar Amount	Lowest Dollar Amount	Number of Awards	Academic/Career Areas and Eligibility Requirements
Nightingale Awards of Pennsylvania Nursing Scholarship	430	$10,000	$6000		Nursing; State: Pennsylvania.
Olive W. Garvey Fellowship Competition	817	$10,000	$1000	6	
Patriot's Pen	779	$10,000	$1000		Talent: writing.
Phillips Foundation Ronald Reagan Future Leaders Scholarship Program	834	$10,000	$2500	10–20	
Pride Foundation/Greater Seattle Business Association Scholarship	741	$10,000	$ 500	90–100	State: Alaska, Idaho, Montana, Oregon, Washington.
Promotion of Excellence Grants Program	227	$10,000	$2000	varies	Education; Civic Affiliation: Phi Kappa Phi.
R.O.S.E. Fund Scholarship Program	836	$10,000	$1000	10–15	
Registered Nurse Education Loan Repayment Program	424	$10,000	$4000	50–70	Nursing; State: California; Studying in California.
RN Education Scholarship Program	424	$10,000	$6000	50–70	Nursing; State: California; Studying in California.
Society for Foodservice Management Scholarship	310	$10,000	$2500		Food Service/Hospitality.
Spencer Risk Management and Insurance Scholarship	355	$10,000	$5000	10–20	Insurance and Actuarial Science.
Spencer Scholarship	355	$10,000	$5000		Insurance and Actuarial Science.
Stephen Phillips Memorial Scholarship Fund	842	$10,000	$3000	150–200	
Stonehouse Golf Youth Scholarship	778	$10,000	$ 500	20	Talent: golf.
Talbots Women's Scholarship Fund	844	$10,000	$1000	5–50	
Technical Minority Scholarship	169	$10,000	$1000	125–150	Chemical Engineering, Computer Science/Data Processing, Electrical Engineering/Electronics, Engineering-Related Technologies, Engineering/Technology, Materials Science, Engineering, and Metallurgy, Mechanical Engineering, Physical Sciences and Math. Limited to ethnic minority students.
Toshiba/NSTA ExploraVision Awards Program	829	$10,000	$5000	16–32	
Veteran's Tribute Scholarship	595	$10,000	$3000	3	Military Service: General.
Worldfest Student Film Award	299	$10,000	$1000	10	Filmmaking/Video.
WRI College Scholarship Program	177	$10,000	$2500		Civil Engineering.
Young American Creative Patriotic Art Awards Program	772	$10,000	$2500	3	Talent: designated field specified by sponsor.
Vermont Incentive Grants	753	$ 9800	$ 500	varies	State: Vermont.
Competitive Cal Grant A	670	$ 9708	$2046	22,500	State: California; Studying in California.
Entitlement Cal Grant A	671	$ 9708	$2046	varies	State: California; Studying in California.
Alberta Centennial Scholarship	687	$ 9000	$1000		State: Alberta.
DeVry Community College Scholarships	806	$ 9000	$1500	varies	

Scholarships, Grants & Prizes At-a-Glance

Award Name	Page Number	Highest Dollar Amount	Lowest Dollar Amount	Number of Awards	Academic/Career Areas and Eligibility Requirements
DeVry High School Community Scholars Award	688	$9000	$1000	4753	Studying in Alberta, Arizona, California, Colorado, Florida, Georgia, Illinois, Missouri, New Jersey, New York, Ohio, Pennsylvania, Texas, Virginia, Washington.
Visby Program: Higher Education and Research	635	$9000	$7500	varies	Nationality: Latvian, Lithuanian, Polish, Russian, Ukrainian.
Alberta Heritage Scholarship Fund Aboriginal Health Careers Bursary	135	$8611	$ 861	20–40	Biology, Dental Health/Services, Health Administration, Health and Medical Sciences, Nursing, Therapy/Rehabilitation; State: Alberta. Limited to American Indian/Alaska Native students.
Edward T. Conroy Memorial Scholarship Program	575	$8550	$7200	70	Military Service: Army; State: Maryland; Studying in Maryland.
Connecticut Independent College Student Grants	684	$8500	$7700	varies	State: Connecticut; Studying in Connecticut.
New Jersey Society of Certified Public Accountants High School Scholarship Program	67	$8500	$6500	15–20	Accounting; State: New Jersey.
North Carolina Student Loan Program for Health, Science, and Mathematics	211	$8500	$3000		Dental Health/Services, Health Administration, Health and Medical Sciences, Nursing, Physical Sciences and Math, Therapy/Rehabilitation; State: North Carolina.
Short-term Student Exchange Promotion Program Scholarship	793	$8244	$5650	1950	
Associate Degree Nursing Scholarship Program	424	$8000	$4000	15–30	Nursing; State: California; Studying in California.
CIRI Foundation Achievement Annual Scholarships	799	$8000	$7000	varies	
Department of Education Scholarship for Programs in China	225	$8000	$ 500	10–20	Education; Talent: foreign language.
Georgia Public Safety Memorial Grant/Law Enforcement Personnel Department Grant	542	$8000	$1000	20–40	Employment Experience: police/firefighting; State: Georgia; Studying in Georgia.
Johnson Controls Foundation Scholarship Program	531	$8000	$2000	45	Corporate Affiliation.
New Jersey War Orphans Tuition Assistance	591	$8000	$2000	varies	Military Service: General; State: New Jersey.
Nursing Education Loan/Scholarship-BSN	426	$8000	$4000	varies	Nursing; State: Mississippi; Studying in Mississippi.
Pat and Jim Host Scholarship	309	$8000	$2000	1	Food Service/Hospitality, Hospitality Management, Travel/Tourism; Studying in Kentucky.
Seneca Nation Higher Education Program	633	$8000	$3000	varies	Limited to American Indian/Alaska Native students.
SPIE Educational Scholarships in Optical Science and Engineering	93	$8000	$1000	30–80	Applied Sciences, Aviation/Aerospace, Chemical Engineering, Electrical Engineering/Electronics, Engineering-Related Technologies, Engineering/Technology, Materials Science, Engineering, and Metallurgy, Mechanical Engineering; Civic Affiliation: International Society for Optical Engineering (SPIE).
YouthForce 2020 Scholarship Program	103	$8000	$2000	5	Architecture, Civil Engineering, Electrical Engineering/Electronics, Mechanical Engineering; State: New York.

Award Name	Page Number	Highest Dollar Amount	Lowest Dollar Amount	Number of Awards	Academic/Career Areas and Eligibility Requirements
Delegate Scholarship Program-Maryland	711	$7950	$ 200	3500	State: Maryland; Studying in Maryland.
Minnesota State Grant Program	715	$7861	$ 100	71,000–75,000	State: Minnesota; Studying in Minnesota.
Environmental Protection Scholarships	164	$7600	$4750	3–5	Chemical Engineering, Civil Engineering, Earth Science, Materials Science, Engineering, and Metallurgy; Studying in Kentucky.
AGC Education and Research Foundation Undergraduate Scholarships	173	$7500	$2500	100	Civil Engineering, Engineering/Technology, Trade/Technical Specialties.
American Legion Department of Pennsylvania State Oratorical Contest	664	$7500	$4000	3	State: Pennsylvania; Talent: public speaking.
Calvin Dawson Memorial Scholarship	560	$7500	$2500	1	Disability: Physically Disabled; State: Florida.
Harold F. Wilkins Scholarship Program	143	$7500	$1000	1–3	Business/Consumer Services, Horticulture/Floriculture.
Legislative Essay Scholarship	687	$7500	$ 750	62–65	State: Delaware.
Legislative Essay Scholarship	686	$7500	$2250	3	State: Delaware.
Leveraged Incentive Grant Program	725	$7500	$ 200	varies	State: New Hampshire; Studying in New Hampshire.
Lotte Lenya Competition for Singers	440	$7500	$3000	varies	Performing Arts; Talent: music/singing.
Outstanding Scholar Recruitment Program	726	$7500	$2500	varies	State: New Jersey; Studying in New Jersey.
Paraprofessional Teacher Preparation Grant	231	$7500	$ 250	varies	Education; State: Massachusetts.
Phelan Art Award in Filmmaking	298	$7500	$2500	1	Filmmaking/Video.
Phelan Art Award in Video	298	$7500	$2500	1–2	Filmmaking/Video.
Soozie Courter Hemophilia Scholarship Program	561	$7500	$2500	19	Disability: Physically Disabled.
William Faulkner-William Wisdom Creative Writing Competition	775	$7500	$ 250	7	Talent: English language, writing.
Women's Architectural Auxiliary Eleanor Allwork Scholarship Grants	98	$7500	$2500	3	Architecture; State: New York; Studying in New York.
Vermont Part-time Student Grants	753	$7350	$ 250	varies	State: Vermont.
Tuition Aid Grant	726	$7272	$ 868	varies	State: New Jersey; Studying in New Jersey.
Freeman Awards for Study in Asia	846	$7000	$3000	varies	
GEAR UP Alaska Scholarship	655	$7000	$3500		State: Alaska.
Higher Education Supplemental Scholarship	631	$7000	$ 500	150	Limited to American Indian/Alaska Native students.
J. Wood Platt Caddie Scholarship Trust	544	$7000	$ 200	250–300	Employment Experience: private club/caddying; Talent: golf.
Kosciuszko Foundation Tuition Scholarship	622	$7000	$1000	100–140	Nationality: Polish; Talent: Polish language.
National Solo Competition	761	$7000	$ 500	26	Talent: music.
SevenSECURE Scholarship	561	$7000	$5000	7	Disability: Physically Disabled.
Sid Richardson Memorial Fund	550	$7000	$ 500	50–60	Employment Experience: designated career field.

Scholarships, Grants & Prizes At-a-Glance

Award Name	Page Number	Highest Dollar Amount	Lowest Dollar Amount	Number of Awards	Academic/Career Areas and Eligibility Requirements
Society of Hispanic Professional Engineers Foundation	168	$7000	$ 500	varies	Chemical Engineering, Civil Engineering, Electrical Engineering/Electronics, Engineering-Related Technologies, Engineering/Technology, Materials Science, Engineering, and Metallurgy, Mechanical Engineering, Natural Sciences, Nuclear Science, Science, Technology, and Society. Limited to Hispanic students.
Twin Towers Orphan Fund	848	$7000	$5000	varies	
Minnesota Indian Scholarship Program	624	$6600	$3300	varies	State: Minnesota; Studying in Minnesota. Limited to American Indian/Alaska Native students.
Indiana National Guard Supplemental Grant	572	$6516	$ 200	503–925	Military Service: Air Force National Guard, Army National Guard; State: Indiana; Studying in Indiana.
Liquitex Excellence in Art Purchase Award Program	112	$6500	$1500	5	Arts.
NBFAA/Security Dealer Youth Scholarship Program	545	$6500	$ 500	32	Employment Experience: fire service, police/firefighting; State: California, Connecticut, Georgia, Indiana, Kentucky, Louisiana, Maryland, Minnesota, New Jersey, New York, North Carolina, Pennsylvania, Tennessee, Virginia, Washington.
Pennsylvania Burglar and Fire Alarm Association Youth Scholarship Program	549	$6500	$ 500	6–8	Employment Experience: police/firefighting; State: Pennsylvania.
Adeline Rosenberg Memorial Prize	769	$6000	$4000	2	Talent: music/singing.
Adult Vocational Training Education Scholarships	611	$6000	$3000	3	Limited to American Indian/Alaska Native students.
AMBUCS Scholars-Scholarships for Therapists	328	$6000	$ 500	300	Health and Medical Sciences, Therapy/Rehabilitation.
American Legion Department of New York State High School Oratorical Contest	663	$6000	$1000	65	State: New York; Talent: public speaking.
Archbold Scholarship Program	327	$6000	$ 600	50	Health and Medical Sciences, Nursing; State: Florida, Georgia.
ASSE-United Parcel Service Scholarship	435	$6000	$4000	4	Occupational Safety and Health; Civic Affiliation: American Society of Safety Engineers.
Davis-Putter Scholarship Fund	805	$6000	$1000	25–30	
GCSAA Scholars Competition	348	$6000	$ 500	varies	Horticulture/Floriculture; Civic Affiliation: Golf Course Superintendents Association of America.
Georgia PROMISE Teacher Scholarship Program	226	$6000	$3000	700–1400	Education; Studying in Georgia.
GMP Memorial Scholarship Program	499	$6000	$4000	8	Civic Affiliation: Glass, Molders, Pottery, Plastics and Allied Workers International Union.
Graco Inc. Scholarship Program	530	$6000	$1500	varies	Corporate Affiliation; Employment Experience: designated career field.
Gulf Coast Hurricane Scholarship	168	$6000	$2000	1–3	Chemical Engineering, Engineering/Technology; State: Alabama, Florida, Louisiana, Mississippi, Texas.
Higher Education Scholarship Program	627	$6000	$ 50	72	Limited to American Indian/Alaska Native students.
IFMA Foundation Scholarships	100	$6000	$1000	10–15	Architecture, Engineering-Related Technologies.

Award Name	Page Number	Highest Dollar Amount	Lowest Dollar Amount	Number of Awards	Academic/Career Areas and Eligibility Requirements
Illinois Department of Public Health Center for Rural Health Nursing Education Scholarship Program	327	$6000	$1500	varies	Health and Medical Sciences, Nursing; State: Illinois.
JVS Jewish Community Scholarship	652	$6000	$ 500	varies	State: California; Religion: Jewish.
Marion Huber Learning Through Listening Awards	513	$6000	$2000	6	Civic Affiliation: Recording for the Blind and Dyslexic; Employment Experience: community service; Disability: Learning Disabled; Talent: leadership.
Mary P. Oenslager Scholastic Achievement Awards	513	$6000	$1000	9	Civic Affiliation: Recording for the Blind and Dyslexic; Employment Experience: community service; Disability: Visually Impaired; Talent: leadership.
Mississippi Health Care Professions Loan/Scholarship Program	328	$6000	$1500	varies	Health and Medical Sciences, Psychology, Therapy/Rehabilitation; State: Mississippi; Studying in Mississippi.
National Minority Junior Golf Scholarship	625	$6000	$1000	varies	Talent: golf. Limited to ethnic minority students.
OFA National Scholarship/Casey Family Scholars	833	$6000	$2000	350	
Robert C. Byrd Honors Scholarship-Arizona	793	$6000	$3000	50–100	Must be in high school.
Robert C. Byrd Honors Scholarship-Arkansas	793	$6000	$3000	62–100	
Robert C. Byrd Honors Scholarship-District of Columbia	688	$6000	$1500	28	State: District of Columbia.
Robert C. Byrd Honors Scholarship-Hawaii	815	$6000	$1500	28	
Senator George J. Mitchell Scholarship Research Institute Scholarships	717	$6000	$2500	130	State: Maine.
Undergraduate Education Scholarships	611	$6000	$3000	12	Limited to American Indian/Alaska Native students.
Victor and Margaret Ball Program	144	$6000	$1500	20	Business/Consumer Services, Horticulture/Floriculture.
Wachovia Citizenship Scholarship	755	$6000	$1000	6	State: Virginia.
Washington Award for Vocational Excellence	756	$5506	$2445	147	State: Washington; Studying in Washington.
Contemporary Record Society National Festival for the Performing Arts Scholarship	767	$5500	$1900	1	Talent: music/singing.
Heartland Scholarship Fund	832	$5500	$3500	varies	
United Parcel Service Diversity Scholarship Program	292	$5500	$4000		Environmental Science, Health and Medical Sciences, Occupational Safety and Health; Civic Affiliation: American Society of Safety Engineers. Limited to ethnic minority students.
Ohio Instructional Grant	732	$5466	$ 78	varies	State: Ohio; Studying in Ohio, Pennsylvania.
BP/IEE Faraday Lecture Scholarship	244	$5240	$3495	1	Electrical Engineering/Electronics.
Academy of Motion Pictures Student Academy Awards	297	$5000	$2000	3–12	Filmmaking/Video.

Scholarships, Grants & Prizes At-a-Glance

Award Name	Page Number	Highest Dollar Amount	Lowest Dollar Amount	Number of Awards	Academic/Career Areas and Eligibility Requirements
Actuarial Scholarships for Minority Students	355	$5000	$ 500	varies	Insurance and Actuarial Science. Limited to ethnic minority students.
Additional ENA Foundation Undergraduate Scholarships	421	$5000	$3000	1–8	Nursing; Civic Affiliation: Emergency Nurses Association.
AFSCME/UNCF Union Scholars Program	604	$5000	$4000	varies	Limited to ethnic minority students.
American Dental Hygienists' Association Institute Research Grant	205	$5000	$1000		Dental Health/Services; Civic Affiliation: American Dental Hygienist's Association.
American Dietetic Association Foundation Scholarship Program	300	$5000	$ 500	186	Food Science/Nutrition; Civic Affiliation: American Dietetic Association.
American Occupational Therapy Foundation State Association Scholarships	321	$5000	$ 250	38	Health and Medical Sciences, Therapy/Rehabilitation; Civic Affiliation: American Occupational Therapy Association.
Annual Senior High Communication Contest	784	$5000	$ 150		Must be in high school.
Apha Delta Kappa Foundation Fine Arts Grants	108	$5000	$1000	6	Arts, Music; Talent: art, music.
Arby's-Big Brothers Big Sisters Scholarship Award	493	$5000	$1000	2	Civic Affiliation: Big Brothers/Big Sisters; Employment Experience: community service.
Ashby B. Carter Memorial Scholarship Program	505	$5000	$2000	3	Civic Affiliation: National Alliance of Postal and Federal Employees.
Asian-American Journalists Association Scholarship	179	$5000	$1000	10–15	Communications, Journalism, Photojournalism/Photography, TV/Radio Broadcasting; Employment Experience: journalism; Talent: photography/photogrammetry/filmmaking, writing.
AXA Foundation Fund Achievement Scholarship	154	$5000	$2000		Business/Consumer Services; State: New York; Talent: leadership. Limited to Black (non-Hispanic) students.
BEEM Foundation Scholarship	401	$5000	$1000	3	Music; State: California.
Biller/Jewish Foundation for Education of Women	651	$5000	$2000	varies	State: New York; Religion: Jewish; Studying in New York.
Black Broadcasters Alliance Scholarship	179	$5000	$3000		Communications. Limited to Black (non-Hispanic) students.
BMI Student Composer Awards	110	$5000	$ 500	10	Arts; Talent: music/singing.
Boys and Girls Clubs of Chicago Scholarships	495	$5000	$3000	varies	Civic Affiliation: Boys or Girls Club; State: Illinois.
Bushrod Campbell and Adah Hall Scholarship	638	$5000	$1000	varies	State: Massachusetts. Limited to Black (non-Hispanic) students.
Calgon, Take Me Away to College Scholarship Competition	844	$5000	$ 500	9	
California Congress of Parents and Teachers, Inc. Scholarship	669	$5000	$ 500	varies	State: California.
Carpe Diem Foundation of Illinois Scholarship Competition	796	$5000	$2500	10–15	
Chairscholars Foundation, Inc. Scholarships	539	$5000	$3000	15–20	Employment Experience: community service; Disability: Hearing Impaired, Physically Disabled, Visually Impaired.
Children, Adult, and Family Services Scholarship	736	$5000	$ 500	varies	State: Oregon; Studying in Oregon.
Christa McAuliffe Teacher Scholarship Loan-Delaware	225	$5000	$1000	1–60	Education; State: Delaware; Studying in Delaware.

Award Name	Page Number	Highest Dollar Amount	Lowest Dollar Amount	Number of Awards	Academic/Career Areas and Eligibility Requirements
Clara Abbott Scholarship Program	529	$5000	$ 500	4000	Corporate Affiliation; Employment Experience: designated career field.
College Scholarship Assistance Program	746	$5000	$ 400	varies	State: Virginia; Studying in Virginia.
Common Knowledge Scholarship	802	$5000	$ 250	5–30	
Connecticut Special Education Teacher Incentive Grant	462	$5000	$2000	varies	Special Education; State: Connecticut; Studying in Connecticut.
Constant Memorial Scholarship for Aquidneck Island Residents	114	$5000	$2000	1–2	Arts, Music; State: Rhode Island; Talent: art, music.
Contemporary Record Society National Competition for Performing Artists	439	$5000	$1500	1	Performing Arts; Talent: music/singing.
Critical Teacher Shortage Student Loan Forgiveness Program-Florida	541	$5000	$2500	varies	Employment Experience: teaching; State: Florida; Studying in Florida.
Culinary Trust Scholarship Program for Culinary Study and Research	302	$5000	$1000	21	Food Science/Nutrition, Food Service/Hospitality; Employment Experience: food service.
Denny's/Hispanic College Fund Scholarship	62	$5000	$ 500	80–100	Accounting, Architecture, Business/Consumer Services, Chemical Engineering, Communications, Computer Science/Data Processing, Economics, Electrical Engineering/Electronics, Engineering-Related Technologies, Engineering/Technology, Graphics/Graphic Arts/Printing, Hospitality Management. Limited to Hispanic students.
Department of Energy Scholarship Program	148	$5000	$ 500	15	Business/Consumer Services, Chemical Engineering, Electrical Engineering/Electronics, Energy and Power Engineering, Engineering-Related Technologies, Engineering/Technology, Environmental Science, Materials Science, Engineering, and Metallurgy, Mechanical Engineering, Natural Resources, Natural Sciences, Nuclear Science.
Diamond State Scholarship	685	$5000	$1250	50	State: Delaware.
Earl Warren Legal Training General Scholarship	377	$5000	$3000	20–25	Law/Legal Services. Limited to Black (non-Hispanic) students.
Edwards Scholarship	690	$5000	$ 250	varies	State: Massachusetts.
El Nuevo Constructor Scholarship Program	99	$5000	$ 500	varies	Architecture, Drafting, Heating, Air-Conditioning, and Refrigeration Mechanics, Industrial Design. Limited to Hispanic students.
Elie Wiesel Prize in Ethics Essay Contest	768	$5000	$ 500	5	Talent: writing.
Elmer O. and Ida Preston Educational Trust Grants and Loans	690	$5000	$ 250	varies	State: Iowa; Studying in Iowa.
Engineering Scholarship	158	$5000	$2000	1–5	Chemical Engineering, Civil Engineering, Electrical Engineering/Electronics, Engineering-Related Technologies, Engineering/Technology, Materials Science, Engineering, and Metallurgy, Mechanical Engineering.
Entertainment Law Initiative Legal Writing Contest	375	$5000	$1500	5	Law/Legal Services.
First in My Family Scholarship Program	616	$5000	$ 500	100–200	Limited to Hispanic students.

Scholarships, Grants & Prizes At-a-Glance

Award Name	Page Number	Highest Dollar Amount	Lowest Dollar Amount	Number of Awards	Academic/Career Areas and Eligibility Requirements
Florida Women's State Golf Association Junior Girls' Scholarship Fund	692	$5000	$2500	1–4	State: Florida; Studying in Florida; Talent: golf.
Ford Sons and Daughters of Employees of Roseburg Forest Products Company Scholarship	533	$5000	$2000	varies	Corporate Affiliation; Employment Experience: designated career field; State: Oregon.
Foundation of Research and Education Undergraduate Merit Scholarships	335	$5000	$1000	40–60	Health Information Management/Technology; Civic Affiliation: American Health Information Management Association.
Foundation of the National Student Nurses' Association General Scholarships	423	$5000	$1000	50–100	Nursing.
Francis Sylvia Zverina Scholarship	348	$5000	$2000	1–3	Horticulture/Floriculture, Landscape Architecture.
Fred Scheigert Scholarship Program	557	$5000	$ 500	1	Disability: Visually Impaired.
Future Teachers Conditional Scholarship and Loan Repayment Program	240	$5000	$ 600	50	Education; State: Washington; Studying in Washington.
George A. Nielsen Public Investor Scholarship	148	$5000	$2500	1–2	Business/Consumer Services, Public Policy and Administration; Employment Experience: designated career field.
Graduate and Professional Scholarship Program-Maryland	210	$5000	$1000	40–200	Dental Health/Services, Health and Medical Sciences, Law/Legal Services, Nursing, Social Services; State: Maryland; Studying in Maryland.
Great Falls Broadcasters Association Scholarship	479	$5000	$2000	1	TV/Radio Broadcasting; State: Montana; Studying in Montana.
HENAAC Scholars Program	290	$5000	$ 500		Engineering-Related Technologies, Materials Science, Engineering, and Metallurgy, Mathematics; Nationality: Hispanic. Limited to Hispanic students.
Herbert Hoover Uncommon Student Award	697	$5000	$ 750	15	State: Iowa; Studying in Iowa.
Herschel C. Price Educational Foundation Scholarships	697	$5000	$ 500	200–300	State: West Virginia.
HHAF Sports Youth Award	616	$5000	$2000	25	Nationality: Hispanic. Limited to Hispanic students.
High School Journalism Workshops for Minorities	360	$5000	$2500	27	Journalism. Limited to ethnic minority students.
Hispanic College Fund Scholarship Program	616	$5000	$1000	600–750	Limited to Hispanic students.
Hispanic Engineer National Achievement Awards Corporation Scholarship Program	122	$5000	$ 500	12–20	Aviation/Aerospace, Biology, Chemical Engineering, Civil Engineering, Computer Science/Data Processing, Electrical Engineering/Electronics, Engineering/Technology, Materials Science, Engineering, and Metallurgy, Mechanical Engineering, Nuclear Science; Nationality: Hispanic. Limited to Hispanic students.
Houston Symphony Ima Hogg Young Artist Competition	771	$5000	$ 300	3	Talent: music.
Howard Rock Foundation Scholarship Program	673	$5000	$2500	3	State: Alaska.
HSF/Camino al Exito Scholarship Program	618	$5000	$2500	varies	Limited to Hispanic students.

Award Name	Page Number	Highest Dollar Amount	Lowest Dollar Amount	Number of Awards	Academic/Career Areas and Eligibility Requirements
ICI Educational Foundation Scholarship Program	62	$5000	$ 500	varies	Accounting, Business/Consumer Services, Computer Science/Data Processing, Engineering/Technology. Limited to Hispanic students.
Indiana Nursing Scholarship Fund	433	$5000	$ 200	490–690	Nursing; State: Indiana; Studying in Indiana.
Instrumentation, Systems, and Automation Society (ISA) Scholarship Program	123	$5000	$ 500	5–15	Aviation/Aerospace, Chemical Engineering, Electrical Engineering/Electronics, Engineering-Related Technologies, Engineering/Technology, Heating, Air-Conditioning, and Refrigeration Mechanics, Mechanical Engineering.
Irish Research Funds	105	$5000	$1000	1–10	Area/Ethnic Studies, Humanities, Social Sciences.
James L. and Genevieve H. Goodwin Memorial Scholarship	684	$5000	$1000	10	State: Connecticut.
Jane M. Klausman Women in Business Scholarships	158	$5000	$4000	5	Business/Consumer Services.
Jaycee War Memorial Fund Scholarship	849	$5000	$1000	25–30	
Jesse Jones, Jr. Scholarship	641	$5000	$2000	4	Limited to Black (non-Hispanic) students.
Jewish Vocational Service Scholarship Program	652	$5000	$ 500		Religion: Jewish.
John Kimball, Jr. Memorial Trust Scholarship Program for the Study of History	339	$5000	$ 250	5–20	History.
Kansas City Initiative Scholarship	642	$5000	$2500	varies	State: Kansas, Missouri. Limited to Black (non-Hispanic) students.
Kapadia Scholarships	283	$5000	$1500	varies	Engineering/Technology.
Kappa Alpha Theta Foundation Named Endowment Grant Program	503	$5000	$ 100	50	Civic Affiliation: Greek Organization.
Keck Foundation Scholarship	849	$5000	$2000	varies	
Kentucky Minority Educator Recruitment and Retention (KMERR) Scholarship	229	$5000	$2500	300	Education; State: Kentucky; Studying in Kentucky. Limited to ethnic minority students.
Kentucky Teacher Scholarship Program	229	$5000	$ 250	600–700	Education; State: Kentucky; Studying in Kentucky.
Kosciuszko Foundation Chopin Piano Competition	439	$5000	$1500	3	Performing Arts; Talent: music/singing.
L. Ron Hubbard's Illustrators of the Future Contest	765	$5000	$ 500	12	Talent: art.
L. Ron Hubbard's Writers of the Future Contest	765	$5000	$ 500	12	Talent: writing.
Legislative Incentives for Future Excellence Program	744	$5000	$2000	varies	State: South Carolina; Studying in South Carolina.
Leveraging Educational Assistance State Partnership Program (LEAP)	698	$5000	$ 400	varies	State: Idaho; Studying in Idaho.
Liederkranz Foundation Scholarship Award for Voice	772	$5000	$1000	14–18	Talent: music/singing.
LINC TELACU Scholarship Program	689	$5000	$ 500	100–150	State: California; Studying in California.

Scholarships, Grants & Prizes At-a-Glance

Award Name	Page Number	Highest Dollar Amount	Lowest Dollar Amount	Number of Awards	Academic/Career Areas and Eligibility Requirements
Lockheed Martin Scholarship Program	164	$5000	$ 500	varies	Chemical Engineering, Computer Science/Data Processing, Electrical Engineering/ Electronics, Energy and Power Engineering, Engineering-Related Technologies, Engineering/Technology, Materials Science, Engineering, and Metallurgy, Military and Defense Studies, Physical Sciences and Math. Limited to Hispanic students.
M & T Bank/ Hispanic College Fund Scholarship Program	63	$5000	$ 500	5–10	Accounting, Business/Consumer Services, Computer Science/Data Processing, Economics, Engineering-Related Technologies, Engineering/Technology; State: Maryland, New York, Pennsylvania, Virginia. Limited to Hispanic students.
Marching Band Scholarships	817	$5000	$1000	4	
Math, Engineering, Science, Business, Education, Computers Scholarships	145	$5000	$ 500	180	Business/Consumer Services, Computer Science/Data Processing, Education, Engineering/Technology, Humanities, Physical Sciences and Math, Science, Technology, and Society, Social Sciences. Limited to American Indian/Alaska Native students.
Michael P. Metcalf Memorial Scholarship	741	$5000	$2000	2–4	State: Rhode Island.
Morris K. Udall Undergraduate Scholarships	294	$5000	$ 350	110	Environmental Science, Public Policy and Administration, Social Services. Limited to American Indian/Alaska Native students.
My Turn Essay Competition	820	$5000	$1000	10	Must be in high school.
NAIW College Scholarship	354	$5000	$2500	varies	Insurance and Actuarial Science.
National Asian-American Journalists Association Newhouse Scholarship	358	$5000	$1000	5	Journalism.
National Competition for Composers' Recordings	767	$5000	$1500	1	Talent: music/singing.
National High School Journalist of the Year/Sister Rita Jeanne Scholarships	182	$5000	$2000	1–6	Communications, Journalism.
National Hispanic Explorers Scholarship Program	93	$5000	$ 500	125–200	Applied Sciences, Aviation/Aerospace, Biology, Chemical Engineering, Civil Engineering, Communications, Computer Science/Data Processing, Earth Science, Electrical Engineering/Electronics, Engineering-Related Technologies, Engineering/Technology, Food Science/Nutrition.
National Leadership Development Grants	614	$5000	$ 500	75	Religion: Methodist. Limited to ethnic minority students.
Native American Journalists Association Scholarships	365	$5000	$ 500	10–14	Journalism; Talent: writing. Limited to American Indian/Alaska Native students.
Native American Leadership in Education (NALE)	145	$5000	$ 500	30	Business/Consumer Services, Education, Humanities, Physical Sciences and Math, Science, Technology, and Society. Limited to American Indian/Alaska Native students.
Network of Executive Women in Hospitality, Inc. Scholarship	101	$5000	$ 500	varies	Architecture, Food Service/Hospitality, Hospitality Management, Interior Design, Landscape Architecture, Travel/Tourism.
Nevada Student Incentive Grant	723	$5000	$ 100	400–800	State: Nevada; Studying in Nevada.

Award Name	Page Number	Highest Dollar Amount	Lowest Dollar Amount	Number of Awards	Academic/Career Areas and Eligibility Requirements
Nevada Women's Fund Scholarships	724	$5000	$ 500	50–80	State: Nevada.
New England Film and Video Festival Awards	297	$5000	$ 250	9–15	Filmmaking/Video; State: Connecticut, Maine, Massachusetts, New Hampshire, New York, Rhode Island, Vermont.
New York Council Navy League Scholarship Fund	578	$5000	$3000	15	Military Service: Coast Guard, Marine Corp, Navy; State: Connecticut, New Jersey, New York.
New York State Tuition Assistance Program	729	$5000	$ 500	350,000–360,000	State: New York; Studying in New York.
North Dakota Board of Nursing Education Loan Program	430	$5000	$2000	30–35	Nursing; State: North Dakota.
Nurse Education Scholarship Loan Program (NESLP)	430	$5000	$ 400	varies	Nursing; State: North Carolina; Studying in North Carolina.
Nurse Scholars Program— Undergraduate (North Carolina)	430	$5000	$1500	600	Nursing; State: North Carolina; Studying in North Carolina.
Oklahoma Educational Foundation for Osteopathic Medicine Endowed Student Scholarship Program	329	$5000	$2500	1–5	Health and Medical Sciences; State: Oklahoma.
Optimist International Essay Contest	832	$5000	$ 650	53–56	
Outdoor Writers Association of America Bodie McDowell Scholarship Award	185	$5000	$1800	3–6	Communications, Filmmaking/Video, Journalism, Literature/English/Writing, Photojournalism/Photography, TV/Radio Broadcasting; Talent: amateur radio, art, photography/photogrammetry/filmmaking.
Paul Douglas Teacher Scholarship (PDTS) Program	228	$5000	$1666		Education.
Police Officers and Firefighters Survivors Education Assistance Program-Alabama	537	$5000	$2000	15–30	Employment Experience: police/firefighting; State: Alabama; Studying in Alabama.
Raymond W. Cannon Memorial Scholarship Program	333	$5000	$2000		Health and Medical Sciences, Law/Legal Services. Limited to Black (non-Hispanic) students.
Regents Professional Opportunity Scholarship	67	$5000	$1000	220	Accounting, Architecture, Dental Health/ Services, Engineering/Technology, Health and Medical Sciences, Interior Design, Landscape Architecture, Law/Legal Services, Nursing, Pharmacy, Psychology, Social Services; State: New York; Studying in New York.
Regents Professional Opportunity Scholarships	729	$5000	$1000	220	State: New York; Studying in New York.
Regional and Restricted Scholarship Award Program	756	$5000	$ 250	200–250	State: Connecticut.
Sallie Mae Fund American Dream Scholarship	643	$5000	$ 500	varies	Limited to Black (non-Hispanic) students.
Screen Actors Guild Foundation/ John L. Dales Scholarship (Transitional)	514	$5000	$3000	varies	Civic Affiliation: Screen Actors' Guild; Employment Experience: designated career field.
Senator George J. Mitchell Scholarship Fund	710	$5000	$2500		State: Maine.

Scholarships, Grants & Prizes At-a-Glance

Award Name	Page Number	Highest Dollar Amount	Lowest Dollar Amount	Number of Awards	Academic/Career Areas and Eligibility Requirements
Sigma Xi Grants-In-Aid of Research	84	$5000	$1000	1–350	Agriculture, Animal/Veterinary Sciences, Biology, Chemical Engineering, Earth Science, Engineering/Technology, Health and Medical Sciences, Mechanical Engineering, Meteorology/Atmospheric Science, Physical Sciences and Math, Science, Technology, and Society, Social Sciences.
SME Corporate Scholars	275	$5000	$1000	varies	Engineering/Technology, Trade/Technical Specialties.
Society of Physics Students Scholarships	448	$5000	$2000	17–22	Physical Sciences and Math; Civic Affiliation: Society of Physics Students.
Society of Plastics Engineers Scholarship Program	168	$5000	$1000	19	Chemical Engineering, Civil Engineering, Electrical Engineering/Electronics, Engineering/Technology, Industrial Design, Materials Science, Engineering, and Metallurgy, Mechanical Engineering, Trade/Technical Specialties.
South Carolina Teacher Loan Program	237	$5000	$2500	1121	Education, Special Education; State: South Carolina; Studying in South Carolina.
TCU Texas Youth Entrepreneur of the Year	749	$5000	$1000	6	State: Texas.
Theta Delta Chi Educational Foundation Inc. Scholarship	847	$5000	$1000		
Tribal Business Management Program (TBM)	55	$5000	$ 500	35	Accounting, Business/Consumer Services, Computer Science/Data Processing, Economics, Electrical Engineering/Electronics, Engineering-Related Technologies, Engineering/Technology, Travel/Tourism. Limited to American Indian/Alaska Native students.
Undergraduate Scholarship	498	$5000	$ 500	15	Civic Affiliation: Greek Organization.
United Agribusiness League Scholarship Program	77	$5000	$1000	10–15	Agribusiness, Agriculture, Animal/Veterinary Sciences, Economics, Food Science/Nutrition, Horticulture/Floriculture, Landscape Architecture.
United Agricultural Benefit Trust Scholarship	77	$5000	$1000	7	Agribusiness, Agriculture, Animal/Veterinary Sciences, Economics, Food Science/Nutrition, Horticulture/Floriculture, Landscape Architecture; Civic Affiliation: United Agribusiness League.
Utah Centennial Opportunity Program for Education	753	$5000	$ 300	2807	State: Utah; Studying in Utah.
Vincent Abate Memorial Scholarship	543	$5000	$1000	1–3	Employment Experience: harness racing.
Warner Norcross and Judd LLP Scholarship for Minority Students	377	$5000	$1000	3	Law/Legal Services. Limited to ethnic minority students.
Willits Foundation Scholarship Program	537	$5000	$1000	10–15	Corporate Affiliation.
Women's Jewelry Association Scholarship Program	471	$5000	$ 500	5–15	Trade/Technical Specialties; Talent: designated field specified by sponsor.
Worldstudio AIGA Scholarships	115	$5000	$1000		Arts.
Worldstudio Foundation Scholarship Program	104	$5000	$1000	30–50	Architecture, Arts, Fashion Design, Filmmaking/Video, Graphics/Graphic Arts/Printing, Industrial Design, Interior Design, Landscape Architecture.

Award Name	Page Number	Highest Dollar Amount	Lowest Dollar Amount	Number of Awards	Academic/Career Areas and Eligibility Requirements
Young Artist Competition	441	$5000	$ 500	9–14	Performing Arts; State: Illinois, Indiana, Iowa, Kansas, Manitoba, Michigan, Minnesota, Missouri, Nebraska, North Dakota, Ontario, South Dakota, Wisconsin; Talent: music.
Missouri College Guarantee Program	717	$4900	$ 100	varies	State: Missouri; Studying in Missouri.
Frank O'Bannon Grant Program	747	$4700	$ 200	38,000–43,660	State: Indiana; Studying in Indiana.
Big 33 Scholarship Foundation, Inc. Scholarships	668	$4500	$ 500	150–200	State: Ohio, Pennsylvania.
Community Foundation for Greater Buffalo Scholarships	679	$4500	$ 200	600–900	State: New York.
North Carolina Veterans Scholarships	587	$4500	$1500		Military Service: General; State: North Carolina.
Teletoon Animation Scholarship Award Competition	114	$4488	$1795	12	Arts, Filmmaking/Video; State: Alberta, British Columbia, Manitoba, New Brunswick, Newfoundland, North West Territories, Nova Scotia, Ontario, Prince Edward Island, Quebec, Saskatchewan.
John Edgar Thomson Foundation Grants	544	$4400	$ 500	varies	Employment Experience: railroad industry.
Kentucky Transportation Cabinet Civil Engineering Scholarship Program	174	$4400	$4000	10–20	Civil Engineering; State: Kentucky; Studying in Kentucky.
Toward Excellence, Access and Success (TEXAS Grant)	749	$4392	$1552	varies	State: Texas; Studying in Texas.
New Jersey Educational Opportunity Fund Grants	212	$4350	$ 200	varies	Dental Health/Services, Health and Medical Sciences; State: New Jersey; Studying in New Jersey.
Persons Case Scholarships	603	$4306	$ 861	5–20	State: Alberta; Studying in Alberta.
State Need Grant	755	$4300	$2200	55,000	State: Washington; Studying in Washington.
Iowa Foster Child Grants	701	$4200	$2000	varies	State: Iowa; Studying in Iowa.
Tennessee Teaching Scholars Program	238	$4200	$1000	30–250	Education; State: Tennessee; Studying in Tennessee.
Canada Millennium Excellence Award Program	608	$4084	$3267	2300	
1st Cavalry Division Association Scholarship	574	$4000	$1000		Military Service: Army.
AACE International Competitive Scholarship	96	$4000	$1000	15–25	Architecture, Aviation/Aerospace, Chemical Engineering, Civil Engineering, Computer Science/Data Processing, Electrical Engineering/Electronics, Engineering-Related Technologies, Engineering/Technology, Mechanical Engineering.
American Society for Enology and Viticulture Scholarships	78	$4000	$ 500	varies	Agriculture, Chemical Engineering, Food Science/Nutrition, Horticulture/Floriculture.
Bridging Scholarships	311	$4000	$2500	40–80	Foreign Language.
California Wine Grape Growers Foundation Scholarship	671	$4000	$1000	2	State: California; Studying in California.
Community Banker Association of Illinois Annual Scholarship Program	679	$4000	$1000	13	State: Illinois.

Scholarships, Grants & Prizes At-a-Glance

Award Name	Page Number	Highest Dollar Amount	Lowest Dollar Amount	Number of Awards	Academic/Career Areas and Eligibility Requirements
Community Banker Association of Illinois Children of Community Banking Scholarship	496	$4000	$1000	1	Civic Affiliation: Community Banker Association of Illinois; Employment Experience: banking; State: Illinois.
Congressional Black Caucus Spouses Education Scholarship Fund	804	$4000	$ 500	200	
Congressional Black Caucus Spouses Health Initiatives	318	$4000	$ 500	200	Health Administration, Health Information Management/Technology, Health and Medical Sciences.
E. Urner Goodman Scholarship	494	$4000	$1000	3–6	Civic Affiliation: Boy Scouts, Order of the Arrow.
Edward D. Hendrickson/SAE Engineering Scholarship	129	$4000	$1000	1	Aviation/Aerospace, Chemical Engineering, Electrical Engineering/Electronics, Engineering-Related Technologies, Engineering/Technology, Materials Science, Engineering, and Metallurgy, Mechanical Engineering.
Federal Junior Duck Stamp Conservation and Design Competition	115	$4000	$1000	3	Arts.
Federal Supplemental Educational Opportunity Grant Program	801	$4000	$ 100		
Firefighter, Ambulance, and Rescue Squad Member Tuition Reimbursement Program-Maryland	300	$4000	$ 200	100–300	Fire Sciences, Health and Medical Sciences, Trade/Technical Specialties; Employment Experience: police/firefighting; State: Maryland; Studying in Maryland.
First State Manufactured Housing Association Scholarship	686	$4000	$2000	2	State: Delaware.
Fraternal Order of Police Associates Scholarship	812	$4000	$ 500	1–2	Must be in high school.
Grant Program for Dependents of Police, Fire, or Correctional Officers	543	$4000	$3000	50–55	Employment Experience: police/firefighting; State: Illinois; Studying in Illinois.
International Association of Fire Chiefs Foundation Scholarship Award	543	$4000	$ 350	10–30	Employment Experience: fire service.
Iowa Tuition Grant Program	701	$4000	$ 100	varies	State: Iowa; Studying in Iowa.
Iowa Vocational Rehabilitation	559	$4000	$ 500	5000	Disability: Hearing Impaired, Learning Disabled, Physically Disabled, Visually Impaired; State: Iowa.
John F. and Anna Lee Stacey Scholarship Fund	112	$4000	$1000	3–5	Arts; Talent: art.
Judith McManus Price Scholarship	481	$4000	$2000	3	Urban and Regional Planning. Limited to American Indian/Alaska Native, Black (non-Hispanic), Hispanic students.
Kaiser Permanente Allied Healthcare Scholarship	326	$4000	$3000	20–40	Health and Medical Sciences, Social Services, Therapy/Rehabilitation; State: California; Studying in California.
Knights of Lithuania National Scholarships	503	$4000	$1000	3–6	Civic Affiliation: Knights of Lithuania; Nationality: Lithuanian; Religion: Roman Catholic.
Lieutenant General Clarence R. Huebner Scholarship Program	574	$4000	$1000	3–6	Military Service: Army.
Lois McMillen Memorial Scholarship Fund	115	$4000	$ 500	varies	Arts; State: Connecticut.

Award Name	Page Number	Highest Dollar Amount	Lowest Dollar Amount	Number of Awards	Academic/Career Areas and Eligibility Requirements
Malcolm Baldrige Scholarship	157	$4000	$2000	1–2	Business/Consumer Services, International Studies; State: Connecticut; Studying in Connecticut.
Melvin Mandell Memorial Scholarship	652	$4000	$1000		State: District of Columbia; Religion: Jewish.
NASA Delaware Space Grant Undergraduate Tuition Scholarship	94	$4000	$1400	6–12	Applied Sciences, Aviation/Aerospace, Chemical Engineering, Civil Engineering, Earth Science, Electrical Engineering/Electronics, Engineering-Related Technologies, Engineering/Technology, Mechanical Engineering, Meteorology/Atmospheric Science, Physical Sciences and Math, Science, Technology, and Society; Studying in Delaware, Pennsylvania.
Part-time Grant Program	747	$4000	$ 50	4680–6700	State: Indiana; Studying in Indiana.
Procter & Gamble Fund Scholarship Competition for Employees' Children	535	$4000	$1000	250	Corporate Affiliation; Employment Experience: designated career field.
Richard and Ethel Koff Memorial Scholarship Fund	402	$4000	$1000	1	Music; State: Massachusetts.
Sigma Delta Chi Scholarships	744	$4000	$3000	4–5	Studying in District of Columbia, Maryland, Virginia; Talent: designated field specified by sponsor, leadership, writing.
Specialty Equipment Market Association Memorial Scholarship Fund	282	$4000	$1000	varies	Engineering/Technology, Trade/Technical Specialties; Talent: automotive.
Travel and Training Fund	781	$4000	$ 500	25–100	Talent: athletics/sports.
Union Plus Credit Card Scholarship Program	484	$4000	$ 500	varies	Civic Affiliation: American Federation of State, County, and Municipal Employees.
Union Plus Scholarship Program	518	$4000	$ 500	110–130	Civic Affiliation: AFL-CIO.
United States Naval Academy Class of 1963 Foundation Grant	599	$4000	$1000		Military Service: Navy.
University Film and Video Association Carole Fielding Student Grants	299	$4000	$1000	5	Filmmaking/Video.
Verizon Foundation Scholarship	646	$4000	$2000		State: New Jersey, New York, Pennsylvania. Limited to Black (non-Hispanic) students.
Vertical Flight Foundation Scholarship	132	$4000	$2000	10–12	Aviation/Aerospace, Electrical Engineering/Electronics, Mechanical Engineering.
Washington National Guard Scholarship Program	572	$4000	$ 200	varies	Military Service: Air Force National Guard, Army National Guard; State: Washington.
Weyerhaeuser Company Foundation Scholarships	537	$4000	$1000	65	Corporate Affiliation.
William Winter Teacher Scholar Loan Program	231	$4000	$ 500	varies	Education; State: Mississippi; Studying in Mississippi.
HOPE—Helping Outstanding Pupils Educationally	694	$3900	$ 300	140,000–170,000	State: Georgia; Studying in Georgia.
International Foodservice Editorial Council Communications Scholarship	182	$3750	$1000	1–6	Communications, Food Science/Nutrition, Food Service/Hospitality, Graphics/Graphic Arts/Printing, Hospitality Management, Journalism, Literature/English/Writing, Photojournalism/Photography, Travel/Tourism; Talent: photography/photogrammetry/filmmaking, writing.

Scholarships, Grants & Prizes At-a-Glance

Award Name	Page Number	Highest Dollar Amount	Lowest Dollar Amount	Number of Awards	Academic/Career Areas and Eligibility Requirements
Osler, Hoskin and Harcourt National Essay Competition	722	$3714	$ 743	3	Studying in Alberta, British Columbia, Manitoba, New Brunswick, Newfoundland, North West Territories, Nova Scotia, Ontario, Prince Edward Island, Quebec, Saskatchewan, Yukon.
Teacher Assistant Scholarship Program	233	$3600	$1200	varies	Education; State: North Carolina; Studying in North Carolina.
American Legion Department of Arkansas Oratorical Contest	660	$3500	$1250	4	State: Arkansas.
American Society of Naval Engineers Scholarship	90	$3500	$2500	8–14	Applied Sciences, Aviation/Aerospace, Civil Engineering, Electrical Engineering/Electronics, Energy and Power Engineering, Engineering/Technology, Marine/Ocean Engineering, Materials Science, Engineering, and Metallurgy, Mechanical Engineering, Nuclear Science, Physical Sciences and Math.
Angus Foundation Scholarships	506	$3500	$1000	20	Civic Affiliation: American Angus Association.
Armenian Students Association of America, Inc. Scholarships	606	$3500	$1000	30	Nationality: Armenian.
Corporate Sponsored Scholarship Program	700	$3500	$ 400	20–70	Studying in Washington.
Foundation Scholarships	743	$3500	$1500	20–30	State: New York.
Kansas National Guard Tuition Assistance Award Program	570	$3500	$ 250	400	Military Service: Air Force National Guard, Army National Guard; State: Kansas; Studying in Kansas.
Minnesota Gay/Lesbian/Bisexual/Transgender Scholarship Fund	825	$3500	$1000	20–30	
Minnesota Nurses Loan Forgiveness Program	328	$3500	$3000	25–35	Health and Medical Sciences, Nursing.
National Federation of Paralegal Associates, Inc. West Scholarship	378	$3500	$1500	2	Law/Legal Services.
Paul and Edith Babson Scholarship	643	$3500	$1000	varies	State: Massachusetts. Limited to Black (non-Hispanic) students.
Twin Cities Graduate MBA Scholarship	65	$3500	$ 500	varies	Accounting, Business/Consumer Services; State: Minnesota; Studying in Minnesota. Limited to Black (non-Hispanic) students.
New Century Scholarship	753	$3400	$1060	145	State: Utah; Studying in Utah.
Pennsylvania State Grants	739	$3300	$ 300	151,000	State: Pennsylvania.
Tennessee Education Lottery Scholarship Program Tennessee HOPE Scholarship	748	$3300	$1650	varies	State: Tennessee; Studying in Tennessee.
South Carolina Tuition Grants Program	745	$3240	$ 100	11,000	State: South Carolina; Studying in South Carolina.
Cal Grant C	670	$3168	$ 576	7761	State: California; Studying in California.
TOPS Opportunity Award	707	$3094	$ 741	varies	State: Louisiana; Studying in Louisiana.
1040 K Race Scholarships	59	$3000	$1000	1–3	Accounting; State: Florida; Studying in Florida. Limited to Black (non-Hispanic) students.
A.T. Cross Scholarship	535	$3000	$1000	varies	Corporate Affiliation; State: Rhode Island.
Actuarial Scholarships for Minority Students	145	$3000	$ 500	20–40	Business/Consumer Services, Mathematics. Limited to American Indian/Alaska Native, Black (non-Hispanic), Hispanic students.
African-American Achievement Scholarship	610	$3000	$2500	9	Nationality: African; State: Massachusetts. Limited to Black (non-Hispanic) students.

Award Name	Page Number	Highest Dollar Amount	Lowest Dollar Amount	Number of Awards	Academic/Career Areas and Eligibility Requirements
American Council of the Blind Scholarships	554	$3000	$ 500	26	Disability: Visually Impaired.
American Foreign Service Association (AFSA) Financial Aid Award Program	484	$3000	$ 500	50–60	Civic Affiliation: American Foreign Service Association; Employment Experience: U.S. Foreign Service.
American Indian Education Foundation Scholarship	605	$3000	$1500	100–150	Limited to American Indian/Alaska Native students.
American Legion Scholarship—Ohio	489	$3000	$2000	15–20	Civic Affiliation: American Legion or Auxiliary.
American Nuclear Society James R. Vogt Scholarship	248	$3000	$2000	1	Engineering/Technology, Nuclear Science.
American Physical Society Corporate-Sponsored Scholarship for Minority Undergraduate Students Who Major in Physics	447	$3000	$ 500		Physical Sciences and Math. Limited to ethnic minority students.
American Physical Society Scholarship for Minority Undergraduate Physics Majors	444	$3000	$2000	20–25	Physical Sciences and Math. Limited to American Indian/Alaska Native, Black (non-Hispanic), Hispanic students.
American Savings Foundation Scholarship	791	$3000	$ 500		
Annual Scholarship Grant Program	306	$3000	$1500		Food Service/Hospitality, Hospitality Management; Disability: Learning Disabled.
Appraisal Institute Educational Scholarship Program	451	$3000	$2000	10	Real Estate.
Arizona Nursery Association Foundation Scholarship	342	$3000	$ 500	12–15	Horticulture/Floriculture.
Arkansas Academic Challenge Scholarship Program	666	$3000	$2000		State: Arkansas; Studying in Arkansas.
Associated General Contractors of America-New York State Chapter Scholarship Program	173	$3000	$2500	10–15	Civil Engineering, Surveying; Surveying Technology, Cartography, or Geographic Information Science, Transportation; State: New York.
Capitol Scholarship Program	684	$3000	$ 500	varies	State: Connecticut; Studying in Connecticut, Delaware, District of Columbia, Maine, Massachusetts, New Hampshire, Pennsylvania, Rhode Island, Vermont.
Charles C. Ely Educational Fund	713	$3000	$1000	varies	State: Massachusetts.
College Bound Last-Dollar Grant	675	$3000	$ 400	90–250	State: Maryland.
College Scholarship Program	617	$3000	$1000	2900–3500	Nationality: Latin American/Caribbean, Mexican, Spanish. Limited to Hispanic students.
Colorado Student Grant	678	$3000	$1500	varies	State: Colorado; Studying in Colorado.
Cottey/Cather Writing Prize	757	$3000	$ 200		State: Iowa, Kansas, Missouri, Nebraska, Wyoming; Talent: writing.
Daughters of the Cincinnati Scholarship	568	$3000	$1000	10	Military Service: Air Force, Army, Coast Guard, Marine Corp, Navy.
Deerfield Plastics/Barker Family Scholarship	529	$3000	$1000	13	Corporate Affiliation; Employment Experience: designated career field; State: Kentucky, Massachusetts.
Delta Delta Delta Graduate Scholarship	497	$3000	$2000	8	Civic Affiliation: Greek Organization; Employment Experience: community service.
Detroit Chapter One-Founding Chapter Scholarship	273	$3000	$1000	3	Engineering/Technology; Studying in Michigan.

Award Name	Page Number	Highest Dollar Amount	Lowest Dollar Amount	Number of Awards	Academic/Career Areas and Eligibility Requirements
Donald Estey Scholarship Fund–Rocky Mountain Chapter	473	$3000	$1000	4	Travel/Tourism; Civic Affiliation: American Society of Travel Agents; Employment Experience: designated career field; State: Colorado, Utah, Wyoming; Studying in Colorado, Utah, Wyoming.
Donaldson Company, Inc. Scholarship Program	529	$3000	$1000		Corporate Affiliation.
Duck Brand Duct Tape "Stuck at Prom" Scholarship Contest	816	$3000	$1000	3	
Eaton Corporation Henry R. Towne Trust Scholarship	530	$3000	$1000	12	Corporate Affiliation.
Elks Emergency Educational Grants	498	$3000	$1000	varies	Civic Affiliation: Elks Club.
EXceL Awards	700	$3000	$2000	6	State: Indiana.
First Data Western Union Foundation Scholarship	811	$3000	$ 500		
Golden Gate Restaurant Association Scholarship Foundation	307	$3000	$1000	1–15	Food Service/Hospitality, Hospitality Management; State: California.
Grand Rapids Combined Theatre Scholarship	694	$3000	$1000	varies	State: Michigan.
Hispanic Association of Colleges and Universities Scholarship Programs	616	$3000	$ 500	200	Limited to Hispanic students.
Hubertus W.V. Willems Scholarship for Male Students	166	$3000	$2000	varies	Chemical Engineering, Engineering-Related Technologies, Physical Sciences and Math; Civic Affiliation: National Association for the Advancement of Colored People. Limited to ethnic minority students.
Institute of Management Accountants Memorial Education Fund Diversity Scholarships	63	$3000	$1000	varies	Accounting; Disability: Physically Disabled.
John C. Santistevan Memorial Scholarship	111	$3000	$1000	varies	Arts. Limited to ethnic minority students.
Joseph H. Bearns Prize in Music	767	$3000	$2000	2	Talent: music.
Kildee Scholarships	82	$3000	$2000	3	Agriculture.
King Olav V Norwegian-American Heritage Fund	106	$3000	$ 250	12–15	Area/Ethnic Studies; Employment Experience: community service, designated career field.
Law Student Essay Competition	375	$3000	$1000	3	Law/Legal Services.
Maryland State Nursing Scholarship and Living Expenses Grant	425	$3000	$ 200	600	Nursing; State: Maryland; Studying in Maryland.
Memorial Foundation for Jewish Culture International Scholarship Program for Community Service	106	$3000	$1000	varies	Area/Ethnic Studies, Education, Religion/Theology, Social Services; Religion: Jewish.
Montana University System Honor Scholarship	718	$3000	$2000	300–400	State: Montana; Studying in Montana.
NAAS II National Scholarship Awards	825	$3000	$ 500	1	
New Jersey Society of Certified Public Accountants College Scholarship Program	66	$3000	$2500	4–45	Accounting; State: New Jersey; Studying in New Jersey.

Award Name	Page Number	Highest Dollar Amount	Lowest Dollar Amount	Number of Awards	Academic/Career Areas and Eligibility Requirements
New Jersey State Golf Association Caddie Scholarship	547	$3000	$1500	200	Employment Experience: private club/caddying; State: New Jersey.
Nursing Student Loan Program	434	$3000	$ 250	150–1800	Nursing; State: Wisconsin; Studying in Wisconsin.
Ohio American Legion Scholarships	510	$3000	$2000	15–18	Civic Affiliation: American Legion or Auxiliary; Military Service: General.
Ordean Scholarship Program	67	$3000	$1500	40–50	Accounting, Education, Nursing, Social Services; State: Minnesota; Studying in Minnesota.
Oregon Collectors Association Bob Hasson Memorial Scholarship	737	$3000	$1500	3	State: Oregon; Studying in Oregon.
Oregon Collectors Association Bob Hasson Memorial Scholarship Fund	734	$3000	$1500	3	State: Oregon; Studying in Oregon.
OSCPA Educational Foundation Scholarship Program	68	$3000	$ 500	50–100	Accounting; State: Oregon; Studying in Oregon.
Pennsylvania Institute of Certified Public Accountants Sophomore Scholarship	68	$3000	$1500	18	Accounting; Studying in Pennsylvania.
Pennsylvania Masonic Youth Foundation Scholarship	512	$3000	$1000	varies	Civic Affiliation: Freemasons; State: Pennsylvania.
PFLAG Scholarship Awards Program	834	$3000	$ 500	5–10	
PHCC Educational Foundation Scholarship Program	103	$3000	$1500	5	Architecture, Business/Consumer Services, Civil Engineering, Engineering-Related Technologies, Engineering/Technology, Heating, Air-Conditioning, and Refrigeration Mechanics, Mechanical Engineering, Trade/Technical Specialties.
Print and Graphics Scholarships	315	$3000	$ 500	200–300	Graphics/Graphic Arts/Printing; Talent: designated field specified by sponsor.
Profile in Courage Essay Contest	819	$3000	$ 500	7	Must be in high school.
Roadway Worker Memorial Scholarship Program	538	$3000	$2000	2–5	Employment Experience: roadway workers.
Roothbert Fund, Inc. Scholarship	837	$3000	$2000	20	
Sara Lee Branded Apparel Scholarships	527	$3000	$1000	varies	Corporate Affiliation.
SARA Student Design Competition	103	$3000	$1000	3	Architecture.
Scholarship for Young Women	847	$3000	$ 500	15	
Scholarship Program for the Blind and Visually Impaired	555	$3000	$1000	15	Disability: Visually Impaired.
Scholarships for Education, Business and Religion	148	$3000	$ 500	varies	Business/Consumer Services, Education, Religion/Theology; State: California.
Seaspace Scholarship Program	458	$3000	$ 500	10–15	Science, Technology, and Society.
Society of Louisiana CPAs Scholarships	69	$3000	$ 500	8–12	Accounting; State: Louisiana; Studying in Louisiana.
Sorantin Young Artist Award	440	$3000	$1000	5–12	Performing Arts; Talent: music/singing.
Student-View Scholarship program	843	$3000	$ 500	1	Must be in high school.
SURFLANT Scholarship	599	$3000	$ 500	varies	Military Service: Navy.
Sussman-Miller Educational Assistance Fund	657	$3000	$ 500	30–40	State: New Mexico.

Scholarships, Grants & Prizes At-a-Glance

Award Name	Page Number	Highest Dollar Amount	Lowest Dollar Amount	Number of Awards	Academic/Career Areas and Eligibility Requirements
Texas History Essay Contest	85	$3000	$1000	3	American Studies, History; Talent: writing.
The Chief Master Sergeants of the Air Force Scholarship Program	568	$3000	$ 500		Military Service: Air Force, Air Force National Guard.
Truckload Carriers Association Scholarship Fund	154	$3000	$1500	18	Business/Consumer Services, Transportation; Employment Experience: designated career field.
Two/Ten International Footwear Foundation Scholarship	552	$3000	$ 200	200–250	Employment Experience: leather/footwear.
U.S. Marine Corps Historical Center Grants	340	$3000	$ 400	5	History, Museum Studies.
Undergraduate Research Program	719	$3000	$ 500	10	Studying in South Carolina.
United Methodist Church Hispanic, Asian, and Native American Scholarship	637	$3000	$1000	200–250	Religion: Methodist. Limited to American Indian/Alaska Native, Asian/Pacific Islander, Hispanic students.
Video Contest for College Students	846	$3000	$ 100	8	
Vincent J. Maiocco Scholarship	685	$3000	$1000	1–4	State: Connecticut.
William P. Willis Scholarship	734	$3000	$2000	32	State: Oklahoma; Studying in Oklahoma.
Writer's Digest Self-Published Book Awards	781	$3000	$ 500	10	Talent: writing.
WSCPA Scholarships for Minority Accounting Majors	72	$3000	$1000	20	Accounting; Studying in Washington.
WSTLA American Justice Essay Scholarship Contest	756	$3000	$1000	3	Studying in Washington.
Youth Scholarship	480	$3000	$1000		TV/Radio Broadcasting.
Critical Teacher Shortage Tuition Reimbursement-Florida	225	$2808	$ 702		Education; Employment Experience: teaching; State: Florida; Studying in Florida.
Academic Scholars Program	733	$2800	$1800	varies	Studying in Oklahoma.
Henry C. McDougal Scholarship	716	$2800	$1200	2–3	State: Missouri; Studying in Missouri.
Kentucky Tuition Grant (KTG)	703	$2800	$ 200	10,000–12,000	State: Kentucky; Studying in Kentucky.
California Farm Bureau Scholarship	73	$2750	$2000	23	Agribusiness, Agriculture; State: California; Studying in California.
Educational Assistance Grants-Maryland	711	$2700	$ 400	11,000–20,000	State: Maryland; Studying in Maryland.
Canada Millennium Bursary	655	$2583	$1937	varies	State: Alberta.
Northern Alberta Development Council Bursary	603	$2583	$1291	125–250	State: Alberta.
ACES Copy Editing Scholarship	382	$2500	$1000		Literature/English/Writing.
Agnes Jones Jackson Scholarship	505	$2500	$1500	varies	Civic Affiliation: National Association for the Advancement of Colored People. Limited to ethnic minority students.
AIAA Undergraduate Scholarship	89	$2500	$2000	30	Applied Sciences, Aviation/Aerospace, Electrical Engineering/Electronics, Engineering/Technology, Materials Science, Engineering, and Metallurgy, Mechanical Engineering, Physical Sciences and Math, Science, Technology, and Society.
Air Traffic Control Association Scholarship	116	$2500	$ 600	7–12	Aviation/Aerospace, Engineering/Technology; Employment Experience: air traffic controller field.

Award Name	Page Number	Highest Dollar Amount	Lowest Dollar Amount	Number of Awards	Academic/Career Areas and Eligibility Requirements
Albert and Florence Newton Nurse Scholarship Newton Fund	429	$2500	$ 250	5–20	Nursing; Studying in Rhode Island.
Albert E. and Florence W. Newton Nurse Scholarship	433	$2500	$ 500	varies	Nursing; Employment Experience: designated career field; State: Rhode Island; Studying in Rhode Island.
Alexander Scholarship Loan Fund	782	$2500	$ 500	varies	Talent: designated field specified by sponsor.
All-Ink.com College Scholarship Program	786	$2500	$1000	5–10	
American Institute of Architects Minority/Disadvantaged Scholarship	97	$2500	$ 500	20	Architecture.
American Institute of Architects/ American Architectural Foundation Minority/ Disadvantaged Scholarships	98	$2500	$ 500	20	Architecture.
American Legion Auxiliary Department of Ohio Department President's Scholarship	582	$2500	$1000	2	Military Service: General; State: Ohio.
American Legion Auxiliary National Presidents Scholarship	485	$2500	$1000	15	Civic Affiliation: American Legion or Auxiliary; Military Service: General; State: Utah.
American Legion Auxiliary National President's Scholarship	581	$2500	$1000	15	Military Service: General; State: Michigan.
American Legion Auxiliary National President's Scholarships	583	$2500	$2000	10	Military Service: General.
American Legion Auxiliary, Department of Idaho National President's Scholarship	579	$2500	$2000	15	Military Service: General; State: Idaho.
American Legion Auxiliary, Department of Oregon National President's Scholarship	582	$2500	$1000	2	Military Service: General; State: Oregon.
American Legion Auxiliary, National President's Scholarship	538	$2500	$1000	3	Employment Experience: community service; Military Service: General; State: North Dakota; Studying in North Dakota.
American Legion Department of Washington Children and Youth Scholarships	490	$2500	$1500	2	Civic Affiliation: American Legion or Auxiliary; Military Service: General; State: Washington; Studying in Washington.
American Orff-Schulwerk Association Research Grant	220	$2500	$ 500	1–2	Education, Music, Performing Arts; Civic Affiliation: American Orff-Schulwerk Association; Employment Experience: designated career field; Talent: music/singing.
Annual James Monroe Scholarship Award	851	$2500	$ 500	3	
Arthur C. Tilley Memorial Scholarship	679	$2500	$ 750	varies	State: Florida.
Artist's Magazine's Annual Art Competition	764	$2500	$ 100	30	Talent: art.
ASCPA University Scholarships	55	$2500	$1000	2–3	Accounting.
Association for Women in Architecture Scholarship	98	$2500	$1000	3	Architecture, Interior Design, Landscape Architecture.

Award Name	Page Number	Highest Dollar Amount	Lowest Dollar Amount	Number of Awards	Academic/Career Areas and Eligibility Requirements
Bank of America Minority Scholarship	146	$2500	$ 750	1	Business/Consumer Services; State: Florida. Limited to ethnic minority students.
BIA Higher Education Grant	618	$2500	$ 50	1–130	Limited to American Indian/Alaska Native students.
Bildner Family Scholarship	638	$2500	$1000		State: New Jersey. Limited to Black (non-Hispanic) students.
Bronislaw Kaper Awards for Young Artists	706	$2500	$ 500	4	State: California; Talent: music.
California Council of the Blind Scholarships	555	$2500	$ 375	varies	Disability: Visually Impaired; State: California.
Charles and Lucille King Family Foundation Scholarships	180	$2500	$1250	10–20	Communications, Filmmaking/Video, TV/Radio Broadcasting.
Claire B. Schultz Memorial Scholarship	679	$2500	$ 750	1–3	State: Florida.
Clem Judd, Jr., Memorial Scholarship	697	$2500	$1000		State: Hawaii.
Colonial Bank Scholarship	610	$2500	$ 750		State: Florida. Limited to ethnic minority students.
Community College Transfer Programs	617	$2500	$1500	varies	Nationality: Hispanic. Limited to Hispanic students.
Community Foundation for Palm Beach and Martin Counties General Scholarship	679	$2500	$ 750	varies	State: Florida.
Congressional Hispanic Caucus Institute Scholarship Awards	611	$2500	$1000	111	Limited to Hispanic students.
Connecticut SPJ Bob Eddy Scholarship Program	359	$2500	$ 750	4	Journalism, Photojournalism/Photography; Talent: writing.
Courtlandt and Gina Miler Scholarship	679	$2500	$ 750	1–3	State: Florida.
Dave Yanis Scholarship Fund	680	$2500	$ 750	varies	State: Florida.
Deloras Jones RN Scholarship Program	425	$2500	$1000		Nursing.
Denise Lynn Padgett Scholarship Fund	680	$2500	$ 750	1	State: Florida.
Donna Jamison Lago Memorial Scholarship	626	$2500	$ 500	9	Must be in high school. Limited to Black (non-Hispanic) students.
Edna Aimes Scholarship	328	$2500	$2000	1–3	Health and Medical Sciences, Pharmacy, Psychology, Public Health; State: New York; Studying in New York.
Emerging Texas Artist Scholarship	114	$2500	$ 500	8–15	Arts; Studying in Texas.
Ernest Frank Scholarship Fund	680	$2500	$ 750	varies	State: Florida.
Felix Morley Journalism Competition	771	$2500	$ 250	6	Talent: writing.
Foundation for Surgical Technology Scholarship Fund	325	$2500	$ 500	5–10	Health and Medical Sciences.
Fulfilling Our Dreams Scholarship Fund	633	$2500	$ 500	50–60	Nationality: Hispanic, Latin American/Caribbean; State: California; Studying in California. Limited to Hispanic students.
George M. Brooker Collegiate Scholarship for Minorities	452	$2500	$1000	3	Real Estate. Limited to ethnic minority students.
German Studies Research Grants	814	$2500	$1500		
Gubelmann Family Foundation Scholarship Fund	680	$2500	$ 750		State: Florida.

Award Name	Page Number	Highest Dollar Amount	Lowest Dollar Amount	Number of Awards	Academic/Career Areas and Eligibility Requirements
H. David Faust Memorial Scholarship	680	$2500	$ 750	1–3	State: Florida.
Harry and Bertha Bronstein Memorial Scholarship	680	$2500	$ 750		State: Florida.
Harry and Rose Howell Scholarship	850	$2500	$2000	1	
High School Scholarship Program	617	$2500	$1000	varies	Nationality: Hispanic. Limited to Hispanic students.
Horticulture Research Institute Timothy Bigelow and Palmer W. Bigelow, Jr. Scholarship	341	$2500	$1500	3	Horticulture/Floriculture, Landscape Architecture; State: Connecticut, Maine, Massachusetts, New Hampshire, Rhode Island, Vermont.
HSF/Society of Hispanic Professional Engineers, Inc. Scholarship Program	174	$2500	$1250	varies	Civil Engineering, Computer Science/Data Processing, Electrical Engineering/ Electronics, Engineering-Related Technologies, Engineering/Technology, Mechanical Engineering, Physical Sciences and Math, Science, Technology, and Society. Limited to Hispanic students.
Humana Foundation Scholarship Program	531	$2500	$1250		Corporate Affiliation.
Hydro Power Contest	247	$2500	$ 500	6–10	Energy and Power Engineering, Hydrology.
Indian American Scholarship Fund	619	$2500	$ 500	3	Nationality: Indian; State: Georgia. Limited to Asian/Pacific Islander students.
Inez Peppers Lovett Scholarship Fund	223	$2500	$ 750	1	Education; State: Florida. Limited to Black (non-Hispanic) students.
Institute of Management Accountants Memorial Education Fund Scholarships	63	$2500	$1000	6–12	Accounting.
International Airlines Travel Agent Network Ronald A. Santana Memorial Foundation	350	$2500	$ 500	2–14	Hospitality Management, Travel/Tourism.
International Order Of The Golden Rule Award of Excellence	313	$2500	$ 500	1–3	Funeral Services/Mortuary Science.
Jennifer Curtis Byler Scholarship for the Study of Public Affairs	184	$2500	$1000	1	Communications, Journalism, Political Science; Employment Experience: designated career field.
Joe Lipper Memorial Scholarship	368	$2500	$1500		Journalism.
Julian and Eunice Cohen Scholarship	681	$2500	$ 750	varies	State: Florida.
Kim Love Satory Scholarship	57	$2500	$ 750	1	Accounting; State: Florida; Talent: English language, leadership.
Koniag Education Foundation Academic/Graduate Scholarship	621	$2500	$ 500	130–170	Limited to American Indian/Alaska Native students.
Korean-American Scholarship Foundation Northeastern Region Scholarships	621	$2500	$1000	60	Nationality: Korean; Studying in Connecticut, Maine, Massachusetts, New Hampshire, New Jersey, New York, Rhode Island, Vermont. Limited to Asian/Pacific Islander students.
Larry Fullerton Photojournalism Scholarship	442	$2500	$ 500	1–2	Photojournalism/Photography; State: Ohio; Studying in Ohio; Talent: photography/photogrammetry/filmmaking.
Law Enforcement Officers' Dependents Scholarship-Arkansas	539	$2500	$2000	27–32	Employment Experience: police/firefighting; State: Arkansas; Studying in Arkansas.

Scholarships, Grants & Prizes At-a-Glance

Award Name	Page Number	Highest Dollar Amount	Lowest Dollar Amount	Number of Awards	Academic/Career Areas and Eligibility Requirements
Legislative Endowment Scholarships	727	$2500	$1000		State: New Mexico; Studying in New Mexico.
Leveraging Educational Assistance Partnership	666	$2500	$ 100	varies	State: Arizona; Studying in Arizona.
Leveraging Educational Assistance Partnership (LEAP)	753	$2500	$ 300	4008	State: Utah; Studying in Utah.
Library Research Grants	107	$2500	$ 500	varies	Art History, Arts; Studying in California; Talent: art.
Lilly Lorenzen Scholarship	761	$2500	$1500	1	Talent: Scandinavian language.
Literacy Initiative Grant Competition	501	$2500	$ 300	varies	Civic Affiliation: Phi Kappa Phi.
Loblolly Scholarship Fund	681	$2500	$ 750		State: Florida.
Maine State Society Foundation Scholarship	711	$2500	$1000	5–10	State: Maine; Studying in Maine.
Marine Corps Scholarship Foundation	597	$2500	$ 500	1000	Military Service: Marine Corp.
Marshall E. McCullough- National Dairy Shrine Scholarships	82	$2500	$1000	2	Agriculture, Animal/Veterinary Sciences.
Mary Rubin and Benjamin M. Rubin Scholarship Fund	673	$2500	$ 500	30–35	State: Maryland.
Massachusetts Gilbert Matching Student Grant Program	426	$2500	$ 200	varies	Nursing; State: Massachusetts; Studying in Massachusetts.
Massachusetts Public Service Grant Program	545	$2500	$ 720	varies	Employment Experience: police/firefighting; State: Massachusetts; Studying in Massachusetts.
Matthew "Bump" Mitchell /Sun-Sentinel Scholarship	681	$2500	$ 750	1	State: Florida.
Maura and William Benjamin Scholarship	681	$2500	$ 750	varies	State: Florida.
Michelin North America Dependent Scholarship	527	$2500	$1000	15	Corporate Affiliation.
Michelin/TIA Scholarships	496	$2500	$1250	3	Civic Affiliation: Tire Industry Association.
Michigan Merit Award	714	$2500	$1000	varies	State: Michigan.
Milton J. Boone Horticultural Scholarship	342	$2500	$ 750	varies	Horticulture/Floriculture; State: Florida.
Minority Undergraduate Retention Grant-Wisconsin	647	$2500	$ 250	varies	State: Wisconsin; Studying in Wisconsin. Limited to ethnic minority students.
National Achievement Scholarship Program	625	$2500	$ 500	800	Must be in high school. Limited to Black (non-Hispanic) students.
National Asphalt Pavement Association Scholarship Program	175	$2500	$ 500	50–150	Civil Engineering.
National Beef Ambassador Program	790	$2500	$ 500	1–3	Must be in high school.
Native American Education Grants	631	$2500	$1500	10–125	Limited to American Indian/Alaska Native students.
New Jersey Society of Architects Scholarship	101	$2500	$1000	varies	Architecture; State: New Jersey.
New Mexico Student Incentive Grant	728	$2500	$ 200		State: New Mexico; Studying in New Mexico.
NOA Vocal Competition/ Legacy Award Program	113	$2500	$ 500	3–8	Arts, Performing Arts; Talent: music, music/singing.

Award Name	Page Number	Highest Dollar Amount	Lowest Dollar Amount	Number of Awards	Academic/Career Areas and Eligibility Requirements
North Carolina 4-H Development Fund Scholarships	674	$2500	$ 500		State: North Carolina.
North Carolina Hispanic College Fund Scholarship	610	$2500	$ 500		Limited to Hispanic students.
Ohio Environmental Science & Engineering Scholarships	295	$2500	$1250	18	Environmental Science; State: Ohio; Studying in Ohio.
Pellegrini Scholarship Grants	636	$2500	$ 500	50	Nationality: Swiss; State: Connecticut, Delaware, New Jersey, New York, Pennsylvania.
Promise of Nursing Scholarship	423	$2500	$1000	varies	Nursing; Studying in California, Florida, Georgia, Illinois, Massachusetts, Michigan, New Jersey, Tennessee, Texas.
Ralph O. Wood Scholarship	681	$2500	$ 750	varies	State: Florida.
Robert Guthrie PKU Scholarship and Awards	563	$2500	$2000	6–12	Disability: Physically Disabled.
Roberta and Stephen R. Weiner Scholarship	681	$2500	$ 750	varies	State: Florida.
Sacramento Bee Journalism Scholarship Program	368	$2500	$1500	16	Journalism; State: California.
Sacramento Bee Scholar Athlete Scholarship	742	$2500	$1000	1–6	State: California.
Scotts Company Scholars Program	348	$2500	$ 500	7	Horticulture/Floriculture.
Society of Physics Students Outstanding Student in Research	515	$2500	$1500	1–2	Civic Affiliation: Society of Physics Students.
South Carolina Need-Based Grants Program	744	$2500	$1250	1–23,485	State: South Carolina; Studying in South Carolina.
Stephen Madry Peck, Jr. Memorial Scholarship	311	$2500	$ 750	1	Foreign Language; State: Florida. Limited to Black (non-Hispanic) students.
Stockholm Scholarship Program	850	$2500	$2000	1	
Student Design Competition	354	$2500	$1000	3–7	Industrial Design.
SuperCollege.com Scholarship	843	$2500	$ 500	1–2	
Surgical Technology Scholarships	324	$2500	$ 500	5–10	Health and Medical Sciences.
Swiss Benevolent Society of Chicago Scholarships	635	$2500	$ 750	30	Nationality: Swiss; State: Illinois, Wisconsin.
Terrill H. Bell Teaching Incentive Loan	239	$2500	$ 900	365	Education; State: Utah; Studying in Utah.
Terry Darby Memorial Scholarship	682	$2500	$ 750	varies	State: Florida; Talent: athletics/sports.
The Air Force Sergeants Association Scholarship	568	$2500	$1500	12	Military Service: Air Force.
Thomas William Bennett Memorial Scholarship	223	$2500	$ 750	varies	Education; State: Florida.
Thoroughbred Horse Racing's United Scholarship Trust	370	$2500	$1000	5	Journalism; State: Washington.
Virginia Tuition Assistance Grant Program (Private Institutions)	746	$2500	$1900	18,600	State: Virginia; Studying in Virginia.
Walter and Adi Blum Scholarship	682	$2500	$ 750	varies	State: Florida.
Washington State Trial Lawyers Association Presidents' Scholarship	756	$2500	$2000	1	State: Washington.
Weitz Company Scholarship	803	$2500	$ 750	varies	Must be in high school.
Wisconsin Higher Education Grants (WHEG)	758	$2500	$ 250	varies	State: Wisconsin; Studying in Wisconsin.

Scholarships, Grants & Prizes At-a-Glance

Award Name	Page Number	Highest Dollar Amount	Lowest Dollar Amount	Number of Awards	Academic/Career Areas and Eligibility Requirements
Angelfire Scholarship	587	$2400	$1000	15	Military Service: General.
Datatel Scholars Foundation Scholarship	805	$2400	$1000	varies	
Glenn Miller Instrumental Scholarship	769	$2400	$1200	2	Talent: music/singing.
Syncrude Higher Education Awards Program	524	$2400	$1783	varies	Corporate Affiliation.
Tennessee Education Lottery Scholarship Program Tennessee HOPE Access Grant	748	$2400	$1575	varies	State: Tennessee; Studying in Tennessee.
American Cancer Society, Florida Division R O C K College Scholarship Program	658	$2300	$1850	150–175	State: Florida; Studying in Florida.
Massachusetts Assistance for Student Success Program	713	$2300	$ 300	25,000–30,000	State: Massachusetts; Studying in Connecticut, District of Columbia, Maine, Massachusetts, New Hampshire, Pennsylvania, Rhode Island, Vermont.
Postsecondary Child Care Grant Program-Minnesota	715	$2300	$ 100	varies	State: Minnesota; Studying in Minnesota.
College Scholarships for Cancer Survivors	658	$2250	$1000	72	State: Indiana, Michigan; Studying in Indiana, Michigan.
Institute of Food Technologists Food Engineering Division Junior/Senior Scholarship	302	$2250	$1000	61	Food Science/Nutrition.
Peter and Alice Koomruian Armenian Education Fund	629	$2250	$1000	5–20	Nationality: Armenian.
Phi Kappa Tau Foundation Scholarships	512	$2250	$1000	20–25	Civic Affiliation: Greek Organization.
Scholarship Incentive Program (ScIP)	686	$2250	$ 700	2	State: Delaware; Studying in Delaware, Pennsylvania.
Student Research Scholarship	334	$2240	$ 640	15	Health and Medical Sciences.
Menominee Indian Tribe Adult Vocational Training Program	623	$2200	$ 100	50–70	Limited to American Indian/Alaska Native students.
Scholarship Incentive Program-Delaware	687	$2200	$ 700	1000–1300	State: Delaware; Studying in Delaware, Pennsylvania.
Alexander Rutherford Scholarships for High School Achievement	602	$2153	$ 344	8400	State: Alberta.
Prairie Baseball Academy Scholarships	657	$2152	$ 430	16–80	Studying in Alberta; Talent: athletics/sports.
Tennessee Student Assistance Award Program	749	$2130	$ 100	26,000	State: Tennessee; Studying in Tennessee.

Profiles of
Scholarships,
Grants & Prizes

Academic Fields/Career Goals

ACCOUNTING

ACCOUNTANCY BOARD OF OHIO   http://acc.ohio.gov

ACCOUNTANCY BOARD OF OHIO EDUCATIONAL ASSISTANCE PROGRAM

Program intended for minority students or students with financial need. Applicant must be enrolled as accounting major at an accredited Ohio college or university in a five-year degree program. Applicant must be an Ohio resident. Please refer to Web site for further details: http://acc.ohio.gov/educasst.html

Academic Fields/Career Goals: Accounting.

Award: Scholarship for use in sophomore, junior, or senior years; not renewable. *Number:* varies. *Amount:* $7700.

Eligibility Requirements: Applicant must be enrolled or expecting to enroll at a four-year institution or university; resident of Ohio and studying in Ohio. Available to U.S. citizens.

Application Requirements: Application, financial need analysis, transcript, FAFSA. *Deadline:* November 15.

Contact: Kay Sedgmer, Scholarship Secretary, Accountancy Board of Ohio
Accountancy Board of Ohio
77 South High Street, 18th Floor
Columbus, OH 43266-0301
Phone: 614-466-4135
Fax: 614-466-2628
E-mail: kay.sedgmer@acc.state.oh.us

ALABAMA SOCIETY OF CERTIFIED PUBLIC ACCOUNTANTS   http://www.ascpa.org

ASCPA EDUCATIONAL FOUNDATION SCHOLARSHIP

Scholarships available for accounting students . Must have completed intermediate accounting courses, must have a "B" average in all accounting courses, must have a "B" average overall, and must have declared a major in accounting.

Academic Fields/Career Goals: Accounting.

Award: Scholarship for use in sophomore, junior, or senior years; not renewable. *Number:* up to 20. *Amount:* up to $1500.

Eligibility Requirements: Applicant must be enrolled or expecting to enroll full-time at an institution or university. Applicant must have 3.0 GPA or higher. Available to U.S. citizens.

Application Requirements: Application, transcript. *Deadline:* varies.

Contact: Diane L. Christy, Communications Director
Alabama Society of Certified Public Accountants
1103 South Perry Street, PO Box 5000
Montgomery, AL 36103
Phone: 334-834-7650
Fax: 334-834-7310
E-mail: dchristy@ascpa.org

ALASKA SOCIETY OF CERTIFIED PUBLIC ACCOUNTANTS   http://www.akcpa.org

PAUL HAGELBARGER MEMORIAL FUND SCHOLARSHIP

Scholarships open to all junior, senior and graduate students who are majoring in accounting and attending four year institutions in Alaska. The number of awards and dollar value of scholarship varies but minimum amount is $2000. Deadline is November 15 and it varies every year.

Academic Fields/Career Goals: Accounting.

Award: Scholarship for use in junior, senior, or graduate years; not renewable. *Number:* 2–3. *Amount:* $2000.

Eligibility Requirements: Applicant must be enrolled or expecting to enroll full-time at an institution or university. Available to U.S. citizens.

Application Requirements: Application, resume, references, transcript. *Deadline:* November 15.

Contact: Linda Plimpton, Executive Director
Alaska Society of Certified Public Accountants
341 West Tudor Road, Suite 105
Anchorage, AK 99503
Phone: 907-562-4334
Fax: 907-562-4025
E-mail: akcpa@ak.net

AMARILLO AREA FOUNDATION   http://www.aaf-hf.org

AMARILLO AREA FOUNDATION SCHOLARSHIPS

Scholarships available to graduating high school seniors from the 26 northernmost counties of the Texas Panhandle. All of the scholarships have specific requirements for items such as: county of residence, gender or race, location of institution of higher education, extra-curricular activities, field of study. For information on specific awards and application please visit Web site: http://www.aaf-hf.org. Application deadline is February 1.

Academic Fields/Career Goals: Accounting; Agriculture; Education; Nursing.

Award: Scholarship for use in freshman, sophomore, junior, or senior years. *Number:* varies. *Amount:* $400–$12,000.

Eligibility Requirements: Applicant must be high school student; planning to enroll or expecting to enroll full-time at a two-year or four-year or technical institution or university and resident of Texas. Available to U.S. citizens.

Application Requirements: Application, financial need analysis, references, test scores, transcript. *Deadline:* February 1.

Contact: Laquita Hurt, Scholarship Coordinator
Amarillo Area Foundation
801 South Fillmore Street, Suite 700
Amarillo, TX 79101
Phone: 806-376-4521
Fax: 806-373-3656
E-mail: laquita@aaf-hf.org

AMERICAN INSTITUTE OF CERTIFIED PUBLIC ACCOUNTANTS   http://www.aicpa.org/

ACCOUNTEMPS/AMERICAN INSTITUTE OF CERTIFIED PUBLIC ACCOUNTANTS STUDENT SCHOLARSHIP

Scholarships are given to students who are declared accounting, finance, or information systems major with an overall and major GPA of at least 3.0. Eligible applicants will have completed at least 30 semester hours. Must be enrolled as a full-time undergraduate student at an accredited college or university in the United States. Must be an AICPA student affiliate member.

Academic Fields/Career Goals: Accounting.

Award: Scholarship for use in freshman, sophomore, junior, senior, graduate, or postgraduate years; not renewable. *Number:* 2. *Amount:* $2500.

Eligibility Requirements: Applicant must be enrolled or expecting to enroll full-time at a two-year or four-year institution or university. Applicant must have 3.0 GPA or higher. Available to U.S. citizens.

American Institute of Certified Public Accountants (continued)

Application Requirements: Application, references, test scores, transcript. *Deadline:* April 1.

Contact: Scholarship Coordinator
American Institute of Certified Public Accountants
1211 Avenue of the Americas
New York, NY 10036-8775
Phone: 212-596-6270
E-mail: educat@aicpa.org

SCHOLARSHIPS FOR MINORITY ACCOUNTING STUDENTS

Scholarships are given to minority students who are declared accounting majors with an overall and major GPA of 3.3. Must be a minority student who has satisfactorily completed at least 30 semester hours (or equivalent) including at least six semester hours in accounting. Must be enrolled as a full-time undergraduate or graduate student at an accredited college or university.

Academic Fields/Career Goals: Accounting.

Award: Scholarship for use in freshman, sophomore, junior, senior, graduate, or postgraduate years; not renewable. *Number:* varies. *Amount:* up to $5000.

Eligibility Requirements: Applicant must be American Indian/Alaska Native, Asian/Pacific Islander, Black (non-Hispanic), or Hispanic and enrolled or expecting to enroll full-time at a four-year institution or university. Available to U.S. citizens.

Application Requirements: Application, essay, financial need analysis, references, transcript. *Deadline:* June 1.

Contact: Scholarship Coordinator
American Institute of Certified Public Accountants
1211 Avenue of the Americas
New York, NY 10036-8775
Phone: 212-596-6270
E-mail: educat@aicpa.org

AMERICAN SOCIETY OF WOMEN ACCOUNTANTS
http://www.aswa.org

AMERICAN SOCIETY OF WOMEN ACCOUNTANTS SCHOLARSHIP

Recipients of The American Society of Women Accountants Scholarship will be chosen from applicants that have completed a minimum of 60 semester hours or 90 quarter hours with a declared major in accounting. Applicants shall be attending an accredited college, university, or professional school of accounting. Please contact local chapter for further details; Chapter Directory is located at http://www.aswa.org

Academic Fields/Career Goals: Accounting.

Award: Scholarship for use in junior, senior, graduate, or postgraduate years; not renewable. *Number:* varies. *Amount:* varies.

Eligibility Requirements: Applicant must be enrolled or expecting to enroll full or part-time at a two-year or four-year or technical institution or university. Available to U.S. and non-U.S. citizens.

Application Requirements: Application, essay, financial need analysis, references, transcript. *Deadline:* varies.

Contact: American Society of Women Accountants
8405 Greensboro Drive, Suite 800
McLean, VA 22102
Phone: 703-506-3265
Fax: 703-506-3266
E-mail: aswa@aswa.org

AMERICAN SOCIETY OF WOMEN ACCOUNTANTS TWO YEAR COLLEGE SCHOLARSHIP

Scholarship for students pursuing an accounting or finance degree in community, state or two year colleges.

Academic Fields/Career Goals: Accounting.

Award: Scholarship for use in senior year. *Number:* 1.

Eligibility Requirements: Applicant must be enrolled or expecting to enroll full-time at a two-year institution. Applicant must have 3.0 GPA or higher. Available to U.S. citizens.

Application Requirements: Application, essay, references, transcript. *Deadline:* varies.

Contact: American Society of Women Accountants
8405 Greensboro Drive, Suite 800
McLean, VA 22102
Phone: 703-506-3265
Fax: 703-506-3266
E-mail: aswa@aswa.org

AMERICAN WOMAN'S SOCIETY OF CERTIFIED PUBLIC ACCOUNTANTS–BOSTON AFFILIATE
http://www.awscpa.org/

AWSCPA AND BOSTON AFFILIATE SCHOLARSHIP

Two scholarships of $1,000 each will be awarded to an undergraduate and/or graduate accounting majors attending college in New England. Must have maintained a cumulative B average.

Academic Fields/Career Goals: Accounting.

Award: Scholarship for use in freshman, sophomore, junior, senior, or graduate years. *Number:* 2. *Amount:* $1000.

Eligibility Requirements: Applicant must be enrolled or expecting to enroll full or part-time at a four-year institution or university. Available to U.S. citizens.

Application Requirements: Application. *Deadline:* April 14.

Contact: Julie Mead, Scholarship Chairperson
American Woman's Society of Certified Public Accountants–
Boston Affiliate
Ziner, Kennedy & Lehan
2300 Crown Colony Drive
Quincy, MA 02169
E-mail: julie.m.mead@aexp.com

AMERICAN WOMAN'S SOCIETY OF CERTIFIED PUBLIC ACCOUNTANTS–GEORGIA AFFILIATE
http://www.awscpa.org

AMERICAN WOMAN'S SOCIETY OF CERTIFIED PUBLIC ACCOUNTANTS-GEORGIA AFFILIATE SCHOLARSHIP

Scholarship available for undergraduate and graduate students enrolled in a Georgia college or university in the field of accounting. Must have either completed or be currently enrolled in Intermediate Accounting II. Must submit essay with application on why you are interested in receiving this scholarship. Deadline for applications is April 30. For information and application contact Scholarship Committee Chair.

Academic Fields/Career Goals: Accounting.

Award: Scholarship for use in freshman, sophomore, junior, senior, or graduate years; not renewable. *Number:* 2. *Amount:* $750.

Eligibility Requirements: Applicant must be enrolled or expecting to enroll at a four-year institution or university and studying in Georgia. Available to U.S. citizens.

Application Requirements: Application, essay, references, transcript. *Deadline:* April 30.

Contact: Amy Knowles-Jones, Scholarship Committee Chair
American Woman's Society of Certified Public Accountants–
Georgia Affiliate
222 Piedmont Avenue, NE
102 Edgemont Drive
LaGrange, GA 30240
Phone: 404-653-1242
Fax: 404-653-1575

ARIZONA SOCIETY OF CERTIFIED PUBLIC ACCOUNTANTS
http://www.ascpa.com

ASCPA HIGH SCHOOL SCHOLARSHIPS

Scholarships awarded to eight high school seniors. Applicants must enroll in an Arizona university or community college as a full-time student in the fall semester. Deadline is January 20.

Academic Fields/Career Goals: Accounting.

Award: Scholarship for use in freshman year; not renewable. *Number:* 8. *Amount:* $1000.

Eligibility Requirements: Applicant must be high school student; planning to enroll or expecting to enroll at a two-year institution and studying in Arizona. Available to U.S. citizens.

Application Requirements: Application, references, transcript. *Deadline:* January 20.

Contact: Heidi Frei, Director of Marketing and Membership
Arizona Society of Certified Public Accountants
2120 North Central Avenue, Suite 100
Phoenix, AZ 85004
Phone: 602-252-4114
Fax: 602-252-1511
E-mail: hfrei@ascpa.com

ASCPA UNIVERSITY SCHOLARSHIPS

Scholarships for accounting majors in Arizona institutions who will begin their senior year and have a 3.5 minimum GPA. Application for the scholarships is done through the accounting department of each of the universities.

Academic Fields/Career Goals: Accounting.

Award: Scholarship for use in senior year. *Number:* 2–3. *Amount:* $1000–$2500.

Eligibility Requirements: Applicant must be enrolled or expecting to enroll at a four-year institution or university. Applicant must have 3.5 GPA or higher. Available to U.S. citizens.

Application Requirements: Application, interview. *Deadline:* varies.

Contact: Heidi Frei, Director of Marketing and Membership
Arizona Society of Certified Public Accountants
2120 North Central Avenue, Suite 100
Phoenix, AZ 85004
Phone: 602-252-4114
Fax: 602-252-1511
E-mail: hfrei@ascpa.com

ASSOCIATION OF CERTIFIED FRAUD EXAMINERS
http://www.acfe.com

RITCHIE-JENNINGS MEMORIAL SCHOLARSHIP

Available to full-time criminal justice and accounting majors only. Please provide transcripts, original essay, and three letters of recommendation, including one from a certified fraud examiner (CFE).

Academic Fields/Career Goals: Accounting; Criminal Justice/Criminology.

Award: Scholarship for use in freshman, sophomore, junior, senior, graduate, or postgraduate years; not renewable. *Number:* 15. *Amount:* $1000.

Eligibility Requirements: Applicant must be enrolled or expecting to enroll full-time at a four-year institution or university. Available to U.S. and non-U.S. citizens.

Application Requirements: Application, essay, interview, references, transcript. *Deadline:* April 30.

Contact: Tony Rolston, Research Editor
Association of Certified Fraud Examiners
The Gregor Building, 716 West Avenue
Austin, TX 78701
Phone: 800-245-3321
Fax: 512-478-9297
E-mail: scholarships@cfenet.com

ASSOCIATION OF LATINO PROFESSIONALS IN FINANCE AND ACCOUNTING
http://www.alpfa.org

HSF-ALPFA SCHOLARSHIPS

One-time award to undergraduate and graduate Hispanic/Latino students pursuing degrees in accounting, finance, and related majors based on financial need and academic performance. Must be enrolled full-time at a U.S. college or university. Minimum 3.0 GPA required. Must be U.S. citizen or legal permanent resident.

Academic Fields/Career Goals: Accounting; Business/Consumer Services.

Award: Scholarship for use in freshman, sophomore, junior, senior, or graduate years; not renewable. *Number:* varies. *Amount:* $1250–$10,000.

Eligibility Requirements: Applicant must be of Hispanic heritage and enrolled or expecting to enroll full-time at a two-year or four-year institution or university. Applicant must have 3.0 GPA or higher. Available to U.S. citizens.

Application Requirements: Application, essay, financial need analysis, references, transcript. *Deadline:* April 30.

Contact: Association of Latino Professionals in Finance and Accounting
National Headquarters, Association of Latino Professionals in Finance and Accounting, 510 West Sixth Street, Suite 400
Los Angeles, CA 90014
Phone: 800-644-4223
Fax: 213-243-0006
E-mail: HCF-Info@hispanicfund.org

CALIFORNIA SOCIETY OF CERTIFIED PUBLIC ACCOUNTANTS
http://www.aicpa.org

AICPA/ACCOUNTEMPS STUDENT SCHOLARSHIP

Financial assistance to two AICPA Student Affiliate members pursuing studies in accounting, finance or information systems. Two awards, each worth $2500. Persons who are already CPAs are not eligible for this scholarship. For more information see Web site: http://www.aicpa.org/download/nolimits/become/ships/AccountempsAICPA_App.pdf

Academic Fields/Career Goals: Accounting; Business/Consumer Services.

Award: Scholarship for use in freshman, sophomore, junior, or senior years; not renewable. *Number:* 2–5. *Amount:* up to $2500.

Eligibility Requirements: Applicant must be enrolled or expecting to enroll full-time at a two-year or four-year institution or university. Applicant must have 3.0 GPA or higher. Available to U.S. citizens.

Application Requirements: Application, references, test scores, transcript. *Deadline:* April 1.

Contact: Kate Wimsatt, Program Administrator
California Society of Certified Public Accountants
AICPA, Academic & Career Development Division, 1211 Avenue of the Americas
New York, NY 10036-8775
Phone: 212-596-6224
Fax: 212-596-6292

SCHOLARSHIPS FOR MINORITY ACCOUNTING STUDENTS

$5000 non-renewable one time award to undergraduate students who have completed at least 30 semester hours or equivalent of college work, with at least six hours in accounting. All applicants must have a minimum overall and accounting GPA of 3.3. Must be enrolled as a full-time student. See Web site for more information: http://www.aicpa.org/nolimits/become/ships/AICPA.htm#aicpa Deadline is June 1.

Academic Fields/Career Goals: Accounting.

Award: Scholarship for use in freshman, sophomore, junior, or senior years; not renewable. *Number:* up to 134. *Amount:* up to $5000.

Eligibility Requirements: Applicant must be American Indian/Alaska Native, Asian/Pacific Islander, Black (non-Hispanic), or Hispanic and enrolled or expecting to enroll full-time at an institution or university. Applicant must have 3.0 GPA or higher. Available to U.S. citizens.

Application Requirements: Application, references, transcript. *Deadline:* June 1.

Contact: Paulette Myeos, Program Administrator
California Society of Certified Public Accountants
AICPA, Academic & Career Development Division, 1211 Avenue of the Americas
New York, NY 10036-8775

CATCHING THE DREAM

TRIBAL BUSINESS MANAGEMENT PROGRAM (TBM)

Renewable scholarships available for Native-American and Alaska Native students to study business administration, economic development, and related subjects, with the goal to provide experts in business management to Native-American tribes in the U.S. Must be at least one-quarter Native-American from a federally recognized, state recognized, or terminated tribe. Must demonstrate high academic achievement, depth of character, leadership,

Catching the Dream (continued)

seriousness of purpose, and service orientation. Application deadlines are March 15, April 15, and September 15.

Academic Fields/Career Goals: Accounting; Business/Consumer Services; Computer Science/Data Processing; Economics; Electrical Engineering/Electronics; Engineering/Technology; Engineering-Related Technologies; Travel/Tourism.

Award: Scholarship for use in freshman, sophomore, junior, senior, or graduate years; renewable. *Number:* up to 35. *Amount:* $500–$5000.

Eligibility Requirements: Applicant must be American Indian/Alaska Native and enrolled or expecting to enroll full-time at a four-year institution or university. Available to U.S. citizens.

Application Requirements: Resume, transcript. *Deadline:* varies.

Contact: Mary Frost, Recruiter
Catching the Dream
8200 Mountain Road, NE, Suite 203
Albuquerque, NM 87110
Phone: 505-262-2351
Fax: 505-262-0534
E-mail: nscholarsh@aol.com

CENTER FOR SCHOLARSHIP ADMINISTRATION   http://www.scholarshipprograms.org

BANK OF AMERICA ADA ABILITIES SCHOLARSHIP

Renewable scholarships are available to students who meet the definition of disabled as defined by the American with Disabilities Act and who reside in states where Bank of America has retail operations. For more details and an application see Web site.

Academic Fields/Career Goals: Accounting; Business/Consumer Services; Computer Science/Data Processing.

Award: Scholarship for use in freshman, sophomore, or junior years; renewable. *Number:* varies. *Amount:* up to $5000.

Eligibility Requirements: Applicant must be age 40 or under and enrolled or expecting to enroll at a two-year or technical institution. Applicant must be hearing impaired, physically disabled, or visually impaired. Applicant must have 2.5 GPA or higher. Available to U.S. citizens.

Application Requirements: Application, essay, financial need analysis, references, transcript. *Deadline:* February 15.

Contact: Sandra Lee, President
Center for Scholarship Administration
PO Box 1465
Taylors, SC 29687-0031
Phone: 864-268-3363
Fax: 864-268-7160
E-mail: sandralee41@bellsouth.net

CENTRAL INTELLIGENCE AGENCY   http://www.cia.gov

CENTRAL INTELLIGENCE AGENCY UNDERGRADUATE SCHOLARSHIP PROGRAM

Highly competitive, need and merit-based award for students with minimum 3.0 GPA, who are interested in working for the Central Intelligence Agency upon graduation. Renewable for four years of undergraduate study. After graduation, must work 3 to 6 years, based on years of sponsorship. Deadlines are August 2 and November 1. Information at Web site: http://www.cia.gov. Must apply in senior year of high school or sophomore year in college.

Academic Fields/Career Goals: Accounting; Business/Consumer Services; Computer Science/Data Processing; Economics; Electrical Engineering/Electronics; Foreign Language; Geography; Graphics/Graphic Arts/Printing; International Studies; Political Science; Surveying; Surveying Technology, Cartography, or Geographic Information Science.

Award: Scholarship for use in freshman, sophomore, junior, or senior years; renewable. *Number:* varies. *Amount:* up to $18,000.

Eligibility Requirements: Applicant must be enrolled or expecting to enroll full-time at a four-year institution or university. Applicant must have 3.0 GPA or higher. Available to U.S. citizens.

Application Requirements: Application, financial need analysis, resume, references, test scores, transcript. *Deadline:* varies.

Contact: Van Patrick, Chief, College Relations
Central Intelligence Agency
Recruitment Center
L 100 LF7
Washington, DC 20505
Phone: 703-613-8388
Fax: 703-613-7676
E-mail: ivanilp0@ucia.gov

CIRI FOUNDATION   http://www.thecirifoundation.org

CARL H. MARRS SCHOLARSHIP FUND

To encourage students seeking an undergraduate degree or graduate degree in business administration, economics, finance, organizational management, accounting, or similar field. Applicant must be Alaska Native student. For more details see Web site: http://www.ciri.com/tcf

Academic Fields/Career Goals: Accounting; Business/Consumer Services; Economics.

Award: Scholarship for use in freshman, sophomore, junior, senior, or graduate years; not renewable. *Number:* varies. *Amount:* up to $20,000.

Eligibility Requirements: Applicant must be enrolled or expecting to enroll full-time at a two-year or four-year institution or university. Available to U.S. citizens.

Application Requirements: Application, essay, references, transcript, proof of eligibility, birth certificate or adoption decree. *Deadline:* June 1.

Contact: Susan Anderson, President/CEO
CIRI Foundation
2600 Cordova Street, Suite 206
Anchorage, AK 99503
Phone: 907-263-5582
Fax: 907-263-5588

COHEN & COMPANY CPAS   http://www.cohencpa.com

COHEN AND COMPANY CPAS SCHOLARSHIP

Offers $500 - $1000 scholarships to outstanding sophomores and juniors majoring in accounting at the following schools in Ohio: Cleveland State University, Baldwin-Wallace College, Case Western Reserve University, John Carroll University, Ohio University, Ohio State University, Miami University, University of Akron, Youngstown State University, Kent State University, and Bowling Green State University.

Academic Fields/Career Goals: Accounting.

Award: Scholarship for use in sophomore or junior years; renewable. *Amount:* $500–$1000.

Eligibility Requirements: Applicant must be enrolled or expecting to enroll full-time at a two-year or four-year institution or university and studying in Ohio. Available to U.S. citizens.

Application Requirements: Application, essay, references. *Deadline:* Continuous.

Contact: Angela Ferenchka, Scholarship coordinator
Cohen & Company CPAs
Cohen & Company CPAs, 1350 Euclid Avenue, Suite 800
Cleveland, OH 44115
Phone: 216-579-1040
Fax: 216-579-0111

COLORADO SOCIETY OF CERTIFIED PUBLIC ACCOUNTANTS EDUCATIONAL FOUNDATION   http://www.cocpa.org

COLORADO COLLEGE AND UNIVERSITY SCHOLARSHIPS

Award of $1000 available to declared accounting majors at Colorado colleges and universities with accredited accounting programs. Must have completed at least 8 semester hours of accounting courses. Overall GPA and accounting GPA must each be at least 3.0. Must be Colorado resident.

Academic Fields/Career Goals: Accounting.

Award: Scholarship for use in junior, senior, graduate, or postgraduate years; not renewable. *Number:* 15–20. *Amount:* $1000.

Eligibility Requirements: Applicant must be enrolled or expecting to enroll full or part-time at a four-year institution or university; resident of Colorado and studying in Colorado. Applicant must have 3.0 GPA or higher. Available to U.S. citizens.

Application Requirements: Application, references, transcript. *Deadline:* varies.

Contact: Gena Mantz, Membership Coordinator
Colorado Society of Certified Public Accountants Educational Foundation
7979 East Tufts Avenue, Suite 500
Denver, CO 80237-2845
Phone: 303-741-8613
Fax: 303-773-2877
E-mail: gmantz@cocpa.org

COLORADO HIGH SCHOOL SCHOLARSHIPS

Scholarships awarded in the Spring each year to outstanding high school seniors who plan to major in accounting.

Academic Fields/Career Goals: Accounting.

Award: Scholarship for use in freshman year. *Amount:* $1000.

Eligibility Requirements: Applicant must be enrolled or expecting to enroll full or part-time at an institution or university; resident of Colorado and studying in Colorado. Applicant must have 3.0 GPA or higher. Available to U.S. citizens.

Application Requirements: Application, test scores, transcript. *Deadline:* March 1.

Contact: Gena Mantz, Membership Coordinator
Colorado Society of Certified Public Accountants Educational Foundation
7979 East Tufts Avenue, Suite 500
Denver, CO 80237-2845
Phone: 303-741-8613
Fax: 303-773-2877
E-mail: gmantz@cocpa.org

ETHNIC DIVERSITY COLLEGE AND UNIVERSITY SCHOLARSHIPS

Award of $1000 for declared accounting major at a Colorado college or university. Must be African-American, Hispanic, Asian-American, American-Indian, or Pacific Islander and have completed at least 8 semester hours of accounting courses. Scholarship is awarded for the fall semester. Must be Colorado resident. Minimum 3.0 GPA required.

Academic Fields/Career Goals: Accounting.

Award: Scholarship for use in sophomore, junior, senior, graduate, or postgraduate years; not renewable. *Number:* 2. *Amount:* $1000.

Eligibility Requirements: Applicant must be American Indian/Alaska Native, Asian/Pacific Islander, Black (non-Hispanic), or Hispanic; enrolled or expecting to enroll full or part-time at a four-year institution or university; resident of Colorado and studying in Colorado. Applicant must have 3.0 GPA or higher. Available to U.S. citizens.

Application Requirements: Application, transcript. *Deadline:* June 30.

Contact: Gena Mantz, Membership Coordinator
Colorado Society of Certified Public Accountants Educational Foundation
7979 East Tufts Avenue, Suite 500
Denver, CO 80237-2845
Phone: 303-741-8613
Fax: 303-773-2877
E-mail: gmantz@cocpa.org

ETHNIC DIVERSITY HIGH SCHOOL SCHOLARSHIPS

Scholarships awarded in the Spring each year to outstanding high school seniors who plan to major in accounting.

Academic Fields/Career Goals: Accounting.

Award: Scholarship for use in freshman year. *Amount:* $1000.

Eligibility Requirements: Applicant must be American Indian/Alaska Native, Asian/Pacific Islander, Black (non-Hispanic), or Hispanic; enrolled or expecting to enroll full or part-time at an institution or university; resident of Colorado and studying in Colorado. Applicant must have 3.0 GPA or higher. Available to U.S. citizens.

Application Requirements: Application, test scores, transcript. *Deadline:* March 1.

Contact: Gena Mantz, Membership Coordinator
Colorado Society of Certified Public Accountants Educational Foundation
7979 East Tufts Avenue, Suite 500
Denver, CO 80237-2845
Phone: 303-741-8613
Fax: 303-773-2877
E-mail: gmantz@cocpa.org

GORDON SCHEER SCHOLARSHIP

Award of $1250 for a declared accounting major attending a college or university in Colorado. Must have completed intermediate accounting. Minimum 3.5 GPA required. Submit application, official transcript, and three references. May reapply. Must be Colorado resident.

Academic Fields/Career Goals: Accounting.

Award: Scholarship for use in sophomore, junior, senior, graduate, or postgraduate years; not renewable. *Number:* 1. *Amount:* $1250.

Eligibility Requirements: Applicant must be enrolled or expecting to enroll full or part-time at a four-year institution or university; resident of Colorado and studying in Colorado. Applicant must have 3.5 GPA or higher. Available to U.S. citizens.

Application Requirements: Application, references, transcript. *Deadline:* June 30.

Contact: Gena Mantz, Membership Coordinator
Colorado Society of Certified Public Accountants Educational Foundation
7979 East Tufts Avenue, Suite 500
Denver, CO 80237-2845
Phone: 303-741-8613
Fax: 303-773-2877
E-mail: gmantz@cocpa.org

COMMUNITY FOUNDATION FOR PALM BEACH AND MARTIN COUNTIES, INC.
http://www.yourcommunityfoundation.org

KIM LOVE SATORY SCHOLARSHIP

For female graduating senior from a Palm Beach or Martin County public or private high school interested in banking and finance. Must provide evidence of strong commitment to community service and involvement. Must demonstrate financial need.

Academic Fields/Career Goals: Accounting.

Award: Scholarship for use in freshman year; not renewable. *Number:* 1. *Amount:* $750–$2500.

Eligibility Requirements: Applicant must be high school student; planning to enroll or expecting to enroll full-time at a four-year institution or university; female; resident of Florida and must have an interest in English language or leadership. Available to U.S. citizens.

Application Requirements: Application, financial need analysis. *Deadline:* February 1.

Contact: Carolyn Jenco, Grants Manager/Scholarship Coordinator
Community Foundation for Palm Beach and Martin Counties, Inc.
700 South Dixie Highway, Suite 200
West Palm Beach, FL 33401
Phone: 561-659-6800
Fax: 561-832-6542
E-mail: cjenco@cfpbmc.org

COMMUNITY FOUNDATION OF WESTERN MASSACHUSETTS
http://www.communityfoundation.org

GREATER SPRINGFIELD ACCOUNTANTS SCHOLARSHIP

Provided to undergraduates pursuing accounting or finance who have completed their sophomore year and are residents of Massachusetts or Hartford County, Connecticut.

Academic Fields/Career Goals: Accounting; Business/Consumer Services.

Award: Scholarship for use in sophomore year; renewable. *Number:* 1–5.

Community Foundation of Western Massachusetts (continued)

Eligibility Requirements: Applicant must be enrolled or expecting to enroll full-time at a two-year or four-year institution and resident of Connecticut or Massachusetts. Available to U.S. citizens.

Application Requirements: Application, financial need analysis, transcript, parent's and student's federal income tax returns, Student Aid Report (SAR). *Deadline:* March 31.

Contact: Dorothy Theriaque, Education Associate
Community Foundation of Western Massachusetts
1500 Main Street, PO Box 15769
Springfield, MA 01115
Phone: 413-732-2858
Fax: 413-733-8565
E-mail: dtheriaque@communityfoundation.org

CONNECTICUT SOCIETY OF CERTIFIED PUBLIC ACCOUNTANTS
http://www.cs-cpa.org

CHILDREN OF CSCPA MEMBERS SCHOLARSHIP PROGRAM

Scholarships of $500 to students majoring in accounting at a Connecticut college or university, who have a parent holding membership in the Connecticut Society of CPAs. Minimum GPA of 3.0 required.

Academic Fields/Career Goals: Accounting.

Award: Scholarship for use in freshman, sophomore, junior, or senior years. *Number:* 5. *Amount:* $500.

Eligibility Requirements: Applicant must be enrolled or expecting to enroll at a four-year institution or university; resident of Connecticut and studying in Connecticut. Available to U.S. citizens.

Application Requirements: Application, transcript. *Deadline:* August 31.

Contact: Ms. Jill Wise, Academic & Student Relations Associate
Connecticut Society of Certified Public Accountants
845 Brook Street, Building Two
Rocky Hill, CT 06067-3405
Phone: 860-258-4800 Ext. 239
Fax: 860-258-4859
E-mail: jillw@cs-cpa.org

CSCPA CANDIDATE'S AWARD

Scholarship of $2500 that assists students in complying with the 150-hour requirement of the Connecticut State Board of Accountancy to sit for the Uniform Certified Public Accountant Examination. An overall GPA of 3.0.

Academic Fields/Career Goals: Accounting.

Award: Scholarship for use in senior, or graduate years. *Number:* 4. *Amount:* $2500.

Eligibility Requirements: Applicant must be enrolled or expecting to enroll at an institution or university; resident of Connecticut and studying in Connecticut. Applicant or parent of applicant must be member of California Teachers Association. Applicant must have 3.0 GPA or higher. Available to U.S. citizens.

Application Requirements: Application, essay, transcript. *Deadline:* August 31.

Contact: Ms. Jill Wise, Academic & Student Relations Associate
Connecticut Society of Certified Public Accountants
845 Brook Street, Building Two
Rocky Hill, CT 06067-3405
Phone: 860-258-4800 Ext. 239
Fax: 860-258-4859
E-mail: jillw@cs-cpa.org

CSCPA JUNIOR AWARD

Scholarship for undergraduate accounting majors at Connecticut colleges or universities recognized by the Connecticut State Board of Accountancy who have completed at least 75 credits (12 of which must be in accounting courses) and have at least two semesters of undergraduate coursework remaining. Students are recommended by their accounting department faculty. Overall GPA of 3.0

Academic Fields/Career Goals: Accounting.

Award: Scholarship for use in junior or senior years. *Number:* 2. *Amount:* $400.

Eligibility Requirements: Applicant must be enrolled or expecting to enroll at a four-year institution or university; resident of Connecticut and studying in Connecticut. Applicant must have 3.0 GPA or higher. Available to U.S. citizens.

Application Requirements: Application, resume, transcript. *Deadline:* March 15.

Contact: Ms. Jill Wise, Academic & Student Relations Associate
Connecticut Society of Certified Public Accountants
845 Brook Street, Building Two
Rocky Hill, CT 06067-3405
Phone: 860-258-4800 Ext. 239
Fax: 860-258-4859
E-mail: jillw@cs-cpa.org

OUTSTANDING COMMUNITY COLLEGE ACCOUNTING STUDENT AWARD

Scholarship for Connecticut community college accounting students who plan to major in accounting at a 4-year Connecticut college or university recognized by the Connecticut State Board of Accountancy. Students are recommended by their accounting department faculty.

Academic Fields/Career Goals: Accounting.

Award: Scholarship for use in freshman, sophomore, junior, or senior years. *Amount:* $400.

Eligibility Requirements: Applicant must be enrolled or expecting to enroll at a four-year institution or university; resident of Connecticut and studying in Connecticut. Available to U.S. citizens.

Application Requirements: Application. *Deadline:* varies.

Contact: Ms. Jill Wise, Academic & Student Relations Associate
Connecticut Society of Certified Public Accountants
845 Brook Street, Building Two
Rocky Hill, CT 06067-3405
Phone: 860-258-4800 Ext. 239
Fax: 860-258-4859
E-mail: jillw@cs-cpa.org

EDUCATIONAL FOUNDATION OF THE MASSACHUSETTS SOCIETY OF CERTIFIED PUBLIC ACCOUNTANT'S
http://www.mscpaonline.org

F. GRANT WAITE, CPA, MEMORIAL SCHOLARSHIP

Scholarship available to undergraduate accounting major who has completed sophomore year. Must demonstrate financial need and superior academic standing. Preference given to married students with children. Deadline is April 19. Information available on Web site at http://www.cpatrack.com.

Academic Fields/Career Goals: Accounting.

Award: Scholarship for use in junior or senior years; not renewable. *Number:* 1. *Amount:* $1000.

Eligibility Requirements: Applicant must be enrolled or expecting to enroll full-time at a four-year institution or university. Available to U.S. citizens.

Application Requirements: Application, financial need analysis, references, transcript. *Deadline:* April 19.

Contact: Barbara M. Iannoni, Academic & Career Development Coordinator
Educational Foundation of the Massachusetts Society of Certified Public Accountant's
105 Chauncy Street
Boston, MA 02111
Phone: 617-556-4000
Fax: 617-556-4126
E-mail: biannoni@mscpaonline.org

KATHLEEN M. PEABODY, CPA, MEMORIAL SCHOLARSHIP

Scholarship available for Massachusetts resident who has completed sophomore year. Must be accounting major with plans to seek an accounting career in Massachusetts. Must demonstrate academic excellence and financial need. Information on Web site at http://www.cpatrack.com.

Academic Fields/Career Goals: Accounting.

Award: Scholarship for use in sophomore, junior, or senior years; not renewable. *Number:* 1. *Amount:* $2500.

Eligibility Requirements: Applicant must be enrolled or expecting to enroll full-time at a four-year institution or university and resident of Massachusetts. Available to U.S. citizens.

Application Requirements: Application, financial need analysis, references, transcript. *Deadline:* March 31.

Contact: Barbara M. Iannoni, Academic & Career Development Coordinator
Educational Foundation of the Massachusetts Society of Certified Public Accountant's
105 Chauncy Street
Boston, MA 02111
Phone: 617-556-4000
Fax: 617-556-4126
E-mail: biannoni@mscpaonline.org

PAYCHEX, INC. ENTREPRENEUR SCHOLARSHIP

Scholarships available to students who are residents of Massachusetts and attending a Massachusetts college or university. Must be an accounting major entering their junior year, have a minimum 3.0 GPA, and demonstrate financial need. Deadline is April 19. Application and information on Web site at http://www.cpatrack.com.

Academic Fields/Career Goals: Accounting.

Award: Scholarship for use in junior year; not renewable. *Number:* 1. *Amount:* $1000.

Eligibility Requirements: Applicant must be enrolled or expecting to enroll full-time at a four-year institution or university; resident of Massachusetts and studying in Massachusetts. Applicant must have 3.0 GPA or higher. Available to U.S. citizens.

Application Requirements: Application, financial need analysis, transcript. *Deadline:* April 19.

Contact: Barbara M. Iannoni, Academic Coordinator
Educational Foundation of the Massachusetts Society of Certified Public Accountant's
105 Chauncy Street
Boston, MA 02111
Phone: 617-556-4000
Fax: 617-556-4126
E-mail: biannoni@mscpaonline.org

STUDENT ESSAY COMPETITION

Prizes available for students enrolled in an undergraduate accounting course at a Massachusetts college or university must submit a paper of no more than 2,000 words on topics such as financial reporting, accounting principles, socio-economic accounting, forensic accounting, interface with computers, auditing, taxation accounting systems, managerial accounting or management services. Visit Web site for specific details: http://www.cpatrack.com.

Academic Fields/Career Goals: Accounting.

Award: Prize for use in freshman, sophomore, junior, or senior years; not renewable. *Number:* 3. *Amount:* $500–$1500.

Eligibility Requirements: Applicant must be enrolled or expecting to enroll at a four-year institution or university and studying in Massachusetts. Available to U.S. citizens.

Application Requirements: Applicant must enter a contest, manuscript, entry form. *Deadline:* March 31.

Contact: Barbara M. Iannoni, Academic & Career Development Coordinator
Educational Foundation of the Massachusetts Society of Certified Public Accountant's
105 Chauncy Street
Boston, MA 02111
Phone: 617-556-4000
Fax: 617-556-4126
E-mail: biannoni@mscpaonline.org

FLORIDA INSTITUTE OF CERTIFIED PUBLIC ACCOUNTANTS   http://www.ficpa.org

FICPA EDUCATIONAL FOUNDATION SCHOLARSHIPS

Scholarship for full-time or part-time (minimum of six (6) credit hours), 4th or 5th year accounting major at participating Florida colleges or universities. See Web site for list of institutions: http://www1.ficpa.org/ficpa/Visitors/Careers/EdFoundation/Scholarships/ Deadline is March 15.

Academic Fields/Career Goals: Accounting.

Award: Scholarship for use in senior year; not renewable. *Number:* up to 80. *Amount:* up to $2000.

Eligibility Requirements: Applicant must be enrolled or expecting to enroll full or part-time at a four-year institution or university; resident of Florida and studying in Florida. Available to U.S. citizens.

Application Requirements: Application, references, transcript. *Deadline:* March 15.

Contact: Betsy Wilson, Program Administrator
Florida Institute of Certified Public Accountants
325 West College Avenue
Tallahassee, FL 32301
Phone: 850-224-2727
Fax: 850-222-8190
E-mail: wilsonb@ficpa.org

1040K RACE SCHOLARSHIPS

Scholarship for an African American who is a permanent resident of Dade County. Must be a full-time, 4th- or 5th-year accounting major at one of these Florida institutions: Barry University, Florida Atlantic University, Florida International University, Florida Memorial College, Nova Southeastern University, St. Thomas University, or University of Miami. Deadline is February 15. See Web site for details: http://www1.ficpa.org/ficpa/Visitors/Careers/EdFoundation/Scholarships/Available

Academic Fields/Career Goals: Accounting.

Award: Scholarship for use in senior year; not renewable. *Number:* up to 2. *Amount:* up to $3000.

Eligibility Requirements: Applicant must be Black (non-Hispanic); enrolled or expecting to enroll full-time at a four-year institution or university; resident of Florida and studying in Florida. Available to U.S. citizens.

Application Requirements: Application, references, transcript. *Deadline:* February 15.

Contact: Betsy Wilson, Program Administrator
Florida Institute of Certified Public Accountants
325 West College Avenue
Tallahassee, FL 32301
Phone: 850-224-2727
Fax: 850-222-8190
E-mail: wilsonb@ficpa.org

FLORIDA INSTITUTE OF CPAS EDUCATIONAL FOUNDATION   http://www.ficpa.org

EDUCATIONAL FOUNDATION SCHOLARSHIPS

Scholarships are for accounting majors who are Florida residents attending Florida college/universities. Applicants must be planning to sit for CPA exam and indicate desire to practice accounting in Florida. Scholarships are granted based on educational achievement, financial need, and demonstrated professional, social, and charitable activities. Citizens of other countries may apply, if planning to work in Florida. Minimum 3.0 GPA required.

Academic Fields/Career Goals: Accounting.

Award: Scholarship for use in senior, or graduate years; not renewable. *Number:* up to 85. *Amount:* up to $2000.

Eligibility Requirements: Applicant must be enrolled or expecting to enroll full or part-time at a four-year institution or university; resident of Florida and studying in Florida. Applicant must have 3.0 GPA or higher. Available to U.S. citizens.

Application Requirements: Application, financial need analysis, references, transcript. *Deadline:* March 15.

Contact: Betsy Wilson, Educational Foundation Assistant
Florida Institute of CPAs Educational Foundation
PO Box 5437
Tallahassee, FL 32314
Phone: 850-224-2727
E-mail: wilsonb@ficpa.org

1040 K RACE SCHOLARSHIPS

Scholarships are for African-American accounting majors who are Florida residents attending Florida colleges/universities. Applicants must be planning to sit for CPA exam and indicate desire to practice accounting in Florida. Scholarships are granted based on educational achievement, financial need

Florida Institute of CPAs Educational Foundation (continued)

and demonstrated professional, social, and charitable activities. Citizens of other countries may apply, if planning to work in Florida. Must be a permanent Dade County resident.

Academic Fields/Career Goals: Accounting.

Award: Scholarship for use in senior, or graduate years; not renewable. *Number:* 1–3. *Amount:* $1000–$3000.

Eligibility Requirements: Applicant must be Black (non-Hispanic); enrolled or expecting to enroll full-time at a four-year institution or university; resident of Florida and studying in Florida. Available to U.S. citizens.

Application Requirements: Application, financial need analysis, references, transcript. *Deadline:* February 15.

Contact: Betsy Wilson, Educational Foundation Assistant
Florida Institute of CPAs Educational Foundation
325 West College Avenue
PO Box 5437
Tallahassee, FL 32314
Phone: 850-224-2727 Ext. 200
Fax: 850-222-8190
E-mail: wilsonb@ficpa.org

GEORGIA SOCIETY OF CERTIFIED PUBLIC ACCOUNTANTS   http://www.gscpa.org

BEN W. BRANNON MEMORIAL SCHOLARSHIP FUND

Scholarship for a rising junior or senior undergraduate accounting major or a graduate student enrolled in a master's level accounting or business administration program at a public or private college or university accredited by the Southern Association of Colleges & Schools. Applicant must demonstrate a commitment to pursuing a career in accounting, be a resident of Georgia, and maintain an overall GPA of 3.0.

Academic Fields/Career Goals: Accounting; Business/Consumer Services.

Award: Scholarship for use in junior, senior, or graduate years. *Number:* 1.

Eligibility Requirements: Applicant must be enrolled or expecting to enroll at a four-year institution or university and resident of Georgia. Applicant must have 3.0 GPA or higher. Available to U.S. citizens.

Application Requirements: Application, driver's license, essay, resume, transcript. *Deadline:* April 15.

Contact: Shelly Grunbaum
Georgia Society of Certified Public Accountants
3353 Peachtree Road NE, Suite 400
Atlanta, GA 30326-1414
Phone: 800-330-8889 Ext. 2956
Fax: 404-237-1291

CHAPTER AWARDED SCHOLARSHIPS

Scholarship for a rising junior or senior undergraduate accounting major or a graduate student enrolled in a master's level accounting or business administration program at a public or private college or university accredited by the Southern Association of Colleges & Schools. Must demonstrate commitment to pursuing a career in accounting, be a resident of Georgia, and maintain an overall GPA of 3.0. To apply for a Chapter Awarded Scholarship, contact your local GSCPA chapter.

Academic Fields/Career Goals: Accounting.

Award: Scholarship for use in junior, senior, or graduate years. *Number:* 1.

Eligibility Requirements: Applicant must be enrolled or expecting to enroll at a four-year institution or university and resident of Georgia. Applicant must have 3.0 GPA or higher. Available to U.S. citizens.

Application Requirements: Application, essay, financial need analysis, resume, test scores. *Deadline:* April 15.

Contact: Shelly Grunbaum
Georgia Society of Certified Public Accountants
3353 Peachtree Road NE, Suite 400
Atlanta, GA 30326-1414
Phone: 800-330-8889 Ext. 2956
Fax: 404-237-1291

CHERRY, BEKAERT AND HOLLAND, LLP ACCOUNTING SCHOLARSHIP

Scholarship for a rising junior or senior undergraduate accounting major or a graduate student enrolled in a master's level accounting or business administration program at a public or private college or university accredited by the Southern Association of Colleges & Schools. Must demonstrate commitment to pursuing a career in accounting, be a resident of Georgia, and maintain an overall GPA of 3.0.

Academic Fields/Career Goals: Accounting.

Award: Scholarship for use in junior, senior, or graduate years. *Number:* 1.

Eligibility Requirements: Applicant must be enrolled or expecting to enroll at a four-year institution or university and resident of Georgia. Applicant must have 3.0 GPA or higher. Available to U.S. citizens.

Application Requirements: Application, driver's license, essay, resume, transcript. *Deadline:* April 15.

Contact: Shelly Grunbaum
Georgia Society of Certified Public Accountants
3353 Peachtree Road NE, Suite 400
Atlanta, GA 30326-1414
Phone: 800-330-8889 Ext. 2956
Fax: 404-237-1291

COLLINS/MOODY - COMPANY SCHOLARSHIP

Scholarship for a rising junior or senior undergraduate accounting major or a graduate student enrolled in a master's level accounting or business administration program at a public or private college or university accredited by the Southern Association of Colleges & Schools. Must demonstrate commitment to pursuing a career in accounting, be a resident of Georgia, and maintain an overall GPA of 3.0.

Academic Fields/Career Goals: Accounting.

Award: Scholarship for use in junior, senior, or graduate years. *Number:* 1.

Eligibility Requirements: Applicant must be enrolled or expecting to enroll at a four-year institution or university and resident of Georgia. Applicant must have 3.0 GPA or higher. Available to U.S. citizens.

Application Requirements: Application, driver's license, essay, resume, transcript. *Deadline:* April 15.

Contact: Shelly Grunbaum
Georgia Society of Certified Public Accountants
3353 Peachtree Road NE, Suite 400
Atlanta, GA 30326-1414
Phone: 800-330-8889 Ext. 2956
Fax: 404-237-1291

EDUCATIONAL FOUNDATION DIRECT SCHOLARSHIPS

Scholarship for a rising junior or senior undergraduate accounting major or a graduate student enrolled in a master's level accounting or business administration program at a public or private college or university accredited by the Southern Association of Colleges & Schools. Must demonstrate commitment to pursuing a career in accounting, be a resident of Georgia, and maintain an overall GPA of 3.0.

Academic Fields/Career Goals: Accounting.

Award: Scholarship for use in junior, senior, or graduate years. *Number:* 1.

Eligibility Requirements: Applicant must be enrolled or expecting to enroll at a four-year institution or university and resident of Georgia. Applicant must have 3.0 GPA or higher. Available to U.S. citizens.

Application Requirements: Application, driver's license, essay, resume, transcript. *Deadline:* April 15.

Contact: Shelly Grunbaum
Georgia Society of Certified Public Accountants
3353 Peachtree Road NE, Suite 400
Atlanta, GA 30326-1414
Phone: 800-330-8889 Ext. 2956
Fax: 404-237-1291

GERTRUDE M. GIGLIOTTI MEMORIAL SCHOLARSHIP

Scholarship for a rising junior or senior undergraduate accounting major or a graduate student enrolled in a master's level accounting or business administration program at a public or private college or university accredited by the Southern Association of Colleges & Schools. Must demonstrate commitment to pursuing a career in accounting, be a resident of Georgia, and maintain an overall GPA of 3.0.

Academic Fields/Career Goals: Accounting.

Award: Scholarship for use in junior, senior, or graduate years.
Number: 1.

Eligibility Requirements: Applicant must be enrolled or expecting to enroll at a four-year institution or university and resident of Georgia. Applicant must have 3.0 GPA or higher. Available to U.S. citizens.

Application Requirements: Application, driver's license, essay, resume, transcript. *Deadline:* April 15.

Contact: Shelly Grunbaum
Georgia Society of Certified Public Accountants
3353 Peachtree Road NE, Suite 400
Atlanta, GA 30326-1414
Phone: 800-330-8889 Ext. 2956
Fax: 404-237-1291

HERMAN, SILVER AND ASSOCIATES SCHOLARSHIP

Scholarship for a rising junior or senior undergraduate accounting major or a graduate student enrolled in a master's level accounting or business administration program at a public or private college or university accredited by the Southern Association of Colleges & Schools. Must demonstrate commitment to pursuing a career in accounting, be a resident of Georgia, and maintain an overall GPA of 3.0.

Academic Fields/Career Goals: Accounting.

Award: Scholarship for use in junior, senior, or graduate years.
Number: 1.

Eligibility Requirements: Applicant must be enrolled or expecting to enroll at a four-year institution or university and resident of Georgia. Applicant must have 3.0 GPA or higher. Available to U.S. citizens.

Application Requirements: Application, driver's license, essay, resume, transcript. *Deadline:* April 15.

Contact: Shelly Grunbaum
Georgia Society of Certified Public Accountants
3353 Peachtree Road NE, Suite 400
Atlanta, GA 30326-1414
Phone: 800-330-8889 Ext. 2956
Fax: 404-237-1291

JULIUS M. JOHNSON MEMORIAL SCHOLARSHIP

Scholarship for a rising junior or senior undergraduate accounting major or a graduate student enrolled in a master's level accounting or business administration program at a public or private college or university accredited by the Southern Association of Colleges & Schools. Must demonstrate commitment to pursuing a career in accounting, be a resident of Georgia, and maintain an overall GPA of 3.0.

Academic Fields/Career Goals: Accounting.

Award: Scholarship for use in junior, senior, or graduate years.
Number: 1.

Eligibility Requirements: Applicant must be enrolled or expecting to enroll at a four-year institution or university and resident of Georgia. Applicant must have 3.0 GPA or higher. Available to U.S. citizens.

Application Requirements: Application, driver's license, essay, resume, transcript. *Deadline:* April 15.

Contact: Shelly Grunbaum
Georgia Society of Certified Public Accountants
3353 Peachtree Road NE, Suite 400
Atlanta, GA 30326-1414
Phone: 800-330-8889 Ext. 2956
Fax: 404-237-1291

PAYCHEX ENTREPRENEUR SCHOLARSHIP

Scholarship for a rising junior or senior undergraduate accounting major or a graduate student enrolled in a master's level accounting or business administration program at a public or private college or university accredited by the Southern Association of Colleges & Schools. Must demonstrate commitment to pursuing a career in accounting, be a resident of Georgia, and maintain an overall GPA of 3.0.

Academic Fields/Career Goals: Accounting.

Award: Scholarship for use in junior, senior, or graduate years.
Number: 1.

Eligibility Requirements: Applicant must be enrolled or expecting to enroll at a four-year institution or university and resident of Georgia. Applicant must have 3.0 GPA or higher. Available to U.S. citizens.

Application Requirements: Application, driver's license, essay, resume, transcript. *Deadline:* April 15.

Contact: Shelly Grunbaum
Georgia Society of Certified Public Accountants
3353 Peachtree Road NE, Suite 400
Atlanta, GA 30326-1414
Phone: 800-330-8889 Ext. 2956
Fax: 404-237-1291

ROBERT H. LANGE MEMORIAL SCHOLARSHIP

Scholarship for a rising junior or senior undergraduate accounting major or a graduate student enrolled in a master's level accounting or business administration program at a public or private college or university accredited by the Southern Association of Colleges & Schools. Must demonstrate commitment to pursuing a career in accounting, be a resident of Georgia, and maintain an overall GPA of 3.0.

Academic Fields/Career Goals: Accounting.

Award: Scholarship for use in junior, senior, or graduate years.
Number: 1.

Eligibility Requirements: Applicant must be enrolled or expecting to enroll at a four-year institution or university and resident of Georgia. Applicant must have 3.0 GPA or higher. Available to U.S. citizens.

Application Requirements: Application, driver's license, essay, resume, transcript. *Deadline:* April 15.

Contact: Shelly Grunbaum
Georgia Society of Certified Public Accountants
3353 Peachtree Road NE, Suite 400
Atlanta, GA 30326-1414
Phone: 800-330-8889 Ext. 2956
Fax: 404-237-1291

THOMAS CONRETE OF GEORGIA SCHOLARSHIP

Scholarship for a rising junior or senior undergraduate accounting major or a graduate student enrolled in a master's level accounting or business administration program at a public or private college or university accredited by the Southern Association of Colleges & Schools. Must demonstrate commitment to pursuing a career in accounting, be a resident of Georgia, and maintain an overall GPA of 3.0.

Academic Fields/Career Goals: Accounting.

Award: Scholarship for use in junior, senior, or graduate years.
Number: 1.

Eligibility Requirements: Applicant must be enrolled or expecting to enroll at a four-year institution or university and resident of Georgia. Applicant must have 3.0 GPA or higher. Available to U.S. citizens.

Application Requirements: Application, driver's license, essay, resume, transcript. *Deadline:* April 15.

Contact: Shelly Grunbaum
Georgia Society of Certified Public Accountants
3353 Peachtree Road NE, Suite 400
Atlanta, GA 30326-1414
Phone: 800-330-8889 Ext. 2956
Fax: 404-237-1291

GOVERNMENT FINANCE OFFICERS ASSOCIATION
http://www.gfoa.org

MINORITIES IN GOVERNMENT FINANCE SCHOLARSHIP

Award given to upper-division undergraduate or graduate student of public administration, governmental accounting, finance, political science, economics, or business administration to recognize outstanding performance by minority student preparing for career in state and local government finance.

Academic Fields/Career Goals: Accounting; Business/Consumer Services; Economics; Political Science; Public Policy and Administration.

Award: Scholarship for use in freshman, sophomore, junior, senior, graduate, or postgraduate years; not renewable. *Number:* 1. *Amount:* $5000.

Eligibility Requirements: Applicant must be American Indian/Alaska Native, Asian/Pacific Islander, Black (non-Hispanic), or Hispanic and enrolled or expecting to enroll full or part-time at a four-year institution or university. Available to U.S. and Canadian citizens.

Application Requirements: Application, essay, resume, references, transcript. *Deadline:* varies.

Contact: Jake Lorentz, Assistant Director
Government Finance Officers Association
Scholarship Committee
203 North LaSalle Street, Suite 2700
Chicago, IL 60601-1210
Phone: 312-977-9700 Ext. 267
Fax: 312-977-4806
E-mail: jlorentz@gfoa.org

GRAND RAPIDS COMMUNITY FOUNDATION
http://www.grfoundation.org

ECONOMIC CLUB OF GRAND RAPIDS BUSINESS STUDY ABROAD SCHOLARSHIP

Financial assistance to students studying business abroad. Individual must be interested in contributing to the growing economic health of the Grand Rapids, Michigan metropolitan area. Refer to Web site for details and application: http://www.grfoundation.org

Academic Fields/Career Goals: Accounting; Business/Consumer Services; Computer Science/Data Processing; Economics; Engineering/Technology; Engineering-Related Technologies; Physical Sciences and Math.

Award: Scholarship for use in sophomore, junior, senior, or graduate years. *Number:* 1. *Amount:* up to $2500.

Eligibility Requirements: Applicant must be enrolled or expecting to enroll at a four-year institution or university and resident of Michigan. Applicant must have 3.0 GPA or higher. Available to U.S. citizens.

Application Requirements: Application, essay, references, transcript. *Deadline:* April 1.

Contact: See Web site.

GREATER WASHINGTON SOCIETY OF CERTIFIED PUBLIC ACCOUNTANTS
http://www.gwscpa.org

GREATER WASHINGTON SOCIETY OF CPAS SCHOLARSHIP

Scholarship available to accounting students. School must offer an accounting degree that qualifies graduates to sit for the CPA exam (must meet the 150-hour rule). Must have at least a 3.0 average in major courses.

Academic Fields/Career Goals: Accounting.

Award: Scholarship for use in senior, or graduate years. *Number:* 2. *Amount:* $5000.

Eligibility Requirements: Applicant must be enrolled or expecting to enroll full or part-time at a four-year institution or university; resident of District of Columbia and studying in District of Columbia. Applicant must have 3.0 GPA or higher. Available to U.S. citizens.

Application Requirements: Application, essay, resume, references, transcript. *Deadline:* July 15.

Contact: Greater Washington Society of Certified Public Accountants
1828 L Street, NW, Suite 900
Washington, DC 20036
Phone: 202-204-8014
Fax: 202-204-8015
E-mail: info@gwscpa.org

HAWAII SOCIETY OF CERTIFIED PUBLIC ACCOUNTANTS
http://www.hscpa.org

HSCPA SCHOLARSHIP PROGRAM FOR ACCOUNTING STUDENTS

Scholarship for Hawaii resident currently attending an accredited Hawaii college or university with 3.0 GPA. Must be majoring, or concentrating, in accounting with the intention to sit for the CPA exam, and have completed an intermediate accounting course. Deadline is January 31. Number of awards vary from year to year.

Academic Fields/Career Goals: Accounting.

Award: Scholarship for use in freshman, sophomore, junior, or senior years; not renewable. *Amount:* $500–$1500.

Eligibility Requirements: Applicant must be enrolled or expecting to enroll full-time at a two-year institution or university. Applicant must have 3.0 GPA or higher. Available to U.S. citizens.

Application Requirements: Application, references, transcript. *Deadline:* January 31.

Contact: Kathy Castillo, Executive Director
Hawaii Society of Certified Public Accountants
900 Fort Street Mall, Suite 850
Honolulu, HI 96813
Phone: 808-537-9475
Fax: 808-537-3520
E-mail: info@hscpa.org

HISPANIC COLLEGE FUND, INC.
http://www.hispanicfund.org

DENNY'S/HISPANIC COLLEGE FUND SCHOLARSHIP

One-time scholarship award open to full-time undergraduates of Hispanic descent pursuing a degree in business or a business-related major with a GPA of 3.0 or better. Eligible students who have applied to the Hispanic College Fund need not re-apply.

Academic Fields/Career Goals: Accounting; Architecture; Business/Consumer Services; Chemical Engineering; Communications; Computer Science/Data Processing; Economics; Electrical Engineering/Electronics; Engineering/Technology; Engineering-Related Technologies; Graphics/Graphic Arts/Printing; Hospitality Management.

Award: Scholarship for use in freshman, sophomore, junior, or senior years; not renewable. *Number:* 80–100. *Amount:* $500–$5000.

Eligibility Requirements: Applicant must be Hispanic and enrolled or expecting to enroll full-time at a two-year or four-year institution or university. Applicant must have 3.0 GPA or higher. Available to U.S. citizens.

Application Requirements: Application, essay, financial need analysis, resume, references, test scores, transcript, college acceptance letter, copy of taxes, copy of Student Aid Report (SAR). *Deadline:* April 15.

Contact: Stina Augustsson, Program Manager
Hispanic College Fund, Inc.
1717 Pennsylvania Avenue, NW, Suite 460
Washington, DC 20006
Phone: 202-296-5400
Fax: 202-296-3774
E-mail: hcf-info@hispanicfund.org

ICI EDUCATIONAL FOUNDATION SCHOLARSHIP PROGRAM

Program intended for undergraduate student pursuing his or her associate's or bachelor's degree in business, computer science, or engineering. Applicant must be U.S. citizen of Hispanic background; May reside in U.S. or Puerto Rico. Must attend college in U.S. or Puerto Rico. Online application only: http://www.hispanicfund.org

Academic Fields/Career Goals: Accounting; Business/Consumer Services; Computer Science/Data Processing; Engineering/Technology.

Award: Scholarship for use in freshman, sophomore, junior, senior, or graduate years; not renewable. *Number:* varies. *Amount:* $500–$5000.

Eligibility Requirements: Applicant must be Hispanic and enrolled or expecting to enroll full-time at a two-year or four-year institution or university. Applicant must have 3.0 GPA or higher. Available to U.S. citizens.

Application Requirements: Application. *Deadline:* April 15.

Contact: Stina Augustsson, Program Manager
Hispanic College Fund, Inc.
1717 Pennsylvania Avenue, NW, Suite 460
Washington, DC 20006
Phone: 202-296-5400
Fax: 202-296-3774
E-mail: hcf-info@hispanicfund.org

M & T BANK/ HISPANIC COLLEGE FUND SCHOLARSHIP PROGRAM

One-time scholarship open to full-time undergraduates of Hispanic descent pursuing a degree in business, accounting, economics, or finance. Must be a U.S. citizen residing in Maryland, Pennsylvania, Virginia, or New York and have a minimum 3.0 GPA. Eligible students who have applied to the Hispanic College Fund need not re-apply.

Academic Fields/Career Goals: Accounting; Business/Consumer Services; Computer Science/Data Processing; Economics; Engineering/Technology; Engineering-Related Technologies.

Award: Scholarship for use in freshman, sophomore, junior, or senior years; not renewable. *Number:* 5–10. *Amount:* $500–$5000.

Eligibility Requirements: Applicant must be Hispanic; enrolled or expecting to enroll full-time at a two-year or four-year institution or university and resident of Maryland, New York, Pennsylvania, or Virginia. Applicant must have 3.0 GPA or higher. Available to U.S. citizens.

Application Requirements: Application, essay, financial need analysis, resume, references, transcript, college acceptance letter, copy of taxes, copy of Student Aid Report (SAR). *Deadline:* April 15.

Contact: Stina Augustsson, Program Manager
Hispanic College Fund, Inc.
1717 Pennsylvania Avenue, NW, Suite 460
Washington, DC 20006
Phone: 202-296-5400
Fax: 202-296-3774
E-mail: hcf-info@hispanicfund.org

ILLINOIS CPA SOCIETY   http://www.icpas.org

HERMAN J. NEAL SCHOLARSHIP

Scholarships of $4000 each available to African-American students who demonstrate strong academic performance in their goal to become a CPA and would benefit from scholarship support. College seniors as well as individuals that have graduated and wish to return to school to complete the coursework needed to become a CPA are encouraged to apply.

Academic Fields/Career Goals: Accounting.

Award: Scholarship for use in senior year. *Number:* 2. *Amount:* $4000.

Eligibility Requirements: Applicant must be Black (non-Hispanic); enrolled or expecting to enroll at a four-year institution or university; resident of Illinois and studying in Illinois. Available to U.S. citizens.

Application Requirements: Application. *Deadline:* varies.

Contact: Veronica Gomez, Manager
Phone: 312-993-0407 Ext. 208

INSTITUTE OF MANAGEMENT ACCOUNTANTS   http://www.imanet.org

INSTITUTE OF MANAGEMENT ACCOUNTANTS MEMORIAL EDUCATION FUND DIVERSITY SCHOLARSHIPS

One-time award for IMA student member pursuing a career in management accounting, financial management, and information technology. Must be U.S. or Canadian citizen. Preference given to minority students, and students with physical disabilities. Application deadline is February 15.

Academic Fields/Career Goals: Accounting.

Award: Scholarship for use in junior, senior, graduate, or postgraduate years; not renewable. *Number:* varies. *Amount:* $1000–$3000.

Eligibility Requirements: Applicant must be enrolled or expecting to enroll full or part-time at a four-year institution or university. Applicant must be physically disabled. Applicant must have 3.0 GPA or higher. Available to U.S. and Canadian citizens.

Application Requirements: Application, essay, resume, references, transcript. *Deadline:* February 15.

Contact: Susan Bender
Phone: 800-638-4427 Ext. 1543
E-mail: students@imanet.org

INSTITUTE OF MANAGEMENT ACCOUNTANTS MEMORIAL EDUCATION FUND SCHOLARSHIPS

Scholarships for IMA undergraduate or graduate student members studying at accredited institutions in the U.S. and Puerto Rico. Must be pursuing a career in management accounting, financial management, or information technology, and have a minimum GPA of 2.8. Awards based on academic merit, IMA participation, strength of recommendations, and quality of written statements.

Academic Fields/Career Goals: Accounting.

Award: Scholarship for use in freshman, sophomore, junior, senior, or graduate years; not renewable. *Number:* 6–12. *Amount:* $1000–$2500.

Eligibility Requirements: Applicant must be enrolled or expecting to enroll full or part-time at a two-year or four-year institution. Applicant must have 3.0 GPA or higher. Available to U.S. citizens.

Application Requirements: Application, essay, resume, references, transcript. *Deadline:* February 15.

Contact: Jodi Ryan, Scholarship Coordinator
Institute of Management Accountants
10 Paragon Drive
Montvale, NJ 07645
Phone: 201-573-9000

STUART CAMERON AND MARGARET MCLEOD MEMORIAL SCHOLARSHIP

Scholarships for IMA undergraduate or graduate student members studying at accredited institutions in the U.S. and Puerto Rico, and carrying 12 credits per semester. Must be pursuing a career in management accounting, financial management, or information technology, and have a minimum GPA of 2.8. Awards based on academic merit, IMA participation, strength of recommendations, and quality of written statements.

Academic Fields/Career Goals: Accounting; Business/Consumer Services.

Award: Scholarship for use in junior or senior years; not renewable. *Number:* 1. *Amount:* up to $5000.

Eligibility Requirements: Applicant must be enrolled or expecting to enroll full or part-time at a two-year or four-year institution. Available to U.S. citizens.

Application Requirements: Application, essay, resume, transcript. *Deadline:* February 15.

Contact: Jodi Ryan, Scholarship Coordinator
Institute of Management Accountants
10 Paragon Drive
Montvale, NJ 07645
Phone: 201-573-9000

KENTUCKY SOCIETY OF CERTIFIED PUBLIC ACCOUNTANTS   http://www.kycpa.org

KENTUCKY SOCIETY OF CERTIFIED PUBLIC ACCOUNTANTS COLLEGE SCHOLARSHIP

Nonrenewable award for accounting majors at a Kentucky college or university. Must rank in upper third of class or have a minimum 3.0 GPA. Must be a Kentucky resident.

Academic Fields/Career Goals: Accounting.

Award: Scholarship for use in sophomore, junior, or senior years; not renewable. *Number:* up to 3. *Amount:* $1000.

Eligibility Requirements: Applicant must be enrolled or expecting to enroll full-time at a two-year or four-year institution or university; resident of Kentucky and studying in Kentucky. Applicant must have 3.0 GPA or higher. Available to U.S. citizens.

Kentucky Society of Certified Public Accountants (continued)

Application Requirements: Application, essay, references, transcript. *Deadline:* February 25.

Contact: Jenni Buckner
    Phone: 502-266-5272
    E-mail: jbuckner@kycpa.org

KENTUCKY SOCIETY OF CERTIFIED PUBLIC ACCOUNTANTS HIGH SCHOOL SCHOLARSHIPS

One-time award for Kentucky high school seniors interested in becoming a certified public accountant. For use full time at a Kentucky four-year institution only. Financial need may be considered when judging equally qualified candidates. Application deadline March 30.

Academic Fields/Career Goals: Accounting.

Award: Scholarship for use in freshman year; not renewable. *Number:* up to 8. *Amount:* $500.

Eligibility Requirements: Applicant must be high school student; planning to enroll or expecting to enroll full-time at a four-year institution or university; resident of Kentucky and studying in Kentucky. Available to U.S. citizens.

Application Requirements: Application, essay, references, transcript, ACT and/or SAT scores. *Deadline:* March 30.

Contact: Chad Sleczkowski, Public Relations Manager
    Kentucky Society of Certified Public Accountants
    1735 Alliant Avenue
    Louisville, KY 40299
    Phone: 502-266-5272
    Fax: 502-261-9512
    E-mail: chads@kycpa.org

LATINO BUSINESS PROFESSIONALS (LBP) OF NORTHERN CALIFORNIA   http://www.lbpbayarea.org

CPA REVIEW COURSE SCHOLARSHIP

Scholarship for an enrolled college student who will graduate with at a minimum, a baccalaureate degree. Must be an LBP student member. Must have a minimum 2.0 GPA. For further information see Web site http://www.lbpbayarea.org.

Academic Fields/Career Goals: Accounting.

Award: Scholarship for use in freshman, sophomore, junior, or senior years. *Amount:* up to $1000.

Eligibility Requirements: Applicant must be enrolled or expecting to enroll at a four-year institution or university. Available to U.S. citizens.

Application Requirements: Application, essay, financial need analysis. *Deadline:* February 17.

Contact: CPA Review Course Scholarship
    Latino Business Professionals (LBP) of Northern California
    PO Box 193296
    1346 The Alameda, No. A-210
    San Jose, CA 95126
    E-mail: LBP.CPA.Scholarships@gmail.com

LAWRENCE P. DOSS SCHOLARSHIP FOUNDATION   http://www.lawrencepdossfnd.org

LAWRENCE P. DOSS SCHOLARSHIP FOUNDATION

Renewable scholarships are available to residents of Michigan who are seniors graduating from a high school in the greater Detroit area. Must be pursuing a degree in accounting, finance, management or business. Financial need considered. For more details see Web site: http://www.lawrencepdossfnd.org

Academic Fields/Career Goals: Accounting; Business/Consumer Services.

Award: Scholarship for use in freshman, sophomore, junior, or senior years; renewable. *Number:* 5. *Amount:* $5000.

Eligibility Requirements: Applicant must be high school student; planning to enroll or expecting to enroll full-time at a four-year institution or university; single and resident of Michigan. Applicant must have 2.5 GPA or higher. Available to U.S. citizens.

Application Requirements: Application, essay, financial need analysis, interview, references, test scores, transcript. *Deadline:* March 15.

Contact: Lawrence P. Doss Scholarship Foundation
    7 Oak Station
    PO Box 351037
    Detroit, MI 48325

MARYLAND ASSOCIATION OF CERTIFIED PUBLIC ACCOUNTANTS EDUCATIONAL FOUNDATION   http://www.tomorrowscpa.org

STUDENT SCHOLARSHIP IN ACCOUNTING MD ASSOCIATION OF CPAS

Award for Maryland residents who will have completed at least 60 credit hours at a Maryland college or university by the time of the award. Must have 3.0 GPA, demonstrate commitment to 150 semester hours of education, and intend to pursue a career as a certified public accountant. Number of awards varies. Must submit accounting department chairman's signature on required statement. Must be a member of the tomorrows CPA program. U.S. citizenship required. See Web site at http://www.tomorrowscpa.org for further details.

Academic Fields/Career Goals: Accounting.

Award: Scholarship for use in junior, senior, or graduate years; renewable. *Number:* up to 20. *Amount:* $1000.

Eligibility Requirements: Applicant must be enrolled or expecting to enroll full-time at a two-year or four-year institution or university; resident of Maryland and studying in Maryland. Applicant must have 3.0 GPA or higher. Available to U.S. citizens.

Application Requirements: Application, financial need analysis, transcript. *Deadline:* April 15.

Contact: Richard Rabicoff, Director of Communications and Marketing
    Phone: 800-782-2036

MICHIGAN ASSOCIATION OF CPAS   http://www.michcpa.org

FIFTH/GRADUATE YEAR STUDENT SCHOLARSHIP

Scholarship for full-time student in senior year, or a student with a combination of education and employment (defined as a minimum of two classes per term and 20 hours per week of employment). Must be majoring in accounting, and a U.S. citizen. Deadline is January 15.

Academic Fields/Career Goals: Accounting.

Award: Scholarship for use in senior year; not renewable. *Number:* 16–22. *Amount:* up to $4000.

Eligibility Requirements: Applicant must be enrolled or expecting to enroll full-time at an institution or university. Available to U.S. citizens.

Application Requirements: Application, essay, financial need analysis, references, transcript. *Deadline:* January 15.

Contact: Michelle Mohan, MACPA Academic Services Specialist
    Michigan Association of CPAs
    5480 Corporate Drive, Suite 200
    Troy, MI 48007-5068
    Phone: 248-267-3700
    Fax: 248-267-3737
    E-mail: macpa@michcpa.org

MINNESOTA SOCIETY OF CERTIFIED PUBLIC ACCOUNTANTS   http://www.mncpa.cor/information/l_index.asp

THE MNCPA SCHOLARSHIP PROGRAM

Scholarships given for graduate study in accounting to students from a Minnesota college or university who passed the CPA exam during the previous year. Must be a sophomore, junior or senior (going on to graduate school). At least a 3.0 GPA in accounting.

Academic Fields/Career Goals: Accounting.

Award: Scholarship for use in sophomore, junior, or senior years. *Amount:* $1000.

Eligibility Requirements: Applicant must be enrolled or expecting to enroll at a four-year institution or university; resident of Minnesota and studying in Minnesota. Applicant must have 3.0 GPA or higher. Available to U.S. citizens.

Application Requirements: Application. *Deadline:* varies.

Contact: MNCPA Scholarship Program
Minnesota Society of Certified Public Accountants
1650 West 82nd Street, Suite 600
Bloomington, MN 55431
Phone: 952-831-2707
Fax: 952-831-7875

MONTANA SOCIETY OF CERTIFIED PUBLIC ACCOUNTANTS   http://www.mscpa.org

MONTANA SOCIETY OF CERTIFIED PUBLIC ACCOUNTANTS SCHOLARSHIP

Scholarship available to one student in each of these four schools: Montana State University Billings, MSU Bozeman, Carroll College, and University of Montana. Must be accouting major, at least a junior standing with at least one semester of coursework remaining, minimum GPA of 2.75 overall and 3.0 in business courses, graduate students eligible. Preference will be given to student members of the MSCPA.

Academic Fields/Career Goals: Accounting.

Award: Scholarship for use in junior, senior, or graduate years. *Number:* 4. *Amount:* $1000.

Eligibility Requirements: Applicant must be enrolled or expecting to enroll at a four-year institution or university; resident of Montana and studying in Montana. Applicant must have 3.0 GPA or higher. Available to U.S. citizens.

Application Requirements: Application. *Deadline:* varies.

Contact: Susan Lively, Administrative Assistant
Montana Society of Certified Public Accountants
PO Box 138
Helena, MT 59624-0138
Phone: 406-442-7301
Fax: 406-443-7278
E-mail: susan@mscpa.org

NATIONAL BLACK MBA ASSOCIATION-TWIN CITIES CHAPTER   http://www.nbmbaatc.org

TWIN CITIES CHAPTER UNDERGRADUATE SCHOLARSHIP

Award for minority students in first, second, third or fourth year full-time in an accredited undergraduate business or management program during the fall semester working toward a bachelors degree. Get application from Web site at http://www.nbmbaatc.org.

Academic Fields/Career Goals: Accounting; Business/Consumer Services.

Award: Scholarship for use in freshman, sophomore, junior, or senior years. *Number:* 5. *Amount:* up to $3500.

Eligibility Requirements: Applicant must be Black (non-Hispanic) and enrolled or expecting to enroll full-time at a four-year institution or university. Available to U.S. citizens.

Application Requirements: Application, essay, transcript. *Deadline:* April 29.

Contact: Janine L. Sanders, Scholarship Chair
National Black MBA Association-Twin Cities Chapter
PO Box 2709
Minneapolis, MN 55402
Phone: 612-626-9762
E-mail: scholar@nbmbaatc.org

TWIN CITIES GRADUATE MBA SCHOLARSHIP

Scholarships for full/part-time outstanding African-American students enrolled in a Minnesota graduate business or management program in the fall or Minnesota residents enrolled in a business or management program in the fall. Resume is required in addition to application which is available on the web at http://www.nbmbaatc.org/scholarships.html.

Academic Fields/Career Goals: Accounting; Business/Consumer Services.

Award: Scholarship for use in senior, or graduate years. *Number:* varies. *Amount:* $500–$3500.

Eligibility Requirements: Applicant must be Black (non-Hispanic); enrolled or expecting to enroll full or part-time at a four-year

institution or university; resident of Minnesota and studying in Minnesota. Available to U.S. citizens.

Application Requirements: Application, essay, photo, resume, transcript. *Deadline:* April 29.

Contact: Janine L. Sanders, Scholarship Chair
National Black MBA Association-Twin Cities Chapter
PO Box 2709
Minneapolis, MN 55402
Phone: 612-626-9762
E-mail: scholar@nbmbaatc.org

NATIONAL CONFERENCE OF CPA PRACTITIONERS, INC.   http://www.nccpap.org

NATIONAL CONFERENCE OF CPA PRACTITIONERS, INC. SCHOLARSHIP

Scholarship awarded to outstanding graduating high school seniors planning to pursue a career as a certified public accountant. Have a GPA of at least 3.3. Deadline is May 1.

Academic Fields/Career Goals: Accounting.

Award: Scholarship for use in freshman year; not renewable. *Amount:* $1000.

Eligibility Requirements: Applicant must be high school student and planning to enroll or expecting to enroll full-time at an institution or university. Applicant must have 3.0 GPA or higher. Available to U.S. citizens.

Application Requirements: Application, transcript. *Deadline:* May 1.

Contact: Scholarship Committee
National Conference of CPA Practitioners, Inc.
22 Jericho Turnpike, Suite 110
Mineola, NY 11501
Phone: 516-333-8282
Fax: 516-333-4099
E-mail: lanak.nccpap@verizon.net

NATIONAL SOCIETY OF ACCOUNTANTS   http://www.nsacct.org

NATIONAL SOCIETY OF ACCOUNTANTS SCHOLARSHIP

Awards available to undergraduate students. Applicants must maintain a 3.0 GPA and have declared a major in accounting. Must submit an appraisal form and transcripts in addition to application. Must be U.S. or Canadian citizen attending an accredited U.S. school. One-time award of $500-$1000.

Academic Fields/Career Goals: Accounting.

Award: Scholarship for use in freshman, sophomore, junior, or senior years; not renewable. *Number:* 36. *Amount:* $500–$1000.

Eligibility Requirements: Applicant must be enrolled or expecting to enroll full or part-time at a two-year or four-year institution or university. Applicant must have 3.0 GPA or higher. Available to U.S. and Canadian citizens.

Application Requirements: Application, transcript, appraisal form. *Deadline:* March 10.

Contact: Susan E. Noell, Director of Education Programs
National Society of Accountants
1010 North Fairfax Street
Alexandria, VA 22314-1574
Phone: 703-549-6400
Fax: 703-549-2984
E-mail: snoell@nsacct.org

NSA LOUIS AND FANNIE SAGER MEMORIAL SCHOLARSHIP AWARD

Up to $1000 will be awarded annually to a graduate of a Virginia public high school who is enrolled as an undergraduate at a Virginia college or university. Applicant must major in accounting. Must submit proof of graduation from a Virginia public school.

Academic Fields/Career Goals: Accounting.

Award: Scholarship for use in freshman, sophomore, junior, or senior years; not renewable. *Number:* 1. *Amount:* $500–$1000.

Eligibility Requirements: Applicant must be high school student; planning to enroll or expecting to enroll full or part-time at a two-year or four-year institution or university; resident of Virginia and studying in Virginia. Applicant must have 3.0 GPA or higher. Available to U.S. and Canadian citizens.

National Society of Accountants (continued)

Application Requirements: Application, transcript, appraisal form. *Deadline:* March 10.

Contact: Susan E. Noell
National Society of Accountants
1010 North Fairfax Street
Alexandria, VA 22314-1574
Phone: 703-549-6400 Ext. 1312
E-mail: snoell@nsacct.org

STANLEY H. STEARMAN SCHOLARSHIP

One award for accounting major who is a relative of an active, retired, or deceased member of National Society of Accountants. Must be citizen of the United States or Canada and attend school in the United States. Minimum GPA of 3.0 required. Not available for freshman year. Submit application, appraisal form, and letter of intent.

Academic Fields/Career Goals: Accounting.

Award: Scholarship for use in freshman, sophomore, junior, senior, or graduate years; renewable. *Number:* 1. *Amount:* up to $2000.

Eligibility Requirements: Applicant must be enrolled or expecting to enroll full or part-time at a two-year or four-year institution or university. Applicant or parent of applicant must be member of National Society of Accountants. Applicant must have 3.0 GPA or higher. Available to U.S. and Canadian citizens.

Application Requirements: Application, essay, transcript, appraisal form. *Deadline:* March 10.

Contact: Susan E. Noell, Director of Education Programs
National Society of Accountants
1010 North Fairfax Street
Alexandria, VA 22314-1574
Phone: 703-549-6400 Ext. 1312
Fax: 703-549-2984
E-mail: snoell@nsacct.org

THE CHARLES EARP MEMORIAL SCHOLARSHIP

Annual award for the student designated as most outstanding of all National Society of Accountants scholarship recipients: an additional stipend of approximately $200 and a beautiful plaque.

Academic Fields/Career Goals: Accounting.

Award: Scholarship for use in freshman, sophomore, junior, or senior years. *Amount:* up to $200.

Eligibility Requirements: Applicant must be enrolled or expecting to enroll at a four-year institution. Available to U.S. citizens.

Application Requirements: Application. *Deadline:* March 10.

Contact: Susan E. Noell
National Society of Accountants
1010 North Fairfax Street
Alexandria, VA 22314-1574
Phone: 703-549-6400 Ext. 1312
E-mail: snoell@nsacct.org

NEBRASKA SOCIETY OF CERTIFIED PUBLIC ACCOUNTANTS
http://www.nescpa.com

NEBRASKA SOCIETY OF CPAS SCHOLARSHIP

Scholarship for junior in a Nebraska college or university. Must be interested in becoming CPA.

Academic Fields/Career Goals: Accounting.

Award: Scholarship for use in junior year. *Amount:* $700–$2000.

Eligibility Requirements: Applicant must be enrolled or expecting to enroll at a four-year institution or university. Available to U.S. citizens.

Application Requirements: Application. *Deadline:* varies.

Contact: Accounting Scholarships
Nebraska Society of Certified Public Accountants
635 South 14th Street, Suite 330
Lincoln, NE 68508
Phone: 402-476-8482
Fax: 402-476-8731
E-mail: society@nescpa.org

NEVADA SOCIETY OF CERTIFIED PUBLIC ACCOUNTANTS
http://www.nevadacpa.org

NEVADA SOCIETY OF CPAS SCHOLARSHIP

Scholarships available for accounting students in one of Nevada's four community colleges, or for juniors or seniors in either University of Nevada, Las Vegas, or University of Nevada, Reno. Must be planning a career in accounting.

Academic Fields/Career Goals: Accounting.

Award: Scholarship for use in freshman, sophomore, junior, or senior years. *Amount:* up to $1500.

Eligibility Requirements: Applicant must be enrolled or expecting to enroll at a four-year institution or university. Available to U.S. citizens.

Application Requirements: Application. *Deadline:* varies.

Contact: Sharon Uithoven, Executive Director
Nevada Society of Certified Public Accountants
5250 Neil Road, Suite 205
Reno, NV 89502
Phone: 775-826-6800 Ext. 104
Fax: 775-826-7942
E-mail: uithoven@nevadacpa.org

NEW HAMPSHIRE SOCIETY OF CERTIFIED PUBLIC ACCOUNTANTS
http://www.nhscpa.org

NEW HAMPSHIRE SOCIETY OF CERTIFIED PUBLIC ACCOUNTANTS SCHOLARSHIP FUND

One-time award for New Hampshire resident majoring full-time in accounting. Must be entering junior or senior year at a four-year college or university or pursuing a master's degree. Transcript and recommendation required. Must apply online at Web site: http://www.nhscpa.org.

Academic Fields/Career Goals: Accounting.

Award: Scholarship for use in junior, senior, or graduate years; not renewable. *Number:* varies. *Amount:* varies.

Eligibility Requirements: Applicant must be enrolled or expecting to enroll full-time at a four-year institution or university and resident of New Hampshire. Available to U.S. citizens.

Application Requirements: Application, references, transcript. *Deadline:* November 1.

Contact: Marlene Gazda, Executive Director
New Hampshire Society of Certified Public Accountants
1750 Elm Street, Suite 403
Manchester, NH 03104
Phone: 603-622-1999
Fax: 603-626-0204

NEW JERSEY SOCIETY OF CERTIFIED PUBLIC ACCOUNTANTS
http://www.njscpa.org

NEW JERSEY SOCIETY OF CERTIFIED PUBLIC ACCOUNTANTS COLLEGE SCHOLARSHIP PROGRAM

Award for college juniors or those entering an accounting-related graduate program. Based upon academic merit. Must be a New Jersey resident attending a four-year New Jersey institution. Must be nominated by accounting department chair or submit application directly. Minimum 3.0 GPA required. Interview required. One-time award of up to $3000.

Academic Fields/Career Goals: Accounting.

Award: Scholarship for use in junior, senior, or graduate years; not renewable. *Number:* 4–45. *Amount:* $2500–$3000.

Eligibility Requirements: Applicant must be enrolled or expecting to enroll full or part-time at a four-year institution or university; resident of New Jersey and studying in New Jersey. Applicant must have 3.0 GPA or higher. Available to U.S. citizens.

Application Requirements: Interview, resume, references, transcript. *Deadline:* varies.

Contact: Janice Amatucci, Student Programs Coordinator
New Jersey Society of Certified Public Accountants
425 Eagle Rock Avenue, Suite 100
Roseland, NJ 07068-1723
Phone: 973-226-4494
Fax: 973-226-7425
E-mail: jamatucci@njscpa.org

NEW JERSEY SOCIETY OF CERTIFIED PUBLIC ACCOUNTANTS HIGH SCHOOL SCHOLARSHIP PROGRAM

This program is open to all NJ high school seniors. Selection is based on a one-hour aptitude exam and the highest scorers on this exam are invited for an interview. The winners receive accounting scholarships to the college of their choice. Five-year awards range in value from $6500-$8500.

Academic Fields/Career Goals: Accounting.

Award: Scholarship for use in freshman, sophomore, junior, senior, or graduate years; renewable. *Number:* 15–20. *Amount:* $6500–$8500.

Eligibility Requirements: Applicant must be high school student; planning to enroll or expecting to enroll full-time at a four-year institution or university and resident of New Jersey. Available to U.S. citizens.

Application Requirements: Interview, test scores. *Deadline:* October 31.

Contact: Janice Amatucci, Student Programs Coordinator
New Jersey Society of Certified Public Accountants
425 Eagle Rock Avenue, Suite 100
Roseland, NJ 07068-1723
Phone: 973-226-4494
Fax: 973-226-7425
E-mail: jamatucci@njscpa.org

NEW YORK STATE EDUCATION DEPARTMENT
http://www.highered.nysed.gov

REGENTS PROFESSIONAL OPPORTUNITY SCHOLARSHIP

Scholarship for New York residents beginning or already enrolled in an approved degree-bearing program of study in New York that leads to licensure in a particular profession. See the Web site for the list of eligible professions. Must be U.S. citizen or permanent resident. Award recipients must agree to practice upon licensure in their profession in New York for 12 months for each annual payment received. Priority given to economically disadvantaged members of minority groups underrepresented in the professions.

Academic Fields/Career Goals: Accounting; Architecture; Dental Health/Services; Engineering/Technology; Health and Medical Sciences; Interior Design; Landscape Architecture; Law/Legal Services; Nursing; Pharmacy; Psychology; Social Services.

Award: Scholarship for use in freshman, sophomore, junior, senior, or graduate years. *Number:* 220. *Amount:* $1000–$5000.

Eligibility Requirements: Applicant must be enrolled or expecting to enroll full-time at a two-year or four-year institution or university; resident of New York and studying in New York. Available to U.S. citizens.

Application Requirements: *Deadline:* May 3.

Contact: Lewis J. Hall, Coordinator
New York State Education Department
Room 1078 EBA
Albany, NY 12234
Phone: 518-486-1319
Fax: 518-486-5346

NEW YORK STATE SOCIETY OF CERTIFIED PUBLIC ACCOUNTANTS FOUNDATION FOR ACCOUNTING EDUCATION
http://www.nysscpa.org

FOUNDATION FOR ACCOUNTING EDUCATION SCHOLARSHIP

Up to 200 $2500 scholarships will be given to college students to encourage them to pursue a career in accounting. Must be a New York resident studying in New York and maintaining a 3.0 GPA.

Academic Fields/Career Goals: Accounting.

Award: Scholarship for use in junior, senior, or graduate years; not renewable. *Number:* 1–200. *Amount:* $2500.

Eligibility Requirements: Applicant must be enrolled or expecting to enroll full or part-time at a four-year institution or university; resident of New York and studying in New York. Applicant must have 3.0 GPA or higher. Available to U.S. citizens.

Application Requirements: Application, financial need analysis, transcript. *Deadline:* August 1.

Contact: Mr. William Pape, Director Member Relations
New York State Society of Certified Public Accountants Foundation for Accounting Education
530 Fifth Avenue, Fifth Floor
18th Floor
New York, NY 10016-5991
Phone: 212-719-8420
Fax: 212-719-3364
E-mail: wpape@nysscpa.org

NORTH DAKOTA SOCIETY OF CERTIFIED PUBLIC ACCOUNTANTS
http://www.ndscpa.org

NORTH DAKOTA SOCIETY OF CERTIFIED PUBLIC ACCOUNTANTS SCHOLARSHIP

Scholarship for undergraduate students enrolled on a full-time basis at a four-year or upper division institution. Graduate students enrolled in a five-year accounting program or in a master's level program in accounting, business administration, finance, or taxation are also eligible.

Academic Fields/Career Goals: Accounting; Business/Consumer Services.

Award: Scholarship for use in freshman, sophomore, junior, senior, or graduate years. *Number:* 1.

Eligibility Requirements: Applicant must be enrolled or expecting to enroll full-time at a four-year institution or university. Available to U.S. citizens.

Application Requirements: Application. *Deadline:* varies.

Contact: North Dakota Society of Certified Public Accountants
2701 South Columbia Road
Grand Forks, ND 58201
Phone: 701-775-7100
Fax: 701-775-7430
E-mail: mail@ndscpa.org

ORDEAN FOUNDATION

ORDEAN SCHOLARSHIP PROGRAM

Renewable award for low-income students who are from Hermantown, Proctor, or Duluth. Students must be fully admitted into social work, management, education, accounting or nursing. Students must work in their designated field in the Duluth area for up to 3 years after graduation. Open to full-time junior or senior undergraduates. Must be U.S. citizens. Minimum 2.5 GPA required.

Academic Fields/Career Goals: Accounting; Education; Nursing; Social Services.

Award: Scholarship for use in junior or senior years; renewable. *Number:* 40–50. *Amount:* $1500–$3000.

Eligibility Requirements: Applicant must be enrolled or expecting to enroll full-time at a four-year institution or university; resident of Minnesota and studying in Minnesota. Applicant must have 2.5 GPA or higher. Available to U.S. citizens.

Application Requirements: Application, financial need analysis, transcript. *Deadline:* Continuous.

Contact: Mrs. Trish Johnson, Assistant Director of Financial Aid
Ordean Foundation
1200 Kenwood Avenue
Duluth, MN 55811
Phone: 218-723-7027
Fax: 218-723-2229
E-mail: tjohnson@css.edu

OREGON STUDENT ASSISTANCE COMMISSION
http://www.osac.state.or.us

HOMESTEAD CAPITAL HOUSING SCHOLARSHIP

Applicant must have graduated from an Oregon high school, be entering at least junior year, have a 2.75 minimum cumulative GPA, and be majoring in one of the following at a four-year Oregon or Washington college: accounting, architecture, community development, construction management, finance, real estate, or engineering (structural, civil, or environmental). Essay required. See Web site: http://www.osac.state.or.us

Academic Fields/Career Goals: Accounting; Architecture; Business/Consumer Services; Civil Engineering; Engineering/Technology; Real Estate.

Award: Scholarship for use in junior or senior years; renewable. *Number:* varies. *Amount:* $500.

Eligibility Requirements: Applicant must be enrolled or expecting to enroll full-time at a four-year institution or university; resident of Oregon and studying in Oregon or Washington. Available to U.S. and non-Canadian citizens.

Application Requirements: Application, essay, financial need analysis, transcript, activity chart. *Deadline:* March 1.

Contact: Director of Grant Programs
Oregon Student Assistance Commission
1500 Valley River Drive, Suite 100
Eugene, OR 97401-7020
Phone: 800-452-8807 Ext. 7395

OSCPA EDUCATIONAL FOUNDATION
http://www.orcpa.org

OSCPA EDUCATIONAL FOUNDATION SCHOLARSHIP PROGRAM

One-time award for students majoring in accounting. Must attend an accredited Oregon college/university or community college on full-time basis. High school seniors must have a minimum 3.5 GPA. College students must have a minimum 3.2 GPA. Must be a U.S. citizen and Oregon resident.

Academic Fields/Career Goals: Accounting.

Award: Scholarship for use in freshman, sophomore, junior, senior, graduate, or postgraduate years; not renewable. *Number:* 50–100. *Amount:* $500–$3000.

Eligibility Requirements: Applicant must be enrolled or expecting to enroll full-time at a two-year or four-year or technical institution or university; resident of Oregon and studying in Oregon. Applicant must have 3.5 GPA or higher. Available to U.S. citizens.

Application Requirements: Application, resume, references, test scores, transcript. *Deadline:* February 13.

Contact: Tonna Hollis, Member Services/Manager
OSCPA Educational Foundation
PO Box 4555
Beaverton, OR 97076-4555
Phone: 503-641-7200 Ext. 29
Fax: 503-626-2942
E-mail: tonna@orcpa.org

PENNSYLVANIA INSTITUTE OF CERTIFIED PUBLIC ACCOUNTANTS
http://www.picpa.org

JOSEPH F. TARICANI MEMORIAL SCHOLARSHIP

To promote the accounting profession and CPA credential, the PICPA awards an one-time award of $1000 to an eligible sophomore in the name of Joseph F. Taricani. Must be enrolled in a post secondary institution in Pennsylvania.

Academic Fields/Career Goals: Accounting.

Award: Scholarship for use in sophomore year; not renewable. *Number:* 1. *Amount:* up to $1000.

Eligibility Requirements: Applicant must be enrolled or expecting to enroll full-time at a two-year or four-year institution or university and studying in Pennsylvania. Applicant must have 3.0 GPA or higher. Available to U.S. and non-U.S. citizens.

Application Requirements: Application, essay, resume, references, test scores, transcript. *Deadline:* March 15.

Contact: Albert E. Trexler, Executive Director
Pennsylvania Institute of Certified Public Accountants
1650 Arch Street, 17th Floor
Philadelphia, PA 19103-2099
Phone: 215-972-6180
E-mail: atrexler@picpa.org

PENNSYLVANIA INSTITUTE OF CERTIFIED PUBLIC ACCOUNTANTS SOPHOMORE SCHOLARSHIP

To promote the accounting profession and CPA credential as an exciting and rewarding career path, the PICPA awards $33,000 annually in new scholarships to full-time sophomore undergraduate students enrolled at Pennsylvania colleges and universities. Minimum 3.0 GPA required.

Academic Fields/Career Goals: Accounting.

Award: Scholarship for use in sophomore year; renewable. *Number:* 18. *Amount:* $1500–$3000.

Eligibility Requirements: Applicant must be enrolled or expecting to enroll full-time at a two-year or four-year institution or university and studying in Pennsylvania. Applicant must have 3.0 GPA or higher. Available to U.S. and non-U.S. citizens.

Application Requirements: Application, essay, resume, references, test scores. *Deadline:* March 15.

Contact: Albert E. Trexler, Executive Director
Pennsylvania Institute of Certified Public Accountants
1650 Arch Street, 17th Floor
Philadelphia, PA 19103-2099
Phone: 215-972-6180
E-mail: atrexler@picpa.org

RHODE ISLAND FOUNDATION
http://www.rifoundation.org

CARL W. CHRISTIANSEN SCHOLARSHIP

Award for Rhode Island residents pursuing study in accounting or related fields.

Academic Fields/Career Goals: Accounting.

Award: Scholarship for use in freshman, sophomore, junior, senior, or graduate years. *Number:* 1–9. *Amount:* $1000.

Eligibility Requirements: Applicant must be enrolled or expecting to enroll full-time at a two-year or four-year institution or university and resident of Rhode Island. Applicant must have 3.0 GPA or higher. Available to U.S. citizens.

Application Requirements: Application. *Deadline:* April 14.

Contact: Raymond Church, Executive Director, RI Society of Public Accountants
Phone: 401-331-5720
E-mail: rchurch@riscpa.org

RHODE ISLAND SOCIETY OF CERTIFIED PUBLIC ACCOUNTANTS
http://www.riscpa.org

RHODE ISLAND SOCIETY OF CERTIFIED PUBLIC ACCOUNTANTS SCHOLARSHIP

Annual scholarship for sophomore or junior majoring in accounting who is a legal resident of Rhode Island and U.S. citizen. Must have interest in career in public accounting, and submit one-page memo outlining that interest. Minimum GPA of 3.0 required. For more information, see Web site: http://www.riscpa.org

Academic Fields/Career Goals: Accounting.

Award: Scholarship for use in sophomore or junior years. *Amount:* up to $200.

Eligibility Requirements: Applicant must be enrolled or expecting to enroll at a four-year institution or university. Available to U.S. citizens.

Application Requirements: Application. *Deadline:* varies.

Contact: Raymond Church
Rhode Island Society of Certified Public Accountants
45 Royal Little Drive
Providence, RI 02904
Phone: 401-331-5720
Fax: 401-454-5780
E-mail: rchurch@riscpa.org

SOCIETY OF LOUISIANA CERTIFIED PUBLIC ACCOUNTANTS
http://www.lcpa.org

SOCIETY OF LOUISIANA CPAS SCHOLARSHIPS

One-time award for accounting majors. Applicant must be a Louisiana resident attending a four-year college or university in Louisiana. For full-time undergraduates entering their junior or senior year, or full-time graduate students. Minimum 2.5 GPA required. Deadline: March 20, varies. Must be U.S. citizen.

Academic Fields/Career Goals: Accounting.

Award: Scholarship for use in junior, senior, or graduate years; not renewable. *Number:* 8–12. *Amount:* $500–$3000.

Eligibility Requirements: Applicant must be enrolled or expecting to enroll full-time at a four-year institution or university; resident of Louisiana and studying in Louisiana. Applicant must have 2.5 GPA or higher. Available to U.S. citizens.

Application Requirements: Application, essay, references, transcript. *Deadline:* March 20.

Contact: Lisa Richardson, Member Services Manager
Society of Louisiana Certified Public Accountants
2400 Veterans Boulevard, Suite 500
Kenner, LA 70062-4739
Phone: 504-904-1139
Fax: 504-469-7930
E-mail: lrichardson@lcpa.org

SOUTH DAKOTA CPA SOCIETY
http://www.sdcpa.org/

EXCELLENCE IN ACCOUNTING SCHOLARSHIP

Scholarships available for senior undergraduate and graduate students majoring in accounting. Must have completed 90 credit hours, demonstrated excellence in academics and leadership potential. Application available online at http://www.sdcpa.org. Deadline is April 15.

Academic Fields/Career Goals: Accounting.

Award: Scholarship for use in senior, or graduate years; renewable. *Number:* 4–10. *Amount:* $500–$1500.

Eligibility Requirements: Applicant must be enrolled or expecting to enroll full-time at a four-year institution or university. Available to U.S. citizens.

Application Requirements: Application, transcript. *Deadline:* April 15.

Contact: Laura Coome, Executive Director
South Dakota CPA Society
PO Box 1798
Sioux Falls, SD 57101
Phone: 605-334-3848

SOUTH DAKOTA RETAILERS ASSOCIATION
http://www.sdra.org

SOUTH DAKOTA RETAILERS ASSOCIATION SCHOLARSHIP PROGRAM

One-time award to assist full-time students studying for a career in retailing. Applicants must have graduated from a South Dakota High School or be enrolled in postsecondary school in South Dakota. One or more awards are given out each year. Deadline is April 2.

Academic Fields/Career Goals: Accounting; Business/Consumer Services; Computer Science/Data Processing; Electrical Engineering/Electronics; Food Service/Hospitality; Graphics/Graphic Arts/Printing; Heating, Air-Conditioning, and Refrigeration Mechanics; Hospitality Management; Interior Design; Law Enforcement/Police Administration; Trade/Technical Specialties; Travel/Tourism.

Award: Scholarship for use in freshman, sophomore, junior, senior, graduate, or postgraduate years; not renewable. *Number:* 1–10. *Amount:* $500–$1000.

Eligibility Requirements: Applicant must be enrolled or expecting to enroll full-time at a two-year or four-year or technical institution or university. Available to U.S. citizens.

Application Requirements: Application, essay, resume, references, transcript. *Deadline:* April 2.

Contact: Donna Leslie, Communications Director
South Dakota Retailers Association
PO Box 638
Pierre, SD 57501
Phone: 800-658-5545
Fax: 605-224-2059
E-mail: dleslie@sdra.org

SUNSHINE LADY FOUNDATION, INC.
http://www.sunshineladyfdn.org

COUNSELOR, ADVOCATE, AND SUPPORT STAFF SCHOLARSHIP PROGRAM

Scholarship for workers in the field of domestic violence. Minimum one year working in the field of DV; Employer recommendation required. For further information view Web site: http://www.sunshineladyfdn.org

Academic Fields/Career Goals: Accounting; Business/Consumer Services; Child and Family Studies; Psychology; Social Sciences; Social Services; Therapy/Rehabilitation; Women's Studies.

Award: Scholarship for use in freshman, sophomore, junior, senior, or graduate years; renewable. *Number:* 50. *Amount:* up to $3000.

Eligibility Requirements: Applicant must be enrolled or expecting to enroll full or part-time at a two-year or four-year or technical institution or university and female. Applicant or parent of applicant must have employment or volunteer experience in human services. Available to U.S. citizens.

Application Requirements: Application, essay, references. *Deadline:* varies.

Contact: Nancy Soward, Program Director
Sunshine Lady Foundation, Inc.
4900 Randall Parkway
Suite H
Wilmington, NC 28403
Phone: 910-397-7742
Fax: 910-397-0023
E-mail: nancy@sunshineladyfdn.org

TENNESSEE SOCIETY OF CPAS
http://www.tncpa.org

TENNESSEE SOCIETY OF CPA SCHOLARSHIP

Scholarships are available only to full-time students who have completed introductory courses in accounting and/or students majoring in accounting. Applicants must be a legal residents of Tennessee.

Academic Fields/Career Goals: Accounting.

Award: Scholarship for use in freshman, sophomore, junior, or senior years. *Amount:* $250–$1000.

Eligibility Requirements: Applicant must be enrolled or expecting to enroll full-time at a four-year institution or university and resident of Tennessee. Available to U.S. citizens.

Application Requirements: Application, financial need analysis, references, transcript. *Deadline:* June 1.

Contact: Connie Rhea, TSCPA Scholarship
Tennessee Society of CPAs
201 Powell Place
Brentwood, TN 37027
Phone: 615-377-3825
E-mail: crhea@tscpa.com

TKE EDUCATIONAL FOUNDATION
http://www.tkefoundation.org

HARRY J. DONNELLY MEMORIAL SCHOLARSHIP

One-time award of $1000 given to a member of Tau Kappa Epsilon pursuing an undergraduate degree in accounting or a graduate degree in law. Applicant should have demonstrated leadership ability within his chapter, campus, or community. Should have 3.0 GPA and plan to be a full-time student the following academic year. Recent head and shoulders photograph must be submitted with application.

TKE Educational Foundation (continued)

Academic Fields/Career Goals: Accounting; Law/Legal Services.

Award: Scholarship for use in freshman, sophomore, junior, senior, or graduate years; not renewable. *Number:* 1. *Amount:* $1000.

Eligibility Requirements: Applicant must be enrolled or expecting to enroll full-time at a four-year institution or university; male and must have an interest in leadership. Applicant must have 3.0 GPA or higher. Available to U.S. and non-U.S. citizens.

Application Requirements: Application, essay, photo, transcript. *Deadline:* May 12.

Contact: Gary A. Reed, President/CEO
TKE Educational Foundation
8645 Founders Road
Indianapolis, IN 46268-1393
Phone: 317-872-6533
Fax: 317-875-8353
E-mail: reedga@tke.org

W. ALLAN HERZOG SCHOLARSHIP

One $3000 award for an undergraduate member of TKE who is a full-time student pursuing a finance or accounting degree. Minimum 2.75 GPA required. Preference given to members of Nu Chapter. Applicant should have record of leadership within chapter and campus organizations. Application deadline is May 12.

Academic Fields/Career Goals: Accounting; Business/Consumer Services.

Award: Scholarship for use in freshman, sophomore, junior, or senior years; not renewable. *Number:* 1. *Amount:* $3000.

Eligibility Requirements: Applicant must be enrolled or expecting to enroll full-time at a four-year institution or university; male and must have an interest in leadership. Available to U.S. and non-U.S. citizens.

Application Requirements: Application, essay, photo, transcript. *Deadline:* May 12.

Contact: Gary A. Reed, President/CEO
TKE Educational Foundation
8645 Founders Road
Indianapolis, IN 46268-1393
Phone: 317-872-6533
Fax: 317-875-8353
E-mail: reedga@tke.org

UNITED NEGRO COLLEGE FUND   http://www.uncf.org

ALLIANT TECHSYSTEMS INTERNSHIP/SCHOLARSHIP

Scholarship is available to undergraduates in their sophomore or junior year. Applicant must be an accounting major enrolled in a UNCF member college or university. Scholarship awardees must participate in a paid summer internship in order to receive the $5000 for the following academic year. Please visit Web site for more information: http://www.uncf.org.

Academic Fields/Career Goals: Accounting.

Award: Scholarship for use in sophomore or junior years. *Number:* varies. *Amount:* $5000.

Eligibility Requirements: Applicant must be Black (non-Hispanic) and enrolled or expecting to enroll at a four-year institution or university. Applicant must have 3.0 GPA or higher. Available to U.S. citizens.

Application Requirements: Application, financial need analysis, FAFSA, Student Aid Report (SAR). *Deadline:* varies.

Contact: Rebecca Bennett, Director, Program Services
United Negro College Fund
8260 Willow Oaks Corporate Drive
Fairfax, VA 22031-8044
Phone: 800-331-2244
E-mail: rbennett@uncf.org

BEST BUY ENTERPRISE EMPLOYEE SCHOLARSHIP

UNCF is partnered with Best Buy to offer this program to UNCF students majoring in business, finance, marketing, or sales. Selected students will receive a $2500 scholarship and an opportunity for an internship at a Best Buy retail store or at a corporate facility. Minimum 3.0 GPA required. Prospective applicants should complete the Student Profile found at Web site: http://www.uncf.org

Academic Fields/Career Goals: Accounting; Business/Consumer Services; Communications; Journalism.

Award: Scholarship for use in freshman, sophomore, junior, or senior years; not renewable. *Amount:* $2500.

Eligibility Requirements: Applicant must be Black (non-Hispanic) and enrolled or expecting to enroll full-time at a four-year institution or university. Applicant must have 3.0 GPA or higher. Available to U.S. citizens.

Application Requirements: Application. *Deadline:* varies.

Contact: Rebecca Bennett, Director, Program Services
United Negro College Fund
8260 Willow Oaks Corporate Drive
Fairfax, VA 22031-8044
Phone: 800-331-2244
E-mail: rbennett@uncf.org

CARDINAL HEALTH SCHOLARSHIP

Scholarship awarded to African-American undergraduate freshmen, sophomores, or juniors attending any four-year accredited college or university. Must be majoring in accounting/finance, information systems, computer science, engineering, chemistry, marketing, purchasing/operations, or pharmacy. Please visit Web site for more information: http://www.uncf.org

Academic Fields/Career Goals: Accounting; Business/Consumer Services; Computer Science/Data Processing; Engineering/Technology; Pharmacy.

Award: Scholarship for use in freshman, sophomore, or junior years; renewable. *Number:* varies. *Amount:* $5000.

Eligibility Requirements: Applicant must be Black (non-Hispanic); enrolled or expecting to enroll at a four-year institution or university and must have an interest in leadership. Applicant must have 3.0 GPA or higher. Available to U.S. citizens.

Application Requirements: Application, financial need analysis, FAFSA, Student Aid Report (SAR). *Deadline:* varies.

Contact: Rebecca Bennett, Director, Program Services
United Negro College Fund
8260 Willow Oaks Corporate Drive
Fairfax, VA 22031-8044
Phone: 800-331-2244
E-mail: rbennett@uncf.org

CARGILL SCHOLARSHIP PROGRAM

Scholarship awarded to undergraduate freshman, sophomore, or junior enrolled in a UNCF member college or university or one of the following institutions: University of Minnesota, Iowa State University, North Carolina A&T State University, and University of Wisconsin-Madison. Please visit Web site for more information: http://www.uncf.org

Academic Fields/Career Goals: Accounting; Agriculture; Animal/Veterinary Sciences; Biology; Chemical Engineering; Computer Science/Data Processing; Food Science/Nutrition; Mechanical Engineering.

Award: Scholarship for use in freshman, sophomore, or junior years. *Number:* varies. *Amount:* $5000.

Eligibility Requirements: Applicant must be Black (non-Hispanic) and enrolled or expecting to enroll at a four-year institution or university. Applicant must have 3.0 GPA or higher. Available to U.S. citizens.

Application Requirements: Application, financial need analysis, FAFSA, Student Aid Report (SAR). *Deadline:* February 28.

Contact: Rebecca Bennett, Director, Program Services
United Negro College Fund
8260 Willow Oaks Corporate Drive
Fairfax, VA 22031-8044
Phone: 800-331-2244
E-mail: rbennett@uncf.org

CON EDISON SCHOLARSHIP

Scholarship available to students majoring in: accounting, computer science, and electrical, mechanical, or nuclear engineering. Applicant must be a resident of New York State. Please visit Web site for more information: http://www.uncf.org

Academic Fields/Career Goals: Accounting; Computer Science/Data Processing; Energy and Power Engineering; Engineering/Technology; Mechanical Engineering.

Award: Scholarship for use in sophomore, junior, or senior years. *Number:* varies. *Amount:* $5000.

Eligibility Requirements: Applicant must be Black (non-Hispanic); enrolled or expecting to enroll at a four-year institution or university and resident of New York. Applicant must have 3.0 GPA or higher. Available to U.S. citizens.

Application Requirements: Application, financial need analysis, FAFSA, Student Aid Report (SAR). *Deadline:* March 15.

Contact: Rebecca Bennett, Director, Program Services
United Negro College Fund
8260 Willow Oaks Corporate Drive
Fairfax, VA 22031-8044
Phone: 800-331-2244
E-mail: rbennett@uncf.org

EMERSON ELECTRIC COMPANY SCHOLARSHIP

Scholarship awards students majoring in: accounting, computer science, engineering, or human resources. Applicant must attend a UNCF member college or university and be a resident of St. Louis, Missouri. Please visit Web site for more information: http://www.uncf.org

Academic Fields/Career Goals: Accounting; Computer Science/Data Processing; Engineering/Technology; Hospitality Management.

Award: Scholarship for use in freshman, sophomore, junior, senior, or graduate years. *Number:* varies. *Amount:* $6000.

Eligibility Requirements: Applicant must be Black (non-Hispanic); enrolled or expecting to enroll at a four-year institution or university and resident of Missouri. Applicant must have 3.0 GPA or higher. Available to U.S. citizens.

Application Requirements: Application, financial need analysis, FAFSA, Student Aid Report (SAR). *Deadline:* varies.

Contact: Rebecca Bennett, Director, Program Services
United Negro College Fund
8260 Willow Oaks Corporate Drive
Fairfax, VA 22031-8044
Phone: 800-331-2244
E-mail: rbennett@uncf.org

FINANCIAL SERVICES INSTITUTION SCHOLARSHIP

Scholarship intended to provide exciting opportunities for students to learn about and be exposed directly to the financial services industry. Applicant must attend a UNCF member college or university. Please visit Web site for more information: http://www.uncf.org

Academic Fields/Career Goals: Accounting; Business/Consumer Services.

Award: Scholarship for use in freshman, sophomore, junior, senior, or graduate years; renewable. *Number:* 1. *Amount:* varies.

Eligibility Requirements: Applicant must be Black (non-Hispanic) and enrolled or expecting to enroll at a four-year institution or university. Applicant must have 2.5 GPA or higher. Available to U.S. citizens.

Application Requirements: Application, financial need analysis, FAFSA, Student Aid Report (SAR). *Deadline:* varies.

Contact: Rebecca Bennett, Director, Program Services
United Negro College Fund
8260 Willow Oaks Corporate Drive
Fairfax, VA 22031-8044
Phone: 800-331-2244
E-mail: rbennett@uncf.org

FORD/UNCF CORPORATE SCHOLARS PROGRAM

Program is designed to provide selected African-American college students with a unique educational opportunity through annual scholarships and a possible paid summer internship with Ford Motor Company offices. Students must be undergraduate sophomores majoring in engineering, finance, accounting, information systems, marketing, computer science, operations management, or electrical engineering at a UNCF member college or university or at a selected historically black college or university. Minimum 3.0 GPA required. Prospective applicants should complete the Student Profile found at Web site: http://www.uncf.org.

Academic Fields/Career Goals: Accounting; Computer Science/Data Processing; Engineering/Technology.

Award: Scholarship for use in sophomore year; not renewable. *Amount:* up to $15,000.

Eligibility Requirements: Applicant must be Black (non-Hispanic); enrolled or expecting to enroll at a four-year institution or university and resident of Michigan. Applicant must have 3.0 GPA or higher. Available to U.S. citizens.

Application Requirements: Application, financial need analysis. *Deadline:* April 30.

Contact: Rebecca Bennett, Director, Program Services
United Negro College Fund
8260 Willow Oaks Corporate Drive
Fairfax, VA 22031-8044
Phone: 800-331-2244
E-mail: rbennett@uncf.org

SPRINT SCHOLARSHIP/INTERNSHIP

Award includes a summer internship and a need-based scholarship to cover educational expenses for junior or senior year. Must major in engineering, business, economics, accounting, math, information systems, computer science/MIS, computer science, electrical engineering, information technology, computer engineering, engineering management, industrial engineering, or statistics. Must have 3.0 GPA. Please visit Web site for more information: http://www.uncf.org

Academic Fields/Career Goals: Accounting; Business/Consumer Services; Computer Science/Data Processing; Economics; Electrical Engineering/Electronics; Engineering/Technology; Physical Sciences and Math.

Award: Scholarship for use in junior or senior years; renewable. *Number:* varies. *Amount:* up to $5000.

Eligibility Requirements: Applicant must be Black (non-Hispanic) and enrolled or expecting to enroll at a four-year institution or university. Applicant must have 3.0 GPA or higher. Available to U.S. citizens.

Application Requirements: Application, financial need analysis, references, transcript, FAFSA, Student Aid Report (SAR). *Deadline:* April 10.

Contact: Sprint/Nextel/UNCF Corporate Scholars Program
United Negro College Fund
8260 Willow Oaks Corporate Drive, PO Box 1435
Fairfax, VA 22031

VIRCHOW, KRAUSE & COMPANY, LLP   http://www.virchowkrause.com

VIRCHOW, KRAUSE AND COMPANY SCHOLARSHIP

Scholarship for a student in each of the Accounting Departments at University of Wisconsin Madison, Whitewater, and La Crosse. The Accounting Department at each school selects a recipient in the accounting program. For more detailed information, please contact Darbie Miller, Human Resources Coordinator at Virchow, Krause & Company, LLP.

Academic Fields/Career Goals: Accounting.

Award: Scholarship for use in freshman, sophomore, junior, or senior years; not renewable. *Number:* up to 3. *Amount:* up to $1000.

Eligibility Requirements: Applicant must be enrolled or expecting to enroll full-time at a two-year or four-year institution or university and studying in Wisconsin. Available to U.S. citizens.

Application Requirements: Application, transcript. *Deadline:* Continuous.

Contact: Darbie Miller, Human Resources Coordinator
Virchow, Krause & Company, LLP
Virchow, Krause & Company, 4600 American Parkway, PO Box 7398
Madison, WI 53707-7398
Phone: 608-240-2474
Fax: 608-249-1411
E-mail: dmiller@virchowkrause.com

VIRGINIA SOCIETY OF CERTIFIED PUBLIC ACCOUNTANTS EDUCATION FOUNDATION   http://www.vscpa.com

VIRGINIA SOCIETY OF CPAS EDUCATIONAL FOUNDATION MINORITY UNDERGRADUATE SCHOLARSHIP

One-time award for a student currently enrolled in a Virginia college or university undergraduate program with the intent to pursue accounting or a

Virginia Society of Certified Public Accountants Education Foundation (continued)

business related field of study. Applicant must have at least six hours of accounting and be currently registered for at least 3 more accounting credit hours. Applicant must be a member of one of the VSCPA-defined minority groups (African-American, Hispanic-American, Native-American or Asian Pacific American). Minimum overall and accounting GPA of 3.0 is required.

Academic Fields/Career Goals: Accounting; Business/Consumer Services.

Award: Scholarship for use in freshman, sophomore, junior, or senior years; not renewable. *Number:* 5. *Amount:* $1500.

Eligibility Requirements: Applicant must be American Indian/Alaska Native, Asian/Pacific Islander, Black (non-Hispanic), or Hispanic; enrolled or expecting to enroll at a two-year or four-year institution or university and studying in Virginia. Applicant must have 3.0 GPA or higher. Available to U.S. citizens.

Application Requirements: Application, essay, resume, references, transcript. *Deadline:* April 15.

Contact: Tracey Zink, Public Relations Coordinator
Virginia Society of Certified Public Accountants Education Foundation
PO Box 4620
Glen Allen, VA 23058-4620
Phone: 800-733-8272
Fax: 804-273-1741
E-mail: tzink@vscpa.com

VIRGINIA SOCIETY OF CPAS EDUCATIONAL FOUNDATION UNDERGRADUATE SCHOLARSHIP

One-time award for a student currently enrolled in a Virginia college or university undergraduate program with the intent to pursue accounting or a business related field of study. Applicant must have at least six hours of accounting and be currently registered for at least 3 more accounting credit hours. Minimum overall and accounting GPA of 3.0 is required.

Academic Fields/Career Goals: Accounting; Business/Consumer Services.

Award: Scholarship for use in freshman, sophomore, junior, or senior years; not renewable. *Number:* 5. *Amount:* $1500.

Eligibility Requirements: Applicant must be enrolled or expecting to enroll at a two-year or four-year institution or university and studying in Virginia. Applicant must have 3.0 GPA or higher. Available to U.S. citizens.

Application Requirements: Application, essay, resume, references, transcript. *Deadline:* April 15.

Contact: Tracey Zink, Public Relations Coordinator
Virginia Society of Certified Public Accountants Education Foundation
PO Box 4620
Glen Allen, VA 23058-4620
Phone: 800-733-8272
Fax: 804-273-1741
E-mail: tzink@vscpa.com

WASHINGTON SOCIETY OF CERTIFIED PUBLIC ACCOUNTANTS   http://www.wscpa.org

WSCPA ACCOUNTING SCHOLARSHIPS

non-renewable tuition scholarships to students majoring in accounting and who have completed their sophomore year at any accredited four-year institution or at least two terms of accounting at any accredited two-year institution in Washington State, with the intent to transfer. Minimum 3.0 GPA required. Deadline is May 1.

Academic Fields/Career Goals: Accounting.

Award: Scholarship for use in sophomore, junior, or senior years; not renewable. *Number:* 8. *Amount:* $500–$1000.

Eligibility Requirements: Applicant must be enrolled or expecting to enroll full or part-time at a two-year or four-year or technical institution and studying in Washington. Applicant must have 3.0 GPA or higher. Available to U.S. citizens.

Application Requirements: Application, essay, financial need analysis, resume, references, transcript. *Deadline:* May 1.

Contact: Mark Peterson, Academic and Student Relations Administrator
Washington Society of Certified Public Accountants
902 140th Avenue, NE
Bellevue, WA 98005-3480
Phone: 425-644-4800
Fax: 425-586-1119
E-mail: mpeterson@wscpa.org

WSCPA SCHOLARSHIPS FOR ACCOUNTING MAJORS

These $1500 need-based scholarships are available to college juniors and seniors majoring in accounting. The one-time award is intended for those studying at a four-year college or university in the state of Washington and may be used for full- or part-time study. Must maintain a 2.75 GPA. Deadline is May 31.

Academic Fields/Career Goals: Accounting.

Award: Scholarship for use in junior or senior years; not renewable. *Number:* up to 11. *Amount:* $1500.

Eligibility Requirements: Applicant must be enrolled or expecting to enroll full or part-time at a four-year institution or university and studying in Washington. Applicant must have 3.0 GPA or higher. Available to U.S. citizens.

Application Requirements: Application, essay, resume, references, transcript. *Deadline:* May 31.

Contact: Mark Peterson, Academic and Student Relations Administrator
Washington Society of Certified Public Accountants
902 140th Avenue, NE
Bellevue, WA 98005-3480
Phone: 425-644-4800
Fax: 425-586-1119
E-mail: mpeterson@wscpa.org

WSCPA SCHOLARSHIPS FOR MINORITY ACCOUNTING MAJORS

Scholarship for $3000 is available to a minority accounting student who will have completed his/her sophomore year by fall of application year at an accredited four-year institution in Washington state. Minimum 3.0 GPA required.

Academic Fields/Career Goals: Accounting.

Award: Scholarship for use in sophomore, junior, or senior years; not renewable. *Number:* up to 20. *Amount:* $1000–$3000.

Eligibility Requirements: Applicant must be enrolled or expecting to enroll full-time at a four-year institution or university and studying in Washington. Applicant must have 3.0 GPA or higher. Available to U.S. citizens.

Application Requirements: Application, essay, financial need analysis, resume, references, transcript. *Deadline:* May 1.

Contact: Mark Peterson, Academic and Student Relations Administrator
Washington Society of Certified Public Accountants
902 140th Avenue, NE
Bellevue, WA 98005-3480
Phone: 425-644-4800
Fax: 425-586-1119
E-mail: mpeterson@wscpa.org

WEST VIRGINIA SOCIETY OF CERTIFIED PUBLIC ACCOUNTANTS   http://www.wvscpa.org

CHARLESTON CHAPTER OF CPA'S ACCOUNTING SCHOLARSHIP FUND

Scholarship for the accounting students residing in the counties that come under the Charleston, West Virginia chapter. Minimum GPA of 3.0 required. Deadline is February 15. Call Susan Hoover at (304) 346-3620 for more information.

Academic Fields/Career Goals: Accounting.

Award: Scholarship for use in junior or senior years; not renewable. *Number:* 1. *Amount:* up to $1000.

Eligibility Requirements: Applicant must be enrolled or expecting to enroll full-time at a two-year institution or university; resident of West Virginia and studying in West Virginia. Applicant must have 3.0 GPA or higher. Available to U.S. citizens.

Application Requirements: Application, essay, references, transcript. *Deadline:* February 15.

Contact: Susan Hoover, Scholarship Coordinator
West Virginia Society of Certified Public Accountants
Greater Kanawha Valley Foundation, 1600 Huntington Square, 900 Lee Street, East
Charleston, WV 25301
Phone: 304-346-3620
Fax: 304-346-3640
E-mail: tgkvf@tgkvf.org

WISS & COMPANY, CPA
http://www.wiss.com

WISS EDWARD W. O'CONNELL MEMORIAL SCHOLARSHIP

Two annual awards to New Jersey high school seniors who will declare a major in accounting. Applicants must have already been accepted into an accredited New Jersey baccalaureate college or university as a matriculating student (full-time or part-time). Students must have a GPA of 3.0 or greater. Must be resident of New Jersey for a minimum of two years. Deadline is April 15. See Web site for application: www.wiss.com

Academic Fields/Career Goals: Accounting.

Award: Scholarship for use in freshman year; not renewable. *Number:* up to 2.

Eligibility Requirements: Applicant must be high school student and planning to enroll or expecting to enroll full or part-time at a four-year institution or university. Applicant must have 3.0 GPA or higher. Available to U.S. citizens.

Application Requirements: Application, essay, references, transcript. *Deadline:* April 15.

Contact: Amy Delman, WISS Edward W. O'Connell Memorial Scholarship Coordinator
Wiss & Company, CPA
354 Eisenhower Parkway
Livingston, NJ 07039
Phone: 973-994-9400
Fax: 973-992-6760

WYOMING SOCIETY OF CERTIFIED PUBLIC ACCOUNTANTS
http://www.wyocpa.org

WYOMING SOCIETY OF CERTIFIED PUBLIC ACCOUNTANTS MEMORIAL SCHOLARSHIPS

Scholarship for senior or fifth year student majoring in accounting. To be used at University of Wyoming or any community college in Wyoming. Deadline is April 1.

Academic Fields/Career Goals: Accounting.

Award: Scholarship for use in senior year; not renewable. *Number:* 1.

Eligibility Requirements: Applicant must be enrolled or expecting to enroll full or part-time at a four-year institution or university and studying in Wyoming. Available to U.S. citizens.

Application Requirements: Application, references, transcript, University of Wyoming or community college academic transcript, short essay discussing future goals and objectives, evidence of work experience and/or extracurricular activities, awards. *Deadline:* April 1.

Contact: Kim Hivko, Student Scholarships
Wyoming Society of Certified Public Accountants
1603 Capitol Avenue, Suite 413
Cheyenne, WY 82001
Phone: 307-634-7039
Fax: 307-634-5110

AFRICAN STUDIES

AMERICAN HISTORICAL ASSOCIATION
http://www.historians.org

WESLEY-LOGAN PRIZE

Prize offered for book on some aspect of the history of dispersion, settlement, adjustment, and return of peoples originally from Africa. Only books of high scholarly and literary merit considered. Copies of book must be sent to each committee member. Refer to Web site (http://www.theaha.org) for names and mailing addresses.

Academic Fields/Career Goals: African Studies; Area/Ethnic Studies; History; Humanities.

Award: Prize for use in freshman, sophomore, junior, senior, graduate, or postgraduate years; not renewable. *Number:* 1. *Amount:* $1000–$1500.

Eligibility Requirements: Applicant must be enrolled or expecting to enroll at an institution or university and must have an interest in writing. Available to U.S. citizens.

Application Requirements: Applicant must enter a contest, books between May and April of the preceding year. *Deadline:* May 15.

Contact: Book Prize Administrator
American Historical Association
400 A Street, SE
Washington, DC 20003
E-mail: aha@theaha.org

CULTURE CONNECTION
http://www.thecultureconnection.com

CULTURE CONNECTION FOUNDATION SCHOLARSHIP

Scholarships available for students in single parent families. May be used for undergraduate or graduate study. Those interested in foreign languages, culture, and ethnic studies are encouraged to apply. Application deadline is August 1.

Academic Fields/Career Goals: African Studies; Anthropology; Area/Ethnic Studies; Art History; Asian Studies; Education; European Studies; Foreign Language; International Studies; Law/Legal Services.

Award: Scholarship for use in freshman, sophomore, junior, senior, or graduate years; renewable. *Number:* 1000. *Amount:* up to $4700.

Eligibility Requirements: Applicant must be enrolled or expecting to enroll full or part-time at a two-year or four-year or technical institution or university and single. Applicant must have 2.5 GPA or higher. Available to U.S. and non-U.S. citizens.

Application Requirements: Application, essay, financial need analysis, interview, references, self-addressed stamped envelope, test scores, transcript, birth certificate, divorce decree. *Deadline:* August 1.

Contact: Anna Leis, National Program Director
Culture Connection
8888 Keystone Crossing, Suite 1300
Indianapolis, IN 46240
Phone: 317-547-7055
E-mail: annaleis@thecultureconnection.com

AGRIBUSINESS

CALIFORNIA FARM BUREAU SCHOLARSHIP FOUNDATION
http://www.cfbf.com/programs/scholar/

CALIFORNIA FARM BUREAU SCHOLARSHIP

Renewable award given to students attending a four-year college or university in California. Applicants must be California residents preparing for a career in the agricultural industry.

Academic Fields/Career Goals: Agribusiness; Agriculture.

Award: Scholarship for use in freshman, sophomore, junior, or senior years; renewable. *Number:* 23. *Amount:* $2000–$2750.

Eligibility Requirements: Applicant must be enrolled or expecting to enroll full-time at a four-year institution or university; resident of California and studying in California. Available to U.S. citizens.

California Farm Bureau Scholarship Foundation (continued)

Application Requirements: Application, essay, interview, references, transcript. *Deadline:* March 1.

Contact: Darlene Licciardo, Scholarship Coordinator
California Farm Bureau Scholarship Foundation
2300 River Plaza Drive
Sacramento, CA 95833
Phone: 916-561-5500
Fax: 916-561-5690
E-mail: dlicciardo@cfbf.com

CHS FOUNDATION   http://www.chsfoundation.org

AGRICULTURE SCHOLARSHIPS

Merit-based awards for students enrolled in agricultural programs at participating vocational or technical and community colleges. Application must be submitted through participating school. School submits ten applications to the CHS Foundation. Recipients are selected in the spring. One-time award of $600. Application must be submitted to the school by the students before February 15.

Academic Fields/Career Goals: Agribusiness; Agriculture.

Award: Scholarship for use in freshman or sophomore years; not renewable. *Number:* up to 81. *Amount:* $600.

Eligibility Requirements: Applicant must be enrolled or expecting to enroll full-time at a two-year or technical institution; resident of Colorado, Idaho, Iowa, Kansas, Minnesota, Montana, Nebraska, North Dakota, Oklahoma, Oregon, South Dakota, Utah, Washington, Wisconsin, or Wyoming and studying in Colorado, Idaho, Iowa, Kansas, Minnesota, Montana, Nebraska, North Dakota, Oklahoma, Oregon, South Dakota, or Utah. Available to U.S. and non-U.S. citizens.

Application Requirements: Application, transcript. *Deadline:* February 15.

Contact: Mary Kaste, Scholarship Director
CHS Foundation
5500 Cenex Drive
Inver Grove Heights, MN 55077
Phone: 651-355-5129
Fax: 651-355-5073
E-mail: mary.kaste@chsinc.com

COOPERATIVE STUDIES SCHOLARSHIPS

Renewable awards for college juniors and seniors attending agricultural colleges of participating universities. Must be enrolled in courses on cooperative principles and business practices. Each university selects a recipient in the spring. If the award is given in the junior year, the student is eligible for an additional $750 in their senior year without reapplying provided that eligibility requirements are met. A maximum of $1500 will be awarded to any one student in the cooperative studies program.

Academic Fields/Career Goals: Agribusiness; Agriculture.

Award: Scholarship for use in junior or senior years; renewable. *Number:* 82. *Amount:* $750–$1500.

Eligibility Requirements: Applicant must be enrolled or expecting to enroll full-time at a four-year institution or university; resident of Colorado, Idaho, Iowa, Kansas, Minnesota, Montana, Nebraska, North Dakota, Oklahoma, Oregon, South Dakota, Utah, Washington, Wisconsin, or Wyoming and studying in Colorado, Idaho, Iowa, Kansas, Minnesota, Montana, Nebraska, North Dakota, Oklahoma, Oregon, South Dakota, or Utah. Available to U.S. and non-U.S. citizens.

Application Requirements: Application, transcript. *Deadline:* April 15.

Contact: Mary Kaste, Scholarship Director
CHS Foundation
5500 Cenex Drive
Inver Grove Heights, MN 55077
Phone: 651-355-5129
Fax: 651-355-5073
E-mail: mary.kaste@chsinc.com

FIRST–FLORICULTURE INDUSTRY RESEARCH AND SCHOLARSHIP TRUST   http://www.firstinfloriculture.org

HAROLD BETTINGER MEMORIAL SCHOLARSHIP

One-time scholarship available to undergraduate or graduate students majoring in horticulture with a business or marketing emphasis, or majoring in business or marketing with a horticulture emphasis. Must have completed one year of study at a four-year institution in the United States or Canada. Minimum GPA of 3.0 required. To apply, applicant must register with lunch-money.com, which is partnering with FIRST to make the application process easier. Fill out one application online at: http://www.firstinfloriculture.org/schl_req_app.htm In addition, submit two letters of recommendation and transcripts via email to: scholarships@firstinfloriculture.org Application deadline is May 1.

Academic Fields/Career Goals: Agribusiness; Agriculture; Business/Consumer Services; Horticulture/Floriculture.

Award: Scholarship for use in freshman, sophomore, junior, or senior years; not renewable. *Number:* 1. *Amount:* $500–$2000.

Eligibility Requirements: Applicant must be enrolled or expecting to enroll full-time at a four-year institution or university. Applicant must have 3.0 GPA or higher. Available to U.S. and Canadian citizens.

Application Requirements: Application, references, transcript. *Deadline:* May 1.

Contact: Bill Willbrandt, Executive Director
FIRST–Floriculture Industry Research and Scholarship Trust
PO Box 280
East Lansing, MI 48826-0280
Phone: 517-333-4617
Fax: 517-333-4494
E-mail: scholarship@firstinfloriculture.org

JACOB VAN NAMEN/VANS MARKETING SCHOLARSHIP

Award open to undergraduates at a four-year college or university in the U.S. or Canada. Must be studying horticulture or a related major and be involved in agribusiness marketing and distribution of floral products. Minimum GPA of 3.0 required. To apply applicant must register with lunch-money.com, which is partnering with FIRST to make the application process easier. Applicant only need to fill out one application online, and there is a link to lunch-money.com from the FIRST Web site: http://www.firstinfloriculture.org/schl_req_app.htm In addition to the application, applicant must submit two letters of recommendation and transcripts via email to: scholarships@firstinfloriculture.org. Application deadline is May 1.

Academic Fields/Career Goals: Agribusiness; Horticulture/Floriculture.

Award: Scholarship for use in sophomore, junior, or senior years; not renewable. *Number:* 1. *Amount:* $500–$2000.

Eligibility Requirements: Applicant must be enrolled or expecting to enroll full-time at a four-year institution or university. Applicant must have 3.0 GPA or higher. Available to U.S. and Canadian citizens.

Application Requirements: Application, references, transcript. *Deadline:* May 1.

Contact: Bill Willbrandt, Executive Director
FIRST–Floriculture Industry Research and Scholarship Trust
PO Box 280
East Lansing, MI 48826-0280
Phone: 517-333-4617
Fax: 517-333-4494
E-mail: scholarship@firstinfloriculture.org

FUHRMANN ORCHARDS

KARL "PETE" FUHRMANN IV MEMORIAL SCHOLARSHIP

One-time award for Ohio residents studying horticulture or agribusiness at any two- or four-year postsecondary institution in the United States. Must be a U.S. citizen. Must be a graduate of an Ohio high school. Write for more information.

Academic Fields/Career Goals: Agribusiness; Horticulture/Floriculture.

Award: Scholarship for use in freshman, sophomore, junior, or senior years; not renewable. *Number:* up to 2. *Amount:* $600–$1000.

Eligibility Requirements: Applicant must be enrolled or expecting to enroll full-time at a two-year or four-year institution and resident of Ohio. Available to U.S. citizens.

Application Requirements: Application, essay, transcript. *Deadline:* April 15.

Contact: Paul W. Fuhrmann, Partner
Fuhrmann Orchards
510 Hansgen-Morgan Road
Wheelersburg, OH 45694
Phone: 614-776-6406
Fax: 614-776-7557

GOLF COURSE SUPERINTENDENTS ASSOCIATION OF AMERICA http://www.gcsaa.org

GOLF COURSE SUPERINTENDENTS ASSOCIATION OF AMERICA STUDENT ESSAY CONTEST

Up to three awards for essays focusing on the golf course management profession. Undergraduates and graduate students pursuing turf grass science, agronomy, or any field related to golf course management may apply. In addition to cash prizes, winning entries may be published or excerpted in Newsline or Golf Course Management magazine. Must be member of GCSAA.

Academic Fields/Career Goals: Agribusiness; Horticulture/Floriculture.

Award: Prize for use in freshman, sophomore, junior, senior, or graduate years; not renewable. *Number:* up to 3. *Amount:* up to $2000.

Eligibility Requirements: Applicant must be enrolled or expecting to enroll full-time at a two-year or four-year institution or university. Applicant or parent of applicant must be member of Golf Course Superintendents Association of America. Available to U.S. and non-U.S. citizens.

Application Requirements: Application, applicant must enter a contest, essay. *Deadline:* March 31.

Contact: Amanda Howard, Employment Administrator
Golf Course Superintendents Association of America
1421 Research Park Drive
Lawrence, KS 66049-3859
Phone: 800-472-7878 Ext. 678
Fax: 785-832-4449
E-mail: ahoward@gcsaa.org

INTERTRIBAL TIMBER COUNCIL http://www.itcnet.org

TRUMAN D. PICARD SCHOLARSHIP

This program is dedicated to assisting Native-American/Native-Alaskan youth seeking careers in natural resources. Graduating senior high school students and those currently attending institutions of higher education are encouraged to apply. A valid Tribal/Alaska Native corporations enrollment card is required. Contact for deadline.

Academic Fields/Career Goals: Agribusiness; Agriculture; Natural Resources.

Award: Scholarship for use in freshman, sophomore, junior, senior, or graduate years; not renewable. *Number:* 10–14. *Amount:* $1200–$1800.

Eligibility Requirements: Applicant must be American Indian/Alaska Native and enrolled or expecting to enroll full-time at a two-year or four-year institution or university. Available to U.S. citizens.

Application Requirements: Application, essay, resume, references, transcript, enrollment card. *Deadline:* March 31.

Contact: Education Committee, Intertribal Timber Council
Intertribal Timber Council
1112 Northeast 21st Avenue
Portland, OR 97232-2114
Phone: 503-282-4296
Fax: 503-282-1274
E-mail: itc1@teleport.com

MAINE DEPARTMENT OF AGRICULTURE, FOOD AND RURAL RESOURCES http://www.maine.gov/agriculture

MAINE RURAL REHABILITATION FUND SCHOLARSHIP PROGRAM

One-time scholarship open to Maine residents enrolled in or accepted by any school, college, or university. Must be full time and demonstrate financial need. Those opting for a Maine institution given preference. Major must lead to an agricultural career. Minimum 2.7 cumulative GPA required, or minimum 3.0 GPA for most recent semester or quarter.

Academic Fields/Career Goals: Agribusiness; Agriculture; Animal/Veterinary Sciences.

Award: Scholarship for use in freshman, sophomore, junior, senior, graduate, or postgraduate years; renewable. *Number:* 10–20. *Amount:* $800–$2000.

Eligibility Requirements: Applicant must be enrolled or expecting to enroll full-time at a two-year or four-year or technical institution or university and resident of Maine. Available to U.S. citizens.

Application Requirements: Application, autobiography, financial need analysis, transcript. *Deadline:* June 15.

Contact: Rod McCormick, Scholarship Coordinator
Maine Department of Agriculture, Food and Rural Resources
28 State House Station
Augusta, ME 04333-0028
Phone: 207-287-7628
Fax: 207-287-7548
E-mail: rod.mccormick@maine.gov

MINNESOTA SOYBEAN RESEARCH AND PROMOTION COUNCIL http://mnsoybean.org

MINNESOTA SOYBEAN RESEARCH AND PROMOTION COUNCIL YOUTH SOYBEAN SCHOLARSHIP

Up to eight $1000 scholarships are available to graduating high school seniors who are residents of Minnesota. Must demonstrate activity in agriculture with plans to study in an agricultural related program. For more details see Web site: http://www.mnsoybean.org.

Academic Fields/Career Goals: Agribusiness; Agriculture; Food Science/Nutrition.

Award: Scholarship for use in freshman year; not renewable. *Number:* up to 8. *Amount:* $1000.

Eligibility Requirements: Applicant must be high school student; planning to enroll or expecting to enroll full or part-time at a two-year or four-year or technical institution or university and resident of Minnesota. Applicant or parent of applicant must have employment or volunteer experience in agriculture or farming. Available to U.S. citizens.

Application Requirements: Application, references, self-addressed stamped envelope, transcript. *Deadline:* March 22.

Contact: J J. Morgan, Scholarship Coordinator
Minnesota Soybean Research and Promotion Council
360 Pierce Avenue, Suite 110
North Mankato, MN 56003
Phone: 888-896-9678
Fax: 507-388-6751
E-mail: jj@mnsoybean.com

NATIONAL DAIRY SHRINE http://www.dairyshrine.org

NDS STUDENT RECOGNITION CONTEST

Awards available to college seniors enrolled in dairy science courses. Applicants must be nominated by their college or university professor and must intend to continue in the dairy field. A college or university may nominate up to two applicants.

Academic Fields/Career Goals: Agribusiness; Agriculture; Animal/Veterinary Sciences; Food Science/Nutrition.

Award: Prize for use in senior year; not renewable. *Number:* 5–10. *Amount:* $500–$1500.

Eligibility Requirements: Applicant must be enrolled or expecting to enroll at a four-year institution or university. Available to U.S. citizens.

Application Requirements: Application, references, transcript, nomination. *Deadline:* March 15.

Contact: Maurice E. Core, Executive Director
National Dairy Shrine
1224 Alton Darby Creek Road
Columbus, OH 43228-4792
Phone: 614-878-5333
Fax: 614-870-2622
E-mail: shrine@cobaselect.com

NATIONAL POTATO COUNCIL WOMEN'S AUXILIARY   http://www.nationalpotatocouncil.org

POTATO INDUSTRY SCHOLARSHIP

The Auxiliary scholarship is for full-time students studying in a potato-related field who desire to work in the potato industry after graduation. Minimum 3.0 GPA required.

Academic Fields/Career Goals: Agribusiness; Agriculture; Food Science/Nutrition; Horticulture/Floriculture.

Award: Scholarship for use in senior, graduate, or postgraduate years; not renewable. *Number:* 2. *Amount:* up to $2000.

Eligibility Requirements: Applicant must be enrolled or expecting to enroll full-time at an institution or university. Applicant must have 3.0 GPA or higher. Available to U.S. citizens.

Application Requirements: Application, essay, resume, references, transcript. *Deadline:* varies.

Contact: John Keeling, Executive Vice President and CEO
National Potato Council Women's Auxiliary
1300 L Street, NW, Suite 910
Washington, DC 20005
Phone: 202-682-9456 Ext. 203
Fax: 202-682-0333
E-mail: johnkeeling@nationalpotatocouncil.org

NATIONAL POULTRY AND FOOD DISTRIBUTORS ASSOCIATION   http://www.npfda.org

NATIONAL POULTRY AND FOOD DISTRIBUTORS ASSOCIATION SCHOLARSHIP FOUNDATION

The scholarships are awarded to full-time students in their junior or senior years at a U.S. college pursuing degrees in poultry science, food science, dietetics, or other related areas of study pertaining to the poultry and food industries.

Academic Fields/Career Goals: Agribusiness; Agriculture; Animal/Veterinary Sciences; Food Science/Nutrition; Food Service/Hospitality; Home Economics.

Award: Scholarship for use in junior or senior years; not renewable. *Number:* 4. *Amount:* $1500–$2000.

Eligibility Requirements: Applicant must be enrolled or expecting to enroll full-time at a four-year institution or university. Available to U.S. and non-U.S. citizens.

Application Requirements: Application, essay, references, transcript. *Deadline:* May 31.

Contact: Kristin McWhorter, Executive Director
Phone: 877-845-1545
Fax: 770-535-7385
E-mail: info@npfda.org

OHIO FARMERS UNION   http://www.ohfarmersunion.org

VIRGIL THOMPSON MEMORIAL SCHOLARSHIP CONTEST

Award available to members of Ohio Farmers Union who are enrolled as full-time college sophomores, juniors or seniors. Must submit an application obtained from OFU and a double-space typed 40-page business plan on "Creating New Ag-Related Opportunities.", including executive summary. Participants must use their own research and data. Awards of $1000 to winner and $500 each to two runners-up

Academic Fields/Career Goals: Agribusiness; Agriculture.

Award: Scholarship for use in sophomore, junior, or senior years. *Number:* 1–3. *Amount:* $500–$1000.

Eligibility Requirements: Applicant must be enrolled or expecting to enroll full-time at a four-year institution or university and resident of Ohio. Applicant or parent of applicant must be member of Ohio Farmers Union. Available to U.S. citizens.

Application Requirements: Application, essay. *Deadline:* December 31.

Contact: Maria Gordon
Ohio Farmers Union
PO Box 363
Ottawa, OH 45875
Phone: 419-523-5300
E-mail: m-gordon@ohfarmersunion.org

PENNSYLVANIA ASSOCIATION OF CONSERVATION DISTRICTS AUXILIARY   http://www.blairconservationdistrict.org

PACD AUXILIARY SCHOLARSHIPS

Award for residents of Pennsylvania who are upperclassmen pursuing a degree program in agricultural and/or environmental science, and/or environmental education. Must be studying at a two- or four-year Pennsylvania institution. Must be U.S. citizens. Submit resume. One-time award of $500.

Academic Fields/Career Goals: Agribusiness; Agriculture; Biology; Environmental Science; Horticulture/Floriculture; Natural Resources.

Award: Scholarship for use in junior or senior years; not renewable. *Number:* 1. *Amount:* $500.

Eligibility Requirements: Applicant must be enrolled or expecting to enroll full or part-time at a two-year or four-year institution or university; resident of Pennsylvania and studying in Pennsylvania. Available to U.S. citizens.

Application Requirements: Application, autobiography, financial need analysis, resume, transcript. *Deadline:* June 13.

Contact: Margaret Angle, District Clerk
Pennsylvania Association of Conservation Districts Auxiliary
1407 Blair Street
Hollidaysburg, PA 16648-2468
Phone: 814-696-0877 Ext. 5
Fax: 814-696-9981
E-mail: Bcd@blairconsevationdistrict.org

SOCIETY FOR RANGE MANAGEMENT   http://www.rangelands.org

MASONIC RANGE SCIENCE SCHOLARSHIP

One award available to applicant pursuing degree in agribusiness, agriculture, animal/veterinary sciences, earth science, natural resources, and range science (or range management). Recipient receives $2000 a year for four years at college or university.

Academic Fields/Career Goals: Agribusiness; Agriculture; Animal/Veterinary Sciences; Earth Science; Natural Resources.

Award: Scholarship for use in freshman or sophomore years; renewable. *Number:* 1. *Amount:* $2000.

Eligibility Requirements: Applicant must be enrolled or expecting to enroll full-time at a four-year institution or university. Available to U.S. and non-U.S. citizens.

Application Requirements: Application, autobiography, essay, references, test scores, transcript. *Deadline:* varies.

Contact: Scholarship Office
Society for Range Management
445 Union Boulevard, Suite 230
Lakewood, CO 80228
Phone: 303-986-3309
Fax: 303-986-3892

SOIL AND WATER CONSERVATION SOCIETY-NEW JERSEY CHAPTER   http://www.geocities.com/njswcs

EDWARD R. HALL SCHOLARSHIP

Two $500 scholarships awarded annually to students attending a New Jersey accredited college or New Jersey residents attending any out-of-state college. Undergraduate students, with the exception of freshmen, are eligible. Must be enrolled in a curriculum related to natural resources. Other areas related to conservation may qualify. Deadline: April 15.

Academic Fields/Career Goals: Agribusiness; Agriculture; Animal/Veterinary Sciences; Biology; Earth Science; Horticulture/Floriculture; Journalism; Materials Science, Engineering, and Metallurgy; Natural Resources; Natural Sciences; Surveying; Surveying Technology, Cartography, or Geographic Information Science.

Award: Scholarship for use in freshman, sophomore, junior, or senior years; not renewable. *Number:* 2. *Amount:* $500.

Eligibility Requirements: Applicant must be enrolled or expecting to enroll full-time at a two-year or four-year institution or university. Available to U.S. and non-U.S. citizens.

Application Requirements: Application, essay, financial need analysis, references, transcript. *Deadline:* April 15.

Contact: Fireman E. Bear Chapter, SWCS, C/O USDA-NRCS
Soil and Water Conservation Society-New Jersey Chapter
220 Davidson Avenue, 4th Floor
Somerset, NJ 08873
Phone: 732-932-9295
E-mail: njswcs@yahoo.com

SOUTH DAKOTA BOARD OF REGENTS
http://www.sdbor.edu

SOUTH DAKOTA BOARD OF REGENTS BJUGSTAD SCHOLARSHIP

Scholarship for graduating North or South Dakota high school senior who is a Native-American. Must demonstrate academic achievement, character and leadership abilities. Submit proof of tribal enrollment. One-time award of $500. Must rank in upper half of class or have a minimum 2.5 GPA. Must be pursuing studies in agriculture, agribusiness, or natural resources.

Academic Fields/Career Goals: Agribusiness; Agriculture; Natural Resources.

Award: Scholarship for use in freshman year; not renewable. *Number:* 1. *Amount:* $500.

Eligibility Requirements: Applicant must be American Indian/Alaska Native; high school student; planning to enroll or expecting to enroll at a two-year or four-year or technical institution or university; resident of North Dakota or South Dakota and must have an interest in leadership. Applicant must have 2.5 GPA or higher. Available to U.S. citizens.

Application Requirements: Application, references, transcript, proof of tribal enrollment. *Deadline:* February 9.

Contact: Scholarship Committee
South Dakota Board of Regents
306 East Capitol Avenue, Suite 200
Pierre, SD 57501-3159

UNITED AGRIBUSINESS LEAGUE
http://www.ual.org

UNITED AGRIBUSINESS LEAGUE SCHOLARSHIP PROGRAM

Award of $1000-$5000 available to students enrolled or planning to enroll in a full-time degree program in agribusiness at a two- or four-year institution. Award is only for students who are studying or residing in the U.S., Canada or Mexico. Minimum 2.5 GPA required. Application deadline varies.

Academic Fields/Career Goals: Agribusiness; Agriculture; Animal/Veterinary Sciences; Economics; Food Science/Nutrition; Horticulture/Floriculture; Landscape Architecture.

Award: Scholarship for use in freshman, sophomore, junior, senior, or graduate years; renewable. *Number:* 10–15. *Amount:* $1000–$5000.

Eligibility Requirements: Applicant must be enrolled or expecting to enroll full-time at a two-year or four-year institution or university. Applicant must have 2.5 GPA or higher. Available to U.S. and non-U.S. citizens.

Application Requirements: Application, essay, financial need analysis, resume, references, test scores, transcript. *Deadline:* March 31.

Contact: UAL/UABT Scholarship Program, United Agribusiness League
United Agribusiness League
54 Corporate Park
Irvine, CA 92606-5105
Phone: 800-223-4590

UNITED AGRICULTURAL BENEFIT TRUST SCHOLARSHIP

Award for an employee, spouse, or child participating in the United Agricultural Benefit Trust health care program. Submit essay that reflects chosen agricultural career path. Submit resume of any educational, work, community, or extracurricular activities that are relevant. Applicant should be a member or affiliated with United Agriculture Benefit Trust.

Academic Fields/Career Goals: Agribusiness; Agriculture; Animal/Veterinary Sciences; Economics; Food Science/Nutrition; Horticulture/Floriculture; Landscape Architecture.

Award: Scholarship for use in freshman, sophomore, junior, or senior years; renewable. *Number:* 7. *Amount:* $1000–$5000.

Eligibility Requirements: Applicant must be enrolled or expecting to enroll full-time at a two-year or four-year institution or university.

Applicant or parent of applicant must be member of United Agribusiness League. Applicant must have 2.5 GPA or higher. Available to U.S. and non-Canadian citizens.

Application Requirements: Application, essay, resume, references, test scores, transcript. *Deadline:* March 31.

Contact: UAL/UABT Scholarship Program, United Agribusiness League
United Agribusiness League
54 Corporate Park
Irvine, CA 92606-5105
Phone: 800-223-4590
Fax: 949-975-1671

AGRICULTURE

AGRILIANCE, LAND O' LAKES, AND CROPLAN GENETICS
http://www.agriliance.com

CAREERS IN AGRICULTURE SCHOLARSHIP PROGRAM

Award of $1000 to twenty high school seniors interested in agriculture-related studies. Must be planning to enroll in a two- or four-year agriculture-related curriculum. The application deadline is March 1.

Academic Fields/Career Goals: Agriculture.

Award: Scholarship for use in freshman year; not renewable. *Number:* 20. *Amount:* $1000.

Eligibility Requirements: Applicant must be high school student and planning to enroll or expecting to enroll full-time at a two-year or four-year institution or university. Available to U.S. citizens.

Application Requirements: Application, essay. *Deadline:* March 1.

Contact: Annette Degnan, Director, Advertising and Communications
Agriliance, Land O' Lakes, and Croplan Genetics
PO Box 64089
St. Paul, MN 55164-0089
Phone: 651-355-5126
E-mail: aldegnan@mbrservices.com

ALBERTA HERITAGE SCHOLARSHIP FUND/ ALBERTA SCHOLARSHIP PROGRAMS
http://www.alis.gov.ab.ca

ALBERTA BARLEY COMMISSION EUGENE BOYKO MEMORIAL SCHOLARSHIP

A CAN$500 scholarship is available for students enrolled in the second or subsequent year of postsecondary study and taking courses with an emphasis on crop production and/or crop processing technology. Must be a Canadian citizen and Alberta resident. Application deadline is August 1. For more details see Web site: http://www.alis.gov.ab.ca

Academic Fields/Career Goals: Agriculture.

Award: Scholarship for use in sophomore, junior, or senior years; not renewable. *Number:* 1. *Amount:* $430.

Eligibility Requirements: Applicant must be enrolled or expecting to enroll full-time at a four-year institution or university and resident of Alberta. Available to Canadian citizens.

Application Requirements: Application. *Deadline:* August 1.

Contact: Stuart Dunn, Manager
Alberta Heritage Scholarship Fund/Alberta Scholarship Programs
4th Floor, 9940 106th Street, Box 28000 Station Main
Edmonton, AB T5J 4R4
Canada
Phone: 780-427-8640
Fax: 780-427-1288
E-mail: scholarships@gov.ab.ca

AMARILLO AREA FOUNDATION
http://www.aaf-hf.org

AMARILLO AREA FOUNDATION SCHOLARSHIPS
• *See page 53*

AMERICAN SOCIETY FOR ENOLOGY AND VITICULTURE
http://www.asev.org

AMERICAN SOCIETY FOR ENOLOGY AND VITICULTURE SCHOLARSHIPS

One-time award for college juniors, seniors, and graduate students residing in North America and enrolled in a program studying viticulture, enology, or any field related to the wine and grape industry. Minimum 3.0 GPA for undergraduates; minimum 3.2 GPA for graduate students. Must be a resident of the U.S., Canada, or Mexico.

Academic Fields/Career Goals: Agriculture; Chemical Engineering; Food Science/Nutrition; Horticulture/Floriculture.

Award: Scholarship for use in junior, senior, or graduate years; not renewable. *Number:* varies. *Amount:* $500–$4000.

Eligibility Requirements: Applicant must be enrolled or expecting to enroll full-time at a four-year institution or university. Applicant must have 3.0 GPA or higher. Available to U.S. and non-U.S. citizens.

Application Requirements: Application, essay, financial need analysis, references, transcript. *Deadline:* March 1.

Contact: Scholarship Committee
American Society for Enology and Viticulture
1784 Picasso Avenue, Suite D
Davis, CA 95616
Phone: 530-753-3142
Fax: 530-753-3318
E-mail: society@asev.org

AMERICAN SOCIETY OF AGRICULTURAL ENGINEERS
http://www.asabe.org

AMERICAN SOCIETY OF AGRICULTURAL AND BIOLOGICAL ENGINEERS FOUNDATION SCHOLARSHIP

One scholarship will be awarded to an undergraduate student member of ASAE who has completed at least one year of undergraduate study and has at least one year of undergraduate study remaining. Must be majoring in agriculture or biological engineering. For more details see Web site: http://www.asae.org.

Academic Fields/Career Goals: Agriculture.

Award: Scholarship for use in sophomore, junior, or senior years; not renewable. *Number:* 1. *Amount:* $1000.

Eligibility Requirements: Applicant must be enrolled or expecting to enroll full-time at a two-year or four-year institution or university. Applicant must have 2.5 GPA or higher. Available to U.S. and Canadian citizens.

Application Requirements: Application, financial need analysis. *Deadline:* March 15.

Contact: Carol Flautt, Scholarship Program
American Society of Agricultural Engineers
2950 Niles Road
St. Joseph, MI 49085
Phone: 269-428-6336
Fax: 269-429-3852
E-mail: flautt@asabe.org

JOHN L. AND SARAH G. MERRIAM SCHOLARSHIP

One scholarship will be awarded to an undergraduate student member of ASAE who has completed at least one year of undergraduate study and has at least one year of undergraduate study remaining. Must be majoring in agriculture or biological engineering with an emphasis on the study of soil and water. For more details see Web site: http://www.asae.org

Academic Fields/Career Goals: Agriculture.

Award: Scholarship for use in sophomore, junior, or senior years; not renewable. *Number:* 1. *Amount:* $1000.

Eligibility Requirements: Applicant must be enrolled or expecting to enroll full-time at a two-year or four-year institution or university. Applicant must have 2.5 GPA or higher. Available to U.S. and Canadian citizens.

Application Requirements: Application, essay. *Deadline:* March 15.

Contact: Carol Flautt, Scholarship Program
American Society of Agricultural Engineers
2950 Niles Road
St. Joseph, MI 49085
Phone: 269-428-6336
Fax: 269-429-3852
E-mail: flautt@asabe.org

WILLIAM J. AND MARIJANE E. ADAMS, JR. SCHOLARSHIP

One-time award for a full-time U.S. or Canadian undergraduate who is a student member of the American Society of Agricultural Engineers and a declared major in biological or agricultural engineering. Must be at least a sophomore and have minimum 2.5 GPA. Must be interested in agricultural machinery product design or development. Write for application procedures.

Academic Fields/Career Goals: Agriculture; Biology.

Award: Scholarship for use in sophomore, junior, or senior years; not renewable. *Number:* 1. *Amount:* $1000.

Eligibility Requirements: Applicant must be enrolled or expecting to enroll full-time at a two-year or four-year institution or university. Applicant must have 2.5 GPA or higher. Available to U.S. and Canadian citizens.

Application Requirements: Application, financial need analysis, references. *Deadline:* March 15.

Contact: Carol Flautt, Scholarship Program
American Society of Agricultural Engineers
2950 Niles Road
St. Joseph, MI 49085-9659
Phone: 269-428-6336
Fax: 269-429-3852
E-mail: flautt@asabe.org

AMERICAN SOCIETY OF AGRONOMY, CROP SCIENCE SOCIETY OF AMERICA, SOIL SCIENCE SOCIETY OF AMERICA
http://www.asa-cssa-sssa.org

CROSS-CULTURAL EXPERIENCE PROGRAM

Award of $1500 open to an undergraduate student majoring in soils, crops, and agronomy, or closely related sciences. The student will have completed their freshman, sophomore, or junior years by the end of spring term 2006. Preference will be given to a student that is a member of an SASES Club. Deadline November 1.

Academic Fields/Career Goals: Agriculture.

Award: Scholarship for use in freshman, sophomore, or junior years; not renewable. *Number:* up to 4. *Amount:* up to $1500.

Eligibility Requirements: Applicant must be enrolled or expecting to enroll full-time at a two-year or four-year institution or university. Available to U.S. and non-U.S. citizens.

Application Requirements: Application, resume, references, letter of interest. *Deadline:* November 1.

Contact: Leann Malison, Program Manager
American Society of Agronomy, Crop Science Society of America, Soil Science Society of America
677 South Segoe Road
Madison, WI 53711
Phone: 608-268-4949
Fax: 608-273-2021
E-mail: lmalison@agronomy.org

FRANCIS AND EVELYN CLARK SOIL BIOLOGY SCHOLARSHIP

Award of $2000 available to graduate student working in the field of soil biology, biochemistry, or microbial ecology. Nominations due March 1, reference letters/final nomination submission due March 8.

Academic Fields/Career Goals: Agriculture.

Award: Scholarship for use in junior or senior years; not renewable. *Number:* up to 5. *Amount:* up to $2000.

Eligibility Requirements: Applicant must be enrolled or expecting to enroll full-time at a two-year or four-year institution or university. Available to U.S. and non-U.S. citizens.

Application Requirements: Application, financial need analysis, resume, references, letter of interest. *Deadline:* March 8.

Contact: Leann Malison, Program Manager
American Society of Agronomy, Crop Science Society of America, Soil Science Society of America
677 South Segoe Road
Madison, WI 53711
Phone: 608-268-4949
Fax: 608-273-2021
E-mail: lmalison@agronomy.org

GERALD O. MOTT SCHOLARSHIP

Scholarship of $2500 is provided to a meritorious graduate student in crop science. Must attend an institution in U.S. and be a CSSA or ASA member. Nominations due March 1, reference letters/final nominationsubmission due March 8.

Academic Fields/Career Goals: Agriculture.

Award: Scholarship for use in junior or senior years; not renewable. *Number:* up to 5. *Amount:* up to $2500.

Eligibility Requirements: Applicant must be enrolled or expecting to enroll full-time at a two-year or four-year institution or university. Available to U.S. citizens.

Application Requirements: Application, essay, resume, bibliography, ASA or CSSA membership number. *Deadline:* March 8.

Contact: Leann Malison, Program Manager
American Society of Agronomy, Crop Science Society of America, Soil Science Society of America
677 South Segoe Road
Madison, WI 53711
Phone: 608-268-4949
Fax: 608-273-2021
E-mail: lmalison@agronomy.org

HANK BEACHELL FUTURE LEADER SCHOLARSHIP

Scholarship for undergraduate students for $3500 plus negotiated travel expenses to the scholarship experience site. Must have completed the sophomore year, must be majoring in agronomy, crop science, soil science, or other related disciplines. Preference will be given to a student that is a member of an SASES affiliated club. Nominations due March 1, reference letters/final nomination submission due March 8.

Academic Fields/Career Goals: Agriculture.

Award: Scholarship for use in sophomore year; not renewable. *Number:* up to 4. *Amount:* up to $3500.

Eligibility Requirements: Applicant must be enrolled or expecting to enroll full-time at a two-year or four-year institution or university. Available to U.S. and non-U.S. citizens.

Application Requirements: Application, resume, references, letter of interest. *Deadline:* March 8.

Contact: Leann Malison, Program Manager
American Society of Agronomy, Crop Science Society of America, Soil Science Society of America
677 South Segoe Road
Madison, WI 53711
Phone: 608-268-4949
Fax: 608-273-2021
E-mail: lmalison@agronomy.org

HARRY J. LARSEN/YARA MEMORIAL SCHOLARSHIP

Scholarship of $5000 provided to a meritorious graduate student in practical soil fertility and crop production. Must have completed at least one year of graduate work leading to a MS or PhD at a U.S.institution. Must be ASA, CSSA, and/or SSSA member. Nominations due March 1, reference letters/final nomination submission due March 8.

Academic Fields/Career Goals: Agriculture.

Award: Scholarship for use in junior or senior years; not renewable. *Number:* up to 6. *Amount:* up to $5000.

Eligibility Requirements: Applicant must be enrolled or expecting to enroll full-time at a two-year or four-year institution or university. Available to U.S. citizens.

Application Requirements: Application, essay, resume, references, bibliography, ASA or CSSA membership number. *Deadline:* March 8.

Contact: Leann Malison, Program Manager
American Society of Agronomy, Crop Science Society of America, Soil Science Society of America
677 South Segoe Road
Madison, WI 53711
Phone: 608-268-4949
Fax: 608-273-2021
E-mail: lmalison@agronomy.org

J. FIELDING REED SCHOLARSHIP

Scholarship of $1000 to honor an outstanding undergraduate senior pursuing a career in soil or plant sciences. Must have GPA of 3.0, must have a history of community and campus leadership activities, specifically in agriculture. Nominations due March 1, reference letters/final nomination submission due March 8.

Academic Fields/Career Goals: Agriculture.

Award: Scholarship for use in senior year; not renewable. *Number:* up to 4. *Amount:* up to $1000.

Eligibility Requirements: Applicant must be enrolled or expecting to enroll full-time at a two-year or four-year institution or university. Applicant must have 3.0 GPA or higher. Available to U.S. and non-U.S. citizens.

Application Requirements: Application, resume, references, letter of interest. *Deadline:* March 8.

Contact: Leann Malison, Program Manager
American Society of Agronomy, Crop Science Society of America, Soil Science Society of America
677 South Segoe Road
Madison, WI 53711
Phone: 608-268-4949
Fax: 608-273-2021
E-mail: lmalison@agronomy.org

CALIFORNIA CITRUS MUTUAL SCHOLARSHIP FOUNDATION   http://www.cacitrusmutual.com

CALIFORNIA CITRUS MUTUAL SCHOLARSHIP

Scholarship for students attending college or university whose family is a member of California Citrus Mutual. Must have a major or minor in agricultural related field.

Academic Fields/Career Goals: Agriculture.

Award: Scholarship for use in freshman, sophomore, junior, senior, or graduate years. *Amount:* up to $2000.

Eligibility Requirements: Applicant must be enrolled or expecting to enroll at a four-year institution or university and resident of California. Available to U.S. citizens.

Application Requirements: Application. *Deadline:* July 3.

Contact: Barbara O'Dell, Executive Assistant
California Citrus Mutual Scholarship Foundation
512 North Kaweah Avenue
Exeter, CA 93221
Phone: 559-592-3790
E-mail: barbara@cacitrusmutual.com

CALIFORNIA FARM BUREAU SCHOLARSHIP FOUNDATION   http://www.cfbf.com/programs/scholar/

CALIFORNIA FARM BUREAU SCHOLARSHIP
• *See page 73*

CALIFORNIA WATER AWARENESS CAMPAIGN   http://www.wateraware.org

CALIFORNIA WATER AWARENESS CAMPAIGN WATER SCHOLAR

To provide economic support to graduating high school and/or junior college students who exhibit an interest or are actively pursuing a career in the water industry.

Academic Fields/Career Goals: Agriculture; Environmental Science; Hydrology; Landscape Architecture; Natural Resources.

Award: Scholarship for use in freshman, sophomore, junior, or senior years; not renewable. *Number:* up to 2. *Amount:* $2500.

California Water Awareness Campaign (continued)

Eligibility Requirements: Applicant must be enrolled or expecting to enroll full-time at a four-year institution or university; resident of California and studying in California. Available to U.S. citizens.

Application Requirements: Application, essay, references, transcript. *Deadline:* March 15.

Contact: Lynne Wichmann, Campaign Coordinator
California Water Awareness Campaign
910 K Street
Sacramento, CA 95814
Phone: 916-325-2596
Fax: 916-325-4849
E-mail: cwac@acwanet.com

CANADIAN RECREATIONAL CANOEING ASSOCIATION http://www.paddlingcanada.com

BILL MASON MEMORIAL SCHOLARSHIP FUND

One-time award for Canadian citizens attending a Canadian college or university. Applicant must at least be a sophomore majoring in an outdoor recreation or environmental studies program. An academic standing of B+ (75%) is required. Applicant must be planning a career in this field. Must also provide history of past involvement and leadership as it pertains to major and career goals. Background in canoeing and kayaking is considered an asset. Application deadline is September 30.

Academic Fields/Career Goals: Agriculture; Anthropology; Earth Science; Environmental Science; Geography; Marine Biology; Natural Resources; Natural Sciences; Oceanography; Recreation, Parks, Leisure Studies; Travel/Tourism.

Award: Scholarship for use in sophomore, junior, or senior years; not renewable. *Number:* 1–2. *Amount:* $743–$1000.

Eligibility Requirements: Applicant must be Canadian citizen; enrolled or expecting to enroll full-time at a two-year or four-year institution or university; resident of Alberta, British Columbia, Manitoba, New Brunswick, Newfoundland, North West Territories, Nova Scotia, Ontario, Prince Edward Island, Quebec, Saskatchewan, or Yukon and studying in Alberta, British Columbia, Manitoba, New Brunswick, Newfoundland, North West Territories, Nova Scotia, Ontario, Prince Edward Island, Quebec, Saskatchewan, or Yukon.

Application Requirements: Application, essay, financial need analysis, transcript, birth certificate, cover letter. *Deadline:* September 30.

Contact: c/o Canadian Recreational Canoeing Association
Canadian Recreational Canoeing Association
446 Main Street W, PO Box 398
Merrickville, ON K0G 1N0
Canada
Phone: 613-269-2910
Fax: 888-252-6292
E-mail: info@paddlingcanada.com

CHS FOUNDATION http://www.chsfoundation.org

AGRICULTURE SCHOLARSHIPS
• *See page 74*

COOPERATIVE STUDIES SCHOLARSHIPS
• *See page 74*

FIRST–FLORICULTURE INDUSTRY RESEARCH AND SCHOLARSHIP TRUST http://www.firstinfloriculture.org

HAROLD BETTINGER MEMORIAL SCHOLARSHIP
• *See page 74*

GARDEN CLUB OF AMERICA http://www.gcamerica.org

GARDEN CLUB OF AMERICA AWARDS FOR SUMMER ENVIRONMENTAL STUDIES

One-time award available to students following their first, second, or third year of college who are majoring in environmental studies, ecology, or related field for credit in a summer course at a U.S. college or university. Submit course plan. For use in summer only. Funds two or more students annually. Application on GCA Web site: http://www.gcamerica.org.

Academic Fields/Career Goals: Agriculture; Earth Science; Meteorology/Atmospheric Science; Natural Resources; Physical Sciences and Math.

Award: Scholarship for use in freshman, sophomore, or junior years; not renewable. *Number:* 2. *Amount:* $1500.

Eligibility Requirements: Applicant must be enrolled or expecting to enroll at a four-year institution. Available to U.S. and non-U.S. citizens.

Application Requirements: Application, essay, references, self-addressed stamped envelope, transcript. *Deadline:* February 10.

Contact: Connie Sutton, Scholarship Committee
Garden Club of America
14 East 60th Street
New York, NY 10022
Phone: 212-753-8287
Fax: 212-753-0134

HEART OF AMERICA RESTAURANTS AND INNS/ MACHINE SHED SCHOLARSHIPS http://www.hoari.com

HEART OF AMERICA RESTAURANTS AND INNS/MACHINE SHED AGRICULTURE SCHOLARSHIP

One-time scholarship for college and university students who major in agriculture or a related field. Applicant must be enrolled in a postsecondary educational institution in Iowa, Illinois, Kansas, Minnesota or Wisconsin. Contact institution's financial aid office for application deadline.

Academic Fields/Career Goals: Agriculture.

Award: Scholarship for use in freshman year; not renewable. *Number:* 19. *Amount:* $1000.

Eligibility Requirements: Applicant must be enrolled or expecting to enroll full-time at a two-year or four-year institution or university and studying in Illinois, Iowa, Kansas, Minnesota, or Wisconsin. Available to U.S. citizens.

Application Requirements: Application. *Deadline:* varies.

Contact: Carmen Darland, Program Contact
Heart of America Restaurants and Inns/Machine Shed Scholarships
1501 River Drive
Moline, IL 61625
Phone: 309-797-9300
Fax: 309-797-8700

ILLINOIS STATE TREASURER'S OFFICE http://www.state.il.us

ILLINOIS STATE TREASURER'S OFFICE EXCELLENCE IN AGRICULTURE SCHOLARSHIP PROGRAM

Scholarships awarded annually to Illinois high school seniors who plan to enroll as full-time students in agriculture or agriculture-related studies in an Illinois institution and be committed to pursuing a career in agriculture or an agriculture-related field.

Academic Fields/Career Goals: Agriculture; Animal/Veterinary Sciences.

Award: Scholarship for use in freshman year; not renewable. *Number:* 5. *Amount:* up to $2500.

Eligibility Requirements: Applicant must be high school student; planning to enroll or expecting to enroll full-time at a two-year or four-year or technical institution or university; resident of Illinois and studying in Illinois. Applicant must have 2.5 GPA or higher. Available to U.S. citizens.

Application Requirements: Application, essay, references, test scores, transcript, goal statement, list of activities. *Deadline:* April 12.

Contact: Judy Baar Topinka, Treasurer
Illinois State Treasurer's Office
300 West Jefferson Street, 3rd Floor
Springfield, IL 62702
Phone: 217-557-6439

INTERTRIBAL TIMBER COUNCIL http://www.itcnet.org

TRUMAN D. PICARD SCHOLARSHIP
• *See page 75*

KENTUCKY NATURAL RESOURCES AND ENVIRONMENTAL PROTECTION CABINET http://www.uky.edu/waterresources

CONSERVATION OF NATURAL RESOURCES SCHOLARSHIP

Scholarship available for a student currently enrolled in college in a Kentucky public institution who has declared a major in the field of agriculture or conservation of natural resources. Must be Kentucky resident.

Academic Fields/Career Goals: Agriculture; Environmental Science; Natural Resources.

Award: Scholarship for use in freshman, sophomore, junior, or senior years; not renewable. *Number:* 1. *Amount:* $1000.

Eligibility Requirements: Applicant must be enrolled or expecting to enroll at a four-year institution or university; resident of Kentucky and studying in Kentucky. Available to U.S. citizens.

Application Requirements: Application, essay, references, transcript. *Deadline:* March 31.

Contact: Kentucky Division of Conservation
Kentucky Natural Resources and Environmental Protection Cabinet
375 Versailles Road
Frankfort, KY 40601
Phone: 502-573-3080
E-mail: steve.coleman@mail.state.ky.us

CONSERVATION OF NATURAL RESOURCES SCHOLARSHIP FOR NONTRADITIONAL STUDENTS

Scholarship available for student at least age 25 pursuing an undergraduate degree in agriculture or a related natural resources field. Must be enrolled in a Kentucky public institution and be a resident of Kentucky.

Academic Fields/Career Goals: Agriculture; Environmental Science; Natural Resources.

Award: Scholarship for use in freshman, sophomore, junior, or senior years; not renewable. *Number:* 1. *Amount:* $1000.

Eligibility Requirements: Applicant must be age 25; enrolled or expecting to enroll at a two-year or four-year institution or university; resident of Kentucky and studying in Kentucky. Available to U.S. citizens.

Application Requirements: Application, essay, references, transcript. *Deadline:* March 31.

Contact: Kentucky Association of Conservation
Kentucky Natural Resources and Environmental Protection Cabinet
375 Versailles Road
Frankfort, KY 40601
Phone: 502-573-3080
E-mail: steve.coleman@mail.state.ky.us

GEORGE R. CRAFTON SCHOLARSHIP

Scholarship available for a high school student applying for enrollment in a Kentucky public institution in the forthcoming year in an area related to agriculture and conservation of natural resources. Must be a Kentucky resident.

Academic Fields/Career Goals: Agriculture; Environmental Science; Natural Resources.

Award: Scholarship for use in freshman year; not renewable. *Number:* 1. *Amount:* $1000.

Eligibility Requirements: Applicant must be high school student; planning to enroll or expecting to enroll at a two-year or four-year institution or university; resident of Kentucky and studying in Kentucky. Available to U.S. citizens.

Application Requirements: Application, essay, references, transcript. *Deadline:* March 31.

Contact: Kentucky Association of Conservation
Kentucky Natural Resources and Environmental Protection Cabinet
375 Versailles Road
Frankfort, KY 40601
Phone: 502-573-3080
E-mail: steve.coleman@mail.state.ky.us

MAINE COMMUNITY FOUNDATION, INC. http://www.mainecf.org

RONALD P. GUERRETTE FUTURE FARMERS OF AMERICA SCHOLARSHIP FUND

Scholarship assistance to a student from Maine. Applicants must be FFA members and have a demonstrated interest and motivation to pursue a career in farming and/or agriculture. Deadline for applications is March 1.

Academic Fields/Career Goals: Agriculture.

Award: Scholarship for use in freshman, sophomore, junior, or senior years; not renewable. *Number:* 1.

Eligibility Requirements: Applicant must be enrolled or expecting to enroll full-time at an institution or university and resident of Maine. Available to U.S. citizens.

Application Requirements: Application, essay, financial need analysis, references, transcript. *Deadline:* March 1.

Contact: Doug Robertson, State FFA Advisor
Maine Community Foundation, Inc.
Department of Education, 23 State House Station
Augusta, ME 04333-0023
Phone: 207-624-6744
Fax: 207-624-6731

MAINE DEPARTMENT OF AGRICULTURE, FOOD AND RURAL RESOURCES http://www.maine.gov/agriculture

MAINE RURAL REHABILITATION FUND SCHOLARSHIP PROGRAM
• See page 75

MASTER BREWERS ASSOCIATION OF THE AMERICAS http://www.mbaa.com

MASTER BREWERS ASSOCIATION OF THE AMERICAS

Renewable award to college students entering their third year of study in a science related to the technical areas of malting and brewing. Must be a child of an MBAA member or person employed at least 5 years in the brewing industry. Minimum 3.0 GPA required.

Academic Fields/Career Goals: Agriculture; Biology; Chemical Engineering; Food Science/Nutrition.

Award: Scholarship for use in junior year; renewable. *Number:* 2. *Amount:* $4000.

Eligibility Requirements: Applicant must be enrolled or expecting to enroll full-time at a four-year institution. Applicant or parent of applicant must have employment or volunteer experience in brewing industry. Applicant must have 3.0 GPA or higher. Available to U.S. and non-U.S. citizens.

Application Requirements: Application, references. *Deadline:* January 16.

Contact: Linda Schmitt, Scholarship Coordinator
Master Brewers Association of the Americas
3340 Pilot Knob Road
St. Paul, MN 55121
Phone: 651-994-3828
Fax: 651-454-0766
E-mail: lschmitt@scisoc.org

MINNESOTA SOYBEAN RESEARCH AND PROMOTION COUNCIL http://mnsoybean.org

MINNESOTA SOYBEAN RESEARCH AND PROMOTION COUNCIL YOUTH SOYBEAN SCHOLARSHIP
• See page 75

MONSANTO AGRIBUSINESS SCHOLARSHIP http://www.monsanto.ca

MONSANTO AGRI-BUSINESS SCHOLARSHIP

Scholarship available to a first year post secondary student who is a Canadian citizen. Must be majoring in the field of agriculture, forestry, business, or biotechnology at a Canadian institution.

Academic Fields/Career Goals: Agriculture; Business/Consumer Services.

Award: Scholarship for use in freshman year. *Amount:* up to $1500.

Monsanto Agribusiness Scholarship (continued)

Eligibility Requirements: Applicant must be enrolled or expecting to enroll at a four-year institution or university. Available to U.S. and Canadian citizens.

Application Requirements: Application, essay, references, transcript. *Deadline:* varies.

Contact: Bob Adamson, Director, Agriculture Biotechnology
Enrichment
Monsanto Agribusiness Scholarship
67 Scurfield Boulevard
Winnipeg, Manitoba R3J 3W2
Canada
Phone: 204-985-1000
Fax: 204-488-1605

NATIONAL COUNCIL OF STATE GARDEN CLUBS, INC. SCHOLARSHIP http://www.gardenclub.org

NATIONAL COUNCIL OF STATE GARDEN CLUBS, INC. SCHOLARSHIP

Scholarship to students for study in agriculture education, horticulture, floriculture, landscape design, botany, biology, plant pathology/science, forestry, agronomy, environmental concerns.

Academic Fields/Career Goals: Agriculture; Biology; Environmental Science; Horticulture/Floriculture.

Award: Scholarship for use in sophomore, junior, senior, or graduate years. *Amount:* $3500.

Eligibility Requirements: Applicant must be enrolled or expecting to enroll full-time at a four-year institution or university. Applicant must have 3.0 GPA or higher. Available to U.S. citizens.

Application Requirements: Application, financial need analysis, references, transcript. *Deadline:* March 1.

Contact: Linda Nelson
National Council of State Garden Clubs, Inc. Scholarship
543 Lakefair Place N
Keizer, OR 97303-3590
Phone: 503-393-4439
E-mail: flwrcellar@msn.com

NATIONAL DAIRY SHRINE http://www.dairyshrine.org

KILDEE SCHOLARSHIPS

Top twenty-five contestants in the three most recent national intercollegiate Dairy Cattle Judging contests are eligible to apply for two $3000 one-time scholarships for graduate study in the field related to dairy cattle production at university of choice. Also the top 25 contestants in the most recent National 4-H & National FFA Dairy Judging contests are eligible to apply for one $2000 Scholarship for undergraduate study in the field related to dairy cattle production at university of choice.

Academic Fields/Career Goals: Agriculture.

Award: Scholarship for use in freshman, sophomore, junior, senior, or graduate years; not renewable. *Number:* 3. *Amount:* $2000–$3000.

Eligibility Requirements: Applicant must be enrolled or expecting to enroll full-time at a four-year institution or university. Available to U.S. and non-U.S. citizens.

Application Requirements: Application, applicant must enter a contest. *Deadline:* March 15.

Contact: Maurice E. Core, Executive Director
National Dairy Shrine
1224 Alton Darby Creek Road
Columbus, OH 43228-9792
Phone: 614-878-5333
Fax: 614-870-2622
E-mail: shrine@cobaselect.com

MARSHALL E. MCCULLOUGH- NATIONAL DAIRY SHRINE SCHOLARSHIPS

Applicant must be a high school senior planning to enter a four-year college or university with intent to major in dairy/animal science with a communications emphasis or agricultural journalism with a dairy/animal science emphasis. One $2500 and one $1000 scholarship are given. Half of the money is awarded during each winner's first college semester, with the second half available following successful completion of the students' sophomore year.

Academic Fields/Career Goals: Agriculture; Animal/Veterinary Sciences.

Award: Scholarship for use in freshman or junior years; not renewable. *Number:* 2. *Amount:* $1000–$2500.

Eligibility Requirements: Applicant must be high school student and planning to enroll or expecting to enroll full-time at a four-year institution or university. Available to U.S. and non-U.S. citizens.

Application Requirements: Application, references, transcript. *Deadline:* March 15.

Contact: Maurice E. Core, Executive Director
National Dairy Shrine
1224 Alton Darby Creek Road
Columbus, OH 43228-9792
E-mail: shrine@cobaselect.com

NATIONAL DAIRY SHRINE LAGER DAIRY SCHOLARSHIP

Scholarship of $1000 is awarded annually to encourage qualified second year dairy students in a two-year agricultural school to pursue careers in the dairy industry.

Academic Fields/Career Goals: Agriculture.

Award: Scholarship for use in sophomore year; not renewable. *Amount:* up to $1000.

Eligibility Requirements: Applicant must be enrolled or expecting to enroll at a two-year institution. Applicant must have 2.5 GPA or higher. Available to U.S. citizens.

Application Requirements: Application, references, transcript. *Deadline:* July 1.

Contact: Maurice Core, Executive Director
National Dairy Shrine
1224 Alton Darby Creek Road
Columbus, OH 43228-9792
Phone: 614-878-5333
Fax: 614-870-2622
E-mail: shrine@cobaselect.com

NATIONAL DAIRY SHRINE/DAIRY MARKETING, INC. MILK MARKETING SCHOLARSHIPS

One-time awards for undergraduate students pursuing careers in marketing of dairy products. Major areas can include: dairy science, animal science, agricultural economics, agricultural communications, agricultural education, general education, food and nutrition, home economics and journalism.

Academic Fields/Career Goals: Agriculture; Animal/Veterinary Sciences; Food Science/Nutrition.

Award: Scholarship for use in sophomore, junior, or senior years; not renewable. *Number:* 7–10. *Amount:* $1000–$1500.

Eligibility Requirements: Applicant must be enrolled or expecting to enroll full-time at a four-year institution or university. Applicant must have 2.5 GPA or higher. Available to U.S. citizens.

Application Requirements: Application, references, transcript. *Deadline:* March 15.

Contact: Maurice E. Core, Executive Director
National Dairy Shrine
1224 Alton Darby Creek Road
Columbus, OH 43228-9792
Phone: 614-878-5333
Fax: 614-870-2622
E-mail: shrine@cobaselect.com

NATIONAL DAIRY SHRINE/KLUSSENDORF SCHOLARSHIP

The scholarship will be granted to a student successfully completing their first, second or third years at a 2-year or 4-year college or university. To be eligible, students must major in a Dairy Science (Animal Science) curriculum with plans to enter the dairy cattle field as a breeder, owner, herdsperson or fitter.

Academic Fields/Career Goals: Agriculture.

Award: Scholarship for use in freshman, sophomore, or junior years; not renewable. *Number:* 1. *Amount:* $1000.

Eligibility Requirements: Applicant must be enrolled or expecting to enroll full-time at a two-year or four-year institution or university. Available to U.S. and non-U.S. citizens.

Application Requirements: Application, applicant must enter a contest, transcript. *Deadline:* March 15.

Contact: Maurice E. Core, Executive Director
National Dairy Shrine
1224 Alton Darby Creek Road
Columbus, OH 43228-9792
Phone: 614-878-5333
Fax: 614-870-2622
E-mail: shrine@cobaselect.com

NDS STUDENT RECOGNITION CONTEST
• *See page 75*

PROGRESSIVE DAIRY PRODUCER AWARD

Two $2000 educational/travel awards for outstanding young dairy producers 21-45 years of age. Open to an individual, couple, or family/multi-partner operation. Must be U.S. citizen.

Academic Fields/Career Goals: Agriculture.

Award: Prize for use in freshman, sophomore, junior, senior, or graduate years; not renewable. *Number:* 2. *Amount:* $2000.

Eligibility Requirements: Applicant must be age 21-45 and enrolled or expecting to enroll at an institution or university. Available to U.S. citizens.

Application Requirements: Application, applicant must enter a contest. *Deadline:* March 15.

Contact: Maurice E. Core, Executive Director
National Dairy Shrine
1224 Alton Darby Creek Road
Columbus, OH 43228-9792
Phone: 614-878-5333
Fax: 614-870-2622
E-mail: shrine@cobaselect.com

NATIONAL GARDEN CLUBS, INC.   http://www.gardenclub.org

NATIONAL GARDEN CLUBS, INC. SCHOLARSHIP PROGRAM

One-time award for full-time students in plant sciences, agriculture and related or allied subjects. Applicants must have at least a 3.25 GPA. Contact Garden Club chairperson in state of residence or write for brochure.

Academic Fields/Career Goals: Agriculture; Biology; Earth Science; Economics; Environmental Science; Horticulture/Floriculture; Landscape Architecture.

Award: Scholarship for use in junior, senior, or graduate years; not renewable. *Number:* 31–34. *Amount:* up to $3500.

Eligibility Requirements: Applicant must be enrolled or expecting to enroll full-time at a four-year institution or university. Available to U.S. citizens.

Application Requirements: Application, financial need analysis, photo, resume, references, transcript. *Deadline:* March 1.

Contact: Linda Nelson, Fourth Vice-President, NGC, Inc
National Garden Clubs, Inc.
543 Lakefair Place N
Keizer, OR 97303-3590
Phone: 503-393-4439
E-mail: flwrcellar@msn.com

NATIONAL POTATO COUNCIL WOMEN'S AUXILIARY   http://www.nationalpotatocouncil.org

POTATO INDUSTRY SCHOLARSHIP
• *See page 76*

NATIONAL POULTRY AND FOOD DISTRIBUTORS ASSOCIATION   http://www.npfda.org

NATIONAL POULTRY AND FOOD DISTRIBUTORS ASSOCIATION SCHOLARSHIP FOUNDATION
• *See page 76*

NEW YORK STATE GRANGE   http://www.nysgrange.com/

HOWARD F. DENISE SCHOLARSHIP

Awards for undergraduates under 21 years old to pursue studies in agriculture. Must be a New York resident with a minimum 3.0 GPA. One-time award of $1000.

Academic Fields/Career Goals: Agriculture.

Award: Scholarship for use in freshman, sophomore, junior, or senior years; not renewable. *Number:* 6. *Amount:* $1000.

Eligibility Requirements: Applicant must be age 20 or under; enrolled or expecting to enroll full-time at a two-year or four-year institution and resident of New York. Applicant must have 3.0 GPA or higher. Available to U.S. citizens.

Application Requirements: Application, financial need analysis, references, transcript. *Deadline:* April 15.

Contact: Ann Hall, Scholarship Chairperson
New York State Grange
100 Grange Place
Cortland, NY 13045
Phone: 607-756-7553
Fax: 607-756-7757
E-mail: nysgrange@nysgrange.com

OHIO 4-H   http://www.ohio4h.org

PAUL A. & ETHEL I. SMITH 4-H SCHOLARSHIP

Nine $2500 scholarships will be awarded. Applicants must be a present or former 4-H member, senior in high school, and planning to enroll as a freshman in the fall at The Ohio State University, ATI or any of its regional campuses, in the College of Food, Agricultural, and Environmental Sciences, including the School of Natural Resources to pursue an education in farming or agriculture.

Academic Fields/Career Goals: Agriculture.

Award: Scholarship for use in freshman year. *Number:* 9. *Amount:* $2500.

Eligibility Requirements: Applicant must be enrolled or expecting to enroll at an institution or university and studying in Ohio. Applicant or parent of applicant must be member of National 4-H. Available to U.S. citizens.

Application Requirements: Application, essay, resume, references, transcript. *Deadline:* January 27.

Contact: Jeff King, Assistant Director
Ohio 4-H
State 4-H Office, Room 25 Agriculture Administration Building
2120 Fyffe Road
Columbus, OH 43210-1084
Phone: 614-292-4444
Fax: 614-292-5937
E-mail: 4hweb@ag.osu.edu

OHIO FARMERS UNION   http://www.ohfarmersunion.org

JOSEPH FITCHER SCHOLARSHIP CONTEST

Scholarship available to member of Ohio Farmers Union who is a high school junior or senior, or enrolled as a college freshman . Participants are to submit an application obtained from OFU and a typed 500 - 1000 word essay on "Agricultural Opportunities in the Future." Award of $1000 to winner and $250 to two runners-up.

Academic Fields/Career Goals: Agriculture.

Award: Scholarship for use in freshman year. *Number:* 1–3. *Amount:* $250–$1000.

Eligibility Requirements: Applicant must be enrolled or expecting to enroll at a four-year institution or university. Applicant or parent of applicant must be member of Ohio Farmers Union. Available to U.S. citizens.

Application Requirements: Application, essay. *Deadline:* December 31.

Contact: Maria Gordon
Ohio Farmers Union
PO Box 363
Ottawa, OH 45875
Phone: 419-523-5300
E-mail: m-gordon@ohfarmersunion.org

Ohio Farmers Union (continued)

VIRGIL THOMPSON MEMORIAL SCHOLARSHIP CONTEST
• See page 76

OREGON SHEEP GROWERS ASSOCIATION
http://www.sheeporegon.com

OREGON SHEEP GROWERS ASSOCIATION MEMORIAL SCHOLARSHIP

One-time award for college students majoring in agricultural science or veterinary medicine pursuing careers in the sheep industry. Must be U.S. citizens and Oregon residents studying at a four-year institution or university. Freshmen are not eligible.

Academic Fields/Career Goals: Agriculture; Animal/Veterinary Sciences.

Award: Scholarship for use in sophomore, junior, senior, or graduate years; not renewable. *Number:* 1–2. *Amount:* $500–$1000.

Eligibility Requirements: Applicant must be enrolled or expecting to enroll full-time at a four-year institution or university and resident of Oregon. Available to U.S. citizens.

Application Requirements: Application, essay, references, transcript. *Deadline:* July 1.

Contact: Scholarship Committee
Oregon Sheep Growers Association
1270 Chemeketa Street, NE
Salem, OR 97301
Phone: 503-364-5462
Fax: 503-585-1921
E-mail: Info@SheepOregon.com

OREGON STUDENT ASSISTANCE COMMISSION
http://www.osac.state.or.us

AGRICULTURAL-WOMEN-IN-NETWORK SCHOLARSHIP

One scholarship for Oregon residents who are agricultural majors with junior or senior undergraduate standing. Must attend a four-year college in Washington, Oregon, or Idaho. Check http://www.osac.state.or.us for more information. Preference for female students.

Academic Fields/Career Goals: Agriculture.

Award: Scholarship for use in junior or senior years; renewable. *Number:* 1. *Amount:* $1000.

Eligibility Requirements: Applicant must be enrolled or expecting to enroll full-time at a four-year institution or university; resident of Oregon and studying in Idaho, Oregon, or Washington. Available to U.S. citizens.

Application Requirements: Application, essay, financial need analysis, transcript, activity chart. *Deadline:* March 1.

Contact: Director of Grant Programs
Oregon Student Assistance Commission
1500 Valley River Drive, Suite 100
Eugene, OR 97401-7020
Phone: 800-452-8807 Ext. 7395

KEY TECHNOLOGY SCHOLARSHIP

Scholarship for graduating high school seniors who reside in Crook, Deschutes, Jackson, Jefferson, Josephine, or Umatilla County, Oregon, or WallaWalla County, Washington. Must have 3.0 GPA and major in engineering or electronics. Dependents of Key employees are given preference. Deadline is March 1.

Academic Fields/Career Goals: Agriculture; Electrical Engineering/Electronics; Engineering/Technology; Mechanical Engineering.

Award: Scholarship for use in freshman, sophomore, junior, or senior years; renewable. *Number:* varies. *Amount:* $500.

Eligibility Requirements: Applicant must be high school student; planning to enroll or expecting to enroll at an institution or university and resident of Oregon or Washington. Applicant must have 3.0 GPA or higher. Available to U.S. citizens.

Application Requirements: Application, essay, financial need analysis, transcript, activities chart. *Deadline:* March 1.

Contact: Director of Grant Programs
Oregon Student Assistance Commission
1500 Valley River Drive, Suite 100
Eugene, OR 97401-7020
Phone: 800-452-8807 Ext. 7395

PENNSYLVANIA ASSOCIATION OF CONSERVATION DISTRICTS AUXILIARY
http://www.blairconservationdistrict.org

PACD AUXILIARY SCHOLARSHIPS
• See page 76

PROFESSIONAL GROUNDS MANAGEMENT SOCIETY
http://www.pgms.org

ANNE SEAMAN PROFESSIONAL GROUNDS MANAGEMENT SOCIETY MEMORIAL SCHOLARSHIP

One-time award for citizens of the U.S. and Canada who are studying to enter the field of grounds management or a closely related field such as agronomy, horticulture, landscape contracting, and irrigation on a full-time basis. Write for further information. Must be sponsored by a PGMS member. The member must write a letter of recommendation for the applicant.

Academic Fields/Career Goals: Agriculture; Civil Engineering; Horticulture/Floriculture; Landscape Architecture.

Award: Scholarship for use in freshman, sophomore, junior, or senior years; not renewable. *Number:* 3. *Amount:* $250–$1500.

Eligibility Requirements: Applicant must be enrolled or expecting to enroll full-time at a two-year or four-year institution. Available to U.S. and Canadian citizens.

Application Requirements: Application, autobiography, financial need analysis, resume, references, transcript. *Deadline:* July 1.

Contact: Heather Waldschmiat, Association Coordinator
Professional Grounds Management Society
720 Light Street
Baltimore, MD 21230-3816
Phone: 410-223-2861
Fax: 410-752-8295
E-mail: pgms@assnhqtrs.com

SIGMA XI, THE SCIENTIFIC RESEARCH SOCIETY
http://www.sigmaxi.org

SIGMA XI GRANTS-IN-AID OF RESEARCH

The program awards grants of up to $1000 to students from all areas of the sciences and engineering. Designated funds from the National Academy of Sciences allow for grants of up to $5000 for astronomy research and $2500 for vision related research. Students use the funding to pay for travel expenses to and from a research site, or for purchase of non-standard laboratory equipment necessary to complete a specific research project.

Academic Fields/Career Goals: Agriculture; Animal/Veterinary Sciences; Biology; Chemical Engineering; Earth Science; Engineering/Technology; Health and Medical Sciences; Mechanical Engineering; Meteorology/Atmospheric Science; Physical Sciences and Math; Science, Technology, and Society; Social Sciences.

Award: Grant for use in freshman, sophomore, junior, senior, or graduate years; not renewable. *Number:* 1–350. *Amount:* $1000–$5000.

Eligibility Requirements: Applicant must be enrolled or expecting to enroll full-time at a four-year institution or university. Available to U.S. and non-U.S. citizens.

Application Requirements: Application, references. *Deadline:* varies.

Contact: Kevin Bowen, Grants Coordinator
Sigma Xi, The Scientific Research Society
99 Alexander Dr, PO Box 13975
Research Triangle Park, NC 27709
Phone: 800-243-6534
E-mail: giar@sigmaxi.org

SOCIETY FOR RANGE MANAGEMENT
http://www.rangelands.org

MASONIC RANGE SCIENCE SCHOLARSHIP
• See page 76

SOIL AND WATER CONSERVATION SOCIETY
http://www.swcs.org

SWCS MELVILLE H. COHEE STUDENT LEADER CONSERVATION SCHOLARSHIP

Provides financial assistance to members of the SWCS who are in their junior or senior year of full-time undergraduate study or are pursuing graduate level studies with a natural resource conservation orientation at properly accredited colleges or universities. Download the application form from the SWCS homepage at http://www.swcs.org

Academic Fields/Career Goals: Agriculture; Economics; Natural Resources; Natural Sciences.

Award: Scholarship for use in junior, senior, or graduate years; not renewable. *Number:* 2. *Amount:* $1000.

Eligibility Requirements: Applicant must be enrolled or expecting to enroll full-time at a four-year institution or university. Applicant must have 3.0 GPA or higher. Available to U.S. and non-U.S. citizens.

Application Requirements: Application, financial need analysis. *Deadline:* February 12.

Contact: Nancy Herselius, Member Services Coordinator
Soil and Water Conservation Society
7515 NE Ankeny Road
Ankeny, IA 50021-9764
Phone: 515-289-2331 Ext. 17
Fax: 515-289-1227
E-mail: nancyh@swcs.org

SOIL AND WATER CONSERVATION SOCIETY-NEW JERSEY CHAPTER
http://www.geocities.com/njswcs

EDWARD R. HALL SCHOLARSHIP
• See page 76

SOUTH DAKOTA BOARD OF REGENTS
http://www.sdbor.edu

SOUTH DAKOTA BOARD OF REGENTS BJUGSTAD SCHOLARSHIP
• See page 77

UNITED AGRIBUSINESS LEAGUE
http://www.ual.org

UNITED AGRIBUSINESS LEAGUE SCHOLARSHIP PROGRAM
• See page 77

UNITED AGRICULTURAL BENEFIT TRUST SCHOLARSHIP
• See page 77

UNITED NEGRO COLLEGE FUND
http://www.uncf.org

CARGILL SCHOLARSHIP PROGRAM
• See page 70

WOMEN GROCERS OF AMERICA
http://www.nationalgrocers.org

MARY MACEY SCHOLARSHIP

Award for students intending to pursue a career in the independent sector of the grocery industry. One-time award for students who have completed freshman year. Submit statement and recommendation from sponsor in the grocery industry. Applicant should have a minimum 2.0 grade point average.

Academic Fields/Career Goals: Agriculture; Business/Consumer Services; Communications; Economics; Food Service/Hospitality.

Award: Scholarship for use in sophomore, junior, senior, graduate, or postgraduate years; not renewable. *Number:* 2. *Amount:* $1000.

Eligibility Requirements: Applicant must be enrolled or expecting to enroll full-time at a two-year or four-year institution or university. Available to U.S. citizens.

Application Requirements: Application, transcript, personal statement. *Deadline:* June 1.

Contact: Anne Wintersteen, Director of Administration
Women Grocers of America
1005 North Glebe Road, Suite 250
Arlington, VA 22201-5758
Phone: 703-516-0700
Fax: 703-516-0115
E-mail: awintersteen@nationalgrocers.org

AMERICAN STUDIES

ORGANIZATION OF AMERICAN HISTORIANS
http://www.oah.org

BINKLEY-STEPHENSON AWARD

One-time award of $500 for the best scholarly article published in the Journal of American History during the preceding calendar year.

Academic Fields/Career Goals: American Studies; History.

Award: Prize for use in freshman, sophomore, junior, senior, graduate, or postgraduate years; not renewable. *Number:* 1. *Amount:* $500.

Eligibility Requirements: Applicant must be enrolled or expecting to enroll at a two-year or four-year or technical institution or university. Available to U.S. and non-U.S. citizens.

Application Requirements: Applicant must enter a contest. *Deadline:* Continuous.

Contact: Estelle Freedman, Committee Chair, Stanford University
Phone: 415-723-2558

SONS OF THE REPUBLIC OF TEXAS
http://www.srttexas.org

TEXAS HISTORY ESSAY CONTEST

Contest for best essay on the history of Texas written by graduating seniors in any high school in the U.S.. History, government and English students are particularly encouraged to participate.

Academic Fields/Career Goals: American Studies; History.

Award: Prize for use in freshman year. *Number:* 3. *Amount:* $1000–$3000.

Eligibility Requirements: Applicant must be high school student; planning to enroll or expecting to enroll at a four-year institution or university and must have an interest in writing. Available to U.S. citizens.

Application Requirements: *Deadline:* February 1.

Contact: Janet Hickl, SRT Administrative Assistant
Sons of the Republic of Texas
1717 8th Street
Bay City, TX 77414
Phone: 979-245-6644
E-mail: srttexas@srttexas.org

THE LINCOLN FORUM
http://www.thelincolnforum.org

PLATT FAMILY SCHOLARSHIP PRIZE ESSAY CONTEST

Scholarship essay contest for full-time students in an American college or university. Entries must contain a minimum of 1500 and a maximum of 5000 words. The essay must be typed and include a works-cited page or bibliography. End notes are suggested but not required. Deadline for entries is July 31.

Academic Fields/Career Goals: American Studies; History.

Award: Scholarship for use in freshman, sophomore, junior, senior, or graduate years. *Number:* 3. *Amount:* $250–$1000.

Eligibility Requirements: Applicant must be enrolled or expecting to enroll full-time at a four-year institution or university and must have an interest in writing. Available to U.S. citizens.

The Lincoln Forum (continued)

Application Requirements: Essay. *Deadline:* July 31.

Contact: Don McCue, Curator
The Lincoln Forum
125 West Vine Street
Redlands, CA 92373
Phone: 909-798-7632
E-mail: archives@akspl.org

ANIMAL/VETERINARY SCIENCES

AMERICAN QUARTER HORSE FOUNDATION (AQHF)
http://www.aqha.org/aqhya

AQHF RACING SCHOLARSHIPS

Must be member of AQHA or AQHYA and intend to pursue a career in the American Quarter Horse racing industry or related field. Recipients receive $2000 per year for four years. Minimum 2.5 GPA required.

Academic Fields/Career Goals: Animal/Veterinary Sciences.

Award: Scholarship for use in freshman, sophomore, junior, or senior years; renewable. *Number:* 5. *Amount:* $8000.

Eligibility Requirements: Applicant must be enrolled or expecting to enroll full-time at a two-year or four-year or technical institution or university. Applicant or parent of applicant must be member of American Quarter Horse Association. Applicant must have 2.5 GPA or higher. Available to U.S. and Canadian citizens.

Application Requirements: Application, essay, financial need analysis, photo, references, transcript. *Deadline:* February 1.

Contact: Laura Owens, Scholarship Coordinator
American Quarter Horse Foundation (AQHF)
2601 I-40 East
Amarillo, TX 79104
Phone: 806-378-5034
Fax: 806-376-1005
E-mail: lowens@aqha.org

AQHF TELEPHONY SCHOLARSHIP FOR SENIOR VETERINARY STUDENTS

$10,000 awarded to member of AQHA in his/her third year of veterinary medicine. Money will be applied to last year of coursework. Minimum 3.0 GPA required. Funding will be applied to student of last year of the veterinary program.

Academic Fields/Career Goals: Animal/Veterinary Sciences.

Award: Scholarship for use in junior, or graduate years; not renewable. *Number:* 1. *Amount:* $5000–$10,000.

Eligibility Requirements: Applicant must be enrolled or expecting to enroll full-time at a four-year institution or university. Applicant or parent of applicant must be member of American Quarter Horse Association. Applicant must have 3.0 GPA or higher. Available to U.S. and Canadian citizens.

Application Requirements: Application, financial need analysis, photo, references, transcript. *Deadline:* February 1.

Contact: Laura Owens
Phone: 806-378-5034
E-mail: lowens@aqha.org

APPALOOSA HORSE CLUB-APPALOOSA YOUTH PROGRAM
http://www.appaloosa.com

LEW AND JOANN EKLUND EDUCATIONAL SCHOLARSHIP

One-time award for college juniors and seniors and graduate students studying a field related to the equine industry. Must be member or dependent of member of the Appaloosa Horse Club. Submit picture and three recommendations. Award based on merit.

Academic Fields/Career Goals: Animal/Veterinary Sciences.

Award: Scholarship for use in junior, senior, or graduate years; not renewable. *Number:* 1. *Amount:* $2000.

Eligibility Requirements: Applicant must be enrolled or expecting to enroll full-time at a four-year institution or university. Applicant or parent of applicant must be member of Appaloosa Horse Club/

Appaloosa Youth Association. Applicant must have 3.5 GPA or higher. Available to U.S. and non-U.S. citizens.

Application Requirements: Application, essay, photo, references, transcript. *Deadline:* June 10.

Contact: Keeley Gant, AYF Coordinator
Appaloosa Horse Club-Appaloosa Youth Program
2720 West Pullman Road
Moscow, ID 83843
Phone: 208-882-5578 Ext. 264
Fax: 208-882-8150
E-mail: aphc@appaloosa.com

ARKANSAS DEPARTMENT OF HIGHER EDUCATION
http://www.arkansashighered.com

ARKANSAS HEALTH EDUCATION GRANT PROGRAM (ARHEG)

Award provides assistance to Arkansas residents pursuing professional degrees in dentistry, optometry, veterinary medicine, podiatry, chiropractic medicine, or osteopathic medicine at out-of-state, accredited institutions (programs that are unavailable in Arkansas).

Academic Fields/Career Goals: Animal/Veterinary Sciences; Dental Health/Services; Health and Medical Sciences.

Award: Grant for use in sophomore, junior, senior, or graduate years; renewable. *Number:* 258–288. *Amount:* $5000–$14,600.

Eligibility Requirements: Applicant must be enrolled or expecting to enroll full-time at a four-year institution or university and resident of Arkansas. Available to U.S. citizens.

Application Requirements: Application, affidavit of Arkansas residency. *Deadline:* Continuous.

Contact: Judy McAinsh, Coordinator, Arkansas Health Education Grant Program
Arkansas Department of Higher Education
114 East Capitol
Little Rock, AR 72201-3818
Phone: 501-371-2013
Fax: 501-371-2002
E-mail: judym@adhe.arknet.edu

ASSOCIATION FOR WOMEN IN SCIENCE EDUCATIONAL FOUNDATION
http://www.awis.org/ed_foundation.html

ASSOCIATION FOR WOMEN IN SCIENCE COLLEGE SCHOLARSHIP

The College Scholarship is for women who plan a career in science as a researcher and/or teacher. Applicants must be high school seniors with a GPA of 3.75 or higher and SAT scores of at least 1200. Open to U.S. citizens only.

Academic Fields/Career Goals: Animal/Veterinary Sciences; Biology; Chemical Engineering; Computer Science/Data Processing; Earth Science; Engineering/Technology; Materials Science, Engineering, and Metallurgy; Mechanical Engineering; Meteorology/Atmospheric Science; Natural Sciences; Nuclear Science; Physical Sciences and Math.

Award: Scholarship for use in freshman year; not renewable. *Number:* 2–10. *Amount:* $100–$1000.

Eligibility Requirements: Applicant must be high school student; planning to enroll or expecting to enroll full-time at a four-year institution or university and female. Available to U.S. citizens.

Application Requirements: Application, essay, references, test scores, transcript. *Deadline:* January 19.

Contact: Barbara Filner, President
Association for Women in Science Educational Foundation
7008 Richard Drive
Bethesda, MD 20817-4838
Phone: 301-229-9243
E-mail: awisedfd@aol.com

ILLINOIS STATE TREASURER'S OFFICE
http://www.state.il.us

ILLINOIS STATE TREASURER'S OFFICE EXCELLENCE IN AGRICULTURE SCHOLARSHIP PROGRAM
• *See page 80*

LOUISIANA OFFICE OF STUDENT FINANCIAL ASSISTANCE
http://www.osfa.state.la.us

ROCKEFELLER STATE WILDLIFE SCHOLARSHIP

Awarded to high school graduates, college undergraduates and graduate students majoring in forestry, wildlife or marine science. Renewable up to five years as an undergraduate and two years as a graduate. Must have at least a 2.5 GPA and have taken the ACT or SAT.

Academic Fields/Career Goals: Animal/Veterinary Sciences; Applied Sciences; Marine Biology; Natural Resources.

Award: Scholarship for use in freshman, sophomore, junior, senior, or graduate years; renewable. *Number:* 60. *Amount:* $1000.

Eligibility Requirements: Applicant must be enrolled or expecting to enroll full-time at a four-year institution or university; resident of Louisiana and studying in Louisiana. Applicant must have 2.5 GPA or higher. Available to U.S. citizens.

Application Requirements: Application, test scores, transcript, FAFSA. *Deadline:* July 1.

Contact: Public Information
Louisiana Office of Student Financial Assistance
PO Box 91202
Baton Rouge, LA 70821-9202
Phone: 800-259-5626 Ext. 1012
Fax: 225-922-0790
E-mail: custserv@osfa.state.la.us

MAINE DEPARTMENT OF AGRICULTURE, FOOD AND RURAL RESOURCES
http://www.maine.gov/agriculture

MAINE RURAL REHABILITATION FUND SCHOLARSHIP PROGRAM
• See page 75

NATIONAL DAIRY SHRINE
http://www.dairyshrine.org

MARSHALL E. MCCULLOUGH- NATIONAL DAIRY SHRINE SCHOLARSHIPS
• See page 82

NATIONAL DAIRY SHRINE/DAIRY MARKETING, INC. MILK MARKETING SCHOLARSHIPS
• See page 82

NDS STUDENT RECOGNITION CONTEST
• See page 75

NATIONAL POULTRY AND FOOD DISTRIBUTORS ASSOCIATION
http://www.npfda.org

NATIONAL POULTRY AND FOOD DISTRIBUTORS ASSOCIATION SCHOLARSHIP FOUNDATION
• See page 76

OREGON SHEEP GROWERS ASSOCIATION
http://www.sheeporegon.com

OREGON SHEEP GROWERS ASSOCIATION MEMORIAL SCHOLARSHIP
• See page 84

OREGON STUDENT ASSISTANCE COMMISSION
http://www.osac.state.or.us

ROYDEN M. BODLEY SCHOLARSHIP

One-time award open to high school graduates who earned their Eagle rank in Boy Scouts of America Cascade Pacific Council. Must major in forestry, wildlife, environment, or related field. Must attend an Oregon college.

Academic Fields/Career Goals: Animal/Veterinary Sciences; Environmental Science; Natural Resources; Natural Sciences.

Award: Scholarship for use in freshman year; renewable. *Number:* 5. *Amount:* $1400.

Eligibility Requirements: Applicant must be enrolled or expecting to enroll full-time at an institution or university; male; resident of Oregon and studying in Oregon. Applicant or parent of applicant must be member of Boy Scouts. Available to U.S. citizens.

Application Requirements: Application, essay, financial need analysis, transcript, activity chart. *Deadline:* March 1.

Contact: Director of Grant Programs
Oregon Student Assistance Commission
1500 Valley River Drive, Suite 100
Eugene, OR 97401-7020
Phone: 800-452-8807 Ext. 7395

SIGMA XI, THE SCIENTIFIC RESEARCH SOCIETY
http://www.sigmaxi.org

SIGMA XI GRANTS-IN-AID OF RESEARCH
• See page 84

SOCIETY FOR RANGE MANAGEMENT
http://www.rangelands.org

MASONIC RANGE SCIENCE SCHOLARSHIP
• See page 76

SOIL AND WATER CONSERVATION SOCIETY-NEW JERSEY CHAPTER
http://www.geocities.com/njswcs

EDWARD R. HALL SCHOLARSHIP
• See page 76

THE AMERICAN KENNEL CLUB
http://www.akc.org

VETERINARY TECHNICIAN STUDENT SCHOLARSHIPS

Scholarship for full-time student at an American Veterinary Medical Association (AVMA) accredited Veterinary Technician school. Must be a NAVTA student member or a member of a NAVTA Student Chapter.

Academic Fields/Career Goals: Animal/Veterinary Sciences.

Award: Scholarship for use in freshman, sophomore, junior, senior, or graduate years. *Number:* 1. *Amount:* up to $2000.

Eligibility Requirements: Applicant must be enrolled or expecting to enroll full-time at a four-year institution or university. Available to U.S. citizens.

Application Requirements: Application, essay, transcript. *Deadline:* May 1.

Contact: Debra Bonnefond
The American Kennel Club
5580 Centerview Drive
Raleigh, NC 27606
Phone: 919-233-9767

UNITED AGRIBUSINESS LEAGUE
http://www.ual.org

UNITED AGRIBUSINESS LEAGUE SCHOLARSHIP PROGRAM
• See page 77

UNITED AGRICULTURAL BENEFIT TRUST SCHOLARSHIP
• See page 77

UNITED NEGRO COLLEGE FUND
http://www.uncf.org

CARGILL SCHOLARSHIP PROGRAM
• See page 70

WILSON ORNITHOLOGICAL SOCIETY
http://www.ummz.lsa.umich.edu/birds/wos.html

GEORGE A. HALL / HAROLD F. MAYFIELD AWARD

One-time award for scientific research on birds. Available to independent researchers without access to funds or facilities at a college or university. Must be a nonprofessional to apply. Submit research proposal.

Academic Fields/Career Goals: Animal/Veterinary Sciences; Biology; Natural Resources.

Award: Grant for use in freshman, sophomore, junior, senior, graduate, or postgraduate years; not renewable. *Number:* 1. *Amount:* $1000.

Eligibility Requirements: Applicant must be enrolled or expecting to enroll at an institution or university. Available to U.S. and non-U.S. citizens.

Wilson Ornithological Society (continued)

Application Requirements: Application, references, proposal. *Deadline:* February 1.

Contact: Leann B. Blem, Scholarship Committee
Wilson Ornithological Society
Virginia Commonwealth University, Department of Biology,
1000 West Cary Street
Richmond, VA 23284-2012
Phone: 804-828-0474
E-mail: lblem@saturn.vcu.edu

PAUL A. STEWART AWARDS

One-time award for studies of bird movements based on banding, analysis of recoveries, and returns of banded birds, or research with an emphasis on economic ornithology. Submit research proposal.

Academic Fields/Career Goals: Animal/Veterinary Sciences; Biology; Natural Resources.

Award: Grant for use in freshman, sophomore, junior, senior, graduate, or postgraduate years; not renewable. *Number:* 1–4. *Amount:* up to $500.

Eligibility Requirements: Applicant must be enrolled or expecting to enroll full or part-time at an institution or university. Available to U.S. and non-U.S. citizens.

Application Requirements: Application, references, proposal. *Deadline:* February 1.

Contact: Leann B. Blem, Scholarship Committee
Wilson Ornithological Society
Virginia Commonwealth University, Department of Biology,
1000 West Cary Street
Richmond, VA 23284-2012
Phone: 804-828-0474
E-mail: lblem@saturn.vcu.edu

ANTHROPOLOGY

AMERICAN SCHOOL OF CLASSICAL STUDIES AT ATHENS
http://www.ascsa.edu.gr

ASCSA SUMMER SESSIONS OPEN SCHOLARSHIPS

Award for graduate and undergraduate students and to middle school, high school, and college teachers. Six-week sessions to travel within Turkey to study sites, monuments, and museums.

Academic Fields/Career Goals: Anthropology; Archaeology; Architecture; Art History; Arts; Historic Preservation and Conservation; History; Humanities; Museum Studies; Near and Middle East Studies; Philosophy; Religion/Theology.

Award: Scholarship for use in senior, graduate, or postgraduate years; not renewable. *Number:* 10.

Eligibility Requirements: Applicant must be enrolled or expecting to enroll full or part-time at a four-year institution or university and must have an interest in designated field specified by sponsor. Available to U.S. and non-U.S. citizens.

Application Requirements: Application, references, transcript. *Deadline:* varies.

Contact: Timothy F Winters, Chair, Committee of Summer Sessions
American School of Classical Studies at Athens
6-8 Charlton Street
Princeton, NJ 08540
Phone: 609-683-0800
Fax: 609-924-0578
E-mail: ascsa@ascsa.org

CANADIAN RECREATIONAL CANOEING ASSOCIATION
http://www.paddlingcanada.com

BILL MASON MEMORIAL SCHOLARSHIP FUND
• See page 80

CULTURE CONNECTION
http://www.thecultureconnection.com

CULTURE CONNECTION FOUNDATION SCHOLARSHIP
• See page 73

EXPLORERS CLUB
http://www.explorers.org

EXPLORATION FUND GRANTS

Grants awarded primarily to graduate students in amounts up to $5000 for the support of exploration and field research. Applications will be judged on the scientific and practical merit of the proposal, the competence of the investigator, and the appropriateness of the budget. Must include signed liability waiver. Applications submitted by e-mail will not be accepted.

Academic Fields/Career Goals: Anthropology; Archaeology; Area/Ethnic Studies; Earth Science; Environmental Science; Natural Sciences; Social Sciences.

Award: Grant for use in freshman, sophomore, junior, senior, or graduate years; not renewable. *Number:* 10–15. *Amount:* $1200.

Eligibility Requirements: Applicant must be enrolled or expecting to enroll at an institution or university. Available to U.S. citizens.

Application Requirements: Application, transcript. *Deadline:* January 13.

Contact: Suzi Zetkus, Administrative Assistant
Explorers Club
46 East 70th Street
New York, NY 10021
Phone: 212-628-8383
Fax: 212-288-4449
E-mail: office@explorers.org

LAMBDA ALPHA NATIONAL COLLEGIATE HONORS SOCIETY FOR ANTHROPOLOGY
http://www.lambdaalpha.com

LAMBDA ALPHA NATIONAL COLLEGIATE HONOR SOCIETY FOR ANTHROPOLOGY NATIONAL DEAN'S LIST AWARD

Award for juniors majoring in anthropology to encourage them to continue their studies in the field. One award of $1000. Deadline: March 1. Must rank in upper half of class or have a minimum 2.5 GPA. For further information applicant should contact the Lambda Alpha faculty sponsor at their own department.

Academic Fields/Career Goals: Anthropology.

Award: Scholarship for use in junior or senior years; not renewable. *Number:* 1. *Amount:* $1000.

Eligibility Requirements: Applicant must be enrolled or expecting to enroll full or part-time at a four-year institution or university. Applicant or parent of applicant must be member of Lambda Alpha National Collegiate Honor Society for Anthropology. Applicant must have 2.5 GPA or higher. Available to U.S. and non-U.S. citizens.

Application Requirements: Application, autobiography, resume, references, transcript. *Deadline:* March 1.

Contact: Dr. B. K. Swartz, Jr., National Executive Secretary
Lambda Alpha National Collegiate Honors Society for Anthropology
Department of Anthropology, Ball State University
Muncie, IN 47306-0435
Phone: 765-289-3667
Fax: 765-285-2163
E-mail: 01bkswartz@bsu.edu

APPLIED SCIENCES

AEA-OREGON COUNCIL
http://aeascholar.ous.edu

AEA- OREGON COUNCIL TECHNOLOGY SCHOLARSHIP PROGRAM

Over 30 scholarships given annually to Oregon high school seniors who plan to major in engineering, computer science or a closely related field and attend one of seven Oregon University system campuses. Must be a U.S. citizen. Deadline is March 3. Must complete application on Web site: http://www.ous.edu/ecs/scholarships

Academic Fields/Career Goals: Applied Sciences; Chemical Engineering; Civil Engineering; Computer Science/Data Processing; Electrical Engineering/Electronics; Engineering/Technology; Materials Science, Engineering, and Metallurgy; Mechanical Engineering.

Award: Scholarship for use in freshman, sophomore, junior, or senior years; renewable. *Number:* 30–35. *Amount:* $2500.

Eligibility Requirements: Applicant must be high school student; planning to enroll or expecting to enroll full-time at an institution or university; resident of Oregon and studying in Oregon. Available to U.S. citizens.

Application Requirements: Application, essay, references, test scores, transcript. *Deadline:* March 3.

Contact: AeA Scholarship, OUS Industry Affairs
AeA-Oregon Council
18640 Northwest Walker Road, Suite 1027
Beaverton, OR 97006-8927
Phone: 503-725-2920
Fax: 503-725-2921
E-mail: aeaschol@capital.ous.edu

AMERICAN INDIAN SCIENCE AND ENGINEERING SOCIETY　　　http://www.aises.org

A.T. ANDERSON MEMORIAL SCHOLARSHIP

Award for full-time students majoring in math or science secondary education, engineering, science, business, medicine, or natural resources. Must be at least one-quarter American-Indian or Alaska Native or have tribal recognition, and be member of AISES. Deadline: June 15. Must have minimum 2.0 GPA.

Academic Fields/Career Goals: Applied Sciences; Biology; Business/Consumer Services; Earth Science; Health and Medical Sciences; Meteorology/Atmospheric Science; Natural Resources; Natural Sciences; Nuclear Science; Physical Sciences and Math.

Award: Scholarship for use in freshman, sophomore, junior, senior, or graduate years; not renewable. *Number:* varies. *Amount:* $1000–$2000.

Eligibility Requirements: Applicant must be American Indian/Alaska Native and enrolled or expecting to enroll full-time at a two-year or four-year institution or university. Available to U.S. citizens.

Application Requirements: Application, essay, financial need analysis, resume, references, transcript, tribal enrollment document. *Deadline:* June 15.

Contact: Scholarship Information
American Indian Science and Engineering Society
PO Box 9828
Albuquerque, NM 87119-9828
Phone: 505-765-1052
Fax: 505-765-5608
E-mail: info@aises.org

BURLINGTON NORTHERN SANTA FE FOUNDATION SCHOLARSHIP

Award for high school senior for study of science, business, education, and health administration. Must reside in Arizona, Colorado, Kansas, Minnesota, Montana, North Dakota, New Mexico, Oklahoma, Oregon, South Dakota, Washington, or San Bernadino County, California. Must be at least one quarter American-Indian or Alaska Native and/or member of federally recognized tribe. Minimum 2.0 GPA required. Must be a current AISES member.

Academic Fields/Career Goals: Applied Sciences; Biology; Business/Consumer Services; Health Administration; Meteorology/Atmospheric Science; Natural Sciences; Nuclear Science; Physical Sciences and Math.

Award: Scholarship for use in freshman, sophomore, junior, or senior years; renewable. *Number:* varies. *Amount:* up to $2500.

Eligibility Requirements: Applicant must be American Indian/Alaska Native; high school student; planning to enroll or expecting to enroll at an institution or university and resident of Arizona, California, Colorado, Kansas, Minnesota, Montana, New Mexico, North Dakota, Oklahoma, Oregon, South Dakota, or Washington. Available to U.S. citizens.

Application Requirements: Application, essay, resume, references, transcript. *Deadline:* April 15.

Contact: Scholarship Information
American Indian Science and Engineering Society
PO Box 9828
Albuquerque, NM 87119-9828
Phone: 505-765-1052
Fax: 505-765-5608
E-mail: info@aises.org

AMERICAN INSTITUTE OF AERONAUTICS AND ASTRONAUTICS　　　http://www.aiaa.org

AIAA UNDERGRADUATE SCHOLARSHIP

Renewable award available to college sophomores, juniors and seniors enrolled full-time in an accredited college/university. Must be AIAA student member or become one prior to receiving award. Course of study must provide entry into some field of science or engineering encompassed by AIAA. Minimum 3.0 GPA required.

Academic Fields/Career Goals: Applied Sciences; Aviation/Aerospace; Electrical Engineering/Electronics; Engineering/Technology; Materials Science, Engineering, and Metallurgy; Mechanical Engineering; Physical Sciences and Math; Science, Technology, and Society.

Award: Scholarship for use in freshman, sophomore, junior, or senior years; renewable. *Number:* 30. *Amount:* $2000–$2500.

Eligibility Requirements: Applicant must be enrolled or expecting to enroll full-time at a two-year or four-year or technical institution or university. Applicant must have 3.0 GPA or higher. Available to U.S. and non-U.S. citizens.

Application Requirements: Application, essay, references, transcript. *Deadline:* January 31.

Contact: Stephen Brock, Student Programs Director
American Institute of Aeronautics and Astronautics
1801 Alexander Bell Drive, Suite 500
Reston, VA 20191
Phone: 703-264-7536
Fax: 703-264-7551
E-mail: stephenb@aiaa.org

AMERICAN METEOROLOGICAL SOCIETY　　　http://www.ametsoc.org/AMS

AMERICAN METEOROLOGICAL SOCIETY INDUSTRY UNDERGRADUATE SCHOLARSHIPS

Renewable scholarship for students entering their junior year of study in the fall, pursuing a degree in atmospheric sciences, oceanography, hydrology, chemistry, computer sciences, mathematics, engineering or physics. Required GPA is 3.52. For further information or application, visit Web site: http://www.ametsoc.org/AMS

Academic Fields/Career Goals: Applied Sciences; Computer Science/Data Processing; Earth Science; Engineering/Technology; Meteorology/Atmospheric Science; Physical Sciences and Math.

Award: Scholarship for use in junior year; renewable. *Number:* varies. *Amount:* $2000.

Eligibility Requirements: Applicant must be enrolled or expecting to enroll full-time at a four-year institution or university. Available to U.S. and non-Canadian citizens.

Application Requirements: Application, essay, references, self-addressed stamped envelope, transcript. *Deadline:* February 13.

Contact: Donna Fernandez, Development Program Coordinator
American Meteorological Society
45 Beacon Street
Boston, MA 02108-3693
Phone: 617-227-2426 Ext. 246
Fax: 617-742-8718
E-mail: dfernand@ametsoc.org

AMERICAN SOCIETY OF HEATING, REFRIGERATING, AND AIR CONDITIONING ENGINEERS, INC. http://www.ashrae.org

AMERICAN SOCIETY OF HEATING, REFRIGERATION, AND AIR CONDITIONING ENGINEERING TECHNOLOGY SCHOLARSHIP

Applicants must have at least one full year of remaining study and must attend full-time. One award to student in engineering technology program leading to associate degree and one award to student in ABET-accredited program leading to bachelor's degree in engineering technology.

Academic Fields/Career Goals: Applied Sciences; Engineering/Technology; Heating, Air-Conditioning, and Refrigeration Mechanics; Trade/Technical Specialties.

Award: Scholarship for use in sophomore, junior, or senior years; not renewable. *Number:* 2. *Amount:* up to $3000.

Eligibility Requirements: Applicant must be enrolled or expecting to enroll full-time at a two-year or four-year institution and must have an interest in leadership. Applicant must have 3.0 GPA or higher. Available to U.S. citizens.

Application Requirements: Application, financial need analysis, references, transcript. *Deadline:* May 1.

Contact: Lois Benedict, Scholarship Administrator
American Society of Heating, Refrigerating, and Air Conditioning Engineers, Inc.
1791 Tullie Circle, NE
Atlanta, GA 30329
Phone: 404-636-8400
Fax: 404-321-5478
E-mail: benedict@ashrae.org

AMERICAN SOCIETY OF NAVAL ENGINEERS http://www.navalengineers.org

AMERICAN SOCIETY OF NAVAL ENGINEERS SCHOLARSHIP

Award for naval engineering students in the final year of an undergraduate program or after one year of graduate study at an accredited institution. Must be full-time student and a U.S. citizen. Must study in specified fields. Minimum 2.5 GPA required. One-time award of $2500 for undergraduates and $3500 for graduate students. No doctoral candidates or candidates who already have an advanced degree. Graduate student applicants are required to be member of the American Society of Naval Engineers.

Academic Fields/Career Goals: Applied Sciences; Aviation/Aerospace; Civil Engineering; Electrical Engineering/Electronics; Energy and Power Engineering; Engineering/Technology; Marine/Ocean Engineering; Materials Science, Engineering, and Metallurgy; Mechanical Engineering; Nuclear Science; Physical Sciences and Math.

Award: Scholarship for use in senior, or graduate years; not renewable. *Number:* 8–14. *Amount:* $2500–$3500.

Eligibility Requirements: Applicant must be enrolled or expecting to enroll full-time at a four-year institution or university. Applicant must have 2.5 GPA or higher. Available to U.S. citizens.

Application Requirements: Application, references, test scores, transcript, graduate student applicants must be members of ASNE. *Deadline:* February 15.

Contact: David Woodbury, Operations Manager
American Society of Naval Engineers
1452 Duke Street
Alexandria, VA 22314
Phone: 703-836-6727
Fax: 703-836-7491
E-mail: scholarships@navalengineers.org

ARRL FOUNDATION, INC. http://www.arrl.org/arrlf/scholgen.html

CHARLES N. FISHER MEMORIAL SCHOLARSHIP

One-time award available to students licensed in any class of amateur radio operators who are majoring in electronics, communications, or a related field. Must be resident of Arizona or California. Must attend regionally accredited institution. Deadline is February 1.

Academic Fields/Career Goals: Applied Sciences; Communications; Electrical Engineering/Electronics; Engineering/Technology; Trade/Technical Specialties.

Award: Scholarship for use in freshman, sophomore, junior, or senior years; not renewable. *Number:* 1. *Amount:* $1000.

Eligibility Requirements: Applicant must be enrolled or expecting to enroll full-time at an institution or university and must have an interest in amateur radio. Available to U.S. citizens.

Application Requirements: Application, transcript. *Deadline:* February 1.

Contact: Mary Hobart, Secretary Foundation
ARRL Foundation, Inc.
225 Main Street
Newington, CT 06111-1494
Phone: 860-594-0397
E-mail: k1mmh@arrl.org

HENRY BROUGHTON, K2AE MEMORIAL SCHOLARSHIP

One award per year (multiple as income permits) to students who are licensed amateur radio operators with a minimum general class license. Must be pursuing baccalaureate course of study in engineering, sciences, or related field at an accredited four-year college or university. Must be home residence within 70 miles of Schenectady, New York. Deadline is February 1.

Academic Fields/Career Goals: Applied Sciences; Engineering-Related Technologies.

Award: Scholarship for use in freshman, sophomore, junior, or senior years; not renewable. *Amount:* $1000.

Eligibility Requirements: Applicant must be enrolled or expecting to enroll full-time at a four-year institution or university; resident of Massachusetts, New York, or Vermont and must have an interest in amateur radio. Available to U.S. citizens.

Application Requirements: Application, transcript. *Deadline:* February 1.

Contact: Mary Hobart, Secretary Foundation
ARRL Foundation, Inc.
225 Main Street
Newington, CT 06111-1494
Phone: 860-594-0397
E-mail: k1mmh@arrl.org

IRVING W. COOK, WA0CGS, SCHOLARSHIP

One-time award to students pursuing a degree in communications, electronics, or related fields who are amateur radio operators. Must be a Kansas resident but may attend school in any state. Deadline is February 1.

Academic Fields/Career Goals: Applied Sciences; Communications; Electrical Engineering/Electronics; Engineering/Technology; Trade/Technical Specialties.

Award: Scholarship for use in freshman, sophomore, junior, or senior years; not renewable. *Number:* 1. *Amount:* $1000.

Eligibility Requirements: Applicant must be enrolled or expecting to enroll full-time at an institution or university and must have an interest in amateur radio. Available to U.S. citizens.

Application Requirements: Application, transcript. *Deadline:* February 1.

Contact: Mary Hobart, Secretary Foundation
ARRL Foundation, Inc.
225 Main Street
Newington, CT 06111-1494
Phone: 860-594-0397
E-mail: k1mmh@arrl.org

MISSISSIPPI SCHOLARSHIP

Available to students pursuing a degree in electronics, communications, or related fields who are licensed in any class of amateur radio operators. Must reside in Mississippi, attend school in Mississippi, and be age 30 or under. Must be a member of the Amateur Radio Relay League. Deadline is February 1.

Academic Fields/Career Goals: Applied Sciences; Communications; Electrical Engineering/Electronics; Engineering/Technology; Trade/Technical Specialties.

Award: Scholarship for use in freshman, sophomore, junior, or senior years; not renewable. *Number:* 1. *Amount:* $500.

Eligibility Requirements: Applicant must be age 30 or under; enrolled or expecting to enroll full-time at an institution or university; resident of Mississippi; studying in Mississippi and must have an interest in amateur radio. Available to U.S. citizens.

Application Requirements: Application, transcript. *Deadline:* February 1.

Contact: Mary Hobart, Secretary Foundation
ARRL Foundation, Inc.
225 Main Street
Newington, CT 06111-1494
Phone: 860-594-0397
E-mail: k1mmh@arrl.org

PAUL AND HELEN L. GRAUER SCHOLARSHIP

Available to students licensed as novice amateur radio operators who are majoring in electronics, communications, or a related field. Preference given to residents of Iowa, Kansas, Missouri, and Nebraska. Pursuit of a baccalaureate or higher degree preferred at an institution in ARRL Midwest Division. Deadline is February 1.

Academic Fields/Career Goals: Applied Sciences; Communications; Electrical Engineering/Electronics; Engineering/Technology; Trade/Technical Specialties.

Award: Scholarship for use in freshman, sophomore, junior, senior, or graduate years; not renewable. *Number:* 1. *Amount:* $1000.

Eligibility Requirements: Applicant must be enrolled or expecting to enroll full-time at a four-year institution or university; studying in Iowa, Kansas, Missouri, or Nebraska and must have an interest in amateur radio. Available to U.S. citizens.

Application Requirements: Application, transcript. *Deadline:* February 1.

Contact: Mary Hobart, Scholarship Director
ARRL Foundation, Inc.
225 Main Street
Newington, CT 06111-1494
Phone: 860-594-0397
E-mail: k1mmh@arrl.org

ASPRS, THE IMAGING AND GEOSPATIAL INFORMATION SOCIETY   http://www.asprs.org

ROBERT E. ALTENHOFEN MEMORIAL SCHOLARSHIP

One-time award is available for undergraduate or graduate study in theoretical photogrammetry. Applicant must supply a sample of work in photogrammetry and a statement of plans for future study in the field. Must be a member of ASPRS. One scholarship of $2000.

Academic Fields/Career Goals: Applied Sciences; Engineering/Technology.

Award: Scholarship for use in freshman, sophomore, junior, senior, or graduate years; not renewable. *Number:* 1. *Amount:* $2000.

Eligibility Requirements: Applicant must be enrolled or expecting to enroll full-time at a two-year or four-year institution or university and must have an interest in photography/photogrammetry/filmmaking. Applicant or parent of applicant must be member of American Society for Photogrammetry and Remote Sensing. Available to U.S. and non-U.S. citizens.

Application Requirements: Application, essay, references, transcript, work sample. *Deadline:* December 1.

Contact: Jesse Winch, Program Manager
ASPRS, The Imaging and Geospatial Information Society
5410 Grosvenor Lane, Suite 210
Bethesda, MD 20814-2160
Phone: 301-493-0290 Ext. 101
Fax: 301-493-0208
E-mail: scholarships@asprs.org

SPACE IMAGING AWARD FOR APPLICATION OF HIGH RESOLUTION DIGITAL SATELLITE IMAGERY

Award for undergraduate or graduate students to stimulate development of applications of digital data through the granting of data for applied research. This is not a cash award. The award consists of data valued at up to $2,000, and a plaque inscribed with the recipient's name and his/her institution. Must be ASPRS member.

Academic Fields/Career Goals: Applied Sciences; Engineering/Technology; Physical Sciences and Math.

Award: Scholarship for use in freshman, sophomore, junior, senior, or graduate years; not renewable. *Number:* 1. *Amount:* up to $2000.

Eligibility Requirements: Applicant must be enrolled or expecting to enroll full-time at a four-year institution or university and must have an interest in photography/photogrammetry/filmmaking. Applicant or parent of applicant must be member of American Society for Photogrammetry and Remote Sensing. Available to U.S. citizens.

Application Requirements: Application, autobiography, references, transcript, proposal. *Deadline:* December 1.

Contact: Jesse Winch, Program Manager
ASPRS, The Imaging and Geospatial Information Society
5410 Grosvenor Lane, Suite 210
Bethesda, MD 20814-2160
Phone: 301-493-0290 Ext. 101
Fax: 301-493-0208
E-mail: scholarships@asprs.org

Z/I IMAGING SCHOLARSHIP

A $2000 scholarship will be awarded to current or prospective graduate students who have graduate-level studies and career goals adjudged to address new and innovative uses of signal processing, image processing techniques and the application of photogrammetry to real-world techniques within the earth imaging industry. Must be a member of ASPRS.

Academic Fields/Career Goals: Applied Sciences; Engineering/Technology; Physical Sciences and Math.

Award: Scholarship for use in senior, or graduate years; not renewable. *Number:* 1. *Amount:* $2000.

Eligibility Requirements: Applicant must be enrolled or expecting to enroll at a four-year institution or university. Available to U.S. citizens.

Application Requirements: Application, essay, references, transcript. *Deadline:* December 1.

Contact: Jesse Winch, Program Manager
ASPRS, The Imaging and Geospatial Information Society
5410 Grosvenor Lane, Suite 210
Bethesda, MD 20814-2160
Phone: 301-493-0290 Ext. 101
Fax: 301-493-0208
E-mail: scholarships@asprs.org

ASSOCIATION OF CALIFORNIA WATER AGENCIES   http://www.acwanet.com

ASSOCIATION OF CALIFORNIA WATER AGENCIES SCHOLARSHIPS

Three $3000 awards available to juniors and seniors who are California residents attending California universities. Must be in a water-related field of study. Applicants can be transferring to a university from a junior college as long as they will be a junior in the fall. Applications available on the Web site: http://www.acwanet.com/news_info/scholarships/index1.asp.

Academic Fields/Career Goals: Applied Sciences; Biology; Civil Engineering; Environmental Science; Hydrology; Natural Resources; Natural Sciences; Surveying; Surveying Technology, Cartography, or Geographic Information Science.

Award: Scholarship for use in junior or senior years; not renewable. *Number:* 3. *Amount:* $3000.

Eligibility Requirements: Applicant must be enrolled or expecting to enroll full-time at a four-year institution or university; resident of California and studying in California. Available to U.S. citizens.

Application Requirements: Application, essay, references, transcript. *Deadline:* April 1.

Contact: La Vonne Watson, Communications Coordinator
Association of California Water Agencies
901 K Street, Suite 100
Sacramento, CA 95814
Phone: 916-441-4545
Fax: 916-325-2316
E-mail: lavonnew@acwanet.com

CLAIR A. HILL SCHOLARSHIP

The Clair A. Hill award scholarship is administered by a different member agency each year. The guidelines vary by administering agency and therefore it is best to contact ACWA for information. Generally, winner is in a water-related field of study. Must be a resident of California enrolled in a California four-year college or university.

Academic Fields/Career Goals: Applied Sciences; Biology; Civil Engineering; Environmental Science; Hydrology; Natural Resources; Natural Sciences; Surveying; Surveying Technology, Cartography, or Geographic Information Science.

Award: Scholarship for use in junior, senior, or graduate years; not renewable. *Number:* 1. *Amount:* $3000.

Eligibility Requirements: Applicant must be enrolled or expecting to enroll full-time at a four-year institution or university; resident of California and studying in California. Available to U.S. citizens.

Application Requirements: Application, essay, references, transcript. *Deadline:* April 1.

Contact: La Vonne Watson, Communications Coordinator
Association of California Water Agencies
910 K Street, Suite 100
Sacramento, CA 95814
Phone: 916-441-4545
Fax: 916-325-2316
E-mail: lavonnew@acwanet.com

ASTRONAUT SCHOLARSHIP FOUNDATION   http://www.astronautscholarship.org

ASTRONAUT SCHOLARSHIP FOUNDATION

Scholarship candidates must be nominated by faculty members. Students may not apply directly for the scholarship. Must be US Citizens. Scholarship nominees must be engineering or natural or applied science students.

Academic Fields/Career Goals: Applied Sciences; Aviation/Aerospace; Biology; Chemical Engineering; Computer Science/Data Processing; Earth Science; Electrical Engineering/Electronics; Engineering-Related Technologies; Materials Science, Engineering, and Metallurgy; Mechanical Engineering; Meteorology/Atmospheric Science.

Award: Scholarship for use in junior, senior, graduate, or postgraduate years; renewable. *Number:* 17. *Amount:* $10,000.

Eligibility Requirements: Applicant must be enrolled or expecting to enroll full-time at a four-year institution or university. Available to U.S. citizens.

Application Requirements: Financial need analysis, references, transcript. *Deadline:* April 15.

Contact: Linn LeBlanc, Executive Director
Astronaut Scholarship Foundation
6225 Vectorspace Boulevard
Titusville, FL 32780
Phone: 321-269-6101 Ext. 6176
Fax: 321-264-9176
E-mail: linnleblanc@astronautscholarship.org

BARRY M. GOLDWATER SCHOLARSHIP AND EXCELLENCE IN EDUCATION FOUNDATION   http://www.act.org/goldwater

BARRY M. GOLDWATER SCHOLARSHIP AND EXCELLENCE IN EDUCATION PROGRAM

One-time award to college juniors and seniors who will pursue advanced degrees in mathematics, natural sciences, or engineering. Students planning to study medicine are eligible if they plan a career in research. Candidates must be nominated by their college or university. Must be U.S. citizens or residents alien demonstrating intent to obtain U.S. citizenship. Minimum 3.0 GPA required. Nomination deadline: February 1. Please visit Web site for further updates. (http://www.act.org/goldwater)

Academic Fields/Career Goals: Applied Sciences; Biology; Chemical Engineering; Civil Engineering; Computer Science/Data Processing; Earth Science; Engineering/Technology; Materials Science, Engineering, and Metallurgy; Mechanical Engineering; Natural Sciences; Nuclear Science; Physical Sciences and Math.

Award: Scholarship for use in sophomore, junior, or senior years; renewable. *Number:* up to 300. *Amount:* up to $7500.

Eligibility Requirements: Applicant must be enrolled or expecting to enroll full-time at a two-year or four-year institution or university. Applicant must have 3.0 GPA or higher. Available to U.S. citizens.

Application Requirements: Application, autobiography, essay, references, transcript, school nomination. *Deadline:* February 1.

Contact: Wanni Spence, Administrative Officer
Barry M. Goldwater Scholarship and Excellence in Education Foundation
6225 Brandon Avenue, Suite 315
Springfield, VA 22150-2519
Phone: 703-756-6012
Fax: 703-756-6015

CHEMICAL INSTITUTE OF CANADA   http://www.cheminst.ca

ALFRED BADER SCHOLARSHIP

Up to three scholarships available to undergraduate seniors who are members of the Canadian Society for Chemistry and who have achieved excellence in organic chemistry or biochemistry. Students must be nominated and submit a project report. U.S. citizens must be enrolled in a Canadian university.

Academic Fields/Career Goals: Applied Sciences.

Award: Scholarship for use in senior year; not renewable. *Number:* 1–3. *Amount:* $1000.

Eligibility Requirements: Applicant must be enrolled or expecting to enroll full-time at an institution or university. Applicant or parent of applicant must be member of Canadian Society for Chemistry. Available to U.S. and Canadian citizens.

Application Requirements: Application, references, transcript. *Deadline:* May 30.

Contact: Student Affairs Manager
Chemical Institute of Canada
130 Slater Street, Suite 550
Ottawa, ON K1P 6E2
Canada
Phone: 613-232-6252 Ext. 223
Fax: 613-232-5862
E-mail: gwilbee@cheminst.ca

DESK AND DERRICK EDUCATIONAL TRUST   http://www.addc.org

DESK AND DERRICK EDUCATIONAL TRUST

Must be a U.S. or Canadian citizen; minimum 3.0 GPA required. Must have financial need, must be enrolled in an energy related major such as oil, gas, allied industries, and alternative energy. Open to full- or part-time junior and senior undergraduates. Applicant must be Desk and Derrick member.

Academic Fields/Career Goals: Applied Sciences; Chemical Engineering; Earth Science; Engineering-Related Technologies; Natural Resources; Natural Sciences; Nuclear Science.

Award: Scholarship for use in junior or senior years; not renewable. *Number:* 7. *Amount:* $750–$1500.

Eligibility Requirements: Applicant must be enrolled or expecting to enroll full or part-time at a four-year institution or university. Applicant must have 3.0 GPA or higher. Available to U.S. and Canadian citizens.

Application Requirements: Application, financial need analysis, transcript. *Deadline:* April 1.

Contact: Cheryl Wootton, Chairman
Desk and Derrick Educational Trust
5153 East 51st Street, Suite 107
Tulsa, OK 74135
Phone: 918-622-1749
Fax: 918-622-1675
E-mail: cwootton@att.net

HERB SOCIETY OF AMERICA   http://www.herbsociety.org

HERB SOCIETY RESEARCH GRANTS

One to five awards of up to $5000. Awards for persons with a proposed program of scientific, academic, or artistic investigation of herbal plants. Must submit a proposal and budget with application by January 31.

Academic Fields/Career Goals: Applied Sciences; Art History; Arts; Biology; Earth Science; Food Science/Nutrition; Health and Medical Sciences; Horticulture/Floriculture; Landscape Architecture; Literature/English/Writing.

Award: Grant for use in freshman, sophomore, junior, senior, graduate, or postgraduate years; not renewable. *Number:* 1–5. *Amount:* up to $5000.

Eligibility Requirements: Applicant must be enrolled or expecting to enroll full or part-time at a two-year or four-year or technical institution or university. Available to U.S. and non-U.S. citizens.

Application Requirements: Application, references, proposal. *Deadline:* January 31.

Contact: The Herb Society of America, Inc. Research Grant
Herb Society of America
9019 Kirtland-Chardon Road
Kirtland, OH 44094
Phone: 440-256-0514
Fax: 440-256-0541
E-mail: herbs@herbsociety.org

HISPANIC COLLEGE FUND, INC. http://www.hispanicfund.org

NATIONAL HISPANIC EXPLORERS SCHOLARSHIP PROGRAM

One-time scholarship award open to full-time undergraduates pursuing a degree in science, math, engineering, or NASA-related major. Must be a U.S. citizen and have a minimum of a 3.0 GPA.

Academic Fields/Career Goals: Applied Sciences; Aviation/Aerospace; Biology; Chemical Engineering; Civil Engineering; Communications; Computer Science/Data Processing; Earth Science; Electrical Engineering/Electronics; Engineering/Technology; Engineering-Related Technologies; Food Science/Nutrition.

Award: Scholarship for use in freshman, sophomore, junior, or senior years; not renewable. *Number:* 125–200. *Amount:* $500–$5000.

Eligibility Requirements: Applicant must be enrolled or expecting to enroll full-time at a two-year or four-year institution or university. Applicant must have 3.0 GPA or higher. Available to U.S. citizens.

Application Requirements: Application, essay, financial need analysis, resume, references, transcript, college acceptance letter, copy of taxes, proof of U.S. citizenship. *Deadline:* April 15.

Contact: Stina Augustsson, Program Manager
Hispanic College Fund, Inc.
1717 Pennsylvania Avenue, NW, Suite 460
Washington, DC 20006
Phone: 202-296-5400
Fax: 202-296-3774
E-mail: hcf-info@hispanicfund.org

INDEPENDENT LABORATORIES INSTITUTE SCHOLARSHIP ALLIANCE http://www.acil.org

INDEPENDENT LABORATORIES INSTITUTE SCHOLARSHIP ALLIANCE

Scholarships are given to full-time undergraduate juniors or seniors, or graduate students majoring in the physical sciences: physics, chemistry, geology, engineering, biology or environmental science. Application deadline is April 7.

Academic Fields/Career Goals: Applied Sciences; Biology; Chemical Engineering; Civil Engineering; Earth Science; Electrical Engineering/Electronics; Engineering/Technology; Engineering-Related Technologies; Fire Sciences; Materials Science, Engineering, and Metallurgy; Mechanical Engineering; Physical Sciences and Math.

Award: Scholarship for use in junior, senior, or graduate years; not renewable. *Number:* 1–2. *Amount:* $1000–$2000.

Eligibility Requirements: Applicant must be enrolled or expecting to enroll full-time at a four-year institution or university. Available to U.S. citizens.

Application Requirements: Application, resume, references, transcript, information on any other scholarship or grant aid applicant is currently receiving. *Deadline:* April 7.

Contact: Janet Allen, Senior Administrator
Independent Laboratories Institute Scholarship Alliance
1629 K Street, NW, Suite 400
Washington, DC 20006-1633
Phone: 202-887-5872 Ext. 204
Fax: 202-887-0021
E-mail: jallen@acil.org

INNOVATION AND SCIENCE COUNCIL OF BRITISH COLUMBIA http://www.scbc.org

PAUL AND HELEN TRUSSEL SCIENCE AND TECHNOLOGY SCHOLARSHIP

CAN $5000 award to a new recipient each year. Student must be enrolled in the sciences and have graduated high school in the Kootenay/Boundary region of British Columbia. Student must be entering 3rd year of studies at a BC or AB post secondary institution. Available to Canadian citizens and landed immigrants.

Academic Fields/Career Goals: Applied Sciences; Biology; Chemical Engineering; Computer Science/Data Processing; Earth Science; Geography; Meteorology/Atmospheric Science; Natural Resources; Natural Sciences; Nuclear Science; Physical Sciences and Math; Science, Technology, and Society.

Award: Scholarship for use in sophomore, junior, senior, graduate, or postgraduate years; renewable. *Number:* 1. *Amount:* $5000–$20,000.

Eligibility Requirements: Applicant must be Canadian citizen; enrolled or expecting to enroll full-time at a two-year or four-year institution or university; resident of British Columbia and studying in Alberta or British Columbia. Applicant must have 3.0 GPA or higher. Available to U.S. and non-U.S. citizens.

Application Requirements: Application, autobiography, references, transcript, proof of citizenship. *Deadline:* May 31.

Contact: BC Innovation Council
Innovation and Science Council of British Columbia
9th Floor, 1188 West Georgia Street
Vancouver, BC V6E 4A2
Canada
Phone: 604-438-2752
Fax: 604-438-6564
E-mail: info@bcinnovationcouncil.com

INTERNATIONAL SOCIETY FOR OPTICAL ENGINEERING-SPIE http://www.spie.org/info/scholarships

SPIE EDUCATIONAL SCHOLARSHIPS IN OPTICAL SCIENCE AND ENGINEERING

Application forms must exhibit demonstrated personal commitment to and involvement of the applicant in the fields of optics, optical science, and engineering, and indicate how the granting of the award will contribute to these fields. Applications will be judged by the SPIE Scholarship Committee on the basis of the long range contribution, which the granting of the award will make to these fields. Must be member of SPIE.

Academic Fields/Career Goals: Applied Sciences; Aviation/Aerospace; Chemical Engineering; Electrical Engineering/Electronics; Engineering/Technology; Engineering-Related Technologies; Materials Science, Engineering, and Metallurgy; Mechanical Engineering.

Award: Scholarship for use in freshman, sophomore, junior, senior, or graduate years; not renewable. *Number:* 30–80. *Amount:* $1000–$8000.

Eligibility Requirements: Applicant must be enrolled or expecting to enroll full-time at a two-year or four-year or technical institution or university. Applicant or parent of applicant must be member of International Society for Optical Engineering (SPIE). Available to U.S. and non-U.S. citizens.

International Society for Optical Engineering-SPIE (continued)

Application Requirements: Application, references, self-addressed stamped envelope. *Deadline:* January 12.

Contact: SPIE Scholarship Committee
International Society for Optical Engineering-SPIE
PO Box 10
Bellingham, WA 98227
Phone: 360-676-3290
Fax: 360-647-1445
E-mail: scholarships@spie.org

LOUISIANA OFFICE OF STUDENT FINANCIAL ASSISTANCE
http://www.osfa.state.la.us

ROCKEFELLER STATE WILDLIFE SCHOLARSHIP
• See page 87

METAVUE CORPORATION
http://www.metavue.com

THE DR. ROBERT RUFFLO SCIENCES PAPER CONTEST

Two scholarhsips a year for undergraduate and graduate students enrolled at an accredited college or university in the U.S. Scholarships are granted for exemplary work in a variety of applied and basic science fields. Work may focus on original research, a research review or critical essay.

Academic Fields/Career Goals: Applied Sciences.

Award: Scholarship for use in freshman, sophomore, junior, senior, or graduate years. *Number:* 2. *Amount:* $500.

Eligibility Requirements: Applicant must be enrolled or expecting to enroll at a two-year or four-year institution or university. Applicant must have 3.0 GPA or higher. Available to U.S. citizens.

Application Requirements: Essay. *Deadline:* June 1.

Contact: Michael Rufflo
Metavue Corporation
1110 Surrey Drive
Sun Prairie, WI 53590
Phone: 608-577-0642
Fax: 512-685-4074
E-mail: rufflo@metavue.com

MIDWEST ROOFING CONTRACTORS ASSOCIATION
http://www.mrca.org

MRCA FOUNDATION SCHOLARSHIP PROGRAM

All candidates for the MRCA Foundation Scholarship must be current, enrolled or intending to enroll in an accredited university, college, community college, or trade school. Applicant must be pursuing a curriculum leading to a career in the construction industry.

Academic Fields/Career Goals: Applied Sciences; Architecture; Business/Consumer Services; Engineering/Technology; Heating, Air-Conditioning, and Refrigeration Mechanics; Materials Science, Engineering, and Metallurgy; Mechanical Engineering; Natural Sciences; Science, Technology, and Society; Surveying; Surveying Technology, Cartography, or Geographic Information Science; Trade/Technical Specialties.

Award: Scholarship for use in freshman, sophomore, junior, senior, or graduate years; renewable. *Number:* 1–5. *Amount:* $500–$1000.

Eligibility Requirements: Applicant must be enrolled or expecting to enroll full or part-time at a two-year or four-year or technical institution or university. Available to U.S. and non-U.S. citizens.

Application Requirements: Application, essay, photo, references, test scores, transcript. *Deadline:* June 20.

Contact: MRCA Foundation
Midwest Roofing Contractors Association
4840 Bob Billings Parkway, Suite 1000
Lawrence, KS 66049-3862

NASA DELAWARE SPACE GRANT CONSORTIUM
http://www.delspace.org

NASA DELAWARE SPACE GRANT UNDERGRADUATE TUITION SCHOLARSHIP

The NASA/DESGC Undergraduate Summer and Undergraduate Tuition Scholarships are awarded annually to encourage and recognize highly qualified undergraduate students interested in careers related to aerospace engineering and space science related fields. All must be enrolled in a DESGC affiliate member college or university. Must be a U.S. citizen.

Academic Fields/Career Goals: Applied Sciences; Aviation/Aerospace; Chemical Engineering; Civil Engineering; Earth Science; Electrical Engineering/Electronics; Engineering/Technology; Engineering-Related Technologies; Mechanical Engineering; Meteorology/Atmospheric Science; Physical Sciences and Math; Science, Technology, and Society.

Award: Scholarship for use in freshman, sophomore, junior, or senior years; not renewable. *Number:* 6–12. *Amount:* $1400–$4000.

Eligibility Requirements: Applicant must be enrolled or expecting to enroll full-time at a two-year or four-year institution or university and studying in Delaware or Pennsylvania. Available to U.S. citizens.

Application Requirements: Application, essay, references, transcript, proof of U.S. citizenship. *Deadline:* April 14.

Contact: Sherry L. Rowland-Perry, Program Coordinator
NASA Delaware Space Grant Consortium
217 Sharp Lab, University of Delaware
Newark, DE 19716-4793
Phone: 302-831-1094
Fax: 302-831-1843
E-mail: desgc@bartol.udel.edu

NASA IDAHO SPACE GRANT CONSORTIUM
http://isgc.uidaho.edu

NASA IDAHO SPACE GRANT CONSORTIUM SCHOLARSHIP PROGRAM

Program awards a $1000 scholarship ($500 each semester) renewable for four years based on GPA (above 3.0), area of study (science/math/engineering or math/science education), full-time status, and attendance at an Idaho institution.

Academic Fields/Career Goals: Applied Sciences; Aviation/Aerospace; Biology; Chemical Engineering; Computer Science/Data Processing; Earth Science; Education; Electrical Engineering/Electronics; Engineering/Technology; Health and Medical Sciences; Physical Sciences and Math; Science, Technology, and Society.

Award: Scholarship for use in freshman, sophomore, junior, or senior years; renewable. *Number:* 1–22. *Amount:* $1000.

Eligibility Requirements: Applicant must be enrolled or expecting to enroll full-time at a two-year or four-year institution or university and studying in Idaho. Applicant must have 3.0 GPA or higher. Available to U.S. citizens.

Application Requirements: Application, essay, resume, references, test scores, transcript. *Deadline:* March 1.

Contact: Jean Teasdale, Director
NASA Idaho Space Grant Consortium
University of Idaho, PO Box 441011
Moscow, ID 83844-1011
Phone: 208-885-4934
Fax: 208-885-1399
E-mail: isgc@uidaho.edu

NASA VERMONT SPACE GRANT CONSORTIUM
http://www.vtspacegrant.org

VERMONT SPACE GRANT CONSORTIUM SCHOLARSHIP PROGRAM

Career goals must be in area related to NASA's interest. Applicant must be resident of Vermont, U.S. citizen, and attend or plan to attend an institution within Vermont. Three scholarships are designated to Native-American recipients. Awards subject to availability of NASA funding. Deadline: March 1.

Academic Fields/Career Goals: Applied Sciences; Aviation/Aerospace; Biology; Earth Science; Engineering/Technology; Engineering-Related Technologies; Health and Medical Sciences; Materials Science,

Engineering, and Metallurgy; Meteorology/Atmospheric Science; Natural Sciences; Physical Sciences and Math; Transportation.

Award: Scholarship for use in freshman, sophomore, junior, or senior years; renewable. *Number:* 10. *Amount:* up to $1500.

Eligibility Requirements: Applicant must be enrolled or expecting to enroll full-time at a two-year or four-year or technical institution or university; resident of Vermont and studying in Vermont. Applicant must have 3.0 GPA or higher. Available to U.S. citizens.

Application Requirements: Application, essay, references, test scores, transcript. *Deadline:* March 1.

Contact: Laurel Zeno, VSGC Grant Administrator/Program
Coordinator
NASA Vermont Space Grant Consortium
Votey Building, University of Vermont, College of Engineering
and Math
Burlington, VT 05405-0156
Phone: 802-656-1429
Fax: 802-656-1102
E-mail: zeno@emba.uvm.edu

NATIONAL INVENTORS HALL OF FAME
http://www.invent.org

COLLEGIATE INVENTORS COMPETITION - GRAND PRIZE

The competition was designed to encourage college students to be active in science, engineering, mathematics, technology and creative invention, while stimulating their problem-solving abilities. This prestigious challenge recognizes the working relationship between a student and his or her advisor who are involved in projects leading to inventions that can be patented. The winning student or student team receives a $25,000 cash prize. The advisors of the winning entries will receive $3000.

Academic Fields/Career Goals: Applied Sciences; Biology; Chemical Engineering; Computer Science/Data Processing; Engineering/Technology; Engineering-Related Technologies; Environmental Science; Health and Medical Sciences; Materials Science, Engineering, and Metallurgy; Physical Sciences and Math.

Award: Prize for use in freshman, sophomore, junior, senior, graduate, or postgraduate years; not renewable. *Number:* 1. *Amount:* up to $25,000.

Eligibility Requirements: Applicant must be enrolled or expecting to enroll full or part-time at a two-year or four-year institution or university. Available to U.S. and non-U.S. citizens.

Application Requirements: Application, applicant must enter a contest, form on Web site. *Deadline:* June 1.

Contact: Ray DePuy, Program Coordinator
National Inventors Hall of Fame
221 South Broadway Street
Akron, OH 44308-1505
Phone: 330-849-6887
Fax: 330-762-6313
E-mail: rdepuy@invent.org

COLLEGIATE INVENTORS COMPETITION FOR UNDERGRADUATE STUDENTS

The Collegiate Inventors Competition is a national competition designed to encourage college students to be active in science, engineering, mathematics, technology, and creative invention, while stimulating their problem solving abilities. This prestigious challenge recognizes the working relationship between a student and their advisor who are involved in projects that can be patented. The prize winning undergraduate student or student-team receives a $10,000 cash prize.

Academic Fields/Career Goals: Applied Sciences; Biology; Chemical Engineering; Computer Science/Data Processing; Engineering/Technology; Engineering-Related Technologies; Environmental Science; Health and Medical Sciences; Materials Science, Engineering, and Metallurgy; Physical Sciences and Math.

Award: Prize for use in freshman, sophomore, junior, or senior years; not renewable. *Number:* 1. *Amount:* up to $10,000.

Eligibility Requirements: Applicant must be enrolled or expecting to enroll full or part-time at a four-year institution or university. Available to U.S. and non-U.S. citizens.

Application Requirements: Application, form available on Web site. *Deadline:* June 1.

Contact: Ray DePuy, Program Coordinator
National Inventors Hall of Fame
221 South Broadway Street
Akron, OH 44308-1505
Phone: 330-849-6887
Fax: 330-762-6313
E-mail: rdepuy@invent.org

SOCIETY FOR MINING, METALLURGY AND EXPLORATION - CENTRAL WYOMING SECTION

COATES, WOLFF, RUSSELL MINING INDUSTRY SCHOLARSHIP

One-time award for Wyoming residents studying mining related fields. Must be full-time undergraduate at sophomore level or above. Minimum 2.5 GPA required. Open to U.S. citizens. Application deadline is December 1.

Academic Fields/Career Goals: Applied Sciences; Chemical Engineering; Civil Engineering; Earth Science; Materials Science, Engineering, and Metallurgy; Mechanical Engineering; Natural Resources; Natural Sciences.

Award: Scholarship for use in sophomore, junior, or senior years; not renewable. *Number:* 3. *Amount:* $1000.

Eligibility Requirements: Applicant must be enrolled or expecting to enroll full-time at a two-year or four-year or technical institution or university and resident of Wyoming. Applicant must have 2.5 GPA or higher. Available to U.S. citizens.

Application Requirements: Application, essay, transcript. *Deadline:* December 1.

Contact: Wayne Heili, Co-Chairman, Scholarship Committee
Society for Mining, Metallurgy and Exploration - Central
Wyoming Section
4210 Deer Run
Casper, WY 82601
Phone: 307-234-5019

SOCIETY OF MEXICAN AMERICAN ENGINEERS AND SCIENTISTS
http://www.maes-natl.org

GRE AND GRADUATE APPLICATIONS WAIVER

Grant serves as a fee waiver for the cost of testing for and applying to graduate school. Must be Mexican-American and a member of the Society of Mexican-American Engineers and Scientists, Inc. (MAES). Minimum GPA of 2.75 required. For more details and an application go to Web site: http://www.maes-natl.org.

Academic Fields/Career Goals: Applied Sciences; Aviation/Aerospace; Biology; Chemical Engineering; Civil Engineering; Earth Science; Electrical Engineering/Electronics; Engineering/Technology; Engineering-Related Technologies; Environmental Science; Science, Technology, and Society.

Award: Grant for use in senior, or graduate years; not renewable. *Number:* 12. *Amount:* $135–$235.

Eligibility Requirements: Applicant must be of Mexican heritage; Hispanic and enrolled or expecting to enroll full or part-time at an institution or university. Available to U.S. citizens.

Application Requirements: Application, essay, resume, test scores, application for graduate school, copy of GRE registration. *Deadline:* varies.

Contact: Gary Cruz, Pagess Director
Society of Mexican American Engineers and Scientists
711 West Bay Area Boulevard, Suite 206
Webster, TX 77598-4051
Phone: 281-557-3677
Fax: 281-557-3757
E-mail: pagess@maes-natl.org

TKE EDUCATIONAL FOUNDATION
http://www.tkefoundation.org

CARROL C. HALL MEMORIAL SCHOLARSHIP

One-time award of $700 given to a full-time undergraduate member of Tau Kappa Epsilon who has demonstrated leadership within chapter, campus, and community. Must be earning a degree in education or science and planning to

TKE Educational Foundation (continued)

become a teacher or pursue a profession in science. Recent head and shoulders photograph must be submitted with application. Minimum 3.0 GPA required.

Academic Fields/Career Goals: Applied Sciences; Biology; Earth Science; Education; Meteorology/Atmospheric Science; Physical Sciences and Math.

Award: Scholarship for use in freshman, sophomore, junior, or senior years; not renewable. *Number:* 1. *Amount:* $700.

Eligibility Requirements: Applicant must be enrolled or expecting to enroll full-time at a four-year institution or university; male and must have an interest in leadership. Applicant must have 3.0 GPA or higher. Available to U.S. and non-U.S. citizens.

Application Requirements: Application, essay, photo, transcript. *Deadline:* May 12.

Contact: Gary A. Reed, President/CEO
TKE Educational Foundation
8645 Founders Road
Indianapolis, IN 46268-1393
Phone: 317-872-6533
Fax: 317-875-8353
E-mail: reedga@tke.org

UNIVERSITIES SPACE RESEARCH ASSOCIATION
http://www.usra.edu

UNIVERSITIES SPACE RESEARCH ASSOCIATION SCHOLARSHIP PROGRAM

Award for full-time undergraduate students attending a 4-year accredited college or university that offers courses leading to a degree in physical sciences or engineering. Applicants must have completed at least two years of college credits by the time the award is received. Must be U.S. citizens. Applicants must be majoring in the physical sciences or engineering. This would include, but is not limited to, aerospace engineering, astronomy, biophysics, chemistry, chemical engineering, computer science, electrical engineering, geophysics, geology, mathematics, mechanical engineering, physics, and space science education. Minimum 3.5 GPA required. Visit Web site at http://www.usra.edu /hq/scholarships/overview.shtml for more information and to download application. No forms will be mailed out.

Academic Fields/Career Goals: Applied Sciences; Aviation/Aerospace; Chemical Engineering; Civil Engineering; Earth Science; Electrical Engineering/Electronics; Engineering/Technology; Materials Science, Engineering, and Metallurgy; Mechanical Engineering; Nuclear Science; Physical Sciences and Math; Science, Technology, and Society.

Award: Scholarship for use in freshman, sophomore, junior, or senior years; not renewable. *Number:* 1–3. *Amount:* $500.

Eligibility Requirements: Applicant must be enrolled or expecting to enroll full-time at a four-year institution or university. Applicant must have 3.5 GPA or higher. Available to U.S. citizens.

Application Requirements: Application, essay, references, transcript. *Deadline:* May 1.

Contact: USRA Scholarship Program
Universities Space Research Association
10211 Wincopin Circle, Suite 500
Columbia, MD 21044-3432
Phone: 410-730-2656
Fax: 410-730-3496
E-mail: info@hq.usra.edu

ARCHAEOLOGY

AMERICAN SCHOOL OF CLASSICAL STUDIES AT ATHENS
http://www.ascsa.edu.gr

ASCSA SUMMER SESSIONS OPEN SCHOLARSHIPS
• See page 88

AMERICAN SCHOOLS OF ORIENTAL RESEARCH (ASOR)
http://www.asor.org

CYPRUS AMERICAN ARCHAEOLOGICAL RESEARCH INSTITUTE HELENA WYLDE AND STUART SWINY FELLOWSHIP

One $750 grant for an upper-level graduate student in a U.S. college or university to pursue a research project relevant to an ongoing field project in Cyprus. Residence at CAARI is mandatory. Submit project statement, work schedule, budget, curriculum vitae, and 2 letters of recommendation. Application deadline: February 1.

Academic Fields/Career Goals: Archaeology; European Studies; Near and Middle East Studies.

Award: Grant for use in junior or senior years; not renewable. *Number:* 1. *Amount:* $750.

Eligibility Requirements: Applicant must be enrolled or expecting to enroll full-time at a four-year institution or university. Available to U.S. citizens.

Application Requirements: Application, references, project statement, work schedule, budget, curriculum vitae. *Deadline:* February 1.

Contact: Alexandra Ratzlaff, Program Coordinator
American Schools of Oriental Research (ASOR)
CAARI at Boston University, 656 Beacon Street, 5th Floor
Boston, MA 02215
Phone: 617-353-6570
Fax: 617-353-6575
E-mail: caari@bu.edu

EXPLORERS CLUB
http://www.explorers.org

EXPLORATION FUND GRANTS
• See page 88

HARVARD TRAVELLERS CLUB

HARVARD TRAVELLERS CLUB GRANTS

Approximately three grants made each year to persons with projects that involve intelligent travel and exploration. The travel must be intimately involved with research and/or exploration. Prefer applications from persons working on advanced degrees.

Academic Fields/Career Goals: Archaeology; Area/Ethnic Studies; Geography; History; Humanities; Natural Sciences.

Award: Grant for use in freshman, sophomore, junior, senior, graduate, or postgraduate years; not renewable. *Number:* 3–4. *Amount:* $500–$1000.

Eligibility Requirements: Applicant must be enrolled or expecting to enroll full or part-time at a four-year institution or university. Available to U.S. and non-U.S. citizens.

Application Requirements: Application, financial need analysis, resume. *Deadline:* February 28.

Contact: George P. Bates, Trustee
Harvard Travellers Club
PO Box 162
Lincoln, MA 01773
Phone: 781-821-0400
Fax: 781-828-4254
E-mail: jessepage@comcast.net

ARCHITECTURE

AACE INTERNATIONAL
http://www.aacei.org

AACE INTERNATIONAL COMPETITIVE SCHOLARSHIP

One-time awards to full-time students pursuing a degree in engineering, construction management, quantity surveying, and related fields. Application deadline is October 15.

Academic Fields/Career Goals: Architecture; Aviation/Aerospace; Chemical Engineering; Civil Engineering; Computer Science/Data Processing; Electrical Engineering/Electronics; Engineering/Technology; Engineering-Related Technologies; Mechanical Engineering.

Award: Scholarship for use in freshman, sophomore, junior, senior, or graduate years; not renewable. *Number:* 15–25. *Amount:* $1000–$4000.

Eligibility Requirements: Applicant must be enrolled or expecting to enroll full-time at a two-year or four-year or technical institution or university. Available to U.S. and non-U.S. citizens.

Application Requirements: Application, essay, transcript. *Deadline:* October 15.

Contact: Charla Miller, Staff Director-Education and Administration
AACE International
209 Prairie Avenue, Suite 100
Morgantown, WV 26501
Phone: 304-296-8444 Ext. 113
Fax: 304-291-5728
E-mail: cmiller@aacei.org

ACI INTERNATIONAL/CONCRETE RESEARCH AND EDUCATION FOUNDATION (CONREF)   http://www.concrete.org

KUMAR MEHTA SCHOLARSHIP

One $3000 award is available for the pursuit of graduate study in a concrete-related field. Recipients must demonstrate ongoing effort to conduct graduate research on sustainable development of concrete. See Web site for more details (http://www.concrete.org).

Academic Fields/Career Goals: Architecture; Civil Engineering; Engineering/Technology; Materials Science, Engineering, and Metallurgy.

Award: Scholarship for use in junior, senior, or graduate years; not renewable. *Number:* 1. *Amount:* $3000.

Eligibility Requirements: Applicant must be enrolled or expecting to enroll full-time at a two-year or four-year institution or university. Available to U.S. and Canadian citizens.

Application Requirements: Application, essay, resume, references, transcript. *Deadline:* November 15.

Contact: Jessie Bournay, Fundraising and Scholarship Assistant
ACI International/Concrete Research and Education Foundation (CONREF)
38800 Country Club Drive
Farmington Hills, MI 48331
Phone: 248-848-3832
Fax: 248-848-3740
E-mail: scholarships@concrete.org

PETER D. COURTOIS CONCRETE CONSTRUCTION SCHOLARSHIP

Two $1000 awards are available for the pursuit of study in a concrete-related field. The student must have senior status in a four-year or longer undergraduate program in engineering, construction, or technology and demonstrate interest and ability to work in the field of concrete construction. See Web site for more details (http://www.concrete.org).

Academic Fields/Career Goals: Architecture; Civil Engineering; Engineering/Technology; Materials Science, Engineering, and Metallurgy.

Award: Scholarship for use in senior year; not renewable. *Number:* 2. *Amount:* $1000.

Eligibility Requirements: Applicant must be enrolled or expecting to enroll at a four-year institution or university. Available to U.S. and Canadian citizens.

Application Requirements: Application, references. *Deadline:* December 15.

Contact: Jessie Bournay, Fundraising and Scholarship Assistant
ACI International/Concrete Research and Education Foundation (CONREF)
38800 Country Club Drive
Farmington Hills, MI 48331
Phone: 248-848-3832
Fax: 248-848-3740
E-mail: scholarships@concrete.org

V. MOHAN MALHOTRA SCHOLARSHIP

One $3000 award is available for the pursuit of graduate study in a concrete-related field. Recipient must be majoring in concrete materials science research. See Web site for more details (http://www.concrete.org).

Academic Fields/Career Goals: Architecture; Civil Engineering; Engineering/Technology; Materials Science, Engineering, and Metallurgy.

Award: Scholarship for use in junior, senior, or graduate years; not renewable. *Number:* 1. *Amount:* $3000.

Eligibility Requirements: Applicant must be enrolled or expecting to enroll full-time at a two-year or four-year institution or university. Available to U.S. and Canadian citizens.

Application Requirements: Application, essay, resume, references, transcript. *Deadline:* November 15.

Contact: Jessie Bournay, Fundraising and Scholarship Assistant
ACI International/Concrete Research and Education Foundation (CONREF)
38800 Country Club Drive
Farmington Hills, MI 48331
Phone: 248-848-3832
Fax: 248-848-3740
E-mail: scholarships@concrete.org

W.R. GRACE SCHOLARSHIP AWARD

One $3000 award is available for the pursuit of graduate study in a concrete-related field. See Web site for more details (http://www.concrete.org).

Academic Fields/Career Goals: Architecture; Civil Engineering; Engineering/Technology; Materials Science, Engineering, and Metallurgy.

Award: Scholarship for use in junior, senior, or graduate years; not renewable. *Number:* 1. *Amount:* $3000.

Eligibility Requirements: Applicant must be enrolled or expecting to enroll full-time at a four-year institution or university. Available to U.S. and Canadian citizens.

Application Requirements: Application, essay, resume, references, transcript. *Deadline:* November 15.

Contact: Jessie Bournay, Fundraising and Scholarship Assistant
ACI International/Concrete Research and Education Foundation (CONREF)
38800 Country Club Drive
Farmington Hills, MI 48331
Phone: 248-848-3832
Fax: 248-848-3740
E-mail: scholarships@concrete.org

AMERICAN ARCHITECTURAL FOUNDATION   http://www.archfoundation.org

AMERICAN INSTITUTE OF ARCHITECTS MINORITY/DISADVANTAGED SCHOLARSHIP

Renewable award for high school seniors and college freshmen who are entering an architecture degree program. Must be nominated by an architect firm, a teacher, dean, or a civic organization director by December. Must include drawing. Deadline for nominations: December 6. Deadline for applications: January 15. Co-sponsored by AIA and AAF.

Academic Fields/Career Goals: Architecture.

Award: Scholarship for use in freshman year; renewable. *Number:* 20. *Amount:* $500–$2500.

Eligibility Requirements: Applicant must be enrolled or expecting to enroll full-time at a four-year institution or university. Available to U.S. citizens.

Application Requirements: Application, financial need analysis, references, test scores, transcript, drawing. *Deadline:* January 15.

Contact: Mary Felber, Director of Scholarship Programs
American Architectural Foundation
1735 New York Avenue, NW
Washington, DC 20006-5292
Phone: 202-626-7511
Fax: 202-626-7509
E-mail: mfelber@archfoundation.org

AMERICAN INSTITUTE OF ARCHITECTS

http://www.aia.org

AMERICAN INSTITUTE OF ARCHITECTS/AMERICAN ARCHITECTURAL FOUNDATION MINORITY/DISADVANTAGED SCHOLARSHIPS

Award to aid high school seniors and college freshmen from minority or disadvantaged backgrounds who are planning to study architecture in an NAAB accredited program. Twenty awards per year, renewable for two additional years. Amounts based on financial need. Must be nominated by either a high school guidance counselor, AIA component, architect, or other individual who is aware of the student's interest and aptitude. Nomination deadline is early December; Applications will be mailed to eligible students. Application deadline is mid-January.

Academic Fields/Career Goals: Architecture.

Award: Scholarship for use in freshman, sophomore, junior, or senior years; renewable. *Number:* up to 20. *Amount:* $500–$2500.

Eligibility Requirements: Applicant must be enrolled or expecting to enroll full-time at a four-year or technical institution or university. Available to U.S. citizens.

Application Requirements: Application, essay, references, transcript, statement of disadvantaged circumstances, a drawing. *Deadline:* January.

Contact: Mary Felber, Scholarship Chair
American Institute of Architects
1735 New York Avenue, NW
Washington, DC 20006-5292
Phone: 202-626-7511
Fax: 202-626-7509
E-mail: mfelber@aia.org

AMERICAN INSTITUTE OF ARCHITECTS, NEW YORK CHAPTER

http://www.aiany.org

THE DOUGLAS HASKELL AWARD FOR STUDENT JOURNALISM

One-time award for architectural students. The Douglas Haskell awards were founded to encourage excellence in writing on architecture and related design fields. Submit ten copies of published article, essay, or journal with 100-word statement of purpose.

Academic Fields/Career Goals: Architecture; Art History; Engineering/Technology; Landscape Architecture.

Award: Prize for use in freshman, sophomore, junior, or senior years; not renewable. *Number:* 1–3. *Amount:* $1000–$2000.

Eligibility Requirements: Applicant must be enrolled or expecting to enroll full or part-time at a two-year or four-year or technical institution or university. Available to U.S. citizens.

Application Requirements: Application, essay, 10 copies of the journal or galleys, 10 copies of a letter from the editor stating the intended date and place of publication, 10 copies of cover page containing a concise statement describing the purpose of the publication. *Deadline:* April 12.

Contact: Marcus Bleyer
American Institute of Architects, New York Chapter
536 LaGuardia Place
New York, NY 10012
Phone: 212-358-6117
E-mail: mbleyer@aiany.org

WOMEN'S ARCHITECTURAL AUXILIARY ELEANOR ALLWORK SCHOLARSHIP GRANTS

Award available to students seeking first professional degree in architecture from an accredited New York school. Must demonstrate financial need. Must be a resident of New York metropolitan area. Must be nominated by Dean of architectural school.

Academic Fields/Career Goals: Architecture.

Award: Scholarship for use in freshman, sophomore, junior, senior, or graduate years; not renewable. *Number:* up to 3. *Amount:* $2500–$7500.

Eligibility Requirements: Applicant must be enrolled or expecting to enroll full-time at an institution or university; resident of New York and studying in New York. Available to U.S. citizens.

Application Requirements: References, self-addressed stamped envelope, student project in an 8.5 x 11 binder (flat artwork only), letter from an architect. *Deadline:* April 14.

Contact: Marcus Bleyer
American Institute of Architects, New York Chapter
536 LaGuardia Place
New York, NY 10012
Phone: 212-358-6117
E-mail: mbleyer@aiany.org

AMERICAN INSTITUTE OF ARCHITECTS, WEST VIRGINIA CHAPTER

http://www.aiawv.org

AIA WEST VIRGINIA SCHOLARSHIP PROGRAM

Applicant must have completed junior year of an accredited undergraduate architectural program or enrolled in an accredited Masters of Architecture program. Select applicants must present a portfolio of work to judging committee. Please refer to Web site for further details: http://www.aiawv.org

Academic Fields/Career Goals: Architecture.

Award: Scholarship for use in senior, or graduate years; not renewable. *Number:* varies. *Amount:* up to $11,000.

Eligibility Requirements: Applicant must be enrolled or expecting to enroll full-time at a four-year institution or university and resident of West Virginia. Available to U.S. citizens.

Application Requirements: Application, resume, references, transcript, personal letter. *Deadline:* May 30.

Contact: Roberta Guffey, Executive Director
American Institute of Architects, West Virginia Chapter
PO Box 813
Charleston, WV 25323
Phone: 304-344-9872
Fax: 304-343-0205
E-mail: roberta.guffey@aiawv.org

AMERICAN SCHOOL OF CLASSICAL STUDIES AT ATHENS

http://www.ascsa.edu.gr

ASCSA SUMMER SESSIONS OPEN SCHOLARSHIPS
• *See page 88*

ASSOCIATION FOR WOMEN IN ARCHITECTURE FOUNDATION

http://www.awa-la.org

ASSOCIATION FOR WOMEN IN ARCHITECTURE SCHOLARSHIP

Must be a California resident or nonresident attending school in California. Must major in architecture or a related field and have completed 1 year (18 units) of schooling. Recipients may reapply. Open to women only. Interview in Los Angeles required. Application deadline is April 28. Applications available the beginning of February.

Academic Fields/Career Goals: Architecture; Interior Design; Landscape Architecture.

Award: Scholarship for use in sophomore, junior, senior, or graduate years; not renewable. *Number:* 3. *Amount:* $1000–$2500.

Eligibility Requirements: Applicant must be enrolled or expecting to enroll full-time at a two-year or four-year or technical institution or university and female. Available to U.S. and non-U.S. citizens.

Application Requirements: Application, essay, financial need analysis, interview, references, self-addressed stamped envelope, transcript. *Deadline:* April 28.

Contact: Nina Briggs, Scholarship Chair
Association for Women in Architecture Foundation
386 Beech Avenue, Unit B4
Torrance, CA 90501-6203
Phone: 310-533-4042
E-mail: ninabriggs@earthlink.net

DALLAS ARCHITECTURAL FOUNDATION-HKS/ JOHN HUMPHRIES MINORITY SCHOLARSHIP   http://www.dallasfoundation.org

DALLAS ARCHITECTURAL FOUNDATION - HARRELL AND HAMILTON SCHOLARSHIP FUND

This program is established to assist students in their final year at one of eight accredited Texas architecture schools, on a rotating basis. Must be a U.S. citizen and permanent resident of Dallas-Fort Worth area. Deadline is March 28.

Academic Fields/Career Goals: Architecture.

Award: Scholarship for use in sophomore year; not renewable. *Amount:* $2500.

Eligibility Requirements: Applicant must be enrolled or expecting to enroll at a four-year institution or university and resident of Texas. Available to U.S. citizens.

Application Requirements: Application. *Deadline:* March 28.

Contact: Dallas Architectural Foundation-HKS/John Humphries
Minority Scholarship
1444 Oak Lawn Avenue, Suite 600
Dallas, TX 75207
Phone: 214-742-3242

DAYTON FOUNDATION   http://www.daytonfoundation.org

AMERICAN INSTITUTE OF ARCHITECTURE (AIA) DAYTON ARCHITECTURAL SCHOLARSHIP FUND

Scholarship to encourage and assist students graduating from high schools in the Dayton/Miami Valley region to pursue a degree in architecture at an accredited college.

Academic Fields/Career Goals: Architecture.

Award: Scholarship for use in freshman year; not renewable. *Number:* up to 2. *Amount:* up to $1000.

Eligibility Requirements: Applicant must be enrolled or expecting to enroll full-time at a two-year or four-year institution or university; resident of Ohio and studying in Connecticut, Florida, Ohio, or Washington. Available to U.S. citizens.

Application Requirements: Application, essay, references, transcript, Student Aid Report (SAR), list of academic achievements, school activities, community service involvement. *Deadline:* varies.

Contact: Diane Timmons, Director Grants and Programs
Dayton Foundation
2300 Kettering Tower
Dayton, OH 45423
E-mail: dtimmons@daytonfoundation.org

FLORIDA EDUCATIONAL FACILITIES PLANNERS' ASSOCIATION   http://www.fefpa.org

FEFPA ASSISTANTSHIP

Scholarship supports full-time juniors, seniors and graduate students enrolled in an accredited four-year Florida university. Must be a resident of Florida with a 3.0 GPA. For more information go to Web site: http://www.fefpa.org

Academic Fields/Career Goals: Architecture; Civil Engineering; Electrical Engineering/Electronics; Engineering/Technology; Engineering-Related Technologies; Landscape Architecture; Mechanical Engineering.

Award: Scholarship for use in sophomore, junior, senior, or graduate years; renewable. *Number:* 2. *Amount:* $3000.

Eligibility Requirements: Applicant must be enrolled or expecting to enroll full-time at a four-year institution or university; resident of Florida and studying in Florida. Applicant must have 3.0 GPA or higher. Available to U.S. and non-U.S. citizens.

Application Requirements: Application, essay, financial need analysis, references, transcript. *Deadline:* July 1.

Contact: Bob Griffith, FEFPA Assistantship, Selection Committee Chair
Florida Educational Facilities Planners' Association
Florida International University, University Park, CSC 236
Miami, FL 33199

HAWAIIAN LODGE, F.& A. M.   http://www.hawaiianlodge.org/

HAWAIIAN LODGE SCHOLARSHIPS

Dedicated to worthy students in the areas of engineering, sciences, Hawaiian studies, and education who would otherwise not be able to attend college.

Academic Fields/Career Goals: Architecture; Biology; Chemical Engineering; Civil Engineering; Computer Science/Data Processing; Dental Health/Services; Electrical Engineering/Electronics; Energy and Power Engineering; Engineering/Technology; Engineering-Related Technologies; Health and Medical Sciences.

Award: Scholarship for use in freshman, sophomore, junior, or senior years; renewable. *Number:* 4–16. *Amount:* $1000.

Eligibility Requirements: Applicant must be high school student; planning to enroll or expecting to enroll full-time at an institution or university and resident of Hawaii. Applicant must have 3.0 GPA or higher. Available to U.S. citizens.

Application Requirements: Application, autobiography, essay, financial need analysis, interview, references, test scores, transcript. *Deadline:* June 1.

Contact: Chairman, Scholarship Committee
Hawaiian Lodge, F.& A. M.
1227 Makiki Street
Honolulu, HI 96814
Phone: 808-979-7809
E-mail: secretary@hawaiianlodge.org

HELLENIC UNIVERSITY CLUB OF PHILADELPHIA   http://www.hucphila.org

THE DIMITRI J. VERVERELLI MEMORIAL SCHOLARSHIP FOR ARCHITECTURE AND/OR ENGINEERING

Scholarship will be awarded to students with outstanding academic qualifications and financial need. Must be enrolled full time in an architecture or engineering degree program at an accredited four-year college or university. High school seniors accepted for enrollment in such a degree program may also apply. Must be of Greek descent, U.S. citizen, and lawful permanent resident of Berks, Bucks, Chester, Delaware, Lancaster, Lehigh, Montgomery, or Philadelphia counties in Pennsylvania; Atlantic, Burlington, Camden, Cape May, Cumberland, Gloucester or Salem counties in New Jersey.

Academic Fields/Career Goals: Architecture; Engineering/Technology.

Award: Scholarship for use in freshman, sophomore, junior, or senior years. *Amount:* $2000.

Eligibility Requirements: Applicant must be of Greek heritage; enrolled or expecting to enroll full-time at a four-year institution or university and resident of New Jersey or Pennsylvania. Available to U.S. citizens.

Application Requirements: Application, financial need analysis. *Deadline:* April 20.

Contact: Zoe Tripolitis, Scholarship Chairman
Hellenic University Club of Philadelphia
PO Box 42199
Philadelphia, PA 19101
Phone: 215-483-7440
E-mail: zoe.tripolitis@arkemagroup.com

HISPANIC COLLEGE FUND, INC.   http://www.hispanicfund.org

DENNY'S/HISPANIC COLLEGE FUND SCHOLARSHIP
• *See page 62*

EL NUEVO CONSTRUCTOR SCHOLARSHIP PROGRAM

Program intended for undergraduate student pursuing his or her associate's or bachelor's degree in a construction related field. Applicant must be a U.S. citizen with Hispanic background. Must attend college or university in U.S. or Puerto Rico. Online application only: http://www.hispanicfund.org

Academic Fields/Career Goals: Architecture; Drafting; Heating, Air-Conditioning, and Refrigeration Mechanics; Industrial Design.

Award: Scholarship for use in freshman, sophomore, junior, or senior years; not renewable. *Number:* varies. *Amount:* $500–$5000.

Hispanic College Fund, Inc. (continued)

Eligibility Requirements: Applicant must be Hispanic and enrolled or expecting to enroll full-time at a two-year or four-year institution or university. Applicant must have 3.0 GPA or higher. Available to U.S. citizens.

Application Requirements: Application. *Deadline:* April 15.

Contact: Stina Augustsson, Program Manager
Hispanic College Fund, Inc.
1717 Pennsylvania Avenue, NW, Suite 460
Washington, DC 20006
Phone: 202-296-5400
Fax: 202-296-3774
E-mail: hcf-info@hispanicfund.org

ILLUMINATING ENGINEERING SOCIETY OF NORTH AMERICA   http://www.iesna.org

ROBERT W. THUNEN MEMORIAL SCHOLARSHIPS

One-time award for juniors, seniors, or graduate students enrolled at four-year colleges and universities in northern California, Nevada, Oregon, or Washington pursuing lighting career. Submit statement describing proposed lighting course work or project and three recommendations, at least one from someone involved professionally or academically with lighting. Curriculum must be accredited by ABET, ACSA, or FIDER.

Academic Fields/Career Goals: Architecture; Engineering/Technology; Engineering-Related Technologies; Interior Design; Performing Arts; TV/Radio Broadcasting.

Award: Scholarship for use in junior, senior, or graduate years; not renewable. *Number:* 2. *Amount:* $2500.

Eligibility Requirements: Applicant must be enrolled or expecting to enroll full-time at a four-year institution or university and studying in California, Nevada, Oregon, or Washington. Available to U.S. and non-U.S. citizens.

Application Requirements: Application, references, transcript. *Deadline:* April 1.

Contact: Chairperson (Thunen Scholarship Committee)
Illuminating Engineering Society of North America
IESNA Golden Gate Section, 1514 Gibbons Drive
Alameda, CA 94501-4001
Phone: 510-864-0204
Fax: 510-864-8511
E-mail: mrcatisbac@aol.com

ILLUMINATING ENGINEERING SOCIETY OF NORTH AMERICA–GOLDEN GATE SECTION   http://www.iesgg.org

ALAN LUCAS MEMORIAL EDUCATIONAL SCHOLARSHIP

Scholarship available to full time student for pursuit of lighting education or research as part of undergraduate, graduate, or doctoral studies. Must attend a four year college or university located in Northern California (including San Luis Obispo, Fresno, and north). Must submit application, statement of purpose, description of work in progress, transcripts, and three recommendations by April 3.

Academic Fields/Career Goals: Architecture; Electrical Engineering/Electronics; Filmmaking/Video; Interior Design.

Award: Scholarship for use in junior, senior, or graduate years; not renewable. *Number:* 1. *Amount:* $1500.

Eligibility Requirements: Applicant must be enrolled or expecting to enroll full-time at a four-year institution or university and studying in California. Available to U.S. citizens.

Application Requirements: Application, references, transcript, statement of purpose, scholar agreement. *Deadline:* April 1.

Contact: Phil Hall, Coordinator
Illuminating Engineering Society of North America–Golden Gate Section
1514 Gibbons Drive
Alameda, CA 94501
Phone: 510-208-5005 Ext. 3030
E-mail: information@iesgg.org

ROBERT W. THUNEN MEMORIAL SCHOLARSHIPS

Scholarships for full-time undergraduate, or graduate study in the lighting field. Must be a junior, senior, or graduate student in a 4-year college or university in Northern Nevada, Northern California, Oregon, or Washington. Must submit a least three letters of recommendation, statement of purpose, transcripts. Applications and complete information can be obtained from Web site: http://www.iesgg.org. Applications must be received by April 1.

Academic Fields/Career Goals: Architecture; Electrical Engineering/Electronics; Filmmaking/Video; Interior Design.

Award: Scholarship for use in junior, senior, or graduate years; not renewable. *Number:* up to 2. *Amount:* $2500.

Eligibility Requirements: Applicant must be enrolled or expecting to enroll full-time at a four-year institution or university and studying in California, Nevada, Oregon, or Washington. Available to U.S. citizens.

Application Requirements: Application, references, transcript, statement of purpose, scholar agreement. *Deadline:* April 1.

Contact: Phil Hall, Coordinator
Illuminating Engineering Society of North America–Golden Gate Section
1514 Gibbons Drive
Alameda, CA 94501
Phone: 510-208-5005 Ext. 3030
E-mail: information@iesgg.org

INTERNATIONAL FACILITY MANAGEMENT ASSOCIATION FOUNDATION   http://www.ifmafoundation.org

IFMA FOUNDATION SCHOLARSHIPS

One-time scholarship of up to $6000 awarded to students currently enrolled in full-time facility management programs. Minimum 3.0 GPA required for undergraduates and 3.5 for graduate students. Application deadline is May 31.

Academic Fields/Career Goals: Architecture; Engineering-Related Technologies.

Award: Scholarship for use in freshman, sophomore, junior, senior, graduate, or postgraduate years; not renewable. *Number:* 10–15. *Amount:* $1000–$6000.

Eligibility Requirements: Applicant must be enrolled or expecting to enroll full-time at a four-year institution or university. Available to U.S. and non-U.S. citizens.

Application Requirements: Application, resume, references, transcript, letter of intent. *Deadline:* May 31.

Contact: Mr. William Rub, Foundation Manager
International Facility Management Association Foundation
1 East Greenway Plaza
Suite 1100
Houston, TX 77046-0194
Phone: 713-623-4362 Ext. 158
Fax: 713-623-6124
E-mail: william.rub@ifma.org

MIDWEST ROOFING CONTRACTORS ASSOCIATION   http://www.mrca.org

MRCA FOUNDATION SCHOLARSHIP PROGRAM
• See page 94

NATIONAL ASSOCIATION OF WOMEN IN CONSTRUCTION   http://nawic.org

NAWIC UNDERGRADUATE SCHOLARSHIPS

One-time award for any student having at least one year of study remaining in a construction-related program leading to an associate or higher degree. Awards range from $500-$2000. Submit application and transcript of grades.

Academic Fields/Career Goals: Architecture; Civil Engineering; Drafting; Electrical Engineering/Electronics; Engineering/Technology; Engineering-Related Technologies; Interior Design; Landscape Architecture; Mechanical Engineering; Trade/Technical Specialties.

Award: Scholarship for use in freshman, sophomore, junior, or senior years; not renewable. *Number:* 40–50. *Amount:* $500–$2000.

Eligibility Requirements: Applicant must be enrolled or expecting to enroll full-time at a two-year or four-year or technical institution or university. Applicant must have 3.0 GPA or higher. Available to U.S. and non-U.S. citizens.

Application Requirements: Application, essay, financial need analysis, interview, transcript. *Deadline:* March 15.

Contact: Scholarship Administrator
National Association of Women in Construction
327 South Adams Street
Fort Worth, TX 76104
E-mail: nawic@nawic.org

NATIONAL FEDERATION OF THE BLIND
http://www.nfb.org

HOWARD BROWN RICKARD SCHOLARSHIP

For legally blind full-time students planning to study architecture, engineering, law, medicine, or natural science. Must submit a letter from National Foundation of the Blind state officer with whom they have discussed their application. May reapply. Based on academic excellence, service to the community, and financial need. One-time award of $3000. Must attend school in the U.S.

Academic Fields/Career Goals: Architecture; Biology; Engineering/Technology; Health and Medical Sciences; Law/Legal Services; Natural Resources; Physical Sciences and Math.

Award: Scholarship for use in freshman, sophomore, junior, or senior years; not renewable. *Number:* 1. *Amount:* $3000.

Eligibility Requirements: Applicant must be enrolled or expecting to enroll full-time at an institution or university. Applicant or parent of applicant must have employment or volunteer experience in community service. Applicant must be visually impaired. Applicant must have 3.5 GPA or higher. Available to U.S. and non-U.S. citizens.

Application Requirements: Application, autobiography, essay, financial need analysis, references, transcript. *Deadline:* March 31.

Contact: Peggy Elliot, Chairman, Scholarship Committee
National Federation of the Blind
805 5th Avenue
Grinnell, IA 50112
Phone: 641-236-3366

NATIONAL INSTITUTE OF BUILDING SCIENCES, MULTIHAZARD MITIGATION COUNCIL
http://www.nibs.org

ARCHITECTURE, CONSTRUCTION, AND ENGINEERING MENTOR PROGRAM SCHOLARSHIPS

Scholarships intended to assist students in starting or completing an undergraduate degree program in a field directly related to architecture, construction, and/or engineering. Accompanying mentor activities will ensure that the students receive instruction in principles and practice of risk management. Three of the scholarships will be awarded to registered members of Federally-recognized Indian tribes.

Academic Fields/Career Goals: Architecture; Civil Engineering; Construction Engineering/Management; Engineering/Technology.

Award: Scholarship for use in freshman, sophomore, junior, or senior years. *Number:* 6. *Amount:* varies.

Eligibility Requirements: Applicant must be enrolled or expecting to enroll full-time at a four-year institution or university. Available to U.S. citizens.

Application Requirements: Application.

Contact: Pamela Mullender, Acting Executive Director, ACE Mentor Program
National Institute of Building Sciences, Multihazard Mitigation Council
National Institute of Building Sciences, 1090 Vermont Avenue, NW, Suite 700
Washington, DC 20005
Phone: 202-898-6396
Fax: 202-289-1092

NETWORK OF EXECUTIVE WOMEN IN HOSPITALITY
http://www.newh.org

NETWORK OF EXECUTIVE WOMEN IN HOSPITALITY, INC. SCHOLARSHIP

Each NEWH chapter provides scholarships for those wishing to enter the hospitality industry and related fields. Awards vary in number and dollar amount for each chapter. Must have completed half the requirements for a degree or certification program in which enrolled. Visit Web site or contact your local chapter for deadlines and further details.

Academic Fields/Career Goals: Architecture; Food Service/Hospitality; Hospitality Management; Interior Design; Landscape Architecture; Travel/Tourism.

Award: Scholarship for use in freshman, sophomore, junior, senior, or graduate years; not renewable. *Number:* varies. *Amount:* $500–$5000.

Eligibility Requirements: Applicant must be enrolled or expecting to enroll full or part-time at a two-year or four-year or technical institution or university. Applicant must have 3.0 GPA or higher. Available to U.S. and non-U.S. citizens.

Application Requirements: Application, financial need analysis, references, transcript. *Deadline:* varies.

Contact: Rebecca Folkerts, local NEWH Chapter
Phone: 800-593-6394

NEW JERSEY SOCIETY OF ARCHITECTS/AIA NEW JERSEY SCHOLARSHIP FOUNDATION
http://www.aia-nj.org/about/scholarship.shtml

NEW JERSEY SOCIETY OF ARCHITECTS SCHOLARSHIP

Award for students with a career interest in architecture who are studying full time at an accredited four-year institution. Must be a resident of New Jersey. Scholarship is for sophomore, junior or senior year, or master's-level study. Must demonstrate financial need or academic achievement. Application deadline is April 30.

Academic Fields/Career Goals: Architecture.

Award: Scholarship for use in sophomore, junior, senior, or graduate years; not renewable. *Number:* varies. *Amount:* $1000–$2500.

Eligibility Requirements: Applicant must be enrolled or expecting to enroll full-time at a two-year or four-year institution or university and resident of New Jersey. Available to U.S. citizens.

Application Requirements: Application, essay, financial need analysis, references, transcript, photos of projects, FAFSA. *Fee:* $5. *Deadline:* April 30.

Contact: Robert Zaccone, President
New Jersey Society of Architects/AIA New Jersey Scholarship Foundation
212 White Avenue
Old Tappan, NJ 07675
Phone: 201-767-9575
Fax: 201-767-5541

NEW YORK STATE EDUCATION DEPARTMENT
http://www.highered.nysed.gov

REGENTS PROFESSIONAL OPPORTUNITY SCHOLARSHIP
• See page 67

ORANGE COUNTY COMMUNITY FOUNDATION
http://www.heef.org

ARCHITECTURE AND ENGINEERING SCHOLARSHIP PROGRAM

Scholarship intended to promote the professions of architecture and engineering. Second year community college transfer students who are residents of Orange County, CA, may apply. Must have a minimum 3.2 GPA and have been accepted into an accredited program in architecture or engineering

Academic Fields/Career Goals: Architecture; Engineering/Technology.

Award: Scholarship for use in sophomore, junior, or senior years; renewable. *Number:* up to 2. *Amount:* up to $2000.

Eligibility Requirements: Applicant must be enrolled or expecting to enroll full-time at a four-year institution or university. Applicant must have 3.5 GPA or higher. Available to U.S. and Canadian citizens.

Application Requirements: Application, essay, self-addressed stamped envelope, transcript. *Deadline:* February 13.

Contact: Rose Garris, Hispanic Education Endowment Fund
Orange County Community Foundation
30 Corporate Park, Suite 410
Irvine, CA 92606
Phone: 949-543-4202 Ext. 23
Fax: 949-553-4211

OREGON STUDENT ASSISTANCE COMMISSION
http://www.osac.state.or.us

GLENN R. AND JUANITA B. STRUBLE SCHOLARSHIP II

One-time award for residents of Benton, Douglas, Jackson, Josephine, Lane, Linn, or Marion counties who are studying arts, engineering, or business management. Minimum 2.75 GPA for graduating high school seniors. Graduate students may be enrolled full or part time in the same majors.

Academic Fields/Career Goals: Architecture; Arts; Business/Consumer Services.

Award: Scholarship for use in freshman, sophomore, junior, senior, or graduate years; renewable. *Number:* 1. *Amount:* $2800.

Eligibility Requirements: Applicant must be enrolled or expecting to enroll full or part-time at an institution or university and resident of Oregon. Available to U.S. citizens.

Application Requirements: Application, essay, financial need analysis, transcript, activities chart. *Deadline:* March 1.

Contact: Director of Grant Programs
Oregon Student Assistance Commission
1500 Valley River Drive, Suite 100
Eugene, OR 97401-7020
Phone: 800-452-8807 Ext. 7395

HOMESTEAD CAPITAL HOUSING SCHOLARSHIP
• See page 68

PARK PEOPLE
http://www.parkpeople.org

THE PARK PEOPLE $2000 SCHOLARSHIP

$2000 scholarships for students pursuing a degree at a Texas university in one of the following fields: architecture with an interest in urban greenery, environmental sciences, horticultural sciences, landscape architecture with an interest in urban greenery, parks and recreation, urban forestry, urban planning. All recipients are required to maintain an overall GPA of at least 2.8.

Academic Fields/Career Goals: Architecture; Environmental Science; Horticulture/Floriculture; Urban and Regional Planning.

Award: Scholarship for use in freshman, sophomore, junior, senior, or graduate years. *Amount:* $2000.

Eligibility Requirements: Applicant must be enrolled or expecting to enroll full-time at a four-year institution or university and studying in Texas. Available to U.S. citizens.

Application Requirements: Application, references, transcript, architecture and landscape architecture students are required to include examples of design work involving urban greenery. *Deadline:* February 10.

Contact: Scholarship Chair
Park People
3015 Richmond, Suite 210
Houston, TX 77098
Phone: 713-942-8429
Fax: 713-942-7275
E-mail: annem@parkpeople.org

PLUMBING-HEATING-COOLING CONTRACTORS ASSOCIATION EDUCATION FOUNDATION
http://www.phccweb.org

BRADFORD WHITE CORPORATION SCHOLARSHIP

Scholarship for students enrolled in either an approved four-year PHCC apprenticeship program or an accredited two-year community college, technical college or trade school.

Academic Fields/Career Goals: Architecture; Business/Consumer Services; Civil Engineering; Engineering/Technology; Engineering-Related Technologies; Heating, Air-Conditioning, and Refrigeration Mechanics; Mechanical Engineering; Trade/Technical Specialties.

Award: Scholarship for use in freshman, sophomore, junior, or senior years. *Number:* 3. *Amount:* $2500.

Eligibility Requirements: Applicant must be enrolled or expecting to enroll at a two-year or four-year or technical institution. Available to U.S. citizens.

Application Requirements: Application. *Deadline:* June 1.

Contact: Program Assistant
Plumbing-Heating-Cooling Contractors Association Education Foundation
PO Box 6808
Falls Church, VA 22040
Phone: 703-237-8100

DELTA FAUCET COMPANY SCHOLARSHIP PROGRAM

Applicants must be sponsored by a member of the National Association of Plumbing-Heating-Cooling Contractors. Applicants must pursue studies in a major related to the plumbing-heating-cooling industry. Visit Web site for additional information.

Academic Fields/Career Goals: Architecture; Business/Consumer Services; Civil Engineering; Engineering/Technology; Engineering-Related Technologies; Heating, Air-Conditioning, and Refrigeration Mechanics; Mechanical Engineering; Trade/Technical Specialties.

Award: Scholarship for use in freshman, sophomore, junior, or senior years; not renewable. *Number:* 6. *Amount:* $2500.

Eligibility Requirements: Applicant must be enrolled or expecting to enroll full or part-time at a four-year institution or university. Applicant must have 2.5 GPA or higher. Available to U.S. and non-U.S. citizens.

Application Requirements: Application, interview, references, test scores, transcript. *Deadline:* June 1.

Contact: Scholarship Administrator
Plumbing-Heating-Cooling Contractors Association Education Foundation
PO Box 6808
Falls Church, VA 22040
Phone: 800-533-7694
Fax: 703-237-7442
E-mail: naphcc@naphcc.org

PHCC EDUCATIONAL FOUNDATION NEED-BASED SCHOLARSHIP

Need-based scholarship worth a maximum of $2500 to a student enrolled in an approved four-year PHCC apprenticeship program, an accredited two-year technical college, community college or trade school or an accredited four-year college or university.

Academic Fields/Career Goals: Architecture; Business/Consumer Services; Civil Engineering; Engineering/Technology; Engineering-Related Technologies; Heating, Air-Conditioning, and Refrigeration Mechanics; Mechanical Engineering; Trade/Technical Specialties.

Award: Scholarship for use in freshman, sophomore, junior, or senior years; not renewable. *Number:* 1. *Amount:* $2500.

Eligibility Requirements: Applicant must be enrolled or expecting to enroll at a two-year or four-year or technical institution or university. Available to U.S. citizens.

Application Requirements: Application. *Deadline:* May 1.

Contact: Scholarship Administrator
Plumbing-Heating-Cooling Contractors Association Education Foundation
PO Box 6808
Falls Church, VA 22040

PHCC EDUCATIONAL FOUNDATION SCHOLARSHIP PROGRAM

Applicants must be sponsored by a member of the National Association of Plumbing-Heating-Cooling Contractors. Applicants must pursue studies in a major related to the plumbing-heating-cooling industry. Visit Web site for additional information.

Academic Fields/Career Goals: Architecture; Business/Consumer Services; Civil Engineering; Engineering/Technology; Engineering-Related Technologies; Heating, Air-Conditioning, and Refrigeration Mechanics; Mechanical Engineering; Trade/Technical Specialties.

Award: Scholarship for use in freshman, sophomore, junior, or senior years; renewable. *Number:* 5. *Amount:* $1500–$3000.

Eligibility Requirements: Applicant must be enrolled or expecting to enroll full or part-time at a two-year or four-year institution or university. Applicant must have 2.5 GPA or higher. Available to U.S. and non-U.S. citizens.

Application Requirements: Application, interview, references, test scores, transcript. *Deadline:* May 1.

Contact: Scholarship Administrator
Plumbing-Heating-Cooling Contractors Association Education Foundation
PO Box 6808
Falls Church, VA 22040
Phone: 800-533-7694
Fax: 703-237-7442
E-mail: naphcc@naphcc.org

SOCIETY OF AMERICAN MILITARY ENGINEERS—VIRGINIA PENINSULA POST
http://posts.same.org/vapeninsula/

THE VIRGINIA PENINSULA POST OF THE SOCIETY OF AMERICAN MILITARY ENGINEERS (S.A.M.E.) SCHOLARSHIP

Scholarships for undergraduate engineering students enrolled in an engineering or architecture program leading to a B.S. degree or equivalent. Must demonstrate commitment to future military service by enrollment in a ROTC program, a commissioning program, or an extended enlistment

Academic Fields/Career Goals: Architecture; Engineering/Technology.

Award: Scholarship for use in sophomore, junior, or senior years. *Amount:* $1000.

Eligibility Requirements: Applicant must be enrolled or expecting to enroll full-time at a four-year institution or university and studying in Virginia. Applicant or parent of applicant must have employment or volunteer experience in community service. Available to U.S. citizens.

Application Requirements: References, transcript. *Deadline:* March 10.

Contact: Jeffrey B. Merz, Scholarship Chair
Society of American Military Engineers—Virginia Peninsula Post
Society of American Military Engineers, 129 Andrews Street, Suite 102
Langley AFB, VA 23665-2769
Phone: 757-764-6579
E-mail: jeffrey.merz@langley.af.mil

SOCIETY OF AMERICAN REGISTERED ARCHITECTS
http://www.sara-national.org

SARA STUDENT DESIGN COMPETITION

One-time award for undergraduate or graduate students attending accredited architectural schools and enrolled in a B.A. or B.S. Architecture or M.Arch. program. Must submit five to ten slides of architectural project. Application deadline varies.

Academic Fields/Career Goals: Architecture.

Award: Prize for use in freshman, sophomore, junior, senior, or graduate years; not renewable. *Number:* up to 3. *Amount:* $1000–$3000.

Eligibility Requirements: Applicant must be enrolled or expecting to enroll at a four-year institution or university. Available to U.S. and non-U.S. citizens.

Application Requirements: Applicant must enter a contest, essay, 5 to 10 slides, project. *Fee:* $15. *Deadline:* May 5.

Contact: Cathie Moscato, Program Administrator
Society of American Registered Architects
PO Box 280
Cosby, TN 37822
Phone: 423-487-0365
Fax: 423-487-0365
E-mail: cathiemoscato@hotmail.com

TURNER CONSTRUCTION COMPANY
http://www.turnerconstruction.com

YOUTHFORCE 2020 SCHOLARSHIP PROGRAM

Award for five graduating high school seniors from New York City schools of $2,000 each year, a total of $8,000 after completing four years of college. As a scholarship recipient, students must maintain a 2.75 grade point average and complete a four-year summer internship at Turner that begins immediately following the first full year of college.

Academic Fields/Career Goals: Architecture; Civil Engineering; Electrical Engineering/Electronics; Mechanical Engineering.

Award: Scholarship for use in freshman year. *Number:* 5. *Amount:* $2000–$8000.

Eligibility Requirements: Applicant must be high school student; planning to enroll or expecting to enroll full-time at an institution or university and resident of New York. Applicant must have 2.5 GPA or higher. Available to U.S. citizens.

Application Requirements: Application, essay, financial need analysis, references, transcript. *Deadline:* May 2.

Contact: Stephanie V. Ansari, Community Affairs Coordinator
Turner Construction Company
375 Hudson Street, 6th Floor
New York, NY 10014

UNICO NATIONAL, INC
http://www.unico.org

THEODORE MAZZA SCHOLARSHIP

Scholarship available to graduating high school senior. Must reside and attend high school within the corporate limits or adjoining suburbs of a city wherein an active chapter of UNICO National is located. Application must be signed by student's principal and properly certified by sponsoring Chapter President and Chapter Secretary. Must have letter of endorsement from President or Scholarship Chairperson of sponsoring Chapter.

Academic Fields/Career Goals: Architecture; Art History; Arts; Music.

Award: Scholarship for use in freshman, sophomore, junior, or senior years; renewable. *Number:* 1. *Amount:* $1500.

Eligibility Requirements: Applicant must be high school student and planning to enroll or expecting to enroll at a four-year institution. Available to U.S. citizens.

Application Requirements: Application, financial need analysis, references, transcript. *Deadline:* varies.

Contact: UNICO National, Inc
UNICO National, Inc
271 US Highway 46 West, Suite A-108
Fairfield, NJ 07004
Phone: 973-808-0035
Fax: 973-808-0043

WAVERLY COMMUNITY HOUSE, INC.
http://www.waverlycomm.com

F. LAMMOT BELIN ARTS SCHOLARSHIP

One-time award to current or former Northeastern Pennsylvania resident artists of outstanding aptitude and promise in the fine arts to further their development into professional artists. "Fine arts" is understood to mean creative, performing, or composing activities in such fields as painting,

Waverly Community House, Inc. (continued)

sculpture, photography, music, drama, dance, literature, and architecture. Application fee: $15. Application deadline: December 15. This grant is not intended for academic tuition.

Academic Fields/Career Goals: Architecture; Arts; Literature/English/ Writing; Music; Performing Arts.

Award: Grant for use in freshman, sophomore, junior, senior, graduate, or postgraduate years; not renewable. *Number:* 1. *Amount:* $10,000.

Eligibility Requirements: Applicant must be enrolled or expecting to enroll at an institution or university and resident of Pennsylvania. Available to U.S. citizens.

Application Requirements: Application, references, tapes (VHS or cassette), CD, or slides. *Fee:* $15. *Deadline:* December 15.

Contact: Chairperson
Waverly Community House, Inc.
1115 North Abington Road
PO Box 142
Waverly, PA 18471
Phone: 570-586-8191
Fax: 570-586-0185
E-mail: info@waverlycomm.com

WEST VIRGINIA SOCIETY OF ARCHITECTS/AIA
http://www.aiawv.org

WEST VIRGINIA SOCIETY OF ARCHITECTS/AIA SCHOLARSHIP

Award for West Virginia resident who has completed at least sixth semester of NAAB-accredited architectural program by May 30. Must submit resume and letter stating need, qualifications, and desire. Deadline: May 30.

Academic Fields/Career Goals: Architecture.

Award: Scholarship for use in junior, senior, graduate, or postgraduate years; not renewable. *Number:* varies. *Amount:* up to $7000.

Eligibility Requirements: Applicant must be enrolled or expecting to enroll at an institution or university and resident of West Virginia. Available to U.S. citizens.

Application Requirements: Application, resume, references, transcript. *Deadline:* May 30.

Contact: Roberta Guffey, Executive Director
West Virginia Society of Architects/AIA
223 Hale Street
Charleston, WV 25323
Phone: 304-344-9872
Fax: 304-343-0205
E-mail: Roberta.Guffey@aiawv.org

WORLDSTUDIO FOUNDATION
http://www.worldstudio.org

WORLDSTUDIO FOUNDATION SCHOLARSHIP PROGRAM

Worldstudio Foundation provides scholarships to minority and economically disadvantaged students who are studying the design/arts disciplines in colleges and universities in the U.S.. Applicant should have a minimum GPA of 2.0

Academic Fields/Career Goals: Architecture; Arts; Fashion Design; Filmmaking/Video; Graphics/Graphic Arts/Printing; Industrial Design; Interior Design; Landscape Architecture.

Award: Scholarship for use in freshman, sophomore, junior, senior, graduate, or postgraduate years; not renewable. *Number:* 30–50. *Amount:* $1000–$5000.

Eligibility Requirements: Applicant must be enrolled or expecting to enroll full-time at a two-year or four-year or technical institution or university. Available to U.S. and non-U.S. citizens.

Application Requirements: Application, essay, financial need analysis, photo, portfolio, references, self-addressed stamped envelope, transcript. *Deadline:* March 19.

Contact: Scholarship Coordinator
Worldstudio Foundation
200 Varick Street, Suite 507
New York, NY 10014
Phone: 212-366-1317 Ext. 18
Fax: 212-807-0024
E-mail: scholarships@worldstudio.org

AREA/ETHNIC STUDIES

AMERICAN HISTORICAL ASSOCIATION
http://www.historians.org

WESLEY-LOGAN PRIZE
• *See page 73*

CANADIAN INSTITUTE OF UKRAINIAN STUDIES
http://www.ualberta.ca/cius/

CANADIAN INSTITUTE OF UKRAINIAN STUDIES RESEARCH GRANTS

Grants for students who pursue Ukrainian and Ukrainian-Canadian studies in history, literature, language, education, social sciences, women's studies, law and library sciences.

Academic Fields/Career Goals: Area/Ethnic Studies; Canadian Studies; European Studies.

Award: Grant for use in freshman, sophomore, junior, or senior years. *Number:* 1.

Eligibility Requirements: Applicant must be enrolled or expecting to enroll full-time at a four-year institution or university.

Application Requirements: Application. *Deadline:* March 1.

Contact: Canadian Institute of Ukrainian Studies
450 Athabasca Hall, University of Alberta
Edmonton, AB T6G 2E8
Canada
Phone: 780-492-2973
Fax: 780-492-4967
E-mail: cius@ualberta.ca

LEO J. KRYSA UNDERGRADUATE SCHOLARSHIP

One-time award for Canadian citizen or landed immigrant to enter their final year of undergraduate study in pursuit of a degree with emphasis on Ukrainian and/or Ukrainian-Canadian studies in the disciplines of education, history, humanities, or social sciences. To be used at any Canadian university for an eight-month period of study. Award is in Canadian dollars.

Academic Fields/Career Goals: Area/Ethnic Studies; Education; History; Humanities; Social Sciences.

Award: Scholarship for use in senior year; not renewable. *Number:* 1. *Amount:* up to $3500.

Eligibility Requirements: Applicant must be Canadian citizen; enrolled or expecting to enroll full-time at a four-year institution or university; resident of Alberta, British Columbia, Manitoba, New Brunswick, Newfoundland, North West Territories, Nova Scotia, Ontario, Prince Edward Island, Quebec, Saskatchewan, or Yukon and studying in Alberta, British Columbia, Manitoba, New Brunswick, Newfoundland, Nova Scotia, Ontario, Prince Edward Island, Quebec, or Saskatchewan.

Application Requirements: Application, references, transcript. *Deadline:* March 1.

Contact: Administrator
Canadian Institute of Ukrainian Studies
University of Alberta
Edmonton, AB T6G 2E8
Canada
Phone: 780-492-2973
Fax: 780-492-4967
E-mail: cius@ualberta.ca

CLAN MACBEAN FOUNDATION
http://www.clanmacbean.net

CLAN MACBEAN FOUNDATION GRANT PROGRAM

Open to men and women of any race, color, creed or nationality. Grant is for course of study or project which reflects direct involvement in the preservation or enhancement of Scottish culture, or an effort that would contribute directly to the improvement of the human family. Applications may be obtained from the foundation. Deadline: May 1.

Academic Fields/Career Goals: Area/Ethnic Studies; Child and Family Studies.

Award: Grant for use in freshman, sophomore, junior, senior, or graduate years; not renewable. *Number:* 3–5. *Amount:* up to $5000.

Eligibility Requirements: Applicant must be enrolled or expecting to enroll full-time at a two-year or four-year institution or university. Available to U.S. and non-U.S. citizens.

Application Requirements: Application, references, transcript. *Deadline:* May 1.

Contact: Raymond Heckethorn, Treasurer
Clan MacBean Foundation
441 Wadsworth Boulevard, Suite 213
Denver, CO 80226
Phone: 303-233-6002
Fax: 303-233-6002
E-mail: macbean@ecentral.com

COSTUME SOCIETY OF AMERICA http://www.costumesocietyamerica.com

ADELE FILENE TRAVEL AWARD

One-time award for Costume Society of America members currently enrolled as students to assist their travel to Costume Society of America national symposium to present either a juried paper or a poster.

Academic Fields/Career Goals: Area/Ethnic Studies; Art History; Arts; Historic Preservation and Conservation; History; Home Economics; Museum Studies; Performing Arts.

Award: Prize for use in freshman, sophomore, junior, senior, or graduate years; not renewable. *Number:* 1–4. *Amount:* $150–$500.

Eligibility Requirements: Applicant must be enrolled or expecting to enroll full or part-time at a two-year or four-year or technical institution or university. Applicant or parent of applicant must be member of Costume Society of America. Available to U.S. and non-U.S. citizens.

Application Requirements: Application, references. *Deadline:* March 1.

Contact: Kim Righi, Program Contact
Costume Society of America
203 Towne Center Drive, PO Box 73
Hillsborough, NJ 08844
Phone: 800-272-9447
E-mail: national.office@costumesocietyamerica.com

STELLA BLUM RESEARCH GRANT

One-time award for members of Costume Society of America with research projects in the field of North American costume which are part of the degree requirement. Must be enrolled at an accredited institution. Submit faculty recommendation. Merit-based award of up to $3000.

Academic Fields/Career Goals: Area/Ethnic Studies; Art History; Arts; Historic Preservation and Conservation; History; Home Economics; Museum Studies; Performing Arts.

Award: Grant for use in freshman, sophomore, junior, senior, or graduate years; not renewable. *Number:* 1. *Amount:* up to $3000.

Eligibility Requirements: Applicant must be enrolled or expecting to enroll full-time at a two-year or four-year or technical institution or university. Applicant or parent of applicant must be member of Costume Society of America. Available to U.S. and non-U.S. citizens.

Application Requirements: Application, essay, references, transcript, proposal of the research project, with the budget analysis, if necessary. *Deadline:* May 1.

Contact: Kim Righi, Program Contact
Costume Society of America
203 Towne Center Drive, PO Box 73
Hillsborough, NJ 08844
Phone: 800-272-9447
E-mail: national.office@costumesocietyamerica.com

CULTURE CONNECTION http://www.thecultureconnection.com

CULTURE CONNECTION FOUNDATION SCHOLARSHIP
• *See page 73*

EXPLORERS CLUB http://www.explorers.org

EXPLORATION FUND GRANTS
• *See page 88*

HARVARD TRAVELLERS CLUB

HARVARD TRAVELLERS CLUB GRANTS
• *See page 96*

IRISH-AMERICAN CULTURAL INSTITUTE http://www.iaci-usa.org

IRISH RESEARCH FUNDS

One-time award for research which has an Irish-American theme in any discipline of humanities and social science. Primary research preferred, but will fund such projects as museum exhibits, curriculum development, and the compilation of bibliographies. Submit proposal.

Academic Fields/Career Goals: Area/Ethnic Studies; Humanities; Social Sciences.

Award: Grant for use in freshman, sophomore, junior, senior, or graduate years; not renewable. *Number:* 1–10. *Amount:* $1000–$5000.

Eligibility Requirements: Applicant must be enrolled or expecting to enroll at an institution or university. Available to U.S. and non-U.S. citizens.

Application Requirements: Application, resume, references. *Deadline:* October 1.

Contact: John Morytko, Director
Irish-American Cultural Institute
1 Lackawanna Place
Morristown, NJ 07960
Phone: 973-605-1991
Fax: 973-605-8875
E-mail: info@iaci-usa.org

JAPANESE GOVERNMENT/THE MONBUSHO SCHOLARSHIP PROGRAM http://www.la.us.emb-japan.go.jp

JAPANESE STUDIES SCHOLARSHIP

One-time award open to undergraduate college/university-enrolled students ages 18 through 29. (university must be outside Japan). One-year course designed to develop Japanese language aptitude and knowledge of the country's culture, areas which the applicant must currently be studying. Scholarship comprises transportation, accommodations, medical expenses, and monthly and arrival allowances. Total number of awards and their dollar value varies, with no specific fixed limits. Info available on Web site: http://www.studyjapan.go.jp/en/ Contact for more information.

Academic Fields/Career Goals: Area/Ethnic Studies.

Award: Scholarship for use in freshman, sophomore, junior, or senior years; not renewable. *Number:* varies. *Amount:* $50,000.

Eligibility Requirements: Applicant must be age 18-29; enrolled or expecting to enroll full-time at a two-year or four-year institution or university and must have an interest in Japanese language. Available to U.S. and non-U.S. citizens.

Application Requirements: Application, autobiography, essay, interview, photo, references, test scores, transcript, medical certificate, certificate of enrollment. *Deadline:* Continuous.

Contact: Japanese Government/The Monbusho Scholarship Program Coordinator
Japanese Government/The Monbusho Scholarship Program
Japanese Government/The Monbusho Scholarship Program, 350 South Grand Avenue, Suite 1700
Los Angeles, CA 90071
Phone: 213-617-6700 Ext. 338
Fax: 213-617-6728
E-mail: info@la-cgjapan.org

KOSCIUSZKO FOUNDATION http://www.kosciuszkofoundation.org

YEAR ABROAD PROGRAM IN POLAND

Grants for upper division and graduate students who wish to study in Poland. Must have letters of recommendation, personal statement, and a physical exam. Covers tuition and provides stipend for housing. Application fee: $50. Minimum 3.0 GPA required. Restricted to U.S. citizens and permanent residents. Check http://www.kosciuszkofoundation.org for complete details. Application is available for download from September through December.

Academic Fields/Career Goals: Area/Ethnic Studies; Foreign Language.

Kosciuszko Foundation (continued)

Award: Scholarship for use in sophomore, junior, senior, or graduate years; not renewable. *Number:* 10. *Amount:* $675–$1350.

Eligibility Requirements: Applicant must be enrolled or expecting to enroll at a four-year institution and must have an interest in Polish language. Applicant must have 3.0 GPA or higher. Available to U.S. citizens.

Application Requirements: Application, interview, photo, references, transcript, personal statement. *Fee:* $50. *Deadline:* December 15.

Contact: Addy Tymczyszyn, Grants Department
Kosciuszko Foundation
15 East 65th Street
New York, NY 10021-6595
Phone: 212-734-2130 Ext. 210

MEMORIAL FOUNDATION FOR JEWISH CULTURE
http://www.mfjc.org

MEMORIAL FOUNDATION FOR JEWISH CULTURE INTERNATIONAL SCHOLARSHIP PROGRAM FOR COMMUNITY SERVICE

The scholarship is open to any individual, regardless of country of origin, who is presently receiving, or plans to undertake, training in a recognized yeshiva, teacher training seminary, school of social work, university or other educational institution. The recipient of the scholarship must commit to serve in a community of need for a minimum of two to three years. The amount of the grant varies, depending on the country in which the student will be trained and other considerations.

Academic Fields/Career Goals: Area/Ethnic Studies; Education; Religion/Theology; Social Services.

Award: Scholarship for use in freshman, sophomore, junior, or senior years; renewable. *Number:* varies. *Amount:* $1000–$3000.

Eligibility Requirements: Applicant must be Jewish and enrolled or expecting to enroll at an institution or university. Available to U.S. and non-U.S. citizens.

Application Requirements: Application, interview, references. *Deadline:* November 30.

Contact: Jerry Hochbaum, Executive Vice President
Memorial Foundation for Jewish Culture
50 Broadway, 34th Floor
New York, NY 10004
Phone: 212-425-6606
Fax: 212-425-6602
E-mail: office@mfjc.org

NATIONAL ITALIAN AMERICAN FOUNDATION
http://www.niaf.org

NATIONAL ITALIAN AMERICAN FOUNDATION CATEGORY II SCHOLARSHIP

Award available to students majoring or minoring in Italian language, Italian Studies, Italian-American Studies or a related field who have outstanding potential and high academic achievements. Minimum 3.25 GPA required. Must be a U.S. citizen and be enrolled in an accredited institution of higher education. Application can only be submitted online. For further information, deadlines, and online application visit Web site: http://www.niaf.org/scholarships/index.asp.

Academic Fields/Career Goals: Area/Ethnic Studies.

Award: Scholarship for use in freshman, sophomore, junior, or senior years; not renewable. *Number:* varies. *Amount:* $2500–$10,000.

Eligibility Requirements: Applicant must be enrolled or expecting to enroll full or part-time at a four-year institution or university and must have an interest in Italian language. Available to U.S. citizens.

Application Requirements: Application, essay, references, transcript. *Deadline:* March 1.

Contact: Michelle Arbeit, Assistant, Education and Culture
National Italian American Foundation
1860 19th Street, NW
Washington, DC 20009
Phone: 202-387-0600
Fax: 202-387-0800
E-mail: marbeit@niaf.org

SONOMA CHAMBOLLE-MUSIGNY SISTER CITIES

HENRI CARDINAUX MEMORIAL SCHOLARSHIP

This cash award is for travel to France. Must have a 3.0 GPA. Must be a resident of California. Must have a permanent address in Sonoma County or attend school in Sonoma County. Applicant must be able to communicate adequately in the French language. Career objective should be related to the fields of viticulture, enology, culinary arts or other profession/vocation for which exposure to the French culture would be relevant.

Academic Fields/Career Goals: Area/Ethnic Studies; Foreign Language.

Award: Scholarship for use in freshman, sophomore, junior, senior, graduate, or postgraduate years; not renewable. *Number:* 1. *Amount:* up to $1500.

Eligibility Requirements: Applicant must be enrolled or expecting to enroll full or part-time at a two-year or four-year or technical institution or university; resident of California and studying in California. Applicant must have 3.0 GPA or higher. Available to U.S. citizens.

Application Requirements: Application, essay, references, transcript. *Deadline:* April 15.

Contact: Ivy Cardinaux, Scholarship Coordinator
Sonoma Chambolle-Musigny Sister Cities
Chamson Scholarship Committee, PO Box 1633
Sonoma, CA 94928-1633
Phone: 707-938-9081
E-mail: icardin@aol.com

SONS OF NORWAY FOUNDATION
http://www.sofn.com

KING OLAV V NORWEGIAN-AMERICAN HERITAGE FUND

Available to American students aging 18 or older interested in studying Norwegian heritage, or any Norwegian students interested in studying American heritage. Selection of applicants is based on a 500-word essay, educational and career goals, community service, work experience, and GPA. Must have minimum 3.0 GPA.

Academic Fields/Career Goals: Area/Ethnic Studies.

Award: Scholarship for use in freshman, sophomore, junior, or senior years; not renewable. *Number:* 12–15. *Amount:* $250–$3000.

Eligibility Requirements: Applicant must be age 18 and enrolled or expecting to enroll full or part-time at a four-year institution or university. Applicant or parent of applicant must have employment or volunteer experience in community service or designated career field. Applicant must have 3.0 GPA or higher. Available to U.S. and non-U.S. citizens.

Application Requirements: Application, essay, references, self-addressed stamped envelope, transcript. *Deadline:* March 1.

Contact: Sons of Norway Foundation
Sons of Norway Foundation
1455 West Lake Street
Minneapolis, MN 55408
Phone: 612-827-3611
Fax: 612-827-0658
E-mail: fraternal@sofn.com

WATERBURY FOUNDATION
http://www.conncf.org/

TADEUSZ SENDZIMIR SCHOLARSHIPS-ACADEMIC YEAR SCHOLARSHIPS

Academic year scholarships of $5000 available for graduate and undergraduate students, preferably of Polish descent, residing in Connecticut, who are studying Polish language, history or culture during the academic year at a college or university in the United States or Poland. Scholarship for exchange study in the United States or Poland.

Academic Fields/Career Goals: Area/Ethnic Studies.

Award: Scholarship for use in freshman, sophomore, junior, senior, or graduate years; not renewable. *Number:* varies. *Amount:* up to $5000.

Eligibility Requirements: Applicant must be enrolled or expecting to enroll at a two-year or four-year institution or university and resident of Connecticut. Available to U.S. and non-U.S. citizens.

Application Requirements: Application, essay, references, transcript. *Deadline:* March 1.

Contact: Josh Carey, Program Officer
Waterbury Foundation
43 Field Street
Waterbury, CT 06702-1216
Phone: 203-753-1315
Fax: 203-756-3054
E-mail: jcarey@conncf.org

TADEUSZ SENDZIMIR SCHOLARSHIPS-SUMMER SCHOOL PROGRAMS

Summer scholarships of $3000 available for graduate and undergraduate students, preferably of Polish descent, residing in Connecticut, who are studying Polish language, history or culture during the academic year at a college or university in the United States or Poland. Scholarship for exchange study in the United States or Poland.

Academic Fields/Career Goals: Area/Ethnic Studies.

Award: Scholarship for use in freshman, sophomore, junior, senior, or graduate years; not renewable. *Number:* varies. *Amount:* up to $3000.

Eligibility Requirements: Applicant must be age 18; enrolled or expecting to enroll at a two-year or four-year institution or university and resident of Connecticut. Available to U.S. and non-U.S. citizens.

Application Requirements: Application, financial need analysis, references, transcript, physician's certificate. *Fee:* $50. *Deadline:* March 1.

Contact: Josh Carey, Program Officer
Waterbury Foundation
43 Field Street
Waterbury, CT 06702-1216
Phone: 203-753-1315
Fax: 203-756-3054
E-mail: jcarey@conncf.org

WELSH NATIONAL GYMANFA GANU ASSOCIATION, INC.   http://www.wngga.org

WNGGA SCHOLARSHIP PROGRAM

One-time award program from which scholarships may be granted to applicants or organization who are enrolled in courses or projects which preserve, develop, and promote the Welsh religious and cultural heritage. Applicant must be U.S. or Canadian citizen. Deadline: March 1.

Academic Fields/Career Goals: Area/Ethnic Studies.

Award: Grant for use in freshman, sophomore, junior, senior, graduate, or postgraduate years; not renewable. *Number:* 5–10. *Amount:* $200–$2000.

Eligibility Requirements: Applicant must be of Welsh heritage and enrolled or expecting to enroll full or part-time at an institution or university. Applicant or parent of applicant must have employment or volunteer experience in designated career field. Available to U.S. and Canadian citizens.

Application Requirements: Application, autobiography, financial need analysis, references, project description, budget. *Deadline:* March 1.

Contact: Myfanwy S. Davies, Chairperson, Scholarship Committee
Welsh National Gymanfa Ganu Association, Inc.
3205 Uplands Drive, Unit 2
Ottawa, ON K1V 9T3
Canada
Phone: 613-526-3019
E-mail: buck@ejsa.com

ART HISTORY

AMERICAN INSTITUTE OF ARCHITECTS, NEW YORK CHAPTER   http://www.aiany.org

THE DOUGLAS HASKELL AWARD FOR STUDENT JOURNALISM
• See page 98

AMERICAN LEGION AUXILIARY, DEPARTMENT OF WASHINGTON   http://www.walegion-aux.org

FLORENCE LEMCKE MEMORIAL SCHOLARSHIP IN FINE ARTS

One-time award for the child of a deceased or living veteran. Must be senior in high school in Washington and planning to pursue an education in the fine arts. Submit statement of veteran's military service. Contact Washington Auxiliary for application. Must be a resident of Washington state.

Academic Fields/Career Goals: Art History; Arts; Humanities; Literature/English/Writing.

Award: Scholarship for use in freshman year; not renewable. *Number:* 1. *Amount:* $300.

Eligibility Requirements: Applicant must be high school student; age 20 or under; planning to enroll or expecting to enroll at an institution or university; resident of Washington and must have an interest in art or writing. Available to U.S. citizens. Applicant or parent must meet one or more of the following requirements: general military experience; retired from active duty; disabled or killed as a result of military service; prisoner of war; or missing in action.

Application Requirements: Application, essay, references, transcript. *Deadline:* April 1.

Contact: Crystal Lawrence, Department Secretary
American Legion Auxiliary, Department of Washington
3600 Ruddell Road
Lacey, WA 98503
Phone: 360-456-5995
Fax: 360-491-7442
E-mail: alawash@qwest.net

AMERICAN SCHOOL OF CLASSICAL STUDIES AT ATHENS   http://www.ascsa.edu.gr

ASCSA SUMMER SESSIONS OPEN SCHOLARSHIPS
• See page 88

COSTUME SOCIETY OF AMERICA   http://www.costumesocietyamerica.com

ADELE FILENE TRAVEL AWARD
• See page 105

STELLA BLUM RESEARCH GRANT
• See page 105

CULTURE CONNECTION   http://www.thecultureconnection.com

CULTURE CONNECTION FOUNDATION SCHOLARSHIP
• See page 73

GETTY GRANT PROGRAM   http://www.getty.edu/grants

LIBRARY RESEARCH GRANTS

Grant intended for scholars at any level who demonstrate compelling need to use materials in Getty Research Library. Applicant's place of residence must be at least 80 or more miles away from Getty Center. Research period may last several days to maximum three months. Grant only supports one research trip to Getty Center. Grantee may reapply after two years; if project is different, grantee may reapply the next year. See Web site at http://www.getty.edu/grants for details.

Academic Fields/Career Goals: Art History; Arts.

Award: Grant for use in freshman, sophomore, junior, senior, graduate, or postgraduate years; renewable. *Number:* varies. *Amount:* $500–$2500.

Eligibility Requirements: Applicant must be enrolled or expecting to enroll full or part-time at an institution or university; studying in California and must have an interest in art. Available to U.S. and non-U.S. citizens.

Getty Grant Program (continued)

Application Requirements: Application, financial need analysis, resume, references, project proposal. *Deadline:* November 1.

Contact: Kathleen Johnson, Program Associate
Getty Grant Program
1200 Getty Center Drive, Suite 800
Los Angeles, CA 90049-1685
Phone: 310-440-7320
Fax: 310-440-7703
E-mail: researchgrants@getty.edu

HERB SOCIETY OF AMERICA   http://www.herbsociety.org

HERB SOCIETY RESEARCH GRANTS
• See page 92

POLISH ARTS CLUB OF BUFFALO SCHOLARSHIP FOUNDATION   http://pacb.bfn.org/about/constitution.html

POLISH ARTS CLUB OF BUFFALO SCHOLARSHIP FOUNDATION TRUST

Provides educational scholarships to students of Polish background who are legal residents of New York. Must be enrolled at the junior level or above in an accredited college or university in NY. Must be a U.S. citizen. Send SASE for more information.

Academic Fields/Career Goals: Art History; Arts; Filmmaking/Video; Humanities; Journalism; Performing Arts.

Award: Scholarship for use in junior, senior, graduate, or postgraduate years; not renewable. *Number:* 1–3. *Amount:* $1000.

Eligibility Requirements: Applicant must be of Polish heritage; enrolled or expecting to enroll full or part-time at a four-year institution or university; resident of New York and studying in New York. Available to U.S. citizens.

Application Requirements: Application, essay, interview, portfolio, resume, references, self-addressed stamped envelope, transcript. *Deadline:* May 15.

Contact: Ann Flansburg, Selection Chair
Polish Arts Club of Buffalo Scholarship Foundation
PO Box 1362
Williamsville, NY 14231-1362
Phone: 716-626-9083
E-mail: donflans123@aol.com

ROBERT H. MOLLOHAN FAMILY CHARITABLE FOUNDATION, INC.   http://www.mollohanfoundation.org

MARY OLIVE EDDY JONES ART SCHOLARSHIP

Scholarship awarded to a rising sophomore or junior seriously interested in pursuing an art-related degree. Applicant must be a West Virginia resident attending a West Virginia college or university.

Academic Fields/Career Goals: Art History; Arts; Graphics/Graphic Arts/Printing.

Award: Scholarship for use in sophomore or junior years; not renewable. *Number:* 1–3. *Amount:* up to $1000.

Eligibility Requirements: Applicant must be enrolled or expecting to enroll full or part-time at a four-year institution or university; resident of West Virginia and studying in West Virginia. Available to U.S. citizens.

Application Requirements: Application, essay, portfolio, resume, references, transcript. *Deadline:* February 6.

Contact: Teah Bayless, Program Manager
Robert H. Mollohan Family Charitable Foundation, Inc.
1000 Technology Drive, Suite 2000
Fairmont, WV 26554
Phone: 304-333-2251
Fax: 304-333-3900
E-mail: tmbayless@wvhtf.org

UNICO NATIONAL, INC   http://www.unico.org

THEODORE MAZZA SCHOLARSHIP
• See page 103

ARTS

ACADEMY OF TELEVISION ARTS AND SCIENCES FOUNDATION   http://www.emmys.tv/foundation

ACADEMY OF TELEVISION ARTS AND SCIENCES COLLEGE TELEVISION AWARDS

Non-U.S. citizens are eligible if they produced their film at a U.S. College. The academy gives 1st, 2nd, and 3rd place awards in the following categories: comedy, drama, music programs, documentary, newscasts, children's programs, traditional animation, and non-traditional animation. Entry forms available September-December.

Academic Fields/Career Goals: Arts; Communications; Filmmaking/Video; Journalism; Performing Arts; Photojournalism/Photography; TV/Radio Broadcasting.

Award: Prize for use in freshman, sophomore, junior, senior, or graduate years; not renewable. *Number:* 25. *Amount:* $500–$2000.

Eligibility Requirements: Applicant must be enrolled or expecting to enroll full-time at a two-year or four-year or technical institution or university. Available to U.S. and non-U.S. citizens.

Application Requirements: Application, applicant must enter a contest, Beta, Beta SP, DVD or VHS copy of film or video; entries longer than one hour will not be accepted and newscasts, magazine shows, comedy and children's program entries must not exceed 30 minutes. *Deadline:* December 15.

Contact: Nancy Robinson, Programs Coordinator
Academy of Television Arts and Sciences Foundation
5220 Lankershim Boulevard
North Hollywood, CA 91601
Phone: 818-754-2839
Fax: 818-761-8524
E-mail: collegeawards@emmys.org

ALLIANCE FOR YOUNG ARTISTS AND WRITERS, INC.   http://www.artandwriting.org

SCHOLASTIC ART AND WRITING AWARDS-ART SECTION

Award for students in grades 7-12. Winners of preliminary judging advance to national level. For further details visit Web site: http://www.artandwriting.org.

Academic Fields/Career Goals: Arts; Literature/English/Writing.

Award: Scholarship for use in freshman, sophomore, junior, or senior years; not renewable. *Number:* 600. *Amount:* $100–$20,000.

Eligibility Requirements: Applicant must be high school student; planning to enroll or expecting to enroll at an institution or university and must have an interest in art. Available to U.S. and Canadian citizens.

Application Requirements: Application, applicant must enter a contest, essay, portfolio, references. *Deadline:* varies.

Contact: Alliance for Young Artists and Writers, Inc.
557 Broadway
New York, NY 10012-1396
Phone: 212-343-6493

ALPHA DELTA KAPPA FOUNDATION   http://www.alphadeltakappa.org

APHA DELTA KAPPA FOUNDATION FINE ARTS GRANTS

Awarded biennially in two categories, Performing Arts and Visual Arts. Next Performing Arts awards will be given in Instrumental Music (strings only) and the next Visual Arts awards will be given in Painting (all media). Applications available after September 1. Deadline for application is April 1. Application fee is $25.

Academic Fields/Career Goals: Arts; Music.

Award: Grant for use in freshman, sophomore, junior, senior, graduate, or postgraduate years; not renewable. *Number:* up to 6. *Amount:* $1000–$5000.

Eligibility Requirements: Applicant must be enrolled or expecting to enroll full or part-time at a four-year institution or university and must have an interest in art or music. Available to U.S. and non-U.S. citizens.

Application Requirements: Application, applicant must enter a contest, references, supporting materials. *Fee:* $25. *Deadline:* April 1.

Contact: Dee Frost, Scholarships and Grants Coordinator
Alpha Delta Kappa Foundation
1615 West 92nd Street
Kansas City, MO 64114-3296
Phone: 816-363-5525
Fax: 816-363-4010
E-mail: headquarters@alphadeltakappa.org

AMERICAN LEGION AUXILIARY, DEPARTMENT OF WASHINGTON
http://www.walegion-aux.org

FLORENCE LEMCKE MEMORIAL SCHOLARSHIP IN FINE ARTS
• *See page 107*

AMERICAN PHILOLOGICAL ASSOCIATION
http://www.apaclassics.org

MINORITY STUDENT SUMMER SCHOLARSHIP

The award supports summer study in the United States, or in Europe, intended to better prepare the recipient for graduate work in classical studies. Please refer to Web site for ethnic heritage specifications and further details: http://www.apaclassics.org

Academic Fields/Career Goals: Arts; Foreign Language; History; Humanities.

Award: Scholarship for use in freshman, sophomore, junior, or senior years; not renewable. *Number:* 1. *Amount:* $3000.

Eligibility Requirements: Applicant must be of African, Chinese, Latin American/Caribbean, Mexican, or Vietnamese heritage; American Indian/Alaska Native, Asian/Pacific Islander, Black (non-Hispanic), or Hispanic and enrolled or expecting to enroll full-time at an institution or university. Available to U.S. and non-U.S. citizens.

Application Requirements: Application, essay, financial need analysis, references, transcript, demonstrated ability in at least one classical language. *Deadline:* February 21.

Contact: Adam Blistein, Executive Director
American Philological Association
University of Pennsylvania, 292 Logan Hall, 249 South 36th Street
Philadelphia, PA 19104-6304
Phone: 215-898-4975
Fax: 215-573-7874
E-mail: apaclassics@sas.upenn.edu

AMERICAN SCHOOL OF CLASSICAL STUDIES AT ATHENS
http://www.ascsa.edu.gr

ASCSA SUMMER SESSIONS OPEN SCHOLARSHIPS
• *See page 88*

ART INSTITUTES
http://www.artinstitutes.edu

NATIONAL ART HONOR SOCIETY SCHOLARSHIP

Senior class members of National Art Honor Society are eligible to compete for these tuition scholarships: 1st Place-$20,000, 2nd Place-$10,000, 3rd Place-$5000, 4th Place: $3000, 5th Place-$2000.

Academic Fields/Career Goals: Arts.

Award: Scholarship for use in freshman, sophomore, junior, or senior years; renewable. *Number:* 5. *Amount:* $2000–$20,000.

Eligibility Requirements: Applicant must be high school student and planning to enroll or expecting to enroll full-time at a technical institution. Available to U.S. citizens.

Application Requirements: Application, applicant must enter a contest, essay, six slides of artwork. *Deadline:* March 1.

Contact: Bill McAnulty, National Art Honor Society Scholarship
Art Institutes
c/o The Art Institute of Pittsburgh, 420 Boulevard of the Allies
Pittsburgh, PA 15219-1328
Phone: 800-275-2470

ARTIST-BLACKSMITH'S ASSOCIATION OF NORTH AMERICA, INC.
http://www.abana.org

ARTIST'S- BLACKSMITH'S ASSOCIATION OF NORTH AMERICA, INC. SCHOLARSHIP PROGRAM

The award is designed to provide financial assistance to ABANA members at all skill levels to assist with the development of their blacksmithing skills and abilities. Applications selected throughout the year. Award money may be used for blacksmith workshops, demonstrations, lectures, etc. Awards granted are not for tuition.

Academic Fields/Career Goals: Arts.

Award: Scholarship for use in freshman year; not renewable. *Number:* 8–10. *Amount:* $200–$1500.

Eligibility Requirements: Applicant must be enrolled or expecting to enroll part-time at a technical institution. Available to U.S. and non-U.S. citizens.

Application Requirements: Application, financial need analysis, photo, resume, references, self-addressed stamped envelope. *Deadline:* varies.

Contact: Lee Ann Mitchell, Central Office Administrator
Artist-Blacksmith's Association of North America, Inc.
PO Box 816
Farmington, GA 30638-0816
Phone: 706-310-1030
Fax: 706-769-7147
E-mail: abana@abana.org

ARTIST'S-BLACKSMITH'S ASSOCIATION OF NORTH AMERICA, INC. AFFILIATE VISITING ARTIST GRANT PROGRAM

Grant is for ABANA Affiliates wishing to bring in demonstrators or other educational opportunities for their membership.

Academic Fields/Career Goals: Arts.

Award: Grant for use in freshman, sophomore, junior, senior, graduate, or postgraduate years; not renewable. *Number:* 8. *Amount:* $600.

Eligibility Requirements: Applicant must be enrolled or expecting to enroll part-time at an institution or university. Available to U.S. and non-U.S. citizens.

Application Requirements: Essay, financial need analysis, photo, resume. *Deadline:* varies.

Contact: Lee Ann Mitchell, Central Office Administrator
Artist-Blacksmith's Association of North America, Inc.
PO Box 816
Farmington, GA 30638-0816
Phone: 706-310-1030
Fax: 706-769-7147
E-mail: abana@abana.org

BEINECKE SCHOLARSHIP PROGRAM
http://www.beineckescholarship.org/

BEINECKE SCHOLARSHIP FOR GRADUATE STUDY

Scholarships are open to students nominated by one of the over 100 institutions that are invited to make a nomination. Unsolicited nominations and/or applications are not accepted. Nomination should be made during the student's junior year. Funds must be used within five years of graduation. For further information visit Web site: http://www.beineckescholarship.org.

Academic Fields/Career Goals: Arts; Humanities; Social Sciences.

Award: Scholarship for use in junior, or graduate years; renewable. *Number:* 18–22. *Amount:* $2000–$30,000.

Eligibility Requirements: Applicant must be enrolled or expecting to enroll full-time at a four-year institution or university. Applicant must have 3.5 GPA or higher. Available to U.S. citizens.

Application Requirements: Application, essay, financial need analysis, references, transcript. *Deadline:* March 1.

Contact: Thomas Parkinson, Program Director
Beinecke Scholarship Program
PO Box 125
Fogelsville, PA 18051-0125
Phone: 610-395-5560
Fax: 610-625-7919
E-mail: beineckescholarship@earthlink.net

BMI FOUNDATION, INC.   http://www.bmi.com

BMI STUDENT COMPOSER AWARDS

One-time award for original composition in classical genre for young student composers who are under age 26 and citizens of the Western Hemisphere. Must submit application and original musical score in early February. Application available at Web site: http://www.bmifoundation.org.

Academic Fields/Career Goals: Arts.

Award: Prize for use in freshman, sophomore, junior, senior, graduate, or postgraduate years; not renewable. *Number:* up to 10. *Amount:* $500–$5000.

Eligibility Requirements: Applicant must be age 26 or under; enrolled or expecting to enroll at a two-year or four-year institution or university and must have an interest in music/singing. Available to U.S. and non-U.S. citizens.

Application Requirements: Application, applicant must enter a contest, self-addressed stamped envelope, original musical score. *Deadline:* varies.

Contact: Mr. Ralph N. Jackson, Director, BMI Student Composer Awards
BMI Foundation, Inc.
320 West 57th Street
New York, NY 10019
Phone: 212-586-2000
Fax: 212-245-8986
E-mail: classical@bmi.com

CALIFORNIA ALLIANCE FOR ARTS EDUCATION (CAAE)   http://www.artsed411.org

EMERGING YOUNG ARTIST AWARDS

Renewable award for California high school seniors studying dance, music, theater or visual arts. For use at a four-year institution or accredited training program. Must demonstrate financial need. Application fee of $10. Application deadline is February 2.

Academic Fields/Career Goals: Arts; Music; Performing Arts.

Award: Scholarship for use in freshman, sophomore, junior, or senior years; renewable. *Number:* up to 12. *Amount:* up to $5000.

Eligibility Requirements: Applicant must be high school student; age 16–19; planning to enroll or expecting to enroll full-time at a four-year institution or university and resident of California. Applicant must have 2.5 GPA or higher. Available to U.S. citizens.

Application Requirements: Application, applicant must enter a contest, essay, financial need analysis, references, performance, work sample. *Fee:* $10. *Deadline:* February 2.

Contact: Peggy Burt, Project Manager
California Alliance for Arts Education (CAAE)
495 East Colorado Boulevard
Pasadena, CA 91101
Phone: 626-578-9315 Ext. 102
Fax: 626-578-9894
E-mail: peggy@artsed411.org

CIRI FOUNDATION   http://www.thecirifoundation.org

CIRI FOUNDATION SUSIE QIMMIQSAK BEVINS ENDOWMENT SCHOLARSHIP FUND

$2000 per semester is offered to Alaska Native Student original enrollees/descendants of Cook Inlet Region, Inc., who are studying the literary, performing, and visual arts. Recipients can reapply every semester. Must be accepted or enrolled in a two- or four-year undergraduate degree or graduate degree program. Deadlines are June 1 and December 1.

Academic Fields/Career Goals: Arts; Literature/English/Writing; Performing Arts.

Award: Scholarship for use in freshman, sophomore, junior, senior, or graduate years; not renewable. *Number:* varies. *Amount:* up to $2000.

Eligibility Requirements: Applicant must be enrolled or expecting to enroll full-time at a two-year or four-year institution or university. Applicant must have 2.5 GPA or higher. Available to U.S. citizens.

Application Requirements: Application, essay, references, transcript, proof of eligibility, birth certificate or adoption decree. *Deadline:* varies.

Contact: Susan Anderson, President/CEO
CIRI Foundation
2600 Cordova Street, Suite 206
Anchorage, AK 99503
Phone: 907-263-5582
Fax: 907-263-5588

COLLEGEBOUND FOUNDATION   http://www.collegeboundfoundation.org

JANET B. SONDHEIM SCHOLARSHIP

Award for Baltimore City public high school graduates. Please see Web site: http://www.collegeboundfoundation.org for complete information on application process. Must major in either fine arts (dance, music, art, drama, photography); or any field of study, but must plan to teach. Minimum GPA of 3.0. Must submit one-page essay on goals and accomplishments and your interest in the arts or teaching. Must submit CollegeBound Competitive Scholarship/Last-Dollar Grant Application.

Academic Fields/Career Goals: Arts; Music; Photojournalism/Photography.

Award: Scholarship for use in freshman, sophomore, junior, or senior years; renewable. *Number:* 1. *Amount:* $500.

Eligibility Requirements: Applicant must be enrolled or expecting to enroll full-time at a two-year or four-year institution or university and resident of Maryland. Applicant must have 3.0 GPA or higher. Available to U.S. citizens.

Application Requirements: Application, essay, financial need analysis, references, transcript, financial aid award letters, Student Aid Report (SAR). *Deadline:* March 19.

Contact: April Bell, Associate Program Director
CollegeBound Foundation
300 Water Street, Suite 300
Baltimore, MD 21202
Phone: 410-783-2905 Ext. 208
Fax: 410-727-5786
E-mail: abell@collegeboundfoundation.org

COSTUME SOCIETY OF AMERICA   http://www.costumesocietyamerica.com

ADELE FILENE TRAVEL AWARD
• See page 105

STELLA BLUM RESEARCH GRANT
• See page 105

ELIZABETH GREENSHIELDS FOUNDATION

ELIZABETH GREENSHIELDS AWARD/GRANT

Award of CAN$12,500 available to candidates working in painting, drawing, printmaking, or sculpture. Work must be representational or figurative. Must submit at least one color slide of each of six works. Must reapply to renew. Applications from self-taught individuals are also accepted.

Academic Fields/Career Goals: Arts.

Award: Grant for use in freshman, sophomore, junior, senior, or graduate years; not renewable. *Number:* 40–60. *Amount:* $10,000–$12,500.

Eligibility Requirements: Applicant must be enrolled or expecting to enroll full or part-time at a two-year or four-year or technical institution or university and must have an interest in art. Available to U.S. and non-U.S. citizens.

Application Requirements: Application, slides. *Deadline:* Continuous.

Contact: Diane Pitcher, Applications Coordinator
Elizabeth Greenshields Foundation
1814 Sherbrooke Street West, Suite 1
Montreal, QC H3H IE4
Canada
Phone: 514-937-9225
Fax: 514-937-0141
E-mail: greenshields@bellnet.ca

GENERAL FEDERATION OF WOMEN'S CLUBS OF MASSACHUSETTS
http://www.gfwcma.org/

GENERAL FEDERATION OF WOMEN'S CLUBS OF MASSACHUSETTS PENNIES FOR ART

Scholarship in art for graduating high school seniors. Must submit letter of endorsement from president of sponsoring General Federation of Women's Clubs of Massachusetts and three examples of original work. Must be resident of Massachusetts.

Academic Fields/Career Goals: Arts.

Award: Scholarship for use in freshman year; not renewable. *Number:* varies. *Amount:* up to $800.

Eligibility Requirements: Applicant must be high school student; planning to enroll or expecting to enroll full-time at a four-year institution or university; resident of Massachusetts and must have an interest in art. Available to U.S. citizens.

Application Requirements: Application, autobiography, essay, portfolio, references, self-addressed stamped envelope. *Deadline:* February 1.

Contact: Kay Doody, Art Chairman
General Federation of Women's Clubs of Massachusetts
PO Box 679
Sudbury, MA 01776-0679
Phone: 978-443-4569
E-mail: kdoody1890@aol.com

GETTY GRANT PROGRAM
http://www.getty.edu/grants

LIBRARY RESEARCH GRANTS
• See page 107

GOLDEN KEY INTERNATIONAL HONOUR SOCIETY
http://www.goldenkey.org

VISUAL AND PERFORMING ARTS ACHIEVEMENT AWARDS

$500 will be awarded to winners in each of the following nine categories: painting, drawing, photography, sculpture, computer-generated art/graphic design/illustration, mixed media, instrumental performance, vocal performance, and dance. Deadline is April 1. See Web site for more information: http://goldenkey.gsu.edu.

Academic Fields/Career Goals: Arts; Graphics/Graphic Arts/Printing.

Award: Prize for use in junior, senior, graduate, or postgraduate years; not renewable. *Number:* 9. *Amount:* $500.

Eligibility Requirements: Applicant must be enrolled or expecting to enroll full or part-time at a four-year institution or university and must have an interest in art. Available to U.S. and non-U.S. citizens.

Application Requirements: Application, artwork. *Deadline:* April 1.

Contact: Scholarship Program Administrators
Golden Key International Honour Society
PO Box 23737
Nashville, TN 37202
Phone: 800-377-2401

HERB SOCIETY OF AMERICA
http://www.herbsociety.org

HERB SOCIETY RESEARCH GRANTS
• See page 92

INSTITUTE FOR HUMANE STUDIES
http://www.theihs.org

FILM AND FICTION SCHOLARSHIP

Scholarship program to support students pursuing degrees in filmmaking or creative writing. Deadline: January 15

Academic Fields/Career Goals: Arts; Filmmaking/Video; Literature/English/Writing.

Award: Scholarship for use in senior, or graduate years; not renewable. *Number:* varies. *Amount:* $3000–$10,000.

Eligibility Requirements: Applicant must be enrolled or expecting to enroll full-time at a four-year institution or university. Available to U.S. and non-U.S. citizens.

Application Requirements: Application, essay. *Deadline:* January 15.

Contact: Institute for Humane Studies
3301 North Fairfax Drive, Suite 440
Arlington, VA 22201-4432
Phone: 703-993-4880
Fax: 703-993-4890
E-mail: ihs@gmu.edu

INTERNATIONAL FURNISHINGS AND DESIGN ASSOCIATION
http://www.ifdaef.org

RUTH CLARK SCHOLARSHIP

Scholarship available to students studying design at an accredited college or design school with a focus on residential furniture design. Applicant must submit five examples of original designs, three of which must be residential furniture examples. May be CD-ROM (pdf format only), slides, photographs, or copies of drawings no larger than 8 1/2"x11". Include five sets of each design example with a short description of each illustration.

Academic Fields/Career Goals: Arts; Industrial Design.

Award: Scholarship for use in sophomore, junior, senior, or graduate years; not renewable. *Number:* 1. *Amount:* $1500.

Eligibility Requirements: Applicant must be enrolled or expecting to enroll full-time at a four-year institution or university. Available to U.S. and non-U.S. citizens.

Application Requirements: Application, essay, references, transcript. *Deadline:* March 31.

Contact: Joan Long, Director of Grants
International Furnishings and Design Association
191 Clarksville Road
Princeton Junction, NJ 08550
Phone: 919-847-3064
Fax: 919-847-3064
E-mail: jlongdesigns@yahoo.com

JACK J. ISGUR FOUNDATION

JACK J. ISGUR FOUNDATION SCHOLARSHIP

Awards scholarships to juniors, seniors, and graduate students with intentions of teaching the humanities in Missouri schools. Applicants interested in teaching in rural schools will take precedence. The deadline is May 1.

Academic Fields/Career Goals: Arts; Education; Humanities; Literature/English/Writing; Music; Performing Arts.

Award: Scholarship for use in junior, senior, graduate, or postgraduate years; not renewable. *Number:* 5–10. *Amount:* $500–$1000.

Eligibility Requirements: Applicant must be enrolled or expecting to enroll full-time at a four-year institution or university. Available to U.S. and non-U.S. citizens.

Application Requirements: Application, references, transcript. *Deadline:* May 1.

Contact: Charles Jensen, Attorney at Law
Jack J. Isgur Foundation
c/o Charles F. Jensen, Stinson, Morrison, Hecker LLP
1201 Walnut Street, 28th Floor
Kansas City, MO 64106
Phone: 816-691-2760
Fax: 816-691-3495
E-mail: cjensen@stinsonmoheck.com

JOHN C. SANTISTEVAN MEMORIAL SCHOLARSHIP
http://www.santistevanart.org

JOHN C. SANTISTEVAN MEMORIAL SCHOLARSHIP

Scholarship available to qualified minority visual arts students from the Metropolitan Los Angeles and surrounding areas. Application deadline varies. Scholarship amount ranges from $1000 to $3000 and number of awards varies every year.

Academic Fields/Career Goals: Arts.

Award: Scholarship for use in freshman, sophomore, junior, or senior years; not renewable. *Number:* varies. *Amount:* $1000–$3000.

Eligibility Requirements: Applicant must be American Indian/Alaska Native, Asian/Pacific Islander, Black (non-Hispanic), or Hispanic and

John C. Santistevan Memorial Scholarship (continued)

enrolled or expecting to enroll full-time at an institution or university. Applicant must have 3.0 GPA or higher. Available to U.S. citizens.

Application Requirements: Application, portfolio. *Deadline:* varies.

Contact: Ivan Houston, President
John C. Santistevan Memorial Scholarship
419 North Larch Mont Boulevard, Number 98
Los Angeles, CA 90004

JOHN F. AND ANNA LEE STACEY SCHOLARSHIP FUND
http://www.nationalcowboymuseum.org

JOHN F. AND ANNA LEE STACEY SCHOLARSHIP FUND

Scholarships for artists who are high school graduates between the ages of 18 and 35, who are U.S. citizens, and whose work is devoted to the classical or conservative tradition of western culture. Awards are for drawing or painting only. Must submit no more than 10 35mm color slides of work. Applications accepted between October 1 and February 1. Contact for further details and application.

Academic Fields/Career Goals: Arts.

Award: Scholarship for use in freshman, sophomore, junior, senior, graduate, or postgraduate years; not renewable. *Number:* 3–5. *Amount:* $1000–$4000.

Eligibility Requirements: Applicant must be age 18-35; enrolled or expecting to enroll full or part-time at a four-year institution or university and must have an interest in art. Available to U.S. citizens.

Application Requirements: Application, applicant must enter a contest, photo, references, 35mm slides. *Deadline:* February 1.

Contact: Ed Muno, Art Curator
John F. and Anna Lee Stacey Scholarship Fund
1700 Northeast 63rd Street
Oklahoma City, OK 73111
Phone: 405-478-2250
Fax: 405-478-4714

JUNIOR ACHIEVEMENT
http://www.ja.org

WALT DISNEY COMPANY FOUNDATION SCHOLARSHIP

Must be a high school senior who completed JA Company Program or JA Economics. Tuition-only scholarship renewable annually for up to four years leading to a bachelor degree in either business administration or fine arts at an accredited college or university. $200 cash accompanies the scholarship each year for incidental fees.

Academic Fields/Career Goals: Arts; Business/Consumer Services.

Award: Scholarship for use in freshman, sophomore, junior, or senior years; renewable. *Number:* 1.

Eligibility Requirements: Applicant must be high school student and planning to enroll or expecting to enroll full-time at a four-year institution or university. Applicant or parent of applicant must be member of Junior Achievement. Available to U.S. and Canadian citizens.

Application Requirements: Application, references, test scores, transcript. *Deadline:* February 1.

Contact: Scholarship Coordinator
Junior Achievement
1 Education Way
Colorado Springs, CO 80906
Phone: 719-535-2954
Fax: 719-540-6175

LINCOLN COMMUNITY FOUNDATION
http://www.lcf.org

HAYMARKET GALLERY EMERGING ARTISTS SCHOLARSHIP

Scholarship for current graduating seniors or current college students enrolled in a qualified accredited college or university in Lancaster County in Nebraska who are pursuing art degrees. Must be residents of Lancaster County, Nebraska and show extraordinary artistic promise.

Academic Fields/Career Goals: Arts.

Award: Scholarship for use in freshman year; not renewable. *Number:* 1. *Amount:* $500–$2000.

Eligibility Requirements: Applicant must be enrolled or expecting to enroll full-time at a two-year or four-year institution or university; resident of Nebraska; studying in Nebraska and must have an interest in art. Available to U.S. citizens.

Application Requirements: Application, portfolio, references. *Deadline:* April 15.

Contact: Debra Shoemaker, Director of Program and Distribution
Lincoln Community Foundation
215 Centennial Mall South, Suite 200
Lincoln, NE 68508
Phone: 402-474-2345
Fax: 402-476-8532
E-mail: debs@lcf.org

LIQUITEX ARTIST MATERIALS PURCHASE AWARD PROGRAM
http://www.liquitex.com

LIQUITEX EXCELLENCE IN ART PURCHASE AWARD PROGRAM

Prizes up to $5000 in cash plus $1,500 in Liquitex products will be awarded to the best art submissions. Submission should be made on 35mm color slides. Void in Quebec or where prohibited by law. For more details see Web site: http://www.liquitex.com.

Academic Fields/Career Goals: Arts.

Award: Prize for use in freshman, sophomore, junior, senior, graduate, or postgraduate years; not renewable. *Number:* 5. *Amount:* $1500–$6500.

Eligibility Requirements: Applicant must be enrolled or expecting to enroll full or part-time at a two-year or four-year or technical institution or university. Available to U.S. and Canadian citizens.

Application Requirements: Application, applicant must enter a contest, 35mm color slides of artwork. *Deadline:* January 15.

Contact: Application available at Web site.

MEDIA ACTION NETWORK FOR ASIAN AMERICANS
http://www.manaa.org

MANAA MEDIA SCHOLARSHIPS FOR ASIAN AMERICAN STUDENTS

One-time award to students pursuing careers in film and television production as writers, directors, producers, and studio executives. Students must have a strong desire to advance a positive and enlightened understanding of the Asian-American experience in mainstream media. See Web site: http://www.manaa.org for application deadline and additional information.

Academic Fields/Career Goals: Arts; Filmmaking/Video; TV/Radio Broadcasting.

Award: Scholarship for use in freshman, sophomore, junior, senior, or graduate years; not renewable. *Number:* 1. *Amount:* $1000.

Eligibility Requirements: Applicant must be Asian/Pacific Islander and enrolled or expecting to enroll full-time at a two-year or four-year or technical institution or university. Available to U.S. citizens.

Application Requirements: Essay, financial need analysis, references, transcript, work sample. *Deadline:* varies.

Contact: MANAA Scholarship
Media Action Network for Asian Americans
PO Box 11105
Burbank, CA 91510
E-mail: manaaletters@yahoo.com.

METAVUE CORPORATION
http://www.metavue.com

THE FW RAUSCH ARTS AND HUMANITIES PAPER CONTEST

Two awards a year to undergraduate students enrolled at an accredited college or university in the U.S. Scholarships are granted for exemplary work in one of a variety of arts- and humanities-related areas the contestant may choose from. Work may focus on research, biography or critical essay.

Academic Fields/Career Goals: Arts; Humanities.

Award: Scholarship for use in freshman, sophomore, junior, or senior years. *Number:* 2. *Amount:* $500.

Eligibility Requirements: Applicant must be enrolled or expecting to enroll at a two-year or four-year institution or university. Applicant must have 3.0 GPA or higher. Available to U.S. citizens.

Application Requirements: Essay. *Deadline:* April 15.

Contact: Michael Rufflo
Metavue Corporation
1110 Surrey Drive
Sun Prairie, WI 53590
Phone: 608-577-0642
Fax: 512-685-4074
E-mail: rufflo@metavue.com

NATIONAL ART MATERIALS TRADE ASSOCIATION   http://www.namta.org

NATIONAL ART MATERIALS TRADE ASSOCIATION ART MAJOR SCHOLARSHIP

One-time award for students majoring or planning to major in the field of art or art education. A NAMTA member must sponsor candidates. Application deadline is April 1. For further details, see Web site at http://www.namta.org or email inquiries to scholarship@namta.org.

Academic Fields/Career Goals: Arts.

Award: Scholarship for use in freshman, sophomore, junior, senior, graduate, or postgraduate years; not renewable. *Number:* 2. *Amount:* $2500.

Eligibility Requirements: Applicant must be enrolled or expecting to enroll full-time at a two-year or four-year or technical institution or university. Available to U.S. and non-U.S. citizens.

Application Requirements: Application, essay, test scores, transcript. *Deadline:* April 1.

Contact: Katharine Coffey, Scholarship Coordinator
National Art Materials Trade Association
15806 Brookway Drive, Suite 300
Huntersville, NC 28078
Phone: 704-892-6244
Fax: 704-892-6247
E-mail: kcoffey@namta.org

NATIONAL FOUNDATION FOR ADVANCEMENT IN THE ARTS   http://www.artsawards.org

ARTS RECOGNITION AND TALENT SEARCH (ARTS)

One-time award for high school seniors or others that are 17-18 years old who show talent in dance, film and video, jazz, music, photography, theater, visual arts, voice, and/or writing. Must submit portfolio, videotape or audiotape, along with application fee. Must be citizens or permanent residents of the U.S., except applicants for the music/jazz discipline.

Academic Fields/Career Goals: Arts; Filmmaking/Video; Literature/English/Writing; Performing Arts; Photojournalism/Photography.

Award: Grant for use in freshman year; not renewable. *Number:* varies. *Amount:* $100–$10,000.

Eligibility Requirements: Applicant must be high school student; age 17-18 and planning to enroll or expecting to enroll full or part-time at a two-year or four-year or technical institution or university. Available to U.S. and non-U.S. citizens.

Application Requirements: Application, applicant must enter a contest, portfolio. *Fee:* $30. *Deadline:* November 1.

Contact: Programs Department
National Foundation for Advancement in the Arts
444 Brickell Avenue, Suite R14
Miami, FL 33133
Phone: 800-970-2787
Fax: 305-377-1149
E-mail: nfaa@nfaa.org

NATIONAL LEAGUE OF AMERICAN PEN WOMEN, INC.   http://www.americanpenwomen.org

NLAPW VIRGINIA LIEBELER BIENNIAL GRANTS FOR MATURE WOMEN (ARTS)

One-time award given in even-numbered years to female artists ages 35 and older who are U.S. citizens to be used to further creative purpose of applicant. Submit three 4x6 or bigger color prints (no slides) of work in any media. For photography, submit three 4x6 prints in color or black and white. All applicants submit statements of background, purpose of grant, and how applicant learned of grant. Application fee of $8. Send self-addressed stamped envelope for further requirements. Deadline for entry is October 1 of odd-numbered year.

Academic Fields/Career Goals: Arts.

Award: Grant for use in freshman, sophomore, junior, senior, graduate, or postgraduate years; not renewable. *Number:* 1. *Amount:* $1000.

Eligibility Requirements: Applicant must be age 35; enrolled or expecting to enroll at an institution or university; female and must have an interest in art or photography/photogrammetry/filmmaking. Available to U.S. citizens.

Application Requirements: Applicant must enter a contest, self-addressed stamped envelope, proof of U.S. citizenship. *Fee:* $8. *Deadline:* October 1.

Contact: NLAPW Virginia Liebeler Biennial Grants for Women
National League of American Pen Women, Inc.
1300 17th Street, NW
Washington, DC 20036-1973

NATIONAL OPERA ASSOCIATION   http://www.noa.org

NOA VOCAL COMPETITION/ LEGACY AWARD PROGRAM

Awards granted based on competitive audition to support study and career development. Singers compete in Scholarship and Artist Division. Legacy Awards are granted for study and career development in any opera-related career to those who further NOA's goal of increased minority participation in the profession.

Academic Fields/Career Goals: Arts; Performing Arts.

Award: Prize for use in freshman, sophomore, junior, senior, graduate, or postgraduate years; not renewable. *Number:* 3–8. *Amount:* $500–$2500.

Eligibility Requirements: Applicant must be age 18-40; enrolled or expecting to enroll full or part-time at a two-year or four-year or technical institution or university and must have an interest in music or music/singing. Available to U.S. and non-U.S. citizens.

Application Requirements: Application, applicant must enter a contest, autobiography, photo, references, audition tape/proposal. *Fee:* $25. *Deadline:* October 15.

Contact: Robert Hansen, Executive Secretary
National Opera Association
PO Box 60869
Canyon, TX 79016-0869
Phone: 806-651-2857
Fax: 806-651-2958
E-mail: hansen@mail.wtamu.edu

NATIONAL SCULPTURE SOCIETY   http://www.nationalsculpture.org

NATIONAL SCULPTURE COMPETITION FOR YOUNG SCULPTORS

For any sculptors age 18-35. Must submit slides of five to ten works with biography. Slides will be returned if self-addressed stamped envelope is included. One medal award and six monetary awards. Deadline in early April. See Web site for details (http://www.nationalsculpture.org).

Academic Fields/Career Goals: Arts.

Award: Prize for use in freshman, sophomore, junior, senior, or graduate years; not renewable. *Number:* 7. *Amount:* $300–$1000.

Eligibility Requirements: Applicant must be age 18-35; enrolled or expecting to enroll full or part-time at an institution or university and must have an interest in art. Available to U.S. citizens.

Application Requirements: Application, applicant must enter a contest, autobiography, self-addressed stamped envelope, slides of work. *Fee:* $35. *Deadline:* April 3.

Contact: Gwen Pier, Executive Director
National Sculpture Society
237 Park Avenue
New York, NY 10017
Phone: 212-764-5645 Ext. 15
Fax: 212-764-5651
E-mail: gwen@nationalsculpture.org

NATIONAL SCULPTURE SOCIETY SCHOLARSHIPS

Scholarships available for students of figurative or representational sculpture. Scholarships are paid directly to the academic institution through which the

National Sculpture Society (continued)

student applies. Applicant must submit 8-10 photographs of at least three different works. Deadline is April of each year.

Academic Fields/Career Goals: Arts.

Award: Scholarship for use in freshman, sophomore, junior, senior, or graduate years; not renewable. *Number:* 1–6. *Amount:* $1000.

Eligibility Requirements: Applicant must be enrolled or expecting to enroll full or part-time at a two-year or four-year or technical institution or university and must have an interest in art. Available to U.S. and non-U.S. citizens.

Application Requirements: Application, financial need analysis, references, self-addressed stamped envelope, transcript, photographs of work. *Deadline:* April.

Contact: Gwen Pier, Executive Director
National Sculpture Society
237 Park Avenue
New York, NY 10017
Phone: 212-764-5645
Fax: 212-764-5651
E-mail: gwen@nationalsculpture.org

ORANGE COUNTY COMMUNITY FOUNDATION   http://www.heef.org

ARTS SCHOLARSHIP PROGRAM

Scholarships awarded to high school students who demonstrate an interest in pursuing an education and/or career in any of the various fields of the arts including the performance of music, drama, dance, and the creativity of visual art such as fine art and graphic design. Deadline is February 13.

Academic Fields/Career Goals: Arts; Performing Arts.

Award: Scholarship for use in freshman year; not renewable. *Number:* 1–2. *Amount:* up to $1000.

Eligibility Requirements: Applicant must be high school student; planning to enroll or expecting to enroll at an institution or university and must have an interest in designated field specified by sponsor or music. Available to U.S. citizens.

Application Requirements: Application, essay, self-addressed stamped envelope, transcript. *Deadline:* February 13.

Contact: Rose Garris, Hispanic Education Endowment Fund
Orange County Community Foundation
30 Corporate Park, Suite 410
Irvine, CA 92606
Phone: 949-543-4202 Ext. 23
Fax: 949-553-4211

OREGON STUDENT ASSISTANCE COMMISSION   http://www.osac.state.or.us

GLENN R. AND JUANITA B. STRUBLE SCHOLARSHIP II
• *See page 102*

POLISH ARTS CLUB OF BUFFALO SCHOLARSHIP FOUNDATION   http://pacb.bfn.org/about/constitution.html

POLISH ARTS CLUB OF BUFFALO SCHOLARSHIP FOUNDATION TRUST
• *See page 108*

RHODE ISLAND FOUNDATION   http://www.rifoundation.org

CONSTANT MEMORIAL SCHOLARSHIP FOR AQUIDNECK ISLAND RESIDENTS

One-time scholarships between $2000 and $5000 are awarded to benefit visual art and/or music major entering his/her sophomore year in college. Applicants must be able to demonstrate financial need and a three year residency in Portsmouth, Middletown, or Newport, RI.

Academic Fields/Career Goals: Arts; Music.

Award: Scholarship for use in sophomore year; not renewable. *Number:* 1–2. *Amount:* $2000–$5000.

Eligibility Requirements: Applicant must be enrolled or expecting to enroll at a four-year institution; resident of Rhode Island and must have an interest in art or music. Available to U.S. citizens.

Application Requirements: Application. *Deadline:* June 9.

Contact: Libby Monahan, Scholarship Coordinator
Rhode Island Foundation
1 Union Station
Providence, RI 02903
Phone: 401-274-4564
Fax: 401-272-1359
E-mail: libbym@rifoundation.org

ROBERT H. MOLLOHAN FAMILY CHARITABLE FOUNDATION, INC.   http://www.mollohanfoundation.org

MARY OLIVE EDDY JONES ART SCHOLARSHIP
• *See page 108*

TELETOON   http://www.teletoon.com

TELETOON ANIMATION SCHOLARSHIP AWARD COMPETITION

Scholarship competition created by TELETOON to encourage creative, original, and imaginative animation by supporting Canadians studying in the animation field or intending to pursue studies in animation. One-time award. Must submit portfolio. Award of CAN$2000–$5000. Deadline is May 20.

Academic Fields/Career Goals: Arts; Filmmaking/Video.

Award: Scholarship for use in freshman, sophomore, junior, senior, graduate, or postgraduate years; not renewable. *Number:* 12. *Amount:* $1795–$4488.

Eligibility Requirements: Applicant must be enrolled or expecting to enroll full-time at a two-year or four-year or technical institution or university and resident of Alberta, British Columbia, Manitoba, New Brunswick, Newfoundland, North West Territories, Nova Scotia, Ontario, Prince Edward Island, Quebec, or Saskatchewan. Available to Canadian citizens.

Application Requirements: Application, applicant must enter a contest, essay, portfolio, transcript. *Deadline:* May 20.

Contact: Denise Vaughan, Senior Coordinator, Public Relations
Teletoon
BCE Place
181 Bay Street, PO Box 787
Toronto M5J 2T3
Canada
Phone: 416-956-2060
Fax: 416-956-2070
E-mail: scholarship@teletoon.com

TEXAS ARTS AND CRAFTS EDUCATIONAL FOUNDATION   http://www.tacef.org

EMERGING TEXAS ARTIST SCHOLARSHIP

Scholarships are awarded as prizes in a juried art exhibit at the Texas State Arts and Crafts Fair. The students are chosen by their art department and attend under their school's banner. The students exhibit and sell their works at the fair. See Web site for details http://www.tacef.org. Must be enrolled in a Texas school.

Academic Fields/Career Goals: Arts.

Award: Scholarship for use in freshman, sophomore, junior, senior, graduate, or postgraduate years; not renewable. *Number:* 8–15. *Amount:* $500–$2500.

Eligibility Requirements: Applicant must be enrolled or expecting to enroll full or part-time at a two-year or four-year institution or university and studying in Texas. Available to U.S. citizens.

Application Requirements: Application, applicant must enter a contest, references, 2 color slides of applicant's work. *Deadline:* March 15.

Contact: Texas Arts and Crafts Educational Foundation
PO Box 291527
Kerrville, TX 78029-1527
Phone: 830-896-5711
E-mail: info@tacef.org

U.S. FISH AND WILDLIFE SERVICE
http://duckstamps.fws.gov

FEDERAL JUNIOR DUCK STAMP CONSERVATION AND DESIGN COMPETITION

Any student in grades K-12, public, private, or home schooled, may enter this competition in all 50 states, the District of Columbia, and U.S. Territories. Teachers will use the curriculum guide which we provide to teach conservation issues to students. Student then does an artistic rendering of one of the North American Migratory Waterfowl and enters it into their state's Junior Duck Stamp Contest. Each state picks one Best of Show to be sent to the National Office in Arlington, VA. A national competition is held in D.C. and one winner is picked. Deadlines: South Carolina January 30, Florida February 21, all other states and territories March 15. Further information is available at: http://duckstamps.fws.gov.

Academic Fields/Career Goals: Arts.

Award: Prize for use in freshman year; not renewable. *Number:* 3. *Amount:* $1000–$4000.

Eligibility Requirements: Applicant must be enrolled or expecting to enroll full or part-time at an institution or university. Available to U.S. citizens.

Application Requirements: Applicant must enter a contest, artistic rendering. *Deadline:* March 15.

Contact: Pat Fisher, Submit entry to State Coordinator, see Web site.
U.S. Fish and Wildlife Service
Federal Duck Stamp Office, 4401 North Fairfax Drive, Suite 4073
Arlington, VA 22203-1622
Phone: 703-358-2007

UNICO NATIONAL, INC
http://www.unico.org

THEODORE MAZZA SCHOLARSHIP
• *See page 103*

UNITED NEGRO COLLEGE FUND
http://www.uncf.org

HOUSTON SYMPHONY/ TOP LADIES SCHOLARSHIP

Scholarship awarded to Iowa residents attending a UNCF member college or university and majoring in art. Minimum 2.5 GPA required. Prospective applicants should complete the Student Profile found at Web site: http://www.uncf.org.

Academic Fields/Career Goals: Arts.

Award: Scholarship for use in junior or senior years; not renewable. *Number:* 1.

Eligibility Requirements: Applicant must be Black (non-Hispanic); enrolled or expecting to enroll at a four-year institution or university and resident of Iowa. Applicant must have 2.5 GPA or higher. Available to U.S. citizens.

Application Requirements: Application, financial need analysis. *Deadline:* Continuous.

Contact: Rebecca Bennett, Director, Program Services
United Negro College Fund
8260 Willow Oaks Corporate Drive
Fairfax, VA 22031-8044
Phone: 800-331-2244
E-mail: rbennett@uncf.org

VARIAZIONE MIXED MEDIA ARTISTS' COLLECTIVE
http://www.zneart.com

LEARNING SCHOLARSHIP

Scholarship available to all high school seniors, undergraduate and graduate students, as well as artists who are not enrolled full time, but enrolled in art classes in order to expand their skills.

Academic Fields/Career Goals: Arts.

Award: Scholarship for use in freshman, sophomore, junior, senior, or graduate years; not renewable. *Amount:* $100.

Eligibility Requirements: Applicant must be enrolled or expecting to enroll full or part-time at a four-year institution or university. Available to U.S. citizens.

Application Requirements: Application, autobiography, financial need analysis. *Deadline:* April 15.

Contact: Zen Learning Scholarship
VariaZioNE Mixed Media Artists' Collective
1152 Crellin Road
Pleasanton, CA 94566

WATERBURY FOUNDATION
http://www.conncf.org/

LOIS MCMILLEN MEMORIAL SCHOLARSHIP FUND

Scholarships to women who are actively pursuing or who would like to pursue an artistic career. Must reside in the Foundation's service area, which is the greater Waterbury area of Connecticut. Awarded for the purpose of attending an accredited college or university or a qualified artists-in-residence program in a chosen artistic field. Preference will be given to artists in the visual arts of painting and design.

Academic Fields/Career Goals: Arts.

Award: Scholarship for use in freshman, sophomore, junior, senior, or graduate years; not renewable. *Number:* varies. *Amount:* $500–$4000.

Eligibility Requirements: Applicant must be enrolled or expecting to enroll at a four-year institution or university; female and resident of Connecticut. Available to U.S. citizens.

Application Requirements: Application, essay, references. *Deadline:* March 1.

Contact: Josh Carey, Program Officer
Waterbury Foundation
43 Field Street
Waterbury, CT 06702-1216
Phone: 203-753-1315
Fax: 203-756-3054
E-mail: jcarey@conncf.org

WAVERLY COMMUNITY HOUSE, INC.
http://www.waverlycomm.com

F. LAMMOT BELIN ARTS SCHOLARSHIP
• *See page 103*

WORLDSTUDIO FOUNDATION
http://www.worldstudio.org

WORLDSTUDIO AIGA SCHOLARSHIPS

Scholarships for minority and economically disadvantaged students who are studying the design/arts disciplines in colleges and universities in the United States.

Academic Fields/Career Goals: Arts.

Award: Scholarship for use in freshman, sophomore, junior, senior, or graduate years. *Amount:* $1000–$5000.

Eligibility Requirements: Applicant must be enrolled or expecting to enroll at a two-year or four-year institution or university. Available to U.S. citizens.

Application Requirements: Application, transcript. *Deadline:* April 14.

Contact: Scholarship Coordinator
Worldstudio Foundation
200 Varick Street, Suite 507
New York, NY 10014
Phone: 212-366-1317 Ext. 18
Fax: 212-807-0024
E-mail: scholarships@worldstudio.org

WORLDSTUDIO FOUNDATION SCHOLARSHIP PROGRAM
• *See page 104*

ASIAN STUDIES

CULTURE CONNECTION
http://www.thecultureconnection.com

CULTURE CONNECTION FOUNDATION SCHOLARSHIP
• *See page 73*

AUDIOLOGY

AUDIOLOGY FOUNDATION OF AMERICA
http://www.audfound.org

AUDIOLOGY FOUNDATION OF AMERICA'S OUTSTANDING AUD STUDENT SCHOLARSHIP

The Audiology Foundation of America's Outstanding AuD Student Award provides funds for students pursuing the Doctor of Audiology (AuD) degree from institutions in the U.S. or Canada and who are entering the third year of an AuD program. Students are recognized for their academic achievement and professional potential.

Academic Fields/Career Goals: Audiology.

Award: Scholarship for use in freshman, sophomore, junior, or senior years; not renewable. *Number:* 2. *Amount:* $4500.

Eligibility Requirements: Applicant must be enrolled or expecting to enroll full-time at a four-year institution or university. Applicant must have 3.5 GPA or higher. Available to U.S. and Canadian citizens.

Application Requirements: Application, essay, photo, references, self-addressed stamped envelope, test scores, transcript, nomination by AuD program director, clinical evaluation forms. *Deadline:* July 15.

Contact: Mary Wilson, Managing Assistant Director
Audiology Foundation of America
8 N 3rd Street, Suite 406
Lafayette, IN 47901-1247
Phone: 765-743-6283
Fax: 765-743-9283
E-mail: mary@audfound.org

SERTOMA INTERNATIONAL
http://www.sertoma.org

SERTOMA COMMUNICATIVE DISORDERS SCHOLARSHIP PROGRAM

Award for graduate students studying audiology and speech-language pathology in the United States and its territories. Minimum 3.2 GPA required. Application deadline is March 30. Further information is available at Web site: http://www.sertoma.org.

Academic Fields/Career Goals: Audiology; Health and Medical Sciences.

Award: Scholarship for use in freshman, sophomore, junior, senior, graduate, or postgraduate years; not renewable. *Number:* 30–40. *Amount:* $1000.

Eligibility Requirements: Applicant must be enrolled or expecting to enroll full-time at a two-year or four-year or technical institution or university. Available to U.S. citizens.

Application Requirements: Application, essay, references, transcript. *Deadline:* March 30.

Contact: Communication Disorders Scholarship
Sertoma International
1912 East Meyer Boulevard
Kansas City, MO 64132
Phone: 816-333-8300
Fax: 816-333-4320
E-mail: infosertoma@sertoma.org

AVIATION/AEROSPACE

AACE INTERNATIONAL
http://www.aacei.org

AACE INTERNATIONAL COMPETITIVE SCHOLARSHIP
• *See page 96*

AIR TRAFFIC CONTROL ASSOCIATION, INC.
http://www.atca.org

AIR TRAFFIC CONTROL ASSOCIATION SCHOLARSHIP

Scholarships for students in programs leading to a bachelor's degree or higher in aviation-related courses of study and for full-time employees engaged in advanced study to improve their skills in air traffic control or aviation. Visit Web site for additional information: http://www.atca.org.

Academic Fields/Career Goals: Aviation/Aerospace; Engineering/Technology.

Award: Scholarship for use in freshman, sophomore, junior, senior, or graduate years; not renewable. *Number:* 7–12. *Amount:* $600–$2500.

Eligibility Requirements: Applicant must be enrolled or expecting to enroll full or part-time at a four-year institution or university. Applicant or parent of applicant must have employment or volunteer experience in air traffic controller field. Available to U.S. citizens.

Application Requirements: Application, autobiography, essay, financial need analysis, references, transcript. *Deadline:* May 1.

Contact: James Crook, Vice President of Operations
Air Traffic Control Association, Inc.
2300 Clarendon Boulevard, Suite 711
Arlington, VA 22201-2302
Phone: 703-522-5717
Fax: 703-527-7251
E-mail: jim.crook@atca.org

AIRCRAFT ELECTRONICS ASSOCIATION EDUCATIONAL FOUNDATION
http://aea.net

BENDIX/KING AVIONICS SCHOLARSHIP

Award for anyone who plans to attend or is attending an accredited school in an avionics or aircraft repair program. Must have minimum 2.5 GPA. One-time award of $1000.

Academic Fields/Career Goals: Aviation/Aerospace.

Award: Scholarship for use in freshman, sophomore, junior, or senior years; not renewable. *Number:* 1. *Amount:* $1000.

Eligibility Requirements: Applicant must be enrolled or expecting to enroll full or part-time at a two-year or four-year or technical institution or university. Applicant must have 2.5 GPA or higher. Available to U.S. and non-U.S. citizens.

Application Requirements: Application, essay, transcript. *Deadline:* February 15.

Contact: Mike Adamson, Educational Foundation Executive Director
Aircraft Electronics Association Educational Foundation
4217 South Hocker Drive
Independence, MO 64055-0963
Phone: 816-373-6565
Fax: 816-478-3100
E-mail: info@aea.net

BUD GLOVER MEMORIAL SCHOLARSHIP

Award for anyone who plans to or is attending an accredited school in an avionics or aircraft repair program. Minimum 2.5 GPA required. One-time award of $1000.

Academic Fields/Career Goals: Aviation/Aerospace; Trade/Technical Specialties.

Award: Scholarship for use in freshman, sophomore, junior, or senior years; not renewable. *Number:* 1. *Amount:* $1000.

Eligibility Requirements: Applicant must be enrolled or expecting to enroll full-time at a two-year or four-year or technical institution or university. Applicant must have 2.5 GPA or higher. Available to U.S. and non-U.S. citizens.

Application Requirements: Application, essay, references, test scores, transcript. *Deadline:* February 15.

Contact: Mike Adamson, Educational Foundation Executive Director
Aircraft Electronics Association Educational Foundation
4217 South Hocker Drive
Independence, MO 64055-0963
Phone: 816-373-6565
Fax: 816-478-3100
E-mail: info@aea.net

CHUCK PEACOCK MEMORIAL SCHOLARSHIP

Award for high school seniors or college students who plan to attend or are attending an accredited school in an aviation management program. Must have minimum 2.5 GPA. One-time award of $1000.

Academic Fields/Career Goals: Aviation/Aerospace.

Award: Scholarship for use in freshman, sophomore, junior, or senior years; not renewable. *Number:* 1. *Amount:* $1000.

Eligibility Requirements: Applicant must be enrolled or expecting to enroll at a two-year or four-year or technical institution or university. Applicant must have 2.5 GPA or higher. Available to U.S. and non-U.S. citizens.

Application Requirements: Application, essay, transcript. *Deadline:* February 15.

Contact: Mike Adamson, Educational Foundation Executive Director
Aircraft Electronics Association Educational Foundation
4217 South Hocker
Independence, MO 64055-0963
Phone: 816-373-6565
Fax: 816-478-3100
E-mail: info@aea.net

DAVID ARVER MEMORIAL SCHOLARSHIP

One-time award for any student who plans to attend an accredited vocational or technical school in Illinois, Indiana, Iowa, Kansas, Michigan, Minnesota, Missouri, Nebraska, North Dakota, South Dakota, or Wisconsin. Must plan to study aviation electronics and have a minimum 2.5 GPA.

Academic Fields/Career Goals: Aviation/Aerospace.

Award: Scholarship for use in freshman, sophomore, junior, or senior years; not renewable. *Number:* 1. *Amount:* $1000.

Eligibility Requirements: Applicant must be enrolled or expecting to enroll full-time at a two-year or four-year or technical institution or university and studying in Illinois, Indiana, Iowa, Kansas, Michigan, Minnesota, Missouri, Nebraska, North Dakota, South Dakota, or Wisconsin. Applicant must have 2.5 GPA or higher. Available to U.S. and non-U.S. citizens.

Application Requirements: Application, essay, references, test scores, transcript. *Deadline:* February 15.

Contact: Mike Adamson, Educational Foundation Executive Director
Aircraft Electronics Association Educational Foundation
4217 South Hocker Drive
Independence, MO 64055-0963
Phone: 816-373-6565
Fax: 816-478-3100
E-mail: info@aea.net

DUTCH AND GINGER ARVER SCHOLARSHIP

Award for anyone who plans to attend or is attending an accredited school in an avionics or aircraft repair program. Must have minimum 2.5 GPA. One-time award of $1000.

Academic Fields/Career Goals: Aviation/Aerospace.

Award: Scholarship for use in freshman, sophomore, junior, or senior years; not renewable. *Number:* 1. *Amount:* $1000.

Eligibility Requirements: Applicant must be enrolled or expecting to enroll full-time at a two-year or four-year or technical institution or university. Applicant must have 2.5 GPA or higher. Available to U.S. and non-U.S. citizens.

Application Requirements: Application, essay, references, test scores, transcript. *Deadline:* February 15.

Contact: Mike Adamson, Educational Foundation Executive Director
Aircraft Electronics Association Educational Foundation
4217 South Hocker Drive
Independence, MO 64055-0963
Phone: 816-373-6565
Fax: 816-478-3100
E-mail: info@aea.net

FIELD AVIATION CO., INC., SCHOLARSHIP

Award for high school seniors and/or college students who plan to or are attending an accredited college/university in an avionics or aircraft repair program. The educational institution must be located in Canada.

Academic Fields/Career Goals: Aviation/Aerospace; Trade/Technical Specialties.

Award: Scholarship for use in freshman, sophomore, junior, or senior years; not renewable. *Number:* 1. *Amount:* $1000.

Eligibility Requirements: Applicant must be enrolled or expecting to enroll full-time at a two-year or four-year or technical institution or university and studying in Alberta, British Columbia, Manitoba, New Brunswick, Newfoundland, North West Territories, Nova Scotia,

Ontario, Prince Edward Island, Quebec, Saskatchewan, or Yukon. Applicant must have 2.5 GPA or higher. Available to U.S. and non-U.S. citizens.

Application Requirements: Application, essay, references, test scores, transcript. *Deadline:* February 15.

Contact: Mike Adamson, Educational Foundation Executive Director
Aircraft Electronics Association Educational Foundation
4217 South Hocker Drive
Independence, MO 64055-0963
Phone: 816-373-6565
Fax: 816-478-3100
E-mail: info@aea.net

GARMIN SCHOLARSHIP

Award for students of avionics or aircraft repair at a college or technical school. One-time award of $2000. Must have minimum 2.5 GPA.

Academic Fields/Career Goals: Aviation/Aerospace.

Award: Scholarship for use in freshman, sophomore, junior, or senior years; not renewable. *Number:* 1. *Amount:* $2000.

Eligibility Requirements: Applicant must be enrolled or expecting to enroll full-time at a two-year or four-year or technical institution or university. Applicant must have 2.5 GPA or higher. Available to U.S. and non-U.S. citizens.

Application Requirements: Application, essay, references, test scores, transcript. *Deadline:* February 15.

Contact: Mike Adamson, Educational Foundation Executive Director
Aircraft Electronics Association Educational Foundation
4217 South Hocker Drive
Independence, MO 64055-0963
Phone: 816-373-6565
Fax: 816-478-3100
E-mail: info@aea.net

JOHNNY DAVIS MEMORIAL SCHOLARSHIP

One-time award for anyone who plans to or is attending school in an avionics or aircraft repair program. Must have minimum 2.5 GPA. One-time award of $1000.

Academic Fields/Career Goals: Aviation/Aerospace.

Award: Scholarship for use in freshman, sophomore, junior, or senior years; not renewable. *Number:* 1. *Amount:* $1000.

Eligibility Requirements: Applicant must be enrolled or expecting to enroll full or part-time at a two-year or four-year or technical institution or university. Applicant must have 2.5 GPA or higher. Available to U.S. and non-U.S. citizens.

Application Requirements: Application, essay, transcript. *Deadline:* February 15.

Contact: Mike Adamson, Educational Foundation Executive Director
Aircraft Electronics Association Educational Foundation
4217 South Hocker Drive
Independence, MO 64055-0963
Phone: 816-373-6565
Fax: 816-478-3100
E-mail: info@aea.net

L-3 AVIONICS SYSTEMS SCHOLARSHIP

Award for high school seniors or college students who plan on or are attending an accredited school in an avionics or aircraft repair program. Must have minimum 2.5 GPA. One-time award of $2500.

Academic Fields/Career Goals: Aviation/Aerospace.

Award: Scholarship for use in freshman, sophomore, junior, or senior years; not renewable. *Number:* 1. *Amount:* $2500.

Eligibility Requirements: Applicant must be enrolled or expecting to enroll at a two-year or four-year or technical institution or university. Applicant must have 2.5 GPA or higher. Available to U.S. and non-U.S. citizens.

Application Requirements: Application, essay, transcript. *Deadline:* February 15.

Aircraft Electronics Association Educational Foundation (continued)

Contact: Mike Adamson, Educational Foundation Executive Director
Aircraft Electronics Association Educational Foundation
4217 South Hocker
Independence, MO 64055-0963
Phone: 816-373-6565
Fax: 816-478-3100
E-mail: info@aea.net

LEE TARBOX MEMORIAL SCHOLARSHIP

Award for students of avionics or aircraft repair at any college or technical school. Minimum 2.5 GPA required. One-time $2500 award.

Academic Fields/Career Goals: Aviation/Aerospace.

Award: Scholarship for use in freshman, sophomore, junior, or senior years; not renewable. *Number:* 1. *Amount:* $2500.

Eligibility Requirements: Applicant must be enrolled or expecting to enroll full-time at a two-year or four-year or technical institution or university. Applicant must have 2.5 GPA or higher. Available to U.S. and non-U.S. citizens.

Application Requirements: Application, essay, references, test scores, transcript. *Deadline:* February 15.

Contact: Mike Adamson, Educational Foundation Executive Director
Aircraft Electronics Association Educational Foundation
4217 South Hocker Drive
Independence, MO 64055-0963
Phone: 816-373-6565
Fax: 816-478-3100
E-mail: info@aea.net

LOWELL GAYLOR MEMORIAL SCHOLARSHIP

Award for anyone who plans to or is attending an accredited school in avionics or aircraft repair program. Minimum 2.5 GPA required. One-time award of $1000.

Academic Fields/Career Goals: Aviation/Aerospace; Trade/Technical Specialties.

Award: Scholarship for use in freshman, sophomore, junior, or senior years; not renewable. *Number:* 1. *Amount:* $1000.

Eligibility Requirements: Applicant must be enrolled or expecting to enroll full-time at a two-year or four-year or technical institution or university. Applicant must have 2.5 GPA or higher. Available to U.S. and non-U.S. citizens.

Application Requirements: Application, essay, references, test scores, transcript. *Deadline:* February 15.

Contact: Mike Adamson, Educational Foundation Executive Director
Aircraft Electronics Association Educational Foundation
4217 South Hocker Drive
Independence, MO 64055-0963
Phone: 816-373-6565
Fax: 816-478-3100
E-mail: info@aea.net

MID-CONTINENT INSTRUMENT SCHOLARSHIP

Award for anyone who plans to attend or is attending an accredited school in an avionics or aircraft repair program. Minimum 2.5 GPA required. One-time award of $1000.

Academic Fields/Career Goals: Aviation/Aerospace.

Award: Scholarship for use in freshman, sophomore, junior, or senior years; not renewable. *Number:* 1. *Amount:* $1000.

Eligibility Requirements: Applicant must be enrolled or expecting to enroll full-time at a two-year or four-year or technical institution or university. Applicant must have 2.5 GPA or higher. Available to U.S. and non-U.S. citizens.

Application Requirements: Application, essay, references, test scores, transcript. *Deadline:* February 15.

Contact: Mike Adamson, Educational Foundation Executive Director
Aircraft Electronics Association Educational Foundation
4217 South Hocker Drive
Independence, MO 64055-0963
Phone: 816-373-6565
Fax: 816-478-3100
E-mail: info@aea.net

MONTE MITCHELL GLOBAL SCHOLARSHIP

Scholarship is available to European students pursuing a degree in aviation maintenance technology, avionics, or aircraft repair at an accredited school located in Europe or the U.S. Minimum 2.5 GPA required.

Academic Fields/Career Goals: Aviation/Aerospace; Trade/Technical Specialties.

Award: Scholarship for use in freshman, sophomore, junior, or senior years; not renewable. *Number:* 1. *Amount:* $1000.

Eligibility Requirements: Applicant must be enrolled or expecting to enroll full-time at a two-year or four-year or technical institution or university. Applicant must have 2.5 GPA or higher. Available to citizens of countries other than the U.S. or Canada.

Application Requirements: Application, essay, references, transcript. *Deadline:* February 15.

Contact: Mike Adamson, Educational Foundation Executive Director
Aircraft Electronics Association Educational Foundation
4217 South Hocker Drive
Independence, MO 64055-0963
Phone: 816-373-6565
Fax: 816-478-3100
E-mail: info@aea.net

PRIVATE PILOT MAGAZINE SCHOLARSHIP

Award for high school seniors or college students who plan to attend or are attending an accredited school in avionics or aircraft repair program. Must have minimum 2.5 GPA. One-time award of $1000.

Academic Fields/Career Goals: Aviation/Aerospace.

Award: Scholarship for use in freshman, sophomore, junior, or senior years; not renewable. *Number:* 1. *Amount:* $1000.

Eligibility Requirements: Applicant must be enrolled or expecting to enroll at a two-year or four-year or technical institution. Applicant must have 2.5 GPA or higher. Available to U.S. and non-U.S. citizens.

Application Requirements: Application, essay, transcript. *Deadline:* February 15.

Contact: Mike Adamson, Educational Foundation Executive Director
Aircraft Electronics Association Educational Foundation
4217 South Hocker
Independence, MO 64055-0963
Phone: 816-373-6565
Fax: 816-478-3100
E-mail: info@aea.net

SPORTY'S PILOT SHOP/CINCINNATI AVIONICS

One-time award available to high school seniors or college students who plan to or are attending an accredited school in avionics or aircraft repair program. Minimum 2.5 GPA required.

Academic Fields/Career Goals: Aviation/Aerospace.

Award: Scholarship for use in freshman, sophomore, junior, or senior years; not renewable. *Number:* 1. *Amount:* $2000.

Eligibility Requirements: Applicant must be enrolled or expecting to enroll full or part-time at a two-year or four-year or technical institution or university. Applicant must have 2.5 GPA or higher. Available to U.S. and non-U.S. citizens.

Application Requirements: Application, essay, references, test scores, transcript. *Deadline:* February 15.

Contact: Mike Adamson, Educational Foundation Executive Director
Aircraft Electronics Association Educational Foundation
4217 South Hocker
Independence, MO 64055-0963
Phone: 816-373-6565
Fax: 816-478-3100
E-mail: info@aea.net

ALASKAN AVIATION SAFETY FOUNDATION
http://www.alaska.net/~etc/aasf/

ALASKAN AVIATION SAFETY FOUNDATION MEMORIAL SCHOLARSHIP FUND

Scholarships for undergraduate or graduate study in aviation. Must be a resident of Alaska and a U.S. citizen. Write for deadlines and details.

Academic Fields/Career Goals: Aviation/Aerospace.

Award: Scholarship for use in sophomore, junior, senior, or graduate years; not renewable. *Number:* 1–3. *Amount:* $500–$750.

Eligibility Requirements: Applicant must be enrolled or expecting to enroll full or part-time at a two-year or four-year or technical institution or university and resident of Alaska. Available to U.S. citizens.

Application Requirements: Application, autobiography, driver's license, financial need analysis, references, test scores, transcript. *Deadline:* varies.

Contact: Scholarship Committee
Alaskan Aviation Safety Foundation
4340 Aircraft Drive
Anchorage, AK 99502
Phone: 907-243-7237

AMERICAN ASSOCIATION OF AIRPORT EXECUTIVES
http://www.aaae.org

AMERICAN ASSOCIATION OF AIRPORT EXECUTIVES FOUNDATION SCHOLARSHIP

$1000 granted each year to juniors or higher who are enrolled in an aviation program and have a minimum 3.0 GPA. Awards based on academic records, financial need, school participation, community activities, work experience, and a personal statement. Must be recommended by school. One student per institution. Multiple recommendations from the same institution will be returned.

Academic Fields/Career Goals: Aviation/Aerospace.

Award: Scholarship for use in junior or senior years; not renewable. *Number:* up to 10. *Amount:* $1000.

Eligibility Requirements: Applicant must be enrolled or expecting to enroll full-time at a four-year institution or university. Applicant must have 3.0 GPA or higher. Available to U.S. citizens.

Application Requirements: Financial need analysis, references, self-addressed stamped envelope, transcript. *Deadline:* May 31.

Contact: Scholarship Coordinator
American Association of Airport Executives
601 Madison Street, Suite 400
Alexandria, VA 22314
Phone: 703-824-0504
Fax: 703-820-1395
E-mail: member.services@airportnet.org

AMERICAN ASSOCIATION OF AIRPORT EXECUTIVES FOUNDATION SCHOLARSHIP-NATIVE AMERICAN

Yearly $1000 grant to a number of Native-American students who are juniors or higher and who are enrolled in an aviation program. Must have a minimum 3.0 GPA. Award based on academic records, financial need, school participation, community activities, work experience, race, and a personal statement. Must be recommended by a school (one student per institution). Multiple recommendations from the same institution will be returned.

Academic Fields/Career Goals: Aviation/Aerospace.

Award: Scholarship for use in junior or senior years; not renewable. *Amount:* $1000.

Eligibility Requirements: Applicant must be American Indian/Alaska Native and enrolled or expecting to enroll full-time at a four-year institution or university. Applicant must have 3.0 GPA or higher. Available to U.S. citizens.

Application Requirements: Financial need analysis, references, self-addressed stamped envelope, transcript. *Deadline:* May 31.

Contact: Scholarship Coordinator
American Association of Airport Executives
601 Madison Street, Suite 400
Alexandria, VA 22314

AMERICAN INSTITUTE OF AERONAUTICS AND ASTRONAUTICS
http://www.aiaa.org

AIAA UNDERGRADUATE SCHOLARSHIP
• See page 89

AMERICAN SOCIETY OF NAVAL ENGINEERS
http://www.navalengineers.org

AMERICAN SOCIETY OF NAVAL ENGINEERS SCHOLARSHIP
• See page 90

AOPA AIR SAFETY FOUNDATION
http://www.aopa.org

AOPA AIR SAFETY FOUNDATION/DONALD BURNSIDE MEMORIAL SCHOLARSHIP

One-time scholarship of $1000 will be given to a U.S. citizen who, without assistance, would find it difficult to obtain a college education. The recipient must be enrolled in and plan to continue a college curriculum leading to a degree in the field of aviation. Must maintain a 3.25 GPA. Visit http://www.aopa.org/asf/scholarship for more information and an application.

Academic Fields/Career Goals: Aviation/Aerospace.

Award: Scholarship for use in junior or senior years; not renewable. *Number:* 1. *Amount:* $1000.

Eligibility Requirements: Applicant must be enrolled or expecting to enroll at a four-year institution or university. Available to U.S. citizens.

Application Requirements: Application, essay, transcript. *Deadline:* March 31.

Contact: Scholarship Coordinator
AOPA Air Safety Foundation
421 Aviation Way
Frederick, MD 21701-4798
Phone: 301-695-2000
Fax: 301-695-2375

AOPA AIR SAFETY FOUNDATION/KOCH CORPORATION SCHOLARSHIP

A $1500 scholarship will be awarded to a deserving U.S. citizen. Recipients will be enrolled in an accredited college or university pursuing a course of study focusing on aviation. Must maintain a 3.25 GPA. Visit http://www.aopa.org/asf/scholarship for more information and an application.

Academic Fields/Career Goals: Aviation/Aerospace.

Award: Scholarship for use in freshman, sophomore, junior, or senior years. *Amount:* $1500.

Eligibility Requirements: Applicant must be enrolled or expecting to enroll at a four-year institution or university. Available to U.S. citizens.

Application Requirements: Application, essay, transcript. *Deadline:* varies.

Contact: Scholarship Coordinator
AOPA Air Safety Foundation
421 Aviation Way
Frederick, MD 21701-4798
Phone: 301-695-2000
Fax: 301-695-2375

AOPA AIR SAFETY FOUNDATION/MCALLISTER MEMORIAL SCHOLARSHIP

One-time scholarship of $1000 will be given to a U.S. citizen who, without assistance, would find it difficult to obtain a college education. The recipient must be enrolled in and plan to continue a college curriculum leading to a degree in the field of aviation. Must maintain a 3.25 GPA. Visit http://www.aopa.org/asf/scholarship for more information and an application.

Academic Fields/Career Goals: Aviation/Aerospace.

Award: Scholarship for use in junior or senior years; not renewable. *Number:* 1. *Amount:* $1000.

Eligibility Requirements: Applicant must be enrolled or expecting to enroll at a four-year institution or university. Available to U.S. citizens.

AOPA Air Safety Foundation (continued)

Application Requirements: Application, essay, self-addressed stamped envelope, transcript. *Deadline:* March 31.

Contact: Mark Sherman, Assistant Professor
AOPA Air Safety Foundation
Department of Aviation, Central Missouri State University, TR Gains 210
Warrensburg, MO 64093
Phone: 660-543-4111

ARMED FORCES COMMUNICATIONS AND ELECTRONICS ASSOCIATION, EDUCATIONAL FOUNDATION   http://www.afcea.org

AFCEA SCHOLARSHIP FOR WORKING PROFESSIONALS

Must be a U.S. citizen currently enrolled as sophomore, junior or senior in an accredited U.S. school. Part time status is defined as enrollment in at least 2 classes per semester at any two- or four-year accredited U.S. college or university with a declared major in a science or technology degree program. Eligible majors include electrical, aerospace, or computer engineering, computer science, computer information systems, physics or mathematics. Overall GPA of 3.4 is required. Deadline is September 15.

Academic Fields/Career Goals: Aviation/Aerospace; Computer Science/Data Processing; Electrical Engineering/Electronics; Engineering/Technology; Physical Sciences and Math.

Award: Scholarship for use in sophomore, junior, or senior years; not renewable. *Number:* varies. *Amount:* $1500.

Eligibility Requirements: Applicant must be enrolled or expecting to enroll part-time at a two-year or four-year institution or university. Available to U.S. citizens.

Application Requirements: Application, references, transcript. *Deadline:* September 15.

Contact: Norma Corrales, Scholarship Coordinator
Phone: 703-631-6149
E-mail: scholarship@afcea.org

ARMED FORCES COMMUNICATIONS AND ELECTRONICS ASSOCIATION ROTC SCHOLARSHIP PROGRAM

Award for ROTC students enrolled in four-year accredited colleges or universities in the U.S. At the time of application students must be sophomore or junior studying electronics or electrical, communications, or aerospace engineering; physics; mathematics; or computer science. Must exhibit academic excellence and potential to serve as officer in the Armed Forces of the U.S. Nominations are submitted by professors of military science, naval science, or aerospace studies by April 1.

Academic Fields/Career Goals: Aviation/Aerospace; Computer Science/Data Processing; Electrical Engineering/Electronics; Engineering/Technology; Physical Sciences and Math.

Award: Scholarship for use in sophomore or junior years; not renewable. *Number:* varies. *Amount:* $2000.

Eligibility Requirements: Applicant must be enrolled or expecting to enroll full-time at a four-year institution or university. Available to U.S. citizens.

Application Requirements: Application, references, transcript. *Deadline:* April 1.

Contact: Fred Rainbow, Vice President and Executive Director
Armed Forces Communications and Electronics Association, Educational Foundation
4400 Fair Lakes Court
Fairfax, VA 22033-3899

ASSOCIATION FOR FACILITIES ENGINEERING (AFE)

ASSOCIATION FOR FACILITIES ENGINEERING CEDAR VALLEY CHAPTER # 132 SCHOLARSHIP

Applicant must be a high school graduate, have a 2.5 or higher GPA, be U.S. citizen, and an Iowa resident. Applicant may be enrolled in any engineering program leading to an AA, BA, or BS degree. Awards are paid directly to the institution in the student's name. Deadline May 1.

Academic Fields/Career Goals: Aviation/Aerospace; Chemical Engineering; Civil Engineering; Electrical Engineering/Electronics; Engineering/Technology; Engineering-Related Technologies; Materials Science, Engineering, and Metallurgy; Mechanical Engineering; Trade/Technical Specialties.

Award: Scholarship for use in freshman, sophomore, junior, or senior years; renewable. *Number:* 1. *Amount:* $500.

Eligibility Requirements: Applicant must be enrolled or expecting to enroll full-time at a two-year or four-year or technical institution or university; resident of Iowa and studying in Iowa. Applicant must have 2.5 GPA or higher. Available to U.S. citizens.

Application Requirements: Application, autobiography, transcript, copy of birth certificate, high school diploma. *Deadline:* May 1.

Contact: Joe Zachar, Special Events Chair
Association for Facilities Engineering (AFE)
1203 Forest Glen Court SE
Cedar Rapids, IA 52403
Phone: 319-364-4740
E-mail: zachar2@aol.com

ASTRONAUT SCHOLARSHIP FOUNDATION   http://www.astronautscholarship.org

ASTRONAUT SCHOLARSHIP FOUNDATION
• See page 92

AVIATION COUNCIL OF PENNSYLVANIA   http://www.acpfly.com

AVIATION COUNCIL OF PENNSYLVANIA SCHOLARSHIP PROGRAM

Awards for Pennsylvania residents to pursue studies at Pennsylvania institutions leading to career as professional pilot or in the fields of aviation technology or aviation management. Awards at discretion of Aviation Council of Pennsylvania. Three to four scholarships ranging from $500 to $1000. Applicants for the aviation management scholarship may attend institutions outside of Pennsylvania.

Academic Fields/Career Goals: Aviation/Aerospace.

Award: Scholarship for use in sophomore, junior, or senior years; not renewable. *Number:* 3–4. *Amount:* $500–$1000.

Eligibility Requirements: Applicant must be enrolled or expecting to enroll full or part-time at a two-year or four-year or technical institution or university; resident of Pennsylvania and studying in Pennsylvania. Available to U.S. citizens.

Application Requirements: Application, financial need analysis, references, transcript. *Deadline:* September 23.

Contact: Robert Rockmaker, Executive Secretary
Aviation Council of Pennsylvania
3111 Arcadia Avenue
Allentown, PA 18103-6903
Phone: 610-797-6911
Fax: 610-797-8238
E-mail: info@acpfly.com

AVIATION DISTRIBUTORS AND MANUFACTURERS ASSOCIATION INTERNATIONAL   http://www.adma.org

ADMA SCHOLARSHIP

Scholarship to provide assistance to students pursuing careers in the aviation field. Those enrolled in an accredited Aviation program may be eligible.

Academic Fields/Career Goals: Aviation/Aerospace.

Award: Scholarship for use in junior or senior years. *Number:* 1. *Amount:* up to $2000.

Eligibility Requirements: Applicant must be enrolled or expecting to enroll full-time at a two-year or four-year institution. Applicant must have 3.0 GPA or higher. Available to U.S. citizens.

Application Requirements: Application, essay, financial need analysis, references, transcript. *Deadline:* March 17.

Contact: ADMA
Aviation Distributors and Manufacturers Association International
100 North 20th Street, 4th Floor
Philadelphia, PA 19103-1443
Phone: 215-564-3484
Fax: 215-963-9785
E-mail: adma@fernley.com

BOY SCOUTS OF AMERICA - MUSKINGUM VALLEY COUNCIL   http://www.learning-for-life.org

NATIONAL AVIATION EXPLORER SCHOLARSHIPS

Scholarships available between $3000 and $10,000 annually to Aviation Explorers pursuing a career in the aviation industry. The intent of these scholarships is to identify and reward those individuals who best exemplify the qualities that lead to success in the aviation industry.

Academic Fields/Career Goals: Aviation/Aerospace.

Award: Scholarship for use in freshman, sophomore, junior, or senior years. *Number:* 5. *Amount:* $3000–$10,000.

Eligibility Requirements: Applicant must be age 18 and enrolled or expecting to enroll at a technical institution. Available to U.S. citizens.

Application Requirements: Application, essay, references. *Deadline:* March 31.

Contact: Boy Scouts of America - Muskingum Valley Council
1325 West Walnut Hill Lane, PO Box 152079
Irving, TX 75015-2079
Phone: 972-580-2433

CIVIL AIR PATROL, USAF AUXILIARY   http://www.capnhq.gov

MAJOR GENERAL LUCAS V. BEAU FLIGHT SCHOLARSHIPS SPONSORED BY THE ORDER OF DAEDALIANS

One-time scholarships of $2100 for active cadets of the Civil Air Patrol who desire a career in military aviation. Award is to be used toward flight training for a private pilot license. Must be 15 1/2-18 1/2 years of age on April 1st of the year for which applying. Must be an active CAP cadet officer. Not open to the general public.

Academic Fields/Career Goals: Aviation/Aerospace.

Award: Scholarship for use in freshman year; not renewable. *Number:* 5. *Amount:* $2100.

Eligibility Requirements: Applicant must be age 16-19; enrolled or expecting to enroll at an institution or university and single. Applicant or parent of applicant must be member of Civil Air Patrol. Available to U.S. citizens.

Application Requirements: Application, essay, interview, photo, references, test scores, transcript. *Deadline:* March 1.

Contact: Kelly Easterly, Assistant Program Manager
Civil Air Patrol, USAF Auxiliary
105 South Hansell Street, Building 714
Maxwell Air Force Base, AL 36112-6332
Phone: 334-953-8640
Fax: 334-953-6699
E-mail: cpr@capnhq.gov

COMMUNITY FOUNDATION OF CAPE COD   http://www.capecodfoundation.org

GEORGE E. PARMENTER AERONAUTICAL SCHOLARSHIP FUND

George E. Parmenter Aeronautical Scholarship Fund awards $1000 annually to a high school senior who has demonstrated a commitment to pursue a career directly related to aeronautics. For more details see Web site: http://www.capecodfoundation.org.

Academic Fields/Career Goals: Aviation/Aerospace.

Award: Scholarship for use in freshman, sophomore, junior, or senior years; not renewable. *Number:* 1. *Amount:* up to $1000.

Eligibility Requirements: Applicant must be high school student; planning to enroll or expecting to enroll full-time at a four-year institution or university and resident of Massachusetts. Available to U.S. citizens.

Application Requirements: Application, essay, financial need analysis, references, test scores, transcript. *Deadline:* April 1.

Contact: Pauline Greenberg, Scholarship Associate
Community Foundation of Cape Cod
259 Willow Street
Yarmouthport, MA 02675
Phone: 508-790-3040
Fax: 508-790-4069
E-mail: pgreenberg@capecodfoundation.org

DAEDALIAN FOUNDATION   http://www.daedalians.org

DAEDALIEAN FOUNDATION MATCHING SCHOLARSHIP PROGRAM

One-time award to students interested in pursuing a career in military aviation. Matching scholars program matches the dollars given by chapters throughout the U.S. Must submit flight/ROTC/CAP recommendation.

Academic Fields/Career Goals: Aviation/Aerospace.

Award: Scholarship for use in freshman, sophomore, junior, or senior years; not renewable. *Number:* 75–80. *Amount:* up to $2000.

Eligibility Requirements: Applicant must be enrolled or expecting to enroll full-time at a two-year or four-year institution or university. Available to U.S. citizens.

Application Requirements: Application, photo, references, test scores, flight/ROTC/CAP recommendation. *Deadline:* Continuous.

Contact: Carole Thomson, Program Executive Secretary
Daedalian Foundation
55 Main Circle, Building 676
Randolph AFB, TX 78148
Phone: 210-945-2113
Fax: 210-945-2112
E-mail: icarus@texas.net

EAA AVIATION FOUNDATION, INC.   http://www.eaa.org

DAVID ALAN QUICK SCHOLARSHIP

Renewable scholarship awarded to an undergraduate junior or senior in good standing. Applicant must be pursuing degree in aerospace or aeronautical engineering at an accredited college or university. Applications may be downloaded from the Web site http://www.eaa.org. Deadline is March 1. Must be an EAA member.

Academic Fields/Career Goals: Aviation/Aerospace.

Award: Scholarship for use in junior or senior years; renewable. *Number:* 1. *Amount:* $1000.

Eligibility Requirements: Applicant must be enrolled or expecting to enroll at a four-year institution or university. Applicant or parent of applicant must be member of Experimental Aircraft Association. Available to U.S. citizens.

Application Requirements: Application, essay, references, transcript. *Fee:* $5. *Deadline:* March 1.

Contact: See Web site for application.

EAA AVIATION ACHIEVEMENT SCHOLARSHIPS

Award for individuals active in recreational aviation endeavors to further their aviation education or training. Two awards in the amount of $500 each. Must submit two or more recommendations. $5 application fee. Please check Web site at http://www.eaa.org for criteria and to download official application. Must be an EAA member.

Academic Fields/Career Goals: Aviation/Aerospace.

Award: Scholarship for use in freshman, sophomore, junior, senior, graduate, or postgraduate years; not renewable. *Number:* 2. *Amount:* $500.

Eligibility Requirements: Applicant must be enrolled or expecting to enroll full or part-time at a two-year or four-year or technical institution or university. Applicant or parent of applicant must be member of Experimental Aircraft Association. Available to U.S. citizens.

EAA Aviation Foundation, Inc. (continued)

Application Requirements: Application, essay, financial need analysis, references, test scores, transcript. *Fee:* $5. *Deadline:* March 1.

Contact: EAA Scholarship Department
EAA Aviation Foundation, Inc.
PO Box 3086
Oshkosh, WI 54903-3086
Phone: 920-426-6823
Fax: 920-426-6560
E-mail: scholarships@eaa.org

H. P. "BUD" MILLIGAN AVIATION SCHOLARSHIP

Renewable scholarship for applicants enrolled in accredited aviation program. Financial need is not a requirement. Must be an EAA member. Applications may be downloaded from the Web site at http://www.eaa.org

Academic Fields/Career Goals: Aviation/Aerospace.

Award: Scholarship for use in freshman, sophomore, junior, or senior years; renewable. *Number:* 1. *Amount:* $1000.

Eligibility Requirements: Applicant must be enrolled or expecting to enroll at a two-year or four-year or technical institution or university. Applicant or parent of applicant must be member of Experimental Aircraft Association. Available to U.S. citizens.

Application Requirements: Application, essay, references, transcript. *Fee:* $5. *Deadline:* March 1.

Contact: See Web site for application.

HANSEN SCHOLARSHIP

Renewable scholarship of $1000 for student enrolled in accredited institution pursuing a degree in aerospace engineering or aeronautical engineering. Student must be in good standing; financial need not a requirement. Must be an EAA member. Applications may be downloaded from the Web site at http://www.eaa.org

Academic Fields/Career Goals: Aviation/Aerospace.

Award: Scholarship for use in freshman, sophomore, junior, or senior years; renewable. *Number:* 1. *Amount:* $1000.

Eligibility Requirements: Applicant must be enrolled or expecting to enroll at a four-year or technical institution or university. Applicant or parent of applicant must be member of Experimental Aircraft Association. Available to U.S. citizens.

Application Requirements: Application, essay, references, transcript. *Fee:* $5. *Deadline:* March 1.

Contact: See Web site for application.

HERBERT L. COX MEMORIAL SCHOLARSHIP

Award for students accepted by or attending an accredited college or university in pursuit of a degree leading to an aviation profession. Must show financial need. Self-supporting students encouraged to apply; recipients encouraged to reapply annually. One award, expected to exceed $500 annually. Must submit two or more recommendations. Deadline is March 1. $5 application fee. Please check Web site http://www.eaa.org for criteria and to download official application. Must be an EAA member.

Academic Fields/Career Goals: Aviation/Aerospace.

Award: Scholarship for use in freshman, sophomore, junior, or senior years; not renewable. *Number:* 1. *Amount:* $500.

Eligibility Requirements: Applicant must be enrolled or expecting to enroll full or part-time at a four-year institution or university. Applicant or parent of applicant must be member of Experimental Aircraft Association. Available to U.S. citizens.

Application Requirements: Application, essay, financial need analysis, references, test scores, transcript. *Fee:* $5. *Deadline:* March 1.

Contact: See Web site for application.

PAYZER SCHOLARSHIP

Must be accepted or enrolled in an accredited college, university, or postsecondary school with an emphasis on technical information. Awarded to an individual who is seeking a major and declares an intention to pursue a professional career in engineering, mathematics, or the physical/biological sciences. Deadline is March 1. $5 application fee. Please check Web site http://www.eaa.org for criteria and to download official application. Must be an EAA member.

Academic Fields/Career Goals: Aviation/Aerospace; Biology; Engineering/Technology; Physical Sciences and Math.

Award: Scholarship for use in freshman, sophomore, junior, senior, or graduate years; not renewable. *Number:* 1. *Amount:* $5000.

Eligibility Requirements: Applicant must be enrolled or expecting to enroll full-time at a four-year institution or university. Applicant or parent of applicant must be member of Experimental Aircraft Association. Available to U.S. citizens.

Application Requirements: Application, essay, references, test scores, transcript. *Fee:* $5. *Deadline:* March 1.

Contact: See Web site for application.

GENERAL AVIATION MANUFACTURERS ASSOCIATION
http://www.gama.aero

EDWARD W. STIMPSON "AVIATION EXCELLENCE" AWARD

One-time scholarship award for students who are graduating from high school and have been accepted to attend aviation college or university in upcoming year. See Web site at http://www.gama.aero for additional details.

Academic Fields/Career Goals: Aviation/Aerospace.

Award: Scholarship for use in freshman or senior years; not renewable. *Number:* 1. *Amount:* $500.

Eligibility Requirements: Applicant must be high school student and planning to enroll or expecting to enroll at an institution or university. Applicant must have 3.0 GPA or higher. Available to U.S. citizens.

Application Requirements: Application, essay, references, transcript. *Deadline:* April 28.

Contact: Bridgette Bailey, Director of Administration
General Aviation Manufacturers Association
1400 K Street, NW, Suite 801
Washington, DC 20005-2485
Phone: 202-393-1500
Fax: 202-842-4063
E-mail: bbailey@gama.aero

HAROLD S. WOOD AWARD FOR EXCELLENCE

One-time scholarship award for a university student who is attending a National Intercollegiate Flying Association (NIFA) school. Must have completed at least one semester of coursework. See Web site at http://www.gama.aero for additional details.

Academic Fields/Career Goals: Aviation/Aerospace.

Award: Scholarship for use in freshman, sophomore, junior, or senior years; not renewable. *Number:* 1. *Amount:* $1000.

Eligibility Requirements: Applicant must be enrolled or expecting to enroll at a four-year institution or university. Applicant must have 3.0 GPA or higher. Available to U.S. citizens.

Application Requirements: Application, references, transcript, nomination. *Deadline:* February 24.

Contact: Bridgette Bailey, Director of Administration
General Aviation Manufacturers Association
1400 K Street, NW, Suite 801
Washington, DC 20005-2485
Phone: 202-393-1500
Fax: 202-842-4063
E-mail: bbailey@gama.aero

HISPANIC COLLEGE FUND, INC.
http://www.hispanicfund.org

NATIONAL HISPANIC EXPLORERS SCHOLARSHIP PROGRAM
• See page 93

HISPANIC ENGINEER NATIONAL ACHIEVEMENT AWARDS CORPORATION (HENAAC)
http://www.henaac.org

HISPANIC ENGINEER NATIONAL ACHIEVEMENT AWARDS CORPORATION SCHOLARSHIP PROGRAM

Scholarships available to Hispanic students maintaining a 3.0 GPA. Must be studying an engineering or science related field. Deadline April 21. For more details and an application go to Web site: http://www.henaac.org

Academic Fields/Career Goals: Aviation/Aerospace; Biology; Chemical Engineering; Civil Engineering; Computer Science/Data Processing; Electrical Engineering/Electronics; Engineering/Technology; Materials Science, Engineering, and Metallurgy; Mechanical Engineering; Nuclear Science.

Award: Scholarship for use in freshman, sophomore, junior, senior, or graduate years; not renewable. *Number:* 12–20. *Amount:* $500–$5000.

Eligibility Requirements: Applicant must be of Hispanic heritage and enrolled or expecting to enroll full-time at a four-year institution or university. Applicant must have 3.0 GPA or higher. Available to U.S. and non-U.S. citizens.

Application Requirements: Application, essay, resume, references, transcript. *Deadline:* April 21.

Contact: Kathy Borunda-Barrera, Scholarship Selection Committee
Hispanic Engineer National Achievement Awards Corporation (HENAAC)
3900 Whiteside Street
Los Angeles, CA 90063
Phone: 323-262-0997
E-mail: kathy@henaac.org

ILLINOIS PILOTS ASSOCIATION   http://www.illinoispilots.com

ILLINOIS PILOTS ASSOCIATION MEMORIAL SCHOLARSHIP

Recipient must be a resident of Illinois established in an Illinois postsecondary institution in a full-time aviation-related program. The applicants will be judged by the scholarship committee and the award (usually $500 annually) will be sent directly to the recipient's school. For further details visit Web site: http://www.illinoispilots.com.

Academic Fields/Career Goals: Aviation/Aerospace.

Award: Scholarship for use in freshman, sophomore, junior, or senior years; not renewable. *Number:* 1. *Amount:* $500.

Eligibility Requirements: Applicant must be enrolled or expecting to enroll full-time at a two-year or four-year or technical institution or university; resident of Illinois and studying in Illinois. Available to U.S. citizens.

Application Requirements: Application, essay, photo, references, transcript. *Deadline:* April 1.

Contact: Ruth Frantz, Scholarship Committee Chairman
Illinois Pilots Association
40W297 Apache Lane
Huntley, IL 60142
Phone: 847-669-3821
Fax: 847-669-3822
E-mail: landings8e@aol.com

INSTRUMENTATION, SYSTEMS, AND AUTOMATION SOCIETY (ISA)   http://www.isa.org

INSTRUMENTATION, SYSTEMS, AND AUTOMATION SOCIETY (ISA) SCHOLARSHIP PROGRAM

The ISA grants scholarships worldwide to full-time students studying in technical fields related to instrumentation systems and automation. Minimum 3.0 GPA required. Applications available at http://www.isa.org

Academic Fields/Career Goals: Aviation/Aerospace; Chemical Engineering; Electrical Engineering/Electronics; Engineering/Technology; Engineering-Related Technologies; Heating, Air-Conditioning, and Refrigeration Mechanics; Mechanical Engineering.

Award: Scholarship for use in sophomore, junior, senior, or graduate years; not renewable. *Number:* 5–15. *Amount:* $500–$5000.

Eligibility Requirements: Applicant must be enrolled or expecting to enroll full-time at a two-year or four-year or technical institution or university. Applicant must have 3.0 GPA or higher. Available to U.S. and non-U.S. citizens.

Application Requirements: Application, essay, references, self-addressed stamped envelope, transcript. *Deadline:* varies.

Contact: Michaela Johnson-Tena, ISA Educational Foundation ÔÇô Scholarship Committee
Instrumentation, Systems, and Automation Society (ISA)
67 Alexander Drive
Research Triangle Park, NC 27709

INTERNATIONAL SOCIETY FOR OPTICAL ENGINEERING-SPIE   http://www.spie.org/info/scholarships

SPIE EDUCATIONAL SCHOLARSHIPS IN OPTICAL SCIENCE AND ENGINEERING

• *See page 93*

INTERNATIONAL SOCIETY OF WOMEN AIRLINE PILOTS (ISA+21)   http://www.iswap.org

INTERNATIONAL SOCIETY OF WOMEN AIRLINE PILOTS AIRLINE SCHOLARSHIPS

Scholarships are available to women who are pursuing careers as airline pilots. All applicants must demonstrate financial need. Must have U.S. FAA Commercial Pilot Certificate with an Instrument Rating and First Class Medical Certificate. AIRLINE Scholarship applicants must have a current FE written. Type Rating awards require an ATP Certificate. Sponsors may stipulate additional requirements. Deadline is December 10.

Academic Fields/Career Goals: Aviation/Aerospace.

Award: Scholarship for use in freshman, sophomore, junior, or senior years; not renewable. *Number:* up to 5. *Amount:* varies.

Eligibility Requirements: Applicant must be age 21; enrolled or expecting to enroll at an institution or university and female. Applicant must have 3.5 GPA or higher. Available to U.S. and non-U.S. citizens.

Application Requirements: Application, autobiography, financial need analysis, interview, photo, resume, references, transcript, copies of all pilot and medical certificates, copy of tax return. *Deadline:* December 10.

Contact: Beverly Sinclair, Scholarship Chairwoman
International Society of Women Airline Pilots (ISA+21)
2457-F South Victor Street
Aurora, CO 80014

INTERNATIONAL SOCIETY OF WOMEN AIRLINE PILOTS FINANCIAL SCHOLARSHIP

Scholarship available to ISA members and nonmembers. Program disburses cash awards towards pilot certificates, ratings, and type ratings to qualifying women. This award is used solely for advanced pilot ratings. All applicants must meet FAA Medical requirements for CLASS I Medical certificate. Visit Web site at http://www.iswap.org for additional information and deadlines.

Academic Fields/Career Goals: Aviation/Aerospace.

Award: Scholarship for use in freshman, sophomore, junior, or senior years; not renewable. *Number:* 1. *Amount:* varies.

Eligibility Requirements: Applicant must be age 21; enrolled or expecting to enroll full-time at an institution or university and female. Applicant must have 3.5 GPA or higher. Available to U.S. and non-U.S. citizens.

Application Requirements: Application, autobiography, financial need analysis, interview, photo, resume, references, transcript, copies of all pilot and medical certificates, copy of tax return. *Deadline:* December 10.

Contact: Beverly Sinclair, Scholarship Chairwoman
International Society of Women Airline Pilots (ISA+21)
2457-F South Victor Street
Aurora, CO 80014

INTERNATIONAL SOCIETY OF WOMEN AIRLINE PILOTS FIORENZA DE BERNARDI MERIT SCHOLARSHIP

Scholarship available to ISA members and nonmembers. Program disburses cash awards towards pilot certificates, ratings, and type ratings to qualifying women. Award for applicants that do not meet the requirements for the Career Scholarship. All applicants must meet FAA Medical requirements for CLASS I Medical certificate. Visit Web site at http://www.iswap.org for additional information and deadlines.

Academic Fields/Career Goals: Aviation/Aerospace.

Award: Scholarship for use in freshman, sophomore, junior, or senior years; not renewable. *Number:* 1. *Amount:* varies.

Eligibility Requirements: Applicant must be age 21; enrolled or expecting to enroll at an institution or university and female. Applicant must have 3.5 GPA or higher. Available to U.S. and non-U.S. citizens.

International Society of Women Airline Pilots (ISA+21) (continued)

Application Requirements: Application, autobiography, financial need analysis, interview, photo, resume, references, transcript, copy of tax returns. *Deadline:* December 10.

Contact: Beverly Sinclair, Scholarship Chairwoman
International Society of Women Airline Pilots (ISA+21)
2457-F South Victor Street
Aurora, CO 80014
E-mail: isa21scholarbev@aol.com

INTERNATIONAL SOCIETY OF WOMEN AIRLINE PILOTS GRACE MCADAMS HARRIS SCHOLARSHIP

Scholarship available to ISA members. Program disburses cash awards towards pilot certificates, ratings, and type ratings to qualifying women. This award may fund any ISA scholarship if the applicant has demonstrated exceptional spirit and attitude under difficult circumstances as it pertains to the field of aviation. All applicants must meet FAA Medical requirements for CLASS I Medical certificate. Visit Web site at http://www.iswap.org for additional information and deadlines.

Academic Fields/Career Goals: Aviation/Aerospace.

Award: Scholarship for use in freshman, sophomore, junior, or senior years; not renewable. *Number:* 1. *Amount:* varies.

Eligibility Requirements: Applicant must be age 21; enrolled or expecting to enroll at an institution or university and female. Applicant must have 3.5 GPA or higher. Available to U.S. and non-U.S. citizens.

Application Requirements: Application, autobiography, financial need analysis, interview, photo, references, transcript, copy of tax returns. *Deadline:* December 10.

Contact: Beverly Sinclair, Scholarship Chairwoman
International Society of Women Airline Pilots (ISA+21)
2457-F South Victor Street
Aurora, CO 80014
E-mail: isa21scholarbev@aol.com

INTERNATIONAL SOCIETY OF WOMEN AIRLINE PILOTS HOLLY MULLENS MEMORIAL SCHOLARSHIP

Scholarship available to ISA members and nonmembers. Program disburses cash awards towards pilot certificates, ratings, and type ratings to qualifying women. Award for single mother applicants. All applicants must meet FAA Medical requirements for CLASS I Medical certificate. Visit Web site at http://www.iswap.org for additional information and deadlines.

Academic Fields/Career Goals: Aviation/Aerospace.

Award: Scholarship for use in freshman, sophomore, junior, or senior years; not renewable. *Number:* 1. *Amount:* varies.

Eligibility Requirements: Applicant must be age 21; enrolled or expecting to enroll at an institution or university and female. Applicant must have 3.5 GPA or higher. Available to U.S. and non-U.S. citizens.

Application Requirements: Application, autobiography, financial need analysis, interview, references, transcript. *Deadline:* December 10.

Contact: Beverly Sinclair, Scholarship Chairwoman
International Society of Women Airline Pilots (ISA+21)
2457-F South Victor Street
Aurora, CO 80014
E-mail: isa21scholarbev@aol.com

INTERNATIONAL SOCIETY OF WOMEN AIRLINE PILOTS NORTH CAROLINA FINANCIAL SCHOLARSHIP

Scholarship available to ISA members and nonmembers. Program disburses cash awards towards pilot certificates, ratings, and type ratings to qualifying women. Must be a North Carolina resident interested in a career with the airline world. All applicants must meet FAA Medical requirements for CLASS I Medical certificate. Visit Web site at http://www.iswap.org for additional information and deadline is December 10.

Academic Fields/Career Goals: Aviation/Aerospace.

Award: Scholarship for use in freshman, sophomore, junior, or senior years; not renewable. *Number:* 1.

Eligibility Requirements: Applicant must be age 21; enrolled or expecting to enroll at an institution or university; female and resident of North Carolina. Applicant must have 3.5 GPA or higher. Available to U.S. and non-U.S. citizens.

Application Requirements: Application, autobiography, financial need analysis, interview, photo, resume, references, transcript, copy of tax return. *Deadline:* December 10.

Contact: Beverly Sinclair, Scholarship Chairwoman
International Society of Women Airline Pilots (ISA+21)
2457-F South Victor Street
Aurora, CO 80014

LINCOLN COMMUNITY FOUNDATION
http://www.lcf.org

LAWRENCE "LARRY" FRAZIER MEMORIAL SCHOLARSHIP

Scholarship for graduating seniors and former graduates of a high school in Nebraska who, upon graduation, intend to pursue a career in the field of aviation, insurance, or law. Applicants must attend a two- or four-year college or university in Nebraska. Preferred applicants will have experience in debate and participated in Girl Scouts or Boy Scouts during her/his youth.

Academic Fields/Career Goals: Aviation/Aerospace; Business/Consumer Services; Law/Legal Services.

Award: Scholarship for use in freshman, sophomore, junior, or senior years; not renewable. *Number:* 1. *Amount:* $500–$2000.

Eligibility Requirements: Applicant must be enrolled or expecting to enroll full-time at a two-year or four-year institution or university; resident of Nebraska and studying in Nebraska. Applicant must have 2.5 GPA or higher. Available to U.S. citizens.

Application Requirements: Application, essay, financial need analysis, test scores, transcript. *Deadline:* April 15.

Contact: Nebraska Chapter, Charter Property Casualty Underwriters, c/o Mark Clymer
Lincoln Community Foundation
Allied Insurance, PO Box 80758
Lincoln, NE 68501

NASA DELAWARE SPACE GRANT CONSORTIUM
http://www.delspace.org

NASA DELAWARE SPACE GRANT UNDERGRADUATE TUITION SCHOLARSHIP
• See page 94

NASA IDAHO SPACE GRANT CONSORTIUM
http://isgc.uidaho.edu

NASA IDAHO SPACE GRANT CONSORTIUM SCHOLARSHIP PROGRAM
• See page 94

NASA MINNESOTA SPACE GRANT CONSORTIUM
http://www.aem.umn.edu/msgc

MINNESOTA SPACE GRANT CONSORTIUM

Between twenty-five and fifty $1000 scholarships are awarded to students registered with MN colleges and universities who belong to the MNSGC consortium. Preference is given to students currently involved in aerospace science or engineering. Minimum 3.0 GPA required. Must be U.S. citizen. For more details see Web site: http://www.aem.umn.edu/msgc or http://calspace.ucsd.edu/spacegrant/

Academic Fields/Career Goals: Aviation/Aerospace; Computer Science/Data Processing; Engineering/Technology; Physical Sciences and Math.

Award: Scholarship for use in sophomore, junior, senior, graduate, or postgraduate years; renewable. *Number:* 25–50. *Amount:* up to $1000.

Eligibility Requirements: Applicant must be enrolled or expecting to enroll full-time at a two-year or four-year institution or university and studying in Minnesota. Applicant must have 3.0 GPA or higher. Available to U.S. citizens.

Application Requirements: Application, references, transcript. *Deadline:* April 1.

Contact: Department of Aerospace Engineering
NASA Minnesota Space Grant Consortium
107 Akerman Hall, 110 Union Street SE
Minneapolis, MN 55455
Phone: 612-626-9295
E-mail: mnsgc@aem.umn.edu

NASA MONTANA SPACE GRANT CONSORTIUM
http://www.spacegrant.montana.edu

MONTANA SPACE GRANT SCHOLARSHIP PROGRAM

Awards are made on a competitive basis to students enrolled in fields of study relevant to the aerospace sciences and engineering. Must be U.S. citizen enrolled as full-time student at a Montana Consortium campus.

Academic Fields/Career Goals: Aviation/Aerospace; Biology; Chemical Engineering; Civil Engineering; Computer Science/Data Processing; Electrical Engineering/Electronics; Engineering/Technology; Mathematics; Mechanical Engineering; Science, Technology, and Society.

Award: Scholarship for use in freshman, sophomore, junior, or senior years; not renewable. *Number:* 15–20. *Amount:* up to $1000.

Eligibility Requirements: Applicant must be enrolled or expecting to enroll full-time at a two-year or four-year institution or university and studying in Montana. Available to U.S. citizens.

Application Requirements: Application, applicant must enter a contest, essay, references, transcript. *Deadline:* April 3.

Contact: Clarice Koby, Program Coordinator
NASA Montana Space Grant Consortium
416 Cobleigh Hall, MSU - Bozeman, PO Box 173835
Bozeman, MT 59717-3835
Phone: 406-994-4223
Fax: 406-994-4452
E-mail: koby@spacegrant.montana.edu

NASA NEBRASKA SPACE GRANT CONSORTIUM
http://nasa.unomaha.edu

NASA NEBRASKA SPACE GRANT

Undergraduate and graduate students attending any of the academic affiliates in Nebraska of the NASA Nebraska Space Grant are eligible for financial assistance in the form of scholarships and fellowships. These funds assist students pursuing research with faculty or coursework in the aerospace and aeronautics fields. Must be U.S. citizen. The numbers and amounts are varies.

Academic Fields/Career Goals: Aviation/Aerospace; Biology; Communications; Computer Science/Data Processing; Earth Science; Electrical Engineering/Electronics; Engineering/Technology; Engineering-Related Technologies; Natural Sciences; Physical Sciences and Math; Science, Technology, and Society; Transportation.

Award: Scholarship for use in freshman, sophomore, junior, senior, or graduate years; not renewable. *Number:* 5. *Amount:* $250–$750.

Eligibility Requirements: Applicant must be enrolled or expecting to enroll full or part-time at a four-year institution or university and studying in Nebraska. Available to U.S. citizens.

Application Requirements: Application, transcript, proof of citizenship. *Deadline:* April 30.

Contact: Mary Fink, Coordinator
NASA Nebraska Space Grant Consortium
Aviation Institute, Allwine Hall 22
6001 Dodge Street
Omaha, NE 68182-0589
Phone: 402-554-3772
Fax: 402-554-3781
E-mail: nasa@unomaha.edu

NASA NEVADA SPACE GRANT CONSORTIUM
http://www.unr.edu/spacegrant

UNIVERSITY AND COMMUNITY COLLEGE SYSTEM OF NEVADA NASA SPACE GRANT AND FELLOWSHIP PROGRAM

Nevada Space Grant provides graduate fellowships and undergraduate scholarship to qualified student majoring in aerospace science, technology and related fields. Must be Nevada resident studying at a Nevada college/university. Minimum 2.5 GPA required.

Academic Fields/Career Goals: Aviation/Aerospace; Chemical Engineering; Computer Science/Data Processing; Electrical Engineering/Electronics; Engineering/Technology; Meteorology/Atmospheric Science; Physical Sciences and Math.

Award: Scholarship for use in freshman, sophomore, junior, or graduate years; renewable. *Number:* 1–20. *Amount:* $2500–$30,000.

Eligibility Requirements: Applicant must be enrolled or expecting to enroll full-time at a two-year or four-year institution or university; resident of Nevada and studying in Nevada. Available to U.S. citizens.

Application Requirements: Application, autobiography, essay, resume, references, transcript, project proposal, budget. *Deadline:* March 15.

Contact: Lori Rountree, Nevada Space Grant Consortium
NASA Nevada Space Grant Consortium
University of Nevada, Reno MS/172
Reno, NV 89557-0138
Phone: 775-784-6261
E-mail: lori@mines.unr.edu

NASA VERMONT SPACE GRANT CONSORTIUM
http://www.vtspacegrant.org

VERMONT SPACE GRANT CONSORTIUM SCHOLARSHIP PROGRAM
• See page 94

NASA VIRGINIA SPACE GRANT CONSORTIUM
http://www.vsgc.odu.edu

AEROSPACE UNDERGRADUATE RESEARCH SCHOLARSHIPS

Scholarships designated for undergraduate students pursuing any field of study with aerospace relevance. Must attend one of the five Virginia Space Grant colleges and universities, with at least two years of undergraduate degree completed. Applicant must have minimum 3.0 GPA. Please refer to Web site for further details: http://www.vsgc.odu.edu

Academic Fields/Career Goals: Aviation/Aerospace.

Award: Scholarship for use in freshman, sophomore, junior, or senior years; not renewable. *Number:* varies. *Amount:* $8500.

Eligibility Requirements: Applicant must be enrolled or expecting to enroll full-time at a four-year institution or university and studying in Virginia. Applicant must have 3.0 GPA or higher. Available to U.S. citizens.

Application Requirements: Application, essay, resume, references, transcript. *Deadline:* February 6.

Contact: Chris Carter, Educational Programs Manager
NASA Virginia Space Grant Consortium
Old Dominion University Peninsula Center
600 Butler Farm Road
Hampton, VA 23666
Phone: 757-766-5210
Fax: 757-766-5205
E-mail: cxcarter@odu.edu

VIRGINIA SPACE GRANT CONSORTIUM COMMUNITY COLLEGE SCHOLARSHIPS

Scholarships designated for Virginia community college students studying technological fields involving aerospace. Applicant must be U.S. citizen with a minimum GPA of 3.0. Please refer to Web site for further details: http://www.vsgc.odu.edu.

Academic Fields/Career Goals: Aviation/Aerospace; Engineering/Technology.

Award: Scholarship for use in freshman, sophomore, junior, graduate, or postgraduate years; not renewable. *Number:* varies. *Amount:* $1500.

Eligibility Requirements: Applicant must be enrolled or expecting to enroll full-time at a two-year or four-year institution or university and studying in Virginia. Applicant must have 3.0 GPA or higher. Available to U.S. citizens.

Application Requirements: Application, essay, resume, references, transcript. *Deadline:* February 27.

Contact: Chris Carter, Educational Programs Manager
NASA Virginia Space Grant Consortium
Old Dominion University Peninsula Center
600 Butler Farm Road
Hampton, VA 23666
Phone: 757-766-5210
Fax: 757-766-5205
E-mail: cxcarter@odu.edu

VIRGINIA SPACE GRANT CONSORTIUM TEACHER EDUCATION SCHOLARSHIPS

Scholarships designated for students enrolled at a Virginia Space Grant college or university in a program that will lead to teacher certification in a

NASA Virginia Space Grant Consortium (continued)

pre-college setting. Students may apply as graduating high school seniors, sophomore community college students or any undergraduate year. Please refer to Web site for further details: http://www.vsgc.odu.edu

Academic Fields/Career Goals: Aviation/Aerospace; Earth Science; Education; Engineering/Technology; Environmental Science; Physical Sciences and Math.

Award: Scholarship for use in sophomore year; not renewable. *Number:* varies. *Amount:* $1000.

Eligibility Requirements: Applicant must be enrolled or expecting to enroll full-time at a two-year or four-year institution or university and studying in Virginia. Applicant must have 3.0 GPA or higher. Available to U.S. citizens.

Application Requirements: Application, essay, resume, references, transcript. *Deadline:* February 27.

Contact: Chris Carter, Educational Programs Manager
NASA Virginia Space Grant Consortium
Old Dominion University Peninsula Center
600 Butler Farm Road
Hampton, VA 23666
Phone: 757-766-5210
Fax: 757-766-5205
E-mail: cxcarter@odu.edu

NASA WEST VIRGINIA SPACE GRANT CONSORTIUM   http://www.nasa.wvu.edu

WEST VIRGINIA SPACE GRANT CONSORTIUM UNDERGRADUATE SCHOLARSHIP PROGRAM

Scholarships intended to support undergraduate students pursuing an aerospace related degree. Students are given opportunities to work with faculty members within their major department on research projects, or students may participate in the Consortium Challenge Program. Please refer to Web site for further details: http://www.nasa.wvu.edu.

Academic Fields/Career Goals: Aviation/Aerospace; Computer Science/Data Processing; Earth Science; Energy and Power Engineering; Engineering/Technology; Engineering-Related Technologies; Environmental Science; Meteorology/Atmospheric Science; Natural Sciences; Nuclear Science; Physical Sciences and Math.

Award: Scholarship for use in freshman, sophomore, junior, or senior years; not renewable. *Number:* varies. *Amount:* $1000–$2000.

Eligibility Requirements: Applicant must be enrolled or expecting to enroll at a four-year institution or university; resident of West Virginia and studying in West Virginia. Available to U.S. citizens.

Application Requirements: Application. *Deadline:* March 3.

Contact: Candey Ramsey, Program Director
NASA West Virginia Space Grant Consortium
PO Box 6070
Morgantown, WV 26506-6070
Phone: 304-293-4099 Ext. 3737
Fax: 304-293-4970
E-mail: candy.ramsey@mail.wvu.edu

NASA WISCONSIN SPACE GRANT CONSORTIUM   http://www.uwgb.edu/WSGC

WISCONSIN SPACE GRANT CONSORTIUM UNDERGRADUATE RESEARCH PROGRAM

One-time award of up to $3500 for a U.S. citizen enrolled full-time, admitted to, or applying to any undergraduate program at a Wisconsin Space Grant Consortium (WSGC) college or university. Award goes to a student to create and implement their own small research study. Minimum 3.0 GPA required. Submit proposal with budget. Application deadline is February 7. Please refer to Web site for more information: http://www.uwgb.edu/wsgc

Academic Fields/Career Goals: Aviation/Aerospace.

Award: Grant for use in freshman, sophomore, junior, or senior years; not renewable. *Number:* varies. *Amount:* up to $3500.

Eligibility Requirements: Applicant must be enrolled or expecting to enroll full-time at a four-year institution or university; resident of Wisconsin and studying in Wisconsin. Applicant must have 3.0 GPA or higher. Available to U.S. citizens.

Application Requirements: Application, references, transcript, proposal with budget. *Deadline:* February 7.

Contact: Thomas Bray, Associate Director of Fellowships
NASA Wisconsin Space Grant Consortium
2420 Nicolet Drive
Green Bay, WI 54311-7001
Phone: 920-465-2108
Fax: 920-465-2376
E-mail: wsgc@uwgb.edu

WISCONSIN SPACE GRANT CONSORTIUM UNDERGRADUATE SCHOLARSHIP PROGRAM

Scholarship of up to $1500 for a U.S. citizen enrolled full-time in, admitted to, or applying to any undergraduate program at a Wisconsin Space Grant Consortium (WSGC) college or university. Awards will be given to students with outstanding potential in programs of aerospace, space science, or other interdisciplinary space-related studies. Minimum 3.0 GPA required. Deadline is February 7. Please refer to Web site for more information: http://www.uwgb.edu/wsgc

Academic Fields/Career Goals: Aviation/Aerospace.

Award: Scholarship for use in freshman, sophomore, junior, or senior years; not renewable. *Number:* varies. *Amount:* up to $1500.

Eligibility Requirements: Applicant must be enrolled or expecting to enroll full-time at a four-year institution or university; resident of Wisconsin and studying in Wisconsin. Applicant must have 3.0 GPA or higher. Available to U.S. citizens.

Application Requirements: Application, essay, references, transcript. *Deadline:* February 7.

Contact: Thomas Bray, Associate Director of Fellowships
NASA Wisconsin Space Grant Consortium
2420 Nicolet Drive
Green Bay, WI 54311-7001
Phone: 920-465-2108
Fax: 920-465-2376
E-mail: wsgc@uwgb.edu

NATIONAL AIR TRANSPORTATION ASSOCIATION FOUNDATION   http://www.nata.aero

DAN L. MEISINGER, SR. MEMORIAL LEARN TO FLY SCHOLARSHIP

A $2500 scholarship is available to students currently enrolled in an aviation program. Must be a high academic achiever. Application must be postmarked by the last Friday in November. For more details see Web site: http://www.nata-online.org

Academic Fields/Career Goals: Aviation/Aerospace.

Award: Scholarship for use in freshman, sophomore, junior, or senior years; not renewable. *Number:* 1. *Amount:* up to $1250.

Eligibility Requirements: Applicant must be age 18; enrolled or expecting to enroll full-time at a four-year institution or university and resident of Illinois, Kansas, or Missouri. Available to U.S. and non-U.S. citizens.

Application Requirements: Application, interview, references, test scores, transcript. *Fee:* $5. *Deadline:* varies.

Contact: Amy Koranda, Manager - Education and Training
National Air Transportation Association Foundation
National Air Transportation Foundation, 4226 King Street
Alexandria, VA 22302
Phone: 703-845-9000
E-mail: akoranda@nata-online.org

JOHN E. GODWIN, JR. MEMORIAL SCHOLARSHIP AWARD

A $2500 scholarship is available to students currently enrolled in an aviation program. Must be a high academic achiever. Application must be postmarked by the last Friday in November. For more details see Web site: http://www.nata-online.org.

Academic Fields/Career Goals: Aviation/Aerospace.

Award: Scholarship for use in freshman, sophomore, junior, or senior years; not renewable. *Number:* 1. *Amount:* up to $2500.

Eligibility Requirements: Applicant must be age 18 and enrolled or expecting to enroll full-time at a four-year institution or university. Available to U.S. and non-U.S. citizens.

Application Requirements: Application, interview, references, test scores, transcript. *Fee:* $5. *Deadline:* varies.

Contact: Amy Koranda, Manager - Education and Training
National Air Transportation Association Foundation
4226 King Street
Alexandria, VA 22302
Phone: 703-845-9000
Fax: 703-845-8176
E-mail: akoranda@nata-online.org

NATA BUSINESS SCHOLARSHIP

Scholarship available for education or training to establish a career in the business aviation industry. Applicable education includes any aviation-related two-year, four-year or graduate degree program at an accredited college or university. Must be 18 years of age or older, be nominated and endorsed by a representative of a Regular or Associate Member Company of the NATA. Application packet postmarked no later than the last Friday in December.

Academic Fields/Career Goals: Aviation/Aerospace.

Award: Scholarship for use in freshman, sophomore, junior, senior, or graduate years. *Amount:* up to $2500.

Eligibility Requirements: Applicant must be enrolled or expecting to enroll at a two-year or four-year institution or university. Available to U.S. citizens.

Application Requirements: Application, essay, resume, transcript. *Fee:* $5. *Deadline:* varies.

Contact: Amy Koranda, Manager - Education and Training
National Air Transportation Association Foundation
4226 King Street
Alexandria, VA 22302
Phone: 703-845-9000
Fax: 703-845-8176
E-mail: akoranda@nata-online.org

PIONEERS OF FLIGHT SCHOLARSHIP PROGRAM

Two $1000 scholarships are available to college students currently enrolled in an aviation program. Must be a high academic achiever. Application must be postmarked by the last Friday in December. For more details see Web site: http://www.nata-online.org.

Academic Fields/Career Goals: Aviation/Aerospace.

Award: Scholarship for use in sophomore or junior years; not renewable. *Number:* 2. *Amount:* up to $1000.

Eligibility Requirements: Applicant must be age 18 and enrolled or expecting to enroll full-time at a four-year institution or university. Available to U.S. and non-U.S. citizens.

Application Requirements: Application, interview, references, test scores, transcript. *Fee:* $5. *Deadline:* varies.

Contact: Gregory Schwab, Chair, Department of Aerospace
Technology, TC 216
National Air Transportation Association Foundation
Indiana State University
Terre Haute, IN 47809
E-mail: aeschwab@isugw.indstate.edu

NATIONAL BUSINESS AVIATION ASSOCIATION, INC.　　　http://www.nbaa.org/scholarships

NBAA INTERNATIONAL OPERATORS SCHOLARSHIP

NBAA International Operators Committee is dedicated to promoting education and training for individuals to increase safety and professionalism. One-time $5000 scholarship offered to one or more recipients for this purpose. Scholarship will be awarded at the Annual International Operators Conference. Include with application: 500 word essay explaining how this scholarship will help the applicant achieve their international aviation career goals, statement of the funds required to achieve these goals, and at least one professional letter of recommendation, preferably from an NBAA Member Company employee. For further information see Web site: http://www.nbaa.org

Academic Fields/Career Goals: Aviation/Aerospace.

Award: Scholarship for use in freshman, sophomore, junior, or senior years; not renewable. *Number:* 1. *Amount:* $5000.

Eligibility Requirements: Applicant must be enrolled or expecting to enroll full-time at a two-year or four-year or technical institution or university. Available to U.S. citizens.

Application Requirements: Application, essay, references. *Deadline:* January 31.

Contact: Jay Evans, Director, Operations
National Business Aviation Association, Inc.
1200 18th Street, NW, Suite 400
Washington, DC 20036-2527
Phone: 202-783-9353
Fax: 202-331-8364
E-mail: info@nbaa.org

NBAA JANICE K. BARDEN SCHOLARSHIP

One-time $1000 scholarship for students officially enrolled in NBAA/UAA (National Business Aviation Association/University Aviation Association) programs. Must be U.S. citizen, officially enrolled in an aviation-related program with 3.0 minimum GPA. Include with application: 250-word essay describing the applicant's interest and goals for a career in the business aviation industry; letter of recommendation from member of aviation department faculty at institution where applicant is enrolled. For further information, and to see a list of NBAA/UAA Member Colleges and Universities, visit Web site: http://www.nbaa.org.

Academic Fields/Career Goals: Aviation/Aerospace.

Award: Scholarship for use in sophomore, junior, senior, graduate, or postgraduate years; not renewable. *Number:* 5. *Amount:* $1000.

Eligibility Requirements: Applicant must be enrolled or expecting to enroll at a two-year or four-year institution or university. Applicant must have 3.0 GPA or higher. Available to U.S. citizens.

Application Requirements: Application, essay, resume, references, transcript. *Deadline:* November 1.

Contact: Jay Evans, Director, Operations
National Business Aviation Association, Inc.
1200 18th Street, NW, Suite 400
Washington, DC 20036-2527
Phone: 202-783-9353
Fax: 202-331-8364
E-mail: info@nbaa.org

NBAA LAWRENCE GINOCCHIO AVIATION SCHOLARSHIP

One-time $5000 scholarship for students officially enrolled in NBAA/UAA (National Business Aviation Association/University Aviation Association) programs. Must be officially enrolled in aviation-related program with 3.0 minimum GPA. Include with application: a 500 to 1,000 word essay describing interest in and goals for a career in the business aviation industry while demonstrating strength of character. Must also have 2 letters of recommendation, including one from member of aviation department faculty at institution where applicant is enrolled. A letter of recommendation from an NBAA Member Company representative is encouraged. For further information, and to see a list of NBAA/UAA Member Colleges and Universities, visit Web site: http://www.nbaa.org

Academic Fields/Career Goals: Aviation/Aerospace.

Award: Scholarship for use in sophomore, junior, senior, or graduate years; not renewable. *Number:* 5. *Amount:* $5000.

Eligibility Requirements: Applicant must be enrolled or expecting to enroll at a four-year institution or university. Applicant must have 3.0 GPA or higher. Available to U.S. citizens.

Application Requirements: Application, essay, resume, references, transcript, proof of enrollment. *Deadline:* August 1.

Contact: Jay Evans, Director, Operations
National Business Aviation Association, Inc.
1200 18th Street, NW, Suite 400
Washington, DC 20036-2527
Phone: 202-783-9353
Fax: 202-331-8364
E-mail: info@nbaa.org

NBAA WILLIAM M. FANNING MAINTENANCE SCHOLARSHIP

One-time award given to two students pursuing careers as maintenance technicians. One award will benefit a student who is currently enrolled in an accredited Airframe and Powerplant (A&P) program at an approved FAR Part 147 school. The second award will benefit an individual who is not currently enrolled but has been accepted into an A&P program. Include with

National Business Aviation Association, Inc. (continued)

application: a 250-word essay describing applicant's interest in and goals for a career in the aviation maintenance field. A letter of recommendation from an NBAA Member Company representative is encouraged.

Academic Fields/Career Goals: Aviation/Aerospace.

Award: Scholarship for use in freshman, sophomore, junior, senior, or graduate years; not renewable. *Number:* 2. *Amount:* $2500.

Eligibility Requirements: Applicant must be enrolled or expecting to enroll full-time at a two-year or four-year or technical institution or university. Available to U.S. citizens.

Application Requirements: Application, essay, resume, references, transcript. *Deadline:* August 1.

Contact: Jay Evans, Director, Operations
National Business Aviation Association, Inc.
1200 18th Street, NW, Suite 400
Washington, DC 20036-2527
Phone: 202-783-9353
Fax: 202-331-8364
E-mail: info@nbaa.org

U.S. AIRCRAFT INSURANCE GROUP PDP SCHOLARSHIP

One-time $1000 scholarship for applicants enrolled full-time in a college or university offering the NBAA (National Business Aviation Association) Professional Development Program (PDP). Must be U.S. citizen, officially enrolled in aviation-related program with 3.0 minimum GPA. Include with application: 250 word essay describing goals for a career in the business aviation flight department. A letter of recommendation from an NBAAA Member Company representative is encouraged. For further information, and to see a list of NBAA/UAA Member Colleges and Universities offering PDP curricula, visit Web site: http://www.nbaa.org.

Academic Fields/Career Goals: Aviation/Aerospace.

Award: Scholarship for use in sophomore, junior, senior, graduate, or postgraduate years; not renewable. *Number:* 3. *Amount:* $1000.

Eligibility Requirements: Applicant must be enrolled or expecting to enroll full-time at a two-year or four-year institution or university and studying in Arizona, Florida, Indiana, Michigan, Missouri, New Jersey, North Dakota, or Oklahoma. Applicant must have 3.0 GPA or higher. Available to U.S. citizens.

Application Requirements: Application, essay, resume, references, transcript, proof of enrollment. *Deadline:* August 1.

Contact: Jay Evans, Director, Operations
National Business Aviation Association, Inc.
1200 18th Street, NW, Suite 400
Washington, DC 20036-2527
Phone: 202-783-9353
Fax: 202-331-8364
E-mail: info@nbaa.org

NINETY-NINES, INC.   http://www.ninety-nines.org

AMELIA EARHART MEMORIAL CAREER SCHOLARSHIP FUND

Scholarships are awarded to members of The Ninety-Nines, Inc., who hold a current medical certificate appropriate for the use of the certificate sought. Applicants must meet the requirements for pilot currency (Flight Review or non-U.S. equivalent) and have financial need. Applicants must agree to complete the course, training and meet the requirements for ratings/certificates specific to the country where training will occur.

Academic Fields/Career Goals: Aviation/Aerospace.

Award: Scholarship for use in freshman, sophomore, junior, or senior years; not renewable. *Number:* varies. *Amount:* varies.

Eligibility Requirements: Applicant must be enrolled or expecting to enroll full-time at an institution or university and female. Available to U.S. and non-U.S. citizens.

Application Requirements: Application, financial need analysis, photo, resume, references. *Deadline:* December 1.

Contact: Charlene H. Falkenberg, Chairman, Permanent Trustee
Ninety-Nines, Inc.
618 South Washington Street
Hobart, IN 46342-5026
Phone: 219-942-8887
Fax: 219-942-8887
E-mail: charf@prodigy.net

NINETY-NINES, SAN FERNANDO VALLEY CHAPTER/VAN NUYS AIRPORT   http://sfv99s.org/

SAN FERNANDO VALLEY CHAPTER OF THE NINETY-NINES CAREER SCHOLARSHIP

Men and women pursuing a career in the aviation field are eligible for a $3,000 scholarship. Must reside in the Greater Los Angeles area and be over 21. Must be a U.S. citizen. Must attend a California school.

Academic Fields/Career Goals: Aviation/Aerospace; Transportation.

Award: Scholarship for use in freshman, sophomore, junior, senior, graduate, or postgraduate years; not renewable. *Number:* 3. *Amount:* $3000.

Eligibility Requirements: Applicant must be age 21; enrolled or expecting to enroll full or part-time at a two-year or four-year or technical institution or university; resident of California and studying in California. Applicant or parent of applicant must have employment or volunteer experience in air traffic controller field or aviation maintenance. Available to U.S. citizens.

Application Requirements: Application, essay, financial need analysis, interview, references, self-addressed stamped envelope, transcript. *Deadline:* April 23.

Contact: Jeanne Fenimore, Co-Chairman
Ninety-Nines, San Fernando Valley Chapter/Van Nuys Airport
PO Box 8160
Van Nuys, CA 91409-8160
Phone: 818-989-0081

OREGON STUDENT ASSISTANCE COMMISSION   http://www.osac.state.or.us

BRIAN L. MOODY MEMORIAL AVIATION SCHOLARSHIP

One-time award for aviation-related studies. Preference is for graduates of high schools in Baker, Grant, Morrow, Umatilla, Union, or Wallowa counties enrolled at least half time. Application deadline is March 1.

Academic Fields/Career Goals: Aviation/Aerospace.

Award: Scholarship for use in freshman, sophomore, junior, or senior years; renewable. *Number:* 2. *Amount:* $1000.

Eligibility Requirements: Applicant must be enrolled or expecting to enroll full or part-time at an institution or university and resident of Oregon. Available to U.S. citizens.

Application Requirements: Application, essay, financial need analysis, transcript, activities chart. *Deadline:* March 1.

Contact: Director of Grant Programs
Oregon Student Assistance Commission
1500 Valley River Drive, Suite 100
Eugene, OR 97401-7020
Phone: 800-452-8807 Ext. 7395

PALWAUKEE AIRPORT PILOTS ASSOCIATION   http://www.pwkpilots.org

PALWAUKEE AIRPORT PILOTS ASSOCIATION SCHOLARSHIP PROGRAM

Scholarship offered to Illinois individuals who are attending accredited programs in Illinois institutions pursuing a course of study in an aviation-related program. Applications on Web site: http://www.pwkpilots.org.

Academic Fields/Career Goals: Aviation/Aerospace.

Award: Scholarship for use in freshman, sophomore, junior, or senior years; not renewable. *Number:* 1. *Amount:* $500–$1000.

Eligibility Requirements: Applicant must be age 18; enrolled or expecting to enroll full or part-time at a two-year or four-year or technical institution or university; resident of Illinois and studying in Illinois. Applicant must have 2.5 GPA or higher. Available to U.S. citizens.

Application Requirements: Application, autobiography, references, transcript. *Deadline:* May 1.

Contact: Raymond Chou, Chairman, Scholarship Committee
Palwaukee Airport Pilots Association
1020 South Plant Road
Wheeling, IL 60090
Phone: 847-537-2580
Fax: 847-537-8183
E-mail: scholarship@pwkpilots.org

PROFESSIONAL AVIATION MAINTENANCE FOUNDATION   http://www.pama.org

PROFESSIONAL AVIATION MAINTENANCE FOUNDATION STUDENT SCHOLARSHIP PROGRAM

For students enrolled in an airframe and power plant licensing program. Must have a B average and have completed 25% of the program. Must reapply each year. Apply after July 1 and until October 31. For more details see Web site: http://www.pama.org.

Academic Fields/Career Goals: Aviation/Aerospace; Trade/Technical Specialties.

Award: Scholarship for use in freshman, sophomore, junior, or senior years; not renewable. *Number:* 10–30. *Amount:* up to $1000.

Eligibility Requirements: Applicant must be enrolled or expecting to enroll at a two-year or four-year or technical institution or university. Applicant must have 3.0 GPA or higher. Available to U.S. and non-U.S. citizens.

Application Requirements: Application, financial need analysis, references, self-addressed stamped envelope, transcript. *Deadline:* November 30.

Contact: Val Quartararo, Director of Membership
Professional Aviation Maintenance Foundation
717 Princess Street
Alexandria, VA 22314
Phone: 703-683-3171
Fax: 703-683-0018
E-mail: hq@pama.org

RHODE ISLAND PILOTS ASSOCIATION   http://www.ripilots.com

RHODE ISLAND PILOTS ASSOCIATION SCHOLARSHIP

A scholarship open to Rhode Island residents to begin or advance a career in aviation.

Academic Fields/Career Goals: Aviation/Aerospace.

Award: Scholarship for use in freshman, sophomore, junior, or senior years; not renewable. *Number:* 2–4. *Amount:* $500–$1000.

Eligibility Requirements: Applicant must be age 16; enrolled or expecting to enroll full or part-time at a two-year or four-year or technical institution and resident of Rhode Island. Available to U.S. citizens.

Application Requirements: Application, essay, financial need analysis, references, test scores, transcript. *Deadline:* February 24.

Contact: Rhode Island Pilots Association Scholarship
Rhode Island Pilots Association
644 Airport Road, Hangar One
Warwick, RI 02886
Phone: 401-568-3497
Fax: 401-568-5392
E-mail: ripaemail@aol.com

SOCIETY OF AUTOMOTIVE ENGINEERS   http://www.sae.org

BMW/SAE ENGINEERING SCHOLARSHIP

Renewable award for high school seniors with a minimum 3.75 GPA. Must be a U.S. citizen pursuing an engineering degree at an accredited four-year institution. Test scores must be in the 90th percentile in both math and verbal. Application should be retrieved from the SAE Web site at http://www.sae.org/students/stuschol.htm.

Academic Fields/Career Goals: Aviation/Aerospace; Chemical Engineering; Electrical Engineering/Electronics; Engineering/

Technology; Engineering-Related Technologies; Materials Science, Engineering, and Metallurgy; Mechanical Engineering.

Award: Scholarship for use in freshman, sophomore, junior, or senior years; renewable. *Number:* 1. *Amount:* up to $6000.

Eligibility Requirements: Applicant must be high school student and planning to enroll or expecting to enroll full-time at a four-year institution or university. Available to U.S. citizens.

Application Requirements: Application, essay, test scores, transcript. *Fee:* $6. *Deadline:* December 1.

Contact: Connie Harnish, SAE Educational Relations
Society of Automotive Engineers
400 Commonwealth Drive
Warrendale, PA 15096-0001
Phone: 724-772-4047
Fax: 724-776-0890
E-mail: connie@sae.org

EDWARD D. HENDRICKSON/SAE ENGINEERING SCHOLARSHIP

Applicants must have a 3.75 grade point average, rank in the 90th percentile in both math and critical reading on SAT I or composite ACT scores, and pursue an engineering degree accredited by ABET. One $4000 scholarship will be awarded at $1000 per year for four years. A 3.0 grade point average and continued engineering enrollment must be maintained to renew the scholarship.

Academic Fields/Career Goals: Aviation/Aerospace; Chemical Engineering; Electrical Engineering/Electronics; Engineering/Technology; Engineering-Related Technologies; Materials Science, Engineering, and Metallurgy; Mechanical Engineering.

Award: Scholarship for use in freshman, sophomore, junior, or senior years; renewable. *Number:* 1. *Amount:* $1000–$4000.

Eligibility Requirements: Applicant must be high school student and planning to enroll or expecting to enroll full-time at a four-year institution or university. Available to U.S. citizens.

Application Requirements: Application, essay, test scores, transcript. *Fee:* $6.

Contact: Connie Harnish, SAE Educational Relations
Society of Automotive Engineers
400 Commonwealth Drive
Warrendale, PA 15096-0001
Phone: 724-772-4047
Fax: 724-776-0890
E-mail: connie@sae.org

TMC/SAE DONALD D. DAWSON TECHNICAL SCHOLARSHIP

Renewable scholarship for high school seniors with a minimum 3.25 GPA. Transfer students from four-year colleges with a minimum 3.0 GPA or students from a postsecondary technical/vocational school with a minimum 3.5 GPA may also apply. Must be pursuing an engineering program at a post secondary institution. Application should be retrieved from SAE Web site http://www.sae.org/students/stuschol.htm

Academic Fields/Career Goals: Aviation/Aerospace; Chemical Engineering; Electrical Engineering/Electronics; Engineering/Technology; Engineering-Related Technologies; Materials Science, Engineering, and Metallurgy; Mechanical Engineering.

Award: Scholarship for use in freshman year; renewable. *Number:* 1. *Amount:* up to $1500.

Eligibility Requirements: Applicant must be enrolled or expecting to enroll full-time at a four-year institution or university. Available to U.S. citizens.

Application Requirements: Application, essay, test scores, transcript. *Fee:* $6. *Deadline:* varies.

Contact: Connie Harnish, SAE Educational Relations
Society of Automotive Engineers
400 Commonwealth Drive
Warrendale, PA 15096-0001
Phone: 724-772-4047
Fax: 724-776-0890
E-mail: connie@sae.org

SOCIETY OF MEXICAN AMERICAN ENGINEERS AND SCIENTISTS   http://www.maes-natl.org

GRE AND GRADUATE APPLICATIONS WAIVER
• See page 95

SOCIETY OF WOMEN ENGINEERS   http://www.swe.org

JUDITH RESNIK MEMORIAL SCHOLARSHIP

One-time award available to aerospace or astronautical engineering major at the sophomore, junior, or senior level. Must be a member of the Society of Women Engineers. Minimum 3.0 GPA required. Deadline: February 1.

Academic Fields/Career Goals: Aviation/Aerospace; Engineering/Technology.

Award: Scholarship for use in sophomore, junior, or senior years; not renewable. *Number:* 1. *Amount:* $2500.

Eligibility Requirements: Applicant must be enrolled or expecting to enroll at a four-year institution or university and female. Applicant or parent of applicant must be member of Society of Women Engineers. Applicant must have 3.0 GPA or higher. Available to U.S. citizens.

Application Requirements: Application, references, self-addressed stamped envelope, transcript. *Deadline:* February 1.

Contact: Suman Pa, Program Coordinator
Society of Women Engineers
230 E Ohio Street, Suite 400
Chicago, IL 60611-3265
Phone: 312-596-5223
Fax: 312-644-8557
E-mail: suman.patil@swe.org

NORTHROP GRUMMAN CORPORATION SCHOLARSHIPS

Scholarships awarded to female undergraduate students majoring in computer engineering, computer science, aeronautical/aerospace engineering, electrical engineering, industrial engineering, mechanical engineering, or manufacturing engineering.

Academic Fields/Career Goals: Aviation/Aerospace; Computer Science/Data Processing; Electrical Engineering/Electronics; Engineering/Technology; Materials Science, Engineering, and Metallurgy; Mechanical Engineering.

Award: Scholarship for use in freshman, junior, or senior years; not renewable. *Number:* 5. *Amount:* $5000.

Eligibility Requirements: Applicant must be enrolled or expecting to enroll full-time at a four-year institution or university and female. Applicant must have 3.0 GPA or higher. Available to U.S. citizens.

Application Requirements: Application. *Deadline:* varies.

Contact: Program Coordinator
E-mail: hq@swe.org

STUDENT PILOT NETWORK   http://www.studentpilot.net

STUDENT PILOT NETWORK-FLIGHT DREAM AWARD

Award is for General Aviation Pilot Flight Training. Open to all persons actively engaged in flight training at a registered SPN flight school. Must be a U.S. or Canadian citizen.

Academic Fields/Career Goals: Aviation/Aerospace.

Award: Grant for use in freshman, sophomore, junior, senior, graduate, or postgraduate years; renewable. *Number:* 1–3. *Amount:* $250–$750.

Eligibility Requirements: Applicant must be enrolled or expecting to enroll full or part-time at a two-year or four-year or technical institution. Available to U.S. and Canadian citizens.

Application Requirements: Application, essay. *Deadline:* November 15.

Contact: Mr. William Terry
Student Pilot Network
1830 Wallace Avenue, Suite 208
St. Charles, IL 60174
E-mail: info@studentpilot.net

TRANSPORTATION CLUBS INTERNATIONAL
http://www.transportationclubinternational.com

ALICE GLAISYER WARFIELD MEMORIAL SCHOLARSHIP

Award is available to currently enrolled students majoring in transportation, logistics, traffic management, or related fields. Available to citizens of the U.S., Canada, and Mexico.

Academic Fields/Career Goals: Aviation/Aerospace; Transportation.

Award: Scholarship for use in freshman, sophomore, junior, senior, graduate, or postgraduate years; not renewable. *Number:* 1. *Amount:* $1000.

Eligibility Requirements: Applicant must be enrolled or expecting to enroll full or part-time at a two-year or four-year or technical institution or university. Available to U.S. and non-U.S. citizens.

Application Requirements: Application, essay, photo, references, transcript. *Deadline:* April 30.

Contact: Bill Blair
Transportation Clubs International
7031 Manchester Street
PO Box 2223
Ocean Shores, WA 98569
E-mail: bblair@zimmerworldwide.com

DENNY LYDIC SCHOLARSHIP

Award is available to currently enrolled college students majoring in transportation, logistics, traffic management, or related fields. Available to citizens of the U.S., Canada, and Mexico.

Academic Fields/Career Goals: Aviation/Aerospace; Transportation.

Award: Scholarship for use in freshman, sophomore, junior, senior, graduate, or postgraduate years; not renewable. *Number:* 1. *Amount:* $500.

Eligibility Requirements: Applicant must be enrolled or expecting to enroll full or part-time at a two-year or four-year or technical institution or university. Available to U.S. and non-U.S. citizens.

Application Requirements: Application, essay, photo, references, transcript. *Deadline:* April 30.

Contact: Bill Blair
Transportation Clubs International
7031 Manchester Street
PO Box 2223
Ocean Shores, WA 98569
E-mail: bblair@zimmerworldwide.com

TEXAS TRANSPORTATION SCHOLARSHIP

Merit-based award for student who is at least a sophomore studying transportation, traffic management, and related fields. Must have been enrolled in a school in Texas during some phase of education (elementary, secondary, high school). Include photo. One-time scholarship of $1000. Submit three references. Available to citizens of the U.S., Canada, and Mexico.

Academic Fields/Career Goals: Aviation/Aerospace; Transportation.

Award: Scholarship for use in sophomore, junior, senior, graduate, or postgraduate years; not renewable. *Number:* 1. *Amount:* $1000.

Eligibility Requirements: Applicant must be enrolled or expecting to enroll full or part-time at a two-year or four-year or technical institution or university. Available to U.S. and non-U.S. citizens.

Application Requirements: Application, essay, photo, references, transcript. *Deadline:* April 30.

Contact: Bill Blair
Transportation Clubs International
7031 Manchester Street
PO Box 2223
Ocean Shores, WA 98569
E-mail: bblair@zimmerworldwide.com

TRANSPORTATION CLUBS INTERNATIONAL CHARLOTTE WOODS SCHOLARSHIP

Award available to enrolled college student majoring in transportation or traffic management. Must be member or dependent of a member of a Transportation Club which is a member of Transportation Clubs International. Must have completed at least one year of post-high school education. One-time award of $1000. Submit three references.

Academic Fields/Career Goals: Aviation/Aerospace; Transportation.

Award: Scholarship for use in freshman, sophomore, junior, senior, graduate, or postgraduate years; not renewable. *Number:* 1. *Amount:* $1000.

Eligibility Requirements: Applicant must be enrolled or expecting to enroll full or part-time at a two-year or four-year or technical institution or university. Applicant or parent of applicant must be member of Transportation Club International. Available to U.S. and non-U.S. citizens.

Application Requirements: Application, essay, photo, references, transcript. *Deadline:* April 30.

Contact: Bill Blair
Transportation Clubs International
15710 JFK Boulevard
Houston, TX 77032
E-mail: bblair@zimmerworldwide.com

TRANSPORTATION CLUBS INTERNATIONAL FRED A. HOOPER MEMORIAL SCHOLARSHIP

Merit-based award is available to currently enrolled college students majoring in traffic management, transportation, physical distribution, logistics, or a related field. Must have completed at least one year of post-high school education. One-time award of $1500. Submit three references. Available to citizens of the U.S., Canada, and Mexico.

Academic Fields/Career Goals: Aviation/Aerospace; Transportation.

Award: Scholarship for use in freshman, sophomore, junior, senior, graduate, or postgraduate years; not renewable. *Number:* 1. *Amount:* $1500.

Eligibility Requirements: Applicant must be enrolled or expecting to enroll full or part-time at a two-year or four-year or technical institution or university. Available to U.S. and non-U.S. citizens.

Application Requirements: Application, essay, photo, references, transcript. *Deadline:* April 30.

Contact: Bill Blair
Transportation Clubs International
7031 Manchester Street
PO Box 2223
Ocean Shores, WA 98569
E-mail: bblair@zimmerworldwide.com

TRANSPORTATION CLUBS INTERNATIONAL GINGER AND FRED DEINES CANADA SCHOLARSHIP

One-time award for student of Canadian heritage attending a four-year college or university in Canada or the U.S. and majoring in transportation, traffic management, logistics, or a related field. Academic merit is considered. Submit three references.

Academic Fields/Career Goals: Aviation/Aerospace; Transportation.

Award: Scholarship for use in freshman, sophomore, junior, senior, graduate, or postgraduate years; not renewable. *Number:* 1.

Eligibility Requirements: Applicant must be of Canadian heritage and enrolled or expecting to enroll full or part-time at a two-year or four-year or technical institution or university. Available to Canadian citizens.

Application Requirements: Application, essay, photo, references, transcript. *Deadline:* April 30.

Contact: Bill Blair
Transportation Clubs International
7031 Manchester Street
PO Box 2223
Ocean Shores, WA 98569
E-mail: bblair@zimmerworldwide.com

TRANSPORTATION CLUBS INTERNATIONAL GINGER AND FRED DEINES MEXICO SCHOLARSHIP

Scholarship for a student of Mexican nationality/residency who is enrolled at an institution in Mexico or the U.S. Must be preparing for a career in transportation. Must have completed at least one year of study. Submit photo and three references.

Academic Fields/Career Goals: Aviation/Aerospace; Transportation.

Award: Scholarship for use in freshman, sophomore, junior, senior, graduate, or postgraduate years; not renewable. *Number:* 1. *Amount:* $1500.

Eligibility Requirements: Applicant must be of Mexican heritage; Hispanic and enrolled or expecting to enroll full or part-time at a two-year or four-year or technical institution or university. Available to U.S. and non-Canadian citizens.

Application Requirements: Application, essay, photo, references, transcript. *Deadline:* April 30.

Contact: Bill Blair
Transportation Clubs International
7031 Manchester Street
PO Box 2223
Ocean Shores, WA 98569
E-mail: bblair@zimmerworldwide.com

UNIVERSITIES SPACE RESEARCH ASSOCIATION
http://www.usra.edu

UNIVERSITIES SPACE RESEARCH ASSOCIATION SCHOLARSHIP PROGRAM
• See page 96

UNIVERSITY AVIATION ASSOCIATION
http://www.aviation.siu.edu

JOSEPH FRASCA EXCELLENCE IN AVIATION SCHOLARSHIP

Established to encourage those who demonstrate the highest level of commitment to and achievement in aviation studies. Applicant must be a junior or senior currently enrolled in a UAA member institution. Must be FAA certified/qualified in either aviation maintenance or flight, have membership in at least one aviation organization, and be involved in aviation activities, projects, and events. Minimum 3.0 GPA required. Deadline is April 10.

Academic Fields/Career Goals: Aviation/Aerospace.

Award: Scholarship for use in junior or senior years; not renewable. *Number:* 2. *Amount:* $1500.

Eligibility Requirements: Applicant must be enrolled or expecting to enroll full or part-time at a four-year institution or university and must have an interest in designated field specified by sponsor. Applicant must have 3.0 GPA or higher. Available to U.S. citizens.

Application Requirements: Application, essay, financial need analysis, references, transcript, FAA certification. *Deadline:* April 10.

Contact: Dr. David A. NewMyer, Department Chair, Aviation Management and Flight
University Aviation Association
Southern Illinois University at Carbondale, College of Applied Sciences and Arts, 1365 Douglas Drive
Carbondale, IL 62901-6623
Phone: 618-453-8898
Fax: 618-453-4850
E-mail: newmyer@siu.edu

PAUL A. WHELAN AVIATION SCHOLARSHIP

One time award of $2000 given to sophomore, junior, senior or graduate. Must be a U.S. citizen. Must be enrolled in University Aviation Association member institution. 2.5 GPA required. FAA certification, membership in aviation related association preferred. Deadline is May 15.

Academic Fields/Career Goals: Aviation/Aerospace.

Award: Scholarship for use in sophomore, junior, or senior years; not renewable. *Amount:* $2000.

Eligibility Requirements: Applicant must be enrolled or expecting to enroll full or part-time at a four-year institution or university. Applicant must have 2.5 GPA or higher. Available to U.S. citizens.

Application Requirements: Application, essay, references, transcript, FAA certification. *Deadline:* May 15.

Contact: David A. NewMyer, Department Chair, Aviation Management and Flight
University Aviation Association
Southern Illinois University at Carbondale, College of Applied Sciences and Arts, 1365 Douglas Drive
Carbondale, IL 62901-6623
Phone: 618-453-8898
Fax: 618-453-7268
E-mail: newmyer@siu.edu

VERTICAL FLIGHT FOUNDATION   http://www.vtol.org

VERTICAL FLIGHT FOUNDATION SCHOLARSHIP

This award is available for undergraduate, graduate, or doctoral study in aerospace, electrical, or mechanical engineering. Undergraduates must be in junior or senior year. Applicants must have an interest in vertical flight technology.

Academic Fields/Career Goals: Aviation/Aerospace; Electrical Engineering/Electronics; Mechanical Engineering.

Award: Scholarship for use in freshman, sophomore, junior, senior, graduate, or postgraduate years; not renewable. *Number:* 10–12. *Amount:* $2000–$4000.

Eligibility Requirements: Applicant must be enrolled or expecting to enroll full-time at a four-year institution or university. Available to U.S. and non-U.S. citizens.

Application Requirements: Application, essay, references, transcript. *Deadline:* February 1.

Contact: Vertical Flight Foundation
Vertical Flight Foundation
217 North Washington Street
Alexandria, VA 22314
Phone: 703-684-6777
Fax: 703-739-9279

WOMEN IN AVIATION, INTERNATIONAL   http://www.wai.org

AIRBUS LEADERSHIP GRANT

Scholarship available to a woman pursuing a degree in an aviation-related field. Applicant must be in sophomore year or above. Must have minimum GPA of 3.0. Must be a member of Women in Aviation, International. Please refer to Web site for further details: http://www.wai.org.

Academic Fields/Career Goals: Aviation/Aerospace.

Award: Scholarship for use in sophomore, junior, senior, graduate, or postgraduate years; not renewable. *Number:* 1. *Amount:* $1000.

Eligibility Requirements: Applicant must be enrolled or expecting to enroll at a two-year or four-year or technical institution or university; female and must have an interest in leadership. Applicant or parent of applicant must be member of Women in Aviation, International. Applicant must have 3.0 GPA or higher. Available to U.S. citizens.

Application Requirements: Application, essay. *Deadline:* varies.

Contact: Kim Wheeler, Scholarship Co-Chair
Women in Aviation, International
101 Corsair Drive, Suite 101
101 Corsair 3647 State Route 503 South
West Alexandria, OH 45381
Phone: 937-839-4647
Fax: 937-839-4645
E-mail: wai@wai.org

CINCINNATI HEART OF IT ALL CHAPTER WOMEN IN AVIATION, INTERNATIONAL ELISHA HALL MEMORIAL SCHOLARSHIP

Scholarship offered to a woman seeking to further her aviation career in flight training, aircraft scheduling or dispatch, aviation management, aviation maintenance, or avionics. Preference will be given to applicants from Cincinnati area. Must be a member of Women in Aviation, International, but does not have to be member of Cincinnati Chapter. Please refer to Web site for further details: http://www.wai.org.

Academic Fields/Career Goals: Aviation/Aerospace.

Award: Scholarship for use in freshman, sophomore, junior, senior, or graduate years; not renewable. *Number:* 1. *Amount:* $1000.

Eligibility Requirements: Applicant must be enrolled or expecting to enroll at a two-year or four-year or technical institution or university and female. Applicant or parent of applicant must be member of Women in Aviation, International. Available to U.S. citizens.

Application Requirements: Application. *Deadline:* varies.

Contact: Kim Wheeler, Scholarship Co-Chair
Women in Aviation, International
101 Corsair Drive, Suite 101
101 Corsair 3647 State Route 503 South
West Alexandria, OH 45381
Phone: 937-839-4647
Fax: 937-839-4645
E-mail: wai@wai.org

DASSAULT FALCON JET CORPORATION SCHOLARSHIP

Scholarship available for a woman pursuing an undergraduate or graduate degree in an aviation-related field. Applicant must be a U.S. citizen with minimum 3.0 GPA. Must be a member of Women in Aviation, International. Please refer to Web site for further details: http://www.wai.org.

Academic Fields/Career Goals: Aviation/Aerospace.

Award: Scholarship for use in freshman, sophomore, junior, senior, or graduate years; not renewable. *Number:* 1. *Amount:* $1000.

Eligibility Requirements: Applicant must be enrolled or expecting to enroll at a two-year or four-year or technical institution or university and female. Applicant or parent of applicant must be member of Women in Aviation, International. Applicant must have 3.0 GPA or higher. Available to U.S. citizens.

Application Requirements: Application, essay. *Deadline:* varies.

Contact: Kim Wheeler, Scholarship Co-Chair
Women in Aviation, International
101 Corsair Drive, Suite 101
101 Corsair 3647 State Route 503 South
West Alexandria, OH 45381
Phone: 937-839-4647
Fax: 937-839-4645
E-mail: wai@wai.org

DELTA AIR LINES AIRCRAFT MAINTENANCE TECHNOLOGY SCHOLARSHIP

Scholarship available to a student currently enrolled in an aviation maintenance technology program, or a degree in aviation maintenance technology. Applicant must be a full-time student with a minimum of two semesters left in program/degree. Must have minimum GPA of 3.0. Must be a member of Women in Aviation, International. Please refer to Web site for further details: http://www.wai.org.

Academic Fields/Career Goals: Aviation/Aerospace.

Award: Scholarship for use in senior, or graduate years; not renewable. *Number:* 1. *Amount:* $5000.

Eligibility Requirements: Applicant must be enrolled or expecting to enroll full-time at a two-year or four-year or technical institution or university. Applicant or parent of applicant must be member of Women in Aviation, International. Applicant must have 3.0 GPA or higher. Available to U.S. and non-U.S. citizens.

Application Requirements: Application, essay. *Deadline:* varies.

Contact: Kim Wheeler, Scholarship Co-Chair
Women in Aviation, International
101 Corsair Drive, Suite 101
101 Corsair 3647 State Route 503 South
West Alexandria, OH 45381
Phone: 937-839-4647
Fax: 937-839-4645
E-mail: wai@wai.org

DELTA AIR LINES ENGINEERING SCHOLARSHIP

Scholarship available for an undergraduate junior or senior enrolled in a BA degree program in aerospace/aeronautical, electrical, or mechanical engineering. Applicant must have minimum GPA of 3.0. Must be a member of Women in Aviation, International. Please refer to Web site for further details: http://www.wai.org.

Academic Fields/Career Goals: Aviation/Aerospace; Electrical Engineering/Electronics; Mechanical Engineering.

Award: Scholarship for use in junior or senior years; not renewable. *Number:* 1. *Amount:* $5000.

Eligibility Requirements: Applicant must be enrolled or expecting to enroll full-time at a two-year or four-year or technical institution or university. Applicant or parent of applicant must be member of Women in Aviation, International. Applicant must have 3.0 GPA or higher. Available to U.S. and non-U.S. citizens.

Application Requirements: Application, essay. *Deadline:* varies.

Contact: Kim Wheeler, Scholarship Co-Chair
Women in Aviation, International
101 Corsair Drive, Suite 101
101 Corsair 3647 State Route 503 South
West Alexandria, OH 45381
Phone: 937-839-4647
Fax: 937-839-4645
E-mail: wai@wai.org

DELTA AIR LINES MAINTENANCE MANAGEMENT/AVIATION BUSINESS MANAGEMENT SCHOLARSHIP

Scholarship available to a full-time student pursuing an associate's degree or BA in aviation maintenance management or aviation business management. Applicant must be within two semesters of degree completion, and have a minimum 3.0 GPA. Must be a member of Women in Aviation, International. Please refer to Web site for further details: http://www.wai.org.

Academic Fields/Career Goals: Aviation/Aerospace.

Award: Scholarship for use in senior year; not renewable. *Number:* 1. *Amount:* $5000.

Eligibility Requirements: Applicant must be enrolled or expecting to enroll full-time at a two-year or four-year or technical institution or university. Applicant or parent of applicant must be member of Women in Aviation, International. Applicant must have 3.0 GPA or higher. Available to U.S. and non-U.S. citizens.

Application Requirements: Application, essay. *Deadline:* varies.

Contact: Kim Wheeler, Scholarship Co-Chair
Women in Aviation, International
101 Corsair Drive, Suite 101
101 Corsair 3647 State Route 503 South
West Alexandria, OH 45381
Phone: 937-839-4647
Fax: 937-839-4645
E-mail: wai@wai.org

DR. MANNY HOROWITZ SCHOLARSHIP

Scholarship available to student pursuing degree in navigation, aircraft scheduling or dispatch, aviation management, aviation maintenance, or avionics. Must be a member of Women in Aviation, International. Please refer to Web site for further details: http://www.wai.org.

Academic Fields/Career Goals: Aviation/Aerospace.

Award: Scholarship for use in freshman, sophomore, junior, senior, or graduate years; not renewable. *Number:* 1. *Amount:* $1000.

Eligibility Requirements: Applicant must be enrolled or expecting to enroll at a two-year or four-year or technical institution or university. Applicant or parent of applicant must be member of Women in Aviation, International. Available to U.S. citizens.

Application Requirements: Application, essay. *Deadline:* varies.

Contact: Kim Wheeler, Scholarship Co-Chair
Women in Aviation, International
101 Corsair Drive, Suite 101
101 Corsair 3647 State Route 503 South
West Alexandria, OH 45381
Phone: 937-839-4647
Fax: 937-839-4645
E-mail: wai@wai.org

GAT WINGS TO THE FUTURE MANAGEMENT SCHOLARSHIP

Scholarship offered to a female student pursuing a degree in an aviation management or business program at an accredited college or university. Applicant must be full-time student with a minimum 3.0 GPA. Must be a member of Women in Aviation, International. Please refer to Web site for further details: http://www.wai.org.

Academic Fields/Career Goals: Aviation/Aerospace.

Award: Scholarship for use in freshman, sophomore, junior, or senior years; not renewable. *Number:* 1. *Amount:* $2500.

Eligibility Requirements: Applicant must be enrolled or expecting to enroll full-time at a two-year or four-year or technical institution or university and female. Applicant or parent of applicant must be member of Women in Aviation, International. Applicant must have 3.0 GPA or higher. Available to U.S. citizens.

Application Requirements: Application. *Deadline:* varies.

Contact: Kim Wheeler, Scholarship Co-Chair
Women in Aviation, International
101 Corsair Drive, Suite 101
101 Corsair 3647 State Route 503 South
West Alexandria, OH 45381
Phone: 937-839-4647
Fax: 937-839-4645
E-mail: wai@wai.org

KEEP FLYING SCHOLARSHIP

Scholarship of up to $3000 available for one or more applicants working on an instrument or multi-engine rating, commercial or initial CFI certificate. Applicant must have private pilot certificate, 100 hours of flight time, and a copy of 70+ applicable written test. Flight training must be completed within one year. Must be a member of Women in Aviation, International. Please refer to Web site for further details: http://www.wai.org.

Academic Fields/Career Goals: Aviation/Aerospace.

Award: Scholarship for use in freshman, sophomore, junior, senior, or graduate years; not renewable. *Number:* varies. *Amount:* up to $3000.

Eligibility Requirements: Applicant must be enrolled or expecting to enroll at a two-year or four-year or technical institution or university. Applicant or parent of applicant must be member of Women in Aviation, International. Available to U.S. citizens.

Application Requirements: Application, essay, references. *Deadline:* varies.

Contact: Kim Wheeler, Scholarship Co-Chair
Women in Aviation, International
101 Corsair Drive, Suite 101
101 Corsair 3647 State Route 503 South
West Alexandria, OH 45381
Phone: 937-839-4647
Fax: 937-839-4645
E-mail: wai@wai.org

PRATT AND WHITNEY MAINTENANCE SCHOLARSHIPS

Six scholarships available to individuals pursuing careers in aviation maintenance. Scholarship includes the option to attend any maintenance course offered by Pratt and Whitney. Must be a member of Women in Aviation, International. Please refer to Web site for further details: http://www.wai.org.

Academic Fields/Career Goals: Aviation/Aerospace.

Award: Scholarship for use in freshman, sophomore, junior, senior, or graduate years; not renewable. *Number:* 6.

Eligibility Requirements: Applicant must be enrolled or expecting to enroll at a two-year or four-year or technical institution or university. Applicant or parent of applicant must be member of Women in Aviation, International. Available to U.S. citizens.

Application Requirements: Application. *Deadline:* varies.

Contact: Kim Wheeler, Scholarship Co-Chair
Women in Aviation, International
101 Corsair Drive, Suite 101
101 Corsair 3647 State Route 503 South
West Alexandria, OH 45381
Phone: 937-839-4647
Fax: 937-839-4645
E-mail: wai@wai.org

PROFESSIONAL PUBLICATIONS SERVICES, INC. CORPORATE AVIATION SCHOLARSHIP

Scholarship available for student pursuing a career in corporate aviation, such as: corporate pilot, scheduler or dispatch, or management of corporate aviation department. Must maintain minimum GPA of 2.0. Must be a member of Women in Aviation, International. Please refer to Web site for further details: http://www.wai.org.

Academic Fields/Career Goals: Aviation/Aerospace.

Award: Scholarship for use in freshman, sophomore, junior, senior, or graduate years; not renewable. *Number:* 1. *Amount:* $1000.

Eligibility Requirements: Applicant must be enrolled or expecting to enroll at a two-year or four-year or technical institution or university. Applicant or parent of applicant must be member of Women in Aviation, International. Available to U.S. citizens.

Women in Aviation, International (continued)

Application Requirements: Application. *Deadline:* varies.

Contact: Kim Wheeler, Scholarship Co-Chair
Women in Aviation, International
101 Corsair Drive, Suite 101
101 Corsair 3647 State Route 503 South
West Alexandria, OH 45381
Phone: 937-839-4647
Fax: 937-839-4645
E-mail: wai@wai.org

ROCKWELL COLLINS ENGINEERING/TECHNICAL SCHOLARSHIP

Scholarship available for full-time student pursuing an engineering or technical degree in an aviation-related career field. Applicant must have minimum GPA of 3.0. Must be a member of Women in Aviation, International. Please refer to Web site for further details: http://www.wai.org.

Academic Fields/Career Goals: Aviation/Aerospace.

Award: Scholarship for use in freshman, sophomore, junior, senior, or graduate years; not renewable. *Number:* 1. *Amount:* $2500.

Eligibility Requirements: Applicant must be enrolled or expecting to enroll full-time at a two-year institution. Applicant or parent of applicant must be member of Women in Aviation, International. Applicant must have 3.0 GPA or higher. Available to U.S. and non-U.S. citizens.

Application Requirements: Application. *Deadline:* varies.

Contact: Kim Wheeler, Scholarship Co-Chair
Women in Aviation, International
101 Corsair Drive, Suite 101
101 Corsair 3647 State Route 503 South
West Alexandria, OH 45381
Phone: 937-839-4647
Fax: 937-839-4645
E-mail: wai@wai.org

THE BOEING CAREER ENHANCEMENT SCHOLARSHIP

Awards scholarship to a woman who wishes to advance her career in aerospace technology or a related management field. Applicants may be full-time or part-time employees currently in the aerospace industry or related field. Also eligible are students pursuing aviation-related degrees that are at the junior level with a minimum GPA of 2.5. Scholarship value to be determined.

Academic Fields/Career Goals: Aviation/Aerospace.

Award: Scholarship for use in junior or senior years. *Number:* 1.

Eligibility Requirements: Applicant must be enrolled or expecting to enroll full or part-time at a four-year institution or university and female. Applicant or parent of applicant must be member of Women in Aviation, International. Applicant must have 2.5 GPA or higher. Available to U.S. and non-U.S. citizens.

Application Requirements: Application. *Deadline:* varies.

Contact: Kim Wheeler, Scholarship Co-Chair
Women in Aviation, International
101 Corsair Drive, Suite 101
101 Corsair 3647 State Route 503 South
West Alexandria, OH 45381
Phone: 937-839-4647
Fax: 937-839-4645
E-mail: wai@wai.org

WOMEN IN AVIATION, INTERNATIONAL ACHIEVEMENT AWARDS

Two scholarships available at $500 each for full-time college or university student, and an individual, not necessarily a student, pursuing an aviation career. Must be a member of Women in Aviation, International. Please refer to Web site for further details: http://www.wai.org.

Academic Fields/Career Goals: Aviation/Aerospace.

Award: Scholarship for use in freshman, sophomore, junior, senior, or graduate years; not renewable. *Number:* 2. *Amount:* $500.

Eligibility Requirements: Applicant must be enrolled or expecting to enroll full-time at a two-year or four-year or technical institution or university. Applicant or parent of applicant must be member of Women in Aviation, International. Available to U.S. citizens.

Application Requirements: Application. *Deadline:* varies.

Contact: Kim Wheeler, Scholarship Co-Chair
Women in Aviation, International
101 Corsair Drive, Suite 101
101 Corsair 3647 State Route 503 South
West Alexandria, OH 45381
Phone: 937-839-4647
Fax: 937-839-4645
E-mail: wai@wai.org

WOMEN IN AVIATION, INTERNATIONAL MANAGEMENT SCHOLARSHIPS

Scholarship available to a female in an aviation management field who has demonstrated traits of leadership, community spirit, and volunteerism. Must be a member of Women in Aviation, International. Please refer to Web site for further details: http://www.wai.org.

Academic Fields/Career Goals: Aviation/Aerospace.

Award: Scholarship for use in freshman, sophomore, junior, senior, or graduate years; not renewable. *Number:* 1. *Amount:* $750.

Eligibility Requirements: Applicant must be enrolled or expecting to enroll at a two-year or four-year or technical institution or university; female and must have an interest in leadership. Applicant or parent of applicant must be member of Women in Aviation, International. Available to U.S. citizens.

Application Requirements: Application. *Deadline:* varies.

Contact: Kim Wheeler, Scholarship Co-Chair
Women in Aviation, International
101 Corsair Drive, Suite 101
101 Corsair 3647 State Route 503 South
West Alexandria, OH 45381
Phone: 937-839-4647
Fax: 937-839-4645
E-mail: wai@wai.org

WOMEN IN CORPORATE AVIATION CAREER SCHOLARSHIPS

Scholarships available to women pursuing a career in corporate aviation. Scholarship may be used toward NBAA Professional Development Program courses, flight training, dispatcher training, or upgrades in aviation education, but cannot be used for general business coursework. Must be a member of Women in Aviation, International. Please refer to Web site for further details: http://www.wai.org.

Academic Fields/Career Goals: Aviation/Aerospace.

Award: Scholarship for use in freshman, sophomore, junior, senior, or graduate years; not renewable. *Number:* 2. *Amount:* $1000.

Eligibility Requirements: Applicant must be enrolled or expecting to enroll at a two-year or four-year or technical institution or university and female. Applicant or parent of applicant must be member of Women in Aviation, International. Available to U.S. citizens.

Application Requirements: Application, financial need analysis. *Deadline:* varies.

Contact: Kim Wheeler, Scholarship Co-Chair
Women in Aviation, International
101 Corsair Drive, Suite 101
101 Corsair 3647 State Route 503 South
West Alexandria, OH 45381
Phone: 937-839-4647
Fax: 937-839-4645
E-mail: wai@wai.org

WOMEN MILITARY AVIATORS, INC. MEMORIAL SCHOLARSHIP

Scholarship available for tuition or flight training for an FAA private pilot rating, or advanced rating at an FAA accredited institution or flight school. Must complete flight training within one year of receiving scholarship funds. Must be a member of Women in Aviation, International. Please refer to Web site for further details: http://www.wai.org.

Academic Fields/Career Goals: Aviation/Aerospace.

Award: Scholarship for use in freshman, sophomore, junior, senior, or graduate years; not renewable. *Number:* 1. *Amount:* $2500.

Eligibility Requirements: Applicant must be enrolled or expecting to enroll at a two-year or four-year or technical institution or university. Applicant or parent of applicant must be member of Women in Aviation, International. Available to U.S. citizens.

Application Requirements: Application, financial need analysis. *Deadline:* varies.

Contact: Kim Wheeler, Scholarship Co-Chair
Women in Aviation, International
101 Corsair Drive, Suite 101
101 Corsair 3647 State Route 503 South
West Alexandria, OH 45381
Phone: 937-839-4647
Fax: 937-839-4645
E-mail: wai@wai.org

BIOLOGY

ALABAMA STATE DEPARTMENT OF EDUCATION
http://www.alsde.edu

MATH AND SCIENCE SCHOLARSHIP PROGRAM FOR ALABAMA TEACHERS

For students pursuing teaching certificates in mathematics, general science, biology, or physics. Applicants must agree to teach for five years (if a position is offered) in a targeted system with critical needs. Renewable if recipient continues to meet the requirements. Minimum 2.5 GPA required. Must attend school in Alabama.

Academic Fields/Career Goals: Biology; Earth Science; Meteorology/Atmospheric Science; Natural Sciences; Physical Sciences and Math.

Award: Forgivable loan for use in junior, senior, or graduate years; renewable. *Amount:* $2000–$12,000.

Eligibility Requirements: Applicant must be enrolled or expecting to enroll full or part-time at a four-year institution or university and studying in Alabama. Applicant must have 2.5 GPA or higher. Available to U.S. citizens.

Application Requirements: Application. *Deadline:* varies.

Contact: Alabama State Department of Education
PO Box 302101
Montgomery, AL 36130-2101
Phone: 334-242-9935

ALBERTA HERITAGE SCHOLARSHIP FUND/ ALBERTA SCHOLARSHIP PROGRAMS
http://www.alis.gov.ab.ca

ALBERTA HERITAGE SCHOLARSHIP FUND ABORIGINAL HEALTH CAREERS BURSARY

Award for aboriginal students in Alberta entering their second or subsequent year of postsecondary education in a health field. Must be Indian, Inuit, or Metis students have been living in Alberta for the last three years, and be enrolled or planning to enroll in a health field at the postsecondary level. Application deadline is May 15.

Academic Fields/Career Goals: Biology; Dental Health/Services; Health Administration; Health and Medical Sciences; Nursing; Therapy/Rehabilitation.

Award: Scholarship for use in sophomore, junior, senior, or graduate years; not renewable. *Number:* 20–40. *Amount:* $861–$8611.

Eligibility Requirements: Applicant must be Canadian citizen; American Indian/Alaska Native; enrolled or expecting to enroll full-time at a two-year or four-year or technical institution or university and resident of Alberta. Applicant must have 2.5 GPA or higher.

Application Requirements: Application, essay, financial need analysis, references, transcript, proof of aboriginal status.. *Deadline:* May 15.

Contact: Stuart Dunn, Manager
Alberta Heritage Scholarship Fund/Alberta Scholarship Programs
4th Floor, 9940 106th Street, Box 28000 Station Main
Edmonton, AB T5J 4R4
Canada
Phone: 780-427-8640
Fax: 780-427-1288
E-mail: scholarships@gov.ab.ca

AMERICAN INDIAN SCIENCE AND ENGINEERING SOCIETY
http://www.aises.org

A.T. ANDERSON MEMORIAL SCHOLARSHIP
• See page 89

BURLINGTON NORTHERN SANTA FE FOUNDATION SCHOLARSHIP
• See page 89

ENVIRONMENTAL PROTECTION AGENCY TRIBAL LANDS ENVIRONMENTAL SCIENCE SCHOLARSHIP

Award for Native-American college juniors, seniors, or graduate students attending an accredited institution and studying full time in biochemistry, biology, chemical engineering, chemistry, entomology, environmental science, hydrology, or environmentally related disciplines. Deadline: June 15. Minimum 2.7 GPA required. Must be a current AISES member.

Academic Fields/Career Goals: Biology; Chemical Engineering; Earth Science; Meteorology/Atmospheric Science; Natural Sciences; Physical Sciences and Math.

Award: Scholarship for use in junior, senior, or graduate years; not renewable. *Number:* varies. *Amount:* up to $4000.

Eligibility Requirements: Applicant must be American Indian/Alaska Native and enrolled or expecting to enroll full-time at a four-year institution or university. Available to U.S. citizens.

Application Requirements: Application, essay, resume, references, transcript. *Deadline:* June 15.

Contact: Scholarship Information
American Indian Science and Engineering Society
PO Box 9828
Albuquerque, NM 87119-9828
Phone: 505-765-1052
Fax: 505-765-5608
E-mail: info@aises.org

AMERICAN SOCIETY OF AGRICULTURAL ENGINEERS
http://www.asabe.org

WILLIAM J. AND MARIJANE E. ADAMS, JR. SCHOLARSHIP
• See page 78

ARKANSAS DEPARTMENT OF HIGHER EDUCATION
http://www.arkansashighered.com

EMERGENCY SECONDARY EDUCATION LOAN PROGRAM

Must be Arkansas resident enrolled full-time in approved Arkansas institution. Renewable award for students majoring in secondary math, chemistry, physics, biology, physical science, general science, special education, or foreign language. Must teach in Arkansas at least five years. Must rank in upper half of class or have a minimum 2.5 GPA.

Academic Fields/Career Goals: Biology; Education; Foreign Language; Physical Sciences and Math; Special Education.

Award: Forgivable loan for use in sophomore, junior, senior, or graduate years; renewable. *Number:* up to 50. *Amount:* up to $2500.

Eligibility Requirements: Applicant must be enrolled or expecting to enroll full-time at a two-year or four-year institution or university; resident of Arkansas and studying in Arkansas. Applicant must have 2.5 GPA or higher. Available to U.S. citizens.

Application Requirements: Application, transcript. *Deadline:* April 1.

Contact: Lillian K. Williams, Assistant Coordinator
Arkansas Department of Higher Education
114 East Capitol
Little Rock, AR 72201
Phone: 501-371-2050
Fax: 501-371-2001

ASSOCIATION FOR IRON AND STEEL TECHNOLOGY
http://www.aist.org

ASSOCIATION FOR IRON AND STEEL TECHNOLOGY OHIO VALLEY CHAPTER SCHOLARSHIP

Scholarship of $1000 per year for up to four years provided that applicant continues to meet requirements and reapplies for scholarship. Applicant must be a dependent of Ohio Valley Chapter member, or Student or Young Professional member. Applicant also must attend or plan to attend an

Association for Iron and Steel Technology (continued)

accredited school full-time and pursue a degree in any of a number of technological fields such as engineering, physics, computer sciences, chemistry or other fields approved by the scholarship committee . Application deadline is January 31 of high school senior year, or of freshman year.

Academic Fields/Career Goals: Biology; Computer Science/Data Processing; Earth Science; Electrical Engineering/Electronics; Engineering/Technology; Engineering-Related Technologies; Environmental Science; Geography; Materials Science, Engineering, and Metallurgy; Physical Sciences and Math.

Award: Scholarship for use in freshman, sophomore, junior, or senior years; not renewable. *Number:* 2. *Amount:* $1000.

Eligibility Requirements: Applicant must be enrolled or expecting to enroll full-time at a four-year institution or university and must have an interest in leadership. Applicant must have 3.0 GPA or higher. Available to U.S. citizens.

Application Requirements: Application, essay, resume, references, transcript, personal statement. *Deadline:* January 31.

Contact: Jeff McKain, Scholarship Chairman
Association for Iron and Steel Technology
11451 Reading Road
Cincinnati, OH 45241
E-mail: jeff.mckain@xtek.com

ASSOCIATION FOR WOMEN IN SCIENCE EDUCATIONAL FOUNDATION   http://www.awis.org/ed_foundation.html

ASSOCIATION FOR WOMEN IN SCIENCE COLLEGE SCHOLARSHIP
• See page 86

ASSOCIATION OF CALIFORNIA WATER AGENCIES   http://www.acwanet.com

ASSOCIATION OF CALIFORNIA WATER AGENCIES SCHOLARSHIPS
• See page 91

CLAIR A. HILL SCHOLARSHIP
• See page 91

ASTRONAUT SCHOLARSHIP FOUNDATION   http://www.astronautscholarship.org

ASTRONAUT SCHOLARSHIP FOUNDATION
• See page 92

BARRY M. GOLDWATER SCHOLARSHIP AND EXCELLENCE IN EDUCATION FOUNDATION   http://www.act.org/goldwater

BARRY M. GOLDWATER SCHOLARSHIP AND EXCELLENCE IN EDUCATION PROGRAM
• See page 92

BUSINESS AND PROFESSIONAL WOMEN'S FOUNDATION   http://www.bpwusa.org

BPW CAREER ADVANCEMENT SCHOLARSHIP PROGRAM FOR WOMEN

Scholarships of $1000 each are awarded for full or part-time study. Applicant must be studying in one of the following fields as biological sciences, teacher education certification, engineering, social science, paralegal studies, humanities, business studies, mathematics, computer science, physical sciences, or for a professional degree (JD, MD, DDS). The Career Advancement Scholarship Program was established to assist women seeking the education necessary for entry or re-entry into the work force, or advancement within a career field. Must be 25 or over. Send self-addressed double-stamped envelope between January 1 and April 1 for application.

Academic Fields/Career Goals: Biology; Computer Science/Data Processing; Dental Health/Services; Education; Engineering/Technology; Engineering-Related Technologies; Health and Medical Sciences; Humanities; Law/Legal Services; Physical Sciences and Math; Social Sciences.

Award: Scholarship for use in freshman, sophomore, junior, senior, or graduate years; not renewable. *Number:* 100–200. *Amount:* $1000.

Eligibility Requirements: Applicant must be age 25; enrolled or expecting to enroll full or part-time at a two-year or four-year or technical institution or university and female. Available to U.S. citizens.

Application Requirements: Application, essay, financial need analysis, references, self-addressed stamped envelope, transcript. *Deadline:* April 15.

Contact: Stefanie Gans, Development and Program Associate
Business and Professional Women's Foundation
1900 M Street, NW, Suite 310
Washington, DC 20036
Phone: 202-777-8990
Fax: 202-861-0298
E-mail: sgans@bpwusa.org

COLLEGEBOUND FOUNDATION   http://www.collegeboundfoundation.org

NATIONAL AQUARIUM IN BALTIMORE HENRY HALL SCHOLARSHIP

Award for Baltimore City public high school graduates 21 years of age or younger. Please see Web site: http://www.collegeboundfoundation.org for complete information on application process. Must have completed at least one year of high school biology, physical science, and algebra and have maintained an 85 average or better in science classes. Must major in biology, engineering, or environmental science and submit a typed one-page essay on why you are pursuing this field of study. Must submit CollegeBound Competitive Scholarship/Last-Dollar Grant Application.

Academic Fields/Career Goals: Biology; Engineering/Technology; Environmental Science.

Award: Scholarship for use in freshman year; not renewable. *Number:* 1–4. *Amount:* $1000.

Eligibility Requirements: Applicant must be age 21 or under; enrolled or expecting to enroll full-time at a two-year or four-year institution or university and resident of Maryland. Available to U.S. citizens.

Application Requirements: Application, essay, financial need analysis, references, transcript, financial aid award letters, Student Aid Report (SAR). *Deadline:* March 19.

Contact: April Bell, Associate Program Director
CollegeBound Foundation
300 Water Street, Suite 300
Baltimore, MD 21202
Phone: 410-783-2905 Ext. 208
Fax: 410-727-5786
E-mail: abell@collegeboundfoundation.org

CONSERVATION FEDERATION OF MISSOURI   http://www.confedmo.org

CHARLES P. BELL CONSERVATION SCHOLARSHIP

Eight scholarships of $250-$600 for Missouri students and/or teachers whose studies or projects are related to natural science, resource conservation, earth resources, or environmental protection. Must be used for study in Missouri. See application for eligibility details.

Academic Fields/Career Goals: Biology; Natural Resources.

Award: Scholarship for use in freshman, sophomore, junior, senior, or graduate years; not renewable. *Number:* 8. *Amount:* $250–$600.

Eligibility Requirements: Applicant must be enrolled or expecting to enroll full-time at a four-year institution or university; resident of Missouri and studying in Missouri. Available to U.S. citizens.

Application Requirements: Application, references, transcript. *Deadline:* January 15.

Contact: Administrative Associate
Conservation Federation of Missouri
728 West Main Street
Jefferson City, MO 65101
Phone: 573-634-2322
Fax: 573-634-8205
E-mail: confedmo@sockets.net

EAA AVIATION FOUNDATION, INC. http://www.eaa.org

PAYZER SCHOLARSHIP
• *See page 122*

ELECTROCHEMICAL SOCIETY, INC. http://www.electrochem.org

DANIEL CUBICCIOTTI STUDENT AWARD OF THE SAN FRANCISCO SECTION OF THE ELECTROCHEMICAL SOCIETY, SPONSORED BY STRUCTURAL INTEGRITY ASSOCIATES

Award for full- or part-time graduate or advanced undergraduate student in a college or university in Northern California. Student will be selected on basis of academic excellence, demonstrated interest in the study or application of electrochemistry and personal characteristics that reflect those of Dr. Dan Cubicciotti. Must be majoring in metallurgy, materials science, chemical engineering, chemistry. Must be nominated by someone familiar with their qualifications; a letter of recommendation from a faculty member from an appropriate department is required.

Academic Fields/Career Goals: Biology; Chemical Engineering; Construction Engineering/Management; Earth Science; Electrical Engineering/Electronics; Energy and Power Engineering; Engineering/Technology; Engineering-Related Technologies; Marine/Ocean Engineering; Materials Science, Engineering, and Metallurgy; Mechanical Engineering; Meteorology/Atmospheric Science.

Award: Scholarship for use in freshman, sophomore, junior, senior, or graduate years. *Number:* 1. *Amount:* $2000.

Eligibility Requirements: Applicant must be enrolled or expecting to enroll full or part-time at a four-year institution or university and studying in California. Available to U.S. and non-U.S. citizens.

Application Requirements: Application, autobiography, resume, references, transcript. *Deadline:* February 15.

Contact: Heidi Rixman, Director of Membership & Development
Electrochemical Society, Inc.
65 South Main Street, Building D
Pennington, NJ 08534-2839
Phone: 609-737-1902 Ext. 126
Fax: 609-737-2743
E-mail: heidi.rixman@electrochem.org

H.H. DOW MEMORIAL STUDENT ACHIEVEMENT AWARD OF THE INDUSTRIAL ELECTROLYSIS AND ELECTROCHEMICAL ENGINEERING DIVISION OF THE ELECTROCHEMICAL SOCIETY, INC.

Award to recognize promising young engineers and scientists in the field of electrochemical engineering and applied electrochemistry. Applicant must be enrolled or accepted for enrollment in a college or university as a graduate student. Must submit description of proposed research project and how it relates to the field of electrochemistry, letter of recommendation from research supervisor, and biography or resume.

Academic Fields/Career Goals: Biology; Chemical Engineering; Construction Engineering/Management; Earth Science; Electrical Engineering/Electronics; Energy and Power Engineering; Engineering/Technology; Engineering-Related Technologies; Marine/Ocean Engineering; Materials Science, Engineering, and Metallurgy; Mechanical Engineering; Meteorology/Atmospheric Science.

Award: Scholarship for use in freshman, sophomore, junior, senior, or graduate years; not renewable. *Number:* 1. *Amount:* $1000.

Eligibility Requirements: Applicant must be enrolled or expecting to enroll at a four-year institution or university. Available to U.S. and non-U.S. citizens.

Application Requirements: Application, resume, references, transcript, description of research project. *Deadline:* September 15.

Contact: Heidi Rixman, Director of Membership & Development
Electrochemical Society, Inc.
65 South Main Street, Building D
Pennington, NJ 08534-2839
Phone: 609-737-1902 Ext. 126
Fax: 609-737-2743
E-mail: heidi.rixman@electrochem.org

STUDENT ACHIEVEMENT AWARDS OF THE INDUSTRIAL ELECTROLYSIS AND ELECTROCHEMICAL ENGINEERING DIVISION OF THE ELECTROCHEMICAL SOCIETY, INC.

Award to recognize promising young engineers and scientists in the field of electrochemical engineering. Applicant must be enrolled in a college or university or accepted for enrollment in a graduate program. Application must include outline of research project to be engaged in during the next year and how it relates to the field of electrochemical engineering and letter of recommendation from research supervisor.

Academic Fields/Career Goals: Biology; Chemical Engineering; Construction Engineering/Management; Earth Science; Electrical Engineering/Electronics; Energy and Power Engineering; Engineering/Technology; Engineering-Related Technologies; Marine/Ocean Engineering; Materials Science, Engineering, and Metallurgy; Mechanical Engineering; Meteorology/Atmospheric Science.

Award: Scholarship for use in freshman, sophomore, junior, senior, or graduate years; not renewable. *Number:* 1. *Amount:* $1000.

Eligibility Requirements: Applicant must be enrolled or expecting to enroll full-time at a four-year institution or university. Available to U.S. and non-U.S. citizens.

Application Requirements: Application, resume, references, transcript, description of proposed research project. *Deadline:* September 15.

Contact: Heidi Rixman, Director of Membership & Development
Electrochemical Society, Inc.
65 South Main Street, Building D
Pennington, NJ 08534-2839
Phone: 609-737-1902 Ext. 126
Fax: 609-737-2743
E-mail: heidi.rixman@electrochem.org

STUDENT RESEARCH AWARDS OF THE BATTERY DIVISION OF THE ELECTROCHEMICAL SOCIETY, INC.

Award to recognize promising young engineers and scientists in the field of electrochemical power sources. Student must be enrolled or have been accepted for enrollment at a college or university.

Academic Fields/Career Goals: Biology; Chemical Engineering; Construction Engineering/Management; Earth Science; Electrical Engineering/Electronics; Energy and Power Engineering; Engineering/Technology; Engineering-Related Technologies; Marine/Ocean Engineering; Materials Science, Engineering, and Metallurgy; Mechanical Engineering; Meteorology/Atmospheric Science.

Award: Scholarship for use in freshman, sophomore, junior, senior, or graduate years; not renewable. *Number:* 1. *Amount:* $1000.

Eligibility Requirements: Applicant must be enrolled or expecting to enroll full-time at a four-year institution or university. Available to U.S. and non-U.S. citizens.

Application Requirements: Application, resume, references, transcript, outline of research project. *Deadline:* March 15.

Contact: Heidi Rixman, Director of Membership & Development
Electrochemical Society, Inc.
65 South Main Street, Building D
Pennington, NJ 08534-2839
Phone: 609-737-1902 Ext. 126
Fax: 609-737-2743
E-mail: heidi.rixman@electrochem.org

FEDERATED GARDEN CLUBS OF CONNECTICUT http://www.ctgardenclubs.org

FEDERATED GARDEN CLUBS OF CONNECTICUT, INC.

One-time award for Connecticut residents pursuing studies in gardening, landscaping, or biology. Minimum 3.0 GPA. Application deadline is July 1.

Academic Fields/Career Goals: Biology; Horticulture/Floriculture; Landscape Architecture.

Award: Scholarship for use in junior, senior, or graduate years; not renewable. *Number:* 2–5. *Amount:* up to $1000.

Eligibility Requirements: Applicant must be enrolled or expecting to enroll full-time at a four-year institution or university and resident of Connecticut. Applicant must have 3.0 GPA or higher. Available to U.S. and non-U.S. citizens.

Application Requirements: Application, autobiography, financial need analysis, references, self-addressed stamped envelope, test scores, transcript. *Deadline:* July 1.

Federated Garden Clubs of Connecticut (continued)

Contact: Mary Gray, Scholarship Chairman
Federated Garden Clubs of Connecticut
14 Business Park Drive
PO Box 854
Branford, CT 06405-0854
Phone: 203-458-2784

GARDEN CLUB OF AMERICA   http://www.gcamerica.org

LOY MCCANDLESS MARKS SCHOLARSHIP IN TROPICAL ORNAMENTAL HORTICULTURE

Award affords a graduate student or advanced undergraduate opportunity to study tropical ornamental horticulture at an appropriate foreign institution specializing in the study of tropical plants. Application on the GCA Web site: http://www.gcamerica.org.

Academic Fields/Career Goals: Biology; Horticulture/Floriculture.

Award: Scholarship for use in sophomore, junior, senior, graduate, or postgraduate years; not renewable. *Number:* 1. *Amount:* $2000.

Eligibility Requirements: Applicant must be enrolled or expecting to enroll at an institution or university. Available to U.S. citizens.

Application Requirements: Application, interview, references, self-addressed stamped envelope, transcript. *Deadline:* January 10.

Contact: Ms. Judy Smith, The Garden Club of America
Garden Club of America
14 East 60th Street
New York, NY 10022-1002
Phone: 212-753-8287
Fax: 212-753-0134

GREAT LAKES COMMISSION   http://www.glc.org

CAROL A. RATZA MEMORIAL SCHOLARSHIP

One-time award to full-time students at a college or university in the Great Lake States (IL, IN, MI, MN, NY, OH, PA, WI) or Canadian provinces of Ontario or Quebec. Must have a demonstrated interest in the environmental or economic applications of electronic communications technology, exhibit academic excellence, and have a sincere appreciation for the Great Lakes and their protection. Refer http://www.glc.org/about/scholarships/scholar.html for more information.

Academic Fields/Career Goals: Biology; Communications; Computer Science/Data Processing; Foreign Language; Graphics/Graphic Arts/Printing; Journalism; Natural Resources; Natural Sciences; Photojournalism/Photography; Science, Technology, and Society; TV/Radio Broadcasting.

Award: Scholarship for use in freshman, sophomore, junior, or senior years; not renewable. *Number:* 1. *Amount:* $1000.

Eligibility Requirements: Applicant must be enrolled or expecting to enroll full-time at a two-year or four-year or technical institution or university; resident of Illinois, Indiana, Michigan, Minnesota, New York, Ohio, Ontario, Pennsylvania, Quebec, or Wisconsin and studying in Illinois, Indiana, Michigan, Minnesota, New York, Ohio, Ontario, Pennsylvania, Quebec, or Wisconsin. Available to U.S. and non-U.S. citizens.

Application Requirements: Application, essay, resume, references, transcript, letter of intent explaining applicant's career goals. *Deadline:* March 31.

Contact: Christine Manninen, Program Manager
Great Lakes Commission
Eisenhower Corporate Park, 2805 South Industrial Highway, Suite 100
Ann Arbor, MI 48104-6791
Phone: 734-971-9135
Fax: 734-971-9150
E-mail: manninen@glc.org

HAWAIIAN LODGE, F.& A. M.   http://www.hawaiianlodge.org/

HAWAIIAN LODGE SCHOLARSHIPS
• See page 99

HERB SOCIETY OF AMERICA   http://www.herbsociety.org

HERB SOCIETY RESEARCH GRANTS
• See page 92

HISPANIC COLLEGE FUND, INC.   http://www.hispanicfund.org

NATIONAL HISPANIC EXPLORERS SCHOLARSHIP PROGRAM
• See page 93

HISPANIC ENGINEER NATIONAL ACHIEVEMENT AWARDS CORPORATION (HENAAC)   http://www.henaac.org

HISPANIC ENGINEER NATIONAL ACHIEVEMENT AWARDS CORPORATION SCHOLARSHIP PROGRAM
• See page 122

INDEPENDENT LABORATORIES INSTITUTE SCHOLARSHIP ALLIANCE   http://www.acil.org

INDEPENDENT LABORATORIES INSTITUTE SCHOLARSHIP ALLIANCE
• See page 93

INNOVATION AND SCIENCE COUNCIL OF BRITISH COLUMBIA   http://www.scbc.org

PAUL AND HELEN TRUSSEL SCIENCE AND TECHNOLOGY SCHOLARSHIP
• See page 93

MASTER BREWERS ASSOCIATION OF THE AMERICAS   http://www.mbaa.com

MASTER BREWERS ASSOCIATION OF THE AMERICAS
• See page 81

MONTANA FEDERATION OF GARDEN CLUBS   http://www.mtfgc.org

LIFE MEMBER MONTANA FEDERATION OF GARDEN CLUBS SCHOLARSHIP

Applicant must be at least a sophomore, majoring in conservation, horticulture, park or forestry, floriculture, greenhouse management, land management, or related subjects. Must be in need of assistance. Must have a potential for a successful future. Must be ranked in upper half of class or have a minimum 2.7 GPA. Must be a Montana resident and all study must be done in Montana. Deadline: May 1.

Academic Fields/Career Goals: Biology; Earth Science; Horticulture/Floriculture; Landscape Architecture.

Award: Scholarship for use in sophomore, junior, or senior years; not renewable. *Number:* 1. *Amount:* $1000.

Eligibility Requirements: Applicant must be enrolled or expecting to enroll full-time at a four-year institution or university; resident of Montana and studying in Montana. Available to U.S. citizens.

Application Requirements: Autobiography, financial need analysis, photo, references, transcript. *Deadline:* May 1.

Contact: Joyce Backa
Montana Federation of Garden Clubs
50 Leonard Street
Craig, MT 59648-8712
Phone: 406-235-4229

NASA IDAHO SPACE GRANT CONSORTIUM   http://isgc.uidaho.edu

NASA IDAHO SPACE GRANT CONSORTIUM SCHOLARSHIP PROGRAM
• See page 94

NASA MONTANA SPACE GRANT CONSORTIUM   http://www.spacegrant.montana.edu

MONTANA SPACE GRANT SCHOLARSHIP PROGRAM
• See page 125

NASA NEBRASKA SPACE GRANT CONSORTIUM
http://nasa.unomaha.edu

NASA NEBRASKA SPACE GRANT
• See page 125

NASA VERMONT SPACE GRANT CONSORTIUM
http://www.vtspacegrant.org

VERMONT SPACE GRANT CONSORTIUM SCHOLARSHIP PROGRAM
• See page 94

NASA/MARYLAND SPACE GRANT CONSORTIUM
http://www.mdspacegrant.org

NASA MARYLAND SPACE GRANT CONSORTIUM UNDERGRADUATE SCHOLARSHIPS

Scholarship for full-time student majoring in (but are not necessarily limited to): the biological and life sciences, chemistry, geological sciences, physics and astronomy, engineering and computer science. Must be a U.S. citizen and a Maryland resident. Enrollment in an affiliate institution of the Maryland Space Grant Consortium is necessary.

Academic Fields/Career Goals: Biology; Computer Science/Data Processing; Engineering/Technology; Humanities; Physical Sciences and Math.

Award: Scholarship for use in freshman, sophomore, junior, or senior years; renewable. *Number:* varies. *Amount:* up to $1000.

Eligibility Requirements: Applicant must be enrolled or expecting to enroll full-time at a four-year institution or university; resident of Maryland and studying in Maryland. Applicant must have 3.0 GPA or higher. Available to U.S. citizens.

Application Requirements: Application, essay, references. *Deadline:* August 15.

Contact: Anna Anikis
NASA/Maryland Space Grant Consortium
Johns Hopkins University, 203 Bloomberg Center for Physics and Astronomy
3400 N Charles Street
Baltimore, MD 21218-2686
Phone: 410-516-7351
Fax: 410-516-4109
E-mail: info@mdspacegrant.org

NATIONAL ASSOCIATION FOR THE ADVANCEMENT OF COLORED PEOPLE
http://www.naacp.org

LOUIS STOKES SCIENCE AND TECHNOLOGY AWARD

Must be an incoming freshman at an Historically Black college or university and major in one of the following: engineering, physics, chemistry, biology, computer science or mathematical science. Freshman must be full-time student and have 2.5 minimum GPA. Award requires financial need. NAACP membership and participation is preferable. Application deadline is April 30.

Academic Fields/Career Goals: Biology; Chemical Engineering; Computer Science/Data Processing; Engineering-Related Technologies; Physical Sciences and Math.

Award: Scholarship for use in freshman year; not renewable. *Number:* varies. *Amount:* $2000.

Eligibility Requirements: Applicant must be American Indian/Alaska Native, Asian/Pacific Islander, Black (non-Hispanic), or Hispanic and enrolled or expecting to enroll full-time at a four-year institution or university. Applicant or parent of applicant must be member of National Association for the Advancement of Colored People. Applicant must have 2.5 GPA or higher. Available to U.S. citizens.

Application Requirements: Application, financial need analysis, references, transcript. *Deadline:* April 30.

Contact: Donna Lakins, Education Department, Scholarship Request
National Association for the Advancement of Colored People
4805 Mt. Hope Drive
Baltimore, MD 21215-3297
Phone: 410-580-5760
Fax: 410-585-1329

NATIONAL ASSOCIATION OF WATER COMPANIES
http://www.nawc.org

J .J. BARR SCHOLARSHIP

Award for a graduating undergraduate senior or graduate student pursuing studies which may lead to a career in the investor owned public water supply business. Must be a U.S. citizen. Write for information and restrictions. One-time award of $5000. Must study in one of the following states: WA, RI, CA, VT, PA, NH, NY, NJ, NC, SC, MA, FL, ME, IL, CT, MO, DE, IN or OH.

Academic Fields/Career Goals: Biology; Business/Consumer Services; Earth Science; Engineering-Related Technologies; Law/Legal Services; Natural Resources.

Award: Scholarship for use in freshman, sophomore, junior, senior, or graduate years; not renewable. *Number:* 1. *Amount:* $5000.

Eligibility Requirements: Applicant must be enrolled or expecting to enroll full or part-time at an institution or university. Available to U.S. citizens.

Application Requirements: Application, essay, references, transcript. *Deadline:* April 1.

Contact: Carlos Villanueva, Marketing and Member Services Manager
National Association of Water Companies
1725 K Street, NW, Suite 1212
Washington, DC 20006
Phone: 202-833-8383
Fax: 202-331-7442
E-mail: carlos@nawc.com

NATIONAL ASSOCIATION OF WATER COMPANIES-NEW JERSEY CHAPTER

NATIONAL ASSOCIATION OF WATER COMPANIES-NEW JERSEY CHAPTER SCHOLARSHIP

For college students interested in a career in the investor-owned water utility industry. Must be U.S. citizen, five-year resident of New Jersey, high school senior or enrolled in a New Jersey college or university. Must maintain a 3.0 GPA.

Academic Fields/Career Goals: Biology; Business/Consumer Services; Communications; Computer Science/Data Processing; Earth Science; Economics; Engineering/Technology; Law/Legal Services; Natural Resources; Physical Sciences and Math; Trade/Technical Specialties.

Award: Scholarship for use in freshman, sophomore, junior, senior, or graduate years; not renewable. *Number:* 1–2. *Amount:* $2500.

Eligibility Requirements: Applicant must be enrolled or expecting to enroll full or part-time at a two-year or four-year institution or university; resident of New Jersey and studying in New Jersey. Applicant must have 3.0 GPA or higher. Available to U.S. citizens.

Application Requirements: Application, essay, references, transcript, 3 recommendation letters. *Deadline:* April 1.

Contact: Gail Brady, Scholarship Committee Chairperson
National Association of Water Companies-New Jersey Chapter
49 Howell Drive
Verona, NJ 07044
Phone: 973-669-5807
Fax: 973-669-8327
E-mail: gbradygbconsult@comcast.net

NATIONAL COUNCIL OF STATE GARDEN CLUBS, INC. SCHOLARSHIP
http://www.gardenclub.org

NATIONAL COUNCIL OF STATE GARDEN CLUBS, INC. SCHOLARSHIP
• See page 82

NATIONAL FEDERATION OF THE BLIND
http://www.nfb.org

HOWARD BROWN RICKARD SCHOLARSHIP
• See page 101

NATIONAL FISH AND WILDLIFE FOUNDATION
http://www.nfwf.org

BUDWEISER CONSERVATION SCHOLARSHIP PROGRAM

One-time award supports and promotes innovative research or study that seeks to respond to today's most pressing conservation issues. This competitive scholarship program is designed to respond to many of the most significant challenges in fish, wildlife, and plant conservation in the United States by providing scholarships to eligible graduate and undergraduate students who are poised to make a significant contribution to the field of conservation.

Academic Fields/Career Goals: Biology; Geography; Natural Resources; Natural Sciences; Political Science; Surveying; Surveying Technology, Cartography, or Geographic Information Science.

Award: Scholarship for use in sophomore, junior, senior, or graduate years; not renewable. *Number:* 10. *Amount:* $10,000.

Eligibility Requirements: Applicant must be age 21 and enrolled or expecting to enroll full-time at a four-year institution or university. Available to U.S. citizens.

Application Requirements: Application, essay, references, transcript, title of proposed research and a short abstract. *Deadline:* January 27.

Contact: Lauren Guite
National Fish and Wildlife Foundation
1120 Connecticut Avenue, NW, Suite 900
Washington, DC 20036
Phone: 202-857-0166
Fax: 202-857-0162

NATIONAL GARDEN CLUBS, INC.
http://www.gardenclub.org

NATIONAL GARDEN CLUBS, INC. SCHOLARSHIP PROGRAM
• See page 83

NATIONAL INSTITUTE OF GENERAL MEDICAL SCIENCES, NATIONAL INSTITUTE OF HEALTH
http://www.nigms.nih.gov

MARC UNDERGRADUATE STUDENT TRAINING IN ACADEMIC RESEARCH U*STAR AWARDS

Scholarships available for minority honors students enrolled in their junior and senior years at participating U*Star universities. Must major in science with the intent to pursue their PhD or MD degrees. Specific details and application are available on Web site: http://www.nigms.nih.gov

Academic Fields/Career Goals: Biology; Computer Science/Data Processing; Natural Sciences.

Award: Scholarship for use in junior, senior, or graduate years; renewable. *Number:* varies. *Amount:* up to $11,232.

Eligibility Requirements: Applicant must be American Indian/Alaska Native, Asian/Pacific Islander, Black (non-Hispanic), or Hispanic; enrolled or expecting to enroll full-time at a four-year institution or university and studying in Alabama, Arizona, California, Colorado, Delaware, Florida, Georgia, Hawaii, Louisiana, Maryland, Minnesota, or Mississippi. Available to U.S. citizens.

Application Requirements: Application. *Deadline:* varies.

Contact: Dr. Adolphus P. Toliver, Chief, MARC Program Branch
National Institute of General Medical Sciences, National Institute of Health
45 Center Drive, Room 2AS.37, MSC 6200
Bethesda, MD 20892-6200
Phone: 301-594-3900
Fax: 301-780-2753
E-mail: tolivera@nigms.nih.gov

NATIONAL INSTITUTES OF HEALTH
http://ugsp.info.nih.gov

NIH UNDERGRADUATE SCHOLARSHIP PROGRAM FOR STUDENTS FROM DISADVANTAGED BACKGROUNDS

The NIH Undergraduate Scholarship Program offers competitive scholarships to exceptional students from disadvantaged backgrounds who are committed to biomedical, behavioral and social science research careers at the NIH. Applicants must be U.S. citizens, nationals, or qualified permanent residents and have a minimum 3.5 GPA.

Academic Fields/Career Goals: Biology; Health and Medical Sciences; Social Sciences.

Award: Scholarship for use in freshman, sophomore, junior, or senior years; renewable. *Number:* 10–20. *Amount:* up to $20,000.

Eligibility Requirements: Applicant must be enrolled or expecting to enroll full-time at a four-year institution or university. Applicant must have 3.5 GPA or higher. Available to U.S. citizens.

Application Requirements: Application, essay, financial need analysis, references, transcript. *Deadline:* February 28.

Contact: NIH Undergraduate Scholarship Program Director
National Institutes of Health
2 Center Drive, Room 2E30, MSC 0230
Bethesda, MD 20892-0230
Phone: 800-528-7689
Fax: 301-480-3123
E-mail: ugsp@nih.gov

NATIONAL INVENTORS HALL OF FAME
http://www.invent.org

COLLEGIATE INVENTORS COMPETITION - GRAND PRIZE
• See page 95

COLLEGIATE INVENTORS COMPETITION FOR UNDERGRADUATE STUDENTS
• See page 95

NEW JERSEY DIVISION OF FISH AND WILDLIFE/NJ CHAPTER OF THE WILDLIFE SOCIETY
http://www.njfishandwildlife.com/cookhmschol.htm

RUSSELL A. COOKINGHAM SCHOLARSHIP

Scholarship to assist qualified students majoring in wildlife/fisheries or conservation education/communications. Conservation education/communications majors must have at least 15 credits in biological sciences. Applicants must have completed at least one-half of the degree requirements for their major. Must be a permanent resident of New Jersey, attending an institution in-state or out-of-state. To apply, send official transcript, 2 letters of recommendation, resume, and cover letter explaining why you should be considered for this scholarship. Deadline is April 1.

Academic Fields/Career Goals: Biology; Communications; Environmental Science; Natural Resources.

Award: Scholarship for use in junior or senior years; not renewable. *Number:* 1. *Amount:* $1000.

Eligibility Requirements: Applicant must be enrolled or expecting to enroll full-time at a four-year institution or university and resident of New Jersey. Available to U.S. citizens.

Application Requirements: Resume, references, transcript, cover letter. *Deadline:* April 1.

Contact: Jim Sciascia, Information and Education Bureau Chief
New Jersey Division of Fish and Wildlife/NJ Chapter of the Wildlife Society
605 Pequest Road
Oxford, NJ 07863
Phone: 609-984-6295
E-mail: jim.sciascia@dep.state.nj.us

OREGON STUDENT ASSISTANCE COMMISSION
http://www.osac.state.or.us

OREGON FOUNDATION FOR BLACKTAIL DEER OUTDOOR AND WILDLIFE SCHOLARSHIP

Award for students majoring in forestry, biology, wildlife science or related fields indicating a serious commitment to careers in wildlife management. Must submit essay on, "Challenges of Wildlife management in coming 10 years." Submit copy of previous year's hunting license. Must be an Oregon resident attending an Oregon institution.

Academic Fields/Career Goals: Biology; Natural Resources; Natural Sciences.

Award: Scholarship for use in freshman, sophomore, junior, or senior years; renewable. *Number:* 4. *Amount:* $500.

Eligibility Requirements: Applicant must be enrolled or expecting to enroll at a four-year institution; resident of Oregon and studying in Oregon. Available to U.S. citizens.

Application Requirements: Application, essay, financial need analysis, references, transcript, hunting license, activities chart. *Deadline:* March 1.

Contact: Director of Grant Programs
Oregon Student Assistance Commission
1500 Valley River Drive, Suite 100
Eugene, OR 97401-7020
Phone: 800-452-8807 Ext. 7395

PENNSYLVANIA ASSOCIATION OF CONSERVATION DISTRICTS AUXILIARY   http://www.blairconservationdistrict.org

PACD AUXILIARY SCHOLARSHIPS
• *See page 76*

RECREATIONAL BOATING INDUSTRIES EDUCATIONAL FOUNDATION   http://www.mbia.org

RECREATIONAL BOATING INDUSTRIES EDUCATIONAL FOUNDATION SCHOLARSHIPS

Scholarships are awarded to students pursuing a degree that will eventually lead to a career in the recreational boating industry. Applicants must be residents of Michigan. Selection will be based on transcript, recommendations, an essay and financial need.

Academic Fields/Career Goals: Biology; Natural Resources; Travel/Tourism.

Award: Scholarship for use in freshman, sophomore, junior, or senior years; not renewable. *Number:* 10–30. *Amount:* $250–$1000.

Eligibility Requirements: Applicant must be enrolled or expecting to enroll full or part-time at a two-year or four-year institution or university and resident of Michigan. Available to U.S. citizens.

Application Requirements: Application, essay, financial need analysis, references, transcript. *Deadline:* March 15.

Contact: Mary Sherman, Administrator
Recreational Boating Industries Educational Foundation
32398 Five Mile Road
Livonia, MI 48154-6109
Phone: 734-261-0123
Fax: 734-261-0880
E-mail: msherm@mbia.org

ROBERT H. MOLLOHAN FAMILY CHARITABLE FOUNDATION, INC.   http://www.mollohanfoundation.org

HIGH TECHNOLOGY SCHOLARS PROGRAM

Scholarship for West Virginia students pursuing a technology-related career and residing in one of the following counties: Barbour, Brooke, Calhoun, Doddridge, Gilmer, Grant, Hancock, Harrison, Marion, Marshall, Mineral, Monongalia, Ohio, Pleasants, Preston, Ritchie, Taylor, Tucker, Tyler, Wetzel, Wood. Scholarship recipients become eligible for a paid internship with a West Virginia business. Students may also apply for debt-forgiveness loans up to $2000 per year.

Academic Fields/Career Goals: Biology; Chemical Engineering; Computer Science/Data Processing; Electrical Engineering/Electronics; Energy and Power Engineering; Engineering/Technology; Engineering-Related Technologies; Mechanical Engineering; Physical Sciences and Math.

Award: Scholarship for use in freshman year; not renewable. *Number:* 1–60. *Amount:* up to $500.

Eligibility Requirements: Applicant must be high school student; planning to enroll or expecting to enroll full or part-time at a four-year institution or university and resident of West Virginia. Applicant must have 3.0 GPA or higher. Available to U.S. citizens.

Application Requirements: Application, essay, resume, references, test scores, transcript. *Deadline:* February 6.

Contact: Teah Bayless, Program Manager
Robert H. Mollohan Family Charitable Foundation, Inc.
1000 Technology Drive, Suite 2000
Fairmont, WV 26554
Phone: 304-333-2251
Fax: 304-333-3900
E-mail: tmbayless@wvhtf.org

ROCKY MOUNTAIN ELK FOUNDATION   http://www.rmef.org

WILDLIFE LEADERSHIP AWARDS

The Rocky Mountain Elk Foundation's (RMEF) Wildlife Leadership Awards program was established in 1990 to recognize, encourage and promote leadership among future wildlife management professionals. RMEF Wildlife Leadership Awards will be presented to up to 10 undergraduate wildlife students. Each award carries a $2000 scholarship, and a one-year membership to the RMEF.

Academic Fields/Career Goals: Biology; Natural Resources.

Award: Scholarship for use in junior or senior years; not renewable. *Number:* 1–10. *Amount:* $2000.

Eligibility Requirements: Applicant must be enrolled or expecting to enroll full-time at a four-year institution or university and must have an interest in designated field specified by sponsor. Available to U.S. and Canadian citizens.

Application Requirements: Application, essay, references. *Deadline:* March 1.

Contact: Denise Wagner
Rocky Mountain Elk Foundation
PO Box 8249
Missoula, MT 59807-8249
Phone: 800-225-5355
Fax: 406-523-4581
E-mail: dwagner@rmef.org

SIGMA XI, THE SCIENTIFIC RESEARCH SOCIETY   http://www.sigmaxi.org

SIGMA XI GRANTS-IN-AID OF RESEARCH
• *See page 84*

SOCIETY FOR INTEGRATIVE AND COMPARATIVE BIOLOGY   http://www.sicb.org

LIBBIE H. HYMAN MEMORIAL SCHOLARSHIP

Scholarship provides assistance to students to take courses or to carry on research on invertebrates at a maritime, freshwater or terrestrial field station. For more information and/or an application go to Web site: http://www.sicb.org.

Academic Fields/Career Goals: Biology.

Award: Scholarship for use in senior, or graduate years; not renewable. *Number:* 1. *Amount:* $750–$1000.

Eligibility Requirements: Applicant must be enrolled or expecting to enroll full or part-time at a four-year institution or university. Available to U.S. and non-U.S. citizens.

Application Requirements: Application, essay, financial need analysis, references, transcript. *Deadline:* March 3.

Contact: Brian Tsukimura, Department of Biology
Society for Integrative and Comparative Biology
Biology Department, Bowdoin College
Brunswick, ME 04011
Phone: 559-278-4244
Fax: 559-278-3963
E-mail: briant@csufresno.edu

SOCIETY FOR MARINE MAMMALOGY   http://www.marinemammalogy.org

FREDERIC FAIRFIELD MEMORIAL FUND AWARD

Award for student scientist who has developed or applied pioneering techniques or research tools for studying marine mammals. Emphasis is on

Society for Marine Mammalogy (continued)

innovative methodology and the potential for making significant advances in our knowledge of marine mammals. All students who indicate a wish to be considered for the award on the Biennial Conference abstract submission form will be considered. Award will be given to a student at each Biennial Conference on the Biology of Marine Mammals

Academic Fields/Career Goals: Biology; Marine Biology.

Award: Scholarship for use in freshman, sophomore, junior, senior, or graduate years. *Number:* 1.

Eligibility Requirements: Applicant must be enrolled or expecting to enroll at a four-year institution or university. Available to U.S. citizens.

Application Requirements: Application. *Deadline:* varies.

Contact: Carol Fairfield, Scholarship Committee Chair
Society for Marine Mammalogy
Awards and Scholarships Committee
49 Eastman Drive South
Laconia, NH 03246
Phone: 603-731-1333
Fax: 603-527-1868
E-mail: carol.fairfield@noaa.gov

SOCIETY OF MEXICAN AMERICAN ENGINEERS AND SCIENTISTS   http://www.maes-natl.org

GRE AND GRADUATE APPLICATIONS WAIVER
• *See page 95*

SOCIETY OF TOXICOLOGY   http://www.toxicology.org

MINORITY UNDERGRADUATE STUDENT AWARDS

Travel funds are provided for members of groups underrepresented in the sciences to attend a special program at the Society of Toxicology Annual Meeting. Must have a 3.0 GPA. Deadline: October 9.

Academic Fields/Career Goals: Biology; Health and Medical Sciences.

Award: Grant for use in freshman, sophomore, junior, or senior years; not renewable. *Number:* 20–50. *Amount:* $1000–$1500.

Eligibility Requirements: Applicant must be American Indian/Alaska Native, Black (non-Hispanic), or Hispanic and enrolled or expecting to enroll full-time at a two-year or four-year institution or university. Applicant must have 3.0 GPA or higher. Available to U.S. citizens.

Application Requirements: Application, essay, resume, references, transcript. *Deadline:* October 9.

Contact: Program Manager
Society of Toxicology
1821 Michael Faraday Drive, Suite 300
Reston, VA 20190
Phone: 703-438-3115
Fax: 703-438-3113

SOIL AND WATER CONSERVATION SOCIETY-NEW JERSEY CHAPTER   http://www.geocities.com/njswcs

EDWARD R. HALL SCHOLARSHIP
• *See page 76*

SOUTHWEST STUDENT SERVICES CORPORATION   http://www.sssc.com/

ANNE LINDEMAN MEMORIAL SCHOLARSHIP

Three $1,000 scholarships are awarded annually to undergraduate students of junior or senior standing who are pursuing a program of study in Education, Social Sciences, or the Health Sciences, at designated Arizona institutions.

Academic Fields/Career Goals: Biology; Dental Health/Services; Education; Food Science/Nutrition; Health and Medical Sciences; Nursing; Social Sciences; Social Services; Special Education; Therapy/Rehabilitation.

Award: Scholarship for use in junior or senior years; not renewable. *Number:* 3. *Amount:* $1000.

Eligibility Requirements: Applicant must be enrolled or expecting to enroll full-time at a four-year institution or university and studying in Arizona. Applicant must have 2.5 GPA or higher. Available to U.S. and non-U.S. citizens.

Application Requirements: Application, essay, resume, references, transcript. *Deadline:* varies.

Contact: Linda Walker, Community Outreach Representative
Southwest Student Services Corporation
PO Box 41150
Mesa, AZ 85274
Phone: 480-461-6566
Fax: 480-461-6595
E-mail: scholarships@sssc.com

TKE EDUCATIONAL FOUNDATION   http://www.tkefoundation.org

CARROL C. HALL MEMORIAL SCHOLARSHIP
• *See page 95*

TURF AND ORNAMENTAL COMMUNICATION ASSOCIATION   http://www.toca.org

TURF AND ORNAMENTAL COMMUNICATORS ASSOCIATION SCHOLARSHIP PROGRAM

One-time award for undergraduate students majoring or minoring in technical communications or a green industry field such as horticulture, plant sciences, botany, or agronomy. The applicant must demonstrate an interest in using this course of study in the field of communications. Applicants must have an overall GPA of 2.5 or 3.0 GPA required in major area of study.

Academic Fields/Career Goals: Biology; Horticulture/Floriculture.

Award: Scholarship for use in freshman, sophomore, junior, or senior years; not renewable. *Number:* 2. *Amount:* up to $1000.

Eligibility Requirements: Applicant must be enrolled or expecting to enroll full-time at a two-year or four-year institution or university. Applicant must have 3.0 GPA or higher. Available to U.S. and non-U.S. citizens.

Application Requirements: Application, essay, portfolio, resume, references, transcript. *Deadline:* March 1.

Contact: Den Gardner, Executive Director
Turf and Ornamental Communication Association
120 West Main Street, Suite 200
PO Box 156
New Prague, MN 56071
Phone: 952-758-6340
Fax: 952-758-5813
E-mail: gard2@aol.com

UNITED NEGRO COLLEGE FUND   http://www.uncf.org

CARGILL SCHOLARSHIP PROGRAM
• *See page 70*

HEINZ ENVIRONMENTAL FELLOWS PROGRAM

Scholarships for UNCF students from Pennsylvania interested in environmental careers. A paid summer internship is included in this award. Minimum 2.5 GPA required. Prospective applicants should complete the Student Profile found at Web site: http://www.uncf.org.

Academic Fields/Career Goals: Biology; Physical Sciences and Math.

Award: Scholarship for use in sophomore year; not renewable. *Amount:* $7500.

Eligibility Requirements: Applicant must be Black (non-Hispanic); enrolled or expecting to enroll at a four-year institution or university and resident of Pennsylvania. Applicant must have 2.5 GPA or higher. Available to U.S. citizens.

Application Requirements: Application, financial need analysis. *Deadline:* Continuous.

Contact: Elvan Gur-Edemen, Senior Program Manager
United Negro College Fund
8260 Willow Oaks Corporate Drive
Fairfax, VA 22031-4511

WYETH SCHOLARSHIP

Must be nominated by financial aid director at the UNCF college. Scholarships for students with 3.0 GPA pursuing science-based or health-related careers. Must be New Jersey resident. Please visit Web site for more information: http://www.uncf.org.

Academic Fields/Career Goals: Biology; Business/Consumer Services; Health and Medical Sciences; Pharmacy; Physical Sciences and Math.

Award: Scholarship for use in freshman, sophomore, junior, or senior years; not renewable. *Amount:* $5000.

Eligibility Requirements: Applicant must be Black (non-Hispanic); enrolled or expecting to enroll at a four-year institution or university and resident of New Jersey. Applicant must have 3.0 GPA or higher. Available to U.S. citizens.

Application Requirements: Application, financial need analysis. *Deadline:* March 8.

Contact: Program Services Department
United Negro College Fund
8260 Willow Oaks Corporate Drive
Fairfax, VA 22031

VIRGINIA BUSINESS AND PROFESSIONAL WOMEN'S FOUNDATION · http://www.bpwva.org

WOMEN IN SCIENCE AND TECHNOLOGY SCHOLARSHIP

One-time award offered to women completing a bachelor's, master's or doctoral degree within two years who are majoring in actuarial science, biology, bio-engineering, chemistry, computer science, dentistry, engineering, mathematics, medicine, physics or similar field. The award may be used for tuition, fees, books, transportation, living expenses, or dependent care. Must be a Virginia resident studying in Virginia.

Academic Fields/Career Goals: Biology; Computer Science/Data Processing; Dental Health/Services; Engineering/Technology; Health and Medical Sciences; Physical Sciences and Math; Science, Technology, and Society.

Award: Scholarship for use in junior, senior, graduate, or postgraduate years; not renewable. *Number:* 1–5. *Amount:* $100–$1000.

Eligibility Requirements: Applicant must be age 18; enrolled or expecting to enroll full or part-time at a four-year institution or university; female; resident of Virginia and studying in Virginia. Available to U.S. citizens.

Application Requirements: Application, essay, financial need analysis, references, transcript. *Deadline:* April 1.

Contact: Sheila Barry-Oliver, Senior Trustee
Virginia Business and Professional Women's Foundation
PO Box 4842
McLean, VA 22103-4842
Phone: 703-759-2081
Fax: 703-759-2053
E-mail: bpwva@advocate.net

WILSON ORNITHOLOGICAL SOCIETY · http://www.ummz.lsa.umich.edu/birds/wos.html

GEORGE A. HALL / HAROLD F. MAYFIELD AWARD
• *See page 87*

PAUL A. STEWART AWARDS
• *See page 88*

BUSINESS/CONSUMER SERVICES

ALL STUDENT LOAN CORPORATION · http://www.allstudentloan.org

ALLSTUDENTLOAN.ORG COLLEGE SCHOLARSHIP PROGRAM

Scholarship for a graduating high school senior or current postsecondary student. Must be an active member of an eligible vocational student organization: Future Business Leaders of America-Phi Beta Lambda, Business Professionals of America or DECA.

Academic Fields/Career Goals: Business/Consumer Services.

Award: Scholarship for use in freshman, sophomore, junior, senior, or graduate years. *Amount:* up to $500.

Eligibility Requirements: Applicant must be enrolled or expecting to enroll at a four-year institution or university. Available to U.S. citizens.

Application Requirements: Application, essay, financial need analysis, FAFSA. *Deadline:* June 1.

Contact: Amy Tien-Gordon, Vice President and Chief Student Lending Officer
ALL Student Loan Corporation
6701 Center Drive West, Suite 500
Los Angeles, CA 90045-1547
Phone: 888-271-9721
Fax: 310-979-4714
E-mail: atien@allstudentloan.org

AMERICAN CONGRESS ON SURVEYING AND MAPPING · http://www.acsm.net

TRI-STATE SURVEYING AND PHOTOGRAMMETRY KRIS M. KUNZE MEMORIAL SCHOLARSHIP

One-time award for students pursuing college-level courses in business administration or business management. Candidates, in order of priority, include professional land surveyors and certified photogrammetrists, land survey interns and students enrolled in a two- or four-year program in surveying and mapping. Must be ACSM member.

Academic Fields/Career Goals: Business/Consumer Services.

Award: Scholarship for use in freshman, sophomore, junior, or senior years; not renewable. *Amount:* $1000.

Eligibility Requirements: Applicant must be enrolled or expecting to enroll full or part-time at a two-year or four-year institution. Applicant or parent of applicant must be member of American Congress on Surveying and Mapping. Available to U.S. citizens.

Application Requirements: Application, essay, references, transcript. *Deadline:* December 1.

Contact: Lilly Matheson, ACSM Awards Department
American Congress on Surveying and Mapping
6 Montgomery Village Avenue, Suite 403
Gaithersburg, MD 20879
Phone: 301-493-0200 Ext. 102
E-mail: lilym@mindspring.com

AMERICAN FLORAL ENDOWMENT · http://www.endowment.org

HAROLD F. WILKINS SCHOLARSHIP PROGRAM

One-time award to aid and encourage students majoring in business, floriculture and ornamental horticulture, to have a floriculture internship outside the U.S. and to aid students who wish to travel to a foreign country to study the floriculture industry (convention, symposium, independent travel programs). Deadlines: March 1 for Fall/Winter training; November 1 for Spring/Summer training.

Academic Fields/Career Goals: Business/Consumer Services; Horticulture/Floriculture.

Award: Scholarship for use in freshman, sophomore, junior, senior, graduate, or postgraduate years; not renewable. *Number:* 1–3. *Amount:* $1000–$7500.

Eligibility Requirements: Applicant must be enrolled or expecting to enroll full-time at a two-year or four-year institution or university. Applicant must have 2.5 GPA or higher. Available to U.S. citizens.

Application Requirements: Application, photo, references, transcript. *Deadline:* varies.

Contact: Amy Lididel, Administrator
American Floral Endowment
PO Box 945
Edwardsville, IL 62025
Phone: 618-692-0045
Fax: 618-692-4045

MOSMILLER SCHOLAR PROGRAM

Award for undergraduate students majoring in business, floriculture, and ornamental horticulture. Ten to sixteen weeks of paid training with floral retailers, wholesalers, and allied trades, in addition to a $2000 grant upon satisfactory completion. Deadlines: March 1 for Fall and Winter training; November 1 for Spring and Summer training.

Academic Fields/Career Goals: Business/Consumer Services; Horticulture/Floriculture.

American Floral Endowment (continued)

Award: Scholarship for use in freshman, sophomore, junior, or senior years; not renewable. *Number: 5–7. Amount: $2000.*

Eligibility Requirements: Applicant must be enrolled or expecting to enroll full-time at a two-year or four-year institution or university. Applicant must have 2.5 GPA or higher. Available to U.S. citizens.

Application Requirements: Application, photo, references, transcript. *Deadline: varies.*

Contact: Amy Lididel, Administrator
American Floral Endowment
11 Glen-Ed Professional Park, PO Box 945
Edwardsville, IL 62034
Phone: 618-692-0045
Fax: 618-692-4045

VICTOR AND MARGARET BALL PROGRAM

Award for undergraduate students majoring in business, floriculture, and ornamental horticulture. A paid training experience for students who are interested in a "production related" career (growing), and up to a $6000 grant upon satisfactory completion of six months of training. Deadlines: March 1 for Fall/Winter training; November 1 for Spring/Summer training.

Academic Fields/Career Goals: Business/Consumer Services; Horticulture/Floriculture.

Award: Scholarship for use in freshman, sophomore, junior, or senior years; not renewable. *Number: 20. Amount: $1500–$6000.*

Eligibility Requirements: Applicant must be enrolled or expecting to enroll full-time at a two-year or four-year institution or university. Applicant must have 2.5 GPA or higher. Available to U.S. citizens.

Application Requirements: Application, photo, references, transcript. *Deadline: varies.*

Contact: Amy Lididel, Administrator
American Floral Endowment
11 Glen-Ed Professional Park, PO Box 945
Edwardsville, IL 62025
Phone: 618-692-0045
Fax: 618-692-4045

AMERICAN INDIAN SCIENCE AND ENGINEERING SOCIETY   http://www.aises.org

A.T. ANDERSON MEMORIAL SCHOLARSHIP
• See page 89

BURLINGTON NORTHERN SANTA FE FOUNDATION SCHOLARSHIP
• See page 89

AMERICAN PUBLIC TRANSPORTATION FOUNDATION   http://www.apta.com

DAN REICHARD JR. SCHOLARSHIP

Scholarship for study towards a career in the business administration/management area of the transit industry. Must be sponsored by APTA member organization and complete internship with APTA member organization. Minimum GPA of 3.0 required.

Academic Fields/Career Goals: Business/Consumer Services; Transportation.

Award: Scholarship for use in sophomore, junior, senior, graduate, or postgraduate years; renewable. *Number: 1. Amount: $2500.*

Eligibility Requirements: Applicant must be enrolled or expecting to enroll full-time at a four-year institution or university. Applicant must have 3.0 GPA or higher. Available to U.S. and Canadian citizens.

Application Requirements: Application, essay, financial need analysis, references, transcript, verification of enrollment for the current semester and copy of the fee schedule from the college/university. *Deadline: June 16.*

Contact: Pamela Boswell, Vice President of Program Management
American Public Transportation Foundation
1666 K Street, NW
Washington, DC 20006-1215
Phone: 202-496-4803
Fax: 202-496-2323
E-mail: pboswell@apta.com

AMERICAN WELDING SOCIETY   http://www.aws.org

JAMES A. TURNER, JR. MEMORIAL SCHOLARSHIP

Award for a full-time student pursuing minimum four-year bachelor's degree in business that will lead to a management career in welding store operations or a welding distributorship. Applicant must be working in this field at least 10 hours per week. Submit verification of employment, a copy of proposed curriculum, and acceptance letter.

Academic Fields/Career Goals: Business/Consumer Services.

Award: Scholarship for use in sophomore, junior, or senior years; renewable. *Number: 1. Amount: $3000.*

Eligibility Requirements: Applicant must be enrolled or expecting to enroll full-time at a four-year institution. Available to U.S. citizens.

Application Requirements: Application, autobiography, financial need analysis, references, transcript. *Deadline: January 15.*

Contact: Vicki Pinsky, Manager Foundation
American Welding Society
550 Northwest Le Jeune Road
Miami, FL 33126
Phone: 800-443-9353 Ext. 212
Fax: 305-443-7559
E-mail: vpinskybw@aws.org

AMERICAN WHOLESALE MARKETERS ASSOCIATION   http://www.awmanet.org

RAY FOLEY MEMORIAL YOUTH EDUCATION FOUNDATION SCHOLARSHIP

Scholarships available to an employee of an AWMA wholesaler member company or the immediate family member of an employee of an AWMA wholesaler member company (spouse, son, or daughter only). Applicant must be enrolled full time in an undergraduate or graduate business program and demonstrate sufficient interest in a career in the convenience products wholesale distribution industry. Application deadline is May 26. For more information, visit the Web site: http://www.awmanet.org/edu/edu-schol.htm

Academic Fields/Career Goals: Business/Consumer Services.

Award: Scholarship for use in freshman, sophomore, junior, senior, or graduate years; not renewable. *Number: 2. Amount: $5000.*

Eligibility Requirements: Applicant must be enrolled or expecting to enroll full-time at a two-year or four-year institution or university. Available to U.S. citizens.

Application Requirements: Application, essay, references. *Deadline: May 26.*

Contact: Kathy Trost, Manager of Education
American Wholesale Marketers Association
2750 Prosperity Avenue, Suite 530
Fairfax, VA 22031
Phone: 800-482-2962 Ext. 648
Fax: 703-573-5738
E-mail: kathyt@awmanet.org.

APICS EDUCATIONAL AND RESEARCH FOUNDATION, INC.   http://www.apics.org

DONALD W. FOGARTY INTERNATIONAL STUDENT PAPER COMPETITION

Annual competition on topics pertaining to resource management only. Must be original work of one or more authors. May submit one paper only. Must be in English. Open to full- and part-time undergraduate and graduate students. High school students ineligible. All queries are directed to Web site. Other queries must submit e-mail address and SASE.

Academic Fields/Career Goals: Business/Consumer Services; Natural Resources.

Award: Prize for use in freshman, sophomore, junior, senior, or graduate years; not renewable. *Number: 58. Amount: $250–$1000.*

Eligibility Requirements: Applicant must be enrolled or expecting to enroll full or part-time at a four-year institution or university. Available to U.S. and non-U.S. citizens.

Application Requirements: Application, applicant must enter a contest, essay, self-addressed stamped envelope. *Deadline:* May 15.

Contact: J . Chisholm, Board of Directors
APICS Educational and Research Foundation, Inc.
5301 Shawnee Road
Alexandria, VA 22312-2317
E-mail: cjames938@aol.com

ARRL FOUNDATION, INC.　　http://www.arrl.org/arrlf/scholgen.html

WILLIAM R. GOLDFARB MEMORIAL SCHOLARSHIP

Award for baccalaureate or post-graduate study in business, computers, medical or nursing, engineering, or sciences. Must be a licensed amateur radio operator. Must demonstrate financial need by submission of a Free Application for Federal Student Aid (FAFSA) Student Aid Report (SAR). Deadline is February 1.

Academic Fields/Career Goals: Business/Consumer Services; Computer Science/Data Processing; Engineering/Technology; Health and Medical Sciences; Natural Sciences; Nursing.

Award: Scholarship for use in freshman, sophomore, junior, senior, or graduate years; not renewable. *Number:* 1. *Amount:* up to $10,000.

Eligibility Requirements: Applicant must be enrolled or expecting to enroll full-time at a four-year institution or university and must have an interest in amateur radio. Available to U.S. citizens.

Application Requirements: Application, financial need analysis, transcript, FAFSA, Student Aid Report (SAR). *Deadline:* February 1.

Contact: Mary Hobart, Secretary Foundation
ARRL Foundation, Inc.
225 Main Street
Newington, CT 06111-1494
Phone: 860-594-0397
E-mail: k1mmh@arrl.org

ASSOCIATION OF LATINO PROFESSIONALS IN FINANCE AND ACCOUNTING　　http://www.alpfa.org

HSF-ALPFA SCHOLARSHIPS
• *See page 55*

CALIFORNIA SOCIETY OF CERTIFIED PUBLIC ACCOUNTANTS　　http://www.aicpa.org

AICPA/ACCOUNTEMPS STUDENT SCHOLARSHIP
• *See page 55*

CASUALTY ACTUARIAL SOCIETY/SOCIETY OF ACTUARIES JOINT COMMITTEE ON MINORITY RECRUITING　　http://www.BeAnActuary.org

ACTUARIAL SCHOLARSHIPS FOR MINORITY STUDENTS

Award for underrepresented minority students planning careers in actuarial science or mathematics. Applicants should have taken the ACT Assessment or the SAT. Number and amount of awards vary with merit and financial need. Must be a U.S. citizen or permanent resident. All scholarship information including application is available online. Do not send award inquiries to address.

Academic Fields/Career Goals: Business/Consumer Services; Mathematics.

Award: Scholarship for use in freshman, sophomore, junior, senior, or graduate years; renewable. *Number:* 20–40. *Amount:* $500–$3000.

Eligibility Requirements: Applicant must be American Indian/Alaska Native, Black (non-Hispanic), or Hispanic and enrolled or expecting to enroll full or part-time at a two-year or four-year institution or university. Applicant must have 3.0 GPA or higher. Available to U.S. and Canadian citizens.

Application Requirements: Application, financial need analysis, references, test scores, transcript, nomination forms. *Deadline:* May 1.

Contact: Summer R. Cole, Minority Scholarship Coordinator
Casualty Actuarial Society/Society of Actuaries Joint Committee on Minority Recruiting
Society of Actuaries, 475 North Martingale Road, Suite 800
Schaumburg, IL 60173-2226
Phone: 847-706-3500

CATCHING THE DREAM

MATH, ENGINEERING, SCIENCE, BUSINESS, EDUCATION, COMPUTERS SCHOLARSHIPS

Renewable scholarships for Native-American students planning to study math, engineering, science, business, education, and computers, or presently studying in these fields. Study of social science, humanities and liberal arts also funded. Scholarships are awarded on merit and on the basis of likelihood of recipient improving the lives of Native American people. Deadlines are March 15, April 15, and September 15. Scholarships are available nationwide.

Academic Fields/Career Goals: Business/Consumer Services; Computer Science/Data Processing; Education; Engineering/Technology; Humanities; Physical Sciences and Math; Science, Technology, and Society; Social Sciences.

Award: Scholarship for use in freshman, sophomore, junior, senior, graduate, or postgraduate years; renewable. *Number:* 180. *Amount:* $500–$5000.

Eligibility Requirements: Applicant must be American Indian/Alaska Native and enrolled or expecting to enroll full-time at a two-year or four-year institution or university. Applicant must have 3.0 GPA or higher. Available to U.S. citizens.

Application Requirements: Application, essay, financial need analysis, photo, references, test scores, transcript, certificate of Indian blood. *Deadline:* April 15.

Contact: Mary Frost, Recruiter
Catching the Dream
8200 Mountain Road, NE Suite 203
Albuquerque, NM 87110
Phone: 505-262-2351
Fax: 505-262-0534
E-mail: nscholarsh@aol.com

NATIVE AMERICAN LEADERSHIP IN EDUCATION (NALE)

Renewable scholarships available for Native-American and Alaska Native students. Must be at least one-quarter Native-American from a federally recognized, state recognized, or terminated tribe. Must be U.S. citizen. Must demonstrate high academic achievement, depth of character, leadership, seriousness of purpose, and service orientation. Application deadlines are March 15, April 15, and September 15.

Academic Fields/Career Goals: Business/Consumer Services; Education; Humanities; Physical Sciences and Math; Science, Technology, and Society.

Award: Scholarship for use in freshman, sophomore, junior, or senior years; renewable. *Number:* up to 30. *Amount:* $500–$5000.

Eligibility Requirements: Applicant must be American Indian/Alaska Native and enrolled or expecting to enroll full-time at a four-year institution or university. Available to U.S. citizens.

Application Requirements: Application, essay, references, transcript. *Deadline:* varies.

Contact: Mary Frost, Recruiter
Catching the Dream
8200 Mountain Road, NE, Suite 203
Albuquerque, NM 87110
Phone: 505-262-2351
Fax: 505-262-0534
E-mail: nscholarsh@aol.com

TRIBAL BUSINESS MANAGEMENT PROGRAM (TBM)
• *See page 55*

CENTER FOR SCHOLARSHIP ADMINISTRATION　　http://www.scholarshipprograms.org

BANK OF AMERICA ADA ABILITIES SCHOLARSHIP
• *See page 56*

CENTRAL INTELLIGENCE AGENCY   http://www.cia.gov

CENTRAL INTELLIGENCE AGENCY UNDERGRADUATE SCHOLARSHIP PROGRAM
• See page 56

CHARLOTTE OBSERVER   http://www.charlotte.com/

CHARLOTTE OBSERVER MINORITY SCHOLARSHIPS

Scholarship is available for minority high school students who are interested in the newspaper business, either in the newsroom or business operations. Applicants must send in samples of their work along with the application. Deadline for submitting application is in December. Must be resident of North Carolina or South Carolina.

Academic Fields/Career Goals: Business/Consumer Services; Journalism.

Award: Scholarship for use in freshman year; not renewable. *Number:* 2. *Amount:* $1000.

Eligibility Requirements: Applicant must be American Indian/Alaska Native, Asian/Pacific Islander, Black (non-Hispanic), or Hispanic; high school student; planning to enroll or expecting to enroll full-time at a four-year institution or university and resident of North Carolina or South Carolina. Available to U.S. citizens.

Application Requirements: Application, essay, interview, resume, references, transcript. *Deadline:* December 27.

Contact: Lyn Belvin, Human Resources Manager
Charlotte Observer
600 South Tyron Street
Charlotte, NC 28202
Phone: 704-358-5726

CIRI FOUNDATION   http://www.thecirifoundation.org

CARL H. MARRS SCHOLARSHIP FUND
• See page 56

COMMUNITY FOUNDATION FOR PALM BEACH AND MARTIN COUNTIES, INC.   http://www.yourcommunityfoundation.org

BANK OF AMERICA MINORITY SCHOLARSHIP

Student member of minority community attending Palm Beach County public or private high school intending to major in business. Must have "C" average or better, financial need, be enrolled in an accredited four year college or university.

Academic Fields/Career Goals: Business/Consumer Services.

Award: Scholarship for use in freshman year; not renewable. *Number:* 1. *Amount:* $750–$2500.

Eligibility Requirements: Applicant must be American Indian/Alaska Native, Asian/Pacific Islander, Black (non-Hispanic), or Hispanic; high school student; planning to enroll or expecting to enroll full-time at a two-year or four-year institution or university and resident of Florida. Available to U.S. citizens.

Application Requirements: Application, financial need analysis, test scores, transcript. *Deadline:* February 1.

Contact: Carolyn Jenco, Grants Manager/Scholarship Coordinator
Community Foundation for Palm Beach and Martin Counties, Inc.
700 South Dixie Highway, Suite 200
West Palm Beach, FL 33401
Phone: 561-659-6800
Fax: 561-832-6542
E-mail: cjenco@cfpbmc.org

COMMUNITY FOUNDATION OF WESTERN MASSACHUSETTS   http://www.communityfoundation.org

GREATER SPRINGFIELD ACCOUNTANTS SCHOLARSHIP
• See page 57

CUBAN AMERICAN NATIONAL FOUNDATION   http://www.canf.org

MAS FAMILY SCHOLARSHIPS

Graduate and undergraduate scholarships in the fields of engineering, business, international relations, economics, communications, and journalism. Applicants must be Cuban-American and have graduated in the top 10% of high school class or have minimum 3.5 college GPA. Selection based on need, academic performance, leadership. Those who have already received awards and maintained high level of performance are given preference over new applicants.

Academic Fields/Career Goals: Business/Consumer Services; Chemical Engineering; Communications; Economics; Electrical Engineering/Electronics; Engineering/Technology; Engineering-Related Technologies; Journalism; Mechanical Engineering; Political Science.

Award: Scholarship for use in freshman, sophomore, junior, or senior years; renewable. *Number:* 10–15. *Amount:* $1000–$10,000.

Eligibility Requirements: Applicant must be of Latin American/Caribbean heritage; enrolled or expecting to enroll full-time at a two-year or four-year institution or university and must have an interest in leadership. Applicant must have 3.5 GPA or higher. Available to U.S. citizens.

Application Requirements: Application, autobiography, essay, financial need analysis, references, test scores, transcript, proof of Cuban descent, admission, statement of need. *Deadline:* March 31.

Contact: Director
Cuban American National Foundation
1312 South West 27th Avenue, 3rd Floor
Miami, FL 33145
Phone: 305-592-7768
Fax: 305-592-7889

DAYTON ADVERTISING CLUB   http://www.daytonadclub.org/scholarship.php

BARBARA S. MILLER MEMORIAL SCHOLARSHIP

Scholarship is available to students studying any of the disciplines related to advertising (marketing, communications, advertising, advertising arts, etc.). Deadline is March 31.

Academic Fields/Career Goals: Business/Consumer Services; Communications.

Award: Scholarship for use in freshman, sophomore, junior, or senior years; not renewable. *Amount:* $750.

Eligibility Requirements: Applicant must be enrolled or expecting to enroll at a four-year institution or university. Available to U.S. citizens.

Application Requirements: Application, essay. *Deadline:* March 31.

Contact: Mike Fariello, Barbara S. Miller Memorial Scholarship
Dayton Advertising Club
PO Box 225
Dayton, OH 45401
Phone: 937-879-3212

DECA (DISTRIBUTIVE EDUCATION CLUBS OF AMERICA)   http://www.deca.org

HARRY A. APPLEGATE SCHOLARSHIP

Available to current DECA members for undergraduate or graduate study. Must major in marketing education, merchandising, and/or management. Nonrenewable award for high school students based on DECA activities, grades, and need. Submit application to state office by state application deadline. National office must receive applications by the second Monday in March.

Academic Fields/Career Goals: Business/Consumer Services; Education; Food Service/Hospitality.

Award: Scholarship for use in freshman, sophomore, junior, senior, or graduate years; not renewable. *Number:* 20–25. *Amount:* up to $1000.

Eligibility Requirements: Applicant must be high school student; planning to enroll or expecting to enroll full or part-time at a two-year or four-year institution or university and must have an interest in leadership. Applicant or parent of applicant must be member of Distribution Ed Club or Future Business Leaders of America. Applicant must have 2.5 GPA or higher. Available to U.S. and Canadian citizens.

Application Requirements: Application, references, test scores, transcript. *Deadline:* March 8.

Contact: Kathy Onion, Marketing Specialist
DECA (Distributive Education Clubs of America)
1908 Association Drive
Reston, VA 20191-4013
Phone: 703-860-5000 Ext. 248
Fax: 703-860-4013
E-mail: kathy_onion@deca.org

FAMILY, CAREER AND COMMUNITY LEADERS OF AMERICA-TEXAS ASSOCIATION http://www.texasfccla.org

FCCLA REGIONAL SCHOLARSHIPS

Five scholarships will be awarded annually to applicants who have been members of the Texas FCCLA. Theme is required on how involvement in FCCLA or family and consumer sciences has prepared you for your future. Applicants should visit the Web site (http://www.texasfccla.org) or write to Texas FCCLA for complete information, submission guidelines, and restrictions.

Academic Fields/Career Goals: Business/Consumer Services; Home Economics.

Award: Scholarship for use in freshman year; not renewable. *Number:* 5. *Amount:* $1000.

Eligibility Requirements: Applicant must be high school student; planning to enroll or expecting to enroll full-time at a four-year institution or university; resident of Texas and studying in Texas. Applicant or parent of applicant must be member of Family, Career and Community Leaders of America. Available to U.S. citizens.

Application Requirements: Application, essay, references, test scores, transcript. *Deadline:* March 1.

Contact: FCCLA Staff
Family, Career and Community Leaders of America-Texas Association
3530 Bee Caves Road, Suite 101
Austin, TX 78746-9616
Phone: 512-306-0099
Fax: 512-306-0041
E-mail: fccla@texasfccla.org

FCCLA TEXAS FARM BUREAU SCHOLARSHIP

Applicant must have been a regional or state FCCLA officer and must be planning to teach home economics/family and consumer sciences. Applicants should visit the Web site (http://www.texasfccla.org) or write to Texas FCCLA for complete information, submission guidelines, and restrictions. Must be a Texas resident and enroll in a Texas institution.

Academic Fields/Career Goals: Business/Consumer Services; Education; Home Economics.

Award: Scholarship for use in freshman year; not renewable. *Number:* 1. *Amount:* $1000.

Eligibility Requirements: Applicant must be high school student; planning to enroll or expecting to enroll full-time at a four-year institution or university; resident of Texas and studying in Texas. Applicant or parent of applicant must be member of Family, Career and Community Leaders of America. Available to U.S. citizens.

Application Requirements: Application, autobiography, essay, references, test scores, transcript. *Deadline:* March 1.

Contact: FCCLA Staff
Family, Career and Community Leaders of America-Texas Association
3530 Bee Caves Road, #101
Austin, TX 78746-9616
Phone: 512-306-0099
Fax: 512-306-0041
E-mail: fccla@texasfccla.org

FIRST–FLORICULTURE INDUSTRY RESEARCH AND SCHOLARSHIP TRUST http://www.firstinfloriculture.org

HAROLD BETTINGER MEMORIAL SCHOLARSHIP
• *See page 74*

FLORIDA BANKERS EDUCATIONAL FOUNDATION http://www.floridabankers.com

FLORIDA BANKERS EDUCATIONAL FOUNDATION SCHOLARSHIP/LOAN

Program has assisted over 2000 students since 1956 and is designed to support the education of future and/or current Florida bankers. Must be enrolled for at least 12 credit hours per year at FBEF participating Florida university. Loan to be paid back if degree is not obtained. Must also work for one year in a Florida bank upon graduation for loan to be forgiven.

Academic Fields/Career Goals: Business/Consumer Services.

Award: Forgivable loan for use in freshman, sophomore, junior, senior, or graduate years; not renewable. *Number:* 10–50. *Amount:* up to $3000.

Eligibility Requirements: Applicant must be enrolled or expecting to enroll full or part-time at a four-year institution or university; resident of Florida; studying in Florida and must have an interest in leadership. Applicant or parent of applicant must have employment or volunteer experience in banking. Applicant must have 2.5 GPA or higher. Available to U.S. citizens.

Application Requirements: Application, driver's license, essay, interview, resume, references, transcript, credit check (for loan). *Deadline:* varies.

Contact: Letty Newton, Director
Florida Bankers Educational Foundation
PO Box 1360
Tallahassee, FL 32302-1360
Phone: 850-224-2265
Fax: 850-224-2423
E-mail: lnewton@flbankers.net

FUKUNAGA SCHOLARSHIP FOUNDATION http://www.servco.com

FUKUNAGA SCHOLARSHIP FOUNDATION

Renewable scholarships available only to Hawaii residents pursuing a business degree at the undergraduate level at an accredited institution. Minimum 3.0 GPA required.

Academic Fields/Career Goals: Business/Consumer Services.

Award: Scholarship for use in freshman, sophomore, junior, or senior years; renewable. *Number:* 12–15. *Amount:* up to $3000.

Eligibility Requirements: Applicant must be enrolled or expecting to enroll full-time at a four-year institution or university and resident of Hawaii. Applicant must have 3.0 GPA or higher. Available to U.S. citizens.

Application Requirements: Application, financial need analysis, references, test scores, transcript, FAFSA, Student Aid Report (SAR). *Deadline:* February 15.

Contact: Sandy Wong, Administrator
Fukunaga Scholarship Foundation
PO Box 2788
Honolulu, HI 96803-2788
Phone: 808-564-1386
Fax: 808-523-3937
E-mail: sandyw@servco.com

GEORGIA SOCIETY OF CERTIFIED PUBLIC ACCOUNTANTS http://www.gscpa.org

BEN W. BRANNON MEMORIAL SCHOLARSHIP FUND
• *See page 60*

GOLDEN KEY INTERNATIONAL HONOUR SOCIETY http://www.goldenkey.org

BUSINESS ACHIEVEMENT AWARD

Applicants will be asked to respond to a problem posed by an honorary member within the discipline. The response will be in the form of a professional business report. One winner will receive a $1000 award. The second place applicant will receive $750 and the third place applicant will receive $500. See Web site for more information: http://goldenkey.gsu.edu.

Academic Fields/Career Goals: Business/Consumer Services.

Golden Key International Honour Society (continued)

Award: Prize for use in junior, senior, graduate, or postgraduate years; not renewable. *Number:* 3. *Amount:* $500–$1000.

Eligibility Requirements: Applicant must be enrolled or expecting to enroll full or part-time at an institution or university. Available to U.S. citizens.

Application Requirements: Application, applicant must enter a contest, essay, references, transcript, business-related report. *Deadline:* March 1.

Contact: Scholarship Program Administrators
Golden Key International Honour Society
PO Box 23737
Nashville, TN 37202-3737
Phone: 800-377-2401
E-mail: scholarships@goldenkey.org

GOVERNMENT FINANCE OFFICERS ASSOCIATION
http://www.gfoa.org

FRANK L. GREATHOUSE GOVERNMENT ACCOUNTING SCHOLARSHIP

One to two scholarships awarded to senior undergraduate students enrolled full-time preparing for a career in state or local government finance. Submit resume. One-time award of $3500.

Academic Fields/Career Goals: Business/Consumer Services; Public Policy and Administration.

Award: Scholarship for use in junior, senior, or postgraduate years; not renewable. *Number:* 1–2. *Amount:* $3500.

Eligibility Requirements: Applicant must be enrolled or expecting to enroll full-time at a two-year or four-year or technical institution or university and must have an interest in designated field specified by sponsor. Available to U.S. and Canadian citizens.

Application Requirements: Application, essay, resume, references, transcript. *Deadline:* varies.

Contact: Jake Lorentz, Assistant Director
Government Finance Officers Association
Scholarship Committee
203 North LaSalle Street, Suite 2700
Chicago, IL 60601-1210
Phone: 312-977-9700 Ext. 267
Fax: 312-977-4806
E-mail: jlorentz@gfoa.org

GEORGE A. NIELSEN PUBLIC INVESTOR SCHOLARSHIP

Award for employee of local government or other public entity who is enrolled or plans to enroll in an undergraduate or graduate program in public administration, finance, business administration, or a related field.

Academic Fields/Career Goals: Business/Consumer Services; Public Policy and Administration.

Award: Scholarship for use in freshman, sophomore, junior, senior, graduate, or postgraduate years; not renewable. *Number:* 1–2. *Amount:* $2500–$5000.

Eligibility Requirements: Applicant must be enrolled or expecting to enroll full or part-time at a four-year institution or university. Applicant or parent of applicant must have employment or volunteer experience in designated career field. Available to U.S. and Canadian citizens.

Application Requirements: Application, essay, resume, references, transcript. *Deadline:* varies.

Contact: Jake Lorentz, Assistant Director
Government Finance Officers Association
Scholarship Committee
203 North LaSalle Street, Suite 2700
Chicago, IL 60601-1210
Phone: 312-977-9700 Ext. 267
Fax: 312-977-4806
E-mail: jlorentz@gfoa.org

MINORITIES IN GOVERNMENT FINANCE SCHOLARSHIP
• *See page 62*

GRAND CHAPTER OF CALIFORNIA-ORDER OF THE EASTERN STAR
http://www.oescal.org

SCHOLARSHIPS FOR EDUCATION, BUSINESS AND RELIGION

$500 to $3000 scholarships are awarded to students residing in California for postsecondary study. These scholarships are awarded for the study of business, education or religion.

Academic Fields/Career Goals: Business/Consumer Services; Education; Religion/Theology.

Award: Scholarship for use in freshman, sophomore, junior, senior, graduate, or postgraduate years; renewable. *Number:* varies. *Amount:* $500–$3000.

Eligibility Requirements: Applicant must be enrolled or expecting to enroll full-time at a two-year or four-year or technical institution or university and resident of California. Applicant must have 3.0 GPA or higher. Available to U.S. citizens.

Application Requirements: Application, financial need analysis, photo, references, self-addressed stamped envelope, transcript, proof of acceptance to college or university. *Deadline:* March 15.

Contact: Sharanne Wick, Grand Secretary
Grand Chapter of California-Order of the Eastern Star
16960 Bastanchury Road, Suite E
Yorba Linda, CA 92886-1711
Phone: 714-986-2380
Fax: 714-986-2385
E-mail: gsecretary@oescal.org

GRAND RAPIDS COMMUNITY FOUNDATION
http://www.grfoundation.org

ECONOMIC CLUB OF GRAND RAPIDS BUSINESS STUDY ABROAD SCHOLARSHIP
• *See page 62*

GREATER KANAWHA VALLEY FOUNDATION
http://www.tgkvf.org

WILLARD H. ERWIN, JR. MEMORIAL SCHOLARSHIP FUND

Award for West Virginia residents who are starting their junior or senior year of undergraduate or graduate studies in a business or health-care finance degree program. Must be enrolled at a college in West Virginia. May apply for two Foundation scholarships but will only be chosen for one. Scholarships are awarded on the basis of financial need and scholastic ability.

Academic Fields/Career Goals: Business/Consumer Services; Health Administration.

Award: Scholarship for use in junior, senior, or graduate years; renewable. *Number:* 1. *Amount:* $500.

Eligibility Requirements: Applicant must be enrolled or expecting to enroll full or part-time at a four-year institution or university; resident of West Virginia and studying in West Virginia. Applicant must have 2.5 GPA or higher. Available to U.S. citizens.

Application Requirements: Application, essay, financial need analysis, references, self-addressed stamped envelope, test scores, transcript. *Deadline:* February 15.

Contact: Susan Hoover, Scholarship Coordinator
Greater Kanawha Valley Foundation
PO Box 3041
Charleston, WV 25331
Phone: 304-346-3620
Fax: 304-346-3640

HISPANIC COLLEGE FUND, INC.
http://www.hispanicfund.org

DENNY'S/HISPANIC COLLEGE FUND SCHOLARSHIP
• *See page 62*

DEPARTMENT OF ENERGY SCHOLARSHIP PROGRAM

Scholarship available to full-time undergraduate students in their sophomore or junior year who are pursuing a degree in business science, engineering or DOE-related major. Must be U.S. citizen, have a minimum 3.0 GPA, and be available to participate in a paid summer internship.

Academic Fields/Career Goals: Business/Consumer Services; Chemical Engineering; Electrical Engineering/Electronics; Energy and Power Engineering; Engineering/Technology; Engineering-Related Technologies; Environmental Science; Materials Science, Engineering, and Metallurgy; Mechanical Engineering; Natural Resources; Natural Sciences; Nuclear Science.

Award: Scholarship for use in freshman, sophomore, junior, or senior years; not renewable. *Number:* 15. *Amount:* $500–$5000.

Eligibility Requirements: Applicant must be enrolled or expecting to enroll full-time at a four-year institution or university. Applicant must have 3.0 GPA or higher. Available to U.S. citizens.

Application Requirements: Application, essay, financial need analysis. *Deadline:* April 15.

Contact: Stina Augustsson, Program Manager
Hispanic College Fund, Inc.
1717 Pennsylvania Avenue, NW, Suite 460
Washington, DC 20006
Phone: 202-296-5400
Fax: 202-296-3774
E-mail: hcf-info@hispanicfund.org

ICI EDUCATIONAL FOUNDATION SCHOLARSHIP PROGRAM
• See page 62

M & T BANK/ HISPANIC COLLEGE FUND SCHOLARSHIP PROGRAM
• See page 63

HISPANIC SCHOLARSHIP FUND   http://www.hsf.net

HSF/GENERAL MOTORS SCHOLARSHIP

Scholarships are available to Hispanic students pursuing a degree in business or engineering at an accredited U.S. four-year college. For more details, deadlines and an application see Web site: http://www.hsf.net

Academic Fields/Career Goals: Business/Consumer Services; Chemical Engineering; Civil Engineering; Electrical Engineering/Electronics; Engineering/Technology; Engineering-Related Technologies; Mechanical Engineering.

Award: Scholarship for use in freshman, sophomore, junior, or senior years; not renewable. *Number:* 83. *Amount:* up to $2500.

Eligibility Requirements: Applicant must be Hispanic and enrolled or expecting to enroll full-time at a four-year institution or university. Applicant must have 3.0 GPA or higher. Available to U.S. citizens.

Application Requirements: Application, essay, financial need analysis, references, transcript, must complete the GM Online Assessment, copy of Student Aid Report (SAR). *Deadline:* June 30.

Contact: Program Officer
Hispanic Scholarship Fund
55 Second Street, Suite 1500
San Francisco, CA 94105
Phone: 877-473-4636
Fax: 415-808-2302

HSF/LITTLE VILLAGE CHAMBER OF COMMERCE AMBASSADORS SCHOLARSHIP PROGRAM

Scholarship for undergraduate and graduate students from the Little Village Community on Chicago's West Side, who are pursuing a degree in business, finance, marketing, and related fields. Minimum cumulative GPA 3.0 on a 4.0 scale (high school seniors) or 2.5 on a 4.0 scale (undergraduate/graduate). Restricted to students from the Little Village Community.

Academic Fields/Career Goals: Business/Consumer Services.

Award: Scholarship for use in freshman, sophomore, junior, senior, or graduate years; not renewable. *Number:* varies. *Amount:* up to $2500.

Eligibility Requirements: Applicant must be Hispanic; enrolled or expecting to enroll full-time at a four-year institution or university and resident of Illinois. Applicant must have 3.0 GPA or higher. Available to U.S. citizens.

Application Requirements: Application, essay, financial need analysis, transcript, copy of Student Aid Report (SAR). *Deadline:* April 30.

Contact: Program Officer
Hispanic Scholarship Fund
55 Second Street, Suite 1500
San Francisco, CA 94105
Phone: 877-473-4636
Fax: 415-808-2302

HSF/TOYOTA SCHOLARSHIP PROGRAM

Scholarships are available to Hispanic students who are entering their freshman year. For more details, deadlines and an application see Web site: http://www.hsf.net

Academic Fields/Career Goals: Business/Consumer Services; Computer Science/Data Processing; Mechanical Engineering.

Award: Scholarship for use in freshman year; not renewable. *Number:* varies. *Amount:* $5000.

Eligibility Requirements: Applicant must be Hispanic; high school student; planning to enroll or expecting to enroll full-time at a two-year or four-year institution or university and studying in California or Texas. Applicant must have 3.0 GPA or higher. Available to U.S. citizens.

Application Requirements: Application, essay, financial need analysis, references, transcript, copy of Student Aid Report (SAR). *Deadline:* October 1.

Contact: Program Officer
Hispanic Scholarship Fund
55 Second Street, Suite 1500
San Francisco, CA 94105
Phone: 877-473-4636
Fax: 415-808-2302

INSTITUTE OF MANAGEMENT ACCOUNTANTS   http://www.imanet.org

STUART CAMERON AND MARGARET MCLEOD MEMORIAL SCHOLARSHIP
• See page 63

JOHN M. AZARIAN MEMORIAL ARMENIAN YOUTH SCHOLARSHIP FUND

JOHN M. AZARIAN MEMORIAL ARMENIAN YOUTH SCHOLARSHIP FUND

Grants awarded to undergraduate students of Armenian descent, attending 4 year college or university within the U.S. full time. Compelling financial need is the main criteria. Minimum 2.5 GPA required. Preference to business majors given. Must be a member of the Armenian church.

Academic Fields/Career Goals: Business/Consumer Services.

Award: Grant for use in freshman, sophomore, junior, or senior years; renewable. *Number:* 3–10. *Amount:* $500–$2000.

Eligibility Requirements: Applicant must be of Armenian heritage and enrolled or expecting to enroll full-time at a four-year institution or university. Applicant must have 2.5 GPA or higher. Available to U.S. citizens.

Application Requirements: Application, autobiography, essay, financial need analysis, references, test scores, transcript. *Deadline:* June 30.

Contact: John Azarian, Jr., President
John M. Azarian Memorial Armenian Youth Scholarship Fund
Azarian Management and Development Company
6 Prospect Street, Suite 1B
Midland Park, NJ 07432
Phone: 201-444-7111
Fax: 201-444-6655
E-mail: azariangrp@aol.com

JORGE MAS CANOSA FREEDOM FOUNDATION   http://www.canf.org

MAS FAMILY SCHOLARSHIP AWARD

Scholarship up to $10,000 per year to any financially needy, Cuban American student who is direct descendant of those who left Cuba or was born in Cuba. Minimum 3.5 GPA in college. Scholarships available only in the fields of engineering, business, international relations, economics, communications and journalism. Deadline is March 31. Write for application.

Jorge Mas Canosa Freedom Foundation (continued)

Academic Fields/Career Goals: Business/Consumer Services; Chemical Engineering; Civil Engineering; Communications; Economics; Electrical Engineering/Electronics; Engineering-Related Technologies; Journalism; Materials Science, Engineering, and Metallurgy; Mechanical Engineering.

Award: Scholarship for use in freshman, sophomore, junior, or senior years; renewable. *Number:* 10. *Amount:* up to $10,000.

Eligibility Requirements: Applicant must be of Latin American/Caribbean heritage; Hispanic and enrolled or expecting to enroll at an institution or university. Applicant must have 3.5 GPA or higher. Available to U.S. citizens.

Application Requirements: Application, autobiography, essay, financial need analysis, test scores, transcript, proof of Cuban descent. *Deadline:* March 31.

Contact: Jorge Mas Canosa Freedom Foundation
Cuban American National Foundation, 1312 Southwest 27th Avenue
Miami, FL 33145
Phone: 305-592-7768

JUNIOR ACHIEVEMENT   http://www.ja.org

WALT DISNEY COMPANY FOUNDATION SCHOLARSHIP
● *See page 112*

LAGRANT FOUNDATION   http://www.lagrantfoundation.org

LAGRANT FOUNDATION SCHOLARSHIP FOR UNDERGRADUATES

Awards are for undergraduate and graduate minority students who are attending accredited four-year institutions and are pursuing careers in the fields of advertising, marketing, and public relations.

Academic Fields/Career Goals: Business/Consumer Services; Communications; Journalism.

Award: Scholarship for use in freshman, sophomore, junior, or senior years; renewable. *Number:* up to 5. *Amount:* up to $5000.

Eligibility Requirements: Applicant must be American Indian/Alaska Native, Asian/Pacific Islander, Black (non-Hispanic), or Hispanic and enrolled or expecting to enroll full-time at a four-year institution or university. Applicant must have 2.5 GPA or higher. Available to U.S. citizens.

Application Requirements: Application, essay, resume, references, transcript. *Deadline:* February 28.

Contact: Melissa Lopez, Program Manager
Lagrant Foundation
626 Wilshire Boulevard, Suite 700
Los Angeles, CA 90017-2920
Phone: 323-469-8680
Fax: 323-469-8683
E-mail: melissalopez@lagrantfoundation.org

LAWRENCE P. DOSS SCHOLARSHIP FOUNDATION   http://www.lawrencepdossfnd.org

LAWRENCE P. DOSS SCHOLARSHIP FOUNDATION
● *See page 64*

LEAGUE OF UNITED LATIN AMERICAN CITIZENS NATIONAL EDUCATIONAL SERVICE CENTERS, INC.   http://www.lnesc.org

GE/LULAC SCHOLARSHIP

Renewable award for minority students who are enrolled as business or engineering majors at accredited colleges or universities in the United States and who will be entering their sophomore year. Must maintain a minimum 3.0 GPA. Selection is based in part on the likelihood of pursuing a career in business or engineering. Application deadline is July 15.

Academic Fields/Career Goals: Business/Consumer Services; Engineering/Technology.

Award: Scholarship for use in sophomore, junior, or senior years; renewable. *Number:* up to 2. *Amount:* up to $5000.

Eligibility Requirements: Applicant must be Hispanic and enrolled or expecting to enroll full-time at a four-year institution or university. Applicant must have 3.0 GPA or higher. Available to U.S. citizens.

Application Requirements: Application, references, transcript, personal statement with career goals. *Deadline:* July 15.

Contact: Lorena Maymi-Garrido, Scholarship Administrator
League of United Latin American Citizens National Educational Service Centers, Inc.
2000 L Street, NW, Suite 610
Washington, DC 20036
Phone: 202-835-9646 Ext. 10
Fax: 202-835-9685
E-mail: lnescaward@aol.com

LINCOLN COMMUNITY FOUNDATION   http://www.lcf.org

LAWRENCE "LARRY" FRAZIER MEMORIAL SCHOLARSHIP
● *See page 124*

LOWE RMP   http://www.dmscholarship.com

CANADIAN DIRECT MARKETING SCHOLARSHIP FOR BUSINESS STUDENTS

Award for students enrolled in a Canadian business school. Award consists of a four-month, paid summer internship, and a $2500 scholarship. Refer to Web site for details: http://www.dmscholarship.com

Academic Fields/Career Goals: Business/Consumer Services.

Award: Scholarship for use in freshman, sophomore, junior, senior, or graduate years; not renewable. *Number:* 1. *Amount:* up to $2500.

Eligibility Requirements: Applicant must be enrolled or expecting to enroll full or part-time at a two-year or four-year institution or university. Available to Canadian citizens.

Application Requirements: Application, applicant must enter a contest, essay, resume, transcript. *Deadline:* March 27.

Contact: DM Scholarship
Lowe RMP
488 Wellington Street W, Suite 200
Toronto, ON M5V 1E3
Canada
E-mail: dmscholarship@draftcanada.com

MARYLAND ASSOCIATION OF PRIVATE COLLEGES AND CAREER SCHOOLS   http://www.mapccs.org

MARYLAND ASSOCIATION OF PRIVATE COLLEGES AND CAREER SCHOOLS SCHOLARSHIP

Awards for study at trade schools only. Must enter school same year high school is completed. For use only in Maryland and by Maryland residents. Write for further information.

Academic Fields/Career Goals: Business/Consumer Services; Computer Science/Data Processing; Dental Health/Services; Engineering/Technology; Food Science/Nutrition; Home Economics; Trade/Technical Specialties; TV/Radio Broadcasting.

Award: Scholarship for use in freshman year; not renewable. *Number:* 50. *Amount:* $500–$19,950.

Eligibility Requirements: Applicant must be high school student; planning to enroll or expecting to enroll full-time at a technical institution; resident of Maryland and studying in Maryland. Available to U.S. citizens.

Application Requirements: Application, references, transcript. *Deadline:* March 17.

Contact: Diane MacDougall, Office Manager
Maryland Association of Private Colleges and Career Schools
PMB 206 1539, Merriet Boulevard
Baltimore, MD 21222
Phone: 410-282-4012
Fax: 410-282-4133
E-mail: matccs@comcast.net

MIDWEST ROOFING CONTRACTORS ASSOCIATION
http://www.mrca.org

MRCA FOUNDATION SCHOLARSHIP PROGRAM
• See page 94

MONSANTO AGRIBUSINESS SCHOLARSHIP
http://www.monsanto.ca

MONSANTO AGRI-BUSINESS SCHOLARSHIP
• See page 81

MRA-THE MANAGEMENT ASSOCIATION
http://www.mranet.org/

MRA INSTITUTE OF MANAGEMENT ENDOWMENT FUND SCHOLARSHIP

Non-renewable scholarship for students preparing for careers in the field of human resources management.

Academic Fields/Career Goals: Business/Consumer Services.

Award: Scholarship for use in freshman, sophomore, junior, or senior years; not renewable. *Number:* 1–2. *Amount:* $1000.

Eligibility Requirements: Applicant must be enrolled or expecting to enroll at a four-year institution or university; resident of Illinois, Iowa, or Wisconsin and studying in Illinois, Iowa, or Wisconsin. Applicant must have 3.0 GPA or higher. Available to U.S. citizens.

Application Requirements: Application, essay, interview, references, transcript, letter from university confirming human resources major. *Deadline:* March 22.

Contact: Leslie Remme, Director of Communications and Technology
MRA-The Management Association
N19 W24400 Riverwood Drive
Waukesha, WI 53188
Phone: 262-696-3528
E-mail: leslier@mranet.org

NATIONAL ASSOCIATION FOR THE ADVANCEMENT OF COLORED PEOPLE
http://www.naacp.org

EARL G. GRAVES NAACP SCHOLARSHIP

One-time award of $5000 to a full-time minority student. Must be an enrolled junior or senior at an accredited college or university in the U.S. as a declared business major, or a graduate student enrolled or accepted in a masters or doctoral program within a business school at an accredited university. Must demonstrate financial need. Application deadline is the April 30.

Academic Fields/Career Goals: Business/Consumer Services.

Award: Scholarship for use in junior, senior, or graduate years; not renewable. *Number:* varies. *Amount:* $5000.

Eligibility Requirements: Applicant must be American Indian/Alaska Native, Asian/Pacific Islander, Black (non-Hispanic), or Hispanic and enrolled or expecting to enroll full-time at a four-year institution or university. Applicant must have 2.5 GPA or higher. Available to U.S. citizens.

Application Requirements: Application, financial need analysis, references, transcript. *Deadline:* April 30.

Contact: Donna Lakins, Education Department, Scholarship Request
National Association for the Advancement of Colored People
4805 Mt. Hope Drive
Baltimore, MD 21215-3297
Phone: 410-580-5760
Fax: 410-585-1329

NATIONAL ASSOCIATION OF INSURANCE WOMEN EDUCATION FOUNDATION

NAIW EDUCATION FOUNDATION PROFESSIONAL SCHOLARSHIP

Professional scholarships are given to applicants with a minimum of two years of experience in the insurance industry. They do not currently need to be employed in the industry. Recipients need to be engaged in a course of study designed to improve their knowledge and skills in performing their employment responsibilities. Scholarships are given three times a year. Application deadlines are March 1, September 1, December 1.

Academic Fields/Career Goals: Business/Consumer Services; Insurance and Actuarial Science.

Award: Scholarship for use in freshman, sophomore, junior, senior, graduate, or postgraduate years; not renewable. *Number:* 10–20. *Amount:* $1000–$2000.

Eligibility Requirements: Applicant must be enrolled or expecting to enroll full or part-time at a two-year or four-year or technical institution or university. Available to U.S. and non-U.S. citizens.

Application Requirements: Application, essay, references, transcript. *Deadline:* varies.

Contact: Billie Sleet, Executive Director
National Association of Insurance Women Education Foundation
5310 East 31st Street, Suite 302
Tulsa, OK 74135
Phone: 918-622-1816
Fax: 918-622-1821
E-mail: foundation@naiwfoundation.org

NATIONAL ASSOCIATION OF WATER COMPANIES
http://www.nawc.org

J.J. BARR SCHOLARSHIP
• See page 139

NATIONAL ASSOCIATION OF WATER COMPANIES-NEW JERSEY CHAPTER

NATIONAL ASSOCIATION OF WATER COMPANIES-NEW JERSEY CHAPTER SCHOLARSHIP
• See page 139

NATIONAL BLACK MBA ASSOCIATION-TWIN CITIES CHAPTER
http://www.nbmbaatc.org

TWIN CITIES CHAPTER UNDERGRADUATE SCHOLARSHIP
• See page 65

TWIN CITIES GRADUATE MBA SCHOLARSHIP
• See page 65

NATIONAL URBAN LEAGUE
http://www.nul.org

BLACK EXECUTIVE EXCHANGE PROGRAM JERRY BARTOW SCHOLARSHIP FUND

Scholarships for undergraduate students at participating Historically Black Colleges and Universities classified as sophomore, junior, or senior, majoring in business, management, technology, or education. Must be available to receive award at BEEP's annual conference. All expenses will be provided by BEEP.

Academic Fields/Career Goals: Business/Consumer Services; Education; Engineering/Technology.

Award: Scholarship for use in sophomore, junior, or senior years; not renewable. *Number:* 2. *Amount:* up to $1500.

Eligibility Requirements: Applicant must be Black (non-Hispanic) and enrolled or expecting to enroll at a four-year institution or university. Applicant must have 2.5 GPA or higher. Available to U.S. citizens.

Application Requirements: Application. *Deadline:* January 15.

Contact: National Urban League
Black Executive Exchange Program Office, National Urban League Inc, 120 Wall Street
New York, NY 10005
Phone: 212-558-5300
Fax: 212-344-5332
E-mail: beep2005@nul.org

NEW ENGLAND EMPLOYEE BENEFITS COUNCIL
http://www.neebc.org

NEW ENGLAND EMPLOYEE BENEFITS COUNCIL SCHOLARSHIP PROGRAM

Renewable award designed to encourage undergraduate or graduate students to pursue a course of study leading to a bachelor's degree or higher in the employee benefits field. Must be a resident of/or studying in Maine, Massachusetts, New Hampshire, Rhode Island, Connecticut or Vermont.

New England Employee Benefits Council (continued)

Academic Fields/Career Goals: Business/Consumer Services.

Award: Scholarship for use in freshman, sophomore, junior, senior, or graduate years; renewable. *Number:* 1–3. *Amount:* up to $5000.

Eligibility Requirements: Applicant must be enrolled or expecting to enroll full-time at a four-year institution or university; resident of Connecticut, Maine, Massachusetts, New Hampshire, Rhode Island, or Vermont and studying in Connecticut, Maine, Massachusetts, New Hampshire, Rhode Island, or Vermont. Available to U.S. citizens.

Application Requirements: Application, essay, references, transcript. *Deadline:* April 1.

Contact: Linda Viens, Office Manager
New England Employee Benefits Council
440 Totten Pond Road
Waltham, MA 02451
Phone: 781-684-8700
Fax: 781-684-9200
E-mail: linda@neebc.org

NORTH DAKOTA SOCIETY OF CERTIFIED PUBLIC ACCOUNTANTS   http://www.ndscpa.org

NORTH DAKOTA SOCIETY OF CERTIFIED PUBLIC ACCOUNTANTS SCHOLARSHIP
• See page 67

ORANGE COUNTY COMMUNITY FOUNDATION   http://www.heef.org

ASSOCIATION OF HISPANIC PROFESSIONALS FOR EDUCATION SCHOLARSHIP

Scholarship awarded to graduating Hispanic high school seniors who are majoring in business administration. Applicants must have a GPA of 3.0 or higher, and be involved in extracurricular activities at school or in the community. Deadline is February 13.

Academic Fields/Career Goals: Business/Consumer Services.

Award: Scholarship for use in freshman year; not renewable. *Number:* 1.

Eligibility Requirements: Applicant must be Hispanic; high school student and planning to enroll or expecting to enroll at an institution or university. Available to U.S. citizens.

Application Requirements: Application, essay, self-addressed stamped envelope, transcript. *Deadline:* February 13.

Contact: Rose Garris, Hispanic Education Endowment Fund
Orange County Community Foundation
30 Corporate Park, Suite 410
Irvine, CA 92606
Phone: 949-543-4202 Ext. 23
Fax: 949-553-4211

UNION BANK OF CALIFORNIA SCHOLARSHIP

Scholarships awarded to Hispanic high school seniors who desire to pursue a major in business, finance, marketing, or economics, who have applied and been accepted to a four-year university, demonstrated financial need through submission of the FAFSA and have attained a cumulative GPA of 3.0. Amount and awards to be determined. Deadline is February 13.

Academic Fields/Career Goals: Business/Consumer Services; Economics.

Award: Scholarship for use in freshman year; not renewable. *Number:* 1.

Eligibility Requirements: Applicant must be Hispanic; high school student and planning to enroll or expecting to enroll at a four-year institution or university. Applicant must have 3.0 GPA or higher. Available to U.S. citizens.

Application Requirements: Application, essay, self-addressed stamped envelope, transcript. *Deadline:* February 13.

Contact: Rose Garris, Hispanic Education Endowment Fund
Orange County Community Foundation
30 Corporate Park, Suite 410
Irvine, CA 92606
Phone: 949-543-4202 Ext. 23
Fax: 949-553-4211

OREGON COMMUNITY FOUNDATION   http://www.ocf1.org/

BULLIVANT HOUSER BAILEY-AFRICAN AMERICAN CHAMBER OF COMMERCE COMMUNITY COLLEGE SCHOLARSHIP FUND

Scholarship for African-American graduates (or the equivalent) of high schools in Multnomah, Washington or Clackamas counties, for use in the pursuit of a postsecondary education at a nonprofit community college in Oregon and Washington. The focus is on students who show academic potential for a course of study related to business or pre-law.

Academic Fields/Career Goals: Business/Consumer Services; Law/Legal Services.

Award: Scholarship for use in freshman year. *Number:* 1.

Eligibility Requirements: Applicant must be Black (non-Hispanic); high school student; planning to enroll or expecting to enroll at a two-year institution; resident of Oregon and studying in Oregon or Washington. Available to U.S. citizens.

Application Requirements: *Deadline:* varies.

Contact: Dianne Causey, Program Associate for Scholarships/Grants
Oregon Community Foundation
1221 South West Yamhill, Suite 100
Portland, OR 97205
Phone: 503-227-6846

OREGON STUDENT ASSISTANCE COMMISSION   http://www.osac.state.or.us

GLENN R. AND JUANITA B. STRUBLE SCHOLARSHIP II
• See page 102

HOMESTEAD CAPITAL HOUSING SCHOLARSHIP
• See page 68

PLUMBING-HEATING-COOLING CONTRACTORS ASSOCIATION EDUCATION FOUNDATION   http://www.phccweb.org

BRADFORD WHITE CORPORATION SCHOLARSHIP
• See page 102

DELTA FAUCET COMPANY SCHOLARSHIP PROGRAM
• See page 102

PHCC EDUCATIONAL FOUNDATION NEED-BASED SCHOLARSHIP
• See page 102

PHCC EDUCATIONAL FOUNDATION SCHOLARSHIP PROGRAM
• See page 103

PROJECT CAMBIO SCHOLARSHIP AWARDS

PROJECT CAMBIO SCHOLARSHIP AWARDS

Scholarship provided to Hispanic women pursuing studies in a business related program. Applicants should have been out of high school and should have been working for at least 5 years.

Academic Fields/Career Goals: Business/Consumer Services.

Award: Scholarship for use in freshman year; not renewable. *Number:* varies. *Amount:* up to $1000.

Eligibility Requirements: Applicant must be Hispanic; enrolled or expecting to enroll full or part-time at a four-year institution or university and female. Available to U.S. citizens.

Application Requirements: Application, essay. *Deadline:* April 30.

Contact: Project Cambio Scholarship Awards
PO Box 3004-227
Corvallis, OR 97339

ROBERT H. MOLLOHAN FAMILY CHARITABLE FOUNDATION, INC. http://www.mollohanfoundation.org

TEAMING TO WIN BUSINESS SCHOLARSHIP

Scholarship for a rising sophomore or junior pursuing a degree in business administration at a West Virginia college or university.

Academic Fields/Career Goals: Business/Consumer Services.

Award: Scholarship for use in sophomore or junior years; not renewable. *Number:* 2. *Amount:* up to $1000.

Eligibility Requirements: Applicant must be enrolled or expecting to enroll full or part-time at a four-year institution or university; resident of West Virginia and studying in West Virginia. Applicant must have 3.0 GPA or higher. Available to U.S. citizens.

Application Requirements: Application, essay, interview, resume, references, test scores, transcript. *Deadline:* February 6.

Contact: Teah Bayless, Program Manager
Robert H. Mollohan Family Charitable Foundation, Inc.
1000 Technology Drive, Suite 2000
Fairmont, WV 26554
Phone: 304-333-2251
Fax: 304-333-3900
E-mail: tmbayless@wvhtf.org

ROYAL BANK NATIVE STUDENTS AWARDS PROGRAM http://www.rbc.com

ROYAL BANK ABORIGINAL STUDENT AWARDS

Award for Canadian Aboriginal student who is status Indian, non-status Indian, Inuit or Métis, accepted or attending college or university in the Directory of Canadian Universities. Must be studying in a financial services discipline (e.g. business, economics, computer science). Award covers maximum of four years at university or two years at college. Must be permanent resident/citizen of Canada.

Academic Fields/Career Goals: Business/Consumer Services; Computer Science/Data Processing; Economics.

Award: Scholarship for use in freshman, sophomore, junior, or senior years; renewable. *Number:* 5. *Amount:* up to $4000.

Eligibility Requirements: Applicant must be Canadian citizen; American Indian/Alaska Native and enrolled or expecting to enroll full-time at a two-year or four-year institution or university.

Application Requirements: Application, essay, financial need analysis, references, transcript. *Deadline:* January 31.

Contact: Coordinator, RBC Financial Group Aboriginal Student Awards
Royal Bank Native Students Awards Program
1 PVM, 10th Floor, W
Montreal, QC H3B 4S6
Canada
E-mail: aboriginalstudentawards@rbc.com

SALES PROFESSIONALS-USA http://www.salesprofessionals-usa.com/

SALES PROFESSIONALS- USA SCHOLARSHIP

Scholarships are awarded to students furthering their degree or obtaining a degree in business or marketing. The scholarships are initiated and awarded by the individual Sales Pros Clubs (located in Colorado, Kansas and Missouri) and are not nationally awarded. A listing of local clubs can be found at http://www.salesprofessionals-usa.com

Academic Fields/Career Goals: Business/Consumer Services.

Award: Scholarship for use in freshman, sophomore, junior, or senior years; not renewable. *Number:* 3–5. *Amount:* $600–$1000.

Eligibility Requirements: Applicant must be enrolled or expecting to enroll full or part-time at a two-year or four-year institution or university; resident of Colorado, Kansas, or Missouri and studying in Colorado, Kansas, or Missouri. Applicant must have 3.0 GPA or higher. Available to U.S. citizens.

Application Requirements: Application, essay. *Deadline:* varies.

Contact: Mary Anne McCubbin, National President
Sales Professionals-USA
PO Box 149
Arvada, CO 80001
Phone: 800-763-7767

SOUTH DAKOTA RETAILERS ASSOCIATION http://www.sdra.org

SOUTH DAKOTA RETAILERS ASSOCIATION SCHOLARSHIP PROGRAM
• See page 69

SOUTHWEST STUDENT SERVICES CORPORATION http://www.sssc.com/

J. WILMAR MIRANDON SCHOLARSHIP

One-time $1000 award to juniors or seniors at Arizona State University, ASU West, University of Arizona, and Northern Arizona University. Applicant should have business as major.

Academic Fields/Career Goals: Business/Consumer Services.

Award: Scholarship for use in junior or senior years. *Amount:* $1000.

Eligibility Requirements: Applicant must be enrolled or expecting to enroll full-time at an institution or university and resident of Arizona. Available to U.S. citizens.

Application Requirements: Application, transcript. *Deadline:* varies.

Contact: Linda Walker, Community Outreach Representative
Southwest Student Services Corporation
PO Box 41150
Mesa, AZ 85274
Phone: 480-461-6566
Fax: 480-461-6595
E-mail: scholarships@sssc.com

SUNSHINE LADY FOUNDATION, INC. http://www.sunshineladyfdn.org

COUNSELOR, ADVOCATE, AND SUPPORT STAFF SCHOLARSHIP PROGRAM
• See page 69

TEXAS FAMILY BUSINESS ASSOCIATION AND SCHOLARSHIP FOUNDATION http://www.texasfamilybusiness.org/tfb6.html

TEXAS FAMILY BUSINESS ASSOCIATION SCHOLARSHIP

Scholarships are awarded to eligible Texas family business members to help them obtain an education in business to insure a greater succession rate of area family businesses, and to help support local colleges and universities by increasing attendance. Applicants must be planning to return to or stay with their family business.

Academic Fields/Career Goals: Business/Consumer Services.

Award: Scholarship for use in freshman, sophomore, junior, or senior years. *Number:* 1.

Eligibility Requirements: Applicant must be enrolled or expecting to enroll at a four-year institution or university and resident of Texas. Available to U.S. citizens.

Application Requirements: Application, essay, transcript. *Deadline:* varies.

Contact: Texas Family Business Association and Scholarship Foundation
558 SPID, Sunrise Mall, Suite 63
Corpus Christi, TX 78412

TKE EDUCATIONAL FOUNDATION http://www.tkefoundation.org

W. ALLAN HERZOG SCHOLARSHIP
• See page 70

TRUCKLOAD CARRIERS ASSOCIATION
http://www.truckload.org

TRUCKLOAD CARRIERS ASSOCIATION SCHOLARSHIP FUND

This scholarship fund is for persons affiliated with the trucking industry and their families to pursue higher education. Special consideration will be given to applicants pursuing transportation or business degrees. Minimum 3.3 GPA required. For junior and senior undergraduate students at four-year college or university. Further information and application deadlines available at Web site http://www.truckload.org.

Academic Fields/Career Goals: Business/Consumer Services; Transportation.

Award: Scholarship for use in junior or senior years; not renewable. *Number:* 18. *Amount:* $1500–$3000.

Eligibility Requirements: Applicant must be enrolled or expecting to enroll full-time at a four-year institution or university. Applicant or parent of applicant must have employment or volunteer experience in designated career field. Available to U.S. citizens.

Application Requirements: Application, essay, financial need analysis, photo, transcript, course schedule including tuition and fees. *Deadline:* May 20.

Contact: Nancy O'Liddy, Scholarship Fund Administrator
Truckload Carriers Association
2200 Mill Road
Alexandria, VA 22314
Phone: 703-838-1950
Fax: 703-836-6610
E-mail: tca@truckload.org

UNITED DAUGHTERS OF THE CONFEDERACY
http://www.hqudc.org

WALTER REED SMITH SCHOLARSHIP

Award for full-time female undergraduate student who is a descendant of a Confederate soldier, studying nutrition, home economics, nursing, business administration, or computer science. Must carry a minimum of 12 credit hours each semester and have a minimum 3.0 GPA. Submit letter of endorsement from sponsoring chapter of the United Daughters of the Confederacy. Scholarship amount for the entire academic year will be sent to college/university.

Academic Fields/Career Goals: Business/Consumer Services; Computer Science/Data Processing; Food Science/Nutrition; Home Economics; Nursing.

Award: Scholarship for use in freshman, sophomore, junior, or senior years; renewable. *Number:* 1–2. *Amount:* $800–$1000.

Eligibility Requirements: Applicant must be enrolled or expecting to enroll full-time at a four-year institution or university and female. Applicant or parent of applicant must be member of United Daughters of the Confederacy. Applicant must have 3.0 GPA or higher. Available to U.S. citizens.

Application Requirements: Application, essay, financial need analysis, photo, references, self-addressed stamped envelope, transcript, confederate ancestor's proof of service. *Deadline:* March 15.

Contact: Robert Kraus, Second Vice President General
United Daughters of the Confederacy
328 North Boulevard
Richmond, VA 23220-4057
Phone: 804-355-1636

UNITED NEGRO COLLEGE FUND
http://www.uncf.org

AXA FOUNDATION FUND ACHIEVEMENT SCHOLARSHIP

Scholarship for New York residents attending a UNCF member college or university. Must declare business-related major. Minimum 3.0 GPA required. Applicants must exemplify high academic achievement, leadership ability, and community service. Prospective applicants should complete the Student Profile found at Web site: http://www.uncf.org.

Academic Fields/Career Goals: Business/Consumer Services.

Award: Scholarship for use in freshman, sophomore, junior, or senior years; not renewable. *Amount:* $2000–$5000.

Eligibility Requirements: Applicant must be Black (non-Hispanic); enrolled or expecting to enroll at a four-year institution or university;

resident of New York and must have an interest in leadership. Applicant must have 3.0 GPA or higher. Available to U.S. citizens.

Application Requirements: Application, financial need analysis. *Deadline:* varies.

Contact: Rebecca Bennett, Director, Program Services
United Negro College Fund
8260 Willow Oaks Corporate Drive
Fairfax, VA 22031-8044
Phone: 800-331-2244
E-mail: rbennett@uncf.org

BEST BUY ENTERPRISE EMPLOYEE SCHOLARSHIP
• See page 70

BOOZ, ALLEN & HAMILTON/WILLIAM F. STASIOR INTERNSHIP

Program available to college juniors majoring in engineering, business, finance, economics, math, science, information systems, or computer science at any of the following UNCF member colleges and universities: Florida A&M, Morehouse, Spelman, Morgan State, Hampton, Howard, Baruch, or Southern University. Minimum 3.3 GPA required. Prospective applicants should complete the Student Profile found at Web site: http://www.uncf.org

Academic Fields/Career Goals: Business/Consumer Services; Computer Science/Data Processing; Earth Science; Engineering/Technology; Physical Sciences and Math.

Award: Scholarship for use in sophomore or junior years; not renewable. *Number:* varies. *Amount:* $10,000.

Eligibility Requirements: Applicant must be Black (non-Hispanic) and enrolled or expecting to enroll full-time at a four-year institution or university. Available to U.S. citizens.

Application Requirements: Application, financial need analysis. *Deadline:* February 29.

Contact: Rebecca Bennett, Director, Program Services
United Negro College Fund
8260 Willow Oaks Corporate Drive
Fairfax, VA 22031-8044
Phone: 800-331-2244
E-mail: rbennett@uncf.org

C.R. BARD SCHOLARSHIP AND INTERNSHIP PROGRAM

Scholarship awards $4000 to undergraduate sophomore majoring in business at a UNCF member college or university. Program provides paid internship during summer at the C. R. Bard headquarters in Murray Hill, New Jersey. Please visit Web site for more information: http://www.uncf.org

Academic Fields/Career Goals: Business/Consumer Services.

Award: Scholarship for use in sophomore year. *Number:* varies. *Amount:* $4000.

Eligibility Requirements: Applicant must be Black (non-Hispanic) and enrolled or expecting to enroll at a four-year institution or university. Applicant must have 3.0 GPA or higher. Available to U.S. citizens.

Application Requirements: Application, financial need analysis, FAFSA, Student Aid Report (SAR). *Deadline:* varies.

Contact: Rebecca Bennett, Director, Program Services
United Negro College Fund
8260 Willow Oaks Corporate Drive
Fairfax, VA 22031-8044
Phone: 800-331-2244
E-mail: rbennett@uncf.org

CARDINAL HEALTH SCHOLARSHIP
• See page 70

CASTLE ROCK FOUNDATION SCHOLARSHIP

Scholarship awarded to students majoring in business or engineering and who attend the following institutions: Bethune-Cookman College, LeMoyne-Owen College, Morehouse College, Shaw University, Spelman College, Tuskegee University, or Xavier University. Please visit Web site for more information: http://www.uncf.org

Academic Fields/Career Goals: Business/Consumer Services; Engineering/Technology.

Award: Scholarship for use in freshman, sophomore, junior, senior, or graduate years. *Number:* 10. *Amount:* $3600.

Eligibility Requirements: Applicant must be Black (non-Hispanic) and enrolled or expecting to enroll at a four-year institution or university. Applicant must have 2.5 GPA or higher. Available to U.S. citizens.

Application Requirements: Application, financial need analysis, FAFSA, Student Aid Report (SAR). *Deadline:* varies.

Contact: Rebecca Bennett, Director, Program Services
United Negro College Fund
8260 Willow Oaks Corporate Drive
Fairfax, VA 22031-8044
Phone: 800-331-2244
E-mail: rbennett@uncf.org

DELL/UNCF CORPORATE SCHOLARS PROGRAM

Program provides rising Texas juniors and seniors with an opportunity to gain valuable internship experience and earn a $10,000 scholarship. Students must attend a UNCF member college or university or an HBCU and major in engineering, business, finance, marketing, computer science/MIS, logistics, human resources, supply chain management, operations management, or electrical engineering. Minimum 3.0 GPA required. Prospective applicants should complete the Student Profile found at Web site: http://www.uncf.org

Academic Fields/Career Goals: Business/Consumer Services; Computer Science/Data Processing; Electrical Engineering/Electronics; Engineering/Technology.

Award: Scholarship for use in sophomore, junior, or graduate years; not renewable. *Amount:* up to $10,000.

Eligibility Requirements: Applicant must be Black (non-Hispanic); enrolled or expecting to enroll full-time at a four-year institution or university and resident of Texas. Applicant must have 3.0 GPA or higher. Available to U.S. citizens.

Application Requirements: Application, financial need analysis. *Deadline:* February 13.

Contact: Rebecca Bennett, Director, Program Services
United Negro College Fund
8260 Willow Oaks Corporate Drive
Fairfax, VA 22031-8044
Phone: 800-331-2244
E-mail: rbennett@uncf.org

FINANCIAL SERVICES INSTITUTION SCHOLARSHIP
• *See page 71*

FLOWERS INDUSTRIES SCHOLARSHIP

Awards given to students majoring in business, marketing, computer science, or food service at one of the following colleges or universities: Bethune-Cookman, Clark Atlanta, Stillman, Virginia Union. Minimum 2.5 GPA required. Prospective applicants should complete the Student Profile found at Web site: http://www.uncf.org.

Academic Fields/Career Goals: Business/Consumer Services; Computer Science/Data Processing; Food Service/Hospitality.

Award: Scholarship for use in junior or senior years; not renewable. *Amount:* $2500.

Eligibility Requirements: Applicant must be Black (non-Hispanic) and enrolled or expecting to enroll at a four-year institution or university. Applicant must have 2.5 GPA or higher. Available to U.S. citizens.

Application Requirements: Application, financial need analysis. *Deadline:* Continuous.

Contact: Rebecca Bennett, Director, Program Services
United Negro College Fund
8260 Willow Oaks Corporate Drive
Fairfax, VA 22031-8044
Phone: 800-331-2244
E-mail: rbennett@uncf.org

KEYCORP SCHOLARS PROGRAM/INTERNSHIP

Scholarship, internship, and mentorship award for college sophomores, juniors, and first year graduate students at a UNCF member college or university who are majoring in finance, marketing, banking, or other business-related subjects. Minimum 3.0 GPA required. Prospective applicants should complete the Student Profile found at Web site: http://www.uncf.org.

Academic Fields/Career Goals: Business/Consumer Services.

Award: Scholarship for use in sophomore, junior, or graduate years; not renewable. *Amount:* up to $7000.

Eligibility Requirements: Applicant must be Black (non-Hispanic) and enrolled or expecting to enroll full-time at a four-year institution or university. Applicant must have 3.0 GPA or higher. Available to U.S. citizens.

Application Requirements: Application, financial need analysis, resume, references, transcript. *Deadline:* February 5.

Contact: Rebecca Bennett, Director, Program Services
United Negro College Fund
8260 Willow Oaks Corporate Drive
Fairfax, VA 22031-8044
Phone: 800-331-2244
E-mail: rbennett@uncf.org

MASTERCARD SCHOLARS PROGRAM

Scholarship awarded covers the cost of tuition, fees, and room and board for students from New York, New Jersey, and Connecticut attending a UNCF member college or university. Students must major in business, finance, accounting, information systems, or marketing. Prospective applicants should complete the Student Profile found at Web site: http://www.uncf.org. Minimum 3.0 GPA required.

Academic Fields/Career Goals: Business/Consumer Services.

Award: Scholarship for use in sophomore or junior years; not renewable. *Amount:* $4500.

Eligibility Requirements: Applicant must be Black (non-Hispanic); enrolled or expecting to enroll at a four-year institution or university and resident of Connecticut, New Jersey, or New York. Applicant must have 3.0 GPA or higher. Available to U.S. citizens.

Application Requirements: Application, financial need analysis. *Deadline:* varies.

Contact: Rebecca Bennett, Director, Program Services
United Negro College Fund
8260 Willow Oaks Corporate Drive
Fairfax, VA 22031-8044
Phone: 800-331-2244
E-mail: rbennett@uncf.org

MAYTAG COMPANY SCHOLARSHIP

Scholarship for students majoring in engineering, business, computer science, or information technology at one of the following colleges or universities: Benedict, Claflin, Lane, LeMoyne-Owen, Morris, Paine, Voorhees, Wilberforce, or a historically black college or university. Minimum 2.5 GPA required. Prospective applicants should complete the Student Profile found at Web site: http://www.uncf.org.

Academic Fields/Career Goals: Business/Consumer Services; Computer Science/Data Processing; Engineering/Technology.

Award: Scholarship for use in freshman, sophomore, junior, or senior years; not renewable. *Amount:* $1250.

Eligibility Requirements: Applicant must be Black (non-Hispanic) and enrolled or expecting to enroll at a four-year institution or university. Applicant must have 2.5 GPA or higher. Available to U.S. citizens.

Application Requirements: Application, financial need analysis. *Deadline:* Continuous.

Contact: Rebecca Bennett, Director, Program Services
United Negro College Fund
8260 Willow Oaks Corporate Drive
Fairfax, VA 22031-8044
Phone: 800-331-2244
E-mail: rbennett@uncf.org

MBIA/WILLIAM O. BAILEY SCHOLARS PROGRAM

Two full-tuition awards given to qualified juniors from New York, New Jersey, or Connecticut with at least a 3.0 GPA and majoring in business or finance who attend a UNCF member college or university. Prospective applicants should complete the Student Profile found at Web site: http://www.uncf.org.

Academic Fields/Career Goals: Business/Consumer Services.

Award: Scholarship for use in junior year; not renewable. *Number:* 2.

Eligibility Requirements: Applicant must be Black (non-Hispanic); enrolled or expecting to enroll full-time at a four-year institution or university and resident of Connecticut, New Jersey, or New York. Applicant must have 3.0 GPA or higher. Available to U.S. citizens.

Application Requirements: Application, financial need analysis. *Deadline:* Continuous.

United Negro College Fund (continued)

Contact: Rebecca Bennett, Director, Program Services
United Negro College Fund
8260 Willow Oaks Corporate Drive
Fairfax, VA 22031-8044
Phone: 800-331-2244
E-mail: rbennett@uncf.org

NORTHEAST UTILITIES SYSTEM SCHOLARSHIP PROGRAM

Scholarships available for African American students enrolled as a sophomore or junior at a participating UNCF college or university. Must be pursuing a degree in engineering, business, information systems, or computer science/MIS. Must complete an internship. Visit Web site for details. http://www.uncf.org

Academic Fields/Career Goals: Business/Consumer Services; Computer Science/Data Processing; Energy and Power Engineering; Engineering/Technology; Engineering-Related Technologies.

Award: Scholarship for use in sophomore or junior years; not renewable. *Number:* varies. *Amount:* $10,000.

Eligibility Requirements: Applicant must be Black (non-Hispanic); enrolled or expecting to enroll at a four-year institution or university and resident of Connecticut or Massachusetts. Applicant must have 3.0 GPA or higher. Available to U.S. citizens.

Application Requirements: Application. *Deadline:* varies.

Contact: Rebecca Bennett, Director, Program Services
United Negro College Fund
8260 Willow Oaks Corporate Drive
Fairfax, VA 22031-8044
Phone: 800-331-2244
E-mail: rbennett@uncf.org

PRINCIPAL FINANCIAL GROUP SCHOLARSHIPS

Scholarships available to students majoring in business, finance, information systems, or banking who are attending a UNCF member college or university. Minimum 2.8 GPA required. Selected students participate in a paid internship in Des Moines, Iowa. Prospective applicants should complete the Student Profile found at Web site: http://www.uncf.org.

Academic Fields/Career Goals: Business/Consumer Services; Computer Science/Data Processing.

Award: Scholarship for use in junior year; not renewable. *Amount:* up to $12,000.

Eligibility Requirements: Applicant must be Black (non-Hispanic) and enrolled or expecting to enroll at an institution or university. Available to U.S. citizens.

Application Requirements: Application, financial need analysis. *Deadline:* March 1.

Contact: Rebecca Bennett, Director, Program Services
United Negro College Fund
8260 Willow Oaks Corporate Drive
Fairfax, VA 22031-8044
Phone: 800-331-2244
E-mail: rbennett@uncf.org

ROCKWELL/UNCF CORPORATE SCHOLARS PROGRAM

Scholarships available for African-American students entering their sophomore year. Must have a minimum 3.0 GPA. Must pursue specified areas of study as well as attend specific universities. See Web site for more information. http://www.uncf.org

Academic Fields/Career Goals: Business/Consumer Services; Earth Science; Electrical Engineering/Electronics; Psychology.

Award: Scholarship for use in sophomore year. *Number:* varies. *Amount:* up to $10,000.

Eligibility Requirements: Applicant must be Black (non-Hispanic); enrolled or expecting to enroll at a four-year institution or university and must have an interest in leadership. Applicant must have 3.0 GPA or higher. Available to U.S. citizens.

Application Requirements: Application, essay, references. *Deadline:* March 1.

Contact: Rebecca Bennett, Director, Program Services
United Negro College Fund
8260 Willow Oaks Corporate Drive
Fairfax, VA 22031-8044
Phone: 800-331-2244
E-mail: rbennett@uncf.org

SBC FOUNDATION SCHOLARSHIP

Award for deserving minority students from Illinois, Indiana, Michigan, Ohio, and Wisconsin. Must be a junior at one of the 39 UNCF member institutions. Must major in business, economics, finance, engineering (IE/EE/ME), or computer science/information technology. Must have 3.0 GPA. Please visit Web site for more information: http://www.uncf.org

Academic Fields/Career Goals: Business/Consumer Services; Computer Science/Data Processing; Economics; Electrical Engineering/Electronics; Engineering/Technology; Mechanical Engineering.

Award: Scholarship for use in junior or senior years; renewable. *Number:* varies. *Amount:* $5000.

Eligibility Requirements: Applicant must be Black (non-Hispanic); enrolled or expecting to enroll at a four-year institution or university and resident of Illinois, Indiana, Michigan, Ohio, or Wisconsin. Applicant must have 3.0 GPA or higher. Available to U.S. citizens.

Application Requirements: Application, financial need analysis, photo, resume, references, transcript, FAFSA, Student Aid Report (SAR). *Deadline:* January 17.

Contact: William Dunham, SBC Foundation Scholarship
United Negro College Fund
8260 Willow Oaks Corporate Drive, PO Box 10444
Fairfax, VA 22031

SBC PACIFIC BELL FOUNDATION SCHOLARSHIP

Scholarships for qualified business-related majors in junior year attending UNCF colleges and universities. Minimum 3.0 GPA required. Prospective applicants should complete the Student Profile found at Web site: http://www.uncf.org. Must be a California resident.

Academic Fields/Career Goals: Business/Consumer Services; Computer Science/Data Processing; Economics; Engineering/Technology.

Award: Scholarship for use in junior year; not renewable. *Amount:* $5000.

Eligibility Requirements: Applicant must be Black (non-Hispanic); enrolled or expecting to enroll at a four-year institution or university and resident of California. Applicant must have 3.0 GPA or higher. Available to U.S. citizens.

Application Requirements: Application, financial need analysis. *Deadline:* Continuous.

Contact: Program Services Department
United Negro College Fund
8260 Willow Oaks Corporate Drive
Fairfax, VA 22031

SOUTHTRUST SCHOLARSHIP

Need-based scholarship available to sophomores and juniors majoring in business who attend a UNCF member college or university. Minimum 3.0 GPA required. Prospective applicants should complete the Student Profile found at Web site: http://www.uncf.org.

Academic Fields/Career Goals: Business/Consumer Services.

Award: Scholarship for use in sophomore or junior years; not renewable. *Amount:* $6250.

Eligibility Requirements: Applicant must be Black (non-Hispanic) and enrolled or expecting to enroll at a four-year institution or university. Applicant must have 3.0 GPA or higher. Available to U.S. citizens.

Application Requirements: Application, essay, financial need analysis, references, transcript. *Deadline:* March 30.

Contact: Rebecca Bennett, Director, Program Services
United Negro College Fund
8260 Willow Oaks Corporate Drive
Fairfax, VA 22031-8044
Phone: 800-331-2244
E-mail: rbennett@uncf.org

SPRINT SCHOLARSHIP/INTERNSHIP
• See page 71

TOYOTA SCHOLARSHIP

Scholarship awarded to students with at least a 3.0 GPA majoring in business, information systems, English, or communications. Students must attend one of the following UNCF member colleges or universities: Clark Atlanta, Morehouse, Morris Brown, Spelman, Tuskegee, or Xavier. Prospective applicants should complete the Student Profile found at Web site: http://www.uncf.org

Academic Fields/Career Goals: Business/Consumer Services; Communications; Literature/English/Writing.

Award: Scholarship for use in freshman year; not renewable. *Amount:* $7500.

Eligibility Requirements: Applicant must be Black (non-Hispanic) and enrolled or expecting to enroll at a four-year institution or university. Applicant must have 3.0 GPA or higher. Available to U.S. citizens.

Application Requirements: Application, financial need analysis. *Deadline:* varies.

Contact: Rebecca Bennett, Director, Program Services
United Negro College Fund
8260 Willow Oaks Corporate Drive
Fairfax, VA 22031-8044
Phone: 800-331-2244
E-mail: rbennett@uncf.org

UPS CORPORATE SCHOLARS PROGRAM/INTERNSHIP

Award consists of both a scholarship and internship. Applicant must be a sophomore or junior undergraduate majoring in marketing, computer science, information technology, or mechanical engineering. Must have 3.0 GPA. Please visit Web site for more information: http://www.uncf.org.

Academic Fields/Career Goals: Business/Consumer Services; Computer Science/Data Processing; Mechanical Engineering.

Award: Scholarship for use in sophomore, junior, or senior years; renewable. *Number:* varies. *Amount:* up to $10,000.

Eligibility Requirements: Applicant must be Black (non-Hispanic) and enrolled or expecting to enroll at a four-year institution or university. Applicant must have 3.0 GPA or higher. Available to U.S. citizens.

Application Requirements: Application, financial need analysis, FAFSA, Student Aid Report (SAR). *Deadline:* February 10.

Contact: Rebecca Bennett, Director, Program Services
United Negro College Fund
8260 Willow Oaks Corporate Drive
Fairfax, VA 22031-8044
Phone: 800-331-2244
E-mail: rbennett@uncf.org

WEYERHAEUSER/UNCF CORPORATE SCHOLARS

Award for sophomores and juniors majoring in forestry, marketing, operations management, electrical engineering, or industrial engineering. Includes paid summer internship. Must have 3.0 GPA. Please visit Web site for more information: http://www.uncf.org.

Academic Fields/Career Goals: Business/Consumer Services; Electrical Engineering/Electronics; Engineering/Technology; Environmental Science; Natural Resources.

Award: Scholarship for use in sophomore, junior, or senior years; renewable. *Number:* varies. *Amount:* $10,000.

Eligibility Requirements: Applicant must be Black (non-Hispanic) and enrolled or expecting to enroll full-time at a four-year institution or university. Applicant must have 3.0 GPA or higher. Available to U.S. citizens.

Application Requirements: Application, essay, financial need analysis, resume, references, transcript, FAFSA, Student Aid Report (SAR). *Deadline:* February 15.

Contact: Weyerhaeuser/UNCF Corporate Scholars Program
United Negro College Fund
PO Box 1435
Alexandria, VA 22313-9998

WM. WRIGLEY, JR. COMPANY SCHOLARS PROGRAM

Must be rising junior or senior at a UNCF member college. Need-based scholarships offered to business, engineering, and chemistry majors with at least a 3.0 GPA. Prospective applicants should complete the Student Profile found at Web site: http://www.uncf.org.

Academic Fields/Career Goals: Business/Consumer Services; Chemical Engineering; Engineering/Technology.

Award: Scholarship for use in sophomore or junior years; not renewable. *Amount:* up to $3000.

Eligibility Requirements: Applicant must be Black (non-Hispanic) and enrolled or expecting to enroll at a four-year institution or university. Applicant must have 3.0 GPA or higher. Available to U.S. citizens.

Application Requirements: Application, financial need analysis. *Deadline:* varies.

Contact: Program Services Department
United Negro College Fund
8260 Willow Oaks Corporate Drive
Fairfax, VA 22031

WYETH SCHOLARSHIP
• See page 142

VIRGINIA SOCIETY OF CERTIFIED PUBLIC ACCOUNTANTS EDUCATION FOUNDATION
http://www.vscpa.com

VIRGINIA SOCIETY OF CPAS EDUCATIONAL FOUNDATION MINORITY UNDERGRADUATE SCHOLARSHIP
• See page 71

VIRGINIA SOCIETY OF CPAS EDUCATIONAL FOUNDATION UNDERGRADUATE SCHOLARSHIP
• See page 72

WATERBURY FOUNDATION
http://www.conncf.org/

MALCOLM BALDRIGE SCHOLARSHIP

One-time award open to undergraduates studying international business or trade. Must be a Connecticut resident enrolled in a Connecticut college. Must be a U.S. citizen.

Academic Fields/Career Goals: Business/Consumer Services; International Studies.

Award: Scholarship for use in freshman, sophomore, junior, or senior years; not renewable. *Number:* 1–2. *Amount:* $2000–$4000.

Eligibility Requirements: Applicant must be enrolled or expecting to enroll at a two-year or four-year institution or university; resident of Connecticut and studying in Connecticut. Available to U.S. citizens.

Application Requirements: Application, essay, financial need analysis, references, transcript. *Deadline:* March 1.

Contact: Josh Carey, Program Officer
Waterbury Foundation
43 Field Street
Waterbury, CT 06702-1216
Phone: 203-753-1315
Fax: 203-756-3054
E-mail: jcarey@conncf.org

WOMEN GROCERS OF AMERICA
http://www.nationalgrocers.org

MARY MACEY SCHOLARSHIP
• See page 85

WOMEN IN LOGISTICS, NORTHERN CALIFORNIA
http://www.womeninlogistics.org

WOMEN IN LOGISTICS SCHOLARSHIP

Award for students who plan to study and eventually pursue a career in a logistics and supply chain management. Must enroll in a California institution. Must be a member of Women in Logistics.

Academic Fields/Career Goals: Business/Consumer Services; Trade/Technical Specialties; Transportation.

Award: Scholarship for use in freshman, sophomore, junior, senior, or graduate years; not renewable. *Number:* 1–3. *Amount:* $500–$1000.

Eligibility Requirements: Applicant must be enrolled or expecting to enroll full or part-time at a two-year or four-year or technical institution or university; female; studying in California and must have

Women in Logistics, Northern California (continued)

an interest in designated field specified by sponsor. Applicant or parent of applicant must be member of Women in Logistics. Available to U.S. and non-U.S. citizens.

Application Requirements: Application, essay, resume, references, transcript. *Deadline:* April 1.

Contact: Dr. Susan Cholette
E-mail: cholette@sfsu.edu

WYOMING TRUCKING ASSOCIATION

WYOMING TRUCKING ASSOCIATION TRUST FUND SCHOLARSHIP

One-time award for Wyoming high school seniors who will enroll at a Wyoming college. Must plan a career in the transportation industry in Wyoming. Course of study includes business and sales management, computer skills, accounting, office procedures and management, communications, mechanics, truck driver training and safety.

Academic Fields/Career Goals: Business/Consumer Services; Communications; Computer Science/Data Processing; Mechanical Engineering; Trade/Technical Specialties; Transportation.

Award: Scholarship for use in freshman, sophomore, junior, or senior years; not renewable. *Number:* 1–10. *Amount:* $250–$960.

Eligibility Requirements: Applicant must be high school student; planning to enroll or expecting to enroll full-time at a two-year or four-year or technical institution or university; resident of Wyoming and studying in Wyoming. Available to U.S. citizens.

Application Requirements: Application, essay, financial need analysis, references, test scores, transcript. *Deadline:* varies.

Contact: Kathy Cundall, Administrative Assistant
Wyoming Trucking Association
Box 1909
Casper, WY 82602-1909
Phone: 307-234-1579
Fax: 307-234-7082
E-mail: wytruck@aol.com

ZONTA INTERNATIONAL FOUNDATION
http://www.zonta.org

JANE M. KLAUSMAN WOMEN IN BUSINESS SCHOLARSHIPS

Awards for female students entering their third or fourth year in an undergraduate business degree. Application available at Web site http://www.zonta.org

Academic Fields/Career Goals: Business/Consumer Services.

Award: Scholarship for use in junior or senior years; not renewable. *Number:* 5. *Amount:* $4000–$5000.

Eligibility Requirements: Applicant must be enrolled or expecting to enroll full-time at a four-year institution or university and female. Available to U.S. and non-U.S. citizens.

Application Requirements: Application, essay, references. *Deadline:* varies.

Contact: Ana Ubides, Foundation Assistant
Zonta International Foundation
557 West Randolph Street
Chicago, IL 60661-2206
Phone: 312-930-5848
Fax: 312-930-0951
E-mail: zontafdtn@zonta.org

CANADIAN STUDIES

CANADIAN INSTITUTE OF UKRAINIAN STUDIES
http://www.ualberta.ca/cius/

CANADIAN INSTITUTE OF UKRAINIAN STUDIES RESEARCH GRANTS
• *See page 104*

CHEMICAL ENGINEERING

AACE INTERNATIONAL
http://www.aacei.org

AACE INTERNATIONAL COMPETITIVE SCHOLARSHIP
• *See page 96*

AEA-OREGON COUNCIL
http://aeascholar.ous.edu

AEA- OREGON COUNCIL TECHNOLOGY SCHOLARSHIP PROGRAM
• *See page 88*

AMERICAN CHEMICAL SOCIETY, RUBBER DIVISION
http://www.rubber.org

AMERICAN CHEMICAL SOCIETY, RUBBER DIVISION UNDERGRADUATE SCHOLARSHIP

Candidate must be majoring in a technical discipline relevant to the rubber industry with a "B" or better overall academic average. Two scholarships are awarded to juniors and seniors enrolled in an accredited college or university in the U.S., Canada, Mexico, India or Brazil.

Academic Fields/Career Goals: Chemical Engineering; Engineering/Technology; Materials Science, Engineering, and Metallurgy; Mechanical Engineering; Science, Technology, and Society.

Award: Scholarship for use in junior or senior years; not renewable. *Number:* 2. *Amount:* $5000.

Eligibility Requirements: Applicant must be enrolled or expecting to enroll full-time at a four-year institution or university. Applicant must have 3.0 GPA or higher. Available to U.S. and non-U.S. citizens.

Application Requirements: Application, essay, interview, references, test scores, transcript. *Deadline:* March 1.

Contact: Victoria George, Education and Publications Manager
American Chemical Society, Rubber Division
250 South Forge Road, PO Box 499
Akron, OH 44325
Phone: 330-972-6938
Fax: 330-920-5269
E-mail: education@rubber.org

AMERICAN COUNCIL OF ENGINEERING COMPANIES OF PENNSYLVANIA (ACEC/PA)
http://www.acecpa.org

ENGINEERING SCHOLARSHIP

Scholarship is available to a fourth-or fifth-year full-time engineering student. Must be U.S. citizen.

Academic Fields/Career Goals: Chemical Engineering; Civil Engineering; Electrical Engineering/Electronics; Engineering/Technology; Engineering-Related Technologies; Materials Science, Engineering, and Metallurgy; Mechanical Engineering.

Award: Scholarship for use in senior, or graduate years; not renewable. *Number:* 1–5. *Amount:* $2000–$5000.

Eligibility Requirements: Applicant must be enrolled or expecting to enroll full-time at a four-year institution or university. Available to U.S. citizens.

Application Requirements: Application, essay, resume, references, transcript. *Deadline:* December 1.

Contact: Laurie Troutman, Administrative Assistant
American Council of Engineering Companies of Pennsylvania (ACEC/PA)
2040 Linglestown Road, Suite 200
Harrisburg, PA 17110
Phone: 717-540-6811
Fax: 717-540-6815
E-mail: laurie@ececta.org

AMERICAN ELECTROPLATERS AND SURFACE FINISHERS SOCIETY
http://www.aesf.org

AMERICAN ELECTROPLATERS AND SURFACE FINISHERS SCHOLARSHIPS

One-time award to students majoring in materials science, chemical engineering, or environmental engineering. Applicant must be a junior or senior undergraduate studying full time. Also open to graduate students.

Academic Fields/Career Goals: Chemical Engineering; Engineering/Technology; Materials Science, Engineering, and Metallurgy.

Award: Scholarship for use in junior, senior, or graduate years; not renewable. *Number:* 5–10. *Amount:* $1500.

Eligibility Requirements: Applicant must be enrolled or expecting to enroll full-time at a four-year institution or university. Available to U.S. and non-U.S. citizens.

Application Requirements: Application, essay, resume, references, transcript. *Deadline:* April 15.

Contact: Janice Williams, Purchasing Manager
American Electroplaters and Surface Finishers Society
Central Florida Research Park
One Thomas Circle, NW, Tenth Floor
Washington, DC 20005
Phone: 407-281-6441
Fax: 407-281-6446
E-mail: janice@aesf.org

AMERICAN INDIAN SCIENCE AND ENGINEERING SOCIETY   http://www.aises.org

ENVIRONMENTAL PROTECTION AGENCY TRIBAL LANDS ENVIRONMENTAL SCIENCE SCHOLARSHIP

• *See page 135*

AMERICAN INSTITUTE OF CHEMICAL ENGINEERS   http://www.aiche.org

CHEME-CAR NATIONAL LEVEL COMPETITION

Each Student Chapter Region may send their first and second place winners to the design competition. Multiple entries from a single school may be permitted at the regional competitions, but only one entry per school is allowed at the national competition.

Academic Fields/Career Goals: Chemical Engineering.

Award: Prize for use in freshman year. *Number:* up to 3. *Amount:* $500–$2000.

Eligibility Requirements: Applicant must be enrolled or expecting to enroll full-time at an institution or university. Available to U.S. citizens.

Application Requirements: Application, applicant must enter a contest, student chapter name, team contact, list of team members, title of entry, description of chemical reaction/drive system, list of chemicals to be used and estimated quantity needed. *Deadline:* varies.

Contact: Prof. David Dixon, Dept Chemistry and Chemical Engineering
American Institute of Chemical Engineers
South Dakota School of Mines and Technology, 501 East Saint Joseph Street
Rapid City, SD 57701
Phone: 605-394-1235
Fax: 605-394-1232
E-mail: david.dixon@sdsmt.edu

DONALD F. AND MILDRED TOPP OTHMER FOUNDATION-NATIONAL SCHOLARSHIP AWARDS

Each year, fifteen national AICHE student members are awarded a scholarship of $1000. Awards are presented on the basis of academic achievement and involvement in student chapter activities. The Student Chapter Advisor must make nominations. Only one nomination will be accepted from each AICHE Student Chapter or Chemical Engineering Club.

Academic Fields/Career Goals: Chemical Engineering.

Award: Scholarship for use in freshman, sophomore, junior, senior, or graduate years; not renewable. *Number:* 15. *Amount:* $1000.

Eligibility Requirements: Applicant must be enrolled or expecting to enroll at a two-year or four-year institution or university. Available to U.S. citizens.

Application Requirements: Application, essay, references, transcript, long-range career plans. *Deadline:* May 10.

Contact: AIChE Awards Administrator
American Institute of Chemical Engineers
3 Park Avenue
New York, NY 10016-5901
Phone: 212-591-7107
Fax: 212-591-8882
E-mail: awards@aiche.org

ENVIRONMENTAL DIVISION GRADUATE STUDENT PAPER AWARD

Three cash prizes recognizing the best graduate student papers on environmental protection through chemical engineering. Graduate student must be primary author and be a member of the American Institute of Chemical Engineers at the time paper is submitted. Paper must describe original research and be suitable for publication in a refereed journal. Must be nominated.

Academic Fields/Career Goals: Chemical Engineering.

Award: Prize for use in freshman, sophomore, junior, senior, or graduate years; not renewable. *Number:* 3. *Amount:* $150–$450.

Eligibility Requirements: Applicant must be enrolled or expecting to enroll at a two-year or four-year institution or university. Available to U.S. citizens.

Application Requirements: Applicant must enter a contest, references, student paper, 5 copies of the nomination package. *Deadline:* October 15.

Contact: Tapas Das
American Institute of Chemical Engineers
125 Mandy Place, NE
Olympia, WA 98516
Phone: 360-456-0573
E-mail: shivaniki@comcast.net

ENVIRONMENTAL DIVISION UNDERGRADUATE STUDENT PAPER AWARD

Cash prizes awarded to full-time undergraduate students who prepare the best original papers based on the results of research or an investigation related to the environment. The work must be performed during the student's undergraduate enrollment, and the paper must be submitted prior to or within six months of graduation. Student must be the sole author of the paper, but faculty guidance is encouraged. Student must be a member of the American Institute of Chemical Engineers Student Chapter. Student's college or university must have an accredited program in chemical engineering. Must be nominated.

Academic Fields/Career Goals: Chemical Engineering.

Award: Prize for use in freshman, sophomore, junior, or senior years; not renewable. *Number:* 3. *Amount:* $100–$300.

Eligibility Requirements: Applicant must be enrolled or expecting to enroll full-time at a two-year or four-year institution or university. Available to U.S. citizens.

Application Requirements: Applicant must enter a contest, references, student paper, 5 copies of the nomination package, work done prior to or within 6 months of graduation. *Deadline:* May 15.

Contact: Tapas Das
American Institute of Chemical Engineers
125 Mandy Place, NE
Olympia, WA 98516
Phone: 360-456-0573
E-mail: shivaniki@comcast.net

JOHN J. MCKETTA UNDERGRADUATE SCHOLARSHIP

A $5000 scholarship will be awarded to a junior or senior student member of AICHE who is planning a career in the chemical engineering process industries. Must maintain a 3.0 GPA. Applicant should show leadership or activity in either the school's AICHE Student Chapter or other university sponsored campus activities. Must attend ABET accredited school in the U.S., Canada, or Mexico.

Academic Fields/Career Goals: Chemical Engineering.

Award: Scholarship for use in junior or senior years; not renewable. *Number:* 1. *Amount:* $5000.

Eligibility Requirements: Applicant must be enrolled or expecting to enroll at a four-year institution or university. Applicant must have 3.0 GPA or higher. Available to U.S. and non-U.S. citizens.

American Institute of Chemical Engineers (continued)

Application Requirements: Application, essay, references. *Deadline:* May 12.

Contact: AIChE Awards Administrator
American Institute of Chemical Engineers
3 Park Avenue
New York, NY 10016
Phone: 212-591-7107
Fax: 212-591-8882
E-mail: awards@aiche.org

MINORITY AFFAIRS COMMITTEE AWARD FOR OUTSTANDING SCHOLASTIC ACHIEVEMENT

Award recognizing the outstanding achievements of a chemical engineering student who serves as a role model for minority students. $1000 award plus $500 travel allowance to attend AICHE meeting. Must be nominated.

Academic Fields/Career Goals: Chemical Engineering.

Award: Scholarship for use in freshman, sophomore, junior, senior, or graduate years; not renewable. *Number:* 1. *Amount:* $1500.

Eligibility Requirements: Applicant must be American Indian/Alaska Native, Asian/Pacific Islander, Black (non-Hispanic), or Hispanic and enrolled or expecting to enroll full-time at a two-year or four-year institution. Applicant must have 3.0 GPA or higher. Available to U.S. citizens.

Application Requirements: Application. *Deadline:* May 15.

Contact: Dr. Emmanuel Dada
American Institute of Chemical Engineers
PO Box 8
Princeton, NJ 08543
Phone: 212-591-7107
E-mail: emmanuel_dada@fmc.com

MINORITY SCHOLARSHIP AWARDS FOR COLLEGE STUDENTS

Award for college undergraduates who are studying chemical engineering. Must be a member of a minority group that is underrepresented in chemical engineering. Must be nominated. Must be an AICHE national student member at the time of application.

Academic Fields/Career Goals: Chemical Engineering.

Award: Scholarship for use in freshman, sophomore, junior, or senior years; renewable. *Number:* up to 10. *Amount:* $1000.

Eligibility Requirements: Applicant must be American Indian/Alaska Native, Asian/Pacific Islander, Black (non-Hispanic), or Hispanic and enrolled or expecting to enroll full-time at a two-year or four-year institution or university. Applicant must have 3.0 GPA or higher. Available to U.S. citizens.

Application Requirements: Application, essay, financial need analysis, references, transcript, career objective. *Deadline:* May 15.

Contact: Dr. Emmanuel Dada
American Institute of Chemical Engineers
PO Box 8
Princeton, NJ 08543
Phone: 212-591-7107
E-mail: emmanuel_dada@fmc.com

MINORITY SCHOLARSHIP AWARDS FOR INCOMING COLLEGE FRESHMEN

Up to ten awards of $1000 for high school graduates who are members of a minority group that is underrepresented in chemical engineering. Must plan to study courses leading to a chemical engineering degree. Must be nominated.

Academic Fields/Career Goals: Chemical Engineering.

Award: Scholarship for use in freshman year; not renewable. *Number:* up to 10. *Amount:* $1000.

Eligibility Requirements: Applicant must be American Indian/Alaska Native, Asian/Pacific Islander, Black (non-Hispanic), or Hispanic; high school student and planning to enroll or expecting to enroll at a four-year institution or university. Applicant must have 3.0 GPA or higher. Available to U.S. citizens.

Application Requirements: Application, essay, financial need analysis, references, transcript, confirmation of minority status. *Deadline:* May 15.

Contact: Dr. Emmanuel Dada
American Institute of Chemical Engineers
PO Box 8
Princeton, NJ 08543
Phone: 212-591-7107
E-mail: emmanuel_dada@fmc.com

NATIONAL STUDENT DESIGN COMPETITION–TEAM (WILLIAM CUNNINGHAM AWARD)

Students solve a chemical engineering design problem devised and judged by chemical engineers from a designated company. The problem's solution requires a wide range of skills in calculation and evaluation of both technical data and economic factors.

Academic Fields/Career Goals: Chemical Engineering.

Award: Prize for use in freshman year. *Number:* 1. *Amount:* up to $600.

Eligibility Requirements: Applicant must be enrolled or expecting to enroll full-time at a technical institution. Available to U.S. citizens.

Application Requirements: Application, individual form for each team member. *Deadline:* June 5.

Contact: AIChE Awards Administrator
American Institute of Chemical Engineers
3 Park Avenue
New York, NY 10016
Phone: 212-591-7107
Fax: 212-591-8882
E-mail: awards@aiche.org

NATIONAL STUDENT DESIGN COMPETITION-INDIVIDUAL

Three cash prizes for student contest problem that typifies a real, working, chemical engineering design situation. Competition booklets are available from Student Chapter advisors. Must be nominated.

Academic Fields/Career Goals: Chemical Engineering.

Award: Prize for use in freshman, sophomore, junior, senior, or graduate years; not renewable. *Number:* 3. *Amount:* $200–$500.

Eligibility Requirements: Applicant must be enrolled or expecting to enroll at a four-year institution or university. Available to U.S. citizens.

Application Requirements: Contest problem that typifies a real, working, chemical engineering design situation. *Deadline:* June 5.

Contact: AIChE Awards Administrator
American Institute of Chemical Engineers
3 Park Avenue
New York, NY 10016
Phone: 212-591-7107
Fax: 212-591-8882
E-mail: awards@aiche.org

NATIONAL STUDENT PAPER COMPETITION

First-place winners from each of the ten Regional Student Paper Competitions present their prize-winning papers during the American Institute of Chemical Engineers meeting in current calendar year. First prize is $500, second prize is $300, and third prize is $200.

Academic Fields/Career Goals: Chemical Engineering.

Award: Prize for use in freshman, sophomore, junior, senior, or graduate years; not renewable. *Number:* 3. *Amount:* $200–$500.

Eligibility Requirements: Applicant must be enrolled or expecting to enroll at a four-year institution or university. Available to U.S. citizens.

Application Requirements: Applicant must enter a contest, student paper, 15-minute paper presentation and 3-5 minute question and answer session. *Deadline:* varies.

Contact: AIChE Awards Administrator
American Institute of Chemical Engineers
3 Park Avenue
New York, NY 10016-5901
Phone: 212-591-7107
Fax: 212-591-8882
E-mail: awards@aiche.org

OUTSTANDING STUDENT CHAPTER ADVISOR AWARD

Award for service and leadership in guiding the activities of an AIChE student chapter in accordance with AIChE principles. Nominations may be made by any AIChE member or student member. Nominations by an entire student chapter acting as a group are encouraged.

Academic Fields/Career Goals: Chemical Engineering.

Award: Prize for use in freshman, sophomore, junior, or senior years. *Number:* 1. *Amount:* up to $1000.

Eligibility Requirements: Applicant must be enrolled or expecting to enroll full-time at a technical institution. Available to U.S. and non-U.S. citizens.

Application Requirements: Application, references, 4 copies of the nomination. *Deadline:* June 1.

Contact: Marvin Borgmeyer
American Institute of Chemical Engineers
PO Box 1607
Baton Rouge, LA 70821-1607
Phone: 225-977-6206
Fax: 225-977-6396

PROCESS DEVELOPMENT DIVISION STUDENT PAPER AWARD

Presented to a full-time graduate or undergraduate student who prepares the best technical paper to describe the results of process development related studies within chemical engineering. Must be carried out while the student is enrolled at a university with an accredited chemical engineering program. Student must be the primary author (faculty advisors may be co-authors). Paper must be suitable for publication in a refereed journal. Student must be a member of AIChE.

Academic Fields/Career Goals: Chemical Engineering.

Award: Prize for use in freshman, sophomore, junior, senior, or graduate years; not renewable. *Number:* 1. *Amount:* $200.

Eligibility Requirements: Applicant must be enrolled or expecting to enroll full-time at a four-year institution or university. Available to U.S. citizens.

Application Requirements: References, original and 5 copies of the nomination form and relevant information. *Deadline:* June 15.

Contact: Cheryl Teich, Engineering Technical Center
American Institute of Chemical Engineers
727 Norristown Road, PO Box 704
Spring House, PA 19477
Phone: 215-619-5342
E-mail: CTeich@rohmhaas.com

REGIONAL STUDENT PAPER COMPETITION

Students present technical papers at the student regional conferences which are held in the spring. Deadlines for regional conferences vary; contact regional host schools for details or look for schedules on Web site (http://www.aiche.org). First prize is $200, second prize is $100, and third prize is $50. First place winner from each region presents the paper at the National Student Paper Competition.

Academic Fields/Career Goals: Chemical Engineering.

Award: Prize for use in freshman, sophomore, junior, senior, or graduate years; not renewable. *Number:* 3. *Amount:* $50–$200.

Eligibility Requirements: Applicant must be enrolled or expecting to enroll at a four-year institution or university. Available to U.S. citizens.

Application Requirements: Applicant must enter a contest, student paper. *Deadline:* varies.

Contact: AIChE Awards Administrator
American Institute of Chemical Engineers
3 Park Avenue
New York, NY 10016-5901
Phone: 212-591-7107
Fax: 212-591-8882
E-mail: awards@aiche.org

SAFETY AND CHEMICAL ENGINEERING EDUCATION (SACHE) STUDENT ESSAY AWARD FOR SAFETY

Two $500 dollar awards will be presented to the individuals submitting the best essays on the topic of chemical process safety. Essays may focus on process safety in education, relevance of safety in undergraduate education, or integrating safety principles into the undergraduate chemical engineering curriculum. The essay must be no more than 1500 words. The student must be an undergraduate student. The student's school must be a member of SACHE.

Academic Fields/Career Goals: Chemical Engineering.

Award: Prize for use in freshman, sophomore, junior, or senior years; not renewable. *Number:* up to 4. *Amount:* $500.

Eligibility Requirements: Applicant must be enrolled or expecting to enroll at a four-year institution or university. Available to U.S. citizens.

Application Requirements: Applicant must enter a contest, essay, report should include separate section titled "inherent safety". *Deadline:* June 5.

Contact: AIChE Awards Administrator
American Institute of Chemical Engineers
3 Park Avenue
New York, NY 10016
Phone: 212-591-7107
Fax: 212-591-8880
E-mail: awards@aiche.org

SAFETY AND HEALTH NATIONAL STUDENT DESIGN COMPETITION AWARD FOR SAFETY

Four $500 awards available for each of the teams or individuals who apply one or more of the following concepts of inherent safety in their designs: a) Design the plant for easier and effective maintainability; b) design the plant with less waste; c) Design the plant with special features that demonstrate inherent safety; d) Include design concepts regarding the entire life cycle. The school must have a student chapter of AIChE.

Academic Fields/Career Goals: Chemical Engineering.

Award: Prize for use in freshman, sophomore, junior, senior, or graduate years; not renewable. *Number:* 4. *Amount:* $500.

Eligibility Requirements: Applicant must be enrolled or expecting to enroll full or part-time at a four-year institution or university. Available to U.S. citizens.

Application Requirements: Application, design. *Deadline:* June 5.

Contact: AIChE Awards Administrator
American Institute of Chemical Engineers
3 Park Avenue
New York, NY 10016
Phone: 212-591-7478
Fax: 212-591-8882
E-mail: awards@aiche.org

W. DAVID SMITH, JR. GRADUATE STUDENT PAPER AWARD

$1500 and a plaque is awarded to an individual for published work on the application of computing and systems technology to chemical engineering. The work must have been done by the individual while pursuing graduate or undergraduate studies in chemical engineering.

Academic Fields/Career Goals: Chemical Engineering.

Award: Prize for use in freshman, sophomore, junior, senior, or graduate years; not renewable. *Number:* 1. *Amount:* $1500.

Eligibility Requirements: Applicant must be enrolled or expecting to enroll at a two-year or four-year institution or university. Available to U.S. citizens.

Application Requirements: Applicant must enter a contest, paper in chemical engineering, computing, and systems technology. *Deadline:* April 15.

Contact: Dr. Karen High
American Institute of Chemical Engineers
School of Chemical Engineering, 423 EN Oklahoma State University
Stillwater, OK 74078
Phone: 405-744-9112
Fax: 405-744-6338
E-mail: high@okstate.edu

AMERICAN SOCIETY FOR CLINICAL LABORATORY SCIENCE
http://www.ascls.org

ASCLS REGION IX CLINICAL LABORATORY SCIENTISTS OF ALASKA SHARON O'MEARA CONTINUING EDUCATION SCHOLARSHIP FUND

Scholarships awarded to students pursuing continuing education in clinical laboratory science or related fields. Students must be a member in good standing of the CLSA and have been a member for at least one year at time of application. Please refer to Web site for further details and application: http://www.clsaonline.org.

American Society for Clinical Laboratory Science (continued)

Academic Fields/Career Goals: Chemical Engineering; Health and Medical Sciences.

Award: Scholarship for use in freshman, sophomore, junior, senior, or graduate years; not renewable. *Number:* 1. *Amount:* varies.

Eligibility Requirements: Applicant must be enrolled or expecting to enroll full or part-time at a two-year or four-year or technical institution or university. Applicant or parent of applicant must be member of American Society for Clinical Laboratory Science. Available to U.S. citizens.

Application Requirements: Application. *Deadline:* varies.

Contact: Karen Martin, CLSA Webmaster
American Society for Clinical Laboratory Science
1536 Porchet Way
Fairbanks, AK 99709
E-mail: webmaster@clsaonline.org

ASCLS REGION VI MISSOURI ORGANIZATION FOR CLINICAL LABORATORY SCIENCE EDUCATION SCHOLARSHIP

Scholarship provides financial assistance to clinical laboratory science or medical laboratory technology students who are beginning or continuing their formal education, or conducting research that directly relates to laboratory science. Applicant must be a member of MOCLS for a minimum of two years. Please refer to Web site for further information and applications: http://www.mocls.org

Academic Fields/Career Goals: Chemical Engineering; Health and Medical Sciences.

Award: Scholarship for use in freshman, sophomore, junior, or graduate years; not renewable. *Number:* 1. *Amount:* varies.

Eligibility Requirements: Applicant must be enrolled or expecting to enroll full or part-time at a two-year or four-year or technical institution or university. Applicant or parent of applicant must be member of American Society for Clinical Laboratory Science. Available to U.S. citizens.

Application Requirements: Application, financial need analysis, references, transcript, proof of enrollment, personal letter. *Deadline:* varies.

Contact: Tom Reddig, Missouri Scholarship Fund Chair
American Society for Clinical Laboratory Science
31 West 59th Street
Kansas City, MO 64113
Phone: 816-931-8686

AMERICAN SOCIETY FOR ENOLOGY AND VITICULTURE
http://www.asev.org

AMERICAN SOCIETY FOR ENOLOGY AND VITICULTURE SCHOLARSHIPS
• See page 78

ASSOCIATION FOR FACILITIES ENGINEERING (AFE)

ASSOCIATION FOR FACILITIES ENGINEERING CEDAR VALLEY CHAPTER # 132 SCHOLARSHIP
• See page 120

ASSOCIATION FOR IRON AND STEEL TECHNOLOGY
http://www.aist.org

ASSOCIATION FOR IRON AND STEEL TECHNOLOGY DAVID H. SAMSON SCHOLARSHIP

Scholarship available for children of AIST members who are Canadian citizens. Scholarship is renewable for up to four years, student must be studying engineering at a Canadian institution or, in the absence of engineering applicants, the award may be made to an eligible student studying chemistry, geology, mathematics, or physics. Application forms and rules may be obtained by writing to scholarship contact.

Academic Fields/Career Goals: Chemical Engineering; Civil Engineering; Electrical Engineering/Electronics; Energy and Power Engineering; Engineering/Technology; Marine/Ocean Engineering; Materials Science, Engineering, and Metallurgy.

Award: Scholarship for use in freshman, sophomore, junior, or senior years; renewable. *Number:* 1. *Amount:* $2000.

Eligibility Requirements: Applicant must be enrolled or expecting to enroll full-time at a four-year institution or university. Available to Canadian citizens.

Application Requirements: Application, references, transcript. *Deadline:* June 30.

Contact: Robert Kneale, AIST Northern Member Chapter Scholarship Chair
Association for Iron and Steel Technology
PO Box 1734
Cambridge, ON N1R 7G8
Canada

ASSOCIATION FOR WOMEN IN SCIENCE EDUCATIONAL FOUNDATION
http://www.awis.org/ed_foundation.html

ASSOCIATION FOR WOMEN IN SCIENCE COLLEGE SCHOLARSHIP
• See page 86

ASTRONAUT SCHOLARSHIP FOUNDATION
http://www.astronautscholarship.org

ASTRONAUT SCHOLARSHIP FOUNDATION
• See page 92

AUTOMOTIVE HALL OF FAME
http://www.automotivehalloffame.org

AUTOMOTIVE HALL OF FAME EDUCATIONAL FUNDS

Over a dozen available awards. Applicant must have a sincere interest in an automotive career. Candidate should maintain a satisfactory academic standing and be enrolled full-time. Financial need is considered but not necessary. Renewable award of varying amounts. Applicants in a four-year program must have completed at least one year of study. Must already be accepted at an accredited college, university, or trade school within the United States at the time of application. High school seniors must submit letter of acceptance. Applicant must send a self-addressed envelope.

Academic Fields/Career Goals: Chemical Engineering; Electrical Engineering/Electronics; Engineering/Technology; Engineering-Related Technologies; Mechanical Engineering; Trade/Technical Specialties.

Award: Scholarship for use in freshman, sophomore, junior, senior, or graduate years; renewable. *Number:* 12. *Amount:* $250–$2000.

Eligibility Requirements: Applicant must be enrolled or expecting to enroll full-time at a two-year or four-year or technical institution or university and must have an interest in automotive. Applicant must have 3.0 GPA or higher. Available to U.S. and Canadian citizens.

Application Requirements: Application, financial need analysis, references, self-addressed stamped envelope, transcript. *Deadline:* May 30.

Contact: Lynne Hall, Scholarship Coordinator
Automotive Hall of Fame
21400 Oakwood Boulevard
Dearborn, MI 48124-4078

BARRY M. GOLDWATER SCHOLARSHIP AND EXCELLENCE IN EDUCATION FOUNDATION
http://www.act.org/goldwater

BARRY M. GOLDWATER SCHOLARSHIP AND EXCELLENCE IN EDUCATION PROGRAM
• See page 92

CHEMICAL INSTITUTE OF CANADA
http://www.cheminst.ca

EDMONTON CHEMICAL ENGINEERING SCHOLARSHIP

One scholarship available to an undergraduate student in chemical engineering entering the second, third, fourth, or fifth year of studies at a Canadian university. Applicants must be members of the Canadian Society for Chemical Engineering. One-time award of CAN$1000 and up to CAN$750 in travel expenses.

Academic Fields/Career Goals: Chemical Engineering.

Award: Scholarship for use in sophomore, junior, or senior years; not renewable. *Number:* 1. *Amount:* $899.

Eligibility Requirements: Applicant must be enrolled or expecting to enroll full-time at an institution or university. Applicant or parent of applicant must be member of Canadian Society for Chemical Engineering. Available to U.S. and Canadian citizens.

Application Requirements: Application, references, transcript. *Deadline:* April 30.

Contact: Student Affairs Manager
Chemical Institute of Canada
130 Slater Street, Suite 550
Ottawa, ON K1P 6E2
Canada
Phone: 613-232-6252 Ext. 223
Fax: 613-232-5862
E-mail: gwilbee@cheminst.ca

SARNIA CHEMICAL ENGINEERING COMMUNITY SCHOLARSHIP

One scholarship available to undergraduate students in chemical engineering about to enter their final year of studies at a Canadian university. Applicants must be members of the Canadian Society for Chemical Engineering. Applications should include evidence of contributions to the Society. One-time award of CAN$1000.

Academic Fields/Career Goals: Chemical Engineering.

Award: Scholarship for use in senior year; not renewable. *Number:* 1. *Amount:* $899.

Eligibility Requirements: Applicant must be enrolled or expecting to enroll full-time at an institution or university. Applicant or parent of applicant must be member of Canadian Society for Chemical Engineering. Available to U.S. and Canadian citizens.

Application Requirements: Application, references, transcript. *Deadline:* April 30.

Contact: Student Affairs Manager
Chemical Institute of Canada
130 Slater Street, Suite 550
Ottawa, ON K1P 6E2
Canada
Phone: 613-232-6252 Ext. 223
Fax: 613-232-5862
E-mail: gwilbee@cheminst.ca

CUBAN AMERICAN NATIONAL FOUNDATION
http://www.canf.org

MAS FAMILY SCHOLARSHIPS
• See page 146

DESK AND DERRICK EDUCATIONAL TRUST
http://www.addc.org

DESK AND DERRICK EDUCATIONAL TRUST
• See page 92

EAST LOS ANGELES COMMUNITY UNION (TELACU) EDUCATION FOUNDATION
http://www.telacu.com

LINC TELACU ENGINEERING AWARD

Scholarships available to low-income applicants from the Greater East Side of Los Angeles. Must be U.S. citizen or permanent resident with Hispanic heritage. Must be a resident of one of the following communities: East Los Angeles, Bell Gardens, Commerce, Huntington Park, Montebello, Monterey Park, Pico Rivera, Santa Ana, South Gate, and the City of Los Angeles. Must be the first generation in their family to achieve a college degree. Must have a record of community service. For sophomores, juniors and seniors only who have completed twelve credits or more of engineering course work at the time of application.

Academic Fields/Career Goals: Chemical Engineering; Computer Science/Data Processing; Electrical Engineering/Electronics; Engineering/Technology; Engineering-Related Technologies; Mechanical Engineering.

Award: Scholarship for use in sophomore, junior, or senior years; not renewable. *Number:* 1. *Amount:* $2500.

Eligibility Requirements: Applicant must be enrolled or expecting to enroll full-time at a four-year institution or university and resident of California. Applicant must have 2.5 GPA or higher. Available to U.S. citizens.

Application Requirements: Application, autobiography, essay, financial need analysis, interview, references, self-addressed stamped envelope, transcript. *Deadline:* April 1.

Contact: Blanca Anchondo, Scholarship Director
East Los Angeles Community Union (TELACU) Education Foundation
5400 East Olympic Boulevard, Suite 300
Los Angeles, CA 90022
Phone: 323-721-1655
Fax: 323-724-3372
E-mail: info@telacu.com

ELECTROCHEMICAL SOCIETY, INC.
http://www.electrochem.org

DANIEL CUBICCIOTTI STUDENT AWARD OF THE SAN FRANCISCO SECTION OF THE ELECTROCHEMICAL SOCIETY, SPONSORED BY STRUCTURAL INTEGRITY ASSOCIATES
• See page 137

H.H. DOW MEMORIAL STUDENT ACHIEVEMENT AWARD OF THE INDUSTRIAL ELECTROLYSIS AND ELECTROCHEMICAL ENGINEERING DIVISION OF THE ELECTROCHEMICAL SOCIETY, INC.
• See page 137

STUDENT ACHIEVEMENT AWARDS OF THE INDUSTRIAL ELECTROLYSIS AND ELECTROCHEMICAL ENGINEERING DIVISION OF THE ELECTROCHEMICAL SOCIETY, INC.
• See page 137

STUDENT RESEARCH AWARDS OF THE BATTERY DIVISION OF THE ELECTROCHEMICAL SOCIETY, INC.
• See page 137

GEORGE BIRD GRINNELL AMERICAN INDIAN FUND
http://www.grinnellfund.org/

AL QOYAWAYMA AWARD

Up to $1000 scholarship for American-Indian/Alaska Native students majoring in either science or engineering in either an undergraduate or graduate program. Must demonstrate an outstanding interest and skill in any one of the arts (visual, performing or written). Applicants must demonstrate financial need, submit personal statement, proof of school enrollment or acceptance, and proof of tribal enrollment. Award of scholarship is totally contingent upon raising the needed funds. Application deadline June 1. Please include self-addressed stamped envelope.

Academic Fields/Career Goals: Chemical Engineering; Civil Engineering; Earth Science; Electrical Engineering/Electronics; Engineering/Technology; Engineering-Related Technologies; Materials Science, Engineering, and Metallurgy; Mechanical Engineering; Science, Technology, and Society.

Award: Scholarship for use in freshman, sophomore, junior, senior, graduate, or postgraduate years; renewable. *Number:* 1. *Amount:* up to $1000.

Eligibility Requirements: Applicant must be American Indian/Alaska Native; enrolled or expecting to enroll full or part-time at a two-year or four-year institution or university and must have an interest in art, music, music/singing, or writing. Available to U.S. citizens.

Application Requirements: Application, essay, financial need analysis, references, self-addressed stamped envelope, transcript, proof of tribal enrollment. *Deadline:* June 1.

Contact: Paula Mintzies, President
George Bird Grinnell American Indian Fund
PO Box 59033
Potomac, MD 20859
Phone: 301-424-2440
Fax: 301-424-8281

HAWAIIAN LODGE, F.& A. M.
http://www.hawaiianlodge.org/

HAWAIIAN LODGE SCHOLARSHIPS
• *See page 99*

HISPANIC COLLEGE FUND, INC.
http://www.hispanicfund.org

DENNY'S/HISPANIC COLLEGE FUND SCHOLARSHIP
• *See page 62*

DEPARTMENT OF ENERGY SCHOLARSHIP PROGRAM
• *See page 148*

LOCKHEED MARTIN SCHOLARSHIP PROGRAM

Program intended for undergraduate student pursuing his or her bachelor's degree in computer science, engineering, or similar major. Applicant must be U.S. citizen with Hispanic background; May reside in U.S. or Puerto Rico. Must attend college or university in U.S. or Puerto Rico. Online application only: http://www.hispanicfund.org

Academic Fields/Career Goals: Chemical Engineering; Computer Science/Data Processing; Electrical Engineering/Electronics; Energy and Power Engineering; Engineering/Technology; Engineering-Related Technologies; Materials Science, Engineering, and Metallurgy; Military and Defense Studies; Physical Sciences and Math.

Award: Scholarship for use in freshman, sophomore, junior, or senior years; not renewable. *Number:* varies. *Amount:* $500–$5000.

Eligibility Requirements: Applicant must be Hispanic and enrolled or expecting to enroll full-time at a four-year institution or university. Applicant must have 3.0 GPA or higher. Available to U.S. citizens.

Application Requirements: Application. *Deadline:* April 15.

Contact: Stina Augustsson, Program Manager
Hispanic College Fund, Inc.
1717 Pennsylvania Avenue, NW, Suite 460
Washington, DC 20006
Phone: 202-296-5400
Fax: 202-296-3774
E-mail: hcf-info@hispanicfund.org

NATIONAL HISPANIC EXPLORERS SCHOLARSHIP PROGRAM
• *See page 93*

HISPANIC ENGINEER NATIONAL ACHIEVEMENT AWARDS CORPORATION (HENAAC)
http://www.henaac.org

HISPANIC ENGINEER NATIONAL ACHIEVEMENT AWARDS CORPORATION SCHOLARSHIP PROGRAM
• *See page 122*

HISPANIC SCHOLARSHIP FUND
http://www.hsf.net

HSF/GENERAL MOTORS SCHOLARSHIP
• *See page 149*

INDEPENDENT LABORATORIES INSTITUTE SCHOLARSHIP ALLIANCE
http://www.acil.org

INDEPENDENT LABORATORIES INSTITUTE SCHOLARSHIP ALLIANCE
• *See page 93*

INNOVATION AND SCIENCE COUNCIL OF BRITISH COLUMBIA
http://www.scbc.org

PAUL AND HELEN TRUSSEL SCIENCE AND TECHNOLOGY SCHOLARSHIP
• *See page 93*

INSTRUMENTATION, SYSTEMS, AND AUTOMATION SOCIETY (ISA)
http://www.isa.org

INSTRUMENTATION, SYSTEMS, AND AUTOMATION SOCIETY (ISA) SCHOLARSHIP PROGRAM
• *See page 123*

INTERNATIONAL SOCIETY FOR OPTICAL ENGINEERING-SPIE
http://www.spie.org/info/scholarships

SPIE EDUCATIONAL SCHOLARSHIPS IN OPTICAL SCIENCE AND ENGINEERING
• *See page 93*

JORGE MAS CANOSA FREEDOM FOUNDATION
http://www.canf.org

MAS FAMILY SCHOLARSHIP AWARD
• *See page 149*

KENTUCKY NATURAL RESOURCES AND ENVIRONMENTAL PROTECTION CABINET
http://www.uky.edu/waterresources

ENVIRONMENTAL PROTECTION SCHOLARSHIPS

Renewable awards for college juniors, seniors, and graduate students for tuition, fees, and room and board at a Kentucky state university. Minimum 2.5 GPA required. Must agree to work full-time for the Kentucky Natural Resources and Environmental Protection Cabinet upon graduation. Interview is required.

Academic Fields/Career Goals: Chemical Engineering; Civil Engineering; Earth Science; Materials Science, Engineering, and Metallurgy.

Award: Scholarship for use in junior, senior, or graduate years; renewable. *Number:* 3–5. *Amount:* $4750–$7600.

Eligibility Requirements: Applicant must be enrolled or expecting to enroll full-time at a four-year institution or university and studying in Kentucky. Applicant must have 2.5 GPA or higher. Available to U.S. and non-U.S. citizens.

Application Requirements: Application, essay, interview, references, transcript, non-U.S. citizens must have valid work permit. *Deadline:* February 15.

Contact: James Kipp, Scholarship Program Coordinator
Kentucky Natural Resources and Environmental Protection Cabinet
233 Mining/Mineral Resources Building
Lexington, KY 40506-0107
Phone: 859-257-1299
Fax: 859-323-1049
E-mail: kipp@uky.edu

LOS ANGELES COUNCIL OF BLACK PROFESSIONAL ENGINEERS
http://www.lablackengineers.org

AL-BEN SCHOLARSHIP FOR ACADEMIC INCENTIVE

Scholarships will be granted for notable academic achievements, interests in engineering, math, or science, and demonstrated desire and commitment to succeed in technical fields. Must be from a minority group that has traditionally been underrepresented in these areas. For more details or an application see Web site: http://www.lablackengineers.org

Academic Fields/Career Goals: Chemical Engineering; Civil Engineering; Computer Science/Data Processing; Electrical Engineering/Electronics; Engineering/Technology; Engineering-Related Technologies; Materials Science, Engineering, and Metallurgy; Mechanical Engineering; Physical Sciences and Math.

Award: Scholarship for use in freshman, sophomore, junior, or senior years; not renewable. *Number:* 2. *Amount:* $500–$1000.

Eligibility Requirements: Applicant must be American Indian/Alaska Native, Asian/Pacific Islander, Black (non-Hispanic), or Hispanic and enrolled or expecting to enroll at an institution or university. Available to U.S. citizens.

Application Requirements: Application, essay, references, transcript. *Deadline:* April 5.

Contact: Los Angeles Council of Black Professional Engineers
PO Box 881029
Los Angeles, CA 90009

AL-BEN SCHOLARSHIP FOR PROFESSIONAL MERIT

Scholarships will be granted for exemplary actions in campus organizations or community activities while maintaining an excellent GPA. Must be from a minority group. For more details or an application see Web site: http://www.lablackengineers.org.

Academic Fields/Career Goals: Chemical Engineering; Civil Engineering; Computer Science/Data Processing; Electrical Engineering/Electronics; Engineering/Technology; Engineering-Related Technologies; Materials Science, Engineering, and Metallurgy; Mechanical Engineering; Physical Sciences and Math.

Award: Scholarship for use in freshman, sophomore, junior, or senior years; not renewable. *Number:* 2. *Amount:* $500–$1000.

Eligibility Requirements: Applicant must be American Indian/Alaska Native, Asian/Pacific Islander, Black (non-Hispanic), or Hispanic and enrolled or expecting to enroll at a four-year institution or university. Available to U.S. citizens.

Application Requirements: Application, essay, references, transcript. *Deadline:* April 5.

Contact: Los Angeles Council of Black Professional Engineers
PO Box 881029
Los Angeles, CA 90009

AL-BEN SCHOLARSHIP FOR SCHOLASTIC ACHIEVEMENT

Scholarships will be granted for superlative scholastic achievements in the academic pursuits of engineering, math, computer or scientific studies. Must be from a minority group that has traditionally been underrepresented in these areas. For more details or an application see Web site: http://www.lablackengineers.org.

Academic Fields/Career Goals: Chemical Engineering; Civil Engineering; Computer Science/Data Processing; Electrical Engineering/Electronics; Engineering/Technology; Engineering-Related Technologies; Materials Science, Engineering, and Metallurgy; Mechanical Engineering; Physical Sciences and Math.

Award: Scholarship for use in freshman, sophomore, junior, or senior years; not renewable. *Number:* 2. *Amount:* $500–$1000.

Eligibility Requirements: Applicant must be American Indian/Alaska Native, Asian/Pacific Islander, Black (non-Hispanic), or Hispanic and enrolled or expecting to enroll at a four-year institution or university. Available to U.S. citizens.

Application Requirements: Application, essay, references, transcript. *Deadline:* April 5.

Contact: Los Angeles Council of Black Professional Engineers
PO Box 881029
Los Angeles, CA 90009

MASTER BREWERS ASSOCIATION OF THE AMERICAS
http://www.mbaa.com

MASTER BREWERS ASSOCIATION OF THE AMERICAS
• See page 81

MEAD WESTVACO CORPORATION
http://www.meadwestvaco.com

WESTVACO/WICKLIFFE SCHOLARSHIP

Scholarship for females. Must be majoring in chemical, pulp, and paper engineering or mechanical engineering; and be a resident of Ballard, Calloway, Carlisle, Fulton, Graves, Hickman, Marshall, or McCracken County in Kentucky or Alexander, Pulaski, or Massac County in Illinois.

Academic Fields/Career Goals: Chemical Engineering; Mechanical Engineering.

Award: Scholarship for use in freshman, sophomore, junior, or senior years. *Number:* 1.

Eligibility Requirements: Applicant must be enrolled or expecting to enroll at a four-year institution or university and female. Available to U.S. citizens.

Application Requirements: *Deadline:* varies.

Contact: Mead Westvaco Corporation
One High Ridge Park
Stamford, CT 06905
Phone: 203-461-7400

MICHIGAN SOCIETY OF PROFESSIONAL ENGINEERS
http://www.michiganspe.org

MICHIGAN SOCIETY OF PROFESSIONAL ENGINEERS UNDESIGNATED GRANT

Grant of $2000 for a top-ranking student enrolled in an ABET-accredited engineering program at a Michigan college or university. Renewal based on academic performance and approval of both the MSPE Scholarship Trust and Dean of School. Must be a member of MSPE student chapter or state member-at-large. Minimum 3.0 GPA required. Must be a Michigan resident.

Academic Fields/Career Goals: Chemical Engineering; Civil Engineering; Electrical Engineering/Electronics; Engineering/Technology; Mechanical Engineering.

Award: Grant for use in freshman, sophomore, junior, or senior years; renewable. *Number:* 1. *Amount:* $2000.

Eligibility Requirements: Applicant must be enrolled or expecting to enroll full-time at an institution or university; resident of Michigan and studying in Michigan. Applicant or parent of applicant must be member of Michigan Society of Professional Engineers. Applicant must have 3.0 GPA or higher. Available to U.S. citizens.

Application Requirements: Application, essay, references, test scores, transcript. *Deadline:* varies.

Contact: Scholarship Coordinator
Michigan Society of Professional Engineers
PO Box 15276
Lansing, MI 48901-5276
Phone: 517-487-9388
Fax: 517-487-0635
E-mail: mspe@voyager.net

MICRON TECHNOLOGY FOUNDATION, INC.
http://www.micron.com

MICRON SCIENCE AND TECHNOLOGY SCHOLARS PROGRAM

Merit-based scholarship for high school seniors who reside in and attend public or private school in Idaho, Utah, Texas, Colorado, or Virginia. Recognizing excellence in academics and leadership. One top prize of $55,000 college scholarship and ten to twelve $16,500 scholarships available each year. Awards will be paid out over 4 years. Must plan to major in computer science, physics, chemistry, material sciences, or electrical, computer, chemical, or mechanical engineering. Combined SAT score of at least 1350 or composite ACT score of at least 30 required.

Academic Fields/Career Goals: Chemical Engineering; Computer Science/Data Processing; Electrical Engineering/Electronics; Engineering/Technology; Engineering-Related Technologies; Materials Science, Engineering, and Metallurgy; Mechanical Engineering; Physical Sciences and Math; Science, Technology, and Society.

Award: Scholarship for use in freshman, sophomore, junior, or senior years; renewable. *Number:* 10–13. *Amount:* $16,500–$55,000.

Eligibility Requirements: Applicant must be high school student; planning to enroll or expecting to enroll full-time at a four-year institution or university; resident of Colorado, Idaho, Texas, Utah, or Virginia and must have an interest in leadership. Applicant must have 3.5 GPA or higher. Available to U.S. citizens.

Application Requirements: Application, essay, interview, references, test scores, transcript. *Deadline:* January 20.

Contact: Lyn Dauffenbach, Scholarship America
Micron Technology Foundation, Inc.
One Scholarship Way, PO Box 297
Saint Peter, MN 56082
Phone: 800-537-4180

NASA DELAWARE SPACE GRANT CONSORTIUM
http://www.delspace.org

NASA DELAWARE SPACE GRANT UNDERGRADUATE TUITION SCHOLARSHIP
• See page 94

NASA IDAHO SPACE GRANT CONSORTIUM
http://isgc.uidaho.edu

NASA IDAHO SPACE GRANT CONSORTIUM SCHOLARSHIP PROGRAM
• See page 94

NASA MONTANA SPACE GRANT CONSORTIUM
http://www.spacegrant.montana.edu

MONTANA SPACE GRANT SCHOLARSHIP PROGRAM
• See page 125

NASA NEVADA SPACE GRANT CONSORTIUM
http://www.unr.edu/spacegrant

UNIVERSITY AND COMMUNITY COLLEGE SYSTEM OF NEVADA NASA SPACE GRANT AND FELLOWSHIP PROGRAM
• See page 125

NATIONAL ASSOCIATION FOR THE ADVANCEMENT OF COLORED PEOPLE
http://www.naacp.org

HUBERTUS W.V. WILLEMS SCHOLARSHIP FOR MALE STUDENTS

Must be male, full-time student, U.S. citizen majoring in one of the following: engineering, chemistry, physics, or mathematical sciences. Graduate student may be full- or part-time and have 2.5 minimum GPA. Graduating high school seniors and undergraduates must have 3.0 minimum GPA. Must demonstrate financial need. Undergraduate scholarship awards $2000; graduate scholarship awards $3000. NAACP membership and participation is highly preferable.

Academic Fields/Career Goals: Chemical Engineering; Engineering-Related Technologies; Physical Sciences and Math.

Award: Scholarship for use in freshman, sophomore, junior, senior, or graduate years; not renewable. *Number:* varies. *Amount:* $2000–$3000.

Eligibility Requirements: Applicant must be American Indian/Alaska Native, Asian/Pacific Islander, Black (non-Hispanic), or Hispanic; enrolled or expecting to enroll full or part-time at a four-year institution or university and male. Applicant or parent of applicant must be member of National Association for the Advancement of Colored People. Available to U.S. citizens.

Application Requirements: Application, financial need analysis, references, transcript. *Deadline:* April 30.

Contact: Donna Lakins, Education Department, Scholarship Request
National Association for the Advancement of Colored People
4805 Mt. Hope Drive
Baltimore, MD 21215-3297
Phone: 410-580-5760
Fax: 410-585-1329

LOUIS STOKES SCIENCE AND TECHNOLOGY AWARD
• See page 139

NATIONAL INVENTORS HALL OF FAME
http://www.invent.org

COLLEGIATE INVENTORS COMPETITION - GRAND PRIZE
• See page 95

COLLEGIATE INVENTORS COMPETITION FOR UNDERGRADUATE STUDENTS
• See page 95

NATIONAL SOCIETY OF PROFESSIONAL ENGINEERS
http://www.nspe.org

MAUREEN L. AND HOWARD N. BLITMAN, PE SCHOLARSHIP TO PROMOTE DIVERSITY IN ENGINEERING

$5000 scholarship to a high school senior entering an ABET-accredited 4-year engineering program. Intended to encourage underrepresented minorities to pursue this challenging and rewarding career.

Academic Fields/Career Goals: Chemical Engineering; Civil Engineering; Electrical Engineering/Electronics; Engineering/Technology; Engineering-Related Technologies; Materials Science, Engineering, and Metallurgy; Mechanical Engineering.

Award: Scholarship for use in freshman or sophomore years; not renewable. *Number:* 1. *Amount:* $5000.

Eligibility Requirements: Applicant must be American Indian/Alaska Native, Black (non-Hispanic), or Hispanic; high school student and planning to enroll or expecting to enroll full-time at a four-year institution or university. Applicant must have 3.5 GPA or higher. Available to U.S. citizens.

Application Requirements: Application, essay, references, test scores, transcript. *Deadline:* March 1.

Contact: Mary K. Maul, Education Manager NSPE
National Society of Professional Engineers
1420 King Street
Alexandria, VA 22314
Phone: 703-684-2833
E-mail: mmaul@nspe.org

NATIONAL SOCIETY OF PROFESSIONAL ENGINEERS/AUXILIARY SCHOLARSHIP

Renewable scholarship for a female student in the amount of $1000 per year for four years. The recipient of this scholarship may attend the college or university of her choice (the program must be accredited by the Engineering Accreditation Commission of the Accreditation Board for Engineering and Technology). The scholarship is awarded strictly on the basis of achievement. Must be a U.S. citizen. Must rank in the upper third of class or have a minimum 3.6 GPA.

Academic Fields/Career Goals: Chemical Engineering; Civil Engineering; Electrical Engineering/Electronics; Engineering/Technology; Engineering-Related Technologies; Materials Science, Engineering, and Metallurgy; Mechanical Engineering.

Award: Scholarship for use in freshman, sophomore, junior, or senior years; renewable. *Number:* 2. *Amount:* $1000.

Eligibility Requirements: Applicant must be high school student; planning to enroll or expecting to enroll full-time at an institution or university and female. Available to U.S. citizens.

Application Requirements: Application, essay, references, test scores, transcript. *Deadline:* December 1.

Contact: Mary Maul, Education Manager
National Society of Professional Engineers
1420 King Street
Alexandria, VA 22314-2794
Phone: 703-684-2833
Fax: 703-836-4875
E-mail: mmaul@nspe.org

PAUL H. ROBBINS HONORARY SCHOLARSHIP

The recipient of this scholarship may attend the college or university of their choice (the program must be accredited by the Engineering Accreditation Commission of the Accreditation Board for Engineering and Technology). The scholarship is awarded strictly on the basis of achievement. Must have GPA of 3.6 or higher and be a member of NSPE. A scholarship renewal report will be required for second-year payment.

Academic Fields/Career Goals: Chemical Engineering; Civil Engineering; Electrical Engineering/Electronics; Engineering/Technology; Engineering-Related Technologies; Materials Science, Engineering, and Metallurgy; Mechanical Engineering.

Award: Scholarship for use in sophomore, junior, or senior years; renewable. *Number:* 1. *Amount:* $5000.

Eligibility Requirements: Applicant must be enrolled or expecting to enroll full-time at a four-year institution or university. Applicant or parent of applicant must be member of National Society of Professional Engineers. Available to U.S. citizens.

Application Requirements: Application, essay, references, test scores, transcript. *Deadline:* December 1.

Contact: Mary Maul, Education Manager
National Society of Professional Engineers
1420 King Street
Alexandria, VA 22314-2794
Phone: 703-684-2833
Fax: 703-836-4875
E-mail: mmaul@nspe.org

PROFESSIONAL ENGINEERS IN INDUSTRY SCHOLARSHIP

Applicants must be sponsored by an NSPE/PEI member. Students must have completed a minimum of two semesters or three quarters of undergraduate engineering studies (or be enrolled in graduate study).

Academic Fields/Career Goals: Chemical Engineering; Civil Engineering; Electrical Engineering/Electronics; Engineering/Technology; Engineering-Related Technologies; Materials Science, Engineering, and Metallurgy; Mechanical Engineering.

Award: Scholarship for use in sophomore, junior, senior, or graduate years; not renewable. *Number:* 1. *Amount:* $2500.

Eligibility Requirements: Applicant must be enrolled or expecting to enroll full-time at a four-year institution or university. Applicant must have 2.5 GPA or higher. Available to U.S. citizens.

Application Requirements: Application, essay, resume, references, transcript, work experience. *Deadline:* April 1.

Contact: Erin Garcia Reyes, Practice Division Manager
National Society of Professional Engineers
1420 King Street
Alexandria, VA 22314
Phone: 703-684-2884
E-mail: egarcia@nspe.org

VIRGINIA HENRY MEMORIAL SCHOLARSHIP

The recipient of this scholarship may attend the college or university of their choice (the program must be accredited by the Engineering Accreditation Commission of the Accreditation Board for Engineering and Technology). The scholarship is awarded strictly on the basis of achievement. Must be female and have 3.6 GPA.

Academic Fields/Career Goals: Chemical Engineering; Civil Engineering; Electrical Engineering/Electronics; Engineering/Technology; Engineering-Related Technologies; Materials Science, Engineering, and Metallurgy; Mechanical Engineering.

Award: Scholarship for use in freshman year; not renewable. *Number:* 1. *Amount:* $1000.

Eligibility Requirements: Applicant must be high school student; planning to enroll or expecting to enroll full-time at a four-year institution and female. Available to U.S. citizens.

Application Requirements: Application, essay, references, test scores, transcript. *Deadline:* December 1.

Contact: Mary Maul, Education Manager
National Society of Professional Engineers
1420 King Street
Alexandria, VA 22314-2794
Phone: 703-684-2833
Fax: 703-836-4875
E-mail: mmaul@nspe.org

OREGON STUDENT ASSISTANCE COMMISSION   http://www.osac.state.or.us

AMERICAN COUNCIL OF ENGINEERING COMPANIES OF OREGON SCHOLARSHIP

Renewable award for students considering a career in the consulting engineering profession. For use at any Oregon four-year college that offers Accreditation Board for engineering and technology accredited programs in chemical, civil, electrical, industrial or mechanical engineering.

Academic Fields/Career Goals: Chemical Engineering; Civil Engineering; Electrical Engineering/Electronics; Engineering-Related Technologies; Mechanical Engineering.

Award: Scholarship for use in freshman, sophomore, junior, or senior years; not renewable. *Number:* varies. *Amount:* $500.

Eligibility Requirements: Applicant must be enrolled or expecting to enroll at a four-year institution or university; resident of Oregon and studying in Oregon. Available to U.S. citizens.

Application Requirements: Application, essay, transcript, activities chart. *Deadline:* March 1.

Contact: Director of Grant Programs
Oregon Student Assistance Commission
1500 Valley River Drive, Suite 100
Eugene, OR 97401-7020
Phone: 800-452-8807 Ext. 7395

ROBERT H. MOLLOHAN FAMILY CHARITABLE FOUNDATION, INC.   http://www.mollohanfoundation.org

HIGH TECHNOLOGY SCHOLARS PROGRAM
• *See page 141*

ROCKY MOUNTAIN COAL MINING INSTITUTE   http://www.rmcmi.org

ROCKY MOUNTAIN COAL MINING INSTITUTE SCHOLARSHIP

Must be full-time college sophomore or junior at time of application, pursuing a degree in mining-related fields or engineering disciplines such as mining, geology, mineral processing, or metallurgy. For residents of Arizona, Colorado, Montana, New Mexico, North Dakota, Texas, Utah, and Wyoming.

Academic Fields/Career Goals: Chemical Engineering; Civil Engineering; Electrical Engineering/Electronics; Engineering/Technology; Mechanical Engineering.

Award: Scholarship for use in sophomore, junior, senior, or graduate years; renewable. *Number:* 16. *Amount:* $2000.

Eligibility Requirements: Applicant must be enrolled or expecting to enroll full-time at a four-year institution or university and resident of Arizona, Colorado, Montana, New Mexico, North Dakota, Texas, Utah, or Wyoming. Available to U.S. citizens.

Application Requirements: Application, interview, references. *Deadline:* February 1.

Contact: Karen Inzano, Executive Director
Rocky Mountain Coal Mining Institute
8057 S Yukon Way
Littleton, CO 80128-5510
Phone: 303-948-3300
Fax: 303-948-1132
E-mail: mail@rmcmi.org

SIGMA XI, THE SCIENTIFIC RESEARCH SOCIETY   http://www.sigmaxi.org

SIGMA XI GRANTS-IN-AID OF RESEARCH
• *See page 84*

SOCIETY FOR MINING, METALLURGY AND EXPLORATION - CENTRAL WYOMING SECTION

COATES, WOLFF, RUSSELL MINING INDUSTRY SCHOLARSHIP
• *See page 95*

SOCIETY OF AUTOMOTIVE ENGINEERS   http://www.sae.org

BMW/SAE ENGINEERING SCHOLARSHIP
• *See page 129*

EDWARD D. HENDRICKSON/SAE ENGINEERING SCHOLARSHIP
• *See page 129*

TMC/SAE DONALD D. DAWSON TECHNICAL SCHOLARSHIP
• *See page 129*

SOCIETY OF HISPANIC PROFESSIONAL ENGINEERS FOUNDATION
http://www.henaac.org

SOCIETY OF HISPANIC PROFESSIONAL ENGINEERS FOUNDATION

Scholarships awarded to Hispanic engineering and science students throughout the U.S. Scholarships are awarded at the beginning of every academic year based upon academic achievement, financial need, involvement in campus and community activities, career goals and counselor recommendations.

Academic Fields/Career Goals: Chemical Engineering; Civil Engineering; Electrical Engineering/Electronics; Engineering/Technology; Engineering-Related Technologies; Materials Science, Engineering, and Metallurgy; Mechanical Engineering; Natural Sciences; Nuclear Science; Science, Technology, and Society.

Award: Scholarship for use in freshman, sophomore, junior, senior, or graduate years; not renewable. *Number:* varies. *Amount:* $500–$7000.

Eligibility Requirements: Applicant must be Hispanic and enrolled or expecting to enroll full-time at an institution or university. Available to U.S. citizens.

Application Requirements: Application, financial need analysis, resume, references. *Deadline:* May 15.

Contact: Kathy Borunda-Barrera, Manager, Scholars Program
Phone: 323-415-9600
Fax: 323-415-7038
E-mail: kathy@henaac.org

SOCIETY OF MEXICAN AMERICAN ENGINEERS AND SCIENTISTS
http://www.maes-natl.org

GRE AND GRADUATE APPLICATIONS WAIVER
• See page 95

SOCIETY OF PLASTICS ENGINEERS (SPE) FOUNDATION
http://www.4spe.com

GULF COAST HURRICANE SCHOLARSHIP

Supplemental financial support available to residents of the Gulf Coast who wish to attend a college, university or technical institute in programs that support the plastics industry.

Academic Fields/Career Goals: Chemical Engineering; Engineering/Technology.

Award: Scholarship for use in freshman, sophomore, junior, or senior years; renewable. *Number:* 1–3. *Amount:* $2000–$6000.

Eligibility Requirements: Applicant must be enrolled or expecting to enroll full or part-time at a two-year or four-year institution or university and resident of Alabama, Florida, Louisiana, Mississippi, or Texas. Available to U.S. citizens.

Application Requirements: Application, essay, financial need analysis, references, transcript. *Deadline:* January 15.

Contact: Gail.R Bristol, Managing Director
Society of Plastics Engineers (SPE) Foundation
14 Fairfield Drive
Brookfield, CT 06804
Phone: 203-740-5447
Fax: 203-775-1157
E-mail: foundation@4spe.org

SOCIETY OF PLASTICS ENGINEERS SCHOLARSHIP PROGRAM

The SPE Foundation offers scholarships to full-time students who have demonstrated or expressed an interest in the plastics industry. They must be majoring in or taking courses that would be beneficial to a career in the plastics industry.

Academic Fields/Career Goals: Chemical Engineering; Civil Engineering; Electrical Engineering/Electronics; Engineering/Technology; Industrial Design; Materials Science, Engineering, and Metallurgy; Mechanical Engineering; Trade/Technical Specialties.

Award: Scholarship for use in freshman, sophomore, junior, senior, or graduate years; not renewable. *Number:* 19. *Amount:* $1000–$5000.

Eligibility Requirements: Applicant must be enrolled or expecting to enroll full-time at a two-year or four-year or technical institution or university. Available to U.S. and non-U.S. citizens.

Application Requirements: Application, essay, financial need analysis, references, transcript. *Deadline:* January 15.

Contact: Gail R. Bristol, Managing Director
Society of Plastics Engineers (SPE) Foundation
14 Fairfield Drive
Brookfield, CT 06804
Phone: 203-740-5447
Fax: 203-775-1157
E-mail: foundation@4spe.org

SOCIETY OF WOMEN ENGINEERS
http://www.swe.org

CHEVRON TEXACO CORPORATION SCHOLARSHIPS

Eight awards open to women who are sophomores or juniors majoring in civil, chemical, mechanical, or petroleum engineering. One-time award of $2000. Must be active SWE student member. Deadline: February 1.

Academic Fields/Career Goals: Chemical Engineering; Civil Engineering; Engineering/Technology; Mechanical Engineering.

Award: Scholarship for use in sophomore or junior years; not renewable. *Number:* 7–8. *Amount:* $2000.

Eligibility Requirements: Applicant must be enrolled or expecting to enroll at a four-year institution or university and female. Applicant or parent of applicant must be member of Society of Women Engineers. Applicant must have 3.5 GPA or higher. Available to U.S. and non-U.S. citizens.

Application Requirements: Application, essay, references, self-addressed stamped envelope, test scores, transcript. *Deadline:* February 1.

Contact: Suman Pa, Program Coordinator
Society of Women Engineers
230 E Ohio Street, Suite 400
Chicago, IL 60611-3265
Phone: 312-596-5223
Fax: 312-644-8557
E-mail: suman.patil@swe.org

DUPONT COMPANY SCHOLARSHIPS

Seven one-time award available to female sophomore, junior, or senior undergraduate students majoring in chemical or mechanical engineering: two are for incoming freshmen. Minimum 3.0 GPA required. Limited to schools in the eastern U.S. Deadline: May 15 for freshman award; February 1 for sophomore, junior, and senior awards.

Academic Fields/Career Goals: Chemical Engineering; Mechanical Engineering.

Award: Scholarship for use in sophomore, junior, or senior years; not renewable. *Number:* 2. *Amount:* $2000.

Eligibility Requirements: Applicant must be enrolled or expecting to enroll full-time at a four-year institution or university and female. Applicant must have 3.0 GPA or higher. Available to U.S. citizens.

Application Requirements: Application, references, self-addressed stamped envelope, test scores, transcript. *Deadline:* varies.

Contact: Suman Pa, Program Coordinator
Society of Women Engineers
230 E Ohio Street, Suite 400
Chicago, IL 60611-3265
Phone: 312-596-5223
Fax: 312-644-8557
E-mail: suman.patil@swe.org

GENERAL MOTORS FOUNDATION UNDERGRADUATE SCHOLARSHIPS

Renewable award for female student entering junior year who is interested in automotive/manufacturing career. Must hold a leadership position in a student organization. Send self-addressed stamped envelope for application. Includes $500 travel grant for SWE National Conference. Must have a 3.5 GPA. Deadline: February 1.

Academic Fields/Career Goals: Chemical Engineering; Electrical Engineering/Electronics; Engineering/Technology; Engineering-Related Technologies; Mechanical Engineering.

Award: Scholarship for use in junior year; renewable. *Number:* 2. *Amount:* $1225.

Eligibility Requirements: Applicant must be enrolled or expecting to enroll full-time at a four-year institution or university; female and must have an interest in leadership. Applicant must have 3.5 GPA or higher. Available to U.S. citizens.

Application Requirements: Application, essay, references, self-addressed stamped envelope, test scores, transcript. *Deadline:* February 1.

Contact: Suman Pa, Program Coordinator
Society of Women Engineers
230 E Ohio Street, Suite 400
Chicago, IL 60611-3265
Phone: 312-596-5223
Fax: 312-644-8557
E-mail: suman.patil@swe.org

TEXAS ENGINEERING FOUNDATION
http://www.tspe.org/

TEXAS SOCIETY OF PROFESSIONAL ENGINEERS (TSPE) REGIONAL SCHOLARSHIPS

One recipient is selected from each of TSPE's five regions. Applicants must be high school seniors maintaining a 3.0 GPA. The deadline is January 15. Must be a resident of Texas and attend a postsecondary institution in Texas, majoring in a field of engineering.

Academic Fields/Career Goals: Chemical Engineering; Civil Engineering; Electrical Engineering/Electronics; Engineering/Technology; Mechanical Engineering.

Award: Scholarship for use in freshman year; not renewable. *Number:* 5. *Amount:* $500.

Eligibility Requirements: Applicant must be high school student; planning to enroll or expecting to enroll full-time at an institution or university; resident of Texas and studying in Texas. Applicant must have 3.0 GPA or higher. Available to U.S. citizens.

Application Requirements: Application, essay, references, transcript. *Deadline:* January 15.

Contact: Krista Weirman, Director of Education Programs
Texas Engineering Foundation
Attention: Programs Director
1001 Congress, Suite 260, PO Box 2145
Austin, TX 78768
Phone: 512-472-9286
Fax: 512-472-2934
E-mail: kristaw@tspe.org

UNITED NEGRO COLLEGE FUND
http://www.uncf.org

CARGILL SCHOLARSHIP PROGRAM
• *See page 70*

MALCOLM PIRNIE, INC. SCHOLARS PROGRAM

Scholarships for UNCF juniors with 3.0 or better GPA majoring in civil, chemical or environmental engineering or one of the environmental sciences. Summer internship is included in program. Prospective applicants should complete the Student Profile found at Web site: http://www.uncf.org.

Academic Fields/Career Goals: Chemical Engineering; Civil Engineering; Computer Science/Data Processing; Earth Science; Natural Resources.

Award: Scholarship for use in junior year; not renewable. *Amount:* $3000.

Eligibility Requirements: Applicant must be Black (non-Hispanic) and enrolled or expecting to enroll at a four-year institution or university. Applicant must have 3.0 GPA or higher. Available to U.S. citizens.

Application Requirements: Application. *Deadline:* February 17.

Contact: Program Services Department
United Negro College Fund
8260 Willow Oaks Corporate Drive
Fairfax, VA 22031

WM. WRIGLEY, JR. COMPANY SCHOLARS PROGRAM
• *See page 157*

UNIVERSITIES SPACE RESEARCH ASSOCIATION
http://www.usra.edu

UNIVERSITIES SPACE RESEARCH ASSOCIATION SCHOLARSHIP PROGRAM
• *See page 96*

UTAH SOCIETY OF PROFESSIONAL ENGINEERS
http://www.uspeonline.com

UTAH SOCIETY OF PROFESSIONAL ENGINEERS SCHOLARSHIP

One-time award for entering freshman pursuing studies in the field of engineering (civil, chemical, electrical, or engineering related technologies.) Minimum 3.5 GPA required. Must be a U.S. citizen and Utah resident attending school in Utah. Application deadline is March 25.

Academic Fields/Career Goals: Chemical Engineering; Civil Engineering; Electrical Engineering/Electronics; Energy and Power Engineering; Engineering/Technology; Mechanical Engineering.

Award: Scholarship for use in freshman year; not renewable. *Number:* 1. *Amount:* $1000.

Eligibility Requirements: Applicant must be high school student; planning to enroll or expecting to enroll full-time at a four-year institution or university; resident of Utah and studying in Utah. Applicant must have 3.5 GPA or higher. Available to U.S. citizens.

Application Requirements: Application, essay, resume, references, test scores, transcript. *Deadline:* March 25.

Contact: Dan Church, Scholarship Chair
Utah Society of Professional Engineers
488 East Winchester Street, Suite 400
Murray, UT 84107
E-mail: churchd@pbworld.com

XEROX
http://www.xerox.com

TECHNICAL MINORITY SCHOLARSHIP

One-time award for minority students enrolled full time in a technical science or engineering discipline. Must be studying at a four-year institution and have a GPA of 3.0 or higher. Available to U.S. citizens and individuals with permanent resident visas. Application deadline is September 15. Further information is available at Web site http://www.xerox.com.

Academic Fields/Career Goals: Chemical Engineering; Computer Science/Data Processing; Electrical Engineering/Electronics; Engineering/Technology; Engineering-Related Technologies; Materials Science, Engineering, and Metallurgy; Mechanical Engineering; Physical Sciences and Math.

Award: Scholarship for use in freshman, sophomore, junior, senior, graduate, or postgraduate years; not renewable. *Number:* 125–150. *Amount:* $1000–$10,000.

Eligibility Requirements: Applicant must be American Indian/Alaska Native, Asian/Pacific Islander, Black (non-Hispanic), or Hispanic and enrolled or expecting to enroll full-time at a four-year institution or university. Applicant must have 3.0 GPA or higher. Available to U.S. citizens.

Application Requirements: Application, resume, transcript. *Deadline:* September 15.

Contact: Ellen Baniak, Director, Staffing Support Services
Xerox
150 State Street, 4th Floor
Rochester, NY 14614
Phone: 585-244-1800 Ext. 4630
Fax: 585-482-3095
E-mail: xtmsp@rballiance.com

CHILD AND FAMILY STUDIES

CLAN MACBEAN FOUNDATION
http://www.clanmacbean.net

CLAN MACBEAN FOUNDATION GRANT PROGRAM
• *See page 104*

KENTUCKY HIGHER EDUCATION ASSISTANCE AUTHORITY (KHEAA)
http://www.kheaa.com

EARLY CHILDHOOD DEVELOPMENT SCHOLARSHIP

Scholarship with conditional service commitment for part-time students currently employed by participating ECD facility or providing training in ECD for an approved organization.

Academic Fields/Career Goals: Child and Family Studies; Education.

Award: Scholarship for use in freshman, sophomore, junior, or senior years; not renewable. *Number:* 900–1000. *Amount:* up to $1400.

Eligibility Requirements: Applicant must be enrolled or expecting to enroll part-time at a four-year institution or university; resident of Kentucky and studying in Kentucky. Available to U.S. citizens.

Application Requirements: Application, resume. *Deadline:* Continuous.

Contact: Early Childhood Development Authority
Kentucky Higher Education Assistance Authority (KHEAA)
275 East Main Street, 2W-E
Frankfort, KY 40621
Phone: 502-564-8099

OHIO 4-H
http://www.ohio4h.org

BEA CLEVELAND 4-H SCHOLARSHIP

One $1000 scholarship to be awarded to a 4-H member who is a senior in high school during the year of application. Applicants must be planning to enroll as a freshman, autumn quarter in the College of Human Ecology, at The Ohio State University or any of its regional campuses.

Academic Fields/Career Goals: Child and Family Studies; Food Science/Nutrition; Home Economics.

Award: Scholarship for use in freshman year. *Number:* 1. *Amount:* $1000.

Eligibility Requirements: Applicant must be enrolled or expecting to enroll at an institution or university and studying in Ohio. Available to U.S. citizens.

Application Requirements: Application, essay, resume, references, transcript. *Deadline:* January 27.

Contact: Jeff King, Assistant Director
Ohio 4-H
State 4-H Office, Room 25 Agriculture Administration Building
2120 Fyffe Road
Columbus, OH 43210-1084
Phone: 614-292-4444
Fax: 614-292-5937
E-mail: 4hweb@ag.osu.edu

MABEL SARBAUGH 4-H SCHOLARSHIP

One $1000 scholarship to be awarded. Applicants must be a 4-H member, senior in high school during the year of application and planning to enroll Autumn Quarter in the College of Human Ecology as a freshman at The Ohio State University or any of its regional campuses.

Academic Fields/Career Goals: Child and Family Studies; Food Science/Nutrition; Home Economics.

Award: Scholarship for use in freshman year. *Number:* 1. *Amount:* $1000.

Eligibility Requirements: Applicant must be enrolled or expecting to enroll at an institution or university and studying in Ohio. Available to U.S. citizens.

Application Requirements: Application, essay, resume, references, transcript. *Deadline:* January 27.

Contact: Jeff King, Assistant Director
Ohio 4-H
State 4-H Office, Room 25 Agriculture Administration Building
2120 Fyffe Road
Columbus, OH 43210-1084
Phone: 614-292-4444
Fax: 614-292-5937
E-mail: 4hweb@ag.osu.edu

SUNSHINE LADY FOUNDATION, INC.
http://www.sunshineladyfdn.org

COUNSELOR, ADVOCATE, AND SUPPORT STAFF SCHOLARSHIP PROGRAM
- *See page 69*

CIVIL ENGINEERING

AACE INTERNATIONAL
http://www.aacei.org

AACE INTERNATIONAL COMPETITIVE SCHOLARSHIP
- *See page 96*

ACI INTERNATIONAL/CONCRETE RESEARCH AND EDUCATION FOUNDATION (CONREF)
http://www.concrete.org

KUMAR MEHTA SCHOLARSHIP
- *See page 97*

PETER D. COURTOIS CONCRETE CONSTRUCTION SCHOLARSHIP
- *See page 97*

V. MOHAN MALHOTRA SCHOLARSHIP
- *See page 97*

W.R. GRACE SCHOLARSHIP AWARD
- *See page 97*

AEA-OREGON COUNCIL
http://aeascholar.ous.edu

AEA- OREGON COUNCIL TECHNOLOGY SCHOLARSHIP PROGRAM
- *See page 88*

AMERICAN COUNCIL OF ENGINEERING COMPANIES OF PENNSYLVANIA (ACEC/PA)
http://www.acecpa.org

ENGINEERING SCHOLARSHIP
- *See page 158*

AMERICAN GROUND WATER TRUST
http://www.agwt.org

AMERICAN GROUND WATER TRUST-AMTROL, INC. SCHOLARSHIP

Award for college/university entry-level students intending to pursue a career in ground water-related field. Must either have completed a science/environmental project involving ground water resources or have had vacation work experience related to the environment and natural resources. Must be U.S. citizen or legal resident with minimum 3.0 GPA. Submit two letters of recommendation and transcript. Deadline: June 1.

Academic Fields/Career Goals: Civil Engineering; Natural Resources.

Award: Scholarship for use in freshman year; not renewable. *Number:* 2. *Amount:* $1000–$2000.

Eligibility Requirements: Applicant must be high school student and planning to enroll or expecting to enroll full-time at a two-year or four-year institution or university. Applicant must have 3.0 GPA or higher. Available to U.S. citizens.

Application Requirements: Application, essay, references, transcript. *Deadline:* June 1.

Contact: Garret Grasskamp, Ground Water Specialist
American Ground Water Trust
PO Box 1796
Concord, NH 03302-1796
Phone: 603-228-5444
Fax: 603-228-6557
E-mail: ggraaskamp@agwt.org

AMERICAN GROUND WATER TRUST-CLAUDE LAVAL CORPORATION THE BEN EVERSON SCHOLARSHIP

For students entering their Freshman year in a full-time academic program of study at a four-year accredited university or college and intending to pursue a career in ground water-related field. Must be U.S. citizen or legal resident with 3.0 GPA or higher. For more information see Web site: http://www.agwt.org.

Academic Fields/Career Goals: Civil Engineering; Natural Resources.

Award: Scholarship for use in freshman year; not renewable. *Number:* 1. *Amount:* $2500.

Eligibility Requirements: Applicant must be high school student and planning to enroll or expecting to enroll full or part-time at a two-year or four-year institution or university. Applicant must have 3.0 GPA or higher. Available to U.S. citizens.

Application Requirements: Application, essay, references, transcript, parent employment verification. *Deadline:* June 1.

Contact: Andrew Stone, Executive Director
American Ground Water Trust
PO Box 1796
Concord, NH 03302-1796
Phone: 603-228-5444
Fax: 603-228-6557
E-mail: astone@agwt.org

AMERICAN PUBLIC TRANSPORTATION FOUNDATION
http://www.apta.com

DONALD C. HYDE ESSAY PROGRAM

Prize awarded for best essay on the subject: "What segment of the public transportation industry interests you and why?" Must be applying for APTF scholarship.

Academic Fields/Career Goals: Civil Engineering; Electrical Engineering/Electronics; Engineering/Technology; Engineering-Related Technologies; Mechanical Engineering; Transportation.

Award: Prize for use in junior, senior, graduate, or postgraduate years; not renewable. *Number:* 1. *Amount:* up to $500.

Eligibility Requirements: Applicant must be enrolled or expecting to enroll full-time at a four-year institution or university. Applicant must have 3.0 GPA or higher. Available to U.S. and Canadian citizens.

Application Requirements: Application, essay, financial need analysis, references, transcript. *Deadline:* June 16.

Contact: Pamela Boswell, Vice President of Program Management
American Public Transportation Foundation
1666 K Street, NW
Washington, DC 20006-1215
Phone: 202-496-4803
Fax: 202-496-2323
E-mail: pboswell@apta.com

JACK GILSTRAP SCHOLARSHIP

Awarded the APTF scholarship to the applicant with the highest score. Must be in public transportation industry-related fields of study. Must be sponsored by AFTA member organization and complete an internship program with a member organization. Minimum 3.0 GPA required.

Academic Fields/Career Goals: Civil Engineering; Electrical Engineering/Electronics; Engineering/Technology; Engineering-Related Technologies; Mechanical Engineering; Transportation.

Award: Scholarship for use in sophomore, junior, senior, graduate, or postgraduate years; renewable. *Number:* 1. *Amount:* $2500.

Eligibility Requirements: Applicant must be enrolled or expecting to enroll full-time at a four-year institution or university. Applicant must have 3.0 GPA or higher. Available to U.S. and Canadian citizens.

Application Requirements: Application, essay, financial need analysis, references, transcript, verification of enrollment for the current semester and copy of the fee schedule from the college/university. *Deadline:* June 16.

Contact: Pamela Boswell, Vice President of Program Management
American Public Transportation Foundation
1666 K Street, NW
Washington, DC 20006-1215
Phone: 202-496-4803
Fax: 202-496-2323
E-mail: pboswell@apta.com

LOUIS T. KLAUDER SCHOLARSHIP

Scholarships for study towards a career in the rail transit industry as an electrical or mechanical engineer. Must be sponsored by APTA member organization and complete internship with APTA member organization. Minimum GPA of 3.0 required.

Academic Fields/Career Goals: Civil Engineering; Electrical Engineering/Electronics; Engineering/Technology; Engineering-Related Technologies; Mechanical Engineering; Transportation.

Award: Scholarship for use in junior, senior, graduate, or postgraduate years; renewable. *Number:* 1. *Amount:* $2500.

Eligibility Requirements: Applicant must be enrolled or expecting to enroll full-time at a four-year institution or university. Applicant must have 3.0 GPA or higher. Available to U.S. and Canadian citizens.

Application Requirements: Application, essay, financial need analysis, references, transcript, verification of enrollment for the current semester and copy of the fee schedule from the college/university. *Deadline:* June 16.

Contact: Pamela Boswell, Vice President of Program Management
American Public Transportation Foundation
1666 K Street, NW
Washington, DC 20006-1215
Phone: 202-496-4803
Fax: 202-496-2323
E-mail: pboswell@apta.com

PARSONS BRINCKERHOFF-JIM LAMMIE SCHOLARSHIP

Scholarship for study in public transportation engineering field. Must be sponsored by APTA member organization and complete internship with APTA member organization. Minimum GPA of 3.0 required.

Academic Fields/Career Goals: Civil Engineering; Electrical Engineering/Electronics; Engineering/Technology; Engineering-Related Technologies; Mechanical Engineering; Transportation.

Award: Scholarship for use in sophomore, junior, senior, graduate, or postgraduate years; renewable. *Number:* 1. *Amount:* $2500.

Eligibility Requirements: Applicant must be enrolled or expecting to enroll full-time at a two-year or four-year institution or university. Applicant must have 3.0 GPA or higher. Available to U.S. and Canadian citizens.

Application Requirements: Application, essay, financial need analysis, references, transcript, verification of enrollment for the current year and copy of the fee schedule from the college/university. *Deadline:* June 16.

Contact: Pamela Boswell, Vice President of Program Management
American Public Transportation Foundation
1666 K Street, NW
Washington, DC 20006-1215
Phone: 202-496-4803
Fax: 202-496-2323
E-mail: pboswell@apta.com

TRANSIT HALL OF FAME SCHOLARSHIP AWARD PROGRAM

Renewable award for undergraduate or graduate students studying transportation or rail transit engineering. Must be sponsored by APTA member organization and complete an internship program with a member organization. Must have a minimum 3.0 GPA and be a U.S. or Canadian citizen.

Academic Fields/Career Goals: Civil Engineering; Electrical Engineering/Electronics; Engineering/Technology; Engineering-Related Technologies; Mechanical Engineering; Transportation.

Award: Scholarship for use in sophomore, junior, senior, graduate, or postgraduate years; renewable. *Number:* 1. *Amount:* up to $2500.

Eligibility Requirements: Applicant must be enrolled or expecting to enroll full-time at a two-year or four-year or technical institution or university. Applicant must have 3.0 GPA or higher. Available to U.S. and Canadian citizens.

CIVIL ENGINEERING

American Public Transportation Foundation (continued)

Application Requirements: Application, essay, financial need analysis, references, transcript, nomination by APTA member, verification of enrollment, copy of the fee schedule from the college/university for the academic year. *Deadline:* June 16.

Contact: Pamela Boswell, Vice President of Program Management
American Public Transportation Foundation
1666 K Street, NW
Washington, DC 20006-1215
Phone: 202-496-4803
Fax: 202-496-4323

AMERICAN SOCIETY OF CIVIL ENGINEERS-MAINE SECTION

AMERICAN SOCIETY OF CIVIL ENGINEERS-MAINE HIGH SCHOOL SCHOLARSHIP

One-time award available to high school student in senior year, pursuing a course of study in civil engineering. Must be resident of Maine. Essay, references and transcript required with application. Deadline is January 31.

Academic Fields/Career Goals: Civil Engineering.

Award: Scholarship for use in freshman year; not renewable. *Number:* 1. *Amount:* $2000.

Eligibility Requirements: Applicant must be high school student; planning to enroll or expecting to enroll full-time at a four-year institution or university and resident of Maine. Available to U.S. citizens.

Application Requirements: Application, essay, references, transcript. *Deadline:* January 31.

Contact: Leslie Corrow, Project Engineer Kleinschmidt Associates
American Society of Civil Engineers-Maine Section
75 Main Street
Pittsfield, ME 04967-0016
Phone: 207-487-3328
Fax: 207-487-3124
E-mail: leslie.corrow@kleinschmidtusa.com

AMERICAN SOCIETY OF NAVAL ENGINEERS   http://www.navalengineers.org

AMERICAN SOCIETY OF NAVAL ENGINEERS SCHOLARSHIP
• *See page 90*

AMERICAN WELDING SOCIETY   http://www.aws.org

ARSHAM AMIRIKIAN ENGINEERING SCHOLARSHIP

Awarded to an undergraduate pursuing a minimum four-year degree in civil engineering or welding-related program at an accredited university. Applicant must be a minimum of eighteen years of age, must have a minimum 3.0 grade point average and must be a citizen of the US. Deadline for application is January 15.

Academic Fields/Career Goals: Civil Engineering; Materials Science, Engineering, and Metallurgy; Trade/Technical Specialties.

Award: Scholarship for use in sophomore, junior, or senior years; not renewable. *Number:* 1. *Amount:* $2500.

Eligibility Requirements: Applicant must be age 18 and enrolled or expecting to enroll full or part-time at a four-year institution. Applicant must have 3.0 GPA or higher. Available to U.S. citizens.

Application Requirements: Application, autobiography, financial need analysis, references, transcript. *Deadline:* January 15.

Contact: Vicki Pinsky, Manager Foundation
American Welding Society
550 Northwest Le Jeune Road
Miami, FL 33126
Phone: 800-443-9353 Ext. 212
Fax: 305-443-7559
E-mail: vpinsky@aws.org

DONALD AND JEAN CLEVELAND-WILLAMETTE VALLEY SECTION SCHOLARSHIP

Award for students pursuing a degree in welding or welding technology. Award granted on an annual basis. For more information, see Web site: http://www.aws.org/foundation. Deadline is March 1.

Academic Fields/Career Goals: Civil Engineering; Engineering-Related Technologies; Materials Science, Engineering, and Metallurgy; Trade/Technical Specialties.

Award: Scholarship for use in freshman, sophomore, junior, senior, graduate, or postgraduate years; renewable. *Number:* 1. *Amount:* $1250.

Eligibility Requirements: Applicant must be enrolled or expecting to enroll at a four-year institution. Available to U.S. citizens.

Application Requirements: Application. *Deadline:* March 1.

Contact: Vicki Pinsky, Manager Foundation
American Welding Society
550 Northwest Le Jeune Road
Miami, FL 33126
Phone: 800-443-9353 Ext. 212
Fax: 305-443-7559
E-mail: vpinsky@aws.org

MATSUO BRIDGE COMPANY, LTD., OF JAPAN SCHOLARSHIP

Awarded to a college junior or senior, or graduate student pursuing a minimum four-year degree in civil engineering, welding engineering, welding engineering technology, or related discipline. Applicant must have a minimum 3.0 overall GPA. Financial need is not required to apply. Must be U.S. citizen.

Academic Fields/Career Goals: Civil Engineering; Engineering/Technology; Engineering-Related Technologies; Trade/Technical Specialties.

Award: Scholarship for use in junior, senior, or graduate years; not renewable. *Number:* 1. *Amount:* $2500.

Eligibility Requirements: Applicant must be age 18 and enrolled or expecting to enroll full or part-time at a two-year or four-year institution or university. Applicant must have 3.0 GPA or higher. Available to U.S. citizens.

Application Requirements: Application, autobiography, financial need analysis, references, transcript. *Deadline:* January 15.

Contact: Vicki Pinsky, Manager Foundation
American Welding Society
550 Northwest Le Jeune Road
Miami, FL 33126
Phone: 800-443-9353 Ext. 212
Fax: 305-443-7559
E-mail: vpinsky@aws.org

ASSOCIATED BUILDERS AND CONTRACTORS SCHOLARSHIP PROGRAM   http://www.abc.org

TRIMMER EDUCATION FOUNDATION SCHOLARSHIPS FOR CONSTRUCTION MANAGEMENT

Scholarships are available to students in a major related to the construction industry. Applicants must be enrolled at an educational institution with an ABC student chapter. For further information, and an application. Applicants must be related undergraduate construction program. Architecture and most engineering programs are excluded, as there are other funds available for these areas. Applicants must have a minimum overall GPA of 2.85. visit Web site: http://www.abc.org.

Academic Fields/Career Goals: Civil Engineering; Electrical Engineering/Electronics; Engineering/Technology; Engineering-Related Technologies; Mechanical Engineering.

Award: Scholarship for use in freshman, sophomore, junior, senior, or graduate years; not renewable. *Number:* 50. *Amount:* up to $1000.

Eligibility Requirements: Applicant must be enrolled or expecting to enroll full-time at a two-year or four-year institution or university. Available to U.S. and non-U.S. citizens.

Application Requirements: Application, essay, financial need analysis, references, transcript. *Deadline:* varies.

Contact: Christine Hess, Director of School to Career
Associated Builders and Contractors Scholarship Program
4250 North Fairfax Drive, 9th Floor
Arlington, VA 22203-1607
Phone: 703-812-2008
Fax: 703-812-8234
E-mail: hess@abc.org

ASSOCIATED GENERAL CONTRACTORS EDUCATION AND RESEARCH FOUNDATION

http://www.agcfoundation.org

AGC EDUCATION AND RESEARCH FOUNDATION GRADUATE SCHOLARSHIPS

Applicants for the Saul Horowitz, Jr. Memorial Graduate Award and Heffner Scholarships for Graduate Students must be college seniors enrolled in an undergraduate construction or civil engineering degree program with plans to pursue a graduate program full-time; or graduate or doctoral students pursuing a construction or civil engineering degree program with at least one academic year remaining. Must maintain a 2.0 GPA. Award is $7,500 in two payments of $3,750. Application and guidelines are available on the web. Deadline: November 1.

Academic Fields/Career Goals: Civil Engineering.

Award: Scholarship for use in senior, graduate, or postgraduate years; not renewable. *Number:* up to 2. *Amount:* up to $7500.

Eligibility Requirements: Applicant must be enrolled or expecting to enroll full-time at a four-year institution or university. Available to U.S. citizens.

Application Requirements: Application, essay, financial need analysis, transcript. *Deadline:* November 1.

Contact: Floretta Slade, Director of Programs
Associated General Contractors Education and Research Foundation
2300 Wilson Boulevard, Suite 400
Arlington, VA 22201
Phone: 703-837-5342
Fax: 703-837-5402
E-mail: sladef@agc.org

AGC EDUCATION AND RESEARCH FOUNDATION UNDERGRADUATE SCHOLARSHIPS

Full-time, four or five-year ABET or ACCE-accredited construction management or construction-related engineering program are eligible to apply. Second-year student at a two year school who is planning to transfer to a four-year program are also eligible.

Academic Fields/Career Goals: Civil Engineering; Engineering/Technology; Trade/Technical Specialties.

Award: Scholarship for use in sophomore, junior, or senior years; renewable. *Number:* up to 100. *Amount:* $2500–$7500.

Eligibility Requirements: Applicant must be enrolled or expecting to enroll full-time at a four-year institution or university. Available to U.S. citizens.

Application Requirements: Application, essay, references, transcript. *Deadline:* November 1.

Contact: Floretta Slade, Director of Programs
Associated General Contractors Education and Research Foundation
2300 Wilson Boulevard, Suite 400
Arlington, VA 22201
Phone: 703-837-5342
Fax: 703-837-5402
E-mail: sladef@agc.org

ASSOCIATED GENERAL CONTRACTORS OF AMERICA-NEW YORK STATE CHAPTER

http://www.agcnys.org

ASSOCIATED GENERAL CONTRACTORS OF AMERICA-NEW YORK STATE CHAPTER SCHOLARSHIP PROGRAM

Program designed to encourage and attract students to the heavy and highway construction industry. Preferred courses of study include civil engineering, construction management and construction technology. Must be a resident of New York. Minimum 2.5 GPA required.

Academic Fields/Career Goals: Civil Engineering; Surveying; Surveying Technology, Cartography, or Geographic Information Science; Transportation.

Award: Scholarship for use in sophomore, junior, senior, or graduate years; not renewable. *Number:* 10–15. *Amount:* $2500–$3000.

Eligibility Requirements: Applicant must be enrolled or expecting to enroll full-time at a two-year or four-year institution or university and resident of New York. Applicant must have 2.5 GPA or higher. Available to U.S. citizens.

Application Requirements: Application, references, transcript. *Deadline:* May 15.

Contact: Liz Elvin, Communications Director
Associated General Contractors of America-New York State Chapter
10 Airline Drive, Suite 203
Albany, NY 12205
Phone: 518-456-1134
Fax: 518-456-1198
E-mail: lelvin@agcnys.org

ASSOCIATION FOR FACILITIES ENGINEERING (AFE)

ASSOCIATION FOR FACILITIES ENGINEERING CEDAR VALLEY CHAPTER # 132 SCHOLARSHIP
• See page 120

ASSOCIATION FOR IRON AND STEEL TECHNOLOGY

http://www.aist.org

ASSOCIATION FOR IRON AND STEEL TECHNOLOGY DAVID H. SAMSON SCHOLARSHIP
• See page 162

ASSOCIATION OF CALIFORNIA WATER AGENCIES

http://www.acwanet.com

ASSOCIATION OF CALIFORNIA WATER AGENCIES SCHOLARSHIPS
• See page 91

CLAIR A. HILL SCHOLARSHIP
• See page 91

BARRY M. GOLDWATER SCHOLARSHIP AND EXCELLENCE IN EDUCATION FOUNDATION

http://www.act.org/goldwater

BARRY M. GOLDWATER SCHOLARSHIP AND EXCELLENCE IN EDUCATION PROGRAM
• See page 92

DALLAS ARCHITECTURAL FOUNDATION-HKS/ JOHN HUMPHRIES MINORITY SCHOLARSHIP

http://www.dallasfoundation.org

JERE W. THOMPSON, JR., SCHOLARSHIP FUND

Renewable scholarships awarded to full-time undergraduate juniors or seniors with a disadvantaged backgrounds, pursuing a degree in civil engineering and closely related disciplines at Texas public colleges and universities. Up to $2000 awarded each semester, beginning with junior year. Must maintain 2.5 GPA. Special consideration given to students from Collin, Dallas, Denton, and Tarrant Counties, Texas Deadline is April 1.

Academic Fields/Career Goals: Civil Engineering.

Award: Scholarship for use in junior or senior years; renewable. *Number:* 2. *Amount:* up to $2000.

Eligibility Requirements: Applicant must be enrolled or expecting to enroll full-time at a four-year institution or university and resident of Texas. Applicant must have 2.5 GPA or higher. Available to U.S. citizens.

Application Requirements: Application. *Deadline:* April 1.

Contact: Cathy McNally, Scholarship Coordinator
Dallas Architectural Foundation-HKS/John Humphries Minority Scholarship
900 Jackson Street, Suite 150
Dallas, TX 75202
Phone: 214-741-9898
Fax: 214-741-9848
E-mail: cmcnally@dallasfoundation.org.

FLORIDA EDUCATIONAL FACILITIES PLANNERS' ASSOCIATION http://www.fefpa.org

FEFPA ASSISTANTSHIP
• See page 99

GEORGE BIRD GRINNELL AMERICAN INDIAN FUND http://www.grinnellfund.org/

AL QOYAWAYMA AWARD
• See page 163

HAWAIIAN LODGE, F.& A. M. http://www.hawaiianlodge.org/

HAWAIIAN LODGE SCHOLARSHIPS
• See page 99

HISPANIC COLLEGE FUND, INC. http://www.hispanicfund.org

NATIONAL HISPANIC EXPLORERS SCHOLARSHIP PROGRAM
• See page 93

HISPANIC ENGINEER NATIONAL ACHIEVEMENT AWARDS CORPORATION (HENAAC) http://www.henaac.org

HISPANIC ENGINEER NATIONAL ACHIEVEMENT AWARDS CORPORATION SCHOLARSHIP PROGRAM
• See page 122

HISPANIC SCHOLARSHIP FUND http://www.hsf.net

HSF/GENERAL MOTORS SCHOLARSHIP
• See page 149

HSF/SOCIETY OF HISPANIC PROFESSIONAL ENGINEERS, INC. SCHOLARSHIP PROGRAM

Scholarship for students of Hispanic heritage pursuing degrees in the engineering, mathematics, science, and computer science fields. All students must be enrolled full-time in a degree seeking program in the U.S. or Puerto Rico.

Academic Fields/Career Goals: Civil Engineering; Computer Science/Data Processing; Electrical Engineering/Electronics; Engineering/Technology; Engineering-Related Technologies; Mechanical Engineering; Physical Sciences and Math; Science, Technology, and Society.

Award: Scholarship for use in freshman, sophomore, junior, senior, or graduate years; not renewable. *Number:* varies. *Amount:* $1250–$2500.

Eligibility Requirements: Applicant must be Hispanic and enrolled or expecting to enroll full-time at an institution or university. Available to U.S. citizens.

Application Requirements: Application, essay, financial need analysis, transcript, copy of Student Aid Report (SAR). *Deadline:* June 15.

Contact: Program Officer
Hispanic Scholarship Fund
55 Second Street, Suite 1500
San Francisco, CA 94105
Phone: 877-473-4636
Fax: 415-808-2302

INDEPENDENT LABORATORIES INSTITUTE SCHOLARSHIP ALLIANCE http://www.acil.org

INDEPENDENT LABORATORIES INSTITUTE SCHOLARSHIP ALLIANCE
• See page 93

JORGE MAS CANOSA FREEDOM FOUNDATION http://www.canf.org

MAS FAMILY SCHOLARSHIP AWARD
• See page 149

KENTUCKY NATURAL RESOURCES AND ENVIRONMENTAL PROTECTION CABINET http://www.uky.edu/waterresources

ENVIRONMENTAL PROTECTION SCHOLARSHIPS
• See page 164

KENTUCKY TRANSPORTATION CABINET http://www.transportation.ky.gov

KENTUCKY TRANSPORTATION CABINET CIVIL ENGINEERING SCHOLARSHIP PROGRAM

Scholarships are available to eligible applicants at 4 universities in Kentucky. Our mission is to continually pursue statewide recruitment and retention of bright, motivated civil engineers in the Kentucky Transportation Cabinet.

Academic Fields/Career Goals: Civil Engineering.

Award: Scholarship for use in freshman, sophomore, junior, senior, or graduate years; renewable. *Number:* 10–20. *Amount:* $4000–$4400.

Eligibility Requirements: Applicant must be enrolled or expecting to enroll full-time at a four-year institution or university; resident of Kentucky and studying in Kentucky. Applicant must have 2.5 GPA or higher. Available to U.S. and non-U.S. citizens.

Application Requirements: Application, essay, interview, references, test scores, transcript. *Deadline:* March 1.

Contact: Jo Anne Tingle, Scholarship Program Manager
Kentucky Transportation Cabinet
Attention: Scholarship Program Manager
SHE's Office, Suite E6-S1-00, 200 Metro Street
Frankfort, KY 40622
Phone: 502-564-3730
Fax: 502-564-2277
E-mail: jo.tingle@ky.gov

LOS ANGELES COUNCIL OF BLACK PROFESSIONAL ENGINEERS http://www.lablackengineers.org

AL-BEN SCHOLARSHIP FOR ACADEMIC INCENTIVE
• See page 164

AL-BEN SCHOLARSHIP FOR PROFESSIONAL MERIT
• See page 165

AL-BEN SCHOLARSHIP FOR SCHOLASTIC ACHIEVEMENT
• See page 165

MICHIGAN SOCIETY OF PROFESSIONAL ENGINEERS http://www.michiganspe.org

MICHIGAN SOCIETY OF PROFESSIONAL ENGINEERS UNDESIGNATED GRANT
• See page 165

MSPE AUXILIARY GRANT FOR UNDERGRADUATE STUDY

One grant of $1000 will be awarded to a student interested in pursuing a career in engineering. Preference is given to a son/daughter of an MSPE member, but is not required to apply.

Academic Fields/Career Goals: Civil Engineering; Engineering/Technology.

Award: Grant for use in freshman, sophomore, junior, or senior years; not renewable. *Number:* 1. *Amount:* $1000.

Eligibility Requirements: Applicant must be enrolled or expecting to enroll full-time at an institution or university; resident of Michigan and studying in Michigan. Applicant must have 3.0 GPA or higher. Available to U.S. citizens.

Application Requirements: Application, essay, references, transcript. *Deadline:* varies.

Contact: Scholarship Coordinator
Michigan Society of Professional Engineers
PO Box 15276
Lansing, MI 48901-5276
Phone: 517-487-9388
Fax: 517-487-0635
E-mail: mspe@voyager.net

NASA DELAWARE SPACE GRANT CONSORTIUM
http://www.delspace.org

NASA DELAWARE SPACE GRANT UNDERGRADUATE TUITION SCHOLARSHIP
• See page 94

NASA MONTANA SPACE GRANT CONSORTIUM
http://www.spacegrant.montana.edu

MONTANA SPACE GRANT SCHOLARSHIP PROGRAM
• See page 125

NATIONAL ASPHALT PAVEMENT ASSOCIATION
http://www.hotmix.org

NATIONAL ASPHALT PAVEMENT ASSOCIATION SCHOLARSHIP PROGRAM

Scholarship provides funding for full-time students majoring in civil engineering, construction management, or construction engineering. Applicant must take at least one course on HMA technology. Please refer to Web site for more details: http://www.hotmix.org/main.htm. Some state restrictions.

Academic Fields/Career Goals: Civil Engineering.

Award: Scholarship for use in freshman, sophomore, junior, senior, or graduate years; renewable. *Number:* 50–150. *Amount:* $500–$2500.

Eligibility Requirements: Applicant must be enrolled or expecting to enroll full-time at a two-year or four-year or technical institution or university. Applicant must have 2.5 GPA or higher. Available to U.S. citizens.

Application Requirements: Application, resume. *Deadline:* varies.

Contact: Carolyn Wilson
Phone: 301-731-4748 Ext. 127
E-mail: cwilson@hotmix.org

NATIONAL ASSOCIATION OF WOMEN IN CONSTRUCTION
http://nawic.org

NAWIC UNDERGRADUATE SCHOLARSHIPS
• See page 100

NATIONAL INSTITUTE OF BUILDING SCIENCES, MULTIHAZARD MITIGATION COUNCIL
http://www.nibs.org

ARCHITECTURE, CONSTRUCTION, AND ENGINEERING MENTOR PROGRAM SCHOLARSHIPS
• See page 101

NATIONAL SOCIETY OF PROFESSIONAL ENGINEERS
http://www.nspe.org

MAUREEN L. AND HOWARD N. BLITMAN, PE SCHOLARSHIP TO PROMOTE DIVERSITY IN ENGINEERING
• See page 166

NATIONAL SOCIETY OF PROFESSIONAL ENGINEERS/AUXILIARY SCHOLARSHIP
• See page 166

PAUL H. ROBBINS HONORARY SCHOLARSHIP
• See page 166

PROFESSIONAL ENGINEERS IN INDUSTRY SCHOLARSHIP
• See page 167

VIRGINIA HENRY MEMORIAL SCHOLARSHIP
• See page 167

NEW ENGLAND WATER WORKS ASSOCIATION
http://www.newwa.org

ELSON T. KILLAM MEMORIAL SCHOLARSHIP

Scholarships are awarded to eligible civil and environmental engineering students on the basis of merit, character, and need. Preference given to those students whose programs are considered by a committee as beneficial to water works practice in New England.

Academic Fields/Career Goals: Civil Engineering.

Award: Scholarship for use in freshman, sophomore, junior, or senior years. *Amount:* up to $1500.

Eligibility Requirements: Applicant must be enrolled or expecting to enroll at a four-year institution or university. Available to U.S. citizens.

Application Requirements: Application, essay, references, transcript. *Deadline:* April 15.

Contact: Thomas MacElhaney, Chair, Scholarship Committee
New England Water Works Association
125 Hopping Brook Road
Holliston, MA 01746
Phone: 617-512-0203
Fax: 978-418-9156
E-mail: Tmacelhaney@concretetank.com

JOSEPH MURPHY SCHOLARSHIP

Scholarships are awarded to eligible civil or environmental engineering or business related science students on the basis of merit, character, and need. Preference given to those students whose programs are considered by a committee as beneficial to water works practice in New England.

Academic Fields/Career Goals: Civil Engineering.

Award: Scholarship for use in freshman, sophomore, junior, or senior years. *Amount:* up to $1500.

Eligibility Requirements: Applicant must be enrolled or expecting to enroll at a four-year institution or university. Available to U.S. citizens.

Application Requirements: Application, essay, references, transcript. *Deadline:* April 15.

Contact: Thomas MacElhaney, Chair, Scholarship Committee
New England Water Works Association
125 Hopping Brook Road
Holliston, MA 01746
Phone: 617-512-0203
Fax: 978-418-9156
E-mail: Tmacelhaney@concretetank.com

NEW ENGLAND WATER WORKS GEORGE E. WATTERS MEMORIAL SCHOLARSHIP.

Scholarships are awarded to eligible students on the basis of merit, character, and need. Preference given to those students' whose programs are considered by a committee as beneficial to water works practice in New England. Must be NEWWA members.

Academic Fields/Career Goals: Civil Engineering; Natural Resources.

Award: Scholarship for use in freshman, sophomore, junior, senior, or postgraduate years; not renewable. *Number:* up to 7. *Amount:* up to $5000.

Eligibility Requirements: Applicant must be enrolled or expecting to enroll full or part-time at a two-year or four-year or technical institution or university. Available to U.S. and non-U.S. citizens.

Application Requirements: Application, essay, references, transcript. *Fee:* $30. *Deadline:* July 15.

Contact: Thomas MacElhaney, Chair, Scholarship Committee
New England Water Works Association
125 Hopping Brook Road
Holliston, MA 01746
Phone: 617-512-0203
Fax: 978-418-9156
E-mail: Tmacelhaney@concretetank.com

THE FRANCIS X. CROWLEY SCHOLARSHIP

Scholarships are awarded to eligible civil engineering and business management students on the basis of merit, character, and need. Preference given to those students whose programs are considered by a committee as beneficial to water works practice in New England.

Academic Fields/Career Goals: Civil Engineering.

Award: Scholarship for use in freshman, sophomore, junior, or senior years. *Amount:* up to $3000.

Eligibility Requirements: Applicant must be enrolled or expecting to enroll at a four-year institution or university. Available to U.S. citizens.

Application Requirements: Application, essay, references, transcript. *Deadline:* April 15.

New England Water Works Association (continued)

Contact: Thomas MacElhaney, Chair, Scholarship Committee
New England Water Works Association
125 Hopping Brook Road
Holliston, MA 01746
Phone: 617-512-0203
Fax: 978-418-9156
E-mail: Tmacelhaney@concretetank.com

OREGON STUDENT ASSISTANCE COMMISSION   http://www.osac.state.or.us

AMERICAN COUNCIL OF ENGINEERING COMPANIES OF OREGON SCHOLARSHIP
• See page 167

HOMESTEAD CAPITAL HOUSING SCHOLARSHIP
• See page 68

PLUMBING-HEATING-COOLING CONTRACTORS ASSOCIATION EDUCATION FOUNDATION   http://www.phccweb.org

BRADFORD WHITE CORPORATION SCHOLARSHIP
• See page 102

DELTA FAUCET COMPANY SCHOLARSHIP PROGRAM
• See page 102

PHCC EDUCATIONAL FOUNDATION NEED-BASED SCHOLARSHIP
• See page 102

PHCC EDUCATIONAL FOUNDATION SCHOLARSHIP PROGRAM
• See page 103

PROFESSIONAL GROUNDS MANAGEMENT SOCIETY   http://www.pgms.org

ANNE SEAMAN PROFESSIONAL GROUNDS MANAGEMENT SOCIETY MEMORIAL SCHOLARSHIP
• See page 84

ROCKY MOUNTAIN COAL MINING INSTITUTE   http://www.rmcmi.org

ROCKY MOUNTAIN COAL MINING INSTITUTE SCHOLARSHIP
• See page 167

SOCIETY FOR MINING, METALLURGY AND EXPLORATION - CENTRAL WYOMING SECTION

COATES, WOLFF, RUSSELL MINING INDUSTRY SCHOLARSHIP
• See page 95

SOCIETY OF HISPANIC PROFESSIONAL ENGINEERS FOUNDATION   http://www.henaac.org

SOCIETY OF HISPANIC PROFESSIONAL ENGINEERS FOUNDATION
• See page 168

SOCIETY OF MEXICAN AMERICAN ENGINEERS AND SCIENTISTS   http://www.maes-natl.org

GRE AND GRADUATE APPLICATIONS WAIVER
• See page 95

SOCIETY OF PLASTICS ENGINEERS (SPE) FOUNDATION   http://www.4spe.com

SOCIETY OF PLASTICS ENGINEERS SCHOLARSHIP PROGRAM
• See page 168

SOCIETY OF WOMEN ENGINEERS   http://www.swe.org

BECHTEL CORPORATION SCHOLARSHIP

Must major in either architectural, civil, electrical, environmental, or mechanical engineering. Must be a member of the Society of Women Engineers. Minimum 3.0 GPA required. Open to sophomores, juniors, and seniors. Deadline: February 1.

Academic Fields/Career Goals: Civil Engineering; Electrical Engineering/Electronics; Engineering/Technology; Mechanical Engineering.

Award: Scholarship for use in sophomore, junior, or senior years; not renewable. *Number:* 2. *Amount:* $1400.

Eligibility Requirements: Applicant must be enrolled or expecting to enroll at a four-year institution or university and female. Applicant or parent of applicant must be member of Society of Women Engineers. Applicant must have 3.0 GPA or higher. Available to U.S. citizens.

Application Requirements: Application, references, self-addressed stamped envelope, transcript. *Deadline:* February 1.

Contact: Suman Pa, Program Coordinator
Society of Women Engineers
230 E Ohio Street, Suite 400
Chicago, IL 60611-3265
Phone: 312-596-5223
Fax: 312-644-8557
E-mail: suman.patil@swe.org

CHEVRON TEXACO CORPORATION SCHOLARSHIPS
• See page 168

TEXAS DEPARTMENT OF TRANSPORTATION   http://www.dot.state.tx.us

CONDITIONAL GRANT PROGRAM

Grants available for up to $6000 ($3000 per semester). Students must be considered economically disadvantaged based on federal guidelines. Must be pursuing a degree in Civil Engineering, Computer Science, Computer Information Systems or Management Information Systems. Must be a Texas resident and study in Texas.

Academic Fields/Career Goals: Civil Engineering; Computer Science/Data Processing.

Award: Grant for use in freshman, sophomore, junior, or senior years; renewable. *Number:* varies. *Amount:* up to $6000.

Eligibility Requirements: Applicant must be American Indian/Alaska Native, Asian/Pacific Islander, Black (non-Hispanic), or Hispanic; enrolled or expecting to enroll full-time at a four-year institution or university; female; resident of Texas and studying in Texas. Applicant must have 2.5 GPA or higher. Available to U.S. citizens.

Application Requirements: Application, essay, interview, references, test scores, transcript. *Deadline:* March 1.

Contact: Minnie Brown, Program Coordinator
Texas Department of Transportation
125 East 11th Street
Austin, TX 78701-2483
Phone: 512-416-4979
Fax: 512-416-4980
E-mail: mbrown2@dot.state.tx.us

TEXAS ENGINEERING FOUNDATION   http://www.tspe.org/

TEXAS SOCIETY OF PROFESSIONAL ENGINEERS (TSPE) REGIONAL SCHOLARSHIPS
• See page 169

TURNER CONSTRUCTION COMPANY   http://www.turnerconstruction.com

YOUTHFORCE 2020 SCHOLARSHIP PROGRAM
• See page 103

UNITED NEGRO COLLEGE FUND   http://www.uncf.org

CDM SCHOLARSHIP/INTERNSHIP

Scholarship open to students attending a UNCF member college or university and majoring in environmental, civil, or electrical engineering. 3.0 GPA required. Prospective applicants should complete the Student Profile found at Web site: http://www.uncf.org.

Academic Fields/Career Goals: Civil Engineering; Electrical Engineering/Electronics; Engineering/Technology.

Award: Scholarship for use in freshman, sophomore, junior, or senior years; not renewable. *Amount:* $5000.

Eligibility Requirements: Applicant must be Black (non-Hispanic) and enrolled or expecting to enroll at a four-year institution or university. Applicant must have 3.0 GPA or higher. Available to U.S. citizens.

Application Requirements: Application. *Deadline:* April 14.

Contact: Rebecca Bennett, Director, Program Services
United Negro College Fund
8260 Willow Oaks Corporate Drive
Fairfax, VA 22031-8044
Phone: 800-331-2244
E-mail: rbennett@uncf.org

CHEVRON/TEXACO SCHOLARS PROGRAM

Scholarship awarded to college sophomores and juniors attending one of six UNCF member colleges and universities (Clark, Atlanta, Morehouse, Morris Brown, Spelman, Tuskegee, or Florida A&M). Applicants must major in civil, mechanical, or petroleum engineering. Minimum 2.5 GPA required. Prospective applicants should complete the Student Profile found at Web site: http://www.uncf.org

Academic Fields/Career Goals: Civil Engineering; Engineering/Technology; Mechanical Engineering.

Award: Scholarship for use in sophomore or junior years; not renewable. *Amount:* up to $3000.

Eligibility Requirements: Applicant must be Black (non-Hispanic) and enrolled or expecting to enroll full-time at a four-year institution or university. Applicant must have 2.5 GPA or higher. Available to U.S. citizens.

Application Requirements: Application, financial need analysis. *Deadline:* February 28.

Contact: Rebecca Bennett, Director, Program Services
United Negro College Fund
8260 Willow Oaks Corporate Drive
Fairfax, VA 22031-8044
Phone: 800-331-2244
E-mail: rbennett@uncf.org

MALCOLM PIRNIE, INC. SCHOLARS PROGRAM
• See page 169

UNIVERSITIES SPACE RESEARCH ASSOCIATION   http://www.usra.edu

UNIVERSITIES SPACE RESEARCH ASSOCIATION SCHOLARSHIP PROGRAM
• See page 96

UTAH SOCIETY OF PROFESSIONAL ENGINEERS   http://www.uspeonline.com

UTAH SOCIETY OF PROFESSIONAL ENGINEERS SCHOLARSHIP
• See page 169

VIRGINIA DEPARTMENT OF TRANSPORTATION   http://www.virginiadot.org

ENGINEER SCHOLARSHIP PROGRAM

Scholarship for a rising sophomore, junior or senior majoring in civil engineering. Must maintain a 2.5 grade point average or above. Applicants must be Virginia resident or attend a Virginia school.

Academic Fields/Career Goals: Civil Engineering.

Award: Scholarship for use in sophomore, junior, or senior years. *Amount:* up to $7000.

Eligibility Requirements: Applicant must be enrolled or expecting to enroll at a four-year institution or university; resident of Virginia and studying in Virginia. Applicant must have 2.5 GPA or higher. Available to U.S. citizens.

Application Requirements: Application. *Deadline:* January 15.

Contact: Scholarship Coordinator
Virginia Department of Transportation
VDOT Learning Center James Monroe Building, 10th Floor
1401 East Broad Street
Richmond, VA 23219-1939
Phone: 804-786-3875
E-mail: mailto:scholarship@Virginiadot.org

WIRE REINFORCEMENT INSTITUTE EDUCATION FOUNDATION   http://www.wirereinforcementinstitute.org

WRI COLLEGE SCHOLARSHIP PROGRAM

Academic scholarships for qualified high school seniors and current undergraduate and graduate level students intending to or presently pursuing four year or graduate level degrees in structural and/or civil engineering at accredited four year universities or colleges.

Academic Fields/Career Goals: Civil Engineering.

Award: Scholarship for use in freshman, sophomore, junior, senior, or graduate years; not renewable. *Amount:* $2500–$10,000.

Eligibility Requirements: Applicant must be enrolled or expecting to enroll at a four-year institution or university. Available to U.S. citizens.

Application Requirements: Application, references, test scores, transcript. *Deadline:* February 1.

Contact: Scholarship Selection Committee
Wire Reinforcement Institute Education Foundation
942 Main Street, Suite 300
Hartford, CT 06103

COMMUNICATIONS

ACADEMY OF TELEVISION ARTS AND SCIENCES FOUNDATION   http://www.emmys.tv/foundation

ACADEMY OF TELEVISION ARTS AND SCIENCES COLLEGE TELEVISION AWARDS
• See page 108

ADC RESEARCH INSTITUTE   http://www.adc.org

JACK SHAHEEN MASS COMMUNICATIONS SCHOLARSHIP AWARD

Awarded to Arab-American students who excel in the communications field (journalism, radio, television or film). Must be a junior or senior undergraduate or graduate student. Must be U.S. citizen. Must have 3.0 GPA.

Academic Fields/Career Goals: Communications; Filmmaking/Video; Journalism; TV/Radio Broadcasting.

Award: Prize for use in junior, senior, or graduate years; not renewable. *Number:* 1. *Amount:* $1000.

Eligibility Requirements: Applicant must be of Arab heritage and enrolled or expecting to enroll at a four-year institution or university. Applicant must have 3.0 GPA or higher. Available to U.S. citizens.

Application Requirements: Essay, references, transcript, copies of original articles, videos, films.

Contact: Marvin Wingfield, Director of Education and Outreach
ADC Research Institute
4201 Connecticut Avenue, NW Suite 300
Washington, DC 20008
Phone: 202-244-2990
Fax: 202-244-3196
E-mail: marvinw@adc.org

ADVERTISING FEDERATION OF FORT WAYNE, INC. http://www.adfedfortwayne.org

ADVERTISING FEDERATION OF FORT WAYNE, INC., SCHOLARSHIP

Applicant must be a full-time college student registered in an advertising or marketing related field. Must be a resident of one of the following Indiana counties: Adams, Allen, Dekalb, Huntington, Kosciusko, LaGrange, Noble, Steuben, Wabash, Wells or Whitley.

Academic Fields/Career Goals: Communications; Filmmaking/Video; Graphics/Graphic Arts/Printing; TV/Radio Broadcasting.

Award: Scholarship for use in sophomore, junior, or senior years; not renewable. *Number:* 1–3. *Amount:* $1000–$1500.

Eligibility Requirements: Applicant must be enrolled or expecting to enroll full-time at a four-year institution and resident of Indiana. Available to U.S. citizens.

Application Requirements: Application. *Deadline:* varies.

Contact: Scholarship Committee
Advertising Federation of Fort Wayne, Inc.
PO Box 10066
Fort Wayne, IN 46850
Phone: 260-427-9106

AMERICAN INSTITUTE OF POLISH CULTURE, INC. http://www.ampolinstitute.org

HARRIET IRSAY SCHOLARSHIP GRANT

Merit-based $1,000 scholarships for students studying communications, public relations, and/or journalism. All U.S. citizens may apply, but preference will be given to U.S. citizens of Polish heritage. Must submit 3 letters of recommendation on appropriate letterhead with application mailed directly to AIPC. For study in United States only. Deadline: March 17. Application fee is $25, now refundable.

Academic Fields/Career Goals: Communications; Journalism.

Award: Scholarship for use in freshman, sophomore, junior, or senior years; not renewable. *Number:* 10–15. *Amount:* $1000.

Eligibility Requirements: Applicant must be enrolled or expecting to enroll full-time at a two-year or four-year institution or university. Available to U.S. citizens.

Application Requirements: Application, resume, references, self-addressed stamped envelope, transcript. *Fee:* $25. *Deadline:* March 17.

Contact: Frances Waxman, Administrative Assistant
American Institute of Polish Culture, Inc.
1440 79th Street Causeway, Suite 117
Miami, FL 33141-4135
Phone: 305-864-2349
Fax: 305-865-5150
E-mail: info@ampolinstitute.org

AMERICAN LEGION, PRESS CLUB OF NEW JERSEY

AMERICAN LEGION PRESS CLUB OF NEW JERSEY AND POST 170 ARTHUR DEHARDT MEMORIAL SCHOLARSHIP

A $500 scholarship will be awarded to two students (one male, one female) entering their freshman year in an accredited four-year college. Eligible applicants will be the son, daughter, grandson, or granddaughter of a current or deceased, card-holding member of the American Legion. Must intend to work toward a degree related to the field of communications.

Academic Fields/Career Goals: Communications; Journalism; Photojournalism/Photography; TV/Radio Broadcasting.

Award: Scholarship for use in freshman year; not renewable. *Number:* 2. *Amount:* $500.

Eligibility Requirements: Applicant must be high school student; planning to enroll or expecting to enroll full-time at a four-year institution; single and resident of New Jersey. Available to U.S. citizens. Applicant or parent must meet one or more of the following requirements: general military experience; retired from active duty; disabled or killed as a result of military service; prisoner of war; or missing in action.

Application Requirements: Application, essay, copy of graduation certificates, DD-214, or honorable discharge of parent or grandparent from whom eligibility is obtained. *Deadline:* July 1.

Contact: Jack W. Kuepfer, Scholarship Chairman ALPC of NJ
American Legion, Press Club of New Jersey
68 Merrill Road
Clifton, NJ 07012-1622
Phone: 973-473-5176

AMERICAN QUARTER HORSE FOUNDATION (AQHF) http://www.aqha.org/aqhya

AQHF JOURNALISM OR COMMUNICATIONS SCHOLARSHIP

Must be member of AQHA or AQHYA who is pursuing a degree in journalism, communications, or a related field. Recipient receives $2000 per year for a four-year degree plan. Minimum 2.5 GPA required.

Academic Fields/Career Goals: Communications; Journalism.

Award: Scholarship for use in freshman, sophomore, junior, or senior years; renewable. *Number:* 1. *Amount:* $8000.

Eligibility Requirements: Applicant must be enrolled or expecting to enroll full-time at a two-year or four-year or technical institution or university. Applicant or parent of applicant must be member of American Quarter Horse Association. Applicant must have 2.5 GPA or higher. Available to U.S. and Canadian citizens.

Application Requirements: Application, essay, financial need analysis, photo, references, transcript. *Deadline:* February 1.

Contact: Laura Owens, Scholarship Coordinator
American Quarter Horse Foundation (AQHF)
2601 I-40 East
Amarillo, TX 79104
Phone: 806-378-5034
Fax: 806-376-1005
E-mail: lowens@aqha.org

ARRL FOUNDATION, INC. http://www.arrl.org/arrlf/scholgen.html

CHARLES N. FISHER MEMORIAL SCHOLARSHIP
• *See page 90*

DR. JAMES L. LAWSON MEMORIAL SCHOLARSHIP

One-time award available to students who are licensed as general amateur radio operators. Preference given to residents of Connecticut, Maine, Massachusetts, New Hampshire, Rhode Island, Vermont, and New York attending school in those states. Preference given to communications or electroncs majors. Deadline is February 1.

Academic Fields/Career Goals: Communications; Electrical Engineering/Electronics.

Award: Scholarship for use in freshman, sophomore, junior, or senior years; not renewable. *Number:* 1. *Amount:* $500.

Eligibility Requirements: Applicant must be enrolled or expecting to enroll full-time at an institution or university and must have an interest in amateur radio. Available to U.S. citizens.

Application Requirements: Application, transcript. *Deadline:* February 1.

Contact: Mary Hobart, Secretary Foundation
ARRL Foundation, Inc.
225 Main Street
Newington, CT 06111-1494
Phone: 860-594-0397
E-mail: k1mmh@arrl.org

FRED R. MCDANIEL MEMORIAL SCHOLARSHIP

Preference given to students with a 3.0 GPA and both residing and attending school in Texas, Oklahoma, Louisiana, Mississippi, New Mexico, or Arkansas. Preference is also given to students in the fields of electronics, communications, or a related field. Must be an amateur radio operator with a general license minimum. One-time award of $500. Deadline is February 1.

Academic Fields/Career Goals: Communications; Electrical Engineering/Electronics.

Award: Scholarship for use in freshman, sophomore, junior, or senior years; not renewable. *Number:* 1. *Amount:* $500.

Eligibility Requirements: Applicant must be enrolled or expecting to enroll full-time at an institution or university and must have an interest in amateur radio. Applicant must have 3.0 GPA or higher. Available to U.S. citizens.

Application Requirements: Application, transcript. *Deadline:* February 1.

Contact: Mary Hobart, Secretary Foundation
ARRL Foundation, Inc.
225 Main Street
Newington, CT 06111-1494
Phone: 860-594-0397
E-mail: k1mmh@arrl.org

IRVING W. COOK, WA0CGS, SCHOLARSHIP
• See page 90

L. PHIL WICKER SCHOLARSHIP

One-time award available to electronics or communications students pursuing a baccalaureate or higher degree who are licensed as general amateur radio operators. Preference given to those residing in North Carolina, South Carolina, Virginia or West Virginia and attending school in ARRL Roanoke Division. Deadline is February 1.

Academic Fields/Career Goals: Communications; Electrical Engineering/Electronics.

Award: Scholarship for use in freshman, sophomore, junior, senior, or graduate years; not renewable. *Number:* 1. *Amount:* $1000.

Eligibility Requirements: Applicant must be enrolled or expecting to enroll full-time at an institution or university; studying in North Carolina, South Carolina, Virginia, or West Virginia and must have an interest in amateur radio. Available to U.S. citizens.

Application Requirements: Application, transcript. *Deadline:* February 1.

Contact: Mary Hobart, Secretary Foundation
ARRL Foundation, Inc.
225 Main Street
Newington, CT 06111-1494
Phone: 860-594-0397
E-mail: k1mmh@arrl.org

MISSISSIPPI SCHOLARSHIP
• See page 90

PAUL AND HELEN L. GRAUER SCHOLARSHIP
• See page 91

PHD ARA SCHOLARSHIP

Award for journalism, computer science, or electronic engineering students who are amateur radio operators. Preference given to students residing in Iowa, Kansas, Missouri, or Nebraska, and those who are children of deceased amateur radio operators. Deadline is February 1.

Academic Fields/Career Goals: Communications; Computer Science/Data Processing; Electrical Engineering/Electronics; Engineering/Technology; Journalism.

Award: Scholarship for use in freshman, sophomore, junior, or senior years; not renewable. *Number:* 1. *Amount:* $1000.

Eligibility Requirements: Applicant must be enrolled or expecting to enroll full-time at an institution or university and must have an interest in amateur radio. Available to U.S. citizens.

Application Requirements: Application, transcript. *Deadline:* February 1.

Contact: Mary Hobart, Secretary Foundation
ARRL Foundation, Inc.
225 Main Street
Newington, CT 06111-1494
Phone: 860-594-0397
E-mail: k1mmh@arrl.org

ASIAN AMERICAN JOURNALISTS ASSOCIATION
http://www.aaja.org

ASIAN-AMERICAN JOURNALISTS ASSOCIATION SCHOLARSHIP

Awards for high school seniors and college students pursuing careers in the news media. Asian heritage is not required. Minimum 2.5 GPA required. Based on scholarship, goals, journalistic ability, financial need, and commitment to the Asian-American community. One-time award of up to $5000. Visit Web site http://www.aaja.org for application and details.

Academic Fields/Career Goals: Communications; Journalism; Photojournalism/Photography; TV/Radio Broadcasting.

Award: Scholarship for use in freshman, sophomore, junior, senior, or graduate years; not renewable. *Number:* 10–15. *Amount:* $1000–$5000.

Eligibility Requirements: Applicant must be enrolled or expecting to enroll full-time at a two-year or four-year institution or university and must have an interest in photography/photogrammetry/filmmaking or writing. Applicant or parent of applicant must have employment or volunteer experience in journalism. Applicant must have 2.5 GPA or higher. Available to U.S. and non-U.S. citizens.

Application Requirements: Application, essay, financial need analysis, resume, references, transcript. *Deadline:* April.

Contact: Brandon Sugiyama, Student Programs Coordinator
Asian American Journalists Association
1182 Market Street, Suite 320
San Francisco, CA 94102
Phone: 415-346-2051 Ext. 102
Fax: 415-346-6343
E-mail: programs@aaja.org

ATLANTA PRESS CLUB, INC.
http://www.atlpressclub.org

ATLANTA PRESS CLUB JOURNALISM SCHOLARSHIP PROGRAM

A one-time award only for students attending a Georgia college accredited by the Southern Association of Colleges and Schools. Must be journalism or communications majors. Based on need and potential for contribution to field. Must interview with selection committee. Must be a U.S. citizen.

Academic Fields/Career Goals: Communications; Journalism; Literature/English/Writing; TV/Radio Broadcasting.

Award: Scholarship for use in freshman, sophomore, junior, or senior years; not renewable. *Number:* 4. *Amount:* $1500.

Eligibility Requirements: Applicant must be enrolled or expecting to enroll full or part-time at a four-year institution or university; studying in Georgia and must have an interest in writing. Available to U.S. citizens.

Application Requirements: Application, essay, interview, portfolio, transcript. *Deadline:* February 15.

Contact: Claire Church, Assistant Director
Atlanta Press Club, Inc.
34 Broad Street, 18th Floor
Atlanta, GA 30303
Phone: 404-577-7377
Fax: 404-223-3706

BLACK BROADCASTERS ALLIANCE
http://www.thebba.org

BLACK BROADCASTERS ALLIANCE SCHOLARSHIP

Scholarship is awarded for African-American students majoring in communications.

Academic Fields/Career Goals: Communications.

Award: Scholarship for use in freshman, sophomore, junior, senior, or graduate years. *Amount:* $3000–$5000.

Eligibility Requirements: Applicant must be Black (non-Hispanic) and enrolled or expecting to enroll at a four-year institution or university. Available to U.S. citizens.

Application Requirements: Application. *Deadline:* varies.

Contact: Eddie Edwards, Chairman
Black Broadcasters Alliance
711 West 40th Street, Suite 330
Baltimore, MD 21211
Phone: 410-662-4536
Fax: 410-662-0816
E-mail: email@thebba.org

CALIFORNIA CHICANO NEWS MEDIA ASSOCIATION (CCNMA) http://www.ccnma.org

JOEL GARCIA MEMORIAL SCHOLARSHIP

Scholarships for Latinos interested in pursuing a career in journalism. Awards based on scholastic achievement, financial need, and community awareness. Submit sample of work. Award for California residents or those attending school in California. Deadline April 3.

Academic Fields/Career Goals: Communications; Journalism; Photojournalism/Photography; TV/Radio Broadcasting.

Award: Scholarship for use in freshman, sophomore, junior, senior, or graduate years; renewable. *Number:* 10–20. *Amount:* $500–$2000.

Eligibility Requirements: Applicant must be of Latin American/ Caribbean heritage; Hispanic; enrolled or expecting to enroll full-time at a two-year or four-year or technical institution or university and resident of California. Available to U.S. and non-U.S. citizens.

Application Requirements: Application, applicant must enter a contest, essay, financial need analysis, interview, portfolio, references, transcript, work samples. *Deadline:* April 3.

Contact: Julio Moran, Executive Director
California Chicano News Media Association (CCNMA)
300 South Grand Avenue, Suite 3950
Los Angeles, CA 90071-8110
Phone: 213-437-4408
Fax: 213-437-4423
E-mail: ccnmainfo@ccnma.org

CANADIAN ASSOCIATION OF BROADCASTERS http://www.cab-acr.ca

RUTH HANCOCK MEMORIAL SCHOLARSHIP

This CAN$1,500 scholarship is awarded annually to 3 students enrolled in a communications course at a Canadian school, who possess strong leadership qualities, natural talent, and a willingness to assist others. Must be a Canadian citizen.

Academic Fields/Career Goals: Communications; TV/Radio Broadcasting.

Award: Scholarship for use in freshman, sophomore, junior, senior, or graduate years; not renewable. *Number:* 3. *Amount:* $1114.

Eligibility Requirements: Applicant must be Canadian citizen; enrolled or expecting to enroll full or part-time at a two-year or four-year institution or university; studying in Alberta, British Columbia, Manitoba, New Brunswick, Newfoundland, North West Territories, Nova Scotia, Ontario, Prince Edward Island, Quebec, Saskatchewan, or Yukon and must have an interest in leadership.

Application Requirements: Application, essay, references. *Deadline:* June 30.

Contact: Vanessa Dewson, Special Events and Projects Coordinator
Canadian Association of Broadcasters
PO Box 627
Station B
Ottawa K1P 5S2
Canada
Phone: 613-233-4035 Ext. 309
Fax: 613-233-6961
E-mail: vdewson@cab-acr.ca

CHARLES & LUCILLE KING FAMILY FOUNDATION, INC. http://www.kingfoundation.org/

CHARLES AND LUCILLE KING FAMILY FOUNDATION SCHOLARSHIPS

Renewable award for college undergraduates at junior or senior level pursuing television, film, or communication studies to further their education. Must attend a four-year undergraduate institution. Minimum 3.0 GPA required to renew scholarship. Must have completed at least two years of study and be currently enrolled in a U.S. college or university. Must submit personal statement with application materials by April 15.

Academic Fields/Career Goals: Communications; Filmmaking/Video; TV/Radio Broadcasting.

Award: Scholarship for use in junior or senior years; renewable. *Number:* 10–20. *Amount:* $1250–$2500.

Eligibility Requirements: Applicant must be enrolled or expecting to enroll full-time at a four-year institution or university. Applicant must have 3.0 GPA or higher. Available to U.S. and non-U.S. citizens.

Application Requirements: Application, essay, financial need analysis, references, transcript. *Deadline:* April 15.

Contact: Michael Donovan, Educational Director
Charles & Lucille King Family Foundation, Inc.
366 Madison Avenue, 10th Floor
New York, NY 10017
Phone: 212-682-2913
Fax: 212-949-0728
E-mail: info@kingfoundation.org

CUBAN AMERICAN NATIONAL FOUNDATION http://www.canf.org

MAS FAMILY SCHOLARSHIPS
• See page 146

DALLAS-FORT WORTH ASSOCIATION OF BLACK COMMUNICATORS http://www.dfwabc.org

FUTURE JOURNALISTS SCHOLARSHIP PROGRAM

Scholarships are available to minority high school seniors and college students pursuing careers in broadcast or print journalism, advertising, public relations, photojournalism, and graphic arts and have permanent residence in Dallas, Tarrant, Denton, Hunt, Collin, or Ellis county, TX. Please see Web site for application and more information: http://www.dfwabc.org

Academic Fields/Career Goals: Communications; Graphics/Graphic Arts/Printing; Journalism; Photojournalism/Photography; TV/Radio Broadcasting.

Award: Scholarship for use in freshman, sophomore, junior, senior, or graduate years; not renewable. *Number:* 12–15. *Amount:* $500–$2000.

Eligibility Requirements: Applicant must be American Indian/Alaska Native, Asian/Pacific Islander, Black (non-Hispanic), or Hispanic; enrolled or expecting to enroll full-time at a four-year institution or university and resident of Texas. Available to U.S. citizens.

Application Requirements: Application, autobiography, essay, photo, portfolio, references. *Deadline:* March 15.

Contact: Ira Hadnot, DFW/ABC Scholarship Chair
Phone: 469-330-9696

DAYTON ADVERTISING CLUB http://www.daytonadclub.org/scholarship.php

BARBARA S. MILLER MEMORIAL SCHOLARSHIP
• See page 146

ELECTRONIC DOCUMENT SYSTEMS FOUNDATION http://www.edsf.org

ELECTRONIC DOCUMENT SYSTEMS FOUNDATION SCHOLARSHIP AWARDS

EDSF Scholarships are awarded to full-time students with a "B" minimum average who are preparing for careers in document preparation; production or distribution; one-to-one marketing; graphic arts and communication; e-commerce; imaging science; printing; web authoring; electronic publishing; computer science; telecommunications or related fields. Application deadline is May 15.

Academic Fields/Career Goals: Communications; Computer Science/ Data Processing; Engineering/Technology; Graphics/Graphic Arts/Printing.

Award: Scholarship for use in freshman, sophomore, junior, senior, or graduate years; not renewable. *Number:* 30–40. *Amount:* $1000–$2000.

Eligibility Requirements: Applicant must be enrolled or expecting to enroll full-time at a two-year or four-year or technical institution or university. Applicant must have 3.0 GPA or higher. Available to U.S. and non-U.S. citizens.

Application Requirements: Application, essay, references, transcript, description of activities and work experience. *Deadline:* May 15.

Contact: Jeanne Mowlds, Executive Director
Electronic Document Systems Foundation
24238 Hawthorne Boulevard
608 Silver Spur Road, Suite 280
Rolling Hills Estates, CA 90274-3616
Phone: 310-265-5510
Fax: 310-265-5588
E-mail: jcmowlds@aol.com

FISHER BROADCASTING COMPANY
http://www.fisherbroadcasting.com

FISHER BROADCASTING, INC., SCHOLARSHIP FOR MINORITIES

Award for minority students enrolled in a broadcast, journalism, or marketing curriculum. For residents of Washington, Oregon, Montana, and Idaho. Attending schools in or out-of-state, or for out-of-state students attending institutions in Washington, Oregon, Montana, or Idaho. Deadline: April 30. Must be in broadcast, marketing or journalism courses. Value and number of awards varies each year.

Academic Fields/Career Goals: Communications; Engineering/ Technology; Journalism; Photojournalism/Photography; TV/Radio Broadcasting.

Award: Scholarship for use in sophomore or junior years; not renewable. *Number:* 2–4. *Amount:* $1000–$10,000.

Eligibility Requirements: Applicant must be American Indian/Alaska Native, Asian/Pacific Islander, Black (non-Hispanic), or Hispanic and enrolled or expecting to enroll full-time at a two-year or four-year or technical institution or university. Applicant must have 2.5 GPA or higher. Available to U.S. citizens.

Application Requirements: Application, essay, financial need analysis, interview, references, transcript. *Deadline:* April 30.

Contact: Annnarie Hitchcock, Human Resources Administrator
Fisher Broadcasting Company
100 4th Avenue North, Suite 510
Seattle, WA 98109
Phone: 206-404-6050
Fax: 206-404-6760

GREAT LAKES COMMISSION
http://www.glc.org

CAROL A. RATZA MEMORIAL SCHOLARSHIP
• *See page 138*

GREATER KANAWHA VALLEY FOUNDATION
http://www.tgkvf.org

WEST VIRGINIA BROADCASTERS ASSOCIATION FUND

Renewable award for students seeking education at a college or university in the field of communications and related areas. Must be a West Virginia resident and maintain at least a 2.5 GPA. Open to employees and family members of station employees that are members of the West Virginia Broadcasters Association. May apply for two Foundation scholarships but will only be chosen for one.

Academic Fields/Career Goals: Communications; Foreign Language; Trade/Technical Specialties; TV/Radio Broadcasting.

Award: Scholarship for use in freshman, sophomore, junior, or senior years; renewable. *Number:* up to 8. *Amount:* $500.

Eligibility Requirements: Applicant must be enrolled or expecting to enroll at a two-year or four-year institution or university and resident of West Virginia. Applicant or parent of applicant must be member of West Virginia Broadcasters Association. Applicant or parent of applicant must have employment or volunteer experience in designated career field. Applicant must have 2.5 GPA or higher. Available to U.S. citizens.

Application Requirements: Application, essay, financial need analysis, references, self-addressed stamped envelope, test scores, transcript. *Deadline:* February 15.

Contact: Susan Hoover, Scholarship Coordinator
Greater Kanawha Valley Foundation
PO Box 3041
Charleston, WV 25331
Phone: 304-346-3620
Fax: 304-346-3640

HISPANIC COLLEGE FUND, INC.
http://www.hispanicfund.org

DENNY'S/HISPANIC COLLEGE FUND SCHOLARSHIP
• *See page 62*

NATIONAL HISPANIC EXPLORERS SCHOLARSHIP PROGRAM
• *See page 93*

INDIANAPOLIS ASSOCIATION OF BLACK JOURNALISTS
http://www.iabj.net

LYNN DEAN FORD IABJ SCHOLARSHIP AWARDS

Scholarship available to full time, African-American students who have been accepted to, or are already matriculated at a four-year college or university. Students must be enrolled in a course of study leading to a career in the media. Must attend college in Indiana or be a graduate of an Indiana high school studying out of state. Information may be obtained from Web site. Deadline: April 28.

Academic Fields/Career Goals: Communications; Journalism; Photojournalism/Photography; TV/Radio Broadcasting.

Award: Scholarship for use in freshman, sophomore, junior, or senior years; not renewable. *Number:* 1. *Amount:* $1000.

Eligibility Requirements: Applicant must be Black (non-Hispanic); enrolled or expecting to enroll full-time at a four-year institution or university and must have an interest in writing. Applicant must have 2.5 GPA or higher. Available to U.S. and non-U.S. citizens.

Application Requirements: Application, essay, portfolio, references. *Deadline:* April 28.

Contact: Courtenay Edelhart, Scholarship Committee Chair
Indianapolis Association of Black Journalists
PO Box 441795
Indianapolis, IN 46244-1795
Phone: 317-388-8163
E-mail: courtenay.edelhart@indystar.com

INTERNATIONAL COMMUNICATIONS INDUSTRIES FOUNDATION
http://www.infocomm.org/foundation

ICIF SCHOLARSHIP FOR DEPENDENTS OF MEMBER ORGANIZATIONS

Scholarship for a spouse, child, stepchild or grandchild of an employee of an INFOCOMM member organization or for an employee of an INFOCOMM member organization. Must be majoring in audiovisual related fields, such as audio, video, audiovisual, electronics, telecommunications, technical theatre, data networking, software development, and information technology Minimum of 2.75 GPA required.

Academic Fields/Career Goals: Communications; Computer Science/ Data Processing; Electrical Engineering/Electronics; Filmmaking/Video.

Award: Scholarship for use in freshman, sophomore, junior, or senior years; not renewable. *Amount:* $1500.

Eligibility Requirements: Applicant must be enrolled or expecting to enroll full-time at a four-year institution or university. Applicant must have 2.5 GPA or higher. Available to U.S. citizens.

International Communications Industries Foundation (continued)

Application Requirements: Application, essay, references, transcript. *Deadline:* May 5.

Contact: Duffy Wilbert, Vice President, Membership
International Communications Industries Foundation
11242 Waples Mill Road, Suite 200
Fairfax, VA 22030
Phone: 703-273-7200 Ext. 3470
Fax: 703-278-8082
E-mail: dwilbert@infocomm.org

INTERNATIONAL COMMUNICATIONS INDUSTRIES FOUNDATION AV SCHOLARSHIP

Scholarship for student majoring in audiovisual related fields such as audio, video, audiovisual, electronics, telecommunications, technical theatre, data networking, software development, information technology. Minimum 2.75 GPA required.

Academic Fields/Career Goals: Communications; Computer Science/Data Processing; Electrical Engineering/Electronics; Filmmaking/Video.

Award: Scholarship for use in freshman, sophomore, junior, or senior years; not renewable. *Amount:* up to $1200.

Eligibility Requirements: Applicant must be enrolled or expecting to enroll full or part-time at a four-year institution or university. Applicant must have 2.5 GPA or higher. Available to U.S. citizens.

Application Requirements: Application, essay, references, transcript. *Deadline:* May 5.

Contact: Duffy Wilbert, Vice President, Membership
International Communications Industries Foundation
11242 Waples Mill Road, Suite 200
Fairfax, VA 22030
Phone: 703-273-7200 Ext. 3470
Fax: 703-278-8082
E-mail: dwilbert@infocomm.org

INTERNATIONAL FOODSERVICE EDITORIAL COUNCIL
http://www.ifec-is-us.com

INTERNATIONAL FOODSERVICE EDITORIAL COUNCIL COMMUNICATIONS SCHOLARSHIP

Applicant must be a full-time student enrolled in an accredited postsecondary educational institution working toward an associate's, bachelor's, or master's degree. Must rank in upper half of class or have a minimum 2.5 GPA. Must have background, education and interests indicating preparedness for entering careers in editorial or public relations in the food-service industry.

Academic Fields/Career Goals: Communications; Food Science/Nutrition; Food Service/Hospitality; Graphics/Graphic Arts/Printing; Hospitality Management; Journalism; Literature/English/Writing; Photojournalism/Photography; Travel/Tourism.

Award: Scholarship for use in freshman, sophomore, junior, senior, graduate, or postgraduate years; not renewable. *Number:* 1–6. *Amount:* $1000–$3750.

Eligibility Requirements: Applicant must be enrolled or expecting to enroll full-time at a two-year or four-year or technical institution or university and must have an interest in photography/photogrammetry/filmmaking or writing. Applicant must have 2.5 GPA or higher. Available to U.S. and non-U.S. citizens.

Application Requirements: Application, essay, references, transcript. *Deadline:* March 15.

Contact: Carol Lally, Executive Director
International Foodservice Editorial Council
PO Box 491
Hyde Park, NY 12538-0491
Phone: 845-229-6973
Fax: 845-229-6993
E-mail: ifec@aol.com

JOHN BAYLISS BROADCAST FOUNDATION
http://www.baylissfoundation.org

JOHN BAYLISS BROADCAST RADIO SCHOLARSHIP

One-time award for college juniors, seniors, or graduate students majoring in broadcast communications with a concentration in radio broadcasting. Must have history of radio-related activities and a GPA of at least 3.0. Essay outlining future broadcasting goals required. Request information by mail, including stamped, self-addressed envelope, or by e-mail rather than by telephone. Must be attending school in U.S. Application is available at Web site: http://www.baylissfoundation.org.

Academic Fields/Career Goals: Communications; Journalism; TV/Radio Broadcasting.

Award: Scholarship for use in junior, senior, or graduate years; not renewable. *Number:* 15. *Amount:* up to $5000.

Eligibility Requirements: Applicant must be enrolled or expecting to enroll full-time at a four-year institution or university. Applicant must have 3.0 GPA or higher. Available to U.S. and Canadian citizens.

Application Requirements: Application, essay, references, self-addressed stamped envelope, transcript. *Deadline:* May 1.

Contact: Chairperson/Bayliss Scholarships, The John Bayliss Broadcast Foundation
John Bayliss Broadcast Foundation
171 17th Street
Pacific Grove, CA 93950
E-mail: info@baylissfoundation.org

JORGE MAS CANOSA FREEDOM FOUNDATION
http://www.canf.org

MAS FAMILY SCHOLARSHIP AWARD
• See page 149

JOURNALISM EDUCATION ASSOCIATION
http://www.jea.org

NATIONAL HIGH SCHOOL JOURNALIST OF THE YEAR/SISTER RITA JEANNE SCHOLARSHIPS

One-time award recognizes the nation's top high school journalists. Open to graduating high school seniors who are planning to study journalism and/or mass communications in college and pursue a career in the field. Applicants must have an advisor who is a JEA member. Minimum 3.0 GPA required. Submit portfolio to state contest coordinator by February 15.

Academic Fields/Career Goals: Communications; Journalism.

Award: Scholarship for use in freshman year; not renewable. *Number:* 1–6. *Amount:* $2000–$5000.

Eligibility Requirements: Applicant must be high school student; age 17-19 and planning to enroll or expecting to enroll full-time at a four-year institution or university. Applicant must have 3.0 GPA or higher. Available to U.S. citizens.

Application Requirements: Application, applicant must enter a contest, essay, photo, portfolio, references, self-addressed stamped envelope, transcript, samples of work. *Deadline:* February 15.

Contact: Connie Fulkerson, Administrative Assistant
Journalism Education Association
103 Kedzie Hall
Manhattan, KS 66506-1505
Phone: 785-532-5532
Fax: 785-532-5563

KATU THOMAS R. DARGAN MINORITY SCHOLARSHIP
http://www.katu.com

THOMAS R. DARGAN MINORITY SCHOLARSHIP

Up to four awards for minority students who are citizens of the United States pursuing broadcast or communications studies. Must be a resident of Oregon or Washington attending an out-of-state institution or be enrolled at a four-year college or university in Oregon or Washington. Minimum 3.0 GPA required. Deadline: April 30.

Academic Fields/Career Goals: Communications; TV/Radio Broadcasting.

Award: Scholarship for use in freshman, sophomore, junior, or senior years; not renewable. *Number:* 1–4. *Amount:* $4000.

Eligibility Requirements: Applicant must be American Indian/Alaska Native, Asian/Pacific Islander, Black (non-Hispanic), or Hispanic and enrolled or expecting to enroll full-time at a four-year institution or university. Applicant must have 3.0 GPA or higher. Available to U.S. citizens.

Application Requirements: Application, essay, financial need analysis, interview, references, transcript. *Deadline:* April 30.

Contact: KATU Thomas R. Dargan Scholarship, c/o Human Resources
KATU Thomas R. Dargan Minority Scholarship
PO Box 2
Portland, OR 97207-0002

LAGRANT FOUNDATION   http://www.lagrantfoundation.org

LAGRANT FOUNDATION SCHOLARSHIP FOR UNDERGRADUATES
• *See page 150*

NASA NEBRASKA SPACE GRANT CONSORTIUM   http://nasa.unomaha.edu

NASA NEBRASKA SPACE GRANT
• *See page 125*

NATIONAL ACADEMY OF TELEVISION ARTS AND SCIENCES   http://www.emmyonline.org/emmy/scholarship.html

NATIONAL ACADEMY OF TELEVISION ARTS AND SCIENCES JOHN CANNON MEMORIAL SCHOLARSHIP

Scholarships distributed over a four-year period with $10,000 awarded prior to the first year of study and three additional awards of $10,000 granted in subsequent years if the recipient demonstrates satisfactory progress towards a degree in a communications-oriented program. Must submit SAT or ACT scores. Must be child or grandchild of NATAS member. Application available on the Web at: http://www.emmyonline.org/emmy/scholr.html.

Academic Fields/Career Goals: Communications; TV/Radio Broadcasting.

Award: Scholarship for use in freshman, sophomore, junior, or senior years; renewable. *Number:* 1. *Amount:* $40,000.

Eligibility Requirements: Applicant must be high school student and planning to enroll or expecting to enroll full-time at a four-year institution. Applicant must have 3.0 GPA or higher. Available to U.S. and non-U.S. citizens.

Application Requirements: Application, essay, references, test scores, transcript. *Deadline:* December 12.

Contact: Luke E. T. Smith, Scholarship Committee
National Academy of Television Arts and Sciences
111 West 57th Street, Suite 600
New York, NY 10019
Phone: 212-586-8424
Fax: 212-246-8129
E-mail: scholarship@natasonline.com

TRUSTEE SCHOLARSHIP PROGRAM

Renewable award for exceptional high school seniors who plan to pursue a baccalaureate degree in communications with an emphasis on any aspect of the television industry. Must attend a four-year college or university. Scholarship is distributed over a four-year period, based on continued eligibility. Application and information available at Web site: http://www.emmyonline.org/emmy/scholarship.html. Application deadline is December 9.

Academic Fields/Career Goals: Communications; TV/Radio Broadcasting.

Award: Scholarship for use in freshman, sophomore, junior, or senior years; renewable. *Number:* 2. *Amount:* $40,000.

Eligibility Requirements: Applicant must be high school student and planning to enroll or expecting to enroll full-time at a four-year institution or university. Applicant must have 3.0 GPA or higher. Available to U.S. and non-U.S. citizens.

Application Requirements: Application, essay, references, test scores, transcript. *Deadline:* December 9.

Contact: Luke E. T. Smith, Scholarship Committee
National Academy of Television Arts and Sciences
111 West 57th Street, Suite 600
New York, NY 10019
Phone: 212-586-8424
Fax: 212-246-8129
E-mail: scholarship@natasonline.com

NATIONAL ASSOCIATION OF BLACK JOURNALISTS   http://www.nabj.org

NABJ SCHOLARSHIP

Scholarship is open to any black student who is currently attending an accredited four-year university. Student must be enrolled as undergraduate or graduate student majoring in journalism (print, radio, online, or television) Minimum 2.5 GPA.

Academic Fields/Career Goals: Communications; Journalism; TV/Radio Broadcasting.

Award: Scholarship for use in freshman, sophomore, junior, or senior years. *Number:* 2. *Amount:* $2500.

Eligibility Requirements: Applicant must be Black (non-Hispanic) and enrolled or expecting to enroll full-time at a four-year institution or university. Applicant must have 2.5 GPA or higher. Available to U.S. citizens.

Contact: Program and Exposition Coordinator
National Association of Black Journalists
8701-A Adelphi Road
Adelphi, MD 20783-1716
Phone: 301-445-7100
Fax: 301-445-7101

NATIONAL ASSOCIATION OF BROADCASTERS   http://www.nab.org

NATIONAL ASSOCIATION OF BROADCASTERS GRANTS FOR RESEARCH IN BROADCASTING

Grants awarded to graduate students and academic personnel for pursuit of research on important issues in the U.S. commercial broadcast industry. Must submit a proposal. One-time awards average $5000. If applicant is graduate student, they must have a recommendation from academic advisor. Please refer to Web site for further details: http://www.nab.org/research/grants/grants.asp.

Academic Fields/Career Goals: Communications; Journalism; TV/Radio Broadcasting.

Award: Grant for use in senior, graduate, or postgraduate years; not renewable. *Number:* 4–6. *Amount:* $5000.

Eligibility Requirements: Applicant must be enrolled or expecting to enroll full-time at a two-year or four-year institution or university. Available to U.S. and non-U.S. citizens.

Application Requirements: Application, references. *Deadline:* January 31.

Contact: Brian Baxter, Research Librarian
National Association of Broadcasters
1771 N Street, NW
Washington, DC 20036-2800
Phone: 202-429-5489
Fax: 202-429-4199
E-mail: bbaxter@nab.org

NATIONAL ASSOCIATION OF WATER COMPANIES-NEW JERSEY CHAPTER

NATIONAL ASSOCIATION OF WATER COMPANIES-NEW JERSEY CHAPTER SCHOLARSHIP
• *See page 139*

NATIONAL GAY AND LESBIAN TASK FORCE   http://www.ngltf.org/about/messenger.htm

NATIONAL GAY AND LESBIAN TASK FORCE MESSENGER-ANDERSON JOURNALISM SCHOLARSHIP

Scholarship with internship program for lesbian, gay, bisexual, and transgender (LGBT) students. Open to high school seniors and undergraduate college students who plan to pursue a degree in journalism or communications at an accredited four-year college or university. Must be a member of NGLTF with minimum GPA of 2.5. Application deadline is February 15.

Academic Fields/Career Goals: Communications; Journalism.

Award: Scholarship for use in freshman, sophomore, junior, or senior years; renewable. *Number:* up to 4. *Amount:* up to $10,000.

National Gay and Lesbian Task Force (continued)

Eligibility Requirements: Applicant must be enrolled or expecting to enroll full-time at a four-year institution or university. Applicant must have 2.5 GPA or higher. Available to U.S. citizens.

Application Requirements: Application, essay, interview, portfolio, resume, references, transcript. *Deadline:* February 15.

Contact: National Gay and Lesbian Task Force
5455 Wilshire Boulevard, Suite 1505
Los Angeles, CA 90036

NATIONAL INSTITUTE FOR LABOR RELATIONS RESEARCH
http://www.nilrr.org

NATIONAL INSTITUTE FOR LABOR RELATIONS RESEARCH WILLIAM B. RUGGLES JOURNALISM SCHOLARSHIP

One-time award for undergraduate or graduate study in journalism or mass communications. Submit 500-word essay on the right-to-work principle. High school seniors accepted into certified journalism school may apply. Deadline: December 31. When corresponding regarding scholarship, please specify "Journalism" or "Ruggles" scholarship.

Academic Fields/Career Goals: Communications; Journalism.

Award: Scholarship for use in freshman, sophomore, junior, senior, or graduate years; not renewable. *Number:* 1. *Amount:* $2000.

Eligibility Requirements: Applicant must be enrolled or expecting to enroll full-time at a four-year institution or university and must have an interest in writing. Available to U.S. and non-U.S. citizens.

Application Requirements: Application, essay, transcript. *Deadline:* December 31.

Contact: Cathy Jones, Scholarship Coordinator
National Institute for Labor Relations Research
5211 Port Royal Road, Suite 510
Springfield, VA 22151
Phone: 703-321-9606
Fax: 703-321-7342
E-mail: research@nilrr.org

NATIONAL SPEAKERS ASSOCIATION
http://www.nsaspeaker.org

NATIONAL SPEAKERS ASSOCIATION SCHOLARSHIP

One-time award for junior, senior, or graduate student majoring or minoring in speech or a directly related field. Must be full-time student at accredited four-year institution with above average academic record. Submit 500-word essay on goals. Application available only on Web site.

Academic Fields/Career Goals: Communications.

Award: Scholarship for use in junior, senior, or graduate years; not renewable. *Number:* 4. *Amount:* $4000.

Eligibility Requirements: Applicant must be enrolled or expecting to enroll full-time at a four-year institution or university. Applicant must have 3.5 GPA or higher. Available to U.S. and non-U.S. citizens.

Application Requirements: Application, essay, references, transcript. *Deadline:* June 1.

Contact: Audrey O'Neal, Scholarship Coordinator
National Speakers Association
1500 South Priest Drive
Tempe, AZ 85281
Phone: 480-968-2552
Fax: 480-968-0911
E-mail: audrey@nsaspeaker.org

NATIONAL STONE, SAND AND GRAVEL ASSOCIATION (NSSGA)
http://www.nssga.org

JENNIFER CURTIS BYLER SCHOLARSHIP FOR THE STUDY OF PUBLIC AFFAIRS

one-time award is open to graduating high school seniors or students already enrolled in a public affairs major in college who are sons or daughters of an aggregates company employee.

Academic Fields/Career Goals: Communications; Journalism; Political Science.

Award: Scholarship for use in freshman, sophomore, junior, or senior years; not renewable. *Number:* 1. *Amount:* $1000–$2500.

Eligibility Requirements: Applicant must be enrolled or expecting to enroll full-time at a four-year institution or university. Applicant or parent of applicant must have employment or volunteer experience in designated career field. Available to U.S. and non-U.S. citizens.

Application Requirements: Application, essay, references, transcript. *Deadline:* May 31.

Contact: Jennifer Curtis Byler Scholarship c/o NSSGA
National Stone, Sand and Gravel Association (NSSGA)
1605 King Street
Arlington, VA 22314
Phone: 703-525-8788
Fax: 703-525-7782
E-mail: info@nssga.org

NATIONAL WRITERS ASSOCIATION FOUNDATION
http://www.nationalwriters.com

NATIONAL WRITERS ASSOCIATION FOUNDATION SCHOLARSHIPS

Scholarships to those with serious interest in any writing field.

Academic Fields/Career Goals: Communications; Filmmaking/Video; Journalism; Literature/English/Writing; Photojournalism/Photography.

Award: Scholarship for use in freshman, sophomore, junior, senior, graduate, or postgraduate years; not renewable. *Number:* 4. *Amount:* $200–$1000.

Eligibility Requirements: Applicant must be enrolled or expecting to enroll full or part-time at a two-year or four-year or technical institution or university and must have an interest in English language, photography/photogrammetry/filmmaking, or writing. Available to U.S. and non-U.S. citizens.

Application Requirements: Application, transcript, writing samples. *Deadline:* December 31.

Contact: Sandy Welchel, Executive Director
National Writers Association Foundation
10940 South Parker Road, Suite 508
Parker, CO 80134
Phone: 303-841-0246
Fax: 303-841-2607
E-mail: info@nationalwriters.com

NEW JERSEY BROADCASTERS ASSOCIATION
http://www.njba.com

MICHAEL S. LIBRETTI SCHOLARSHIP

Scholarships for undergraduate students in broadcasting, communication and journalism. Must be a New Jersey resident.

Academic Fields/Career Goals: Communications; Journalism; TV/Radio Broadcasting.

Award: Scholarship for use in freshman, sophomore, junior, or senior years. *Amount:* up to $2500.

Eligibility Requirements: Applicant must be enrolled or expecting to enroll full-time at a four-year institution or university and resident of New Jersey. Available to U.S. citizens.

Application Requirements: *Deadline:* April.

Contact: New Jersey Broadcasters Association
Broadcast House
348 Applegarth Road
Cranbury, NJ 08512
Phone: 888-652-2366
E-mail: njba@njba.com

NEW JERSEY DIVISION OF FISH AND WILDLIFE/NJ CHAPTER OF THE WILDLIFE SOCIETY
http://www.njfishandwildlife.com/cookhmschol.htm

RUSSELL A. COOKINGHAM SCHOLARSHIP
• *See page 140*

OREGON ASSOCIATION OF BROADCASTERS
http://www.theoab.org

OAB BROADCAST SCHOLARSHIP

One-time award for students to begin or continue their education in broadcast and related studies. Must have a 3.0 GPA. Must be a resident of Oregon studying in Oregon.

Academic Fields/Career Goals: Communications; Journalism; TV/Radio Broadcasting.

Award: Scholarship for use in freshman, sophomore, junior, or senior years; not renewable. *Number:* 6. *Amount:* $1000.

Eligibility Requirements: Applicant must be high school student; planning to enroll or expecting to enroll full-time at a two-year or four-year institution; resident of Oregon and studying in Oregon. Applicant must have 3.0 GPA or higher. Available to U.S. citizens.

Application Requirements: Application, autobiography, essay, financial need analysis, resume, references, transcript. *Deadline:* March 2.

Contact: Bill Johnstone, President and CEO
Oregon Association of Broadcasters
7150 Southwest Hampton Street, Suite 240
Portland, OR 97223-8366
Phone: 503-443-2299
Fax: 503-443-2488
E-mail: theoab@theoab.org

OUTDOOR WRITERS ASSOCIATION OF AMERICA
http://www.owaa.org/

OUTDOOR WRITERS ASSOCIATION OF AMERICA BODIE MCDOWELL SCHOLARSHIP AWARD

One-time award for college juniors, seniors, and graduate level candidates who demonstrate outdoor communication talent and intend to make a career in this field. Applicants are nominated by their institution. One applicant per school in both graduate and undergraduate designations. Must submit examples of outdoor communications work.

Academic Fields/Career Goals: Communications; Filmmaking/Video; Journalism; Literature/English/Writing; Photojournalism/Photography; TV/Radio Broadcasting.

Award: Scholarship for use in junior, senior, or graduate years; not renewable. *Number:* 3–6. *Amount:* $1800–$5000.

Eligibility Requirements: Applicant must be enrolled or expecting to enroll full or part-time at a four-year institution or university and must have an interest in amateur radio, art, photography/photogrammetry/filmmaking, or writing. Available to U.S. and non-U.S. citizens.

Application Requirements: Application, essay, references, transcript.

Contact: Executive Director
Outdoor Writers Association of America
121 Hickory Street, Suite 1
Missoula, MT 59801
Phone: 406-728-7434
Fax: 406-728-7445
E-mail: owaa@montana.com

PRINTING INDUSTRIES OF WISCONSIN EDUCATION FOUNDATION SCHOLARSHIPS
http://www.piw.org

PAGEL GRAPHIC ARTS SCHOLARSHIP FUND

Scholarship available for all age groups who are attending school in Wisconsin and pursuing some form of higher education in the print communications industry.

Academic Fields/Career Goals: Communications; Journalism.

Award: Scholarship for use in freshman, sophomore, junior, or senior years. *Amount:* $500–$1000.

Eligibility Requirements: Applicant must be enrolled or expecting to enroll full or part-time at a four-year institution or university; resident of Wisconsin and studying in Wisconsin. Available to U.S. citizens.

Application Requirements: Application. *Deadline:* March 15.

Contact: Bob Carlson
Printing Industries of Wisconsin Education Foundation Scholarships
PO Box 34
Elm Grove, WI 53122-0034
Phone: 262-789-8484

PUBLIC RELATIONS STUDENT SOCIETY OF AMERICA
http://www.prssa.org

PUBLIC RELATIONS SOCIETY OF AMERICA MULTICULTURAL AFFAIRS SCHOLARSHIP

One-time award for members of principal minority group who are in their junior or senior year at an accredited four-year college or university. Must have at least a 3.0 GPA and be preparing for career in public relations or communications. Two scholarships at $1500 each. Must be a full-time student and U.S. citizen. Application deadline is April 14.

Academic Fields/Career Goals: Communications.

Award: Scholarship for use in freshman, sophomore, junior, or senior years; not renewable. *Number:* 2. *Amount:* $1500.

Eligibility Requirements: Applicant must be American Indian/Alaska Native, Asian/Pacific Islander, Black (non-Hispanic), or Hispanic and enrolled or expecting to enroll full-time at a four-year institution or university. Applicant must have 3.0 GPA or higher. Available to U.S. citizens.

Application Requirements: Application, essay, financial need analysis, references, transcript. *Deadline:* April 14.

Contact: Jeneen Garcia, Director of Education
Public Relations Student Society of America
33 Maiden Lane, 11th Floor
New York, NY 10038-5150
Phone: 212-460-1466
Fax: 212-995-0757
E-mail: jeneen.garcia@prsa.org

RADIO-TELEVISION NEWS DIRECTORS ASSOCIATION AND FOUNDATION
http://www.rtndf.org/

ABE SCHECTER GRADUATE SCHOLARSHIP

Available to any graduate student pursuing a career in electronic news, electronic news teaching, or research. Submit one-page essay detailing past merits and career objective, letter of endorsement, and one to three examples of work, not to exceed 15 minutes total. One-time award of $2000. Application deadline is May 8.

Academic Fields/Career Goals: Communications; Journalism; TV/Radio Broadcasting.

Award: Scholarship for use in sophomore, junior, senior, or graduate years; not renewable. *Number:* 1. *Amount:* $2000.

Eligibility Requirements: Applicant must be enrolled or expecting to enroll full-time at a four-year institution or university. Available to U.S. and non-U.S. citizens.

Application Requirements: Application, essay, resume, references. *Deadline:* May 8.

Contact: Karen Jackson-Bullitt, Manager, Education Programs
Radio-Television News Directors Association and Foundation
1600 K Street, NW, Suite 700
Washington, DC 20006-2838
Phone: 202-467-5218
Fax: 202-223-4007
E-mail: karenb@rtndf.org

CAROLE SIMPSON SCHOLARSHIP

Award for minority sophomore, junior, or senior undergraduate student enrolled in an electronic journalism program. Submit one to three examples of reporting or producing skills on audiocassette tape or videotape, totaling 15 minutes or less, with scripts. One-time award of $2000. Entries must be postmarked by May 10.

Academic Fields/Career Goals: Communications; Journalism; TV/Radio Broadcasting.

Radio-Television News Directors Association and Foundation (continued)

Award: Scholarship for use in sophomore, junior, senior, or graduate years; not renewable. *Number:* 1. *Amount:* $2000.

Eligibility Requirements: Applicant must be American Indian/Alaska Native, Asian/Pacific Islander, Black (non-Hispanic), or Hispanic; enrolled or expecting to enroll full-time at a four-year institution or university and must have an interest in photography/photogrammetry/filmmaking or writing. Available to U.S. and non-U.S. citizens.

Application Requirements: Application, essay, resume, references, video or audio tape of work. *Deadline:* May 8.

Contact: Karen Jackson-Bullitt, Project Coordinator
Radio-Television News Directors Association and Foundation
1600 K Street, NW, Suite 700
Washington, DC 20006
Phone: 202-467-5218
Fax: 202-223-4007
E-mail: karenb@rtndf.org

KEN KASHIWAHARA SCHOLARSHIP

One-time award of $2500 for minority sophomore, junior, or senior whose career objective is electronic journalism. Submit one to three examples showing reporting or producing skills on audiocassette or VHS, with scripts. Entries must be postmarked by May 10.

Academic Fields/Career Goals: Communications; Journalism; TV/Radio Broadcasting.

Award: Scholarship for use in sophomore, junior, senior, or graduate years; not renewable. *Number:* 1. *Amount:* $2500.

Eligibility Requirements: Applicant must be American Indian/Alaska Native, Asian/Pacific Islander, Black (non-Hispanic), or Hispanic and enrolled or expecting to enroll full-time at a four-year institution or university. Available to U.S. and non-U.S. citizens.

Application Requirements: Application, essay, resume, references, video or audio tape of work. *Deadline:* May 8.

Contact: Karen Jackson-Bullitt, Manager, Education Programs
Radio-Television News Directors Association and Foundation
1600 K Street, NW, Suite 700
Washington, DC 20006-2838
Phone: 202-467-5218
Fax: 202-223-4007
E-mail: karenb@rtndf.org

LOU AND CAROLE PRATO SPORTS REPORTING SCHOLARSHIP

One-time tuition grant of $1000 is given to a deserving student with strong writing skills who is planning a career as a sports reporter in television or radio.

Academic Fields/Career Goals: Communications; Journalism; TV/Radio Broadcasting.

Award: Grant for use in sophomore, junior, senior, or graduate years; not renewable. *Number:* 1. *Amount:* $1000.

Eligibility Requirements: Applicant must be enrolled or expecting to enroll full-time at a four-year institution or university. Available to U.S. and non-U.S. citizens.

Application Requirements: Application, essay, resume, references. *Deadline:* May 8.

Contact: Karen Jackson-Bullitt, Manager, Education Programs
Radio-Television News Directors Association and Foundation
1600 K Street, NW, Suite 700
Washington, DC 20006-2838
Phone: 202-467-5218
Fax: 202-223-4007
E-mail: karenb@rtndf.org

MIKE REYNOLDS $1,000 SCHOLARSHIP

Scholarship for undergraduate student demonstrating need for financial assistance and by indicating media-related jobs held and contributions made to funding his or her own education. Applicants must submit a copy of their FAFSA Student Aid Report (SAR) as a part of the application.

Academic Fields/Career Goals: Communications; Journalism; TV/Radio Broadcasting.

Award: Scholarship for use in sophomore, junior, senior, or graduate years; not renewable. *Number:* 1. *Amount:* $1000.

Eligibility Requirements: Applicant must be American Indian/Alaska Native, Asian/Pacific Islander, Black (non-Hispanic), or Hispanic and enrolled or expecting to enroll full-time at a four-year institution or university. Available to U.S. and non-U.S. citizens.

Application Requirements: Application, essay, financial need analysis, resume, references, video or audio tape of work. *Deadline:* May 8.

Contact: Karen Jackson-Bullitt, Manager, Education Programs
Radio-Television News Directors Association and Foundation
1600 K Street, NW, Suite 700
Washington, DC 20006-2838
Phone: 202-467-5218
Fax: 202-223-4007
E-mail: karenb@rtndf.org

PRESIDENT'S $2500 SCHOLARSHIP

Two awards of $2500 given in honor of former RTNDA Presidents for college sophomores, juniors and seniors.

Academic Fields/Career Goals: Communications; Journalism; TV/Radio Broadcasting.

Award: Scholarship for use in sophomore, junior, or senior years; not renewable. *Number:* 2. *Amount:* $2500.

Eligibility Requirements: Applicant must be enrolled or expecting to enroll full-time at a four-year institution or university. Available to U.S. and non-U.S. citizens.

Application Requirements: Application, essay, resume, references, video or audio tape of work. *Deadline:* May 8.

Contact: Karen Jackson-Bullitt, Manager, Education Programs
Radio-Television News Directors Association and Foundation
1600 K Street, NW, Suite 700
Washington, DC 20006-2838
Phone: 202-467-5218
Fax: 202-223-4007
E-mail: karenb@rtndf.org

RHODE ISLAND FOUNDATION
http://www.rifoundation.org

RDW GROUP, INC. MINORITY SCHOLARSHIP FOR COMMUNICATIONS

One-time award to provide support to minority students who wish to pursue a course of study in communications at the undergraduate or graduate level. Must be a Rhode Island resident.

Academic Fields/Career Goals: Communications.

Award: Scholarship for use in freshman, sophomore, junior, senior, or graduate years; not renewable. *Number:* 1. *Amount:* $2000.

Eligibility Requirements: Applicant must be American Indian/Alaska Native, Asian/Pacific Islander, Black (non-Hispanic), or Hispanic; enrolled or expecting to enroll full-time at an institution or university and resident of Rhode Island. Available to U.S. citizens.

Application Requirements: Application, essay, self-addressed stamped envelope, transcript. *Deadline:* April 28.

Contact: Libby Monahan, Scholarship Coordinator
Rhode Island Foundation
1 Union Station
Providence, RI 02903
Phone: 401-274-4564
Fax: 401-272-1359
E-mail: libbym@rifoundation.org

SOCIETY FOR TECHNICAL COMMUNICATION
http://www.stc.org

SOCIETY FOR TECHNICAL COMMUNICATION SCHOLARSHIP PROGRAM

Applicants must have completed at least one year of postsecondary education. Applicants must be full-time students. They may either be graduate students working toward a master's or doctorate degree, or undergraduate students working toward a bachelor's degree. Students should have at least one full year of academic work remaining. They should be studying communication of information about technical subjects. Two awards available for undergraduate students, two available for graduate students.

Academic Fields/Career Goals: Communications; Engineering-Related Technologies.

Award: Scholarship for use in sophomore, junior, senior, or graduate years; not renewable. *Number:* up to 4. *Amount:* up to $1500.

Eligibility Requirements: Applicant must be enrolled or expecting to enroll full-time at a four-year institution or university. Available to U.S. and non-U.S. citizens.

Application Requirements: Application, essay, references, transcript. *Deadline:* February 15.

Contact: Buffy Bennett, Special Projects Director
Society for Technical Communication
901 North Stuart Street, Suite 904
Arlington, VA 22203-1822
Phone: 703-522-4114
Fax: 703-522-2075
E-mail: stc@stc.org

SOCIETY FOR TECHNICAL COMMUNICATION–LONE STAR CHAPTER   http://www.stc-dfw.org

LONE STAR COMMUNITY SCHOLARSHIPS

Scholarship for graduate or undergraduate student working toward a degree or certificate in the technical communication field. Must be a member of Society for Technical Communication or living or attending school in STC Region 5. For further information see Web site http://www.stc-dfw.org

Academic Fields/Career Goals: Communications.

Award: Scholarship for use in freshman, sophomore, junior, senior, or graduate years. *Number:* 1.

Eligibility Requirements: Applicant must be enrolled or expecting to enroll at a four-year institution or university. Available to U.S. citizens.

Application Requirements: Application, references, transcript, copy of degree/certificate plan. *Deadline:* March 15.

Contact: Ann Balaban, Scholarship Chair
Society for Technical Communication–Lone Star Chapter
PO Box 515065
Dallas, TX 75251-5065
Phone: 214-526-0828
E-mail: scholarships@stc-dfw.org

SOCIETY OF PROFESSIONAL JOURNALISTS-SOUTH FLORIDA CHAPTER   http://www.spjsofla.net/

GARTH REEVES, JR. MEMORIAL SCHOLARSHIPS

Scholarships for senior high school students, undergraduate, and graduate minority students preparing for a news career. Must be a South Florida resident. Amount is determined by need; minimum award is $500. One-time award, renewable upon application. Academic performance and quality of work for student or professional news media is considered.

Academic Fields/Career Goals: Communications; Journalism.

Award: Scholarship for use in freshman, sophomore, junior, senior, or graduate years; not renewable. *Number:* 1–3. *Amount:* $500.

Eligibility Requirements: Applicant must be American Indian/Alaska Native, Asian/Pacific Islander, Black (non-Hispanic), or Hispanic; enrolled or expecting to enroll full or part-time at a two-year or four-year institution or university; resident of Florida and must have an interest in designated field specified by sponsor. Applicant must have 3.0 GPA or higher. Available to U.S. citizens.

Application Requirements: Application, financial need analysis, references, self-addressed stamped envelope, transcript, examples of applicant's journalism.

Contact: Oline Cogdill, Chair, Scholarship Committee
Society of Professional Journalists-South Florida Chapter
200 East Las Olas Boulevard
Fort Lauderdale, FL 33301
Phone: 954-356-4886
E-mail: ocogdill@sun-sentinel.com

TEXAS ASSOCIATION OF BROADCASTERS   http://www.tab.org

BELO TEXAS BROADCAST EDUCATION FOUNDATION SCHOLARSHIP

Scholarship of $2000 to a junior or senior student enrolled in a fully accredited program of instruction that emphasizes radio or television broadcasting or communications at a four-year college or university in Texas.

Academic Fields/Career Goals: Communications; TV/Radio Broadcasting.

Award: Scholarship for use in junior or senior years. *Amount:* $2000.

Eligibility Requirements: Applicant must be enrolled or expecting to enroll full-time at a four-year institution or university and studying in Texas. Applicant must have 3.0 GPA or higher. Available to U.S. citizens.

Application Requirements: Application, essay, references. *Deadline:* May 5.

Contact: Craig Bean, Public Service Manager
Texas Association of Broadcasters
502 East 11th Street, Suite 200
Austin, TX 78701
Phone: 512-322-9944
Fax: 512-322-0522
E-mail: craig@tab.org

BONNER MCLANE TEXAS BROADCAST EDUCATION FOUNDATION SCHOLARSHIP

Scholarship of $2000 to a junior or senior student enrolled in a fully accredited program of instruction that emphasizes radio or television broadcasting or communications at a four-year college or university in Texas.

Academic Fields/Career Goals: Communications; TV/Radio Broadcasting.

Award: Scholarship for use in junior or senior years. *Amount:* $2000.

Eligibility Requirements: Applicant must be enrolled or expecting to enroll full-time at a four-year institution or university and studying in Texas. Applicant must have 3.0 GPA or higher. Available to U.S. citizens.

Application Requirements: Application, essay, references. *Deadline:* May 5.

Contact: Craig Bean, Public Service Manager
Texas Association of Broadcasters
502 East 11th Street, Suite 200
Austin, TX 78701
Phone: 512-322-9944
Fax: 512-322-0522
E-mail: craig@tab.org

STUDENT TEXAS BROADCAST EDUCATION FOUNDATION SCHOLARSHIP

Scholarship of $2000 to a student enrolled in a program of instruction that emphasizes radio or television broadcasting or communications at a two-year or technical school in Texas.

Academic Fields/Career Goals: Communications; TV/Radio Broadcasting.

Award: Scholarship for use in freshman or sophomore years. *Amount:* $2000.

Eligibility Requirements: Applicant must be enrolled or expecting to enroll full-time at a two-year or technical institution and studying in Texas. Applicant must have 3.0 GPA or higher. Available to U.S. citizens.

Application Requirements: Application, essay, references. *Deadline:* May 5.

Contact: Craig Bean, Public Service Manager
Texas Association of Broadcasters
502 East 11th Street, Suite 200
Austin, TX 78701
Phone: 512-322-9944
Fax: 512-322-0522
E-mail: craig@tab.org

TOM REIFF TEXAS BROADCAST EDUCATION FOUNDATION SCHOLARSHIP

Scholarship of $2000 to an upcoming junior or senior student enrolled in a fully accredited program of instruction that emphasizes radio or television broadcasting or communications at a four-year college or university in Texas.

Academic Fields/Career Goals: Communications; TV/Radio Broadcasting.

Award: Scholarship for use in junior or senior years. *Amount:* $2000.

Texas Association of Broadcasters (continued)

Eligibility Requirements: Applicant must be enrolled or expecting to enroll full-time at a four-year institution or university and studying in Texas. Applicant must have 3.0 GPA or higher. Available to U.S. citizens.

Application Requirements: Application, essay, references. *Deadline:* May 5.

Contact: Craig Bean, Public Service Manager
Texas Association of Broadcasters
502 East 11th Street, Suite 200
Austin, TX 78701
Phone: 512-322-9944
Fax: 512-322-0522
E-mail: craig@tab.org

UNDERGRADUATE TEXAS BROADCAST EDUCATION FOUNDATION SCHOLARSHIP

Scholarship of $2000 to a freshman or sophomore student enrolled in a fully accredited program of instruction that emphasizes radio or television broadcasting or communications at a four-year college or university in Texas.

Academic Fields/Career Goals: Communications; TV/Radio Broadcasting.

Award: Scholarship for use in freshman or sophomore years. *Amount:* $2000.

Eligibility Requirements: Applicant must be enrolled or expecting to enroll full-time at a four-year institution or university and studying in Texas. Applicant must have 3.0 GPA or higher. Available to U.S. citizens.

Application Requirements: Application, essay, references. *Deadline:* May 5.

Contact: Craig Bean, Public Service Manager
Texas Association of Broadcasters
502 East 11th Street, Suite 200
Austin, TX 78701
Phone: 512-322-9944
Fax: 512-322-0522
E-mail: craig@tab.org

VANN KENNEDY TEXAS BROADCAST EDUCATION FOUNDATION SCHOLARSHIP

Scholarship of $2000 to a student enrolled in a fully accredited program of instruction that emphasizes radio or television broadcasting or communications at a college or university in Texas.

Academic Fields/Career Goals: Communications; TV/Radio Broadcasting.

Award: Scholarship for use in freshman, sophomore, junior, senior, or graduate years. *Amount:* $2000.

Eligibility Requirements: Applicant must be enrolled or expecting to enroll full-time at a two-year or four-year institution or university and studying in Texas. Applicant must have 3.0 GPA or higher. Available to U.S. citizens.

Application Requirements: Application, essay, references. *Deadline:* May 5.

Contact: Craig Bean, Public Service Manager
Texas Association of Broadcasters
502 East 11th Street, Suite 200
Austin, TX 78701
Phone: 512-322-9944
Fax: 512-322-0522
E-mail: craig@tab.org

TEXAS GRIDIRON CLUB, INC.   http://www.spjfw.org

TEXAS GRIDIRON CLUB SCHOLARSHIPS

Awards for college juniors, seniors, or graduate students majoring in newspaper, photojournalism, or broadcast fields. Must submit work samples. Minimum grant $500. Recipient must be a Texas resident or going to school in Texas.

Academic Fields/Career Goals: Communications; Journalism; Photojournalism/Photography; TV/Radio Broadcasting.

Award: Scholarship for use in freshman, sophomore, junior, senior, or graduate years; not renewable. *Number:* 10–15. *Amount:* $500–$1500.

Eligibility Requirements: Applicant must be enrolled or expecting to enroll full or part-time at a four-year institution or university. Available to U.S. and non-U.S. citizens.

Application Requirements: Application, essay, financial need analysis, references, transcript, work samples. *Deadline:* February 22.

Contact: Angie Summers, Scholarships Coordinator
Texas Gridiron Club, Inc.
709 Houston Street
Arlington, TX 76012

TEXAS OUTDOOR WRITERS ASSOCIATION   http://www.towa.org/

TEXAS OUTDOOR WRITERS ASSOCIATION SCHOLARSHIP

Annual merit award available to students attending an accredited Texas college or university preparing for a career which would incorporate communications skills about the outdoors, environmental conservation, or resource management. Minimum 2.5 GPA required. Submit writing/photo samples.

Academic Fields/Career Goals: Communications; Environmental Science; Natural Resources.

Award: Scholarship for use in freshman, sophomore, junior, senior, graduate, or postgraduate years; not renewable. *Number:* 2. *Amount:* $1000–$1500.

Eligibility Requirements: Applicant must be enrolled or expecting to enroll full or part-time at a four-year institution or university; resident of Texas; studying in Texas and must have an interest in writing. Applicant must have 2.5 GPA or higher. Available to U.S. citizens.

Application Requirements: Application, references, transcript, writing/photo samples. *Deadline:* December 31.

Contact: Chester Moore Jr., Scholarship Chair
Texas Outdoor Writers Association
101 Broad Street
Orange, TX 77630
Phone: 409-882-0945
E-mail: cmoorehunt@gt.rr.com

TKE EDUCATIONAL FOUNDATION   http://www.tkefoundation.org

GEORGE W. WOOLERY MEMORIAL SCHOLARSHIP

This scholarship is available to initiated undergraduate members of Tau Kappa Epsilon who are full-time students in good standing pursuing a degree in communications or marketing with a cumulative GPA of 2.50 or higher and a record of leadership within the TKE chapter and on campus. Preference will first be given to members of Beta-Sigma Chapter, but if no qualified candidate applies, the award will be open to any member of TKE.

Academic Fields/Career Goals: Communications.

Award: Scholarship for use in freshman, sophomore, junior, or senior years; not renewable. *Number:* 1. *Amount:* up to $600.

Eligibility Requirements: Applicant must be enrolled or expecting to enroll full-time at a four-year institution or university; male and must have an interest in leadership. Applicant must have 2.5 GPA or higher. Available to U.S. and non-U.S. citizens.

Application Requirements: Application, essay, photo, transcript. *Deadline:* May 12.

Contact: Gary Reed, President/CEO
TKE Educational Foundation
8645 Founders Road
Indianapolis, IN 46131
Phone: 317-872-6533
Fax: 317-875-8353
E-mail: reedga@tke.org

UNITED METHODIST COMMUNICATIONS
http://www.umcom.org/

LEONARD M. PERRYMAN COMMUNICATIONS SCHOLARSHIP FOR ETHNIC MINORITY STUDENTS

One-time award to assist United Methodist ethnic minority students who are college juniors or seniors intending to pursue careers in religious communications. Submit examples of work. Contact for complete information.

Academic Fields/Career Goals: Communications; Journalism; Photojournalism/Photography; Religion/Theology; TV/Radio Broadcasting.

Award: Scholarship for use in freshman, sophomore, junior, or senior years; not renewable. *Number:* 1. *Amount:* $2500.

Eligibility Requirements: Applicant must be Methodist; American Indian/Alaska Native, Asian/Pacific Islander, Black (non-Hispanic), or Hispanic and enrolled or expecting to enroll full-time at a four-year institution or university. Available to U.S. and non-U.S. citizens.

Application Requirements: Application, essay, photo, references, transcript. *Deadline:* March 15.

Contact: Amelia Tucker-Shaw, Coordinator
United Methodist Communications
810 12th Avenue, South
Nashville, TN 37202-4744
Phone: 888-278-4862
E-mail: atucker-shaw@umcom.org

UNITED NEGRO COLLEGE FUND
http://www.uncf.org

BEST BUY ENTERPRISE EMPLOYEE SCHOLARSHIP
• See page 70

C-SPAN SCHOLARSHIP PROGRAM

Scholarship for students majoring in communications, journalism, political science, english, history, or radio/TV/film. Applicant must be undergraduate sophomore or junior attending a UNCF member college or university. Program offers a paid summer internship. Please visit Web site for more information: http://www.uncf.org

Academic Fields/Career Goals: Communications; History; Journalism; Library and Information Sciences; Political Science; TV/Radio Broadcasting.

Award: Scholarship for use in sophomore or junior years. *Number:* varies. *Amount:* $2000.

Eligibility Requirements: Applicant must be Black (non-Hispanic) and enrolled or expecting to enroll at a four-year institution or university. Applicant must have 3.0 GPA or higher. Available to U.S. citizens.

Application Requirements: Application, financial need analysis, FAFSA, Student Aid Report (SAR). *Deadline:* April 7.

Contact: Rebecca Bennett, Director, Program Services
United Negro College Fund
8260 Willow Oaks Corporate Drive
Fairfax, VA 22031-8044
Phone: 800-331-2244
E-mail: rbennett@uncf.org

READER'S DIGEST SCHOLARSHIP

Scholarships for UNCF students majoring in journalism, English or communications. Minimum 3.0 GPA required. Prospective applicants should complete the Student Profile found at Web site: http://www.uncf.org.

Academic Fields/Career Goals: Communications; Journalism; Literature/English/Writing.

Award: Scholarship for use in junior or senior years; not renewable. *Amount:* $5000.

Eligibility Requirements: Applicant must be Black (non-Hispanic) and enrolled or expecting to enroll at a four-year institution or university. Applicant must have 3.0 GPA or higher. Available to U.S. citizens.

Application Requirements: Application, financial need analysis, photo, references, transcript, published writing sample. *Deadline:* November 18.

Contact: Program Services Department
United Negro College Fund
8260 Willow Oaks Corporate Drive
Fairfax, VA 22031

TOYOTA SCHOLARSHIP
• See page 157

VALLEY PRESS CLUB
http://www.valleypressclub.com/

VALLEY PRESS CLUB SCHOLARSHIPS, THE REPUBLICAN SCHOLARSHIP; PHOTOJOURNALISM SCHOLARSHIP, CHANNEL 22 SCHOLARSHIP

Nonrenewable award for graduating high school seniors from northern Connecticut and western Massachusetts interested in television journalism, photojournalism, broadcast journalism, or print journalism. Based on scholarship and financial need Must submit an autobiographical news story, not an essay.

Academic Fields/Career Goals: Communications; Journalism; Photojournalism/Photography; TV/Radio Broadcasting.

Award: Scholarship for use in freshman or senior years; not renewable. *Number:* up to 4. *Amount:* $1000.

Eligibility Requirements: Applicant must be high school student; planning to enroll or expecting to enroll full-time at a two-year or four-year institution or university; resident of Connecticut or Massachusetts and must have an interest in photography/ photogrammetry/filmmaking or writing. Available to U.S. citizens.

Application Requirements: Application, financial need analysis, interview, references, test scores, transcript, autobiographical news story. *Deadline:* April 1.

Contact: Robert McClellan, Scholarship committee chair
Valley Press Club
PO Box 5475
Springfield, MA 01101
Phone: 413-783-3355

VIRGINIA ASSOCIATION OF BROADCASTERS
http://www.vabonline.com

VIRGINIA ASSOCIATION OF BROADCASTERS SCHOLARSHIP AWARD

Scholarships are available to entering juniors and seniors majoring in mass communications-related courses. Must either be a resident of Virginia or go to a Virginia college or university. Must be U.S. citizen and enrolled full-time.

Academic Fields/Career Goals: Communications.

Award: Scholarship for use in junior or senior years; renewable. *Number:* 4. *Amount:* $500–$1000.

Eligibility Requirements: Applicant must be age 20 and enrolled or expecting to enroll full-time at a four-year institution or university. Available to U.S. citizens.

Application Requirements: Application, essay, financial need analysis, transcript. *Deadline:* February 15.

Contact: Ruby Seal, Director of Administration
Virginia Association of Broadcasters
630 Country Green Lane
Charlottesville, VA 22902
Phone: 434-977-3716
Fax: 434-979-2439
E-mail: ruby@easterassociates.com

WASHINGTON NEWS COUNCIL
http://www.wanewscouncil.org/

DICK LARSEN SCHOLARSHIP PROGRAM

One-time award for a student at a Washington state four-year public or private college with a serious interest in a career in communications-journalism, public relations, politics, or a related field. Must be resident of Washington state and U.S. citizen. See Web site for more information.

Academic Fields/Career Goals: Communications; Journalism; Political Science.

Award: Scholarship for use in sophomore, junior, senior, or graduate years; not renewable. *Number:* 1. *Amount:* $1000–$2000.

Eligibility Requirements: Applicant must be enrolled or expecting to enroll full-time at a four-year institution or university; resident of Washington and studying in Washington. Available to U.S. citizens.

Washington News Council (continued)

Application Requirements: Application, essay, financial need analysis, references, transcript, 3 samples of work. *Deadline:* May 31.

Contact: Scholarship Committee
Washington News Council
PO Box 3672
Seattle, WA 98124-3672

HERB ROBINSON SCHOLARSHIP PROGRAM

One-time award to a graduating Washington state high school senior who is entering a four-year public or private college or university in Washington. Must have a serious interest in a career in communications-journalism, public relations, politics or a related field. Must be resident of Washington state and a U.S. citizen. See Web site for more information.

Academic Fields/Career Goals: Communications; Journalism; Political Science.

Award: Scholarship for use in freshman, or graduate years. *Number:* 1. *Amount:* $1000.

Eligibility Requirements: Applicant must be high school student; planning to enroll or expecting to enroll full-time at a four-year institution or university; resident of Washington and studying in Washington. Available to U.S. citizens.

Application Requirements: Application, essay, financial need analysis, references, transcript. *Deadline:* May 31.

Contact: John Hamer, Executive Director
Washington News Council
PO Box 3672
Seattle, WA 98124-3672
Phone: 206-262-9793
Fax: 206-464-7902
E-mail: jhamer@wanewscouncil.org

WMTW-TV 8-AUBURN, MAINE   http://www.wmtw.com

BOB ELLIOT- WMTW-TV 8 JOURNALISM SCHOLARSHIP

Non-renewable scholarship awards $1500 to one graduating high school senior within the WMTW-TV 8 viewing area who plans to major in journalism, communications or a related area of study.

Academic Fields/Career Goals: Communications; Journalism; TV/Radio Broadcasting.

Award: Scholarship for use in freshman year; not renewable. *Number:* 1. *Amount:* up to $1500.

Eligibility Requirements: Applicant must be high school student; planning to enroll or expecting to enroll full-time at an institution or university and resident of Maine. Available to U.S. citizens.

Application Requirements: Application, essay, references, transcript. *Deadline:* March 27.

Contact: David Butta, Bob Elliot-WMTW-TV8 Journalism Scholarship
WMTW-TV 8-Auburn, Maine
WMTW-TV 8, PO Box 8
Auburn, ME 04211-0008
Phone: 207-514-1317

WOMEN GROCERS OF AMERICA   http://www.nationalgrocers.org

MARY MACEY SCHOLARSHIP
• See page 85

WOMEN'S BASKETBALL COACHES ASSOCIATION   http://www.wbca.org

ROBIN ROBERTS/WBCA SPORTS COMMUNICATIONS SCHOLARSHIP AWARD

One-time award for female student athletes who have completed their eligibility and plan to go to graduate school. Must major in communications. Must be nominated by the head coach of women's basketball who is a member of the WBCA.

Academic Fields/Career Goals: Communications; Journalism.

Award: Scholarship for use in freshman, sophomore, junior, senior, graduate, or postgraduate years; not renewable. *Number:* 1. *Amount:* $2000.

Eligibility Requirements: Applicant must be enrolled or expecting to enroll full or part-time at a four-year institution or university; female and must have an interest in athletics/sports. Available to U.S. and non-U.S. citizens.

Application Requirements: Application, references, statistics. *Deadline:* February 7.

Contact: Kristen Miller, Manager of Office Administration and Awards
Women's Basketball Coaches Association
4646 Lawrenceville Highway
Lilburn, GA 30247-3620
Phone: 770-279-8027 Ext. 102
Fax: 770-279-6290
E-mail: kmiller@wbca.org

WYOMING TRUCKING ASSOCIATION

WYOMING TRUCKING ASSOCIATION TRUST FUND SCHOLARSHIP
• See page 158

COMPUTER SCIENCE/DATA PROCESSING

AACE INTERNATIONAL   http://www.aacei.org

AACE INTERNATIONAL COMPETITIVE SCHOLARSHIP
• See page 96

AEA-OREGON COUNCIL   http://aeascholar.ous.edu

AEA- OREGON COUNCIL TECHNOLOGY SCHOLARSHIP PROGRAM
• See page 88

ALICE L. HALTOM EDUCATIONAL FUND   http://www.alhef.org

ALICE L. HALTOM EDUCATIONAL FUND SCHOLARSHIP

Award for students pursuing a career in information and records management. Up to $1000 for those in an associate degree program. Up to $2000 for students in a baccalaureate or advanced degree program. Application deadline is May 1.

Academic Fields/Career Goals: Computer Science/Data Processing; Library and Information Sciences.

Award: Scholarship for use in freshman, sophomore, junior, senior, or graduate years. *Number:* varies. *Amount:* $1000–$2000.

Eligibility Requirements: Applicant must be enrolled or expecting to enroll at a two-year or four-year institution or university. Available to U.S. and non-U.S. citizens.

Application Requirements: Application, references, transcript. *Deadline:* May 1.

Contact: Alice L. Haltom Educational Fund
PO Box 1794
Houston, TX 77251
E-mail: info@alhef.org

AMERICAN FOUNDATION FOR THE BLIND   http://www.afb.org/scholarships.asp

PAUL W. RUCKES SCHOLARSHIP

Scholarship of $1,000 to an undergraduate or graduate student studying in the field of engineering or in computer, physical, or life sciences. For more information and application requirements, please visit www.afb.org/scholarships.asp

Academic Fields/Career Goals: Computer Science/Data Processing; Electrical Engineering/Electronics; Engineering/Technology; Engineering/Technology; Natural Sciences; Near and Middle East Studies; Physical Sciences and Math.

Award: Scholarship for use in freshman, sophomore, junior, or senior years; not renewable. *Number:* 1. *Amount:* up to $1000.

Eligibility Requirements: Applicant must be enrolled or expecting to enroll full or part-time at a two-year or four-year institution or university. Applicant must be visually impaired. Available to U.S. citizens.

Application Requirements: Application, essay, references, transcript, proof of post-secondary acceptance and legal blindness. *Deadline:* March 31.

Contact: Alina Vayntrub, Information Center
American Foundation for the Blind
11 Penn Plaza, Suite 300
New York, NY 10001
Phone: 212-502-7661
Fax: 212-502-7771
E-mail: afbinfo@afb.net

AMERICAN METEOROLOGICAL SOCIETY   http://www.ametsoc.org/AMS

AMERICAN METEOROLOGICAL SOCIETY INDUSTRY UNDERGRADUATE SCHOLARSHIPS
• *See page 89*

AMERICAN SOCIETY FOR INFORMATION SCIENCE AND TECHNOLOGY   http://www.asis.org

JOHN WILEY & SONS BEST JASIST PAPER AWARD

Award of $1500 to recognize the best refereed paper published in the volume year of the JASIT preceding the ASIST annual meeting. John Wiley & Sons, Inc., shall contribute $500 towards travel expenses to attend the ASIST annual meeting. All papers published in the volume year of JASIST preceding the ASIST annual meeting are eligible for the award. No nomination procedure is used for this award. All eligible papers are considered.

Academic Fields/Career Goals: Computer Science/Data Processing; Library and Information Sciences.

Award: Prize for use in freshman, sophomore, junior, senior, graduate, or postgraduate years; not renewable. *Number:* 1. *Amount:* $1500.

Eligibility Requirements: Applicant must be enrolled or expecting to enroll at an institution or university. Available to U.S. citizens.

Application Requirements: *Deadline:* varies.

Contact: Awards Coordinator
American Society for Information Science and Technology
1320 Fenwick Lane, Suite 510
Silver Spring, MD 20910-3602
Phone: 301-495-0900
Fax: 301-495-0810
E-mail: asis@asis.org

ARMED FORCES COMMUNICATIONS AND ELECTRONICS ASSOCIATION, EDUCATIONAL FOUNDATION   http://www.afcea.org

AFCEA SCHOLARSHIP FOR WORKING PROFESSIONALS
• *See page 120*

AFCEA SGT. JEANNETTE L. WINTERS, USMC MEMORIAL SCHOLARSHIP

Applications are requested from men and women currently on active duty in the U.S. Marine Corps or U.S. Marine Corps men and women veterans who are honorably discharged and currently attending four-year colleges or universities in the U.S. Applications will be accepted from qualified sophomore, junior, and senior undergraduate students enrolled either part-time or full-time in an eligible degree program.

Academic Fields/Career Goals: Computer Science/Data Processing; Electrical Engineering/Electronics; Engineering/Technology; Physical Sciences and Math.

Award: Scholarship for use in sophomore, junior, or senior years; not renewable. *Number:* varies. *Amount:* $2000.

Eligibility Requirements: Applicant must be enrolled or expecting to enroll full or part-time at a four-year institution or university. Applicant must have 3.0 GPA or higher. Available to U.S. citizens. Applicant must have served in the Marine Corps.

Application Requirements: Application, references, transcript.
Deadline: September 1.

Contact: Norma Corrales
Armed Forces Communications and Electronics Association, Educational Foundation
4400 Fair Lakes Court
Fairfax, VA 22033
Phone: 703-631-6149
E-mail: scholarship@afcea.org

AFCEA/LOCKHEED MARTIN ORINCON IT SCHOLARSHIP

One-time award for active duty military personnel or veterans, their spouses or dependents who meet the general criteria for the General Paige Scholarship or civilians who meet the general criteria for the General Wickham Scholarship are eligible, provided the school they are attending is an accredited four-year college or university in the greater San Diego, California geographical area. Must be a sophomore or junior at the time of application.

Academic Fields/Career Goals: Computer Science/Data Processing; Electrical Engineering/Electronics; Engineering/Technology; Physical Sciences and Math.

Award: Scholarship for use in sophomore or junior years; not renewable. *Number:* varies. *Amount:* $3000.

Eligibility Requirements: Applicant must be enrolled or expecting to enroll full-time at a four-year institution or university and studying in California. Available to U.S. citizens. Applicant must have general military experience.

Application Requirements: Application, references, transcript.
Deadline: April 1.

Contact: Armed Forces Communications and Electronics Association, Educational Foundation
4400 Fair Lakes Court
Fairfax, VA 22033
Phone: 703-631-6149

ARMED FORCES COMMUNICATIONS AND ELECTRONICS ASSOCIATION EDUCATIONAL FOUNDATION DISTANCE-LEARNING SCHOLARSHIP

Candidates must be enrolled full time in an eligible undergraduate degree-granting online program that is affiliated with a major, accredited 4-year college or university in the U.S. GPA of 3.5 overall required.

Academic Fields/Career Goals: Computer Science/Data Processing; Electrical Engineering/Electronics; Engineering/Technology.

Award: Scholarship for use in sophomore, junior, or senior years; not renewable. *Number:* varies. *Amount:* $1500.

Eligibility Requirements: Applicant must be enrolled or expecting to enroll full-time at a four-year institution or university. Applicant must have 3.5 GPA or higher. Available to U.S. citizens.

Application Requirements: Application, references, transcript.
Deadline: May 1.

Contact: Norma Corrales
Armed Forces Communications and Electronics Association, Educational Foundation
4400 Fair Lakes Court
Fairfax, VA 22033
Phone: 703-631-6149
E-mail: scholarship@afcea.org

ARMED FORCES COMMUNICATIONS AND ELECTRONICS ASSOCIATION GENERAL EMMETT PAIGE SCHOLARSHIP

Award for persons on active duty in the uniformed military services or veterans, and their spouses or dependents. Must be enrolled full-time in four-year, accredited U.S. college or university and studying electrical engineering, computer science, computer engineering, physics, or mathematics. Must have a GPA of at least 3.4. Graduating high school seniors not eligible to apply, but veterans attending college full-time as freshman are eligible. All other applicants must be sophomores or juniors when applying. Spouses or dependents must be a sophomore or junior at the time of application. Deadline: March 1.

Academic Fields/Career Goals: Computer Science/Data Processing; Electrical Engineering/Electronics; Engineering/Technology; Physical Sciences and Math.

Award: Scholarship for use in freshman, sophomore, junior, or senior years; not renewable. *Number:* varies. *Amount:* $2000.

Armed Forces Communications and Electronics Association, Educational Foundation (continued)

Eligibility Requirements: Applicant must be enrolled or expecting to enroll full-time at a four-year institution or university. Available to U.S. citizens. Applicant must have general military experience.

Application Requirements: Application, references, transcript. *Deadline:* March 1.

Contact: Armed Forces Communications and Electronics Association, Educational Foundation
4400 Fair Lakes Court
Fairfax, VA 22033-3899
E-mail: scholarship@afcea.org

ARMED FORCES COMMUNICATIONS AND ELECTRONICS ASSOCIATION GENERAL JOHN A. WICKHAM SCHOLARSHIP

Award for U.S. citizens enrolled full-time in four-year, accredited colleges or universities in the U.S. and studying electrical engineering, computer science, computer engineering, physics, or mathematics. At time of application, must be a sophomore or junior with GPA of at least 3.5. Deadline: April 1.

Academic Fields/Career Goals: Computer Science/Data Processing; Electrical Engineering/Electronics; Engineering/Technology; Physical Sciences and Math.

Award: Scholarship for use in sophomore or junior years; not renewable. *Number:* varies. *Amount:* $2000.

Eligibility Requirements: Applicant must be enrolled or expecting to enroll full-time at a four-year institution or university. Applicant must have 3.5 GPA or higher. Available to U.S. citizens.

Application Requirements: Application, references, transcript. *Deadline:* April 1.

Contact: Armed Forces Communications and Electronics Association, Educational Foundation
4400 Fair Lakes Court
Fairfax, VA 22033-3899
E-mail: scholarship@afcea.org

ARMED FORCES COMMUNICATIONS AND ELECTRONICS ASSOCIATION ROTC SCHOLARSHIP PROGRAM
• *See page 120*

ARRL FOUNDATION, INC.   http://www.arrl.org/arrlf/scholgen.html

PHD ARA SCHOLARSHIP
• *See page 179*

WILLIAM R. GOLDFARB MEMORIAL SCHOLARSHIP
• *See page 145*

ASSOCIATION FOR IRON AND STEEL TECHNOLOGY   http://www.aist.org

ASSOCIATION FOR IRON AND STEEL TECHNOLOGY OHIO VALLEY CHAPTER SCHOLARSHIP
• *See page 135*

ASSOCIATION FOR WOMEN IN COMPUTING— HOUSTON   http://www.awchouston.org

KATHI BOWLES SCHOLARSHIP FOR WOMEN IN COMPUTING

Award of one or more scholarships for women interested in pursuing a technology degree who are graduating from high school, currently enrolled in a technology program at an accredited four year university or pursuing a master's degree. Award is of $7000. Minimum GPA of 3.0 required. Must be a U.S. citizen or permanent resident. Deadline is March 31.

Academic Fields/Career Goals: Computer Science/Data Processing; Engineering/Technology.

Award: Scholarship for use in freshman, sophomore, junior, or senior years; not renewable. *Number:* 1–2. *Amount:* up to $7000.

Eligibility Requirements: Applicant must be enrolled or expecting to enroll full-time at a four-year institution and female. Applicant must have 3.0 GPA or higher. Available to U.S. citizens.

Application Requirements: Application, essay, resume, references, transcript. *Deadline:* March 31.

Contact: Jan Whitehead, Scholarship Committee
Association for Women in Computing— Houston
PO Box 421316
Houston, TX 77242-1316
Phone: 713-222-0955
E-mail: scholarship@awchouston.org

ASSOCIATION FOR WOMEN IN SCIENCE EDUCATIONAL FOUNDATION   http://www.awis.org/ed_foundation.html

ASSOCIATION FOR WOMEN IN SCIENCE COLLEGE SCHOLARSHIP
• *See page 86*

ASTRONAUT SCHOLARSHIP FOUNDATION   http://www.astronautscholarship.org

ASTRONAUT SCHOLARSHIP FOUNDATION
• *See page 92*

BARRY M. GOLDWATER SCHOLARSHIP AND EXCELLENCE IN EDUCATION FOUNDATION   http://www.act.org/goldwater

BARRY M. GOLDWATER SCHOLARSHIP AND EXCELLENCE IN EDUCATION PROGRAM
• *See page 92*

BUSINESS AND PROFESSIONAL WOMEN'S FOUNDATION   http://www.bpwusa.org

BPW CAREER ADVANCEMENT SCHOLARSHIP PROGRAM FOR WOMEN
• *See page 136*

CATCHING THE DREAM

MATH, ENGINEERING, SCIENCE, BUSINESS, EDUCATION, COMPUTERS SCHOLARSHIPS
• *See page 145*

TRIBAL BUSINESS MANAGEMENT PROGRAM (TBM)
• *See page 55*

CENTER FOR SCHOLARSHIP ADMINISTRATION   http://www.scholarshipprograms.org

BANK OF AMERICA ADA ABILITIES SCHOLARSHIP
• *See page 56*

CENTRAL INTELLIGENCE AGENCY   http://www.cia.gov

CENTRAL INTELLIGENCE AGENCY UNDERGRADUATE SCHOLARSHIP PROGRAM
• *See page 56*

EAST LOS ANGELES COMMUNITY UNION (TELACU) EDUCATION FOUNDATION   http://www.telacu.com

LINC TELACU ENGINEERING AWARD
• *See page 163*

ELECTRONIC DOCUMENT SYSTEMS FOUNDATION   http://www.edsf.org

ELECTRONIC DOCUMENT SYSTEMS FOUNDATION SCHOLARSHIP AWARDS
• *See page 180*

GRAND RAPIDS COMMUNITY FOUNDATION   http://www.grfoundation.org

ECONOMIC CLUB OF GRAND RAPIDS BUSINESS STUDY ABROAD SCHOLARSHIP
• *See page 62*

GREAT LAKES COMMISSION
http://www.glc.org

CAROL A. RATZA MEMORIAL SCHOLARSHIP
• See page 138

HAWAIIAN LODGE, F.& A. M.
http://www.hawaiianlodge.org/

HAWAIIAN LODGE SCHOLARSHIPS
• See page 99

HISPANIC COLLEGE FUND, INC.
http://www.hispanicfund.org

DENNY'S/HISPANIC COLLEGE FUND SCHOLARSHIP
• See page 62

ICI EDUCATIONAL FOUNDATION SCHOLARSHIP PROGRAM
• See page 62

LOCKHEED MARTIN SCHOLARSHIP PROGRAM
• See page 164

M & T BANK/ HISPANIC COLLEGE FUND SCHOLARSHIP PROGRAM
• See page 63

NATIONAL HISPANIC EXPLORERS SCHOLARSHIP PROGRAM
• See page 93

HISPANIC ENGINEER NATIONAL ACHIEVEMENT AWARDS CORPORATION (HENAAC)
http://www.henaac.org

HISPANIC ENGINEER NATIONAL ACHIEVEMENT AWARDS CORPORATION SCHOLARSHIP PROGRAM
• See page 122

HISPANIC SCHOLARSHIP FUND
http://www.hsf.net

HSF/SOCIETY OF HISPANIC PROFESSIONAL ENGINEERS, INC. SCHOLARSHIP PROGRAM
• See page 174

HSF/TOYOTA SCHOLARSHIP PROGRAM
• See page 149

INNOVATION AND SCIENCE COUNCIL OF BRITISH COLUMBIA
http://www.scbc.org

PAUL AND HELEN TRUSSEL SCIENCE AND TECHNOLOGY SCHOLARSHIP
• See page 93

INTERNATIONAL COMMUNICATIONS INDUSTRIES FOUNDATION
http://www.infocomm.org/foundation

ICIF SCHOLARSHIP FOR DEPENDENTS OF MEMBER ORGANIZATIONS
• See page 181

INTERNATIONAL COMMUNICATIONS INDUSTRIES FOUNDATION AV SCHOLARSHIP
• See page 182

LOS ANGELES COUNCIL OF BLACK PROFESSIONAL ENGINEERS
http://www.lablackengineers.org

AL-BEN SCHOLARSHIP FOR ACADEMIC INCENTIVE
• See page 164

AL-BEN SCHOLARSHIP FOR PROFESSIONAL MERIT
• See page 165

AL-BEN SCHOLARSHIP FOR SCHOLASTIC ACHIEVEMENT
• See page 165

MARYLAND ASSOCIATION OF PRIVATE COLLEGES AND CAREER SCHOOLS
http://www.mapccs.org

MARYLAND ASSOCIATION OF PRIVATE COLLEGES AND CAREER SCHOOLS SCHOLARSHIP
• See page 150

MICRON TECHNOLOGY FOUNDATION, INC.
http://www.micron.com

MICRON SCIENCE AND TECHNOLOGY SCHOLARS PROGRAM
• See page 165

NASA IDAHO SPACE GRANT CONSORTIUM
http://isgc.uidaho.edu

NASA IDAHO SPACE GRANT CONSORTIUM SCHOLARSHIP PROGRAM
• See page 94

NASA MINNESOTA SPACE GRANT CONSORTIUM
http://www.aem.umn.edu/msgc

MINNESOTA SPACE GRANT CONSORTIUM
• See page 124

NASA MONTANA SPACE GRANT CONSORTIUM
http://www.spacegrant.montana.edu

MONTANA SPACE GRANT SCHOLARSHIP PROGRAM
• See page 125

NASA NEBRASKA SPACE GRANT CONSORTIUM
http://nasa.unomaha.edu

NASA NEBRASKA SPACE GRANT
• See page 125

NASA NEVADA SPACE GRANT CONSORTIUM
http://www.unr.edu/spacegrant

UNIVERSITY AND COMMUNITY COLLEGE SYSTEM OF NEVADA NASA SPACE GRANT AND FELLOWSHIP PROGRAM
• See page 125

NASA WEST VIRGINIA SPACE GRANT CONSORTIUM
http://www.nasa.wvu.edu

WEST VIRGINIA SPACE GRANT CONSORTIUM UNDERGRADUATE SCHOLARSHIP PROGRAM
• See page 126

NASA/MARYLAND SPACE GRANT CONSORTIUM
http://www.mdspacegrant.org

NASA MARYLAND SPACE GRANT CONSORTIUM UNDERGRADUATE SCHOLARSHIPS
• See page 139

NATIONAL ASSOCIATION FOR THE ADVANCEMENT OF COLORED PEOPLE
http://www.naacp.org

LOUIS STOKES SCIENCE AND TECHNOLOGY AWARD
• See page 139

NATIONAL ASSOCIATION OF WATER COMPANIES-NEW JERSEY CHAPTER

NATIONAL ASSOCIATION OF WATER COMPANIES-NEW JERSEY CHAPTER SCHOLARSHIP
• See page 139

NATIONAL FEDERATION OF THE BLIND
http://www.nfb.org

NATIONAL FEDERATION OF THE BLIND COMPUTER SCIENCE SCHOLARSHIP

One-time award for students who are legally blind and studying computer science. Must submit recommendation from state officer of National Federation of the Blind. Award based on financial need, minimum 3.5 GPA, scholarship, and community service. Must attend school in U.S.

Academic Fields/Career Goals: Computer Science/Data Processing.

Award: Scholarship for use in freshman, sophomore, junior, or senior years; not renewable. *Number:* 1. *Amount:* $3000.

National Federation of the Blind (continued)

Eligibility Requirements: Applicant must be enrolled or expecting to enroll at an institution or university. Applicant or parent of applicant must have employment or volunteer experience in community service. Applicant must be visually impaired. Applicant must have 3.5 GPA or higher. Available to U.S. and non-U.S. citizens.

Application Requirements: Application, autobiography, essay, financial need analysis, references, transcript. *Deadline:* March 31.

Contact: Peggy Elliot, Chairman, Scholarship Committee
National Federation of the Blind
805 5th Avenue
Grinnell, IA 50112
Phone: 641-236-3366

NATIONAL INSTITUTE OF GENERAL MEDICAL SCIENCES, NATIONAL INSTITUTE OF HEALTH   http://www.nigms.nih.gov

MARC UNDERGRADUATE STUDENT TRAINING IN ACADEMIC RESEARCH U*STAR AWARDS
• See page 140

NATIONAL INVENTORS HALL OF FAME   http://www.invent.org

COLLEGIATE INVENTORS COMPETITION - GRAND PRIZE
• See page 95

COLLEGIATE INVENTORS COMPETITION FOR UNDERGRADUATE STUDENTS
• See page 95

NATIONAL SECURITY AGENCY   http://www.nsa.gov

NATIONAL SECURITY AGENCY STOKES EDUCATIONAL SCHOLARSHIP PROGRAM

Renewable awards for high school students planning to attend a four-year undergraduate institution to study foreign languages, computer science, math, electrical engineering, or computer engineering. Must be at least 16 to apply. Must be a U.S. citizen. Minimum 3.0 GPA required, and minimum SAT score of 1100. For application visit Web site: http://www.nsa.gov/programs/employ/index.html.

Academic Fields/Career Goals: Computer Science/Data Processing; Electrical Engineering/Electronics; Foreign Language; Physical Sciences and Math.

Award: Scholarship for use in freshman, sophomore, junior, or senior years; renewable. *Number:* 10–30. *Amount:* varies.

Eligibility Requirements: Applicant must be high school student; age 16 and planning to enroll or expecting to enroll full-time at a four-year institution. Applicant must have 3.0 GPA or higher. Available to U.S. citizens.

Application Requirements: Application, essay, interview, resume, references, test scores, transcript. *Deadline:* November 30.

Contact: Ceil O'Connor, Program Manager
National Security Agency
Attn: STOKES, 9800 Savage Road, Suite 6779
Fort Meade, MD 20755-6779
Phone: 866-672-4473
Fax: 410-854-3002
E-mail: cmoconn@nsa.gov

OREGON STUDENT ASSISTANCE COMMISSION   http://www.osac.state.or.us

HOWARD VOLLUM AMERICAN INDIAN SCHOLARSHIP

Renewable award for American-Indian residents of Clackamas, Multnomah, or Washington County in Oregon, or of Clark County in Washington. For study of science, computer science, engineering or mathematics. Must submit certification of tribal enrollment or American-Indian ancestry. Preference for those who have demonstrated commitment to the American-Indian community.

Academic Fields/Career Goals: Computer Science/Data Processing; Engineering/Technology; Physical Sciences and Math.

Award: Scholarship for use in freshman, sophomore, junior, or senior years; renewable. *Number:* 5. *Amount:* $3000.

Eligibility Requirements: Applicant must be American Indian/Alaska Native; enrolled or expecting to enroll at an institution or university and resident of Oregon or Washington. Available to U.S. citizens.

Application Requirements: Application, essay, transcript, Tribal enrollment card, Johnson O'Malley Student Eligibility Form. *Deadline:* March 1.

Contact: Director of Grant Programs
Oregon Student Assistance Commission
1500 Valley River Drive, Suite 100
Eugene, OR 97401-7020
Phone: 800-452-8807 Ext. 7395

MENTOR GRAPHICS SCHOLARSHIP

One-time award for computer science, computer engineering, or electrical engineering majors entering junior or senior year at a four-year institution. Preference for one award to female, African-American, Native-American, or Hispanic applicant.

Academic Fields/Career Goals: Computer Science/Data Processing; Electrical Engineering/Electronics.

Award: Scholarship for use in junior or senior years; not renewable. *Number:* 4. *Amount:* $2000.

Eligibility Requirements: Applicant must be enrolled or expecting to enroll full-time at a four-year institution or university and resident of Oregon. Available to U.S. citizens.

Application Requirements: Application, essay, financial need analysis, references, transcript, activity chart. *Deadline:* March 1.

Contact: Director of Grant Programs
Oregon Student Assistance Commission
1500 Valley River Drive, Suite 100
Eugene, OR 97401-7020
Phone: 800-452-8807 Ext. 7395

ROBERT H. MOLLOHAN FAMILY CHARITABLE FOUNDATION, INC.   http://www.mollohanfoundation.org

HIGH TECHNOLOGY SCHOLARS PROGRAM
• See page 141

ROYAL BANK NATIVE STUDENTS AWARDS PROGRAM   http://www.rbc.com

ROYAL BANK ABORIGINAL STUDENT AWARDS
• See page 153

SOCIETY OF WOMEN ENGINEERS   http://www.swe.org

AGILENT MENTORING SCHOLARSHIP

One $1000 scholarship for undergraduate sophomore or junior studying biological engineering, computer engineering, computer science, electrical engineering, or mechanical engineering.

Academic Fields/Career Goals: Computer Science/Data Processing; Electrical Engineering/Electronics; Engineering/Technology; Mechanical Engineering.

Award: Scholarship for use in sophomore or junior years; not renewable. *Number:* 1. *Amount:* $1000.

Eligibility Requirements: Applicant must be enrolled or expecting to enroll full-time at a four-year institution or university and female. Applicant must have 3.0 GPA or higher. Available to U.S. citizens.

Application Requirements: Application. *Deadline:* February 1.

Contact: Kim Wheeler
E-mail: hq@swe.org

DELL COMPUTER CORPORATION SCHOLARSHIPS

Awarded to entering female juniors and seniors majoring in computer science, computer engineering, electrical engineering, or mechanical engineering who demonstrate financial need and maintain a minimum 3.0 GPA. Deadline: February 1.

Academic Fields/Career Goals: Computer Science/Data Processing; Electrical Engineering/Electronics; Engineering/Technology; Mechanical Engineering.

Award: Scholarship for use in junior or senior years; not renewable. *Number:* 2. *Amount:* $2250.

Eligibility Requirements: Applicant must be enrolled or expecting to enroll at a four-year institution or university and female. Applicant must have 3.0 GPA or higher. Available to U.S. and non-U.S. citizens.

Application Requirements: Application, essay, financial need analysis, references, self-addressed stamped envelope, test scores, transcript. *Deadline:* February 1.

Contact: Suman Pa, Program Coordinator
Society of Women Engineers
230 E Ohio Street, Suite 400
Chicago, IL 60611-3265
Phone: 312-596-5223
Fax: 312-644-8557
E-mail: suman.patil@swe.org

GUIDANT CORPORATION SCHOLARSHIP

Two $5000 scholarships available to undergraduate seniors majoring in chemical engineering, computer engineering, computer science, electrical engineering, industrial engineering, mechanical engineering, manufacturing engineering, and materials science and engineering.

Academic Fields/Career Goals: Computer Science/Data Processing; Electrical Engineering/Electronics; Engineering/Technology; Engineering-Related Technologies; Materials Science, Engineering, and Metallurgy; Mechanical Engineering.

Award: Scholarship for use in senior year; not renewable. *Number:* 2. *Amount:* $5000.

Eligibility Requirements: Applicant must be enrolled or expecting to enroll full-time at a four-year institution or university and female. Applicant must have 3.0 GPA or higher. Available to U.S. citizens.

Application Requirements: Application. *Deadline:* February 1.

Contact: Suman Pa, Program Coordinator
Society of Women Engineers
230 E Ohio Street, Suite 400
Chicago, IL 60611-3265
Phone: 312-596-5223
Fax: 312-644-8557
E-mail: suman.patil@swe.org

LYDIA I. PICKUP MEMORIAL SCHOLARSHIP

Available to female sophomore, junior, or senior undergraduate student or graduate student. For graduate education to advance applicant's career in engineering or computer science. Minimum 3.0 GPA required. Deadline: February 1.

Academic Fields/Career Goals: Computer Science/Data Processing; Engineering/Technology.

Award: Scholarship for use in freshman, sophomore, junior, senior, or graduate years; not renewable. *Number:* 1. *Amount:* $2000.

Eligibility Requirements: Applicant must be enrolled or expecting to enroll at a four-year institution or university and female. Applicant must have 3.0 GPA or higher. Available to U.S. citizens.

Application Requirements: Application, references, self-addressed stamped envelope, transcript. *Deadline:* February 1.

Contact: Suman Pa, Program Coordinator
Society of Women Engineers
230 E Ohio Street, Suite 400
Chicago, IL 60611-3265
Phone: 312-596-5223
Fax: 312-644-8557
E-mail: suman.patil@swe.org

MICROSOFT CORPORATION SCHOLARSHIPS

Scholarships for female computer engineering or computer science students in sophomore, junior, senior year, or first year master's degree students. Must exhibit career interest in the field of computer software. Minimum 3.5 GPA required. Deadline: February 1.

Academic Fields/Career Goals: Computer Science/Data Processing.

Award: Scholarship for use in sophomore, junior, senior, or graduate years; renewable. *Number:* 2. *Amount:* $2500.

Eligibility Requirements: Applicant must be enrolled or expecting to enroll at a four-year institution or university and female. Applicant must have 3.5 GPA or higher. Available to U.S. citizens.

Application Requirements: Application, essay, references, self-addressed stamped envelope, test scores, transcript. *Deadline:* February 1.

Contact: Suman Pa, Program Coordinator
Society of Women Engineers
230 E Ohio Street, Suite 400
Chicago, IL 60611-3265
Phone: 312-596-5223
Fax: 312-644-8557
E-mail: suman.patil@swe.org

NORTHROP GRUMMAN CORPORATION SCHOLARSHIPS
• See page 130

SWE BALTIMORE-WASHINGTON SECTION SCHOLARSHIPS

Must be enrolled as an undergraduate or graduate engineering student in an ABET-accredited engineering or computer science within the Baltimore-Washington region. Please see the Web site for more details: http://www.swe-bws.org

Academic Fields/Career Goals: Computer Science/Data Processing; Engineering/Technology.

Award: Scholarship for use in freshman, sophomore, junior, senior, or graduate years; not renewable. *Number:* 5. *Amount:* varies.

Eligibility Requirements: Applicant must be enrolled or expecting to enroll at a four-year institution or university; female and studying in District of Columbia, Maryland, or Virginia. Applicant must have 3.0 GPA or higher. Available to U.S. citizens.

Application Requirements: Application, essay, photo, references, transcript. *Deadline:* March 1.

Contact: Kathleen Hufnagel, Scholarship Chair
Society of Women Engineers
1601 Barnstead Drive
Reston, VA 20194
E-mail: scholarships@swe-bws.org

SWE BATON ROUGE SECTION SCHOLARSHIPS

Applicant must be planning to attend college in the following fall semester for engineering or computer science. Applications available from high school guidance counselor.

Academic Fields/Career Goals: Computer Science/Data Processing; Engineering/Technology.

Award: Scholarship for use in freshman year; not renewable. *Number:* 6–7. *Amount:* $1000.

Eligibility Requirements: Applicant must be high school student; planning to enroll or expecting to enroll at a four-year institution; female and resident of Louisiana. Available to U.S. citizens.

Application Requirements: Application, test scores, transcript. *Deadline:* varies.

Contact: Donna Scott, Scholarship Chair
Phone: 225-473-5801
E-mail: swebrouge@hotmail.com

SWE CALIFORNIA GOLDEN GATE SECTION SCHOLARSHIPS

Scholarships awarded to female entering freshmen pursuing degrees in engineering, computer science, physical science, or mathematics. Applicants must be attending high school, or living within the boundaries of the Golden Gate Section. Counties include: San Francisco, Marin, Napa, Sonoma, San Mateo counties and parts of Contra Costa and Alameda counties.

Academic Fields/Career Goals: Computer Science/Data Processing; Engineering/Technology; Physical Sciences and Math.

Award: Scholarship for use in freshman year; not renewable. *Number:* 10–15. *Amount:* $500–$1000.

Eligibility Requirements: Applicant must be high school student; planning to enroll or expecting to enroll at an institution or university; female and resident of California. Available to U.S. citizens.

Application Requirements: Application, essay, references. *Deadline:* April 19.

Society of Women Engineers (continued)

Contact: Lisa M. Duncan, SWE-GGS Scholarship Chair
Society of Women Engineers
2625 Alcatraz Avenue, PO Box 356
Berkeley, CA 94705
Phone: 510-242-2554

SWE CONNECTICUT SECTION JEAN R. BEERS SCHOLARSHIP

Scholarship awarded to undergraduate sophomore, junior, or senior pursuing Bachelor of Science degree in engineering, mathematics, computers, or science. Applicant must attend school or live within the boundaries of the Connecticut Section.

Academic Fields/Career Goals: Computer Science/Data Processing; Engineering/Technology; Physical Sciences and Math.

Award: Scholarship for use in freshman, sophomore, junior, or senior years; not renewable. *Number:* varies. *Amount:* $1500.

Eligibility Requirements: Applicant must be enrolled or expecting to enroll at a four-year institution or university; female and resident of Connecticut. Available to U.S. citizens.

Application Requirements: Application, essay, financial need analysis. *Deadline:* January 31.

Contact: SWE-CT Scholarship Committee Program Chair
Society of Women Engineers
PO Box 305
Greens Farms, CT 06838
E-mail: swect@sbcglobal.net

SWE GREATER NEW ORLEANS SECTION SCHOLARSHIP

Scholarships available to women pursuing baccalaureate or graduate degree in an ABET accredited or SWE approved schools for engineering, or CSAB/ABET accredited schools, or SWE approved schools for computer science. Available to students from the following parishes: Jefferson, Lafourche, Orleans, Plaqremines, St. Bernard, St. Charles, St. James, St. John, St. Tammany, Tangipahoa, or Terrebonne.

Academic Fields/Career Goals: Computer Science/Data Processing; Engineering/Technology.

Award: Scholarship for use in freshman, sophomore, junior, senior, or graduate years; not renewable. *Number:* 1. *Amount:* varies.

Eligibility Requirements: Applicant must be enrolled or expecting to enroll at a four-year institution or university; female and resident of Louisiana. Available to U.S. citizens.

Application Requirements: Application. *Deadline:* March 31.

Contact: Jaime Lewis
Phone: 504-465-6827

SOCIETY OF WOMEN ENGINEERS - DALLAS SECTION   http://www.dallaswe.org

NATIONAL SOCIETY OF WOMEN ENGINEERS SCHOLARSHIPS

Financial assistance for women admitted to accredited baccalaureate or graduate programs in preparation for careers in engineering, engineering technology and computer science. Minimum GPA of 3.5 for freshman applicants and 3.0 for sophomore, junior, senior, and graduate applicants. Application deadline is May 15.

Academic Fields/Career Goals: Computer Science/Data Processing; Engineering/Technology.

Award: Scholarship for use in freshman, sophomore, junior, or senior years. *Amount:* $1000.

Eligibility Requirements: Applicant must be enrolled or expecting to enroll full-time at a two-year or four-year institution or university and female. Available to U.S. citizens.

Application Requirements: Application, essay, references, transcript, statement of acceptance or good standing. *Deadline:* May 15.

Contact: Scholarship Selection Committee, Society of Women Engineers
Society of Women Engineers - Dallas Section
230 East Ohio Street, Suite 400
Chicago, IL 60611-3265
E-mail: scholarshipapplication@swe.org

SOCIETY OF WOMEN ENGINEERS - ROCKY MOUNTAIN SECTION   http://www.swe.org

SOCIETY OF WOMEN ENGINEERS-ROCKY MOUNTAIN SECTION SCHOLARSHIP PROGRAM

One-time award for female high school seniors in Colorado and Wyoming who intend to enroll in engineering or computer science at an ABET-accredited college or university in those states. Female college students who have already enrolled in those programs may also apply. For more information visit http://www.swe.org and look for local scholarships. Deadline is February 1.

Academic Fields/Career Goals: Computer Science/Data Processing; Engineering/Technology.

Award: Scholarship for use in freshman, sophomore, junior, senior, or graduate years; not renewable. *Number:* 3–5. *Amount:* $500–$1000.

Eligibility Requirements: Applicant must be enrolled or expecting to enroll full-time at a four-year institution or university; female; resident of Colorado or Wyoming and studying in Colorado or Wyoming. Applicant must have 3.5 GPA or higher. Available to U.S. and non-U.S. citizens.

Application Requirements: Application, essay, resume, references, test scores, transcript. *Deadline:* February 1.

Contact: Barbara Kontogiannis, SWE-RMS Scholarship Chair
Society of Women Engineers - Rocky Mountain Section
8646 South Cresthill Lane
Highlands Ranch, CO 80130-3969
Phone: 303-971-5213
E-mail: barbekon@stanfordalumni.org

SOCIETY OF WOMEN ENGINEERS - TWIN TIERS SECTION   http://www.swetwintiers.org

SOCIETY OF WOMEN ENGINEERS - TWIN TIERS SECTION SCHOLARSHIP

Applicants must reside or attend school in the Twin Tiers SWE section of New York. This is limited to zip codes that begin with 148, 149, 169 and residents of Bradford County, Pennsylvania. Applicant must be accepted or enrolled in an undergraduate degree program in engineering or computer science at an ABET-, CSAB- or SWE-accredited school. Please refer to Web site for specific details http://www.swetwintiers.org/

Academic Fields/Career Goals: Computer Science/Data Processing; Engineering/Technology.

Award: Scholarship for use in freshman, sophomore, or junior years; not renewable. *Number:* 5. *Amount:* $1500.

Eligibility Requirements: Applicant must be enrolled or expecting to enroll at an institution or university and female. Available to U.S. citizens.

Application Requirements: Application, essay, references, self-addressed stamped envelope, transcript, letter of acceptance, resume, personal information, achievements. *Deadline:* March 25.

Contact: Valerie Mis, Scholarship Chair
Society of Women Engineers - Twin Tiers Section
PO Box 798
Corning, NY 14830
Phone: 607-974-8846
E-mail: misvr@corning.com

SOUTH DAKOTA RETAILERS ASSOCIATION   http://www.sdra.org

SOUTH DAKOTA RETAILERS ASSOCIATION SCHOLARSHIP PROGRAM

• See page 69

TEXAS DEPARTMENT OF TRANSPORTATION   http://www.dot.state.tx.us

CONDITIONAL GRANT PROGRAM

• See page 176

UNITED DAUGHTERS OF THE CONFEDERACY

http://www.hqudc.org

WALTER REED SMITH SCHOLARSHIP
• See page 154

UNITED NEGRO COLLEGE FUND

http://www.uncf.org

ACCENTURE SCHOLARSHIP

Applicant must be enrolled at one of the following schools: Morehouse College, Spelman College, Howard University, Florida A&M, North Carolina A&T, and Prairie View A&M University. Please visit Web site for more information: http://www.uncf.org

Academic Fields/Career Goals: Computer Science/Data Processing; Engineering/Technology.

Award: Scholarship for use in sophomore or junior years; not renewable. *Number:* 5. *Amount:* $2000.

Eligibility Requirements: Applicant must be enrolled or expecting to enroll at a four-year institution or university. Applicant must have 3.0 GPA or higher. Available to U.S. citizens.

Application Requirements: Application, financial need analysis, FAFSA, Student Aid Report (SAR). *Deadline:* varies.

Contact: Rebecca Bennett, Director, Program Services
United Negro College Fund
8260 Willow Oaks Corporate Drive
Fairfax, VA 22031-8044
Phone: 800-331-2244
E-mail: rbennett@uncf.org

BOOZ, ALLEN & HAMILTON/WILLIAM F. STASIOR INTERNSHIP
• See page 154

CARDINAL HEALTH SCHOLARSHIP
• See page 70

CARGILL SCHOLARSHIP PROGRAM
• See page 70

CISCO/UNCF SCHOLARS PROGRAM

Scholarship provides financial support for African-American electrical engineering or computer science majors attending specific UNCF member college or university. Minimum 3.2 GPA required. Prospective applicants should complete the Student Profile found at Web site: http://www.uncf.org

Academic Fields/Career Goals: Computer Science/Data Processing; Electrical Engineering/Electronics.

Award: Scholarship for use in sophomore year; not renewable. *Amount:* $4000.

Eligibility Requirements: Applicant must be Black (non-Hispanic) and enrolled or expecting to enroll full-time at a four-year institution or university. Available to U.S. citizens.

Application Requirements: Application, financial need analysis. *Deadline:* April 15.

Contact: Rebecca Bennett, Director, Program Services
United Negro College Fund
8260 Willow Oaks Corporate Drive
Fairfax, VA 22031-8044
Phone: 800-331-2244
E-mail: rbennett@uncf.org

CON EDISON SCHOLARSHIP
• See page 70

DELL/UNCF CORPORATE SCHOLARS PROGRAM
• See page 155

EMERSON ELECTRIC COMPANY SCHOLARSHIP
• See page 71

FLOWERS INDUSTRIES SCHOLARSHIP
• See page 155

FORD/UNCF CORPORATE SCHOLARS PROGRAM
• See page 71

KODAK ENGINEERING EXCELLENCE PROGRAM SCHOLARSHIP

Scholarships for engineering or computer science majors attending a UNCF member college or university. Minimum 3.0 GPA required. Prospective applicants should complete the Student Profile found at Web site: http://www.uncf.org.

Academic Fields/Career Goals: Computer Science/Data Processing; Engineering/Technology.

Award: Scholarship for use in junior year; not renewable. *Amount:* $4800.

Eligibility Requirements: Applicant must be Black (non-Hispanic) and enrolled or expecting to enroll at a four-year institution or university. Applicant must have 3.0 GPA or higher. Available to U.S. citizens.

Application Requirements: Application, financial need analysis, photo, resume, references, transcript. *Deadline:* February 24.

Contact: Rebecca Bennett, Director, Program Services
United Negro College Fund
8260 Willow Oaks Corporate Drive
Fairfax, VA 22031-8044
Phone: 800-331-2244
E-mail: rbennett@uncf.org

MALCOLM PIRNIE, INC. SCHOLARS PROGRAM
• See page 169

MAYTAG COMPANY SCHOLARSHIP
• See page 155

NORTHEAST UTILITIES SYSTEM SCHOLARSHIP PROGRAM
• See page 156

PRINCIPAL FINANCIAL GROUP SCHOLARSHIPS
• See page 156

SBC FOUNDATION SCHOLARSHIP
• See page 156

SBC PACIFIC BELL FOUNDATION SCHOLARSHIP
• See page 156

SPRINT SCHOLARSHIP/INTERNSHIP
• See page 71

TRW INFORMATION TECHNOLOGY MINORITY SCHOLARSHIP

Award for sophomore and junior minority college students majoring in engineering, computer science, and other information sciences at Howard University, George Mason University, Morgan State, Virginia Polytechnic Institute, or Pennsylvania State. Must have 3.0 GPA. Please visit Web site for more information: http://www.uncf.org

Academic Fields/Career Goals: Computer Science/Data Processing; Engineering/Technology.

Award: Scholarship for use in sophomore, junior, or senior years; renewable. *Number:* varies. *Amount:* $3000.

Eligibility Requirements: Applicant must be Black (non-Hispanic) and enrolled or expecting to enroll at a four-year institution or university. Applicant must have 3.0 GPA or higher. Available to U.S. citizens.

Application Requirements: Application, financial need analysis, FAFSA, Student Aid Report (SAR). *Deadline:* varies.

Contact: Rebecca Bennett, Director, Program Services
United Negro College Fund
8260 Willow Oaks Corporate Drive
Fairfax, VA 22031-8044
Phone: 800-331-2244
E-mail: rbennett@uncf.org

UPS CORPORATE SCHOLARS PROGRAM/INTERNSHIP
• See page 157

USENIX ASSOCIATION SCHOLARSHIP

Applicants should be majors in computer science, or information systems. Students must have 3.5 GPA to qualify. Prospective applicants should complete the Student Profile found at Web site: http://www.uncf.org.

Academic Fields/Career Goals: Computer Science/Data Processing.

United Negro College Fund (continued)

Award: Scholarship for use in freshman, sophomore, junior, senior, or graduate years; not renewable. *Amount:* up to $10,000.

Eligibility Requirements: Applicant must be Black (non-Hispanic) and enrolled or expecting to enroll at a four-year institution or university. Applicant must have 3.5 GPA or higher. Available to U.S. citizens.

Application Requirements: Application, financial need analysis. *Deadline:* Continuous.

Contact: Program Services Department
United Negro College Fund
8260 Willow Oaks Corporate Drive
Fairfax, VA 22031

VIRGINIA BUSINESS AND PROFESSIONAL WOMEN'S FOUNDATION   http://www.bpwva.org

WOMEN IN SCIENCE AND TECHNOLOGY SCHOLARSHIP
• See page 143

WYOMING TRUCKING ASSOCIATION

WYOMING TRUCKING ASSOCIATION TRUST FUND SCHOLARSHIP
• See page 158

XEROX   http://www.xerox.com

TECHNICAL MINORITY SCHOLARSHIP
• See page 169

CONSTRUCTION ENGINEERING/ MANAGEMENT

ELECTROCHEMICAL SOCIETY, INC.   http://www.electrochem.org

DANIEL CUBICCIOTTI STUDENT AWARD OF THE SAN FRANCISCO SECTION OF THE ELECTROCHEMICAL SOCIETY, SPONSORED BY STRUCTURAL INTEGRITY ASSOCIATES
• See page 137

H.H. DOW MEMORIAL STUDENT ACHIEVEMENT AWARD OF THE INDUSTRIAL ELECTROLYSIS AND ELECTROCHEMICAL ENGINEERING DIVISION OF THE ELECTROCHEMICAL SOCIETY, INC.
• See page 137

STUDENT ACHIEVEMENT AWARDS OF THE INDUSTRIAL ELECTROLYSIS AND ELECTROCHEMICAL ENGINEERING DIVISION OF THE ELECTROCHEMICAL SOCIETY, INC.
• See page 137

STUDENT RESEARCH AWARDS OF THE BATTERY DIVISION OF THE ELECTROCHEMICAL SOCIETY, INC.
• See page 137

NATIONAL INSTITUTE OF BUILDING SCIENCES, MULTIHAZARD MITIGATION COUNCIL   http://www.nibs.org

ARCHITECTURE, CONSTRUCTION, AND ENGINEERING MENTOR PROGRAM SCHOLARSHIPS
• See page 101

COSMETOLOGY

JOE FRANCIS HAIRCARE SCHOLARSHIP FOUNDATION   http://www.joefrancis.com

JOE FRANCIS HAIRCARE SCHOLARSHIP PROGRAM

Scholarships are awarded for $1000 each, with a minimum of sixteen scholarships awarded annually. Applicants are evaluated for their potential to successfully complete school, their financial need, and their commitment to a long-term career in cosmetology. The deadline is June 1. Must be U.S. citizen and enrolled in school by Fall of award year.

Academic Fields/Career Goals: Cosmetology.

Award: Scholarship for use in freshman or sophomore years; not renewable. *Number:* 16. *Amount:* $1000.

Eligibility Requirements: Applicant must be enrolled or expecting to enroll full- or part-time at a technical institution. Available to U.S. citizens.

Application Requirements: Application, essay, financial need analysis, references. *Deadline:* June 1.

Contact: Joe Francis Haircare Scholarship Foundation
Joe Francis Haircare Scholarship Foundation
PO Box 50625
Minneapolis, MN 55405
Phone: 651-769-1757

CRIMINAL JUSTICE/CRIMINOLOGY

ALBERTA HERITAGE SCHOLARSHIP FUND/ ALBERTA SCHOLARSHIP PROGRAMS   http://www.alis.gov.ab.ca

ROBERT C. CARSON MEMORIAL BURSARY

Award for Alberta residents who are full-time students enrolled in the second year of either Law Enforcement or Criminal Justice. The qualifying Alberta institutions are: Lethbridge Community College, Mount Royal College, Grant MacEwan College, the University of Calgary or the University of Alberta. Applicant must be nominated by the educational institution they are attending. Preference will be given to non-sponsored aboriginal students. Deadline: October 1.

Academic Fields/Career Goals: Criminal Justice/Criminology; Law Enforcement/Police Administration; Law/Legal Services.

Award: Scholarship for use in sophomore year; not renewable. *Number:* 5. *Amount:* $430.

Eligibility Requirements: Applicant must be Canadian citizen; enrolled or expecting to enroll full-time at an institution or university; resident of Alberta and studying in Alberta. Applicant must have 2.5 GPA or higher.

Application Requirements: Application. *Deadline:* October 1.

Contact: Stuart Dunn, Manager
Alberta Heritage Scholarship Fund/Alberta Scholarship Programs
4th Floor, 9940 106th Street, Box 28000 Station Main
Edmonton, AB T5J 4R4
Canada
Phone: 780-427-8640
Fax: 780-427-1288
E-mail: scholarships@gov.ab.ca

AMERICAN CRIMINAL JUSTICE ASSOCIATION- LAMBDA ALPHA EPSILON   http://www.acjalae.org

AMERICAN CRIMINAL JUSTICE ASSOCIATION-LAMBDA ALPHA EPSILON NATIONAL SCHOLARSHIP

Awarded only to members of the American Criminal Justice Association. One-time award of $100-$400. Members may reapply each year. Must have minimum 3.0 GPA. Must pursue studies in law/legal services, criminal justice/law, or the social sciences. Application deadline is December 31.

Academic Fields/Career Goals: Criminal Justice/Criminology; Law/ Legal Services; Social Sciences.

Award: Scholarship for use in freshman, sophomore, junior, senior, or graduate years; not renewable. *Number:* 9. *Amount:* $100–$400.

Eligibility Requirements: Applicant must be enrolled or expecting to enroll full- or part-time at a two-year or four-year institution or university. Applicant or parent of applicant must be member of American Criminal Justice Association. Applicant must have 3.0 GPA or higher. Available to U.S. citizens.

Application Requirements: Application, references, transcript. *Deadline:* December 31.

Contact: Karen Campbell, Executive Secretary
American Criminal Justice Association-Lambda Alpha Epsilon
PO Box 601047
Sacramento, CA 95860-1047
Phone: 916-484-6553
Fax: 916-488-2227
E-mail: acjalae@aol.com

AMERICAN SOCIETY OF CRIMINOLOGY
http://www.ASC41.com

AMERICAN SOCIETY OF CRIMINOLOGY GENE CARTE STUDENT PAPER COMPETITION

Award for full-time undergraduate or graduate students. Must submit a conceptual or empirical paper on a subject directly relating to criminology. Papers must be 7500 words or less. Visit Web site for additional information.

Academic Fields/Career Goals: Criminal Justice/Criminology; Law Enforcement/Police Administration; Law/Legal Services; Social Sciences.

Award: Prize for use in freshman, sophomore, junior, senior, or graduate years; not renewable. *Number:* 3. *Amount:* $200–$500.

Eligibility Requirements: Applicant must be enrolled or expecting to enroll full-time at a four-year institution or university and must have an interest in writing. Available to U.S. citizens.

Application Requirements: Applicant must enter a contest, essay. *Deadline:* April 15.

Contact: William Wells, Crime Studies Center, Southern Illinois University
American Society of Criminology
Mail Code 4504
Carbondale, IL 62901-4504
Phone: 618-453-6362
Fax: 618-453-6377
E-mail: wwells@siu.edu

ASSOCIATION OF CERTIFIED FRAUD EXAMINERS
http://www.acfe.com

RITCHIE-JENNINGS MEMORIAL SCHOLARSHIP
• *See page 55*

CONNECTICUT ASSOCIATION OF WOMEN POLICE

CONNECTICUT ASSOCIATION OF WOMEN POLICE SCHOLARSHIP

Available to Connecticut residents graduating from an accredited high school, entering a college or university in CT as a criminal justice major. The deadline is April 30.

Academic Fields/Career Goals: Criminal Justice/Criminology; Law Enforcement/Police Administration.

Award: Scholarship for use in freshman year; not renewable. *Number:* 1–3. *Amount:* $200–$500.

Eligibility Requirements: Applicant must be high school student; planning to enroll or expecting to enroll full-time at a two-year or four-year institution or university; resident of Connecticut; studying in Connecticut and must have an interest in designated field specified by sponsor. Available to U.S. citizens.

Application Requirements: Application, essay, financial need analysis, references, transcript. *Deadline:* April 30.

Contact: Scholarship Committee
Connecticut Association of Women Police
PO Box 1653
Hartford, CT 06144

INDIANA SHERIFFS' ASSOCIATION
http://www.indianasheriffs.org

INDIANA SHERIFFS' ASSOCIATION SCHOLARSHIP PROGRAM

Applicant must be an Indiana resident majoring in a criminal justice/law enforcement field at an Indiana college or university. Must be a member or dependent child or grandchild of a member of the Indiana Sheriffs' Association. Must be a full time student with at least 12 credit hours.

Academic Fields/Career Goals: Criminal Justice/Criminology; Law Enforcement/Police Administration.

Award: Scholarship for use in freshman, sophomore, junior, or senior years; not renewable. *Number:* up to 40. *Amount:* up to $500.

Eligibility Requirements: Applicant must be enrolled or expecting to enroll full-time at a two-year or four-year institution or university; resident of Indiana and studying in Indiana. Applicant or parent of applicant must be member of Indiana Sheriffs' Association. Available to U.S. citizens.

Application Requirements: Application, essay, test scores, transcript, SAT scores. *Deadline:* April 1.

Contact: Laura Vest, Administrative Assistant
Indiana Sheriffs' Association
PO Box 19127
Indianapolis, IN 46219
Phone: 317-356-3633
Fax: 317-356-3996
E-mail: laura_vest@hotmail.com

MISSOURI SHERIFFS' ASSOCIATION
http://www.mosheriffs.com

JOHN DENNIS SCHOLARSHIP

For college freshmen attending a Missouri college or university majoring in criminal justice. Award is based on financial need. Students must be in upper one-third of their graduating class and participate in extracurricular activities. Must be a Missouri resident.

Academic Fields/Career Goals: Criminal Justice/Criminology.

Award: Scholarship for use in freshman year; not renewable. *Number:* 16. *Amount:* $500.

Eligibility Requirements: Applicant must be high school student; planning to enroll or expecting to enroll full-time at a four-year institution or university; resident of Missouri and studying in Missouri. Applicant must have 3.0 GPA or higher. Available to U.S. citizens.

Application Requirements: Application, essay, financial need analysis, test scores. *Deadline:* January 31.

Contact: Karen Logan, Administrative Assistant
Missouri Sheriffs' Association
6605 Business 50 West
Jefferson City, MO 65109-6307
Phone: 573-635-5925 Ext. 10
Fax: 573-635-2128
E-mail: karen@mosheriffs.com

NATIONAL BLACK POLICE ASSOCIATION
http://www.blackpolice.org

ALPHONSO DEAL SCHOLARSHIP AWARD

One-time award available to students interested in law enforcement or related fields. Must be a graduating high school senior accepted into a college or university and have at least a 2.5 GPA.

Academic Fields/Career Goals: Criminal Justice/Criminology; Law Enforcement/Police Administration; Law/Legal Services; Social Sciences; Social Services.

Award: Scholarship for use in freshman year; not renewable. *Number:* 2. *Amount:* $500.

Eligibility Requirements: Applicant must be high school student and planning to enroll or expecting to enroll full-time at a four-year institution or university. Applicant must have 2.5 GPA or higher. Available to U.S. citizens.

Application Requirements: Application, autobiography, photo, references, transcript, letter of acceptance. *Deadline:* June 1.

Contact: Ronald Hampton, Executive Director
National Black Police Association
3251 Mt. Pleasant Street, NW
Washington, DC 20010-2103
Phone: 202-986-2070
Fax: 202-986-0410
E-mail: nbpanatofc@worldnet.att.net

NORTH CAROLINA POLICE CORPS
http://www.ncpolicecorps.org

NORTH CAROLINA POLICE CORPS SCHOLARSHIP

Selected participants must attend a four-year institution full-time. May receive up to $6667 per year with a maximum of $30,000. Must complete 24-week training course receiving $450 per week while in residence and serve four years in selected law enforcement agency. Must have physical, background investigation, drug test, and psychological evaluation.

Academic Fields/Career Goals: Criminal Justice/Criminology; Law Enforcement/Police Administration.

Award: Scholarship for use in freshman, sophomore, junior, senior, or graduate years; renewable. *Number:* 15–30.

Eligibility Requirements: Applicant must be enrolled or expecting to enroll full-time at a four-year institution or university. Available to U.S. citizens.

Application Requirements: Application, autobiography, essay, interview, photo, references, test scores, transcript. *Deadline:* varies.

Contact: Pat Watson
North Carolina Police Corps
NC Department of Crime Control and Public Safety, 309 Chapanoke Road
Raleigh, NC 27603
Phone: 919-773-2823
Fax: 919-773-2845

NORTH CAROLINA STATE EDUCATION ASSISTANCE AUTHORITY
http://www.ncseaa.edu

NORTH CAROLINA SHERIFFS' ASSOCIATION UNDERGRADUATE CRIMINAL JUSTICE SCHOLARSHIPS

One-time award for full-time North Carolina resident undergraduate students majoring in criminal justice at a University of North Carolina school. Priority given to child of any North Carolina law enforcement officer. Letter of recommendation from county sheriff required.

Academic Fields/Career Goals: Criminal Justice/Criminology; Law Enforcement/Police Administration.

Award: Scholarship for use in freshman, sophomore, junior, or senior years; not renewable. *Number:* up to 10. *Amount:* $1000–$2000.

Eligibility Requirements: Applicant must be enrolled or expecting to enroll full-time at a two-year or four-year institution or university; resident of North Carolina and studying in North Carolina. Applicant or parent of applicant must have employment or volunteer experience in police/firefighting. Available to U.S. citizens.

Application Requirements: Application, financial need analysis, references, transcript, statement of career goals. *Deadline:* Continuous.

Contact: Bill Carswell, Manager of Scholarship and Grant Division
North Carolina State Education Assistance Authority
PO Box 14103
Research Triangle Park, NC 27709
Phone: 919-549-8614
Fax: 919-248-4687
E-mail: carswellb@ncseaa.edu

CULINARY ARTS

AMERICAN ACADEMY OF CHEFS
http://www.acfchefs.org

CHAINE DES ROTISSEURS SCHOLARSHIPS

Scholarship available to exemplary student currently enrolled in an accredited, postsecondary school of culinary arts, or other postsecondary culinary training program acceptable to the AAC.

Academic Fields/Career Goals: Culinary Arts.

Award: Scholarship for use in freshman, sophomore, junior, or senior years. *Amount:* up to $1000.

Eligibility Requirements: Applicant must be enrolled or expecting to enroll full-time at a two-year or four-year institution. Available to U.S. citizens.

Application Requirements: Application, financial need analysis, references, transcript. *Deadline:* December 1.

Contact: John Minniti, President
American Academy of Chefs
180 Center Place Way
St. Augustine, FL 32095
Phone: 904-824-4468

ART INSTITUTES
http://www.artinstitutes.edu

BEST TEEN CHEF CULINARY SCHOLARSHIP COMPETITION

Competition for high school seniors planning to pursue a career in culinary arts at The Art Institutes of their choice. Minimum of 10 semi-finalists will be chosen from each participating Art Institute school to compete in regional cook-offs. Winners will advance to national cook-off competition. Full and partial scholarships awarded. Applicant must be a graduating high school senior with a 2.0 minimum cumulative GPA.

Academic Fields/Career Goals: Culinary Arts.

Award: Scholarship for use in freshman, sophomore, junior, or senior years; renewable. *Number:* 10–18. *Amount:* $2000–$30,000.

Eligibility Requirements: Applicant must be high school student and planning to enroll or expecting to enroll full-time at a technical institution. Available to U.S. citizens.

Application Requirements: Application, applicant must enter a contest, essay, transcript, menu and recipes. *Deadline:* February 11.

Contact: Art Institutes
210 Sixth Avenue, 33rd Floor
Pittsburgh, PA 15222-2603
Phone: 888-542-2600

CAREERS THROUGH CULINARY ARTS PROGRAM, INC.
http://www.ccap.org

CAREERS THROUGH CULINARY ARTS PROGRAM COOKING COMPETITION FOR SCHOLARSHIPS

Cooking competition with finalists receiving a scholarship. Must be a senior in a C-CAP-designated partner high school in Arizona, Tidewater Virginia, or the cities of Boston, Chicago, Los Angeles, New York, Philadelphia or Washington, DC. Must demonstrate mastery of select culinary skills. 25 from each area are chosen as finalists and receive scholarships ranging from $1000 to $78,000.

Academic Fields/Career Goals: Culinary Arts.

Award: Scholarship for use in freshman, sophomore, junior, or senior years; not renewable. *Number:* 88–95. *Amount:* $1000–$78,000.

Eligibility Requirements: Applicant must be high school student; planning to enroll or expecting to enroll full or part-time at a two-year or four-year or technical institution or university and resident of Arizona, California, District of Columbia, Illinois, Massachusetts, New York, Pennsylvania, or Virginia. Available to U.S. and non-U.S. citizens.

Application Requirements: Application, applicant must enter a contest, essay, interview, references, test scores, transcript, cooking competition. *Deadline:* varies.

Contact: Mei Campanella, College Advisor
Careers Through Culinary Arts Program, Inc.
250 West 57th Street, Suite 2015
New York, NY 10107
Phone: 212-974-7111
Fax: 212-974-7117
E-mail: mcampanella@ccapinc.org

CHARLIE TROTTER'S CULINARY EDUCATION FOUNDATION
http://www.charlietrotters.com

CHARLIE TROTTER'S CULINARY EDUCATION SCHOLARSHIP

Scholarships for students who are seeking careers in the culinary arts and working with Chicago-area youth to promote the quest for education as well as an interest in cooking and food. Must be a resident of Illinois. Deadline is May 1.

Academic Fields/Career Goals: Culinary Arts.

Award: Scholarship for use in junior or senior years; not renewable. *Number:* 1.

Eligibility Requirements: Applicant must be enrolled or expecting to enroll full-time at a two-year or four-year institution or university and resident of Illinois. Available to U.S. and non-Canadian citizens.

Application Requirements: Application, essay, references, transcript. *Deadline:* May 1.

Contact: Charlie TrotterÔÇÖs Culinary Education Foundation
Charlie Trotter Culinary Education Foundation
816 West Armitage Avenue
Chicago, IL 60614
Phone: 773-248-6228
Fax: 773-248-6088
E-mail: info@charlietrotters.com

CHEF2CHEF SCHOLARSHIP FUND   http://chef2chef.net

THE CHEF2CHEF CULINARY STUDENT GRANT

Awards to students attending an accredited culinary school or institute. Based on demonstrated financial need, participation in online culinary forum, essay.

Academic Fields/Career Goals: Culinary Arts.

Award: Scholarship for use in freshman, sophomore, junior, or senior years. *Number:* up to 30. *Amount:* up to $1000.

Eligibility Requirements: Applicant must be enrolled or expecting to enroll at a four-year institution or university. Available to U.S. and non-U.S. citizens.

Application Requirements: Application, essay, financial need analysis, references. *Deadline:* varies.

Contact: David Nelson, Program Manager
Chef2Chef Scholarship Fund
1360 Indian Trail Number 13
Attention: Culinary Grant Application
Steamboat Springs, CO 80487
Phone: 970-871-6115
Fax: 480-474-1669
E-mail: dnelson@chef2chef.net

FUTURE CULINARIAN OF AMERICA SCHOLARSHIP FOUNDATION   http://216.170.94.24/contact.html

FUTURE CULINARIAN OF AMERICA SCHOLARSHIP

Scholarships from $3000 to $10,000 awarded on a competitive and needs basis to qualified applicants. All scholarships are available to culinary students who are attending, or who have been accepted by, accredited, postsecondary, degree granting culinary schools and have completed that school's application process.

Academic Fields/Career Goals: Culinary Arts.

Award: Scholarship for use in freshman or sophomore years. *Amount:* $3000–$10,000.

Eligibility Requirements: Applicant must be enrolled or expecting to enroll full-time at a two-year or four-year or technical institution or university. Applicant must have 3.5 GPA or higher. Available to U.S. citizens.

Application Requirements: Application, references, transcript. *Deadline:* varies.

Contact: Future Culinarian of America Scholarship Foundation
PO Box 19249
Birmingham, AL 35219-9249
Phone: 888-211-8150

INTERNATIONAL CAKE EXPLORATION SOCIETE (ICES)   http://www.ices.org

INTERNATIONAL CAKE EXPLORATION SOCIETE SCHOLARSHIP

Scholarships will be paid only to the teacher/schools on the ICES Approved Teacher list. Must be able to work with different types of icing: butter cream, royal, rolled fondant etc.

Academic Fields/Career Goals: Culinary Arts.

Award: Scholarship for use in freshman, sophomore, junior, or senior years. *Number:* 1.

Eligibility Requirements: Applicant must be enrolled or expecting to enroll at a technical institution. Available to U.S. citizens.

Application Requirements: Application, photo, references. *Deadline:* varies.

Contact: Jo Puhak, Scholarship Chairman
International Cake Exploration Societe (ICES)
316 Chalet Drive
Millersville, MD 21108-0561

JAMES BEARD FOUNDATION, INC.   http://www.jamesbeard.org

ALLEN SUSSER SCHOLARSHIP

Scholarships for high-school seniors planning to enroll or students currently enrolled at the Florida Culinary Institute (West Palm Beach), Johnson & Wales University (North Miami, FL), Florida International University (Miami, FL) or the School of Culinary Arts at The Art Institute of Florida (Fort Lauderdale). Must be residents of Dade, Palm Beach, or Broward counties and substantiate residency.

Academic Fields/Career Goals: Culinary Arts.

Award: Scholarship for use in freshman, sophomore, junior, or senior years; not renewable. *Number:* 1. *Amount:* up to $2000.

Eligibility Requirements: Applicant must be enrolled or expecting to enroll full-time at a two-year or technical institution and resident of Florida. Available to U.S. citizens.

Application Requirements: Application, essay, financial need analysis, references, transcript. *Deadline:* April 15.

Contact: Caroline Stuart, Scholarship Director
James Beard Foundation, Inc.
167 West 12th Street
New York, NY 10011
Phone: 212-675-4984 Ext. 311
Fax: 212-645-1438
E-mail: jamesbeardfound@hotmail.com

AMERICAN RESTAURANT SCHOLARSHIP

Scholarships available for students who plan to enroll or are already enrolled at a licensed or accredited culinary school, and are residents of Florida, Kansas, Missouri, or Pennsylvania.

Academic Fields/Career Goals: Culinary Arts.

Award: Scholarship for use in freshman, sophomore, junior, senior, or graduate years; not renewable. *Number:* up to 2. *Amount:* up to $4500.

Eligibility Requirements: Applicant must be enrolled or expecting to enroll full-time at an institution or university and studying in Florida, Kansas, Missouri, or Pennsylvania. Available to U.S. and non-U.S. citizens.

Application Requirements: Application, essay, financial need analysis, references, transcript. *Deadline:* April 15.

Contact: Caroline Stuart, Scholarship Director
James Beard Foundation, Inc.
167 West 12th Street
New York, NY 10011
Phone: 212-675-4984 Ext. 311
Fax: 212-645-1438
E-mail: jamesbeardfound@hotmail.com

CHARLIE TROTTER SCHOLARSHIP

Awards available for students who plan to enroll or are already enrolled at a licensed or accredited culinary school, and reside in Illinois and substantiate residency. Up to two awards of $5000 each and one award of $2000.

Academic Fields/Career Goals: Culinary Arts.

Award: Scholarship for use in freshman, sophomore, junior, or senior years; not renewable. *Number:* up to 3. *Amount:* up to $5000.

Eligibility Requirements: Applicant must be enrolled or expecting to enroll full-time at a technical institution and resident of Illinois. Available to U.S. citizens.

Application Requirements: Application, essay, financial need analysis, references, transcript. *Deadline:* April 15.

James Beard Foundation, Inc. (continued)

Contact: Caroline Stuart, Scholarship Director
James Beard Foundation, Inc.
167 West 12th Street
New York, NY 10011
Phone: 212-675-4984 Ext. 311
Fax: 212-645-1438
E-mail: jamesbeardfound@hotmail.com

CIROC GRAPE CHEFS OF AMERICA CULINARY SCHOLARSHIPS

Scholarships for students enrolled or planning to enroll at a licensed or accredited culinary school. Must be a resident of Chicago, New York, Los Angeles, San Francisco, Miami, or Atlanta and substantiate residency, be at least 21 years of age or older, and not be employees of alcoholic beverage retailers, wholesalers, distributors, or employees of Diageo. Effort will be made to grant at least one (1) award per geographic region.

Academic Fields/Career Goals: Culinary Arts.

Award: Scholarship for use in freshman, sophomore, junior, senior, or graduate years; not renewable. *Number:* up to 6. *Amount:* up to $5000.

Eligibility Requirements: Applicant must be age 21 and enrolled or expecting to enroll full-time at an institution or university. Available to U.S. and non-U.S. citizens.

Application Requirements: Application, essay, financial need analysis, references, transcript. *Deadline:* April 15.

Contact: Caroline Stuart, Scholarship Director
James Beard Foundation, Inc.
167 West 12th Street
New York, NY 10011
Phone: 212-675-4984 Ext. 311
Fax: 212-645-1438
E-mail: jamesbeardfound@hotmail.com

CLAY TRIPLETTE SCHOLARSHIP

Scholarship for deserving students who want to pursue a baking and pastry degree. Up to 2 awards $5,000 per award Applicants must plan to enroll or already be enrolled in an accredited baking or pastry studies program at a licensed or accredited culinary school.

Academic Fields/Career Goals: Culinary Arts.

Award: Scholarship for use in freshman, sophomore, junior, or senior years; not renewable. *Number:* up to 2. *Amount:* up to $5000.

Eligibility Requirements: Applicant must be enrolled or expecting to enroll full-time at a technical institution. Available to U.S. citizens.

Application Requirements: Application, essay, financial need analysis, references, transcript. *Deadline:* April 15.

Contact: Caroline Stuart, Scholarship Director
James Beard Foundation, Inc.
167 West 12th Street
New York, NY 10011
Phone: 212-675-4984 Ext. 311
Fax: 212-645-1438
E-mail: jamesbeardfound@hotmail.com

DESEO AT THE WESTIN SCHOLARSHIP

Scholarship for residents of Arizona who can substantiate residency, who have participated in the Arizona Careers Through Culinary Arts (C-CAP) program, and have been recommended by Arizona C-CAP.

Academic Fields/Career Goals: Culinary Arts.

Award: Scholarship for use in freshman, sophomore, junior, or senior years; not renewable. *Number:* 1. *Amount:* up to $3750.

Eligibility Requirements: Applicant must be enrolled or expecting to enroll full-time at a technical institution. Available to U.S. citizens.

Application Requirements: Application, essay, financial need analysis, references, transcript. *Deadline:* April 15.

Contact: Caroline Stuart, Scholarship Director
James Beard Foundation, Inc.
167 West 12th Street
New York, NY 10011
Phone: 212-675-4984 Ext. 311
Fax: 212-645-1438
E-mail: jamesbeardfound@hotmail.com

GENE HOVIS MEMORIAL SCHOLARSHIP

Scholarship available for African-American female student who is planning to enroll or currently enrolled at a licensed or accredited culinary school. Must submit a 500-word essay on culinary goals and how this scholarship will help to attain them.

Academic Fields/Career Goals: Culinary Arts.

Award: Scholarship for use in freshman, sophomore, junior, or senior years; not renewable. *Number:* 1. *Amount:* up to $4000.

Eligibility Requirements: Applicant must be Black (non-Hispanic); enrolled or expecting to enroll full-time at a technical institution and female. Available to U.S. citizens.

Application Requirements: Application, essay, financial need analysis, references, transcript. *Deadline:* April 15.

Contact: Caroline Stuart, Scholarship Director
James Beard Foundation, Inc.
167 West 12th Street
New York, NY 10011
Phone: 212-675-4984 Ext. 311
Fax: 212-645-1438
E-mail: jamesbeardfound@hotmail.com

SANFORD D'AMATO SCHOLARSHIP

Scholarship for students who plan to enroll or are already enrolled in the ACF (American Culinary Federation) apprenticeship program through Milwaukee Area Technical College and ACF Chefs of Milwaukee or WCTI Technical College, and reside in Milwaukee, WI, county and substantiate residency.

Academic Fields/Career Goals: Culinary Arts.

Award: Scholarship for use in freshman year; not renewable. *Number:* 1. *Amount:* up to $1000.

Eligibility Requirements: Applicant must be enrolled or expecting to enroll full-time at a technical institution. Available to U.S. citizens.

Application Requirements: Application, essay, financial need analysis, references, transcript. *Deadline:* April 15.

Contact: Caroline Stuart, Scholarship Director
James Beard Foundation, Inc.
167 West 12th Street
New York, NY 10011
Phone: 212-675-4984 Ext. 311
Fax: 212-645-1438
E-mail: jamesbeardfound@hotmail.com

ST. REGIS HOUSTON SCHOLARSHIP

Scholarship available for students who plan to enroll or are already enrolled at a licensed or accredited culinary school, and reside in the greater Houston, TX area and substantiate residency.

Academic Fields/Career Goals: Culinary Arts.

Award: Scholarship for use in freshman year; not renewable. *Number:* 1. *Amount:* up to $2500.

Eligibility Requirements: Applicant must be enrolled or expecting to enroll full-time at a technical institution and resident of Texas. Available to U.S. citizens.

Application Requirements: Application, essay, financial need analysis, references, transcript. *Deadline:* April 15.

Contact: Caroline Stuart, Scholarship Director
James Beard Foundation, Inc.
167 West 12th Street
New York, NY 10011
Phone: 212-675-4984 Ext. 311
Fax: 212-645-1438
E-mail: jamesbeardfound@hotmail.com

THE PALACE RESTAURANT IN THE CINCINNATIAN HOTEL CULINARY SCHOLARSHIP

Award available for student who plans to enroll or is already enrolled at a licensed or accredited culinary school. Must submit a 500-word essay describing culinary goals.

Academic Fields/Career Goals: Culinary Arts.

Award: Scholarship for use in freshman, sophomore, junior, or senior years; not renewable. *Number:* 1. *Amount:* up to $1500.

Eligibility Requirements: Applicant must be enrolled or expecting to enroll full-time at a technical institution. Available to U.S. citizens.

Application Requirements: Application, essay, financial need analysis, references, transcript. *Deadline:* April 15.

Contact: Caroline Stuart, Scholarship Director
James Beard Foundation, Inc.
167 West 12th Street
New York, NY 10011
Phone: 212-675-4984 Ext. 311
Fax: 212-645-1438
E-mail: jamesbeardfound@hotmail.com

THE PETER CAMERON SCHOLARSHIP

Scholarships for high school seniors planning to enroll at a licensed or accredited culinary school who have a minimum GPA of 3.0.

Academic Fields/Career Goals: Culinary Arts.

Award: Scholarship for use in freshman year; not renewable. *Number:* 1. *Amount:* up to $5000.

Eligibility Requirements: Applicant must be high school student and planning to enroll or expecting to enroll full-time at an institution or university. Applicant must have 3.0 GPA or higher. Available to U.S. and non-U.S. citizens.

Application Requirements: Application, essay, financial need analysis, references, transcript. *Deadline:* April 15.

Contact: Caroline Stuart, Scholarship Director
James Beard Foundation, Inc.
167 West 12th Street
New York, NY 10011
Phone: 212-675-4984 Ext. 311
Fax: 212-645-1438
E-mail: jamesbeardfound@hotmail.com

LES DAMES D'ESCOFFIER   http://www.lesdames.ca/scholarship.htm

LES DAMES D'ESCOFFIER SCHOLARSHIP

Scholarships for women of all ages who want to begin basic training in the areas of food, wine, hospitality, nutrition, food technology, the arts of the table, and other fields; and to women seeking to refine their skills in these fields. Must be British Columbia residents. Deadline is March 31. Two $2500 scholarships to the Northwest Culinary Academy of Vancouver; A $10000 scholarship to The Art Institute of Vancouver, Dubrulle Culinary Arts.

Academic Fields/Career Goals: Culinary Arts; Food Science/Nutrition.

Award: Scholarship for use in freshman year; renewable. *Number:* 3. *Amount:* $2500–$10,000.

Eligibility Requirements: Applicant must be enrolled or expecting to enroll full or part-time at a technical institution or university and female. Available to U.S. and non-U.S. citizens.

Application Requirements: Application, essay, references, self-addressed stamped envelope, transcript, check or money order for the $30 non-refundable processing fee, made payable to Les Dames d'Escoffier, British Columbia Chapter. *Deadline:* March 31.

Contact: Greg Jewell, Executive Director
Les Dames d'Escoffier
KBC MPI Headquarters, PO Box 4961
Louisville, KY 40204
Phone: 502-456-1851
Fax: 502-456-1821
E-mail: gjewell@aecmanagement.com

OREGON STUDENT ASSISTANCE COMMISSION   http://www.osac.state.or.us

OREGON WINE BROTHERHOOD SCHOLARSHIP

One-time award for students majoring in oenology, viticulture, or culinary arts with an emphasis on wine. Must attend Chemeketa Community College, Oregon State University, or University of California, Davis. Minimum 3.0 GPA. Application deadline is March 1.

Academic Fields/Career Goals: Culinary Arts; Food Science/Nutrition.

Award: Scholarship for use in freshman, sophomore, junior, or senior years; renewable. *Number:* varies. *Amount:* $500.

Eligibility Requirements: Applicant must be enrolled or expecting to enroll full-time at a two-year institution or university; resident of Oregon and studying in California or Oregon. Applicant must have 3.0 GPA or higher. Available to U.S. citizens.

Application Requirements: Application, essay, financial need analysis, transcript, activities chart. *Deadline:* March 1.

Contact: Director of Grant Programs
Oregon Student Assistance Commission
1500 Valley River Drive, Suite 100
Eugene, OR 97401-7020
Phone: 800-452-8807 Ext. 7395

DENTAL HEALTH/SERVICES

ACADEMY OF LDS DENTISTS   http://www.academyofldsdentists.com

ACADEMY OF LDS DENTISTS SCHOLARSHIP

Awards available to dental students who are Latter Day Saints and having difficulty meeting the financial demands of dental school.

Academic Fields/Career Goals: Dental Health/Services.

Award: Scholarship for use in freshman, sophomore, or junior years. *Amount:* $10,000.

Eligibility Requirements: Applicant must be enrolled or expecting to enroll at a four-year institution. Available to U.S. and non-U.S. citizens.

Application Requirements: Application. *Deadline:* varies.

Contact: Steve Trost
Academy of LDS Dentists
136 Harman Building
Provo, UT 84602
Phone: 801-422-4853
Fax: 801-422-0730
E-mail: cw136@byu.edu

ALBERTA HERITAGE SCHOLARSHIP FUND/ ALBERTA SCHOLARSHIP PROGRAMS   http://www.alis.gov.ab.ca

ALBERTA HERITAGE SCHOLARSHIP FUND ABORIGINAL HEALTH CAREERS BURSARY

• *See page 135*

AMERICAN ACADEMY OF ORAL AND MAXILLOFACIAL RADIOLOGY   http://www.aaomr.org

CHARLES R. MORRIS STUDENT RESEARCH AWARD

One-time award plus additional benefits for dental or dental hygiene students who present the results of research in oral and maxillofacial radiology conducted while a full-time pre-doctoral or undergraduate students. The manuscript must be accompanied by a nomination from the institution in which the research was carried out.

American Academy of Oral and Maxillofacial Radiology (continued)

Academic Fields/Career Goals: Dental Health/Services.

Award: Grant for use in junior, senior, or graduate years; not renewable. *Number:* 1. *Amount:* $1000.

Eligibility Requirements: Applicant must be enrolled or expecting to enroll full-time at a four-year institution or university. Available to U.S. and non-U.S. citizens.

Application Requirements: Application, references, manuscript. *Deadline:* June 16.

Contact: J. Sean Hubar, Program Coordinator
American Academy of Oral and Maxillofacial Radiology
LSU School of Dentistry, 1100 Florida Avenue
New Orleans, LA 70119
Phone: 504-619-8623
Fax: 504-619-8741
E-mail: jhubar@lsumc.edu

AMERICAN DENTAL ASSISTANTS ASSOCIATION   http://www.dentalassistant.org

JULIETTE A. SOUTHARD/ORAL B LABORATORIES SCHOLARSHIP

Leadership-based award available to students enrolled in an ADAA dental assistant's program. Proof of acceptance into ADAA program and two letters of reference are required. ADAA membership required.

Academic Fields/Career Goals: Dental Health/Services.

Award: Scholarship for use in freshman, sophomore, junior, or senior years; not renewable. *Number:* 10. *Amount:* $500.

Eligibility Requirements: Applicant must be enrolled or expecting to enroll full or part-time at an institution or university and must have an interest in leadership. Applicant or parent of applicant must be member of American Dental Assistants Association. Available to U.S. citizens.

Application Requirements: Application, essay, financial need analysis, references, transcript. *Deadline:* January 31.

Contact: Dennis Marrell, Staff Assistant
American Dental Assistants Association
35 East Wacker Drive, Suite 1730
Chicago, IL 60601-2211
Phone: 312-541-1550 Ext. 200
Fax: 312-541-1496
E-mail: adaa1@aol.com

AMERICAN DENTAL ASSOCIATION (ADA) FOUNDATION   http://www.adafoundation.org

AMERICAN DENTAL ASSOCIATION FOUNDATION DENTAL ASSISTING SCHOLARSHIP PROGRAM

Applicant must be enrolled full-time with a minimum of twelve hours as an entering student in an accredited dental assistant program. Submit autobiographical sketch. Must be a U.S. citizen and have at least a 3.0 GPA on a 4.0 scale. One-time award of $1000. Applicant may obtain application materials from financial aid officer of school where he or she is currently enrolled.

Academic Fields/Career Goals: Dental Health/Services.

Award: Scholarship for use in freshman year; not renewable. *Number:* varies. *Amount:* $1000.

Eligibility Requirements: Applicant must be enrolled or expecting to enroll full-time at a two-year or four-year or technical institution. Applicant must have 3.0 GPA or higher. Available to U.S. citizens.

Application Requirements: Application, autobiography, essay, financial need analysis, references. *Deadline:* October 31.

Contact: Rose L. Famularo
American Dental Association (ADA) Foundation
211 East Chicago Avenue, 12th Floor
Chicago, IL 60611

AMERICAN DENTAL ASSOCIATION FOUNDATION DENTAL HYGIENE SCHOLARSHIP PROGRAM

Must be enrolled full-time with a minimum of twelve hours as a final-year student at an accredited dental hygiene program. Must be U.S. citizen with minimum 3.0 GPA on a 4.0 scale. Submit autobiographical statement. Applicant may obtain application materials from financial aid officer of school he or she is currently enrolled.

Academic Fields/Career Goals: Dental Health/Services.

Award: Scholarship for use in senior year; not renewable. *Number:* varies. *Amount:* $1000.

Eligibility Requirements: Applicant must be enrolled or expecting to enroll full-time at a two-year or four-year institution or university. Applicant must have 3.0 GPA or higher. Available to U.S. citizens.

Application Requirements: Application, autobiography, essay, financial need analysis, references. *Deadline:* August 15.

Contact: Rose Famularo
American Dental Association (ADA) Foundation
211 East Chicago Avenue, 12th Floor
Chicago, IL 60611

AMERICAN DENTAL ASSOCIATION FOUNDATION DENTAL LAB TECHNOLOGY SCHOLARSHIP

Must be enrolled full-time with a minimum of twelve hours as a last-year student at an accredited dental laboratory technology program. Must be U.S. citizen with a minimum 3.0 GPA on a 4.0 scale. Submit autobiographical statement. Applicant may obtain application materials from financial aid officer of school he or she is currently enrolled.

Academic Fields/Career Goals: Dental Health/Services.

Award: Scholarship for use in senior year; not renewable. *Number:* varies. *Amount:* $1000.

Eligibility Requirements: Applicant must be enrolled or expecting to enroll full-time at a two-year or four-year or technical institution. Applicant must have 3.0 GPA or higher. Available to U.S. citizens.

Application Requirements: Application, autobiography, essay, financial need analysis, references. *Deadline:* September 15.

Contact: Rose Famularo
American Dental Association (ADA) Foundation
211 East Chicago Avenue, 12th Floor
Chicago, IL 60611

AMERICAN DENTAL ASSOCIATION FOUNDATION DENTAL STUDENT SCHOLARSHIP PROGRAM

One-time award for second-year students at an accredited dental school. Must have 3.0 GPA based on a 4.0 scale, and be enrolled full-time (minimum of twelve hours). Must show financial need and be a U.S. citizen. Applicant may obtain application materials from financial aid officer of school he or she is currently enrolled.

Academic Fields/Career Goals: Dental Health/Services.

Award: Scholarship for use in sophomore, or graduate years; not renewable. *Number:* varies. *Amount:* $2500.

Eligibility Requirements: Applicant must be enrolled or expecting to enroll full-time at a four-year institution or university. Applicant must have 3.0 GPA or higher. Available to U.S. citizens.

Application Requirements: Application, autobiography, essay, financial need analysis, references. *Deadline:* July 31.

Contact: Rose Famularo
American Dental Association (ADA) Foundation
211 East Chicago Avenue, 12th Floor
Chicago, IL 60611

AMERICAN DENTAL ASSOCIATION FOUNDATION MINORITY DENTAL STUDENT SCHOLARSHIP PROGRAM

For second year students of a minority group that are underrepresented in dental school enrollment. Based on financial need and academic achievement. Must be U.S. citizen and full-time-student, minimum twelve hours. Must have minimum 3.0 GPA on a 4.0 scale. Applicant must be enrolled in a dental school accredited by the Commission on Dental Accreditation. Applicant may obtain application materials from financial aid officer of school he or she is currently enrolled.

Academic Fields/Career Goals: Dental Health/Services.

Award: Scholarship for use in sophomore, or graduate years; not renewable. *Number:* varies. *Amount:* $2500.

Eligibility Requirements: Applicant must be American Indian/Alaska Native, Black (non-Hispanic), or Hispanic and enrolled or expecting to enroll full-time at a four-year institution or university. Applicant must have 3.0 GPA or higher. Available to U.S. citizens.

Application Requirements: Application, autobiography, essay, financial need analysis, references. *Deadline:* July 31.

Contact: Rose Famularo
American Dental Association (ADA) Foundation
211 East Chicago Avenue, 12th Floor
Chicago, IL 60611

AMERICAN DENTAL EDUCATION ASSOCIATION/ WARNER LAMBERT   http://www.adea.org

ADEA/ORAL-B LABORATORIES SCHOLARSHIP

Scholarship awarded to support dental hygiene students who are pursuing education beyond the associate's degree and who have an interest in an academic career. Must be an individual member of the American Dental Education Association. Deadline is December 9.

Academic Fields/Career Goals: Dental Health/Services.

Award: Scholarship for use in freshman, sophomore, junior, senior, or graduate years; not renewable. *Number:* 2. *Amount:* $2000.

Eligibility Requirements: Applicant must be enrolled or expecting to enroll full or part-time at a four-year institution or university. Applicant or parent of applicant must be member of American Dental Education Association. Available to U.S. citizens.

Application Requirements: Application, references, transcript, copy of a valid license, personal statement, letters of nomination. *Deadline:* December 9.

Contact: Monique Morgan, ADEA/Listerine Scholarships
American Dental Education Association/Warner Lambert
1400 K Street, NW, Suite 1100
Washington, DC 20005
Phone: 202-289-7201
E-mail: morganm@adea.org

ADEA/SIGMA PHI ALPHA LINDA DEVORE SCHOLARSHIP

Scholarship awarded to an individual pursuing allied dental education study at the bachelor's, masters or doctoral degree level. Must be a member of the American Dental Education Association. Deadline is December 9.

Academic Fields/Career Goals: Dental Health/Services.

Award: Scholarship for use in freshman, sophomore, junior, senior, or graduate years; not renewable. *Number:* 1. *Amount:* $1000.

Eligibility Requirements: Applicant must be enrolled or expecting to enroll full or part-time at a two-year or four-year institution or university. Applicant or parent of applicant must be member of American Dental Education Association. Available to U.S. citizens.

Application Requirements: Application, references, transcript, personal statement. *Deadline:* December 9.

Contact: Monique Morgan, ADEA/Listerine Scholarships
American Dental Education Association/Warner Lambert
1400 K Street, NW, Suite 1100
Washington, DC 20005
Phone: 202-289-7201
E-mail: morganm@adea.org

AMERICAN DENTAL HYGIENISTS' ASSOCIATION (ADHA) INSTITUTE   http://www.adha.org/

ADHA INSTITUTE GENERAL SCHOLARSHIPS

One-time award to students enrolled in an accredited dental hygiene program in the United States. Must be a full-time student with a minimum 3.0 GPA and completed one year in a dental hygiene curriculum. Submit a Career Goals statements. Must enclose a copy of SADHA or ADHA membership card with application. Merit scholarships also awarded. Please refer to Web site for further details http://www.adha.org

Academic Fields/Career Goals: Dental Health/Services.

Award: Scholarship for use in freshman, sophomore, junior, senior, or graduate years; not renewable. *Number:* up to 34. *Amount:* up to $2000.

Eligibility Requirements: Applicant must be enrolled or expecting to enroll full-time at a two-year or four-year institution or university. Applicant or parent of applicant must be member of American Dental Hygienist's Association. Applicant must have 3.0 GPA or higher. Available to U.S. citizens.

Application Requirements: Application, financial need analysis, references. *Deadline:* May 1.

Contact: Scholarship Information
American Dental Hygienists' Association (ADHA) Institute
444 North Michigan Avenue, Suite 3400
Chicago, IL 60611
Phone: 800-735-4916
Fax: 312-467-1806
E-mail: institute@adha.net

AMERICAN DENTAL HYGIENISTS' ASSOCIATION INSTITUTE MINORITY SCHOLARSHIP

Nonrenewable awards for members of minority groups currently underrepresented in dental hygiene, including males. Must have a minimum 3.0 GPA, have completed one year of a dental hygiene curriculum, and show financial need of at least $1500. ADHA of SADHA membership required. Must be a U.S. citizen. Please refer to Web site for details http://www.adha.org

Academic Fields/Career Goals: Dental Health/Services.

Award: Scholarship for use in freshman, sophomore, junior, senior, or graduate years; not renewable. *Number:* 2. *Amount:* $1500–$2000.

Eligibility Requirements: Applicant must be American Indian/Alaska Native, Asian/Pacific Islander, Black (non-Hispanic), or Hispanic and enrolled or expecting to enroll full-time at a two-year or four-year institution or university. Applicant or parent of applicant must be member of American Dental Hygienist's Association. Applicant must have 3.0 GPA or higher. Available to U.S. citizens.

Application Requirements: Application, financial need analysis, references. *Deadline:* May 1.

Contact: Scholarship Information
American Dental Hygienists' Association (ADHA) Institute
444 North Michigan Avenue, Suite 3400
Chicago, IL 60611

AMERICAN DENTAL HYGIENISTS' ASSOCIATION INSTITUTE RESEARCH GRANT

One-time award for a licensed dental hygienist or a student pursuing a dental hygiene degree to promote the oral health of the public by improving dental hygiene education and practice. Must submit research proposal. ADHA membership required. Must be a U.S. citizen. Please refer to Web site for further details http://www.adha.org

Academic Fields/Career Goals: Dental Health/Services.

Award: Grant for use in freshman, sophomore, junior, senior, or graduate years; not renewable. *Amount:* $1000–$5000.

Eligibility Requirements: Applicant must be enrolled or expecting to enroll at a four-year institution. Applicant or parent of applicant must be member of American Dental Hygienist's Association. Applicant must have 3.0 GPA or higher. Available to U.S. citizens.

Application Requirements: Application, references, proposal. *Deadline:* January 30.

Contact: Executive Administrator
American Dental Hygienists' Association (ADHA) Institute
444 North Michigan Avenue, Suite 3400
Chicago, IL 60611

AMERICAN DENTAL HYGIENISTS' ASSOCIATION PART-TIME SCHOLARSHIP

Awarded to a dental student pursuing a certificate, associate, baccalaureate, or graduate degree on a part-time basis. Minimum 3.0 GPA required. Submit application and financial need analysis form. ADHA membership required. Eligible after freshman year. Must be a U.S. citizen. Please refer to Web site for further details http://www.adha.org

Academic Fields/Career Goals: Dental Health/Services.

Award: Scholarship for use in freshman, sophomore, junior, senior, or graduate years; not renewable. *Number:* 1. *Amount:* $1500.

Eligibility Requirements: Applicant must be enrolled or expecting to enroll part-time at a two-year or four-year institution or university. Applicant or parent of applicant must be member of American Dental Hygienist's Association. Applicant must have 3.0 GPA or higher. Available to U.S. citizens.

Application Requirements: Application, financial need analysis, references. *Deadline:* May 1.

American Dental Hygienists' Association (ADHA) Institute (continued)

Contact: Scholarship Information
American Dental Hygienists' Association (ADHA) Institute
444 North Michigan Avenue, Suite 3400
Chicago, IL 60611

COLGATE "BRIGHT SMILES, BRIGHT FUTURES" MINORITY SCHOLARSHIP

One-time award to a member of a minority group currently underrepresented in dental hygiene programs, including men. Minimum 3.0 GPA required. For use after first year of study. ADHA or SADHA membership required. Must be a U.S. citizen. Please refer to Web site for further details http://www.adha.org

Academic Fields/Career Goals: Dental Health/Services.

Award: Scholarship for use in freshman, sophomore, junior, or senior years; not renewable. *Number:* 2. *Amount:* $1500.

Eligibility Requirements: Applicant must be American Indian/Alaska Native, Asian/Pacific Islander, Black (non-Hispanic), or Hispanic and enrolled or expecting to enroll full-time at a two-year or four-year institution or university. Applicant or parent of applicant must be member of American Dental Hygienist's Association. Applicant must have 3.0 GPA or higher. Available to U.S. citizens.

Application Requirements: Application, financial need analysis, references. *Deadline:* May 1.

Contact: Scholarship Information
American Dental Hygienists' Association (ADHA) Institute
444 North Michigan Avenue, Suite 3400
Chicago, IL 60611

DR. ALFRED C. FONES SCHOLARSHIP

One-time award to an applicant in the baccalaureate or graduate degree categories who intends to become a dental hygiene teacher/educator. ADHA membership required. Must be a U.S. citizen and have a minimum 3.5 GPA. Please refer to Web site for further details http://www.adha.org

Academic Fields/Career Goals: Dental Health/Services.

Award: Scholarship for use in freshman, sophomore, junior, senior, or graduate years; not renewable. *Number:* 1. *Amount:* $1500.

Eligibility Requirements: Applicant must be enrolled or expecting to enroll full-time at a four-year institution or university. Applicant or parent of applicant must be member of American Dental Hygienist's Association. Applicant must have 3.5 GPA or higher. Available to U.S. citizens.

Application Requirements: Application, financial need analysis, references. *Deadline:* May 1.

Contact: Scholarship Information
American Dental Hygienists' Association (ADHA) Institute
444 North Michigan Avenue, Suite 3400
Chicago, IL 60611

DR. HAROLD HILLENBRAND SCHOLARSHIP

Awarded to a candidate who demonstrates specific academic excellence and outstanding clinical performance, in addition to having a minimum dental hygiene cumulative GPA of 3.5. Must demonstrate financial need of at least $1500. One-time award. ADHA membership required. Must be a U.S. citizen. Please refer to Web site for further details http://www.adha.org

Academic Fields/Career Goals: Dental Health/Services.

Award: Scholarship for use in freshman, sophomore, junior, or senior years; not renewable. *Number:* 1. *Amount:* $1500.

Eligibility Requirements: Applicant must be enrolled or expecting to enroll full-time at a two-year or four-year institution or university. Applicant or parent of applicant must be member of American Dental Hygienist's Association. Applicant must have 3.5 GPA or higher. Available to U.S. citizens.

Application Requirements: Application, financial need analysis, references. *Deadline:* May 1.

Contact: Scholarship Information
American Dental Hygienists' Association (ADHA) Institute
444 North Michigan Avenue, Suite 3400
Chicago, IL 60611

IRENE E. NEWMAN SCHOLARSHIP

One-time award to a candidate who has three years of a bachelor's degree in dental hygiene completed or is currently enrolled in a graduate degree program, and demonstrates potential in public health or community dental health. 3.0 GPA required. ADHA membership required. Must be a U.S. citizen. Please refer to Web site for further details http://www.adha.org

Academic Fields/Career Goals: Dental Health/Services.

Award: Scholarship for use in freshman, sophomore, junior, senior, or graduate years; not renewable. *Number:* 1. *Amount:* $1500.

Eligibility Requirements: Applicant must be enrolled or expecting to enroll full-time at a four-year institution or university. Applicant or parent of applicant must be member of American Dental Hygienist's Association. Applicant must have 3.0 GPA or higher. Available to U.S. citizens.

Application Requirements: Application, financial need analysis, references. *Deadline:* May 1.

Contact: Scholarship Information
American Dental Hygienists' Association (ADHA) Institute
444 North Michigan Avenue, Suite 3400
Chicago, IL 60611

MARGARET E. SWANSON SCHOLARSHIP

Awarded to a candidate who is pursuing a dental career and who demonstrates exceptional organizational leadership potential. Award is merit-based. Freshmen are not eligible. One-time award of up to $1500. Minimum 3.0 GPA required. ADHA membership required. Must be a U.S. citizen. Please refer to Web site for further details http://www.adha.org

Academic Fields/Career Goals: Dental Health/Services.

Award: Scholarship for use in sophomore, junior, senior, or graduate years; not renewable. *Number:* 1. *Amount:* up to $1500.

Eligibility Requirements: Applicant must be enrolled or expecting to enroll full-time at a two-year or four-year institution or university and must have an interest in leadership. Applicant or parent of applicant must be member of American Dental Hygienist's Association. Applicant must have 3.0 GPA or higher. Available to U.S. citizens.

Application Requirements: Application, financial need analysis, references. *Deadline:* May 1.

Contact: Scholarship Information
American Dental Hygienists' Association (ADHA) Institute
444 North Michigan Avenue, Suite 3400
Chicago, IL 60611

MARSH AFFINITY GROUP SERVICES SCHOLARSHIP

One-time award to full-time student pursuing a baccalaureate degree in dental hygiene. Minimum 3.0 GPA required. Sponsored by Marsh Affinity Group Services, a service of Seabury and Smith. Must submit a copy of SADHA or ADHA membership card with application. Please refer to Web site for further details http://www.adha.org

Academic Fields/Career Goals: Dental Health/Services.

Award: Scholarship for use in freshman, sophomore, junior, or senior years; not renewable. *Amount:* up to $2000.

Eligibility Requirements: Applicant must be enrolled or expecting to enroll full-time at a four-year institution or university. Applicant or parent of applicant must be member of American Dental Hygienist's Association. Applicant must have 3.0 GPA or higher. Available to U.S. citizens.

Application Requirements: Application, essay, financial need analysis, references. *Deadline:* May 1.

Contact: Scholarship Information
American Dental Hygienists' Association (ADHA) Institute
444 North Michigan Avenue, Suite 3400
Chicago, IL 60611
Phone: 800-735-4916
Fax: 312-467-1806
E-mail: institute@adha.net

ORAL-B LABORATORIES DENTAL HYGIENE SCHOLARSHIP

One-time award to full-time student at the baccalaureate degree level who demonstrates an intent to encourage professional excellence and scholarship, promote quality research, and support dental hygiene through public and private education. Minimum 3.5 GPA required. Sponsored by Oral-B Laboratories. Must submit a copy of SADHA or ADHA membership card with application. Please refer to Web site for further details http://www.adha.org

Academic Fields/Career Goals: Dental Health/Services.

Award: Scholarship for use in freshman, sophomore, junior, or senior years; not renewable. *Number:* 2. *Amount:* up to $2000.

Eligibility Requirements: Applicant must be enrolled or expecting to enroll full-time at a four-year institution or university. Applicant or parent of applicant must be member of American Dental Hygienist's Association. Applicant must have 3.5 GPA or higher. Available to U.S. citizens.

Application Requirements: Application, essay, financial need analysis, references. *Deadline:* May 1.

Contact: Scholarship Information
American Dental Hygienists' Association (ADHA) Institute
444 North Michigan Avenue, Suite 3400
Chicago, IL 60611
Phone: 800-735-4916
Fax: 312-467-1806
E-mail: institute@adha.net

SIGMA PHI ALPHA UNDERGRADUATE SCHOLARSHIP

Awarded to an outstanding candidate who is pursuing an associate certificate or baccalaureate degree in dental hygiene at an accredited dental hygiene school with an active chapter of Sigma Phi Alpha Dental Hygiene Honor Society. One-time award. Minimum 3.5 GPA required. ADHA membership required. Must be a U.S. citizen. Please refer to Web site for further details http://www.adha.org

Academic Fields/Career Goals: Dental Health/Services.

Award: Scholarship for use in freshman, sophomore, junior, or senior years; not renewable. *Number:* 1. *Amount:* $1000.

Eligibility Requirements: Applicant must be enrolled or expecting to enroll full-time at a two-year or four-year institution. Applicant or parent of applicant must be member of American Dental Hygienist's Association. Applicant must have 3.5 GPA or higher. Available to U.S. citizens.

Application Requirements: Application, financial need analysis, references, transcript. *Deadline:* May 1.

Contact: Scholarship Information
American Dental Hygienists' Association (ADHA) Institute
444 North Michigan Avenue, Suite 3400
Chicago, IL 60611

WILMA MOTLEY CALIFORNIA MERIT SCHOLARSHIP

One-time award to full-time students pursuing an associate/certificate or baccalaureate degree in an accredited dental hygiene program within the state of California. Must demonstrate leadership experience. Minimum 3.5 GPA required. Award is based on merit. Must submit a copy of SADHA or ADHA membership card with application. Please refer to Web site for further details http://www.adha.org

Academic Fields/Career Goals: Dental Health/Services.

Award: Scholarship for use in freshman, sophomore, junior, or senior years; not renewable. *Number:* 1. *Amount:* up to $2000.

Eligibility Requirements: Applicant must be enrolled or expecting to enroll full-time at a two-year or four-year institution or university and studying in California. Applicant or parent of applicant must be member of American Dental Hygienist's Association. Applicant must have 3.5 GPA or higher. Available to U.S. citizens.

Application Requirements: Application, references. *Deadline:* May 1.

Contact: Scholarship Information
American Dental Hygienists' Association (ADHA) Institute
444 North Michigan Avenue, Suite 3400
Chicago, IL 60611
Phone: 800-735-4916
Fax: 312-467-1806
E-mail: institute@adha.net

AMERICAN LEGION AUXILIARY, DEPARTMENT OF WYOMING

PAST PRESIDENTS PARLEY HEALTH CARE SCHOLARSHIP

Scholarship is of $300 which is available for student in the human health care field. Must be a resident of Wyoming, a U.S. citizen, and attend a school in Wyoming. Minimum 3.5 GPA required. Deadline for application is June 1.

Academic Fields/Career Goals: Dental Health/Services; Health and Medical Sciences; Nursing; Therapy/Rehabilitation.

Award: Scholarship for use in sophomore year; not renewable. *Number:* 1–2. *Amount:* $300.

Eligibility Requirements: Applicant must be enrolled or expecting to enroll full-time at a two-year or four-year or technical institution or university; resident of Wyoming and studying in Wyoming. Applicant must have 3.5 GPA or higher. Available to U.S. citizens.

Application Requirements: Application, financial need analysis, transcript. *Deadline:* June 1.

Contact: Sonja Wright, Department Secretary
American Legion Auxiliary, Department of Wyoming
PO Box 2198
Gillette, WY 82717
Phone: 307-686-7137
Fax: 307-686-7137
E-mail: sonja@vcn.com

AMERICAN MEDICAL TECHNOLOGISTS   http://www.amt1.com

AMERICAN MEDICAL TECHNOLOGISTS STUDENT SCHOLARSHIP

One-time award for the undergraduate study of medical technology, medical laboratory technician, office laboratory technician, phlebotomy, or medical, dental assisting. Must attend an accredited institution. Preference to those with financial need. To request application write to AMT stating educational interest/goal. Include SASE. Deadline: April 1.

Academic Fields/Career Goals: Dental Health/Services; Health and Medical Sciences.

Award: Scholarship for use in freshman, sophomore, junior, or senior years; not renewable. *Number:* 5. *Amount:* up to $500.

Eligibility Requirements: Applicant must be enrolled or expecting to enroll at a four-year institution or university. Available to U.S. citizens.

Application Requirements: Application, essay, financial need analysis, references, self-addressed stamped envelope, transcript. *Deadline:* April 1.

Contact: Linda Kujbida, Scholarship Coordinator
American Medical Technologists
710 Higgins Road
Park Ridge, IL 60068-5765
Phone: 847-823-5169
Fax: 847-823-0458
E-mail: amtmail@aol.com

ARKANSAS DEPARTMENT OF HIGHER EDUCATION   http://www.arkansashighered.com

ARKANSAS HEALTH EDUCATION GRANT PROGRAM (ARHEG)
• See page 86

BECA FOUNDATION, INC.   http://www.becafoundation.org

ALICE NEWELL JOSLYN MEDICAL FUND

Scholarships to full-time Latino students entering the medical/health care profession and living or attending college in San Diego County. Financial need, scholastic determination and community/cultural awareness are considered. Awarded for four years annually contingent on scholastic progress.

Academic Fields/Career Goals: Dental Health/Services; Health and Medical Sciences; Nursing; Therapy/Rehabilitation.

Award: Scholarship for use in freshman, sophomore, junior, senior, or graduate years; renewable. *Number:* varies. *Amount:* $500–$2000.

Eligibility Requirements: Applicant must be of Hispanic heritage and enrolled or expecting to enroll full-time at a four-year institution or university. Applicant must have 2.5 GPA or higher. Available to U.S. citizens.

Application Requirements: Application, essay, financial need analysis, references, transcript. *Deadline:* March 2.

Contact: Ana Garcia, Operations Manager
BECA Foundation, Inc.
830 E Grand Avenue
Suite B
Escondido, CA 92025
Phone: 760-741-8246

BETHESDA LUTHERAN HOMES AND SERVICES, INC.
http://www.blhs.org

DEVELOPMENTAL DISABILITIES SCHOLASTIC ACHIEVEMENT SCHOLARSHIP FOR LUTHERAN COLLEGE STUDENTS

One-time award for Lutheran college students who have completed sophomore year in studies related to developmental disabilities. Awards of up to $1500. 3.0 GPA required.

Academic Fields/Career Goals: Dental Health/Services; Education; Health Administration; Health and Medical Sciences; Health Information Management/Technology; Humanities; Social Services; Special Education; Therapy/Rehabilitation.

Award: Scholarship for use in sophomore or junior years; not renewable. *Number:* 1–3. *Amount:* up to $1500.

Eligibility Requirements: Applicant must be Lutheran and enrolled or expecting to enroll full-time at a four-year institution or university. Applicant must have 3.0 GPA or higher. Available to U.S. and Canadian citizens.

Application Requirements: Application, autobiography, essay, references, transcript. *Deadline:* March 15.

Contact: Thomas Heuer, Coordinator, Outreach Programs and Services
Bethesda Lutheran Homes and Services, Inc.
National Christian Resource Center, 600 Hoffmann Drive
Watertown, WI 53094-6294
Phone: 920-261-3050 Ext. 4449
Fax: 920-262-6513
E-mail: theuer@blhs.org

BUSINESS AND PROFESSIONAL WOMEN'S FOUNDATION
http://www.bpwusa.org

BPW CAREER ADVANCEMENT SCHOLARSHIP PROGRAM FOR WOMEN
• See page 136

DELAWARE STATE DENTAL SOCIETY
http://www.delawarestatedentalsociety.org

G. LAYTON GRIER SCHOLARSHIP

Three awards for Delaware residents to study dentistry. Freshmen are not eligible. Must be a U.S. citizen. Write for more information. One-time award of $1000. Student must have successfully completed the first year of dental school.

Academic Fields/Career Goals: Dental Health/Services.

Award: Scholarship for use in sophomore, or graduate years; not renewable. *Number:* 3. *Amount:* $1000.

Eligibility Requirements: Applicant must be enrolled or expecting to enroll full-time at a four-year institution or university and resident of Delaware. Available to U.S. citizens.

Application Requirements: Application, autobiography, driver's license, financial need analysis, interview, references, transcript, proof of residency. *Deadline:* March 1.

Contact: Scholarship Coordinator
Delaware State Dental Society
1925 Layering Avenue
Wilmington, DE 19806
Phone: 302-654-4335

FLORIDA DENTAL HEALTH FOUNDATION
http://www.floridadental.org

DENTAL ASSISTING SCHOLARSHIPS

One-time award for dental assistant study. Must be resident of Florida for at least three years. Must have minimum 2.5 GPA and references from an accredited dental assistant's school. Application available on Web site.

Academic Fields/Career Goals: Dental Health/Services.

Award: Scholarship for use in freshman, sophomore, junior, or senior years; not renewable. *Number:* 10–15. *Amount:* $200–$300.

Eligibility Requirements: Applicant must be enrolled or expecting to enroll full or part-time at a two-year or technical institution; resident of Florida and studying in Florida. Applicant must have 2.5 GPA or higher. Available to U.S. citizens.

Application Requirements: Application, references, transcript. *Deadline:* Continuous.

Contact: Cheri Sutherland, Secretary
Florida Dental Health Foundation
1111 East Tennessee Street
Tallahassee, FL 32308-6914
Phone: 850-681-3629 Ext. 119
Fax: 850-681-0116
E-mail: csutherland@floridadental.org

DENTAL HYGIENE SCHOLARSHIPS

Award for dental hygienist study. Must have minimum 2.5 GPA. Must be Florida resident for at least three years. Application deadlines are May 1 for Fall awards and November 1 for Spring awards. May reapply. Application available on Web site: http://www.floridadental.org

Academic Fields/Career Goals: Dental Health/Services.

Award: Scholarship for use in freshman or sophomore years; not renewable. *Number:* 15–20. *Amount:* $200–$500.

Eligibility Requirements: Applicant must be enrolled or expecting to enroll full or part-time at a two-year or technical institution; resident of Florida and studying in Florida. Applicant must have 2.5 GPA or higher. Available to U.S. citizens.

Application Requirements: Application, references, transcript. *Deadline:* varies.

Contact: Cheri Sutherland, Secretary
Florida Dental Health Foundation
1111 East Tennessee Street
Tallahassee, FL 32308-6914
Phone: 850-681-3629 Ext. 119
Fax: 850-681-0116
E-mail: csutherland@floridadental.org

HAWAIIAN LODGE, F.& A. M.
http://www.hawaiianlodge.org/

HAWAIIAN LODGE SCHOLARSHIPS
• See page 99

HEALTH PROFESSIONS EDUCATION FOUNDATION
http://www.healthprofessions.ca.gov

HEALTH PROFESSIONS EDUCATION SCHOLARSHIP PROGRAM

The scholarship is awarded to students pursuing a career as a dentist, dental hygienist, nurse practitioner, certified nurse midwife, or physician assistant. Eligible scholarship applicants may receive $10,000 per year in financial assistance. Applicants must agree to practice in a medically underserved area of California for a minimum of two years. Deadline: March 24. Must be a resident of CA and U.S. citizen. Minimum 2.0 GPA.

Academic Fields/Career Goals: Dental Health/Services; Health and Medical Sciences; Nursing.

Award: Scholarship for use in senior, graduate, or postgraduate years; not renewable. *Number:* 10–15. *Amount:* $5000–$10,000.

Eligibility Requirements: Applicant must be enrolled or expecting to enroll full or part-time at an institution or university; resident of California and studying in California. Available to U.S. citizens.

Application Requirements: Application, driver's license, financial need analysis, references, transcript, graduation date verification form, Student Aid Report (SAR). *Deadline:* March 24.

Contact: Carlos Rodriguez, Program Director
Health Professions Education Foundation
818 K Street, Suite 210
Sacramento, CA 95814
Phone: 916-324-6500
Fax: 916-324-6585

HELLENIC UNIVERSITY CLUB OF PHILADELPHIA
http://www.hucphila.org

THE NICHOLAS S. HETOS, DDS, MEMORIAL GRADUATE SCHOLARSHIP

The Nicholas S. Hetos, DDS, Memorial Graduate Scholarship in the amount of $2000 will be awarded to a senior undergraduate or graduate student with financial need pursuing studies leading to a Doctor of Dental Medicine (D.M.D.) or Doctor of Dental Surgery (D.D.S.) Degree.

Academic Fields/Career Goals: Dental Health/Services.

Award: Scholarship for use in senior, or graduate years. *Amount:* $2000.

Eligibility Requirements: Applicant must be of Greek heritage; enrolled or expecting to enroll full-time at a four-year institution or university and resident of New Jersey or Pennsylvania. Available to U.S. citizens.

Application Requirements: Application. *Deadline:* April 20.

Contact: Zoe Tripolitis, Scholarship Chairman
Hellenic University Club of Philadelphia
PO Box 42199
Philadelphia, PA 19101
Phone: 215-483-7440
E-mail: zoe.tripolitis@arkemagroup.com

HISPANIC DENTAL ASSOCIATION   http://www.hdassoc.org

DR. JUAN D. VILLARREAL/ HISPANIC DENTAL ASSOCIATION FOUNDATION

Scholarship offered to Hispanic U.S. students who have been accepted into or are currently enrolled in an accredited dental or dental hygiene program in the state of Texas. The awarding of these scholarships will obligate the grantees to complete the current year of their dental or dental hygiene program. Scholastic achievement, leadership skills, community service and commitment to improving the health of the Hispanic community will all be considered. Deadlines are July 1 for dental students and July 15 for dental hygiene students.

Academic Fields/Career Goals: Dental Health/Services.

Award: Scholarship for use in freshman, sophomore, junior, or senior years; not renewable. *Number:* varies. *Amount:* $500–$1000.

Eligibility Requirements: Applicant must be of Hispanic heritage; enrolled or expecting to enroll full-time at a two-year or four-year institution; resident of Texas and studying in Texas. Available to U.S. citizens.

Application Requirements: Application, transcript. *Deadline:* varies.

Contact: Liz Valdivia, Office Manager
Hispanic Dental Association
7138 South Avers Avenue
Chicago, IL 60629
Phone: 800-852-7921
Fax: 773-284-8312
E-mail: lvaldivia@hdassoc.org

INDIAN HEALTH SERVICES, UNITED STATES DEPARTMENT OF HEALTH AND HUMAN SERVICES   http://www.ihs.gov

INDIAN HEALTH SERVICE HEALTH PROFESSIONS PRE-GRADUATE SCHOLARSHIPS

Renewable scholarship available to Native-American students. Minimum 2.0 GPA required. Award averages $18,500. New applicants must first submit to Area Scholarship Coordinator. Must enroll in courses leading to a bachelor degree in the areas of pre-medicine or pre-dentistry, and intend to serve Indian people upon completion of professional healthcare education. Priority is given to students in their junior and senior years. Contact office for more information.

Academic Fields/Career Goals: Dental Health/Services; Health and Medical Sciences.

Award: Scholarship for use in freshman, sophomore, junior, or senior years; renewable. *Number:* varies. *Amount:* $18,500.

Eligibility Requirements: Applicant must be American Indian/Alaska Native and enrolled or expecting to enroll full or part-time at a two-year or four-year or technical institution or university. Available to U.S. citizens.

Application Requirements: Application, applicant must enter a contest, essay, references, transcript, proof of descent. *Deadline:* February 28.

Contact: Jeff Brien, Acting Chief, Scholarship Branch
Indian Health Services, United States Department of Health and Human Services
801 Thompson Avenue, Suite 120
Rockville, MD 20852
Phone: 301-443-6197
Fax: 301-443-6048

INTERNATIONAL ORDER OF THE KING'S DAUGHTERS AND SONS   http://www.iokds.org

HEALTH CAREERS SCHOLARSHIP

Award for students preparing for careers in medicine, dentistry, pharmacy, physical or occupational therapy, and medical technologies. Student must be a U.S. or Canadian citizen, enrolled full-time in a school accredited in the field involved and located in the U.S. or Canada. For all students, except those preparing for an RN degree, application must be for at least the third year of college. RN students must have completed the first year of schooling. Pre-medicine students are not eligible to apply. For those students seeking degrees of MD or DDS application must be for at least the second year of medical or dental school. Each applicant must supply proof of acceptance in the school involved. There is no age limit.

Academic Fields/Career Goals: Dental Health/Services; Health and Medical Sciences; Nursing; Therapy/Rehabilitation.

Award: Scholarship for use in sophomore, junior, senior, or graduate years; not renewable. *Number:* 40–50. *Amount:* $500–$1000.

Eligibility Requirements: Applicant must be enrolled or expecting to enroll full-time at a four-year institution or university. Available to U.S. and Canadian citizens.

Application Requirements: Application, photo, resume, references, self-addressed stamped envelope, transcript, itemized budget. *Deadline:* April 1.

Contact: Director, Health Careers Department
International Order of the King's Daughters and Sons
PO Box 1017
Chautauqua, NY 14722-1017
Phone: 716-357-4951

JEWISH FOUNDATION FOR EDUCATION OF WOMEN   http://www.jfew.org

SCHOLARSHIP PROGRAM FOR FORMER SOVIET UNION EMIGRES TRAINING IN THE HEALTH SCIENCES

Scholarships for female from the former Soviet Union who are studying for careers in medicine, dentistry, dental hygiene, nursing, pharmacy, occupational therapy, physician assistant programs, and physical therapy. Must live within 50 miles of New York City. Must demonstrate financial need and a good academic record. Deadline is June 15.

Academic Fields/Career Goals: Dental Health/Services; Health and Medical Sciences; Nursing; Therapy/Rehabilitation.

Award: Scholarship for use in freshman, sophomore, junior, senior, or graduate years; renewable. *Number:* varies. *Amount:* up to $5000.

Eligibility Requirements: Applicant must be of former Soviet Union heritage; enrolled or expecting to enroll full-time at a four-year institution or university; female and resident of Connecticut, New Jersey, or New York. Available to U.S. and non-Canadian citizens.

Application Requirements: Application, financial need analysis, transcript. *Deadline:* June 15.

Contact: Marge Goldwater, Executive Director
Jewish Foundation for Education of Women
135 East 64th Street
New York, NY 10021
Phone: 212-288-3931
Fax: 212-288-5798
E-mail: fdnscholar@aol.com

MARIN EDUCATION FUND
http://www.marineducationfund.org

GOLDMAN FAMILY FUND, NEW LEADER SCHOLARSHIP

Applicant for scholarship must attend one of the Bay Area public universities (California State University, Howard; San Francisco State University; San Jose State University; Sonoma State University; University of California at Berkeley). Must be studying social sciences, human services, health-related fields, or public service and have completed at least 30 hours at that university. Must be undergraduate upper division student, demonstrate financial need and high academic achievement.

Academic Fields/Career Goals: Dental Health/Services; Food Science/Nutrition; Health Administration; Health and Medical Sciences; Health Information Management/Technology; Nursing; Social Sciences; Social Services; Therapy/Rehabilitation.

Award: Scholarship for use in freshman, sophomore, junior, or senior years; renewable. *Amount:* $6000.

Eligibility Requirements: Applicant must be enrolled or expecting to enroll full or part-time at a four-year institution or university and studying in California. Applicant must have 3.5 GPA or higher. Available to U.S. and non-U.S. citizens.

Application Requirements: Application, financial need analysis, interview, transcript, proof of enrollment. *Deadline:* March 15.

Contact: Marin Education Fund
Marin Education Fund
781 Lincoln Avenue, Suite 140
San Rafael, CA 94901
Phone: 415-459-4240
Fax: 415-459-0527
E-mail: info@marineducationfund.org

MARYLAND ASSOCIATION OF PRIVATE COLLEGES AND CAREER SCHOOLS
http://www.mapccs.org

MARYLAND ASSOCIATION OF PRIVATE COLLEGES AND CAREER SCHOOLS SCHOLARSHIP
• See page 150

MARYLAND HIGHER EDUCATION COMMISSION
http://www.mhec.state.md.us

GRADUATE AND PROFESSIONAL SCHOLARSHIP PROGRAM-MARYLAND

Graduate and professional scholarships provide need-based financial assistance to students attending a Maryland school of medicine, dentistry, law, pharmacy, social work, or nursing. Funds are provided to specific Maryland colleges and universities. Students must demonstrate financial need and be Maryland residents. Contact institution financial aid office for more information.

Academic Fields/Career Goals: Dental Health/Services; Health and Medical Sciences; Law/Legal Services; Nursing; Social Services.

Award: Scholarship for use in freshman, sophomore, junior, senior, graduate, or postgraduate years; renewable. *Number:* 40–200. *Amount:* $1000–$5000.

Eligibility Requirements: Applicant must be enrolled or expecting to enroll full or part-time at a four-year institution or university; resident of Maryland and studying in Maryland. Available to U.S. citizens.

Application Requirements: Application, financial need analysis. *Deadline:* March 1.

Contact: institution financial aid office

MISSOURI DEPARTMENT OF HEALTH AND SENIOR SERVICES
http://www.dhss.mo.gov

PRIMARY CARE RESOURCE INITIATIVE FOR MISSOURI LOAN PROGRAM

Forgivable loans for Missouri residents attending Missouri institutions pursuing a degree as a primary care physician or dentist, studying for a bachelors degree as a dental hygienist, or a master of science degree in nursing leading to certification as an Advanced Practice Nurse. To be forgiven participant must work in a Missouri health professional shortage area.

Academic Fields/Career Goals: Dental Health/Services; Health and Medical Sciences; Nursing.

Award: Forgivable loan for use in freshman, sophomore, junior, senior, graduate, or postgraduate years; not renewable. *Number:* varies. *Amount:* $3000–$25,000.

Eligibility Requirements: Applicant must be enrolled or expecting to enroll full or part-time at a four-year institution or university; resident of Missouri and studying in Missouri. Available to U.S. citizens.

Application Requirements: Application, driver's license. *Deadline:* July 1.

Contact: Kristie Frank, Health Program Representative
Missouri Department of Health and Senior Services
PO Box 570
Jefferson City, MO 65102-0570
Phone: 800-891-7415
Fax: 573-522-8146
E-mail: frank@dhss.mo.gov

NEBRASKA HEALTH AND HUMAN SERVICES SYSTEM, OFFICE OF RURAL HEALTH
http://www.hhs.state.ne.us

RURAL HEALTH STUDENT LOAN PROGRAM

Must be enrolled or accepted for enrollment in medical or dental school at Creighton University or University of Nebraska Medical Center, or in Physician Assistant Program at a Nebraska college. Students must agree to practice one year in a shortage area for each year a scholarship is awarded, and to specialize in family practice, general surgery, internal medicine, pediatrics, obstetrics/gynecology, or psychiatry. Applications accepted April 1 to June 1. Must be a Nebraska resident.

Academic Fields/Career Goals: Dental Health/Services; Health and Medical Sciences.

Award: Forgivable loan for use in freshman, sophomore, junior, senior, or graduate years; not renewable. *Amount:* $5000–$20,000.

Eligibility Requirements: Applicant must be enrolled or expecting to enroll at a four-year institution or university; resident of Nebraska and studying in Nebraska. Applicant or parent of applicant must have employment or volunteer experience in designated career field. Available to U.S. citizens.

Application Requirements: Application, interview. *Deadline:* varies.

Contact: Nebraska Health and Human Services System, Office of Rural Health
301 Centennial Mall South, PO Box 95044
Lincoln, NE 68509
Phone: 402-471-2337
Fax: 402-471-0180

NEW MEXICO COMMISSION ON HIGHER EDUCATION
http://www.hed.state.nm.us

ALLIED HEALTH STUDENT LOAN PROGRAM-NEW MEXICO

Renewable loans for New Mexico residents enrolled in an undergraduate allied health program. Loans can be forgiven through service in a medically underserved area or can be repaid. Penalties apply for failure to provide service. May borrow up to $12,000 per year for four years.

Academic Fields/Career Goals: Dental Health/Services; Health and Medical Sciences; Nursing; Social Sciences; Therapy/Rehabilitation.

Award: Forgivable loan for use in freshman, sophomore, junior, or senior years; renewable. *Number:* 1–40. *Amount:* up to $12,000.

Eligibility Requirements: Applicant must be enrolled or expecting to enroll full or part-time at a two-year or four-year institution or university; resident of New Mexico and studying in New Mexico. Available to U.S. citizens.

Application Requirements: Application, financial need analysis, transcript, FAFSA. *Deadline:* July 1.

Contact: Ofelia Morales, Director of Financial Aid
New Mexico Commission on Higher Education
1068 Cerrillos Road, PO Box 15910
Santa Fe, NM 87505
Phone: 505-476-6506
E-mail: ofelia.morales@state.nm.us

NEW YORK STATE EDUCATION DEPARTMENT
http://www.highered.nysed.gov

REGENTS PROFESSIONAL OPPORTUNITY SCHOLARSHIP
• See page 67

NORTH CAROLINA STATE EDUCATION ASSISTANCE AUTHORITY
http://www.ncseaa.edu

NORTH CAROLINA STUDENT LOAN PROGRAM FOR HEALTH, SCIENCE, AND MATHEMATICS

Renewable award for North Carolina residents studying health-related fields, or science or math education. Based on merit, need, and promise of service as a health professional or educator in an underserved area of North Carolina. Need two co-signers. Submit surety statement.

Academic Fields/Career Goals: Dental Health/Services; Health Administration; Health and Medical Sciences; Nursing; Physical Sciences and Math; Therapy/Rehabilitation.

Award: Forgivable loan for use in freshman, junior, senior, or graduate years; renewable. *Amount:* $3000–$8500.

Eligibility Requirements: Applicant must be enrolled or expecting to enroll full-time at a two-year or four-year institution or university and resident of North Carolina. Available to U.S. citizens.

Application Requirements: Application, financial need analysis, transcript. *Deadline:* June 1.

Contact: Edna Williams, Manager, Selection and Origination, HSM Loan Program
North Carolina State Education Assistance Authority
PO Box 14223
Research Triangle Park, NC 27709
Phone: 800-700-1775 Ext. 313
E-mail: eew@ncseaa.edu

OREGON STUDENT ASSISTANCE COMMISSION
http://www.osac.state.or.us

JEANNETTE MOWERY SCHOLARSHIP

Award for Oregon graduate students pursuing a course of study in law, medicine or dentistry. Must attend Oregon law schools or Oregon Health Sciences University.

Academic Fields/Career Goals: Dental Health/Services; Health and Medical Sciences; Law/Legal Services.

Award: Scholarship for use in freshman, sophomore, junior, senior, or graduate years; renewable. *Number:* varies. *Amount:* $500.

Eligibility Requirements: Applicant must be enrolled or expecting to enroll full-time at a two-year or four-year institution or university; resident of Oregon and studying in Oregon. Available to U.S. citizens.

Application Requirements: Application, essay, financial need analysis, references, transcript, activity chart. *Deadline:* March 1.

Contact: Director of Grant Programs
Oregon Student Assistance Commission
1500 Valley River Drive, Suite 100
Eugene, OR 97401-7020
Phone: 800-452-8807 Ext. 7395

PNC BANK TRUST DEPARTMENT

H. FLETCHER BROWN SCHOLARSHIP

Renewable award based on academic performance, test scores, financial need, and interview. Applicant's family income must be below $75,000. Awards are made in spring of senior year of high school or spring of senior year of college. Must be pursuing studies in engineering, chemistry, law, medicine (limited to those pursuing MD or DO degree), or dentistry. Must have been born in Delaware and be a Delaware resident. Birth certificate required for documentation. Class rank must be in the upper 20 percentile. Applicant must maintain a 2.5 GPA in order to keep scholarship.

Academic Fields/Career Goals: Dental Health/Services; Engineering/Technology; Health and Medical Sciences; Law/Legal Services; Physical Sciences and Math.

Award: Scholarship for use in freshman, or graduate years; renewable. *Number:* 1–2. *Amount:* varies.

Eligibility Requirements: Applicant must be enrolled or expecting to enroll full-time at a four-year institution and resident of Delaware. Applicant must have 2.5 GPA or higher. Available to U.S. citizens.

Application Requirements: Application, financial need analysis, interview, photo, references, test scores, transcript. *Deadline:* April 15.

Contact: Donald W. Davis, Vice President
PNC Bank Trust Department
222/16 Delaware Avenue, PO Box 791
Wilmington, DE 19899
Phone: 302-429-1186
Fax: 302-429-5658

SOUTHWEST STUDENT SERVICES CORPORATION
http://www.sssc.com/

ANNE LINDEMAN MEMORIAL SCHOLARSHIP
• See page 142

UNITED STATES PUBLIC HEALTH SERVICE - HEALTH RESOURCES AND SERVICES ADMINISTRATION, BUREAU OF HEALTH
http://bhpr.hrsa.gov/dsa

HEALTH RESOURCES AND SERVICES ADMINISTRATION-BUREAU OF HEALTH PROFESSIONS SCHOLARSHIPS FOR DISADVANTAGED STUDENTS

Scholarships to full-time students from disadvantaged backgrounds enrolled in health professions and nursing programs. Institution must apply for funding. One-time award. Students must contact financial aid office to apply. School must be eligible to receive SDS funds.

Academic Fields/Career Goals: Dental Health/Services; Health and Medical Sciences; Nursing; Therapy/Rehabilitation.

Award: Scholarship for use in freshman, sophomore, junior, senior, or graduate years; not renewable. *Amount:* varies.

Eligibility Requirements: Applicant must be enrolled or expecting to enroll full-time at a two-year or four-year institution or university. Available to U.S. citizens.

Application Requirements: Application, financial need analysis. *Deadline:* Continuous.

Contact: Andrea Stampone, Scholarship Coordinator
United States Public Health Service - Health Resources and Services Administration, Bureau of Health
Division of Health Careers Diversity Development, Parklawn Building, Room 8-34, 5600 Fishers Lane
Rockville, MD 20857
Phone: 301-443-4776
Fax: 301-446-0846

UNIVERSITY OF MEDICINE AND DENTISTRY OF NJ SCHOOL OF OSTEOPATHIC MEDICINE
http://www.umdnj.edu

MARTIN LUTHER KING PHYSICIAN/DENTIST SCHOLARSHIPS

Renewable award available to New Jersey residents enrolled full-time in a medical or dental program. Several scholarships are available. Dollar amount varies. Must be a former or current EOF recipient, a minority or from a disadvantaged background. Applicant must attend a New Jersey institution and apply for financial aid.

Academic Fields/Career Goals: Dental Health/Services; Health and Medical Sciences.

Award: Scholarship for use in freshman, sophomore, junior, senior, or graduate years; renewable. *Number:* varies. *Amount:* varies.

Eligibility Requirements: Applicant must be enrolled or expecting to enroll full-time at a four-year institution or university; resident of New Jersey and studying in New Jersey. Available to U.S. citizens.

University of Medicine and Dentistry of NJ School of Osteopathic Medicine (continued)

Application Requirements: Application, financial need analysis. *Deadline:* Continuous.

Contact: Glenn Lang, EOF Executive Director
University of Medicine and Dentistry of NJ School of Osteopathic Medicine
20 West State Street, 7th Floor, PO Box 542
Trenton, NJ 08625-0542
Phone: 609-984-2709
Fax: 609-633-8420
E-mail: glang@che.state.nj.us

NEW JERSEY EDUCATIONAL OPPORTUNITY FUND GRANTS

Grants up to $4350 per year. Must be a New Jersey resident for at least twelve consecutive months and attend a New Jersey institution. Must be from a disadvantaged background as defined by EOF guidelines. EOF grant applicants must also apply for financial aid. EOF recipients may qualify for the Martin Luther King Physician/Dentistry Scholarships for graduate study at a professional institution.

Academic Fields/Career Goals: Dental Health/Services; Health and Medical Sciences.

Award: Grant for use in freshman, sophomore, junior, senior, or graduate years; renewable. *Number:* varies. *Amount:* $200–$4350.

Eligibility Requirements: Applicant must be enrolled or expecting to enroll full-time at a four-year institution or university; resident of New Jersey and studying in New Jersey. Available to U.S. citizens.

Application Requirements: Application, financial need analysis. *Deadline:* Continuous.

Contact: Glenn Lang, EOF Executive Director
University of Medicine and Dentistry of NJ School of Osteopathic Medicine
40 East Laurel Road, Primary Care Center 119, PO Box 542
Trenton, NJ 08625-0542
Phone: 609-984-2709
Fax: 609-292-7225
E-mail: glang@che.state.nj.us

VIRGINIA BUSINESS AND PROFESSIONAL WOMEN'S FOUNDATION   http://www.bpwva.org

WOMEN IN SCIENCE AND TECHNOLOGY SCHOLARSHIP
• See page 143

DRAFTING

HISPANIC COLLEGE FUND, INC.   http://www.hispanicfund.org

EL NUEVO CONSTRUCTOR SCHOLARSHIP PROGRAM
• See page 99

NATIONAL ASSOCIATION OF WOMEN IN CONSTRUCTION   http://nawic.org

NAWIC UNDERGRADUATE SCHOLARSHIPS
• See page 100

PROFESSIONAL CONSTRUCTION ESTIMATORS ASSOCIATION   http://www.pcea.org

TED WILSON MEMORIAL SCHOLARSHIP FOUNDATION

Scholarship available to students wishing to pursue a career in the construction industry. Currently available in the following states: NC, SC, VA, GA, and FL.

Academic Fields/Career Goals: Drafting; Electrical Engineering/Electronics; Engineering/Technology; Heating, Air-Conditioning, and Refrigeration Mechanics; Landscape Architecture; Mechanical Engineering; Surveying; Surveying Technology, Cartography, or Geographic Information Science.

Award: Scholarship for use in freshman, sophomore, junior, or graduate years; not renewable. *Number:* 5. *Amount:* up to $1500.

Eligibility Requirements: Applicant must be enrolled or expecting to enroll full-time at a two-year or four-year or technical institution and studying in Florida, Georgia, North Carolina, South Carolina, or Virginia. Available to U.S. and non-U.S. citizens.

Application Requirements: Application, financial need analysis, references, transcript. *Deadline:* March 15.

Contact: Kim Ellis, National Office Manager
Professional Construction Estimators Association
PO Box 680336
Charlotte, NC 28216-0336
Phone: 704-987-9978
E-mail: pcea@pcea.org

EARTH SCIENCE

ALABAMA STATE DEPARTMENT OF EDUCATION   http://www.alsde.edu

MATH AND SCIENCE SCHOLARSHIP PROGRAM FOR ALABAMA TEACHERS
• See page 135

ALASKA GEOLOGICAL SOCIETY, INC.   http://www.alaskageology.org/scholarship

ALASKA GEOLOGICAL SOCIETY SCHOLARSHIP

Scholarship available for full-time junior/senior undergraduate or graduate student (taking at least 12 undergraduate credit hours or 9 graduate credit hours) at an Alaska university with academic emphasis (major or minor) in earth sciences.

Academic Fields/Career Goals: Earth Science.

Award: Scholarship for use in freshman, sophomore, junior, senior, or graduate years. *Amount:* varies.

Eligibility Requirements: Applicant must be enrolled or expecting to enroll full-time at a four-year institution or university and studying in Alaska. Available to U.S. citizens.

Application Requirements: Application, references, transcript, cover letter. *Deadline:* April 1.

Contact: Micaela Weeks
Phone: 907-564-5635
E-mail: laryn.smith@bp.com

AMERICAN INDIAN SCIENCE AND ENGINEERING SOCIETY   http://www.aises.org

A.T. ANDERSON MEMORIAL SCHOLARSHIP
• See page 89

ENVIRONMENTAL PROTECTION AGENCY TRIBAL LANDS ENVIRONMENTAL SCIENCE SCHOLARSHIP
• See page 135

AMERICAN METEOROLOGICAL SOCIETY   http://www.ametsoc.org/AMS

AMERICAN METEOROLOGICAL SOCIETY INDUSTRY UNDERGRADUATE SCHOLARSHIPS
• See page 89

ARIZONA HYDROLOGICAL SOCIETY   http://www.azhydrosoc.org

ARIZONA HYDROLOGICAL SURVEY STUDENT SCHOLARSHIP

One-time award to outstanding undergraduate or graduate students that have demonstrated academic excellence in water resources related fields as a means of encouraging them to continue to develop as water resources professionals. Must be a resident of Arizona and be enrolled in a postsecondary Arizona institution.

Academic Fields/Career Goals: Earth Science; Natural Resources; Nuclear Science; Physical Sciences and Math; Science, Technology, and Society; Surveying; Surveying Technology, Cartography, or Geographic Information Science.

Award: Scholarship for use in sophomore, junior, senior, or graduate years; not renewable. *Number:* 3. *Amount:* $1500.

Eligibility Requirements: Applicant must be enrolled or expecting to enroll full-time at a two-year or technical institution or university; resident of Arizona and studying in Arizona. Available to U.S. citizens.

Application Requirements: Application, essay, financial need analysis, references, transcript. *Deadline:* June 30.

Contact: Aregai Tecle, Professor
Arizona Hydrological Society
Northern Arizona University School of Forestry, PO Box 15018
Flagstaff, AZ 86011
Phone: 928-523-6642
E-mail: aregai.tecle@nau.edu

ASSOCIATION FOR IRON AND STEEL
TECHNOLOGY   http://www.aist.org

ASSOCIATION FOR IRON AND STEEL TECHNOLOGY OHIO VALLEY CHAPTER SCHOLARSHIP
• *See page 135*

ASSOCIATION FOR WOMEN GEOSCIENTISTS,
PUGET SOUND CHAPTER   http://www.awg.org

PUGET SOUND CHAPTER SCHOLARSHIP

Scholarship for undergraduate women committed to completing a bachelor's degree and pursuing a career or graduate work in the geosciences, including geology, environmental/engineering geology, geochemistry, geophysics, and hydrology. Must be sophomore, junior, or senior woman enrolled in a university or 2-year college in western Washington State, west of the Columbia and Okanogan Rivers. Must have minimum 3.2 GPA. Must be a U.S. citizen or permanent resident. Please refer to Web site for further information: http://www.scn.org/psawg.

Academic Fields/Career Goals: Earth Science; Physical Sciences and Math.

Award: Scholarship for use in freshman, sophomore, junior, or senior years; not renewable. *Number:* 1. *Amount:* $1000.

Eligibility Requirements: Applicant must be enrolled or expecting to enroll full-time at a two-year or four-year institution or university; female and studying in Washington. Applicant must have 3.0 GPA or higher. Available to U.S. citizens.

Application Requirements: Essay, financial need analysis, references, transcript. *Deadline:* varies.

Contact: Lynn Hultgrien
Association for Women Geoscientists, Puget Sound Chapter
Association for Women Geoscientists,Puget Sound Chapter,
PO Box 4229
Kent, WA 98089
Phone: 206-543-9024

ASSOCIATION FOR WOMEN IN
SCIENCE EDUCATIONAL
FOUNDATION   http://www.awis.org/ed_foundation.html

ASSOCIATION FOR WOMEN IN SCIENCE COLLEGE SCHOLARSHIP
• *See page 86*

AWIS KIRSTEN R. LORENTZEN AWARD IN PHYSICS

Award for female undergraduate students, to be used in their junior or senior year of study. Must be studying toward a degree in physics or geoscience and excel in both academic and non-academic pursuits. Applicants must be U.S. citizens, studying in the United States.

Academic Fields/Career Goals: Earth Science; Physical Sciences and Math.

Award: Scholarship for use in sophomore or junior years; not renewable. *Number:* 1. *Amount:* $1000.

Eligibility Requirements: Applicant must be enrolled or expecting to enroll full-time at a four-year institution or university and female. Available to U.S. citizens.

Application Requirements: Application, essay, references, transcript. *Deadline:* February 3.

Contact: Barbara Filner, President
Association for Women in Science Educational Foundation
7008 Richard Drive
Bethesda, MD 20817-4838
Phone: 301-229-9243
E-mail: awisedfd@aol.com

ASSOCIATION OF ENGINEERING
GEOLOGISTS   http://www.aegweb.org

MARLIAVE FUND

Several scholarships to support graduate and undergraduate students studying engineering geology and geological engineering. One-time awards.

Academic Fields/Career Goals: Earth Science; Engineering/Technology; Engineering-Related Technologies.

Award: Scholarship for use in senior, or graduate years; not renewable. *Number:* varies. *Amount:* up to $1000.

Eligibility Requirements: Applicant must be enrolled or expecting to enroll full-time at a four-year institution or university. Available to U.S. citizens.

Application Requirements: Application, resume, transcript. *Deadline:* April 15.

Contact: Paul Santi, Scholarship Coordinator
Association of Engineering Geologists
Department of Geology and Geological Engineering, Berthoud Hall
Golden, CO 80401
Phone: 303-216-2714

TILFORD FUND

For undergraduate students, the scholarship goes toward the cost of a geology field camp course or senior thesis field research. For graduate students, the scholarship would apply to field research. Must be a student member of AEG.

Academic Fields/Career Goals: Earth Science.

Award: Scholarship for use in freshman, sophomore, junior, senior, or graduate years; not renewable. *Number:* 2–4. *Amount:* up to $1000.

Eligibility Requirements: Applicant must be enrolled or expecting to enroll full-time at a four-year institution or university. Applicant or parent of applicant must be member of Association of Engineering Geologists. Available to U.S. citizens.

Application Requirements: Application, essay, references, transcript. *Deadline:* varies.

Contact: Deb Green Tilford, Chairman
Association of Engineering Geologists
NRT Scholarship Committee, 79 Forest Lane
Placitas, NM 87043
E-mail: tilgreen@aol.com

ASTRONAUT SCHOLARSHIP
FOUNDATION   http://www.astronautscholarship.org

ASTRONAUT SCHOLARSHIP FOUNDATION
• *See page 92*

BARRY M. GOLDWATER SCHOLARSHIP AND
EXCELLENCE IN EDUCATION
FOUNDATION   http://www.act.org/goldwater

BARRY M. GOLDWATER SCHOLARSHIP AND EXCELLENCE IN EDUCATION PROGRAM
• *See page 92*

CALIFORNIA GROUNDWATER
ASSOCIATION   http://www.groundh2o.org

CALIFORNIA GROUNDWATER ASSOCIATION SCHOLARSHIP

Award for California residents who demonstrate an interest in some facet of groundwater technology. One to two $1000 awards. Must use for study in California. Submit letter of recommendation. Deadline: April 1.

Academic Fields/Career Goals: Earth Science; Natural Resources.

California Groundwater Association (continued)

Award: Scholarship for use in freshman, sophomore, junior, or senior years; not renewable. *Number:* 1–2. *Amount:* $1000.

Eligibility Requirements: Applicant must be enrolled or expecting to enroll full or part-time at a two-year or four-year or technical institution or university; resident of California and studying in California. Available to U.S. citizens.

Application Requirements: Application, essay, references, transcript. *Deadline:* April 1.

Contact: Mike Mortensson, Executive Director
California Groundwater Association
PO Box 14369
Santa Rosa, CA 95402
Phone: 707-578-4408
Fax: 707-546-4906
E-mail: wellguy@groundh2o.org

CANADIAN RECREATIONAL CANOEING ASSOCIATION   http://www.paddlingcanada.com

BILL MASON MEMORIAL SCHOLARSHIP FUND
• See page 80

DESK AND DERRICK EDUCATIONAL TRUST   http://www.addc.org

DESK AND DERRICK EDUCATIONAL TRUST
• See page 92

ELECTROCHEMICAL SOCIETY, INC.   http://www.electrochem.org

DANIEL CUBICCIOTTI STUDENT AWARD OF THE SAN FRANCISCO SECTION OF THE ELECTROCHEMICAL SOCIETY, SPONSORED BY STRUCTURAL INTEGRITY ASSOCIATES
• See page 137

H.H. DOW MEMORIAL STUDENT ACHIEVEMENT AWARD OF THE INDUSTRIAL ELECTROLYSIS AND ELECTROCHEMICAL ENGINEERING DIVISION OF THE ELECTROCHEMICAL SOCIETY, INC.
• See page 137

STUDENT ACHIEVEMENT AWARDS OF THE INDUSTRIAL ELECTROLYSIS AND ELECTROCHEMICAL ENGINEERING DIVISION OF THE ELECTROCHEMICAL SOCIETY, INC.
• See page 137

STUDENT RESEARCH AWARDS OF THE BATTERY DIVISION OF THE ELECTROCHEMICAL SOCIETY, INC.
• See page 137

EXPLORERS CLUB   http://www.explorers.org

EXPLORATION FUND GRANTS
• See page 88

GARDEN CLUB OF AMERICA   http://www.gcamerica.org

GARDEN CLUB OF AMERICA AWARDS FOR SUMMER ENVIRONMENTAL STUDIES
• See page 80

GEORGE BIRD GRINNELL AMERICAN INDIAN FUND   http://www.grinnellfund.org/

AL QOYAWAYMA AWARD
• See page 163

HERB SOCIETY OF AMERICA   http://www.herbsociety.org

HERB SOCIETY RESEARCH GRANTS
• See page 92

HISPANIC COLLEGE FUND, INC.   http://www.hispanicfund.org

NATIONAL HISPANIC EXPLORERS SCHOLARSHIP PROGRAM
• See page 93

INDEPENDENT LABORATORIES INSTITUTE SCHOLARSHIP ALLIANCE   http://www.acil.org

INDEPENDENT LABORATORIES INSTITUTE SCHOLARSHIP ALLIANCE
• See page 93

INNOVATION AND SCIENCE COUNCIL OF BRITISH COLUMBIA   http://www.scbc.org

PAUL AND HELEN TRUSSEL SCIENCE AND TECHNOLOGY SCHOLARSHIP
• See page 93

INTERNATIONAL ASSOCIATION OF GREAT LAKES RESEARCH   http://www.iaglr.org

PAUL W. RODGERS SCHOLARSHIP

Award given to any senior undergraduate, masters or doctoral student who wishes to pursue a future in research, conservation, education, communication, management, or other knowledge-based activity pertaining to the Great Lakes. Deadline is March 1.

Academic Fields/Career Goals: Earth Science; Education; Environmental Science; Hydrology; Marine Biology; Natural Resources; Natural Sciences.

Award: Scholarship for use in senior, or graduate years; not renewable. *Number:* 1. *Amount:* $2000.

Eligibility Requirements: Applicant must be enrolled or expecting to enroll full-time at a four-year institution or university. Available to U.S. citizens.

Application Requirements: Application, references, transcript. *Deadline:* March 1.

Contact: Wendy Foster
International Association of Great Lakes Research
Attention: Business Office
2205 Commonwealth Boulevard
Ann Arbor, MI 48105
Phone: 734-665-5503
Fax: 734-741-2055
E-mail: office@iaglr.org

KENTUCKY NATURAL RESOURCES AND ENVIRONMENTAL PROTECTION CABINET   http://www.uky.edu/waterresources

ENVIRONMENTAL PROTECTION SCHOLARSHIPS
• See page 164

MINERALOGICAL SOCIETY OF AMERICA   http://www.minsocam.org

MINERALOGICAL SOCIETY OF AMERICA-GRANT FOR STUDENT RESEARCH IN MINERALOGY AND PETROLOGY

A $5000 grant for research in mineralogy and petrology. Selection based on qualifications of applicant; quality, innovativeness, and scientific significance of the research; and likelihood of project success. Application available on Web site at http://www.minsocam.org.

Academic Fields/Career Goals: Earth Science; Gemology; Museum Studies; Natural Resources; Natural Sciences; Physical Sciences and Math.

Award: Grant for use in freshman, sophomore, junior, senior, or graduate years; not renewable. *Number:* 2. *Amount:* $5000.

Eligibility Requirements: Applicant must be enrolled or expecting to enroll full-time at a four-year institution or university. Available to U.S. and non-U.S. citizens.

Application Requirements: Application. *Deadline:* June 1.

Contact: Dr. J. Alexander Speer
Mineralogical Society of America
1015 Eighteenth Street, NW, Suite 601
Washington, DC 20036-5212
Phone: 703-652-9950
Fax: 703-652-9951
E-mail: j_a_speer@minsocam.org

MINERALOGY SOCIETY OF AMERICA-GRANT FOR RESEARCH IN CRYSTALLOGRAPHY

A $5000 grant for research in crystallography. Award selection based on qualifications of applicant; quality, innovativeness, and scientific significance of proposed research; and likelihood of project success. Application available on Web site at http://www.minsocam.org. For applicants between the ages of 25-35.

Academic Fields/Career Goals: Earth Science; Gemology; Materials Science, Engineering, and Metallurgy; Museum Studies; Natural Resources; Natural Sciences; Physical Sciences and Math.

Award: Grant for use in junior, senior, or graduate years; not renewable. *Number:* 1. *Amount:* $5000.

Eligibility Requirements: Applicant must be age 25-35 and enrolled or expecting to enroll full-time at a four-year institution or university. Available to U.S. and non-U.S. citizens.

Application Requirements: Application. *Deadline:* June 1.

Contact: J. Alexander Speer
Mineralogical Society of America
1015 Eighteenth Street, NW, Suite 601
Washington, DC 20036-5212
Phone: 703-652-9950
Fax: 703-652-9950
E-mail: j_a_speer@minsocam.org

MONTANA FEDERATION OF GARDEN CLUBS   http://www.mtfgc.org

LIFE MEMBER MONTANA FEDERATION OF GARDEN CLUBS SCHOLARSHIP
• *See page 138*

NASA DELAWARE SPACE GRANT CONSORTIUM   http://www.delspace.org

NASA DELAWARE SPACE GRANT UNDERGRADUATE TUITION SCHOLARSHIP
• *See page 94*

NASA IDAHO SPACE GRANT CONSORTIUM   http://isgc.uidaho.edu

NASA IDAHO SPACE GRANT CONSORTIUM SCHOLARSHIP PROGRAM
• *See page 94*

NASA NEBRASKA SPACE GRANT CONSORTIUM   http://nasa.unomaha.edu

NASA NEBRASKA SPACE GRANT
• *See page 125*

NASA VERMONT SPACE GRANT CONSORTIUM   http://www.vtspacegrant.org

VERMONT SPACE GRANT CONSORTIUM SCHOLARSHIP PROGRAM
• *See page 94*

NASA VIRGINIA SPACE GRANT CONSORTIUM   http://www.vsgc.odu.edu

VIRGINIA SPACE GRANT CONSORTIUM TEACHER EDUCATION SCHOLARSHIPS
• *See page 125*

NASA WEST VIRGINIA SPACE GRANT CONSORTIUM   http://www.nasa.wvu.edu

WEST VIRGINIA SPACE GRANT CONSORTIUM UNDERGRADUATE SCHOLARSHIP PROGRAM
• *See page 126*

NATIONAL ASSOCIATION OF GEOSCIENCE TEACHERS–FAR WESTERN SECTION   http://www.nagt-fws.org

NATIONAL ASSOCIATION OF GEOSCIENCE TEACHERS - FAR WESTERN SECTION SCHOLARSHIP

Academically superior students currently enrolled in school in Hawaii, Nevada, or California are eligible to apply for one of three $500 scholarships to the school of their choice. High school senior or community college students enrolling full time (12 quarter units) in a bachelor's degree program in geology at a four year institution. Undergraduate geology majors enrolling in an upper division field geology course of approximately 30 field mapping days.

Academic Fields/Career Goals: Earth Science.

Award: Scholarship for use in freshman, sophomore, junior, senior, or graduate years. *Amount:* $500.

Eligibility Requirements: Applicant must be enrolled or expecting to enroll at a four-year institution or university and studying in California, Hawaii, or Nevada. Available to U.S. citizens.

Application Requirements: Application, references, transcript. *Deadline:* March 1.

Contact: Mike Martin
National Association of Geoscience Teachers–Far Western Section
c/o Martin Luther King High School
9301 Wood Road
Riverside, CA 92508

NATIONAL ASSOCIATION OF WATER COMPANIES   http://www.nawc.org

J .J. BARR SCHOLARSHIP
• *See page 139*

NATIONAL ASSOCIATION OF WATER COMPANIES-NEW JERSEY CHAPTER

NATIONAL ASSOCIATION OF WATER COMPANIES-NEW JERSEY CHAPTER SCHOLARSHIP
• *See page 139*

NATIONAL GARDEN CLUBS, INC.   http://www.gardenclub.org

NATIONAL GARDEN CLUBS, INC. SCHOLARSHIP PROGRAM
• *See page 83*

OZARKA NATURAL SPRING WATER   http://www.ozarkawater.com

STATEWIDE SCHOLARSHIPS

Scholarships offered to qualified students who are currently enrolled or planning to enroll in the earth/environmental sciences program at a public or private, not-for-profit, four-year college or university program.

Academic Fields/Career Goals: Earth Science; Environmental Science.

Award: Scholarship for use in freshman, sophomore, or junior years. *Number:* up to 2. *Amount:* up to $10,000.

Eligibility Requirements: Applicant must be enrolled or expecting to enroll full-time at a four-year institution or university and resident of Texas. Applicant must have 3.0 GPA or higher. Available to U.S. citizens.

Ozarka Natural Spring Water (continued)

Application Requirements: Application, essay, transcript. *Deadline:* April 17.

Contact: David Feckley, Scholarship Committee
Ozarka Natural Spring Water
3265 FM 2869
Hawkins, TX 75765
E-mail: edcfund@texas.net

SIGMA XI, THE SCIENTIFIC RESEARCH SOCIETY
http://www.sigmaxi.org

SIGMA XI GRANTS-IN-AID OF RESEARCH
• *See page 84*

SOCIETY FOR MINING, METALLURGY AND EXPLORATION - CENTRAL WYOMING SECTION

COATES, WOLFF, RUSSELL MINING INDUSTRY SCHOLARSHIP
• *See page 95*

SOCIETY FOR RANGE MANAGEMENT
http://www.rangelands.org

MASONIC RANGE SCIENCE SCHOLARSHIP
• *See page 76*

SOCIETY OF MEXICAN AMERICAN ENGINEERS AND SCIENTISTS
http://www.maes-natl.org

GRE AND GRADUATE APPLICATIONS WAIVER
• *See page 95*

SOIL AND WATER CONSERVATION SOCIETY
http://www.swcs.org

DONALD A. WILLIAMS SCHOLARSHIP SOIL CONSERVATION SCHOLARSHIP

Provides financial assistance to members of SWCS who are currently employed but who wish to improve their technical or administrative competence in a conservation-related field through course work at an accredited college or through a program of special study. Download the application form from the SWCS homepage at http://www.swcs.org

Academic Fields/Career Goals: Earth Science; Natural Resources; Natural Sciences.

Award: Scholarship for use in freshman, sophomore, junior, or senior years; not renewable. *Number:* up to 3. *Amount:* $1500.

Eligibility Requirements: Applicant must be enrolled or expecting to enroll at a four-year institution or university. Applicant or parent of applicant must be member of Soil and Water Conservation Society. Applicant or parent of applicant must have employment or volunteer experience in designated career field. Available to U.S. and non-U.S. citizens.

Application Requirements: Application, financial need analysis, budget. *Deadline:* February 12.

Contact: Nancy Herselius, Member Services Coordinator
Soil and Water Conservation Society
7515 NE Ankeny Road
Ankeny, IA 50021-9764
Phone: 515-289-2331 Ext. 17
Fax: 515-289-1227
E-mail: nancyh@swcs.org

SOIL AND WATER CONSERVATION SOCIETY-NEW JERSEY CHAPTER
http://www.geocities.com/njswcs

EDWARD R. HALL SCHOLARSHIP
• *See page 76*

TKE EDUCATIONAL FOUNDATION
http://www.tkefoundation.org

CARROL C. HALL MEMORIAL SCHOLARSHIP
• *See page 95*

TIMOTHY L. TASCHWER SCHOLARSHIP

Scholarship available to an undergraduate member of Tau Kappa Epsilon who is a full-time student of at least sophomore year standing, with a cumulative grade point average of 2.75 or higher. Applicant must be pursuing a degree in natural resources, earth sciences or related subjects and have a record of active TKE chapter leadership involvement.

Academic Fields/Career Goals: Earth Science; Natural Resources.

Award: Scholarship for use in sophomore, junior, or senior years. *Amount:* $500.

Eligibility Requirements: Applicant must be enrolled or expecting to enroll full-time at a four-year institution or university. Available to U.S. and Canadian citizens.

Application Requirements: Application, photo, transcript. *Deadline:* May 12.

Contact: Gary Reed, President/CEO
TKE Educational Foundation
8645 Founders Road
Indianapolis, IN 46131
Phone: 317-872-6533
Fax: 317-875-8353
E-mail: reedga@tke.org

UNITED NEGRO COLLEGE FUND
http://www.uncf.org

BOOZ, ALLEN & HAMILTON/WILLIAM F. STASIOR INTERNSHIP
• *See page 154*

MALCOLM PIRNIE, INC. SCHOLARS PROGRAM
• *See page 169*

ROCKWELL/UNCF CORPORATE SCHOLARS PROGRAM
• *See page 156*

UNIVERSITIES SPACE RESEARCH ASSOCIATION
http://www.usra.edu

UNIVERSITIES SPACE RESEARCH ASSOCIATION SCHOLARSHIP PROGRAM
• *See page 96*

ECONOMICS

ASSOCIATION TO UNITE THE DEMOCRACIES
http://www.iaud.org

MAYME AND HERBERT FRANK EDUCATIONAL FUND

Award of $500-$2000 for graduate scholars interested in federalism to pursue the study of federalism and international integration. Must provide thesis, evidence of relevant course work, and/or independent project research. Deadlines are April 1 for Fall term and October 1 for Spring term.

Academic Fields/Career Goals: Economics; European Studies; International Studies; Peace and Conflict Studies; Political Science.

Award: Scholarship for use in freshman, sophomore, junior, senior, or graduate years; not renewable. *Number:* 1–15. *Amount:* $500–$2000.

Eligibility Requirements: Applicant must be enrolled or expecting to enroll full or part-time at an institution or university. Available to U.S. and Canadian citizens.

Application Requirements: Application, essay, transcript. *Deadline:* varies.

Contact: Robert Frantz, President and CEO
Association to Unite the Democracies
PO Box 77164
Washington, DC 20013-7164
Phone: 202-220-1388
Fax: 202-220-1389
E-mail: atunite@unionnow.org

CATCHING THE DREAM

TRIBAL BUSINESS MANAGEMENT PROGRAM (TBM)
• See page 55

CENTRAL INTELLIGENCE AGENCY   http://www.cia.gov

CENTRAL INTELLIGENCE AGENCY UNDERGRADUATE SCHOLARSHIP PROGRAM
• See page 56

CIRI FOUNDATION   http://www.thecirifoundation.org

CARL H. MARRS SCHOLARSHIP FUND
• See page 56

CUBAN AMERICAN NATIONAL FOUNDATION   http://www.canf.org

MAS FAMILY SCHOLARSHIPS
• See page 146

FUND FOR AMERICAN STUDIES   http://www.tfas.org

ECONOMIC JOURNALISM AWARD

One-time award for the magazine or newspaper writer (or team of writers) who has done the most to shape public opinion by giving the public a better understanding of economic theory and reality. Multiple entries may be submitted, but no more than 20 stories per entry should be included. Entry deadline is March 15. See Web site at http://www.tfas.org for further information.

Academic Fields/Career Goals: Economics; Journalism.

Award: Prize for use in freshman, sophomore, junior, senior, or graduate years; not renewable. *Number:* 1. *Amount:* $5000.

Eligibility Requirements: Applicant must be enrolled or expecting to enroll at an institution or university. Available to U.S. citizens.

Application Requirements: Application, portfolio. *Deadline:* March 15.

Contact: Steve Slattery, Vice President of Programs
Fund for American Studies
1706 New Hampshire Avenue, NW
Washington, DC 20009
Phone: 202-986-0384
Fax: 202-986-8930
E-mail: sslattery@tfas.org

GOVERNMENT FINANCE OFFICERS ASSOCIATION   http://www.gfoa.org

MINORITIES IN GOVERNMENT FINANCE SCHOLARSHIP
• See page 62

GRAND RAPIDS COMMUNITY FOUNDATION   http://www.grfoundation.org

ECONOMIC CLUB OF GRAND RAPIDS BUSINESS STUDY ABROAD SCHOLARSHIP
• See page 62

HARRY S. TRUMAN LIBRARY INSTITUTE   http://www.trumanlibrary.org

HARRY S. TRUMAN LIBRARY INSTITUTE UNDERGRADUATE STUDENT GRANT

Award to support an undergraduate senior writing a thesis on a Truman-related topic to come to the Library and conduct research. Intended to offset expenses incurred for that purpose only. With application, student must include a description of, and rationale for, the project and indicate how the research experience will contribute to the student's future development as a scholar or in an applied field. Deadline: December 1. Project description and proposal not to exceed five pages in length. Letter of support from faculty adviser required.

Academic Fields/Career Goals: Economics; Historic Preservation and Conservation; History; Political Science.

Award: Grant for use in freshman, sophomore, junior, or senior years; not renewable. *Number:* 1. *Amount:* up to $1000.

Eligibility Requirements: Applicant must be enrolled or expecting to enroll at a four-year institution or university and studying in Missouri. Available to U.S. and non-U.S. citizens.

Application Requirements: Application, references, project description and proposal, faculty letter of support. *Deadline:* December 1.

Contact: Lisa Sullivan, Grants Administrator
Harry S. Truman Library Institute
500 West U.S. Highway 24
Independence, MO 64050-1798
Phone: 816-268-8248
Fax: 816-268-8299
E-mail: lisa.sullivan@nara.gov

HISPANIC COLLEGE FUND, INC.   http://www.hispanicfund.org

DENNY'S/HISPANIC COLLEGE FUND SCHOLARSHIP
• See page 62

M & T BANK/ HISPANIC COLLEGE FUND SCHOLARSHIP PROGRAM
• See page 63

JORGE MAS CANOSA FREEDOM FOUNDATION   http://www.canf.org

MAS FAMILY SCHOLARSHIP AWARD
• See page 149

JUNIOR ACHIEVEMENT OF MAINE   http://maine.ja.org

NATIONAL ASSOCIATION OF INSURANCE WOMEN/JUNIOR ACHIEVEMENT OF MAINE SCHOLARSHIP

One-time award for a Maine high school student enrolled in a Junior Achievement high school program or who has taught a JA class in a lower grade. Also available to a college student who has taught a JA class. Recommendations and a minimum 3.0 GPA necessary. Deadline: March 15.

Academic Fields/Career Goals: Economics.

Award: Scholarship for use in freshman, sophomore, junior, or senior years; not renewable. *Number:* 1. *Amount:* $1000.

Eligibility Requirements: Applicant must be enrolled or expecting to enroll full-time at a two-year or four-year or technical institution or university and resident of Maine. Applicant or parent of applicant must be member of Junior Achievement. Applicant or parent of applicant must have employment or volunteer experience in community service. Applicant must have 3.0 GPA or higher. Available to U.S. citizens.

Application Requirements: Application, essay, resume, references, transcript. *Deadline:* March 15.

Contact: Anne Washburne, Program and Council Operations Director
Junior Achievement of Maine
90 Bridge Street, Suite 120
Westbrook, ME 04092
Phone: 207-591-9005
Fax: 207-591-9007
E-mail: program@jamaine.org

NATIONAL ASSOCIATION OF WATER COMPANIES-NEW JERSEY CHAPTER

NATIONAL ASSOCIATION OF WATER COMPANIES-NEW JERSEY CHAPTER SCHOLARSHIP
• See page 139

NATIONAL GARDEN CLUBS, INC.   http://www.gardenclub.org

NATIONAL GARDEN CLUBS, INC. SCHOLARSHIP PROGRAM
• See page 83

NATIONAL SOCIETY DAUGHTERS OF THE AMERICAN REVOLUTION   http://www.dar.org

NATIONAL SOCIETY DAUGHTERS OF THE AMERICAN REVOLUTION ENID HALL GRISWOLD MEMORIAL SCHOLARSHIP

For college juniors and seniors majoring in political science, history, government, or economics. Applicants need not be DAR members but must

National Society Daughters of the American Revolution (continued)

submit letter of sponsorship from local chapter and financial need form from parents. Merit-based. Must submit self-addressed stamped envelope to be considered. Deadline is February 15.

Academic Fields/Career Goals: Economics; History; Political Science.

Award: Scholarship for use in junior or senior years; not renewable. *Number:* 1–5. *Amount:* $1000.

Eligibility Requirements: Applicant must be enrolled or expecting to enroll at a four-year institution or university. Applicant must have 3.0 GPA or higher. Available to U.S. citizens.

Application Requirements: Application, essay, financial need analysis, references, self-addressed stamped envelope, test scores, transcript. *Deadline:* February 15.

Contact: Committee Services Office, Scholarship
National Society Daughters of the American Revolution
1776 D Street, NW
Washington, DC 20006-5392

ORANGE COUNTY COMMUNITY FOUNDATION   http://www.heef.org

UNION BANK OF CALIFORNIA SCHOLARSHIP
• *See page 152*

ROYAL BANK NATIVE STUDENTS AWARDS PROGRAM   http://www.rbc.com

ROYAL BANK ABORIGINAL STUDENT AWARDS
• *See page 153*

SOIL AND WATER CONSERVATION SOCIETY   http://www.swcs.org

SWCS MELVILLE H. COHEE STUDENT LEADER CONSERVATION SCHOLARSHIP
• *See page 85*

UNITED AGRIBUSINESS LEAGUE   http://www.ual.org

UNITED AGRIBUSINESS LEAGUE SCHOLARSHIP PROGRAM
• *See page 77*

UNITED AGRICULTURAL BENEFIT TRUST SCHOLARSHIP
• *See page 77*

UNITED NEGRO COLLEGE FUND   http://www.uncf.org

SBC FOUNDATION SCHOLARSHIP
• *See page 156*

SBC PACIFIC BELL FOUNDATION SCHOLARSHIP
• *See page 156*

SPRINT SCHOLARSHIP/INTERNSHIP
• *See page 71*

WOMEN GROCERS OF AMERICA   http://www.nationalgrocers.org

MARY MACEY SCHOLARSHIP
• *See page 85*

EDUCATION

ALBERTA HERITAGE SCHOLARSHIP FUND/ ALBERTA SCHOLARSHIP PROGRAMS   http://www.alis.gov.ab.ca

ANNA AND JOHN KOLESAR MEMORIAL SCHOLARSHIPS

One scholarship will be awarded to the applicant with the highest academic average in three designated subjects as shown on an Alberta Education Transcript. Applicants must be Alberta residents, planning to enroll in a Faculty of Education, and from a family where neither parent has a university degree.

Academic Fields/Career Goals: Education; Special Education.

Award: Scholarship for use in freshman or sophomore years; not renewable. *Number:* 1. *Amount:* $1033.

Eligibility Requirements: Applicant must be Canadian citizen; high school student; planning to enroll or expecting to enroll full-time at a two-year or four-year institution or university and resident of Alberta. Applicant must have 3.0 GPA or higher.

Application Requirements: Application, transcript. *Deadline:* July 1.

Contact: Stuart Dunn, Manager
Alberta Heritage Scholarship Fund/Alberta Scholarship Programs
4th Floor, 9940 106th Street, Box 28000 Station Main
Edmonton, AB T5J 4R4
Canada
Phone: 780-427-8640
Fax: 780-422-4516
E-mail: scholarships@gov.ab.ca

LANGUAGES IN TEACHER EDUCATION SCHOLARSHIPS

Scholarships of CAN$2500 for education students in Alberta institutions with a specialty in languages other than English. Students must be nominated by their Alberta postsecondary institution. Nomination deadline is March 1.

Academic Fields/Career Goals: Education; Foreign Language.

Award: Scholarship for use in freshman, sophomore, junior, or senior years. *Number:* 13. *Amount:* $2152.

Eligibility Requirements: Applicant must be enrolled or expecting to enroll full-time at an institution or university and studying in Alberta. Available to U.S. and Canadian citizens.

Application Requirements: Nomination by institution.

Contact: Stuart Dunn, Manager
Alberta Heritage Scholarship Fund/Alberta Scholarship Programs
4th Floor, 9940 106th Street, Box 28000 Station Main
Edmonton, AB T5J 4R4
Canada
Phone: 780-427-8640
Fax: 780-427-1288
E-mail: scholarships@gov.ab.ca

ALPHA DELTA KAPPA FOUNDATION   http://www.alphadeltakappa.org

INTERNATIONAL TEACHER EDUCATION SCHOLARSHIP

Enables women from foreign countries to study for their master's degree in the United States. Applicants must be single with no dependents, age 20-35, non-U.S. citizens residing outside the U.S., have at least one year of college completed, and plan to enter the teaching profession.

Academic Fields/Career Goals: Education.

Award: Scholarship for use in sophomore, junior, senior, or graduate years; renewable. *Number:* up to 7. *Amount:* up to $10,000.

Eligibility Requirements: Applicant must be age 20-35; enrolled or expecting to enroll full-time at a four-year institution or university and single female. Applicant must have 3.5 GPA or higher. Available to Canadian and non-U.S. citizens.

Application Requirements: Application, autobiography, financial need analysis, photo, references, test scores, transcript, certificates of health from physician and dentist, TOEFL scores, college acceptance. *Deadline:* January 1.

Contact: Dee Frost, Scholarships and Grants Coordinator
Alpha Delta Kappa Foundation
1615 West 92nd Street
Kansas City, MO 64114-3296
Phone: 816-363-5525
Fax: 816-363-4010
E-mail: headquarters@alphadeltakappa.org

ALPHA KAPPA ALPHA   http://www.akaeaf.org

AKA EDUCATIONAL ADVANCEMENT FOUNDATION MERIT SCHOLARSHIP

Scholarships for students demonstrating exceptional academic achievement. Applicant must have completed a minimum of one year in a degree granting institution and be continuing their program in that institution. Must have GPA of 3.0 or higher and show evidence of leadership by participation in community or campus activities.

Academic Fields/Career Goals: Education.

Award: Scholarship for use in sophomore, junior, or senior years. *Amount:* up to $1000.

Eligibility Requirements: Applicant must be enrolled or expecting to enroll at a four-year institution or university. Applicant must have 3.0 GPA or higher. Available to U.S. citizens.

Application Requirements: Application. *Deadline:* January 15.

Contact: Linda M. White, President
Alpha Kappa Alpha
5656 South Stony Island Avenue
Chicago, IL 60637
Phone: 773-947-0026
E-mail: akaeaf@aol.com

AMARILLO AREA FOUNDATION   http://www.aaf-hf.org

AMARILLO AREA FOUNDATION SCHOLARSHIPS
• *See page 53*

AMERICAN ASSOCIATION FOR HEALTH EDUCATION   http://www.aahperd.org/aahe

AMERICAN ASSOCIATION FOR HEALTH EDUCATION WILLIAM M. KANE SCHOLARSHIP

Award for undergraduate student enrolled in health education program. Must submit resume, essay, and three letters of recommendation. One-time award of $1000. Deadline: December 1. For study in U.S. and U.S. territories. Minimum 3.5 GPA required.

Academic Fields/Career Goals: Education; Health and Medical Sciences.

Award: Scholarship for use in freshman, sophomore, junior, or senior years; not renewable. *Number:* 1. *Amount:* $1000.

Eligibility Requirements: Applicant must be enrolled or expecting to enroll full-time at a four-year institution or university. Applicant must have 3.5 GPA or higher. Available to U.S. citizens.

Application Requirements: Application, essay, resume, references, transcript. *Deadline:* November 15.

Contact: Linda M. Moore, Program Administrator
American Association for Health Education
1900 Association Drive
Reston, VA 20191-1599
Phone: 703-476-3437
Fax: 703-476-6638
E-mail: aahe@aahperd.org

AMERICAN FEDERATION OF TEACHERS   http://www.aft.org

ROBERT G. PORTER SCHOLARS PROGRAM-AFT MEMBERS

Non-renewable grant provides continuing education for school teachers, paraprofessionals and school-related personnel, higher education faculty and professionals, employees of state and local governments, nurses and other health professionals. Must be member of the American Federation of Teachers for at least one year.

Academic Fields/Career Goals: Education; Health and Medical Sciences; Special Education.

Award: Grant for use in freshman, sophomore, junior, senior, or graduate years; not renewable. *Number:* 4–10. *Amount:* $1000.

Eligibility Requirements: Applicant must be enrolled or expecting to enroll full or part-time at a four-year institution or university. Available to U.S. citizens.

Application Requirements: Application, essay. *Deadline:* March 31.

Contact: Bernadette Bailey, Scholarship Coordinator
American Federation of Teachers
555 New Jersey Avenue, NW
Washington, DC 20001
Phone: 202-879-4481
Fax: 202-879-4406
E-mail: bbailey@aft.org

AMERICAN FOUNDATION FOR THE BLIND   http://www.afb.org/scholarships.asp

DELTA GAMMA FOUNDATION FLORENCE MARGARET HARVEY MEMORIAL SCHOLARSHIP

The Delta Gamma Foundation Florence Margaret Harvey Memorial Scholarship provides one (1) scholarship of $1,000 to an undergraduate or graduate student who has exhibited academic excellence, and is studying in the field of rehabilitation and/or education of persons who are blind or visually impaired. For additional information and application requirements, refer to Web site: www.afb.org/scholarships.asp

Academic Fields/Career Goals: Education; Therapy/Rehabilitation.

Award: Scholarship for use in freshman, sophomore, junior, or senior years; not renewable. *Number:* 1. *Amount:* up to $1000.

Eligibility Requirements: Applicant must be enrolled or expecting to enroll full or part-time at a two-year or four-year institution or university. Applicant must be visually impaired. Available to U.S. citizens.

Application Requirements: Application, essay, references, transcript, proof of post-secondary acceptance and legal blindness. *Deadline:* March 31.

Contact: Alina Vayntrub, Departmental Assistant, Information Center
American Foundation for the Blind
11 Penn Plaza, Suite 300
New York, NY 10001
Phone: 212-502-7661
Fax: 212-502-7771
E-mail: afbinfo@afb.net

RUDOLPH DILLMAN MEMORIAL SCHOLARSHIP

The Rudolph Dillman Memorial Scholarship is a one-time award not open to previous recipients. It provides four (4) scholarships of $2,500 each to undergraduate or graduate students who are studying in the field of rehabilitation and/or education of persons who are blind or visually impaired. One of these grants is specifically for a student who meets all requirements and submits evidence of economic need. For additional information and application requirements, visit www.afb.org/scholarships.asp

Academic Fields/Career Goals: Education; Therapy/Rehabilitation.

Award: Scholarship for use in freshman, sophomore, junior, senior, or graduate years; not renewable. *Number:* up to 4. *Amount:* up to $2500.

Eligibility Requirements: Applicant must be enrolled or expecting to enroll full or part-time at a two-year or four-year institution or university. Applicant must be visually impaired. Available to U.S. citizens.

Application Requirements: Application, essay, financial need analysis, references, transcript, proof of legal blindness, acceptance letter. *Deadline:* March 31.

Contact: Information Center
American Foundation for the Blind
American Foundation for the Blind Scholarship Committee, 11 Penn Plaza, Suite 300
New York, NY 10001
Phone: 212-502-7661
Fax: 212-502-7771
E-mail: afbinfo@afb.net

AMERICAN LEGION AUXILIARY, DEPARTMENT OF IOWA   http://www.ialegion.org/ala

HARRIET HOFFMAN MEMORIAL SCHOLARSHIP FOR TEACHER TRAINING

One-time award for Iowa residents attending Iowa institutions who are the children, grandchildren, or great-grandchildren of veterans. Must be studying education. Preference given to descendants of deceased veterans.

Academic Fields/Career Goals: Education.

Award: Scholarship for use in freshman, sophomore, junior, or senior years; not renewable. *Number:* 1. *Amount:* $400.

Eligibility Requirements: Applicant must be enrolled or expecting to enroll full or part-time at a four-year institution or university; resident of Iowa and studying in Iowa. Available to U.S. citizens. Applicant or parent must meet one or more of the following requirements: general

American Legion Auxiliary, Department of Iowa (continued)

military experience; retired from active duty; disabled or killed as a result of military service; prisoner of war; or missing in action.

Application Requirements: Application, autobiography, essay, financial need analysis, photo, references, self-addressed stamped envelope, test scores, transcript. *Deadline:* June 1.

Contact: Marlene Valentine, Secretary/Treasurer
American Legion Auxiliary, Department of Iowa
720 Lyon Street
Des Moines, IA 50309
Phone: 515-282-7987
Fax: 515-282-7583

AMERICAN MONTESSORI SOCIETY
http://www.amshq.org

AMERICAN MONTESSORI SOCIETY TEACHER EDUCATION SCHOLARSHIP FUND

One-time award for aspiring Montessori teacher candidates. Must study full time and be under age 20. Submit verification that applicant has been accepted into the AMS program.

Academic Fields/Career Goals: Education.

Award: Scholarship for use in freshman, sophomore, or junior years; not renewable. *Number:* 5–20. *Amount:* varies.

Eligibility Requirements: Applicant must be age 19 or under and enrolled or expecting to enroll full-time at a two-year or four-year institution or university. Available to U.S. and non-U.S. citizens.

Application Requirements: Application, autobiography, essay, financial need analysis, references. *Deadline:* May 1.

Contact: Dottie Sweet Feldman, Fund Administrator
American Montessori Society
2720 Sonata Drive
Columbus, OH 43209
Phone: 614-237-2975
E-mail: dssf@juno.com

AMERICAN ORFF-SCHULWERK ASSOCIATION
http://www.aosa.org

AMERICAN ORFF-SCHULWERK ASSOCIATION RESEARCH GRANT

Nonrenewable award to graduate students with work experience in music, who are also members of AOSA, for projects that promote the philosophy and the Orff-Schulwerk processes developed by Carl Orff and Gunild Keetman. Must be U.S. citizen or U.S. resident for past five years. Deadlines are January 15 and July 15.

Academic Fields/Career Goals: Education; Music; Performing Arts.

Award: Grant for use in freshman, sophomore, junior, senior, graduate, or postgraduate years; not renewable. *Number:* 1–2. *Amount:* $500–$2500.

Eligibility Requirements: Applicant must be enrolled or expecting to enroll full or part-time at an institution or university and must have an interest in music/singing. Applicant or parent of applicant must be member of American Orff-Schulwerk Association. Applicant or parent of applicant must have employment or volunteer experience in designated career field. Available to U.S. citizens.

Application Requirements: Application, references, self-addressed stamped envelope. *Deadline:* varies.

Contact: Cindi Wobig, Executive Director
American Orff-Schulwerk Association
PO Box 391089
Cleveland, OH 44139-8089
Phone: 440-543-5366
Fax: 440-543-2687
E-mail: aosahdq@msn.com

GUNILD KEETMAN ASSISTANCE FUND

Scholarship for graduate students interested in furthering their growth in Orff-Schulwerk through teacher training courses. Must be a U.S. citizen or U.S. resident for past five years, a member of AOSA for last two years, and have financial need.

Academic Fields/Career Goals: Education; Performing Arts.

Award: Scholarship for use in freshman, sophomore, junior, senior, graduate, or postgraduate years; not renewable. *Number:* 1–15. *Amount:* $500–$2000.

Eligibility Requirements: Applicant must be enrolled or expecting to enroll full or part-time at an institution or university and must have an interest in music/singing. Applicant or parent of applicant must be member of American Orff-Schulwerk Association. Applicant or parent of applicant must have employment or volunteer experience in designated career field. Available to U.S. citizens.

Application Requirements: Application, financial need analysis, references. *Deadline:* January 15.

Contact: Cindi Wobig, Executive Director
American Orff-Schulwerk Association
PO Box 391089
Cleveland, OH 44139-8089
Phone: 440-543-5366
Fax: 440-543-2687
E-mail: aosahdq@msn.com

AMERICAN QUARTER HORSE FOUNDATION (AQHF)
http://www.aqha.org/aqhya

AQHF EDUCATION OR NURSING SCHOLARSHIP

Must be current member of AQHA or AQHYA and pursuing a career in education or nursing. Recipient receives $2500 per year for four years. Minimum 2.5 GPA required.

Academic Fields/Career Goals: Education; Nursing.

Award: Scholarship for use in freshman year; renewable. *Number:* 1. *Amount:* $10,000.

Eligibility Requirements: Applicant must be enrolled or expecting to enroll full-time at a two-year or four-year or technical institution or university. Applicant or parent of applicant must be member of American Quarter Horse Association. Applicant must have 2.5 GPA or higher. Available to U.S. and Canadian citizens.

Application Requirements: Application, financial need analysis, photo, references, transcript. *Deadline:* February 1.

Contact: Laura Owens, Scholarship Coordinator
American Quarter Horse Foundation (AQHF)
2601 I-40 East
Amarillo, TX 79104
Phone: 806-378-5034
Fax: 806-376-1005
E-mail: lowens@aqha.org

ARCTIC INSTITUTE OF NORTH AMERICA
http://www.arctic.ucalgary.ca

JIM BOURQUE SCHOLARSHIP

One-time award to Canadian Aboriginal student enrolled in postsecondary training in education, environmental studies, traditional knowledge or telecommunications. Must submit, in 500 words or less, a description of their intended program of study and reasons for their choice of program.

Academic Fields/Career Goals: Education; Natural Resources; Natural Sciences.

Award: Scholarship for use in freshman, sophomore, junior, or senior years; not renewable. *Number:* 1. *Amount:* $868.

Eligibility Requirements: Applicant must be Canadian citizen and enrolled or expecting to enroll full-time at an institution or university.

Application Requirements: Essay, financial need analysis, references, transcript, proof of enrollment in, or application to, a post secondary institution. *Deadline:* July 18.

Contact: Dr. Benoit Beauchamp
Arctic Institute of North America
Arctic Institute of North America, University of Calgary, 2500 University Drive, NW
Calgary, AB T2N 1N4
Canada
Phone: 403-220-7515
Fax: 403-282-4609

ARIZONA BUSINESS EDUCATION ASSOCIATION
http://www.azbea.org

ABEA STUDENT TEACHER SCHOLARSHIPS

Scholarships awarded to future business education teachers. Must be member of ABEA. Deadline is April 9.

Academic Fields/Career Goals: Education.

Award: Scholarship for use in sophomore, junior, or senior years; not renewable. *Number:* up to 3. *Amount:* up to $500.

Eligibility Requirements: Applicant must be enrolled or expecting to enroll at a four-year institution or university. Available to U.S. citizens.

Application Requirements: Application, resume, references, transcript. *Deadline:* April 9.

Contact: Shirley Eittreim, Scholarships Committee Chair
Arizona Business Education Association
Northland Pioneer College, PO Box 610
Holbrook, AZ 86025
Phone: 928-532-6151
E-mail: sjeittreim@cybertrails.com

ARKANSAS DEPARTMENT OF HIGHER EDUCATION
http://www.arkansashighered.com

ARKANSAS MINORITY TEACHER SCHOLARS PROGRAM

Renewable award for Native-American, African-American, Hispanic and Asian-American students who have completed at least sixty semester hours and are enrolled full-time in a teacher education program in Arkansas. Award may be renewed for one year. Must be Arkansas resident with minimum 2.5 GPA. Must teach for three to five years in Arkansas to repay scholarship funds received. Must pass PPST exam.

Academic Fields/Career Goals: Education.

Award: Forgivable loan for use in junior or senior years; renewable. *Number:* up to 100. *Amount:* up to $5000.

Eligibility Requirements: Applicant must be American Indian/Alaska Native, Asian/Pacific Islander, Black (non-Hispanic), or Hispanic; enrolled or expecting to enroll full-time at a four-year institution or university; resident of Arkansas and studying in Arkansas. Applicant must have 2.5 GPA or higher. Available to U.S. citizens.

Application Requirements: Application, transcript. *Deadline:* June 1.

Contact: Lillian Williams, Assistant Coordinator
Arkansas Department of Higher Education
114 East Capitol
Little Rock, AR 72201
Phone: 501-371-2050
Fax: 501-371-2001

EMERGENCY SECONDARY EDUCATION LOAN PROGRAM
• See page 135

BETHESDA LUTHERAN HOMES AND SERVICES, INC.
http://www.blhs.org

DEVELOPMENTAL DISABILITIES SCHOLASTIC ACHIEVEMENT SCHOLARSHIP FOR LUTHERAN COLLEGE STUDENTS
• See page 208

BROWN FOUNDATION FOR EDUCATIONAL EQUITY, EXCELLENCE, AND RESEARCH
http://www.brownvboard.org/foundatn/sclrbroc.htm

BROWN SCHOLAR

Renewable scholarship award to college student entering junior year who is admitted to teacher education program at a four-year college or university. Applicants must be minority student. Minimum 3.0 GPA required. Award paid at $500 per semester for up to four semesters.

Academic Fields/Career Goals: Education.

Award: Scholarship for use in junior or senior years; renewable. *Number:* varies. *Amount:* $1000.

Eligibility Requirements: Applicant must be American Indian/Alaska Native, Asian/Pacific Islander, Black (non-Hispanic), or Hispanic and enrolled or expecting to enroll full-time at a four-year institution or university. Applicant must have 3.0 GPA or higher. Available to U.S. citizens.

Application Requirements: Application, essay, references, transcript. *Deadline:* March 30.

Contact: Chelsey Smith, Staff/Administrative Assistant
Brown Foundation for Educational Equity, Excellence, and Research
PO Box 4862
Topeka, KS 66604
Phone: 785-235-3939
Fax: 785-235-1001
E-mail: brownfound@juno.com

LUCINDA TODD BOOK SCHOLARSHIP

Book award of $300 to graduating high school senior planning to pursue teacher education at four-year college or university. Award paid to institution for books. Applicants must be minority student. Minimum 3.0 GPA required.

Academic Fields/Career Goals: Education.

Award: Scholarship for use in freshman year; not renewable. *Number:* varies. *Amount:* $300.

Eligibility Requirements: Applicant must be American Indian/Alaska Native, Asian/Pacific Islander, Black (non-Hispanic), or Hispanic; high school student and planning to enroll or expecting to enroll full or part-time at a four-year institution or university. Applicant must have 3.0 GPA or higher. Available to U.S. citizens.

Application Requirements: Application, references, transcript. *Deadline:* March 30.

Contact: Chelsey Smith, Staff/Administrative Assistant
Brown Foundation for Educational Equity, Excellence, and Research
PO Box 4862
Topeka, KS 66604
Phone: 785-235-3939
Fax: 785-235-1001
E-mail: brownfound@juno.com

BUSINESS AND PROFESSIONAL WOMEN'S FOUNDATION
http://www.bpwusa.org

BPW CAREER ADVANCEMENT SCHOLARSHIP PROGRAM FOR WOMEN
• See page 136

CALIFORNIA STATE PARENT-TEACHER ASSOCIATION
http://www.capta.org

CONTINUING EDUCATION - CREDENTIAL TEACHERS AND COUNSELORS SCHOLARSHIP

Scholarships are available annually from the California State PTA for continuing education use, including summer study, from January 1 through December 31. Applicant must be a member of a PTA/PTSA unit in good standing and teach or have a counseling position at that PTA/PTSA school. Deadline November 15.

Academic Fields/Career Goals: Education.

Award: Scholarship for use in freshman, or graduate years; renewable. *Amount:* up to $500.

Eligibility Requirements: Applicant must be enrolled or expecting to enroll full-time at an institution or university and resident of California. Available to U.S. citizens.

Application Requirements: Application, essay, references, copy of membership card. *Deadline:* November 15.

Contact: Becky Reece, Scholarship and Award Chairman
California State Parent-Teacher Association
930 Georgia Street
Los Angeles, CA 90015-1322
Phone: 213-620-1100
Fax: 213-620-1411

CALIFORNIA TEACHERS ASSOCIATION (CTA)
http://www.cta.org

L. GORDON BITTLE MEMORIAL SCHOLARSHIP

Three $2000 awards annually to active Student California Teachers Association (SCTA) members for study in a teacher preparatory program. Students may reapply each year. Applications available in October and due February 16th. Not available to those who are currently working in public schools as members of CTA.

Academic Fields/Career Goals: Education.

Award: Scholarship for use in freshman, sophomore, junior, senior, or graduate years; not renewable. *Number:* 3. *Amount:* $2000.

Eligibility Requirements: Applicant must be enrolled or expecting to enroll full-time at a two-year or four-year institution or university; resident of California and studying in California. Available to U.S. and non-U.S. citizens.

Application Requirements: Application, essay, references, transcript. *Deadline:* January 27.

Contact: Janeya Collins, Scholarship Coordinator
California Teachers Association (CTA)
PO Box 921
Burlingame, CA 94011-0921
Phone: 650-552-5468
Fax: 650-552-5001
E-mail: scholarships@cta.org

MARTIN LUTHER KING, JR. MEMORIAL SCHOLARSHIP

For ethnic minority members of the California Teachers Association, their dependent children, and ethnic minority members of Student California Teachers Association who want to pursue degrees or credentials in public education. Applications available in January and due March 15.

Academic Fields/Career Goals: Education.

Award: Scholarship for use in freshman, sophomore, junior, senior, or graduate years; not renewable. *Number:* 100–150. *Amount:* $1000–$2000.

Eligibility Requirements: Applicant must be American Indian/Alaska Native, Asian/Pacific Islander, Black (non-Hispanic), or Hispanic and enrolled or expecting to enroll full-time at a two-year or four-year institution or university. Applicant or parent of applicant must be member of California Teachers Association. Available to U.S. and non-U.S. citizens.

Application Requirements: Application, essay, financial need analysis, references. *Deadline:* March 15.

Contact: Janeya Collins, Scholarship Coordinator
California Teachers Association (CTA)
PO Box 921
Burlingame, CA 94011-0921
Phone: 650-552-5468
Fax: 650-552-5001
E-mail: scholarships@cta.org

CANADIAN INSTITUTE OF UKRAINIAN STUDIES
http://www.ualberta.ca/cius/

LEO J. KRYSA UNDERGRADUATE SCHOLARSHIP
• *See page 104*

CATCHING THE DREAM

MATH, ENGINEERING, SCIENCE, BUSINESS, EDUCATION, COMPUTERS SCHOLARSHIPS
• *See page 145*

NATIVE AMERICAN LEADERSHIP IN EDUCATION (NALE)
• *See page 145*

COLLEGE FOUNDATION OF NORTH CAROLINA, INC
http://www.cfnc.org

DOTTIE MARTIN TEACHERS SCHOLARSHIP

Annual scholarship of $500 is designed for any student presently enrolled in a college or university and studying the field of education. Recent high school graduates are not eligible to apply.

Academic Fields/Career Goals: Education.

Award: Scholarship for use in freshman, sophomore, junior, senior, graduate, or postgraduate years. *Number:* 2–3. *Amount:* up to $500.

Eligibility Requirements: Applicant must be enrolled or expecting to enroll at a two-year or four-year or technical institution or university. Available to U.S. citizens.

Application Requirements: Application. *Deadline:* June 1.

Contact: Joyce Glass
College Foundation of North Carolina, Inc
4413 Driftwood Drive
Clemmons, NC 27012
Phone: 336-766-0067
E-mail: fwglass@earthlink.net

COLLEGEBOUND FOUNDATION
http://www.collegeboundfoundation.org

ALICE G. PINDERHUGHES SCHOLARSHIP

Award for Baltimore City public high school graduates. Please see Web site: http://www.collegeboundfoundation.org for complete information on application process. Must major in education and plan to teach in grades K-12. Minimum GPA of 3.0, must have financial need. Must submit one-page essay describing a teacher who has made an impact on you. Must submit CollegeBound Competitive Scholarship/Last-Dollar Grant Application.

Academic Fields/Career Goals: Education.

Award: Scholarship for use in freshman, sophomore, junior, or senior years; renewable. *Number:* 1. *Amount:* $500.

Eligibility Requirements: Applicant must be enrolled or expecting to enroll full-time at a two-year or four-year institution or university and resident of Maryland. Applicant must have 3.0 GPA or higher. Available to U.S. citizens.

Application Requirements: Application, essay, financial need analysis, references, transcript, financial aid award letters, Student Aid Report (SAR). *Deadline:* March 19.

Contact: April Bell, Associate Program Director
CollegeBound Foundation
300 Water Street, Suite 300
Baltimore, MD 21202
Phone: 410-783-2905 Ext. 208
Fax: 410-727-5786
E-mail: abell@collegeboundfoundation.org

SHEILA Z. KOLMAN MEMORIAL SCHOLARSHIP

Award for Baltimore City public high school graduates. Please see Web site: http://www.collegeboundfoundation.org for complete information on application process. Must submit College Bound Competitive Scholarship/Last-Dollar Grant Application. Minimum GPA of 2.5 required, demonstrable financial need. Submit 500-1000 word essay on how a teacher affected your life in a positive way. Must major or minor in education.

Academic Fields/Career Goals: Education.

Award: Scholarship for use in freshman year; not renewable. *Number:* 1. *Amount:* $1000.

Eligibility Requirements: Applicant must be enrolled or expecting to enroll full-time at a four-year institution or university and resident of Maryland. Applicant must have 2.5 GPA or higher. Available to U.S. citizens.

Application Requirements: Application, essay, financial need analysis, references, transcript, financial aid award letters, Student Aid Report (SAR). *Deadline:* March 19.

Contact: April Bell, Associate Program Director
CollegeBound Foundation
300 Water Street, Suite 300
Baltimore, MD 21202
Phone: 410-783-2905 Ext. 208
Fax: 410-727-5786
E-mail: abell@collegeboundfoundation.org

COMMISSION FRANCO-AMERICAINE D'ECHANGES UNIVERSITAIRES ET CULTURELS
http://www.fulbright-france.org

FULBRIGHT PROGRAM

Fulbright program offered to senior scholars, advanced students, professionals and exchange teachers to carry out research, and/or lecture, study or teach in the U.S. or France. Program provides grants to approximately 100 nationals from both countries. Applicants must submit proof of their affiliation with their host institution. Grant is only available to American and French citizens. For French citizens, photo must accompany application. Application deadlines: August 1 (for U.S. applicants) and December 15 (for French applicants). For more information, see Web site: http://www.fulbright-france.org.

Academic Fields/Career Goals: Education.

Award: Grant for use in senior, graduate, or postgraduate years; not renewable. *Number:* 80–100. *Amount:* $1000–$20,000.

Eligibility Requirements: Applicant must be enrolled or expecting to enroll full or part-time at a four-year institution or university. Applicant or parent of applicant must have employment or volunteer experience in teaching. Available to U.S. and non-Canadian citizens.

Application Requirements: Application, essay, interview, photo, references, test scores, transcript. *Deadline:* varies.

Contact: Amy Tondu, Program Officer
Commission Franco-Americaine d'Echanges Universitaires et Culturels
Fulbright Commission
9 Rue Chardin
Paris 75016
France
Phone: 33-1-44145364
Fax: 33-1-42880479
E-mail: atondu@fulbright-france.org

COMMON KNOWLEDGE SCHOLARSHIP FOUNDATION
http://www.cksf.org

FUTURE TEACHER OF AMERICA SCHOLARSHIP

Multiple-choice, Internet-based quiz competition that tests student's knowledge in core subjects associated with teaching. Open to 9-11 grade high school students in the United States interested in teaching/education as a career. Contest dates are; 1: December 4 - 9 and 2: May 7 - 12. For more information and online registration check Web site: www.cksf.org

Academic Fields/Career Goals: Education.

Award: Scholarship for use in freshman year; not renewable. *Number:* 2. *Amount:* $250.

Eligibility Requirements: Applicant must be high school student and planning to enroll or expecting to enroll at a four-year institution or university. Available to U.S. citizens.

Application Requirements: Applicant must enter a contest. *Deadline:* varies.

Contact: Daryl Hulce, President
Common Knowledge Scholarship Foundation
PO Box 290361
Davie, FL 33329-0361
Phone: 954-262-8553
Fax: 954-262-3940
E-mail: hulce@cksf.org

COMMUNITY FOUNDATION FOR PALM BEACH AND MARTIN COUNTIES, INC.
http://www.yourcommunityfoundation.org

INEZ PEPPERS LOVETT SCHOLARSHIP FUND

African-American Palm Beach County graduating senior interested in pursuing a career in elementary education. Must have 3.0 GPA or better and demonstrate financial need.

Academic Fields/Career Goals: Education.

Award: Scholarship for use in freshman year; not renewable. *Number:* 1. *Amount:* $750–$2500.

Eligibility Requirements: Applicant must be Black (non-Hispanic); high school student; planning to enroll or expecting to enroll full-time at a four-year institution or university; female and resident of Florida. Applicant must have 3.0 GPA or higher. Available to U.S. citizens.

Application Requirements: Application, financial need analysis, transcript. *Deadline:* February 1.

Contact: Carolyn Jenco, Grants Manager/Scholarship Coordinator
Community Foundation for Palm Beach and Martin Counties, Inc.
700 South Dixie Highway, Suite 200
West Palm Beach, FL 33401
Phone: 561-659-6800
Fax: 561-832-6542
E-mail: cjenco@cfpbmc.org

THOMAS WILLIAM BENNETT MEMORIAL SCHOLARSHIP

Scholarship is awarded to a high school senior, in public or private school, planning on pursuing a career in education, preferably teaching reading skills. Must have 2.5 GPA or better. Must be a resident of Palm Beach or Martin County. Deadline is February 1. Applications are available online: http://www.yourcommunityfoundation.org

Academic Fields/Career Goals: Education.

Award: Scholarship for use in freshman year; not renewable. *Number:* varies. *Amount:* $750–$2500.

Eligibility Requirements: Applicant must be high school student; planning to enroll or expecting to enroll at a four-year institution or university and resident of Florida. Applicant must have 2.5 GPA or higher. Available to U.S. citizens.

Application Requirements: Application. *Deadline:* February 1.

Contact: Carolyn Jenco, Grants Manager/Scholarship Coordinator
Community Foundation for Palm Beach and Martin Counties, Inc.
700 South Dixie Highway, Suite 200
West Palm Beach, FL 33401
Phone: 561-659-6800
Fax: 561-832-6542
E-mail: cjenco@cfpbmc.org

COMMUNITY FOUNDATION OF WESTERN MASSACHUSETTS
http://www.communityfoundation.org

MARGARET E. AND AGNES K. O'DONNELL SCHOLARSHIP FUND

For graduating seniors of Northampton High School and Smith Vocational High School, and for students of the College of Our Lady of the Elms and Fitchburg State College majoring in education.

Academic Fields/Career Goals: Education.

Award: Scholarship for use in freshman year; renewable. *Number:* up to 17. *Amount:* $1000–$1800.

Eligibility Requirements: Applicant must be enrolled or expecting to enroll full-time at a four-year institution or university and resident of Massachusetts. Available to U.S. citizens.

Application Requirements: Application, financial need analysis, transcript, parent and student federal income tax returns, GPA. *Deadline:* March 31.

Contact: Dorothy Theriaque, Education Associate
Community Foundation of Western Massachusetts
1500 Main Street, PO Box 15769
Springfield, MA 01115
Phone: 413-732-2858
Fax: 413-733-8565
E-mail: dtheriaque@communityfoundation.org

CONFEDERATED TRIBES OF GRAND RONDE
http://www.grandronde.org

EULA PETITE MEMORIAL EDUCATION SCHOLARSHIPS

Available to any enrolled member of the Confederated Tribes of Grand Ronde. Available to education majors only. Renewable for six terms/four semesters of continuous study. Intended for last two years of undergraduate study, or any two years of graduate study.

Academic Fields/Career Goals: Education.

Award: Scholarship for use in junior, senior, or graduate years; renewable. *Number:* 1. *Amount:* $7000.

Confederated Tribes of Grand Ronde (continued)

Eligibility Requirements: Applicant must be American Indian/Alaska Native and enrolled or expecting to enroll full or part-time at a two-year or four-year institution or university. Available to U.S. and non-U.S. citizens.

Application Requirements: Application, essay, references, test scores, transcript, verification of Tribal enrollment. *Deadline:* April 30.

Contact: Tribal Scholarship Coordinator
Confederated Tribes of Grand Ronde
9615 Grand Ronde Road
Grand Ronde, OR 97347
Phone: 800-422-0232 Ext. 2275
Fax: 503-879-2286
E-mail: education@grandronde.org

CONNECTICUT ASSOCIATION FOR HEALTH, PHYSICAL EDUCATION, RECREATION AND DANCE
http://www.ctahperd.org

MARY BENEVENTO CAHPERD SCHOLARSHIP

Scholarship awarded to a graduating high school senior who plans to engage in the professional studies of health education, physical education, recreation, or dance. Must be resident of Connecticut and plan to attend a university or four-year college in Connecticut.

Academic Fields/Career Goals: Education; Sports-related.

Award: Scholarship for use in freshman year; not renewable. *Number:* 1–2. *Amount:* $1000.

Eligibility Requirements: Applicant must be high school student; planning to enroll or expecting to enroll full-time at a four-year institution or university; resident of Connecticut and studying in Connecticut. Available to U.S. citizens.

Application Requirements: Application, essay, references, test scores, transcript. *Deadline:* April 1.

Contact: Jodie Hellmann, CAHPERD Scholarship Chair
Connecticut Association for Health, Physical Education, Recreation and Dance
376 Old Woodbury Road
Southbury, CT 06488
Phone: 203-264-7921
E-mail: jahellmann@yahoo.com

CONNECTICUT DEPARTMENT OF HIGHER EDUCATION
http://www.ctdhe.org

MINORITY TEACHER INCENTIVE GRANT PROGRAM

Program provides up to $5000 a year for two years of full-time study in a teacher preparation program, for the junior or senior year at a Connecticut college or university. Applicant must be African American, Hispanic/Latino, Asian American or Native American heritage, and be nominated by the Education Dean.

Academic Fields/Career Goals: Education.

Award: Grant for use in junior or senior years; not renewable. *Amount:* $5000.

Eligibility Requirements: Applicant must be American Indian/Alaska Native, Asian/Pacific Islander, Black (non-Hispanic), or Hispanic and enrolled or expecting to enroll full-time at a four-year institution or university. Available to U.S. citizens.

Application Requirements: Application, transcript. *Deadline:* October 1.

Contact: John Siegrist, Director, Financial Aid Office
Connecticut Department of Higher Education
61 Woodland Street
Hartford, CT 06105-2326
Phone: 860-947-1855
Fax: 860-947-1311
E-mail: jsiegrist@ctdhe.org

CONNECTICUT EDUCATION FOUNDATION, INC.
http://www.cea.org

SCHOLARSHIP FOR MINORITY COLLEGE STUDENTS

An award for qualified minority candidates who have been accepted into a teacher preparation program at an accredited Connecticut college or university. Must have a 2.75 GPA.

Academic Fields/Career Goals: Education.

Award: Scholarship for use in freshman, sophomore, junior, or senior years; not renewable. *Number:* varies. *Amount:* up to $750.

Eligibility Requirements: Applicant must be American Indian/Alaska Native, Asian/Pacific Islander, Black (non-Hispanic), or Hispanic; enrolled or expecting to enroll full-time at a two-year or four-year institution or university and studying in Connecticut. Available to U.S. citizens.

Application Requirements: Application, essay, references, transcript, income verification, letter of acceptance, copy of Student Aid Report (SAR). *Deadline:* May 1.

Contact: Phil Apruzzese, President
Connecticut Education Foundation, Inc.
21 Oak Street, Suite 500
Hartford, CT 06106
Phone: 860-525-5641
Fax: 860-725-6323
E-mail: phila@cea.org

SCHOLARSHIP FOR MINORITY HIGH SCHOOL STUDENTS

Award for qualified minority candidates who have been accepted into an accredited two or four-year Connecticut college or university and intend to enter the teaching profession. Must have 2.75 GPA.

Academic Fields/Career Goals: Education.

Award: Scholarship for use in freshman year; not renewable. *Number:* varies. *Amount:* up to $500.

Eligibility Requirements: Applicant must be American Indian/Alaska Native, Asian/Pacific Islander, Black (non-Hispanic), or Hispanic; enrolled or expecting to enroll at a two-year or four-year institution or university and studying in Connecticut. Available to U.S. citizens.

Application Requirements: Application, essay, references, transcript, letter of acceptance, income verification, copy of Student Aid Report (SAR). *Deadline:* May 1.

Contact: Phil Apruzzese, President
Connecticut Education Foundation, Inc.
21 Oak Street, Suite 500
Hartford, CT 06106
Phone: 860-525-5641
Fax: 860-725-6323
E-mail: phila@cea.org

CONTINENTAL SOCIETY, DAUGHTERS OF INDIAN WARS

CONTINENTAL SOCIETY, DAUGHTERS OF INDIAN WARS SCHOLARSHIP

Award for certified Indian tribal member enrolled in an undergraduate degree program in education or social service. Must maintain minimum 3.0 GPA and work with Native-American after college; work must be on a reservation. Preference given to those in or entering junior year.

Academic Fields/Career Goals: Education; Social Services.

Award: Scholarship for use in freshman, sophomore, junior, senior, or graduate years; not renewable. *Number:* 1. *Amount:* $5000.

Eligibility Requirements: Applicant must be American Indian/Alaska Native and enrolled or expecting to enroll full-time at a two-year or four-year institution. Applicant must have 3.0 GPA or higher. Available to U.S. and Canadian citizens.

Application Requirements: Application, autobiography, essay, financial need analysis, references, transcript, list of extracurricular activities and achievements. *Deadline:* June 15.

Contact: Donald Trolinger, Scholarship Chairperson
Continental Society, Daughters of Indian Wars
61300 East 10010 Road
Miami, OK 74357-4726
Phone: 918-542-5772
Fax: 918-540-0664
E-mail: ottawahillpt@neok.com

COUNCIL FOR INTERNATIONAL EDUCATIONAL EXCHANGE
http://www.ciee.org/study

DEPARTMENT OF EDUCATION SCHOLARSHIP FOR PROGRAMS IN CHINA

Scholarships offered to students who are pursuing Chinese language programs in China. Must be a U.S. citizen enrolled in a CIEE program. Students must have the equivalent of two years study in Chinese language documented. Deadlines are April 1 and November 1. For more details see Web site: http://www.ciee.org/study/scholarships.aspx#china

Academic Fields/Career Goals: Education.

Award: Scholarship for use in junior, senior, or graduate years; not renewable. *Number:* 10–20. *Amount:* $500–$8000.

Eligibility Requirements: Applicant must be enrolled or expecting to enroll full-time at a two-year or four-year institution or university and must have an interest in foreign language. Applicant must have 3.0 GPA or higher. Available to U.S. citizens.

Application Requirements: Application, essay, financial need analysis, references, transcript. *Deadline:* varies.

Contact: Kate Dunkerley, Senior Program Coordinator-Grants Program
Council for International Educational Exchange
3 Copley Place, 2nd Floor
Boston, MA 02116
Phone: 800-448-9944 Ext. 368
Fax: 617-247-2911
E-mail: kdunkerley@ciee.org

CULTURE CONNECTION
http://www.thecultureconnection.com

CULTURE CONNECTION FOUNDATION SCHOLARSHIP
• *See page 73*

DECA (DISTRIBUTIVE EDUCATION CLUBS OF AMERICA)
http://www.deca.org

HARRY A. APPLEGATE SCHOLARSHIP
• *See page 146*

DELAWARE HIGHER EDUCATION COMMISSION
http://www.doe.k12.de.us

CHRISTA MCAULIFFE TEACHER SCHOLARSHIP LOAN-DELAWARE

Award for Delaware residents who are pursuing teaching careers. Must agree to teach in Delaware public schools as repayment of loan. Minimum award is $1000 and is renewable for up to four years. Available only at Delaware colleges. Based on academic merit. Must be ranked in upper half of class, and have a score of 1050 on SAT or 25 on the ACT.

Academic Fields/Career Goals: Education.

Award: Forgivable loan for use in freshman, sophomore, junior, or senior years; renewable. *Number:* 1–60. *Amount:* $1000–$5000.

Eligibility Requirements: Applicant must be enrolled or expecting to enroll full-time at a four-year institution or university; resident of Delaware and studying in Delaware. Applicant must have 2.5 GPA or higher. Available to U.S. citizens.

Application Requirements: Application, essay, test scores, transcript. *Deadline:* March 31.

Contact: Donna Myers, Field Agent/Program Administrator
Delaware Higher Education Commission
820 North French Street, 5th Floor
Wilmington, DE 19711-3509
Phone: 302-577-3240
Fax: 302-577-6765
E-mail: dmyers@doe.k12.de.us

FAMILY, CAREER AND COMMUNITY LEADERS OF AMERICA-TEXAS ASSOCIATION
http://www.texasfccla.org

FCCLA TEXAS FARM BUREAU SCHOLARSHIP
• *See page 147*

FLORIDA DEPARTMENT OF EDUCATION
http://www.floridastudentfinancialaid.org

CRITICAL TEACHER SHORTAGE TUITION REIMBURSEMENT-FLORIDA

One-time awards for full-time Florida public school employees who are certified to teach in Florida and are teaching, or preparing to teach, in critical teacher shortage subject areas. Must earn minimum grade of 3.0 in approved courses. May receive tuition reimbursement up to 9 semester hours or equivalent per academic year, not to exceed $78 per semester hour, for maximum 36 hours. Must be resident of Florida.

Academic Fields/Career Goals: Education.

Award: Scholarship for use in freshman, sophomore, junior, senior, or graduate years; not renewable. *Amount:* $702–$2808.

Eligibility Requirements: Applicant must be enrolled or expecting to enroll at a two-year or four-year institution or university; resident of Florida and studying in Florida. Applicant or parent of applicant must have employment or volunteer experience in teaching. Applicant must have 3.0 GPA or higher. Available to U.S. citizens.

Application Requirements: Application. *Deadline:* September 15.

Contact: Barb Dombrowski, Education Director, Policy and Training
Florida Department of Education
Office of Student Financial Assistance
1940 North Monroe, Suite 70
Tallahassee, FL 32303-4759
Phone: 850-410-5191
Fax: 850-488-5966
E-mail: barb.dombrowski@fldoe.org

GENERAL FEDERATION OF WOMEN'S CLUBS OF MASSACHUSETTS
http://www.gfwcma.org/

GENERAL FEDERATION OF WOMEN'S CLUBS OF MASSACHUSETTS MUSIC SCHOLARSHIP

Scholarship for study in music (including piano), music education, and music therapy. Must include letter of endorsement from president of the sponsoring General Federation of Women's Clubs of Massachusetts. Audition required. For high school seniors who are Massachusetts residents.

Academic Fields/Career Goals: Education; Music; Performing Arts; Therapy/Rehabilitation.

Award: Scholarship for use in freshman year; not renewable. *Number:* varies. *Amount:* up to $800.

Eligibility Requirements: Applicant must be high school student; planning to enroll or expecting to enroll full-time at an institution or university; resident of Massachusetts and must have an interest in music/singing. Available to U.S. citizens.

Application Requirements: Application, essay, interview, references, self-addressed stamped envelope, transcript. *Deadline:* February 1.

Contact: Virginia Williams, Music Chairperson, GFWC of Massachusetts
General Federation of Women's Clubs of Massachusetts
PO Box 679
Sudbury, MA 01776-0679
Phone: 978-443-4569
E-mail: dlvtwillialms@aol.com

NEWTONVILLE WOMAN'S CLUB SCHOLARSHIPS

Award for Massachusetts high school seniors enrolling in a four-year institution. Must be in a teacher training program and seeking certification to teach. Interview is required. One-time award of $600. Must also include a letter of endorsement from the president of the sponsoring General Federation of Women's Clubs of Massachusetts in the community of applicant's legal residence.

Academic Fields/Career Goals: Education.

Award: Scholarship for use in freshman year; not renewable. *Number:* 1. *Amount:* $600.

Eligibility Requirements: Applicant must be high school student; planning to enroll or expecting to enroll full-time at a four-year institution or university and resident of Massachusetts. Available to U.S. citizens.

General Federation of Women's Clubs of Massachusetts (continued)

Application Requirements: Application, autobiography, essay, interview, references, self-addressed stamped envelope, transcript. *Deadline:* March 1.

Contact: Jane Howard, Scholarship Chairperson
General Federation of Women's Clubs of Massachusetts
PO Box 679
Sudbury, MA 01776-0679
Phone: 978-444-9105

GEORGIA ASSOCIATION OF EDUCATORS http://www.gae.org

GAE GFIE SCHOLARSHIP FOR ASPIRING TEACHERS

Scholarships will be awarded to graduating seniors who currently attend a fully accredited public Georgia high school and will attend a fully accredited Georgia college or university within the next 12 months. Must have a 3.0 GPA. Must submit three letters of recommendation. Must have plans to enter the teaching profession.

Academic Fields/Career Goals: Education.

Award: Scholarship for use in freshman year; not renewable. *Number:* 10–20. *Amount:* $1000.

Eligibility Requirements: Applicant must be high school student; planning to enroll or expecting to enroll at a two-year or four-year institution or university; resident of Georgia and studying in Georgia. Applicant must have 3.0 GPA or higher. Available to U.S. citizens.

Application Requirements: Application, transcript. *Deadline:* March 15.

Contact: Sally Bennett, Professional Development Specialist
Georgia Association of Educators
100 Crescent Centre Parkway Suite 500
Tucker, GA 30084-7049
Phone: 678-837-1103
E-mail: sally.bennett@gae.org

GEORGIA STUDENT FINANCE COMMISSION http://www.gsfc.org

GEORGIA PROMISE TEACHER SCHOLARSHIP PROGRAM

Renewable, forgivable loans for junior undergraduates at Georgia colleges who have been accepted for enrollment into a teacher education program leading to initial certification. Minimum cumulative 3.0 GPA required. Recipient must teach at a Georgia public school for one year for each $1500 awarded. Available to seniors for renewal only. Write for deadlines.

Academic Fields/Career Goals: Education.

Award: Forgivable loan for use in junior or senior years; renewable. *Number:* 700–1400. *Amount:* $3000–$6000.

Eligibility Requirements: Applicant must be enrolled or expecting to enroll full or part-time at a four-year institution or university and studying in Georgia. Applicant must have 3.0 GPA or higher. Available to U.S. citizens.

Application Requirements: Application, transcript, Selective Service registration, official certification to be admitted into an approved teacher education program in Georgia. *Deadline:* Continuous.

Contact: Stan DeWitt, Manager of Teacher Scholarships
Georgia Student Finance Commission
2082 East Exchange Place, Suite 100
Tucker, GA 30084
Phone: 770-724-9060
Fax: 770-724-9031
E-mail: stand@gsfc.org

GOLDEN APPLE FOUNDATION http://www.goldenapple.org

GOLDEN APPLE SCHOLARS OF ILLINOIS

100 scholars are selected annually. Scholars receive $7,000 a year for four years. Applicants must be between 17 and 21 and maintain a GPA of 2.5. Eligible applicants must be residents of Illinois studying in Illinois. The deadline is December 1. Recipients must agree to teach in high-need Illinois schools.

Academic Fields/Career Goals: Education.

Award: Forgivable loan for use in freshman, sophomore, junior, or senior years; not renewable. *Number:* up to 100. *Amount:* $7000.

Eligibility Requirements: Applicant must be age 17-21; enrolled or expecting to enroll full-time at a four-year institution or university; resident of Illinois and studying in Illinois. Applicant must have 2.5 GPA or higher. Available to U.S. and non-U.S. citizens.

Application Requirements: Application, autobiography, essay, interview, photo, references, test scores, transcript. *Deadline:* December 1.

Contact: Pat Kilduff, Director of Recruitment and Placement
Golden Apple Foundation
8 South Michigan Avenue, Suite 700
Chicago, IL 60603-3318
Phone: 312-407-0006
Fax: 312-407-0344
E-mail: kilduff@goldenapple.org

GOLDEN KEY INTERNATIONAL HONOUR SOCIETY http://www.goldenkey.org

EDUCATION ACHIEVEMENT AWARDS

Applicants will be asked to create an original thematic unit comprised of individual lesson plans. One winner will receive a $1000 award. The second place applicant will receive $750 and the third place applicant will receive $500. See Web site for more information: http://goldenkey.gsu.edu. Deadline is March 1.

Academic Fields/Career Goals: Education.

Award: Prize for use in junior, senior, graduate, or postgraduate years; not renewable. *Number:* 3. *Amount:* $500–$1000.

Eligibility Requirements: Applicant must be enrolled or expecting to enroll at an institution or university. Available to U.S. citizens.

Application Requirements: Application, applicant must enter a contest, essay, references, transcript. *Deadline:* March 1.

Contact: Scholarship Program Administrators
Golden Key International Honour Society
PO Box 23737
Nashville, TN 37202-3737
Phone: 800-377-2401
E-mail: scholarships@goldenkey.org

GRAND CHAPTER OF CALIFORNIA-ORDER OF THE EASTERN STAR http://www.oescal.org

SCHOLARSHIPS FOR EDUCATION, BUSINESS AND RELIGION
• *See page 148*

GREATER KANAWHA VALLEY FOUNDATION http://www.tgkvf.org

JOSEPH C. BASILE, II, MEMORIAL SCHOLARSHIP FUND

Award for residents of West Virginia who are majoring in education. Must be an undergraduate at a college or university in West Virginia. Award based on financial need. May apply for only two Foundation scholarships but will only be chosen for one.

Academic Fields/Career Goals: Education.

Award: Scholarship for use in freshman, sophomore, junior, or senior years; not renewable. *Number:* 1. *Amount:* $1000.

Eligibility Requirements: Applicant must be enrolled or expecting to enroll at a two-year or four-year institution or university; resident of West Virginia and studying in West Virginia. Applicant must have 2.5 GPA or higher. Available to U.S. citizens.

Application Requirements: Application, essay, financial need analysis, references, self-addressed stamped envelope, test scores, transcript. *Deadline:* February 15.

Contact: Susan Hoover, Scholarship Coordinator
Greater Kanawha Valley Foundation
PO Box 3041
Charleston, WV 25331
Phone: 304-346-3620
Fax: 304-346-3640

HAWAII EDUCATION ASSOCIATION
http://www.heaed.com/

FAITH C. AI LAI HEA STUDENT TEACHER SCHOLARSHIP

$5000 scholarship established for student teachers who are enrolled in a full-time undergraduate or post-baccalaureate program in accredited institution of higher learning. Minimum 3.5 GPA required. Preference to students in or from Hawaii.

Academic Fields/Career Goals: Education.

Award: Scholarship for use in freshman, sophomore, junior, senior, graduate, or postgraduate years; not renewable. *Number:* 2. *Amount:* $5000.

Eligibility Requirements: Applicant must be enrolled or expecting to enroll full-time at a four-year institution or university. Applicant must have 3.5 GPA or higher. Available to U.S. citizens.

Application Requirements: Application, autobiography, financial need analysis, photo, references, transcript. *Deadline:* April 11.

Contact: Faith C. Ai Lai HEA Student Teacher Scholarship Committee
Hawaii Education Association
1649 Kalakaua Avenue
Honolulu, HI 96826-2494
Phone: 808-949-6657
Fax: 808-944-2032
E-mail: hea.office@heaed.com

FAITH C. AI LAI HEA UNDERGRADUATE SCHOLARSHIP

Scholarship has been established for education majors, students in or from state of Hawaii with GPA of 3.5 or better, full-time undergraduate students. $2000 a school year. $1000 will be sent at beginning of each semester.

Academic Fields/Career Goals: Education.

Award: Scholarship for use in freshman, sophomore, junior, or senior years; not renewable. *Number:* 4. *Amount:* $2000.

Eligibility Requirements: Applicant must be enrolled or expecting to enroll full-time at a four-year institution or university and resident of Hawaii. Applicant must have 3.5 GPA or higher. Available to U.S. citizens.

Application Requirements: Application, autobiography, financial need analysis, photo, references, transcript. *Deadline:* April 11.

Contact: Faith C. Ai Lai HEA Scholarship Committee
Hawaii Education Association
1649 Kalakaua Avenue
Honolulu, HI 96826-2494
Phone: 808-949-6657
Fax: 808-944-2032
E-mail: hea.office@heaed.com

HAWAII EDUCATION ASSOCIATION STUDENT TEACHER SCHOLARSHIP

Scholarship available to children of HEA members. Intent is to minimize the need for employment during student teaching semester. Must be enrolled full-time in an undergraduate or post-baccalaureate program in accredited institution of higher learning.

Academic Fields/Career Goals: Education.

Award: Scholarship for use in senior, graduate, or postgraduate years; not renewable. *Number:* 2. *Amount:* $3000.

Eligibility Requirements: Applicant must be enrolled or expecting to enroll full-time at a four-year institution or university. Applicant or parent of applicant must be member of Hawaii Education Association. Available to U.S. citizens.

Application Requirements: Application, autobiography, financial need analysis, photo, references, transcript. *Deadline:* April 4.

Contact: Hawaii Education Association
Hawaii Education Association
1649 Kalakaua Avenue
Honolulu, HI 96826-2494
Phone: 808-949-6657
Fax: 808-944-2032
E-mail: hea.office@heaed.com

MAY AND HUBERT EVERLY HEA SCHOLARSHIP

Scholarship for education majors who intend to teach in state of Hawaii at K-12 level. Undergraduate student in two- or four-year college/university. $1000 scholarship paid beginning of each semester.

Academic Fields/Career Goals: Education.

Award: Scholarship for use in freshman, sophomore, junior, or senior years; not renewable. *Number:* 1. *Amount:* $1000.

Eligibility Requirements: Applicant must be enrolled or expecting to enroll full-time at a two-year or four-year institution or university and studying in Hawaii. Applicant must have 3.0 GPA or higher. Available to U.S. citizens.

Application Requirements: Application, autobiography, financial need analysis, photo, references, transcript. *Deadline:* April 4.

Contact: May and Hubert Everly HEA Scholarship Committee
Hawaii Education Association
1649 Kalakaua Avenue
Honolulu, HI 96826-2494
Phone: 808-949-6657
Fax: 808-944-2032
E-mail: hea.office@heaed.com

HONOR SOCIETY OF PHI KAPPA PHI
http://www.phikappaphi.org

PROMOTION OF EXCELLENCE GRANTS PROGRAM

Grants up to $10,000 will be awarded to Phi Kappa Phi member-led teams for projects designed to establish or implement programs that promote academic excellence in higher education or designed to achieve greater clarity and further scientific understanding about some aspect of the promotion of academic excellence. Total number of available awards and the dollar value varies. For more details see Web site: http://www.phikappaphi.org

Academic Fields/Career Goals: Education.

Award: Grant for use in freshman, sophomore, junior, senior, graduate, or postgraduate years; not renewable. *Number:* varies. *Amount:* $2000–$10,000.

Eligibility Requirements: Applicant must be enrolled or expecting to enroll at an institution or university. Applicant or parent of applicant must be member of Phi Kappa Phi. Available to U.S. and non-U.S. citizens.

Application Requirements: Application. *Deadline:* January 27.

Contact: Theresa Bard, Programs Coordinator
Honor Society of Phi Kappa Phi
305 French House, Highland Road, Louisiana State University
Baton Rouge, LA 70893-6000
Phone: 225-388-4917 Ext. 13
Fax: 225-388-4900
E-mail: awards@phikappaphi.org

IDAHO STATE BOARD OF EDUCATION
http://www.boardofed.idaho.gov

EDUCATION INCENTIVE LOAN FORGIVENESS CONTRACT-IDAHO

Renewable award assists Idaho residents enrolling in teacher education or nursing programs within state. Must rank in top 15% of high school graduating class, have a 3.0 GPA or above, and agree to work in Idaho for two years. Deadlines vary. Contact financial aid office at institution of choice.

Academic Fields/Career Goals: Education; Nursing.

Award: Forgivable loan for use in freshman, sophomore, junior, or senior years; renewable. *Number:* 13–45. *Amount:* varies.

Eligibility Requirements: Applicant must be enrolled or expecting to enroll full-time at a two-year or four-year institution or university; resident of Idaho and studying in Idaho. Applicant must have 3.0 GPA or higher. Available to U.S. citizens.

Application Requirements: Application, test scores, transcript. *Deadline:* varies.

Contact: Dana Kelly, Program Manager
Idaho State Board of Education
PO Box 83720
Boise, ID 83720-0037
Phone: 208-332-1574
E-mail: dana.kelly@osbe.idaho.gov

ILLINOIS CONGRESS OF PARENTS AND TEACHERS
http://www.illinoispta.org

LILLIAN E. GLOVER ILLINOIS PTA SCHOLARSHIP PROGRAM

This scholarship is for a student studying in the field of education or an education-related degree program, which requires certification from Illinois State Board of Education. Must be an Illinois resident. Must rank in upper quarter of class. Award for high school seniors graduating from any Illinois public high school. Applications available at every public high school in the counseling office/career center starting in January, or see Web site: http://www.illinoispta.org.

Academic Fields/Career Goals: Education.

Award: Scholarship for use in freshman year; not renewable. *Number:* 44. *Amount:* $750–$1500.

Eligibility Requirements: Applicant must be high school student; planning to enroll or expecting to enroll full-time at a four-year institution or university and resident of Illinois. Available to U.S. citizens.

Application Requirements: Application, essay, photo, references, self-addressed stamped envelope, transcript. *Deadline:* March 1.

Contact: Dianne Schorr, Scholarship Chairman
Illinois Congress of Parents and Teachers
901 South Spring Street
Springfield, IL 62704
Phone: 800-877-9617
Fax: 217-528-9490
E-mail: DianneSchorr@aol.com

ILLINOIS STUDENT ASSISTANCE COMMISSION (ISAC)
http://www.collegezone.org

ILLINOIS FUTURE TEACHERS CORPS PROGRAM

Scholarships available for students planning to become teachers in Illinois. Students must be Illinois residents, enrolled or accepted as a junior or above in a Teacher Education Program at an Illinois college or university. By receiving award, students agree to teach for 5 years at either a public, private, or parochial Illinois preschool, or at a public elementary or secondary school. For an application and further information, visit http://www.collegezone.com

Academic Fields/Career Goals: Education.

Award: Forgivable loan for use in junior, senior, or graduate years; renewable. *Number:* 1150. *Amount:* up to $15,000.

Eligibility Requirements: Applicant must be enrolled or expecting to enroll full or part-time at a four-year institution or university; resident of Illinois and studying in Illinois. Applicant must have 2.5 GPA or higher. Available to U.S. citizens.

Application Requirements: Application, financial need analysis, FAFSA. *Deadline:* March 1.

Contact: College Zone Counselor
Illinois Student Assistance Commission (ISAC)
1755 Lake Cook Road
Deerfield, IL 60015-5209
Phone: 800-899-4722
E-mail: collegezone@isac.org

MINORITY TEACHERS OF ILLINOIS SCHOLARSHIP PROGRAM

Award for minority students planning to teach at an approved Illinois preschool, elementary, or secondary school. Deadline: March 1. Must be Illinois resident.

Academic Fields/Career Goals: Education; Special Education.

Award: Forgivable loan for use in freshman, sophomore, junior, senior, graduate, or postgraduate years; renewable. *Number:* 450–550. *Amount:* up to $5000.

Eligibility Requirements: Applicant must be American Indian/Alaska Native, Asian/Pacific Islander, Black (non-Hispanic), or Hispanic; enrolled or expecting to enroll full or part-time at a two-year or four-year institution or university; resident of Illinois and studying in Illinois. Applicant must have 2.5 GPA or higher. Available to U.S. citizens.

Application Requirements: Application. *Deadline:* March 1.

Contact: College Zone Counselor
Illinois Student Assistance Commission (ISAC)
1755 Lake Cook Road
Deerfield, IL 60015-5209
Phone: 800-899-4722
E-mail: collegezone@isac.org

PAUL DOUGLAS TEACHER SCHOLARSHIP (PDTS) PROGRAM

Program enables and encourages outstanding high school graduates to pursue teaching careers at the preschool, elementary or secondary school level by providing financial assistance.

Academic Fields/Career Goals: Education.

Award: Scholarship for use in freshman year; not renewable. *Amount:* $1666–$5000.

Eligibility Requirements: Applicant must be enrolled or expecting to enroll full-time at an institution or university. Available to U.S. citizens.

Application Requirements: Application, financial need analysis. *Deadline:* August 1.

Contact: College Zone Counselor
Illinois Student Assistance Commission (ISAC)
1755 Lake Cook Road
Deerfield, IL 60015-5209
Phone: 800-899-4722
E-mail: collegezone@isac.org

INDIANA RETIRED TEACHER'S ASSOCIATION (IRTA)
http://www.retiredteachers.org

INDIANA RETIRED TEACHERS ASSOCIATION FOUNDATION SCHOLARSHIP

Scholarship available to college sophomores or juniors who are enrolled full-time in an education program at an Indiana college or university for a first baccalaureate degree. The applicant must be the child, grandchild, legal dependent or spouse of an active, retired or deceased member of the Indiana State Teachers Retirement Fund.

Academic Fields/Career Goals: Education.

Award: Scholarship for use in sophomore, junior, or senior years; not renewable. *Number:* 8. *Amount:* $1200.

Eligibility Requirements: Applicant must be enrolled or expecting to enroll full-time at a four-year institution or university; resident of Indiana and studying in Indiana. Applicant or parent of applicant must be member of Indiana State Teachers Association. Applicant or parent of applicant must have employment or volunteer experience in teaching. Applicant must have 2.5 GPA or higher. Available to U.S. citizens.

Application Requirements: Application, essay, financial need analysis, references, transcript. *Deadline:* February 22.

Contact: Joan Grubbs, Executive Assistant
Indiana Retired Teacher's Association (IRTA)
150 West Market Street, Suite 610
Indianapolis, IN 46204-2812
Phone: 888-454-9333
Fax: 317-637-9671
E-mail: irta@iquest.net

INTERNATIONAL ASSOCIATION OF GREAT LAKES RESEARCH
http://www.iaglr.org

PAUL W. RODGERS SCHOLARSHIP
• See page 214

INTERNATIONAL TECHNOLOGY EDUCATION ASSOCIATION
http://www.iteaconnect.org/index.html

INTERNATIONAL TECHNOLOGY EDUCATION ASSOCIATION UNDERGRADUATE SCHOLARSHIP

Award available to undergraduate student majoring in technology education teacher preparation. The award is based upon interest in teaching, academic ability and faculty recommendations.

Academic Fields/Career Goals: Education; Engineering/Technology.

Award: Scholarship for use in freshman, sophomore, or junior years. *Amount:* $1000.

Eligibility Requirements: Applicant must be enrolled or expecting to enroll full or part-time at an institution or university. Applicant must have 2.5 GPA or higher. Available to U.S. and non-U.S. citizens.

Application Requirements: Application, resume, references, transcript. *Deadline:* December 1.

Contact: Barbara Mongold, Scholarship Committee
International Technology Education Association
Undergraduate Scholarship Committee
1914 Association Drive, Suite 201
Reston, VA 20191-1539
Phone: 703-860-2100
Fax: 703-860-0353
E-mail: iteaordr@iris.org

TSA SPONSORED ITEA SCHOLARSHIP

Scholarship to support the technology education profession by encouraging TSA students to pursue careers as K-12 technology teachers.

Academic Fields/Career Goals: Education; Engineering/Technology.

Award: Scholarship for use in freshman year. *Number:* 1–3. *Amount:* $500.

Eligibility Requirements: Applicant must be high school student and planning to enroll or expecting to enroll full or part-time at an institution or university. Available to U.S. and non-U.S. citizens.

Application Requirements: Application, essay, references, SAT score and/or ACT score, high school class rank (indicate how many in class). *Deadline:* December 31.

Contact: Barbara Mongold, Scholarship Committee
International Technology Education Association
Undergraduate Scholarship Committee
1914 Association Drive, Suite 201
Reston, VA 20191-1539
Phone: 703-860-2100
Fax: 703-860-0353
E-mail: iteaordr@iris.org

IOWA COLLEGE STUDENT AID COMMISSION
http://www.iowacollegeaid.org

IOWA TEACHER FORGIVABLE LOAN PROGRAM

Forgivable loan assists students who will teach in Iowa secondary schools. Must be an Iowa resident attending an Iowa postsecondary institution. Contact for additional information.

Academic Fields/Career Goals: Education.

Award: Forgivable loan for use in freshman, sophomore, junior, or senior years; not renewable. *Number:* varies. *Amount:* $2686.

Eligibility Requirements: Applicant must be enrolled or expecting to enroll full or part-time at a four-year institution or university; resident of Iowa and studying in Iowa. Applicant or parent of applicant must have employment or volunteer experience in teaching. Available to U.S. citizens.

Application Requirements: Application, financial need analysis. *Deadline:* Continuous.

Contact: Brenda Easter, Special Programs Administrator
Iowa College Student Aid Commission
200 10th Street, 4th Floor
Des Moines, IA 50309-3609
Phone: 515-242-3380
Fax: 515-242-3388
E-mail: icsac@max.state.ia.us

JACK J. ISGUR FOUNDATION

JACK J. ISGUR FOUNDATION SCHOLARSHIP
• See page 111

KENTUCKY DEPARTMENT OF EDUCATION
http://www.kde.state.ky.us

KENTUCKY MINORITY EDUCATOR RECRUITMENT AND RETENTION (KMERR) SCHOLARSHIP

Scholarship for minority teacher candidates who rank in the upper half of their class or have a minimum 2.5 GPA. Must be a U.S. citizen and Kentucky resident enrolled in one of Kentucky's eight public institutions. Must teach one semester in Kentucky for each semester the scholarship is received.

Academic Fields/Career Goals: Education.

Award: Forgivable loan for use in freshman, sophomore, junior, senior, or graduate years; renewable. *Number:* 300. *Amount:* $2500–$5000.

Eligibility Requirements: Applicant must be American Indian/Alaska Native, Asian/Pacific Islander, Black (non-Hispanic), or Hispanic; enrolled or expecting to enroll full-time at a two-year or four-year institution or university; resident of Kentucky and studying in Kentucky. Applicant must have 2.5 GPA or higher. Available to U.S. citizens.

Application Requirements: Application, essay, references, test scores, transcript. *Deadline:* Continuous.

Contact: Robby Morton, Director
Kentucky Department of Education
500 Mero Street, 17th Floor
Frankfort, KY 40601
Phone: 502-564-1479
Fax: 502-564-6952
E-mail: rmorton@kde.state.ky.us

KENTUCKY HIGHER EDUCATION ASSISTANCE AUTHORITY (KHEAA)
http://www.kheaa.com

EARLY CHILDHOOD DEVELOPMENT SCHOLARSHIP
• See page 170

KENTUCKY TEACHER SCHOLARSHIP PROGRAM

Award for Kentucky resident attending Kentucky institutions and pursuing initial teacher certification. Must teach one semester for each semester of award received. In critical shortage areas, must teach one semester for every two semesters of award received. Repayment obligation if teaching requirement not met. Submit Free Application for Federal Student Aid and Teacher Scholarship Application by May 1.

Academic Fields/Career Goals: Education.

Award: Forgivable loan for use in freshman, sophomore, junior, senior, or graduate years; renewable. *Number:* 600–700. *Amount:* $250–$5000.

Eligibility Requirements: Applicant must be enrolled or expecting to enroll full-time at a two-year or four-year institution or university; resident of Kentucky and studying in Kentucky. Available to U.S. citizens.

Application Requirements: Application, financial need analysis. *Deadline:* May 1.

Contact: Tim Phelps, Student Aid Branch Manager
Kentucky Higher Education Assistance Authority (KHEAA)
PO Box 798
Frankfort, KY 40602
Phone: 502-696-7393
Fax: 502-696-7496
E-mail: tphelps@kheaa.com

LINCOLN COMMUNITY FOUNDATION
http://www.lcf.org

DALE E. SIEFKES SCHOLARSHIP

Scholarship for a junior or senior attending any college or university in Nebraska. Must be pursuing studies in education and demonstrate financial need. Minimum 3.80 GPA required. Application deadline: April 15.

Academic Fields/Career Goals: Education.

Award: Scholarship for use in junior or senior years; not renewable. *Number:* 1. *Amount:* $500–$2000.

Eligibility Requirements: Applicant must be enrolled or expecting to enroll full-time at a two-year or four-year or technical institution or university and studying in Nebraska. Available to U.S. citizens.

Lincoln Community Foundation (continued)

Application Requirements: Application, essay, financial need analysis, test scores, transcript. *Deadline:* April 15.

Contact: Debra Shoemaker, Director of Program and Distribution
Lincoln Community Foundation
215 Centennial Mall South, Suite 200
Lincoln, NE 68508
Phone: 402-474-2345
Fax: 402-476-8532
E-mail: debs@lcf.org

NEBRASKA RURAL COMMUNITY SCHOOLS ASSOCIATION SCHOLARSHIP

Scholarships are for students attending schools in Nebraska holding current memberships in NRCSA. Must major in education and demonstrate financial need. Applicants should also demonstrate academic achievement, leadership, character, and initiative. Preferred students will be involved in extracurricular activities. Must be a resident of Nebraska.

Academic Fields/Career Goals: Education.

Award: Scholarship for use in freshman year; not renewable. *Number:* 6. *Amount:* $500–$1000.

Eligibility Requirements: Applicant must be high school student; planning to enroll or expecting to enroll full-time at a two-year or four-year institution or university; resident of Nebraska and studying in Nebraska. Applicant must have 3.5 GPA or higher. Available to U.S. citizens.

Application Requirements: Application, essay, financial need analysis, references. *Deadline:* February 10.

Contact: Debra Shoemaker, Director of Program and Distribution
Lincoln Community Foundation
215 Centennial Mall South, Suite 200
Lincoln, NE 68508
Phone: 402-474-2345
Fax: 402-476-8532
E-mail: debs@lcf.org

MARION D. AND EVA S. PEEPLES FOUNDATION TRUST SCHOLARSHIP PROGRAM   http://www.jccf.org

MARION A. AND EVA S. PEEPLES SCHOLARSHIPS

Award for study in nursing, dietetics, and teaching in industrial arts. Applicant must reapply each year for renewal. Recipient must maintain 2.5 GPA and take at least 12 credit hours per semester. Minimum 1100 on SAT if high school student. Must be Indiana resident and attending an Indiana school. Deadline: February 15 if applicant is a high school student residing in Johnson County; March 1 if applicant is residing outside Johnson County.

Academic Fields/Career Goals: Education; Engineering/Technology; Food Science/Nutrition; Nursing; Trade/Technical Specialties.

Award: Scholarship for use in freshman, sophomore, junior, or senior years; renewable. *Number:* 15–30. *Amount:* $500–$2000.

Eligibility Requirements: Applicant must be enrolled or expecting to enroll full-time at a two-year or four-year or technical institution or university; resident of Indiana and studying in Indiana. Applicant must have 2.5 GPA or higher. Available to U.S. citizens.

Application Requirements: Application, autobiography, financial need analysis, interview, references, self-addressed stamped envelope, test scores, transcript. *Deadline:* February 15.

Contact: Ms. Kelley Peters, Scholarship Director
Marion D. and Eva S. Peeples Foundation Trust Scholarship Program
398 South Main Street, PO Box 217
Franklin, IN 46131
Phone: 317-738-2213
Fax: 317-738-9113
E-mail: kelleyp@jccf.org

MARYLAND HIGHER EDUCATION COMMISSION   http://www.mhec.state.md.us

CHILD CARE PROVIDER PROGRAM-MARYLAND

Forgivable loan provides assistance for Maryland undergraduates attending a Maryland institution and pursuing studies in a child development program or an early childhood education program. Must serve as a professional day care provider in Maryland for one year for each year award received. Must maintain minimum 2.0 GPA. Contact for further information.

Academic Fields/Career Goals: Education.

Award: Forgivable loan for use in freshman, sophomore, junior, or senior years; renewable. *Number:* 100–150. *Amount:* $500–$2000.

Eligibility Requirements: Applicant must be enrolled or expecting to enroll full or part-time at a two-year or four-year institution or university; resident of Maryland and studying in Maryland. Available to U.S. citizens.

Application Requirements: Application, transcript. *Deadline:* June 15.

Contact: Margaret Crutchley, Office of Student Financial Assistance
Maryland Higher Education Commission
839 Bestgate Road, Suite 400
Annapolis, MD 21401-3013
Phone: 410-260-4545
Fax: 410-260-3203
E-mail: ofsamail@mhec.state.md.us

DISTINGUISHED SCHOLAR-TEACHER EDUCATION AWARDS

Up to $3,000 award for Maryland high school seniors who have received the Distinguished Scholar Award. Recipient must enroll as a full-time undergraduate in a Maryland institution and pursue a program of study leading to a Maryland teaching certificate. Must maintain annual 3.0 GPA for renewal. Must teach in a Maryland public school one year for each year award is received.

Academic Fields/Career Goals: Education.

Award: Forgivable loan for use in freshman, sophomore, junior, or senior years; renewable. *Number:* 20–80. *Amount:* up to $3000.

Eligibility Requirements: Applicant must be high school student; planning to enroll or expecting to enroll full-time at a two-year or four-year institution or university; resident of Maryland and studying in Maryland. Applicant must have 3.0 GPA or higher. Available to U.S. citizens.

Application Requirements: Application, test scores, transcript, must be recipient of the Distinguished Scholar Award. *Deadline:* July 1.

Contact: Monica Tipton, Office of Student Financial Assistance
Maryland Higher Education Commission
839 Bestgate Road, Suite 400
Annapolis, MD 21401-3013
Phone: 410-260-4568
Fax: 410-260-3200
E-mail: ofsamail@mhec.state.md.us

JANET L. HOFFMANN LOAN ASSISTANCE REPAYMENT PROGRAM

Provides assistance for repayment of loan debt to Maryland residents working full-time in nonprofit organizations and state or local governments. Must submit Employment Verification Form and Lender Verification Form.

Academic Fields/Career Goals: Education; Law/Legal Services; Nursing; Social Services; Therapy/Rehabilitation.

Award: Grant for use in freshman, sophomore, junior, senior, or graduate years; not renewable. *Number:* up to 400. *Amount:* up to $7500.

Eligibility Requirements: Applicant must be enrolled or expecting to enroll at an institution or university; resident of Maryland and studying in Maryland. Available to U.S. citizens.

Application Requirements: Application, transcript, IRS 1040 form. *Deadline:* September 30.

Contact: Marie Janiszewski, Office of Student Financial Assistance
Maryland Higher Education Commission
839 Bestgate Road, Suite 400
Annapolis, MD 21401
Phone: 410-260-4569
Fax: 410-260-3203
E-mail: ofsamail@mhec.state.md.us

SHARON CHRISTA MCAULIFFE TEACHER EDUCATION-CRITICAL SHORTAGE GRANT PROGRAM

Renewable awards for Maryland residents who are college juniors, seniors, or graduate students enrolled in a Maryland teacher education program. Must agree to enter profession in a subject designated as a critical shortage area. Must teach in Maryland for one year for each award year. Renewable for one year.

Academic Fields/Career Goals: Education.

Award: Forgivable loan for use in junior, senior, or graduate years; renewable. *Number:* up to 137. *Amount:* $200–$17,000.

Eligibility Requirements: Applicant must be enrolled or expecting to enroll full or part-time at a four-year institution or university; resident of Maryland and studying in Maryland. Applicant must have 3.0 GPA or higher. Available to U.S. citizens.

Application Requirements: Application, essay, resume, transcript. *Deadline:* December 31.

Contact: Margaret Crutchley, Office of Student Financial Assistance
Maryland Higher Education Commission
839 Bestgate Road, Suite 400
Annapolis, MD 21401-3013
Phone: 410-260-4545
Fax: 410-260-3203
E-mail: ofsamail@mhec.state.md.us

MASSACHUSETTS OFFICE OF STUDENT FINANCIAL ASSISTANCE   http://www.osfa.mass.edu

PARAPROFESSIONAL TEACHER PREPARATION GRANT

Grant providing financial aid assistance to Massachusetts residents who are currently employed as paraprofessionals in Massachusetts public schools and wish to obtain higher education and become certified as full time teachers.

Academic Fields/Career Goals: Education.

Award: Grant for use in freshman, sophomore, junior, or senior years. *Number:* varies. *Amount:* $250–$7500.

Eligibility Requirements: Applicant must be enrolled or expecting to enroll full or part-time at a two-year or four-year institution or university and resident of Massachusetts. Available to U.S. citizens.

Application Requirements: Application. *Deadline:* varies.

Contact: Clantha McCurdy, Associate Vice Chancellor
Massachusetts Office of Student Financial Assistance
454 Broadway, Suite 200
Revere, MA 02151
Phone: 617-727-9420
Fax: 617-727-0667
E-mail: cmccurdy@osfa.mass.edu

TOMORROW'S TEACHERS SCHOLARSHIP PROGRAM

Tuition waver for graduating high school senior ranking in top 25% of class. Must be a resident of Massachusetts and pursue a bachelor's degree at a public college or university in the Commonwealth. Must commit to teach for four years in a Massachusetts public school. Scholarship Program provides payment of full tuition and required fees at eligible public colleges and universities.

Academic Fields/Career Goals: Education.

Award: Scholarship for use in freshman, sophomore, junior, or senior years; renewable. *Number:* varies. *Amount:* varies.

Eligibility Requirements: Applicant must be high school student; planning to enroll or expecting to enroll full-time at a four-year institution or university; resident of Massachusetts and studying in Massachusetts. Applicant must have 3.5 GPA or higher. Available to U.S. citizens.

Application Requirements: Application, essay, references, transcript. *Deadline:* February 15.

Contact: Alison Leary
Massachusetts Office of Student Financial Assistance
454 Broadway, Suite 200
Revere, MA 02151
Phone: 617-727-9420
Fax: 617-727-0667
E-mail: osfa@osfa.mass.edu

MEMORIAL FOUNDATION FOR JEWISH CULTURE   http://www.mfjc.org

MEMORIAL FOUNDATION FOR JEWISH CULTURE INTERNATIONAL SCHOLARSHIP PROGRAM FOR COMMUNITY SERVICE

• *See page 106*

MISSISSIPPI STATE STUDENT FINANCIAL AID   http://www.mississippiuniversities.com

CRITICAL NEEDS TEACHER LOAN/SCHOLARSHIP

Eligible applicants will agree to employment immediately upon degree completion as a full-time classroom teacher in a public school located in a critical teacher shortage area in the state of Mississippi. Must verify the intention to pursue a first bachelor's degree in teacher education. Award covers tuition and required fees, average cost of room and meals plus a $500 allowance for books. Must be enrolled at a Mississippi college or university.

Academic Fields/Career Goals: Education; Psychology; Therapy/Rehabilitation.

Award: Forgivable loan for use in junior or senior years; not renewable. *Number:* 1.

Eligibility Requirements: Applicant must be enrolled or expecting to enroll full or part-time at a four-year institution or university and studying in Mississippi. Applicant must have 2.5 GPA or higher. Available to U.S. citizens.

Application Requirements: Application, test scores, transcript. *Deadline:* March 31.

Contact: Mississippi Student Financial Aid
Mississippi State Student Financial Aid
3825 Ridgewood Road
Jackson, MS 39211-6453
Phone: 800-327-2980
E-mail: sfa@ihl.state.ms.us

WILLIAM WINTER TEACHER SCHOLAR LOAN PROGRAM

Awarded to Mississippi residents pursuing a teaching career. Must be enrolled full-time in a program leading to a Class A certification and maintain a 2.5 GPA. Must agree to teach one year for each year award is received.

Academic Fields/Career Goals: Education.

Award: Forgivable loan for use in junior or senior years; renewable. *Number:* varies. *Amount:* $500–$4000.

Eligibility Requirements: Applicant must be enrolled or expecting to enroll full-time at a two-year or four-year institution or university; resident of Mississippi and studying in Mississippi. Applicant must have 2.5 GPA or higher. Available to U.S. citizens.

Application Requirements: Application, driver's license, references, transcript. *Deadline:* March 31.

Contact: Board of Trustees
Mississippi State Student Financial Aid
3825 Ridgewood Road
Jackson, MS 39211-6453

MISSOURI DEPARTMENT OF ELEMENTARY AND SECONDARY EDUCATION   http://www.dese.mo.gov

MISSOURI MINORITY TEACHING SCHOLARSHIP

Award may be used any year up to four years at an approved, participating Missouri institution. Scholarship is for minority Missouri residents in teaching programs. Recipients must commit to teach for five years in a Missouri public elementary or secondary school. Graduate students must teach math or science. Otherwise, award must be repaid.

Academic Fields/Career Goals: Education.

Award: Scholarship for use in freshman, sophomore, junior, senior, or graduate years; renewable. *Number:* 100. *Amount:* up to $3000.

Eligibility Requirements: Applicant must be American Indian/Alaska Native, Asian/Pacific Islander, Black (non-Hispanic), or Hispanic; enrolled or expecting to enroll full-time at a two-year or four-year institution or university; resident of Missouri and studying in Missouri. Applicant must have 3.0 GPA or higher. Available to U.S. citizens.

Application Requirements: Application, essay, financial need analysis, resume, references, test scores, transcript. *Deadline:* February 15.

Missouri Department of Elementary and Secondary Education (continued)

Contact: Laura Harrison, Administrative Assistant
Missouri Department of Elementary and Secondary Education
PO Box 480
Jefferson City, MO 65102-0480
Phone: 573-751-1668
Fax: 573-526-3580
E-mail: laura.harrison@dese.mo.gov

MISSOURI TEACHER EDUCATION SCHOLARSHIP (GENERAL)

Nonrenewable award for Missouri high school seniors or Missouri resident college students. Must attend approved teacher training program at a participating Missouri institution. Must rank in top 15 % of high school class on ACT/SAT. Merit-based award. Recipients must commit to teach in Missouri for five years at a public elementary or secondary school or award must be repaid.

Academic Fields/Career Goals: Education.

Award: Scholarship for use in freshman, sophomore, junior, or senior years; not renewable. *Number:* 200–240. *Amount:* up to $2000.

Eligibility Requirements: Applicant must be enrolled or expecting to enroll full-time at a two-year or four-year institution or university; resident of Missouri and studying in Missouri. Applicant must have 3.5 GPA or higher. Available to U.S. citizens.

Application Requirements: Application, essay, resume, references, test scores, transcript. *Deadline:* February 15.

Contact: Laura Harrison, Administrative Assistant II
Missouri Department of Elementary and Secondary Education
PO Box 480
Jefferson City, MO 65102-0480
Phone: 573-751-1668
Fax: 573-526-3580
E-mail: laura.harrison@dese.mo.gov

NASA IDAHO SPACE GRANT CONSORTIUM
http://isgc.uidaho.edu

NASA IDAHO SPACE GRANT CONSORTIUM SCHOLARSHIP PROGRAM
• See page 94

NASA VIRGINIA SPACE GRANT CONSORTIUM
http://www.vsgc.odu.edu

VIRGINIA SPACE GRANT CONSORTIUM TEACHER EDUCATION SCHOLARSHIPS
• See page 125

NATIONAL ASSOCIATION FOR THE ADVANCEMENT OF COLORED PEOPLE
http://www.naacp.org

NAACP LILLIAN AND SAMUEL SUTTON EDUCATION SCHOLARSHIP

Must be an education major, full-time student, and be enrolled in accredited college in the U.S.. Graduating high school seniors and undergraduate students must have 2.5 minimum GPA. Graduate students must have 3.0 and can be full- or part-time. Undergraduate scholarship awards $1000; graduate scholarship awards $2000. NAACP membership and participation is preferable, copy of NAACP membership card or receipt of membership is needed. Application deadline is April 30.

Academic Fields/Career Goals: Education.

Award: Scholarship for use in freshman, sophomore, junior, senior, or graduate years; not renewable. *Number:* varies. *Amount:* $1000–$2000.

Eligibility Requirements: Applicant must be American Indian/Alaska Native, Asian/Pacific Islander, Black (non-Hispanic), or Hispanic and enrolled or expecting to enroll full or part-time at a four-year institution or university. Applicant or parent of applicant must be member of National Association for the Advancement of Colored People. Available to U.S. citizens.

Application Requirements: Application, financial need analysis, references, transcript. *Deadline:* April 30.

Contact: Donna Lakins, Education Department, Scholarship Request
National Association for the Advancement of Colored People
4805 Mt. Hope Drive
Baltimore, MD 21215-3297
Phone: 410-580-5760
Fax: 410-585-1329

THURGOOD MARSHALL SCHOLARSHIP FUND

Scholarship for full-time students at historically Black public colleges, universities; 3.0 GPA, ACT score at least 24, or SAT combined verbal/math score of at least 1,000 required.

Academic Fields/Career Goals: Education.

Award: Scholarship for use in freshman, sophomore, junior, or senior years. *Amount:* $4000.

Eligibility Requirements: Applicant must be American Indian/Alaska Native, Asian/Pacific Islander, Black (non-Hispanic), or Hispanic and enrolled or expecting to enroll full-time at a four-year institution or university. Available to U.S. citizens.

Application Requirements: Application. *Deadline:* May 1.

Contact: The Thurgood Marshall Scholarship Fund
National Association for the Advancement of Colored People
100 Park Avenue, 10th Floor
New York, NY 10017

NATIONAL FEDERATION OF THE BLIND
http://www.nfb.org

NATIONAL FEDERATION OF THE BLIND EDUCATOR OF TOMORROW AWARD

Award for students who are legally blind and pursuing teaching careers. Must submit recommendation from state officer of National Federation of the Blind. Awards based on academic excellence, service to the community, and financial need. May reapply. Must attend school in U.S. Must be planning a career in elementary, secondary, or postsecondary teaching

Academic Fields/Career Goals: Education.

Award: Scholarship for use in freshman, sophomore, junior, or senior years; not renewable. *Number:* 1. *Amount:* $3000.

Eligibility Requirements: Applicant must be enrolled or expecting to enroll at an institution or university. Applicant or parent of applicant must have employment or volunteer experience in community service. Applicant must be visually impaired. Applicant must have 3.5 GPA or higher. Available to U.S. and non-U.S. citizens.

Application Requirements: Application, autobiography, essay, financial need analysis, references, transcript. *Deadline:* March 31.

Contact: Peggy Elliot, Chairman, Scholarship Committee
National Federation of the Blind
805 Fifth Avenue
Grinnell, IA 50112
Phone: 641-236-3366

NATIONAL INSTITUTE FOR LABOR RELATIONS RESEARCH
http://www.nilrr.org

APPLEGATE/JACKSON/PARKS FUTURE TEACHER SCHOLARSHIP

Scholarship available to all education majors currently attending school. Award is based on an essay demonstrating knowledge of and interest in compulsory unionism in education. When corresponding regarding scholarship, please specify "Education" or "Future Teacher Scholarship". High school seniors accepted into a teacher education program may apply.

Academic Fields/Career Goals: Education; Special Education.

Award: Scholarship for use in freshman, sophomore, junior, senior, or graduate years; not renewable. *Number:* 1. *Amount:* $1000.

Eligibility Requirements: Applicant must be enrolled or expecting to enroll full or part-time at a two-year or four-year institution or university. Available to U.S. citizens.

Application Requirements: Application, applicant must enter a contest, essay, transcript. *Deadline:* December 31.

Contact: Cathy Jones, Scholarship Coordinator
National Institute for Labor Relations Research
5211 Port Royal Road
Springfield, VA 22151
Phone: 703-321-9606
Fax: 703-321-7342
E-mail: research@nilrr.org

NATIONAL URBAN LEAGUE   http://www.nul.org

BLACK EXECUTIVE EXCHANGE PROGRAM JERRY BARTOW SCHOLARSHIP FUND

• *See page 151*

NEW HAMPSHIRE POSTSECONDARY EDUCATION COMMISSION   http://www.state.nh.us/postsecondary

WORKFORCE INCENTIVE PROGRAM

The Workforce Incentive Program links higher education with critical workforce needs. There are two components to the program: an incentive for students to study in particular areas (forgivable loan) and assistance for employees in critical workforce shortage areas (loan repayment). Critical shortage areas are: nursing, special education, and foreign language education. Please refer to Web site for further details: http://www.state.nh.us/postsecondary

Academic Fields/Career Goals: Education; Foreign Language; Nursing; Special Education.

Award: Forgivable loan for use in freshman, sophomore, junior, senior, graduate, or postgraduate years. *Number:* varies. *Amount:* varies.

Eligibility Requirements: Applicant must be enrolled or expecting to enroll at an institution or university and studying in New Hampshire. Available to U.S. citizens.

Application Requirements: Application. *Deadline:* varies.

Contact: Judith A Knapp, Scholarship Coordinator
New Hampshire Postsecondary Education Commission
3 Barrell Court, Suite 300
Concord, NH 03301-8543
Phone: 603-271-2555
Fax: 603-271-2696
E-mail: jknapp@pec.state.nh.us

NORTH CAROLINA ASSOCIATION OF EDUCATORS   http://www.ncae.org

MARY MORROW-EDNA RICHARDS SCHOLARSHIP

One-time award for junior year of study in four-year education degree program. Preference given to members of the student branch of the North Carolina Association of Educators. Must be North Carolina resident attending a North Carolina institution. Must agree to teach in North Carolina for two years after graduation. Must be a junior in college when application is filed. Deadline is second Monday in January.

Academic Fields/Career Goals: Education.

Award: Forgivable loan for use in junior or senior years; not renewable. *Number:* 3. *Amount:* up to $1000.

Eligibility Requirements: Applicant must be enrolled or expecting to enroll full-time at a four-year institution or university; resident of North Carolina and studying in North Carolina. Available to U.S. citizens.

Application Requirements: Application, essay, financial need analysis, references, transcript. *Deadline:* varies.

Contact: Jackie Vaughn, Morrow/Richards Scholarship Coordinator
North Carolina Association of Educators
700 South Salisbury Street
Raleigh, NC 27611
Phone: 919-832-3000 Ext. 216
Fax: 919-839-8229
E-mail: jvaughn@nea.org

NORTH CAROLINA STATE EDUCATION ASSISTANCE AUTHORITY   http://www.ncseaa.edu

TEACHER ASSISTANT SCHOLARSHIP PROGRAM

Funding to attend a public or private four-year college or university in North Carolina with an approved teacher education program. Applicant must be employed full-time as a teacher assistant in an instructional area while pursuing licensure and maintain employment to remain eligible. Refer to Web site for further details: http://www.ncseaa.edu/tas.htm

Academic Fields/Career Goals: Education.

Award: Scholarship for use in freshman, sophomore, junior, or senior years; renewable. *Number:* varies. *Amount:* $1200–$3600.

Eligibility Requirements: Applicant must be enrolled or expecting to enroll full-time at a four-year institution or university; resident of North Carolina and studying in North Carolina. Applicant must have 2.5 GPA or higher. Available to U.S. citizens.

Application Requirements: Application, FAFSA. *Deadline:* March 31.

Contact: Bill Carswell, Manager of Scholarship and Grant Division
North Carolina State Education Assistance Authority
PO Box 14103
Research Triangle Park, NC 27709
Phone: 919-549-8614
Fax: 919-248-4687
E-mail: carswellb@ncseaa.edu

NORTH CAROLINA TEACHING FELLOWS COMMISSION   http://www.teachingfellows.org

NORTH CAROLINA TEACHING FELLOWS SCHOLARSHIP PROGRAM

Renewable award for North Carolina high school seniors pursuing teaching careers. Must agree to teach in a North Carolina public or government school for four years or repay award. Must attend one of the 14 approved schools in North Carolina. Merit-based. Must interview at the local level and at the regional level as a finalist. Application available online only: http://www.teachingfellows.org.

Academic Fields/Career Goals: Education.

Award: Forgivable loan for use in freshman, sophomore, junior, or senior years; renewable. *Number:* up to 500. *Amount:* $6500.

Eligibility Requirements: Applicant must be high school student; planning to enroll or expecting to enroll full-time at a four-year institution; resident of North Carolina and studying in North Carolina. Applicant must have 3.5 GPA or higher. Available to U.S. citizens.

Application Requirements: Application, essay, interview, references, test scores, transcript. *Deadline:* varies.

Contact: Sherry Woodruff, Program Officer
North Carolina Teaching Fellows Commission
3739 National Drive, Suite 210
Raleigh, NC 27612
Phone: 919-781-6833 Ext. 103
Fax: 919-781-6527
E-mail: tfellows@ncforum.org

NORTH DAKOTA UNIVERSITY SYSTEM   http://www.ndus.nodak.edu

NORTH DAKOTA TEACHER SHORTAGE LOAN FORGIVENESS PROGRAM

Forgivable loan for individuals who received their education degree from a North Dakota public institution and teach in North Dakota at grade levels and/or content areas identified by the Department of Public Instruction as having a teacher shortage. Funding recipients are eligible to have indebtedness reduced for up to $1000 per year for every consecutive year they teach in a teacher shortage area for up to three years. Applications are available on Web site: http://www.ndus.nodak.edu/students/financial-aid

Academic Fields/Career Goals: Education.

Award: Forgivable loan for use in freshman, sophomore, junior, or senior years; renewable. *Number:* 100–175. *Amount:* up to $1000.

Eligibility Requirements: Applicant must be enrolled or expecting to enroll at a four-year institution or university; resident of North Dakota and studying in North Dakota. Applicant or parent of applicant must have employment or volunteer experience in teaching. Available to U.S. citizens.

North Dakota University System (continued)

Application Requirements: Application, financial need analysis. *Deadline:* April 1.

Contact: Peggy Wipf
North Dakota University System
600 East Boulevard Avenue, Department 215
Bismarck, ND 58505-0230
Phone: 701-328-4114

OKLAHOMA STATE REGENTS FOR HIGHER EDUCATION
http://www.okhighered.org

FUTURE TEACHER SCHOLARSHIP-OKLAHOMA

Open to outstanding Oklahoma high school graduates who agree to teach in shortage areas. Must rank in top 15% of graduating class or score above 85th percentile on ACT or similar test, or be accepted in an educational program. Students nominated by institution. Reapply to renew. Must attend college/university in Oklahoma. Contact institution's financial aid office for application deadline.

Academic Fields/Career Goals: Education.

Award: Scholarship for use in freshman, sophomore, junior, senior, or graduate years; renewable. *Number:* varies. *Amount:* $500–$1500.

Eligibility Requirements: Applicant must be enrolled or expecting to enroll full or part-time at a two-year or four-year institution or university; resident of Oklahoma and studying in Oklahoma. Available to U.S. citizens.

Application Requirements: Application, essay, test scores, transcript.

Contact: Scholarship Programs Coordinator
Oklahoma State Regents for Higher Education
PO Box 108850
Oklahoma City, OK 73101-8850
Phone: 800-858-1840
Fax: 405-225-9230

ORDEAN FOUNDATION

ORDEAN SCHOLARSHIP PROGRAM
• See page 67

OREGON PTA
http://www.oregonpta.org

TEACHER EDUCATION SCHOLARSHIP

Applicants must be attending an Oregon public college or university that trains teachers or transfers education credits. Applicants must be an Oregon resident.

Academic Fields/Career Goals: Education.

Award: Scholarship for use in freshman, sophomore, junior, or senior years; not renewable. *Number:* 4–10. *Amount:* up to $500.

Eligibility Requirements: Applicant must be enrolled or expecting to enroll full or part-time at a two-year or four-year institution or university; resident of Oregon and studying in Oregon. Available to U.S. citizens.

Application Requirements: Application, autobiography, essay, references, self-addressed stamped envelope, test scores, transcript. *Deadline:* March 10.

Contact: Jeanine Sinnott, TES Chair
Oregon PTA
123 Northeast 3rd Suite 235
Portland, OR 97232
Phone: 503-286-5193
E-mail: purplecat@coho.com

OREGON STUDENT ASSISTANCE COMMISSION
http://www.osac.state.or.us

ALPHA DELTA KAPPA/HARRIET SIMMONS SCHOLARSHIP

One-time award for elementary and secondary education majors entering their senior year, or graduate students enrolled in a fifth-year program leading to a teaching certificate. Visit Web site http://www.osac.state.or.us for more information.

Academic Fields/Career Goals: Education.

Award: Scholarship for use in senior, or graduate years; not renewable. *Number:* 1. *Amount:* $690.

Eligibility Requirements: Applicant must be enrolled or expecting to enroll full-time at a four-year institution or university and resident of Oregon. Available to U.S. citizens.

Application Requirements: Application, essay, financial need analysis, transcript, activity chart. *Deadline:* March 1.

Contact: Director of Grant Programs
Oregon Student Assistance Commission
1500 Valley River Drive, Suite 100
Eugene, OR 97401-7020
Phone: 800-452-8807 Ext. 7395

FRIENDS OF OREGON STUDENTS SCHOLARSHIP

Preference will be given for non-traditional students (older, returning, single parent) who are working and will continue to work 20+ hours per week while attending college at least three-quarters time. Must be pursuing careers in the helping professions (health, education, social work, environmental or public service areas). Finalists to attend interview.

Academic Fields/Career Goals: Education; Health and Medical Sciences; Social Services.

Award: Scholarship for use in freshman, sophomore, junior, or senior years; renewable. *Number:* 28. *Amount:* $2426.

Eligibility Requirements: Applicant must be enrolled or expecting to enroll at a four-year institution and resident of Oregon. Applicant or parent of applicant must have employment or volunteer experience in designated career field. Applicant must have 2.5 GPA or higher. Available to U.S. citizens.

Application Requirements: Application, essay, financial need analysis, interview, references, transcript, activity chart. *Deadline:* March 1.

Contact: Director of Grant Programs
Oregon Student Assistance Commission
1500 Valley River Drive, Suite 100
Eugene, OR 97401-7020
Phone: 800-452-8807 Ext. 7395

HARRIET A. SIMMONS SCHOLARSHIP

Scholarship available for elementary and secondary education majors entering senior, fifth year, or graduate students in fifth year. Must be a resident of Oregon. Deadline is March 1.

Academic Fields/Career Goals: Education.

Award: Scholarship for use in senior, or graduate years; not renewable. *Number:* varies. *Amount:* $500.

Eligibility Requirements: Applicant must be enrolled or expecting to enroll full-time at a four-year institution or university and resident of Oregon. Available to U.S. citizens.

Application Requirements: Application, essay, financial need analysis, transcript, activities chart. *Deadline:* March 1.

Contact: Director of Grant Programs
Oregon Student Assistance Commission
1500 Valley River Drive, Suite 100
Eugene, OR 97401-7020
Phone: 800-452-8807 Ext. 7395

JAMES CARLSON MEMORIAL SCHOLARSHIP

One-time award for elementary or secondary education majors entering senior or fifth year, or graduate students in fifth year for elementary or secondary certificate. Priority given to African-American, Asian, Hispanic, Native-American ethnic groups; dependents of Oregon Education Association members, and others committed to teaching autistic children.

Academic Fields/Career Goals: Education; Special Education.

Award: Scholarship for use in senior, or graduate years; not renewable. *Number:* 3. *Amount:* $1300.

Eligibility Requirements: Applicant must be enrolled or expecting to enroll full-time at a four-year institution and resident of Oregon. Available to U.S. citizens.

Application Requirements: Application, essay, financial need analysis, transcript, activity chart. *Deadline:* March 1.

Contact: Director of Grant Programs
Oregon Student Assistance Commission
1500 Valley River Drive, Suite 100
Eugene, OR 97401-7020
Phone: 800-452-8807 Ext. 7395

MARIAN DU PUY MEMORIAL SCHOLARSHIP

One-time award for students accepted in teacher education programs. Must be enrolled or planning to enroll in full-time undergraduate study as a college junior or above with the career goal of becoming a teacher. Minimum 3.0 GPA. For use at Oregon four-year colleges only. Must be graduate of high schools in Multnomah, Clackamas, or Washington counties.

Academic Fields/Career Goals: Education.

Award: Scholarship for use in junior or senior years; renewable. *Number:* varies. *Amount:* $500.

Eligibility Requirements: Applicant must be enrolled or expecting to enroll full-time at a four-year institution or university; resident of Oregon and studying in Oregon. Applicant must have 3.0 GPA or higher. Available to U.S. citizens.

Application Requirements: Application, essay, financial need analysis, transcript, activities chart. *Deadline:* March 1.

Contact: Director of Grant Programs
Oregon Student Assistance Commission
1500 Valley River Drive, Suite 100
Eugene, OR 97401-7020
Phone: 800-452-8807 Ext. 7395

NETTIE HANSELMAN JAYNES SCHOLARSHIP

One-time award for elementary and secondary education majors entering their senior or fifth year. Graduate students in their fifth year for elementary or secondary certificate also may apply. Application deadline is March 1.

Academic Fields/Career Goals: Education.

Award: Scholarship for use in senior, or graduate years; not renewable. *Number:* 1. *Amount:* $890.

Eligibility Requirements: Applicant must be enrolled or expecting to enroll full-time at a four-year institution or university and resident of Oregon. Available to U.S. citizens.

Application Requirements: Application, essay, financial need analysis, transcript, activities chart. *Deadline:* March 1.

Contact: Director of Grant Programs
Oregon Student Assistance Commission
1500 Valley River Drive, Suite 100
Eugene, OR 97401-7020
Phone: 800-452-8807 Ext. 7395

OREGON EDUCATION ASSOCIATION SCHOLARSHIP

Scholarship open to graduating seniors of any Oregon public high school. Must plan to complete baccalaureate degree and teaching certification at an Oregon college. Renewable with satisfactory academic progress.

Academic Fields/Career Goals: Education.

Award: Scholarship for use in freshman, sophomore, junior, or senior years; renewable. *Number:* 5. *Amount:* $800.

Eligibility Requirements: Applicant must be high school student; planning to enroll or expecting to enroll at an institution or university; resident of Oregon and studying in Oregon. Available to U.S. citizens.

Application Requirements: Application, essay, transcript, activity chart. *Deadline:* March 1.

Contact: Director of Grant Programs
Oregon Student Assistance Commission
1500 Valley River Drive, Suite 100
Eugene, OR 97401-7020
Phone: 800-452-8807 Ext. 7935

PAGE FOUNDATION, INC.   http://www.pagefoundation.org

PROFESSIONAL ASSOCIATION OF GEORGIA EDUCATORS FOUNDATION SCHOLARSHIP PROGRAM

Each scholarship is a one-time cash award of $1000, payable to the recipient's college or university. Eligible applicants will be residents of Georgia studying education-related courses at an accredited college or university. Scholarships are given to juniors, seniors, undergraduates and teachers returning for a graduate degree. For more information go to http://www.pagefoundation.org. Applicant must be a PAGE or SPAGE member. Application due April 30.

Academic Fields/Career Goals: Education.

Award: Scholarship for use in junior, senior, graduate, or postgraduate years; not renewable. *Number:* 8–15. *Amount:* $1000.

Eligibility Requirements: Applicant must be enrolled or expecting to enroll full or part-time at a two-year or four-year institution and resident of Georgia. Applicant must have 3.0 GPA or higher. Available to U.S. citizens.

Application Requirements: Application, essay, references, transcript. *Deadline:* April 30.

Contact: Michelle Crawford, Scholarships Coordinator
PAGE Foundation, Inc.
PO Box 942270
Atlanta, GA 31141-2270
Phone: 770-216-8555
Fax: 770-216-9672
E-mail: mcrawford@pagefoundation.org

STUDENT PROFESSIONAL ASSOCIATION OF GEORGIA EDUCATORS SCHOLARSHIPS

One-time awards available to SPAGE members. Must be an upcoming junior or senior or graduate student. Must agree to teach in Georgia for three years. Must have a 3.0 GPA or higher.

Academic Fields/Career Goals: Education.

Award: Scholarship for use in junior, senior, or graduate years. *Amount:* up to $1000.

Eligibility Requirements: Applicant must be enrolled or expecting to enroll full-time at a four-year institution or university. Applicant must have 3.0 GPA or higher. Available to U.S. citizens.

Application Requirements: Application, essay, references, transcript. *Deadline:* varies.

Contact: Michelle Crawford, Scholarships Coordinator
PAGE Foundation, Inc.
PO Box 942270
Atlanta, GA 31141-2270
Phone: 770-216-8555
Fax: 770-216-9672
E-mail: mcrawford@pagefoundation.org

PENNSYLVANIA HIGHER EDUCATION ASSISTANCE AGENCY   http://www.pheaa.org

QUALITY EARLY EDUCATION LOAN FORGIVENESS PROGRAM

Forgivable loan available to graduates working in Pennsylvania in the field of Early Childhood Education. Applicants must be employed full-time by a Pennsylvania Department of Public Welfare-approved child daycare center or group child daycare home. Applicants cannot have a gross annual income of more than $23,000 from employment in a Pennsylvania Department of Public Welfare-approved child daycare center or group child daycare home.

Academic Fields/Career Goals: Education.

Award: Forgivable loan for use in freshman, sophomore, junior, or senior years. *Amount:* up to $3300.

Eligibility Requirements: Applicant must be enrolled or expecting to enroll at a two-year or four-year or technical institution or university and resident of Pennsylvania. Available to U.S. citizens.

Application Requirements: Application.

Contact: Keith New, Director of Communications and Press Office
Pennsylvania Higher Education Assistance Agency
1200 N 7th Street
Harrisburg, PA 17102-1444
Phone: 717-720-2509
Fax: 717-720-3903
E-mail: knew@pheaa.org

PI LAMBDA THETA, INC.   http://www.pilambda.org

DISTINGUISHED STUDENT SCHOLAR AWARD

The Distinguished Student Scholar Award is presented in recognition of an education major who has displayed leadership potential and a strong dedication to education. Award given out in odd years. Minimum 3.5 GPA required.

Pi Lambda Theta, Inc. (continued)

Academic Fields/Career Goals: Education.

Award: Prize for use in freshman, sophomore, junior, or senior years; not renewable. *Number:* 1. *Amount:* $500.

Eligibility Requirements: Applicant must be enrolled or expecting to enroll full or part-time at a four-year institution or university and must have an interest in leadership. Applicant or parent of applicant must have employment or volunteer experience in community service. Applicant must have 3.5 GPA or higher. Available to U.S. and non-U.S. citizens.

Application Requirements: Application, resume, references, transcript, two letters of support from faculty members other than the nominator, letter of endorsement from the nominee's chapter. *Deadline:* February 10.

Contact: Pam Todd, Manager, Member Services
Pi Lambda Theta, Inc.
4101 East 3rd Street, PO Box 6626
Bloomington, IN 47407-6626
Phone: 812-339-3411
Fax: 812-339-3462
E-mail: endowment@pilambda.org

GRADUATE STUDENT SCHOLAR AWARD

The Graduate Student Scholar Award is presented in recognition of an outstanding graduate student who is an education major. Award given out in odd years. Minimum 3.5 GPA required.

Academic Fields/Career Goals: Education.

Award: Prize for use in senior, or graduate years; not renewable. *Number:* 1. *Amount:* $1000.

Eligibility Requirements: Applicant must be enrolled or expecting to enroll full or part-time at a four-year institution or university and must have an interest in leadership. Applicant or parent of applicant must have employment or volunteer experience in community service. Applicant must have 3.5 GPA or higher. Available to U.S. and non-U.S. citizens.

Application Requirements: Application, essay, resume, references, transcript, letter of endorsement from nominee's chapter. *Deadline:* February 10.

Contact: Pam Todd, Manager, Member Services
Pi Lambda Theta, Inc.
4101 East 3rd Street, PO Box 6626
Bloomington, IN 47407-6626
Phone: 812-339-3411
Fax: 812-339-3462
E-mail: pam@pilambda.org

STUDENT SUPPORT SCHOLARSHIP

This scholarship is available to current members of Pi Lambda Theta who will be a full-time or part-time student enrolled in a minimum of three semester hours at a regionally accredited institution during the year following the award. Minimum 3.5 GPA required.

Academic Fields/Career Goals: Education.

Award: Scholarship for use in sophomore, junior, senior, graduate, or postgraduate years; not renewable. *Number:* 1–6. *Amount:* $750.

Eligibility Requirements: Applicant must be enrolled or expecting to enroll full or part-time at a two-year or four-year or technical institution or university. Applicant must have 3.5 GPA or higher. Available to U.S. and non-U.S. citizens.

Application Requirements: Application, essay, transcript. *Deadline:* February 10.

Contact: Pam Todd, Manager, Member Services
Pi Lambda Theta, Inc.
4101 East 3rd Street, PO Box 6626
Bloomington, IN 47407-6626
Phone: 812-339-3411
Fax: 812-339-3462
E-mail: root@pilambda.org

SARAH KLENKE MEMORIAL TEACHING SCHOLARSHIP

SARAH KLENKE MEMORIAL TEACHING SCHOLARSHIP PROGRAM

Scholarship for graduating senior or high school graduate enrolling in a two- or four-year college or university with a desire to major in education. Preference given to the average student: GPA between 2.0 and 3.0. Participation in JROTC, softball, or baseball is required.

Academic Fields/Career Goals: Education.

Award: Scholarship for use in freshman year. *Number:* 2. *Amount:* up to $1000.

Eligibility Requirements: Applicant must be enrolled or expecting to enroll full-time at a two-year or four-year institution or university. Available to U.S. citizens.

Application Requirements: Application, essay, references. *Deadline:* March 15.

Contact: c/o Aaron Klenke
Sarah Klenke Memorial Teaching Scholarship
3131 Glade Springs
Kingwood, TX 77339

SIGMA ALPHA IOTA PHILANTHROPIES, INC.   http://www.sai-national.org

SIGMA ALPHA IOTA PHILANTHROPIES UNDERGRADUATE SCHOLARSHIPS

One-time award to undergraduate members of SAI who are freshman, sophomores or juniors. For use in sophomore, junior, or senior year. Must be female over 18 years of age studying performing arts or performing arts education. Contact local chapter for further details. 12 scholarships of $1500 each and 3 scholarships of $2000 each .

Academic Fields/Career Goals: Education; Performing Arts.

Award: Scholarship for use in sophomore, junior, or senior years; not renewable. *Number:* 15. *Amount:* $1500–$2000.

Eligibility Requirements: Applicant must be age 19; enrolled or expecting to enroll full-time at a four-year institution or university; female and must have an interest in music/singing. Available to U.S. and non-U.S. citizens.

Application Requirements: Application, essay, financial need analysis, references, transcript. *Deadline:* March 15.

Contact: Eleanor Tapscott, Project Director
Sigma Alpha Iota Philanthropies, Inc.
One Tunnel Road
Asheville, NC 28805
Phone: 828-251-0606
Fax: 828-251-0644
E-mail: webmaster@sai-national.org

SIGMA ALPHA IOTA VISUALLY IMPAIRED SCHOLARSHIP

One-time award offered yearly for member of SAI who is visually impaired, and a member of a college or alumnae chapter. Submit fifteen-minute tape or evidence of work in composition, musicology, or research. One scholarship of $1000. Application fee: $25.

Academic Fields/Career Goals: Education; Music; Performing Arts.

Award: Scholarship for use in freshman, sophomore, junior, senior, or graduate years; not renewable. *Number:* 1. *Amount:* $1000.

Eligibility Requirements: Applicant must be enrolled or expecting to enroll full or part-time at a four-year institution or university; female and must have an interest in music/singing. Applicant must be visually impaired. Available to U.S. and non-U.S. citizens.

Application Requirements: Application, essay, references, transcript, tape. *Fee:* $25. *Deadline:* March 15.

Contact: Karen Louise Gearreald, Director
Sigma Alpha Iota Philanthropies, Inc.
One Tunnel Road
Asheville, NC 28805
Phone: 828-251-0606
Fax: 828-251-0644
E-mail: hadley@exis.net

SOCIAL SCIENCES AND HUMANITIES RESEARCH COUNCIL OF CANADA
http://www.sshrc.ca

RESEARCH DEVELOPMENT INITIATIVE

The broad purpose of the program is to support research that is in its initial stages by supporting the development of new ways of analyzing, structuring, integrating, and transferring knowledge in the humanities and the social sciences. Application deadlines: December 15, April 7, and October 7. For more details and an application see Web site: http://www.sshrc.ca

Academic Fields/Career Goals: Education; Humanities; Social Sciences.

Award: Grant for use in freshman, sophomore, junior, senior, graduate, or postgraduate years; not renewable. *Number:* varies. *Amount:* $40,000.

Eligibility Requirements: Applicant must be enrolled or expecting to enroll at a four-year institution or university. Available to Canadian citizens.

Application Requirements: Application. *Deadline:* varies.

Contact: Garry Pinard, Program Officer
Social Sciences and Humanities Research Council of Canada
350 Albert Street, PO Box 1610
Ottawa, ON K1P 6G4
Canada
Phone: 613-992-5129
Fax: 613-947-0223
E-mail: garry.pinard@sshrc.ca

SOUTH CAROLINA STUDENT LOAN CORPORATION
http://www.slc.sc.edu

SOUTH CAROLINA TEACHER LOAN PROGRAM

One-time awards for South Carolina residents attending four-year postsecondary institutions in South Carolina. Recipients must teach in the South Carolina public school system in a critical-need area after graduation. 20% of loan forgiven for each year of service. Write for additional requirements.

Academic Fields/Career Goals: Education; Special Education.

Award: Forgivable loan for use in freshman, sophomore, junior, senior, or graduate years; not renewable. *Number:* up to 1121. *Amount:* $2500–$5000.

Eligibility Requirements: Applicant must be enrolled or expecting to enroll full or part-time at a four-year institution or university; resident of South Carolina and studying in South Carolina. Applicant must have 3.0 GPA or higher. Available to U.S. citizens.

Application Requirements: Application, test scores. *Deadline:* June 1.

Contact: Jennifer Jones-Gaddy, Vice President
South Carolina Student Loan Corporation
PO Box 21487
Columbia, SC 29221
Phone: 803-798-0916
Fax: 803-772-9410
E-mail: jgaddy@slc.sc.edu

SOUTH DAKOTA BOARD OF REGENTS
http://www.sdbor.edu

HAINES MEMORIAL SCHOLARSHIP

One-time scholarship for South Dakota public university students who are sophomores, juniors, or seniors having at least a 2.5 GPA and majoring in a teacher education program. Include resume with application. Must be South Dakota resident.

Academic Fields/Career Goals: Education.

Award: Scholarship for use in sophomore, junior, or senior years; not renewable. *Number:* 1. *Amount:* $2150.

Eligibility Requirements: Applicant must be enrolled or expecting to enroll at an institution or university; resident of South Dakota and studying in South Dakota. Applicant must have 2.5 GPA or higher. Available to U.S. citizens.

Application Requirements: Application, autobiography, essay, resume. *Deadline:* February 9.

Contact: Scholarship Committee
South Dakota Board of Regents
306 East Capitol Avenue, Suite 200
Pierre, SD 57501-3159

SOUTH DAKOTA BOARD OF REGENTS ANNIS I. FOWLER/KADEN SCHOLARSHIP

Scholarship for graduating South Dakota high school seniors to pursue a career in elementary education at a South Dakota public university. University must be one of the following: BHSU, BSU, NSU or USD. Applicants must have a cumulative GPA of 3.0 after three years of high school. One-time award.

Academic Fields/Career Goals: Education.

Award: Scholarship for use in freshman year; not renewable. *Number:* 2. *Amount:* $1000.

Eligibility Requirements: Applicant must be high school student; planning to enroll or expecting to enroll at an institution or university; resident of South Dakota and studying in South Dakota. Applicant must have 3.0 GPA or higher. Available to U.S. citizens.

Application Requirements: Application, essay, references, test scores, transcript. *Deadline:* February 19.

Contact: Scholarship Committee
South Dakota Board of Regents
306 East Capitol Avenue, Suite 200
Pierre, SD 57501-3159

SOUTHWEST STUDENT SERVICES CORPORATION
http://www.sssc.com/

ANNE LINDEMAN MEMORIAL SCHOLARSHIP
• See page 142

STATE COUNCIL OF HIGHER EDUCATION FOR VIRGINIA
http://www.schev.edu

HIGHER EDUCATION TEACHER ASSISTANCE PROGRAM

Need-based scholarship for Virginia residents enrolled in a K-12 teacher preparation program in a participating Virginia college or university. Must be nominated by a faculty member in the Education Department at the institution. Applications must be obtained from and returned to the financial aid office at the participating institution.

Academic Fields/Career Goals: Education; Special Education.

Award: Scholarship for use in freshman, sophomore, junior, or senior years; renewable. *Number:* varies. *Amount:* $1000–$2000.

Eligibility Requirements: Applicant must be enrolled or expecting to enroll full-time at a two-year or four-year institution or university; resident of Virginia and studying in Virginia. Applicant must have 2.5 GPA or higher. Available to U.S. citizens.

Application Requirements: Application, financial need analysis, references, FAFSA.

Contact: Lee Andes, Assistant Director for Financial Aid
State Council of Higher Education for Virginia
James Monroe Building, 10th Floor
101 North 14th Street
Richmond, VA 23219
Phone: 804-225-2614
Fax: 804-225-2604
E-mail: leeandes@schev.edu

SOUTHSIDE VIRGINIA TOBACCO TEACHER SCHOLARSHIP/LOAN

Need-based scholarship for Southside Virginia natives to pursue a degree in K-12 teacher education in any four-year U.S. institution and then return to the Southside region to live and work. Must teach in Southside Virginia public school for scholarship/loan forgiveness.

Academic Fields/Career Goals: Education.

Award: Forgivable loan for use in freshman, sophomore, junior, or senior years; renewable. *Number:* varies. *Amount:* up to $4000.

Eligibility Requirements: Applicant must be enrolled or expecting to enroll full or part-time at a two-year or four-year institution or university and resident of Virginia. Available to U.S. citizens.

State Council of Higher Education for Virginia (continued)

Application Requirements: Application, financial need analysis, FAFSA.

Contact: Christine Fields
State Council of Higher Education for Virginia
PO Box 1987
Abingdon, VA 24212
Phone: 276-619-4376 Ext. 4002

STATE OF WYOMING, ADMINISTERED BY UNIVERSITY OF WYOMING

http://www.uwyo.edu/scholarships

SUPERIOR STUDENT IN EDUCATION SCHOLARSHIP-WYOMING

Available to Wyoming high school graduates who have demonstrated high academic achievement and plan to teach in Wyoming public schools. Award is for tuition at Wyoming institutions. Must maintain 3.0 GPA.

Academic Fields/Career Goals: Education.

Award: Scholarship for use in freshman, sophomore, junior, or senior years; renewable. *Number:* 16–80. *Amount:* varies.

Eligibility Requirements: Applicant must be enrolled or expecting to enroll full-time at a two-year or four-year institution or university; resident of Wyoming and studying in Wyoming. Applicant must have 3.0 GPA or higher. Available to U.S. citizens.

Application Requirements: Application, references, test scores, transcript. *Deadline:* October 31.

Contact: Joel Anne Berrigan, Assistant Director, Scholarships
State of Wyoming, administered by University of Wyoming
Student Financial Aid, Department 3335, 1000 East University Avenue
Laramie, WY 82071-3335
Phone: 307-766-2117
Fax: 307-766-3800
E-mail: finaid@uwyo.edu

TENNESSEE EDUCATION ASSOCIATION

http://www.teateachers.org

TEA DON SAHLI-KATHY WOODALL FUTURE TEACHERS OF AMERICA SCHOLARSHIP

Scholarship is available to a high school senior planning to major in education, attending a high school which has an FTA Chapter affiliated with TEA, and planning to enroll in a Tennessee college.

Academic Fields/Career Goals: Education.

Award: Scholarship for use in freshman year; not renewable. *Number:* 1. *Amount:* $1000.

Eligibility Requirements: Applicant must be high school student; planning to enroll or expecting to enroll full-time at a four-year institution or university; resident of Tennessee and studying in Tennessee. Applicant must have 3.0 GPA or higher. Available to U.S. citizens.

Application Requirements: Application, essay, financial need analysis, references, transcript, statement of income. *Deadline:* March 1.

Contact: Jeanette DeMain, Administrative Assistant
Tennessee Education Association
801 Second Avenue North
Nashville, TN 37201-1099
Phone: 615-242-8392
Fax: 615-259-4581
E-mail: jdemain@tea.nea.org

TEA DON SAHLI-KATHY WOODALL MINORITY SCHOLARSHIP

Scholarship is available to a minority high school senior planning to major in education and planning to enroll in a Tennessee college. Application must be made by an FTA Chapter, or by the student with the recommendation of an active TEA member.

Academic Fields/Career Goals: Education.

Award: Scholarship for use in freshman year; not renewable. *Number:* 1. *Amount:* $1000.

Eligibility Requirements: Applicant must be American Indian/Alaska Native, Asian/Pacific Islander, Black (non-Hispanic), or Hispanic; high

school student; planning to enroll or expecting to enroll full-time at a four-year institution or university; resident of Tennessee and studying in Tennessee. Applicant must have 3.0 GPA or higher. Available to U.S. citizens.

Application Requirements: Application, essay, financial need analysis, references, transcript, statement of income. *Deadline:* March 1.

Contact: Jeanette DeMain, Administrative Assistant
Tennessee Education Association
801 Second Avenue North
Nashville, TN 37201-1099
Phone: 615-242-8392
Fax: 615-259-4581
E-mail: jdemain@tea.nea.org

TEA DON SAHLI-KATHY WOODALL UNDERGRADUATE SCHOLARSHIP

Scholarship is available to undergraduate students who are student TEA members. Application must be made through the local STEA Chapter.

Academic Fields/Career Goals: Education.

Award: Scholarship for use in freshman, sophomore, junior, or senior years; not renewable. *Number:* 4. *Amount:* $500–$1000.

Eligibility Requirements: Applicant must be enrolled or expecting to enroll full or part-time at a four-year institution or university; resident of Tennessee and studying in Tennessee. Applicant or parent of applicant must be member of Tennessee Education Association. Applicant must have 3.0 GPA or higher. Available to U.S. citizens.

Application Requirements: Application, essay, financial need analysis, references, transcript, statement of income. *Deadline:* March 1.

Contact: Jeanette DeMain, Administrative Assistant
Tennessee Education Association
801 Second Avenue North
Nashville, TN 37201-1099
Phone: 615-242-8392
Fax: 615-259-4581
E-mail: jdemain@tea.nea.org

TENNESSEE STUDENT ASSISTANCE CORPORATION

http://www.state.tn.us/tsac

CHRISTA MCAULIFFE SCHOLARSHIP PROGRAM

Scholarship to assist and support Tennessee students who have demonstrated a commitment to a career in educating the youth of Tennessee. The scholarship is offered to college seniors for a period of one academic year.

Academic Fields/Career Goals: Education.

Award: Scholarship for use in senior year. *Amount:* up to $1000.

Eligibility Requirements: Applicant must be enrolled or expecting to enroll at a four-year institution or university and studying in Tennessee. Available to U.S. citizens.

Application Requirements: Application. *Deadline:* April 1.

Contact: Naomi Derryberry, Grant and Scholarship Administrator
Tennessee Student Assistance Corporation
404 James Robertson Parkway, Suite 1950
Parkway Towers
Nashville, TN 37243-0820
Phone: 800-342-1663
Fax: 615-741-6101
E-mail: tsac.aidinfo@state.tn.us

TENNESSEE TEACHING SCHOLARS PROGRAM

Forgivable loan for college juniors, seniors, and college graduates admitted to an education program in Tennessee with a minimum GPA of 2.75. Students must commit to teach in a Tennessee public school one year for each year of the award.

Academic Fields/Career Goals: Education.

Award: Forgivable loan for use in junior, senior, or graduate years; not renewable. *Number:* 30–250. *Amount:* $1000–$4200.

Eligibility Requirements: Applicant must be enrolled or expecting to enroll full or part-time at a four-year institution or university; resident of Tennessee and studying in Tennessee. Available to U.S. citizens.

Application Requirements: Application, references, test scores, transcript, letter of intent. *Deadline:* April 15.

Contact: Mike McCormack, Scholarship Administrator
Tennessee Student Assistance Corporation
Parkway Towers, Suite 1950
Nashville, TN 37243-0820
Phone: 615-741-1346
Fax: 615-741-6101
E-mail: mike.mccormack@state.tn.us

THE EDUCATION PARTNERSHIP
http://www.edpartnership.org

LOUIS FEINSTEIN MEMORIAL SCHOLARSHIPS

For students who are interested in a teaching career and best exemplify the qualities of brotherhood, compassion, integrity, leadership, and a determination to make a positive difference in the lives of others. Students will receive benefits including an $8000 scholarship for those attending Rhode Island colleges and universities, and $2000 to all scholars upon graduation. Only high school juniors may apply. Application deadline is June 30.

Academic Fields/Career Goals: Education.

Award: Scholarship for use in freshman, sophomore, junior, or senior years; renewable. *Number:* 10–20. *Amount:* $10,000.

Eligibility Requirements: Applicant must be high school student; age 16-17; planning to enroll or expecting to enroll full-time at a two-year or four-year institution or university and studying in Rhode Island. Applicant must have 2.5 GPA or higher. Available to U.S. citizens.

Application Requirements: Application, essay, interview, references, test scores, transcript. *Deadline:* June 30.

Contact: Keturah Johnson, Scholarships and Communications
Coordinator
The Education Partnership
345 South Main Street
Providence, RI 02903
Phone: 401-331-5222 Ext. 112
Fax: 401-331-1659
E-mail: kjohnson@edpartnership.org

TKE EDUCATIONAL FOUNDATION
http://www.tkefoundation.org

CARROL C. HALL MEMORIAL SCHOLARSHIP
• *See page 95*

FRANCIS J. FLYNN MEMORIAL SCHOLARSHIP

Award of $1400 for an undergraduate member of TKE who is a full-time student pursuing a degree in mathematics or education. Minimum 2.75 GPA required. Leadership within chapter or campus organizations recognized. Preference will be given to members of Theta-Sigma Chapter. Application deadline: May 12.

Academic Fields/Career Goals: Education; Physical Sciences and Math.

Award: Scholarship for use in freshman, sophomore, junior, or senior years; not renewable. *Number:* 1. *Amount:* $1400.

Eligibility Requirements: Applicant must be enrolled or expecting to enroll full-time at a four-year institution or university; male and must have an interest in leadership. Available to U.S. and non-U.S. citizens.

Application Requirements: Application, essay, photo, transcript. *Deadline:* May 12.

Contact: Gary A. Reed, President/CEO
TKE Educational Foundation
8645 Founders Road
Indianapolis, IN 46268-1393
Phone: 317-872-6533
Fax: 317-875-8353
E-mail: reedga@tke.org

UNITED NEGRO COLLEGE FUND
http://www.uncf.org

WINSTON-SALEM/FORSYTH COUNTY PUBLIC SCHOOLS SCHOLARSHIP

Award to a graduating high school senior in one of the eight regular high schools in the Winston-Salem/Forsyth County, NC area, who plans to pursue a career in education. Please visit Web site for more information: http://www.uncf.org.

Academic Fields/Career Goals: Education.

Award: Scholarship for use in freshman, sophomore, junior, or senior years; renewable. *Number:* 1. *Amount:* $5000.

Eligibility Requirements: Applicant must be Black (non-Hispanic); high school student; planning to enroll or expecting to enroll at an institution or university and resident of North Carolina. Applicant must have 2.5 GPA or higher. Available to U.S. citizens.

Application Requirements: Application, financial need analysis, FAFSA, Student Aid Report (SAR). *Deadline:* varies.

Contact: Rebecca Bennett, Director, Program Services
United Negro College Fund
8260 Willow Oaks Corporate Drive
Fairfax, VA 22031-8044
Phone: 800-331-2244
E-mail: rbennett@uncf.org

UTAH STATE BOARD OF REGENTS
http://www.utahsbr.edu/

TERRILL H. BELL TEACHING INCENTIVE LOAN

Designed to provide financial assistance to outstanding Utah students pursuing a degree in education. The incentive loan funds full-time tuition and general fees for eight semesters. After graduation/certification the loan may be forgiven if the recipient teaches in a Utah public school or accredited private school (K-12). Loan forgiveness is done on a year-for-year basis. For more details see Web site: http://www.utahsbr.edu

Academic Fields/Career Goals: Education.

Award: Forgivable loan for use in freshman, sophomore, junior, senior, or graduate years; renewable. *Number:* 365. *Amount:* $900–$2500.

Eligibility Requirements: Applicant must be enrolled or expecting to enroll full-time at a two-year or four-year institution or university; resident of Utah and studying in Utah. Available to U.S. citizens.

Application Requirements: Application, essay, references, test scores, transcript. *Deadline:* varies.

Contact: Charles Downer, Compliance Officer
Utah State Board of Regents
Board of Regents Building, the Gateway
60 South 400 West
Salt Lake City, UT 84101-1284
Phone: 801-321-7221
Fax: 801-366-8470
E-mail: cdowner@utahsbr.edu

VERMONT TEACHER DIVERSITY SCHOLARSHIP PROGRAM
http://www.templeton.vsc.edu/teacherdiversity/

VERMONT TEACHER DIVERSITY SCHOLARSHIP PROGRAM

Loan forgiveness program for students from diverse racial and ethnic backgrounds who attend college in Vermont with a goal of becoming public school teachers. After three years of teaching in the Vermont public school system, they may receive up to $12,000 in loan forgiveness. Preference will be given to residents of Vermont. Application and information available on Web site: http://templeton.vsc.edu/teacherdiversity. Applications are due in April or November.

Academic Fields/Career Goals: Education.

Award: Forgivable loan for use in freshman, sophomore, junior, senior, or graduate years; not renewable. *Number:* up to 4. *Amount:* up to $4000.

Eligibility Requirements: Applicant must be American Indian/Alaska Native, Asian/Pacific Islander, Black (non-Hispanic), or Hispanic; enrolled or expecting to enroll full or part-time at a four-year institution or university and studying in Vermont. Available to U.S. citizens.

Application Requirements: Application, resume, references, transcript. *Deadline:* April 6.

Contact: Ms. Phyl Newbeck, Director
Vermont Teacher Diversity Scholarship Program
PO Box 359
Waterbury, VT 05676-0359
Phone: 802-241-3379
Fax: 802-241-3369

WASHINGTON HIGHER EDUCATION COORDINATING BOARD   http://www.hecb.wa.gov

FUTURE TEACHERS CONDITIONAL SCHOLARSHIP AND LOAN REPAYMENT PROGRAM

This program is designed to encourage outstanding students and paraprofessionals to become teachers. In return for conditional scholarships or loan repayments, participants agree to teach in Washington K-12 schools. Additional consideration is given to individuals seeking certification or additional endorsements in teacher subject shortage areas, as well as to individuals with demonstrated bilingual ability. Must be residents of Washington and attend an institution in Washington.

Academic Fields/Career Goals: Education.

Award: Forgivable loan for use in freshman, sophomore, junior, or senior years; renewable. *Number:* 50. *Amount:* $600–$5000.

Eligibility Requirements: Applicant must be enrolled or expecting to enroll full or part-time at a two-year or four-year institution or university; resident of Washington and studying in Washington. Available to U.S. citizens.

Application Requirements: Application, essay, references, transcript, bilingual verification (if applicable). *Deadline:* October 15.

Contact: Mary Knutson, Program Coordinator
Washington Higher Education Coordinating Board
917 Lakeridge Way, SW, PO Box 43430
Olympia, WA 98504-3430
Phone: 360-753-7800
Fax: 360-753-7808
E-mail: futureteachers@hecb.wa.gov

WISCONSIN CONGRESS OF PARENTS AND TEACHERS, INC.

BROOKMIRE-HASTINGS SCHOLARSHIPS

One-time award to graduating high school seniors from Wisconsin public schools. Must pursue a degree in education. High school must have an active PTA in good standing of the Wisconsin PTA.

Academic Fields/Career Goals: Education; Special Education.

Award: Scholarship for use in freshman year; not renewable. *Number:* up to 2. *Amount:* $500.

Eligibility Requirements: Applicant must be high school student; planning to enroll or expecting to enroll full-time at a four-year institution and resident of Wisconsin. Available to U.S. citizens.

Application Requirements: Application, essay, interview, references, transcript. *Deadline:* February 10.

Contact: Kim Schwantes, Executive Administrator
Wisconsin Congress of Parents and Teachers, Inc.
4797 Hayes Road, Suite 2
Madison, WI 53704-3256

WISCONSIN MATHEMATICS COUNCIL, INC.   http://www.wismath.org

ARNE ENGEBRETSEN WISCONSIN MATHEMATICS COUNCIL SCHOLARSHIP

Scholarship for Wisconsin high school senior who is planning to study mathematics education and teach mathematics at K-12 level.

Academic Fields/Career Goals: Education; Mathematics.

Award: Scholarship for use in freshman year; not renewable. *Number:* 1. *Amount:* $1200.

Eligibility Requirements: Applicant must be high school student; planning to enroll or expecting to enroll full-time at a four-year institution or university and resident of Wisconsin. Available to U.S. citizens.

Application Requirements: Application, essay, resume, references, transcript. *Deadline:* varies.

Contact: Denise Pheifer, Executive Director
Wisconsin Mathematics Council, Inc.
W175 N11117 Stonewood Drive, Suite 204
Germantown, WI 53022
Phone: 262-242-9418
Fax: 262-242-1862
E-mail: wismath@execpc.com

ETHEL A. NEIJAHR WISCONSIN MATHEMATICS COUNCIL SCHOLARSHIP

Scholarship for a Wisconsin resident who is currently enrolled in teacher education programs in a Wisconsin institution studying mathematics education. Minimum GPA of 3.0 required.

Academic Fields/Career Goals: Education; Mathematics.

Award: Scholarship for use in junior, senior, or graduate years; not renewable. *Number:* 1. *Amount:* $1200.

Eligibility Requirements: Applicant must be enrolled or expecting to enroll full-time at a four-year institution or university; resident of Wisconsin and studying in Wisconsin. Applicant must have 3.0 GPA or higher. Available to U.S. citizens.

Application Requirements: Application, essay, resume, references, transcript. *Deadline:* March 1.

Contact: Denise Pheifer, Executive Director
Wisconsin Mathematics Council, Inc.
W175 N11117 Stonewood Drive, Suite 204
Germantown, WI 53022
Phone: 262-242-9418
Fax: 262-242-1862
E-mail: wismath@execpc.com

SISTER MARY PETRONIA VAN STRATEN WISCONSIN MATHEMATICS COUNCIL SCHOLARSHIP

Scholarship for a Wisconsin resident who is currently enrolled in teacher education programs in Wisconsin institution studying mathematics education. Minimum GPA of 3.0 required.

Academic Fields/Career Goals: Education; Mathematics.

Award: Scholarship for use in junior, senior, or graduate years; not renewable. *Number:* 1. *Amount:* $1200.

Eligibility Requirements: Applicant must be enrolled or expecting to enroll full-time at a four-year institution or university; resident of Wisconsin and studying in Wisconsin. Applicant must have 3.0 GPA or higher. Available to U.S. citizens.

Application Requirements: Application, essay, resume, references, transcript. *Deadline:* March 1.

Contact: Denise Pheifer, Executive Director
Wisconsin Mathematics Council, Inc.
W175 N11117 Stonewood Drive, Suite 204
Germantown, WI 53022
Phone: 262-242-9418
Fax: 262-242-1862
E-mail: wismath@execpc.com

WOMEN BAND DIRECTORS INTERNATIONAL   http://www.womenbanddirectors.org

GLADYS STONE WRIGHT SCHOLARSHIP

One-time award for women instrumental music majors enrolled in a four-year institution. Applicants must be working toward a degree in music education with the intention of becoming a band director. Merit-based.

Academic Fields/Career Goals: Education; Music; Performing Arts.

Award: Scholarship for use in freshman, sophomore, junior, senior, or graduate years; not renewable. *Number:* 1. *Amount:* $300.

Eligibility Requirements: Applicant must be enrolled or expecting to enroll full-time at a four-year institution or university; female and must have an interest in music/singing. Applicant must have 3.0 GPA or higher. Available to U.S. and non-U.S. citizens.

Application Requirements: Application, essay, financial need analysis, photo, resume, references, self-addressed stamped envelope, transcript. *Deadline:* December 1.

Contact: Women Band Directors International
292 Band Hall, Louisiana State University
Baton Rouge, LA 70803

HELEN MAY BULTER MEMORIAL SCHOLARSHIP

One-time award for women instrumental music majors enrolled in a four-year institution. Applicants must be working toward a degree in music education with the intention of becoming a band director. Merit-based.

Academic Fields/Career Goals: Education; Music; Performing Arts.

Award: Scholarship for use in freshman, sophomore, junior, senior, or graduate years; not renewable. *Number:* 1. *Amount:* $300.

Eligibility Requirements: Applicant must be enrolled or expecting to enroll full-time at a four-year institution or university; female and must have an interest in music/singing. Applicant must have 3.0 GPA or higher. Available to U.S. and non-U.S. citizens.

Application Requirements: Application, essay, financial need analysis, photo, resume, references, self-addressed stamped envelope, transcript. *Deadline:* December 1.

Contact: Women Band Directors International
292 Band Hall, Louisiana State University
Baton Rouge, LA 70803

MARTHA ANN STARK MEMORIAL SCHOLARSHIP

One-time award for a woman college student who demonstrates outstanding contributions to bands and band music. Must be pursuing a major in music education and plan to become a band director. Merit-based. Must have a 3.0 GPA.

Academic Fields/Career Goals: Education; Music; Performing Arts.

Award: Scholarship for use in freshman, sophomore, junior, or senior years; not renewable. *Number:* 1. *Amount:* $300.

Eligibility Requirements: Applicant must be enrolled or expecting to enroll full-time at a four-year institution or university; female and must have an interest in music/singing. Applicant must have 3.0 GPA or higher. Available to U.S. and non-U.S. citizens.

Application Requirements: Application, essay, financial need analysis, photo, resume, references, self-addressed stamped envelope, transcript. *Deadline:* December 1.

Contact: Diane Gorzycki, WBDI Scholarship Chair
Women Band Directors International
7424 Whistlestop Drive
Austin, TX 78749
E-mail: dgorzycki@austin.rr.com

MUSIC TECHNOLOGY SCHOLARSHIP

One-time award of $500. Student must be able to demonstrate the use of incorporation of music technology. Applicants must be working toward a degree in music education with the intention of becoming a band director.

Academic Fields/Career Goals: Education; Music; Performing Arts.

Award: Scholarship for use in freshman, sophomore, junior, senior, or graduate years; not renewable. *Number:* 1. *Amount:* $500.

Eligibility Requirements: Applicant must be enrolled or expecting to enroll full-time at a four-year institution or university; female and must have an interest in music/singing. Applicant must have 3.0 GPA or higher. Available to U.S. and non-U.S. citizens.

Application Requirements: Application, essay, financial need analysis, photo, resume, references, self-addressed stamped envelope, transcript. *Deadline:* December 1.

Contact: Linda Moorhouse, Associate Director of Bands
Women Band Directors International
292 Band Hall, Louisiana State University
Baton Rouge, LA 70803
Phone: 225-578-2384
Fax: 225-578-4693
E-mail: moorhous@lsu.edu

VOLKWEIN MEMORIAL SCHOLARSHIP

One-time award for women instrumental music majors enrolled in a four-year institution. Applicants must be working toward a degree in music education with the intention of becoming a band director. Merit-based. Must have a 3.0 GPA.

Academic Fields/Career Goals: Education; Music; Performing Arts.

Award: Scholarship for use in freshman, sophomore, junior, senior, or graduate years; not renewable. *Number:* 1. *Amount:* $300.

Eligibility Requirements: Applicant must be enrolled or expecting to enroll full-time at a four-year institution or university; female and must have an interest in music/singing. Applicant must have 3.0 GPA or higher. Available to U.S. and non-U.S. citizens.

Application Requirements: Application, essay, financial need analysis, photo, resume, references, self-addressed stamped envelope, transcript. *Deadline:* December 1.

Contact: Diane Gorzycki, WBDI Scholarship Chair
Women Band Directors International
7424 Whistlestop Drive
Austin, TX 78749
E-mail: dgorzycki@austin.rr.com

YES I CAN! FOUNDATION   http://www.yesican.org

SARA CONLON MEMORIAL SCHOLARSHIP AWARD

Scholarship available to a student with a disability who is also a member of an ethnic minority group, such as African-American, Hispanic, Native American or Asian. Applicant must demonstrate gifted and/or talented abilities in any one or more of the following categories: general intellectual ability, specific academic aptitude, creativity, leadership, visual or performing arts, and be committed to pursuing major in Education.

Academic Fields/Career Goals: Education.

Award: Scholarship for use in freshman, sophomore, junior, or senior years. *Amount:* up to $500.

Eligibility Requirements: Applicant must be American Indian/Alaska Native, Asian/Pacific Islander, Black (non-Hispanic), or Hispanic and enrolled or expecting to enroll full-time at a four-year institution or university. Applicant must be hearing impaired, learning disabled, physically disabled, or visually impaired. Available to U.S. citizens.

Application Requirements: Application, financial need analysis, references, transcript, proof of disability. *Deadline:* varies.

Contact: Jessa Foor, Program Development Specialist
Yes I Can! Foundation
1110 North Glebe Road, Suite 300
Arlington, VA 22201
Phone: 703-245-0607
Fax: 703-620-4334
E-mail: yesican@cec.sped.org

ZETA PHI BETA SORORITY, INC. NATIONAL EDUCATIONAL FOUNDATION   http://www.zphib1920.org

ISABEL M. HERSON SCHOLARSHIP IN EDUCATION

Scholarships available for graduate or undergraduate students enrolled in a degree program in either elementary or secondary education. Award for full-time study for one academic year. See Web site for additional information and application: http://www.zphib1920.org

Academic Fields/Career Goals: Education.

Award: Scholarship for use in freshman, sophomore, junior, senior, or graduate years; not renewable. *Number:* varies. *Amount:* $500–$1000.

Eligibility Requirements: Applicant must be enrolled or expecting to enroll full-time at a four-year institution or university. Available to U.S. citizens.

Application Requirements: Application, essay, references, transcript, proof of enrollment. *Deadline:* February 1.

Contact: Cheryl Williams, National Second Vice President
Zeta Phi Beta Sorority, Inc. National Educational Foundation
1734 New Hampshire Avenue, NW
Washington, DC 20009-2595
Fax: 318-631-4028
E-mail: 2ndanti@zphib1920.org

ELECTRICAL ENGINEERING/ ELECTRONICS

AACE INTERNATIONAL   http://www.aacei.org

AACE INTERNATIONAL COMPETITIVE SCHOLARSHIP
• *See page 96*

AEA-OREGON COUNCIL   http://aeascholar.ous.edu

AEA- OREGON COUNCIL TECHNOLOGY SCHOLARSHIP PROGRAM
• *See page 88*

AMERICAN COUNCIL OF ENGINEERING COMPANIES OF PENNSYLVANIA (ACEC/PA)   http://www.acecpa.org

ENGINEERING SCHOLARSHIP
• *See page 158*

AMERICAN FOUNDATION FOR THE BLIND   http://www.afb.org/scholarships.asp

PAUL W. RUCKES SCHOLARSHIP
• *See page 190*

AMERICAN INSTITUTE OF AERONAUTICS AND ASTRONAUTICS   http://www.aiaa.org

AIAA UNDERGRADUATE SCHOLARSHIP
• *See page 89*

AMERICAN PUBLIC TRANSPORTATION FOUNDATION   http://www.apta.com

DONALD C. HYDE ESSAY PROGRAM
• *See page 171*

JACK GILSTRAP SCHOLARSHIP
• *See page 171*

LOUIS T. KLAUDER SCHOLARSHIP
• *See page 171*

PARSONS BRINCKERHOFF-JIM LAMMIE SCHOLARSHIP
• *See page 171*

TRANSIT HALL OF FAME SCHOLARSHIP AWARD PROGRAM
• *See page 171*

AMERICAN SOCIETY OF HEATING, REFRIGERATING, AND AIR CONDITIONING ENGINEERS, INC.   http://www.ashrae.org

ALWIN B. NEWTON SCHOLARSHIP FUND

For full-time studies relating to heating, refrigeration, and air conditioning engineering. Must be for an ABET-accredited program. Minimum 3.0 GPA required. Character, leadership ability and potential service to the HVAC and/or refrigeration profession are considered in selection process.

Academic Fields/Career Goals: Electrical Engineering/Electronics; Engineering/Technology; Heating, Air-Conditioning, and Refrigeration Mechanics; Mechanical Engineering; Trade/Technical Specialties.

Award: Scholarship for use in sophomore, junior, or senior years; not renewable. *Number:* 1. *Amount:* $3000.

Eligibility Requirements: Applicant must be enrolled or expecting to enroll full-time at a four-year institution or university and must have an interest in leadership. Applicant must have 3.0 GPA or higher. Available to U.S. citizens.

Application Requirements: Application, financial need analysis, references, transcript. *Deadline:* February 1.

Contact: Lois Benedict, Scholarship Administrator
    American Society of Heating, Refrigerating, and Air Conditioning Engineers, Inc.
    1791 Tullie Circle, NE
    Atlanta, GA 30329
    Phone: 404-636-8400
    Fax: 404-321-5478
    E-mail: benedict@ashrae.org

REUBEN TRANE SCHOLARSHIP

Two-year scholarship for full-time study in heating, refrigerating, and air conditioning. Recipient awarded $5000 each year for two years in an ABET-accredited program. Applicant must have two years remaining in undergraduate study. Minimum 3.0 GPA required.

Academic Fields/Career Goals: Electrical Engineering/Electronics; Heating, Air-Conditioning, and Refrigeration Mechanics; Mechanical Engineering; Trade/Technical Specialties.

Award: Scholarship for use in sophomore, junior, or senior years; renewable. *Number:* up to 2. *Amount:* up to $10,000.

Eligibility Requirements: Applicant must be enrolled or expecting to enroll full-time at a four-year institution or university. Applicant must have 3.0 GPA or higher. Available to U.S. citizens.

Application Requirements: Application, financial need analysis, references, transcript. *Deadline:* December 1.

Contact: Lois Benedict, Scholarship Administrator
    American Society of Heating, Refrigerating, and Air Conditioning Engineers, Inc.
    1791 Tullie Circle, NE
    Atlanta, GA 30329
    Phone: 404-636-8400
    Fax: 404-321-5478
    E-mail: benedict@ashrae.org

AMERICAN SOCIETY OF NAVAL ENGINEERS   http://www.navalengineers.org

AMERICAN SOCIETY OF NAVAL ENGINEERS SCHOLARSHIP
• *See page 90*

ARMED FORCES COMMUNICATIONS AND ELECTRONICS ASSOCIATION, EDUCATIONAL FOUNDATION   http://www.afcea.org

AFCEA SCHOLARSHIP FOR WORKING PROFESSIONALS
• *See page 120*

AFCEA SGT. JEANNETTE L. WINTERS, USMC MEMORIAL SCHOLARSHIP
• *See page 191*

AFCEA/LOCKHEED MARTIN ORINCON IT SCHOLARSHIP
• *See page 191*

ARMED FORCES COMMUNICATIONS AND ELECTRONICS ASSOCIATION EDUCATIONAL FOUNDATION DISTANCE-LEARNING SCHOLARSHIP
• *See page 191*

ARMED FORCES COMMUNICATIONS AND ELECTRONICS ASSOCIATION GENERAL EMMETT PAIGE SCHOLARSHIP
• *See page 191*

ARMED FORCES COMMUNICATIONS AND ELECTRONICS ASSOCIATION GENERAL JOHN A. WICKHAM SCHOLARSHIP
• *See page 192*

ARMED FORCES COMMUNICATIONS AND ELECTRONICS ASSOCIATION ROTC SCHOLARSHIP PROGRAM
• *See page 120*

ARRL FOUNDATION, INC.   http://www.arrl.org/arrlf/scholgen.html

CHARLES N. FISHER MEMORIAL SCHOLARSHIP
• *See page 90*

DR. JAMES L. LAWSON MEMORIAL SCHOLARSHIP
• *See page 178*

EARL I. ANDERSON SCHOLARSHIP

Award for students in electronic engineering or related technical field. Students must be amateur radio operators and members of the American Radio Relay League. Preference given to students who reside and attend classes in Illinois, Indiana, Michigan, or Florida.

Academic Fields/Career Goals: Electrical Engineering/Electronics.

Award: Scholarship for use in freshman, sophomore, junior, or senior years; not renewable. *Number: 3. Amount:* $1250.

Eligibility Requirements: Applicant must be enrolled or expecting to enroll full-time at an institution or university and must have an interest in amateur radio. Applicant or parent of applicant must be member of American Radio Relay League. Available to U.S. citizens.

Application Requirements: Application, transcript. *Deadline:* February 1.

Contact: Mary Hobart, Secretary Foundation
ARRL Foundation, Inc.
225 Main Street
Newington, CT 06111-1494
Phone: 860-594-0397
E-mail: k1mmh@arrl.org

EDMOND A. METZGER SCHOLARSHIP

Scholarship for undergraduate or graduate students who are licensed amateur radio operators, novice minimum. Applicants must be electrical engineering students and members of the Amateur Radio Relay League. Must reside in Illinois, Indiana, or Wisconsin and attend a school in those states.

Academic Fields/Career Goals: Electrical Engineering/Electronics.

Award: Scholarship for use in freshman, sophomore, junior, senior, or graduate years; not renewable. *Number: 1. Amount:* $500.

Eligibility Requirements: Applicant must be enrolled or expecting to enroll full-time at an institution or university; studying in Illinois, Indiana, or Wisconsin and must have an interest in amateur radio. Applicant or parent of applicant must be member of American Radio Relay League. Available to U.S. and Canadian citizens.

Application Requirements: Application, transcript. *Deadline:* February 1.

Contact: Mary Hobbart, Secretary Foundation
ARRL Foundation, Inc.
225 Main Street
Newington, CT 06111-1494
Phone: 860-594-0397
E-mail: k1mmh@arrl.org

FRED R. MCDANIEL MEMORIAL SCHOLARSHIP
• *See page 178*

IRVING W. COOK, WA0CGS, SCHOLARSHIP
• *See page 90*

L. PHIL WICKER SCHOLARSHIP
• *See page 179*

MISSISSIPPI SCHOLARSHIP
• *See page 90*

PAUL AND HELEN L. GRAUER SCHOLARSHIP
• *See page 91*

PERRY F. HADLOCK MEMORIAL SCHOLARSHIP

For students licensed as technicians pursuing an electrical or electronics engineering degree. Preference given to students attending Clarkson University, Potsdam, New York or open to all Atlantic and Hudson Divisions. Pursue a bachelor's or higher degree. Preference to electrical and electronics engineering majors. Deadline is February 1.

Academic Fields/Career Goals: Electrical Engineering/Electronics.

Award: Scholarship for use in freshman, sophomore, junior, senior, or graduate years; not renewable. *Number: 1. Amount:* $2000.

Eligibility Requirements: Applicant must be enrolled or expecting to enroll full-time at a four-year institution or university and must have an interest in amateur radio. Available to U.S. citizens.

Application Requirements: Application, transcript. *Deadline:* February 1.

Contact: Mary Hobart, Secretary Foundation
ARRL Foundation, Inc.
225 Main Street
Newington, CT 06111-1494
Phone: 860-594-0397
E-mail: k1mmh@arrl.org

PHD ARA SCHOLARSHIP
• *See page 179*

ASSOCIATED BUILDERS AND CONTRACTORS SCHOLARSHIP PROGRAM   http://www.abc.org

TRIMMER EDUCATION FOUNDATION SCHOLARSHIPS FOR CONSTRUCTION MANAGEMENT
• *See page 172*

ASSOCIATION FOR FACILITIES ENGINEERING (AFE)

ASSOCIATION FOR FACILITIES ENGINEERING CEDAR VALLEY CHAPTER # 132 SCHOLARSHIP
• *See page 120*

ASSOCIATION FOR IRON AND STEEL TECHNOLOGY   http://www.aist.org

ASSOCIATION FOR IRON AND STEEL TECHNOLOGY DAVID H. SAMSON SCHOLARSHIP
• *See page 162*

ASSOCIATION FOR IRON AND STEEL TECHNOLOGY OHIO VALLEY CHAPTER SCHOLARSHIP
• *See page 135*

ASTRONAUT SCHOLARSHIP FOUNDATION   http://www.astronautscholarship.org

ASTRONAUT SCHOLARSHIP FOUNDATION
• *See page 92*

AUTOMOTIVE HALL OF FAME   http://www.automotivehalloffame.org

AUTOMOTIVE HALL OF FAME EDUCATIONAL FUNDS
• *See page 162*

CATCHING THE DREAM

TRIBAL BUSINESS MANAGEMENT PROGRAM (TBM)
• *See page 55*

CENTRAL INTELLIGENCE AGENCY   http://www.cia.gov

CENTRAL INTELLIGENCE AGENCY UNDERGRADUATE SCHOLARSHIP PROGRAM
• *See page 56*

CUBAN AMERICAN NATIONAL FOUNDATION   http://www.canf.org

MAS FAMILY SCHOLARSHIPS
• *See page 146*

EAST LOS ANGELES COMMUNITY UNION (TELACU) EDUCATION FOUNDATION   http://www.telacu.com

LINC TELACU ENGINEERING AWARD
• *See page 163*

ELECTROCHEMICAL SOCIETY, INC.
http://www.electrochem.org

DANIEL CUBICCIOTTI STUDENT AWARD OF THE SAN FRANCISCO SECTION OF THE ELECTROCHEMICAL SOCIETY, SPONSORED BY STRUCTURAL INTEGRITY ASSOCIATES
• See page 137

H.H. DOW MEMORIAL STUDENT ACHIEVEMENT AWARD OF THE INDUSTRIAL ELECTROLYSIS AND ELECTROCHEMICAL ENGINEERING DIVISION OF THE ELECTROCHEMICAL SOCIETY, INC.
• See page 137

STUDENT ACHIEVEMENT AWARDS OF THE INDUSTRIAL ELECTROLYSIS AND ELECTROCHEMICAL ENGINEERING DIVISION OF THE ELECTROCHEMICAL SOCIETY, INC.
• See page 137

STUDENT RESEARCH AWARDS OF THE BATTERY DIVISION OF THE ELECTROCHEMICAL SOCIETY, INC.
• See page 137

FLORIDA EDUCATIONAL FACILITIES PLANNERS' ASSOCIATION
http://www.fefpa.org

FEFPA ASSISTANTSHIP
• See page 99

GEORGE BIRD GRINNELL AMERICAN INDIAN FUND
http://www.grinnellfund.org/

AL QOYAWAYMA AWARD
• See page 163

HAWAIIAN LODGE, F.& A. M.
http://www.hawaiianlodge.org/

HAWAIIAN LODGE SCHOLARSHIPS
• See page 99

HISPANIC COLLEGE FUND, INC.
http://www.hispanicfund.org

DENNY'S/HISPANIC COLLEGE FUND SCHOLARSHIP
• See page 62

DEPARTMENT OF ENERGY SCHOLARSHIP PROGRAM
• See page 148

LOCKHEED MARTIN SCHOLARSHIP PROGRAM
• See page 164

NATIONAL HISPANIC EXPLORERS SCHOLARSHIP PROGRAM
• See page 93

HISPANIC ENGINEER NATIONAL ACHIEVEMENT AWARDS CORPORATION (HENAAC)
http://www.henaac.org

HISPANIC ENGINEER NATIONAL ACHIEVEMENT AWARDS CORPORATION SCHOLARSHIP PROGRAM
• See page 122

HISPANIC SCHOLARSHIP FUND
http://www.hsf.net

HSF/GENERAL MOTORS SCHOLARSHIP
• See page 149

HSF/SOCIETY OF HISPANIC PROFESSIONAL ENGINEERS, INC. SCHOLARSHIP PROGRAM
• See page 174

ILLUMINATING ENGINEERING SOCIETY OF NORTH AMERICA–GOLDEN GATE SECTION
http://www.iesgg.org

ALAN LUCAS MEMORIAL EDUCATIONAL SCHOLARSHIP
• See page 100

ROBERT W. THUNEN MEMORIAL SCHOLARSHIPS
• See page 100

INDEPENDENT LABORATORIES INSTITUTE SCHOLARSHIP ALLIANCE
http://www.acil.org

INDEPENDENT LABORATORIES INSTITUTE SCHOLARSHIP ALLIANCE
• See page 93

INSTITUTION OF ELECTRICAL ENGINEERS
http://www.iee.org

BP/IEE FARADAY LECTURE SCHOLARSHIP

Award to assist outstanding students, embarking on an IEE-accredited Meng degree course, to obtain professional qualifications in electrical, electronic, IT, manufacturing or related engineering, in the U.K. or Ireland.

Academic Fields/Career Goals: Electrical Engineering/Electronics.

Award: Scholarship for use in freshman year; renewable. *Number:* 1. *Amount:* $3495–$5240.

Eligibility Requirements: Applicant must be high school student and planning to enroll or expecting to enroll full-time at an institution or university. Available to U.S. and non-U.S. citizens.

Application Requirements: Application, interview, photo, references, test scores. *Deadline:* June 30.

Contact: Scholarships and Prizes
Institution of Electrical Engineers
Michael Faraday House
Six Hills Way, Stevenage
Hertfordshire SG1 2AY
United Kingdom
Phone: 44 0 1438 765 694
Fax: 44 0 1438 765 660
E-mail: scholarships@iee.org.uk

IEE JUBILEE SCHOLARSHIP

Award to assist outstanding students, embarking on an IEE-accredited MEng degree course, to obtain professional qualifications in electrical, electronic, IT, manufacturing or related engineering, in the UK or Ireland.

Academic Fields/Career Goals: Electrical Engineering/Electronics.

Award: Scholarship for use in freshman year; renewable. *Number:* 12. *Amount:* $1750.

Eligibility Requirements: Applicant must be high school student and planning to enroll or expecting to enroll full-time at an institution or university. Available to U.S. and non-U.S. citizens.

Application Requirements: Application, interview, photo, references, test scores. *Deadline:* June 30.

Contact: Scholarships and Prizes
Institution of Electrical Engineers
Michael Faraday House
Six Hills Way, Stevenage
Hertfordshire SG1 2AY
United Kingdom
Phone: 44 0 1438 765 694
Fax: 44 0 1438 765 660
E-mail: scholarships@iee.org.uk

INSTRUMENTATION, SYSTEMS, AND AUTOMATION SOCIETY (ISA)
http://www.isa.org

INSTRUMENTATION, SYSTEMS, AND AUTOMATION SOCIETY (ISA) SCHOLARSHIP PROGRAM
• See page 123

INTERNATIONAL COMMUNICATIONS INDUSTRIES FOUNDATION
http://www.infocomm.org/foundation

ICIF SCHOLARSHIP FOR DEPENDENTS OF MEMBER ORGANIZATIONS
• See page 181

INTERNATIONAL COMMUNICATIONS INDUSTRIES FOUNDATION AV SCHOLARSHIP
• See page 182

INTERNATIONAL SOCIETY FOR OPTICAL ENGINEERING-SPIE   http://www.spie.org/info/scholarships

SPIE EDUCATIONAL SCHOLARSHIPS IN OPTICAL SCIENCE AND ENGINEERING
• See page 93

JORGE MAS CANOSA FREEDOM FOUNDATION   http://www.canf.org

MAS FAMILY SCHOLARSHIP AWARD
• See page 149

KOREAN-AMERICAN SCIENTISTS AND ENGINEERS ASSOCIATION   http://www.ksea.org

KSEA SCHOLARSHIPS

Award for undergraduate or graduate Korean-American students majoring in science, engineering or related fields. Must be a member of KSEA. Two scholarships are reserved for women. Application deadline is February 15. See Web site at http://www.ksea.org for further details.

Academic Fields/Career Goals: Electrical Engineering/Electronics; Engineering/Technology; Engineering-Related Technologies; Science, Technology, and Society.

Award: Scholarship for use in freshman, sophomore, junior, senior, or graduate years; not renewable. *Number:* varies. *Amount:* $1000.

Eligibility Requirements: Applicant must be of Korean heritage and enrolled or expecting to enroll full-time at a two-year or four-year institution or university. Applicant or parent of applicant must be member of Korean-American Scientists and Engineers Association. Available to U.S. citizens.

Application Requirements: Application, essay, resume, references, transcript. *Deadline:* February 15.

Contact: KSEA Scholarships
Korean-American Scientists and Engineers Association
1952 Gallows Road, Suite 300
Vienna, VA 22182
Phone: 703-748-1221
Fax: 703-748-1331
E-mail: sejong@ksea.org

LOS ANGELES COUNCIL OF BLACK PROFESSIONAL ENGINEERS   http://www.lablackengineers.org

AL-BEN SCHOLARSHIP FOR ACADEMIC INCENTIVE
• See page 164

AL-BEN SCHOLARSHIP FOR PROFESSIONAL MERIT
• See page 165

AL-BEN SCHOLARSHIP FOR SCHOLASTIC ACHIEVEMENT
• See page 165

MICHIGAN SOCIETY OF PROFESSIONAL ENGINEERS   http://www.michiganspe.org

MICHIGAN SOCIETY OF PROFESSIONAL ENGINEERS UNDESIGNATED GRANT
• See page 165

MICRON TECHNOLOGY FOUNDATION, INC.   http://www.micron.com

MICRON SCIENCE AND TECHNOLOGY SCHOLARS PROGRAM
• See page 165

NASA DELAWARE SPACE GRANT CONSORTIUM   http://www.delspace.org

NASA DELAWARE SPACE GRANT UNDERGRADUATE TUITION SCHOLARSHIP
• See page 94

NASA IDAHO SPACE GRANT CONSORTIUM   http://isgc.uidaho.edu

NASA IDAHO SPACE GRANT CONSORTIUM SCHOLARSHIP PROGRAM
• See page 94

NASA MONTANA SPACE GRANT CONSORTIUM   http://www.spacegrant.montana.edu

MONTANA SPACE GRANT SCHOLARSHIP PROGRAM
• See page 125

NASA NEBRASKA SPACE GRANT CONSORTIUM   http://nasa.unomaha.edu

NASA NEBRASKA SPACE GRANT
• See page 125

NASA NEVADA SPACE GRANT CONSORTIUM   http://www.unr.edu/spacegrant

UNIVERSITY AND COMMUNITY COLLEGE SYSTEM OF NEVADA NASA SPACE GRANT AND FELLOWSHIP PROGRAM
• See page 125

NATIONAL ASSOCIATION OF WOMEN IN CONSTRUCTION   http://nawic.org

NAWIC UNDERGRADUATE SCHOLARSHIPS
• See page 100

NATIONAL SECURITY AGENCY   http://www.nsa.gov

NATIONAL SECURITY AGENCY STOKES EDUCATIONAL SCHOLARSHIP PROGRAM
• See page 194

NATIONAL SOCIETY OF PROFESSIONAL ENGINEERS   http://www.nspe.org

MAUREEN L. AND HOWARD N. BLITMAN, PE SCHOLARSHIP TO PROMOTE DIVERSITY IN ENGINEERING
• See page 166

NATIONAL SOCIETY OF PROFESSIONAL ENGINEERS/AUXILIARY SCHOLARSHIP
• See page 166

PAUL H. ROBBINS HONORARY SCHOLARSHIP
• See page 166

PROFESSIONAL ENGINEERS IN INDUSTRY SCHOLARSHIP
• See page 167

VIRGINIA HENRY MEMORIAL SCHOLARSHIP
• See page 167

OREGON STUDENT ASSISTANCE COMMISSION   http://www.osac.state.or.us

AMERICAN COUNCIL OF ENGINEERING COMPANIES OF OREGON SCHOLARSHIP
• See page 167

KEY TECHNOLOGY SCHOLARSHIP
• See page 84

MENTOR GRAPHICS SCHOLARSHIP
• See page 194

PROFESSIONAL CONSTRUCTION ESTIMATORS ASSOCIATION   http://www.pcea.org

TED WILSON MEMORIAL SCHOLARSHIP FOUNDATION
• See page 212

ROBERT H. MOLLOHAN FAMILY CHARITABLE FOUNDATION, INC. http://www.mollohanfoundation.org

HIGH TECHNOLOGY SCHOLARS PROGRAM
• See page 141

ROCKY MOUNTAIN COAL MINING INSTITUTE http://www.rmcmi.org

ROCKY MOUNTAIN COAL MINING INSTITUTE SCHOLARSHIP
• See page 167

SOCIETY OF AUTOMOTIVE ENGINEERS http://www.sae.org

BMW/SAE ENGINEERING SCHOLARSHIP
• See page 129

EDWARD D. HENDRICKSON/SAE ENGINEERING SCHOLARSHIP
• See page 129

TMC/SAE DONALD D. DAWSON TECHNICAL SCHOLARSHIP
• See page 129

SOCIETY OF HISPANIC PROFESSIONAL ENGINEERS FOUNDATION http://www.henaac.org

SOCIETY OF HISPANIC PROFESSIONAL ENGINEERS FOUNDATION
• See page 168

SOCIETY OF MANUFACTURING ENGINEERS EDUCATION FOUNDATION http://www.sme.org

WILLIAM E. WEISEL SCHOLARSHIP FUND

Must be full-time undergraduate student enrolled in a degree engineering or technology program in the United States or Canada and must be seeking a career in robotics or automated systems used in manufacturing. Candidates will also be considered which are seeking a career in robotics for use in the medical field. Must have completed a minimum of 30 college credit hours. Minimum GPA of 3.5 is required.

Academic Fields/Career Goals: Electrical Engineering/Electronics; Engineering/Technology; Mechanical Engineering; Trade/Technical Specialties.

Award: Scholarship for use in freshman, sophomore, junior, or senior years; not renewable. *Number:* 1. *Amount:* $1000.

Eligibility Requirements: Applicant must be enrolled or expecting to enroll full-time at a four-year institution or university. Applicant must have 3.5 GPA or higher. Available to U.S. and Canadian citizens.

Application Requirements: Essay, resume, references, transcript. *Deadline:* February 1.

Contact: Cindy Monzon, Program Coordinator
Society of Manufacturing Engineers Education Foundation
1 SME Drive
PO Box 930
Dearborn, MI 48121-0930
Phone: 313-271-1500 Ext. 1707
Fax: 313-240-6095
E-mail: monzcyn@sme.org

SOCIETY OF MEXICAN AMERICAN ENGINEERS AND SCIENTISTS http://www.maes-natl.org

GRE AND GRADUATE APPLICATIONS WAIVER
• See page 95

SOCIETY OF PLASTICS ENGINEERS (SPE) FOUNDATION http://www.4spe.com

SOCIETY OF PLASTICS ENGINEERS SCHOLARSHIP PROGRAM
• See page 168

SOCIETY OF WOMEN ENGINEERS http://www.swe.org

AGILENT MENTORING SCHOLARSHIP
• See page 194

BECHTEL CORPORATION SCHOLARSHIP
• See page 176

BERTHA LAMME MEMORIAL SCHOLARSHIP

One $1200 scholarship for entering freshman pursuing electrical engineering degree.

Academic Fields/Career Goals: Electrical Engineering/Electronics.

Award: Scholarship for use in freshman year; not renewable. *Number:* 1. *Amount:* $1200.

Eligibility Requirements: Applicant must be enrolled or expecting to enroll full-time at a four-year institution or university and female. Applicant must have 3.5 GPA or higher. Available to U.S. citizens.

Application Requirements: Application. *Deadline:* May 15.

Contact: Suman Pa, Program Coordinator
Society of Women Engineers
230 E Ohio Street, Suite 400
Chicago, IL 60611-3265
Phone: 312-596-5223
Fax: 312-644-8557
E-mail: suman.patil@swe.org

DAIMLER CHRYSLER CORPORATION SCHOLARSHIP

Renewable award for entering female sophomore majoring in mechanical or electrical engineering at an accredited school. Applicants must have minimum 3.0 GPA. Must be active contributor to and supporter of Society of Women Engineers. Must be U.S. citizen. Deadline: February 1.

Academic Fields/Career Goals: Electrical Engineering/Electronics; Mechanical Engineering.

Award: Scholarship for use in sophomore year; renewable. *Number:* 1. *Amount:* $2000.

Eligibility Requirements: Applicant must be enrolled or expecting to enroll at a four-year institution or university and female. Applicant or parent of applicant must be member of Society of Women Engineers. Applicant must have 3.0 GPA or higher. Available to U.S. citizens.

Application Requirements: Application, essay, references, self-addressed stamped envelope, test scores, transcript. *Deadline:* February 1.

Contact: Suman Pa, Program Coordinator
Society of Women Engineers
230 E Ohio Street, Suite 400
Chicago, IL 60611-3265
Phone: 312-596-5223
Fax: 312-644-8557
E-mail: suman.patil@swe.org

DELL COMPUTER CORPORATION SCHOLARSHIPS
• See page 194

GENERAL MOTORS FOUNDATION UNDERGRADUATE SCHOLARSHIPS
• See page 168

GUIDANT CORPORATION SCHOLARSHIP
• See page 195

LOCKHEED AERONAUTICS COMPANY SCHOLARSHIPS

Two $1000 scholarships for entering female juniors majoring in electrical or mechanical engineering. One scholarship for each major. Minimum 3.5 GPA required. Application deadline is February 1.

Academic Fields/Career Goals: Electrical Engineering/Electronics; Mechanical Engineering.

Award: Scholarship for use in junior year; not renewable. *Number:* 2. *Amount:* $1000.

Eligibility Requirements: Applicant must be enrolled or expecting to enroll full-time at a four-year institution or university and female. Applicant must have 3.5 GPA or higher. Available to U.S. and non-U.S. citizens.

Application Requirements: Application, essay, references, self-addressed stamped envelope, test scores, transcript. *Deadline:* February 1.

Contact: Suman Pa, Program Coordinator
Society of Women Engineers
230 E Ohio Street, Suite 400
Chicago, IL 60611-3265
Phone: 312-596-5223
Fax: 312-644-8557
E-mail: suman.patil@swe.org

NORTHROP GRUMMAN CORPORATION SCHOLARSHIPS
• *See page 130*

SOUTH DAKOTA RETAILERS ASSOCIATION   http://www.sdra.org

SOUTH DAKOTA RETAILERS ASSOCIATION SCHOLARSHIP PROGRAM
• *See page 69*

TEXAS ENGINEERING FOUNDATION   http://www.tspe.org/

TEXAS SOCIETY OF PROFESSIONAL ENGINEERS (TSPE) REGIONAL SCHOLARSHIPS
• *See page 169*

TURNER CONSTRUCTION COMPANY   http://www.turnerconstruction.com

YOUTHFORCE 2020 SCHOLARSHIP PROGRAM
• *See page 103*

UNITED NEGRO COLLEGE FUND   http://www.uncf.org

CDM SCHOLARSHIP/INTERNSHIP
• *See page 177*

CISCO/UNCF SCHOLARS PROGRAM
• *See page 197*

DELL/UNCF CORPORATE SCHOLARS PROGRAM
• *See page 155*

ROCKWELL/UNCF CORPORATE SCHOLARS PROGRAM
• *See page 156*

SBC FOUNDATION SCHOLARSHIP
• *See page 156*

SPRINT SCHOLARSHIP/INTERNSHIP
• *See page 71*

WEYERHAEUSER/UNCF CORPORATE SCHOLARS
• *See page 157*

UNIVERSITIES SPACE RESEARCH ASSOCIATION   http://www.usra.edu

UNIVERSITIES SPACE RESEARCH ASSOCIATION SCHOLARSHIP PROGRAM
• *See page 96*

UTAH SOCIETY OF PROFESSIONAL ENGINEERS   http://www.uspeonline.com

UTAH SOCIETY OF PROFESSIONAL ENGINEERS SCHOLARSHIP
• *See page 169*

VERTICAL FLIGHT FOUNDATION   http://www.vtol.org

VERTICAL FLIGHT FOUNDATION SCHOLARSHIP
• *See page 132*

WOMEN IN AVIATION, INTERNATIONAL   http://www.wai.org

DELTA AIR LINES ENGINEERING SCHOLARSHIP
• *See page 132*

XEROX   http://www.xerox.com

TECHNICAL MINORITY SCHOLARSHIP
• *See page 169*

ENERGY AND POWER ENGINEERING

AMERICAN SOCIETY OF NAVAL ENGINEERS   http://www.navalengineers.org

AMERICAN SOCIETY OF NAVAL ENGINEERS SCHOLARSHIP
• *See page 90*

ASSOCIATION FOR IRON AND STEEL TECHNOLOGY   http://www.aist.org

ASSOCIATION FOR IRON AND STEEL TECHNOLOGY DAVID H. SAMSON SCHOLARSHIP
• *See page 162*

ELECTROCHEMICAL SOCIETY, INC.   http://www.electrochem.org

DANIEL CUBICCIOTTI STUDENT AWARD OF THE SAN FRANCISCO SECTION OF THE ELECTROCHEMICAL SOCIETY, SPONSORED BY STRUCTURAL INTEGRITY ASSOCIATES
• *See page 137*

H.H. DOW MEMORIAL STUDENT ACHIEVEMENT AWARD OF THE INDUSTRIAL ELECTROLYSIS AND ELECTROCHEMICAL ENGINEERING DIVISION OF THE ELECTROCHEMICAL SOCIETY, INC.
• *See page 137*

STUDENT ACHIEVEMENT AWARDS OF THE INDUSTRIAL ELECTROLYSIS AND ELECTROCHEMICAL ENGINEERING DIVISION OF THE ELECTROCHEMICAL SOCIETY, INC.
• *See page 137*

STUDENT RESEARCH AWARDS OF THE BATTERY DIVISION OF THE ELECTROCHEMICAL SOCIETY, INC.
• *See page 137*

HANDS-ON! PROJECTS/HYDRO POWER CONTEST   http://users.rcn.com/hands-on/hydro/contest.html

HYDRO POWER CONTEST

Scholarship awards are presented to winners in two categories of an engineering competition. Winners must design, build, and submit for testing a device that converts the potential energy contained in water into mechanical power. Contestants may compete in either power or efficiency categories, or both. Application fee is $20. Deadline is June 1.

Academic Fields/Career Goals: Energy and Power Engineering; Hydrology.

Award: Scholarship for use in freshman, sophomore, junior, senior, or graduate years; not renewable. *Number:* 6–10. *Amount:* $500–$2500.

Eligibility Requirements: Applicant must be enrolled or expecting to enroll full-time at a two-year or four-year or technical institution or university. Available to U.S. and non-U.S. citizens.

Application Requirements: Application, applicant must enter a contest, transcript. *Fee:* $20. *Deadline:* June 1.

Contact: Michael Coates, Administrator
Hands-on! Projects/Hydro Power Contest
9 Mayflower Road
Northborough, MA 01532
Phone: 508-351-6023
Fax: 508-351-6023
E-mail: hands-on@rcn.com

HAWAIIAN LODGE, F.& A. M.   http://www.hawaiianlodge.org/

HAWAIIAN LODGE SCHOLARSHIPS
• *See page 99*

HISPANIC COLLEGE FUND, INC.   http://www.hispanicfund.org

DEPARTMENT OF ENERGY SCHOLARSHIP PROGRAM
• *See page 148*

Hispanic College Fund, Inc. (continued)

LOCKHEED MARTIN SCHOLARSHIP PROGRAM
• *See page 164*

NASA WEST VIRGINIA SPACE GRANT CONSORTIUM
http://www.nasa.wvu.edu

WEST VIRGINIA SPACE GRANT CONSORTIUM UNDERGRADUATE SCHOLARSHIP PROGRAM
• *See page 126*

ROBERT H. MOLLOHAN FAMILY CHARITABLE FOUNDATION, INC.
http://www.mollohanfoundation.org

HIGH TECHNOLOGY SCHOLARS PROGRAM
• *See page 141*

UNITED NEGRO COLLEGE FUND
http://www.uncf.org

CON EDISON SCHOLARSHIP
• *See page 70*

NORTHEAST UTILITIES SYSTEM SCHOLARSHIP PROGRAM
• *See page 156*

UTAH SOCIETY OF PROFESSIONAL ENGINEERS
http://www.uspeonline.com

UTAH SOCIETY OF PROFESSIONAL ENGINEERS SCHOLARSHIP
• *See page 169*

ENGINEERING/TECHNOLOGY

AACE INTERNATIONAL
http://www.aacei.org

AACE INTERNATIONAL COMPETITIVE SCHOLARSHIP
• *See page 96*

ACI INTERNATIONAL/CONCRETE RESEARCH AND EDUCATION FOUNDATION (CONREF)
http://www.concrete.org

KUMAR MEHTA SCHOLARSHIP
• *See page 97*

PETER D. COURTOIS CONCRETE CONSTRUCTION SCHOLARSHIP
• *See page 97*

V. MOHAN MALHOTRA SCHOLARSHIP
• *See page 97*

W.R. GRACE SCHOLARSHIP AWARD
• *See page 97*

AEA-OREGON COUNCIL
http://aeascholar.ous.edu

AEA- OREGON COUNCIL TECHNOLOGY SCHOLARSHIP PROGRAM
• *See page 88*

AIR TRAFFIC CONTROL ASSOCIATION, INC.
http://www.atca.org

AIR TRAFFIC CONTROL ASSOCIATION SCHOLARSHIP
• *See page 116*

AMERICAN CHEMICAL SOCIETY, RUBBER DIVISION
http://www.rubber.org

AMERICAN CHEMICAL SOCIETY, RUBBER DIVISION UNDERGRADUATE SCHOLARSHIP
• *See page 158*

AMERICAN COUNCIL OF ENGINEERING COMPANIES OF PENNSYLVANIA (ACEC/PA)
http://www.acecpa.org

ENGINEERING SCHOLARSHIP
• *See page 158*

AMERICAN ELECTROPLATERS AND SURFACE FINISHERS SOCIETY
http://www.aesf.org

AMERICAN ELECTROPLATERS AND SURFACE FINISHERS SCHOLARSHIPS
• *See page 158*

AMERICAN FOUNDATION FOR THE BLIND
http://www.afb.org/scholarships.asp

PAUL W. RUCKES SCHOLARSHIP
• *See page 190*

PAUL W. RUCKES SCHOLARSHIP
• *See page 190*

AMERICAN INSTITUTE OF AERONAUTICS AND ASTRONAUTICS
http://www.aiaa.org

AIAA UNDERGRADUATE SCHOLARSHIP
• *See page 89*

AMERICAN INSTITUTE OF ARCHITECTS, NEW YORK CHAPTER
http://www.aiany.org

THE DOUGLAS HASKELL AWARD FOR STUDENT JOURNALISM
• *See page 98*

AMERICAN METEOROLOGICAL SOCIETY
http://www.ametsoc.org/AMS

AMERICAN METEOROLOGICAL SOCIETY INDUSTRY UNDERGRADUATE SCHOLARSHIPS
• *See page 89*

AMERICAN NUCLEAR SOCIETY
http://www.ans.org

AMERICAN NUCLEAR SOCIETY JAMES R. VOGT SCHOLARSHIP

One-time award for juniors, seniors, and first-year graduate students enrolled or proposing research in radio-analytical or analytical application of nuclear science. Check "Vogt" box for this one-time award. Must be U.S. citizen or permanent resident. Application available at Web site: http://www.ans.org.

Academic Fields/Career Goals: Engineering/Technology; Nuclear Science.

Award: Scholarship for use in freshman, sophomore, junior, senior, or graduate years; not renewable. *Number:* 1. *Amount:* $2000–$3000.

Eligibility Requirements: Applicant must be enrolled or expecting to enroll full-time at a four-year institution or university. Available to U.S. citizens.

Application Requirements: Application, references, transcript. *Deadline:* February 1.

Contact: Scholarship Coordinator
American Nuclear Society
555 North Kensington Avenue
La Grange Park, IL 60526
Phone: 708-352-6611
Fax: 708-352-0499
E-mail: outreach@ans.org

AMERICAN NUCLEAR SOCIETY OPERATIONS AND POWER SCHOLARSHIP

Must be at least an entering junior enrolled in a program leading to a degree in nuclear science, nuclear engineering, or a nuclear-related field. One-time award for a U.S. citizen or permanent resident. Application available at Web site: http://www.ans.org.

Academic Fields/Career Goals: Engineering/Technology; Nuclear Science.

Award: Scholarship for use in freshman, sophomore, junior, or senior years; not renewable. *Number:* 1–21. *Amount:* $2500.

Eligibility Requirements: Applicant must be enrolled or expecting to enroll at a four-year institution or university. Available to U.S. citizens.

Application Requirements: Application, references, transcript. *Deadline:* February 1.

Contact: Scholarship Coordinator
American Nuclear Society
555 North Kensington Avenue
La Grange Park, IL 60526
Phone: 708-352-6611
Fax: 708-352-0499
E-mail: outreach@ans.org

AMERICAN NUCLEAR SOCIETY UNDERGRADUATE SCHOLARSHIPS

One-time award for students who have completed at least one year of a four-year nuclear science or nuclear engineering or nuclear-related program. Must be sponsored by ANS member or branch. Must be U.S. citizen or permanent resident. Application available at Web site: http://www.ans.org.

Academic Fields/Career Goals: Engineering/Technology; Nuclear Science.

Award: Scholarship for use in freshman, sophomore, junior, or senior years; not renewable. *Number:* 1–21. *Amount:* $2000.

Eligibility Requirements: Applicant must be enrolled or expecting to enroll full-time at a four-year institution or university. Available to U.S. citizens.

Application Requirements: Application, references, transcript. *Deadline:* February 1.

Contact: Scholarship Coordinator
American Nuclear Society
555 North Kensington Avenue
La Grange Park, IL 60526
Phone: 708-352-6611
Fax: 708-352-0499
E-mail: outreach@ans.org

CHARLES (TOMMY) THOMAS MEMORIAL SCHOLARSHIP DIVISION SCHOLARSHIP

Must be at least an entering junior enrolled in a course of study relating to a degree in nuclear science, nuclear engineering, or a nuclear-related field. One-time award for U.S. citizen or permanent resident. Must be enrolled in a U.S. institution. Student must be pursuing a degree in a discipline related to the environmental sciences. Application available at Web site: http://www.ans.org.

Academic Fields/Career Goals: Engineering/Technology; Nuclear Science.

Award: Scholarship for use in freshman, sophomore, junior, or senior years; not renewable. *Number:* 1–21. *Amount:* $2000.

Eligibility Requirements: Applicant must be enrolled or expecting to enroll full-time at a four-year institution or university. Available to U.S. citizens.

Application Requirements: Application, references, transcript. *Deadline:* February 1.

Contact: Scholarship Coordinator
American Nuclear Society
555 North Kensington Avenue
La Grange Park, IL 60526
Phone: 708-352-6611
Fax: 708-352-0499
E-mail: outreach@ans.org

DECOMMISSIONING, DECONTAMINATION, AND REUTILIZATION SCHOLARSHIP

For undergraduate student associated with decommissioning/decontamination of nuclear facilities, management/characterization of nuclear waste, or environmental restoration. Application available at Web site. Must be a U.S. citizen enrolled in a U.S. school. Student will join the American Nuclear Society. Applicants are required to submit a brief essay discussing the importance of some aspect of decommissioning, decontamination, and reutilization to the future of the nuclear field.

Academic Fields/Career Goals: Engineering/Technology; Nuclear Science.

Award: Scholarship for use in freshman, sophomore, junior, or senior years; not renewable. *Number:* 1–21. *Amount:* $2000.

Eligibility Requirements: Applicant must be enrolled or expecting to enroll full-time at a four-year institution or university and must have an interest in designated field specified by sponsor. Available to U.S. citizens.

Application Requirements: Application, essay, references, transcript. *Deadline:* February 1.

Contact: Scholarship Coordinator
American Nuclear Society
555 North Kensington Avenue
La Grange Park, IL 60526
Phone: 708-352-6611
Fax: 708-352-0499
E-mail: outreach@ans.org

DELAYED EDUCATION FOR WOMEN SCHOLARSHIPS

One-time award is to enable mature women whose formal studies in nuclear science, nuclear engineering, or related fields have been delayed or interrupted at least one year. Must be U.S. citizen or permanent resident in a four-year program. Application available at Web site: http://www.ans.org.

Academic Fields/Career Goals: Engineering/Technology; Nuclear Science.

Award: Scholarship for use in freshman, sophomore, junior, or senior years; not renewable. *Number:* 1. *Amount:* $3500.

Eligibility Requirements: Applicant must be enrolled or expecting to enroll full-time at a four-year institution or university and female. Applicant must have 2.5 GPA or higher. Available to U.S. citizens.

Application Requirements: Application, financial need analysis, references, transcript. *Deadline:* February 1.

Contact: Scholarship Coordinator
American Nuclear Society
555 North Kensington Avenue
La Grange Park, IL 60526
Phone: 708-352-6611
Fax: 708-352-0499
E-mail: outreach@ans.org

JOHN AND MURIEL LANDIS SCHOLARSHIP AWARDS

One-time award for undergraduate and graduate study in nuclear engineering or nuclear-related field. Must have greater than average financial need or be educationally disadvantaged and be nominated by ANS member. Must be U.S. citizen or permanent resident. Application available at Web site: http://www.ans.org.

Academic Fields/Career Goals: Engineering/Technology; Nuclear Science.

Award: Scholarship for use in freshman, sophomore, junior, senior, or graduate years; not renewable. *Number:* 1–8. *Amount:* $3500.

Eligibility Requirements: Applicant must be enrolled or expecting to enroll at a four-year institution or university. Available to U.S. and non-U.S. citizens.

Application Requirements: Application, financial need analysis, references, transcript. *Deadline:* February 1.

Contact: Scholarship Coordinator
American Nuclear Society
555 North Kensington Avenue
La Grange Park, IL 60526
Phone: 708-352-6611
Fax: 708-352-0469
E-mail: outreach@ans.org

JOHN R. LAMARSH SCHOLARSHIP

One-time award for a maximum of four scholarships for students who have completed one year in a course of study leading to a degree in nuclear science, nuclear engineering, or a nuclear-related field and who will be sophomores in the upcoming academic year; and a maximum of 21 scholarships for students who have completed two or more years and will be entering as juniors or seniors. Must be sponsored by the ANS and be a U.S. citizen or permanent resident.

Academic Fields/Career Goals: Engineering/Technology; Nuclear Science.

Award: Scholarship for use in freshman, sophomore, junior, or senior years; not renewable. *Number:* 1–21. *Amount:* $2000.

American Nuclear Society (continued)

Eligibility Requirements: Applicant must be enrolled or expecting to enroll at a four-year institution or university. Available to U.S. citizens.

Application Requirements: Application, references, transcript. *Deadline:* February 1.

Contact: Scholarship Coordinator
American Nuclear Society
555 North Kensington Avenue
La Grange Park, IL 60526
Phone: 708-352-6611
Fax: 708-352-0499
E-mail: outreach@ans.org

JOSEPH R. DIETRICH SCHOLARSHIP

One-time award of a maximum of four scholarships for students who have completed one year in a course of study leading to a degree in nuclear science, nuclear engineering, or a nuclear-related field and who will be sophomores in the upcoming academic year; and a maximum of 21 scholarships for students who have completed two or more years and will be entering as juniors or seniors. Must be sponsored by the ANS and be a U.S. citizen or permanent resident.

Academic Fields/Career Goals: Engineering/Technology; Nuclear Science.

Award: Scholarship for use in freshman, sophomore, junior, or senior years; not renewable. *Number:* 1–21. *Amount:* $2000.

Eligibility Requirements: Applicant must be enrolled or expecting to enroll at a four-year institution or university. Available to U.S. citizens.

Application Requirements: Application, references, transcript. *Deadline:* February 1.

Contact: Scholarship Coordinator
American Nuclear Society
555 North Kensington Avenue
La Grange Park, IL 60526
Phone: 708-352-6611
Fax: 708-352-0499
E-mail: outreach@ans.org

ROBERT G. LACY SCHOLARSHIP

Scholarship awards a maximum of four scholarships for students who have completed one year in a course of study leading to a degree in nuclear science, nuclear engineering, or a nuclear-related field and who will be sophomores in the upcoming academic year; and a maximum of 21 scholarships for students who have completed two or more years and will be entering as juniors or seniors.

Academic Fields/Career Goals: Engineering/Technology; Nuclear Science.

Award: Scholarship for use in freshman, sophomore, junior, or senior years. *Number:* 1–21.

Eligibility Requirements: Applicant must be enrolled or expecting to enroll full-time at a four-year institution or university. Available to U.S. citizens.

Application Requirements: Application, references, transcript. *Deadline:* February 1.

Contact: Scholarship Coordinator
American Nuclear Society
555 North Kensington Avenue
La Grange Park, IL 60526
Phone: 708-352-6611
Fax: 708-352-0499
E-mail: outreach@ans.org

ROBERT T. (BOB) LINER SCHOLARSHIP

Scholarship awards a maximum of four scholarships for students who have completed one year in a course of study leading to a degree in nuclear science, nuclear engineering, or a nuclear-related field and who will be sophomores in the upcoming academic year; and a maximum of 21 scholarships for students who have completed two or more years and will be entering as juniors or seniors.

Academic Fields/Career Goals: Engineering/Technology; Nuclear Science.

Award: Scholarship for use in freshman, sophomore, junior, or senior years. *Number:* 1–21.

Eligibility Requirements: Applicant must be enrolled or expecting to enroll full-time at a four-year institution or university. Available to U.S. citizens.

Application Requirements: Application, references, transcript. *Deadline:* February 1.

Contact: Scholarship Coordinator
American Nuclear Society
555 North Kensington Avenue
La Grange Park, IL 60526
Phone: 708-352-6611
Fax: 708-352-0499
E-mail: outreach@ans.org

AMERICAN PUBLIC TRANSPORTATION FOUNDATION
http://www.apta.com

DONALD C. HYDE ESSAY PROGRAM
• See page 171

JACK GILSTRAP SCHOLARSHIP
• See page 171

LOUIS T. KLAUDER SCHOLARSHIP
• See page 171

PARSONS BRINCKERHOFF-JIM LAMMIE SCHOLARSHIP
• See page 171

TRANSIT HALL OF FAME SCHOLARSHIP AWARD PROGRAM
• See page 171

AMERICAN RAILWAY ENGINEERING AND MAINTENANCE OF WAY ASSOCIATION
http://www.arema.org

AREMA MICHAEL R. GARCIA SCHOLARSHIP

Award for students enrolled in a four or five year program leading to a bachelor's degree in engineering or engineering technology. This scholarship is for students who are married and/or are supporting a family while enrolled as a student. Deadline is March 15.

Academic Fields/Career Goals: Engineering/Technology.

Award: Scholarship for use in freshman, sophomore, junior, or senior years; not renewable. *Amount:* $1000.

Eligibility Requirements: Applicant must be enrolled or expecting to enroll full-time at a four-year institution or university. Available to U.S. citizens.

Application Requirements: Application, resume, references, transcript, cover letter. *Deadline:* March 15.

Contact: Stacy Elder, AREMA Educational Foundation Undergraduate Scholar
American Railway Engineering and Maintenance of Way Association
10003 Derekwood Lane
Suite 210
Lanham, MD 20706
Phone: 301-459-3200 Ext. 706
Fax: 301-459-8077
E-mail: selder@arema.org

AREMA UNDERGRADUATE SCHOLARSHIPS

Scholarships are awarded to engineering students who have a potential interest in railway engineering careers. Must have at least a 2.00 GPA. Deadline is March 15.

Academic Fields/Career Goals: Engineering/Technology.

Award: Scholarship for use in freshman, sophomore, junior, or senior years; not renewable. *Amount:* $1000.

Eligibility Requirements: Applicant must be enrolled or expecting to enroll full-time at a four-year institution or university. Available to U.S. citizens.

Application Requirements: Application, resume, references, transcript, cover letter. *Deadline:* March 15.

Contact: AREMA Scholarship Committee
American Railway Engineering and Maintenance of Way Association
10003 Derekwood Lane, Suite 210
Lanham, MD 20706

AMERICAN SOCIETY OF AGRICULTURAL ENGINEERS
http://www.asabe.org

AMERICAN SOCIETY OF AGRICULTURAL AND BIOLOGICAL ENGINEERS STUDENT ENGINEER OF THE YEAR SCHOLARSHIP

Award for engineering undergraduate student in the U.S. or Canada. Must be active student member of the American Society of Agricultural Engineers. Write for more information and special application procedures. One-time award of $1000. Must have completed one year of school, and must submit paper titled "My Goals in the Engineering Profession."

Academic Fields/Career Goals: Engineering/Technology.

Award: Scholarship for use in sophomore, junior, or senior years; not renewable. *Number:* 1. *Amount:* $1000.

Eligibility Requirements: Applicant must be enrolled or expecting to enroll at a two-year or four-year institution or university. Applicant must have 3.0 GPA or higher. Available to U.S. and Canadian citizens.

Application Requirements: Application, essay, references. *Deadline:* March 15.

Contact: Carol Flautt, Scholarship Program
American Society of Agricultural Engineers
2950 Niles Road
St. Joseph, MI 49085
Phone: 269-428-6336
Fax: 269-429-3852
E-mail: flautt@asabe.org

AMERICAN SOCIETY OF CERTIFIED ENGINEERING TECHNICIANS
http://www.ascet.org

AMERICAN SOCIETY OF CERTIFIED ENGINEERING TECHNICIANS SMALL CASH GRANT

Award designed to provide financial assistance to high school seniors who will enter an engineering technology program following high school graduation. Must be U.S. citizen. Must be a student, certified, regular, registered or associate member of ASCET. Application deadline is April 1.

Academic Fields/Career Goals: Engineering/Technology.

Award: Grant for use in freshman year; not renewable. *Number:* up to 4. *Amount:* $100.

Eligibility Requirements: Applicant must be high school student and planning to enroll or expecting to enroll full or part-time at a two-year or four-year or technical institution or university. Available to U.S. citizens.

Application Requirements: Application, references, transcript. *Deadline:* April 1.

Contact: Tim Latham, General Manager
American Society of Certified Engineering Technicians
PO Box 1536
Brandon, MS 39043
Phone: 601-824-8991
E-mail: Tim-Latham@ascet.org

JOSEPH C. JOHNSON MEMORIAL GRANT

The Joseph C. Johnson Memorial Grant is a $750 award given to qualified applicants in order to offset the cost of tuition, books and lab fees. Applicant must be an American citizen or a legal resident of the country in which the applicant is currently living, as well as be either a student, certified, regular, registered or associate member of ASCET. Student must be enrolled in an engineering technology program. For further information, visit http://www.ascet.org

Academic Fields/Career Goals: Engineering/Technology.

Award: Grant for use in freshman, sophomore, junior, or senior years; not renewable. *Number:* 1. *Amount:* $750.

Eligibility Requirements: Applicant must be enrolled or expecting to enroll full or part-time at a two-year or four-year or technical institution or university. Applicant must have 3.0 GPA or higher. Available to U.S. citizens.

Application Requirements: Application, financial need analysis, references, transcript. *Deadline:* April 1.

Contact: Tim Latham, General Manager
American Society of Certified Engineering Technicians
PO Box 1536
Brandon, MS 39043
Phone: 601-824-8991
E-mail: Tim-Latham@ascet.org

JOSEPH M. PARISH MEMORIAL GRANT

The Joseph M. Parish Memorial Grant will be awarded to a student in the amount of $500 to be used to offset the cost of tuition, books and lab fees. Applicant must be a student member of ASCET and be an American citizen or a legal resident of the country in which the applicant is currently living. The award will be given to full time students enrolled in an engineering technology program; students pursuing a B.S. degree in Engineering are not eligible for this grant. For more information, visit http://www.ascet.org

Academic Fields/Career Goals: Engineering/Technology.

Award: Grant for use in sophomore or senior years; not renewable. *Number:* 1. *Amount:* up to $500.

Eligibility Requirements: Applicant must be enrolled or expecting to enroll full-time at a two-year or four-year institution. Applicant must have 3.0 GPA or higher. Available to U.S. citizens.

Application Requirements: Application, financial need analysis. *Deadline:* April 1.

Contact: Tim Latham, General Manager
American Society of Certified Engineering Technicians
PO Box 1536
Brandon, MS 39043
Phone: 601-824-8991
E-mail: Tim-Latham@ascet.org

AMERICAN SOCIETY OF HEATING, REFRIGERATING, AND AIR CONDITIONING ENGINEERS, INC.
http://www.ashrae.org

ALWIN B. NEWTON SCHOLARSHIP FUND
• See page 242

AMERICAN SOCIETY OF HEATING, REFRIGERATION, AND AIR CONDITIONING ENGINEERING TECHNOLOGY SCHOLARSHIP
• See page 90

ASHRAE MEMORIAL SCHOLARSHIP

One-time $3000 award for full-time study in hearing, ventilating, refrigeration, and air conditioning in an ABET-accredited program at an accredited school. Submit letter of recommendation from a professor or faculty adviser and two letters of recommendation from individuals familiar with the applicant's character, accomplishments, and likelihood of success in the HVAC and/or refrigeration industry. Applicants must have at least one full year of remaining study.

Academic Fields/Career Goals: Engineering/Technology; Engineering-Related Technologies; Heating, Air-Conditioning, and Refrigeration Mechanics; Trade/Technical Specialties.

Award: Scholarship for use in sophomore, junior, or senior years; not renewable. *Number:* 1. *Amount:* $3000.

Eligibility Requirements: Applicant must be enrolled or expecting to enroll full-time at a four-year institution or university. Applicant must have 3.0 GPA or higher. Available to U.S. citizens.

Application Requirements: Application, financial need analysis, references, transcript. *Deadline:* December 1.

American Society of Heating, Refrigerating, and Air Conditioning Engineers, Inc. (continued)

Contact: Lois Benedict, Scholarship Administrator
American Society of Heating, Refrigerating, and Air Conditioning Engineers, Inc.
1791 Tullie Circle, NE
Atlanta, GA 30329
Phone: 404-636-8400
Fax: 404-321-5478
E-mail: benedict@ashrae.org

ASHRAE REGION IV BENNY BOOTLE SCHOLARSHIP

One-time award to full-time engineering student enrolled in ABET-accredited program. Minimum 3.0 GPA required. Must study in North Carolina, South Carolina or Georgia.

Academic Fields/Career Goals: Engineering/Technology; Heating, Air-Conditioning, and Refrigeration Mechanics.

Award: Scholarship for use in sophomore, junior, or senior years; not renewable. *Number:* 1. *Amount:* up to $3000.

Eligibility Requirements: Applicant must be enrolled or expecting to enroll full-time at a four-year institution or university and studying in Georgia, North Carolina, or South Carolina. Applicant must have 3.0 GPA or higher. Available to U.S. citizens.

Application Requirements: Application, financial need analysis, references, transcript. *Deadline:* December 1.

Contact: Lois Benedict, Scholarship Administrator
American Society of Heating, Refrigerating, and Air Conditioning Engineers, Inc.
1791 Tullie Circle, NE
Atlanta, GA 30329
Phone: 404-636-8400
Fax: 404-321-5478
E-mail: benedict@ashrae.org

ASHRAE REGION VIII SCHOLARSHIP

One-time award to qualified engineering students enrolled full-time in an ABET-accredited program. Minimum 3.0 GPA required. Must study in Arkansas, Louisiana, Texas, Oklahoma or Mexico.

Academic Fields/Career Goals: Engineering/Technology; Heating, Air-Conditioning, and Refrigeration Mechanics.

Award: Scholarship for use in sophomore, junior, or senior years; not renewable. *Number:* 1. *Amount:* up to $3000.

Eligibility Requirements: Applicant must be enrolled or expecting to enroll full-time at a four-year institution or university and studying in Arkansas, Louisiana, Oklahoma, or Texas. Applicant must have 3.0 GPA or higher. Available to U.S. citizens.

Application Requirements: Application, financial need analysis, references, transcript. *Deadline:* December 1.

Contact: Lois Benedict, Scholarship Administrator
American Society of Heating, Refrigerating, and Air Conditioning Engineers, Inc.
1791 Tullie Circle, NE
Atlanta, GA 30329
Phone: 404-636-8400
Fax: 404-321-5478
E-mail: benedict@ashrae.org

ASHRAE SCHOLARSHIPS

One-time, $3000 award for full-time study in heating, ventilating, refrigeration, and air conditioning in an ABET-accredited program at an accredited school. Submit letter of recommendation from a professor or faculty adviser and two letters of recommendation from individuals familiar with the applicant's character, accomplishments, and likelihood of success in the HVAC and/or refrigeration industry. Applicants must have at least one full year of remaining study.

Academic Fields/Career Goals: Engineering/Technology; Engineering-Related Technologies; Heating, Air-Conditioning, and Refrigeration Mechanics; Trade/Technical Specialties.

Award: Scholarship for use in sophomore, junior, or senior years; not renewable. *Number:* up to 2. *Amount:* $3000.

Eligibility Requirements: Applicant must be enrolled or expecting to enroll full-time at a four-year institution or university and must have an interest in leadership. Applicant must have 3.0 GPA or higher. Available to U.S. citizens.

Application Requirements: Application, financial need analysis, references, transcript. *Deadline:* December 1.

Contact: Lois Benedict, Scholarship Administrator
American Society of Heating, Refrigerating, and Air Conditioning Engineers, Inc.
1791 Tullie Circle, NE
Atlanta, GA 30329
Phone: 404-636-8400
Fax: 404-321-5478
E-mail: benedict@ashrae.org

HENRY ADAMS SCHOLARSHIP

One-time $3000 award for full-time study in heating, ventilating, refrigeration, and air conditioning in an ABET-accredited program at an accredited school. Submit letter of recommendation from a professor or faculty adviser and two letters of recommendation from individuals familiar with the applicant's character, accomplishments, and likelihood of success in the HVAC and/or refrigeration industry. Applicants must have at least one full year of remaining study.

Academic Fields/Career Goals: Engineering/Technology; Engineering-Related Technologies; Heating, Air-Conditioning, and Refrigeration Mechanics; Trade/Technical Specialties.

Award: Scholarship for use in sophomore, junior, or senior years; not renewable. *Number:* 1. *Amount:* $3000.

Eligibility Requirements: Applicant must be enrolled or expecting to enroll full-time at a four-year institution and must have an interest in leadership. Applicant must have 3.0 GPA or higher. Available to U.S. citizens.

Application Requirements: Application, financial need analysis, references, transcript. *Deadline:* December 1.

Contact: Lois Benedict, Scholarship Administrator
American Society of Heating, Refrigerating, and Air Conditioning Engineers, Inc.
1791 Tullie Circle, NE
Atlanta, GA 30329
Phone: 404-636-8400
Fax: 404-321-5478
E-mail: benedict@ashrae.org

AMERICAN SOCIETY OF MECHANICAL ENGINEERS (ASME INTERNATIONAL)　　　http://www.asme.org

AMERICAN SOCIETY OF MECHANICAL ENGINEERS FOUNDATION SCHOLARSHIP

Award for college juniors and seniors who are members of the American Society of Mechanical Engineers. Must be pursuing studies in a mechanical engineering, mechanical engineering technology, or related program. There are no geographic or citizenship limitations. Application is available online: http://www.asme.org/education/enged/aid.

Academic Fields/Career Goals: Engineering/Technology; Mechanical Engineering.

Award: Scholarship for use in sophomore, junior, or senior years; not renewable. *Number:* up to 16. *Amount:* up to $1500.

Eligibility Requirements: Applicant must be enrolled or expecting to enroll full-time at a two-year or four-year institution or university. Available to U.S. and non-U.S. citizens.

Application Requirements: Application, essay, financial need analysis, references, self-addressed stamped envelope, transcript, must be ASME student members. *Deadline:* March 15.

Contact: Maisha Phillips, Coordinator, Student Development ASME
American Society of Mechanical Engineers (ASME International)
3 Park Avenue
New York, NY 10016-5990
Phone: 212-591-8131
Fax: 212-591-7143
E-mail: phillipsm@asme.org

AMERICAN SOCIETY OF NAVAL ENGINEERS
http://www.navalengineers.org

AMERICAN SOCIETY OF NAVAL ENGINEERS SCHOLARSHIP
• See page 90

AMERICAN WELDING SOCIETY
http://www.aws.org

AIRGAS-TERRY JARVIS MEMORIAL SCHOLARSHIP

Award for a full-time undergraduate pursuing a minimum four-year degree in welding engineering or welding engineering technology. Must have a minimum 2.8 overall GPA with a 3.0 GPA in engineering courses. Priority given to applicants residing or attending school in Florida, Georgia, or Alabama.

Academic Fields/Career Goals: Engineering/Technology; Engineering-Related Technologies; Trade/Technical Specialties.

Award: Scholarship for use in sophomore, junior, or senior years; renewable. *Number:* 1. *Amount:* $2500.

Eligibility Requirements: Applicant must be age 18 and enrolled or expecting to enroll full-time at a four-year institution. Applicant must have 3.0 GPA or higher. Available to U.S. and Canadian citizens.

Application Requirements: Application, autobiography, essay, financial need analysis, references, transcript. *Deadline:* January 15.

Contact: Vicki Pinsky, Manager Foundation
American Welding Society
550 Northwest Le Jeune Road
Miami, FL 33126
Phone: 800-443-9353 Ext. 212
Fax: 305-443-7559
E-mail: vpinsky@aws.org

AMERICAN WELDING SOCIETY INTERNATIONAL SCHOLARSHIP

Award for full-time international students pursuing a bachelor's degree or equivalent in a welding or related field of study. Applicant must have completed at least one year of welding or related field of study at a baccalaureate degree-granting institution and be in the top 20 percent of that institution's grading system. Scholarship not available for students residing in Canada, Mexico, or United States. For more information see Web site: http://www.aws.org/foundation

Academic Fields/Career Goals: Engineering/Technology; Engineering-Related Technologies; Trade/Technical Specialties.

Award: Scholarship for use in freshman, sophomore, junior, or senior years; renewable. *Number:* 1. *Amount:* up to $2500.

Eligibility Requirements: Applicant must be enrolled or expecting to enroll full-time at a four-year institution or university. Available to citizens of countries other than the U.S. or Canada.

Application Requirements: Application, essay, resume, references, transcript, proof of citizenship. *Deadline:* April 1.

Contact: Vicki Pinsky, Manager Foundation
American Welding Society
550 Northwest Le Jeune Road
Miami, FL 33126
Phone: 800-443-9353 Ext. 212
Fax: 305-443-7559
E-mail: vpinsky@aws.org

DONALD AND SHIRLEY HASTINGS SCHOLARSHIP

Award for undergraduate pursuing a four-year degree either full-time or part-time in welding engineering or welding engineering technology. Priority will be given to welding engineering students. Preference is given to students residing or attending school in California or Ohio. Submit copy of proposed curriculum. Must rank in upper half of class or have a minimum GPA of 2.5. Must also include acceptance letter. Deadline is January 15.

Academic Fields/Career Goals: Engineering/Technology; Materials Science, Engineering, and Metallurgy.

Award: Scholarship for use in freshman, sophomore, junior, or senior years. *Number:* 1. *Amount:* $2500.

Eligibility Requirements: Applicant must be age 18 and enrolled or expecting to enroll full or part-time at a four-year institution. Applicant must have 2.5 GPA or higher. Available to U.S. citizens.

Application Requirements: Application, autobiography, financial need analysis, references, transcript, proof of financial need. *Deadline:* January 15.

Contact: Vicki Pinsky, Manager Foundation
American Welding Society
550 Northwest Le Jeune Road
Miami, FL 33126
Phone: 800-443-9353 Ext. 212
Fax: 305-443-7559
E-mail: vpinsky@aws.org

DONALD F. HASTINGS SCHOLARSHIP

Award for undergraduate pursuing a four-year degree either full-time or part-time in welding engineering or welding engineering technology. Priority will be given to welding engineering students. Preference given to students residing or attending school in California or Ohio. Submit copy of proposed curriculum. Must rank in upper half of class or have a minimum GPA of 2.5. Also include acceptance letter.

Academic Fields/Career Goals: Engineering/Technology; Engineering-Related Technologies; Trade/Technical Specialties.

Award: Scholarship for use in sophomore, junior, or senior years; renewable. *Number:* 1. *Amount:* $2500.

Eligibility Requirements: Applicant must be enrolled or expecting to enroll full or part-time at a four-year institution. Applicant must have 2.5 GPA or higher. Available to U.S. citizens.

Application Requirements: Application, autobiography, financial need analysis, references, transcript. *Deadline:* January 15.

Contact: Vicki Pinsky, Manager Foundation
American Welding Society
550 Northwest Le Jeune Road
Miami, FL 33126
Phone: 800-443-9353 Ext. 212
Fax: 305-443-7559
E-mail: vpinsky@aws.org

EDWARD J. BRADY MEMORIAL SCHOLARSHIP

Award for an undergraduate pursuing a four-year degree either full-time or part-time in welding engineering or welding engineering technology. Priority given to welding engineering students. Submit a letter of reference indicating previous hands-on experience, a copy of proposed curriculum, and an acceptance letter. Must have minimum 2.5 GPA. Deadline: January 15.

Academic Fields/Career Goals: Engineering/Technology; Engineering-Related Technologies; Trade/Technical Specialties.

Award: Scholarship for use in sophomore, junior, or senior years; renewable. *Number:* 1. *Amount:* $2500.

Eligibility Requirements: Applicant must be age 18 and enrolled or expecting to enroll full or part-time at a four-year institution. Applicant must have 2.5 GPA or higher. Available to U.S. citizens.

Application Requirements: Application, autobiography, essay, financial need analysis, references, transcript. *Deadline:* January 15.

Contact: Vicki Pinsky, Manager Foundation
American Welding Society
550 Northwest Le Jeune Road
Miami, FL 33126
Phone: 800-443-9353 Ext. 212
Fax: 305-443-7559
E-mail: vpinsky@aws.org

HOWARD E. ADKINS MEMORIAL SCHOLARSHIP

Award for a full-time junior or senior in welding engineering or welding engineering technology. Preference to welding engineering students and those residing or attending school in Wisconsin or Kentucky. Must have at least 3.2 GPA in engineering, scientific, and technical subjects and a 2.8 GPA overall. No financial need is required to apply. Award may be granted a maximum of two years. Reapply each year. Submit copy of proposed curriculum and an acceptance letter.

Academic Fields/Career Goals: Engineering/Technology; Engineering-Related Technologies; Trade/Technical Specialties.

Award: Scholarship for use in junior or senior years; renewable. *Number:* 1. *Amount:* $2500.

Eligibility Requirements: Applicant must be age 18 and enrolled or expecting to enroll full-time at a four-year institution. Applicant must have 3.5 GPA or higher. Available to U.S. citizens.

American Welding Society (continued)

Application Requirements: Application, autobiography, essay, references, transcript. *Deadline:* January 15.

Contact: Vicki Pinsky, Manager Foundation
American Welding Society
550 Northwest Le Jeune Road
Miami, FL 33126
Phone: 800-443-9353 Ext. 212
Fax: 305-443-7559
E-mail: vpinsky@aws.org

ILLINOIS TOOL WORKS WELDING COMPANIES SCHOLARSHIP

Two awards of $3000 each are available for undergraduate students who will be seniors in a four-year bachelors degree in welding engineering technology or welding engineering. Applicant must be U.S. citizen planning to attend a U.S. institution and have a minimum 3.0 GPA. Priority given to students attending Ferris State University, exhibit a strong interest in welding equipment and have prior work experience in the welding equipment field. Application deadline is January 15. For more information see http://www.aws.org/foundation

Academic Fields/Career Goals: Engineering/Technology; Engineering-Related Technologies; Trade/Technical Specialties.

Award: Scholarship for use in senior year; not renewable. *Number:* 2. *Amount:* $3000.

Eligibility Requirements: Applicant must be age 18 and enrolled or expecting to enroll full or part-time at a four-year institution or university. Applicant must have 3.0 GPA or higher. Available to U.S. citizens.

Application Requirements: Application, transcript. *Deadline:* January 15.

Contact: Vicki Pinsky, Manager Foundation
American Welding Society
550 Northwest Le Jeune Road
Miami, FL 33126
Phone: 800-443-9353 Ext. 212
Fax: 305-443-7559
E-mail: vpinsky@aws.org

JOHN C. LINCOLN MEMORIAL SCHOLARSHIP

Award for an undergraduate pursuing a four-year degree either full time or part time in engineering or welding engineering technology. Priority given to welding engineering students. Priority will be given to those individuals residing or attending school in the states of Ohio or Arizona. Applicant must have a minimum 2.5 overall grade point average. Proof of financial need is required to qualify. Deadline is January 15.

Academic Fields/Career Goals: Engineering/Technology; Engineering-Related Technologies; Trade/Technical Specialties.

Award: Scholarship for use in sophomore, junior, or senior years; renewable. *Number:* 1. *Amount:* $2500.

Eligibility Requirements: Applicant must be age 18 and enrolled or expecting to enroll full or part-time at a four-year institution. Applicant must have 2.5 GPA or higher. Available to U.S. citizens.

Application Requirements: Application, autobiography, financial need analysis, references, transcript. *Deadline:* January 15.

Contact: Vicki Pinsky, Manager Foundation
American Welding Society
550 Northwest Le Jeune Road
Miami, FL 33126
Phone: 800-443-9353 Ext. 212
Fax: 305-443-7559
E-mail: vpinsky@aws.org

MATSUO BRIDGE COMPANY, LTD., OF JAPAN SCHOLARSHIP

• See page 172

MILLER ELECTRIC INTERNATIONAL WORLD SKILLS COMPETITION SCHOLARSHIP

Applicant must compete in the National Skills USA-VICA Competition for Welding, and advance to the AWS Weld Trials at the AWS International Welding and Fabricating Exposition and Convention, which is held on a bi-annual basis. The winner of the U.S. Weld Trial Competition will receive the following: The Miller Electric Mfg. Co. Scholarship for $10,000 and runner up $1000. For additional information, see Web site: http://www.aws.org/foundation

Academic Fields/Career Goals: Engineering/Technology; Trade/Technical Specialties.

Award: Scholarship for use in freshman, sophomore, junior, senior, graduate, or postgraduate years; renewable. *Number:* 1. *Amount:* $1000–$10,000.

Eligibility Requirements: Applicant must be enrolled or expecting to enroll full or part-time at an institution or university. Available to U.S. citizens.

Application Requirements: Applicant must enter a contest. *Deadline:* varies.

Contact: Vicki Pinsky, Manager Foundation
American Welding Society
550 Northwest Le Jeune Road
Miami, FL 33126
Phone: 800-443-9353 Ext. 212
Fax: 305-443-7559
E-mail: vpinsky@aws.org

PRAXAIR INTERNATIONAL SCHOLARSHIP

Award for a full-time student demonstrating leadership and pursuing a four-year degree in welding engineering or welding engineering technology. Priority given to welding engineering students. Must be a U.S. or Canadian citizen. Financial need is not required. Must have minimum 2.5 GPA. Application deadline is January 15.

Academic Fields/Career Goals: Engineering/Technology; Engineering-Related Technologies; Trade/Technical Specialties.

Award: Scholarship for use in sophomore, junior, or senior years; renewable. *Number:* 1. *Amount:* $2500.

Eligibility Requirements: Applicant must be age 18 and enrolled or expecting to enroll full-time at a four-year institution. Applicant must have 2.5 GPA or higher. Available to U.S. and Canadian citizens.

Application Requirements: Application, autobiography, financial need analysis, references, transcript. *Deadline:* January 15.

Contact: Vicki Pinsky, Manager Foundation
American Welding Society
550 Northwest Le Jeune Road
Miami, FL 33126
Phone: 800-443-9353 Ext. 212
Fax: 305-443-7559
E-mail: vpinsky@aws.org

RESISTANCE WELDER MANUFACTURERS' ASSOCIATION SCHOLARSHIP

Award of $2500 to provide financial assistance to those individuals who express an interest in the resistance welding process while pursuing a career in welding engineering. Available to U. S. and Canadian citizens. Must be a junior in a four-year program only and must maintain a minimum 3.0 GPA. Deadline is October 1.

Academic Fields/Career Goals: Engineering/Technology; Materials Science, Engineering, and Metallurgy.

Award: Scholarship for use in junior year; not renewable. *Number:* 1. *Amount:* $2500.

Eligibility Requirements: Applicant must be enrolled or expecting to enroll full-time at a four-year institution. Available to U.S. and Canadian citizens.

Application Requirements: Application, essay, resume, transcript. *Deadline:* October 1.

Contact: Vicki Pinsky, Manager Foundation
American Welding Society
550 Northwest Le Jeune Road
Miami, FL 33126
Phone: 800-443-9353 Ext. 212
Fax: 305-443-7559
E-mail: vpinsky@aws.org

ROBERT L. PEASLEE DETROIT BRAZING AND SOLDERING DIVISION SCHOLARSHIP

Award of $2500 to provide financial assistance to those individuals attending an accredited engineering college or university with an emphasis on brazing and soldering applications. Must be eighteen years of age, must be at least a college junior, must have minimum 3.0 GPA. Deadline is January 15.

Academic Fields/Career Goals: Engineering/Technology; Materials Science, Engineering, and Metallurgy.

Award: Scholarship for use in junior year; renewable. *Number:* 1. *Amount:* $2500.

Eligibility Requirements: Applicant must be age 18 and enrolled or expecting to enroll full-time at a four-year institution. Applicant must have 3.0 GPA or higher. Available to U.S. and Canadian citizens.

Application Requirements: Application, financial need analysis, resume, references, transcript, statement of unmet financial need. *Deadline:* January 15.

Contact: Vicki Pinsky, Manager Foundation
American Welding Society
550 Northwest Le Jeune Road
Miami, FL 33126
Phone: 800-443-9353 Ext. 212
Fax: 305-443-7559
E-mail: vpinsky@aws.org

WILLIAM B. HOWELL MEMORIAL SCHOLARSHIP

Awarded to a full-time undergraduate student pursuing a minimum four-year degree in a welding program at an accredited university. Priority will be given to those individuals residing or attending schools in the state of Florida, Michigan, and Ohio. Minimum 2.5 GPA required.

Academic Fields/Career Goals: Engineering/Technology; Engineering-Related Technologies; Trade/Technical Specialties.

Award: Scholarship for use in sophomore, junior, or senior years; renewable. *Number:* 1. *Amount:* $2500.

Eligibility Requirements: Applicant must be age 18 and enrolled or expecting to enroll full-time at a four-year institution. Applicant must have 2.5 GPA or higher. Available to U.S. citizens.

Application Requirements: Application, autobiography, essay, financial need analysis, references, transcript. *Deadline:* January 15.

Contact: Vicki Pinsky, Manager Foundation
American Welding Society
550 Northwest Le Jeune Road
Miami, FL 33126
Phone: 305-443-9353 Ext. 212
Fax: 305-443-7559
E-mail: vpinsky@aws.org

ARMED FORCES COMMUNICATIONS AND ELECTRONICS ASSOCIATION, EDUCATIONAL FOUNDATION   http://www.afcea.org

AFCEA SCHOLARSHIP FOR WORKING PROFESSIONALS
• *See page 120*

AFCEA SGT. JEANNETTE L. WINTERS, USMC MEMORIAL SCHOLARSHIP
• *See page 191*

AFCEA/LOCKHEED MARTIN ORINCON IT SCHOLARSHIP
• *See page 191*

ARMED FORCES COMMUNICATIONS AND ELECTRONICS ASSOCIATION EDUCATIONAL FOUNDATION DISTANCE-LEARNING SCHOLARSHIP
• *See page 191*

ARMED FORCES COMMUNICATIONS AND ELECTRONICS ASSOCIATION GENERAL EMMETT PAIGE SCHOLARSHIP
• *See page 191*

ARMED FORCES COMMUNICATIONS AND ELECTRONICS ASSOCIATION GENERAL JOHN A. WICKHAM SCHOLARSHIP
• *See page 192*

ARMED FORCES COMMUNICATIONS AND ELECTRONICS ASSOCIATION ROTC SCHOLARSHIP PROGRAM
• *See page 120*

VICE ADMIRAL JERRY O. TUTTLE, USN (RET.) AND MRS. BARBARA A. TUTTLE SCIENCE AND TECHNOLOGY SCHOLARSHIP

Candidate must be a U.S. citizen enrolled in a technology-related field and be a sophomore or junior at the time of application. Primary consideration will be given to military enlisted candidates.

Academic Fields/Career Goals: Engineering/Technology; Engineering-Related Technologies; Science, Technology, and Society.

Award: Scholarship for use in sophomore or junior years; not renewable. *Number:* varies. *Amount:* $2000.

Eligibility Requirements: Applicant must be enrolled or expecting to enroll full-time at a four-year or technical institution or university. Available to U.S. citizens.

Application Requirements: Application, references, transcript. *Deadline:* October 15.

Contact: Norma Corrales
Armed Forces Communications and Electronics Association, Educational Foundation
4400 Fair Lakes Court
Fairfax, VA 22033
Phone: 703-631-6149
E-mail: scholarship@afcea.org

ARRL FOUNDATION, INC.   http://www.arrl.org/arrlf/scholgen.html

CHARLES N. FISHER MEMORIAL SCHOLARSHIP
• *See page 90*

IRVING W. COOK, WA0CGS, SCHOLARSHIP
• *See page 90*

MISSISSIPPI SCHOLARSHIP
• *See page 90*

PAUL AND HELEN L. GRAUER SCHOLARSHIP
• *See page 91*

PHD ARA SCHOLARSHIP
• *See page 179*

WILLIAM R. GOLDFARB MEMORIAL SCHOLARSHIP
• *See page 145*

ASM MATERIALS EDUCATION FOUNDATION   http://www.asminternational.org

ASM MATERIALS EDUCATION FOUNDATION SCHOLARSHIPS

Twelve awards of $1000 for student members of ASM International studying metallurgy or materials engineering. Must have completed at least one year of college to apply. Award is based on merit; financial need is not considered.

Academic Fields/Career Goals: Engineering/Technology; Materials Science, Engineering, and Metallurgy.

Award: Scholarship for use in freshman, sophomore, junior, or senior years; not renewable. *Number:* 12. *Amount:* $1000.

Eligibility Requirements: Applicant must be enrolled or expecting to enroll full-time at a four-year institution or university. Applicant or parent of applicant must be member of ASM International. Available to U.S. and non-U.S. citizens.

Application Requirements: Application, essay, photo, references, transcript. *Deadline:* May 1.

Contact: Pergentina Deatherage, Administrator, Foundation Programs
ASM Materials Education Foundation
9639 Kinsman Road
Materials Park, OH 44073-0002
Phone: 440-338-5151
Fax: 440-338-4634
E-mail: jdeather@asminternational.org

ASM OUTSTANDING SCHOLARS AWARDS

Three awards of $2000 for student members of ASM International studying metallurgy or materials science and engineering. Must have completed at least one year of college to apply. Awards are merit-based; financial need is not considered.

Academic Fields/Career Goals: Engineering/Technology; Materials Science, Engineering, and Metallurgy.

Award: Scholarship for use in sophomore, junior, or senior years; not renewable. *Number:* 3. *Amount:* $2000.

ASM Materials Education Foundation (continued)

Eligibility Requirements: Applicant must be enrolled or expecting to enroll full-time at a four-year institution or university. Applicant or parent of applicant must be member of ASM International. Available to U.S. and non-U.S. citizens.

Application Requirements: Application, essay, photo, references, transcript. *Deadline:* May 1.

Contact: Pergentina Deatherage, Administrator, Foundation Programs
ASM Materials Education Foundation
9639 Kinsman Road
Materials Park, OH 44073-0002
Phone: 440-338-5151
Fax: 440-338-4634

EDWARD J. DULIS SCHOLARSHIP

Award of $1500 for student members of ASM International studying metallurgy or materials science and engineering. Must have completed at least one year of college to apply. Award is merit based; financial need is not considered.

Academic Fields/Career Goals: Engineering/Technology; Materials Science, Engineering, and Metallurgy.

Award: Scholarship for use in freshman, sophomore, junior, or senior years; not renewable. *Number:* 1. *Amount:* $1500.

Eligibility Requirements: Applicant must be enrolled or expecting to enroll full-time at an institution or university. Applicant or parent of applicant must be member of ASM International. Available to U.S. and non-U.S. citizens.

Application Requirements: Application, photo, references, transcript. *Deadline:* May 1.

Contact: Pergentina Deatherage, Administrator, Foundation Programs
ASM Materials Education Foundation
9639 Kinsman Road
Materials Park, OH 44073-0002
Phone: 440-338-5151
Fax: 440-338-4634

GEORGE A. ROBERTS SCHOLARSHIP

Seven awards for college juniors or seniors studying metallurgy or materials engineering in North America. Applicants must be student members of ASM International. Awards based on need, interest in field, academics, and character.

Academic Fields/Career Goals: Engineering/Technology; Materials Science, Engineering, and Metallurgy.

Award: Scholarship for use in junior or senior years; not renewable. *Number:* 7. *Amount:* $6000.

Eligibility Requirements: Applicant must be enrolled or expecting to enroll full-time at an institution or university. Applicant or parent of applicant must be member of ASM International. Available to U.S. and non-U.S. citizens.

Application Requirements: Application, essay, financial need analysis, photo, references, transcript. *Deadline:* May 1.

Contact: Pergentina Deatherage, Administrator, Foundation Programs
ASM Materials Education Foundation
9639 Kinsman Road
Materials Park, OH 44073-0002
Phone: 440-338-5151
Fax: 440-338-4634

JOHN M. HANIAK SCHOLARSHIP

Award for student members of ASM International studying metallurgy or materials science and engineering. Must have completed at least one year of college to apply. Award is merit based; financial need is not considered.

Academic Fields/Career Goals: Engineering/Technology; Materials Science, Engineering, and Metallurgy.

Award: Scholarship for use in freshman, sophomore, junior, or senior years; not renewable. *Number:* 1. *Amount:* $1500.

Eligibility Requirements: Applicant must be enrolled or expecting to enroll full-time at a four-year institution or university. Applicant or parent of applicant must be member of ASM International. Available to U.S. and non-U.S. citizens.

Application Requirements: Application, essay, references, self-addressed stamped envelope, transcript. *Deadline:* May 1.

Contact: Pergentina Deatherage, Administrator, Foundation Programs
ASM Materials Education Foundation
9639 Kinsman Road
Materials Park, OH 44073-0002
Phone: 440-338-5151
Fax: 440-338-4634

NICHOLAS J. GRANT SCHOLARSHIP

Full tuition for student member of ASM International studying metallurgy or materials science and engineering. Must have completed first two years of college at a North American university. Must provide proof of financial status.

Academic Fields/Career Goals: Engineering/Technology; Materials Science, Engineering, and Metallurgy.

Award: Scholarship for use in junior or senior years; not renewable. *Number:* 1. *Amount:* varies.

Eligibility Requirements: Applicant must be enrolled or expecting to enroll full-time at an institution or university. Applicant or parent of applicant must be member of ASM International. Available to U.S. and non-U.S. citizens.

Application Requirements: Application, essay, financial need analysis, photo, references, transcript. *Deadline:* May 1.

Contact: Pergentina Deatherage, Administrator, Foundation Programs
ASM Materials Education Foundation
9639 Kinsman Road
Materials Park, OH 44073-0002

WILLIAM P. WOODSIDE FOUNDER'S SCHOLARSHIP

Award for college junior or senior studying metallurgy or materials engineering in North America. Must be a student member of ASM International. Award based on need, interest in field, academics, and character. Scholarship covers full tuition up to $10,000.

Academic Fields/Career Goals: Engineering/Technology; Materials Science, Engineering, and Metallurgy.

Award: Scholarship for use in junior or senior years; not renewable. *Number:* 1. *Amount:* up to $10,000.

Eligibility Requirements: Applicant must be enrolled or expecting to enroll full-time at an institution or university. Applicant or parent of applicant must be member of ASM International. Available to U.S. and non-U.S. citizens.

Application Requirements: Application, essay, financial need analysis, photo, references, transcript. *Deadline:* May 1.

Contact: Pergentina Deatherage, Administrator, Foundation Programs
ASM Materials Education Foundation
9639 Kinsman Road
Materials Park, OH 44073-0002
Phone: 440-338-5151
Fax: 440-338-4634

ASPRS, THE IMAGING AND GEOSPATIAL INFORMATION SOCIETY
http://www.asprs.org

ROBERT E. ALTENHOFEN MEMORIAL SCHOLARSHIP
• See page 91

SPACE IMAGING AWARD FOR APPLICATION OF HIGH RESOLUTION DIGITAL SATELLITE IMAGERY
• See page 91

Z/I IMAGING SCHOLARSHIP
• See page 91

ASSOCIATED BUILDERS AND CONTRACTORS SCHOLARSHIP PROGRAM
http://www.abc.org

TRIMMER EDUCATION FOUNDATION SCHOLARSHIPS FOR CONSTRUCTION MANAGEMENT
• See page 172

ASSOCIATED GENERAL CONTRACTORS EDUCATION AND RESEARCH FOUNDATION   http://www.agcfoundation.org

AGC EDUCATION AND RESEARCH FOUNDATION UNDERGRADUATE SCHOLARSHIPS
• See page 173

ASSOCIATION FOR FACILITIES ENGINEERING (AFE)

ASSOCIATION FOR FACILITIES ENGINEERING CEDAR VALLEY CHAPTER # 132 SCHOLARSHIP
• See page 120

ASSOCIATION FOR IRON AND STEEL TECHNOLOGY   http://www.aist.org

AIST ALFRED B. GLOSSBRENNER AND JOHN KLUSCH SCHOLARSHIPS

Scholarship intended to award high school senior who plans on pursuing degree in metallurgy or engineering. Student must have previous academic excellence in science courses. Applicant must be a dependent of a AIST Northeastern Ohio Chapter member.

Academic Fields/Career Goals: Engineering/Technology; Materials Science, Engineering, and Metallurgy.

Award: Scholarship for use in freshman, sophomore, junior, or senior years; not renewable. *Number:* 2. *Amount:* $1000.

Eligibility Requirements: Applicant must be high school student; planning to enroll or expecting to enroll full-time at a four-year institution or university and must have an interest in leadership. Available to U.S. citizens.

Application Requirements: Application, essay, resume, references, transcript. *Deadline:* April 30.

Contact: Michael D. Hickman, Section Secretary, AIST Canton Section
Association for Iron and Steel Technology
PO Box 2657, 22831 East State Street
Alliance, OH 44601

AIST WILLIAM E. SCHWABE MEMORIAL SCHOLARSHIP

One time scholarship of $1500 will be awarded to an undergraduate student enrolled full-time and majoring in the field of engineering, metallurgy or materials science program at an accredited North American university.

Academic Fields/Career Goals: Engineering/Technology; Materials Science, Engineering, and Metallurgy.

Award: Scholarship for use in freshman, sophomore, junior, or senior years. *Number:* 1. *Amount:* $1500.

Eligibility Requirements: Applicant must be enrolled or expecting to enroll full-time at a four-year institution or university. Applicant must have 3.0 GPA or higher. Available to U.S. citizens.

Application Requirements: Application, essay, resume, references, transcript. *Deadline:* April 18.

Contact: Lori Wharrey, Board Administrator
Association for Iron and Steel Technology
186 Thorn Hill Road
Warrendale, PA 15086-7528
Phone: 724-776-6040 Ext. 621
Fax: 724-776-0430
E-mail: lwharrey@aist.org

ASSOCIATION FOR IRON AND STEEL TECHNOLOGY DAVID H. SAMSON SCHOLARSHIP
• See page 162

ASSOCIATION FOR IRON AND STEEL TECHNOLOGY MIDWEST CHAPTER BETTY MCKERN SCHOLARSHIP

Scholarship will be awarded to a graduating female high school senior, or undergraduate freshman, sophomore, or junior enrolled in a fully AIST accredited college or university. Applicant must be in good academic standing. Applicant must be a dependent of an AIST Midwest Chapter member.

Academic Fields/Career Goals: Engineering/Technology.

Award: Scholarship for use in freshman, sophomore, or junior years; not renewable. *Number:* 1. *Amount:* $2500.

Eligibility Requirements: Applicant must be enrolled or expecting to enroll full-time at a four-year institution or university and female. Available to U.S. citizens.

Application Requirements: Application, essay, references, transcript. *Deadline:* May 15.

Contact: Michael Heaney, Division Manager Maintenance and Engineering, ISG Indiana Harbor
Association for Iron and Steel Technology
3001 Dickey Road
East Chicago, IN 46312

ASSOCIATION FOR IRON AND STEEL TECHNOLOGY MIDWEST CHAPTER DON NELSON SCHOLARSHIP

One scholarship will be awarded to a graduating high school senior, or undergraduate freshman, sophomore or junior enrolled in a fully AIST accredited college or university. Applicant must be in good academic standing. Applicant must be a dependent of an AIST Midwest Chapter member.

Academic Fields/Career Goals: Engineering/Technology.

Award: Scholarship for use in freshman, sophomore, or junior years; not renewable. *Number:* 1. *Amount:* $750.

Eligibility Requirements: Applicant must be enrolled or expecting to enroll full-time at a four-year institution or university. Available to U.S. citizens.

Application Requirements: Application, essay, references, transcript. *Deadline:* May 15.

Contact: Michael Heaney, Division Manager Maintenance and Engineering, ISG Indiana Harbor
Association for Iron and Steel Technology
3001 Dickey Road
East Chicago, IN 46312

ASSOCIATION FOR IRON AND STEEL TECHNOLOGY MIDWEST CHAPTER ENGINEERING SCHOLARSHIP

Two four-year $1000 scholarships will be awarded to graduating high school senior, or undergraduate freshman, sophomore, or junior enrolled in a fully AIST accredited college or university. Applicant must be in good academic standing. Applicant must be a dependent of an AIST Midwest Chapter member.

Academic Fields/Career Goals: Engineering/Technology.

Award: Scholarship for use in freshman, sophomore, or junior years; renewable. *Number:* 2. *Amount:* $1000.

Eligibility Requirements: Applicant must be enrolled or expecting to enroll full-time at a four-year institution or university. Available to U.S. citizens.

Application Requirements: Application, essay, references, transcript. *Deadline:* May 15.

Contact: Michael Heaney, Division Manager Maintenance and Engineering, ISG Indiana Harbor
Association for Iron and Steel Technology
3001 Dickey Road
East Chicago, IN 46312

ASSOCIATION FOR IRON AND STEEL TECHNOLOGY MIDWEST CHAPTER JACK GILL SCHOLARSHIP

Scholarship will be awarded to a graduating high school senior, or undergraduate freshman, sophomore, or junior enrolled in a fully AIST accredited college or university. Applicant must be in good academic standing. Applicant must be a dependent of an AIST Midwest Chapter member.

Academic Fields/Career Goals: Engineering/Technology.

Award: Scholarship for use in freshman, sophomore, or junior years; not renewable. *Number:* 1. *Amount:* $2500.

Eligibility Requirements: Applicant must be enrolled or expecting to enroll full-time at a four-year institution or university. Available to U.S. citizens.

Application Requirements: Application, essay, references, transcript. *Deadline:* May 15.

Association for Iron and Steel Technology (continued)

Contact: Michael Heaney, Division Manager Maintenance and
Engineering, ISG Indiana Harbor
Association for Iron and Steel Technology
3001 Dickey Road
East Chicago, IN 46312

ASSOCIATION FOR IRON AND STEEL TECHNOLOGY MIDWEST CHAPTER MEL NICKEL SCHOLARSHIP

Scholarship will be awarded to a graduating high school senior, or undergraduate freshman, sophomore or junior enrolled in a fully AIST accredited college or university. Applicant must be in good academic standing. Applicant must be a dependent of an AIST Midwest Chapter member.

Academic Fields/Career Goals: Engineering/Technology.

Award: Scholarship for use in freshman, sophomore, or junior years; not renewable. *Number:* 1. *Amount:* $2500.

Eligibility Requirements: Applicant must be enrolled or expecting to enroll full-time at a four-year institution or university. Available to U.S. citizens.

Application Requirements: Application, essay, references, transcript. *Deadline:* May 15.

Contact: Michael Heaney, Division Manager Maintenance and
Engineering, ISG Indiana Harbor
Association for Iron and Steel Technology
3001 Dickey Road
East Chicago, IN 46312

ASSOCIATION FOR IRON AND STEEL TECHNOLOGY NATIONAL MERIT SCHOLARSHIP

Scholarship of $2000 per year, renewable for up to four years, for sons and daughters of AIST members in good standing who have qualified as a semifinalist in the National Merit Scholarship competition.

Academic Fields/Career Goals: Engineering/Technology; Materials Science, Engineering, and Metallurgy.

Award: Scholarship for use in freshman, sophomore, junior, or senior years; renewable. *Number:* 1. *Amount:* $2000.

Eligibility Requirements: Applicant must be high school student and planning to enroll or expecting to enroll full-time at a four-year institution or university. Available to U.S. citizens.

Application Requirements: References, test scores, transcript, National Merit Scholarship semi-finalist.

Contact: Lori Wharrey, Board Administrator
Association for Iron and Steel Technology
186 Thorn Hill Road
Warrendale, PA 15086-7528
Phone: 724-776-6040 Ext. 621
Fax: 724-776-0430
E-mail: lwharrey@aist.org

ASSOCIATION FOR IRON AND STEEL TECHNOLOGY NORTHWEST MEMBER CHAPTER SCHOLARSHIP

Scholarships available to encourage a Pacific Northwest area student to prepare for a career in engineering. Must be the child, grandchild, spouse, or niece/nephew of a member in good standing of the AIST Northwest Member Chapter. Award based on academic achievements in science projects in chemistry, mathematics, and physics. Application forms may be obtained by writing to: The Secretary, AIST Member Chapter. Applications are to be returned by registered mail to the same address by June 15.

Academic Fields/Career Goals: Engineering/Technology; Materials Science, Engineering, and Metallurgy.

Award: Scholarship for use in freshman, sophomore, junior, or senior years; not renewable. *Number:* 2. *Amount:* $1000.

Eligibility Requirements: Applicant must be enrolled or expecting to enroll full or part-time at a four-year institution or university. Available to U.S. citizens.

Application Requirements: Application. *Deadline:* June 15.

Contact: Gerardo Giraldo, Secretary-Treasurer Northwest Chapter
Association for Iron and Steel Technology
c/o Nucor Steel Seattle, Inc., Washington Steel Division, 2424
Southwest Andover Street
Seattle, WA 98106-1100
Phone: 206-933-2245
Fax: 206-933-2207
E-mail: gerry.giraldo@nucor-seattle.com

ASSOCIATION FOR IRON AND STEEL TECHNOLOGY OHIO VALLEY CHAPTER SCHOLARSHIP
• See page 135

ASSOCIATION FOR IRON AND STEEL TECHNOLOGY PITTSBURGH CHAPTER SCHOLARSHIP

Scholarships available for children and grandchildren (natural, step, adopted, or ward), or spouse of a member in good standing of the Pittsburgh Member Chapter. Applicant must be a high school senior or currently enrolled undergraduate preparing for a career in engineering or metallurgy. Application and guidelines on Web site: http://www.aist.org/chapters/mc_pittsburgh_scholar.htm. Completed applications are to be returned by registered mail to scholarship contact postmarked no later than May 31.

Academic Fields/Career Goals: Engineering/Technology; Materials Science, Engineering, and Metallurgy.

Award: Scholarship for use in freshman, sophomore, junior, or senior years; not renewable. *Number:* 2. *Amount:* $2500.

Eligibility Requirements: Applicant must be enrolled or expecting to enroll full-time at a four-year institution or university. Available to U.S. citizens.

Application Requirements: Application, essay. *Deadline:* June 15.

Contact: Paul D. Conley, Pittsburgh Chapter AIST
Association for Iron and Steel Technology
100 River Road
Brackenridge, PA 15014-1597

ASSOCIATION FOR IRON AND STEEL TECHNOLOGY SOUTHEAST MEMBER CHAPTER SCHOLARSHIP

Scholarship for children, stepchildren, grandchildren, or spouse of active Southeast Chapter members who are pursuing a career in engineering, the sciences, or other majors relating to iron and steel production. Awarded based on SAT and ACT scores, consideration will be given for extra-curricular activities and the essay. Students may reapply for the scholarship each year for their term of college. Applications available by writing Chapter Secretary. Additional information on Web site: http://www.aist.org/chapters/mc_southeast_scholar_guidelines.htm.

Academic Fields/Career Goals: Engineering/Technology; Materials Science, Engineering, and Metallurgy.

Award: Scholarship for use in freshman, sophomore, junior, or senior years; renewable. *Number:* 1. *Amount:* $1000.

Eligibility Requirements: Applicant must be enrolled or expecting to enroll full or part-time at a four-year institution or university. Available to U.S. citizens.

Application Requirements: Application, essay, test scores. *Deadline:* July 30.

Contact: Mike Hutson, AIST Southeast Chapter Secretary
Association for Iron and Steel Technology
803 Floyd Street
Kings Mountain, NC 29086
Phone: 704-730-8320
Fax: 704-730-8321
E-mail: mike@johnhutsoncompany.com

ASSOCIATION FOR WOMEN IN COMPUTING— HOUSTON   http://www.awchouston.org

KATHI BOWLES SCHOLARSHIP FOR WOMEN IN COMPUTING
• See page 192

ASSOCIATION FOR WOMEN IN SCIENCE EDUCATIONAL FOUNDATION   http://www.awis.org/ed_foundation.html

ASSOCIATION FOR WOMEN IN SCIENCE COLLEGE SCHOLARSHIP
• See page 86

ASSOCIATION OF ENGINEERING GEOLOGISTS
http://www.aegweb.org

MARLIAVE FUND
• See page 213

AUTOMOTIVE HALL OF FAME
http://www.automotivehalloffame.org

AUTOMOTIVE HALL OF FAME EDUCATIONAL FUNDS
• See page 162

BARRY M. GOLDWATER SCHOLARSHIP AND EXCELLENCE IN EDUCATION FOUNDATION
http://www.act.org/goldwater

BARRY M. GOLDWATER SCHOLARSHIP AND EXCELLENCE IN EDUCATION PROGRAM
• See page 92

BOYS AND GIRLS CLUBS OF GREATER SAN DIEGO
http://www.sdyouth.org

SPENCE REESE SCHOLARSHIP FUND

Renewable scholarship for graduating male high school seniors in U.S. with minimum 2.5 GPA. For study of law, medicine, engineering, and political science. Application fee: $10. Based on academic ability, financial need, and character. Required to attend a personal interview in San Diego, California. Travel expenses for the interview will be reimbursed by the Scholarship Foundation.

Academic Fields/Career Goals: Engineering/Technology; Health and Medical Sciences; Law/Legal Services; Political Science.

Award: Scholarship for use in freshman, sophomore, junior, or senior years; renewable. *Number:* 4. *Amount:* $2000.

Eligibility Requirements: Applicant must be high school student; age 20 or under; planning to enroll or expecting to enroll full-time at a four-year institution or university and male. Applicant must have 2.5 GPA or higher. Available to U.S. citizens.

Application Requirements: Application, financial need analysis, interview, self-addressed stamped envelope, test scores, transcript. *Fee:* $10. *Deadline:* April 15.

Contact: Jean Pilley, Scholarship Coordinator
Boys and Girls Clubs of Greater San Diego
4635 Clairemont Mesa Boulevard
San Diego, CA 92117
Phone: 619-298-3520
Fax: 619-298-3615
E-mail: bgcsandiego@yahoo.com

BUSINESS AND PROFESSIONAL WOMEN'S FOUNDATION
http://www.bpwusa.org

BPW CAREER ADVANCEMENT SCHOLARSHIP PROGRAM FOR WOMEN
• See page 136

CATCHING THE DREAM

MATH, ENGINEERING, SCIENCE, BUSINESS, EDUCATION, COMPUTERS SCHOLARSHIPS
• See page 145

TRIBAL BUSINESS MANAGEMENT PROGRAM (TBM)
• See page 55

COLLEGEBOUND FOUNDATION
http://www.collegeboundfoundation.org

DR. FREEMAN A. HRABOWSKI, III SCHOLARSHIP

Award for Baltimore City public high school graduates. Please see Web site: http://www.collegeboundfoundation.org for complete information on application process. Must major in field of mathematics and/or science/technology, minimum GPA of 3.0. Must apply for CollegeBound Competitive Scholarship/Last-Dollar Grant. Preference given to students attending a Maryland university.

Academic Fields/Career Goals: Engineering/Technology; Mathematics.

Award: Scholarship for use in freshman, sophomore, junior, or senior years; renewable. *Number:* 1. *Amount:* $1500.

Eligibility Requirements: Applicant must be enrolled or expecting to enroll full-time at a two-year or four-year institution or university and resident of Maryland. Applicant must have 3.0 GPA or higher. Available to U.S. citizens.

Application Requirements: Application, financial need analysis, references, transcript, financial aid award letters, Student Aid Report (SAR). *Deadline:* March 19.

Contact: April Bell, Associate Program Director
CollegeBound Foundation
300 Water Street, Suite 300
Baltimore, MD 21202
Phone: 410-783-2905 Ext. 208
Fax: 410-727-5786
E-mail: abell@collegeboundfoundation.org

GEORGE V. MCGOWAN SCHOLARSHIP

Award for Baltimore City public high school graduates. Please see Web site: http://www.collegeboundfoundation.org for complete information on application process. Must major in engineering, have a cumulative GPA of 3.0 or better, and combined SAT score of 1000. Preference given to students who attend a Maryland university. Must complete and return CollegeBound/Competitive Scholarship/Last-Dollar Grant Application.

Academic Fields/Career Goals: Engineering/Technology.

Award: Scholarship for use in freshman, sophomore, junior, or senior years; renewable. *Number:* 1. *Amount:* $1500.

Eligibility Requirements: Applicant must be enrolled or expecting to enroll full-time at a two-year or four-year institution or university and resident of Maryland. Applicant must have 3.0 GPA or higher. Available to U.S. citizens.

Application Requirements: Application, financial need analysis, references, transcript, financial aid award letters, Student Aid Report (SAR). *Deadline:* March 19.

Contact: April Bell, Associate Program Director
CollegeBound Foundation
300 Water Street, Suite 300
Baltimore, MD 21202
Phone: 410-783-2905 Ext. 208
Fax: 410-727-5786
E-mail: abell@collegeboundfoundation.org

NATIONAL AQUARIUM IN BALTIMORE HENRY HALL SCHOLARSHIP
• See page 136

CUBAN AMERICAN NATIONAL FOUNDATION
http://www.canf.org

MAS FAMILY SCHOLARSHIPS
• See page 146

DAYTON FOUNDATION
http://www.daytonfoundation.org

R.C. APPENZELLER FAMILY ENDOWMENT FUND

Awarded as renewable scholarships to students pursuing a career in engineering at an accredited college or university.

Academic Fields/Career Goals: Engineering/Technology.

Award: Scholarship for use in freshman, sophomore, junior, or senior years; renewable. *Number:* 1. *Amount:* up to $1000.

Eligibility Requirements: Applicant must be enrolled or expecting to enroll full-time at a two-year or four-year institution or university. Available to U.S. citizens.

Application Requirements: Application, financial need analysis, references, transcript. *Deadline:* varies.

Contact: Diane Timmons, Director Grants and Programs
Dayton Foundation
2300 Kettering Tower
Dayton, OH 45423
Phone: 937-225-9966
E-mail: dtimmons@daytonfoundation.org

DEVRY, INC.　　　　　　　　http://www.devry.edu

CISCO SCHOLARSHIP-HIGH SCHOOL GRADUATES

Award of $1200 per semester for high school graduates who successfully completed IT Essentials I or II, or CCNA Semester prior to entering a DeVry Institute. Must apply within one year from high school graduation.

Academic Fields/Career Goals: Engineering/Technology; Engineering-Related Technologies; Health Information Management/Technology.

Award: Scholarship for use in freshman year; not renewable. *Amount:* $1200–$10,800.

Eligibility Requirements: Applicant must be enrolled or expecting to enroll full-time at a technical institution. Available to U.S. and Canadian citizens.

Application Requirements: Application. *Deadline:* Continuous.

Contact: Thonie Simpson, National HS Program Manager
　　　　　DeVry, Inc.
　　　　　1 Tower Lane
　　　　　Oakbrook Terrace, IL 60181-4624
　　　　　Phone: 630-706-3122
　　　　　Fax: 630-574-1696
　　　　　E-mail: outreach@devry.edu

EAA AVIATION FOUNDATION, INC.　http://www.eaa.org

PAYZER SCHOLARSHIP
• See page 122

EAST LOS ANGELES COMMUNITY UNION (TELACU) EDUCATION FOUNDATION　　　　　http://www.telacu.com

LINC TELACU ENGINEERING AWARD
• See page 163

ELECTROCHEMICAL SOCIETY, INC.　　　　　　　http://www.electrochem.org

DANIEL CUBICCIOTTI STUDENT AWARD OF THE SAN FRANCISCO SECTION OF THE ELECTROCHEMICAL SOCIETY, SPONSORED BY STRUCTURAL INTEGRITY ASSOCIATES
• See page 137

H.H. DOW MEMORIAL STUDENT ACHIEVEMENT AWARD OF THE INDUSTRIAL ELECTROLYSIS AND ELECTROCHEMICAL ENGINEERING DIVISION OF THE ELECTROCHEMICAL SOCIETY, INC.
• See page 137

STUDENT ACHIEVEMENT AWARDS OF THE INDUSTRIAL ELECTROLYSIS AND ELECTROCHEMICAL ENGINEERING DIVISION OF THE ELECTROCHEMICAL SOCIETY, INC.
• See page 137

STUDENT RESEARCH AWARDS OF THE BATTERY DIVISION OF THE ELECTROCHEMICAL SOCIETY, INC.
• See page 137

ELECTRONIC DOCUMENT SYSTEMS FOUNDATION　　　　　　　http://www.edsf.org

ELECTRONIC DOCUMENT SYSTEMS FOUNDATION SCHOLARSHIP AWARDS
• See page 180

ENGINEERS FOUNDATION OF OHIO　　　　　http://www.ohioengineer.com

C. MERRILL BARBER, P.E., MEMORIAL SCHOLARSHIP

Scholarship availables for graduating high school senior, residing in Ohio, entering an accredited engineering college or university. Minimum GPA of 3.0 required. Renewable for three years. Not available for the year 2006.

Academic Fields/Career Goals: Engineering/Technology.

Award: Scholarship for use in freshman year; renewable. *Number:* 1. *Amount:* up to $1000.

Eligibility Requirements: Applicant must be enrolled or expecting to enroll full-time at a four-year institution or university; resident of Ohio and studying in Ohio. Applicant must have 3.0 GPA or higher. Available to U.S. citizens.

Application Requirements: Application, test scores.

Contact: Pam McClure, Manager of Administration
　　　　　Engineers Foundation of Ohio
　　　　　4795 Evanswood Drive, Suite 201
　　　　　Columbus, OH 43229-7216
　　　　　Phone: 614-846-1177
　　　　　Fax: 614-846-1131
　　　　　E-mail: ospe@iwaynet.net

CYRIL W. NEFF, P.E., P.S., MEMORIAL SCHOLARSHIP

Scholarship for graduating high school senior students from Cuyahoga, Lorain, Lake, Geauga, Medina and Ashtabula counties only, and entering Ohio colleges or the University of Notre Dame.

Academic Fields/Career Goals: Engineering/Technology.

Award: Scholarship for use in freshman year. *Number:* 1. *Amount:* up to $2500.

Eligibility Requirements: Applicant must be enrolled or expecting to enroll at a four-year institution or university; resident of Ohio and studying in Ohio. Applicant must have 3.0 GPA or higher. Available to U.S. citizens.

Application Requirements: Application, financial need analysis, test scores. *Deadline:* varies.

Contact: Pam McClure, Manager of Administration
　　　　　Engineers Foundation of Ohio
　　　　　4795 Evanswood Drive, Suite 201
　　　　　Columbus, OH 43229-7216
　　　　　Phone: 614-846-1177
　　　　　Fax: 614-846-1131
　　　　　E-mail: ospe@iwaynet.net

ENGINEERS FOUNDATION OF OHIO GENERAL FUND SCHOLARSHIP

Applicant must be college junior or senior at the end of the academic year in which the application is submitted. Must be enrolled full-time at an Ohio college or university in a curriculum leading to a BS degree in engineering or its equivalent. Minimum GPA of 3.0 required.

Academic Fields/Career Goals: Engineering/Technology.

Award: Scholarship for use in junior or senior years. *Number:* 1. *Amount:* up to $1000.

Eligibility Requirements: Applicant must be enrolled or expecting to enroll full-time at a four-year institution or university; resident of Ohio and studying in Ohio. Applicant must have 3.0 GPA or higher. Available to U.S. citizens.

Application Requirements: Application, test scores.

Contact: Pam McClure, Manager of Administration
　　　　　Engineers Foundation of Ohio
　　　　　4795 Evanswood Drive, Suite 201
　　　　　Columbus, OH 43229-7216
　　　　　Phone: 614-846-1177
　　　　　Fax: 614-846-1131
　　　　　E-mail: ospe@iwaynet.net

G. BROOKS EARNEST-OHIO SOCIETY OF PROFESSIONAL ENGINEERS, CLEVELAND CHAPTER MEMORIAL SCHOLARSHIP

Scholarship open to students from Ashtabula, Cuyahoga, Geauga or Lake county; entering Case Western Reserve University or Cleveland State University. Renewable for three years. Not available for the year 2006.

Academic Fields/Career Goals: Engineering/Technology.

Award: Scholarship for use in freshman year; renewable. *Number:* 1. *Amount:* up to $1000.

Eligibility Requirements: Applicant must be enrolled or expecting to enroll full-time at a four-year institution or university; resident of Ohio and studying in Ohio. Applicant must have 3.0 GPA or higher. Available to U.S. citizens.

Application Requirements: Application, test scores. *Deadline:* varies.

The beginning of the right column (above CYRIL W. NEFF) continues the C. MERRILL BARBER entry:

Eligibility Requirements: Applicant must be enrolled or expecting to enroll full-time at a four-year institution or university; resident of Ohio and studying in Ohio. Applicant must have 3.0 GPA or higher. Available to U.S. citizens.

Application Requirements: Application, test scores.

Contact: Pam McClure, Manager of Administration
　　　　　Engineers Foundation of Ohio
　　　　　4795 Evanswood Drive, Suite 201
　　　　　Columbus, OH 43229-7216
　　　　　Phone: 614-846-1177
　　　　　Fax: 614-846-1131
　　　　　E-mail: ospe@iwaynet.net

Contact: Pam McClure, Manager of Administration
Engineers Foundation of Ohio
4795 Evanswood Drive, Suite 201
Columbus, OH 43229-7216
Phone: 614-846-1177
Fax: 614-846-1131
E-mail: ospe@iwaynet.net

HOMER T. BORTON, P.E., SCHOLARSHIP

Renewable scholarship for students who were accepted for enrollment at an Ohio college or university.

Academic Fields/Career Goals: Engineering/Technology.

Award: Scholarship for use in freshman year; renewable. *Number:* 1. *Amount:* up to $1000.

Eligibility Requirements: Applicant must be enrolled or expecting to enroll full-time at a four-year institution or university; resident of Ohio and studying in Ohio. Applicant must have 3.0 GPA or higher. Available to U.S. citizens.

Application Requirements: Application, test scores. *Deadline:* varies.

Contact: Pam McClure, Manager of Administration
Engineers Foundation of Ohio
4795 Evanswood Drive, Suite 201
Columbus, OH 43229-7216
Phone: 614-846-1177
Fax: 614-846-1131
E-mail: ospe@iwaynet.net

LLOYD A. CHACEY, P.E.-OHIO SOCIETY OF PROFESSIONAL ENGINEERS MEMORIAL SCHOLARSHIP

Scholarship available for a son, daughter, brother, sister, niece, nephew, spouse or grandchild of a current member of the Ohio Society of Professional Engineers, or of a deceased member who was in good standing at the time of his or her death. Must be enrolled full-time at an Ohio college or university in a curriculum leading to a BS degree in engineering or its equivalent.

Academic Fields/Career Goals: Engineering/Technology.

Award: Scholarship for use in junior year; renewable. *Number:* 1. *Amount:* up to $2000.

Eligibility Requirements: Applicant must be enrolled or expecting to enroll full-time at a four-year institution or university and resident of Ohio. Applicant must have 3.0 GPA or higher. Available to U.S. citizens.

Application Requirements: Application, financial need analysis, test scores. *Deadline:* varies.

Contact: Pam McClure, Manager of Administration
Engineers Foundation of Ohio
4795 Evanswood Drive, Suite 201
Columbus, OH 43229-7216
Phone: 614-846-1177
Fax: 614-846-1131
E-mail: ospe@iwaynet.net

MELVIN BAUER, P.E., P.S.-OHIO SOCIETY OF PROFESSIONAL ENGINEERS NORTH CENTRAL -MEMORIAL SCHOLARSHIP

Scholarship available for graduating high school seniors interested in engineering who are from Ashland, Richland, Wayne and Crawford counties, entering Ohio Colleges.

Academic Fields/Career Goals: Engineering/Technology.

Award: Scholarship for use in freshman year; not renewable. *Number:* 1. *Amount:* up to $500.

Eligibility Requirements: Applicant must be enrolled or expecting to enroll full-time at a four-year institution or university; resident of Ohio and studying in Ohio. Applicant must have 3.0 GPA or higher. Available to U.S. citizens.

Application Requirements: Application, test scores. *Deadline:* varies.

Contact: Pam McClure, Manager of Administration
Engineers Foundation of Ohio
4795 Evanswood Drive, Suite 201
Columbus, OH 43229-7216
Phone: 614-846-1177
Fax: 614-846-1131
E-mail: ospe@iwaynet.net

RAYMOND H. FULLER, P.E., MEMORIAL SCHOLARSHIP

Scholarship to promote the engineering profession to young people. Recipients must be accepted for enrollment at an Ohio college or university.

Academic Fields/Career Goals: Engineering/Technology.

Award: Scholarship for use in freshman year; not renewable. *Number:* 1. *Amount:* up to $1000.

Eligibility Requirements: Applicant must be enrolled or expecting to enroll full-time at a four-year institution or university; resident of Ohio and studying in Ohio. Applicant must have 3.0 GPA or higher. Available to U.S. citizens.

Application Requirements: Application, financial need analysis, test scores. *Deadline:* varies.

Contact: Pam McClure, Manager of Administration
Engineers Foundation of Ohio
4795 Evanswood Drive, Suite 201
Columbus, OH 43229-7216
Phone: 614-846-1177
Fax: 614-846-1131
E-mail: ospe@iwaynet.net

FISHER BROADCASTING COMPANY   http://www.fisherbroadcasting.com

FISHER BROADCASTING, INC., SCHOLARSHIP FOR MINORITIES
• *See page 181*

FLORIDA EDUCATIONAL FACILITIES PLANNERS' ASSOCIATION   http://www.fefpa.org

FEFPA ASSISTANTSHIP
• *See page 99*

GEORGE BIRD GRINNELL AMERICAN INDIAN FUND   http://www.grinnellfund.org/

AL QOYAWAYMA AWARD
• *See page 163*

GERMAN ACADEMIC EXCHANGE SERVICE (DAAD)   http://www.daad.org

HIGH-TECH IN OLD MUNICH

Grant offers opportunity for engineering students with beginning and advanced language skills to study during the summer at TU Munchen. Open to second, third and fourth year students enrolled full time at an accredited university or college in the U.S. or Canada. Must be U.S. or Canadian citizen or permanent resident. Minimum of one semester of college German or equivalent required. Deadline: March 15.

Academic Fields/Career Goals: Engineering/Technology.

Award: Grant for use in sophomore, junior, or senior years; not renewable. *Number:* 30. *Amount:* $1800.

Eligibility Requirements: Applicant must be enrolled or expecting to enroll full-time at a four-year institution or university and must have an interest in German language. Available to U.S. and Canadian citizens.

Application Requirements: Application, essay, resume, references, transcript. *Deadline:* March 15.

Contact: German Academic Exchange Service (DAAD)
871 United Nations Plaza
New York, NY 10017
Phone: 212-758-3223
Fax: 212-755-5780
E-mail: daadny@daad.org

GOLDEN KEY INTERNATIONAL HONOUR SOCIETY
http://www.goldenkey.org

ENGINEERING/ TECHNOLOGY ACHIEVEMENT AWARD

Applicants will be asked to respond to a problem posed by an honorary member within discipline. One winner will receive a $1000 award. The second place applicant will receive $750 and the third place applicant will receive $500. See Web site for more information: http://goldenkey.gsu.edu.

Academic Fields/Career Goals: Engineering/Technology.

Award: Prize for use in junior, senior, graduate, or postgraduate years; not renewable. *Number:* 3. *Amount:* $500–$1000.

Eligibility Requirements: Applicant must be enrolled or expecting to enroll full or part-time at an institution or university. Available to U.S. citizens.

Application Requirements: Application, applicant must enter a contest, essay, references, transcript. *Deadline:* March 1.

Contact: Scholarship Program Administrators
Golden Key International Honour Society
PO Box 23737
Nashville, TN 37202-3737
Phone: 800-377-2401
E-mail: scholarships@goldenkey.org

FORD MOTOR COMPANY ENGINEERING AND LEADERSHIP SCHOLARSHIP

This scholarship provides opportunities for engineering majors and furthers the interests of one of the Society's key partners, Ford Motor Company. One U.S. $10,000 scholarship. Deadline is April 1.

Academic Fields/Career Goals: Engineering/Technology.

Award: Scholarship for use in junior or senior years; not renewable. *Number:* 1. *Amount:* $10,000.

Eligibility Requirements: Applicant must be enrolled or expecting to enroll full-time at an institution or university. Applicant or parent of applicant must be member of Golden Key National Honor Society. Applicant must have 3.5 GPA or higher. Available to U.S. and non-U.S. citizens.

Application Requirements: Application, essay, resume, transcript. *Deadline:* April 1.

Contact: Scholarship Program Administrators
Golden Key International Honour Society
PO Box 23737
Nashville, TN 37202
Phone: 800-377-2401

GRAND RAPIDS COMMUNITY FOUNDATION
http://www.grfoundation.org

ECONOMIC CLUB OF GRAND RAPIDS BUSINESS STUDY ABROAD SCHOLARSHIP
• See page 62

GREATER KANAWHA VALLEY FOUNDATION
http://www.tgkvf.org

MATH AND SCIENCE SCHOLARSHIP

Awarded to students pursuing a degree in math, science or engineering at any accredited college or university. For purposes of this Fund, science shall include chemistry, physics, biology and other scientific fields. Scholarships are awarded for one or more years. May apply for two Foundation scholarships but will only be chosen for one. Must be a resident of West Virginia.

Academic Fields/Career Goals: Engineering/Technology; Physical Sciences and Math; Science, Technology, and Society.

Award: Scholarship for use in freshman, sophomore, junior, or senior years; renewable. *Number:* 1. *Amount:* $500.

Eligibility Requirements: Applicant must be enrolled or expecting to enroll full-time at a four-year institution or university and resident of West Virginia. Applicant must have 2.5 GPA or higher. Available to U.S. citizens.

Application Requirements: Application, essay, financial need analysis, references, transcript, IRS 1040 form. *Deadline:* February 15.

Contact: Susan Hoover, Scholarship Coordinator
Greater Kanawha Valley Foundation
PO Box 3041
Charleston, WV 25331
Phone: 304-346-3620
Fax: 304-346-3640

HAWAIIAN LODGE, F.& A. M.
http://www.hawaiianlodge.org/

HAWAIIAN LODGE SCHOLARSHIPS
• See page 99

HELLENIC UNIVERSITY CLUB OF PHILADELPHIA
http://www.hucphila.org

THE DIMITRI J. VERVERELLI MEMORIAL SCHOLARSHIP FOR ARCHITECTURE AND/OR ENGINEERING
• See page 99

HISPANIC COLLEGE FUND, INC.
http://www.hispanicfund.org

DENNY'S/HISPANIC COLLEGE FUND SCHOLARSHIP
• See page 62

DEPARTMENT OF ENERGY SCHOLARSHIP PROGRAM
• See page 148

ICI EDUCATIONAL FOUNDATION SCHOLARSHIP PROGRAM
• See page 62

LOCKHEED MARTIN SCHOLARSHIP PROGRAM
• See page 164

M & T BANK/ HISPANIC COLLEGE FUND SCHOLARSHIP PROGRAM
• See page 63

NATIONAL HISPANIC EXPLORERS SCHOLARSHIP PROGRAM
• See page 93

HISPANIC ENGINEER NATIONAL ACHIEVEMENT AWARDS CORPORATION (HENAAC)
http://www.henaac.org

HISPANIC ENGINEER NATIONAL ACHIEVEMENT AWARDS CORPORATION SCHOLARSHIP PROGRAM
• See page 122

HISPANIC SCHOLARSHIP FUND
http://www.hsf.net

HSF/GENERAL MOTORS SCHOLARSHIP
• See page 149

HSF/SOCIETY OF HISPANIC PROFESSIONAL ENGINEERS, INC. SCHOLARSHIP PROGRAM
• See page 174

ILLINOIS SOCIETY OF PROFESSIONAL ENGINEERS
http://www.ilspe.com

ILLINOIS SOCIETY OF PROFESSIONAL ENGINEERS ADVANTAGE AWARD/FOUNDATION SCHOLARSHIP

Applicant must be son or daughter of ISPE member in good standing and attend an Illinois university approved by the Accreditation Board of Engineering. Applicant must be at least a junior at the approved university. Engineering technology students are not eligible. Application deadline is January 31. Required essay must address why applicant wishes to become a professional engineer. Must have a "B" average.

Academic Fields/Career Goals: Engineering/Technology.

Award: Scholarship for use in junior or senior years; not renewable. *Number:* 1. *Amount:* $1200.

Eligibility Requirements: Applicant must be enrolled or expecting to enroll at an institution or university and studying in Illinois. Available to U.S. citizens.

Application Requirements: Application, essay, references, transcript. *Deadline:* January 31.

Contact: Illinois Society of Professional Engineers
600 South Second, Suite 403
Springfield, IL 62704
E-mail: info@ilspe.com

ILLINOIS SOCIETY OF PROFESSIONAL ENGINEERS/MELVIN E. AMSTUTZ MEMORIAL AWARD

Applicant must attend an Illinois university approved by the Accreditation Board of Engineering. Applicant must be at least a junior in university he or she attends, and must prove financial need. Engineering technology students are not eligible. Application deadline is January 31. Essay must address why applicant wishes to become a professional engineer. Must have a "B" average.

Academic Fields/Career Goals: Engineering/Technology.

Award: Scholarship for use in junior or senior years; not renewable. *Number:* 1. *Amount:* $1500.

Eligibility Requirements: Applicant must be enrolled or expecting to enroll at an institution or university and studying in Illinois. Available to U.S. citizens.

Application Requirements: Application, essay, financial need analysis, references. *Deadline:* January 31.

Contact: Illinois Society of Professional Engineers
600 South Second, Suite 403
Springfield, IL 62704
E-mail: info@ilspe.com

ILLINOIS SOCIETY OF PROFESSIONAL ENGINEERS/PEPPY MOLDOVAN MEMORIAL AWARD

Applicant must be female engineering student enrolled as a sophomore at a specified Illinois college or university. Applicant must be accepted at an accredited Illinois university.

Academic Fields/Career Goals: Engineering/Technology.

Award: Scholarship for use in sophomore, junior, or senior years. *Number:* 1. *Amount:* $1000.

Eligibility Requirements: Applicant must be enrolled or expecting to enroll at a two-year or four-year institution; female and studying in Illinois. Available to U.S. citizens.

Application Requirements: Application, essay, resume, references, transcript. *Deadline:* January 31.

Contact: Illinois Society of Professional Engineers
600 South Second, Suite 403
Springfield, IL 62704
E-mail: info@ilspe.com

ILLUMINATING ENGINEERING SOCIETY OF NORTH AMERICA   http://www.iesna.org

ROBERT W. THUNEN MEMORIAL SCHOLARSHIPS
• See page 100

INDEPENDENT LABORATORIES INSTITUTE SCHOLARSHIP ALLIANCE   http://www.acil.org

INDEPENDENT LABORATORIES INSTITUTE SCHOLARSHIP ALLIANCE
• See page 93

INDIANA SOCIETY OF PROFESSIONAL ENGINEERS   http://www.indspe.org

INDIANA ENGINEERING SCHOLARSHIP

Award for Indiana resident who attends an Indiana educational institution, or commutes daily to a school outside Indiana. Applicant must have accrued the minimum of one-half the credits required for an undergraduate ABET accredited engineering degree. For details and an application visit Web site: http://indspe.org.

Academic Fields/Career Goals: Engineering/Technology.

Award: Scholarship for use in freshman, sophomore, junior, or senior years; not renewable. *Number:* 3. *Amount:* $750.

Eligibility Requirements: Applicant must be enrolled or expecting to enroll full-time at an institution or university; resident of Indiana and studying in Indiana. Available to U.S. citizens.

Application Requirements: Application, interview, references, transcript. *Deadline:* May 1.

Contact: Indiana Society of Professional Engineers
PO Box 20806
Indianapolis, IN 46220
Phone: 317-255-2267
Fax: 317-255-2530
E-mail: lhowe@indy.net

INSTITUTE OF INDUSTRIAL ENGINEERS   http://www.iienet.org

A.O. PUTNAM MEMORIAL SCHOLARSHIP

One-time award for industrial engineering undergraduates at four-year accredited institutions. Applicants must be members of the Institute of Industrial Engineers, have a 3.4 GPA, and be nominated by a department head by November 15. Priority given to students who have demonstrated an interest in management consulting.

Academic Fields/Career Goals: Engineering/Technology.

Award: Scholarship for use in freshman, sophomore, junior, or senior years; not renewable. *Number:* 1. *Amount:* $600.

Eligibility Requirements: Applicant must be enrolled or expecting to enroll full-time at a four-year institution or university. Applicant or parent of applicant must be member of Institute of Industrial Engineers. Available to U.S. and non-U.S. citizens.

Application Requirements: Application, references, transcript, nomination. *Deadline:* November 15.

Contact: Sherry Richards, Chapter Operations Assistant
Institute of Industrial Engineers
3577 Parkway Lane
Suite 200
Norcross, GA 30092-2988
Phone: 770-449-0461 Ext. 118
Fax: 770-263-8532
E-mail: srichards@iienet.org

C.B. GAMBRELL UNDERGRADUATE SCHOLARSHIP

One-time award for undergraduate industrial engineering students who are U.S. citizens graduated from a U.S. high school with a class standing above freshman level in an ABET accredited IE program. Must be a member of Industrial Engineers, have a minimum GPA of 3.4, and be nominated by a department head.

Academic Fields/Career Goals: Engineering/Technology.

Award: Scholarship for use in sophomore, junior, or senior years; not renewable. *Number:* 1. *Amount:* $600.

Eligibility Requirements: Applicant must be enrolled or expecting to enroll full-time at a four-year institution or university. Applicant or parent of applicant must be member of Institute of Industrial Engineers. Available to U.S. citizens.

Application Requirements: Application, references, nomination. *Deadline:* November 15.

Contact: Sherry Richards, Chapter Operations Assistant
Institute of Industrial Engineers
3577 Parkway Lane
Suite 200
Norcross, GA 30092-2988
Phone: 770-449-0461 Ext. 118
Fax: 770-263-8532
E-mail: srichards@iienet.org

DWIGHT D. GARDNER SCHOLARSHIP

Scholarship of $1000 for undergraduate students enrolled in any school in the U.S. and its territories, Canada, and Mexico, provided the school's engineering program or equivalent is accredited by an agency recognized by IIE and the student is pursuing a course of study in industrial engineering. Must be an IIE member and have minimum 3.4 GPA. Must be nominated.

Academic Fields/Career Goals: Engineering/Technology.

Award: Scholarship for use in freshman, sophomore, junior, or senior years; not renewable. *Number:* 2. *Amount:* $1000.

Eligibility Requirements: Applicant must be enrolled or expecting to enroll full-time at a four-year institution or university. Applicant or

Institute of Industrial Engineers (continued)

parent of applicant must be member of Institute of Industrial Engineers. Available to U.S. and non-U.S. citizens.

Application Requirements: Application, essay, financial need analysis, references, transcript, nomination. *Deadline:* November 15.

Contact: Sherry Richards, Chapter Operations Assistant
Institute of Industrial Engineers
3577 Parkway Lane
Suite 200
Norcross, GA 30092-2988
Phone: 770-449-0461 Ext. 118
Fax: 770-263-8532
E-mail: srichards@iienet.org

IIE COUNCIL OF FELLOWS UNDERGRADUATE SCHOLARSHIP

Awards to undergraduate students enrolled in any school in the U.S. and its territories, Canada and Mexico, provided the school's engineering program or equivalent is accredited by an agency recognized by IIE and the student is pursuing a course of study in industrial engineering. Must be IIE member and have minimum 3.4 GPA. Write to IIE Headquarters to obtain application form.

Academic Fields/Career Goals: Engineering/Technology.

Award: Scholarship for use in freshman, sophomore, junior, or senior years; not renewable. *Amount:* $1000.

Eligibility Requirements: Applicant must be enrolled or expecting to enroll full-time at a four-year institution or university. Applicant or parent of applicant must be member of Institute of Industrial Engineers. Available to U.S. and non-U.S. citizens.

Application Requirements: Application. *Deadline:* November 15.

Contact: Sherry Richards, Chapter Operations Assistant
Institute of Industrial Engineers
3577 Parkway Lane
Suite 200
Norcross, GA 30092-2988
Phone: 770-449-0461 Ext. 118
Fax: 770-263-8532
E-mail: srichards@iienet.org

LISA ZAKEN AWARD FOR EXCELLENCE

Award for undergraduate and graduate students enrolled in any school, and pursuing a course of study in industrial engineering. Award is intended to recognize excellence in scholarly activities and leadership related to the industrial engineering profession on campus.

Academic Fields/Career Goals: Engineering/Technology.

Award: Prize for use in freshman, sophomore, junior, senior, or graduate years. *Amount:* $600.

Eligibility Requirements: Applicant must be enrolled or expecting to enroll full-time at an institution or university. Applicant or parent of applicant must be member of Institute of Industrial Engineers. Available to U.S. and non-U.S. citizens.

Application Requirements: Application, essay, references, nomination. *Deadline:* February 15.

Contact: Sherry Richards, Chapter Operations Assistant
Institute of Industrial Engineers
3577 Parkway Lane
Suite 200
Norcross, GA 30092-2988
Phone: 770-449-0461 Ext. 118
Fax: 770-263-8532
E-mail: srichards@iienet.org

MARVIN MUNDEL MEMORIAL SCHOLARSHIP

Scholarship awarded to undergraduate students enrolled in any school in the U.S., Canada, or Mexico with an accredited industrial engineering program. Priority given to students who have demonstrated an interest in work measurement and methods engineering. Must be active Institute members with 3.4 GPA or above. Must be nominated by department head or faculty adviser.

Academic Fields/Career Goals: Engineering/Technology.

Award: Scholarship for use in freshman, sophomore, junior, or senior years; not renewable. *Amount:* $600.

Eligibility Requirements: Applicant must be enrolled or expecting to enroll at a four-year institution or university. Applicant or parent of applicant must be member of Institute of Industrial Engineers. Available to U.S. and non-U.S. citizens.

Application Requirements: Application, nomination. *Deadline:* November 15.

Contact: Sherry Richards, Chapter Operations Assistant
Institute of Industrial Engineers
3577 Parkway Lane
Suite 200
Norcross, GA 30092-2988
Phone: 770-449-0461 Ext. 118
Fax: 770-263-8532
E-mail: srichards@iienet.org

UNITED PARCEL SERVICE SCHOLARSHIP FOR FEMALE STUDENTS

One-time award for female undergraduate students enrolled at any school in the U.S., Canada, or Mexico in an industrial engineering program. Must be a member of Institute of Industrial Engineers, have a minimum GPA of 3.4, and be nominated by a department head.

Academic Fields/Career Goals: Engineering/Technology.

Award: Scholarship for use in freshman, sophomore, junior, or senior years; not renewable. *Number:* 1. *Amount:* $4000.

Eligibility Requirements: Applicant must be enrolled or expecting to enroll full-time at a four-year or technical institution or university and female. Applicant or parent of applicant must be member of Institute of Industrial Engineers. Available to U.S. and non-U.S. citizens.

Application Requirements: Application, references, transcript, nomination. *Deadline:* November 15.

Contact: Sherry Richards, Chapter Operations Assistant
Institute of Industrial Engineers
3577 Parkway Lane
Suite 200
Norcross, GA 30092-2988
Phone: 770-449-0461 Ext. 118
Fax: 770-263-8532
E-mail: srichards@iienet.org

UPS SCHOLARSHIP FOR MINORITY STUDENTS

One-time award for minority undergraduate students enrolled at any school in the U.S., Canada, or Mexico in an industrial engineering program. Must be a member of Institute of Industrial Engineers, have minimum GPA of 3.4, and be nominated by a department head.

Academic Fields/Career Goals: Engineering/Technology.

Award: Scholarship for use in freshman, sophomore, junior, or senior years; not renewable. *Number:* varies. *Amount:* $4000.

Eligibility Requirements: Applicant must be American Indian/Alaska Native, Asian/Pacific Islander, Black (non-Hispanic), or Hispanic and enrolled or expecting to enroll at a four-year or technical institution or university. Applicant or parent of applicant must be member of Institute of Industrial Engineers. Available to U.S. and non-U.S. citizens.

Application Requirements: Application, references, transcript, nomination. *Deadline:* November 15.

Contact: Sherry Richards, Chapter Operations Assistant
Institute of Industrial Engineers
3577 Parkway Lane
Suite 200
Norcross, GA 30092-2988
Phone: 770-449-0461 Ext. 118
Fax: 770-263-8532
E-mail: srichards@iienet.org

INSTRUMENTATION, SYSTEMS, AND AUTOMATION SOCIETY (ISA) http://www.isa.org

INSTRUMENTATION, SYSTEMS, AND AUTOMATION SOCIETY (ISA) SCHOLARSHIP PROGRAM

• *See page 123*

INTERNATIONAL SOCIETY FOR OPTICAL ENGINEERING-SPIE   http://www.spie.org/info/scholarships

MICHAEL KIDGER MEMORIAL SCHOLARSHIP IN OPTICAL DESIGN

Scholarship to be awarded to a student of optical design. The candidate must have at least one year after the award to complete his or her chosen course of study.

Academic Fields/Career Goals: Engineering/Technology.

Award: Scholarship for use in junior year. *Amount:* up to $5000.

Eligibility Requirements: Applicant must be enrolled or expecting to enroll at a four-year institution or university. Available to U.S. citizens.

Application Requirements: Application, references, summary (5 pages maximum) of academic background and interest in pursuing training or research in optical design, limited supporting material may be attached. *Deadline:* February 28.

Contact: David Williamson
International Society for Optical Engineering-SPIE
PO Box 10
Bellingham, WA 98227-0010
E-mail: education@spie.org

SPIE EDUCATIONAL SCHOLARSHIPS IN OPTICAL SCIENCE AND ENGINEERING
• *See page 93*

INTERNATIONAL TECHNOLOGY EDUCATION ASSOCIATION   http://www.iteaconnect.org/index.html

INTERNATIONAL TECHNOLOGY EDUCATION ASSOCIATION UNDERGRADUATE SCHOLARSHIP
• *See page 228*

INTERNATIONAL TECHNOLOGY EDUCATION ASSOCIATION UNDERGRADUATE SCHOLARSHIP IN TECHNOLOGY EDUCATION

A scholarship for undergraduate students pursuing a degree in technology education/technological studies. Applicants must be members of the Association.

Academic Fields/Career Goals: Engineering/Technology.

Award: Scholarship for use in freshman, sophomore, or junior years; not renewable. *Number:* 3. *Amount:* $1000.

Eligibility Requirements: Applicant must be enrolled or expecting to enroll full-time at a four-year institution or university. Applicant or parent of applicant must be member of International Technology Education Association. Applicant must have 2.5 GPA or higher. Available to U.S. and non-U.S. citizens.

Application Requirements: Application, resume, references, transcript. *Deadline:* December 1.

Contact: Barbara Mongold, Undergraduate Scholarship Committee
International Technology Education Association
1914 Association Drive, Suite 201
Reston, VA 20191
Phone: 703-860-2100
Fax: 703-860-0353
E-mail: iteaordr@iris.org

MALEY/FOUNDATION FOR TECHNOLOGY EDUCATION SCHOLARSHIP

One-time award for K-12 technology teachers who are pursuing graduate study full or part time. Applicants must be members of the Association. Application deadline is December 1.

Academic Fields/Career Goals: Engineering/Technology.

Award: Scholarship for use in freshman, sophomore, junior, senior, or graduate years; not renewable. *Number:* 1. *Amount:* $1000.

Eligibility Requirements: Applicant must be enrolled or expecting to enroll full or part-time at an institution or university. Applicant or parent of applicant must be member of International Technology Education Association. Applicant or parent of applicant must have employment or volunteer experience in teaching. Available to U.S. and non-U.S. citizens.

Application Requirements: Application, resume, references, transcript, documentation of acceptance into graduate school. *Deadline:* December 1.

Contact: Barbara Mongold, Scholarship Committee
International Technology Education Association
Undergraduate Scholarship Committee
1914 Association Drive, Suite 201
Reston, VA 20191-1539
Phone: 703-860-2100
Fax: 703-860-0353
E-mail: iteaordr@iris.org

TSA SPONSORED ITEA SCHOLARSHIP
• *See page 229*

INTERNATIONAL UNION OF ELECTRONIC, ELECTRICAL, SALARIED, MACHINE, AND FURNITURE WORKERS-CWA   http://www.iue-cwa.org

DAVID J. FITZMAURICE ENGINEERING SCHOLARSHIP

One award for a student whose parent or grandparent is a member of the IUE-CWA. Applicant must be pursuing undergraduate engineering degree. Submit family financial status form with application. One-time award of $2000.

Academic Fields/Career Goals: Engineering/Technology.

Award: Scholarship for use in freshman, sophomore, junior, senior, or graduate years; not renewable. *Number:* 1. *Amount:* $2000.

Eligibility Requirements: Applicant must be enrolled or expecting to enroll full-time at a two-year or four-year or technical institution or university. Applicant or parent of applicant must be member of International Union of Electronic, Electrical, Salaries, Machine and Furniture Workers. Available to U.S. citizens.

Application Requirements: Application, essay, financial need analysis, references, test scores, transcript. *Deadline:* March 31.

Contact: Trudy Humphrey, Director
International Union of Electronic, Electrical, Salaried, Machine, and Furniture Workers-CWA
501 3rd Street, NW
Washington, DC 20001
Phone: 202-434-9591
Fax: 202-434-1252
E-mail: thumphrey@cwa-union.org

KOREAN-AMERICAN SCIENTISTS AND ENGINEERS ASSOCIATION   http://www.ksea.org

KSEA SCHOLARSHIPS
• *See page 245*

LEAGUE OF UNITED LATIN AMERICAN CITIZENS NATIONAL EDUCATIONAL SERVICE CENTERS, INC.   http://www.lnesc.org

GE/LULAC SCHOLARSHIP
• *See page 150*

GM/LULAC SCHOLARSHIP

Renewable award for minority students who are pursuing an undergraduate degree in engineering at an accredited college or university. Must maintain a minimum 3.0 GPA. Selection is based in part on the likelihood of pursuing a successful career in engineering. Application deadline is July 15.

Academic Fields/Career Goals: Engineering/Technology.

Award: Scholarship for use in freshman, sophomore, junior, or senior years; renewable. *Number:* up to 20. *Amount:* up to $2000.

Eligibility Requirements: Applicant must be Hispanic and enrolled or expecting to enroll full-time at a four-year institution or university. Applicant must have 3.0 GPA or higher. Available to U.S. citizens.

League of United Latin American Citizens National Educational Service Centers, Inc. (continued)

Application Requirements: Application, essay, references, transcript. *Deadline:* July 15.

Contact: Lorena Maymi-Garrido, Scholarship Administrator
League of United Latin American Citizens National Educational
Service Centers, Inc.
2000 L Street, NW, Suite 610
Washington, DC 20036
Phone: 202-835-9646 Ext. 10
Fax: 202-835-9685
E-mail: lnescaward@aol.com

LOS ANGELES COUNCIL OF BLACK PROFESSIONAL ENGINEERS   http://www.lablackengineers.org

AL-BEN SCHOLARSHIP FOR ACADEMIC INCENTIVE
• *See page 164*

AL-BEN SCHOLARSHIP FOR PROFESSIONAL MERIT
• *See page 165*

AL-BEN SCHOLARSHIP FOR SCHOLASTIC ACHIEVEMENT
• *See page 165*

MAINE SOCIETY OF PROFESSIONAL ENGINEERS

MAINE SOCIETY OF PROFESSIONAL ENGINEERS VERNON T. SWAINE-ROBERT E. CHUTE SCHOLARSHIP

Nonrenewable scholarship for full-time study for freshmen only. Must be a Maine resident. Deadline: March 1. Application can also be obtained by sending email to rgmglads@twi.net

Academic Fields/Career Goals: Engineering/Technology; Engineering-Related Technologies.

Award: Scholarship for use in freshman year; not renewable. *Number:* 1–2. *Amount:* $1500.

Eligibility Requirements: Applicant must be enrolled or expecting to enroll full-time at a four-year institution or university; resident of Maine and studying in Maine. Applicant must have 2.5 GPA or higher. Available to U.S. citizens.

Application Requirements: Application, essay, interview, references, self-addressed stamped envelope, test scores, transcript. *Deadline:* March 1.

Contact: Robert G. Martin, Scholarship Committee Chairman
Maine Society of Professional Engineers
RRI Box 70
Belgrade, ME 04917
Phone: 207-495-2244
E-mail: rgmglads@twi.net

MARION D. AND EVA S. PEEPLES FOUNDATION TRUST SCHOLARSHIP PROGRAM   http://www.jccf.org

MARION A. AND EVA S. PEEPLES SCHOLARSHIPS
• *See page 230*

MARYLAND ASSOCIATION OF PRIVATE COLLEGES AND CAREER SCHOOLS   http://www.mapccs.org

MARYLAND ASSOCIATION OF PRIVATE COLLEGES AND CAREER SCHOOLS SCHOLARSHIP
• *See page 150*

MICHIGAN SOCIETY OF PROFESSIONAL ENGINEERS   http://www.michiganspe.org

MICHIGAN SOCIETY OF PROFESSIONAL ENGINEERS UNDESIGNATED GRANT
• *See page 165*

MSPE AUXILIARY GRANT FOR UNDERGRADUATE STUDY
• *See page 174*

MICRON TECHNOLOGY FOUNDATION, INC.   http://www.micron.com

MICRON SCIENCE AND TECHNOLOGY SCHOLARS PROGRAM
• *See page 165*

MIDWEST ROOFING CONTRACTORS ASSOCIATION   http://www.mrca.org

MRCA FOUNDATION SCHOLARSHIP PROGRAM
• *See page 94*

MINERALS, METALS, AND MATERIALS SOCIETY (TMS)   http://www.tms.org

TMS J. KEITH BRIMACOMBE PRESIDENTIAL SCHOLARSHIP

One award of $5000 for a Minerals, Metals, and Materials Society student member who is an undergraduate student(sophomore and junior) majoring in metallurgical engineering, materials science and engineering, or minerals processing/extraction programs. $1000 travel stipend for recipient to attend the TMS Annual Banquet to formally receive scholarship.

Academic Fields/Career Goals: Engineering/Technology; Engineering-Related Technologies; Materials Science, Engineering, and Metallurgy.

Award: Scholarship for use in freshman, sophomore, junior, or senior years; not renewable. *Number:* 1. *Amount:* $5000.

Eligibility Requirements: Applicant must be enrolled or expecting to enroll full-time at a four-year institution. Applicant must have 2.5 GPA or higher. Available to U.S. and non-U.S. citizens.

Application Requirements: Application, essay, references, transcript. *Deadline:* March 15.

Contact: TMS Student Awards Program
Minerals, Metals, and Materials Society (TMS)
184 Thorn Hill Road
Warrendale, PA 15086
Phone: 724-776-9000 Ext. 259
Fax: 724-776-3770

TMS OUTSTANDING STUDENT PAPER CONTEST-UNDERGRADUATE

Two prizes for essays on global or national issues, as well as technical research papers. Metallurgy or materials science papers will be considered. Applicants must be TMS student members or include completed membership application with dues payment and essay to become eligible. Submit one entry per student. Prize includes cash and travel expenses.

Academic Fields/Career Goals: Engineering/Technology; Engineering-Related Technologies; Materials Science, Engineering, and Metallurgy.

Award: Prize for use in freshman, sophomore, junior, or senior years; not renewable. *Number:* 2. *Amount:* $500–$1000.

Eligibility Requirements: Applicant must be enrolled or expecting to enroll full-time at a four-year institution. Available to U.S. and non-U.S. citizens.

Application Requirements: Application, essay. *Deadline:* May 1.

Contact: TMS Student Awards Program
Minerals, Metals, and Materials Society (TMS)
184 Thorn Hill Road
Warrendale, PA 15086
Phone: 724-776-9000 Ext. 259
Fax: 724-776-3770

TMS/EMPMD GILBERT CHIN SCHOLARSHIP

Award of $2000 to a TMS student member who is a college undergraduate studying subjects in relation to electronic, magnetic, and/or photonic materials. Only to sophomore and junior undergraduate applicants. Enrolled full-time in a program that includes the study of electronic materials. An additional $500 travel award for recipient to attend the TMS Annual Meeting to accept award.

Academic Fields/Career Goals: Engineering/Technology; Engineering-Related Technologies; Materials Science, Engineering, and Metallurgy.

Award: Scholarship for use in freshman, sophomore, junior, or senior years; not renewable. *Number:* 1. *Amount:* $2000.

Eligibility Requirements: Applicant must be enrolled or expecting to enroll full-time at a four-year institution. Available to U.S. and non-U.S. citizens.

Application Requirements: Application, essay, references, transcript. *Deadline:* March 15.

Contact: TMS Student Awards Program
Minerals, Metals, and Materials Society (TMS)
184 Thorn Hill Road
Warrendale, PA 15086
Phone: 724-776-9000 Ext. 259
Fax: 724-776-3770
E-mail: students@tms.org.

TMS/EPD SCHOLARSHIP

Four awards of $2000 for TMS student members majoring in the extraction and processing of materials. It is given to college sophomore and juniors enrolled full-time in a program relating to the extraction and processing of minerals, metals, and materials. Recipients are given the opportunity to select up to five Extraction and Processing Division-sponsored conference proceedings or textbooks to be donated to the recipient's college/university in his/her name.

Academic Fields/Career Goals: Engineering/Technology; Engineering-Related Technologies; Materials Science, Engineering, and Metallurgy.

Award: Scholarship for use in freshman, sophomore, junior, or senior years; not renewable. *Number:* 4. *Amount:* $2000.

Eligibility Requirements: Applicant must be enrolled or expecting to enroll full-time at a four-year institution. Available to U.S. and non-U.S. citizens.

Application Requirements: Application, essay, references, transcript. *Deadline:* March 15.

Contact: TMS Student Awards Program
Minerals, Metals, and Materials Society (TMS)
184 Thorn Hill Road
Warrendale, PA 15086
Phone: 724-776-9000 Ext. 259
Fax: 724-776-3770

TMS/INTERNATIONAL SYMPOSIUM ON SUPERALLOYS SCHOLARSHIP PROGRAM

Two awards of $2000 for undergraduate(sophomore and junior) and graduate student member of TMS majoring in metallurgy, materials science and engineering, or materials processing/extraction programs. Preference given to students pursuing a curriculum/career in superalloys. Scholarship will be awarded at the TMS Fall Conference.

Academic Fields/Career Goals: Engineering/Technology; Engineering-Related Technologies; Materials Science, Engineering, and Metallurgy.

Award: Scholarship for use in sophomore, junior, or graduate years; not renewable. *Number:* 2. *Amount:* $2000.

Eligibility Requirements: Applicant must be enrolled or expecting to enroll full-time at a four-year institution or university. Available to U.S. and non-U.S. citizens.

Application Requirements: Application, essay, references, transcript. *Deadline:* March 15.

Contact: TMS Student Awards Program
Minerals, Metals, and Materials Society (TMS)
184 Thorn Hill Road
Warrendale, PA 15086
Phone: 724-776-9000 Ext. 259
Fax: 724-776-3770

TMS/LMD SCHOLARSHIP PROGRAM

Three awards of $4000 for undergraduate TMS student members majoring in the study of non-ferrous metallurgy. Preference given to juniors and seniors enrolled full-time in a non-ferrous metallurgy program, and to individuals who have participated in a relevant industrial co-op program. Recipients are given the opportunity of selecting up to $300 in Light Metals Division-sponsored conference proceedings or textbooks to be donated to the recipient's college/university library in his/her name.

Academic Fields/Career Goals: Engineering/Technology; Engineering-Related Technologies; Materials Science, Engineering, and Metallurgy.

Award: Scholarship for use in freshman, sophomore, junior, or senior years; not renewable. *Number:* 3. *Amount:* $4000.

Eligibility Requirements: Applicant must be enrolled or expecting to enroll full-time at a four-year institution. Available to U.S. and non-U.S. citizens.

Application Requirements: Application, essay, references, transcript. *Deadline:* March 15.

Contact: TMS Student Awards Program
Minerals, Metals, and Materials Society (TMS)
184 Thorn Hill Road
Warrendale, PA 15086
Phone: 724-776-9000 Ext. 259
Fax: 724-776-3770

TMS/STRUCTURAL MATERIALS DIVISION SCHOLARSHIP

Two awards of $2500 for TMS student members who are undergraduates(sophomore and junior) majoring in materials science and engineering or physical metallurgy. Recipient will be given $500 in travel expenses to the TMS Annual Meeting to accept his/her award. Preference given to seniors enrolled full time in an engineering program relating to the structure, property, and processing of materials.

Academic Fields/Career Goals: Engineering/Technology; Engineering-Related Technologies; Materials Science, Engineering, and Metallurgy.

Award: Scholarship for use in freshman, sophomore, junior, or senior years; not renewable. *Number:* 2. *Amount:* $2500.

Eligibility Requirements: Applicant must be enrolled or expecting to enroll full-time at a four-year institution. Available to U.S. and non-U.S. citizens.

Application Requirements: Application, essay, references, transcript. *Deadline:* March 15.

Contact: TMS Student Awards Program
Minerals, Metals, and Materials Society (TMS)
184 Thorn Hill Road
Warrendale, PA 15086
Phone: 724-776-9000 Ext. 259
Fax: 724-776-3770

NASA DELAWARE SPACE GRANT CONSORTIUM
http://www.delspace.org

NASA DELAWARE SPACE GRANT UNDERGRADUATE TUITION SCHOLARSHIP
• See page 94

NASA IDAHO SPACE GRANT CONSORTIUM
http://isgc.uidaho.edu

NASA IDAHO SPACE GRANT CONSORTIUM SCHOLARSHIP PROGRAM
• See page 94

NASA MINNESOTA SPACE GRANT CONSORTIUM
http://www.aem.umn.edu/msgc

MINNESOTA SPACE GRANT CONSORTIUM
• See page 124

NASA MONTANA SPACE GRANT CONSORTIUM
http://www.spacegrant.montana.edu

MONTANA SPACE GRANT SCHOLARSHIP PROGRAM
• See page 125

NASA NEBRASKA SPACE GRANT CONSORTIUM
http://nasa.unomaha.edu

NASA NEBRASKA SPACE GRANT
• See page 125

NASA NEVADA SPACE GRANT CONSORTIUM
http://www.unr.edu/spacegrant

UNIVERSITY AND COMMUNITY COLLEGE SYSTEM OF NEVADA NASA SPACE GRANT AND FELLOWSHIP PROGRAM
• See page 125

NASA VERMONT SPACE GRANT CONSORTIUM
http://www.vtspacegrant.org

VERMONT SPACE GRANT CONSORTIUM SCHOLARSHIP PROGRAM
• See page 94

NASA VIRGINIA SPACE GRANT CONSORTIUM
http://www.vsgc.odu.edu

VIRGINIA SPACE GRANT CONSORTIUM COMMUNITY COLLEGE SCHOLARSHIPS
* See page 125

VIRGINIA SPACE GRANT CONSORTIUM TEACHER EDUCATION SCHOLARSHIPS
* See page 125

NASA WEST VIRGINIA SPACE GRANT CONSORTIUM
http://www.nasa.wvu.edu

WEST VIRGINIA SPACE GRANT CONSORTIUM UNDERGRADUATE SCHOLARSHIP PROGRAM
* See page 126

NASA/MARYLAND SPACE GRANT CONSORTIUM
http://www.mdspacegrant.org

NASA MARYLAND SPACE GRANT CONSORTIUM UNDERGRADUATE SCHOLARSHIPS
* See page 139

NATIONAL ACTION COUNCIL FOR MINORITIES IN ENGINEERING-NACME, INC.
http://www.nacme.org

NACME SCHOLARS PROGRAM

Renewable award for African-American, American-Indian, or Latino student enrolled in a baccalaureate engineering program. Must attend an ABET-accredited institution full-time and complete one semester with a minimum 2.7 GPA. Must be a U.S. citizen. Award money is given to participating institutions who select applicants and disperse funds. Check Web site for details: http://www.nacme.org

Academic Fields/Career Goals: Engineering/Technology.

Award: Scholarship for use in freshman, sophomore, junior, or senior years; renewable. *Number:* varies. *Amount:* up to $5000.

Eligibility Requirements: Applicant must be American Indian/Alaska Native, Black (non-Hispanic), or Hispanic and enrolled or expecting to enroll full-time at a four-year institution or university. Available to U.S. citizens.

Application Requirements: Application, financial need analysis, references. *Deadline:* Continuous.

Contact: Aileen M. Walter, Director, Scholar Management
National Action Council for Minorities in Engineering-NACME, Inc.
440 Hamilton Avenue, Suite 302
White Plains, NY 10601
Phone: 914-539-4010

NACME/NASA SPACE STATION ENGINEERING SCHOLARS PROGRAM

Scholarships available for applicants attending designated minority institutions. Must have a minimum 3.0 GPA and pursue studies in engineering. Must demonstrate financial need and have earned no more than 39 credit hours. Check Web site for details http://www.nacme.org

Academic Fields/Career Goals: Engineering/Technology.

Award: Scholarship for use in freshman, sophomore, junior, or senior years; renewable. *Number:* 1. *Amount:* varies.

Eligibility Requirements: Applicant must be enrolled or expecting to enroll full-time at a four-year institution or university. Applicant must have 3.0 GPA or higher. Available to U.S. citizens.

Application Requirements: Application, financial need analysis. *Deadline:* Continuous.

Contact: Laurel Lichtenberger, Undergraduate Student Programs
National Action Council for Minorities in Engineering-NACME, Inc.
Mail Code XA-D
Kennedy Space Center, FL 32899
Phone: 321-867-4036
Fax: 321-867-7242
E-mail: laurel.lichtenberger-1@ksc.nasa.gov

NATIONAL ASSOCIATION OF WATER COMPANIES-NEW JERSEY CHAPTER

NATIONAL ASSOCIATION OF WATER COMPANIES-NEW JERSEY CHAPTER SCHOLARSHIP
* See page 139

NATIONAL ASSOCIATION OF WOMEN IN CONSTRUCTION
http://nawic.org

NAWIC UNDERGRADUATE SCHOLARSHIPS
* See page 100

NATIONAL FEDERATION OF THE BLIND
http://www.nfb.org

HOWARD BROWN RICKARD SCHOLARSHIP
* See page 101

NATIONAL INSTITUTE OF BUILDING SCIENCES, MULTIHAZARD MITIGATION COUNCIL
http://www.nibs.org

ARCHITECTURE, CONSTRUCTION, AND ENGINEERING MENTOR PROGRAM SCHOLARSHIPS
* See page 101

NATIONAL INVENTORS HALL OF FAME
http://www.invent.org

COLLEGIATE INVENTORS COMPETITION - GRAND PRIZE
* See page 95

COLLEGIATE INVENTORS COMPETITION FOR UNDERGRADUATE STUDENTS
* See page 95

NATIONAL OCEANIC AND ATMOSPHERIC ADMINISTRATION
http://see.orau.org

NATIONAL OCEANIC AND ATMOSPHERIC ADMINISTRATION EDUCATIONAL PARTNERSHIP PROGRAM WITH MINORITY SERVING INSTITUTIONS UNDERGRADUATE SCHOLARSHIP

Scholarships for junior and senior year students attending minority serving institutions pursuing degrees in areas related to the National Oceanic and Atmospheric Administration. Must be U.S. citizen. Tuition and fees paid ($4000 maximum).

Academic Fields/Career Goals: Engineering/Technology; Environmental Science; Geography; Marine Biology; Mathematics; Meteorology/Atmospheric Science; Meteorology/Atmospheric Science; Oceanography; Physical Sciences and Math.

Award: Scholarship for use in junior or senior years. *Amount:* up to $4650.

Eligibility Requirements: Applicant must be Black (non-Hispanic) or Hispanic and enrolled or expecting to enroll full or part-time at a four-year institution or university. Available to U.S. citizens.

Application Requirements: Application. *Deadline:* Continuous.

Contact: Carl Wheeler, Program Manager
National Oceanic and Atmospheric Administration
c/o ORISE
120 Badger Avenue, PO Box 117
Oak Ridge, TN 37831-0117
Phone: 865-241-6704
E-mail: Wheelerc@orau.gov

NATIONAL SOCIETY OF PROFESSIONAL ENGINEERS
http://www.nspe.org

DOMINICK SARCI MEMORIAL SCHOLARSHIP

Scholarship awards $1500 to a senior at any high school who will be attending an ABET-accredited engineering program at a U.S. college/university in the Fall 2006 Semester. Deadline is March 1.

Academic Fields/Career Goals: Engineering/Technology.

Award: Scholarship for use in freshman, sophomore, junior, senior, graduate, or postgraduate years; not renewable. *Number:* 2. *Amount:* $1500.

Eligibility Requirements: Applicant must be enrolled or expecting to enroll at a two-year or four-year or technical institution or university. Available to U.S. citizens.

Application Requirements: Application, references, self-addressed stamped envelope. *Deadline:* March 1.

Contact: Bronx Chapter - NYSSPE
National Society of Professional Engineers
PO Box 126
Bronx, NY 10471-0126

MAUREEN L. AND HOWARD N. BLITMAN, PE SCHOLARSHIP TO PROMOTE DIVERSITY IN ENGINEERING
• See page 166

NATIONAL SOCIETY OF PROFESSIONAL ENGINEERS/AUXILIARY SCHOLARSHIP
• See page 166

PAUL H. ROBBINS HONORARY SCHOLARSHIP
• See page 166

PROFESSIONAL ENGINEERS IN INDUSTRY SCHOLARSHIP
• See page 167

VIRGINIA HENRY MEMORIAL SCHOLARSHIP
• See page 167

WILLIAM H. BAILEY JR. MEMORIAL SCHOLARSHIP

Scholarship of $1000 to an African-American college student who is a resident of the Bronx, NY and who has completed one year of engineering coursework at an ABET-accredited engineering program at a U.S. college/university. Deadline is March 1.

Academic Fields/Career Goals: Engineering/Technology.

Award: Scholarship for use in freshman, sophomore, junior, senior, graduate, or postgraduate years; not renewable. *Number:* 1. *Amount:* $1000.

Eligibility Requirements: Applicant must be Black (non-Hispanic); enrolled or expecting to enroll full-time at a two-year or four-year or technical institution or university and resident of New York. Available to U.S. citizens.

Application Requirements: Application, references, transcript. *Deadline:* March 1.

Contact: Scholarship Co-ordinate
National Society of Professional Engineers
PO Box 126
Bronx, NY 10471-0126

NATIONAL STONE, SAND AND GRAVEL ASSOCIATION (NSSGA)   http://www.nssga.org

BARRY K. WENDT MEMORIAL SCHOLARSHIP

Restricted to a student in an engineering school who plans to pursue a career in the aggregates industry. One-time award for full-time students attending a four-year college or university.

Academic Fields/Career Goals: Engineering/Technology; Engineering-Related Technologies.

Award: Scholarship for use in freshman, sophomore, junior, or senior years; not renewable. *Number:* 1. *Amount:* up to $2500.

Eligibility Requirements: Applicant must be enrolled or expecting to enroll full-time at a four-year institution or university. Available to U.S. and non-U.S. citizens.

Application Requirements: Application, essay, references, transcript. *Deadline:* April 30.

Contact: Wendt Memorial Scholarship Committee, c/o NSSGA
National Stone, Sand and Gravel Association (NSSGA)
1605 King Street
Arlington, VA 22314
Phone: 703-525-8788
Fax: 703-525-7782
E-mail: info@nssga.org

NATIONAL URBAN LEAGUE   http://www.nul.org

BLACK EXECUTIVE EXCHANGE PROGRAM JERRY BARTOW SCHOLARSHIP FUND
• See page 151

NEW YORK STATE EDUCATION DEPARTMENT   http://www.highered.nysed.gov

REGENTS PROFESSIONAL OPPORTUNITY SCHOLARSHIP
• See page 67

ORANGE COUNTY COMMUNITY FOUNDATION   http://www.heef.org

ARCHITECTURE AND ENGINEERING SCHOLARSHIP PROGRAM
• See page 102

OREGON STUDENT ASSISTANCE COMMISSION   http://www.osac.state.or.us

HOMESTEAD CAPITAL HOUSING SCHOLARSHIP
• See page 68

HOWARD VOLLUM AMERICAN INDIAN SCHOLARSHIP
• See page 194

KEY TECHNOLOGY SCHOLARSHIP
• See page 84

PLASTICS INSTITUTE OF AMERICA   http://www.plasticsinstitute.org/

PLASTICS PIONEERS SCHOLARSHIPS

Financial grants awarded to undergraduate students needing help in their education expenses to enter into a full-time career in any and all segments of the plastics industry, with emphasis on "hands on" participation in the many fields where members of the Plastics Pioneers Association have spent their professional years. Applicants must be U.S. citizens.

Academic Fields/Career Goals: Engineering/Technology; Engineering-Related Technologies; Materials Science, Engineering, and Metallurgy; Trade/Technical Specialties.

Award: Scholarship for use in freshman, sophomore, junior, or senior years; renewable. *Number:* 30–40. *Amount:* $1500.

Eligibility Requirements: Applicant must be enrolled or expecting to enroll full or part-time at a two-year or four-year or technical institution. Available to U.S. citizens.

Application Requirements: Application, essay, references, transcript. *Deadline:* April 1.

Contact: Aldo Crugnola, Executive Director
Plastics Institute of America
333 Aiken Street
Lowell, MA 01854
Phone: 978-934-2575
Fax: 978-459-9420
E-mail: pia@uml.edu

PLUMBING-HEATING-COOLING CONTRACTORS ASSOCIATION EDUCATION FOUNDATION   http://www.phccweb.org

BRADFORD WHITE CORPORATION SCHOLARSHIP
• See page 102

DELTA FAUCET COMPANY SCHOLARSHIP PROGRAM
• See page 102

PHCC EDUCATIONAL FOUNDATION NEED-BASED SCHOLARSHIP
• See page 102

PHCC EDUCATIONAL FOUNDATION SCHOLARSHIP PROGRAM
• See page 103

PNC BANK TRUST DEPARTMENT

H. FLETCHER BROWN SCHOLARSHIP
• See page 211

PROFESSIONAL CONSTRUCTION ESTIMATORS ASSOCIATION http://www.pcea.org

TED WILSON MEMORIAL SCHOLARSHIP FOUNDATION
• See page 212

ROBERT H. MOLLOHAN FAMILY CHARITABLE FOUNDATION, INC. http://www.mollohanfoundation.org

HIGH TECHNOLOGY SCHOLARS PROGRAM
• See page 141

ROCKY MOUNTAIN COAL MINING INSTITUTE http://www.rmcmi.org

ROCKY MOUNTAIN COAL MINING INSTITUTE SCHOLARSHIP
• See page 167

SIGMA XI, THE SCIENTIFIC RESEARCH SOCIETY http://www.sigmaxi.org

SIGMA XI GRANTS-IN-AID OF RESEARCH
• See page 84

SOCIETY FOR IMAGING SCIENCE AND TECHNOLOGY http://www.imaging.org/

RAYMOND DAVIS SCHOLARSHIP

Award available to an undergraduate junior or senior or graduate student enrolled full-time in an accredited program of photographic, imaging science or engineering. Minimum award is $1000. Applications processed between October 15 and December 15 only.

Academic Fields/Career Goals: Engineering/Technology; Physical Sciences and Math.

Award: Scholarship for use in junior, senior, or graduate years; not renewable. *Number:* 1–2. *Amount:* $1000.

Eligibility Requirements: Applicant must be enrolled or expecting to enroll full-time at a four-year institution or university. Available to U.S. citizens.

Application Requirements: Application, autobiography, references, transcript. *Deadline:* December 15.

Contact: Donna Smith, Production Manager
Society for Imaging Science and Technology
7003 Kilworth Lane
Springfield, VA 22151
Phone: 703-642-9090 Ext. 17
Fax: 703-642-9094
E-mail: info@imaging.org

SOCIETY OF AMERICAN MILITARY ENGINEERS— VIRGINIA PENINSULA POST http://posts.same.org/vapeninsula/

THE VIRGINIA PENINSULA POST OF THE SOCIETY OF AMERICAN MILITARY ENGINEERS (S.A.M.E.) SCHOLARSHIP
• See page 103

SOCIETY OF AUTOMOTIVE ENGINEERS http://www.sae.org

BMW/SAE ENGINEERING SCHOLARSHIP
• See page 129

DETROIT SECTION SAE TECHNICAL SCHOLARSHIP

Applicants must be a child or grandchild of a current SAE Detroit Section member and intend to enroll in a two- or four-year engineering or science program at an accredited college or university. A minimum 3.0 grade point average and 1200 SAT i or 28 ACT composite score and demonstrated financial need is required.

Academic Fields/Career Goals: Engineering/Technology; Engineering-Related Technologies; Science, Technology, and Society.

Award: Scholarship for use in freshman, sophomore, junior, or senior years; renewable. *Number:* 1. *Amount:* up to $2500.

Eligibility Requirements: Applicant must be high school student and planning to enroll or expecting to enroll full-time at a two-year or

four-year institution or university. Applicant or parent of applicant must be member of Society of Automotive Engineers. Applicant must have 3.0 GPA or higher. Available to U.S. citizens.

Application Requirements: Application, financial need analysis, test scores, transcript. *Deadline:* December 1.

Contact: Connie Harnish, SAE Educational Relations
Society of Automotive Engineers
400 Commonwealth Drive
Warrendale, PA 15096-0001
Phone: 724-772-4047
E-mail: connie@sae.org

EDWARD D. HENDRICKSON/SAE ENGINEERING SCHOLARSHIP
• See page 129

FRED M. YOUNG SR./SAE ENGINEERING SCHOLARSHIP

Renewable scholarship for student enrolled in an ABET-accredited engineering program. Must have 3.75 GPA, rank in the 90th percentile in both math and verbal on SAT or composite ACT scores. A 3.0 GPA and continued engineering enrollment must be maintained to renew scholarship. Application should be retrieved from the SAE Web site at http://www.sae.org/students/stuschol.htm

Academic Fields/Career Goals: Engineering/Technology.

Award: Scholarship for use in freshman, sophomore, junior, senior, or graduate years; renewable. *Number:* 1. *Amount:* up to $1000.

Eligibility Requirements: Applicant must be enrolled or expecting to enroll full-time at a four-year institution or university. Available to U.S. citizens.

Application Requirements: Application, essay, test scores, transcript. *Deadline:* varies.

Contact: Connie Harnish, SAE Educational Relations
Society of Automotive Engineers
400 Commonwealth Drive
Warrendale, PA 15096
Phone: 724-772-4047
E-mail: connie@sae.org

RALPH K. HILLQUIST HONORARY SAE SCHOLARSHIP

Non-renewable scholarship for university juniors with a minimum 3.0 GPA. Must have a declared major in mechanical or automotive-related engineering. Preference given to those with studies related to noise and vibration. Application should be retrieved from the SAE Web site http://www.sae.org/students/stuschol.htm

Academic Fields/Career Goals: Engineering/Technology; Engineering-Related Technologies; Mechanical Engineering.

Award: Scholarship for use in junior year; not renewable. *Number:* 1. *Amount:* $1000.

Eligibility Requirements: Applicant must be enrolled or expecting to enroll full-time at a four-year institution or university. Applicant must have 3.0 GPA or higher. Available to U.S. citizens.

Application Requirements: Application. *Deadline:* February 1.

Contact: Connie Harnish, SAE Educational Relations
Society of Automotive Engineers
400 Commonwealth Drive
Warrendale, PA 15096-0001
Phone: 724-772-4047
E-mail: connie@sae.org

SAE BALTIMORE SECTION BILL BRUBAKER SCHOLARSHIP

Non-renewable scholarship for any family member of a member of Baltimore SAE or any high school senior accepted to an engineering university in Maryland.

Academic Fields/Career Goals: Engineering/Technology.

Award: Scholarship for use in freshman year; not renewable. *Number:* 1. *Amount:* up to $1000.

Eligibility Requirements: Applicant must be enrolled or expecting to enroll full-time at a four-year institution or university. Applicant or parent of applicant must be member of Society of Automotive Engineers. Available to U.S. citizens.

Application Requirements: Application, essay, resume, transcript. *Deadline:* May 10.

Contact: Rich Bechtold
Society of Automotive Engineers
5400 Thunder Hill Road
Columbia, MD 21045
Phone: 410-997-1282
E-mail: RLBechtold@aol.com

SAE LONG TERM MEMBER SPONSORED SCHOLARSHIP

One-time award for SAE student member who will be entering the senior year of undergraduate engineering studies. The scholarship will be awarded purely on the basis of the student's support for SAE and its programs. GPA is not a determining factor. Application deadline is April 1.

Academic Fields/Career Goals: Engineering/Technology.

Award: Scholarship for use in freshman, sophomore, junior, or senior years; not renewable. *Amount:* up to $1000.

Eligibility Requirements: Applicant must be enrolled or expecting to enroll at a four-year institution. Applicant or parent of applicant must be member of Society of Automotive Engineers. Available to U.S. citizens.

Application Requirements: Application, references. *Deadline:* April 1.

Contact: Connie Harnish, SAE Educational Relations
Society of Automotive Engineers
400 Commonwealth Drive
Warrendale, PA 15096
Phone: 724-772-4047
E-mail: connie@sae.org

SAE WILLIAM G. BELFREY MEMORIAL GRANT

Non-renewable grant for university juniors at a Canadian university enrolled in a mobility-related engineering discipline. Must be a Canadian citizen. Application should be retrieved from SAE Web site http://www.sae.org/students/stuschol.htm

Academic Fields/Career Goals: Engineering/Technology; Engineering-Related Technologies.

Award: Grant for use in junior or senior years. *Number:* 1. *Amount:* up to $1000.

Eligibility Requirements: Applicant must be enrolled or expecting to enroll full-time at a four-year institution or university. Available to Canadian citizens.

Application Requirements: Application, essay, resume, references, transcript. *Deadline:* April 1.

Contact: Connie Harnish, SAE Educational Relations
Society of Automotive Engineers
400 Commonwealth Drive
Warrendale, PA 15096-0001
Phone: 724-772-4047
E-mail: connie@sae.org

TAU BETA PI/SAE ENGINEERING SCHOLARSHIP

Merit-based award given to top-ranking candidates pursuing an accredited engineering program. Award is for freshman year only. Must have 3.75 GPA and rank in the 90th percentile in both math and verbal for SAT scores or for composite ACT scores. Application should be retrieved from the SAE Web site at http://www.sae.org/students/stuschol.htm

Academic Fields/Career Goals: Engineering/Technology.

Award: Scholarship for use in freshman year; not renewable. *Number:* 6. *Amount:* up to $1000.

Eligibility Requirements: Applicant must be high school student and planning to enroll or expecting to enroll at a four-year institution. Available to U.S. citizens.

Application Requirements: Application, essay, test scores, transcript. *Deadline:* varies.

Contact: Connie Harnish, SAE Educational Relations
Society of Automotive Engineers
400 Commonwealth Drive
Warrendale, PA 15096
Phone: 724-772-4047
E-mail: connie@sae.org

TMC/SAE DONALD D. DAWSON TECHNICAL SCHOLARSHIP
• See page 129

YANMAR/SAE SCHOLARSHIP

Eligible applicants will be citizens of North America (U.S., Canada, Mexico) and will be entering their junior year of undergraduate engineering or enrolled in a postgraduate engineering or related science program. Applicants must be pursuing a course of study or research related to the conservation of energy in transportation, agriculture, construction, and power generation. Emphasis will be placed on research or study related to the internal combustion engine. Application should be retrieved from the SAE Web site at http://www.sae.org/students/stuschol.htm

Academic Fields/Career Goals: Engineering/Technology; Engineering-Related Technologies; Materials Science, Engineering, and Metallurgy; Mechanical Engineering.

Award: Scholarship for use in senior, graduate, or postgraduate years; renewable. *Number:* 1. *Amount:* up to $1000.

Eligibility Requirements: Applicant must be Canadian or Mexican citizen and enrolled or expecting to enroll full-time at a four-year institution or university. Available to U.S. and Canadian citizens.

Application Requirements: Application, essay, self-addressed stamped envelope, test scores, transcript. *Deadline:* April 1.

Contact: Connie Harnish, SAE Educational Relations
Society of Automotive Engineers
400 Commonwealth Drive
Warrendale, PA 15096
Phone: 724-772-4047
E-mail: connie@sae.org

SOCIETY OF BROADCAST ENGINEERS, INC.   http://www.sbe.org

ROBERT GREENBERG/HAROLD E. ENNES SCHOLARSHIP FUND AND ENNES EDUCATIONAL FOUNDATION BROADCAST TECHNOLOGY SCHOLARSHIP

Merit-based awards for undergraduate students to study the technical aspects of broadcast engineering. Students should apply as high school senior or college freshman and may use the award for a two- or four-year college or university program. One-time award of $1000.

Academic Fields/Career Goals: Engineering/Technology; Engineering-Related Technologies; TV/Radio Broadcasting.

Award: Scholarship for use in freshman, sophomore, junior, or senior years; not renewable. *Number:* 3. *Amount:* $1000.

Eligibility Requirements: Applicant must be enrolled or expecting to enroll full-time at a two-year or four-year institution or university. Applicant must have 3.0 GPA or higher. Available to U.S. and Canadian citizens.

Application Requirements: Application, autobiography, essay, references, self-addressed stamped envelope, transcript. *Deadline:* July 1.

Contact: Linda Baun, Certification Director
Society of Broadcast Engineers, Inc.
9102 North Meridian Street, Suite 150
Indianapolis, IN 46260
Phone: 317-846-9000
Fax: 317-846-9120
E-mail: lbaun@sbe.org

SOCIETY OF HISPANIC PROFESSIONAL ENGINEERS FOUNDATION   http://www.henaac.org

SOCIETY OF HISPANIC PROFESSIONAL ENGINEERS FOUNDATION
• See page 168

SOCIETY OF MANUFACTURING ENGINEERS EDUCATION FOUNDATION   http://www.sme.org

ALBERT E. WISCHMEYER MEMORIAL SCHOLARSHIP AWARD

One-time award supports two scholarships of at least $1900 each. Applicants must be residents of Western New York State (West of Interstate 81), graduating high school seniors or current undergraduate students enrolled in an accredited degree program in manufacturing engineering, manufacturing

Society of Manufacturing Engineers Education Foundation (continued)

engineering technology or mechanical technology. Applicants must plan to attend a college or university in New York State and have an overall minimum GPA of 3.0.

Academic Fields/Career Goals: Engineering/Technology.

Award: Scholarship for use in freshman, sophomore, junior, or senior years; not renewable. *Number:* 2. *Amount:* $1900.

Eligibility Requirements: Applicant must be enrolled or expecting to enroll full-time at a four-year institution or university; resident of New York and studying in New York. Applicant must have 3.0 GPA or higher. Available to U.S. citizens.

Application Requirements: Application, essay, resume, references, transcript. *Deadline:* February 1.

Contact: Cindy Monzon, Program Coordinator
Society of Manufacturing Engineers Education Foundation
1 SME Drive
PO Box 930
Dearborn, MI 48121-0930
Phone: 313-271-1500 Ext. 1707
Fax: 313-240-6095
E-mail: monzcyn@sme.org

ARTHUR AND GLADYS CERVENKA SCHOLARSHIP AWARD

One-time award to full-time students enrolled in a degree program in manufacturing engineering or technology. Preference given to students attending a Florida institution. Must have completed a minimum of thirty college credit hours. Minimum 3.0 GPA required.

Academic Fields/Career Goals: Engineering/Technology.

Award: Scholarship for use in freshman, sophomore, junior, or senior years; not renewable. *Number:* 1. *Amount:* $1250.

Eligibility Requirements: Applicant must be enrolled or expecting to enroll full-time at a four-year institution or university. Applicant must have 3.0 GPA or higher. Available to U.S. citizens.

Application Requirements: Application, essay, resume, references, transcript. *Deadline:* February 1.

Contact: Cindy Monzon, Program Coordinator
Society of Manufacturing Engineers Education Foundation
1 SME Drive
PO Box 930
Dearborn, MI 48121-0930
Phone: 313-271-1500 Ext. 1707
Fax: 313-240-6095
E-mail: monzcyn@sme.org

CATERPILLAR SCHOLARS AWARD FUND

Supports five one-time scholarships of $2000 each for full-time students enrolled in a manufacturing engineering program. Minority applicants may apply as incoming freshmen. Applicants must have an overall minimum GPA of 3.0 on a 4.0 scale.

Academic Fields/Career Goals: Engineering/Technology.

Award: Scholarship for use in freshman, sophomore, junior, or senior years; not renewable. *Number:* 5. *Amount:* $2000.

Eligibility Requirements: Applicant must be enrolled or expecting to enroll full-time at a four-year institution or university. Applicant must have 3.0 GPA or higher. Available to U.S. citizens.

Application Requirements: Application, essay, references, transcript. *Deadline:* February 1.

Contact: Cindy Monzon, Program Coordinator
Society of Manufacturing Engineers Education Foundation
1 SME Drive
PO Box 930
Dearborn, MI 48121-0930
Phone: 313-271-1500 Ext. 1707
Fax: 313-240-6095
E-mail: monzcyn@sme.org

CHAPTER 31 - PEORIA SCHOLARSHIP

Scholarship available for students seeking a bachelor's degree in manufacturing engineering, industrial engineering, manufacturing technology or a manufacturing related degree program at either Bradley University (Peoria, Illinois) or Illinois State University (Normal, Illinois).

Academic Fields/Career Goals: Engineering/Technology.

Award: Scholarship for use in freshman, sophomore, junior, or senior years. *Number:* 1. *Amount:* $1250.

Eligibility Requirements: Applicant must be enrolled or expecting to enroll full-time at a four-year institution or university. Applicant must have 3.0 GPA or higher. Available to U.S. citizens.

Application Requirements: Application. *Deadline:* varies.

Contact: Cindy Monzon, Program Coordinator
Society of Manufacturing Engineers Education Foundation
1 SME Drive
PO Box 930
Dearborn, MI 48121-0930
Phone: 313-271-1500 Ext. 1707
Fax: 313-240-6095
E-mail: monzcyn@sme.org

CHAPTER 4 LAWRENCE A. WACKER MEMORIAL SCHOLARSHIP

Two one-time awards available to full-time students. One scholarship will be granted to a graduating high school senior and the other will be granted to a current undergraduate student. Students must be enrolled in or accepted to a degree program in manufacturing, mechanical or industrial engineering at a college or university in the state of Wisconsin. All applicants must have a GPA of 3.0 or better on a 4.0 scale.

Academic Fields/Career Goals: Engineering/Technology.

Award: Scholarship for use in freshman, sophomore, junior, or senior years; not renewable. *Number:* 2. *Amount:* $1500.

Eligibility Requirements: Applicant must be enrolled or expecting to enroll full-time at a four-year institution or university and studying in Wisconsin. Applicant must have 3.0 GPA or higher. Available to U.S. citizens.

Application Requirements: Application, essay, resume, references, transcript. *Deadline:* February 1.

Contact: Cindy Monzon, Program Coordinator
Society of Manufacturing Engineers Education Foundation
1 SME Drive
PO Box 930
Dearborn, MI 48121-0930
Phone: 313-271-1500 Ext. 1707
Fax: 313-240-6095
E-mail: monzcyn@sme.org

CLINTON J. HELTON MANUFACTURING SCHOLARSHIP AWARD FUND

One-time award to full-time students enrolled in a degree program in manufacturing engineering or technology at one of the following institutions: Colorado State University, University of Colorado-all campuses. Applicants must possess an overall minimum GPA of 3.3.

Academic Fields/Career Goals: Engineering/Technology; Trade/Technical Specialties.

Award: Scholarship for use in freshman, sophomore, junior, or senior years. *Number:* 1. *Amount:* $3500.

Eligibility Requirements: Applicant must be enrolled or expecting to enroll full-time at a four-year institution or university and studying in Colorado. Available to U.S. citizens.

Application Requirements: *Deadline:* February 1.

Contact: Cindy Monzon, Program Coordinator
Society of Manufacturing Engineers Education Foundation
1 SME Drive
PO Box 930
Dearborn, MI 48121-0930
Phone: 313-271-1500 Ext. 1707
Fax: 313-240-6095
E-mail: monzcyn@sme.org

CONNIE AND ROBERT T. GUNTER SCHOLARSHIP

One-time award for full-time undergraduate student attending Georgia Institute of Technology, Georgia Southern College, or Southern College of Technology and enrolled in a degree program in manufacturing engineering or manufacturing engineering technology. Must have minimum 3.5 GPA and have completed at least thirty college credit hours. One-time award of $1200. Must submit application cover sheet and resume.

Academic Fields/Career Goals: Engineering/Technology.

Award: Scholarship for use in freshman, sophomore, junior, or senior years; not renewable. *Number:* 1. *Amount:* $1200.

Eligibility Requirements: Applicant must be enrolled or expecting to enroll full-time at a four-year institution or university and studying in Georgia. Applicant must have 3.5 GPA or higher. Available to U.S. citizens.

Application Requirements: Application, essay, resume, references, transcript. *Deadline:* February 1.

Contact: Cindy Monzon, Program Coordinator
Society of Manufacturing Engineers Education Foundation
1 SME Drive
PO Box 930
Dearborn, MI 48121-0930
Phone: 313-271-1500 Ext. 1707
Fax: 313-240-6095
E-mail: monzcyn@sme.org

DETROIT CHAPTER ONE-FOUNDING CHAPTER SCHOLARSHIP

Three annual awards of at least $1000 each, will be available in each of the following: associate degree and equivalent, baccalaureate degree and graduate degree programs. Minimum GPA of 3.0 is required. Must be undergraduate or graduate student enrolled in a manufacturing engineering or technology program at one of the sponsored institutions and be a member in good standing of their SME Student Chapter.

Academic Fields/Career Goals: Engineering/Technology.

Award: Scholarship for use in freshman, sophomore, junior, senior, or graduate years; not renewable. *Number:* 3. *Amount:* $1000–$3000.

Eligibility Requirements: Applicant must be enrolled or expecting to enroll full or part-time at a two-year or four-year institution or university and studying in Michigan. Applicant must have 3.0 GPA or higher. Available to U.S. citizens.

Application Requirements: Application, references. *Deadline:* February 1.

Contact: Cindy Monzon, Program Coordinator
Society of Manufacturing Engineers Education Foundation
1 SME Drive
PO Box 930
Dearborn, MI 48121-0930
Phone: 313-271-1500 Ext. 1707
Fax: 313-240-6095
E-mail: monzcyn@sme.org

DIRECTOR'S SCHOLARSHIP AWARD

One-time award for full-time undergraduate students enrolled in a manufacturing degree program in the U.S. or Canada. Must have completed thirty college credit hours. Minimum 3.5 GPA required. Preference given to students who demonstrate leadership skills.

Academic Fields/Career Goals: Engineering/Technology.

Award: Scholarship for use in freshman, sophomore, junior, or senior years; not renewable. *Number:* 2. *Amount:* $5000.

Eligibility Requirements: Applicant must be enrolled or expecting to enroll full-time at a four-year institution or university and must have an interest in leadership. Applicant must have 3.5 GPA or higher. Available to U.S. citizens.

Application Requirements: Application, essay, resume, references, transcript. *Deadline:* February 1.

Contact: Cindy Monzon, Program Coordinator
Society of Manufacturing Engineers Education Foundation
1 SME Drive
PO Box 930
Dearborn, MI 48121-0930
Phone: 313-271-1500 Ext. 1707
Fax: 313-240-6095
E-mail: monzcyn@sme.org

DOWNRIVER DETROIT CHAPTER 198 SCHOLARSHIP

One-time award for an individual seeking an associate's degree, bachelor's degree, or graduate degree in manufacturing, mechanical or industrial engineering, engineering technology, or industrial technology at an accredited public or private college or university in Michigan. Applicants must have a minimum GPA of 2.5. Preference is given to applicants who are a child or grandchild of a current SME Downriver Chapter No. 198 member, a member of its student chapter, or a Michigan resident.

Academic Fields/Career Goals: Engineering/Technology; Industrial Design; Mechanical Engineering; Trade/Technical Specialties.

Award: Scholarship for use in freshman, sophomore, junior, senior, or graduate years. *Number:* 1. *Amount:* $1200.

Eligibility Requirements: Applicant must be enrolled or expecting to enroll full-time at a two-year or four-year institution or university and studying in Michigan. Applicant must have 2.5 GPA or higher. Available to U.S. citizens.

Application Requirements: *Deadline:* February 1.

Contact: Cindy Monzon, Program Coordinator
Society of Manufacturing Engineers Education Foundation
1 SME Drive
PO Box 930
Dearborn, MI 48121-0930
Phone: 313-271-1500 Ext. 1707
Fax: 313-240-6095
E-mail: monzcyn@sme.org

E. WAYNE KAY COMMUNITY COLLEGE SCHOLARSHIP AWARD

One-time award to full-time students enrolled at an accredited community college or trade school which offers programs in manufacturing or closely related field in the U.S. or Canada. Minimum GPA of 3.0 required. Must have less than 60 college credit hours and seeking a career in manufacturing engineering or technology.

Academic Fields/Career Goals: Engineering/Technology; Trade/Technical Specialties.

Award: Scholarship for use in freshman or sophomore years; not renewable. *Number:* 1. *Amount:* $1000.

Eligibility Requirements: Applicant must be enrolled or expecting to enroll full-time at a two-year or technical institution. Applicant must have 3.0 GPA or higher. Available to U.S. citizens.

Application Requirements: Application, essay, resume, references, transcript. *Deadline:* February 1.

Contact: Cindy Monzon, Program Coordinator
Society of Manufacturing Engineers Education Foundation
1 SME Drive
PO Box 930
Dearborn, MI 48121-0930
Phone: 313-271-1500 Ext. 1707
Fax: 313-240-6095
E-mail: monzcyn@sme.org

E. WAYNE KAY CO-OP SCHOLARSHIP

Two $2500 awards for full-time students enrolled in a manufacturing engineering or technology co-op program at an accredited college or university. Minimum 3.0 GPA required. Must have completed a minimum of 30 college credit hours.

Academic Fields/Career Goals: Engineering/Technology.

Award: Scholarship for use in freshman, sophomore, junior, or senior years; not renewable. *Number:* 2. *Amount:* $2500.

Eligibility Requirements: Applicant must be enrolled or expecting to enroll full-time at a four-year institution or university. Applicant must have 3.0 GPA or higher. Available to U.S. and non-U.S. citizens.

Application Requirements: Application, essay, references, transcript. *Deadline:* February 1.

Contact: Cindy Monzon, Program Coordinator
Society of Manufacturing Engineers Education Foundation
1 SME Drive
PO Box 930
Dearborn, MI 48121-0930
Phone: 313-271-1500 Ext. 1707
Fax: 313-240-6095
E-mail: monzcyn@sme.org

E. WAYNE KAY SCHOLARSHIP

Award for full-time undergraduate study in manufacturing engineering and manufacturing technology. Must have minimum 3.0 GPA. Submit transcript, essay, references, application cover sheet, and statement letter with resume. One-time award of $2500. Must have completed a minimum of 30 college credit hours.

Society of Manufacturing Engineers Education Foundation (continued)

Academic Fields/Career Goals: Engineering/Technology; Trade/Technical Specialties.

Award: Scholarship for use in freshman, sophomore, junior, or senior years; not renewable. *Number:* 10. *Amount:* $2500.

Eligibility Requirements: Applicant must be enrolled or expecting to enroll full-time at a four-year institution or university. Applicant must have 3.0 GPA or higher. Available to U.S. and Canadian citizens.

Application Requirements: Application, essay, resume, references, transcript. *Deadline:* February 1.

Contact: Cindy Monzon, Program Coordinator
Society of Manufacturing Engineers Education Foundation
1 SME Drive
PO Box 930
Dearborn, MI 48121-0930
Phone: 313-271-1500 Ext. 1707
Fax: 313-240-6095
E-mail: monzcyn@sme.org

EDWARD S. ROTH MANUFACTURING ENGINEERING SCHOLARSHIP

Awarded to a graduating high school senior, a current full time undergraduate or graduate student enrolled in an accredited four-year degree program in manufacturing engineering at a sponsored ABET accredited school. Minimum GPA of 3.0 and be a U.S. citizen. Preferences will be given to students demonstrating financial need, minority students, and students participating in a Co-Op program. The top three applications will be sent to Mr. and Mrs. Roth for final selection.

Academic Fields/Career Goals: Engineering/Technology.

Award: Scholarship for use in freshman, sophomore, junior, senior, or graduate years; not renewable. *Number:* 1. *Amount:* $2500.

Eligibility Requirements: Applicant must be enrolled or expecting to enroll full-time at a four-year institution or university and studying in California, Florida, Illinois, Massachusetts, Minnesota, Ohio, Texas, or Utah. Applicant must have 3.0 GPA or higher. Available to U.S. citizens.

Application Requirements: Application, interview. *Deadline:* February 1.

Contact: Cindy Monzon, Program Coordinator
Society of Manufacturing Engineers Education Foundation
1 SME Drive
PO Box 930
Dearborn, MI 48121-0930
Phone: 313-271-1500 Ext. 1707
Fax: 313-240-6095
E-mail: monzcyn@sme.org

FORT WAYNE CHAPTER 56 SCHOLARSHIP

One-time award for an individual seeking an associate's degree, bachelor's degree, or graduate degree in manufacturing, mechanical or industrial engineering, engineering technology, or industrial technology at an accredited public or private college or university in Indiana. Applicants must have a minimum GPA of 2.5. Preference given to applicants who are a child or grandchild of a current SME Fort Wayne Chapter No. 56 member, a member of its student chapter, or an Indiana resident.

Academic Fields/Career Goals: Engineering/Technology; Industrial Design; Mechanical Engineering; Trade/Technical Specialties.

Award: Scholarship for use in freshman, sophomore, junior, senior, or graduate years. *Number:* 3. *Amount:* $2000.

Eligibility Requirements: Applicant must be enrolled or expecting to enroll full-time at a two-year or four-year institution or university and studying in Indiana. Applicant must have 2.5 GPA or higher. Available to U.S. citizens.

Application Requirements: *Deadline:* February 1.

Contact: Cindy Monzon, Program Coordinator
Society of Manufacturing Engineers Education Foundation
1 SME Drive
PO Box 930
Dearborn, MI 48121-0930
Phone: 313-271-1500 Ext. 1707
Fax: 313-240-6095
E-mail: monzcyn@sme.org

GUILIANO MAZZETTI SCHOLARSHIP AWARD

One-time award available to full-time students enrolled in a degree program in manufacturing engineering or technology in the U.S. or Canada. Must have completed a minimum of thirty college credit hours. Minimum GPA of 3.0 required.

Academic Fields/Career Goals: Engineering/Technology.

Award: Scholarship for use in freshman, sophomore, junior, or senior years; not renewable. *Number:* 2. *Amount:* $1500.

Eligibility Requirements: Applicant must be enrolled or expecting to enroll full-time at a four-year institution or university. Applicant must have 3.0 GPA or higher. Available to U.S. and Canadian citizens.

Application Requirements: Application, essay, resume, references, transcript. *Deadline:* February 1.

Contact: Cindy Monzon, Program Coordinator
Society of Manufacturing Engineers Education Foundation
1 SME Drive
PO Box 930
Dearborn, MI 48121-0930
Phone: 313-271-1500 Ext. 1707
Fax: 313-240-6095
E-mail: monzcyn@sme.org

KALAMAZOO CHAPTER 116-ROSCOE DOUGLAS MEMORIAL SCHOLARSHIP AWARD

Scholarship to full-time undergraduate students enrolled in a degree program in manufacturing, engineering or technology at one of the sponsored Michigan institutions. Minimum GPA of 3.0 required. Must have completed a minimum of 30 college credit hours.

Academic Fields/Career Goals: Engineering/Technology.

Award: Scholarship for use in freshman, sophomore, junior, or senior years; not renewable. *Number:* 1. *Amount:* $1500.

Eligibility Requirements: Applicant must be enrolled or expecting to enroll full-time at a four-year institution or university and studying in Michigan. Applicant must have 3.0 GPA or higher. Available to U.S. citizens.

Application Requirements: Application. *Deadline:* February 1.

Contact: Cindy Monzon, Program Coordinator
Society of Manufacturing Engineers Education Foundation
1 SME Drive
PO Box 930
Dearborn, MI 48121-0930
Phone: 313-271-1500 Ext. 1707
Fax: 313-240-6095
E-mail: monzcyn@sme.org

LUCILE B. KAUFMAN WOMEN'S SCHOLARSHIP

Scholarships available for female full-time undergraduate students enrolled in a degree program in manufacturing engineering, technology or a closely related field in the United States or Canada.

Academic Fields/Career Goals: Engineering/Technology.

Award: Scholarship for use in freshman, sophomore, junior, or senior years. *Number:* 2. *Amount:* $1500.

Eligibility Requirements: Applicant must be enrolled or expecting to enroll full-time at a four-year institution or university and female. Applicant must have 3.0 GPA or higher. Available to U.S. and Canadian citizens.

Application Requirements: Application.

Contact: Cindy Monzon, Program Coordinator
Society of Manufacturing Engineers Education Foundation
1 SME Drive
PO Box 930
Dearborn, MI 48121-0930
Phone: 313-271-1500 Ext. 1707
Fax: 313-240-6095
E-mail: monzcyn@sme.org

MYRTLE AND EARL WALKER SCHOLARSHIP FUND

One-time award for students seeking a career in manufacturing engineering or technology who have completed at least 15 credit hours or one semester. Must have minimum 3.0 GPA. Submit application cover sheet, resume, transcript, essay, references, and statement of career goals.

Academic Fields/Career Goals: Engineering/Technology; Trade/Technical Specialties.

Award: Scholarship for use in freshman, sophomore, junior, or senior years; not renewable. *Number:* 25. *Amount:* $1000.

Eligibility Requirements: Applicant must be enrolled or expecting to enroll full-time at a two-year or four-year or technical institution or university. Applicant must have 3.0 GPA or higher. Available to U.S. and Canadian citizens.

Application Requirements: Application, essay, resume, references, transcript. *Deadline:* February 1.

Contact: Cindy Monzon, Program Coordinator
Society of Manufacturing Engineers Education Foundation
1 SME Drive
PO Box 930
Dearborn, MI 48121-0930
Phone: 313-271-1500 Ext. 1707
Fax: 313-240-6095
E-mail: monzcyn@sme.org

NORTH CENTRAL REGION 9 SCHOLARSHIP

Award to a full-time student enrolled in a manufacturing, mechanical, or industrial engineering degree program in North Central Region 9 (Iowa, Minnesota, Nebraska, North Dakota, South Dakota, Wisconsin, and the upper peninsula of Michigan). Applicants must have a 3.0 GPA. Preference will be given to North Central Region 9 members and their family members and to residents of the states in North Central Region 9.

Academic Fields/Career Goals: Engineering/Technology; Industrial Design; Mechanical Engineering; Trade/Technical Specialties.

Award: Scholarship for use in freshman, sophomore, junior, or senior years. *Number:* 1. *Amount:* $1000.

Eligibility Requirements: Applicant must be enrolled or expecting to enroll full-time at a four-year institution or university and studying in Iowa, Michigan, Minnesota, Nebraska, North Dakota, South Dakota, or Wisconsin. Applicant must have 3.0 GPA or higher. Available to U.S. citizens.

Application Requirements: *Deadline:* February 1.

Contact: Cindy Monzon, Program Coordinator
Society of Manufacturing Engineers Education Foundation
1 SME Drive
PO Box 930
Dearborn, MI 48121-0930
Phone: 313-271-1500 Ext. 1707
Fax: 313-240-6095
E-mail: monzcyn@sme.org

PHOENIX CHAPTER 67 SCHOLARSHIP

Award for a high school senior who plans on enrolling in a manufacturing program technology or manufacturing technology program or an undergraduate student enrolled in a manufacturing engineering technology, manufacturing technology, industrial technology, or closely related program at an accredited college or university in Arizona. Applicants must have an overall GPA of 2.5 and a GPA of 3.0 in their manufacturing courses to continue their eligibility in subsequent years.

Academic Fields/Career Goals: Engineering/Technology; Industrial Design; Mechanical Engineering; Trade/Technical Specialties.

Award: Scholarship for use in freshman, sophomore, junior, or senior years. *Number:* 1. *Amount:* $1000.

Eligibility Requirements: Applicant must be enrolled or expecting to enroll full-time at a two-year or four-year institution or university and studying in Arizona. Applicant must have 2.5 GPA or higher. Available to U.S. citizens.

Application Requirements: *Deadline:* February 1.

Contact: Cindy Monzon, Program Coordinator
Society of Manufacturing Engineers Education Foundation
1 SME Drive
PO Box 930
Dearborn, MI 48121-0930
Phone: 313-271-1500 Ext. 1707
Fax: 313-240-6095
E-mail: monzcyn@sme.org

ST. LOUIS CHAPTER NO. 17 SCHOLARSHIP FUND

Award for undergraduates pursuing studies in manufacturing engineering or industrial technology. Must attend an approved institution with a student chapter of the Society of Manufacturing Engineers, sponsored by St. Louis Chapter Number 17. One-time award of $1000. Award based on merit. Submit application cover sheet and resume. Must rank in upper quarter of class or have minimum GPA of 3.5.

Academic Fields/Career Goals: Engineering/Technology.

Award: Scholarship for use in freshman, sophomore, junior, or senior years; not renewable. *Number:* 4. *Amount:* $1000.

Eligibility Requirements: Applicant must be enrolled or expecting to enroll full-time at a two-year or four-year institution or university and studying in Illinois or Missouri. Applicant must have 3.0 GPA or higher. Available to U.S. and Canadian citizens.

Application Requirements: Application, essay, resume, references, transcript. *Deadline:* February 1.

Contact: Cindy Monzon, Program Coordinator
Society of Manufacturing Engineers Education Foundation
1 SME Drive
PO Box 930
Dearborn, MI 48121-0930
Phone: 313-271-1500 Ext. 1707
Fax: 313-240-6095
E-mail: monzcyn@sme.org

SME CORPORATE SCHOLARS

Award to full-time students enrolled in a degree program in manufacturing engineering or technology in United States or Canada. Applicants must have an overall GPA of 3.0.

Academic Fields/Career Goals: Engineering/Technology; Trade/Technical Specialties.

Award: Scholarship for use in freshman, sophomore, junior, or senior years. *Number:* varies. *Amount:* $1000–$5000.

Eligibility Requirements: Applicant must be enrolled or expecting to enroll full-time at a four-year institution or university. Applicant must have 3.0 GPA or higher. Available to U.S. citizens.

Application Requirements: *Deadline:* February 1.

Contact: Cindy Monzon, Program Coordinator
Society of Manufacturing Engineers Education Foundation
1 SME Drive
PO Box 930
Dearborn, MI 48121-0930
Phone: 313-271-1500 Ext. 1707
Fax: 313-240-6095
E-mail: monzcyn@sme.org

SME FAMILY SCHOLARSHIP

Three scholarships awarded to children or grandchildren of Society of Manufacturing Engineers members. Must be graduating high school senior planning to pursue full-time studies for an undergraduate degree in manufacturing engineering, manufacturing engineering technology, or a closely related engineering study at an accredited college or university. Undergraduate students must have completed 30 credit hours. Minimum GPA of 3.0 and SAT score of 1000 required, or ACT score of 21.

Academic Fields/Career Goals: Engineering/Technology.

Award: Scholarship for use in freshman, sophomore, junior, or senior years; renewable. *Number:* 3. *Amount:* $5000–$20,000.

Society of Manufacturing Engineers Education Foundation (continued)

Eligibility Requirements: Applicant must be enrolled or expecting to enroll full-time at a four-year institution or university. Applicant must have 3.0 GPA or higher. Available to U.S. and non-U.S. citizens.

Application Requirements: Application, essay, resume, references, test scores, transcript. *Deadline:* February 1.

Contact: Cindy Monzon, Program Coordinator
Society of Manufacturing Engineers Education Foundation
1 SME Drive
PO Box 930
Dearborn, MI 48121-0930
Phone: 313-271-1500 Ext. 1707
Fax: 313-240-6095
E-mail: monzcyn@sme.org

WALT BARTRAM MEMORIAL EDUCATION AWARD

Scholarship available for graduating high school seniors who commit to enroll in, or full-time college or university students pursuing a degree in, manufacturing engineering or a closely related field within the areas of New Mexico, Arizona or Southern California and be a resident there. Must be a current SME Chapter member, except high school students who may apply without any SME member relationship.

Academic Fields/Career Goals: Engineering/Technology.

Award: Scholarship for use in freshman year. *Number:* 1. *Amount:* $1500.

Eligibility Requirements: Applicant must be high school student; planning to enroll or expecting to enroll at an institution or university and resident of Arizona or New Mexico. Applicant must have 3.5 GPA or higher. Available to U.S. citizens.

Application Requirements: Application.

Contact: Cindy Monzon, Program Coordinator
Society of Manufacturing Engineers Education Foundation
1 SME Drive
PO Box 930
Dearborn, MI 48121-0930
Phone: 313-271-1500 Ext. 1707
Fax: 313-240-6095
E-mail: monzcyn@sme.org

WAYNE KAY HIGH SCHOOL SCHOLARSHIP

Two awards for up to $2500 each for two years as follows: $1000 for first year and renewable for $1500 for second year, based on academic excellence and career path. Must be graduating high school seniors who commit to enroll in manufacturing engineering or technology program at an accredited college or university as a full-time freshman in the current summer or full semester. Minimum 3.0 GPA required.

Academic Fields/Career Goals: Engineering/Technology.

Award: Scholarship for use in freshman year; renewable. *Number:* 2. *Amount:* up to $2500.

Eligibility Requirements: Applicant must be high school student and planning to enroll or expecting to enroll full-time at a four-year institution or university. Applicant must have 3.0 GPA or higher. Available to U.S. and non-U.S. citizens.

Application Requirements: Application, essay, references, transcript. *Deadline:* February 1.

Contact: Cindy Monzon, Program Coordinator
Society of Manufacturing Engineers Education Foundation
1 SME Drive
PO Box 930
Dearborn, MI 48121-0930
Phone: 313-271-1500 Ext. 1707
Fax: 313-240-6095
E-mail: monzcyn@sme.org

WICHITA CHAPTER 52 SCHOLARSHIP

Award for an individual seeking an associate's degree, bachelor's degree, or graduate degree in manufacturing, mechanical or industrial engineering, engineering technology, or industrial technology at an accredited public or private college or university in Kansas. Applicants must have a minimum GPA of 2.5. Preference given to applicants who are a relative of a current SME Wichita Chapter No. 52 member or a Kansas resident.

Academic Fields/Career Goals: Engineering/Technology; Industrial Design; Mechanical Engineering; Trade/Technical Specialties.

Award: Scholarship for use in freshman, sophomore, junior, senior, or graduate years. *Number:* 1. *Amount:* $1000.

Eligibility Requirements: Applicant must be enrolled or expecting to enroll full-time at a two-year or four-year institution or university and studying in Kansas. Applicant must have 2.5 GPA or higher. Available to U.S. citizens.

Application Requirements: *Deadline:* February 1.

Contact: Cindy Monzon, Program Coordinator
Society of Manufacturing Engineers Education Foundation
1 SME Drive
PO Box 930
Dearborn, MI 48121-0930
Phone: 313-271-1500 Ext. 1707
Fax: 313-240-6095
E-mail: monzcyn@sme.org

WILLIAM E. WEISEL SCHOLARSHIP FUND
• *See page 246*

SOCIETY OF MEXICAN AMERICAN ENGINEERS AND SCIENTISTS   http://www.maes-natl.org

GRE AND GRADUATE APPLICATIONS WAIVER
• *See page 95*

SOCIETY OF NAVAL ARCHITECTS & MARINE ENGINEERS   http://www.sname.org

SOCIETY OF NAVAL ARCHITECTS AND MARINE ENGINEERS UNDERGRADUATE SCHOLARSHIPS

These scholarships are open to U.S. and Canadian citizens studying toward a degree in naval architecture, marine engineering, ocean engineering or marine industry-related fields at an approved school. Must be nominated by school. Applicants must be entering their junior or senior year and must be a member of the Society at the time of the award. For more information visit Web site at http://www.sname.org.

Academic Fields/Career Goals: Engineering/Technology; Marine/Ocean Engineering.

Award: Scholarship for use in junior or senior years; not renewable. *Number:* varies. *Amount:* up to $2000.

Eligibility Requirements: Applicant must be enrolled or expecting to enroll at a four-year institution or university. Available to U.S. and Canadian citizens.

Application Requirements: Nomination. *Deadline:* May 1.

Contact: Chairman, Scholarships Committee
Society of Naval Architects & Marine Engineers
601 Pavonia Avenue
Jersey City, NJ 07306
Phone: 201-798-4800
Fax: 201-798-4975
E-mail: efaustino@sname.org

SOCIETY OF PETROLEUM ENGINEERS   http://www.spe.org

GUS ARCHIE MEMORIAL SCHOLARSHIPS

Renewable award for high school seniors planning to enroll in a petroleum engineering degree program at a four-year institution. Must have minimum 3.5 GPA.

Academic Fields/Career Goals: Engineering/Technology.

Award: Scholarship for use in freshman, sophomore, junior, or senior years; renewable. *Amount:* $5000.

Eligibility Requirements: Applicant must be high school student and planning to enroll or expecting to enroll full-time at a four-year institution or university. Applicant must have 3.5 GPA or higher. Available to U.S. and non-U.S. citizens.

Application Requirements: Application, autobiography, financial need analysis, photo, references, test scores, transcript. *Deadline:* April 30.

Contact: Tom Whipple, Professional Development Manager
Society of Petroleum Engineers
PO Box 833836
Richardson, TX 75083
Phone: 972-952-9452
Fax: 972-952-9435
E-mail: twhipple@spe.org

SOCIETY OF PLASTICS ENGINEERS (SPE) FOUNDATION
http://www.4spe.com

GULF COAST HURRICANE SCHOLARSHIP
• See page 168

SOCIETY OF PLASTICS ENGINEERS SCHOLARSHIP PROGRAM
• See page 168

SOCIETY OF WOMEN ENGINEERS
http://www.swe.org

ADMIRAL GRACE MURRAY HOPPER MEMORIAL SCHOLARSHIP

Scholarships for female freshmen entering the study of engineering in a four-year program. Must attend an ABET-accredited or SWE-approved school and have minimum GPA of 3.5. Five one-time awards of $1000 each. Deadline: May 15.

Academic Fields/Career Goals: Engineering/Technology.

Award: Scholarship for use in freshman year; not renewable. *Number:* 5. *Amount:* $1000.

Eligibility Requirements: Applicant must be high school student; planning to enroll or expecting to enroll full-time at a four-year institution or university and female. Applicant must have 3.5 GPA or higher. Available to U.S. and non-U.S. citizens.

Application Requirements: Application, essay, self-addressed stamped envelope, test scores, transcript. *Deadline:* May 15.

Contact: Suman Pa, Program Coordinator
Society of Women Engineers
230 E Ohio Street, Suite 400
Chicago, IL 60611-3265
Phone: 312-596-5223
Fax: 312-644-8557
E-mail: suman.patil@swe.org

ADOBE SYSTEMS COMPUTER SCIENCE SCHOLARSHIP

Two scholarships available to female engineering students in junior or senior year. Must have 3.0 GPA. Preference given to students attending selected schools in the San Francisco Bay area.

Academic Fields/Career Goals: Engineering/Technology.

Award: Scholarship for use in junior or senior years. *Number:* 2. *Amount:* $1500–$2000.

Eligibility Requirements: Applicant must be enrolled or expecting to enroll at a four-year institution or university and female. Applicant must have 3.0 GPA or higher. Available to U.S. citizens.

Application Requirements: Application, references, self-addressed stamped envelope, transcript. *Deadline:* February 1.

Contact: Suman Pa, Program Coordinator
Society of Women Engineers
230 E Ohio Street, Suite 400
Chicago, IL 60611-3265
Phone: 312-596-5223
Fax: 312-644-8557
E-mail: suman.patil@swe.org

AGILENT MENTORING SCHOLARSHIP
• See page 194

ANNE MAUREEN WHITNEY BARROW MEMORIAL SCHOLARSHIP

One award for a female undergraduate entering an engineering or engineering technology degree program. Must have a minimum 3.5 GPA. Send self-addressed stamped envelope for application. Renewable award of $5000. Deadline: May 15 for freshmen and February 1 for sophomores, juniors, and seniors.

Academic Fields/Career Goals: Engineering/Technology.

Award: Scholarship for use in freshman, sophomore, junior, or senior years; renewable. *Number:* 1. *Amount:* $5000.

Eligibility Requirements: Applicant must be enrolled or expecting to enroll full-time at a four-year institution or university and female. Applicant must have 3.5 GPA or higher. Available to U.S. and non-U.S. citizens.

Application Requirements: Application, essay, references, self-addressed stamped envelope, test scores, transcript. *Deadline:* varies.

Contact: Suman Pa, Program Coordinator
Society of Women Engineers
230 E Ohio Street, Suite 400
Chicago, IL 60611-3265
Phone: 312-596-5223
Fax: 312-644-8557
E-mail: suman.patil@swe.org

ARIZONA SECTION SCHOLARSHIP

Two scholarships for use in freshman year who are either residents of Arizona or attending a school in that state. Must be studying an engineering related field. Deadline: May 15. Minimum 3.5 GPA required.

Academic Fields/Career Goals: Engineering/Technology; Engineering-Related Technologies.

Award: Scholarship for use in freshman year; not renewable. *Number:* 2. *Amount:* $1000.

Eligibility Requirements: Applicant must be high school student; planning to enroll or expecting to enroll full-time at a two-year or four-year institution or university and female. Applicant must have 3.5 GPA or higher. Available to U.S. citizens.

Application Requirements: Application, essay, references, self-addressed stamped envelope, test scores, transcript. *Deadline:* May 15.

Contact: Suman Pa, Program Coordinator
Society of Women Engineers
230 E Ohio Street, Suite 400
Chicago, IL 60611-3265
Phone: 312-596-5223
Fax: 312-644-8557
E-mail: suman.patil@swe.org

B.J. HARROD SCHOLARSHIP

Two $1500 awards made to an incoming female freshman majoring in engineering. Deadline for application is May 15.

Academic Fields/Career Goals: Engineering/Technology.

Award: Scholarship for use in freshman year; not renewable. *Number:* 2. *Amount:* $1500.

Eligibility Requirements: Applicant must be high school student; planning to enroll or expecting to enroll full-time at a two-year or four-year institution or university and female. Applicant must have 3.5 GPA or higher. Available to U.S. and non-U.S. citizens.

Application Requirements: Application, essay, references, self-addressed stamped envelope, test scores, transcript. *Deadline:* May 15.

Contact: Suman Pa, Program Coordinator
Society of Women Engineers
230 E Ohio Street, Suite 400
Chicago, IL 60611-3265
Phone: 312-596-5223
Fax: 312-644-8557
E-mail: suman.patil@swe.org

B.K. KRENZER MEMORIAL REENTRY SCHOLARSHIP

Preference is given to degreed female engineers desiring to return to the workforce following a period of temporary retirement. Recipients may be entering any year of an engineering program, undergraduate or graduate, as full-time or part-time students. Applicants must have been out of the engineering job market as well as out of school for a minimum of two years. Deadline: May 15.

Academic Fields/Career Goals: Engineering/Technology.

Award: Scholarship for use in freshman, sophomore, junior, senior, or graduate years; not renewable. *Number:* 1. *Amount:* $2000.

Eligibility Requirements: Applicant must be enrolled or expecting to enroll full or part-time at a two-year or four-year or technical institution or university and female. Applicant must have 3.5 GPA or higher. Available to U.S. and non-U.S. citizens.

Society of Women Engineers (continued)

Application Requirements: Application, essay, references, self-addressed stamped envelope, test scores, transcript. *Deadline:* May 15.

Contact: Suman Pa, Program Coordinator
Society of Women Engineers
230 E Ohio Street, Suite 400
Chicago, IL 60611-3265
Phone: 312-596-5223
Fax: 312-644-8557
E-mail: suman.patil@swe.org

BECHTEL CORPORATION SCHOLARSHIP

• *See page 176*

CATERPILLAR, INC. SCHOLARSHIP

Three $2400 scholarships awarded to undergraduate and graduate students studying engineering. Must be U.S. citizen or authorized to work in the United States. Must have minimum 2.8 GPA.

Academic Fields/Career Goals: Engineering/Technology.

Award: Scholarship for use in freshman, sophomore, junior, senior, or graduate years; not renewable. *Number:* 3. *Amount:* $2400.

Eligibility Requirements: Applicant must be enrolled or expecting to enroll full-time at a four-year institution or university and female. Available to U.S. citizens.

Application Requirements: Application. *Deadline:* February 1.

Contact: Suman Pa, Program Coordinator
Society of Women Engineers
230 E Ohio Street, Suite 400
Chicago, IL 60611-3265
Phone: 312-596-5223
Fax: 312-644-8557
E-mail: suman.patil@swe.org

CHEVRON TEXACO CORPORATION SCHOLARSHIPS

• *See page 168*

COLUMBIA RIVER SECTION SCHOLARSHIPS

Scholarships available to students attending University of Portland, Portland State University, or Oregon Institute of Technology or a transfer student from an Oregon or Southwest Washington community college planning on pursuing an engineering degree at one of those schools.

Academic Fields/Career Goals: Engineering/Technology.

Award: Scholarship for use in freshman, sophomore, junior, senior, or graduate years; not renewable. *Number:* 6. *Amount:* $300–$750.

Eligibility Requirements: Applicant must be enrolled or expecting to enroll full-time at a two-year or four-year institution or university; female and studying in Oregon or Washington. Applicant must have 2.5 GPA or higher. Available to U.S. citizens.

Application Requirements: Application. *Deadline:* March 1.

Contact: Karina Wagner, Scholarship Chair
E-mail: scholarship@swe-columbia-river.org

DELL COMPUTER CORPORATION SCHOLARSHIPS

• *See page 194*

DOROTHY LEMKE HOWARTH SCHOLARSHIPS

Scholarship awarded to entering female sophomore students in engineering who are U.S. citizens attending a four-year institution. Send self-addressed stamped envelope for more information. Must have minimum 3.0 GPA. Five one-time awards of $2000 each. Deadline: February 1.

Academic Fields/Career Goals: Engineering/Technology.

Award: Scholarship for use in sophomore year; not renewable. *Number:* 5. *Amount:* $2000.

Eligibility Requirements: Applicant must be enrolled or expecting to enroll at a four-year institution or university and female. Applicant must have 3.0 GPA or higher. Available to U.S. citizens.

Application Requirements: Application, essay, references, self-addressed stamped envelope, test scores, transcript. *Deadline:* February 1.

Contact: Suman Pa, Program Coordinator
Society of Women Engineers
230 E Ohio Street, Suite 400
Chicago, IL 60611-3265
Phone: 312-596-5223
Fax: 312-644-8557
E-mail: suman.patil@swe.org

DOROTHY M. AND EARL S. HOFFMAN SCHOLARSHIP

Renewable three-year scholarship for female freshman engineering students. Must have minimum 3.5 GPA. Preference given to students at Bucknell University and Rensselaer Polytechnic University.

Academic Fields/Career Goals: Engineering/Technology.

Award: Scholarship for use in freshman year; renewable. *Number:* 5. *Amount:* $3000.

Eligibility Requirements: Applicant must be high school student; planning to enroll or expecting to enroll full-time at a four-year institution or university and female. Applicant must have 3.5 GPA or higher. Available to U.S. citizens.

Application Requirements: Application, references, self-addressed stamped envelope, transcript. *Deadline:* May 15.

Contact: Suman Pa, Program Coordinator
Society of Women Engineers
230 E Ohio Street, Suite 400
Chicago, IL 60611-3265
Phone: 312-596-5223
Fax: 312-644-8557
E-mail: suman.patil@swe.org

DOROTHY MORRIS SCHOLARSHIP

One $1000 scholarship available to graduate of New Jersey high school. Must be U.S. citizen.

Academic Fields/Career Goals: Engineering/Technology.

Award: Scholarship for use in sophomore, junior, or senior years; not renewable. *Number:* 1. *Amount:* $1000.

Eligibility Requirements: Applicant must be enrolled or expecting to enroll full-time at a four-year institution or university and female. Applicant must have 3.0 GPA or higher. Available to U.S. citizens.

Application Requirements: Application. *Deadline:* February 1.

Contact: Suman Pa, Program Coordinator
Society of Women Engineers
230 E Ohio Street, Suite 400
Chicago, IL 60611-3265
Phone: 312-596-5223
Fax: 312-644-8557
E-mail: suman.patil@swe.org

ELECTRONICS FOR IMAGING (EFI) SCHOLARSHIPS

Four scholarships available to female engineering students in sophomore, junior, senior year, and graduate study. Preference given to students attending selected schools in the San Francisco Bay area.

Academic Fields/Career Goals: Engineering/Technology.

Award: Scholarship for use in sophomore, junior, senior, or graduate years. *Number:* 4. *Amount:* $4000.

Eligibility Requirements: Applicant must be enrolled or expecting to enroll full-time at a four-year institution or university and female. Applicant must have 3.0 GPA or higher. Available to U.S. citizens.

Application Requirements: Application, references, self-addressed stamped envelope, transcript. *Deadline:* February 1.

Contact: Suman Pa, Program Coordinator
Society of Women Engineers
230 E Ohio Street, Suite 400
Chicago, IL 60611-3265
Phone: 312-596-5223
Fax: 312-644-8557
E-mail: suman.patil@swe.org

ELECTRONICS FOR IMAGING SCHOLARSHIP

Four $4000 scholarships available to female sophomore, junior, and senior undergraduate engineering students.

Academic Fields/Career Goals: Engineering/Technology.

Award: Scholarship for use in freshman, sophomore, junior, senior, or graduate years; not renewable. *Number:* 4. *Amount:* $4000.

Eligibility Requirements: Applicant must be enrolled or expecting to enroll full-time at a four-year institution or university and female. Applicant must have 3.0 GPA or higher. Available to U.S. citizens.

Application Requirements: Application. *Deadline:* February 1.

Contact: Suman Pa, Program Coordinator
Society of Women Engineers
230 E Ohio Street, Suite 400
Chicago, IL 60611-3265
Phone: 312-596-5223
Fax: 312-644-8557
E-mail: suman.patil@swe.org

EXELON SCHOLARSHIP

One $1000 scholarship for entering freshman pursuing engineering degree.

Academic Fields/Career Goals: Engineering/Technology.

Award: Scholarship for use in freshman year; not renewable. *Number:* 1. *Amount:* $1000.

Eligibility Requirements: Applicant must be enrolled or expecting to enroll full-time at a four-year institution or university and female. Applicant must have 3.5 GPA or higher. Available to U.S. citizens.

Application Requirements: Application. *Deadline:* May 15.

Contact: Suman Pa, Program Coordinator
Society of Women Engineers
230 E Ohio Street, Suite 400
Chicago, IL 60611-3265
Phone: 312-596-5223
Fax: 312-644-8557
E-mail: suman.patil@swe.org

FORD MOTOR COMPANY SCHOLARSHIP

One $1000 scholarship will be awarded to a female student studying engineering. Eligible applicants will be sophomores and juniors demonstrating leadership qualities.

Academic Fields/Career Goals: Engineering/Technology.

Award: Scholarship for use in sophomore or junior years; not renewable. *Number:* 2. *Amount:* $1000.

Eligibility Requirements: Applicant must be enrolled or expecting to enroll at a four-year institution or university; female and must have an interest in leadership. Applicant must have 3.5 GPA or higher. Available to U.S. citizens.

Application Requirements: Application, references, self-addressed stamped envelope, transcript. *Deadline:* February 1.

Contact: Suman Pa, Program Coordinator
Society of Women Engineers
230 E Ohio Street, Suite 400
Chicago, IL 60611-3265
Phone: 312-596-5223
Fax: 312-644-8557
E-mail: suman.patil@swe.org

GENERAL ELECTRIC FOUNDATION SCHOLARSHIP

Renewable award for outstanding women engineering students. Renewable for three years with continued academic achievement. Send self-addressed stamped envelope for more information. Must be U.S. citizen. Must have a minimum 3.5 GPA. Deadline: May 15.

Academic Fields/Career Goals: Engineering/Technology.

Award: Scholarship for use in freshman year; renewable. *Number:* 3. *Amount:* $1000–$1250.

Eligibility Requirements: Applicant must be high school student; planning to enroll or expecting to enroll at a four-year institution or university and female. Applicant must have 3.5 GPA or higher. Available to U.S. citizens.

Application Requirements: Application, essay, references, self-addressed stamped envelope, test scores, transcript. *Deadline:* May 15.

Contact: Suman Pa, Program Coordinator
Society of Women Engineers
230 E Ohio Street, Suite 400
Chicago, IL 60611-3265
Phone: 312-596-5223
Fax: 312-644-8557
E-mail: suman.patil@swe.org

GENERAL ELECTRIC WOMEN'S NETWORK SCHOLARSHIP

Thirteen $2425 scholarships available to undergraduate sophomores, juniors, and seniors studying engineering. Must be U.S. citizen.

Academic Fields/Career Goals: Engineering/Technology.

Award: Scholarship for use in sophomore, junior, or senior years; not renewable. *Number:* 13. *Amount:* $2425.

Eligibility Requirements: Applicant must be enrolled or expecting to enroll full-time at a four-year institution or university and female. Applicant must have 3.0 GPA or higher. Available to U.S. citizens.

Application Requirements: Application. *Deadline:* February 1.

Contact: Suman Pa, Program Coordinator
Society of Women Engineers
230 E Ohio Street, Suite 400
Chicago, IL 60611-3265
Phone: 312-596-5223
Fax: 312-644-8557
E-mail: suman.patil@swe.org

GENERAL MOTORS FOUNDATION UNDERGRADUATE SCHOLARSHIPS
• See page 168

GUIDANT CORPORATION SCHOLARSHIP
• See page 195

IVY PARKER MEMORIAL SCHOLARSHIP

One-time award for female engineering major. Must be in junior or senior year and have a minimum 3.0 GPA. Selection also based on financial need. Deadline: February 1.

Academic Fields/Career Goals: Engineering/Technology.

Award: Scholarship for use in junior or senior years; not renewable. *Number:* 1. *Amount:* $2500.

Eligibility Requirements: Applicant must be enrolled or expecting to enroll at a four-year institution or university and female. Applicant must have 3.0 GPA or higher. Available to U.S. citizens.

Application Requirements: Application, financial need analysis, references, self-addressed stamped envelope, transcript. *Deadline:* February 1.

Contact: Suman Pa, Program Coordinator
Society of Women Engineers
230 E Ohio Street, Suite 400
Chicago, IL 60611-3265
Phone: 312-596-5223
Fax: 312-644-8557
E-mail: suman.patil@swe.org

JUDITH RESNIK MEMORIAL SCHOLARSHIP
• See page 130

LILIAN MOLLER GILBRETH SCHOLARSHIP

One award for college junior or senior female engineering student. Must be a U.S. citizen and possess outstanding potential demonstrated by achievement. Send self-addressed stamped envelope for application. One-time award of $6000. Must rank in upper third of class or have a minimum GPA of 3.0. Deadline: February 1.

Academic Fields/Career Goals: Engineering/Technology.

Award: Scholarship for use in junior or senior years; not renewable. *Number:* 1. *Amount:* $6000.

Eligibility Requirements: Applicant must be enrolled or expecting to enroll at a four-year institution or university and female. Applicant must have 3.0 GPA or higher. Available to U.S. citizens.

Application Requirements: Application, essay, references, self-addressed stamped envelope, test scores, transcript. *Deadline:* February 1.

Society of Women Engineers (continued)

Contact: Suman Pa, Program Coordinator
Society of Women Engineers
230 E Ohio Street, Suite 400
Chicago, IL 60611-3265
Phone: 312-596-5223
Fax: 312-644-8557
E-mail: suman.patil@swe.org

LOCKHEED-MARTIN CORPORATION SCHOLARSHIPS

Two $3000 scholarships awarded to female incoming freshmen majoring in engineering. Minimum 3.5 GPA required. Deadline for application is May 15.

Academic Fields/Career Goals: Engineering/Technology.

Award: Scholarship for use in freshman year; not renewable. *Number:* 2. *Amount:* $3000.

Eligibility Requirements: Applicant must be enrolled or expecting to enroll full-time at a four-year institution or university and female. Applicant must have 3.5 GPA or higher. Available to U.S. and non-U.S. citizens.

Application Requirements: Application, essay, references, self-addressed stamped envelope, test scores, transcript. *Deadline:* May 15.

Contact: Suman Pa, Program Coordinator
Society of Women Engineers
230 E Ohio Street, Suite 400
Chicago, IL 60611-3265
Phone: 312-596-5223
Fax: 312-644-8557
E-mail: suman.patil@swe.org

LYDIA I. PICKUP MEMORIAL SCHOLARSHIP

• See page 195

MASWE MEMORIAL SCHOLARSHIP

Four $2000 awards for female engineering students who are sophomores, juniors, or seniors in college. Must be U.S. citizens and have minimum 3.0 GPA. Send self-addressed stamped envelope for application. Selection also based on financial need. Deadline: February 1.

Academic Fields/Career Goals: Engineering/Technology.

Award: Scholarship for use in sophomore, junior, or senior years; not renewable. *Number:* 4. *Amount:* $2000.

Eligibility Requirements: Applicant must be enrolled or expecting to enroll at a four-year institution or university and female. Applicant must have 3.0 GPA or higher. Available to U.S. citizens.

Application Requirements: Application, essay, financial need analysis, self-addressed stamped envelope, test scores, transcript. *Deadline:* February 1.

Contact: Suman Pa, Program Coordinator
Society of Women Engineers
230 E Ohio Street, Suite 400
Chicago, IL 60611-3265
Phone: 312-596-5223
Fax: 312-644-8557
E-mail: suman.patil@swe.org

MERIDITH THOMS MEMORIAL SCHOLARSHIP

Renewable award available to female engineering majors. Minimum 3.0 GPA required. Must be in ABET-accredited engineering program at SWE-approved colleges and universities.

Academic Fields/Career Goals: Engineering/Technology.

Award: Scholarship for use in sophomore, junior, or senior years; renewable. *Number:* 6. *Amount:* $2000.

Eligibility Requirements: Applicant must be enrolled or expecting to enroll at a four-year institution or university and female. Applicant must have 3.0 GPA or higher. Available to U.S. citizens.

Application Requirements: Application, references, self-addressed stamped envelope, test scores, transcript. *Deadline:* February 1.

Contact: Suman Pa, Program Coordinator
Society of Women Engineers
230 E Ohio Street, Suite 400
Chicago, IL 60611-3265
Phone: 312-596-5223
Fax: 312-644-8557
E-mail: suman.patil@swe.org

MINNESOTA SWE SECTION SCHOLARSHIP

Applicants must be undergraduate juniors or seniors at an accredited engineering program attending a Minnesota, North Dakota, or South Dakota school. Applicants judged on potential to succeed as engineer, communication skills, extracurricular activities, community involvement or leadership skills, demonstration of work experience and success, and academic excellence.

Academic Fields/Career Goals: Engineering/Technology.

Award: Scholarship for use in junior or senior years; not renewable. *Number:* 1. *Amount:* $750.

Eligibility Requirements: Applicant must be enrolled or expecting to enroll at a four-year institution or university; female and studying in Minnesota, North Dakota, or South Dakota. Available to U.S. citizens.

Application Requirements: Application. *Deadline:* March 15.

Contact: Naomi Brill
Phone: 651-636-8676
E-mail: nbrill323@yahoo.com

NEW JERSEY SCHOLARSHIP

Award granted to female New Jersey resident majoring in engineering. Available to incoming freshman. Minimum 3.5 GPA required. Application deadline is May 15.

Academic Fields/Career Goals: Engineering/Technology.

Award: Scholarship for use in freshman year; not renewable. *Number:* 1. *Amount:* $1500.

Eligibility Requirements: Applicant must be enrolled or expecting to enroll full-time at a four-year institution or university; female and resident of New Jersey. Applicant must have 3.5 GPA or higher. Available to U.S. citizens.

Application Requirements: Application, essay, references, self-addressed stamped envelope, test scores, transcript. *Deadline:* May 15.

Contact: Suman Pa, Program Coordinator
Society of Women Engineers
230 E Ohio Street, Suite 400
Chicago, IL 60611-3265
Phone: 312-596-5223
Fax: 312-644-8557
E-mail: suman.patil@swe.org

NORTHROP GRUMMAN CORPORATION SCHOLARSHIPS

• See page 130

OLIVE LYNN SALEMBIER SCHOLARSHIP

One $2000 award for female students entering any undergraduate or graduate year as full- or part-time students. Applicants must have been out of the engineering job market as well as out of school for a minimum of two years. Application deadline is May 15.

Academic Fields/Career Goals: Engineering/Technology.

Award: Scholarship for use in freshman, sophomore, junior, senior, or graduate years; not renewable. *Number:* 1. *Amount:* $2000.

Eligibility Requirements: Applicant must be enrolled or expecting to enroll full or part-time at a four-year institution or university and female. Applicant must have 3.5 GPA or higher. Available to U.S. citizens.

Application Requirements: Application, essay, references, self-addressed stamped envelope, test scores, transcript. *Deadline:* May 15.

Contact: Suman Pa, Program Coordinator
Society of Women Engineers
230 E Ohio Street, Suite 400
Chicago, IL 60611-3265
Phone: 312-596-5223
Fax: 312-644-8557
E-mail: suman.patil@swe.org

PAST PRESIDENTS SCHOLARSHIPS

Two $1500 awards offered to female undergraduate or graduate students majoring in engineering. Minimum 3.0 GPA required. Must be U.S. citizen. Deadline: February 1.

Academic Fields/Career Goals: Engineering/Technology.

Award: Scholarship for use in sophomore, junior, senior, or graduate years; renewable. *Number:* 2. *Amount:* $1500.

Eligibility Requirements: Applicant must be enrolled or expecting to enroll full-time at a four-year institution or university and female. Applicant must have 3.0 GPA or higher. Available to U.S. citizens.

Application Requirements: Application, essay, references, self-addressed stamped envelope, test scores, transcript. *Deadline:* February 1.

Contact: Suman Pa, Program Coordinator
Society of Women Engineers
230 E Ohio Street, Suite 400
Chicago, IL 60611-3265
Phone: 312-596-5223
Fax: 312-644-8557
E-mail: suman.patil@swe.org

ROCKWELL AUTOMATION SCHOLARSHIP

One-time award available to female engineering major. Must be in junior year and have a minimum 3.5 GPA. Must have demonstrated leadership potential. Underrepresented group preferred. Deadline: February 1.

Academic Fields/Career Goals: Engineering/Technology.

Award: Scholarship for use in junior year; not renewable. *Number:* 2. *Amount:* $2500.

Eligibility Requirements: Applicant must be enrolled or expecting to enroll full-time at a four-year institution or university; female and must have an interest in leadership. Applicant must have 3.0 GPA or higher. Available to U.S. citizens.

Application Requirements: Application, references, self-addressed stamped envelope, transcript. *Deadline:* February 1.

Contact: Suman Pa, Program Coordinator
Society of Women Engineers
230 E Ohio Street, Suite 400
Chicago, IL 60611-3265
Phone: 312-596-5223
Fax: 312-644-8557
E-mail: suman.patil@swe.org

SUSAN MISZKOWITZ MEMORIAL SCHOLARSHIP

One $1000 scholarship available to undergraduate sophomore, junior, or senior studying engineering.

Academic Fields/Career Goals: Engineering/Technology.

Award: Scholarship for use in sophomore, junior, or senior years; not renewable. *Number:* 1. *Amount:* $1000.

Eligibility Requirements: Applicant must be enrolled or expecting to enroll full-time at a four-year institution or university and female. Applicant must have 3.0 GPA or higher. Available to U.S. citizens.

Application Requirements: Application. *Deadline:* February 1.

Contact: Suman Pa, Program Coordinator
Society of Women Engineers
230 E Ohio Street, Suite 400
Chicago, IL 60611-3265
Phone: 312-596-5223
Fax: 312-644-8557
E-mail: suman.patil@swe.org

SWE BALTIMORE-WASHINGTON SECTION SCHOLARSHIPS
• See page 195

SWE BATON ROUGE SECTION SCHOLARSHIPS
• See page 195

SWE CALIFORNIA GOLDEN GATE SECTION SCHOLARSHIPS
• See page 195

SWE CALIFORNIA SANTA CLARA VALLEY SECTION SCHOLARSHIP

Applicant must plan to attend school full time in the fall next year and plan to attend a four or five year baccalaureate program or an advanced degree program. Applicant must attend school or be a permanent resident in the South San Francisco Bay Area. Please the see Web site for more details: http://www.swe-goldenwest.org/scvs/www/index.htm

Academic Fields/Career Goals: Engineering/Technology.

Award: Scholarship for use in freshman, sophomore, junior, senior, or graduate years; not renewable. *Number:* 10–15. *Amount:* $500–$1000.

Eligibility Requirements: Applicant must be enrolled or expecting to enroll full-time at a four-year institution or university; female and resident of California. Available to U.S. citizens.

Application Requirements: Application. *Deadline:* varies.

Contact: Melissa Tumbleson, Scholarship Chair
Phone: 510-559-9252
E-mail: melissa.tumbleson@comcast.net

SWE CHICAGO REGIONAL SECTION SCHOLARSHIPS

Scholarship for first-year, reentry, or transfer student in undergraduate engineering degree program. Must be accepted into accredited university for following fall semester. Applications available at Web site: http://www.iit.edu/~swe-chi

Academic Fields/Career Goals: Engineering/Technology.

Award: Scholarship for use in freshman, sophomore, junior, or senior years; not renewable. *Number:* 1. *Amount:* varies.

Eligibility Requirements: Applicant must be enrolled or expecting to enroll at a four-year institution or university and female. Available to U.S. citizens.

Application Requirements: Application, essay. *Deadline:* April 15.

Contact: Laurel Jasek, Scholarship Committee Chair
Society of Women Engineers
PO Box 95525
Palatine, IL 60095-0525
E-mail: swe-crs@swe.org

SWE CONNECTICUT SECTION JEAN R. BEERS SCHOLARSHIP
• See page 196

SWE FLORIDA SPACE COAST SECTION SCHOLARSHIP

One or more awards of $1000 to entering freshman within the counties served by the Section.

Academic Fields/Career Goals: Engineering/Technology.

Award: Scholarship for use in freshman, sophomore, junior, or senior years; not renewable. *Number:* 1. *Amount:* $1000.

Eligibility Requirements: Applicant must be enrolled or expecting to enroll at a four-year institution or university; female; resident of Florida and studying in Florida. Available to U.S. citizens.

Application Requirements: Application. *Deadline:* varies.

Contact: Donna Ware, Scholarship Committee
Society of Women Engineers
PO Box 1297
Cape Canaveral, FL 32920
E-mail: donna.ware@lmco.com

SWE GREATER NEW ORLEANS SECTION SCHOLARSHIP
• See page 196

SWE LEHIGH VALLEY SECTION SCHOLARSHIP

Applicants must be female graduating high school seniors, within the Lehigh Valley Section, planning on attending an ABET-accredited college or university in the following fall semester.

Academic Fields/Career Goals: Engineering/Technology.

Award: Scholarship for use in freshman year; not renewable. *Number:* varies. *Amount:* $1000.

Eligibility Requirements: Applicant must be high school student; planning to enroll or expecting to enroll at an institution or university; female; resident of Pennsylvania and must have an interest in leadership. Available to U.S. citizens.

Society of Women Engineers (continued)

Application Requirements: Application, proof of acceptance. *Deadline:* April 15.

Contact: Amy Holovaty
Phone: 610-481-5317
E-mail: holovaam@apci.com

SWE SOUTHWEST IDAHO SECTION SCHOLARSHIP

Applicant must be female high school senior resident of Southwest Idaho planning to attend an engineering program. Must plan on attending a five year program at an ABET-accredited engineering program.

Academic Fields/Career Goals: Engineering/Technology.

Award: Scholarship for use in freshman year; not renewable. *Number:* varies. *Amount:* varies.

Eligibility Requirements: Applicant must be enrolled or expecting to enroll full or part-time at a four-year institution or university; female and resident of Idaho. Available to U.S. citizens.

Application Requirements: Application, essay. *Deadline:* varies.

Contact: Alonna Albertus, Scholarship Co-chair
E-mail: alonna.albertus@hp.com

SWE ST. LOUIS SCHOLARSHIP

One $500 scholarship will be awarded to an entering sophomore, junior, or senior undergraduate student, or a graduate student attending one of the following colleges/universities: Southern Illinois University, Parks College of Engineering and Aviation, St. Louis University, University of Missouri, or Washington University. Must be SWE student member.

Academic Fields/Career Goals: Engineering/Technology.

Award: Scholarship for use in sophomore, junior, senior, or graduate years; not renewable. *Number:* 1. *Amount:* $500.

Eligibility Requirements: Applicant must be enrolled or expecting to enroll at a four-year institution or university; female and studying in Illinois or Missouri. Applicant or parent of applicant must be member of Society of Women Engineers. Available to U.S. citizens.

Application Requirements: Application. *Deadline:* varies.

Contact: Heidi Houghton
Phone: 618-583-1343
E-mail: Heidi.Houghton@swe.org

WILLAMETTE VALLEY SECTION MARTINA TESTA MEMORIAL SCHOLARSHIP

Applicant must be female graduating high school senior planning on pursuing an engineering baccalaureate degree at an ABET-accredited school.

Academic Fields/Career Goals: Engineering/Technology.

Award: Scholarship for use in freshman year; not renewable. *Number:* 1. *Amount:* $1000.

Eligibility Requirements: Applicant must be high school student; planning to enroll or expecting to enroll at a four-year institution or university; female and resident of Oregon. Available to U.S. citizens.

Application Requirements: Application. *Deadline:* varies.

Contact: Marilyn McGettigan, Scholarship Committee Chair
Society of Women Engineers
PO Box 576
Corvallis, OR 97339-0576

SOCIETY OF WOMEN ENGINEERS - DALLAS SECTION   http://www.dallaswe.org

FRESHMAN ENGINEERING SCHOLARSHIP FOR DALLAS WOMEN

Scholarship for freshman women pursuing a degree in engineering. Applicant must be a Texas resident. Deadline is May 15. Please refer to Web site for further details: http://www.dallaswe.org

Academic Fields/Career Goals: Engineering/Technology.

Award: Scholarship for use in freshman year; not renewable. *Number:* 2. *Amount:* $500.

Eligibility Requirements: Applicant must be high school student; planning to enroll or expecting to enroll full-time at a four-year institution or university; female and resident of Texas. Available to U.S. citizens.

Application Requirements: Application, financial need analysis, references, confirmation of enrollment. *Deadline:* May 15.

Contact: SWE - Dallas Section
Society of Women Engineers - Dallas Section
PO Box 852022
Richardson, TX 75085-2022

NATIONAL SOCIETY OF WOMEN ENGINEERS SCHOLARSHIPS
• See page 196

SOCIETY OF WOMEN ENGINEERS - ROCKY MOUNTAIN SECTION   http://www.swe.org

SOCIETY OF WOMEN ENGINEERS-ROCKY MOUNTAIN SECTION SCHOLARSHIP PROGRAM
• See page 196

SOCIETY OF WOMEN ENGINEERS - TWIN TIERS SECTION   http://www.swetwintiers.org

SOCIETY OF WOMEN ENGINEERS - TWIN TIERS SECTION SCHOLARSHIP
• See page 196

SPECIALTY EQUIPMENT MARKET ASSOCIATION   http://www.sema.org

SPECIALTY EQUIPMENT MARKET ASSOCIATION MEMORIAL SCHOLARSHIP FUND

Scholarship for higher education in the automotive field. All applicants must be attending a U.S. institution. For further details visit Web site: http://www.sema.org.

Academic Fields/Career Goals: Engineering/Technology; Trade/Technical Specialties.

Award: Scholarship for use in freshman, sophomore, junior, senior, or graduate years; not renewable. *Number:* varies. *Amount:* $1000–$4000.

Eligibility Requirements: Applicant must be enrolled or expecting to enroll full-time at a two-year or four-year or technical institution or university and must have an interest in automotive. Applicant must have 2.5 GPA or higher. Available to U.S. and non-U.S. citizens.

Application Requirements: Application, essay, photo, references, self-addressed stamped envelope, transcript. *Deadline:* May 31.

Contact: SEMA Memorial Scholarship Fund
Specialty Equipment Market Association
1575 South Valley Vista Drive
Diamond Bar, CA 91765
Phone: 909-396-0289
E-mail: sema@sema.org

TAU BETA PI ASSOCIATION   http://www.tbp.org

TAU BETA PI SCHOLARSHIP PROGRAM

One-time award for initiated members of Tau Beta Pi in their senior year of full-time undergraduate engineering study. Submit application and two letters of recommendation. Contact for complete details or visit http://www.tbp.org.

Academic Fields/Career Goals: Engineering/Technology.

Award: Scholarship for use in freshman, sophomore, junior, or senior years; not renewable. *Number:* 30–50. *Amount:* $2000.

Eligibility Requirements: Applicant must be enrolled or expecting to enroll full-time at a four-year institution or university. Applicant or parent of applicant must be member of Tau Beta Pi Association. Applicant must have 3.5 GPA or higher. Available to U.S. and non-U.S. citizens.

Application Requirements: Application, references. *Deadline:* March 1.

Contact: D. Stephen Pierre, Jr., Director of Fellowships
Tau Beta Pi Association
PO Box 2697
Knoxville, TN 37901-2697
Fax: 334-694-2310
E-mail: dspierre@southernco.com

TEXAS ENGINEERING FOUNDATION
http://www.tspe.org/

TEXAS SOCIETY OF PROFESSIONAL ENGINEERS (TSPE) REGIONAL SCHOLARSHIPS
• See page 169

TRIANGLE EDUCATION FOUNDATION
http://www.triangle.org

KAPADIA SCHOLARSHIPS

One-time award for active members of the Triangle Fraternity. Must be full-time, male students who have completed at least one year of study at the college level. Must be majoring in an engineering program and have at least a 3.0 GPA. Preference given to members of the Zoroastrian religion.

Academic Fields/Career Goals: Engineering/Technology.

Award: Scholarship for use in freshman, sophomore, junior, senior, or graduate years; not renewable. *Number:* varies. *Amount:* $1500–$5000.

Eligibility Requirements: Applicant must be enrolled or expecting to enroll full-time at a four-year institution or university and male. Applicant must have 3.0 GPA or higher. Available to U.S. and non-U.S. citizens.

Application Requirements: Application, essay, financial need analysis, references, self-addressed stamped envelope, transcript. *Deadline:* February 15.

Contact: Scott Bova, Administrative Assistant
Triangle Education Foundation
120 South Center Street
Plainfield, IN 46168
Phone: 317-837-9641
Fax: 317-837-9042
E-mail: sbova@triangle.org

SEVCIK SCHOLARSHIP

One-time award for active member of the Triangle Fraternity. Must be full-time male student who has completed at least two full academic years of school. Minimum 3.0 GPA. Preference to minority students and Ohio State undergraduates who are engineering majors. Application must be postmarked by Feb 15. Further information available at Web site http://www.triangle.org

Academic Fields/Career Goals: Engineering/Technology.

Award: Scholarship for use in freshman, sophomore, junior, or senior years; not renewable. *Number:* 1. *Amount:* up to $1000.

Eligibility Requirements: Applicant must be American Indian/Alaska Native, Asian/Pacific Islander, Black (non-Hispanic), or Hispanic; enrolled or expecting to enroll full-time at a four-year institution or university and male. Applicant must have 3.0 GPA or higher. Available to U.S. citizens.

Application Requirements: Application, essay, financial need analysis, references, self-addressed stamped envelope, transcript. *Deadline:* February 15.

Contact: Scott Bova, President
Triangle Education Foundation
120 South Center Street
Plainfield, IN 46168-1214
Phone: 317-705-9803
Fax: 317-837-9642
E-mail: sbova@triangle.org

UNITED NEGRO COLLEGE FUND
http://www.uncf.org

ACCENTURE SCHOLARSHIP
• See page 197

BATTELLE SCHOLARS PROGRAM

Scholarship for students from central Ohio attending a UNCF member college or university. Please visit Web site for more information: http://www.uncf.org

Academic Fields/Career Goals: Engineering/Technology.

Award: Scholarship for use in junior year. *Number:* varies. *Amount:* $10,000.

Eligibility Requirements: Applicant must be Black (non-Hispanic); enrolled or expecting to enroll at a four-year institution or university and resident of Ohio. Applicant must have 3.0 GPA or higher. Available to U.S. citizens.

Application Requirements: Application, financial need analysis, FAFSA, Student Aid Report (SAR). *Deadline:* varies.

Contact: Rebecca Bennett, Director, Program Services
United Negro College Fund
8260 Willow Oaks Corporate Drive
Fairfax, VA 22031-8044
Phone: 800-331-2244
E-mail: rbennett@uncf.org

BOOZ, ALLEN & HAMILTON/WILLIAM F. STASIOR INTERNSHIP
• See page 154

CARDINAL HEALTH SCHOLARSHIP
• See page 70

CARTER AND BURGESS SCHOLARSHIP

Scholarship awarded to a student majoring in engineering, who also attends a UNCF member college or university. Must be a resident of Ft Worth, Texas. Please visit Web site for more information: http://www.uncf.org

Academic Fields/Career Goals: Engineering/Technology.

Award: Scholarship for use in freshman, sophomore, junior, senior, or graduate years; renewable. *Number:* 1. *Amount:* varies.

Eligibility Requirements: Applicant must be Black (non-Hispanic); enrolled or expecting to enroll at a four-year institution or university and resident of Texas. Applicant must have 2.5 GPA or higher. Available to U.S. citizens.

Application Requirements: Application, financial need analysis, FAFSA, Student Aid Report (SAR). *Deadline:* varies.

Contact: Rebecca Bennett, Director, Program Services
United Negro College Fund
8260 Willow Oaks Corporate Drive
Fairfax, VA 22031-8044
Phone: 800-331-2244
E-mail: rbennett@uncf.org

CASTLE ROCK FOUNDATION SCHOLARSHIP
• See page 154

CDM SCHOLARSHIP/INTERNSHIP
• See page 177

CHEVRON/TEXACO SCHOLARS PROGRAM
• See page 177

CON EDISON SCHOLARSHIP
• See page 70

DELL/UNCF CORPORATE SCHOLARS PROGRAM
• See page 155

EMERSON ELECTRIC COMPANY SCHOLARSHIP
• See page 71

FORD/UNCF CORPORATE SCHOLARS PROGRAM
• See page 71

GILBANE SCHOLARSHIP/INTERNSHIP

Scholarship provides up to $5000 in financial assistance after students have completed a paid summer internship program. Applicants must be Pennsylvania residents majoring in engineering at a UNCF member college or university. Minimum 2.5 GPA required. Prospective applicants should complete the Student Profile found at Web site: http://www.uncf.org

Academic Fields/Career Goals: Engineering/Technology.

Award: Scholarship for use in sophomore or junior years; not renewable. *Amount:* up to $5000.

Eligibility Requirements: Applicant must be Black (non-Hispanic); enrolled or expecting to enroll full-time at a four-year institution or university and resident of Delaware or Pennsylvania. Applicant must have 2.5 GPA or higher. Available to U.S. citizens.

Application Requirements: Application, financial need analysis. *Deadline:* February 17.

United Negro College Fund (continued)

Contact: Rebecca Bennett, Director, Program Services
United Negro College Fund
8260 Willow Oaks Corporate Drive
Fairfax, VA 22031-8044
Phone: 800-331-2244
E-mail: rbennett@uncf.org

KODAK ENGINEERING EXCELLENCE PROGRAM SCHOLARSHIP
• *See page 197*

MAYTAG COMPANY SCHOLARSHIP
• *See page 155*

NORTHEAST UTILITIES SYSTEM SCHOLARSHIP PROGRAM
• *See page 156*

SBC FOUNDATION SCHOLARSHIP
• *See page 156*

SBC PACIFIC BELL FOUNDATION SCHOLARSHIP
• *See page 156*

SPRINT SCHOLARSHIP/INTERNSHIP
• *See page 71*

TRW INFORMATION TECHNOLOGY MINORITY SCHOLARSHIP
• *See page 197*

WEYERHAEUSER/UNCF CORPORATE SCHOLARS
• *See page 157*

WM. WRIGLEY, JR. COMPANY SCHOLARS PROGRAM
• *See page 157*

UNIVERSITIES SPACE RESEARCH ASSOCIATION
http://www.usra.edu

UNIVERSITIES SPACE RESEARCH ASSOCIATION SCHOLARSHIP PROGRAM
• *See page 96*

UTAH SOCIETY OF PROFESSIONAL ENGINEERS
http://www.uspeonline.com

UTAH SOCIETY OF PROFESSIONAL ENGINEERS SCHOLARSHIP
• *See page 169*

VIRGINIA BUSINESS AND PROFESSIONAL WOMEN'S FOUNDATION
http://www.bpwva.org

WOMEN IN SCIENCE AND TECHNOLOGY SCHOLARSHIP
• *See page 143*

WINDSTAR FOUNDATION
http://www.wstar.org

WINDSTAR ENVIRONMENTAL STUDIES SCHOLARSHIPS

Two $500 scholarships for qualified undergraduates entering their junior or senior year of college, and one $1000 scholarship for graduate students entering their second year of graduate school.

Academic Fields/Career Goals: Engineering/Technology; Environmental Health.

Award: Scholarship for use in junior, senior, or graduate years. *Amount:* $500–$1000.

Eligibility Requirements: Applicant must be enrolled or expecting to enroll at an institution or university. Applicant must have 3.0 GPA or higher. Available to U.S. citizens.

Application Requirements: Application, essay, transcript. *Deadline:* June 1.

Contact: Gene Hall, Environmental Studies Scholarship
Windstar Foundation
c/o CU Museum of Natural History, University of Colorado
Campus Box 265
Boulder, CO 80309-0265
Phone: 970-927-5430
Fax: 866-927-5430
E-mail: biodivers@yahoo.com

WISCONSIN SOCIETY OF PROFESSIONAL ENGINEERS
http://www.wspe.org

WISCONSIN SOCIETY OF PROFESSIONAL ENGINEERS SCHOLARSHIPS

One-time award for students pursuing full-time study in engineering. Must be a Wisconsin resident and have a minimum GPA of 3.0. Application deadline is December 15.

Academic Fields/Career Goals: Engineering/Technology.

Award: Scholarship for use in freshman, junior, or senior years; not renewable. *Number:* 3. *Amount:* $1000–$1500.

Eligibility Requirements: Applicant must be enrolled or expecting to enroll full-time at a four-year institution or university and resident of Wisconsin. Applicant must have 3.0 GPA or higher. Available to U.S. and non-U.S. citizens.

Application Requirements: Application, essay, references, self-addressed stamped envelope, test scores, transcript. *Deadline:* December 15.

Contact: Annette Hess, Executive Director
Wisconsin Society of Professional Engineers
7044 South 13th Street
Oak Creek, WI 53154
Phone: 414-768-8000 Ext. 119
E-mail: wspe@wspe.org

XEROX
http://www.xerox.com

TECHNICAL MINORITY SCHOLARSHIP
• *See page 169*

ENGINEERING-RELATED TECHNOLOGIES

AACE INTERNATIONAL
http://www.aacei.org

AACE INTERNATIONAL COMPETITIVE SCHOLARSHIP
• *See page 96*

AMERICAN COUNCIL OF ENGINEERING COMPANIES OF PENNSYLVANIA (ACEC/PA)
http://www.acecpa.org

ENGINEERING SCHOLARSHIP
• *See page 158*

AMERICAN INDIAN SCIENCE AND ENGINEERING SOCIETY
http://www.aises.org

GENERAL MOTORS ENGINEERING SCHOLARSHIP

A $3000 scholarship will be given to a current AISES member. Must be a member of an American-Indian Tribe or otherwise be considered to be an American-Indian by the tribe with which affiliation is claimed. Must maintain a 3.0 GPA.

Academic Fields/Career Goals: Engineering-Related Technologies.

Award: Scholarship for use in freshman, sophomore, junior, senior, or graduate years; not renewable. *Number:* varies. *Amount:* up to $3000.

Eligibility Requirements: Applicant must be American Indian/Alaska Native and enrolled or expecting to enroll full-time at a four-year institution or university. Applicant must have 3.0 GPA or higher. Available to U.S. citizens.

Application Requirements: Application, essay, resume, references, transcript. *Deadline:* June 15.

Contact: Shirley Lacourse, Scholarship Information
American Indian Science and Engineering Society
PO Box 9828
Albuquerque, NM 87119-9828
Phone: 505-765-1052
Fax: 505-765-5608
E-mail: info@aises.org

HENRY RODRIGUEZ RECLAMATION COLLEGE SCHOLARSHIP AND INTERNSHIP

A $5000 scholarship will be given to a current AISES member. Must be enrolled full time in an accredited college or university. Must agree to serve an eight- to ten-week paid internship with the Bureau of Reclamation prior to graduation. Must maintain a 2.5 GPA. Must be seeking a BA in engineering or science, relating to water resources or an environmentally-related field. Must be a member of a Federally recognized Indian tribe.

Academic Fields/Career Goals: Engineering-Related Technologies; Environmental Science; Natural Resources; Natural Sciences.

Award: Scholarship for use in freshman, sophomore, junior, or senior years; renewable. *Number:* varies. *Amount:* up to $5000.

Eligibility Requirements: Applicant must be enrolled or expecting to enroll full-time at a four-year institution or university. Applicant must have 2.5 GPA or higher. Available to U.S. citizens.

Application Requirements: Application, essay, resume, references, transcript. *Deadline:* June 15.

Contact: Shirley Lacourse, Scholarship Information
American Indian Science and Engineering Society
PO Box 9828
Albuquerque, NM 87119-9828
Phone: 505-765-1052
Fax: 505-765-5608
E-mail: info@aises.org

AMERICAN PUBLIC TRANSPORTATION FOUNDATION   http://www.apta.com

DONALD C. HYDE ESSAY PROGRAM
• See page 171

JACK GILSTRAP SCHOLARSHIP
• See page 171

LOUIS T. KLAUDER SCHOLARSHIP
• See page 171

PARSONS BRINCKERHOFF-JIM LAMMIE SCHOLARSHIP
• See page 171

TRANSIT HALL OF FAME SCHOLARSHIP AWARD PROGRAM
• See page 171

AMERICAN SOCIETY OF HEATING, REFRIGERATING, AND AIR CONDITIONING ENGINEERS, INC.   http://www.ashrae.org

ASHRAE MEMORIAL SCHOLARSHIP
• See page 251

ASHRAE SCHOLARSHIPS
• See page 252

DUANE HANSON SCHOLARSHIP

One-time $3000 award for full-time study in heating, ventilating, refrigeration, and air conditioning in an ABET-accredited program at an accredited school. Submit letter of recommendation from a professor or faculty adviser and two letters of recommendation from individuals familiar with the applicant's character, accomplishments, and likelihood of success in the HVAC and/or refrigeration industry. Applicants must have at least one full year of remaining study.

Academic Fields/Career Goals: Engineering-Related Technologies; Heating, Air-Conditioning, and Refrigeration Mechanics; Trade/Technical Specialties.

Award: Scholarship for use in sophomore, junior, or senior years; not renewable. *Number:* 1. *Amount:* $3000.

Eligibility Requirements: Applicant must be enrolled or expecting to enroll full-time at a four-year institution or university. Applicant must have 3.0 GPA or higher. Available to U.S. citizens.

Application Requirements: Application, financial need analysis, references, transcript. *Deadline:* December 1.

Contact: Lois Benedict, Scholarship Administrator
American Society of Heating, Refrigerating, and Air Conditioning Engineers, Inc.
1791 Tullie Circle, NE
Atlanta, GA 30329
Phone: 404-636-8400
Fax: 404-321-5478
E-mail: benedict@ashrae.org

HENRY ADAMS SCHOLARSHIP
• See page 252

AMERICAN WELDING SOCIETY   http://www.aws.org

AIRGAS JERRY BAKER SCHOLARSHIP

Awarded to full-time undergraduate pursuing a minimum four-year degree in welding engineering or welding engineering technology. Applicant must be a minimum of eighteen years of age, must have 3.0 grade point average. Priority will be given to those individuals residing or attending school in the states of Alabama, Georgia or Florida. Application deadline is January 15.

Academic Fields/Career Goals: Engineering-Related Technologies; Trade/Technical Specialties.

Award: Scholarship for use in sophomore, junior, or senior years; not renewable. *Number:* 1. *Amount:* $2500.

Eligibility Requirements: Applicant must be age 18 and enrolled or expecting to enroll full-time at a four-year institution. Applicant must have 3.0 GPA or higher. Available to U.S. and Canadian citizens.

Application Requirements: Application, autobiography, financial need analysis, references, transcript. *Deadline:* January 15.

Contact: Vicki Pinsky, Manager Foundation
American Welding Society
550 Northwest Le Jeune Road
Miami, FL 33126
Phone: 800-443-9353 Ext. 212
Fax: 305-443-7559
E-mail: vpinsky@aws.org

AIRGAS-TERRY JARVIS MEMORIAL SCHOLARSHIP
• See page 253

AMERICAN WELDING SOCIETY DISTRICT SCHOLARSHIP PROGRAM

Award for students in vocational training, community college, or a degree program in welding or a related field of study. Applicants must be high school graduates or equivalent. Must reside in the U.S. and attend a U.S. institution. Recipients may reapply. Must include personal statement of career goals. Also must rank in upper half of class or have a minimum GPA of 2.5.

Academic Fields/Career Goals: Engineering-Related Technologies; Trade/Technical Specialties.

Award: Scholarship for use in freshman, sophomore, junior, or senior years; not renewable. *Number:* 66–150. *Amount:* $500–$1000.

Eligibility Requirements: Applicant must be age 18 and enrolled or expecting to enroll full or part-time at a two-year or four-year or technical institution or university. Available to U.S. and non-U.S. citizens.

Application Requirements: Application, autobiography, financial need analysis, transcript. *Deadline:* March 1.

Contact: Nazdhia Prado-Pulido, Foundation Associate
American Welding Society
550 Northwest Le Jeune Road
Miami, FL 33126
Phone: 800-443-9353 Ext. 250
Fax: 305-443-7559
E-mail: nprado-pulido@aws.org

AMERICAN WELDING SOCIETY INTERNATIONAL SCHOLARSHIP
• See page 253

American Welding Society (continued)

DONALD AND JEAN CLEVELAND-WILLAMETTE VALLEY SECTION SCHOLARSHIP
• *See page 172*

DONALD F. HASTINGS SCHOLARSHIP
• *See page 253*

EDWARD J. BRADY MEMORIAL SCHOLARSHIP
• *See page 253*

HOWARD E. ADKINS MEMORIAL SCHOLARSHIP
• *See page 253*

ILLINOIS TOOL WORKS WELDING COMPANIES SCHOLARSHIP
• *See page 254*

JOHN C. LINCOLN MEMORIAL SCHOLARSHIP
• *See page 254*

MATSUO BRIDGE COMPANY, LTD., OF JAPAN SCHOLARSHIP
• *See page 172*

PRAXAIR INTERNATIONAL SCHOLARSHIP
• *See page 254*

WILLIAM A. AND ANN M. BROTHERS SCHOLARSHIP

Awarded to a full-time undergraduate pursuing a bachelor's degree in welding or welding-related program at an accredited university. Applicant must have a minimum 2.5 overall grade point average. Deadline is January 15.

Academic Fields/Career Goals: Engineering-Related Technologies; Trade/Technical Specialties.

Award: Scholarship for use in sophomore, junior, or senior years; not renewable. *Number:* 1. *Amount:* $2500.

Eligibility Requirements: Applicant must be age 18 and enrolled or expecting to enroll full-time at a four-year institution. Applicant must have 2.5 GPA or higher. Available to U.S. citizens.

Application Requirements: Application, autobiography, financial need analysis, references, transcript, proof of financial need. *Deadline:* January 15.

Contact: Vicki Pinsky, Manager Foundation
American Welding Society
550 Northwest Le Jeune Road
Miami, FL 33126
Phone: 800-443-9353 Ext. 212
Fax: 305-443-7559
E-mail: vpinsky@aws.org

WILLIAM B. HOWELL MEMORIAL SCHOLARSHIP
• *See page 255*

ARMED FORCES COMMUNICATIONS AND ELECTRONICS ASSOCIATION, EDUCATIONAL FOUNDATION http://www.afcea.org

VICE ADMIRAL JERRY O. TUTTLE, USN (RET.) AND MRS. BARBARA A. TUTTLE SCIENCE AND TECHNOLOGY SCHOLARSHIP
• *See page 255*

ARRL FOUNDATION, INC. http://www.arrl.org/arrlf/scholgen.html

HENRY BROUGHTON, K2AE MEMORIAL SCHOLARSHIP
• *See page 90*

ASSOCIATED BUILDERS AND CONTRACTORS SCHOLARSHIP PROGRAM http://www.abc.org

TRIMMER EDUCATION FOUNDATION SCHOLARSHIPS FOR CONSTRUCTION MANAGEMENT
• *See page 172*

ASSOCIATION FOR FACILITIES ENGINEERING (AFE)

ASSOCIATION FOR FACILITIES ENGINEERING CEDAR VALLEY CHAPTER # 132 SCHOLARSHIP
• *See page 120*

ASSOCIATION FOR IRON AND STEEL TECHNOLOGY http://www.aist.org

ASSOCIATION FOR IRON AND STEEL TECHNOLOGY OHIO VALLEY CHAPTER SCHOLARSHIP
• *See page 135*

ASSOCIATION OF ENGINEERING GEOLOGISTS http://www.aegweb.org

MARLIAVE FUND
• *See page 213*

ASTRONAUT SCHOLARSHIP FOUNDATION http://www.astronautscholarship.org

ASTRONAUT SCHOLARSHIP FOUNDATION
• *See page 92*

AUTOMOTIVE HALL OF FAME http://www.automotivehalloffame.org

AUTOMOTIVE HALL OF FAME EDUCATIONAL FUNDS
• *See page 162*

BUSINESS AND PROFESSIONAL WOMEN'S FOUNDATION http://www.bpwusa.org

BPW CAREER ADVANCEMENT SCHOLARSHIP PROGRAM FOR WOMEN
• *See page 136*

CATCHING THE DREAM

TRIBAL BUSINESS MANAGEMENT PROGRAM (TBM)
• *See page 55*

CUBAN AMERICAN NATIONAL FOUNDATION http://www.canf.org

MAS FAMILY SCHOLARSHIPS
• *See page 146*

DESK AND DERRICK EDUCATIONAL TRUST http://www.addc.org

DESK AND DERRICK EDUCATIONAL TRUST
• *See page 92*

DEVRY, INC. http://www.devry.edu

CISCO SCHOLARSHIP-HIGH SCHOOL GRADUATES
• *See page 260*

EAST LOS ANGELES COMMUNITY UNION (TELACU) EDUCATION FOUNDATION http://www.telacu.com

LINC TELACU ENGINEERING AWARD
• *See page 163*

ELECTROCHEMICAL SOCIETY, INC. http://www.electrochem.org

DANIEL CUBICCIOTTI STUDENT AWARD OF THE SAN FRANCISCO SECTION OF THE ELECTROCHEMICAL SOCIETY, SPONSORED BY STRUCTURAL INTEGRITY ASSOCIATES
• *See page 137*

H.H. DOW MEMORIAL STUDENT ACHIEVEMENT AWARD OF THE INDUSTRIAL ELECTROLYSIS AND ELECTROCHEMICAL ENGINEERING DIVISION OF THE ELECTROCHEMICAL SOCIETY, INC.
• *See page 137*

STUDENT ACHIEVEMENT AWARDS OF THE INDUSTRIAL ELECTROLYSIS AND ELECTROCHEMICAL ENGINEERING DIVISION OF THE ELECTROCHEMICAL SOCIETY, INC.
• *See page 137*

STUDENT RESEARCH AWARDS OF THE BATTERY DIVISION OF THE ELECTROCHEMICAL SOCIETY, INC.
• *See page 137*

FLORIDA EDUCATIONAL FACILITIES PLANNERS' ASSOCIATION   http://www.fefpa.org

FEFPA ASSISTANTSHIP
• *See page 99*

GEORGE BIRD GRINNELL AMERICAN INDIAN FUND   http://www.grinnellfund.org/

AL QOYAWAYMA AWARD
• *See page 163*

GRAND RAPIDS COMMUNITY FOUNDATION   http://www.grfoundation.org

ECONOMIC CLUB OF GRAND RAPIDS BUSINESS STUDY ABROAD SCHOLARSHIP
• *See page 62*

HAWAIIAN LODGE, F.& A. M.   http://www.hawaiianlodge.org/

HAWAIIAN LODGE SCHOLARSHIPS
• *See page 99*

HISPANIC COLLEGE FUND, INC.   http://www.hispanicfund.org

DENNY'S/HISPANIC COLLEGE FUND SCHOLARSHIP
• *See page 62*

DEPARTMENT OF ENERGY SCHOLARSHIP PROGRAM
• *See page 148*

LOCKHEED MARTIN SCHOLARSHIP PROGRAM
• *See page 164*

M & T BANK/ HISPANIC COLLEGE FUND SCHOLARSHIP PROGRAM
• *See page 63*

NATIONAL HISPANIC EXPLORERS SCHOLARSHIP PROGRAM
• *See page 93*

HISPANIC SCHOLARSHIP FUND   http://www.hsf.net

HSF/GENERAL MOTORS SCHOLARSHIP
• *See page 149*

HSF/SOCIETY OF HISPANIC PROFESSIONAL ENGINEERS, INC. SCHOLARSHIP PROGRAM
• *See page 174*

ILLUMINATING ENGINEERING SOCIETY OF NORTH AMERICA   http://www.iesna.org

ROBERT W. THUNEN MEMORIAL SCHOLARSHIPS
• *See page 100*

INDEPENDENT LABORATORIES INSTITUTE SCHOLARSHIP ALLIANCE   http://www.acil.org

INDEPENDENT LABORATORIES INSTITUTE SCHOLARSHIP ALLIANCE
• *See page 93*

INSTITUTION OF ELECTRICAL ENGINEERS   http://www.iee.org

IEE ENGINEERING DEGREE SCHOLARSHIPS FOR WOMEN

Award to encourage women students in their final year of college or sixth form to enter the engineering profession.

Academic Fields/Career Goals: Engineering-Related Technologies.

Award: Scholarship for use in freshman year; renewable. *Number:* 10. *Amount:* up to $1750.

Eligibility Requirements: Applicant must be high school student; planning to enroll or expecting to enroll full-time at an institution or university and female. Available to U.S. and non-U.S. citizens.

Application Requirements: Application, photo, references, test scores. *Deadline:* June 30.

Contact: Scholarships and Prizes
Institution of Electrical Engineers
Michael Faraday House
Six Hills Way, Stevenage
Hertfordshire SG1 2AY
United Kingdom
Phone: 44 0 1438 765 694
Fax: 44 0 1438 765 660
E-mail: scholarships@iee.org.uk

IEE FUNDING UNDERGRADUATES TO STUDY ENGINEERING (FUSE) SCHOLARSHIP

Award to assist students of high ability in need of financial support, who are in their penultimate year of college, or are about to commence an IEE-accredited degree course in the UK or Ireland. Applicants must be receiving a DfES loan or grant.

Academic Fields/Career Goals: Engineering-Related Technologies.

Award: Scholarship for use in freshman year; renewable. *Number:* 20–50. *Amount:* $1750.

Eligibility Requirements: Applicant must be high school student and planning to enroll or expecting to enroll full-time at an institution or university. Available to U.S. and non-U.S. citizens.

Application Requirements: Application, financial need analysis, photo, references, test scores. *Deadline:* June 30.

Contact: Scholarships and Prizes
Institution of Electrical Engineers
Michael Faraday House
Six Hills Way, Stevenage
Hertfordshire SG1 2AY
United Kingdom
Phone: 44 0 1438 765 694
Fax: 44 0 1438 765 660
E-mail: scholarships@iee.org.uk

INSTRUMENTATION, SYSTEMS, AND AUTOMATION SOCIETY (ISA)   http://www.isa.org

INSTRUMENTATION, SYSTEMS, AND AUTOMATION SOCIETY (ISA) SCHOLARSHIP PROGRAM
• *See page 123*

INTERNATIONAL FACILITY MANAGEMENT ASSOCIATION FOUNDATION   http://www.ifmafoundation.org

IFMA FOUNDATION SCHOLARSHIPS
• *See page 100*

INTERNATIONAL SOCIETY FOR OPTICAL ENGINEERING-SPIE   http://www.spie.org/info/scholarships

BACUS SCHOLARSHIP

Scholarship is available to a full-time undergraduate or graduate student in the field of microlithography with an emphasis on optical tooling and/or semiconductor manufacturing technologies. Applicants must not be full-time employees in industry, government, or academia, and must be presenting an accepted paper at an SPIE-sponsored meeting.

Academic Fields/Career Goals: Engineering-Related Technologies.

Award: Scholarship for use in freshman, sophomore, junior, senior, or graduate years. *Number:* 1. *Amount:* $2500.

Eligibility Requirements: Applicant must be enrolled or expecting to enroll full-time at a four-year institution or university. Available to U.S. citizens.

International Society for Optical Engineering-SPIE (continued)

Application Requirements: Application, references, written support from a Chair.

Contact: Pascale Barnett, SPIE Scholarship Coordinator
International Society for Optical Engineering-SPIE
PO Box 10
Bellingham, WA 98227-0010
Phone: 360-676-3290
Fax: 360-647-1445
E-mail: scholarships@spie.org

LASER TECHNOLOGY, ENGINEERING AND APPLICATIONS SCHOLARSHIP

Scholarship awarded to full-time students in recognition of scholarly achievement in laser technology, engineering, or applications. Applicants must not be full-time employees in industry, government, or academia, and must be presenting an accepted paper at an SPIE-sponsored meeting.

Academic Fields/Career Goals: Engineering-Related Technologies.

Award: Scholarship for use in freshman, sophomore, junior, or senior years. *Number:* 1.

Eligibility Requirements: Applicant must be enrolled or expecting to enroll full-time at a four-year institution. Available to U.S. citizens.

Application Requirements: Application, references.

Contact: SPIE Scholarship Committee
International Society for Optical Engineering-SPIE
PO Box 10
Bellingham, WA 98227-0010
Phone: 360-685-5452
Fax: 360-647-1445
E-mail: scholarships@spie.org

SPIE EDUCATIONAL SCHOLARSHIPS IN OPTICAL SCIENCE AND ENGINEERING

• *See page 93*

WILLIAM H. PRICE SCHOLARSHIP

Scholarship awarded to a full-time graduate or undergraduate student in the field of optical design and engineering. Must not be full-time employees in industry, government, or academia. Applicants must be presenting an accepted paper at an SPIE-sponsored meeting.

Academic Fields/Career Goals: Engineering-Related Technologies.

Award: Scholarship for use in freshman, sophomore, junior, senior, or graduate years. *Number:* 1.

Eligibility Requirements: Applicant must be enrolled or expecting to enroll at a four-year institution or university. Available to U.S. citizens.

Application Requirements: Application, references.

Contact: SPIE Scholarship Committee
International Society for Optical Engineering-SPIE
PO Box 10
Bellingham, WA 98227-0010
Phone: 360-685-5452
Fax: 360-647-1445
E-mail: scholarships@spie.org

JORGE MAS CANOSA FREEDOM FOUNDATION
http://www.canf.org

MAS FAMILY SCHOLARSHIP AWARD
• *See page 149*

KOREAN-AMERICAN SCIENTISTS AND ENGINEERS ASSOCIATION
http://www.ksea.org

KSEA SCHOLARSHIPS
• *See page 245*

LOS ANGELES COUNCIL OF BLACK PROFESSIONAL ENGINEERS
http://www.lablackengineers.org

AL-BEN SCHOLARSHIP FOR ACADEMIC INCENTIVE
• *See page 164*

AL-BEN SCHOLARSHIP FOR PROFESSIONAL MERIT
• *See page 165*

AL-BEN SCHOLARSHIP FOR SCHOLASTIC ACHIEVEMENT
• *See page 165*

MAINE SOCIETY OF PROFESSIONAL ENGINEERS

MAINE SOCIETY OF PROFESSIONAL ENGINEERS VERNON T. SWAINE-ROBERT E. CHUTE SCHOLARSHIP
• *See page 266*

MICRON TECHNOLOGY FOUNDATION, INC.
http://www.micron.com

MICRON SCIENCE AND TECHNOLOGY SCHOLARS PROGRAM
• *See page 165*

MINERALS, METALS, AND MATERIALS SOCIETY (TMS)
http://www.tms.org

TMS J. KEITH BRIMACOMBE PRESIDENTIAL SCHOLARSHIP
• *See page 266*

TMS OUTSTANDING STUDENT PAPER CONTEST-UNDERGRADUATE
• *See page 266*

TMS/EMPMD GILBERT CHIN SCHOLARSHIP
• *See page 266*

TMS/EPD SCHOLARSHIP
• *See page 267*

TMS/INTERNATIONAL SYMPOSIUM ON SUPERALLOYS SCHOLARSHIP PROGRAM
• *See page 267*

TMS/LMD SCHOLARSHIP PROGRAM
• *See page 267*

TMS/STRUCTURAL MATERIALS DIVISION SCHOLARSHIP
• *See page 267*

NASA DELAWARE SPACE GRANT CONSORTIUM
http://www.delspace.org

NASA DELAWARE SPACE GRANT UNDERGRADUATE TUITION SCHOLARSHIP
• *See page 94*

NASA NEBRASKA SPACE GRANT CONSORTIUM
http://nasa.unomaha.edu

NASA NEBRASKA SPACE GRANT
• *See page 125*

NASA RHODE ISLAND SPACE GRANT CONSORTIUM
http://www.planetary.brown.edu/RI_Space_Grant

NASA RHODE ISLAND SPACE GRANT CONSORTIUM OUTREACH SCHOLARSHIP FOR UNDERGRADUATE STUDENTS

Scholarship for undergraduate students attending a Rhode Island Space Grant Consortium participating institution studying in any space-related field of science, math, engineering, or other field with applications in space study. Recipients are expected to devote a maximum of 8 hours per week to outreach activities in science education for K-12 children and teachers. See Web site for additional information: http://www.spacegrant.brown.edu

Academic Fields/Career Goals: Engineering-Related Technologies; Mathematics; Science, Technology, and Society.

Award: Scholarship for use in freshman, sophomore, junior, or senior years; not renewable. *Number:* up to 2. *Amount:* up to $4000.

Eligibility Requirements: Applicant must be enrolled or expecting to enroll full-time at a four-year institution or university and studying in Rhode Island. Applicant must have 3.0 GPA or higher. Available to U.S. citizens.

Application Requirements: Application, essay, resume, references, transcript. *Deadline:* March 1.

Contact: Dorcas Metcalf, Program Manager
NASA Rhode Island Space Grant Consortium
Brown University, Box 1846
Providence, RI 02912
Phone: 401-863-1151
Fax: 401-863-1242
E-mail: dorcas_metcalf@brown.edu

NASA VERMONT SPACE GRANT CONSORTIUM
http://www.vtspacegrant.org

VERMONT SPACE GRANT CONSORTIUM SCHOLARSHIP PROGRAM
• *See page 94*

NASA WEST VIRGINIA SPACE GRANT CONSORTIUM
http://www.nasa.wvu.edu

WEST VIRGINIA SPACE GRANT CONSORTIUM UNDERGRADUATE SCHOLARSHIP PROGRAM
• *See page 126*

NATIONAL ASSOCIATION FOR THE ADVANCEMENT OF COLORED PEOPLE
http://www.naacp.org

HUBERTUS W.V. WILLEMS SCHOLARSHIP FOR MALE STUDENTS
• *See page 166*

LOUIS STOKES SCIENCE AND TECHNOLOGY AWARD
• *See page 139*

NATIONAL ASSOCIATION OF WATER COMPANIES
http://www.nawc.org

J .J. BARR SCHOLARSHIP
• *See page 139*

NATIONAL ASSOCIATION OF WOMEN IN CONSTRUCTION
http://nawic.org

NAWIC UNDERGRADUATE SCHOLARSHIPS
• *See page 100*

NATIONAL INVENTORS HALL OF FAME
http://www.invent.org

COLLEGIATE INVENTORS COMPETITION - GRAND PRIZE
• *See page 95*

COLLEGIATE INVENTORS COMPETITION FOR UNDERGRADUATE STUDENTS
• *See page 95*

NATIONAL SOCIETY OF PROFESSIONAL ENGINEERS
http://www.nspe.org

MAUREEN L. AND HOWARD N. BLITMAN, PE SCHOLARSHIP TO PROMOTE DIVERSITY IN ENGINEERING
• *See page 166*

NATIONAL SOCIETY OF PROFESSIONAL ENGINEERS/AUXILIARY SCHOLARSHIP
• *See page 166*

PAUL H. ROBBINS HONORARY SCHOLARSHIP
• *See page 166*

PROFESSIONAL ENGINEERS IN INDUSTRY SCHOLARSHIP
• *See page 167*

VIRGINIA HENRY MEMORIAL SCHOLARSHIP
• *See page 167*

NATIONAL STONE, SAND AND GRAVEL ASSOCIATION (NSSGA)
http://www.nssga.org

BARRY K. WENDT MEMORIAL SCHOLARSHIP
• *See page 269*

OREGON STUDENT ASSISTANCE COMMISSION
http://www.osac.state.or.us

AMERICAN COUNCIL OF ENGINEERING COMPANIES OF OREGON SCHOLARSHIP
• *See page 167*

PLASTICS INSTITUTE OF AMERICA
http://www.plasticsinstitute.org/

PLASTICS PIONEERS SCHOLARSHIPS
• *See page 269*

PLUMBING-HEATING-COOLING CONTRACTORS ASSOCIATION EDUCATION FOUNDATION
http://www.phccweb.org

BRADFORD WHITE CORPORATION SCHOLARSHIP
• *See page 102*

DELTA FAUCET COMPANY SCHOLARSHIP PROGRAM
• *See page 102*

PHCC EDUCATIONAL FOUNDATION NEED-BASED SCHOLARSHIP
• *See page 102*

PHCC EDUCATIONAL FOUNDATION SCHOLARSHIP PROGRAM
• *See page 103*

ROBERT H. MOLLOHAN FAMILY CHARITABLE FOUNDATION, INC.
http://www.mollohanfoundation.org

HIGH TECHNOLOGY SCHOLARS PROGRAM
• *See page 141*

SOCIETY FOR TECHNICAL COMMUNICATION
http://www.stc.org

SOCIETY FOR TECHNICAL COMMUNICATION SCHOLARSHIP PROGRAM
• *See page 186*

SOCIETY OF AUTOMOTIVE ENGINEERS
http://www.sae.org

BMW/SAE ENGINEERING SCHOLARSHIP
• *See page 129*

DETROIT SECTION SAE TECHNICAL SCHOLARSHIP
• *See page 270*

EDWARD D. HENDRICKSON/SAE ENGINEERING SCHOLARSHIP
• *See page 129*

RALPH K. HILLQUIST HONORARY SAE SCHOLARSHIP
• *See page 270*

SAE WILLIAM G. BELFREY MEMORIAL GRANT
• *See page 271*

TMC/SAE DONALD D. DAWSON TECHNICAL SCHOLARSHIP
• *See page 129*

YANMAR/SAE SCHOLARSHIP
• *See page 271*

SOCIETY OF BROADCAST ENGINEERS, INC.
http://www.sbe.org

ROBERT GREENBERG/HAROLD E. ENNES SCHOLARSHIP FUND AND ENNES EDUCATIONAL FOUNDATION BROADCAST TECHNOLOGY SCHOLARSHIP
• *See page 271*

SOCIETY OF HISPANIC PROFESSIONAL ENGINEERS FOUNDATION
http://www.henaac.org

HENAAC SCHOLARS PROGRAM

Applicants must be student leaders majoring in engineering, math, computer science or material science. Applicants must be of Hispanic origin and/or must significantly participate in and promote organizations and activites in the Hispanic Community.

Academic Fields/Career Goals: Engineering-Related Technologies; Materials Science, Engineering, and Metallurgy; Mathematics.

Award: Scholarship for use in freshman, sophomore, junior, senior, or graduate years. *Amount:* $500–$5000.

Eligibility Requirements: Applicant must be of Hispanic heritage and enrolled or expecting to enroll at a four-year institution or university. Applicant must have 3.0 GPA or higher. Available to U.S. citizens.

Application Requirements: Application, essay, resume, references, transcript. *Deadline:* April 21.

Contact: Kathy Borunda Barrera
Society of Hispanic Professional Engineers Foundation
HENAAC, ATTN: Scholarship Selection Committee, 3900 Whiteside Street
Los Angeles, CA 90063
Phone: 323-262-0997
E-mail: kathy@henaac.org

SOCIETY OF HISPANIC PROFESSIONAL ENGINEERS FOUNDATION
• See page 168

SOCIETY OF MEXICAN AMERICAN ENGINEERS AND SCIENTISTS
http://www.maes-natl.org

GRE AND GRADUATE APPLICATIONS WAIVER
• See page 95

SOCIETY OF WOMEN ENGINEERS
http://www.swe.org

ARIZONA SECTION SCHOLARSHIP
• See page 277

GENERAL MOTORS FOUNDATION UNDERGRADUATE SCHOLARSHIPS
• See page 168

GUIDANT CORPORATION SCHOLARSHIP
• See page 195

SOLE - THE INTERNATIONAL LOGISTICS SOCIETY
http://www.sole.org

LOGISTICS EDUCATION FOUNDATION SCHOLARSHIP

One-time award for students enrolled in a program of study in logistics. Must have a minimum 3.0 GPA. Submit transcript and references with application.

Academic Fields/Career Goals: Engineering-Related Technologies.

Award: Scholarship for use in freshman, sophomore, junior, senior, or graduate years; not renewable. *Number:* 5–10. *Amount:* up to $1000.

Eligibility Requirements: Applicant must be enrolled or expecting to enroll full-time at a four-year institution or university. Applicant must have 3.0 GPA or higher. Available to U.S. and non-U.S. citizens.

Application Requirements: Application, references, transcript. *Deadline:* May 15.

Contact: Chairman, Scholarships Committee
SOLE - The International Logistics Society
8100 Professional Place, Suite 111
Hyattsville, MD 20785
Phone: 301-459-8446
Fax: 301-459-1522
E-mail: solehq@erols.com

TAG AND LABEL MANUFACTURERS INSTITUTE, INC.
http://www.tlmi.com

TLMI 4 YEAR COLLEGES/FULL-TIME STUDENTS SCHOLARSHIP

TLMI offers six $5000 scholarships annually to qualified junior and senior undergraduates. Applicant must demonstrate interest in entering the tag and label industry. Minimum 3.0 GPA required.

Academic Fields/Career Goals: Engineering-Related Technologies; Flexography; Graphics/Graphic Arts/Printing.

Award: Scholarship for use in sophomore, junior, or senior years; renewable. *Number:* 6. *Amount:* $5000.

Eligibility Requirements: Applicant must be enrolled or expecting to enroll full-time at a four-year institution or university. Applicant must have 3.0 GPA or higher. Available to U.S. and Canadian citizens.

Application Requirements: Application, autobiography, interview, portfolio, resume, references, transcript. *Deadline:* March 31.

Contact: Karen Planz
Tag and Label Manufacturers Institute, Inc.
40 Shuman Boulevard, Suite 295
Naperville, IL 60563
Phone: 800-533-8564
E-mail: office@tlmi.com

UNITED NEGRO COLLEGE FUND
http://www.uncf.org

NORTHEAST UTILITIES SYSTEM SCHOLARSHIP PROGRAM
• See page 156

XEROX
http://www.xerox.com

TECHNICAL MINORITY SCHOLARSHIP
• See page 169

ENTOMOLOGY

ENTOMOLOGICAL FOUNDATION
http://www.entfdn.org

BIOQUIP UNDERGRADUATE SCHOLARSHIP

Scholarships for students enrolled as an undergraduate in entomology at a college or university in the United States, Mexico or Canada in the fall prior to the application deadline. Scholarship amount $2000.

Academic Fields/Career Goals: Entomology.

Award: Scholarship for use in freshman, sophomore, junior, or senior years; not renewable. *Amount:* $2000.

Eligibility Requirements: Applicant must be enrolled or expecting to enroll full or part-time at a four-year institution or university. Available to U.S. and Canadian citizens.

Application Requirements: Application, references, transcript. *Deadline:* July 1.

Contact:
Phone: 301-731-4535
Fax: 301-731-4538
E-mail: esa@entsoc.org

ENTOMOLOGICAL SOCIETY OF AMERICA
http://www.entsoc.org

BIOQUIP UNDERGRADUATE SCHOLARSHIP

Award to assist students in obtaining a degree in entomology or pursuing a career as an entomologist. Must have accumulated a minimum of ninety college credit hours by September 1 following the application deadline, and either completed two junior-level entomology courses or have a research project in entomology.

Academic Fields/Career Goals: Entomology.

Award: Scholarship for use in freshman, sophomore, junior, or senior years. *Amount:* $2000.

Eligibility Requirements: Applicant must be enrolled or expecting to enroll at a four-year institution or university. Available to U.S. and Canadian citizens.

Application Requirements: Essay, resume, transcript. *Deadline:* July 1.

Contact: Lisa Spurlock, Awards Administrator
E-mail: awards@entsoc.org

THE INTERNATIONAL CONGRESS ON INSECT NEUROCHEMISTRY AND NEUROPHYSIOLOGY (ICINN) STUDENT RECOGNITION AWARD IN INSECT PHYSIOLOGY, BIOCHEMISTRY, TOXICOLOGY, AND MOLECULAR BIOLOGY

Award for innovative research in the areas of insect physiology, biochemistry, toxicology, and molecular biology in the broad sense. The award amount varies. Must have demonstrated excellence in the advancement of basic or applied entomological research on the undergraduate or graduate level.

Academic Fields/Career Goals: Entomology.

Award: Prize for use in freshman, sophomore, junior, senior, or postgraduate years. *Number:* 1. *Amount:* varies.

Eligibility Requirements: Applicant must be enrolled or expecting to enroll at a four-year institution or university. Applicant or parent of applicant must be member of Entomological Society of America. Available to U.S. and non-U.S. citizens.

Application Requirements: Essay, resume, references, transcript. *Deadline:* July 1.

Contact: Melodie Dziduch, Foundation Awards Administrator
Phone: 301-459-9082
E-mail: melodie@entfdn.org

ENVIRONMENTAL HEALTH

COLLEGE BOARD/ROBERT WOOD JOHNSON FOUNDATION YES PROGRAM

http://www.collegeboard.com/yes

YOUNG EPIDEMIOLOGY SCHOLARS COMPETITION

YES Competition for students is open to high school juniors and seniors who are citizens or permanent residents (holding a Green Card) of the United States and enrolled in a high school in the United States, Puerto Rico, Guam, U.S. Virgin Islands, American Samoa, Midway, Wake or the Mariana Islands, or in Department of Defense or American/International Schools abroad. Home schooled students are also eligible.

Academic Fields/Career Goals: Environmental Health; Public Health.

Award: Prize for use in freshman year. *Amount:* $1000–$50,000.

Eligibility Requirements: Applicant must be high school student; planning to enroll or expecting to enroll at an institution or university. Available to U.S. citizens.

Application Requirements: Application. *Deadline:* varies.

Contact: The College Board
College Board/Robert Wood Johnson Foundation YES Program
11911 Freedom Drive, Suite 300
Reston, VA 20190
Phone: 800-626-9795 Ext. 5932
E-mail: yes@collegeboard.org

DELAWARE HIGHER EDUCATION COMMISSION

http://www.doe.k12.de.us

DELAWARE SOLID WASTE AUTHORITY JOHN P. "PAT" HEALY SCHOLARSHIP

Scholarships given to residents of Delaware who are high school seniors or freshmen or sophomores in college. Must be majoring in either environmental engineering or environmental sciences in a Delaware college. Must file the Free Application for Federal Student Aid (FAFSA). Scholarships are automatically renewed for three years if a 3.0 GPA is maintained. Deadline: March 15.

Academic Fields/Career Goals: Environmental Health.

Award: Scholarship for use in freshman or sophomore years; renewable. *Number:* 1. *Amount:* $2000.

Eligibility Requirements: Applicant must be enrolled or expecting to enroll full-time at a two-year or four-year institution or university; resident of Delaware and studying in Delaware. Applicant must have 3.0 GPA or higher. Available to U.S. citizens.

Application Requirements: Application, financial need analysis, FAFSA. *Deadline:* March 15.

Contact: Donna Myers, Field Agent/Program Administrator
Delaware Higher Education Commission
820 North French Street, 5th Floor
Wilmington, DE 19711-3509
Phone: 302-577-3240
Fax: 302-577-6765
E-mail: dmyers@doe.k12.de.us

FLORIDA ENVIRONMENTAL HEALTH ASSOCIATION

http://www.feha.org/scholar.htm

FLORIDA ENVIRONMENTAL HEALTH ASSOCIATION SCHOLARSHIP

Scholarships offered to students interested in pursuing a career in the field of environmental health or to enhance an existing career in environmental health. Applicant must be a member of FEHA in good standing.

Academic Fields/Career Goals: Environmental Health.

Award: Scholarship for use in junior, senior, or postgraduate years. *Amount:* $500.

Eligibility Requirements: Applicant must be enrolled or expecting to enroll at a four-year institution or university. Applicant must have 2.5 GPA or higher. Available to U.S. citizens.

Application Requirements: Application, references, transcript. *Deadline:* June 23.

Contact: Michelle Kearney, Feha Scholarship Committee
E-mail: michelle_kearney@doh.state.fl.us

SAEMS - SOUTHERN ARIZONA ENVIRONMENTAL MANAGEMENT SOCIETY

http://www.saems.org

ENVIRONMENTAL SCHOLARSHIPS

Applicant must be a student in any accredited Southern Arizona college or university. Student must have a minimum GPA of 2.5 or be a full- or part-time student and plan on pursuing a career in the environmental arena.

Academic Fields/Career Goals: Environmental Health.

Award: Scholarship for use in freshman, sophomore, junior, senior, or graduate years; not renewable. *Number:* 2. *Amount:* up to $3000.

Eligibility Requirements: Applicant must be enrolled or expecting to enroll full or part-time at a two-year or four-year institution or university and studying in Arizona. Applicant must have 2.5 GPA or higher. Available to U.S. and non-U.S. citizens.

Application Requirements: Application, essay, interview. *Deadline:* March 15.

Contact: Dan Uthe, Scholarship Committee Chair
SAEMS - Southern Arizona Environmental Management Society
PO Box 41433
Tucson, AZ 85717
Phone: 520-791-5630
Fax: 520-791-5346
E-mail: dan.uthe@tucsonaz.com

WINDSTAR FOUNDATION

http://www.wstar.org

WINDSTAR ENVIRONMENTAL STUDIES SCHOLARSHIPS
• See page 284

WISCONSIN ASSOCIATION FOR FOOD PROTECTION

http://www.wafp-wi.org

E.H. MARTH FOOD AND ENVIRONMENTAL SCHOLARSHIP

Scholarship to promote and sustain interest in fields of study that may lead to a career in dairy, food, or environmental sanitation. One scholarship is awarded per year and previous applicants and recipients may reapply.

Academic Fields/Career Goals: Environmental Health.

Award: Scholarship for use in freshman, sophomore, junior, or senior years. *Amount:* $1000.

Eligibility Requirements: Applicant must be enrolled or expecting to enroll at a four-year institution or university; resident of Wisconsin and studying in Wisconsin. Available to U.S. citizens.

Application Requirements: Application, references, transcript. *Deadline:* July 1.

Contact: Wisconsin Association for Food Protection
c/o George Nelson, 1207 Main Street East
Menomie, WI 54751

ENVIRONMENTAL SCIENCE

AIR & WASTE MANAGEMENT ASSOCIATION– ALLEGHENY MOUNTAIN SECTION
http://www.ams-awma.org

ALLEGHENY MOUNTAIN SECTION AIR & WASTE MANAGEMENT ASSOCIATION SCHOLARSHIP

Scholarships for qualified students enrolled in an undergraduate program leading to a career in a field related directly to the environment. Open to undergraduate students currently enrolled or high school students accepted full-time in a four-(4) year college or university program in Western Pennsylvania or West Virginia. Applicants should have at least a ôBö average or a 3.0.

Academic Fields/Career Goals: Environmental Science.

Award: Scholarship for use in freshman, sophomore, junior, or senior years; not renewable. *Number:* up to 2. *Amount:* up to $1500.

Eligibility Requirements: Applicant must be enrolled or expecting to enroll full-time at a four-year institution or university; resident of Pennsylvania or West Virginia and studying in Pennsylvania or West Virginia. Applicant must have 3.0 GPA or higher. Available to U.S. citizens.

Application Requirements: Application, essay, resume, references, transcript, plan of study. *Deadline:* March 30.

Contact: David Testa, Scholarship Chair
Air & Waste Management Association–Allegheny Mountain Section
c/o Calgon Carbon Corporation, PO Box 717
Pittsburgh, PA 15230-0717
Phone: 412-787-6803
E-mail: dtesta@calgoncarbon-us.com

AIR & WASTE MANAGEMENT ASSOCIATION– COASTAL PLAINS CHAPTER
http://www.awmacoastalplains.org

COASTAL PLAINS CHAPTER OF THE AIR AND WASTE MANAGEMENT ASSOCIATION ENVIRONMENTAL STEWARD SCHOLARSHIP

Five scholarships will be awarded for the students who pursue their career in environmental science or physical science. Two $800 Scholarship for University of West Florida, One for Pensacola Junior College, one for Okaloosa-Walton Community College and one for Gulf Coast Community College.

Academic Fields/Career Goals: Environmental Science; Physical Sciences and Math.

Award: Scholarship for use in freshman, sophomore, junior, or senior years; not renewable. *Number:* 5. *Amount:* $800.

Eligibility Requirements: Applicant must be enrolled or expecting to enroll full-time at a two-year or four-year institution or university. Applicant must have 2.5 GPA or higher. Available to U.S. citizens.

Application Requirements: Application, essay, references. *Deadline:* varies.

Contact: Dwain G. Waters, Treasurer
Air & Waste Management Association–Coastal Plains Chapter
1 Energy Place
Pensacola, FL 32520-0328
Phone: 850-444-6527
Fax: 850-444-6217
E-mail: Gdwaters@southernco.com

AMERICAN INDIAN SCIENCE AND ENGINEERING SOCIETY
http://www.aises.org

HENRY RODRIGUEZ RECLAMATION COLLEGE SCHOLARSHIP AND INTERNSHIP
• See page 285

AMERICAN METEOROLOGICAL SOCIETY
http://www.ametsoc.org/AMS

CARL W. KREITZBERG ENDOWED SCHOLARSHIP

Scholarships are awarded to college juniors and seniors in atmospheric and related sciences programs at accredited U.S. institutions. Required GPA is 3.25 and above.

Academic Fields/Career Goals: Environmental Science; Meteorology/ Atmospheric Science.

Award: Scholarship for use in junior or senior years; not renewable. *Amount:* up to $2000.

Eligibility Requirements: Applicant must be enrolled or expecting to enroll full-time at a two-year or four-year institution or university and must have an interest in designated field specified by sponsor. Available to U.S. citizens.

Application Requirements: Application, essay, references, transcript. *Deadline:* February 10.

Contact: Donna Fernandez, Development Program Coordinator
American Meteorological Society
45 Beacon Street
Boston, MA 02108-3693
Phone: 617-227-2426 Ext. 246
Fax: 617-742-8718
E-mail: dfernand@ametsoc.org

AMERICAN SOCIETY OF SAFETY ENGINEERS (ASSE) FOUNDATION
http://www.asse.org

UNITED PARCEL SERVICE DIVERSITY SCHOLARSHIP PROGRAM

Two one-time awards available to minority ethnic or racial group students pursuing an undergraduate degree full-time in occupational safety, health, or environment. Must be an ASSE member, a U.S. citizen, and have a minimum 3.25 GPA. Recommendation by a safety faculty member required. Deadline is December 1.

Academic Fields/Career Goals: Environmental Science; Health and Medical Sciences; Occupational Safety and Health.

Award: Scholarship for use in freshman, sophomore, junior, or senior years; not renewable. *Amount:* $4000–$5500.

Eligibility Requirements: Applicant must be American Indian/Alaska Native, Asian/Pacific Islander, Black (non-Hispanic), or Hispanic and enrolled or expecting to enroll full-time at a two-year or four-year or technical institution or university. Applicant or parent of applicant must be member of American Society of Safety Engineers. Available to U.S. citizens.

Application Requirements: Application, essay, financial need analysis, references, transcript. *Deadline:* December 1.

Contact: Mary Goranson, Scholarship Coordinator
American Society of Safety Engineers (ASSE) Foundation
1800 East Oakton Street
Des Plaines, IL 60018
Phone: 847-768-3412

ASSOCIATION FOR IRON AND STEEL TECHNOLOGY
http://www.aist.org

ASSOCIATION FOR IRON AND STEEL TECHNOLOGY OHIO VALLEY CHAPTER SCHOLARSHIP
• See page 135

ASSOCIATION OF CALIFORNIA WATER AGENCIES
http://www.acwanet.com

ASSOCIATION OF CALIFORNIA WATER AGENCIES SCHOLARSHIPS
• See page 91

CLAIR A. HILL SCHOLARSHIP
• See page 91

AUDUBON SOCIETY OF WESTERN PENNSYLVANIA
http://www.aswp.org

BEULAH FREY ENVIRONMENTAL SCHOLARSHIP

Scholarship available to high school seniors from Allegheny, Armstrong, south Butler, Beaver, north Fayette, northeast Washington, and Westmoreland counties pursuing studies in the Environmental and Natural Sciences. Students who are applying to a two or four-year college to further their studies in an environmentally-related field are eligible to apply.

Academic Fields/Career Goals: Environmental Science; Natural Sciences.

Award: Scholarship for use in freshman year; not renewable. *Number:* 1–2. *Amount:* $1000.

Eligibility Requirements: Applicant must be high school student; planning to enroll or expecting to enroll full-time at a four-year institution or university and resident of Pennsylvania. Available to U.S. citizens.

Application Requirements: Application, essay, references, test scores, transcript. *Deadline:* March 31.

Contact: Trisha O'Neill, Director of Education
Audubon Society of Western Pennsylvania
614 Dorseyville Road
Pittsburgh, PA 15238
Phone: 412-963-6100
Fax: 412-963-6761
E-mail: toneill@aswp.org

CALIFORNIA WATER AWARENESS CAMPAIGN
http://www.wateraware.org

CALIFORNIA WATER AWARENESS CAMPAIGN WATER SCHOLAR
• See page 79

CANADIAN RECREATIONAL CANOEING ASSOCIATION
http://www.paddlingcanada.com

BILL MASON MEMORIAL SCHOLARSHIP FUND
• See page 80

COLLEGEBOUND FOUNDATION
http://www.collegeboundfoundation.org

NATIONAL AQUARIUM IN BALTIMORE HENRY HALL SCHOLARSHIP
• See page 136

DOGRIB TREATY 11 SCHOLARSHIP COMMITTEE
http://www.dt11sc.ca

FRANCIS BLACKDUCK MEMORIAL "STRONG LIKE TWO PEOPLE" AWARDS

Award for students of Dogrib ancestry enrolled in either college, university, or technical school with a major in environmental studies or natural resources sciences/technologies. Preference will be given to individuals who are able to speak fluently in both Dogrib and English.

Academic Fields/Career Goals: Environmental Science; Natural Resources.

Award: Scholarship for use in freshman, sophomore, junior, senior, or graduate years. *Number:* 2. *Amount:* $500.

Eligibility Requirements: Applicant must be enrolled or expecting to enroll at a two-year or four-year or technical institution or university. Available to U.S. and Canadian citizens.

Application Requirements: Application, transcript. *Deadline:* July 15.

Contact: Morven MacPherson, Post Secondary Student Support Coordinator
Dogrib Treaty 11 Scholarship Committee
c/o CJBRHS
PO Box 1
Rae-Edzo X0E 0Y0
Canada
Phone: 867-371-3815
Fax: 867-371-3813
E-mail: morvenm@dogrib.net

ENVIRONMENTAL PROFESSIONALS' ORGANIZATION OF CONNECTICUT
http://www.epoc.org

EPOC ENVIRONMENTAL SCHOLARSHIP FUND

Scholarships awarded annually to junior, senior, and graduate level students (full or part time) enrolled in accepted programs of study leading the student to become an environmental professional in Connecticut.

Academic Fields/Career Goals: Environmental Science.

Award: Scholarship for use in junior or senior years; not renewable. *Number:* 2–3.

Eligibility Requirements: Applicant must be enrolled or expecting to enroll full or part-time at a two-year or four-year institution or university. Available to U.S. citizens.

Application Requirements: Application, transcript. *Deadline:* varies.

Contact: John Figurelli, Scholarship Committee Chair
Environmental Professionals' Organization of Connecticut
PO Box 176
Amston, CT 06231-0176
Phone: 860-228-2492
Fax: 860-228-4902

EXPLORERS CLUB
http://www.explorers.org

EXPLORATION FUND GRANTS
• See page 88

FRIENDS OF THE FRELINGHUYSEN ARBORETUM
http://www.arboretumfriends.org

BENJAMIN C. BLACKBURN SCHOLARSHIP

One-time award for college undergraduates and graduate students who are pursuing degrees in horticulture, landscape architecture, or environmental studies. Must be a U.S. citizen and New Jersey resident. Must have minimum 3.0 GPA.

Academic Fields/Career Goals: Environmental Science; Horticulture/Floriculture; Landscape Architecture; Natural Resources.

Award: Scholarship for use in freshman, sophomore, junior, senior, or graduate years; not renewable. *Number:* 1. *Amount:* $5000.

Eligibility Requirements: Applicant must be enrolled or expecting to enroll full-time at a two-year or four-year institution or university and resident of New Jersey. Applicant must have 3.0 GPA or higher. Available to U.S. citizens.

Application Requirements: Application, essay, references, transcript. *Deadline:* April 17.

Contact: Dorothy Hennessey, Scholarship Chairman
Friends of the Frelinghuysen Arboretum
53 East Hanover Avenue
PO Box 1295
Morristown, NJ 07962-1295
Phone: 973-326-7603
Fax: 973-644-9627

HISPANIC COLLEGE FUND, INC.
http://www.hispanicfund.org

DEPARTMENT OF ENERGY SCHOLARSHIP PROGRAM
• See page 148

INSTITUTE OF ENVIRONMENTAL SCIENCES AND TECHNOLOGY (IEST)
http://www.iest.org

EUGENE BORSON SCHOLARSHIP

Annual award of $500 for the best original technical paper(s) written by a student in a topic related to the environmental sciences in connection with controlled environments, particularly through contamination control and nanotechnologies, in which products and equipment are manufactured, processed, or tested. See Web site: http://www.iest.org/technical/scholarships/BorsonProcedures.pdf.

Academic Fields/Career Goals: Environmental Science.

Award: Scholarship for use in sophomore year; not renewable. *Number:* 1. *Amount:* up to $500.

Institute of Environmental Sciences and Technology (IEST) (continued)

Eligibility Requirements: Applicant must be enrolled or expecting to enroll full-time at a two-year or four-year institution or university. Applicant must have 3.0 GPA or higher. Available to U.S. citizens.

Application Requirements: Application, references, transcript. *Deadline:* March 15.

Contact: Roberta Burrows, Director, Communication Services
Institute of Environmental Sciences and Technology (IEST)
5005 Newport Drive, Suite 506
Rolling Meadows, IL 60008-3841
Phone: 847-255-1561 Ext. 20
Fax: 847-255-1699
E-mail: iest@iest.org

PARK ESPENSCHADE MEMORIAL SCHOLARSHIP

Annual award of $500 for the best original technical paper(s) written by a student in a topic related to the environmental sciences. Must be in sophomore year or above in an accredited institution. Must have minimum GPA of 3.0. Deadline is March 15.

Academic Fields/Career Goals: Environmental Science.

Award: Scholarship for use in sophomore year; not renewable. *Number:* 1. *Amount:* $500.

Eligibility Requirements: Applicant must be enrolled or expecting to enroll full-time at a two-year or four-year institution or university. Applicant must have 3.0 GPA or higher. Available to U.S. citizens.

Application Requirements: Application, essay, references, transcript, copy of student ID, completed permission to publish form. *Deadline:* March 15.

Contact: Roberta Burrows, Director, Communication Services
Institute of Environmental Sciences and Technology (IEST)
5005 Newport Drive, Suite 506
Rolling Meadows, IL 60008-3841
Phone: 847-255-1561 Ext. 20
Fax: 847-255-1699
E-mail: iest@iest.org

INTERNATIONAL ASSOCIATION OF GREAT LAKES RESEARCH http://www.iaglr.org

PAUL W. RODGERS SCHOLARSHIP
• See page 214

KENTUCKY NATURAL RESOURCES AND ENVIRONMENTAL PROTECTION CABINET http://www.uky.edu/waterresources

CONSERVATION OF NATURAL RESOURCES SCHOLARSHIP
• See page 81

CONSERVATION OF NATURAL RESOURCES SCHOLARSHIP FOR NONTRADITIONAL STUDENTS
• See page 81

GEORGE R. CRAFTON SCHOLARSHIP
• See page 81

MAINE COMMUNITY FOUNDATION, INC. http://www.mainecf.org

R.V. "GADABOUT" GADDIS CHARITABLE FUND

Award available to Maine high school graduates who are college juniors or seniors majoring in outdoor writing or a related environmental field. Deadline is April 1. For more information, see Web site: http://www.mainecf.org/

Academic Fields/Career Goals: Environmental Science.

Award: Scholarship for use in junior or senior years. *Number:* 1.

Eligibility Requirements: Applicant must be enrolled or expecting to enroll at a two-year or four-year institution or university and resident of Maine. Available to U.S. citizens.

Application Requirements: Application, essay, financial need analysis, copy of college financial aid offer. *Deadline:* April 1.

Contact: Jean Warren, Scholarship Coordinator
Maine Community Foundation, Inc.
R.V. Gadabout Gaddis Scholarship Fund, c/o Maine Community Foundation, 245 Main Street
Ellsworth, ME 04605
Phone: 207-667-9735
Fax: 207-667-0447
E-mail: info@mainecf.org

MANITOBA FORESTRY ASSOCIATION http://www.mbforestryassoc.ca

DR. ALAN BEAVEN FORESTRY SCHOLARSHIP

Awarded annually to a Manitoba resident, selected by a committee of Association members. Must be a recent graduate of high school and entering first year forestry at a Canadian university or technical school. Scholarship of $500 will be paid, in the student's name, to the university or school as part of the tuition.

Academic Fields/Career Goals: Environmental Science; Natural Resources.

Award: Scholarship for use in freshman year. *Amount:* $500.

Eligibility Requirements: Applicant must be enrolled or expecting to enroll at an institution or university and resident of Manitoba. Available to U.S. and Canadian citizens.

Application Requirements: Application, references, transcript. *Deadline:* July 31.

Contact: Manitoba Forestry Association
900 Corydon Avenue
Winnipeg R3M 0Y4
Canada
Phone: 204-453-3182
Fax: 204-477-5765
E-mail: mfainc@mts.net

MISSISSIPPI STATE STUDENT FINANCIAL AID http://www.mississippiuniversities.com

GULF COAST RESEARCH LABORATORY MINORITY SUMMER GRANT

Grants to minority freshmen, sophomore, junior, or senior student at a Mississippi college or university majoring in marine and environmental sciences.

Academic Fields/Career Goals: Environmental Science.

Award: Grant for use in freshman, sophomore, junior, or senior years. *Number:* 1.

Eligibility Requirements: Applicant must be American Indian/Alaska Native, Asian/Pacific Islander, Black (non-Hispanic), or Hispanic; enrolled or expecting to enroll full-time at a four-year institution or university; resident of Mississippi and studying in Mississippi. Available to U.S. citizens.

Application Requirements: Application, transcript. *Deadline:* March 31.

Contact: Mississippi Student Financial Aid
Mississippi State Student Financial Aid
3825 Ridgewood Road
Jackson, MS 39211-6453
Phone: 800-327-2980
E-mail: sfa@ihl.state.ms.us

MORRIS K. UDALL FOUNDATION http://www.udall.gov

MORRIS K. UDALL UNDERGRADUATE SCHOLARSHIPS

80 scholarships of up to $5000 and 50 honorable mentions of $350 awarded to applicants on the basis of merit. Awarded to sophomore and junior-level college students. Applicants should have demonstrated commitment to careers related to the environment or to careers related to tribal public policy or health care.

Academic Fields/Career Goals: Environmental Science; Public Policy and Administration; Social Services.

Award: Scholarship for use in sophomore or junior years. *Number:* up to 110. *Amount:* $350–$5000.

Eligibility Requirements: Applicant must be American Indian/Alaska Native and enrolled or expecting to enroll at a four-year institution or university. Available to U.S. citizens.

Application Requirements: Application, test scores, transcript. *Deadline:* March 3.

Contact: Melissa Millage, Program Manager
Morris K. Udall Foundation
130 South Scott Avenue, Suite 3350
Tucson, AZ 85701-1922
Phone: 520-670-5529
E-mail: millage@udall.gov

NASA VIRGINIA SPACE GRANT CONSORTIUM   http://www.vsgc.odu.edu

VIRGINIA SPACE GRANT CONSORTIUM TEACHER EDUCATION SCHOLARSHIPS
• See page 125

NASA WEST VIRGINIA SPACE GRANT CONSORTIUM   http://www.nasa.wvu.edu

WEST VIRGINIA SPACE GRANT CONSORTIUM UNDERGRADUATE SCHOLARSHIP PROGRAM
• See page 126

NATIONAL COUNCIL OF STATE GARDEN CLUBS, INC. SCHOLARSHIP   http://www.gardenclub.org

NATIONAL COUNCIL OF STATE GARDEN CLUBS, INC. SCHOLARSHIP
• See page 82

NATIONAL GARDEN CLUBS, INC.   http://www.gardenclub.org

NATIONAL GARDEN CLUBS, INC. SCHOLARSHIP PROGRAM
• See page 83

NATIONAL INVENTORS HALL OF FAME   http://www.invent.org

COLLEGIATE INVENTORS COMPETITION - GRAND PRIZE
• See page 95

COLLEGIATE INVENTORS COMPETITION FOR UNDERGRADUATE STUDENTS
• See page 95

NATIONAL OCEANIC AND ATMOSPHERIC ADMINISTRATION   http://see.orau.org

NATIONAL OCEANIC AND ATMOSPHERIC ADMINISTRATION EDUCATIONAL PARTNERSHIP PROGRAM WITH MINORITY SERVING INSTITUTIONS UNDERGRADUATE SCHOLARSHIP
• See page 268

NATIONAL SAFETY COUNCIL   http://www.cshema.org

CAMPUS SAFETY, HEALTH AND ENVIRONMENTAL MANAGEMENT ASSOCIATION SCHOLARSHIP AWARD PROGRAM

One $2000 scholarship, to encourage the study of safety and environmental management, is available to full-time undergraduate or graduate students in all majors/disciplines. Submit application, transcript, and essay by March 31 deadline. Information and application available at CSHEMA's Web site: http://www.cshema.org

Academic Fields/Career Goals: Environmental Science; Occupational Safety and Health.

Award: Scholarship for use in freshman, sophomore, junior, senior, or graduate years; not renewable. *Number:* 1. *Amount:* $2000.

Eligibility Requirements: Applicant must be enrolled or expecting to enroll full-time at a four-year institution or university. Available to U.S. and Canadian citizens.

Application Requirements: Application, essay, transcript. *Deadline:* March 31.

Contact: Scholarship Committee
National Safety Council
1121 Spring Lake Drive
Itasca, IL 60143-3201
Phone: 630-775-2227
Fax: 630-285-1613

NEW JERSEY DIVISION OF FISH AND WILDLIFE/NJ CHAPTER OF THE WILDLIFE SOCIETY   http://www.njfishandwildlife.com/cookhmschol.htm

RUSSELL A. COOKINGHAM SCHOLARSHIP
• See page 140

OHIO ACADEMY OF SCIENCE/OHIO ENVIRONMENTAL EDUCATION FUND   http://www.ohiosci.org

OHIO ENVIRONMENTAL SCIENCE & ENGINEERING SCHOLARSHIPS

Merit-based, non-renewable, tuition-only scholarships given to undergraduate students admitted to Ohio state or private colleges and universities who can demonstrate their knowledge and commitment to careers in environmental sciences or environmental engineering. Must be in their final year of a program in a two-year or four-year institution. Sophomores in a four-year institution are not eligible. Deadline is June 1.

Academic Fields/Career Goals: Environmental Science.

Award: Scholarship for use in senior year; not renewable. *Number:* 18. *Amount:* $1250–$2500.

Eligibility Requirements: Applicant must be enrolled or expecting to enroll full or part-time at a two-year or four-year institution or university; resident of Ohio and studying in Ohio. Applicant must have 3.0 GPA or higher. Available to U.S. citizens.

Application Requirements: Application, essay, resume, references, self-addressed stamped envelope, transcript. *Deadline:* June 1.

Contact: Mr. Lynn E. Elfner, CEO
Ohio Academy of Science/Ohio Environmental Education Fund
1500 West Third Avenue, Suite 228
Columbus, OH 43212-2817
Phone: 614-488-2228
Fax: 614-488-7629
E-mail: oas@iwaynet.net

OREGON STUDENT ASSISTANCE COMMISSION   http://www.osac.state.or.us

ROYDEN M. BODLEY SCHOLARSHIP
• See page 87

OZARKA NATURAL SPRING WATER   http://www.ozarkawater.com

STATEWIDE SCHOLARSHIPS
• See page 215

PARK PEOPLE   http://www.parkpeople.org

THE PARK PEOPLE $2000 SCHOLARSHIP
• See page 102

PENNSYLVANIA ASSOCIATION OF CONSERVATION DISTRICTS AUXILIARY   http://www.blairconservationdistrict.org

PACD AUXILIARY SCHOLARSHIPS
• See page 76

PENNSYLVANIA FISH AND BOAT COMMISSION   http://sites.state.pa.us/Fish

RALPH W. ABELE CONSERVATION SCHOLARSHIP

Scholarships to assist worthy young men and women in pursuing their education at approved institutions of higher learning in one of the environmental disciplines, such as fisheries, forestry, ecology, wildlife

Pennsylvania Fish and Boat Commission (continued)

management or environmental resource management. Awarded without regard to the race, color, creed, sex or national origin of the applicant. Scholarships have been awarded in the amount of $1000 and $500 per year.

Academic Fields/Career Goals: Environmental Science; Natural Resources.

Award: Scholarship for use in freshman, sophomore, junior, senior, or graduate years. *Amount:* $500–$1000.

Eligibility Requirements: Applicant must be enrolled or expecting to enroll at a four-year institution or university and resident of Pennsylvania. Available to U.S. citizens.

Application Requirements: Application. *Deadline:* varies.

Contact: Joe Greene, Treasurer
　　　　　Pennsylvania Fish and Boat Commission
　　　　　PO Box 67000
　　　　　Harrisburg, PA 17106-7000

SOCIETY OF MEXICAN AMERICAN ENGINEERS AND SCIENTISTS　　http://www.maes-natl.org

GRE AND GRADUATE APPLICATIONS WAIVER
• *See page 95*

TEXAS OUTDOOR WRITERS ASSOCIATION　　http://www.towa.org/

TEXAS OUTDOOR WRITERS ASSOCIATION SCHOLARSHIP
• *See page 188*

UNITED NEGRO COLLEGE FUND　　http://www.uncf.org

WEYERHAEUSER/UNCF CORPORATE SCHOLARS
• *See page 157*

VIRGINIA ASSOCIATION OF SOIL AND WATER CONSERVATION DISTRICTS EDUCATIONAL FOUNDATION, INC.　　http://www.fauquiercounty.gov

VASWCD EDUCATIONAL FOUNDATION, INC. SCHOLARSHIP AWARDS PROGRAM

Scholarship for full-time students enrolled in or applied to a college undergraduate or graduate level curriculum. Must have class ranking in the top 20% of his or her graduating class or a 3.0 or greater GPA. Most recent official high school or college transcript must accompany the application. Must demonstrate active interest in conservation. Scholarship recipients need to reapply to their individual SWCD for scholarship consideration in ensuing years.

Academic Fields/Career Goals: Environmental Science; Natural Resources.

Award: Scholarship for use in freshman, sophomore, junior, senior, or graduate years. *Number:* 4. *Amount:* $1000.

Eligibility Requirements: Applicant must be enrolled or expecting to enroll full-time at a four-year institution or university and resident of Virginia. Applicant must have 3.0 GPA or higher. Available to U.S. citizens.

Application Requirements: Application, essay, financial need analysis, references, transcript. *Deadline:* March 1.

Contact: Jennifer Krick, District Manager
　　　　　Virginia Association of Soil and Water Conservation Districts
　　　　　　Educational Foundation, Inc.
　　　　　John Marshall Soil and Water
　　　　　98 Alexandria Pike, Suite 31
　　　　　Warrenton, VA 20186
　　　　　Phone: 540-347-3120 Ext. 116
　　　　　Fax: 540-349-0878
　　　　　E-mail: jennifer.krick@va.nacdnet.net

EUROPEAN STUDIES

AMERICAN SCHOOLS OF ORIENTAL RESEARCH (ASOR)　　http://www.asor.org

CYPRUS AMERICAN ARCHAEOLOGICAL RESEARCH INSTITUTE HELENA WYLDE AND STUART SWINY FELLOWSHIP
• *See page 96*

ASSOCIATION TO UNITE THE DEMOCRACIES　　http://www.iaud.org

MAYME AND HERBERT FRANK EDUCATIONAL FUND
• *See page 216*

CANADIAN INSTITUTE OF UKRAINIAN STUDIES　　http://www.ualberta.ca/cius/

CANADIAN INSTITUTE OF UKRAINIAN STUDIES RESEARCH GRANTS
• *See page 104*

CULTURE CONNECTION　　http://www.thecultureconnection.com

CULTURE CONNECTION FOUNDATION SCHOLARSHIP
• *See page 73*

GERMAN ACADEMIC EXCHANGE SERVICE (DAAD)　　http://www.daad.org

GERMAN ACADEMIC EXCHANGE INFORMATION VISITS

Grants worth 430 Euros are available for an information visit of 7 to 12 days to groups of 10 to 15 students, accompanied by a faculty member. The purpose of this program is to increase the knowledge of specific German subjects and institutions within the framework of an academic study tour. Preference will be given to groups with a homogeneous academic background. Tours cannot be funded during July and August and between December and January 8. Application should reach DAAD New York at least six months before beginning date of planned visit.

Academic Fields/Career Goals: European Studies; German Studies.

Award: Grant for use in junior, senior, or graduate years; not renewable. *Number:* 10–15.

Eligibility Requirements: Applicant must be enrolled or expecting to enroll at an institution or university. Available to U.S. and Canadian citizens.

Application Requirements: Application. *Deadline:* Continuous.

Contact: German Academic Exchange Service (DAAD)
　　　　　871 United Nations Plaza
　　　　　New York, NY 10017
　　　　　Phone: 212-758-3223
　　　　　Fax: 212-755-5780
　　　　　E-mail: daadny@daad.org

FASHION DESIGN

OREGON STUDENT ASSISTANCE COMMISSION　　http://www.osac.state.or.us

FASHION GROUP INTERNATIONAL OF PORTLAND SCHOLARSHIP

Award for Oregon residents planning to pursue a career in a fashion-related field. Must be enrolled at least half-time at the sophomore or higher level. Minimum GPA of 3.0 required. Semifinalists will be interviewed in Portland. Must attend college in Oregon, Washington, California, or Idaho.

Academic Fields/Career Goals: Fashion Design.

Award: Scholarship for use in sophomore, junior, or senior years; renewable. *Number:* 5. *Amount:* $1500.

Eligibility Requirements: Applicant must be enrolled or expecting to enroll full or part-time at a two-year or four-year institution or university; resident of Oregon and studying in California, Idaho, Oregon, or Washington. Applicant must have 3.0 GPA or higher. Available to U.S. citizens.

Application Requirements: Application, essay, financial need analysis, interview, references, transcript, activity chart. *Deadline:* March 1.

Contact: Director of Grant Programs
Oregon Student Assistance Commission
1500 Valley River Drive, Suite 100
Eugene, OR 97401-7020
Phone: 800-452-8807 Ext. 7395

WORLDSTUDIO
FOUNDATION   http://www.worldstudio.org

WORLDSTUDIO FOUNDATION SCHOLARSHIP PROGRAM
• *See page 104*

FILMMAKING/VIDEO

ACADEMY FOUNDATION OF THE ACADEMY OF MOTION PICTURE ARTS AND
SCIENCES   http://www.oscars.org/saa

ACADEMY OF MOTION PICTURE STUDENT ACADEMY AWARD-HONORARY FOREIGN FILM

One award is given to an applicant from an institution outside the U.S. and a member of CILECT. Applications are limited to one per school, per year. Visit Web site for applications: http://www.oscars.org/saa

Academic Fields/Career Goals: Filmmaking/Video.

Award: Prize for use in freshman, sophomore, junior, senior, or graduate years; not renewable. *Number:* 1. *Amount:* $1000.

Eligibility Requirements: Applicant must be enrolled or expecting to enroll full-time at a four-year institution or university.

Application Requirements: Application, applicant must enter a contest, self-addressed stamped envelope, 16mm, 35mm, 70mm, or digital betacam format film or tape. *Deadline:* March 24.

Contact: Richard Miller, Awards Administration Director
Academy Foundation of the Academy of Motion Picture Arts
and Sciences
8949 Wilshire Boulevard
Beverly Hills, CA 90211-1972
Phone: 310-247-3000
Fax: 310-859-9619
E-mail: rmiller@oscars.org

ACADEMY OF MOTION PICTURES STUDENT ACADEMY AWARDS

Available to students who have made a narrative, documentary, alternative, or animated film of up to sixty minutes within the curricular structure of an accredited college or university. Initial entry must be on 1/2 inch VHS tape. 16mm or larger format print or digital betacam tape required for further rounds. Prizes awarded in four categories. Each category awards Gold ($5000), Silver ($3000), and Bronze ($2000). Visit Web site for details and application (http://www.oscars.org/saa).

Academic Fields/Career Goals: Filmmaking/Video.

Award: Prize for use in freshman, sophomore, junior, senior, or graduate years; not renewable. *Number:* 3–12. *Amount:* $2000–$5000.

Eligibility Requirements: Applicant must be enrolled or expecting to enroll full-time at a two-year or four-year institution or university. Available to U.S. and non-U.S. citizens.

Application Requirements: Application, applicant must enter a contest, 16mm or larger format film print or an NTSC Digital Betacam version of the entry (BetaSP format is not acceptable). *Deadline:* April 1.

Contact: Richard Miller, Awards Administration Director
Academy Foundation of the Academy of Motion Picture Arts
and Sciences
8949 Wilshire Boulevard
Beverly Hills, CA 90211-1972
Phone: 310-247-3000 Ext. 129
Fax: 310-859-9619
E-mail: rmiller@oscars.org

ACADEMY OF TELEVISION ARTS AND SCIENCES
FOUNDATION   http://www.emmys.tv/foundation

ACADEMY OF TELEVISION ARTS AND SCIENCES COLLEGE TELEVISION AWARDS
• *See page 108*

ADC RESEARCH INSTITUTE   http://www.adc.org

JACK SHAHEEN MASS COMMUNICATIONS SCHOLARSHIP AWARD
• *See page 177*

ADVERTISING FEDERATION OF FORT WAYNE,
INC.   http://www.adfedfortwayne.org

ADVERTISING FEDERATION OF FORT WAYNE, INC., SCHOLARSHIP
• *See page 178*

CHARLES & LUCILLE KING FAMILY FOUNDATION,
INC.   http://www.kingfoundation.org/

CHARLES AND LUCILLE KING FAMILY FOUNDATION SCHOLARSHIPS
• *See page 180*

ILLUMINATING ENGINEERING SOCIETY OF
NORTH AMERICA–GOLDEN GATE
SECTION   http://www.iesgg.org

ALAN LUCAS MEMORIAL EDUCATIONAL SCHOLARSHIP
• *See page 100*

ROBERT W. THUNEN MEMORIAL SCHOLARSHIPS
• *See page 100*

INSTITUTE FOR HUMANE
STUDIES   http://www.theihs.org

FILM AND FICTION SCHOLARSHIP
• *See page 111*

INTERNATIONAL COMMUNICATIONS INDUSTRIES
FOUNDATION   http://www.infocomm.org/foundation

ICIF SCHOLARSHIP FOR DEPENDENTS OF MEMBER ORGANIZATIONS
• *See page 181*

INTERNATIONAL COMMUNICATIONS INDUSTRIES FOUNDATION AV SCHOLARSHIP
• *See page 182*

MEDIA ACTION NETWORK FOR ASIAN
AMERICANS   http://www.manaa.org

MANAA MEDIA SCHOLARSHIPS FOR ASIAN AMERICAN STUDENTS
• *See page 112*

NATIONAL FOUNDATION FOR ADVANCEMENT IN
THE ARTS   http://www.artsawards.org

ARTS RECOGNITION AND TALENT SEARCH (ARTS)
• *See page 113*

NATIONAL WRITERS ASSOCIATION
FOUNDATION   http://www.nationalwriters.com

NATIONAL WRITERS ASSOCIATION FOUNDATION SCHOLARSHIPS
• *See page 184*

NEW ENGLAND FILM AND VIDEO FESTIVAL

NEW ENGLAND FILM AND VIDEO FESTIVAL AWARDS

One-time film and video awards available to students who are residents of New England or upstate New York. Must be U.S. citizen. Application fee of $25.

Academic Fields/Career Goals: Filmmaking/Video.

Award: Prize for use in freshman, sophomore, junior, or senior years; not renewable. *Number:* 9–15. *Amount:* $250–$5000.

New England Film and Video Festival (continued)

Eligibility Requirements: Applicant must be enrolled or expecting to enroll full or part-time at a two-year or four-year institution or university and resident of Connecticut, Maine, Massachusetts, New Hampshire, New York, Rhode Island, or Vermont. Available to U.S. citizens.

Application Requirements: Application, applicant must enter a contest, driver's license, photo. *Fee:* $25. *Deadline:* November 15.

Contact: Sandra Sullivan, Festival Co-director
New England Film and Video Festival
119 Braintree Street, Box 159, Suite 104
Boston, MA 02134
Phone: 617-783-9241 Ext. 12
Fax: 617-783-4368
E-mail: festival@bfvf.org

OUTDOOR WRITERS ASSOCIATION OF AMERICA http://www.owaa.org/

OUTDOOR WRITERS ASSOCIATION OF AMERICA BODIE MCDOWELL SCHOLARSHIP AWARD
• *See page 185*

PHI DELTA THETA EDUCATIONAL FOUNDATION http://phideltatheta.org

FRANCIS D. LYON SCHOLARSHIPS

Program run in the honor of Francis D. Lyon who had a distinguished motion picture and television career as a film editor, director, and producer. Both undergraduate and graduate students are invited to apply. Applicants must be pursuing a filmmaking career.

Academic Fields/Career Goals: Filmmaking/Video.

Award: Scholarship for use in freshman, sophomore, junior, senior, graduate, or postgraduate years; not renewable. *Number:* 2. *Amount:* up to $3000.

Eligibility Requirements: Applicant must be enrolled or expecting to enroll full-time at a four-year institution or university. Available to U.S. and non-U.S. citizens.

Application Requirements: Application, essay, photo, references, transcript. *Deadline:* March 15.

Contact: Carmalieta Jenkins, Assistant to the President
Phi Delta Theta Educational Foundation
2 South Campus Avenue
Oxford, OH 45056-1801
Phone: 513-523-6966
Fax: 513-523-9200
E-mail: carmalieta@phideltatheta.org

POLISH ARTS CLUB OF BUFFALO SCHOLARSHIP FOUNDATION http://pacb.bfn.org/about/constitution.html

POLISH ARTS CLUB OF BUFFALO SCHOLARSHIP FOUNDATION TRUST
• *See page 108*

RHODE ISLAND FOUNDATION http://www.rifoundation.org

RHODE ISLAND EDSAL ADVERTISING SCHOLARSHIP

One-time award for a Rhode Island resident with an advertising-related major who intends to pursue a career in advertising, public relations, marketing, graphic design, film, or broadcast production. Must be a college sophomore or above.

Academic Fields/Career Goals: Filmmaking/Video; Graphics/Graphic Arts/Printing; TV/Radio Broadcasting.

Award: Scholarship for use in freshman, sophomore, junior, or senior years; not renewable. *Number:* 1. *Amount:* $1500.

Eligibility Requirements: Applicant must be enrolled or expecting to enroll full or part-time at a four-year institution and resident of Rhode Island. Available to U.S. citizens.

Application Requirements: Application, financial need analysis, references, self-addressed stamped envelope, transcript. *Deadline:* April 28.

Contact: Scholarship Coordinator
Rhode Island Foundation
1 Union Station
Providence, RI 02903
Phone: 401-274-4564
Fax: 401-272-1359

SAN FRANCISCO FOUNDATION http://www.sff.org

PHELAN ART AWARD IN FILMMAKING

Award presented in every even-numbered year to recognize achievement in filmmaking. Must have been born in California, but need not be a current resident. Applicants must provide a copy of their birth certificate with their application. This award is not a scholarship. See Web site at http://www.sff.org for further information and deadlines.

Academic Fields/Career Goals: Filmmaking/Video.

Award: Prize for use in freshman, sophomore, junior, senior, graduate, or postgraduate years; not renewable. *Number:* 1. *Amount:* $2500–$7500.

Eligibility Requirements: Applicant must be enrolled or expecting to enroll at an institution or university. Available to U.S. citizens.

Application Requirements: Application, applicant must enter a contest, self-addressed stamped envelope. *Deadline:* varies.

Contact: Art Awards Coordinator
San Francisco Foundation
225 Bush Street, Suite 500
San Francisco, CA 94104
Phone: 415-733-8500

PHELAN ART AWARD IN VIDEO

Award presented in every even-numbered year to recognize achievement in video. Must have been born in California, but need not be a current resident. Applicants must provide a copy of their birth certificates with their application. This award is not a scholarship. See Web site at http://www.sff.org for further information and deadlines.

Academic Fields/Career Goals: Filmmaking/Video.

Award: Prize for use in freshman, sophomore, junior, senior, graduate, or postgraduate years; not renewable. *Number:* 1–2. *Amount:* $2500–$7500.

Eligibility Requirements: Applicant must be enrolled or expecting to enroll at an institution or university. Available to U.S. citizens.

Application Requirements: Application, applicant must enter a contest, self-addressed stamped envelope. *Deadline:* varies.

Contact: Art Awards Coordinator
San Francisco Foundation
225 Bush Street, Suite 500
San Francisco, CA 94104
Phone: 415-733-8500

SOCIETY OF MOTION PICTURE AND TELEVISION ENGINEERS http://www.smpte.org

LOU WOLF MEMORIAL SCHOLARSHIP

Award for full-time students enrolled in an accredited high school, two-year or four-year college or university. Must be members of Society of Motion Picture and Television Engineers.

Academic Fields/Career Goals: Filmmaking/Video.

Award: Scholarship for use in freshman, sophomore, junior, senior, or graduate years. *Amount:* up to $2000.

Eligibility Requirements: Applicant must be enrolled or expecting to enroll full-time at a two-year or four-year institution or university. Applicant or parent of applicant must be member of Society of Motion Picture and Television Engineers. Available to U.S. citizens.

Application Requirements: Application, references, transcript. *Deadline:* June 1.

Contact: Sally-Ann D'Amato, Society of Motion Picture and Television
Engineers
Society of Motion Picture and Television Engineers
3 Barker Avenue
White Plains, NY 10601
Phone: 914-761-1100
E-mail: sdamato@smpte.org

STUDENT PAPER AWARD

Contest for best paper by a current Student Member of SMPTE. Paper must deal with some technical phase of motion pictures, television, photographic instrumentation, or their closely allied arts and sciences. For more information see Web site: http://www.smpte.org.

Academic Fields/Career Goals: Filmmaking/Video.

Award: Prize for use in freshman, sophomore, junior, senior, graduate, or postgraduate years. *Number:* 1.

Eligibility Requirements: Applicant must be enrolled or expecting to enroll at a four-year institution or university. Applicant or parent of applicant must be member of Society of Motion Picture and Television Engineers. Available to U.S. citizens.

Application Requirements: Application, essay, student ID card. *Deadline:* July 1.

Contact: Sally-Ann D'Amato, Society of Motion Picture and Television
Engineers
Society of Motion Picture and Television Engineers
3 Barker Avenue
White Plains, NY 10601
Phone: 914-761-1100
E-mail: sdamato@smpte.org

TELETOON   http://www.teletoon.com

TELETOON ANIMATION SCHOLARSHIP AWARD COMPETITION
• *See page 114*

UNIVERSITY FILM AND VIDEO ASSOCIATION   http://www.ufva.org

UNIVERSITY FILM AND VIDEO ASSOCIATION CAROLE FIELDING STUDENT GRANTS

Up to $4000 is available for production grants in narrative, documentary, experimental, new-media/installation, or animation. Up to $1000 is available for grants in research. Applicant must be sponsored by a faculty person who is an active member of the University Film and Video Association. Fifty percent of award distributed upon completion of project.

Academic Fields/Career Goals: Filmmaking/Video.

Award: Grant for use in freshman, sophomore, junior, senior, or graduate years; not renewable. *Number:* up to 5. *Amount:* $1000–$4000.

Eligibility Requirements: Applicant must be enrolled or expecting to enroll full or part-time at a two-year or four-year institution. Available to U.S. and non-U.S. citizens.

Application Requirements: Application, essay, resume, references, project description, budget. *Deadline:* varies.

Contact: Prof. Robert Johnson, Jr., Chair, Carole Fielding Grants
University Film and Video Association
Framingham State College, 100 State Street
Framingham, MA 01701-9101
Phone: 508-626-4684
Fax: 508-626-4847
E-mail: rjohnso@frc.mass.edu

WOMEN IN FILM AND TELEVISION (WIFT)   http://www.wif.org

WIF FOUNDATION SCHOLARSHIP

Scholarships for female students based on their academic standing, artistic talents and commitment to a film-based curriculum with special consideration for financial need, regardless of age, ethnicity or religious affiliation. Scholarships to such schools as UCLA, USC, Chapman University and AFI are available to female students who are already enrolled and have been nominated by instructors and faculty at respective schools Contact your advisors if you have questions about available scholarships.

Academic Fields/Career Goals: Filmmaking/Video.

Award: Scholarship for use in freshman, sophomore, junior, or senior years; not renewable. *Number:* up to 3. *Amount:* up to $1000.

Eligibility Requirements: Applicant must be enrolled or expecting to enroll part-time at a two-year or four-year or technical institution or university and female. Available to U.S. citizens.

Application Requirements: Application, essay, financial need analysis, references, transcript. *Deadline:* March 4.

Contact: Gayle Nachlix, WIF Foundation Scholarship Coordinator
Women in Film and Television (WIFT)
8857 West Olympic Boulevard, Suite 201
Beverly Hills, CA 90211
Phone: 310-657-5144

WORLDFEST INTERNATIONAL FILM AND VIDEO FESTIVAL   http://www.worldfest.org

WORLDFEST STUDENT FILM AWARD

This is a cash award program for student films, both shorts and features. Film must be entered into the Worldfest International Film and Video Festival by December 15 to be considered for an award. Application fee is $45. Entry form available on Web site: http://worldfest.org.

Academic Fields/Career Goals: Filmmaking/Video.

Award: Prize for use in freshman, sophomore, junior, senior, or graduate years; not renewable. *Number:* 10. *Amount:* $1000–$10,000.

Eligibility Requirements: Applicant must be enrolled or expecting to enroll full or part-time at a two-year or four-year or technical institution or university. Available to U.S. and non-U.S. citizens.

Application Requirements: Application, applicant must enter a contest, film/tape entry. *Fee:* $45. *Deadline:* December 15.

Contact: Hunter Todd, Executive Director
Worldfest International Film and Video Festival
PO Box 56566
Houston, TX 77256-6566
Phone: 713-965-9955
Fax: 713-965-9960
E-mail: mail@worldfest.org

WORLDSTUDIO FOUNDATION   http://www.worldstudio.org

WORLDSTUDIO FOUNDATION SCHOLARSHIP PROGRAM
• *See page 104*

FIRE SCIENCES

BOY SCOUTS OF AMERICA - MUSKINGUM VALLEY COUNCIL   http://www.learning-for-life.org

INTERNATIONAL ASSOCIATION OF FIRE CHIEFS FOUNDATION SCHOLARSHIP

Annual scholarship program which awards $500 to Explorers who are pursuing a career in the fire sciences.

Academic Fields/Career Goals: Fire Sciences.

Award: Scholarship for use in freshman year. *Number:* 2. *Amount:* $500.

Eligibility Requirements: Applicant must be enrolled or expecting to enroll at an institution or university. Available to U.S. citizens.

Application Requirements: Application, essay, photo, references, transcript. *Deadline:* July 1.

Contact: Boy Scouts of America - Muskingum Valley Council
PO Box 152079
Irving, TX 75015-2079

INDEPENDENT LABORATORIES INSTITUTE SCHOLARSHIP ALLIANCE   http://www.acil.org

INDEPENDENT LABORATORIES INSTITUTE SCHOLARSHIP ALLIANCE
• *See page 93*

INTERNATIONAL ASSOCIATION OF ARSON INVESTIGATORS EDUCATIONAL FOUNDATION, INC.
http://www.fire-investigators.org/

JOHN CHARLES WILSON SCHOLARSHIP

One-time award to members in good standing of IAAI or the immediate family of a member or must be sponsored by an IAAI member. Must enroll or plan to enroll full-time in an accredited college or university that offers courses in police, fire sciences, or any arson investigation-related field. Application available at Web site. Deadline is February 15.

Academic Fields/Career Goals: Fire Sciences; Law Enforcement/Police Administration.

Award: Scholarship for use in freshman, sophomore, junior, senior, or graduate years; not renewable. *Number:* 5–10. *Amount:* $500–$1000.

Eligibility Requirements: Applicant must be enrolled or expecting to enroll full-time at a two-year or four-year institution or university. Available to U.S. and non-U.S. citizens.

Application Requirements: Application, essay, references, transcript. *Deadline:* February 15.

Contact: Marsha Sipes, Office Manager
International Association of Arson Investigators Educational Foundation, Inc.
12770 Boenker Road
Bridgeton, MO 63044
Phone: 314-739-4224
Fax: 314-739-4219
E-mail: iaai@firearson.com

LEARNING FOR LIFE
http://www.learning-for-life.org

INTERNATIONAL ASSOCIATIONS OF FIRE CHIEFS FOUNDATION SCHOLARSHIP

The International Association of Fire Chiefs Foundation coordinates a yearly $500 scholarship program to assist Explorers in pursuing a career in the fire sciences. Applicant must be younger than 21 years of age. For more information visit http://www.learning-for-life.org/exploring

Academic Fields/Career Goals: Fire Sciences.

Award: Scholarship for use in freshman, sophomore, junior, or senior years; not renewable. *Number:* 1. *Amount:* $500.

Eligibility Requirements: Applicant must be age 20 or under and enrolled or expecting to enroll full-time at a four-year institution. Available to U.S. citizens.

Application Requirements: Application, essay, references, transcript. *Deadline:* July 1.

Contact: Learning for Life
S210, PO Box 152079
Irving, TX 75015-2079

MARYLAND HIGHER EDUCATION COMMISSION
http://www.mhec.state.md.us

FIREFIGHTER, AMBULANCE, AND RESCUE SQUAD MEMBER TUITION REIMBURSEMENT PROGRAM-MARYLAND

Award intended to reimburse members of rescue organizations serving Maryland communities for tuition costs of course work towards a degree or certificate in fire service or medical technology. Must attend a two- or four-year school in Maryland. Minimum 2.0 GPA.

Academic Fields/Career Goals: Fire Sciences; Health and Medical Sciences; Trade/Technical Specialties.

Award: Scholarship for use in freshman, sophomore, junior, or senior years; not renewable. *Number:* 100–300. *Amount:* $200–$4000.

Eligibility Requirements: Applicant must be enrolled or expecting to enroll full or part-time at a two-year or four-year institution or university; resident of Maryland and studying in Maryland. Applicant or parent of applicant must have employment or volunteer experience in police/firefighting. Available to U.S. citizens.

Application Requirements: Application, transcript. *Deadline:* July 1.

Contact: Gerrie Rogers, Office of Student Financial Assistance
Maryland Higher Education Commission
839 Bestgate Road, Suite 400
Annapolis, MD 21401-3013
Phone: 410-260-4574
Fax: 410-260-3203
E-mail: ofsamail@mhec.state.md.us

FLEXOGRAPHY

TAG AND LABEL MANUFACTURERS INSTITUTE, INC.
http://www.tlmi.com

TLMI 4 YEAR COLLEGES/FULL-TIME STUDENTS SCHOLARSHIP
• See page 290

TLMI SCHOLARSHIP GRANT FOR STUDENTS OF 2 YEAR COLLEGES

One-time award of $1000 to students enrolled full-time in a flexographic printing degree program at a two-year college or technical school.

Academic Fields/Career Goals: Flexography.

Award: Scholarship for use in freshman or sophomore years. *Number:* 4. *Amount:* $1000.

Eligibility Requirements: Applicant must be enrolled or expecting to enroll full-time at a two-year institution. Applicant must have 3.0 GPA or higher. Available to U.S. citizens.

Application Requirements: Application, transcript, statement including personal information about applicant, financial circumstances, career and/or educational goals, employment experience, and reasons why they should be selection for this award. *Deadline:* March 31.

Contact: Scholarship Committee
Tag and Label Manufacturers Institute, Inc.
40 Shuman Boulevard, Suite 295
Naperville, IL 60563

FOOD SCIENCE/NUTRITION

AMERICAN ASSOCIATION OF CEREAL CHEMISTS
http://www.aaccnet.org

UNDERGRADUATE SCHOLARSHIP AWARD

One-time award to encourage scholastically outstanding undergraduate students in academic preparation for a career in grain-based food science and technology, and to attract and encourage outstanding students to enter the field of grain-based food science and technology. Must be AACC member. Minimum 3.0 GPA required. Application must be submitted to AACC by March 1.

Academic Fields/Career Goals: Food Science/Nutrition.

Award: Scholarship for use in junior or senior years; not renewable. *Number:* up to 15. *Amount:* $1000–$2000.

Eligibility Requirements: Applicant must be enrolled or expecting to enroll full-time at a four-year institution or university. Applicant must have 3.0 GPA or higher. Available to U.S. and non-U.S. citizens.

Application Requirements: Application, essay, references, transcript. *Deadline:* March 1.

Contact: Linda Schmitt, Scholarship Coordinator
American Association of Cereal Chemists
3340 Pilot Knob Road
St. Paul, MN 55121-2097
Phone: 651-994-3828
Fax: 651-454-0766
E-mail: lschmitt@scisoc.org

AMERICAN DIETETIC ASSOCIATION
http://www.eatright.org

AMERICAN DIETETIC ASSOCIATION FOUNDATION SCHOLARSHIP PROGRAM

ADAF scholarships are available for undergraduate and graduate students enrolled in programs, including dietetic internships, preparing for entry to dietetics practice as well as dietetics professionals engaged in continuing education at the graduate level. Scholarship funds are provided by many state dietetic associations, dietetic practice groups, past ADA leaders and corporate donors. All scholarships require ADA membership. Details available on Web site http://www.eatright.org.

Academic Fields/Career Goals: Food Science/Nutrition.

Award: Scholarship for use in sophomore, junior, senior, graduate, or postgraduate years; not renewable. *Number:* 186. *Amount:* $500–$5000.

Eligibility Requirements: Applicant must be enrolled or expecting to enroll full or part-time at a two-year or four-year institution. Applicant or parent of applicant must be member of American Dietetic Association. Available to U.S. citizens.

Application Requirements: Application, essay, financial need analysis, references, transcript. *Deadline:* February 15.

Contact: Education Team
Phone: 800-877-1600 Ext. 5400
E-mail: education@eatright.org

AMERICAN INSTITUTE OF WINE AND FOOD-PACIFIC NORTHWEST CHAPTER

CULINARY, VINIFERA, AND HOSPITALITY SCHOLARSHIP

One-time award available to residents of Washington State. Must be enrolled full-time in an accredited culinary, vinifera, or hospitality program in Washington State. Must have completed two years. Minimum 3.0 GPA required.

Academic Fields/Career Goals: Food Science/Nutrition; Food Service/Hospitality; Hospitality Management.

Award: Scholarship for use in freshman, sophomore, or junior years; not renewable. *Number:* 1–2. *Amount:* $1000–$2000.

Eligibility Requirements: Applicant must be enrolled or expecting to enroll full-time at a four-year or technical institution or university; resident of Washington and studying in Washington. Applicant must have 3.0 GPA or higher. Available to U.S. and non-U.S. citizens.

Application Requirements: Application, essay, references. *Deadline:* Continuous.

Contact: Brad Sturman, Scholarship Coordinator
American Institute of Wine and Food-Pacific Northwest Chapter
224 18th Avenue
Kirkland, WA 98033
Phone: 206-679-6228

AMERICAN SOCIETY FOR ENOLOGY AND VITICULTURE   http://www.asev.org

AMERICAN SOCIETY FOR ENOLOGY AND VITICULTURE SCHOLARSHIPS
• See page 78

ASSOCIATION FOR FOOD AND DRUG OFFICIALS   http://www.afdo.org

ASSOCIATION FOR FOOD AND DRUG OFFICIALS SCHOLARSHIP FUND

A $1500 scholarship for students in their third or fourth year of college/university who have demonstrated a desire for a career in research, regulatory work, quality control, or teaching in an area related to some aspect of food, drugs, or consumer products safety. Minimum 3.0 GPA required in first two years of undergraduate study. For further information, visit Web site: http://www.afdo.org

Academic Fields/Career Goals: Food Science/Nutrition.

Award: Scholarship for use in junior or senior years; not renewable. *Number:* 2. *Amount:* $1500.

Eligibility Requirements: Applicant must be enrolled or expecting to enroll full-time at a four-year institution or university. Applicant must have 3.0 GPA or higher. Available to U.S. citizens.

Application Requirements: Application, essay, references, transcript. *Deadline:* February 1.

Contact: Leigh Ann Stamdaugh, Administrative/Special Projects Assistant
Association for Food and Drug Officials
2550 Kingston Road, Suite 311
York, PA 17402
Phone: 717-757-2888
Fax: 717-755-8089
E-mail: afdo@afdo.org

CHILD NUTRITION FOUNDATION   http://www.asfsa.org

NANCY CURRY SCHOLARSHIP

Scholarship assists members of the American School Food Service Association and their dependents to pursue educational and career advancement in school foodservice or child nutrition.

Academic Fields/Career Goals: Food Science/Nutrition; Food Service/Hospitality.

Award: Scholarship for use in freshman, sophomore, junior, senior, or graduate years; not renewable. *Number:* 1. *Amount:* $1000.

Eligibility Requirements: Applicant must be enrolled or expecting to enroll full or part-time at a two-year or four-year or technical institution or university. Applicant or parent of applicant must be member of American School Food Service Association. Applicant or parent of applicant must have employment or volunteer experience in food service. Applicant must have 3.0 GPA or higher. Available to U.S. citizens.

Application Requirements: Application, essay, resume, references, test scores, transcript, proof of enrollment. *Deadline:* April 15.

Contact: Ruth O'Brien, Scholarship Manager
Child Nutrition Foundation
700 South Washington Street, Suite 300
Alexandria, VA 22314
Phone: 703-739-3900 Ext. 150

PROFESSIONAL GROWTH SCHOLARSHIP

Scholarships for child nutrition professionals pursuing graduate education in a food science management or nutrition-related field of study.

Academic Fields/Career Goals: Food Science/Nutrition; Food Service/Hospitality.

Award: Scholarship for use in freshman, sophomore, junior, senior, or graduate years; not renewable. *Number:* varies. *Amount:* varies.

Eligibility Requirements: Applicant must be enrolled or expecting to enroll full or part-time at a two-year or four-year or technical institution or university. Applicant or parent of applicant must be member of American School Food Service Association. Applicant or parent of applicant must have employment or volunteer experience in food service. Applicant must have 3.5 GPA or higher. Available to U.S. citizens.

Application Requirements: Application, essay, resume, references, transcript, proof of enrollment, official program requirement. *Deadline:* April 15.

Contact: Ruth O'Brien, Scholarship Manager
Child Nutrition Foundation
700 South Washington Street, Suite 300
Alexandria, VA 22314
Phone: 703-739-3900 Ext. 150
Fax: 703-739-3915
E-mail: robrien@asfsa.org

SCHWAN'S FOOD SERVICE SCHOLARSHIP

Program is designed to assist members of the American School Food Service Association and their dependents as they pursue educational advancement in the field of child nutrition.

Academic Fields/Career Goals: Food Science/Nutrition; Food Service/Hospitality.

Award: Scholarship for use in freshman, sophomore, junior, senior, or graduate years; not renewable. *Number:* 50–60. *Amount:* $150–$1000.

Eligibility Requirements: Applicant must be enrolled or expecting to enroll full or part-time at a two-year or four-year or technical institution or university. Applicant or parent of applicant must be

Child Nutrition Foundation (continued)

member of American School Food Service Association. Applicant or parent of applicant must have employment or volunteer experience in food service. Applicant must have 2.5 GPA or higher. Available to U.S. citizens.

Application Requirements: Application, essay, resume, references, transcript, proof of enrollment, official program requirements. *Deadline:* April 15.

Contact: Ruth O'Brien, Scholarship Manager
Child Nutrition Foundation
700 South Washington Street, Suite 300
Alexandria, VA 22314
Phone: 703-739-3900 Ext. 150
E-mail: robrien@asfsa.org

CULINARY TRUST   http://www.iacpfoundation.org

CULINARY TRUST SCHOLARSHIP PROGRAM FOR CULINARY STUDY AND RESEARCH

Scholarships for beginning students, continuing education, culinary professionals, and independent research. Applicants must have at least two years of food service experience (paid, volunteer, or combination of both), a minimum 3.0 GPA and write an essay. There is a $25 application fee.

Academic Fields/Career Goals: Food Science/Nutrition; Food Service/Hospitality.

Award: Scholarship for use in freshman, sophomore, junior, senior, graduate, or postgraduate years; not renewable. *Number:* 21. *Amount:* $1000–$5000.

Eligibility Requirements: Applicant must be enrolled or expecting to enroll full or part-time at a two-year or four-year or technical institution or university. Applicant or parent of applicant must have employment or volunteer experience in food service. Applicant must have 3.0 GPA or higher. Available to U.S. and non-U.S. citizens.

Application Requirements: Application, essay, interview, references, transcript. *Fee:* $25. *Deadline:* December 15.

Contact: Trina Gribbins, Director of Administration
Culinary Trust
304 West Liberty Street, Suite 201
Louisville, KY 40202-3068
Phone: 502-581-9786 Ext. 264
Fax: 502-589-3602
E-mail: tgribbins@hqtrs.com

HERB SOCIETY OF AMERICA   http://www.herbsociety.org

HERB SOCIETY RESEARCH GRANTS
• See page 92

HISPANIC COLLEGE FUND, INC.   http://www.hispanicfund.org

NATIONAL HISPANIC EXPLORERS SCHOLARSHIP PROGRAM
• See page 93

INSTITUTE OF FOOD TECHNOLOGISTS   http://www.ift.org

INSTITUTE OF FOOD TECHNOLOGISTS FOOD ENGINEERING DIVISION JUNIOR/SENIOR SCHOLARSHIP

One-time award for junior or senior level students in an Institute of Food Technologists approved program, with demonstrated intent to pursue professional activities in food science or food technology. Submit recommendation. Applications must be sent to department head of educational institution, not IFT.

Academic Fields/Career Goals: Food Science/Nutrition.

Award: Scholarship for use in sophomore, junior, or senior years; not renewable. *Number:* 61. *Amount:* $1000–$2250.

Eligibility Requirements: Applicant must be enrolled or expecting to enroll at a four-year institution or university. Available to U.S. citizens.

Application Requirements: Application, references, transcript. *Deadline:* February 1.

Contact: Administrator
Institute of Food Technologists
525 West Van Buren Street, Suite 1000
Chicago, IL 60607
Phone: 312-782-8424
Fax: 312-782-8348

INSTITUTE OF FOOD TECHNOLOGISTS FRESHMAN SCHOLARSHIPS

Twenty-four awards for scholastically outstanding high school graduates or seniors entering college in an approved four-year program in food sciences or technology. Program must be approved by Institute of Food Technologists Education Committee. Submit application to head of college. Merit-based, one-time award of $1000-$1500.

Academic Fields/Career Goals: Food Science/Nutrition.

Award: Scholarship for use in freshman year; not renewable. *Number:* 24. *Amount:* $1000–$1500.

Eligibility Requirements: Applicant must be enrolled or expecting to enroll full-time at a four-year institution or university. Applicant must have 3.5 GPA or higher. Available to U.S. and non-U.S. citizens.

Application Requirements: Application, references, transcript. *Deadline:* February 15.

Contact: Administrator
Institute of Food Technologists
525 West Van Buren Street, Suite 1000
Chicago, IL 60607
Phone: 312-782-8424
Fax: 312-782-8348

INSTITUTE OF FOOD TECHNOLOGISTS QUALITY ASSURANCE DIVISION JUNIOR/SENIOR SCHOLARSHIPS

One-time award for college juniors and seniors who are taking or have taken a course in quality assurance and have demonstrated an interest in the quality assurance area. Submit recommendation. Applications must be sent to department head of educational institution, not IFT.

Academic Fields/Career Goals: Food Science/Nutrition.

Award: Scholarship for use in junior or senior years; not renewable. *Number:* 2. *Amount:* $2000.

Eligibility Requirements: Applicant must be enrolled or expecting to enroll at a four-year institution. Available to U.S. citizens.

Application Requirements: Application, references, transcript. *Deadline:* February 1.

Contact: Administrator
Institute of Food Technologists
525 West Van Buren Street, Suite 1000
Chicago, IL 60607
Phone: 312-782-8424
Fax: 312-782-8348

INSTITUTE OF FOOD TECHNOLOGISTS SOPHOMORE SCHOLARSHIPS

Twenty-two awards available to college freshmen for use in sophomore year. Applicants must major in food science or food technology in a four-year Institute of Food Technologists Education Committee-approved program and have a 2.5 GPA. One-time award of $1000. Applications must be submitted to the department head of educational institution.

Academic Fields/Career Goals: Food Science/Nutrition.

Award: Scholarship for use in freshman or sophomore years; not renewable. *Number:* 22. *Amount:* $1000.

Eligibility Requirements: Applicant must be enrolled or expecting to enroll full-time at a four-year institution or university. Applicant must have 2.5 GPA or higher. Available to U.S. citizens.

Application Requirements: Application, references, transcript. *Deadline:* March 1.

Contact: Administrator
Institute of Food Technologists
525 West Van Buren Street, Suite 1000
Chicago, IL 60607
Phone: 312-782-8424
Fax: 312-782-8348

INSTITUTE OF FOOD TECHNOLOGISTS/MASTER FOODS USA UNDERGRADUATE MENTORED SCHOLARSHIP

Mentored scholarships available for students from a minority group pursuing studies in Food Science. Must have a 3.0 GPA. Deadline is June 1.

Academic Fields/Career Goals: Food Science/Nutrition.

Award: Scholarship for use in freshman, sophomore, junior, or senior years; renewable. *Number:* 7. *Amount:* $4000.

Eligibility Requirements: Applicant must be American Indian/Alaska Native, Asian/Pacific Islander, Black (non-Hispanic), or Hispanic and enrolled or expecting to enroll at a two-year or four-year institution or university. Applicant must have 3.0 GPA or higher. Available to U.S. citizens.

Application Requirements: Application, test scores. *Deadline:* June 1.

Contact: Ms. Elizabeth Plummer, Manager of Foundation
Development
Institute of Food Technologists
525 West Van Buren Street, Suite 1000
Chicago, IL 60607
Phone: 312-782-8424 Ext. 226
Fax: 312-416-7919
E-mail: ejplummer@ift.org

INTERNATIONAL FOODSERVICE EDITORIAL COUNCIL
http://www.ifec-is-us.com

INTERNATIONAL FOODSERVICE EDITORIAL COUNCIL COMMUNICATIONS SCHOLARSHIP

• See page 182

JAMES BEARD FOUNDATION, INC.
http://www.jamesbeard.org

AAA FIVE DIAMOND SCHOLARSHIP

One-time award towards tuition at an accredited culinary school of the applicant's choice. Must submit a 500 word essay on culinary goals and how this scholarship can help attain them. Candidates must demonstrate a strong commitment to the culinary arts, an exceptional academic or work record, and financial need. See Web site at http://www.jamesbeard.org for further details.

Academic Fields/Career Goals: Food Science/Nutrition.

Award: Scholarship for use in freshman, sophomore, junior, senior, or graduate years; not renewable. *Number:* 1. *Amount:* $5000.

Eligibility Requirements: Applicant must be enrolled or expecting to enroll at an institution or university. Available to U.S. and non-U.S. citizens.

Application Requirements: Application, essay, financial need analysis, references, transcript. *Deadline:* April 15.

Contact: Caroline Stuart, Scholarship Director
James Beard Foundation, Inc.
167 West 12th Street
New York, NY 10011
Phone: 212-675-4984 Ext. 311
Fax: 212-645-1438
E-mail: jamesbeardfound@hotmail.com

ARTIE CUTLER MEMORIAL SCHOLARSHIP

One-time award towards tuition at an accredited culinary school of student's choice. Applicant must submit a 500 word essay on culinary goals and how this scholarship can help attain them. Candidates must demonstrate a strong commitment to the culinary arts, an exceptional academic or work record, and financial need. See Web site at http://www.jamesbeard.org for further details.

Academic Fields/Career Goals: Food Science/Nutrition.

Award: Scholarship for use in freshman, sophomore, junior, senior, or graduate years; not renewable. *Number:* 1. *Amount:* $4000.

Eligibility Requirements: Applicant must be enrolled or expecting to enroll at an institution or university. Available to U.S. and non-U.S. citizens.

Application Requirements: Application, essay, financial need analysis, references, transcript. *Deadline:* April 15.

Contact: Caroline Stuart, Scholarship Director
James Beard Foundation, Inc.
167 West 12th Street
New York, NY 10011
Phone: 212-675-4984 Ext. 311
Fax: 212-645-1438
E-mail: jamesbeardfound@hotmail.com

BECOMING A CHEF SCHOLARSHIP

One-time award towards tuition at an accredited culinary school of student's choice. Candidates must demonstrate a strong commitment to the culinary arts, an exceptional academic or work record, and financial need. See Web site at http://www.jamesbeard.org for further details.

Academic Fields/Career Goals: Food Science/Nutrition.

Award: Scholarship for use in freshman, sophomore, junior, senior, or graduate years; not renewable. *Number:* 1. *Amount:* $1000.

Eligibility Requirements: Applicant must be enrolled or expecting to enroll at an institution or university. Available to U.S. and non-U.S. citizens.

Application Requirements: Application, essay, financial need analysis, references, transcript. *Deadline:* April 15.

Contact: Caroline Stuart, Scholarship Director
James Beard Foundation, Inc.
167 West 12th Street
New York, NY 10011
Phone: 212-675-4984 Ext. 311
Fax: 212-645-1438
E-mail: jamesbeardfound@hotmail.com

BRYAN CLOSE POLO GRILL SCHOLARSHIP

One-time award towards tuition at an accredited culinary school of student's choice. Applicant must be a resident of Oklahoma and have had at least one year of culinary experience. Candidates must demonstrate a strong commitment to the culinary arts, an exceptional academic or work record, and financial need. See Web site at http://www.jamesbeard.org for further details.

Academic Fields/Career Goals: Food Science/Nutrition.

Award: Scholarship for use in freshman, sophomore, junior, senior, or graduate years; not renewable. *Number:* 4. *Amount:* $500–$1000.

Eligibility Requirements: Applicant must be enrolled or expecting to enroll at an institution or university and resident of Arkansas, Kansas, Louisiana, Mississippi, Oklahoma, or Texas. Available to U.S. and non-U.S. citizens.

Application Requirements: Application, essay, financial need analysis, references, transcript. *Deadline:* April 15.

Contact: Caroline Stuart, Scholarship Director
James Beard Foundation, Inc.
167 West 12th Street
New York, NY 10011
Phone: 212-675-4984 Ext. 311
Fax: 212-645-1438
E-mail: jamesbeardfound@hotmail.com

DANA CAMPBELL MEMORIAL SCHOLARSHIP

Scholarship for $2000 awarded to an applicant with career interests in food journalism who is in his/her second or third year in an accredited bachelor degree program in journalism or a food-related curriculum. Must be resident of a "Southern" state within the Southern Living readership area (Alabama, Florida, Georgia, North Carolina, South Carolina, Louisiana, Virginia, Arkansas, Texas, Mississippi, Kentucky, Maryland, Missouri, Oklahoma, West Virginia, or Delaware) and substantiate residency. The scholarship recipient will also be considered for an internship at Southern Living. See Web site at http://www.jamesbeard.org for further details.

Academic Fields/Career Goals: Food Science/Nutrition.

Award: Scholarship for use in sophomore or junior years; not renewable. *Number:* 1. *Amount:* $2000.

James Beard Foundation, Inc. (continued)

Eligibility Requirements: Applicant must be enrolled or expecting to enroll at a four-year institution or university and resident of Alabama, Arkansas, Delaware, Florida, Georgia, Kentucky, Louisiana, Maryland, Mississippi, Missouri, North Carolina, Oklahoma, South Carolina, Texas, or Virginia. Available to U.S. and non-U.S. citizens.

Application Requirements: Application, essay, financial need analysis, references, transcript. *Deadline:* April 15.

Contact: Caroline Stuart, Scholarship Director
James Beard Foundation, Inc.
167 West 12th Street
New York, NY 10011
Phone: 212-675-4984 Ext. 311
Fax: 212-645-1438
E-mail: jamesbeardfound@hotmail.com

DAVID EDGCUMBE SCHOLARSHIP

One-time award towards tuition for a beginning student interested in teaching in the culinary field. Applicant must have a high school diploma or equivalent. Candidates must demonstrate a strong commitment to the culinary arts, an exceptional academic or work record, and financial need. See Web site at http://www.jamesbeard.org for further details.

Academic Fields/Career Goals: Food Science/Nutrition.

Award: Scholarship for use in freshman year; not renewable. *Number:* 1. *Amount:* $1000.

Eligibility Requirements: Applicant must be enrolled or expecting to enroll at an institution or university. Available to U.S. and non-U.S. citizens.

Application Requirements: Application, essay, financial need analysis, references, transcript. *Deadline:* April 15.

Contact: Caroline Stuart, Scholarship Director
James Beard Foundation, Inc.
167 West 12th Street
New York, NY 10011
Phone: 212-675-4984 Ext. 311
Fax: 212-645-1438
E-mail: jamesbeardfound@hotmail.com

GINO COFACCI MEMORIAL SCHOLARSHIP

One-time award towards tuition for foreign culinary education. Applicant must have applied for an extensive culinary course. Approval of the course is at the discretion of the James Beard Foundation scholarship committee. Candidates must demonstrate a strong commitment to the culinary arts, an exceptional academic or work record, and financial need. See Web site at http://www.jamesbeard.org for further details.

Academic Fields/Career Goals: Food Science/Nutrition.

Award: Scholarship for use in freshman, sophomore, junior, senior, or graduate years; not renewable. *Number:* 1. *Amount:* $1000.

Eligibility Requirements: Applicant must be enrolled or expecting to enroll at an institution or university. Available to U.S. and non-U.S. citizens.

Application Requirements: Application, essay, financial need analysis, references, transcript. *Deadline:* April 15.

Contact: Caroline Stuart, Scholarship Director
James Beard Foundation, Inc.
167 West 12th Street
New York, NY 10011
Phone: 212-675-4984 Ext. 311
Fax: 212-645-1438
E-mail: jamesbeardfound@hotmail.com

JAMES BEARD FOUNDATION GENERAL SCHOLARSHIPS

One-time award towards tuition at an accredited culinary school of student's choice. The amount of each scholarship will be at the discretion of the James Beard Foundation scholarship committee. Candidates must demonstrate a strong commitment to the culinary arts, an exceptional academic or work record, and financial need. See Web site at http://www.jamesbeard.org for further details.

Academic Fields/Career Goals: Food Science/Nutrition.

Award: Scholarship for use in freshman, sophomore, junior, senior, or graduate years; not renewable. *Number:* up to 50. *Amount:* $1000–$2000.

Eligibility Requirements: Applicant must be enrolled or expecting to enroll at an institution or university. Available to U.S. and non-U.S. citizens.

Application Requirements: Application, essay, financial need analysis, references, transcript. *Deadline:* April 15.

Contact: Caroline Stuart, Scholarship Director
James Beard Foundation, Inc.
167 West 12th Street
New York, NY 10011
Phone: 212-675-4984 Ext. 311
Fax: 212-645-1438
E-mail: jamesbeardfound@hotmail.com

LA TOQUE SCHOLARSHIP

Scholarship for $3000 toward tuition at an accredited culinary school of the student's choice. See Web site at http://www.jamesbeard.org for further details.

Academic Fields/Career Goals: Food Science/Nutrition.

Award: Scholarship for use in freshman, sophomore, junior, senior, or graduate years; not renewable. *Number:* 1. *Amount:* $3000.

Eligibility Requirements: Applicant must be enrolled or expecting to enroll at an institution or university. Available to U.S. and non-U.S. citizens.

Application Requirements: Application, essay, financial need analysis, references, transcript. *Deadline:* May 1.

Contact: Caroline Stuart, Scholarship Director
James Beard Foundation, Inc.
167 West 12th Street
New York, NY 10011
Phone: 212-675-4984 Ext. 311
Fax: 212-645-1438
E-mail: jamesbeardfound@hotmail.com

PETER KUMP MEMORIAL SCHOLARSHIP

One-time award towards tuition at an accredited or licensed culinary school of student's choice. Applicant must submit a 500 word essay on culinary goals and how this scholarship can help attain them. Candidates must demonstrate a strong commitment to the culinary arts, an exceptional academic or work record, and financial need. See Web site at http://www.jamesbeard.org for further details.

Academic Fields/Career Goals: Food Science/Nutrition.

Award: Scholarship for use in freshman year; not renewable. *Number:* 1. *Amount:* $5000.

Eligibility Requirements: Applicant must be high school student and planning to enroll or expecting to enroll at an institution or university. Applicant must have 3.5 GPA or higher. Available to U.S. and non-U.S. citizens.

Application Requirements: Application, essay, financial need analysis, references, transcript. *Deadline:* April 15.

Contact: Caroline Stuart, Scholarship Director
James Beard Foundation, Inc.
167 West 12th Street
New York, NY 10011
Phone: 212-675-4984 Ext. 311
Fax: 212-645-1438
E-mail: jamesbeardfound@hotmail.com

SIA'S SCHOLARSHIP

One-time award towards tuition at an accredited culinary school. Applicant must be from Georgia, Louisiana or Texas. Applicant must be finishing the first year or beginning the second year of a minimum two-year program at an accredited culinary school. Applicant must submit a 500 word essay on their culinary goals and how this scholarship can help to attain them. See Web site at http://www.jamesbeard.org for further details.

Academic Fields/Career Goals: Food Science/Nutrition.

Award: Scholarship for use in sophomore, junior, or senior years; not renewable. *Number:* 1. *Amount:* $5000.

Eligibility Requirements: Applicant must be enrolled or expecting to enroll at a two-year institution and resident of Georgia, Louisiana, or Texas. Available to U.S. and non-U.S. citizens.

Application Requirements: Application, essay, financial need analysis, references, transcript. *Deadline:* April 15.

Contact: Caroline Stuart, Scholarship Director
James Beard Foundation, Inc.
167 West 12th Street
New York, NY 10011
Phone: 212-675-4984 Ext. 311
Fax: 212-645-1438
E-mail: jamesbeardfound@hotmail.com

WALLY JOE SCHOLARSHIP

One-time award towards tuition at an accredited culinary school for applicants who are residents of Mississippi, Tennessee, Arkansas, or Louisiana. Candidates must demonstrate a strong commitment to the culinary arts, an exceptional academic or work record, and financial need. See Web site at http://www.jamesbeard.org for further details.

Academic Fields/Career Goals: Food Science/Nutrition.

Award: Scholarship for use in freshman, sophomore, junior, senior, or graduate years; not renewable. *Number:* 2. *Amount:* $2000.

Eligibility Requirements: Applicant must be enrolled or expecting to enroll at an institution or university and resident of Alaska, Louisiana, Mississippi, or Tennessee. Available to U.S. and non-U.S. citizens.

Application Requirements: Application, essay, financial need analysis, references, transcript. *Deadline:* April 15.

Contact: Caroline Stuart, Scholarship Director
James Beard Foundation, Inc.
167 West 12th Street
New York, NY 10011
Phone: 212-675-4984 Ext. 311
Fax: 212-645-1438
E-mail: jamesbeardfound@hotmail.com

LES DAMES D'ESCOFFIER   http://www.lesdames.ca/scholarship.htm

LES DAMES D'ESCOFFIER SCHOLARSHIP
• See page 203

MAINE SCHOOL FOOD SERVICE ASSOCIATION (MSFSA)

SCHOLARSHIP OF THE MAINE SCHOOL FOOD SERVICE ASSOCIATION

Awarded to students from Maine enrolling in nutrition or culinary arts. It is also available to employees of school nutrition programs wishing to continue their education. Applicant can be a high school senior, college student, or member of MSFSA. Applicant must be attending an institution in Maine.

Academic Fields/Career Goals: Food Science/Nutrition; Food Service/Hospitality; Home Economics; Hospitality Management; Trade/Technical Specialties.

Award: Scholarship for use in freshman, sophomore, junior, or senior years; not renewable. *Number:* 1–4. *Amount:* $300–$1200.

Eligibility Requirements: Applicant must be enrolled or expecting to enroll full or part-time at a two-year or four-year or technical institution or university; resident of Maine and studying in Maine. Available to U.S. citizens.

Application Requirements: Application, essay, references, transcript. *Deadline:* May 1.

Contact: Kathleen Civiello, Education Committee Chair, MSFSA
Professional Development
Maine School Food Service Association (MSFSA)
166 Connecticut Avenue
Millinocket, ME 04462
Phone: 207-723-9906
Fax: 207-723-6410
E-mail: civijk@prexar.com

MARIN EDUCATION FUND   http://www.marineducationfund.org

GOLDMAN FAMILY FUND, NEW LEADER SCHOLARSHIP
• See page 210

MARION D. AND EVA S. PEEPLES FOUNDATION TRUST SCHOLARSHIP PROGRAM   http://www.jccf.org

MARION A. AND EVA S. PEEPLES SCHOLARSHIPS
• See page 230

MARYLAND ASSOCIATION OF PRIVATE COLLEGES AND CAREER SCHOOLS   http://www.mapccs.org

MARYLAND ASSOCIATION OF PRIVATE COLLEGES AND CAREER SCHOOLS SCHOLARSHIP
• See page 150

MASTER BREWERS ASSOCIATION OF THE AMERICAS   http://www.mbaa.com

MASTER BREWERS ASSOCIATION OF THE AMERICAS
• See page 81

MINNESOTA SOYBEAN RESEARCH AND PROMOTION COUNCIL   http://mnsoybean.org

MINNESOTA SOYBEAN RESEARCH AND PROMOTION COUNCIL YOUTH SOYBEAN SCHOLARSHIP
• See page 75

NATIONAL DAIRY SHRINE   http://www.dairyshrine.org

NATIONAL DAIRY SHRINE/DAIRY MARKETING, INC. MILK MARKETING SCHOLARSHIPS
• See page 82

NDS STUDENT RECOGNITION CONTEST
• See page 75

NATIONAL POTATO COUNCIL WOMEN'S AUXILIARY   http://www.nationalpotatocouncil.org

POTATO INDUSTRY SCHOLARSHIP
• See page 76

NATIONAL POULTRY AND FOOD DISTRIBUTORS ASSOCIATION   http://www.npfda.org

NATIONAL POULTRY AND FOOD DISTRIBUTORS ASSOCIATION SCHOLARSHIP FOUNDATION
• See page 76

OHIO 4-H   http://www.ohio4h.org

BEA CLEVELAND 4-H SCHOLARSHIP
• See page 170

MABEL SARBAUGH 4-H SCHOLARSHIP
• See page 170

OREGON STUDENT ASSISTANCE COMMISSION   http://www.osac.state.or.us

OREGON WINE BROTHERHOOD SCHOLARSHIP
• See page 203

SOUTHWEST STUDENT SERVICES CORPORATION   http://www.sssc.com/

ANNE LINDEMAN MEMORIAL SCHOLARSHIP
• See page 142

TEXAS ELECTRIC CO-OP, INC.   http://www.texas-ec.org

ANN LANE HOME ECONOMICS SCHOLARSHIP

Award for graduating high school member of a local family, career, and community leaders of America, Texas Association chapter. Minimum GPA of 2.5. Include a 250-word essay on "The Role of the Homemaker" and two letters of recommendation. Must attend a Texas institution. Merit-based. One-time scholarship of $1000.

Academic Fields/Career Goals: Food Science/Nutrition; Food Service/Hospitality; Home Economics.

Texas Electric Co-Op, Inc. (continued)

Award: Scholarship for use in freshman year; not renewable. *Number:* 1. *Amount:* $1000.

Eligibility Requirements: Applicant must be high school student; planning to enroll or expecting to enroll full-time at a two-year or four-year or technical institution or university; resident of Texas and studying in Texas. Applicant or parent of applicant must be member of Family, Career and Community Leaders of America. Applicant must have 2.5 GPA or higher. Available to U.S. citizens.

Application Requirements: Application, essay, financial need analysis, photo, references, test scores, transcript. *Deadline:* March 1.

Contact: Tiffin Wortham, Vice President of Member services
Texas Electric Co-Op, Inc.
2550 South IH-35
Austin, TX 78704
Phone: 512-454-0311

UNITED AGRIBUSINESS LEAGUE   http://www.ual.org

UNITED AGRIBUSINESS LEAGUE SCHOLARSHIP PROGRAM
• *See page 77*

UNITED AGRICULTURAL BENEFIT TRUST SCHOLARSHIP
• *See page 77*

UNITED DAUGHTERS OF THE CONFEDERACY   http://www.hqudc.org

WALTER REED SMITH SCHOLARSHIP
• *See page 154*

UNITED NEGRO COLLEGE FUND   http://www.uncf.org

CARGILL SCHOLARSHIP PROGRAM
• *See page 70*

FOOD SERVICE/HOSPITALITY

AMERICAN CULINARY FEDERATION   http://www.acfchefs.org

AMERICAN ACADEMY OF CHEFS CHAINE DES ROTISSEURS SCHOLARSHIP

One-time award to exemplary students currently enrolled in a full-time two-year culinary program. Must have completed a grading or marking period. Deadline is December 1.

Academic Fields/Career Goals: Food Service/Hospitality.

Award: Scholarship for use in freshman, sophomore, or postgraduate years; not renewable. *Number:* 10. *Amount:* $1000.

Eligibility Requirements: Applicant must be enrolled or expecting to enroll full-time at a two-year or technical institution. Available to U.S. citizens.

Application Requirements: Application, references, transcript. *Deadline:* December 1.

Contact: Member Services Center
American Culinary Federation
180 Carter Place Way
St. Augustine, FL 32095
Phone: 904-824-4468
Fax: 904-825-4758

AMERICAN HOTEL AND LODGING EDUCATIONAL FOUNDATION   http://www.ahlef.org

ANNUAL SCHOLARSHIP GRANT PROGRAM

Students are selected for this award by their school. Available to full-time students who have compled at least one or two years of a hospitality-related degree, are U.S. citizens or have permanent U.S. resident status. Minimum GPA of 3.0

Academic Fields/Career Goals: Food Service/Hospitality; Hospitality Management.

Award: Scholarship for use in sophomore, junior, or senior years. *Amount:* $1500–$3000.

Eligibility Requirements: Applicant must be enrolled or expecting to enroll at a two-year or four-year institution. Applicant must be learning disabled. Available to U.S. citizens.

Application Requirements: Application. *Deadline:* May 1.

Contact: Crystal Hammond
American Hotel and Lodging Educational Foundation
1201 New York Avenue, NW, Suite 600
Washington, DC 20005-3931
Phone: 202-289-3188
Fax: 202-289-3199
E-mail: chammond@ahlef.org

AMERICAN INSTITUTE OF WINE AND FOOD- PACIFIC NORTHWEST CHAPTER

CULINARY, VINIFERA, AND HOSPITALITY SCHOLARSHIP
• *See page 301*

CALIFORNIA RESTAURANT ASSOCIATION EDUCATIONAL FOUNDATION   http://www.calrest.org

ACADEMIC SCHOLARSHIP FOR HIGH SCHOOL SENIORS

Scholarships awarded to high school seniors to support their education in the restaurant and/or food service industry. Applicants must be seniors who are citizens of the United States, its territories (American Samoa, Guam, Puerto Rico, and U.S. Virgin Islands) or permanent resident aliens attending school in the United States, deadline is April 21.

Academic Fields/Career Goals: Food Service/Hospitality.

Award: Scholarship for use in freshman year; not renewable. *Amount:* $2000.

Eligibility Requirements: Applicant must be high school student and planning to enroll or expecting to enroll at a two-year or four-year or technical institution or university. Available to U.S. citizens.

Application Requirements: Application, essay, references. *Deadline:* April 21.

Contact: NRAEF Scholarships and Mentoring Program
California Restaurant Association Educational Foundation
175 West Jackson Boulevard, Suite 1500
Chicago, IL 60604-2814
Phone: 312-715-1010 Ext. 744
Fax: 312-566-9733
E-mail: scholars@nraef.org

ACADEMIC SCHOLARSHIP FOR UNDERGRADUATE STUDENTS

Scholarships awarded to college students to support their education in the restaurant and food service industry. Minimum 2.75 GPA required. Individuals must be citizens of the United States, its territories (American Samoa, Guam, Puerto Rico, and U.S. Virgin Islands). Deadline varies.

Academic Fields/Career Goals: Food Service/Hospitality.

Award: Scholarship for use in freshman, sophomore, junior, or senior years. *Amount:* $2000.

Eligibility Requirements: Applicant must be enrolled or expecting to enroll at a four-year institution or university. Available to U.S. citizens.

Application Requirements: Application, essay, references, transcript. *Deadline:* varies.

Contact: Wendy Armour
California Restaurant Association Educational Foundation
1011 10th Street
Sacramento, CA 95814
Phone: 800-765-4842 Ext. 2728
Fax: 916-447-6182
E-mail: warmour@calrest.org

CHILD NUTRITION FOUNDATION   http://www.asfsa.org

NANCY CURRY SCHOLARSHIP
• *See page 301*

PROFESSIONAL GROWTH SCHOLARSHIP
• *See page 301*

SCHWAN'S FOOD SERVICE SCHOLARSHIP
• See page 301

CULINARY TRUST   http://www.iacpfoundation.org

CULINARY TRUST SCHOLARSHIP PROGRAM FOR CULINARY STUDY AND RESEARCH
• See page 302

DECA (DISTRIBUTIVE EDUCATION CLUBS OF AMERICA)   http://www.deca.org

HARRY A. APPLEGATE SCHOLARSHIP
• See page 146

GOLDEN GATE RESTAURANT ASSOCIATION   http://www.ggra.org

GOLDEN GATE RESTAURANT ASSOCIATION SCHOLARSHIP FOUNDATION

One-time award for any student pursuing a food service degree at a 501(c)(3) institution, or institutions approved by the Board of Trustees. California residency and personal interview in San Francisco is required. Minimum GPA of 2.75 required. Write for further information.

Academic Fields/Career Goals: Food Service/Hospitality; Hospitality Management.

Award: Scholarship for use in freshman, sophomore, junior, or senior years; not renewable. *Number:* 1–15. *Amount:* $1000–$3000.

Eligibility Requirements: Applicant must be enrolled or expecting to enroll full or part-time at a two-year or four-year or technical institution or university and resident of California. Available to U.S. citizens.

Application Requirements: Application, essay, financial need analysis, interview, references, transcript. *Deadline:* March 31.

Contact: Donnalyn Murphy, Scholarship Coordinator
Golden Gate Restaurant Association
120 Montgomery Street, Suite 1280
San Francisco, CA 94104
Phone: 415-781-5348 Ext. 812
Fax: 415-781-3925
E-mail: administration@ggra.org

INTERNATIONAL EXECUTIVE HOUSEKEEPERS ASSOCIATION   http://www.ieha.org

INTERNATIONAL EXECUTIVE HOUSEKEEPERS EDUCATIONAL FOUNDATION

Award for students planning careers in the area of facilities management. Must be enrolled in IEHA-approved courses at a participating college or university. One-time award of up to $800. Must be a member of IEHA.

Academic Fields/Career Goals: Food Service/Hospitality; Home Economics; Horticulture/Floriculture; Trade/Technical Specialties.

Award: Scholarship for use in freshman, sophomore, junior, or senior years; not renewable. *Number:* 10. *Amount:* up to $800.

Eligibility Requirements: Applicant must be enrolled or expecting to enroll full or part-time at a two-year or four-year or technical institution or university and must have an interest in designated field specified by sponsor. Applicant or parent of applicant must be member of International Executive Housekeepers Association. Available to U.S. citizens.

Application Requirements: Application, essay, transcript. *Deadline:* January 10.

Contact: Beth Risinger, CEO/Executive Director
International Executive Housekeepers Association
1001 Eastwind Drive, Suite 301
Westerville, OH 43081-3361
Phone: 800-200-6342
Fax: 614-895-7166
E-mail: excel@ieha.org

INTERNATIONAL FOOD SERVICE EXECUTIVES ASSOCIATION   http://www.ifsea.com

WORTHY GOAL SCHOLARSHIP FUND

Scholarships to assist individuals in receiving food service management or vocational training beyond high school. Applicant must be enrolled or accepted as full-time student in a food service related major for the fall term following the award.

Academic Fields/Career Goals: Food Service/Hospitality.

Award: Scholarship for use in freshman, sophomore, junior, senior, or graduate years; not renewable. *Number:* 15. *Amount:* $1000–$1500.

Eligibility Requirements: Applicant must be enrolled or expecting to enroll full-time at a two-year or four-year or technical institution or university. Available to U.S. and non-U.S. citizens.

Application Requirements: Essay, financial need analysis, references, transcript, financial statement summary, work experience documentation. *Deadline:* February 1.

Contact: Ed H. Manley, Scholarship Chairperson
International Food Service Executives Association
2609 Surfwood Drive
Las Vegas, NV 89128
Phone: 702-838-8821
Fax: 702-838-8853
E-mail: hq@ifsea.com

INTERNATIONAL FOODSERVICE EDITORIAL COUNCIL   http://www.ifec-is-us.com

INTERNATIONAL FOODSERVICE EDITORIAL COUNCIL COMMUNICATIONS SCHOLARSHIP
• See page 182

MAINE SCHOOL FOOD SERVICE ASSOCIATION (MSFSA)

SCHOLARSHIP OF THE MAINE SCHOOL FOOD SERVICE ASSOCIATION
• See page 305

MISSOURI TRAVEL COUNCIL   http://www.missouritravel.com

MISSOURI TRAVEL COUNCIL TOURISM SCHOLARSHIP

One-time award for Missouri resident pursuing a hospitality related major such as hotel/restaurant management, parks and recreation, etc. Applicant must be currently enrolled in an accredited college or university in the State of Missouri. Selection based on essay, GPA, community involvement, academic activities, and hospitality-related experience.

Academic Fields/Career Goals: Food Service/Hospitality; Hospitality Management; Travel/Tourism.

Award: Scholarship for use in freshman, sophomore, junior, or senior years; not renewable. *Number:* 2. *Amount:* $1000.

Eligibility Requirements: Applicant must be enrolled or expecting to enroll full-time at a two-year or four-year or technical institution or university; resident of Missouri and studying in Missouri. Applicant must have 3.0 GPA or higher. Available to U.S. citizens.

Application Requirements: Application, essay, transcript. *Deadline:* November 1.

Contact: Pat Amick, Executive Director
Missouri Travel Council
204 East High Street
Jefferson City, MO 65101-3287
Phone: 573-636-2814
Fax: 573-636-5783
E-mail: pamick@sockets.net

NATIONAL POULTRY AND FOOD DISTRIBUTORS ASSOCIATION   http://www.npfda.org

NATIONAL POULTRY AND FOOD DISTRIBUTORS ASSOCIATION SCHOLARSHIP FOUNDATION
• See page 76

NATIONAL RESTAURANT ASSOCIATION EDUCATIONAL FOUNDATION
http://www.nraef.org

COCA-COLA SALUTE TO EXCELLENCE SCHOLARSHIP AWARD

Scholarship for a student currently enrolled in college who has completed at least one semester in a restaurant and/or foodservice-related program. Application deadline is March 10.

Academic Fields/Career Goals: Food Service/Hospitality.

Award: Scholarship for use in freshman, sophomore, junior, senior, graduate, or postgraduate years; not renewable. *Amount:* up to $2000.

Eligibility Requirements: Applicant must be enrolled or expecting to enroll at a two-year or four-year or technical institution or university. Applicant or parent of applicant must have employment or volunteer experience in food service. Available to U.S. citizens.

Application Requirements: Application, essay, transcript. *Deadline:* March 10.

Contact: Dalilah Ramos, Scholarship Program Specialist
National Restaurant Association Educational Foundation
175 West Jackson Boulevard
Suite 1500
Chicago, IL 60604-2702
Phone: 800-765-2122
Fax: 312-566-9733
E-mail: dramos@foodtrain.org

NATIONAL RESTAURANT ASSOCIATION EDUCATIONAL FOUNDATION PROFESSIONAL DEVELOPMENT SCHOLARSHIP FOR EDUCATORS

For restaurant and food service educators who want to complement classroom time with hands-on operational professional development. Applicants must be full-time educators of a restaurant and foodservice-related program in a secondary or postsecondary school. See Web site: http://www.nraef.org for application and details.

Academic Fields/Career Goals: Food Service/Hospitality.

Award: Scholarship for use in junior, senior, graduate, or postgraduate years; not renewable. *Number:* varies. *Amount:* up to $1500.

Eligibility Requirements: Applicant must be enrolled or expecting to enroll full-time at a two-year or four-year institution or university. Applicant or parent of applicant must have employment or volunteer experience in food service. Applicant must have 3.0 GPA or higher. Available to U.S. citizens.

Application Requirements: Application, references. *Deadline:* February 17.

Contact: Emilee N. Rogan, Director, Scholarship Program
National Restaurant Association Educational Foundation
175 West Jackson Boulevard, Suite 1500
Chicago, IL 60604-2702
Phone: 800-765-2122 Ext. 780
Fax: 312-715-1362
E-mail: scholars@foodtrain.org

NATIONAL RESTAURANT ASSOCIATION EDUCATIONAL FOUNDATION UNDERGRADUATE SCHOLARSHIPS FOR COLLEGE STUDENTS

This scholarship is awarded to college students who have demonstrated a commitment to both postsecondary hospitality education and to a career in the industry with 750 hours of industry work experience. Must have a 2.75 GPA, and be enrolled for a full academic term for the school year beginning in fall. For application and further details visit Web site: http://nraef.org.

Academic Fields/Career Goals: Food Service/Hospitality.

Award: Scholarship for use in sophomore, junior, or senior years; not renewable. *Number:* 159–200. *Amount:* $2000.

Eligibility Requirements: Applicant must be enrolled or expecting to enroll full-time at an institution or university. Applicant or parent of applicant must have employment or volunteer experience in food service. Available to U.S. citizens.

Application Requirements: Application, essay, transcript. *Deadline:* varies.

Contact: Dalilah Ramos, Scholarship Program Specialist
National Restaurant Association Educational Foundation
175 West Jackson Boulevard
Suite 1500
Chicago, IL 60604-2702
Phone: 800-765-2122
Fax: 312-566-9733
E-mail: dramos@foodtrain.org

NATIONAL RESTAURANT ASSOCIATION EDUCATIONAL FOUNDATION UNDERGRADUATE SCHOLARSHIPS FOR HIGH SCHOOL SENIORS

This scholarship is awarded to high school students who have demonstrated a commitment to both postsecondary hospitality education and to a career in the industry. Must have two hundred and fifty hours of industry experience, age 17-19 with a 2.75 GPA.

Academic Fields/Career Goals: Food Service/Hospitality.

Award: Scholarship for use in freshman year; not renewable. *Number:* 50–100. *Amount:* $2000.

Eligibility Requirements: Applicant must be high school student; age 17-19 and planning to enroll or expecting to enroll full-time at an institution or university. Applicant or parent of applicant must have employment or volunteer experience in food service. Available to U.S. citizens.

Application Requirements: Application, essay, references, transcript, letter of acceptance. *Deadline:* April 21.

Contact: Dalilah Ramos, Scholarship Program Specialist
National Restaurant Association Educational Foundation
175 West Jackson Boulevard
Suite 1500
Chicago, IL 60604-2702
Phone: 800-765-2122
Fax: 312-566-9733
E-mail: dramos@foodtrain.org

PROSTART® NATIONAL CERTIFICATE OF ACHIEVEMENT SCHOLARSHIP

For high school junior and senior students who have earned Pro Start National Certificate of Achievement and are continuing their education in a restaurant or foodservice program. For application and details visit Web site: http://nraef.org

Academic Fields/Career Goals: Food Service/Hospitality.

Award: Scholarship for use in freshman, sophomore, junior, or senior years; not renewable. *Number:* varies. *Amount:* up to $2000.

Eligibility Requirements: Applicant must be high school student and planning to enroll or expecting to enroll full or part-time at a two-year or four-year or technical institution. Available to U.S. citizens.

Application Requirements: Application. *Deadline:* August 16.

Contact: Dalilah Ramos, Scholarship Program Specialist
National Restaurant Association Educational Foundation
175 West Jackson Boulevard
Suite 1500
Chicago, IL 60604-2702
Phone: 800-765-2122
Fax: 312-566-9733
E-mail: dramos@foodtrain.org

NATIONAL TOURISM FOUNDATION
http://www.ntfonline.org

CLEVELAND LEGACY I AND II SCHOLARSHIP AWARDS

Award for Ohio residents pursuing travel and tourism studies. Must be enrolled full time in two- or four-year institution. Minimum 3.0 GPA required. Submit resume.

Academic Fields/Career Goals: Food Service/Hospitality; Hospitality Management; Travel/Tourism.

Award: Scholarship for use in freshman, sophomore, junior, or senior years; not renewable. *Number:* 1. *Amount:* $1000.

Eligibility Requirements: Applicant must be enrolled or expecting to enroll full-time at a two-year or four-year institution or university and resident of Ohio. Applicant must have 3.0 GPA or higher. Available to U.S. citizens.

Application Requirements: Application, essay, resume, references, transcript. *Deadline:* May 10.

Contact: Michelle Gorin, Projects Coordinator
National Tourism Foundation
546 East Main Street
Lexington, KY 40508-3071
Phone: 800-682-8886
Fax: 859-226-4437
E-mail: michelle.gorin@ntastaff.com

NEW HORIZONS KATHY LE TARTE SCHOLARSHIP

One $1000 scholarship awarded to an undergraduate student entering his or her junior year of study. Applicant must be enrolled in a tourism-related program at an accredited four-year college or university. Must have minimum 3.0 GPA. Applicant must be Michigan resident. Please refer to Web site for further details: http://www.ntfonline.org

Academic Fields/Career Goals: Food Service/Hospitality; Hospitality Management; Travel/Tourism.

Award: Scholarship for use in freshman, sophomore, junior, or senior years; not renewable. *Number:* 1. *Amount:* $1000.

Eligibility Requirements: Applicant must be enrolled or expecting to enroll full-time at a two-year or four-year institution or university and resident of Michigan. Applicant must have 3.0 GPA or higher. Available to U.S. citizens.

Application Requirements: Application, essay, resume, references, transcript. *Deadline:* May 10.

Contact: Michelle Gorin, Projects Coordinator
National Tourism Foundation
546 East Main Street
Lexington, KY 40508-3071
Phone: 800-682-8886
Fax: 859-226-4437
E-mail: michelle.gorin@ntastaff.com

PAT AND JIM HOST SCHOLARSHIP

Award for students who have a degree emphasis in a travel and tourism related field. Must maintain a 3.0 GPA for renewal. Application deadline is May 10.

Academic Fields/Career Goals: Food Service/Hospitality; Hospitality Management; Travel/Tourism.

Award: Scholarship for use in freshman, sophomore, junior, or senior years; renewable. *Number:* 1. *Amount:* $2000–$8000.

Eligibility Requirements: Applicant must be enrolled or expecting to enroll full-time at a four-year institution or university and studying in Kentucky. Applicant must have 3.0 GPA or higher. Available to U.S. citizens.

Application Requirements: Application, essay, resume, references, transcript. *Deadline:* May 10.

Contact: Michelle Gorin, Projects Coordinator
National Tourism Foundation
546 East Main Street
Lexington, KY 40508-3071
Phone: 800-682-8886
Fax: 859-226-4437
E-mail: michelle.gorin@ntastaff.com

SOCIETIE DES CASINOS DU QUEBEC SCHOLARSHIP

Award for resident of Quebec who is pursuing travel and tourism studies. May attend a four-year college or university. Minimum 3.0 GPA required.

Academic Fields/Career Goals: Food Service/Hospitality; Hospitality Management; Travel/Tourism.

Award: Scholarship for use in freshman, sophomore, junior, or senior years; not renewable. *Number:* 1. *Amount:* $1000.

Eligibility Requirements: Applicant must be enrolled or expecting to enroll full-time at a two-year or four-year institution and resident of Quebec. Applicant must have 3.0 GPA or higher. Available to U.S. and Canadian citizens.

Application Requirements: Application, essay, resume, references, transcript. *Deadline:* May 10.

Contact: Michelle Gorin, Projects Coordinator
National Tourism Foundation
546 East Main Street
Lexington, KY 40508-3071
Phone: 800-682-8886
Fax: 859-226-4437
E-mail: michelle.gorin@ntastaff.com

TAMPA, HILLSBOROUGH LEGACY SCHOLARSHIP

One-time award for Florida resident who is pursuing studies in travel and tourism. Must attend a Florida college or university. Minimum 3.0 GPA required.

Academic Fields/Career Goals: Food Service/Hospitality; Hospitality Management; Travel/Tourism.

Award: Scholarship for use in freshman, sophomore, junior, or senior years; not renewable. *Number:* 1. *Amount:* $1000.

Eligibility Requirements: Applicant must be enrolled or expecting to enroll full-time at a two-year or four-year institution or university; resident of Florida and studying in Florida. Applicant must have 3.0 GPA or higher. Available to U.S. citizens.

Application Requirements: Application, essay, resume, references, transcript. *Deadline:* May 10.

Contact: Michelle Gorin, Projects Coordinator
National Tourism Foundation
546 East Main Street
Lexington, KY 40508-3071
Phone: 800-682-8886
Fax: 859-226-4437
E-mail: michelle.gorin@ntastaff.com

TAUCK SCHOLARS SCHOLARSHIPS

Four undergraduate scholarships awarded to students entering their sophomore or junior years of study in travel and tourism-related degrees. Applicants will receive $3000 over two years; $1500 awarded first year and $1500 awarded the following year. Must have minimum 3.0 GPA. Please refer to Web site for further details: http://www.ntfonline.org

Academic Fields/Career Goals: Food Service/Hospitality; Hospitality Management; Travel/Tourism.

Award: Scholarship for use in sophomore or junior years; renewable. *Number:* 4. *Amount:* $3000.

Eligibility Requirements: Applicant must be enrolled or expecting to enroll at a two-year or four-year institution or university. Applicant must have 3.0 GPA or higher. Available to U.S. citizens.

Application Requirements: Application, essay, resume, references, transcript. *Deadline:* May 10.

Contact: Michelle Gorin, Projects Coordinator
Phone: 800-682-8886
Fax: 859-226-4437
E-mail: michelle.gorin@ntastaff.com

TULSA SCHOLARSHIP AWARDS

Scholarship for Oklahoma residents pursuing travel and tourism studies. Must be a college junior or senior enrolled in an Oklahoma four-year institution. Minimum 3.0 GPA required. Submit resume. One-time award of $500.

Academic Fields/Career Goals: Food Service/Hospitality; Hospitality Management; Travel/Tourism.

Award: Scholarship for use in freshman, sophomore, junior, or senior years; not renewable. *Number:* 1. *Amount:* $500.

Eligibility Requirements: Applicant must be enrolled or expecting to enroll full-time at a four-year institution or university; resident of Oklahoma and studying in Oklahoma. Applicant must have 3.0 GPA or higher. Available to U.S. citizens.

Application Requirements: Application, essay, resume, references, transcript. *Deadline:* May 10.

National Tourism Foundation (continued)

Contact: Michelle Gorin, Projects Coordinator
National Tourism Foundation
546 East Main Street
Lexington, KY 40508-3071
Phone: 800-682-8886
Fax: 859-226-4437
E-mail: michelle.gorin@ntastaff.com

YELLOW RIBBON SCHOLARSHIP

Scholarship for residents of North America with physical or sensory disabilities who are pursuing travel and tourism studies in a North American institution. Must be entering postsecondary education with a minimum 3.0 GPA or must be maintaining at least a 2.5 GPA at college level. Submit resume. One-time award of $2500. Must submit an essay explaining how applicant plans to utilize his or her education in making a career in travel and tourism.

Academic Fields/Career Goals: Food Service/Hospitality; Hospitality Management; Travel/Tourism.

Award: Scholarship for use in freshman, sophomore, junior, or senior years; not renewable. *Number:* 1. *Amount:* $2500.

Eligibility Requirements: Applicant must be enrolled or expecting to enroll full-time at a two-year or four-year institution or university. Applicant must be hearing impaired, physically disabled, or visually impaired. Applicant must have 3.0 GPA or higher. Available to U.S. and Canadian citizens.

Application Requirements: Application, essay, resume, references, transcript. *Deadline:* May 10.

Contact: Michelle Gorin, Projects Coordinator
National Tourism Foundation
546 East Main Street
Lexington, KY 40508-3071
Phone: 800-682-8886
Fax: 859-226-4437
E-mail: michelle.gorin@ntastaff.com

NETWORK OF EXECUTIVE WOMEN IN HOSPITALITY
http://www.newh.org

NETWORK OF EXECUTIVE WOMEN IN HOSPITALITY, INC. SCHOLARSHIP
• See page 101

SOCIETY FOR FOODSERVICE MANAGEMENT
http://www.sfm-online.org

SOCIETY FOR FOODSERVICE MANAGEMENT SCHOLARSHIP

Scholarship for high school seniors interested in pursuing a career in the food service industry. Minimum of 2.7 GPA and acceptance into a full time postsecondary program required.

Academic Fields/Career Goals: Food Service/Hospitality.

Award: Scholarship for use in freshman year. *Amount:* $2500–$10,000.

Eligibility Requirements: Applicant must be high school student and planning to enroll or expecting to enroll full-time at an institution or university. Available to U.S. citizens.

Application Requirements: Application, references, transcript. *Deadline:* varies.

Contact: Greg Hobby, STC Scholarship Committee
Society for Foodservice Management
304 West Liberty Street, Suite 201
Louisville, KY 40202
Phone: 503-583-3783
Fax: 502-589-3602
E-mail: ghobby@hqtrs.com

SOUTH DAKOTA RETAILERS ASSOCIATION
http://www.sdra.org

SOUTH DAKOTA RETAILERS ASSOCIATION SCHOLARSHIP PROGRAM
• See page 69

TEXAS ELECTRIC CO-OP, INC.
http://www.texas-ec.org

ANN LANE HOME ECONOMICS SCHOLARSHIP
• See page 305

UNITED NEGRO COLLEGE FUND
http://www.uncf.org

FLOWERS INDUSTRIES SCHOLARSHIP
• See page 155

WOMEN GROCERS OF AMERICA
http://www.nationalgrocers.org

MARY MACEY SCHOLARSHIP
• See page 85

FOREIGN LANGUAGE

ACL/NJCL NATIONAL LATIN EXAM
http://www.nle.org

NATIONAL LATIN EXAM SCHOLARSHIP

Applications for the $1000 scholarships are mailed to gold medal winners in Latin III-IV Prose, III-IV Poetry, or Latin V-VI who are high school seniors. Applicants must agree to take at least one year of Latin or classical Greek in college.

Academic Fields/Career Goals: Foreign Language.

Award: Scholarship for use in freshman, sophomore, junior, senior, or graduate years; renewable. *Number:* 21. *Amount:* $1000.

Eligibility Requirements: Applicant must be high school student; planning to enroll or expecting to enroll full-time at a two-year or four-year institution or university and must have an interest in Greek language or Latin language. Available to U.S. and non-U.S. citizens.

Application Requirements: Application, applicant must enter a contest, essay, test scores, transcript. *Fee:* $4. *Deadline:* January 27.

Contact: Jane Hall, Co-Chair
ACL/NJCL National Latin Exam
Mary Washington College
1301 College Avenue
Fredericksburg, VA 22401
Phone: 888-378-7721
Fax: 540-654-1567
E-mail: jhhall@nle.org

ALBERTA HERITAGE SCHOLARSHIP FUND/ ALBERTA SCHOLARSHIP PROGRAMS
http://www.alis.gov.ab.ca

LANGUAGES IN TEACHER EDUCATION SCHOLARSHIPS
• See page 218

ALPHA MU GAMMA, THE NATIONAL COLLEGIATE FOREIGN LANGUAGE SOCIETY
http://www.lacitycollege.edu

NATIONAL ALPHA MU GAMMA SCHOLARSHIPS

One-time award to student members of Alpha Mu Gamma with a minimum 3.5 GPA who plan to continue study of a foreign language. Must participate in a national scholarship competition. Apply through local chapter advisers. Freshmen are not eligible. Must submit copy of Alpha Mu Gamma membership certificate. Can study overseas if part of his/her school program.

Academic Fields/Career Goals: Foreign Language.

Award: Scholarship for use in sophomore, junior, senior, graduate, or postgraduate years; not renewable. *Number:* 3. *Amount:* up to $750.

Eligibility Requirements: Applicant must be enrolled or expecting to enroll full or part-time at a two-year or four-year institution or university. Applicant or parent of applicant must be member of Alpha Mu Gamma. Applicant must have 3.5 GPA or higher. Available to U.S. and non-U.S. citizens.

Application Requirements: Application, applicant must enter a contest, essay, references, transcript, photocopy of ALPHA MU GAMMA Full Membership. *Deadline:* February 1.

Contact: Hisham Malek, Scholarship Coordinator
Alpha Mu Gamma, The National Collegiate Foreign Language Society
855 North Vermont Avenue
Los Angeles, CA 90029
Phone: 323-644-9752
Fax: 323-644-9752
E-mail: amgnat@lacitycollege.edu

AMERICAN CLASSICAL LEAGUE/NATIONAL JUNIOR CLASSICAL LEAGUE   http://www.aclclassics.org

NATIONAL JUNIOR CLASSICAL LEAGUE SCHOLARSHIP

This one-time award is available to graduating high school seniors who are members of the Junior Classical League. Preference is given to students who plan to major in the classics. Number and value of awards vary.

Academic Fields/Career Goals: Foreign Language; Humanities.

Award: Scholarship for use in freshman year; not renewable. *Number:* 7. *Amount:* $1000–$1500.

Eligibility Requirements: Applicant must be high school student; planning to enroll or expecting to enroll full-time at a two-year or four-year institution or university and must have an interest in foreign language. Applicant or parent of applicant must be member of Junior Classical League. Available to U.S. and non-U.S. citizens.

Application Requirements: Application, essay, references, transcript. *Deadline:* May 1.

Contact: Geri Dutra, Administrator
American Classical League/National Junior Classical League
Miami University, 422 Wells Mill Drive
Oxford, OH 45066
Phone: 513-529-7741
Fax: 513-529-7742
E-mail: info@aclclassics.org

AMERICAN PHILOLOGICAL ASSOCIATION   http://www.apaclassics.org

MINORITY STUDENT SUMMER SCHOLARSHIP
• *See page 109*

ARKANSAS DEPARTMENT OF HIGHER EDUCATION   http://www.arkansashighered.com

EMERGENCY SECONDARY EDUCATION LOAN PROGRAM
• *See page 135*

ASSOCIATION OF TEACHERS OF JAPANESE BRIDGING CLEARINGHOUSE FOR STUDY ABROAD IN JAPAN   http://www.colorado.edu

BRIDGING SCHOLARSHIPS

Scholarships for U.S. students studying in Japan on semester or year-long programs. Deadlines are April 5 and October 5.

Academic Fields/Career Goals: Foreign Language.

Award: Scholarship for use in freshman, sophomore, junior, or senior years; not renewable. *Number:* 40–80. *Amount:* $2500–$4000.

Eligibility Requirements: Applicant must be enrolled or expecting to enroll full-time at a two-year or four-year institution or university. Available to U.S. citizens.

Application Requirements: Application, essay, financial need analysis, references, transcript.

Contact: Susan Schmidt, Executive Director
Association of Teachers of Japanese Bridging Clearinghouse for Study Abroad in Japan
Campus Box 279, 240 Humanities Building, University of Colorado
Boulder, CO 80309-0279
Phone: 303-492-5487
Fax: 303-492-5856
E-mail: atj@colorado.edu

CENTRAL INTELLIGENCE AGENCY   http://www.cia.gov

CENTRAL INTELLIGENCE AGENCY UNDERGRADUATE SCHOLARSHIP PROGRAM
• *See page 56*

COMMUNITY FOUNDATION FOR PALM BEACH AND MARTIN COUNTIES, INC.   http://www.yourcommunityfoundation.org

STEPHEN MADRY PECK, JR. MEMORIAL SCHOLARSHIP

African-American student, high achiever in French or Spanish as a second language. College applicant with goal of pursuing a major or minor in French or Spanish language or culture. Martin and Palm Beach County residents only.

Academic Fields/Career Goals: Foreign Language.

Award: Scholarship for use in freshman year; not renewable. *Number:* 1. *Amount:* $750–$2500.

Eligibility Requirements: Applicant must be Black (non-Hispanic); high school student; planning to enroll or expecting to enroll full-time at a four-year institution or university and resident of Florida. Available to U.S. citizens.

Application Requirements: Application, financial need analysis. *Deadline:* February 1.

Contact: Carolyn Jenco, Grants Manager/Scholarship Coordinator
Community Foundation for Palm Beach and Martin Counties, Inc.
700 South Dixie Highway, Suite 200
West Palm Beach, FL 33401
Phone: 561-659-6800
Fax: 561-832-6542
E-mail: cjenco@cfpbmc.org

CULTURE CONNECTION   http://www.thecultureconnection.com

CULTURE CONNECTION FOUNDATION SCHOLARSHIP
• *See page 73*

DONALD KEENE CENTER OF JAPANESE CULTURE   http://www.donaldkeenecenter.org/

JAPAN-U.S. FRIENDSHIP COMMISSION PRIZE FOR THE TRANSLATION OF JAPANESE LITERATURE

The Donald Keene Center of Japanese Culture offers an annual prize for translation of a work of classical Japanese literature into English and a prize for translation of a work of modern Japanese literature into English. To qualify, works must be book-length translations of Japanese literary works: novels, collections of short stories, literary essays, memoirs, drama or poetry.

Academic Fields/Career Goals: Foreign Language.

Award: Prize for use in freshman, sophomore, junior, senior, graduate, or postgraduate years; not renewable. *Number:* up to 2. *Amount:* up to $5000.

Eligibility Requirements: Applicant must be enrolled or expecting to enroll at an institution or university. Available to U.S. and non-U.S. citizens.

Application Requirements: Application, applicant must enter a contest, resume, 7 copies of book-length manuscript or published book. *Deadline:* February 1.

Contact: Yurika Kurakata, Associate Director
Donald Keene Center of Japanese Culture
Columbia University, 507 Kent Hall
New York, NY 10027
Phone: 212-854-5036
Fax: 212-854-4019
E-mail: donald-keene-center@columbia.edu

GREAT LAKES COMMISSION   http://www.glc.org

CAROL A. RATZA MEMORIAL SCHOLARSHIP
• *See page 138*

GREATER KANAWHA VALLEY FOUNDATION
http://www.tgkvf.org

WEST VIRGINIA BROADCASTERS ASSOCIATION FUND
• See page 181

JAPAN STUDIES SCHOLARSHIP FOUNDATION COMMITTEE

JAPAN STUDIES SCHOLARSHIP

Two $1500 awards for residents of Northern or Central California and Nevada who are currently enrolled sophomore, junior or senior students studying or researching Japanese culture, language, or Japan-U.S. relations. Must attend an award ceremony in August.

Academic Fields/Career Goals: Foreign Language; International Studies; Social Sciences.

Award: Scholarship for use in sophomore, junior, or senior years; not renewable. *Number:* 2. *Amount:* $1500.

Eligibility Requirements: Applicant must be enrolled or expecting to enroll full-time at a four-year institution or university and resident of California or Nevada. Available to U.S. citizens.

Application Requirements: Application, transcript. *Deadline:* May 5.

Contact: H. Takahashi, Senior Education Coordinator
Japan Studies Scholarship Foundation Committee
c/o Japan Information Center, 50 Fremont Street, Suite 2200
San Francisco, CA 94105
Phone: 415-346-2461
E-mail: education@cgjsf.org

KLINGON LANGUAGE INSTITUTE
http://www.kli.org

KOR MEMORIAL SCHOLARSHIP

Scholarship for undergraduate or graduate student in a program leading to a degree in a field of language study. Instructions for applying are at the Web site only: http://www.kli.org/scholarship. Must send application materials by mail as instructed.

Academic Fields/Career Goals: Foreign Language.

Award: Scholarship for use in sophomore, junior, senior, or graduate years; not renewable. *Number:* 1. *Amount:* $500.

Eligibility Requirements: Applicant must be enrolled or expecting to enroll full-time at a four-year institution or university and must have an interest in foreign language. Available to U.S. citizens.

Application Requirements: Application, resume, references, nominating letter from chair, head, or dean, statement of goals. *Deadline:* June 1.

Contact: Klingon Language Institute
PO Box 634
Flourtown, PA 19031

KOSCIUSZKO FOUNDATION
http://www.kosciuszkofoundation.org

YEAR ABROAD PROGRAM IN POLAND
• See page 105

NATIONAL FEDERATION OF THE BLIND
http://www.nfb.org

MICHAEL AND MARIE MARUCCI SCHOLARSHIP

One-time award for students who are legally blind and pursuing full-time studies in the U.S. Must be studying a foreign language or comparative literature; pursuing a degree in history, geography, or political science with a concentration in international studies; or majoring in any other discipline that includes study abroad. Must also show competency in a foreign language.

Academic Fields/Career Goals: Foreign Language; History; International Studies; Literature/English/Writing; Political Science.

Award: Scholarship for use in freshman, sophomore, junior, or senior years; not renewable. *Number:* 1. *Amount:* $5000.

Eligibility Requirements: Applicant must be enrolled or expecting to enroll full-time at a four-year institution or university. Applicant must be visually impaired. Available to U.S. citizens.

Application Requirements: Application, essay, financial need analysis, references, transcript. *Deadline:* March 31.

Contact: Peggy Elliott, Chairman
National Federation of the Blind
805 Fifth Avenue
Grinnell, IA 50112
Phone: 641-236-3366
E-mail: delliott@pcpartner.net

NATIONAL SECURITY AGENCY
http://www.nsa.gov

NATIONAL SECURITY AGENCY STOKES EDUCATIONAL SCHOLARSHIP PROGRAM
• See page 194

NEW HAMPSHIRE POSTSECONDARY EDUCATION COMMISSION
http://www.state.nh.us/postsecondary

WORKFORCE INCENTIVE PROGRAM
• See page 233

NORWICH JUBILEE ESPERANTO FOUNDATION
http://www.esperanto.org/uk/nojef/index.htm

TRAVEL GRANTS

Fluency in the Esperanto language is essential. Applicants must have arranged to visit an approved Esperanto conference or other venue abroad. Non-Britons must have arranged to lecture or speak informally in at least one British Esperanto club or similar venue. Preference to non-Britons whose native language is not English.

Academic Fields/Career Goals: Foreign Language.

Award: Grant for use in freshman, sophomore, junior, senior, or graduate years; not renewable. *Number:* 1–20. *Amount:* $64–$1600.

Eligibility Requirements: Applicant must be age 26 or under; enrolled or expecting to enroll full or part-time at a two-year or four-year or technical institution or university and must have an interest in Spanish language. Available to U.S. and non-U.S. citizens.

Application Requirements: Application, essay, references. *Deadline:* Continuous.

Contact: Dr. Kathleen M. Hall
Norwich Jubilee Esperanto Foundation
37 Granville Court, Cheney Lane
Oxford OX3 0HS
United Kingdom

ROTARY FOUNDATION OF ROTARY INTERNATIONAL
http://www.rotary.org

ROTARY FOUNDATION CULTURAL AMBASSADORIAL SCHOLARSHIP

One-time award funds three or six months (depending on availability through sponsoring Rotary district) of intensive language study and cultural immersion abroad. Applicant must have completed at least two years of university course work and one year in proposed language of study. Application through local Rotary club. Appearances before clubs required during award period. Applications deadlines vary locally between March through August. See Web site at http://www.rotary.org for updated info.

Academic Fields/Career Goals: Foreign Language.

Award: Scholarship for use in junior, senior, or graduate years; not renewable. *Number:* 150–250. *Amount:* $12,000–$19,000.

Eligibility Requirements: Applicant must be enrolled or expecting to enroll full-time at a two-year institution or university and must have an interest in leadership. Available to U.S. and non-U.S. citizens.

Application Requirements: Application, autobiography, essay, interview, resume, references, transcript. *Deadline:* varies.

Contact: Resource Development Assistant
Rotary Foundation of Rotary International
1560 Sherman Avenue
Evanston, IL 60201
Phone: 847-866-4459
Fax: 847-866-4459
E-mail: scholarshipinquiries@rotary.org

SONOMA CHAMBOLLE-MUSIGNY SISTER CITIES

HENRI CARDINAUX MEMORIAL SCHOLARSHIP
• *See page 106*

FUNERAL SERVICES/MORTUARY SCIENCE

AMERICAN BOARD OF FUNERAL SERVICE EDUCATION   http://www.abfse.org/html/dir-listing.html

AMERICAN BOARD OF FUNERAL SERVICE EDUCATION SCHOLARSHIPS

One-time award for U.S. citizens who are currently enrolled in and have completed at least one term of study in an accredited funeral science education program. Application deadlines are mid-March and mid-September. For more details see Web site: http//www.abfse.org.

Academic Fields/Career Goals: Funeral Services/Mortuary Science.

Award: Scholarship for use in freshman, sophomore, junior, or senior years; not renewable. *Number:* 50. *Amount:* $250–$500.

Eligibility Requirements: Applicant must be enrolled or expecting to enroll at a two-year or four-year institution or university. Available to U.S. citizens.

Application Requirements: Application, essay, financial need analysis, references, transcript. *Deadline:* varies.

Contact: Dr. Michael Smith
American Board of Funeral Service Education
3432 Ashland Avenue, Suite U
St. Joseph, MO 64506
Phone: 816-233-3747
Fax: 816-233-3793
E-mail: exdir@abfse.org

ILLINOIS FUNERAL DIRECTORS ASSOCIATION   http://www.ifda.org

ILLINOIS FUNERAL DIRECTORS ASSOCIATION SCHOLARSHIPS

Award for Illinois residents attending a two-year or four-year mortuary service program in Illinois. Open to students at the sophomore level. Must be U.S. citizens. Minimum 3.5 GPA required. Write for application deadline. One-time award of $750. Must be recommended by school.

Academic Fields/Career Goals: Funeral Services/Mortuary Science.

Award: Scholarship for use in sophomore year; not renewable. *Number:* 12. *Amount:* $750.

Eligibility Requirements: Applicant must be enrolled or expecting to enroll full-time at a two-year or four-year institution; resident of Illinois and studying in Illinois. Applicant must have 3.5 GPA or higher. Available to U.S. citizens.

Application Requirements: Application. *Deadline:* varies.

Contact: Paul Dixon, Executive Director
Illinois Funeral Directors Association
215 South Grand Avenue West
Springfield, IL 62704
Phone: 217-525-2000
Fax: 217-525-8342
E-mail: info@ifda.org

INTERNATIONAL ORDER OF THE GOLDEN RULE   http://www.ogr.org

INTERNATIONAL ORDER OF THE GOLDEN RULE AWARD OF EXCELLENCE

One-time scholarship for mortuary science students to prepare for a career in funeral service. Must be enrolled in a mortuary science degree program at an accredited mortuary school. Deadline is October 1. Minimum 3.0 GPA required.

Academic Fields/Career Goals: Funeral Services/Mortuary Science.

Award: Scholarship for use in freshman, sophomore, junior, or senior years; not renewable. *Number:* 1–3. *Amount:* $500–$2500.

Eligibility Requirements: Applicant must be enrolled or expecting to enroll full or part-time at a two-year or four-year or technical institution. Applicant must have 3.0 GPA or higher. Available to U.S. and non-U.S. citizens.

Application Requirements: Application, essay, financial need analysis, transcript. *Deadline:* October 1.

Contact: International Order of the Golden Rule, Education Department
International Order of the Golden Rule
PO Box 28689
St. Louis, MO 63146-1189
Phone: 800-637-8030
Fax: 314-209-1289
E-mail: info@ogr.org

MISSOURI FUNERAL DIRECTOR'S ASSOCIATION   http://www.mofda.org/

MISSOURI FUNERAL DIRECTORS ASSOCIATION SCHOLARSHIPS

Available to Missouri residents pursuing a career in funeral services/mortuary science. Minimum 3.0 GPA required. Application deadline is October 15.

Academic Fields/Career Goals: Funeral Services/Mortuary Science.

Award: Scholarship for use in freshman, sophomore, junior, or senior years; not renewable. *Number:* 3–4. *Amount:* $500–$1000.

Eligibility Requirements: Applicant must be enrolled or expecting to enroll full-time at a two-year or four-year institution and resident of Missouri. Applicant must have 3.0 GPA or higher. Available to U.S. citizens.

Application Requirements: Application, essay, financial need analysis, references, test scores, transcript. *Deadline:* October 15.

Contact: Sherry L. Anderson, Executive Director
Missouri Funeral Director's Association
PO Box 104688
Jefferson City, MO 65110
Phone: 573-635-1661
Fax: 573-635-9494

WALLACE S. AND WILMA K. LAUGHLIN FOUNDATION TRUST

WALLACE S. AND WILMA K. LAUGHLIN SCHOLARSHIP

Scholarships for Nebraska students entering mortuary science programs in order to become a licensed funeral director. Must be U.S. citizen. Must be high school graduate. Application deadline June 30.

Academic Fields/Career Goals: Funeral Services/Mortuary Science.

Award: Scholarship for use in freshman, sophomore, junior, or senior years; not renewable. *Number:* up to 4. *Amount:* $1000.

Eligibility Requirements: Applicant must be enrolled or expecting to enroll full-time at a two-year or four-year institution or university and resident of Nebraska. Available to U.S. citizens.

Application Requirements: Application, financial need analysis, interview, references, transcript. *Deadline:* June 30.

Contact: Leo Seger, President, Nebraska Funeral Directors Association
Wallace S. and Wilma K. Laughlin Foundation Trust
6000 South 58th Street, Suite B
Lincoln, NE 68516
Phone: 402-423-8900
Fax: 402-420-9716
E-mail: segerfh@morcomm.net

GEMOLOGY

MINERALOGICAL SOCIETY OF AMERICA   http://www.minsocam.org

MINERALOGICAL SOCIETY OF AMERICA-GRANT FOR STUDENT RESEARCH IN MINERALOGY AND PETROLOGY
• *See page 214*

MINERALOGY SOCIETY OF AMERICA-GRANT FOR RESEARCH IN CRYSTALLOGRAPHY
• *See page 215*

GEOGRAPHY

ASSOCIATION FOR IRON AND STEEL TECHNOLOGY
http://www.aist.org

ASSOCIATION FOR IRON AND STEEL TECHNOLOGY OHIO VALLEY CHAPTER SCHOLARSHIP
• See page 135

CANADIAN RECREATIONAL CANOEING ASSOCIATION
http://www.paddlingcanada.com

BILL MASON MEMORIAL SCHOLARSHIP FUND
• See page 80

CENTRAL INTELLIGENCE AGENCY
http://www.cia.gov

CENTRAL INTELLIGENCE AGENCY UNDERGRADUATE SCHOLARSHIP PROGRAM
• See page 56

GAMMA THETA UPSILON-INTERNATIONAL GEOGRAPHIC HONOR SOCIETY
http://gtuhonors.org/

BUZZARD- MAXFIELD- RICHASON AND RECHLIN SCHOLARSHIP

Award is granted to a student who is a GTU member, majoring in geography, will be a junior or senior undergraduate in the fall and who has been accepted into a graduate program in geography. Deadline is May 1.

Academic Fields/Career Goals: Geography.

Award: Scholarship for use in junior, senior, or graduate years; not renewable. *Amount:* $500.

Eligibility Requirements: Applicant must be enrolled or expecting to enroll full-time at a two-year or four-year institution or university. Applicant must have 3.0 GPA or higher. Available to U.S. and non-U.S. citizens.

Application Requirements: Application, references, transcript. *Deadline:* May 1.

Contact: Dr. Howard G. Johnson
Gamma Theta Upsilon-International Geographic Honor Society
206 Martin Hall, Jacksonville State University
Jacksonville, AL 36265

CHRISTOPHERSON GEOSYSTEMS SCHOLARSHIP

Scholarship for undergraduate or graduate study in geosystems. Applicant must be a member of Gamma Theta Upsilon prior to submitting the application form. Must submit publishable term paper on geosystems. Deadline is June 1.

Academic Fields/Career Goals: Geography.

Award: Scholarship for use in freshman, sophomore, junior, senior, or graduate years; not renewable. *Amount:* $500.

Eligibility Requirements: Applicant must be enrolled or expecting to enroll full-time at a two-year or four-year institution or university. Applicant must have 3.0 GPA or higher. Available to U.S. and non-U.S. citizens.

Application Requirements: Application, references, transcript, term papers. *Deadline:* June 1.

Contact: Dr. Howard G. Johnson
Gamma Theta Upsilon-International Geographic Honor Society
206 Martin Hall, Jacksonville State University
Jacksonville, AL 36265

GTU JOHN WILEY-STRAHLER PHYSICAL GEOGRAPHY SCHOLARSHIP

Scholarship for undergraduate or graduate study in physical geography. Applicant must be a member of Gamma Theta Upsilon prior to submitting the application form. Must submit publishable term paper on physical geography. Deadline is June 1.

Academic Fields/Career Goals: Geography.

Award: Scholarship for use in freshman, sophomore, junior, senior, or graduate years; not renewable. *Amount:* $500.

Eligibility Requirements: Applicant must be enrolled or expecting to enroll full-time at a two-year or four-year institution or university. Applicant must have 3.0 GPA or higher. Available to U.S. and non-U.S. citizens.

Application Requirements: Application, references, transcript, term papers. *Deadline:* June 1.

Contact: Dr. Howard G. Johnson
Gamma Theta Upsilon-International Geographic Honor Society
206 Martin Hall, Jacksonville State University
Jacksonville, AL 36265

ROWNTREE LEWIS PRICE AND WYCOFF SCHOLARSHIP

Scholarship for undergraduate or graduate study in regional geography. Applicant must be a member of Gamma Theta Upsilon prior to submitting the application form. Must submit publishable term paper on regional geography. Deadline is June 1.

Academic Fields/Career Goals: Geography.

Award: Scholarship for use in freshman, sophomore, junior, senior, or graduate years; not renewable. *Amount:* $500.

Eligibility Requirements: Applicant must be enrolled or expecting to enroll full-time at a two-year or four-year institution or university. Applicant must have 3.0 GPA or higher. Available to U.S. and non-U.S. citizens.

Application Requirements: Application, references, transcript, term papers. *Deadline:* June 1.

Contact: Dr. Howard G. Johnson
Gamma Theta Upsilon-International Geographic Honor Society
206 Martin Hall, Jacksonville State University
Jacksonville, AL 36265

HARVARD TRAVELLERS CLUB

HARVARD TRAVELLERS CLUB GRANTS
• See page 96

INNOVATION AND SCIENCE COUNCIL OF BRITISH COLUMBIA
http://www.scbc.org

PAUL AND HELEN TRUSSEL SCIENCE AND TECHNOLOGY SCHOLARSHIP
• See page 93

NATIONAL FISH AND WILDLIFE FOUNDATION
http://www.nfwf.org

BUDWEISER CONSERVATION SCHOLARSHIP PROGRAM
• See page 140

NATIONAL OCEANIC AND ATMOSPHERIC ADMINISTRATION
http://see.orau.org

NATIONAL OCEANIC AND ATMOSPHERIC ADMINISTRATION EDUCATIONAL PARTNERSHIP PROGRAM WITH MINORITY SERVING INSTITUTIONS UNDERGRADUATE SCHOLARSHIP
• See page 268

GERMAN STUDIES

GERMAN ACADEMIC EXCHANGE SERVICE (DAAD)
http://www.daad.org

GERMAN ACADEMIC EXCHANGE INFORMATION VISITS
• See page 296

GRAPHICS/GRAPHIC ARTS/ PRINTING

ADVERTISING FEDERATION OF FORT WAYNE, INC.
http://www.adfedfortwayne.org

ADVERTISING FEDERATION OF FORT WAYNE, INC., SCHOLARSHIP
• See page 178

ART INSTITUTES
http://www.artinstitutes.edu

NATIONAL POSTER DESIGN CONTEST

Graphic design competition for high school seniors who are interested in pursuing a career in design. Competition winners receive tuition scholarships at The Art Institutes location they have chosen to attend. Students should submit work that shows an understanding of the specified theme "Life is Better with Art in it", basic design concepts, and development of a "design eye".

Academic Fields/Career Goals: Graphics/Graphic Arts/Printing.

Award: Scholarship for use in freshman, sophomore, junior, or senior years; renewable. *Number:* 10. *Amount:* $2000–$25,000.

Eligibility Requirements: Applicant must be high school student and planning to enroll or expecting to enroll full-time at a technical institution. Available to U.S. citizens.

Application Requirements: Application, applicant must enter a contest, transcript, 35mm slide of work. *Deadline:* February 10.

Contact: Michael Maki, Vice President for Academic Affairs
Art Institutes
210 Sixth Ave, 32nd Floor
Pittsburgh, PA 15222-2598
Phone: 888-624-0300

CENTRAL INTELLIGENCE AGENCY
http://www.cia.gov

CENTRAL INTELLIGENCE AGENCY UNDERGRADUATE SCHOLARSHIP PROGRAM
• *See page 56*

DALLAS-FORT WORTH ASSOCIATION OF BLACK COMMUNICATORS
http://www.dfwabc.org

FUTURE JOURNALISTS SCHOLARSHIP PROGRAM
• *See page 180*

ELECTRONIC DOCUMENT SYSTEMS FOUNDATION
http://www.edsf.org

ELECTRONIC DOCUMENT SYSTEMS FOUNDATION SCHOLARSHIP AWARDS
• *See page 180*

GOLDEN KEY INTERNATIONAL HONOUR SOCIETY
http://www.goldenkey.org

VISUAL AND PERFORMING ARTS ACHIEVEMENT AWARDS
• *See page 111*

GREAT LAKES COMMISSION
http://www.glc.org

CAROL A. RATZA MEMORIAL SCHOLARSHIP
• *See page 138*

HALLMARK GRAPHIC ARTS SCHOLARSHIP

HALLMARK GRAPHIC ARTS SCHOLARSHIP

Scholarship available to students who are enrolled full-time at one of the seven colleges or universities designated by the Gravure Education Foundation as a Gravure Resource Center. Applicant must be a college junior. Must have a GPA of 3.0 or better and be active in sports, clubs, community participation, or volunteer activity.

Academic Fields/Career Goals: Graphics/Graphic Arts/Printing.

Award: Scholarship for use in junior or senior years. *Amount:* up to $1500.

Eligibility Requirements: Applicant must be enrolled or expecting to enroll at a four-year institution or university. Applicant must have 3.0 GPA or higher. Available to U.S. citizens.

Application Requirements: Application, essay. *Deadline:* varies.

Contact: Laura Wayland-Smith Hatch, Director
Hallmark Graphic Arts Scholarship
c/o Gravure Education Foundation
107 East Sutton Place
Wilmington, DE 19810
Phone: 315-589-8879
E-mail: lwshatch@gaa.org

HISPANIC COLLEGE FUND, INC.
http://www.hispanicfund.org

DENNY'S/HISPANIC COLLEGE FUND SCHOLARSHIP
• *See page 62*

INTERNATIONAL FOODSERVICE EDITORIAL COUNCIL
http://www.ifec-is-us.com

INTERNATIONAL FOODSERVICE EDITORIAL COUNCIL COMMUNICATIONS SCHOLARSHIP
• *See page 182*

MAINE GRAPHICS ARTS ASSOCIATION

MAINE GRAPHICS ART ASSOCIATION

Scholarship for Maine high school students majoring in graphic arts at any university. Submit transcript and references with application. One-time award.

Academic Fields/Career Goals: Graphics/Graphic Arts/Printing.

Award: Scholarship for use in freshman, sophomore, junior, or senior years; not renewable. *Number:* up to 20. *Amount:* $100–$500.

Eligibility Requirements: Applicant must be high school student; planning to enroll or expecting to enroll full or part-time at an institution or university and resident of Maine. Available to U.S. citizens.

Application Requirements: Application, references, transcript. *Deadline:* May 15.

Contact: Angie Dougherty, Director
Maine Graphics Arts Association
PO Box 874
Auburn, ME 04212-0874
Phone: 207-883-3083
Fax: 207-883-3158
E-mail: edpougher@maine.rr.com

NEW ENGLAND PRINTING AND PUBLISHING COUNCIL
http://www.ppcne.org

NEW ENGLAND GRAPHIC ARTS SCHOLARSHIP

Applicants must be residents of New England who have admission to an accredited two-year vocational or technical college or a four-year college or university that offers a degree program related to printing or graphic arts. Renewable for up to four years if student maintains a 2.5 GPA.

Academic Fields/Career Goals: Graphics/Graphic Arts/Printing.

Award: Scholarship for use in freshman, sophomore, junior, or senior years; renewable. *Number:* 75–80. *Amount:* $1500–$2000.

Eligibility Requirements: Applicant must be enrolled or expecting to enroll full-time at a two-year or four-year institution or university and resident of Connecticut, Maine, Massachusetts, New Hampshire, Rhode Island, or Vermont. Applicant must have 2.5 GPA or higher. Available to U.S. citizens.

Application Requirements: Application, financial need analysis, test scores, transcript. *Deadline:* May 15.

Contact: Kurt Drescher, Scholarship Chair
New England Printing and Publishing Council
PO Box 593
Reading, MA 01867-0218
Phone: 781-944-1116
Fax: 781-944-3905

PRINT AND GRAPHIC SCHOLARSHIP FOUNDATION
http://www.gain.net

PRINT AND GRAPHICS SCHOLARSHIPS

Applicant must be interested in a career in graphic communications, printing technology, printing management, or publishing. Must have and maintain a 3.0 cumulative GPA. Selection based on academic record, class rank, recommendations, biographical information and extracurricular activities. Deadline for high school students is March 1 and April 1 for enrolled college students. Award available to citizens outside U.S. as long as they are attending a U.S. institution. Application may be obtained from Web site http://www.pgsf.org and may be submitted between November 1 and April 1.

Print and Graphic Scholarship Foundation (continued)

Academic Fields/Career Goals: Graphics/Graphic Arts/Printing.

Award: Scholarship for use in freshman, sophomore, junior, senior, or graduate years; renewable. *Number:* 200–300. *Amount:* $500–$3000.

Eligibility Requirements: Applicant must be enrolled or expecting to enroll full-time at a two-year or four-year or technical institution or university and must have an interest in designated field specified by sponsor. Applicant must have 3.0 GPA or higher. Available to U.S. and non-U.S. citizens.

Application Requirements: Application, essay, references, self-addressed stamped envelope, test scores, transcript. *Deadline:* varies.

Contact: Bernadine Eckert, Program Administrator
Print and Graphic Scholarship Foundation
Printing Industries of America/Graphic Arts Technical Foundation
200 Deer Run Road
Sewickley, PA 15143-2600
Phone: 412-741-6860
Fax: 412-741-2311
E-mail: pgsf@gatf.org

PRINTING AND IMAGING ASSOCIATION OF MIDAMERICA   http://www.piamidam.org

CLAMPITT PAPER/HENRY PHILLIPS MEMORIAL SCHOLARSHIP

Award for a student who is a Texas or Oklahoma resident. Must be enrolled in an accredited two- or four-year print technology or management program.

Academic Fields/Career Goals: Graphics/Graphic Arts/Printing.

Award: Scholarship for use in freshman year. *Amount:* up to $1000.

Eligibility Requirements: Applicant must be enrolled or expecting to enroll full-time at a two-year or four-year institution. Available to U.S. citizens.

Application Requirements: Application, references, transcript. *Deadline:* March 1.

Contact: Clampitt Paper/Henry Phillips Memorial Scholarship
Printing and Imaging Association of MidAmerica
c/o PIA-MidAmerica, 8828 North Stemmons, Suite 505
Dallas, TX 75247
Phone: 214-630-8871 Ext. 205
E-mail: dodier@piamidam.org

PRINTING INDUSTRIES OF MICHIGAN, INC. SCHOLARSHIP   http://www.print.org

PRINTING INDUSTRIES OF MICHIGAN SCHOLARSHIP FUND

Scholarship for student who is going to enroll in a college or university graphic arts program or to a student currently enrolled and pursuing a career in the graphic communications industry. Applicants must live in Michigan. deadline is April 1 of each year:

Academic Fields/Career Goals: Graphics/Graphic Arts/Printing.

Award: Scholarship for use in freshman or sophomore years. *Number:* 1.

Eligibility Requirements: Applicant must be enrolled or expecting to enroll full-time at a two-year or four-year institution or university and resident of Michigan. Available to U.S. citizens.

Application Requirements: Application. *Deadline:* April 1.

Contact: Scholarship Committee
Printing Industries of Michigan, Inc. Scholarship
23815 Northwestern Highway, Suite 2700
Southfield, MI 48075-7713

PRINTING INDUSTRIES OF WISCONSIN EDUCATION FOUNDATION SCHOLARSHIPS   http://www.piw.org

MADISON AREA CLUB OF PRINTING HOUSE CRAFTSMEN SCHOLARSHIP

Scholarship is available not only to high school graduates entering the graphic arts area, but also to the those endeavoring to increase their skills through added education. The scholarship is open to students who live within the territory of the Madison Area Club.

Academic Fields/Career Goals: Graphics/Graphic Arts/Printing.

Award: Scholarship for use in freshman, sophomore, junior, senior, or graduate years; not renewable. *Amount:* $1000.

Eligibility Requirements: Applicant must be enrolled or expecting to enroll full or part-time at a two-year or four-year institution or university. Available to U.S. citizens.

Application Requirements: Application, references. *Deadline:* March 10.

Contact: Doug Mackenzie
Printing Industries of Wisconsin Education Foundation Scholarships
Stoughton High School, 600 Llincoln Avenue
Stoughton, WI 53589
Phone: 608-877-5781
Fax: 608-877-5619
E-mail: mackedo@mail.stoughton.k12.wi.us

PRINTING INDUSTRY OF MINNESOTA EDUCATION FOUNDATION   http://www.pimn.org

PRINTING INDUSTRY OF MINNESOTA EDUCATION FOUNDATION SCHOLARSHIP FUND

The PIMEF offers $1000 renewable scholarships to full-time students enrolled in two- or four-year institutions and technical colleges offering degrees in the print communications discipline. Applicant must be a Minnesota resident and be committed to a career in the print communications industry. Minimum 3.0 GPA required. Priority given to children of PIM member company employees.

Academic Fields/Career Goals: Graphics/Graphic Arts/Printing.

Award: Scholarship for use in freshman, sophomore, junior, or senior years; renewable. *Number:* 10–15. *Amount:* $1000.

Eligibility Requirements: Applicant must be enrolled or expecting to enroll full-time at a two-year or four-year or technical institution or university; resident of Minnesota and studying in Minnesota, New York, or Wisconsin. Applicant must have 3.0 GPA or higher. Available to U.S. citizens.

Application Requirements: Application, autobiography, essay, references, test scores, transcript, copy of college admission form, proof of admission. *Deadline:* April 15.

Contact: Carla Steuck, Director of Education Services
Printing Industry of Minnesota Education Foundation
2829 University Avenue SE, Suite 750
Minneapolis, MN 55414-3248
Phone: 612-379-6012
Fax: 612-379-6030
E-mail: csteuck@pimn.org

RHODE ISLAND FOUNDATION   http://www.rifoundation.org

RHODE ISLAND EDSAL ADVERTISING SCHOLARSHIP
• See page 298

ROBERT H. MOLLOHAN FAMILY CHARITABLE FOUNDATION, INC.   http://www.mollohanfoundation.org

MARY OLIVE EDDY JONES ART SCHOLARSHIP
• See page 108

SOUTH DAKOTA RETAILERS ASSOCIATION   http://www.sdra.org

SOUTH DAKOTA RETAILERS ASSOCIATION SCHOLARSHIP PROGRAM
• See page 69

TAG AND LABEL MANUFACTURERS INSTITUTE, INC.   http://www.tlmi.com

TLMI 4 YEAR COLLEGES/FULL-TIME STUDENTS SCHOLARSHIP
• See page 290

TEXAS GRAPHIC ARTS EDUCATIONAL FOUNDATION SCHOLARSHIPS

TEXAS GRAPHIC ARTS EDUCATIONAL FOUNDATION SCHOLARSHIPS

Scholarships for graduating high school seniors from Texas or secondary graphic arts students from Texas or studying in Texas. Must be in programs recognized as graphic communications oriented.

Academic Fields/Career Goals: Graphics/Graphic Arts/Printing.

Award: Scholarship for use in freshman, sophomore, junior, senior, or graduate years. *Amount:* $500–$1000.

Eligibility Requirements: Applicant must be enrolled or expecting to enroll at a four-year institution or university and studying in Texas. Available to U.S. citizens.

Application Requirements: Application. *Deadline:* varies.

Contact: Jim Weinstein, Director, Texas Graphic Arts Educational Foundation
Texas Graphic Arts Educational Foundation Scholarships
1720 Regal Row, Suite 150
Dallas, TX 75235
Phone: 214-630-8277
Fax: 214-637-1508

WORLDSTUDIO FOUNDATION

http://www.worldstudio.org

WORLDSTUDIO FOUNDATION SCHOLARSHIP PROGRAM
• *See page 104*

HEALTH ADMINISTRATION

ALBERTA HERITAGE SCHOLARSHIP FUND/ ALBERTA SCHOLARSHIP PROGRAMS

http://www.alis.gov.ab.ca

ALBERTA HERITAGE SCHOLARSHIP FUND ABORIGINAL HEALTH CAREERS BURSARY
• *See page 135*

AMERICAN INDIAN SCIENCE AND ENGINEERING SOCIETY

http://www.aises.org

BURLINGTON NORTHERN SANTA FE FOUNDATION SCHOLARSHIP
• *See page 89*

AMERICAN SOCIETY OF RADIOLOGIC TECHNOLOGISTS EDUCATION AND RESEARCH FOUNDATION

http://www.asrt.org

JEANETTE C. AND ISADORE N. STERN SCHOLARSHIP

Open to ASRT members only who are certificate, undergraduate or graduate students. Must have ASRT, ARRT registered/unrestricted state license, and must have worked in the radiological sciences profession for at least one year in the past five years. Sponsored in conjunction with E-Z-EM Inc.

Academic Fields/Career Goals: Health Administration; Health and Medical Sciences; Health Information Management/Technology.

Award: Scholarship for use in freshman, sophomore, junior, senior, or graduate years; not renewable. *Number:* up to 10. *Amount:* up to $1000.

Eligibility Requirements: Applicant must be enrolled or expecting to enroll full or part-time at a two-year or four-year or technical institution or university. Available to U.S. and non-U.S. citizens.

Application Requirements: Application, essay, financial need analysis, resume, references. *Deadline:* February 1.

Contact: Phelosha Collaros, Development Officer
American Society of Radiologic Technologists Education and Research Foundation
15000 Central Avenue, SE
Albuquerque, NM 87123-3917
Phone: 505-298-4500 Ext. 1233
Fax: 505-298-5063
E-mail: pcollaros@asrt.org

SIEMENS SCHOLAR AWARD

Open to ASRT members only who are undergraduate or graduate students. Must have ARRT registered/unrestricted state license, and must have worked in the radiologic sciences profession for at least one year in the past five years. Sponsored in conjunction with Seimen's Medical-Oncology Care Systems. Renewal of scholarship is only allowed twice.

Academic Fields/Career Goals: Health Administration; Health and Medical Sciences; Health Information Management/Technology; Radiology.

Award: Scholarship for use in freshman, sophomore, junior, senior, or graduate years; renewable. *Number:* 1. *Amount:* up to $3000.

Eligibility Requirements: Applicant must be enrolled or expecting to enroll full-time at a four-year institution or university. Available to U.S. and non-U.S. citizens.

Application Requirements: Application, essay, financial need analysis, resume, references, application must be completed in black ink, letter verifying employment. *Deadline:* February 1.

Contact: Phelosha Collaros, Development Officer
American Society of Radiologic Technologists Education and Research Foundation
15000 Central Avenue, SE
Albuquerque, NM 87123-3917
Phone: 505-298-4500 Ext. 1233
Fax: 505-298-5063
E-mail: pcollaros@asrt.org

BETHESDA LUTHERAN HOMES AND SERVICES, INC.

http://www.blhs.org

DEVELOPMENTAL DISABILITIES SCHOLASTIC ACHIEVEMENT SCHOLARSHIP FOR LUTHERAN COLLEGE STUDENTS
• *See page 208*

CANADIAN SOCIETY FOR MEDICAL LABORATORY SCIENCE

http://www.csmls.org

E.V. BOOTH SCHOLARSHIP AWARD

This fund was established to assist CSMLS members in fulfilling their vision of achieving university level education in the medical laboratory sciences. One-time award of CAN$500. Must be a Canadian citizen.

Academic Fields/Career Goals: Health Administration; Health and Medical Sciences; Health Information Management/Technology.

Award: Scholarship for use in freshman, sophomore, junior, senior, or graduate years; not renewable. *Number:* 2. *Amount:* $449.

Eligibility Requirements: Applicant must be Canadian citizen and enrolled or expecting to enroll full or part-time at a four-year institution or university. Applicant or parent of applicant must be member of Canadian Society for Medical Laboratory Science.

Application Requirements: Application, financial need analysis, self-addressed stamped envelope, transcript. *Deadline:* April 1.

Contact: Lynn Zehr, Executive Assistant
Canadian Society for Medical Laboratory Science
PO Box 2830 LCDI
Hamilton, ON L8N 3N8
Canada
Phone: 905-528-8642 Ext. 12
Fax: 905-528-4968
E-mail: lzehr@csmls.org

CONGRESSIONAL BLACK CAUCUS SPOUSES PROGRAM   http://www.cbcfinc.org

CONGRESSIONAL BLACK CAUCUS SPOUSES HEALTH INITIATIVES

Award made to students who reside or attend school in a congressional district represented by an African-American member of Congress. Awards scholarships to academically talented and highly motivated students who intend to pursue full-time undergraduate, graduate or doctoral degrees in health related areas. Minimum 2.5 GPA required. Contact the congressional office in the appropriate district for information and applications. Visit http://www.cbcfinc.org for a list of district offices. Any correspondence sent to the CBC Foundation Office at Pennsylvania Avenue will be discarded and may disqualify applicant for the award.

Academic Fields/Career Goals: Health Administration; Health and Medical Sciences; Health Information Management/Technology.

Award: Scholarship for use in freshman, sophomore, junior, senior, or graduate years; renewable. *Number:* 200. *Amount:* $500–$4000.

Eligibility Requirements: Applicant must be enrolled or expecting to enroll full-time at a two-year or four-year institution or university. Applicant must have 2.5 GPA or higher. Available to U.S. citizens.

Application Requirements: Application, essay, financial need analysis, interview, photo, references, transcript. *Deadline:* May 1.

Contact: Appropriate Congressional District Office
Phone: 202-263-2836

GREATER KANAWHA VALLEY FOUNDATION   http://www.tgkvf.org

WILLARD H. ERWIN, JR. MEMORIAL SCHOLARSHIP FUND
• See page 148

HEALTHCARE INFORMATION AND MANAGEMENT SYSTEMS SOCIETY FOUNDATION   http://www.himss.org

HIMSS FOUNDATION SCHOLARSHIP PROGRAM

One-time award available to undergraduate (junior level or higher), Management Engineering student (junior level or higher), graduate, or PhD candidate. Given for academic excellence and the potential for future leadership in the health care information and management systems industry. Must be full-time student and a member of HIMSS.

Academic Fields/Career Goals: Health Administration; Health and Medical Sciences; Health Information Management/Technology; Science, Technology, and Society.

Award: Scholarship for use in freshman, sophomore, junior, senior, graduate, or postgraduate years; renewable. *Number:* 3–5. *Amount:* $5000.

Eligibility Requirements: Applicant must be enrolled or expecting to enroll full-time at a two-year or four-year institution or university. Applicant or parent of applicant must be member of Healthcare Information and Management Systems Society. Available to U.S. and non-U.S. citizens.

Application Requirements: Application, autobiography, essay, photo, resume, references, transcript. *Deadline:* October 1.

Contact: Betty Sanders, Member Relations Coordinator
Healthcare Information and Management Systems Society Foundation
230 East Ohio, Suite 500
Chicago, IL 60611
Phone: 312-915-9269
Fax: 312-664-6143
E-mail: bsanders@himss.org

INDIAN HEALTH SERVICES, UNITED STATES DEPARTMENT OF HEALTH AND HUMAN SERVICES   http://www.ihs.gov

INDIAN HEALTH SERVICE HEALTH PROFESSIONS PRE-PROFESSIONAL SCHOLARSHIP

Renewable scholarship available for full-or part-time undergraduate study. Minimum 2.0 GPA required. Award averages $18,500. First time applicants must submit application to Area Scholarship Coordinator. Must be Native-Americans. Must enroll in courses that are either compensatory or pre-professional; required in order to qualify for entrance into a health professions program. Must be a member of federally recognized tribe.

Academic Fields/Career Goals: Health Administration; Health and Medical Sciences; Nursing; Therapy/Rehabilitation.

Award: Scholarship for use in freshman, sophomore, junior, or senior years; renewable. *Number:* varies. *Amount:* $18,500.

Eligibility Requirements: Applicant must be American Indian/Alaska Native and enrolled or expecting to enroll full or part-time at a two-year or four-year or technical institution or university. Available to U.S. citizens.

Application Requirements: Application, applicant must enter a contest, essay, references, transcript, proof of descent. *Deadline:* February 28.

Contact: Jeff Brien, Acting Chief, Scholarship Branch
Indian Health Services, United States Department of Health and Human Services
801 Thompson Avenue, Suite 120
Rockville, MD 20852
Phone: 301-443-6197
Fax: 301-443-6048

MARIN EDUCATION FUND   http://www.marineducationfund.org

GOLDMAN FAMILY FUND, NEW LEADER SCHOLARSHIP
• See page 210

NORTH CAROLINA STATE EDUCATION ASSISTANCE AUTHORITY   http://www.ncseaa.edu

NORTH CAROLINA STUDENT LOAN PROGRAM FOR HEALTH, SCIENCE, AND MATHEMATICS
• See page 211

ROSCOE POUND INSTITUTE   http://www.roscoepound.org

ELAINE OSBORNE JACOBSON AWARD FOR WOMEN WORKING IN HEALTH CARE LAW

For female law students who, through academics and career experience, demonstrate commitment to advocacy for health-care needs of women, elderly, the disabled, and children. One-time award of $3000. Must study in North America.

Academic Fields/Career Goals: Health Administration; Health and Medical Sciences; Law/Legal Services.

Award: Prize for use in freshman, sophomore, junior, senior, or graduate years; not renewable. *Number:* 1. *Amount:* $3000.

Eligibility Requirements: Applicant must be enrolled or expecting to enroll full or part-time at a four-year institution or university and female. Available to U.S. and non-U.S. citizens.

Application Requirements: Application, autobiography, essay, resume, references. *Deadline:* varies.

Contact: Kimberly Kornegay, Program Assistant
Roscoe Pound Institute
1054 31st Street NW, Suite 260
Washington, DC 20007-4499
Phone: 202-965-3500 Ext. 385
Fax: 202-965-0355
E-mail: pound@roscoepound.org

VIRGINIA SOCIETY OF HEALTHCARE HR ADMINISTRATION

VIRGINIA SOCIETY FOR HEALTHCARE HUMAN RESOURCES ADMINISTRATION SCHOLARSHIP

One-time award to a deserving junior, senior, or graduate student to promote and encourage excellence in the practice of healthcare human resources management in the State of Virginia. Award only available to Virginia residents who have an interest in healthcare, specifically Human Resources Administration. Must study in Virginia.

Academic Fields/Career Goals: Health Administration.

Award: Scholarship for use in junior, senior, or graduate years; not renewable. *Number:* 1. *Amount:* $1000.

Eligibility Requirements: Applicant must be enrolled or expecting to enroll full or part-time at a four-year institution or university; resident of Virginia and studying in Virginia. Available to U.S. citizens.

Application Requirements: Application, autobiography, references, transcript. *Deadline:* August 15.

Contact: Janice S. Gibbs, Assistant Director of Human Resources
Virginia Society of Healthcare HR Administration
2800 Godwin Boulevard
Suffolk, VA 23434
Phone: 757-934-4602
Fax: 757-934-4414
E-mail: jgibbs@obic.com

HEALTH AND MEDICAL SCIENCES

ALBERTA HERITAGE SCHOLARSHIP FUND/ ALBERTA SCHOLARSHIP PROGRAMS   http://www.alis.gov.ab.ca

ALBERTA HERITAGE SCHOLARSHIP FUND ABORIGINAL HEALTH CAREERS BURSARY
• See page 135

AMERICAN ASSOCIATION FOR HEALTH EDUCATION   http://www.aahperd.org/aahe

AMERICAN ASSOCIATION FOR HEALTH EDUCATION WILLIAM M. KANE SCHOLARSHIP
• See page 219

AMERICAN COLLEGE OF SPORTS MEDICINE   http://www.acsm.org

RAY AND ROSALEE WEISS RESEARCH ENDOWMENT

Grant will be given to one student who plans to focus on the physical, mental, and emotional benefits of physical activity. Grant money must be used for applied research. Applicants must be a member of ACSM. Please refer to Web site for further information: http://www.acsm.org.

Academic Fields/Career Goals: Health and Medical Sciences; Sports-related.

Award: Grant for use in freshman, sophomore, junior, senior, or graduate years; not renewable. *Number:* 1. *Amount:* $1500.

Eligibility Requirements: Applicant must be enrolled or expecting to enroll full-time at a four-year institution or university. Applicant or parent of applicant must be member of American College of Sports Medicine. Available to U.S. and non-U.S. citizens.

Application Requirements: Application, essay, financial need analysis, resume. *Deadline:* January 30.

Contact: Megan Wayne, Research and Advancement Coordinator
American College of Sports Medicine
PO Box 1440
Indianapolis, IN 46206-1440
Phone: 317-637-9200
Fax: 317-634-7817
E-mail: mwayne@acsm.org

AMERICAN FEDERATION OF TEACHERS   http://www.aft.org

ROBERT G. PORTER SCHOLARS PROGRAM-AFT MEMBERS
• See page 219

AMERICAN FOUNDATION FOR PHARMACEUTICAL EDUCATION   http://www.afpenet.org

AMERICAN ASSOCIATION OF PHARMACEUTICAL SCIENTISTS GATEWAY SCHOLARSHIP PROGRAM

Awards of $4500 for research project, $500 to attend AAPS Annual Meeting. To encourage students to undertake pre-professional or undergraduate degree research experience. Letter from faculty sponsor and one other faculty member, official transcript, and test scores required. May be used in sophomore, junior, or senior year, or in last three years of PharmD program.

Academic Fields/Career Goals: Health and Medical Sciences.

Award: Scholarship for use in sophomore, junior, senior, or graduate years; renewable. *Number:* up to 15. *Amount:* up to $5000.

Eligibility Requirements: Applicant must be enrolled or expecting to enroll full-time at an institution or university. Available to U.S. citizens.

Application Requirements: Application, references, test scores, transcript. *Deadline:* January 27.

Contact: Robert M. Bachman, President
American Foundation for Pharmaceutical Education
One Church Street, Suite 202
Rockville, MD 20850
Phone: 301-738-2160
Fax: 301-738-2161

AMERICAN INDIAN SCIENCE AND ENGINEERING SOCIETY   http://www.aises.org

A.T. ANDERSON MEMORIAL SCHOLARSHIP
• See page 89

AMERICAN LEGION AUXILIARY, DEPARTMENT OF ARIZONA   http://www.azlegion.org/majorp~2.htm

AMERICAN LEGION AUXILIARY DEPARTMENT OF ARIZONA HEALTH CARE OCCUPATION SCHOLARSHIPS

Award for Arizona residents enrolled at an institution in Arizona that awards degree or certificate in health occupations. Preference given to an immediate family member of a veteran. Must be a U.S. citizen and Arizona resident for at least one year.

Academic Fields/Career Goals: Health and Medical Sciences.

Award: Scholarship for use in freshman, sophomore, junior, or senior years; not renewable. *Amount:* $300.

Eligibility Requirements: Applicant must be enrolled or expecting to enroll full-time at a two-year or four-year institution or university; resident of Arizona and studying in Arizona. Available to U.S. citizens.

Application Requirements: Application, autobiography, essay, financial need analysis, photo, references, test scores, transcript. *Deadline:* May 15.

Contact: Department Secretary and Treasurer
American Legion Auxiliary, Department of Arizona
4701 North 19th Avenue, Suite 100
Phoenix, AZ 85015-3727
Phone: 602-241-1080
Fax: 602-604-9640
E-mail: amlegauxaz@mcleodusa.net

AMERICAN LEGION AUXILIARY, DEPARTMENT OF MICHIGAN   http://www.michalaux.org

MEDICAL CAREER SCHOLARSHIP

Award for training in Michigan as registered nurse, licensed practical nurse, physical therapist, respiratory therapist, or any medical career. Must be child, grandchild, great-grandchild, wife, or widow of honorably discharged or deceased veteran who has served during eligibility dates for American Legion membership. Must be Michigan resident attending a Michigan school.

Academic Fields/Career Goals: Health and Medical Sciences; Nursing; Therapy/Rehabilitation.

Award: Scholarship for use in freshman year; not renewable. *Number:* 5–20. *Amount:* $500.

Eligibility Requirements: Applicant must be enrolled or expecting to enroll full or part-time at a two-year or four-year or technical institution or university; resident of Michigan and studying in Michigan. Applicant must have 3.5 GPA or higher. Available to U.S. citizens. Applicant or parent must meet one or more of the following requirements: general military experience; retired from active duty; disabled or killed as a result of military service; prisoner of war; or missing in action.

American Legion Auxiliary, Department of Michigan (continued)

Application Requirements: Application, financial need analysis, references, test scores, transcript, veteran's discharge papers, copy of pages 1 and 2 of federal income tax return. *Deadline:* March 15.

Contact: Ms. Priscilla Kelsey, Chairman
American Legion Auxiliary, Department of Michigan
212 North Verlinden Avenue
Lansing, MI 48915
Phone: 517-371-4720 Ext. 19
Fax: 517-371-2401
E-mail: michalaux@voyager.net

AMERICAN LEGION AUXILIARY, DEPARTMENT OF MINNESOTA

AMERICAN LEGION AUXILIARY DEPARTMENT OF MINNESOTA PAST PRESIDENT PARLEY HEALTH CARE SCHOLARSHIP

One-time $1000 award for American Legion Auxiliary Department of Minnesota member of at least three years who is needy and deserving, to begin or continue education in any phase of the health care field. Must be a Minnesota resident, attend a vocational or postsecondary institution and maintain at least a C average in school.

Academic Fields/Career Goals: Health and Medical Sciences.

Award: Scholarship for use in freshman, sophomore, junior, or senior years; not renewable. *Number:* up to 3. *Amount:* $1000.

Eligibility Requirements: Applicant must be enrolled or expecting to enroll at a two-year or four-year or technical institution or university; resident of Minnesota and studying in Minnesota. Applicant or parent of applicant must be member of American Legion or Auxiliary. Available to U.S. citizens.

Application Requirements: Application, financial need analysis. *Deadline:* March 15.

Contact: Eleanor Johnson, Executive Secretary
American Legion Auxiliary, Department of Minnesota
State Veterans Service Building, 20 West 12th Street
St. Paul, MN 55155
Phone: 651-224-7634
Fax: 651-224-5243

AMERICAN LEGION AUXILIARY, DEPARTMENT OF TEXAS
http://www.alatexas.org

AMERICAN LEGION AUXILIARY, DEPARTMENT OF TEXAS PAST PRESIDENT'S PARLEY MEDICAL SCHOLARSHIP

Scholarships available for full-time students pursuing studies in human health care. Must be a resident of Texas. Must be a veteran or child, grandchild, great grandchild of a veteran who served in the Armed Forces during period of eligibility. For specific details and application contact your local American Legion Auxiliary unit. Deadline is May 1.

Academic Fields/Career Goals: Health and Medical Sciences.

Award: Scholarship for use in freshman, sophomore, junior, senior, graduate, or postgraduate years; not renewable. *Number:* varies. *Amount:* $500.

Eligibility Requirements: Applicant must be enrolled or expecting to enroll full-time at a two-year or four-year or technical institution or university and resident of Texas. Available to U.S. citizens. Applicant or parent must meet one or more of the following requirements: Army experience; retired from active duty; disabled or killed as a result of military service; prisoner of war; or missing in action.

Application Requirements: Application, financial need analysis, photo, references, self-addressed stamped envelope, transcript, letter stating qualifications and intentions. *Deadline:* May 1.

Contact: Paula Raney, Department Secretary
American Legion Auxiliary, Department of Texas
3401 Ed Bluestein Boulevard, Suite 200
Austin, TX 78721-2902
Phone: 512-476-7278
Fax: 512-482-8391

AMERICAN LEGION AUXILIARY, DEPARTMENT OF WYOMING

PAST PRESIDENTS PARLEY HEALTH CARE SCHOLARSHIP
• *See page 207*

AMERICAN MEDICAL ASSOCIATION FOUNDATION
http://www.ama-assn.org

AMA FOUNDATION NATIONAL SCHOLARSHIP

An annual scholarship of $10,000 will be awarded to a medical student based on academic excellence and/or financial need. Students must be nominated by the office of the dean. Dean's office may nominate 1-3 students based on size of enrollment.

Academic Fields/Career Goals: Health and Medical Sciences.

Award: Scholarship for use in senior, or graduate years. *Number:* 1. *Amount:* up to $10,000.

Eligibility Requirements: Applicant must be enrolled or expecting to enroll full-time at an institution or university. Available to U.S. citizens.

Application Requirements: Application, financial need analysis, references. *Deadline:* varies.

Contact: Dina Lindenberg, AMA Foundation
American Medical Association Foundation
515 North State Street
Chicago, IL 60610
Phone: 312-464-4193
Fax: 312-464-4142
E-mail: Dina.Lindenberg@ama-assn.org

JERRY L. PETTIS MEMORIAL SCHOLARSHIP

One-time award for junior or senior year medical student with a demonstrated interest in the communication of science. Submit letter of nomination from dean, letter and curriculum vitae from student, letter from supportive professional, and any other materials to support nomination.

Academic Fields/Career Goals: Health and Medical Sciences.

Award: Scholarship for use in junior, senior, or graduate years; not renewable. *Number:* 1. *Amount:* up to $2500.

Eligibility Requirements: Applicant must be enrolled or expecting to enroll full-time at an institution or university. Available to U.S. citizens.

Application Requirements: Application, autobiography, resume, references. *Deadline:* January 31.

Contact: Rita M. Palulonis, AMA Foundation
American Medical Association Foundation
515 North State Street
Chicago, IL 60610
Phone: 312-464-4200
Fax: 312-464-4142
E-mail: scholarships@ama-assn.org

JOHNSON F. HAMMOND, MD MEMORIAL SCHOLARSHIP

An annual scholarship of $3000 will be awarded to a medical student of high moral character and outstanding achievement with demonstrated interest and involvement in medical journalism. Must submit letter of nomination from the office of the dean.

Academic Fields/Career Goals: Health and Medical Sciences.

Award: Scholarship for use in freshman, sophomore, junior, senior, graduate, or postgraduate years; not renewable. *Number:* 1. *Amount:* $3000.

Eligibility Requirements: Applicant must be enrolled or expecting to enroll full-time at an institution or university. Available to U.S. citizens.

Application Requirements: Autobiography, portfolio, resume, references, letter of nomination from Dean. *Deadline:* February 15.

Contact: Kathleen MacArthur, Executive Director
American Medical Association Foundation
515 North State Street
Chicago, IL 60610
Phone: 312-464-5852
Fax: 312-464-4142
E-mail: scholarships@ama-assn.org

ROCK SLEYSTER MEMORIAL SCHOLARSHIP

Available to school-nominated seniors studying medicine who aspire to specialize in psychiatry. Must be enrolled at an accredited U.S. or Canadian school that grants the MD. Minimum 3.0 GPA required. Must be U.S. citizen. One-time award of $2500.

Academic Fields/Career Goals: Health and Medical Sciences.

Award: Scholarship for use in senior, or graduate years; not renewable. *Number:* 20. *Amount:* $2500.

Eligibility Requirements: Applicant must be enrolled or expecting to enroll full-time at an institution or university. Applicant must have 3.0 GPA or higher. Available to U.S. citizens.

Application Requirements: Application, autobiography, essay, financial need analysis, references, transcript. *Deadline:* varies.

Contact: Director of Financial Aid
American Medical Association Foundation
515 North State Street
Chicago, IL 60610
Phone: 312-464-4200
Fax: 312-464-4142
E-mail: financialaid@siumed.edu

AMERICAN MEDICAL TECHNOLOGISTS
http://www.amt1.com

AMERICAN MEDICAL TECHNOLOGISTS STUDENT SCHOLARSHIP
• *See page 207*

AMERICAN OCCUPATIONAL THERAPY FOUNDATION, INC.
http://www.aotf.org

AMERICAN OCCUPATIONAL THERAPY FOUNDATION STATE ASSOCIATION SCHOLARSHIPS

Awards offered at the American Occupational Therapy Foundation state association level for study leading to associate, baccalaureate and graduate degrees in occupational therapy. Must be an AOTF member. Requirements vary by state. See Web site at http://www.aotf.org for further details. Application deadline is January 15.

Academic Fields/Career Goals: Health and Medical Sciences; Therapy/Rehabilitation.

Award: Scholarship for use in freshman, sophomore, junior, senior, or graduate years; not renewable. *Number:* up to 38. *Amount:* $250–$5000.

Eligibility Requirements: Applicant must be enrolled or expecting to enroll full or part-time at a two-year or four-year institution or university. Applicant or parent of applicant must be member of American Occupational Therapy Association. Available to U.S. citizens.

Application Requirements: Application, essay, financial need analysis, references, transcript, Curriculum Director's statement. *Deadline:* January 15.

Contact: Jane Huntington, Scholarship Coordinator
American Occupational Therapy Foundation, Inc.
PO Box 31220
Bethesda, MD 20824-1220
Phone: 301-652-6611
Fax: 301-656-3620
E-mail: jhuntington@aotf.org

CARLOTTA WELLES SCHOLARSHIP

Award for study leading to an occupational therapy assistant degree at an accredited institution. Must be a member of the American Occupational Therapy Association. Application deadline is January 15.

Academic Fields/Career Goals: Health and Medical Sciences; Therapy/Rehabilitation.

Award: Scholarship for use in sophomore year; not renewable. *Number:* varies. *Amount:* $500.

Eligibility Requirements: Applicant must be enrolled or expecting to enroll full-time at a two-year institution. Applicant or parent of applicant must be member of American Occupational Therapy Association. Available to U.S. citizens.

Application Requirements: Application, essay, financial need analysis, references, transcript, Curriculum Director's statement. *Deadline:* January 15.

Contact: Jane Huntington, Scholarship Coordinator
American Occupational Therapy Foundation, Inc.
PO Box 31220
Bethesda, MD 20824-1220
Phone: 301-652-6611
Fax: 301-656-3620

FLORENCE WOOD/ARKANSAS OCCUPATIONAL THERAPY ASSOCIATION SCHOLARSHIP

One scholarship of $500 to an Arkansas resident enrolled in an accredited occupational therapy educational program in Arkansas. Application deadline is January 15.

Academic Fields/Career Goals: Health and Medical Sciences; Therapy/Rehabilitation.

Award: Scholarship for use in junior, senior, or graduate years; not renewable. *Number:* 1. *Amount:* $500.

Eligibility Requirements: Applicant must be enrolled or expecting to enroll full or part-time at a two-year or four-year or technical institution or university; resident of Arkansas and studying in Arkansas. Available to U.S. citizens.

Application Requirements: Application, essay, financial need analysis, references, transcript, Curriculum Director's statement. *Deadline:* January 15.

Contact: Jane Huntington, Scholarship Coordinator
American Occupational Therapy Foundation, Inc.
4720 Montgomery Lane, PO Box 31220
Bethesda, MD 20824
Phone: 301-652-6611 Ext. 2550
Fax: 301-656-3620
E-mail: jhuntington@aotf.org

AMERICAN OPTOMETRIC FOUNDATION
http://www.aaopt.org

VISTAKON AWARD OF EXCELLENCE IN CONTACT LENS PATIENT CARE

Open to any fourth-year student attending any school or college of optometry. Must have 3.0 GPA. Student's knowledge of subject matter and skillful, professional clinical contact lens patient care are considered. School makes selection and sends application to AOF.

Academic Fields/Career Goals: Health and Medical Sciences.

Award: Scholarship for use in senior, or graduate years; not renewable. *Number:* 19. *Amount:* $1000.

Eligibility Requirements: Applicant must be enrolled or expecting to enroll full-time at a four-year institution or university. Applicant must have 3.0 GPA or higher. Available to U.S. and non-U.S. citizens.

Application Requirements: Application, references. *Deadline:* September 1.

Contact: Kristal Watkins
American Optometric Foundation
6110 Executive Boulevard, Suite 506
Rockville, MD 20852
Phone: 301-984-4734
Fax: 301-984-4737
E-mail: christine@aaoptom.org

AMERICAN PHYSICAL THERAPY ASSOCIATION
http://www.apta.org

MINORITY SCHOLARSHIP AWARD FOR ACADEMIC EXCELLENCE IN PHYSICAL THERAPY

Scholarships available to minority students enrolled in their final year of an accredited physical therapy program. All application material must be received by December 1. Information is available on Web site http://www.apta.org.

Academic Fields/Career Goals: Health and Medical Sciences.

American Physical Therapy Association (continued)

Award: Scholarship for use in senior year; not renewable. *Number:* varies. *Amount:* up to $5000.

Eligibility Requirements: Applicant must be American Indian/Alaska Native, Asian/Pacific Islander, Black (non-Hispanic), or Hispanic and enrolled or expecting to enroll at a four-year institution or university. Available to U.S. citizens.

Application Requirements: Application, essay, resume, references, transcript, 1 original, 6 copies. *Deadline:* December 1.

Contact: Eva King, Assistant to the Director
American Physical Therapy Association
1111 N Fairfax Street
Alexandria, VA 22314-1488
Phone: 800-999-2782 Ext. 3144
E-mail: evaking@apta.org

MINORITY SCHOLARSHIP AWARD FOR ACADEMIC EXCELLENCE-PHYSICAL THERAPIST ASSISTANT

Scholarships available for minority students enrolled in the final year of an accredited physical therapist assistant program. All material must be received by December 1. Information and application is available on Web site http://www.apta.org

Academic Fields/Career Goals: Health and Medical Sciences.

Award: Scholarship for use in senior year; not renewable. *Number:* varies. *Amount:* up to $2000.

Eligibility Requirements: Applicant must be American Indian/Alaska Native, Asian/Pacific Islander, Black (non-Hispanic), or Hispanic and enrolled or expecting to enroll at a four-year institution or university. Available to U.S. citizens.

Application Requirements: Application, essay, resume, references, transcript, 1 original, 6 copies. *Deadline:* December 1.

Contact: Eva King, Assistant to the Director
American Physical Therapy Association
1111 N Fairfax Street
Alexandria, VA 22314-1488
Phone: 800-999-2782 Ext. 3144
E-mail: evaking@apta.org

AMERICAN RESPIRATORY CARE FOUNDATION
http://www.arcfoundation.org

JIMMY A. YOUNG MEMORIAL EDUCATION RECOGNITION AWARD

Award available to undergraduate minority students studying respiratory care at an American Medical Association-approved institution. Submit letters of recommendation and a paper on a respiratory care topic. Must have a minimum 3.0 GPA. One-time award of up to $1000.

Academic Fields/Career Goals: Health and Medical Sciences; Therapy/Rehabilitation.

Award: Prize for use in freshman, sophomore, junior, or senior years; not renewable. *Number:* 1. *Amount:* up to $1000.

Eligibility Requirements: Applicant must be American Indian/Alaska Native, Asian/Pacific Islander, Black (non-Hispanic), or Hispanic and enrolled or expecting to enroll full or part-time at a two-year or four-year or technical institution or university. Applicant must have 3.0 GPA or higher. Available to U.S. citizens.

Application Requirements: Application, references, transcript, paper on respiratory care topic. *Deadline:* June 19.

Contact: Jill Nelson, Administrative Coordinator
American Respiratory Care Foundation
9425 North MacArthur Boulevard, Suite 100
Irving, TX 75063-4706
Phone: 972-243-2272
Fax: 972-484-2720
E-mail: info@arcfoundation.org

MORTON B. DUGGAN, JR. MEMORIAL EDUCATION RECOGNITION AWARD

Award for students with a minimum 3.0 GPA enrolled in an American Medical Association-approved respiratory care program. Must be U.S. citizen or permanent resident. Need proof of college enrollment. Submit an original referenced paper on respiratory care. Preference given to Georgia and South Carolina residents. One-time merit-based award of $1000 plus airfare, registration to AARC Congress, and one night's lodging.

Academic Fields/Career Goals: Health and Medical Sciences; Therapy/Rehabilitation.

Award: Prize for use in freshman, sophomore, junior, or senior years; not renewable. *Number:* 1. *Amount:* $1000.

Eligibility Requirements: Applicant must be enrolled or expecting to enroll full or part-time at a two-year or four-year or technical institution or university. Applicant must have 3.0 GPA or higher. Available to U.S. and non-U.S. citizens.

Application Requirements: Application, references, transcript, paper on respiratory care. *Deadline:* June 19.

Contact: Jill Nelson, Administrative Coordinator
American Respiratory Care Foundation
9425 North MacArthur Boulevard, Suite 100
Irving, TX 75063-4706
Phone: 972-243-2272
Fax: 972-484-2720
E-mail: info@arcfoundation.org

NBRC/AMP ROBERT M. LAWRENCE, MD, EDUCATION RECOGNITION AWARD

Merit-based award to third- or fourth-year student with a minimum 3.0 GPA, enrolled in accredited undergraduate respiratory therapy program. Submit proof of enrollment, original paper on some aspect of respiratory care, and original 1200 word essay on how this award will assist the applicant in reaching the objective of a degree and the ultimate goal of leadership in health care.

Academic Fields/Career Goals: Health and Medical Sciences; Therapy/Rehabilitation.

Award: Prize for use in junior or senior years; not renewable. *Number:* 1. *Amount:* up to $2500.

Eligibility Requirements: Applicant must be enrolled or expecting to enroll full or part-time at a four-year institution or university. Applicant must have 3.0 GPA or higher. Available to U.S. and non-U.S. citizens.

Application Requirements: Application, essay, references, transcript, paper on respiratory care. *Deadline:* June 19.

Contact: Jill Nelson, Administrative Coordinator
American Respiratory Care Foundation
9425 North MacArthur Boulevard, Suite 100
Irving, TX 75063-4706
Phone: 972-243-2272
Fax: 972-484-2720
E-mail: info@arcfoundation.org

NBRC/AMP WILLIAM W. BURGIN, MD EDUCATION RECOGNITION AWARD

Merit-based award for second-year students enrolled in an accredited respiratory therapy program leading to an associate degree. Minimum GPA of 3.0 required. Submit an original referenced paper on some aspect of respiratory care and an original essay of at least 1200 words describing how the award will assist applicant in attaining career objective.

Academic Fields/Career Goals: Health and Medical Sciences; Therapy/Rehabilitation.

Award: Prize for use in sophomore year; not renewable. *Number:* 1. *Amount:* up to $2500.

Eligibility Requirements: Applicant must be enrolled or expecting to enroll full or part-time at a two-year or four-year institution or university. Applicant must have 3.0 GPA or higher. Available to U.S. and non-U.S. citizens.

Application Requirements: Application, essay, references, transcript, paper on respiratory care. *Deadline:* June 19.

Contact: Jill Nelson, Administrative Coordinator
American Respiratory Care Foundation
9425 North MacArthur Boulevard, Suite 100
Irving, TX 75063-4706
Phone: 972-243-2272
Fax: 972-484-2720
E-mail: info@arcfoundation.org

SEPRACOR ACHIEVEMENT AWARD FOR EXCELLENCE IN PULMONARY DISEASE STATE MANAGEMENT

One-time award to recognize achievement in respiratory therapy and other disease state management. Must be a member of the American Association for Respiratory Care.

Academic Fields/Career Goals: Health and Medical Sciences; Therapy/Rehabilitation.

Award: Prize for use in freshman, sophomore, junior, senior, graduate, or postgraduate years; not renewable. *Number:* 1. *Amount:* up to $2500.

Eligibility Requirements: Applicant must be enrolled or expecting to enroll at an institution or university. Applicant or parent of applicant must have employment or volunteer experience in designated career field. Available to U.S. and non-U.S. citizens.

Application Requirements: References, curriculum vitae. *Deadline:* June 19.

Contact: Jill Nelson, Administrative Coordinator
American Respiratory Care Foundation
9425 North MacArthur Boulevard, Suite 100
Irving, TX 75063-4706
Phone: 972-243-2272
Fax: 972-484-2720
E-mail: info@arcfoundation.org

AMERICAN SOCIETY FOR CLINICAL LABORATORY SCIENCE
http://www.ascls.org

ASCLS REGION II VIRGINIA SOCIETY FOR CLINICAL LABORATORY SCIENCE SCHOLARSHIPS

One $500 scholarship available to a clinical laboratory student in his or her final year of study. Applicant must be in their final clinical year in an accredited CLS/MT, CLT/MLT, cytology, or histology program. Must attend program within Commonwealth of Virginia. Please refer to Web site for further information and application: http://www.rscls.vavalleyweb.com.

Academic Fields/Career Goals: Health and Medical Sciences.

Award: Scholarship for use in senior year; not renewable. *Number:* 1. *Amount:* $500.

Eligibility Requirements: Applicant must be enrolled or expecting to enroll at a four-year institution or university and studying in Virginia. Available to U.S. citizens.

Application Requirements: Application, financial need analysis, references, transcript. *Deadline:* varies.

Contact: Shirley Jenkins
E-mail: shirley.jenkins@mjh.org

ASCLS REGION IV OHIO SOCIETY FOR CLINICAL LABORATORY SCIENCE GERALDINE DIEBLER/STELLA GRIFFIN AWARD

One scholarship available to a student enrolled in a clinical laboratory science curriculum. Award may be used for freshman year through clinical year of program. Applicant must be a permanent resident of Ohio from the Akron, Canton, and Steubenville areas. Must have minimum 2.5 GPA. Please refer to Web site for further information and application: http://www/oscls.com.

Academic Fields/Career Goals: Health and Medical Sciences.

Award: Scholarship for use in freshman, sophomore, junior, or senior years; not renewable. *Number:* 1. *Amount:* $1000.

Eligibility Requirements: Applicant must be enrolled or expecting to enroll at a four-year institution or university and resident of Ohio. Applicant must have 2.5 GPA or higher. Available to U.S. citizens.

Application Requirements: Application, financial need analysis, references, transcript, personal statement. *Deadline:* May 15.

Contact: Sondra Sutherland, CLT & PBT Program Director
American Society for Clinical Laboratory Science
Jefferson Community College, 4000 Sunset Boulevard.
Steubenville, OH 43952
Phone: 740-264-5591 Ext. 165
Fax: 740-264-9504
E-mail: ssutherlan@jcc.edu

ASCLS REGION IV OHIO SOCIETY FOR CLINICAL LABORATORY SCIENCE STELLA GRIFFIN MEMORIAL SCHOLARSHIP

One scholarship available to a student enrolled in a clinical laboratory science curriculum. Award may be used for freshman year through clinical year of program. Applicant must be a permanent resident of Ohio with a minimum 2.5 GPA. Please refer to Web site for further information and application: http://www.oscls.com

Academic Fields/Career Goals: Health and Medical Sciences.

Award: Scholarship for use in freshman, sophomore, junior, or senior years; not renewable. *Number:* 1. *Amount:* $1000.

Eligibility Requirements: Applicant must be enrolled or expecting to enroll at a four-year institution or university and resident of Ohio. Applicant must have 2.5 GPA or higher. Available to U.S. citizens.

Application Requirements: Application, financial need analysis, references, transcript, personal statement. *Deadline:* May 15.

Contact: Rose Ann Crawford, Scholarship Committee Chair
American Society for Clinical Laboratory Science
529 Tammery Drive
Tallmadge, OH 44278-3033
Phone: 330-344-6256
E-mail: rac529@hotmail.com

ASCLS REGION IX CLINICAL LABORATORY SCIENTISTS OF ALASKA SHARON O'MEARA CONTINUING EDUCATION SCHOLARSHIP FUND
• See page 161

ASCLS REGION VI MISSOURI ORGANIZATION FOR CLINICAL LABORATORY SCIENCE EDUCATION SCHOLARSHIP
• See page 162

AMERICAN SOCIETY OF RADIOLOGIC TECHNOLOGISTS EDUCATION AND RESEARCH FOUNDATION
http://www.asrt.org

JEANETTE C. AND ISADORE N. STERN SCHOLARSHIP
• See page 317

JERMAN-CAHOON STUDENT SCHOLARSHIP

Merit Scholarship for certificate or undergraduate students. Must have completed at least one semester in the Radiological Sciences to apply. Financial need is a factor. Requirements include 3.0 GPA, recommendation and 450-500 word essay.

Academic Fields/Career Goals: Health and Medical Sciences; Radiology.

Award: Scholarship for use in freshman, sophomore, or junior years; not renewable. *Number:* 3. *Amount:* $2500.

Eligibility Requirements: Applicant must be enrolled or expecting to enroll full or part-time at a two-year or four-year or technical institution or university. Applicant must have 3.0 GPA or higher. Available to U.S. citizens.

Application Requirements: Application, essay, financial need analysis, references, transcript, application must be completed in dark ink, essay must be double-spaced and in 12-point font. *Deadline:* February 1.

Contact: Phelosha Collaros, Development Officer
American Society of Radiologic Technologists Education and Research Foundation
15000 Central Avenue, SE
Albuquerque, NM 87123-3917
Phone: 505-298-4500 Ext. 1233
Fax: 505-298-5063
E-mail: pcollaros@asrt.org

ROYCE OSBORN MINORITY STUDENT SCHOLARSHIP

Minority scholarship for certificate or undergraduate students. Must have completed at least one semester in the Radiologic Sciences to apply. Financial need is a factor. Requirements include 3.0 GPA, recommendation, and 450-500 word essay.

American Society of Radiologic Technologists Education and Research Foundation (continued)

Academic Fields/Career Goals: Health and Medical Sciences; Radiology.

Award: Scholarship for use in freshman, sophomore, or junior years; renewable. *Number:* 5. *Amount:* $4000.

Eligibility Requirements: Applicant must be American Indian/Alaska Native, Asian/Pacific Islander, Black (non-Hispanic), or Hispanic and enrolled or expecting to enroll full or part-time at a two-year or four-year or technical institution or university. Available to U.S. citizens.

Application Requirements: Application, essay, financial need analysis, references, transcript. *Deadline:* February 1.

Contact: Phelosha Collaros, Development Officer
American Society of Radiologic Technologists Education and Research Foundation
15000 Central Avenue, SE
Albuquerque, NM 87123-3917
Phone: 505-298-4500 Ext. 1233
Fax: 505-298-5063
E-mail: pcollaros@asrt.org

SIEMENS SCHOLAR AWARD
• *See page 317*

VARIAN RADIATION THERAPY STUDENT SCHOLARSHIP

Merit Scholarship for undergraduate or certificate students accepted or enrolled in a Radiation Therapy Program. Financial need is a factor. Requirements include 3.0 GPA, recommendation and 450-500 word essay. Sponsored in conjunction with Varian Oncology Systems. Can apply twice only.

Academic Fields/Career Goals: Health and Medical Sciences; Radiology.

Award: Scholarship for use in freshman, sophomore, or junior years; renewable. *Number:* up to 11. *Amount:* $5000.

Eligibility Requirements: Applicant must be enrolled or expecting to enroll full or part-time at a two-year or four-year or technical institution or university. Applicant must have 3.0 GPA or higher. Available to U.S. citizens.

Application Requirements: Application, essay, financial need analysis, references, transcript. *Deadline:* February 1.

Contact: Phelosha Collaros, Development Officer
American Society of Radiologic Technologists Education and Research Foundation
15000 Central Avenue, SE
Albuquerque, NM 87123-3917
Phone: 505-298-4500 Ext. 1233
Fax: 505-298-5063
E-mail: pcollaros@asrt.org

AMERICAN SOCIETY OF SAFETY ENGINEERS (ASSE) FOUNDATION   http://www.asse.org
UNITED PARCEL SERVICE DIVERSITY SCHOLARSHIP PROGRAM
• *See page 292*

ARKANSAS DEPARTMENT OF HIGHER EDUCATION   http://www.arkansashighered.com
ARKANSAS HEALTH EDUCATION GRANT PROGRAM (ARHEG)
• *See page 86*

ARRL FOUNDATION, INC.   http://www.arrl.org/arrlf/scholgen.html
WILLIAM R. GOLDFARB MEMORIAL SCHOLARSHIP
• *See page 145*

ASSOCIATED MEDICAL SERVICES, INC.   http://www.ams-inc.on.ca
ASSOCIATED MEDICAL SERVICES, INC. HANNAH STUDENTSHIP

Studentships available to undergraduate students who are Canadian citizens or permanent residents. Research must be done at a Canadian university and limited to the study of health, disease, or medicine. Studentship limited to three months. Deadline is February 1. Information is available on Web site: http://www.ams-inc.on.ca

Academic Fields/Career Goals: Health and Medical Sciences.

Award: Grant for use in freshman, sophomore, junior, or senior years. *Number:* 1–10. *Amount:* up to $4532.

Eligibility Requirements: Applicant must be Canadian citizen; enrolled or expecting to enroll at a four-year institution or university and studying in Alberta, British Columbia, Manitoba, New Brunswick, Newfoundland, North West Territories, Nova Scotia, Prince Edward Island, Quebec, Saskatchewan, or Yukon.

Application Requirements: Application, references, transcript, ethics certificate. *Deadline:* February 1.

Contact: Dr. Peter L. Twohig
Associated Medical Services, Inc.
c/o Gorsebrook Research Institute, Saint Mary's University, 923 Robie Street
Halifax B3H 3C3
Canada

ASSOCIATION OF SURGICAL TECHNOLOGISTS   http://www.ast.org
SURGICAL TECHNOLOGY SCHOLARSHIPS

The scholarship is to encourage and reward educational excellence and need demonstrated by surgical technology students.

Academic Fields/Career Goals: Health and Medical Sciences.

Award: Scholarship for use in freshman or sophomore years; not renewable. *Number:* 5–10. *Amount:* $500–$2500.

Eligibility Requirements: Applicant must be enrolled or expecting to enroll full-time at a two-year or technical institution. Applicant must have 3.5 GPA or higher. Available to U.S. and non-U.S. citizens.

Application Requirements: Application, essay, financial need analysis, references, self-addressed stamped envelope, transcript. *Deadline:* April 1.

Contact: Karen Ludwig, Director of Publishing-Association of Surgical Technologists
Association of Surgical Technologists
7108-C South Alton Way
Centennial, CO 80112-2106
Phone: 303-694-9130 Ext. 224
Fax: 303-694-9169
E-mail: kludwig@ast.org

THOMSON DELMAR LEARNING SURGICAL TECHNOLOGY SCHOLARSHIP

Award available to a student in CAAHEP-accredited program. Must have a 2.5 GPA. See Web site for more information http://www.ast.org

Academic Fields/Career Goals: Health and Medical Sciences.

Award: Scholarship for use in freshman, sophomore, junior, or senior years; not renewable. *Number:* 1. *Amount:* up to $1000.

Eligibility Requirements: Applicant must be enrolled or expecting to enroll full-time at a two-year or technical institution. Applicant must have 2.5 GPA or higher. Available to U.S. and Canadian citizens.

Application Requirements: Application, essay, references, self-addressed stamped envelope, transcript, course fee schedule. *Deadline:* April 1.

Contact: Karen Ludwig, AST Education Department
Association of Surgical Technologists
7108-C South Alton Way
Centennial, CO 80112-2106
Phone: 303-694-9130
Fax: 303-694-9196
E-mail: kludwig@ast.org

BECA FOUNDATION, INC.   http://www.becafoundation.org

ALICE NEWELL JOSLYN MEDICAL FUND
• *See page 207*

BETHESDA LUTHERAN HOMES AND SERVICES, INC.   http://www.blhs.org

DEVELOPMENTAL DISABILITIES SCHOLASTIC ACHIEVEMENT SCHOLARSHIP FOR LUTHERAN COLLEGE STUDENTS
• *See page 208*

BOYS AND GIRLS CLUBS OF GREATER SAN DIEGO   http://www.sdyouth.org

SPENCE REESE SCHOLARSHIP FUND
• *See page 259*

BRITISH COLUMBIA MINISTRY OF ADVANCED EDUCATION   http://www.aved.gov.bc.ca/

LOAN FORGIVENESS PROGRAM FOR NURSES, DOCTORS, MIDWIVES, AND PHARMACISTS

Loans to nursing, medical, midwifery, and pharmacy students from the British Columbia Ministry of Advanced Education will be forgiven at a rate of 33% per every year of service in a underprivileged or rural area of British Columbia. Three years of service will be rewarded with complete forgiveness of the loan. Must be Canadian. Must have graduated from a postsecondary institution with BC student loans in August 2000, or later. For more information, see Web site: www.aved.gov.bc.ca/studentservices

Academic Fields/Career Goals: Health and Medical Sciences; Nursing; Pharmacy.

Award: Forgivable loan for use in freshman, sophomore, junior, senior, or graduate years; renewable. *Number:* 1. *Amount:* varies.

Eligibility Requirements: Applicant must be enrolled or expecting to enroll at a two-year or four-year institution or university. Available to Canadian citizens.

Application Requirements: Application, transcript. *Deadline:* Continuous.

Contact: Student Services Branch
British Columbia Ministry of Advanced Education
Stn Prov Govt
Victoria, BC V8W 9H7
Canada
Phone: 250-387-6100

BUREAU OF HEALTH PROFESSIONS   http://nhsc.bhpr.hrsa.gov/members/scholars/

NATIONAL HEALTH SERVICE CORPS SCHOLARSHIP PROGRAM

Federal scholarships for U.S. citizens pursuing allopathic (MD) or osteopathic (DO) medicine, dentistry, family nurse practitioner, nurse midwifery, or physician assistant education. Two-year to four-year service commitment required. Scholarship includes tuition, fees, monthly stipends, and payment for educational expenses. Monthly stipend is taxable. Federal income tax only withheld from monthly stipend. Call 1-800-221-9393 for the application.

Academic Fields/Career Goals: Health and Medical Sciences; Nursing.

Award: Scholarship for use in freshman, sophomore, junior, or graduate years; renewable. *Number:* 200–300. *Amount:* $67,500–$135,000.

Eligibility Requirements: Applicant must be enrolled or expecting to enroll full-time at a four-year institution or university. Available to U.S. citizens.

Application Requirements: Application, interview. *Deadline:* March 31.

Contact: Sonya Shorter, Application and Award Branch
Bureau of Health Professions
5600 Fishers Lane, Room 8A-55
Rockville, MD 20857
Phone: 301-594-4404
Fax: 301-594-4981
E-mail: sshorter@hrsa.gov

BUSINESS AND PROFESSIONAL WOMEN'S FOUNDATION   http://www.bpwusa.org

BPW CAREER ADVANCEMENT SCHOLARSHIP PROGRAM FOR WOMEN
• *See page 136*

CANADIAN SOCIETY FOR MEDICAL LABORATORY SCIENCE   http://www.csmls.org

E.V. BOOTH SCHOLARSHIP AWARD
• *See page 317*

CAROL WELCH MEMORIAL SCHOLARSHIP FUND

CAROL WELCH MEMORIAL SCHOLARSHIP

Scholarships for healthcare-related fields of study. Applicants must be at least a sophomore in college, enrolled in an eligible program.

Academic Fields/Career Goals: Health and Medical Sciences.

Award: Scholarship for use in sophomore, junior, or senior years. *Number:* 1.

Eligibility Requirements: Applicant must be enrolled or expecting to enroll at a four-year institution or university. Available to U.S. citizens.

Application Requirements: *Deadline:* May 1.

Contact: Carol Welch Memorial Scholarship Fund
San Pablo Campus Service League
2000 Vale Road
San Pablo, CA 94806

CONGRESSIONAL BLACK CAUCUS SPOUSES PROGRAM   http://www.cbcfinc.org

CONGRESSIONAL BLACK CAUCUS SPOUSES HEALTH INITIATIVES
• *See page 318*

FEDERATION OF STRAIGHT CHIROPRACTORS AND ORGANIZATIONS   http://www.straightchiropractic.org

SYLVA ASHWORTH SCHOLARSHIP

Scholarship is open to single mothers enrolled in chiropractic college. Must submit an essay, maximum 2 pages, double spaced. Include verification of single mother status (i.e. note from the Registrar). Deadline is April 1. See Web site for essay topic: http://www.straightchiropractic.com/index.php?file=sylva.htm

Academic Fields/Career Goals: Health and Medical Sciences.

Award: Scholarship for use in freshman, sophomore, junior, senior, or graduate years; not renewable. *Number:* 1. *Amount:* up to $1000.

Eligibility Requirements: Applicant must be enrolled or expecting to enroll full or part-time at an institution or university and female. Available to U.S. citizens.

Application Requirements: Essay, applicant's contact information, school and trimester should be included on the cover sheet, verification of single mother status (note from the registrar). *Deadline:* April 1.

Contact: Renee Hillman, Administrative Assistant
Federation of Straight Chiropractors and Organizations
2276 Wassergass Road
Hellertown, PA 18055
Phone: 800-521-9856
Fax: 610-838-3031
E-mail: fsco@juno.com

FOUNDATION FOR SURGICAL TECHNOLOGY   http://www.ffst.org

FOUNDATION FOR SURGICAL TECHNOLOGY SCHOLARSHIP FUND

Scholarships available for students who are currently enrolled in a CAAHEP-accredited surgical technology program. Must be preparing for a career as a surgical technologist. 3.0 GPA is required. One-time award valued from $500 upwards, which varies from year to year . Applicant must be selected by sponsoring institution. Visit Web site for more information.

Academic Fields/Career Goals: Health and Medical Sciences.

Award: Scholarship for use in freshman, sophomore, junior, or senior years; not renewable. *Number:* 5–10. *Amount:* $500–$2500.

Foundation for Surgical Technology (continued)

Eligibility Requirements: Applicant must be enrolled or expecting to enroll full-time at a two-year or four-year or technical institution or university. Applicant must have 3.0 GPA or higher. Available to U.S. and non-U.S. citizens.

Application Requirements: Application, financial need analysis, references, transcript. *Deadline:* April 1.

Contact: Karen Ludwig, Director of Publishing
Foundation for Surgical Technology
6 West Drive Creek Circle
Littleton, CO 80120
Phone: 303-694-9130 Ext. 224
Fax: 303-694-9169

GENERAL FEDERATION OF WOMEN'S CLUBS OF MASSACHUSETTS   http://www.gfwcma.org/

CATHERINE E. PHILBIN SCHOLARSHIP

One scholarship of $500 will be awarded to a graduate or undergraduate student studying public health. Eligible applicants will be residents of Massachusetts. Along with the application, students must send a personal statement of no more than 500 words addressing professional goals and financial need.

Academic Fields/Career Goals: Health and Medical Sciences.

Award: Scholarship for use in freshman, sophomore, junior, senior, or graduate years; not renewable. *Number:* 1. *Amount:* $500.

Eligibility Requirements: Applicant must be enrolled or expecting to enroll full-time at a two-year or four-year institution or university and resident of Massachusetts. Available to U.S. citizens.

Application Requirements: Application, essay, references, transcript. *Deadline:* March 1.

Contact: Jane Howard, Scholarship Chairman, GFWC of MA
General Federation of Women's Clubs of Massachusetts
PO Box 679
Sudbury, MA 01776-0679

GEORGIA COUNCIL OF CHIROPRACTIC   http://www.georgiachiropractic.org

DR. RICHARD W. KIMBROUGH MEMORIAL SCHOLARSHIP

Award to full-time chiropractic student who is a member of the Georgia Council of Chiropratic. Must have GPA of 2.5. Several awards totalling $1000.

Academic Fields/Career Goals: Health and Medical Sciences.

Award: Scholarship for use in freshman, sophomore, junior, senior, or graduate years. *Amount:* $1000.

Eligibility Requirements: Applicant must be enrolled or expecting to enroll full-time at an institution or university. Applicant must have 2.5 GPA or higher. Available to U.S. citizens.

Application Requirements: Application, essay, transcript. *Deadline:* varies.

Contact: Georgia Council of Chiropractic
1755 The Triangle Building, Suite 260
PO Box 1623
Atlanta, GA 30339
Phone: 678-627-0494
Fax: 678-627-0493

GREATER KANAWHA VALLEY FOUNDATION   http://www.tgkvf.org

NICHOLAS AND MARY AGNES TRIVILLIAN MEMORIAL SCHOLARSHIP FUND

Renewable award for West Virginia residents pursuing medical or pharmacy programs. Must show financial need and academic merit. For more information, contact address below. May apply for two Foundation scholarships but will only be chosen for one.

Academic Fields/Career Goals: Health and Medical Sciences.

Award: Scholarship for use in freshman, sophomore, junior, senior, or graduate years; renewable. *Number:* up to 29. *Amount:* $1000.

Eligibility Requirements: Applicant must be enrolled or expecting to enroll at a four-year institution or university and resident of West Virginia. Applicant must have 2.5 GPA or higher. Available to U.S. citizens.

Application Requirements: Application, essay, financial need analysis, references, self-addressed stamped envelope, test scores, transcript. *Deadline:* February 15.

Contact: Susan Hoover, Scholarship Coordinator
Greater Kanawha Valley Foundation
PO Box 3041
Charleston, WV 25331
Phone: 304-346-3620
Fax: 304-346-3640

HAWAIIAN LODGE, F.& A. M.   http://www.hawaiianlodge.org/

HAWAIIAN LODGE SCHOLARSHIPS
- *See page 99*

HEALTH PROFESSIONS EDUCATION FOUNDATION   http://www.healthprofessions.ca.gov

HEALTH PROFESSIONS EDUCATION SCHOLARSHIP PROGRAM
- *See page 208*

KAISER PERMANENTE ALLIED HEALTHCARE SCHOLARSHIP

One-time award to all students enrolled in or accepted to California accredited allied health education programs. Scholarship up to $4000. Deadlines: March 24 and September 11. More information on http://www.healthprofessions.ca.gov/Applications/17AlliedHealthcareApplicationDEC05.pdf

Academic Fields/Career Goals: Health and Medical Sciences; Social Services; Therapy/Rehabilitation.

Award: Scholarship for use in freshman, sophomore, junior, or senior years; not renewable. *Number:* 20–40. *Amount:* $3000–$4000.

Eligibility Requirements: Applicant must be enrolled or expecting to enroll full or part-time at a two-year or four-year or technical institution or university; resident of California and studying in California. Available to U.S. citizens.

Application Requirements: Application, autobiography, financial need analysis, resume, references, transcript. *Deadline:* varies.

Contact: Carlos Rodriguez, Program Director
Health Professions Education Foundation
818 K Street, Suite 210
Sacramento, CA 95814
Phone: 916-324-6500
Fax: 916-324-6585

HEALTHCARE INFORMATION AND MANAGEMENT SYSTEMS SOCIETY FOUNDATION   http://www.himss.org

HIMSS FOUNDATION SCHOLARSHIP PROGRAM
- *See page 318*

HELLENIC UNIVERSITY CLUB OF PHILADELPHIA   http://www.hucphila.org

THE DR. PETER A. THEODOS MEMORIAL GRADUATE SCHOLARSHIP

Scholarship in the amount of $2500 will be awarded to a senior undergraduate or graduate student with financial need pursuing studies leading to a Doctor of Medicine (M.D.) Degree.

Academic Fields/Career Goals: Health and Medical Sciences.

Award: Scholarship for use in senior, or graduate years. *Amount:* $2500.

Eligibility Requirements: Applicant must be of Greek heritage; enrolled or expecting to enroll full-time at a four-year institution or university and resident of New Jersey or Pennsylvania. Available to U.S. citizens.

Application Requirements: Application. *Deadline:* April 20.

Contact: Zoe Tripolitis, Scholarship Chairman
Hellenic University Club of Philadelphia
PO Box 42199
Philadelphia, PA 19101
Phone: 215-483-7440
E-mail: zoe.tripolitis@arkemagroup.com

HERB SOCIETY OF AMERICA   http://www.herbsociety.org

HERB SOCIETY RESEARCH GRANTS
• *See page 92*

ILLINOIS STUDENT ASSISTANCE COMMISSION (ISAC)   http://www.collegezone.org

ILLINOIS DEPARTMENT OF PUBLIC HEALTH CENTER FOR RURAL HEALTH ALLIED HEALTH CARE PROFESSIONAL SCHOLARSHIP PROGRAM

Scholarship for Illinois students studying to be a nurse practitioner, physician assistant, or certified nurse midwife. Funding available for up to two years. Must fulfill an obligation to practice full-time in a designated shortage area as an allied healthcare professional in Illinois for one year for each year of scholarship funding. Failure to fulfill the obligation will require repayment to the state three times the amount of the scholarship received for each unfulfilled year of obligation plus 7% interest per year.

Academic Fields/Career Goals: Health and Medical Sciences.

Award: Scholarship for use in freshman, sophomore, junior, or senior years; renewable. *Number:* 20. *Amount:* $7500–$15,000.

Eligibility Requirements: Applicant must be enrolled or expecting to enroll full or part-time at a two-year or four-year institution or university and resident of Illinois. Available to U.S. citizens.

Application Requirements: Application, copy of Student Aid Report (SAR), letter of acceptance. *Deadline:* June 30.

Contact: Marcia Franklin, Department of Public Health
Illinois Student Assistance Commission (ISAC)
535 West Jefferson Street
Springfield, IL 62761
Phone: 217-782-1624

ILLINOIS DEPARTMENT OF PUBLIC HEALTH CENTER FOR RURAL HEALTH NURSING EDUCATION SCHOLARSHIP PROGRAM

Scholarship for Illinois students pursuing a certificate, diploma, or degree in nursing and demonstrating financial need. Scholarship provides up to four years of financial aid in return for full-or part-time employment as a licensed practical or registered nurse in Illinois upon graduation. Must remain employed in Illinois for a period equivalent to the educational time that was supported by the scholarship. Application deadline is May 31.

Academic Fields/Career Goals: Health and Medical Sciences; Nursing.

Award: Scholarship for use in freshman, sophomore, junior, or senior years; renewable. *Number:* varies. *Amount:* $1500–$6000.

Eligibility Requirements: Applicant must be enrolled or expecting to enroll full or part-time at a two-year or four-year institution or university and resident of Illinois. Available to U.S. citizens.

Application Requirements: Application, financial need analysis, transcript. *Deadline:* May 31.

Contact: Nursing Education Scholarship Program
Illinois Student Assistance Commission (ISAC)
535 West Jefferson Street
Springfield, IL 62761-0001
Phone: 212-782-1624

INDIAN HEALTH SERVICES, UNITED STATES DEPARTMENT OF HEALTH AND HUMAN SERVICES   http://www.ihs.gov

INDIAN HEALTH SERVICE HEALTH PROFESSIONS PRE-GRADUATE SCHOLARSHIPS
• *See page 209*

INDIAN HEALTH SERVICE HEALTH PROFESSIONS PRE-PROFESSIONAL SCHOLARSHIP
• *See page 318*

INTERNATIONAL ORDER OF THE KING'S DAUGHTERS AND SONS   http://www.iokds.org

HEALTH CAREERS SCHOLARSHIP
• *See page 209*

J.D. ARCHBOLD MEMORIAL HOSPITAL   http://www.archbold.org

ARCHBOLD SCHOLARSHIP PROGRAM

Service cancelable loan awarded for a clinical degree. Awarded to residents of Southwest Georgia and North Florida. Specific clinical degree may vary, depending on need in area. Must agree to full-time employment for one to three years upon graduation.

Academic Fields/Career Goals: Health and Medical Sciences; Nursing.

Award: Forgivable loan for use in freshman, sophomore, junior, or senior years; not renewable. *Number:* 50. *Amount:* $600–$6000.

Eligibility Requirements: Applicant must be enrolled or expecting to enroll full or part-time at a two-year or four-year or technical institution or university and resident of Florida or Georgia. Available to U.S. citizens.

Application Requirements: Application, interview, transcript. *Deadline:* Continuous.

Contact: Donna McMillan, Education Coordinator
J.D. Archbold Memorial Hospital
PO Box 1018
Thomasville, GA 31799
Phone: 229-228-2795
Fax: 229-228-8584

JEWISH FOUNDATION FOR EDUCATION OF WOMEN   http://www.jfew.org

SCHOLARSHIP PROGRAM FOR FORMER SOVIET UNION EMIGRES TRAINING IN THE HEALTH SCIENCES
• *See page 209*

LADIES AUXILIARY TO THE VETERANS OF FOREIGN WARS, DEPARTMENT OF MAINE

FRANCIS L. BOOTH MEDICAL SCHOLARSHIP SPONSORED BY LAVFW DEPARTMENT OF MAINE

Award for an undergraduate student majoring in the field of medicine who has a parent or grandparent who is a member of the Maine VFW or VFW auxiliary.

Academic Fields/Career Goals: Health and Medical Sciences; Humanities; Nursing; Therapy/Rehabilitation.

Award: Scholarship for use in freshman, sophomore, junior, or senior years; not renewable. *Number:* 1. *Amount:* $1000.

Eligibility Requirements: Applicant must be enrolled or expecting to enroll full-time at a four-year institution or university. Applicant or parent of applicant must be member of Veterans of Foreign Wars or Auxiliary. Applicant must have 3.0 GPA or higher. Available to U.S. citizens.

Application Requirements: Application, financial need analysis, resume, references, transcript. *Deadline:* March 1.

Contact: Linda Bracket, President

MARIN EDUCATION FUND   http://www.marineducationfund.org

GOLDMAN FAMILY FUND, NEW LEADER SCHOLARSHIP
• *See page 210*

MARYLAND HIGHER EDUCATION COMMISSION   http://www.mhec.state.md.us

FIREFIGHTER, AMBULANCE, AND RESCUE SQUAD MEMBER TUITION REIMBURSEMENT PROGRAM-MARYLAND
• *See page 300*

GRADUATE AND PROFESSIONAL SCHOLARSHIP PROGRAM-MARYLAND
• *See page 210*

MENTAL HEALTH ASSOCIATION IN NEW YORK STATE, INC.
http://www.mhanys.org

EDNA AIMES SCHOLARSHIP

One-time award for individuals studying the prevention and treatment of mental illness and the promotion of mental health. Must be a New York resident attending a New York four-year institution. Application deadline is April 15.

Academic Fields/Career Goals: Health and Medical Sciences; Pharmacy; Psychology; Public Health.

Award: Scholarship for use in junior, senior, or graduate years; not renewable. *Number:* 1–3. *Amount:* $2000–$2500.

Eligibility Requirements: Applicant must be enrolled or expecting to enroll full-time at a four-year institution or university; resident of New York and studying in New York. Available to U.S. and non-U.S. citizens.

Application Requirements: Application, essay, resume, references, transcript, demonstrated financial need, personal statement, work experience. *Deadline:* April 15.

Contact: Lillian Lasher, Administrative Assistant
Mental Health Association in New York State, Inc.
194 Washington Avenue, Suite 415
Albany, NY 12210
Phone: 518-434-0439 Ext. 22
Fax: 518-427-8676
E-mail: llasher@mhanys.org

MINNESOTA DEPARTMENT OF HEALTH
http://www.health.state.mn.us

MINNESOTA NURSES LOAN FORGIVENESS PROGRAM

This program offers loan repayment to registered nurse and licensed practical nurse students who agree to practice in a Minnesota nursing home or an Intermediate Care Facility for persons with mental retardation for a minimum 3-year/4-year service obligation after completion of training. Candidates must apply while still in school.

Academic Fields/Career Goals: Health and Medical Sciences; Nursing.

Award: Forgivable loan for use in freshman, sophomore, junior, or senior years; not renewable. *Number:* 25–35. *Amount:* $3000–$3500.

Eligibility Requirements: Applicant must be enrolled or expecting to enroll full or part-time at a two-year or four-year or technical institution or university. Available to U.S. citizens.

Application Requirements: Application, essay, resume. *Deadline:* December 1.

Contact: Karen Welter
Minnesota Department of Health
121 East Seventh Place, Suite 460, PO Box 64975
St. Paul, MN 55164-0975
Phone: 651-282-6302
Fax: 651-297-5808
E-mail: karen.welter@health.state.mn.us

MISSISSIPPI STATE STUDENT FINANCIAL AID
http://www.mississippiuniversities.com

MISSISSIPPI HEALTH CARE PROFESSIONS LOAN/SCHOLARSHIP PROGRAM

Renewable award for junior and senior undergraduates studying psychology, speech pathology or occupational therapy. Must be Mississippi residents attending four-year universities in Mississippi. Must fulfill work obligation in Mississippi or pay back as loan. Renewable award for graduate student enrolled in physical therapy.

Academic Fields/Career Goals: Health and Medical Sciences; Psychology; Therapy/Rehabilitation.

Award: Forgivable loan for use in junior, senior, or graduate years; renewable. *Number:* varies. *Amount:* $1500–$6000.

Eligibility Requirements: Applicant must be enrolled or expecting to enroll full-time at a four-year institution or university; resident of Mississippi and studying in Mississippi. Available to U.S. citizens.

Application Requirements: Application, driver's license, references, transcript. *Deadline:* March 31.

Contact: Susan Eckels, Program Administrator
Mississippi State Student Financial Aid
3825 Ridgewood Road
Jackson, MS 39211-6453
Phone: 601-432-6997
E-mail: sme@ihl.state.ms.us

MISSOURI DEPARTMENT OF HEALTH AND SENIOR SERVICES
http://www.dhss.mo.gov

ACES/PRIMO PROGRAM

Program of the Missouri Area Health Education Centers (MAHEC) And the Primary Care Resource Initiative for Missouri students interested in Primary Care. Applicant should have a minimum GPA of 3.0

Academic Fields/Career Goals: Health and Medical Sciences.

Award: Forgivable loan for use in freshman, sophomore, junior, or senior years; not renewable. *Amount:* up to $5000.

Eligibility Requirements: Applicant must be enrolled or expecting to enroll full-time at an institution or university. Applicant must have 3.0 GPA or higher. Available to U.S. citizens.

Application Requirements: Application. *Deadline:* July 1.

Contact: Jan Shipley, Programs Director
Missouri Department of Health and Senior Services
1101 Yuane Ave
Rolla, MO 65401
Phone: 573-364-4797
Fax: 573-364-8972

PRIMARY CARE RESOURCE INITIATIVE FOR MISSOURI LOAN PROGRAM
• See page 210

NASA IDAHO SPACE GRANT CONSORTIUM
http://isgc.uidaho.edu

NASA IDAHO SPACE GRANT CONSORTIUM SCHOLARSHIP PROGRAM
• See page 94

NASA VERMONT SPACE GRANT CONSORTIUM
http://www.vtspacegrant.org

VERMONT SPACE GRANT CONSORTIUM SCHOLARSHIP PROGRAM
• See page 94

NATIONAL AMBUCS, INC.
http://www.ambucs.com

AMBUCS SCHOLARS-SCHOLARSHIPS FOR THERAPISTS

Scholarships are open to students who are U.S. citizens at a junior level or above in college. Must be enrolled in an accredited program by the appropriate health therapy profession authority in physical therapy, occupational therapy, speech-language pathology, or audiology and must demonstrate a financial need. Application available on Web site at http://www.ambucs.com. Paper applications are not accepted.

Academic Fields/Career Goals: Health and Medical Sciences; Therapy/Rehabilitation.

Award: Scholarship for use in junior, senior, graduate, or postgraduate years; not renewable. *Number:* 300. *Amount:* $500–$6000.

Eligibility Requirements: Applicant must be enrolled or expecting to enroll full-time at a four-year institution or university. Available to U.S. citizens.

Application Requirements: Application, essay, financial need analysis, enrollment certification form. *Deadline:* April 15.

Contact: Janice Blankenship, Scholarship Coordinator
National AMBUCS, Inc.
PO Box 5127
High Point, NC 27262
Phone: 336-869-2166
Fax: 336-887-8451
E-mail: janiceb@ambucs.com

NATIONAL ATHLETIC TRAINERS' ASSOCIATION RESEARCH AND EDUCATION FOUNDATION   http://www.natafoundation.org

NATIONAL ATHLETIC TRAINER'S ASSOCIATION RESEARCH AND EDUCATION FOUNDATION SCHOLARSHIP PROGRAM

One-time award available to full-time students who are members of NATA. Minimum 3.2 GPA required. Open to undergraduate upperclassmen and graduate/post-graduate students. Deadline is February 10.

Academic Fields/Career Goals: Health and Medical Sciences; Health Information Management/Technology; Sports-related; Therapy/Rehabilitation.

Award: Scholarship for use in junior, senior, graduate, or postgraduate years; not renewable. *Number:* 55–70. *Amount:* $2000.

Eligibility Requirements: Applicant must be enrolled or expecting to enroll full-time at a four-year institution or university. Available to U.S. and non-U.S. citizens.

Application Requirements: Application, essay, references, transcript. *Deadline:* February 10.

Contact: Barbara Niland, Scholarship Coordinator
　　　National Athletic Trainers' Association Research and Education
　　　　Foundation
　　　2952 Stemmons Freeway, Suite 200
　　　Dallas, TX 75247
　　　Phone: 214-637-6282 Ext. 151
　　　Fax: 214-637-2206
　　　E-mail: barbara@nata.org

NATIONAL COMMUNITY PHARMACIST ASSOCIATION (NCPA) FOUNDATION   http://www.ncpanet.org

NATIONAL COMMUNITY PHARMACIST ASSOCIATION FOUNDATION PRESIDENTIAL SCHOLARSHIP

Scholarship for student members of NCPA who are full-time pharmacy students at an accredited U.S. school of pharmacy. Based on academic achievement and leadership qualities. Submit resume and curriculum vitae with application. Application deadline is March 1. One-time award of up to $2000 for college juniors and seniors.

Academic Fields/Career Goals: Health and Medical Sciences.

Award: Scholarship for use in junior or senior years; not renewable. *Number:* up to 15. *Amount:* up to $2000.

Eligibility Requirements: Applicant must be enrolled or expecting to enroll full-time at a four-year institution or university. Applicant must have 2.5 GPA or higher. Available to U.S. citizens.

Application Requirements: Application, essay, resume, references, transcript. *Deadline:* March 1.

Contact: Yulanda Slade, Administrative Assistant
　　　National Community Pharmacist Association (NCPA) Founda-
　　　　tion
　　　100 Daingerfield Road
　　　Alexandria, VA 22314
　　　Phone: 703-683-8200
　　　Fax: 703-683-3619

NATIONAL FEDERATION OF THE BLIND   http://www.nfb.org

HOWARD BROWN RICKARD SCHOLARSHIP
• *See page 101*

NATIONAL INSTITUTES OF HEALTH   http://ugsp.info.nih.gov

NIH UNDERGRADUATE SCHOLARSHIP PROGRAM FOR STUDENTS FROM DISADVANTAGED BACKGROUNDS
• *See page 140*

NATIONAL INVENTORS HALL OF FAME   http://www.invent.org

COLLEGIATE INVENTORS COMPETITION - GRAND PRIZE
• *See page 95*

COLLEGIATE INVENTORS COMPETITION FOR UNDERGRADUATE STUDENTS
• *See page 95*

NATIONAL SOCIETY DAUGHTERS OF THE AMERICAN REVOLUTION   http://www.dar.org

NATIONAL SOCIETY DAUGHTERS OF THE AMERICAN REVOLUTION IRENE AND DAISY MACGREGOR MEMORIAL SCHOLARSHIP

Renewable award to students who are accepted into an accredited school of medicine and who are planning to pursue an MD degree or study psychiatric nursing. Must obtain letter of sponsorship from local DAR chapter. Must be a U.S. citizen. Must submit self-addressed stamped envelope to be considered. Deadline is April 15.

Academic Fields/Career Goals: Health and Medical Sciences; Nursing.

Award: Scholarship for use in freshman, sophomore, junior, senior, or graduate years; renewable. *Number:* 2. *Amount:* $5000.

Eligibility Requirements: Applicant must be enrolled or expecting to enroll at a four-year institution or university. Available to U.S. citizens.

Application Requirements: Application, references, self-addressed stamped envelope, test scores, transcript. *Deadline:* April 15.

Contact: Committee Services Office, Scholarship
　　　National Society Daughters of the American Revolution
　　　1776 D Street, NW
　　　Washington, DC 20006-5392

NEBRASKA HEALTH AND HUMAN SERVICES SYSTEM, OFFICE OF RURAL HEALTH   http://www.hhs.state.ne.us

RURAL HEALTH STUDENT LOAN PROGRAM
• *See page 210*

NEW MEXICO COMMISSION ON HIGHER EDUCATION   http://www.hed.state.nm.us

ALLIED HEALTH STUDENT LOAN PROGRAM-NEW MEXICO
• *See page 210*

NEW YORK STATE EDUCATION DEPARTMENT   http://www.highered.nysed.gov

REGENTS PROFESSIONAL OPPORTUNITY SCHOLARSHIP
• *See page 67*

NORTH CAROLINA STATE EDUCATION ASSISTANCE AUTHORITY   http://www.ncseaa.edu

NORTH CAROLINA STUDENT LOAN PROGRAM FOR HEALTH, SCIENCE, AND MATHEMATICS
• *See page 211*

OKLAHOMA EDUCATIONAL FOUNDATION FOR OSTEOPATHIC MEDICINE   http://www.okosteo.org/

OKLAHOMA EDUCATIONAL FOUNDATION FOR OSTEOPATHIC MEDICINE ENDOWED STUDENT SCHOLARSHIP PROGRAM

Nonrenewable award available to students attending osteopathic colleges. Applications are reviewed yearly. Write for specific deadlines. Must be Oklahoma resident.

Academic Fields/Career Goals: Health and Medical Sciences.

Award: Scholarship for use in freshman, sophomore, junior, senior, or graduate years; not renewable. *Number:* 1–5. *Amount:* $2500–$5000.

Eligibility Requirements: Applicant must be enrolled or expecting to enroll full-time at a four-year institution or university and resident of Oklahoma. Available to U.S. citizens.

Oklahoma Educational Foundation for Osteopathic Medicine (continued)

Application Requirements: Application, essay, financial need analysis, photo, references, transcript. *Deadline:* varies.

Contact: Dorothy Prophet, Foundation Administrator
Oklahoma Educational Foundation for Osteopathic Medicine
4848 North Lincoln Boulevard
Oklahoma City, OK 73105-3335
Phone: 405-528-4848
Fax: 405-528-6102
E-mail: dorothy@okosteo.org

ONS FOUNDATION   http://www.ons.org

ONS FOUNDATION NURSING OUTCOMES RESEARCH GRANT

One grant for a registered nurse actively involved in some aspect of cancer patient care, education, or research. Award to be used to support research. Research must be clinically focused. One-time award of $7500. Deadline: November 1.

Academic Fields/Career Goals: Health and Medical Sciences; Nursing.

Award: Grant for use in junior, senior, graduate, or postgraduate years; not renewable. *Number:* 1. *Amount:* $7500.

Eligibility Requirements: Applicant must be enrolled or expecting to enroll at an institution or university. Applicant or parent of applicant must have employment or volunteer experience in designated career field. Available to U.S. citizens.

Application Requirements: Application. *Deadline:* November 1.

Contact: Bonny Revo, Executive Assistant
ONS Foundation
125 Enterprise Drive
Pittsburgh, PA 15275
Phone: 412-859-6100
Fax: 412-859-6162
E-mail: brevo@ons.org

ONS FOUNDATION ONCOLOGY NURSING SOCIETY RESEARCH GRANT

One grant for a registered nurse actively involved in some aspect of cancer patient care, education, or research. Award to be used to support research. Research must be clinically focused. One-time award of $10,000. Deadline: November 1.

Academic Fields/Career Goals: Health and Medical Sciences; Nursing.

Award: Grant for use in junior, senior, graduate, or postgraduate years; not renewable. *Number:* 1. *Amount:* $10,000.

Eligibility Requirements: Applicant must be enrolled or expecting to enroll at an institution or university. Applicant or parent of applicant must have employment or volunteer experience in designated career field. Available to U.S. citizens.

Application Requirements: Application. *Deadline:* November 1.

Contact: Bonny Revo, Executive Assistant
ONS Foundation
125 Enterprise Drive
Pittsburgh, PA 15275
Phone: 412-859-6100
Fax: 412-859-6162
E-mail: brevo@ons.org

ORANGE COUNTY COMMUNITY FOUNDATION   http://www.heef.org

HEALTHCARE EDUCATION SCHOLARSHIP FUND

Scholarship awarded to Hispanic high school seniors who demonstrate an interest in pursuing an education and/or career in any of the various fields of healthcare. Deadline is February 13.

Academic Fields/Career Goals: Health and Medical Sciences.

Award: Scholarship for use in freshman year; not renewable. *Number:* 1–2. *Amount:* up to $1000.

Eligibility Requirements: Applicant must be Hispanic; high school student and planning to enroll or expecting to enroll at an institution or university. Available to U.S. citizens.

Application Requirements: Application, essay, self-addressed stamped envelope, transcript. *Deadline:* February 13.

Contact: Rose Garris, Hispanic Education Endowment Fund
Orange County Community Foundation
30 Corporate Park, Suite 410
Irvine, CA 92606
Phone: 949-543-4202 Ext. 23
Fax: 949-553-4211

OREGON COMMUNITY FOUNDATION   http://www.ocf1.org/

DR. FRANZ AND KATHRYN STENZEL FUND

Scholarships for Oregon residents, for use in the pursuit of a postsecondary education, with a focus on three types of students: (a) those pursuing any type of undergraduate degree, (b) those pursing a nursing education through a two-year, four-year or graduate program, and (3) medical students.

Academic Fields/Career Goals: Health and Medical Sciences; Nursing.

Award: Scholarship for use in freshman, sophomore, junior, senior, or graduate years. *Number:* 1.

Eligibility Requirements: Applicant must be enrolled or expecting to enroll full-time at a four-year institution or university; resident of Oregon and studying in Oregon. Available to U.S. citizens.

Application Requirements: *Deadline:* varies.

Contact: Dianne Causey, Program Associate for Scholarships/Grants
Oregon Community Foundation
1221 South West Yamhill, Suite 100
Portland, OR 97205
Phone: 503-227-6846
Fax: 503-274-7771
E-mail: info@ocf1.org

GAYLE AND HARVEY RUBIN SCHOLARSHIP FUND

Scholarship for Oregon residents who are studying, or who plan to study, medicine or law. Must be enrolled in or accepted for enrollment in a full-time graduate course of study, working toward either an MD, DDM, of JD degree at an eligible institution.

Academic Fields/Career Goals: Health and Medical Sciences; Law/Legal Services.

Award: Scholarship for use in freshman, sophomore, junior, senior, or graduate years. *Number:* 1.

Eligibility Requirements: Applicant must be enrolled or expecting to enroll full-time at a four-year institution or university and resident of Oregon. Available to U.S. citizens.

Application Requirements: *Deadline:* varies.

Contact: Dianne Causey, Program Associate for Scholarships/Grants
Oregon Community Foundation
1221 South West Yamhill, Suite 100
Portland, OR 97205
Phone: 503-227-6846

OREGON STUDENT ASSISTANCE COMMISSION   http://www.osac.state.or.us

FRIENDS OF OREGON STUDENTS SCHOLARSHIP
• *See page 234*

JEANNETTE MOWERY SCHOLARSHIP
• *See page 211*

LAWRENCE R. FOSTER MEMORIAL SCHOLARSHIP

One-time award to students enrolled or planning to enroll in a public health degree program. First preference given to those working in the public health field and those pursuing a graduate degree in public health. Undergraduates entering junior or senior year health programs may apply if seeking a public health career, and not private practice. Prefer applicants from diverse cultures. Must provide 3 references. Additional essay required. Must be resident of Oregon.

Academic Fields/Career Goals: Health and Medical Sciences.

Award: Scholarship for use in junior, senior, graduate, or postgraduate years; renewable. *Number:* 6. *Amount:* $4167.

Eligibility Requirements: Applicant must be enrolled or expecting to enroll full or part-time at a four-year institution or university and resident of Oregon. Available to U.S. citizens.

Application Requirements: Application, essay, financial need analysis, references, transcript, activity chart. *Deadline:* March 1.

Contact: Director of Grant Programs
Oregon Student Assistance Commission
1500 Valley River Drive, Suite 100
Eugene, OR 97401-7020
Phone: 800-452-8807 Ext. 7395

MARION A. LINDEMAN SCHOLARSHIP

Award for Willamette View employees who have completed one or more years of service as Certified Nurses Assistants or nursing staff members. Must pursue a degree or certification in nursing; speech, physical or occupational therapy or other health-related fields.

Academic Fields/Career Goals: Health and Medical Sciences; Nursing; Therapy/Rehabilitation.

Award: Scholarship for use in freshman, sophomore, junior, or senior years; renewable. *Number:* 1.

Eligibility Requirements: Applicant must be enrolled or expecting to enroll full or part-time at a two-year or four-year institution and resident of Oregon. Applicant or parent of applicant must have employment or volunteer experience in designated career field. Available to U.S. citizens.

Application Requirements: Application, essay, financial need analysis, references, transcript, activity chart. *Deadline:* March 1.

Contact: Director of Grant Programs
Oregon Student Assistance Commission
1500 Valley River Drive, Suite 100
Eugene, OR 97401-7020
Phone: 800-452-8807 Ext. 7395

OUM CHIROPRACTOR PROGRAM
http://www.oumchiropractor.com

WELLNESS WORKS SCHOLARSHIP

Scholarships twice each year, in November and in May. Must be currently enrolled in one of the US Colleges of Chiropractic. Must submit best idea in the form of an essay, marketing campaign, or storyboard (typed in Word or PowerPoint, 500 words or less) for marketing chiropractic care nationally as proactive health maintenance. See Web site for more information at: http://www.oumchiropractor.com

Academic Fields/Career Goals: Health and Medical Sciences.

Award: Scholarship for use in freshman, sophomore, junior, senior, or graduate years; not renewable. *Number:* 1.

Eligibility Requirements: Applicant must be enrolled or expecting to enroll at a four-year institution or university. Available to U.S. citizens.

Application Requirements: Application, essay, photo, transcript. *Deadline:* varies.

Contact: OUM Wellness Works Scholarship Program
OUM Chiropractor Program
110 Westwood Place
Brentwood, TN 37027

PACERS FOUNDATION, INC.
http://www.pacersfoundation.org

LINDA CRAIG MEMORIAL SCHOLARSHIP PRESENTED BY ST. VINCENT SPORTS MEDICINE

Scholarship presented by St. Vincent Sports Medicine is for currently-enrolled juniors and seniors with declared majors of medicine, sports medicine, and/or physical therapy. Students must have completed at least 4 semesters and attend a school in Indiana. Minimum 3.0 GPA required.

Academic Fields/Career Goals: Health and Medical Sciences; Sports-related; Therapy/Rehabilitation.

Award: Scholarship for use in junior, senior, graduate, or postgraduate years; renewable. *Number:* 1–2. *Amount:* $2000.

Eligibility Requirements: Applicant must be enrolled or expecting to enroll full-time at a two-year or four-year institution or university. Applicant must have 3.0 GPA or higher. Available to U.S. citizens.

Application Requirements: Application, essay, references, transcript. *Deadline:* March 1.

Contact: Sarah Baird, Coordinator
Pacers Foundation, Inc.
125 South Pennsylvania Street
Indianapolis, IN 46204
Phone: 317-917-2864
Fax: 317-917-2599
E-mail: foundation@pacers.com

PHYSICIAN ASSISTANT FOUNDATION
http://www.aapa.org

PHYSICIAN ASSISTANT FOUNDATION ANNUAL SCHOLARSHIP

One-time award for student members of the American Academy of Physician Assistants enrolled in an ARC PA-accredited physician assistant program. Award based on financial need, academic achievement, and goals. Must submit two passport-type photographs for promotional reasons.

Academic Fields/Career Goals: Health and Medical Sciences.

Award: Scholarship for use in junior or senior years; not renewable. *Number:* 50–75. *Amount:* $2000.

Eligibility Requirements: Applicant must be enrolled or expecting to enroll full or part-time at a two-year or four-year institution or university. Applicant or parent of applicant must be member of American Academy of Physicians Assistants. Available to U.S. and non-U.S. citizens.

Application Requirements: Application, essay, financial need analysis, photo, transcript. *Deadline:* February 1.

Contact: PA Foundation Scholarship Committee
Physician Assistant Foundation
950 North Washington Street
Alexandria, VA 22304
Phone: 703-836-2276
Fax: 703-684-1924

PILOT INTERNATIONAL FOUNDATION
http://www.pilotinternational.org

PILOT INTERNATIONAL FOUNDATION RUBY NEWHALL MEMORIAL SCHOLARSHIP

Scholarship available to international students for study in the United States or Canada. Applicant must have visa or green card. Application deadline is February 15.

Academic Fields/Career Goals: Health and Medical Sciences; Nursing; Psychology; Special Education; Therapy/Rehabilitation.

Award: Scholarship for use in freshman, sophomore, junior, or senior years; not renewable. *Number:* 1. *Amount:* varies.

Eligibility Requirements: Applicant must be enrolled or expecting to enroll full or part-time at a two-year or four-year or technical institution. Applicant must have 3.0 GPA or higher. Available to Canadian and non-U.S. citizens.

Application Requirements: Application, essay, financial need analysis, references, self-addressed stamped envelope, transcript, visa or F1 status. *Deadline:* February 15.

Contact: Jennifer Overbay, Foundation Services Director
Pilot International Foundation
PO Box 4844
Macon, GA 31208-5600
Phone: 478-743-7403
Fax: 478-743-2173
E-mail: pifinfo@pilothq.org

PILOT INTERNATIONAL FOUNDATION SCHOLARSHIP PROGRAM

Scholarship program for undergraduate students preparing for a career helping those with brain related disorders or disabilities. Applicant must have visa or green card.

Academic Fields/Career Goals: Health and Medical Sciences; Nursing; Psychology; Special Education; Therapy/Rehabilitation.

Award: Scholarship for use in freshman, sophomore, junior, or senior years; not renewable. *Number:* 1. *Amount:* varies.

Eligibility Requirements: Applicant must be enrolled or expecting to enroll full or part-time at a two-year or four-year or technical

Pilot International Foundation (continued)

institution or university. Applicant must have 3.0 GPA or higher. Available to U.S. and non-U.S. citizens.

Application Requirements: Application, essay, financial need analysis, references, self-addressed stamped envelope, transcript, visa or F1 status. *Deadline:* February 15.

Contact: Jennifer Overbay, Foundation Services Director
Pilot International Foundation
PO Box 4844
Macon, GA 31208-5600
Phone: 478-743-7403
Fax: 478-743-2173
E-mail: pifinfo@pilothq.org

PILOT INTERNATIONAL FOUNDATION/LIFELINE SCHOLARSHIP PROGRAM

Scholarship program is for graduate or undergraduate students preparing for a second career, re-entering the job market, or obtaining additional training in their current field. The career path must pertain to assisting those with brain related disorders or disabilities. Applicant must have visa or green card.

Academic Fields/Career Goals: Health and Medical Sciences; Nursing; Psychology; Special Education; Therapy/Rehabilitation.

Award: Scholarship for use in freshman, sophomore, junior, senior, or graduate years; not renewable. *Number:* 1. *Amount:* varies.

Eligibility Requirements: Applicant must be enrolled or expecting to enroll full or part-time at a two-year or four-year or technical institution or university. Applicant must have 3.0 GPA or higher. Available to U.S. and non-U.S. citizens.

Application Requirements: Application, essay, financial need analysis, references, self-addressed stamped envelope, transcript, visa or F1 status. *Deadline:* February 15.

Contact: Jennifer Overbay, Foundation Services Director
Pilot International Foundation
PO Box 4844
Macon, GA 31208-5600
Phone: 478-743-7403
Fax: 478-743-2173
E-mail: pifinfo@pilothq.org

PNC BANK TRUST DEPARTMENT

H. FLETCHER BROWN SCHOLARSHIP
• See page 211

ROBERT WOOD JOHNSON FOUNDATION AND THE COLLEGE BOARD http://www.collegeboard.com/yes/fs/atc.html

YOUNG EPIDEMIOLOGY SCHOLARS COMPETITION

YES Competition offers college scholarship awards to high school juniors and seniors who conduct outstanding research projects that apply epidemiological methods of analysis to a health-related issue.

Academic Fields/Career Goals: Health and Medical Sciences.

Award: Scholarship for use in freshman year; not renewable. *Number:* up to 120. *Amount:* $15,000–$50,000.

Eligibility Requirements: Applicant must be high school student and planning to enroll or expecting to enroll full-time at an institution or university. Available to U.S. citizens.

Application Requirements: Application. *Deadline:* February 1.

Contact: Jennifer Topiel, Associate Director, Public Affairs
Robert Wood Johnson Foundation and the College Board
Young Epidemiology Scholars Competition
45 Columbus Avenue
New York, NY 10023-6992
Phone: 212-713-8183
Fax: 212-713-8184
E-mail: jtopiel@collegeboard.org

ROSCOE POUND INSTITUTE http://www.roscoepound.org

ELAINE OSBORNE JACOBSON AWARD FOR WOMEN WORKING IN HEALTH CARE LAW
• See page 318

SERTOMA INTERNATIONAL http://www.sertoma.org

SERTOMA COMMUNICATIVE DISORDERS SCHOLARSHIP PROGRAM
• See page 116

SIGMA XI, THE SCIENTIFIC RESEARCH SOCIETY http://www.sigmaxi.org

SIGMA XI GRANTS-IN-AID OF RESEARCH
• See page 84

SOCIETY FOR APPLIED ANTHROPOLOGY http://www.sfaa.net

PETER KONG-MING NEW STUDENT PRIZE

Prize awarded for SFAA's annual student research competition in the applied social and behavioral sciences. The issue of research question should be in the domain of health care or human services (broadly construed). The winner of the competition will receive a cash prize of $1000, a crystal trophy, and travel funds to attend the annual meeting of the SFAA. For more details, see Web site at http://www.sfaa.net

Academic Fields/Career Goals: Health and Medical Sciences; Social Sciences.

Award: Prize for use in freshman, sophomore, junior, senior, or graduate years; not renewable. *Number:* 1–3. *Amount:* $100–$1000.

Eligibility Requirements: Applicant must be enrolled or expecting to enroll full or part-time at a two-year or four-year institution or university. Available to U.S. and non-U.S. citizens.

Application Requirements: Application, applicant must enter a contest, manuscript. *Deadline:* December 31.

Contact: J.T. May, Executive Director
Society for Applied Anthropology
PO Box 2436
Oklahoma City, OK 73101-2436
Phone: 405-843-5113
Fax: 405-843-8553
E-mail: info@sfaa.net

SOCIETY OF NUCLEAR MEDICINE http://www.snm.org

PAUL COLE SCHOLARSHIP

One-time award for students of nuclear medicine technology at a two- or four-year institution. Academic merit considered. Minimum 2.5 GPA required. Application must be submitted by program director on behalf of the student. Please see Web site: http://www.snm.org for more information and application.

Academic Fields/Career Goals: Health and Medical Sciences; Nuclear Science.

Award: Scholarship for use in freshman, sophomore, junior, or senior years; not renewable. *Number:* 24. *Amount:* $1000.

Eligibility Requirements: Applicant must be enrolled or expecting to enroll full or part-time at a two-year or four-year institution or university. Applicant must have 2.5 GPA or higher. Available to U.S. and Canadian citizens.

Application Requirements: Application, essay, references, transcript. *Deadline:* October 15.

Contact: SNMTS Committee on Awards, Development Office
Society of Nuclear Medicine
1850 Samuel Morse Drive
Reston, VA 20190

SOCIETY OF TOXICOLOGY http://www.toxicology.org

MINORITY UNDERGRADUATE STUDENT AWARDS
• See page 142

SOUTHWEST STUDENT SERVICES CORPORATION
http://www.sssc.com/

ANNE LINDEMAN MEMORIAL SCHOLARSHIP
• See page 142

SUBURBAN HOSPITAL HEALTHCARE SYSTEM
http://www.suburbanhospital.org

SUBURBAN HOSPITAL HEALTHCARE SYSTEM SCHOLARSHIP

Award to students pursuing heath care-related careers. Must be resident of Maryland, Virginia, Washington, D.C. Employment/volunteer experience in a health care-related environment is preferred. Minimum 2.5 GPA required. Deadline: April 21.

Academic Fields/Career Goals: Health and Medical Sciences; Nursing; Therapy/Rehabilitation.

Award: Scholarship for use in junior or senior years; not renewable. *Number:* varies. *Amount:* up to $5000.

Eligibility Requirements: Applicant must be enrolled or expecting to enroll full or part-time at a two-year or four-year institution or university; resident of District of Columbia, Maryland, or Virginia and studying in District of Columbia, Maryland, or Virginia. Applicant must have 2.5 GPA or higher. Available to U.S. citizens.

Application Requirements: Application, essay, interview, references, self-addressed stamped envelope, transcript, proof of enrollment in good standing. *Deadline:* April 21.

Contact: Charmaine Williams, Manager, Employee Relations
Suburban Hospital Healthcare System
Human Resources Department, 8600 Old Georgetown Road
Bethesda, MD 20814-1497
Phone: 301-896-3795
Fax: 301-897-1339

TEXAS HIGHER EDUCATION COORDINATING BOARD
http://www.collegefortexans.com

OUTSTANDING RURAL SCHOLAR PROGRAM

Award enables rural communities to sponsor a student going into health professions. The students must agree to work in that community once they receive their degree. Must be Texas resident entering a Texas institution on a full-time basis. Must demonstrate financial need.

Academic Fields/Career Goals: Health and Medical Sciences.

Award: Scholarship for use in freshman, sophomore, junior, or senior years; renewable. *Number:* 1. *Amount:* varies.

Eligibility Requirements: Applicant must be enrolled or expecting to enroll full-time at a four-year institution or university; resident of Texas and studying in Texas. Applicant must have 3.0 GPA or higher. Available to U.S. citizens.

Application Requirements: Application, financial need analysis, transcript, nomination. *Deadline:* varies.

Contact: Office of Rural Community Affairs
Texas Higher Education Coordinating Board
PO Drawer 1708
Austin, TX 78767
Phone: 512-479-8891
E-mail: grantinfo@thecb.state.tx.us

TRIANGLE COMMUNITY FOUNDATION
http://www.trianglecf.org

GERTRUDE B. ELION MENTORED MEDICAL STUDENT RESEARCH AWARDS

An annual award of $10,000 to women, enrolled as full-time students, and should have completed at least one year of medical school prior to the start of the award.

Academic Fields/Career Goals: Health and Medical Sciences.

Award: Prize for use in sophomore, junior, or senior years. *Amount:* $10,000.

Eligibility Requirements: Applicant must be enrolled or expecting to enroll full-time at a four-year institution or university and female. Available to U.S. citizens.

Application Requirements: Application, resume, references. *Deadline:* April 20.

Contact: Linda Depo, Philanthropic Services Associate
Triangle Community Foundation
4813 Emperor Boulevard
Cambridge Hall
Durham, NC 27703
Phone: 919-474-8370
Fax: 919-949-9208
E-mail: linda@trianglecf.org

TUBERCULOSIS ASSOCIATION OF OHIO COUNTY
http://www.tboc.org

DR. WILLIAM J. STEGER SCHOLARSHIP AWARDS

Award for students who are residents of Ohio, Marshall, Brooke, Wetzel, Tyler, and Hancock counties in West Virginia and Belmont county in Ohio. Must be enrolled in respiratory care programs at designated West Virginia institutions. Submit application, financial aid forms, and references. Write or email for more information. Scholarship reverts to loan if students do not practice respiratory therapy in designated areas.

Academic Fields/Career Goals: Health and Medical Sciences; Therapy/Rehabilitation.

Award: Scholarship for use in freshman, sophomore, junior, or senior years; not renewable. *Number:* varies. *Amount:* up to $2000.

Eligibility Requirements: Applicant must be enrolled or expecting to enroll full-time at a two-year or four-year institution or university; resident of Ohio or West Virginia and studying in West Virginia. Available to U.S. citizens.

Application Requirements: Application, financial need analysis, references, transcript. *Deadline:* Continuous.

Contact: Scholarship Director
Tuberculosis Association of Ohio County
90 16th Street
Wheeling, WV 26003
Phone: 304-233-0640

UNITED NEGRO COLLEGE FUND
http://www.uncf.org

RAYMOND W. CANNON MEMORIAL SCHOLARSHIP PROGRAM

Must be nominated by financial aid director at the UNCF college. Available to students majoring in pharmacy or pre-law who have demonstrated leadership in high school and college. Prospective applicants should complete the Student Profile found at Web site: http://www.uncf.org.

Academic Fields/Career Goals: Health and Medical Sciences; Law/Legal Services.

Award: Scholarship for use in junior year; not renewable. *Amount:* $2000–$5000.

Eligibility Requirements: Applicant must be Black (non-Hispanic) and enrolled or expecting to enroll at a four-year institution or university. Applicant must have 2.5 GPA or higher. Available to U.S. citizens.

Application Requirements: Application, financial need analysis. *Deadline:* Continuous.

Contact: Program Services Department
United Negro College Fund
8260 Willow Oaks Corporate Drive
Fairfax, VA 22031

SODEXHO SCHOLARSHIP

Award available to incoming freshmen attending historically black colleges and universities. Must major in nursing, social work, political science, community development, or other related health disciplines. Must demonstrate leadership abilities. Minimum GPA of 3.0. Please visit Web site for more information: http://www.uncf.org

Academic Fields/Career Goals: Health and Medical Sciences; Nursing; Political Science; Social Services.

Award: Scholarship for use in freshman, sophomore, junior, or senior years; renewable. *Number:* varies. *Amount:* up to $3500.

Eligibility Requirements: Applicant must be Black (non-Hispanic); high school student and planning to enroll or expecting to enroll at a four-year institution or university. Applicant must have 3.0 GPA or higher. Available to U.S. citizens.

United Negro College Fund (continued)

Application Requirements: Application, financial need analysis, references, transcript, FAFSA, Student Aid Report (SAR). *Deadline:* August 22.

> **Contact:** Annette Singletary, Senior Program Manager
> United Negro College Fund
> 8260 Willow Oaks Corporate Drive
> Fairfax, VA 22031
> *Phone:* 800-331-2244

WYETH SCHOLARSHIP
• *See page 142*

UNITED STATES PUBLIC HEALTH SERVICE - HEALTH RESOURCES AND SERVICES ADMINISTRATION, BUREAU OF HEALTH
http://bhpr.hrsa.gov/dsa

HEALTH RESOURCES AND SERVICES ADMINISTRATION-BUREAU OF HEALTH PROFESSIONS SCHOLARSHIPS FOR DISADVANTAGED STUDENTS
• *See page 211*

UNIVERSITY OF MEDICINE AND DENTISTRY OF NJ SCHOOL OF OSTEOPATHIC MEDICINE
http://www.umdnj.edu

MARTIN LUTHER KING PHYSICIAN/DENTIST SCHOLARSHIPS
• *See page 211*

NEW JERSEY EDUCATIONAL OPPORTUNITY FUND GRANTS
• *See page 212*

VESALIUS TRUST FOR VISUAL COMMUNICATION IN THE HEALTH SCIENCES
http://www.vesalius.org

CHARLOTTE S. HOLT FUND

Scholarship awarded annually to students who have completed one year of their medical illustration curriculum. Applicants are judged on their background, education and support personnel as well as their graduate research project proposal.

Academic Fields/Career Goals: Health and Medical Sciences.

Award: Scholarship for use in sophomore, junior, senior, or graduate years. *Number:* 1.

Eligibility Requirements: Applicant must be enrolled or expecting to enroll at a four-year institution or university. Available to U.S. citizens.

Application Requirements: Application, financial need analysis, portfolio, test scores, transcript. *Deadline:* varies.

> **Contact:** Lisa Warren, Executive Director
> Vesalius Trust for Visual Communication in the Health Sciences
> 20751 West Chartwell Drive
> Kildeer, IL 60047
> *Phone:* 847-540-8671
> *Fax:* 847-540-8681
> *E-mail:* vesaliustrust@aol.com

STUDENT RESEARCH SCHOLARSHIP

Scholarships available to students currently enrolled in a undergraduate or graduate school program of bio-communications (medical illustration) who have completed one full year of the curriculum. Deadline is the first Friday of November.

Academic Fields/Career Goals: Health and Medical Sciences.

Award: Scholarship for use in sophomore, junior, senior, or graduate years; not renewable. *Number:* 15. *Amount:* $640–$2240.

Eligibility Requirements: Applicant must be enrolled or expecting to enroll full or part-time at a four-year institution or university. Available to U.S. and non-U.S. citizens.

Application Requirements: Application, autobiography, portfolio, references, transcript. *Deadline:* varies.

> **Contact:** Wendy Hiller Gee, VT Student Grants and Scholarships, c/o Krames
> Vesalius Trust for Visual Communication in the Health Sciences
> 1100 Grundy Lane
> San Bruno, CA 94066
> *Phone:* 650-244-4320
> *E-mail:* wendy.hillergee@krames.com

VIRGINIA BUSINESS AND PROFESSIONAL WOMEN'S FOUNDATION
http://www.bpwva.org

WOMEN IN SCIENCE AND TECHNOLOGY SCHOLARSHIP
• *See page 143*

WASHINGTON HOSPITAL HEALTHCARE SYSTEM
http://www.whhs.com

MEDICAL STAFF SCHOLARSHIP

Scholarship awarded to high school students who are pursuing careers in the health sciences field. Applications are accepted between January and mid-March of each year.

Academic Fields/Career Goals: Health and Medical Sciences.

Award: Scholarship for use in freshman year. *Number:* 2. *Amount:* $1500.

Eligibility Requirements: Applicant must be high school student; age 22 or under and planning to enroll or expecting to enroll at an institution or university. Applicant must have 2.5 GPA or higher. Available to U.S. citizens.

Application Requirements: Application, interview, references, transcript. *Deadline:* March 15.

> **Contact:**
> *Phone:* 510-791-3446

WASHINGTON STATE ENVIRONMENTAL HEALTH ASSOCIATION
http://www.wseha.org/

CIND M. TRESER MEMORIAL SCHOLARSHIP PROGRAM

Scholarships are available for undergraduate students pursuing a major in environmental health or related science and intending to practice environmental health. Must be a resident of Washington. For more details see Web site: http://www.wseha.org.

Academic Fields/Career Goals: Health and Medical Sciences.

Award: Scholarship for use in freshman, sophomore, junior, or senior years; not renewable. *Number:* 1. *Amount:* $1000.

Eligibility Requirements: Applicant must be enrolled or expecting to enroll full-time at a two-year or four-year institution or university and resident of Washington. Available to U.S. citizens.

Application Requirements: Application, references, transcript. *Deadline:* March 15.

> **Contact:** Charles Treser, WSEHA Scholarships Committee Chair
> Washington State Environmental Health Association
> 3045 Northwest 57th Street
> Seattle, WA 98107
> *Phone:* 206-616-2097
> *Fax:* 206-543-8123
> *E-mail:* ctreser@u.washington.edu

ZETA PHI BETA SORORITY, INC. NATIONAL EDUCATIONAL FOUNDATION
http://www.zphib1920.org

S. EVELYN LEWIS MEMORIAL SCHOLARSHIP IN MEDICAL HEALTH SCIENCES

Scholarships available for graduate or undergraduate women enrolled in a program leading to a degree in medicine or health sciences. Must be a full-time student. See Web site for information and application: http://www.zphib1920.org

Academic Fields/Career Goals: Health and Medical Sciences.

Award: Scholarship for use in freshman, sophomore, junior, senior, or graduate years; not renewable. *Number:* varies. *Amount:* $500–$1000.

Eligibility Requirements: Applicant must be enrolled or expecting to enroll full-time at a four-year institution or university and female. Available to U.S. citizens.

Application Requirements: Application, essay, references, transcript, proof of enrollment. *Deadline:* February 1.

Contact: Cheryl Williams, National Second Vice President
Zeta Phi Beta Sorority, Inc. National Educational Foundation
1734 New Hampshire Avenue, NW
Washington, DC 20009-2595
Fax: 318-631-4028
E-mail: 2ndanti@zphib1920.org

HEALTH INFORMATION MANAGEMENT/TECHNOLOGY

AMERICAN HEALTH INFORMATION MANAGEMENT ASSOCIATION/FOUNDATION OF RESEARCH AND EDUCATION   http://www.ahima.org

FOUNDATION OF RESEARCH AND EDUCATION UNDERGRADUATE MERIT SCHOLARSHIPS

Multiple scholarships for undergraduate Health Information Management students. One standard application for all available scholarships. Applicant must have a minimum cumulative GPA of 3.0 (out of 4.0) or 4.0 (out of 5.0). Applications can be downloaded at http://www.ahima.org. Must be a member of AHIMA.

Academic Fields/Career Goals: Health Information Management/Technology.

Award: Scholarship for use in freshman, sophomore, junior, senior, graduate, or postgraduate years; not renewable. *Number:* 40–60. *Amount:* $1000–$5000.

Eligibility Requirements: Applicant must be enrolled or expecting to enroll full or part-time at a two-year or four-year or technical institution or university. Applicant or parent of applicant must be member of American Health Information Management Association. Applicant must have 3.0 GPA or higher. Available to U.S. and non-U.S. citizens.

Application Requirements: Application, essay, references, transcript. *Deadline:* April 28.

Contact: Donor Relations and Grants Associate
American Health Information Management Association/ Foundation of Research and Education
233 North Michigan Avenue, Suite 2150
Chicago, IL 60601-5800
Phone: 312-233-1100
E-mail: fore@ahima.org

AMERICAN SOCIETY OF RADIOLOGIC TECHNOLOGISTS EDUCATION AND RESEARCH FOUNDATION   http://www.asrt.org

JEANETTE C. AND ISADORE N. STERN SCHOLARSHIP
• See page 317

SIEMENS SCHOLAR AWARD
• See page 317

BETHESDA LUTHERAN HOMES AND SERVICES, INC.   http://www.blhs.org

DEVELOPMENTAL DISABILITIES SCHOLASTIC ACHIEVEMENT SCHOLARSHIP FOR LUTHERAN COLLEGE STUDENTS
• See page 208

CANADIAN SOCIETY FOR MEDICAL LABORATORY SCIENCE   http://www.csmls.org

E.V. BOOTH SCHOLARSHIP AWARD
• See page 317

CONGRESSIONAL BLACK CAUCUS SPOUSES PROGRAM   http://www.cbcfinc.org

CONGRESSIONAL BLACK CAUCUS SPOUSES HEALTH INITIATIVES
• See page 318

DEVRY, INC.   http://www.devry.edu

CISCO SCHOLARSHIP-HIGH SCHOOL GRADUATES
• See page 260

HEALTHCARE INFORMATION AND MANAGEMENT SYSTEMS SOCIETY FOUNDATION   http://www.himss.org

HIMSS FOUNDATION SCHOLARSHIP PROGRAM
• See page 318

MARIN EDUCATION FUND   http://www.marineducationfund.org

GOLDMAN FAMILY FUND, NEW LEADER SCHOLARSHIP
• See page 210

NATIONAL ATHLETIC TRAINERS' ASSOCIATION RESEARCH AND EDUCATION FOUNDATION   http://www.natafoundation.org

NATIONAL ATHLETIC TRAINER'S ASSOCIATION RESEARCH AND EDUCATION FOUNDATION SCHOLARSHIP PROGRAM
• See page 329

NATIONAL STRENGTH AND CONDITIONING ASSOCIATION   http://www.nsca-lift.org

GNC NUTRITION RESEARCH GRANT

GNC sponsors this nutrition based research grant. The purpose of the project must fall within the mission of the NSCA. Applicant must submit: cover letter, abstract, proposal, itemized budget, "Human Subject Consent Form," and proof of institutional review board approval, and abbreviated vitae of faculty co-investigator. Please refer to Web site for further details: http://www.nsca-lift.org

Academic Fields/Career Goals: Health Information Management/ Technology; Sports-related; Therapy/Rehabilitation.

Award: Grant for use in junior, senior, or graduate years; not renewable. *Number:* 1. *Amount:* up to $2500.

Eligibility Requirements: Applicant must be enrolled or expecting to enroll full-time at a four-year institution or university. Applicant or parent of applicant must be member of National Strength and Conditioning Association. Available to U.S. and non-U.S. citizens.

Application Requirements: Application, references, transcript, abstract, proposal, itemized budget, time schedule, consent form, vitae of faculty co-investigator. *Deadline:* March 15.

Contact: Karri Baker, Membership Director
National Strength and Conditioning Association
PO Box 9908
Colorado Springs, CO 80932-0908
Phone: 719-632-6722
Fax: 719-632-6367
E-mail: foundation@nsca-lift.org

NATIONAL STRENGTH AND CONDITIONING ASSOCIATION CHALLENGE SCHOLARSHIP

One-time award for undergraduate or graduate students in strength and conditioning-related fields. Must be NSCA member for at least one year prior to the application deadline of March 15. Submit resume, cover letter, and 500-word essay outlining course of study, career goals, and financial need. Please see Web site for further details: http://www.nsca-lift.org

Academic Fields/Career Goals: Health Information Management/ Technology; Sports-related; Therapy/Rehabilitation.

Award: Scholarship for use in freshman, sophomore, junior, senior, or graduate years; not renewable. *Number:* 1–12. *Amount:* $1000.

Eligibility Requirements: Applicant must be enrolled or expecting to enroll full-time at a two-year or four-year institution or university. Applicant or parent of applicant must be member of National Strength and Conditioning Association. Available to U.S. and non-U.S. citizens.

National Strength and Conditioning Association (continued)

Application Requirements: Application, essay, financial need analysis, photo, resume, references, transcript. *Deadline:* March 15.

Contact: Karri Baker, Membership Director
National Strength and Conditioning Association
1885 Bob Johnson Drive
Colorado Springs, CO 80906-4000
Phone: 719-632-6722
Fax: 719-632-6367
E-mail: foundation@nsca-lift.org

NATIONAL STRENGTH AND CONDITIONING ASSOCIATION HIGH SCHOOL SCHOLARSHIP

One-time award to high school seniors preparing to enter college. Must demonstrate acceptance into an accredited institution and intention to graduate with a degree in a strength and conditioning field. Minimum 3.0 GPA required. Must be a member of NCSA. Please see Web site for further details: http://www.nsca-lift.org

Academic Fields/Career Goals: Health Information Management/Technology; Sports-related; Therapy/Rehabilitation.

Award: Scholarship for use in freshman year; not renewable. *Number:* 1–2. *Amount:* $1000.

Eligibility Requirements: Applicant must be high school student and planning to enroll or expecting to enroll full-time at a four-year institution or university. Applicant or parent of applicant must be member of National Strength and Conditioning Association. Applicant must have 3.0 GPA or higher. Available to U.S. and non-U.S. citizens.

Application Requirements: Application, essay, references, transcript, letter of acceptance. *Deadline:* March 15.

Contact: Karri Baker, Membership Director
National Strength and Conditioning Association
1885 Bob Johnson Drive
Colorado Springs, CO 80906-4000
Phone: 719-632-6722
Fax: 719-632-6367
E-mail: foundation@nsca-lift.org

NATIONAL STRENGTH AND CONDITIONING ASSOCIATION UNDERGRADUATE RESEARCH GRANT

One-time award for undergraduate research in strength and conditioning. Maximum award is $1500 (overhead costs are not supported). The purpose of the project should fall within the mission of the NSCA. Must be a NSCA member. Application deadline is March 15. Please refer to Web site for further details: http://www.nsca-lift.org

Academic Fields/Career Goals: Health Information Management/Technology; Sports-related; Therapy/Rehabilitation.

Award: Grant for use in freshman, sophomore, junior, or senior years; not renewable. *Number:* 1–3. *Amount:* up to $1500.

Eligibility Requirements: Applicant must be enrolled or expecting to enroll full-time at a four-year institution or university. Applicant or parent of applicant must be member of National Strength and Conditioning Association. Available to U.S. and non-U.S. citizens.

Application Requirements: Application, essay, financial need analysis, photo, resume, references, transcript, proposal, abstract, itemized budget. *Deadline:* March 15.

Contact: Karri Baker, Membership Director
National Strength and Conditioning Association
1885 Bob Johnson Drive
Colorado Springs, CO 80906-4000
Phone: 719-632-6722
Fax: 719-632-6367
E-mail: foundation@nsca-lift.org

NATIONAL STRENGTH AND CONDITIONING ASSOCIATION WOMEN'S SCHOLARSHIP

This scholarship is designed to encourage women, ages 17 and older, to enter into the field of strength and conditioning. Please refer to Web site for further details: http://www.nsca-lift.org

Academic Fields/Career Goals: Health Information Management/Technology; Sports-related; Therapy/Rehabilitation.

Award: Scholarship for use in freshman, sophomore, junior, senior, or graduate years; not renewable. *Number:* 1–2. *Amount:* $1000.

Eligibility Requirements: Applicant must be age 17; enrolled or expecting to enroll full-time at a two-year or four-year institution or university and female. Applicant or parent of applicant must be member of National Strength and Conditioning Association. Available to U.S. and non-U.S. citizens.

Application Requirements: Application, essay, resume, references, transcript. *Deadline:* March 15.

Contact: Karri Baker, Membership Director
National Strength and Conditioning Association
1885 Bob Johnson Drive
Colorado Springs, CO 80906-4000
Phone: 719-632-6722
Fax: 719-632-6367
E-mail: foundation@nsca-lift.org

NSCA MINORITY SCHOLARSHIP

This scholarship is designed to encourage minorities, ages 17 and older, to enter into the field of strength and conditioning. Please refer to Web site for further details: http://www.nsca-lift.org

Academic Fields/Career Goals: Health Information Management/Technology; Sports-related; Therapy/Rehabilitation.

Award: Scholarship for use in freshman, sophomore, junior, senior, or graduate years; not renewable. *Number:* 1–2. *Amount:* $1000.

Eligibility Requirements: Applicant must be American Indian/Alaska Native, Asian/Pacific Islander, Black (non-Hispanic), or Hispanic; age 17 and enrolled or expecting to enroll full-time at a two-year or four-year institution or university. Applicant or parent of applicant must be member of National Strength and Conditioning Association. Available to U.S. and non-U.S. citizens.

Application Requirements: Application, essay, resume, references, transcript. *Deadline:* March 15.

Contact: Karri Baker, Membership Director
National Strength and Conditioning Association
PO Box 9908
Colorado Springs, CO 80932-0908
Phone: 719-632-6722
Fax: 719-632-6367
E-mail: foundation@nsca-lift.org

POWER SYSTEMS PROFESSIONAL SCHOLARSHIP

One-time award for students in pursuit of a career as a strength and conditioning coach. Submit letter of application, resume, transcripts, and 500-word essay outlining career goals and objectives. Must be a member of National Strength and Conditioning Association. Please refer to Web site for further details: http://www.nsca-lift.org

Academic Fields/Career Goals: Health Information Management/Technology; Sports-related; Therapy/Rehabilitation.

Award: Scholarship for use in freshman, sophomore, junior, senior, or graduate years; not renewable. *Number:* 1. *Amount:* $1000.

Eligibility Requirements: Applicant must be enrolled or expecting to enroll full-time at a four-year institution or university. Applicant or parent of applicant must be member of National Strength and Conditioning Association. Available to U.S. and non-U.S. citizens.

Application Requirements: Application, essay, photo, resume, references, transcript. *Deadline:* March 15.

Contact: Karri Baker, Membership Director
National Strength and Conditioning Association
1885 Bob Johnson Drive
Colorado Springs, CO 80906-4000
Phone: 719-632-6722
Fax: 719-632-6367
E-mail: foundation@nsca-lift.org

WASHINGTON HOSPITAL HEALTHCARE SYSTEM
http://www.whhs.com

SERVICE LEAGUE VOLUNTEER SCHOLARSHIP

Scholarship awarded to students who are pursuing studies in a health-related field. Must be a full time student. Deadline is April 1.

Academic Fields/Career Goals: Health Information Management/Technology.

Award: Scholarship for use in freshman, sophomore, junior, or senior years; renewable. *Number:* 2. *Amount:* $1000.

Eligibility Requirements: Applicant must be age 22 or under and enrolled or expecting to enroll full-time at a four-year institution or university. Applicant must have 2.5 GPA or higher. Available to U.S. citizens.

Application Requirements: Application, interview, references, transcript. *Deadline:* April 1.

Contact: Dr. Jacob Eapen, Secretary
Washington Hospital Healthcare System
2000 Mowry Avenue
Fremont, CA 94538
Phone: 510-491-3417
Fax: 510-491-3496

HEATING, AIR-CONDITIONING, AND REFRIGERATION MECHANICS

AMERICAN SOCIETY OF HEATING, REFRIGERATING, AND AIR CONDITIONING ENGINEERS, INC.
http://www.ashrae.org

ALWIN B. NEWTON SCHOLARSHIP FUND
• See page 242

AMERICAN SOCIETY OF HEATING, REFRIGERATION, AND AIR CONDITIONING ENGINEERING TECHNOLOGY SCHOLARSHIP
• See page 90

ASHRAE MEMORIAL SCHOLARSHIP
• See page 251

ASHRAE REGION IV BENNY BOOTLE SCHOLARSHIP
• See page 252

ASHRAE REGION VIII SCHOLARSHIP
• See page 252

ASHRAE SCHOLARSHIPS
• See page 252

DUANE HANSON SCHOLARSHIP
• See page 285

HENRY ADAMS SCHOLARSHIP
• See page 252

REUBEN TRANE SCHOLARSHIP
• See page 242

HISPANIC COLLEGE FUND, INC.
http://www.hispanicfund.org

EL NUEVO CONSTRUCTOR SCHOLARSHIP PROGRAM
• See page 99

INSTRUMENTATION, SYSTEMS, AND AUTOMATION SOCIETY (ISA)
http://www.isa.org

INSTRUMENTATION, SYSTEMS, AND AUTOMATION SOCIETY (ISA) SCHOLARSHIP PROGRAM
• See page 123

MIDWEST ROOFING CONTRACTORS ASSOCIATION
http://www.mrca.org

MRCA FOUNDATION SCHOLARSHIP PROGRAM
• See page 94

PLUMBING-HEATING-COOLING CONTRACTORS ASSOCIATION EDUCATION FOUNDATION
http://www.phccweb.org

BRADFORD WHITE CORPORATION SCHOLARSHIP
• See page 102

DELTA FAUCET COMPANY SCHOLARSHIP PROGRAM
• See page 102

PHCC EDUCATIONAL FOUNDATION NEED-BASED SCHOLARSHIP
• See page 102

PHCC EDUCATIONAL FOUNDATION SCHOLARSHIP PROGRAM
• See page 103

PROFESSIONAL CONSTRUCTION ESTIMATORS ASSOCIATION
http://www.pcea.org

TED WILSON MEMORIAL SCHOLARSHIP FOUNDATION
• See page 212

SOUTH DAKOTA RETAILERS ASSOCIATION
http://www.sdra.org

SOUTH DAKOTA RETAILERS ASSOCIATION SCHOLARSHIP PROGRAM
• See page 69

HISTORIC PRESERVATION AND CONSERVATION

AMERICAN SCHOOL OF CLASSICAL STUDIES AT ATHENS
http://www.ascsa.edu.gr

ASCSA SUMMER SESSIONS OPEN SCHOLARSHIPS
• See page 88

COSTUME SOCIETY OF AMERICA
http://www.costumesocietyamerica.com

ADELE FILENE TRAVEL AWARD
• See page 105

STELLA BLUM RESEARCH GRANT
• See page 105

GEORGIA TRUST FOR HISTORIC PRESERVATION
http://www.georgiatrust.org

GEORGIA TRUST FOR HISTORIC PRESERVATION SCHOLARSHIP

Each year, the Trust awards two $1000 scholarships to encourage the study of historic preservation and related fields. Recipients are chosen on the basis of leadership and academic achievement. Applicants must be residents of Georgia enrolled in an accredited Georgia institution. A GPA of 3.0 is required.

Academic Fields/Career Goals: Historic Preservation and Conservation.

Award: Scholarship for use in freshman, sophomore, junior, senior, or graduate years; not renewable. *Number:* 2. *Amount:* $1000.

Eligibility Requirements: Applicant must be enrolled or expecting to enroll full-time at a four-year institution or university; resident of Georgia and studying in Georgia. Applicant must have 3.0 GPA or higher. Available to U.S. citizens.

Application Requirements: Application, essay, resume, references, transcript. *Deadline:* February 1.

Contact: Scholarship Coordinator
Georgia Trust for Historic Preservation
1516 Peachtree Street, NW
Atlanta, GA 30309
Phone: 404-881-9980
Fax: 404-875-2205
E-mail: info@georgiatrust.org

HARRY S. TRUMAN LIBRARY INSTITUTE
http://www.trumanlibrary.org

HARRY S. TRUMAN LIBRARY INSTITUTE UNDERGRADUATE STUDENT GRANT
See page 217

NATIONAL SOCIETY DAUGHTERS OF THE AMERICAN REVOLUTION
http://www.dar.org

NATIONAL SOCIETY DAUGHTERS OF THE AMERICAN REVOLUTION J. E. CALDWELL CENTENNIAL SCHOLARSHIP

Nonrenewable award for graduate students pursuing an education in historic preservation. Based on academic excellence, commitment to field of study, and need. Applicant must be U.S. citizen and be sponsored by DAR chapter (need not be member). Must submit self-addressed stamped envelope to be considered. Deadline is February 15.

Academic Fields/Career Goals: Historic Preservation and Conservation; History.

Award: Scholarship for use in freshman, sophomore, junior, senior, or graduate years; not renewable. *Number:* 2. *Amount:* $2000.

Eligibility Requirements: Applicant must be enrolled or expecting to enroll at a four-year institution or university. Applicant must have 3.5 GPA or higher. Available to U.S. citizens.

Application Requirements: Application, essay, financial need analysis, references, self-addressed stamped envelope, transcript. *Deadline:* February 15.

Contact: Committee Services Office, Scholarship
National Society Daughters of the American Revolution
1775 D Street, NW
Washington, DC 20006-5392

HISTORY

AMERICAN HISTORICAL ASSOCIATION
http://www.historians.org

WESLEY-LOGAN PRIZE
• *See page 73*

AMERICAN PHILOLOGICAL ASSOCIATION
http://www.apaclassics.org

MINORITY STUDENT SUMMER SCHOLARSHIP
• *See page 109*

AMERICAN SCHOOL OF CLASSICAL STUDIES AT ATHENS
http://www.ascsa.edu.gr

ASCSA SUMMER SESSIONS OPEN SCHOLARSHIPS
• *See page 88*

CANADIAN INSTITUTE OF UKRAINIAN STUDIES
http://www.ualberta.ca/cius/

LEO J. KRYSA UNDERGRADUATE SCHOLARSHIP
• *See page 104*

COLLEGEBOUND FOUNDATION
http://www.collegeboundfoundation.org

DECATUR H. MILLER SCHOLARSHIP

Award for Baltimore City public high school graduates. Please see Web site: http://www.collegeboundfoundation.org for complete information on application process. Must major in political science, history, or pre-law. Minimum GPA of 3.0, SAT score of 1100. Preference given to students who plan to enter law school. Must submit CollegeBound Competitive Scholarship/Last-Dollar Grant Application.

Academic Fields/Career Goals: History; Law/Legal Services; Political Science.

Award: Scholarship for use in freshman, sophomore, junior, or senior years; renewable. *Number:* 1. *Amount:* $1500.

Eligibility Requirements: Applicant must be enrolled or expecting to enroll full-time at a two-year or four-year institution or university and resident of Maryland. Applicant must have 3.0 GPA or higher. Available to U.S. citizens.

Application Requirements: Application, financial need analysis, references, transcript, financial aid award letters, Student Aid Report (SAR). *Deadline:* March 19.

Contact: April Bell, Associate Program Director
CollegeBound Foundation
300 Water Street, Suite 300
Baltimore, MD 21202
Phone: 410-783-2905 Ext. 208
Fax: 410-727-5786
E-mail: abell@collegeboundfoundation.org

COSTUME SOCIETY OF AMERICA
http://www.costumesocietyamerica.com

ADELE FILENE TRAVEL AWARD
• *See page 105*

STELLA BLUM RESEARCH GRANT
• *See page 105*

HARRY S. TRUMAN LIBRARY INSTITUTE
http://www.trumanlibrary.org

HARRY S. TRUMAN LIBRARY INSTITUTE UNDERGRADUATE STUDENT GRANT
• *See page 217*

HARVARD TRAVELLERS CLUB

HARVARD TRAVELLERS CLUB GRANTS
• *See page 96*

NATIONAL FEDERATION OF THE BLIND
http://www.nfb.org

MICHAEL AND MARIE MARUCCI SCHOLARSHIP
• *See page 312*

NATIONAL SOCIETY DAUGHTERS OF THE AMERICAN REVOLUTION
http://www.dar.org

NATIONAL SOCIETY DAUGHTERS OF THE AMERICAN REVOLUTION AMERICAN HISTORY SCHOLARSHIP

For graduating high school seniors planning to major in U.S. history at a four-year institution. Must submit a DAR sponsorship letter from local chapter and financial need form from parents. Application deadline: February 1. Merit-based. Must submit self-addressed stamped envelope to be considered. Contact state chairman.

Academic Fields/Career Goals: History.

Award: Scholarship for use in freshman, sophomore, junior, or senior years; renewable. *Number:* 1–3. *Amount:* up to $2000.

Eligibility Requirements: Applicant must be high school student and planning to enroll or expecting to enroll at a four-year institution. Applicant or parent of applicant must be member of Daughters of the American Revolution. Applicant must have 3.0 GPA or higher. Available to U.S. and non-U.S. citizens.

Application Requirements: Application, essay, financial need analysis, references, self-addressed stamped envelope, test scores, transcript. *Deadline:* February 1.

Contact: State Chairman, DAR Scholarship
National Society Daughters of the American Revolution
1776 D Street, NW
Washington, DC 20006-5392
Phone: 202-879-3292 Ext. 292

NATIONAL SOCIETY DAUGHTERS OF THE AMERICAN REVOLUTION ENID HALL GRISWOLD MEMORIAL SCHOLARSHIP
• *See page 217*

NATIONAL SOCIETY DAUGHTERS OF THE AMERICAN REVOLUTION J. E. CALDWELL CENTENNIAL SCHOLARSHIP
• *See page 338*

NEW JERSEY HISTORICAL COMMISSION
http://www.state.nj.us/state/history/grants.html

RICHARD G. MCCORMICK PRIZE

Award to the author of an outstanding book on New Jersey history published during the preceding two years. Offered only in odd-numbered years. Nomination form is on the Web site. Must be nominated.

Academic Fields/Career Goals: History.

Award: Prize for use in freshman, sophomore, junior, senior, graduate, or postgraduate years; not renewable. *Number:* 1. *Amount:* $1000.

Eligibility Requirements: Applicant must be enrolled or expecting to enroll at an institution or university. Available to U.S. citizens.

Application Requirements: Application, nomination, 1 copy of book. *Deadline:* January 2.

Contact: Mary Murrin, Director, Grants Program
New Jersey Historical Commission
Attention: Grants and Prizes
225 W State Street, PO Box 305
Trenton, NJ 08625-0305
Phone: 609-984-0954
Fax: 609-633-8168
E-mail: mary.murrin@sos.state.nj.us

ORGANIZATION OF AMERICAN HISTORIANS
http://www.oah.org

BINKLEY-STEPHENSON AWARD
• *See page 85*

PHI ALPHA THETA HISTORY HONOR SOCIETY, INC.
http://www.phialphatheta.org

PHI ALPHA THETA PAPER PRIZES

$300 prize for best graduate student paper, $250 prize for best undergraduate paper, and four $250 prizes for either graduate or undergraduate papers. All applicants must be members of Phi Alpha Theta. Deadline is July 1.

Academic Fields/Career Goals: History.

Award: Prize for use in freshman, sophomore, junior, senior, or graduate years; not renewable. *Number:* 6. *Amount:* $250–$300.

Eligibility Requirements: Applicant must be enrolled or expecting to enroll full-time at a four-year institution or university. Applicant must have 3.0 GPA or higher. Available to U.S. and non-U.S. citizens.

Application Requirements: Applicant must enter a contest, essay, references. *Deadline:* July 1.

Contact: Dr. Clayton Drees
Phi Alpha Theta History Honor Society, Inc.
1584 Wesleyan Drive
Norfolk, VA 23502-5599
E-mail: cdrees@vwc.edu

PHI ALPHA THETA WORLD HISTORY ASSOCIATION PAPER PRIZE

One undergraduate and one graduate-level prize for papers examining any historical issue with global implications (for example: exchange or interchange of cultures, comparison of civilizations or cultures). This is a joint award with the World History Association. Must be a member of the World History Association or Phi Alpha Theta. Paper must have been composed while enrolled at an accredited college or university. Must send in 2 copies of paper along with professor's letter. Deadline is August 15.

Academic Fields/Career Goals: History.

Award: Prize for use in freshman, sophomore, junior, senior, or graduate years; not renewable. *Number:* 2. *Amount:* $400.

Eligibility Requirements: Applicant must be enrolled or expecting to enroll full-time at a four-year institution or university. Applicant must have 3.0 GPA or higher. Available to U.S. and non-U.S. citizens.

Application Requirements: Essay, 2 copies of paper, abstract, letter from faculty member. *Deadline:* August 15.

Contact: Prof. Alfred J. Andrea
Phi Alpha Theta History Honor Society, Inc.
Department of History, The University of Vermont
Burlington, VT 05405-0164

PHI ALPHA THETA/WESTERN FRONT ASSOCIATION PAPER PRIZE

Essay competition available to full-time undergraduate members of Phi Alpha Theta. The paper must be from 12 to 15 typed pages and must address the American experience in World War I, dealing with virtually any aspect of American involvement during the period from 1912 (Second Moroccan Crisis) to 1924 (Dawes Plan). Primary source material must be used. For further details visit Web site: http://www.phialphatheta.org/awards2.htm.

Academic Fields/Career Goals: History.

Award: Prize for use in freshman, sophomore, junior, or senior years; not renewable. *Number:* 1. *Amount:* $700.

Eligibility Requirements: Applicant must be enrolled or expecting to enroll full-time at a four-year institution or university. Applicant must have 3.0 GPA or higher. Available to U.S. and non-U.S. citizens.

Application Requirements: Applicant must enter a contest, essay, disk containing electronic copy of paper and cover letter. *Deadline:* December 3.

Contact: Prof. Graydon A. Tunstall, Jr.
Phi Alpha Theta History Honor Society, Inc.
4202 East Fowler Ave, SOC107
Tampa, FL 33620-8100
Phone: 813-974-8212
Fax: 813-974-8215
E-mail: phialpha@phialphatheta.org

SONS OF THE REPUBLIC OF TEXAS
http://www.srttexas.org

TEXAS HISTORY ESSAY CONTEST
• *See page 85*

SOUTHERN BAPTIST HISTORICAL LIBRARY AND ARCHIVES
http://www.sbhla.org

LYNN E. MAY, JR. STUDY GRANT

Grants to assist researchers (graduate students, college and seminary professors, historians, and other writers) with travel and research costs related to research in the Southern Baptist Historical Library and Archives.

Academic Fields/Career Goals: History; Religion/Theology.

Award: Grant for use in junior, senior, graduate, or postgraduate years; not renewable. *Number:* 8–10. *Amount:* $500–$750.

Eligibility Requirements: Applicant must be enrolled or expecting to enroll full or part-time at a two-year or four-year institution or university and studying in Tennessee. Available to U.S. and non-U.S. citizens.

Application Requirements: Application, references. *Deadline:* April 1.

Contact: Bill Sumners, Director
Southern Baptist Historical Library and Archives
901 Commerce Street, Suite 400
Nashville, TN 37203-3630

THE LINCOLN FORUM
http://www.thelincolnforum.org

PLATT FAMILY SCHOLARSHIP PRIZE ESSAY CONTEST
• *See page 85*

TOPSFIELD HISTORICAL SOCIETY
http://www.topsfieldhistory.org

JOHN KIMBALL, JR. MEMORIAL TRUST SCHOLARSHIP PROGRAM FOR THE STUDY OF HISTORY

For tuition, books, and other educational and research expenses to undergraduate and graduate students, as well as college, university, and graduate school instructors and professors who have excelled in, and/or have a passion for, the study of history and related disciplines, and who reside in, or have a substantial connection to Topsfield, Massachusetts.

Academic Fields/Career Goals: History.

Topsfield Historical Society (continued)

Award: Grant for use in freshman, sophomore, junior, senior, graduate, or postgraduate years; not renewable. *Number:* 5–20. *Amount:* $250–$5000.

Eligibility Requirements: Applicant must be enrolled or expecting to enroll full or part-time at a two-year or four-year institution or university. Available to U.S. citizens.

Application Requirements: Application. *Deadline:* May 15.

Contact: Norman Isler, President
Topsfield Historical Society
PO Box 323
Topsfield, MA 01983
Phone: 978-887-9724
Fax: 978-887-0185
E-mail: nisler@verizon.net

UNITED DAUGHTERS OF THE CONFEDERACY   http://www.hqudc.org

HELEN JAMES BREWER SCHOLARSHIP

Award for full-time undergraduate student who is a descendant of a Confederate soldier, sailor or marine. Must be from Alabama, Florida, Georgia, South Carolina, Tennessee or Virginia. Recipient must be enrolled in an accredited college or university and studying Southern history and literature. Must be a member or former member of the Children of the Confederacy. Minimum 3.0 GPA. Submit letter of endorsement from sponsoring chapter of the United Daughters of the Confederacy. Please refer to Web site for further details: http://www.hqudc.org

Academic Fields/Career Goals: History; Literature/English/Writing.

Award: Scholarship for use in freshman, sophomore, junior, or senior years; renewable. *Number:* 1–2. *Amount:* $800–$1000.

Eligibility Requirements: Applicant must be enrolled or expecting to enroll full-time at a four-year institution or university and resident of Alabama, Florida, Georgia, South Carolina, Tennessee, or Virginia. Applicant or parent of applicant must be member of United Daughters of the Confederacy. Applicant must have 3.0 GPA or higher. Available to U.S. citizens.

Application Requirements: Application, essay, financial need analysis, photo, references, self-addressed stamped envelope, transcript, confederate ancestor's proof of service. *Deadline:* March 15.

Contact: Robert Kraus, Second Vice President General
United Daughters of the Confederacy
328 North Boulevard
Richmond, VA 23220-4057
Phone: 804-355-1636

UNITED NEGRO COLLEGE FUND   http://www.uncf.org

C-SPAN SCHOLARSHIP PROGRAM
• *See page 189*

UNITED STATES MARINE CORPS HISTORICAL CENTER   http://www.hqinet001.hqmc.usmc.mil

U.S. MARINE CORPS HISTORICAL CENTER GRANTS

Research grants for graduate-level and advanced study in Marine Corps history and related fields. Must submit preliminary letter outlining qualifications and a topic or request for a topic. Pending approval, applicants must submit a writing sample, transcripts, and a formal application. Program gives preference to pre1975 period topics. A portion of the research can be done in Washington, D.C. Applications considered year-round.

Academic Fields/Career Goals: History; Museum Studies.

Award: Grant for use in freshman, sophomore, junior, senior, graduate, or postgraduate years; not renewable. *Number:* up to 5. *Amount:* $400–$3000.

Eligibility Requirements: Applicant must be enrolled or expecting to enroll full-time at an institution or university. Available to U.S. and non-U.S. citizens.

Application Requirements: Application, resume, references, transcript, writing sample. *Deadline:* Continuous.

Contact: Coordinator, Grants and Fellowships
United States Marine Corps Historical Center
3079 Moreell Avenue
Quantico, VA 22134

HOME ECONOMICS

COSTUME SOCIETY OF AMERICA   http://www.costumesocietyamerica.com

ADELE FILENE TRAVEL AWARD
• *See page 105*

STELLA BLUM RESEARCH GRANT
• *See page 105*

FAMILY, CAREER AND COMMUNITY LEADERS OF AMERICA-TEXAS ASSOCIATION   http://www.texasfccla.org

C.J. DAVIDSON SCHOLARSHIP FOR FCCLA

Scholarships are available to outstanding members of the Texas FCCLA. $1000 is awarded per semester and will be continued for eight straight semesters if recipients remain eligible. Applicants should visit the Web site (http://www.texasfccla.org) or write to Texas FCCLA for complete information, submission guidelines, and restrictions.

Academic Fields/Career Goals: Home Economics.

Award: Scholarship for use in freshman, sophomore, junior, or senior years; renewable. *Number:* 10. *Amount:* $1000.

Eligibility Requirements: Applicant must be high school student; planning to enroll or expecting to enroll full-time at a four-year institution or university; single; resident of Texas and studying in Texas. Applicant or parent of applicant must be member of Family, Career and Community Leaders of America. Applicant must have 2.5 GPA or higher. Available to U.S. citizens.

Application Requirements: Application, essay, references, test scores, transcript. *Deadline:* March 1.

Contact: FCCLA Staff
Family, Career and Community Leaders of America-Texas Association
3530 Bee Caves Road, #101
Austin, TX 78746-9616
Phone: 512-306-0099
Fax: 512-306-0041
E-mail: fccla@texasfccla.org

FCCLA HOUSTON LIVESTOCK SHOW AND RODEO SCHOLARSHIP

Ten, four-year $10,000 scholarships to be awarded to outstanding members of the Texas FCCLA. Applicants should visit the Web site (http://www.texasfccla.org) or write to Texas FCCLA for complete information, submission guidelines, and restrictions. Minimum 3.5 GPA required. Must be Texas resident and attend a Texas institution.

Academic Fields/Career Goals: Home Economics.

Award: Scholarship for use in freshman, sophomore, junior, or senior years; not renewable. *Number:* 10. *Amount:* $10,000.

Eligibility Requirements: Applicant must be high school student; planning to enroll or expecting to enroll full-time at a four-year institution or university; resident of Texas and studying in Texas. Applicant or parent of applicant must be member of Family, Career and Community Leaders of America. Applicant must have 3.5 GPA or higher. Available to U.S. citizens.

Application Requirements: Application, essay, photo, references, test scores, transcript. *Deadline:* March 1.

Contact: FCCLA Staff
Family, Career and Community Leaders of America-Texas Association
3530 Bee Caves Road, Suite 101
Austin, TX 78746-9616
Phone: 512-306-0099
Fax: 512-306-0041
E-mail: fccla@texasfccla.org

FCCLA REGIONAL SCHOLARSHIPS
• See page 147

FCCLA TEXAS FARM BUREAU SCHOLARSHIP
• See page 147

INTERNATIONAL EXECUTIVE HOUSEKEEPERS ASSOCIATION http://www.ieha.org

INTERNATIONAL EXECUTIVE HOUSEKEEPERS EDUCATIONAL FOUNDATION
• See page 307

MAINE SCHOOL FOOD SERVICE ASSOCIATION (MSFSA)

SCHOLARSHIP OF THE MAINE SCHOOL FOOD SERVICE ASSOCIATION
• See page 305

MARYLAND ASSOCIATION OF PRIVATE COLLEGES AND CAREER SCHOOLS http://www.mapccs.org

MARYLAND ASSOCIATION OF PRIVATE COLLEGES AND CAREER SCHOOLS SCHOLARSHIP
• See page 150

NATIONAL POULTRY AND FOOD DISTRIBUTORS ASSOCIATION http://www.npfda.org

NATIONAL POULTRY AND FOOD DISTRIBUTORS ASSOCIATION SCHOLARSHIP FOUNDATION
• See page 76

OHIO 4-H http://www.ohio4h.org

BEA CLEVELAND 4-H SCHOLARSHIP
• See page 170

MABEL SARBAUGH 4-H SCHOLARSHIP
• See page 170

TEXAS ELECTRIC CO-OP, INC. http://www.texas-ec.org

ANN LANE HOME ECONOMICS SCHOLARSHIP
• See page 305

UNITED DAUGHTERS OF THE CONFEDERACY http://www.hqudc.org

WALTER REED SMITH SCHOLARSHIP
• See page 154

HORTICULTURE/FLORICULTURE

ALABAMA GOLF COURSE SUPERINTENDENTS ASSOCIATION http://www.agcsa.org/

ALABAMA GOLF COURSE SUPERINTENDENT'S ASSOCIATION'S DONNIE ARTHUR MEMORIAL SCHOLARSHIP

One-time award for students majoring in agriculture with an emphasis on turfgrass management. Must have a minimum 2.0 GPA. Application deadline is September 30.

Academic Fields/Career Goals: Horticulture/Floriculture.

Award: Scholarship for use in freshman, sophomore, junior, or senior years; not renewable. *Number:* 2. *Amount:* $1000.

Eligibility Requirements: Applicant must be enrolled or expecting to enroll full-time at a two-year or four-year institution or university. Available to U.S. and non-U.S. citizens.

Application Requirements: Application, essay, transcript. *Deadline:* September 30.

Contact: Scholarship Committee Claimer
Alabama Golf Course Superintendents Association
PO Box 661214
Birmingham, AL 35266-1214
E-mail: agcsa@charter.net

AMERICAN FLORAL ENDOWMENT http://www.endowment.org

HAROLD F. WILKINS SCHOLARSHIP PROGRAM
• See page 143

MOSMILLER SCHOLAR PROGRAM
• See page 143

VICTOR AND MARGARET BALL PROGRAM
• See page 144

AMERICAN NURSERY AND LANDSCAPE ASSOCIATION http://www.anla.org/research

ANLA NATIONAL SCHOLARSHIP ENDOWMENT-USREY FAMILY SCHOLARSHIP

Award for students accredited undergraduate or graduate landscape horticulture program or related discipline at a two- or four-year institution. The applicant must be a student enrolled in a California state university or college. Preference given to applicants who plan to work within the industry. Must have a minimum 2.5 GPA.

Academic Fields/Career Goals: Horticulture/Floriculture; Landscape Architecture.

Award: Scholarship for use in sophomore, junior, senior, graduate, or postgraduate years; not renewable. *Number:* 1. *Amount:* $1000–$1500.

Eligibility Requirements: Applicant must be enrolled or expecting to enroll full-time at a two-year or four-year or technical institution or university and studying in California. Applicant must have 2.5 GPA or higher. Available to U.S. and non-U.S. citizens.

Application Requirements: Application, essay, financial need analysis, references, transcript. *Deadline:* April 1.

Contact: Teresa Jodon, Endowment Program Administrator
American Nursery and Landscape Association
1000 Vermont Avenue, NW, Suite 300
Washington, DC 20005
Phone: 202-789-2900 Ext. 3014
Fax: 202-789-1893
E-mail: hriresearch@anla.org

CARVILLE M. AKEHURST MEMORIAL SCHOLARSHIP

Scholarship is available to resident of Maryland, Virginia, or West Virginia. Applicant must be enrolled in an accredited undergraduate or graduate landscape/ horticulture program or related discipline at a two- or four-year institution and must have minimum 3.0 GPA. Application deadline April 1.

Academic Fields/Career Goals: Horticulture/Floriculture; Landscape Architecture.

Award: Scholarship for use in junior, senior, or graduate years; not renewable. *Number:* 1–2. *Amount:* $1000.

Eligibility Requirements: Applicant must be enrolled or expecting to enroll full-time at a two-year or four-year institution or university and resident of Maryland, Virginia, or West Virginia. Applicant must have 3.0 GPA or higher. Available to U.S. citizens.

Application Requirements: Application, essay, financial need analysis, resume, references, transcript. *Deadline:* April 1.

Contact: Teresa Jodon, Endowment Program Administrator
American Nursery and Landscape Association
1000 Vermont Avenue, NW, Suite 300
Washington, DC 20005
Phone: 202-789-5980 Ext. 3014
Fax: 202-789-1893
E-mail: tjodon@anla.org

HORTICULTURE RESEARCH INSTITUTE TIMOTHY BIGELOW AND PALMER W. BIGELOW, JR. SCHOLARSHIP

Award for students who are enrolled in accredited undergraduate or graduate landscape/horticulture program. Must be resident of Connecticut, Maine, Massachusetts, New Hampshire, Rhode Island, or Vermont. Undergraduates must have a GPA of 2.25; graduate students, 3.0. Financial need, desire to work in nursery industry are factors. Deadline: April 1.

Academic Fields/Career Goals: Horticulture/Floriculture; Landscape Architecture.

American Nursery and Landscape Association (continued)

Award: Scholarship for use in sophomore, junior, senior, or graduate years; not renewable. *Number:* 3. *Amount:* $1500–$2500.

Eligibility Requirements: Applicant must be enrolled or expecting to enroll full-time at an institution or university and resident of Connecticut, Maine, Massachusetts, New Hampshire, Rhode Island, or Vermont. Available to U.S. and non-U.S. citizens.

Application Requirements: Application, essay, financial need analysis, references, transcript. *Deadline:* April 1.

Contact: Teresa Jodon, Endowment Program Administrator
American Nursery and Landscape Association
1000 Vermont Street, NW, Suite 300
Washington, DC 20005
Phone: 202-789-5980 Ext. 3014
Fax: 202-789-1893
E-mail: hriresearch@anla.org

SPRING MEADOW NURSERY SCHOLARSHIP

Scholarship for the full-time study of horticulture or landscape architecture students in undergraduate or graduate landscape horticulture program or related discipline at a two- or four-year institution. Applicant must have minimum 2.5 GPA. Application deadline is April 1.

Academic Fields/Career Goals: Horticulture/Floriculture; Landscape Architecture.

Award: Scholarship for use in freshman, sophomore, junior, senior, or graduate years; not renewable. *Number:* 1–2. *Amount:* $1000–$1500.

Eligibility Requirements: Applicant must be enrolled or expecting to enroll full-time at a two-year or four-year or technical institution or university. Applicant must have 2.5 GPA or higher. Available to U.S. and Canadian citizens.

Application Requirements: Application, essay, financial need analysis, resume, references, transcript. *Deadline:* April 1.

Contact: Teresa Jodon, Endowment Program Administrator
American Nursery and Landscape Association
1000 Vermont Avenue, NW, Suite 300
Washington, DC 20005-4914
Phone: 202-789-5980 Ext. 3014
Fax: 202-789-1893
E-mail: tjodon@anla.org

AMERICAN SOCIETY FOR ENOLOGY AND VITICULTURE   http://www.asev.org

AMERICAN SOCIETY FOR ENOLOGY AND VITICULTURE SCHOLARSHIPS
• See page 78

ARIZONA NURSERY ASSOCIATION   http://www.azna.org

ARIZONA NURSERY ASSOCIATION FOUNDATION SCHOLARSHIP

Provides research grants and scholarships for the green industry. Application deadline is April 15. Applicant must be an Arizona resident currently or planning to be enrolled in a horticultural related curriculum at an Arizona university, community college, or continuing education program. See Web site for further details: http://www.azna.org

Academic Fields/Career Goals: Horticulture/Floriculture.

Award: Scholarship for use in freshman, sophomore, junior, senior, or postgraduate years; not renewable. *Number:* 12–15. *Amount:* $500–$3000.

Eligibility Requirements: Applicant must be enrolled or expecting to enroll full or part-time at a two-year or four-year or technical institution or university. Available to U.S. and non-U.S. citizens.

Application Requirements: Application, references, transcript. *Deadline:* April 15.

Contact: Cheryl Goar, Executive Director
Arizona Nursery Association
1430 West Broadway
Suite A-180
Tempe, AZ 85282
Phone: 480-966-1610
Fax: 480-966-0923
E-mail: cgoar@azna.org

COMMUNITY FOUNDATION FOR PALM BEACH AND MARTIN COUNTIES, INC.   http://www.yourcommunityfoundation.org

MILTON J. BOONE HORTICULTURAL SCHOLARSHIP

Scholarship awarded to graduating senior in high school, or returning student to the pursuit of Horticultural studies. Restricted to residents of Palm Beach or Martin County. Deadline is February 1. Applications available online http://www.yourcommunityfoundation.org

Academic Fields/Career Goals: Horticulture/Floriculture.

Award: Scholarship for use in freshman year; not renewable. *Number:* varies. *Amount:* $750–$2500.

Eligibility Requirements: Applicant must be enrolled or expecting to enroll at a four-year institution or university and resident of Florida. Available to U.S. citizens.

Application Requirements: Application, financial need analysis. *Deadline:* February 1.

Contact: Carolyn Jenco, Grants Manager/Scholarship Coordinator
Community Foundation for Palm Beach and Martin Counties, Inc.
700 South Dixie Highway, Suite 200
West Palm Beach, FL 33401
Phone: 561-659-6800
Fax: 561-832-6542
E-mail: cjenco@cfpbmc.org

CONNECTICUT NURSERYMEN'S FOUNDATION, INC.

CONNECTICUT NURSERYMEN'S FOUNDATION, INC. SCHOLARSHIPS

Award to graduating high school seniors or preparatory school graduates who will enter college in the fall semester, majoring in horticulture, landscape design, or nursery management. This award is renewable for up to four years. Must be a resident of Connecticut and a U.S. citizen. Deadline: March 15. Minimum 2.5 GPA required.

Academic Fields/Career Goals: Horticulture/Floriculture; Landscape Architecture.

Award: Scholarship for use in freshman year; renewable. *Number:* 1. *Amount:* $5000.

Eligibility Requirements: Applicant must be high school student; planning to enroll or expecting to enroll full-time at a two-year or four-year institution or university and resident of Connecticut. Applicant must have 2.5 GPA or higher. Available to U.S. citizens.

Application Requirements: Application, financial need analysis, interview, references, test scores, transcript. *Deadline:* March 15.

Contact: Michael D. Johnson, Financial Coordinator
Connecticut Nurserymen's Foundation, Inc.
888 Summer Hill Road
Madison, CT 06443
Phone: 203-421-3055
Fax: 203-421-5189

FEDERATED GARDEN CLUBS OF CONNECTICUT   http://www.ctgardenclubs.org

FEDERATED GARDEN CLUBS OF CONNECTICUT, INC.
• See page 137

FIRST–FLORICULTURE INDUSTRY RESEARCH AND SCHOLARSHIP TRUST   http://www.firstinfloriculture.org

BALL HORTICULTURAL COMPANY SCHOLARSHIP

Award open to undergraduates entering junior or senior year at a four-year college or university in the U.S. or Canada. Must be studying horticulture or a related field and intend to pursue a career in commercial floriculture. To apply applicant must register with lunch-money.com, which is partnering with FIRST to make the application process easier. Applicant only need to fill out one application online, and there is a link to lunch-money.com from the FIRST Web site: http://www.firstinfloriculture.org/schl_req_app.htm. In addition to the application, applicant must submit two letters of recommendation and transcripts via email to: scholarships@firstinfloriculture.org. Application deadline is May 1.

Academic Fields/Career Goals: Horticulture/Floriculture.

Award: Scholarship for use in junior or senior years; not renewable. *Number:* 1. *Amount:* $500–$2000.

Eligibility Requirements: Applicant must be enrolled or expecting to enroll at a four-year institution or university. Applicant must have 3.0 GPA or higher. Available to U.S. and Canadian citizens.

Application Requirements: Application, references, transcript. *Deadline:* May 1.

Contact: Bill Willbrandt, Scholarship Information
FIRST–Floriculture Industry Research and Scholarship Trust
PO Box 280
East Lansing, MI 48826-0280
Phone: 517-333-4617
Fax: 517-333-4494
E-mail: scholarship@firstinfloriculture.org

BARBARA CARLSON SCHOLARSHIP

Award open to undergraduates or graduates studying horticulture or a related major at a four-year college or university in the U.S. or Canada. For students interested in interning or working for public gardens. Must have a career interest in horticulture. To apply applicant must register with lunch-money.com, which is partnering with FIRST to make the application process easier. Applicant only need to fill out one application online, and there is a link to lunch-money.com from the FIRST Web site: http://www.firstinfloriculture.org/schl_req_app.htm In addition to the application, applicant must submit two letters of recommendation and transcripts via email to: scholarships@firstinfloriculture.org. Application deadline is May 1.

Academic Fields/Career Goals: Horticulture/Floriculture.

Award: Scholarship for use in sophomore, junior, senior, or graduate years; not renewable. *Number:* 1. *Amount:* $500–$2000.

Eligibility Requirements: Applicant must be enrolled or expecting to enroll full-time at a four-year institution or university. Applicant or parent of applicant must have employment or volunteer experience in designated career field. Applicant must have 3.0 GPA or higher. Available to U.S. and Canadian citizens.

Application Requirements: Application, references, transcript. *Deadline:* May 1.

Contact: Bill Willbrandt, Scholarship Information
FIRST–Floriculture Industry Research and Scholarship Trust
PO Box 280
East Lansing, MI 48826-0280
Phone: 517-333-4617
Fax: 517-333-4494
E-mail: scholarship@firstinfloriculture.org

BUD OHLMAN SCHOLARSHIP

Award available for student studying horticulture at a U.S. or Canadian institution with career goal of becoming a bedding plant grower for an established business. Minimum GPA of 3.0 required. To apply you must register with lunch-money.com, which is partnering with FIRST to make the application process easier. You only need to fill out one application online, and there is a link to lunch-money.com from the FIRST Web site: http://www.firstinfloriculture.org/schl_req_app.htm In addition to the application, you must submit two letters of recommendation and transcripts via email to: scholarships@firstinfloriculture.org. Application deadline is May 1.

Academic Fields/Career Goals: Horticulture/Floriculture.

Award: Scholarship for use in junior or senior years; not renewable. *Number:* 1. *Amount:* $500–$2000.

Eligibility Requirements: Applicant must be enrolled or expecting to enroll at a four-year institution or university. Applicant must have 3.0 GPA or higher. Available to U.S. and Canadian citizens.

Application Requirements: Application, references, transcript. *Deadline:* May 1.

Contact: Bill Willbrandt, Executive Director
FIRST–Floriculture Industry Research and Scholarship Trust
PO Box 280
East Lansing, MI 48826-0280
Phone: 517-333-4617
Fax: 517-333-4494
E-mail: scholarship@firstinfloriculture.org

CARL F. DEITZ MEMORIAL SCHOLARSHIP

One-time award available to undergraduate horticulture or related majors at a four-year institution in the U.S. or Canada who have a career interest in horticultural allied trades. Must have completed one year of study. Minimum 3.0 GPA required. To apply you must register with lunch-money.com, which is partnering with FIRST to make the application process easier. Complete the application online at: http://www.firstinfloriculture.org/schl_req_app.htm In addition, you must submit two letters of recommendation and transcripts via email to: scholarships@firstinfloriculture.org. Application deadline is May 1.

Academic Fields/Career Goals: Horticulture/Floriculture.

Award: Scholarship for use in sophomore, junior, or senior years; not renewable. *Number:* 1. *Amount:* $500–$2000.

Eligibility Requirements: Applicant must be enrolled or expecting to enroll full-time at a four-year institution or university. Applicant must have 3.0 GPA or higher. Available to U.S. and Canadian citizens.

Application Requirements: Application, references, transcript. *Deadline:* May 1.

Contact: Bill Willbrandt, Executive Director
FIRST–Floriculture Industry Research and Scholarship Trust
PO Box 280
East Lansing, MI 48826-0280
Phone: 517-333-4617
Fax: 517-333-4494
E-mail: scholarship@firstinfloriculture.org

DOSATRON INTERNATIONAL, INC., SCHOLARSHIP

Award open to upper-level undergraduates or graduates studying horticulture or a related major at a four-year college or university in the U.S. or Canada. Must have interest in floriculture production, with a career goal to work in a greenhouse environment. Minimum GPA of 3.0 required. To apply applicant must register with lunch-money.com, which is partnering with FIRST to make the application process easier. Applicant only need to fill out one application online, and there is a link to lunch-money.com from the FIRST Web site: http://www.firstinfloriculture.org/schl_req_app.htm In addition to the application, applicant must submit two letters of recommendation and transcripts via email to: scholarships@firstinfloriculture.org. Application deadline is May 1.

Academic Fields/Career Goals: Horticulture/Floriculture.

Award: Scholarship for use in junior, senior, or graduate years; not renewable. *Number:* 1. *Amount:* $500–$2000.

Eligibility Requirements: Applicant must be enrolled or expecting to enroll full-time at a four-year institution or university. Applicant must have 3.0 GPA or higher. Available to U.S. and Canadian citizens.

Application Requirements: Application, references, transcript. *Deadline:* May 1.

Contact: Bill Willbrandt, Executive Director
FIRST–Floriculture Industry Research and Scholarship Trust
PO Box 280
East Lansing, MI 48826-0280
Phone: 517-333-4617
Fax: 517-333-4494
E-mail: scholarship@firstinfloriculture.org

EARL DEDMAN MEMORIAL SCHOLARSHIP

Award available to students from the Northwest area of the U.S. who are undergraduates studying horticulture or a related subject at a four-year college or university in the U.S. or Canada. Must intend to pursue a career as a greenhouse grower. Minimum GPA of 3.0 required. To apply you must register with lunch-money.com, which is partnering with FIRST to make the application process easier. You only need to fill out one application online, and there is a link to lunch-money.com from the FIRST Web site: http://www.firstinfloriculture.org/schl_req_app.htm In addition to the application, you must submit two letters of recommendation and transcripts via email to: scholarships@firstinfloriculture.org. Application deadline is May 1.

Academic Fields/Career Goals: Horticulture/Floriculture.

FIRST–Floriculture Industry Research and Scholarship Trust (continued)

Award: Scholarship for use in junior or senior years; not renewable. *Number:* 1. *Amount:* $500–$2000.

Eligibility Requirements: Applicant must be enrolled or expecting to enroll full-time at a four-year institution or university. Applicant must have 3.0 GPA or higher. Available to U.S. and Canadian citizens.

Application Requirements: Application, references, transcript. *Deadline:* May 1.

Contact: Bill Willbrandt, Executive Director
FIRST–Floriculture Industry Research and Scholarship Trust
PO Box 280
East Lansing, MI 48826-0280
Phone: 517-333-4417
Fax: 517-333-4494
E-mail: scholarship@firstinfloriculture.org

ECKE FAMILY SCHOLARSHIP

Award available to students entering junior or senior year at a four-year college or university in the U.S. or Canada. Must be studying horticulture or a related field and intend to pursue a career in production floriculture. Minimum GPA of 3.0 required. To apply you must register with lunch-money.com, which is partnering with FIRST to make the application process easier. You only need to fill out one application online, and there is a link to lunch-money.com from the FIRST Web site: http://www.firstinfloriculture.org/schl_req_app.htm In addition to the application, you must submit two letters of recommendation and transcripts via email to: scholarships@firstinfloriculture.org. Application deadline is May 1.

Academic Fields/Career Goals: Horticulture/Floriculture.

Award: Scholarship for use in junior or senior years; not renewable. *Number:* 1. *Amount:* $500–$2000.

Eligibility Requirements: Applicant must be enrolled or expecting to enroll full-time at a four-year institution or university. Applicant must have 3.0 GPA or higher. Available to U.S. and Canadian citizens.

Application Requirements: Application, references, transcript. *Deadline:* May 1.

Contact: Bill Willbrandt, Executive Director
FIRST–Floriculture Industry Research and Scholarship Trust
PO Box 280
East Lansing, MI 48826-0280
Phone: 517-333-4617
Fax: 517-333-4494
E-mail: scholarship@firstinfloriculture.org

ED MARKHAM INTERNATIONAL SCHOLARSHIP

Award open to undergraduates or graduates studying horticulture or a related major at a four-year college or university in the U.S. or Canada. For students who wish to further their understanding of domestic and international marketing through international horticultural related study, work, or travel. Minimum GPA of 3.0 required. To apply you must register with lunch-money.com, which is partnering with FIRST to make the application process easier. You only need to fill out one application online, and there is a link to lunch-money.com from the FIRST Web site: http://www.firstinfloriculture.org/schl_req_app.htm In addition to the application, applicant must submit two letters of recommendation and transcripts via email to: scholarships@firstinfloriculture.org. Application deadline is May 1.

Academic Fields/Career Goals: Horticulture/Floriculture.

Award: Scholarship for use in sophomore, junior, senior, or graduate years; not renewable. *Number:* 1. *Amount:* $500–$2000.

Eligibility Requirements: Applicant must be enrolled or expecting to enroll full-time at a four-year institution or university. Applicant must have 3.0 GPA or higher. Available to U.S. and Canadian citizens.

Application Requirements: Application, references, transcript. *Deadline:* May 1.

Contact: Bill Willbrandt, Executive Director
FIRST–Floriculture Industry Research and Scholarship Trust
PO Box 280
East Lansing, MI 48826-0280
Phone: 517-333-4617
Fax: 517-333-4494
E-mail: scholarship@firstinfloriculture.org

FRAN JOHNSON SCHOLARSHIP FOR NON-TRADITIONAL STUDENTS

One-time scholarship for graduate/undergraduate pursuing a degree in floriculture at a U.S. or Canadian institution who has been out of school for at least five years and is now reentering a program. Must have specific interest in bedding plants/floral crops. Send photo with application. To apply you must register with lunch-money.com, which is partnering with FIRST to make the application process easier. You only need to fill out one application online, and there is a link to lunch-money.com from the FIRST Web site: http://www.firstinfloriculture.org/schl_req_app.htm In addition to the application, you must submit two letters of recommendation and transcripts via email to: scholarships@firstinfloriculture.org. Application deadline is May 1.

Academic Fields/Career Goals: Horticulture/Floriculture.

Award: Scholarship for use in freshman, sophomore, junior, senior, or graduate years; not renewable. *Number:* 1. *Amount:* $500–$2000.

Eligibility Requirements: Applicant must be enrolled or expecting to enroll full-time at a four-year institution or university. Available to U.S. and Canadian citizens.

Application Requirements: Application, references, transcript. *Deadline:* May 1.

Contact: Bill Willbrandt, Executive Director
FIRST–Floriculture Industry Research and Scholarship Trust
PO Box 280
East Lansing, MI 48826-0280
Phone: 517-333-4617
Fax: 517-333-4494
E-mail: scholarship@firstinfloriculture.org

HAROLD BETTINGER MEMORIAL SCHOLARSHIP
• See page 74

JACOB VAN NAMEN/VANS MARKETING SCHOLARSHIP
• See page 74

JAMES BRIDENBAUGH MEMORIAL SCHOLARSHIP

Award open to students in sophomore, junior, and senior year at a four-year college or university in the U.S. or Canada. Must be studying horticulture or a related field and intend to pursue a career in floral design and marketing of fresh flowers and plants. Minimum GPA of 3.0 required. To apply you must register with lunch-money.com, which is partnering with FIRST to make the application process easier. You only need to fill out one application online, and there is a link to lunch-money.com from the FIRST Web site: http://www.firstinfloriculture.org/schl_req_app.htm In addition to the application, you must submit two letters of recommendation and transcripts via email to: scholarships@firstinfloriculture.org. Application deadline is May 1.

Academic Fields/Career Goals: Horticulture/Floriculture.

Award: Scholarship for use in sophomore, junior, or senior years; not renewable. *Number:* 1. *Amount:* $500–$2000.

Eligibility Requirements: Applicant must be enrolled or expecting to enroll full-time at a four-year institution or university. Applicant must have 3.0 GPA or higher. Available to U.S. and Canadian citizens.

Application Requirements: Application, applicant must enter a contest, references, transcript. *Deadline:* May 1.

Contact: Bill Willbrandt, Executive Director
FIRST–Floriculture Industry Research and Scholarship Trust
PO Box 280
East Lansing, MI 48826-0280
Phone: 517-333-4617
Fax: 517-333-4494
E-mail: scholarship@firstinfloriculture.org

JAMES RATHMELL, JR. MEMORIAL SCHOLARSHIP

One scholarship available to upper-level undergraduate or graduate student at a four-year institution in the U.S. or Canada who plans to engage in a work-study program outside the country for at least six months in the field of floriculture or horticulture. Minimum 3.0 GPA required. Submit letter of invitation from host country. To apply you must register with lunch-money.

com, which is partnering with FIRST to make the application process easier. Complete the application online at: http://www.firstinfloriculture.org/schl_req_app.htm In addition, you must submit two letters of recommendation and transcripts via email to: scholarships@firstinfloriculture.org. Application deadline is May 1.

Academic Fields/Career Goals: Horticulture/Floriculture.

Award: Scholarship for use in junior, senior, or graduate years; not renewable. *Number:* 1. *Amount:* $500–$2000.

Eligibility Requirements: Applicant must be enrolled or expecting to enroll full-time at a four-year institution or university. Applicant must have 3.0 GPA or higher. Available to U.S. and Canadian citizens.

Application Requirements: Application, references, transcript. *Deadline:* May 1.

Contact: Bill Willbrandt, Executive Director
FIRST–Floriculture Industry Research and Scholarship Trust
PO Box 280
East Lansing, MI 48826-0280
Phone: 517-333-4617
Fax: 517-333-4494
E-mail: scholarship@firstinfloriculture.org

JIM PERRY/HOLDEN L. BETTINGER SCHOLARSHIP

Award for vocational students in a one- or two-year program in the U.S. or Canada who intend to become a grower or greenhouse manager. Minimum GPA of 3.0 required. To apply you must register with lunch-money.com, which is partnering with FIRST to make the application process easier. You only need to fill out one application online, and there is a link to lunch-money.com from the FIRST Web site: http://www.firstinfloriculture.org/schl_req_app.htm In addition to the application, you must submit two letters of recommendation and transcripts via email to: scholarships@firstinfloriculture.org. Application deadline is May 1.

Academic Fields/Career Goals: Horticulture/Floriculture.

Award: Scholarship for use in freshman or sophomore years; not renewable. *Number:* 1. *Amount:* $500–$2000.

Eligibility Requirements: Applicant must be enrolled or expecting to enroll full or part-time at a two-year or four-year or technical institution or university. Applicant must have 3.0 GPA or higher. Available to U.S. and Canadian citizens.

Application Requirements: Application, references, transcript. *Deadline:* May 1.

Contact: Bill Willbrandt, Executive Director
FIRST–Floriculture Industry Research and Scholarship Trust
PO Box 280
East Lansing, MI 48826-0280
Phone: 517-333-4617
Fax: 517-333-4494
E-mail: scholarship@firstinfloriculture.org

JOHN HOLDEN MEMORIAL VOCATIONAL SCHOLARSHIP

Award open to vocational students in a one- or two-year program in an institution in the U.S. or Canada. Must be studying horticulture or a related field and intend to pursue a career as a grower or greenhouse manager. Minimum GPA of 3.0 required. To apply you must register with lunch-money.com, which is partnering with FIRST to make the application process easier. You only need to fill out one application online, and there is a link to lunch-money.com from the FIRST Web site: http://www.firstinfloriculture.org/schl_req_app.htm In addition to the application, you must submit two letters of recommendation and transcripts via email to: scholarships@firstinfloriculture.org. Application deadline is May 1.

Academic Fields/Career Goals: Horticulture/Floriculture.

Award: Scholarship for use in freshman or sophomore years; not renewable. *Number:* 1. *Amount:* $500–$2000.

Eligibility Requirements: Applicant must be enrolled or expecting to enroll full-time at a two-year or four-year or technical institution or university. Applicant must have 3.0 GPA or higher. Available to U.S. and Canadian citizens.

Application Requirements: Application, references, transcript. *Deadline:* May 1.

Contact: Bill Willbrandt, Executive Director
FIRST–Floriculture Industry Research and Scholarship Trust
PO Box 280
East Lansing, MI 48826-0280
Phone: 517-333-4617
Fax: 517-333-4494
E-mail: scholarship@firstinfloriculture.org

JOHN L. TOMASOVIC, SR., SCHOLARSHIP

Award for student pursuing career in horticulture at a U.S. or Canadian school. Special consideration for financial need and grade point average between 3.0 and 3.5. To apply you must register with lunch-money.com, which is partnering with FIRST to make the application process easier. You only need to fill out one application online, and there is a link to lunch-money.com from the FIRST Web site: http://www.firstinfloriculture.org/schl_req_app.htm In addition to the application, you must submit two letters of recommendation and transcripts via email to: scholarships@firstinfloriculture.org. Application deadline is May 1.

Academic Fields/Career Goals: Horticulture/Floriculture.

Award: Scholarship for use in sophomore, junior, senior, or graduate years; not renewable. *Number:* 1. *Amount:* $500–$2000.

Eligibility Requirements: Applicant must be enrolled or expecting to enroll full-time at a four-year institution or university. Applicant must have 3.0 GPA or higher. Available to U.S. and Canadian citizens.

Application Requirements: Application, financial need analysis, references, transcript. *Deadline:* May 1.

Contact: Bill Willbrandt, Executive Director
FIRST–Floriculture Industry Research and Scholarship Trust
PO Box 280
East Lansing, MI 48826-0280
Phone: 517-333-4617
Fax: 517-333-4494
E-mail: scholarship@firstinfloriculture.org

LEONARD BETTINGER SCHOLARSHIP

Award open to vocational students in a one- or two-year program in an institution in the U.S. or Canada. Must be studying horticulture or a related field and intend to pursue a career as a grower or greenhouse manager. Minimum GPA of 3.0 required. To apply you must register with lunch-money.com, which is partnering with FIRST to make the application process easier. You only need to fill out one application online, and there is a link to lunch-money.com from the FIRST Web site: http://www.firstinfloriculture.org/schl_req_app.htm In addition to the application, you must submit two letters of recommendation and transcripts via email to: scholarships@firstinfloriculture.org. Application deadline is May 1.

Academic Fields/Career Goals: Horticulture/Floriculture.

Award: Scholarship for use in freshman or sophomore years; not renewable. *Number:* 1. *Amount:* $500–$2000.

Eligibility Requirements: Applicant must be enrolled or expecting to enroll full-time at a two-year or four-year or technical institution or university. Applicant must have 3.0 GPA or higher. Available to U.S. and Canadian citizens.

Application Requirements: Application, references, transcript. *Deadline:* May 1.

Contact: Bill Willbrandt, Executive Director
FIRST–Floriculture Industry Research and Scholarship Trust
PO Box 280
East Lansing, MI 48826-0280
Phone: 517-333-4617
Fax: 517-333-4494
E-mail: scholarship@firstinfloriculture.org

LONG ISLAND FLOWER GROWERS SCHOLARSHIP

Award for a horticulture student from Long Island studying commercial horticulture in a two- or four-year college or university in the U.S. or Canada. Minimum GPA of 3.0 required. To apply you must register with lunch-money.com, which is partnering with FIRST to make the application process easier. You only need to fill out one application online, and there is a link to lunch-money.com from the FIRST Web site: http://www.firstinfloriculture.org/schl_req_app.htm In addition to the application, you must submit two letters of recommendation and transcripts via email to: scholarships@firstinfloriculture.org. Application deadline is May 1.

Academic Fields/Career Goals: Horticulture/Floriculture.

FIRST–Floriculture Industry Research and Scholarship Trust (continued)

Award: Scholarship for use in sophomore, junior, or senior years; not renewable. *Number:* 1. *Amount:* $500–$2000.

Eligibility Requirements: Applicant must be enrolled or expecting to enroll full-time at a two-year or four-year institution or university and resident of New York. Applicant must have 3.0 GPA or higher. Available to U.S. and Canadian citizens.

Application Requirements: Application, references, transcript. *Deadline:* May 1.

Contact: Bill Willbrandt, Executive Director
FIRST–Floriculture Industry Research and Scholarship Trust
PO Box 280
East Lansing, MI 48826-0280
Phone: 517-333-4617
Fax: 517-333-4494
E-mail: scholarship@firstinfloriculture.org

NATIONAL GREENHOUSE MANUFACTURERS ASSOCIATION SCHOLARSHIP

Scholarship targets students majoring in horticulture and bioengineering or the equivalent. Must be at least a junior at an accredited four-year college in the U.S. or Canada. Minimum GPA of 3.0 required. To apply you must register with lunch-money.com, which is partnering with FIRST to make the application process easier. You only need to fill out one application online, and there is a link to lunch-money.com from the FIRST Web site: http://www.firstinfloriculture.org/schl_req_app.htm In addition to the application, you must submit two letters of recommendation and transcripts via email to: scholarships@firstinfloriculture.org. Application deadline is May 1.

Academic Fields/Career Goals: Horticulture/Floriculture.

Award: Scholarship for use in junior or senior years; not renewable. *Amount:* $500–$2000.

Eligibility Requirements: Applicant must be enrolled or expecting to enroll full or part-time at a four-year institution or university. Applicant must have 3.0 GPA or higher. Available to U.S. and Canadian citizens.

Application Requirements: Application, references, transcript. *Deadline:* May 1.

Contact: Bill Willbrandt, Executive Director
FIRST–Floriculture Industry Research and Scholarship Trust
PO Box 280
East Lansing, MI 48826-0280
Phone: 517-333-4617
Fax: 517-333-4494
E-mail: scholarship@firstinfloriculture.org

NORM MOLL SCHOLARSHIP

Award available to students from Ohio, preferably northwestern Ohio, who are majoring in horticulture or related field and are attending Ohio State University or OSU Agricultural Technical Institute. Minimum GPA of 3.0 required. To apply you must register with lunch-money.com, which is partnering with FIRST to make the application process easier. You only need to fill out one application online, and there is a link to lunch-money.com from the FIRST Web site: http://www.firstinfloriculture.org/schl_req_app.htm In addition to the application, you must submit two letters of recommendation and transcripts via email to: scholarships@firstinfloriculture.org. Application deadline is May 1.

Academic Fields/Career Goals: Horticulture/Floriculture.

Award: Scholarship for use in sophomore, junior, or senior years; not renewable. *Number:* 1. *Amount:* $500–$2000.

Eligibility Requirements: Applicant must be enrolled or expecting to enroll full-time at a four-year or technical institution or university; resident of Ohio and studying in Ohio. Applicant must have 3.0 GPA or higher. Available to U.S. and Canadian citizens.

Application Requirements: Application, references, transcript. *Deadline:* May 1.

Contact: Bill Willbrandt, Executive Director
FIRST–Floriculture Industry Research and Scholarship Trust
PO Box 280
East Lansing, MI 48826-0280
Phone: 517-333-4617
Fax: 517-333-4494
E-mail: scholarship@firstinfloriculture.org

PARIS FRACASSO PRODUCTION FLORICULTURE SCHOLARSHIP

Award open to undergraduates entering junior or senior year at a four-year college or university in the U.S. or Canada. Must be studying horticulture or a related major and intend to pursue a career in floriculture production. Minimum GPA of 3.0 required. To apply applicant must register with lunch-money.com, which is partnering with FIRST to make the application process easier. Applicant only need to fill out one application online, and there is a link to lunch-money.com from the FIRST Web site: http://www.firstinfloriculture.org/schl_req_app.htm In addition to the application, applicant must submit two letters of recommendation and transcripts via email to: scholarships@firstinfloriculture.org. Application deadline is May 1.

Academic Fields/Career Goals: Horticulture/Floriculture.

Award: Scholarship for use in junior or senior years; not renewable. *Number:* 1. *Amount:* $500–$2000.

Eligibility Requirements: Applicant must be enrolled or expecting to enroll full-time at a four-year institution or university. Applicant must have 3.0 GPA or higher. Available to U.S. and Canadian citizens.

Application Requirements: Application, references, transcript. *Deadline:* May 1.

Contact: Bill Willbrandt, Executive Director
FIRST–Floriculture Industry Research and Scholarship Trust
PO Box 280
East Lansing, MI 48826-0280
Phone: 517-333-4617
Fax: 517-333-4494
E-mail: scholarship@firstinfloriculture.org

RICHARD E. BARRETT SCHOLARSHIP

Scholarship available for student pursuing a career in research and/or education in horticulture at a U.S. or Canadian institution. Minimum GPA of 3.0 required. To apply you must register with lunch-money.com, which is partnering with FIRST to make the application process easier. You only need to fill out one application online, and there is a link to lunch-money.com from the FIRST Web site: http://www.firstinfloriculture.org/schl_req_app.htm In addition to the application, you must submit two letters of recommendation and transcripts via email to: scholarships@firstinfloriculture.org. Application deadline is May 1.

Academic Fields/Career Goals: Horticulture/Floriculture.

Award: Scholarship for use in sophomore, junior, senior, or graduate years; not renewable. *Number:* 1. *Amount:* $500–$2000.

Eligibility Requirements: Applicant must be enrolled or expecting to enroll full-time at a four-year institution or university. Applicant must have 3.0 GPA or higher. Available to U.S. and Canadian citizens.

Application Requirements: Application, references, transcript. *Deadline:* May 1.

Contact: Bill Willbrandt, Executive Director
FIRST–Floriculture Industry Research and Scholarship Trust
PO Box 280
East Lansing, MI 48826-0280
Phone: 517-333-4617
Fax: 517-333-4494
E-mail: scholarship@firstinfloriculture.org

SEED COMPANIES SCHOLARSHIP

Award open to undergraduates entering junior or senior year at a four-year college or university in the U.S. or Canada, as well as to graduate students. Must be studying horticulture or a related field and intend to pursue a career in the seed industry in research, sales, breeding or marketing. Minimum GPA of 3.0 required. To apply applicant must register with lunch-money.com, which is partnering with FIRST to make the application process easier. Applicant only need to fill out one application online, and there is a link to lunch-money.com from the FIRST Web site: http://www.firstinfloriculture.org/schl_req_app.htm In addition to the application, applicant must submit two letters of recommendation and transcripts via email to: scholarships@firstinfloriculture.org. Application deadline is May 1.

Academic Fields/Career Goals: Horticulture/Floriculture.

Award: Scholarship for use in junior, senior, or graduate years; not renewable. *Number:* 1. *Amount:* $500–$2000.

Eligibility Requirements: Applicant must be enrolled or expecting to enroll full-time at a four-year institution or university. Applicant must have 3.0 GPA or higher. Available to U.S. and Canadian citizens.

Application Requirements: Application, references, transcript. *Deadline:* May 1.

Contact: Bill Willbrandt, Executive Director
FIRST–Floriculture Industry Research and Scholarship Trust
PO Box 280
East Lansing, MI 48826-0280
Phone: 517-333-4617
Fax: 517-333-4494
E-mail: scholarship@firstinfloriculture.org

SOUTHEAST GREENHOUSE CONFERENCE SCHOLARSHIP

Award available to students studying horticulture at a college or university in one of the following states: Alabama, Florida, Georgia, North Carolina, South Carolina, Tennessee, or Virginia. Minimum GPA of 3.0 required. To apply you must register with lunch-money.com, which is partnering with FIRST to make the application process easier. You only need to fill out one application online, and there is a link to lunch-money.com from the FIRST Web site: http://www.firstinfloriculture.org/schl_req_app.htm In addition to the application, you must submit two letters of recommendation and transcripts via email to: scholarships@firstinfloriculture.org. Application deadline is May 1.

Academic Fields/Career Goals: Horticulture/Floriculture.

Award: Scholarship for use in junior, senior, or graduate years; not renewable. *Number:* 1. *Amount:* $500–$2000.

Eligibility Requirements: Applicant must be enrolled or expecting to enroll full-time at a four-year institution or university and studying in Alabama, Florida, Georgia, North Carolina, South Carolina, Tennessee, or Virginia. Applicant must have 3.0 GPA or higher. Available to U.S. and Canadian citizens.

Application Requirements: Application, references, transcript. *Deadline:* May 1.

Contact: Bill Willbrandt, Executive Director
FIRST–Floriculture Industry Research and Scholarship Trust
PO Box 280
East Lansing, MI 48826-0280
Phone: 517-333-4617
Fax: 517-333-4494
E-mail: scholarship@firstinfloriculture.org

WESTERN MICHIGAN GREENHOUSE ASSOCIATION SCHOLARSHIP

Award available to a student from Michigan who is studying commercial horticulture at a four-year college or university in the U.S. or Canada. Minimum GPA of 3.0 required. To apply you must register with lunch-money.com, which is partnering with FIRST to make the application process easier. You only need to fill out one application online, and there is a link to lunch-money.com from the FIRST Web site: http://www.firstinfloriculture.org/schl_req_app.htm In addition to the application, you must submit two letters of recommendation and transcripts via email to: scholarships@firstinfloriculture.org. Application deadline is May 1.

Academic Fields/Career Goals: Horticulture/Floriculture.

Award: Scholarship for use in sophomore, junior, or senior years; not renewable. *Number:* 1. *Amount:* $500–$2000.

Eligibility Requirements: Applicant must be enrolled or expecting to enroll at a four-year institution or university and resident of Michigan. Applicant must have 3.0 GPA or higher. Available to U.S. and Canadian citizens.

Application Requirements: Application, references, transcript. *Deadline:* May 1.

Contact: Bill Willbrandt, Executive Director
FIRST–Floriculture Industry Research and Scholarship Trust
PO Box 280
East Lansing, MI 48826-0280
Phone: 517-333-4617
Fax: 517-333-4494
E-mail: scholarship@firstinfloriculture.org

FRIENDS OF THE FRELINGHUYSEN ARBORETUM
http://www.arboretumfriends.org

BENJAMIN C. BLACKBURN SCHOLARSHIP
• See page 293

FUHRMANN ORCHARDS

KARL "PETE" FUHRMANN IV MEMORIAL SCHOLARSHIP
• See page 74

GARDEN CLUB OF AMERICA
http://www.gcamerica.org

GARDEN CLUB OF AMERICA SUMMER SCHOLARSHIP IN FIELD BOTANY

For students wishing to pursue summer studies doing work in the field. Field work to be done in any of the 50 United States. Work may award academic credit. Application available on the GCA Web site: http://www.gcamerica.org

Academic Fields/Career Goals: Horticulture/Floriculture.

Award: Scholarship for use in freshman, sophomore, junior, senior, graduate, or postgraduate years. *Number:* 1. *Amount:* $1500.

Eligibility Requirements: Applicant must be enrolled or expecting to enroll at a two-year or four-year institution or university. Available to U.S. citizens.

Application Requirements: Application, essay, references, transcript. *Deadline:* February 1.

Contact: Ms. Judy Smith
Garden Club of America
14 East 60th Street
New York, NY 10022-1002
Phone: 212-753-8287
Fax: 212-753-0134

JOAN K. HUNT AND RACHEL M. HUNT SUMMER SCHOLARSHIP IN FIELD BOTANY

The purpose of this scholarship is to promote the awareness of the importance of botany to horticulture. Study must be in any one of the 50 states of the U.S. Preference is given to undergraduates. For more details and an application visit Web site: http://www.gcamerica.org

Academic Fields/Career Goals: Horticulture/Floriculture.

Award: Scholarship for use in freshman, sophomore, junior, senior, or postgraduate years. *Number:* 1. *Amount:* up to $1500.

Eligibility Requirements: Applicant must be enrolled or expecting to enroll at a two-year or four-year institution or university. Available to U.S. citizens.

Application Requirements: *Deadline:* February 1.

Contact: Ms. Judy Smith
Garden Club of America
14 East 60th Street
New York, NY 10022-1002
Phone: 212-753-8287
Fax: 212-753-0134

KATHARINE M. GROSSCUP SCHOLARSHIP

Several scholarships available to college juniors, seniors, and graduate students studying horticulture or related fields. Preference given to students from Ohio, Pennsylvania, West Virginia, Michigan, Indiana, and Kentucky. One-time award of up to $3000. Application on GCA Web site: http://www.gcamerica.org.

Academic Fields/Career Goals: Horticulture/Floriculture.

Award: Scholarship for use in sophomore, junior, senior, or graduate years; not renewable. *Number:* 1–3. *Amount:* up to $3000.

Eligibility Requirements: Applicant must be enrolled or expecting to enroll at an institution or university. Available to U.S. citizens.

Application Requirements: Application, interview, references, self-addressed stamped envelope, transcript. *Deadline:* February 1.

Contact: Nancy Stevenson, Scholarship Administrator
Garden Club of America
Cleveland Botanical Garden, 11030 East Boulevard
Cleveland, OH 44106
Fax: 216-721-2056

Garden Club of America (continued)

LOY MCCANDLESS MARKS SCHOLARSHIP IN TROPICAL ORNAMENTAL HORTICULTURE
• See page 138

GOLDEN STATE BONSAI FEDERATION
http://www.gsbf-bonsai.org

HORTICULTURE SCHOLARSHIPS

Scholarship for study towards a certificate in ornamental horticulture from an accredited school. Applicant must be a current member of a GSBF member Club and have a letter of recommendation from either their GSBF member Club President, or a responsible spokesperson from GSBF.

Academic Fields/Career Goals: Horticulture/Floriculture.

Award: Scholarship for use in freshman, sophomore, junior, senior, graduate, or postgraduate years. *Amount:* up to $400.

Eligibility Requirements: Applicant must be enrolled or expecting to enroll at a two-year or four-year or technical institution or university. Available to U.S. citizens.

Application Requirements: Application, references. *Deadline:* varies.

Contact: Abe Far, President
Golden State Bonsai Federation
2451 Galahad Road
San Diego, CA 92123
Phone: 619-234-3434
E-mail: abefar@cox.net

GOLF COURSE SUPERINTENDENTS ASSOCIATION OF AMERICA
http://www.gcsaa.org

GCSAA SCHOLARS COMPETITION

For outstanding students planning careers in golf course management. Must be full-time college undergraduates currently enrolled in a two-year or more accredited program related to golf course management and have completed one year of program. Must be member of GCSAA.

Academic Fields/Career Goals: Horticulture/Floriculture.

Award: Scholarship for use in freshman, sophomore, junior, or senior years; not renewable. *Number:* varies. *Amount:* $500–$6000.

Eligibility Requirements: Applicant must be enrolled or expecting to enroll full-time at a two-year or four-year institution or university. Applicant or parent of applicant must be member of Golf Course Superintendents Association of America. Available to U.S. and non-U.S. citizens.

Application Requirements: Application, essay, references, transcript. *Deadline:* June 1.

Contact: Amanda Howard, Employment Administrator
Golf Course Superintendents Association of America
1421 Research Park Drive
Lawrence, KS 66049-3859
Phone: 800-472-7878 Ext. 678
Fax: 785-832-4449
E-mail: ahoward@gcsaa.org

GOLF COURSE SUPERINTENDENTS ASSOCIATION OF AMERICA STUDENT ESSAY CONTEST
• See page 75

SCOTTS COMPANY SCHOLARS PROGRAM

The Scotts Company Scholars Program was developed by the Scotts Company in cooperation with The Environmental Institute for Golf to offer education and employment opportunities to students interested in pursuing a career in the "green industry." Students from diverse ethnic, cultural and socioeconomic backgrounds will be considered for judging. Must be a graduating high school senior or freshman, sophomore, or junior in college. Graduating high school seniors must attach a letter of college acceptance to application.

Academic Fields/Career Goals: Horticulture/Floriculture.

Award: Scholarship for use in freshman, sophomore, junior, or senior years; not renewable. *Number:* up to 7. *Amount:* $500–$2500.

Eligibility Requirements: Applicant must be enrolled or expecting to enroll full-time at a two-year or four-year or technical institution or university. Available to U.S. and non-U.S. citizens.

Application Requirements: Application, essay, references, transcript. *Deadline:* March 1.

Contact: Amanda Howard, Employment Administrator
Golf Course Superintendents Association of America
1421 Research Park Drive
Lawrence, KS 66049-3859
Phone: 800-472-7878 Ext. 678
Fax: 785-832-4449
E-mail: ahoward@gcsaa.org

HERB SOCIETY OF AMERICA
http://www.herbsociety.org

HERB SOCIETY RESEARCH GRANTS
• See page 92

HERB SOCIETY OF AMERICA, WESTERN RESERVE UNIT
http://www.herbsociety.org

FRANCIS SYLVIA ZVERINA SCHOLARSHIP

Awards are given to needy students who plan a career in horticulture or related field. Preference will be given to applicants whose horticultural career goals involve teaching, research, or work in the public or nonprofit sector, such as public gardens, botanical gardens, parks, arboreta, city planning, public education, and awareness.

Academic Fields/Career Goals: Horticulture/Floriculture; Landscape Architecture.

Award: Scholarship for use in sophomore, junior, or senior years; not renewable. *Number:* 1–3. *Amount:* $2000–$5000.

Eligibility Requirements: Applicant must be enrolled or expecting to enroll full or part-time at a four-year institution or university. Available to U.S. citizens.

Application Requirements: Application, essay, references, transcript. *Deadline:* March 15.

Contact: Dr. Jane Cavanaugh, Committee Chair
Herb Society of America, Western Reserve Unit
2293 Stanford Drive
Wickliffe, OH 44092
Phone: 440-943-0947
E-mail: jancavan@sbcglobal.net

WESTERN RESERVE HERB SOCIETY SCHOLARSHIP

Awards are given to needy students who plan a career in horticulture or related field. Preference will be given to applicants whose horticultural career goals involve teaching, research, or work in the public or nonprofit sector, such as public gardens, botanical gardens, parks, arboreta, city planning, public education and awareness.

Academic Fields/Career Goals: Horticulture/Floriculture; Landscape Architecture.

Award: Scholarship for use in sophomore, junior, senior, or graduate years; not renewable. *Number:* 1–3. *Amount:* $1000–$2000.

Eligibility Requirements: Applicant must be enrolled or expecting to enroll full or part-time at a four-year institution or university and resident of Ohio. Available to U.S. citizens.

Application Requirements: Application, essay, references, transcript. *Deadline:* March 15.

Contact: Dr. Jane Cavanaugh, Committee Chair
Herb Society of America, Western Reserve Unit
2293 Stanford Drive
Wickliffe, OH 44092
Phone: 440-943-0947
E-mail: jancavan@sbcglobal.net

INTERNATIONAL EXECUTIVE HOUSEKEEPERS ASSOCIATION
http://www.ieha.org

INTERNATIONAL EXECUTIVE HOUSEKEEPERS EDUCATIONAL FOUNDATION
• See page 307

JOSEPH SHINODA MEMORIAL SCHOLARSHIP FOUNDATION
http://www.shinodascholarship.org

JOSEPH SHINODA MEMORIAL SCHOLARSHIP

One-time award for undergraduates in accredited colleges and universities. Must be furthering their education in the field of floriculture (production, distribution, research, or retail). Deadline is March 30.

Academic Fields/Career Goals: Horticulture/Floriculture.

Award: Scholarship for use in freshman, sophomore, junior, or senior years; not renewable. *Number:* 10–20. *Amount:* up to $1000.

Eligibility Requirements: Applicant must be enrolled or expecting to enroll full-time at a four-year institution or university and must have an interest in designated field specified by sponsor. Available to U.S. and non-U.S. citizens.

Application Requirements: Application, essay, financial need analysis, photo, references, transcript. *Deadline:* March 30.

Contact: Prof. Virginia R. Walter, Joseph Shinoda Memorial
Scholarship Foundation Inc, C/O Horticulture and Crop
Science Department
Joseph Shinoda Memorial Scholarship Foundation
California Polytechnic State University
San Luis Obispo, CA 93407
Phone: 805-756-2897
E-mail: vwalter@calpoly.edu

LANDSCAPE ARCHITECTURE FOUNDATION
http://www.LAprofession.org

LAF/CLASS FUND ORNAMENTAL HORTICULTURE PROGRAM

Three $1,000 scholarships to juniors and/or seniors enrolled in an ornamental horticulture curriculum

Academic Fields/Career Goals: Horticulture/Floriculture.

Award: Prize for use in junior or senior years. *Number:* 3. *Amount:* $1000.

Eligibility Requirements: Applicant must be enrolled or expecting to enroll full or part-time at an institution or university and studying in California. Available to U.S. citizens.

Application Requirements: Application, essay, references. *Deadline:* February 15.

Contact: Ron Figura, Project Manager
Landscape Architecture Foundation
818 18th Street, NW
Suite 810
Washington, DC 20006
Phone: 202-331-7070 Ext. 10
Fax: 202-331-7079
E-mail: rfigura@lafoundation.org

LANDSCAPE ARCHITECTURE FOUNDATION/CALIFORNIA LANDSCAPE ARCHITECTURE STUDENT FUND UNIVERSITY SCHOLARSHIP PROGRAM

Nonrenewable scholarship for students continuing to study landscape architecture in California. Based on financial need and commitment to profession.

Academic Fields/Career Goals: Horticulture/Floriculture; Landscape Architecture.

Award: Scholarship for use in junior or senior years; not renewable. *Number:* 6. *Amount:* $2000.

Eligibility Requirements: Applicant must be enrolled or expecting to enroll full or part-time at a four-year institution or university and studying in California. Available to U.S. citizens.

Application Requirements: Application, financial need analysis, references. *Deadline:* February 15.

Contact: Ron Figura, Project Manager
Landscape Architecture Foundation
818 18th Street, NW
Suite 810
Washington, DC 20006
Phone: 202-331-7070 Ext. 10
Fax: 202-331-7079
E-mail: rfigura@lafoundation.org

MONTANA FEDERATION OF GARDEN CLUBS
http://www.mtfgc.org

LIFE MEMBER MONTANA FEDERATION OF GARDEN CLUBS SCHOLARSHIP
• See page 138

NATIONAL GARDEN CLUBS SCHOLARSHIP

Scholarship for a college student majoring in some branch of horticulture. Applicants must have sophomore or higher standing and be a legal resident of Montana.

Academic Fields/Career Goals: Horticulture/Floriculture.

Award: Scholarship for use in sophomore, junior, or senior years. *Amount:* up to $3500.

Eligibility Requirements: Applicant must be enrolled or expecting to enroll full-time at a four-year institution or university and resident of Montana. Available to U.S. citizens.

Application Requirements: Application, financial need analysis. *Deadline:* February 28.

Contact: Margaret S. Yaw
Montana Federation of Garden Clubs
2603 Spring Creek Drive
Bozeman, MT 59715-3621
Phone: 406-587-3621

NATIONAL COUNCIL OF STATE GARDEN CLUBS, INC. SCHOLARSHIP
http://www.gardenclub.org

NATIONAL COUNCIL OF STATE GARDEN CLUBS, INC. SCHOLARSHIP
• See page 82

NATIONAL GARDEN CLUBS, INC.
http://www.gardenclub.org

NATIONAL GARDEN CLUBS, INC. SCHOLARSHIP PROGRAM
• See page 83

NATIONAL POTATO COUNCIL WOMEN'S AUXILIARY
http://www.nationalpotatocouncil.org

POTATO INDUSTRY SCHOLARSHIP
• See page 76

PARK PEOPLE
http://www.parkpeople.org

THE PARK PEOPLE $2000 SCHOLARSHIP
• See page 102

PENNSYLVANIA ASSOCIATION OF CONSERVATION DISTRICTS AUXILIARY
http://www.blairconservationdistrict.org

PACD AUXILIARY SCHOLARSHIPS
• See page 76

PROFESSIONAL GROUNDS MANAGEMENT SOCIETY
http://www.pgms.org

ANNE SEAMAN PROFESSIONAL GROUNDS MANAGEMENT SOCIETY MEMORIAL SCHOLARSHIP
• See page 84

SOIL AND WATER CONSERVATION SOCIETY-NEW JERSEY CHAPTER
http://www.geocities.com/njswcs

EDWARD R. HALL SCHOLARSHIP
• See page 76

TURF AND ORNAMENTAL COMMUNICATION ASSOCIATION
http://www.toca.org

TURF AND ORNAMENTAL COMMUNICATORS ASSOCIATION SCHOLARSHIP PROGRAM
• See page 142

UNITED AGRIBUSINESS LEAGUE http://www.ual.org

UNITED AGRIBUSINESS LEAGUE SCHOLARSHIP PROGRAM
• See page 77

UNITED AGRICULTURAL BENEFIT TRUST SCHOLARSHIP
• See page 77

HOSPITALITY MANAGEMENT

AMERICAN HOTEL AND LODGING EDUCATIONAL FOUNDATION http://www.ahlef.org

AMERICAN EXPRESS SCHOLARSHIP PROGRAM

Award for hotel employees of American Hotel and Lodging Association member properties and their dependents. For full- and part-time students in undergraduate program leading to degree in hospitality management. Must be employed at hotel which is a property of AH&LA. Complete appropriate application, and submit copy of college curriculum and IRS 1040 form. Deadline: May 1. Application available at Web site: http://www.ahlef.org.

Academic Fields/Career Goals: Hospitality Management.

Award: Scholarship for use in freshman, sophomore, junior, or senior years; not renewable. *Number:* varies. *Amount:* $500–$2000.

Eligibility Requirements: Applicant must be enrolled or expecting to enroll full or part-time at a two-year or four-year institution or university. Applicant or parent of applicant must have employment or volunteer experience in hospitality/hotel administration/operations. Available to U.S. citizens.

Application Requirements: Application, essay, financial need analysis, transcript. *Deadline:* May 1.

Contact: Crystal Hammond, Manager of Foundation Programs
American Hotel and Lodging Educational Foundation
1201 New York Avenue, NW, Suite 600
Washington, DC 20005-3931
Phone: 202-289-3188
Fax: 202-289-3199
E-mail: chammond@ahlef.org

ANNUAL SCHOLARSHIP GRANT PROGRAM
• See page 306

LODGING MANAGEMENT PROGRAM SCHOLARSHIPS

Scholarships established to recognize the achievements of high school students who have successfully completed both years of the LMP high school curriculum and to encourage their further studies in an accredited undergraduate hospitality management degree-granting program or in an educational institute distance learning course or professional certification.

Academic Fields/Career Goals: Hospitality Management.

Award: Scholarship for use in freshman year. *Number:* 1.

Eligibility Requirements: Applicant must be enrolled or expecting to enroll at a two-year institution. Available to U.S. citizens.

Application Requirements: Application.

Contact: Crystal Hammond
American Hotel and Lodging Educational Foundation
1201 New York Avenue, NW, Suite 600
Washington, DC 20005-3197

AMERICAN INSTITUTE OF WINE AND FOOD-PACIFIC NORTHWEST CHAPTER

CULINARY, VINIFERA, AND HOSPITALITY SCHOLARSHIP
• See page 301

CLUB FOUNDATION http://www.clubfoundation.org

STUDENT SCHOLARSHIP PROGRAM

Candidates must be actively seeking a managerial career in the private club industry and currently attending an accredited four-year college or university. Individual must have completed his/her freshman year and be enrolled full-time for the following year. Also, candidate must have achieved and continue to maintain a GPA of at least 2.5 on a 4.0 scale, or 4.5 on a 6.0 scale.

Academic Fields/Career Goals: Hospitality Management.

Award: Scholarship for use in sophomore, junior, or senior years; not renewable. *Number:* 2. *Amount:* $2500.

Eligibility Requirements: Applicant must be enrolled or expecting to enroll full-time at a four-year institution or university. Applicant must have 2.5 GPA or higher. Available to U.S. citizens.

Application Requirements: Application, essay, resume, references, self-addressed stamped envelope, transcript. *Deadline:* April 14.

Contact: Rhonda Schaver, Manager, Administration and Scholarship Programs
Club Foundation
1733 King Street
Alexandria, VA 22314
Phone: 703-739-9500 Ext. 301
Fax: 703-739-0124
E-mail: schaverr@clubfoundation.org

GOLDEN GATE RESTAURANT ASSOCIATION http://www.ggra.org

GOLDEN GATE RESTAURANT ASSOCIATION SCHOLARSHIP FOUNDATION
• See page 307

HAWAII HOTEL AND LODGING ASSOCIATION http://www.hawaiihotels.org

R.W. BOB HOLDEN SCHOLARSHIP

One $500 award for student attending or planning to attend an accredited university or college in Hawaii majoring in hotel management. Must be Hawaii resident and have a minimum 3.0 GPA.

Academic Fields/Career Goals: Hospitality Management; Travel/Tourism.

Award: Scholarship for use in freshman, sophomore, junior, senior, or graduate years; not renewable. *Number:* 1–5. *Amount:* $500.

Eligibility Requirements: Applicant must be enrolled or expecting to enroll full-time at a two-year or four-year institution or university; resident of Hawaii and studying in Hawaii. Applicant must have 3.0 GPA or higher. Available to U.S. and non-U.S. citizens.

Application Requirements: Application, autobiography, driver's license, essay, photo, references, transcript. *Deadline:* July 1.

Contact: Naomi Kanna, Director of Membership Services
Hawaii Hotel and Lodging Association
2250 Kalakaua Avenue, Suite 404-4
Honolulu, HI 96815-2564
Phone: 808-923-0407
Fax: 808-924-3843
E-mail: hha@hawaiihotels.org

HISPANIC COLLEGE FUND, INC. http://www.hispanicfund.org

DENNY'S/HISPANIC COLLEGE FUND SCHOLARSHIP
• See page 62

INTERNATIONAL AIRLINES TRAVEL AGENT NETWORK http://www.iatan.org

INTERNATIONAL AIRLINES TRAVEL AGENT NETWORK RONALD A. SANTANA MEMORIAL FOUNDATION

The IATAN Foundation provides scholarships annually to individuals who are interested in pursuing or enhancing their careers in travel. The IATAN Foundation was established in memory of the late Ronald A. Santana, IATAN former Board member, to continue his dedication and tireless efforts toward the education of travel agents.

Academic Fields/Career Goals: Hospitality Management; Travel/Tourism.

Award: Scholarship for use in freshman, sophomore, junior, senior, or graduate years; not renewable. *Number:* 2–14. *Amount:* $500–$2500.

Eligibility Requirements: Applicant must be age 17 and enrolled or expecting to enroll full or part-time at a two-year or four-year or technical institution or university. Available to U.S. citizens.

Application Requirements: Application, essay, resume, references, transcript. *Deadline:* April 15.

Contact: Denise Ladouceur, President
International Airlines Travel Agent Network
PO Box 2988
Plattsburgh, NY 12901-0999
Phone: 877-734-2826

INTERNATIONAL EXECUTIVE HOUSEKEEPERS ASSOCIATION
http://www.ieha.org

INTERNATIONAL EXECUTIVE HOUSEKEEPERS ASSOCIATION EDUCATIONAL FOUNDATION SPARTAN SCHOLARSHIP

Award available to I.E.H.A. members and their immediate families. Scholarship will be awarded to the best qualified candidate as determined by I.E.H.A.'s Education Committee.

Academic Fields/Career Goals: Hospitality Management.

Award: Scholarship for use in freshman, sophomore, junior, or senior years; not renewable. *Amount:* $1500.

Eligibility Requirements: Applicant must be enrolled or expecting to enroll at a four-year institution or university. Applicant or parent of applicant must be member of International Executive Housekeepers Association. Available to U.S. citizens.

Application Requirements: Application, financial need analysis. *Deadline:* January.

Contact: I.E.H.A. Scholarship Selection Committee
International Executive Housekeepers Association
1001 Eastwind Drive, Suite 301
Westerville, OH 43081-3361
Phone: 800-200-6342
Fax: 614-895-1248

INTERNATIONAL FOODSERVICE EDITORIAL COUNCIL
http://www.ifec-is-us.com

INTERNATIONAL FOODSERVICE EDITORIAL COUNCIL COMMUNICATIONS SCHOLARSHIP
• *See page 182*

MAINE SCHOOL FOOD SERVICE ASSOCIATION (MSFSA)

SCHOLARSHIP OF THE MAINE SCHOOL FOOD SERVICE ASSOCIATION
• *See page 305*

MISSOURI TRAVEL COUNCIL
http://www.missouritravel.com

MISSOURI TRAVEL COUNCIL TOURISM SCHOLARSHIP
• *See page 307*

NATIONAL TOURISM FOUNDATION
http://www.ntfonline.org

ACADEMY OF TRAVEL AND TOURISM SCHOLARSHIPS

One $500 scholarship award to a graduating high school senior planning to attend accredited postsecondary education tourism-related program. Applicant must be completing senior year of high school at Academy of Travel and Tourism location. Each academy may submit most qualified student. Please refer to Web site for further details: http://www.ntfonline.org

Academic Fields/Career Goals: Hospitality Management; Political Science; Travel/Tourism.

Award: Scholarship for use in freshman year; not renewable. *Number:* 1. *Amount:* $500.

Eligibility Requirements: Applicant must be high school student and planning to enroll or expecting to enroll at a two-year or four-year institution or university. Applicant must have 3.0 GPA or higher. Available to U.S. citizens.

Application Requirements: Application, essay, resume, references. *Deadline:* May 10.

Contact: Michelle Gorin, Projects Coordinator
National Tourism Foundation
546 East Main Street
Lexington, KY 40508-3071
Phone: 800-682-8886
Fax: 859-226-4437
E-mail: michelle.gorin@ntastaff.com

CLEVELAND LEGACY I AND II SCHOLARSHIP AWARDS
• *See page 308*

NEW HORIZONS KATHY LE TARTE SCHOLARSHIP
• *See page 309*

PAT AND JIM HOST SCHOLARSHIP
• *See page 309*

SOCIETIE DES CASINOS DU QUEBEC SCHOLARSHIP
• *See page 309*

TAMPA, HILLSBOROUGH LEGACY SCHOLARSHIP
• *See page 309*

TAUCK SCHOLARS SCHOLARSHIPS
• *See page 309*

TULSA SCHOLARSHIP AWARDS
• *See page 309*

YELLOW RIBBON SCHOLARSHIP
• *See page 310*

NETWORK OF EXECUTIVE WOMEN IN HOSPITALITY
http://www.newh.org

NETWORK OF EXECUTIVE WOMEN IN HOSPITALITY, INC. SCHOLARSHIP
• *See page 101*

SOUTH DAKOTA RETAILERS ASSOCIATION
http://www.sdra.org

SOUTH DAKOTA RETAILERS ASSOCIATION SCHOLARSHIP PROGRAM
• *See page 69*

UNITED NEGRO COLLEGE FUND
http://www.uncf.org

EMERSON ELECTRIC COMPANY SCHOLARSHIP
• *See page 71*

HUMANITIES

ALBERTA HERITAGE SCHOLARSHIP FUND/ ALBERTA SCHOLARSHIP PROGRAMS
http://www.alis.gov.ab.ca

LOIS HOLE HUMANITIES AND SOCIAL SCIENCES SCHOLARSHIP

Award of CAN$ 5000 for students enrolled full-time in the second or subsequent year of postsecondary study in the Faculty of Humanities or the Faculty of Social Sciences, at the University of Alberta, the University of Calgary, the University of Lethbridge, and Athabasca University. Application deadline is October 15 - University of Alberta, November 15 - University of Lethbridge, the University of Calgary and Athabasca University.

Academic Fields/Career Goals: Humanities; Social Sciences.

Award: Scholarship for use in freshman year; not renewable. *Number:* 4. *Amount:* $4305.

Eligibility Requirements: Applicant must be enrolled or expecting to enroll full-time at an institution or university; resident of Alberta and studying in Alberta. Available to U.S. and Canadian citizens.

Alberta Heritage Scholarship Fund/Alberta Scholarship Programs
(continued)

Application Requirements: Application. *Deadline:* varies.

Contact: Stuart Dunn, Manager
Alberta Heritage Scholarship Fund/Alberta Scholarship Programs
4th Floor, 9940 106 Street, Box 28000 Station Main
Edmonton, AB T5J 4R4
Canada
Phone: 780-427-8640
Fax: 780-427-1288
E-mail: scholarships@gov.ab.ca

AMERICAN CLASSICAL LEAGUE/NATIONAL JUNIOR CLASSICAL LEAGUE   http://www.aclclassics.org

NATIONAL JUNIOR CLASSICAL LEAGUE SCHOLARSHIP
* See page 311

AMERICAN HISTORICAL ASSOCIATION   http://www.historians.org

WESLEY-LOGAN PRIZE
* See page 73

AMERICAN LEGION AUXILIARY, DEPARTMENT OF WASHINGTON   http://www.walegion-aux.org

FLORENCE LEMCKE MEMORIAL SCHOLARSHIP IN FINE ARTS
* See page 107

AMERICAN PHILOLOGICAL ASSOCIATION   http://www.apaclassics.org

MINORITY STUDENT SUMMER SCHOLARSHIP
* See page 109

AMERICAN SCHOOL OF CLASSICAL STUDIES AT ATHENS   http://www.ascsa.edu.gr

ASCSA SUMMER SESSIONS OPEN SCHOLARSHIPS
* See page 88

BEINECKE SCHOLARSHIP PROGRAM   http://www.beineckescholarship.org/

BEINECKE SCHOLARSHIP FOR GRADUATE STUDY
* See page 109

BETHESDA LUTHERAN HOMES AND SERVICES, INC.   http://www.blhs.org

DEVELOPMENTAL DISABILITIES SCHOLASTIC ACHIEVEMENT SCHOLARSHIP FOR LUTHERAN COLLEGE STUDENTS
* See page 208

BUSINESS AND PROFESSIONAL WOMEN'S FOUNDATION   http://www.bpwusa.org

BPW CAREER ADVANCEMENT SCHOLARSHIP PROGRAM FOR WOMEN
* See page 136

CANADIAN INSTITUTE OF UKRAINIAN STUDIES   http://www.ualberta.ca/cius/

LEO J. KRYSA UNDERGRADUATE SCHOLARSHIP
* See page 104

CATCHING THE DREAM

MATH, ENGINEERING, SCIENCE, BUSINESS, EDUCATION, COMPUTERS SCHOLARSHIPS
* See page 145

NATIVE AMERICAN LEADERSHIP IN EDUCATION (NALE)
* See page 145

CHINESE HISTORICAL SOCIETY OF SOUTHERN CALIFORNIA

CHSSC SCHOLARSHIP AWARD

$1000 scholarship is offered to a deserving full-time student in southern California who demonstrates strong interest in Chinese American studies in humanities or social sciences. Deadline is March 12.

Academic Fields/Career Goals: Humanities; Social Sciences.

Award: Scholarship for use in freshman, sophomore, junior, senior, or graduate years; not renewable. *Number:* 1–2. *Amount:* $1000.

Eligibility Requirements: Applicant must be enrolled or expecting to enroll full-time at a four-year institution or university; resident of California and studying in California. Applicant must have 3.0 GPA or higher. Available to U.S. and non-U.S. citizens.

Application Requirements: Application, essay, financial need analysis, interview, references, transcript. *Deadline:* March 12.

Contact: CHSSC Scholarship Committee
Chinese Historical Society of Southern California
415 Bernard Street
Los Angeles, CA 90012-1703

DELAWARE DEPARTMENT OF EDUCATION   http://www.doe.k12.de.us

CHARLES L. HEBNER MEMORIAL SCHOLARSHIP

Award for legal residents of Delaware who plan to enroll full-time at the University of Delaware or Delaware State University. Must pursue their career in humanities or social sciences. Must have combined score of 1350 on the SAT. Full tuition, fees, room, board, and books at the University of Delaware or Delaware State University. Renewable for up to three additional years. One award every year per school. Deadline is March 13.

Academic Fields/Career Goals: Humanities; Social Sciences.

Award: Scholarship for use in freshman, sophomore, junior, senior, graduate, or postgraduate years; renewable. *Number:* 1.

Eligibility Requirements: Applicant must be enrolled or expecting to enroll full-time at a two-year or four-year or technical institution or university; resident of Delaware and studying in Delaware. Available to U.S. citizens.

Application Requirements: Application, transcript. *Deadline:* March 13.

Contact: Maureen Laffey, Director
Delaware Department of Education
Carvel State Office Building, 820 North French Street
Wilmington, DE 19801
Phone: 302-577-5240
Fax: 302-577-6765
E-mail: dedoe@doe.k12.de.us

HARVARD TRAVELLERS CLUB

HARVARD TRAVELLERS CLUB GRANTS
* See page 96

IRISH-AMERICAN CULTURAL INSTITUTE   http://www.iaci-usa.org

IRISH RESEARCH FUNDS
* See page 105

JACK J. ISGUR FOUNDATION

JACK J. ISGUR FOUNDATION SCHOLARSHIP
* See page 111

LADIES AUXILIARY TO THE VETERANS OF FOREIGN WARS, DEPARTMENT OF MAINE

FRANCIS L. BOOTH MEDICAL SCHOLARSHIP SPONSORED BY LAVFW DEPARTMENT OF MAINE
* See page 327

METAVUE CORPORATION   http://www.metavue.com

THE FW RAUSCH ARTS AND HUMANITIES PAPER CONTEST
* See page 112

NASA/MARYLAND SPACE GRANT CONSORTIUM
http://www.mdspacegrant.org

NASA MARYLAND SPACE GRANT CONSORTIUM UNDERGRADUATE SCHOLARSHIPS
• See page 139

NATIONAL FEDERATION OF THE BLIND
http://www.nfb.org

NATIONAL FEDERATION OF THE BLIND HUMANITIES SCHOLARSHIP

One-time award for full-time postsecondary study in the humanities (art, English, foreign languages, history, philosophy, or religion) for students who are legally blind. Must submit recommendation from state officer of National Federation of the Blind. Based on academic excellence, service to the community, and financial need. May reapply. Must attend school in U.S.

Academic Fields/Career Goals: Humanities.

Award: Scholarship for use in freshman, sophomore, junior, or senior years; not renewable. *Number:* 1. *Amount:* $3000.

Eligibility Requirements: Applicant must be enrolled or expecting to enroll full-time at a two-year or four-year institution or university. Applicant or parent of applicant must have employment or volunteer experience in community service. Applicant must be visually impaired. Applicant must have 3.5 GPA or higher. Available to U.S. and non-U.S. citizens.

Application Requirements: Application, autobiography, essay, financial need analysis, references, transcript, letter from the State President or other officer of the National Federation of the Blind. *Deadline:* March 31.

Contact: Peggy Elliot, Chairman, Scholarship Committee
National Federation of the Blind
805 Fifth Avenue
Grinnell, IA 50112-1653
Phone: 641-236-3369

POLISH ARTS CLUB OF BUFFALO SCHOLARSHIP FOUNDATION
http://pacb.bfn.org/about/constitution.html

POLISH ARTS CLUB OF BUFFALO SCHOLARSHIP FOUNDATION TRUST
• See page 108

POLISH HERITAGE ASSOCIATION OF MARYLAND

ROBERT P. PULA MEMORIAL SCHOLARSHIP

Scholarship will be awarded to a student whose major is in the humanities, social sciences, literature, or Polish studies. Must be of Polish descent (at least two Polish grandparents), a U.S. citizen, and resident of Maryland. Application deadline is March 31.

Academic Fields/Career Goals: Humanities; Literature/English/Writing; Social Sciences.

Award: Scholarship for use in freshman, sophomore, junior, or senior years; not renewable. *Number:* 1. *Amount:* up to $1500.

Eligibility Requirements: Applicant must be of Polish heritage and enrolled or expecting to enroll full-time at a two-year institution or university. Available to U.S. citizens.

Application Requirements: Application, essay, financial need analysis, interview, transcript. *Deadline:* March 31.

Contact: Thomas Hollowak
Phone: 410-837-4268
E-mail: thollowak@ubalt.edu

SOCIAL SCIENCES AND HUMANITIES RESEARCH COUNCIL OF CANADA
http://www.sshrc.ca

RESEARCH DEVELOPMENT INITIATIVE
• See page 237

UNITED NEGRO COLLEGE FUND
http://www.uncf.org

MCCLARE FAMILY TRUST SCHOLARSHIP

Scholarship for college freshmen majoring in the humanities with an interest in English literature. Must attend UNCF member institution. Information on Web site http://www.uncf.org

Academic Fields/Career Goals: Humanities.

Award: Scholarship for use in freshman year; renewable. *Number:* 1. *Amount:* varies.

Eligibility Requirements: Applicant must be Black (non-Hispanic) and enrolled or expecting to enroll at a four-year institution or university. Applicant must have 3.0 GPA or higher. Available to U.S. citizens.

Application Requirements: Application, financial need analysis, FAFSA. *Deadline:* varies.

Contact: Rebecca Bennett, Director, Program Services
United Negro College Fund
8260 Willow Oaks Corporate Drive
Fairfax, VA 22031-8044
Phone: 800-331-2244
E-mail: rbennett@uncf.org

HYDROLOGY

ASSOCIATION OF CALIFORNIA WATER AGENCIES
http://www.acwanet.com

ASSOCIATION OF CALIFORNIA WATER AGENCIES SCHOLARSHIPS
• See page 91

CLAIR A. HILL SCHOLARSHIP
• See page 91

CALIFORNIA WATER AWARENESS CAMPAIGN
http://www.wateraware.org

CALIFORNIA WATER AWARENESS CAMPAIGN WATER SCHOLAR
• See page 79

HANDS-ON! PROJECTS/HYDRO POWER CONTEST
http://users.rcn.com/hands-on/hydro/contest.html

HYDRO POWER CONTEST
• See page 247

INTERNATIONAL ASSOCIATION OF GREAT LAKES RESEARCH
http://www.iaglr.org

PAUL W. RODGERS SCHOLARSHIP
• See page 214

INDUSTRIAL DESIGN

HISPANIC COLLEGE FUND, INC.
http://www.hispanicfund.org

EL NUEVO CONSTRUCTOR SCHOLARSHIP PROGRAM
• See page 99

INDUSTRIAL DESIGNERS SOCIETY OF AMERICA
http://www.idsa.org

INDUSTRIAL DESIGNERS SOCIETY OF AMERICA UNDERGRADUATE SCHOLARSHIP

One-time award to a U.S. citizen or permanent U.S. resident currently enrolled in an industrial design program. Must submit 20 visual examples of work and study full-time. Reference URL: http://new.idsa.org/webmodules/articles/anmviewer.asp?a=120&z=99

Academic Fields/Career Goals: Industrial Design.

Award: Scholarship for use in junior year; not renewable. *Number:* 2. *Amount:* $1000–$2000.

Eligibility Requirements: Applicant must be enrolled or expecting to enroll full-time at a four-year institution or university. Applicant must have 3.0 GPA or higher. Available to U.S. citizens.

Industrial Designers Society of America (continued)

Application Requirements: Application, references, transcript. *Deadline:* May 1.

Contact: Max Taylor, Executive Assistant
Industrial Designers Society of America
45195 Business Court, Suite 250
Dulles, VA 20166
Phone: 703-707-6000
Fax: 703-787-8501
E-mail: maxt@idsa.org

INTERNATIONAL FURNISHINGS AND DESIGN ASSOCIATION
http://www.ifdaef.org

RUTH CLARK SCHOLARSHIP
• *See page 111*

INTERNATIONAL HOUSEWARES ASSOCIATION
http://www.housewares.org

STUDENT DESIGN COMPETITION

Prizes awarded to full-time students enrolled in a degree program for industrial design at a U.S. college. Must design a housewares project according to specified guidelines. Must call to obtain entry form. Details on Web site: http://www.ifpte.org

Academic Fields/Career Goals: Industrial Design.

Award: Prize for use in freshman, sophomore, junior, or senior years; not renewable. *Number:* 3–7. *Amount:* $1000–$2500.

Eligibility Requirements: Applicant must be enrolled or expecting to enroll full-time at a four-year institution or university. Available to U.S. and non-U.S. citizens.

Application Requirements: Application, applicant must enter a contest, entry form, drawings, slides. *Deadline:* December 30.

Contact: Victoria Matranga, Design Programs Coordinator
International Housewares Association
6400 Shafer Court, Suite 650
Rosemont, IL 60018
Phone: 847-692-0136
Fax: 847-292-4211
E-mail: vmatranga@housewares.org

SOCIETY OF MANUFACTURING ENGINEERS EDUCATION FOUNDATION
http://www.sme.org

DOWNRIVER DETROIT CHAPTER 198 SCHOLARSHIP
• *See page 273*

FORT WAYNE CHAPTER 56 SCHOLARSHIP
• *See page 274*

NORTH CENTRAL REGION 9 SCHOLARSHIP
• *See page 275*

PHOENIX CHAPTER 67 SCHOLARSHIP
• *See page 275*

WICHITA CHAPTER 52 SCHOLARSHIP
• *See page 276*

SOCIETY OF PLASTICS ENGINEERS (SPE) FOUNDATION
http://www.4spe.com

SOCIETY OF PLASTICS ENGINEERS SCHOLARSHIP PROGRAM
• *See page 168*

WORLDSTUDIO FOUNDATION
http://www.worldstudio.org

WORLDSTUDIO FOUNDATION SCHOLARSHIP PROGRAM
• *See page 104*

INSURANCE AND ACTUARIAL SCIENCE

CASUALTY ACTUARIES OF THE SOUTHEAST
http://www.casact.org

CASUALTY ACTUARIES OF THE SOUTHEAST SCHOLARSHIP PROGRAM

Scholarships available for undergraduate students in the southeastern states for the study of actuarial science. Must be studying in one of the following states: Alabama, Arkansas, Florida, Georgia, Kentucky, Louisiana, Mississippi, North Carolina, South Carolina, Tennessee, or Virginia. See Web site: http://www.casact.org/affiliates/case/scholarmemo.htm for information and application form and evaluation and recommendation form.

Academic Fields/Career Goals: Insurance and Actuarial Science.

Award: Scholarship for use in sophomore, junior, or senior years; not renewable. *Number:* 1. *Amount:* $1000.

Eligibility Requirements: Applicant must be enrolled or expecting to enroll full-time at a four-year institution or university and studying in Alabama, Arkansas, Florida, Georgia, Kentucky, Louisiana, Michigan, North Carolina, South Carolina, Tennessee, or Virginia. Available to U.S. citizens.

Application Requirements: Application, evaluation and recommendation form.

Contact: Mr. Michael Miller
Casualty Actuaries of the Southeast
3500 Lenox Road, Suite 900
Altanta, GA 30326-4238
Phone: 404-365-1549
E-mail: michael.miller@towersperrin.com

MISSOURI INSURANCE EDUCATION FOUNDATION
http://www.mief.org/hsapp.htm

MISSOURI INSURANCE EDUCATION FOUNDATION SCHOLARSHIP

One $2000 scholarship to honor Lawrence Leggett, and five $1500 Missouri Insurance Education Foundation Scholarships available to college students in junior or senior year of a college or university. Must be Missouri residents. Application deadline is March 31.

Academic Fields/Career Goals: Insurance and Actuarial Science.

Award: Scholarship for use in junior or senior years. *Number:* 1–5. *Amount:* $1500–$2000.

Eligibility Requirements: Applicant must be enrolled or expecting to enroll full-time at a four-year institution or university; resident of Missouri and studying in Missouri. Applicant must have 2.5 GPA or higher. Available to U.S. citizens.

Application Requirements: Application, financial need analysis, references, transcript. *Deadline:* March 31.

Contact: William Bennett, Scholarship Chairman
Missouri Insurance Education Foundation
PO Box 1654
Jefferson City, MO 65102
Phone: 573-893-4234
E-mail: miis@midamerica.net

NATIONAL ASSOCIATION OF INSURANCE WOMEN EDUCATION FOUNDATION

NAIW COLLEGE SCHOLARSHIP

Award available to student seeking bachelor degree or higher with a major in insurance, risk management, or actuarial science. Must have completed two insurance, actuarial or risk management-related courses. Must have completed third year of college and have a minimum 3.75 GPA. Deadline is March 1.

Academic Fields/Career Goals: Insurance and Actuarial Science.

Award: Scholarship for use in sophomore, junior, senior, or graduate years; not renewable. *Number:* varies. *Amount:* $2500–$5000.

Eligibility Requirements: Applicant must be enrolled or expecting to enroll full or part-time at a four-year institution or university. Available to U.S. citizens.

Application Requirements: Application, essay, references, transcript. *Deadline:* March 1.

Contact: Billie Sleet, Executive Director
National Association of Insurance Women Education Foundation
5310 East 31st Street, Suite 302
Tulsa, OK 74135
Phone: 918-622-1816
Fax: 918-622-1821
E-mail: foundation@naiwfoundation.org

NAIW EDUCATION FOUNDATION PROFESSIONAL SCHOLARSHIP
• *See page 151*

SOCIETY OF ACTUARIES http://www.soa.org

ACTUARIAL SCHOLARSHIPS FOR MINORITY STUDENTS

Award for minority students at the undergraduate or graduate level pursuing an actuarial career. Amount based on merit and individual need. Must be U.S. citizen or permanent resident. Recipients receive an additional $500 for each actuarial exam passed. Application deadline is April 15. See Web site at http://www.beanactuary.org for further details.

Academic Fields/Career Goals: Insurance and Actuarial Science.

Award: Scholarship for use in freshman, sophomore, junior, senior, or graduate years; not renewable. *Number:* varies. *Amount:* $500–$5000.

Eligibility Requirements: Applicant must be American Indian/Alaska Native, Asian/Pacific Islander, Black (non-Hispanic), or Hispanic and enrolled or expecting to enroll full-time at a four-year institution or university. Available to U.S. and non-U.S. citizens.

Application Requirements: Application, financial need analysis, transcript. *Deadline:* April 15.

Contact: Minority Scholarship Coordinator
Society of Actuaries
475 North Martingale Road, Suite 600
Schaumburg, IL 60173-2226
Phone: 847-706-3500
E-mail: sparker@soa.org

SPENCER EDUCATIONAL FOUNDATION, INC. http://www.spencered.org

SPENCER RISK MANAGEMENT AND INSURANCE SCHOLARSHIP

Scholarship awarded to full- or part-time students interested in risk management/insurance studies. Student must retain 3.3 GPA or higher. Please refer to Web site for further details: http://www.spencer.org.

Academic Fields/Career Goals: Insurance and Actuarial Science.

Award: Scholarship for use in sophomore, junior, senior, or graduate years; renewable. *Number:* 10–20. *Amount:* $5000–$10,000.

Eligibility Requirements: Applicant must be enrolled or expecting to enroll full or part-time at a four-year institution or university. Available to U.S. and non-U.S. citizens.

Application Requirements: Application, essay, resume, references, transcript. *Deadline:* varies.

Contact: Angela Sabatino, Secretary and Foundation Administrator
Spencer Educational Foundation, Inc.
1065 Avenue of the Americas, 13th Floor
New York, NY 10018-5637
Phone: 212-655-6223
Fax: 212-655-6044
E-mail: asabatino@rims.org

SPENCER SCHOLARSHIP

Scholarship is available to outstanding applicants who are focused on a career in risk management, insurance, and related disciplines. Deadline is January 31.

Academic Fields/Career Goals: Insurance and Actuarial Science.

Award: Scholarship for use in junior, senior, graduate, or postgraduate years; renewable. *Amount:* $5000–$10,000.

Eligibility Requirements: Applicant must be enrolled or expecting to enroll full-time at a two-year or four-year institution or university. Available to U.S. citizens.

Application Requirements: Application, resume, references, transcript. *Deadline:* January 31.

Contact: Angela Sabatino, Secretary and Foundation Administrator
Spencer Educational Foundation, Inc.
655 Third Avenue, 2nd Floor
New York, NY 10017
Phone: 212-655-6223
Fax: 212-655-6044
E-mail: asabatino@rims.org

INTERIOR DESIGN

AMERICAN SOCIETY OF INTERIOR DESIGNERS (ASID) EDUCATION FOUNDATION, INC. http://www.asid.org

ASID EDUCATIONAL FOUNDATION/IRENE WINIFRED ENO GRANT

Provides financial assistance to individuals or groups engaged in the creation of an educational program(s) or an interior design research project dedicated to health, safety, and welfare. The grant will be awarded on the basis of the project description, breakdown of potential use of funds, and the marketing plan for the use/distribution of the end product of the project. The grant is open to students, educators, interior design practitioners, institutions, or other interior design-related groups.

Academic Fields/Career Goals: Interior Design.

Award: Grant for use in freshman, sophomore, junior, senior, graduate, or postgraduate years. *Number:* 1. *Amount:* $1000.

Eligibility Requirements: Applicant must be enrolled or expecting to enroll at an institution or university. Available to U.S. citizens.

Application Requirements: Application. *Deadline:* March 31.

Contact: American Society of Interior Designers (ASID) Education Foundation, Inc.
608 Massachusetts Avenue, NE
Washington, DC 20002-6006
Phone: 202-546-3480
Fax: 202-546-3240
E-mail: education@asid.org

ASID EDUCATIONAL FOUNDATION/JOEL POLSKY ACADEMIC ACHIEVEMENT AWARD

Awarded to recognize an outstanding undergraduate or graduate student's interior design research or thesis project. Research papers or doctoral and master's thesis should address such interior design topics as educational research, behavioral science, business practice, design process, theory, or technical subjects.

Academic Fields/Career Goals: Interior Design.

Award: Prize for use in freshman, sophomore, junior, senior, or graduate years. *Number:* 1. *Amount:* $1000.

Eligibility Requirements: Applicant must be enrolled or expecting to enroll at an institution or university. Available to U.S. citizens.

Application Requirements: Application, references. *Deadline:* March 31.

Contact: American Society of Interior Designers (ASID) Education Foundation, Inc.
608 Massachusetts Avenue, NE
Washington, DC 20002-6006
Phone: 202-546-3480
Fax: 202-546-3240
E-mail: education@asid.org

ASID EDUCATIONAL FOUNDATION/YALE R. BURGE COMPETITION

Open to all students in their final years of undergraduate study enrolled in at least a three-year program of interior design. The competition is designed to encourage students to seriously plan their portfolios. Portfolio components, submitted on slides, may be as few as eight, but are not to exceed 12. Judges will evaluate presentation skills, design and planning competency, and conceptual creativity.

Academic Fields/Career Goals: Interior Design.

Award: Prize for use in senior year. *Number:* 1. *Amount:* $750.

American Society of Interior Designers (ASID) Education Foundation, Inc.
(continued)

Eligibility Requirements: Applicant must be enrolled or expecting to enroll at an institution or university. Available to U.S. citizens.

Application Requirements: Application, applicant must enter a contest, portfolio. *Fee:* $10. *Deadline:* March 31.

Contact: American Society of Interior Designers (ASID) Education
Foundation, Inc.
608 Massachusetts Avenue, NE
Washington, DC 20002-6006
Phone: 202-546-3480
Fax: 202-546-3240
E-mail: education@asid.org

ASSOCIATION FOR WOMEN IN ARCHITECTURE FOUNDATION   http://www.awa-la.org

ASSOCIATION FOR WOMEN IN ARCHITECTURE SCHOLARSHIP
• *See page 98*

ILLUMINATING ENGINEERING SOCIETY OF NORTH AMERICA   http://www.iesna.org

ROBERT W. THUNEN MEMORIAL SCHOLARSHIPS
• *See page 100*

ILLUMINATING ENGINEERING SOCIETY OF NORTH AMERICA–GOLDEN GATE SECTION   http://www.iesgg.org

ALAN LUCAS MEMORIAL EDUCATIONAL SCHOLARSHIP
• *See page 100*

ROBERT W. THUNEN MEMORIAL SCHOLARSHIPS
• *See page 100*

INTERNATIONAL FURNISHINGS AND DESIGN ASSOCIATION   http://www.ifdaef.org

CHARLES D. MAYO SCHOLARSHIP

Scholarship available to students studying interior design and the related fields of the home furnishings and design industry. Award of $1000 to full-time student. Applicant does not have to be IFDA student member. Applicant must submit 300-500 word essay explaining future plans and goals, indicating why they believe that they are deserving of this award. Decision based upon student's academic achievement, awards and accomplishments, future plans and goals, and letter of recommendation.

Academic Fields/Career Goals: Interior Design; Trade/Technical Specialties.

Award: Scholarship for use in freshman, sophomore, junior, or senior years; not renewable. *Number:* 1. *Amount:* $1000.

Eligibility Requirements: Applicant must be enrolled or expecting to enroll full-time at a two-year or four-year or technical institution or university. Available to U.S. and non-U.S. citizens.

Application Requirements: Application, essay, references, transcript. *Deadline:* March 31.

Contact: Joan Long, Director of Grants
International Furnishings and Design Association
191 Clarksville Road
Princeton Junction, NJ 08550
Phone: 919-847-3064
Fax: 919-847-3064
E-mail: jlongdesigns@yahoo.com

IFDA STUDENT SCHOLARSHIP

Scholarship available to students studying interior design and the related fields of the home furnishings and design industry. Award of $3000 to full-time student. Applicant must be IFDA student member. Applicant must submit 300-500 word essay explaining why they joined IFDA, discuss future plans and goals, and indicate why they are deserving of this award. Decision based upon student's academic achievement, awards and accomplishments, future plans and goals, and letter of recommendation.

Academic Fields/Career Goals: Interior Design; Trade/Technical Specialties.

Award: Scholarship for use in freshman, sophomore, junior, or senior years; not renewable. *Number:* 1. *Amount:* $1500.

Eligibility Requirements: Applicant must be enrolled or expecting to enroll full-time at a two-year or four-year or technical institution or university. Available to U.S. and non-U.S. citizens.

Application Requirements: Application, essay, references, transcript. *Deadline:* March 31.

Contact: Joan Long, Director of Grants
International Furnishings and Design Association
191 Clarksville Road
Princeton Junction, NJ 08550
Phone: 919-847-3064
Fax: 919-847-3064
E-mail: jlongdesigns@yahoo.com

NATIONAL ASSOCIATION OF WOMEN IN CONSTRUCTION   http://nawic.org

NAWIC UNDERGRADUATE SCHOLARSHIPS
• *See page 100*

NETWORK OF EXECUTIVE WOMEN IN HOSPITALITY   http://www.newh.org

NETWORK OF EXECUTIVE WOMEN IN HOSPITALITY, INC. SCHOLARSHIP
• *See page 101*

NEW YORK STATE EDUCATION DEPARTMENT   http://www.highered.nysed.gov

REGENTS PROFESSIONAL OPPORTUNITY SCHOLARSHIP
• *See page 67*

SOUTH DAKOTA RETAILERS ASSOCIATION   http://www.sdra.org

SOUTH DAKOTA RETAILERS ASSOCIATION SCHOLARSHIP PROGRAM
• *See page 69*

WORLDSTUDIO FOUNDATION   http://www.worldstudio.org

WORLDSTUDIO FOUNDATION SCHOLARSHIP PROGRAM
• *See page 104*

INTERNATIONAL STUDIES

ARRL FOUNDATION, INC.   http://www.arrl.org/arrlf/scholgen.html

DONALD RIEBHOFF MEMORIAL SCHOLARSHIP

One $1000 award available to students with a Technician Class license for radio operation. Must be pursuing a baccalaureate or higher degree in international studies at any accredited institution above the high school level. Must be an ARRL member. Deadline is February 1.

Academic Fields/Career Goals: International Studies.

Award: Scholarship for use in freshman, sophomore, junior, senior, or graduate years; not renewable. *Number:* 1. *Amount:* $1000.

Eligibility Requirements: Applicant must be enrolled or expecting to enroll full-time at a four-year institution or university and must have an interest in amateur radio. Applicant or parent of applicant must be member of American Radio Relay League. Available to U.S. citizens.

Application Requirements: Application, transcript. *Deadline:* February 1.

Contact: Mary Hobart, Secretary Foundation
ARRL Foundation, Inc.
225 Main Street
Newington, CT 06111-1494
Phone: 860-594-0397
E-mail: k1mmh@arrl.org

ASSOCIATION TO UNITE THE DEMOCRACIES
http://www.iaud.org

MAYME AND HERBERT FRANK EDUCATIONAL FUND
• See page 216

CENTRAL INTELLIGENCE AGENCY
http://www.cia.gov

CENTRAL INTELLIGENCE AGENCY UNDERGRADUATE SCHOLARSHIP PROGRAM
• See page 56

CULTURE CONNECTION
http://www.thecultureconnection.com

CULTURE CONNECTION FOUNDATION SCHOLARSHIP
• See page 73

JAPAN STUDIES SCHOLARSHIP FOUNDATION COMMITTEE

JAPAN STUDIES SCHOLARSHIP
• See page 312

NATIONAL FEDERATION OF THE BLIND
http://www.nfb.org

MICHAEL AND MARIE MARUCCI SCHOLARSHIP
• See page 312

PACIFIC AND ASIAN AFFAIRS COUNCIL
http://www.paachawaii.org

PAAC SCHOLARSHIP

Scholarships available for college, study abroad, and other educational opportunities. Must be a student in Hawaii public or private high school involved in PAAC activities. Contact PAAC organization in local high school for more information.

Academic Fields/Career Goals: International Studies.

Award: Scholarship for use in freshman, sophomore, junior, or senior years; not renewable. *Number:* 5. *Amount:* $100–$1000.

Eligibility Requirements: Applicant must be high school student; planning to enroll or expecting to enroll at a two-year or four-year or technical institution or university and resident of Hawaii. Available to U.S. citizens.

Application Requirements: Application. *Deadline:* April 14.

Contact: Natasha Chappel, High School Program Coordinator
Pacific and Asian Affairs Council
1601 East-West Road, 4th Floor
Honolulu, HI 96848-1601
Phone: 808-944-7759
Fax: 808-944-7785
E-mail: hs@paachawaii.org

WATERBURY FOUNDATION
http://www.conncf.org/

MALCOLM BALDRIGE SCHOLARSHIP
• See page 157

JOURNALISM

ACADEMY OF TELEVISION ARTS AND SCIENCES FOUNDATION
http://www.emmys.tv/foundation

ACADEMY OF TELEVISION ARTS AND SCIENCES COLLEGE TELEVISION AWARDS
• See page 108

ADC RESEARCH INSTITUTE
http://www.adc.org

JACK SHAHEEN MASS COMMUNICATIONS SCHOLARSHIP AWARD
• See page 177

AMERICAN INSTITUTE OF POLISH CULTURE, INC.
http://www.ampolinstitute.org

HARRIET IRSAY SCHOLARSHIP GRANT
• See page 178

AMERICAN LEGION, PRESS CLUB OF NEW JERSEY

AMERICAN LEGION PRESS CLUB OF NEW JERSEY AND POST 170 ARTHUR DEHARDT MEMORIAL SCHOLARSHIP
• See page 178

AMERICAN QUARTER HORSE FOUNDATION (AQHF)
http://www.aqha.org/aqhya

AQHF JOURNALISM OR COMMUNICATIONS SCHOLARSHIP
• See page 178

ARRL FOUNDATION, INC.
http://www.arrl.org/arrlf/scholgen.html

PHD ARA SCHOLARSHIP
• See page 179

ASIAN AMERICAN JOURNALISTS ASSOCIATION
http://www.aaja.org

AAJA/COX FOUNDATION SCHOLARSHIP

Awards of up to $2500 to students pursuing careers in print, broadcast, or photo journalism. Deadline is April.

Academic Fields/Career Goals: Journalism; TV/Radio Broadcasting.

Award: Scholarship for use in freshman, sophomore, junior, senior, graduate, or postgraduate years; not renewable. *Number:* 1. *Amount:* up to $2500.

Eligibility Requirements: Applicant must be enrolled or expecting to enroll full-time at a two-year or four-year or technical institution or university. Applicant must have 2.5 GPA or higher. Available to U.S. and non-U.S. citizens.

Application Requirements: Application, essay, financial need analysis, resume, references, transcript. *Deadline:* April.

Contact: Brandon Sugiyama, Student Program Coordinator
Asian American Journalists Association
1182 Market Street, Suite 320
San Francisco, CA 94102
Phone: 415-346-2051 Ext. 102
Fax: 415-346-6343
E-mail: brandons@aaja.org

ASIAN-AMERICAN JOURNALISTS ASSOCIATION SCHOLARSHIP
• See page 179

MARY MOY QUAN ING MEMORIAL SCHOLARSHIP AWARD

One-time award for a deserving high school senior for undergraduate study. Must intend to pursue a journalism career and must show a commitment to the Asian-American community. One-time award of up to $1500. Visit Web site http://www.aaja.org for application and details. Deadline is April.

Academic Fields/Career Goals: Journalism.

Award: Scholarship for use in freshman year; not renewable. *Number:* 1. *Amount:* up to $2000.

Eligibility Requirements: Applicant must be high school student; planning to enroll or expecting to enroll full-time at a two-year or four-year institution and must have an interest in writing. Applicant must have 2.5 GPA or higher. Available to U.S. and non-U.S. citizens.

Asian American Journalists Association (continued)

Application Requirements: Application, essay, financial need analysis, resume, references, transcript. *Deadline:* April.

Contact: Brandon Sugiyama, Student Programs Coordinator
Asian American Journalists Association
1182 Market Street, Suite 320
San Francisco, CA 94102
Phone: 415-346-2051
Fax: 415-346-6343
E-mail: programs@aaja.org

MINORU YASUI MEMORIAL SCHOLARSHIP AWARD

One-time award for a promising Asian undergraduate male who will pursue a broadcasting career. For use at an accredited two- or four-year institution. One-time award of $2000. Visit Web site http://www.aaja.org for application and details. Deadline is April.

Academic Fields/Career Goals: Journalism; TV/Radio Broadcasting.

Award: Scholarship for use in freshman, sophomore, junior, or senior years; not renewable. *Number:* 1. *Amount:* $2000.

Eligibility Requirements: Applicant must be Asian/Pacific Islander; enrolled or expecting to enroll full-time at a two-year or four-year institution or university and male. Applicant must have 2.5 GPA or higher. Available to U.S. and non-U.S. citizens.

Application Requirements: Application, essay, financial need analysis, resume, references, transcript. *Deadline:* April.

Contact: Brandon Sugiyama, Student Programs Coordinator
Asian American Journalists Association
1182 Market Street, Suite 320
San Francisco, CA 94102
Phone: 415-346-2051 Ext. 102
Fax: 415-346-6343
E-mail: programs@aaja.org

NATIONAL ASIAN-AMERICAN JOURNALISTS ASSOCIATION NEWHOUSE SCHOLARSHIP

One-time award for high school seniors and college students who plan to or are currently enrolled in a journalism program at any two- or four-year postsecondary institution. Up to $5000 awarded. Scholarship awardees will be eligible for summer internships with a Newhouse publication. Applicants from underrepresented Asian Pacific American groups including Vietnamese, Hmong, Cambodians, and other Southeast Asians, South Asians, and Pacific Islanders are especially encouraged. Visit Web site: http://www.aaja.org for application and details.

Academic Fields/Career Goals: Journalism.

Award: Scholarship for use in freshman, sophomore, junior, or senior years; not renewable. *Number:* up to 5. *Amount:* $1000–$5000.

Eligibility Requirements: Applicant must be enrolled or expecting to enroll full-time at a two-year or four-year institution or university. Applicant must have 2.5 GPA or higher. Available to U.S. and non-U.S. citizens.

Application Requirements: Application, essay, financial need analysis, resume, references, transcript. *Deadline:* April.

Contact: Brandon Sugiyama, Student Programs Coordinator
Asian American Journalists Association
1182 Market Street, Suite 320
San Francisco, CA 94102
Phone: 415-346-2051 Ext. 102
Fax: 415-346-6343
E-mail: programs@aaja.org

VINCENT CHIN MEMORIAL SCHOLARSHIP

AAJA will award $5000 to a journalism student committed to keeping Vincent Chin's memory alive. Minimum GPA of 2.5. Deadline is April.

Academic Fields/Career Goals: Journalism.

Award: Scholarship for use in freshman, sophomore, junior, senior, graduate, or postgraduate years; not renewable. *Number:* 1. *Amount:* up to $5000.

Eligibility Requirements: Applicant must be enrolled or expecting to enroll full-time at a two-year or four-year or technical institution or university. Applicant must have 2.5 GPA or higher. Available to U.S. and non-U.S. citizens.

Application Requirements: Application, essay, financial need analysis, resume, references, transcript. *Deadline:* April.

Contact: Brandon Sugiyama, Student Program Coordinator
Asian American Journalists Association
1182 Market Street, Suite 320
San Francisco, CA 94102
Phone: 415-346-2051 Ext. 102
Fax: 415-346-6343
E-mail: brandons@aaja.org

ASSOCIATED PRESS   http://www.aptra.org

ASSOCIATED PRESS TELEVISION/RADIO ASSOCIATION-CLETE ROBERTS JOURNALISM SCHOLARSHIP AWARDS

Award for college undergraduates and graduate students studying in California or Nevada and pursuing careers in broadcast journalism. Please submit application, references, and examples of broadcast-related work. Email for application to shughes@nbc3.com. One-time award of $1500.

Academic Fields/Career Goals: Journalism; TV/Radio Broadcasting.

Award: Scholarship for use in freshman, sophomore, junior, senior, or graduate years; not renewable. *Number:* 3. *Amount:* $1500.

Eligibility Requirements: Applicant must be enrolled or expecting to enroll full-time at a two-year or four-year institution or university and studying in California or Nevada. Available to U.S. citizens.

Application Requirements: Application, references. *Deadline:* December 10.

Contact: Rachel Ambrose, CA-NV Broadcast Editor
Associated Press
221 South Figueroa Street, Suite 300
Los Angeles, CA 90012
Phone: 213-626-1200
Fax: 213-346-0200
E-mail: rambrose@ap.org

KATHRYN DETTMAN MEMORIAL JOURNALISM SCHOLARSHIP

One-time $1500 award for broadcast journalism students, enrolled at a California or Nevada college or university. Submit entry form and examples of broadcast-related work. Email for application to shughes@nbc3.com. Application deadline: December 10.

Academic Fields/Career Goals: Journalism; TV/Radio Broadcasting.

Award: Scholarship for use in freshman, sophomore, junior, or senior years; not renewable. *Number:* 1–4. *Amount:* $1500.

Eligibility Requirements: Applicant must be enrolled or expecting to enroll at a two-year or four-year institution or university and studying in California or Nevada. Available to U.S. citizens.

Application Requirements: Application. *Deadline:* December 10.

Contact: Rachel Ambrose, CA-NV Broadcast Editor
Associated Press
221 South Figueroa Street
Los Angeles, CA 90012
Phone: 213-626-1200
Fax: 213-346-0200
E-mail: rambrose@ap.org

ASSOCIATED PRESS TELEVISION-RADIO ASSOCIATION OF CALIFORNIA AND NEVADA   http://www.aptra.org

APTRA-CLETE ROBERTS MEMORIAL JOURNALISM SCHOLARSHIP AWARD

Open to students pursuing a career in broadcast journalism. Applications must be typed.

Academic Fields/Career Goals: Journalism; TV/Radio Broadcasting.

Award: Scholarship for use in sophomore, junior, or senior years; not renewable. *Number:* 1. *Amount:* up to $1500.

Eligibility Requirements: Applicant must be enrolled or expecting to enroll at a two-year or four-year institution; resident of California or Nevada and studying in California or Nevada. Available to U.S. citizens.

Application Requirements: Application, essay, examples of broadcast-related work preferred. *Deadline:* December 9.

Contact: Roberta Gonzales, Scholarship Application Contact
Associated Press Television-Radio Association of California and Nevada
CBS 5 TV, 855 Battery Street
San Francisco, CA 94111

APTRA-KATHRYN DETTMAN MEMORIAL SCHOLARSHIP

Open to students pursuing a career in broadcast journalism. Must be a college student currently enrolled at a California or Nevada college or university. Applications must be typed. No e-mail or faxes will be accepted.

Academic Fields/Career Goals: Journalism; TV/Radio Broadcasting.

Award: Scholarship for use in sophomore, junior, or senior years; not renewable. *Number:* 1. *Amount:* up to $1500.

Eligibility Requirements: Applicant must be enrolled or expecting to enroll at a two-year or four-year institution or university; resident of California or Nevada and studying in California or Nevada. Available to U.S. citizens.

Application Requirements: Application, examples of broadcast-related work preferred. *Deadline:* December 9.

Contact: Roberta Gonzales, Scholarship Application Contact
Associated Press Television-Radio Association of California and Nevada
CBS 5 TV, 855 Battery Street
San Francisco, CA 94111

ATLANTA PRESS CLUB, INC.   http://www.atlpressclub.org

ATLANTA PRESS CLUB JOURNALISM SCHOLARSHIP PROGRAM
• See page 179

CALIFORNIA CHICANO NEWS MEDIA ASSOCIATION (CCNMA)   http://www.ccnma.org

JOEL GARCIA MEMORIAL SCHOLARSHIP
• See page 180

CANADIAN ASSOCIATION OF BROADCASTERS   http://www.cab-acr.ca

JIM ALLARD BROADCAST JOURNALISM SCHOLARSHIP

This CAN$2,500 scholarship is awarded annually to aspiring broadcasters enrolled in broadcast journalism courses at a Canadian college or university. The award is given to the student who best combines academic achievement with natural talent. Must be a Canadian citizen.

Academic Fields/Career Goals: Journalism; TV/Radio Broadcasting.

Award: Scholarship for use in freshman, sophomore, junior, senior, or graduate years; not renewable. *Number:* 1. *Amount:* $1857.

Eligibility Requirements: Applicant must be Canadian citizen; enrolled or expecting to enroll full or part-time at a two-year or four-year institution or university; studying in Alberta, British Columbia, Manitoba, New Brunswick, Newfoundland, North West Territories, Nova Scotia, Ontario, Prince Edward Island, Quebec, Saskatchewan, or Yukon and must have an interest in leadership.

Application Requirements: Application, essay, references. *Deadline:* June 30.

Contact: Vanessa Dewson, Special Events and Projects Coordinator
Canadian Association of Broadcasters
PO Box 627
Station B
Ottawa K1P 5S2
Canada
Phone: 613-233-4035 Ext. 309
Fax: 613-233-6961
E-mail: vdewson@cab-acr.ca

CANADIAN PRESS   http://www.cp.org

GIL PURCELL MEMORIAL JOURNALISM SCHOLARSHIP FOR NATIVE CANADIANS

The designed to encourage native Canadian students to enter the field of journalism in Canada. Award for Aboriginal Canadians (status or non-status Indian, Metis, or Inuit) who are pursuing postsecondary studies and intend to work in the field of journalism.

Academic Fields/Career Goals: Journalism.

Award: Scholarship for use in freshman, sophomore, junior, senior, graduate, or postgraduate years; not renewable. *Number:* 1. *Amount:* $3424.

Eligibility Requirements: Applicant must be of Canadian heritage and Canadian citizen; American Indian/Alaska Native and enrolled or expecting to enroll full-time at a four-year institution or university.

Application Requirements: Application, interview, resume. *Deadline:* November 15.

Contact: Paul Woods, Director of Human Resources
Canadian Press
36 King Street East
Toronto M5C 2L9
Canada
Phone: 416-507-2133
Fax: 416-507-2033
E-mail: pwoods@cp.org

CHARLOTTE OBSERVER   http://www.charlotte.com/

CHARLOTTE OBSERVER MINORITY SCHOLARSHIPS
• See page 146

CHIPS QUINN SCHOLARS   http://www.chipsquinn.org

CHIPS QUINN SCHOLARSHIP

Scholarship available for college juniors, seniors or graduates with journalism majors.

Academic Fields/Career Goals: Journalism.

Award: Scholarship for use in junior, senior, or graduate years. *Amount:* up to $1000.

Eligibility Requirements: Applicant must be enrolled or expecting to enroll at a four-year institution or university. Available to U.S. citizens.

Application Requirements: Application, essay, photo, resume, references, transcript. *Deadline:* October 15.

Contact: Karen Catone, Director
Chips Quinn Scholars
Freedom Forum, 1101 Wilson Boulevard
Arlington, VA 22209
Phone: 703-284-3934
E-mail: kcatone@freedomforum.org

CONNECTICUT CHAPTER OF SOCIETY OF PROFESSIONAL JOURNALISTS   http://www.ctspj.org

CONNECTICUT SPJ BOB EDDY SCHOLARSHIP PROGRAM

One-time award for college junior or senior planning a career in journalism. Must be a Connecticut resident attending a four-year college or any student attending a four-year college in Connecticut. Information available from February 1 to April 14.

Academic Fields/Career Goals: Journalism; Photojournalism/Photography.

Award: Scholarship for use in junior or senior years; not renewable. *Number:* 4. *Amount:* $750–$2500.

Eligibility Requirements: Applicant must be enrolled or expecting to enroll full-time at a four-year institution and must have an interest in writing. Available to U.S. and non-U.S. citizens.

Connecticut Chapter of Society of Professional Journalists (continued)

Application Requirements: Application, essay, financial need analysis, transcript. *Deadline:* April 12.

Contact: Debra Estock, Scholarship Committee Chairman
Connecticut Chapter of Society of Professional Journalists
71 Kenwood Avenue
Fairfield, CT 06430
Phone: 203-255-2127
E-mail: destock963@aol.com

CUBAN AMERICAN NATIONAL FOUNDATION
http://www.canf.org

MAS FAMILY SCHOLARSHIPS
• *See page 146*

DALLAS-FORT WORTH ASSOCIATION OF BLACK COMMUNICATORS
http://www.dfwabc.org

FUTURE JOURNALISTS SCHOLARSHIP PROGRAM
• *See page 180*

DOW JONES NEWSPAPER FUND
http://djnewspaperfund.dowjones.com

DOW JONES-SPORTS EDITING PROGRAM

Award to encourage students to consider sports copy editing as a career in by providing training, paid summer internships and scholarship grants. Must pursue their career in newspaper journalism. Deadline is November 1.

Academic Fields/Career Goals: Journalism.

Award: Scholarship for use in junior or senior years; not renewable. *Number:* 12. *Amount:* $1000.

Eligibility Requirements: Applicant must be enrolled or expecting to enroll full-time at a two-year or four-year institution or university. Available to U.S. and non-U.S. citizens.

Application Requirements: Application, essay, portfolio, resume, references, transcript. *Deadline:* November 1.

Contact: Linda Waller Shockley, Deputy Director
Dow Jones Newspaper Fund
PO Box 300
Princeton, NJ 08543-0300
Phone: 609-452-2820
Fax: 609-520-5804
E-mail: newsfund@wsj.dowjones.com

HIGH SCHOOL JOURNALISM WORKSHOPS FOR MINORITIES

Award to encourage minority high school students to consider careers in journalism by providing an opportunity to work with professional journalists and instructors on reporting, writing and editing a student newspaper.

Academic Fields/Career Goals: Journalism.

Award: Grant for use in freshman year. *Number:* 27. *Amount:* $2500–$5000.

Eligibility Requirements: Applicant must be American Indian/Alaska Native, Asian/Pacific Islander, Black (non-Hispanic), or Hispanic and enrolled or expecting to enroll full-time at an institution or university. Available to U.S. and Canadian citizens.

Application Requirements: Application, essay, portfolio, resume, references, transcript. *Deadline:* October 1.

Contact: Linda Waller Shockley, Deputy Director
Dow Jones Newspaper Fund
PO Box 300
Princeton, NJ 08543-0300
Phone: 609-452-2820
Fax: 609-520-5804
E-mail: newsfund@wsj.dowjones.com

ELLEN MASIN PERSINA/NATIONAL PRESS CLUB SCHOLARSHIP FOR MINORITIES IN JOURNALISM
http://npc.press.org

PERSINA SCHOLARSHIP FOR MINORITIES IN JOURNALISM

Scholarship of $20,000 ($5000 per year) awarded to a talented minority student planning to pursue a career in journalism. Applicant must be a high school senior. Must have a 2.75 or better GPA. Must have applied to or been accepted by a college or university for the upcoming year.

Academic Fields/Career Goals: Journalism.

Award: Scholarship for use in freshman year. *Amount:* up to $5000.

Eligibility Requirements: Applicant must be American Indian/Alaska Native, Asian/Pacific Islander, Black (non-Hispanic), or Hispanic and enrolled or expecting to enroll at an institution or university. Available to U.S. citizens.

Application Requirements: Application, essay, financial need analysis, references, transcript. *Deadline:* March 1.

Contact: John Bloom, General Manager
Ellen Masin Persina/National Press Club Scholarship for Minorities in Journalism
529 14th Street, NW
Washington, DC 20045
Phone: 202-662-7500
Fax: 202-662-7512
E-mail: jbloom@press.org

FISHER BROADCASTING COMPANY
http://www.fisherbroadcasting.com

FISHER BROADCASTING, INC., SCHOLARSHIP FOR MINORITIES
• *See page 181*

FREEDOM FORUM
http://www.freedomforum.org

AL NEUHARTH FREE SPIRIT SCHOLARSHIP

One-time award for high school seniors interested in pursuing a career in journalism. Must be actively involved in high school journalism and demonstrate qualities such as being a visionary, an innovative leader, an entrepreneur or a courageous achiever. Deadline is October 15. See Web site at http://www.freedomforum.org for further information.

Academic Fields/Career Goals: Journalism.

Award: Scholarship for use in freshman year; not renewable. *Number:* up to 102. *Amount:* $1000.

Eligibility Requirements: Applicant must be high school student and planning to enroll or expecting to enroll full-time at an institution or university. Available to U.S. citizens.

Application Requirements: Application, essay, photo, references, transcript, sample of journalistic work. *Deadline:* October 15.

Contact: Diana Leckie, Administrator
Freedom Forum
1101 Wilson Boulevard
Arlington, VA 22209
Phone: 703-528-0800

CHIPS QUINN SCHOLARS PROGRAM

One-time award for students of color who are college juniors, seniors or recent graduates. Must have a definite interest in print journalism as a career. Award requires paid internship. Applicants may be nominated by their schools, by newspaper editors or by direct application with supporting letters of endorsement. Deadline is October 15. See Web site at http://www.freedomforum.org for further information.

Academic Fields/Career Goals: Journalism.

Award: Scholarship for use in junior or senior years; not renewable. *Number:* 75. *Amount:* up to $1000.

Eligibility Requirements: Applicant must be American Indian/Alaska Native, Asian/Pacific Islander, Black (non-Hispanic), or Hispanic and enrolled or expecting to enroll full-time at a four-year institution or university. Available to U.S. citizens.

Application Requirements: Application, essay, photo, portfolio, resume, references, transcript, valid driver's license. *Deadline:* October 15.

Contact: Karen Catone, Director
Freedom Forum
1101 Wilson Boulevard
Arlington, VA 22209
Phone: 703-284-3934
Fax: 703-284-3543
E-mail: kcatone@freedomforum.org

FUND FOR AMERICAN STUDIES   http://www.tfas.org

ECONOMIC JOURNALISM AWARD
• *See page 217*

FUNDACION EDUCATIVA CARLOS M. CASTANEDA   http://www.fecmc.org

THE CARLOS M. CASTANEDA JOURNALISM SCHOLARSHIP

One-year scholarship to a Spanish-speaking individual for graduate studies in journalism. Scholarships are renewable after reviewing the student's grade point average (minimum 3.0) and general performance. An undergraduate major in journalism is not necessary, but his undergraduate curriculum should include history and liberal arts courses and must master the Spanish language.

Academic Fields/Career Goals: Journalism.

Award: Scholarship for use in freshman, sophomore, junior, or senior years; renewable. *Amount:* $7000.

Eligibility Requirements: Applicant must be enrolled or expecting to enroll at a four-year institution. Applicant must have 3.0 GPA or higher. Available to U.S. citizens.

Application Requirements: Autobiography, essay, resume, references, portfolio with 3 published stories. *Deadline:* March 15.

Contact: Fundacion Educativa Carlos M. Castaneda, FECMC
Journalism Scholarship
Fundacion Educativa Carlos M. Castaneda
1925 Brickell Avenue, D-1108
Miami, FL 33129
Phone: 305-859-9617
E-mail: fundacion_educativa_cmc@yahoo.com

GEORGIA PRESS EDUCATIONAL FOUNDATION, INC.   http://www.gapress.org

AMERICAN PRESS INSTITUTE SCHOLARSHIP

This scholarship is for employees who work at a Georgia Press Association member newspaper in good standing.

Academic Fields/Career Goals: Journalism.

Award: Scholarship for use in freshman, sophomore, junior, senior, graduate, or postgraduate years; not renewable. *Amount:* $2500.

Eligibility Requirements: Applicant must be enrolled or expecting to enroll at a two-year or four-year institution or university and resident of Georgia. Applicant or parent of applicant must be member of American Federation of State, County, and Municipal Employees. Available to U.S. citizens.

Application Requirements: Application, photo, transcript. *Deadline:* July 1.

Contact: Ali Garrett, Manager
Georgia Press Educational Foundation, Inc.
3066 Mercer University Drive, Suite 200
Atlanta, GA 30341-4137
Phone: 770-454-6776
Fax: 770-454-6778
E-mail: agarrett@gapress.org

DURWOOD MCALISTER SCHOLARSHIP

Scholarship awarded annually to an outstanding student majoring in print journalism at a Georgia college or university. Deadline is February 1.

Academic Fields/Career Goals: Journalism.

Award: Scholarship for use in freshman, sophomore, junior, senior, graduate, or postgraduate years; not renewable. *Amount:* $500–$1500.

Eligibility Requirements: Applicant must be enrolled or expecting to enroll at a two-year or four-year or technical institution or university; resident of Georgia and must have an interest in writing. Available to U.S. citizens.

Application Requirements: Application, essay, photo, references, transcript. *Deadline:* February 1.

Contact: Ali Garrett, Manager
Georgia Press Educational Foundation, Inc.
3066 Mercer University Drive, Suite 200
Atlanta, GA 30341-4137
Phone: 770-454-6776
Fax: 770-454-6778
E-mail: agarrett@gapress.org

GEORGIA PRESS EDUCATIONAL FOUNDATION SCHOLARSHIPS

One-time awards to Georgia high school seniors and college undergraduates. Based on prior interest in newspaper journalism. Must be recommended by high school counselor, professor, and/or Georgia Press Educational Foundation member. Must reside and attend school in Georgia. Application deadline is February 1.

Academic Fields/Career Goals: Journalism.

Award: Scholarship for use in freshman, sophomore, junior, or senior years; not renewable. *Number:* 20. *Amount:* $500–$1500.

Eligibility Requirements: Applicant must be enrolled or expecting to enroll full-time at a two-year or four-year institution or university; resident of Georgia; studying in Georgia and must have an interest in writing. Applicant must have 2.5 GPA or higher. Available to U.S. citizens.

Application Requirements: Application, financial need analysis, photo, references, test scores, transcript. *Deadline:* February 1.

Contact: Ali Garrett
Georgia Press Educational Foundation, Inc.
3066 Mercer University Drive, Suite 200
Atlanta, GA 30341-4137
Phone: 770-454-6776
Fax: 770-454-6778

KIRK SUTLIVE SCHOLARSHIP

Scholarship awarded anually to a junior or senior majoring in either the news-editorial or public relations sequence. Deadline is February 1.

Academic Fields/Career Goals: Journalism.

Award: Scholarship for use in junior or senior years; not renewable. *Amount:* $500–$1500.

Eligibility Requirements: Applicant must be enrolled or expecting to enroll full-time at a four-year institution or university. Available to U.S. citizens.

Application Requirements: Application, essay, financial need analysis, photo, transcript. *Deadline:* February 1.

Contact: Ali Garrett, Manager
Georgia Press Educational Foundation, Inc.
3066 Mercer University Drive, Suite 200
Atlanta, GA 30341-4137
Phone: 770-454-6776
Fax: 770-454-6778
E-mail: agarrett@gapress.org

MORRIS NEWSPAPER CORPORATION SCHOLARSHIP

Scholarship awarded annually to an outstanding print journalism student. Applications are submitted through newspapers in the Morris Newspaper Corporation chain and recipients are named by the Foundation.

Academic Fields/Career Goals: Journalism.

Award: Scholarship for use in freshman, sophomore, junior, or senior years; not renewable. *Amount:* $500–$1500.

Eligibility Requirements: Applicant must be enrolled or expecting to enroll at a technical institution; resident of Georgia and must have an interest in writing. Available to U.S. citizens.

Application Requirements: Application, essay, photo, references, transcript. *Deadline:* February 1.

Georgia Press Educational Foundation, Inc. (continued)

Contact: Ali Garrett, Manager
Georgia Press Educational Foundation, Inc.
3066 Mercer University Drive, Suite 200
Atlanta, GA 30341-4137
Phone: 770-454-6776
Fax: 770-454-6778
E-mail: agarrett@gapress.org

WILLIAM C. ROGERS SCHOLARSHIP

Scholarship awarded to a junior or senior majoring in the news-editorial sequence. Deadline is February 1.

Academic Fields/Career Goals: Journalism.

Award: Scholarship for use in junior or senior years. *Amount:* $500–$1500.

Eligibility Requirements: Applicant must be enrolled or expecting to enroll at a four-year institution or university; resident of Georgia and must have an interest in writing. Available to U.S. citizens.

Application Requirements: Application, essay, photo, references, transcript. *Deadline:* February 1.

Contact: Ali Garrett, Manager
Georgia Press Educational Foundation, Inc.
3066 Mercer University Drive, Suite 200
Atlanta, GA 30341-4137
Phone: 770-454-6776
Fax: 770-454-6778
E-mail: agarrett@gapress.org

GREAT LAKES COMMISSION   http://www.glc.org

CAROL A. RATZA MEMORIAL SCHOLARSHIP
• See page 138

INDIANA BROADCASTERS ASSOCIATION   http://www.indianabroadcasters.org

INDIANA BROADCASTERS FOUNDATION SCHOLARSHIP

Must be majoring in broadcasting, electronic media, or journalism. Must maintain a 3.0 GPA and be a resident of Indiana. One-time award for full-time undergraduate study in Indiana.

Academic Fields/Career Goals: Journalism; TV/Radio Broadcasting.

Award: Scholarship for use in freshman, sophomore, junior, or senior years; not renewable. *Number:* up to 14. *Amount:* $500–$2000.

Eligibility Requirements: Applicant must be high school student; planning to enroll or expecting to enroll full-time at a two-year or four-year or technical institution or university; resident of Indiana and studying in Indiana. Applicant must have 3.0 GPA or higher. Available to U.S. citizens.

Application Requirements: Application, essay, references, transcript. *Deadline:* March 27.

Contact: Gwen C. Piening, Scholarship Administrator
Indiana Broadcasters Association
3003 East 98th Street, Suite 161
Indianapolis, IN 46280
Phone: 317-573-0119
Fax: 317-573-0895
E-mail: indba@aol.com

INDIANAPOLIS ASSOCIATION OF BLACK JOURNALISTS   http://www.iabj.net

LYNN DEAN FORD IABJ SCHOLARSHIP AWARDS
• See page 181

INTERNATIONAL FOODSERVICE EDITORIAL COUNCIL   http://www.ifec-is-us.com

INTERNATIONAL FOODSERVICE EDITORIAL COUNCIL COMMUNICATIONS SCHOLARSHIP
• See page 182

JIM ELDER GOOD SPORT FUND   http://www.jimelder.org

JOURNALISM AND BROADCASTING SCHOLARSHIPS

Scholarships available for junior and senior college students at Arkansas universities for journalism and broadcasting. Scholarship amount $3000/year.

Academic Fields/Career Goals: Journalism; TV/Radio Broadcasting.

Award: Scholarship for use in junior or senior years. *Amount:* $3000.

Eligibility Requirements: Applicant must be enrolled or expecting to enroll at an institution or university and studying in Arkansas. Available to U.S. citizens.

Application Requirements: Application. *Deadline:* varies.

Contact: Jim Elder Good Sport Fund
PO Box 444
Little Rock, AR 72203
Phone: 501-766-6444
E-mail: info@jimelder.org

JOHN BAYLISS BROADCAST FOUNDATION   http://www.baylissfoundation.org

JOHN BAYLISS BROADCAST RADIO SCHOLARSHIP
• See page 182

JOHN M. WILL MEMORIAL SCHOLARSHIP FOUNDATION

HEARIN-CHANDLER JOURNALISM SCHOLARSHIP

Scholarship for residents of Mobile, Baldwin, Escambia, Clarke, Conecuh, Washington, and Monroe counties in Alabama; Santa Rosa and Escambia counties in Florida; George and Jackson counties in Mississippi. For full-time journalism study, leading to a degree, at a regionally accredited institution. Applicant may be a high school senior, college student, or practicing journalist.

Academic Fields/Career Goals: Journalism.

Award: Scholarship for use in freshman, sophomore, junior, or senior years; not renewable. *Number:* 1. *Amount:* $5000.

Eligibility Requirements: Applicant must be enrolled or expecting to enroll full-time at a four-year institution or university; resident of Alabama, Florida, or Mississippi and must have an interest in writing. Available to U.S. citizens.

Application Requirements: Application, essay, interview, portfolio, references, transcript. *Deadline:* varies.

Contact: William Holman, II, Secretary of Foundation
John M. Will Memorial Scholarship Foundation
PO Box 290
Mobile, AL 36601
Phone: 251-405-1300
Fax: 251-432-6843

JOHN M. WILL JOURNALISM SCHOLARSHIP

Scholarship for residents of Mobile, Baldwin, Escambia, Clarke, Conecuh, Washington, and Monroe counties in Alabama; Santa Rosa and Escambia counties in Florida; George and Jackson counties in Mississippi. For full-time journalism study at a regionally accredited institution. Applicant may be high school senior, college student, or practicing journalist.

Academic Fields/Career Goals: Journalism.

Award: Scholarship for use in freshman, sophomore, junior, or senior years; not renewable. *Number:* 1. *Amount:* $3000.

Eligibility Requirements: Applicant must be enrolled or expecting to enroll full-time at a four-year institution or university; resident of Alabama, Florida, or Mississippi and must have an interest in writing. Available to U.S. citizens.

Application Requirements: Application, essay, interview, portfolio, references, transcript. *Deadline:* March 31.

Contact: William Holman, II, Secretary of Foundation
John M. Will Memorial Scholarship Foundation
PO Box 290
Mobile, AL 36601
Phone: 251-405-1300
Fax: 251-432-6843

JORGE MAS CANOSA FREEDOM FOUNDATION
http://www.canf.org

MAS FAMILY SCHOLARSHIP AWARD
• See page 149

JOURNALISM EDUCATION ASSOCIATION
http://www.jea.org

NATIONAL HIGH SCHOOL JOURNALIST OF THE YEAR/SISTER RITA JEANNE SCHOLARSHIPS
• See page 182

KANSAS CITY STAR
http://www.kcstar.com

ERNEST HEMINGWAY WRITING AWARDS

Four scholarships of $2500 will be awarded to high school students who work for their school newspaper. Students must plan to enroll in an accredited college or university. Applications should be accompanied by writing samples or clips from the newspaper. Eligible applicants will be United States citizens. The deadline is January 15.

Academic Fields/Career Goals: Journalism.

Award: Scholarship for use in freshman, sophomore, junior, or senior years; not renewable. *Number:* 4. *Amount:* $2500.

Eligibility Requirements: Applicant must be high school student and planning to enroll or expecting to enroll full-time at a two-year or four-year institution or university. Available to U.S. citizens.

Application Requirements: Application, mounted samples of writing. *Deadline:* January 15.

Contact: Lisa Lopez, Administrative Assistant
Kansas City Star
1729 Grand Boulevard
Kansas City, MO 64108
Phone: 816-234-4907
Fax: 816-234-4876
E-mail: llopez@kcstar.com

LAGRANT FOUNDATION
http://www.lagrantfoundation.org

LAGRANT FOUNDATION SCHOLARSHIP FOR UNDERGRADUATES
• See page 150

LANDMARK COMMUNICATIONS, INC.
http://www.landmarkcom.com/employment/scholarships.php

LANDMARK SCHOLARS PROGRAM

Scholarship of $10,000, two paid summer internships, and a full-time paid internship for at least one year after graduation is available to minority students. Applicants must be college sophomores and first preference is given to students with ties to the Mid-Atlantic states. Must be enrolled full-time in a 4-year degree program, minimum GPA of 2.5 required.

Academic Fields/Career Goals: Journalism.

Award: Scholarship for use in sophomore year. *Number:* 1. *Amount:* up to $10,000.

Eligibility Requirements: Applicant must be American Indian/Alaska Native, Asian/Pacific Islander, Black (non-Hispanic), or Hispanic and enrolled or expecting to enroll at a four-year institution or university. Applicant must have 2.5 GPA or higher. Available to U.S. citizens.

Application Requirements: Application, essay, financial need analysis, references, transcript, work samples.. *Deadline:* January 1.

Contact: Ann Morris, Managing Editor/Scholarship coordinator
Landmark Communications, Inc.
Greensboro News & Record, 200 East Market Street
Greensboro, NC 27401
Phone: 336-373-7000
E-mail: amorris@news-record.com

MAINE COMMUNITY FOUNDATION, INC.
http://www.mainecf.org

GUY P. GANNETT SCHOLARSHIP FUND

Scholarships available to graduates of Maine high schools pursuing a major in journalism or a field reasonably related. Renewable throughout their post secondary and graduate education. Deadline is May 1.

Academic Fields/Career Goals: Journalism.

Award: Scholarship for use in freshman year; renewable.

Eligibility Requirements: Applicant must be enrolled or expecting to enroll full-time at an institution or university and resident of Maine. Available to U.S. citizens.

Application Requirements: Application, essay, financial need analysis, references, transcript. *Deadline:* May 1.

Contact: Amy Pollien, Program Administrator
Maine Community Foundation, Inc.
Guy P. Gannett Scholarship Fund, Maine Community Foundation, 245 Main Street
Ellsworth, ME 04605
Phone: 877-700-6800
E-mail: info@mainecf.org

MISSISSIPPI PRESS ASSOCIATION EDUCATION FOUNDATION
http://www.mspress.org/foundation/

MISSISSIPPI PRESS ASSOCIATION EDUCATION FOUNDATION SCHOLARSHIP

The Mississippi Press Association Education Foundation annually offers $1000 ($500 per semester) scholarships to qualified students enrolled in print journalism, and who are residents of Mississippi. The recipient who maintains a 3.0 GPA, and submits proof of summer internship, will be eligible to continue the scholarship for his/her following year. Total value of the scholarship can be as much as $4000 when awarded to an upcoming freshman who remains qualified throughout their four years of print journalism education.

Academic Fields/Career Goals: Journalism.

Award: Scholarship for use in freshman, sophomore, junior, or senior years; renewable. *Number:* 2. *Amount:* $1000.

Eligibility Requirements: Applicant must be enrolled or expecting to enroll full-time at a two-year or four-year institution or university; resident of Mississippi and studying in Mississippi. Applicant must have 3.0 GPA or higher. Available to U.S. citizens.

Application Requirements: Application, references, sample of work. *Deadline:* April 1.

Contact: Scholarship Coordinator
Mississippi Press Association Education Foundation
351 Edgewood Terrace
Jackson, MS 39206
Phone: 601-981-3060
Fax: 601-981-3676
E-mail: foundation@mspress.org

NATIONAL ACADEMY OF TELEVISION ARTS AND SCIENCES-NATIONAL CAPITAL/CHESAPEAKE BAY CHAPTER
http://www.natasdc.org/home.html

THE BETTY ENDICOTT/NTA-NCCB STUDENT SCHOLARSHIP

Scholarship for a full-time college student pursuing a career in communication, television or broadcast journalism. Must be enrolled in an accredited 4-year college or university in Maryland, Virginia or Washington, D.C. Minimum GPA of 3.0 required.

Academic Fields/Career Goals: Journalism; TV/Radio Broadcasting.

Award: Scholarship for use in sophomore or junior years. *Number:* 1. *Amount:* $5000.

Eligibility Requirements: Applicant must be enrolled or expecting to enroll full-time at a four-year institution or university and studying in District of Columbia, Maryland, Virginia, or Washington. Applicant must have 3.0 GPA or higher. Available to U.S. citizens.

Application Requirements: Application, essay, resume, references, transcript. *Deadline:* varies.

Contact: Dianne Bruno, Administrator
National Academy of Television Arts and Sciences-National Capital/Chesapeake Bay Chapter
Attention: Student Affairs Committee
9405 Russell Road
Silver Spring, MD 20910
Phone: 301-587-3993
Fax: 301-587-3993

NATIONAL ASSOCIATION OF BLACK JOURNALISTS
http://www.nabj.org

ALLISON FISHER SCHOLARSHIP

Available to any African-American student who is currently attending an accredited university. Must be majoring in print journalism and maintain a 3.0 GPA. Recipient will attend NABJ convention and participate in mentor program. Previous NABJ scholarship winners not eligible. Must be NABJ member before award.

Academic Fields/Career Goals: Journalism.

Award: Scholarship for use in freshman, sophomore, junior, senior, or graduate years; not renewable. *Number:* 1. *Amount:* $2500.

Eligibility Requirements: Applicant must be Black (non-Hispanic) and enrolled or expecting to enroll at a four-year institution or university. Applicant must have 3.0 GPA or higher. Available to U.S. citizens.

Application Requirements: Autobiography, references, proof of enrollment. *Deadline:* April 30.

Contact: Warren J. Paul, Media Instructor/Program Associate
National Association of Black Journalists
8701-A Adelphi Road
Adelphi, MD 20783-1716
Phone: 301-445-7100 Ext. 108
Fax: 301-445-7101

GERALD BOYD/ROBIN STONE NON-SUSTAINING SCHOLARSHIP

One-time scholarship is open to any African-American student who is currently enrolled in an accredited four-year institution. Must be enrolled as an undergraduate or graduate student and maintain a 3.0 GPA. Major must be in print journalism. Must be NABJ member before award.

Academic Fields/Career Goals: Journalism.

Award: Scholarship for use in freshman, sophomore, junior, senior, or graduate years; not renewable. *Number:* 1. *Amount:* $2500.

Eligibility Requirements: Applicant must be Black (non-Hispanic) and enrolled or expecting to enroll full-time at a four-year institution. Applicant must have 3.0 GPA or higher. Available to U.S. citizens.

Application Requirements: Application, essay, photo, references, transcript, 6 samples of work. *Deadline:* April 30.

Contact: Warren J. Paul, Media Institute Program Associate
National Association of Black Journalists
8701-A Adelphi Road
Adelphi, MD 20783
Phone: 301-445-7100 Ext. 108
Fax: 301-445-7101
E-mail: warren@nabj.org

NABJ SCHOLARSHIP
• *See page 183*

NATIONAL ASSOCIATION OF BLACK JOURNALISTS AND NEWHOUSE FOUNDATION SCHOLARSHIP

Renewable award for African-American high school seniors planning to attend an accredited four-year college or university and major in journalism. Minimum 3.0 GPA required. Summer internship also required. Submit work sample and autobiography with application. Recipients attend NABJ convention and participate in mentor program. Must be NABJ member before award.

Academic Fields/Career Goals: Journalism.

Award: Scholarship for use in freshman, sophomore, junior, or senior years; renewable. *Number:* 2. *Amount:* $5000–$10,000.

Eligibility Requirements: Applicant must be Black (non-Hispanic); high school student; planning to enroll or expecting to enroll full-time at a four-year institution or university and must have an interest in writing. Applicant must have 3.0 GPA or higher. Available to U.S. citizens.

Application Requirements: Application, autobiography, essay, interview, references, transcript. *Deadline:* April 30.

Contact: Program and Exposition Coordinator
National Association of Black Journalists
8701-A Adelphi Road
Adelphi, MD 20783-1716
Phone: 301-445-7100 Ext. 109
Fax: 301-445-7101

NATIONAL ASSOCIATION OF BLACK JOURNALISTS NON-SUSTAINING SCHOLARSHIP AWARDS

One-time award for African-American college students attending a four-year institution and majoring in journalism. Minimum 2.5 GPA required. Submit letter from adviser, work sample, autobiography, resume, and photo with application. Recipient will attend NABJ convention and participate in mentor program. Previous NABJ scholarship winners not eligible. Must be NABJ member before award.

Academic Fields/Career Goals: Journalism; Photojournalism/Photography; TV/Radio Broadcasting.

Award: Scholarship for use in freshman, sophomore, junior, or senior years; not renewable. *Number:* 10. *Amount:* $2500.

Eligibility Requirements: Applicant must be Black (non-Hispanic); enrolled or expecting to enroll full-time at a four-year institution or university and must have an interest in writing. Applicant must have 2.5 GPA or higher. Available to U.S. citizens.

Application Requirements: Application, autobiography, photo, references, transcript, proof of enrollment. *Deadline:* April 30.

Contact: Ryan Williams, Program and Exposition Coordinator
National Association of Black Journalists
8701-A Adelphi Road
Adelphi, MD 20783-1716
Phone: 301-445-7100 Ext. 109
Fax: 301-445-7101

NATIONAL ASSOCIATION OF BROADCASTERS
http://www.nab.org

NATIONAL ASSOCIATION OF BROADCASTERS GRANTS FOR RESEARCH IN BROADCASTING
• *See page 183*

NATIONAL GAY AND LESBIAN TASK FORCE
http://www.ngltf.org/about/messenger.htm

NATIONAL GAY AND LESBIAN TASK FORCE MESSENGER-ANDERSON JOURNALISM SCHOLARSHIP
• *See page 183*

NATIONAL INSTITUTE FOR LABOR RELATIONS RESEARCH
http://www.nilrr.org

NATIONAL INSTITUTE FOR LABOR RELATIONS RESEARCH WILLIAM B. RUGGLES JOURNALISM SCHOLARSHIP
• *See page 184*

NATIONAL PRESS FOUNDATION
http://www.mindspring.com/~us009848/id1.htm

THE EVERT CLARK/SETH PAYNE AWARD

Award to encourage young science writers by recognizing outstanding reporting and writing in any field of science. Deadline is June 30.

Academic Fields/Career Goals: Journalism; Literature/English/Writing.

Award: Prize for use in freshman, sophomore, junior, or senior years; not renewable. *Amount:* $1000.

Eligibility Requirements: Applicant must be age 30 or under and enrolled or expecting to enroll at a four-year institution or university. Available to U.S. citizens.

Application Requirements: Application. *Deadline:* June 30.

Contact: Clark/Payne Award
National Press Foundation
1211 Connecticut Avenue, Suite 310
Washington, DC 20036

NATIONAL SCHOLASTIC PRESS ASSOCIATION

http://www.studentpress.org

NSPA JOURNALISM HONOR ROLL SCHOLARSHIP

For seniors pursuing a career in journalism. Must have achieved a GPA of 3.75 or higher.

Academic Fields/Career Goals: Journalism.

Award: Scholarship for use in freshman year; not renewable. *Number:* 1–3. *Amount:* $1000.

Eligibility Requirements: Applicant must be high school student and planning to enroll or expecting to enroll full or part-time at a four-year institution or university. Applicant must have 3.5 GPA or higher. Available to U.S. and non-U.S. citizens.

Application Requirements: Application, essay, references, transcript, NSPA membership required. *Deadline:* February 15.

Contact: Mary Erickson, Critique Coordinator
National Scholastic Press Association
2221 University Avenue SE, Suite 121
Minneapolis, MN 55414
Phone: 612-625-8335
Fax: 612-626-0720
E-mail: info@studentpress.org

NATIONAL SOCIETY OF NEWSPAPER COLUMNISTS

http://www.columnists.com

COLUMNIST SCHOLARSHIP CONTEST

Scholarship available to undergraduates (including seniors) who write bylined general interest or editorial page columns that appear in the print or on-line editions of college newspapers. Specialized columnists, such as movie reviewers and sports commentators, are not eligible. Columns carrying dual by-lines are eligible but only one prize will be awarded.

Academic Fields/Career Goals: Journalism.

Award: Prize for use in sophomore, junior, or senior years; not renewable. *Number:* up to 2. *Amount:* $500–$1000.

Eligibility Requirements: Applicant must be enrolled or expecting to enroll full-time at an institution or university. Available to U.S. citizens.

Application Requirements: Application, applicant must enter a contest. *Deadline:* March 1.

Contact: Russell Frank, NSNC Education Committee Chair
National Society of Newspaper Columnists
College of Communications, Carnegie Building, Penn State University
University Park, PA 16802
Phone: 814-863-6415
Fax: 814-863-8161
E-mail: rfrank@psu.edu

NATIONAL STONE, SAND AND GRAVEL ASSOCIATION (NSSGA)

http://www.nssga.org

JENNIFER CURTIS BYLER SCHOLARSHIP FOR THE STUDY OF PUBLIC AFFAIRS

• See page 184

NATIONAL WRITERS ASSOCIATION FOUNDATION

http://www.nationalwriters.com

NATIONAL WRITERS ASSOCIATION FOUNDATION SCHOLARSHIPS

• See page 184

NATIVE AMERICAN JOURNALISTS ASSOCIATION

http://www.naja.com

NATIVE AMERICAN JOURNALISTS ASSOCIATION SCHOLARSHIPS

Applicants must have proof of tribal association. Send cover letter, letters of reference, and work samples with application. Financial need considered. One-time award for undergraduate study leading to journalism career at accredited colleges and universities. Applicants must be current members of Native-American Journalists Association or may join at time of application.

Academic Fields/Career Goals: Journalism.

Award: Scholarship for use in freshman, sophomore, junior, senior, or graduate years; not renewable. *Number:* 10–14. *Amount:* $500–$5000.

Eligibility Requirements: Applicant must be American Indian/Alaska Native; enrolled or expecting to enroll full-time at a two-year or four-year institution or university and must have an interest in writing. Applicant must have 2.5 GPA or higher. Available to U.S. and Canadian citizens.

Application Requirements: Application, driver's license, essay, financial need analysis, interview, photo, portfolio, resume, references, test scores, transcript. *Deadline:* April 1.

Contact: Kim Baca, Interim Executive Director
Native American Journalists Association
555 Dakota Street
Vermillion, SD 57069
Phone: 605-677-5282
E-mail: kim@naja.com

NEBRASKA PRESS ASSOCIATION

http://www.nebpress.com

NEBRASKA PRESS ASSOCIATION FOUNDATION, INC., SCHOLARSHIP

Award for graduates of Nebraska high schools who have a minimum GPA of 2.5 and are enrolled or planning to enroll in programs in Nebraska colleges or universities leading to careers in print journalism. Two to four awards of $1250. Deadline: March 8.

Academic Fields/Career Goals: Journalism; Photojournalism/Photography.

Award: Scholarship for use in freshman, sophomore, junior, or senior years; not renewable. *Number:* 2–4. *Amount:* $1250.

Eligibility Requirements: Applicant must be enrolled or expecting to enroll full-time at a four-year institution or university; resident of Nebraska and studying in Nebraska. Applicant must have 2.5 GPA or higher. Available to U.S. citizens.

Application Requirements: Application, references. *Deadline:* March 8.

Contact: Allen Beermann, Executive Director
Nebraska Press Association
845 S Street
Lincoln, NE 68508-1226
Phone: 402-476-2851
Fax: 402-476-2942
E-mail: nebpress@nebpress.com

NEW JERSEY BROADCASTERS ASSOCIATION

http://www.njba.com

MICHAEL S. LIBRETTI SCHOLARSHIP

• See page 184

NEWSPAPER GUILD-CWA

http://www.newsguild.org

DAVID S. BARR AWARD

For their journalistic achievements and to encourage young journalists to focus on issues of social justice, one $500 award will be given to a graduating high school senior and one $1500 award will be given to a college student. For application and more details see Web site: http://www.newguild.org.

Academic Fields/Career Goals: Journalism.

Award: Scholarship for use in freshman, sophomore, junior, or senior years; not renewable. *Number:* up to 2. *Amount:* $500–$1500.

Eligibility Requirements: Applicant must be enrolled or expecting to enroll full or part-time at an institution or university. Available to U.S. and Canadian citizens.

Application Requirements: Application. *Deadline:* varies.

Contact: The Newspaper Guild-Communication Workers of America
Newspaper Guild-CWA
503 3rd Street, NW, Suite 250
Washington, DC 20001

NORTHWEST JOURNALISTS OF COLOR

http://www.aajaseattle.org

NORTHWEST JOURNALISTS OF COLOR SCHOLARSHIP

One-time award for Washington state high school and college students seeking careers in journalism. Must be an undergraduate enrolled in an

Northwest Journalists of Color (continued)

accredited college or university or a senior in high school. Must be Asian-American, African-American, Native-American, or Latino. Application deadline is May 3.

Academic Fields/Career Goals: Journalism.

Award: Scholarship for use in freshman, sophomore, junior, senior, or graduate years; not renewable. *Number:* 1–6. *Amount:* $250–$1000.

Eligibility Requirements: Applicant must be American Indian/Alaska Native, Asian/Pacific Islander, Black (non-Hispanic), or Hispanic; enrolled or expecting to enroll full-time at a two-year or four-year or technical institution or university and resident of Washington. Applicant must have 2.5 GPA or higher. Available to U.S. citizens.

Application Requirements: Application, essay, financial need analysis, references, transcript, work samples. *Deadline:* May 3.

Contact: Lori Matsukawa, Scholarship Coordinator
Northwest Journalists of Color
333 Dexter Avenue North
Seattle, WA 98109
Phone: 206-448-3853
Fax: 206-448-4525
E-mail: lmatsukawa@king5.com

OHIO NEWSPAPERS FOUNDATION   http://www.ohionews.org/foundation.html

HAROLD K. DOUTHIT SCHOLARSHIP

A $1000 scholarship will be awarded to a northern Ohio high school senior who plans to pursue a newspaper journalism career. Applicants must be enrolled in a high school in Cuyahoga, Lorain, Huron, Erie, Wood, Geauge, Sandusky, Ottawa, or Lucas County. The applicant must be enrolled in an accredited Ohio college or university at the time the award is distributed. A minimum high school GPA of 3.0 (B) is required.

Academic Fields/Career Goals: Journalism.

Award: Scholarship for use in freshman year; not renewable. *Number:* 1. *Amount:* $1000.

Eligibility Requirements: Applicant must be high school student; planning to enroll or expecting to enroll full-time at an institution or university; resident of Ohio and studying in Ohio. Applicant must have 3.0 GPA or higher. Available to U.S. citizens.

Application Requirements: Application, autobiography, financial need analysis, references, transcript. *Deadline:* March 31.

Contact: Kathleen Pouliot, Secretary
Ohio Newspapers Foundation
1335 Dublin Road, Suite 216-B
Columbus, OH 43215-7038
Phone: 614-486-6677
Fax: 614-486-4940
E-mail: kpouliot@ohionews.org

OHIO NEWSPAPER WOMEN'S SCHOLARSHIP

Scholarship available to a female student who is enrolled as a junior or senior in an Ohio college or university and majoring in journalism or an equivalent degree program.

Academic Fields/Career Goals: Journalism.

Award: Scholarship for use in junior or senior years. *Amount:* $1000.

Eligibility Requirements: Applicant must be enrolled or expecting to enroll full-time at a four-year institution or university and female. Available to U.S. citizens.

Application Requirements: Application, references, test scores, transcript. *Deadline:* March 31.

Contact: Kathleen Pouliot, Secretary
Ohio Newspapers Foundation
1335 Dublin Road, Suite 216-B
Columbus, OH 43215-7038
Phone: 614-486-6677
Fax: 614-486-4940
E-mail: kpouliot@ohionews.org

OHIO NEWSPAPERS FOUNDATION MINORITY SCHOLARSHIP

Three $1500 scholarships will be awarded to minority high school seniors who plan to pursue a newspaper journalism career. Applicants must be enrolled in an accredited Ohio college or university. A minimum high school GPA of 2.5 (C+) is required. Applicants must be African-American, Hispanic, Asian-American or American-Indian.

Academic Fields/Career Goals: Journalism.

Award: Scholarship for use in freshman year; not renewable. *Number:* 3. *Amount:* $1500.

Eligibility Requirements: Applicant must be American Indian/Alaska Native, Asian/Pacific Islander, Black (non-Hispanic), or Hispanic; high school student; planning to enroll or expecting to enroll full-time at an institution or university; resident of Ohio and studying in Ohio. Applicant must have 2.5 GPA or higher. Available to U.S. citizens.

Application Requirements: Application, autobiography, essay, transcript. *Deadline:* March 31.

Contact: Kathleen Pouliot, Secretary
Ohio Newspapers Foundation
1335 Dublin Road, Suite 216-B
Columbus, OH 43215-7038
Phone: 614-486-6677
Fax: 614-486-4940
E-mail: kpouliot@ohionews.org

OHIO NEWSPAPERS FOUNDATION UNIVERSITY JOURNALISM SCHOLARSHIP

A $1500 scholarship will be awarded to a student who is enrolled in an Ohio college or university who is majoring in journalism or equivalent degree program. Applicants are not limited to, but preference will be given to students demonstrating a career commitment to newspaper journalism. A minimum GPA of 2.5 (C+) is required. Applicants must be sophomore, junior, or senior.

Academic Fields/Career Goals: Journalism.

Award: Scholarship for use in sophomore, junior, or senior years; not renewable. *Number:* 1. *Amount:* $1500.

Eligibility Requirements: Applicant must be enrolled or expecting to enroll full-time at a four-year institution or university; resident of Ohio and studying in Ohio. Applicant must have 2.5 GPA or higher. Available to U.S. citizens.

Application Requirements: Application, autobiography, essay, references, transcript. *Deadline:* March 31.

Contact: Kathleen Pouliot, Secretary
Ohio Newspapers Foundation
1335 Dublin Road, Suite 216-B
Columbus, OH 43215-7038
Phone: 614-486-6677
Fax: 614-486-4940
E-mail: kpouliot@ohionews.org

OREGON ASSOCIATION OF BROADCASTERS   http://www.theoab.org

OAB BROADCAST SCHOLARSHIP
• See page 185

OREGON COMMUNITY FOUNDATION   http://www.ocf1.org/

JACKSON FOUNDATION JOURNALISM SCHOLARSHIP FUND

Scholarship for students attending an Oregon college or university and majoring in, or with emphasis on, journalism.

Academic Fields/Career Goals: Journalism.

Award: Scholarship for use in freshman, sophomore, junior, or senior years. *Number:* 1.

Eligibility Requirements: Applicant must be enrolled or expecting to enroll at a four-year institution or university; resident of Oregon and studying in Oregon. Available to U.S. citizens.

Application Requirements: *Deadline:* varies.

Contact: Dianne Causey, Program Associate for Scholarships/Grants
Oregon Community Foundation
1221 South West Yamhill, Suite 100
Portland, OR 97205
Phone: 503-227-6846
Fax: 503-274-7771
E-mail: info@ocf1.org

OREGON STUDENT ASSISTANCE COMMISSION
http://www.osac.state.or.us

ENTERCOM PORTLAND RADIO SCHOLARSHIP FUND

Awards for residents of Clackamas, Multnomah, Washington, or Yamhill Counties in Oregon or Clark County, Washington. Award for the study of broadcasting or journalism at the undergraduate level. One-time award.

Academic Fields/Career Goals: Journalism; TV/Radio Broadcasting.

Award: Scholarship for use in freshman, junior, or senior years; renewable. *Number:* varies. *Amount:* $500.

Eligibility Requirements: Applicant must be enrolled or expecting to enroll full-time at a four-year institution or university and resident of Oregon or Washington. Available to U.S. citizens.

Application Requirements: Application, essay, financial need analysis, test scores, transcript, activity chart. *Deadline:* March 1.

Contact: Director of Grant Programs
Oregon Student Assistance Commission
1500 Valley River Drive, Suite 100
Eugene, OR 97401-7020
Phone: 800-452-8807 Ext. 7395

JACKSON FOUNDATION JOURNALISM SCHOLARSHIP

Award for graduates of Oregon high schools pursuing a major in journalism. Must be enrolled in an Oregon college.

Academic Fields/Career Goals: Journalism.

Award: Scholarship for use in freshman, sophomore, junior, or senior years; renewable. *Number:* 7. *Amount:* $1429.

Eligibility Requirements: Applicant must be enrolled or expecting to enroll at a two-year or four-year institution or university; resident of Oregon and studying in Oregon. Available to U.S. citizens.

Application Requirements: Application, essay, financial need analysis, references, transcript, activity chart. *Deadline:* March 1.

Contact: Director of Grant Programs
Oregon Student Assistance Commission
1500 Valley River Drive, Suite 100
Eugene, OR 97401-7020
Phone: 800-452-8807 Ext. 7395

MARK HASS JOURNALISM AWARD

One-time award for journalism majors who are graduating Oregon high school seniors and college undergraduates. Visit Web site http://www.osac.state.or.us for application procedures, requirements and deadlines.

Academic Fields/Career Goals: Journalism.

Award: Scholarship for use in freshman, sophomore, junior, or senior years; not renewable. *Number:* 1. *Amount:* $1000.

Eligibility Requirements: Applicant must be enrolled or expecting to enroll at an institution or university and resident of Oregon. Available to U.S. citizens.

Application Requirements: Application, essay, financial need analysis, references, transcript, activity chart. *Deadline:* March 1.

Contact: Director of Grant Programs
Oregon Student Assistance Commission
1500 Valley River Drive, Suite 100
Eugene, OR 97401-7020
Phone: 800-452-8807 Ext. 7395

OUTDOOR WRITERS ASSOCIATION OF AMERICA
http://www.owaa.org/

OUTDOOR WRITERS ASSOCIATION OF AMERICA BODIE MCDOWELL SCHOLARSHIP AWARD
• See page 185

OVERSEAS PRESS CLUB FOUNDATION
http://www.opcofamerica.org

OVERSEAS PRESS CLUB FOUNDATION SCHOLARSHIPS

Students who aspire to become foreign correspondents are asked to write an essay of no more than 500 words concentrating on an area of the world or an international issue that is in keeping with the applicant's interest. It can be in the form of a story, news analysis, or a traditional essay. Must be studying at an American college or university. Application deadline is December 1.

Academic Fields/Career Goals: Journalism.

Award: Scholarship for use in freshman, sophomore, junior, senior, or graduate years; not renewable. *Number:* 12. *Amount:* $2000.

Eligibility Requirements: Applicant must be enrolled or expecting to enroll full or part-time at a two-year or four-year institution or university. Available to U.S. and non-U.S. citizens.

Application Requirements: Applicant must enter a contest, autobiography, essay, resume. *Deadline:* December 1.

Contact: William J. Holstein, President
Overseas Press Club Foundation
40 West 45th Street
New York, NY 10036
Phone: 212-626-9220
Fax: 212-626-9210
E-mail: foundation@opcofamerica.org

PHILADELPHIA ASSOCIATION OF BLACK JOURNALISTS
http://www.pabj.org

PHILADELPHIA ASSOCIATION OF BLACK JOURNALISTS SCHOLARSHIP

One-time award available to African-American high school students interested in becoming journalists. Must have a 2.5 GPA. All applicants must state their intention to pursue journalism careers

Academic Fields/Career Goals: Journalism.

Award: Scholarship for use in freshman or senior years; not renewable. *Number:* 2. *Amount:* up to $1000.

Eligibility Requirements: Applicant must be Black (non-Hispanic); high school student; planning to enroll or expecting to enroll full-time at a four-year institution or university; resident of Delaware and must have an interest in writing. Applicant must have 2.5 GPA or higher. Available to U.S. citizens.

Application Requirements: Application, autobiography, essay, references, transcript. *Deadline:* May 1.

Contact: Manny Smith, PABJ Scholarship Committee member
Philadelphia Association of Black Journalists
PO Box 8232
Philadelphia, PA 19101
E-mail: manuelsmith@gmail.com

PHILADELPHIA TRIBUNE SCHOLARSHIP

Scholarship for African American students who are residents of the City of Philadelphia. High school students can apply. Deadline is May 15.

Academic Fields/Career Goals: Journalism.

Award: Scholarship for use in freshman, sophomore, junior, or senior years. *Number:* up to 5. *Amount:* up to $1000.

Eligibility Requirements: Applicant must be Black (non-Hispanic); high school student; planning to enroll or expecting to enroll full-time at an institution or university and resident of Pennsylvania. Applicant must have 2.5 GPA or higher. Available to U.S. citizens.

Application Requirements: Application, essay, references. *Deadline:* May 15.

Contact: Nia Ngina Meeks, Scholarship coordinator
Philadelphia Association of Black Journalists
PO Box 8232
Philadelphia, PA 19101
Phone: 215-492-2980
Fax: 215-492-2990
E-mail: nmeeks@pasenate.com

POLISH ARTS CLUB OF BUFFALO SCHOLARSHIP FOUNDATION
http://pacb.bfn.org/about/constitution.html

POLISH ARTS CLUB OF BUFFALO SCHOLARSHIP FOUNDATION TRUST
• See page 108

PRINTING INDUSTRIES OF WISCONSIN EDUCATION FOUNDATION SCHOLARSHIPS
http://www.piw.org

PAGEL GRAPHIC ARTS SCHOLARSHIP FUND
• See page 185

QUILL AND SCROLL FOUNDATION
http://www.uiowa.edu/~quill-sc

EDWARD J. NELL MEMORIAL SCHOLARSHIP IN JOURNALISM

Merit-based award for high school seniors planning to major in journalism. Must have won a National Quill and Scroll Writing Award or a Photography or Yearbook Excellence contest. Entry forms available from journalism adviser or Quill and Scroll. Must rank in upper third of class or have a minimum 3.0 GPA.

Academic Fields/Career Goals: Journalism.

Award: Scholarship for use in freshman year; not renewable. *Number:* 8–10. *Amount:* $500–$1500.

Eligibility Requirements: Applicant must be high school student; planning to enroll or expecting to enroll full-time at a four-year institution or university and must have an interest in photography/ photogrammetry/filmmaking or writing. Applicant must have 3.0 GPA or higher. Available to U.S. citizens.

Application Requirements: Application, essay, photo, references, self-addressed stamped envelope, test scores, transcript. *Deadline:* May 10.

Contact: Richard Johns, Executive Director
Quill and Scroll Foundation
312 WSSH, School of Journalism
Iowa City, IA 52242-1528
Phone: 319-335-3321
Fax: 319-335-5210
E-mail: quill-scroll@uiowa.edu

RADIO-TELEVISION NEWS DIRECTORS ASSOCIATION AND FOUNDATION
http://www.rtndf.org/

ABE SCHECTER GRADUATE SCHOLARSHIP
• See page 185

CAROLE SIMPSON SCHOLARSHIP
• See page 185

KEN KASHIWAHARA SCHOLARSHIP
• See page 186

LOU AND CAROLE PRATO SPORTS REPORTING SCHOLARSHIP
• See page 186

MIKE REYNOLDS $1,000 SCHOLARSHIP
• See page 186

PRESIDENT'S $2500 SCHOLARSHIP
• See page 186

SACRAMENTO BEE
http://www.sacbee.com

SACRAMENTO BEE JOURNALISM SCHOLARSHIP PROGRAM

The Sacramento Bee Journalism Scholarship Program is for graduating high school seniors, and college students pursuing careers in the newspaper business. Applicants and recipients must reside in the Sacramento region.

Academic Fields/Career Goals: Journalism.

Award: Scholarship for use in senior year; not renewable. *Number:* up to 16. *Amount:* $1500–$2500.

Eligibility Requirements: Applicant must be enrolled or expecting to enroll full-time at a four-year institution or university and resident of California. Applicant must have 3.0 GPA or higher. Available to U.S. citizens.

Application Requirements: Application, autobiography, essay, financial need analysis, photo, portfolio, resume, references, transcript. *Deadline:* January 31.

Contact: Cathy Rodriguez, Public Affairs Representative
Sacramento Bee
2100 Q Street
Sacramento, CA 95816
Phone: 916-321-1880
Fax: 916-321-1783
E-mail: crodriguez@sacbee.com

SAN DIEGO PRESS CLUB SCHOLARSHIP FOUNDATION
http://www.sdpressclub.com/foundation

JOE LIPPER MEMORIAL SCHOLARSHIP

Scholarship for journalism students. The candidates are selected based on GPA, participation in community service, and media-related internships.

Academic Fields/Career Goals: Journalism.

Award: Scholarship for use in freshman, sophomore, junior, or senior years. *Amount:* $1500–$2500.

Eligibility Requirements: Applicant must be enrolled or expecting to enroll full-time at a four-year institution or university. Available to U.S. citizens.

Application Requirements: Application, essay. *Deadline:* varies.

Contact: Denis Vedder
San Diego Press Club Scholarship Foundation
PO Box 82571
San Diego, CA 92138-2571
Phone: 760-434-2957
E-mail: thevedders@sbcglobal.net

SANTA CLARA UNIVERSITY SCHOOL OF LAW - COMPUTER AND HIGH TECHNOLOGY LAW JOURNAL
http://www.scu.edu/techlaw

SANTA CLARA UNIVERSITY SCHOOL OF LAW COMPUTER AND HIGH TECHNOLOGY LAW JOURNAL COMMENT CONTEST

Current law students in the U.S. may submit a comment involving research and analysis on law and technology. Topic changes annually. Please call or visit Web site for deadline and more information.

Academic Fields/Career Goals: Journalism; Law/Legal Services.

Award: Prize for use in senior, or graduate years; not renewable. *Number:* 3. *Amount:* $1000–$2000.

Eligibility Requirements: Applicant must be enrolled or expecting to enroll full or part-time at a two-year institution or university. Available to U.S. citizens.

Application Requirements: Applicant must enter a contest, essay, 3 copies of essay, cover letter, disk with essay. *Deadline:* June 15.

Contact: Senior Comments Editor
Santa Clara University School of Law - Computer and High Technology Law Journal
500 El Camino Real
Santa Clara, CA 95053-0421
Phone: 408-554-4197
E-mail: ndpope@scu.edu

SEATTLE POST-INTELLIGENCER
http://www.seattlepi.com

BOBBI MCCALLUM MEMORIAL SCHOLARSHIP

Scholarship is available to junior and senior college women from a Washington state university who have an interest in print journalism. Submit clips of published stories with transcripts, financial need analysis, application, and two letters of recommendation. Must be a Washington resident. Submit only questions through email. Applications must be mailed.

Academic Fields/Career Goals: Journalism.

Award: Scholarship for use in junior or senior years; not renewable. *Number:* 1. *Amount:* $1000.

Eligibility Requirements: Applicant must be enrolled or expecting to enroll full or part-time at a four-year institution; female; resident of Washington and studying in Washington. Applicant must have 3.0 GPA or higher. Available to U.S. citizens.

Application Requirements: Application, financial need analysis, portfolio, resume, references, transcript. *Deadline:* April 1.

Contact: Janet Grimley, Assistant Managing Editor
Seattle Post-Intelligencer
PO Box 1909
Seattle, WA 98111
Phone: 206-448-8316
Fax: 206-448-8305
E-mail: janetgrimley@seattlep-i.com

SOCIETY OF PROFESSIONAL JOURNALISTS MARYLAND PRO CHAPTER   http://www.saber.towson.edu/~bhalle/scholarship.html

MARYLAND SPJ PRO CHAPTER COLLEGE SCHOLARSHIP

Scholarships for journalism students whose regular home residence is in Maryland, but may attend colleges or universities outside Maryland in nearby Virginia, D.C. or Pennsylvania. Membership in local campus chapters or journalism clubs, societies or radio/TV groups should be listed.

Academic Fields/Career Goals: Journalism.

Award: Scholarship for use in freshman, sophomore, junior, or senior years; not renewable. *Number:* 1.

Eligibility Requirements: Applicant must be enrolled or expecting to enroll full or part-time at a four-year institution or university and resident of Maryland. Available to U.S. citizens.

Application Requirements: Application, essay, financial need analysis, references, transcript, awards or honors received. *Deadline:* May 9.

Contact: Sue Kopen, Katcef
Society of Professional Journalists Maryland Pro Chapter
402 Fox Hollow Lane
Annapolis, MD 21403
Phone: 301-405-7526
E-mail: susiekk@aol.com

SOCIETY OF PROFESSIONAL JOURNALISTS, LOS ANGELES CHAPTER   http://www.spj.org/losangeles

BILL FARR SCHOLARSHIP

Awards are available to a student who is either a resident of Los Angeles, Ventura or Orange counties or is enrolled at a university in one of those three California counties. Must have completed sophomore year and be enrolled in or accepted to a journalism program. Application deadline is April 15.

Academic Fields/Career Goals: Journalism.

Award: Scholarship for use in junior, senior, or graduate years; not renewable. *Number:* 1. *Amount:* $500–$1000.

Eligibility Requirements: Applicant must be enrolled or expecting to enroll full-time at a four-year institution or university and resident of California. Available to U.S. citizens.

Application Requirements: Application, essay, financial need analysis, resume, references, work samples. *Deadline:* April 15.

Contact: Daniel Garvey, Scholarship Chairman
Society of Professional Journalists, Los Angeles Chapter
1250 Bellflower
Long Beach, CA 90840
Phone: 562-985-5779

CARL GREENBERG SCHOLARSHIP

Awards are available to a student who is either a resident of Los Angeles, Ventura or Orange counties or is enrolled at a university in one of those three California counties. Must have completed sophomore year and be enrolled in or accepted to an investigative or political journalism program. Application deadline is April 15.

Academic Fields/Career Goals: Journalism.

Award: Scholarship for use in junior, senior, or graduate years; not renewable. *Number:* 1. *Amount:* up to $1000.

Eligibility Requirements: Applicant must be enrolled or expecting to enroll full-time at a four-year institution or university and resident of California. Available to U.S. citizens.

Application Requirements: Application, essay, financial need analysis, resume, references, work samples. *Deadline:* April 15.

Contact: Daniel Garvey, Scholarship Chairman
Society of Professional Journalists, Los Angeles Chapter
1250 Bellflower
Long Beach, CA 90840
Phone: 562-985-5779

HELEN JOHNSON SCHOLARSHIP

Awards are available to a student who is a resident of Los Angeles, Ventura or Orange counties or is enrolled at a university in one of those three California counties. Must have completed sophomore year and be enrolled in or accepted to a broadcast journalism program. Application deadline is April 15.

Academic Fields/Career Goals: Journalism; TV/Radio Broadcasting.

Award: Scholarship for use in junior, senior, or graduate years; not renewable. *Number:* 1. *Amount:* $500–$1000.

Eligibility Requirements: Applicant must be enrolled or expecting to enroll full-time at a four-year institution or university and resident of California. Available to U.S. citizens.

Application Requirements: Application, essay, financial need analysis, resume, references, work samples. *Deadline:* April 15.

Contact: Daniel Garvey, Scholarship Chairman
Society of Professional Journalists, Los Angeles Chapter
1250 Bellflower
Long Beach, CA 90840
Phone: 562-985-5779

KEN INOUYE SCHOLARSHIP

Awards are available to a minority student who is either a resident of Los Angeles, Ventura or Orange counties or is enrolled at a university in one of those three California counties. Must have completed sophomore year and be enrolled in or accepted to a journalism program. Application deadline is April 15.

Academic Fields/Career Goals: Journalism.

Award: Scholarship for use in junior, senior, or graduate years; renewable. *Number:* 1. *Amount:* $500–$1000.

Eligibility Requirements: Applicant must be American Indian/Alaska Native, Asian/Pacific Islander, Black (non-Hispanic), or Hispanic; enrolled or expecting to enroll full-time at a four-year institution or university and resident of California. Available to U.S. citizens.

Application Requirements: Application, essay, financial need analysis, resume, references, work samples. *Deadline:* April 15.

Contact: Daniel Garvey, Scholarship Chairman
Society of Professional Journalists, Los Angeles Chapter
1250 Bellflower
Long Beach, CA 90840
Phone: 562-985-5779

SOCIETY OF PROFESSIONAL JOURNALISTS-SOUTH FLORIDA CHAPTER   http://www.spjsofla.net/

GARTH REEVES, JR. MEMORIAL SCHOLARSHIPS
• See page 187

SOIL AND WATER CONSERVATION SOCIETY-NEW JERSEY CHAPTER   http://www.geocities.com/njswcs

EDWARD R. HALL SCHOLARSHIP
• See page 76

SOUTH ASIAN JOURNALISTS ASSOCIATION (SAJA)   http://www.saja.org

SAJA JOURNALISM SCHOLARSHIP

Scholarships for students of South Asian descent (includes Bangladesh, Bhutan, India, Maldives, Nepal, Pakistan and Sri Lanka, Indo-Caribbean). Must be interested in pursuing journalism. Applicant must be a high school senior, undergraduate student or graduate-level student.

Academic Fields/Career Goals: Journalism.

Award: Scholarship for use in freshman, sophomore, junior, senior, or graduate years. *Amount:* $1000–$1500.

Eligibility Requirements: Applicant must be Asian/Pacific Islander and enrolled or expecting to enroll at a four-year institution or university. Available to U.S. citizens.

Application Requirements: Application, essay, financial need analysis, photo, references. *Deadline:* April 1.

Contact: Sudeep Reddy, Student Committee and Scholarships
South Asian Journalists Association (SAJA)
Columbia Graduate School of Journalism
2950 Broadway
New York, NY 10027
Phone: 212-854-0191
E-mail: sreddy@dallasnews.com

SOUTH CAROLINA PRESS ASSOCIATION FOUNDATION
http://www.scpress.org

SOUTH CAROLINA PRESS ASSOCIATION FOUNDATION NEWSPAPER SCHOLARSHIPS

Renewable award for students entering junior year at a South Carolina institution. Based on grades, journalistic activities in college, and recommendations. Must agree to work in the newspaper field for two years after graduation or repay as loan.

Academic Fields/Career Goals: Journalism.

Award: Forgivable loan for use in junior year; renewable. *Number:* up to 3. *Amount:* up to $1000.

Eligibility Requirements: Applicant must be enrolled or expecting to enroll full-time at a four-year institution and studying in South Carolina. Available to U.S. and non-U.S. citizens.

Application Requirements: Application, essay, financial need analysis, portfolio, resume, references, transcript. *Deadline:* January 1.

Contact: William C. Rogers, Secretary
South Carolina Press Association Foundation
PO Box 11429
Columbia, SC 29211-1429
Phone: 803-750-9561
Fax: 803-551-0903

TEXAS GRIDIRON CLUB, INC.
http://www.spjfw.org

TEXAS GRIDIRON CLUB SCHOLARSHIPS
• See page 188

THE CHRONICLE OF HIGHER EDUCATION
http://www.chronicle.com

DAVID W. MILLER AWARD FOR STUDENT JOURNALISTS

Award for undergraduate students studying journalism. Applicants may be students in any country. For further information see Web site: http://www.chronicle.com

Academic Fields/Career Goals: Journalism.

Award: Prize for use in freshman, sophomore, junior, or senior years. *Amount:* up to $2500.

Eligibility Requirements: Applicant must be enrolled or expecting to enroll at a four-year institution or university. Available to U.S. and non-U.S. citizens.

Application Requirements: Application, essay. *Deadline:* June 1.

Contact: The Chronicle of Higher Education
The Chronicle of Higher Education, 1255 23rd Street, NW
Washington, DC 20037
E-mail: milleraward@chronicle.com

UNITED METHODIST COMMUNICATIONS
http://www.umcom.org/

LEONARD M. PERRYMAN COMMUNICATIONS SCHOLARSHIP FOR ETHNIC MINORITY STUDENTS
• See page 189

UNITED NEGRO COLLEGE FUND
http://www.uncf.org

BEST BUY ENTERPRISE EMPLOYEE SCHOLARSHIP
• See page 70

C-SPAN SCHOLARSHIP PROGRAM
• See page 189

READER'S DIGEST SCHOLARSHIP
• See page 189

VALLEY PRESS CLUB
http://www.valleypressclub.com/

VALLEY PRESS CLUB SCHOLARSHIPS, THE REPUBLICAN SCHOLARSHIP; PHOTOJOURNALISM SCHOLARSHIP, CHANNEL 22 SCHOLARSHIP
• See page 189

WASHINGTON NEWS COUNCIL
http://www.wanewscouncil.org/

DICK LARSEN SCHOLARSHIP PROGRAM
• See page 189

HERB ROBINSON SCHOLARSHIP PROGRAM
• See page 190

WASHINGTON PRESS CLUB FOUNDATION
http://www.wpcf.org

WASHINGTON PRESS CLUB FOUNDATION SCHOLARSHIPS

Renewable scholarships to students of journalism in four-year college or university. See Web site for information and application: http://www.press.org/programs/awards.cfm

Academic Fields/Career Goals: Journalism.

Award: Scholarship for use in freshman, sophomore, junior, or senior years; renewable. *Number:* 1.

Eligibility Requirements: Applicant must be enrolled or expecting to enroll full-time at a four-year institution or university. Available to U.S. citizens.

Contact: Washington Press Club Foundation
National Press Club Building
Suite 115, 529 14th Street, NW
Washington, DC 20045

WASHINGTON THOROUGHBRED FOUNDATION
http://www.washingtonthoroughbred.com

THOROUGHBRED HORSE RACING'S UNITED SCHOLARSHIP TRUST

Awards for those majoring in an equine industry-related field of study or journalism. One renewable scholarship and three one-time grants. Must describe in writing, on video, audiotape, or film how the expansion of gaming in Washington state has affected the thoroughbred industry. See Web site at http://www.washingtonthoroughbred.com for application and further information. Deadline is February 1.

Academic Fields/Career Goals: Journalism.

Award: Scholarship for use in freshman, sophomore, junior, or senior years; not renewable. *Number:* up to 5. *Amount:* $1000–$2500.

Eligibility Requirements: Applicant must be enrolled or expecting to enroll full-time at a four-year institution or university and resident of Washington. Available to U.S. citizens.

Application Requirements: Application, essay, interview. *Deadline:* February 1.

Contact: Ralph Vacca, THRUST Scholarship Committee, c/o
Washington Thoroughbred Breeders Association
Washington Thoroughbred Foundation
PO Box 1499
Auburn, WA 98071-1499
Phone: 253-288-7878

WMTW-TV 8-AUBURN, MAINE
http://www.wmtw.com

BOB ELLIOT- WMTW-TV 8 JOURNALISM SCHOLARSHIP
• See page 190

WOMEN'S BASKETBALL COACHES ASSOCIATION
http://www.wbca.org

ROBIN ROBERTS/WBCA SPORTS COMMUNICATIONS SCHOLARSHIP AWARD
• See page 190

LANDSCAPE ARCHITECTURE

AMERICAN INSTITUTE OF ARCHITECTS, NEW YORK CHAPTER
http://www.aiany.org

THE DOUGLAS HASKELL AWARD FOR STUDENT JOURNALISM
• See page 98

AMERICAN NURSERY AND LANDSCAPE ASSOCIATION
http://www.anla.org/research

ANLA NATIONAL SCHOLARSHIP ENDOWMENT-USREY FAMILY SCHOLARSHIP
• See page 341

CARVILLE M. AKEHURST MEMORIAL SCHOLARSHIP
• See page 341

HORTICULTURE RESEARCH INSTITUTE TIMOTHY BIGELOW AND PALMER W. BIGELOW, JR. SCHOLARSHIP
• See page 341

SPRING MEADOW NURSERY SCHOLARSHIP
• See page 342

ASSOCIATION FOR WOMEN IN ARCHITECTURE FOUNDATION
http://www.awa-la.org

ASSOCIATION FOR WOMEN IN ARCHITECTURE SCHOLARSHIP
• See page 98

CALIFORNIA WATER AWARENESS CAMPAIGN
http://www.wateraware.org

CALIFORNIA WATER AWARENESS CAMPAIGN WATER SCHOLAR
• See page 79

CONNECTICUT NURSERYMEN'S FOUNDATION, INC.

CONNECTICUT NURSERYMEN'S FOUNDATION, INC. SCHOLARSHIPS
• See page 342

FEDERATED GARDEN CLUBS OF CONNECTICUT
http://www.ctgardenclubs.org

FEDERATED GARDEN CLUBS OF CONNECTICUT, INC.
• See page 137

FLORIDA EDUCATIONAL FACILITIES PLANNERS' ASSOCIATION
http://www.fefpa.org

FEFPA ASSISTANTSHIP
• See page 99

FRIENDS OF THE FRELINGHUYSEN ARBORETUM
http://www.arboretumfriends.org

BENJAMIN C. BLACKBURN SCHOLARSHIP
• See page 293

HERB SOCIETY OF AMERICA
http://www.herbsociety.org

HERB SOCIETY RESEARCH GRANTS
• See page 92

HERB SOCIETY OF AMERICA, WESTERN RESERVE UNIT
http://www.herbsociety.org

FRANCIS SYLVIA ZVERINA SCHOLARSHIP
• See page 348

WESTERN RESERVE HERB SOCIETY SCHOLARSHIP
• See page 348

LANDSCAPE ARCHITECTURE FOUNDATION
http://www.LAprofession.org

ASLA COUNCIL OF FELLOWS SCHOLARSHIP

Scholarship to aid promising students with unmet financial need. Special consideration given to economically disadvantaged and under-represented populations in the study of landscape architecture. Applicants seeking special consideration for the diversity scholarship should indicate and identify their association with a specific ethnic or cultural group in their cover sheet under the Additional Comments section (see General Submission Guidelines).

Academic Fields/Career Goals: Landscape Architecture.

Award: Scholarship for use in junior or senior years. *Number:* 2. *Amount:* $4000.

Eligibility Requirements: Applicant must be enrolled or expecting to enroll full or part-time at an institution or university. Applicant or parent of applicant must be member of Lambda Alpha National Collegiate Honor Society for Anthropology. Available to U.S. citizens.

Application Requirements: Application, essay, financial need analysis, references. *Deadline:* February 15.

Contact: Ron Figura, Project Manager
Landscape Architecture Foundation
818 18th Street, NW
Suite 810
Washington, DC 20006
Phone: 202-331-7070 Ext. 10
Fax: 202-331-7079
E-mail: rfigura@lafoundation.org

COURTLAND PAUL SCHOLARSHIP

Scholarship for undergraduate students in the final two years of study in Landscape Architecture Accreditation Board-accredited schools. Applicants must demonstrate financial need, be U.S. citizen, and have a minimum GPA of C.

Academic Fields/Career Goals: Landscape Architecture.

Award: Scholarship for use in junior or senior years. *Amount:* $5000.

Eligibility Requirements: Applicant must be enrolled or expecting to enroll full or part-time at an institution or university. Available to U.S. and non-U.S. citizens.

Application Requirements: Application, essay, references. *Deadline:* February 15.

Contact: Ron Figura, Project Manager
Landscape Architecture Foundation
818 18th Street, NW
Suite 810
Washington, DC 20006
Phone: 202-331-7070 Ext. 10
Fax: 202-331-7079
E-mail: rfigura@lafoundation.org

HAWAII CHAPTER/DAVID T. WOOLSEY SCHOLARSHIP

One-time award of $2000 in memory of David T. Woolsey provides funds for a third, fourth, fifth-year, or graduate student in landscape architecture from Hawaii. Must submit three 8x10 photographs of design work. Must include record of Hawaii residency.

Academic Fields/Career Goals: Landscape Architecture.

Award: Scholarship for use in junior, senior, or graduate years; not renewable. *Number:* 1. *Amount:* $2000.

Eligibility Requirements: Applicant must be enrolled or expecting to enroll at a four-year institution and resident of Hawaii. Available to U.S. citizens.

Application Requirements: Application, autobiography, essay, financial need analysis, references, photos of work, proof of Hawaii residency. *Deadline:* February 15.

Contact: Ron Figura, Project Manager
Landscape Architecture Foundation
818 18th Street, NW
Suite 810
Washington, DC 20006
Phone: 202-331-7070 Ext. 10
Fax: 202-331-7079
E-mail: rfigura@lafoundation.org

LANDSCAPE ARCHITECTURE FOUNDATION/CALIFORNIA LANDSCAPE ARCHITECTURAL STUDENT FUND SCHOLARSHIPS PROGRAM

Nonrenewable scholarships for students continuing degree program in landscape architecture at eligible institution in California. Based on financial need and commitment to profession.

Academic Fields/Career Goals: Landscape Architecture.

Award: Scholarship for use in freshman, sophomore, junior, or senior years; not renewable. *Number:* 4. *Amount:* $1000.

Eligibility Requirements: Applicant must be enrolled or expecting to enroll at a four-year institution or university and studying in California. Available to U.S. citizens.

Landscape Architecture Foundation (continued)

Application Requirements: Application, financial need analysis, references. *Deadline:* February 15.

Contact: Ron Figura, Project Manager
Landscape Architecture Foundation
818 18th Street, NW
Suite 810
Washington, DC 20006
Phone: 202-331-7070 Ext. 10
Fax: 202-331-7079
E-mail: rfigura@lafoundation.org

LANDSCAPE ARCHITECTURE FOUNDATION/CALIFORNIA LANDSCAPE ARCHITECTURE STUDENT FUND UNIVERSITY SCHOLARSHIP PROGRAM
• *See page 349*

RAIN BIRD COMPANY SCHOLARSHIP

One-time need-based award for student in final two years of undergraduate study in landscape architecture. 300-word essay on career goals and how recipient will contribute to the advancement of the profession is required.

Academic Fields/Career Goals: Landscape Architecture.

Award: Scholarship for use in junior or senior years; not renewable. *Number:* 1. *Amount:* $2500.

Eligibility Requirements: Applicant must be enrolled or expecting to enroll at a four-year institution or university. Available to U.S. and non-U.S. citizens.

Application Requirements: Application, essay, financial need analysis, references. *Deadline:* February 15.

Contact: Ron Figura, Project Manager
Landscape Architecture Foundation
818 18th Street, NW
Suite 810
Washington, DC 20006
Phone: 202-331-7070 Ext. 10
Fax: 202-331-7079
E-mail: rfigura@lafoundation.org

THE EDSA MINORITY SCHOLARSHIP

Scholarship for African American, Hispanic, Native American and minority students of other cultural and ethnic backgrounds to continue their landscape architecture education as they enter into their final two years of undergraduate study.

Academic Fields/Career Goals: Landscape Architecture.

Award: Scholarship for use in junior or senior years. *Amount:* $3500.

Eligibility Requirements: Applicant must be American Indian/Alaska Native, Asian/Pacific Islander, Black (non-Hispanic), or Hispanic and enrolled or expecting to enroll full or part-time at an institution or university. Available to U.S. citizens.

Application Requirements: Application, essay, references, three 8¢ x 11 work samples in either jpg or PDF format. *Deadline:* February 15.

Contact: Ron Figura, Project Manager
Landscape Architecture Foundation
818 18th Street, NW
Suite 810
Washington, DC 20006
Phone: 202-331-7070 Ext. 10
Fax: 202-331-7079
E-mail: rfigura@lafoundation.org

MONTANA FEDERATION OF GARDEN CLUBS
http://www.mtfgc.org

LIFE MEMBER MONTANA FEDERATION OF GARDEN CLUBS SCHOLARSHIP
• *See page 138*

NATIONAL ASSOCIATION OF WOMEN IN CONSTRUCTION
http://nawic.org

NAWIC UNDERGRADUATE SCHOLARSHIPS
• *See page 100*

NATIONAL GARDEN CLUBS, INC.
http://www.gardenclub.org

NATIONAL GARDEN CLUBS, INC. SCHOLARSHIP PROGRAM
• *See page 83*

NETWORK OF EXECUTIVE WOMEN IN HOSPITALITY
http://www.newh.org

NETWORK OF EXECUTIVE WOMEN IN HOSPITALITY, INC. SCHOLARSHIP
• *See page 101*

NEW YORK STATE EDUCATION DEPARTMENT
http://www.highered.nysed.gov

REGENTS PROFESSIONAL OPPORTUNITY SCHOLARSHIP
• *See page 67*

PROFESSIONAL CONSTRUCTION ESTIMATORS ASSOCIATION
http://www.pcea.org

TED WILSON MEMORIAL SCHOLARSHIP FOUNDATION
• *See page 212*

PROFESSIONAL GROUNDS MANAGEMENT SOCIETY
http://www.pgms.org

ANNE SEAMAN PROFESSIONAL GROUNDS MANAGEMENT SOCIETY MEMORIAL SCHOLARSHIP
• *See page 84*

UNITED AGRIBUSINESS LEAGUE
http://www.ual.org

UNITED AGRIBUSINESS LEAGUE SCHOLARSHIP PROGRAM
• *See page 77*

UNITED AGRICULTURAL BENEFIT TRUST SCHOLARSHIP
• *See page 77*

WORLDSTUDIO FOUNDATION
http://www.worldstudio.org

WORLDSTUDIO FOUNDATION SCHOLARSHIP PROGRAM
• *See page 104*

LAW ENFORCEMENT/POLICE ADMINISTRATION

ALBERTA HERITAGE SCHOLARSHIP FUND/ALBERTA SCHOLARSHIP PROGRAMS
http://www.alis.gov.ab.ca

ROBERT C. CARSON MEMORIAL BURSARY
• *See page 198*

AMERICAN SOCIETY OF CRIMINOLOGY
http://www.ASC41.com

AMERICAN SOCIETY OF CRIMINOLOGY GENE CARTE STUDENT PAPER COMPETITION
• *See page 199*

BOY SCOUTS OF AMERICA - MUSKINGUM VALLEY COUNCIL
http://www.learning-for-life.org

ATFAR SCHOLARSHIP

Scholarships to assist Explorers whose well-rounded performance in academics, exploring and other activities indicate an exceptional potential to pursue undergraduate studies in preparation for entering the law enforcement profession.

Academic Fields/Career Goals: Law Enforcement/Police Administration.

Award: Scholarship for use in freshman, sophomore, junior, or senior years. *Amount:* $1000.

Eligibility Requirements: Applicant must be enrolled or expecting to enroll at a four-year institution or university. Available to U.S. citizens.

Application Requirements: Application, essay, references, transcript. *Deadline:* March 15.

Contact: Boy Scouts of America - Muskingum Valley Council
PO Box 152079, 1325 West Walnut Hill Lane
Irving, TX 75015-2039

FEDERAL CRIMINAL INVESTIGATORS' SERVICE AWARD

Volunteer service award consisting of a plaque, a U.S. savings bond and recognition in the association's newsletter. Must be Explorer Scout who has made a significant contribution in service as a volunteer in the activities of the sponsoring law enforcement department or agency.

Academic Fields/Career Goals: Law Enforcement/Police Administration.

Award: Prize for use in freshman, sophomore, junior, or senior years. *Amount:* $500.

Eligibility Requirements: Applicant must be enrolled or expecting to enroll at a technical institution. Available to U.S. citizens.

Application Requirements: Nomination form, endorsement letter. *Deadline:* March 31.

Contact: Boy Scouts of America - Muskingum Valley Council
1325 West Walnut Hill Lane, PO Box 152079
Irving, TX 75015-2079

SHERYL A. HORAK MEMORIAL SCHOLARSHIP

One-time merit-based $1000 scholarship. The number of scholarships awarded depends upon the yield of the endowment. The award also includes a plaque and pin. The recognition will be presented at the national law enforcement explorer conference or a local ceremony.

Academic Fields/Career Goals: Law Enforcement/Police Administration.

Award: Scholarship for use in freshman, sophomore, junior, or senior years. *Amount:* $1000.

Eligibility Requirements: Applicant must be enrolled or expecting to enroll at a four-year institution or university. Available to U.S. citizens.

Application Requirements: Application, essay, photo, references, transcript. *Deadline:* March 31.

Contact: Boy Scouts of America - Muskingum Valley Council
1325 West Walnut Hill Lane, PO Box 152079
Irving, TX 75015-2079

CONNECTICUT ASSOCIATION OF WOMEN POLICE

CONNECTICUT ASSOCIATION OF WOMEN POLICE SCHOLARSHIP
• See page 199

ILLINOIS POLICE CORPS

ILLINOIS POLICE CORPS SCHOLARSHIP

Scholarships available for students seeking careers in law enforcement. Must agree to commit to four years of employment with a participating Illinois law enforcement agency. Check Web site for updated information on available funding, application, and requirements: http://www.ptb.state.il.us/policecorps/default.html

Academic Fields/Career Goals: Law Enforcement/Police Administration.

Award: Scholarship for use in freshman, sophomore, junior, senior, or graduate years. *Number:* 10. *Amount:* $7500–$10,000.

Eligibility Requirements: Applicant must be enrolled or expecting to enroll full-time at a four-year institution or university. Applicant must have 2.5 GPA or higher. Available to U.S. citizens.

Application Requirements: Application, driver's license, interview, references, transcript. *Deadline:* Continuous.

Contact: Illinois Police Corps
Illinois Police Corps
1 University Circle
Macomb, IL 61455
Phone: 309-298-3350
Fax: 309-298-2515

INDIANA SHERIFFS' ASSOCIATION   http://www.indianasheriffs.org

INDIANA SHERIFFS' ASSOCIATION SCHOLARSHIP PROGRAM
• See page 199

INTERNATIONAL ASSOCIATION OF ARSON INVESTIGATORS EDUCATIONAL FOUNDATION, INC.   http://www.fire-investigators.org/

JOHN CHARLES WILSON SCHOLARSHIP
• See page 300

LEARNING FOR LIFE   http://www.learning-for-life.org

BUREAU OF ALCOHOL, TOBACCO, FIREARMS AND EXPLOSIVES SCHOLARSHIP-LAW ENFORCEMENT

As part of the Learning for Life-Exploring Program the ATFRA Scholarships are presented every even-numbered year to Law Enforcement Explorers whose achievements reflect the high degree of motivation, commitment, and community concern that epitomizes the law enforcement profession. For more information visit Web site http://www.learning-for-life.org/exploring. Applicant must be younger than 21 years of age.

Academic Fields/Career Goals: Law Enforcement/Police Administration.

Award: Scholarship for use in freshman, sophomore, junior, or senior years; not renewable. *Number:* 2. *Amount:* $1000.

Eligibility Requirements: Applicant must be age 20 or under and enrolled or expecting to enroll full-time at a two-year or four-year institution or university. Available to U.S. citizens.

Application Requirements: Application, essay, references, transcript. *Deadline:* March 15.

Contact: Learning for Life
1325 West Walnut Hill Lane, Sum 310
PO Box 152079
Irving, TX 75015-2079
Phone: 972-580-2433

CAPTAIN JAMES J. REGAN SCHOLARSHIP

The National Technical Investigators Association presents two one-time $500 scholarships annually. Criteria include academic record, leadership, extracurricular activities, and a personal statement on "What significance I place on a technical background in law enforcement." Applicant must be younger than 21 years of age. For more information visit http://www.learning-for-life.org/exploring

Academic Fields/Career Goals: Law Enforcement/Police Administration.

Award: Scholarship for use in freshman, sophomore, junior, or senior years; not renewable. *Number:* 2. *Amount:* $500.

Eligibility Requirements: Applicant must be age 20 or under and enrolled or expecting to enroll full-time at a four-year institution or university. Available to U.S. citizens.

Application Requirements: Application, essay, references, transcript. *Deadline:* March 31.

Contact: Learning for Life
1325 West Walnut Hill Lane, Sum 310
PO Box 152079
Irving, TX 75015-2079
Phone: 972-580-2433

DEA DRUG ABUSE PREVENTION SERVICE AWARDS

The DEA Drug Abuse Prevention Service Award consists of an engraved plaque and a $1,000 award, which will be presented in recognition of "an act or actions representing a contribution of outstanding service in drug abuse prevention." For more information visit http://www.learning-for-life.org/exploring. Applicant must be younger than 21 years of age.

Academic Fields/Career Goals: Law Enforcement/Police Administration.

Award: Prize for use in freshman, sophomore, junior, or senior years; not renewable. *Number:* 1. *Amount:* $1000.

Learning for Life (continued)

Eligibility Requirements: Applicant must be age 20 or under; enrolled or expecting to enroll full-time at an institution or university and must have an interest in designated field specified by sponsor. Available to U.S. citizens.

Application Requirements: Application. *Deadline:* March 31.

Contact: National Law Enforcement Scholarships and Awards
Learning for Life
1325 West Walnut Hill Lane, PO Box 152079
Irving, TX 75015-2079
Phone: 972-580-2433

FEDERAL CRIMINAL INVESTIGATORS' SERVICE AWARD

Federal Investigators Association recognizes Explorers who render outstanding service to law enforcement agencies with a $500 U.S. Savings bond and plaque. Please visit Web site http://www.learning-for-life.org/exploring for information and application. Applicant must be younger than 21 years of age.

Academic Fields/Career Goals: Law Enforcement/Police Administration.

Award: Prize for use in freshman, sophomore, junior, or senior years; not renewable. *Number:* varies. *Amount:* $500.

Eligibility Requirements: Applicant must be age 20 or under and enrolled or expecting to enroll at an institution or university. Available to U.S. citizens.

Application Requirements: Application. *Deadline:* varies.

Contact: National Law Enforcement Scholarships and Awards
Learning for Life
1325 West Walnut Hill Lane, PO Box 152079
Irving, TX 75015-2079
Phone: 972-580-2433

FLOYD BORING AWARD

The director of the U.S. Secret Service presents two scholarships annually to a law enforcement Explorer whose achievements reflect the high degree of motivation, commitment, and community concern that epitomizes the law enforcement profession. Applicant must be younger than 21 years of age. For more information visit http://www.learning-for-life.org/exploring

Academic Fields/Career Goals: Law Enforcement/Police Administration.

Award: Scholarship for use in freshman, sophomore, junior, or senior years; not renewable. *Number:* 2. *Amount:* $2000.

Eligibility Requirements: Applicant must be age 20 or under and enrolled or expecting to enroll full-time at a four-year institution or university. Available to U.S. citizens.

Application Requirements: Application, essay, photo, references, transcript. *Deadline:* varies.

Contact: Learning for Life
1325 West Walnut Hill Lane, Sum 310
PO Box 152079
Irving, TX 75015-2079
Phone: 972-580-2433

SHERYL A. HORAK MEMORIAL SCHOLARSHIP

This merit-based award involves a $1000, one-time scholarship. The number of scholarships awarded depends upon the yield of the endowment. The award also includes a plaque and pin. Applicant must be younger than 21 years of age.

Academic Fields/Career Goals: Law Enforcement/Police Administration.

Award: Scholarship for use in freshman, sophomore, junior, or senior years; not renewable. *Number:* 1–2. *Amount:* $1000.

Eligibility Requirements: Applicant must be age 20 or under and enrolled or expecting to enroll full-time at a two-year or four-year institution or university. Available to U.S. citizens.

Application Requirements: Application, essay, photo, references, transcript. *Deadline:* varies.

Contact: National Law Enforcement Scholarships and Awards
Learning for Life
1325 West Walnut Hill Lane, PO Box 152079
Irving, TX 75015-2079

NATIONAL BLACK POLICE ASSOCIATION   http://www.blackpolice.org

ALPHONSO DEAL SCHOLARSHIP AWARD

• *See page 199*

NORTH CAROLINA POLICE CORPS   http://www.ncpolicecorps.org

NORTH CAROLINA POLICE CORPS SCHOLARSHIP

• *See page 200*

NORTH CAROLINA STATE EDUCATION ASSISTANCE AUTHORITY   http://www.ncseaa.edu

NORTH CAROLINA SHERIFFS' ASSOCIATION UNDERGRADUATE CRIMINAL JUSTICE SCHOLARSHIPS

• *See page 200*

SOUTH DAKOTA RETAILERS ASSOCIATION   http://www.sdra.org

SOUTH DAKOTA RETAILERS ASSOCIATION SCHOLARSHIP PROGRAM

• *See page 69*

UTAH POLICE CORPS   http://www.policecorps.utah.gov

UTAH POLICE CORPS SCHOLARSHIP PROGRAM

Once accepted into this program we will pay up to $7500 per academic year for a degree with any major. Years completed before acceptance into our program are reimbursed for a total of up to $15,000. Students must attend and pass our police training academy and complete four years with one of Utah's sponsoring law enforcement agencies.

Academic Fields/Career Goals: Law Enforcement/Police Administration.

Award: Scholarship for use in freshman, sophomore, junior, senior, graduate, or postgraduate years; renewable. *Number:* 30. *Amount:* $7500–$15,000.

Eligibility Requirements: Applicant must be enrolled or expecting to enroll full-time at a four-year institution or university. Available to U.S. citizens.

Application Requirements: Application, autobiography, driver's license, interview, photo, resume, references, test scores, transcript. *Deadline:* Continuous.

Contact: Arlene Bobowski, Office Specialist
Utah Police Corps
4525 S 2700 W
Salt Lake City, UT 84119-1775
Phone: 801-965-4650
Fax: 801-965-4292
E-mail: abobowski@utah.gov

LAW/LEGAL SERVICES

ALBERTA HERITAGE SCHOLARSHIP FUND/ ALBERTA SCHOLARSHIP PROGRAMS   http://www.alis.gov.ab.ca

ROBERT C. CARSON MEMORIAL BURSARY

• *See page 198*

ALLIANCE DEFENSE FUND   http://www.alliancedefensefund.org

WILLIAM PEW RELIGIOUS FREEDOM SCHOLARSHIP COMPETITION

One-time award for law students of any faith currently enrolled at an American law school. Must submit an essay. See Web site at http://www.alliancedefensefund.org for topic and further details. Deadline is April 1.

Academic Fields/Career Goals: Law/Legal Services.

Award: Scholarship for use in freshman, sophomore, junior, or senior years; not renewable. *Number:* 3. *Amount:* up to $2500.

Eligibility Requirements: Applicant must be enrolled or expecting to enroll full or part-time at a four-year institution or university. Available to U.S. and non-U.S. citizens.

Application Requirements: Applicant must enter a contest, essay. *Deadline:* April 1.

Contact: Application available at Web site.
        E-mail: pewscholarship@alliancedefensefund.org

AMERICAN ASSOCIATION OF LAW LIBRARIES   http://www.aallnet.org/

TYPE I: LIBRARY DEGREE FOR LAW SCHOOL GRADUATES

One-time award for graduates of law school who are degree candidates in an accredited library school. Preference given to AALL members and to those with law library experience. Based on need.

Academic Fields/Career Goals: Law/Legal Services; Library and Information Sciences.

Award: Scholarship for use in freshman, sophomore, junior, senior, or graduate years; not renewable. *Number:* 1. *Amount:* varies.

Eligibility Requirements: Applicant must be enrolled or expecting to enroll full or part-time at a four-year institution or university. Available to U.S. and non-U.S. citizens.

Application Requirements: Application, essay, financial need analysis, references, self-addressed stamped envelope, transcript. *Deadline:* April 1.

Contact: Rachel Shaevel, Membership Coordinator
        American Association of Law Libraries
        53 West Jackson Boulevard, Suite 940
        Chicago, IL 60604-3695
        Phone: 312-939-4764 Ext. 10
        Fax: 312-431-1097
        E-mail: membership@aall.org

AMERICAN CRIMINAL JUSTICE ASSOCIATION- LAMBDA ALPHA EPSILON   http://www.acjalae.org

AMERICAN CRIMINAL JUSTICE ASSOCIATION-LAMBDA ALPHA EPSILON NATIONAL SCHOLARSHIP
• *See page 198*

AMERICAN JUDGES ASSOCIATION   http://aja.ncsc.dni.us/

LAW STUDENT ESSAY COMPETITION

This is an essay competition for full-time law students studying at accredited law schools in the United States, Canada, and Mexico. A review committee rates the entries on their quality and their interest to the judiciary. Essays must be original and unpublished. 1st place: $3000. 2nd place: $1500. 3rd place: $1000.

Academic Fields/Career Goals: Law/Legal Services.

Award: Prize for use in freshman, sophomore, junior, senior, or graduate years; not renewable. *Number:* 3. *Amount:* $1000–$3000.

Eligibility Requirements: Applicant must be enrolled or expecting to enroll full-time at an institution or university. Available to U.S. and non-U.S. citizens.

Application Requirements: Application, applicant must enter a contest, essay. *Deadline:* June 1.

Contact: Shelley Rockwell, Association Management Specialist
        American Judges Association
        300 Newport Avenue, PO Box 8798
        Williamsburg, VA 23187-8798
        Phone: 757-259-1841
        Fax: 757-259-1520
        E-mail: srockwell@ncsc.dni.us

AMERICAN SOCIETY OF CRIMINOLOGY   http://www.ASC41.com

AMERICAN SOCIETY OF CRIMINOLOGY GENE CARTE STUDENT PAPER COMPETITION
• *See page 199*

BLACK ENTERTAINMENT AND SPORTS LAWYERS ASSOCIATION, INC.   http://www.besla.org

BESLA SCHOLARSHIP LEGAL WRITING COMPETITION

Scholarship awarded for the best 1000-word, or two-page essay on a compelling legal issue facing the entertainment or sports industry. Essay must be written by law school student who has completed at least one full year at an accredited law school. Minimum GPA of 2.8 required.

Academic Fields/Career Goals: Law/Legal Services.

Award: Scholarship for use in freshman, sophomore, junior, senior, or graduate years. *Amount:* $1500.

Eligibility Requirements: Applicant must be enrolled or expecting to enroll at a four-year institution or university. Available to U.S. citizens.

Application Requirements: Application, essay, transcript. *Deadline:* October 1.

Contact: Phyllicia Hatton
        Black Entertainment and Sports Lawyers Association, Inc.
        PO Box 441485
        Fort Washington, MD 20749-1485
        Phone: 301-248-1818
        Fax: 301-248-0700
        E-mail: BESLAmailbox@aol.com

BOYS AND GIRLS CLUBS OF GREATER SAN DIEGO   http://www.sdyouth.org

SPENCE REESE SCHOLARSHIP FUND
• *See page 259*

BUSINESS AND PROFESSIONAL WOMEN'S FOUNDATION   http://www.bpwusa.org

BPW CAREER ADVANCEMENT SCHOLARSHIP PROGRAM FOR WOMEN
• *See page 136*

CHICAGO CHAPTER OF RECORDING ACADEMY

ENTERTAINMENT LAW INITIATIVE LEGAL WRITING CONTEST

One-time award open to law students currently enrolled at an ABA accredited law school. Manuscript must identify a compelling legal issue confronting the music industry and propose a resolution. Applicants must register their names and contact information by January 2 to be eligible to enter the contest. Write for further information.

Academic Fields/Career Goals: Law/Legal Services.

Award: Prize for use in freshman, sophomore, junior, senior, or graduate years; not renewable. *Number:* 5. *Amount:* $1500–$5000.

Eligibility Requirements: Applicant must be enrolled or expecting to enroll at a four-year institution or university. Available to U.S. citizens.

Application Requirements: Application, essay, transcript. *Deadline:* varies.

Contact: Cole Sternberg, ELI Project Coordinator
        Chicago Chapter of Recording Academy
        3402 Pico Boulevard
        Santa Monica, CA 90405
        Phone: 310-392-3777
        E-mail: coles@grammy.com

COLLEGEBOUND FOUNDATION   http://www.collegeboundfoundation.org

DECATUR H. MILLER SCHOLARSHIP
• *See page 338*

JEANETTE R. WOLMAN SCHOLARSHIP

Award for Baltimore City public high school graduates. Please see Web site: http://www.collegeboundfoundation.org for complete information on application process. Must major in pre-law, social work or a field that focuses on child advocacy. Minimum GPA of 3.0. Must submit CollegeBound Competitive Scholarship/Last-Dollar Grant Application.

Academic Fields/Career Goals: Law/Legal Services; Social Sciences.

Award: Scholarship for use in freshman, sophomore, junior, or senior years; renewable. *Number:* 1. *Amount:* $500.

CollegeBound Foundation (continued)

Eligibility Requirements: Applicant must be enrolled or expecting to enroll full-time at a two-year or four-year institution or university and resident of Maryland. Applicant must have 3.0 GPA or higher. Available to U.S. citizens.

Application Requirements: Application, financial need analysis, transcript, financial aid award letters, Student Aid Report (SAR). *Deadline:* March 19.

Contact: April Bell, Associate Program Director
CollegeBound Foundation
300 Water Street, Suite 300
Baltimore, MD 21202
Phone: 410-783-2905 Ext. 208
Fax: 410-727-5786
E-mail: abell@collegeboundfoundation.org

COUNTY PROSECUTORS ASSOCIATION OF NEW JERSEY FOUNDATION

ANDREW K. RUOTOLO, JR. MEMORIAL SCHOLARSHIP

One-time award for New Jersey resident pursuing legal studies at a New Jersey law school or graduate school. Must be a U.S. citizen. Must exhibit an interest in and commitment to, enhancing the rights and well-being of children through child advocacy programs.

Academic Fields/Career Goals: Law/Legal Services.

Award: Scholarship for use in freshman, sophomore, junior, senior, graduate, or postgraduate years; not renewable. *Number:* 1. *Amount:* $2500.

Eligibility Requirements: Applicant must be enrolled or expecting to enroll full or part-time at a four-year institution or university; resident of New Jersey and studying in New Jersey. Available to U.S. citizens.

Application Requirements: Application, financial need analysis, interview. *Deadline:* June 15.

Contact: Theodore Romankow, Union County Prosecutor
County Prosecutors Association of New Jersey Foundation
Union County Prosecutors Office
32 Rahway Avenue
Elizabeth, NJ 07202
Phone: 908-527-4506

HARRY Y. COTTON MEMORIAL SCHOLARSHIP

One-time award for New Jersey resident accepted for admission to law school. Must have an interest in pursuing a career as a prosecutor with an emphasis on domestic violence or hate crimes prosecutions. Must attend law school in New Jersey.

Academic Fields/Career Goals: Law/Legal Services.

Award: Scholarship for use in freshman, sophomore, junior, senior, graduate, or postgraduate years; not renewable. *Number:* 1. *Amount:* $2500.

Eligibility Requirements: Applicant must be enrolled or expecting to enroll at a four-year institution or university; resident of New Jersey and studying in New Jersey. Available to U.S. citizens.

Application Requirements: Application, financial need analysis, interview. *Deadline:* June 15.

Contact: Theodore Romankow, Union County Prosecutor
County Prosecutors Association of New Jersey Foundation
Union County Prosecutors Office
32 Rahway Avenue
Elizabeth, NJ 07202
Phone: 908-527-4506

OSCAR W. RITTENHOUSE MEMORIAL SCHOLARSHIP

One-time award for New Jersey residents pursuing legal studies at a New Jersey accredited law school. Must be U.S. citizens. Must have an interest in pursuing a career as a prosecutor.

Academic Fields/Career Goals: Law/Legal Services.

Award: Scholarship for use in freshman, sophomore, junior, senior, graduate, or postgraduate years; not renewable. *Number:* 1. *Amount:* $2500.

Eligibility Requirements: Applicant must be enrolled or expecting to enroll full or part-time at a four-year institution or university; resident of New Jersey and studying in New Jersey. Available to U.S. citizens.

Application Requirements: Application, financial need analysis, interview. *Deadline:* June 15.

Contact: Theodore Romankow, Union County Prosecutor
County Prosecutors Association of New Jersey Foundation
Union County Prosecutors Office
32 Rahway Avenue
Elizabeth, NJ 07202
Phone: 908-527-4506

CULTURE CONNECTION
http://www.thecultureconnection.com

CULTURE CONNECTION FOUNDATION SCHOLARSHIP
• See page 73

FEDERAL CIRCUIT BAR ASSOCIATION
http://www.fedcirbar.org

GILES SUTHERLAND RICH MEMORIAL SCHOLARSHIP

Scholarship available to a law student showing financial need and academic promise, either in undergraduate studies or in law school. Deadline is April 28.

Academic Fields/Career Goals: Law/Legal Services.

Award: Scholarship for use in freshman, sophomore, junior, senior, or graduate years. *Amount:* up to $10,000.

Eligibility Requirements: Applicant must be enrolled or expecting to enroll at a four-year institution or university. Available to U.S. and non-U.S. citizens.

Application Requirements: Application, essay, financial need analysis. *Deadline:* April 28.

Contact: Stephen Peterson, Past President, The Federal Circuit Bar Association, c/o Finnegan, Henderson Farabow, Garrett, & Dunner
Federal Circuit Bar Association
901New York Avenue, NW
Washington, DC 20001-4413

WILLIAM S. BULLINGER SCHOLARSHIP

Scholarship available to a law student showing financial need and academic promise, either in undergraduate studies or in law school. Deadline is April 28.

Academic Fields/Career Goals: Law/Legal Services.

Award: Scholarship for use in freshman, sophomore, junior, senior, or graduate years. *Number:* 5. *Amount:* $5000.

Eligibility Requirements: Applicant must be enrolled or expecting to enroll at a four-year institution or university. Available to U.S. citizens.

Application Requirements: Application, essay, financial need analysis. *Deadline:* April 28.

Contact: Stephen Peterson, Past President, The Federal Circuit Bar Association, c/o Finnegan, Henderson Farabow, Garrett, & Dunner
Federal Circuit Bar Association
901 New York Avenue, NW
Washington, DC 20001-4413

FEMINIST JURISPRUDENCE ESSAY CONTEST
http://www.nd.edu

NOTRE DAME LAW SCHOOL FEMINIST JURISPRUDENCE WRITING COMPETITION

U.S. and Canadian law students are invited to submit essays (not to exceed 50 pages) within the category of feminist jurisprudence. Co-authoring is allowed. The winning author(s) will be invited to Notre Dame Law School to receive the award.

Academic Fields/Career Goals: Law/Legal Services.

Award: Prize for use in freshman, sophomore, junior, or senior years; not renewable. *Number:* 1. *Amount:* $1000.

Eligibility Requirements: Applicant must be enrolled or expecting to enroll full or part-time at a four-year institution or university. Available to U.S. and Canadian citizens.

Application Requirements: Application, applicant must enter a contest, essay. *Deadline:* June 1.

Contact: Teresa Godwin Phelps
Feminist Jurisprudence Essay Contest
PO Box 780
Notre Dame, IN 46556
Phone: 574-631-5763
Fax: 574-631-3980
E-mail: Teresa.G.Phelps.1@nd.edu

FOLEY AND LARDNER LLP   http://www.foleyrecruiting.com

FOLEY & LARDNER MINORITY SCHOLARSHIP PROGRAM

Scholarship for minority students in their first year of law school at participating institutions: Duke, Florida, Georgetown, Michigan, Northwestern, Stanford, UCLA and Wisconsin. One scholarship awarded at each school. Contact financial aid office at the participating schools for application.

Academic Fields/Career Goals: Law/Legal Services.

Award: Scholarship for use in freshman, or graduate years; not renewable. *Number:* 8. *Amount:* up to $5000.

Eligibility Requirements: Applicant must be American Indian/Alaska Native, Asian/Pacific Islander, Black (non-Hispanic), or Hispanic; enrolled or expecting to enroll full-time at a four-year institution and studying in California, District of Columbia, Florida, Illinois, Michigan, North Carolina, or Wisconsin. Available to U.S. citizens.

Application Requirements: Application, resume, transcript. *Deadline:* September 27.

Contact: Nancy Sennett, Office Managing Partner
Foley and Lardner LLP
Firstar Center
777 East Wisconsin Avenue
Milwaukee, WI 53202-5367
Phone: 414-271-2400
Fax: 414-297-4900
E-mail: nsennett@foley.com

GRAND RAPIDS COMMUNITY FOUNDATION   http://www.grfoundation.org

WARNER NORCROSS AND JUDD LLP SCHOLARSHIP FOR MINORITY STUDENTS

Financial assistance to students who are residents of Michigan, or attend a college/university/vocational school in Michigan, and are of racial and ethnic minority heritage pursuing a career in law, paralegal, or a legal secretarial program. Law school scholarship ($5000), paralegal scholarship ($2000), legal secretary scholarship ($1000). Refer to Web site for details and an application.

Academic Fields/Career Goals: Law/Legal Services.

Award: Scholarship for use in freshman, sophomore, junior, senior, or graduate years; not renewable. *Number:* up to 3. *Amount:* $1000–$5000.

Eligibility Requirements: Applicant must be American Indian/Alaska Native, Asian/Pacific Islander, Black (non-Hispanic), or Hispanic and enrolled or expecting to enroll at a two-year or four-year institution or university. Applicant must have 2.5 GPA or higher. Available to U.S. citizens.

Application Requirements: Application, essay, financial need analysis, references, transcript. *Deadline:* April 15.

Contact: See Web site.

GREATER KANAWHA VALLEY FOUNDATION   http://www.tgkvf.org

BERNICE PICKINS PARSONS FUND

Renewable award open to students pursuing education or training in the fields of library science, nursing and paraprofessional training in the legal field. May apply for two foundation scholarships, but will only be chosen for one. Grant based on financial need. Must be a resident of West Virginia.

Academic Fields/Career Goals: Law/Legal Services; Library and Information Sciences; Nursing.

Award: Grant for use in freshman, sophomore, junior, or senior years; renewable. *Number:* 10. *Amount:* $500.

Eligibility Requirements: Applicant must be enrolled or expecting to enroll full-time at a four-year institution or university and resident of West Virginia. Applicant must have 2.5 GPA or higher. Available to U.S. citizens.

Application Requirements: Application, essay, financial need analysis, references, self-addressed stamped envelope, test scores, transcript. *Deadline:* February 15.

Contact: Susan Hoover, Scholarship Coordinator
Greater Kanawha Valley Foundation
PO Box 3041
Charleston, WV 25331
Phone: 304-346-3620
Fax: 304-346-3640
E-mail: shoover@tgkvf.org

INTER-AMERICAN BAR ASSOCIATION   http://www.iaba.org

LAW STUDENT'S BEST PAPER AWARD

Prizes awarded for the three best papers presented to the IABA by law students in the Americas. Paper may be prepared in English, Spanish, Portuguese or French. Submit proof of law school enrollment. Contact for topics.

Academic Fields/Career Goals: Law/Legal Services.

Award: Prize for use in freshman, sophomore, junior, senior, graduate, or postgraduate years; not renewable. *Number:* 3. *Amount:* $400–$800.

Eligibility Requirements: Applicant must be enrolled or expecting to enroll full or part-time at a four-year institution or university. Available to U.S. and non-U.S. citizens.

Application Requirements: Applicant must enter a contest, essay, proof of enrollment in law school. *Deadline:* May 28.

Contact: Patricia De La Riva, Office Manager
Inter-American Bar Association
1211 Connecticut Avenue, NW, Suite 202
Washington, DC 20036
Phone: 202-466-5944 Ext. 13
Fax: 202-466-5946
E-mail: iaba@iaba.org

LINCOLN COMMUNITY FOUNDATION   http://www.lcf.org

LAWRENCE "LARRY" FRAZIER MEMORIAL SCHOLARSHIP
• See page 124

MARYLAND HIGHER EDUCATION COMMISSION   http://www.mhec.state.md.us

GRADUATE AND PROFESSIONAL SCHOLARSHIP PROGRAM-MARYLAND
• See page 210

JANET L. HOFFMANN LOAN ASSISTANCE REPAYMENT PROGRAM
• See page 230

NAACP LEGAL DEFENSE AND EDUCATIONAL FUND, INC.   http://www.naacpldf.org/scholarships

EARL WARREN LEGAL TRAINING GENERAL SCHOLARSHIP

Renewable award to first year law students who have a well-defined interest in civil rights and community services. Application must be requested in writing by March 15. Application deadline is March 30.

Academic Fields/Career Goals: Law/Legal Services.

Award: Scholarship for use in freshman, or graduate years; renewable. *Number:* 20–25. *Amount:* $3000–$5000.

Eligibility Requirements: Applicant must be Black (non-Hispanic) and enrolled or expecting to enroll at a two-year or four-year institution. Available to U.S. citizens.

NAACP Legal Defense and Educational Fund, Inc. (continued)

Application Requirements: Application. *Deadline:* March 30.

Contact: Micheal Bagley, Program Director
NAACP Legal Defense and Educational Fund, Inc.
99 Hudson Street, Suite 1600
New York, NY 10013
Phone: 212-965-2225
Fax: 212-219-1595

SHEARMAN AND STERLING SCHOLARSHIP PROGRAM

Renewable award for first-year African American law student. Application must be requested in writing by March 15. Application deadline is March 30.

Academic Fields/Career Goals: Law/Legal Services.

Award: Scholarship for use in freshman, or graduate years; renewable. *Number:* 2. *Amount:* $15,000.

Eligibility Requirements: Applicant must be Black (non-Hispanic) and enrolled or expecting to enroll full-time at an institution or university. Available to U.S. citizens.

Application Requirements: Application. *Deadline:* March 30.

Contact: Micheal Bagley, Program Director
NAACP Legal Defense and Educational Fund, Inc.
99 Hudson Street, Suite 1600
New York, NY 10013
Phone: 212-965-2225
Fax: 212-219-1595

NATIONAL ASSOCIATION OF WATER COMPANIES   http://www.nawc.org

J .J. BARR SCHOLARSHIP
• *See page 139*

NATIONAL ASSOCIATION OF WATER COMPANIES-NEW JERSEY CHAPTER

NATIONAL ASSOCIATION OF WATER COMPANIES-NEW JERSEY CHAPTER SCHOLARSHIP
• *See page 139*

NATIONAL BLACK LAW STUDENTS ASSOCIATION   http://www.nblsa.org

NBLS NELSON MANDELA SCHOLARSHIP

Scholarships are available to law students who are entering their first year of law school. Must submit a proposal geared toward an area of law as it is reflected in the annual NBLSA convention theme. For more details see Web site: http://www.nblsa.org

Academic Fields/Career Goals: Law/Legal Services.

Award: Scholarship for use in freshman, or graduate years; not renewable. *Number:* 6. *Amount:* $1000.

Eligibility Requirements: Applicant must be Black (non-Hispanic) and enrolled or expecting to enroll full-time at a four-year institution or university. Available to U.S. and non-U.S. citizens.

Application Requirements: Application, essay, resume, references, transcript, proposal. *Deadline:* November 1.

Contact: Rashage Green, NBLSA Education Chair
National Black Law Students Association
PO Box 40401
St.Paul, MN 55104

SANDY BROWN MEMORIAL SCHOLARSHIP

Two awards of not less than $500 for rising second or third year African-American law students. Applicants must write an essay on the NBLSA's annual convention theme. For more details see Web site: http://www.nblsa.org

Academic Fields/Career Goals: Law/Legal Services.

Award: Scholarship for use in sophomore, junior, or graduate years; not renewable. *Number:* 2. *Amount:* $500.

Eligibility Requirements: Applicant must be Black (non-Hispanic) and enrolled or expecting to enroll full-time at a four-year institution or university. Available to U.S. citizens.

Application Requirements: Application, applicant must enter a contest, essay. *Deadline:* November 1.

Contact: Rashage Green, NBLSA Education Chair
National Black Law Students Association
PO Box 40401
St. Paul, MN 55104

NATIONAL BLACK POLICE ASSOCIATION   http://www.blackpolice.org

ALPHONSO DEAL SCHOLARSHIP AWARD
• *See page 199*

NATIONAL FEDERATION OF PARALEGAL ASSOCIATIONS, INC. (NFPA)   http://www.paralegals.org

NATIONAL FEDERATION OF PARALEGAL ASSOCIATES, INC. WEST SCHOLARSHIP

Paralegal scholarship. Minimum GPA of 3.0 required. Application deadline is February 1.

Academic Fields/Career Goals: Law/Legal Services.

Award: Scholarship for use in freshman, sophomore, junior, senior, graduate, or postgraduate years; not renewable. *Number:* 2. *Amount:* $1500–$3500.

Eligibility Requirements: Applicant must be enrolled or expecting to enroll full or part-time at a two-year or four-year or technical institution or university. Applicant must have 3.0 GPA or higher. Available to U.S. and non-U.S. citizens.

Application Requirements: Application, essay, references, transcript. *Deadline:* February 1.

Contact: National Federation of Paralegal Associations, Inc. (NFPA)
2517 Eastlake
PO Box 2016
Edmonds, WA 98020
Phone: 425-967-0045
Fax: 425-771-9588
E-mail: info@paralegals.org

NATIONAL FEDERATION OF THE BLIND   http://www.nfb.org

HOWARD BROWN RICKARD SCHOLARSHIP
• *See page 101*

NEW YORK STATE EDUCATION DEPARTMENT   http://www.highered.nysed.gov

REGENTS PROFESSIONAL OPPORTUNITY SCHOLARSHIP
• *See page 67*

OREGON COMMUNITY FOUNDATION   http://www.ocf1.org/

BULLIVANT HOUSER BAILEY-AFRICAN AMERICAN CHAMBER OF COMMERCE COMMUNITY COLLEGE SCHOLARSHIP FUND
• *See page 152*

GAYLE AND HARVEY RUBIN SCHOLARSHIP FUND
• *See page 330*

OREGON STUDENT ASSISTANCE COMMISSION   http://www.osac.state.or.us

JEANNETTE MOWERY SCHOLARSHIP
• *See page 211*

PITTSBURGH INTELLECTUAL PROPERTY LAW ASSOCIATION   http://www.pgh-net.com/pipla/index.html

PIPLA INTELLECTUAL PROPERTY LAW STUDENT LEADERSHIP SCHOLARSHIP

Two $1000 awards will be given, one to a law student at the University of Pittsburgh and the other to a law student at Duquesne. Applicant must have completed at least three courses in the Intellectual Property elective course concentration and must have demonstrated leadership.

Academic Fields/Career Goals: Law/Legal Services.

Award: Scholarship for use in freshman, or graduate years. *Number:* 2. *Amount:* $1000.

Eligibility Requirements: Applicant must be enrolled or expecting to enroll at an institution or university. Available to U.S. citizens.

Application Requirements: Application. *Deadline:* February 17.

Contact: Pittsburgh Intellectual Property Law Association, Student Leadership Committee Chairman
Pittsburgh Intellectual Property Law Association
700 Koppers Building, 436 Seventh Avenue
Pittsburgh, PA 15219-1818

PNC BANK TRUST DEPARTMENT

H. FLETCHER BROWN SCHOLARSHIP
• *See page 211*

PUERTO RICAN LEGAL DEFENSE AND EDUCATION FUND   http://www.prldef.org

PUERTO RICAN BAR ASSOCIATION SCHOLARSHIP AWARD

One-time award for Latino students attending law school in the U.S. Selection is based on financial need and academic promise. Must be in a JD degree program in an ABA-approved law school.

Academic Fields/Career Goals: Law/Legal Services.

Award: Scholarship for use in freshman, sophomore, or graduate years; not renewable. *Number:* 5. *Amount:* $2000.

Eligibility Requirements: Applicant must be of Hispanic heritage and enrolled or expecting to enroll full or part-time at an institution or university. Applicant must have 2.5 GPA or higher. Available to U.S. citizens.

Application Requirements: Application, essay, financial need analysis, resume, references, transcript, IRS 1040 form. *Deadline:* March 4.

Contact: Sonji Patrick, Director, Education Division
Puerto Rican Legal Defense and Education Fund
99 Hudson Street, 14th Floor
New York, NY 10013
Phone: 212-739-7496
Fax: 212-431-4276
E-mail: education@prldef.org

ROSCOE POUND INSTITUTE   http://www.roscoepound.org

ELAINE OSBORNE JACOBSON AWARD FOR WOMEN WORKING IN HEALTH CARE LAW
• *See page 318*

ROSCOE HOGAN ENVIRONMENTAL LAW ESSAY CONTEST

Honors law students' writing abilities in the area of environmental law. See the Web site for current topic, deadlines and more information: http://www.roscoepound.org.

Academic Fields/Career Goals: Law/Legal Services.

Award: Prize for use in freshman, sophomore, junior, senior, or graduate years; not renewable. *Number:* 1. *Amount:* up to $5000.

Eligibility Requirements: Applicant must be enrolled or expecting to enroll full-time at a four-year institution or university. Available to U.S. and non-U.S. citizens.

Application Requirements: Application, applicant must enter a contest, essay. *Deadline:* varies.

Contact: Kimberly Kornegay, Program Assistant
Roscoe Pound Institute
1054 31st Street, NW, Suite 260
Washington, DC 20007
Phone: 202-965-3500 Ext. 385
Fax: 202-965-0355
E-mail: pound@roscoepound.org

SANTA CLARA UNIVERSITY SCHOOL OF LAW - COMPUTER AND HIGH TECHNOLOGY LAW JOURNAL   http://www.scu.edu/techlaw

SANTA CLARA UNIVERSITY SCHOOL OF LAW COMPUTER AND HIGH TECHNOLOGY LAW JOURNAL COMMENT CONTEST
• *See page 368*

THURGOOD MARSHALL SCHOLARSHIP FUND   http://www.thurgoodmarshallfund.org

THE SIDNEY B. WILLIAMS, JR. INTELLECTUAL PROPERTY LAW SCHOOL SCHOLARSHIP

Law scholarship of $10,000 will be awarded to a minority student developing a career in intellectual property law or holding a past or present, full or part-time, position in an area related to intellectual property law.

Academic Fields/Career Goals: Law/Legal Services.

Award: Scholarship for use in freshman, sophomore, junior, senior, or graduate years; renewable. *Amount:* up to $10,000.

Eligibility Requirements: Applicant must be Black (non-Hispanic) and enrolled or expecting to enroll full or part-time at a four-year institution or university. Available to U.S. citizens.

Application Requirements: Application, financial need analysis, interview, resume, references, transcript. *Deadline:* February 26.

Contact: Paul Allen
Thurgood Marshall Scholarship Fund
90 Williams Street, Suite 1203
New York, NY 10038
Phone: 212-573-8888
E-mail: pallen@tmsf.org

TKE EDUCATIONAL FOUNDATION   http://www.tkefoundation.org

HARRY J. DONNELLY MEMORIAL SCHOLARSHIP
• *See page 69*

TOWNSEND AND TOWNSEND AND CREW LLP   http://www.townsend.com/

TOWNSEND AND TOWNSEND AND CREW LLP DIVERSITY SCHOLARSHIP PROGRAM

Scholarships for students in good standing at ABA -accredited law schools who are women and/or members of racial minorities.Must demonstrate a commitment to pursuing a career in patent law in a city in which Townsend and Townsend and Crew has an office. Scholarships are not renewable, but recipients may reapply for a successive academic year. Each year the Firm awards one scholarship per school. Financial need is not a consideration.

Academic Fields/Career Goals: Law/Legal Services.

Award: Scholarship for use in freshman, sophomore, junior, senior, or graduate years; not renewable. *Amount:* $2000.

Eligibility Requirements: Applicant must be American Indian/Alaska Native, Asian/Pacific Islander, Black (non-Hispanic), or Hispanic; enrolled or expecting to enroll at a four-year institution or university and female. Available to U.S. citizens.

Application Requirements: Application, interview, resume, references, transcript, proof of enrollment at one of the listed law schools. *Deadline:* September 1.

Contact: Lindy Yurich
Townsend and Townsend and Crew LLP
Two Embarcadero Center, 8th Floor
San Francisco, CA 94111-3834
Phone: 415-576-0200
Fax: 415-576-0300
E-mail: mvyurich@townsend.com

UNITED NEGRO COLLEGE FUND   http://www.uncf.org

RAYMOND W. CANNON MEMORIAL SCHOLARSHIP PROGRAM
• *See page 333*

WILEY MANUEL LAW FOUNDATION

WILEY MANUEL LAW FOUNDATION SCHOLARSHIP

Scholarships for Northern California law students who best exemplify the qualities of the late Justice Wiley. Award amount varies.

Academic Fields/Career Goals: Law/Legal Services.

Award: Scholarship for use in freshman, sophomore, junior, senior, or graduate years. *Number:* 1.

Eligibility Requirements: Applicant must be enrolled or expecting to enroll at a four-year institution or university; resident of California and studying in California. Available to U.S. citizens.

Application Requirements: Application. *Deadline:* April 15.

Contact: Sara Butler
    E-mail: viteris@uchastings.edu

LIBRARY AND INFORMATION SCIENCES

ALICE L. HALTOM EDUCATIONAL FUND
http://www.alhef.org

ALICE L. HALTOM EDUCATIONAL FUND SCHOLARSHIP
• See page 190

AMERICAN ASSOCIATION OF LAW LIBRARIES
http://www.aallnet.org/

LAW LIBRARIANS IN CONTINUING EDUCATION COURSES

Awarded to law librarians with a degree from an accredited library or law school who are registrants in continuing education courses related to law librarianship. Application deadlines are February 1, April 1, and October 1.

Academic Fields/Career Goals: Library and Information Sciences.

Award: Scholarship for use in freshman, sophomore, junior, senior, or graduate years; not renewable. *Number:* varies. *Amount:* $500.

Eligibility Requirements: Applicant must be enrolled or expecting to enroll full or part-time at a four-year institution or university. Applicant or parent of applicant must be member of American Association of Law Librarians. Applicant or parent of applicant must have employment or volunteer experience in designated career field. Available to U.S. and non-U.S. citizens.

Application Requirements: Application, essay, financial need analysis, references, self-addressed stamped envelope, course description. *Deadline:* varies.

Contact: Rachel Shaevel, Membership Coordinator
    American Association of Law Libraries
    53 West Jackson Boulevard, Suite 940
    Chicago, IL 60604-3695
    Phone: 312-939-4764 Ext. 10
    Fax: 312-431-1097
    E-mail: membership@aall.org

TYPE I: LIBRARY DEGREE FOR LAW SCHOOL GRADUATES
• See page 375

TYPE III: LIBRARY DEGREE FOR NON-LAW SCHOOL GRADUATES

One-time award for college graduate with meaningful law library experience who is a degree candidate in an accredited library school. Preference given to AALL members. Based on need.

Academic Fields/Career Goals: Library and Information Sciences.

Award: Scholarship for use in freshman, sophomore, junior, senior, or graduate years; not renewable. *Number:* varies. *Amount:* varies.

Eligibility Requirements: Applicant must be enrolled or expecting to enroll full or part-time at a four-year institution or university. Applicant or parent of applicant must be member of American Association of Law Librarians. Available to U.S. and non-U.S. citizens.

Application Requirements: Application, essay, financial need analysis, references, self-addressed stamped envelope, transcript. *Deadline:* April 1.

Contact: Rachel Shaevel, Membership Coordinator
    American Association of Law Libraries
    53 West Jackson Boulevard, Suite 940
    Chicago, IL 60604-3695
    Phone: 312-939-4764 Ext. 10
    Fax: 312-431-1097
    E-mail: membership@aall.org

AMERICAN SOCIETY FOR INFORMATION SCIENCE AND TECHNOLOGY
http://www.asis.org

JOHN WILEY & SONS BEST JASIST PAPER AWARD
• See page 191

BLACK CAUCUS OF THE AMERICAN LIBRARY ASSOCIATION
http://www.bcala.org

E.J. JOSEY SCHOLARSHIP AWARD

Two unrestricted grants of $2000 to be awarded annually to African-American students enrolled in, or accepted by, ALA accredited programs. Applicants are judged on the basis of application essays of 1000 to 1200 words discussing issues, problems, or challenges facing library service to minority populations such as African-Americans, and other supporting documentation submitted for review by the scholarship committee.

Academic Fields/Career Goals: Library and Information Sciences.

Award: Scholarship for use in freshman, sophomore, junior, senior, or graduate years; not renewable. *Number:* 2. *Amount:* $2000.

Eligibility Requirements: Applicant must be Black (non-Hispanic) and enrolled or expecting to enroll full-time at a four-year institution or university. Available to U.S. and non-U.S. citizens.

Application Requirements: Essay. *Deadline:* December 13.

Contact: Ismail Abdullahi, Chair of the E. J. Josey Scholarship
    Committee, School of Library & Information
    Black Caucus of the American Library Association
    Clark Atlanta University, James P. Brawley Drive
    Atlanta, GA 30314
    E-mail: abdull@cau.edu

CALIFORNIA LIBRARY ASSOCIATION
http://www.cla-net.org

THE BEGUN SCHOLARSHIP

Award to support continuing library school students who have demonstrated a commitment to becoming young adult librarians in a California public library. Must be currently enrolled in an ALA-accredited master's of library and information science or information studies program in California. Must be U.S. citizens and California resident. Must maintain minimum 3.0 GPA. Deadline: July 15.

Academic Fields/Career Goals: Library and Information Sciences.

Award: Scholarship for use in freshman year; not renewable. *Number:* 1. *Amount:* $3000.

Eligibility Requirements: Applicant must be enrolled or expecting to enroll full-time at an institution or university and resident of California. Applicant must have 3.0 GPA or higher. Available to U.S. citizens.

Application Requirements: Application, autobiography, essay, resume, references.

Contact: Laura Fisher, Office Coordinator
    California Library Association
    717 20th Street, Suite 200
    Sacramento, CA 95814
    Phone: 916-447-8541
    Fax: 916-447-8394
    E-mail: info@cla-net.org

CALIFORNIA SCHOOL LIBRARY ASSOCIATION
http://www.schoollibrary.org

LIBRARY MEDIA TEACHER SCHOLARSHIP IN HONOR OF GENE WHITE AND THE MARTHA DEAN CHILDREN

Scholarships are made available to assist those persons seeking preparation leading toward a degree or credential which will qualify the individual to work as a professional in the library media field in a school setting. For more details and an application see Web site: http://www.schoollibrary.org.

Academic Fields/Career Goals: Library and Information Sciences.

Award: Scholarship for use in junior, senior, or graduate years; not renewable. *Number:* 5. *Amount:* up to $1500.

Eligibility Requirements: Applicant must be enrolled or expecting to enroll full-time at a two-year or four-year institution or university. Available to U.S. citizens.

Application Requirements: Application, references. *Deadline:* March 11.

Contact: Alison Steinberg, President
California School Library Association
4926 Field St
San Diego, CA 92110
Phone: 619-628-5110
E-mail: aliphred@earthlink.net

GREATER KANAWHA VALLEY FOUNDATION
http://www.tgkvf.org

BERNICE PICKINS PARSONS FUND
• *See page 377*

IDAHO LIBRARY ASSOCIATION
http://www.idaholibraries.org

IDAHO LIBRARY ASSOCIATION GARDNER HANKS SCHOLARSHIP

Scholarship for students who are beginning or continuing formal library education, pursuing a Masters of Library Science degree or Media Generalist certification. Must be an ILA member.

Academic Fields/Career Goals: Library and Information Sciences.

Award: Scholarship for use in freshman, sophomore, junior, or senior years. *Number:* 1.

Eligibility Requirements: Applicant must be enrolled or expecting to enroll full-time at a four-year institution or university. Applicant or parent of applicant must be member of Idaho Library Association. Available to U.S. citizens.

Application Requirements: Application, financial need analysis, references. *Deadline:* September 1.

Contact: Wayne Gunter, Chairperson, Scholarships, Recruitment and Awards
Idaho Library Association
PO Box 8533
Moscow, ID 83843
Phone: 208-263-6930 Ext. 208
Fax: 208-263-8320
E-mail: wayne@ebcl.lib.id.us

IDAHO LIBRARY ASSOCIATION LIBRARY SCIENCE SCHOLARSHIPS

One-time award for students studying library science. Must be a member of the Idaho Library Association. Must be a resident of Idaho.

Academic Fields/Career Goals: Library and Information Sciences.

Award: Scholarship for use in freshman, sophomore, junior, senior, or graduate years; not renewable. *Number:* 2–6. *Amount:* $100–$500.

Eligibility Requirements: Applicant must be enrolled or expecting to enroll full or part-time at a two-year or four-year institution or university and resident of Idaho. Applicant or parent of applicant must be member of Idaho Library Association. Available to U.S. and non-U.S. citizens.

Application Requirements: Application, essay, resume, references. *Deadline:* September 1.

Contact: Wayne Gunter, Chairperson, Recruitment & Awards Committee
Idaho Library Association
East Bonner County Free Library District, 1407 Cedar Street
Sandpoint, ID 83864-2052

INDIANA LIBRARY FEDERATION
http://www.ilfonline.org

AIME SCHOLARSHIP FUND

Scholarships are provided for undergraduate or graduate students entering or currently enrolled in a program to receive educational certification in the field of School Library Media Services. For more details see Web site: http://www.ilfonline.org.

Academic Fields/Career Goals: Library and Information Sciences.

Award: Scholarship for use in freshman, sophomore, junior, senior, or graduate years; not renewable. *Number:* varies. *Amount:* up to $500.

Eligibility Requirements: Applicant must be enrolled or expecting to enroll at a four-year institution or university. Available to U.S. citizens.

Application Requirements: Application, references, transcript. *Deadline:* December 31.

Contact: Application available at Web site.

PENNSYLVANIA LIBRARY ASSOCIATION
http://www.palibraries.org

BRODART/PENNSYLVANIA LIBRARY ASSOCIATION UNDERGRADUATE SCHOLARSHIP GRANT

Applicant must be enrolled in a state certified institution and must complete a minimum of 3 credits in library science courses leading to state certification. Credits must be completed during the summer session or academic year (September through May) which begins the year of the scholarship award.

Academic Fields/Career Goals: Library and Information Sciences.

Award: Scholarship for use in freshman, sophomore, junior, or senior years; not renewable. *Number:* varies. *Amount:* up to $2000.

Eligibility Requirements: Applicant must be enrolled or expecting to enroll full or part-time at a two-year or four-year institution or university; resident of Pennsylvania and studying in Pennsylvania. Available to U.S. citizens.

Application Requirements: Application, references. *Deadline:* May 15.

Contact: Ellen Wharton, Administrative Assistant
Pennsylvania Library Association
220 Cumberland Parkway, Suite 10
Mechanicsburg, PA 17055-5683
Phone: 717-766-7663
Fax: 717-766-5440
E-mail: ellen@palibraries.org

SPECIAL LIBRARIES ASSOCIATION
http://www.sla.org

SPECIAL LIBRARIES ASSOCIATION AFFIRMATIVE ACTION SCHOLARSHIP

One scholarship available to graduating college seniors and master's candidates. Must be United States citizen or permanent resident and a member of a minority group and be enrolled in a library science program. May be used for tuition or any research-related costs. One-time award of $6000.

Academic Fields/Career Goals: Library and Information Sciences.

Award: Scholarship for use in senior, or graduate years; not renewable. *Number:* 1. *Amount:* $6000.

Eligibility Requirements: Applicant must be American Indian/Alaska Native, Asian/Pacific Islander, Black (non-Hispanic), or Hispanic and enrolled or expecting to enroll full or part-time at a four-year institution or university. Available to U.S. citizens.

Special Libraries Association (continued)

Application Requirements: Application, essay, financial need analysis, interview, references, test scores, transcript. *Deadline:* October 31.

Contact: Diana Gonzales, Membership Coordinator
Special Libraries Association
331 South Patrick Street
Alexandria, VA 22314-3501
Phone: 703-647-4900
Fax: 703-647-4901
E-mail: sla@sla.org

SPECIAL LIBRARIES ASSOCIATION SCHOLARSHIP

Up to three scholarships available to graduating college seniors and master's candidates enrolled in a program for library science. May be used for tuition, fees, research, and other related costs. Members of SLA preferred. One-time awards of $6000 each.

Academic Fields/Career Goals: Library and Information Sciences.

Award: Scholarship for use in senior, or graduate years; not renewable. *Number:* up to 3. *Amount:* $6000.

Eligibility Requirements: Applicant must be enrolled or expecting to enroll full or part-time at a four-year institution or university. Available to U.S. citizens.

Application Requirements: Application, essay, financial need analysis, interview, references, test scores, transcript. *Deadline:* October 31.

Contact: Diana Gonzales, Membership Coordinator
Special Libraries Association
331 South Patrick Street
Alexandria, VA 22314-3501
Phone: 703-647-4900
Fax: 703-647-4901
E-mail: sla@sla.org

UNITED NEGRO COLLEGE FUND   http://www.uncf.org

C-SPAN SCHOLARSHIP PROGRAM
• See page 189

LITERATURE/ENGLISH/WRITING

ACTORS THEATRE OF LOUISVILLE   http://www.actorstheatre.org

NATIONAL TEN MINUTE PLAY CONTEST

Writers from across the country compete for prizes by submitting short plays (10 pages or less). Plays are considered for our annual Apprentice Showcase, The Humana Festival of New American Plays and the $1000 Heideman Award. Must be U.S. citizen. Deadline is November 1.

Academic Fields/Career Goals: Literature/English/Writing.

Award: Prize for use in freshman, sophomore, junior, senior, or graduate years; not renewable. *Number:* 1. *Amount:* $1000.

Eligibility Requirements: Applicant must be enrolled or expecting to enroll full or part-time at a two-year or four-year or technical institution or university. Available to U.S. citizens.

Application Requirements: Applicant must enter a contest. *Deadline:* November 1.

Contact: Mervin Antonio, New Play Development Director
Actors Theatre of Louisville
316 West Main Street
Louisville, KY 40202-4218
Phone: 502-584-1265 Ext. 3033
Fax: 502-561-3300

AIM MAGAZINE SHORT STORY CONTEST   http://www.aimmagazine.org

AMERICA'S INTERCULTURAL MAGAZINE (AIM) SHORT STORY CONTEST

Short fiction award for a previously unpublished story that embodies our goal of furthering the brotherhood of man through the written word. Proof that people from different racial/ethnic backgrounds are more alike than they are different. Maximum length 4000 words. Story should not moralize. August 15 is deadline.

Academic Fields/Career Goals: Literature/English/Writing.

Award: Prize for use in freshman, sophomore, junior, senior, or graduate years; not renewable. *Number:* 1. *Amount:* $75–$100.

Eligibility Requirements: Applicant must be enrolled or expecting to enroll at a two-year or four-year or technical institution or university. Available to U.S. and Canadian citizens.

Application Requirements: Applicant must enter a contest. *Deadline:* August 15.

Contact: Mark Boone, Fiction Editor
Aim Magazine Short Story Contest
PO Box 1174
Maywood, IL 60153
Phone: 708-344-4414

ALLIANCE FOR YOUNG ARTISTS AND WRITERS, INC.   http://www.artandwriting.org

SCHOLASTIC ART AND WRITING AWARDS-ART SECTION
• See page 108

AMERICAN COPY EDITORS SOCIETY   http://www.copydesk.org

ACES COPY EDITING SCHOLARSHIP

Several scholarships each year for $2500 and students who are not chosen as an Aubespin scholar are automatically eligible for ACES' other scholarships, at $1000 each. Open to students who will be juniors, seniors or graduate students in the fall, and graduating students who will take full-time copy editing jobs or internships. Deadline is October 15.

Academic Fields/Career Goals: Literature/English/Writing.

Award: Scholarship for use in junior, senior, or graduate years; not renewable. *Amount:* $1000–$2500.

Eligibility Requirements: Applicant must be enrolled or expecting to enroll full-time at an institution or university. Applicant must have 2.5 GPA or higher. Available to U.S. citizens.

Application Requirements: Application, essay, references, list of course work relevant to copy editing, copy of a story edited by the applicant. *Deadline:* October 15.

Contact: Kathy Schenck, Assistant Managing Editor
American Copy Editors Society
333 West State Street
Milwaukee, WI 53203
Phone: 414-224-2237

AMERICAN FOUNDATION FOR THE BLIND   http://www.afb.org/scholarships.asp

R.L. GILLETTE SCHOLARSHIP

The R. L. Gillette Scholarship offers two (2) scholarships of $1,000 each to women who are enrolled in a four-year undergraduate degree program in literature or music. In addition to the general requirements, applicants must submit a performance tape not to exceed 30 minutes, or a creative writing sample. For additional information and application requirements, refer to Web site: www.afb.org/scholarships.asp

Academic Fields/Career Goals: Literature/English/Writing; Music.

Award: Scholarship for use in freshman, sophomore, junior, or senior years; not renewable. *Number:* up to 2. *Amount:* up to $1000.

Eligibility Requirements: Applicant must be enrolled or expecting to enroll full-time at a four-year institution or university and female. Applicant must be visually impaired. Available to U.S. citizens.

Application Requirements: Application, essay, financial need analysis, references, transcript, performance tape (not to exceed 30 minutes) or creative writing sample, proof of legal blindness, acceptance letter. *Deadline:* March 31.

Contact: Alina Vayntrub, Departmental Assistant, Information Center
American Foundation for the Blind
11 Penn Plaza, Suite 300
New York, NY 10001
Phone: 212-502-7661
Fax: 212-502-7771
E-mail: afbinfo@afb.net

AMERICAN LEGION AUXILIARY, DEPARTMENT OF WASHINGTON
http://www.walegion-aux.org

FLORENCE LEMCKE MEMORIAL SCHOLARSHIP IN FINE ARTS
• See page 107

AMY LOWELL POETRY TRAVELING SCHOLARSHIP TRUST
http://www.amylowell.org

AMY LOWELL POETRY TRAVELING SCHOLARSHIP

The Amy Lowell Poetry Traveling Scholarship awards a scholarship each year to a poet of American birth. Upon acceptance, the recipient agrees to spend one year outside the continent of North America in a place deemed by the recipient suitable to advance the art of poetry. At the end of the year, the recipient shall submit at least three poems for consideration by the trust's committee. Application request deadline is October 1. Application submission deadline is October 15. For additional information visit Web site: http://www.amylowell.org

Academic Fields/Career Goals: Literature/English/Writing.

Award: Scholarship for use in freshman, sophomore, junior, senior, graduate, or postgraduate years; not renewable. *Number:* 1. *Amount:* $40,000.

Eligibility Requirements: Applicant must be enrolled or expecting to enroll at a two-year or four-year or technical institution or university. Available to U.S. citizens.

Application Requirements: Application, applicant must enter a contest, poetry sample. *Deadline:* October 15.

Contact: Pearl Bell, Trust Administrator
Amy Lowell Poetry Traveling Scholarship Trust
Two International Place
Boston, MA 02110
Phone: 617-248-5000
Fax: 617-248-4000

ATLANTA PRESS CLUB, INC.
http://www.atlpressclub.org

ATLANTA PRESS CLUB JOURNALISM SCHOLARSHIP PROGRAM
• See page 179

BIBLIOGRAPHICAL SOCIETY OF AMERICA
http://www.bibsocamer.org

JUSTIN G. SCHILLER PRIZE FOR BIBLIOGRAPHICAL WORK IN PRE-20TH-CENTURY CHILDREN'S BOOKS

Award for bibliographic work in the field of childrens books printed before 1901. Winner will receive a cash award and a year's membership in the Society.

Academic Fields/Career Goals: Literature/English/Writing.

Award: Prize for use in freshman, sophomore, junior, or senior years; not renewable. *Number:* 1. *Amount:* up to $2000.

Eligibility Requirements: Applicant must be enrolled or expecting to enroll at an institution or university. Available to U.S. and non-U.S. citizens.

Application Requirements: Application, applicant must enter a contest, resume, documentation regarding the approval of a thesis or dissertation or confirming the date of publication. *Deadline:* September 1.

Contact: Michele Randall, Executive Secretary
Bibliographical Society of America
PO Box 1537, Lenox Hill Station
New York, NY 10021
Phone: 212-452-2710
Fax: 212-452-2710
E-mail: bsa@bibsocamer.org

CENTER FOR LESBIAN AND GAY STUDIES (C.L.A.G.S.)
http://www.clags.org

CENTER FOR GAY AND LESBIAN STUDIES UNDERGRADUATE PAPER AWARDS

A cash prize of $250 will be awarded to the best paper written in a CUNY or SUNY undergraduate class on a topic related to gay, lesbian, bisexual, queer, or transgender experiences. Essays should be between 15 and 50 pages, well thought-out and fully realized.

Academic Fields/Career Goals: Literature/English/Writing; Social Sciences.

Award: Prize for use in freshman, sophomore, junior, or senior years; not renewable. *Number:* 1. *Amount:* $250.

Eligibility Requirements: Applicant must be enrolled or expecting to enroll full or part-time at a four-year institution or university; resident of New York and studying in New York. Available to U.S. and non-U.S. citizens.

Application Requirements: Applicant must enter a contest, essay. *Deadline:* June 1.

Contact: Lavelle Porter, Office Staff
Center for Lesbian and Gay Studies (C.L.A.G.S.)
365 Fifth Avenue, Room 7115
New York, NY 10016
Phone: 212-817-1955
Fax: 212-817-1567
E-mail: clags@gc.cuny.edu

CIRI FOUNDATION
http://www.thecirifoundation.org

CIRI FOUNDATION SUSIE QIMMIQSAK BEVINS ENDOWMENT SCHOLARSHIP FUND
• See page 110

CULTURAL FELLOWSHIP GRANTS

Applicant must be accepted or enrolled in a seminar or conference that is accredited, authorized, or approved by the CIRI Foundation. May reapply each quarter until grant cap is reached and may reapply the following year. Must be Alaska Native Student, CIRI original enrollee, or descendant. Award is intended to encourage applicants in perpetuating and transmitting the visual, literary, and performing arts of Alaska's first people. Application deadlines are March 31, June 30, September 30, and December 1.

Academic Fields/Career Goals: Literature/English/Writing; Performing Arts.

Award: Grant for use in freshman, sophomore, junior, senior, graduate, or postgraduate years; not renewable. *Number:* varies. *Amount:* up to $500.

Eligibility Requirements: Applicant must be age 18 and enrolled or expecting to enroll full or part-time at a two-year or four-year institution or university. Applicant must have 2.5 GPA or higher. Available to U.S. citizens.

Application Requirements: Application, essay, references, transcript, proof of eligibility, birth certificate or adoption decree. *Deadline:* varies.

Contact: Susan Anderson, President/CEO
CIRI Foundation
2600 Cordova Street, Suite 206
Anchorage, AK 99503
Phone: 907-263-5582
Fax: 907-263-5588
E-mail: tcf@ciri.com

GUIDEPOSTS MAGAZINE
http://www.guideposts.com

GUIDEPOSTS YOUNG WRITER'S CONTEST

Entrants must be either a high school junior or senior. Submit a first-person story about a memorable or moving experience; story must be a true personal experience of the writer. Authors of top ten manuscripts receive a scholarship. First Prize: $10,000; Second Prize: $8,000; Third Prize: $6,000; Fourth Prize: $4,000; Fifth Prize: $3,000; Sixth through Tenth Prizes: $1,000; Eleventh through Twentieth Prizes receive $250 gift certificate for college supplies. The deadline is the Monday before Thanksgiving.

Academic Fields/Career Goals: Literature/English/Writing.

Award: Prize for use in freshman year; not renewable. *Number:* 20. *Amount:* $250–$10,000.

Eligibility Requirements: Applicant must be high school student and planning to enroll or expecting to enroll full or part-time at a two-year or four-year or technical institution or university. Available to U.S. and non-U.S. citizens.

Application Requirements: Applicant must enter a contest, manuscript (maximum 1500 words). *Deadline:* varies.

Contact: Christine Pisani, Secretary
GUIDEPOSTS Magazine
16 East 34th Street, 21st Floor
New York, NY 10016
Phone: 212-251-8100
Fax: 212-684-1311
E-mail: cpisani@guideposts.org

HERB SOCIETY OF AMERICA
http://www.herbsociety.org

HERB SOCIETY RESEARCH GRANTS
• See page 92

INSTITUTE FOR HUMANE STUDIES
http://www.theihs.org

FILM AND FICTION SCHOLARSHIP
• See page 111

INTERNATIONAL FOODSERVICE EDITORIAL COUNCIL
http://www.ifec-is-us.com

INTERNATIONAL FOODSERVICE EDITORIAL COUNCIL COMMUNICATIONS SCHOLARSHIP
• See page 182

JACK J. ISGUR FOUNDATION

JACK J. ISGUR FOUNDATION SCHOLARSHIP
• See page 111

LAMBDA IOTA TAU, COLLEGE LITERATURE HONOR SOCIETY
http://www.bsu.edu/csh/english/undergraduate/lit/

LAMBDA IOTA TAU LITERATURE SCHOLARSHIP

Scholarships for members of Lambda Iota Tau who are pursuing the study of literature. Must be nominated by chapter sponsor and have 3.5 GPA. Must be an initiated member of Lambda Iota Tau.

Academic Fields/Career Goals: Literature/English/Writing.

Award: Scholarship for use in freshman, sophomore, junior, senior, graduate, or postgraduate years; not renewable. *Number:* 2. *Amount:* $1000.

Eligibility Requirements: Applicant must be enrolled or expecting to enroll full-time at a two-year or four-year institution or university. Applicant must have 3.5 GPA or higher. Available to U.S. and non-U.S. citizens.

Application Requirements: Application, essay, references. *Deadline:* May 31.

Contact: Prof. Bruce Hozeski, Executive Secretary/Treasurer
Lambda Iota Tau, College Literature Honor Society
Ball State University Department of English
2000 West University Avenue
Muncie, IN 47306-0460
Phone: 765-285-8584
Fax: 765-285-3765
E-mail: bhozeski@bsu.edu

NATIONAL FEDERATION OF THE BLIND
http://www.nfb.org

MICHAEL AND MARIE MARUCCI SCHOLARSHIP
• See page 312

NATIONAL FOUNDATION FOR ADVANCEMENT IN THE ARTS
http://www.artsawards.org

ARTS RECOGNITION AND TALENT SEARCH (ARTS)
• See page 113

NATIONAL PRESS FOUNDATION
http://www.mindspring.com/~us009848/id1.htm

THE EVERT CLARK/SETH PAYNE AWARD
• See page 364

NATIONAL WRITERS ASSOCIATION FOUNDATION
http://www.nationalwriters.com

NATIONAL WRITERS ASSOCIATION FOUNDATION SCHOLARSHIPS
• See page 184

OREGON STUDENT ASSISTANCE COMMISSION
http://www.osac.state.or.us

SEHAR SALEHA AHMAD AND ABRAHIM EKRAMULLAH ZAFAR FOUNDATION SCHOLARSHIP

Available to Oregon high school graduates. Award open to students majoring in English. Preference given to females. Minimum 3.5 GPA required.

Academic Fields/Career Goals: Literature/English/Writing.

Award: Scholarship for use in freshman year; renewable. *Number:* varies. *Amount:* $500.

Eligibility Requirements: Applicant must be high school student; planning to enroll or expecting to enroll full-time at an institution or university and resident of Oregon. Applicant must have 3.5 GPA or higher. Available to U.S. citizens.

Application Requirements: Application, essay, financial need analysis, references, transcript, activity chart. *Deadline:* March 1.

Contact: Director of Grant Programs
Oregon Student Assistance Commission
1500 Valley River Drive, Suite 100
Eugene, OR 97401-7020
Phone: 800-452-8807 Ext. 7395

OUTDOOR WRITERS ASSOCIATION OF AMERICA
http://www.owaa.org/

OUTDOOR WRITERS ASSOCIATION OF AMERICA BODIE MCDOWELL SCHOLARSHIP AWARD
• See page 185

PLAYWRIGHTS' CENTER
http://www.pwcenter.org

MANY VOICES RESIDENCY PROGRAM

The Playwrights' Center's Many Voices programs enrich the American theater by offering playwriting residencies to artists of color. Must be U.S. citizen.

Academic Fields/Career Goals: Literature/English/Writing.

Award: Grant for use in freshman, sophomore, junior, senior, graduate, or postgraduate years; not renewable. *Number:* 8. *Amount:* $1200–$2000.

Eligibility Requirements: Applicant must be American Indian/Alaska Native, Asian/Pacific Islander, Black (non-Hispanic), or Hispanic;

enrolled or expecting to enroll full or part-time at a two-year or four-year or technical institution or university; resident of Minnesota; studying in Minnesota and must have an interest in writing. Available to U.S. citizens.

Application Requirements: Application, resume, writing sample. *Deadline:* July 31.

Contact: Stacey Parshall, Many Voices Coordinator
Playwrights' Center
2301 Franklin Avenue East
Minneapolis, MN 55406
Phone: 612-332-7481 Ext. 10
Fax: 612-332-6037
E-mail: staceyp@pwcenter.org

POLISH HERITAGE ASSOCIATION OF MARYLAND

ROBERT P. PULA MEMORIAL SCHOLARSHIP
• See page 353

UNITED DAUGHTERS OF THE CONFEDERACY   http://www.hqudc.org

HELEN JAMES BREWER SCHOLARSHIP
• See page 340

UNITED NEGRO COLLEGE FUND   http://www.uncf.org

READER'S DIGEST SCHOLARSHIP
• See page 189

TOYOTA SCHOLARSHIP
• See page 157

WAVERLY COMMUNITY HOUSE, INC.   http://www.waverlycomm.com

F. LAMMOT BELIN ARTS SCHOLARSHIP
• See page 103

WILLA CATHER FOUNDATION   http://www.willacather.org

NORMA ROSS WALTER SCHOLARSHIP

Applicants must be prospective first-year college women students who have been or plan to be graduated from Nebraska high schools. Must major in English at any accredited college or university. Must have a minimum 3.0 GPA. Deadline is January 31.

Academic Fields/Career Goals: Literature/English/Writing.

Award: Scholarship for use in freshman year; not renewable. *Number:* 1. *Amount:* up to $1000.

Eligibility Requirements: Applicant must be enrolled or expecting to enroll full-time at a four-year institution or university; female and resident of Nebraska. Applicant must have 3.0 GPA or higher. Available to U.S. citizens.

Application Requirements: Application, essay, portfolio, references, test scores, transcript. *Deadline:* January 31.

Contact: Betty Kort, Executive Director
Willa Cather Foundation
413 North Webster Street
Red Cloud, NE 68970
Phone: 402-746-2653
Fax: 402-746-2652
E-mail: bkort@gpcom.net

MARINE BIOLOGY

CANADIAN RECREATIONAL CANOEING ASSOCIATION   http://www.paddlingcanada.com

BILL MASON MEMORIAL SCHOLARSHIP FUND
• See page 80

FLORIDA SEA GRANT   http://www.flseagrant.org

AYLESWORTH AND OLD SALT SCHOLARSHIPS

Scholarships available for undergraduate: two years (beginning junior year); master's: two years; and doctoral: three years. The maximum award can be in the amount of 65 percent of the annual official university or college tuition or $4000, whichever is lower.

Academic Fields/Career Goals: Marine Biology.

Award: Scholarship for use in junior, senior, or graduate years. *Number:* 80. *Amount:* up to $4000.

Eligibility Requirements: Applicant must be enrolled or expecting to enroll at a four-year institution or university and studying in Florida. Available to U.S. citizens.

Application Requirements: Application, financial need analysis, resume, transcript. *Deadline:* November 5.

Contact: James C. Cato, Director
Florida Sea Grant
PO Box 110400
Gainesville, FL 32611-0400
Phone: 352-392-5870
Fax: 352-392-5113

SKOCH SCHOLARSHIP

Scholarship of $1000 is presented each year to a Florida high school senior who plans to major in a coastal-related field of study at a Florida university or college.

Academic Fields/Career Goals: Marine Biology.

Award: Scholarship for use in freshman year. *Amount:* $1000.

Eligibility Requirements: Applicant must be enrolled or expecting to enroll at an institution or university and studying in Florida. Available to U.S. citizens.

Application Requirements: Application. *Deadline:* varies.

Contact: James Cato, Director
Florida Sea Grant
University of Florida, Building 803 McCarty Drive
PO Box 110400
Gainesville, FL 32611-0400
Phone: 352-392-5870
Fax: 352-392-5113
E-mail: jccato@ufl.edu

INTERNATIONAL ASSOCIATION OF GREAT LAKES RESEARCH   http://www.iaglr.org

PAUL W. RODGERS SCHOLARSHIP
• See page 214

LOUISIANA OFFICE OF STUDENT FINANCIAL ASSISTANCE   http://www.osfa.state.la.us

ROCKEFELLER STATE WILDLIFE SCHOLARSHIP
• See page 87

MARINE TECHNOLOGY SOCIETY   http://www.mtsociety.org

CHARLES H. BUSSMAN UNDERGRADUATE SCHOLARSHIP

Scholarship for undergraduate students enrolled full time in a marine-related field. Must be student members of Marine Technology Society.

Academic Fields/Career Goals: Marine Biology; Marine/Ocean Engineering; Oceanography.

Award: Scholarship for use in freshman, sophomore, junior, or senior years. *Amount:* up to $2500.

Eligibility Requirements: Applicant must be enrolled or expecting to enroll at a four-year institution or university. Available to U.S. citizens.

Marine Technology Society (continued)

Application Requirements: Application, autobiography, references, transcript. *Deadline:* April 17.

Contact: Daniel Schwartz, Vice President of Education and Research
Marine Technology Society
5565 Sterrett Place, Suite 108
Columbia, MD 21044
Phone: 410-884-5330
Fax: 410-884-9060
E-mail: schwartz@ocean.washington.edu

JOHN C. BAJUS SCHOLARSHIP

Scholarship available to undergraduate and graduate students enrolled full time in a marine-related field. Must be a MTS student member with demonstrated commitment to community service/volunteer activities.

Academic Fields/Career Goals: Marine Biology; Marine/Ocean Engineering; Occupational Safety and Health.

Award: Scholarship for use in freshman, sophomore, junior, senior, or graduate years. *Amount:* up to $1000.

Eligibility Requirements: Applicant must be enrolled or expecting to enroll full-time at a four-year institution or university. Available to U.S. citizens.

Application Requirements: Application, autobiography, references, transcript. *Deadline:* April 17.

Contact: Daniel Schwartz, Vice President of Education and Research
Marine Technology Society
5565 Sterrett Place, Suite 108
Columbia, MD 21044
Phone: 410-884-5330
Fax: 410-884-9060
E-mail: schwartz@ocean.washington.edu

THE MTS STUDENT SCHOLARSHIP

Scholarships available to both Marine Technology Society members and non-members, undergraduates, and graduate students enrolled full time in a marine-related field. High school seniors who have been accepted into a full-time undergraduate program in a marine-related field are also eligible to apply.

Academic Fields/Career Goals: Marine Biology; Marine/Ocean Engineering; Occupational Safety and Health.

Award: Scholarship for use in freshman, sophomore, junior, senior, or graduate years. *Amount:* up to $2000.

Eligibility Requirements: Applicant must be enrolled or expecting to enroll full-time at a four-year institution or university. Available to U.S. citizens.

Application Requirements: Application, autobiography, references, transcript. *Deadline:* April 17.

Contact: Daniel Schwartz, Vice President of Education and Research
Marine Technology Society
5565 Sterrett Place, Suite 108
Columbia, MD 21044
Phone: 410-884-5330
Fax: 410-884-9060
E-mail: schwartz@ocean.washington.edu

NATIONAL OCEANIC AND ATMOSPHERIC ADMINISTRATION
http://see.orau.org

NATIONAL OCEANIC AND ATMOSPHERIC ADMINISTRATION EDUCATIONAL PARTNERSHIP PROGRAM WITH MINORITY SERVING INSTITUTIONS UNDERGRADUATE SCHOLARSHIP
• *See page 268*

SOCIETY FOR MARINE MAMMALOGY
http://www.marinemammalogy.org

FREDERIC FAIRFIELD MEMORIAL FUND AWARD
• *See page 141*

MARINE/OCEAN ENGINEERING

AMERICAN SOCIETY OF NAVAL ENGINEERS
http://www.navalengineers.org

AMERICAN SOCIETY OF NAVAL ENGINEERS SCHOLARSHIP
• *See page 90*

ASSOCIATION FOR IRON AND STEEL TECHNOLOGY
http://www.aist.org

ASSOCIATION FOR IRON AND STEEL TECHNOLOGY DAVID H. SAMSON SCHOLARSHIP
• *See page 162*

ELECTROCHEMICAL SOCIETY, INC.
http://www.electrochem.org

DANIEL CUBICCIOTTI STUDENT AWARD OF THE SAN FRANCISCO SECTION OF THE ELECTROCHEMICAL SOCIETY, SPONSORED BY STRUCTURAL INTEGRITY ASSOCIATES
• *See page 137*

H.H. DOW MEMORIAL STUDENT ACHIEVEMENT AWARD OF THE INDUSTRIAL ELECTROLYSIS AND ELECTROCHEMICAL ENGINEERING DIVISION OF THE ELECTROCHEMICAL SOCIETY, INC.
• *See page 137*

STUDENT ACHIEVEMENT AWARDS OF THE INDUSTRIAL ELECTROLYSIS AND ELECTROCHEMICAL ENGINEERING DIVISION OF THE ELECTROCHEMICAL SOCIETY, INC.
• *See page 137*

STUDENT RESEARCH AWARDS OF THE BATTERY DIVISION OF THE ELECTROCHEMICAL SOCIETY, INC.
• *See page 137*

MARINE TECHNOLOGY SOCIETY
http://www.mtsociety.org

CHARLES H. BUSSMAN UNDERGRADUATE SCHOLARSHIP
• *See page 385*

JOHN C. BAJUS SCHOLARSHIP
• *See page 386*

ROV SCHOLARSHIP

Scholarships for undergraduate and graduate students interested in remotely operated vehicles or underwater work that furthers the use of ROVs. Must be a Marine Technology Society member.

Academic Fields/Career Goals: Marine/Ocean Engineering.

Award: Scholarship for use in freshman, sophomore, junior, senior, or graduate years. *Amount:* up to $10,000.

Eligibility Requirements: Applicant must be enrolled or expecting to enroll full-time at a four-year institution or university. Available to U.S. citizens.

Application Requirements: Application, autobiography, essay, references, transcript. *Deadline:* April 17.

Contact: Chuck Richards, Chair, ROV Scholarship Committee
Marine Technology Society
c/o C.A. Richards and Associates Inc, 777 North Eldridge Parkway, Suite 280
Houston, TX 77079

THE MTS STUDENT SCHOLARSHIP
• *See page 386*

THE PAROS-DIGIQUARTZ SCHOLARSHIP

Scholarships available to both Marine Technology Society members and non-members, undergraduates, and graduate students enrolled full time in a marine-related field with an interest in marine instrumentation. High school seniors who have been accepted into a full-time undergraduate program in a marine-related field are also eligible to apply.

Academic Fields/Career Goals: Marine/Ocean Engineering.

Award: Scholarship for use in freshman, sophomore, junior, senior, or graduate years. *Amount:* up to $2000.

Eligibility Requirements: Applicant must be enrolled or expecting to enroll full-time at a four-year institution or university. Available to U.S. citizens.

Application Requirements: Application, autobiography, references, transcript. *Deadline:* April 17.

Contact: Daniel Schwartz, Vice President of Education and Research
Marine Technology Society
5565 Sterrett Place, Suite 108
Columbia, MD 21044
Phone: 410-884-5330
Fax: 410-884-9060
E-mail: schwartz@ocean.washington.edu

SOCIETY OF NAVAL ARCHITECTS & MARINE ENGINEERS   http://www.sname.org

SOCIETY OF NAVAL ARCHITECTS AND MARINE ENGINEERS UNDERGRADUATE SCHOLARSHIPS

MATERIALS SCIENCE, ENGINEERING, AND METALLURGY

ACI INTERNATIONAL/CONCRETE RESEARCH AND EDUCATION FOUNDATION (CONREF)   http://www.concrete.org

KUMAR MEHTA SCHOLARSHIP

PETER D. COURTOIS CONCRETE CONSTRUCTION SCHOLARSHIP

V. MOHAN MALHOTRA SCHOLARSHIP

W.R. GRACE SCHOLARSHIP AWARD

AEA-OREGON COUNCIL   http://aeascholar.ous.edu

AEA- OREGON COUNCIL TECHNOLOGY SCHOLARSHIP PROGRAM

AMERICAN CHEMICAL SOCIETY, RUBBER DIVISION   http://www.rubber.org

AMERICAN CHEMICAL SOCIETY, RUBBER DIVISION UNDERGRADUATE SCHOLARSHIP

AMERICAN COUNCIL OF ENGINEERING COMPANIES OF PENNSYLVANIA (ACEC/PA)   http://www.acecpa.org

ENGINEERING SCHOLARSHIP

AMERICAN ELECTROPLATERS AND SURFACE FINISHERS SOCIETY   http://www.aesf.org

AMERICAN ELECTROPLATERS AND SURFACE FINISHERS SCHOLARSHIPS

AMERICAN INSTITUTE OF AERONAUTICS AND ASTRONAUTICS   http://www.aiaa.org

AIAA UNDERGRADUATE SCHOLARSHIP

AMERICAN SOCIETY OF NAVAL ENGINEERS   http://www.navalengineers.org

AMERICAN SOCIETY OF NAVAL ENGINEERS SCHOLARSHIP

AMERICAN WELDING SOCIETY   http://www.aws.org

ARSHAM AMIRIKIAN ENGINEERING SCHOLARSHIP

DONALD AND JEAN CLEVELAND-WILLAMETTE VALLEY SECTION SCHOLARSHIP

DONALD AND SHIRLEY HASTINGS SCHOLARSHIP

RESISTANCE WELDER MANUFACTURERS' ASSOCIATION SCHOLARSHIP

ROBERT L. PEASLEE DETROIT BRAZING AND SOLDERING DIVISION SCHOLARSHIP

ASM MATERIALS EDUCATION FOUNDATION   http://www.asminternational.org

ASM MATERIALS EDUCATION FOUNDATION SCHOLARSHIPS

ASM OUTSTANDING SCHOLARS AWARDS

EDWARD J. DULIS SCHOLARSHIP

GEORGE A. ROBERTS SCHOLARSHIP

JOHN M. HANIAK SCHOLARSHIP

NICHOLAS J. GRANT SCHOLARSHIP

WILLIAM P. WOODSIDE FOUNDER'S SCHOLARSHIP

ASSOCIATION FOR FACILITIES ENGINEERING (AFE)

ASSOCIATION FOR FACILITIES ENGINEERING CEDAR VALLEY CHAPTER # 132 SCHOLARSHIP

ASSOCIATION FOR IRON AND STEEL TECHNOLOGY   http://www.aist.org

AIST ALFRED B. GLOSSBRENNER AND JOHN KLUSCH SCHOLARSHIPS

AIST WILLIAM E. SCHWABE MEMORIAL SCHOLARSHIP

ASSOCIATION FOR IRON AND STEEL TECHNOLOGY BALTIMORE CHAPTER SCHOLARSHIP

Scholarship for Baltimore Chapter area high school seniors or currently enrolled undergraduate students pursuing a career in engineering or metallurgy. Must be the child, grandchild, or spouse of a member of the Baltimore Chapter of AIST. Student may reapply each year for the term of their college education. Information and application available on Web site: http://www.aist.org/chapters/mc_baltimore_scholar.htm

Academic Fields/Career Goals: Materials Science, Engineering, and Metallurgy.

Award: Scholarship for use in freshman, sophomore, junior, or senior years; not renewable. *Number:* 1. *Amount:* $1500.

Eligibility Requirements: Applicant must be enrolled or expecting to enroll full-time at a four-year institution or university. Available to U.S. citizens.

Association for Iron and Steel Technology (continued)

Application Requirements: Application, essay, test scores, transcript. *Deadline:* April 30.

Contact: Thomas Russo, AIST Baltimore Member Chapter
Scholarships/Division Manager Steelmaking
Association for Iron and Steel Technology
5111 North Point Boulevard
Sparrows Point, MD 21219-1014

ASSOCIATION FOR IRON AND STEEL TECHNOLOGY BENJAMIN F. FAIRLESS SCHOLARSHIP

Scholarships available to students of metallurgy, metallurgical engineering, or materials science, who have a genuine interest in a career in ferrous related industries as demonstrated by an internship, co-op, or related experience or who have plans to pursue such experiences during college. Student may apply after first term of freshman year of college and must join the AIST at the student rate. The Web site contains further information.

Academic Fields/Career Goals: Materials Science, Engineering, and Metallurgy.

Award: Scholarship for use in freshman, sophomore, junior, or senior years; not renewable. *Number:* 2. *Amount:* $2000.

Eligibility Requirements: Applicant must be enrolled or expecting to enroll full-time at a four-year institution or university and must have an interest in leadership. Applicant must have 3.0 GPA or higher. Available to U.S. and non-U.S. citizens.

Application Requirements: Application, essay, resume, references, transcript. *Deadline:* April 18.

Contact: Lori Wharrey, Board Administrator
Association for Iron and Steel Technology
186 Thorn Hill Road
Warrendale, PA 15086-7528
Phone: 724-776-6040 Ext. 621
Fax: 724-776-0430
E-mail: lwharrey@aist.org

ASSOCIATION FOR IRON AND STEEL TECHNOLOGY DAVID H. SAMSON SCHOLARSHIP
• See page 162

ASSOCIATION FOR IRON AND STEEL TECHNOLOGY FERROUS METALLURGY EDUCATION TODAY (FEMET)

Scholarship/internship to provide incentive for students to become involved in the steel industry. Each recipient is awarded $5000 in their junior year, a paid summer internship with a North American steel company between junior and senior year, and $5000 toward senior year tuition. Must be enrolled full-time in metallurgy or materials science program at an accredited North American University. For more information call or email scholarship contact.

Academic Fields/Career Goals: Materials Science, Engineering, and Metallurgy.

Award: Scholarship for use in junior or senior years; not renewable. *Number:* 10. *Amount:* $5000.

Eligibility Requirements: Applicant must be enrolled or expecting to enroll full-time at a four-year institution or university. Applicant must have 3.0 GPA or higher. Available to U.S. citizens.

Application Requirements: Application, essay, resume, references, transcript.

Contact: B. V. Lakshminarayana
Phone: 202-452-7143
E-mail: blakshmi@steel.org

ASSOCIATION FOR IRON AND STEEL TECHNOLOGY NATIONAL MERIT SCHOLARSHIP
• See page 258

ASSOCIATION FOR IRON AND STEEL TECHNOLOGY NORTHWEST MEMBER CHAPTER SCHOLARSHIP
• See page 258

ASSOCIATION FOR IRON AND STEEL TECHNOLOGY OHIO VALLEY CHAPTER SCHOLARSHIP
• See page 135

ASSOCIATION FOR IRON AND STEEL TECHNOLOGY PITTSBURGH CHAPTER SCHOLARSHIP
• See page 258

ASSOCIATION FOR IRON AND STEEL TECHNOLOGY RONALD E. LINCOLN SCHOLARSHIP

Scholarship available to students of metallurgy, metallurgical engineering, or materials science, who have a genuine interest in a career in ferrous related industries as demonstrated by an internship, co-op, or related experience or who have plans to pursue such experiences during college. Student may apply after first term of freshman year of college and must join the AIST at the student rate. The Web site contains further information.

Academic Fields/Career Goals: Materials Science, Engineering, and Metallurgy.

Award: Scholarship for use in freshman, sophomore, junior, or senior years; not renewable. *Number:* 2. *Amount:* $2000.

Eligibility Requirements: Applicant must be enrolled or expecting to enroll full-time at a four-year institution or university and must have an interest in leadership. Applicant must have 3.0 GPA or higher. Available to U.S. and non-U.S. citizens.

Application Requirements: Application, essay, resume, references, transcript. *Deadline:* April 18.

Contact: Lori Wharrey, Board Administrator
Association for Iron and Steel Technology
186 Thorn Hill Road
Warrendale, PA 15086-7528
Phone: 724-776-6040 Ext. 621
Fax: 724-776-0430
E-mail: lwharrey@aist.org

ASSOCIATION FOR IRON AND STEEL TECHNOLOGY SOUTHEAST MEMBER CHAPTER SCHOLARSHIP
• See page 258

ASSOCIATION FOR IRON AND STEEL TECHNOLOGY WILLY KORF MEMORIAL SCHOLARSHIP

Scholarships available to students of metallurgy, metallurgical engineering, or materials science, who have a genuine interest in a career in ferrous related industries as demonstrated by an internship, co-op, or related experience or who have plans to pursue such experiences during college. Student may apply at first term of freshman year of college and must join the AIST at the student rate. The Web site contains further information.

Academic Fields/Career Goals: Materials Science, Engineering, and Metallurgy.

Award: Scholarship for use in sophomore, junior, or senior years; not renewable. *Number:* 3. *Amount:* $2000.

Eligibility Requirements: Applicant must be enrolled or expecting to enroll full-time at a four-year institution or university and must have an interest in leadership. Applicant must have 3.0 GPA or higher. Available to U.S. and non-U.S. citizens.

Application Requirements: Application, essay, resume, references, transcript, demonstrated interest in the iron and steel industry. *Deadline:* April 18.

Contact: Ms. Lori Wharrey, AIST Board Administrator
Association for Iron and Steel Technology
186 Thorn Hill Road
Warrendale, PA 15086
Phone: 724-776-6040 Ext. 621
E-mail: lwharrey@aist.org

ASSOCIATION FOR WOMEN IN SCIENCE EDUCATIONAL FOUNDATION   http://www.awis.org/ed_foundation.html

ASSOCIATION FOR WOMEN IN SCIENCE COLLEGE SCHOLARSHIP
• See page 86

ASTRONAUT SCHOLARSHIP FOUNDATION   http://www.astronautscholarship.org

ASTRONAUT SCHOLARSHIP FOUNDATION
• See page 92

BARRY M. GOLDWATER SCHOLARSHIP AND EXCELLENCE IN EDUCATION FOUNDATION
http://www.act.org/goldwater

BARRY M. GOLDWATER SCHOLARSHIP AND EXCELLENCE IN EDUCATION PROGRAM
• See page 92

ELECTROCHEMICAL SOCIETY, INC.
http://www.electrochem.org

DANIEL CUBICCIOTTI STUDENT AWARD OF THE SAN FRANCISCO SECTION OF THE ELECTROCHEMICAL SOCIETY, SPONSORED BY STRUCTURAL INTEGRITY ASSOCIATES
• See page 137

H.H. DOW MEMORIAL STUDENT ACHIEVEMENT AWARD OF THE INDUSTRIAL ELECTROLYSIS AND ELECTROCHEMICAL ENGINEERING DIVISION OF THE ELECTROCHEMICAL SOCIETY, INC.
• See page 137

STUDENT ACHIEVEMENT AWARDS OF THE INDUSTRIAL ELECTROLYSIS AND ELECTROCHEMICAL ENGINEERING DIVISION OF THE ELECTROCHEMICAL SOCIETY, INC.
• See page 137

STUDENT RESEARCH AWARDS OF THE BATTERY DIVISION OF THE ELECTROCHEMICAL SOCIETY, INC.
• See page 137

GEORGE BIRD GRINNELL AMERICAN INDIAN FUND
http://www.grinnellfund.org/

AL QOYAWAYMA AWARD
• See page 163

H.H. HARRIS FOUNDATION
http://www.afsinc.org

H.H. HARRIS FOUNDATION ANNUAL SCHOLARSHIP

Scholarships averaging $1000 will be awarded to students and professionals in the metallurgical and casting of metals field who are U.S. citizens. For more details see Web site: http://www.afsinc.org. Deadline is June 30.

Academic Fields/Career Goals: Materials Science, Engineering, and Metallurgy.

Award: Scholarship for use in freshman, sophomore, junior, senior, graduate, or postgraduate years; not renewable. *Amount:* $500.

Eligibility Requirements: Applicant must be enrolled or expecting to enroll full or part-time at a four-year institution or university. Available to U.S. citizens.

Application Requirements: Application, references. *Deadline:* June 30.

Contact: John Hough, Trustee
H.H. Harris Foundation
30 South Wacker Drive, Suite 2300
Chicago, IL 60606
Fax: 312-346-0904
E-mail: johnHH@aol.com

HISPANIC COLLEGE FUND, INC.
http://www.hispanicfund.org

DEPARTMENT OF ENERGY SCHOLARSHIP PROGRAM
• See page 148

LOCKHEED MARTIN SCHOLARSHIP PROGRAM
• See page 164

HISPANIC ENGINEER NATIONAL ACHIEVEMENT AWARDS CORPORATION (HENAAC)
http://www.henaac.org

HISPANIC ENGINEER NATIONAL ACHIEVEMENT AWARDS CORPORATION SCHOLARSHIP PROGRAM
• See page 122

INDEPENDENT LABORATORIES INSTITUTE SCHOLARSHIP ALLIANCE
http://www.acil.org

INDEPENDENT LABORATORIES INSTITUTE SCHOLARSHIP ALLIANCE
• See page 93

INTERNATIONAL SOCIETY FOR OPTICAL ENGINEERING-SPIE
http://www.spie.org/info/scholarships

SPIE EDUCATIONAL SCHOLARSHIPS IN OPTICAL SCIENCE AND ENGINEERING
• See page 93

JORGE MAS CANOSA FREEDOM FOUNDATION
http://www.canf.org

MAS FAMILY SCHOLARSHIP AWARD
• See page 149

KENTUCKY NATURAL RESOURCES AND ENVIRONMENTAL PROTECTION CABINET
http://www.uky.edu/waterresources

ENVIRONMENTAL PROTECTION SCHOLARSHIPS
• See page 164

LOS ANGELES COUNCIL OF BLACK PROFESSIONAL ENGINEERS
http://www.lablackengineers.org

AL-BEN SCHOLARSHIP FOR ACADEMIC INCENTIVE
• See page 164

AL-BEN SCHOLARSHIP FOR PROFESSIONAL MERIT
• See page 165

AL-BEN SCHOLARSHIP FOR SCHOLASTIC ACHIEVEMENT
• See page 165

MAINE METAL PRODUCTS ASSOCIATION
http://www.maine-metals.org

MAINE METAL PRODUCTS ASSOCIATION SCHOLARSHIP PROGRAM

MMPA offers scholarship awards to individuals seeking postsecondary education in the metal trades/precision manufacturing field of study. Any Maine student or worker can apply for tuition assistance at any Maine institute of higher learning. Special awards are also available.

Academic Fields/Career Goals: Materials Science, Engineering, and Metallurgy; Mechanical Engineering; Trade/Technical Specialties.

Award: Scholarship for use in freshman, sophomore, junior, senior, graduate, or postgraduate years; renewable. *Number:* 15–25. *Amount:* $250–$1000.

Eligibility Requirements: Applicant must be enrolled or expecting to enroll full or part-time at a two-year or four-year or technical institution or university; resident of Maine and studying in Maine. Applicant must have 2.5 GPA or higher. Available to U.S. citizens.

Application Requirements: Application, essay, references, transcript. *Deadline:* June 1.

Contact: Lisa Martin, Executive Director
Maine Metal Products Association
28 Stroudwater Street, Suite 4
Westbrook, ME 04092
Phone: 207-854-2153
Fax: 207-854-3865
E-mail: info@maine-metals.org

MICRON TECHNOLOGY FOUNDATION, INC.
http://www.micron.com

MICRON SCIENCE AND TECHNOLOGY SCHOLARS PROGRAM
• See page 165

MIDWEST ROOFING CONTRACTORS ASSOCIATION
http://www.mrca.org

MRCA FOUNDATION SCHOLARSHIP PROGRAM
• See page 94

MINERALOGICAL SOCIETY OF AMERICA
http://www.minsocam.org

MINERALOGY SOCIETY OF AMERICA-GRANT FOR RESEARCH IN CRYSTALLOGRAPHY
- *See page 215*

MINERALS, METALS, AND MATERIALS SOCIETY (TMS)
http://www.tms.org

TMS J. KEITH BRIMACOMBE PRESIDENTIAL SCHOLARSHIP
- *See page 266*

TMS OUTSTANDING STUDENT PAPER CONTEST-UNDERGRADUATE
- *See page 266*

TMS/EMPMD GILBERT CHIN SCHOLARSHIP
- *See page 266*

TMS/EPD SCHOLARSHIP
- *See page 267*

TMS/INTERNATIONAL SYMPOSIUM ON SUPERALLOYS SCHOLARSHIP PROGRAM
- *See page 267*

TMS/LMD SCHOLARSHIP PROGRAM
- *See page 267*

TMS/STRUCTURAL MATERIALS DIVISION SCHOLARSHIP
- *See page 267*

NASA VERMONT SPACE GRANT CONSORTIUM
http://www.vtspacegrant.org

VERMONT SPACE GRANT CONSORTIUM SCHOLARSHIP PROGRAM
- *See page 94*

NATIONAL INVENTORS HALL OF FAME
http://www.invent.org

COLLEGIATE INVENTORS COMPETITION - GRAND PRIZE
- *See page 95*

COLLEGIATE INVENTORS COMPETITION FOR UNDERGRADUATE STUDENTS
- *See page 95*

NATIONAL SOCIETY OF PROFESSIONAL ENGINEERS
http://www.nspe.org

MAUREEN L. AND HOWARD N. BLITMAN, PE SCHOLARSHIP TO PROMOTE DIVERSITY IN ENGINEERING
- *See page 166*

NATIONAL SOCIETY OF PROFESSIONAL ENGINEERS/AUXILIARY SCHOLARSHIP
- *See page 166*

PAUL H. ROBBINS HONORARY SCHOLARSHIP
- *See page 166*

PROFESSIONAL ENGINEERS IN INDUSTRY SCHOLARSHIP
- *See page 167*

VIRGINIA HENRY MEMORIAL SCHOLARSHIP
- *See page 167*

PLASTICS INSTITUTE OF AMERICA
http://www.plasticsinstitute.org/

PLASTICS PIONEERS SCHOLARSHIPS
- *See page 269*

SOCIETY FOR MINING, METALLURGY AND EXPLORATION - CENTRAL WYOMING SECTION

COATES, WOLFF, RUSSELL MINING INDUSTRY SCHOLARSHIP
- *See page 95*

SOCIETY OF AUTOMOTIVE ENGINEERS
http://www.sae.org

BMW/SAE ENGINEERING SCHOLARSHIP
- *See page 129*

EDWARD D. HENDRICKSON/SAE ENGINEERING SCHOLARSHIP
- *See page 129*

TMC/SAE DONALD D. DAWSON TECHNICAL SCHOLARSHIP
- *See page 129*

YANMAR/SAE SCHOLARSHIP
- *See page 271*

SOCIETY OF HISPANIC PROFESSIONAL ENGINEERS FOUNDATION
http://www.henaac.org

HENAAC SCHOLARS PROGRAM
- *See page 290*

SOCIETY OF HISPANIC PROFESSIONAL ENGINEERS FOUNDATION
- *See page 168*

SOCIETY OF PLASTICS ENGINEERS (SPE) FOUNDATION
http://www.4spe.com

SOCIETY OF PLASTICS ENGINEERS SCHOLARSHIP PROGRAM
- *See page 168*

SOCIETY OF WOMEN ENGINEERS
http://www.swe.org

GUIDANT CORPORATION SCHOLARSHIP
- *See page 195*

NORTHROP GRUMMAN CORPORATION SCHOLARSHIPS
- *See page 130*

SOIL AND WATER CONSERVATION SOCIETY-NEW JERSEY CHAPTER
http://www.geocities.com/njswcs

EDWARD R. HALL SCHOLARSHIP
- *See page 76*

UNIVERSITIES SPACE RESEARCH ASSOCIATION
http://www.usra.edu

UNIVERSITIES SPACE RESEARCH ASSOCIATION SCHOLARSHIP PROGRAM
- *See page 96*

XEROX
http://www.xerox.com

TECHNICAL MINORITY SCHOLARSHIP
- *See page 169*

MATHEMATICS

CALIFORNIA MATHEMATICS COUNCIL - SOUTH
http://www.cmc-math.org

CALIFORNIA MATHEMATICS COUNCIL - SOUTH SECONDARY EDUCATION SCHOLARSHIPS

Scholarships awarded to students enrolled in accredited Southern California secondary education (math major) credential programs. Applicants must be members of the California Math Council-South. Application deadline is January 31. For more information check the Web site: www.cmc-math.org

Academic Fields/Career Goals: Mathematics.

Award: Scholarship for use in freshman, sophomore, junior, or senior years; renewable. *Amount:* $100–$1000.

Eligibility Requirements: Applicant must be enrolled or expecting to enroll full or part-time at a four-year institution or university and studying in California. Available to U.S. and non-U.S. citizens.

Application Requirements: Application, essay, references, transcript. *Deadline:* January 31.

Contact: Dr. Sid Kolpas, Professor of Mathematics
California Mathematics Council - South
CMC-SS Scholarship Committee
1500 North Verdugo Road
Glendale, CA 91208-2894
Phone: 818-240-1000 Ext. 5378
Fax: 818-551-5282
E-mail: sjkolpas@sprintmail.com

CASUALTY ACTUARIAL SOCIETY/SOCIETY OF ACTUARIES JOINT COMMITTEE ON MINORITY RECRUITING   http://www.BeAnActuary.org

ACTUARIAL SCHOLARSHIPS FOR MINORITY STUDENTS
• *See page 145*

COLLEGEBOUND FOUNDATION   http://www.collegeboundfoundation.org

DR. FREEMAN A. HRABOWSKI, III SCHOLARSHIP
• *See page 259*

NASA MONTANA SPACE GRANT CONSORTIUM   http://www.spacegrant.montana.edu

MONTANA SPACE GRANT SCHOLARSHIP PROGRAM
• *See page 125*

NASA RHODE ISLAND SPACE GRANT CONSORTIUM   http://www.planetary.brown.edu/RI_Space_Grant

NASA RHODE ISLAND SPACE GRANT CONSORTIUM OUTREACH SCHOLARSHIP FOR UNDERGRADUATE STUDENTS
• *See page 288*

NATIONAL OCEANIC AND ATMOSPHERIC ADMINISTRATION   http://see.orau.org

NATIONAL OCEANIC AND ATMOSPHERIC ADMINISTRATION EDUCATIONAL PARTNERSHIP PROGRAM WITH MINORITY SERVING INSTITUTIONS UNDERGRADUATE SCHOLARSHIP
• *See page 268*

SOCIETY OF HISPANIC PROFESSIONAL ENGINEERS FOUNDATION   http://www.henaac.org

HENAAC SCHOLARS PROGRAM
• *See page 290*

WISCONSIN MATHEMATICS COUNCIL, INC.   http://www.wismath.org

ARNE ENGEBRETSEN WISCONSIN MATHEMATICS COUNCIL SCHOLARSHIP
• *See page 240*

ETHEL A. NEIJAHR WISCONSIN MATHEMATICS COUNCIL SCHOLARSHIP
• *See page 240*

SISTER MARY PETRONIA VAN STRATEN WISCONSIN MATHEMATICS COUNCIL SCHOLARSHIP
• *See page 240*

MECHANICAL ENGINEERING

AACE INTERNATIONAL   http://www.aacei.org

AACE INTERNATIONAL COMPETITIVE SCHOLARSHIP
• *See page 96*

AEA-OREGON COUNCIL   http://aeascholar.ous.edu

AEA- OREGON COUNCIL TECHNOLOGY SCHOLARSHIP PROGRAM
• *See page 88*

AMERICAN CHEMICAL SOCIETY, RUBBER DIVISION   http://www.rubber.org

AMERICAN CHEMICAL SOCIETY, RUBBER DIVISION UNDERGRADUATE SCHOLARSHIP
• *See page 158*

AMERICAN COUNCIL OF ENGINEERING COMPANIES OF PENNSYLVANIA (ACEC/PA)   http://www.acecpa.org

ENGINEERING SCHOLARSHIP
• *See page 158*

AMERICAN INSTITUTE OF AERONAUTICS AND ASTRONAUTICS   http://www.aiaa.org

AIAA UNDERGRADUATE SCHOLARSHIP
• *See page 89*

AMERICAN PUBLIC TRANSPORTATION FOUNDATION   http://www.apta.com

DONALD C. HYDE ESSAY PROGRAM
• *See page 171*

JACK GILSTRAP SCHOLARSHIP
• *See page 171*

LOUIS T. KLAUDER SCHOLARSHIP
• *See page 171*

PARSONS BRINCKERHOFF-JIM LAMMIE SCHOLARSHIP
• *See page 171*

TRANSIT HALL OF FAME SCHOLARSHIP AWARD PROGRAM
• *See page 171*

AMERICAN SOCIETY OF HEATING, REFRIGERATING, AND AIR CONDITIONING ENGINEERS, INC.   http://www.ashrae.org

ALWIN B. NEWTON SCHOLARSHIP FUND
• *See page 242*

REUBEN TRANE SCHOLARSHIP
• *See page 242*

AMERICAN SOCIETY OF MECHANICAL ENGINEERS (ASME INTERNATIONAL)   http://www.asme.org

AMERICAN SOCIETY OF MECHANICAL ENGINEERS FOUNDATION SCHOLARSHIP
• *See page 252*

AMERICAN SOCIETY OF MECHANICAL ENGINEERS SOLID WASTE PROCESSING DIVISION UNDERGRADUATE SCHOLARSHIP

One undergraduate scholarship available for study at North American colleges and universities with established programs in solid waste management. Award is divided equally between the student and the school.

Academic Fields/Career Goals: Mechanical Engineering.

Award: Scholarship for use in sophomore, junior, or senior years; not renewable. *Number:* 1. *Amount:* $2000.

Eligibility Requirements: Applicant must be enrolled or expecting to enroll full-time at a four-year institution or university. Available to U.S. and non-U.S. citizens.

American Society of Mechanical Engineers (ASME International) (continued)

Application Requirements: Application, essay, references, transcript. *Deadline:* June 5.

Contact: Elio Manes, Senior Manager
American Society of Mechanical Engineers (ASME International)
3 Park Avenue
New York, NY 10016-5990
Phone: 212-591-7797
Fax: 212-591-7671
E-mail: manese@asme.org

AMERICAN SOCIETY OF MECHANICAL ENGINEERS/FIRST ROBOTICS COMPETITION SCHOLARSHIP

Seven $5000 scholarships to graduating high school seniors who are members of a FIRST Robotics Competition. Must be planning to enroll no later than the fall semester following high school graduation in an ABET-accredited or substantially equivalent mechanical engineering or mechanical engineering technology program. ASME does not accept applications directly from students for this program. Students must be nominated by ASME members involved with FIRST teams. Nomination postmark deadline: March 1.

Academic Fields/Career Goals: Mechanical Engineering.

Award: Scholarship for use in freshman year; not renewable. *Number:* 7. *Amount:* $5000.

Eligibility Requirements: Applicant must be high school student and planning to enroll or expecting to enroll full-time at a four-year institution or university. Available to U.S. citizens.

Application Requirements: Applicant must enter a contest, financial need analysis, transcript, nominated letter from ASME member. *Deadline:* March 1.

Contact: Mel Torre, Director of Communication
American Society of Mechanical Engineers (ASME International)
3 Park Avenue
New York, NY 10016-5990
Phone: 212-591-8157
Fax: 212-591-7143
E-mail: torrec@asme.org

F.W. "BEICH" BEICHLEY SCHOLARSHIP

One-time award for college juniors and seniors who are members of the American Society of Mechanical Engineers. Must be attending a four-year institution and pursuing studies in mechanical engineering or mechanical engineering technology. Application available online http://www.asme.org/education/enged/aid.

Academic Fields/Career Goals: Mechanical Engineering.

Award: Scholarship for use in junior or senior years; not renewable. *Number:* 1. *Amount:* $2000.

Eligibility Requirements: Applicant must be enrolled or expecting to enroll full-time at a two-year or four-year institution or university. Available to U.S. citizens.

Application Requirements: Application, essay, financial need analysis, references, self-addressed stamped envelope, transcript, must be ASME student members. *Deadline:* March 15.

Contact: Maisha Phillips, Coordinator, Student Development ASME
American Society of Mechanical Engineers (ASME International)
3 Park Avenue
New York, NY 10016-5990
Phone: 212-591-8131
Fax: 212-591-7143
E-mail: phillipsm@asme.org

FRANK WILLIAM AND DOROTHY GIVEN MILLER SCHOLARSHIP

Award for college juniors and seniors who are members of the American Society of Mechanical Engineers. Must be attending a four-year institution in North America and pursuing studies in mechanical engineering or mechanical engineering technology. Must be a U.S. citizen, or North American resident. Application available online http://www.asme.org/education/enged/aid.

Academic Fields/Career Goals: Mechanical Engineering.

Award: Scholarship for use in sophomore, junior, or senior years; not renewable. *Number:* 2. *Amount:* $1500.

Eligibility Requirements: Applicant must be enrolled or expecting to enroll full-time at a four-year institution or university. Available to U.S. citizens.

Application Requirements: Application, essay, financial need analysis, references, self-addressed stamped envelope, transcript, applicants must be ASME student members. *Deadline:* March 15.

Contact: Maisha Phillips, Coordinator, Student Development ASME
American Society of Mechanical Engineers (ASME International)
3 Park Avenue
New York, NY 10016-5990
Phone: 212-591-8131
Fax: 212-591-7143
E-mail: phillipsm@asme.org

GARLAND DUNCAN SCHOLARSHIP

Award for college juniors and seniors who are members of the American Society of Mechanical Engineers. Must be enrolled at a four-year college or university and pursuing studies in mechanical engineering or mechanical engineering technology in the U.S. Application available online http://www.asme.org/education/enged/aid

Academic Fields/Career Goals: Mechanical Engineering.

Award: Scholarship for use in junior or senior years; not renewable. *Number:* up to 2. *Amount:* up to $3500.

Eligibility Requirements: Applicant must be enrolled or expecting to enroll full-time at a two-year or four-year institution or university. Available to U.S. and non-U.S. citizens.

Application Requirements: Application, essay, financial need analysis, references, self-addressed stamped envelope, transcript, applicants must be ASME student members. *Deadline:* March 15.

Contact: Maisha Phillips, Coordinator, Student Development ASME
American Society of Mechanical Engineers (ASME International)
3 Park Avenue
New York, NY 10016-5990
Phone: 212-591-8131
Fax: 212-591-7143
E-mail: phillipsm@asme.org

JOHN AND ELSA GRACIK SCHOLARSHIPS

Award for college undergraduates enrolled or enrolling in a mechanical engineering or related program. Must be a U.S. citizen and a member of the American Society of Mechanical Engineers. Application available online http://www.asme.org/education/enged/aid

Academic Fields/Career Goals: Mechanical Engineering.

Award: Scholarship for use in sophomore, junior, or senior years; not renewable. *Number:* up to 18. *Amount:* $1500.

Eligibility Requirements: Applicant must be enrolled or expecting to enroll full-time at a two-year or four-year institution or university. Available to U.S. citizens.

Application Requirements: Application, essay, financial need analysis, references, self-addressed stamped envelope, transcript, applicants must be ASME student members. *Deadline:* March 15.

Contact: Maisha Phillips, Coordinator, Student Development ASME
American Society of Mechanical Engineers (ASME International)
3 Park Avenue
New York, NY 10016-5990
Phone: 212-591-8131
Fax: 212-591-7143
E-mail: PhillipsM@asme.org

KENNETH ANDREW ROE SCHOLARSHIP

Award for college juniors and seniors who are members of the American Society of Mechanical Engineers. Must be a U.S. citizen and North American resident. Must be pursuing studies in an ABET-accredited mechanical engineering or mechanical engineering technology program. Application available online http://www.asme.org/education/enged/aid

Academic Fields/Career Goals: Mechanical Engineering.

Award: Scholarship for use in junior or senior years; not renewable. *Number:* 1. *Amount:* $10,000.

Eligibility Requirements: Applicant must be enrolled or expecting to enroll full-time at a two-year or four-year institution or university. Available to U.S. citizens.

Application Requirements: Application, essay, financial need analysis, references, self-addressed stamped envelope, transcript, applicants must be ASME student members. *Deadline:* March 15.

Contact: Maisha Phillips, Coordinator, Student Development ASME
American Society of Mechanical Engineers (ASME International)
3 Park Avenue
New York, NY 10016-5990
Phone: 212-591-8131
Fax: 212-591-7143
E-mail: phillipsm@asme.org

MELVIN R. GREEN SCHOLARSHIP

Award for college juniors and seniors who are members of the American Society of Mechanical Engineers. Must be enrolled at a four-year college or university, and pursuing studies in mechanical engineering or mechanical engineering technology. Application is available online http://www.asme.org/education/enged/aid

Academic Fields/Career Goals: Mechanical Engineering.

Award: Scholarship for use in junior or senior years; not renewable. *Number:* up to 2. *Amount:* up to $3500.

Eligibility Requirements: Applicant must be enrolled or expecting to enroll full-time at a two-year or four-year institution or university. Available to U.S. and non-U.S. citizens.

Application Requirements: Application, essay, financial need analysis, references, self-addressed stamped envelope, transcript, applicants must be ASME student members. *Deadline:* March 15.

Contact: Maisha Phillips, Coordinator, Student Development ASME
American Society of Mechanical Engineers (ASME International)
3 Park Avenue
New York, NY 10016-5990
Phone: 212-591-8131
Fax: 212-591-7143
E-mail: phillipsm@asme.org

ROBERT F. SAMMATARO PRESSURE VESSELS AND PIPING DIVISION MEMORIAL SCHOLARSHIP

One award of $1000 scholarship to an ASME student member, preferably with an interest in pressure vessels and piping. Must be U.S. citizen. Deadline: March 15. Application available online: http://www.asme.org/education/enged/aid

Academic Fields/Career Goals: Mechanical Engineering.

Award: Scholarship for use in sophomore, junior, or senior years; not renewable. *Number:* 1. *Amount:* $1000.

Eligibility Requirements: Applicant must be enrolled or expecting to enroll full-time at a four-year institution or university. Available to U.S. citizens.

Application Requirements: Application, essay, financial need analysis, references, transcript. *Deadline:* March 15.

Contact: Maisha Phillips, Coordinator, Student Development ASME
American Society of Mechanical Engineers (ASME International)
3 Park Avenue
New York, NY 10016-5990
Phone: 212-591-8131
Fax: 212-591-7143
E-mail: phillipsm@asme.org

WILLIAM J. & MARIJANE E. ADAMS, JR. SCHOLARSHIP

Award for student with a minimum 2.5 GPA who is at least a sophomore and attends a college or university in ASME Region IX (California, Nevada, and Hawaii). Must be pursuing studies in mechanical engineering or mechanical engineering technology and demonstrate special interest in product development and design. Must be a member of the American Society of Mechanical Engineers. Application available online: http://www.asme.org/education/enged/aid

Academic Fields/Career Goals: Mechanical Engineering.

Award: Scholarship for use in sophomore, junior, or senior years; not renewable. *Number:* 1. *Amount:* $2500.

Eligibility Requirements: Applicant must be enrolled or expecting to enroll full-time at a two-year or four-year institution or university and studying in California, Hawaii, or Nevada. Applicant must have 2.5 GPA or higher. Available to U.S. citizens.

Application Requirements: Application, essay, financial need analysis, references, self-addressed stamped envelope, transcript. *Deadline:* March 15.

Contact: Maisha Phillips, Coordinator, Student Development ASME
American Society of Mechanical Engineers (ASME International)
3 Park Avenue
New York, NY 10016-5990
Phone: 212-591-8131
Fax: 212-591-7143
E-mail: phillipsm@asme.org

AMERICAN SOCIETY OF MECHANICAL ENGINEERS AUXILIARY, INC.   http://www.asme.org

AGNES MALAKATE KEZIOS SCHOLARSHIP

Available to college juniors for use in final year at a four-year college. Five-year students may apply in fourth year. Must be majoring in mechanical engineering, be member of a student section of ASME (if available), and exhibit leadership values. Must be a U.S. citizen enrolled in a college/university in the U.S. that has ABET-accreditation.

Academic Fields/Career Goals: Mechanical Engineering.

Award: Scholarship for use in junior or senior years; not renewable. *Number:* varies. *Amount:* up to $2000.

Eligibility Requirements: Applicant must be enrolled or expecting to enroll full-time at a four-year institution or university. Available to U.S. citizens.

Application Requirements: Application, autobiography, references, transcript. *Deadline:* March 15.

Contact: Alverta Cover, Undergraduate Scholarships
American Society of Mechanical Engineers Auxiliary, Inc.
5425 Caldwell Mill Road
Birmingham, AL 35242
Phone: 205-991-6109
E-mail: undergradauxsch@asme.org

ALLEN J. BALDWIN SCHOLARSHIP

Available to college juniors for use in final year at a four-year college. Five-year students may apply in fourth year. Must be majoring in mechanical engineering, be member of a student section of ASME (if available), and exhibit leadership values. Must be U.S. citizen enrolled in a college/university in the U.S. that has ABET-accreditation.

Academic Fields/Career Goals: Mechanical Engineering.

Award: Scholarship for use in junior or senior years; not renewable. *Number:* varies. *Amount:* up to $2000.

Eligibility Requirements: Applicant must be enrolled or expecting to enroll full-time at a four-year institution or university. Available to U.S. citizens.

Application Requirements: Application, autobiography, financial need analysis, references, self-addressed stamped envelope, transcript. *Deadline:* March 15.

Contact: Alverta Cover, Undergraduate Scholarships
American Society of Mechanical Engineers Auxiliary, Inc.
5425 Caldwell Mill Road
Birmingham, AL 35242
Phone: 205-991-6109
E-mail: undergradauxsch@asme.org

AMERICAN SOCIETY OF MECHANICAL ENGINEERS-AMERICAN SOCIETY OF MECHANICAL ENGINEERS AUXILIARY FIRST CLARKE SCHOLARSHIP

Scholarships available for high school seniors only, who are active on FIRST teams. Applicant must be a member or nominated by a member of ASME or ASME Auxiliary . Must enroll full time in an ABET accredited mechanical engineering or mechanical engineering technology program.

Academic Fields/Career Goals: Mechanical Engineering.

Award: Scholarship for use in freshman year; not renewable. *Number:* up to 10. *Amount:* up to $5000.

Eligibility Requirements: Applicant must be high school student and planning to enroll or expecting to enroll full-time at a four-year institution or university. Available to U.S. citizens.

American Society of Mechanical Engineers Auxiliary, Inc. (continued)

Application Requirements: Application, financial need analysis, resume, transcript, nomination letter from an ASME member, ASME Auxiliary member, or student member. *Deadline:* March 15.

Contact: Maisha Phillips, ASME Auxiliary FIRST Clarke Scholarship
American Society of Mechanical Engineers Auxiliary, Inc.
3 Park Avenue, 23-E5
New York, NY 10016-5990
Phone: 800-843-2763
E-mail: PhillipsM@asme.org

BERNA LOU CARTWRIGHT SCHOLARSHIP

Available to college juniors for use in final year at a four-year college. Five-year students may apply in fourth year. Must be majoring in mechanical engineering, be member of a student section of ASME (if available), and exhibit leadership values. Must be a U.S. citizen enrolled in a college/ university in the U.S. that has ABET-accreditation.

Academic Fields/Career Goals: Mechanical Engineering.

Award: Scholarship for use in junior or senior years; not renewable. *Number:* 2–10. *Amount:* up to $2000.

Eligibility Requirements: Applicant must be enrolled or expecting to enroll full-time at a four-year institution or university and must have an interest in leadership. Available to U.S. citizens.

Application Requirements: Application, autobiography, references, self-addressed stamped envelope, transcript. *Deadline:* March 15.

Contact: Alverta Cover, Undergraduate Scholarships
American Society of Mechanical Engineers Auxiliary, Inc.
5425 Caldwell Mill Road
Birmingham, AL 35242
Phone: 205-991-6109
E-mail: undergradauxsch@asme.org

SYLVIA W. FARNY SCHOLARSHIP

One-time awards of $2000 to ASME student members for the final year of undergraduate study in mechanical engineering. Must be a U.S. citizen enrolled in a college/university in the U.S. that has ABET-accreditation.

Academic Fields/Career Goals: Mechanical Engineering.

Award: Scholarship for use in junior or senior years; not renewable. *Number:* 2–10. *Amount:* $2000.

Eligibility Requirements: Applicant must be enrolled or expecting to enroll full-time at a four-year institution or university. Available to U.S. citizens.

Application Requirements: Application, references, transcript. *Deadline:* March 15.

Contact: Alverta Cover, Undergraduate Scholarships
American Society of Mechanical Engineers Auxiliary, Inc.
5425 Caldwell Mill Road
Birmingham, AL 35242
Phone: 205-991-6109
E-mail: covera@asme.org

AMERICAN SOCIETY OF NAVAL ENGINEERS
http://www.navalengineers.org

AMERICAN SOCIETY OF NAVAL ENGINEERS SCHOLARSHIP
• See page 90

ASSOCIATED BUILDERS AND CONTRACTORS SCHOLARSHIP PROGRAM
http://www.abc.org

TRIMMER EDUCATION FOUNDATION SCHOLARSHIPS FOR CONSTRUCTION MANAGEMENT
• See page 172

ASSOCIATION FOR FACILITIES ENGINEERING (AFE)

ASSOCIATION FOR FACILITIES ENGINEERING CEDAR VALLEY CHAPTER # 132 SCHOLARSHIP
• See page 120

ASSOCIATION FOR WOMEN IN SCIENCE EDUCATIONAL FOUNDATION
http://www.awis.org/ed_foundation.html

ASSOCIATION FOR WOMEN IN SCIENCE COLLEGE SCHOLARSHIP
• See page 86

ASTRONAUT SCHOLARSHIP FOUNDATION
http://www.astronautscholarship.org

ASTRONAUT SCHOLARSHIP FOUNDATION
• See page 92

AUTOMOTIVE HALL OF FAME
http://www.automotivehalloffame.org

AUTOMOTIVE HALL OF FAME EDUCATIONAL FUNDS
• See page 162

BARRY M. GOLDWATER SCHOLARSHIP AND EXCELLENCE IN EDUCATION FOUNDATION
http://www.act.org/goldwater

BARRY M. GOLDWATER SCHOLARSHIP AND EXCELLENCE IN EDUCATION PROGRAM
• See page 92

CUBAN AMERICAN NATIONAL FOUNDATION
http://www.canf.org

MAS FAMILY SCHOLARSHIPS
• See page 146

EAST LOS ANGELES COMMUNITY UNION (TELACU) EDUCATION FOUNDATION
http://www.telacu.com

LINC TELACU ENGINEERING AWARD
• See page 163

ELECTROCHEMICAL SOCIETY, INC.
http://www.electrochem.org

DANIEL CUBICCIOTTI STUDENT AWARD OF THE SAN FRANCISCO SECTION OF THE ELECTROCHEMICAL SOCIETY, SPONSORED BY STRUCTURAL INTEGRITY ASSOCIATES
• See page 137

H.H. DOW MEMORIAL STUDENT ACHIEVEMENT AWARD OF THE INDUSTRIAL ELECTROLYSIS AND ELECTROCHEMICAL ENGINEERING DIVISION OF THE ELECTROCHEMICAL SOCIETY, INC.
• See page 137

STUDENT ACHIEVEMENT AWARDS OF THE INDUSTRIAL ELECTROLYSIS AND ELECTROCHEMICAL ENGINEERING DIVISION OF THE ELECTROCHEMICAL SOCIETY, INC.
• See page 137

STUDENT RESEARCH AWARDS OF THE BATTERY DIVISION OF THE ELECTROCHEMICAL SOCIETY, INC.
• See page 137

FLORIDA EDUCATIONAL FACILITIES PLANNERS' ASSOCIATION
http://www.fefpa.org

FEFPA ASSISTANTSHIP
• See page 99

GEORGE BIRD GRINNELL AMERICAN INDIAN FUND
http://www.grinnellfund.org/

AL QOYAWAYMA AWARD
• See page 163

HISPANIC COLLEGE FUND, INC.
http://www.hispanicfund.org

DEPARTMENT OF ENERGY SCHOLARSHIP PROGRAM
• See page 148

HISPANIC ENGINEER NATIONAL ACHIEVEMENT AWARDS CORPORATION (HENAAC)
http://www.henaac.org

HISPANIC ENGINEER NATIONAL ACHIEVEMENT AWARDS CORPORATION SCHOLARSHIP PROGRAM

HISPANIC SCHOLARSHIP FUND
http://www.hsf.net

HSF/GENERAL MOTORS SCHOLARSHIP

HSF/SOCIETY OF HISPANIC PROFESSIONAL ENGINEERS, INC. SCHOLARSHIP PROGRAM

HSF/TOYOTA SCHOLARSHIP PROGRAM

INDEPENDENT LABORATORIES INSTITUTE SCHOLARSHIP ALLIANCE
http://www.acil.org

INDEPENDENT LABORATORIES INSTITUTE SCHOLARSHIP ALLIANCE

INSTRUMENTATION, SYSTEMS, AND AUTOMATION SOCIETY (ISA)
http://www.isa.org

INSTRUMENTATION, SYSTEMS, AND AUTOMATION SOCIETY (ISA) SCHOLARSHIP PROGRAM

INTERNATIONAL SOCIETY FOR OPTICAL ENGINEERING-SPIE
http://www.spie.org/info/scholarships

SPIE EDUCATIONAL SCHOLARSHIPS IN OPTICAL SCIENCE AND ENGINEERING

JORGE MAS CANOSA FREEDOM FOUNDATION
http://www.canf.org

MAS FAMILY SCHOLARSHIP AWARD

LOS ANGELES COUNCIL OF BLACK PROFESSIONAL ENGINEERS
http://www.lablackengineers.org

AL-BEN SCHOLARSHIP FOR ACADEMIC INCENTIVE

AL-BEN SCHOLARSHIP FOR PROFESSIONAL MERIT

AL-BEN SCHOLARSHIP FOR SCHOLASTIC ACHIEVEMENT

MAINE EDUCATION SERVICES
http://www.mesfoundation.com/

MAINE METAL PRODUCTS ASSOCIATION SCHOLARSHIP

Awards available for individuals who have demonstrated an outstanding record and overall potential to attend an institution of higher learning majoring in: Mechanical Engineering, Machine Tool Technician, Sheet Metal Fabrication, Welding, CADCAM for Metals Industry Restricted to the study of metal working trades.

Academic Fields/Career Goals: Mechanical Engineering; Trade/Technical Specialties.

Award: Scholarship for use in freshman year; renewable. *Amount:* $250–$1000.

Eligibility Requirements: Applicant must be enrolled or expecting to enroll full or part-time at a technical institution and resident of Maine. Available to U.S. citizens.

Application Requirements: Application, financial need analysis, references, transcript. *Deadline:* June 1.

Contact: Kim Benjamin, Vice President of Operations
Maine Education Services
One City Center
11th Floor
Portland, ME 04101
Phone: 207-791-3600
Fax: 207-791-3616
E-mail: kbenjamin@mesfoundation.com

MAINE METAL PRODUCTS ASSOCIATION
http://www.maine-metals.org

MAINE METAL PRODUCTS ASSOCIATION SCHOLARSHIP PROGRAM

MEAD WESTVACO CORPORATION
http://www.meadwestvaco.com

WESTVACO/WICKLIFFE SCHOLARSHIP

MICHIGAN SOCIETY OF PROFESSIONAL ENGINEERS
http://www.michiganspe.org

MICHIGAN SOCIETY OF PROFESSIONAL ENGINEERS UNDESIGNATED GRANT

MICRON TECHNOLOGY FOUNDATION, INC.
http://www.micron.com

MICRON SCIENCE AND TECHNOLOGY SCHOLARS PROGRAM

MIDWEST ROOFING CONTRACTORS ASSOCIATION
http://www.mrca.org

MRCA FOUNDATION SCHOLARSHIP PROGRAM

NASA DELAWARE SPACE GRANT CONSORTIUM
http://www.delspace.org

NASA DELAWARE SPACE GRANT UNDERGRADUATE TUITION SCHOLARSHIP

NASA MONTANA SPACE GRANT CONSORTIUM
http://www.spacegrant.montana.edu

MONTANA SPACE GRANT SCHOLARSHIP PROGRAM

NATIONAL ASSOCIATION OF WOMEN IN CONSTRUCTION
http://nawic.org

NAWIC UNDERGRADUATE SCHOLARSHIPS

NATIONAL SOCIETY OF PROFESSIONAL ENGINEERS
http://www.nspe.org

MAUREEN L. AND HOWARD N. BLITMAN, PE SCHOLARSHIP TO PROMOTE DIVERSITY IN ENGINEERING

NATIONAL SOCIETY OF PROFESSIONAL ENGINEERS/AUXILIARY SCHOLARSHIP

PAUL H. ROBBINS HONORARY SCHOLARSHIP

PROFESSIONAL ENGINEERS IN INDUSTRY SCHOLARSHIP

National Society of Professional Engineers (continued)

VIRGINIA HENRY MEMORIAL SCHOLARSHIP
- *See page 167*

OREGON STUDENT ASSISTANCE COMMISSION
http://www.osac.state.or.us

AMERICAN COUNCIL OF ENGINEERING COMPANIES OF OREGON SCHOLARSHIP
- *See page 167*

KEY TECHNOLOGY SCHOLARSHIP
- *See page 84*

PLUMBING-HEATING-COOLING CONTRACTORS ASSOCIATION EDUCATION FOUNDATION
http://www.phccweb.org

BRADFORD WHITE CORPORATION SCHOLARSHIP
- *See page 102*

DELTA FAUCET COMPANY SCHOLARSHIP PROGRAM
- *See page 102*

PHCC EDUCATIONAL FOUNDATION NEED-BASED SCHOLARSHIP
- *See page 102*

PHCC EDUCATIONAL FOUNDATION SCHOLARSHIP PROGRAM
- *See page 103*

PROFESSIONAL CONSTRUCTION ESTIMATORS ASSOCIATION
http://www.pcea.org

TED WILSON MEMORIAL SCHOLARSHIP FOUNDATION
- *See page 212*

ROBERT H. MOLLOHAN FAMILY CHARITABLE FOUNDATION, INC.
http://www.mollohanfoundation.org

HIGH TECHNOLOGY SCHOLARS PROGRAM
- *See page 141*

ROCKY MOUNTAIN COAL MINING INSTITUTE
http://www.rmcmi.org

ROCKY MOUNTAIN COAL MINING INSTITUTE SCHOLARSHIP
- *See page 167*

SIGMA XI, THE SCIENTIFIC RESEARCH SOCIETY
http://www.sigmaxi.org

SIGMA XI GRANTS-IN-AID OF RESEARCH
- *See page 84*

SOCIETY FOR MINING, METALLURGY AND EXPLORATION - CENTRAL WYOMING SECTION

COATES, WOLFF, RUSSELL MINING INDUSTRY SCHOLARSHIP
- *See page 95*

SOCIETY OF AUTOMOTIVE ENGINEERS
http://www.sae.org

BMW/SAE ENGINEERING SCHOLARSHIP
- *See page 129*

EDWARD D. HENDRICKSON/SAE ENGINEERING SCHOLARSHIP
- *See page 129*

RALPH K. HILLQUIST HONORARY SAE SCHOLARSHIP
- *See page 270*

TMC/SAE DONALD D. DAWSON TECHNICAL SCHOLARSHIP
- *See page 129*

YANMAR/SAE SCHOLARSHIP
- *See page 271*

SOCIETY OF HISPANIC PROFESSIONAL ENGINEERS FOUNDATION
http://www.henaac.org

SOCIETY OF HISPANIC PROFESSIONAL ENGINEERS FOUNDATION
- *See page 168*

SOCIETY OF MANUFACTURING ENGINEERS EDUCATION FOUNDATION
http://www.sme.org

DOWNRIVER DETROIT CHAPTER 198 SCHOLARSHIP
- *See page 273*

FORT WAYNE CHAPTER 56 SCHOLARSHIP
- *See page 274*

NORTH CENTRAL REGION 9 SCHOLARSHIP
- *See page 275*

PHOENIX CHAPTER 67 SCHOLARSHIP
- *See page 275*

WICHITA CHAPTER 52 SCHOLARSHIP
- *See page 276*

WILLIAM E. WEISEL SCHOLARSHIP FUND
- *See page 246*

SOCIETY OF PLASTICS ENGINEERS (SPE) FOUNDATION
http://www.4spe.com

SOCIETY OF PLASTICS ENGINEERS SCHOLARSHIP PROGRAM
- *See page 168*

SOCIETY OF WOMEN ENGINEERS
http://www.swe.org

AGILENT MENTORING SCHOLARSHIP
- *See page 194*

BECHTEL CORPORATION SCHOLARSHIP
- *See page 176*

CHEVRON TEXACO CORPORATION SCHOLARSHIPS
- *See page 168*

DAIMLER CHRYSLER CORPORATION SCHOLARSHIP
- *See page 246*

DELL COMPUTER CORPORATION SCHOLARSHIPS
- *See page 194*

DUPONT COMPANY SCHOLARSHIPS
- *See page 168*

GENERAL MOTORS FOUNDATION UNDERGRADUATE SCHOLARSHIPS
- *See page 168*

GUIDANT CORPORATION SCHOLARSHIP
- *See page 195*

LOCKHEED AERONAUTICS COMPANY SCHOLARSHIPS
- *See page 246*

NORTHROP GRUMMAN CORPORATION SCHOLARSHIPS
- *See page 130*

TEXAS ENGINEERING FOUNDATION
http://www.tspe.org/

TEXAS SOCIETY OF PROFESSIONAL ENGINEERS (TSPE) REGIONAL SCHOLARSHIPS
- *See page 169*

TURNER CONSTRUCTION COMPANY
http://www.turnerconstruction.com

YOUTHFORCE 2020 SCHOLARSHIP PROGRAM
- *See page 103*

UNITED NEGRO COLLEGE FUND
http://www.uncf.org

CARGILL SCHOLARSHIP PROGRAM
- *See page 70*

CHEVRON/TEXACO SCHOLARS PROGRAM
• See page 177

CON EDISON SCHOLARSHIP
• See page 70

SBC FOUNDATION SCHOLARSHIP
• See page 156

UPS CORPORATE SCHOLARS PROGRAM/INTERNSHIP
• See page 157

UNIVERSITIES SPACE RESEARCH ASSOCIATION
http://www.usra.edu

UNIVERSITIES SPACE RESEARCH ASSOCIATION SCHOLARSHIP PROGRAM
• See page 96

UTAH SOCIETY OF PROFESSIONAL ENGINEERS
http://www.uspeonline.com

UTAH SOCIETY OF PROFESSIONAL ENGINEERS SCHOLARSHIP
• See page 169

VERTICAL FLIGHT FOUNDATION
http://www.vtol.org

VERTICAL FLIGHT FOUNDATION SCHOLARSHIP
• See page 132

WOMEN IN AVIATION, INTERNATIONAL
http://www.wai.org

DELTA AIR LINES ENGINEERING SCHOLARSHIP
• See page 132

WYOMING TRUCKING ASSOCIATION

WYOMING TRUCKING ASSOCIATION TRUST FUND SCHOLARSHIP
• See page 158

XEROX
http://www.xerox.com

TECHNICAL MINORITY SCHOLARSHIP
• See page 169

METEOROLOGY/ATMOSPHERIC SCIENCE

ALABAMA FUNERAL DIRECTORS ASSOCIATION, INC.
http://www.nfda.org/careers/scholar/index.html

ALABAMA FUNERAL DIRECTORS ASSOCIATION SCHOLARSHIP

Two $1,000 scholarships available to students who are resident of Alabama with an associate's degree or its credit hour equivalent, a portion of which is in funeral service education.

Academic Fields/Career Goals: Meteorology/Atmospheric Science.

Award: Scholarship for use in freshman, sophomore, junior, or senior years; not renewable. *Number:* 2. *Amount:* $1000.

Eligibility Requirements: Applicant must be enrolled or expecting to enroll full or part-time at an institution or university and resident of Alabama. Available to U.S. citizens.

Application Requirements: Application. *Deadline:* varies.

Contact: Alabama Funeral Directors Association, Inc.
PO Box 241281
Montgomery, AL 36124-1281
Phone: 334-277-9565
Fax: 334-277-8028

ALABAMA STATE DEPARTMENT OF EDUCATION
http://www.alsde.edu

MATH AND SCIENCE SCHOLARSHIP PROGRAM FOR ALABAMA TEACHERS
• See page 135

AMERICAN INDIAN SCIENCE AND ENGINEERING SOCIETY
http://www.aises.org

A.T. ANDERSON MEMORIAL SCHOLARSHIP
• See page 89

BURLINGTON NORTHERN SANTA FE FOUNDATION SCHOLARSHIP
• See page 89

ENVIRONMENTAL PROTECTION AGENCY TRIBAL LANDS ENVIRONMENTAL SCIENCE SCHOLARSHIP
• See page 135

AMERICAN METEOROLOGICAL SOCIETY
http://www.ametsoc.org/AMS

AMERICAN METEOROLOGICAL SOCIETY 75TH ANNIVERSARY SCHOLARSHIP

Award for full-time college juniors and seniors majoring in atmospheric or related oceanic and hydrologic sciences. Must be enrolled at a U.S. institution. Cumulative GPA of 3.25 required. One-time award of $2000.

Academic Fields/Career Goals: Meteorology/Atmospheric Science.

Award: Scholarship for use in junior or senior years; not renewable. *Number:* 13. *Amount:* $2000.

Eligibility Requirements: Applicant must be enrolled or expecting to enroll full-time at a two-year or four-year institution or university. Available to U.S. citizens.

Application Requirements: Application, essay, references, transcript. *Deadline:* February 13.

Contact: Donna Fernandez, Development Program Coordinator
American Meteorological Society
45 Beacon Street
Boston, MA 02108-3693
Phone: 617-227-2426 Ext. 246
Fax: 617-742-8718
E-mail: dfernand@ametsoc.org

AMERICAN METEOROLOGICAL SOCIETY DR. PEDRO GRAU UNDERGRADUATE SCHOLARSHIP

Award for full-time college juniors and seniors majoring in atmospheric or related oceanic and hydrologic sciences. Must be enrolled at a U.S. institution. Cumulative GPA of 3.25 required. One-time award of $2500.

Academic Fields/Career Goals: Meteorology/Atmospheric Science.

Award: Scholarship for use in junior or senior years; not renewable. *Number:* 1. *Amount:* up to $2500.

Eligibility Requirements: Applicant must be enrolled or expecting to enroll full-time at a two-year or four-year institution or university. Available to U.S. citizens.

Application Requirements: Application, essay, references, transcript. *Deadline:* February 10.

Contact: Donna Fernandez, Development Program Coordinator
American Meteorological Society
45 Beacon Street
Boston, MA 02108-3693
Phone: 617-227-2426 Ext. 246
Fax: 617-742-8718
E-mail: dfernand@ametsoc.org

AMERICAN METEOROLOGICAL SOCIETY HOWARD H. HANKS, JR. METEOROLOGICAL SCHOLARSHIP

Award for college juniors and seniors majoring in atmospheric or related oceanic and hydrologic sciences. Must be enrolled full-time at a U.S. institution with a 3.25 cumulative GPA. U.S. citizenship required. One-time award of $700.

Academic Fields/Career Goals: Meteorology/Atmospheric Science.

Award: Scholarship for use in junior or senior years; not renewable. *Number:* varies. *Amount:* $700.

Eligibility Requirements: Applicant must be enrolled or expecting to enroll full-time at a four-year institution. Available to U.S. citizens.

American Meteorological Society (continued)

Application Requirements: Application, essay, references, transcript. *Deadline:* February 13.

Contact: Donna Fernandez, Development Program Coordinator
American Meteorological Society
45 Beacon Street
Boston, MA 02108-3693
Phone: 617-227-2426 Ext. 246
Fax: 617-742-8718
E-mail: dfernand@ametsoc.org

AMERICAN METEOROLOGICAL SOCIETY HOWARD T. ORVILLE METEOROLOGY SCHOLARSHIP

One-time award for college juniors and seniors majoring in atmospheric or related oceanic and hydrologic sciences. Must be enrolled full-time at a U.S. institution with a 3.25 cumulative GPA.

Academic Fields/Career Goals: Meteorology/Atmospheric Science.

Award: Scholarship for use in junior or senior years; not renewable. *Number:* varies. *Amount:* up to $5000.

Eligibility Requirements: Applicant must be enrolled or expecting to enroll full-time at an institution or university. Available to U.S. citizens.

Application Requirements: Application, essay, references, transcript. *Deadline:* February 13.

Contact: Donna Fernandez, Development Program Coordinator
American Meteorological Society
45 Beacon Street
Boston, MA 02108-3693
Phone: 617-227-2426 Ext. 246
Fax: 617-742-8718
E-mail: dfernand@ametsoc.org

AMERICAN METEOROLOGICAL SOCIETY INDUSTRY UNDERGRADUATE SCHOLARSHIPS
• See page 89

AMERICAN METEOROLOGICAL SOCIETY MARK J. SCHROEDER SCHOLARSHIP IN METEOROLOGY

Award for full-time college juniors and seniors majoring in atmospheric or related oceanic and hydrologic sciences. Must be enrolled at a U.S. institution and demonstrate financial need. Cumulative GPA of 3.25 is required.

Academic Fields/Career Goals: Meteorology/Atmospheric Science.

Award: Scholarship for use in junior or senior years; not renewable. *Number:* varies. *Amount:* up to $5000.

Eligibility Requirements: Applicant must be enrolled or expecting to enroll full-time at a two-year or four-year institution or university. Available to U.S. citizens.

Application Requirements: Application, essay, financial need analysis, references, transcript. *Deadline:* February 13.

Contact: Donna Fernandez, Development Program Coordinator
American Meteorological Society
45 Beacon Street
Boston, MA 02108-3693
Phone: 617-227-2426 Ext. 246
Fax: 617-742-8718
E-mail: dfernand@ametsoc.org

AMERICAN METEOROLOGICAL SOCIETY RICHARD AND HELEN HAGEMEYER SCHOLARSHIP

Award for full-time college juniors and seniors majoring in atmospheric or related oceanic and hydrologic sciences. Must be enrolled at a U.S. institution. Cumulative GPA of 3.25 is required. One-time award of $3000.

Academic Fields/Career Goals: Meteorology/Atmospheric Science.

Award: Scholarship for use in junior or senior years; not renewable. *Number:* 1. *Amount:* $3000.

Eligibility Requirements: Applicant must be enrolled or expecting to enroll full-time at a two-year or four-year institution or university. Available to U.S. citizens.

Application Requirements: Application, essay, references, transcript. *Deadline:* February 10.

Contact: Donna Fernandez, Development Program Coordinator
American Meteorological Society
45 Beacon Street
Boston, MA 02108-3693
Phone: 617-227-2426 Ext. 246
Fax: 617-742-8718
E-mail: dfernand@ametsoc.org

AMERICAN METEOROLOGICAL SOCIETY WERNER A. BAUM UNDERGRADUATE SCHOLARSHIP

Award for full-time college juniors and seniors majoring in atmospheric or related oceanic and hydrologic sciences. Must be enrolled at a U.S. institution and demonstrate financial need. Cumulative GPA of 3.25 is required. One-time award of $5000.

Academic Fields/Career Goals: Meteorology/Atmospheric Science.

Award: Scholarship for use in junior or senior years; not renewable. *Number:* varies. *Amount:* $5000.

Eligibility Requirements: Applicant must be enrolled or expecting to enroll full-time at a two-year or four-year institution or university. Available to U.S. citizens.

Application Requirements: Application, essay, financial need analysis, references, transcript. *Deadline:* February 13.

Contact: Donna Fernandez, Development Program Coordinator
American Meteorological Society
45 Beacon Street
Boston, MA 02108-3693
Phone: 617-227-2426 Ext. 246
Fax: 617-742-8718
E-mail: dfernand@ametsoc.org

AMERICAN METEOROLOGICAL SOCIETY/INDUSTRY MINORITY SCHOLARSHIPS

Two-year scholarships of $3000 per year for minority students entering their freshman year of college. Must plan to pursue careers in the atmospheric and related oceanic and hydrologic sciences. Must be U.S. citizen or permanent resident to apply.

Academic Fields/Career Goals: Meteorology/Atmospheric Science.

Award: Scholarship for use in freshman year; not renewable. *Number:* varies. *Amount:* up to $3000.

Eligibility Requirements: Applicant must be American Indian/Alaska Native, Asian/Pacific Islander, Black (non-Hispanic), or Hispanic; high school student and planning to enroll or expecting to enroll full-time at a two-year or four-year institution or university. Available to U.S. citizens.

Application Requirements: Application, references, test scores, transcript. *Deadline:* February 10.

Contact: Donna Fernandez, Development Program Coordinator
American Meteorological Society
45 Beacon Street
Boston, MA 02108-3693
Phone: 617-227-2426 Ext. 246
Fax: 617-742-8718
E-mail: dfernand@ametsoc.org

CARL W. KREITZBERG ENDOWED SCHOLARSHIP
• See page 292

ETHAN AND ALLAN MURPHY MEMORIAL SCHOLARSHIP

Award for full-time college juniors and seniors majoring in atmospheric or related oceanic and hydrologic science. Must show clear intent to make the atmospheric or related sciences a career. Must be enrolled in an accredited U.S. institution. Minimum 3.25 GPA required.

Academic Fields/Career Goals: Meteorology/Atmospheric Science.

Award: Scholarship for use in junior or senior years; not renewable. *Number:* varies. *Amount:* $2000.

Eligibility Requirements: Applicant must be enrolled or expecting to enroll full-time at a two-year or four-year institution or university. Available to U.S. citizens.

Application Requirements: Application, essay, references, transcript. *Deadline:* February 10.

Contact: Donna Fernandez, Development Program Coordinator
American Meteorological Society
45 Beacon Street
Boston, MA 02108-3693
Phone: 617-227-2426 Ext. 246
Fax: 617-742-8718
E-mail: dfernand@ametsoc.org

FATHER JAMES B. MACELWANE ANNUAL AWARDS

Available to enrolled undergraduates who submit a paper on a phase of atmospheric sciences with a statement from a supervisor on the student's original contribution to the work. Minimum 3.0 GPA required. No more than two students from any one institution may enter papers in one contest. Must submit letter from department head or faculty member confirming applicant's undergraduate status and paper's originality.

Academic Fields/Career Goals: Meteorology/Atmospheric Science.

Award: Prize for use in freshman, sophomore, junior, or senior years; not renewable. *Number:* 1. *Amount:* up to $300.

Eligibility Requirements: Applicant must be enrolled or expecting to enroll at a four-year institution. Applicant must have 3.0 GPA or higher. Available to U.S. citizens.

Application Requirements: Applicant must enter a contest, essay, references, letter of application. *Deadline:* June 11.

Contact: Donna Fernandez, Development Program Coordinator
American Meteorological Society
45 Beacon Street
Boston, MA 02108-3693
Phone: 617-227-2426 Ext. 246
Fax: 617-742-8718
E-mail: dfernand@ametsoc.org

GEORGE S. BENTON SCHOLARSHIP

Scholarships are awarded to college juniors and seniors at accredited U.S. institutions for study in atmospheric sciences. Required GPA is 3.25 and above.

Academic Fields/Career Goals: Meteorology/Atmospheric Science.

Award: Scholarship for use in junior or senior years; not renewable. *Amount:* up to $3500.

Eligibility Requirements: Applicant must be enrolled or expecting to enroll full-time at a two-year or four-year institution or university. Available to U.S. citizens.

Application Requirements: Application, financial need analysis, resume, transcript. *Deadline:* February 10.

Contact: Donna Fernandez, Development Program Coordinator
American Meteorological Society
45 Beacon Street
Boston, MA 02108-3693
Phone: 617-227-2426 Ext. 246
Fax: 617-742-8718
E-mail: dfernand@ametsoc.org

GUILLERMO SALAZAR RODRIGUES SCHOLARSHIP

Award for full-time college juniors and seniors majoring in atmospheric or related oceanic and hydrologic science. Must show clear intent to make the atmospheric or related sciences a career. Must be enrolled in an accredited U.S. institution. Minimum 3.25 GPA required.

Academic Fields/Career Goals: Meteorology/Atmospheric Science.

Award: Scholarship for use in junior or senior years; not renewable. *Number:* 1. *Amount:* up to $2500.

Eligibility Requirements: Applicant must be enrolled or expecting to enroll at a two-year or four-year institution or university. Available to U.S. citizens.

Application Requirements: Application, essay, references, transcript. *Deadline:* February 10.

Contact: Donna Fernandez, Development Program Coordinator
American Meteorological Society
45 Beacon Street
Boston, MA 02108-3693
Phone: 617-227-2426 Ext. 246
Fax: 617-742-8718
E-mail: dfernand@ametsoc.org

JOHN R. HOPE SCHOLARSHIP

Award for full-time college juniors and seniors majoring in atmospheric or related oceanic and hydrologic science. Must show clear intent to make the atmospheric or related science a career. Minimum 3.25 GPA required. Must be enrolled in an accredited U.S. institution.

Academic Fields/Career Goals: Meteorology/Atmospheric Science.

Award: Scholarship for use in junior or senior years; not renewable. *Number:* varies. *Amount:* up to $2500.

Eligibility Requirements: Applicant must be enrolled or expecting to enroll full-time at a two-year or four-year institution or university. Available to U.S. citizens.

Application Requirements: Application, essay, references, transcript. *Deadline:* February 10.

Contact: Donna Fernandez, Development Program Coordinator
American Meteorological Society
45 Beacon Street
Boston, MA 02108-3693
Phone: 617-227-2426 Ext. 246
Fax: 617-742-8718
E-mail: dfernand@ametsoc.org

LOREN W. CROW SCHOLARSHIP

One-time award for college juniors and seniors who are majoring in atmospheric or related oceanic and hydrologic sciences. Must be enrolled full-time at a U.S. institution with a 3.25 GPA. Must be a U.S. citizen.

Academic Fields/Career Goals: Meteorology/Atmospheric Science.

Award: Scholarship for use in junior or senior years; not renewable. *Number:* varies. *Amount:* up to $2000.

Eligibility Requirements: Applicant must be enrolled or expecting to enroll at a two-year or four-year institution or university. Available to U.S. citizens.

Application Requirements: Application, essay, references, transcript. *Deadline:* February 10.

Contact: Donna Fernandez, Development Program Coordinator
American Meteorological Society
45 Beacon Street
Boston, MA 02108-3693
Phone: 617-227-2426 Ext. 246
Fax: 617-742-8718
E-mail: dfernand@ametsoc.org

OM AND SARASWATI BAHETHI SCHOLARSHIP

Assists students pursuing degrees in the atmospheric and related sciences. Minimum GPA of 3.25 required.

Academic Fields/Career Goals: Meteorology/Atmospheric Science.

Award: Scholarship for use in junior or senior years; not renewable. *Number:* 1. *Amount:* up to $2000.

Eligibility Requirements: Applicant must be enrolled or expecting to enroll full-time at a two-year or four-year institution or university. Available to U.S. citizens.

Application Requirements: Application, essay, references, transcript. *Deadline:* February 10.

Contact: Donna Fernandez, Development Program Coordinator
American Meteorological Society
45 Beacon Street
Boston, MA 02108-3693
Phone: 617-227-2426 Ext. 246
Fax: 617-742-8718
E-mail: dfernand@ametsoc.org

ASSOCIATION FOR WOMEN IN SCIENCE EDUCATIONAL FOUNDATION   http://www.awis.org/ed_foundation.html

ASSOCIATION FOR WOMEN IN SCIENCE COLLEGE SCHOLARSHIP
• *See page 86*

ASTRONAUT SCHOLARSHIP FOUNDATION   http://www.astronautscholarship.org

ASTRONAUT SCHOLARSHIP FOUNDATION
• *See page 92*

ELECTROCHEMICAL SOCIETY, INC.   http://www.electrochem.org

DANIEL CUBICCIOTTI STUDENT AWARD OF THE SAN FRANCISCO SECTION OF THE ELECTROCHEMICAL SOCIETY, SPONSORED BY STRUCTURAL INTEGRITY ASSOCIATES
• *See page 137*

H.H. DOW MEMORIAL STUDENT ACHIEVEMENT AWARD OF THE INDUSTRIAL ELECTROLYSIS AND ELECTROCHEMICAL ENGINEERING DIVISION OF THE ELECTROCHEMICAL SOCIETY, INC.
• *See page 137*

STUDENT ACHIEVEMENT AWARDS OF THE INDUSTRIAL ELECTROLYSIS AND ELECTROCHEMICAL ENGINEERING DIVISION OF THE ELECTROCHEMICAL SOCIETY, INC.
• *See page 137*

STUDENT RESEARCH AWARDS OF THE BATTERY DIVISION OF THE ELECTROCHEMICAL SOCIETY, INC.
• *See page 137*

GARDEN CLUB OF AMERICA   http://www.gcamerica.org

GARDEN CLUB OF AMERICA AWARDS FOR SUMMER ENVIRONMENTAL STUDIES
• *See page 80*

INNOVATION AND SCIENCE COUNCIL OF BRITISH COLUMBIA   http://www.scbc.org

PAUL AND HELEN TRUSSEL SCIENCE AND TECHNOLOGY SCHOLARSHIP
• *See page 93*

NASA DELAWARE SPACE GRANT CONSORTIUM   http://www.delspace.org

NASA DELAWARE SPACE GRANT UNDERGRADUATE TUITION SCHOLARSHIP
• *See page 94*

NASA NEVADA SPACE GRANT CONSORTIUM   http://www.unr.edu/spacegrant

UNIVERSITY AND COMMUNITY COLLEGE SYSTEM OF NEVADA NASA SPACE GRANT AND FELLOWSHIP PROGRAM
• *See page 125*

NASA VERMONT SPACE GRANT CONSORTIUM   http://www.vtspacegrant.org

VERMONT SPACE GRANT CONSORTIUM SCHOLARSHIP PROGRAM
• *See page 94*

NASA WEST VIRGINIA SPACE GRANT CONSORTIUM   http://www.nasa.wvu.edu

WEST VIRGINIA SPACE GRANT CONSORTIUM UNDERGRADUATE SCHOLARSHIP PROGRAM
• *See page 126*

NATIONAL OCEANIC AND ATMOSPHERIC ADMINISTRATION   http://see.orau.org

NATIONAL OCEANIC AND ATMOSPHERIC ADMINISTRATION EDUCATIONAL PARTNERSHIP PROGRAM WITH MINORITY SERVING INSTITUTIONS UNDERGRADUATE SCHOLARSHIP
• *See page 268*

NATIONAL OCEANIC AND ATMOSPHERIC ADMINISTRATION EDUCATIONAL PARTNERSHIP PROGRAM WITH MINORITY SERVING INSTITUTIONS UNDERGRADUATE SCHOLARSHIP
• *See page 268*

SIGMA XI, THE SCIENTIFIC RESEARCH SOCIETY   http://www.sigmaxi.org

SIGMA XI GRANTS-IN-AID OF RESEARCH
• *See page 84*

TKE EDUCATIONAL FOUNDATION   http://www.tkefoundation.org

CARROL C. HALL MEMORIAL SCHOLARSHIP
• *See page 95*

MILITARY AND DEFENSE STUDIES

HISPANIC COLLEGE FUND, INC.   http://www.hispanicfund.org

LOCKHEED MARTIN SCHOLARSHIP PROGRAM
• *See page 164*

MUSEUM STUDIES

AMERICAN SCHOOL OF CLASSICAL STUDIES AT ATHENS   http://www.ascsa.edu.gr

ASCSA SUMMER SESSIONS OPEN SCHOLARSHIPS
• *See page 88*

COSTUME SOCIETY OF AMERICA   http://www.costumesocietyamerica.com

ADELE FILENE TRAVEL AWARD
• *See page 105*

STELLA BLUM RESEARCH GRANT
• *See page 105*

MINERALOGICAL SOCIETY OF AMERICA   http://www.minsocam.org

MINERALOGICAL SOCIETY OF AMERICA-GRANT FOR STUDENT RESEARCH IN MINERALOGY AND PETROLOGY
• *See page 214*

MINERALOGY SOCIETY OF AMERICA-GRANT FOR RESEARCH IN CRYSTALLOGRAPHY
• *See page 215*

UNITED STATES MARINE CORPS HISTORICAL CENTER   http://www.hqinet001.hqmc.usmc.mil

U.S. MARINE CORPS HISTORICAL CENTER GRANTS
• *See page 340*

MUSIC

ALPHA DELTA KAPPA FOUNDATION   http://www.alphadeltakappa.org

APHA DELTA KAPPA FOUNDATION FINE ARTS GRANTS
• *See page 108*

AMERICAN COLLEGE OF MUSICIANS/NATIONAL GUILD OF PIANO TEACHERS   http://www.pianoguild.com

AMERICAN COLLEGE OF MUSICIANS/NATIONAL GUILD OF PIANO TEACHERS 200-DOLLAR SCHOLARSHIPS

Available only to student affiliate members who have participated in National Guild of Piano Teachers auditions over a ten-year period. Must be sponsored by Guild member. Contact American College of Musicians for more information.

Academic Fields/Career Goals: Music.

Award: Scholarship for use in freshman, sophomore, junior, or senior years; not renewable. *Number:* 150. *Amount:* $200.

Eligibility Requirements: Applicant must be enrolled or expecting to enroll full-time at a two-year or four-year or technical institution or university. Applicant or parent of applicant must be member of American College of Musicians. Available to U.S. and non-U.S. citizens.

Application Requirements: Application, test scores. *Deadline:* September 15.

Contact: Pat McCabe, Scholarship Coordinator, Scholarship Committee
American College of Musicians/National Guild of Piano Teachers
PO Box 1807, 808 Rio Grande
Austin, TX 78767-1807
Phone: 512-478-5775
E-mail: ngpt@aol.com

AMERICAN FOUNDATION FOR THE BLIND   http://www.afb.org/scholarships.asp

R.L. GILLETTE SCHOLARSHIP
• See page 382

AMERICAN LEGION, DEPARTMENT OF KANSAS   http://www.ksamlegion.org

MUSIC COMMITTEE SCHOLARSHIP

One-time award open to a high school senior or college freshman or sophomore. Must be used at an approved Kansas university or college. Must major or minor in music. Write for more information.

Academic Fields/Career Goals: Music; Performing Arts.

Award: Scholarship for use in freshman or sophomore years; not renewable. *Number:* 1. *Amount:* $1000.

Eligibility Requirements: Applicant must be enrolled or expecting to enroll at a two-year or four-year or technical institution or university; studying in Kansas and must have an interest in music/singing. Available to U.S. citizens.

Application Requirements: Application, financial need analysis, photo, references, transcript. *Deadline:* February 15.

Contact: Scholarship Administrator
American Legion, Department of Kansas
1314 Southwest Topeka Boulevard
Topeka, KS 66612-1886

AMERICAN MUSICOLOGICAL SOCIETY   http://www.ams-net.org

MINORITY TRAVEL FUND AWARD

Award for promising minority undergraduates and terminal masters degree candidates who are considering graduate work toward a doctorate in music. Award is to help cover travel expenses to the AMS annual conference. Deadline October 11. See Web site for more information http://www.ams-net.org

Academic Fields/Career Goals: Music.

Award: Grant for use in freshman, sophomore, junior, senior, or graduate years; not renewable. *Number:* varies. *Amount:* varies.

Eligibility Requirements: Applicant must be American Indian/Alaska Native, Asian/Pacific Islander, Black (non-Hispanic), or Hispanic and enrolled or expecting to enroll at a four-year institution or university. Available to U.S. citizens.

Application Requirements: Application, autobiography, references. *Deadline:* October 11.

Contact: Martha Feldman, Chair of the Committee
American Musicological Society
201 South 34th Street
Philadelphia, PA 19104-6313
Phone: 215-573-3673
E-mail: rore@uchicago.edu

AMERICAN ORFF-SCHULWERK ASSOCIATION   http://www.aosa.org

AMERICAN ORFF-SCHULWERK ASSOCIATION RESEARCH GRANT
• See page 220

BEEM FOUNDATION FOR THE ADVANCEMENT OF MUSIC   http://www.beemfoundation.org

BEEM FOUNDATION SCHOLARSHIP

Competition for excellence in the performance of vocal or instrumental music. Awarded to talented music students of Southern California.

Academic Fields/Career Goals: Music.

Award: Scholarship for use in freshman, sophomore, junior, senior, or graduate years; not renewable. *Number:* up to 3. *Amount:* $1000–$5000.

Eligibility Requirements: Applicant must be age 25 or under; enrolled or expecting to enroll full-time at an institution or university and resident of California. Available to U.S. citizens.

Application Requirements: Application, applicant must enter a contest, photo, resume, transcript. *Deadline:* May 2.

Contact: Bette Cox, President
BEEM Foundation for the Advancement of Music
3864 Grayburn Avenue
Los Angeles, CA 90008-1941
Phone: 323-291-7252
Fax: 323-291-7752
E-mail: bette.cox@beemfoundation.com

BMI FOUNDATION, INC.   http://www.bmi.com

JOHN LENNON SCHOLARSHIP PROGRAM

Scholarships available to songwriters and composers from music schools, universities and youth orchestras. Also submissions from the Music Educators National Conference are solicited. The submitted work must be an original song with lyrics accompanied by whatever instrumentation is chosen by the applicant.

Academic Fields/Career Goals: Music.

Award: Scholarship for use in freshman, sophomore, junior, senior, graduate, or postgraduate years; not renewable. *Number:* up to 3. *Amount:* $5000–$10,000.

Eligibility Requirements: Applicant must be age 15-24 and enrolled or expecting to enroll at a two-year or four-year or technical institution or university. Available to U.S. citizens.

Application Requirements: Application, applicant must enter a contest, CD or audio tape of a song written by the applicant with original words and music, 3 typed copies of the lyric. *Deadline:* January 20.

Contact: Ralph N. Jackson, President
BMI Foundation, Inc.
320 West 57th Street
New York, NY 10019
Phone: 212-586-2000
Fax: 212-245-8986
E-mail: info@bmifoundation.org

PEERMUSIC LATIN SCHOLARSHIP

Award for the best song or instrumental work in any Latin genre. The competition is open to songwriters and composers who are current students at colleges and universities. Submitted work must be an original. Applicants must not have had any musical work commercially recorded or distributed.

Academic Fields/Career Goals: Music.

Award: Scholarship for use in freshman, sophomore, junior, senior, graduate, or postgraduate years; not renewable. *Number:* 1. *Amount:* up to $5000.

BMI Foundation, Inc. (continued)

Eligibility Requirements: Applicant must be age 16-24 and enrolled or expecting to enroll at a two-year or four-year or technical institution or university. Available to U.S. citizens.

Application Requirements: Application, applicant must enter a contest, CD of original song or instrumental work, 3 typed lyric sheets. *Deadline:* January 13.

Contact: Ralph N. Jackson, President
BMI Foundation, Inc.
320 West 57th Street
New York, NY 10019
Phone: 212-586-2000
Fax: 212-245-8986

CALIFORNIA ALLIANCE FOR ARTS EDUCATION (CAAE)   http://www.artsed411.org

EMERGING YOUNG ARTIST AWARDS
• See page 110

CHOPIN FOUNDATION OF THE UNITED STATES   http://www.chopin.org

CHOPIN FOUNDATION OF THE UNITED STATES SCHOLARSHIP

Program aimed to help young American pianists to continue their piano education. Award(s) are available to students between ages 14 to 17 whose field of study is music and whose major is piano. Renewable for up to four years. Students will be assisted in preparing to qualify for the American National Chopin Piano Competition. Must be U.S. citizen or legal resident. Award based on performance of F. Chopin's required repertoire.

Academic Fields/Career Goals: Music; Performing Arts.

Award: Scholarship for use in freshman year; renewable. *Number:* up to 10. *Amount:* up to $1000.

Eligibility Requirements: Applicant must be age 14-17; enrolled or expecting to enroll full or part-time at an institution or university and must have an interest in music. Available to U.S. citizens.

Application Requirements: Application, applicant must enter a contest, references, 20-30 minute audio tape of Chopin's work. *Fee:* $25. *Deadline:* February 15.

Contact: Jadwiga Gewert, Executive Director
Chopin Foundation of the United States
1440 79th Street Causeway, Suite 117
Miami, FL 33141
Phone: 305-868-0624
Fax: 305-865-5150
E-mail: info@chopin.org

COLLEGEBOUND FOUNDATION   http://www.collegeboundfoundation.org

JANET B. SONDHEIM SCHOLARSHIP
• See page 110

COMMUNITY FOUNDATION OF CAPE COD   http://www.capecodfoundation.org

RICHARD AND ETHEL KOFF MEMORIAL SCHOLARSHIP FUND

Richard & Ethel Koff Memorial Scholarship Fund provides four-year scholarships to graduating seniors from the greater Barnstable area intending to further their education in the field of music. For more details see Web site: http://www.capecodfoundation.org.

Academic Fields/Career Goals: Music.

Award: Scholarship for use in freshman, sophomore, or junior years; renewable. *Number:* 1. *Amount:* $1000–$4000.

Eligibility Requirements: Applicant must be high school student; planning to enroll or expecting to enroll full-time at an institution or university and resident of Massachusetts. Available to U.S. citizens.

Application Requirements: Application, essay, financial need analysis, references, test scores, transcript. *Deadline:* April 1.

Contact: Pauline Greenberg, Scholarship Associate
Community Foundation of Cape Cod
259 Willow Street
Yarmouthport, MA 02675
Phone: 508-790-3040
Fax: 508-790-4069
E-mail: pgreenberg@capecodfoundation.org

DAYTON FOUNDATION   http://www.daytonfoundation.org

MU PHI EPSILON SCHOLARSHIP FUND

Scholarship to assist individuals in furthering their music studies. Should be enrolled full time at Wright State University, University of Dayton, Central State University, Sinclair Community College, Wilberforce University or Cedarville University.

Academic Fields/Career Goals: Music.

Award: Scholarship for use in sophomore or junior years; not renewable. *Number:* 1. *Amount:* up to $1000.

Eligibility Requirements: Applicant must be enrolled or expecting to enroll full-time at a two-year or four-year institution or university. Applicant must have 3.0 GPA or higher. Available to U.S. citizens.

Application Requirements: Application, essay, references, transcript. *Deadline:* March 1.

Contact: Diane Timmons, Director Grants and Programs
Dayton Foundation
2300 Kettering Tower
Dayton, OH 45423
Phone: 937-225-9966
E-mail: dtimmons@daytonfoundation.org

DELTA OMICRON INTERNATIONAL MUSIC FRATERNITY/DELTA OMICRON FOUNDATION, INC.   http://delta-omicron.org

SUMMER MUSIC SCHOLARSHIPS

Seven $500 awards for summer music workshops. Open to Delta Omicron members in good standing. Must be at least 16 years old. Deadline: March 31.

Academic Fields/Career Goals: Music.

Award: Scholarship for use in freshman, sophomore, junior, senior, graduate, or postgraduate years; not renewable. *Number:* 7. *Amount:* $500.

Eligibility Requirements: Applicant must be age 16; enrolled or expecting to enroll full or part-time at a two-year or four-year institution or university and must have an interest in music or music/singing. Available to U.S. and non-U.S. citizens.

Application Requirements: Application, references. *Deadline:* March 31.

Contact: Michelle A. May, Chair, Rotating Grants and Summer Scholarships
Delta Omicron International Music Fraternity/Delta Omicron Foundation, Inc.
1635 West Boston Boulevard
Detroit, MI 48206
Phone: 313-865-1149
Fax: 313-965-0868
E-mail: maybiz@aol.com

GENERAL FEDERATION OF WOMEN'S CLUBS OF MASSACHUSETTS   http://www.gfwcma.org/

DORCHESTER WOMEN'S CLUB SCHOLARSHIP

Scholarship for major in voice. Must submit letter of endorsement from president of the sponsoring General Federation of Women's Clubs of Massachusetts and personal statement of no more than 500 words addressing professional goals and financial need. Audition required. Must be a Massachusetts resident.

Academic Fields/Career Goals: Music; Performing Arts.

Award: Scholarship for use in freshman, sophomore, junior, or senior years; not renewable. *Number:* 1. *Amount:* $500.

Eligibility Requirements: Applicant must be enrolled or expecting to enroll full-time at an institution or university; resident of Massachusetts and must have an interest in music/singing. Available to U.S. citizens.

Application Requirements: Application, applicant must enter a contest, autobiography, interview, references, self-addressed stamped envelope, transcript. *Deadline:* February 1.

Contact: Virginia Williams, Chairman Music Program, GFWC of MA
General Federation of Women's Clubs of Massachusetts
PO Box 679
Sudbury, MA 01776-0679
Phone: 978-443-4569
E-mail: joaheart@attbi.com

GENERAL FEDERATION OF WOMEN'S CLUBS OF MASSACHUSETTS MUSIC SCHOLARSHIP
• See page 225

HOUSTON SYMPHONY http://www.houstonsymphony.org

HOUSTON SYMPHONY LEAGUE CONCERTO COMPETITION

Competition is open to student musicians 18 years of age or younger who have not yet graduated from high school and who play any standard orchestral instrument or piano. Must live within a 75-mile radius of Houston and submit a screening CD or tape of one movement of their concerto.

Academic Fields/Career Goals: Music.

Award: Prize for use in freshman year; not renewable. *Number:* up to 3. *Amount:* $250–$1000.

Eligibility Requirements: Applicant must be high school student; age 18 or under and planning to enroll or expecting to enroll at an institution or university. Available to U.S. citizens.

Application Requirements: Application, applicant must enter a contest, references, CD or cassette. *Fee:* $25. *Deadline:* November 18.

Contact: Carol Wilson, Education Coordinator
Houston Symphony
615 Louisiana, Suite 102
Houston, TX 77002
Phone: 713-238-1449
Fax: 713-224-0453
E-mail: e&o@houstonsymphony.org

INTERNATIONALER MUSIKWETTBEWERB http://www.ard-musikwettbewerb.de

INTERNATIONAL MUSIC COMPETITION OF THE ARD MUNICH

Twelve prizes will be awarded at the International Music Competition of the ARD Munich. The competition is held annually in September. Prizes are awarded in various categories.

Academic Fields/Career Goals: Music.

Award: Prize for use in senior, or graduate years; not renewable. *Number:* 12.

Eligibility Requirements: Applicant must be age 20-29 and enrolled or expecting to enroll at an institution or university. Available to U.S. and non-U.S. citizens.

Application Requirements: Application, applicant must enter a contest, references. *Fee:* $80. *Deadline:* May 2.

Contact: Ingeborg Krause, Head of Organization
Internationaler Musikwettbewerb
Bayerischer Rundfink
Munich 80300
Germany
Phone: 49-89-5900247
Fax: 49-89-5900357
E-mail: ard.musikwettbewerb@brnet.de

JACK J. ISGUR FOUNDATION

JACK J. ISGUR FOUNDATION SCHOLARSHIP
• See page 111

NATIONAL ASSOCIATION OF PASTORAL MUSICIANS http://www.npm.org

DAN SCHUTTE SCHOLARSHIP

Award for students pursuing studies related to the field of pastoral music. Applicant must intend to work at least two years in the field of pastoral music following graduation or program completion. Must submit applicant's definition of pastoral music, description of talents and previous experience, and a 5 minute performance cassette of applicant's choir/ensemble. Applicant must be a member of NPM.

Academic Fields/Career Goals: Music; Religion/Theology.

Award: Scholarship for use in freshman, sophomore, junior, senior, or graduate years; not renewable. *Amount:* $1000.

Eligibility Requirements: Applicant must be enrolled or expecting to enroll full or part-time at a two-year or four-year institution or university and must have an interest in music/singing. Available to U.S. and non-U.S. citizens.

Application Requirements: Application, essay, financial need analysis, resume, references, tape of performance. *Deadline:* March 3.

Contact: Kathleen Haley, Scholarship Department
National Association of Pastoral Musicians
962 Wayne Avenue
Suite 210
Silver Spring, MD 20910-4461
Phone: 240-247-3000
Fax: 240-247-3001
E-mail: npmsing@npm.org

ELAINE RENDLER-RENE DOSOGNE-GEORGETOWN CHORALE SCHOLARSHIP

Award for students pursuing studies related to the field of pastoral music. Applicant must intend to work at least two years in the field of pastoral music following graduation or program completion. Must submit applicant's definition of "pastoral music," description of talents and previous experience, and a 5-minute performance cassette or applicant's choir ensemble. Applicant must be a member of NPM.

Academic Fields/Career Goals: Music; Religion/Theology.

Award: Scholarship for use in freshman, sophomore, junior, senior, graduate, or postgraduate years; not renewable. *Number:* 1. *Amount:* $1000.

Eligibility Requirements: Applicant must be enrolled or expecting to enroll full or part-time at a two-year or four-year or technical institution or university and must have an interest in music/singing. Available to U.S. and non-U.S. citizens.

Application Requirements: Application, essay, financial need analysis, resume, references, tape of performance. *Deadline:* March 3.

Contact: Scholarship Department
National Association of Pastoral Musicians
962 Wayne Avenue, Suite 210
Silver Spring, MD 20910
Phone: 240-247-3000
Fax: 240-247-3001
E-mail: npmsing@npm.org

FUNK FAMILY MEMORIAL SCHOLARSHIP

Award for students pursuing studies related to the field of pastoral music. Applicant must intend to work at least two years in the field of pastoral music following graduation or program completion. Must submit applicant's definition of "pastoral music," description of talents and previous experience, and a 5-minute performance cassette of applicant's choir ensemble. Applicant must be a member of NPM.

Academic Fields/Career Goals: Music; Religion/Theology.

Award: Scholarship for use in freshman, sophomore, junior, senior, graduate, or postgraduate years; not renewable. *Number:* 1. *Amount:* $1000.

Eligibility Requirements: Applicant must be enrolled or expecting to enroll full or part-time at a two-year or four-year or technical institution or university and must have an interest in music/singing. Available to U.S. and non-U.S. citizens.

Application Requirements: Application, essay, financial need analysis, resume, references, tape of performance. *Deadline:* March 3.

National Association of Pastoral Musicians (continued)

Contact: Scholarship Department
National Association of Pastoral Musicians
962 Wayne Avenue, Suite 210
Silver Spring, MD 20910
Phone: 240-247-3000
Fax: 240-247-3001
E-mail: npmsing@npm.org

GIA PUBLICATION PASTORAL MUSICIAN SCHOLARSHIP

Award for students pursuing studies related to the field of pastoral music. Applicant must intend to work at least two years in the field of pastoral music following graduation or program completion. Must submit applicant's definition of "pastoral music," description of talents and previous experience, and a 5-minute performance cassette of applicant's choir/ensemble. Applicant must be a member of NPM.

Academic Fields/Career Goals: Music; Religion/Theology.

Award: Scholarship for use in freshman, sophomore, junior, senior, graduate, or postgraduate years; not renewable. *Number:* 1. *Amount:* $2000.

Eligibility Requirements: Applicant must be enrolled or expecting to enroll full or part-time at a two-year or four-year or technical institution or university and must have an interest in music/singing. Available to U.S. and non-U.S. citizens.

Application Requirements: Application, essay, financial need analysis, resume, references, tape of performance. *Deadline:* March 3.

Contact: Scholarship Department
National Association of Pastoral Musicians
962 Wayne Avenue, Suite 210
Silver Spring, MD 20910
Phone: 240-247-3000
Fax: 240-247-3001
E-mail: npmsing@npm.org

MUSONICS SCHOLARSHIP

Award for students pursuing studies related to the field of pastoral music. Applicant must intend to work at least two years in the field of pastoral music following graduation or program completion. Must submit applicant's definition of "pastoral music," description of talents and previous experience, and a 5-minute performance cassette of applicant's choir/ensemble. Applicant must be a member of NPM.

Academic Fields/Career Goals: Music; Religion/Theology.

Award: Scholarship for use in freshman, sophomore, junior, senior, graduate, or postgraduate years; not renewable. *Number:* 1. *Amount:* $2500.

Eligibility Requirements: Applicant must be enrolled or expecting to enroll full or part-time at a two-year or four-year or technical institution or university and must have an interest in music/singing. Available to U.S. and non-U.S. citizens.

Application Requirements: Application, essay, financial need analysis, resume, references, tape of performance. *Deadline:* March 3.

Contact: Scholarship Department
National Association of Pastoral Musicians
962 Wayne Avenue, Suite 210
Silver Spring, MD 20910
Phone: 240-247-3000
Fax: 240-247-3001
E-mail: npmsing@npm.org

NATIONAL ASSOCIATION OF PASTORAL MUSICIANS MEMBERS' SCHOLARSHIP

Award for students pursuing studies related to the field of pastoral music. Applicant must intend to work at least two years in the field of pastoral music following graduation or program completion. Must submit applicant's definition of "pastoral music," description of talents and previous experience, and a 5-minute performance cassette of applicant's choir/ensemble. Applicant must be a member of NPM.

Academic Fields/Career Goals: Music; Religion/Theology.

Award: Scholarship for use in freshman, sophomore, junior, senior, graduate, or postgraduate years; not renewable. *Number:* 1. *Amount:* up to $4500.

Eligibility Requirements: Applicant must be enrolled or expecting to enroll full or part-time at a two-year or four-year or technical institution or university and must have an interest in music/singing. Available to U.S. and non-U.S. citizens.

Application Requirements: Application, essay, financial need analysis, resume, references, tape of performance. *Deadline:* March 3.

Contact: Scholarship Department
National Association of Pastoral Musicians
962 Wayne Avenue, Suite 210
Silver Spring, MD 20910
Phone: 240-247-3000
Fax: 240-247-3001
E-mail: npmsing@npm.org

NPM BOARD OF DIRECTORS SCHOLARSHIP

Award for students pursuing studies related to the field of pastoral music. Applicant must intend to work at least two years in the field of pastoral music following graduation or program completion. Must submit applicant's definition of "pastoral music," description of talents and previous experience, and a 5 minute performance cassette of applicant's choir/ensemble. Applicant must be a member of NPM.

Academic Fields/Career Goals: Music; Religion/Theology.

Award: Scholarship for use in freshman, sophomore, junior, senior, or graduate years; not renewable. *Amount:* $2000.

Eligibility Requirements: Applicant must be enrolled or expecting to enroll full or part-time at a two-year or four-year institution or university and must have an interest in music/singing. Available to U.S. and non-U.S. citizens.

Application Requirements: Application, essay, financial need analysis, resume, references, tape of performance. *Deadline:* March 3.

Contact: Kathleen Haley, Scholarship Department
National Association of Pastoral Musicians
962 Wayne Avenue
Suite 210
Silver Spring, MD 20910-4461
Phone: 240-247-3000
Fax: 240-247-3001
E-mail: npmsing@npm.org

NPM COMPOSERS AND AUTHORS SCHOLARSHIP

Award for students pursuing studies related to the field of pastoral music. Applicant must intend to work at least two years in the field of pastoral music following graduation or program completion. Must submit applicant's definition of "pastoral music," description of talents and previous experience, and a 5 minute performance cassette of applicant's choir/ensemble. Applicant must be a member of NPM.

Academic Fields/Career Goals: Music; Religion/Theology.

Award: Scholarship for use in freshman, sophomore, junior, senior, or graduate years; not renewable. *Amount:* $1750.

Eligibility Requirements: Applicant must be enrolled or expecting to enroll full or part-time at a two-year or four-year institution or university and must have an interest in music/singing. Available to U.S. and non-U.S. citizens.

Application Requirements: Application, essay, financial need analysis, resume, references, tape of performance. *Deadline:* March 3.

Contact: Kathleen Haley, Scholarship Department
National Association of Pastoral Musicians
962 Wayne Avenue
Suite 210
Silver Spring, MD 20910-4461
Phone: 240-247-3000
Fax: 240-247-3001
E-mail: npmsing@npm.org

NPM KOINONIA/BOARD OF DIRECTORS SCHOLARSHIP

Awards for students pursuing studies related to the field of pastoral music. Applicant must intend to work at least two years in the field of pastoral music following graduation or program completion. Must submit applicant's definition of "pastoral music", description of talents and previous experience, and a five-minute performance cassette of applicant's choir/ensemble. Applicant must be a member of NPM.

Academic Fields/Career Goals: Music; Religion/Theology.

Award: Scholarship for use in freshman, sophomore, junior, senior, or graduate years; not renewable. *Number:* 2. *Amount:* up to $3500.

Eligibility Requirements: Applicant must be enrolled or expecting to enroll full or part-time at a two-year or four-year or technical institution or university and must have an interest in music/singing. Available to U.S. and non-U.S. citizens.

Application Requirements: Application, essay, financial need analysis, resume, references. *Deadline:* March 3.

Contact: Scholarship Department
National Association of Pastoral Musicians
962 Wayne Avenue, Suite 210
Silver Spring, MD 20910
Phone: 240-247-3000
Fax: 240-247-3001

NPM MIAMI VALLEY CATHOLIC CHURCH MUSICIANS SCHOLARSHIP

Award for students pursuing studies related to the field of pastoral music. Applicant must intend to work at least two years in the field of pastoral music following graduation or program completion. Must submit applicant's definition of "pastoral music," description of talents and previous experience, and a 5 minute performance cassette of applicant's choir/ensemble. Applicant must be a member of NPM.

Academic Fields/Career Goals: Music; Religion/Theology.

Award: Scholarship for use in freshman, sophomore, junior, senior, or graduate years; not renewable. *Amount:* $1250.

Eligibility Requirements: Applicant must be enrolled or expecting to enroll full or part-time at a two-year or four-year institution or university and must have an interest in music/singing. Available to U.S. and non-U.S. citizens.

Application Requirements: Application, essay, financial need analysis, resume, references, tape of performance. *Deadline:* March 3.

Contact: Kathleen Haley, Scholarship Department
National Association of Pastoral Musicians
962 Wayne Avenue
Suite 210
Silver Spring, MD 20910-4461
Phone: 240-247-3000
Fax: 240-247-3001
E-mail: npmsing@npm.org

NPM PERROT SCHOLARSHIP

Award for students pursuing studies related to the field of pastoral music. Applicant must intend to work at least two years in the field of pastoral music following graduation or program completion. Must submit applicant's definition of "pastoral music," description of talents and previous experience, and a 5-minute performance cassette of applicant's choir/ensemble. Applicant must be member of NPM.

Academic Fields/Career Goals: Music; Religion/Theology.

Award: Scholarship for use in freshman, sophomore, junior, senior, graduate, or postgraduate years; not renewable. *Number:* 1. *Amount:* $3500.

Eligibility Requirements: Applicant must be enrolled or expecting to enroll full or part-time at a two-year or four-year or technical institution or university. Available to U.S. and non-U.S. citizens.

Application Requirements: Application, essay, financial need analysis, resume, references, tape of performance. *Deadline:* March 3.

Contact: Scholarship Department
National Association of Pastoral Musicians
962 Wayne Avenue, Suite 210
Silver Spring, MD 20910
Phone: 240-247-3000
Fax: 240-247-3001

OREGON CATHOLIC PRESS SCHOLARSHIP

Award for students pursuing studies related to the field of pastoral music. Applicant must intend to work at least two years in the field of pastoral music following graduation or program completion. Must submit applicant's definition of "pastoral music," description of talents and previous experience, and a 5 minute performance cassette of applicant's choir/ensemble. Applicant must be a member of NPM.

Academic Fields/Career Goals: Music; Religion/Theology.

Award: Scholarship for use in freshman, sophomore, junior, senior, graduate, or postgraduate years; not renewable. *Number:* 1. *Amount:* $1500.

Eligibility Requirements: Applicant must be enrolled or expecting to enroll full or part-time at a two-year or four-year or technical institution or university and must have an interest in music/singing. Available to U.S. and non-U.S. citizens.

Application Requirements: Application, essay, financial need analysis, resume, references, tape of performance. *Deadline:* March 3.

Contact: Scholarship Department
National Association of Pastoral Musicians
962 Wayne Avenue, Suite 210
Silver Spring, MD 20910
Phone: 240-247-3000
Fax: 240-247-3001
E-mail: npmsing@npm.org

PALUCH FAMILY FOUNDATION/WORLD LIBRARY PUBLICATIONS SCHOLARSHIP

Award for students pursuing studies related to the field of pastoral music. Applicant must intend to work at least two years in the field of pastoral music following graduation or program completion. Must submit applicant's definition of "pastoral music", description of talents and previous experience, and a 5-minute performance cassette of applicant's choir/ensemble. Applicant must be a member of NPM.

Academic Fields/Career Goals: Music; Religion/Theology.

Award: Scholarship for use in freshman, sophomore, junior, senior, graduate, or postgraduate years; not renewable. *Number:* 1. *Amount:* $2500.

Eligibility Requirements: Applicant must be enrolled or expecting to enroll full or part-time at a two-year or four-year or technical institution or university and must have an interest in music/singing. Available to U.S. and non-U.S. citizens.

Application Requirements: Application, essay, financial need analysis, resume, references, tape of performance. *Deadline:* March 3.

Contact: Scholarship Department
National Association of Pastoral Musicians
962 Wayne Avenue, Suite 210
Silver Spring, MD 20910
Phone: 240-247-3000
Fax: 240-247-3001
E-mail: npmsing@npm.org

STEVEN C. WARNER SCHOLARSHIP

Award for students pursuing studies related to the field of pastoral music. Applicant must intend to work at least two years in the field of pastoral music following graduation or program completion. Must submit applicant's definition of pastoral music, description of talents and previous experience, and a 5 minute performance cassette of applicant's choir/ensemble. Applicant must be a member of NPM.

Academic Fields/Career Goals: Music; Religion/Theology.

Award: Scholarship for use in freshman, sophomore, junior, senior, or graduate years; not renewable. *Amount:* $500.

Eligibility Requirements: Applicant must be enrolled or expecting to enroll full or part-time at a two-year or four-year institution or university and must have an interest in music/singing. Available to U.S. and non-U.S. citizens.

Application Requirements: Application, essay, financial need analysis, resume, references, tape of performance. *Deadline:* March 3.

Contact: Kathleen Haley, Scholarship Department
National Association of Pastoral Musicians
962 Wayne Avenue
Suite 210
Silver Spring, MD 20910-4461
Phone: 240-247-3000
Fax: 240-247-3001
E-mail: npmsing@npm.org

NATIONAL FOUNDATION FOR ADVANCEMENT IN THE ARTS
http://www.artsawards.org

ASTRAL CAREER GRANT

Award available to those pursuing music and dance. Must be U.S. citizens or permanent residents. One-time award. Music applicants must be vocalists, composers or pianists, while dance applicants must be ballet dancers or choreographers.

Academic Fields/Career Goals: Music; Performing Arts.

Award: Grant for use in freshman, sophomore, junior, or senior years; not renewable. *Number:* 8–12. *Amount:* $200–$250.

Eligibility Requirements: Applicant must be enrolled or expecting to enroll part-time at an institution or university. Available to U.S. and non-U.S. citizens.

Application Requirements: Application, autobiography, essay, financial need analysis, portfolio, resume, references, self-addressed stamped envelope, transcript. *Deadline:* Continuous.

Contact: Programs Department
National Foundation for Advancement in the Arts
444 Brickell Avenue, Suite R14
Miami, FL 33133
Phone: 800-970-2787 Ext. 33
Fax: 305-377-1149
E-mail: nfaa@nfaa.org

NATIONAL GUILD OF COMMUNITY SCHOOLS OF THE ARTS
http://www.nationalguild.org

YOUNG COMPOSERS AWARDS

Applicant must send an original classical or jazz musical composition. Must be ages 13-18 and a U.S. or Canadian resident in either school music program or private program. Submit four copies of work and certification by teacher with $15 check. One-time award of $250-$1000.

Academic Fields/Career Goals: Music; Performing Arts.

Award: Prize for use in freshman year; not renewable. *Number:* 4. *Amount:* $250–$1000.

Eligibility Requirements: Applicant must be high school student; age 13-18; planning to enroll or expecting to enroll full-time at an institution or university and must have an interest in music/singing. Available to U.S. and non-U.S. citizens.

Application Requirements: Application, applicant must enter a contest, composition manuscripts. *Fee:* $15. *Deadline:* April 14.

Contact: Carissa Reddick, YCA Coordinator
National Guild of Community Schools of the Arts
The Hartt School Community Division, University of Hartford,
200 Bloomfield Avenue
West Hartford, CT 06117
Phone: 860-768-7768 Ext. 8558
Fax: 860-768-4777
E-mail: youngcomp@hartford.edu

RHODE ISLAND FOUNDATION
http://www.rifoundation.org

BACH ORGAN AND KEYBOARD SCHOLARSHIP FUND

For organ or keyboard musicians attending four-year colleges and universities. Applicants must demonstrate good grades and financial need. Must include music tape. Must be Rhode Island residents attending college as a music major.

Academic Fields/Career Goals: Music.

Award: Scholarship for use in freshman, sophomore, junior, senior, graduate, or postgraduate years; renewable. *Number:* 1–3. *Amount:* $300–$1000.

Eligibility Requirements: Applicant must be enrolled or expecting to enroll full-time at a two-year or four-year institution or university; resident of Rhode Island and must have an interest in music/singing. Available to U.S. citizens.

Application Requirements: Application, financial need analysis, references, self-addressed stamped envelope, transcript. *Deadline:* June 9.

Contact: Libby Monahan, Scholarship Coordinator
Rhode Island Foundation
1 Union Station
Providence, RI 02903
Phone: 401-274-4564
Fax: 401-272-1359

CONSTANT MEMORIAL SCHOLARSHIP FOR AQUIDNECK ISLAND RESIDENTS
• *See page 114*

SIGMA ALPHA IOTA PHILANTHROPIES, INC.
http://www.sai-national.org

SIGMA ALPHA IOTA GRADUATE PERFORMANCE AWARDS

One-time award offered triennially to SAI members over 20 who are pursuing graduate study in field of music performance. Winners perform at national convention. Submit tape with required repertoire. Contact chapter for details. Two awards in each category (vocal; keyboard and percussion; strings; wind and brass) ranging from $1500 to $2000. Application fee: $25.

Academic Fields/Career Goals: Music; Performing Arts.

Award: Prize for use in freshman, sophomore, junior, senior, or graduate years; not renewable. *Number:* 8. *Amount:* $1500–$2000.

Eligibility Requirements: Applicant must be age 21; enrolled or expecting to enroll at a four-year institution or university; female and must have an interest in music/singing. Available to U.S. and non-U.S. citizens.

Application Requirements: Application, applicant must enter a contest, essay, references, transcript, tape. *Fee:* $25. *Deadline:* March 15.

Contact: Dr. Emily White, Project Director
Sigma Alpha Iota Philanthropies, Inc.
One Tunnel Road
Asheville, NC 28805
Phone: 828-251-0606
Fax: 828-251-0644
E-mail: webmaster@sai-national.org

SIGMA ALPHA IOTA JAZZ PERFORMANCE AWARDS

Award for a college-initiated member of Sigma Alpha Iota who is enrolled in an undergraduate or graduate program in jazz studies or jazz performance at the time of application. Applicant must be no older than age 32 on March 15, 2006.

Academic Fields/Career Goals: Music.

Award: Prize for use in freshman, sophomore, junior, senior, or graduate years. *Number:* 2. *Amount:* $1500–$2000.

Eligibility Requirements: Applicant must be age 32 or under; enrolled or expecting to enroll full or part-time at a four-year institution or university; female and must have an interest in music/singing. Available to U.S. and non-U.S. citizens.

Application Requirements: Application, essay. *Fee:* $25. *Deadline:* March 15.

Contact: Margie Halinski, Director
Sigma Alpha Iota Philanthropies, Inc.
One Tunnel Road
Asheville, NC 28805
Phone: 828-251-0606
Fax: 828-251-0644
E-mail: mhalinski@yahoo.com

SIGMA ALPHA IOTA JAZZ STUDIES SCHOLARSHIP

Award for an initiated member of Sigma Alpha Iota in good financial standing with the Fraternity. Scholarship must be applied toward study leading to a music degree with an emphasis in Jazz Studies.

Academic Fields/Career Goals: Music.

Award: Scholarship for use in freshman, sophomore, junior, or senior years. *Amount:* $1500.

Eligibility Requirements: Applicant must be enrolled or expecting to enroll at a four-year institution or university; female and must have an interest in music/singing. Available to U.S. and non-U.S. citizens.

Application Requirements: Application, references, transcript. *Fee:* $25. *Deadline:* March 15.

Contact: Margie Halinski, Project Director
Sigma Alpha Iota Philanthropies, Inc.
One Tunnel Road
Asheville, NC 28805
Phone: 828-251-0606
Fax: 828-251-0644
E-mail: mhalinski@yahoo.com

SIGMA ALPHA IOTA MUSIC BUSINESS/TECHNOLOGY SCHOLARSHIP

Tuition scholarship for an initiated member of Sigma Alpha Iota in good financial standing with the Fraternity. Must be enrolled full time in a bachelor's degree program and entering the junior or senior year of study in Fall 2006. Minimum GPA of 3.0 required.

Academic Fields/Career Goals: Music.

Award: Scholarship for use in junior or senior years. *Amount:* $2000.

Eligibility Requirements: Applicant must be enrolled or expecting to enroll full-time at a four-year institution or university; female and must have an interest in music/singing. Applicant must have 3.0 GPA or higher. Available to U.S. and non-U.S. citizens.

Application Requirements: Application, references, transcript, statement of purpose, including career goals. *Fee:* $25. *Deadline:* March 15.

Contact: Kim L. Wangler, Director
Sigma Alpha Iota Philanthropies, Inc.
One Tunnel Road
Asheville, NC 28805
Phone: 828-251-0606
Fax: 828-251-0644
E-mail: wanglerkl@appstate.edu

SIGMA ALPHA IOTA MUSIC THERAPY SCHOLARSHIP

One-time award offered yearly for undergraduate and graduate members of SAI who have completed two years in music therapy training at a university approved by the American Music Therapy Association. Contact local chapter for further information. Application fee: $25.

Academic Fields/Career Goals: Music; Therapy/Rehabilitation.

Award: Scholarship for use in freshman, sophomore, junior, senior, or graduate years; not renewable. *Number:* 1. *Amount:* $1000.

Eligibility Requirements: Applicant must be enrolled or expecting to enroll full-time at a four-year institution or university; female and must have an interest in music/singing. Available to U.S. and non-U.S. citizens.

Application Requirements: Application, essay, references, transcript. *Fee:* $25. *Deadline:* March 15.

Contact: Michelle Gaddis Kennemer, Director
Sigma Alpha Iota Philanthropies, Inc.
One Tunnel Road
Asheville, NC 28805
Phone: 828-251-0606
Fax: 828-251-0644
E-mail: jmichelle17@hotmail.com

SIGMA ALPHA IOTA PHILANTHROPIES UNDERGRADUATE PERFORMANCE SCHOLARSHIPS

Award offered triennially for female SAI members in freshman, sophomore or junior year in voice; keyboard and percussion; strings; winds and brass. Winners perform at national convention. Must submit tape with required repertoire. Consult local chapter for details. Four one-time scholarships of $1500. Application fee: $25.

Academic Fields/Career Goals: Music; Performing Arts.

Award: Scholarship for use in freshman, sophomore, junior, or senior years; not renewable. *Number:* 4. *Amount:* $1500.

Eligibility Requirements: Applicant must be enrolled or expecting to enroll full-time at a four-year institution or university; female and must have an interest in music/singing. Available to U.S. and non-U.S. citizens.

Application Requirements: Application, applicant must enter a contest, essay, references, transcript, audio tape. *Fee:* $25. *Deadline:* March 15.

Contact: Dr. Emily White, Director
Sigma Alpha Iota Philanthropies, Inc.
One Tunnel Road
Asheville, NC 28805
Phone: 828-251-0606
Fax: 828-251-0644
E-mail: hornstein1@aol.com

SIGMA ALPHA IOTA SUMMER MUSIC SCHOLARSHIPS IN THE U.S. OR ABROAD

One-time award for use at summer music programs in the U.S. or abroad. Must be a member of SAI and accepted by the summer music program. Contact local chapter for details. Application fee: $25.

Academic Fields/Career Goals: Music; Performing Arts.

Award: Scholarship for use in freshman, sophomore, junior, or senior years; not renewable. *Number:* 5. *Amount:* up to $1000.

Eligibility Requirements: Applicant must be enrolled or expecting to enroll full-time at a four-year institution or university; female and must have an interest in music/singing. Available to U.S. and non-U.S. citizens.

Application Requirements: Application, essay. *Fee:* $25. *Deadline:* March 15.

Contact: Mary Jennings, Director
Sigma Alpha Iota Philanthropies, Inc.
One Tunnel Road
Asheville, NC 28805
Phone: 828-251-0606
Fax: 828-251-0644
E-mail: maryj10101@aol.com

SIGMA ALPHA IOTA VISUALLY IMPAIRED SCHOLARSHIP
• See page 236

UNICO NATIONAL, INC   http://www.unico.org

THEODORE MAZZA SCHOLARSHIP
• See page 103

WAVERLY COMMUNITY HOUSE, INC.   http://www.waverlycomm.com

F. LAMMOT BELIN ARTS SCHOLARSHIP
• See page 103

WOMEN BAND DIRECTORS INTERNATIONAL   http://www.womenbanddirectors.org

CHARLOTTE PLUMMER OWEN MEMORIAL SCHOLARSHIP

Scholarship available to support young college women presently preparing to be band directors.

Academic Fields/Career Goals: Music; Performing Arts.

Award: Scholarship for use in junior or senior years. *Number:* 1. *Amount:* $300.

Eligibility Requirements: Applicant must be enrolled or expecting to enroll full-time at a four-year institution or university and female. Available to U.S. citizens.

Application Requirements: Application, photo, transcript.

Contact: Diane Gorzycki, WBDI Scholarship Chair
Women Band Directors International
292 Band Hall-Louisiana State University
Baton Rouge, LA 70803
E-mail: dgorzycki@austin.rr.com

GLADYS STONE WRIGHT SCHOLARSHIP
• See page 240

HELEN MAY BULTER MEMORIAL SCHOLARSHIP
• See page 241

MARTHA ANN STARK MEMORIAL SCHOLARSHIP
• See page 241

MUSIC TECHNOLOGY SCHOLARSHIP
• See page 241

Women Band Directors International (continued)

VOLKWEIN MEMORIAL SCHOLARSHIP
• *See page 241*

NATURAL RESOURCES

AMERICAN GROUND WATER TRUST
http://www.agwt.org

AMERICAN GROUND WATER TRUST-AMTROL, INC. SCHOLARSHIP
• *See page 170*

AMERICAN GROUND WATER TRUST-CLAUDE LAVAL CORPORATION THE BEN EVERSON SCHOLARSHIP
• *See page 170*

AMERICAN INDIAN SCIENCE AND ENGINEERING SOCIETY
http://www.aises.org

A.T. ANDERSON MEMORIAL SCHOLARSHIP
• *See page 89*

HENRY RODRIGUEZ RECLAMATION COLLEGE SCHOLARSHIP AND INTERNSHIP
• *See page 285*

AMERICAN WATER RESOURCES ASSOCIATION
http://www.awra.org

RICHARD A. HERBERT MEMORIAL SCHOLARSHIP

There are two scholarships: one for full-time undergraduate student working toward his/her first undergraduate degree and enrolled in a program related to water resources. One is for full-time graduate student enrolled in a program relating to water resources. All applicants must be national AWRA members.

Academic Fields/Career Goals: Natural Resources.

Award: Scholarship for use in freshman, sophomore, junior, senior, or graduate years; not renewable. *Number:* 2. *Amount:* up to $2000.

Eligibility Requirements: Applicant must be enrolled or expecting to enroll full-time at a four-year institution or university. Available to U.S. and non-U.S. citizens.

Application Requirements: Application, essay, references, transcript. *Deadline:* April 24.

Contact: American Water Resources Association
4 West Federal Street, PO Box 1626
Middleburg, VA 20118
Phone: 540-687-8390
Fax: 540-687-8395
E-mail: info@awra.org

APICS EDUCATIONAL AND RESEARCH FOUNDATION, INC.
http://www.apics.org

DONALD W. FOGARTY INTERNATIONAL STUDENT PAPER COMPETITION
• *See page 144*

ARCTIC INSTITUTE OF NORTH AMERICA
http://www.arctic.ucalgary.ca

JIM BOURQUE SCHOLARSHIP
• *See page 220*

ARIZONA HYDROLOGICAL SOCIETY
http://www.azhydrosoc.org

ARIZONA HYDROLOGICAL SURVEY STUDENT SCHOLARSHIP
• *See page 212*

ASSOCIATION OF CALIFORNIA WATER AGENCIES
http://www.acwanet.com

ASSOCIATION OF CALIFORNIA WATER AGENCIES SCHOLARSHIPS
• *See page 91*

CLAIR A. HILL SCHOLARSHIP
• *See page 91*

CALIFORNIA GROUNDWATER ASSOCIATION
http://www.groundh2o.org

CALIFORNIA GROUNDWATER ASSOCIATION SCHOLARSHIP
• *See page 213*

CALIFORNIA WATER AWARENESS CAMPAIGN
http://www.wateraware.org

CALIFORNIA WATER AWARENESS CAMPAIGN WATER SCHOLAR
• *See page 79*

CANADIAN RECREATIONAL CANOEING ASSOCIATION
http://www.paddlingcanada.com

BILL MASON MEMORIAL SCHOLARSHIP FUND
• *See page 80*

CONSERVATION FEDERATION OF MISSOURI
http://www.confedmo.org

CHARLES P. BELL CONSERVATION SCHOLARSHIP
• *See page 136*

DESK AND DERRICK EDUCATIONAL TRUST
http://www.addc.org

DESK AND DERRICK EDUCATIONAL TRUST
• *See page 92*

DOGRIB TREATY 11 SCHOLARSHIP COMMITTEE
http://www.dt11sc.ca

FRANCIS BLACKDUCK MEMORIAL "STRONG LIKE TWO PEOPLE" AWARDS
• *See page 293*

FRIENDS OF THE FRELINGHUYSEN ARBORETUM
http://www.arboretumfriends.org

BENJAMIN C. BLACKBURN SCHOLARSHIP
• *See page 293*

GARDEN CLUB OF AMERICA
http://www.gcamerica.org

FRANCES M. PEACOCK SCHOLARSHIP FOR NATIVE BIRD HABITAT

One-time scholarship available to a college senior or graduate student to study habitat related issues to benefit endangered bird species.

Academic Fields/Career Goals: Natural Resources.

Award: Scholarship for use in senior, or graduate years; not renewable. *Number:* 1. *Amount:* $4000.

Eligibility Requirements: Applicant must be enrolled or expecting to enroll at a four-year institution or university. Available to U.S. citizens.

Application Requirements: Application, essay, references, self-addressed stamped envelope, budget. *Deadline:* January 15.

Contact: Scott Sutcliffe, Associate Director
Garden Club of America
Cornell Lab of Ornithology, 159 Sapsucker Woods Road
Ithaca, NY 14850
Fax: 607-254-2415
E-mail: lh17@cornell.edu

GARDEN CLUB OF AMERICA AWARDS FOR SUMMER ENVIRONMENTAL STUDIES
• *See page 80*

GREAT LAKES COMMISSION
http://www.glc.org

CAROL A. RATZA MEMORIAL SCHOLARSHIP
• *See page 138*

HISPANIC COLLEGE FUND, INC.
http://www.hispanicfund.org

DEPARTMENT OF ENERGY SCHOLARSHIP PROGRAM
• See page 148

INDIANA WILDLIFE FEDERATION ENDOWMENT
http://indianawildlife.org/

CHARLES A. HOLT INDIANA WILDLIFE FEDERATION ENDOWMENT SCHOLARSHIP

A $1000 scholarship will be awarded to an Indiana resident accepted for the study or already enrolled for the study of resource conservation or environmental education at the undergraduate level. For more details see Web site: http://www.indianawildlife.org.

Academic Fields/Career Goals: Natural Resources.

Award: Scholarship for use in sophomore, junior, or senior years; not renewable. *Number:* 1. *Amount:* $1000.

Eligibility Requirements: Applicant must be enrolled or expecting to enroll full-time at a four-year institution or university; resident of Indiana and studying in Indiana. Available to U.S. citizens.

Application Requirements: Application, essay, references. *Deadline:* April 30.

Contact: Application available at Web site.

INNOVATION AND SCIENCE COUNCIL OF BRITISH COLUMBIA
http://www.scbc.org

PAUL AND HELEN TRUSSEL SCIENCE AND TECHNOLOGY SCHOLARSHIP
• See page 93

INTERNATIONAL ASSOCIATION OF GREAT LAKES RESEARCH
http://www.iaglr.org

PAUL W. RODGERS SCHOLARSHIP
• See page 214

INTERTRIBAL TIMBER COUNCIL
http://www.itcnet.org

TRUMAN D. PICARD SCHOLARSHIP
• See page 75

KENTUCKY NATURAL RESOURCES AND ENVIRONMENTAL PROTECTION CABINET
http://www.uky.edu/waterresources

CONSERVATION OF NATURAL RESOURCES SCHOLARSHIP
• See page 81

CONSERVATION OF NATURAL RESOURCES SCHOLARSHIP FOR NONTRADITIONAL STUDENTS
• See page 81

GEORGE R. CRAFTON SCHOLARSHIP
• See page 81

LOUISIANA OFFICE OF STUDENT FINANCIAL ASSISTANCE
http://www.osfa.state.la.us

ROCKEFELLER STATE WILDLIFE SCHOLARSHIP
• See page 87

MAINE CAMPGROUND OWNERS ASSOCIATION
http://www.campmaine.com

MAINE CAMPGROUND OWNERS ASSOCIATION SCHOLARSHIP

One-time award of $500 to a Maine resident pursuing a career in outdoor recreation. Must have completed one year of study and have a GPA of at least 2.5. Application deadline is March 29.

Academic Fields/Career Goals: Natural Resources; Recreation, Parks, Leisure Studies.

Award: Scholarship for use in sophomore, junior, senior, graduate, or postgraduate years; not renewable. *Number:* 1–2. *Amount:* $500.

Eligibility Requirements: Applicant must be enrolled or expecting to enroll at a two-year or four-year or technical institution or university and resident of Maine. Applicant must have 2.5 GPA or higher. Available to U.S. citizens.

Application Requirements: Application, essay, financial need analysis, transcript. *Deadline:* March 29.

Contact: Richard Abare, Executive Director
Maine Campground Owners Association
10 Falcon Road, Suite 1
Lewiston, ME 04240
Phone: 207-782-5874
Fax: 207-782-4497
E-mail: info@campmaine.com

MANITOBA FORESTRY ASSOCIATION
http://www.mbforestryassoc.ca

DR. ALAN BEAVEN FORESTRY SCHOLARSHIP
• See page 294

MINERALOGICAL SOCIETY OF AMERICA
http://www.minsocam.org

MINERALOGICAL SOCIETY OF AMERICA-GRANT FOR STUDENT RESEARCH IN MINERALOGY AND PETROLOGY
• See page 214

MINERALOGY SOCIETY OF AMERICA-GRANT FOR RESEARCH IN CRYSTALLOGRAPHY
• See page 215

NATIONAL ASSOCIATION OF WATER COMPANIES
http://www.nawc.org

J .J. BARR SCHOLARSHIP
• See page 139

NATIONAL ASSOCIATION OF WATER COMPANIES-NEW JERSEY CHAPTER

NATIONAL ASSOCIATION OF WATER COMPANIES-NEW JERSEY CHAPTER SCHOLARSHIP
• See page 139

NATIONAL FEDERATION OF THE BLIND
http://www.nfb.org

HOWARD BROWN RICKARD SCHOLARSHIP
• See page 101

NATIONAL FISH AND WILDLIFE FOUNDATION
http://www.nfwf.org

BUDWEISER CONSERVATION SCHOLARSHIP PROGRAM
• See page 140

NEW ENGLAND WATER WORKS ASSOCIATION
http://www.newwa.org

NEW ENGLAND WATER WORKS GEORGE E. WATTERS MEMORIAL SCHOLARSHIP.
• See page 175

NEW JERSEY DIVISION OF FISH AND WILDLIFE/NJ CHAPTER OF THE WILDLIFE SOCIETY
http://www.njfishandwildlife.com/cookhmschol.htm

RUSSELL A. COOKINGHAM SCHOLARSHIP
• See page 140

OREGON STUDENT ASSISTANCE COMMISSION
http://www.osac.state.or.us

OREGON FOUNDATION FOR BLACKTAIL DEER OUTDOOR AND WILDLIFE SCHOLARSHIP
• See page 140

Oregon Student Assistance Commission (continued)

ROYDEN M. BODLEY SCHOLARSHIP
• See page 87

PARK PEOPLE   http://www.parkpeople.org

THE PARK PEOPLE $4000 SCHOLARSHIP

A $4000 scholarship is offered to a student pursuing a degree in forestry at a Texas university. All recipients are required to maintain an overall GPA of at least 2.8 and must be full-time students during each semester covered by the award.

Academic Fields/Career Goals: Natural Resources.

Award: Scholarship for use in freshman, sophomore, junior, senior, or graduate years. *Amount:* $4000.

Eligibility Requirements: Applicant must be enrolled or expecting to enroll full-time at a four-year institution or university and studying in Texas. Available to U.S. citizens.

Application Requirements: Application, references, transcript. *Deadline:* February 10.

Contact: Scholarship Chair
          Park People
          3015 Richmond, Suite 210
          Houston, TX 77098
          Phone: 713-942-8429
          Fax: 713-942-7275
          E-mail: annem@parkpeople.org

PENNSYLVANIA ASSOCIATION OF CONSERVATION DISTRICTS AUXILIARY   http://www.blairconservationdistrict.org

PACD AUXILIARY SCHOLARSHIPS
• See page 76

PENNSYLVANIA FISH AND BOAT COMMISSION   http://sites.state.pa.us/Fish

RALPH W. ABELE CONSERVATION SCHOLARSHIP
• See page 295

RAILWAY TIE ASSOCIATION   http://www.rta.org

JOHN MABRY FORESTRY SCHOLARSHIP

One-time award to potential forestry industry leaders. Open to junior and senior undergraduates who will be enrolled in accredited forestry schools. Applications reviewed with emphasis on leadership qualities, career objectives, scholastic achievement, and financial need. Application deadline is June 30.

Academic Fields/Career Goals: Natural Resources.

Award: Scholarship for use in junior or senior years; not renewable. *Number:* 2. *Amount:* $1250.

Eligibility Requirements: Applicant must be enrolled or expecting to enroll full-time at a four-year institution or university. Available to U.S. and Canadian citizens.

Application Requirements: Application, autobiography, essay, references, transcript. *Deadline:* June 30.

Contact: Debbie Corallo, Administrator
          Railway Tie Association
          115 Commerce Drive, Suite C
          Fayetteville, GA 30214
          Phone: 770-460-5553
          Fax: 770-460-5573
          E-mail: ties@rta.org

RECREATIONAL BOATING INDUSTRIES EDUCATIONAL FOUNDATION   http://www.mbia.org

RECREATIONAL BOATING INDUSTRIES EDUCATIONAL FOUNDATION SCHOLARSHIPS
• See page 141

ROCKY MOUNTAIN ELK FOUNDATION   http://www.rmef.org

WILDLIFE LEADERSHIP AWARDS
• See page 141

SOCIETY FOR MINING, METALLURGY AND EXPLORATION - CENTRAL WYOMING SECTION

COATES, WOLFF, RUSSELL MINING INDUSTRY SCHOLARSHIP
• See page 95

SOCIETY FOR RANGE MANAGEMENT   http://www.rangelands.org

MASONIC RANGE SCIENCE SCHOLARSHIP
• See page 76

SOIL AND WATER CONSERVATION SOCIETY   http://www.swcs.org

DONALD A. WILLIAMS SCHOLARSHIP SOIL CONSERVATION SCHOLARSHIP
• See page 216

SWCS MELVILLE H. COHEE STUDENT LEADER CONSERVATION SCHOLARSHIP
• See page 85

SOIL AND WATER CONSERVATION SOCIETY-MISSOURI SHOW-ME CHAPTER   http://www.swcs.missouri.edu/scholarships.htm

MELVILLE H. COHEE STUDENT LEADER CONSERVATION SCHOLARSHIP

Scholarship provides financial assistance to members of SWCS who are in their junior or senior year of full-time undergraduate study or are pursuing graduate level studies with a natural resource conservation orientation at accredited colleges or universities.

Academic Fields/Career Goals: Natural Resources.

Award: Scholarship for use in junior, senior, or postgraduate years. *Number:* 2. *Amount:* $1000.

Eligibility Requirements: Applicant must be enrolled or expecting to enroll full-time at a four-year institution or university. Applicant or parent of applicant must be member of Soil and Water Conservation Society. Applicant must have 3.0 GPA or higher. Available to U.S. and non-U.S. citizens.

Application Requirements: Application, references, transcript.

Contact: Bev Maltsberger, Scholarship Administrator
          Soil and Water Conservation Society-Missouri Show-Me Chapter
          4125 Mitchell Avenue
          St. Joseph, MO 64507
          Phone: 816-279-1691
          E-mail: maltsbergerb@missouri.edu

SWCS/BETTY BROEMMELSIEK SCHOLARSHIP

Financial assistance for students wishing to pursue studies with a natural resource conservation orientation. Scholarship is for students who attended high school in Missouri. Need not be an SWCS member. Applications must be postmarked by November 28.

Academic Fields/Career Goals: Natural Resources.

Award: Scholarship for use in freshman, sophomore, junior, or senior years. *Number:* 2. *Amount:* $500–$1000.

Eligibility Requirements: Applicant must be enrolled or expecting to enroll full-time at a four-year institution or university and studying in Missouri. Available to U.S. citizens.

Application Requirements: Essay, references, transcript, list of leadership positions. *Deadline:* November 28.

Contact: Beverly Maltsberger, Buchanan County Extension Center
          Soil and Water Conservation Society-Missouri Show-Me Chapter
          4125 Mitchell Avenue, PO Box 7077
          St. Joseph, MO 64507-7077
          Phone: 816-279-1691
          E-mail: maltsbergerb@missouri.edu

SOIL AND WATER CONSERVATION SOCIETY-NEW JERSEY CHAPTER
http://www.geocities.com/njswcs

EDWARD R. HALL SCHOLARSHIP
• See page 76

SOUTH DAKOTA BOARD OF REGENTS
http://www.sdbor.edu

SOUTH DAKOTA BOARD OF REGENTS BJUGSTAD SCHOLARSHIP
• See page 77

TEXAS OUTDOOR WRITERS ASSOCIATION
http://www.towa.org/

TEXAS OUTDOOR WRITERS ASSOCIATION SCHOLARSHIP
• See page 188

TKE EDUCATIONAL FOUNDATION
http://www.tkefoundation.org

TIMOTHY L. TASCHWER SCHOLARSHIP
• See page 216

UNITED NEGRO COLLEGE FUND
http://www.uncf.org

MALCOLM PIRNIE, INC. SCHOLARS PROGRAM
• See page 169

MELLON ECOLOGY PROGRAM (S.E.E.D.S)

Program gives minority students exposure to research in ecology and ecology-related careers. Must attend a UNCF member college or university. Prospective applicants should complete the Student Profile found at Web site: http://www.uncf.org.

Academic Fields/Career Goals: Natural Resources.

Award: Scholarship for use in freshman, sophomore, junior, or senior years; not renewable. *Number:* 1.

Eligibility Requirements: Applicant must be Black (non-Hispanic) and enrolled or expecting to enroll at a four-year institution or university. Available to U.S. citizens.

Application Requirements: Application, financial need analysis. *Deadline:* Continuous.

Contact: Rebecca Bennett, Director, Program Services
United Negro College Fund
8260 Willow Oaks Corporate Drive
Fairfax, VA 22031-8044
Phone: 800-331-2244
E-mail: rbennett@uncf.org

WEYERHAEUSER/UNCF CORPORATE SCHOLARS
• See page 157

UNITED STATES ENVIRONMENTAL PROTECTION AGENCY
http://www.epa.gov

NATIONAL NETWORK FOR ENVIRONMENTAL MANAGEMENT STUDIES FELLOWSHIP

The NNEMS Fellowship Program is designed to provide undergraduate and graduate students with research opportunities at one of EPA's facilities nationwide. EPA awards approximately 40 NNEMS fellowships per year. Selected students receive a stipend for performing their research project. EPA develops an annual catalog of research projects available for student application. Submit a complete application package as described in the annual catalog. Minimum 3.0 GPA required.

Academic Fields/Career Goals: Natural Resources.

Award: Grant for use in freshman, sophomore, junior, senior, or graduate years; not renewable. *Number:* 35–40.

Eligibility Requirements: Applicant must be enrolled or expecting to enroll full or part-time at a two-year or four-year institution or university. Applicant must have 3.0 GPA or higher. Available to U.S. citizens.

Application Requirements: Application, applicant must enter a contest, resume, references, transcript. *Deadline:* January 26.

Contact: Mr. Michael Baker, Acting Director
United States Environmental Protection Agency
Office of Environmental Education, 1200 Pennsylvania Avenue, NW (1704A)
Washington, DC 20460
Phone: 202-564-0446
E-mail: baker.michael@epa.gov

VIRGINIA ASSOCIATION OF SOIL AND WATER CONSERVATION DISTRICTS EDUCATIONAL FOUNDATION, INC.
http://www.fauquiercounty.gov

VASWCD EDUCATIONAL FOUNDATION, INC. SCHOLARSHIP AWARDS PROGRAM
• See page 296

WILSON ORNITHOLOGICAL SOCIETY
http://www.ummz.lsa.umich.edu/birds/wos.html

GEORGE A. HALL / HAROLD F. MAYFIELD AWARD
• See page 87

PAUL A. STEWART AWARDS
• See page 88

NATURAL SCIENCES

ALABAMA STATE DEPARTMENT OF EDUCATION
http://www.alsde.edu

MATH AND SCIENCE SCHOLARSHIP PROGRAM FOR ALABAMA TEACHERS
• See page 135

AMERICAN FOUNDATION FOR THE BLIND
http://www.afb.org/scholarships.asp

PAUL W. RUCKES SCHOLARSHIP
• See page 190

AMERICAN INDIAN SCIENCE AND ENGINEERING SOCIETY
http://www.aises.org

A.T. ANDERSON MEMORIAL SCHOLARSHIP
• See page 89

BURLINGTON NORTHERN SANTA FE FOUNDATION SCHOLARSHIP
• See page 89

ENVIRONMENTAL PROTECTION AGENCY TRIBAL LANDS ENVIRONMENTAL SCIENCE SCHOLARSHIP
• See page 135

HENRY RODRIGUEZ RECLAMATION COLLEGE SCHOLARSHIP AND INTERNSHIP
• See page 285

ARCTIC INSTITUTE OF NORTH AMERICA
http://www.arctic.ucalgary.ca

JIM BOURQUE SCHOLARSHIP
• See page 220

ARRL FOUNDATION, INC.
http://www.arrl.org/arrlf/scholgen.html

WILLIAM R. GOLDFARB MEMORIAL SCHOLARSHIP
• See page 145

ASSOCIATION FOR WOMEN IN SCIENCE EDUCATIONAL FOUNDATION
http://www.awis.org/ed_foundation.html

ASSOCIATION FOR WOMEN IN SCIENCE COLLEGE SCHOLARSHIP
• See page 86

ASSOCIATION OF CALIFORNIA WATER AGENCIES
http://www.acwanet.com

ASSOCIATION OF CALIFORNIA WATER AGENCIES SCHOLARSHIPS
• See page 91

CLAIR A. HILL SCHOLARSHIP
• See page 91

AUDUBON SOCIETY OF WESTERN PENNSYLVANIA
http://www.aswp.org

BEULAH FREY ENVIRONMENTAL SCHOLARSHIP
• See page 293

BARRY M. GOLDWATER SCHOLARSHIP AND EXCELLENCE IN EDUCATION FOUNDATION
http://www.act.org/goldwater

BARRY M. GOLDWATER SCHOLARSHIP AND EXCELLENCE IN EDUCATION PROGRAM
• See page 92

CANADIAN RECREATIONAL CANOEING ASSOCIATION
http://www.paddlingcanada.com

BILL MASON MEMORIAL SCHOLARSHIP FUND
• See page 80

DESK AND DERRICK EDUCATIONAL TRUST
http://www.addc.org

DESK AND DERRICK EDUCATIONAL TRUST
• See page 92

EXPLORERS CLUB
http://www.explorers.org

EXPLORATION FUND GRANTS
• See page 88

YOUTH ACTIVITY FUND

Award given to college students or high school students pursuing a research project in the field of science. Applicants must have two letters of recommendation, one-page description of project, and a budget or plan.

Academic Fields/Career Goals: Natural Sciences; Science, Technology, and Society.

Award: Grant for use in freshman, sophomore, junior, or senior years; not renewable. *Number:* 10–15. *Amount:* $500–$1500.

Eligibility Requirements: Applicant must be enrolled or expecting to enroll at an institution or university. Available to U.S. citizens.

Application Requirements: Application, essay, financial need analysis, references, all applications must be submitted in hard copy by postal mail. *Deadline:* February 13.

Contact: Suzi Zetkus, Administrative Assistant
Explorers Club
46 East 70th Street
New York, NY 10021
Phone: 212-628-8383
Fax: 212-288-4449

GREAT LAKES COMMISSION
http://www.glc.org

CAROL A. RATZA MEMORIAL SCHOLARSHIP
• See page 138

HARVARD TRAVELLERS CLUB

HARVARD TRAVELLERS CLUB GRANTS
• See page 96

HISPANIC COLLEGE FUND, INC.
http://www.hispanicfund.org

DEPARTMENT OF ENERGY SCHOLARSHIP PROGRAM
• See page 148

INNOVATION AND SCIENCE COUNCIL OF BRITISH COLUMBIA
http://www.scbc.org

PAUL AND HELEN TRUSSEL SCIENCE AND TECHNOLOGY SCHOLARSHIP
• See page 93

INTERNATIONAL ASSOCIATION OF GREAT LAKES RESEARCH
http://www.iaglr.org

PAUL W. RODGERS SCHOLARSHIP
• See page 214

MIDWEST ROOFING CONTRACTORS ASSOCIATION
http://www.mrca.org

MRCA FOUNDATION SCHOLARSHIP PROGRAM
• See page 94

MINERALOGICAL SOCIETY OF AMERICA
http://www.minsocam.org

MINERALOGICAL SOCIETY OF AMERICA-GRANT FOR STUDENT RESEARCH IN MINERALOGY AND PETROLOGY
• See page 214

MINERALOGY SOCIETY OF AMERICA-GRANT FOR RESEARCH IN CRYSTALLOGRAPHY
• See page 215

NASA NEBRASKA SPACE GRANT CONSORTIUM
http://nasa.unomaha.edu

NASA NEBRASKA SPACE GRANT
• See page 125

NASA VERMONT SPACE GRANT CONSORTIUM
http://www.vtspacegrant.org

VERMONT SPACE GRANT CONSORTIUM SCHOLARSHIP PROGRAM
• See page 94

NASA WEST VIRGINIA SPACE GRANT CONSORTIUM
http://www.nasa.wvu.edu

WEST VIRGINIA SPACE GRANT CONSORTIUM UNDERGRADUATE SCHOLARSHIP PROGRAM
• See page 126

NATIONAL FISH AND WILDLIFE FOUNDATION
http://www.nfwf.org

BUDWEISER CONSERVATION SCHOLARSHIP PROGRAM
• See page 140

NATIONAL INSTITUTE OF GENERAL MEDICAL SCIENCES, NATIONAL INSTITUTE OF HEALTH
http://www.nigms.nih.gov

*MARC UNDERGRADUATE STUDENT TRAINING IN ACADEMIC RESEARCH U*STAR AWARDS*
• See page 140

OREGON STUDENT ASSISTANCE COMMISSION
http://www.osac.state.or.us

OREGON FOUNDATION FOR BLACKTAIL DEER OUTDOOR AND WILDLIFE SCHOLARSHIP
• See page 140

ROYDEN M. BODLEY SCHOLARSHIP
• See page 87

POLANKI, POLISH WOMEN'S CULTURAL CLUB
http://www.polanki.org

COPERNICUS AWARD

Award to a student of Polish heritage who is an outstanding student in a science field. Applicants must be college juniors, seniors, or graduate students and must be Wisconsin residents or attend college in Wisconsin. Successful applicants will should have a GPA of 3.0.

Academic Fields/Career Goals: Natural Sciences; Physical Sciences and Math.

Award: Scholarship for use in junior, senior, or graduate years. *Number:* 1. *Amount:* $500–$1000.

Eligibility Requirements: Applicant must be of Polish heritage and enrolled or expecting to enroll at a four-year institution or university. Available to U.S. citizens.

Application Requirements: Application, transcript. *Deadline:* March 1.

Contact: Susan Mikos
Polanki, Polish Women's Cultural Club
of Milwaukee, Wisconsin, U.S.A.
4160 South 1st Street
PO Box 341458
Milwaukee, WI 53234
Phone: 414-332-1728
E-mail: polanki@polanki.org

SOCIETY FOR MINING, METALLURGY AND EXPLORATION - CENTRAL WYOMING SECTION

COATES, WOLFF, RUSSELL MINING INDUSTRY SCHOLARSHIP
• See page 95

SOCIETY OF HISPANIC PROFESSIONAL ENGINEERS FOUNDATION
http://www.henaac.org

SOCIETY OF HISPANIC PROFESSIONAL ENGINEERS FOUNDATION
• See page 168

SOIL AND WATER CONSERVATION SOCIETY
http://www.swcs.org

DONALD A. WILLIAMS SCHOLARSHIP SOIL CONSERVATION SCHOLARSHIP
• See page 216

SWCS MELVILLE H. COHEE STUDENT LEADER CONSERVATION SCHOLARSHIP
• See page 85

SOIL AND WATER CONSERVATION SOCIETY-NEW JERSEY CHAPTER
http://www.geocities.com/njswcs

EDWARD R. HALL SCHOLARSHIP
• See page 76

NEAR AND MIDDLE EAST STUDIES

AMERICAN FOUNDATION FOR THE BLIND
http://www.afb.org/scholarships.asp

PAUL W. RUCKES SCHOLARSHIP
• See page 190

AMERICAN SCHOOL OF CLASSICAL STUDIES AT ATHENS
http://www.ascsa.edu.gr

ASCSA SUMMER SESSIONS OPEN SCHOLARSHIPS
• See page 88

AMERICAN SCHOOLS OF ORIENTAL RESEARCH (ASOR)
http://www.asor.org

CYPRUS AMERICAN ARCHAEOLOGICAL RESEARCH INSTITUTE HELENA WYLDE AND STUART SWINY FELLOWSHIP
• See page 96

NUCLEAR SCIENCE

AMERICAN INDIAN SCIENCE AND ENGINEERING SOCIETY
http://www.aises.org

A.T. ANDERSON MEMORIAL SCHOLARSHIP
• See page 89

BURLINGTON NORTHERN SANTA FE FOUNDATION SCHOLARSHIP
• See page 89

AMERICAN NUCLEAR SOCIETY
http://www.ans.org

AMERICAN NUCLEAR SOCIETY JAMES R. VOGT SCHOLARSHIP
• See page 248

AMERICAN NUCLEAR SOCIETY OPERATIONS AND POWER SCHOLARSHIP
• See page 248

AMERICAN NUCLEAR SOCIETY UNDERGRADUATE SCHOLARSHIPS
• See page 249

ANS INCOMING FRESHMAN SCHOLARSHIP

Scholarship for graduating high-school seniors who have enrolled full time in college courses and are pursuing a degree in nuclear engineering or intent to pursue a degree in nuclear engineering. Scholarships will be awarded based on an applicant's high school academic achievement and course of undergraduate study.

Academic Fields/Career Goals: Nuclear Science.

Award: Scholarship for use in freshman year. *Number:* 1–5. *Amount:* up to $2000.

Eligibility Requirements: Applicant must be enrolled or expecting to enroll full-time at a four-year institution or university. Available to U.S. citizens.

Application Requirements: Application, essay, references, transcript. *Deadline:* April 1.

Contact: Scholarship Coordinator
American Nuclear Society
555 North Kensington Avenue
La Grange Park, IL 60526
Phone: 708-352-6611
Fax: 708-352-0499
E-mail: outreach@ans.org

CHARLES (TOMMY) THOMAS MEMORIAL SCHOLARSHIP DIVISION SCHOLARSHIP
• See page 249

DECOMMISSIONING, DECONTAMINATION, AND REUTILIZATION SCHOLARSHIP
• See page 249

DELAYED EDUCATION FOR WOMEN SCHOLARSHIPS
• See page 249

JOHN AND MURIEL LANDIS SCHOLARSHIP AWARDS
• See page 249

JOHN R. LAMARSH SCHOLARSHIP
• See page 249

JOSEPH R. DIETRICH SCHOLARSHIP
• See page 250

RAYMOND DISALVO SCHOLARSHIP

Scholarship awards a maximum of four scholarships for students who have completed one year in a course of study leading to a degree in nuclear science, nuclear engineering, or a nuclear-related field and who will be sophomores in

American Nuclear Society (continued)

the upcoming academic year; and a maximum of 21 scholarships for students who have completed two or more years and will be entering as juniors or seniors.

Academic Fields/Career Goals: Nuclear Science.

Award: Scholarship for use in freshman, sophomore, junior, or senior years. *Number:* 1–21.

Eligibility Requirements: Applicant must be enrolled or expecting to enroll full-time at a four-year institution or university. Available to U.S. citizens.

Application Requirements: Application, references, transcript. *Deadline:* February 1.

Contact: Scholarship Coordinator
American Nuclear Society
555 North Kensington Avenue
La Grange Park, IL 60526
Phone: 708-352-6611
Fax: 708-352-0499
E-mail: outreach@ans.org

ROBERT G. LACY SCHOLARSHIP
• *See page 250*

ROBERT T. (BOB) LINER SCHOLARSHIP
• *See page 250*

AMERICAN SOCIETY OF NAVAL ENGINEERS
http://www.navalengineers.org

AMERICAN SOCIETY OF NAVAL ENGINEERS SCHOLARSHIP
• *See page 90*

ARIZONA HYDROLOGICAL SOCIETY
http://www.azhydrosoc.org

ARIZONA HYDROLOGICAL SURVEY STUDENT SCHOLARSHIP
• *See page 212*

ASSOCIATION FOR WOMEN IN SCIENCE EDUCATIONAL FOUNDATION
http://www.awis.org/ed_foundation.html

ASSOCIATION FOR WOMEN IN SCIENCE COLLEGE SCHOLARSHIP
• *See page 86*

BARRY M. GOLDWATER SCHOLARSHIP AND EXCELLENCE IN EDUCATION FOUNDATION
http://www.act.org/goldwater

BARRY M. GOLDWATER SCHOLARSHIP AND EXCELLENCE IN EDUCATION PROGRAM
• *See page 92*

DESK AND DERRICK EDUCATIONAL TRUST
http://www.addc.org

DESK AND DERRICK EDUCATIONAL TRUST
• *See page 92*

HISPANIC COLLEGE FUND, INC.
http://www.hispanicfund.org

DEPARTMENT OF ENERGY SCHOLARSHIP PROGRAM
• *See page 148*

HISPANIC ENGINEER NATIONAL ACHIEVEMENT AWARDS CORPORATION (HENAAC)
http://www.henaac.org

HISPANIC ENGINEER NATIONAL ACHIEVEMENT AWARDS CORPORATION SCHOLARSHIP PROGRAM
• *See page 122*

INNOVATION AND SCIENCE COUNCIL OF BRITISH COLUMBIA
http://www.scbc.org

PAUL AND HELEN TRUSSEL SCIENCE AND TECHNOLOGY SCHOLARSHIP
• *See page 93*

NASA WEST VIRGINIA SPACE GRANT CONSORTIUM
http://www.nasa.wvu.edu

WEST VIRGINIA SPACE GRANT CONSORTIUM UNDERGRADUATE SCHOLARSHIP PROGRAM
• *See page 126*

SOCIETY OF HISPANIC PROFESSIONAL ENGINEERS FOUNDATION
http://www.henaac.org

SOCIETY OF HISPANIC PROFESSIONAL ENGINEERS FOUNDATION
• *See page 168*

SOCIETY OF NUCLEAR MEDICINE
http://www.snm.org

PAUL COLE SCHOLARSHIP
• *See page 332*

UNIVERSITIES SPACE RESEARCH ASSOCIATION
http://www.usra.edu/hq/scholarships/overview.shtml

UNIVERSITIES SPACE RESEARCH ASSOCIATION SCHOLARSHIP PROGRAM
• *See page 96*

NURSING

ABORIGINAL NURSES ASSOCIATION OF CANADA
http://www.anac.on.ca

NORTHERN ONTARIO ABORIGINAL NURSES AWARD

Award to provide financial assistance to a student of Aboriginal ancestry enrolled in a Registered Nursing program, whose goal upon graduation is to work and provide assistance to those people living in an Aboriginal community or a remote community in Northern Ontario. Applicant must be a member of the ANAC. Must be Aboriginal, Metis or Inuit, and must provide photocopies of Indian Status card, or evidence of Metis or Inuit status.

Academic Fields/Career Goals: Nursing.

Award: Scholarship for use in freshman, sophomore, junior, or senior years; not renewable. *Number:* 2. *Amount:* $500.

Eligibility Requirements: Applicant must be enrolled or expecting to enroll full or part-time at a two-year or technical institution or university. Available to U.S. and Canadian citizens.

Application Requirements: Application, essay, references, transcript. *Deadline:* December 15.

Contact: Doris Fox, Administrative Assistant
Aboriginal Nurses Association of Canada
56 Sparks Street, Suite 502
Ottawa K1P 5A9
Canada
Phone: 613-724-4677
Fax: 613-724-4718

ALBERTA HERITAGE SCHOLARSHIP FUND/ ALBERTA SCHOLARSHIP PROGRAMS
http://www.alis.gov.ab.ca

ALBERTA HERITAGE SCHOLARSHIP FUND ABORIGINAL HEALTH CAREERS BURSARY
• *See page 135*

AMARILLO AREA FOUNDATION
http://www.aaf-hf.org

AMARILLO AREA FOUNDATION SCHOLARSHIPS
• *See page 53*

AMERICAN ASSOCIATION OF CRITICAL-CARE NURSES (AACN)

http://www.aacn.org

AACN EDUCATIONAL ADVANCEMENT SCHOLARSHIPS-BSN COMPLETION

Award for juniors and seniors currently enrolled in a nursing program accredited by State Board of Nursing. Must be AACN member with active RN license who is currently or has recently worked in critical care. Must have 3.0 GPA. Supports RN members completing a baccalaureate degree in nursing. Student may only receive award a maximum of two times. Application deadline is April 1.

Academic Fields/Career Goals: Nursing.

Award: Scholarship for use in junior or senior years; not renewable. *Number:* 50–100. *Amount:* $1500.

Eligibility Requirements: Applicant must be enrolled or expecting to enroll full or part-time at a four-year institution or university. Applicant or parent of applicant must be member of American Association of Critical Care Nurses. Applicant or parent of applicant must have employment or volunteer experience in designated career field. Applicant must have 3.0 GPA or higher. Available to U.S. and Canadian citizens.

Application Requirements: Application, essay, transcript, verification of critical care experience. *Deadline:* April 1.

Contact: Lisa Mynes, Member Relations and Services Specialist
American Association of Critical-Care Nurses (AACN)
101 Columbia
Aliso Viejo, CA 92656
Phone: 949-362-2000
Fax: 949-362-2020
E-mail: lisa.mynes@aacn.org

AMERICAN ASSOCIATION OF NEUROSCIENCE NURSES

http://www.aann.org

NEUROSCIENCE NURSING FOUNDATION SCHOLARSHIP

Scholarship available for registered nurse to attend an NLN accredited school. Submit letter of school acceptance along with application, transcript, and copy of current RN license. Applicants should have diploma or AD

Academic Fields/Career Goals: Nursing.

Award: Scholarship for use in freshman, sophomore, junior, senior, or graduate years; not renewable. *Number:* varies. *Amount:* $1500.

Eligibility Requirements: Applicant must be enrolled or expecting to enroll at a two-year or four-year institution or university. Applicant must have 3.0 GPA or higher. Available to U.S. citizens.

Application Requirements: Application, transcript, letter of acceptance. *Deadline:* January 15.

Contact: NNF Scholarship Programs
American Association of Neuroscience Nurses
4700 West Lake Avenue
Glenview, IL 60025-1485
Phone: 888-557-2266
E-mail: info@aann.org

AMERICAN LEGION AUXILIARY, DEPARTMENT OF ARIZONA

http://www.azlegion.org/majorp~2.htm

AMERICAN LEGION AUXILIARY DEPARTMENT OF ARIZONA NURSES' SCHOLARSHIPS

Award for Arizona residents enrolled in their second year at an institution in Arizona awarding degree as a registered nurse. Preference given to immediate family member of a veteran. Must be a U.S. citizen and resident of Arizona for one year.

Academic Fields/Career Goals: Nursing.

Award: Scholarship for use in sophomore, junior, or senior years; not renewable. *Amount:* $400.

Eligibility Requirements: Applicant must be enrolled or expecting to enroll full-time at a two-year or four-year institution or university; resident of Arizona and studying in Arizona. Available to U.S. citizens.

Application Requirements: Application, autobiography, essay, financial need analysis, photo, references, test scores, transcript. *Deadline:* May 15.

Contact: Department Secretary and Treasurer
American Legion Auxiliary, Department of Arizona
4701 North 19th Avenue, Suite 100
Phoenix, AZ 85015-3727
Phone: 602-241-1080
Fax: 602-604-9640
E-mail: amlegauxaz@mcleodusa.net

AMERICAN LEGION AUXILIARY, DEPARTMENT OF ARKANSAS

AMERICAN LEGION AUXILIARY DEPARTMENT OF ARKANSAS NURSE SCHOLARSHIP

One-time award for Arkansas residents who are the children of veterans who served during eligibility dates for membership. Must attend nursing program in Arkansas. Open to high school seniors. Must complete 1,000-word essay entitled "What my country's flag means to me." Contact local American Legion Auxiliary.

Academic Fields/Career Goals: Nursing.

Award: Scholarship for use in freshman or senior years; not renewable. *Number:* 1. *Amount:* $500.

Eligibility Requirements: Applicant must be high school student; planning to enroll or expecting to enroll full-time at a two-year or four-year or technical institution or university; resident of Arkansas and studying in Arkansas. Available to U.S. citizens. Applicant or parent must meet one or more of the following requirements: general military experience; retired from active duty; disabled or killed as a result of military service; prisoner of war; or missing in action.

Application Requirements: Application, essay, financial need analysis, references, self-addressed stamped envelope, test scores, transcript, copy of veteran discharge papers, branch of service, dates of service, DD Form 214. *Deadline:* March 1.

Contact: Department Secretary
American Legion Auxiliary, Department of Arkansas
1415 West 7th Street
Little Rock, AR 72201
Phone: 501-374-5836

AMERICAN LEGION AUXILIARY, DEPARTMENT OF IDAHO

AMERICAN LEGION AUXILIARY, DEPARTMENT OF IDAHO NURSING SCHOLARSHIP

Scholarship available to veterans or the children of veterans who are majoring in nursing. Applicants must be 17-35 years of age and residents of Idaho for five years prior to applying. One-time award of $750.

Academic Fields/Career Goals: Nursing.

Award: Scholarship for use in freshman, sophomore, junior, or senior years; not renewable. *Number:* 1. *Amount:* $750.

Eligibility Requirements: Applicant must be age 17-35; enrolled or expecting to enroll full-time at an institution or university and resident of Idaho. Available to U.S. citizens. Applicant or parent must meet one or more of the following requirements: general military experience; retired from active duty; disabled or killed as a result of military service; prisoner of war; or missing in action.

Application Requirements: Application, financial need analysis, photo, references, self-addressed stamped envelope, transcript. *Deadline:* May 15.

Contact: Mary Chase, Secretary
American Legion Auxiliary, Department of Idaho
905 South Warren Street
Boise, ID 83706-3825
Phone: 208-342-7066
Fax: 208-342-7066
E-mail: idalegionaux@msn.com

AMERICAN LEGION AUXILIARY, DEPARTMENT OF IOWA
http://www.ialegion.org/ala

M.V. MCCRAE MEMORIAL NURSES SCHOLARSHIP

One-time award available to the child of an Iowa American Legion Post member or Iowa American Legion Auxiliary Unit member. Award is for full-time study in accredited nursing program. Must be U.S. citizen and Iowa resident. Must attend an Iowa institution.

Academic Fields/Career Goals: Nursing.

Award: Scholarship for use in freshman, sophomore, junior, or senior years; not renewable. *Number:* 1. *Amount:* $400.

Eligibility Requirements: Applicant must be enrolled or expecting to enroll full or part-time at a two-year or four-year institution or university; resident of Iowa and studying in Iowa. Applicant or parent of applicant must be member of American Legion or Auxiliary. Available to U.S. citizens. Applicant or parent must meet one or more of the following requirements: general military experience; retired from active duty; disabled or killed as a result of military service; prisoner of war; or missing in action.

Application Requirements: Application, autobiography, essay, financial need analysis, photo, references, self-addressed stamped envelope, test scores, transcript. *Deadline:* June 1.

Contact: Marlene Valentine, Secretary/Treasurer
American Legion Auxiliary, Department of Iowa
720 Lyon Street
Des Moines, IA 50309
Phone: 515-282-7987
Fax: 515-282-7583

AMERICAN LEGION AUXILIARY, DEPARTMENT OF MICHIGAN
http://www.michalaux.org

MEDICAL CAREER SCHOLARSHIP
• *See page 319*

AMERICAN LEGION AUXILIARY, DEPARTMENT OF MISSOURI

PAST PRESIDENTS PARLEY SCHOLARSHIP-MISSOURI

A $500 scholarship is awarded to high school graduate who has chosen to study nursing. $250 will be awarded each semester upon receipt of verification from the college that student is enrolled. The applicant must be a resident of Missouri and a member of a veteran's family. The applicant must be validated by the sponsoring unit. Check with sponsoring unit for details on required recommendation letters.

Academic Fields/Career Goals: Nursing.

Award: Scholarship for use in freshman year; not renewable. *Number:* 1. *Amount:* $500.

Eligibility Requirements: Applicant must be high school student; planning to enroll or expecting to enroll full-time at a two-year or four-year or technical institution or university and resident of Missouri. Applicant or parent of applicant must be member of American Legion or Auxiliary. Available to U.S. citizens. Applicant or parent must meet one or more of the following requirements: general military experience; retired from active duty; disabled or killed as a result of military service; prisoner of war; or missing in action.

Application Requirements: Application, photo. *Deadline:* March 1.

Contact: Mary Doerhoff, Department Secretary/Treasurer
American Legion Auxiliary, Department of Missouri
600 Ellis Boulevard
Jefferson City, MO 65101-1615
Phone: 573-636-9133
Fax: 573-635-3467
E-mail: dptmoala@socket.net

AMERICAN LEGION AUXILIARY, DEPARTMENT OF NEBRASKA

AMERICAN LEGION AUXILIARY DEPARTMENT OF NEBRASKA NURSE'S GIFT TUITION SCHOLARSHIP

One-time scholarship for Nebraska resident who is a veteran or a child of a veteran who served in the Armed Forces during dates of eligibility for American Legion membership. Proof of enrollment in nursing program at eligible institution required. Must rank in upper third of class or have a minimum 3.0 GPA.

Academic Fields/Career Goals: Nursing.

Award: Scholarship for use in freshman, sophomore, junior, or senior years; not renewable. *Number:* 1–20. *Amount:* $200–$400.

Eligibility Requirements: Applicant must be enrolled or expecting to enroll full-time at a two-year or four-year institution or university and resident of Nebraska. Applicant must have 3.0 GPA or higher. Available to U.S. citizens. Applicant or parent must meet one or more of the following requirements: general military experience; retired from active duty; disabled or killed as a result of military service; prisoner of war; or missing in action.

Application Requirements: Application, essay, financial need analysis, references, test scores, transcript. *Deadline:* March 26.

Contact: Terry Walker, Department Secretary
American Legion Auxiliary, Department of Nebraska
PO Box 5227
Lincoln, NE 68505
Phone: 402-466-1808
Fax: 402-466-0182
E-mail: neaux@alltel.net

AMERICAN LEGION AUXILIARY DEPARTMENT OF NEBRASKA PRACTICAL NURSE SCHOLARSHIP

Nonrenewable scholarship for a veteran or a child of a veteran who served in the Armed Forces during dates of eligibility for American Legion membership. For full-time undergraduate study toward nursing degree at eligible institution. Must be a Nebraska resident. Must rank in upper third of class or have a minimum 3.0 GPA.

Academic Fields/Career Goals: Nursing.

Award: Scholarship for use in freshman, sophomore, junior, or senior years; not renewable. *Number:* 1–3. *Amount:* $200–$400.

Eligibility Requirements: Applicant must be enrolled or expecting to enroll full-time at a two-year or four-year institution or university and resident of Nebraska. Applicant must have 3.0 GPA or higher. Available to U.S. citizens. Applicant or parent must meet one or more of the following requirements: general military experience; retired from active duty; disabled or killed as a result of military service; prisoner of war; or missing in action.

Application Requirements: Application, essay, financial need analysis, references, test scores, transcript. *Deadline:* March 26.

Contact: Terry Walker, Department Secretary
American Legion Auxiliary, Department of Nebraska
PO Box 5227
Lincoln, NE 68505
Phone: 402-466-1808
Fax: 402-466-0182
E-mail: neaux@alltel.net

AMERICAN LEGION AUXILIARY, DEPARTMENT OF NEW MEXICO

AMERICAN LEGION AUXILIARY DEPARTMENT OF NEW MEXICO PAST PRESIDENT PARLEY NURSES SCHOLARSHIP

Scholarship available to children of veterans who served in the Armed Forces during the eligibility dates for American Legion membership. Must be New Mexico resident, high school senior, and in pursuit of a nursing degree full-time at an accredited institution. One-time award of $250. Must be U.S. citizen.

Academic Fields/Career Goals: Nursing.

Award: Scholarship for use in freshman, sophomore, junior, or senior years; not renewable. *Number:* 1. *Amount:* $250.

Eligibility Requirements: Applicant must be high school student; planning to enroll or expecting to enroll full-time at an institution or university and resident of New Mexico. Available to U.S. citizens. Applicant or parent must meet one or more of the following requirements: general military experience; retired from active duty; disabled or killed as a result of military service; prisoner of war; or missing in action.

Application Requirements: Application, essay, references, self-addressed stamped envelope, transcript. *Deadline:* March 1.

Contact: Loreen Jorgensen, Scholarship Director
American Legion Auxiliary, Department of New Mexico
1215 Mountain Road, NE
Albuquerque, NM 87102
Phone: 505-242-9918
Fax: 505-247-0478

AMERICAN LEGION AUXILIARY, DEPARTMENT OF NORTH DAKOTA   http://www.ndlegion.org

AMERICAN LEGION AUXILIARY DEPARTMENT OF NORTH DAKOTA PAST PRESIDENT'S PARLEY NURSES' SCHOLARSHIP

One-time award for North Dakota resident who is the child, grandchild, or great-grandchild of a member of the American Legion or Auxiliary. Must be a graduate of a North Dakota high school and attending a nursing program in North Dakota. A minimum 2.5 GPA is required.

Academic Fields/Career Goals: Nursing.

Award: Scholarship for use in freshman, sophomore, junior, or senior years; not renewable. *Number:* 5. *Amount:* $500.

Eligibility Requirements: Applicant must be enrolled or expecting to enroll full or part-time at a two-year or four-year institution or university; resident of North Dakota and studying in North Dakota. Applicant or parent of applicant must be member of American Legion or Auxiliary. Applicant must have 2.5 GPA or higher. Available to U.S. citizens. Applicant or parent must meet one or more of the following requirements: general military experience; retired from active duty; disabled or killed as a result of military service; prisoner of war; or missing in action.

Application Requirements: Application, autobiography, essay, financial need analysis, self-addressed stamped envelope, test scores, transcript. *Deadline:* May 15.

Contact: Myrna Ronholm, Department Secretary
American Legion Auxiliary, Department of North Dakota
PO Box 1060
Jamestown, ND 58402-1060
Phone: 701-253-5992

AMERICAN LEGION AUXILIARY, DEPARTMENT OF OHIO

AMERICAN LEGION AUXILIARY DEPARTMENT OF OHIO PAST PRESIDENT'S PARLEY NURSES' SCHOLARSHIP

One-time award worth $300-$500 for Ohio residents who are the children or grandchildren of a veteran, living or deceased. Must enroll or be enrolled in a nursing program. Application requests must be received by May 1.

Academic Fields/Career Goals: Nursing.

Award: Scholarship for use in freshman, sophomore, junior, or senior years; not renewable. *Number:* 15–20. *Amount:* $300–$500.

Eligibility Requirements: Applicant must be enrolled or expecting to enroll full-time at a two-year or four-year institution or university and resident of Ohio. Available to U.S. citizens. Applicant or parent must meet one or more of the following requirements: general military experience; retired from active duty; disabled or killed as a result of military service; prisoner of war; or missing in action.

Application Requirements: Application, references. *Deadline:* May 1.

Contact: Reva McClure, Scholarship Coordinator
American Legion Auxiliary, Department of Ohio
PO Box 2760
Zanesville, OH 43702-2760
Phone: 740-452-8245
Fax: 740-452-2620
E-mail: ala_pam@rrohio.com

AMERICAN LEGION AUXILIARY, DEPARTMENT OF OREGON

AMERICAN LEGION AUXILIARY DEPARTMENT OF OREGON NURSES SCHOLARSHIP

One-time award for Oregon residents entering their freshman year who are the children of veterans who served during eligibility dates for American Legion membership. Must enroll in a nursing program. Contact local units for application.

Academic Fields/Career Goals: Nursing.

Award: Scholarship for use in freshman year; renewable. *Number:* 1. *Amount:* $1500.

Eligibility Requirements: Applicant must be enrolled or expecting to enroll at a four-year institution or university and resident of Oregon. Available to U.S. citizens. Applicant or parent must meet one or more of the following requirements: general military experience; retired from active duty; disabled or killed as a result of military service; prisoner of war; or missing in action.

Application Requirements: Application, financial need analysis, interview, transcript. *Deadline:* May 1.

Contact: Pat Calhoun-Floren, Secretary
American Legion Auxiliary, Department of Oregon
PO Box 1730
Wilsonville, OR 97070
Phone: 503-682-3162
Fax: 503-685-5008

AMERICAN LEGION AUXILIARY, DEPARTMENT OF WASHINGTON   http://www.walegion-aux.org

MARGARITE MCALPIN NURSE'S SCHOLARSHIP

One award for a child or grandchild of a veteran pursuing an education in nursing or have served in the Armed Forces. May be a high school senior or an enrolled nursing student. Submit a brief statement of military service of veteran parent or grandparent. For Washington residents. One-time award of $300.

Academic Fields/Career Goals: Nursing.

Award: Scholarship for use in freshman, sophomore, junior, senior, or graduate years; not renewable. *Number:* 1. *Amount:* $300.

Eligibility Requirements: Applicant must be enrolled or expecting to enroll at a four-year institution or university and resident of Washington. Available to U.S. citizens. Applicant or parent must meet one or more of the following requirements: general military experience; retired from active duty; disabled or killed as a result of military service; prisoner of war; or missing in action.

Application Requirements: Application, autobiography, essay, financial need analysis, references, transcript. *Deadline:* April 1.

Contact: Crystal Lawrence, Department Secretary
American Legion Auxiliary, Department of Washington
3600 Ruddell Road
Lacey, WA 98503
Phone: 360-456-5995
Fax: 360-491-7442
E-mail: alawash@qwest.net

AMERICAN LEGION AUXILIARY, DEPARTMENT OF WISCONSIN   http://www.amlegionauxwi.org

PAST PRESIDENTS PARLEY REGISTERED NURSE SCHOLARSHIP

One-time award of $1000. Applicant must be in nursing school or have positive acceptance to an accredited hospital or university registered nursing program. Applicant must be a daughter, son, wife, or widow of a veteran. Granddaughters and great-granddaughters of veterans who are auxiliary members may also apply. Must send with completed application: certification of an American Legion Auxiliary Unit President, copy of proof that veteran was in service (i.e. discharge papers), letters of recommendation, transcripts, and essay. Must have minimum 3.5 GPA, show financial need, and be a resident of Wisconsin. Refer questions to Department Secretary, (608) 745-0124. Applications available on Web site: http://www.legion-aux.org

Academic Fields/Career Goals: Nursing.

Award: Scholarship for use in freshman, sophomore, junior, senior, or graduate years; not renewable. *Number:* 3. *Amount:* $1000.

American Legion Auxiliary, Department of Wisconsin (continued)

Eligibility Requirements: Applicant must be enrolled or expecting to enroll full or part-time at a technical institution or university and resident of Wisconsin. Applicant or parent of applicant must be member of American Legion or Auxiliary. Applicant must have 3.5 GPA or higher. Available to U.S. citizens.

Application Requirements: Application, essay, financial need analysis, references, transcript. *Deadline:* March 15.

Contact: Kim Henderson, Scholarship Information
American Legion Auxiliary, Department of Wisconsin
PO Box 140
Portage, WI 53901-0140
Phone: 608-745-0124
Fax: 608-745-1947

AMERICAN LEGION AUXILIARY, DEPARTMENT OF WYOMING

PAST PRESIDENTS PARLEY HEALTH CARE SCHOLARSHIP
• See page 207

AMERICAN LEGION, DEPARTMENT OF KANSAS
http://www.ksamlegion.org

HOBBLE (LPN) NURSING SCHOLARSHIP

This is an outright grant of $300 (payable one time) at the start of the first semester, awarded only upon acceptance and verification of enrollment by the scholarship winner in an accredited Kansas school which awards a diploma for Licensed Practical Nursing (LPN). The applicant must have attained the age of 18 prior to taking the Kansas State Board Examination. The scholarship will be awarded to an individual who is both qualified and in need of financial aid.

Academic Fields/Career Goals: Nursing.

Award: Scholarship for use in freshman year; not renewable. *Number:* 1. *Amount:* $300.

Eligibility Requirements: Applicant must be age 18; enrolled or expecting to enroll at a two-year or four-year institution; resident of Kansas and studying in Kansas. Available to U.S. citizens.

Application Requirements: Application, financial need analysis, photo, references. *Deadline:* February 15.

Contact: Scholarship Administrator
American Legion, Department of Kansas
1314 Southwest Topeka Boulevard
Topeka, KS 66612-1886

AMERICAN LEGION, DEPARTMENT OF MISSOURI
http://www.missourilegion.org

M.D. "JACK" MURPHY MEMORIAL SCHOLARSHIP

One-time award for a single Missouri resident who wants to further their education in the field of nursing. Should be at least 18. Must be a dependent child or grandchild of a Missouri veteran.

Academic Fields/Career Goals: Nursing.

Award: Scholarship for use in freshman or sophomore years; renewable. *Number:* 1. *Amount:* $750.

Eligibility Requirements: Applicant must be age 18; enrolled or expecting to enroll full-time at a four-year institution or university; single and resident of Missouri. Available to U.S. citizens. Applicant or parent must meet one or more of the following requirements: general military experience; retired from active duty; disabled or killed as a result of military service; prisoner of war; or missing in action.

Application Requirements: Application, financial need analysis, test scores. *Deadline:* April 20.

Contact: Mr. John Doane, Chairman
American Legion, Department of Missouri
PO Box 179
Jefferson City, MO 65102-0179
Phone: 417-924-8186
Fax: 573-893-2980

AMERICAN LEGION, EIGHT AND FORTY
http://www.legion.org

EIGHT & FORTY LUNG AND RESPIRATORY DISEASE NURSING SCHOLARSHIP FUND

Available to registered nurses with work experience who are taking courses leading to full-time employment in lung or respiratory disease nursing and teaching. Candidates should have proven leadership qualities in emergency situations.

Academic Fields/Career Goals: Nursing.

Award: Scholarship for use in junior, senior, or graduate years; not renewable. *Number:* 20–25. *Amount:* $2500.

Eligibility Requirements: Applicant must be enrolled or expecting to enroll full or part-time at a four-year institution or university and must have an interest in leadership. Available to U.S. citizens.

Application Requirements: Application, references, transcript, applicant must be employed in a clinic, hospital, or health department. *Deadline:* May 15.

Contact: Program Administrator
American Legion, Eight and Forty
PO Box 1055
Indianapolis, IN 46206-1055

AMERICAN NEPHROLOGY NURSES' ASSOCIATION
http://www.annanurse.org

ABBOTT/PAMELA BALZER CAREER MOBILITY SCHOLARSHIP

Scholarships available to support qualified ANNA members, minimum two years membership, in the pursuit of either a BSN or advanced degree in nursing that will enhance their nephrology nursing practice. Deadline is October 15. Details on Web site http://www.annanurse.org

Academic Fields/Career Goals: Nursing.

Award: Scholarship for use in junior, senior, graduate, or postgraduate years; not renewable. *Number:* 1. *Amount:* $2500.

Eligibility Requirements: Applicant must be enrolled or expecting to enroll full or part-time at a two-year or four-year institution or university. Applicant or parent of applicant must be member of American Nephrology Nurses' Association. Applicant or parent of applicant must have employment or volunteer experience in designated career field. Available to U.S. citizens.

Application Requirements: Application, essay, references, transcript, eligibility documentation, acceptance letter. *Deadline:* October 15.

Contact: Charlotte Thomas-Hawkins, American Nephrology Nurses' Association
American Nephrology Nurses' Association
East Holly Avenue
Box 56
Pitman, NJ 08071-0056
Phone: 856-256-2320
Fax: 856-589-7463
E-mail: anna@ajj.com

AMERICAN NEPHROLOGY NURSES' ASSOCIATION AMERICAN REGENT CAREER MOBILITY SCHOLARSHIP

Scholarships available to support qualified ANNA members in the pursuit of either a BSN or advanced degree in nursing that will enhance nephrology nursing practice. Deadline is October 15. Details on Web. http://www.annanurse.org

Academic Fields/Career Goals: Nursing.

Award: Scholarship for use in junior, senior, graduate, or postgraduate years; not renewable. *Number:* 1. *Amount:* $2000.

Eligibility Requirements: Applicant must be enrolled or expecting to enroll full or part-time at a two-year or four-year institution or university. Applicant or parent of applicant must be member of American Nephrology Nurses' Association. Applicant or parent of applicant must have employment or volunteer experience in designated career field. Available to U.S. citizens.

Application Requirements: Application, essay, references, transcript, eligibility documentation, acceptance letter. *Deadline:* October 15.

Contact: Charlotte Thomas-Hawkins, American Nephrology Nurses' Association
American Nephrology Nurses' Association
East Holly Avenue
Box 56
Pitman, NJ 08071-0056
Phone: 856-256-2320
Fax: 856-589-7463
E-mail: anna@ajj.com

AMERICAN NEPHROLOGY NURSES' ASSOCIATION AMGEN CAREER MOBILITY SCHOLARSHIP

Scholarships available to support qualified ANNA members in the pursuit of either a BSN or advanced degree in nursing that will enhance nephrology nursing practice. Deadline is October 15. For more details visit the Web site http://www.annanurse.org

Academic Fields/Career Goals: Nursing.

Award: Scholarship for use in junior, senior, graduate, or postgraduate years; not renewable. *Number:* 1. *Amount:* $2500.

Eligibility Requirements: Applicant must be enrolled or expecting to enroll full or part-time at a two-year or four-year institution or university. Applicant or parent of applicant must be member of American Nephrology Nurses' Association. Applicant or parent of applicant must have employment or volunteer experience in designated career field. Available to U.S. citizens.

Application Requirements: Application, essay, references, transcript, eligibility documentation, acceptance letter. *Deadline:* October 15.

Contact: Charlotte Thomas-Hawkins, American Nephrology Nurses' Association
American Nephrology Nurses' Association
East Holly Avenue
Box 56
Pitman, NJ 08071-0056
Phone: 856-256-2320
Fax: 856-589-7463
E-mail: anna@ajj.com

AMERICAN NEPHROLOGY NURSES' ASSOCIATION ANTHONY J. JANETTI, INC. CAREER MOBILITY SCHOLARSHIP

Scholarships available to support qualified ANNA members in the pursuit of either a BSN or advanced degree in nursing that will enhance nephrology nursing practice. Deadline is October 15. For details visit the Web site http://www.annanurse.org

Academic Fields/Career Goals: Nursing.

Award: Scholarship for use in junior, senior, graduate, or postgraduate years; not renewable. *Number:* 1. *Amount:* up to $2500.

Eligibility Requirements: Applicant must be enrolled or expecting to enroll at a two-year or four-year institution or university. Applicant or parent of applicant must be member of American Nephrology Nurses' Association. Applicant or parent of applicant must have employment or volunteer experience in designated career field. Available to U.S. citizens.

Application Requirements: Application, essay, references, transcript, eligibility documentation, letter of acceptance. *Deadline:* October 15.

Contact: Charlotte Thomas-Hawkins, American Nephrology Nurses' Association
American Nephrology Nurses' Association
East Holly Avenue
Box 56
Pitman, NJ 08071-0056
Phone: 856-256-2320
Fax: 856-589-7463
E-mail: anna@ajj.com

AMERICAN NEPHROLOGY NURSES' ASSOCIATION CAREER MOBILITY SCHOLARSHIP

Scholarships available to support qualified ANNA members, minimum two years, in the pursuit of either BSN or advanced degrees in nursing that will enhance their nephrology nursing practice. Must be accepted or enrolled in baccalaureate or higher degree program in nursing. Details on Web site http://www.annanurse.org

Academic Fields/Career Goals: Nursing.

Award: Scholarship for use in junior, senior, graduate, or postgraduate years; not renewable. *Number:* 5. *Amount:* $2000.

Eligibility Requirements: Applicant must be enrolled or expecting to enroll full or part-time at a two-year or four-year institution or university. Applicant or parent of applicant must be member of American Nephrology Nurses' Association. Applicant or parent of applicant must have employment or volunteer experience in designated career field. Available to U.S. citizens.

Application Requirements: Application, essay, references, transcript, eligibility documentation, acceptance letter. *Deadline:* October 15.

Contact: Charlotte Thomas-Hawkins, American Nephrology Nurses' Association
American Nephrology Nurses' Association
East Holly Avenue
Box 56
Pitman, NJ 08071-0056
Phone: 856-256-2320
Fax: 856-589-7463
E-mail: anna@ajj.com

AMERICAN NEPHROLOGY NURSES' ASSOCIATION NNCC CAREER MOBILITY SCHOLARSHIP

Scholarships available for qualified ANNA members who are certified nephrology nurses, or certified dialysis nurse in the pursuit of a BSN or advanced degree in nursing. The applicant must hold a current credential as a Certified Nephrology Nurse (CNN) or Certified Dialysis Nurse (CDN) administered by the Nephrology Nursing Certification Commission (NNCC). Deadline is October 15. Details on Web. http://www.annanurse.org

Academic Fields/Career Goals: Nursing.

Award: Scholarship for use in junior, senior, graduate, or postgraduate years. *Number:* 3. *Amount:* $2000.

Eligibility Requirements: Applicant must be enrolled or expecting to enroll full or part-time at a two-year or four-year institution or university. Applicant or parent of applicant must be member of American Nephrology Nurses' Association. Applicant or parent of applicant must have employment or volunteer experience in designated career field. Available to U.S. citizens.

Application Requirements: Application, essay, references, transcript, eligibility documentation, letter of acceptance. *Deadline:* October 15.

Contact: Charlotte Thomas-Hawkins, American Nephrology Nurses' Association
American Nephrology Nurses' Association
East Holly Avenue
Box 56
Pitman, NJ 08071-0056
Phone: 856-256-2320
Fax: 856-589-7463
E-mail: anna@ajj.com

AMERICAN NEPHROLOGY NURSES' ASSOCIATION WATSON PHARMA, INC. CAREER MOBILITY SCHOLARSHIP

Scholarships available to support qualified ANNA members in the pursuit of either a BSN or advanced degree in nursing that will enhance nephrology nursing practice. Deadline is October 15. For details visit the Web site http://www.annanurse.org

Academic Fields/Career Goals: Nursing.

Award: Scholarship for use in junior, senior, graduate, or postgraduate years; not renewable. *Number:* 1. *Amount:* $2500.

Eligibility Requirements: Applicant must be enrolled or expecting to enroll full or part-time at a two-year or four-year institution or university. Applicant or parent of applicant must be member of American Nephrology Nurses' Association. Applicant or parent of applicant must have employment or volunteer experience in designated career field. Available to U.S. citizens.

Application Requirements: Application, essay, references, transcript, eligibility documentation, letter of acceptance. *Deadline:* October 15.

American Nephrology Nurses' Association (continued)

Contact: Charlotte Thomas-Hawkins, American Nephrology Nurses'
Association
American Nephrology Nurses' Association
East Holly Avenue
Box 56
Pitman, NJ 08071-0056
Phone: 856-256-2320
Fax: 856-589-7463
E-mail: anna@ajj.com

AMERICAN QUARTER HORSE FOUNDATION
(AQHF)   http://www.aqha.org/aqhya

AQHF EDUCATION OR NURSING SCHOLARSHIP
• *See page 220*

ARRL FOUNDATION,
INC.   http://www.arrl.org/arrlf/scholgen.html

WILLIAM R. GOLDFARB MEMORIAL SCHOLARSHIP
• *See page 145*

ASSOCIATION OF PERI-OPERATIVE REGISTERED
NURSES   http://www.aorn.org/foundation

ASSOCIATION OF PERI-OPERATIVE REGISTERED NURSES

Applicant must be an RN and a member of AORN for twelve consecutive
months to apply for a scholarship for an advanced degree. Recipients may
reapply. Amount and number of one-time awards vary. Minimum 3.0 GPA
required. Must be pursuing studies in nursing. Students working toward their
RN need not be members of AORN. Applicants must be U.S. citizen or legal
resident. See Web site: http://www.aorn.org for application and further details

Academic Fields/Career Goals: Nursing.

Award: Scholarship for use in freshman, sophomore, junior, senior, or
graduate years; not renewable. *Number:* varies. *Amount:* varies.

Eligibility Requirements: Applicant must be enrolled or expecting to
enroll full or part-time at a two-year or four-year institution or
university. Applicant or parent of applicant must be member of
Association of Operating Room Nurses. Applicant must have 3.0 GPA
or higher. Available to U.S. citizens.

Application Requirements: Application, essay, transcript. *Deadline:*
June 1.

Contact: Ingrid Bendzsa, Scholarship Coordinator
Association of Peri-Operative Registered Nurses
2170 South Parker Road, Suite 300
Denver, CO 80231
Phone: 800-755-2676 Ext. 328
Fax: 303-755-4219
E-mail: ibendzsa@aorn.org

BECA FOUNDATION, INC.   http://www.becafoundation.org

ALICE NEWELL JOSLYN MEDICAL FUND
• *See page 207*

BETHESDA LUTHERAN HOMES AND SERVICES,
INC.   http://www.blhs.org

*NURSING SCHOLASTIC ACHIEVEMENT SCHOLARSHIP FOR LUTHERAN
COLLEGE STUDENTS*

One-time award for college nursing students with minimum 3.0 GPA who are
Lutheran and have completed the sophomore year of a four-year nursing
program or one year of a two-year nursing program. Must be interested in
working with people with developmental disabilities. Awards of up to $1500.

Academic Fields/Career Goals: Nursing.

Award: Scholarship for use in sophomore, junior, senior, or graduate
years; not renewable. *Number:* 1–3. *Amount:* up to $1500.

Eligibility Requirements: Applicant must be Lutheran and enrolled or
expecting to enroll full-time at a two-year or four-year institution or
university. Applicant must have 3.0 GPA or higher. Available to U.S.
and Canadian citizens.

Application Requirements: Application, autobiography, essay,
references, transcript. *Deadline:* March 15.

Contact: Thomas Heuer, Coordinator, Outreach Programs and Services
Bethesda Lutheran Homes and Services, Inc.
National Christian Resource Center, 600 Hoffmann Drive
Watertown, WI 53094-6294
Phone: 920-261-3050 Ext. 4449
Fax: 920-262-6513
E-mail: theuer@blhs.org

BRITISH COLUMBIA MINISTRY OF ADVANCED
EDUCATION   http://www.aved.gov.bc.ca/

*LOAN FORGIVENESS PROGRAM FOR NURSES, DOCTORS, MIDWIVES,
AND PHARMACISTS*
• *See page 325*

BUREAU OF HEALTH
PROFESSIONS   http://nhsc.bhpr.hrsa.gov/members/scholars/

NATIONAL HEALTH SERVICE CORPS SCHOLARSHIP PROGRAM
• *See page 325*

CALIFORNIA STATE PARENT-TEACHER
ASSOCIATION   http://www.capta.org

CONTINUING EDUCATION FOR SCHOOL NURSES SCHOLARSHIP

Available annually from the California State PTA for continuing education
use at Board of Registered Nurses-(BRN) approved institutions and/or
providers from Jan 1 through Dec 31. Applicant must be a member of a
PTA/PTSA unit in good standing and have an assignment in at least one
PTA/PTSA school. Deadline Nov 15.

Academic Fields/Career Goals: Nursing.

Award: Scholarship for use in freshman, sophomore, junior, senior, or
graduate years; renewable. *Amount:* up to $500.

Eligibility Requirements: Applicant must be high school student;
planning to enroll or expecting to enroll full-time at a two-year or
four-year or technical institution or university and resident of
California. Available to U.S. citizens.

Application Requirements: Application, essay, references, copy of
membership card. *Deadline:* November 15.

Contact: Becky Reece, Scholarship and Award Chairman
California State Parent-Teacher Association
930 Georgia Street
Los Angeles, CA 90015-1322
Phone: 213-620-1100
Fax: 213-620-1411

CHILDREN'S HOSPITAL OF
ATLANTA   http://www.choa.org/

CHANCES SCHOLARSHIP PROGRAM

Scholarship available for students accepted into a nursing program for the RN
degree. Upon graduation from nursing school, recipients will be committed to
work as a Registered Nurse for Children's Hospital of Atlanta for 18 months
for each academic year of support received. A verified minimum 2.8 GPA is
required.

Academic Fields/Career Goals: Nursing.

Award: Scholarship for use in freshman, sophomore, junior, or senior
years. *Amount:* up to $16,000.

Eligibility Requirements: Applicant must be enrolled or expecting to
enroll at a four-year institution. Available to U.S. citizens.

Application Requirements: Application, essay, resume, references. *Deadline:* April 1.

Contact: Bobbette Loyd, Program Coordinator
Children's Hospital of Atlanta
Children's Healthcare of Atlanta, Human Resources, 1600 Tullie
Circle, NE
Atlanta, GA 30329-2321
Phone: 404-785-7211

OPPORTUNITIES SCHOLARSHIP PROGRAM

Scholarship available for an individual admitted, enrolled, and classified as a nursing student in a matriculated status at an eligible institution. Upon graduation from nursing school, recipients will be committed to work as a full-time Registered Nurse at Children's Hospital of Atlanta for one year for each year of support received. A verified minimum 2.8 GPA (high school or college) is required Must be fluent in two or more languages, one of which must be English

Academic Fields/Career Goals: Nursing.

Award: Scholarship for use in freshman, sophomore, junior, or senior years. *Amount:* up to $10,000.

Eligibility Requirements: Applicant must be enrolled or expecting to enroll at a four-year institution or university. Available to U.S. citizens.

Application Requirements: Application, essay, resume, references. *Deadline:* May 1.

Contact: Bobbette Loyd, Program Coordinator
Children's Hospital of Atlanta
Children's Healthcare of Atlanta, 1600 Tullie Circle, NE
Atlanta, GA 30329
Phone: 404-785-7211

COMMON KNOWLEDGE SCHOLARSHIP FOUNDATION   http://www.cksf.org

THE NATIONAL NURSING SCHOLARSHIP

Quiz based on nursing curriculum. The majority of the questions were written by nurses, faculty and nursing students. This program is available to college nursing students in the United States. For more information and online registration check Web site: www.cksf.org

Academic Fields/Career Goals: Nursing.

Award: Scholarship for use in freshman, sophomore, junior, or senior years; not renewable. *Number:* up to 4. *Amount:* $250.

Eligibility Requirements: Applicant must be enrolled or expecting to enroll at a two-year or four-year institution. Available to U.S. citizens.

Application Requirements: Applicant must enter a contest.

Contact: Daryl Hulce, President
Common Knowledge Scholarship Foundation
PO Box 290361
Davie, FL 33329-0361
Phone: 954-262-8553
Fax: 954-262-3940
E-mail: hulce@cksf.org

COMMUNITY FOUNDATION OF WESTERN MASSACHUSETTS   http://www.communityfoundation.org

ELEANOR M. MORRISSEY SCHOLARSHIP

Scholarship provided to graduating seniors of Berkshire, Franklin, Hampden, and Hampshire counties who are pursuing a career in nursing.

Academic Fields/Career Goals: Nursing.

Award: Scholarship for use in freshman year; not renewable. *Number:* 1.

Eligibility Requirements: Applicant must be high school student and planning to enroll or expecting to enroll full-time at an institution or university. Available to U.S. citizens.

Application Requirements: Application, financial need analysis, transcript, parent's and student's federal income tax returns, Student Aid Report (SAR). *Deadline:* March 31.

Contact: Dorothy Theriaque, Education Associate
Community Foundation of Western Massachusetts
1500 Main Street, PO Box 15769
Springfield, MA 01115
Phone: 413-732-2858
Fax: 413-733-8565
E-mail: dtheriaque@communityfoundation.org

DANISH SISTERHOOD OF AMERICA   http://www.danishsisterhood.org/

ELIZABETH GARDE NURSING SCHOLARSHIP

One-time award for student seeking to be in the medical profession. Must be a member of the Danish Sisterhood of America or be a son or daughter of a member. Minimum GPA of 3.0. Write for further details.

Academic Fields/Career Goals: Nursing.

Award: Scholarship for use in freshman, sophomore, junior, senior, graduate, or postgraduate years; not renewable. *Number:* 1. *Amount:* $850.

Eligibility Requirements: Applicant must be enrolled or expecting to enroll at a two-year or four-year or technical institution or university. Applicant or parent of applicant must be member of Danish Sisterhood of America. Applicant must have 3.0 GPA or higher. Available to U.S. and non-U.S. citizens.

Application Requirements: Application. *Deadline:* February 28.

Contact: Lizette Burtis, National Trustee Scholarship Chairperson
Danish Sisterhood of America
7874 Rayside Ave
Burnaby V5E 2L3
Canada

DEMOCRATIC NURSING ORGANIZATION OF SOUTH AFRICA   http://www.denosa.org.za

DEMOCRATIC NURSING ORGANIZATION OF SOUTH AFRICA STUDY FUND

Awards granted annually to members of DENOSA who are enrolled for postsecondary studies. Must have been member of DENOSA for three years. Must study in South Africa. Deadline is January 31.

Academic Fields/Career Goals: Nursing.

Award: Grant for use in freshman, sophomore, junior, or senior years; not renewable. *Number:* varies. *Amount:* varies.

Eligibility Requirements: Applicant must be enrolled or expecting to enroll full or part-time at a four-year or technical institution or university. Available to citizens of countries other than the U.S. or Canada.

Application Requirements: Application. *Deadline:* January 31.

Contact: Thembeka Gwagwa, Executive Director
Democratic Nursing Organization of South Africa
PO Box 1280
Pretoria 0001
South Africa
Phone: 27-12-3432315
Fax: 27-12-3440750
E-mail: info@denosa.org.za

EMERGENCY NURSES ASSOCIATION (ENA) FOUNDATION   http://www.ena.org/foundation

ADDITIONAL ENA FOUNDATION UNDERGRADUATE SCHOLARSHIPS

Scholarships available to nurses (RN, LPN, LVN) who are pursuing baccalaureate degrees in nursing. Applicants must be ENA members for a minimum of twelve months prior to applying.

Academic Fields/Career Goals: Nursing.

Award: Scholarship for use in freshman, sophomore, junior, or senior years. *Number:* 1–8. *Amount:* $3000–$5000.

Eligibility Requirements: Applicant must be enrolled or expecting to enroll at a four-year institution or university. Applicant or parent of applicant must be member of Emergency Nurses Association. Available to U.S. and non-U.S. citizens.

Application Requirements: Application, references, transcript. *Deadline:* June 1.

Contact: Ellen Siciliano, Development Manager
Emergency Nurses Association (ENA) Foundation
915 Lee Street
Des Plaines, IL 60016-6569
Phone: 847-460-4100
Fax: 847-460-4004
E-mail: foundation@ena.org

CHARLES KUNZ MEMORIAL UNDERGRADUATE SCHOLARSHIP

Scholarship awarded to a nurse (RN, LPN or LVN) who is pursuing a baccalaureate degree in nursing. Applicants must be ENA members for a minimum of twelve months prior to applying.

Academic Fields/Career Goals: Nursing.

Award: Scholarship for use in freshman, sophomore, junior, or senior years. *Number:* 1. *Amount:* $3000.

Eligibility Requirements: Applicant must be enrolled or expecting to enroll at a four-year institution or university. Applicant or parent of applicant must be member of Emergency Nurses Association. Available to U.S. and non-U.S. citizens.

Application Requirements: Application, references, transcript. *Deadline:* June 1.

Contact: Ellen Siciliano, Development Manager
Emergency Nurses Association (ENA) Foundation
915 Lee Street
Des Plaines, IL 60016-6569
Phone: 847-460-4100
Fax: 847-460-4004
E-mail: foundation@ena.org

ENA FOUNDATION CEN UNDERGRADUATE SCHOLARSHIP

Scholarship awarded to a nurse (RN, LPN, LVN) with a current CEN who is pursuing a baccalaureate degree in nursing. Applicants must be ENA members for a minimum of twelve months prior to applying.

Academic Fields/Career Goals: Nursing.

Award: Scholarship for use in freshman, sophomore, junior, or senior years. *Number:* 1. *Amount:* $2000.

Eligibility Requirements: Applicant must be enrolled or expecting to enroll at a four-year institution or university. Applicant or parent of applicant must be member of Emergency Nurses Association. Available to U.S. and non-U.S. citizens.

Application Requirements: Application, references, transcript. *Deadline:* June 1.

Contact: Ellen Siciliano, Development Manager
Emergency Nurses Association (ENA) Foundation
915 Lee Street
Des Plaines, IL 60016-6569
Phone: 847-460-4100
Fax: 847-460-4004
E-mail: foundation@ena.org

MARGARET MILLER MEMORIAL UNDERGRADUATE SCHOLARSHIP

Scholarship toward tuition costs for a nurse (RN, LPN, or LVN) in pursuit of a baccalaureate degree in nursing. Applicants must be ENA members for a minimum of twelve months prior to applying.

Academic Fields/Career Goals: Nursing.

Award: Scholarship for use in freshman, sophomore, junior, or senior years. *Number:* 1. *Amount:* $2000.

Eligibility Requirements: Applicant must be enrolled or expecting to enroll at a four-year institution or university. Applicant or parent of applicant must be member of Emergency Nurses Association. Available to U.S. and non-U.S. citizens.

Application Requirements: Application, references, transcript. *Deadline:* June 1.

Contact: Ellen Siciliano, Development Manager
Emergency Nurses Association (ENA) Foundation
915 Lee Street
Des Plaines, IL 60016-6569
Phone: 847-460-4100
Fax: 847-460-4004
E-mail: foundation@ena.org

MONSTER NON-RN UNDERGRADUATE SCHOLARSHIP

Scholarship available to a nursing student who is currently a non-RN nurse studying to obtain an undergraduate degree in nursing. Applicants need not be ENA members to apply, however, applicants must be members of the National Student Nurses Association.

Academic Fields/Career Goals: Nursing.

Award: Scholarship for use in freshman, sophomore, junior, or senior years. *Number:* 1. *Amount:* $2500.

Eligibility Requirements: Applicant must be enrolled or expecting to enroll at a four-year institution or university. Applicant or parent of applicant must be member of Screen Actors' Guild. Available to U.S. and non-U.S. citizens.

Application Requirements: Application, references, transcript. *Deadline:* June 1.

Contact: Ellen Siciliano, Development Manager
Emergency Nurses Association (ENA) Foundation
915 Lee Street
Des Plaines, IL 60016-6569
Phone: 847-460-4100
Fax: 847-460-4004
E-mail: foundation@ena.org

FOUNDATION OF THE NATIONAL STUDENT NURSES' ASSOCIATION
http://www.nsna.org

BREAKTHROUGH TO NURSING SCHOLARSHIPS FOR RACIAL/ETHNIC MINORITIES

Available to minority students enrolled in nursing or pre-nursing programs. Awards based on need, scholarship, and health-related activities. Application fee of $10. Send self-addressed stamped envelope with two stamps along with application request. One-time award of $1000-$2000. Application available at Web site.

Academic Fields/Career Goals: Nursing.

Award: Scholarship for use in freshman, sophomore, junior, or senior years; not renewable. *Number:* 5. *Amount:* $1000–$2000.

Eligibility Requirements: Applicant must be American Indian/Alaska Native, Asian/Pacific Islander, Black (non-Hispanic), or Hispanic and enrolled or expecting to enroll at an institution or university. Available to U.S. citizens.

Application Requirements: Application, financial need analysis, self-addressed stamped envelope, transcript. *Fee:* $10. *Deadline:* January 13.

Contact: Application available at Web site.
E-mail: receptionist@nsna.org

FOUNDATION OF THE NATIONAL STUDENT NURSES' ASSOCIATION CAREER MOBILITY SCHOLARSHIP

One-time award open to registered nurses enrolled in program leading to a BA in nursing or licensed practical or vocational nurses enrolled in a program leading to licensure as a registered nurse. Submit copy of license. Application fee: $10. Send self-addressed stamped envelope.

Academic Fields/Career Goals: Nursing.

Award: Scholarship for use in freshman, sophomore, junior, or senior years; not renewable. *Number:* varies. *Amount:* $1000–$2000.

Eligibility Requirements: Applicant must be enrolled or expecting to enroll at an institution or university. Applicant or parent of applicant must have employment or volunteer experience in community service, designated career field, or helping handicapped. Available to U.S. citizens.

Application Requirements: Application, financial need analysis, self-addressed stamped envelope, transcript. *Fee:* $10. *Deadline:* January 13.

Contact: Application available at Web site.
E-mail: receptionist@nsna.org

FOUNDATION OF THE NATIONAL STUDENT NURSES' ASSOCIATION GENERAL SCHOLARSHIPS

One-time award for National Student Nurses' Association members and nonmembers enrolled in nursing programs leading to RN license. Based on need, academic ability, and health-related nursing school or community involvement. Send self-addressed stamped envelope with two stamps for application. Graduating high school seniors are not eligible.

Academic Fields/Career Goals: Nursing.

Award: Scholarship for use in freshman, sophomore, junior, or senior years; not renewable. *Number:* 50–100. *Amount:* $1000–$5000.

Eligibility Requirements: Applicant must be enrolled or expecting to enroll full-time at a two-year or four-year institution or university. Applicant must have 2.5 GPA or higher. Available to U.S. citizens.

Application Requirements: Application, financial need analysis, self-addressed stamped envelope, transcript. *Fee:* $10. *Deadline:* January 13.

Contact: Application available at Web site.
E-mail: receptionist@nsna.org

FOUNDATION OF THE NATIONAL STUDENT NURSES' ASSOCIATION SPECIALTY SCHOLARSHIP

One-time award available to students currently enrolled in a state-approved school of nursing or pre-nursing. Must have interest in a specialty area of nursing. Send self-addressed stamped envelope with two stamps for application. Application fee: $10.

Academic Fields/Career Goals: Nursing.

Award: Scholarship for use in freshman, sophomore, junior, or senior years; not renewable. *Number:* varies. *Amount:* $1000–$2000.

Eligibility Requirements: Applicant must be enrolled or expecting to enroll at an institution or university. Applicant or parent of applicant must have employment or volunteer experience in community service or helping handicapped. Available to U.S. citizens.

Application Requirements: Application, financial need analysis, self-addressed stamped envelope, transcript. *Fee:* $10. *Deadline:* January 13.

Contact: Application available at Web site.
E-mail: receptionist@nsna.org

PROMISE OF NURSING SCHOLARSHIP

For applicants attending nursing school in California, South Florida, Georgia, Illinois, Massachusetts, Michigan, New Jersey, Tennessee, or Dallas/Fort Worth Texas. For an application and further details visit Web site: http://www.nsna.org

Academic Fields/Career Goals: Nursing.

Award: Scholarship for use in freshman, sophomore, junior, or senior years. *Number:* varies. *Amount:* $1000–$2500.

Eligibility Requirements: Applicant must be enrolled or expecting to enroll at an institution or university and studying in California, Florida, Georgia, Illinois, Massachusetts, Michigan, New Jersey, Tennessee, or Texas. Available to U.S. citizens.

Application Requirements: Application, transcript. *Fee:* $10. *Deadline:* January 13.

Contact: Scholarship Chairperson
Foundation of the National Student Nurses' Association
45 Main Street, Suite 606
Brooklyn, NY 11201
Phone: 718-210-0705
E-mail: receptionist@nsna.org

GENERAL FEDERATION OF WOMEN'S CLUBS OF MASSACHUSETTS   http://www.gfwcma.org/

GRADUATE STUDY IN CANCER RESEARCH OR NURSE PRACTITIONER

Graduate scholarship for women pursuing cancer research or nurse practitioner studies and maintaining legal residence in Massachusetts for at least five years. Deadline is March 1.

Academic Fields/Career Goals: Nursing.

Award: Scholarship for use in freshman, sophomore, junior, senior, graduate, or postgraduate years. *Amount:* $3000.

Eligibility Requirements: Applicant must be enrolled or expecting to enroll at a two-year or four-year or technical institution or university; female and resident of Massachusetts. Available to U.S. citizens.

Application Requirements: Application, essay, resume, references, transcript. *Deadline:* March 1.

Contact: June McSweeney, Chairman of Trustees, GFWC Of MA Headquarters
General Federation of Women's Clubs of Massachusetts
PO Box 679
Sudbury, MA 01776-0679
E-mail: JuneMcS@aol.com

GREATER KANAWHA VALLEY FOUNDATION   http://www.tgkvf.org

BERNICE PICKINS PARSONS FUND
• See page 377

ELEANORA G. WYLIE SCHOLARSHIP FUND FOR NURSING

Awarded to persons to attend any accredited college or university, with preference given to applicants pursuing a nursing education, either at the undergraduate or graduate level, or, specifically, in the broad field of gerontology. May apply for two Foundation scholarships but will only be chosen for one. Must be a resident of West Virginia.

Academic Fields/Career Goals: Nursing.

Award: Scholarship for use in freshman, sophomore, junior, senior, or graduate years; renewable. *Number:* 1. *Amount:* $500.

Eligibility Requirements: Applicant must be enrolled or expecting to enroll full-time at a four-year institution or university and resident of West Virginia. Applicant must have 2.5 GPA or higher. Available to U.S. citizens.

Application Requirements: Application, essay, financial need analysis, references, transcript, IRS 1040 form. *Deadline:* February 15.

Contact: Susan Hoover, Scholarship Coordinator
Greater Kanawha Valley Foundation
PO Box 3041
Charleston, WV 25331
Phone: 304-346-3620
Fax: 304-346-3640

GUSTAVUS B. CAPITO FUND

Scholarships awarded to students who show financial need and are seeking education in nursing at any accredited college or university with a nursing program in West Virginia. Scholarships are awarded for one or more years. May apply for two Foundation scholarships but will only be chosen for one. Must be a resident of West Virginia.

Academic Fields/Career Goals: Nursing.

Award: Scholarship for use in freshman, sophomore, junior, or senior years; renewable. *Number:* 6. *Amount:* $1000.

Eligibility Requirements: Applicant must be enrolled or expecting to enroll full-time at a two-year or four-year institution or university; resident of West Virginia and studying in West Virginia. Applicant must have 2.5 GPA or higher. Available to U.S. citizens.

Application Requirements: Application, essay, financial need analysis, references, transcript, IRS 1040 form. *Deadline:* February 15.

Contact: Susan Hoover, Scholarship Coordinator
Greater Kanawha Valley Foundation
PO Box 3041
Charleston, WV 25331
Phone: 304-346-3620
Fax: 304-346-3640

HAVANA NATIONAL BANK, TRUSTEE   http://www.havanabank.com

MCFARLAND CHARITABLE NURSING SCHOLARSHIP

For registered nursing students only. Must sign contract obliging student to work in Havana, Illinois for two years for each year of funding or repay award with interest and liquidated damages. Submit test scores, essay, transcripts,

Havana National Bank, Trustee (continued)

references, financial need analysis, and autobiography with application. Preference given to local residents. GPA is an important consideration in selection.

Academic Fields/Career Goals: Nursing.

Award: Forgivable loan for use in freshman, sophomore, junior, senior, graduate, or postgraduate years; renewable. *Number:* 3–5. *Amount:* $1000–$15,000.

Eligibility Requirements: Applicant must be enrolled or expecting to enroll full-time at a two-year or four-year institution or university. Available to U.S. and non-U.S. citizens.

Application Requirements: Application, autobiography, essay, financial need analysis, interview, photo, references, test scores, transcript. *Deadline:* April 1.

Contact: Larry Thomson, Vice President and Senior Trust Officer
Havana National Bank, Trustee
PO Box 200
Havana, IL 62644
Phone: 309-543-3361
Fax: 309-543-3441
E-mail: info@havanabank.com

HEALTH PROFESSIONS EDUCATION FOUNDATION   http://www.healthprofessions.ca.gov

ASSOCIATE DEGREE NURSING SCHOLARSHIP PROGRAM

One-time award to nursing students accepted to or enrolled in associate degree nursing programs and who agree to obtain a BSN at a nursing program in California within five years of obtaining an ADN. Eligible applicants may receive up to $8000 per year in financial assistance. Deadlines: March 24 and September 11. Must be a resident of California. Minimum 2.0 GPA.

Academic Fields/Career Goals: Nursing.

Award: Scholarship for use in freshman or sophomore years; not renewable. *Number:* 15–30. *Amount:* $4000–$8000.

Eligibility Requirements: Applicant must be enrolled or expecting to enroll full or part-time at a two-year or technical institution or university; resident of California and studying in California. Available to U.S. citizens.

Application Requirements: Application, driver's license, financial need analysis, references, transcript, graduation date verification form, verification of language fluency. *Deadline:* varies.

Contact: Carlos Rodriguez, Program Director
Health Professions Education Foundation
818 K Street, Suite 210
Sacramento, CA 95814
Phone: 916-324-6500
Fax: 916-324-6585
E-mail: cgray@oshpd.state.ca.us

CENTRAL VALLEY NURSING SCHOLARSHIP

One-time award for California residents studying nursing at a California institution. Scholarship is part of the Central Valley Nursing Work Force Diversity Initiative. Minimum 2.0 GPA. Application deadlines are March 26 and October 9.

Academic Fields/Career Goals: Nursing.

Award: Scholarship for use in freshman, sophomore, junior, senior, graduate, or postgraduate years; not renewable. *Number:* 90–140. *Amount:* $8000–$12,000.

Eligibility Requirements: Applicant must be enrolled or expecting to enroll full or part-time at a two-year or four-year or technical institution or university; resident of California and studying in California. Available to U.S. citizens.

Application Requirements: Application, driver's license, financial need analysis, transcript. *Deadline:* varies.

Contact: Carlos Rodriguez, Program Director
Health Professions Education Foundation
818 K Street, Suite 210
Sacramento, CA 95814
Phone: 916-324-6500

HEALTH PROFESSIONS EDUCATION SCHOLARSHIP PROGRAM
• See page 208

REGISTERED NURSE EDUCATION LOAN REPAYMENT PROGRAM

Repays governmental and commercial loans that were obtained for tuition expenses, books, equipment, and reasonable living expenses associated with attending college. In return for the repayment of educational debt, loan repayment recipients are required to practice full time in direct patient care in a medically underserved area or county health facility. Deadlines: March 24 and September 11. Must be resident of CA

Academic Fields/Career Goals: Nursing.

Award: Grant for use in senior, or postgraduate years; not renewable. *Number:* 50–70. *Amount:* $4000–$10,000.

Eligibility Requirements: Applicant must be enrolled or expecting to enroll full or part-time at a four-year institution or university; resident of California and studying in California. Available to U.S. citizens.

Application Requirements: Application, driver's license, financial need analysis, references, transcript. *Deadline:* varies.

Contact: Monique Voss, Program Director
Health Professions Education Foundation
818 K Street, Suite 210
Sacramento, CA 95814
Phone: 916-324-6500
Fax: 916-324-6585
E-mail: mvoss@oshpd.state.ca.us

RN EDUCATION SCHOLARSHIP PROGRAM

One-time award to nursing students accepted to or enrolled in baccalaureate degree nursing programs in California. Eligible applicants may receive up to $10,000 per year in financial assistance. Deadlines: March 24 and September 11. Must be resident of California and a U.S. citizen. Minimum 2.0 GPA.

Academic Fields/Career Goals: Nursing.

Award: Scholarship for use in freshman, sophomore, junior, or senior years; not renewable. *Number:* 50–70. *Amount:* $6000–$10,000.

Eligibility Requirements: Applicant must be enrolled or expecting to enroll full or part-time at a four-year or technical institution or university; resident of California and studying in California. Available to U.S. citizens.

Application Requirements: Application, essay, financial need analysis, references, transcript, employment verification form, proof of RN license, verification of language fluency. *Deadline:* varies.

Contact: Monique Voss, Program Director
Health Professions Education Foundation
818 K Street, Suite 210
Sacramento, CA 95814
Phone: 916-324-6500
Fax: 916-324-6585
E-mail: mvoss@oshpd.state.ca.us

IDAHO STATE BOARD OF EDUCATION   http://www.boardofed.idaho.gov

EDUCATION INCENTIVE LOAN FORGIVENESS CONTRACT-IDAHO
• See page 227

ILLINOIS NURSES ASSOCIATION   http://www.illinoisnurses.com

SONNE SCHOLARSHIP

One-time award for up to $1500 available to nursing students. Funds may be used to cover tuition, fees, or any other cost encountered by students enrolled in Illinois state-approved nursing program. Award limited to U.S. citizens who are residents of Illinois. Minimum 2.5 GPA required.

Academic Fields/Career Goals: Nursing.

Award: Scholarship for use in freshman, sophomore, junior, or senior years; not renewable. *Number:* 2–4. *Amount:* $1000–$1500.

Eligibility Requirements: Applicant must be enrolled or expecting to enroll full-time at a four-year institution or university; resident of Illinois and studying in Illinois. Applicant must have 2.5 GPA or higher. Available to U.S. citizens.

Application Requirements: Application, essay, financial need analysis, references, transcript. *Deadline:* May 1.

Contact: Sonne Scholarship Committee
Illinois Nurses Association
105 West Adams Street, Suite 2101
Chicago, IL 60603

ILLINOIS STUDENT ASSISTANCE COMMISSION (ISAC)   http://www.collegezone.org

ILLINOIS DEPARTMENT OF PUBLIC HEALTH CENTER FOR RURAL HEALTH NURSING EDUCATION SCHOLARSHIP PROGRAM
• *See page 327*

INDIAN HEALTH SERVICES, UNITED STATES DEPARTMENT OF HEALTH AND HUMAN SERVICES   http://www.ihs.gov

HEALTH PROFESSIONS PREPARATORY SCHOLARSHIP PROGRAM

Renewable scholarship available for undergraduate, graduate, or doctoral study in health professions and allied health professions programs. Minimum 2.0 GPA required. Award averages $18,500. New applicants must first submit to Area Scholarship Coordinator. There are service obligations and payback requirements that the recipient incurs upon acceptance of the scholarship funding. Contact office for more information.

Academic Fields/Career Goals: Nursing; Pharmacy; Social Services.

Award: Scholarship for use in freshman, sophomore, junior, senior, or graduate years; renewable. *Number:* up to 393. *Amount:* $18,500.

Eligibility Requirements: Applicant must be American Indian/Alaska Native and enrolled or expecting to enroll full or part-time at a two-year or four-year or technical institution or university. Available to U.S. citizens.

Application Requirements: Application, applicant must enter a contest, essay, references, transcript, proof of descent. *Deadline:* February 28.

Contact: Jeff Brien, Acting Chief, Scholarship Branch
Indian Health Services, United States Department of Health and Human Services
801 Thompson Avenue, Suite 120
Rockville, MD 20852
Phone: 301-443-6197
Fax: 301-443-6048

INDIAN HEALTH SERVICE HEALTH PROFESSIONS PRE-PROFESSIONAL SCHOLARSHIP
• *See page 318*

INDIANA HEALTH CARE FOUNDATION   http://www.ihca.org

INDIANA HEALTH CARE FOUNDATION NURSING SCHOLARSHIP

One-time award of up to $1500 for Indiana residents studying nursing at an institution in Indiana, Ohio, Kentucky, Illinois or Michigan. Minimum 2.5 GPA. Application deadline May 1.

Academic Fields/Career Goals: Nursing.

Award: Scholarship for use in freshman, sophomore, junior, senior, graduate, or postgraduate years; not renewable. *Number:* varies. *Amount:* $750–$1500.

Eligibility Requirements: Applicant must be enrolled or expecting to enroll full or part-time at a two-year or four-year or technical institution or university; resident of Indiana and studying in Illinois, Indiana, Kentucky, Michigan, or Ohio. Applicant must have 2.5 GPA or higher. Available to U.S. citizens.

Application Requirements: Application, essay, interview, references, transcript. *Deadline:* May 1.

Contact: Indiana Health Care Foundation
Indiana Health Care Foundation
One North Capitol Avenue, Suite 1115
Indianapolis, IN 46204
Phone: 317-636-6406

INTERNATIONAL ORDER OF THE KING'S DAUGHTERS AND SONS   http://www.iokds.org

HEALTH CAREERS SCHOLARSHIP
• *See page 209*

J.D. ARCHBOLD MEMORIAL HOSPITAL   http://www.archbold.org

ARCHBOLD SCHOLARSHIP PROGRAM
• *See page 327*

JEWISH FOUNDATION FOR EDUCATION OF WOMEN   http://www.jfew.org

SCHOLARSHIP PROGRAM FOR FORMER SOVIET UNION EMIGRES TRAINING IN THE HEALTH SCIENCES
• *See page 209*

KAISER PERMANENTE   http://financialaid.kp.org

DELORAS JONES RN SCHOLARSHIP PROGRAM

Scholarships for nursing students in California. Must have a undergraduate cumulative GPA of at least 2.50. Graduate/doctoral students must have a 3.00 GPA.

Academic Fields/Career Goals: Nursing.

Award: Scholarship for use in freshman, sophomore, junior, senior, or graduate years. *Amount:* $1000–$2500.

Eligibility Requirements: Applicant must be enrolled or expecting to enroll at a four-year institution or university. Applicant must have 2.5 GPA or higher. Available to U.S. citizens.

Application Requirements: Application, financial need analysis, copy of federal income tax return. *Deadline:* varies.

Contact: Pauline Tsai
Kaiser Permanente
Deloras Jones RN Scholarship Program
1800 Harrison Street, 5th Floor
Oakland, CA 94612
Phone: 510-987-9869
E-mail: pauline.b.tsai@kp.org

LADIES AUXILIARY TO THE VETERANS OF FOREIGN WARS, DEPARTMENT OF MAINE

FRANCIS L. BOOTH MEDICAL SCHOLARSHIP SPONSORED BY LAVFW DEPARTMENT OF MAINE
• *See page 327*

MARIN EDUCATION FUND   http://www.marineducationfund.org

GOLDMAN FAMILY FUND, NEW LEADER SCHOLARSHIP
• *See page 210*

MARION D. AND EVA S. PEEPLES FOUNDATION TRUST SCHOLARSHIP PROGRAM   http://www.jccf.org

MARION A. AND EVA S. PEEPLES SCHOLARSHIPS
• *See page 230*

MARYLAND HIGHER EDUCATION COMMISSION   http://www.mhec.state.md.us

GRADUATE AND PROFESSIONAL SCHOLARSHIP PROGRAM-MARYLAND
• *See page 210*

JANET L. HOFFMANN LOAN ASSISTANCE REPAYMENT PROGRAM
• *See page 230*

MARYLAND STATE NURSING SCHOLARSHIP AND LIVING EXPENSES GRANT

Renewable grant for Maryland residents enrolled in a two or four-year Maryland institution nursing degree program. Recipients must agree to serve as a full-time nurse in a Maryland shortage area and must maintain a 3.0 GPA in college. Application deadline is June 30. Submit Free Application for Federal Student Aid.

Maryland Higher Education Commission (continued)

Academic Fields/Career Goals: Nursing.

Award: Forgivable loan for use in freshman, sophomore, junior, senior, or graduate years; renewable. *Number:* up to 600. *Amount:* $200–$3000.

Eligibility Requirements: Applicant must be enrolled or expecting to enroll full-time at a two-year or four-year institution or university; resident of Maryland and studying in Maryland. Applicant must have 3.0 GPA or higher. Available to U.S. citizens.

Application Requirements: Application, financial need analysis, transcript, FAFSA. *Deadline:* June 30.

Contact: Marie Janiszewski, Office of Student Financial Assistance
Maryland Higher Education Commission
839 Bestgate Road, Suite 400
Annapolis, MD 21401-3013
Phone: 410-260-4569
Fax: 410-260-3203
E-mail: ofsamail@mhec.state.md.us

TUITION REDUCTION FOR NON-RESIDENT NURSING STUDENTS

Forgivable loan is available to nonresidents of Maryland who attend a two-year or four-year public institution in Maryland. The loan will be renewed provided student maintains academic requirements designated by institution attended. Loan recipient must agree to serve as a full-time nurse in a hospital or related institution for an equal amount of years as tuition was paid by Maryland Higher Education Commission. Loan recipient will pay tuition of Maryland resident.

Academic Fields/Career Goals: Nursing.

Award: Forgivable loan for use in freshman, sophomore, junior, or senior years; renewable. *Number:* 1. *Amount:* varies.

Eligibility Requirements: Applicant must be enrolled or expecting to enroll full or part-time at a two-year or four-year institution and studying in Maryland. Available to U.S. citizens.

Application Requirements: Application. *Deadline:* varies.

Contact: Financial Aid Office of your school

MASSACHUSETTS OFFICE OF STUDENT FINANCIAL ASSISTANCE   http://www.osfa.mass.edu

MASSACHUSETTS GILBERT MATCHING STUDENT GRANT PROGRAM

Must be permanent Massachusetts resident for at least one year and attending an independent, regionally accredited Massachusetts school or school of nursing full time. File the Free Application for Federal Student Aid after January 1. Contact college financial aid office for complete details and deadlines.

Academic Fields/Career Goals: Nursing.

Award: Grant for use in freshman, sophomore, junior, or senior years; not renewable. *Number:* varies. *Amount:* $200–$2500.

Eligibility Requirements: Applicant must be enrolled or expecting to enroll full-time at a four-year institution or university; resident of Massachusetts and studying in Massachusetts. Available to U.S. citizens.

Application Requirements: Financial need analysis, FAFSA. *Deadline:* varies.

Contact: College Financial Aid Office

MICHIGAN BUREAU OF STUDENT FINANCIAL ASSISTANCE   http://www.michigan.gov/studentaid

MICHIGAN NURSING SCHOLARSHIP

For students enrolled in an LPN, associate degree in nursing, or bachelor of science in nursing programs. Colleges determine application procedure and select recipients. Recipients must fulfill in-state work commitment or repay scholarship.

Academic Fields/Career Goals: Nursing.

Award: Scholarship for use in freshman, sophomore, junior, or senior years; renewable. *Number:* varies. *Amount:* up to $4000.

Eligibility Requirements: Applicant must be enrolled or expecting to enroll full or part-time at a two-year or four-year institution or university; resident of Michigan and studying in Michigan. Available to U.S. citizens.

Application Requirements: *Deadline:* varies.

Contact: Program Director
Michigan Bureau of Student Financial Assistance
PO Box 30462
Lansing, MI 48909-7962
Phone: 888-447-2687
E-mail: osg@michigan.gov

MICHIGAN LEAGUE FOR NURSING   http://www.michleaguenursing.org

NURSING STUDENT SCHOLARSHIP

One-time award for students who have completed at least one year of a nursing program or are continuing with undergraduate degree at a Michigan institution. Must have GPA of 2.0 or better. Scholarships of variable number and amount. Must be a resident of Michigan. Deadline: January 6.

Academic Fields/Career Goals: Nursing.

Award: Scholarship for use in sophomore, junior, or senior years; not renewable. *Number:* up to 4. *Amount:* $500.

Eligibility Requirements: Applicant must be enrolled or expecting to enroll at a two-year or four-year institution; resident of Michigan and studying in Michigan. Available to U.S. citizens.

Application Requirements: Application, essay, references, transcript. *Deadline:* January 6.

Contact: Carole Stacy, Managing Director
Michigan League for Nursing
2410 Woodlake Drive, Suite 440
Okemos, MI 48864
Phone: 517-347-8091
Fax: 517-347-4096
E-mail: cstacy@mhc.org

MINNESOTA DEPARTMENT OF HEALTH   http://www.health.state.mn.us

MINNESOTA NURSES LOAN FORGIVENESS PROGRAM
• See page 328

MINORITY NURSE MAGAZINE   http://www.minoritynurse.com

MINORITY NURSE MAGAZINE SCHOLARSHIP PROGRAM

Scholarships to help academically excellent, financially needy racial and ethnic minority nursing students complete a BSN degree.

Academic Fields/Career Goals: Nursing.

Award: Scholarship for use in junior, senior, or graduate years; not renewable. *Number:* 4. *Amount:* $500–$1000.

Eligibility Requirements: Applicant must be American Indian/Alaska Native, Asian/Pacific Islander, Black (non-Hispanic), or Hispanic and enrolled or expecting to enroll full or part-time at a four-year institution or university. Applicant must have 3.0 GPA or higher. Available to U.S. citizens.

Application Requirements: Application, essay, financial need analysis, references, transcript. *Deadline:* June 15.

Contact: Ms. Pam Chwedyk, Senior Editor/Editorial Manager
Minority Nurse Magazine
211 West Wacker Drive, Suite 900
Chicago, IL 60606
Phone: 312-525-3095
Fax: 312-429-3336
E-mail: pchwedyk@alloyeducation.com

MISSISSIPPI STATE STUDENT FINANCIAL AID   http://www.mississippiuniversities.com

NURSING EDUCATION LOAN/SCHOLARSHIP-BSN

Renewable award for Mississippi undergraduates in junior or senior year pursuing nursing programs in Mississippi in order to earn BSN degree. Include transcript and references with application. Must agree to employment in professional nursing (patient care) in Mississippi.

Academic Fields/Career Goals: Nursing.

Award: Forgivable loan for use in junior or senior years; renewable. *Number:* varies. *Amount:* $4000–$8000.

Eligibility Requirements: Applicant must be enrolled or expecting to enroll full or part-time at a four-year institution or university; resident of Mississippi and studying in Mississippi. Applicant must have 2.5 GPA or higher. Available to U.S. citizens.

Application Requirements: Application, driver's license, financial need analysis, references, transcript. *Deadline:* March 31.

Contact: Board of Trustees
Mississippi State Student Financial Aid
3825 Ridgewood Road
Jackson, MS 39211-6453

MISSOURI DEPARTMENT OF HEALTH AND SENIOR SERVICES   http://www.dhss.mo.gov

PRIMARY CARE RESOURCE INITIATIVE FOR MISSOURI LOAN PROGRAM
• See page 210

NATIONAL ASSOCIATION OF DIRECTORS OF NURSING ADMINISTRATION IN LONG TERM CARE   http://www.nadona.org

NATIONAL ASSOCIATION OF DIRECTORS OF NURSING ADMINISTRATION IN LONG TERM CARE-UPWARD BOUND SCHOLARSHIP

Financial assistance to nurses who are currently employed in long-term care and are interested in pursuing higher education, with a career focus on long-term care. Must be an RN, LPN, or a certified nursing assistant and be currently accepted or enrolled in one of the following programs: a LPN or RN program, an accredited RN program or undergraduate health care management program, a baccalaureate or master's degree program in nursing or gerontology.

Academic Fields/Career Goals: Nursing.

Award: Scholarship for use in freshman, sophomore, junior, senior, or graduate years. *Number:* 1.

Eligibility Requirements: Applicant must be enrolled or expecting to enroll at a four-year institution or university. Available to U.S. citizens.

Application Requirements: Application. *Deadline:* varies.

Contact: Education/Scholarship Committee
National Association of Directors of Nursing Administration in Long Term Care
NADONA Caring Scholarship
10999 Reed Hartman Highway, Suite 233
Cincinnati, OH 45242
Phone: 513-791-3679
Fax: 513-791-3699
E-mail: info@nadona.org

NATIONAL BLACK NURSES ASSOCIATION, INC.   http://www.nbna.org

AETNA SCHOLARSHIP

Scholarships available to nursing students with at least one year of program left for completion. Must be an active member of the National Black Nurses Association. Must demonstrate involvement in African-American community. Send self-addressed stamped envelope for application.

Academic Fields/Career Goals: Nursing.

Award: Scholarship for use in freshman, sophomore, junior, or senior years; not renewable. *Number:* 1–2. *Amount:* $500–$2000.

Eligibility Requirements: Applicant must be enrolled or expecting to enroll full or part-time at a two-year or four-year institution or university. Applicant or parent of applicant must be member of National Black Nurses' Association. Applicant or parent of applicant must have employment or volunteer experience in community service. Available to U.S. and non-U.S. citizens.

Application Requirements: Application, essay, photo, references, self-addressed stamped envelope, transcript. *Deadline:* April 15.

Contact: Scholarship Committee
National Black Nurses Association, Inc.
8360 Fenton Street, Suite 330
Silver Spring, MD 20910-3803
Phone: 301-589-3200
Fax: 301-589-3223
E-mail: nbna@erols.com

DR. HILDA RICHARDS SCHOLARSHIP

Scholarships available to nursing students with at least one year of program left for completion. Must be an active member of the National Black Nurses Association at student rate of $35. Must demonstrate involvement in African-American community. Send self-addressed stamped envelope for application.

Academic Fields/Career Goals: Nursing.

Award: Scholarship for use in freshman, sophomore, junior, or senior years; not renewable. *Number:* 1–2. *Amount:* $500–$2000.

Eligibility Requirements: Applicant must be enrolled or expecting to enroll full or part-time at a two-year or four-year institution or university. Applicant or parent of applicant must be member of National Black Nurses' Association. Applicant or parent of applicant must have employment or volunteer experience in community service. Available to U.S. and non-U.S. citizens.

Application Requirements: Application, essay, photo, references, self-addressed stamped envelope, transcript. *Deadline:* April 15.

Contact: Scholarship Committee
National Black Nurses Association, Inc.
8360 Fenton Street, Suite 330
Silver Spring, MD 20910-3803
Phone: 301-589-3200
Fax: 301-589-3223
E-mail: nbna@erols.com

DR. LAURANNE SAMS SCHOLARSHIP

Scholarships available to nursing students with at least one year of program left for completion. Must be an active member of National Black Nurses Association. Student membership is $35. Must demonstrate involvement in African-American community. Send self-addressed stamped envelope for application.

Academic Fields/Career Goals: Nursing.

Award: Scholarship for use in freshman, sophomore, junior, or senior years; not renewable. *Number:* 1–2. *Amount:* $500–$2000.

Eligibility Requirements: Applicant must be enrolled or expecting to enroll full or part-time at a two-year or four-year institution or university. Applicant or parent of applicant must be member of National Black Nurses' Association. Applicant or parent of applicant must have employment or volunteer experience in community service. Available to U.S. and non-U.S. citizens.

Application Requirements: Application, essay, photo, references, self-addressed stamped envelope, transcript. *Deadline:* April 15.

Contact: Scholarship Committee
National Black Nurses Association, Inc.
8360 Fenton Street, Suite 330
Silver Spring, MD 20910-3803
Phone: 301-589-3200
Fax: 301-589-3223
E-mail: nbna@erols.com

KAISER PERMANENTE SCHOOL OF ANESTHESIA SCHOLARSHIP

Scholarship available to nursing students with an least one full year of program left for completion. Must be an active member of the National Black Nurses Association at the student rate of $35. Must demonstrate involvement in the African-American community. Send self-addressed envelope for application.

Academic Fields/Career Goals: Nursing.

Award: Scholarship for use in freshman, sophomore, junior, or senior years; not renewable. *Number:* 1–2. *Amount:* $500–$2000.

Eligibility Requirements: Applicant must be enrolled or expecting to enroll full or part-time at a two-year or four-year institution or university. Applicant or parent of applicant must be member of

National Black Nurses Association, Inc. (continued)

National Black Nurses' Association. Applicant or parent of applicant must have employment or volunteer experience in community service. Available to U.S. and non-U.S. citizens.

Application Requirements: Application, essay, photo, references, self-addressed stamped envelope, transcript. *Deadline:* April 15.

Contact: Scholarship Committee
National Black Nurses Association, Inc.
8360 Fenton Street, Suite 330
Silver Spring, MD 20910-3803
Phone: 301-589-3200
Fax: 301-589-3223
E-mail: nbna@erols.com

MARTHA R. DUDLEY LVN/LPN SCHOLARSHIP

Scholarships available to nursing students with at least one year of program left for completion. Must be an active member of the National Black Nurses Association. Must demonstrate involvement in African-American community. Send self-addressed stamped envelope for application.

Academic Fields/Career Goals: Nursing.

Award: Scholarship for use in freshman, sophomore, or junior years; not renewable. *Number:* 1–2. *Amount:* $500–$2000.

Eligibility Requirements: Applicant must be Black (non-Hispanic) and enrolled or expecting to enroll full or part-time at a four-year institution or university. Applicant or parent of applicant must be member of National Black Nurses' Association. Applicant or parent of applicant must have employment or volunteer experience in community service. Available to U.S. and non-U.S. citizens.

Application Requirements: Application, essay, photo, references, self-addressed stamped envelope. *Deadline:* April 15.

Contact: Scholarship Committee
National Black Nurses Association, Inc.
8360 Fenton Street, Suite 330
Silver Spring, MD 20910-3803
Phone: 301-589-3200
Fax: 301-589-3223
E-mail: nbna@erols.com

MAYO FOUNDATIONS SCHOLARSHIP

Scholarships available to nursing students with at least one year of program left for completion. Must be an active member of the National Black Nurses Association at student rate of $35. Must demonstrate involvement in African-American community. Send self-addressed stamped envelope for application.

Academic Fields/Career Goals: Nursing.

Award: Scholarship for use in freshman, sophomore, junior, or senior years; not renewable. *Number:* 1–2. *Amount:* $500–$2000.

Eligibility Requirements: Applicant must be enrolled or expecting to enroll full or part-time at a two-year or four-year or technical institution or university. Applicant or parent of applicant must be member of National Black Nurses' Association. Applicant or parent of applicant must have employment or volunteer experience in community service. Available to U.S. and non-U.S. citizens.

Application Requirements: Application, essay, photo, references, self-addressed stamped envelope, transcript. *Deadline:* April 15.

Contact: Scholarship Committee
National Black Nurses Association, Inc.
8360 Fenton Street, Suite 330
Silver Spring, MD 20910-3803
Phone: 301-589-3200
Fax: 301-589-3223
E-mail: nbna@erols.com

NBNA BOARD OF DIRECTORS SCHOLARSHIP

Scholarships for licensed persons who are members of National Black Nurses Association who are enrolled at an accredited school of nursing pursuing a bachelor's or advanced degree. Requires transcript, letter of recommendation from local chapter and school of nursing, and self-addressed stamped envelope. Must show evidence of involvement in African-American community. Student NBNA fee-$35. Must have at least one full year of school remaining.

Academic Fields/Career Goals: Nursing.

Award: Scholarship for use in freshman, sophomore, junior, senior, or graduate years; not renewable. *Number:* 1–2. *Amount:* $500–$2000.

Eligibility Requirements: Applicant must be enrolled or expecting to enroll full or part-time at a two-year or four-year institution or university. Applicant or parent of applicant must be member of National Black Nurses' Association. Applicant or parent of applicant must have employment or volunteer experience in community service. Available to U.S. and non-U.S. citizens.

Application Requirements: Application, essay, photo, references, self-addressed stamped envelope, transcript. *Deadline:* April 15.

Contact: Scholarship Committee
National Black Nurses Association, Inc.
8360 Fenton Street, Suite 330
Silver Spring, MD 20910-3803
Phone: 301-589-3200
Fax: 301-589-3223
E-mail: nbna@erols.com

NURSING SPECTRUM SCHOLARSHIP

Scholarships available to nursing students with at least one year of program left for completion. Must be an active member of the National Black Nurses Association. Must demonstrate involvement in African-American community. Send self-addressed stamped envelope for application.

Academic Fields/Career Goals: Nursing.

Award: Scholarship for use in freshman, sophomore, junior, or senior years; not renewable. *Number:* 1–2. *Amount:* $500–$2000.

Eligibility Requirements: Applicant must be enrolled or expecting to enroll full or part-time at a two-year or four-year institution or university. Applicant or parent of applicant must be member of National Black Nurses' Association. Applicant or parent of applicant must have employment or volunteer experience in community service. Available to U.S. and non-U.S. citizens.

Application Requirements: Application, essay, photo, references, self-addressed stamped envelope, transcript. *Deadline:* April 15.

Contact: Scholarship Committee
National Black Nurses Association, Inc.
8360 Fenton Street, Suite 330
Silver Spring, MD 20910-3803
Phone: 301-589-3200
Fax: 301-589-3223
E-mail: nbna@erols.com

NATIONAL SOCIETY DAUGHTERS OF THE AMERICAN REVOLUTION   http://www.dar.org

NATIONAL SOCIETY DAUGHTERS OF THE AMERICAN REVOLUTION CAROLINE E. HOLT NURSING SCHOLARSHIPS

Nonrenewable award for undergraduate nursing students. Must be U.S. citizen. Need not be DAR member but must submit a letter of sponsorship from local chapter and a financial need form from parents. Award is merit-based. Deadlines: February 15 and August 15. Must submit self-addressed stamped envelope to be considered.

Academic Fields/Career Goals: Nursing.

Award: Scholarship for use in freshman, sophomore, junior, or senior years; not renewable. *Amount:* $500.

Eligibility Requirements: Applicant must be enrolled or expecting to enroll at a two-year or four-year institution or university. Applicant must have 3.0 GPA or higher. Available to U.S. citizens.

Application Requirements: Application, essay, financial need analysis, references, self-addressed stamped envelope, test scores, transcript. *Deadline:* varies.

Contact: Committee Services Office, Scholarship
National Society Daughters of the American Revolution
1776 D Street, NW
Washington, DC 20006-5392

NATIONAL SOCIETY DAUGHTERS OF THE AMERICAN REVOLUTION IRENE AND DAISY MACGREGOR MEMORIAL SCHOLARSHIP
• See page 329

NATIONAL SOCIETY DAUGHTERS OF THE AMERICAN REVOLUTION MADELINE PICKETT (HALBERT) COGSWELL NURSING SCHOLARSHIP

Nonrenewable award for undergraduate nursing students. Must be eligible for membership in NSDAR through relationship to NSDAR, Sons of the Revolution, or DAR member. DAR member number must be included. Must be sponsored by a local chapter. Apply by February 15 or August 15. Must submit self-addressed stamped envelope to be considered.

Academic Fields/Career Goals: Nursing.

Award: Scholarship for use in freshman, sophomore, junior, or senior years; not renewable. *Number:* 7–10. *Amount:* $500.

Eligibility Requirements: Applicant must be enrolled or expecting to enroll at a two-year or four-year institution or university. Applicant or parent of applicant must be member of Daughters of the American Revolution. Applicant must have 3.0 GPA or higher. Available to U.S. citizens.

Application Requirements: Application, essay, financial need analysis, references, self-addressed stamped envelope, test scores, transcript. *Deadline:* varies.

Contact: Committee Services Office, Scholarship
National Society Daughters of the American Revolution
1776 D Street, NW
Washington, DC 20006-5392

NATIONAL SOCIETY DAUGHTERS OF THE AMERICAN REVOLUTION MILDRED NUTTING NURSING SCHOLARSHIP

Nonrenewable award for undergraduate nursing students. Must be a U.S. citizen. Need not be a DAR member but must submit a letter of sponsorship from local chapter and a financial need form from parents. Deadlines: February 15 and August 15. Must submit a self-addressed stamped envelope to be considered. Preference will be given to candidates from the greater Lowell, MA area.

Academic Fields/Career Goals: Nursing.

Award: Scholarship for use in freshman, sophomore, junior, or senior years; not renewable. *Number:* varies. *Amount:* $500.

Eligibility Requirements: Applicant must be enrolled or expecting to enroll at a two-year or four-year institution or university. Applicant must have 3.0 GPA or higher. Available to U.S. citizens.

Application Requirements: Application, essay, financial need analysis, references, self-addressed stamped envelope, test scores, transcript. *Deadline:* varies.

Contact: Committee Services Office, Scholarship
National Society Daughters of the American Revolution
1776 D Street, NW
Washington, DC 20006-5392

NATIONAL SOCIETY OF THE COLONIAL DAMES OF AMERICA

AMERICAN INDIAN NURSE SCHOLARSHIP AWARDS

Renewable award of $500 to $1500 per semester for Native American nursing student with minimum 2.5 GPA in an accredited nursing program within two years of completing courses. Applicant may also be a graduating high school student accepted in a nursing program. Must be full-time student with financial need not receiving Indian Health Service Scholarship and recommended by college.

Academic Fields/Career Goals: Nursing.

Award: Scholarship for use in freshman, sophomore, junior, senior, graduate, or postgraduate years; renewable. *Number:* 10–15. *Amount:* $500–$1500.

Eligibility Requirements: Applicant must be American Indian/Alaska Native and enrolled or expecting to enroll full-time at a two-year or four-year or technical institution or university. Applicant must have 2.5 GPA or higher. Available to U.S. citizens.

Application Requirements: Application, autobiography, financial need analysis, photo, references, transcript. *Deadline:* Continuous.

Contact:

NEW HAMPSHIRE POSTSECONDARY EDUCATION COMMISSION
http://www.state.nh.us/postsecondary

WORKFORCE INCENTIVE PROGRAM
• See page 233

NEW MEXICO COMMISSION ON HIGHER EDUCATION
http://www.hed.state.nm.us

ALLIED HEALTH STUDENT LOAN PROGRAM-NEW MEXICO
• See page 210

NURSING STUDENT LOAN-FOR-SERVICE PROGRAM

Award for New Mexico residents accepted or enrolled in nursing program at New Mexico public postsecondary institution. Must practice as nurse in designated health professional shortage area in New Mexico. Award dependent upon financial need but may not exceed $12,000. Deadline: July 1.

Academic Fields/Career Goals: Nursing.

Award: Forgivable loan for use in freshman, sophomore, junior, or senior years; not renewable. *Amount:* up to $12,000.

Eligibility Requirements: Applicant must be enrolled or expecting to enroll full or part-time at a two-year or four-year institution; resident of New Mexico and studying in New Mexico. Available to U.S. citizens.

Application Requirements: Application, financial need analysis, transcript, FAFSA, letter of acceptance. *Deadline:* July 1.

Contact: Ofelia Morales, Director of Financial Aid
New Mexico Commission on Higher Education
1068 Cerrillos Road, PO Box 15910
Santa Fe, NM 87505
Phone: 505-476-6506
E-mail: ofelia.morales@state.nm.us

NEW YORK STATE EDUCATION DEPARTMENT
http://www.highered.nysed.gov

REGENTS PROFESSIONAL OPPORTUNITY SCHOLARSHIP
• See page 67

NEW YORK STATE GRANGE
http://www.nysgrange.com/

JUNE GILL NURSING SCHOLARSHIP

One annual scholarship award to verified NYS Grange member pursuing a career in nursing. Selection based on verification of NYS Grange membership and enrollment in a nursing program, as well as applicant's career statement, academic records, and financial need. Payment made after successful completion of one term.

Academic Fields/Career Goals: Nursing.

Award: Scholarship for use in freshman, sophomore, junior, or senior years; not renewable. *Number:* 1. *Amount:* varies.

Eligibility Requirements: Applicant must be enrolled or expecting to enroll at a two-year or four-year institution and resident of New York. Applicant or parent of applicant must be member of Grange Association. Available to U.S. citizens.

Application Requirements: Application, financial need analysis. *Deadline:* varies.

Contact: Ann Hall, Scholarship Chairperson
New York State Grange
100 Grange Place
Cortland, NY 13045
Phone: 607-756-7553
Fax: 607-756-7757
E-mail: nysgrange@nysgrange.com

NEWTON NURSE SCHOLARS RHODE ISLAND FOUNDATION
http://northwesthealthcare.org

ALBERT AND FLORENCE NEWTON NURSE SCHOLARSHIP NEWTON FUND

For schools in Rhode Island only. Ascribes funds to: registered nurses seeking BS degree in nursing; senior nursing students in final year of education to become a registered nurse; registered nurses with BS degree seeking graduate degree; programs selected which are targeted to increase the availability of new registered nurses. Application deadlines: April 1 and October 1.

Newton Nurse Scholars Rhode Island Foundation (continued)

Academic Fields/Career Goals: Nursing.

Award: Scholarship for use in junior, senior, or graduate years; not renewable. *Number:* 5–20. *Amount:* $250–$2500.

Eligibility Requirements: Applicant must be enrolled or expecting to enroll full or part-time at a two-year or four-year institution or university and studying in Rhode Island. Available to U.S. and non-U.S. citizens.

Application Requirements: Application, essay, financial need analysis.

Contact: Libby Monahan
Newton Nurse Scholars Rhode Island Foundation
1 Union Station
Providence, RI 02903
Phone: 401-274-4564

NIGHTINGALE AWARDS OF PENNSYLVANIA
http://www.nightingaleawards.org

NIGHTINGALE AWARDS OF PENNSYLVANIA NURSING SCHOLARSHIP

Scholarships for students who are studying nursing at the basic or advanced level and intend to practice in Pennsylvania. Regardless of the type of nursing program, all candidates accepted into or presently enrolled in accredited nursing programs in Pennsylvania may apply. Scholarships are awarded to students who enter professional nursing programs, practical nursing programs, and advanced degree programs.

Academic Fields/Career Goals: Nursing.

Award: Scholarship for use in freshman, sophomore, junior, senior, or graduate years. *Amount:* $6000–$10,000.

Eligibility Requirements: Applicant must be enrolled or expecting to enroll full-time at a four-year institution or university and resident of Pennsylvania. Available to U.S. citizens.

Application Requirements: Application, references, test scores, transcript. *Deadline:* January 31.

Contact: Nightingale Awards of Pennsylvania
2090 Linglestown Road, Suite 107
Harrisburg, PA 17110
E-mail: nightingale@pronursingresources.com

NORTH CAROLINA STATE EDUCATION ASSISTANCE AUTHORITY
http://www.ncseaa.edu

NORTH CAROLINA STUDENT LOAN PROGRAM FOR HEALTH, SCIENCE, AND MATHEMATICS
• See page 211

NURSE EDUCATION SCHOLARSHIP LOAN PROGRAM (NESLP)

Must be U.S. citizen and North Carolina resident. Award available through financial aid offices of North Carolina colleges and universities that offer nurse education programs to prepare students for licensure in the state as LPN or RN. Recipients enter contract with the State of North Carolina to work full time as a licensed nurse. Loans not repaid through service must be repaid in cash. Award based upon financial need. Maximum award for students enrolled in Associate Degree Nursing and Practical Nurse Education programs is $3000. Maximum award for students enrolled in a Baccalaureate program is $5000.

Academic Fields/Career Goals: Nursing.

Award: Forgivable loan for use in freshman, sophomore, junior, or senior years; renewable. *Number:* varies. *Amount:* $400–$5000.

Eligibility Requirements: Applicant must be enrolled or expecting to enroll at a four-year institution or university; resident of North Carolina and studying in North Carolina. Available to U.S. citizens.

Application Requirements: Application, financial need analysis. *Deadline:* Continuous.

Contact: Bill Carswell, Manager of Scholarship and Grant Division
North Carolina State Education Assistance Authority
PO Box 14103
Research Triangle Park, NC 27709
Phone: 919-549-8614
Fax: 919-248-4687
E-mail: carswellb@ncseaa.edu

NURSE SCHOLARS PROGRAM—UNDERGRADUATE (NORTH CAROLINA)

Forgivable loans to residents of North Carolina who have gained full acceptance to a North Carolina institution of higher education that offers a nursing program. Must apply to the North Carolina State Education and Welfare division. Must serve as a registered nurse in North Carolina for one year for each year of funding. Minimum 3.0 GPA required. Amount of award is based upon type of nursing education sought.

Academic Fields/Career Goals: Nursing.

Award: Forgivable loan for use in freshman, sophomore, junior, or senior years; renewable. *Number:* up to 600. *Amount:* $1500–$5000.

Eligibility Requirements: Applicant must be enrolled or expecting to enroll full-time at a two-year or four-year institution or university; resident of North Carolina and studying in North Carolina. Applicant must have 3.0 GPA or higher. Available to U.S. citizens.

Application Requirements: Application, essay, references, test scores, transcript. *Deadline:* May 3.

Contact: Bill Carswell, Manager of Scholarship and Grant Division
North Carolina State Education Assistance Authority
PO Box 14103
Research Triangle Park, NC 27709
Phone: 919-549-8614
Fax: 919-248-4687
E-mail: carswellb@ncseaa.edu

NORTH DAKOTA BOARD OF NURSING

NORTH DAKOTA BOARD OF NURSING EDUCATION LOAN PROGRAM

One-time loan for North Dakota residents pursuing a nursing degree. Must sign repayment note agreeing to repay loan by nursing employment in North Dakota after graduation. Repayment rate is $1 per hour of employment. For juniors, seniors, and graduate students.

Academic Fields/Career Goals: Nursing.

Award: Forgivable loan for use in freshman, sophomore, junior, senior, or graduate years; not renewable. *Number:* 30–35. *Amount:* $2000–$5000.

Eligibility Requirements: Applicant must be enrolled or expecting to enroll full or part-time at a two-year or four-year institution or university and resident of North Dakota. Applicant must have 2.5 GPA or higher. Available to U.S. citizens.

Application Requirements: Application, financial need analysis, references, transcript. *Fee:* $15. *Deadline:* July 1.

Contact: Constance Kalanek, Executive Director
North Dakota Board of Nursing
919 South 7th Street, Suite 504
Bismarck, ND 58504-5881
Phone: 701-328-9777
Fax: 701-328-9785
E-mail: executivedir@nbdon.org

ONS FOUNDATION
http://www.ons.org

ONS FOUNDATION ETHNIC MINORITY BACHELOR'S SCHOLARSHIP

Three scholarships available to registered nurses with a demonstrated interest in oncology nursing. Must be currently enrolled in an undergraduate program at an NLN-accredited school, and must currently hold a license to practice as a registered nurse. Must be minority student who has not received any BA grants previously from ONF. One-time award of $2000. Deadline: February 1.

Academic Fields/Career Goals: Nursing.

Award: Scholarship for use in freshman, sophomore, junior, or senior years; not renewable. *Number:* 3. *Amount:* $2000.

Eligibility Requirements: Applicant must be American Indian/Alaska Native, Asian/Pacific Islander, Black (non-Hispanic), or Hispanic and enrolled or expecting to enroll full or part-time at a four-year institution or university. Applicant or parent of applicant must have employment or volunteer experience in designated career field. Available to U.S. citizens.

Application Requirements: Application, transcript. *Fee:* $5. *Deadline:* February 1.

Contact: Bonny Revo, Executive Assistant
ONS Foundation
125 Enterprise Drive
Pittsburgh, PA 15275
Phone: 412-859-6100
Fax: 412-859-6162
E-mail: brevo@ons.org

ONS FOUNDATION JOSH GOTTHEIL MEMORIAL BONE MARROW TRANSPLANT CAREER DEVELOPMENT AWARDS

Several awards available to any professional registered nurse for practice of bone marrow transplant nursing by providing financial assistance to continue education that will further professional goals or to supplement tuition in a bachelor's or master's program. Submit examples of contributions to BMT nursing. Four awards of $2000 each. Deadline: December 1.

Academic Fields/Career Goals: Nursing.

Award: Scholarship for use in freshman, sophomore, junior, senior, or graduate years; not renewable. *Number:* 4. *Amount:* $2000.

Eligibility Requirements: Applicant must be enrolled or expecting to enroll full or part-time at a four-year institution or university. Applicant or parent of applicant must have employment or volunteer experience in designated career field. Available to U.S. and non-U.S. citizens.

Application Requirements: Application, essay, resume, references. *Deadline:* December 1.

Contact: Bonny Revo, Executive Assistant
ONS Foundation
125 Enterprise Drive
Pittsburgh, PA 15275
Phone: 412-859-6100
Fax: 412-859-6162
E-mail: brevo@ons.org

ONS FOUNDATION NURSING OUTCOMES RESEARCH GRANT
• *See page 330*

ONS FOUNDATION ONCOLOGY NURSING SOCIETY RESEARCH GRANT
• *See page 330*

ONS FOUNDATION ROBERTA PIERCE SCOFIELD BACHELOR'S SCHOLARSHIPS

Three awards to improve oncology nursing by assisting registered nurses in furthering their education. Must be currently enrolled in an undergraduate nursing degree program at an NLN-accredited school of nursing and must hold a current license to practice as a registered nurse. One-time award of $2000. Deadline: February 1.

Academic Fields/Career Goals: Nursing.

Award: Scholarship for use in freshman, sophomore, junior, or senior years; not renewable. *Number:* 3. *Amount:* $2000.

Eligibility Requirements: Applicant must be enrolled or expecting to enroll full or part-time at a four-year institution or university. Applicant or parent of applicant must have employment or volunteer experience in designated career field. Available to U.S. citizens.

Application Requirements: Application, transcript. *Fee:* $5. *Deadline:* February 1.

Contact: Bonny Revo, Executive Assistant
ONS Foundation
125 Enterprise Drive
Pittsburgh, PA 15275
Phone: 412-859-6100
Fax: 412-859-6162
E-mail: brevo@ons.org

ONS FOUNDATION/ONCOLOGY NURSING CERTIFICATION CORPORATION BACHELOR'S SCHOLARSHIPS

Ten awards to improve oncology nursing by assisting registered nurses in furthering their education. Must be currently enrolled in an undergraduate nursing degree program at an NLN-accredited school of nursing and must have a current license to practice as a registered nurse. One-time award of $2000. Deadline: February 1.

Academic Fields/Career Goals: Nursing.

Award: Scholarship for use in freshman, sophomore, junior, or senior years; not renewable. *Number:* 10. *Amount:* $2000.

Eligibility Requirements: Applicant must be enrolled or expecting to enroll full or part-time at a four-year institution or university. Applicant or parent of applicant must have employment or volunteer experience in designated career field. Available to U.S. citizens.

Application Requirements: Application, transcript. *Fee:* $5. *Deadline:* February 1.

Contact: Bonny Revo, Executive Assistant
ONS Foundation
125 Enterprise Drive
Pittsburgh, PA 15275
Phone: 412-859-6100
Fax: 412-859-6162
E-mail: brevo@ons.org

ONS FOUNDATION/PEARL MOORE CAREER DEVELOPMENT AWARDS

Several awards to reward a professional staff nurse for meritorious practice by providing financial assistance to continue education. Must possess or be pursuing a BSN and be employed as a staff nurse with two years' oncology practice. Three awards of $3000 each. Deadline: December 1.

Academic Fields/Career Goals: Nursing.

Award: Scholarship for use in freshman, sophomore, junior, or senior years; not renewable. *Number:* 3. *Amount:* $3000.

Eligibility Requirements: Applicant must be enrolled or expecting to enroll at a four-year institution or university. Applicant or parent of applicant must have employment or volunteer experience in designated career field. Available to U.S. citizens.

Application Requirements: Application, autobiography, references. *Deadline:* December 1.

Contact: Bonny Revo, Executive Assistant
ONS Foundation
125 Enterprise Drive
Pittsburgh, PA 15275
Phone: 412-859-6100
Fax: 412-859-6162
E-mail: brevo@ons.org

ORDEAN FOUNDATION

ORDEAN SCHOLARSHIP PROGRAM
• *See page 67*

OREGON COMMUNITY FOUNDATION
http://www.ocf1.org/

DR. FRANZ AND KATHRYN STENZEL FUND
• *See page 330*

NLN ELLA MCKINNEY SCHOLARSHIP FUND

Award for graduates (or the equivalent) of high schools in Oregon, for use in the pursuit of an undergraduate or graduate nursing education at a nonprofit college or university in Oregon accredited by the NLN Accrediting Commission.

Academic Fields/Career Goals: Nursing.

Award: Scholarship for use in freshman, sophomore, junior, senior, or graduate years. *Number:* 1.

Eligibility Requirements: Applicant must be enrolled or expecting to enroll at a four-year institution or university; resident of Oregon and studying in Oregon. Available to U.S. citizens.

Application Requirements: *Deadline:* varies.

Contact: Dianne Causey, Program Associate for Scholarships/Grants
Oregon Community Foundation
1221 South West Yamhill, Suite 100
Portland, OR 97205
Phone: 503-227-6846

OREGON NURSES ASSOCIATION

http://www.oregonrn.org/

ONF-SMITH EDUCATION SCHOLARSHIP

Award for nursing students enrolled in an undergraduate or graduate program in Oregon. RN recipients must be current ONA members. Non-RN recipients of the baccalaureate scholarship must join the nurses association in their state of residence upon graduation. Application deadline is February 28.

Academic Fields/Career Goals: Nursing.

Award: Scholarship for use in freshman, sophomore, junior, senior, or graduate years; not renewable. *Number:* 3. *Amount:* $1000.

Eligibility Requirements: Applicant must be enrolled or expecting to enroll full-time at a four-year institution or university and studying in Oregon. Applicant must have 3.0 GPA or higher. Available to U.S. citizens.

Application Requirements: Application.

Contact: Oregon Nurses Association
18765 South West Boones Ferry Road, Suite 200
Tualatin, OR 97062
Phone: 503-293-0011

OREGON STUDENT ASSISTANCE COMMISSION

http://www.osac.state.or.us

BERTHA P. SINGER NURSES SCHOLARSHIP

Available to Oregon residents pursuing a nursing career. Must have at least a 3.0 GPA and attend a college or university in Oregon. Must have completed one year of undergraduate study. One-time award of $1000. Proof of enrollment in 3rd year of 4-year nursing degree program or 2nd year of a 2-year associate degree nursing program is required. (Transcripts not sufficient.) U.S. Bancorp employees, their children, or close relatives are not eligible.

Academic Fields/Career Goals: Nursing.

Award: Scholarship for use in sophomore, junior, senior, or graduate years; renewable. *Number:* 23. *Amount:* $1000.

Eligibility Requirements: Applicant must be enrolled or expecting to enroll at a two-year or four-year institution or university; resident of Oregon and studying in Oregon. Applicant must have 3.0 GPA or higher. Available to U.S. citizens.

Application Requirements: Application, essay, financial need analysis, test scores, transcript. *Deadline:* March 1.

Contact: Director of Grant Programs
Oregon Student Assistance Commission
1500 Valley River Drive, Suite 100
Eugene, OR 97401-7020
Phone: 800-452-8807 Ext. 7395

FRANKS FOUNDATION SCHOLARSHIP

Award for graduating high school seniors with a minimum 2.5 GPA and college students with a minimum 2.0 GPA. Must major in nursing or theology. First preference: residents of Deschutes, Crook, or Jefferson Counties. Second preference: residents of Harney, Lake, Grant, and Klamath Counties. U.S. Bancorp employees and relatives ineligible.

Academic Fields/Career Goals: Nursing; Religion/Theology.

Award: Scholarship for use in freshman, sophomore, junior, senior, or graduate years; not renewable. *Number:* 22. *Amount:* $1023.

Eligibility Requirements: Applicant must be enrolled or expecting to enroll at an institution or university and resident of Oregon. Available to U.S. citizens.

Application Requirements: Application, essay, financial need analysis, transcript, activity chart. *Deadline:* March 1.

Contact: Director of Grant Programs
Oregon Student Assistance Commission
1500 Valley River Drive, Suite 100
Eugene, OR 97401-7020
Phone: 800-452-8807 Ext. 7395

MARION A. LINDEMAN SCHOLARSHIP
• See page 331

WALTER AND MARIE SCHMIDT SCHOLARSHIP

Scholarship available to a student who is enrolled or planning to enroll in a program of training to become a registered nurse. Applicants must submit an additional essay describing their desire to pursue a nursing career in geriatrics. U.S. Bancorp employees and their relatives are not eligible.

Academic Fields/Career Goals: Nursing.

Award: Scholarship for use in freshman or sophomore years; renewable. *Number:* 33. *Amount:* $939.

Eligibility Requirements: Applicant must be enrolled or expecting to enroll full or part-time at a two-year or four-year institution and resident of Oregon. Available to U.S. citizens.

Application Requirements: Application, essay, financial need analysis, references, transcript, activity chart. *Deadline:* March 1.

Contact: Director of Grant Programs
Oregon Student Assistance Commission
1500 Valley River Drive, Suite 100
Eugene, OR 97401-7020
Phone: 800-452-8807 Ext. 7395

PENNSYLVANIA HIGHER EDUCATION ASSISTANCE AGENCY

http://www.pheaa.org

LOAN FORGIVENESS PROGRAM FOR STATE VETERANS HOMES NURSES

Forgivable loans for nursing education. Must have full-time employment as a direct care nurse, within three months of graduation, at one of State Veterans Homes. Applicants must complete qualifying program of study between November 17, 2005 and December 31, 2006 leading to certification as a Licensed Practical Nurse within PA Registered Nurse within PA.

Academic Fields/Career Goals: Nursing.

Award: Forgivable loan for use in senior year. *Amount:* up to $10,000.

Eligibility Requirements: Applicant must be enrolled or expecting to enroll at an institution or university and resident of Pennsylvania. Available to U.S. citizens.

Application Requirements: Application. *Deadline:* December 31.

Contact: Pennsylvania Higher Education Assistance Agency
AES Lender School Team, PO Box 2461
Harrisburg, PA 17105-2461

NURSING LOAN FORGIVENESS FOR HEALTHIER FUTURES PROGRAM

Forgivable loans for nursing education. Applicants must pass the Pennsylvania State Board of Nursing examination, and begin full-time employment within three months of graduation as a direct patient care nurse at an approved, participating Pennsylvania facility, or within one year, as a nurse educator in an approved participating Pennsylvania postsecondary education program.

Academic Fields/Career Goals: Nursing.

Award: Forgivable loan for use in freshman, sophomore, junior, or senior years. *Amount:* up to $12,500.

Eligibility Requirements: Applicant must be enrolled or expecting to enroll at an institution or university and resident of Pennsylvania. Available to U.S. citizens.

Application Requirements: Application. *Deadline:* December 31.

Contact: Pennsylvania Higher Education Assistance Agency
American Education Services, Nursing Loan Forgiveness for Healthier Futures Program, Lender School Team, PO Box 2461
Harrisburg, PA 17105-2461
Phone: 800-859-5442
Fax: 717-720-3916

PILOT INTERNATIONAL FOUNDATION

http://www.pilotinternational.org

PILOT INTERNATIONAL FOUNDATION RUBY NEWHALL MEMORIAL SCHOLARSHIP
• See page 331

PILOT INTERNATIONAL FOUNDATION SCHOLARSHIP PROGRAM
• See page 331

PILOT INTERNATIONAL FOUNDATION/LIFELINE SCHOLARSHIP PROGRAM
• See page 332

RHODE ISLAND FOUNDATION
http://www.rifoundation.org

ALBERT E. AND FLORENCE W. NEWTON NURSE SCHOLARSHIP

To benefit practicing nurses (RN's) enrolled in an accredited BSN program in Rhode Island. Renewable award. Must be a Rhode Island resident and beginning junior year or higher. Must have proof of nursing license. Deadline: April 17.

Academic Fields/Career Goals: Nursing.

Award: Scholarship for use in junior, senior, graduate, or postgraduate years; renewable. *Number:* varies. *Amount:* $500–$2500.

Eligibility Requirements: Applicant must be enrolled or expecting to enroll full or part-time at an institution or university; resident of Rhode Island and studying in Rhode Island. Applicant or parent of applicant must have employment or volunteer experience in designated career field. Available to U.S. citizens.

Application Requirements: Application, financial need analysis, self-addressed stamped envelope, transcript. *Deadline:* April 17.

Contact: Libby Monahan, Scholarship Coordinator
Rhode Island Foundation
1 Union Station
Providence, RI 02903
Phone: 401-274-4564
Fax: 401-272-1359
E-mail: libbym@rifoundation.org

SOUTHWEST STUDENT SERVICES CORPORATION
http://www.sssc.com/

ANNE LINDEMAN MEMORIAL SCHOLARSHIP
• See page 142

STATE STUDENT ASSISTANCE COMMISSION OF INDIANA (SSACI)
http://www.in.gov/ssaci

INDIANA NURSING SCHOLARSHIP FUND

Need-based tuition funding for nursing students enrolled full- or part-time at an eligible Indiana institution. Must be a U.S. citizen and an Indiana resident and have a minimum 2.0 GPA or meet the minimum requirements for the nursing program. Upon graduation, recipients must practice as a nurse in an Indiana health care setting for two years.

Academic Fields/Career Goals: Nursing.

Award: Scholarship for use in freshman, sophomore, junior, or senior years; not renewable. *Number:* 490–690. *Amount:* $200–$5000.

Eligibility Requirements: Applicant must be enrolled or expecting to enroll full or part-time at a two-year or four-year institution or university; resident of Indiana and studying in Indiana. Available to U.S. citizens.

Application Requirements: Application, financial need analysis, FAFSA. *Deadline:* Continuous.

Contact: Yvonne Heflin, Director, Special Programs
State Student Assistance Commission of Indiana (SSACI)
150 West Market Street, Suite 500
Indianapolis, IN 46204-2805
Phone: 317-232-2350
Fax: 317-232-3260

SUBURBAN HOSPITAL HEALTHCARE SYSTEM
http://www.suburbanhospital.org

SUBURBAN HOSPITAL HEALTHCARE SYSTEM SCHOLARSHIP
• See page 333

ULMAN CANCER FUND FOR YOUNG ADULTS
http://www.ulmanfund.org/

BARBARA PALO FOSTER MEMORIAL SCHOLARSHIP

Scholarship for people who have lost a parent to cancer or have a parent with cancer and are seeking or receiving postsecondary education in the field of nursing.

Academic Fields/Career Goals: Nursing.

Award: Scholarship for use in freshman, sophomore, junior, or senior years. *Amount:* up to $1000.

Eligibility Requirements: Applicant must be age 16-39 and enrolled or expecting to enroll full or part-time at a four-year institution or university. Available to U.S. citizens.

Application Requirements: Application. *Deadline:* April 1.

Contact: Fay Baker, Scholarship Coordinator
Ulman Cancer Fund for Young Adults
4725 Dorsey Hall Drive, Suite A
PO Box 505
Ellicott City, MD 21042
Phone: 410-964-0202
Fax: 410-964-0402
E-mail: scholarship@ulmanfund.org

UNITED DAUGHTERS OF THE CONFEDERACY
http://www.hqudc.org

PHOEBE PEMBER MEMORIAL SCHOLARSHIP

Award for full-time undergraduate student who is a descendant of a Confederate soldier enrolled in a School of Nursing. Must carry a minimum of 12 credit hours each semester and have a minimum 3.0 GPA. Submit letter of endorsement from sponsoring Chapter of the United Daughters of the Confederacy. Scholarship amount for the entire academic year will be sent to college/university.

Academic Fields/Career Goals: Nursing.

Award: Scholarship for use in freshman, sophomore, junior, or senior years; renewable. *Number:* 1–2. *Amount:* $800–$1000.

Eligibility Requirements: Applicant must be enrolled or expecting to enroll full-time at a four-year institution or university. Applicant or parent of applicant must be member of United Daughters of the Confederacy. Applicant must have 3.0 GPA or higher. Available to U.S. citizens.

Application Requirements: Application, essay, financial need analysis, photo, references, self-addressed stamped envelope, transcript, confederate ancestor's proof of service. *Deadline:* March 15.

Contact: Robert Kraus, Second Vice President General
United Daughters of the Confederacy
328 North Boulevard
Richmond, VA 23220-4057
Phone: 804-355-1636

WALTER REED SMITH SCHOLARSHIP
• See page 154

UNITED NEGRO COLLEGE FUND
http://www.uncf.org

SODEXHO SCHOLARSHIP
• See page 333

UNITED STATES PUBLIC HEALTH SERVICE - HEALTH RESOURCES AND SERVICES ADMINISTRATION, BUREAU OF HEALTH
http://bhpr.hrsa.gov/dsa

HEALTH RESOURCES AND SERVICES ADMINISTRATION-BUREAU OF HEALTH PROFESSIONS SCHOLARSHIPS FOR DISADVANTAGED STUDENTS
• See page 211

VIRGINIA DEPARTMENT OF HEALTH, OFFICE OF HEALTH POLICY AND PLANNING
http://www.vdh.virginia.gov

MARY MARSHALL PRACTICAL NURSING SCHOLARSHIPS

Award for practical nursing students who are Virginia residents. Must attend a nursing program in Virginia. Recipient must agree to work in Virginia after graduation. Minimum 3.0 GPA required. Recipients may reapply up to three years for an award.

Academic Fields/Career Goals: Nursing.

Award: Scholarship for use in freshman, sophomore, junior, or senior years; not renewable. *Number:* varies. *Amount:* $100–$1200.

Eligibility Requirements: Applicant must be enrolled or expecting to enroll full or part-time at a two-year or technical institution; resident of Virginia and studying in Virginia. Applicant must have 3.0 GPA or higher. Available to U.S. citizens.

Application Requirements: Application, financial need analysis, references, transcript. *Deadline:* June 30.

Contact: Norma Marrin, Business Manager/Policy Analyst
Virginia Department of Health, Office of Health Policy and Planning
PO Box 2448
Richmond, VA 23218-2448
Phone: 804-864-7433
Fax: 804-864-7440
E-mail: norma.marrin@vdh.virginia.gov

MARY MARSHALL REGISTERED NURSING PROGRAM SCHOLARSHIPS

Award for registered nursing students who are Virginia residents. Must attend a nursing program in Virginia. Recipient must agree to work in Virginia after graduation. Minimum 3.0 GPA required. Recipient may reapply up to three years for an award.

Academic Fields/Career Goals: Nursing.

Award: Scholarship for use in freshman, sophomore, junior, or senior years; not renewable. *Number:* 60–100. *Amount:* $100–$1200.

Eligibility Requirements: Applicant must be enrolled or expecting to enroll full or part-time at a two-year or four-year institution or university; resident of Virginia and studying in Virginia. Applicant must have 3.0 GPA or higher. Available to U.S. citizens.

Application Requirements: Application, financial need analysis, references, transcript. *Deadline:* June 30.

Contact: Norma Marrin, Business Manager/Policy Analyst
Virginia Department of Health, Office of Health Policy and Planning
PO Box 2448
Richmond, VA 23218-2448
Phone: 804-864-7433
Fax: 804-864-7440
E-mail: norma.marrin@vdh.virginia.gov

WISCONSIN HIGHER EDUCATIONAL AIDS BOARD
http://www.heab.state.wi.us

NURSING STUDENT LOAN PROGRAM

Provides forgivable loans to students enrolled in a nursing program. Must be a Wisconsin resident studying in Wisconsin. Application deadline is last day on which student is enrolled. Please refer to Web site for further details: http://www.heab.state.wi.us

Academic Fields/Career Goals: Nursing.

Award: Forgivable loan for use in freshman, sophomore, junior, or senior years; renewable. *Number:* 150–1800. *Amount:* $250–$3000.

Eligibility Requirements: Applicant must be enrolled or expecting to enroll full or part-time at a two-year or four-year or technical institution or university; resident of Wisconsin and studying in Wisconsin. Available to U.S. citizens.

Application Requirements: Application, financial need analysis.

Contact: Cindy Lehrman, Program Coordinator
Wisconsin Higher Educational Aids Board
PO Box 7885
Madison, WI 53707-7885
Phone: 608-267-2209
Fax: 608-267-2808
E-mail: cindy.lehrman@heab.state.wi.us

WISCONSIN LEAGUE FOR NURSING, INC.
http://www.cuw.edu/AdultEd_Graduate/programs/nursing/wln

NURSING SCHOLARSHIP FOR HIGH SCHOOL SENIORS

One scholarship for a Wisconsin high school senior who will be pursing a professional nursing career. The senior must have been accepted by a Wisconsin NLN accredited school of nursing, have financial need, demonstrate scholastic excellence and leadership potential. Contact the WLN office by mail to request an application.

Academic Fields/Career Goals: Nursing.

Award: Scholarship for use in freshman year; not renewable. *Number:* 1. *Amount:* $500.

Eligibility Requirements: Applicant must be high school student; planning to enroll or expecting to enroll full-time at a two-year or four-year institution or university; resident of Wisconsin and studying in Wisconsin. Available to U.S. citizens.

Application Requirements: Application, financial need analysis. *Deadline:* March 1.

Contact: Mary Ann Tanner, Administrative Secretary
Wisconsin League for Nursing, Inc.
PO Box 107
Long Lake, WI 54542-0107
Phone: 414-332-6271

WISCONSIN LEAGUE FOR NURSING INC., SCHOLARSHIP

One-time award for Wisconsin residents who have completed half of an accredited Wisconsin school of nursing program. Financial need of student must be demonstrated. Contact for additional information.

Academic Fields/Career Goals: Nursing.

Award: Scholarship for use in junior, senior, or graduate years; not renewable. *Number:* 12. *Amount:* $500–$1000.

Eligibility Requirements: Applicant must be enrolled or expecting to enroll full-time at a two-year or four-year or technical institution or university; resident of Wisconsin and studying in Wisconsin. Available to U.S. citizens.

Application Requirements: Application, financial need analysis. *Deadline:* March 1.

Contact: Mary Ann Tanner, Administrative Secretary
Wisconsin League for Nursing, Inc.
PO Box 107
Long Lake, WI 54542-0107
Phone: 414-332-6271

OCCUPATIONAL SAFETY AND HEALTH

AMERICAN SOCIETY OF SAFETY ENGINEERS (ASSE) FOUNDATION
http://www.asse.org

AMERICA RESPONDS MEMORIAL SCHOLARSHIP

One $1000 scholarship will be awarded to a student pursuing an undergraduate degree in occupational safety and health or a closely related field. Must have completed 60 semester hours and maintain at least a 3.2 GPA. Eligible applicants will be members of American Society of Safety Engineers.

Academic Fields/Career Goals: Occupational Safety and Health.

Award: Scholarship for use in freshman, sophomore, junior, or senior years; not renewable. *Number:* 1. *Amount:* up to $1000.

Eligibility Requirements: Applicant must be enrolled or expecting to enroll full-time at a two-year or four-year or technical institution or university. Applicant or parent of applicant must be member of American Society of Safety Engineers. Available to U.S. citizens.

Application Requirements: Application, essay, financial need analysis, references, transcript. *Deadline:* December 1.

Contact: Mary Goranson, Scholarship Coordinator
American Society of Safety Engineers (ASSE) Foundation
1800 East Oakton Street
Des Plaines, IL 60018
Phone: 847-768-3412
E-mail: mgoranson@asse.org

ASSE-EDWIN P. GRANBERRY, JR. DISTINGUISHED SERVICE AWARD SCHOLARSHIP

Scholarships for students pursuing an under graduate degree in occupational safety. Completion of at least 60 current semester hours and minimum GPA of 3.0 required. Deadline is December 1. ASSE student membership is required.

Academic Fields/Career Goals: Occupational Safety and Health.

Award: Scholarship for use in sophomore, junior, or senior years; not renewable. *Number:* 1. *Amount:* up to $1000.

Eligibility Requirements: Applicant must be enrolled or expecting to enroll full-time at a four-year institution or university. Applicant or parent of applicant must be member of American Society of Safety Engineers. Applicant must have 3.0 GPA or higher. Available to U.S. citizens.

Application Requirements: Application, essay, references, transcript. *Deadline:* December 1.

Contact: Mary Goranson, Scholarship Coordinator
American Society of Safety Engineers (ASSE) Foundation
1800 East Oakton Street
Des Plaines, IL 60018
Phone: 847-768-3435
E-mail: mgoranson@asse.org

ASSE-GULF COAST PAST PRESIDENTS SCHOLARSHIP

One $1000 scholarship will be awarded to a part- or full-time student pursuing an undergraduate degree in occupational safety and health or a closely related field. Must have completed 60 semester hours and maintain at least a 3.2 GPA. ASSE general or professional membership required if applicant is a part-time student.

Academic Fields/Career Goals: Occupational Safety and Health.

Award: Scholarship for use in junior or senior years; not renewable. *Number:* up to 2. *Amount:* up to $1000.

Eligibility Requirements: Applicant must be enrolled or expecting to enroll part-time at a four-year institution or university. Applicant or parent of applicant must be member of American Society of Safety Engineers. Available to U.S. citizens.

Application Requirements: Application, essay, financial need analysis, references, transcript. *Deadline:* December 1.

Contact: Mary Goranson, Scholarship Coordinator
American Society of Safety Engineers (ASSE) Foundation
1800 East Oakton Street
Des Plaines, IL 60018
Phone: 847-768-3412
E-mail: mgoranson@asse.org

ASSE-MARSH RISK CONSULTING SCHOLARSHIP

For students pursuing an undergraduate degree in occupational safety. Completion of at least 60 credit hours and minimum GPA of 3.0 required. Deadline is December 1.

Academic Fields/Career Goals: Occupational Safety and Health.

Award: Scholarship for use in junior or senior years; not renewable. *Number:* 1. *Amount:* up to $5000.

Eligibility Requirements: Applicant must be enrolled or expecting to enroll full-time at a four-year institution or university. Applicant or parent of applicant must be member of American Society of Safety Engineers. Applicant must have 3.0 GPA or higher. Available to U.S. and non-U.S. citizens.

Application Requirements: Application, essay, references, transcript. *Deadline:* December 1.

Contact: Mary Goranson, Scholarship Coordinator
American Society of Safety Engineers (ASSE) Foundation
1800 East Oakton Street
Des Plaines, IL 60018
Phone: 847-768-3435
E-mail: mgoranson@asse.org

ASSE-REGION IV/EDWIN P. GRANBERRY SCHOLARSHIP

One $1000 scholarship will be awarded to a student pursuing an undergraduate degree in occupational safety and health or a closely related field. Must reside in the ASSE Region IV area (Louisiana, Alabama, Mississippi, Georgia, Florida, Puerto Rico or United States Virgin Islands). Natives of Region IV attending school elsewhere are also eligible. Must have completed 60 semester hours and maintain at least a 3.2 GPA. Eligible applicants will be members of American Society of Safety Engineers.

Academic Fields/Career Goals: Occupational Safety and Health.

Award: Scholarship for use in freshman, sophomore, junior, or senior years; not renewable. *Number:* 1. *Amount:* up to $1000.

Eligibility Requirements: Applicant must be enrolled or expecting to enroll full-time at a two-year or four-year institution or university. Applicant or parent of applicant must be member of American Society of Safety Engineers. Available to U.S. citizens.

Application Requirements: Application, essay, financial need analysis, references, transcript. *Deadline:* December 1.

Contact: Mary Goranson, Scholarship Coordinator
American Society of Safety Engineers (ASSE) Foundation
1800 East Oakton Street
Des Plaines, IL 60018
Phone: 847-768-3412

ASSE-UNITED PARCEL SERVICE SCHOLARSHIP

Scholarships for students pursuing a four-year BS or BA degree in occupational safety and health or related area (i.e. safety engineering, safety management, systems safety, environmental science, industrial hygiene, ergonomics, fire science or other related safety, health, or environmental program). Completion of at least 60 current semester hours and a minimum 3.0 GPA is required. Deadline: December 1.

Academic Fields/Career Goals: Occupational Safety and Health.

Award: Scholarship for use in freshman, sophomore, junior, or senior years; not renewable. *Number:* 4. *Amount:* $4000–$6000.

Eligibility Requirements: Applicant must be enrolled or expecting to enroll full-time at a four-year institution or university. Applicant or parent of applicant must be member of American Society of Safety Engineers. Applicant must have 3.0 GPA or higher. Available to U.S. and non-U.S. citizens.

Application Requirements: Application, essay, references, transcript. *Deadline:* December 1.

Contact: Mary Goranson, Scholarship Coordinator
American Society of Safety Engineers (ASSE) Foundation
1800 East Oakton Street
Des Plaines, IL 60018
Phone: 847-768-3412
E-mail: mgoranson@asse.org

FORD MOTOR COMPANY SCHOLARSHIP-UNDERGRADUATE

For women pursuing an undergraduate degree in occupational safety. Completion of at least 60 current semester hours and minimum GPA of 3.0 required. Deadline is December 1.

Academic Fields/Career Goals: Occupational Safety and Health.

Award: Scholarship for use in junior or senior years; not renewable. *Number:* up to 3. *Amount:* up to $3375.

Eligibility Requirements: Applicant must be enrolled or expecting to enroll full-time at a four-year institution or university and female. Applicant or parent of applicant must be member of American Society of Safety Engineers. Applicant must have 3.0 GPA or higher. Available to U.S. and non-U.S. citizens.

Application Requirements: Application, essay, references, transcript. *Deadline:* December 1.

OCCUPATIONAL SAFETY AND HEALTH

American Society of Safety Engineers (ASSE) Foundation (continued)

Contact: Mary Goranson, Scholarship Coordinator
American Society of Safety Engineers (ASSE) Foundation
1800 East Oakton Street
Des Plaines, IL 60018
Phone: 847-768-3435
E-mail: mgoranson@asse.org

GEORGIA CHAPTER OF ASSE ANNUAL SCHOLARSHIP

One $1000 scholarship will be awarded to a student pursuing an undergraduate degree in occupational safety and health or a closely related field. Student must reside in a county that is within the ASSE Georgia Chapter or be enrolled in a college or university within Georgia. Must have completed 60 semester hours and maintain at least a 3.2 GPA. Eligible applicants will be members of American Society of Safety Engineers.

Academic Fields/Career Goals: Occupational Safety and Health.

Award: Scholarship for use in junior or senior years; not renewable. *Number:* 1. *Amount:* up to $1000.

Eligibility Requirements: Applicant must be enrolled or expecting to enroll full-time at a four-year institution or university. Applicant or parent of applicant must be member of American Society of Safety Engineers. Applicant must have 3.0 GPA or higher. Available to U.S. citizens.

Application Requirements: Application, essay, financial need analysis, references, transcript. *Deadline:* December 1.

Contact: Mary Goranson, Scholarship Coordinator
American Society of Safety Engineers (ASSE) Foundation
1800 East Oakton Street
Des Plaines, IL 60018
Phone: 847-768-3412
E-mail: mgoranson@asse.org

GOLD COUNTRY SECTION AND REGION II SCHOLARSHIP

One $1000 scholarship for students pursuing an undergraduate or graduate degree in occupational safety and health or a closely related field. Student residing within region II (MT,ID, WY, CO, UT, NV, AZ, NM) area will have priority on this award. ASSE student membership required.

Academic Fields/Career Goals: Occupational Safety and Health.

Award: Scholarship for use in freshman, sophomore, junior, senior, or graduate years; not renewable. *Number:* 1. *Amount:* up to $1000.

Eligibility Requirements: Applicant must be enrolled or expecting to enroll full-time at an institution or university. Applicant or parent of applicant must be member of American Society of Safety Engineers. Applicant must have 3.0 GPA or higher. Available to U.S. citizens.

Application Requirements: Application, financial need analysis, transcript. *Deadline:* December 1.

Contact: Mary Goranson, Scholarship Coordinator
American Society of Safety Engineers (ASSE) Foundation
1800 East Oakton Street
Des Plaines, IL 60018
Phone: 847-768-3412
E-mail: mgoranson@asse.org

HAROLD F. POLSTON SCHOLARSHIP

Scholarship for students pursuing undergraduate or graduate degree in occupational safety and health or a closely related field. Priority will be given to students that belong to the Middle Tennessee Chapter.

Academic Fields/Career Goals: Occupational Safety and Health.

Award: Scholarship for use in freshman or sophomore years; not renewable. *Number:* 1. *Amount:* up to $2000.

Eligibility Requirements: Applicant must be enrolled or expecting to enroll full-time at a two-year or four-year institution. Applicant must have 3.0 GPA or higher. Available to U.S. citizens.

Application Requirements: Application, financial need analysis, references, transcript. *Deadline:* December 1.

Contact: Mary Goranson, Scholarship Coordinator
American Society of Safety Engineers (ASSE) Foundation
1800 East Oakton Street
Des Plaines, IL 60018
Phone: 847-768-3412
E-mail: mgoranson@asse.org

HARRY TABACK 9/11 MEMORIAL SCHOLARSHIP

Scholarship for students pursuing an undergraduate or graduate degree in occupational safety and health or a closely related field. Student must be a natural born United States citizen.

Academic Fields/Career Goals: Occupational Safety and Health.

Award: Scholarship for use in freshman or sophomore years; not renewable. *Number:* 1. *Amount:* up to $1000.

Eligibility Requirements: Applicant must be enrolled or expecting to enroll full-time at a two-year or four-year institution. Applicant must have 3.0 GPA or higher. Available to U.S. citizens.

Application Requirements: Application, financial need analysis, references, transcript. *Deadline:* December 1.

Contact: Mary Goranson, Scholarship Coordinator
American Society of Safety Engineers (ASSE) Foundation
1800 East Oakton Street
Des Plaines, IL 60018
Phone: 847-768-3412
E-mail: mgoranson@asse.org

LIBERTY MUTUAL SCHOLARSHIP

One $3000 scholarship for students pursuing an undergraduate degree in occupational safety and health or a closely related field. ASSE student membership required.

Academic Fields/Career Goals: Occupational Safety and Health.

Award: Scholarship for use in freshman or sophomore years; not renewable. *Number:* 1. *Amount:* up to $3000.

Eligibility Requirements: Applicant must be enrolled or expecting to enroll full-time at a two-year or four-year institution. Applicant or parent of applicant must be member of American Society of Safety Engineers. Applicant must have 3.0 GPA or higher. Available to U.S. citizens.

Application Requirements: Application, financial need analysis, transcript. *Deadline:* December 1.

Contact: Mary Goranson, Scholarship Coordinator
American Society of Safety Engineers (ASSE) Foundation
1800 East Oakton Street
Des Plaines, IL 60018
Phone: 847-768-3412
E-mail: mgoranson@asse.org

NORTHEASTERN ILLINOIS CHAPTER SCHOLARSHIP

One $2500 scholarship for students pursuing an undergraduate or graduate degree in occupational safety and health or a closely related field. Students attending school in the Northeastern Illinois region, including Illinois and Wisconsin have priority on this award. ASSE student membership required.

Academic Fields/Career Goals: Occupational Safety and Health.

Award: Scholarship for use in freshman, sophomore, junior, senior, or graduate years; not renewable. *Number:* 1. *Amount:* up to $2500.

Eligibility Requirements: Applicant must be enrolled or expecting to enroll full-time at a two-year or four-year institution. Applicant or parent of applicant must be member of American Society of Safety Engineers. Applicant must have 3.0 GPA or higher. Available to U.S. citizens.

Application Requirements: Application, financial need analysis, transcript. *Deadline:* December 1.

Contact: Mary Goranson, Scholarship Coordinator
American Society of Safety Engineers (ASSE) Foundation
1800 East Oakton Street
Des Plaines, IL 60018
Phone: 847-768-3412
E-mail: mgoranson@asse.org

SCOTT DOMINGUEZ-CRATERS OF THE MOON SCHOLARSHIP

For part-or full-time students pursuing an undergraduate or graduate degree in occupational safety and health or a closely related field. Students residing within the Craters of the Moon Chapter, Idaho, and Region II (MT, ID, WY, CO, UT, NV, AZ, NM) will have priority on this award. ASSE student membership required. For further information see Web site: http://www.asse.org/foundation.htm

Academic Fields/Career Goals: Occupational Safety and Health.

Award: Scholarship for use in freshman, sophomore, junior, senior, or graduate years; not renewable. *Number:* 1. *Amount:* up to $1000.

Eligibility Requirements: Applicant must be enrolled or expecting to enroll full or part-time at a two-year or four-year institution. Applicant or parent of applicant must be member of American Society of Safety Engineers. Applicant must have 3.0 GPA or higher. Available to U.S. citizens.

Application Requirements: Application, financial need analysis, transcript. *Deadline:* December 1.

Contact: Mary Goranson, Scholarship Coordinator
American Society of Safety Engineers (ASSE) Foundation
1800 East Oakton Street
Des Plaines, IL 60018
Phone: 847-768-3412
E-mail: mgoranson@asse.org

UNITED PARCEL SERVICE DIVERSITY SCHOLARSHIP PROGRAM
• *See page 292*

MARINE TECHNOLOGY SOCIETY
http://www.mtsociety.org

JOHN C. BAJUS SCHOLARSHIP
• *See page 386*

THE MTS STUDENT SCHOLARSHIP
• *See page 386*

NATIONAL ENVIRONMENTAL HEALTH ASSOCIATION/AMERICAN ACADEMY OF SANITARIANS
http://www.neha.org

NATIONAL ENVIRONMENTAL HEALTH ASSOCIATION/AMERICAN ACADEMY OF SANITARIANS SCHOLARSHIP

One-time award for college juniors, seniors, and graduate students pursuing studies in environmental health sciences or public health. Undergraduates must be enrolled full-time in an approved program that is accredited by the Environmental Health Accreditation Council (EHAC) or a NEHA institutional/educational or sustaining member school. Graduate students must be enrolled full-time in a graduate program at a recognized college or university with a declared curriculum in EH science and/or public health.

Academic Fields/Career Goals: Occupational Safety and Health; Public Health.

Award: Scholarship for use in freshman, sophomore, junior, or senior years; renewable. *Number:* 3–4. *Amount:* $1000–$2000.

Eligibility Requirements: Applicant must be enrolled or expecting to enroll full-time at a two-year or four-year institution or university. Available to U.S. citizens.

Application Requirements: Application, references, transcript. *Deadline:* February 1.

Contact: Scholarship Coordinator
National Environmental Health Association/American Academy of Sanitarians
720 South Colorado Boulevard, Suite 970
Denver, CO 80246-1904
Phone: 303-756-9090
Fax: 303-691-9490
E-mail: cdimmitt@neha.org

NATIONAL SAFETY COUNCIL
http://www.cshema.org

CAMPUS SAFETY, HEALTH AND ENVIRONMENTAL MANAGEMENT ASSOCIATION SCHOLARSHIP AWARD PROGRAM
• *See page 295*

OCEANOGRAPHY

CANADIAN RECREATIONAL CANOEING ASSOCIATION
http://www.paddlingcanada.com

BILL MASON MEMORIAL SCHOLARSHIP FUND
• *See page 80*

MARINE TECHNOLOGY SOCIETY
http://www.mtsociety.org

CHARLES H. BUSSMAN UNDERGRADUATE SCHOLARSHIP
• *See page 385*

NATIONAL OCEANIC AND ATMOSPHERIC ADMINISTRATION
http://see.orau.org

NATIONAL OCEANIC AND ATMOSPHERIC ADMINISTRATION EDUCATIONAL PARTNERSHIP PROGRAM WITH MINORITY SERVING INSTITUTIONS UNDERGRADUATE SCHOLARSHIP
• *See page 268*

WOMAN'S NATIONAL FARM AND GARDEN ASSOCIATION
http://www.wnfga.org

WARREN, SANDERS, MCNAUGHTON OCEANOGRAPHIC SCHOLARSHIP

Scholarship for graduate study in oceanography. For information and application contact Scholarship Coordinator.

Academic Fields/Career Goals: Oceanography.

Award: Scholarship for use in freshman, sophomore, junior, senior, graduate, or postgraduate years; not renewable. *Number:* 1. *Amount:* $1000–$1500.

Eligibility Requirements: Applicant must be enrolled or expecting to enroll at a four-year institution or university. Available to U.S. citizens.

Application Requirements: Resume, references, transcript. *Deadline:* May 25.

Contact: Markie Phillips
Woman's National Farm and Garden Association
83 Webster Road
Weston, MA 02493
Phone: 781-899-3990

PEACE AND CONFLICT STUDIES

ASSOCIATION TO UNITE THE DEMOCRACIES
http://www.iaud.org

MAYME AND HERBERT FRANK EDUCATIONAL FUND
• *See page 216*

MENNONITE EDUCATION AGENCY
http://www.mennoniteeducation.org

RACIAL/ETHNIC LEADERSHIP EDUCATION (RELE)

One-time grant for underrepresented minorities (especially people of color) who are not part of a recognized associate group in the Mennonite Church.

Academic Fields/Career Goals: Peace and Conflict Studies; Religion/Theology.

Award: Grant for use in freshman, sophomore, junior, or senior years; not renewable. *Number:* 2–3. *Amount:* $500.

Eligibility Requirements: Applicant must be American Indian/Alaska Native, Asian/Pacific Islander, Black (non-Hispanic), or Hispanic and enrolled or expecting to enroll full or part-time at a two-year or four-year institution or university. Available to U.S. and Canadian citizens.

Mennonite Education Agency (continued)

Application Requirements: Application, financial need analysis, references. *Deadline:* Continuous.

Contact: Lisa Heinz, Associate Director, Finance
Mennonite Education Agency
500 South Main Street
PO Box 1142
Elkhart, IN 46515-1142
Phone: 574-642-3164
Fax: 574-642-4863

UNITED STATES INSTITUTE OF PEACE
http://www.usip.org/

NATIONAL PEACE ESSAY CONTEST

Essay contest designed to have students research and write about international peace and conflict resolution. Topic changes yearly. State winners are invited to Washington, D.C. for the awards program. Deadline varies, usually end of January. Must be enrolled in a U.S. high school.

Academic Fields/Career Goals: Peace and Conflict Studies.

Award: Scholarship for use in freshman year; not renewable. *Number:* 50. *Amount:* $1000–$10,000.

Eligibility Requirements: Applicant must be high school student and planning to enroll or expecting to enroll full or part-time at a two-year or four-year institution or university. Available to U.S. citizens.

Application Requirements: Application, applicant must enter a contest, essay. *Deadline:* varies.

Contact: Contest Coordinator, Education Program
United States Institute of Peace
1200 17th Street, NW, 2nd Floor
Washington, DC 20036-3011
Phone: 202-457-3854
Fax: 202-429-6063
E-mail: essay_contest@usip.org

PERFORMING ARTS

ACADEMY OF TELEVISION ARTS AND SCIENCES FOUNDATION
http://www.emmys.tv/foundation

ACADEMY OF TELEVISION ARTS AND SCIENCES COLLEGE TELEVISION AWARDS
• See page 108

AMERICAN LEGION, DEPARTMENT OF KANSAS
http://www.ksamlegion.org

MUSIC COMMITTEE SCHOLARSHIP
• See page 401

AMERICAN ORFF-SCHULWERK ASSOCIATION
http://www.aosa.org

AMERICAN ORFF-SCHULWERK ASSOCIATION RESEARCH GRANT
• See page 220

GUNILD KEETMAN ASSISTANCE FUND
• See page 220

CALIFORNIA ALLIANCE FOR ARTS EDUCATION (CAAE)
http://www.artsed411.org

EMERGING YOUNG ARTIST AWARDS
• See page 110

CASE WESTERN RESERVE UNIVERSITY
http://www.cwru.edu/artsci/thtr

MARC A. KLEIN PLAYWRIGHT AWARD

Annual competition among student playwrights with cash award of $1000. Play receives a full main stage production. Contact Department of Theater Arts for application; Playwrights must be enrolled at an American college or university.

Academic Fields/Career Goals: Performing Arts.

Award: Scholarship for use in freshman, sophomore, junior, senior, or graduate years; renewable. *Number:* 1–4. *Amount:* $1000–$20,000.

Eligibility Requirements: Applicant must be enrolled or expecting to enroll full-time at a four-year institution or university. Available to U.S. and non-U.S. citizens.

Application Requirements: Application, audition or portfolio. *Deadline:* varies.

Contact: John Orlock, Chair

CHOPIN FOUNDATION OF THE UNITED STATES
http://www.chopin.org

CHOPIN FOUNDATION OF THE UNITED STATES SCHOLARSHIP
• See page 402

CIRI FOUNDATION
http://www.thecirifoundation.org

CIRI FOUNDATION SUSIE QIMMIQSAK BEVINS ENDOWMENT SCHOLARSHIP FUND
• See page 110

CULTURAL FELLOWSHIP GRANTS
• See page 383

CLARICE SMITH PERFORMING ARTS CENTER AT MARYLAND
http://www.claricesmithcenter.umd.edu

WILLIAM KAPELL INTERNATIONAL PIANO COMPETITION AND FESTIVAL

Quadrennial international piano competition for ages 18-31. $80 application fee. Competition takes place at the Clarice Smith Performing Arts Center at the University of Maryland. Next competition will be in 2007.

Academic Fields/Career Goals: Performing Arts.

Award: Prize for use in freshman, sophomore, junior, senior, graduate, or postgraduate years; not renewable. *Number:* up to 12. *Amount:* $1000–$20,000.

Eligibility Requirements: Applicant must be age 18-31; enrolled or expecting to enroll at an institution or university and must have an interest in music. Available to U.S. and non-U.S. citizens.

Application Requirements: Application, applicant must enter a contest, autobiography, photo, portfolio, references, CD of performance. *Fee:* $80. *Deadline:* December 1.

Contact: Christopher Patton, Coordinator
Clarice Smith Performing Arts Center at Maryland
Suite 3800, University of Maryland
College Park, MD 20742-1625
Phone: 301-405-8174
Fax: 301-405-5977
E-mail: kapell@deans.umd.edu

CONGRESSIONAL BLACK CAUCUS SPOUSES PROGRAM
http://www.cbcfinc.org

CONGRESSIONAL BLACK CAUCUS SPOUSES PERFORMING ARTS SCHOLARSHIP

Award made to students who reside or attend school in a congressional district represented by an African-American member of Congress. Must be full-time student enrolled in a performing arts program. Minimum 2.5 GPA required. Contact the congressional office in the appropriate district for information and applications. See http://www.cbcfinc.org for a list of district offices.

Academic Fields/Career Goals: Performing Arts.

Award: Scholarship for use in freshman, sophomore, junior, senior, graduate, or postgraduate years; not renewable. *Number:* 10. *Amount:* $3000.

Eligibility Requirements: Applicant must be enrolled or expecting to enroll full-time at a two-year or four-year or technical institution or university. Applicant must have 2.5 GPA or higher. Available to U.S. citizens.

Application Requirements: Application, essay, financial need analysis, interview, photo, references, transcript, video of performance. *Deadline:* May 1.

Contact: Appropriate Congressional District Office
Phone: 202-263-2836

CONTEMPORARY RECORD SOCIETY
http://www.crsnews.org

CONTEMPORARY RECORD SOCIETY NATIONAL COMPETITION FOR PERFORMING ARTISTS

Applicant may submit one performance tape of varied length with each application. May use any number of instrumentalists and voices. First prize is commercial distribution of winner's recording. Application fee is $50. Submit self-addressed stamped envelope for application. Deadline: March 10.

Academic Fields/Career Goals: Performing Arts.

Award: Prize for use in freshman, sophomore, junior, senior, or graduate years; not renewable. *Number:* 1. *Amount:* $1500–$5000.

Eligibility Requirements: Applicant must be enrolled or expecting to enroll at an institution or university and must have an interest in music/singing. Available to U.S. and non-U.S. citizens.

Application Requirements: Application, applicant must enter a contest, autobiography, resume, references, self-addressed stamped envelope. *Fee:* $50. *Deadline:* March 10.

Contact: Administrative Assistant
Contemporary Record Society
724 Winchester Road
Broomall, PA 19008
Phone: 610-544-5920
Fax: 610-544-5921
E-mail: crsnews@verizon.net

COSTUME SOCIETY OF AMERICA
http://www.costumesocietyamerica.com

ADELE FILENE TRAVEL AWARD
• *See page 105*

STELLA BLUM RESEARCH GRANT
• *See page 105*

DONNA REED FOUNDATION FOR THE PERFORMING ARTS
http://www.donnareed.org

DONNA REED PERFORMING ARTS SCHOLARSHIPS

Three scholarships awarded to division finalists in acting, musical theatre, and vocal. Six awards are given to second level winners, two in each division. Must be a graduating high school senior. To remain eligible, you must be attending an accredited postsecondary or approved program of study. Finalists will compete at the Donna Reed Festival in Iowa during the third week of June.

Academic Fields/Career Goals: Performing Arts.

Award: Scholarship for use in freshman year; not renewable. *Number:* up to 6. *Amount:* $200–$1000.

Eligibility Requirements: Applicant must be high school student and planning to enroll or expecting to enroll full-time at a two-year or four-year or technical institution or university. Available to U.S. and non-U.S. citizens.

Application Requirements: Application, applicant must enter a contest, video/audio tape, CD, DVD for 3 minutes. *Fee:* $25. *Deadline:* June 1.

Contact: Gwen Ecklund, Executive Director
Donna Reed Foundation for the Performing Arts
1305 Broadway
Denison, IA 51442
Phone: 712-263-3334
Fax: 712-263-8026
E-mail: gwen@donnareed.org

GENERAL FEDERATION OF WOMEN'S CLUBS OF MASSACHUSETTS
http://www.gfwcma.org/

DORCHESTER WOMEN'S CLUB SCHOLARSHIP
• *See page 402*

GENERAL FEDERATION OF WOMEN'S CLUBS OF MASSACHUSETTS MUSIC SCHOLARSHIP
• *See page 225*

GINA BACHAUER INTERNATIONAL PIANO FOUNDATION
http://www.bachauer.com

GINA BACHAUER INTERNATIONAL ARTISTS PIANO COMPETITION AWARD

Piano competition sponsored every four years. Includes solo, and orchestral performances. Prizes include cash awards, concerts, CD recording, and residency in various countries. Submit birth certificate copy, passport copy, tapes of last two year's programs, and audition tape. May also audition live.

Academic Fields/Career Goals: Performing Arts.

Award: Prize for use in freshman, sophomore, junior, senior, graduate, or postgraduate years; not renewable. *Number:* 6. *Amount:* $600–$30,000.

Eligibility Requirements: Applicant must be age 19-32; enrolled or expecting to enroll at an institution or university and must have an interest in music/singing. Available to U.S. and non-U.S. citizens.

Application Requirements: Application, applicant must enter a contest, autobiography, driver's license, essay, photo, resume, tapes, passport and birth certificate copies. *Fee:* $75. *Deadline:* November 15.

Contact: Paul Pollei, Artistic Director
Gina Bachauer International Piano Foundation
138 West Broadway Suite 220
Salt Lake City, UT 84101-1664
Phone: 801-297-4250
Fax: 801-521-9202
E-mail: gina@bachauer.com

ILLUMINATING ENGINEERING SOCIETY OF NORTH AMERICA
http://www.iesna.org

ROBERT W. THUNEN MEMORIAL SCHOLARSHIPS
• *See page 100*

JACK J. ISGUR FOUNDATION

JACK J. ISGUR FOUNDATION SCHOLARSHIP
• *See page 111*

KOSCIUSZKO FOUNDATION
http://www.kosciuszkofoundation.org

KOSCIUSZKO FOUNDATION CHOPIN PIANO COMPETITION

Three awards for students majoring or planning to major in piano studies who are between the ages of 16 and 22. Must submit recital program of at least 60-75 minutes. Live audition and $35 fee required. Must be U.S. citizen or full-time international student in the U.S. with valid visa.

Academic Fields/Career Goals: Performing Arts.

Award: Prize for use in freshman, sophomore, junior, or senior years; not renewable. *Number:* 3. *Amount:* $1500–$5000.

Eligibility Requirements: Applicant must be age 16-22; enrolled or expecting to enroll full or part-time at a four-year institution or university and must have an interest in music/singing. Available to U.S. citizens.

Application Requirements: Application, applicant must enter a contest, photo, references, curriculum vitae, proof of age. *Fee:* $35. *Deadline:* varies.

Contact: Tom Pniewski, Director of Cultural Programs
Kosciuszko Foundation
15 East 65th Street
New York, NY 10021-6595
Phone: 212-734-2130
Fax: 212-628-4552
E-mail: tompkf@aol.com

KURT WEILL FOUNDATION FOR MUSIC
http://www.kwf.org

LOTTE LENYA COMPETITION FOR SINGERS

The Lotte Lenya Competition for Singers exists to recognize excellence in the performance of music for the theater, including opera, operetta, and American musical theater. Applicants should contact the Foundation for more information.

Academic Fields/Career Goals: Performing Arts.

Award: Prize for use in freshman, sophomore, junior, senior, graduate, or postgraduate years; not renewable. *Number:* varies. *Amount:* $3000–$7500.

Eligibility Requirements: Applicant must be age 32 or under; enrolled or expecting to enroll at an institution or university and must have an interest in music/singing. Available to U.S. and Canadian citizens.

Application Requirements: Application, applicant must enter a contest, audition. *Deadline:* January 23.

Contact: Carolyn Weber, Director of Program Administration and
Business Affairs
Kurt Weill Foundation for Music
7 East 20th Street
New York, NY 10003-1106
Phone: 212-505-5240
Fax: 212-353-9663

MIDLAND COMMUNITY THEATER
http://www.mctmidland.org

MADEIRA SHANER SCHOLARSHIP

Available to freshman and sophomore students who are U. S. citizens and residents of Midland, Texas. Intended for those pursuing a career in the performing arts. Minimum 3.0 GPA. Application deadline: June 30.

Academic Fields/Career Goals: Performing Arts.

Award: Scholarship for use in freshman or sophomore years; not renewable. *Number:* 2–3. *Amount:* $1000.

Eligibility Requirements: Applicant must be enrolled or expecting to enroll full-time at a four-year institution or university and resident of Texas. Applicant must have 3.0 GPA or higher. Available to U.S. citizens.

Application Requirements: Application. *Deadline:* June 30.

Contact: Georganne Payne, Director of Business Operations and
Development
Midland Community Theater
2000 West Wadley
Midland, TX 79705
Phone: 432-682-2544 Ext. 3006
E-mail: georganne@mctmidland.org

NATIONAL FOUNDATION FOR ADVANCEMENT IN THE ARTS
http://www.artsawards.org

ARTS RECOGNITION AND TALENT SEARCH (ARTS)
• See page 113

ASTRAL CAREER GRANT
• See page 406

NATIONAL GUILD OF COMMUNITY SCHOOLS OF THE ARTS
http://www.nationalguild.org

YOUNG COMPOSERS AWARDS
• See page 406

NATIONAL OPERA ASSOCIATION
http://www.noa.org

NOA VOCAL COMPETITION/ LEGACY AWARD PROGRAM
• See page 113

ORANGE COUNTY COMMUNITY FOUNDATION
http://www.heef.org

ARTS SCHOLARSHIP PROGRAM
• See page 114

POLISH ARTS CLUB OF BUFFALO SCHOLARSHIP FOUNDATION
http://pacb.bfn.org/about/constitution.html

POLISH ARTS CLUB OF BUFFALO SCHOLARSHIP FOUNDATION TRUST
• See page 108

SAN ANGELO SYMPHONY SOCIETY
http://www.sanangelosymphony.org

SORANTIN YOUNG ARTIST AWARD

Prizes awarded to vocalists under 31 and pianists and instrumentalists under 28 in four categories namely piano, vocal, strings, and instrumental. Overall winner will appear with the San Angelo Symphony Orchestra. Application fee of $50 is required.

Academic Fields/Career Goals: Performing Arts.

Award: Prize for use in freshman, sophomore, junior, senior, graduate, or postgraduate years; not renewable. *Number:* 5–12. *Amount:* $1000–$3000.

Eligibility Requirements: Applicant must be age 27 or under; enrolled or expecting to enroll at a two-year or four-year institution or university and must have an interest in music/singing. Available to U.S. and non-U.S. citizens.

Application Requirements: Application, applicant must enter a contest, autobiography, photo, photocopy of a birth certificate, driver's license or passport for proof of age.. *Fee:* $50. *Deadline:* varies.

Contact: Claire Simons
San Angelo Symphony Society
PO Box 5922
San Angelo, TX 76902-5922
Phone: 325-658-5877
Fax: 325-653-1045
E-mail: receptionist@sanangelosymphony.org

SIGMA ALPHA IOTA PHILANTHROPIES, INC.
http://www.sai-national.org

SIGMA ALPHA IOTA GRADUATE PERFORMANCE AWARDS
• See page 406

SIGMA ALPHA IOTA PHILANTHROPIES UNDERGRADUATE PERFORMANCE SCHOLARSHIPS
• See page 407

SIGMA ALPHA IOTA PHILANTHROPIES UNDERGRADUATE SCHOLARSHIPS
• See page 236

SIGMA ALPHA IOTA SUMMER MUSIC SCHOLARSHIPS IN THE U.S. OR ABROAD
• See page 407

SIGMA ALPHA IOTA VISUALLY IMPAIRED SCHOLARSHIP
• See page 236

VSA ARTS
http://www.vsarts.org

VSA ARTS-PANASONIC YOUNG SOLOIST AWARD

Musical performance competition for persons 25 and under with disabilities. One-time award of $5000. Submit audio or videotape of performance. Contact VSA arts for information and application materials. (TTY) 202-737-0645.

Academic Fields/Career Goals: Performing Arts.

Award: Scholarship for use in freshman, sophomore, junior, or senior years; not renewable. *Number:* 2. *Amount:* $5000.

Eligibility Requirements: Applicant must be age 25 or under; enrolled or expecting to enroll full or part-time at an institution or university and must have an interest in music/singing. Applicant must be hearing impaired, learning disabled, physically disabled, or visually impaired. Available to U.S. citizens.

Application Requirements: Application, applicant must enter a contest, autobiography, audition tape. *Deadline:* November 1.

Contact: Elena Widder, Director of Performing Arts
VSA arts
818 Connecticut Avenue, NW, Suite 600
Washington, DC 20006
Phone: 800-933-8721
Fax: 202-737-0725
E-mail: info@vsarts.org

VSA ARTS-ROSEMARY KENNEDY INTERNATIONAL YOUNG SOLOIST AWARD

Musical performance for persons 25 and under with disabilities. Submit audio or videotape of performance. Contact VSA arts for information and application materials.

Academic Fields/Career Goals: Performing Arts.

Award: Scholarship for use in freshman, sophomore, junior, or senior years; not renewable. *Number:* 2. *Amount:* $5000.

Eligibility Requirements: Applicant must be age 25 or under; enrolled or expecting to enroll full or part-time at an institution or university and must have an interest in music/singing. Applicant must be hearing impaired, learning disabled, physically disabled, or visually impaired. Available to Canadian and non-U.S. citizens.

Application Requirements: Application, applicant must enter a contest, autobiography, audio or video tape of the performance. *Deadline:* November 1.

Contact: Elena Widder, Director of Performing Arts
VSA arts
818 Connecticut Avenue, NW, Suite 600
Washington, DC 20006
Phone: 800-933-8721
Fax: 202-737-0725
E-mail: info@vsarts.org

WAMSO-MINNESOTA ORCHESTRA VOLUNTEER ASSOCIATION   http://www.wamso.org

YOUNG ARTIST COMPETITION

Created in 1956, the contest is designed to discover and encourage exceptional young talented musicians ages 15-26 through a regional competition. Applicants submit taped performances. From that group, selected participants compete in the semi-finals with finalists advancing to the last round. Applicant must play an instrument which has a permanent chair in the Minnesota orchestra. Only students or legal residents of Michigan, Minnesota, Iowa, Illinois, Kansas, Missouri, Nebraska, North Dakota, South Dakota, Indiana, Wisconsin, Ontario, and Manitoba are eligible. Application fee is $65.

Academic Fields/Career Goals: Performing Arts.

Award: Prize for use in freshman, sophomore, junior, senior, graduate, or postgraduate years; not renewable. *Number:* 9–14. *Amount:* $500–$5000.

Eligibility Requirements: Applicant must be age 15-26; enrolled or expecting to enroll at an institution or university; resident of Illinois, Indiana, Iowa, Kansas, Manitoba, Michigan, Minnesota, Missouri, Nebraska, North Dakota, Ontario, South Dakota, or Wisconsin and must have an interest in music. Available to U.S. and non-U.S. citizens.

Application Requirements: Application, applicant must enter a contest, taped performance of specific repertoire. *Fee:* $65. *Deadline:* September 15.

Contact: YAC Chair
WAMSO-Minnesota Orchestra Volunteer Association
Orchestra Hall
1111 Nicollet Mall
Minneapolis, MN 55403-2477
Phone: 612-371-5654
Fax: 612-371-7176
E-mail: wamso@mnorch.org

WAVERLY COMMUNITY HOUSE, INC.   http://www.waverlycomm.com

F. LAMMOT BELIN ARTS SCHOLARSHIP
• *See page 103*

WOMEN BAND DIRECTORS INTERNATIONAL   http://www.womenbanddirectors.org

CHARLOTTE PLUMMER OWEN MEMORIAL SCHOLARSHIP
• *See page 407*

GLADYS STONE WRIGHT SCHOLARSHIP
• *See page 240*

HELEN MAY BULTER MEMORIAL SCHOLARSHIP
• *See page 241*

MARTHA ANN STARK MEMORIAL SCHOLARSHIP
• *See page 241*

MUSIC TECHNOLOGY SCHOLARSHIP
• *See page 241*

VOLKWEIN MEMORIAL SCHOLARSHIP
• *See page 241*

PHARMACY

ALBERTA HERITAGE SCHOLARSHIP FUND/ ALBERTA SCHOLARSHIP PROGRAMS   http://www.alis.gov.ab.ca

NORTHERN ALBERTA DEVELOPMENT COUNCIL BURSARY FOR PHARMACY STUDENTS

Bursaries of CAN$ 3000 for one year of study to encourage students from northern Alberta to obtain a postsecondary education. Must be a resident of Alberta based on Students Finance Regulations, enrolled in a four year pharmacy degree program leading to a BSc in Pharmacy, plan to live and work in northern Alberta upon completion of your studies and not be in default of a provincial student loan.

Academic Fields/Career Goals: Pharmacy.

Award: Scholarship for use in freshman, sophomore, junior, or senior years; not renewable. *Number:* up to 125. *Amount:* up to $2583.

Eligibility Requirements: Applicant must be enrolled or expecting to enroll full-time at a four-year institution; resident of Alberta and studying in Alberta. Available to U.S. and Canadian citizens.

Application Requirements: Application. *Deadline:* May 15.

Contact: Carol Vesak, Bursary Coordinator
Alberta Heritage Scholarship Fund/Alberta Scholarship Programs
2nd Floor, Provincial Building, 9621-96 Avenue, PO Box 900-14
Peace River, AB T8S 1T4
Canada
Phone: 780-624-6545
E-mail: nadc.bursary@gov.ab.ca

AMERICAN FOUNDATION FOR PHARMACEUTICAL EDUCATION   http://www.afpenet.org

PHI LAMBDA SIGMA-GLAXO WELLCOME-AFPE FIRST YEAR GRADUATE SCHOLARSHIP

Applicant must be in final year of pharmacy college BS or PharmD program and be a member of Phi Lambda Sigma. Recipient will be invited to attend award ceremony during the Annual Meeting of Phi Lambda Sigma, held during the annual meeting of the American Pharmaceutical Association. U.S. citizenship or permanent resident status is required.

Academic Fields/Career Goals: Pharmacy.

Award: Scholarship for use in senior, or postgraduate years; not renewable. *Number:* 1. *Amount:* $7500.

Eligibility Requirements: Applicant must be enrolled or expecting to enroll full-time at an institution or university. Available to U.S. citizens.

Application Requirements: Application, essay, resume, references, test scores, transcript. *Deadline:* February 1.

Contact: Mary Euler, R.Ph., Executive Director, Phi Lambda Sigma
Leadership Society
American Foundation for Pharmaceutical Education
5005 Rockhill Road
Kansas City, MO 64110

AMERICAN PHARMACY SERVICES CORPORATION FOUNDATION FOR EDUCATION AND RESEARCH, INC.
http://www.apscnet.com

AMERICAN PHARMACY SERVICES CORPORATION SCHOLARSHIP/LOAN

Forgivable loan available to students who have successfully completed the requirement of a pre-pharmacy curriculum and have been accepted into an accredited pharmacy school. Must be committed to independent pharmacy practice and upon graduation and licensure must accept a pharmacist position in a APSC member pharmacy to pay off their loan in four years of full-time employment. Selection for loan is based on academic record, personal characteristics management potential and interest in independent pharmacy. Must maintain a grade point average equal to "C". Application deadline July 15 for fall semester; November 15 for spring semester. For application and information see Web site: http://www.apscnet.com

Academic Fields/Career Goals: Pharmacy.

Award: Forgivable loan for use in freshman, sophomore, junior, senior, or graduate years; renewable. *Number:* varies. *Amount:* up to $3000.

Eligibility Requirements: Applicant must be enrolled or expecting to enroll at an institution or university. Available to U.S. citizens.

Application Requirements: Application, financial need analysis, references, transcript. *Deadline:* varies.

Contact: Teresa Doris, Program Director
American Pharmacy Services Corporation Foundation for Education and Research, Inc.
102 Enterprise Drive
Frankfort, KY 40601
Phone: 502-695-8899
Fax: 502-695-9912
E-mail: teresa@apscnet.com

BRITISH COLUMBIA MINISTRY OF ADVANCED EDUCATION
http://www.aved.gov.bc.ca/

LOAN FORGIVENESS PROGRAM FOR NURSES, DOCTORS, MIDWIVES, AND PHARMACISTS
• See page 325

INDIAN HEALTH SERVICES, UNITED STATES DEPARTMENT OF HEALTH AND HUMAN SERVICES
http://www.ihs.gov

HEALTH PROFESSIONS PREPARATORY SCHOLARSHIP PROGRAM
• See page 425

MENTAL HEALTH ASSOCIATION IN NEW YORK STATE, INC.
http://www.mhanys.org

EDNA AIMES SCHOLARSHIP
• See page 328

NEW YORK STATE EDUCATION DEPARTMENT
http://www.highered.nysed.gov

REGENTS PROFESSIONAL OPPORTUNITY SCHOLARSHIP
• See page 67

UNITED NEGRO COLLEGE FUND
http://www.uncf.org

CARDINAL HEALTH SCHOLARSHIP
• See page 70

CVS/PHARMACY SCHOLARSHIP

Scholarship awarded to undergraduate junior or senior enrolled in a pharmacy major. Applicant must attend school in the Washington, D. C. area or in Detroit, Michigan. Must have minimum 2.8 GPA. Please visit Web site for more information: http://www.uncf.org

Academic Fields/Career Goals: Pharmacy.

Award: Scholarship for use in junior or senior years. *Number:* varies. *Amount:* $2000.

Eligibility Requirements: Applicant must be Black (non-Hispanic); enrolled or expecting to enroll at a four-year institution or university and studying in District of Columbia or Michigan. Available to U.S. citizens.

Application Requirements: Application, financial need analysis, FAFSA, Student Aid Report (SAR). *Deadline:* varies.

Contact: Rebecca Bennett, Director, Program Services
United Negro College Fund
8260 Willow Oaks Corporate Drive
Fairfax, VA 22031-8044
Phone: 800-331-2244
E-mail: rbennett@uncf.org

WYETH SCHOLARSHIP
• See page 142

PHILOSOPHY

AMERICAN SCHOOL OF CLASSICAL STUDIES AT ATHENS
http://www.ascsa.edu.gr

ASCSA SUMMER SESSIONS OPEN SCHOLARSHIPS
• See page 88

PHOTOJOURNALISM/ PHOTOGRAPHY

ACADEMY OF TELEVISION ARTS AND SCIENCES FOUNDATION
http://www.emmys.tv/foundation

ACADEMY OF TELEVISION ARTS AND SCIENCES COLLEGE TELEVISION AWARDS
• See page 108

AMERICAN LEGION, PRESS CLUB OF NEW JERSEY

AMERICAN LEGION PRESS CLUB OF NEW JERSEY AND POST 170 ARTHUR DEHARDT MEMORIAL SCHOLARSHIP
• See page 178

ASIAN AMERICAN JOURNALISTS ASSOCIATION
http://www.aaja.org

ASIAN-AMERICAN JOURNALISTS ASSOCIATION SCHOLARSHIP
• See page 179

CALIFORNIA CHICANO NEWS MEDIA ASSOCIATION (CCNMA)
http://www.ccnma.org

JOEL GARCIA MEMORIAL SCHOLARSHIP
• See page 180

COLLEGEBOUND FOUNDATION
http://www.collegeboundfoundation.org

JANET B. SONDHEIM SCHOLARSHIP
• See page 110

CONNECTICUT CHAPTER OF SOCIETY OF PROFESSIONAL JOURNALISTS
http://www.ctspj.org

CONNECTICUT SPJ BOB EDDY SCHOLARSHIP PROGRAM
• See page 359

DALLAS-FORT WORTH ASSOCIATION OF BLACK COMMUNICATORS
http://www.dfwabc.org

FUTURE JOURNALISTS SCHOLARSHIP PROGRAM
• See page 180

DAYTON FOUNDATION
http://www.daytonfoundation.org

LARRY FULLERTON PHOTOJOURNALISM SCHOLARSHIP

One-time scholarship for Ohio resident pursuing career in photojournalism. Must have experience and submit examples of work. Award for use at an Ohio two- or four-year college or university. High school students are ineligible. For use in sophomore, junior or senior year. Minimum 2.5 GPA required. Must be U.S. citizen.

Academic Fields/Career Goals: Photojournalism/Photography.

Award: Scholarship for use in sophomore, junior, or senior years; not renewable. *Number:* 1–2. *Amount:* $500–$2500.

Eligibility Requirements: Applicant must be enrolled or expecting to enroll full-time at a two-year or four-year institution or university; resident of Ohio; studying in Ohio and must have an interest in photography/photogrammetry/filmmaking. Applicant must have 2.5 GPA or higher. Available to U.S. citizens.

Application Requirements: Application, financial need analysis, portfolio, transcript, slide portfolio. *Deadline:* January 31.

Contact: Diane Timmons, Director of Grants and Programs
Dayton Foundation
2300 Kettering Tower
Dayton, OH 45423
Phone: 937-222-0410
Fax: 937-222-0636
E-mail: dtimmons@daytonfoundation.org

FISHER BROADCASTING COMPANY
http://www.fisherbroadcasting.com

FISHER BROADCASTING, INC., SCHOLARSHIP FOR MINORITIES
• *See page 181*

GREAT LAKES COMMISSION
http://www.glc.org

CAROL A. RATZA MEMORIAL SCHOLARSHIP
• *See page 138*

INDIANAPOLIS ASSOCIATION OF BLACK JOURNALISTS
http://www.iabj.net

LYNN DEAN FORD IABJ SCHOLARSHIP AWARDS
• *See page 181*

INTERNATIONAL FOODSERVICE EDITORIAL COUNCIL
http://www.ifec-is-us.com

INTERNATIONAL FOODSERVICE EDITORIAL COUNCIL COMMUNICATIONS SCHOLARSHIP
• *See page 182*

NATIONAL ASSOCIATION OF BLACK JOURNALISTS
http://www.nabj.org

NATIONAL ASSOCIATION OF BLACK JOURNALISTS NON-SUSTAINING SCHOLARSHIP AWARDS
• *See page 364*

VISUAL TASK FORCE SCHOLARSHIP

Scholarship available to African American students attending an accredited four-year college or university and majoring in visual journalism. Minimum 3.0 GPA required. Must be NABJ member before award.

Academic Fields/Career Goals: Photojournalism/Photography.

Award: Scholarship for use in freshman, sophomore, junior, senior, or graduate years. *Number:* 2. *Amount:* $1250.

Eligibility Requirements: Applicant must be Black (non-Hispanic) and enrolled or expecting to enroll full-time at a four-year institution or university. Applicant must have 3.0 GPA or higher. Available to U.S. citizens.

Application Requirements: *Deadline:* April 30.

Contact: Program and Exposition Coordinator
National Association of Black Journalists
8701-A Adelphi Road
Adelphi, MD 20783-1716
Phone: 301-445-7100
Fax: 301-445-7101

NATIONAL FOUNDATION FOR ADVANCEMENT IN THE ARTS
http://www.artsawards.org

ARTS RECOGNITION AND TALENT SEARCH (ARTS)
• *See page 113*

NATIONAL PRESS PHOTOGRAPHERS FOUNDATION, INC.
http://www.nppa.org

BOB EAST SCHOLARSHIP

Award of $2000 for applicant who is either an undergraduate in the first three and one-half years of college or is planning to pursue postgraduate work and offers indication of acceptance in such a program. Portfolio must include at least five single images in addition to a picture story. Award is chosen primarily on portfolio quality.

Academic Fields/Career Goals: Photojournalism/Photography.

Award: Scholarship for use in freshman, sophomore, junior, or senior years; not renewable. *Number:* 1. *Amount:* $2000.

Eligibility Requirements: Applicant must be enrolled or expecting to enroll full-time at a four-year institution or university. Available to U.S. citizens.

Application Requirements: Application, financial need analysis, portfolio, self-addressed stamped envelope, transcript. *Deadline:* March 1.

Contact: Chuck Fadely
National Press Photographers Foundation, Inc.
The Miami Herald, One Herald Plaza
Miami, FL 33132
Phone: 305-376-2015
E-mail: info@nppa.org

NATIONAL PRESS PHOTOGRAPHERS FOUNDATION STILL PHOTOGRAPHER SCHOLARSHIP

Award of $2000 for students who have completed one year at a four-year college or university having photojournalism courses. Applicant must be pursuing a bachelor's degree and must have at least one-half year of undergraduate schooling remaining at the time of award.

Academic Fields/Career Goals: Photojournalism/Photography.

Award: Scholarship for use in sophomore, junior, or senior years; not renewable. *Number:* 1. *Amount:* $2000.

Eligibility Requirements: Applicant must be enrolled or expecting to enroll full-time at a four-year institution or university. Available to U.S. citizens.

Application Requirements: Application, financial need analysis, portfolio, self-addressed stamped envelope, transcript. *Deadline:* March 1.

Contact: Bill Sanders, Photo Editor
E-mail: wsanders@citizen-times.com

NATIONAL PRESS PHOTOGRAPHERS FOUNDATION TELEVISION NEWS SCHOLARSHIP

Award of $1000 for student enrolled in a four-year college or university having courses in TV news photojournalism. Applicant must be pursuing a bachelor's degree and be in his/her junior or senior year at the time of award. Submit entry form, biographical sketch, and videotape samples of work.

Academic Fields/Career Goals: Photojournalism/Photography; TV/Radio Broadcasting.

Award: Scholarship for use in junior or senior years; not renewable. *Number:* 1. *Amount:* $1000.

Eligibility Requirements: Applicant must be enrolled or expecting to enroll full-time at a four-year institution or university. Available to U.S. citizens.

Application Requirements: Application, autobiography, essay, financial need analysis, portfolio, references, self-addressed stamped envelope, transcript. *Deadline:* March 1.

Contact: Ed Dooks
National Press Photographers Foundation, Inc.
5 Mohawk Drive
Lexington, MA 02421-6217
E-mail: dooks@verizon.net

REID BLACKBURN SCHOLARSHIP

Award of $2000 for a student who has completed one year of a photojournalism program at a four-year college or university in preparation for a bachelor's degree. Must have at least one-half year of undergraduate schooling remaining at time of award. The philosophy and goals statement is particularly important in this selection.

Academic Fields/Career Goals: Photojournalism/Photography.

National Press Photographers Foundation, Inc. (continued)

Award: Scholarship for use in sophomore, junior, or senior years; not renewable. *Number:* 1. *Amount:* $2000.

Eligibility Requirements: Applicant must be enrolled or expecting to enroll full-time at a four-year institution or university. Available to U.S. citizens.

Application Requirements: Application, essay, financial need analysis, portfolio, self-addressed stamped envelope, transcript. *Deadline:* March 1.

Contact: Jeremiah Coughlan, Staff Photographer
National Press Photographers Foundation, Inc.
The Columbian, 701 West 8th Street
Vancouver, WA 98660
Phone: 360-694-3391
E-mail: coughlan@attbi.com

NATIONAL WRITERS ASSOCIATION FOUNDATION   http://www.nationalwriters.com

NATIONAL WRITERS ASSOCIATION FOUNDATION SCHOLARSHIPS
• See page 184

NEBRASKA PRESS ASSOCIATION   http://www.nebpress.com

NEBRASKA PRESS ASSOCIATION FOUNDATION, INC., SCHOLARSHIP
• See page 365

OUTDOOR WRITERS ASSOCIATION OF AMERICA   http://www.owaa.org/

OUTDOOR WRITERS ASSOCIATION OF AMERICA BODIE MCDOWELL SCHOLARSHIP AWARD
• See page 185

TEXAS GRIDIRON CLUB, INC.   http://www.spjfw.org

TEXAS GRIDIRON CLUB SCHOLARSHIPS
• See page 188

UNITED METHODIST COMMUNICATIONS   http://www.umcom.org/

LEONARD M. PERRYMAN COMMUNICATIONS SCHOLARSHIP FOR ETHNIC MINORITY STUDENTS
• See page 189

VALLEY PRESS CLUB   http://www.valleypressclub.com/

VALLEY PRESS CLUB SCHOLARSHIPS, THE REPUBLICAN SCHOLARSHIP; PHOTOJOURNALISM SCHOLARSHIP, CHANNEL 22 SCHOLARSHIP
• See page 189

PHYSICAL SCIENCES AND MATH

AIR & WASTE MANAGEMENT ASSOCIATION– COASTAL PLAINS CHAPTER   http://www.awmacoastalplains.org

COASTAL PLAINS CHAPTER OF THE AIR AND WASTE MANAGEMENT ASSOCIATION ENVIRONMENTAL STEWARD SCHOLARSHIP
• See page 292

ALABAMA STATE DEPARTMENT OF EDUCATION   http://www.alsde.edu

MATH AND SCIENCE SCHOLARSHIP PROGRAM FOR ALABAMA TEACHERS
• See page 135

AMERICAN FOUNDATION FOR THE BLIND   http://www.afb.org/scholarships.asp

PAUL W. RUCKES SCHOLARSHIP
• See page 190

AMERICAN INDIAN SCIENCE AND ENGINEERING SOCIETY   http://www.aises.org

A.T. ANDERSON MEMORIAL SCHOLARSHIP
• See page 89

BURLINGTON NORTHERN SANTA FE FOUNDATION SCHOLARSHIP
• See page 89

ENVIRONMENTAL PROTECTION AGENCY TRIBAL LANDS ENVIRONMENTAL SCIENCE SCHOLARSHIP
• See page 135

AMERICAN INSTITUTE OF AERONAUTICS AND ASTRONAUTICS   http://www.aiaa.org

AIAA UNDERGRADUATE SCHOLARSHIP
• See page 89

AMERICAN LEGION, DEPARTMENT OF MARYLAND   http://www.mdlegion.org

AMERICAN LEGION DEPARTMENT OF MARYLAND MATH-SCIENCE SCHOLARSHIP

Scholarship for study in math or the sciences. Must be a Maryland resident and the dependent child of a veteran. Must submit essay, financial need analysis, and transcript with application. Nonrenewable award for freshman. Application available on Web site: http://mdlegion.org. Deadline is March 31.

Academic Fields/Career Goals: Physical Sciences and Math.

Award: Scholarship for use in freshman year; not renewable. *Number:* 1. *Amount:* $500.

Eligibility Requirements: Applicant must be high school student; planning to enroll or expecting to enroll full-time at a two-year or four-year institution and resident of Maryland. Available to U.S. citizens. Applicant or parent must meet one or more of the following requirements: general military experience; retired from active duty; disabled or killed as a result of military service; prisoner of war; or missing in action.

Application Requirements: Application, essay, financial need analysis, transcript. *Deadline:* March 31.

Contact: Thomas Davis, Department Adjutant
American Legion, Department of Maryland
101 North Gay, Room E
Baltimore, MD 21202
Phone: 410-752-1405
Fax: 410-752-3822
E-mail: tom@mdlegion.org

AMERICAN METEOROLOGICAL SOCIETY   http://www.ametsoc.org/AMS

AMERICAN METEOROLOGICAL SOCIETY INDUSTRY UNDERGRADUATE SCHOLARSHIPS
• See page 89

AMERICAN PHYSICAL SOCIETY   http://www.aps.org

AMERICAN PHYSICAL SOCIETY SCHOLARSHIP FOR MINORITY UNDERGRADUATE PHYSICS MAJORS

One-time award for high school seniors, college freshmen and sophomores planning to major in physics. Must be African-American, Hispanic, or Native-American. Must be a U.S. citizen or a legal resident. For legal residents, a copy of alien registration card is required. Deadline for application is the first Friday in February.

Academic Fields/Career Goals: Physical Sciences and Math.

Award: Scholarship for use in freshman or sophomore years; not renewable. *Number:* 20–25. *Amount:* $2000–$3000.

Eligibility Requirements: Applicant must be American Indian/Alaska Native, Black (non-Hispanic), or Hispanic and enrolled or expecting to enroll full-time at a two-year or four-year institution or university. Available to U.S. citizens.

Application Requirements: Application, essay, references, test scores, transcript. *Deadline:* February.

Contact: Arlene Modeste Knowles, Scholarship Administrator
American Physical Society
One Physics Ellipse
College Park, MD 20740
Phone: 301-209-3232
Fax: 301-209-0865
E-mail: knowles@aps.org

AMERICAN SOCIETY OF NAVAL ENGINEERS
http://www.navalengineers.org

AMERICAN SOCIETY OF NAVAL ENGINEERS SCHOLARSHIP
* See page 90

ARIZONA HYDROLOGICAL SOCIETY
http://www.azhydrosoc.org

ARIZONA HYDROLOGICAL SURVEY STUDENT SCHOLARSHIP
* See page 212

ARKANSAS DEPARTMENT OF HIGHER EDUCATION
http://www.arkansashighered.com

EMERGENCY SECONDARY EDUCATION LOAN PROGRAM
* See page 135

ARMED FORCES COMMUNICATIONS AND ELECTRONICS ASSOCIATION, EDUCATIONAL FOUNDATION
http://www.afcea.org

AFCEA SCHOLARSHIP FOR WORKING PROFESSIONALS
* See page 120

AFCEA SGT. JEANNETTE L. WINTERS, USMC MEMORIAL SCHOLARSHIP
* See page 191

AFCEA/LOCKHEED MARTIN ORINCON IT SCHOLARSHIP
* See page 191

ARMED FORCES COMMUNICATIONS AND ELECTRONICS ASSOCIATION GENERAL EMMETT PAIGE SCHOLARSHIP
* See page 191

ARMED FORCES COMMUNICATIONS AND ELECTRONICS ASSOCIATION GENERAL JOHN A. WICKHAM SCHOLARSHIP
* See page 192

ARMED FORCES COMMUNICATIONS AND ELECTRONICS ASSOCIATION ROTC SCHOLARSHIP PROGRAM
* See page 120

ASPRS, THE IMAGING AND GEOSPATIAL INFORMATION SOCIETY
http://www.asprs.org

SPACE IMAGING AWARD FOR APPLICATION OF HIGH RESOLUTION DIGITAL SATELLITE IMAGERY
* See page 91

Z/I IMAGING SCHOLARSHIP
* See page 91

ASSOCIATION FOR IRON AND STEEL TECHNOLOGY
http://www.aist.org

ASSOCIATION FOR IRON AND STEEL TECHNOLOGY OHIO VALLEY CHAPTER SCHOLARSHIP
* See page 135

ASSOCIATION FOR WOMEN GEOSCIENTISTS, PUGET SOUND CHAPTER
http://www.awg.org

PUGET SOUND CHAPTER SCHOLARSHIP
* See page 213

ASSOCIATION FOR WOMEN IN MATHEMATICS
http://www.awm-math.org

ALICE T. SCHAFER MATHEMATICS PRIZE FOR EXCELLENCE IN MATHEMATICS BY AN UNDERGRADUATE WOMAN

One-time merit award for women undergraduates in the math field. Based on quality of performance in math courses and special programs, ability to work independently, interest in math, and performance in competitions. Must be nominated by professor or adviser.

Academic Fields/Career Goals: Physical Sciences and Math.

Award: Prize for use in freshman, sophomore, junior, or senior years; not renewable. *Number:* 1. *Amount:* $250–$1000.

Eligibility Requirements: Applicant must be enrolled or expecting to enroll full-time at a four-year institution or university and female. Available to U.S. citizens.

Application Requirements: References, transcript, 5 complete copies of nominations. *Deadline:* October 1.

Contact: Dawn V. Wheeler, Director of Marketing
Association for Women in Mathematics
4114 Computer and Space Sciences Building
College Park, MD 20742-2461
E-mail: awm@math.umd.edu

ASSOCIATION FOR WOMEN IN SCIENCE EDUCATIONAL FOUNDATION
http://www.awis.org/ed_foundation.html

ASSOCIATION FOR WOMEN IN SCIENCE COLLEGE SCHOLARSHIP
* See page 86

AWIS KIRSTEN R. LORENTZEN AWARD IN PHYSICS
* See page 213

BARRY M. GOLDWATER SCHOLARSHIP AND EXCELLENCE IN EDUCATION FOUNDATION
http://www.act.org/goldwater

BARRY M. GOLDWATER SCHOLARSHIP AND EXCELLENCE IN EDUCATION PROGRAM
* See page 92

BUSINESS AND PROFESSIONAL WOMEN'S FOUNDATION
http://www.bpwusa.org

BPW CAREER ADVANCEMENT SCHOLARSHIP PROGRAM FOR WOMEN
* See page 136

CATCHING THE DREAM

MATH, ENGINEERING, SCIENCE, BUSINESS, EDUCATION, COMPUTERS SCHOLARSHIPS
* See page 145

NATIVE AMERICAN LEADERSHIP IN EDUCATION (NALE)
* See page 145

EAA AVIATION FOUNDATION, INC.
http://www.eaa.org

PAYZER SCHOLARSHIP
* See page 122

GARDEN CLUB OF AMERICA
http://www.gcamerica.org

GARDEN CLUB OF AMERICA AWARDS FOR SUMMER ENVIRONMENTAL STUDIES
* See page 80

GRAND RAPIDS COMMUNITY FOUNDATION
http://www.grfoundation.org

ECONOMIC CLUB OF GRAND RAPIDS BUSINESS STUDY ABROAD SCHOLARSHIP
* See page 62

GREATER KANAWHA VALLEY FOUNDATION
http://www.tgkvf.org

MATH AND SCIENCE SCHOLARSHIP
• *See page 262*

HACH SCIENTIFIC FOUNDATION
http://www.hachscientificfoundation.org

HACH SCIENTIFIC FOUNDATION SCHOLARSHIPS

Scholarship for undergraduate student who is majoring in chemistry. Must have a minimum GPA of 3.0 and a citizen of the U.S.

Academic Fields/Career Goals: Physical Sciences and Math.

Award: Scholarship for use in freshman, sophomore, junior, or senior years; renewable. *Amount:* up to $6000.

Eligibility Requirements: Applicant must be enrolled or expecting to enroll full-time at a four-year institution or university. Applicant must have 3.0 GPA or higher. Available to U.S. citizens.

Application Requirements: Application, financial need analysis. *Deadline:* varies.

Contact: Hach Scientific Foundation Scholarship
Hach Scientific Foundation
Hach Scientific Foundation
Loveland, CO 80538
Phone: 970-461-1871
Fax: 970-461-1876
E-mail: brycehach@hachscientificfoundation.org

HISPANIC COLLEGE FUND, INC.
http://www.hispanicfund.org

LOCKHEED MARTIN SCHOLARSHIP PROGRAM
• *See page 164*

HISPANIC SCHOLARSHIP FUND
http://www.hsf.net

HSF/SOCIETY OF HISPANIC PROFESSIONAL ENGINEERS, INC. SCHOLARSHIP PROGRAM
• *See page 174*

INDEPENDENT LABORATORIES INSTITUTE SCHOLARSHIP ALLIANCE
http://www.acil.org

INDEPENDENT LABORATORIES INSTITUTE SCHOLARSHIP ALLIANCE
• *See page 93*

INNOVATION AND SCIENCE COUNCIL OF BRITISH COLUMBIA
http://www.scbc.org

PAUL AND HELEN TRUSSEL SCIENCE AND TECHNOLOGY SCHOLARSHIP
• *See page 93*

LOS ANGELES COUNCIL OF BLACK PROFESSIONAL ENGINEERS
http://www.lablackengineers.org

AL-BEN SCHOLARSHIP FOR ACADEMIC INCENTIVE
• *See page 164*

AL-BEN SCHOLARSHIP FOR PROFESSIONAL MERIT
• *See page 165*

AL-BEN SCHOLARSHIP FOR SCHOLASTIC ACHIEVEMENT
• *See page 165*

MICRON TECHNOLOGY FOUNDATION, INC.
http://www.micron.com

MICRON SCIENCE AND TECHNOLOGY SCHOLARS PROGRAM
• *See page 165*

MINERALOGICAL SOCIETY OF AMERICA
http://www.minsocam.org

MINERALOGICAL SOCIETY OF AMERICA-GRANT FOR STUDENT RESEARCH IN MINERALOGY AND PETROLOGY
• *See page 214*

MINERALOGY SOCIETY OF AMERICA-GRANT FOR RESEARCH IN CRYSTALLOGRAPHY
• *See page 215*

NASA DELAWARE SPACE GRANT CONSORTIUM
http://www.delspace.org

NASA DELAWARE SPACE GRANT UNDERGRADUATE TUITION SCHOLARSHIP
• *See page 94*

NASA IDAHO SPACE GRANT CONSORTIUM
http://isgc.uidaho.edu

NASA IDAHO SPACE GRANT CONSORTIUM SCHOLARSHIP PROGRAM
• *See page 94*

NASA MINNESOTA SPACE GRANT CONSORTIUM
http://www.aem.umn.edu/msgc

MINNESOTA SPACE GRANT CONSORTIUM
• *See page 124*

NASA NEBRASKA SPACE GRANT CONSORTIUM
http://nasa.unomaha.edu

NASA NEBRASKA SPACE GRANT
• *See page 125*

NASA NEVADA SPACE GRANT CONSORTIUM
http://www.unr.edu/spacegrant

UNIVERSITY AND COMMUNITY COLLEGE SYSTEM OF NEVADA NASA SPACE GRANT AND FELLOWSHIP PROGRAM
• *See page 125*

NASA VERMONT SPACE GRANT CONSORTIUM
http://www.vtspacegrant.org

VERMONT SPACE GRANT CONSORTIUM SCHOLARSHIP PROGRAM
• *See page 94*

NASA VIRGINIA SPACE GRANT CONSORTIUM
http://www.vsgc.odu.edu

VIRGINIA SPACE GRANT CONSORTIUM TEACHER EDUCATION SCHOLARSHIPS
• *See page 125*

NASA WEST VIRGINIA SPACE GRANT CONSORTIUM
http://www.nasa.wvu.edu

WEST VIRGINIA SPACE GRANT CONSORTIUM UNDERGRADUATE SCHOLARSHIP PROGRAM
• *See page 126*

NASA/MARYLAND SPACE GRANT CONSORTIUM
http://www.mdspacegrant.org

NASA MARYLAND SPACE GRANT CONSORTIUM UNDERGRADUATE SCHOLARSHIPS
• *See page 139*

NATIONAL ASSOCIATION FOR THE ADVANCEMENT OF COLORED PEOPLE
http://www.naacp.org

HUBERTUS W.V. WILLEMS SCHOLARSHIP FOR MALE STUDENTS
• *See page 166*

LOUIS STOKES SCIENCE AND TECHNOLOGY AWARD
• *See page 139*

NATIONAL ASSOCIATION OF WATER COMPANIES-NEW JERSEY CHAPTER

NATIONAL ASSOCIATION OF WATER COMPANIES-NEW JERSEY CHAPTER SCHOLARSHIP
• *See page 139*

NATIONAL FEDERATION OF THE BLIND
http://www.nfb.org

HOWARD BROWN RICKARD SCHOLARSHIP
• See page 101

NATIONAL INVENTORS HALL OF FAME
http://www.invent.org

COLLEGIATE INVENTORS COMPETITION - GRAND PRIZE
• See page 95

COLLEGIATE INVENTORS COMPETITION FOR UNDERGRADUATE STUDENTS
• See page 95

NATIONAL OCEANIC AND ATMOSPHERIC ADMINISTRATION
http://see.orau.org

NATIONAL OCEANIC AND ATMOSPHERIC ADMINISTRATION EDUCATIONAL PARTNERSHIP PROGRAM WITH MINORITY SERVING INSTITUTIONS UNDERGRADUATE SCHOLARSHIP
• See page 268

NATIONAL SECURITY AGENCY
http://www.nsa.gov

NATIONAL SECURITY AGENCY STOKES EDUCATIONAL SCHOLARSHIP PROGRAM
• See page 194

NATIONAL SOCIETY OF BLACK PHYSICISTS
http://www.nsbp.org

AMERICAN PHYSICAL SOCIETY CORPORATE-SPONSORED SCHOLARSHIP FOR MINORITY UNDERGRADUATE STUDENTS WHO MAJOR IN PHYSICS

Scholarship available for minority undergraduate students majoring in physics. Award of $2000 per year for new corporate scholars, and $3000 per year for renewal students. In addition, each physics department that hosts one or more APS minority undergraduate scholars and assigns a mentor for their student/s will receive a $500 award for programs to encourage minority students.

Academic Fields/Career Goals: Physical Sciences and Math.

Award: Scholarship for use in freshman or sophomore years. *Amount:* $500–$3000.

Eligibility Requirements: Applicant must be American Indian/Alaska Native, Asian/Pacific Islander, Black (non-Hispanic), or Hispanic and enrolled or expecting to enroll full or part-time at a four-year institution or university. Available to U.S. citizens.

Application Requirements: Application, references, transcript. *Deadline:* December 1.

Contact: Kennedy Reed, Scholarship Chairman
National Society of Black Physicists
6704G Lee Highway
Arlington, VA 22205
Phone: 703-536-4207
Fax: 703-536-4203
E-mail: scholarships@nsbp.org

ELMER S. IMES SCHOLARSHIP IN PHYSICS

Graduating high school seniors and undergraduate students already enrolled in college as physics majors may apply for the scholarship. U.S citizenship is required.

Academic Fields/Career Goals: Physical Sciences and Math.

Award: Scholarship for use in freshman, sophomore, junior, or senior years; not renewable. *Number:* 1. *Amount:* $1000.

Eligibility Requirements: Applicant must be enrolled or expecting to enroll full-time at a four-year institution or university. Available to U.S. and non-U.S. citizens.

Application Requirements: Application, autobiography, essay, resume, references, transcript. *Deadline:* varies.

Contact: Kennedy Reed, Scholarship Chairman
National Society of Black Physicists
6704G Lee Highway
Arlington, VA 22205
Phone: 703-536-4207
Fax: 703-536-4203
E-mail: scholarships@nsbp.org

HARVEY WASHINGTON BANKS SCHOLARSHIP IN ASTRONOMY

One-time scholarship for student majoring in physics. Application available on Web site: http://www.nsbp.org

Academic Fields/Career Goals: Physical Sciences and Math.

Award: Scholarship for use in freshman, sophomore, junior, or senior years; not renewable. *Number:* 1. *Amount:* $1000.

Eligibility Requirements: Applicant must be enrolled or expecting to enroll full-time at a four-year institution or university. Available to U.S. citizens.

Application Requirements: Application, essay, references, transcript. *Deadline:* December 1.

Contact: Kennedy Reed, Scholarship Chairman
National Society of Black Physicists
6704G Lee Highway
Arlington, VA 22205
Phone: 703-536-4207
Fax: 703-536-4203
E-mail: scholarships@nsbp.org

MICHAEL P. ANDERSON SCHOLARSHIP IN SPACE SCIENCE

One-time scholarship for student majoring in physics. Application available on Web site: http://www.nsbp.org

Academic Fields/Career Goals: Physical Sciences and Math.

Award: Scholarship for use in freshman, sophomore, junior, or senior years; not renewable. *Number:* 1. *Amount:* $1000.

Eligibility Requirements: Applicant must be enrolled or expecting to enroll full-time at a four-year institution or university. Available to U.S. citizens.

Application Requirements: Application, essay, references, transcript. *Deadline:* December 1.

Contact: Kennedy Reed, Scholarship Chairman
National Society of Black Physicists
6704G Lee Highway
Arlington, VA 22205
Phone: 703-536-4207
Fax: 703-536-4203
E-mail: scholarships@nsbp.org

NATIONAL SOCIETY OF BLACK PHYSICISTS AND LAWRENCE LIVERMORE NATIONAL LIBRARY UNDERGRADUATE SCHOLARSHIP

Scholarship is available to graduating high school seniors and undergraduate students enrolled in a physics major. Scholarship is renewable up to four years if student maintains a 3.0 GPA and remains a physics major. Student required to intern one summer during scholarship period at Lawrence Livermore National Library. Application available on Web site: http://www.nsbp.org

Academic Fields/Career Goals: Physical Sciences and Math.

Award: Scholarship for use in freshman, sophomore, junior, or senior years; renewable. *Number:* 1. *Amount:* $5000.

Eligibility Requirements: Applicant must be enrolled or expecting to enroll full-time at a four-year institution or university. Applicant must have 3.0 GPA or higher. Available to U.S. citizens.

Application Requirements: Application, essay, references, transcript. *Deadline:* December 1.

National Society of Black Physicists (continued)

Contact: Kennedy Reed, Scholarship Chairman
National Society of Black Physicists
6704G Lee Highway
Arlington, VA 22205
Phone: 703-536-4207
Fax: 703-536-4203
E-mail: scholarships@nsbp.org

RONALD E. MCNAIR SCHOLARSHIP IN SPACE AND OPTICAL PHYSICS

One-time scholarship for students majoring in physics. Application available on Web site: http://www.nsbp.org

Academic Fields/Career Goals: Physical Sciences and Math.

Award: Scholarship for use in freshman, sophomore, junior, or senior years; not renewable. *Number:* 1. *Amount:* $1000.

Eligibility Requirements: Applicant must be enrolled or expecting to enroll full-time at a four-year institution or university. Available to U.S. citizens.

Application Requirements: Application, essay, references, transcript. *Deadline:* December 1.

Contact: Kennedy Reed, Scholarship Chairman
National Society of Black Physicists
6704G Lee Highway
Arlington, VA 22205
Phone: 703-536-4207
Fax: 703-536-4203
E-mail: scholarships@nsbp.org

WALTER SAMUEL MCAFEE SCHOLARSHIP IN SPACE PHYSICS

One-time scholarship for student majoring in physics. Application available on Web site: http://www.nsbp.org

Academic Fields/Career Goals: Physical Sciences and Math.

Award: Scholarship for use in freshman, sophomore, junior, or senior years; not renewable. *Number:* 1. *Amount:* $1000.

Eligibility Requirements: Applicant must be enrolled or expecting to enroll full-time at a four-year institution or university. Available to U.S. citizens.

Application Requirements: Application, essay, references, transcript. *Deadline:* December 1.

Contact: Kennedy Reed, Scholarship Chairman
National Society of Black Physicists
6704G Lee Highway
Arlington, VA 22205
Phone: 703-536-4207
Fax: 703-536-4203
E-mail: scholarships@nsbp.org

WILLIE HOBBS MOORE, HARRY L. MORRISON, AND ARTHUR B.C. WALKER PHYSICS SCHOLARSHIPS

Scholarships are intended for undergraduate physics majors in their junior or senior year of college. Student should apply as a sophomore or junior. Application available on Web site: http://www.nsbp.org

Academic Fields/Career Goals: Physical Sciences and Math.

Award: Scholarship for use in sophomore, junior, or senior years; not renewable. *Number:* 3. *Amount:* $1000.

Eligibility Requirements: Applicant must be enrolled or expecting to enroll full-time at a four-year institution or university. Available to U.S. citizens.

Application Requirements: Application, essay, references, transcript. *Deadline:* December 1.

Contact: Kennedy Reed, Scholarship Chairman
National Society of Black Physicists
6704G Lee Highway
Arlington, VA 22205
Phone: 703-536-4207
Fax: 703-536-4203
E-mail: scholarships@nsbp.org

NORTH CAROLINA STATE EDUCATION ASSISTANCE AUTHORITY   http://www.ncseaa.edu

NORTH CAROLINA STUDENT LOAN PROGRAM FOR HEALTH, SCIENCE, AND MATHEMATICS
• *See page 211*

OREGON STUDENT ASSISTANCE COMMISSION   http://www.osac.state.or.us

HOWARD VOLLUM AMERICAN INDIAN SCHOLARSHIP
• *See page 194*

PNC BANK TRUST DEPARTMENT

H. FLETCHER BROWN SCHOLARSHIP
• *See page 211*

POLANKI, POLISH WOMEN'S CULTURAL CLUB   http://www.polanki.org

COPERNICUS AWARD
• *See page 413*

ROBERT H. MOLLOHAN FAMILY CHARITABLE FOUNDATION, INC.   http://www.mollohanfoundation.org

HIGH TECHNOLOGY SCHOLARS PROGRAM
• *See page 141*

SIGMA XI, THE SCIENTIFIC RESEARCH SOCIETY   http://www.sigmaxi.org

SIGMA XI GRANTS-IN-AID OF RESEARCH
• *See page 84*

SOCIETY FOR IMAGING SCIENCE AND TECHNOLOGY   http://www.imaging.org/

RAYMOND DAVIS SCHOLARSHIP
• *See page 270*

SOCIETY OF PHYSICS STUDENTS   http://www.spsnational.org

SOCIETY OF PHYSICS STUDENTS SCHOLARSHIPS

Scholarships available to Society of Physics Students (SPS) members. Award based on scholarship and/or need, and SPS participation. For more details visit: http://www.spsnational.org

Academic Fields/Career Goals: Physical Sciences and Math.

Award: Scholarship for use in sophomore, junior, or senior years; not renewable. *Number:* 17–22. *Amount:* $2000–$5000.

Eligibility Requirements: Applicant must be enrolled or expecting to enroll full-time at a two-year or four-year institution or university. Applicant or parent of applicant must be member of Society of Physics Students. Available to U.S. and non-U.S. citizens.

Application Requirements: Application, references, transcript. *Deadline:* February 15.

Contact: SPS Scholarship Committee
Society of Physics Students
One Physics Ellipse
College Park, MD 20740
Phone: 301-209-3007
Fax: 301-209-0839
E-mail: sps@aip.org

SOCIETY OF WOMEN ENGINEERS   http://www.swe.org

SWE CALIFORNIA GOLDEN GATE SECTION SCHOLARSHIPS
• *See page 195*

SWE CONNECTICUT SECTION JEAN R. BEERS SCHOLARSHIP
• *See page 196*

TKE EDUCATIONAL FOUNDATION
http://www.tkefoundation.org

CARROL C. HALL MEMORIAL SCHOLARSHIP
• See page 95

FRANCIS J. FLYNN MEMORIAL SCHOLARSHIP
• See page 239

UNITED NEGRO COLLEGE FUND
http://www.uncf.org

BOOZ, ALLEN & HAMILTON/WILLIAM F. STASIOR INTERNSHIP
• See page 154

HEINZ ENVIRONMENTAL FELLOWS PROGRAM
• See page 142

SPRINT SCHOLARSHIP/INTERNSHIP
• See page 71

WYETH SCHOLARSHIP
• See page 142

UNIVERSITIES SPACE RESEARCH ASSOCIATION
http://www.usra.edu/hq/scholarships/overview.shtml

UNIVERSITIES SPACE RESEARCH ASSOCIATION SCHOLARSHIP PROGRAM
• See page 96

VIRGINIA BUSINESS AND PROFESSIONAL WOMEN'S FOUNDATION
http://www.bpwva.org

WOMEN IN SCIENCE AND TECHNOLOGY SCHOLARSHIP
• See page 143

XEROX
http://www.xerox.com

TECHNICAL MINORITY SCHOLARSHIP
• See page 169

POLITICAL SCIENCE

AMERICAN FEDERATION OF STATE, COUNTY, AND MUNICIPAL EMPLOYEES
http://www.afscme.org

JERRY CLARK MEMORIAL SCHOLARSHIP

Renewable award for a student majoring in political science for his or her junior and senior years of study. Must be a child of an AFSCME member. The recipient also will be given the opportunity to intern at the International Union headquarters. Minimum 3.0 GPA required. Once awarded, the scholarship will be renewed for the senior year provided the student remains enrolled full-time as a political science major. See Web site at http://www.afscme.org for further details. Application deadline is July 1.

Academic Fields/Career Goals: Political Science.

Award: Scholarship for use in sophomore, junior, or senior years; renewable. *Number:* 1. *Amount:* $10,000.

Eligibility Requirements: Applicant must be enrolled or expecting to enroll full-time at a four-year institution or university. Applicant or parent of applicant must be member of American Federation of State, County, and Municipal Employees. Applicant must have 3.0 GPA or higher. Available to U.S. citizens.

Application Requirements: Application, transcript. *Deadline:* July 1.

Contact: Genevieve Marcus, Scholarship Coordinator
American Federation of State, County, and Municipal Employees
1625 L Street, NW
Washington, DC 20036
Phone: 202-429-1250
Fax: 202-429-1272

AMERICAN LEGION AUXILIARY, DEPARTMENT OF ARIZONA
http://www.azlegion.org/majorp~2.htm

AMERICAN LEGION AUXILIARY DEPARTMENT OF ARIZONA WILMA HOYAL-MAXINE CHILTON MEMORIAL SCHOLARSHIP

Annual scholarship to a student in second year or higher in one of the three state universities in Arizona. Must be enrolled in a program of study in political science, public programs, or special education. Must be a citizen of United States and of Arizona for at least one year. Honorably discharged veterans or immediate family members are given preference.

Academic Fields/Career Goals: Political Science; Public Policy and Administration; Social Services; Special Education.

Award: Scholarship for use in sophomore, junior, senior, graduate, or postgraduate years; not renewable. *Number:* 1. *Amount:* $400.

Eligibility Requirements: Applicant must be enrolled or expecting to enroll full-time at a two-year or four-year institution or university; resident of Arizona and studying in Arizona. Available to U.S. citizens.

Application Requirements: Application, autobiography, essay, financial need analysis, photo, references, test scores, transcript. *Deadline:* May 15.

Contact: Barbara Matteson, Department Secretary and Treasurer
American Legion Auxiliary, Department of Arizona
4701 North 19th Avenue, Suite 100
Phoenix, AZ 85015-3727
Phone: 602-241-1080
Fax: 602-604-9640
E-mail: amlegauxaz@mcleodusa.net

ASSOCIATION TO UNITE THE DEMOCRACIES
http://www.iaud.org

MAYME AND HERBERT FRANK EDUCATIONAL FUND
• See page 216

BOYS AND GIRLS CLUBS OF GREATER SAN DIEGO
http://www.sdyouth.org

SPENCE REESE SCHOLARSHIP FUND
• See page 259

CENTRAL INTELLIGENCE AGENCY
http://www.cia.gov

CENTRAL INTELLIGENCE AGENCY UNDERGRADUATE SCHOLARSHIP PROGRAM
• See page 56

COLLEGEBOUND FOUNDATION
http://www.collegeboundfoundation.org

DECATUR H. MILLER SCHOLARSHIP
• See page 338

CUBAN AMERICAN NATIONAL FOUNDATION
http://www.canf.org

MAS FAMILY SCHOLARSHIPS
• See page 146

GOVERNMENT FINANCE OFFICERS ASSOCIATION
http://www.gfoa.org

MINORITIES IN GOVERNMENT FINANCE SCHOLARSHIP
• See page 62

HARRY S. TRUMAN LIBRARY INSTITUTE
http://www.trumanlibrary.org

HARRY S. TRUMAN LIBRARY INSTITUTE UNDERGRADUATE STUDENT GRANT
• See page 217

NATIONAL FEDERATION OF THE BLIND
http://www.nfb.org

MICHAEL AND MARIE MARUCCI SCHOLARSHIP
• See page 312

NATIONAL FISH AND WILDLIFE FOUNDATION
http://www.nfwf.org

BUDWEISER CONSERVATION SCHOLARSHIP PROGRAM
• *See page 140*

NATIONAL SOCIETY DAUGHTERS OF THE AMERICAN REVOLUTION
http://www.dar.org

NATIONAL SOCIETY DAUGHTERS OF THE AMERICAN REVOLUTION ENID HALL GRISWOLD MEMORIAL SCHOLARSHIP
• *See page 217*

NATIONAL STONE, SAND AND GRAVEL ASSOCIATION (NSSGA)
http://www.nssga.org

JENNIFER CURTIS BYLER SCHOLARSHIP FOR THE STUDY OF PUBLIC AFFAIRS
• *See page 184*

NATIONAL TOURISM FOUNDATION
http://www.ntfonline.org

ACADEMY OF TRAVEL AND TOURISM SCHOLARSHIPS
• *See page 351*

TKE EDUCATIONAL FOUNDATION
http://www.tkefoundation.org

BRUCE B. MELCHERT SCHOLARSHIP

One-time award of $500 given to an undergraduate member of Tau Kappa Epsilon with sophomore, junior, or senior standing. Applicant must be pursuing a degree in political science or government and have a record of leadership within his fraternity and other campus organizations. Should have as a goal to serve in a political or government position. Recent head and shoulders photograph must be submitted with application. Minimum 3.0 GPA required.

Academic Fields/Career Goals: Political Science.

Award: Scholarship for use in sophomore, junior, or senior years; not renewable. *Number:* 1. *Amount:* $500.

Eligibility Requirements: Applicant must be enrolled or expecting to enroll full-time at a four-year institution or university; male and must have an interest in leadership. Applicant must have 3.0 GPA or higher. Available to U.S. and non-U.S. citizens.

Application Requirements: Application, essay, photo, transcript. *Deadline:* May 12.

Contact: Gary A. Reed, President/CEO
TKE Educational Foundation
8645 Founders Road
Indianapolis, IN 46268-1393
Phone: 317-872-6533
Fax: 317-875-8353
E-mail: reedga@tke.org

UNITED NEGRO COLLEGE FUND
http://www.uncf.org

C-SPAN SCHOLARSHIP PROGRAM
• *See page 189*

SODEXHO SCHOLARSHIP
• *See page 333*

WASHINGTON NEWS COUNCIL
http://www.wanewscouncil.org/

DICK LARSEN SCHOLARSHIP PROGRAM
• *See page 189*

HERB ROBINSON SCHOLARSHIP PROGRAM
• *See page 190*

PSYCHOLOGY

MENTAL HEALTH ASSOCIATION IN NEW YORK STATE, INC.
http://www.mhanys.org

EDNA AIMES SCHOLARSHIP
• *See page 328*

MISSISSIPPI STATE STUDENT FINANCIAL AID
http://www.mississippiuniversities.com

CRITICAL NEEDS TEACHER LOAN/SCHOLARSHIP
• *See page 231*

MISSISSIPPI HEALTH CARE PROFESSIONS LOAN/SCHOLARSHIP PROGRAM
• *See page 328*

NEW YORK STATE EDUCATION DEPARTMENT
http://www.highered.nysed.gov

REGENTS PROFESSIONAL OPPORTUNITY SCHOLARSHIP
• *See page 67*

PI LAMBDA THETA, INC.
http://www.pilambda.org

JANET ISHIKAWA-DANIEL FULLMER SCHOLARSHIP IN COUNSELING

The scholarship provides $1000 to outstanding students pursuing graduate degrees in counseling or counseling psychology. Applicant should display leadership potential and be involved in extracurricular activities. Must have a cumulative GPA of at least 3.5 during the junior or senior years of the undergraduate degree program and, if applicable, in all courses taken while enrolled in a graduate program is required.

Academic Fields/Career Goals: Psychology.

Award: Scholarship for use in freshman, sophomore, junior, senior, or graduate years; not renewable. *Number:* 1. *Amount:* $1000.

Eligibility Requirements: Applicant must be enrolled or expecting to enroll full or part-time at an institution or university. Applicant must have 3.5 GPA or higher. Available to U.S. and non-U.S. citizens.

Application Requirements: Application, resume, references, transcript. *Deadline:* February 10.

Contact: Ellen Mills, Controller
Pi Lambda Theta, Inc.
PO Box 6626
Bloomington, IN 47407-6626
Phone: 812-339-3411
Fax: 812-339-3462
E-mail: ellen@pilambda.org

PILOT INTERNATIONAL FOUNDATION
http://www.pilotinternational.org

PILOT INTERNATIONAL FOUNDATION RUBY NEWHALL MEMORIAL SCHOLARSHIP
• *See page 331*

PILOT INTERNATIONAL FOUNDATION SCHOLARSHIP PROGRAM
• *See page 331*

PILOT INTERNATIONAL FOUNDATION/LIFELINE SCHOLARSHIP PROGRAM
• *See page 332*

SUNSHINE LADY FOUNDATION, INC.
http://www.sunshineladyfdn.org

COUNSELOR, ADVOCATE, AND SUPPORT STAFF SCHOLARSHIP PROGRAM
• *See page 69*

UNITED NEGRO COLLEGE FUND
http://www.uncf.org

ROCKWELL/UNCF CORPORATE SCHOLARS PROGRAM
• *See page 156*

PUBLIC HEALTH

COLLEGE BOARD/ROBERT WOOD JOHNSON FOUNDATION YES PROGRAM
http://www.collegeboard.com/yes

YOUNG EPIDEMIOLOGY SCHOLARS COMPETITION
• See page 291

MENTAL HEALTH ASSOCIATION IN NEW YORK STATE, INC.
http://www.mhanys.org

EDNA AIMES SCHOLARSHIP
• See page 328

NATIONAL ENVIRONMENTAL HEALTH ASSOCIATION/AMERICAN ACADEMY OF SANITARIANS
http://www.neha.org

NATIONAL ENVIRONMENTAL HEALTH ASSOCIATION/AMERICAN ACADEMY OF SANITARIANS SCHOLARSHIP
• See page 437

PUBLIC POLICY AND ADMINISTRATION

AMERICAN LEGION AUXILIARY, DEPARTMENT OF ARIZONA
http://www.azlegion.org/majorp~2.htm

AMERICAN LEGION AUXILIARY DEPARTMENT OF ARIZONA WILMA HOYAL-MAXINE CHILTON MEMORIAL SCHOLARSHIP
• See page 449

GOVERNMENT FINANCE OFFICERS ASSOCIATION
http://www.gfoa.org

FRANK L. GREATHOUSE GOVERNMENT ACCOUNTING SCHOLARSHIP
• See page 148

GEORGE A. NIELSEN PUBLIC INVESTOR SCHOLARSHIP
• See page 148

MINORITIES IN GOVERNMENT FINANCE SCHOLARSHIP
• See page 62

MARYLAND HIGHER EDUCATION COMMISSION
http://www.mhec.state.md.us

WILLIAM DONALD SCHAEFER SCHOLARSHIP

Scholarship for current high school seniors, full-time degree seeking undergraduate and graduate students who are accepted for admission or are currently enrolled at an eligible institution in Maryland that offers courses of study, training, or other educational activities that are designed to prepare individuals for a career in public service.

Academic Fields/Career Goals: Public Policy and Administration.

Award: Scholarship for use in freshman, sophomore, junior, senior, or graduate years; renewable. *Amount:* up to $8500.

Eligibility Requirements: Applicant must be enrolled or expecting to enroll full-time at a two-year or four-year institution or university; resident of Maryland and studying in Maryland. Available to U.S. citizens.

Application Requirements: Application, financial need analysis, FAFSA. *Deadline:* March 1.

Contact: Office of Student Financial Assistance
Maryland Higher Education Commission
839 Bestgate Road, Suite 400
Annapolis, MD 21401-3013
Phone: 410-260-4565
E-mail: lasplin@mhec.state.md.us

MORRIS K. UDALL FOUNDATION
http://www.udall.gov

MORRIS K. UDALL UNDERGRADUATE SCHOLARSHIPS
• See page 294

RADIOLOGY

AMERICAN SOCIETY OF RADIOLOGIC TECHNOLOGISTS EDUCATION AND RESEARCH FOUNDATION
http://www.asrt.org

JERMAN-CAHOON STUDENT SCHOLARSHIP
• See page 323

ROYCE OSBORN MINORITY STUDENT SCHOLARSHIP
• See page 323

SIEMENS SCHOLAR AWARD
• See page 317

VARIAN RADIATION THERAPY STUDENT SCHOLARSHIP
• See page 324

REAL ESTATE

APPRAISAL INSTITUTE
http://www.appraisalinstitute.org

APPRAISAL INSTITUTE EDUCATIONAL SCHOLARSHIP PROGRAM

Award available to racial, ethnic and gender groups underrepresented in real estate appraisal or allied field, and to those who are disabled. Minimum 2.5 GPA required. Must demonstrate financial need.

Academic Fields/Career Goals: Real Estate.

Award: Scholarship for use in freshman, sophomore, junior, senior, or graduate years; not renewable. *Number:* up to 10. *Amount:* $2000–$3000.

Eligibility Requirements: Applicant must be enrolled or expecting to enroll full or part-time at a two-year or four-year institution or university. Applicant must have 2.5 GPA or higher. Available to U.S. and non-U.S. citizens.

Application Requirements: Application, essay, financial need analysis, references, transcript. *Deadline:* March 15.

Contact: Olivia Carreon, Project Coordinator
Appraisal Institute
c/o Appraisal Institute, 550 West Van Buren Street
Chicago, IL 60607
Phone: 312-335-4100
E-mail: ocarreon@appraisalinstitute.org

EDUCATIONAL SCHOLARSHIP PROGRAM

Scholarships for minorities including women, American Indians or Alaska Natives, Asians, Black or African Americans, Hispanics or Latinos, and Native Hawaiians or other Pacific Islanders. Must be full or part-time students enrolled in real estate courses within a degree granting college/university or junior college/university. Must have proof of a cumulative grade point average of no less than 2.5

Academic Fields/Career Goals: Real Estate.

Award: Scholarship for use in freshman, sophomore, junior, or senior years. *Amount:* up to $1000.

Eligibility Requirements: Applicant must be American Indian/Alaska Native, Asian/Pacific Islander, Black (non-Hispanic), or Hispanic; enrolled or expecting to enroll at a two-year or four-year institution or university and female. Applicant must have 2.5 GPA or higher. Available to U.S. citizens.

Application Requirements: Application, essay, photo, references, transcript. *Deadline:* April 15.

Contact: Wendy Woodburn
Appraisal Institute
Appraisal Institute, 550 West Van Buren Street, Suite 1000
Chicago, IL 60607
Phone: 312-335-4191
Fax: 312-335-4196
E-mail: wwoodburn@appraisalinstitute.org

ILLINOIS REAL ESTATE EDUCATIONAL
FOUNDATION   http://www.illinoisrealtor.org

ILLINOIS REAL ESTATE EDUCATIONAL FOUNDATION ACADEMIC SCHOLARSHIPS

Awards for Illinois residents attending an accredited two- or four-year junior college, college or university in Illinois. Must have completed 30 college credit hours and be pursuing a degree with an emphasis in real estate. Must be a U.S. citizen. Minimum scholarship amount is $500.

Academic Fields/Career Goals: Real Estate.

Award: Scholarship for use in freshman, sophomore, junior, or senior years; not renewable. *Number:* varies. *Amount:* up to $2000.

Eligibility Requirements: Applicant must be enrolled or expecting to enroll full-time at a two-year or four-year institution or university; resident of Illinois and studying in Illinois. Available to U.S. citizens.

Application Requirements: Application, essay, interview, references, transcript. *Deadline:* April 1.

Contact: Stephen Sundquist, General Manager
Illinois Real Estate Educational Foundation
3180 Adloff Lane
Springfield, IL 62703-9451
Phone: 217-529-2600
Fax: 217-529-3904
E-mail: ssundquist@ilreef.org

THOMAS F. SEAY SCHOLARSHIP

Minimum $500 award to students pursuing a degree with an emphasis in real estate. Must be a U.S. citizen and attending any accredited U.S. college or university full-time. Must have completed at least 30 college credit hours. Minimum 3.5 GPA required.

Academic Fields/Career Goals: Real Estate.

Award: Scholarship for use in freshman, sophomore, junior or senior years; not renewable. *Number:* varies. *Amount:* $500–$2000.

Eligibility Requirements: Applicant must be enrolled or expecting to enroll full-time at a two-year or four-year institution or university. Applicant must have 3.5 GPA or higher. Available to U.S. citizens.

Application Requirements: Application, essay, interview, references, transcript. *Deadline:* April 1.

Contact: Stephen Sundquist, General Manager
Illinois Real Estate Educational Foundation
3180 Adloff Lane
Springfield, IL 62703
Phone: 217-529-2600
Fax: 217-529-3904
E-mail: ssundquist@ilreef.org

INSTITUTE OF REAL ESTATE MANAGEMENT
FOUNDATION   http://www.irem.org

GEORGE M. BROOKER COLLEGIATE SCHOLARSHIP FOR MINORITIES

One-time award for minority college juniors, seniors, and graduate students who are U.S. citizens and are committed to a career in real estate, specifically real estate management. Must have a minimum GPA of 3.0. Application deadline is March 31.

Academic Fields/Career Goals: Real Estate.

Award: Scholarship for use in junior, senior, or graduate years; not renewable. *Number:* up to 3. *Amount:* $1000–$2500.

Eligibility Requirements: Applicant must be American Indian/Alaska Native, Asian/Pacific Islander, Black (non-Hispanic), or Hispanic and enrolled or expecting to enroll full-time at a four-year institution or university. Applicant must have 3.0 GPA or higher. Available to U.S. citizens.

Application Requirements: Application, essay, interview, references, transcript. *Deadline:* March 31.

Contact: Kimberly Holmes, Foundation Administrator
Institute of Real Estate Management Foundation
430 North Michigan Avenue, 7th Floor
Chicago, IL 60611-4090
Phone: 312-329-6008
Fax: 312-410-7908
E-mail: foundatn@irem.org

INTERNATIONAL COUNCIL OF SHOPPING
CENTERS EDUCATIONAL
FOUNDATION   http://www.icsc.org

ICSC JOHN. T RIORDAN PROFESSIONAL EDUCATION SCHOLARSHIP

Award for higher education for shopping center professionals. Must be a official ICSC member in good standing, actively employed in the shopping center industry for a minimum of one year, or recent graduate of college/university with coursework emphasis in real estate; or a graduate of REAP or Inroads programs within the past 18 months prior to year end when the application is submitted. Deadline is March 15.

Academic Fields/Career Goals: Real Estate.

Award: Scholarship for use in freshman year; not renewable. *Number:* 1.

Eligibility Requirements: Applicant must be enrolled or expecting to enroll full-time at an institution or university. Available to U.S. and non-U.S. citizens.

Application Requirements: Application, essay, resume, references, statement describing any past ICSC participation. *Deadline:* March 15.

Contact: Sarah Ritchie, Educational Foundation Manager
International Council of Shopping Centers Educational Foundation
1221 Avenue of the Americas, 41st Floor
New York,, NY 10020-1099
Phone: 646-728-3800
Fax: 732-694-1676
E-mail: edfoundation@icsc.org

NEW JERSEY ASSOCIATION OF
REALTORS   http://www.njar.com

NEW JERSEY ASSOCIATION OF REALTORS EDUCATIONAL FOUNDATION SCHOLARSHIP PROGRAM

One-time awards for New Jersey residents who are high school seniors, college undergraduates, or graduate students pursuing studies in real estate or allied fields. Preference to students considering a career in real estate. Must be member of NJAR or relative of a member. Selected candidates are interviewed in June. Must be a U.S. citizen.

Academic Fields/Career Goals: Real Estate.

Award: Scholarship for use in freshman, sophomore, junior, senior, or graduate years; not renewable. *Number:* 20. *Amount:* $1000–$2000.

Eligibility Requirements: Applicant must be enrolled or expecting to enroll full-time at a four-year institution or university and resident of New Jersey. Available to U.S. citizens.

Application Requirements: Application, essay, financial need analysis, interview, transcript. *Deadline:* April 25.

Contact: Diane Hatley, Educational Foundation
New Jersey Association of Realtors
PO Box 2098
Edison, NJ 08818
Phone: 732-494-5616
Fax: 732-494-4723

OREGON STUDENT ASSISTANCE
COMMISSION   http://www.osac.state.or.us

HOMESTEAD CAPITAL HOUSING SCHOLARSHIP
• See page 68

RECREATION, PARKS, LEISURE STUDIES

AMERICAN ALLIANCE FOR HEALTH, PHYSICAL
EDUCATION, RECREATION AND
DANCE   http://www.aahperd.org

ROBERT W. CRAWFORD STUDENT LITERARY AWARD

Award for writing excellence recognizes an undergraduate or graduate student enrolled or majoring in recreation, parks, and leisure studies at an accredited university, college, or community college. Manuscripts must be related to parks, recreation, and leisure to be eligible. Deadline is January 2 and varies every year.

Academic Fields/Career Goals: Recreation, Parks, Leisure Studies.

Award: Scholarship for use in freshman, sophomore, junior, senior, or graduate years; not renewable. *Number:* 2. *Amount:* $500.

Eligibility Requirements: Applicant must be enrolled or expecting to enroll full or part-time at a two-year or four-year institution or university. Available to U.S. and non-U.S. citizens.

Application Requirements: Application, essay, resume, faculty sponsor, sample evaluation sheets. *Deadline:* January 2.

Contact: Program Coordinator
American Alliance for Health, Physical Education, Recreation
and Dance
1900 Association Drive
Reston, VA 20191
Phone: 703-476-3432
Fax: 703-476-9527
E-mail: aalr@aahperd.org

CANADIAN RECREATIONAL CANOEING ASSOCIATION   http://www.paddlingcanada.com

BILL MASON MEMORIAL SCHOLARSHIP FUND
• *See page 80*

MAINE CAMPGROUND OWNERS ASSOCIATION   http://www.campmaine.com

MAINE CAMPGROUND OWNERS ASSOCIATION SCHOLARSHIP
• *See page 409*

RELIGION/THEOLOGY

AMERICAN SCHOOL OF CLASSICAL STUDIES AT ATHENS   http://www.ascsa.edu.gr

ASCSA SUMMER SESSIONS OPEN SCHOLARSHIPS
• *See page 88*

BANK OF AMERICA

WILLIAM HEATH EDUCATION SCHOLARSHIP FOR MINISTERS, PRIESTS AND MISSIONARIES

One-time award available to male students who are graduates from a high school in Alabama, Florida, Georgia, Kentucky, Louisiana, Maryland, Mississippi, North Carolina, South Carolina, Tennessee, Virginia, or West Virginia. Students must be under age 35 and pursuing an undergraduate or graduate degree in order to serve in the ministry, as a missionary or as a social worker. Primary consideration is given to those candidates who are of the Methodist or Episcopalian denominations.

Academic Fields/Career Goals: Religion/Theology; Social Services.

Award: Scholarship for use in sophomore, junior, senior, or graduate years; not renewable. *Amount:* $100–$350.

Eligibility Requirements: Applicant must be Episcopalian or Methodist; age 35 or under; enrolled or expecting to enroll full or part-time at a two-year or four-year institution or university; male and resident of Alabama, Florida, Georgia, Kentucky, Louisiana, Maryland, Mississippi, North Carolina, South Carolina, Tennessee, Virginia, or West Virginia. Available to U.S. citizens.

Application Requirements: Application, essay, references, transcript, copy of high school diploma, birth certificate. *Deadline:* June 30.

Contact: Lori J. Nichols, Relationship Associate
Bank of America
600 Cleveland Street, 3rd Floor
Clearwater, FL 33755
Phone: 727-298-5935
Fax: 727-298-5940
E-mail: lori.j.nichols@bankofamerica.com

CATHOLIC KNIGHTS OF AMERICA   http://www.catholicknights.org

VOCATIONAL SCHOLARSHIP PROGRAM

Vocational scholarships are available for qualifying men and women seeking to enter Roman Catholic religious life. Enrollment in an accredited educational institute is a must. Religious activities, financial need and recommendation by the church are considered when selecting scholarship winners. Minimum 2.5 GPA required. Applicant must not be married.

Academic Fields/Career Goals: Religion/Theology; Social Services.

Award: Grant for use in freshman, sophomore, junior, senior, or graduate years; renewable. *Number:* 5–12. *Amount:* $100–$250.

Eligibility Requirements: Applicant must be Roman Catholic; enrolled or expecting to enroll full-time at a four-year institution or university; single and resident of Arkansas, Indiana, Iowa, Louisiana, Missouri, New Mexico, Ohio, Pennsylvania, Tennessee, Texas, or Wisconsin. Applicant must have 2.5 GPA or higher. Available to U.S. citizens.

Application Requirements: Application, essay, financial need analysis, references. *Deadline:* May 1.

Contact: Christina Knott, Fraternal Communications Supervisor
Catholic Knights of America
4545 Oleapha Avenue
St. Louis, MO 63139
Phone: 314-446-2991
Fax: 314-351-9937
E-mail: christina.knott@catholicknights.org

CATHOLIC WORKMAN   http://www.fcsla.com

FIRST CATHOLIC SLOVAK LADIES ASSOCIATION SEMINARIAN (COLLEGE) SCHOLARSHIP

Fraternal Scholarship award for study at an accredited college or university in the United States or Canada. The candidate must be in a program leading to a bachelor's degree. Full time students working toward a two-year associate degree are eligible. For more information check the Web site: www.fcsla.com

Academic Fields/Career Goals: Religion/Theology.

Award: Scholarship for use in freshman, sophomore, junior, or senior years. *Number:* 15–55. *Amount:* $1250–$1750.

Eligibility Requirements: Applicant must be enrolled or expecting to enroll full-time at a two-year or four-year institution or university. Available to U.S. and non-U.S. citizens.

Application Requirements: Application, autobiography, transcript, letter of acceptance. *Deadline:* March 1.

Contact: Lenore Krava, Executive Secretary
Catholic Workman
24950 Chagrin Boulevard
Beachwood, OH 44122-5634
Phone: 216-464-8015
Fax: 216-464-9260
E-mail: info@fcsla.com

DISCIPLES OF CHRIST HOMELAND MINISTRIES   http://www.discipleshomemissions.org

DAVID TAMOTSU KAGIWADA MEMORIAL SCHOLARSHIP

$2000 scholarship available to Asian-American ministerial students. Must be a member of the Christian Church (Disciples of Christ), demonstrate financial need, have a C+ average, be a full-time student, and be under care of a regional Commission on the Ministry. Application may be submitted electronically. Deadline March 15.

Academic Fields/Career Goals: Religion/Theology.

Award: Scholarship for use in freshman, sophomore, junior, or senior years; not renewable. *Number:* varies. *Amount:* $2000.

Eligibility Requirements: Applicant must be Disciple of Christ; Asian/Pacific Islander and enrolled or expecting to enroll full-time at a two-year or four-year institution or university. Applicant must have 2.5 GPA or higher. Available to U.S. citizens.

Disciples of Christ Homeland Ministries (continued)

Application Requirements: Application, financial need analysis, references, transcript. *Deadline:* March 15.

Contact: Shaina Vardis, Administrative Assistant
Disciples of Christ Homeland Ministries
PO Box 1986
Indianapolis, IN 46206-1986
Phone: 317-713-2666
Fax: 317-635-4426
E-mail: svardis@dhm.disciples.org

DISCIPLE CHAPLAINS' SCHOLARSHIP

$2000 scholarship available to first year seminarians. Must be a member of the Christian Church (Disciples of Christ), demonstrate financial need, have a C+ average, be a full-time student, and be under the care of a regional Commission on the Ministry. Application may be submitted electronically. Deadline March 15.

Academic Fields/Career Goals: Religion/Theology.

Award: Scholarship for use in freshman year; not renewable. *Number:* varies. *Amount:* $2000.

Eligibility Requirements: Applicant must be Disciple of Christ and enrolled or expecting to enroll full-time at an institution or university. Applicant must have 2.5 GPA or higher. Available to U.S. and non-U.S. citizens.

Application Requirements: Application, financial need analysis, references, transcript. *Deadline:* March 15.

Contact: Shaina Vardis, Administrative Assistant
Disciples of Christ Homeland Ministries
PO Box 1986
Indianapolis, IN 46206-1986
Phone: 317-713-2666
Fax: 317-635-4426
E-mail: svardis@dhm.disciples.org

EDWIN G. AND LAURETTA M. MICHAEL SCHOLARSHIP

$2000 scholarship available to ministers' wives. Must be a member of the Christian Church (Disciples of Christ), demonstrate financial need, have a C+ average, be a full-time student, and be under the care of a regional Commission on the Ministry. Application may be submitted electronically. Deadline March 15.

Academic Fields/Career Goals: Religion/Theology.

Award: Scholarship for use in freshman, sophomore, junior, or senior years; not renewable. *Number:* varies. *Amount:* $2000.

Eligibility Requirements: Applicant must be Disciple of Christ; enrolled or expecting to enroll full-time at a two-year or four-year institution or university and married female. Applicant must have 2.5 GPA or higher. Available to U.S. and non-U.S. citizens.

Application Requirements: Application, financial need analysis, references, transcript. *Deadline:* March 15.

Contact: Shaina Vardis, Administrative Assistant
Disciples of Christ Homeland Ministries
PO Box 1986
Indianapolis, IN 46206-1986
Phone: 317-713-2666
Fax: 317-635-4426
E-mail: svardis@dhm.disciples.org

KATHERINE J. SHUTZE MEMORIAL SCHOLARSHIP

$2000 scholarship available to female seminary students. Must be a member of the Christian Church (Disciples of Christ), demonstrate financial need, have a C+ average, be a full-time student, and be under the care of a regional Commission on the Ministry. Application may be submitted electronically. Deadline March 15.

Academic Fields/Career Goals: Religion/Theology.

Award: Scholarship for use in freshman, sophomore, junior, or senior years; not renewable. *Number:* varies. *Amount:* $2000.

Eligibility Requirements: Applicant must be Disciple of Christ; enrolled or expecting to enroll full-time at an institution or university and female. Applicant must have 2.5 GPA or higher. Available to U.S. and non-U.S. citizens.

Application Requirements: Application, financial need analysis, references, transcript. *Deadline:* March 15.

Contact: Shaina Vardis, Administrative Assistant
Disciples of Christ Homeland Ministries
PO Box 1986
Indianapolis, IN 46206-1986
Phone: 317-713-2666
Fax: 317-635-4426
E-mail: svardis@dhm.disciples.org

ROWLEY/MINISTERIAL EDUCATION SCHOLARSHIP

$2000 scholarship available to seminary students preparing for the ministry. Must be a member of the Christian Church (Disciples of Christ), demonstrate financial need, have a C+ average, be a full-time student and be under the care of a regional Commission on the Ministry. Application may be submitted electronically. Deadline March 15.

Academic Fields/Career Goals: Religion/Theology.

Award: Scholarship for use in freshman, sophomore, junior, senior, or graduate years; not renewable. *Number:* varies. *Amount:* $2000.

Eligibility Requirements: Applicant must be Disciple of Christ and enrolled or expecting to enroll full-time at a two-year or four-year institution or university. Applicant must have 2.5 GPA or higher. Available to U.S. and non-U.S. citizens.

Application Requirements: Application, financial need analysis, references, transcript. *Deadline:* March 15.

Contact: Shaina Vardis, Administrative Assistant
Disciples of Christ Homeland Ministries
PO Box 1986
Indianapolis, IN 46206-1986
Phone: 317-713-2666
Fax: 317-635-4426
E-mail: svardis@dhm.disciples.org

STAR SUPPORTER SCHOLARSHIP/LOAN

Scholarships in the form of forgivable loans are available to Black/African-Americans preparing for ministry. One year of full-time professional ministry reduces loan by one third. Three years of service repays loan. Must be member of the Christian Church (Disciples of Christ), have a C+ average, demonstrate financial need, be a full-time student in an accredited school or seminary and be under the care of a regional Commission on the Ministry. Application may be submitted electronically. Deadline March 15.

Academic Fields/Career Goals: Religion/Theology.

Award: Forgivable loan for use in freshman, sophomore, junior, or senior years; not renewable. *Number:* varies. *Amount:* $2000.

Eligibility Requirements: Applicant must be Disciple of Christ; Black (non-Hispanic) and enrolled or expecting to enroll full-time at a two-year or four-year institution or university. Applicant must have 2.5 GPA or higher. Available to U.S. citizens.

Application Requirements: Application, financial need analysis, references, transcript. *Deadline:* March 15.

Contact: Shaina Vardis, Administrative Assistant
Disciples of Christ Homeland Ministries
PO Box 1986
Indianapolis, IN 46206-1986
Phone: 317-713-2666
Fax: 317-635-4426
E-mail: svardis@dhm.disciples.org

ED E. AND GLADYS HURLEY FOUNDATION

ED E. AND GLADYS HURLEY FOUNDATION SCHOLARSHIP

The Hurley Foundation provides scholarships (maximum of $1000/year per student) to worthy and deserving young men and women, residing in any state, who wish to study at a school within the State of Texas to become ministers, missionaries or religious workers of the Protestant faith. Contact institution's financial aid office for more information.

Academic Fields/Career Goals: Religion/Theology.

Award: Scholarship for use in freshman, sophomore, junior, senior, graduate, or postgraduate years; not renewable. *Number:* 100–150. *Amount:* up to $1000.

Eligibility Requirements: Applicant must be Protestant; enrolled or expecting to enroll full or part-time at a two-year or four-year institution or university; resident of Arkansas, Louisiana, or Texas and studying in Texas. Available to U.S. citizens.

Application Requirements: Application, financial need analysis, references. *Deadline:* April 30.

Contact: Financial Aid Office at school for application

FIRST PRESBYTERIAN CHURCH
http://www.firstchurchtulsa.org

ELSA EVERETT MEMORIAL TRUST FUND

Scholarships for students from First Presbyterian Church who are studying for the ministry or Christian education work. Deadline is April 15.

Academic Fields/Career Goals: Religion/Theology.

Award: Scholarship for use in freshman, sophomore, junior, senior, graduate, or postgraduate years; not renewable. *Amount:* $500–$2000.

Eligibility Requirements: Applicant must be Presbyterian and enrolled or expecting to enroll full-time at a two-year or four-year or technical institution or university. Available to U.S. citizens.

Application Requirements: Application, financial need analysis, interview, references, transcript. *Deadline:* April 15.

Contact: Tonye Briscoe, Administrative Assistant
First Presbyterian Church
706 South Boston Avenue
Tulsa, OK 74119-1629
Phone: 918-584-4701
Fax: 918-584-5233
E-mail: tbriscoe@firstchurchtulsa.org

FIRST PRESBYTERIAN CHURCH SCHOLARSHIP PROGRAM

Awards to students pursuing full-time study at an accredited college, university or seminary. Preference given to church members in Tulsa, East Oklahoma, Synod of Sun, and at-large. Minimum 2.0 GPA. Must be a communicant member of the Presbyterian Church (U.S.A.).

Academic Fields/Career Goals: Religion/Theology.

Award: Scholarship for use in freshman, sophomore, junior, senior, or graduate years; not renewable. *Number:* 3–5. *Amount:* $500–$2000.

Eligibility Requirements: Applicant must be Presbyterian and enrolled or expecting to enroll full-time at a four-year institution or university. Available to U.S. citizens.

Application Requirements: Application, financial need analysis, interview, references, transcript. *Deadline:* April 15.

Contact: Tonye Briscoe, Administrative Assistant
First Presbyterian Church
709 South Boston Avenue
Tulsa, OK 74119-1629
Phone: 918-584-4701 Ext. 240
Fax: 918-584-5233
E-mail: tbriscoe@firstchurchtulsa.org

ULLERY CHARITABLE TRUST FUND

Awards to assist students pursuing full-time Christian work with the Presbyterian Church. Must be a member of the Presbyterian Church, preference given to members of the First Presbyterian Church, Tulsa, OK. Deadline is April 15.

Academic Fields/Career Goals: Religion/Theology.

Award: Scholarship for use in freshman year. *Amount:* $500–$2000.

Eligibility Requirements: Applicant must be Presbyterian and enrolled or expecting to enroll full-time at an institution or university. Available to U.S. citizens.

Application Requirements: Application, financial need analysis, interview, references, transcript. *Deadline:* April 15.

Contact: Tonye Briscoe, Administrative Assistant
First Presbyterian Church
706 South Boston Avenue
Tulsa, OK 74119-1629
Phone: 918-584-4701
Fax: 918-584-5233
E-mail: tbriscoe@firstchurchtulsa.org

GRAND CHAPTER OF CALIFORNIA-ORDER OF THE EASTERN STAR
http://www.oescal.org

SCHOLARSHIPS FOR EDUCATION, BUSINESS AND RELIGION
• See page 148

INTERNATIONAL ORDER OF THE KING'S DAUGHTERS AND SONS
http://www.iokds.org

INTERNATIONAL ORDER OF THE KING'S DAUGHTERS AND SONS STUDENT MINISTRY SCHOLARSHIP

Merit-based award available to graduate students, with a minimum 3.0 GPA, who are pursuing a career in the ministry, Master of Divinity only. School or seminary must be accredited by Association of Theological Schools in the U.S. or Canada. Offered to U.S. and Canadian citizens only. Send self-addressed stamped envelope with application request. Submit cassette of two five-minute discussions. Several one-time awards ranging from $500 to $1000. Application requests accepted January 1-March 31 only.

Academic Fields/Career Goals: Religion/Theology.

Award: Scholarship for use in freshman, sophomore, junior, senior, or graduate years; not renewable. *Number:* 30–36. *Amount:* $500–$1000.

Eligibility Requirements: Applicant must be Christian and enrolled or expecting to enroll full-time at an institution or university. Applicant must have 3.0 GPA or higher. Available to U.S. and Canadian citizens.

Application Requirements: Application, autobiography, essay, financial need analysis, photo, references, self-addressed stamped envelope, transcript, budget. *Deadline:* April 30.

Contact: Director, Student Ministry Department
International Order of the King's Daughters and Sons
PO Box 1017
Chautauqua, NY 14722-1017
Phone: 716-357-4951

MARY E. BIVINS FOUNDATION
http://www.bivinsfoundation.org

MARY E. BIVINS RELIGIOUS SCHOLARSHIP

Scholarships provided to individuals who are permanent residents of the Texas Panhandle pursuing an undergraduate or graduate degree in a field preparing them to preach the Christian religion. Write for details.

Academic Fields/Career Goals: Religion/Theology.

Award: Scholarship for use in freshman, sophomore, junior, senior, or graduate years; not renewable. *Number:* 50–75. *Amount:* $1000–$2000.

Eligibility Requirements: Applicant must be Christian; enrolled or expecting to enroll full-time at a two-year or four-year institution or university and resident of Texas. Applicant must have 2.5 GPA or higher. Available to U.S. citizens.

Application Requirements: Application, essay, references, test scores, transcript, proof of residence. *Deadline:* varies.

Contact: Mary E. Bivins Foundation
Mary E. Bivins Foundation
PO Box 1727
Amarillo, TX 79105-1727
E-mail: info@bivinsfoundations.org

MEMORIAL FOUNDATION FOR JEWISH CULTURE
http://www.mfjc.org

MEMORIAL FOUNDATION FOR JEWISH CULTURE INTERNATIONAL SCHOLARSHIP PROGRAM FOR COMMUNITY SERVICE
• See page 106

MENNONITE EDUCATION AGENCY
http://www.mennoniteeducation.org

RACIAL/ETHNIC LEADERSHIP EDUCATION (RELE)
• See page 437

NATIONAL ASSOCIATION OF PASTORAL MUSICIANS
http://www.npm.org

DAN SCHUTTE SCHOLARSHIP
• See page 403

National Association of Pastoral Musicians (continued)

ELAINE RENDLER-RENE DOSOGNE-GEORGETOWN CHORALE SCHOLARSHIP
• See page 403

FUNK FAMILY MEMORIAL SCHOLARSHIP
• See page 403

GIA PUBLICATION PASTORAL MUSICIAN SCHOLARSHIP
• See page 404

MUSONICS SCHOLARSHIP
• See page 404

NATIONAL ASSOCIATION OF PASTORAL MUSICIANS MEMBERS' SCHOLARSHIP
• See page 404

NPM BOARD OF DIRECTORS SCHOLARSHIP
• See page 404

NPM COMPOSERS AND AUTHORS SCHOLARSHIP
• See page 404

NPM KOINONIA/BOARD OF DIRECTORS SCHOLARSHIP
• See page 404

NPM MIAMI VALLEY CATHOLIC CHURCH MUSICIANS SCHOLARSHIP
• See page 405

NPM PERROT SCHOLARSHIP
• See page 405

OREGON CATHOLIC PRESS SCHOLARSHIP
• See page 405

PALUCH FAMILY FOUNDATION/WORLD LIBRARY PUBLICATIONS SCHOLARSHIP
• See page 405

STEVEN C. WARNER SCHOLARSHIP
• See page 405

OREGON STUDENT ASSISTANCE COMMISSION   http://www.osac.state.or.us

FRANKS FOUNDATION SCHOLARSHIP
• See page 432

SOUTHERN BAPTIST HISTORICAL LIBRARY AND ARCHIVES   http://www.sbhla.org

LYNN E. MAY, JR. STUDY GRANT
• See page 339

UNITED METHODIST CHURCH   http://www.umc.org

ERNEST AND EURICE MILLER BASS SCHOLARSHIP FUND

One-time award for undergraduate student enrolled at an accredited institution and entering United Methodist Church ministry as a deacon or elder. Must be an active member of United Methodist Church for at least one year. Merit-based award. Minimum 3.0 GPA required.

Academic Fields/Career Goals: Religion/Theology.

Award: Scholarship for use in freshman, sophomore, junior, or senior years; not renewable. *Number:* 55–60. *Amount:* $800–$1000.

Eligibility Requirements: Applicant must be Methodist and enrolled or expecting to enroll full-time at a two-year or four-year institution or university. Applicant must have 3.0 GPA or higher. Available to U.S. citizens.

Application Requirements: Application, essay, references, transcript. *Deadline:* June 1.

Contact: Patti J. Zimmerman, Scholarships Administrator
United Methodist Church
PO Box 34007
Nashville, TN 37203-0007
Phone: 615-340-7344
E-mail: pzimmer@gbhem.org

UNITED METHODIST COMMUNICATIONS   http://www.umcom.org/

LEONARD M. PERRYMAN COMMUNICATIONS SCHOLARSHIP FOR ETHNIC MINORITY STUDENTS
• See page 189

SCIENCE, TECHNOLOGY, AND SOCIETY

AMERICAN CHEMICAL SOCIETY, RUBBER DIVISION   http://www.rubber.org

AMERICAN CHEMICAL SOCIETY, RUBBER DIVISION UNDERGRADUATE SCHOLARSHIP
• See page 158

AMERICAN INSTITUTE OF AERONAUTICS AND ASTRONAUTICS   http://www.aiaa.org

AIAA UNDERGRADUATE SCHOLARSHIP
• See page 89

ARIZONA HYDROLOGICAL SOCIETY   http://www.azhydrosoc.org

ARIZONA HYDROLOGICAL SURVEY STUDENT SCHOLARSHIP
• See page 212

ARMED FORCES COMMUNICATIONS AND ELECTRONICS ASSOCIATION, EDUCATIONAL FOUNDATION   http://www.afcea.org

VICE ADMIRAL JERRY O. TUTTLE, USN (RET.) AND MRS. BARBARA A. TUTTLE SCIENCE AND TECHNOLOGY SCHOLARSHIP
• See page 255

CATCHING THE DREAM

MATH, ENGINEERING, SCIENCE, BUSINESS, EDUCATION, COMPUTERS SCHOLARSHIPS
• See page 145

NATIVE AMERICAN LEADERSHIP IN EDUCATION (NALE)
• See page 145

COMMON KNOWLEDGE SCHOLARSHIP FOUNDATION   http://www.cksf.org

THE CHEMISTRY COMMON KNOWLEDGE CHALLENGE

Quiz questions from introductory and intermediate level chemistry courses. Participants for scholarship money based on taking a series of short multiple-choice quizzes. For more information and online registration check Web site: www.cksf.org

Academic Fields/Career Goals: Science, Technology, and Society.

Award: Prize for use in freshman, sophomore, junior, or senior years; not renewable. *Number:* 2. *Amount:* $125.

Eligibility Requirements: Applicant must be enrolled or expecting to enroll at a two-year or four-year institution. Available to U.S. citizens.

Application Requirements: Applicant must enter a contest. *Deadline:* varies.

Contact: Daryl Hulce, President
Common Knowledge Scholarship Foundation
PO Box 290361
Davie, FL 33329-0361
Phone: 954-262-8553
Fax: 954-262-3940
E-mail: hulce@cksf.org

EXPLORERS CLUB   http://www.explorers.org

YOUTH ACTIVITY FUND
• See page 412

GEORGE BIRD GRINNELL AMERICAN INDIAN FUND
http://www.grinnellfund.org/

AL QOYAWAYMA AWARD
• See page 163

GREAT LAKES COMMISSION
http://www.glc.org

CAROL A. RATZA MEMORIAL SCHOLARSHIP
• See page 138

GREATER KANAWHA VALLEY FOUNDATION
http://www.tgkvf.org

MATH AND SCIENCE SCHOLARSHIP
• See page 262

HACKENSACK RIVERKEEPER
http://www.hackensackriverkeeper.org

THE RON VELLEKAMP ENVIRONMENTAL SCHOLARSHIP

Scholarship available to a high school senior who either attends a high school located within the Hackensack River Watershed or resides within the boundaries of the Hackensack River Watershed and plans to pursue a career in environmental protection. Must be nominated by high school and have been accepted by an accredited college or university for a program in natural sciences or other appropriate subject .

Academic Fields/Career Goals: Science, Technology, and Society.

Award: Scholarship for use in freshman year. *Amount:* up to $1000.

Eligibility Requirements: Applicant must be enrolled or expecting to enroll at an institution or university; resident of New Jersey and studying in New Jersey. Available to U.S. citizens.

Application Requirements: Application, essay, transcript, letter of acceptance from college or university. *Deadline:* April 22.

Contact: Lisa Ryan
Hackensack Riverkeeper
231 Main Street
Hackensack, NJ 07601-7304
Phone: 201-968-0808
E-mail: lisaryan@hackensackriverkeeper.org

HEALTHCARE INFORMATION AND MANAGEMENT SYSTEMS SOCIETY FOUNDATION
http://www.himss.org

HIMSS FOUNDATION SCHOLARSHIP PROGRAM
• See page 318

HISPANIC SCHOLARSHIP FUND
http://www.hsf.net

HSF/SOCIETY OF HISPANIC PROFESSIONAL ENGINEERS, INC. SCHOLARSHIP PROGRAM
• See page 174

INNOVATION AND SCIENCE COUNCIL OF BRITISH COLUMBIA
http://www.scbc.org

PAUL AND HELEN TRUSSEL SCIENCE AND TECHNOLOGY SCHOLARSHIP
• See page 93

KOREAN-AMERICAN SCIENTISTS AND ENGINEERS ASSOCIATION
http://www.ksea.org

KSEA SCHOLARSHIPS
• See page 245

MICRON TECHNOLOGY FOUNDATION, INC.
http://www.micron.com

MICRON SCIENCE AND TECHNOLOGY SCHOLARS PROGRAM
• See page 165

MIDWEST ROOFING CONTRACTORS ASSOCIATION
http://www.mrca.org

MRCA FOUNDATION SCHOLARSHIP PROGRAM
• See page 94

NASA DELAWARE SPACE GRANT CONSORTIUM
http://www.delspace.org

NASA DELAWARE SPACE GRANT UNDERGRADUATE TUITION SCHOLARSHIP
• See page 94

NASA IDAHO SPACE GRANT CONSORTIUM
http://isgc.uidaho.edu

NASA IDAHO SPACE GRANT CONSORTIUM SCHOLARSHIP PROGRAM
• See page 94

NASA MONTANA SPACE GRANT CONSORTIUM
http://www.spacegrant.montana.edu

MONTANA SPACE GRANT SCHOLARSHIP PROGRAM
• See page 125

NASA NEBRASKA SPACE GRANT CONSORTIUM
http://nasa.unomaha.edu

NASA NEBRASKA SPACE GRANT
• See page 125

NASA RHODE ISLAND SPACE GRANT CONSORTIUM
http://www.planetary.brown.edu/RI_Space_Grant

NASA RHODE ISLAND SPACE GRANT CONSORTIUM OUTREACH SCHOLARSHIP FOR UNDERGRADUATE STUDENTS
• See page 288

PENNSYLVANIA HIGHER EDUCATION ASSISTANCE AGENCY
http://www.pheaa.org

NEW ECONOMY TECHNOLOGY SCHOLARSHIP (NETS)-SCITECH SCHOLARSHIPS

Scholarship for undergraduate studying in approved science or technology fields. Recipients of these scholarships must agree to work full-time in Pennsylvania following graduation, one year for each year that a scholarship award is received. Funds under this program will be awarded on a first-come, first-served basis.

Academic Fields/Career Goals: Science, Technology, and Society.

Award: Scholarship for use in sophomore, junior, or senior years; renewable. *Amount:* up to $3000.

Eligibility Requirements: Applicant must be enrolled or expecting to enroll full-time at a four-year institution or university; resident of Pennsylvania and studying in Pennsylvania. Applicant must have 3.0 GPA or higher. Available to U.S. citizens.

Application Requirements: Application. *Deadline:* varies.

Contact: Pennsylvania Higher Education Assistance Agency
New Economy Technology Scholarship Program, PHEAA State Grant and Special Programs, 1200 North 7th St
Harrisburg, PA 17102-1444
Phone: 800-692-7392

NEW ECONOMY TECHNOLOGY SCHOLARSHIP-TECHNOLOGY SCHOLARSHIPS

Scholarships make financial aid available if you are an undergraduate studying in approved science or technology fields. Recipients of these scholarships must agree to work full-time in Pennsylvania following graduation, one year for each year that a scholarship award is received. funds under this program will be awarded on a first-come, first-served basis.

Academic Fields/Career Goals: Science, Technology, and Society.

Award: Scholarship for use in freshman, sophomore, junior, or senior years. *Amount:* up to $1000.

Eligibility Requirements: Applicant must be enrolled or expecting to enroll full or part-time at a two-year or four-year institution; resident of Pennsylvania and studying in Pennsylvania. Applicant must have 3.0 GPA or higher. Available to U.S. citizens.

Pennsylvania Higher Education Assistance Agency (continued)

Application Requirements: Application. *Deadline:* varies.

Contact: Pennsylvania Higher Education Assistance Agency
New Economy Technology Scholarship Program, PHEAA State
Grant and Special Programs, 1200 North 7th St
Harrisburg, PA 17102-1444
Phone: 800-692-7392

SEASPACE, INC.   http://www.seaspace.org

SEASPACE SCHOLARSHIP PROGRAM

One-time award open to college junior/senior or graduate students pursuing degrees in the marine/aquatic sciences. Must be enrolled full-time with a minimum overall GPA of 3.3/4.0. Must be enrolled in an accredited U.S. institution. Must demonstrate financial need.

Academic Fields/Career Goals: Science, Technology, and Society.

Award: Scholarship for use in junior, senior, or graduate years; not renewable. *Number:* 10–15. *Amount:* $500–$3000.

Eligibility Requirements: Applicant must be enrolled or expecting to enroll full-time at a four-year institution or university. Available to U.S. and non-U.S. citizens.

Application Requirements: Application, financial need analysis, self-addressed stamped envelope, transcript. *Deadline:* February 1.

Contact: Carolyn Peterson, Scholarship Committee Co-Chair
Seaspace, Inc.
PO Box 3753
Houston, TX 77253-3753
Phone: 713-467-6675
E-mail: sscholarship@piovere.com

SIGMA XI, THE SCIENTIFIC RESEARCH SOCIETY   http://www.sigmaxi.org

SIGMA XI GRANTS-IN-AID OF RESEARCH
• *See page 84*

SOCIETY OF AUTOMOTIVE ENGINEERS   http://www.sae.org

DETROIT SECTION SAE TECHNICAL SCHOLARSHIP
• *See page 270*

SOCIETY OF HISPANIC PROFESSIONAL ENGINEERS FOUNDATION   http://www.henaac.org

SOCIETY OF HISPANIC PROFESSIONAL ENGINEERS FOUNDATION
• *See page 168*

SOCIETY OF MEXICAN AMERICAN ENGINEERS AND SCIENTISTS   http://www.maes-natl.org

GRE AND GRADUATE APPLICATIONS WAIVER
• *See page 95*

UNIVERSITIES SPACE RESEARCH ASSOCIATION   http://www.usra.edu

UNIVERSITIES SPACE RESEARCH ASSOCIATION SCHOLARSHIP PROGRAM
• *See page 96*

VIRGINIA BUSINESS AND PROFESSIONAL WOMEN'S FOUNDATION   http://www.bpwva.org

WOMEN IN SCIENCE AND TECHNOLOGY SCHOLARSHIP
• *See page 143*

SOCIAL SCIENCES

ALBERTA HERITAGE SCHOLARSHIP FUND/ ALBERTA SCHOLARSHIP PROGRAMS   http://www.alis.gov.ab.ca

LOIS HOLE HUMANITIES AND SOCIAL SCIENCES SCHOLARSHIP
• *See page 351*

AMERICAN CRIMINAL JUSTICE ASSOCIATION-LAMBDA ALPHA EPSILON   http://www.acjalae.org

AMERICAN CRIMINAL JUSTICE ASSOCIATION-LAMBDA ALPHA EPSILON NATIONAL SCHOLARSHIP
• *See page 198*

AMERICAN SOCIETY OF CRIMINOLOGY   http://www.ASC41.com

AMERICAN SOCIETY OF CRIMINOLOGY GENE CARTE STUDENT PAPER COMPETITION
• *See page 199*

BEINECKE SCHOLARSHIP PROGRAM   http://www.beineckescholarship.org/

BEINECKE SCHOLARSHIP FOR GRADUATE STUDY
• *See page 109*

BUSINESS AND PROFESSIONAL WOMEN'S FOUNDATION   http://www.bpwusa.org

BPW CAREER ADVANCEMENT SCHOLARSHIP PROGRAM FOR WOMEN
• *See page 136*

CANADIAN INSTITUTE OF UKRAINIAN STUDIES   http://www.ualberta.ca/cius/

LEO J. KRYSA UNDERGRADUATE SCHOLARSHIP
• *See page 104*

CATCHING THE DREAM

MATH, ENGINEERING, SCIENCE, BUSINESS, EDUCATION, COMPUTERS SCHOLARSHIPS
• *See page 145*

CENTER FOR LESBIAN AND GAY STUDIES (C.L.A.G.S.)   http://www.clags.org

CENTER FOR GAY AND LESBIAN STUDIES UNDERGRADUATE PAPER AWARDS
• *See page 383*

CHINESE HISTORICAL SOCIETY OF SOUTHERN CALIFORNIA

CHSSC SCHOLARSHIP AWARD
• *See page 352*

COLLEGEBOUND FOUNDATION   http://www.collegeboundfoundation.org

JEANETTE R. WOLMAN SCHOLARSHIP
• *See page 375*

DELAWARE DEPARTMENT OF EDUCATION   http://www.doe.k12.de.us

CHARLES L. HEBNER MEMORIAL SCHOLARSHIP
• *See page 352*

EXPLORERS CLUB   http://www.explorers.org

EXPLORATION FUND GRANTS
• *See page 88*

IRISH-AMERICAN CULTURAL INSTITUTE
http://www.iaci-usa.org

IRISH RESEARCH FUNDS
• See page 105

JAPAN STUDIES SCHOLARSHIP FOUNDATION COMMITTEE

JAPAN STUDIES SCHOLARSHIP
• See page 312

MARIN EDUCATION FUND
http://www.marineducationfund.org

GOLDMAN FAMILY FUND, NEW LEADER SCHOLARSHIP
• See page 210

NATIONAL BLACK POLICE ASSOCIATION
http://www.blackpolice.org

ALPHONSO DEAL SCHOLARSHIP AWARD
• See page 199

NATIONAL INSTITUTES OF HEALTH
http://ugsp.info.nih.gov

NIH UNDERGRADUATE SCHOLARSHIP PROGRAM FOR STUDENTS FROM DISADVANTAGED BACKGROUNDS
• See page 140

NEW MEXICO COMMISSION ON HIGHER EDUCATION
http://www.hed.state.nm.us

ALLIED HEALTH STUDENT LOAN PROGRAM-NEW MEXICO
• See page 210

ORGONE BIOPHYSICAL RESEARCH LABORATORY
http://www.orgonelab.org

LOU HOCHBERG AWARDS

Awards granted for the following: university theses and dissertations ($1000), university/college essays ($500), and high school essays ($500); university thesis/dissertation research improvement and implementation grants ($1500); outstanding research and journalism. Must focus upon the social aspects of the discoveries of Wilhelm Reich.

Academic Fields/Career Goals: Social Sciences.

Award: Prize for use in freshman, sophomore, junior, senior, graduate, or postgraduate years; renewable. *Number:* 2–4. *Amount:* $500–$1500.

Eligibility Requirements: Applicant must be enrolled or expecting to enroll full or part-time at a two-year or four-year or technical institution or university. Available to U.S. and non-U.S. citizens.

Application Requirements: Applicant must enter a contest, transcript, photocopy of student ID. *Deadline:* Continuous.

Contact: The Orgone Biophysical Research Laboratory
Orgone Biophysical Research Laboratory
PO Box 1148
Ashland, OR 97520
Phone: 541-552-0118
Fax: 541-552-0118
E-mail: info@orgonelab.org

PARAPSYCHOLOGY FOUNDATION
http://www.parapsychology.org

CHARLES T. AND JUDITH A. TART STUDENT INCENTIVE

An annual incentive award to promote the research of an undergraduate or graduate student who shows dedication to work within parapsychology. For more details see Web site: http://www.parapsychology.org

Academic Fields/Career Goals: Social Sciences.

Award: Scholarship for use in freshman, sophomore, junior, senior, or graduate years; not renewable. *Number:* 1. *Amount:* $500.

Eligibility Requirements: Applicant must be enrolled or expecting to enroll full-time at an institution or university. Available to U.S. citizens.

Application Requirements: Application, essay, references, transcript. *Deadline:* November 15.

Contact: Director of Library
Parapsychology Foundation
PO Box 1562
New York, NY 10021-0043
E-mail: office@parapsychology.org

EILEEN J. GARRETT SCHOLARSHIP FOR PARAPSYCHOLOGICAL RESEARCH

Applicants must evince academic interest in the science of parapsychology through research, term papers, and courses for which credit was received. Those with only a general interest will not be considered. Visit Web site for additional information.

Academic Fields/Career Goals: Social Sciences.

Award: Scholarship for use in freshman, sophomore, junior, senior, graduate, or postgraduate years; not renewable. *Number:* 1. *Amount:* $3000.

Eligibility Requirements: Applicant must be enrolled or expecting to enroll full-time at an institution or university. Available to U.S. citizens.

Application Requirements: Application, essay, references, transcript. *Deadline:* July 15.

Contact: Lisette Coly, Director of Library
Parapsychology Foundation
PO Box 1562
New York, NY 10021-0043
E-mail: office@parapsychology.org

POLISH HERITAGE ASSOCIATION OF MARYLAND

ROBERT P. PULA MEMORIAL SCHOLARSHIP
• See page 353

SIGMA XI, THE SCIENTIFIC RESEARCH SOCIETY
http://www.sigmaxi.org

SIGMA XI GRANTS-IN-AID OF RESEARCH
• See page 84

SOCIAL SCIENCES AND HUMANITIES RESEARCH COUNCIL OF CANADA
http://www.sshrc.ca

RESEARCH DEVELOPMENT INITIATIVE
• See page 237

SOCIETY FOR APPLIED ANTHROPOLOGY
http://www.sfaa.net

DEL JONES MEMORIAL TRAVEL AWARD

Travel grants of $500 are available for students to attend the annual meeting of the Society. The Society seeks to achieve greater diversity in its programs and activities, and the award is directed toward increasing the participation of African Americans in the annual meeting program. For more details see Web site: http://www.sfaa.net

Academic Fields/Career Goals: Social Sciences.

Award: Grant for use in freshman, sophomore, junior, senior, or graduate years; not renewable. *Number:* 2. *Amount:* up to $500.

Eligibility Requirements: Applicant must be Black (non-Hispanic) and enrolled or expecting to enroll full or part-time at a two-year or four-year institution or university. Available to U.S. and non-U.S. citizens.

Society for Applied Anthropology (continued)

Application Requirements: Application, applicant must enter a contest, paper abstract and written statement. *Deadline:* January 17.

Contact: J.T. May, Executive Director
Society for Applied Anthropology
PO Box 2436
Oklahoma City, OK 73101-2436
Phone: 405-843-5113
Fax: 405-843-8553
E-mail: info@sfaa.net

EDWARD H. AND ROSAMUND B. SPICER TRAVEL AWARD

Two travel grants of $500 are awarded to students who meet the eligibility qualifications. The awards are for the students to attend and participate in the SFAA annual meeting. The award's purpose is to further the maturation of students in the social sciences, both intellectually and practically. For more details, see Web site: http://www.sfaa.net

Academic Fields/Career Goals: Social Sciences.

Award: Prize for use in freshman, sophomore, junior, or senior years; not renewable. *Number:* 2. *Amount:* up to $500.

Eligibility Requirements: Applicant must be enrolled or expecting to enroll full or part-time at a two-year or four-year institution or university. Available to U.S. and non-U.S. citizens.

Application Requirements: Application, applicant must enter a contest, paper abstract and written statement. *Deadline:* January 17.

Contact: J.T. May, Executive Director
Society for Applied Anthropology
PO Box 2436
Oklahoma City, OK 73101-2436
Phone: 405-843-5113
Fax: 405-843-8553
E-mail: info@sfaa.net

PETER KONG-MING NEW STUDENT PRIZE
• See page 332

SOUTHWEST STUDENT SERVICES CORPORATION
http://www.sssc.com/

ANNE LINDEMAN MEMORIAL SCHOLARSHIP
• See page 142

SUNSHINE LADY FOUNDATION, INC.
http://www.sunshineladyfdn.org

COUNSELOR, ADVOCATE, AND SUPPORT STAFF SCHOLARSHIP PROGRAM
• See page 69

SOCIAL SERVICES

AMERICAN LEGION AUXILIARY, DEPARTMENT OF ARIZONA
http://www.azlegion.org/majorp~2.htm

AMERICAN LEGION AUXILIARY DEPARTMENT OF ARIZONA WILMA HOYAL-MAXINE CHILTON MEMORIAL SCHOLARSHIP
• See page 449

BANK OF AMERICA

WILLIAM HEATH EDUCATION SCHOLARSHIP FOR MINISTERS, PRIESTS AND MISSIONARIES
• See page 453

BETHESDA LUTHERAN HOMES AND SERVICES, INC.
http://www.blhs.org

DEVELOPMENTAL DISABILITIES AWARENESS AWARDS FOR LUTHERAN HIGH SCHOOL STUDENTS

Award available to students interested in the developmental disabilities field. Students must complete two activities from a suggested list, which, together with the application process, are designed to promote the student's knowledge

of careers in the field of developmental disabilities services. Up to three awards are given - $250, $150, $100. For more information visit Web site at : http://www.blhs.org

Academic Fields/Career Goals: Social Services; Special Education.

Award: Scholarship for use in freshman year. *Amount:* $100–$250.

Eligibility Requirements: Applicant must be high school student and planning to enroll or expecting to enroll at an institution or university. Applicant must have 3.0 GPA or higher. Available to U.S. citizens.

Application Requirements: Application, essay, references, transcript. *Deadline:* March 15.

Contact: Thomas Heuer, Coordinator, Outreach Programs and Services
Bethesda Lutheran Homes and Services, Inc.
National Christian Resource Center
600 Hoffmann Drive
Watertown, WI 53094
Phone: 800-369-4636 Ext. 4449
Fax: 920-262-6513
E-mail: theuer@blhs.org

DEVELOPMENTAL DISABILITIES SCHOLASTIC ACHIEVEMENT SCHOLARSHIP FOR LUTHERAN COLLEGE STUDENTS
• See page 208

CATHOLIC KNIGHTS OF AMERICA
http://www.catholicknights.org

VOCATIONAL SCHOLARSHIP PROGRAM
• See page 453

CONTINENTAL SOCIETY, DAUGHTERS OF INDIAN WARS

CONTINENTAL SOCIETY, DAUGHTERS OF INDIAN WARS SCHOLARSHIP
• See page 224

HEALTH PROFESSIONS EDUCATION FOUNDATION
http://www.healthprofessions.ca.gov

KAISER PERMANENTE ALLIED HEALTHCARE SCHOLARSHIP
• See page 326

INDIAN HEALTH SERVICES, UNITED STATES DEPARTMENT OF HEALTH AND HUMAN SERVICES
http://www.ihs.gov

HEALTH PROFESSIONS PREPARATORY SCHOLARSHIP PROGRAM
• See page 425

MARIN EDUCATION FUND
http://www.marineducationfund.org

GOLDMAN FAMILY FUND, NEW LEADER SCHOLARSHIP
• See page 210

MARYLAND HIGHER EDUCATION COMMISSION
http://www.mhec.state.md.us

GRADUATE AND PROFESSIONAL SCHOLARSHIP PROGRAM-MARYLAND
• See page 210

JANET L. HOFFMANN LOAN ASSISTANCE REPAYMENT PROGRAM
• See page 230

MEMORIAL FOUNDATION FOR JEWISH CULTURE
http://www.mfjc.org

MEMORIAL FOUNDATION FOR JEWISH CULTURE INTERNATIONAL SCHOLARSHIP PROGRAM FOR COMMUNITY SERVICE
• See page 106

MORRIS K. UDALL FOUNDATION
http://www.udall.gov

MORRIS K. UDALL UNDERGRADUATE SCHOLARSHIPS
• See page 294

NATIONAL BLACK POLICE ASSOCIATION
http://www.blackpolice.org

ALPHONSO DEAL SCHOLARSHIP AWARD
• *See page 199*

NEW YORK STATE EDUCATION DEPARTMENT
http://www.highered.nysed.gov

REGENTS PROFESSIONAL OPPORTUNITY SCHOLARSHIP
• *See page 67*

ORDEAN FOUNDATION

ORDEAN SCHOLARSHIP PROGRAM
• *See page 67*

OREGON STUDENT ASSISTANCE COMMISSION
http://www.osac.state.or.us

FRIENDS OF OREGON STUDENTS SCHOLARSHIP
• *See page 234*

SOUTHWEST STUDENT SERVICES CORPORATION
http://www.sssc.com/

ANNE LINDEMAN MEMORIAL SCHOLARSHIP
• *See page 142*

SUNSHINE LADY FOUNDATION, INC.
http://www.sunshineladyfdn.org

COUNSELOR, ADVOCATE, AND SUPPORT STAFF SCHOLARSHIP PROGRAM
• *See page 69*

UNITED COMMUNITY SERVICES FOR WORKING FAMILIES

TED BRICKER SCHOLARSHIP

One-time award available to child of a union member who is a parent or guardian. Must be a resident of Pennsylvania. Must submit essay that is clear, concise, persuasive, and shows a commitment to the community. Application deadline is June 30.

Academic Fields/Career Goals: Social Services.

Award: Scholarship for use in freshman year; not renewable. *Number:* 1. *Amount:* up to $500.

Eligibility Requirements: Applicant must be high school student; planning to enroll or expecting to enroll full-time at a four-year institution or university and resident of Pennsylvania. Applicant or parent of applicant must be member of AFL-CIO. Applicant or parent of applicant must have employment or volunteer experience in community service. Available to U.S. citizens.

Application Requirements: Application, essay, financial need analysis, transcript. *Deadline:* June 30.

Contact: United Community Services for Working Families
Medrick Hall, 950 Weiser Street
Reading, PA 19601
E-mail: unionscholarships@aesSuccess.org

UNITED NEGRO COLLEGE FUND
http://www.uncf.org

FANNIE MAE FOUNDATION SCHOLARSHIP

Scholarship benefits 12 students pursuing careers in the fields of housing and community development. Must attend UNCF member college or university or Benedict College, Bethune-Cookman College, Johnson C. Smith University, LeMoyne-Owen College, or Morris Brown College. Minimum 3.0 GPA required. Prospective applicants should complete the Student Profile found at Web site: http://www.uncf.org.

Academic Fields/Career Goals: Social Services.

Award: Scholarship for use in junior year; not renewable. *Number:* 12.

Eligibility Requirements: Applicant must be Black (non-Hispanic) and enrolled or expecting to enroll at a four-year institution or university. Applicant must have 3.0 GPA or higher. Available to U.S. citizens.

Application Requirements: Application, financial need analysis.
Deadline: November 5.

Contact: Rebecca Bennett, Director, Program Services
United Negro College Fund
8260 Willow Oaks Corporate Drive
Fairfax, VA 22031-8044
Phone: 800-331-2244
E-mail: rbennett@uncf.org

SODEXHO SCHOLARSHIP
• *See page 333*

SPECIAL EDUCATION

ALBERTA HERITAGE SCHOLARSHIP FUND/ALBERTA SCHOLARSHIP PROGRAMS
http://www.alis.gov.ab.ca

ANNA AND JOHN KOLESAR MEMORIAL SCHOLARSHIPS
• *See page 218*

AMERICAN FEDERATION OF TEACHERS
http://www.aft.org

ROBERT G. PORTER SCHOLARS PROGRAM-AFT MEMBERS
• *See page 219*

AMERICAN LEGION AUXILIARY, DEPARTMENT OF ARIZONA
http://www.azlegion.org/majorp~2.htm

AMERICAN LEGION AUXILIARY DEPARTMENT OF ARIZONA WILMA HOYAL-MAXINE CHILTON MEMORIAL SCHOLARSHIP
• *See page 449*

ARC OF WASHINGTON TRUST FUND
http://www.arcwa.org

ARC OF WASHINGTON TRUST FUND STIPEND PROGRAM

Stipends of up to $5000 will be awarded to upper division or graduate students in schools in the states of Washington, Alaska, Oregon or Idaho. Applicants must have a demonstrated interest in the field of mental retardation. The application can be downloaded from the Web site: http://www.arcwa.org.

Academic Fields/Career Goals: Special Education.

Award: Scholarship for use in junior, senior, graduate, or postgraduate years; not renewable. *Number:* 1–8. *Amount:* $5000.

Eligibility Requirements: Applicant must be enrolled or expecting to enroll full-time at a four-year institution or university and studying in Alaska, Idaho, Oregon, or Washington. Available to U.S. and non-U.S. citizens.

Application Requirements: Application, autobiography, essay, references, transcript. *Deadline:* February 28.

Contact: Neal Lessenger, Secretary
ARC of Washington Trust Fund
2600 Martin Way East, Suite B
PO Box 27028
Olympia, WA 98506
Phone: 206-363-2206
E-mail: arcwatrust@msn.com

ARKANSAS DEPARTMENT OF HIGHER EDUCATION
http://www.arkansashighered.com

EMERGENCY SECONDARY EDUCATION LOAN PROGRAM
• *See page 135*

BETHESDA LUTHERAN HOMES AND SERVICES, INC.
http://www.blhs.org

DEVELOPMENTAL DISABILITIES AWARENESS AWARDS FOR LUTHERAN HIGH SCHOOL STUDENTS
• *See page 460*

Bethesda Lutheran Homes and Services, Inc. (continued)

DEVELOPMENTAL DISABILITIES SCHOLASTIC ACHIEVEMENT SCHOLARSHIP FOR LUTHERAN COLLEGE STUDENTS
• *See page 208*

CONNECTICUT DEPARTMENT OF HIGHER EDUCATION
http://www.ctdhe.org

CONNECTICUT SPECIAL EDUCATION TEACHER INCENTIVE GRANT

Renewable award for upper-level undergraduates or graduate students in special education programs. Must be in a program at a Connecticut college or university, or be a Connecticut resident enrolled in an approved out-of-state program. Priority is placed on minority and bilingual candidates. Application deadline is October 1. Must be nominated by the education dean of institution attended.

Academic Fields/Career Goals: Special Education.

Award: Grant for use in junior, senior, or graduate years; renewable. *Number:* varies. *Amount:* $2000–$5000.

Eligibility Requirements: Applicant must be enrolled or expecting to enroll full or part-time at a four-year institution or university; resident of Connecticut and studying in Connecticut. Available to U.S. citizens.

Application Requirements: Application. *Deadline:* October 1.

Contact: John Siegrist, Director, Financial Aid Office
Connecticut Department of Higher Education
61 Woodland Street
Hartford, CT 06105-2326
Phone: 860-947-1855
Fax: 860-947-1311
E-mail: jsiegrist@ctdhe.org

ILLINOIS STUDENT ASSISTANCE COMMISSION (ISAC)
http://www.collegezone.org

ILLINOIS SPECIAL EDUCATION TEACHER TUITION WAIVER

Tuition waiver for up to four years for Illinois teacher or student pursuing a career in special education. Must be enrolled in an eligible Illinois institution and seeking certification in any area of special education. Must teach in Illinois for two years upon gaining certification.

Academic Fields/Career Goals: Special Education.

Award: Forgivable loan for use in freshman, sophomore, junior, senior, or graduate years; renewable. *Number:* up to 250.

Eligibility Requirements: Applicant must be enrolled or expecting to enroll at a four-year institution or university; resident of Illinois and studying in Illinois. Available to U.S. citizens.

Application Requirements: Application. *Deadline:* March 1.

Contact: College Zone Counselor
Illinois Student Assistance Commission (ISAC)
1755 Lake Cook Road
Deerfield, IL 60015-5209
Phone: 800-899-4722
E-mail: collegezone@isac.org

MINORITY TEACHERS OF ILLINOIS SCHOLARSHIP PROGRAM
• *See page 228*

NATIONAL INSTITUTE FOR LABOR RELATIONS RESEARCH
http://www.nilrr.org

APPLEGATE/JACKSON/PARKS FUTURE TEACHER SCHOLARSHIP
• *See page 232*

NEW HAMPSHIRE POSTSECONDARY EDUCATION COMMISSION
http://www.state.nh.us/postsecondary

WORKFORCE INCENTIVE PROGRAM
• *See page 233*

OREGON STUDENT ASSISTANCE COMMISSION
http://www.osac.state.or.us

JAMES CARLSON MEMORIAL SCHOLARSHIP
• *See page 234*

PILOT INTERNATIONAL FOUNDATION
http://www.pilotinternational.org

PILOT INTERNATIONAL FOUNDATION RUBY NEWHALL MEMORIAL SCHOLARSHIP
• *See page 331*

PILOT INTERNATIONAL FOUNDATION SCHOLARSHIP PROGRAM
• *See page 331*

PILOT INTERNATIONAL FOUNDATION/LIFELINE SCHOLARSHIP PROGRAM
• *See page 332*

SOUTH CAROLINA STUDENT LOAN CORPORATION
http://www.slc.sc.edu

SOUTH CAROLINA TEACHER LOAN PROGRAM
• *See page 237*

SOUTHWEST STUDENT SERVICES CORPORATION
http://www.sssc.com/

ANNE LINDEMAN MEMORIAL SCHOLARSHIP
• *See page 142*

STATE COUNCIL OF HIGHER EDUCATION FOR VIRGINIA
http://www.schev.edu

HIGHER EDUCATION TEACHER ASSISTANCE PROGRAM
• *See page 237*

WISCONSIN CONGRESS OF PARENTS AND TEACHERS, INC.

BROOKMIRE-HASTINGS SCHOLARSHIPS
• *See page 240*

SPORTS-RELATED

AMERICAN COLLEGE OF SPORTS MEDICINE
http://www.acsm.org

RAY AND ROSALEE WEISS RESEARCH ENDOWMENT
• *See page 319*

CONNECTICUT ASSOCIATION FOR HEALTH, PHYSICAL EDUCATION, RECREATION AND DANCE
http://www.ctahperd.org

MARY BENEVENTO CAHPERD SCHOLARSHIP
• *See page 224*

NATIONAL ATHLETIC TRAINERS' ASSOCIATION RESEARCH AND EDUCATION FOUNDATION
http://www.natafoundation.org

NATIONAL ATHLETIC TRAINER'S ASSOCIATION RESEARCH AND EDUCATION FOUNDATION SCHOLARSHIP PROGRAM
• *See page 329*

NATIONAL STRENGTH AND CONDITIONING ASSOCIATION
http://www.nsca-lift.org

GNC NUTRITION RESEARCH GRANT
• *See page 335*

NATIONAL STRENGTH AND CONDITIONING ASSOCIATION CHALLENGE SCHOLARSHIP
• *See page 335*

NATIONAL STRENGTH AND CONDITIONING ASSOCIATION HIGH SCHOOL SCHOLARSHIP
• *See page 336*

NATIONAL STRENGTH AND CONDITIONING ASSOCIATION UNDERGRADUATE RESEARCH GRANT
• *See page 336*

NATIONAL STRENGTH AND CONDITIONING ASSOCIATION WOMEN'S SCHOLARSHIP
• See page 336

NSCA MINORITY SCHOLARSHIP
• See page 336

POWER SYSTEMS PROFESSIONAL SCHOLARSHIP
• See page 336

PACERS FOUNDATION, INC.   http://www.pacersfoundation.org

LINDA CRAIG MEMORIAL SCHOLARSHIP PRESENTED BY ST. VINCENT SPORTS MEDICINE
• See page 331

PHOENIX SUNS CHARITIES/SUN STUDENTS SCHOLARSHIP   http://www.nba.com/suns

QWEST LEADERSHIP CHALLENGE

A male and female from each participating high school will be chosen to compete in the Qwest Leadership Challenge. Upon completion of 30 volunteer hours for a nonprofit or educational organization, each participating school will receive a check from Qwest and the Phoenix Suns for $500 to be donated to its nonprofit organization of choice. In addition, two student-athletes will be chosen to receive $5,000 scholarships.

Academic Fields/Career Goals: Sports-related.

Award: Scholarship for use in freshman year. *Number:* 2. *Amount:* $5000.

Eligibility Requirements: Applicant must be high school student; planning to enroll or expecting to enroll at an institution or university; resident of Arizona and must have an interest in athletics/sports. Available to U.S. citizens.

Contact: Phoenix Suns Partnership Activation
Phoenix Suns Charities/Sun Students Scholarship
PO Box 1369
Phoenix, AZ 85001
Phone: 602-379-7987
E-mail: dpreuss@suns.com

PI LAMBDA THETA, INC.   http://www.pilambda.org

TOBIN SORENSON PHYSICAL EDUCATION SCHOLARSHIP

The Tobin Sorenson Scholarship provides $1000 for tuition to an outstanding student who intends to pursue a career at the K-12 level as a physical education teacher, adaptive physical education teacher, coach, recreational therapist, dance therapist, or similar professional focusing on teaching the knowledge and use of the human body. Awarded in odd years only. Minimum 3.5 GPA required.

Academic Fields/Career Goals: Sports-related; Therapy/Rehabilitation.

Award: Scholarship for use in sophomore, or graduate years; not renewable. *Number:* 1. *Amount:* $1000.

Eligibility Requirements: Applicant must be enrolled or expecting to enroll full or part-time at a two-year or four-year institution or university. Applicant must have 3.5 GPA or higher. Available to U.S. and non-U.S. citizens.

Application Requirements: Application, resume, references, transcript. *Deadline:* February 10.

Contact: Ellen Mills, Controller
Pi Lambda Theta, Inc.
4101 East 3rd Street, PO Box 6626
Bloomington, IN 47407-6626
Phone: 812-339-3411
Fax: 812-339-3462
E-mail: ellen@pilambda.org

WOMEN'S SPORTS FOUNDATION   http://www.womenssportsfoundation.org

LINDA RIDDLE/SGMA SCHOLARSHIP

One-time award for female high school seniors entering a two- or four-year college. Provides female athletes of limited financial means the opportunity to pursue their sport in addition to their college studies. Minimum GPA 3.5. Must be a U.S. citizen.

Academic Fields/Career Goals: Sports-related.

Award: Scholarship for use in freshman year; not renewable. *Number:* 1–10. *Amount:* $1500.

Eligibility Requirements: Applicant must be high school student; planning to enroll or expecting to enroll full-time at a two-year or four-year institution or university; female and must have an interest in athletics/sports. Applicant must have 3.5 GPA or higher. Available to U.S. citizens.

Application Requirements: Application, essay, financial need analysis, references, transcript. *Deadline:* December 1.

Contact: Monica Garrett, Senior Programs Manager
Women's Sports Foundation
Eisenhower Park
East Meadow, NY 11554
Phone: 516-542-4700
Fax: 516-542-4716
E-mail: wosport@aol.com

SURVEYING; SURVEYING TECHNOLOGY, CARTOGRAPHY, OR GEOGRAPHIC INFORMATION SCIENCE

AMERICAN CONGRESS ON SURVEYING AND MAPPING   http://www.acsm.net

ACSM FELLOWS SCHOLARSHIP

One-time award available to a student with a junior or higher standing in any ACSM discipline. Must be ACSM member.

Academic Fields/Career Goals: Surveying; Surveying Technology, Cartography, or Geographic Information Science.

Award: Scholarship for use in freshman, sophomore, junior, or senior years; not renewable. *Amount:* $2000.

Eligibility Requirements: Applicant must be enrolled or expecting to enroll at a four-year institution. Applicant or parent of applicant must be member of American Congress on Surveying and Mapping. Available to U.S. citizens.

Application Requirements: Application, essay, references, transcript. *Deadline:* December 1.

Contact: Lilly Matheson, ACSM Awards Department
American Congress on Surveying and Mapping
6 Montgomery Village Avenue, Suite 403
Gaithersburg, MD 20879
Phone: 301-493-0200 Ext. 102
E-mail: lilym@mindspring.com

AMERICAN ASSOCIATION FOR GEODETIC SURVEYING JOSEPH F. DRACUP SCHOLARSHIP AWARD

Award for students enrolled in four-year degree program in surveying. Preference given to applicants from programs with significant focus on geodetic surveying. Must be ACSM member.

Academic Fields/Career Goals: Surveying; Surveying Technology, Cartography, or Geographic Information Science.

Award: Scholarship for use in freshman, sophomore, junior, or senior years; not renewable. *Number:* 1. *Amount:* $2000.

Eligibility Requirements: Applicant must be enrolled or expecting to enroll at a four-year institution or university. Applicant or parent of applicant must be member of American Congress on Surveying and Mapping. Available to U.S. citizens.

American Congress on Surveying and Mapping (continued)

Application Requirements: Application, essay, references, transcript. *Deadline:* December 1.

Contact: Lilly Matheson, ACSM Awards Department
American Congress on Surveying and Mapping
6 Montgomery Village Avenue, Suite 403
Gaithersburg, MD 20879
Phone: 301-493-0200 Ext. 102
E-mail: lilym@mindspring.com

BERNTSEN INTERNATIONAL SCHOLARSHIP IN SURVEYING

Award for students enrolled in four-year degree program in surveying, or in closely-related degree program, such as geomatics or surveying engineering. Award funded by Berntsen International, Inc. Must be ACSM member.

Academic Fields/Career Goals: Surveying; Surveying Technology, Cartography, or Geographic Information Science.

Award: Scholarship for use in freshman, sophomore, junior, or senior years; not renewable. *Number:* 1. *Amount:* $1500.

Eligibility Requirements: Applicant must be enrolled or expecting to enroll at a four-year institution or university. Applicant or parent of applicant must be member of American Congress on Surveying and Mapping. Available to U.S. citizens.

Application Requirements: Application, essay, references, transcript. *Deadline:* December 1.

Contact: Lilly Matheson, ACSM Awards Department
American Congress on Surveying and Mapping
6 Montgomery Village Avenue, Suite 403
Gaithersburg, MD 20879
Phone: 301-493-0200 Ext. 102
E-mail: lilym@mindspring.com

BERNTSEN INTERNATIONAL SCHOLARSHIP IN SURVEYING TECHNOLOGY

Award of $500 for students enrolled in a two-year degree program in surveying technology. For U.S. study only. Must be a member of the American Congress on Surveying and Mapping. Contact for further information.

Academic Fields/Career Goals: Surveying; Surveying Technology, Cartography, or Geographic Information Science.

Award: Scholarship for use in freshman or sophomore years; not renewable. *Amount:* $500.

Eligibility Requirements: Applicant must be enrolled or expecting to enroll at a two-year institution. Applicant or parent of applicant must be member of American Congress on Surveying and Mapping. Available to U.S. citizens.

Application Requirements: Application, essay, references, transcript. *Deadline:* December 1.

Contact: Lilly Matheson, ACSM Awards Department
American Congress on Surveying and Mapping
6 Montgomery Village Avenue, Suite 403
Gaithersburg, MD 20879
Phone: 301-493-0200 Ext. 102
E-mail: lilym@mindspring.com

CADY MCDONNELL MEMORIAL SCHOLARSHIP

Award of $1000 for female surveying student. Must be a resident of one of the following western states: Alaska, Arizona, California, Colorado, Hawaii, Idaho, Montana, Nevada, New Mexico, Oregon, Utah, Washington, and Wyoming. Must provide proof of legal home residence and be a member of the American Congress on Surveying and Mapping.

Academic Fields/Career Goals: Surveying; Surveying Technology, Cartography, or Geographic Information Science.

Award: Scholarship for use in freshman, sophomore, junior, or senior years; not renewable. *Number:* 1. *Amount:* $1000.

Eligibility Requirements: Applicant must be enrolled or expecting to enroll full or part-time at a two-year or four-year institution or university; female and resident of Alaska, Arizona, California, Colorado, Hawaii, Idaho, Montana, Nevada, New Mexico, Oregon, Utah, Washington, or Wyoming. Applicant or parent of applicant must be member of American Congress on Surveying and Mapping. Available to U.S. citizens.

Application Requirements: Application, essay, references, transcript. *Deadline:* December 1.

Contact: Lilly Matheson, ACSM Awards Department
American Congress on Surveying and Mapping
6 Montgomery Village Avenue, Suite 403
Gaithersburg, MD 20879
Phone: 301-493-0200 Ext. 102
E-mail: lilym@mindspring.com

CARTOGRAPHY AND GEOGRAPHIC INFORMATION SOCIETY SCHOLARSHIP

Award of $1000 for a member of the American Congress on Surveying and Mapping studying cartography or geographic information science. Preference given to undergraduates with junior or senior standing. Contact for further information. Must be ACSM member.

Academic Fields/Career Goals: Surveying; Surveying Technology, Cartography, or Geographic Information Science.

Award: Scholarship for use in freshman, sophomore, junior, senior, or graduate years; not renewable. *Number:* 1. *Amount:* $1000.

Eligibility Requirements: Applicant must be enrolled or expecting to enroll full-time at a two-year or four-year institution. Applicant or parent of applicant must be member of American Congress on Surveying and Mapping. Available to U.S. citizens.

Application Requirements: Application, essay, references, transcript. *Deadline:* December 1.

Contact: Lilly Matheson, ACSM Awards Department
American Congress on Surveying and Mapping
6 Montgomery Village Avenue, Suite 403
Gaithersburg, MD 20879
Phone: 301-493-0200 Ext. 102
E-mail: lilym@mindspring.com

NATIONAL SOCIETY OF PROFESSIONAL SURVEYORS BOARD OF GOVERNORS SCHOLARSHIP

Award available to student enrolled in surveying program entering junior year of study at four-year institution. Minimum 3.0 GPA required. Must be ACSM member.

Academic Fields/Career Goals: Surveying; Surveying Technology, Cartography, or Geographic Information Science.

Award: Scholarship for use in junior year; not renewable. *Amount:* up to $1000.

Eligibility Requirements: Applicant must be enrolled or expecting to enroll full or part-time at a two-year or four-year institution or university. Applicant or parent of applicant must be member of American Congress on Surveying and Mapping. Applicant must have 3.0 GPA or higher. Available to U.S. and non-U.S. citizens.

Application Requirements: Application, essay, references, transcript. *Deadline:* December 1.

Contact: Pat Canfield, Executive Administrator
American Congress on Surveying and Mapping
6 Montgomery Village Avenue, Suite 403
Gaithersburg, MD 20879
Phone: 240-632-9716 Ext. 113
Fax: 240-632-1321
E-mail: pat.canfield@acsm.net

NATIONAL SOCIETY OF PROFESSIONAL SURVEYORS FOR EQUAL OPPORTUNITY/MARY FEINDT SCHOLARSHIP

Award available to female members of ACSM. Applicants must be enrolled in a four-year degree program in a surveying and mapping curriculum in the U.S..

Academic Fields/Career Goals: Surveying; Surveying Technology, Cartography, or Geographic Information Science.

Award: Scholarship for use in freshman, sophomore, junior, or senior years; not renewable. *Number:* 1. *Amount:* $1000.

Eligibility Requirements: Applicant must be enrolled or expecting to enroll full-time at a four-year institution or university and female. Applicant or parent of applicant must be member of American Congress on Surveying and Mapping. Available to U.S. citizens.

Application Requirements: Application, essay, references, transcript. *Deadline:* December 1.

Contact: Pat Canfield, Executive Coordinator
American Congress on Surveying and Mapping
6 Montgomery Village Avenue, Suite 403
Gaithersburg, MD 20879
Phone: 240-632-9716
Fax: 240-632-1321
E-mail: pat.canfield@acsm.net

NATIONAL SOCIETY OF PROFESSIONAL SURVEYORS SCHOLARSHIPS

Award recognizes outstanding students enrolled full-time in undergraduate surveying program. Must be ACSM member.

Academic Fields/Career Goals: Surveying; Surveying Technology, Cartography, or Geographic Information Science.

Award: Scholarship for use in freshman, sophomore, junior, or senior years; not renewable. *Number:* 2. *Amount:* $1000.

Eligibility Requirements: Applicant must be enrolled or expecting to enroll full-time at a four-year institution or university. Applicant or parent of applicant must be member of American Congress on Surveying and Mapping. Available to U.S. citizens.

Application Requirements: Application, essay, references, transcript. *Deadline:* December 1.

Contact: Lilly Matheson, ACSM Awards Department
American Congress on Surveying and Mapping
6 Montgomery Village Avenue, Suite 403
Gaithersburg, MD 20879
Phone: 301-493-0200 Ext. 102
E-mail: lilym@mindspring.com

NETTIE DRACUP MEMORIAL SCHOLARSHIP

Award for undergraduate student enrolled in geodetic surveying at an accredited college or university. Must be U.S. citizen. Must be ACSM member.

Academic Fields/Career Goals: Surveying; Surveying Technology, Cartography, or Geographic Information Science.

Award: Scholarship for use in freshman, sophomore, junior, or senior years; not renewable. *Number:* 1. *Amount:* $2000.

Eligibility Requirements: Applicant must be enrolled or expecting to enroll at a four-year institution or university. Applicant or parent of applicant must be member of American Congress on Surveying and Mapping. Available to U.S. citizens.

Application Requirements: Application, essay, financial need analysis, references, transcript. *Deadline:* December 1.

Contact: Lilly Matheson, ACSM Awards Department
American Congress on Surveying and Mapping
6 Montgomery Village Avenue, Suite 403
Gaithersburg, MD 20879
Phone: 301-493-0200 Ext. 102
E-mail: lilym@mindspring.com

SCHONSTEDT SCHOLARSHIP IN SURVEYING

Award preference given to applicants with junior or senior standing. Award sponsored by Schonstedt Instrument Company. Schonstedt donates magnetic locator to surveying program at each recipient's school. Must be ACSM member.

Academic Fields/Career Goals: Surveying; Surveying Technology, Cartography, or Geographic Information Science.

Award: Scholarship for use in freshman, sophomore, junior, or senior years; not renewable. *Number:* 2. *Amount:* $1500.

Eligibility Requirements: Applicant must be enrolled or expecting to enroll at a four-year institution or university. Applicant or parent of applicant must be member of American Congress on Surveying and Mapping. Available to U.S. citizens.

Application Requirements: Application, essay, references, transcript. *Deadline:* December 1.

Contact: Lilly Matheson, ACSM Awards Department
American Congress on Surveying and Mapping
6 Montgomery Village Avenue, Suite 403
Gaithersburg, MD 20879
Phone: 301-493-0200 Ext. 102
E-mail: lilym@mindspring.com

ARIZONA HYDROLOGICAL SOCIETY
http://www.azhydrosoc.org

ARIZONA HYDROLOGICAL SURVEY STUDENT SCHOLARSHIP
• See page 212

ASSOCIATED GENERAL CONTRACTORS OF AMERICA-NEW YORK STATE CHAPTER
http://www.agcnys.org

ASSOCIATED GENERAL CONTRACTORS OF AMERICA-NEW YORK STATE CHAPTER SCHOLARSHIP PROGRAM
• See page 173

ASSOCIATION OF CALIFORNIA WATER AGENCIES
http://www.acwanet.com

ASSOCIATION OF CALIFORNIA WATER AGENCIES SCHOLARSHIPS
• See page 91

CLAIR A. HILL SCHOLARSHIP
• See page 91

CENTRAL INTELLIGENCE AGENCY
http://www.cia.gov

CENTRAL INTELLIGENCE AGENCY UNDERGRADUATE SCHOLARSHIP PROGRAM
• See page 56

MIDWEST ROOFING CONTRACTORS ASSOCIATION
http://www.mrca.org

MRCA FOUNDATION SCHOLARSHIP PROGRAM
• See page 94

NATIONAL FISH AND WILDLIFE FOUNDATION
http://www.nfwf.org

BUDWEISER CONSERVATION SCHOLARSHIP PROGRAM
• See page 140

OREGON STUDENT ASSISTANCE COMMISSION
http://www.osac.state.or.us

PROFESSIONAL LAND SURVEYORS OF OREGON SCHOLARSHIPS

Award for sophomores or above enrolled in course of study leading to land-surveying career. Community college applicants must intend to transfer to four-year college. Oregon colleges only. Applicants must intend to take Fundamentals of Land Surveying exam. Additional essay stating education/career goals and their relation to land surveying is required.

Academic Fields/Career Goals: Surveying; Surveying Technology, Cartography, or Geographic Information Science.

Award: Scholarship for use in sophomore, junior, or senior years; renewable. *Number:* 5. *Amount:* $1600.

Eligibility Requirements: Applicant must be enrolled or expecting to enroll full-time at a four-year institution or university; resident of Oregon and studying in Oregon. Available to U.S. citizens.

Application Requirements: Application, essay, financial need analysis, references, transcript, activity chart. *Deadline:* March 1.

Contact: Director of Grant Programs
Oregon Student Assistance Commission
1500 Valley River Drive, Suite 100
Eugene, OR 97401-7020
Phone: 800-452-8807 Ext. 7395

PROFESSIONAL CONSTRUCTION ESTIMATORS ASSOCIATION
http://www.pcea.org

TED WILSON MEMORIAL SCHOLARSHIP FOUNDATION
• See page 212

SOIL AND WATER CONSERVATION SOCIETY-NEW JERSEY CHAPTER
http://www.geocities.com/njswcs

EDWARD R. HALL SCHOLARSHIP
• See page 76

THERAPY/REHABILITATION

ALBERTA HERITAGE SCHOLARSHIP FUND/ ALBERTA SCHOLARSHIP PROGRAMS
http://www.alis.gov.ab.ca

ALBERTA HERITAGE SCHOLARSHIP FUND ABORIGINAL HEALTH CAREERS BURSARY
• See page 135

AMERICAN ART THERAPY ASSOCIATION
http://www.arttherapy.org

MYRA LEVICK SCHOLARSHIP FUND

Scholarship available to students who can demonstrate financial need, acceptance into an AATA-approved art therapy program, and an undergraduate GPA of at least 3.0. Applicants must be a active student member of AATA.

Academic Fields/Career Goals: Therapy/Rehabilitation.

Award: Scholarship for use in freshman, sophomore, junior, or senior years. *Number:* 3.

Eligibility Requirements: Applicant must be enrolled or expecting to enroll at a four-year institution or university. Applicant must have 3.0 GPA or higher.

Application Requirements: Application, essay, references, transcript, proof of acceptance or enrollment in an AATA approved graduate art therapy program. *Deadline:* June 15.

Contact: American Art Therapy Association
American Art Therapy Association, 5999 Stevenson Avenue
Alexandria, VA 22304
Phone: 888-290-0878

AMERICAN FOUNDATION FOR THE BLIND
http://www.afb.org/scholarships.asp

DELTA GAMMA FOUNDATION FLORENCE MARGARET HARVEY MEMORIAL SCHOLARSHIP
• See page 219

RUDOLPH DILLMAN MEMORIAL SCHOLARSHIP
• See page 219

AMERICAN LEGION AUXILIARY, DEPARTMENT OF MICHIGAN
http://www.michalaux.org

MEDICAL CAREER SCHOLARSHIP
• See page 319

AMERICAN LEGION AUXILIARY, DEPARTMENT OF WYOMING

PAST PRESIDENTS PARLEY HEALTH CARE SCHOLARSHIP
• See page 207

AMERICAN OCCUPATIONAL THERAPY FOUNDATION, INC.
http://www.aotf.org

AMERICAN OCCUPATIONAL THERAPY FOUNDATION STATE ASSOCIATION SCHOLARSHIPS
• See page 321

CARLOTTA WELLES SCHOLARSHIP
• See page 321

FLORENCE WOOD/ARKANSAS OCCUPATIONAL THERAPY ASSOCIATION SCHOLARSHIP
• See page 321

AMERICAN RESPIRATORY CARE FOUNDATION
http://www.arcfoundation.org

JIMMY A. YOUNG MEMORIAL EDUCATION RECOGNITION AWARD
• See page 322

MORTON B. DUGGAN, JR. MEMORIAL EDUCATION RECOGNITION AWARD
• See page 322

NBRC/AMP ROBERT M. LAWRENCE, MD, EDUCATION RECOGNITION AWARD
• See page 322

NBRC/AMP WILLIAM W. BURGIN, MD EDUCATION RECOGNITION AWARD
• See page 322

SEPRACOR ACHIEVEMENT AWARD FOR EXCELLENCE IN PULMONARY DISEASE STATE MANAGEMENT
• See page 323

BECA FOUNDATION, INC.
http://www.becafoundation.org

ALICE NEWELL JOSLYN MEDICAL FUND
• See page 207

BETHESDA LUTHERAN HOMES AND SERVICES, INC.
http://www.blhs.org

DEVELOPMENTAL DISABILITIES SCHOLASTIC ACHIEVEMENT SCHOLARSHIP FOR LUTHERAN COLLEGE STUDENTS
• See page 208

GENERAL FEDERATION OF WOMEN'S CLUBS OF MASSACHUSETTS
http://www.gfwcma.org/

GENERAL FEDERATION OF WOMEN'S CLUBS OF MASSACHUSETTS MUSIC SCHOLARSHIP
• See page 225

HEALTH PROFESSIONS EDUCATION FOUNDATION
http://www.healthprofessions.ca.gov

KAISER PERMANENTE ALLIED HEALTHCARE SCHOLARSHIP
• See page 326

INDIAN HEALTH SERVICES, UNITED STATES DEPARTMENT OF HEALTH AND HUMAN SERVICES
http://www.ihs.gov

INDIAN HEALTH SERVICE HEALTH PROFESSIONS PRE-PROFESSIONAL SCHOLARSHIP
• See page 318

INTERNATIONAL ORDER OF THE KING'S DAUGHTERS AND SONS
http://www.iokds.org

HEALTH CAREERS SCHOLARSHIP
• See page 209

JEWISH FOUNDATION FOR EDUCATION OF WOMEN
http://www.jfew.org

SCHOLARSHIP PROGRAM FOR FORMER SOVIET UNION EMIGRES TRAINING IN THE HEALTH SCIENCES
• See page 209

LADIES AUXILIARY TO THE VETERANS OF FOREIGN WARS, DEPARTMENT OF MAINE

FRANCIS L. BOOTH MEDICAL SCHOLARSHIP SPONSORED BY LAVFW DEPARTMENT OF MAINE
• See page 327

MARIN EDUCATION FUND
http://www.marineducationfund.org

GOLDMAN FAMILY FUND, NEW LEADER SCHOLARSHIP
• See page 210

MARYLAND HIGHER EDUCATION COMMISSION
http://www.mhec.state.md.us

JANET L. HOFFMANN LOAN ASSISTANCE REPAYMENT PROGRAM
• See page 230

PHYSICAL AND OCCUPATIONAL THERAPISTS AND ASSISTANTS GRANT PROGRAM

For Maryland residents training as physical, occupational therapists or therapy assistants at Maryland postsecondary institutions. Recipients must provide one year of service for each full, or partial, year of award. Service must be to handicapped children in a Maryland facility that has, or accommodates and provides services to, such children. Minimum 2.0 GPA.

Academic Fields/Career Goals: Therapy/Rehabilitation.

Award: Forgivable loan for use in freshman, sophomore, junior, senior, or graduate years; renewable. *Number:* up to 10. *Amount:* up to $2000.

Eligibility Requirements: Applicant must be enrolled or expecting to enroll full-time at a two-year or four-year institution or university; resident of Maryland and studying in Maryland. Available to U.S. citizens.

Application Requirements: Application, transcript. *Deadline:* July 1.

Contact: Gerrie Rogers, Office of Student Financial Assistance
Maryland Higher Education Commission
839 Bestgate Road, Suite 400
Annapolis, MD 21401
Phone: 410-260-4574
Fax: 410-260-3203
E-mail: ssamail@mhec.state.md.us

MISSISSIPPI STATE STUDENT FINANCIAL AID
http://www.mississippiuniversities.com

CRITICAL NEEDS TEACHER LOAN/SCHOLARSHIP
• See page 231

MISSISSIPPI HEALTH CARE PROFESSIONS LOAN/SCHOLARSHIP PROGRAM
• See page 328

NATIONAL AMBUCS, INC.
http://www.ambucs.com

AMBUCS SCHOLARS-SCHOLARSHIPS FOR THERAPISTS
• See page 328

NATIONAL ATHLETIC TRAINERS' ASSOCIATION RESEARCH AND EDUCATION FOUNDATION
http://www.natafoundation.org

NATIONAL ATHLETIC TRAINER'S ASSOCIATION RESEARCH AND EDUCATION FOUNDATION SCHOLARSHIP PROGRAM
• See page 329

NATIONAL SOCIETY DAUGHTERS OF THE AMERICAN REVOLUTION
http://www.dar.org

NATIONAL SOCIETY DAUGHTERS OF THE AMERICAN REVOLUTION MEDICAL OCCUPATIONAL THERAPY SCHOLARSHIPS

Nonrenewable award for students of physical or occupational therapy. Must be U.S. citizen sponsored by local DAR chapter. Award based on merit. Obtain list of local chapters from NSDAR. Deadlines: February 15 and August 15. Must submit self-addressed stamped envelope to be considered.

Academic Fields/Career Goals: Therapy/Rehabilitation.

Award: Scholarship for use in freshman, sophomore, junior, or senior years; not renewable. *Number:* 20. *Amount:* $500.

Eligibility Requirements: Applicant must be enrolled or expecting to enroll at a two-year or four-year institution. Applicant must have 3.0 GPA or higher. Available to U.S. citizens.

Application Requirements: Application, essay, financial need analysis, references, self-addressed stamped envelope, test scores, transcript. *Deadline:* varies.

Contact: Committee Services Office, Scholarship
National Society Daughters of the American Revolution
1776 D Street, NW
Washington, DC 20006-5392

NATIONAL STRENGTH AND CONDITIONING ASSOCIATION
http://www.nsca-lift.org

GNC NUTRITION RESEARCH GRANT
• See page 335

NATIONAL STRENGTH AND CONDITIONING ASSOCIATION CHALLENGE SCHOLARSHIP
• See page 335

NATIONAL STRENGTH AND CONDITIONING ASSOCIATION HIGH SCHOOL SCHOLARSHIP
• See page 336

NATIONAL STRENGTH AND CONDITIONING ASSOCIATION UNDERGRADUATE RESEARCH GRANT
• See page 336

NATIONAL STRENGTH AND CONDITIONING ASSOCIATION WOMEN'S SCHOLARSHIP
• See page 336

NSCA MINORITY SCHOLARSHIP
• See page 336

POWER SYSTEMS PROFESSIONAL SCHOLARSHIP
• See page 336

NEW MEXICO COMMISSION ON HIGHER EDUCATION
http://www.hed.state.nm.us

ALLIED HEALTH STUDENT LOAN PROGRAM-NEW MEXICO
• See page 210

NORTH CAROLINA STATE EDUCATION ASSISTANCE AUTHORITY
http://www.ncseaa.edu

NORTH CAROLINA STUDENT LOAN PROGRAM FOR HEALTH, SCIENCE, AND MATHEMATICS
• See page 211

OREGON STUDENT ASSISTANCE COMMISSION
http://www.osac.state.or.us

MARION A. LINDEMAN SCHOLARSHIP
• See page 331

PACERS FOUNDATION, INC.
http://www.pacersfoundation.org

LINDA CRAIG MEMORIAL SCHOLARSHIP PRESENTED BY ST. VINCENT SPORTS MEDICINE
• See page 331

PI LAMBDA THETA, INC.
http://www.pilambda.org

TOBIN SORENSON PHYSICAL EDUCATION SCHOLARSHIP
• See page 463

PILOT INTERNATIONAL FOUNDATION
http://www.pilotinternational.org

PILOT INTERNATIONAL FOUNDATION RUBY NEWHALL MEMORIAL SCHOLARSHIP
• See page 331

PILOT INTERNATIONAL FOUNDATION SCHOLARSHIP PROGRAM
• See page 331

PILOT INTERNATIONAL FOUNDATION/LIFELINE SCHOLARSHIP PROGRAM
• See page 332

SIGMA ALPHA IOTA PHILANTHROPIES, INC.
http://www.sai-national.org

SIGMA ALPHA IOTA MUSIC THERAPY SCHOLARSHIP
• See page 407

SOUTHWEST STUDENT SERVICES CORPORATION
http://www.sssc.com/

ANNE LINDEMAN MEMORIAL SCHOLARSHIP
• See page 142

SUBURBAN HOSPITAL HEALTHCARE SYSTEM
http://www.suburbanhospital.org

SUBURBAN HOSPITAL HEALTHCARE SYSTEM SCHOLARSHIP
• See page 333

SUNSHINE LADY FOUNDATION, INC.
http://www.sunshineladyfdn.org

COUNSELOR, ADVOCATE, AND SUPPORT STAFF SCHOLARSHIP PROGRAM
• See page 69

TUBERCULOSIS ASSOCIATION OF OHIO COUNTY
http://www.tboc.org

DR. WILLIAM J. STEGER SCHOLARSHIP AWARDS
• See page 333

UNITED STATES DEPARTMENT OF EDUCATION, REHABILITATION SERVICES ADMINISTRATION
http://www.ed.gov

REHABILITATION TRAINING PROGRAM SCHOLARSHIP

RSA Scholarships are provided by colleges and universities receiving RSA training grants. Eligible students are generally full-time undergraduate or graduate students in training programs related to rehabilitation. Upon graduation, students must work for a state or nonprofit rehabilitation organization for two years for each year of assistance received. College or university sets criteria and application fee. Many universities with scholarship funds can be found at the following Web site: http://www.ed.gov/students/college/aid/rehab/index.html

Academic Fields/Career Goals: Therapy/Rehabilitation.

Award: Scholarship for use in freshman, sophomore, junior, senior, or graduate years; not renewable. *Number:* 1. *Amount:* varies.

Eligibility Requirements: Applicant must be enrolled or expecting to enroll full-time at a two-year or four-year institution or university. Available to U.S. citizens.

Application Requirements: Application. *Deadline:* Continuous.

Contact: Rehabilitation Training Program
United States Department of Education, Rehabilitation Services Administration
Division of Resource Development, 330 C Street, SW
Washington, DC 20202-2649
Phone: 202-205-8926
Fax: 202-260-0723

UNITED STATES PUBLIC HEALTH SERVICE - HEALTH RESOURCES AND SERVICES ADMINISTRATION, BUREAU OF HEALTH
http://bhpr.hrsa.gov/dsa

HEALTH RESOURCES AND SERVICES ADMINISTRATION-BUREAU OF HEALTH PROFESSIONS SCHOLARSHIPS FOR DISADVANTAGED STUDENTS
• See page 211

TRADE/TECHNICAL SPECIALTIES

AIRCRAFT ELECTRONICS ASSOCIATION EDUCATIONAL FOUNDATION
http://aea.net

BUD GLOVER MEMORIAL SCHOLARSHIP
• See page 116

FIELD AVIATION CO., INC., SCHOLARSHIP
• See page 117

LOWELL GAYLOR MEMORIAL SCHOLARSHIP
• See page 118

MONTE MITCHELL GLOBAL SCHOLARSHIP
• See page 118

ALBERTA HERITAGE SCHOLARSHIP FUND/ ALBERTA SCHOLARSHIP PROGRAMS
http://www.alis.gov.ab.ca

ALBERTA APPRENTICESHIP AND INDUSTRY TRAINING SCHOLARSHIPS

Award of CAN$ 1000 to recognize the excellence of Alberta apprentices in a trade, and trainees in a designated occupation, and to encourage recipients to complete their apprenticeship or occupational training programs. Must be a Canadian citizen or landed immigrant, an Alberta resident as defined by Alberta Scholarship Programs. Application deadline is July 31.

Academic Fields/Career Goals: Trade/Technical Specialties.

Award: Scholarship for use in freshman year. *Number:* 165. *Amount:* $861.

Eligibility Requirements: Applicant must be enrolled or expecting to enroll full-time at a technical institution. Available to U.S. and Canadian citizens.

Application Requirements: Application, financial need analysis. *Deadline:* July 31.

Contact: Stuart Dunn, Manager
Alberta Heritage Scholarship Fund/Alberta Scholarship Programs
4th Floor, 9940 106th Street, Box 28000 Station Main
Edmonton, AB T5J 4R4
Canada
Phone: 780-427-8640
Fax: 780-427-1288
E-mail: scholarships@gov.ab.ca

AMERICAN LEGION, DEPARTMENT OF PENNSYLVANIA
http://www.pa-legion.com

ROBERT W. VALIMONT ENDOWMENT FUND SCHOLARSHIP (PART II)

Scholarships for any Pennsylvania high school senior seeking admission to a two-year college, post-high school trade/technical school, or training program. Must attend school in Pennsylvania. Continuation of award is based on grades. Renewable award of $600. Number of awards varies from year to year. Membership in an American Legion post in Pennsylvania is not required, but it must be documented if it does apply.

Academic Fields/Career Goals: Trade/Technical Specialties.

Award: Scholarship for use in freshman or sophomore years; renewable. *Amount:* $600.

Eligibility Requirements: Applicant must be high school student; planning to enroll or expecting to enroll full-time at a two-year or technical institution; resident of Pennsylvania and studying in Pennsylvania. Applicant must have 2.5 GPA or higher. Available to U.S. citizens.

Application Requirements: Application, financial need analysis, test scores, transcript. *Deadline:* May 30.

Contact: James H. Hales, Jr., Department Commander
American Legion, Department of Pennsylvania
PO Box 2324
Harrisburg, PA 17105-2324
Phone: 717-730-9100
Fax: 717-975-2836
E-mail: hq@pa-legion.com

AMERICAN SOCIETY OF HEATING, REFRIGERATING, AND AIR CONDITIONING ENGINEERS, INC.
http://www.ashrae.org

ALWIN B. NEWTON SCHOLARSHIP FUND
• See page 242

AMERICAN SOCIETY OF HEATING, REFRIGERATION, AND AIR CONDITIONING ENGINEERING TECHNOLOGY SCHOLARSHIP
• See page 90

ASHRAE MEMORIAL SCHOLARSHIP
• See page 251

ASHRAE SCHOLARSHIPS
• See page 252

DUANE HANSON SCHOLARSHIP
• See page 285

HENRY ADAMS SCHOLARSHIP
• See page 252

REUBEN TRANE SCHOLARSHIP
• See page 242

AMERICAN WELDING SOCIETY   http://www.aws.org

AIRGAS JERRY BAKER SCHOLARSHIP
• See page 285

AIRGAS-TERRY JARVIS MEMORIAL SCHOLARSHIP
• See page 253

AMERICAN WELDING SOCIETY DISTRICT SCHOLARSHIP PROGRAM
• See page 285

AMERICAN WELDING SOCIETY INTERNATIONAL SCHOLARSHIP
• See page 253

ARSHAM AMIRIKIAN ENGINEERING SCHOLARSHIP
• See page 172

DONALD AND JEAN CLEVELAND-WILLAMETTE VALLEY SECTION SCHOLARSHIP
• See page 172

DONALD F. HASTINGS SCHOLARSHIP
• See page 253

EDWARD J. BRADY MEMORIAL SCHOLARSHIP
• See page 253

HOWARD E. ADKINS MEMORIAL SCHOLARSHIP
• See page 253

ILLINOIS TOOL WORKS WELDING COMPANIES SCHOLARSHIP
• See page 254

JOHN C. LINCOLN MEMORIAL SCHOLARSHIP
• See page 254

MATSUO BRIDGE COMPANY, LTD., OF JAPAN SCHOLARSHIP
• See page 172

MILLER ELECTRIC INTERNATIONAL WORLD SKILLS COMPETITION SCHOLARSHIP
• See page 254

PRAXAIR INTERNATIONAL SCHOLARSHIP
• See page 254

WILLIAM A. AND ANN M. BROTHERS SCHOLARSHIP
• See page 286

WILLIAM B. HOWELL MEMORIAL SCHOLARSHIP
• See page 255

ARRL FOUNDATION, INC.   http://www.arrl.org/arrlf/scholgen.html

CHARLES N. FISHER MEMORIAL SCHOLARSHIP
• See page 90

IRVING W. COOK, WA0CGS, SCHOLARSHIP
• See page 90

MISSISSIPPI SCHOLARSHIP
• See page 90

PAUL AND HELEN L. GRAUER SCHOLARSHIP
• See page 91

ASSOCIATED GENERAL CONTRACTORS EDUCATION AND RESEARCH FOUNDATION   http://www.agcfoundation.org

AGC EDUCATION AND RESEARCH FOUNDATION UNDERGRADUATE SCHOLARSHIPS
• See page 173

ASSOCIATION FOR FACILITIES ENGINEERING (AFE)

ASSOCIATION FOR FACILITIES ENGINEERING CEDAR VALLEY CHAPTER # 132 SCHOLARSHIP
• See page 120

AUTOMOTIVE HALL OF FAME   http://www.automotivehalloffame.org

AUTOMOTIVE HALL OF FAME EDUCATIONAL FUNDS
• See page 162

BOY SCOUTS OF AMERICA - MUSKINGUM VALLEY COUNCIL   http://www.learning-for-life.org

AFL-CIO SKILL TRADES SCHOLARSHIP

Two $1,000 scholarships available annually to Explorers to help them support their education toward a career in skilled trades.

Academic Fields/Career Goals: Trade/Technical Specialties.
Award: Scholarship for use in freshman year. *Number:* 2. *Amount:* $1000.
Eligibility Requirements: Applicant must be enrolled or expecting to enroll at a technical institution. Available to U.S. citizens.
Application Requirements: Application, driver's license, photo, references. *Deadline:* April 30.
Contact: Boy Scouts of America - Muskingum Valley Council
S120, PO Box 152079
Irving, TX 75015-2079

COLLEGE FOUNDATION OF NORTH CAROLINA, INC   http://www.cfnc.org

PROGRESS ENERGY SCHOLARSHIP PROGRAM

Scholarship for a North Carolina resident enrolled, or planning to enroll as a full-time student in a course of study leading to a two-year technical degree at Cape Fear Community College, Fayetteville Technical Community College, or Wake Technical Community College in an approved major. Three colleges receive $15,000 to be divided among recipients.

Academic Fields/Career Goals: Trade/Technical Specialties.
Award: Scholarship for use in freshman, sophomore, junior, or senior years; renewable.
Eligibility Requirements: Applicant must be enrolled or expecting to enroll full-time at a four-year institution or university and resident of North Carolina. Available to U.S. citizens.
Application Requirements: Application.
Contact: College Foundation of North Carolina, Inc
PO Box 41966
Raleigh, NC 27629-1966
Phone: 888-234-6400
E-mail: programinformation@CFNC.org

WACHOVIA TECHNICAL SCHOLARSHIP PROGRAM

Scholarships are offered to students enrolled in two year technical programs. Recipient must be enrolled full time in the second year of a two-year technical program at a North Carolina community college. There is no special application form for the scholarship.

Academic Fields/Career Goals: Trade/Technical Specialties.
Award: Scholarship for use in sophomore year. *Number:* up to 113. *Amount:* up to $500.

College Foundation of North Carolina, Inc (continued)

Eligibility Requirements: Applicant must be enrolled or expecting to enroll full-time at a two-year institution and studying in North Carolina. Available to U.S. citizens.

Contact: College Foundation of North Carolina, Inc
PO Box 41966
Raleigh, NC 27629-1966
Phone: 888-234-6400
E-mail: programinformation@CFNC.org

DATATEL, INC.   http://www.datatel.com/dsf

NANCY GOODHUE LYNCH SCHOLARSHIP

For any undergraduate student in an Information Technology curriculum program. Applicant must attend a Datatel client institution. Completed applications must be submitted by January 31.

Academic Fields/Career Goals: Trade/Technical Specialties.

Award: Scholarship for use in freshman, sophomore, junior, or senior years; not renewable. *Number:* 2. *Amount:* $2500.

Eligibility Requirements: Applicant must be enrolled or expecting to enroll full or part-time at a two-year or four-year or technical institution or university. Available to U.S. and non-U.S. citizens.

Application Requirements: Application, essay, references, transcript. *Deadline:* January 31.

Contact: Marissa Solis, Project Leader
Datatel, Inc.
4375 Fair Lakes Court
Fairfax, VA 22033
Phone: 800-486-4332
Fax: 703-968-4573
E-mail: scholars@datatel.com

GREATER KANAWHA VALLEY FOUNDATION   http://www.tgkvf.org

WEST VIRGINIA BROADCASTERS ASSOCIATION FUND
• *See page 181*

INTERNATIONAL EXECUTIVE HOUSEKEEPERS ASSOCIATION   http://www.ieha.org

INTERNATIONAL EXECUTIVE HOUSEKEEPERS EDUCATIONAL FOUNDATION
• *See page 307*

INTERNATIONAL FURNISHINGS AND DESIGN ASSOCIATION   http://www.ifdaef.org

CHARLES D. MAYO SCHOLARSHIP
• *See page 356*

IFDA STUDENT SCHOLARSHIP
• *See page 356*

LEARNING FOR LIFE   http://www.learning-for-life.org

AFL-CIO SKILLED TRADES EXPLORING SCHOLARSHIPS

Two $1000 scholarships annually to Explorers to help them support their education toward a career in skilled trades.

Academic Fields/Career Goals: Trade/Technical Specialties.

Award: Scholarship for use in freshman year. *Number:* up to 2. *Amount:* $1000.

Eligibility Requirements: Applicant must be enrolled or expecting to enroll at a technical institution. Available to U.S. citizens.

Application Requirements: Application, transcript. *Deadline:* April 30.

Contact: Learning for Life National Office
Learning for Life
S210, PO Box 152079
Irving, TX 75015-2079

MAINE EDUCATION SERVICES   http://www.mesfoundation.com/

MAINE METAL PRODUCTS ASSOCIATION SCHOLARSHIP
• *See page 395*

MAINE METAL PRODUCTS ASSOCIATION   http://www.maine-metals.org

MAINE METAL PRODUCTS ASSOCIATION SCHOLARSHIP PROGRAM
• *See page 389*

MAINE SCHOOL FOOD SERVICE ASSOCIATION (MSFSA)

SCHOLARSHIP OF THE MAINE SCHOOL FOOD SERVICE ASSOCIATION
• *See page 305*

MARION D. AND EVA S. PEEPLES FOUNDATION TRUST SCHOLARSHIP PROGRAM   http://www.jccf.org

MARION A. AND EVA S. PEEPLES SCHOLARSHIPS
• *See page 230*

MARYLAND ASSOCIATION OF PRIVATE COLLEGES AND CAREER SCHOOLS   http://www.mapccs.org

MARYLAND ASSOCIATION OF PRIVATE COLLEGES AND CAREER SCHOOLS SCHOLARSHIP
• *See page 150*

MARYLAND HIGHER EDUCATION COMMISSION   http://www.mhec.state.md.us

FIREFIGHTER, AMBULANCE, AND RESCUE SQUAD MEMBER TUITION REIMBURSEMENT PROGRAM-MARYLAND
• *See page 300*

MIDWEST ROOFING CONTRACTORS ASSOCIATION   http://www.mrca.org

MRCA FOUNDATION SCHOLARSHIP PROGRAM
• *See page 94*

NATIONAL ASSOCIATION OF WATER COMPANIES-NEW JERSEY CHAPTER

NATIONAL ASSOCIATION OF WATER COMPANIES-NEW JERSEY CHAPTER SCHOLARSHIP
• *See page 139*

NATIONAL ASSOCIATION OF WOMEN IN CONSTRUCTION   http://nawic.org

NAWIC CONSTRUCTION TRADES SCHOLARSHIP

Scholarship for women pursuing a trade apprenticeship program. Only for students attending school in the United States or Canada.

Academic Fields/Career Goals: Trade/Technical Specialties.

Award: Scholarship for use in freshman, sophomore, junior, or senior years. *Amount:* $1000–$2000.

Eligibility Requirements: Applicant must be enrolled or expecting to enroll full-time at a technical institution and female. Available to U.S. and Canadian citizens.

Application Requirements: Application, essay.

Contact: Scholarship Administrator
National Association of Women in Construction
327 South Adams Street
Fort Worth, TX 76104
E-mail: nawic@nawic.org

NAWIC UNDERGRADUATE SCHOLARSHIPS
• *See page 100*

PLASTICS INSTITUTE OF AMERICA
http://www.plasticsinstitute.org/

PLASTICS PIONEERS SCHOLARSHIPS
• *See page 269*

PLUMBING-HEATING-COOLING CONTRACTORS ASSOCIATION EDUCATION FOUNDATION
http://www.phccweb.org

BRADFORD WHITE CORPORATION SCHOLARSHIP
• *See page 102*

DELTA FAUCET COMPANY SCHOLARSHIP PROGRAM
• *See page 102*

PHCC EDUCATIONAL FOUNDATION NEED-BASED SCHOLARSHIP
• *See page 102*

PHCC EDUCATIONAL FOUNDATION SCHOLARSHIP PROGRAM
• *See page 103*

PROFESSIONAL AVIATION MAINTENANCE FOUNDATION
http://www.pama.org

PROFESSIONAL AVIATION MAINTENANCE FOUNDATION STUDENT SCHOLARSHIP PROGRAM
• *See page 129*

SOCIETY OF MANUFACTURING ENGINEERS EDUCATION FOUNDATION
http://www.sme.org

CLINTON J. HELTON MANUFACTURING SCHOLARSHIP AWARD FUND
• *See page 272*

DOWNRIVER DETROIT CHAPTER 198 SCHOLARSHIP
• *See page 273*

E. WAYNE KAY COMMUNITY COLLEGE SCHOLARSHIP AWARD
• *See page 273*

E. WAYNE KAY SCHOLARSHIP
• *See page 273*

FORT WAYNE CHAPTER 56 SCHOLARSHIP
• *See page 274*

MYRTLE AND EARL WALKER SCHOLARSHIP FUND
• *See page 275*

NORTH CENTRAL REGION 9 SCHOLARSHIP
• *See page 275*

PHOENIX CHAPTER 67 SCHOLARSHIP
• *See page 275*

SME CORPORATE SCHOLARS
• *See page 275*

WICHITA CHAPTER 52 SCHOLARSHIP
• *See page 276*

WILLIAM E. WEISEL SCHOLARSHIP FUND
• *See page 246*

SOCIETY OF PLASTICS ENGINEERS (SPE) FOUNDATION
http://www.4spe.com

SOCIETY OF PLASTICS ENGINEERS SCHOLARSHIP PROGRAM
• *See page 168*

SOUTH DAKOTA RETAILERS ASSOCIATION
http://www.sdra.org

SOUTH DAKOTA RETAILERS ASSOCIATION SCHOLARSHIP PROGRAM
• *See page 69*

SPECIALTY EQUIPMENT MARKET ASSOCIATION
http://www.sema.org

SPECIALTY EQUIPMENT MARKET ASSOCIATION MEMORIAL SCHOLARSHIP FUND
• *See page 282*

WOMEN IN LOGISTICS, NORTHERN CALIFORNIA
http://www.womeninlogistics.org

WOMEN IN LOGISTICS SCHOLARSHIP
• *See page 157*

WOMEN'S JEWELRY ASSOCIATION
http://www.womensjewelry.org

WOMEN'S JEWELRY ASSOCIATION SCHOLARSHIP PROGRAM

Program is designed to encourage talented female students and help support their studies in the jewelry field. Applicants required to submit original drawings of their jewelry designs.

Academic Fields/Career Goals: Trade/Technical Specialties.

Award: Scholarship for use in freshman, sophomore, junior, senior, graduate, or postgraduate years; not renewable. *Number:* 5–15. *Amount:* $500–$5000.

Eligibility Requirements: Applicant must be enrolled or expecting to enroll full or part-time at a two-year or four-year or technical institution or university; female and must have an interest in designated field specified by sponsor. Available to U.S. citizens.

Application Requirements: Application, essay, portfolio, references, transcript. *Deadline:* varies.

Contact: Gillian Schultz, Scholarship Committee
Women's Jewelry Association
373 Route 46 West, Building E, Suite 215
Fairfield, NJ 07004
Phone: 973-575-7190
Fax: 973-575-1445
E-mail: info@womensjewelry.org

WYOMING TRUCKING ASSOCIATION

WYOMING TRUCKING ASSOCIATION TRUST FUND SCHOLARSHIP
• *See page 158*

TRANSPORTATION

AMERICAN PUBLIC TRANSPORTATION FOUNDATION
http://www.apta.com

DAN REICHARD JR. SCHOLARSHIP
• *See page 144*

DONALD C. HYDE ESSAY PROGRAM
• *See page 171*

DR. GEORGE M. SMERK SCHOLARSHIP

Scholarship for study towards a career in career in public transit management. Must be sponsored by APTA member organization. Minimum GPA of 3.0 required.

Academic Fields/Career Goals: Transportation.

Award: Scholarship for use in sophomore, junior, or senior years; not renewable. *Number:* 1. *Amount:* up to $2500.

Eligibility Requirements: Applicant must be enrolled or expecting to enroll full-time at an institution or university. Applicant must have 3.0 GPA or higher. Available to U.S. citizens.

American Public Transportation Foundation (continued)

Application Requirements: Application, essay, financial need analysis, references, test scores, transcript, verification of enrollment for the fall semester, copy of the fee schedule from the college/university. *Deadline:* June 16.

Contact: Pamela Boswell, Vice President of Program Management
American Public Transportation Foundation
1666 K Street, NW
Washington, DC 20006-1215
Phone: 202-496-4803
Fax: 202-496-2323
E-mail: pboswell@apta.com

JACK GILSTRAP SCHOLARSHIP
• See page 171

LOUIS T. KLAUDER SCHOLARSHIP
• See page 171

PARSONS BRINCKERHOFF-JIM LAMMIE SCHOLARSHIP
• See page 171

TRANSIT HALL OF FAME SCHOLARSHIP AWARD PROGRAM
• See page 171

ASSOCIATED GENERAL CONTRACTORS OF AMERICA-NEW YORK STATE CHAPTER   http://www.agcnys.org

ASSOCIATED GENERAL CONTRACTORS OF AMERICA-NEW YORK STATE CHAPTER SCHOLARSHIP PROGRAM
• See page 173

NASA NEBRASKA SPACE GRANT CONSORTIUM   http://nasa.unomaha.edu

NASA NEBRASKA SPACE GRANT
• See page 125

NASA VERMONT SPACE GRANT CONSORTIUM   http://www.vtspacegrant.org

VERMONT SPACE GRANT CONSORTIUM SCHOLARSHIP PROGRAM
• See page 94

NATIONAL CUSTOMS BROKERS AND FORWARDERS ASSOCIATION OF AMERICA   http://www.ncbfaa.org

NATIONAL CUSTOMS BROKERS AND FORWARDERS ASSOCIATION OF AMERICA SCHOLARSHIP AWARD

One-time award for employees of NCBFAA member organizations and their children. Must be studying transportation logistics or international trade full time. Minimum 2.5 GPA. Application deadline is March 3.

Academic Fields/Career Goals: Transportation.

Award: Scholarship for use in freshman, sophomore, junior, senior, graduate, or postgraduate years; not renewable. *Number:* 1. *Amount:* $5000.

Eligibility Requirements: Applicant must be enrolled or expecting to enroll full-time at a four-year institution. Applicant or parent of applicant must have employment or volunteer experience in customs broker. Applicant must have 2.5 GPA or higher. Available to U.S. citizens.

Application Requirements: Application, essay, resume, references, letter from member. *Deadline:* March 3.

Contact: Tom Mathers, Director Communications
National Customs Brokers and Forwarders Association of America
1200 18th Street, NW, Suite 901
Washington, DC 20036
Phone: 202-466-0222
Fax: 202-466-0226
E-mail: tom@ncbfaa.org

NINETY-NINES, SAN FERNANDO VALLEY CHAPTER/VAN NUYS AIRPORT   http://sfv99s.org/

SAN FERNANDO VALLEY CHAPTER OF THE NINETY-NINES CAREER SCHOLARSHIP
• See page 128

TRANSPORTATION CLUBS INTERNATIONAL   http://www.transportationclubsinternational.com

ALICE GLAISYER WARFIELD MEMORIAL SCHOLARSHIP
• See page 130

DENNY LYDIC SCHOLARSHIP
• See page 130

TEXAS TRANSPORTATION SCHOLARSHIP
• See page 130

TRANSPORTATION CLUBS INTERNATIONAL CHARLOTTE WOODS SCHOLARSHIP
• See page 130

TRANSPORTATION CLUBS INTERNATIONAL FRED A. HOOPER MEMORIAL SCHOLARSHIP
• See page 131

TRANSPORTATION CLUBS INTERNATIONAL GINGER AND FRED DEINES CANADA SCHOLARSHIP
• See page 131

TRANSPORTATION CLUBS INTERNATIONAL GINGER AND FRED DEINES MEXICO SCHOLARSHIP
• See page 131

TRUCKLOAD CARRIERS ASSOCIATION   http://www.truckload.org

TRUCKLOAD CARRIERS ASSOCIATION SCHOLARSHIP FUND
• See page 154

WOMEN IN LOGISTICS, NORTHERN CALIFORNIA   http://www.womeninlogistics.org

WOMEN IN LOGISTICS SCHOLARSHIP
• See page 157

WYOMING TRUCKING ASSOCIATION

WYOMING TRUCKING ASSOCIATION TRUST FUND SCHOLARSHIP
• See page 158

TRAVEL/TOURISM

AMERICAN SOCIETY OF TRAVEL AGENTS (ASTA) FOUNDATION   http://www.astanet.com

AMERICAN EXPRESS TRAVEL SCHOLARSHIP

Candidate must be enrolled in a travel or tourism program in either a two- or four-year college or university or proprietary travel school. Must write 500-word essay on student's view of travel industry's future. Merit-based. Award criteria subject to change. Contact ASTA Foundation for more information, or visit Web site: http://www.astanet.com/education/edu_scholarships.asp. Minimum 2.5 GPA required.

Academic Fields/Career Goals: Travel/Tourism.

Award: Scholarship for use in freshman, sophomore, junior, or senior years; not renewable. *Number:* 1. *Amount:* varies.

Eligibility Requirements: Applicant must be Canadian citizen and enrolled or expecting to enroll full or part-time at a two-year or four-year or technical institution. Applicant must have 2.5 GPA or higher. Available to U.S. and Canadian citizens.

Application Requirements: Application, driver's license, essay, resume, references, transcript. *Deadline:* August 16.

Contact: Verlette Mitchell, Manager
American Society of Travel Agents (ASTA) Foundation
1101 King Street
Alexandria, VA 22314-2187
Phone: 703-739-8721
Fax: 703-684-8319
E-mail: scholarship@astahq.com

ARIZONA CHAPTER GOLD SCHOLARSHIP

One-time award for college undergraduates who are Arizona residents pursuing a travel or tourism degree at a four-year Arizona institution. Freshmen are not eligible. Must submit essay on career plans and interests. Write for application by sending a self-addressed stamped business size envelope or go to http://www.astanet.com for requirements and an application. Minimum 2.5 GPA required.

Academic Fields/Career Goals: Travel/Tourism.

Award: Scholarship for use in sophomore, junior, or senior years; not renewable. *Number:* 1. *Amount:* $3000.

Eligibility Requirements: Applicant must be enrolled or expecting to enroll full or part-time at a four-year institution or university; resident of Arizona and studying in Arizona. Applicant or parent of applicant must have employment or volunteer experience in designated career field. Applicant must have 2.5 GPA or higher. Available to U.S. and non-U.S. citizens.

Application Requirements: Application, driver's license, essay, references, transcript. *Deadline:* August 16.

Contact: Verlette Mitchell, Manager
American Society of Travel Agents (ASTA) Foundation
1101 King Street
Alexandria, VA 22314-2187
Phone: 703-739-8721
Fax: 703-684-8319
E-mail: scholarship@astahq.com

DONALD ESTEY SCHOLARSHIP FUND-ROCKY MOUNTAIN CHAPTER

One-time award for travel professionals or students in industry training programs. If professional, must be affiliated with the American Society of Travel Agents Rocky Mountain Chapter. Students are not required to be members of ASTA, but must have letter of recommendation from ASTA Rocky Mountain Chapter. Must be Colorado, Utah, or Wyoming resident. Visit Web site: http://www.astanet.com for requirements, application, and deadlines.

Academic Fields/Career Goals: Travel/Tourism.

Award: Scholarship for use in freshman, sophomore, junior, or senior years; not renewable. *Number:* 4. *Amount:* $1000–$3000.

Eligibility Requirements: Applicant must be enrolled or expecting to enroll full or part-time at a two-year or technical institution; resident of Colorado, Utah, or Wyoming and studying in Colorado, Utah, or Wyoming. Applicant or parent of applicant must be member of American Society of Travel Agents. Applicant or parent of applicant must have employment or volunteer experience in designated career field. Available to U.S. citizens.

Application Requirements: Application, driver's license, financial need analysis, references, test scores, transcript. *Deadline:* August 16.

Contact: Verlette Mitchell, Manager
American Society of Travel Agents (ASTA) Foundation
1101 King Street
Alexandria, VA 22314-2187
Phone: 703-739-8721
Fax: 703-684-8319
E-mail: scholarship@astahq.com

GEORGE REINKE SCHOLARSHIPS

For a student enrolled in proprietary travel school or junior college in a travel agent training program. Applicant must write a 500-word essay on career goals in the travel or tourism industry. Go to Web site (http://www.astanet.com) for requirements and an application. Two deadlines per year.

Academic Fields/Career Goals: Travel/Tourism.

Award: Scholarship for use in sophomore, junior, or senior years; not renewable. *Number:* up to 6. *Amount:* $2000.

Eligibility Requirements: Applicant must be enrolled or expecting to enroll full or part-time at a two-year or technical institution. Applicant or parent of applicant must have employment or volunteer experience in designated career field. Applicant must have 2.5 GPA or higher. Available to U.S. citizens.

Application Requirements: Application, driver's license, essay, references, transcript. *Deadline:* varies.

Contact: Verlette Mitchell, Manager
American Society of Travel Agents (ASTA) Foundation
1101 King Street
Alexandria, VA 22314-2187
Phone: 703-739-8721
Fax: 703-684-8319
E-mail: scholarship@astahq.com

HEALY SCHOLARSHIP

One-time award for a college undergraduate pursuing a travel or tourism degree. Must submit essay suggesting improvements for the travel industry. Go to http://www.astanet.com for requirements and an application. Must attend an institution in the U.S. or Canada. Minimum 2.5 GPA required.

Academic Fields/Career Goals: Travel/Tourism.

Award: Scholarship for use in freshman, sophomore, junior, or senior years; not renewable. *Number:* 1. *Amount:* $2000.

Eligibility Requirements: Applicant must be enrolled or expecting to enroll full or part-time at a four-year institution or university. Applicant must have 2.5 GPA or higher. Available to U.S. and Canadian citizens.

Application Requirements: Application, driver's license, essay, references, self-addressed stamped envelope, transcript. *Deadline:* August 16.

Contact: Verlette Mitchell, Manager
American Society of Travel Agents (ASTA) Foundation
1101 King Street
Alexandria, VA 22314-2187
Phone: 703-739-8721
Fax: 703-684-8319
E-mail: scholarship@astahq.com

HOLLAND-AMERICA LINE WESTOURS SCHOLARSHIPS

Students must write 500-word essay on the future of the cruise industry and must be enrolled in travel or tourism program at a two- or four-year college or proprietary travel school. Go to http://www.astanet.com for requirements and an application form. Minimum 2.5 GPA required.

Academic Fields/Career Goals: Travel/Tourism.

Award: Scholarship for use in freshman, sophomore, junior, or senior years; not renewable. *Number:* 2. *Amount:* $3000.

Eligibility Requirements: Applicant must be enrolled or expecting to enroll full or part-time at a two-year or four-year or technical institution or university. Applicant or parent of applicant must have employment or volunteer experience in designated career field or hospitality/hotel administration/operations. Applicant must have 2.5 GPA or higher. Available to U.S. citizens.

Application Requirements: Application, driver's license, essay, financial need analysis, resume, references, transcript, topic of research, name and phone number of project contact, sponsor school details. *Deadline:* August 16.

Contact: Verlette Mitchell, Manager
American Society of Travel Agents (ASTA) Foundation
1101 King Street
Alexandria, VA 22314-2187
Phone: 703-739-8721
Fax: 703-684-8319
E-mail: scholarship@astahq.com

JOHN HJORTH SCHOLARSHIP FUND-SAN DIEGO CHAPTER

One-time award for travel professionals working for an agency that is a member of American Society of Travel Agents' San Diego Chapter. Provides support for employees to further education in travel and tourism. Go to http://www.astanet.com for requirements and an application form.

Academic Fields/Career Goals: Travel/Tourism.

Award: Scholarship for use in freshman, sophomore, junior, senior, or graduate years; not renewable. *Number:* 3. *Amount:* $250.

American Society of Travel Agents (ASTA) Foundation (continued)

Eligibility Requirements: Applicant must be enrolled or expecting to enroll full or part-time at a technical institution and resident of California. Applicant or parent of applicant must be member of American Society of Travel Agents. Applicant or parent of applicant must have employment or volunteer experience in designated career field. Available to U.S. citizens.

Application Requirements: Application, essay, references. *Deadline:* August 16.

Contact: Verlette Mitchell, Manager
American Society of Travel Agents (ASTA) Foundation
1101 King Street
Alexandria, VA 22314-2187
Phone: 703-739-8721
Fax: 703-684-8319
E-mail: scholarship@astahq.com

JOSEPH R. STONE SCHOLARSHIPS

One-time award for high school senior or college undergraduate pursuing a travel or tourism degree. Must have a parent in the industry and proof of employment. Must submit 500-word essay explaining career goals. Go to http://www.astanet.com for requirements and an application form. Minimum 2.5 GPA required.

Academic Fields/Career Goals: Travel/Tourism.

Award: Scholarship for use in freshman, sophomore, junior, or senior years; not renewable. *Number:* 3. *Amount:* $2400.

Eligibility Requirements: Applicant must be enrolled or expecting to enroll full or part-time at a four-year institution or university. Applicant or parent of applicant must be member of American Society of Travel Agents. Applicant or parent of applicant must have employment or volunteer experience in designated career field. Applicant must have 2.5 GPA or higher. Available to U.S. and Canadian citizens.

Application Requirements: Application, essay, references, transcript. *Deadline:* August 16.

Contact: Verlette Mitchell, Manager
American Society of Travel Agents (ASTA) Foundation
1101 King Street
Alexandria, VA 22314-2187
Phone: 703-739-8721
Fax: 703-684-8319
E-mail: scholarship@astahq.com

NANCY STEWART SCHOLARSHIP FUND-ALLEGHENY CHAPTER

One-time award for travel professionals working for an agency that is a member of American Society of Travel Agents' Allegheny Chapter. Applicant must be Pennsylvania resident. The applicant must also have at least three years of travel industry experience. Provides support for employees to further education in travel and tourism. Go to http://www.astanet.com for requirements and an application form.

Academic Fields/Career Goals: Travel/Tourism.

Award: Scholarship for use in freshman year; not renewable. *Number:* 3. *Amount:* $400.

Eligibility Requirements: Applicant must be enrolled or expecting to enroll part-time at a technical institution and resident of Pennsylvania. Applicant or parent of applicant must be member of American Society of Travel Agents. Applicant or parent of applicant must have employment or volunteer experience in designated career field. Available to U.S. citizens.

Application Requirements: Application, essay, references. *Deadline:* August 16.

Contact: Verlette Mitchell, Manager
American Society of Travel Agents (ASTA) Foundation
1101 King Street
Alexandria, VA 22314-2187
Phone: 703-739-8721
Fax: 703-684-8319
E-mail: scholarship@astahq.com

NORTHERN CALIFORNIA CHAPTER RICHARD EPPING SCHOLARSHIP

Merit-based award for residents of northern California or northern Nevada who are attending school in the same area. Submit 500-word essay on desire

for travel or tourism career. Go to http://www.astanet.com for requirements and an application. Minimum 2.5 GPA required.

Academic Fields/Career Goals: Travel/Tourism.

Award: Scholarship for use in freshman, sophomore, junior, or senior years; not renewable. *Number:* 1. *Amount:* $2000.

Eligibility Requirements: Applicant must be enrolled or expecting to enroll full or part-time at a two-year or four-year or technical institution or university; resident of California or Nevada and studying in California or Nevada. Applicant must have 2.5 GPA or higher. Available to U.S. citizens.

Application Requirements: Application, essay, references, transcript. *Deadline:* August 16.

Contact: Verlette Mitchell, Manager
American Society of Travel Agents (ASTA) Foundation
1101 King Street
Alexandria, VA 22314-2187
Phone: 703-739-8721
Fax: 703-684-8319
E-mail: scholarship@astahq.com

ORANGE COUNTY CHAPTER/HARRY JACKSON SCHOLARSHIP FUND

One-time award for California residents enrolled in a travel related program. Must be a member of the American Society of Travel Agents and pursuing a career in the travel industry. Go to http://www.astanet.com for requirements and an application form.

Academic Fields/Career Goals: Travel/Tourism.

Award: Scholarship for use in freshman year; not renewable. *Number:* varies. *Amount:* $250–$2000.

Eligibility Requirements: Applicant must be enrolled or expecting to enroll full or part-time at a technical institution and resident of California. Applicant or parent of applicant must be member of American Society of Travel Agents. Applicant or parent of applicant must have employment or volunteer experience in designated career field. Available to U.S. citizens.

Application Requirements: Application, financial need analysis, references, transcript. *Deadline:* August 16.

Contact: Verlette Mitchell, Manager
American Society of Travel Agents (ASTA) Foundation
1101 King Street
Alexandria, VA 22314-2187
Phone: 703-739-8721
Fax: 703-684-8319
E-mail: scholarship@astahq.com

PACIFIC NORTHWEST CHAPTER-WILLIAM HUNT SCHOLARSHIP FUND

One-time award for travel professionals who are members or employees of American Society of Travel Agents member organizations in the Oregon or Pacific Northwest Chapters. Must be a resident of and studying in one of the following states: Alaska, Idaho, Montana, Oregon, or Washington. Must be pursuing a certificate or diploma in travel or tourism. Please visit Web site http://www.astanet.com for updated information.

Academic Fields/Career Goals: Travel/Tourism.

Award: Scholarship for use in freshman year; not renewable. *Number:* 3. *Amount:* $200–$1000.

Eligibility Requirements: Applicant must be enrolled or expecting to enroll full or part-time at a two-year or four-year or technical institution and resident of Alaska, Idaho, Montana, Oregon, or Washington. Applicant or parent of applicant must be member of American Society of Travel Agents. Applicant or parent of applicant must have employment or volunteer experience in designated career field. Available to U.S. citizens.

Application Requirements: Application, essay, references. *Deadline:* August 16.

Contact: Verlette Mitchell, Manager
American Society of Travel Agents (ASTA) Foundation
1101 King Street
Alexandria, VA 22314-2187
Phone: 703-739-8721
Fax: 703-684-8319
E-mail: scholarship@astahq.com

PRINCESS CRUISES AND PRINCESS TOURS SCHOLARSHIP

Merit-based award for student accepted or enrolled as an undergraduate in a travel or tourism program. Submit 300-word essay on two features cruise ships will need to offer passengers in the next ten years. Go to http://www.astanet.com for requirements and an application form. Minimum 2.5 GPA required.

Academic Fields/Career Goals: Travel/Tourism.

Award: Scholarship for use in freshman, sophomore, junior, or senior years; not renewable. *Number:* 2. *Amount:* $2000.

Eligibility Requirements: Applicant must be enrolled or expecting to enroll full or part-time at a two-year or four-year or technical institution or university. Applicant must have 2.5 GPA or higher. Available to U.S. and non-U.S. citizens.

Application Requirements: Application, essay, references, transcript. *Deadline:* August 16.

Contact: Verlette Mitchell, Manager
American Society of Travel Agents (ASTA) Foundation
1101 King Street
Alexandria, VA 22314-2187
Phone: 703-739-8721
Fax: 703-684-8319
E-mail: scholarship@astahq.com

SOUTHEAST AMERICAN SOCIETY OF TRAVEL AGENTS CHAPTER SCHOLARSHIP

One-time award for active or associate members of the Southeast Chapter of American Society of Travel Agents. Must be resident of and studying in one of the following states: Alabama, Georgia, Kentucky, Louisiana, Mississippi, North Carolina, South Carolina, or Tennessee. Must have minimum two years experience in travel industry. Must complete ICTA course within three years and complete each of the four courses for CTE certification. Check http://www.astanet.com for requirements and an application form.

Academic Fields/Career Goals: Travel/Tourism.

Award: Scholarship for use in freshman year; not renewable. *Number:* 6. *Amount:* $350.

Eligibility Requirements: Applicant must be enrolled or expecting to enroll part-time at a technical institution; resident of Alabama, Georgia, Kentucky, Louisiana, Mississippi, North Carolina, South Carolina, or Tennessee and studying in Alabama, Georgia, Louisiana, Mississippi, North Carolina, South Carolina, or Tennessee. Applicant or parent of applicant must be member of American Society of Travel Agents. Applicant or parent of applicant must have employment or volunteer experience in designated career field. Applicant must have 2.5 GPA or higher. Available to U.S. citizens.

Application Requirements: Application, references, letter of interest or of need, proof of course certification. *Deadline:* August 16.

Contact: Verlette Mitchell, Manager
American Society of Travel Agents (ASTA) Foundation
1101 King Street
Alexandria, VA 22314-2187
Phone: 703-739-8721
Fax: 703-684-8319
E-mail: scholarship@astahq.com

SOUTHERN CALIFORNIA CHAPTER/PLEASANT HAWAIIAN HOLIDAYS SCHOLARSHIP

Two awards for students pursuing travel or tourism degrees. One award given to student attending college in southern California, and one award given to a student attending school anywhere in the U.S. If an insufficient number of qualified southern California applicants is received, then both awards may be given to students enrolled anywhere in the U.S. Applicant must be U.S. citizens. Please go to http://www.astanet.com for requirements and an application form. Minimum 2.5 GPA required.

Academic Fields/Career Goals: Travel/Tourism.

Award: Scholarship for use in freshman, sophomore, junior, or senior years; not renewable. *Number:* 2. *Amount:* $2500.

Eligibility Requirements: Applicant must be enrolled or expecting to enroll full or part-time at a four-year institution or university. Applicant must have 2.5 GPA or higher. Available to U.S. citizens.

Application Requirements: Application, essay, references, transcript. *Deadline:* August 16.

Contact: Verlette Mitchell, Manager
American Society of Travel Agents (ASTA) Foundation
1101 King Street
Alexandria, VA 22314-2187
Phone: 703-739-8721
Fax: 703-684-8319
E-mail: scholarship@astahq.com

STAN AND LEONE POLLARD SCHOLARSHIPS

Available to a person re-entering the job market. Must be enrolled in a travel or tourism curriculum at a proprietary travel school or junior college. Go to Web site (http://www.astanet.com) for requirements and an application form. Scholarships are awarded twice each year.

Academic Fields/Career Goals: Travel/Tourism.

Award: Scholarship for use in freshman, sophomore, or junior years; not renewable. *Number:* 2. *Amount:* $2000.

Eligibility Requirements: Applicant must be enrolled or expecting to enroll full or part-time at a two-year or technical institution. Applicant must have 2.5 GPA or higher. Available to U.S. and Canadian citizens.

Application Requirements: Application, essay, references, transcript. *Deadline:* August 16.

Contact: Verlette Mitchell, Manager
American Society of Travel Agents (ASTA) Foundation
1101 King Street
Alexandria, VA 22314-2187
Phone: 703-739-8721
Fax: 703-684-8319
E-mail: scholarship@astahq.com

CANADIAN RECREATIONAL CANOEING ASSOCIATION
http://www.paddlingcanada.com

BILL MASON MEMORIAL SCHOLARSHIP FUND
• See page 80

CATCHING THE DREAM

TRIBAL BUSINESS MANAGEMENT PROGRAM (TBM)
• See page 55

HAWAII HOTEL AND LODGING ASSOCIATION
http://www.hawaiihotels.org

R.W. BOB HOLDEN SCHOLARSHIP
• See page 350

INTERNATIONAL AIRLINES TRAVEL AGENT NETWORK
http://www.iatan.org

INTERNATIONAL AIRLINES TRAVEL AGENT NETWORK RONALD A. SANTANA MEMORIAL FOUNDATION
• See page 350

INTERNATIONAL FOODSERVICE EDITORIAL COUNCIL
http://www.ifec-is-us.com

INTERNATIONAL FOODSERVICE EDITORIAL COUNCIL COMMUNICATIONS SCHOLARSHIP
• See page 182

MISSOURI TRAVEL COUNCIL
http://www.missouritravel.com

MISSOURI TRAVEL COUNCIL TOURISM SCHOLARSHIP
• See page 307

NATIONAL TOURISM FOUNDATION
http://www.ntfonline.org

ACADEMY OF TRAVEL AND TOURISM SCHOLARSHIPS
• See page 351

CLEVELAND LEGACY I AND II SCHOLARSHIP AWARDS
• See page 308

NEW HORIZONS KATHY LE TARTE SCHOLARSHIP
• See page 309

PAT AND JIM HOST SCHOLARSHIP
• See page 309

SOCIETIE DES CASINOS DU QUEBEC SCHOLARSHIP
• See page 309

TAMPA, HILLSBOROUGH LEGACY SCHOLARSHIP
• See page 309

TAUCK SCHOLARS SCHOLARSHIPS
• See page 309

TULSA SCHOLARSHIP AWARDS
• See page 309

YELLOW RIBBON SCHOLARSHIP
• See page 310

NETWORK OF EXECUTIVE WOMEN IN HOSPITALITY
http://www.newh.org

NETWORK OF EXECUTIVE WOMEN IN HOSPITALITY, INC. SCHOLARSHIP
• See page 101

RECREATIONAL BOATING INDUSTRIES EDUCATIONAL FOUNDATION
http://www.mbia.org

RECREATIONAL BOATING INDUSTRIES EDUCATIONAL FOUNDATION SCHOLARSHIPS
• See page 141

SOUTH DAKOTA RETAILERS ASSOCIATION
http://www.sdra.org

SOUTH DAKOTA RETAILERS ASSOCIATION SCHOLARSHIP PROGRAM
• See page 69

TV/RADIO BROADCASTING

ACADEMY OF TELEVISION ARTS AND SCIENCES FOUNDATION
http://www.emmys.tv/foundation

ACADEMY OF TELEVISION ARTS AND SCIENCES COLLEGE TELEVISION AWARDS
• See page 108

ADC RESEARCH INSTITUTE
http://www.adc.org

JACK SHAHEEN MASS COMMUNICATIONS SCHOLARSHIP AWARD
• See page 177

ADVERTISING FEDERATION OF FORT WAYNE, INC.
http://www.adfedfortwayne.org

ADVERTISING FEDERATION OF FORT WAYNE, INC., SCHOLARSHIP
• See page 178

ALABAMA BROADCASTERS ASSOCIATION
http://www.al-ba.com/scholarship.html

ALABAMA BROADCASTERS ASSOCIATION SCHOLARSHIP

Scholarship available to Alabama residents studying broadcasting at any accredited Alabama college or university. This will include two-year junior colleges and technical colleges.

Academic Fields/Career Goals: TV/Radio Broadcasting.

Award: Scholarship for use in junior or senior years. *Number:* 4. *Amount:* $2500.

Eligibility Requirements: Applicant must be enrolled or expecting to enroll at a two-year or four-year institution or university and resident of Alabama. Available to U.S. citizens.

Application Requirements: Application, references. *Deadline:* March 31.

Contact: Alabama Broadcasters Association
2180 Parkway Lake Drive
Hoover, AL 35244
Phone: 205-982-5001
Fax: 205-982-0015

AMERICAN LEGION, PRESS CLUB OF NEW JERSEY

AMERICAN LEGION PRESS CLUB OF NEW JERSEY AND POST 170 ARTHUR DEHARDT MEMORIAL SCHOLARSHIP
• See page 178

ASIAN AMERICAN JOURNALISTS ASSOCIATION
http://www.aaja.org

AAJA/COX FOUNDATION SCHOLARSHIP
• See page 357

ASIAN-AMERICAN JOURNALISTS ASSOCIATION SCHOLARSHIP
• See page 179

MINORU YASUI MEMORIAL SCHOLARSHIP AWARD
• See page 358

ASSOCIATED PRESS
http://www.aptra.org

ASSOCIATED PRESS TELEVISION/RADIO ASSOCIATION-CLETE ROBERTS JOURNALISM SCHOLARSHIP AWARDS
• See page 358

KATHRYN DETTMAN MEMORIAL JOURNALISM SCHOLARSHIP
• See page 358

ASSOCIATED PRESS TELEVISION-RADIO ASSOCIATION OF CALIFORNIA AND NEVADA
http://www.aptra.org

APTRA-CLETE ROBERTS MEMORIAL JOURNALISM SCHOLARSHIP AWARD
• See page 358

APTRA-KATHYRN DETTMAN MEMORIAL SCHOLARSHIP
• See page 359

ATLANTA PRESS CLUB, INC.
http://www.atlpressclub.org

ATLANTA PRESS CLUB JOURNALISM SCHOLARSHIP PROGRAM
• See page 179

CALIFORNIA BROADCASTERS FOUNDATION
http://www.cabroadcasters.org

CALIFORNIA BROADCASTERS FOUNDATION INTERN SCHOLARSHIP

Two $500 scholarships to radio interns and two $500 scholarships to television interns each semester. Any enrolled college student working as an intern at any California Broadcasters Foundation or Association member radio or television station. No minimum hours per week requirements. Immediate family of current Foundation Board Members are not eligible. Deadline is June 18(Fall), December 10(Spring).

Academic Fields/Career Goals: TV/Radio Broadcasting.

Award: Scholarship for use in freshman, sophomore, junior, or senior years; not renewable. *Number:* up to 8. *Amount:* $500.

Eligibility Requirements: Applicant must be enrolled or expecting to enroll full or part-time at an institution or university and resident of California. Available to U.S. citizens.

Application Requirements: Application, essay, references. *Deadline:* varies.

Contact: Mark Powers, Program Manager
California Broadcasters Foundation
915 L Street, Suite 1150
Sacramento, CA 95814
Phone: 916-444-2237

CALIFORNIA CHICANO NEWS MEDIA ASSOCIATION (CCNMA)　http://www.ccnma.org

JOEL GARCIA MEMORIAL SCHOLARSHIP
• *See page 180*

CANADIAN ASSOCIATION OF BROADCASTERS　http://www.cab-acr.ca

JIM ALLARD BROADCAST JOURNALISM SCHOLARSHIP
• *See page 359*

RUTH HANCOCK MEMORIAL SCHOLARSHIP
• *See page 180*

CHARLES & LUCILLE KING FAMILY FOUNDATION, INC.　http://www.kingfoundation.org/

CHARLES AND LUCILLE KING FAMILY FOUNDATION SCHOLARSHIPS
• *See page 180*

CIRI FOUNDATION　http://www.thecirifoundation.org

CAP LATHROP SCHOLARSHIP PROGRAM

Applicants should plan to work in the broadcast/telecommunications industry in Alaska upon completion of the academic degree. One-time award to full-time student. Must be Native American Student. Minimum 3.0 GPA required. For more details see Web site: http://www.ciri.com/tcf.

Academic Fields/Career Goals: TV/Radio Broadcasting.

Award: Scholarship for use in freshman, sophomore, junior, senior, or graduate years; not renewable. *Number:* varies. *Amount:* $3500.

Eligibility Requirements: Applicant must be American Indian/Alaska Native and enrolled or expecting to enroll full-time at a two-year or four-year institution or university. Applicant must have 3.0 GPA or higher. Available to U.S. citizens.

Application Requirements: Application, photo, references, transcript, statement of purpose, proof of eligibility, proof of name change if different from birth certificate or previous applications, proof of acceptance/enrollment. *Deadline:* June 1.

Contact: Susan Anderson, President/CEO
CIRI Foundation
3600 San Jeronimo Drive, Suite 256
Anchorage, AK 99508-2870
Phone: 907-793-3575
Fax: 907-793-3585
E-mail: tcf@thecirifoundation.org

COLORADO BROADCASTERS ASSOCIATION　http://www.e-cba.org

CONTINUING EDUCATION SCHOLARSHIP PROGRAM

Scholarship available to a fulltime employee of a Colorado broadcast station and a resident of Colorado.

Academic Fields/Career Goals: TV/Radio Broadcasting.

Award: Scholarship for use in freshman, sophomore, junior, or senior years. *Amount:* up to $3000.

Eligibility Requirements: Applicant must be enrolled or expecting to enroll at a technical institution and resident of Colorado. Available to U.S. citizens.

Application Requirements: Application. *Deadline:* varies.

Contact: Marilyn Hogan, CBA Scholarships
Colorado Broadcasters Association
PO Box 2369
2042 Boreas Pass Road
Breckenridge, CO 80424
Phone: 970-547-1388
Fax: 970-547-1384
E-mail: cobroadcasters@earthlink.net

VOCATIONAL SCHOOL SCHOLARSHIP PROGRAM

Scholarship open to students at any accredited professional training school offering programs in broadcasting or some other aspect of professional media education that explicitly prepares students for careers in broadcasting. Applicants must be residents of Colorado.

Academic Fields/Career Goals: TV/Radio Broadcasting.

Award: Scholarship for use in freshman, sophomore, junior, or senior years. *Amount:* up to $1000.

Eligibility Requirements: Applicant must be enrolled or expecting to enroll at a technical institution and resident of Colorado. Available to U.S. citizens.

Application Requirements: Application, references. *Deadline:* February 10.

Contact: Marilyn Hogan, CBA Scholarships
Colorado Broadcasters Association
PO Box 2369
2042 Boreas Pass Road
Breckenridge, CO 80424
Phone: 970-547-1388
Fax: 970-547-1384
E-mail: cobroadcasters@earthlink.net

DALLAS-FORT WORTH ASSOCIATION OF BLACK COMMUNICATORS　http://www.dfwabc.org

FUTURE JOURNALISTS SCHOLARSHIP PROGRAM
• *See page 180*

ELKS NATIONAL FOUNDATION　http://www.elks.org/enf

ELKS EAGLE SCOUT AWARDS

Four $8,000 scholarships ($2,000 per year), and four $4,000 scholarships ($1,000 per year). To registered Scouts who have achieved the rank of Eagle, have a SAT score of at least 1090 and/or equivalent ACT score of 26, be graduating from high school during the year they are applying, and have financial need.

Academic Fields/Career Goals: TV/Radio Broadcasting.

Award: Prize for use in freshman year. *Number:* up to 8. *Amount:* $1000–$2000.

Eligibility Requirements: Applicant must be enrolled or expecting to enroll at an institution or university and male. Applicant or parent of applicant must be member of Boy Scouts. Available to U.S. citizens.

Application Requirements: Application, financial need analysis, test scores, SAT score of at least 1090 and/or equivalent ACT score of 26. *Deadline:* October.

Contact: The National Office
Elks National Foundation
Boy Scouts of America, PO Box 152079
Irving, TX 75015-2079
Phone: 972-580-2000

FISHER BROADCASTING COMPANY　http://www.fisherbroadcasting.com

FISHER BROADCASTING, INC., SCHOLARSHIP FOR MINORITIES
• *See page 181*

GREAT LAKES COMMISSION　http://www.glc.org

CAROL A. RATZA MEMORIAL SCHOLARSHIP
• *See page 138*

GREATER KANAWHA VALLEY FOUNDATION
http://www.tgkvf.org

WEST VIRGINIA BROADCASTERS ASSOCIATION FUND
• See page 181

HAWAII ASSOCIATION OF BROADCASTERS, INC.
http://www.hawaiibroadcasters.com

HAWAII ASSOCIATION OF BROADCASTERS SCHOLARSHIP

Scholarship for full-time college student with the career goal of working in the broadcast industry in Hawaii upon graduation. Must be a senior in high school or a student currently enrolled in college. Minimum GPA of 2.5 required.

Academic Fields/Career Goals: TV/Radio Broadcasting.

Award: Scholarship for use in freshman, sophomore, junior, or senior years. Amount: $3500.

Eligibility Requirements: Applicant must be enrolled or expecting to enroll at a two-year or four-year institution or university. Applicant must have 2.5 GPA or higher. Available to U.S. citizens.

Application Requirements: Application, references. Deadline: April 15.

Contact: HAB Scholarship Committee
Hawaii Association of Broadcasters, Inc.
PO Box 22112
Honolulu, HI 96823-2112
Phone: 808-599-1455
Fax: 808-599-7784

IDAHO STATE BROADCASTERS ASSOCIATION
http://www.idahobroadcasters.org

WAYNE C. CORNILS MEMORIAL SCHOLARSHIP

Scholarship for students enrolled in an Idaho school on a full-time basis. Must be majoring in broadcasting related field. Must have GPA of 2.0 if in the first two years of school and a GPA of 2.5 in the last two years of school.

Academic Fields/Career Goals: TV/Radio Broadcasting.

Award: Scholarship for use in freshman, sophomore, junior, or senior years. Amount: up to $1000.

Eligibility Requirements: Applicant must be high school student; planning to enroll or expecting to enroll full-time at a four-year institution and studying in Idaho. Available to U.S. citizens.

Application Requirements: Application, essay, references, transcript. Deadline: March 15.

Contact: Connie Searles, President
Idaho State Broadcasters Association
270 North 27th Street, Suite B
Boise, ID 83702
Phone: 208-345-3072
Fax: 208-343-8046
E-mail: connies@cyberhighway.net

ILLUMINATING ENGINEERING SOCIETY OF NORTH AMERICA
http://www.iesna.org

ROBERT W. THUNEN MEMORIAL SCHOLARSHIPS
• See page 100

INDIANA BROADCASTERS ASSOCIATION
http://www.indianabroadcasters.org

INDIANA BROADCASTERS FOUNDATION SCHOLARSHIP
• See page 362

INDIANAPOLIS ASSOCIATION OF BLACK JOURNALISTS
http://www.iabj.net

LYNN DEAN FORD IABJ SCHOLARSHIP AWARDS
• See page 181

JIM ELDER GOOD SPORT FUND
http://www.jimelder.org

JOURNALISM AND BROADCASTING SCHOLARSHIPS
• See page 362

JOHN BAYLISS BROADCAST FOUNDATION
http://www.baylissfoundation.org

JOHN BAYLISS BROADCAST RADIO SCHOLARSHIP
• See page 182

KATU THOMAS R. DARGAN MINORITY SCHOLARSHIP
http://www.katu.com

THOMAS R. DARGAN MINORITY SCHOLARSHIP
• See page 182

LIN TELEVISION CORPORATION
http://www.lintv.com

LINTV MINORITY SCHOLARSHIP

Scholarship to help educate and train outstanding minority candidates who seek to enter the television broadcast field. Must have a minimum 3.0 cumulative GPA and be a declared major in journalism or related broadcast field at an accredited university or college. Must be a sophomore or have completed sufficient semester hours or similar educational units to be within 2 years of receiving an undergraduate bachelor's degree. Deadline: March 15

Academic Fields/Career Goals: TV/Radio Broadcasting.

Award: Scholarship for use in sophomore year; not renewable. Number: 1.

Eligibility Requirements: Applicant must be American Indian/Alaska Native, Asian/Pacific Islander, Black (non-Hispanic), or Hispanic and enrolled or expecting to enroll full-time at a two-year or four-year institution or university. Applicant must have 3.0 GPA or higher. Available to U.S. citizens.

Application Requirements: Application, transcript. Deadline: March 15.

Contact: Gail Brekke, Scholarship Coordinator
Lin Television Corporation
8 Elm Street
New Haven, CT 06510
Phone: 203-784-8958
E-mail: gail.brekke@lintv.com

LOUISIANA ASSOCIATION OF BROADCASTERS
http://www.broadcasters.org

BROADCAST SCHOLARSHIP PROGRAM

Scholarship worth $2000 given to students enrolled and attending classes, full-time, in a fully accredited broadcast curriculum at a Louisiana four-year college. Must be a Louisiana resident and maintain a minimum 2.5 GPA. Previous LAB Scholarship Award winners are eligible. Deadline is February 1.

Academic Fields/Career Goals: TV/Radio Broadcasting.

Award: Scholarship for use in junior or senior years; not renewable. Number: 1–3. Amount: up to $2000.

Eligibility Requirements: Applicant must be enrolled or expecting to enroll full-time at a four-year institution; resident of Louisiana and studying in Louisiana. Applicant must have 2.5 GPA or higher. Available to U.S. citizens.

Application Requirements: Application, financial need analysis, references, transcript. Deadline: February 1.

Contact: Louise L. Munson, Scholarship Coordinator
Louisiana Association of Broadcasters
660 Florida Boulevard
Baton Rouge, LA 70801
Phone: 225-267-4522
Fax: 225-267-4329
E-mail: lmunson@broadcasters.org

MARYLAND ASSOCIATION OF PRIVATE COLLEGES AND CAREER SCHOOLS
http://www.mapccs.org

MARYLAND ASSOCIATION OF PRIVATE COLLEGES AND CAREER SCHOOLS SCHOLARSHIP
• See page 150

MASSACHUSETTS BROADCASTERS ASSOCIATION
http://www.massbroadcasters.org

MBA STUDENT BROADCASTER SCHOLARSHIP

Scholarship available to students who are permanent residents of Massachusetts and are in the process of enrolling, or are currently enrolled, at an accredited institution of higher learning in a program in radio and television broadcasting. Such institutions may include vocational schools, 2 or 4 year colleges or universities in the U.S. Must be full-time student.

Academic Fields/Career Goals: TV/Radio Broadcasting.

Award: Scholarship for use in freshman, sophomore, junior, or senior years. *Amount:* $1500.

Eligibility Requirements: Applicant must be enrolled or expecting to enroll full-time at a two-year or four-year or technical institution or university. Available to U.S. citizens.

Application Requirements: Application, financial need analysis, references, transcript. *Deadline:* April 7.

Contact: Massachusetts Broadcasters Association
43 Riverside Avenue, Suite 401
Medford, MA 02155
Phone: 800-471-1875
Fax: 800-471-1876

MEDIA ACTION NETWORK FOR ASIAN AMERICANS
http://www.manaa.org

MANAA MEDIA SCHOLARSHIPS FOR ASIAN AMERICAN STUDENTS
• See page 112

MICHIGAN ASSOCIATION OF BROADCASTERS FOUNDATION
http://www.michmab.com

WXYZ-TV BROADCASTING SCHOLARSHIP

One-time $1000 scholarship to assist students who are actively pursuing a career in a broadcast-related field. No limit on the number of awards within the program. Interested applicants should send a cover letter, resume, letters of recommendation, and an essay (200-300 words). The scholarship is open to Michigan residents currently attending college within the state Michigan.

Academic Fields/Career Goals: TV/Radio Broadcasting.

Award: Scholarship for use in freshman year; not renewable. *Amount:* up to $1000.

Eligibility Requirements: Applicant must be enrolled or expecting to enroll full-time at a two-year or four-year institution or university; resident of Michigan and studying in Michigan. Available to U.S. citizens.

Application Requirements: Application, autobiography, essay, references, 200-300 word essay explaining applicant's career goals. *Deadline:* Continuous.

Contact: Karole White, Michigan High School and College Broadcast Awards coordinator
Michigan Association of Broadcasters Foundation
819 North Washington Avenue
Lansing, MI 48906
Phone: 517-484-7444
Fax: 517-484-5810
E-mail: mabf@michmab.com

MINNESOTA BROADCASTERS ASSOCIATION
http://www.minnesotabroadcasters.com

JAMES J. WYCHOR SCHOLARSHIP

One-time scholarships to Minnesota residents interested in broadcasting who are planning to enter broadcasting or other work in electronic media. Minimum 3.0 GPA is required. Application deadline is May 31. Submit proof of enrollment at an accredited postsecondary institution.

Academic Fields/Career Goals: TV/Radio Broadcasting.

Award: Scholarship for use in freshman, sophomore, junior, senior, or graduate years; not renewable. *Number:* 10. *Amount:* $1500.

Eligibility Requirements: Applicant must be enrolled or expecting to enroll full-time at a four-year institution or university; resident of Minnesota and must have an interest in designated field specified by sponsor. Applicant must have 3.0 GPA or higher. Available to U.S. citizens.

Application Requirements: Application, essay, references, transcript. *Deadline:* May 31.

Contact: Minnesota Broadcasters Association
3033 Excelsior Boulevard, Suite 301
Minneapolis, MN 55416
E-mail: meischen@minnesotabroadcasters.com

MISSISSIPPI ASSOCIATION OF BROADCASTERS
http://www.msbroadcasters.org

MISSISSIPPI ASSOCIATION OF BROADCASTERS SCHOLARSHIP

Scholarship available to a student enrolled in a fully accredited broadcast curriculum at a Mississippi two- or four-year college.

Academic Fields/Career Goals: TV/Radio Broadcasting.

Award: Scholarship for use in freshman, sophomore, junior, or senior years. *Amount:* $4000.

Eligibility Requirements: Applicant must be enrolled or expecting to enroll full-time at a two-year or four-year institution or university; resident of Mississippi and studying in Mississippi. Available to U.S. citizens.

Application Requirements: Application, financial need analysis, references, extracurricular activities and community involvement also considered. *Deadline:* May 1.

Contact: Mississippi Association of Broadcasters
855 South Pear Orchard Road, Suite 403
Ridgeland, MS 39157
Phone: 601-957-9121
Fax: 601-957-9175
E-mail: email@msbroadcasters.org

MISSOURI BROADCASTERS ASSOCIATION SCHOLARSHIP PROGRAM
http://www.mbaweb.org

MISSOURI BROADCASTERS ASSOCIATION SCHOLARSHIP

Scholarship for a Missouri resident enrolled or planning to enroll in a broadcast or related curriculum, which provides training and expertise applicable to a broadcast operation. Must maintain a GPA of at least 3.0 or equivalent. Multiple awards may be assigned each year and the amount of the scholarship will vary.

Academic Fields/Career Goals: TV/Radio Broadcasting.

Award: Scholarship for use in freshman, sophomore, junior, or senior years. *Number:* 1.

Eligibility Requirements: Applicant must be high school student; planning to enroll or expecting to enroll full-time at an institution or university; resident of Missouri and studying in Missouri. Applicant must have 3.0 GPA or higher. Available to U.S. citizens.

Application Requirements: Application, financial need analysis, references. *Deadline:* March 31.

Contact: Scholarship Committee
Missouri Broadcasters Association Scholarship Program
PO Box 104445
Jefferson City, MO 65110-4445
Phone: 573-636-6692
Fax: 573-634-8258
E-mail: mba@mbaweb.org

MONTANA BROADCASTERS ASSOCIATION
http://www.mtbroadcasters.org

GREAT FALLS BROADCASTERS ASSOCIATION SCHOLARSHIP

Scholarship available to a student who has graduated from a north-central Montana high school (Cascade, Meagher, Judith Basin, Fergus, Choteau, Teton, Pondera, Glacier, Toole, Liberty, Hill, Blaine, Phillips, and Valley counties) and is enrolled as at least a second year student in radio-TV at any public or private Montana college or university.

Academic Fields/Career Goals: TV/Radio Broadcasting.

Award: Scholarship for use in senior year; not renewable. *Number:* 1. *Amount:* $2000-$5000.

Montana Broadcasters Association (continued)

Eligibility Requirements: Applicant must be enrolled or expecting to enroll full-time at a two-year or four-year institution or university; resident of Montana and studying in Montana. Available to U.S. citizens.

Application Requirements: Application, essay, references, transcript. *Deadline:* March 15.

Contact: Gregory McDonald, Scholarship Coordinator
Montana Broadcasters Association
HC 70 PO Box 90
Bonner, MT 59823
Phone: 406-244-4622
Fax: 406-244-5518
E-mail: mba@mtbroadcasters.org

NATIONAL ACADEMY OF TELEVISION ARTS AND SCIENCES   http://www.emmyonline.org/emmy/scholarship.html

NATIONAL ACADEMY OF TELEVISION ARTS AND SCIENCES JOHN CANNON MEMORIAL SCHOLARSHIP
• See page 183

TRUSTEE SCHOLARSHIP PROGRAM
• See page 183

NATIONAL ACADEMY OF TELEVISION ARTS AND SCIENCES-NATIONAL CAPITAL/CHESAPEAKE BAY CHAPTER   http://www.natasdc.org/home.html

THE BETTY ENDICOTT/NTA-NCCB STUDENT SCHOLARSHIP
• See page 363

NATIONAL ASSOCIATION OF BLACK JOURNALISTS   http://www.nabj.org

NABJ SCHOLARSHIP
• See page 183

NATIONAL ASSOCIATION OF BLACK JOURNALISTS NON-SUSTAINING SCHOLARSHIP AWARDS
• See page 364

NATIONAL ASSOCIATION OF BROADCASTERS   http://www.nab.org

NATIONAL ASSOCIATION OF BROADCASTERS GRANTS FOR RESEARCH IN BROADCASTING
• See page 183

NATIONAL PRESS PHOTOGRAPHERS FOUNDATION, INC.   http://www.nppa.org

NATIONAL PRESS PHOTOGRAPHERS FOUNDATION TELEVISION NEWS SCHOLARSHIP
• See page 443

NEW JERSEY BROADCASTERS ASSOCIATION   http://www.njba.com

MICHAEL S. LIBRETTI SCHOLARSHIP
• See page 184

NORTH CAROLINA ASSOCIATION OF BROADCASTERS   http://www.ncbroadcast.com/scholarships.htm

NCAB SCHOLARSHIP

Scholarship for the child of an employee of a member station or company who is entering or already enrolled in a North Carolina college or university with an interest in broadcasting. Must be no younger than 17 and no older than 20 years of age. Applicants required to submit information on their academic performance and work experience and write a short essay about why they are interested in pursuing a career in the broadcast industry.

Academic Fields/Career Goals: TV/Radio Broadcasting.

Award: Scholarship for use in freshman year; not renewable. *Number:* up to 2. *Amount:* up to $2500.

Eligibility Requirements: Applicant must be high school student; age 17-20 and planning to enroll or expecting to enroll full-time at a two-year or four-year institution or university. Available to U.S. citizens.

Application Requirements: Application, essay, references, transcript, academic history, awards and honors, work history, extracurricular activities. *Deadline:* March 17.

Contact: JoAnn Davis, NCAB Scholarship coordinator
North Carolina Association of Broadcasters
North Carolina Association of Broadcasters, PO Box 627
Raleigh, NC 27602
Phone: 919-821-7300

OREGON ASSOCIATION OF BROADCASTERS   http://www.theoab.org

OAB BROADCAST SCHOLARSHIP
• See page 185

OREGON STUDENT ASSISTANCE COMMISSION   http://www.osac.state.or.us

ENTERCOM PORTLAND RADIO SCHOLARSHIP FUND
• See page 367

OUTDOOR WRITERS ASSOCIATION OF AMERICA   http://www.owaa.org/

OUTDOOR WRITERS ASSOCIATION OF AMERICA BODIE MCDOWELL SCHOLARSHIP AWARD
• See page 185

RADIO-TELEVISION NEWS DIRECTORS ASSOCIATION AND FOUNDATION   http://www.rtndf.org/

ABE SCHECTER GRADUATE SCHOLARSHIP
• See page 185

CAROLE SIMPSON SCHOLARSHIP
• See page 185

KEN KASHIWAHARA SCHOLARSHIP
• See page 186

LOU AND CAROLE PRATO SPORTS REPORTING SCHOLARSHIP
• See page 186

MIKE REYNOLDS $1,000 SCHOLARSHIP
• See page 186

PRESIDENT'S $2500 SCHOLARSHIP
• See page 186

RHODE ISLAND FOUNDATION   http://www.rifoundation.org

RHODE ISLAND EDSAL ADVERTISING SCHOLARSHIP
• See page 298

SOCIETY OF BROADCAST ENGINEERS, INC.   http://www.sbe.org

ROBERT GREENBERG/HAROLD E. ENNES SCHOLARSHIP FUND AND ENNES EDUCATIONAL FOUNDATION BROADCAST TECHNOLOGY SCHOLARSHIP
• See page 271

YOUTH SCHOLARSHIP

Award available to senior in high school with a serious interest in pursuing studies leading to a career in broadcast engineering or closely related field.

Academic Fields/Career Goals: TV/Radio Broadcasting.

Award: Scholarship for use in freshman year. *Amount:* $1000–$3000.

Eligibility Requirements: Applicant must be high school student and planning to enroll or expecting to enroll full-time at a four-year institution or university. Available to U.S. citizens.

Application Requirements: Application, autobiography, transcript, written statement of education plans after high school. *Deadline:* July 1.

Contact: Linda Baun, Certification Director
Society of Broadcast Engineers, Inc.
9102 North Meridian Street
Suite 150
Indianapolis, IN 46260
Phone: 317-846-9000
Fax: 317-846-9120
E-mail: lbaun@sbe.org

SOCIETY OF PROFESSIONAL JOURNALISTS, LOS ANGELES CHAPTER http://www.spj.org/losangeles

HELEN JOHNSON SCHOLARSHIP
• *See page 369*

TEXAS ASSOCIATION OF BROADCASTERS http://www.tab.org

BELO TEXAS BROADCAST EDUCATION FOUNDATION SCHOLARSHIP
• *See page 187*

BONNER MCLANE TEXAS BROADCAST EDUCATION FOUNDATION SCHOLARSHIP
• *See page 187*

STUDENT TEXAS BROADCAST EDUCATION FOUNDATION SCHOLARSHIP
• *See page 187*

TOM REIFF TEXAS BROADCAST EDUCATION FOUNDATION SCHOLARSHIP
• *See page 187*

UNDERGRADUATE TEXAS BROADCAST EDUCATION FOUNDATION SCHOLARSHIP
• *See page 188*

VANN KENNEDY TEXAS BROADCAST EDUCATION FOUNDATION SCHOLARSHIP
• *See page 188*

TEXAS GRIDIRON CLUB, INC. http://www.spjfw.org

TEXAS GRIDIRON CLUB SCHOLARSHIPS
• *See page 188*

UNITED METHODIST COMMUNICATIONS http://www.umcom.org/

LEONARD M. PERRYMAN COMMUNICATIONS SCHOLARSHIP FOR ETHNIC MINORITY STUDENTS
• *See page 189*

UNITED NEGRO COLLEGE FUND http://www.uncf.org

C-SPAN SCHOLARSHIP PROGRAM
• *See page 189*

VALLEY PRESS CLUB http://www.valleypressclub.com/

VALLEY PRESS CLUB SCHOLARSHIPS, THE REPUBLICAN SCHOLARSHIP; PHOTOJOURNALISM SCHOLARSHIP, CHANNEL 22 SCHOLARSHIP
• *See page 189*

WMTW-TV 8-AUBURN, MAINE http://www.wmtw.com

BOB ELLIOT- WMTW-TV 8 JOURNALISM SCHOLARSHIP
• *See page 190*

WOWT-TV- OMAHA, NEBRASKA http://www.wowt.com

WOWT-TV BROADCASTING SCHOLARSHIP PROGRAM

Annual scholarship for high school graduates in the Channel 6 viewing area of Nebraska who are pursuing a career in broadcasting. Student must have a minimum grade point average of 3.0 upon graduation and pursuing further education at an accredited educational institution.

Academic Fields/Career Goals: TV/Radio Broadcasting.

Award: Scholarship for use in freshman year; not renewable. *Number:* up to 2. *Amount:* up to $1000.

Eligibility Requirements: Applicant must be high school student and planning to enroll or expecting to enroll full-time at a four-year institution or university. Applicant must have 3.0 GPA or higher. Available to U.S. citizens.

Application Requirements: Application, essay, interview, references, transcript, interviews held April 1-15 at Channel 6 studios. *Deadline:* March 15.

Contact: Gail Lee, WOWT TV Broadcasting Scholarship Coordinator
WOWT-TV- Omaha, Nebraska
3501 Farnam Street
Omaha, NE 68131
Phone: 402-346-6666
Fax: 402-233-7880

YOUNG AMERICAN BROADCASTERS SCHOLARSHIP http://www.youngamericanbroadcasters.org

YOUNG AMERICAN BROADCASTERS SCHOLARSHIP

Program is dedicated to reaching an ethnically diverse college population and encouraging them in regard to radio and Internet broadcasting.

Academic Fields/Career Goals: TV/Radio Broadcasting.

Award: Scholarship for use in sophomore, junior, or senior years; not renewable. *Amount:* up to $5000.

Eligibility Requirements: Applicant must be enrolled or expecting to enroll at an institution or university. Available to U.S. citizens.

Application Requirements: Application, applicant must enter a contest. *Deadline:* varies.

Contact: Young American Broadcasters Scholarship
1030 15th Street, NW Suite 1028
Washington, DC 20005
Phone: 202-408-8255
Fax: 202-408-5188

URBAN AND REGIONAL PLANNING

AMERICAN PLANNING ASSOCIATION http://www.planning.org

JUDITH MCMANUS PRICE SCHOLARSHIP

Scholarship available for Undergraduate or graduate women and minority students enrolled in degree programs in planning or a closely related field. Must demonstrate a genuine financial need. Deadline is April 30. Details on Web site: http://www.planning.org

Academic Fields/Career Goals: Urban and Regional Planning.

Award: Scholarship for use in freshman, sophomore, junior, senior, or graduate years; not renewable. *Number:* 3. *Amount:* $2000–$4000.

Eligibility Requirements: Applicant must be American Indian/Alaska Native, Black (non-Hispanic), or Hispanic; enrolled or expecting to enroll at a four-year institution or university and female. Available to U.S. citizens.

Application Requirements: Application, financial need analysis, resume, references, transcript. *Deadline:* April 30.

Contact: Kriss Blank, Leadership Affairs Associate
American Planning Association
122 South Michigan Avenue, Suite 1600
Chicago, IL 60603
Phone: 312-786-6722
Fax: 312-786-6727
E-mail: kblank@planning.org

CONNECTICUT CHAPTER OF THE AMERICAN PLANNING ASSOCIATION http://www.ccapa.org

DIANA DONALD SCHOLARSHIP

The Diana Donald Scholarship is available to Connecticut residents or students attending schools in Connecticut. Applicants must be enrolled in a graduate or undergraduate program in city planning or a closely related field.

Connecticut Chapter of the American Planning Association (continued)

Academic Fields/Career Goals: Urban and Regional Planning.

Award: Scholarship for use in freshman, sophomore, junior, senior, or graduate years; not renewable. *Number:* 1. *Amount:* $1000.

Eligibility Requirements: Applicant must be enrolled or expecting to enroll full-time at an institution or university; resident of Connecticut and studying in Connecticut. Available to U.S. and non-U.S. citizens.

Application Requirements: Application, essay, financial need analysis, references, transcript. *Deadline:* March 10.

Contact: Michael Piscitelli
Connecticut Chapter of the American Planning Association
City Planning Department, 165 Church Street, 5th Floor
New Haven, CT 06510
Phone: 203-946-7814

PARK PEOPLE   http://www.parkpeople.org

THE PARK PEOPLE $2000 SCHOLARSHIP
• *See page 102*

WOMEN'S STUDIES

SUNSHINE LADY FOUNDATION, INC.   http://www.sunshineladyfdn.org

COUNSELOR, ADVOCATE, AND SUPPORT STAFF SCHOLARSHIP PROGRAM
• *See page 69*

Nonacademic/Noncareer Criteria

CIVIC, PROFESSIONAL, SOCIAL, OR UNION AFFILIATION

AIR LINE PILOTS ASSOCIATION, INTERNATIONAL
http://www.alpa.org

AIR LINE PILOTS ASSOCIATION SCHOLARSHIP PROGRAM

Four-year scholarship for children of medically retired, long-term disabled, or deceased pilot members of the Air Line Pilots Association. High school seniors may apply. Scholarship awards $3000 a year for four years. Minimum 3.0 GPA required. For undergraduate use.

Award: Scholarship for use in freshman, sophomore, junior, or senior years; renewable. *Number:* 1. *Amount:* $3000.

Eligibility Requirements: Applicant must be enrolled or expecting to enroll full-time at a four-year institution or university. Applicant or parent of applicant must be member of Airline Pilots Association. Applicant must have 3.0 GPA or higher. Available to U.S. and Canadian citizens.

Application Requirements: Application, financial need analysis, transcript. *Deadline:* April 1.

Contact: Janice Redden, Scholarship Program Manager
Air Line Pilots Association, International
1625 Massachusetts Avenue, NW
Washington, DC 20036

ALBERTA HERITAGE SCHOLARSHIP FUND/ ALBERTA SCHOLARSHIP PROGRAMS
http://www.alis.gov.ab.ca

BOYS AND GIRLS CLUB OF ALBERTA SCHOLARSHIPS

A CAN$500 scholarship is available to assist members of the Boys and Girls club pursue higher education. Candidates must be 24 years of age or younger, be current or former members of a Boys and Girls Club in Alberta and enrolled or planning to enroll full time in a postsecondary program. Must be a Canadian citizen or landed immigrant, and Alberta resident. Application deadline is July 1. For more details see Web site: http://www.alis.gov.ab.ca

Award: Scholarship for use in freshman, sophomore, junior, or senior years; not renewable. *Number:* 3. *Amount:* $430.

Eligibility Requirements: Applicant must be age 24 or under; enrolled or expecting to enroll full-time at a two-year or four-year or technical institution or university and resident of Alberta. Applicant or parent of applicant must be member of Boys or Girls Club. Available to Canadian citizens.

Application Requirements: Application, references, transcript. *Deadline:* July 1.

Contact: Stuart Dunn, Manager
Alberta Heritage Scholarship Fund/Alberta Scholarship Programs
4th Floor, 9940 106th Street, Box 28000 Station Main
Edmonton, AB T5J 4R4
Canada
Phone: 780-427-8640
Fax: 780-427-1288
E-mail: scholarships@gov.ab.ca

AMERICAN ASSOCIATION OF BIOANALYSTS
http://www.aab.org

DAVID BIRENBAUM SCHOLARSHIP FUND

One-time award based on merit for associate members or dependents of members of the American Association of Bioanalysts for study in any discipline for any academic year. Submit two character references.

Award: Scholarship for use in freshman, sophomore, junior, senior, graduate, or postgraduate years; not renewable. *Number:* 1–10. *Amount:* $500.

Eligibility Requirements: Applicant must be enrolled or expecting to enroll full or part-time at a two-year or four-year or technical institution or university. Applicant or parent of applicant must be member of American Association of Bioanalysts. Applicant must have 2.5 GPA or higher. Available to U.S. and non-U.S. citizens.

Application Requirements: Application, essay, financial need analysis, references, transcript. *Deadline:* March 15.

Contact: Leann Hampton, Administrator
American Association of Bioanalysts
906 Locust Street, Suite 1100
St. Louis, MO 63101-1419
Phone: 314-241-1445
Fax: 314-241-1449

AMERICAN BOWLING CONGRESS
http://www.bowl.com

CHUCK HALL STAR OF TOMORROW SCHOLARSHIP

Award is available to male, amateur bowlers 21 and under. Must be a high school senior or undergraduate student. Merit is taken into account as well. Minimum GPA of 2.50 is required. The award is $1,500 which is renewable for up to three years. Application deadline is October 1. Must be a member of YABA or ABC in good standing.

Award: Scholarship for use in freshman, sophomore, junior, or senior years; renewable. *Number:* 1. *Amount:* $1500.

Eligibility Requirements: Applicant must be age 21 or under; enrolled or expecting to enroll full or part-time at a two-year or four-year or technical institution or university; male and must have an interest in bowling. Applicant or parent of applicant must be member of Young American Bowling Alliance. Applicant must have 2.5 GPA or higher. Available to U.S. and Canadian citizens.

Application Requirements: Application, essay, references, self-addressed stamped envelope, transcript. *Deadline:* October 1.

Contact: Ed Gocha, Scholarship Administrator
American Bowling Congress
5301 South 76th Street
Greendale, WI 53129-1192
Phone: 800-514-2695 Ext. 3343
Fax: 414-421-3014
E-mail: egocha@bowlinginc.com

AMERICAN FEDERATION OF STATE, COUNTY, AND MUNICIPAL EMPLOYEES
http://www.afscme.org

AMERICAN FEDERATION OF STATE, COUNTY, AND MUNICIPAL EMPLOYEES SCHOLARSHIP PROGRAM

Award for family dependents of American Federation of State, County, and Municipal Employees members. Must be a graduating high school senior planning to pursue postsecondary education at a four-year institution. Submit

American Federation of State, County, and Municipal Employees (continued)

proof of parent's membership. Transcript and essay on what AFSCME has meant to my family must accompany application. Renewable award of $2000.

Award: Scholarship for use in freshman, sophomore, junior, or senior years; renewable. *Number:* 10. *Amount:* $2000.

Eligibility Requirements: Applicant must be high school student and planning to enroll or expecting to enroll full-time at a four-year institution or university. Applicant or parent of applicant must be member of American Federation of State, County, and Municipal Employees. Available to U.S. citizens.

Application Requirements: Application, essay, references, test scores, transcript. *Deadline:* December 31.

Contact: Genevieve Marcus, Scholarship Coordinator
American Federation of State, County, and Municipal Employees
1625 L Street, NW
Washington, DC 20036
Phone: 202-429-1250
Fax: 202-429-1272

UNION PLUS CREDIT CARD SCHOLARSHIP PROGRAM

One-time award for AFSCME members, their spouses and dependent children. Graduate students and grandchildren are not eligible. Members need not be AFSCME Advantage Union Plus credit cardholders to apply. Further information available at Web site http://www.afscme.org. Application deadline is January 31.

Award: Scholarship for use in freshman, sophomore, junior, or senior years; not renewable. *Number:* varies. *Amount:* $500–$4000.

Eligibility Requirements: Applicant must be enrolled or expecting to enroll at a two-year or four-year or technical institution. Applicant or parent of applicant must be member of American Federation of State, County, and Municipal Employees. Available to U.S. citizens.

Application Requirements: Application, autobiography, essay, references, transcript. *Deadline:* January 31.

Contact: Genevieve Marcus, Scholarship Coordinator
American Federation of State, County, and Municipal Employees
1625 L Street, NW
Washington, DC 20036
Phone: 202-429-1250
Fax: 202-429-1272

AMERICAN FOREIGN SERVICE ASSOCIATION
http://www.afsa.org

AMERICAN FOREIGN SERVICE ASSOCIATION (AFSA) FINANCIAL AID AWARD PROGRAM

Need-based financial aid scholarship program open to children whose parents are in the U.S. Government Foreign Service. Must attend a U.S. school full-time and maintain a C average. Must maintain a satisfactory academic record of 2.0 GPA. Children whose parents are in the military and international students are not eligible.

Award: Scholarship for use in freshman, sophomore, junior, or senior years; renewable. *Number:* 50–60. *Amount:* $500–$3000.

Eligibility Requirements: Applicant must be enrolled or expecting to enroll full-time at a two-year or four-year or technical institution or university and single. Applicant or parent of applicant must be member of American Foreign Service Association. Applicant or parent of applicant must have employment or volunteer experience in U.S. government foreign service. Available to U.S. citizens.

Application Requirements: Application, financial need analysis, transcript, CSS profile. *Deadline:* February 6.

Contact: Lori Dec, Scholarship Administrator
American Foreign Service Association
2101 E Street, NW
Washington, DC 20037
Phone: 202-944-4045
Fax: 202-338-6820
E-mail: dec@afsa.org

AMERICAN FOREIGN SERVICE ASSOCIATION (AFSA)/AAFSW MERIT AWARD PROGRAM

One-time award for a high school senior whose parent is a U.S. Government Foreign Service employee. Must maintain a satisfactory academic record 2.0

GPA. Parent must be a member of AFSA or AAFSW. Children of military parents or international students are not eligible. Award based upon academic and artistic achievements of the applicant.

Award: Prize for use in freshman year; not renewable. *Number:* 6–15. *Amount:* $500–$1500.

Eligibility Requirements: Applicant must be high school student; planning to enroll or expecting to enroll full-time at an institution or university and single. Applicant or parent of applicant must be member of American Foreign Service Association. Applicant or parent of applicant must have employment or volunteer experience in U.S. government foreign service. Available to U.S. citizens.

Application Requirements: Application, essay, references, self-addressed stamped envelope, test scores, transcript. *Deadline:* February 6.

Contact: Lori Dec, Scholarship Administrator
American Foreign Service Association
2101 E Street, NW
Washington, DC 20037
Phone: 202-944-4045
Fax: 202-338-6820
E-mail: dec@afsa.org

AMERICAN LEGION AUXILIARY, DEPARTMENT OF CONNECTICUT

AMERICAN LEGION AUXILIARY DEPARTMENT OF CONNECTICUT MEMORIAL EDUCATIONAL GRANT

Half the number of grants awarded to children of veterans who are also residents of CT. Remaining grants awarded to child or grandchild of a member (or member at time of death) of the CT Departments of the American Legion /American Legion Auxiliary, regardless of residency; or are members of the CT Departments of the American Legion Auxiliary/Sons of the American Legion, regardless of residency. Contact local unit President. Must include list of community service activities.

Award: Grant for use in freshman, sophomore, junior, or senior years; not renewable. *Number:* 4. *Amount:* $500.

Eligibility Requirements: Applicant must be age 16-23 and enrolled or expecting to enroll full-time at a two-year or four-year or technical institution or university. Applicant or parent of applicant must be member of American Legion or Auxiliary. Available to U.S. citizens. Applicant or parent must meet one or more of the following requirements: general military experience; retired from active duty; disabled or killed as a result of military service; prisoner of war; or missing in action.

Application Requirements: Application, financial need analysis, references, self-addressed stamped envelope, transcript. *Deadline:* April 3.

Contact: Local Unit President
American Legion Auxiliary, Department of Connecticut
PO Box 208
287 West Street
Rocky Hill, CT 06067

AMERICAN LEGION AUXILIARY, DEPARTMENT OF FLORIDA
http://www.floridalegion.org

AMERICAN LEGION AUXILIARY DEPARTMENT OF FLORIDA MEMORIAL SCHOLARSHIP

Scholarship for a member, daughter, or granddaughter of a member of Florida American Legion Auxiliary with a minimum three-year membership. Award for Florida resident for undergraduate study in Florida school. Minimum 2.5 GPA required.

Award: Scholarship for use in freshman, sophomore, junior, or senior years; renewable. *Number:* varies. *Amount:* $500–$1000.

Eligibility Requirements: Applicant must be enrolled or expecting to enroll full-time at a two-year or four-year or technical institution or university; female; resident of Florida and studying in Florida. Applicant or parent of applicant must be member of American Legion or Auxiliary. Applicant must have 2.5 GPA or higher. Available to U.S. citizens.

Application Requirements: Application, financial need analysis, references, transcript. *Deadline:* January 1.

Contact: Marie Mahoney, Department Secretary and Treasurer
American Legion Auxiliary, Department of Florida
PO Box 547917
Orlando, FL 32854-7917
Phone: 407-293-7411
Fax: 407-299-6522
E-mail: alaflorida@aol.com

AMERICAN LEGION AUXILIARY, DEPARTMENT OF MISSOURI

AMERICAN LEGION AUXILIARY MISSOURI STATE NATIONAL PRESIDENT'S SCHOLARSHIP

State-level award. Missouri Legion Auxiliary offers two $500 scholarships. To be eligible, applicant must complete 50 hours of community service during their high school years. Sponsoring Unit and Department must validate application. Applicant must be Missouri resident.

Award: Scholarship for use in freshman, sophomore, junior, or senior years; not renewable. *Number:* 2. *Amount:* $500.

Eligibility Requirements: Applicant must be enrolled or expecting to enroll full-time at a two-year or four-year or technical institution or university and resident of Missouri. Applicant or parent of applicant must be member of American Legion or Auxiliary. Applicant or parent of applicant must have employment or volunteer experience in community service. Available to U.S. citizens. Applicant or parent must meet one or more of the following requirements: general military experience; retired from active duty; disabled or killed as a result of military service; prisoner of war; or missing in action.

Application Requirements: Application. *Deadline:* March 1.

Contact: Mary Doerhoff

LELA MURPHY SCHOLARSHIP

$500 scholarship for high school graduate. $250 will be awarded each semester. Applicant must be Missouri resident and the granddaughter or great-granddaughter of a living or deceased Auxiliary member. Sponsoring Unit and Department must validate application. Application deadline is March 1.

Award: Scholarship for use in freshman year; not renewable. *Number:* 1. *Amount:* $500.

Eligibility Requirements: Applicant must be high school student; planning to enroll or expecting to enroll at a two-year or four-year or technical institution or university; female and resident of Missouri. Applicant or parent of applicant must be member of American Legion or Auxiliary. Available to U.S. citizens. Applicant or parent must meet one or more of the following requirements: general military experience; retired from active duty; disabled or killed as a result of military service; prisoner of war; or missing in action.

Application Requirements: Application. *Deadline:* March 1.

Contact: Mary Doerhoff, Department Secretary/Treasurer
American Legion Auxiliary, Department of Missouri
600 Ellis Boulevard
Jefferson City, MO 65101-1615
Phone: 573-636-9133
Fax: 573-635-3467
E-mail: dptmoala@socket.net

AMERICAN LEGION AUXILIARY, DEPARTMENT OF NEBRASKA

AMERICAN LEGION AUXILIARY DEPARTMENT OF NEBRASKA PRESIDENT'S SCHOLARSHIP FOR JUNIOR MEMBERS

One-time prize for female resident of Nebraska who has been entered into the National President's Scholarship for Junior Members and does not win at the national level. Must be in grades 9-12. Must rank in upper third of class or have a minimum 3.0 GPA.

Award: Prize for use in freshman year; not renewable. *Number:* 1. *Amount:* $200.

Eligibility Requirements: Applicant must be high school student; planning to enroll or expecting to enroll full-time at a two-year or four-year or technical institution or university; female and resident of Nebraska. Applicant or parent of applicant must be member of American Legion or Auxiliary. Applicant must have 3.0 GPA or higher. Available to U.S. citizens.

Application Requirements: Application, financial need analysis, references, transcript. *Deadline:* March 15.

Contact: Terry Walker, Department Secretary
American Legion Auxiliary, Department of Nebraska
PO Box 5227
Lincoln, NE 68505
Phone: 402-466-1808
Fax: 402-466-0182
E-mail: neaux@alltel.net

RUBY PAUL CAMPAIGN FUND SCHOLARSHIP

One-time award for Nebraska residents who are children, grandchildren, or great-grandchildren of an American Legion Auxiliary member, or who have been members of the American Legion, American Legion Auxiliary, or Sons of the American Legion or Auxiliary for two years prior to application. Must rank in upper third of class or have a minimum 3.0 GPA.

Award: Scholarship for use in freshman year; not renewable. *Number:* 1–3. *Amount:* $100–$300.

Eligibility Requirements: Applicant must be enrolled or expecting to enroll full-time at a two-year or four-year or technical institution or university and resident of Nebraska. Applicant or parent of applicant must be member of American Legion or Auxiliary. Applicant must have 3.0 GPA or higher. Available to U.S. citizens. Applicant or parent must meet one or more of the following requirements: general military experience; retired from active duty; disabled or killed as a result of military service; prisoner of war; or missing in action.

Application Requirements: Application, essay, financial need analysis, references, test scores, transcript. *Deadline:* March 26.

Contact: Terry Walker, Department Secretary
American Legion Auxiliary, Department of Nebraska
PO Box 5227
Lincoln, NE 68505
Phone: 402-466-1808
Fax: 402-466-0182
E-mail: neaux@alltel.net

AMERICAN LEGION AUXILIARY, DEPARTMENT OF UTAH
http://www.legion-aux.org

AMERICAN LEGION AUXILIARY NATIONAL PRESIDENTS SCHOLARSHIP

Scholarships available for graduating high school seniors. Must be a resident of Utah, a U.S. citizen and the direct descendant of a veteran.

Award: Scholarship for use in freshman year; not renewable. *Number:* up to 15. *Amount:* $1000–$2500.

Eligibility Requirements: Applicant must be high school student; planning to enroll or expecting to enroll full-time at a two-year or four-year or technical institution or university; single and resident of Utah. Applicant or parent of applicant must be member of American Legion or Auxiliary. Available to U.S. citizens. Applicant must have general military experience.

Application Requirements: Application, essay, references, test scores, transcript, statement of parent's military service. *Deadline:* March 1.

Contact: Marsha Knight, Department Secretary
American Legion Auxiliary, Department of Utah
455 East 400 South, Suite 50
Salt Lake City, UT 84111
Phone: 801-539-1015
Fax: 801-521-9191
E-mail: utahlegion@aol.com

AMERICAN LEGION AUXILIARY, DEPARTMENT OF WISCONSIN
http://www.amlegionauxwi.org

DELLA VAN DEUREN MEMORIAL SCHOLARSHIP

One-time award of $1000. For a student to qualify, the mother of the applicant or the applicant must be a member of an Auxiliary unit. Must send with completed application: certification of an American Legion Auxiliary Unit President, copy of proof that veteran was in service (i.e. discharge papers), letters of recommendation, transcripts, and essay. Must have minimum 3.5 GPA, show financial need, and be a resident of Wisconsin.

American Legion Auxiliary, Department of Wisconsin (continued)

Refer questions to Department Secretary, (608) 745-0124. Applications available on Web site: http://www.legion-aux.org

Award: Scholarship for use in freshman, sophomore, junior, senior, or graduate years; not renewable. *Number:* 2. *Amount:* $1000.

Eligibility Requirements: Applicant must be enrolled or expecting to enroll full or part-time at a four-year institution or university and resident of Wisconsin. Applicant or parent of applicant must be member of American Legion or Auxiliary. Applicant must have 3.5 GPA or higher. Available to U.S. citizens.

Application Requirements: Application, essay, financial need analysis, references, transcript. *Deadline:* March 15.

Contact: Kim Henderson, Scholarship Information
American Legion Auxiliary, Department of Wisconsin
PO Box 140
Portage, WI 53901-0140
Phone: 608-745-0124
Fax: 608-745-1947

H.S. AND ANGELINA LEWIS SCHOLARSHIPS

One-time award of $1000. Applicant must be a daughter, son, wife, or widow of a veteran. Granddaughters and great-granddaughters of veterans who are auxiliary members may also apply. Must send with completed application: certification of an American Legion Auxiliary Unit President, copy of proof that veteran was in service (i.e. discharge papers), letters of recommendation, transcripts and essay. Must have minimum 3.5 GPA, show financial need, and be a resident of Wisconsin. Refer questions to Department Secretary, (608) 745-0124. Applications available on Web site: http://www.legion-aux.org

Award: Scholarship for use in freshman, sophomore, junior, senior, or graduate years; not renewable. *Number:* 6. *Amount:* $1000.

Eligibility Requirements: Applicant must be enrolled or expecting to enroll full or part-time at a four-year institution or university and resident of Wisconsin. Applicant or parent of applicant must be member of American Legion or Auxiliary. Applicant must have 3.5 GPA or higher. Available to U.S. citizens.

Application Requirements: Application, essay, financial need analysis, references, transcript. *Deadline:* March 15.

Contact: Kim Henderson, Scholarship Information
American Legion Auxiliary, Department of Wisconsin
2930 American Legion Drive
PO Box 140
Portage, WI 53901-0140
Phone: 608-745-0124
Fax: 608-745-1947
E-mail: membership@amlegionauxwi.org

MERIT AND MEMORIAL SCHOLARSHIPS

One-time award of $1000. Applicant must be a daughter, son, wife, or widow of a veteran. Granddaughters and great granddaughters of veterans who are auxiliary members may also apply. Must send with completed application: certification of an American Legion Auxiliary Unit President, copy of proof that veteran was in service (i.e. discharge papers), letters of recommendation, transcripts, and essay. Must have minimum 3.5 GPA, show financial need, and be a resident of Wisconsin. Refer questions to Department Secretary, (608) 745-0124. Applications available on Web site: http://www.legion-aux.org

Award: Scholarship for use in freshman, sophomore, junior, senior, or graduate years; not renewable. *Number:* 6. *Amount:* $1000.

Eligibility Requirements: Applicant must be enrolled or expecting to enroll full or part-time at a four-year institution or university and resident of Wisconsin. Applicant or parent of applicant must be member of American Legion or Auxiliary. Applicant must have 3.5 GPA or higher. Available to U.S. citizens.

Application Requirements: Application, essay, financial need analysis, references, transcript. *Deadline:* March 15.

Contact: Kim Henderson, Scholarship Information
American Legion Auxiliary, Department of Wisconsin
PO Box 140
Portage, WI 53901-0140
Phone: 608-745-0124
Fax: 608-745-1947

PAST PRESIDENTS PARLEY HEALTH CAREER SCHOLARSHIPS

One-time award of $750. Course of study need not be a four-year program. Hospital, university, or technical school program is acceptable. Applicant must be a daughter, son, wife, or widow of a veteran. Granddaughters and great-granddaughters of veterans who are auxiliary members may also apply. Must send with completed application: certification of an American Legion Auxiliary Unit President, copy of proof that veteran was in service (i.e. discharge papers), letters of recommendation, transcripts, and essay. Must have minimum 3.5 GPA, show financial need, and be a resident of Wisconsin. Refer questions to Department Secretary, (608) 745-0124. Applications available on Web site: http://www.legion-aux.org

Award: Scholarship for use in freshman, sophomore, junior, or senior years; not renewable. *Number:* 2. *Amount:* $1000.

Eligibility Requirements: Applicant must be enrolled or expecting to enroll full or part-time at a two-year or four-year or technical institution or university and resident of Wisconsin. Applicant or parent of applicant must be member of American Legion or Auxiliary. Applicant must have 3.5 GPA or higher. Available to U.S. citizens.

Application Requirements: Application, essay, financial need analysis, references, transcript. *Deadline:* March 15.

Contact: Kim Henderson, Scholarship Information
American Legion Auxiliary, Department of Wisconsin
PO Box 140
Portage, WI 53901-0140
Phone: 608-745-0124
Fax: 608-745-1947

STATE PRESIDENT'S SCHOLARSHIPS

One-time award of $1000. In order for student to qualify, the mother of the applicant or the applicant must be a member of an Auxiliary unit. Must send with completed application: certification of an American Legion Auxiliary Unit President, copy of proof that veteran was in service (i.e. discharge papers), letters of recommendation, transcripts, and essay. Must have minimum 3.5 GPA, show financial need, and be a resident of Wisconsin. Refer questions to Department Secretary, (608) 745-0124. Applications available on Web site: http://www.legion-aux.org.

Award: Scholarship for use in freshman, sophomore, junior, senior, or graduate years; not renewable. *Number:* 3. *Amount:* $1000.

Eligibility Requirements: Applicant must be enrolled or expecting to enroll full or part-time at a four-year institution or university and resident of Wisconsin. Applicant or parent of applicant must be member of American Legion or Auxiliary. Applicant must have 3.5 GPA or higher. Available to U.S. citizens.

Application Requirements: Application, essay, financial need analysis, references, transcript. *Deadline:* March 15.

Contact: Kim Henderson, Scholarship Information
American Legion Auxiliary, Department of Wisconsin
PO Box 140
Portage, WI 53901-0140
Phone: 608-745-0124
Fax: 608-745-1947

AMERICAN LEGION AUXILIARY, NATIONAL HEADQUARTERS   http://www.legion-aux.org

AMERICAN LEGION AUXILIARY GIRL SCOUT ACHIEVEMENT AWARD

One scholarship available to recipients of Girl Scout Gold Award. Must be active in religious institution and have received appropriate religious emblem, Cadet or Senior Scout level. Must show practical citizenship in religious institution, community, and school. One-time award of $1000.

Award: Scholarship for use in freshman year; not renewable. *Number:* 1. *Amount:* $1000.

Eligibility Requirements: Applicant must be high school student; planning to enroll or expecting to enroll full-time at a two-year or four-year institution or university and female. Applicant or parent of applicant must be member of Girl Scouts. Applicant or parent of applicant must have employment or volunteer experience in community service. Available to U.S. and non-U.S. citizens.

Application Requirements: Application, applicant must enter a contest, essay, references, self-addressed stamped envelope, test scores, transcript. *Deadline:* February 10.

Contact: Department Secretary
American Legion Auxiliary, National Headquarters
777 North Meridian Street, 3rd Floor
Indianapolis, IN 46204-1189
Phone: 317-955-3845
Fax: 317-955-3884
E-mail: youthprog@legion-aux.org

AMERICAN LEGION AUXILIARY NON-TRADITIONAL STUDENTS SCHOLARSHIPS

One-time award for a student returning to the classroom after some period of time in which his/her formal schooling was interrupted or a student who has had at least one year of college and is in need of financial assistance to pursue an undergraduate degree. Must be a member of the American Legion, American Legion Auxiliary or Sons of the American Legion. One scholarship will be awarded per division.

Award: Scholarship for use in freshman, sophomore, junior, or senior years; not renewable. *Amount:* $1000.

Eligibility Requirements: Applicant must be enrolled or expecting to enroll full-time at a two-year or four-year or technical institution or university. Applicant or parent of applicant must be member of American Legion or Auxiliary. Available to U.S. citizens.

Application Requirements: Application, essay, references, test scores, transcript, statement of the military service of parent or parents. *Deadline:* March 1.

Contact: Department Secretary
American Legion Auxiliary, National Headquarters
777 North Meridian Street, 3rd Floor
Indianapolis, IN 46204-1189
Phone: 317-955-3853
Fax: 317-955-3884
E-mail: aef@legion-aux.org

AMERICAN LEGION AUXILIARY SPIRIT OF YOUTH SCHOLARSHIPS FOR JUNIOR MEMBERS

Renewable awards available to graduating high school seniors. Must be women and current junior members of the American Legion Auxiliary, with a three-year membership history. Students should apply through local chapter. Leadership considered.

Award: Scholarship for use in freshman, sophomore, junior, or senior years; renewable. *Number:* 1. *Amount:* $1000.

Eligibility Requirements: Applicant must be high school student; planning to enroll or expecting to enroll full-time at a four-year institution or university and female. Applicant or parent of applicant must be member of American Legion or Auxiliary. Available to U.S. and non-U.S. citizens.

Application Requirements: Application, essay, references, self-addressed stamped envelope, test scores, transcript. *Deadline:* March 1.

Contact: Department Secretary
American Legion Auxiliary, National Headquarters
777 North Meridian Street, 3rd Floor
Indianapolis, IN 46204-1189
Phone: 317-955-3853
Fax: 317-955-3884
E-mail: aef@legion-aux.org

AMERICAN LEGION, DEPARTMENT OF IDAHO   http://home.mindspring.com/~idlegion

AMERICAN LEGION, DEPARTMENT OF IDAHO SCHOLARSHIP

One-time award of up to $500 for residents of Idaho studying at an Idaho institution. Minimum 2.5 GPA. Application deadline is July 1.

Award: Scholarship for use in freshman year; not renewable. *Amount:* $300–$500.

Eligibility Requirements: Applicant must be high school student; planning to enroll or expecting to enroll full-time at a technical institution or university; single; resident of Idaho and studying in Idaho. Applicant or parent of applicant must be member of American

Legion or Auxiliary. Applicant must have 2.5 GPA or higher. Available to U.S. citizens. Applicant or parent must meet one or more of the following requirements: general military experience; retired from active duty; disabled or killed as a result of military service; prisoner of war; or missing in action.

Application Requirements: Application, autobiography, financial need analysis, references, self-addressed stamped envelope, transcript. *Deadline:* July 1.

Contact: Terry Niles, Department Adjunct
American Legion, Department of Idaho
901 Warren Street
Boise, ID 83706-3825
Phone: 208-342-7061
Fax: 208-342-1964
E-mail: adj@idaholegion.com

AMERICAN LEGION, DEPARTMENT OF ILLINOIS   http://www.illegion.org

AMERICAN ESSAY CONTEST SCHOLARSHIP

Students in 8th, 9th, 10th, 11th, and 12th grades of any accredited Illinois high school. Must write a 500-word essay on selected topic

Award: Scholarship for use in freshman year; not renewable. *Amount:* $50–$75.

Eligibility Requirements: Applicant must be high school student; planning to enroll or expecting to enroll full-time at an institution or university and resident of Illinois. Applicant or parent of applicant must be member of American Legion or Auxiliary. Available to U.S. citizens.

Application Requirements: Application, applicant must enter a contest, essay. *Deadline:* February 2.

Contact: Bill Bechtel, Assistant Adjutant
American Legion, Department of Illinois
PO Box 2910
Bloomington, IL 61702
Phone: 309-663-0361
Fax: 309-663-5783

AMERICAN LEGION, DEPARTMENT OF ILLINOIS SCHOLARSHIPS

Twenty $1000 scholarships for graduating students of Illinois high schools. May be used at any accredited college, university, trade or technical school. Applicant must be a child or grandchild of members of the American Legion Illinois. Awards will be based on academic merit and financial need. Applications available September 15 and must be returned prior to March 15.

Award: Scholarship for use in freshman year; not renewable. *Number:* up to 20. *Amount:* $1000.

Eligibility Requirements: Applicant must be high school student; planning to enroll or expecting to enroll full or part-time at a two-year or four-year or technical institution or university; resident of Illinois and studying in Illinois. Applicant or parent of applicant must be member of American Legion or Auxiliary. Available to U.S. citizens.

Application Requirements: Application, financial need analysis, photo, test scores, transcript. *Deadline:* March 15.

Contact: Bill Bechtel, Assistant Adjutant
American Legion, Department of Illinois
PO Box 2910
Bloomington, IL 61702
Phone: 309-663-0361
Fax: 309-663-5783

AMERICAN LEGION, DEPARTMENT OF ILLINOIS, BOY SCOUT/ EXPLORER SCHOLARSHIP

Scholarship for a graduating high school senior who is a qualified senior Boy Scout or Explorer and a resident of Illinois. Must write a 500-word essay on Legion's Americanism and Boy Scout programs. Deadline: April 30.

Award: Scholarship for use in freshman year; not renewable. *Number:* up to 5. *Amount:* $200–$1000.

Eligibility Requirements: Applicant must be high school student; planning to enroll or expecting to enroll full or part-time at a two-year or four-year or technical institution or university and resident of Illinois. Applicant or parent of applicant must be member of Boy Scouts. Available to U.S. citizens.

American Legion, Department of Illinois (continued)

Application Requirements: Application, applicant must enter a contest, essay. *Deadline:* April 30.

Contact: Bill Bechtel, Assistant Adjutant
American Legion, Department of Illinois
PO Box 2910
Bloomington, IL 61702
Phone: 309-663-0361
Fax: 309-663-5783

AMERICAN LEGION, DEPARTMENT OF IOWA
http://www.ialegion.org

AMERICAN LEGION DEPARTMENT OF IOWA EAGLE SCOUT OF THE YEAR SCHOLARSHIP

Three one-time award for Eagle Scouts who are residents of Iowa. Must be a high school student with minimum 2.5 GPA.

Award: Scholarship for use in freshman year; not renewable. *Number:* 4. *Amount:* $250–$1000.

Eligibility Requirements: Applicant must be high school student; planning to enroll or expecting to enroll full-time at a two-year or four-year institution or university; male and resident of Iowa. Applicant or parent of applicant must be member of Boy Scouts. Applicant must have 2.5 GPA or higher. Available to U.S. citizens.

Application Requirements: Application. *Deadline:* March 1.

Contact: Program Director
American Legion, Department of Iowa
720 Lyon Street
Des Moines, IA 50309
Phone: 515-282-5068

AMERICAN LEGION, DEPARTMENT OF KANSAS
http://www.ksamlegion.org

ALBERT M. LAPPIN SCHOLARSHIP

Scholarship for children of the members of Kansas American Legion or its Auxiliary. Membership has to have been active for the past three years. The children of deceased members are also eligible if parents' dues were paid up at time of death. Must be high school senior or college freshman or sophomore. Must use award at a Kansas college, university, or trade school.

Award: Scholarship for use in freshman or sophomore years; not renewable. *Number:* 1. *Amount:* $1000.

Eligibility Requirements: Applicant must be enrolled or expecting to enroll at a two-year or four-year or technical institution or university and studying in Kansas. Applicant or parent of applicant must be member of American Legion or Auxiliary. Available to U.S. citizens. Applicant or parent must meet one or more of the following requirements: general military experience; retired from active duty; disabled or killed as a result of military service; prisoner of war; or missing in action.

Application Requirements: Application, essay, financial need analysis, photo, transcript. *Deadline:* February 15.

Contact: Scholarship Administrator
American Legion, Department of Kansas
1314 Southwest Topeka Boulevard
Topeka, KS 66612-1886

HUGH A. SMITH SCHOLARSHIP FUND

Scholarship available to children of the Kansas American Legion or its Auxiliary members. Membership has to have been active for the past three years. Children of deceased members are also eligible if parents' dues were paid at time of death. Open to a high school senior or college freshman or sophomore. Award must be used at a Kansas university, college, or trade school. The applicant must be an average or better student scholastically, and must show a high school transcript with GPA.

Award: Scholarship for use in freshman or sophomore years; not renewable. *Number:* 1. *Amount:* $500.

Eligibility Requirements: Applicant must be enrolled or expecting to enroll at a two-year or four-year or technical institution or university and studying in Kansas. Applicant or parent of applicant must be member of American Legion or Auxiliary. Available to U.S. citizens. Applicant or parent must meet one or more of the following

requirements: general military experience; retired from active duty; disabled or killed as a result of military service; prisoner of war; or missing in action.

Application Requirements: Application, financial need analysis, photo, references, transcript. *Deadline:* February 15.

Contact: Scholarship Administrator
American Legion, Department of Kansas
1314 Southwest Topeka Boulevard
Topeka, KS 66612-1886

ROSEDALE POST 346 SCHOLARSHIP

Available to high school seniors, college level freshmen, or sophomores who are in need of educational assistance, and are enrolled or intend to enroll in an approved school located in the state of Kansas. The applicant must be the son or daughter of a veteran; the parent(s) must have been a member of the Kansas American Legion and/or Legion Auxiliary for the past three years. The sons or daughters of deceased members in either organization are also eligible if the parent's dues were paid up at the time of death. The applicant must be an average or better student scholastically.

Award: Scholarship for use in freshman or sophomore years; not renewable. *Number:* 2. *Amount:* $1500.

Eligibility Requirements: Applicant must be enrolled or expecting to enroll at a two-year or four-year or technical institution or university and studying in Kansas. Applicant or parent of applicant must be member of American Legion or Auxiliary. Available to U.S. citizens. Applicant or parent must meet one or more of the following requirements: general military experience; retired from active duty; disabled or killed as a result of military service; prisoner of war; or missing in action.

Application Requirements: Application, financial need analysis, photo, references, transcript. *Deadline:* February 15.

Contact: Scholarship Administrator
American Legion, Department of Kansas
1314 Southwest Topeka Boulevard
Topeka, KS 66612-1886

TED AND NORA ANDERSON SCHOLARSHIPS

Scholarship for children of American Legion or Auxiliary members. Must be high school seniors or college freshmen or sophomores. Scholarship for use at an approved Kansas college, university, or trade school. Must be Kansas resident.

Award: Scholarship for use in freshman or sophomore years; not renewable. *Number:* 4. *Amount:* $500.

Eligibility Requirements: Applicant must be enrolled or expecting to enroll at a two-year or four-year or technical institution or university; resident of Kansas and studying in Kansas. Applicant or parent of applicant must be member of American Legion or Auxiliary. Available to U.S. citizens. Applicant or parent must meet one or more of the following requirements: general military experience; retired from active duty; disabled or killed as a result of military service; prisoner of war; or missing in action.

Application Requirements: Application, financial need analysis, photo, references, transcript. *Deadline:* February 15.

Contact: Scholarship Administrator
American Legion, Department of Kansas
1314 Southwest Topeka Boulevard
Topeka, KS 66612-1886

AMERICAN LEGION, DEPARTMENT OF MAINE

JAMES V. DAY SCHOLARSHIP

One-time $500 award for a Maine resident whose parent is a member of the American Legion in Maine. Must be a U.S. citizen. Based on character and financial need. Minimum 2.5 GPA required.

Award: Scholarship for use in freshman, sophomore, junior, or senior years; not renewable. *Number:* 1. *Amount:* $500.

Eligibility Requirements: Applicant must be enrolled or expecting to enroll full-time at a two-year or four-year or technical institution or university and resident of Maine. Applicant or parent of applicant must be member of American Legion or Auxiliary. Applicant must have 2.5 GPA or higher. Available to U.S. citizens. Applicant or parent must meet one or more of the following requirements: general military experience; retired from active duty; disabled or killed as a result of military service; prisoner of war; or missing in action.

Application Requirements: Application, financial need analysis, references, transcript. *Deadline:* May 1.

Contact: Paul L'Heureux
American Legion, Department of Maine
12 Sherwood Drive, PO Box 900
Auburn, ME 04210

AMERICAN LEGION, DEPARTMENT OF MINNESOTA

AMERICAN LEGION DEPARTMENT OF MINNESOTA MEMORIAL SCHOLARSHIP

Scholarship available to Minnesota residents who are dependents of members of the Minnesota American Legion or Auxiliary. Award for study at a Minnesota institution or neighboring state with reciprocating agreement. One-time award of $500.

Award: Scholarship for use in freshman, sophomore, junior, or senior years; not renewable. *Number:* 6. *Amount:* $500.

Eligibility Requirements: Applicant must be enrolled or expecting to enroll full or part-time at a two-year or four-year or technical institution or university; resident of Minnesota and studying in Iowa, Minnesota, North Dakota, South Dakota, or Wisconsin. Applicant or parent of applicant must be member of American Legion or Auxiliary. Applicant must have 2.5 GPA or higher. Available to U.S. citizens. Applicant or parent must meet one or more of the following requirements: general military experience; retired from active duty; disabled or killed as a result of military service; prisoner of war; or missing in action.

Application Requirements: Application, essay, financial need analysis, references, transcript. *Deadline:* April 1.

Contact: Jennifer Kelley, Program Coordinator
American Legion, Department of Minnesota
20 West 12th Street, Room 300-A
St. Paul, MN 55155
Phone: 651-291-1800
Fax: 651-291-1057
E-mail: department@mnlegion.org

MINNESOTA LEGIONNAIRES INSURANCE TRUST SCHOLARSHIP

Scholarship for Minnesota residents who are veterans or dependents of veterans. Award for study at a Minnesota institution or neighboring state with reciprocating agreement. One-time award of $500. All applications must be approved and recommended by a post of the American Legion.

Award: Scholarship for use in sophomore, junior, or senior years; not renewable. *Number:* 3. *Amount:* $500.

Eligibility Requirements: Applicant must be enrolled or expecting to enroll full or part-time at a two-year or four-year or technical institution or university; resident of Minnesota and studying in Iowa, Minnesota, North Dakota, South Dakota, or Wisconsin. Applicant or parent of applicant must be member of American Legion or Auxiliary. Applicant must have 2.5 GPA or higher. Available to U.S. citizens. Applicant or parent must meet one or more of the following requirements: general military experience; retired from active duty; disabled or killed as a result of military service; prisoner of war; or missing in action.

Application Requirements: Application, essay, financial need analysis, references, transcript. *Deadline:* April 1.

Contact: Jennifer Kelley, Program Coordinator
American Legion, Department of Minnesota
20 West 12th Street, Room 300-A
St. Paul, MN 55155
Phone: 651-291-1800
Fax: 651-291-1057
E-mail: department@mnlegion.org

AMERICAN LEGION, DEPARTMENT OF MISSOURI
http://www.missourilegion.org

CHARLES L. BACON MEMORIAL SCHOLARSHIP

One-time $500 award given to current members of the American Legion, American Legion Auxiliary, Sons of the American Legion or the descendant of

CIVIC, PROFESSIONAL, SOCIAL, OR UNION AFFILIATION

a member of any of these organizations. Applicant must be under 21, not married, and must use scholarship as full-time student at accredited college or university. Applicant must be Missouri resident. Must submit proof of American Legion membership.

Award: Scholarship for use in freshman year; not renewable. *Number:* 2. *Amount:* $500.

Eligibility Requirements: Applicant must be age 20 or under; enrolled or expecting to enroll full-time at a four-year institution or university; single and resident of Missouri. Applicant or parent of applicant must be member of American Legion or Auxiliary. Available to U.S. citizens. Applicant or parent must meet one or more of the following requirements: general military experience; retired from active duty; disabled or killed as a result of military service; prisoner of war; or missing in action.

Application Requirements: Application, financial need analysis, test scores. *Deadline:* April 20.

Contact: Mr. John Doane, Chairman
American Legion, Department of Missouri
PO Box 179
Jefferson City, MO 65102
Phone: 417-924-8186
Fax: 573-893-2980

AMERICAN LEGION, DEPARTMENT OF NEBRASKA

MAYNARD JENSEN AMERICAN LEGION MEMORIAL SCHOLARSHIP

Scholarship for dependents or grandchildren of members, prisoner-of-war, missing-in-action veterans, killed-in-action veterans, or any deceased veterans of the American Legion. One-time award is based on academic achievement and financial need for Nebraska residents attending Nebraska institutions. Several scholarships of $500 each. Must have minimum 2.5 GPA and must submit school certification of GPA.

Award: Scholarship for use in freshman, sophomore, junior, or senior years; not renewable. *Number:* 1–10. *Amount:* $500.

Eligibility Requirements: Applicant must be enrolled or expecting to enroll full-time at a two-year or four-year or technical institution or university; resident of Nebraska and studying in Nebraska. Applicant or parent of applicant must be member of American Legion or Auxiliary. Applicant must have 2.5 GPA or higher. Available to U.S. citizens. Applicant or parent must meet one or more of the following requirements: general military experience; retired from active duty; disabled or killed as a result of military service; prisoner of war; or missing in action.

Application Requirements: Application, financial need analysis. *Deadline:* March 1.

Contact: Burdette Burkhart, Activities Director
American Legion, Department of Nebraska
PO Box 5205
Lincoln, NE 68505-0205
Phone: 402-464-6338
Fax: 402-464-6330
E-mail: actdirlegion@alltel.net

AMERICAN LEGION, DEPARTMENT OF OHIO
http://www.ohioamericanlegion.org

AMERICAN LEGION SCHOLARSHIP—OHIO

For descendants of Ohio Legionnaires only. Nonrenewable award for full-time study only. Must rank in upper third of class or have a minimum 3.0 GPA. Must include descendancy proofs. Deadline: April 15.

Award: Scholarship for use in freshman, sophomore, junior, or senior years; not renewable. *Number:* 15–20. *Amount:* $2000–$3000.

Eligibility Requirements: Applicant must be enrolled or expecting to enroll at a two-year or four-year or technical institution or university. Applicant or parent of applicant must be member of American Legion or Auxiliary. Applicant must have 3.5 GPA or higher. Available to U.S. and non-U.S. citizens.

Peterson's Scholarships, Grants & Prizes 2007 **489**

American Legion, Department of Ohio (continued)

Application Requirements: Application, test scores, transcript, proof of decendency. *Deadline:* April 15.

Contact: Donald Lanthorn, Service Director
American Legion, Department of Ohio
PO Box 8007
Delaware, OH 43015-8007
Phone: 740-362-7478
Fax: 740-362-1429
E-mail: dlanthorn@iwaynet.net

AMERICAN LEGION, DEPARTMENT OF PENNSYLVANIA   http://www.pa-legion.com

JOSEPH P. GAVENONIS COLLEGE SCHOLARSHIP (PLAN I)

Scholarships for Pennsylvania residents seeking a four-year degree from a Pennsylvania college or university. Must be the child of a member of a Pennsylvania American Legion post. Must be a graduating high school senior. Award amount and number of awards determined annually. Renewable award. Must maintain 2.5 GPA in college.

Award: Scholarship for use in freshman, sophomore, junior, or senior years; renewable. *Amount:* $500–$1000.

Eligibility Requirements: Applicant must be high school student; planning to enroll or expecting to enroll full-time at a four-year institution or university; resident of Pennsylvania and studying in Pennsylvania. Applicant or parent of applicant must be member of American Legion or Auxiliary. Applicant must have 2.5 GPA or higher. Available to U.S. citizens.

Application Requirements: Application, financial need analysis, test scores, transcript. *Deadline:* May 30.

Contact: James H. Hales, Jr., Department Commander
American Legion, Department of Pennsylvania
PO Box 2324
Harrisburg, PA 17105-2324
Phone: 717-730-9100
Fax: 717-975-2836
E-mail: hq@pa-legion.com

AMERICAN LEGION, DEPARTMENT OF VERMONT   http://www.legionvthq.com/

AMERICAN LEGION EAGLE SCOUT OF THE YEAR

Awarded to the Boy Scout chosen for outstanding service to his religious institution, school, and community. Must receive the Eagle Scout Award and reside in Vermont.

Award: Scholarship for use in freshman year; not renewable. *Number:* 1. *Amount:* $1000.

Eligibility Requirements: Applicant must be high school student; planning to enroll or expecting to enroll at an institution or university and resident of Vermont. Applicant or parent of applicant must be member of Boy Scouts. Applicant or parent of applicant must have employment or volunteer experience in community service. Available to U.S. citizens.

Application Requirements: Application, photo. *Deadline:* March 1.

Contact: Richard Gray, Boy Scout Committee Chairman
American Legion, Department of Vermont
PO Box 396
Montpelier, VT 05601-0396
Phone: 802-223-7131
Fax: 802-223-0318
E-mail: alvt@sover.net

AMERICAN LEGION, DEPARTMENT OF WASHINGTON   http://www.walegion.org

AMERICAN LEGION DEPARTMENT OF WASHINGTON CHILDREN AND YOUTH SCHOLARSHIPS

One-time award for the son or daughter of a Washington American Legion or Auxiliary member, living or deceased. Must be high school senior planning to attend an accredited institution of higher education in Washington. Award based on need. Must be Washington resident.

Award: Scholarship for use in freshman year; not renewable. *Number:* 2. *Amount:* $1500–$2500.

Eligibility Requirements: Applicant must be high school student; planning to enroll or expecting to enroll full-time at an institution or university; resident of Washington and studying in Washington. Applicant or parent of applicant must be member of American Legion or Auxiliary. Available to U.S. citizens. Applicant or parent must meet one or more of the following requirements: general military experience; retired from active duty; disabled or killed as a result of military service; prisoner of war; or missing in action.

Application Requirements: Application, financial need analysis, transcript. *Deadline:* April 1.

Contact: Thomas Conner, Administrative Assistant
American Legion, Department of Washington
PO Box 3917
Lacey, WA 98509-3917
E-mail: tomal@qwest.net

AMERICAN LEGION, DEPARTMENT OF WEST VIRGINIA

WILLIAM F. "BILL" JOHNSON MEMORIAL SCHOLARSHIP SPONSORED BY SONS OF THE AMERICAN LEGION

Essay based on a different question each year. Award given second semester of college providing winner has passing grades first semester. Must be a resident of West Virginia and the child or grandchild of a member of The American Legion. Deadline is March 15.

Award: Scholarship for use in freshman year; not renewable. *Number:* 1. *Amount:* $1000.

Eligibility Requirements: Applicant must be high school student; planning to enroll or expecting to enroll full-time at a two-year or four-year institution or university and resident of West Virginia. Applicant or parent of applicant must be member of American Legion or Auxiliary. Available to U.S. citizens. Applicant or parent must meet one or more of the following requirements: general military experience; retired from active duty; disabled or killed as a result of military service; prisoner of war; or missing in action.

Application Requirements: Application, essay, transcript. *Deadline:* March 15.

Contact: Miles Epling, State Adjutant
American Legion, Department of West Virginia
2016 Kanawha Boulevard East
Charleston, WV 25311-3191
Phone: 304-343-7591
Fax: 304-343-7592
E-mail: wvlegion@aol.com

AMERICAN LEGION, NATIONAL HEADQUARTERS   http://www.legion.org

AMERICAN LEGION NATIONAL HEADQUARTERS EAGLE SCOUT OF THE YEAR

Several scholarships for registered Eagle Scouts of American Legion-sponsored troops or American Legion families. Must be active in religious institution and have rendered outstanding school, community, and church service. Four one-time awards of $2500-$10,000. Applicant must be in high school and be at least 15 years old and no older than 18 years old.

Award: Scholarship for use in freshman, sophomore, junior, or senior years; not renewable. *Number:* 4. *Amount:* $2500–$10,000.

Eligibility Requirements: Applicant must be high school student; age 15-18; planning to enroll or expecting to enroll full-time at a four-year institution or university and male. Applicant or parent of applicant must be member of American Legion or Auxiliary or Boy Scouts. Applicant or parent of applicant must have employment or volunteer experience in community service. Available to U.S. citizens.

Application Requirements: Application, essay, references, transcript. *Deadline:* March 1.

Contact: Michael Buss, Assistant Director
American Legion, National Headquarters
PO Box 1055
Indianapolis, IN 46206-1055
Phone: 317-630-1249
Fax: 317-630-1369
E-mail: acy@legion.org

AMERICAN POSTAL WORKERS UNION
http://www.apwu.org

VOCATIONAL SCHOLARSHIP PROGRAM

A scholarship for a child, grandchild, stepchild, or legally adopted child of an active member, Retiree's Department member, or deceased member of the American Postal Workers Union. Applicant must be a senior attending high school who plans on attending an accredited vocational school or community college vocational program as a full-time student. The award is $1000 per year consecutively or until completion of the course, with the total not exceeding $3000. For additional information see Web site http://www.apwu.org

Award: Scholarship for use in freshman or sophomore years. *Number:* 1. *Amount:* $1000.

Eligibility Requirements: Applicant must be high school student and planning to enroll or expecting to enroll at a two-year or technical institution. Applicant or parent of applicant must be member of American Postal Workers Union. Applicant or parent of applicant must have employment or volunteer experience in federal/postal service. Available to U.S. citizens.

Application Requirements: Application, transcript. *Deadline:* March 15.

Contact: Terry Stapleton, Secretary/Treasurer
American Postal Workers Union
1300 L Street, NW
Washington, DC 20005
Phone: 202-842-4215
Fax: 202-842-8530

AMERICAN QUARTER HORSE FOUNDATION (AQHF)
http://www.aqha.org/aqhya

AMERICAN QUARTER HORSE FOUNDATION YOUTH SCHOLARSHIPS

$8000 scholarships to AQHYA members who have belonged for three or more years. The recipient will receive $2000 per year for four years. Minimum 2.5 GPA required. Members must apply during their senior year of high school or home school equivalency. Applicants must rank within the upper 25% of their high school graduating class. Students currently enrolled as a first year college freshman are not eligible for consideration.

Award: Scholarship for use in freshman, sophomore, junior, or senior years; renewable. *Number:* 1–30. *Amount:* $8000.

Eligibility Requirements: Applicant must be high school student and planning to enroll or expecting to enroll full-time at a two-year or four-year or technical institution or university. Applicant or parent of applicant must be member of American Quarter Horse Association. Applicant must have 2.5 GPA or higher. Available to U.S. and Canadian citizens.

Application Requirements: Application, financial need analysis, photo, references, transcript. *Deadline:* February 1.

Contact: Laura Owens, Scholarship Coordinator
American Quarter Horse Foundation (AQHF)
2601 I-40 East
Amarillo, TX 79104
Phone: 806-378-5034
Fax: 806-376-1005
E-mail: lowens@aqha.org

AQHF WORKING STUDENT SCHOLARSHIP

Must be member of AQHA or AQHYA who plans to work a minimum of 200 hours per school year. Recipient receives $2000 per year for a four-year degree plan. Minimum 2.5 GPA required.

Award: Scholarship for use in freshman year; renewable. *Number:* 1. *Amount:* $2000.

Eligibility Requirements: Applicant must be enrolled or expecting to enroll full-time at a two-year or four-year or technical institution or

university. Applicant or parent of applicant must be member of American Quarter Horse Association. Applicant must have 2.5 GPA or higher. Available to U.S. and Canadian citizens.

Application Requirements: Application, financial need analysis, photo, references, transcript. *Deadline:* February 1.

Contact: Laura Owens, Scholarship Coordinator
American Quarter Horse Foundation (AQHF)
2601 I-40 East
Amarillo, TX 79104
Phone: 806-376-5181
Fax: 806-376-1005
E-mail: lowens@aqha.org

ARIZONA QUARTER HORSE YOUTH RACING SCHOLARSHIP

Renewable scholarship to a current AQHA or AQHYA member who lives in the state of Arizona. The recipient will receive $500 per year. Must be a full-time undergraduate. Minimum 2.5 GPA required.

Award: Scholarship for use in freshman or sophomore years; renewable. *Number:* 1. *Amount:* $500.

Eligibility Requirements: Applicant must be enrolled or expecting to enroll full-time at a two-year or four-year or technical institution or university and resident of Arizona. Applicant or parent of applicant must be member of American Quarter Horse Association. Applicant must have 2.5 GPA or higher. Available to U.S. citizens.

Application Requirements: Application, driver's license, financial need analysis, photo, references, transcript, copy of driver's license or voter registration. *Deadline:* February 1.

Contact: Laura Owens, Scholarship Coordinator
American Quarter Horse Foundation (AQHF)
2601 I-40 East
Amarillo, TX 79104
Phone: 806-378-5034
Fax: 806-376-1005
E-mail: lowens@aqha.org

DR. GERALD O'CONNOR MICHIGAN SCHOLARSHIP

Must be current member of AQHA or AQHYA who lives in Michigan. Recipient receives $500 per year for a four-year degree plan. This scholarship is awarded every four years. Minimum 2.5 GPA required.

Award: Scholarship for use in freshman, sophomore, junior, or senior years; renewable. *Number:* 1. *Amount:* $2000.

Eligibility Requirements: Applicant must be enrolled or expecting to enroll full-time at a two-year or four-year or technical institution or university and resident of Michigan. Applicant or parent of applicant must be member of American Quarter Horse Association. Applicant must have 2.5 GPA or higher. Available to U.S. citizens.

Application Requirements: Application, driver's license, financial need analysis, photo, references, transcript, copy of driver's license or voter registration. *Deadline:* February 1.

Contact: Laura Owens, Scholarship Coordinator
American Quarter Horse Foundation (AQHF)
2601 I-40 East
Amarillo, TX 79104
Phone: 806-378-5034
Fax: 806-376-1005
E-mail: lowens@aqha.org

EXCELLENCE IN EQUINE/AGRICULTURAL INVOLVEMENT SCHOLARSHIP

$25,000 scholarship to a current Member of AQHYA or AQHA from a farming or ranching family who exemplifies the qualities developed through a lifetime involvement with horses and agriculture. The recipient will receive $6250 per year for a four-year degree plan if recipient maintains a 3.5 GPA.

Award: Scholarship for use in freshman, sophomore, junior, or senior years; renewable. *Number:* 1. *Amount:* $25,000.

Eligibility Requirements: Applicant must be enrolled or expecting to enroll full-time at a two-year or four-year or technical institution or university. Applicant or parent of applicant must be member of American Quarter Horse Association. Applicant or parent of applicant must have employment or volunteer experience in farming. Applicant must have 2.5 GPA or higher. Available to U.S. and Canadian citizens.

Application Requirements: Application, financial need analysis, photo, references, transcript, telephone interview. *Deadline:* February 1.

American Quarter Horse Foundation (AQHF) (continued)

Contact: Laura Owens, Scholarship Coordinator
American Quarter Horse Foundation (AQHF)
2601 I-40 East
Amarillo, TX 79104
Phone: 806-378-5034
Fax: 806-376-1005
E-mail: lowens@aqha.org

FARM AND RANCH HERITAGE SCHOLARSHIP

$12,500 scholarship to current AQHYA or AQHA Members from farm or ranch backgrounds. The recipients will receive $3,125 per year for a four-year degree plan if the recipient maintains a 3.0 GPA.

Award: Scholarship for use in freshman, sophomore, junior, or senior years; renewable. *Number:* 1–2. *Amount:* $12,500.

Eligibility Requirements: Applicant must be enrolled or expecting to enroll full-time at a two-year or four-year or technical institution or university. Applicant or parent of applicant must be member of American Quarter Horse Association. Applicant or parent of applicant must have employment or volunteer experience in farming. Applicant must have 3.0 GPA or higher. Available to U.S. and Canadian citizens.

Application Requirements: Application, financial need analysis, photo, references, transcript. *Deadline:* February 1.

Contact: Laura Owens, Scholarship Coordinator
American Quarter Horse Foundation (AQHF)
2601 I-40 East
Amarillo, TX 79104
Phone: 806-378-5034
Fax: 806-376-1005
E-mail: lowens@aqha.org

GUY STOOPS MEMORIAL PROFESSIONAL HORSEMEN'S FAMILY SCHOLARSHIP

$500 will be awarded to the child of an AQHA Professional Horseman. Applicant must be AQHA member for three or more years. Minimum 2.5 GPA.

Award: Scholarship for use in freshman or sophomore years; renewable. *Number:* 2. *Amount:* $500.

Eligibility Requirements: Applicant must be enrolled or expecting to enroll full-time at a two-year or four-year or technical institution or university. Applicant or parent of applicant must be member of American Quarter Horse Association or Professional Horsemen Association. Applicant or parent of applicant must have employment or volunteer experience in designated career field. Applicant must have 2.5 GPA or higher. Available to U.S. and Canadian citizens.

Application Requirements: Application, financial need analysis, photo, references, transcript. *Deadline:* February 1.

Contact: Laura Owens
Phone: 806-378-5034
E-mail: lowens@aqha.org

INDIANA QUARTER HORSE YOUTH SCHOLARSHIP

$1000 scholarship to a current AQHYA member who lives in the state of Indiana. The recipient will receive $1000 for one year. Minimum 2.5 GPA required.

Award: Scholarship for use in freshman, sophomore, junior, or senior years; not renewable. *Number:* 1. *Amount:* $1000.

Eligibility Requirements: Applicant must be enrolled or expecting to enroll full-time at a two-year or four-year or technical institution or university and resident of Indiana. Applicant or parent of applicant must be member of American Quarter Horse Association. Applicant must have 2.5 GPA or higher. Available to U.S. citizens.

Application Requirements: Application, driver's license, financial need analysis, photo, references, transcript, copy of driver's license or voter registration. *Deadline:* February 1.

Contact: Laura Owens, Scholarship Coordinator
American Quarter Horse Foundation (AQHF)
2601 I-40 East
Amarillo, TX 79104
Phone: 806-378-5034
Fax: 806-376-1005
E-mail: lowens@aqha.org

JOAN CAIN FLORIDA QUARTER HORSE YOUTH SCHOLARSHIP

$1000 awarded to AQHA member from Florida. Minimum 2.5 GPA. Must be member of Florida Quarter Horse Youth Association.

Award: Scholarship for use in freshman, sophomore, junior, or senior years; renewable. *Number:* 1. *Amount:* $1000.

Eligibility Requirements: Applicant must be enrolled or expecting to enroll full-time at a two-year or four-year or technical institution or university and resident of Florida. Applicant or parent of applicant must be member of American Quarter Horse Association. Applicant must have 2.5 GPA or higher. Available to U.S. citizens.

Application Requirements: Application, driver's license, photo, references, transcript, membership card, copy of driver's license or voter registration. *Deadline:* February 1.

Contact: Laura Owens
Phone: 806-378-5034
E-mail: lowens@aqha.org

NEBRASKA QUARTER HORSE YOUTH SCHOLARSHIP

$2000 scholarship to a current AQHYA Member who lives in the state of Nebraska. The recipient will receive $500 per year for a four-year degree plan. Members may apply during their senior year of high school or while enrolled at an accredited college, university or vocational school. Applicants must provide evidence of a minimum cumulative 2.5 grade point average.

Award: Scholarship for use in freshman, sophomore, junior, or senior years; renewable. *Number:* 1. *Amount:* $2000.

Eligibility Requirements: Applicant must be enrolled or expecting to enroll full-time at a two-year or four-year or technical institution or university and resident of Nebraska. Applicant or parent of applicant must be member of American Quarter Horse Association. Applicant must have 2.5 GPA or higher. Available to U.S. citizens.

Application Requirements: Application, driver's license, financial need analysis, photo, references, transcript. *Deadline:* February 1.

Contact: Laura Owens, Scholarship Coordinator
American Quarter Horse Foundation (AQHF)
2601 I-40 East
Amarillo, TX 79104
Phone: 806-378-5034
Fax: 806-376-1005
E-mail: lowens@aqha.org

RAY MELTON MEMORIAL VIRGINIA QUARTER HORSE YOUTH SCHOLARSHIP

Must be member of AQHA or AQHYA who resides in Virginia. Recipient receives $500 for one year. Minimum 2.5 GPA required.

Award: Scholarship for use in freshman, sophomore, junior, or senior years; renewable. *Number:* 1. *Amount:* $500.

Eligibility Requirements: Applicant must be enrolled or expecting to enroll full-time at a two-year or four-year or technical institution or university and resident of Virginia. Applicant or parent of applicant must be member of American Quarter Horse Association. Applicant must have 2.5 GPA or higher. Available to U.S. citizens.

Application Requirements: Application, driver's license, financial need analysis, photo, references, transcript, copy of driver's license or voter registration. *Deadline:* February 1.

Contact: Laura Owens, Scholarship Coordinator
American Quarter Horse Foundation (AQHF)
2601 I-40 East
Amarillo, TX 79104
Phone: 806-378-5034
Fax: 806-376-1005
E-mail: lowens@aqha.org

SWAYZE WOODRUFF SCHOLARSHIP

Must be member of AQHA or AQHYA who resides in Alabama, Tennessee, Louisiana, Mississippi, or Arkansas. Recipient receives $2000 per year for four-year degree plan. Must be renewed annually.

Award: Scholarship for use in freshman year; renewable. *Number:* 1. *Amount:* $8000.

Eligibility Requirements: Applicant must be enrolled or expecting to enroll full-time at a two-year or four-year or technical institution or university and resident of Alabama, Arkansas, Louisiana, Mississippi, or Tennessee. Applicant or parent of applicant must be member of American Quarter Horse Association. Applicant must have 2.5 GPA or higher. Available to U.S. citizens.

Application Requirements: Application, driver's license, financial need analysis, photo, references, transcript, copy of driver's license or voter registration. *Deadline:* February 1.

Contact: Laura Owens, Scholarship Coordinator
American Quarter Horse Foundation (AQHF)
2601 I-40 East
Amarillo, TX 79104
Phone: 806-378-5034
Fax: 806-376-1005
E-mail: lowens@aqha.org

AMERICAN SOCIETY OF TRAVEL AGENTS (ASTA) FOUNDATION   http://www.astanet.com

ARIZONA CHAPTER DEPENDENT/EMPLOYEE MEMBERSHIP SCHOLARSHIP

One-time award for dependents of active members or employees of an American Society of Travel Agents member in Arizona. Major in travel and tourism is not required. Must be resident of Arizona. Submit proof of employment and membership, as well as a 500-word essay on career goals. Must attend Arizona institution. For requirements and an application form, visit Web site: http://www.astanet.com/education/edu_scholarships.asp. Minimum 2.5 GPA required.

Award: Scholarship for use in junior or senior years; not renewable. *Number:* 1. *Amount:* $1500.

Eligibility Requirements: Applicant must be enrolled or expecting to enroll full or part-time at a two-year or four-year institution or university; resident of Arizona and studying in Arizona. Applicant or parent of applicant must be member of American Society of Travel Agents. Applicant or parent of applicant must have employment or volunteer experience in designated career field. Applicant must have 2.5 GPA or higher. Available to U.S. citizens.

Application Requirements: Application, driver's license, essay, references, transcript. *Deadline:* August 16.

Contact: Verlette Mitchell, Manager
American Society of Travel Agents (ASTA) Foundation
1101 King Street
Alexandria, VA 22314-2187
Phone: 703-739-8721
Fax: 703-684-8319
E-mail: scholarship@astahq.com

AMERICAN WATER SKI EDUCATIONAL FOUNDATION   http://www.waterskihalloffame.com

AMERICAN WATER SKI EDUCATIONAL FOUNDATION SCHOLARSHIP

Six awards for incoming college sophomores through incoming seniors who are members of U.S.A Waterski. Award based upon academics, leadership, extracurricular activities, recommendations, and financial need. One-time award of $1500.

Award: Scholarship for use in freshman, sophomore, junior, or senior years; not renewable. *Number:* 6. *Amount:* $1500.

Eligibility Requirements: Applicant must be enrolled or expecting to enroll full-time at a two-year or four-year institution and must have an interest in leadership. Applicant or parent of applicant must be member of USA Water Ski. Available to U.S. citizens.

Application Requirements: Application, essay, financial need analysis, references, transcript. *Deadline:* April 1.

Contact: Carole Lowe, Scholarship Director
American Water Ski Educational Foundation
1251 Holy Cow Road
Polk City, FL 33868-8200
Phone: 863-324-2472
Fax: 863-324-3996
E-mail: awsefhalloffame@cs.com

AMVETS AUXILIARY   http://www.amvetsaux.org

AMVETS NATIONAL LADIES AUXILIARY SCHOLARSHIP

One-time award of up to $1000 for a member of AMVETS or the Auxiliary. Applicant may also be the family member of a member. Award for full-time study at any accredited U.S. institution. Minimum 2.5 GPA required.

Award: Scholarship for use in sophomore, junior, or senior years; not renewable. *Number:* 7. *Amount:* $750–$1000.

Eligibility Requirements: Applicant must be enrolled or expecting to enroll full-time at a two-year or four-year or technical institution or university. Applicant or parent of applicant must be member of AMVETS Auxiliary. Applicant must have 2.5 GPA or higher. Available to U.S. citizens.

Application Requirements: Application, essay, references, transcript. *Deadline:* June 1.

Contact: Scholarship Officer
AMVETS Auxiliary
4647 Forbes Boulevard
Lanham, MD 20706-4380
Phone: 301-459-6255
Fax: 877-726-8387

APPALOOSA HORSE CLUB-APPALOOSA YOUTH PROGRAM   http://www.appaloosa.com

APPALOOSA YOUTH EDUCATIONAL SCHOLARSHIPS

Applicants must be members or dependents of members of the Appaloosa Youth Association or Appaloosa Horse Club. Based on academics, leadership, sportsmanship, and horsemanship. Send picture with application.

Award: Scholarship for use in freshman, sophomore, junior, senior, or graduate years; not renewable. *Number:* 6–8. *Amount:* $1000.

Eligibility Requirements: Applicant must be enrolled or expecting to enroll full-time at a two-year or four-year institution or university and must have an interest in animal/agricultural competition or leadership. Applicant or parent of applicant must be member of Appaloosa Horse Club/Appaloosa Youth Association. Applicant must have 2.5 GPA or higher. Available to U.S. citizens.

Application Requirements: Application, essay, photo, references, test scores, transcript. *Deadline:* June 10.

Contact: Keeley Gant, AYF Coordinator
Appaloosa Horse Club-Appaloosa Youth Program
2720 West Pullman Road
Moscow, ID 83843
Phone: 208-882-5578 Ext. 264
Fax: 208-882-8150
E-mail: aphc@appaloosa.com

ARBY'S FOUNDATION, BIG BROTHERS BIG SISTERS OF AMERICA   http://www.bbbsa.org

ARBY'S-BIG BROTHERS BIG SISTERS SCHOLARSHIP AWARD

Designed to assist exemplary high school students from low and middle-income families. Applicants must be or have been a Little Brother or Little Sister in the Big Brothers or Big Sisters program. Write for more information. Merit considered. Renewable scholarships of up to $5000. Must rank in upper half of class or have a minimum 2.5 GPA.

Award: Scholarship for use in freshman year; renewable. *Number:* 2. *Amount:* $1000–$5000.

Eligibility Requirements: Applicant must be enrolled or expecting to enroll full-time at a two-year or four-year institution or university. Applicant or parent of applicant must be member of Big Brothers/Big Sisters. Applicant or parent of applicant must have employment or volunteer experience in community service. Applicant must have 2.5 GPA or higher. Available to U.S. citizens.

Arby's Foundation, Big Brothers Big Sisters of America (continued)

Application Requirements: Application, essay, financial need analysis, photo, references, test scores, transcript. *Deadline:* March 31.

Contact: Robin Palley, Vice President Of Business Development
Arby's Foundation, Big Brothers Big Sisters of America
230 North 13th Street
Philadelphia, PA 19107
Phone: 215-567-7000
Fax: 215-567-0394
E-mail: national@bbbsa.org

ARRL FOUNDATION, INC.   http://www.arrl.org/arrlf/scholgen.html

IRARC MEMORIAL/JOSEPH P. RUBINO, WA4MMD, SCHOLARSHIP

Need-based award available to students who are licensed amateur radio operators. Residence in Brevard County, Florida preferred, Florida residence required. Must maintain 2.5 GPA and pursue undergraduate degree or electronic technician certification.

Award: Scholarship for use in freshman, sophomore, junior, or senior years; not renewable. *Number:* varies. *Amount:* $750.

Eligibility Requirements: Applicant must be enrolled or expecting to enroll full-time at a two-year or four-year or technical institution or university; resident of Florida and must have an interest in amateur radio. Applicant or parent of applicant must be member of American Radio Relay League. Applicant must have 2.5 GPA or higher. Available to U.S. citizens.

Application Requirements: Application, financial need analysis, transcript. *Deadline:* February 1.

Contact: Mary Hobart, Secretary Foundation
ARRL Foundation, Inc.
225 Main Street
Newington, CT 06111-1494
Phone: 860-594-0397
E-mail: k1mmh@arrl.org

YANKEE CLIPPER CONTEST CLUB, INC. YOUTH SCHOLARSHIP

One-time award available to students who are licensed as general class or higher amateur radio operators and who live or attend college in the 175-mile radius of YCCC Center. Qualifying area includes all of MA, RI, CT and Long Island NY, most of VT and NH, portions of ME, eastern NY, and extreme north-eastern sections of PA and NJ.

Award: Scholarship for use in freshman, sophomore, junior, or senior years; not renewable. *Number:* 1. *Amount:* $1500–$2000.

Eligibility Requirements: Applicant must be enrolled or expecting to enroll full-time at a two-year or four-year or technical institution or university and must have an interest in amateur radio. Applicant or parent of applicant must be member of American Radio Relay League. Available to U.S. citizens.

Application Requirements: Application, transcript. *Deadline:* February 1.

Contact: Mary Hobart, Secretary Foundation
ARRL Foundation, Inc.
225 Main Street
Newington, CT 06111-1494
Phone: 860-594-0397
E-mail: k1mmh@arrl.org

YOU'VE GOT A FRIEND IN PENNSYLVANIA SCHOLARSHIP

One-time award available to students who are licensed as general amateur radio operators and who are members of the American Radio Relay League. Residents of Pennsylvania preferred.

Award: Scholarship for use in freshman, sophomore, junior, or senior years; not renewable. *Number:* 1. *Amount:* $1000.

Eligibility Requirements: Applicant must be enrolled or expecting to enroll full-time at a two-year or four-year or technical institution or university and must have an interest in amateur radio. Applicant or parent of applicant must be member of American Radio Relay League. Available to U.S. citizens.

Application Requirements: Application, transcript. *Deadline:* February 1.

Contact: Mary Hobart, Secretary Foundation
ARRL Foundation, Inc.
225 Main Street
Newington, CT 06111-1494
Phone: 860-594-0397
E-mail: k1mmh@arrl.org

ASSOCIATION OF AMERICAN GEOGRAPHERS   http://www.aag.org

ANNE U. WHITE FUND

Grants are available to AAG members who have held membership for at least two years. Must submit a summary of results no later then twelve months after receiving award. For more details see Web site: http://www.aag.org/Grantsawards/Annewhitefund.html

Award: Grant for use in freshman, sophomore, junior, senior, graduate, or postgraduate years; not renewable. *Number:* 6. *Amount:* $1000–$1500.

Eligibility Requirements: Applicant must be enrolled or expecting to enroll at a four-year institution or university. Applicant or parent of applicant must be member of Association of American Geographers. Available to U.S. citizens.

Application Requirements: Application, essay, 9 completed applications. *Deadline:* December 31.

Contact: Ehsan M. Khater
Association of American Geographers
AAG Office, 1710 16th Street, NW
Washington, DC 20009-3198
Phone: 202-234-1450
Fax: 202-234-2744
E-mail: ekhater@aag.org

BOY SCOUTS OF AMERICA/ORDER OF THE ARROW

E. URNER GOODMAN SCHOLARSHIP

Renewable aid to members of Order of the Arrow planning professional career with Boy Scouts. Submit 250 to 500-word essay on reasons for pursuing Boy Scouts of America career, proof of college acceptance for undergraduate study, and resume. Merit-based award.

Award: Scholarship for use in freshman, sophomore, junior, or senior years; renewable. *Number:* 3–6. *Amount:* $1000–$4000.

Eligibility Requirements: Applicant must be enrolled or expecting to enroll full-time at a four-year institution and male. Applicant or parent of applicant must be member of Boy Scouts or Order of the Arrow. Applicant must have 2.5 GPA or higher. Available to U.S. citizens.

Application Requirements: Application, autobiography, essay, photo, resume, references, self-addressed stamped envelope, test scores, transcript. *Deadline:* January 15.

Contact: Clyde Mayer, National Director
Boy Scouts of America/Order of the Arrow
1325 West Walnut Hill Lane
Irving, TX 75038-3008
Phone: 972-580-2438
Fax: 972-580-2399
E-mail: cmayer@netbsa.org

BOYS & GIRLS CLUBS OF AMERICA   http://www.bgca.org

BOYS & GIRLS CLUBS OF AMERICA NATIONAL YOUTH OF THE YEAR AWARD

This nonrenewable award is available to youths 14-18 who have been active members of their Boys Club or Girls Club for at least one year. Contact local club for nomination form. Minimum 3.0 GPA required. Must be nominated by local club.

Award: Scholarship for use in freshman, sophomore, junior, or senior years; not renewable. *Number:* 5. *Amount:* up to $10,000.

Eligibility Requirements: Applicant must be high school student; age 14-18; planning to enroll or expecting to enroll full or part-time at a two-year or four-year or technical institution; single and must have an interest in leadership. Applicant or parent of applicant must be member of Boys or Girls Club. Applicant must have 3.0 GPA or higher. Available to U.S. citizens.

Application Requirements: Application, essay, interview, references. *Deadline:* varies.

Contact: Kelvin Davis, Program Services Director
Boys & Girls Clubs of America
1230 West Peachtree Street, NW
Atlanta, GA 30309

BOYS AND GIRLS CLUBS OF CHICAGO
http://www.bgcc.org

BOYS AND GIRLS CLUBS OF CHICAGO SCHOLARSHIPS

Boys and Girls Clubs of Chicago scholarships are awarded to graduating high school seniors who are local Club members. Scholarships are based upon academic achievement, Club involvement, financial need, and personal interviews. Students are asked to maintain their grades, seek internships and job opportunities, and lend guidance to younger children.

Award: Scholarship for use in freshman, sophomore, junior, or senior years; renewable. *Number:* varies. *Amount:* $3000–$5000.

Eligibility Requirements: Applicant must be high school student; planning to enroll or expecting to enroll full or part-time at a two-year or four-year or technical institution or university and resident of Illinois. Applicant or parent of applicant must be member of Boys or Girls Club. Applicant must have 2.5 GPA or higher. Available to U.S. citizens.

Contact: LaKesha Nelson, Project Director
Boys and Girls Clubs of Chicago
550 West Van Buren Street, Suite 350
Chicago, IL 60607
Phone: 312-235-8000
Fax: 312-427-4110
E-mail: lnelson@bgcc.org

BUFFALO AFL-CIO COUNCIL

AFL-CIO COUNCIL OF BUFFALO SCHOLARSHIP

One-time award of $1000 for a high school senior who is a son or daughter of a member of a local union affiliated with the Buffalo AFL-CIO Council. Must be a New York resident and use award for study in New York. Write for more information. March deadline.

Award: Scholarship for use in freshman year; not renewable. *Number:* 1. *Amount:* $1000.

Eligibility Requirements: Applicant must be high school student; planning to enroll or expecting to enroll full-time at a two-year or four-year institution; resident of New York and studying in New York. Applicant or parent of applicant must be member of AFL-CIO. Available to U.S. citizens.

Application Requirements: Application, essay, references, transcript. *Deadline:* March 14.

Contact: Scholarship Director
Buffalo AFL-CIO Council
295 Main Street
Buffalo, NY 14203
Phone: 716-852-0375
Fax: 716-855-1802

CALIFORNIA GRANGE FOUNDATION
http://www.californiagrange.org

CALIFORNIA GRANGE FOUNDATION SCHOLARSHIP

Scholarship program available for Grange members residing in California who wish to attend a higher institution of learning of their choice. Visit Web site for additional information and to download scholarship applications.

Award: Scholarship for use in freshman, sophomore, junior, or senior years; renewable. *Number:* 5–15. *Amount:* $500–$1000.

Eligibility Requirements: Applicant must be enrolled or expecting to enroll full or part-time at a two-year or four-year or technical institution or university and resident of California. Applicant or parent of applicant must be member of Grange Association. Available to U.S. citizens.

Application Requirements: Application, financial need analysis, references, transcript. *Deadline:* April 1.

Contact: California Grange Foundation
2101 Stockton Boulevard
Sacramento, CA 95817
Phone: 916-454-5805
Fax: 916-739-8189

CALIFORNIA TEACHERS ASSOCIATION (CTA)
http://www.cta.org

CALIFORNIA TEACHERS ASSOCIATION SCHOLARSHIP FOR DEPENDENT CHILDREN

Twenty-five $2000 scholarships for study in higher education awarded annually. Twenty-three provided by California Teachers Association; one provided by D. A. Weber Scholarship Fund for student attending continuation high school; and one provided by Ralph J. Flynn Memorial Fund. Must be dependent child of active, retired, or deceased member of California Teachers Association. Applications available in October.

Award: Scholarship for use in freshman, sophomore, junior, or senior years; not renewable. *Number:* 25. *Amount:* $2000.

Eligibility Requirements: Applicant must be enrolled or expecting to enroll full-time at a two-year or four-year or technical institution or university. Applicant or parent of applicant must be member of California Teachers Association. Applicant must have 3.0 GPA or higher. Available to U.S. citizens.

Application Requirements: Application, essay, references, transcript. *Deadline:* January 27.

Contact: Janeya Collins, Scholarship Coordinator
California Teachers Association (CTA)
PO Box 921
Burlingame, CA 94011-0921
Phone: 650-552-5468
Fax: 650-552-5001
E-mail: scholarships@cta.org

CALIFORNIA TEACHERS ASSOCIATION SCHOLARSHIP FOR MEMBERS

Must be an active member of California Teachers Association (including members working on an emergency credential). Available for study in a degree, credential, or graduate program. Deadline is January 27. Visit http://www.cta.org/InsideCTA/TrainingHR/ScholarshipPrograms.htm for more information.

Award: Scholarship for use in freshman, sophomore, junior, senior, or graduate years; not renewable. *Number:* 5. *Amount:* $2000.

Eligibility Requirements: Applicant must be enrolled or expecting to enroll full-time at an institution or university. Applicant or parent of applicant must be member of California Teachers Association. Applicant must have 3.0 GPA or higher. Available to U.S. citizens.

Application Requirements: Application, essay, references, transcript. *Deadline:* January 27.

Contact: Janeya Collins, Scholarship Coordinator
California Teachers Association (CTA)
PO Box 921
Burlingame, CA 94011-0921
Phone: 650-552-5468
E-mail: scholarships@cta.org

CATHOLIC KOLPING SOCIETY OF AMERICA
http://www.kolping.org

FATHER KREWITT SCHOLARSHIP

Scholarship based on an essay of 500 words on a specific topic selected by the board of the Kolping Society. Must be a member of the Kolping Society, or a child or grandchild of a member. Further information and application available at Web site: http://www.kolping.org. Application deadline is February 28.

Award: Scholarship for use in freshman, sophomore, junior, senior, or graduate years; not renewable. *Number:* 1. *Amount:* up to $1000.

Eligibility Requirements: Applicant must be Roman Catholic and enrolled or expecting to enroll full-time at a two-year or four-year or technical institution or university. Applicant or parent of applicant must be member of Catholic Kolping Society of America. Available to U.S. citizens.

Catholic Kolping Society of America (continued)

Application Requirements: Application, applicant must enter a contest, essay. *Deadline:* February 28.

Contact: Patricia Farkas, National Administrator
Catholic Kolping Society of America
9 East 8th Street
Clifton, NJ 07011
Phone: 877-659-7237
E-mail: PatFarkas@aol.com

CENTER FOR SCHOLARSHIP ADMINISTRATION   http://www.scholarshipprograms.org

GREENVILLE AREA PERSONNEL ASSOCIATION WALTER L. MARTIN MEMORIAL SCHOLARSHIP PROGRAM

One-time award to dependent children of GAPA members. Financial need is not a consideration. For more details see the Web site.

Award: Scholarship for use in freshman, sophomore, junior, or senior years; not renewable. *Number:* varies. *Amount:* $1000.

Eligibility Requirements: Applicant must be enrolled or expecting to enroll full-time at a two-year or four-year or technical institution or university. Applicant or parent of applicant must be member of Greenville Area Personnel Association. Applicant must have 2.5 GPA or higher. Available to U.S. citizens.

Application Requirements: Application, essay, references, transcript. *Deadline:* March 1.

Contact: Sandra Lee, President
Center for Scholarship Administration
PO Box 1465
Taylors, SC 29687-0031
Phone: 864-268-3363
Fax: 864-268-7160
E-mail: sandralee41@bellsouth.net

MICHELIN/TIA SCHOLARSHIPS

Renewable scholarships are available to qualified employees and dependent children of qualified employees of tire dealers who are members of the Tire Industry Association. For more details and an application see Web site: http://www.scholarshipprograms.org

Award: Scholarship for use in freshman, sophomore, junior, or senior years; renewable. *Number:* 3. *Amount:* $1250–$2500.

Eligibility Requirements: Applicant must be enrolled or expecting to enroll full-time at a two-year or four-year or technical institution or university. Applicant or parent of applicant must be member of Tire Industry Association. Applicant must have 3.0 GPA or higher. Available to U.S. citizens.

Application Requirements: Application, essay, references, transcript. *Deadline:* March 31.

Contact: Sandra Lee, President
Center for Scholarship Administration
PO Box 1465
Taylors, SC 29687-0031
Phone: 864-268-3363
Fax: 864-268-7160
E-mail: sandralee41@bellsouth.net

NATIONAL ASSOCIATION OF FOOD EQUIPMENT DEALERS, INC. SCHOLARSHIP

Non-renewable scholarships are available to the dependent children of qualified employees of NAFED dealers. Contact NAFED owner for more detailed information on additional criteria.

Award: Scholarship for use in senior year; not renewable. *Number:* 1. *Amount:* $5000.

Eligibility Requirements: Applicant must be enrolled or expecting to enroll full-time at a two-year or four-year or technical institution or university. Applicant or parent of applicant must be member of National Association of Food Equipment Dealers. Applicant must have 3.0 GPA or higher. Available to U.S. citizens.

Application Requirements: Application, essay, references, transcript. *Deadline:* February 15.

Contact: Sandra Lee, President
Center for Scholarship Administration
PO Box 1465
Taylors, SC 29687-0031
Phone: 864-268-3363
Fax: 864-268-7160
E-mail: sandralee41@bellsouth.net

CIVIL AIR PATROL, USAF AUXILIARY   http://www.capnhq.gov

CIVIL AIR PATROL ACADEMIC SCHOLARSHIPS

One-time $250-$1000 award for active members of the Civil Air Patrol to pursue undergraduate, graduate, or trade or technical education. Must be a current CAP member. Significant restrictions apply. Not open to the general public. Contact for further details.

Award: Scholarship for use in freshman, sophomore, junior, senior, or graduate years; not renewable. *Number:* up to 40. *Amount:* $250–$1000.

Eligibility Requirements: Applicant must be enrolled or expecting to enroll full-time at a two-year or four-year or technical institution or university. Applicant or parent of applicant must be member of Civil Air Patrol. Available to U.S. citizens.

Application Requirements: Application, essay, photo, resume, references, test scores, transcript. *Deadline:* January 31.

Contact: Kelly Easterly, Assistant Program Manager
Civil Air Patrol, USAF Auxiliary
105 South Hansell Street, Building 714
Maxwell Air Force Base, AL 36112-6332
Phone: 334-953-8640
Fax: 334-953-6699
E-mail: cpr@capnhq.gov

COMCAST LEADERS AND ACHIEVERS SCHOLARSHIP PROGRAM   http://www.comcast.com

COMCAST LEADERS AND ACHIEVERS SCHOLARSHIP

Awards for full-time seniors attending high school in an eligible community served by Comcast Cable. Must have a GPA of 2.8 or higher and demonstrate leadership abilities in school activities. High school principals must submit nominations to Scholarship Program Administrators by February 10.

Award: Scholarship for use in freshman year; not renewable. *Amount:* $1000.

Eligibility Requirements: Applicant must be high school student and planning to enroll or expecting to enroll full-time at an institution or university. Applicant or parent of applicant must be member of Community Banker Association of Illinois. Available to U.S. citizens.

Application Requirements: Application. *Deadline:* December 19.

Contact: Comcast Leaders and Achievers Scholarship Program
c/o Scholarship Managers
407 South White Horse Pike
Audubon, NJ 08106

COMMUNITY BANKER ASSOCIATION OF ILLINOIS   http://www.cbai.com

COMMUNITY BANKER ASSOCIATION OF ILLINOIS CHILDREN OF COMMUNITY BANKING SCHOLARSHIP

Also known as William C. Harris Memorial Scholarship. Eligible Illinois community banks can submit one name for each $1000 they have donated to the CBAI Foundation. Children of eligible community bankers and part-time bank employees entering freshman year of higher education are eligible. Winner determined by drawing. Must be Illinois resident.

Award: Scholarship for use in freshman year; not renewable. *Number:* 1. *Amount:* $1000–$4000.

Eligibility Requirements: Applicant must be high school student; planning to enroll or expecting to enroll full-time at a two-year or four-year or technical institution or university and resident of Illinois. Applicant or parent of applicant must be member of Community Banker Association of Illinois. Applicant or parent of applicant must have employment or volunteer experience in banking. Available to U.S. citizens.

Application Requirements: *Deadline:* August 15.

COMMUNITY FOUNDATION OF WESTERN MASSACHUSETTS
http://www.communityfoundation.org

HORACE HILL SCHOLARSHIP

Scholarships are given to children or grandchildren of a member of the Springfield Newspapers' 25-Year Club. For more information or application visit http://www.communityfoundation.org.

Award: Scholarship for use in freshman, sophomore, junior, senior, or graduate years; renewable. *Number:* 4. *Amount:* up to $550.

Eligibility Requirements: Applicant must be enrolled or expecting to enroll full or part-time at a two-year or four-year institution or university. Applicant or parent of applicant must be member of Springfield Newspaper 25-Year Club. Applicant or parent of applicant must have employment or volunteer experience in journalism. Available to U.S. citizens.

Application Requirements: Application, financial need analysis, transcript, parent and student federal income tax returns. *Deadline:* March 31.

Contact: Dorothy Theriaque, Education Associate
Community Foundation of Western Massachusetts
1500 Main Street, PO Box 15769
Springfield, MA 01115
Phone: 413-732-2858
Fax: 413-733-8565
E-mail: dtheriaque@communityfoundation.org

DANISH SISTERHOOD OF AMERICA
http://www.danishsisterhood.org/

BETTY HANSEN CONTINUING EDUCATION GRANT

Grant is available to part-time students for use at any level, including community education classes. Must be a member of the Danish Sisterhood of America.

Award: Grant for use in freshman, sophomore, junior, or senior years; renewable. *Number:* up to 10. *Amount:* up to $500.

Eligibility Requirements: Applicant must be enrolled or expecting to enroll part-time at an institution or university. Applicant or parent of applicant must be member of Danish Sisterhood of America. Available to U.S. and non-U.S. citizens.

Application Requirements: Application. *Deadline:* varies.

Contact: Lizette Burtis, National Trustee Scholarship Chairperson
Danish Sisterhood of America
7874 Rayside Ave
Burnaby V5E 2L3
Canada

NATIONAL SCHOLARSHIP, MILDRED SORENSEN, OLGA CHRISTENSEN AND BETTY HANSEN SCHOLARSHIPS

One-time awards for full-time, postsecondary students who are members, or a son or daughter of members of the Danish Sisterhood of America. Candidates must have a minimum 2.5 GPA. Write for further details.

Award: Scholarship for use in freshman, sophomore, junior, or senior years; not renewable. *Number:* up to 12. *Amount:* $500–$1000.

Eligibility Requirements: Applicant must be enrolled or expecting to enroll full or part-time at a two-year or four-year or technical institution or university. Applicant or parent of applicant must be member of Danish Sisterhood of America. Applicant must have 2.5 GPA or higher. Available to U.S. and non-U.S. citizens.

Application Requirements: Application, references, test scores, transcript. *Deadline:* February 28.

Contact: Lizette Burtis, National Trustee Scholarship Chairman
Danish Sisterhood of America
3020 Santa Juanita Court
Santa Rosa, CA 95405

DAVIS-ROBERTS SCHOLARSHIP FUND, INC.

DAVIS-ROBERTS SCHOLARSHIPS

Renewable award to assist Demolays and Jobs Daughters in the state of Wyoming with their education, providing they are attending or planning to attend school full-time. Must submit letter from Chapter Dad or Bethel Guardian and photo.

Award: Scholarship for use in freshman, sophomore, junior, senior, or graduate years; renewable. *Number:* 3–5. *Amount:* $350–$1000.

Eligibility Requirements: Applicant must be enrolled or expecting to enroll full-time at a two-year or four-year or technical institution or university and resident of Wyoming. Applicant or parent of applicant must be member of Demolay or Jobs Daughters. Applicant must have 2.5 GPA or higher. Available to U.S. citizens.

Application Requirements: Application, essay, financial need analysis, photo, references, transcript. *Deadline:* June 15.

Contact: Gary Skillern, Secretary
Davis-Roberts Scholarship Fund, Inc.
PO Box 20645
Cheyenne, WY 82003
Phone: 307-632-0491

DELTA DELTA DELTA FOUNDATION
http://www.tridelta.org

DELTA DELTA DELTA GRADUATE SCHOLARSHIP

Scholarship awarded to alumnae members attending graduate school. All scholarship winners must complete application materials provided by the Foundation. All applicants must be highly involved in TriDelta and in their communities, and they must also have achieved academic excellence.

Award: Scholarship for use in freshman, sophomore, junior, senior, or graduate years; not renewable. *Number:* 8. *Amount:* $2000–$3000.

Eligibility Requirements: Applicant must be enrolled or expecting to enroll full-time at an institution or university and female. Applicant or parent of applicant must have employment or volunteer experience in community service. Available to U.S. citizens.

Application Requirements: Application, financial need analysis, references, transcript, personal statement. *Deadline:* February 15.

Contact: Laura Allen, Foundation Manager of Scholarships and Financial Services
Delta Delta Delta Foundation
PO Box 5987
Arlington, TX 76005
Phone: 817-633-8001
Fax: 817-652-0212
E-mail: lallen@trideltaeo.org

DELTA DELTA DELTA UNDERGRADUATE SCHOLARSHIP

One-time award based on academic achievement, campus, chapter, and community involvement. Any initiated sophomore or junior member in good-standing of Delta Delta Delta may apply. Application and information available at Web site http://www.tridelta.org.

Award: Scholarship for use in sophomore, junior, or senior years; not renewable. *Number:* 48–50. *Amount:* $500–$1500.

Eligibility Requirements: Applicant must be enrolled or expecting to enroll full-time at a four-year institution or university and single female. Applicant or parent of applicant must have employment or volunteer experience in community service. Available to U.S. citizens.

Application Requirements: Application, references, transcript, alumna adviser check-off, personal statement. *Deadline:* February 15.

Contact: Laura Allen, Foundation Manager of Scholarships and Financial Services
Delta Delta Delta Foundation
PO Box 5987
Arlington, TX 76005
Phone: 817-633-8001
Fax: 817-652-0212
E-mail: lallen@trideltaeo.org

DELTA GAMMA FOUNDATION

http://www.deltagamma.org

DELTA GAMMA FOUNDATION SCHOLARSHIPS

Award for initiated members of the Delta Gamma Fraternity. Must be female. Applicants must have completed three semesters or five quarters of college with a minimum 3.0 GPA. Must be active in campus, community, and chapter activities. Freshmen are ineligible. One-time award of $1000.

Award: Scholarship for use in sophomore, junior, or senior years; not renewable. *Number:* 150–175. *Amount:* $1000.

Eligibility Requirements: Applicant must be enrolled or expecting to enroll full-time at a four-year institution or university and female. Applicant must have 3.0 GPA or higher. Available to U.S. and Canadian citizens.

Application Requirements: Application, autobiography, essay, photo, references, self-addressed stamped envelope, transcript. *Deadline:* March 1.

Contact: Kathleen Williams, Assistant Development Director
Delta Gamma Foundation
3250 Riverside Drive, PO Box 21397
Columbus, OH 43221-0397
Phone: 614-481-8169 Ext. 324
E-mail: kathleen@deltagamma.org

DELTA PHI EPSILON EDUCATIONAL FOUNDATION

http://www.dphie.org

DELTA PHI EPSILON EDUCATIONAL FOUNDATION GRANT

Scholarships are available to members and sons/daughters of members of Delta Phi Epsilon for graduate and undergraduate programs. Eligibility is based on academic achievement, recommendations and financial need.

Award: Grant for use in freshman, sophomore, junior, senior, or graduate years; not renewable. *Number:* 6–8. *Amount:* $1000.

Eligibility Requirements: Applicant must be enrolled or expecting to enroll full-time at a four-year institution or university. Available to U.S. and non-U.S. citizens.

Application Requirements: Application, autobiography, essay, financial need analysis, photo, references, transcript. *Deadline:* March 1.

Contact: Felicia Ausbury, Executive Director
Delta Phi Epsilon Educational Foundation
16A Worthington Drive
Maryland Heights, MO 63043
Phone: 314-275-2626
Fax: 314-275-2655
E-mail: fausbury@dphie.org

DELTA SIGMA PI

http://www.dspnet.org

UNDERGRADUATE SCHOLARSHIP

Must be a member of Delta Sigma Pi in good standing with at least one full semester or quarter of college remaining. Awarded in the fall.

Award: Scholarship for use in sophomore, junior, or senior years; not renewable. *Number:* up to 15. *Amount:* $500–$5000.

Eligibility Requirements: Applicant must be enrolled or expecting to enroll full-time at a four-year institution or university. Available to U.S. citizens.

Application Requirements: Application, financial need analysis, references, transcript, description of fraternity, campus, community involvement. *Deadline:* June 30.

Contact: Bill Schilling, Executive Director
Delta Sigma Pi
330 South Campus Avenue, PO Box 230
Oxford, OH 45056-0230
Phone: 513-523-1907
Fax: 513-523-7292
E-mail: bill@dspnet.org

EASTERN ORTHODOX COMMITTEE ON SCOUTING

http://www.eocs.org

EASTERN ORTHODOX COMMITTEE ON SCOUTING SCHOLARSHIPS

One-time award for high school seniors planning to attend a four-year institution. Must be a registered member of a Boy or Girl Scout unit, an Eagle Scout or Gold Award recipient, active member of an Eastern Orthodox Church, and recipient of the Alpha Omega religious award.

Award: Scholarship for use in freshman year; not renewable. *Number:* 3. *Amount:* up to $1000.

Eligibility Requirements: Applicant must be Eastern Orthodox; high school student; planning to enroll or expecting to enroll full-time at a four-year institution and single. Applicant or parent of applicant must be member of Boy Scouts or Girl Scouts. Available to U.S. citizens.

Application Requirements: Application, autobiography, references, self-addressed stamped envelope, test scores, transcript. *Deadline:* May 1.

Contact: George Boulukos, Scholarship Chairman
Eastern Orthodox Committee on Scouting
862 Guy Lombardo Avenue
Freeport, NY 11520
Phone: 516-868-4050
Fax: 516-868-4052
E-mail: geobou03@aol.com

ELKS GOLD AWARD SCHOLARSHIPS/GIRL SCOUTS OF THE USA

http://www.gsusa.org

ELKS NATIONAL FOUNDATION GOLD AWARD SCHOLARSHIPS

Eight awards given annually to Gold Award recipients selected by the Girl Scouts of America. One girl from each Girl Scout Service area will receive a $6000 scholarship ($1500 per year). Must be a high school senior planning full-time undergraduate study. Contact the Girl Scout Council or visit Web site: http://www.girlscouts.org for information and applications. Deadlines vary per Council.

Award: Scholarship for use in freshman, sophomore, junior, or senior years; renewable. *Number:* 8. *Amount:* $6000.

Eligibility Requirements: Applicant must be high school student; planning to enroll or expecting to enroll full-time at a two-year or four-year institution or university and female. Applicant or parent of applicant must be member of Girl Scouts. Available to U.S. citizens.

Application Requirements: Application, applicant must enter a contest, autobiography, financial need analysis, references, transcript. *Deadline:* varies.

Contact: Melissa Algranati, Membership and Program Services Contact
Elks Gold Award Scholarships/Girl Scouts of the USA
420 Fifth Avenue
New York, NY 10018-2798
Phone: 212-852-8553 Ext. 5720
Fax: 212-852-6515

ELKS NATIONAL FOUNDATION

http://www.elks.org/enf

ELKS EMERGENCY EDUCATIONAL GRANTS

Grant available to children of Elks who are deceased or totally incapacitated. Applicants for the one-year, renewable awards must be unmarried, under the age of 23, be a full-time undergraduate student, and demonstrate financial need. Contact ENF for an application. Deadline between July 1 and December 31 of the academic year for which assistance is desired. Visit Web site at http://www.elks.org (keyword: scholarship).

Award: Grant for use in freshman, sophomore, junior, or senior years; renewable. *Number:* varies. *Amount:* $1000–$3000.

Eligibility Requirements: Applicant must be age 23 or under; enrolled or expecting to enroll full-time at a two-year or four-year or technical institution or university and single. Applicant or parent of applicant must be member of Elks Club. Available to U.S. citizens.

Application Requirements: Application, essay, financial need analysis, references, self-addressed stamped envelope, transcript. *Deadline:* December 31.

Contact: Jeannine Kunz, Program Coordinator
Elks National Foundation
2750 North Lakeview Avenue
Chicago, IL 60614-1889
Phone: 773-755-4732
Fax: 773-755-4733
E-mail: scholarships@elks.org

ELKS NATIONAL FOUNDATION LEGACY AWARDS

Up to five hundred $1000 one-year scholarships for children and grandchildren of Elks in good standing. Parent or grandparent must have been an Elk for two years. Contact local Elks Lodge for an application or send a SASE to Foundation or see home page (http://www.elks.org, keyword: scholarship). Deadline is January 13.

Award: Scholarship for use in freshman year; not renewable. *Number:* up to 500. *Amount:* $1000.

Eligibility Requirements: Applicant must be high school student and planning to enroll or expecting to enroll full-time at a two-year or four-year institution or university. Applicant or parent of applicant must be member of Elks Club. Available to U.S. citizens.

Application Requirements: Application, essay, references, self-addressed stamped envelope, test scores, transcript. *Deadline:* January 13.

Contact: Jeannine Kunz, Scholarship Coordinator
Elks National Foundation
2750 North Lakeview Avenue
Chicago, IL 60614-1889
Phone: 773-755-4732
Fax: 773-755-4733
E-mail: scholarship@elks.org

FEDERATION OF AMERICAN CONSUMERS AND TRAVELERS
http://www.fact-org.org

FEDERATION OF AMERICAN CONSUMERS AND TRAVELERS GRADUATING HIGH SCHOOL SENIOR SCHOLARSHIP

A minimum of one $10,000 scholarship and one $2500 scholarship are given to graduating high school seniors. Eligible applicants will be a member or the child or grandchild of a member of FACT. Awards are designed for the so-called average" student. These funds are for the young man or woman who may never have made the honor roll or who did not excel on the athletic field and wants to obtain a higher education, but is all too often overlooked by other scholarship sources. For more information visit http://www.fact-org.org

Award: Scholarship for use in freshman, sophomore, junior, or senior years; not renewable. *Number:* 2. *Amount:* $2500–$10,000.

Eligibility Requirements: Applicant must be high school student and planning to enroll or expecting to enroll full-time at a two-year or four-year institution or university. Applicant or parent of applicant must be member of Federation of American Consumers and Travelers. Available to U.S. citizens.

Application Requirements: Application, autobiography, essay, references, test scores, transcript. *Deadline:* January 15.

Contact: Vicki Rolens, Managing Director
Federation of American Consumers and Travelers
PO Box 104
Edwardsville, IL 62025
Phone: 800-872-3228
Fax: 618-656-5369
E-mail: vrolens@fact-org.org

FLEET RESERVE ASSOCIATION
http://www.fra.org

FLEET RESERVE ASSOCIATION SCHOLARSHIP

Dependent children/grandchildren and spouses of members in good standing of the Fleet Reserve Association or deceased while in aforementioned status, and member of the FRA may be eligible for up to $5000. Selection is based on financial need, academic standing, character and leadership qualities. Deadline: April 15. FRA members may access applications on Web site: http://www.fra.org/

Award: Scholarship for use in freshman, sophomore, junior, or senior years; not renewable. *Number:* up to 6. *Amount:* up to $5000.

Eligibility Requirements: Applicant must be enrolled or expecting to enroll full-time at a two-year or four-year institution or university and must have an interest in leadership. Applicant or parent of applicant must be member of Fleet Reserve Association/Auxiliary. Applicant must have 3.0 GPA or higher. Available to U.S. citizens. Applicant or parent must meet one or more of the following requirements: Coast Guard, Marine Corps, or Navy experience; retired from active duty; disabled or killed as a result of military service; prisoner of war; or missing in action.

Application Requirements: Application, essay, financial need analysis, references, test scores, transcript. *Deadline:* April 15.

Contact: Scholarship Administrator
Fleet Reserve Association
125 North West Street
Alexandria, VA 22314-2754
E-mail: fra@fra.org

GLASS, MOLDERS, POTTERY, PLASTICS AND ALLIED WORKERS INTERNATIONAL UNION
http://www.gmpiu.org

GMP MEMORIAL SCHOLARSHIP PROGRAM

Eight $6000 scholarships will be awarded to the sons and daughters of members of the Glass, Molders, Pottery, Plastics, and Allied Workers International Union. Scholarships can be renewed for up to four years. For more details see Web site: http://www.gmpiu.org.

Award: Scholarship for use in freshman, sophomore, junior, or senior years; renewable. *Number:* up to 8. *Amount:* $4000–$6000.

Eligibility Requirements: Applicant must be high school student and planning to enroll or expecting to enroll full-time at a four-year institution or university. Applicant or parent of applicant must be member of Glass, Molders, Pottery, Plastics and Allied Workers International Union. Available to U.S. citizens.

Application Requirements: Application. *Deadline:* November 1.

Contact: Bruce R. Smith, International Secretary-Treasurer
Glass, Molders, Pottery, Plastics and Allied Workers International Union
608 East Baltimore Pike, PO Box 607
Media, PA 19063
Phone: 610-892-0143
Fax: 610-892-9657

GOLDEN KEY INTERNATIONAL HONOUR SOCIETY
http://www.goldenkey.org

GEICO LIFE SCHOLARSHIP

Ten $1000 awards will be given to returning students in recognition of academic excellence while balancing additional responsibilities. Must have completed at least twelve undergraduate credits in the previous year. See Web site for more information: http://goldenkey.gsu.edu. Deadline is April 1.

Award: Scholarship for use in junior or senior years; not renewable. *Number:* 10. *Amount:* $1000.

Eligibility Requirements: Applicant must be enrolled or expecting to enroll full or part-time at an institution or university. Applicant or parent of applicant must be member of Golden Key National Honor Society. Available to U.S. citizens.

Application Requirements: Application, essay, references, transcript. *Deadline:* April 1.

Contact: Scholarship Program Administrators
Golden Key International Honour Society
PO Box 23737
Nashville, TN 37202
Phone: 800-377-2401

GOLDEN KEY STUDY ABROAD SCHOLARSHIPS

Ten $1000 scholarships will be awarded twice a year to assist student in the pursuit of a study abroad program. Deadlines are April 15 and October 15.

Award: Scholarship for use in junior or senior years; not renewable. *Number:* 10. *Amount:* $1000.

Golden Key International Honour Society (continued)

Eligibility Requirements: Applicant must be enrolled or expecting to enroll full-time at a four-year institution or university. Applicant or parent of applicant must be member of Golden Key National Honor Society. Available to U.S. citizens.

Application Requirements: Application, essay, transcript. *Deadline:* varies.

Contact: Scholarship Program Administrators
Golden Key International Honour Society
PO Box 23737
Nashville, TN 37202-3737
Phone: 800-377-2401
E-mail: scholarships@goldenkey.org

INTERNATIONAL STUDENT LEADERS AWARD

The International Student Leader Award is designed to recognize one talented Golden Key member for outstanding commitment to Golden Key, as well as for campus and community leadership and academic achievement. The recipient of the award will receive $1000. Winners for the Regional Student Leader Awards will then be considered as candidates for the International Student Leader Award. Deadline is June 1.

Award: Scholarship for use in junior, senior, graduate, or postgraduate years; not renewable. *Number:* 1. *Amount:* $1000.

Eligibility Requirements: Applicant must be enrolled or expecting to enroll at an institution or university and must have an interest in leadership. Applicant or parent of applicant must be member of Golden Key National Honor Society. Available to U.S. and non-U.S. citizens.

Application Requirements: Application, applicant must enter a contest, essay, resume, references. *Deadline:* June 1.

Contact: Scholarship Program Administrators
Golden Key International Honour Society
PO Box 23737
Nashville, TN 37202-3737
Phone: 800-377-2401
E-mail: scholarships@goldenkey.org

GOLF COURSE SUPERINTENDENTS ASSOCIATION OF AMERICA
http://www.gcsaa.org

GOLF COURSE SUPERINTENDENTS ASSOCIATION OF AMERICA LEGACY AWARD

Awards of $1500 for the children or grandchildren of Golf Course Superintendents Association of America members. Graduating high school seniors must attach a letter of acceptance to their application.

Award: Scholarship for use in freshman, sophomore, junior, senior, or graduate years; not renewable. *Number:* 20. *Amount:* $1500.

Eligibility Requirements: Applicant must be enrolled or expecting to enroll full-time at a two-year or four-year or technical institution or university. Applicant or parent of applicant must be member of Golf Course Superintendents Association of America. Available to U.S. and non-U.S. citizens.

Application Requirements: Application, essay, references, transcript. *Deadline:* April 15.

Contact: Amanda Howard, Employment Administrator
Golf Course Superintendents Association of America
1421 Research Park Drive
Lawrence, KS 66049-3859
Phone: 800-472-7878 Ext. 678
Fax: 785-832-4449
E-mail: ahoward@gcsaa.org

JOSEPH S. GARSHE COLLEGIATE GRANT PROGRAM

Renewable award available to children/step children of GCSAA members for use at an accredited college or trade school. Applicant must be a graduating high school senior and be accepted at an institution of higher learning for the upcoming year.

Award: Scholarship for use in freshman or sophomore years; renewable. *Number:* 1. *Amount:* $2500.

Eligibility Requirements: Applicant must be high school student and planning to enroll or expecting to enroll full-time at a two-year or

four-year or technical institution or university. Applicant or parent of applicant must be member of Golf Course Superintendents Association of America. Available to U.S. and non-U.S. citizens.

Application Requirements: Application, essay, transcript. *Deadline:* March 15.

Contact: Amanda Howard, Employment Administrator
Golf Course Superintendents Association of America
1421 Research Park Drive
Lawrence, KS 66049-3859
Phone: 800-472-7878 Ext. 4424
Fax: 785-832-4449
E-mail: ahoward@gcsaa.org

GRAPHIC COMMUNICATIONS INTERNATIONAL UNION
http://www.gciu.org/

A.J. DEANDRADE SCHOLARSHIP PROGRAM

Program is open to dependents of Graphic Communications International Union members. Must be a graduating high school senior. The deadline is February 16. Award is payable at $500 a year for four years.

Award: Scholarship for use in freshman, sophomore, junior, or senior years; renewable. *Number:* 10. *Amount:* $2000.

Eligibility Requirements: Applicant must be high school student and planning to enroll or expecting to enroll full-time at a four-year institution or university. Applicant or parent of applicant must be member of Graphic Communication International Union. Available to U.S. and Canadian citizens.

Application Requirements: Application, essay, references, test scores, transcript. *Deadline:* February 16.

Contact: Graphic Communications International Union
1900 L Street NW
Washington, DC 20036
Phone: 202-462-1400
Fax: 202-721-0641

HAWAII EDUCATION ASSOCIATION
http://www.heaed.com/

HAWAII EDUCATION ASSOCIATION HIGH SCHOOL STUDENT SCHOLARSHIP

Scholarship available to high school seniors planning on attending four-year college/university. Must be children of HEA members. Membership must be for at least one year.

Award: Scholarship for use in freshman year; not renewable. *Number:* 5. *Amount:* $1000.

Eligibility Requirements: Applicant must be high school student; planning to enroll or expecting to enroll full-time at a four-year institution or university and resident of Hawaii. Applicant or parent of applicant must be member of Hawaii Education Association. Available to U.S. citizens.

Application Requirements: Application, autobiography, financial need analysis, photo, references, transcript. *Deadline:* April 4.

Contact: HEA Scholarship Committee
Hawaii Education Association
1649 Kalakaua Avenue
Honolulu, HI 96826-2494
Phone: 808-949-6657
Fax: 808-944-2032
E-mail: hea.office@heaed.com

HEBREW IMMIGRANT AID SOCIETY
http://www.hias.org

HEBREW IMMIGRANT AID SOCIETY SCHOLARSHIP AWARDS COMPETITION

Must be Hebrew Immigrant Aid Society-assisted refugee who came to the U.S. after January 1, 1992. Must have completed two semesters at a U.S. high school, college, or graduate school. Application and information are available at Web site http://www.hias.org. Applications will only be accepted online. Applications must be submitted by midnight of March 15.

Award: Scholarship for use in freshman, sophomore, junior, senior, or graduate years; not renewable. *Number:* 70–90. *Amount:* $1500.

Eligibility Requirements: Applicant must be enrolled or expecting to enroll full or part-time at a two-year or four-year or technical institution or university. Applicant or parent of applicant must be member of Hebrew Immigrant Aid Society. Available to U.S. citizens.

Application Requirements: Application, applicant must enter a contest, essay, financial need analysis, test scores, transcript. *Deadline:* March 15.

Contact: Amy Greenstein, Program Contact
Hebrew Immigrant Aid Society
333 Seventh Avenue, 16th Floor
New York, NY 10001-5004
Phone: 212-613-1358
Fax: 212-697-4483
E-mail: scholarship@hias.org

HONOR SOCIETY OF PHI KAPPA PHI   http://www.phikappaphi.org

LITERACY INITIATIVE GRANT COMPETITION

Grants up to $2500 will be awarded to Phi Kappa Phi members for projects relating to literacy. These projects should fulfill the spirit of volunteerism and community. The total number of awards vary for each year. For more details see Web site: http://www.phikappaphi.org/Web/Scholarships/literacy/literacy_instructions.html

Award: Grant for use in freshman, sophomore, junior, senior, graduate, or postgraduate years; not renewable. *Number:* varies. *Amount:* $300–$2500.

Eligibility Requirements: Applicant must be enrolled or expecting to enroll at an institution or university. Applicant or parent of applicant must be member of Phi Kappa Phi. Available to U.S. and non-U.S. citizens.

Application Requirements: Application, financial need analysis. *Deadline:* February 1.

Contact: Theresa Bard, Programs Coordinator
Honor Society of Phi Kappa Phi
305 French House, Highland Road, Louisiana State University
Baton Rouge, LA 70893-6000
Phone: 225-388-4917 Ext. 13
Fax: 225-388-4900
E-mail: awards@phikappaphi.org

INTERNATIONAL CHEMICAL WORKERS UNION   http://www.icwuc.org

WALTER L. MITCHELL MEMORIAL AWARDS

Award available to children of International Chemical Workers Union members. Applicants must be starting their freshman year of college.

Award: Grant for use in freshman year; not renewable. *Number:* 13. *Amount:* $1000–$1500.

Eligibility Requirements: Applicant must be enrolled or expecting to enroll full-time at a two-year or four-year or technical institution or university. Applicant or parent of applicant must be member of International Chemical Workers Union. Available to U.S. and non-U.S. citizens.

Application Requirements: Application, autobiography, test scores, transcript. *Deadline:* April 25.

Contact: International Chemical Workers Union Council
International Chemical Workers Union
1655 West Market Street
Akron, OH 44313
Phone: 330-926-1444
Fax: 330-926-0816
E-mail: agreen@icwuc.org

INTERNATIONAL FEDERATION OF PROFESSIONAL AND TECHNICAL ENGINEERS   http://www.ifpte.org

INTERNATIONAL FEDERATION OF PROFESSIONAL AND TECHNICAL ENGINEERS ANNUAL SCHOLARSHIP

IFPTE annual scholarships are open to high school seniors who have demonstrated academic achievement and service to their school and community. Only children or grandchildren of IFPTE members are eligible. Must be a U.S. or Canadian citizen.

Award: Scholarship for use in freshman or senior years; not renewable. *Number:* 3. *Amount:* $1500.

Eligibility Requirements: Applicant must be high school student and planning to enroll or expecting to enroll full-time at a two-year or four-year or technical institution or university. Applicant or parent of applicant must be member of International Federation of Professional and Technical Engineers. Available to U.S. and Canadian citizens.

Application Requirements: Application, essay, references, transcript. *Deadline:* March 15.

Contact: Candace M. Rhett, Communications Representative
International Federation of Professional and Technical Engineers
8630 Fenton Street, Suite 400
Silver Spring, MD 20910
Phone: 301-565-9016
Fax: 301-565-0018
E-mail: crhett@ifpte.org

INTERNATIONAL UNION OF ELECTRONIC, ELECTRICAL, SALARIED, MACHINE, AND FURNITURE WORKERS-CWA   http://www.iue-cwa.org

CWA JOE BEIRNE FOUNDATION SCHOLARSHIP PROGRAM

Two-year scholarships, to be paid at the rate of $3000 annually to Communication Workers of America members, their spouses, children, and grandchildren (including dependents of laid-off, retired or deceased CWA members). A second-year award is contingent on academic accomplishment of the first year. No specific studies are required. Scholarship winners may pursue whatever courses they wish. Winner chosen by lottery drawing.

Award: Scholarship for use in freshman, sophomore, junior, senior, or graduate years; not renewable. *Number:* up to 30. *Amount:* $3000.

Eligibility Requirements: Applicant must be enrolled or expecting to enroll at a two-year or four-year institution or university. Applicant or parent of applicant must be member of AFL-CIO. Available to U.S. and Canadian citizens.

Application Requirements: Application, essay. *Deadline:* March 31.

Contact: Trudy Humphrey, Director
International Union of Electronic, Electrical, Salaried, Machine, and Furniture Workers-CWA
501 3rd Street, NW
Washington, DC 20001
Phone: 202-434-9591
Fax: 202-434-1252
E-mail: thumphrey@cwa-union.org

IUE-CWA INTERNATIONAL BRUCE VAN ESS SCHOLARSHIP

Scholarship available to all IUE-CWA members and employees and their children and grandchildren. Must be accepted for admission or enrolled as a full-time student. All study must be completed at the undergraduate level. Deadline is March 31.

Award: Scholarship for use in freshman, sophomore, junior, senior, or graduate years; not renewable. *Number:* 1. *Amount:* $2500.

Eligibility Requirements: Applicant must be enrolled or expecting to enroll full-time at a two-year or four-year or technical institution or university. Applicant or parent of applicant must be member of International Union of Electronic, Electrical, Salaries, Machine and Furniture Workers. Available to U.S. citizens.

Application Requirements: Application, essay, financial need analysis, references, test scores, transcript. *Deadline:* March 31.

Contact: Trudy Humphrey, Director
International Union of Electronic, Electrical, Salaried, Machine, and Furniture Workers-CWA
501 3rd Street, NW
Washington, DC 20001
Phone: 202-434-9591
Fax: 202-434-1252
E-mail: thumphrey@cwa-union.org

PAUL JENNINGS SCHOLARSHIP AWARD

One award for a student whose parent or grandparent is or has been a local union elected official. Families of full-time international union officers are not eligible. Submit family financial status form with application.

International Union of Electronic, Electrical, Salaried, Machine, and Furniture Workers-CWA (continued)

Award: Scholarship for use in freshman, sophomore, junior, senior, or graduate years; not renewable. *Number:* 1. *Amount:* $3000.

Eligibility Requirements: Applicant must be enrolled or expecting to enroll full-time at a two-year or four-year or technical institution or university. Applicant or parent of applicant must be member of International Union of Electronic, Electrical, Salaries, Machine and Furniture Workers. Available to U.S. citizens.

Application Requirements: Application, essay, financial need analysis, references, test scores, transcript. *Deadline:* March 31.

Contact: Trudy Humphrey, Director
International Union of Electronic, Electrical, Salaried, Machine, and Furniture Workers-CWA
501 3rd Street, NW
Washington, DC 20001
Phone: 202-434-9591
Fax: 202-434-1252
E-mail: thumphrey@cwa-union.org

WILLIE RUDD SCHOLARSHIP

One-time award available to all IUE-CWA members and employees and their children and grandchildren. Applicant must be accepted for admission or already enrolled as a full-time student at an accredited college or university, nursing or technical school offering college credit courses. All study must be completed at the undergraduate level. Application deadline is March 31.

Award: Scholarship for use in freshman, sophomore, junior, senior, or graduate years; not renewable. *Number:* 1. *Amount:* $1000.

Eligibility Requirements: Applicant must be enrolled or expecting to enroll full-time at a four-year or technical institution or university. Applicant or parent of applicant must be member of International Union of Electronic, Electrical, Salaries, Machine and Furniture Workers. Available to U.S. citizens.

Application Requirements: Application, essay, financial need analysis, references, test scores, transcript. *Deadline:* March 31.

Contact: Trudy Humphrey, Director
International Union of Electronic, Electrical, Salaried, Machine, and Furniture Workers-CWA
501 3rd Street, NW
Washington, DC 20001
Phone: 202-434-9591
Fax: 202-434-1252
E-mail: thumphrey@cwa-union.org

JAYCEE WAR MEMORIAL FUND
http://www.usjaycees.org/

CHARLES FORD SCHOLARSHIP

One (1) scholarship awarded annually. Available to an active member of the Jaycees who wishes to return to a college or university to complete his or her formal education. Applicant must be a citizen of the U.S., possess academic potential and leadership qualities, and show financial need. The scholarship is a one-time award of $2500 sent directly to the recipient's college or university of choice.

Award: Scholarship for use in freshman, sophomore, junior, or senior years; not renewable. *Number:* 1. *Amount:* $2500.

Eligibility Requirements: Applicant must be age 21-40 and enrolled or expecting to enroll full or part-time at a four-year institution or university. Applicant or parent of applicant must be member of Jaycees. Applicant must have 3.0 GPA or higher. Available to U.S. citizens.

Application Requirements: Application, financial need analysis, self-addressed stamped envelope, transcript. *Fee:* $5. *Deadline:* March 1.

Contact: Ford Scholarship
Jaycee War Memorial Fund
PO Box 7
Tulsa, OK 74114-1116
Phone: 918-584-2481
Fax: 918-584-4422

THOMAS WOOD BALDRIDGE SCHOLARSHIP

Members of the Junior Chamber of Commerce organization (Jaycees) or immediate family members or descendents of a former Jaycee member are

eligible to apply. Applicants must possess academic potential, leadership qualities, and show financial need. Application deadline is March 1. Send $5 application fee and self-addressed stamped envelope. Must be U.S. citizen.

Award: Scholarship for use in freshman, sophomore, junior, or senior years; not renewable. *Number:* 1. *Amount:* $3000.

Eligibility Requirements: Applicant must be enrolled or expecting to enroll full or part-time at a two-year or four-year or technical institution or university. Applicant or parent of applicant must be member of Jaycees. Applicant must have 3.0 GPA or higher. Available to U.S. citizens.

Application Requirements: Application, financial need analysis, self-addressed stamped envelope, transcript. *Fee:* $5. *Deadline:* March 1.

Contact: Baldridge Scholarship
Jaycee War Memorial Fund
4 West 21st Street, PO Box 7
Tulsa, OK 74114-1114
Phone: 918-584-2481
Fax: 918-584-4422

JUNIOR ACHIEVEMENT
http://www.ja.org

JUNIOR ACHIEVEMENT JOE FRANCOMANO SCHOLARSHIP

Renewable award to high school seniors who have demonstrated academic achievement, leadership skills, and financial need. May be used at any accredited postsecondary educational institution for any field of study resulting in a baccalaureate degree. Must have completed JA Company Program or JA Economics. Award split for 4 years and $5000 paid every year.

Award: Scholarship for use in freshman, sophomore, junior, or senior years; not renewable. *Number:* 1. *Amount:* up to $20,000.

Eligibility Requirements: Applicant must be high school student; planning to enroll or expecting to enroll full-time at a four-year institution or university and must have an interest in leadership. Applicant or parent of applicant must be member of Junior Achievement. Applicant must have 3.0 GPA or higher. Available to U.S. and Canadian citizens.

Application Requirements: Application, essay, financial need analysis, references, transcript. *Deadline:* February 1.

Contact: Scholarships Coordinator
Junior Achievement
1 Education Way
Colorado Springs, CO 80906
Phone: 719-540-8000
Fax: 719-540-6299
E-mail: scholarships@ja.org

JUNIOR ACHIEVEMENT OFFICE DEPOT SCHOLARSHIP

One-time award to high school graduating seniors seeking a degree from an accredited postsecondary educational institution. Must demonstrate academic achievement and leadership skills. Must have completed a Junior Achievement program. Minimum 3.0 GPA required.

Award: Scholarship for use in freshman year; not renewable. *Number:* up to 7. *Amount:* up to $10,000.

Eligibility Requirements: Applicant must be high school student; planning to enroll or expecting to enroll full-time at a four-year institution or university and must have an interest in leadership. Applicant or parent of applicant must be member of Junior Achievement. Applicant must have 3.0 GPA or higher. Available to U.S. and Canadian citizens.

Application Requirements: Application, essay, financial need analysis, references, test scores, transcript. *Deadline:* February 27.

Contact: Scholarship/Education Department
Junior Achievement
1 Education Way
Colorado Springs, CO 80906
Phone: 719-540-8000
Fax: 719-540-6299

KAPPA ALPHA THETA FOUNDATION
http://www.kappaalphatheta.org

KAPPA ALPHA THETA FOUNDATION MERIT BASED SCHOLARSHIP PROGRAM

Foundation scholarships are awarded to either graduate or undergraduate members of Kappa Alpha Theta. All scholarships are merit-based. Application postmark date is February 1. Applications may be downloaded from the Web site or may be obtained by calling 1-888-526-1870 ext. 119.

Award: Scholarship for use in freshman, sophomore, junior, senior, graduate, or postgraduate years; not renewable. *Number:* 120–150. *Amount:* $1000–$10,000.

Eligibility Requirements: Applicant must be enrolled or expecting to enroll full or part-time at a four-year institution or university and female. Available to U.S. and non-U.S. citizens.

Application Requirements: Application, resume, references, transcript. *Deadline:* February 1.

Contact: Cindy Thoennes, Coordinator of Programs
Kappa Alpha Theta Foundation
8740 Founders Road
Indianapolis, IN 46268
Phone: 317-876-1870 Ext. 119
Fax: 317-876-1925
E-mail: cthoennes@kappaalphatheta.org

KAPPA ALPHA THETA FOUNDATION NAMED ENDOWMENT GRANT PROGRAM

The Kappa Alpha Theta Foundation Named Endowment Grant program was established to provide monies for undergraduate and alumna members of the Fraternity for leadership training and non-degree educational opportunities. Individual Thetas, collegiate or alumna undergraduate, and college and alumnae chapters may apply for grant. Applications may be downloaded from the Web site. Application is due 90 days prior to event, workshop, or program.

Award: Grant for use in freshman, sophomore, junior, or senior years; not renewable. *Number:* up to 50. *Amount:* $100–$5000.

Eligibility Requirements: Applicant must be enrolled or expecting to enroll at an institution or university and female. Available to U.S. and non-U.S. citizens.

Application Requirements: Application, resume, references, budget, proposal, narrative. *Deadline:* Continuous.

Contact: Cindy Thoennes, Coordinator of Programs
Kappa Alpha Theta Foundation
8740 Founders Road
Indianapolis, IN 46268
Phone: 317-876-1870 Ext. 119
Fax: 317-876-1925
E-mail: cthoennes@kappaalphatheta.org

KAPPA GAMMA PI   http://www.kappagammapi.org

ELENA LUCREZIA CORNARO PISCOPIA SCHOLARSHIP FOR GRADUATE STUDIES

One-time awards for graduate studies are open to members of Kappa Gamma Pi, the National Catholic College Graduate Honor Society. They are awarded annually and may be applied as needed for graduate expenses at any accredited university. Deadline: April 20.

Award: Scholarship for use in freshman, sophomore, junior, senior, graduate, or postgraduate years; not renewable. *Number:* 2–4. *Amount:* $3000.

Eligibility Requirements: Applicant must be enrolled or expecting to enroll full or part-time at an institution or university. Available to U.S. and non-U.S. citizens.

Application Requirements: Application, essay, financial need analysis, references. *Deadline:* April 20.

Contact: Susan Smith Jaros, Cornaro Scholarship Chair
Kappa Gamma Pi
160 Rosedale Place
Rossford, OH 43460
Fax: 419-696-7341
E-mail: susan_jaros@mhsnr.org

KNIGHTS OF COLUMBUS   http://www.kofc.org

FOURTH DEGREE PRO DEO AND PRO PATRIA (CANADA)

Renewable scholarships for members of Canadian Knights of Columbus councils and their children who are entering first year of study for baccalaureate degree. Based on academic excellence.

Award: Scholarship for use in freshman year; renewable. *Number:* 12. *Amount:* $1500.

Eligibility Requirements: Applicant must be Roman Catholic; Canadian citizen and enrolled or expecting to enroll full-time at a four-year institution. Applicant or parent of applicant must be member of Knights of Columbus. Applicant must have 3.0 GPA or higher.

Application Requirements: Application, autobiography, references, test scores, transcript. *Deadline:* May 1.

Contact: Donald Barry, Director of Scholarship Aid
Knights of Columbus
PO Box 1670
New Haven, CT 06507-0901
Phone: 203-752-4332
Fax: 203-752-4103

FRANCIS P. MATTHEWS AND JOHN E. SWIFT EDUCATIONAL TRUST SCHOLARSHIPS

Available to dependent children of Knights of Columbus who died or became permanently and totally disabled while in military service during a time of conflict, from a cause connected with military service, or as the result of criminal violence while in the performance of their duties as full-time law enforcement officers or firemen. The scholarship is awarded at a Catholic college and includes the amount not covered by other financial aid for tuition, room, board, books and fees.

Award: Scholarship for use in freshman, sophomore, junior, or senior years; renewable. *Number:* 1–4. *Amount:* varies.

Eligibility Requirements: Applicant must be Roman Catholic and enrolled or expecting to enroll full-time at a four-year institution. Applicant or parent of applicant must be member of Knights of Columbus. Applicant must have 2.5 GPA or higher. Available to U.S. and non-U.S. citizens.

Application Requirements: Application. *Deadline:* Continuous.

Contact: Donald Barry, Director of Scholarship Aid
Knights of Columbus
PO Box 1670
New Haven, CT 06507-0901
Phone: 203-752-4332
Fax: 203-752-4103

JOHN W. MC DEVITT (FOURTH DEGREE) SCHOLARSHIPS

Renewable scholarship for students entering freshman year at a Catholic college or university. Applicant must submit Pro Deo and Pro Patria Scholarship application. Must be a member or wife, son, or daughter of a member of the Knights of Columbus. Minimum 3.0 GPA required.

Award: Scholarship for use in freshman year; renewable. *Number:* 36. *Amount:* $1500.

Eligibility Requirements: Applicant must be Roman Catholic and enrolled or expecting to enroll full-time at a two-year or four-year institution or university. Applicant or parent of applicant must be member of Knights of Columbus. Applicant must have 3.0 GPA or higher. Available to U.S. citizens.

Application Requirements: Application, autobiography, references, test scores, transcript. *Deadline:* March 1.

Contact: Donald Barry, Director of Scholarship Aid
Knights of Columbus
PO Box 1670
New Haven, CT 06507-0901
Phone: 203-752-4332
Fax: 203-752-4103

KNIGHTS OF LITHUANIA   http://www.knightsoflithuania.com

KNIGHTS OF LITHUANIA NATIONAL SCHOLARSHIPS

Awards available only for members of the Knights of Lithuania with a minimum of two years of prior membership. Minimum 2.5 GPA required.

Award: Scholarship for use in freshman, sophomore, junior, senior, graduate, or postgraduate years; not renewable. *Number:* 3–6. *Amount:* $1000–$4000.

Eligibility Requirements: Applicant must be Roman Catholic; of Lithuanian heritage and enrolled or expecting to enroll full or part-time at a four-year institution or university. Applicant or parent of applicant must be member of Knights of Lithuania. Applicant must have 2.5 GPA or higher. Available to U.S. citizens.

Knights of Lithuania (continued)

Application Requirements: Application, essay, financial need analysis, photo, references, self-addressed stamped envelope, test scores, transcript. *Deadline:* June 15.

Contact: John Baltrus, Chairperson
Knights of Lithuania
118 Vine Street
Jefferson Hills, PA 15025-4034
Phone: 412-233-2764
E-mail: jonaspb@verizon.net

LADIES AUXILIARY OF THE FLEET RESERVE ASSOCIATION   http://www.la-fra.org

ALLIE MAE ODEN MEMORIAL SCHOLARSHIP

Scholarships are given to the children/grandchildren of members of the FRA or LA FRA. Deadline is April 15. Selections are based on financial need, academic standing, character, and leadership qualities. Must be sponsored by a FRA member (living or deceased) in good standing.

Award: Scholarship for use in freshman, sophomore, junior, senior, graduate, or postgraduate years; not renewable. *Number:* varies. *Amount:* varies.

Eligibility Requirements: Applicant must be enrolled or expecting to enroll at a two-year or four-year institution or university. Applicant or parent of applicant must be member of Fleet Reserve Association/Auxiliary. Available to U.S. citizens. Applicant or parent must meet one or more of the following requirements: Coast Guard, Marine Corps, or Navy experience; retired from active duty; disabled or killed as a result of military service; prisoner of war; or missing in action.

Application Requirements: Application, transcript. *Deadline:* April 15.

Contact: Scholarship Administrator
Ladies Auxiliary of the Fleet Reserve Association
125 North West Street
Alexandria, VA 22314-2754
Phone: 858-748-5190
E-mail: powaydick@webtu.net

LADIES AUXILIARY TO THE VETERANS OF FOREIGN WARS   http://www.ladiesauxvfw.com

JUNIOR GIRLS SCHOLARSHIP PROGRAM

High school awards available to girls under 17 who have been members of Junior Girls Unit of Ladies Auxiliary for one year. Awards based on scholastic aptitude, participation in Junior Girls Unit, and school activities. Two one-time scholarships at $5000 and $10,000.

Award: Scholarship for use in freshman, sophomore, junior, or senior years; renewable. *Number:* up to 2. *Amount:* $5000–$10,000.

Eligibility Requirements: Applicant must be high school student; age 13-16; planning to enroll or expecting to enroll full-time at a two-year or four-year or technical institution; single female and must have an interest in leadership. Applicant or parent of applicant must be member of Veterans of Foreign Wars or Auxiliary. Applicant must have 3.0 GPA or higher. Available to U.S. citizens.

Application Requirements: Application, applicant must enter a contest, references, transcript. *Deadline:* March 11.

Contact: Judith Millick, Administrator of Programs
Ladies Auxiliary to the Veterans of Foreign Wars
406 West 34th Street, 10th Floor
Kansas City, MO 64111
Phone: 816-561-8655 Ext. 19
Fax: 816-931-4753
E-mail: jmillick@vfw.org

MILITARY BENEFIT ASSOCIATION   http://www.militarybenefit.org

MILITARY BENEFIT ASSOCIATION SCHOLARSHIP

Applicants for the scholarship must be dependent children of members of the Military Benefit Association. They must maintain a 2.5 or higher cumulative GPA or the equivalent. Applicants must have a high school degree or GED and plan to enroll in a full-time undergraduate course of study at an accredited two- or four-year college, university or vocational-technical school by fall of the year in which the award is granted.

Award: Scholarship for use in freshman, sophomore, junior, or senior years. *Number:* 5. *Amount:* $2000.

Eligibility Requirements: Applicant must be enrolled or expecting to enroll full-time at a two-year or four-year institution or university. Applicant or parent of applicant must be member of Minnesota Medical Association. Applicant or parent of applicant must have employment or volunteer experience in migrant worker. Applicant must have 2.5 GPA or higher. Available to U.S. citizens.

Application Requirements: Application, transcript. *Deadline:* February 15.

Contact: Military Benefit Association
PO Box 221110
Chantilly, VA 20153-1110
Phone: 800-336-0100

MINNESOTA AFL-CIO   http://www.mnaflcio.org

BILL PETERSON SCHOLARSHIP

Scholarship available to union member, spouse, or dependent to attend a postsecondary institution. Local must have participated or made a donation to the Bill Peterson Golf Tournament. See Web site for additional information. http://www.mnaflcio.org

Award: Scholarship for use in freshman, sophomore, junior, or senior years; not renewable. *Number:* 20. *Amount:* $1000.

Eligibility Requirements: Applicant must be enrolled or expecting to enroll at a two-year or four-year or technical institution or university; resident of Minnesota and studying in Minnesota. Applicant or parent of applicant must be member of AFL-CIO. Available to U.S. citizens.

Application Requirements: Application, essay. *Deadline:* April 1.

Contact: Jim Geelan, Organizing Director
Minnesota AFL-CIO
175 Aurora Avenue
St. Paul, MN 55103
Phone: 651-227-7647
Fax: 651-227-3801
E-mail: tgeelan@mnaflcio.org

MARTIN DUFFY ADULT LEARNER SCHOLARSHIP AWARD

Scholarship available for union members affiliated with the Minnesota AFL-CIO or the Minnesota Joint Council 32. May be used at any postsecondary institution in Minnesota. Deadline is April 30. Information available on Web site at http://www.mnaflcio.org

Award: Scholarship for use in freshman, sophomore, junior, or senior years; not renewable. *Number:* 4. *Amount:* $500.

Eligibility Requirements: Applicant must be enrolled or expecting to enroll at a two-year or four-year or technical institution or university; resident of Minnesota and studying in Minnesota. Applicant or parent of applicant must be member of AFL-CIO. Available to U.S. citizens.

Application Requirements: Application. *Deadline:* April 30.

Contact: Jim Geelan, Organizing Director
Minnesota AFL-CIO
175 Aurora Avenue
St. Paul, MN 55103
Phone: 651-227-7647
Fax: 651-227-3801
E-mail: tgeelan@mnaflcio.org

MINNESOTA AFL-CIO SCHOLARSHIPS

Must be attending a college or university located within the state of Minnesota. Applicant must have a parent or legal guardian who has held for a period of one year membership in a local union which is an affiliate of the Minnesota AFL-CIO. Winners are selected by lot. Academic eligibility based on a straight "B" average or better. See Web site (http://www.mnaflcio.org) for information and application.

Award: Scholarship for use in freshman year; not renewable. *Number:* up to 5. *Amount:* $1000.

Eligibility Requirements: Applicant must be high school student; planning to enroll or expecting to enroll full-time at a two-year or four-year or technical institution or university and studying in

Minnesota. Applicant or parent of applicant must be member of AFL-CIO. Applicant must have 3.0 GPA or higher. Available to U.S. and non-U.S. citizens.

Application Requirements: Application, transcript. *Deadline:* May 1.

Contact: Jim Geelan, Organizing Director
Minnesota AFL-CIO
175 Aurora Avenue
St. Paul, MN 55103
Phone: 651-227-7647
Fax: 651-227-3801
E-mail: tgeelan@mnaflcio.org

NATIONAL ALLIANCE OF POSTAL AND FEDERAL EMPLOYEES (NAPFE)   http://www.napfe.com

ASHBY B. CARTER MEMORIAL SCHOLARSHIP PROGRAM

Scholarship for the dependents of members of National Allaince of Postal and Federal Employees. Applicant should be a high school senior and should have taken the aptitude test of College Board Entrance Examination.

Award: Scholarship for use in freshman year. *Number:* 3. *Amount:* $2000–$5000.

Eligibility Requirements: Applicant must be high school student and planning to enroll or expecting to enroll full-time at an institution or university. Applicant or parent of applicant must be member of National Alliance of Postal and Federal Employees. Available to U.S. citizens.

Application Requirements: Application. *Deadline:* varies.

Contact: Melissa Jeffries-Stewart, Director
National Alliance of Postal and Federal Employees (NAPFE)
1628 11th Street, NW
Washington, DC 20001
Phone: 202-939-6325 Ext. 239
Fax: 202-939-6389
E-mail: headquarters@napfe.org

NATIONAL ASSOCIATION FOR THE ADVANCEMENT OF COLORED PEOPLE   http://www.naacp.org

AGNES JONES JACKSON SCHOLARSHIP

Must be current NAACP member, citizen of U.S., and enrolled full-time in accredited college. Graduating high school seniors and undergraduate students must have minimum 2.5 GPA. Graduate students must have 3.0 GPA and be full- or part-time. Must also demonstrate financial need. Must not have reached 25 years of age. Undergraduate scholarship awards $1500, graduate awards $2500. Deadline is April 30.

Award: Scholarship for use in freshman, sophomore, junior, senior, or graduate years; not renewable. *Number:* varies. *Amount:* $1500–$2500.

Eligibility Requirements: Applicant must be American Indian/Alaska Native, Asian/Pacific Islander, Black (non-Hispanic), or Hispanic; age 24 or under and enrolled or expecting to enroll full or part-time at a four-year institution or university. Applicant or parent of applicant must be member of National Association for the Advancement of Colored People. Available to U.S. citizens.

Application Requirements: Application, financial need analysis, references, transcript, evidence of NAACP membership. *Deadline:* April 30.

Contact: Donna Lakins, Education Department, Scholarship Request
National Association for the Advancement of Colored People
4805 Mt. Hope Drive
Baltimore, MD 21215-3297
Phone: 410-580-5760
Fax: 410-585-1329

ROY WILKINS SCHOLARSHIP

One-time award of $500 to $1000. Must be full-time freshman entering into accredited U.S. college. Must be U.S. citizen and have minimum 2.5 GPA. NAACP membership and participation is preferable.

Award: Scholarship for use in freshman year; not renewable. *Number:* varies. *Amount:* $500–$1000.

Eligibility Requirements: Applicant must be American Indian/Alaska Native, Asian/Pacific Islander, Black (non-Hispanic), or Hispanic; high

school student and planning to enroll or expecting to enroll full-time at a four-year institution or university. Applicant or parent of applicant must be member of National Association for the Advancement of Colored People. Applicant must have 2.5 GPA or higher. Available to U.S. citizens.

Application Requirements: Application, financial need analysis, references, transcript. *Deadline:* April 30.

Contact: Donna Lakins, Education Department, Scholarship Request
National Association for the Advancement of Colored People
4805 Mt. Hope Drive
Baltimore, MD 21215-3297
Phone: 410-580-5760
Fax: 410-585-1329

NATIONAL ASSOCIATION OF ENERGY SERVICE COMPANIES   http://www.aesc.net

ASSOCIATION OF ENERGY SERVICE COMPANIES SCHOLARSHIP PROGRAM

Applicant must be the legal dependant of an employee from an AESC member company, or an employee. Dependants of company officers are not eligible. Must submit application to local AESC Chapter Chairman. Application must include ACT or SAT test scores.

Award: Scholarship for use in freshman, sophomore, or junior years; renewable. *Number:* 1.

Eligibility Requirements: Applicant must be enrolled or expecting to enroll at a two-year or four-year or technical institution or university. Applicant or parent of applicant must be member of Association of Energy Service Companies. Available to U.S. citizens.

Application Requirements: Application, essay, test scores, transcript. *Deadline:* March 14.

Contact: Darla Eggleston, Administrative Assistant
National Association of Energy Service Companies
10200 Richmond Avenue
Suite 253
Houston, TX 77042
Phone: 800-692-0771
Fax: 713-781-7542
E-mail: degggleston@aesc.net

NATIONAL ASSOCIATION OF SECONDARY SCHOOL PRINCIPALS   http://www.principals.org

NATIONAL HONOR SOCIETY SCHOLARSHIPS

One-time award available only to high school seniors who are National Honor Society members, for use at an accredited two- or four-year college or university in the U.S. Based on outstanding scholarship, leadership, service, and character. Application fee $6. Contact school counselor or NHS chapter adviser. Minimum 3.0 GPA.

Award: Scholarship for use in freshman year; not renewable. *Number:* 200. *Amount:* $1000.

Eligibility Requirements: Applicant must be high school student and planning to enroll or expecting to enroll full-time at a two-year or four-year institution or university. Applicant or parent of applicant must be member of National Honor Society. Applicant must have 3.0 GPA or higher. Available to U.S. and non-Canadian citizens.

Application Requirements: Application, essay, references, test scores, transcript. *Fee:* $6. *Deadline:* January 19.

Contact: local school's NHS chapter adviser

NATIONAL BETA CLUB   http://www.betaclub.org

NATIONAL BETA CLUB SCHOLARSHIP

Applicant must be in 12th grade and a member of the National Beta Club. Must be nominated by school chapter of the National Beta Club, therefore, applications will not be sent to the individual students. Renewable and nonrenewable awards available. Contact school Beta Club sponsor for more information.

Award: Scholarship for use in freshman year; renewable. *Number:* 208. *Amount:* $1000–$15,000.

Eligibility Requirements: Applicant must be high school student and planning to enroll or expecting to enroll full-time at a two-year or

National Beta Club (continued)

four-year institution or university. Applicant or parent of applicant must be member of National Beta Club. Available to U.S. citizens.

Application Requirements: Application, essay, references, test scores, transcript. *Deadline:* December 10.

Contact: Charles Tillotson, Executive Director
National Beta Club
151 Beta Club Way
Spartanburg, SC 29306-3012
Phone: 800-845-8281 Ext. 123
Fax: 864-542-9300
E-mail: ctillotson@betaclub.org

NATIONAL FOSTER PARENT ASSOCIATION   http://www.nfpainc.org

NATIONAL FOSTER PARENT ASSOCIATION SCHOLARSHIP

Award for high school senior who will be entering first year of college, comparable education, or training program. Five $1000 awards, three for foster children currently in foster care with an NFPA member family, and one each for birth and adopted children of foster parents. NFPA family membership required ($35 membership fee).

Award: Scholarship for use in freshman year; not renewable. *Number:* 5. *Amount:* $1000.

Eligibility Requirements: Applicant must be high school student; age 17 and planning to enroll or expecting to enroll full-time at a two-year or four-year or technical institution or university. Applicant or parent of applicant must be member of National Foster Parent Association. Available to U.S. citizens.

Application Requirements: Application, autobiography, essay, financial need analysis, photo, references, test scores, transcript. *Deadline:* March 31.

Contact: Karen Jorgenson, Executive Director
National Foster Parent Association
7512 Stanich Avenue, Suite 6
Gig Harbor, WA 98335
Phone: 253-853-4000
Fax: 253-853-4001
E-mail: info@nfpainc.org

NATIONAL FRATERNAL SOCIETY OF THE DEAF   http://www.nfsd.com

NATIONAL FRATERNAL SOCIETY OF THE DEAF SCHOLARSHIPS

Provides scholarship to cover room and board, tuition and/or fees. Applicants must be members of the NFSD for one full year and in a postsecondary program or ready to enter one as a full-time student.

Award: Scholarship for use in freshman, sophomore, junior, senior, graduate, or postgraduate years; not renewable. *Number:* 5. *Amount:* $1000.

Eligibility Requirements: Applicant must be enrolled or expecting to enroll full-time at a two-year or four-year institution or university. Applicant or parent of applicant must be member of National Fraternal Society of the Deaf. Available to U.S. citizens.

Application Requirements: Application, photo, references, transcript. *Deadline:* July 1.

Contact: Scholarship Information
National Fraternal Society of the Deaf
1118 South 6th Street
Springfield, IL 62703
Phone: 217-789-7429
Fax: 217-789-7489
E-mail: thefrat@nfsd.com

NATIONAL JUNIOR ANGUS ASSOCIATION   http://www.njaa.info

ANGUS FOUNDATION SCHOLARSHIPS

Applicants must have at one time been a National Junior Angus Association member and must currently be a junior, regular or life member of the American Angus Association. Must be applied to undergraduate studies in

any field. Applicants must have a minimum 2.0 GPA. See Web site for further information and to download application.

Award: Scholarship for use in freshman, sophomore, junior, or senior years; not renewable. *Number:* 20. *Amount:* $1000–$3500.

Eligibility Requirements: Applicant must be age 25 or under and enrolled or expecting to enroll full-time at a two-year or four-year or technical institution or university. Applicant or parent of applicant must be member of American Angus Association. Available to U.S. citizens.

Application Requirements: Application, references, transcript. *Deadline:* May 1.

Contact: James Fisher, Director of Activities and Junior Activities
National Junior Angus Association
3201 Frederick Avenue
St. Joseph, MO 64506
Phone: 816-383-5100
Fax: 816-233-9703
E-mail: jfisher@angus.org

NATIONAL MILITARY INTELLIGENCE ASSOCIATION   http://www.nmia.org/Scholarship.html

NATIONAL MILITARY INTELLIGENCE ASSOCIATION SCHOLARSHIP

One-time award for the dependent children of NMIA members pursuing an undergraduate degree. Award is based on merit. Must be a U.S. citizen. Minimum 3.0 GPA is required. Application deadline is November 1. Information on Web site at http://www.nmia.org.

Award: Scholarship for use in freshman, sophomore, junior, or senior years; not renewable. *Number:* 1–3. *Amount:* $1000.

Eligibility Requirements: Applicant must be enrolled or expecting to enroll full-time at a four-year institution or university. Applicant or parent of applicant must be member of National Military Intelligence Association. Applicant must have 3.0 GPA or higher. Available to U.S. citizens.

Application Requirements: Application, test scores. *Deadline:* November 1.

Contact: National Military Intelligence Association
PO Box 489
Hamilton, VA 20159

NATIONAL RIFLE ASSOCIATION   http://www.nrahq.org

JEANNE E. BRAY MEMORIAL SCHOLARSHIP PROGRAM

Renewable award of up to $2000 for dependent of NRA member who is a current full-time commissioned peace officer, an officer killed in the line of duty, a retired peace officer, or a peace officer disabled as a result of an incident occurring in the line of duty. Intended for full-time study. Minimum 2.5 GPA required.

Award: Scholarship for use in freshman, sophomore, junior, or senior years; renewable. *Number:* varies. *Amount:* up to $2000.

Eligibility Requirements: Applicant must be enrolled or expecting to enroll full-time at a two-year or four-year institution or university. Applicant or parent of applicant must be member of National Rifle Association. Applicant must have 2.5 GPA or higher. Available to U.S. citizens.

Application Requirements: Application, essay, references, test scores, transcript. *Deadline:* November 15.

Contact: National Rifle Association of America
National Rifle Association
11250 Waples Mill Road
Fairfax, VA 22030
Phone: 703-267-1354
Fax: 703-267-3743

NATIONAL SOCIETY DAUGHTERS OF THE AMERICAN REVOLUTION   http://www.dar.org

NATIONAL SOCIETY DAUGHTERS OF THE AMERICAN REVOLUTION LILLIAN AND ARTHUR DUNN SCHOLARSHIP

These renewable awards are available to graduating high school seniors whose mothers are active members of the DAR. Must include DAR member number. Must be sponsored by DAR chapter. Awards based on scholarship, need, and commitment to field of study. Must submit self-addressed stamped envelope to be considered. Deadline is February 15.

Award: Scholarship for use in freshman, sophomore, junior, senior, or graduate years; renewable. *Number:* 4. *Amount:* $2000.

Eligibility Requirements: Applicant must be high school student and planning to enroll or expecting to enroll at a four-year institution or university. Applicant or parent of applicant must be member of Daughters of the American Revolution. Applicant must have 3.0 GPA or higher. Available to U.S. citizens.

Application Requirements: Application, essay, financial need analysis, references, self-addressed stamped envelope, test scores, transcript. *Deadline:* February 15.

Contact: Committee Services Office, Scholarship
National Society Daughters of the American Revolution
1776 D Street, NW
Washington, DC 20006-5392

NATIONAL UNION OF PUBLIC AND GENERAL EMPLOYEES
http://www.nupge.ca

SCHOLARSHIP FOR ABORIGINAL CANADIANS

Award for Aboriginal Canadian students who plan to enter the first year of a Canadian college or university and who are children or foster children of a member of the National Union of Public and General Employees. Must write a 750-1000-word essay on "The importance of quality public services in enhancing the quality of life of Aboriginal Canadians".

Award: Scholarship for use in freshman year. *Number:* 1. *Amount:* $1500.

Eligibility Requirements: Applicant must be of Canadian heritage and Canadian citizen; high school student; planning to enroll or expecting to enroll full-time at a four-year institution or university and studying in Alberta, British Columbia, Manitoba, New Brunswick, Newfoundland, North West Territories, Nova Scotia, Ontario, Prince Edward Island, Quebec, Saskatchewan, or Yukon. Applicant or parent of applicant must be member of National Union of Public and General Employees.

Application Requirements: Application, applicant must enter a contest, essay. *Deadline:* June 30.

Contact: Louise Trepanier
National Union of Public and General Employees
15 Auriga Drive
Nepean K2E 1B7
Canada
Phone: 613-228-9800
Fax: 613-228-9801
E-mail: ltrepanier@nupge.ca

SCHOLARSHIP FOR VISIBLE MINORITIES

Award for first-year Canadian students who are, by race or color, in a visible minority and who are children or foster children of a member of the National Union of Public and General Employees. Must write a 750-1000-word essay on "The importance of quality public services in enhancing the quality of life of visible minorities".

Award: Scholarship for use in freshman year. *Number:* 1. *Amount:* $1500.

Eligibility Requirements: Applicant must be Canadian citizen; American Indian/Alaska Native, Asian/Pacific Islander, Black (non-Hispanic), or Hispanic; high school student; planning to enroll or expecting to enroll full-time at a four-year institution or university and studying in Alberta, British Columbia, Manitoba, New Brunswick, Newfoundland, North West Territories, Nova Scotia, Ontario, Prince Edward Island, Quebec, Saskatchewan, or Yukon. Applicant or parent of applicant must be member of National Union of Public and General Employees.

Application Requirements: Application, applicant must enter a contest, essay. *Deadline:* June 30.

Contact: Louise Trepanier
National Union of Public and General Employees
15 Auriga Drive
Nepean K2E 1B7
Canada
Phone: 613-228-9800
Fax: 613-228-9801
E-mail: ltrepanier@nupge.ca

TERRY FOX MEMORIAL SCHOLARSHIP

Award for Canadian students with disabilities who plan to enter the first year of a Canadian college or university and who are the children or foster children of a member of the National Union of Public and General Employees. Must write a 750-1000-word essay on: "The importance of quality public services in enhancing the quality of life of people with disabilities".

Award: Scholarship for use in freshman year. *Number:* 1. *Amount:* $1500.

Eligibility Requirements: Applicant must be Canadian citizen; high school student; planning to enroll or expecting to enroll full-time at a four-year institution or university and studying in Alberta, British Columbia, Manitoba, New Brunswick, Newfoundland, North West Territories, Nova Scotia, Ontario, Prince Edward Island, Quebec, Saskatchewan, or Yukon. Applicant or parent of applicant must be member of National Union of Public and General Employees. Applicant must be hearing impaired, learning disabled, physically disabled, or visually impaired.

Application Requirements: Application, applicant must enter a contest, essay. *Deadline:* June 30.

Contact: Louise Trepanier
National Union of Public and General Employees
15 Auriga Drive
Nepean K2E 1B7
Canada
Phone: 613-228-9800
Fax: 613-228-9801
E-mail: ltrepanier@nupge.ca

TOMMY DOUGLAS SCHOLARSHIP

Award for first-year students at a Canadian college or university who are children or foster children of members of National Union of Public and General Employees. Must write an essay on the topic: "How Tommy Douglas contributed to making Canada a more just and equitable society".

Award: Scholarship for use in freshman year. *Number:* 1. *Amount:* $1500.

Eligibility Requirements: Applicant must be Canadian citizen; high school student; planning to enroll or expecting to enroll full-time at an institution or university and studying in Alberta, British Columbia, Manitoba, New Brunswick, Newfoundland, North West Territories, Nova Scotia, Ontario, Prince Edward Island, Quebec, Saskatchewan, or Yukon. Applicant or parent of applicant must be member of National Union of Public and General Employees.

Application Requirements: Application, applicant must enter a contest, essay. *Deadline:* June 30.

Contact: Louise Trepanier
National Union of Public and General Employees
15 Auriga Drive
Nepean K2E 1B7
Canada
Phone: 613-228-9800
Fax: 613-228-9801
E-mail: ltrepanier@nupge.ca

NATSO FOUNDATION
http://www.natsofoundation.org

BILL MOON SCHOLARSHIP

Available to employees or dependents of NATSO-affiliated truckstops/travel plazas. Visit Web site at http://www.natsofoundation.org for additional information.

Award: Scholarship for use in freshman, sophomore, junior, senior, or graduate years; not renewable. *Number:* 5–12. *Amount:* up to $2500.

Eligibility Requirements: Applicant must be enrolled or expecting to enroll full or part-time at a two-year or four-year institution or university. Applicant or parent of applicant must be member of

NATSO Foundation (continued)

NATSO Foundation. Applicant or parent of applicant must have employment or volunteer experience in designated career field. Available to U.S. and non-U.S. citizens.

Application Requirements: Application, essay, financial need analysis, references, transcript, signature from employer. *Deadline:* April 14.

Contact: Heather Mooney, Bill Moon Scholarship Committee
NATSO Foundation
60 Main Street
Farmington, CT 06032

NEBRASKA DECA   http://www.nedeca.org

NEBRASKA DECA LEADERSHIP SCHOLARSHIP

For applicants who intend to pursue a full-time two-year or four-year course of study in a marketing or business-related field. Applicant must be active in DECA and involved in community service activities.

Award: Scholarship for use in freshman year; not renewable. *Number:* 2–6. *Amount:* $250–$500.

Eligibility Requirements: Applicant must be enrolled or expecting to enroll full-time at a two-year or four-year or technical institution or university and resident of Nebraska. Applicant or parent of applicant must be member of Distribution Ed Club or Future Business Leaders of America. Applicant must have 2.5 GPA or higher. Available to U.S. citizens.

Application Requirements: Application, essay, resume, references, test scores, transcript, DECA participation and accomplishment documents. *Deadline:* February 1.

Contact: Scholarship Review Committee
Nebraska DECA
301 Centennial Mall South
Lincoln, NE 68509-4987
Phone: 402-471-4803
E-mail: nedeca@nedeca.org

NEW YORK STATE AFL-CIO   http://www.nysaflcio.org

NEW YORK STATE AFL-CIO SCHOLARSHIP

Applicant must be a New York State high school graduate, planning to enroll in a New York state postsecondary school. Parent or guardian must be a member of a union affiliated with the NYS AFL-CIO. Must be accepted in a course of study in labor relations or a related field. Renewable award for $8000 ($2000 per year). Application deadline is May 1.

Award: Scholarship for use in freshman, sophomore, junior, or senior years; renewable. *Number:* 1. *Amount:* $2000.

Eligibility Requirements: Applicant must be high school student; planning to enroll or expecting to enroll full-time at a two-year or four-year or technical institution or university; resident of New York and studying in New York. Applicant or parent of applicant must be member of AFL-CIO. Available to U.S. citizens.

Application Requirements: Application, essay, references. *Deadline:* May 1.

Contact: Gary Duesberg, Education Director
New York State AFL-CIO
New York State AFL-CIO, 100 South Swan Street
Albany, NY 12210-1939
Phone: 518-436-8516 Ext. 244

NEW YORK STATE GRANGE   http://www.nysgrange.com/

SUSAN W. FREESTONE EDUCATION AWARD

Grants are for members of Junior Grange and Subordinate Grange in New York State. Students must enroll in an approved two or four-year college in New York State. Second grants available with reapplication. Minimum 2.5 GPA required.

Award: Scholarship for use in freshman, sophomore, junior, or senior years; renewable. *Amount:* $500–$1000.

Eligibility Requirements: Applicant must be enrolled or expecting to enroll full-time at a two-year or four-year institution; resident of New York and studying in New York. Applicant or parent of applicant must be member of Grange Association. Applicant must have 2.5 GPA or higher. Available to U.S. citizens.

Application Requirements: Application, financial need analysis, references, transcript. *Deadline:* April 15.

Contact: Ann Hall, Scholarship Chairperson
New York State Grange
100 Grange Place
Cortland, NY 13045
Phone: 607-756-7553
Fax: 607-756-7757
E-mail: nysgrange@nysgrange.com

NEW YORK STATE SOCIETY OF PROFESSIONAL ENGINEERS   http://www.nysspe.org

NYSSPE-PAST OFFICERS' SCHOLARSHIP

Scholarship awarded to the child of a NYSSPE member in the amount of $1000. Based on academic achievement. GPA of 3.6 or higher.

Award: Scholarship for use in freshman, sophomore, junior, or senior years; not renewable. *Number:* 1. *Amount:* $1000.

Eligibility Requirements: Applicant must be enrolled or expecting to enroll full-time at an institution or university. Applicant or parent of applicant must be member of New York State Society of Professional Engineers. Available to U.S. citizens.

Application Requirements: Application, essay, references, test scores, transcript. *Deadline:* December 1.

Contact: NYSSPE
New York State Society of Professional Engineers
RPI Technology Park, 385 Jordan Road
Troy, NY 12180
Phone: 518-283-7490
E-mail: jamiller@nysspe.org

NON COMMISSIONED OFFICERS ASSOCIATION (NCOA)   http://www.ncoausa.org

NON-COMMISSIONED OFFICERS ASSOCIATION SCHOLARSHIPS

Awards for children and spouses of members of the Non-Commissioned Officers Association. Must be full-time student. Deadline is March 31. Children of members must be under age 25 to receive initial grant. Applicant must maintain 3.0 GPA for renewal.

Award: Scholarship for use in freshman, sophomore, junior, or senior years; renewable. *Number:* 16. *Amount:* $900–$1000.

Eligibility Requirements: Applicant must be age 24 or under and enrolled or expecting to enroll full-time at a four-year institution. Applicant or parent of applicant must be member of Non Commissioned Officers Association. Applicant must have 3.0 GPA or higher. Available to U.S. citizens.

Application Requirements: Application, autobiography, essay, references, test scores, transcript. *Deadline:* March 31.

Contact: Hilda Atkinson, Scholarship Department
Non Commissioned Officers Association (NCOA)
PO Box 33610
San Antonio, TX 78265-3610
Phone: 210-653-6161 Ext. 261
Fax: 210-637-3337
E-mail: hatkinso@ncoausa.org

NORTH EAST ROOFING EDUCATIONAL FOUNDATION   http://www.nerca.org

NORTH EAST ROOFING EDUCATIONAL FOUNDATION SCHOLARSHIP

Applicants must be a member of NERCA, their employees, or their respective immediate family. Immediate family is defined as self, spouse, or child. The child may be natural, legally, adopted or a stepchild. Also must be a high school senior or graduate who plans to enroll in a full-time undergraduate course of study at an accredited two-year or four-year college, university, or vocational-technical school.

Award: Scholarship for use in freshman, sophomore, junior, or senior years; not renewable. *Number:* 4–5. *Amount:* up to $1500.

Eligibility Requirements: Applicant must be enrolled or expecting to enroll full or part-time at a two-year or four-year or technical institution or university. Applicant or parent of applicant must be member of National Roofing Contractors Association. Applicant or parent of applicant must have employment or volunteer experience in designated career field. Available to U.S. and Canadian citizens.

Application Requirements: Application, references, self-addressed stamped envelope, transcript. *Deadline:* April 30.

Contact: North East Roofing Educational Foundation
150, Grossman Drive Suite 313
Braintree, MA 02184
Phone: 781-849-3220
Fax: 781-849 Ext. 3223

NORTHEAST FRESH FOODS ALLIANCE
http://www.neffa.com

NORTHEAST FRESH FOODS ALLIANCE SCHOLARSHIP AWARDS PROGRAM

The scholarship is available to graduating seniors who are employed, or whose parents are employed, by a Northeast Fresh Foods Alliance member company. Please refer to the Web site for further details: http://www.neffa.com

Award: Scholarship for use in freshman or senior years; not renewable. *Number:* 15–20. *Amount:* $500.

Eligibility Requirements: Applicant must be high school student and planning to enroll or expecting to enroll full-time at a two-year or four-year or technical institution or university. Applicant or parent of applicant must be member of Northeast Fresh Foods Alliance. Applicant or parent of applicant must have employment or volunteer experience in food service. Available to U.S. citizens.

Application Requirements: Application, essay, references, transcript. *Deadline:* varies.

Contact: Andrea L. Walker, Executive Director
Northeast Fresh Foods Alliance
1189R North Main Street
Randolph, MA 02368
Phone: 781-963-9726
Fax: 781-963-5829
E-mail: andrea@neffa.com

NORTHEASTERN LOGGERS' ASSOCIATION, INC.
http://www.loggertraining.com

NORTHEASTERN LOGGERS' ASSOCIATION SCHOLARSHIPS

Scholarships available to those whose family belongs to the Northeastern Loggers' Association or whose family member is an employee of the Industrial and Associate Members of the Northeastern Loggers' Association. Must submit paper on topic of "What it means to grow up in the forest industry." Deadline: March 31.

Award: Scholarship for use in freshman, sophomore, junior, or senior years; not renewable. *Number:* 8. *Amount:* $500–$1000.

Eligibility Requirements: Applicant must be enrolled or expecting to enroll full-time at a two-year or four-year or technical institution or university and must have an interest in designated field specified by sponsor. Applicant or parent of applicant must be member of Northeastern Loggers Association. Available to U.S. and non-U.S. citizens.

Application Requirements: Application, essay, transcript. *Deadline:* March 31.

Contact: Mona Lincoln, Director, Training and Safety
Northeastern Loggers' Association, Inc.
PO Box 69
Old Forge, NY 13420-0069
Phone: 315-369-3078
Fax: 315-369-3736
E-mail: mona@loggertraining.com

OHIO 4-H
http://www.ohio4h.org

ALL AMERICAN YOUTH HORSE SHOW FOUNDATION 4-H SCHOLARSHIP

One $1500 scholarship to be awarded. Applicants must be high school seniors and current 4-H horse members planning to enroll in the fall at any accredited post secondary institution in any course of study.

Award: Scholarship for use in freshman year. *Number:* 1. *Amount:* $1500.

Eligibility Requirements: Applicant must be enrolled or expecting to enroll at an institution or university. Applicant or parent of applicant must be member of National 4-H. Available to U.S. citizens.

Application Requirements: Application, essay, resume, references, transcript. *Deadline:* January 27.

Contact: Jeff King, Assistant Director
Ohio 4-H
State 4-H Office, Room 25 Agriculture Administration Building
2120 Fyffe Road
Columbus, OH 43210-1084
Phone: 614-292-4444
Fax: 614-292-5937
E-mail: 4hweb@ag.osu.edu

CHARLES & GWYENNA LIFER 4-H SCHOLARSHIP

One $1000 scholarship to be awarded. Applicants must be 4-H members, seniors in high school during year of application, and planning to enroll autumn quarter at the Ohio State University main campus in Columbus with a major in the area of agriculture or natural resources. Secondary eligibility will be given to seniors planning to attend the Agricultural Technical Institute (ATI) located in Wooster, Ohio. Preference will be given to applicants from Richland, Knox, and Monroe counties.

Award: Scholarship for use in freshman year. *Number:* 1. *Amount:* $1000.

Eligibility Requirements: Applicant must be enrolled or expecting to enroll at an institution or university and studying in Ohio. Applicant or parent of applicant must be member of National 4-H. Available to U.S. citizens.

Application Requirements: Application, financial need analysis, resume, references, transcript. *Deadline:* January 27.

Contact: Jeff King, Assistant Director
Ohio 4-H
State 4-H Office, Room 25 Agriculture Administration Building
2120 Fyffe Road
Columbus, OH 43210-1084
Phone: 614-292-4444
Fax: 614-292-5937
E-mail: 4hweb@ag.osu.edu

MARY E. BORDER OHIO SCHOLARSHIP

Two $1000 scholarships to be awarded. Applicants must be high school seniors and current 4-H members planning to enroll in the fall at any accredited post secondary institution in any course of study.

Award: Scholarship for use in freshman year. *Number:* 2. *Amount:* $1000.

Eligibility Requirements: Applicant must be enrolled or expecting to enroll at an institution or university. Applicant or parent of applicant must be member of National 4-H. Available to U.S. citizens.

Application Requirements: Application, essay, resume, references, transcript. *Deadline:* January 27.

Contact: Jeff King, Assistant Director
Ohio 4-H
State 4-H Office, Room 25 Agriculture Administration Building
2120 Fyffe Road
Columbus, OH 43210-1084
Phone: 614-292-4444
Fax: 614-292-5937
E-mail: 4hweb@ag.osu.edu

MR. & MRS. G. DEMING SEYMOUR 4-H SCHOLARSHIP

One $1000 scholarship will be awarded. Applicants must be a present or former 4-H member, senior in high school, and planning to enroll as a freshman in the fall at The Ohio State University, Agricultural Technical Institute (ATI), or any of its regional campuses, in any academic area. Preference will be given to Richland County applicants.

Award: Scholarship for use in freshman year. *Number:* 1. *Amount:* $1000.

Eligibility Requirements: Applicant must be enrolled or expecting to enroll at an institution or university and studying in Ohio. Applicant or parent of applicant must be member of National 4-H. Available to U.S. citizens.

Application Requirements: Application, essay, resume, references, transcript. *Deadline:* January 27.

Ohio 4-H (continued)

Contact: Jeff King, Assistant Director
Ohio 4-H
State 4-H Office, Room 25 Agriculture Administration Building
2120 Fyffe Road
Columbus, OH 43210-1084
Phone: 614-292-4444
Fax: 614-292-5937
E-mail: 4hweb@ag.osu.edu

OHIO AMERICAN LEGION   http://ohioamericanlegion.org

OHIO AMERICAN LEGION SCHOLARSHIPS

One-time award for full-time students attending accredited institution. Open to students of any postsecondary academic year. Must have minimum 3.0 GPA. Deadline April 15. Must be a member of the American Legion, a direct descendent of a Legionnaire (living or deceased), or surviving spouse or child of a deceased U.S. military person who died on active duty or of injuries received on active duty.

Award: Scholarship for use in freshman, sophomore, junior, or senior years; not renewable. *Number:* 15–18. *Amount:* $2000–$3000.

Eligibility Requirements: Applicant must be enrolled or expecting to enroll full-time at a two-year or four-year or technical institution or university. Applicant or parent of applicant must be member of American Legion or Auxiliary. Applicant must have 3.0 GPA or higher. Available to U.S. and non-U.S. citizens. Applicant or parent must meet one or more of the following requirements: general military experience; retired from active duty; disabled or killed as a result of military service; prisoner of war; or missing in action.

Application Requirements: Application, transcript. *Deadline:* April 15.

Contact: Donald Lanthorn, Service Director
Ohio American Legion
60 Big Run Road, PO Box 8007
Delaware, OH 43015
Phone: 740-362-7478
Fax: 740-362-1429
E-mail: dlanthorn@iwaynet.net

OHIO CIVIL SERVICE EMPLOYEES ASSOCIATION   http://www.ocsea.org

LES BEST SCHOLARSHIP

Twelve scholarships worth up to $1000 will be awarded to eligible union members, spouses and their dependent children. For more details see Web site: http://www.ocsea.org.

Award: Scholarship for use in freshman, sophomore, junior, or senior years; not renewable. *Number:* 8–12. *Amount:* $250–$1000.

Eligibility Requirements: Applicant must be enrolled or expecting to enroll full or part-time at a two-year or four-year or technical institution or university and resident of Ohio. Applicant or parent of applicant must be member of Ohio Civil Service Employee Association. Available to U.S. citizens.

Application Requirements: Application, essay, references, transcript, proof of enrollment. *Deadline:* April 2.

Contact: Les Best Scholarship Program
Ohio Civil Service Employees Association
390 Worthington Road, Suite A
Westerville, OH 43082-8331
Phone: 614-865-4740
Fax: 614-865-4777

OKLAHOMA ALUMNI & ASSOCIATES OF FHA, HERO AND FCCLA, INC.   http://www.okfccla.org

OKLAHOMA ALUMNI & ASSOCIATES OF FHA, HERO AND FCCLA, INC. SCHOLARSHIP

Financial aid for academically promising FCCLA members who will be pursuing a postsecondary education. Must be a resident of Oklahoma, show financial need, minimum GPA of 3.0 required.

Award: Scholarship for use in freshman year; not renewable. *Number:* 2. *Amount:* $1000.

Eligibility Requirements: Applicant must be high school student; planning to enroll or expecting to enroll full-time at a two-year or four-year or technical institution or university and resident of Oklahoma. Applicant or parent of applicant must be member of Family, Career and Community Leaders of America. Applicant must have 3.0 GPA or higher. Available to U.S. citizens.

Application Requirements: Application, essay, references, transcript. *Deadline:* March 1.

Contact: Denise Morris, State FCCLA Adviser
Oklahoma Alumni & Associates of FHA, HERO and FCCLA, Inc.
1500 West Seventh Avenue
Stillwater, OK 74074
Phone: 405-743-5467
Fax: 405-743-6809
E-mail: dmorr@okcareertech.org

OREGON STUDENT ASSISTANCE COMMISSION   http://www.osac.state.or.us

AFSCME: AMERICAN FEDERATION OF STATE, COUNTY, AND MUNICIPAL EMPLOYEES LOCAL 1724 SCHOLARSHIP

Award for active, laid-off, retired, or disabled members in good standing or spouses (including life partners and their children), natural children, stepchildren, or grandchildren of active, laid-off retired, disabled, or deceased members in good standing. Qualifying members must have been active in AFSCME Local 1724 one year or more as of March 1 of the year in which the scholarship application is filed, or a member one year or more preceding the date of layoff, death, disability.

Award: Scholarship for use in freshman, sophomore, junior, senior, or graduate years; not renewable. *Number:* 3. *Amount:* $667.

Eligibility Requirements: Applicant must be enrolled or expecting to enroll full or part-time at a four-year institution and resident of Oregon. Applicant or parent of applicant must be member of American Federation of State, County, and Municipal Employees. Available to U.S. citizens.

Application Requirements: Application, essay, financial need analysis, references, transcript, activity chart. *Deadline:* March 1.

Contact: Director of Grant Programs
Oregon Student Assistance Commission
1500 Valley River Drive, Suite 100
Eugene, OR 97401-7020
Phone: 800-452-8807 Ext. 7395

AFSCME: AMERICAN FEDERATION OF STATE, COUNTY, AND MUNICIPAL EMPLOYEES LOCAL 75 SCHOLARSHIP

One-time award for active, laid-off, retired, or disabled members in good standing or spouses (including life partners and their children), natural children, or grandchildren of active, laid-off, retired, disabled, or deceased members in good standing. Qualifying members must have been active in AFSCME Local 75 one year or more as of March 1 of the year in which the scholarship application is filed or have been a member one year or more preceding the date of layoff, death, disability, or retirement. Part-time enrollment (minimum six credit hours) will be considered, but only for active members, spouses (or life partners), or laid-off members. Additional essay required. College students must have minimum cumulative 2.5 GPA; graduating high school seniors must have minimum 3.0 GPA and combined achievement test scores of 1100+.

Award: Scholarship for use in freshman, sophomore, junior, senior, or graduate years; renewable. *Number:* 6. *Amount:* $583.

Eligibility Requirements: Applicant must be American Indian/Alaska Native, Asian/Pacific Islander, Black (non-Hispanic), or Hispanic; enrolled or expecting to enroll full or part-time at an institution or university and resident of Oregon. Applicant or parent of applicant must be member of American Federation of State, County, and Municipal Employees. Applicant must be hearing impaired, learning disabled, physically disabled, or visually impaired. Available to U.S. citizens. Applicant or parent must meet one or more of the following requirements: general military experience; retired from active duty; disabled or killed as a result of military service; prisoner of war; or missing in action.

Application Requirements: Application, autobiography, driver's license, essay, financial need analysis, interview, photo, portfolio, resume, references, self-addressed stamped envelope, test scores, transcript, activity chart. *Deadline:* March 1.

Contact: Director of Grant Programs
Oregon Student Assistance Commission
1500 Valley River Drive, Suite 100
Eugene, OR 97401-7020
Phone: 800-452-8807 Ext. 7395

INTERNATIONAL BROTHERHOOD OF ELECTRICAL WORKERS LOCAL 280 SCHOLARSHIP

Scholarship available for children or grandchildren of active or retired members of IBEW Local 280 who are residents of Oregon. Not based on financial need. Deadline is March 1.

Award: Scholarship for use in freshman, sophomore, junior, or senior years; not renewable. *Number:* varies. *Amount:* $500.

Eligibility Requirements: Applicant must be enrolled or expecting to enroll at an institution or university and resident of Oregon. Applicant or parent of applicant must be member of International Brotherhood of Electrical Workers. Available to U.S. citizens.

Application Requirements: Application, essay, transcript, activities chart. *Deadline:* March 1.

Contact: Director of Grant Programs
Oregon Student Assistance Commission
1500 Valley River Drive, Suite 100
Eugene, OR 97401-7020
Phone: 800-452-8807 Ext. 7395

INTERNATIONAL UNION OF OPERATING ENGINEERS LOCAL 701 SCHOLARSHIP

Scholarship available for graduating high school seniors who are children of Local 701 members. Not based on financial need. Deadline is March 1.

Award: Scholarship for use in freshman year; not renewable. *Number:* varies. *Amount:* $500.

Eligibility Requirements: Applicant must be high school student; planning to enroll or expecting to enroll at an institution or university and resident of Oregon. Applicant or parent of applicant must be member of International Union of Operating Engineers. Available to U.S. citizens.

Application Requirements: Application, essay, transcript, activities chart. *Deadline:* March 1.

Contact: Director of Grant Programs
Oregon Student Assistance Commission
1500 Valley River Drive, Suite 100
Eugene, OR 97401-7020
Phone: 800-452-8807 Ext. 7395

OREGON PUBLISHING COMPANY/HILLIARD SCHOLARSHIP

Available for graduating high school seniors who are members of the Prospective Gents Club of the Bridge Builders organization. Must be in the process of completing requirements for Bridge Builders "Rites of Passage Program." Automatically renewable upon volunteer service to Bridge Builders Program.

Award: Scholarship for use in freshman year; renewable. *Number:* 1. *Amount:* $2500.

Eligibility Requirements: Applicant must be high school student; planning to enroll or expecting to enroll at a four-year institution and resident of Oregon. Available to U.S. citizens.

Application Requirements: Application, essay, financial need analysis, references, transcript, activity chart. *Deadline:* March 1.

Contact: Director of Grant Programs
Oregon Student Assistance Commission
1500 Valley River Drive, Suite 100
Eugene, OR 97401-7020
Phone: 800-452-8807 Ext. 7395

OREGON STATE FISCAL ASSOCIATION SCHOLARSHIP

One-time award for OSFA members or their children. Members may enroll part-time and must study public administration, finance, economics, or related fields. Children of members must enroll full-time and may enter any program of study. Must be enrolled in an Oregon college.

Award: Scholarship for use in freshman, sophomore, junior, senior, or graduate years; renewable. *Number:* 2. *Amount:* $500.

Eligibility Requirements: Applicant must be enrolled or expecting to enroll full or part-time at a two-year or four-year institution; resident of Oregon and studying in Oregon. Applicant or parent of applicant must be member of Oregon State Fiscal Association. Available to U.S. citizens.

Application Requirements: Application, essay, financial need analysis, references, transcript, activity chart. *Deadline:* March 1.

Contact: Director of Grant Programs
Oregon Student Assistance Commission
1500 Valley River Drive, Suite 100
Eugene, OR 97401-7020
Phone: 800-452-8807 Ext. 7395

TEAMSTERS CLYDE C. CROSBY/JOSEPH M. EDGAR MEMORIAL SCHOLARSHIP

One-time scholarship available for a graduating high school senior with a minimum 3.0 cumulative GPA who is a child, or dependent stepchild of an active, retired, disabled, or deceased member of local union affiliated with Teamsters 37. Member must have been active for at least one year. Award may be received for a maximum of twelve quarters.

Award: Scholarship for use in freshman, sophomore, junior, or senior years; renewable. *Number:* 2. *Amount:* $500.

Eligibility Requirements: Applicant must be high school student; planning to enroll or expecting to enroll at an institution or university and resident of Oregon. Applicant or parent of applicant must be member of Teamsters. Applicant or parent of applicant must have employment or volunteer experience in designated career field. Applicant must have 3.0 GPA or higher. Available to U.S. citizens.

Application Requirements: Application, essay, financial need analysis, transcript, activity chart. *Deadline:* March 1.

Contact: Director of Grant Programs
Oregon Student Assistance Commission
1500 Valley River Drive, Suite 100
Eugene, OR 97401-7020
Phone: 800-452-8807 Ext. 7395

TEAMSTERS COUNCIL 37 FEDERAL CREDIT UNION SCHOLARSHIP

One-time award for members or dependents of Council #37 credit union who are active, retired, disabled or deceased members of teamsters Joint Council #37. Members must have been active in local affiliated with Council for at least one year. Must be enrolled at least half-time in college and have cumulative GPA between 2.0 and 3.0. Contact for application requirements and deadlines.

Award: Scholarship for use in freshman, sophomore, junior, senior, or graduate years; not renewable. *Number:* 1. *Amount:* $1000.

Eligibility Requirements: Applicant must be enrolled or expecting to enroll full or part-time at a two-year or four-year institution and resident of Oregon. Applicant or parent of applicant must be member of Teamsters. Applicant or parent of applicant must have employment or volunteer experience in designated career field. Available to U.S. citizens.

Application Requirements: Application, essay, financial need analysis, references, transcript, activity chart, additional essay topic: The Importance of Preserving the Right to Strike in a Free Enterprise System. *Deadline:* March 1.

Contact: Director of Grant Programs
Oregon Student Assistance Commission
1500 Valley River Drive, Suite 100
Eugene, OR 97401-7020
Phone: 800-452-8807 Ext. 7395

TEAMSTERS LOCAL 305 SCHOLARSHIP

Graduating high school seniors who are children or dependent stepchildren of active, retired, disabled, or deceased members of Local 305 of the Joint Council of Teamsters #37. Members must have been active at least 1 year. Not based on financial need. Deadline is March 1.

Award: Scholarship for use in freshman, sophomore, junior, or senior years; renewable. *Number:* varies. *Amount:* $500.

Eligibility Requirements: Applicant must be high school student; planning to enroll or expecting to enroll at an institution or university

Oregon Student Assistance Commission (continued)

and resident of Oregon. Applicant or parent of applicant must be member of Teamsters. Available to U.S. citizens.

Application Requirements: Application, essay, transcript, activities chart. *Deadline:* March 1.

Contact: Director of Grant Programs
Oregon Student Assistance Commission
1500 Valley River Drive, Suite 100
Eugene, OR 97401-7020
Phone: 800-452-8807 Ext. 7395

PARENTS WITHOUT PARTNERS INTERNATIONAL SCHOLARSHIP PROGRAM   http://www.parentswithoutpartners.org

PARENTS WITHOUT PARTNERS INTERNATIONAL SCHOLARSHIP PROGRAM

Up to ten scholarships between $250 and $500 will be given to the children of members of Parents Without Partners. Must be a U.S. or Canadian citizen between 20 and 25. Application can be downloaded from the following Web site: http://parentswithoutpartners.org.

Award: Scholarship for use in freshman, sophomore, junior, or senior years; not renewable. *Number:* 10. *Amount:* $250–$500.

Eligibility Requirements: Applicant must be age 20-25 and enrolled or expecting to enroll full-time at a two-year or four-year or technical institution or university. Applicant or parent of applicant must be member of Parents Without Partners. Available to U.S. and Canadian citizens.

Application Requirements: Application, applicant must enter a contest, essay, references, transcript. *Deadline:* March 15.

Contact: Ann Willard, Scholarship Chair
Parents Without Partners International Scholarship Program
1737 Ridgemont Drive
Tuscaloosa, AL 35404
Phone: 205-553-3974
E-mail: gaewillard@aol.com

PENNSYLVANIA AFL-CIO   http://www.paaflcio.org

PA AFL-CIO UNIONISM IN AMERICA ESSAY CONTEST

Contest consists of three categories: high school seniors, student currently attending an accredited post secondary institution and affiliated members attending an accredited post secondary institution. Requirements: Completed application form, 1500-word essay, three references (one from a labor organization member). Three award levels in each category: 1st - $2000; 2nd - $1000; 3rd - $500. Must be a resident of Pennsylvania and a U.S. citizen.

Award: Prize for use in freshman, sophomore, junior, or senior years; not renewable. *Number:* 9. *Amount:* $500–$2000.

Eligibility Requirements: Applicant must be enrolled or expecting to enroll full-time at a two-year or four-year or technical institution or university and resident of Pennsylvania. Applicant or parent of applicant must be member of AFL-CIO. Available to U.S. citizens.

Application Requirements: Application, applicant must enter a contest, essay, references, hard copy and CD copy of the essay. *Deadline:* January 31.

Contact: Carl Dillinger, Education Director
Pennsylvania AFL-CIO
231 State Street
Harrisburg, PA 17101-1110
Phone: 717-231-2843
Fax: 717-238-5441
E-mail: cdillinger@paaflcio.org

PENNSYLVANIA FEDERATION OF DEMOCRATIC WOMEN, INC.   http://www.pfdw.org

PENNSYLVANIA FEDERATION OF DEMOCRATIC WOMEN, INC. ANNUAL SCHOLARSHIP AWARDS

Scholarships for any female resident of Pennsylvania who is a student in the junior class of an accredited college or university and is a registered Democrat. Applicants must possess a Democratic Party family background or be an active participant in activities of the Democratic Party.

Award: Scholarship for use in junior or senior years; not renewable. *Number:* 5–6. *Amount:* up to $1000.

Eligibility Requirements: Applicant must be enrolled or expecting to enroll full-time at a four-year institution or university; female and resident of Pennsylvania. Applicant or parent of applicant must be member of Democratic Party. Available to U.S. citizens.

Application Requirements: Application, essay, financial need analysis, references, transcript. *Deadline:* varies.

Contact: Marianne McManus, Scholarship Committee
Pennsylvania Federation of Democratic Women, Inc.
PO Box 86
York, PA 17405-0086
Phone: 717-732-2011

PENNSYLVANIA YOUTH FOUNDATION   http://www.pagrandlodge.org/pmyf

PENNSYLVANIA MASONIC YOUTH FOUNDATION SCHOLARSHIP

Grants for child, stepchild, grandchild, sibling, or dependent of a member in good standing of a Pennsylvania Masonic Lodge. Applicant must be high school graduate or high school senior who is pursuing a college education. Minimum GPA 3.0. Deadline March 15.

Award: Grant for use in freshman, sophomore, junior, or senior years; not renewable. *Number:* varies. *Amount:* $1000–$3000.

Eligibility Requirements: Applicant must be enrolled or expecting to enroll full-time at a two-year or four-year or technical institution or university and resident of Pennsylvania. Applicant or parent of applicant must be member of Freemasons. Applicant must have 3.0 GPA or higher. Available to U.S. citizens.

Application Requirements: Application, financial need analysis, transcript. *Deadline:* March 15.

Contact: Executive Director, PA Youth Foundation
Pennsylvania Youth Foundation
1244 Bainbridge Road
Elizabethtown, PA 17022
E-mail: pyf@pagrandlodge.org

PHI KAPPA TAU FOUNDATION   http://www.phikappatau.org/

PHI KAPPA TAU FOUNDATION SCHOLARSHIPS

Scholarship program is based on academic performance, chapter leadership, campus activities, community service, and recommendation letters. Candidates must be initiated members of Phi Kappa Tau Fraternity in good standing.

Award: Scholarship for use in sophomore, junior, senior, graduate, or postgraduate years; not renewable. *Number:* 20–25. *Amount:* $1000–$2250.

Eligibility Requirements: Applicant must be enrolled or expecting to enroll full or part-time at a four-year institution or university and male. Applicant must have 3.0 GPA or higher. Available to U.S. and non-U.S. citizens.

Application Requirements: Application, essay, photo, resume, references, transcript, chapter leadership. *Deadline:* April 1.

Contact: Bethany A. Deines, Director of Development
Phi Kappa Tau Foundation
5221 Morning Sun Road
Oxford, OH 45056
Phone: 513-523-4193
Fax: 513-524-4812
E-mail: badeines@phikappatau.org

PHI SIGMA PI NATIONAL HONOR FRATERNITY   http://www.phisigmapi.org

RICHARD CECIL TODD AND CLAUDA PENNOCK TODD TRIPOD SCHOLARSHIP

The purpose of this scholarship is to promote the future academic opportunity of brothers (members) of Phi Sigma Pi National Honor Fraternity who have excelled in embodying the ideals of scholarship, leadership, and fellowship. One-time award for full-time student, sophomore level or higher, with minimum 3.0 GPA.

Award: Scholarship for use in sophomore, junior, senior, graduate, or postgraduate years; not renewable. *Number:* 1. *Amount:* up to $1500.

Eligibility Requirements: Applicant must be enrolled or expecting to enroll full-time at a four-year institution or university. Applicant must have 3.0 GPA or higher. Available to U.S. and non-U.S. citizens.

Application Requirements: Application, autobiography, essay, references, transcript. *Deadline:* April 15.

Contact: Suzanne Schaffer, Executive Director
Phi Sigma Pi National Honor Fraternity
2119 Ambassador Circle
Lancaster, PA 17603
Phone: 717-299-4710
Fax: 717-390-3054
E-mail: schaffer@phisigmapi.org

PONY OF THE AMERICAS CLUB   http://www.poac.org

PONY OF THE AMERICAS SCHOLARSHIP

Two to four renewable awards that may be used for any year or any institution but must be for full-time undergraduate study. Application and transcript required. Deadline: June 1. Award restricted to those who have interest in animal or agricultural competition and active involvement in Pony of the Americas.

Award: Scholarship for use in freshman, sophomore, junior, or senior years; not renewable. *Number:* 2–4. *Amount:* $500–$1000.

Eligibility Requirements: Applicant must be enrolled or expecting to enroll full-time at a two-year or four-year or technical institution or university and must have an interest in animal/agricultural competition. Applicant or parent of applicant must be member of Pony of the Americas Club. Available to U.S. and non-U.S. citizens.

Application Requirements: Application, autobiography, essay, references, transcript. *Deadline:* June 1.

Contact: Lynda Corn, Scholarship Administrator
Pony of the Americas Club
5240 Elmwood Avenue
Indianapolis, IN 46203
Phone: 317-788-0107
Fax: 317-788-8974
E-mail: lyndac@poac.org

PROFESSIONAL BOWLERS ASSOCIATION   http://www.pba.com

PROFESSIONAL BOWLERS ASSOCIATION BILLY WELU MEMORIAL SCHOLARSHIP

One-time award available to a currently enrolled student who demonstrates outstanding academic and bowling achievement. Must be a member of YABA, WIBC, or ABC. Must have minimum 2.5 GPA.

Award: Scholarship for use in freshman, sophomore, junior, or senior years; not renewable. *Number:* 1. *Amount:* $1000.

Eligibility Requirements: Applicant must be enrolled or expecting to enroll full or part-time at an institution or university and must have an interest in bowling. Applicant or parent of applicant must be member of Young American Bowling Alliance. Applicant must have 2.5 GPA or higher. Available to U.S. and non-U.S. citizens.

Application Requirements: Application, essay, references, transcript. *Deadline:* May 31.

Contact: Bowling Scholarship Administrator
Professional Bowlers Association
719 Second Avenue, Suite 701
Seattle, WA 98104
Phone: 206-332-9688
Fax: 206-332-9722

PROFESSIONAL HORSEMEN'S SCHOLARSHIP FUND, INC.   http://www.nationalpha.com/

PROFESSIONAL HORSEMEN'S SCHOLARSHIP FUND

Award for members of Professional Horsemen Association. Applicants must reapply after first year, for additional funds. Children of members are also eligible. Applicants must be full-time students attending a two- or four-year college or institution. Financial need is considered.

Award: Scholarship for use in freshman, sophomore, junior, senior, or graduate years; renewable. *Number:* 8–15. *Amount:* $1000–$1500.

Eligibility Requirements: Applicant must be enrolled or expecting to enroll full-time at a two-year or four-year or technical institution or university. Applicant or parent of applicant must be member of Professional Horsemen Association. Available to U.S. citizens.

Application Requirements: Application, autobiography, financial need analysis, references, transcript. *Deadline:* July 1.

Contact: Ann Grenci, Chairperson
Professional Horsemen's Scholarship Fund, Inc.
204 Old Sleepy Hollow Road
Pleasantville, NY 10570
Phone: 591-694-6893
Fax: 561-694-2254

PROJECT BEST SCHOLARSHIP FUND   http://www.projectbest.com

PROJECT BEST SCHOLARSHIP

Awards for employees or children or spouses of employees working for a company or labor union in the construction industry that is affiliated with Project BEST. Must be a resident of West Virginia, Pennsylvania, or Ohio and attend a West Virginia or Ohio postsecondary institution. Must be a U.S. citizen. One-time award of $1000 or $2000.

Award: Scholarship for use in freshman, sophomore, junior, senior, or graduate years; renewable. *Number:* 11–22. *Amount:* $1000–$2000.

Eligibility Requirements: Applicant must be enrolled or expecting to enroll full-time at a two-year or four-year institution or university; resident of Ohio, Pennsylvania, or West Virginia and studying in Ohio or West Virginia. Applicant or parent of applicant must be member of AFL-CIO. Applicant or parent of applicant must have employment or volunteer experience in construction. Available to U.S. citizens.

Application Requirements: Application. *Deadline:* Continuous.

Contact: Mary Jo Klempa, Director
Project BEST Scholarship Fund
21 Armory Drive
Wheeling, WV 26003
Phone: 304-242-0520
Fax: 304-242-7261
E-mail: best2003@swave.net

RECORDING FOR THE BLIND & DYSLEXIC   http://www.rfbd.org

MARION HUBER LEARNING THROUGH LISTENING AWARDS

One-time award presented to outstanding high school seniors with learning disabilities in recognition of extraordinary leadership, scholarship, enterprise, and service to others. Candidates must be registered with the Recording for the Blind & Dyslexic for at least one year prior to the filing date of March 1.

Award: Prize for use in freshman year; not renewable. *Number:* 6. *Amount:* $2000–$6000.

Eligibility Requirements: Applicant must be high school student; planning to enroll or expecting to enroll full-time at a two-year or four-year or technical institution or university and must have an interest in leadership. Applicant or parent of applicant must be member of Recording for the Blind and Dyslexic. Applicant or parent of applicant must have employment or volunteer experience in community service. Applicant must be learning disabled. Applicant must have 3.0 GPA or higher. Available to U.S. citizens.

Application Requirements: Application, essay, references, transcript. *Deadline:* March 1.

Contact: Strategic Communications Department
Recording for the Blind & Dyslexic
20 Roszel Road
Princeton, NJ 08540-5443
Phone: 609-520-3044
Fax: 609-520-7990

MARY P. OENSLAGER SCHOLASTIC ACHIEVEMENT AWARDS

Awards for legally blind college seniors, awarded on basis of leadership, scholarship, enterprise, and service to others. Candidates must be registered with Recording for the Blind & Dyslexic for at least one year prior to filing

Recording for the Blind & Dyslexic (continued)

date of February 21 and have an overall GPA of 3.0 or equivalent. Applicants need not plan to continue their education beyond a bachelor's degree.

Award: Prize for use in senior, or graduate years; not renewable. *Number:* 9. *Amount:* $1000–$6000.

Eligibility Requirements: Applicant must be enrolled or expecting to enroll full-time at a four-year institution or university and must have an interest in leadership. Applicant or parent of applicant must be member of Recording for the Blind and Dyslexic. Applicant or parent of applicant must have employment or volunteer experience in community service. Applicant must be visually impaired. Applicant must have 3.0 GPA or higher. Available to U.S. citizens.

Application Requirements: Application, essay, references, transcript. *Deadline:* March 1.

Contact: Strategic Communications Department
Recording for the Blind & Dyslexic
20 Roszel Road
Princeton, NJ 08540-5443
Phone: 866-520-3044
Fax: 609-520-7990

RESERVE OFFICERS ASSOCIATION OF THE US   http://www.roa.org

HENRY J. REILLY MEMORIAL SCHOLARSHIP-HIGH SCHOOL SENIORS AND FIRST YEAR FRESHMEN

Award for high school seniors or college freshmen who are children or grandchildren of active members of the Reserve Officers Association. Must demonstrate leadership, have minimum 3.0 GPA and 1250 on the SAT. One-time award of $500. Must submit sponsor verification. College freshmen must submit college transcript. Must be U.S. citizen.

Award: Scholarship for use in freshman, sophomore, or junior years; not renewable. *Number:* 25–50. *Amount:* $500.

Eligibility Requirements: Applicant must be enrolled or expecting to enroll full-time at a four-year institution or university and must have an interest in leadership. Applicant or parent of applicant must be member of Reserve Officers Association. Applicant must have 3.0 GPA or higher. Available to U.S. citizens. Applicant or parent must meet one or more of the following requirements: general military experience; retired from active duty; disabled or killed as a result of military service; prisoner of war; or missing in action.

Application Requirements: Application, essay, test scores, transcript, sponsor verification. *Deadline:* April 10.

Contact: Mickey Hagen, Coordinator of Applications
Reserve Officers Association of the US
1 Constitution Avenue, NE
Washington, DC 20002-5655
Phone: 202-479-2200
Fax: 202-479-0416
E-mail: mhagen@roa.org

HENRY J. REILLY MEMORIAL UNDERGRADUATE SCHOLARSHIP PROGRAM FOR COLLEGE ATTENDEES

Award for members and children or grandchildren of members of the Reserve Officers Association or its Auxiliary. Must be 26 years old or younger and enrolled at an accredited four-year institution. Must submit sponsor verification. One-time award of $500. Minimum 3.0 GPA required. Submit SAT or ACT scores; contact for score requirements. Must be U.S. citizen.

Award: Scholarship for use in freshman, sophomore, junior, or senior years; not renewable. *Number:* 25–35. *Amount:* $500.

Eligibility Requirements: Applicant must be age 26 or under and enrolled or expecting to enroll full-time at a two-year or four-year institution or university. Applicant or parent of applicant must be member of Reserve Officers Association. Applicant must have 3.0 GPA or higher. Available to U.S. citizens. Applicant or parent must meet one or more of the following requirements: general military experience; retired from active duty; disabled or killed as a result of military service; prisoner of war; or missing in action.

Application Requirements: Application, essay, test scores, transcript, sponsor verification. *Deadline:* April 10.

Contact: Mickey Hagen, Coordinator of Applications
Reserve Officers Association of the US
1 Constitution Avenue, NE
Washington, DC 20002-5655
Phone: 202-479-2200
Fax: 202-479-0416
E-mail: mhagen@roa.org

SCREEN ACTORS GUILD FOUNDATION   http://www.sagfoundation.org/

SCREEN ACTORS GUILD FOUNDATION/JOHN L. DALES SCHOLARSHIP (TRANSITIONAL)

Award for Guild members and children of members. The member applying must have been a member in good standing for ten years. Member's lifetime gross income in Guild's jurisdiction must total $30,000.

Award: Scholarship for use in freshman, sophomore, junior, senior, or graduate years; not renewable. *Number:* varies. *Amount:* $3000–$5000.

Eligibility Requirements: Applicant must be enrolled or expecting to enroll full-time at a two-year or four-year institution or university. Applicant or parent of applicant must be member of Screen Actors' Guild. Applicant or parent of applicant must have employment or volunteer experience in designated career field. Available to U.S. citizens.

Application Requirements: Application, essay, financial need analysis, resume, references, test scores, transcript. *Deadline:* March 15.

Contact: Davidson Lloyd, Administrative Director
Screen Actors Guild Foundation
5757 Wilshire Boulevard, 7th Floor
Los Angeles, CA 90036-3600
Phone: 323-549-6649
Fax: 323-549-6710
E-mail: dlloyd@sag.org

SECOND BOMBARDMENT ASSOCIATION

SECOND BOMBARDMENT ASSOCIATION SCHOLARSHIP

Award for children of members of the Second Bombardment Wing of the U.S. Air Force. Write for more information. Must attend a four-year postsecondary institution. Program is administered by Air Force Aid in Washington, D.C. Documentation must be submitted to them.

Award: Scholarship for use in freshman, sophomore, junior, senior, graduate, or postgraduate years; renewable. *Number:* 2. *Amount:* $1000.

Eligibility Requirements: Applicant must be enrolled or expecting to enroll full-time at a four-year institution or university. Applicant or parent of applicant must be member of Second Bombardment Association. Available to U.S. and non-U.S. citizens. Applicant or parent must meet one or more of the following requirements: Air Force experience; retired from active duty; disabled or killed as a result of military service; prisoner of war; or missing in action.

Application Requirements: Application. *Deadline:* Continuous.

Contact: Second Bombardment Association
1745 Jefferson Davis Highway, Suite 202
Arlington, VA 22202

SERVICE EMPLOYEES INTERNATIONAL UNION - CALIFORNIA STATE COUNCIL OF SERVICE EMPLOYEES   http://www.seiuca.org

CHARLES HARDY MEMORIAL SCHOLARSHIP AWARDS

Renewable $1000 award for California residents. For full-time study only. Deadline is in mid-March. Must be SEIU members or children of members. Membership must be for three continuous years as of September 1, 2001. For recent affiliates to SEIU, you must have been a member of your association for three years. Download application at Web site (http://www.seiu.org) and take online union history test (open book).

Award: Scholarship for use in freshman year; renewable. *Number:* 1–4. *Amount:* $1000.

Eligibility Requirements: Applicant must be enrolled or expecting to enroll full-time at a two-year or four-year institution or university and resident of California. Applicant or parent of applicant must be member of Service Employees International Union. Applicant or parent of applicant must have employment or volunteer experience in designated career field. Available to U.S. citizens.

Application Requirements: Application, online test. *Deadline:* March 15.

Contact: SEIU-Scholarship Committee
Service Employees International Union - California State Council of Service Employees
1313 L Street, NW
Washington, DC 20005
Phone: 800-846-1561

SLOVAK GYMNASTIC UNION SOKOL, USA

SLOVAK GYMNASTIC UNION SOKOL, USA/MILAN GETTING SCHOLARSHIP

Available to members of SOKOL, U.S.A who have been in good standing for at least three years. Must have plans to attend college. Renewable for a maximum of four years, based upon academic achievement. Minimum GPA 2.5 required.

Award: Scholarship for use in freshman, sophomore, junior, or senior years; renewable. *Number:* 4–8. *Amount:* $500.

Eligibility Requirements: Applicant must be high school student and planning to enroll or expecting to enroll full-time at a four-year institution. Applicant or parent of applicant must be member of SOKOL, USA. Applicant must have 2.5 GPA or higher. Available to U.S. citizens.

Application Requirements: Application, references, transcript. *Deadline:* April 15.

Contact: Slovak Gymnastic Union SOKOL, USA
276 Prospect Street, PO Box 189
East Orange, NJ 07019

SOCIETY OF PHYSICS STUDENTS   http://www.spsnational.org

SOCIETY OF PHYSICS STUDENTS OUTSTANDING STUDENT IN RESEARCH

$500 stipend, plus expenses paid to present research (undergraduate) at the International Conference of Physics Students; location is abroad, varies each year. $500 is also awarded to Society of Physics Students chapter. Available to members of the Society of Physics Students. More details visit: http://www.spsnational.org

Award: Prize for use in freshman, sophomore, junior, or senior years; not renewable. *Number:* 1–2. *Amount:* $1500–$2500.

Eligibility Requirements: Applicant must be enrolled or expecting to enroll full-time at a two-year or four-year institution or university. Applicant or parent of applicant must be member of Society of Physics Students. Available to U.S. and non-U.S. citizens.

Application Requirements: Application, references, abstract. *Deadline:* April 15.

Contact: SPS Secretary
Society of Physics Students
One Physics Ellipse
College Park, MD 20740
Phone: 301-209-3007
Fax: 301-209-0839
E-mail: sps@aip.org

SOCIETY OF PHYSICS STUDENTS PEGGY DIXON 2-YEAR COLLEGE SCHOLARSHIP

Scholarship available to Society of Physics Students (SPS) members. Award based on scholarship and/or need, and SPS participation. For more details visit Web site: http://www.spsnational.org

Award: Scholarship for use in junior, or graduate years; not renewable. *Number:* 1. *Amount:* $2000.

Eligibility Requirements: Applicant must be enrolled or expecting to enroll at a two-year institution. Applicant or parent of applicant must be member of Society of Physics Students. Available to U.S. and non-U.S. citizens.

Application Requirements: Application, financial need analysis, transcript. *Deadline:* February 15.

Contact: SPS Secretary
Society of Physics Students
1 Physics Ellipse
College Park, MD 20740-3843
Phone: 301-209-3007
Fax: 301-209-0839
E-mail: sps@aip.org

SONS OF NORWAY FOUNDATION   http://www.sofn.com

ASTRID G. CATES AND MYRTLE BEINHAUER SCHOLARSHIP FUNDS

Merit and need-based award available to students ages 17 to 22 who are members, children, or grandchildren of members of the Sons of Norway. School transcript required. Financial need is key criterion for award. Must have minimum 3.0 GPA. One-time award of $500 to $750.

Award: Scholarship for use in freshman, sophomore, junior, or senior years; not renewable. *Number:* 6. *Amount:* $500–$750.

Eligibility Requirements: Applicant must be of Norwegian heritage; age 17-22 and enrolled or expecting to enroll at a two-year or four-year or technical institution or university. Applicant or parent of applicant must be member of Mutual Benefit Society. Applicant must have 3.0 GPA or higher. Available to U.S. citizens.

Application Requirements: Application, essay, financial need analysis, references, self-addressed stamped envelope, test scores, transcript. *Deadline:* March 1.

Contact: Sons of Norway Foundation
Sons of Norway Foundation
1455 West Lake Street
Minneapolis, MN 55408-2666
Phone: 612-827-3611
Fax: 612-827-0658
E-mail: fraternal@sofn.com

SOUTH CAROLINA STATE EMPLOYEES ASSOCIATION   http://www.SCSEA.com

RICHLAND/LEXINGTON SCSEA SCHOLARSHIP

Scholarships available to SCSEA members or their relatives, with priority given to Richland-Lexington Chapter members, spouses and/or children of Chapter members. The awardees must be currently enrolled at a recognized and accredited college, university, trade school or other institute of higher learning and must have completed at least one academic semester/quarter.

Award: Scholarship for use in sophomore, junior, senior, graduate, or postgraduate years. *Number:* 3. *Amount:* $750.

Eligibility Requirements: Applicant must be enrolled or expecting to enroll at a two-year or four-year institution or university and resident of South Carolina. Applicant or parent of applicant must be member of Society of Architectural Historians. Available to U.S. citizens.

Application Requirements: Application, essay, transcript. *Deadline:* April 1.

Contact: South Carolina State Employees Association
PO Box 8447
Columbia, SC 29202-8447
Phone: 803-765-0680
Fax: 803-779-6558

TENNESSEE EDUCATION ASSOCIATION   http://www.teateachers.org

TEA DON SAHLI-KATHY WOODALL SONS AND DAUGHTERS SCHOLARSHIP

Scholarship is available to a TEA member's child who is a high school senior, undergraduate or graduate student, and is planning to enroll, or is already enrolled, in a Tennessee college.

Award: Scholarship for use in freshman, sophomore, junior, senior, or graduate years; not renewable. *Number:* 1. *Amount:* $1000.

Eligibility Requirements: Applicant must be enrolled or expecting to enroll full-time at a four-year institution or university; resident of Tennessee and studying in Tennessee. Applicant or parent of applicant must be member of Tennessee Education Association. Applicant must have 3.0 GPA or higher. Available to U.S. citizens.

Tennessee Education Association (continued)

Application Requirements: Application, essay, financial need analysis, references, transcript, statement of income. *Deadline:* March 1.

Contact: Jeanette DeMain, Administrative Assistant
Tennessee Education Association
801 Second Avenue North
Nashville, TN 37201-1099
Phone: 615-242-8392
Fax: 615-259-4581
E-mail: jdemain@tea.nea.org

TEXAS AFL-CIO   http://www.aflcio.org

TEXAS AFL-CIO SCHOLARSHIP PROGRAM

Award for sons or daughters of affiliated union members. Selection by testing or interview process. Fifteen one-time awards of $1000. Deadline: January 31. Applicant must be a graduating high school senior and Texas resident.

Award: Scholarship for use in freshman year; not renewable. *Number:* 15. *Amount:* $1000.

Eligibility Requirements: Applicant must be high school student; planning to enroll or expecting to enroll full-time at a two-year or four-year or technical institution or university and resident of Texas. Applicant or parent of applicant must be member of AFL-CIO. Available to U.S. citizens.

Application Requirements: Application, essay, financial need analysis, interview, photo, test scores, transcript. *Deadline:* January 31.

Contact: Edward Sills, Director of Communications
Texas AFL-CIO
Education Department
PO Box 12727
Austin, TX 78711
Phone: 512-477-6195
E-mail: ed@texasflcio.org

TKE EDUCATIONAL FOUNDATION   http://www.tkefoundation.org

ALL-TKE ACADEMIC TEAM RECOGNITION AND JOHN A. COURSON TOP SCHOLAR AWARD

One-time award given to full-time male students who are active members of Tau Kappa Epsilon with junior or senior standing. Candidates should be able to maintain excellent academic standing while making positive contributions to chapter, campus, and community. Top Scholar Award will be selected from All-TKE academic team. Recent head and shoulders photograph must be submitted with application.

Award: Scholarship for use in junior or senior years; not renewable. *Number:* 10. *Amount:* up to $3000.

Eligibility Requirements: Applicant must be enrolled or expecting to enroll full-time at a four-year institution or university; male and must have an interest in leadership. Applicant must have 3.5 GPA or higher. Available to U.S. and non-U.S. citizens.

Application Requirements: Application, photo, transcript. *Deadline:* February 24.

Contact: Gary A. Reed, President/CEO
TKE Educational Foundation
8645 Founders Road
Indianapolis, IN 46268-1393
Phone: 317-872-6533
Fax: 317-875-8353
E-mail: reedga@tke.org

CANADIAN TKE SCHOLARSHIP

This scholarship is available to an undergraduate Teke who has been initiated into a Canadian TKE chapter and has demonstrated leadership qualities within the Fraternity and the campus community, while maintaining a good academic record.

Award: Scholarship for use in freshman, sophomore, junior, or senior years; not renewable. *Number:* 1. *Amount:* $200.

Eligibility Requirements: Applicant must be enrolled or expecting to enroll full-time at a four-year institution or university; male and must have an interest in leadership. Available to U.S. and non-U.S. citizens.

Application Requirements: Application, essay, photo, transcript. *Deadline:* May 15.

Contact: Gary Reed, President/CEO
TKE Educational Foundation
8645 Founders Road
Indianapolis, IN 46131
Phone: 317-872-6533
Fax: 317-875-8353
E-mail: reedga@tke.org

CHARLES WALGREEN, JR. SCHOLARSHIP

Award is given in recognition of outstanding leadership, as demonstrated by an individual's activities and accomplishments within the chapter, on campus and in the community, while maintaining a good academic record. All initiated undergraduate members of TKE, in good standing with a cumulative GPA of 3.0 or higher, are eligible to apply.

Award: Scholarship for use in freshman, sophomore, junior, or senior years; not renewable. *Number:* 1. *Amount:* $2500.

Eligibility Requirements: Applicant must be enrolled or expecting to enroll full-time at a four-year institution or university; male and must have an interest in leadership. Applicant must have 3.0 GPA or higher. Available to U.S. and non-U.S. citizens.

Application Requirements: Application, essay, photo, transcript. *Deadline:* May 12.

Contact: Gary Reed, President/CEO
TKE Educational Foundation
8645 Founders Road
Indianapolis, IN 46131
Phone: 317-872-6533
Fax: 317-875-8353
E-mail: reedga@tke.org

DONALD A. FISHER MEMORIAL SCHOLARSHIP

One-time award of $1500 given to an undergraduate member of Tau Kappa Epsilon who has demonstrated leadership ability within his chapter, campus, or community. Must be a full-time student in good standing with a GPA of 2.5 or higher. Recent head and shoulders photograph must be submitted with application.

Award: Scholarship for use in freshman, sophomore, junior, or senior years; not renewable. *Number:* 1. *Amount:* $1500.

Eligibility Requirements: Applicant must be enrolled or expecting to enroll full-time at a four-year institution or university; male and must have an interest in leadership. Applicant must have 2.5 GPA or higher. Available to U.S. and non-U.S. citizens.

Application Requirements: Application, essay, photo, transcript. *Deadline:* May 12.

Contact: Gary A. Reed, President/CEO
TKE Educational Foundation
8645 Founders Road
Indianapolis, IN 46268-1393
Phone: 317-872-6533
Fax: 317-875-8353
E-mail: reedga@tke.org

DWAYNE R. WOERPEL MEMORIAL LEADERSHIP AWARD

An award available to an undergraduate Tau Kappa Epsilon member who is a full-time student and graduate of the TKE Leadership Academy. Applicants should have demonstrated leadership qualities in service to the Fraternity and to the civic and religious community while maintaining a 3.0 GPA or higher.

Award: Scholarship for use in freshman, sophomore, junior, or senior years; not renewable. *Number:* 1. *Amount:* $500.

Eligibility Requirements: Applicant must be enrolled or expecting to enroll full-time at a four-year institution or university; male and must have an interest in leadership. Applicant must have 3.0 GPA or higher. Available to U.S. and non-U.S. citizens.

Application Requirements: Application, essay, photo, transcript. *Deadline:* May 12.

Contact: Gary Reed, President/CEO
TKE Educational Foundation
8645 Founders Road
Indianapolis, IN 46131
Phone: 317-872-6533
Fax: 317-875-8353
E-mail: reedga@tke.org

ELMER AND DORIS SCHMITZ SR. MEMORIAL SCHOLARSHIP

One-time award of $600 given to an undergraduate member of Tau Kappa Epsilon from Wisconsin who has demonstrated leadership ability within his chapter, campus, or community. Must be a full-time student in good standing with a GPA of 2.5 or higher. Recent head and shoulders photograph must be submitted with application.

Award: Scholarship for use in freshman, sophomore, junior, or senior years; not renewable. *Number:* 1. *Amount:* $600.

Eligibility Requirements: Applicant must be enrolled or expecting to enroll full-time at a four-year institution or university; male; resident of Wisconsin and must have an interest in leadership. Applicant must have 2.5 GPA or higher. Available to U.S. and non-U.S. citizens.

Application Requirements: Application, essay, photo, transcript. *Deadline:* May 12.

Contact: Gary A. Reed, President/CEO
TKE Educational Foundation
8645 Founders Road
Indianapolis, IN 46268-1393
Phone: 317-872-6533
Fax: 317-875-8353
E-mail: reedga@tke.org

EUGENE C. BEACH MEMORIAL SCHOLARSHIP

One-time award of $400 given to an undergraduate member of Tau Kappa Epsilon who has demonstrated leadership ability within his chapter, campus, or community. Must be a full-time student in good standing with a GPA of 2.5 or higher. Recent head and shoulders photograph must be submitted with application.

Award: Scholarship for use in freshman, sophomore, junior, or senior years; not renewable. *Number:* 1. *Amount:* $400.

Eligibility Requirements: Applicant must be enrolled or expecting to enroll full-time at a four-year institution or university; male and must have an interest in leadership. Applicant must have 2.5 GPA or higher. Available to U.S. and non-U.S. citizens.

Application Requirements: Application, essay, photo, transcript. *Deadline:* May 12.

Contact: Gary A. Reed, President/CEO
TKE Educational Foundation
8645 Founders Road
Indianapolis, IN 46268-1393
Phone: 317-872-6533
Fax: 317-875-8353
E-mail: reedga@tke.org

J. RUSSEL SALSBURY MEMORIAL SCHOLARSHIP

One-time award of $300 given to an undergraduate member of Tau Kappa Epsilon who has demonstrated leadership ability within his chapter, campus, or community. Must be a full-time student in good standing with a GPA of 2.5 or higher. Recent head and shoulders photograph must be submitted with application.

Award: Scholarship for use in freshman, sophomore, junior, or senior years; not renewable. *Number:* 1. *Amount:* $300.

Eligibility Requirements: Applicant must be enrolled or expecting to enroll full-time at a four-year institution or university; male and must have an interest in leadership. Applicant must have 2.5 GPA or higher. Available to U.S. and non-U.S. citizens.

Application Requirements: Application, essay, photo, transcript. *Deadline:* May 12.

Contact: Gary A. Reed, President/CEO
TKE Educational Foundation
8645 Founders Road
Indianapolis, IN 46268-1393
Phone: 317-872-6533
Fax: 317-875-8353
E-mail: reedga@tke.org

MICHAEL J. MORIN MEMORIAL SCHOLARSHIP

One-time award for any undergraduate member of Tau Kappa Epsilon who has demonstrated leadership capacity within his chapter, on campus or the community. Must have a cumulative GPA of 2.5 or higher and be a full-time student in good standing.

Award: Scholarship for use in freshman, sophomore, junior, or senior years; not renewable. *Number:* 1. *Amount:* $500.

Eligibility Requirements: Applicant must be enrolled or expecting to enroll full-time at a four-year institution or university; male and must have an interest in leadership. Applicant must have 2.5 GPA or higher. Available to U.S. and non-U.S. citizens.

Application Requirements: Application, essay, photo, transcript. *Deadline:* May 12.

Contact: Gary Reed, President/CEO
TKE Educational Foundation
8645 Founders Road
Indianapolis, IN 46131
Phone: 317-872-6533
Fax: 317-875-8353
E-mail: reedga@tke.org

MILES GRAY MEMORIAL SCHOLARSHIP

One-time award of $500 given to an undergraduate member of Tau Kappa Epsilon who has demonstrated leadership ability within his chapter, campus, or community. Must be a full-time student in good standing with a GPA of 2.5 or higher. Recent head and shoulders photograph must be submitted with application.

Award: Scholarship for use in freshman, sophomore, junior, or senior years; not renewable. *Number:* 1. *Amount:* $500.

Eligibility Requirements: Applicant must be enrolled or expecting to enroll full-time at a four-year institution or university; male and must have an interest in leadership. Applicant must have 2.5 GPA or higher. Available to U.S. and non-U.S. citizens.

Application Requirements: Application, essay, photo, transcript. *Deadline:* May 12.

Contact: Gary A. Reed, President/CEO
TKE Educational Foundation
8645 Founders Road
Indianapolis, IN 46268-1393
Phone: 317-872-6533
Fax: 317-875-8353
E-mail: reedga@tke.org

RONALD REAGAN LEADERSHIP AWARD

One-time award of $2000 for initiated undergraduate member of Tau Kappa Epsilon, given in recognition of outstanding leadership, as demonstrated by activities and accomplishments within chapter, on campus, and in community. Must be a full-time student in good standing. Recent head and shoulders photograph must be submitted with application. Recipient required to attend official fraternity function to accept award.

Award: Scholarship for use in freshman, sophomore, junior, or senior years; not renewable. *Number:* 1. *Amount:* $2000.

Eligibility Requirements: Applicant must be enrolled or expecting to enroll full-time at a four-year institution or university; male and must have an interest in leadership. Applicant must have 3.0 GPA or higher. Available to U.S. and non-U.S. citizens.

Application Requirements: Application, essay, photo, transcript. *Deadline:* May 12.

TKE Educational Foundation (continued)

Contact: Gary A. Reed, President/CEO
TKE Educational Foundation
8645 Founders Road
Indianapolis, IN 46268-1393
Phone: 317-872-6533
Fax: 317-875-8353
E-mail: reedga@tke.org

T.J. SCHMITZ SCHOLARSHIP

Award for an initiated undergraduate member of TKE. Must be a full-time student in good standing with a minimum cumulative GPA of 2.5. Must have demonstrated leadership capability within chapter, campus, or community. Application deadline: May 12.

Award: Scholarship for use in freshman, sophomore, junior, or senior years; not renewable. *Number:* 1. *Amount:* $800.

Eligibility Requirements: Applicant must be enrolled or expecting to enroll full-time at an institution or university; male and must have an interest in leadership. Applicant must have 2.5 GPA or higher. Available to U.S. and non-U.S. citizens.

Application Requirements: Application, essay, photo, transcript. *Deadline:* May 12.

Contact: Gary A. Reed, President/CEO
TKE Educational Foundation
8645 Founders Road
Indianapolis, IN 46268-1393
Phone: 317-872-6533
Fax: 317-875-8353
E-mail: reedga@tke.org

WALLACE MCCAULEY MEMORIAL SCHOLARSHIP

One-time award to undergraduate member of Tau Kappa Epsilon with junior or senior standing. Must have demonstrated understanding of the importance of good alumni relations. Must have excelled in the development, promotion, and execution of programs which increase alumni contact, awareness, and participation in fraternity activities.

Award: Scholarship for use in junior or senior years; not renewable. *Number:* 1. *Amount:* $600.

Eligibility Requirements: Applicant must be enrolled or expecting to enroll full-time at a four-year institution or university; male and must have an interest in leadership. Available to U.S. and non-U.S. citizens.

Application Requirements: Application, essay, photo, transcript. *Deadline:* May 12.

Contact: Gary A. Reed, President/CEO
TKE Educational Foundation
8645 Founders Road
Indianapolis, IN 46268-1393
Phone: 317-872-6533
Fax: 317-875-8353
E-mail: reedga@tke.org

WILLIAM V. MUSE SCHOLARSHIP

Award of $700 given to undergraduate member of Tau Kappa Epsilon who has completed at least 30 semester hours of course work. Applicant should demonstrate leadership within chapter and maintain 3.0 GPA. Preference given to members of Epsilon-Upsilon Chapter.

Award: Scholarship for use in freshman, sophomore, junior, or senior years; not renewable. *Number:* 1. *Amount:* $700.

Eligibility Requirements: Applicant must be enrolled or expecting to enroll full-time at a four-year institution or university; male and must have an interest in leadership. Applicant must have 3.0 GPA or higher. Available to U.S. and non-U.S. citizens.

Application Requirements: Application, essay, photo, transcript. *Deadline:* May 12.

Contact: Gary A. Reed, President/CEO
TKE Educational Foundation
8645 Founders Road
Indianapolis, IN 46268-1393
Phone: 317-872-6533
Fax: 317-875-8353
E-mail: reedga@tke.org

WILLIAM WILSON MEMORIAL SCHOLARSHIP

One-time award given to undergraduate member of Tau Kappa Epsilon with junior or senior standing. Must have demonstrated understanding of the importance of good alumni relations. Must have excelled in the development, promotion, and execution of programs which increase alumni contact, awareness, and participation in fraternity activities.

Award: Scholarship for use in junior or senior years; not renewable. *Number:* 1. *Amount:* $600.

Eligibility Requirements: Applicant must be enrolled or expecting to enroll full-time at a four-year institution or university; male and must have an interest in leadership. Available to U.S. and non-U.S. citizens.

Application Requirements: Application, essay, photo, transcript. *Deadline:* May 12.

Contact: Gary A. Reed, President/CEO
TKE Educational Foundation
8645 Founders Road
Indianapolis, IN 46268-1393
Phone: 317-872-6533
Fax: 317-875-8353
E-mail: reedga@tke.org

UNION PLUS SCHOLARSHIP PROGRAM   http://www.unionplus.org

UNION PLUS SCHOLARSHIP PROGRAM

One-time cash award for AFL-CIO union members, their spouses or dependent children. Based upon academic achievement, character, leadership, career goals, social awareness and financial need. Must be from Canada or U.S. including Puerto Rico. Members must download application from Web site http://www.unionplus.org. Applications are available from September 1 to January 15.

Award: Scholarship for use in freshman, sophomore, junior, or senior years; not renewable. *Number:* 110–130. *Amount:* $500–$4000.

Eligibility Requirements: Applicant must be enrolled or expecting to enroll full or part-time at a two-year or four-year or technical institution or university. Applicant or parent of applicant must be member of AFL-CIO. Available to U.S. and Canadian citizens.

Application Requirements: Application, essay, financial need analysis, references, test scores, transcript. *Deadline:* January 31.

Contact: Union Plus Scholarship Program
1125 15th Street, NW, Suite 300
Washington, DC 20005

UNITED COMMUNITY SERVICES FOR WORKING FAMILIES

RONALD LORAH MEMORIAL SCHOLARSHIP

One-time award available to a union member, spouse of a union member, or child of a union member. Must be a resident of Pennsylvania. Must submit essay that is clear, concise, persuasive and show an understanding of unions. Application deadline is July 23.

Award: Scholarship for use in freshman, sophomore, junior, or senior years; not renewable. *Number:* 1. *Amount:* $500–$1000.

Eligibility Requirements: Applicant must be enrolled or expecting to enroll full-time at a two-year or four-year or technical institution or university and resident of Pennsylvania. Applicant or parent of applicant must be member of AFL-CIO. Available to U.S. citizens.

Application Requirements: Application, essay, financial need analysis. *Deadline:* July 23.

Contact: United Community Services for Working Families
Labor Advisory Committee of Reading and Berks County,
Berkshire Plaza Boulevard, Suite V-1 529 Reading Avenue
West Reading, PA 19611
E-mail: unionscholarships@aesSuccess.org

UNITED DAUGHTERS OF THE CONFEDERACY

http://www.hqudc.org

ADMIRAL RAPHAEL SEMMES SCHOLARSHIP

Renewable award for undergraduate student who is a descendant of a Confederate soldier, sailor or marine. Must be enrolled in an accredited college or university and carry a minimum of 12 credit hours each semester. Minimum 3.0 GPA required. Submit letter of endorsement from sponsoring chapter of the United Daughters of the Confederacy. Scholarship amount for the entire academic year will be sent to college/university.

Award: Scholarship for use in freshman, sophomore, junior, or senior years; renewable. *Number: 1–2. Amount: $800–$1000.*

Eligibility Requirements: Applicant must be enrolled or expecting to enroll full-time at a four-year institution or university. Applicant or parent of applicant must be member of United Daughters of the Confederacy. Applicant must have 3.0 GPA or higher. Available to U.S. citizens.

Application Requirements: Application, essay, financial need analysis, photo, references, self-addressed stamped envelope, transcript, confederate ancestor's proof of service. *Deadline:* March 15.

Contact: Robert Kraus, Second Vice President General
United Daughters of the Confederacy
328 North Boulevard
Richmond, VA 23220-4057
Phone: 804-355-1636

BARBARA JACKSON SICHEL MEMORIAL SCHOLARSHIP

Renewable award for undergraduate student who is a descendant of a Confederate soldier, sailor or marine. Must be enrolled in an accredited college or university and carry a minimum of 12 credit hours each semester. Minimum of 3.0 GPA required. Submit a letter of endorsement from sponsoring Chapter of the United Daughters of the Confederacy. Please refer to Web site for further details: http://www.hqudc.org

Award: Scholarship for use in freshman, sophomore, junior, or senior years; renewable. *Number: 1–2. Amount: $800–$1000.*

Eligibility Requirements: Applicant must be enrolled or expecting to enroll full-time at a four-year institution or university. Applicant or parent of applicant must be member of United Daughters of the Confederacy. Applicant must have 3.0 GPA or higher. Available to U.S. citizens.

Application Requirements: Application, essay, financial need analysis, photo, references, self-addressed stamped envelope, transcript, proof of confederate ancestor's service. *Deadline:* March 15.

Contact: Robert Kraus, Second Vice President General
United Daughters of the Confederacy
328 North Boulevard
Richmond, VA 23220-4057
Phone: 804-355-1636

CHARLOTTE M. F. BENTLEY / NEW YORK CHAPTER 103 SCHOLARSHIP

Renewable award for undergraduate student who is a descendant of a Confederate soldier, sailor or marine. Must be enrolled in an accredited college or university and carry a minimum of 12 credit hours each semester. Minimum of 3.0 GPA required. Submit a letter of endorsement from sponsoring Chapter of the United Daughters of the Confederacy. Preference given to UDC and C of C members from New York. Please refer to Web site for further details: http://www.hqudc.org

Award: Scholarship for use in freshman, sophomore, junior, or senior years; renewable. *Number: 1–2. Amount: $800–$1000.*

Eligibility Requirements: Applicant must be enrolled or expecting to enroll full-time at a four-year institution or university. Applicant or parent of applicant must be member of United Daughters of the Confederacy. Applicant must have 3.0 GPA or higher. Available to U.S. citizens.

Application Requirements: Application, essay, financial need analysis, photo, references, self-addressed stamped envelope, transcript, proof of confederate ancestor's service. *Deadline:* March 15.

Contact: Robert Kraus, Second Vice President General
United Daughters of the Confederacy
328 North Boulevard
Richmond, VA 23220-4057
Phone: 804-355-1636

CODY BACHMAN SCHOLARSHIP

Renewable award for undergraduate student who is a descendant of a Confederate soldier, sailor or marine. Must be enrolled in an accredited college or university and carry a minimum of 12 credit hours each semester. Minimum 3.0 GPA required. Submit letter of endorsement from sponsoring chapter of the United Daughters of the Confederacy. Please refer to Web site for further details: http://www.hqudc.org

Award: Scholarship for use in freshman, sophomore, junior, or senior years; renewable. *Number: 1–2. Amount: $800–$1000.*

Eligibility Requirements: Applicant must be enrolled or expecting to enroll full-time at a four-year institution or university. Applicant or parent of applicant must be member of United Daughters of the Confederacy. Applicant must have 3.0 GPA or higher. Available to U.S. citizens.

Application Requirements: Application, essay, financial need analysis, photo, references, self-addressed stamped envelope, transcript. *Deadline:* March 15.

Contact: Robert Kraus, Second Vice President General
United Daughters of the Confederacy
328 North Boulevard
Richmond, VA 23220-4057
Phone: 804-355-1636

CORA BELL WESLEY MEMORIAL SCHOLARSHIP

Renewable award for undergraduate student who is a descendant of a Confederate soldier, sailor or marine. Must be enrolled in an accredited college or university and carry a minimum of 12 credit hours each semester. Minimum 3.0 GPA required. Submit letter of endorsement from sponsoring chapter of the United Daughters of the Confederacy. Scholarship amount for the entire academic year will be sent to college/university.

Award: Scholarship for use in freshman, sophomore, junior, or senior years; renewable. *Number: 1–2. Amount: $800–$1000.*

Eligibility Requirements: Applicant must be enrolled or expecting to enroll full-time at a four-year institution or university. Applicant or parent of applicant must be member of United Daughters of the Confederacy. Applicant must have 3.0 GPA or higher. Available to U.S. citizens.

Application Requirements: Application, essay, financial need analysis, photo, references, self-addressed stamped envelope, transcript, confederate ancestor's proof of service. *Deadline:* March 15.

Contact: Robert Kraus, Second Vice President General
United Daughters of the Confederacy
328 North Boulevard
Richmond, VA 23220-4057
Phone: 804-355-1636

CORNELIA BRANCH STONE SCHOLARSHIP

Renewable award for undergraduate student who is a descendant of a Confederate soldier, sailor or marine. Must be enrolled in an accredited college or university and carry a minimum of 12 credit hours each semester. Minimum of 3.0 GPA required. Submit a letter of endorsement from sponsoring Chapter of the United Daughters of the Confederacy. Scholarship amount for the entire academic year will be sent to college/university.

Award: Scholarship for use in freshman, sophomore, junior, or senior years; renewable. *Number: 1–2. Amount: $800–$1000.*

Eligibility Requirements: Applicant must be enrolled or expecting to enroll full-time at a four-year institution or university. Applicant or parent of applicant must be member of United Daughters of the Confederacy. Applicant must have 3.0 GPA or higher. Available to U.S. citizens.

Application Requirements: Application, essay, financial need analysis, photo, references, self-addressed stamped envelope, transcript, confederate ancestor's proof of service. *Deadline:* March 15.

United Daughters of the Confederacy (continued)

Contact: Robert Kraus, Second Vice President General
United Daughters of the Confederacy
328 North Boulevard
Richmond, VA 23220-4057
Phone: 804-355-1636

DAVID STEPHEN WYLIE SCHOLARSHIP

Renewable award for undergraduate student who is a descendant of a Confederate soldier, sailor or marine. Must be enrolled in an accredited college or university and carry a minimum of 12 credit hours each semester. Minimum 3.0 GPA required. Submit letter of endorsement from sponsoring chapter of the United Daughters of the Confederacy. Scholarship amount for the entire academic year will be sent to college/university.

Award: Scholarship for use in freshman, sophomore, junior, or senior years; renewable. *Number:* 1–2. *Amount:* $800–$1000.

Eligibility Requirements: Applicant must be enrolled or expecting to enroll full-time at a four-year institution or university. Applicant or parent of applicant must be member of United Daughters of the Confederacy. Applicant must have 3.0 GPA or higher. Available to U.S. citizens.

Application Requirements: Application, essay, financial need analysis, photo, references, self-addressed stamped envelope, transcript, confederate ancestor's proof of service. *Deadline:* March 15.

Contact: Robert Kraus, Second Vice President General
United Daughters of the Confederacy
328 North Boulevard
Richmond, VA 23220-4057
Phone: 804-355-1636

DOROTHY WILLIAMS SCHOLARSHIP

Renewable award for undergraduate student who is a descendant of a Confederate soldier, sailor or marine. Must be enrolled in an accredited college or university and carry a minimum of 12 credit hours each semester. Minimum 3.0 GPA required. Submit a letter of endorsement from sponsoring chapter of the United Daughters of the Confederacy. Scholarship amount for the entire academic year will be sent to college/university.

Award: Scholarship for use in freshman, sophomore, junior, or senior years; renewable. *Number:* 1–2. *Amount:* $800–$1000.

Eligibility Requirements: Applicant must be enrolled or expecting to enroll full-time at a four-year institution or university. Applicant or parent of applicant must be member of United Daughters of the Confederacy. Applicant must have 3.0 GPA or higher. Available to U.S. citizens.

Application Requirements: Application, essay, financial need analysis, photo, references, self-addressed stamped envelope, transcript, confederate ancestor's proof of service. *Deadline:* March 15.

Contact: Robert Kraus, Second Vice President General
United Daughters of the Confederacy
328 North Boulevard
Richmond, VA 23220-4057
Phone: 804-355-1636

ELIZABETH AND WALLACE KINGSBURY SCHOLARSHIP

Award for full-time undergraduate student who is a descendant of a Confederate soldier, studying at an accredited college or university and carrying a minimum of 12 credit hours each semester. Must have been a member of the Children of the Confederacy for a minimum of three years. Minimum 3.0 GPA required. Scholarship amount for the entire academic year will be sent to college/university.

Award: Scholarship for use in freshman, sophomore, junior, or senior years; renewable. *Number:* 1–2. *Amount:* $800–$1000.

Eligibility Requirements: Applicant must be enrolled or expecting to enroll full-time at a four-year institution or university. Applicant or parent of applicant must be member of United Daughters of the Confederacy. Applicant must have 3.0 GPA or higher. Available to U.S. citizens.

Application Requirements: Application, essay, financial need analysis, photo, references, self-addressed stamped envelope, transcript, confederate ancestor's proof of service. *Deadline:* March 15.

Contact: Robert Kraus, Second Vice President General
United Daughters of the Confederacy
328 North Boulevard
Richmond, VA 23220-4057
Phone: 804-355-1636

GERTRUDE BOTTS-SAUCIER SCHOLARSHIP

Award for full-time undergraduate student who is a descendant of a Confederate soldier, sailor or marine. Must be from Texas, Mississippi or Louisiana. Must carry a minimum of 12 credit hours each semester and have a minimum 3.0 GPA. Submit letter of endorsement from sponsoring chapter of the United Daughters of the Confederacy. Scholarship amount for the entire academic year will be sent to college/university.

Award: Scholarship for use in freshman, sophomore, junior, or senior years; renewable. *Number:* 1–2. *Amount:* $800–$1000.

Eligibility Requirements: Applicant must be enrolled or expecting to enroll full-time at a four-year institution or university and resident of Louisiana, Mississippi, or Texas. Applicant or parent of applicant must be member of United Daughters of the Confederacy. Applicant must have 3.0 GPA or higher. Available to U.S. citizens.

Application Requirements: Application, essay, financial need analysis, photo, references, self-addressed stamped envelope, transcript, confederate ancestor's proof of service. *Deadline:* March 15.

Contact: Robert Kraus, Second Vice President General
United Daughters of the Confederacy
328 North Boulevard
Richmond, VA 23220-4057
Phone: 804-355-1636

HECTOR W. CHURCH SCHOLARSHIP

Renewable award for undergraduate student who is a descendant of a Confederate soldier, sailor or marine. Must be enrolled in an accredited college or university and carry a minimum of 12 credit hours each semester. Minimum of 3.0 GPA required. Submit letter of endorsement from sponsoring chapter of the United Daughters of the Confederacy. Scholarship amount for the entire academic year will be sent to college/university.

Award: Scholarship for use in freshman, sophomore, junior, or senior years; renewable. *Number:* 1–5. *Amount:* $800–$1000.

Eligibility Requirements: Applicant must be enrolled or expecting to enroll full-time at a four-year institution or university. Applicant or parent of applicant must be member of United Daughters of the Confederacy. Applicant must have 3.0 GPA or higher. Available to U.S. citizens.

Application Requirements: Application, essay, financial need analysis, photo, references, self-addressed stamped envelope, transcript, confederate ancestor's proof of service. *Deadline:* March 15.

Contact: Mrs. Robert C. Kraus, Second Vice president General
United Daughters of the Confederacy
239 Deerfield Lane
Franklin, NC 28734-0112

HENRY CLAY DARSEY SCHOLARSHIP

Renewable award for undergraduate student who is a descendant of a Confederate soldier, sailor or marine. Must be enrolled in an accredited college or university and carry a minimum of 12 credit hours each semester. Minimum 3.0 GPA required. Submit letter of endorsement from sponsoring Chapter of the United Daughters of the Confederacy. Scholarship amount for the entire academic year will be sent to college/university.

Award: Scholarship for use in freshman, sophomore, junior, or senior years; renewable. *Number:* 1–2. *Amount:* $800–$1000.

Eligibility Requirements: Applicant must be enrolled or expecting to enroll full-time at a four-year institution or university. Applicant or parent of applicant must be member of United Daughters of the Confederacy. Applicant must have 3.0 GPA or higher. Available to U.S. citizens.

Application Requirements: Application, essay, financial need analysis, photo, references, self-addressed stamped envelope, transcript, confederate ancestor's proof of service. *Deadline:* March 15.

Contact: Robert Kraus, Second Vice President General
United Daughters of the Confederacy
328 North Boulevard
Richmond, VA 23220-4057
Phone: 804-355-1636

JANET B. SEIPPEL SCHOLARSHIP

Renewable award for undergraduate student who is a descendant of a Confederate soldier, sailor or marine. Must be enrolled in an accredited college or university and carry a minimum of 12 credit hours each semester. Minimum of 3.0 GPA required. Submit a letter of endorsement from sponsoring chapter of the United Daughters of the Confederacy. Scholarship amount for the entire academic year will be sent to college/university.

Award: Scholarship for use in freshman, sophomore, junior, or senior years; renewable. *Number:* 1–2. *Amount:* $800–$1000.

Eligibility Requirements: Applicant must be enrolled or expecting to enroll full-time at a four-year institution or university. Applicant or parent of applicant must be member of United Daughters of the Confederacy. Applicant must have 3.0 GPA or higher. Available to U.S. citizens.

Application Requirements: Application, essay, financial need analysis, photo, references, self-addressed stamped envelope, transcript, confederate ancestor's proof of service. *Deadline:* March 15.

Contact: Robert Kraus, Second Vice President General
United Daughters of the Confederacy
328 North Boulevard
Richmond, VA 23220-4057
Phone: 804-355-1636

LOLA B. CURRY SCHOLARSHIP

Award for full-time student from Alabama who is a descendant of a Confederate soldier. Must be enrolled in an accredited college or university in Alabama and carry a minimum of 12 credit hours each semester. Minimum 3.0 GPA required. Submit letter of endorsement from sponsoring chapter of the United Daughters of the Confederacy. Scholarship amount for the entire academic year will be sent to college/university.

Award: Scholarship for use in freshman, sophomore, junior, or senior years; renewable. *Number:* 1–2. *Amount:* $800–$1000.

Eligibility Requirements: Applicant must be enrolled or expecting to enroll full-time at a four-year institution or university; resident of Alabama and studying in Alabama. Applicant or parent of applicant must be member of United Daughters of the Confederacy. Applicant must have 3.0 GPA or higher. Available to U.S. citizens.

Application Requirements: Application, essay, financial need analysis, photo, references, self-addressed stamped envelope, transcript, confederate ancestor's proof of service. *Deadline:* March 15.

Contact: Robert Kraus, Second Vice President General
United Daughters of the Confederacy
328 North Boulevard
Richmond, VA 23220-4057
Phone: 804-355-1636

M. B. POPPENHEIM MEMORIAL SCHOLARSHIP

Renewable award for undergraduate student who is a descendant of a Confederate soldier, sailor or marine. Must be enrolled in an accredited college or university and carry a minimum of 12 credit hours each semester. Minimum 3.0 GPA required. Submit a letter of endorsement from sponsoring Chapter of the United Daughters of the Confederacy. Scholarship amount for the entire academic year will be sent to college/university.

Award: Scholarship for use in freshman, sophomore, junior, or senior years; renewable. *Number:* 1–2. *Amount:* $800–$1000.

Eligibility Requirements: Applicant must be enrolled or expecting to enroll full-time at a four-year institution or university. Applicant or parent of applicant must be member of United Daughters of the Confederacy. Applicant must have 3.0 GPA or higher. Available to U.S. citizens.

Application Requirements: Application, essay, financial need analysis, photo, references, self-addressed stamped envelope, transcript, confederate ancestor's proof of service. *Deadline:* March 15.

Contact: Robert Kraus, Second Vice President General
United Daughters of the Confederacy
328 North Boulevard
Richmond, VA 23220-4057
Phone: 804-355-1636

MAJOR MADISON BELL SCHOLARSHIP

Renewable award for undergraduate student who is a descendant of a Confederate soldier, sailor or marine. Must be enrolled in an accredited college or university and carry a minimum of 12 credit hours each semester. Minimum 3.0 GPA required. Submit letter of endorsement from sponsoring chapter of the United Daughters of the Confederacy. Scholarship amount for the entire academic year will be sent to college/university.

Award: Scholarship for use in freshman, sophomore, junior, or senior years; renewable. *Number:* 1–2. *Amount:* $800–$1000.

Eligibility Requirements: Applicant must be enrolled or expecting to enroll full-time at a four-year institution or university. Applicant or parent of applicant must be member of United Daughters of the Confederacy. Applicant must have 3.0 GPA or higher. Available to U.S. citizens.

Application Requirements: Application, essay, financial need analysis, photo, references, self-addressed stamped envelope, transcript, confederate ancestor's proof of service. *Deadline:* March 15.

Contact: Mrs. Robert C. Kraus, Second Vice President General
United Daughters of the Confederacy
239 Deerfield Lane
Franklin, NC 28734-0112

MATTHEW FONTAINE MAURY SCHOLARSHIP

Renewable award for undergraduate student who is a descendant of a Confederate soldier, sailor or marine. Must be enrolled in an accredited college or university and carry a minimum of 12 credit hours each semester. Minimum 3.0 GPA required. Submit letter of endorsement from sponsoring Chapter of the United Daughters of the Confederacy. Scholarship amount for the entire academic year will be sent to college/university.

Award: Scholarship for use in freshman, sophomore, junior, or senior years; renewable. *Number:* 1–2. *Amount:* $800–$1000.

Eligibility Requirements: Applicant must be enrolled or expecting to enroll full-time at a four-year institution or university. Applicant or parent of applicant must be member of United Daughters of the Confederacy. Applicant must have 3.0 GPA or higher. Available to U.S. citizens.

Application Requirements: Application, essay, financial need analysis, photo, references, self-addressed stamped envelope, transcript, confederate ancestor's proof of service. *Deadline:* March 15.

Contact: Robert Kraus, Second Vice President General
United Daughters of the Confederacy
328 North Boulevard
Richmond, VA 23220-4057
Phone: 804-355-1636

MRS. ELLA M. FRANKLIN SCHOLARSHIP

Renewable award for undergraduate student who is a descendant of a Confederate soldier, sailor, or marine. Must be enrolled in an accredited college or university and carry a minimum of 12 credit hours each semester. Minimum 3.0 GPA required. Submit letter of endorsement from sponsoring chapter of the United Daughters of the Confederacy. Scholarship amount for the entire academic year will be sent to college/university.

Award: Scholarship for use in freshman, sophomore, junior, or senior years; renewable. *Number:* 1–2. *Amount:* $800–$1000.

Eligibility Requirements: Applicant must be enrolled or expecting to enroll full-time at a four-year institution or university. Applicant or parent of applicant must be member of United Daughters of the Confederacy. Applicant must have 3.0 GPA or higher. Available to U.S. citizens.

Application Requirements: Application, essay, financial need analysis, photo, references, self-addressed stamped envelope, transcript, confederate ancestor's proof of service. *Deadline:* March 15.

United Daughters of the Confederacy (continued)

Contact: Robert Kraus, Second Vice President General
United Daughters of the Confederacy
328 North Boulevard
Richmond, VA 23220-4057
Phone: 804-355-1636

MRS. L. H. RAINES MEMORIAL SCHOLARSHIP

Renewable award for undergraduate student who is a descendant of a Confederate solider, sailor or marine. Must be enrolled in an accredited college or university and carry a minimum of 12 credit hours each semester. Minimum 3.0 GPA required. Submit letter of endorsement from sponsoring chapter of the United Daughters of the Confederacy. Scholarship amount for the entire academic year will be sent to college/university.

Award: Scholarship for use in freshman, sophomore, junior, or senior years; renewable. *Number:* 1–2. *Amount:* $800–$1000.

Eligibility Requirements: Applicant must be enrolled or expecting to enroll full-time at a four-year institution or university. Applicant or parent of applicant must be member of United Daughters of the Confederacy. Applicant must have 3.0 GPA or higher. Available to U.S. citizens.

Application Requirements: Application, essay, financial need analysis, photo, references, self-addressed stamped envelope, transcript, confederate ancestor's proof of service. *Deadline:* March 15.

Contact: Robert Kraus, Second Vice President General
United Daughters of the Confederacy
328 North Boulevard
Richmond, VA 23220-4057
Phone: 804-355-1636

S.A. CUNNINGHAM SCHOLARSHIP

Renewable award for undergraduate student who is a descendant of a Confederate soldier, sailor or marine. Must be enrolled in an accredited college or university and carry a minimum of 12 credit hours each semester. Minimum 3.0 GPA required. Submit letter of endorsement from sponsoring Chapter of the United Daughters of the Confederacy. Scholarship amount for the entire academic year will be sent to college/university.

Award: Scholarship for use in freshman, sophomore, junior, or senior years; renewable. *Number:* 1–2. *Amount:* $800–$1000.

Eligibility Requirements: Applicant must be enrolled or expecting to enroll full-time at a four-year institution or university. Applicant or parent of applicant must be member of United Daughters of the Confederacy. Applicant must have 3.0 GPA or higher. Available to U.S. citizens.

Application Requirements: Application, essay, financial need analysis, photo, references, self-addressed stamped envelope, transcript, confederate ancestor's proof of service. *Deadline:* March 15.

Contact: Mrs. Robert C. Kraus, Second Vice President General
United Daughters of the Confederacy
239 Deerfield Lane
Franklin, NC 28734-0112

STONEWALL JACKSON SCHOLARSHIP

Renewable award for undergraduate student who is a descendant of a Confederate soldier, sailor or marine. Must be enrolled in an accredited college or university and carry a minimum of 12 credit hours each semester. Minimum 3.0 GPA required. Submit letter of endorsement from sponsoring Chapter of the United Daughters of the Confederacy. Scholarship amount for the entire academic year will be sent to college/university.

Award: Scholarship for use in freshman, sophomore, junior, or senior years; renewable. *Number:* 1–2. *Amount:* $800–$1000.

Eligibility Requirements: Applicant must be enrolled or expecting to enroll full-time at a four-year institution or university. Applicant or parent of applicant must be member of United Daughters of the Confederacy. Applicant must have 3.0 GPA or higher. Available to U.S. citizens.

Application Requirements: Application, essay, financial need analysis, photo, references, self-addressed stamped envelope, transcript, confederate ancestor's proof of service. *Deadline:* March.

Contact: Robert Kraus, Second Vice President General
United Daughters of the Confederacy
328 North Boulevard
Richmond, VA 23220-4057
Phone: 804-355-1636

WINNIE DAVIS-CHILDREN OF THE CONFEDERACY SCHOLARSHIP

Award for full-time undergraduate student who is a descendant of a Confederate soldier, enrolled in an accredited college or university and carrying a minimum of 12 credit hours each semester. Recipient must be, or have been until age of 18, a participating member of the Children of the Confederacy and approved by the Third Vice President General. Minimum 3.0 GPA required. Scholarship amount for the entire academic year will be sent to college/university.

Award: Scholarship for use in freshman, sophomore, junior, or senior years; renewable. *Number:* 1–2. *Amount:* $800–$1000.

Eligibility Requirements: Applicant must be enrolled or expecting to enroll full-time at a four-year institution or university. Applicant or parent of applicant must be member of United Daughters of the Confederacy. Applicant must have 3.0 GPA or higher. Available to U.S. citizens.

Application Requirements: Application, driver's license, essay, financial need analysis, photo, portfolio, resume, references, self-addressed stamped envelope, transcript, confederate ancestor's proof of service. *Deadline:* March 15.

Contact: Robert Kraus, Second Vice President General
United Daughters of the Confederacy
328 North Boulevard
Richmond, VA 23220-4057
Phone: 804-355-1636

UNITED FOOD AND COMMERCIAL WORKERS INTERNATIONAL UNION   http://www.ufcw.org

JAMES A. SUFFRIDGE UNITED FOOD AND COMMERCIAL WORKERS SCHOLARSHIP PROGRAM

Scholarships available to graduating high school seniors during the specific program year. Must be a member of UFCW or the dependent of a UFCW member. Scholarship is disbursed over a four-year period of undergraduate study. Seven renewable awards of $4000 each.

Award: Scholarship for use in freshman, sophomore, junior, or senior years; renewable. *Number:* 7. *Amount:* $4000.

Eligibility Requirements: Applicant must be high school student; age 20 or under and planning to enroll or expecting to enroll full-time at a four-year institution. Applicant or parent of applicant must be member of United Food and Commercial Workers. Available to U.S. and Canadian citizens.

Application Requirements: Application, test scores, transcript. *Deadline:* March 15.

Contact: Amri Joyner, Scholarship Coordinator
United Food and Commercial Workers International Union
1775 K Street, NW
Washington, DC 20006
Phone: 202-223-3111
Fax: 202-466-1587
E-mail: scholarship@ufcw.org

UNITED STATES JUNIOR CHAMBER OF COMMERCE   http://www.usjaycees.org

JAYCEE CHARLES R. FORD SCHOLARSHIP

One-time award of $2500 available to active members of Jaycee wishing to return to college to complete his/her formal education. Must be U.S. citizen, possess academic potential and leadership qualities and show financial need. To receive an application, send $5 application fee and self-addressed stamped envelope between July 1 and February 1.

Award: Scholarship for use in freshman, sophomore, junior, or senior years; not renewable. *Number:* 1. *Amount:* $2500.

Eligibility Requirements: Applicant must be enrolled or expecting to enroll at a two-year or four-year institution or university. Applicant or parent of applicant must be member of Jaycees. Available to U.S. citizens.

Application Requirements: Application, financial need analysis, self-addressed stamped envelope. *Fee:* $5. *Deadline:* April 1.

Contact: Karen Fitzgerald, Customer Service/Data Processing
United States Junior Chamber of Commerce
PO Box 7
Tulsa, OK 74102-0007
Phone: 918-584-2484
Fax: 918-584-4422
E-mail: customerservice@usjaycees.org

JAYCEE THOMAS WOOD BALDRIDGE SCHOLARSHIP

One-time award of $3000 available to a Jaycee immediate family member or a descendent of a Jaycee member. Must be U.S. citizen, possess academic potential and leadership qualities and show financial need. To receive an application, send $5 application fee and self-addressed stamped envelope between July 1 and February 1.

Award: Scholarship for use in freshman, sophomore, junior, or senior years; not renewable. *Number:* 1. *Amount:* $3000.

Eligibility Requirements: Applicant must be enrolled or expecting to enroll at a two-year or four-year institution or university. Applicant or parent of applicant must be member of Jaycees. Available to U.S. citizens.

Application Requirements: Application, financial need analysis, self-addressed stamped envelope. *Fee:* $5. *Deadline:* April 1.

Contact: Karen Fitzgerald, Customer Service/Data Processing
United States Junior Chamber of Commerce
PO Box 7
Tulsa, OK 74102-0007
Phone: 918-584-2484
Fax: 918-584-4422
E-mail: customerservice@usjaycees.org

UTILITY WORKERS UNION OF AMERICA
http://www.uwua.net/

UTILITY WORKERS UNION OF AMERICA SCHOLARSHIP AWARDS PROGRAM

Renewable award for high school juniors who are children of active members of the Utility Workers Union of America. Must take the Preliminary SAT National Merit Scholarship Qualifying Test in junior year and plan to enter college in the fall after high school graduation.

Award: Scholarship for use in freshman, sophomore, junior, or senior years; renewable. *Number:* 2. *Amount:* $500–$2000.

Eligibility Requirements: Applicant must be high school student and planning to enroll or expecting to enroll full-time at a four-year institution or university. Applicant or parent of applicant must be member of Utility Workers Union of America. Available to U.S. citizens.

Application Requirements: Application. *Deadline:* January 1.

Contact: Rosanna Farley, Office Manager
Utility Workers Union of America
815 16th Street, NW
Washington, DC 20006
Phone: 202-974-8200
Fax: 202-974-8201
E-mail: rfarley@aflcio.org

WESTERN FRATERNAL LIFE ASSOCIATION
http://www.wflains.com

WESTERN FRATERNAL LIFE ASSOCIATION NATIONAL SCHOLARSHIP

Ten national scholarships will be awarded annually for up to $1000 to qualified members attending college or vocational programs. Traditional and non-traditional students are eligible. Must be a WFLA member in good standing for two years prior to the application deadline. A member is an individual who has life insurance or an annuity with WFLA. High school seniors may apply. Members who are qualified for the National Scholarship may also qualify for 3 state scholarships and the NFCA's scholarship.

Award: Scholarship for use in freshman, sophomore, junior, or senior years; renewable. *Number:* 10. *Amount:* $500–$1000.

Eligibility Requirements: Applicant must be enrolled or expecting to enroll full-time at a two-year or four-year or technical institution or

university. Applicant or parent of applicant must be member of Western Fraternal Life Association. Available to U.S. citizens.

Application Requirements: Application, driver's license, essay, references, test scores, transcript. *Deadline:* March 1.

Contact: Linda Grove, Fraternal Manager
Western Fraternal Life Association
1900 1st Avenue NE
Cedar Rapids, IA 52402-5372
Phone: 877-935-2467
Fax: 319-363-8806
E-mail: lgrove@wflains.com

WOMEN'S INTERNATIONAL BOWLING CONGRESS
http://www.bowl.com

ALBERTA E. CROWE STAR OF TOMORROW AWARD

Renewable award for a U.S. or Canadian female high school or college student who competes in the sport of bowling. Must be a current YABA or WIBC member in good standing. Must be younger than 22 years old. Minimum 2.5 GPA required. Deadline is October 1.

Award: Scholarship for use in freshman, sophomore, junior, or senior years; renewable. *Number:* 1. *Amount:* $1500.

Eligibility Requirements: Applicant must be age 21 or under; enrolled or expecting to enroll at an institution or university; female and must have an interest in bowling. Applicant or parent of applicant must be member of Young American Bowling Alliance. Applicant must have 2.5 GPA or higher. Available to U.S. and Canadian citizens.

Application Requirements: Application, essay, references, transcript. *Deadline:* October 1.

Contact: Ed Gocha, Manager of Smart Scholarship
Women's International Bowling Congress
5301 South 76th Street
Greendale, WI 53129-1192
Phone: 800-514-2695 Ext. 3343
Fax: 414-421-3013
E-mail: egocha@bowlinginc.com

WYOMING FARM BUREAU FEDERATION
http://www.wyfb.org

KING-LIVINGSTON SCHOLARSHIP

One-time award given to graduates of Wyoming high schools. Must attend a Wyoming junior college or the University of Wyoming. Minimum 2.5 GPA required. Applicant's family must be a current member of the Wyoming Farm Bureau. Deadline is March 1.

Award: Scholarship for use in freshman, sophomore, junior, senior, or graduate years; not renewable. *Number:* 1. *Amount:* $750.

Eligibility Requirements: Applicant must be enrolled or expecting to enroll at a two-year or four-year institution or university; resident of Wyoming and studying in Wyoming. Applicant or parent of applicant must be member of Wyoming Farm Bureau. Applicant must have 2.5 GPA or higher. Available to U.S. citizens.

Application Requirements: Application, financial need analysis, photo, resume, references, transcript. *Deadline:* March 1.

Contact: Ellen Westbrook, Executive Secretary
Wyoming Farm Bureau Federation
931 Boulder Drive
Laramie, WY 82070
Phone: 307-721-7719
Fax: 307-721-7790
E-mail: ewestbrook@mwfbi.com

WYOMING FARM BUREAU CONTINUING EDUCATION SCHOLARSHIPS

Award to students attending a two-year college in Wyoming or the University of Wyoming. Must be a resident of Wyoming and applicant's family must be a current member of the Wyoming Farm Bureau. Applicants must submit at least two semesters of college grade transcripts. Freshmen must submit first semester grades and proof of enrollment in second semester. Minimum 2.5 GPA. Deadline is March 1.

Award: Scholarship for use in freshman, sophomore, junior, senior, or graduate years. *Number:* 3. *Amount:* $500.

Wyoming Farm Bureau Federation (continued)

Eligibility Requirements: Applicant must be enrolled or expecting to enroll at a two-year or four-year institution or university; resident of Wyoming and studying in Wyoming. Applicant or parent of applicant must be member of Wyoming Farm Bureau. Applicant must have 2.5 GPA or higher. Available to U.S. citizens.

Application Requirements: Application, financial need analysis, photo, resume, references, transcript. *Deadline:* March 1.

Contact: Ellen Westbrook, Executive Secretary
Wyoming Farm Bureau Federation
931 Boulder Drive
Laramie, WY 82070
Phone: 307-721-7719
Fax: 307-721-7790
E-mail: ewestbrook@mwfbi.com

WYOMING FARM BUREAU FEDERATION SCHOLARSHIPS

Five $500 scholarships will be given to graduates of Wyoming high schools. Eligible candidates will be enrolled in a two-year college in Wyoming or the University of Wyoming and must have a minimum 2.5 GPA. Applicant's family should be current member of the Wyoming Farm Bureau Federation. Deadline: March 1.

Award: Scholarship for use in freshman, sophomore, junior, senior, or graduate years; not renewable. *Number:* 5. *Amount:* $500.

Eligibility Requirements: Applicant must be enrolled or expecting to enroll at a two-year or four-year institution or university; resident of Wyoming and studying in Wyoming. Applicant or parent of applicant must be member of Wyoming Farm Bureau. Applicant must have 2.5 GPA or higher. Available to U.S. citizens.

Application Requirements: Application, financial need analysis, photo, resume, references, transcript. *Deadline:* March 1.

Contact: Ellen Westbrook, Executive Secretary
Wyoming Farm Bureau Federation
931 Boulder Drive
Laramie, WY 82070
Phone: 307-721-7719
Fax: 307-721-7790
E-mail: ewestbrook@mwfbi.com

YOUNG AMERICAN BOWLING ALLIANCE (YABA)
http://www.bowl.com

GIFT FOR LIFE SCHOLARSHIP

One-time award for high school students who compete in the sport of bowling. Minimum 2.0 GPA required. Must demonstrate financial need. Must be a member in good standing of YABA. Application deadline is April 1.

Award: Scholarship for use in freshman year; not renewable. *Number:* 12. *Amount:* $1000.

Eligibility Requirements: Applicant must be high school student; planning to enroll or expecting to enroll full-time at a two-year or four-year or technical institution or university and must have an interest in bowling. Applicant or parent of applicant must be member of Young American Bowling Alliance. Available to U.S. citizens.

Application Requirements: Application, essay, financial need analysis, references. *Deadline:* April 1.

Contact: Young American Bowling Alliance (YABA)
5301 South 76th Street
Greendale, WI 53129
Phone: 800-514-2695 Ext. 3318
E-mail: egocha@bowlinginc.com

PEPSI-COLA YOUTH BOWLING CHAMPIONSHIPS

Awarded to members of the Young American Bowling Alliance. Must win state or provincial tournaments to be eligible for international championships. U.S. citizens abroad may participate through military affiliate. Application fee varies by state. Contact Youth Director at local bowling center.

Award: Scholarship for use in freshman, sophomore, junior, or senior years; not renewable. *Number:* 292. *Amount:* $500–$2000.

Eligibility Requirements: Applicant must be enrolled or expecting to enroll full or part-time at an institution or university and must have an interest in bowling. Applicant or parent of applicant must be member of Young American Bowling Alliance. Available to U.S. and non-U.S. citizens.

Application Requirements: Application, applicant must enter a contest. *Deadline:* February 28.

Contact: Karen Richter, Smart Accounts Administrator
Young American Bowling Alliance (YABA)
5301 South 76th Street
Greendale, WI 53129-1192
Phone: 800-514-2695 Ext. 3318
Fax: 414-423-3014
E-mail: kricht@bowlinginc.com

CORPORATE AFFILIATION

ADMINISTRATIVE MANAGEMENT SERVICES (AMS)
http://home.cogeco.ca

DAIMLER CHRYSLER SCHOLARSHIP PROGRAM

Student must be graduating from final high school year and be enrolling in first year of a three- to four-year degree program. Twelve students are chosen based on academic performance, extracurricular activities, and community service. Once in the program they could be eligible for four awards as long as a "B" average is maintained on a full workload. Open to Canadian citizens who are dependents of employees of Daimler Chrysler Canada, Inc.

Award: Scholarship for use in freshman, sophomore, junior, or senior years; renewable. *Number:* 12. *Amount:* $743–$1000.

Eligibility Requirements: Applicant must be Canadian citizen; high school student and planning to enroll or expecting to enroll full-time at an institution or university. Applicant or parent of applicant must be affiliated with Daimler Chrysler Canada, Inc.. Applicant must have 3.0 GPA or higher.

Application Requirements: Application, autobiography, references, transcript. *Deadline:* April 30.

Contact: Donna Burnett, Scholarship Coordinator
Administrative Management Services (AMS)
829 Norwest Road, Suite 412
Kingston, ON K7P 2N3
Canada
Phone: 613-634-4350
Fax: 613-634-4209
E-mail: chrisb7@cogeco.ca

SYNCRUDE HIGHER EDUCATION AWARDS PROGRAM

Awarded to Canadian students enrolled in a program that involves a minimum of two years full-time study. Students could qualify for four awards at the undergraduate level and two years at the graduate or professional level as long as they are under 25 years of age. Awards may be held at the community college level for a maximum of two years. Must be a dependent of a Syncrude Canada, Inc., employee & Northward Development Ltd., employee

Award: Scholarship for use in freshman, sophomore, junior, senior, or graduate years; renewable. *Number:* varies. *Amount:* $1783–$2400.

Eligibility Requirements: Applicant must be Canadian citizen; age 24 or under and enrolled or expecting to enroll full-time at a two-year or technical institution or university. Applicant or parent of applicant must be affiliated with Syncrude Canada, Inc..

Application Requirements: Application, transcript. *Deadline:* November 15.

Contact: Donna Burnett, Awards Coordinator
Administrative Management Services (AMS)
Suite 412,829 Norwest Road
Kingston, ON K7P 2M3
Canada
Phone: 613-634-4350
Fax: 613-634-4209
E-mail: chrisb7@cogeco.ca

ALBERTA HERITAGE SCHOLARSHIP FUND/ ALBERTA SCHOLARSHIP PROGRAMS

http://www.alis.gov.ab.ca

ALBERTA HERITAGE SCHOLARSHIP FUND CANA SCHOLARSHIPS

Award to recognize and reward exceptional academic achievement of children of CANA or ACE Construction for the last two consecutive years. Must be Alberta resident entering second or subsequent year of study at an eligible institution. Application deadline is October 31.

Award: Scholarship for use in sophomore, junior, or senior years; not renewable. *Number:* 3. *Amount:* $861–$1291.

Eligibility Requirements: Applicant must be Canadian citizen; enrolled or expecting to enroll full-time at a two-year or four-year institution or university and resident of Alberta. Applicant or parent of applicant must be affiliated with CANA. Applicant must have 2.5 GPA or higher.

Application Requirements: Application, transcript. *Deadline:* October 31.

Contact: Stuart Dunn, Manager
Alberta Heritage Scholarship Fund/Alberta Scholarship Programs
4th Floor, 9940 106th Street, Box 28000 Station Main
Edmonton, AB T5J 4R4
Canada
Phone: 780-427-8640
Fax: 780-427-1288
E-mail: scholarships@gov.ab.ca

STREAM-FLO/MASTER FLO SCHOLARSHIPS

Two CAN$3000 scholarships are available to recognize exceptional academic achievement at the high school level of sons and daughters of Stream-Flo Industries Ltd., Master Flo Valve, Inc., and ERC Industries employees. Application deadline is July 31. For more details see Web site: http://www.alis.gov.ab.ca

Award: Scholarship for use in freshman year; not renewable. *Number:* 2. *Amount:* $2583.

Eligibility Requirements: Applicant must be high school student; planning to enroll or expecting to enroll full-time at a four-year or technical institution or university and studying in Alberta, British Columbia, or Saskatchewan. Applicant or parent of applicant must be affiliated with Stream-Flo Industries Ltd.. Available to Canadian citizens.

Application Requirements: Application. *Deadline:* July 31.

Contact: Stuart Dunn, Manager
Alberta Heritage Scholarship Fund/Alberta Scholarship Programs
4th Floor, 9940 106th Street, Box 28000 Station Main
Edmonton, AB T5J 4R4
Canada
Phone: 780-427-8640
Fax: 780-427-1288
E-mail: scholarships@gov.ab.ca

BUTLER MANUFACTURING COMPANY

http://www.butlermfg.com

BUTLER MANUFACTURING COMPANY FOUNDATION SCHOLARSHIP PROGRAM

Award for high school seniors who are the children of full-time employees of Butler Manufacturing Company and its subsidiaries. Award is renewable for up to four years. Must enroll full-time and stay in upper half of class.

Award: Scholarship for use in freshman year; renewable. *Number:* 8. *Amount:* $2500.

Eligibility Requirements: Applicant must be high school student and planning to enroll or expecting to enroll full-time at a two-year institution. Applicant or parent of applicant must be affiliated with Butler Manufacturing Company. Available to U.S. and Canadian citizens.

Application Requirements: Application, essay, financial need analysis, references, test scores, transcript. *Deadline:* February 18.

Contact: Barbara Fay, Foundation Administrator
Butler Manufacturing Company
PO Box 419917
1540 Genessee Street
Kansas City, MO 64102
Phone: 816-968-3208
Fax: 816-968-6501
E-mail: blfay@butlermfg.org

CENTER FOR SCHOLARSHIP ADMINISTRATION

http://www.scholarshipprograms.org

BI-LO JOHN ROHALEY SCHOLARSHIP

Nonrenewable scholarships are available to associates of BI-LO who have had a minimum of one-year of service averaging 15 hours a week. For more details and an application, see Web site.

Award: Scholarship for use in freshman, sophomore, junior, or senior years; not renewable. *Number:* 3. *Amount:* $2000.

Eligibility Requirements: Applicant must be enrolled or expecting to enroll full-time at a two-year or four-year or technical institution or university. Applicant or parent of applicant must be affiliated with BI-LO. Available to U.S. citizens.

Application Requirements: Application, essay, financial need analysis, references, transcript. *Deadline:* February 15.

Contact: Sandra Lee, President
Center for Scholarship Administration
PO Box 1465
Taylors, SC 29687-0031
Phone: 864-268-3363
Fax: 864-268-7160
E-mail: sandralee41@bellsouth.net

BONITZ (BILL ROGERS) SCHOLARSHIP

Renewable scholarships are for dependent children of qualified employees of Bonitz group of companies. For more details and an application, see Human Resources Manager at Bonitz of South Carolina.

Award: Scholarship for use in freshman, sophomore, junior, or senior years; renewable. *Number:* 1. *Amount:* up to $3000.

Eligibility Requirements: Applicant must be age 21 or under and enrolled or expecting to enroll full-time at a two-year or four-year or technical institution or university. Applicant or parent of applicant must be affiliated with Bonitz. Applicant must have 2.5 GPA or higher. Available to U.S. citizens.

Application Requirements: Application, essay, financial need analysis, references, transcript. *Deadline:* December 1.

Contact: Sandra Lee, President
Center for Scholarship Administration
PO Box 1465
Taylors, SC 29687-0031
Phone: 864-268-3363
Fax: 864-268-7160
E-mail: sandralee41@bellsouth.net

CARDINAL LOGISTICS MANAGEMENT, INC. SCHOLARSHIPS

Renewable scholarships are for dependent children of qualified employees of Cardinal Logistics Management, Inc. Contact the Human Resources Manager at Cardinal Logistics Management, Inc. for deadlines and more detailed information on additional criteria.

Award: Scholarship for use in freshman, sophomore, junior, or senior years; renewable. *Number:* 1. *Amount:* $2000.

Eligibility Requirements: Applicant must be enrolled or expecting to enroll full-time at a four-year institution or university and single. Applicant or parent of applicant must be affiliated with Cardinal Logistic Management. Applicant must have 2.5 GPA or higher. Available to U.S. citizens.

Application Requirements: Application, essay, references, transcript. *Deadline:* January 1.

Center for Scholarship Administration (continued)

Contact: Sandra Lee, President
Center for Scholarship Administration
PO Box 1465
Taylors, SC 29687-0031
Phone: 864-268-3363
Fax: 864-268-7160
E-mail: sandralee41@bellsouth.net

CARRIS SCHOLARSHIPS

Nonrenewable scholarships are for dependent children of qualified employees of Carris Financial Corporation. For more details and an application, see Web site: http://www.scholarshipprograms.org

Award: Scholarship for use in freshman, sophomore, junior, or senior years; not renewable. *Number:* up to 25. *Amount:* up to $2000.

Eligibility Requirements: Applicant must be enrolled or expecting to enroll full-time at a two-year or four-year or technical institution or university. Applicant or parent of applicant must be affiliated with Carris Financial Corporation. Available to U.S. citizens.

Application Requirements: Application, essay, financial need analysis, references, transcript. *Deadline:* March 1.

Contact: Sandra Lee, President
Center for Scholarship Administration
PO Box 1465
Taylors, SC 29687-0031
Phone: 864-268-3363
Fax: 864-268-7160
E-mail: sandralee41@bellsouth.net

CONSOLIDATED SYSTEMS, INC. BILL ROGERS SCHOLARSHIP

Renewable scholarships are for dependent children of qualified employees of Consolidated Systems, Inc. who are on hourly payroll. Contact the Human Resources Manager for deadlines and more detailed information on additional criteria.

Award: Scholarship for use in freshman, sophomore, or junior years; renewable. *Number:* 1. *Amount:* $2000.

Eligibility Requirements: Applicant must be age 25 or under and enrolled or expecting to enroll full-time at a two-year or four-year or technical institution or university. Applicant or parent of applicant must be affiliated with Consolidation Systems, Inc.. Available to U.S. citizens.

Application Requirements: Application, essay, references, transcript. *Deadline:* February 15.

Contact: Sandra Lee, President
Center for Scholarship Administration
PO Box 1465
Taylors, SC 29687-0031
Phone: 864-268-3363
Fax: 864-268-7160
E-mail: sandralee41@bellsouth.net

CONSOLIDATED SYSTEMS, INC. THOMAS C. MEREDITH SCHOLARSHIP

Renewable scholarships are for dependent children of qualified employees of Consolidated Systems, Inc. who are on salaried payroll. Contact the Human Resources Manager for deadlines and more detailed information on additional criteria.

Award: Scholarship for use in freshman, sophomore, or junior years; renewable. *Number:* 1. *Amount:* $2000.

Eligibility Requirements: Applicant must be age 25 or under and enrolled or expecting to enroll full-time at a two-year or four-year or technical institution or university. Applicant or parent of applicant must be affiliated with Consolidation Systems, Inc.. Available to U.S. citizens.

Application Requirements: Application, essay, references, transcript. *Deadline:* February 15.

Contact: Sandra Lee, President
Center for Scholarship Administration
PO Box 1465
Taylors, SC 29687-0031
Phone: 864-268-3363
Fax: 864-268-7160
E-mail: sandralee41@bellsouth.net

DAN RIVER FOUNDATION SCHOLARSHIP

Renewable scholarships are for dependent children of qualified employees of Dan River, Inc. For more details and an application see Web site: http://www.scholarshipprograms.org

Award: Scholarship for use in freshman, sophomore, junior, or senior years; renewable. *Number:* varies. *Amount:* up to $2000.

Eligibility Requirements: Applicant must be enrolled or expecting to enroll at a two-year or four-year institution or university. Applicant or parent of applicant must be affiliated with Dan River, Inc.. Applicant must have 2.5 GPA or higher. Available to U.S. citizens.

Application Requirements: Application, essay, financial need analysis, references, transcript. *Deadline:* April 30.

Contact: Sandra Lee, President
Center for Scholarship Administration
PO Box 1465
Taylors, SC 29687-0031
Phone: 864-268-3363
Fax: 864-268-7160
E-mail: sandralee41@bellsouth.net

DELTA APPAREL, INC. SCHOLARSHIP

Renewable scholarships are for dependent children of qualified employees of Delta Apparel, Inc. Contact the Human Resources Manager for deadlines and more detailed information on additional criteria.

Award: Scholarship for use in freshman, sophomore, junior, or senior years; renewable. *Number:* varies. *Amount:* $1000.

Eligibility Requirements: Applicant must be enrolled or expecting to enroll at a two-year or four-year or technical institution or university. Applicant or parent of applicant must be affiliated with Delta Apparel, Inc.. Applicant must have 2.5 GPA or higher. Available to U.S. citizens.

Application Requirements: Application, essay, financial need analysis, references, transcript. *Deadline:* March 31.

Contact: Sandra Lee, President
Center for Scholarship Administration
PO Box 1465
Taylors, SC 29687-0031
Phone: 864-268-3363
Fax: 864-268-7160
E-mail: sandralee41@bellsouth.net

FLEXIBLE TECHNOLOGIES, INC. SCHOLARSHIPS

Renewable scholarships are for dependent children of qualified employees of Flexible Technologies, Inc. Must maintain a 2.5 GPA to continue to receive the scholarship. Contact the Human Resources Manager for deadlines and more detailed information on additional criteria.

Award: Scholarship for use in freshman, sophomore, junior, or senior years; renewable. *Number:* 2. *Amount:* $2000.

Eligibility Requirements: Applicant must be high school student and planning to enroll or expecting to enroll full-time at a four-year institution or university. Applicant or parent of applicant must be affiliated with Flexible Technologies, Inc.. Applicant must have 2.5 GPA or higher. Available to U.S. and Canadian citizens.

Application Requirements: Application, essay, references, transcript. *Deadline:* March 31.

Contact: Sandra Lee, President
Center for Scholarship Administration
PO Box 1465
Taylors, SC 29687-0031
Phone: 864-268-3363
Fax: 864-268-7160
E-mail: sandralee41@bellsouth.net

LUCILLE P. AND EDWARD C. GILES FOUNDATION SCHOLARSHIPS

Renewable scholarships are available for dependent children or dependent grandchildren of qualified employees of Caraustar Industries, Inc. For more details and an application see Web site: http://www.scholarshipprograms.org

Award: Scholarship for use in freshman, sophomore, junior, senior, or graduate years; renewable. *Number:* varies. *Amount:* up to $6000.

Eligibility Requirements: Applicant must be enrolled or expecting to enroll full-time at a two-year or four-year or technical institution or university. Applicant or parent of applicant must be affiliated with Caraustar Industries, Inc.. Available to U.S. citizens.

Application Requirements: Application, essay, financial need analysis, references, transcript. *Deadline:* February 15.

Contact: Sandra Lee, President
Center for Scholarship Administration
PO Box 1465
Taylors, SC 29687-0031
Phone: 864-268-3363
Fax: 864-268-7160
E-mail: sandralee41@bellsouth.net

MICHELIN NORTH AMERICA DEPENDENT SCHOLARSHIP

A renewable award for dependent children of qualified Michelin North America employees. Applicant must be unmarried and age 23 or younger. For more details see Web site.

Award: Scholarship for use in freshman, sophomore, junior, or senior years; renewable. *Number:* up to 15. *Amount:* $1000–$2500.

Eligibility Requirements: Applicant must be age 23 or under; enrolled or expecting to enroll full-time at a two-year or four-year or technical institution or university and single. Applicant or parent of applicant must be affiliated with Michelin North America. Applicant must have 3.0 GPA or higher. Available to U.S. citizens.

Application Requirements: Application, essay, references, transcript. *Deadline:* March 1.

Contact: Sandra Lee, President
Center for Scholarship Administration
PO Box 1465
Taylors, SC 29687-0031
Phone: 864-268-3363
Fax: 864-268-7160
E-mail: sandralee41@bellsouth.net

MILLIKEN & COMPANY SCHOLARSHIP

Renewable scholarships are available to eligible associates or to dependent children of eligible associates of Milliken & Company. Must attend any private, accredited, four-year, not-for-profit, tax-free institution by federal statute (501) c (3) located in Georgia, New York, North Carolina or South Carolina. For more details and an application see Web site: http://www.scholarshipprograms.org

Award: Scholarship for use in freshman, sophomore, junior, or senior years; renewable. *Number:* up to 9. *Amount:* up to $5000.

Eligibility Requirements: Applicant must be enrolled or expecting to enroll at an institution or university and studying in Georgia, New York, North Carolina, or South Carolina. Applicant or parent of applicant must be affiliated with Milliken & Company. Available to U.S. citizens.

Application Requirements: Application, essay, references, transcript. *Deadline:* February 15.

Contact: Sandra Lee, President
Center for Scholarship Administration
PO Box 1465
Taylors, SC 29687-0031
Phone: 864-268-3363
Fax: 864-268-7160
E-mail: sandralee41@bellsouth.net

SARA LEE BRANDED APPAREL SCHOLARSHIPS

Renewable scholarships are available to dependent children of qualified employees of Sara Lee Corporation. Award amounts are determined from the costs at the college. For more details and an application see Web site: http://www.scholarshipprograms.org

Award: Scholarship for use in freshman, sophomore, junior, or senior years; renewable. *Number:* varies. *Amount:* $1000–$3000.

Eligibility Requirements: Applicant must be age 24 or under; enrolled or expecting to enroll full-time at a two-year or four-year or technical institution or university and single. Applicant or parent of applicant must be affiliated with Sara Lee Corporation. Available to U.S. citizens.

Application Requirements: Application, essay, financial need analysis, references, transcript. *Deadline:* March 15.

Contact: Sandra Lee, President
Center for Scholarship Administration
PO Box 1465
Taylors, SC 29687-0031
Phone: 864-268-3363
Fax: 864-268-7160
E-mail: sandralee41@bellsouth.net

SONOCO SCHOLARSHIP

Renewable scholarships are available to dependent children of qualified employees of Sonoco. For more details and an application see Web site: http://www.scholarshipprograms.org

Award: Scholarship for use in freshman, sophomore, junior, or senior years; renewable. *Number:* 10. *Amount:* $2000.

Eligibility Requirements: Applicant must be high school student and planning to enroll or expecting to enroll full-time at a four-year institution or university. Applicant or parent of applicant must be affiliated with Sonoco. Available to U.S. citizens.

Application Requirements: Application, essay, financial need analysis, references, transcript. *Deadline:* February 15.

Contact: Sandra Lee, President
Center for Scholarship Administration
PO Box 1465
Taylors, SC 29687-0031
Phone: 864-268-3363
Fax: 864-268-7160
E-mail: sandralee41@bellsouth.net

SPARTANBURG AUTOMOTIVE, INC. SCHOLARSHIPS

Renewable scholarships are available to dependent children of qualified employees of Spartanburg Automotive, Inc. Contact the Human Resources Manager for more detailed information on additional criteria.

Award: Scholarship for use in freshman year; renewable. *Number:* varies. *Amount:* $1000.

Eligibility Requirements: Applicant must be high school student and planning to enroll or expecting to enroll full-time at a two-year or four-year or technical institution or university. Applicant or parent of applicant must be affiliated with Spartanburg Automotive, Inc.. Available to U.S. citizens.

Application Requirements: Application, essay, references, transcript. *Deadline:* May 15.

Contact: Sandra Lee, President
Center for Scholarship Administration
PO Box 1465
Taylors, SC 29687-0031
Phone: 864-268-3363
Fax: 864-268-7160
E-mail: sandralee41@bellsouth.net

SPARTANBURG STAINLESS PRODUCTS, INC. SCHOLARSHIP

Renewable scholarships are available to dependent children of qualified employees of Spartanburg Stainless Products, Inc. Contact the Human Resources Manager for more detailed information on additional criteria.

Award: Scholarship for use in freshman year; renewable. *Number:* varies. *Amount:* $1000.

Eligibility Requirements: Applicant must be high school student and planning to enroll or expecting to enroll full-time at a two-year or four-year or technical institution or university. Applicant or parent of applicant must be affiliated with Spartanburg Stainless Products, Inc.. Available to U.S. citizens.

Application Requirements: Application, essay, references, transcript. *Deadline:* March 31.

Center for Scholarship Administration (continued)

Contact: Sandra Lee, President
Center for Scholarship Administration
PO Box 1465
Taylors, SC 29687-0031
Phone: 864-268-3363
Fax: 864-268-7160
E-mail: sandralee41@bellsouth.net

STRATA MARKETING, INC. SCHOLARSHIP PROGRAM

One-time award for dependent children of Strata Marketing Inc. employees. The scholarships are for 25% of annual tuition up to $8000 each.

Award: Scholarship for use in freshman, sophomore, junior, or senior years; not renewable. *Number:* up to 3. *Amount:* up to $8000.

Eligibility Requirements: Applicant must be age 24 or under; enrolled or expecting to enroll full-time at a four-year institution or university and single. Applicant or parent of applicant must be affiliated with Strata Marketing, Inc.. Applicant must have 3.0 GPA or higher. Available to U.S. citizens.

Application Requirements: Application, essay, references, transcript. *Deadline:* March 15.

Contact: Sandra Lee, President
Center for Scholarship Administration
PO Box 1465
Taylors, SC 29687-0031
Phone: 864-268-3363
Fax: 864-268-7160
E-mail: sandralee41@bellsouth.net

SUBWAY OF SOUTH CAROLINA SCHOLARSHIP

Non-renewable scholarships are available to qualified employees and dependent children of qualified employees of Subway of South Carolina. For more details and an application see Web site: http://www.scholarshipprograms.org

Award: Scholarship for use in freshman year; not renewable. *Number:* 10. *Amount:* $1000.

Eligibility Requirements: Applicant must be enrolled or expecting to enroll full-time at a two-year or four-year or technical institution or university. Applicant or parent of applicant must be affiliated with Subway. Available to U.S. citizens.

Application Requirements: Application. *Deadline:* January 31.

Contact: Sandra Lee, President
Center for Scholarship Administration
PO Box 1465
Taylors, SC 29687-0031
Phone: 864-268-3363
Fax: 864-268-7160
E-mail: sandralee41@bellsouth.net

SUBWAY SCHOLARSHIPS

Non-renewable scholarships are available to qualified employees of Subway. For more details and an application see Web site: http://www.scholarshipprograms.org

Award: Scholarship for use in freshman, sophomore, junior, or senior years; not renewable. *Number:* varies. *Amount:* $1000.

Eligibility Requirements: Applicant must be enrolled or expecting to enroll full-time at a two-year or four-year institution or university. Applicant or parent of applicant must be affiliated with Subway. Available to U.S. citizens.

Application Requirements: Application, essay, references, transcript. *Deadline:* November 30.

Contact: Sandra Lee, President
Center for Scholarship Administration
PO Box 1465
Taylors, SC 29687-0031
Phone: 864-268-3363
Fax: 864-268-7160
E-mail: sandralee41@bellsouth.net

TIETEX INTERNATIONAL SCHOLARSHIP

Renewable scholarships are available to the dependent children of employees of Teitex International. Contact the Human Resources Manager for more detailed information on additional criteria.

Award: Scholarship for use in freshman, sophomore, junior, or senior years; renewable. *Number:* varies. *Amount:* $1500.

Eligibility Requirements: Applicant must be high school student and planning to enroll or expecting to enroll full-time at a four-year institution or university. Applicant or parent of applicant must be affiliated with Teitex International. Available to U.S. citizens.

Application Requirements: Application, essay, references, transcript. *Deadline:* February 15.

Contact: Sandra Lee, President
Center for Scholarship Administration
PO Box 1465
Taylors, SC 29687-0031
Phone: 864-268-3363
Fax: 864-268-7160
E-mail: sandralee41@bellsouth.net

TUPPERWARE U.S., INC. SCHOLARSHIP

Non-renewable scholarships are available to the dependent children of qualified associates of Tupperware U.S., Inc. Contact the Human Resources Advisor for more detailed information on additional criteria.

Award: Scholarship for use in freshman year; not renewable. *Number:* varies. *Amount:* $1000–$10,500.

Eligibility Requirements: Applicant must be high school student and planning to enroll or expecting to enroll full-time at a two-year or four-year or technical institution or university. Applicant or parent of applicant must be affiliated with Tupperware U.S., Inc.. Available to U.S. citizens.

Application Requirements: Application, essay, financial need analysis, references, transcript. *Deadline:* March 1.

Contact: Sandra Lee, President
Center for Scholarship Administration
PO Box 1465
Taylors, SC 29687-0031
Phone: 864-268-3363
Fax: 864-268-7160
E-mail: sandralee41@bellsouth.net

WACHOVIA DEPENDENT SCHOLARSHIPS

Renewable scholarships are available to dependent children of qualified employees of Wachovia. For more details and an application see Web site: http://www.scholarshipprograms.org

Award: Scholarship for use in freshman, sophomore, junior, or senior years; renewable. *Number:* 100. *Amount:* up to $4000.

Eligibility Requirements: Applicant must be high school student; planning to enroll or expecting to enroll full-time at a four-year institution or university and single. Applicant or parent of applicant must be affiliated with Wachovia Bank. Applicant must have 3.0 GPA or higher. Available to U.S. citizens.

Application Requirements: Application, essay, financial need analysis, references, transcript. *Deadline:* March 15.

Contact: Sandra Lee, President
Center for Scholarship Administration
PO Box 1465
Taylors, SC 29687-0031
Phone: 864-268-3363
Fax: 864-268-7160
E-mail: sandralee41@bellsouth.net

CHESAPEAKE CORPORATION FOUNDATION
http://www.cskcorp.com

CHESAPEAKE CORPORATION FOUNDATION SCHOLARSHIP PROGRAM FOR CHESAPEAKE EMPLOYEES' CHILDREN

Award of up to $3,500 per academic year for up to four years to help finance the college education of outstanding sons and daughters of Chesapeake Corporation employees.

Award: Scholarship for use in freshman, sophomore, junior, or senior years; renewable. *Number:* 1–2. *Amount:* up to $3500.

Eligibility Requirements: Applicant must be high school student and planning to enroll or expecting to enroll full-time at a four-year institution or university. Applicant or parent of applicant must be affiliated with Chesapeake Corporation. Applicant or parent of applicant must have employment or volunteer experience in designated career field. Available to U.S. and non-Canadian citizens.

Application Requirements: Application, autobiography, test scores, transcript. *Deadline:* November 14.

Contact: J. P. Causey, Jr., President
Chesapeake Corporation Foundation
PO Box 2350
Richmond, VA 23218
Phone: 804-697-1000
Fax: 804-697-1199

CHICK-FIL-A, INC.

CHICK-FIL-A LEADERSHIP SCHOLARSHIP

Scholarships available to current employees of Chick-fil-A restaurants. Must show proof of enrollment in technical school, two- or four-year college or university. Must demonstrate solid work ethic, be actively involved in school or community activities, and possess strong leadership abilities. Must apply with approval of a Unit Operator accompanied by their letter of recommendation. Letter of recommendation from non-work-related individual also required.

Award: Scholarship for use in freshman year; not renewable. *Number:* 975. *Amount:* $1000.

Eligibility Requirements: Applicant must be high school student and planning to enroll or expecting to enroll at a two-year or four-year or technical institution. Applicant or parent of applicant must be affiliated with Chick-Fil-A, Inc.. Applicant or parent of applicant must have employment or volunteer experience in food service. Available to U.S. citizens.

Application Requirements: Application, references, transcript. *Deadline:* Continuous.

Contact:

S. TRUETT CATHY SCHOLAR AWARDS

This award is given to the top 25 Chick-fil-A Leadership Scholarship recipients each year.

Award: Scholarship for use in freshman year; not renewable. *Number:* up to 25. *Amount:* up to $1000.

Eligibility Requirements: Applicant must be enrolled or expecting to enroll full or part-time at a two-year or four-year or technical institution. Applicant or parent of applicant must be affiliated with Chick-Fil-A, Inc.. Available to U.S. citizens.

Application Requirements: *Deadline:* Continuous.

Contact:

CLARA ABBOTT FOUNDATION   http://clara.abbott.com

CLARA ABBOTT SCHOLARSHIP PROGRAM

Scholarships are available to the children of Abbott Laboratories' employees and retirees. Must be under 29 years of age and planning to attend an accredited undergraduate program. Must reapply each year. Requirements: Completed application, copies of W2 and IRS 1040 form, and student's most recent grade report. Based on financial need. The deadline is the second Monday of December.

Award: Grant for use in freshman, sophomore, junior, or senior years; not renewable. *Number:* 4000. *Amount:* $500–$5000.

Eligibility Requirements: Applicant must be age 17-28 and enrolled or expecting to enroll full or part-time at a two-year or four-year or technical institution or university. Applicant or parent of applicant must be affiliated with Abbott Laboratories. Applicant or parent of applicant must have employment or volunteer experience in designated career field. Available to U.S. and non-U.S. citizens.

Application Requirements: Application, financial need analysis, transcript, copy of W-2 forms, copy of 1040 forms. *Deadline:* varies.

Contact: Kate O'Brian, Scholarship Coordinator
Clara Abbott Foundation
200 Abbott Park Road, D579, J37
Abbott Park, IL 60064
Phone: 847-935-8196
Fax: 847-938-6511
E-mail: jo.jakubowicz@abbott.com

COMMUNITY FOUNDATION OF WESTERN MASSACHUSETTS   http://www.communityfoundation.org

DEERFIELD PLASTICS/BARKER FAMILY SCHOLARSHIP

Established by the Barker family for the children of employees of the former Deerfield Plastics.

Award: Scholarship for use in freshman, sophomore, junior, senior, or graduate years; not renewable. *Number:* up to 13. *Amount:* $1000–$3000.

Eligibility Requirements: Applicant must be enrolled or expecting to enroll full or part-time at a two-year or four-year institution or university and resident of Kentucky or Massachusetts. Applicant or parent of applicant must be affiliated with Deerfield Plastics. Applicant or parent of applicant must have employment or volunteer experience in designated career field. Available to U.S. citizens.

Application Requirements: Application, financial need analysis, transcript, parent and student federal income tax returns. *Deadline:* March 31.

Contact: Dorothy Theriaque, Education Associate
Community Foundation of Western Massachusetts
1500 Main Street, PO Box 15769
Springfield, MA 01115
Phone: 413-732-2858
Fax: 413-733-8565
E-mail: dtheriaque@communityfoundation.org

DEMOLAY FOUNDATION INCORPORATED   http://www.demolay.org

FRANK S. LAND SCHOLARSHIP

Scholarship is designed to be awarded to members of DeMolay International, who have not yet reached the age of 21, to assist in financing their education. Must be U.S. resident.

Award: Scholarship for use in freshman, sophomore, junior, or senior years; not renewable. *Number:* 10–15. *Amount:* $800.

Eligibility Requirements: Applicant must be age 21 or under; enrolled or expecting to enroll full-time at a two-year or four-year institution or university and male. Applicant or parent of applicant must be affiliated with DeMolay. Available to U.S. citizens.

Application Requirements: Application, references, self-addressed stamped envelope, transcript. *Deadline:* April 1.

Contact: Jeffrey Kitsmiller, Executive Director
DeMolay Foundation Incorporated
10200 Northwest Ambassador Drive
Kansas City, MO 64153
Phone: 800-336-6529
Fax: 816-891-9062
E-mail: news@demolay.org

DONALDSON COMPANY   http://www.donaldson.com

DONALDSON COMPANY, INC. SCHOLARSHIP PROGRAM

Scholarships for children of U.S. employees of Donaldson Company, Inc. Any form of accredited postsecondary education is eligible. Application deadline is March 15.

Award: Scholarship for use in freshman, sophomore, junior, or senior years; renewable. *Amount:* $1000–$3000.

Eligibility Requirements: Applicant must be enrolled or expecting to enroll full-time at a two-year or four-year or technical institution or university. Applicant or parent of applicant must be affiliated with Donaldson Company. Available to U.S. citizens.

Application Requirements: Application, essay, financial need analysis, references, transcript. *Deadline:* March 15.

Contact: Norm Linnell, Vice President, General Counsel, and Secretary
Donaldson Company
PO Box 1299
Minneapolis, MN 55440
Phone: 952-887-3631
Fax: 952-887-3005
E-mail: nlinnell@mail.donaldson.com

DUKE ENERGY CORPORATION
http://www.duke-energy.com

DUKE ENERGY SCHOLARS PROGRAM

The scholarship is for undergraduate study at accredited, two-year technical schools or community colleges and/or four-year colleges or universities in the U.S. and Canada who are children of eligible employees and retirees of Duke Energy and its subsidiaries. Fifteen four-year scholarships of up to $20,000 and five $1000 awards given annually. Recipients selected by 5-member outside committee.

Award: Scholarship for use in freshman, sophomore, junior, or senior years; renewable. *Number:* 20. *Amount:* $1000–$20,000.

Eligibility Requirements: Applicant must be high school student and planning to enroll or expecting to enroll full-time at a two-year or four-year or technical institution or university. Applicant or parent of applicant must be affiliated with Duke Energy Corporation. Available to U.S. and non-U.S. citizens.

Application Requirements: Application, autobiography, essay, financial need analysis, references, test scores, transcript. *Deadline:* December 1.

Contact: Celia Beam, Scholarship Administrator
Duke Energy Corporation
526 South Church Street
PO Box 1244
Charlotte, NC 28202-1904
Phone: 704-382-5544
Fax: 704-382-3553
E-mail: chbeam@duke-energy.com

EATON CORPORATION
http://www.eaton.com

EATON CORPORATION HENRY R. TOWNE TRUST SCHOLARSHIP

Award for children of employees of the Eaton Corporation and its subsidiaries. Applicant must be junior in high school taking October PSAT. Renewable award of $1000 to $3000 depending upon financial need.

Award: Scholarship for use in freshman year; renewable. *Number:* 12. *Amount:* $1000–$3000.

Eligibility Requirements: Applicant must be high school student and planning to enroll or expecting to enroll full-time at a four-year institution. Applicant or parent of applicant must be affiliated with Eaton Corporation. Available to U.S. citizens.

Application Requirements: Application. *Deadline:* varies.

Contact: Mildred Neumann, Scholarship Coordinator
Eaton Corporation
Eaton Center
1111 Superior Avenue
Cleveland, OH 44114-2584
Phone: 216-523-4354
Fax: 216-479-7354
E-mail: mildredneumann@eaton.com

GANNETT FOUNDATION
http://www.gannettfoundation.org

GANNETT FOUNDATION/MADELYN P. JENNINGS SCHOLARSHIP AWARD

One-time awards for high school students whose parents are current full-time Gannett Company employees. Must be planning to attend a 4-year college or university for full-time study in the fall after graduation. Students must meet all requirements for participation in the National Merit Scholarship Program and take the PSAT/NMSQT in their junior year of high school. Application deadline is January 1 of applicant's junior year of high school. Call for application and information.

Award: Scholarship for use in freshman year; not renewable. *Number:* 12. *Amount:* $3000.

Eligibility Requirements: Applicant must be high school student and planning to enroll or expecting to enroll full-time at a four-year institution or university. Applicant or parent of applicant must be affiliated with Gannett Company, Inc.. Available to U.S. citizens.

Application Requirements: Application, test scores, PSAT/NMSQT. *Deadline:* January 1.

Contact: Gannett Foundation/Madelyn P. Jennings Scholarship Awards, c/o Benefits Department, Gannett Co., Inc.
Gannett Foundation
7950 Jones Branch Drive
McLean, VA 22107

GATEWAY PRESS, INC. OF LOUISVILLE
http://www.gatewaypressinc.com

GATEWAY PRESS SCHOLARSHIP

Scholarship for graduating high school seniors whose parents have been employees of Gateway Press Inc for a minimum of 5 years. Applicant must be accepted at a college or university and maintain a minimum GPA of 2.25.

Award: Scholarship for use in freshman year; renewable. *Amount:* up to $3000.

Eligibility Requirements: Applicant must be enrolled or expecting to enroll full-time at an institution or university. Applicant or parent of applicant must be affiliated with Gateway Press Inc.. Available to U.S. citizens.

Application Requirements: Application. *Deadline:* January 1.

Contact: Chris "Kit" Georgehead, Human Resources Manager
Gateway Press, Inc. of Louisville
4500 Robards Lane
Louisville, KY 40218
Phone: 502-454-0431
Fax: 502-459-7930
E-mail: kit@gatewaypressinc.com

GRACO, INC.
http://www.graco.com

DAVID A. KOCH SCHOLARSHIP

Three awards of $7500 (one for athletic achievement) for children of Graco employees with at least one year of company service. Award based on academics, financial need, and tuition costs. Candidate must be under 26 years of age.

Award: Scholarship for use in freshman, sophomore, junior, senior, or graduate years; not renewable. *Number:* 3. *Amount:* $7500.

Eligibility Requirements: Applicant must be age 26 or under and enrolled or expecting to enroll full-time at a two-year or four-year or technical institution or university. Applicant or parent of applicant must be affiliated with Graco, Inc.. Applicant or parent of applicant must have employment or volunteer experience in designated career field. Available to U.S. and non-U.S. citizens.

Application Requirements: Application, financial need analysis, test scores, transcript. *Deadline:* March 15.

Contact: Kristin Ridley, Grants Administration Manager
Graco, Inc.
PO Box 1441
Minneapolis, MN 55440-1441
Phone: 612-623-6684
Fax: 612-623-6944

GRACO INC. SCHOLARSHIP PROGRAM

Renewable award for children of Graco employees under 26 years of age pursuing undergraduate or graduate education. Awards are based upon academics, financial need, and tuition costs. Submit transcripts, test scores, and financial need analysis with application.

Award: Scholarship for use in freshman, sophomore, junior, senior, or graduate years; renewable. *Number:* varies. *Amount:* $1500–$6000.

Eligibility Requirements: Applicant must be age 26 or under and enrolled or expecting to enroll full-time at a two-year or four-year or technical institution or university. Applicant or parent of applicant must be affiliated with Graco, Inc.. Applicant or parent of applicant must have employment or volunteer experience in designated career field. Available to U.S. and non-U.S. citizens.

Application Requirements: Application, financial need analysis, test scores, transcript. *Deadline:* March 15.

Contact: Kristin Ridley, Grants Administration Manager
Graco, Inc.
PO Box 1441
Minneapolis, MN 55440-1441
Phone: 612-623-6684
Fax: 612-623-6944

HORMEL FOODS CORPORATION http://www.hormel.com

HORMEL FOODS SCHOLARSHIP

College scholarships worth up to $3000. Must apply in junior year of high school. Scholarships are renewable for up to four years. Must be the child of a Hormel Food employee or retiree. Must submit PSAT scores.

Award: Scholarship for use in freshman, sophomore, junior, or senior years; not renewable. *Number:* up to 15. *Amount:* $2000.

Eligibility Requirements: Applicant must be high school student and planning to enroll or expecting to enroll full-time at a four-year institution or university. Applicant or parent of applicant must be affiliated with Hormel Foods Corporation. Available to U.S. citizens.

Application Requirements: Application, test scores. *Deadline:* January 10.

Contact: Julie Craven, Vice President Corporate communications
Hormel Foods Corporation
1 Hormel Place
Austin, MN 55912
Phone: 507-437-5345

HUMANA FOUNDATION

HUMANA FOUNDATION SCHOLARSHIP PROGRAM

Up to 75 scholarships are given to full-time undergraduate students. Eligible applicants must be under 25 and a United States citizen. The deadline is February 1. Must be a dependent of a Humana employee.

Award: Scholarship for use in freshman, sophomore, or junior years; renewable. *Amount:* $1250–$2500.

Eligibility Requirements: Applicant must be age 25 or under and enrolled or expecting to enroll full-time at a two-year or four-year institution. Applicant or parent of applicant must be affiliated with Humana Foundation. Available to U.S. citizens.

Application Requirements: Application, references, transcript. *Deadline:* February 1.

Contact: Charles Jackson, Program Manager
Humana Foundation
500 West Main Street, Room 208
Louisville, KY 40202
Phone: 502-580-1245
Fax: 502-580-1256
E-mail: cjackson@humana.com

JOHNSON CONTROLS, INC. http://www.johnsoncontrols.com

JOHNSON CONTROLS FOUNDATION SCHOLARSHIP PROGRAM

Available to high school seniors who are children of Johnson Controls, Inc., employees. 20 one-time awards of $2000 and 25 renewable scholarships of $2000 a year for up to four years. Application deadline is last Friday in March.

Award: Scholarship for use in freshman, sophomore, junior, or senior years; renewable. *Number:* up to 45. *Amount:* $2000–$8000.

Eligibility Requirements: Applicant must be high school student and planning to enroll or expecting to enroll full-time at a four-year institution. Applicant or parent of applicant must be affiliated with Johnson Controls, Inc.. Applicant must have 3.0 GPA or higher. Available to U.S. citizens.

Application Requirements: Application, transcript. *Deadline:* March.

Contact: Marlene Griffith, Human Resources Administration Coordinator
Johnson Controls, Inc.
5757 North Green Bay Avenue, X-46
Milwaukee, WI 53209
Phone: 414-524-2425
Fax: 414-524-2299

KINGSBURY CORPORATION http://www.kingsburycorp.com/

KINGSBURY FUND SCHOLARSHIPS

Up to three scholarships available to sons and daughters of Kingsbury Corporation employees. Must be a student in good standing, demonstrate leadership and good citizenship, be active in school affairs or have a part-time job, and establish a financial need. Renewable awards of $2000 each.

Award: Scholarship for use in freshman, sophomore, junior, or senior years; renewable. *Number:* 1–3. *Amount:* $2000.

Eligibility Requirements: Applicant must be enrolled or expecting to enroll full-time at a two-year or four-year institution or university and must have an interest in leadership. Applicant or parent of applicant must be affiliated with Kingsbury Corporation. Applicant or parent of applicant must have employment or volunteer experience in designated career field. Applicant must have 2.5 GPA or higher. Available to U.S. citizens.

Application Requirements: Application, essay, financial need analysis, references, transcript. *Deadline:* April 28.

Contact: Linda Prize, Executive Assistant
Kingsbury Corporation
80 Laurel Street
Keene, NH 03431-4207
Phone: 603-352-5212
Fax: 603-352-8789

KOHLER COMPANY http://www.kohler.com

KOHLER COMPANY COLLEGE SCHOLARSHIP

Renewable award for college-bound children of Kohler and its U.S. and Canadian subsidiary employees. High school students who are Kohler employees are also eligible. Scholarships are valued at $1500 per year. Scholarships are accepted from December 1 to February 15.

Award: Scholarship for use in freshman, sophomore, junior, or senior years; renewable. *Number:* 21. *Amount:* $1500.

Eligibility Requirements: Applicant must be high school student and planning to enroll or expecting to enroll full-time at a two-year or four-year institution or university. Applicant or parent of applicant must be affiliated with Kohler Company. Available to U.S. and Canadian citizens.

Application Requirements: Application, references, test scores, transcript. *Deadline:* February 15.

Contact: Lynn Kulow, Senior Communication Specialist-Corporate Giving and Civic Services
Kohler Company
444 Highland Drive
Kohler, WI 53044
Phone: 920-457-4441
Fax: 920-457-9064
E-mail: lynn.kulow@kohler.com

MAINE COMMUNITY FOUNDATION, INC. http://www.mainecf.org

LAWRENCE AND LOUISE ROBBINS SCHOLARSHIP FUND

Scholarship is for employees or retirees of the Robbins Lumber Company of Searsmont or their children or grandchildren to pursue post secondary education. Recipients will be selected on the basis of academic achievement, personal aspirations, and contributions to school and the community. Deadline is May 1.

Award: Scholarship for use in freshman, sophomore, junior, or senior years; renewable. *Number:* up to 2. *Amount:* up to $500.

Eligibility Requirements: Applicant must be high school student and planning to enroll or expecting to enroll full-time at an institution or university. Applicant or parent of applicant must be affiliated with Robbins Lumber Company. Available to U.S. citizens.

Maine Community Foundation, Inc. (continued)

Application Requirements: Application, essay, transcript. *Deadline:* May 1.

Contact: Douglas C. Fortin, Controller
Maine Community Foundation, Inc.
Robbins Lumber Inc., PO Box 9
Searsmont, ME 04973
Phone: 207-342-5221
Fax: 207-342-5201

NATIONAL ART MATERIALS TRADE ASSOCIATION
http://www.namta.org

NATIONAL ART MATERIALS TRADE ASSOCIATION ACADEMIC SCHOLARSHIP

Five scholarships awarded to an employee or relative of a National Art Materials Trade Association member firm. Submit transcript, test scores, and essay with application. One-time award of $1000. Application deadline is Mar 15. For further details, see Web site at http://www.namta.org or email inquiries to scholarship@namta.org.

Award: Scholarship for use in freshman, sophomore, junior, senior, graduate, or postgraduate years; not renewable. *Number:* 2–5. *Amount:* $1000.

Eligibility Requirements: Applicant must be enrolled or expecting to enroll full-time at a two-year or four-year or technical institution or university. Applicant or parent of applicant must be affiliated with National Art Materials Trade Association. Available to U.S. and non-U.S. citizens.

Application Requirements: Application, essay, test scores, transcript. *Deadline:* March 15.

Contact: Katharine Coffey, Scholarship Coordinator
National Art Materials Trade Association
15806 Brookway Drive, Suite 300
Huntersville, NC 28078
Phone: 704-892-6244
Fax: 704-892-6247
E-mail: kcoffey@namta.org

NEW HAMPSHIRE FOOD INDUSTRIES EDUCATION FOUNDATION
http://www.grocers.org

NEW HAMPSHIRE FOOD INDUSTRY SCHOLARSHIPS

The scholarships are one-time, non-renewable awards of $1000. The purpose is to assist students who are employees or children of employees working for New Hampshire Grocers Association members. More information on http://www.grocers.org/pages/17/index.htm

Award: Scholarship for use in freshman, sophomore, junior, senior, or graduate years; not renewable. *Number:* 20. *Amount:* $1000.

Eligibility Requirements: Applicant must be enrolled or expecting to enroll full-time at a two-year or four-year or technical institution or university. Applicant or parent of applicant must be affiliated with New Hampshire Grocers Association member companies. Available to U.S. and non-U.S. citizens.

Application Requirements: Application, essay, references, test scores, transcript. *Deadline:* April 1.

Contact: John M. Dumais, Secretary/Treasurer
New Hampshire Food Industries Education Foundation
110 Stark Street
Manchester, NH 03101-1977
Phone: 603-669-9333 Ext. 110
Fax: 603-623-1137
E-mail: scholarships@grocers.org

OMNOVA SOLUTIONS FOUNDATION
http://www.omnova.com

NATIONAL MERIT SCHOLARSHIPS FUNDED BY OMNOVA SOLUTIONS FOUNDATION

Awarded to children of Omnova Solutions employees only. Preliminary SAT or National Merit Scholarship Qualifying Test scores required. Test should be taken two years prior to high school graduation. Renewable award is for undergraduate study at an accredited four-year college or university. Deadline is January 1.

Award: Scholarship for use in freshman, sophomore, junior, or senior years; renewable. *Number:* 3. *Amount:* $500–$2000.

Eligibility Requirements: Applicant must be high school student and planning to enroll or expecting to enroll full-time at a four-year institution or university. Applicant or parent of applicant must be affiliated with Omnova Solutions. Available to U.S. citizens.

Application Requirements: Application, test scores. *Deadline:* January 1.

Contact: S. Theresa Carter, Director
Omnova Solutions Foundation
175 Ghent Road
Fairlawn, OH 44333-3300
Phone: 330-869-4289
Fax: 330-869-4345
E-mail: theresa.carter@omnova.com

OREGON STUDENT ASSISTANCE COMMISSION
http://www.osac.state.or.us

A. VICTOR ROSENFELD SCHOLARSHIP

One-time award for children of employees of Calbag Metals, Portland, who have worked for that company for three years prior to the March 1 scholarship deadline.

Award: Scholarship for use in freshman, sophomore, junior, or senior years; renewable. *Number:* 1. *Amount:* $1000.

Eligibility Requirements: Applicant must be enrolled or expecting to enroll at a four-year institution and resident of Oregon. Applicant or parent of applicant must be affiliated with Calbag Metals. Applicant or parent of applicant must have employment or volunteer experience in designated career field. Available to U.S. citizens.

Application Requirements: Application, essay, financial need analysis, references, transcript, activity chart. *Deadline:* March 1.

Contact: Director of Grant Programs
Oregon Student Assistance Commission
1500 Valley River Drive, Suite 100
Eugene, OR 97401-7020
Phone: 800-452-8807 Ext. 7395

ALBINA FUEL COMPANY SCHOLARSHIP

One scholarship available to a dependent child of a current Albina Fuel Company employee. The employee must have been employed for at least one full year as of October 1 prior to the scholarship deadline. One-time award.

Award: Scholarship for use in freshman, sophomore, junior, or senior years; renewable. *Number:* 3. *Amount:* $1000.

Eligibility Requirements: Applicant must be enrolled or expecting to enroll at an institution or university and resident of Oregon. Applicant or parent of applicant must be affiliated with Albina Fuel Company. Applicant or parent of applicant must have employment or volunteer experience in designated career field. Available to U.S. citizens.

Application Requirements: Application, essay, transcript, activity chart. *Deadline:* March 1.

Contact: Director of Grant Programs
Oregon Student Assistance Commission
1500 Valley River Drive, Suite 100
Eugene, OR 97401-7020
Phone: 800-452-8807 Ext. 7395

BANK OF THE CASCADES SCHOLARSHIP

One-time award for employees or natural, adopted, or step children between the ages of 17 and 25 of current Bank of the Cascades employees. Children must be high school graduates with minimum 3.0 GPA. Employees must have been continuously employed at Bank of the Cascades for one year at no fewer than 20 hours per week as of the March 1 scholarship deadline. For use at Oregon colleges only. Children of Bank of the Cascades officers are not eligible.

Award: Scholarship for use in freshman, sophomore, junior, or senior years; renewable. *Number:* varies. *Amount:* $500.

Eligibility Requirements: Applicant must be age 17-25; enrolled or expecting to enroll full-time at an institution or university; resident of

Oregon and studying in Oregon. Applicant or parent of applicant must be affiliated with Bank of the Cascades. Applicant must have 3.0 GPA or higher. Available to U.S. citizens.

Application Requirements: Application, essay, financial need analysis, transcript, activities chart. *Deadline:* March 1.

Contact: Director of Grant Programs
Oregon Student Assistance Commission
1500 Valley River Drive, Suite 100
Eugene, OR 97401-7020
Phone: 800-452-8807 Ext. 7395

BLUE HERON PAPER EMPLOYEE DEPENDENTS SCHOLARSHIP

Renewable award for children, grandchildren, and legal dependents (twenty two years old and under) of active Blue Heron Paper (formerly Smurfit Newsprint) employees. Must be employed with company at least one year.

Award: Scholarship for use in freshman, sophomore, junior, or senior years; renewable. *Number:* 1. *Amount:* $1750.

Eligibility Requirements: Applicant must be age 22 or under; enrolled or expecting to enroll at a four-year institution and resident of Oregon. Applicant or parent of applicant must be affiliated with Blue Heron Paper. Available to U.S. citizens.

Application Requirements: Application, essay, references, transcript, activity chart. *Deadline:* March 1.

Contact: Director of Grant Programs
Oregon Student Assistance Commission
1500 Valley River Drive, Suite 100
Eugene, OR 97401-7020
Phone: 800-452-8807 Ext. 7395

DAN KONNIE MEMORIAL DEPENDENTS SCHOLARSHIP

Renewable award for graduating high school seniors who are children of Swanson Brothers Lumber Co. employees. Must be enrolled in a U.S. public college. Must be an Oregon resident.

Award: Scholarship for use in freshman year; renewable. *Number:* 19. *Amount:* $2000.

Eligibility Requirements: Applicant must be enrolled or expecting to enroll full-time at a four-year institution and resident of Oregon. Applicant or parent of applicant must be affiliated with Swanson Brothers Lumber Company. Available to U.S. citizens.

Application Requirements: Application, essay, references, transcript, activity chart. *Deadline:* March 1.

Contact: Director of Grant Programs
Oregon Student Assistance Commission
1500 Valley River Drive, Suite 100
Eugene, OR 97401-7020
Phone: 800-452-8807 Ext. 7395

ESSEX SCHOLARSHIP

One-time award for employees of Essex General Construction Inc., or their children. Must be between the ages of 17 and 25. Qualifying children must be high school graduates or GED recipients. Qualifying employees must have been continuously employed at Essex for at least one year for at least 20 hours per week as of the March 1 scholarship deadline.

Award: Scholarship for use in freshman, sophomore, junior, or senior years; renewable. *Number:* 1. *Amount:* $5000.

Eligibility Requirements: Applicant must be age 17-25; enrolled or expecting to enroll at an institution or university and resident of Oregon. Applicant or parent of applicant must be affiliated with Essex General Construction. Available to U.S. citizens.

Application Requirements: Application, essay, financial need analysis, transcript, activities chart. *Deadline:* March 1.

Contact: Director of Grant Programs
Oregon Student Assistance Commission
1500 Valley River Drive, Suite 100
Eugene, OR 97401-7020
Phone: 800-452-8807 Ext. 7395

FORD SONS AND DAUGHTERS OF EMPLOYEES OF ROSEBURG FOREST PRODUCTS COMPANY SCHOLARSHIP

Renewable award for legal dependents of employees of Roseburg Forest Products Co. Must be twenty one years of age or younger. Qualifying parents must have been employees a minimum of eighteen months prior to the March 1 deadline.

Award: Scholarship for use in freshman, sophomore, junior, or senior years; renewable. *Number:* varies. *Amount:* $2000–$5000.

Eligibility Requirements: Applicant must be age 21 or under; enrolled or expecting to enroll full-time at a two-year or four-year institution and resident of Oregon. Applicant or parent of applicant must be affiliated with Roseburg Forest Products. Applicant or parent of applicant must have employment or volunteer experience in designated career field. Available to U.S. citizens.

Application Requirements: Application, essay, references, transcript, activity chart. *Deadline:* March 1.

Contact: Director of Grant Programs
Oregon Student Assistance Commission
1500 Valley River Drive, Suite 100
Eugene, OR 97401-7020
Phone: 800-452-8807 Ext. 7395

GLENN JACKSON SCHOLARS SCHOLARSHIPS (OCF)

Award for graduating high school seniors who are dependents of employees or retirees of Oregon Department of Transportation or Parks and Recreation Department. Employees must have worked in their department at least three years. Award for maximum twelve undergraduate quarters or six quarters at a two-year institution. Must be U.S. citizen or permanent resident. Visit Web site (http://www.osac.state.or.us) for more details.

Award: Scholarship for use in freshman, sophomore, junior, or senior years; renewable. *Number:* 2. *Amount:* $2500.

Eligibility Requirements: Applicant must be high school student; planning to enroll or expecting to enroll at a four-year institution and resident of Oregon. Applicant or parent of applicant must be affiliated with Oregon Department of Transportation Parks and Recreation. Applicant or parent of applicant must have employment or volunteer experience in designated career field. Available to U.S. citizens.

Application Requirements: Application, essay, financial need analysis, references, transcript, activity chart. *Deadline:* March 1.

Contact: Director of Grant Programs
Oregon Student Assistance Commission
1500 Valley River Drive, Suite 100
Eugene, OR 97401-7020
Phone: 800-452-8807 Ext. 7395

MC GARRY MACHINE INC. SCHOLARSHIP

One-time award for employees or dependents of employees of McGarry Machine who are high school graduates or GED recipients enrolling at least half-time in college. Contact Web site http://www.osac.state.or.us for further information.

Award: Scholarship for use in freshman, sophomore, junior, senior, or graduate years; renewable. *Number:* varies. *Amount:* $500.

Eligibility Requirements: Applicant must be enrolled or expecting to enroll full or part-time at a four-year institution and resident of Oregon. Applicant or parent of applicant must be affiliated with McGarry Machine, Inc.. Applicant or parent of applicant must have employment or volunteer experience in designated career field. Available to U.S. citizens.

Application Requirements: Application, essay, references, transcript, activity chart. *Deadline:* March 1.

Contact: Director of Grant Programs
Oregon Student Assistance Commission
1500 Valley River Drive, Suite 100
Eugene, OR 97401-7020
Phone: 800-452-8807 Ext. 7395

NORTHWEST AUTOMATIC VENDING ASSOCIATION SCHOLARSHIP

Awarded to graduating high school seniors who are either children or grandchildren of members or associate members of Northwest Automatic Vending Association.

Award: Scholarship for use in freshman year; not renewable. *Number:* 1.

Eligibility Requirements: Applicant must be high school student and planning to enroll or expecting to enroll at an institution or university. Applicant or parent of applicant must be affiliated with Northwest Automatic Vending Association. Available to U.S. citizens.

Application Requirements: Application, essay, financial need analysis, transcript, activities chart. *Deadline:* March 1.

Oregon Student Assistance Commission (continued)

Contact: Director of Grant Programs
Oregon Student Assistance Commission
1500 Valley River Drive, Suite 100
Eugene, OR 97401-7020
Phone: 800-452-8807 Ext. 7395

OREGON TRUCKING ASSOCIATION SCHOLARSHIP

One scholarship available to a child of an Oregon Trucking Association member, or child of employee of member. Applicants must be Oregon residents who are graduating high school seniors from an Oregon high school. One-time award.

Award: Scholarship for use in freshman year; not renewable. *Number:* 4. *Amount:* $750.

Eligibility Requirements: Applicant must be high school student; planning to enroll or expecting to enroll at a four-year institution and resident of Oregon. Applicant or parent of applicant must be affiliated with Oregon Trucking Association. Applicant or parent of applicant must have employment or volunteer experience in designated career field. Available to U.S. citizens.

Application Requirements: Application, essay, financial need analysis, references, transcript, activity chart. *Deadline:* March 1.

Contact: Director of Grant Programs
Oregon Student Assistance Commission
1500 Valley River Drive, Suite 100
Eugene, OR 97401-7020
Phone: 800-452-8807 Ext. 7395

PACIFICSOURCE SCHOLARSHIP

One-time award for high school graduates or GED recipients between the ages of 17 and 25 who are the natural, adopted, or step children of PacificSource employees. Employee must have been continuously employed at PacificSource for at least two years at no fewer than 20 hours per week. Minimum 3.0 GPA. Children of PacificSource officers are not eligible to participate.

Award: Scholarship for use in freshman, sophomore, junior, or senior years; renewable. *Number:* varies. *Amount:* $500.

Eligibility Requirements: Applicant must be age 17-25; enrolled or expecting to enroll full-time at an institution or university and resident of Oregon. Applicant or parent of applicant must be affiliated with PacificSource. Applicant must have 3.0 GPA or higher. Available to U.S. citizens.

Application Requirements: Application, essay, transcript, activities chart. *Deadline:* March 1.

Contact: Director of Grant Programs
Oregon Student Assistance Commission
1500 Valley River Drive, Suite 100
Eugene, OR 97401-7020
Phone: 800-452-8807 Ext. 7395

REED'S FUEL AND TRUCKING COMPANY SCHOLARSHIP

One-time award for dependents of Reed's employees who have been employed at least one year prior to deadline. Must attend a college or a university in Oregon and have minimum cumulative 2.5 GPA. Employees may enroll part time. Dependents must enroll full time.

Award: Scholarship for use in freshman, sophomore, junior, or senior years; renewable. *Number:* 1. *Amount:* $500.

Eligibility Requirements: Applicant must be enrolled or expecting to enroll full or part-time at a two-year or four-year institution; resident of Oregon and studying in Oregon. Applicant or parent of applicant must be affiliated with Reeds Fuel and Trucking Company. Applicant or parent of applicant must have employment or volunteer experience in designated career field. Applicant must have 2.5 GPA or higher. Available to U.S. citizens.

Application Requirements: Application, essay, references, transcript, activity chart. *Deadline:* March 1.

Contact: Director of Grant Programs
Oregon Student Assistance Commission
1500 Valley River Drive, Suite 100
Eugene, OR 97401-7020
Phone: 800-452-8807 Ext. 7395

RICHARD F. BRENTANO MEMORIAL SCHOLARSHIP

One-time award for legal dependents of Waste Control Systems Inc., and subsidiaries. Employees must be employed at least one year as of application deadline. Must be 24 years old or less, 26 years old for dependents entering U.S. Armed Forces directly from high school.

Award: Scholarship for use in freshman, sophomore, junior, or senior years; not renewable. *Number:* 9. *Amount:* $1417.

Eligibility Requirements: Applicant must be age 26 or under; enrolled or expecting to enroll at a four-year institution and resident of Oregon. Applicant or parent of applicant must be affiliated with Waste Control Systems, Inc.. Available to U.S. citizens.

Application Requirements: Application, essay, references, transcript, activity chart. *Deadline:* March 1.

Contact: Director of Grant Programs
Oregon Student Assistance Commission
1500 Valley River Drive, Suite 100
Eugene, OR 97401-7020
Phone: 800-452-8807 Ext. 7395

ROBERT D. FORSTER SCHOLARSHIP

One scholarship available to a dependent child of a Walsh Construction Co. employee who has completed 1000 hours or more in each of three consecutive fiscal years. Award may be received for a maximum of twelve quarters of undergraduate study and may only be used at four-year colleges.

Award: Scholarship for use in freshman, sophomore, junior, or senior years; renewable. *Number:* 1. *Amount:* $2500.

Eligibility Requirements: Applicant must be enrolled or expecting to enroll at a four-year institution or university and resident of Oregon. Applicant or parent of applicant must be affiliated with Walsh Construction Company. Applicant or parent of applicant must have employment or volunteer experience in designated career field. Available to U.S. citizens.

Application Requirements: Application, essay, financial need analysis, references, transcript, activity chart. *Deadline:* March 1.

Contact: Director of Grant Programs
Oregon Student Assistance Commission
1500 Valley River Drive, Suite 100
Eugene, OR 97401-7020
Phone: 800-452-8807 Ext. 7395

ROGER W. EMMONS MEMORIAL SCHOLARSHIP

One scholarship available to a graduating Oregon high school senior who is a child or grandchild of an employee (for at least three years) of member of the Oregon Refuse and Recycling Association.

Award: Scholarship for use in freshman year; renewable. *Number:* 3. *Amount:* $1000.

Eligibility Requirements: Applicant must be high school student; planning to enroll or expecting to enroll full-time at a four-year institution and resident of Oregon. Applicant or parent of applicant must be affiliated with Oregon Refuse and Recycling Association. Applicant or parent of applicant must have employment or volunteer experience in designated career field. Available to U.S. citizens.

Application Requirements: Application, essay, references, transcript, activity chart. *Deadline:* March 1.

Contact: Director of Grant Programs
Oregon Student Assistance Commission
1500 Valley River Drive, Suite 100
Eugene, OR 97401-7020
Phone: 800-452-8807 Ext. 7395

SP NEWSPRINT COMPANY, NEWBERG MILL, EMPLOYEE DEPENDENTS SCHOLARSHIP

One-time award available to children, grandchildren, legal dependents (22 years old and under) of active SP Newsprint Co., Newberg Mill employees. Age limit extended by years served to maximum age of 26 for those entering armed services directly from high school. Employees must be employed by the company at least one year. At least one award is for community colleges.

Award: Scholarship for use in freshman, sophomore, junior, or senior years; renewable. *Number:* 9. *Amount:* $1667.

Eligibility Requirements: Applicant must be age 26 or under; enrolled or expecting to enroll full-time at a two-year institution or university and resident of Oregon. Applicant or parent of applicant must be affiliated with SP Newsprint Company. Applicant or parent of applicant must have employment or volunteer experience in designated career field. Available to U.S. citizens.

Application Requirements: Application, essay, financial need analysis, references, transcript, activity chart. *Deadline:* March 1.

Contact: Director of Grant Programs
Oregon Student Assistance Commission
1500 Valley River Drive, Suite 100
Eugene, OR 97401-7020
Phone: 800-452-8807 Ext. 7395

STIMSON LUMBER COMPANY SCHOLARSHIP

Award for dependents of Stimson employees who are graduating seniors from accredited high school. Non-renewable scholarships available for two- or four-year colleges. Four-year scholarships renewable with minimum 2.7 cumulative GPA.

Award: Scholarship for use in freshman year. *Number:* 19. *Amount:* $1947.

Eligibility Requirements: Applicant must be enrolled or expecting to enroll at a two-year or four-year institution or university and resident of Oregon. Applicant or parent of applicant must be affiliated with Stimson Lumber Company. Applicant or parent of applicant must have employment or volunteer experience in designated career field. Available to U.S. citizens.

Application Requirements: Application, essay, financial need analysis, references, transcript, activity chart. *Deadline:* March 1.

Contact: Director of Grant Programs
Oregon Student Assistance Commission
1500 Valley River Drive, Suite 100
Eugene, OR 97401-7020
Phone: 800-452-8807 Ext. 7395

TAYLOR MADE LABELS SCHOLARSHIP

Award available to a child, grandchild or legal dependent (22 years of age and under) of an active employee of Taylor Made Label Company. Employee must have been employed by Taylor Made for a minimum of one year as of scholarship deadline.

Award: Scholarship for use in freshman, sophomore, junior, or senior years; renewable. *Number:* varies. *Amount:* $500.

Eligibility Requirements: Applicant must be age 22 or under; enrolled or expecting to enroll at a four-year institution and resident of Oregon. Applicant or parent of applicant must be affiliated with Taylor Made Label Company. Applicant or parent of applicant must have employment or volunteer experience in designated career field. Available to U.S. citizens.

Application Requirements: Application, essay, financial need analysis, references, transcript, activity chart. *Deadline:* March 1.

Contact: Director of Grant Programs
Oregon Student Assistance Commission
1500 Valley River Drive, Suite 100
Eugene, OR 97401-7020
Phone: 800-452-8807 Ext. 7395

WALTER DAVIES SCHOLARSHIP

Award for U.S. Bancorp employees or employees' natural or adopted children. Must be Oregon high school graduates.

Award: Scholarship for use in freshman, sophomore, junior, or senior years; renewable. *Number:* 38. *Amount:* $1529.

Eligibility Requirements: Applicant must be enrolled or expecting to enroll at a four-year institution and resident of Oregon. Applicant or parent of applicant must be affiliated with U.S. Bancorp. Available to U.S. citizens.

Application Requirements: Application, essay, financial need analysis, references, transcript, activity chart. *Deadline:* March 1.

Contact: Director of Grant Programs
Oregon Student Assistance Commission
1500 Valley River Drive, Suite 100
Eugene, OR 97401-7020
Phone: 800-452-8807 Ext. 7395

WOODARD FAMILY SCHOLARSHIP

Scholarships are available to employees and children of employees of Kimwood Corporation or Middlefield Estates. Applicants must have graduated from a U.S. high school. Awards may be used at Oregon colleges only, and may be received for a maximum of twelve quarters of undergraduate study.

Award: Scholarship for use in freshman, sophomore, junior, or senior years; renewable. *Number:* varies. *Amount:* $500.

Eligibility Requirements: Applicant must be enrolled or expecting to enroll full-time at a two-year or four-year institution; resident of Oregon and studying in Oregon. Applicant or parent of applicant must be affiliated with Kimwood Corporation or Middlefield Village. Applicant or parent of applicant must have employment or volunteer experience in designated career field. Available to U.S. citizens.

Application Requirements: Application, essay, financial need analysis, references, transcript. *Deadline:* March 1.

Contact: Director of Grant Programs
Oregon Student Assistance Commission
1500 Valley River Drive, Suite 100
Eugene, OR 97401-7020
Phone: 800-452-8807 Ext. 7395

PROCTER & GAMBLE FUND   http://www.pg.com

PROCTER & GAMBLE FUND SCHOLARSHIP COMPETITION FOR EMPLOYEES' CHILDREN

Award for high school seniors who are dependents of eligible employees, including deceased employees, and retirees of Procter and Gamble Company. Deadline: January 15 of applicant's senior year of high school.

Award: Scholarship for use in freshman year; not renewable. *Number:* up to 250. *Amount:* $1000–$4000.

Eligibility Requirements: Applicant must be high school student and planning to enroll or expecting to enroll full-time at a two-year or four-year or technical institution or university. Applicant or parent of applicant must be affiliated with Procter & Gamble Company. Applicant or parent of applicant must have employment or volunteer experience in designated career field. Available to U.S. citizens.

Application Requirements: Application, applicant must enter a contest, essay, references, test scores, transcript. *Deadline:* November 15.

Contact: Tawnia True, Coordinator, P&G Employee Scholarship Fund
Procter & Gamble Fund
PO Box 599
Cincinnati, OH 45201-0599
Phone: 513-983-2139
Fax: 513-983-2173
E-mail: pgfund.im@pg.com

RHODE ISLAND FOUNDATION   http://www.rifoundation.org

A.T. CROSS SCHOLARSHIP

Numerous scholarships available to children of full-time employees of A.T. Cross Company. Renewable. Must be Rhode Island resident.

Award: Scholarship for use in freshman, sophomore, junior, senior, or graduate years; renewable. *Number:* varies. *Amount:* $1000–$3000.

Eligibility Requirements: Applicant must be enrolled or expecting to enroll full-time at an institution or university and resident of Rhode Island. Applicant or parent of applicant must be affiliated with A.T. Cross. Available to U.S. citizens.

Application Requirements: Application, self-addressed stamped envelope. *Deadline:* May 12.

Contact: Kathleen Agostinelli
Rhode Island Foundation
One Albion Road
Lincoln, RI 02865
Phone: 401-335-8484

SHELBY ENERGY COOPERATIVE
http://www.shelbyenergy.com

SHELBY ENERGY COOPERATIVE SCHOLARSHIPS

Scholarships for high school seniors in central Kentucky whose parents or guardians are Shelby Energy members. Award based on financial need, academic excellence, community and school involvement, and the essay submitted.

Award: Scholarship for use in freshman year. *Number:* 6. *Amount:* $1000.

Eligibility Requirements: Applicant must be high school student and planning to enroll or expecting to enroll full-time at an institution or university. Applicant or parent of applicant must be affiliated with Shelby Energy. Available to U.S. citizens.

Application Requirements: Application, financial need analysis. *Deadline:* April 10.

Contact: Marketing Department
Shelby Energy Cooperative
620 Old Finchville Road
Shelbyville, KY 40065
Phone: 502-633-4420
Fax: 502-633-2387
E-mail: shelbyenergy@shelbyenergy.com

TEAMSTERS LOCAL UNION 326

JOSEPH B. SHAFFERMAN, SR. MEMORIAL SCHOLARSHIP FUND

Scholarships for student members of General Teamsters Local Union 326. For undergraduate study at college or university, non-academic or certificate programs are not eligible.

Award: Scholarship for use in freshman, sophomore, junior, or senior years. *Number:* 1.

Eligibility Requirements: Applicant must be enrolled or expecting to enroll at a four-year institution or university. Applicant or parent of applicant must be affiliated with Teamsters #326. Available to U.S. citizens.

Application Requirements: Application. *Deadline:* February 16.

Contact: Teamsters Local Union 326
Teamsters Local Union 326
451 E New Churchmans Road
New Castle, DE 19720

UNITED NEGRO COLLEGE FUND
http://www.uncf.org

KFC SCHOLARS PROGRAM

Award for KFC corporate or franchise employee who has at least one year of work experience with KFC and who wishes to pursue a bachelor's degree in business management, computer sciences, or liberal arts at a UNCF institution. Must have a 3.0 GPA, be an employee in good standing, and have an unmet financial need.

Award: Scholarship for use in freshman, sophomore, junior, or senior years; renewable. *Number:* 1. *Amount:* varies.

Eligibility Requirements: Applicant must be enrolled or expecting to enroll at a four-year institution or university. Applicant or parent of applicant must be affiliated with Kentucky Fried Chicken. Applicant must have 2.5 GPA or higher. Available to U.S. citizens.

Application Requirements: Application, essay, transcript. *Deadline:* varies.

Contact: Rebecca Bennett, Director, Program Services
United Negro College Fund
8260 Willow Oaks Corporate Drive
Fairfax, VA 22031-8044
Phone: 800-331-2244
E-mail: rbennett@uncf.org

LEON JACKSON, JR. SCHOLARSHIP

Award for current UNCF employees who desire to return to school to complete their associate, undergraduate, or graduate education. Please see Web site for more information: http://www.uncf.org

Award: Scholarship for use in freshman, sophomore, junior, senior, graduate, or postgraduate years; renewable. *Number:* up to 2. *Amount:* up to $2500.

Eligibility Requirements: Applicant must be Black (non-Hispanic) and enrolled or expecting to enroll full or part-time at a two-year or four-year institution or university. Applicant or parent of applicant must be affiliated with United Negro College Fund. Applicant must have 2.5 GPA or higher. Available to U.S. citizens.

Application Requirements: Application, essay, financial need analysis, references, transcript, FAFSA, Student Aid Report (SAR). *Deadline:* varies.

Contact: Rebecca Bennett, Director, Program Services
United Negro College Fund
8260 Willow Oaks Corporate Drive
Fairfax, VA 22031-8044
Phone: 800-331-2244
E-mail: rbennett@uncf.org

WAL-MART FOUNDATION
http://www.walmartfoundation.org

WAL-MART ASSOCIATE SCHOLARSHIPS

Awards for college-bound high school seniors who work for Wal-Mart or whose parents are part-time Wal-Mart associates or have not been with the company for one year. Based on ACT or SAT scores, counselor recommendations, transcripts, class rank, activities, and financial need. One-time award of up to $2000. For use at an accredited two- or four-year U.S. institution.

Award: Scholarship for use in freshman year; not renewable. *Number:* 150–300. *Amount:* up to $2000.

Eligibility Requirements: Applicant must be high school student and planning to enroll or expecting to enroll full-time at a two-year or four-year institution. Applicant or parent of applicant must be affiliated with Wal-Mart Foundation. Applicant or parent of applicant must have employment or volunteer experience in designated career field. Available to U.S. citizens.

Application Requirements: Application, test scores, transcript, federal income tax return. *Deadline:* February 1.

Contact: Jenny Harral
Wal-Mart Foundation
702 Southwest 8th Street
Bentonville, AR 72716-0150
Phone: 800-530-9925
Fax: 501-273-6850

WAL-MART HIGHER REACH SCHOLARSHIP

For non-traditional students who have been employed full-time by Wal-Mart for at least a year by February 1 and out of high school for 1 year . Award is based on financial need, academic record, essay, and job performance. Applications are available from each location personnel office in November.

Award: Scholarship for use in freshman, sophomore, junior, or senior years; not renewable. *Number:* varies. *Amount:* $500–$2000.

Eligibility Requirements: Applicant must be enrolled or expecting to enroll part-time at a two-year or four-year institution or university. Applicant or parent of applicant must be affiliated with Wal-Mart Foundation. Applicant or parent of applicant must have employment or volunteer experience in designated career field. Available to U.S. citizens.

Application Requirements: Application, essay, financial need analysis, references, transcript, job performance appraisal. *Deadline:* February 1.

Contact: Emmy Hardin, Program Coordinator
Wal-Mart Foundation
702 Southwest 8th Street
Bentonville, AR 72716-9002
Phone: 800-530-9925
Fax: 501-273-6850

WALTON FAMILY FOUNDATION SCHOLARSHIP

Award for high-school seniors who are children of a Wal-Mart associate who has been employed as a full-time associate for at least one year. $10000 undergraduate scholarship payable over four years. Must submit latest federal income tax return. Contact a member of Wal-Mart management for an application starting in November each year.

Award: Scholarship for use in freshman, sophomore, junior, or senior years; renewable. *Number:* 100–120. *Amount:* up to $10,000.

Eligibility Requirements: Applicant must be high school student and planning to enroll or expecting to enroll full-time at a two-year or four-year institution or university. Applicant or parent of applicant must be affiliated with Wal-Mart Foundation. Available to U.S. citizens.

Application Requirements: Application, financial need analysis, test scores, transcript, federal income tax return. *Deadline:* February 1.

Contact: Jenny Harral
Wal-Mart Foundation
702 Southwest 8th Street
Bentonville, AR 72716-0150
Phone: 800-530-9925
Fax: 501-273-6850

WALTON FAMILY FOUNDATION

http://www.wffhome.com

WALTON FAMILY FOUNDATION SCHOLARSHIP

Scholarship for the son/daughter of a full time Wal-Mart Associate employee. Must be a graduating high school senior. Must have a minimum 22 ACT or 1030 combined SAT score.

Award: Scholarship for use in freshman year. *Amount:* up to $10,000.

Eligibility Requirements: Applicant must be high school student and planning to enroll or expecting to enroll full-time at an institution or university. Applicant or parent of applicant must be affiliated with Wal-Mart Foundation. Available to U.S. citizens.

Application Requirements: Application, proposal. *Deadline:* varies.

Contact: Walton Family Foundation Scholarship Program
Walton Family Foundation
PO Box 2030
Bentonville, AR 72712
Phone: 479-464-1570
Fax: 479-464-1580

WEYERHAEUSER COMPANY FOUNDATION

http://www.weyerhaeuser.com/

WEYERHAEUSER COMPANY FOUNDATION SCHOLARSHIPS

Renewable awards for children of Weyerhaeuser Company employees. Must apply by January 15 of senior year in high school.

Award: Scholarship for use in freshman or senior years; renewable. *Number:* 65. *Amount:* $1000–$4000.

Eligibility Requirements: Applicant must be high school student and planning to enroll or expecting to enroll full-time at a two-year or four-year or technical institution. Applicant or parent of applicant must be affiliated with Weyerhauser Company. Available to U.S. citizens.

Application Requirements: Application. *Deadline:* January 15.

Contact: Penny Paul, Program Manager
Weyerhaeuser Company Foundation
EC-22A8
PO Box 9777
Federal Way, WA 98063-9777
Phone: 253-924-2629
Fax: 253-924-3658

WILLITS FOUNDATION

WILLITS FOUNDATION SCHOLARSHIP PROGRAM

Renewable awards for children of full-time C. R. Bard, Inc., employees only. Children of Bard officers are not eligible. For domestic Bard branches only. Must be pursuing, or planning to pursue, full-time postsecondary studies in the year in which the application is made.

Award: Scholarship for use in freshman, sophomore, junior, senior, graduate, or postgraduate years; renewable. *Number:* 10–15. *Amount:* $1000–$5000.

Eligibility Requirements: Applicant must be enrolled or expecting to enroll full-time at a four-year institution or university. Applicant or parent of applicant must be affiliated with C.R. Bard, Inc.. Available to U.S. citizens.

Application Requirements: Application, essay, photo, references, test scores, transcript. *Deadline:* March 1.

Contact: Linda Hrevnack, Program Manager
Willits Foundation
730 Central Avenue
Murray Hill, NJ 07974
Phone: 908-277-8182
Fax: 908-277-8098

EMPLOYMENT EXPERIENCE

A.W. BODINE-SUNKIST GROWERS, INC.

http://www.sunkist.com

A.W. BODINE-SUNKIST MEMORIAL SCHOLARSHIP

Renewable award for undergraduate study for applicants whose family derives most of its income from the agriculture industry in Arizona or California. Award is based on minimum 2.7 GPA and financial need.

Award: Scholarship for use in freshman, sophomore, junior, or senior years; renewable. *Number:* 20. *Amount:* $2000.

Eligibility Requirements: Applicant must be enrolled or expecting to enroll full-time at a four-year institution and resident of Arizona or California. Applicant or parent of applicant must have employment or volunteer experience in agriculture. Available to U.S. citizens.

Application Requirements: Application, essay, financial need analysis, references, test scores, transcript. *Deadline:* April 30.

Contact: Claire Smith, Scholarship Administrator
A.W. Bodine-Sunkist Growers, Inc.
PO Box 7888
Van Nuys, CA 91409-7888
Phone: 818-986-4800
Fax: 818-379-7511

AIR TRAFFIC CONTROL ASSOCIATION, INC.

http://www.atca.org

BUCKINGHAM MEMORIAL SCHOLARSHIP

Scholarships granted to children of air traffic control specialists pursuing a bachelor's degree or higher in any course of study. Must be the child, natural or by adoption, of a person serving, or having served as an air traffic control specialist, be it with the U.S. Government, U.S. Military, or in a private facility in the U.S.

Award: Scholarship for use in freshman, sophomore, junior, senior, or graduate years; not renewable. *Number:* 2–4. *Amount:* $1000–$1500.

Eligibility Requirements: Applicant must be enrolled or expecting to enroll full or part-time at a four-year institution or university. Applicant or parent of applicant must have employment or volunteer experience in air traffic controller field. Available to U.S. citizens.

Application Requirements: Application, autobiography, essay, financial need analysis, references, transcript. *Deadline:* May 1.

Contact: James Crook, Vice President of Operations
Air Traffic Control Association, Inc.
2300 Clarendon Boulevard, Suite 711
Arlington, VA 22201-2302
Phone: 703-522-5717
Fax: 703-527-7251
E-mail: jim.crook@atca.org

ALABAMA COMMISSION ON HIGHER EDUCATION

http://www.ache.state.al.us

POLICE OFFICERS AND FIREFIGHTERS SURVIVORS EDUCATION ASSISTANCE PROGRAM-ALABAMA

Provides tuition, fees, books, and supplies to dependents of full-time police officers and firefighters killed in the line of duty. Must attend any Alabama public college as an undergraduate. Must be Alabama resident. Renewable.

Award: Grant for use in freshman, sophomore, junior, or senior years; renewable. *Number:* 15–30. *Amount:* $2000–$5000.

Eligibility Requirements: Applicant must be enrolled or expecting to enroll full or part-time at a two-year or four-year or technical institution or university; single; resident of Alabama and studying in

Alabama Commission on Higher Education (continued)

Alabama. Applicant or parent of applicant must have employment or volunteer experience in police/firefighting. Available to U.S. citizens.

Application Requirements: Application, transcript. *Deadline:* Continuous.

Contact: William Wall, Associate Executive Director for Student
Assistance, ACHE
Alabama Commission on Higher Education
PO Box 302000
Montgomery, AL 36130-2000
Phone: 334-242-2273
Fax: 334-242-0268
E-mail: wwall@ache.state.al.us

ALLAINET
CORPORATION   http://www.allainet.com/ANET/index.html

PROJECT HIGHER

Online recruiting program for creative, focused, service-minded college students in North America to work while completing college tuition-free. Must contact project through Web site: http://www.weblo.com/projecthire and complete the tasks assigned online during a 33-day period. Twelve winning candidates will receive salary, performance bonuses, college tuition, and comprehensive training programs. Registration deadline is February 28.

Award: Scholarship for use in freshman, sophomore, junior, senior, graduate, or postgraduate years; not renewable. *Number:* 12. *Amount:* up to $43,000.

Eligibility Requirements: Applicant must be enrolled or expecting to enroll full or part-time at a four-year institution or university. Applicant or parent of applicant must have employment or volunteer experience in community service. Available to U.S. and non-U.S. citizens.

Application Requirements: Application. *Deadline:* February 28.

Contact: Allainet Corporation
426 Tremblay Road
Ottawa K1V 0C5
Canada

AMERICAN FOREIGN SERVICE
ASSOCIATION   http://www.afsa.org

AMERICAN FOREIGN SERVICE ASSOCIATION (AFSA) FINANCIAL AID AWARD PROGRAM
• See page 484

AMERICAN FOREIGN SERVICE ASSOCIATION (AFSA)/AAFSW MERIT AWARD PROGRAM
• See page 484

AMERICAN LEGION AUXILIARY, DEPARTMENT OF
MISSOURI

AMERICAN LEGION AUXILIARY MISSOURI STATE NATIONAL PRESIDENT'S SCHOLARSHIP
• See page 485

AMERICAN LEGION AUXILIARY, DEPARTMENT OF
NORTH DAKOTA   http://www.ndlegion.org

AMERICAN LEGION AUXILIARY, NATIONAL PRESIDENT'S SCHOLARSHIP

Three division scholarships for children of veterans who served in the Armed Forces during eligible dates for American Legion membership. Must be U.S. citizen and a high school senior with a minimum 2.5 GPA. Must be entered by local American Legion Auxiliary Unit. Contact local Unit President. National Headquarters Web site: http://www.legion-aux.org.

Award: Scholarship for use in freshman year; not renewable. *Number:* 3. *Amount:* $1000–$2500.

Eligibility Requirements: Applicant must be high school student; planning to enroll or expecting to enroll full-time at a four-year institution or university; resident of North Dakota and studying in North Dakota. Applicant or parent of applicant must have employment or volunteer experience in community service. Applicant must have 2.5 GPA or higher. Available to U.S. citizens. Applicant or parent must

meet one or more of the following requirements: general military experience; retired from active duty; disabled or killed as a result of military service; prisoner of war; or missing in action.

Application Requirements: Application, essay, financial need analysis, references, test scores, transcript, 50 hours voluntary service. *Deadline:* March 1.

Contact: Alice Carlson, Education Chairman
American Legion Auxiliary, Department of North Dakota
6422 Northeast 122nd Avenue
Lankin, ND 58250-9761
Phone: 701-593-6332

AMERICAN LEGION AUXILIARY, NATIONAL
HEADQUARTERS   http://www.legion-aux.org

AMERICAN LEGION AUXILIARY GIRL SCOUT ACHIEVEMENT AWARD
• See page 486

AMERICAN LEGION, DEPARTMENT OF
VERMONT   http://www.legionvthq.com/

AMERICAN LEGION EAGLE SCOUT OF THE YEAR
• See page 490

AMERICAN LEGION, NATIONAL
HEADQUARTERS   http://www.legion.org

AMERICAN LEGION NATIONAL HEADQUARTERS EAGLE SCOUT OF THE YEAR
• See page 490

AMERICAN POSTAL WORKERS
UNION   http://www.apwu.org

VOCATIONAL SCHOLARSHIP PROGRAM
• See page 491

AMERICAN QUARTER HORSE FOUNDATION
(AQHF)   http://www.aqha.org/aqhya

EXCELLENCE IN EQUINE/AGRICULTURAL INVOLVEMENT SCHOLARSHIP
• See page 491

FARM AND RANCH HERITAGE SCHOLARSHIP
• See page 492

GUY STOOPS MEMORIAL PROFESSIONAL HORSEMEN'S FAMILY SCHOLARSHIP
• See page 492

AMERICAN SOCIETY OF TRAVEL AGENTS (ASTA)
FOUNDATION   http://www.astanet.com

ARIZONA CHAPTER DEPENDENT/EMPLOYEE MEMBERSHIP SCHOLARSHIP
• See page 493

AMERICAN TRAFFIC SAFETY SERVICES
FOUNDATION   http://www.atssa.com

ROADWAY WORKER MEMORIAL SCHOLARSHIP PROGRAM

One-time scholarship providing financial assistance for post-high school education to the children of roadway workers killed or permanently disabled in work zones, including mobile operations and the installation of roadway safety features or to the parents or legal guardians of such children. 200-word essay required. Applicant must explain reasons for wanting to continue education.

Award: Scholarship for use in freshman, sophomore, junior, or senior years; not renewable. *Number:* 2–5. *Amount:* $2000–$3000.

Eligibility Requirements: Applicant must be enrolled or expecting to enroll full or part-time at a two-year or four-year or technical institution or university. Applicant or parent of applicant must have employment or volunteer experience in roadway worker. Available to U.S. citizens.

Application Requirements: Application, essay, financial need analysis, references, transcript, 200-word statement. *Deadline:* February 15.

Contact: Foundation Director
American Traffic Safety Services Foundation
15 Riverside Parkway, Suite 100
Fredericksburg, VA 22406
Phone: 540-368-1701
Fax: 540-368 Ext. 1717

ARBY'S FOUNDATION, BIG BROTHERS BIG SISTERS OF AMERICA   http://www.bbbsa.org

ARBY'S-BIG BROTHERS BIG SISTERS SCHOLARSHIP AWARD
• *See page 493*

ARKANSAS DEPARTMENT OF HIGHER EDUCATION   http://www.arkansashighered.com

LAW ENFORCEMENT OFFICERS' DEPENDENTS SCHOLARSHIP-ARKANSAS

For dependents, under 23 years old, of Arkansas law-enforcement officers killed or permanently disabled in the line of duty. Renewable award is a waiver of tuition, fees, and room at two- or four-year Arkansas institution. Submit birth certificate, death certificate, and claims commission report of findings of fact. Proof of disability from State Claims Commission may also be submitted.

Award: Scholarship for use in freshman, sophomore, junior, or senior years; renewable. *Number:* 27–32. *Amount:* $2000–$2500.

Eligibility Requirements: Applicant must be age 22 or under; enrolled or expecting to enroll full or part-time at a two-year or four-year or technical institution or university; resident of Arkansas and studying in Arkansas. Applicant or parent of applicant must have employment or volunteer experience in police/firefighting. Available to U.S. citizens.

Application Requirements: Application. *Deadline:* Continuous.

Contact: Lillian Williams, Assistant Coordinator
Arkansas Department of Higher Education
114 East Capitol
Little Rock, AR 72201
Phone: 501-371-2050
Fax: 501-371-2001
E-mail: lillianw@adhe.arknet.edu

CALIFORNIA CORRECTIONAL PEACE OFFICERS ASSOCIATION   http://www.ccpoa.org

CALIFORNIA CORRECTIONAL PEACE OFFICERS ASSOCIATION JOE HARPER SCHOLARSHIP

A scholarship program for immediate relatives and/or correctional officers in California.

Award: Scholarship for use in freshman, sophomore, junior, senior, or graduate years; not renewable. *Number:* 100. *Amount:* $1000.

Eligibility Requirements: Applicant must be enrolled or expecting to enroll full or part-time at a two-year or four-year or technical institution or university and resident of California. Applicant or parent of applicant must have employment or volunteer experience in designated career field. Applicant must have 3.5 GPA or higher. Available to U.S. citizens.

Application Requirements: Application, autobiography, essay, financial need analysis, photo, references, test scores, transcript. *Deadline:* April 30.

Contact: Marcia Bartlett, Bookkeeper
California Correctional Peace Officers Association
755 Riverpoint Drive, Suite 200
West Sacremento, CA 95605
Phone: 916-372-6060
Fax: 916-372-6623

CALIFORNIA TABLE GRAPE COMMISSION   http://www.freshcaliforniagrapes.com

CALIFORNIA TABLE GRAPE FARM WORKERS SCHOLARSHIP PROGRAM

Applicants must be high school graduates who plan to attend any college or university in California. The applicant, a parent, or a legal guardian must have worked in the California table grape harvest during the last season. School activities, personal references, and financial need are considered. Must be U.S. citizen. Application deadline is mid-March every year.

Award: Scholarship for use in freshman, sophomore, junior, or senior years; not renewable. *Number:* 3. *Amount:* $16,000.

Eligibility Requirements: Applicant must be enrolled or expecting to enroll full-time at a four-year institution or university and studying in California. Applicant or parent of applicant must have employment or volunteer experience in designated career field. Available to U.S. citizens.

Application Requirements: Application, essay, references, test scores, transcript. *Deadline:* March 17.

Contact: Amy Boam, Scholarship Coordinator
California Table Grape Commission
392 West Fallbrook, Suite 101
Fresno, CA 93711-6150
Phone: 559-447-8350
Fax: 559-447-9184

CHAIRSCHOLARS FOUNDATION, INC.   http://www.chairscholars.org

CHAIRSCHOLARS FOUNDATION, INC. SCHOLARSHIPS

Award for students who are severely physically challenged. Applicants may be high school seniors or college freshmen. Must be outstanding citizen with history of public service. Minimum 3.5 GPA required. Ten to twelve renewable awards of $5000. Must be under 21 years old.

Award: Scholarship for use in freshman or sophomore years; renewable. *Number:* 15–20. *Amount:* $3000–$5000.

Eligibility Requirements: Applicant must be age 21 or under and enrolled or expecting to enroll full-time at a two-year or four-year or technical institution or university. Applicant or parent of applicant must have employment or volunteer experience in community service. Applicant must be hearing impaired, physically disabled, or visually impaired. Applicant must have 3.5 GPA or higher. Available to U.S. citizens.

Application Requirements: Application, autobiography, essay, financial need analysis, photo, portfolio, resume, references, self-addressed stamped envelope, test scores, transcript, parents' tax return from previous year. *Deadline:* February 28.

Contact: Hugo Keim
Chairscholars Foundation, Inc.
16101 Carencia Lane
Odessa, FL 33556
Phone: 813-920-2737
E-mail: hugokeim@earthlink.net

CHESAPEAKE CORPORATION FOUNDATION   http://www.cskcorp.com

CHESAPEAKE CORPORATION FOUNDATION SCHOLARSHIP PROGRAM FOR CHESAPEAKE EMPLOYEES' CHILDREN
• *See page 528*

CHICK-FIL-A, INC.

CHICK-FIL-A LEADERSHIP SCHOLARSHIP
• *See page 529*

CIVIL SERVICE EMPLOYEES INSURANCE COMPANY   http://www.cseinsurance.com

YOUTH AUTOMOBILE SAFETY SCHOLARSHIP ESSAY COMPETITION FOR CHILDREN OF PUBLIC EMPLOYEES

Applicants must be residents of California, Arizona, Utah, or Nevada with minimum 3.0 GPA. Awards are for children of full-time or retired public employees. Letter of acceptance required.

Award: Scholarship for use in freshman year; not renewable. *Number:* 1–10. *Amount:* $500.

Eligibility Requirements: Applicant must be high school student; planning to enroll or expecting to enroll full-time at a two-year or four-year or technical institution or university and resident of Arizona, California, Nevada, or Utah. Applicant or parent of applicant must

Civil Service Employees Insurance Company (continued)

have employment or volunteer experience in designated career field. Applicant must have 3.0 GPA or higher. Available to U.S. citizens.

Application Requirements: Application, essay, references, transcript. *Deadline:* April 7.

Contact: Jonathan Kaban, Project Coordinator, Scholarship Contest
Civil Service Employees Insurance Company
PO Box 8041
Walnut Creek, CA 94956-8041
Phone: 925-817-6496
Fax: 925-817-6489
E-mail: jkaban@cse-insurance.com

CLARA ABBOTT FOUNDATION   http://www.clara.abbott.com

CLARA ABBOTT SCHOLARSHIP PROGRAM
• *See page 529*

COLLEGE ASSISTANCE MIGRANT PROGRAM   http://www.stedwards.edu/camp/program/index.html

COLLEGE ASSISTANCE MIGRANT PROGRAM AT ST. EDWARD'S UNIVERSITY

The purpose of CAMP is to provide migrant/seasonal farm workers who have completed high school requirements an opportunity to work toward a four-year baccalaureate degree. This program offers the eligible student financial, academic, and other supportive assistance necessary for successful completion of the first two semesters of college. Must be U.S. citizen. Application deadline is March 1.

Award: Grant for use in freshman year; not renewable. *Number:* 40. *Amount:* $500–$23,000.

Eligibility Requirements: Applicant must be enrolled or expecting to enroll full-time at an institution or university. Applicant or parent of applicant must have employment or volunteer experience in agriculture. Available to U.S. citizens.

Application Requirements: Application, essay, financial need analysis, references, test scores, transcript, certification of migrant eligibility. *Deadline:* March 1.

Contact: Esther Quinones Yacono, Director
College Assistance Migrant Program
3001 South Congress Avenue
Austin, TX 78704
Phone: 512-448-8625
Fax: 512-464-8830
E-mail: esthery@admin.stedwards.edu

COMMUNITY BANKER ASSOCIATION OF ILLINOIS

COMMUNITY BANKER ASSOCIATION OF ILLINOIS CHILDREN OF COMMUNITY BANKING SCHOLARSHIP
• *See page 496*

COMMUNITY FOUNDATION OF WESTERN MASSACHUSETTS   http://www.communityfoundation.org

DEERFIELD PLASTICS/BARKER FAMILY SCHOLARSHIP
• *See page 529*

HORACE HILL SCHOLARSHIP
• *See page 497*

CONNECTICUT POLICE CORPS   http://www.post.state.ct.us

CONNECTICUT POLICE CORPS PROGRAM

Students may choose to study criminal justice, or may pursue degrees in other fields. Scholarships awarded post graduation from accredited 4-year colleges and universities and after completing Police Corps training. Eligible for $30,000. One-half is paid at end of training; one-half after 12 months of service.

Award: Scholarship for use in freshman, sophomore, junior, senior, or graduate years; renewable. *Number:* 10. *Amount:* $10,000.

Eligibility Requirements: Applicant must be enrolled or expecting to enroll full-time at a four-year institution or university. Applicant or

parent of applicant must have employment or volunteer experience in police/firefighting. Available to U.S. citizens.

Application Requirements: Application. *Deadline:* varies.

Contact: David Swenson, Director
Connecticut Police Corps
Connecticut Police Academy
48 Haley Crescent Drive
Groton, CT 06340
Phone: 860-536-4791
Fax: 860-536-4797
E-mail: ctpolicecorps@aol.com

COUNTY PROSECUTORS ASSOCIATION OF NEW JERSEY FOUNDATION

JOHN S. STAMLER MEMORIAL SCHOLARSHIP

One-time award for New Jersey resident and sworn law enforcement officer seeking educational advancement on a college or graduate level to improve his or her effectiveness as a law enforcement officer. Must also demonstrate financial need.

Award: Scholarship for use in freshman, sophomore, junior, senior, or graduate years; not renewable. *Number:* 1. *Amount:* $2500.

Eligibility Requirements: Applicant must be enrolled or expecting to enroll full or part-time at a two-year or four-year institution or university; resident of New Jersey and studying in New Jersey. Applicant or parent of applicant must have employment or volunteer experience in police/firefighting. Available to U.S. citizens.

Application Requirements: Application, financial need analysis, interview. *Deadline:* June 15.

Contact: Theodore Romankow, Union County Prosecutor
County Prosecutors Association of New Jersey Foundation
Union County Prosecutors Office
32 Rahway Avenue
Elizabeth, NJ 07202
Phone: 908-527-4506

DALLAS MORNING NEWS   http://www.dallasnews.com

DALLAS MORNING NEWS ANNUAL TEENAGE CITIZENSHIP TRIBUTE

Award recognizes high school seniors who have achieved the highest standards of citizenship in their schools and communities. All 12th grade students in Dallas, Collin, Denton, Ellis, Hunt, Kaufman, Parker, Rockwall, and Tarrant counties are eligible. Nominees must demonstrate qualities of leadership, initiative, good judgment, and responsibility. Volunteer service in the community is essential. Must have minimum 2.5 GPA. For more details see Web site: http://tact.dallasnews.com.

Award: Scholarship for use in freshman year; not renewable. *Number:* 20. *Amount:* $500–$2000.

Eligibility Requirements: Applicant must be high school student; planning to enroll or expecting to enroll full-time at a four-year institution or university; resident of Texas and must have an interest in leadership. Applicant or parent of applicant must have employment or volunteer experience in community service. Applicant must have 2.5 GPA or higher. Available to U.S. citizens.

Application Requirements: Application, interview, references. *Deadline:* February 10.

Contact: Monica Egert-Smith, Community Services Programs Coordinator
Dallas Morning News
PO Box 655237
Dallas, TX 75265-5237
Phone: 214-977-7256
E-mail: megert@dallasnews.com

DELAWARE HIGHER EDUCATION COMMISSION   http://www.doe.k12.de.us

EDUCATIONAL BENEFITS FOR CHILDREN OF DECEASED MILITARY AND STATE POLICE

Renewable award for Delaware residents who are children of state or military police who were killed in the line of duty. Must attend a Delaware institution unless program of study is not available. Funds cover tuition and fees at Delaware institutions. The amount varies at non-Delaware institutions. Must submit proof of service and related death. Must be ages 16-24 at time of application. Deadline is three weeks before classes begin.

Award: Grant for use in freshman, sophomore, junior, or senior years; renewable. *Number:* 1–10. *Amount:* $6255.

Eligibility Requirements: Applicant must be age 16-24; enrolled or expecting to enroll full-time at a two-year or four-year institution or university and resident of Delaware. Applicant or parent of applicant must have employment or volunteer experience in police/firefighting. Available to U.S. citizens. Applicant or parent must meet one or more of the following requirements: general military experience; retired from active duty; disabled or killed as a result of military service; prisoner of war; or missing in action.

Application Requirements: Application, verification of service-related death. *Deadline:* Continuous.

Contact: Donna Myers, Field Agent/Program Administrator
Delaware Higher Education Commission
820 North French Street, 5th Floor
Wilmington, DE 19711-3509
Phone: 302-577-3240
Fax: 302-577-6765
E-mail: dmyers@doe.k12.de.us

DELTA DELTA DELTA FOUNDATION   http://www.tridelta.org

DELTA DELTA DELTA GRADUATE SCHOLARSHIP
• *See page 497*

DELTA DELTA DELTA UNDERGRADUATE SCHOLARSHIP
• *See page 497*

DISABLED AMERICAN VETERANS   http://www.dav.org

JESSE BROWN MEMORIAL YOUTH SCHOLARSHIP PROGRAM

Designed to encourage youth volunteers to become active in Department of Veterans Affairs Voluntary Services (VAVS) programs. Scholarship is awarded annually to outstanding youth volunteers who are very active in VAVS activities.

Award: Scholarship for use in freshman, sophomore, junior, senior, graduate, or postgraduate years; renewable. *Number:* 12. *Amount:* $5000–$15,000.

Eligibility Requirements: Applicant must be age 21 or under and enrolled or expecting to enroll full-time at a two-year or four-year or technical institution or university. Applicant or parent of applicant must have employment or volunteer experience in helping handicapped. Available to U.S. citizens.

Application Requirements: Application, essay, 100 hours of volunteer activity at VA medical facility. *Deadline:* varies.

Contact: Arthur Wilson, President
Disabled American Veterans
807 Maine Avenue, SW
Washington, DC 20024
Phone: 202-233-3318

EXPLOSIVE ORDNANCE DISPOSAL MEMORIAL COMMITTEE   http://www.eodmemorial.org

EXPLOSIVE ORDNANCE DISPOSAL MEMORIAL SCHOLARSHIP

Award based on academic merit, community involvement, and financial need for the children and spouses of Explosive Ordnance Disposal technicians. This scholarship is for students enrolled or planning to enroll full-time as an undergraduate in a U.S. accredited two year, four year, or vocational school. Applications are only available on the Web site at http://www.eodmemorial.org

Award: Scholarship for use in freshman, sophomore, junior, or senior years; not renewable. *Number:* 20–60. *Amount:* $1500–$2000.

Eligibility Requirements: Applicant must be enrolled or expecting to enroll full-time at a four-year or technical institution or university. Applicant or parent of applicant must have employment or volunteer experience in explosive ordnance disposal. Available to U.S. citizens. Applicant or parent must meet one or more of the following requirements: general military experience; retired from active duty; disabled or killed as a result of military service; prisoner of war; or missing in action.

Application Requirements: Application, financial need analysis, transcript. *Deadline:* March 1.

Contact: Mary McKinley, Administrator
Explosive Ordnance Disposal Memorial Committee
PO Box 594
Niceville, FL 32588
Phone: 850-729-2401
Fax: 850-729-2401
E-mail: admin@eodmemorial.org

FEDERAL EMPLOYEE EDUCATION AND ASSISTANCE FUND   http://www.feea.org

FEEA SCHOLARSHIPS

One-time award for students enrolled in an accredited postsecondary school in a course of study that will lead to a two-year, four-year or graduate degree. Must be a current civilian federal or postal employee with at least three years of federal service, or a dependent family member (children and spouses). Minimum 3.0 GPA required.

Award: Scholarship for use in freshman, sophomore, junior, senior, or graduate years; not renewable. *Number:* varies. *Amount:* $350–$1200.

Eligibility Requirements: Applicant must be enrolled or expecting to enroll full or part-time at a two-year or four-year institution or university. Applicant or parent of applicant must have employment or volunteer experience in federal/postal service. Applicant must have 3.0 GPA or higher. Available to U.S. and non-U.S. citizens.

Application Requirements: Application, essay, references, self-addressed stamped envelope, test scores, transcript. *Deadline:* March 28.

Contact: Stephen Bauer, Director
Federal Employee Education and Assistance Fund
8441 West Bowles Avenue, Suite 200
Littleton, CO 80123-9501
Phone: 303-933-7580
Fax: 303-933-7587

FINANCE AUTHORITY OF MAINE   http://www.famemaine.com

TUITION WAIVER PROGRAMS

Provides tuition waivers for children and spouses of EMS personnel, firefighters, and law enforcement officers who have been killed in the line of duty and for students who were foster children under the custody of the Department of Human Services when they graduated from high school. Waivers valid at the University of Maine System, the Maine Technical College System, and Maine Maritime Academy.

Award: Grant for use in freshman, sophomore, junior, or senior years; not renewable. *Number:* 1. *Amount:* varies.

Eligibility Requirements: Applicant must be enrolled or expecting to enroll at an institution or university; resident of Maine and studying in Maine. Applicant or parent of applicant must have employment or volunteer experience in designated career field or police/firefighting. Available to U.S. citizens.

Application Requirements: Application, letter from the Department of Human Services documenting that applicant is in their custody and residing in foster care at the time of graduation from high school or its equivalent. *Deadline:* Continuous.

Contact: Trisha Malloy, Program Officer
Finance Authority of Maine
5 Community Drive
Augusta, ME 04332
Phone: 207-623-3263
Fax: 207-623-0095
E-mail: trisha@famemaine.com

FLORIDA DEPARTMENT OF EDUCATION   http://www.floridastudentfinancialaid.org

CRITICAL TEACHER SHORTAGE STUDENT LOAN FORGIVENESS PROGRAM-FLORIDA

Eligible Florida teachers may receive up to $5000 for repayment of undergraduate and graduate educational loans, which lead to certification in

Florida Department of Education (continued)

critical teacher shortage subject area. Must teach full-time at a Florida public school in a critical area for a minimum of ninety days to be eligible. Visit Web site for further information.

Award: Forgivable loan for use in freshman, sophomore, junior, senior, or graduate years; renewable. *Number:* varies. *Amount:* $2500–$5000.

Eligibility Requirements: Applicant must be enrolled or expecting to enroll at a two-year or four-year institution or university; resident of Florida and studying in Florida. Applicant or parent of applicant must have employment or volunteer experience in teaching. Available to U.S. citizens.

Application Requirements: Application, transcript. *Deadline:* July 15.

Contact: Barb Dombrowski, Education Director, Policy and Training
Florida Department of Education
Office of Student Financial Assistance
1940 North Monroe, Suite 70
Tallahassee, FL 32303-4759
Phone: 850-410-5191
Fax: 850-488-5966
E-mail: barb.dombrowski@fldoe.org

GEORGIA STUDENT FINANCE COMMISSION
http://www.gsfc.org

GEORGIA PUBLIC SAFETY MEMORIAL GRANT/LAW ENFORCEMENT PERSONNEL DEPARTMENT GRANT

Award for children of Georgia law enforcement officers, prison guards, or fire fighters killed or permanently disabled in the line of duty. Must attend an accredited postsecondary Georgia school. Complete the Law Enforcement Personnel Dependents application.

Award: Grant for use in freshman, sophomore, junior, or senior years; renewable. *Number:* 20–40. *Amount:* $1000–$8000.

Eligibility Requirements: Applicant must be enrolled or expecting to enroll full-time at a two-year or four-year or technical institution or university; resident of Georgia and studying in Georgia. Applicant or parent of applicant must have employment or volunteer experience in police/firefighting. Available to U.S. citizens.

Application Requirements: Application, financial need analysis, Selective Service registration. *Deadline:* Continuous.

Contact: William Flook, Director of Scholarships and Grants Division
Georgia Student Finance Commission
2082 East Exchange Place, Suite 100
Tucker, GA 30084
Phone: 770-724-9052
Fax: 770-724-9031
E-mail: billf@gsfc.org

GRACO, INC.
http://www.graco.com

DAVID A. KOCH SCHOLARSHIP
• See page 530

GRACO INC. SCHOLARSHIP PROGRAM
• See page 530

GREATER KANAWHA VALLEY FOUNDATION
http://www.tgkvf.org

SCPA SCHOLARSHIP FUND

Renewable award for West Virginia residents who are full time-students with minimum 2.5 GPA. Applicant must have parent who is employed or has been previously employed by the coal industry in southern West Virginia. Include employer's name and address. May apply for two Foundation scholarships but will only be chosen for one. Scholarships are awarded on a financial need basis and may be awarded for one or more years.

Award: Scholarship for use in freshman, sophomore, junior, or senior years; renewable. *Number:* 9–11. *Amount:* $1000.

Eligibility Requirements: Applicant must be enrolled or expecting to enroll full-time at a four-year institution or university and resident of West Virginia. Applicant or parent of applicant must have employment or volunteer experience in coal industry. Applicant must have 2.5 GPA or higher. Available to U.S. citizens.

Application Requirements: Application, essay, financial need analysis, references, self-addressed stamped envelope, test scores, transcript. *Deadline:* February 15.

Contact: Susan Hoover, Scholarship Coordinator
Greater Kanawha Valley Foundation
PO Box 3041
Charleston, WV 25331
Phone: 304-346-3620
Fax: 304-346-3640

WEST VIRGINIA GOLF ASSOCIATION FUND

Awarded to students at any accredited West Virginia college or university. This fund is open to individuals who meet the following criteria: 1) have played golf in WV as an amateur for recreation or competition or 2) have been or are presently employed in WV as a caddie, groundskeeper, bag boy, etc. Must also include a reference by a coach, golf professional or employer and an essay explaining how the game of golf has made an impact in applicant's life. Scholarships are awarded with a commitment of one year. May apply for two Foundation scholarships but will only be chosen for one.

Award: Scholarship for use in freshman, sophomore, junior, or senior years; not renewable. *Number:* 2. *Amount:* $1000.

Eligibility Requirements: Applicant must be enrolled or expecting to enroll full-time at a four-year institution or university; resident of West Virginia and studying in West Virginia. Applicant or parent of applicant must have employment or volunteer experience in private club/caddying. Applicant must have 2.5 GPA or higher. Available to U.S. citizens.

Application Requirements: Application, essay, references, transcript, IRS 1040 form. *Deadline:* February 15.

Contact: Susan Hoover, Scholarship Coordinator
Greater Kanawha Valley Foundation
PO Box 3041
Charleston, WV 25331
Phone: 304-346-3620
Fax: 304-346-3640

HARNESS HORSE YOUTH FOUNDATION
http://www.hhyf.org

CHARLES BRADLEY MEMORIAL SCHOLARSHIP

One-time award for full-time undergraduates between the ages of 18-24. Open to children of licensed pari-mutuel harness racing officials. Minimum 2.5 GPA required. Must be U.S. or Canadian citizen. Total number of available awards and the dollar value varies each year.

Award: Scholarship for use in freshman, sophomore, junior, or senior years; not renewable. *Number:* 1–3. *Amount:* $250–$500.

Eligibility Requirements: Applicant must be age 18-24 and enrolled or expecting to enroll full-time at a two-year or four-year or technical institution or university. Applicant or parent of applicant must have employment or volunteer experience in harness racing. Applicant must have 2.5 GPA or higher. Available to U.S. and Canadian citizens.

Application Requirements: Application, essay, references, transcript, page 1 of parents' IRS form. *Deadline:* April 30.

Contact: Ellen Taylor, Executive Director
Harness Horse Youth Foundation
16575 Carey Road
Westfield, IN 46074
Phone: 317-867-5877
Fax: 317-867-5896
E-mail: ellen@hhyf.org

DOUG BROWN SCHOLARSHIP

One-time award for full-time undergraduates between the ages of 18-24. Open to children whose parents are actively involved in harness racing. Must be a Canadian citizen. Minimum 2.5 GPA required.

Award: Scholarship for use in freshman, sophomore, junior, or senior years; not renewable. *Number:* 1. *Amount:* $3500.

Eligibility Requirements: Applicant must be age 18-24 and enrolled or expecting to enroll full-time at a two-year or four-year or technical institution or university. Applicant or parent of applicant must have employment or volunteer experience in harness racing. Applicant must have 2.5 GPA or higher. Available to Canadian citizens.

Application Requirements: Application, essay, references, transcript, page 1 of parents' IRS form. *Deadline:* April 30.

Contact: Ellen Taylor, Executive Director
Harness Horse Youth Foundation
16575 Carey Road
Westfield, IN 46074
Phone: 317-867-5877
Fax: 317-867-5896
E-mail: ellen@hhyf.org

VINCENT ABATE MEMORIAL SCHOLARSHIP

One-time award for full-time undergraduates between the ages of 18-24. Open to children whose parents are employees of The Meadowlands or Freehold Raceway. Minimum 2.5 GPA required. Must be U.S. citizen.

Award: Scholarship for use in freshman, sophomore, junior, or senior years; not renewable. *Number:* 1–3. *Amount:* $1000–$5000.

Eligibility Requirements: Applicant must be age 18-24 and enrolled or expecting to enroll full-time at a two-year or four-year or technical institution or university. Applicant or parent of applicant must have employment or volunteer experience in harness racing. Applicant must have 2.5 GPA or higher. Available to U.S. citizens.

Application Requirements: Application, essay, references, transcript, page 1 of parents' IRS form. *Deadline:* April 30.

Contact: Ellen Taylor, Executive Director
Harness Horse Youth Foundation
16575 Carey Road
Westfield, IN 46074
Phone: 317-867-5877
Fax: 317-867-5896
E-mail: ellen@hhyf.org

HARNESS TRACKS OF AMERICA, INC.   http://www.harnesstracks.com

HARNESS TRACKS OF AMERICA SCHOLARSHIP

One-time, merit-based award for students actively involved in harness racing or the children of licensed drivers, trainers, breeders, or caretakers, living or deceased. Based on financial need, academic merit, and active harness racing involvement by applicant or family member. High school seniors may apply for the following school year award. For further details visit Web site: http://www.harnesstracks.com.

Award: Scholarship for use in freshman, sophomore, junior, senior, or graduate years; not renewable. *Number:* up to 6. *Amount:* $7500–$10,000.

Eligibility Requirements: Applicant must be enrolled or expecting to enroll full-time at a two-year or four-year or technical institution or university. Applicant or parent of applicant must have employment or volunteer experience in harness racing. Available to U.S. and non-U.S. citizens.

Application Requirements: Application, essay, financial need analysis, transcript, IRS 1040 for for parents and/or applicant. *Deadline:* June 15.

Contact: Jessica Carner, Editorial Coordinator
Harness Tracks of America, Inc.
4640 East Sunrise Drive, Suite 200
Tucson, AZ 85718
Phone: 520-529-2525
Fax: 520-529-3235
E-mail: info@harnesstracks.com

IDAHO STATE BOARD OF EDUCATION   http://www.boardofed.idaho.gov

PUBLIC SAFETY OFFICER DEPENDENT SCHOLARSHIP

Scholarship for dependents of full-time Idaho public safety officers who were killed or disabled in the line of duty. Recipients will attend an Idaho postsecondary institution with a full waiver of fees.

Award: Scholarship for use in freshman year; renewable. *Amount:* $1000.

Eligibility Requirements: Applicant must be enrolled or expecting to enroll at an institution or university; resident of Idaho and studying in Idaho. Applicant or parent of applicant must have employment or volunteer experience in police/firefighting. Available to U.S. citizens.

Application Requirements: Application.

Contact: Dana Kelly, Program Manager
Idaho State Board of Education
PO Box 83720
Boise, ID 83720-0037
Phone: 208-332-1574
E-mail: dana.kelly@osbe.idaho.gov

ILLINOIS STUDENT ASSISTANCE COMMISSION (ISAC)   http://www.collegezone.org

GRANT PROGRAM FOR DEPENDENTS OF POLICE, FIRE, OR CORRECTIONAL OFFICERS

Award for dependents of police, fire, and corrections officers killed or disabled in line of duty. Provides for tuition and fees at approved Illinois institutions. Must be resident of Illinois. Continuous deadline. Provide proof of status. For information and application, go to Web site: http://www.collegezone.

Award: Grant for use in freshman, sophomore, junior, senior, graduate, or postgraduate years; renewable. *Number:* 50–55. *Amount:* $3000–$4000.

Eligibility Requirements: Applicant must be enrolled or expecting to enroll at a two-year or four-year or technical institution or university; resident of Illinois and studying in Illinois. Applicant or parent of applicant must have employment or volunteer experience in police/firefighting. Available to U.S. citizens.

Application Requirements: Application, proof of status. *Deadline:* Continuous.

Contact: College Zone Counselor
Illinois Student Assistance Commission (ISAC)
1755 Lake Cook Road
Deerfield, IL 60015-5209
Phone: 800-899-4722
E-mail: collegezone@isac.org

INDIANA POLICE CORPS   http://www.in.gov/cji/policecorps

SCHOLARSHIPS FOR DEPENDENTS OF FALLEN OFFICERS

Scholarships are available to the dependents of officers who have been killed in the line of duty. For more details and an application see Web site: http://www.in.gov/cji/policecorps.

Award: Scholarship for use in freshman, sophomore, junior, or senior years; renewable. *Number:* varies. *Amount:* up to $30,000.

Eligibility Requirements: Applicant must be enrolled or expecting to enroll at a two-year or four-year or technical institution or university. Applicant or parent of applicant must have employment or volunteer experience in police/firefighting. Available to U.S. citizens.

Application Requirements: Application, request for scholarship payment. *Deadline:* Continuous.

Contact: Application available at Web site.

INTERNATIONAL ASSOCIATION OF FIRE CHIEFS FOUNDATION   http://www.iafcf.org

INTERNATIONAL ASSOCIATION OF FIRE CHIEFS FOUNDATION SCHOLARSHIP AWARD

One-time award open to any person who is an active member (volunteer or paid) of an emergency or fire department. Must be studying at a recognized institution of higher education. Application deadline is August 1.

Award: Scholarship for use in freshman, sophomore, junior, senior, graduate, or postgraduate years; not renewable. *Number:* 10–30. *Amount:* $350–$4000.

Eligibility Requirements: Applicant must be enrolled or expecting to enroll full or part-time at a two-year or four-year or technical institution or university. Applicant or parent of applicant must have employment or volunteer experience in fire service. Available to U.S. and non-U.S. citizens.

International Association of Fire Chiefs Foundation (continued)

Application Requirements: Application, essay. *Deadline:* August 1.

Contact: Patricia Hessenauer
International Association of Fire Chiefs Foundation
PO Box 1818
Windermere, FL 34786
Phone: 571-344-5410
E-mail: iafcfoun@msn.com

INTERNATIONAL ASSOCIATION OF FIRE FIGHTERS

http://www.iaff.org

W.H. "HOWIE" MCCLENNAN SCHOLARSHIP

Fund was established to provide financial assistance to sons, daughters, and legally adopted children of IAFF members killed in the line of duty who are planning to attend an institution of higher learning.

Award: Scholarship for use in freshman, sophomore, junior, senior, or graduate years; renewable. *Number:* 20–25. *Amount:* $2500.

Eligibility Requirements: Applicant must be enrolled or expecting to enroll full or part-time at a two-year or four-year or technical institution or university. Applicant or parent of applicant must have employment or volunteer experience in police/firefighting. Available to U.S. and Canadian citizens.

Application Requirements: Application, essay, references, transcript. *Deadline:* February 1.

Contact: Office of the McClennan Scholarship General President
International Association of Fire Fighters
1750 New York Avenue, NW
Washington, DC 20006
Phone: 202-737-8484
Fax: 202-737-8418

J. WOOD PLATT CADDIE SCHOLARSHIP TRUST

http://www.gapgolf.org

J. WOOD PLATT CADDIE SCHOLARSHIP TRUST

Renewable award for high school seniors or college undergraduates who have caddied at least one year at a member club of the Golf Association of Philadelphia. Submit transcript and financial need analysis with application. Interview required. Deadline is April 25.

Award: Scholarship for use in freshman, sophomore, junior, senior, or graduate years; renewable. *Number:* 250–300. *Amount:* $200–$7000.

Eligibility Requirements: Applicant must be enrolled or expecting to enroll full-time at a two-year or four-year institution or university and must have an interest in golf. Applicant or parent of applicant must have employment or volunteer experience in private club/caddying. Available to U.S. and non-U.S. citizens.

Application Requirements: Application, financial need analysis, interview, references, test scores, transcript. *Deadline:* April 25.

Contact: Robert Caucci, Program Administrator
J. Wood Platt Caddie Scholarship Trust
PO Box 808
Southeastern, PA 19399-0808
Phone: 610-687-2340 Ext. 21
Fax: 610-687-2082

JOHN EDGAR THOMSON FOUNDATION

JOHN EDGAR THOMSON FOUNDATION GRANTS

Must be the daughter of a deceased railroad employee. Employee (mother/father) must have been actively employed at time of death. Recipients of disability, sick leave, workman's compensation are considered eligible. Monthly grant is available until the age of 22, as long as recipient is in college full-time, earning at least 12 credits. Termination at age 22 or upon graduation, whichever comes first. Recipient must remain unmarried. Based upon financial need. Submit birth certificate.

Award: Grant for use in freshman, sophomore, junior, or senior years; renewable. *Number:* varies. *Amount:* $500–$4400.

Eligibility Requirements: Applicant must be age 21 or under; enrolled or expecting to enroll full-time at a two-year or four-year or technical institution or university and single female. Applicant or parent of applicant must have employment or volunteer experience in railroad industry. Available to U.S. citizens.

Application Requirements: Application, financial need analysis, interview, photo, references, transcript, birth certificate. *Deadline:* Continuous.

Contact: Sheila Cohen, Director
John Edgar Thomson Foundation
201 South 18th Street, Suite 318
Philadelphia, PA 19103
Phone: 215-545-6083
Fax: 215-545-6083

KINGSBURY CORPORATION

http://www.kingsburycorp.com/

KINGSBURY FUND SCHOLARSHIPS

• See page 531

LINCOLN COMMUNITY FOUNDATION

http://www.lcf.org

GEORGE WATTERS-NEBRASKA PETROLEUM MARKETERS ASSOCIATION SCHOLARSHIP

Scholarship for any Nebraska high school graduating senior to attend any two- or four-year postsecondary institution in Nebraska. Must be in upper 33% of class, and demonstrate academic achievement and leadership. Sponsored by Nebraska Petroleum Marketers who makes the selection process and determines application deadline. Applicants must be the son or daughter of any Nebraska Petroleum Marketer and Convenience Store Association member, or the son or daughter of a Nebraska Petroleum Marketers and Convenience Store Association's full- or part-time employee.

Award: Scholarship for use in freshman year; not renewable. *Number:* 3. *Amount:* $500–$2000.

Eligibility Requirements: Applicant must be high school student; planning to enroll or expecting to enroll full-time at a two-year or four-year or technical institution or university; resident of Nebraska; studying in Nebraska and must have an interest in leadership. Applicant or parent of applicant must have employment or volunteer experience in designated career field. Applicant must have 3.0 GPA or higher. Available to U.S. citizens.

Application Requirements: Application, references, transcript. *Deadline:* March 1.

Contact: Grafton and Associates Certified Public Accountants
Lincoln Community Foundation
8101 O Street, Suite 200
Lincoln, NE 68510

HARRY AND LENORA RICHARDSON-NATIONAL ASSOCIATION OF POSTMASTERS OF THE UNITED STATES SCHOLARSHIP

Scholarship for a graduating senior who is the child, grandchild, or member of the Nebraska Chapter, National Association of Postmaster of the United States or the Nebraska Branch, National League of Postmasters of the United States. Applicants must demonstrate academic achievement and participation in extracurricular and community activities. Must be a Nebraska resident. Must attend a Nebraska college or university.

Award: Scholarship for use in freshman year; not renewable. *Number:* 1. *Amount:* $500–$2000.

Eligibility Requirements: Applicant must be high school student; planning to enroll or expecting to enroll full-time at a two-year or four-year institution or university; resident of Nebraska and studying in Nebraska. Applicant or parent of applicant must have employment or volunteer experience in federal/postal service. Applicant must have 2.5 GPA or higher. Available to U.S. citizens.

Application Requirements: Application, autobiography, references, transcript. *Deadline:* April 1.

Contact: Betty Mapes, Scholarship Chairman
Lincoln Community Foundation
PO Box 333
Fullerton, NE 68638

HARRY AND LENORA RICHARDSON-NEBRASKA BRANCH OF THE NATIONAL LEAGUE OF POSTMASTERS SCHOLARSHIP

Scholarship for a graduating senior who is the child, grandchild, or member of the Nebraska Chapter, National Association of Postmasters of the United

States, or the Nebraska Branch, National League of Postmasters of the United States. Applicants must demonstrate academic achievement and participation in extracurricular and community activities. Must be a Nebraska resident. Must attend a Nebraska college or university.

Award: Scholarship for use in freshman year; not renewable. *Number:* 1. *Amount:* $500–$2000.

Eligibility Requirements: Applicant must be high school student; planning to enroll or expecting to enroll full-time at a two-year or four-year institution or university; resident of Nebraska and studying in Nebraska. Applicant or parent of applicant must have employment or volunteer experience in federal/postal service. Applicant must have 2.5 GPA or higher. Available to U.S. citizens.

Application Requirements: Application, autobiography, references, transcript. *Deadline:* March 15.

Contact: Sharleen Miller, Scholarship Chair
Lincoln Community Foundation
85342 488th Avenue
Chambers, NE 68725

LOUIS C. AND AMY E. NUERNBERGER MEMORIAL SCHOLARSHIP

Scholarship for high school graduates who have been employed at the Wakefield Health Care Center in Wakefield, NE for at least one year.

Award: Scholarship for use in freshman, sophomore, junior, or senior years; renewable. *Number:* 1. *Amount:* $500–$2000.

Eligibility Requirements: Applicant must be enrolled or expecting to enroll full-time at a two-year or four-year or technical institution or university and resident of Nebraska. Applicant or parent of applicant must have employment or volunteer experience in designated career field. Applicant must have 2.5 GPA or higher. Available to U.S. citizens.

Application Requirements: Application, essay, test scores, transcript. *Deadline:* April 1.

Contact: Administrator, Wakefield Health Care Center
Lincoln Community Foundation
306 Ash Street
Wakefield, NE 68784

THOMAS C. WOODS, JR. MEMORIAL SCHOLARSHIP

Scholarships are for graduating seniors or former graduates of any high school in the following counties in Nebraska: Adams, Butler, Cass, Clay, Fillmore, Gage, Hamilton, Jefferson, Johnson, Lancaster, Nemaha, Nucholls, Otoe, Pawnee, Polk, Richardson, Saline, Saunders, Seward, Thayer, Webster, and York. Applicants must be qualified dependents of current ALLTEL employees. Must attend a college/universities in Nebraska. Minimum 2.5 GPA required.

Award: Scholarship for use in freshman, sophomore, junior, or senior years; not renewable. *Number:* 10–15. *Amount:* $500–$2000.

Eligibility Requirements: Applicant must be enrolled or expecting to enroll full-time at a two-year or four-year institution or university; resident of Nebraska and studying in Nebraska. Applicant or parent of applicant must have employment or volunteer experience in designated career field. Applicant must have 2.5 GPA or higher. Available to U.S. citizens.

Application Requirements: Application, essay, financial need analysis, test scores. *Deadline:* April 17.

Contact: Debra Shoemaker, Director of Program and Distribution
Lincoln Community Foundation
215 Centennial Mall South, Suite 200
Lincoln, NE 68508
Phone: 402-474-2345
Fax: 402-476-8532
E-mail: debs@lcf.org

MASSACHUSETTS OFFICE OF STUDENT FINANCIAL ASSISTANCE   http://www.osfa.mass.edu

MASSACHUSETTS PUBLIC SERVICE GRANT PROGRAM

Scholarships for children and/or spouses of deceased members of fire, police, and corrections departments who were killed in the line of duty. For Massachusetts residents attending Massachusetts institutions. Applicant should have not received a prior bachelors degree or its equivalent

Award: Grant for use in freshman, sophomore, junior, or senior years; not renewable. *Number:* varies. *Amount:* $720–$2500.

Eligibility Requirements: Applicant must be enrolled or expecting to enroll full-time at a four-year institution or university; resident of Massachusetts and studying in Massachusetts. Applicant or parent of applicant must have employment or volunteer experience in police/firefighting. Available to U.S. citizens.

Application Requirements: Application, financial need analysis, FAFSA. *Deadline:* May 1.

Contact: Alison Leary
Massachusetts Office of Student Financial Assistance
454 Broadway, Suite 200
Revere, MA 02151
Phone: 617-727-9420
Fax: 617-727-0667
E-mail: osfa@osfa.mass.edu

MILITARY BENEFIT ASSOCIATION   http://www.militarybenefit.org

MILITARY BENEFIT ASSOCIATION SCHOLARSHIP
• See page 504

MINNESOTA HIGHER EDUCATION SERVICES OFFICE   http://www.getreadyforcollege.org

SAFETY OFFICERS' SURVIVOR GRANT PROGRAM

Grant for eligible survivors of Minnesota public safety officers killed in the line of duty. Safety officers who have been permanently or totally disabled in the line of duty are also eligible. Must be used at a Minnesota institution participating in State Grant Program. Write for details. Must submit proof of death or disability and Public Safety Officers Benefit Fund Certificate. Must apply each year. Can be renewed for four years.

Award: Grant for use in freshman, sophomore, junior, or senior years; renewable. *Amount:* up to $9208.

Eligibility Requirements: Applicant must be age 23 or under; enrolled or expecting to enroll full or part-time at a two-year or four-year or technical institution or university; resident of Minnesota and studying in Minnesota. Applicant or parent of applicant must have employment or volunteer experience in police/firefighting. Available to U.S. citizens.

Application Requirements: Application, proof of death/disability. *Deadline:* Continuous.

Contact: Minnesota Higher Education Services Office
1450 Energy Park Drive, Suite 350
St. Paul, MN 55108-5227
Phone: 651-642-0567 Ext. 1

NATIONAL BURGLAR AND FIRE ALARM ASSOCIATION   http://www.alarm.org

NBFAA/SECURITY DEALER YOUTH SCHOLARSHIP PROGRAM

Scholarship program provides cash college scholarship awards to deserving sons or daughters of police and fire officials. Applicants should contact state NBFAA chapters. For more information visit our Web site at http://www.alarm.org

Award: Scholarship for use in freshman year; not renewable. *Number:* 32. *Amount:* $500–$6500.

Eligibility Requirements: Applicant must be high school student; age 15-20; planning to enroll or expecting to enroll full-time at a four-year institution or university and resident of California, Connecticut, Georgia, Indiana, Kentucky, Louisiana, Maryland, Minnesota, New Jersey, New York, North Carolina, Pennsylvania, Tennessee, Virginia, or Washington. Applicant or parent of applicant must have employment or volunteer experience in fire service or police/firefighting. Available to U.S. and non-Canadian citizens.

Application Requirements: Application, essay, test scores, transcript. *Deadline:* March 1.

Contact: Rick Ostopowicz, Communications Manager
National Burglar and Fire Alarm Association
8380 Colesville Road, Suite 750
Silver Spring, MD 20910
Phone: 301-585-1855 Ext. 133
Fax: 301-585-1866
E-mail: communications@alarm.org

NATIONAL FEDERATION OF THE BLIND

http://www.nfb.org

E. U. PARKER SCHOLARSHIP

Award for students who are legally blind and pursuing full-time postsecondary education at a United States institution. Applicant must submit recommendation from state officer of the National Federation of the Blind. Award based on academic excellence, service to the community, and financial need. One-time award of $3000.

Award: Scholarship for use in freshman, sophomore, junior, or senior years; not renewable. *Number:* 1. *Amount:* $3000.

Eligibility Requirements: Applicant must be enrolled or expecting to enroll full-time at a four-year institution or university. Applicant or parent of applicant must have employment or volunteer experience in community service. Applicant must be visually impaired. Available to U.S. citizens.

Application Requirements: Application, autobiography, essay, financial need analysis, references, transcript. *Deadline:* March 31.

Contact: Peggy Elliot, Chairman, Scholarship Committee
National Federation of the Blind
805 Fifth Avenue
Grinnell, IA 50112
Phone: 641-236-3366

HERMIONE GRANT CALHOUN SCHOLARSHIP

Award for full-time female undergraduate and graduate students who are legally blind and planning to study for a degree. Need minimum 2.5 GPA. Must submit a letter from state officer of National Federation of the Blind with whom they have discussed their application. May reapply. Must attend school in the U.S. Award based on academic excellence, service to the community, and financial need.

Award: Scholarship for use in freshman, sophomore, junior, senior, or graduate years; not renewable. *Number:* 1. *Amount:* $3000.

Eligibility Requirements: Applicant must be enrolled or expecting to enroll full-time at a four-year institution or university and female. Applicant or parent of applicant must have employment or volunteer experience in community service. Applicant must be visually impaired. Applicant must have 2.5 GPA or higher. Available to U.S. and non-U.S. citizens.

Application Requirements: Application, autobiography, essay, financial need analysis, references, transcript. *Deadline:* March 31.

Contact: Peggy Elliot, Chairman, Scholarship Committee
National Federation of the Blind
805 Fifth Avenue
Grinnell, IA 50112
Phone: 641-236-3366

JENNICA FERGUSON MEMORIAL SCHOLARSHIP

One-time award for students who are legally blind and pursuing full-time secondary education in the U.S. Applicant must send a letter from a State officer of the National Federation of the Blind with whom they have discussed their application. Award is based on academic excellence, financial need and service to the community.

Award: Scholarship for use in freshman, sophomore, junior, or senior years; not renewable. *Number:* 1. *Amount:* $5000.

Eligibility Requirements: Applicant must be enrolled or expecting to enroll full-time at a four-year institution or university. Applicant or parent of applicant must have employment or volunteer experience in community service. Applicant must be visually impaired. Available to U.S. citizens.

Application Requirements: Application, essay, financial need analysis, references, transcript. *Deadline:* March 31.

Contact: Peggy Elliott, Chairman
National Federation of the Blind
805 Fifth Avenue
Grinnell, IA 50112
Phone: 641-236-3366
E-mail: delliott@pcpartner.net

KENNETH JERNIGAN SCHOLARSHIP

One-time award for full-time postsecondary study for students who are legally blind. Applicants must submit recommendation from state officer of National Federation of the Blind. Award based on academic excellence, service to the community, and financial need. Must attend school in the U.S. Sponsored by the American Action Fund for Blind Children and Adults.

Award: Scholarship for use in freshman, sophomore, junior, or senior years; not renewable. *Number:* 1. *Amount:* $10,000–$12,000.

Eligibility Requirements: Applicant must be enrolled or expecting to enroll full-time at a four-year institution or university. Applicant or parent of applicant must have employment or volunteer experience in community service. Applicant must be visually impaired. Applicant must have 3.5 GPA or higher. Available to U.S. and non-U.S. citizens.

Application Requirements: Application, autobiography, essay, financial need analysis, references, transcript. *Deadline:* March 31.

Contact: Peggy Elliot, Chairman, Scholarship Committee
National Federation of the Blind
805 5th Avenue
Grinnell, IA 50112
Phone: 641-236-3366

KUCHLER-KILLIAN MEMORIAL SCHOLARSHIP

Award for legally blind full-time students. Applicants must submit a letter from a state officer of National Federation of the Blind with whom they have discussed their application. May reapply each year. Award based on scholarship and service. Must attend school in U.S.

Award: Scholarship for use in freshman, sophomore, junior, or senior years; not renewable. *Number:* 1. *Amount:* $3000.

Eligibility Requirements: Applicant must be enrolled or expecting to enroll full-time at a four-year institution or university. Applicant or parent of applicant must have employment or volunteer experience in community service. Applicant must be visually impaired. Available to U.S. and non-U.S. citizens.

Application Requirements: Application, autobiography, essay, financial need analysis, references, transcript. *Deadline:* March 31.

Contact: Peggy Elliot, Chairman, Scholarship Committee
National Federation of the Blind
805 Fifth Avenue
Grinnell, IA 50112
Phone: 641-236-3366

MELVA T. OWEN MEMORIAL SCHOLARSHIP

For full-time students in a degree program who are legally blind and who are not pursuing a degree in religious studies. Must submit letter from the National Federation of the Blind state officer with whom they have discussed their application. Based on academic excellence, service to the community, and financial need. Must attend school in the U.S.

Award: Scholarship for use in freshman, sophomore, junior, or senior years; not renewable. *Number:* 1. *Amount:* $10,000.

Eligibility Requirements: Applicant must be enrolled or expecting to enroll full-time at a four-year institution or university. Applicant or parent of applicant must have employment or volunteer experience in community service. Applicant must be visually impaired. Applicant must have 3.5 GPA or higher. Available to U.S. and non-U.S. citizens.

Application Requirements: Application, autobiography, essay, financial need analysis, references, transcript. *Deadline:* March 31.

Contact: Peggy Elliot, Chairman, Scholarship Committee
National Federation of the Blind
805 Fifth Avenue
Grinnell, IA 50112
Phone: 641-236-3366

SALLY S. JACOBSEN SCHOLARSHIP

One-time award for students who are legally blind and pursuing full-time studies in the U.S. Applicant must send a letter from a state officer of the National Federation of the Blind with whom they have discussed their application. Award based on academic excellence, financial need and service to the community.

Award: Scholarship for use in freshman, sophomore, junior, or senior years; not renewable. *Number:* 1. *Amount:* $5000.

Eligibility Requirements: Applicant must be enrolled or expecting to enroll full-time at an institution or university. Applicant or parent of applicant must have employment or volunteer experience in community service. Applicant must be visually impaired. Available to U.S. citizens.

Application Requirements: Application, essay, financial need analysis, references, transcript. *Deadline:* March 31.

Contact: Peggy Elliott, Chairman
National Federation of the Blind
805 Fifth Avenue
Grinnell, IA 50112
Phone: 641-236-3366
E-mail: delliott@pcpartner.net

NATSO FOUNDATION http://www.natsofoundation.org

BILL MOON SCHOLARSHIP
• See page 507

NEVADA POLICE CORPS http://www.nevadapolicecorps.state.nv.us

NEVADA POLICE CORPS SCHOLARSHIP FOR DEPENDENT CHILDREN OF OFFICERS SLAIN IN THE LINE OF DUTY

Scholarships available for dependent children of officers slain in the line of duty. Apply to agency in which parent served. Check Web site for participating states and additional information http://www.ojp.usdoj.gov/opc/ee/

Award: Scholarship for use in freshman, sophomore, junior, or senior years. *Number:* varies. *Amount:* up to $15,000.

Eligibility Requirements: Applicant must be enrolled or expecting to enroll at a two-year or four-year or technical institution or university. Applicant or parent of applicant must have employment or volunteer experience in police/firefighting. Available to U.S. citizens.

Application Requirements: Application. *Deadline:* varies.

Contact: Greg Befort, Director
Nevada Police Corps
WNCC, Cedar Building Room 309-312
2201 West College Parkway
Carson City, NV 89703
Phone: 775-684-8720
Fax: 775-684-8775
E-mail: gbefort@post.state.nv.us

NEW JERSEY HIGHER EDUCATION STUDENT ASSISTANCE AUTHORITY http://www.hesaa.org

LAW ENFORCEMENT OFFICER MEMORIAL SCHOLARSHIP

Scholarships for full-time undergraduate study at approved New Jersey institutions for the dependent children of New Jersey law enforcement officers killed in the line of duty. Value of scholarship established annually.

Award: Scholarship for use in freshman, sophomore, junior, or senior years; renewable. *Number:* 1. *Amount:* varies.

Eligibility Requirements: Applicant must be enrolled or expecting to enroll full-time at a four-year institution or university; resident of New Jersey and studying in New Jersey. Applicant or parent of applicant must have employment or volunteer experience in police/firefighting. Available to U.S. citizens.

Application Requirements: Application. *Deadline:* varies.

Contact: Carol Muka, Assistant Director of Grants and Scholarships
New Jersey Higher Education Student Assistance Authority
PO Box 540
Trenton, NJ 08625
Phone: 800-792-8670
Fax: 609-588-2228

SURVIVOR TUITION BENEFITS PROGRAM

Program will pay the full tuition for eligible applicants attending two and four-year public colleges and universities as either half-time or full-time students. Eligibility for this program is limited to a period of 8 years from the date of death of the member in the case of a surviving spouse, and 8 years following graduation from high school in the case of a child. Deadline: October 1 for Fall and March 1 for Spring.

Award: Scholarship for use in freshman, sophomore, junior, or senior years; renewable. *Number:* varies.

Eligibility Requirements: Applicant must be enrolled or expecting to enroll full or part-time at a two-year or four-year institution or university; resident of New Jersey and studying in New Jersey.

Applicant or parent of applicant must have employment or volunteer experience in police/firefighting. Available to U.S. citizens.

Application Requirements: Application. *Deadline:* varies.

Contact: Carol Muka, Scholarship Coordinator
New Jersey Higher Education Student Assistance Authority
PO Box 540
Trenton, NJ 08625
Phone: 800-792-8670
Fax: 609-588-2228

NEW JERSEY STATE GOLF ASSOCIATION http://www.njsga.org

NEW JERSEY STATE GOLF ASSOCIATION CADDIE SCHOLARSHIP

Applicants for this scholarship must reside in New Jersey, have a minimum 2.5 GPA, and have been for at least one year at a member club of the New Jersey State Golf Association. Scholarship award is based on grades, test scores, references, and financial need. Award renewable for undergraduate use.

Award: Scholarship for use in freshman, sophomore, junior, or senior years; renewable. *Number:* 200. *Amount:* $1500–$3000.

Eligibility Requirements: Applicant must be enrolled or expecting to enroll full-time at a two-year or four-year institution or university and resident of New Jersey. Applicant or parent of applicant must have employment or volunteer experience in private club/caddying. Applicant must have 2.5 GPA or higher. Available to U.S. citizens.

Application Requirements: Application, financial need analysis, references, test scores, transcript. *Deadline:* May 1.

Contact: Education Director
New Jersey State Golf Association
PO Box 6947
Freehold, NJ 07728
Phone: 732-780-4822
Fax: 732-780-4822
E-mail: j.o.petersen@att.net

NEW YORK STATE HIGHER EDUCATION SERVICES CORPORATION http://www.hesc.com/

NEW YORK MEMORIAL SCHOLARSHIPS FOR FAMILIES OF DECEASED POLICE OFFICERS, FIRE FIGHTERS AND PEACE OFFICERS

Renewable scholarship for families of New York police officers, peace officers or firefighters who died in the line of duty. Must be a New York resident pursuing undergraduate study at a SUNY college or university.

Award: Scholarship for use in freshman, sophomore, junior, or senior years; renewable. *Number:* 1. *Amount:* varies.

Eligibility Requirements: Applicant must be enrolled or expecting to enroll full-time at a four-year institution or university; resident of New York and studying in New York. Applicant or parent of applicant must have employment or volunteer experience in police/firefighting. Available to U.S. citizens.

Application Requirements: Application, financial need analysis. *Deadline:* May 1.

Contact: Student Information
New York State Higher Education Services Corporation
99 Washington Avenue, Room 1320
Albany, NY 12255

NORTH CAROLINA BAR ASSOCIATION http://www.ncbar.org

NORTH CAROLINA BAR ASSOCIATION YOUNG LAWYERS DIVISION SCHOLARSHIP

For children of North Carolina law enforcement officers killed or permanently disabled in the line of duty. Must apply for the first time before 27th birthday.

Award: Scholarship for use in freshman, graduate, or postgraduate years; renewable. *Number:* varies. *Amount:* up to $2000.

Eligibility Requirements: Applicant must be age 26 or under; enrolled or expecting to enroll full-time at a two-year or four-year or technical institution or university and resident of North Carolina. Applicant or

North Carolina Bar Association (continued)

parent of applicant must have employment or volunteer experience in police/firefighting. Available to U.S. citizens.

Application Requirements: Application, financial need analysis, photo, test scores, transcript. *Deadline:* April 3.

Contact: Jacquelyn Terrell-Fountain, Assistant Director of Sections, YLD Staff Liaison
North Carolina Bar Association
PO Box 3688
Cary, NC 27519
Phone: 919-677-0561
Fax: 919-677-0761
E-mail: jterrell@ncbar.org

NORTH EAST ROOFING EDUCATIONAL FOUNDATION   http://www.nerca.org

NORTH EAST ROOFING EDUCATIONAL FOUNDATION SCHOLARSHIP
• *See page 508*

NORTHEAST FRESH FOODS ALLIANCE   http://www.neffa.com

NORTHEAST FRESH FOODS ALLIANCE SCHOLARSHIP AWARDS PROGRAM
• *See page 509*

OHIO BOARD OF REGENTS   http://www.regents.state.oh.us

OHIO SAFETY OFFICERS COLLEGE MEMORIAL FUND

Renewable award covering up to full tuition is available to children and surviving spouses of peace officers and fire fighters killed in the line of duty in any state. Children must be under 26 years of age. Must be an Ohio resident and enroll full-time or part-time at an Ohio college or university.

Award: Scholarship for use in freshman, sophomore, junior, or senior years; renewable. *Number:* 50–65. *Amount:* varies.

Eligibility Requirements: Applicant must be age 25 or under; enrolled or expecting to enroll full or part-time at a two-year or four-year institution or university; resident of Ohio and studying in Ohio. Applicant or parent of applicant must have employment or volunteer experience in police/firefighting. Available to U.S. citizens.

Application Requirements: *Deadline:* Continuous.

Contact: Barbara Metheney, Program Administrator
Ohio Board of Regents
30 East Broad Street, 36th Floor
Columbus, OH 43215-3414
Phone: 614-752-9535
Fax: 614-752-5903
E-mail: bmethene@regents.state.oh.us

OREGON STUDENT ASSISTANCE COMMISSION   http://www.osac.state.or.us

A. VICTOR ROSENFELD SCHOLARSHIP
• *See page 532*

ALBINA FUEL COMPANY SCHOLARSHIP
• *See page 532*

CARPENTERS AND JOINERS LOCAL 2130 SCHOLARSHIP

One-time award open to graduating high school seniors in Columbia, Washington, or Yamhill counties, or to college students from households with at least one union member. Preference given to applicants whose legal guardians are rank-and-file members of local carpenter unions. Must have a minimum cumulative 2.5 GPA. Essay required. See Web site for details. (http://www.osac.state.or.us).

Award: Scholarship for use in freshman or sophomore years; not renewable. *Number:* 1. *Amount:* $750.

Eligibility Requirements: Applicant must be enrolled or expecting to enroll at an institution or university and resident of Oregon. Applicant or parent of applicant must have employment or volunteer experience in designated career field. Applicant must have 2.5 GPA or higher. Available to U.S. citizens.

Application Requirements: Application, essay, financial need analysis, transcript, activity chart. *Deadline:* March 1.

Contact: Director of Grant Programs
Oregon Student Assistance Commission
1500 Valley River Drive, Suite 100
Eugene, OR 97401-7020

FORD SONS AND DAUGHTERS OF EMPLOYEES OF ROSEBURG FOREST PRODUCTS COMPANY SCHOLARSHIP
• *See page 533*

GLENN JACKSON SCHOLARS SCHOLARSHIPS (OCF)
• *See page 533*

MC GARRY MACHINE INC. SCHOLARSHIP
• *See page 533*

OREGON AFL-CIO SCHOLARSHIP

One-time award for graduating Oregon high school seniors. Must write essay. Preference given to applicants from union families. Visit Web site (http://www.osac.state.or.us) for details.

Award: Scholarship for use in freshman year; not renewable. *Number:* 4. *Amount:* $1513.

Eligibility Requirements: Applicant must be high school student; planning to enroll or expecting to enroll full or part-time at a two-year or four-year or technical institution or university and resident of Oregon. Applicant or parent of applicant must have employment or volunteer experience in designated career field. Available to U.S. citizens.

Application Requirements: Application, essay, financial need analysis, test scores, transcript, activity chart. *Deadline:* March 1.

Contact: Director of Grant Programs
Oregon Student Assistance Commission
1500 Valley River Drive, Suite 100
Eugene, OR 97401-7020
Phone: 800-452-8807 Ext. 7395

OREGON DUNGENESS CRAB COMMISSION SCHOLARSHIP

One scholarship available to graduating high school senior who is a dependent of licensed Oregon Dungeness Crab fisherman or crew member. One-time award. Identify name of vessel in place of work site.

Award: Scholarship for use in freshman year; not renewable. *Number:* 2. *Amount:* $500.

Eligibility Requirements: Applicant must be high school student; planning to enroll or expecting to enroll at an institution or university and resident of Oregon. Applicant or parent of applicant must have employment or volunteer experience in designated career field. Available to U.S. citizens.

Application Requirements: Application, essay, financial need analysis, transcript, activity chart, name of vessel in place of worksite in membership section. *Deadline:* March 1.

Contact: Oregon Student Assistance Commission
1500 Valley River Drive, Suite 100
Eugene, OR 97401-7020
Phone: 800-452-8807 Ext. 7395

OREGON OCCUPATIONAL SAFETY AND HEALTH DIVISION WORKERS MEMORIAL SCHOLARSHIP

Available to Oregon residents who are the dependents or spouses of an Oregon worker who was killed or permanently disabled on the job. Submit essay of 500 words or less titled "How has the injury or death of your parent or spouse affected or influenced your decision to further your education?" See Web site for more details. (http://www.osac.state.or.us)

Award: Scholarship for use in freshman, sophomore, junior, senior, or graduate years; renewable. *Number:* 1. *Amount:* $4786.

Eligibility Requirements: Applicant must be enrolled or expecting to enroll full-time at a four-year institution or university and resident of Oregon. Applicant or parent of applicant must have employment or volunteer experience in designated career field. Available to U.S. citizens.

Application Requirements: Application, essay, financial need analysis, test scores, transcript, workers compensation claim number. *Deadline:* March 1.

Contact: Director of Grant Programs
Oregon Student Assistance Commission
1500 Valley River Drive, Suite 100
Eugene, OR 97401-7020
Phone: 800-452-8807 Ext. 7395

OREGON SALMON COMMISSION SCHOLARSHIP

One-time award open to graduating high school seniors. Must be a dependent of a licensed Oregon salmon fisherman. Must be a resident of Oregon. Should place name of vessel in place of worksite in membership section of application.

Award: Scholarship for use in freshman year; not renewable. *Number:* 2. *Amount:* $500.

Eligibility Requirements: Applicant must be high school student; planning to enroll or expecting to enroll at an institution or university and resident of Oregon. Applicant or parent of applicant must have employment or volunteer experience in designated career field. Available to U.S. citizens.

Application Requirements: Application, essay, financial need analysis, transcript, activity chart. *Deadline:* March 1.

Contact: Director of Grant Programs
Oregon Student Assistance Commission
1500 Valley River Drive, Suite 100
Eugene, OR 97401-7020
Phone: 800-452-8807 Ext. 7395

OREGON TRAWL COMMISSION SCHOLARSHIP

One-time award for graduating high school seniors and college students who are dependents of licensed Oregon Trawl fishermen or crew. Visit Web site (http://www.osac.state.or.us) for more details.

Award: Scholarship for use in freshman, sophomore, junior, or senior years; renewable. *Number:* 2. *Amount:* $500.

Eligibility Requirements: Applicant must be enrolled or expecting to enroll at an institution or university and resident of Oregon. Applicant or parent of applicant must have employment or volunteer experience in designated career field. Available to U.S. citizens.

Application Requirements: Application, essay, financial need analysis, references, transcript, activity chart. *Deadline:* March 1.

Contact: Director of Grant Programs
Oregon Student Assistance Commission
1500 Valley River Drive, Suite 100
Eugene, OR 97401-7020
Phone: 800-452-8807 Ext. 7395

OREGON TRUCKING ASSOCIATION SCHOLARSHIP

• *See page 534*

PENDLETON POSTAL WORKERS SCHOLARSHIP

One-time award for graduating high school seniors who are children or grandchildren of active, retired or deceased members of Pendleton APWU Local 110 at least one year preceding application deadline. Contact for application requirements and deadlines. Essay required "What has the labor movement accomplished historically for working people?"

Award: Scholarship for use in freshman year; not renewable. *Number:* varies. *Amount:* $500.

Eligibility Requirements: Applicant must be high school student; planning to enroll or expecting to enroll at a four-year institution and resident of Oregon. Applicant or parent of applicant must have employment or volunteer experience in designated career field. Available to U.S. citizens.

Application Requirements: Application, essay, references, transcript, activity chart. *Deadline:* March 1.

Contact: Director of Grant Programs
Oregon Student Assistance Commission
1500 Valley River Drive, Suite 100
Eugene, OR 97401-7020
Phone: 800-452-8807 Ext. 7395

REED'S FUEL AND TRUCKING COMPANY SCHOLARSHIP

• *See page 534*

ROBERT D. FORSTER SCHOLARSHIP

• *See page 534*

ROGER W. EMMONS MEMORIAL SCHOLARSHIP

• *See page 534*

SP NEWSPRINT COMPANY, NEWBERG MILL, EMPLOYEE DEPENDENTS SCHOLARSHIP

• *See page 534*

STIMSON LUMBER COMPANY SCHOLARSHIP

• *See page 535*

TAYLOR MADE LABELS SCHOLARSHIP

• *See page 535*

TEAMSTERS CLYDE C. CROSBY/JOSEPH M. EDGAR MEMORIAL SCHOLARSHIP

• *See page 511*

TEAMSTERS COUNCIL 37 FEDERAL CREDIT UNION SCHOLARSHIP

• *See page 511*

TYKESON FAMILY SCHOLARSHIP

Renewable award available to children aged 23 years and under of full-time employees who have been employed for at least two years prior to March 1 of application year. Companies included are: Bend Cable Communications LLC, Central Oregon Cable Advertising LLC, or Tykeson/Associates Enterprises. Must attend an Oregon college. See Web site for more information. (http://www.osac.state.or.us)

Award: Scholarship for use in freshman, sophomore, junior, or senior years; renewable. *Number:* 1. *Amount:* $2000.

Eligibility Requirements: Applicant must be age 23 or under; enrolled or expecting to enroll at a four-year institution; resident of Oregon and studying in Oregon. Applicant or parent of applicant must have employment or volunteer experience in designated career field. Available to U.S. citizens.

Application Requirements: Application, essay, financial need analysis, references, transcript, activity chart. *Deadline:* March 1.

Contact: Director of Grant Programs
Oregon Student Assistance Commission
1500 Valley River Drive, Suite 100
Eugene, OR 97401-7020
Phone: 800-452-8807 Ext. 7395

WILLETT AND MARGUERITE LAKE SCHOLARSHIP

Scholarship awards children, stepchildren and grandchildren of current employees of Bonita Pioneer Packaging Company who have been employed by the company 2 years as of the March 1 scholarship deadline.

Award: Scholarship for use in freshman, sophomore, junior, senior, or graduate years; renewable. *Number:* varies. *Amount:* $500.

Eligibility Requirements: Applicant must be enrolled or expecting to enroll at an institution or university and resident of Hawaii or Oregon. Applicant or parent of applicant must have employment or volunteer experience in designated career field. Available to U.S. citizens.

Application Requirements: Application, essay, financial need analysis, transcript, activity chart. *Deadline:* March 1.

Contact: Director of Grant Programs
Oregon Student Assistance Commission
1500 Valley River Drive, Suite 100
Eugene, OR 97401-7020
Phone: 800-452-8807 Ext. 7395

WOODARD FAMILY SCHOLARSHIP

• *See page 535*

PENNSYLVANIA BURGLAR AND FIRE ALARM ASSOCIATION
http://www.pbfaa.com

PENNSYLVANIA BURGLAR AND FIRE ALARM ASSOCIATION YOUTH SCHOLARSHIP PROGRAM

Non-renewable scholarships available to sons and daughters of active Pennsylvania police and fire personnel, and volunteer fire department personnel for full-time study at a two-or four-year college, or university. Regional awards of $500 in each of the 5 geographic regions; state awards of $1000 first prize, $500 second prize; national awards of $6500 first place and $3500 second place. Must be a senior in a Pennsylvania high school. Call or email state office for application and information.

Pennsylvania Burglar and Fire Alarm Association (continued)

Award: Scholarship for use in freshman year; not renewable. *Number:* 6–8. *Amount:* $500–$6500.

Eligibility Requirements: Applicant must be high school student; planning to enroll or expecting to enroll full-time at a two-year or four-year institution or university and resident of Pennsylvania. Applicant or parent of applicant must have employment or volunteer experience in police/firefighting. Available to U.S. citizens.

Application Requirements: Application, essay, resume, test scores, transcript. *Deadline:* March 1.

Contact: Dale Eller, Executive Director
Pennsylvania Burglar and Fire Alarm Association
PO Box 8264
Erie, PA 16505-0264
Phone: 814-838-3093
Fax: 814-838-5127
E-mail: info@pbfaa.com

PI LAMBDA THETA, INC. http://www.pilambda.org

NADEEN BURKEHOLDER WILLIAMS MUSIC SCHOLARSHIP

The scholarship provides $1000 to an outstanding K-12 teacher who is pursuing a graduate degree at an accredited college or university and who is either a music education teacher or applies music systematically in teaching another subject. Minimum 3.5 GPA required.

Award: Scholarship for use in freshman, sophomore, junior, senior, or graduate years; not renewable. *Number:* 1–5. *Amount:* $1000.

Eligibility Requirements: Applicant must be enrolled or expecting to enroll full or part-time at a four-year institution or university and must have an interest in music. Applicant or parent of applicant must have employment or volunteer experience in teaching. Applicant must have 3.5 GPA or higher. Available to U.S. and non-U.S. citizens.

Application Requirements: Application, essay, portfolio, resume, references. *Deadline:* February 10.

Contact: Pam Todd, Manager, Member Services
Pi Lambda Theta, Inc.
4101 East 3rd Street, PO Box 6626
Bloomington, IN 47407-6626
Phone: 812-339-3411
Fax: 812-339-3462
E-mail: endowment@pilambda.org

PROCTER & GAMBLE FUND http://www.pg.com

PROCTER & GAMBLE FUND SCHOLARSHIP COMPETITION FOR EMPLOYEES' CHILDREN
• *See page 535*

PROJECT BEST SCHOLARSHIP FUND http://www.projectbest.com

PROJECT BEST SCHOLARSHIP
• *See page 513*

RECORDING FOR THE BLIND & DYSLEXIC http://www.rfbd.org

MARION HUBER LEARNING THROUGH LISTENING AWARDS
• *See page 513*

MARY P. OENSLAGER SCHOLASTIC ACHIEVEMENT AWARDS
• *See page 513*

SALVATORE TADDONIO FAMILY FOUNDATION

TADDONIO SCHOLARSHIP

Award is given to students who are residents of Colorado and attend Colorado institutions. Minimum 3.0 GPA required. Must submit evidence of community service.

Award: Scholarship for use in freshman, sophomore, junior, or senior years; renewable. *Number:* 6–10. *Amount:* $500–$1500.

Eligibility Requirements: Applicant must be enrolled or expecting to enroll full-time at a two-year or four-year institution or university; resident of Colorado and studying in Colorado. Applicant or parent of

applicant must have employment or volunteer experience in community service. Applicant must have 3.0 GPA or higher. Available to U.S. citizens.

Application Requirements: Application, essay, transcript, record of volunteer work. *Deadline:* varies.

Contact: Samuel Cheris, Trustee
Salvatore Taddonio Family Foundation
6161 South Syracuse Way, Suite 100
Greenwood Village, CO 80111-4707
Phone: 303-632-7212
E-mail: cheriss@bwn.net

SCOTTISH RITE CHARITABLE FOUNDATION OF CANADA http://www.srcf.ca

SCOTTISH RITE CHARITABLE FOUNDATION COLLEGE BURSARIES

Up to $2000 award for full-time students enrolled in their second or third year of study at a recognized community college. Applicants must be in a program leading to certification in the field of intellectual impairment. Must submit summary of past involvement in this field. Must be a Canadian citizen. Bursary is available to one qualified student from each province and territory. Write or visit Web site for additional details.

Award: Grant for use in freshman, sophomore, junior, or senior years; not renewable. *Number:* up to 13. *Amount:* up to $1486.

Eligibility Requirements: Applicant must be Canadian citizen; enrolled or expecting to enroll full-time at a two-year or four-year institution; resident of Alberta, British Columbia, Manitoba, New Brunswick, Newfoundland, North West Territories, Nova Scotia, Ontario, Prince Edward Island, Quebec, Saskatchewan, or Yukon and studying in Alberta, British Columbia, Manitoba, New Brunswick, Newfoundland, North West Territories, Nova Scotia, Ontario, Prince Edward Island, Quebec, Saskatchewan, or Yukon. Applicant or parent of applicant must have employment or volunteer experience in helping handicapped.

Application Requirements: Application, essay, resume, references, transcript. *Deadline:* June 30.

Contact: The Awards Committee, Scottish Rite Charitable Foundation of Canada
Scottish Rite Charitable Foundation of Canada
4 Queen Street South
Hamilton, ON L8P 3R3
Canada
Phone: 905-522-0033
Fax: 905-522-3716

SCREEN ACTORS GUILD FOUNDATION http://www.sagfoundation.org/

SCREEN ACTORS GUILD FOUNDATION/JOHN L. DALES SCHOLARSHIP (TRANSITIONAL)
• *See page 514*

SERVICE EMPLOYEES INTERNATIONAL UNION - CALIFORNIA STATE COUNCIL OF SERVICE EMPLOYEES http://www.seiuca.org

CHARLES HARDY MEMORIAL SCHOLARSHIP AWARDS
• *See page 514*

SID RICHARDSON MEMORIAL FUND http://www.sidrichardson.org

SID RICHARDSON MEMORIAL FUND

Applicants Must be children or grandchildren of persons presently employed (or retired) at a Sid Bass/Richardson company or its subsidiaries. Employee must have a minimum of three years of full-time employment at one of the following companies: Barbnet Investment Co., Perry R. Bass, Inc., Bass Enterprises Production Company, Richardson Energy Marketing Services, Sid Richardson Carbon Company, Sid Richardson Energy Services, Sid Richardson Energy Services-JAL, Sid W. Richardson Foundation.

Award: Scholarship for use in freshman, sophomore, junior, senior, graduate, or postgraduate years; not renewable. *Number:* 50–60. *Amount:* $500–$7000.

Eligibility Requirements: Applicant must be enrolled or expecting to enroll full-time at a two-year or four-year or technical institution or university. Applicant or parent of applicant must have employment or volunteer experience in designated career field. Available to U.S. and non-U.S. citizens.

Application Requirements: Application, essay, financial need analysis, resume, references, test scores, transcript. *Deadline:* March 31.

Contact: Valleau Wilkie Jr, Executive Vice-President
Sid Richardson Memorial Fund
Sid W. Richardson Foundation
309 Main Street
Fort Worth, TX 76102
Phone: 817-336-0494
Fax: 817-332-2176

STATE FARM COMPANIES/YOUTH SERVICE AMERICA   http://www.ysa.org/awards/

HARRIS WOFFORD AWARDS

Awards recognize extraordinary achievements in three categories: Youth (ages 5-25), Organization (nonprofit, corporate, foundation), and Media (organization or individual) for actively contributing towards, "making service and service-learning the common expectation and common experience of every young person."

Award: Grant for use in freshman, sophomore, junior, senior, graduate, or postgraduate years. *Amount:* $500.

Eligibility Requirements: Applicant must be enrolled or expecting to enroll at a two-year or four-year or technical institution or university. Applicant or parent of applicant must have employment or volunteer experience in community service. Available to U.S. citizens.

Application Requirements: Application. *Deadline:* October 12.

Contact:
Phone: 202-296-2992 Ext. 11
E-mail: woffordawards@ysa.org

TAILHOOK EDUCATIONAL FOUNDATION   http://www.tailhook.org

TAILHOOK EDUCATIONAL FOUNDATION SCHOLARSHIP

Applicant must be a high school graduate and the natural or adopted son or daughter of a current or former Naval Aviator, Naval Flight Officer, or Naval Air crewman. Individuals or children of individuals serving or having served on board a U.S. Navy Aircraft Carrier in ship's company or the Air Wing also eligible.

Award: Scholarship for use in freshman, sophomore, junior, or senior years; renewable. *Number:* 20. *Amount:* up to $2000.

Eligibility Requirements: Applicant must be enrolled or expecting to enroll full-time at a two-year or four-year institution or university. Applicant or parent of applicant must have employment or volunteer experience in designated career field. Applicant must have 3.0 GPA or higher. Available to U.S. and non-U.S. citizens. Applicant or parent must meet one or more of the following requirements: Coast Guard, Marine Corps, or Navy experience; retired from active duty; disabled or killed as a result of military service; prisoner of war; or missing in action.

Application Requirements: Application, driver's license, essay, references, self-addressed stamped envelope, test scores, transcript, proof of eligibility. *Deadline:* March 15.

Contact: Jim Carroll, Administrative Officer
Tailhook Educational Foundation
PO Box 26626
San Diego, CA 92196
Phone: 800-269-8267
Fax: 858-578-8839
E-mail: thookassn@aol.com

TENNESSEE STUDENT ASSISTANCE CORPORATION   http://www.state.tn.us/tsac

DEPENDENT CHILDREN SCHOLARSHIP PROGRAM

Scholarship aid for Tennessee residents who are dependent children of a Tennessee law enforcement officer, fireman, or an emergency medical service technician who has been killed or totally and permanently disabled while performing duties within the scope of such employment. The scholarship awarded to full-time undergraduate students for a maximum of four academic years or the period required for the completion of the program of study.

Award: Scholarship for use in freshman, sophomore, junior, or senior years. *Number:* 1.

Eligibility Requirements: Applicant must be enrolled or expecting to enroll at a four-year institution or university and resident of Tennessee. Applicant or parent of applicant must have employment or volunteer experience in police/firefighting. Available to U.S. citizens.

Application Requirements: Application, FAFSA. *Deadline:* July 15.

Contact: Naomi Derryberry, Grant and Scholarship Administrator
Tennessee Student Assistance Corporation
404 James Robertson Parkway, Suite 1950
Parkway Towers
Nashville, TN 37243-0820
Phone: 800-342-1663
Fax: 615-741-6101
E-mail: tsac.aidinfo@state.tn.us

THE HITACHI FOUNDATION   http://www.hitachifoundation.org

YOSHIYAMA AWARD FOR EXEMPLARY SERVICE TO THE COMMUNITY

Award for high school seniors based on their community service activities. Must be nominated by someone familiar with their service. Submit nomination form, letter of nomination, and two supporting letters by April 1.

Award: Prize for use in freshman year; not renewable. *Number:* 8–12. *Amount:* $5000.

Eligibility Requirements: Applicant must be high school student; planning to enroll or expecting to enroll full-time at an institution or university and single. Applicant or parent of applicant must have employment or volunteer experience in community service. Available to U.S. citizens.

Application Requirements: References, nomination form, letter of nomination. *Deadline:* April 1.

Contact: Assistant Coordinator
The Hitachi Foundation
1509 22nd Street, NW
Washington, DC 20037-1098
Phone: 202-457-0588
Fax: 202-296-1098

TUITION EXCHANGE, INC.   http://www.tuitionexchange.org

TUITION EXCHANGE SCHOLARSHIPS

The Tuition Exchange is an association of 540 colleges and universities awarding over 3,700 full or substantial scholarships each year for children and other family members of faculty and staff employed at participating institutions. Application procedures and deadlines vary per school. Contact Tuition Exchange Liaison Officer at home institution for details. See Web site for complete list of participating institutions: http://www.tuitionexchange.org

Award: Scholarship for use in freshman, sophomore, junior, senior, graduate, or postgraduate years; renewable. *Number:* 3400–4000. *Amount:* $10,000–$20,800.

Eligibility Requirements: Applicant must be enrolled or expecting to enroll full or part-time at a two-year or four-year institution or university. Applicant or parent of applicant must have employment or volunteer experience in designated career field. Available to U.S. and non-U.S. citizens.

Application Requirements: Application. *Deadline:* varies.

Contact: Robert L. Norris, President
Tuition Exchange, Inc.
1743 Connecticut Avenue, NW
Washington, DC 20009-1108
Phone: 202-518-0135
Fax: 202-518-0137
E-mail: rnorris@tuitionexchange.org

TWO TEN FOOTWEAR FOUNDATION
http://www.twoten.org

TWO/TEN INTERNATIONAL FOOTWEAR FOUNDATION SCHOLARSHIP

Renewable, merit and need-based award available to students who have 500 hours work experience in footwear, leather, or allied industries during year of application, or have a parent employed in one of these fields for at least two years. Must have proof of employment and maintain 2.0 GPA.

Award: Scholarship for use in freshman, sophomore, junior, or senior years; renewable. *Number:* 200–250. *Amount:* $200–$3000.

Eligibility Requirements: Applicant must be enrolled or expecting to enroll full or part-time at a two-year or four-year or technical institution or university. Applicant or parent of applicant must have employment or volunteer experience in leather/footwear. Available to U.S. citizens.

Application Requirements: Application, essay, financial need analysis, references, transcript. *Deadline:* January 1.

Contact: Catherine Nelson, Scholarship Director
Two Ten Footwear Foundation
1466 Main Street
Waltham, MA 02451-1623
Phone: 781-736-1503
Fax: 781-736-1555
E-mail: scholarship@twoten.org

UNITED STATES SUBMARINE VETERANS, INC.
http://ussvcf.org/scolyrs.htm

UNITED STATES SUBMARINE VETERANS INC. NATIONAL SCHOLARSHIP PROGRAM

Sponsor must be a "Qualified Submarine" member in good standing as a Base Member or Member-at-Large (MAL). Program is awarded to those who have financial needs, 2.5 GPA and essay. Open to son, daughter, stepchildren, grandchildren of qualified member. Can apply each year until 23rd birthday. Applicants must be between the ages of 17-23 and must be unmarried.

Award: Scholarship for use in freshman, sophomore, junior, or senior years; not renewable. *Number:* 2–18. *Amount:* $750–$1500.

Eligibility Requirements: Applicant must be age 17-23; enrolled or expecting to enroll full-time at a two-year or four-year or technical institution and single. Applicant or parent of applicant must have employment or volunteer experience in seafaring. Applicant must have 2.5 GPA or higher. Available to U.S. citizens. Applicant or parent must meet one or more of the following requirements: Navy experience; retired from active duty; disabled or killed as a result of military service; prisoner of war; or missing in action.

Application Requirements: Application, essay, financial need analysis, references, test scores, transcript. *Deadline:* April 15.

Contact: Paul William Orstad, USSVI National Scholarship Chairman
United States Submarine Veterans, Inc.
30 Surrey Lane
Norwich, CT 06369-6541
Phone: 860-889-4750
Fax: 860-334-6457
E-mail: hogan343@aol.com

WAL-MART FOUNDATION
http://www.walmartfoundation.org

WAL-MART ASSOCIATE SCHOLARSHIPS
• See page 536

WAL-MART HIGHER REACH SCHOLARSHIP
• See page 536

WESTERN GOLF ASSOCIATION-EVANS SCHOLARS FOUNDATION
http://www.evansscholarsfoundation.com

CHICK EVANS CADDIE SCHOLARSHIP

Full tuition and housing awards to high school seniors who have worked at least two years as caddies at a Western Golf Association member club. Must demonstrate need, have outstanding character, maintain a B average in college preparation classes and rank in top 25% of graduating class. Apply after July 15th following junior year. Applications must be received by September 30.

Award: Scholarship for use in freshman, sophomore, junior, or senior years; renewable. *Number:* 200. *Amount:* varies.

Eligibility Requirements: Applicant must be high school student; planning to enroll or expecting to enroll full-time at a four-year institution and studying in Colorado, Illinois, Indiana, Kansas, Michigan, Minnesota, Missouri, Ohio, Oregon, Pennsylvania, Washington, or Wisconsin. Applicant or parent of applicant must have employment or volunteer experience in private club/caddying. Applicant must have 3.5 GPA or higher. Available to U.S. citizens.

Application Requirements: Application, essay, financial need analysis, interview, references, test scores, transcript. *Deadline:* September 30.

Contact: Scholarship Committee
Western Golf Association-Evans Scholars Foundation
One Briar Road
Golf, IL 60029
Phone: 847-724-4600
Fax: 847-724-7133
E-mail: evansscholars@wgaesf.com

ZONTA INTERNATIONAL FOUNDATION
http://www.zonta.org

YOUNG WOMEN IN PUBLIC AFFAIRS AWARD

One-time award for pre-college women with a commitment to the volunteer sector and evidence of volunteer leadership achievements. Must be 16-20 years of age with a career interest in public affairs, public policy and community organizations. Further information and application available at Web site http://www.zonta.org.

Award: Scholarship for use in freshman year; not renewable. *Number:* varies. *Amount:* $500–$1000.

Eligibility Requirements: Applicant must be high school student; age 16-20; planning to enroll or expecting to enroll at a four-year institution or university and female. Applicant or parent of applicant must have employment or volunteer experience in community service. Available to U.S. citizens.

Application Requirements: Application, references. *Deadline:* varies.

Contact: Ana Ubides, Foundation Assistant
Zonta International Foundation
557 West Randolph Street
Chicago, IL 60661-2206
Phone: 312-930-5848
Fax: 312-930-0951
E-mail: zontafdtn@zonta.org

IMPAIRMENT

ALEXANDER GRAHAM BELL ASSOCIATION FOR THE DEAF AND HARD OF HEARING
http://www.agbell.org

ALLIE RANEY HUNT SCHOLARSHIP

Award available to undergraduate born with profound or severe hearing loss (of at least 60 dB), or who experienced hearing loss before acquiring language. Must be accepted or enrolled in a mainstream college or university as a full-time student and must use spoken communication as primary mode of communication. Must submit audiogram and letters of recommendation. Application is available at Web site: http://www.agbell.org

Award: Scholarship for use in freshman, sophomore, junior, or senior years; not renewable. *Number:* 1. *Amount:* $2000.

Eligibility Requirements: Applicant must be enrolled or expecting to enroll full-time at a four-year institution or university. Applicant must be hearing impaired. Available to U.S. citizens.

Application Requirements: Application, references, transcript, current audiological report. *Deadline:* April 15.

Contact: Financial Aid Coordinator
Alexander Graham Bell Association for the Deaf and Hard of Hearing
3417 Volta Place, NW
Washington, DC 20007-2778
E-mail: financialaid@agbell.org

BENNION FAMILY SCHOLARSHIP

Award available to undergraduate born with profound or severe hearing loss (of at least 60 dB), or who experienced hearing loss before acquiring language. Must be accepted or enrolled in a mainstream college or university as a full-time student and must use spoken communication as primary mode of communication. Must submit audiogram and letters of recommendation. Application is available at Web site: http://www.agbell.org

Award: Scholarship for use in freshman, sophomore, junior, or senior years; not renewable. *Number:* 1. *Amount:* $2000.

Eligibility Requirements: Applicant must be enrolled or expecting to enroll full-time at a four-year institution or university. Applicant must be hearing impaired. Available to U.S. citizens.

Application Requirements: Application, references, transcript, current audiological report. *Deadline:* April 15.

Contact: Financial Aid Coordinator
Alexander Graham Bell Association for the Deaf and Hard of Hearing
3417 Volta Place, NW
Washington, DC 20007-2778
E-mail: financialaid@agbell.org

DEAF AND HARD OF HEARING SECTION SCHOLARSHIP FUND

Award available to undergraduate born with profound or severe hearing loss (of at least 60 dB), or who experienced hearing loss before acquiring language. Must be accepted or enrolled in a college or university that primarily enrolls students with normal hearing as a full-time student and must use spoken communication as primary mode of communication. Must be member in good standing of AG Bell and member of the DHHS. Must submit audiogram and letters of recommendation. Application is available at Web site: http://www.agbell.org

Award: Scholarship for use in freshman, sophomore, or junior years; not renewable. *Number:* 2. *Amount:* $1000.

Eligibility Requirements: Applicant must be enrolled or expecting to enroll full-time at a four-year institution or university. Applicant must be hearing impaired. Available to U.S. citizens.

Application Requirements: Application, references, transcript, current audiological report. *Deadline:* April 15.

Contact: Financial Aid Coordinator
Alexander Graham Bell Association for the Deaf and Hard of Hearing
3417 Volta Place, NW
Washington, DC 20007-2778
E-mail: financialaid@agbell.org

ELSIE M. BELL GROSVENOR SCHOLARSHIP

Award available to undergraduate born with profound or severe hearing loss (of at least 60 dB), or who experienced hearing loss before acquiring language. Must be accepted or enrolled in a mainstream college or university in the Washington, D.C. area as a full-time student and must use spoken communication as primary mode of communication. Must submit audiogram and letters of recommendation. Application is available at Web site: http://www.agbell.org

Award: Scholarship for use in freshman, sophomore, junior, or senior years; not renewable. *Number:* 1. *Amount:* $2000.

Eligibility Requirements: Applicant must be enrolled or expecting to enroll full-time at a four-year institution or university and resident of District of Columbia. Applicant must be hearing impaired. Available to U.S. citizens.

Application Requirements: Application, references, transcript, current audiological report. *Deadline:* April 15.

Contact: Financial Aid Coordinator
Alexander Graham Bell Association for the Deaf and Hard of Hearing
3417 Volta Place, NW
Washington, DC 20007-2778
E-mail: financialaid@agbell.org

FEDERATION OF JEWISH WOMEN'S ORGANIZATION SCHOLARSHIP

Award available to undergraduate born with profound or severe hearing loss (of at least 60 dB), or who experienced hearing loss before acquiring language. Must be accepted or enrolled in a mainstream college or university as a full-time student and must use spoken communication as primary mode of communication. Must submit audiogram and letters of recommendation. Application is available at Web site: http://www.agbell.org

Award: Scholarship for use in freshman, sophomore, junior, or senior years; not renewable. *Number:* 1. *Amount:* $2000.

Eligibility Requirements: Applicant must be enrolled or expecting to enroll full-time at a four-year institution or university. Applicant must be hearing impaired. Available to U.S. citizens.

Application Requirements: Application, references, transcript, current audiological report. *Deadline:* April 15.

Contact: Financial Aid Coordinator
Alexander Graham Bell Association for the Deaf and Hard of Hearing
3417 Volta Place, NW
Washington, DC 20007-2778
E-mail: financialaid@agbell.org

LADIES AUXILIARY NATIONAL RURAL LETTER CARRIERS SCHOLARSHIP

Award available to undergraduate born with profound or severe hearing loss (of at least 60 dB), or who experienced hearing loss before acquiring language. Must be accepted or enrolled in a mainstream college or university as a full-time student and must use spoken communication as primary mode of communication. Must submit audiogram and letters of recommendation. Application is available at Web site: http://www.agbell.org

Award: Scholarship for use in freshman, sophomore, junior, or senior years; not renewable. *Number:* 1. *Amount:* $2000.

Eligibility Requirements: Applicant must be enrolled or expecting to enroll full-time at a four-year institution or university. Applicant must be hearing impaired. Available to U.S. citizens.

Application Requirements: Application, references, transcript, current audiological report. *Deadline:* April 15.

Contact: Financial Aid Coordinator
Alexander Graham Bell Association for the Deaf and Hard of Hearing
3417 Volta Place, NW
Washington, DC 20007-2778
E-mail: financialaid@agbell.org

LUCILLE B. ABT SCHOLARSHIP

Award available to undergraduate born with profound or severe hearing loss (of at least 60 dB), or who experienced hearing loss before acquiring language. Must use speech or speech reading as a primary mode of communication and be accepted or enrolled full-time in a college or university that primarily enrolls students with normal hearing. Must submit audiogram and letters of recommendation. Application is available at Web site: http://www.agbell.org

Award: Scholarship for use in freshman, sophomore, junior, or senior years; not renewable. *Number:* 10. *Amount:* $5000.

Eligibility Requirements: Applicant must be enrolled or expecting to enroll full-time at a four-year institution or university. Applicant must be hearing impaired. Available to U.S. citizens.

Application Requirements: Application, references, transcript, current audiological report. *Deadline:* April 15.

Contact: Financial Aid Coordinator
Alexander Graham Bell Association for the Deaf and Hard of Hearing
3417 Volta Place, NW
Washington, DC 20007-2778
E-mail: financialaid@agbell.org

ROBERT H. WEITBRECHT SCHOLARSHIP

Award available to undergraduate born with profound or severe hearing loss (of at least 60 dB), or who experienced hearing loss before acquiring language.

Alexander Graham Bell Association for the Deaf and Hard of Hearing (continued)

Must use speech or speech reading as a primary mode of communication and be accepted or enrolled full-time in a college or university that primarily enrolls students with normal hearing. Priority given to those studying engineering or science. Must submit audiogram and letters of recommendation. Application is available at Web site: http://www.agbell.org

Award: Scholarship for use in freshman, sophomore, junior, or senior years; not renewable. *Number:* 1. *Amount:* $2000.

Eligibility Requirements: Applicant must be enrolled or expecting to enroll full-time at a four-year institution or university. Applicant must be hearing impaired. Available to U.S. citizens.

Application Requirements: Application, references, transcript, current audiological report. *Deadline:* April 15.

Contact: Financial Aid Coordinator
Alexander Graham Bell Association for the Deaf and Hard of Hearing
3417 Volta Place, NW
Washington, DC 20007-2778
E-mail: financialaid@agbell.org

SAMUEL M. AND GERTRUDE G. LEVY SCHOLARSHIP FUND

Award available to undergraduate born with profound or severe hearing loss (of at least 60 dB), or who experienced hearing loss before acquiring language. Must use speech or speech reading as a primary mode of communication and be accepted or enrolled full-time in a college or university that primarily enrolls students with normal hearing. Must submit audiogram and letters of recommendation. Application is available at Web site: http://www.agbell.org

Award: Scholarship for use in freshman, sophomore, junior, or senior years; not renewable. *Number:* 1. *Amount:* $2000.

Eligibility Requirements: Applicant must be enrolled or expecting to enroll full-time at a four-year institution or university. Applicant must be hearing impaired. Available to U.S. citizens.

Application Requirements: Application, references, transcript, current audiological report. *Deadline:* April 15.

Contact: Financial Aid Coordinator
Alexander Graham Bell Association for the Deaf and Hard of Hearing
3417 Volta Place, NW
Washington, DC 20007-2778
E-mail: financialaid@agbell.org

VOLTA SCHOLARSHIP FUND

Award available to undergraduate born with profound or severe hearing loss (of at least 60 dB), or who experienced hearing loss before acquiring language. Must use speech or speech reading as a primary mode of communication and be accepted or enrolled full-time in a college or university that primarily enrolls students with normal hearing. Must submit audiogram and letters of recommendation. Application is available at Web site: http://www.agbell.org

Award: Scholarship for use in freshman, sophomore, junior, or senior years; not renewable. *Number:* 1. *Amount:* $2000.

Eligibility Requirements: Applicant must be enrolled or expecting to enroll full-time at a four-year institution or university. Applicant must be hearing impaired. Available to U.S. citizens.

Application Requirements: Application, references, transcript, current audiological report. *Deadline:* April 15.

Contact: Financial Aid Coordinator
Alexander Graham Bell Association for the Deaf and Hard of Hearing
3417 Volta Place, NW
Washington, DC 20007-2778
E-mail: financialaid@agbell.org

WALTER W. AND THELMA C. HISSEY COLLEGE SCHOLARSHIP FUND

Award available to undergraduate or graduate student born with profound or severe hearing loss (of at least 60 dB), or who experienced hearing loss before acquiring language. Must use speech or speech reading as a primary mode of communication and be accepted or enrolled full-time in a college or university that primarily enrolls students with normal hearing. Must submit audiogram and letters of recommendation. Application is available at Web site: http://www.agbell.org

Award: Scholarship for use in freshman, sophomore, junior, senior, or graduate years; not renewable. *Number:* 2. *Amount:* $5000.

Eligibility Requirements: Applicant must be enrolled or expecting to enroll full-time at a four-year institution or university. Applicant must be hearing impaired. Available to U.S. citizens.

Application Requirements: Application, references, transcript, current audiological report. *Deadline:* April 15.

Contact: Financial Aid Coordinator
Alexander Graham Bell Association for the Deaf and Hard of Hearing
3417 Volta Place, NW
Washington, DC 20007-2778
E-mail: financialaid@agbell.org

AMERICAN ACADEMY OF ALLERGY, ASTHMA AND IMMUNOLOGY
http://www.aaaai.org

AWARD OF EXCELLENCE ASTHMA SCHOLARSHIP PROGRAM

One-time award to high school seniors with asthma who are furthering their education in a postsecondary school. Must demonstrate academic excellence. Must be a U.S. citizen. Application deadline generally the first week of January. Check Web site for updated information. http://www.aaaai.org.

Award: Scholarship for use in freshman year; not renewable. *Number:* 56. *Amount:* $100–$1000.

Eligibility Requirements: Applicant must be high school student and planning to enroll or expecting to enroll full-time at a two-year or four-year or technical institution or university. Applicant must be physically disabled. Available to U.S. and Canadian citizens.

Application Requirements: Application, essay, references, transcript, only online applications will be accepted. *Deadline:* varies.

Contact: John Augustyniak
American Academy of Allergy, Asthma and Immunology
555 East Wells Street, Suite 1100
Milwaukee, WI 53202-3823
Phone: 414-272-6071
Fax: 414-272-6070
E-mail: jaugustyniak@aaaai.org

AMERICAN COUNCIL OF THE BLIND
http://www.acb.org

AMERICAN COUNCIL OF THE BLIND SCHOLARSHIPS

Merit-based award available to undergraduate, graduate, vocational or technical students who are legally blind in both eyes. Submit certificate of legal blindness and proof of acceptance at an accredited postsecondary institution.

Award: Scholarship for use in freshman, sophomore, junior, senior, or graduate years; renewable. *Number:* 26. *Amount:* $500–$3000.

Eligibility Requirements: Applicant must be enrolled or expecting to enroll full-time at a four-year or technical institution or university. Applicant must be visually impaired. Applicant must have 3.5 GPA or higher. Available to U.S. citizens.

Application Requirements: Application, autobiography, essay, references, transcript, evidence of legal blindness. *Deadline:* March 1.

Contact: Terry Pacheco, Affiliate and Membership Services
American Council of the Blind
1155 15th Street, NW, Suite 1004
Washington, DC 20005
Phone: 202-467-5081
Fax: 202-467-5085
E-mail: info@acb.org

AMERICAN FOUNDATION FOR THE BLIND
http://www.afb.org/scholarships.asp

FERDINAND TORRES SCHOLARSHIP

The Ferdinand Torres Scholarship provides one (1) scholarship of $1,500 to a full-time undergraduate or graduate student who presents evidence of economic need. To be eligible the applicant must reside in the U.S., but need not be a citizen of the U.S. Preference will be given to applicants residing in the New York City metropolitan area and new immigrants to the U.S. For additional information and application requirements, visit: www.afb.org/scholarships.asp

Award: Scholarship for use in freshman, sophomore, junior, or senior years; not renewable. *Number:* 1. *Amount:* up to $1500.

Eligibility Requirements: Applicant must be enrolled or expecting to enroll full-time at a two-year or four-year institution or university. Applicant must be visually impaired. Available to U.S. and non-U.S. citizens.

Application Requirements: Application, essay, financial need analysis, references, transcript, proof of acceptance in an accredited full-time undergraduate or graduate program, evidence of economic need, proof of legal blindness. *Deadline:* March 31.

Contact: Information Center
American Foundation for the Blind
American Foundation for the Blind Scholarship Committee, 11
Penn Plaza, Suite 300
New York, NY 10001
Phone: 212-502-7661
Fax: 212-502-7771
E-mail: afbinfo@afb.net

ASSOCIATION FOR EDUCATION AND REHABILITATION OF THE BLIND AND VISUALLY IMPAIRED
http://www.aerbvi.org

WILLIAM AND DOROTHY FERREL SCHOLARSHIP

Nonrenewable scholarship given in even years for postsecondary education leading to career in services for blind or visually impaired. Applicant must submit proof of legal blindness or visual field impairment of 20% or less. Refer to Web site for details and application: http://www.aerbui.org.

Award: Scholarship for use in freshman, sophomore, junior, senior, graduate, or postgraduate years; not renewable. *Number:* 2. *Amount:* $500.

Eligibility Requirements: Applicant must be enrolled or expecting to enroll at a two-year or four-year institution or university. Applicant must be visually impaired. Available to U.S. citizens.

Application Requirements: Application. *Deadline:* March 15.

Contact: Barbara Sherr
Association for Education and Rehabilitation of the Blind and
Visually Impaired
1703 North Beauregard Street, Suite 440
Alexandria, VA 22311-1717
Phone: 703-671-4500 Ext. 201
E-mail: bsherr@aerbvi.org

ASSOCIATION OF BLIND CITIZENS
http://www.blindcitizens.org

REGGIE JOHNSON MEMORIAL SCHOLARSHIP

Award for high school or college student who is legally blind. High school or college transcript, certificate of legal blindness, or a letter from your opthalmologist required. Must submit two letters of reference and a disk copy of your biographical sketch.

Award: Scholarship for use in freshman, sophomore, junior, senior, or graduate years. *Amount:* $1000–$2000.

Eligibility Requirements: Applicant must be enrolled or expecting to enroll full-time at a four-year institution or university. Applicant must be visually impaired. Available to U.S. citizens.

Application Requirements: Application, autobiography, references, transcript, certificate of legal blindness or a letter from an ophthalmologist. *Deadline:* April 15.

Contact: John Oliveira, President
Association of Blind Citizens
PO Box 246
Holbrook, MA 02343
Phone: 781-961-1023
Fax: 781-961-0004
E-mail: scholarship@blindcitizens.org

SCHOLARSHIP PROGRAM FOR THE BLIND AND VISUALLY IMPAIRED

One-time award provides assistance to blind and visually impaired students. Awards can be applied to offset tuition or for blindness-related expenses. Association offers eleven $1000 scholarships, three $2000 scholarships, and one $3000 scholarship. Visit http://www.blindcitizens.org and follow instructions to apply online. Application deadline is April 15.

Award: Scholarship for use in freshman, sophomore, junior, senior, graduate, or postgraduate years; not renewable. *Number:* up to 15. *Amount:* $1000–$3000.

Eligibility Requirements: Applicant must be enrolled or expecting to enroll full or part-time at a two-year or four-year or technical institution or university. Applicant must be visually impaired. Available to U.S. citizens.

Application Requirements: Application, autobiography, references, transcript, medical certificate of blindness. *Deadline:* April 15.

Contact: Association of Blind Citizens
PO Box 246
Holbrook, MA 02343
Phone: 781-961-1023
Fax: 781-961-0004
E-mail: scholarship@assocofblindcitizens.org

ASTHMA AND ALLERGY FOUNDATION OF AMERICA (AAFA) GREATER KANSAS CITY CHAPTER
http://www.aafakc.org

BERRI MITCHEL MEMORIAL SCHOLARSHIP

The Berri Mitchel Memorial Scholarship provides four scholarships to greater Kansas City area high school seniors who have a history of asthma, have succeeded academically, and have shown an interest in their school and community. Application deadline is March 1.

Award: Scholarship for use in freshman year; not renewable. *Number:* 4. *Amount:* $1000.

Eligibility Requirements: Applicant must be high school student; planning to enroll or expecting to enroll full or part-time at a two-year or technical institution and resident of Kansas or Missouri. Applicant must be physically disabled. Available to U.S. citizens.

Application Requirements: Application, essay, references, transcript. *Deadline:* March 1.

Contact: Michelle Cook, Director of Community Education
Asthma and Allergy Foundation of America (AAFA) Greater
Kansas City Chapter
9140 Ward Parkway, Suite 120
Kansas City, MO 64114
Phone: 816-333-6608
Fax: 816-333-6684
E-mail: info@aafakc.org

CALIFORNIA COUNCIL OF THE BLIND
http://www.ccbnet.org

CALIFORNIA COUNCIL OF THE BLIND SCHOLARSHIPS

Scholarships available to blind student applicants who are California residents entering or continuing studies at an accredited California college, university, or vocational training school. Must be a full-time student registered for at least twelve units for the entire academic year. Applications must be typed and all blanks must be filled in to be considered for scholarship. Applications available at Web site (http://www.ccbnet.org.)

Award: Scholarship for use in freshman, sophomore, junior, senior, graduate, or postgraduate years; not renewable. *Number:* varies. *Amount:* $375–$2500.

Eligibility Requirements: Applicant must be enrolled or expecting to enroll full-time at a two-year or four-year or technical institution or university and resident of California. Applicant must be visually impaired. Available to U.S. citizens.

Application Requirements: Application, financial need analysis, interview, references, transcript, proof of blindness from a doctor or rehabilitation agency. *Deadline:* June 15.

Contact: Colette Davis, Scholarship Chair
California Council of the Blind
2879 East Alden Place
Anaheim, CA 92806
Phone: 714-630-8098
Fax: 714-666-2494

CHAIRSCHOLARS FOUNDATION, INC.
http://www.chairscholars.org

CHAIRSCHOLARS FOUNDATION, INC. SCHOLARSHIPS
• See page 539

CHRISTIAN RECORD SERVICES, INC.
http://www.christianrecord.org

CHRISTIAN RECORD SERVICES INC. SCHOLARSHIPS

One-time award for legally blind or blind college undergraduates. Submit application, essay-autobiography, photo, references, and financial information by April 1.

Award: Scholarship for use in freshman, sophomore, junior, or senior years; not renewable. *Number:* 7–15. *Amount:* $250–$500.

Eligibility Requirements: Applicant must be enrolled or expecting to enroll full-time at a two-year or four-year institution or university. Applicant must be visually impaired. Available to U.S. citizens.

Application Requirements: Application, autobiography, essay, financial need analysis, photo, references. *Deadline:* April 1.

Contact: Melisa Welch, Assistant to Treasurer
Christian Record Services, Inc.
4444 South 52nd Street
Lincoln, NE 68516-1302
Phone: 402-488-0981 Ext. 213
Fax: 402-488-7582
E-mail: info@christianrecord.org

COLLEGE WOMEN'S ASSOCIATION OF JAPAN
http://www.cwaj.org

SCHOLARSHIP FOR THE VISUALLY IMPAIRED TO STUDY ABROAD

Scholarship for visually impaired Japanese nationals or permanent residents of Japan; who have been accepted into an undergraduate or graduate degree program at an accredited English-speaking university or research institution. Former recipients of CWAJ awards and members of CWAJ are ineligible. Deadline October 28.

Award: Scholarship for use in freshman, sophomore, junior, senior, or postgraduate years; not renewable. *Number:* 1. *Amount:* $23,318.

Eligibility Requirements: Applicant must be of Japanese heritage and Japanese citizen and enrolled or expecting to enroll at a four-year institution or university. Applicant must be visually impaired. Available to U.S. and non-U.S. citizens.

Application Requirements: Application, essay, references, test scores, transcript. *Fee:* $8. *Deadline:* October 28.

Contact: CWAJ Scholarship Committee
College Women's Association of Japan
2-24-13-1202 Kami-Osaki
Shinagawa-ku
Tokyo 141-0021
Japan
Phone: 81-03-3491-2091
Fax: 81-03-3491-2092
E-mail: scholarship@cwaj.org

SCHOLARSHIP FOR THE VISUALLY IMPAIRED TO STUDY IN JAPAN

Scholarship for visually impaired Japanese or permanent resident students for graduate or undergraduate study in Japan. Former recipients of CWAJ awards and members of CWAJ are ineligible.

Award: Scholarship for use in freshman, sophomore, junior, senior, or postgraduate years; not renewable. *Number:* 1. *Amount:* $16,960.

Eligibility Requirements: Applicant must be of Japanese heritage and Japanese citizen and enrolled or expecting to enroll at a four-year institution or university. Applicant must be visually impaired. Available to U.S. and non-U.S. citizens.

Application Requirements: Application, essay, references, self-addressed stamped envelope, transcript. *Fee:* $8. *Deadline:* October 28.

Contact: CWAJ Scholarship Committee
Phone: 81-03-3491-2091
Fax: 81-03-3491-2092
E-mail: scholarship@cwaj.org

COLLEGEBOUND FOUNDATION
http://www.collegeboundfoundation.org

ERICA LYNNE E. DURANT MEMORIAL SCHOLARSHIP

Award for Baltimore City public high school senior. Please see Web site: http://www.collegeboundfoundation.org for complete information on application process. Must submit CollegeBound Competitive Scholarship/Last-Dollar Grant Application. Must be physically challenged or learning disabled, provide proof of disability from a licensed professional. Must submit essay on how your disability has enriched your life and be available for an interview.

Award: Scholarship for use in freshman year; not renewable. *Number:* 1. *Amount:* $500.

Eligibility Requirements: Applicant must be high school student; planning to enroll or expecting to enroll full-time at a two-year or four-year institution or university; resident of Maryland and studying in Maryland. Applicant must be learning disabled or physically disabled. Available to U.S. citizens.

Application Requirements: Application, essay, financial need analysis, interview, references, transcript, financial aid award letters, Student Aid Report (SAR). *Deadline:* March 19.

Contact: April Bell, Associate Program Director
CollegeBound Foundation
300 Water Street, Suite 300
Baltimore, MD 21202
Phone: 410-783-2905 Ext. 208
Fax: 410-727-5786
E-mail: abell@collegeboundfoundation.org

COMMUNITY FOUNDATION OF CAPE COD
http://www.capecodfoundation.org

FRANK X. AND MARY E. WENY SCHOLARSHIP FUND

Frank X. and Mary E. Weny Scholarship Fund is awarded to a graduating senior from Cape Cod who is living with diabetes. Financial need will also be considered. For more details see Web site: http://www.capecodfoundation.org.

Award: Scholarship for use in freshman year; not renewable. *Number:* 1. *Amount:* up to $8000.

Eligibility Requirements: Applicant must be high school student; planning to enroll or expecting to enroll full-time at a two-year or four-year or technical institution or university and resident of Massachusetts. Applicant must be physically disabled. Available to U.S. citizens.

Application Requirements: Application, essay, financial need analysis, references, test scores, transcript, doctor's note. *Deadline:* April 1.

Contact: Kristin O'Malley, Program Officer/Scholarship Associate
Community Foundation of Cape Cod
259 Willow Street
Yarmouthport, MA 02675
Phone: 508-790-3040
Fax: 508-790-4069
E-mail: komalley@capecodfoundation.org

COUNCIL FOR INTERNATIONAL EDUCATIONAL EXCHANGE
http://www.ciee.org/study

ROBERT B. BAILEY III MINORITY SCHOLARSHIPS FOR EDUCATION ABROAD

One-time award for students from underrepresented groups in study abroad participating in Council for International Educational Exchange (CIEE)-administered overseas program. Application deadlines: April 1 and November 1. Applicant must be self-identified as belonging to an underrepresented group in study abroad.

Award: Scholarship for use in freshman, sophomore, junior, or senior years; not renewable. *Number:* 15–300. *Amount:* $500.

Eligibility Requirements: Applicant must be American Indian/Alaska Native, Asian/Pacific Islander, Black (non-Hispanic), or Hispanic and enrolled or expecting to enroll full-time at an institution or university. Applicant must be hearing impaired, learning disabled, physically disabled, or visually impaired. Applicant must have 3.5 GPA or higher. Available to U.S. citizens.

Application Requirements: Application, essay, financial need analysis, references, transcript. *Deadline:* varies.

Contact: Kate Dunkerley, Senior Program Coordinator-Grants
Program
Council for International Educational Exchange
3 Copley Place, 2nd Floor
Boston, MA 02116
Phone: 800-448-9944 Ext. 368
Fax: 617-247-2911
E-mail: kdunkerley@ciee.org

COUNCIL OF CITIZENS WITH LOW VISION INTERNATIONAL C/O AMERICAN COUNCIL OF THE BLIND
http://www.cclvi.org

FRED SCHEIGERT SCHOLARSHIP PROGRAM

Scholarships are available to full-time undergraduate students who are visually impaired. Must maintain a 3.0 GPA. For more details, specific requirements, and an application go to Web site: http://www.cclvi.org.

Award: Scholarship for use in freshman, sophomore, junior, or senior years; renewable. *Number:* 1. *Amount:* $500–$5000.

Eligibility Requirements: Applicant must be enrolled or expecting to enroll full-time at a four-year institution or university. Applicant must be visually impaired. Applicant must have 3.0 GPA or higher. Available to U.S. citizens.

Application Requirements: Application, essay, references, transcript. *Deadline:* April 15.

Contact: Bernice Kandarian
Council of Citizens with Low Vision International c/o American
Council of the Blind
2211 Latham Street, Suite 120
Mountain View, CA 94040-1652
Phone: 650-969-1688
E-mail: bernice@tsoft.net

COURAGE CENTER, VOCATIONAL SERVICES DEPARTMENT
http://www.courage.org

SCHOLARSHIP FOR PEOPLE WITH DISABILITIES

Award provides financial assistance to students with sensory or physical disabilities. May reapply each year. Applicant must be pursuing educational goals or technical expertise beyond high school. Must be U.S. citizen and resident of Minnesota, or participate in Courage Center Services. Indication of extracurricular work and volunteer history must be submitted along with application form.

Award: Scholarship for use in freshman, sophomore, junior, or senior years; not renewable. *Number:* varies. *Amount:* $500–$1000.

Eligibility Requirements: Applicant must be enrolled or expecting to enroll full-time at a two-year or four-year or technical institution or university and resident of Minnesota. Applicant must be hearing impaired, physically disabled, or visually impaired. Available to U.S. citizens.

Application Requirements: Application, essay, financial need analysis, interview. *Deadline:* May 31.

Contact: Nancy Robinow, Administrative Assistant
Courage Center, Vocational Services Department
3915 Golden Valley Road
Minneapolis, MN 55422-4298
Phone: 763-520-0553
Fax: 763-520-0577
E-mail: nrobinow@courage.org

CYSTIC FIBROSIS SCHOLARSHIP FOUNDATION
http://www.cfscholarship.org

CYSTIC FIBROSIS SCHOLARSHIP

Awards for young adults with cystic fibrosis to be used to further their education after high school. Awards may be used for tuition, books and fees. Awards are for one year. Students may reapply in subsequent years.

Award: Scholarship for use in freshman, sophomore, junior, or senior years; renewable. *Number:* 40–50. *Amount:* $1000.

Eligibility Requirements: Applicant must be enrolled or expecting to enroll full or part-time at a two-year or four-year or technical institution or university. Applicant must be physically disabled. Available to U.S. citizens.

Application Requirements: Application, essay, financial need analysis, references, test scores, transcript. *Deadline:* March 17.

Contact: Mary K. Bottorff, President
Cystic Fibrosis Scholarship Foundation
2814 Grant Street
Evanston, IL 60201
Phone: 847-328-0127
Fax: 847-328-0127
E-mail: mkbcfsf@aol.com

DISABLEDPERSON INC. COLLEGE SCHOLARSHIP
http://www.disABLEDperson.com

DISABLEDPERSON INC. COLLEGE SCHOLARSHIP AWARD

Essay contest for disabled persons who are enrolled as full-time students in a 2- or 4-year accredited college or university. Length of the essay must not exceed 1000 words.

Award: Prize for use in freshman, sophomore, junior, or senior years. *Amount:* up to $500.

Eligibility Requirements: Applicant must be enrolled or expecting to enroll full-time at a two-year or four-year institution or university. Applicant must be hearing impaired, learning disabled, physically disabled, or visually impaired. Available to U.S. citizens.

Application Requirements: Application, applicant must enter a contest, essay, transcript, proof of disability. *Deadline:* varies.

Contact:
Phone: 760-420-1269
E-mail: disabledpersons@aol.com

EAR FOUNDATION MINNIE PEARL SCHOLARSHIP PROGRAM
http://www.earfoundation.org

MINNIE PEARL SCHOLARSHIP PROGRAM

Renewable scholarship for full-time college students with a severe to profound bilateral hearing loss. Initially, recipients must be high school seniors with at least a 3.0 GPA. Renewals based upon maintenance of GPA.

Award: Scholarship for use in freshman year; renewable. *Number:* 1–5. *Amount:* $2500.

Eligibility Requirements: Applicant must be high school student and planning to enroll or expecting to enroll full-time at an institution or university. Applicant must be hearing impaired. Applicant must have 3.0 GPA or higher. Available to U.S. citizens.

Application Requirements: Application, essay, photo, references, self-addressed stamped envelope, transcript. *Deadline:* February 15.

Contact: Minnie Pearl Scholarship Program, The EAR Foundation
Ear Foundation Minnie Pearl Scholarship Program
955 Woodland Street.
Nashville, TN 37203
Phone: 615-627-2724
Fax: 615-627-2728
E-mail: info@earfoundation.org

EDMONTON COMMUNITY FOUNDATION
http://www.DollarsForLearners.com

CHARMAINE LETOURNEAU FUND

Annual award to a deaf or hard of hearing person who will attend an academic or training program at a qualified postsecondary institution. Must be resident of Alberta at time of application. The amount of the award varies each year.

Award: Prize for use in freshman, sophomore, junior, or senior years. *Number:* 1. *Amount:* $500–$1000.

Eligibility Requirements: Applicant must be Canadian citizen and enrolled or expecting to enroll at a four-year institution or university. Applicant must be hearing impaired. Available to U.S. and Canadian citizens.

Edmonton Community Foundation (continued)

Application Requirements: Application, interview, references, personal letter, medical documentation of hearing loss. *Deadline:* May 31.

Contact: Reg Basken, Scholarships Officer
Edmonton Community Foundation
710 Royal Bank Building, 9910-103 Street NW
10117 Jasper Avenue
Edmonton T5K 2V7
Canada
Phone: 780-426-0015
Fax: 780-425-0121
E-mail: info@dollarsforlearners.com

EPILEPSY FOUNDATION OF IDAHO
http://www.epilepsyidaho.org

GREGORY W. GILE MEMORIAL SCHOLARSHIP PROGRAM

Applicant must be a graduate of an Idaho high school, either entering or continuing school and pursuing an academic or vocational undergraduate degree or certificate. Must be a resident of Idaho. Application deadline is March 15.

Award: Scholarship for use in freshman, sophomore, junior, senior, or graduate years; not renewable. *Number:* 1. *Amount:* $1000–$1500.

Eligibility Requirements: Applicant must be enrolled or expecting to enroll full-time at a two-year or four-year or technical institution or university and resident of Idaho. Applicant must be physically disabled. Available to U.S. and non-U.S. citizens.

Application Requirements: Application, essay, references. *Deadline:* March 15.

Contact: Epilepsy Foundation of Idaho
Epilepsy Foundation of Idaho
310 West Idaho Street
Boise, ID 83702

MARK MUSIC MEMORIAL SCHOLARSHIP

One-time award to promote educational opportunities for Idaho residents with epilepsy. Applicant must be a high school graduate or hold an equivalent certificate, and be either entering or continuing school and pursuing an academic or vocational undergraduate degree or certificate. Application deadline is March 15.

Award: Scholarship for use in freshman, sophomore, junior, senior, or graduate years; not renewable. *Number:* 1. *Amount:* $500.

Eligibility Requirements: Applicant must be enrolled or expecting to enroll full-time at a two-year or four-year or technical institution or university and resident of Idaho. Applicant must be physically disabled. Available to U.S. and non-U.S. citizens.

Application Requirements: Application, essay, references. *Deadline:* March 15.

Contact: Epilepsy Foundation of Idaho
Epilepsy Foundation of Idaho
310 West Idaho Street
Boise, ID 83702

GREAT LAKES HEMOPHILIA FOUNDATION
http://www.glhf.org/scholar.htm

EDUCATION AND TRAINING ASSISTANCE PROGRAM

This scholarship not only targets the traditional college and vocational students, but also looks at retraining adults with bleeding disorders who are finding it difficult to function in their chosen field because of health complications. It also targets parents of children with bleeding disorders who through career advancement can better meet the financial needs of caring for their child.

Award: Scholarship for use in freshman, sophomore, junior, senior, graduate, or postgraduate years; not renewable. *Number:* 5–6. *Amount:* $500–$2000.

Eligibility Requirements: Applicant must be enrolled or expecting to enroll full or part-time at a two-year or four-year or technical institution or university and resident of Wisconsin. Applicant must be physically disabled. Available to U.S. citizens.

Application Requirements: Application, essay, references, self-addressed stamped envelope, transcript. *Deadline:* May 1.

Contact: Tammy Molter
Great Lakes Hemophilia Foundation
PO Box 0704
Milwaukee, WI 53201-0704
Phone: 414-257-0200
Fax: 414-257-1225
E-mail: info@glhf.org

GLHF INDIVIDUAL CLASS SCHOLARSHIP

Scholarship available to members of the Wisconsin bleeding disorder community: individuals with a bleeding disorder and their immediate families. Provides funding assistance for tuition and enrollment fees relevant to continuing education in a non-traditional or non-degree format.

Award: Scholarship for use in freshman, sophomore, junior, or senior years. *Amount:* up to $500.

Eligibility Requirements: Applicant must be enrolled or expecting to enroll full or part-time at a technical institution. Applicant must be physically disabled. Available to U.S. citizens.

Application Requirements: Application. *Deadline:* varies.

Contact: Tammy Molter
Great Lakes Hemophilia Foundation
PO Box 0704
Milwaukee, WI 53201-0704
Phone: 414-257-0200
Fax: 414-257-1225
E-mail: info@glhf.org

HEMOPHILIA HEALTH SERVICES
http://www.hemophiliahealth.com

HEMOPHILIA HEALTH SERVICES MEMORIAL SCHOLARSHIP

One-time award open to full-time students with hemophilia or another bleeding disorder. Scholarship may be used at any accredited, nonprofit college, university, or vocational/technical school. Selection based on academic achievement in relation to tested ability, involvement in extracurricular and community activities, and financial need. For an application visit the Web site at http://www.hemophiliahealth.com. Deadline is May 1.

Award: Scholarship for use in freshman, sophomore, junior, senior, graduate, or postgraduate years; not renewable. *Number:* 7–10. *Amount:* $1500–$2000.

Eligibility Requirements: Applicant must be enrolled or expecting to enroll full-time at a two-year or four-year or technical institution or university. Applicant must be physically disabled. Available to U.S. citizens.

Application Requirements: Application, essay, financial need analysis, references, test scores, transcript, physician certification form. *Deadline:* May 1.

Contact: Sally Johnson, Special Program Coordinator
Hemophilia Health Services
6820 Charlotte Pike
Nashville, TN 37209-4234
Phone: 615-850-5175
Fax: 615-352-2588
E-mail: scholarship@hemophiliahealth.com

SCOTT TARBELL SCHOLARSHIP

This scholarship is designed to help full- and part-time students pursue an education in the technical fields of computer science and mathematics. Deadline is May 1. For an application visit the Web site at http://www.hemophiliahealth.com

Award: Scholarship for use in freshman, sophomore, junior, senior, graduate, or postgraduate years; not renewable. *Number:* 1–2. *Amount:* $1500–$2000.

Eligibility Requirements: Applicant must be enrolled or expecting to enroll full or part-time at a two-year or four-year or technical institution or university. Applicant must be physically disabled. Available to U.S. citizens.

Application Requirements: Application, essay, financial need analysis, references, test scores, transcript, doctor certification form. *Deadline:* May 1.

Contact: Sally Johnson, Special Programs Coordinator
Hemophilia Health Services
6820 Charlotte Pike
Nashville, TN 37209-4234
Phone: 615-850-5175
Fax: 615-352-2588
E-mail: scholarship@hemophiliahealth.com

IDAHO STATE BOARD OF EDUCATION
http://www.boardofed.idaho.gov

IDAHO MINORITY AND "AT RISK" STUDENT SCHOLARSHIP

Renewable award for Idaho residents who are disabled or members of a minority group and have financial need. Must attend one of eight postsecondary institutions in the state for undergraduate study. Deadlines vary by institution. Must be a U.S. citizen and be a graduate of an Idaho high school. Contact college financial aid office.

Award: Scholarship for use in freshman, sophomore, junior, or senior years; renewable. *Number:* 35–40. *Amount:* $3000.

Eligibility Requirements: Applicant must be American Indian/Alaska Native, Black (non-Hispanic), or Hispanic; enrolled or expecting to enroll full-time at a two-year or four-year or technical institution or university; resident of Idaho and studying in Idaho. Applicant must be hearing impaired, physically disabled, or visually impaired. Available to U.S. citizens.

Application Requirements: Application, financial need analysis, transcript. *Deadline:* varies.

Contact: Dana Kelly, Program Manager
Idaho State Board of Education
PO Box 83720
Boise, ID 83720-0037
Phone: 208-332-1574
E-mail: dana.kelly@osbe.idaho.gov

ILLINOIS COUNCIL OF THE BLIND
http://www.icbonline.org

FLOYD CARGILL SCHOLARSHIP

Award for a visually impaired Illinois resident attending or planning to attend an Illinois college. One-time award of $750. Deadline: June 15.

Award: Scholarship for use in freshman, sophomore, junior, or senior years; not renewable. *Number:* 1. *Amount:* $750.

Eligibility Requirements: Applicant must be enrolled or expecting to enroll full-time at a two-year or four-year or technical institution or university; resident of Illinois and studying in Illinois. Applicant must be visually impaired. Applicant must have 2.5 GPA or higher. Available to U.S. citizens.

Application Requirements: Application, autobiography, references, test scores, transcript. *Deadline:* June 15.

Contact: Maggie Uorich, Office Manager
Illinois Council of the Blind
PO Box 1336
Springfield, IL 62705
Phone: 217-523-4967
Fax: 217-523-4302
E-mail: icb@icbonline.org

IMMUNE DEFICIENCY FOUNDATION
http://www.primaryimmune.org

IMMUNE DEFICIENCY FOUNDATION SCHOLARSHIP

One-time award available to individuals diagnosed with a primary immune deficiency disease. Must submit medical verification of diagnosis. Available for study at the undergraduate level at any postsecondary institution. Must be U.S. citizen.

Award: Scholarship for use in freshman, sophomore, junior, or senior years; not renewable. *Number:* 30–40. *Amount:* $750–$2000.

Eligibility Requirements: Applicant must be enrolled or expecting to enroll full-time or part-time at a two-year or four-year or technical institution or university. Applicant must be physically disabled. Available to U.S. citizens.

Application Requirements: Application, autobiography, essay, financial need analysis, references, medical verification of diagnosis. *Deadline:* March 31.

Contact: Tamara Brown, Medical Programs Manager
Immune Deficiency Foundation
40 West Chesapeake Avenue, Suite 308
Towson, MD 21204
Phone: 800-296-4433
Fax: 410-321-9165
E-mail: tb@primaryimmune.org

IOWA DIVISION OF VOCATIONAL REHABILITATION SERVICES
http://www.ivrs.iowa.gov

IOWA VOCATIONAL REHABILITATION

Provides vocational rehabilitation services to individuals with disabilities who need these services in order to maintain, retain, or obtain employment compatible with their disabilities. Must be Iowa resident.

Award: Grant for use in freshman, sophomore, junior, senior, graduate, or postgraduate years; renewable. *Number:* up to 5000. *Amount:* $500–$4000.

Eligibility Requirements: Applicant must be enrolled or expecting to enroll full or part-time at a two-year or four-year or technical institution or university and resident of Iowa. Applicant must be hearing impaired, learning disabled, physically disabled, or visually impaired. Available to U.S. and non-U.S. citizens.

Application Requirements: Application, interview. *Deadline:* Continuous.

Contact: Ralph Childers, Policy and Workforce Initiatives Coordinator
Iowa Division of Vocational Rehabilitation Services
Division of Vocational Rehabilitation Services
510 East 12th Street
Des Moines, IA 50319
Phone: 515-281-4151
Fax: 515-281-4703
E-mail: ralph.childers@iowa.gov

JEWISH GUILD FOR THE BLIND
http://66.40.142.226/index.asp

GUILDSCHOLAR AWARD

Annual scholarship program for college bound high school students who are legally blind. Applications will be accepted from students at the start of their senior year.

Award: Scholarship for use in freshman year. *Number:* 12–15. *Amount:* up to $15,000.

Eligibility Requirements: Applicant must be enrolled or expecting to enroll full or part-time at a four-year institution or university. Applicant must be visually impaired. Available to U.S. citizens.

Application Requirements: Application, references, transcript, proof of legal blindness, proof of U.S. citizenship, personal statement. *Deadline:* September 11.

Contact: Gordon Rovins
Jewish Guild for the Blind
15 West 65th Street
New York, NY 10023
Phone: 212-769-7801
E-mail: guildscholar@jgb.org

KENTUCKY DEPARTMENT OF VOCATIONAL REHABILITATION
http://ovr.ky.gov/index.htm

KENTUCKY DEPARTMENT OF VOCATIONAL REHABILITATION

Kentucky Department of Vocational Rehabilitation provides services necessary to secure employment. Eligible individual must possess physical or mental impairment that results in a substantial impediment to employment; benefit from vocational rehabilitation services in terms of an employment outcome; and require vocational rehabilitation services to prepare for, enter, or retain employment.

Kentucky Department of Vocational Rehabilitation (continued)

Award: Grant for use in freshman, sophomore, junior, senior, graduate, or postgraduate years; renewable. *Number:* varies. *Amount:* varies.

Eligibility Requirements: Applicant must be enrolled or expecting to enroll full or part-time at a two-year or four-year or technical institution or university. Applicant must be learning disabled or physically disabled. Available to U.S. and non-U.S. citizens.

Application Requirements: Application, financial need analysis, interview, transcript. *Deadline:* Continuous.

Contact: Charles Tuckett, Program Administrator
Kentucky Department of Vocational Rehabilitation
209 Street Clair Street
Frankfort, KY 40601
Phone: 502-595-3423
Fax: 502-564-6745
E-mail: marianu.spencer@mail.state.ky.us

LA KELLEY COMMUNICATIONS

http://www.kelleycom.com

ARTISTIC ENDEAVORS SCHOLARSHIP

Person with hemophilia or VWD not necessarily attending college. Scholarship can be used for producing a play, writing a book, painting, publishing or another artistic endeavor. Imagination and portfolio required.

Award: Scholarship for use in freshman, sophomore, junior, or senior years; not renewable. *Amount:* $1500.

Eligibility Requirements: Applicant must be enrolled or expecting to enroll at a four-year institution or university and must have an interest in art or writing. Applicant must be physically disabled. Available to U.S. citizens.

Application Requirements: Application. *Deadline:* April 1.

Contact: Sandy Aultman
LA Kelley Communications
1405 W. Pinhook Road, Suite 101
Lafayette, LA 70503
Phone: 337-261-9787
Fax: 337-261-1787

CALVIN DAWSON MEMORIAL SCHOLARSHIP

Scholarship for Florida resident with bleeding disorder attending a college, university or trade school. Award amount and number varies.

Award: Scholarship for use in freshman, sophomore, junior, senior, or graduate years. *Number:* 1. *Amount:* $2500–$7500.

Eligibility Requirements: Applicant must be enrolled or expecting to enroll full or part-time at a two-year or four-year or technical institution or university and resident of Florida. Applicant must be physically disabled. Available to U.S. citizens.

Application Requirements: Application. *Deadline:* April 30.

Contact: Hemophilia Foundation of Greater Florida
LA Kelley Communications
1350 North Orange Avenue, Suite 227
Winter Park, FL 32789
Phone: 800-293-6527

ERIC DOSTIE MEMORIAL COLLEGE SCHOLARSHIP

Awarded to a person with a bleeding disorder (their sibling or child) to attend any accredited college or university. Must be a U.S. citizen. Applicant may reapply.

Award: Scholarship for use in freshman, sophomore, junior, senior, or graduate years; not renewable. *Number:* up to 10. *Amount:* $1000.

Eligibility Requirements: Applicant must be enrolled or expecting to enroll full-time at a two-year or four-year institution or university. Applicant must be physically disabled. Applicant must have 2.5 GPA or higher. Available to U.S. citizens.

Application Requirements: Application, essay, photo, references, test scores, transcript. *Deadline:* March 1.

Contact: Scholarship Administrator
LA Kelley Communications
41093 County Center Drive
Temecula, CA 92591
Phone: 800-323-6832 Ext. 1300
Fax: 951-296-2565

HEMOPHILIA FEDERATION OF AMERICA

Person with hemophilia or VWD attending any accredited two- or four-year college, university or vocation/technical school in the U.S.

Award: Scholarship for use in freshman, sophomore, junior, or senior years. *Number:* 1–3. *Amount:* $1500.

Eligibility Requirements: Applicant must be enrolled or expecting to enroll full or part-time at a two-year or four-year or technical institution or university. Applicant must be physically disabled. Available to U.S. citizens.

Application Requirements: Application. *Deadline:* April 1.

Contact: Sandy Aultman
LA Kelley Communications
1045 West Pinhook Road, Suite 101
Lafayette, LA 70503
Phone: 337-261-9787
Fax: 337-261-1787

HEMOPHILIA FOUNDATION OF MICHIGAN ACADEMIC SCHOLARSHIP

Award available to person, or immediate family member, with hemophilia or other inherited bleeding disorder residing in Michigan.

Award: Scholarship for use in freshman, sophomore, junior, or senior years. *Number:* 2. *Amount:* $1500.

Eligibility Requirements: Applicant must be enrolled or expecting to enroll at a four-year institution or university and resident of Michigan. Applicant must be physically disabled. Available to U.S. citizens.

Application Requirements: Application. *Deadline:* varies.

Contact: HFM Academic Assistance
LA Kelley Communications
905 West Eisenhower Circle, Suite 107
Ann Arbor, MI 48103
Phone: 734-332-4226
Fax: 734-332-4204

HEMOPHILIA HEALTH SERVICES MEMORIAL SCHOLARSHIP FUND

Award available to full-time undergraduate and graduate students with hemophilia, von Willebrand disease, and other factor deficiencies. Applicants must be U.S. citizens and demonstrate financial need, academic achievement in relation to tested ability, and involvement in extracurricular and community.

Award: Scholarship for use in freshman, sophomore, junior, senior, or graduate years. *Amount:* $1500.

Eligibility Requirements: Applicant must be enrolled or expecting to enroll full-time at an institution or university. Applicant must be physically disabled. Available to U.S. citizens.

Application Requirements: *Deadline:* May 1.

Contact: Scholarship Committee
LA Kelley Communications
6820 Charlotte Pike
Nashville, TN 37209-4234
Phone: 800-800-6606 Ext. 5175
Fax: 615-352-2588

KEVIN CHILD SCHOLARSHIP

Award available to person with hemophilia or VWD. Must be a high school senior planning to attend college, university or vocational school, or a college student pursuing postsecondary education.

Award: Scholarship for use in freshman, sophomore, junior, or senior years. *Amount:* $500–$1000.

Eligibility Requirements: Applicant must be enrolled or expecting to enroll at a two-year or four-year or technical institution or university. Applicant must be physically disabled. Available to U.S. citizens.

Application Requirements: *Deadline:* June 27.

Contact: Dept. of Finance, Administration & MIS
LA Kelley Communications
116 West 32nd Street, 11th Floor
New York, NY 10001-3212
Phone: 212-328-3700

LAWRENCE MADEIROS MEMORIAL SCHOLARSHIP

Award available to high school students with a bleeding disorder or other chronic disorder. Applicants must be accepted at, or currently enrolled in, an accredited college or university.

Award: Scholarship for use in freshman year. *Amount:* $1000.

Eligibility Requirements: Applicant must be enrolled or expecting to enroll full-time at a two-year or four-year institution or university. Applicant must be physically disabled. Available to U.S. citizens.

Application Requirements: Application. *Deadline:* June 16.

Contact: Carol Madeiros
LA Kelley Communications
485 Bunker Hill Road
Mayfield, NY 12117
Phone: 518-863-2668
Fax: 518-863-6126
E-mail: lamspintacular@aol.com

MICHAEL BENDIX SUTTON FOUNDATION

Two $2,000 scholarships for persons with hemophilia pursuing pre-law study.

Award: Scholarship for use in freshman, sophomore, junior, or senior years. *Number:* 2. *Amount:* $2000.

Eligibility Requirements: Applicant must be enrolled or expecting to enroll full-time at an institution or university. Applicant must be physically disabled. Available to U.S. citizens.

Application Requirements: Application. *Deadline:* March 30.

Contact: Marion B. Sutton
LA Kelley Communications
300 Maritime Avenue
White Plains, NY 10601

MIKE HYLTON AND RON NIEDERMAN MEMORIAL SCHOLARSHIPS

Scholarship for men or immediate family member with hemophilia or other bleeding disorder pursuing postsecondary education at a college, university, trade or technical school.

Award: Scholarship for use in freshman, sophomore, junior, or senior years. *Number:* 10. *Amount:* $1000.

Eligibility Requirements: Applicant must be enrolled or expecting to enroll full-time at a two-year or four-year or technical institution or university. Applicant must be physically disabled. Available to U.S. citizens.

Application Requirements: Application. *Deadline:* April 30.

Contact: Linda Leigh Sulser, Scholarship Committee
LA Kelley Communications
900 Avenida Acaso, Suite A
Camarillo, CA 93012
Phone: 877-376-4968
Fax: 805-482-6324
E-mail: scholarships@factorsupport.com

MILLIE GONZALEZ MEMORIAL SCHOLARSHIP

Scholarship for women or immediate family member with hemophilia or other bleeding disorder pursuing postsecondary education at a college, university, trade or technical school.

Award: Scholarship for use in freshman, sophomore, junior, or senior years. *Number:* 5. *Amount:* $1000.

Eligibility Requirements: Applicant must be enrolled or expecting to enroll full-time at a two-year or four-year or technical institution or university. Applicant must be physically disabled. Available to U.S. citizens.

Application Requirements: Application. *Deadline:* April 30.

Contact: Linda Leigh Sulser, Scholarship Committee Liaison
LA Kelley Communications
900 Avenida Acaso, Suite A
Camarillo, CA 93012
Phone: 877-376-4968

RACHEL WARNER SCHOLARSHIP

Scholarship for person with bleeding disorder.

Award: Scholarship for use in freshman, sophomore, junior, senior, graduate, or postgraduate years.

Eligibility Requirements: Applicant must be enrolled or expecting to enroll at a two-year or four-year or technical institution or university. Applicant must be physically disabled. Available to U.S. citizens.

Application Requirements: *Deadline:* May 1.

Contact: The Committee of Ten Thousand
LA Kelley Communications
236 Massachusetts Avenue, Suite 609
Washington, DC 20002
Phone: 800-488-2688
Fax: 202-543-6720

SEVENSECURE SCHOLARSHIP

Award available to patients with factor VIII or FIX deficiency with inhibitors, who are customers of Novo Nordisk, Inc., and are enrolled full time at a vocational school, college or graduate school.

Award: Scholarship for use in freshman, sophomore, junior, senior, or graduate years. *Number:* 7. *Amount:* $5000–$7000.

Eligibility Requirements: Applicant must be enrolled or expecting to enroll full-time at an institution or university. Applicant must be physically disabled. Available to U.S. citizens.

Application Requirements: Application.

Contact: Stephanie Allan, Office Manager/Kelley Communications
LA Kelley Communications
68 East Main Street, Suite 102
Georgetown, MA 01833
Phone: 978-352-7657
Fax: 978-352-6254
E-mail: info@kelleycom.com

SIBLING CONTINUING EDUCATION SCHOLARSHIP

Award of $1500 for use in furthering the education of school-age child with a blood clotting disorder.

Award: Scholarship for use in freshman year. *Amount:* $1500.

Eligibility Requirements: Applicant must be enrolled or expecting to enroll at a four-year institution or university. Applicant must be physically disabled. Available to U.S. citizens.

Application Requirements: Application. *Deadline:* April 1.

Contact: Sandy Aultman
LA Kelley Communications
1045 West Pinhook Road, Suite 101
Lafayette, LA 70503
Phone: 337-261-9787
Fax: 337-261-1787

SOOZIE COURTER HEMOPHILIA SCHOLARSHIP PROGRAM

Scholarship for Students with hemophilia A or B. Must be a high school senior or recipient of a graduate equivalency diploma (GED), or currently enrolled in an accredited junior college, college (undergraduate or graduate), or vocational school.

Award: Scholarship for use in freshman, sophomore, junior, senior, or graduate years. *Number:* 19. *Amount:* $2500–$7500.

Eligibility Requirements: Applicant must be enrolled or expecting to enroll full-time at a two-year or four-year institution or university. Applicant must be physically disabled. Available to U.S. citizens.

Application Requirements: *Deadline:* April 15.

Contact: The Resource Group
LA Kelley Communications
345 Hudson Street, 4th Floor
New York, NY 10014-7475
Phone: 888-999-2349

LIGHTHOUSE INTERNATIONAL

http://www.lighthouse.org

SCHOLARSHIP AWARDS

One-time award designed to reward excellence, recognize accomplishments, and to help students who are blind or partially sighted achieve their career goals. There are 4 categories: college bound, undergraduate, graduate, adult undergraduate II. Students must be legally blind, U.S. citizens, enrolled in an accredited program of study. Applicants must be a resident of and attend

Lighthouse International (continued)

school in one of these states: New York, Connecticut, Massachusetts, New Jersey, Rhode Island, Maine, New Hampshire, Pennsylvania, Vermont, Delaware, Maryland, and Washington, D.C.

Award: Prize for use in freshman, sophomore, junior, senior, graduate, or postgraduate years; not renewable. *Number:* 4. *Amount:* up to $5000.

Eligibility Requirements: Applicant must be enrolled or expecting to enroll full-time at a four-year institution or university; resident of Connecticut, Delaware, District of Columbia, Florida, Maine, Maryland, Massachusetts, New Hampshire, New Jersey, New York, North Carolina, Pennsylvania, Rhode Island, Vermont, or West Virginia and studying in Connecticut, Delaware, District of Columbia, Maine, Maryland, Massachusetts, New Hampshire, New Jersey, New York, Pennsylvania, Rhode Island, or Vermont. Applicant must be visually impaired. Available to U.S. citizens.

Application Requirements: Application, essay, references, transcript, proof of U.S. citizenship, proof of legal blindness. *Deadline:* March 31.

Contact: Kelly Boyle, Scholarships Program
Lighthouse International
The Sol and Lillian Goldman Building, 111 East 59th Street
New York, NY 10022-1202
Phone: 212-821-9428
E-mail: kboyle@lighthouse.org

LILLY REINTEGRATION PROGRAMS

LILLY REINTEGRATION SCHOLARSHIP

Scholarships available to students diagnosed with schizophrenia, bi-polar, schizophreniform, or a schizoaffective disorder. Must be currently receiving medical treatment for the disease, including medications and psychiatric follow-up. Must also be U.S. citizen and actively involved in rehabilitative or reintegration efforts. Applicants must be at least 18 years of age. For information and application, use e-mail at lillyscholarships@reintigration.com

Award: Scholarship for use in freshman, sophomore, junior, senior, graduate, or postgraduate years; not renewable. *Number:* 70–100. *Amount:* varies.

Eligibility Requirements: Applicant must be age 18 and enrolled or expecting to enroll full or part-time at a two-year or four-year or technical institution or university. Applicant must be physically disabled. Available to U.S. citizens.

Application Requirements: Application, essay, references, transcript. *Deadline:* January 31.

Contact: Lilly Secretariat
Lilly Reintegration Programs
PMB 1167, 734 North LaSalle Street
Chicago, IL 60610
Phone: 800-809-8202
E-mail: lillyscholarships@reintegration.com

LOUISE C. NACCA MEMORIAL FOR EDUCATIONAL AID FOR THE HANDICAPPED TRUST

LOUISE NACCA MEMORIAL TRUST

One-time award available to student who has a visual, hearing or physical impairment. May be used at any postsecondary institution. Must be a U.S. citizen. Must demonstrate financial need.

Award: Scholarship for use in freshman, sophomore, junior, senior, or graduate years; not renewable. *Number:* varies. *Amount:* up to $5000.

Eligibility Requirements: Applicant must be enrolled or expecting to enroll full or part-time at a two-year or four-year or technical institution or university and resident of New Jersey. Applicant must be hearing impaired, physically disabled, or visually impaired. Available to U.S. citizens.

Application Requirements: Application, financial need analysis. *Deadline:* varies.

Contact: Board Director
Louise C. Nacca Memorial for Educational Aid for the Handicapped Trust
7 Sanford Avenue
Belleville, NJ 07109

NATIONAL CENTER FOR LEARNING DISABILITIES, INC.
http://www.ld.org

ANNE FORD SCHOLARSHIP

A $10,000 award given to a high school senior of high merit with an identified learning disability who is pursuing an undergraduate degree. The ideal candidate is a person who has faced the challenges of having a learning disability and who, through perseverance and academic endeavor, has created a life of purpose and achievement. Visit Web site at http://www.ld.org for deadline information.

Award: Scholarship for use in freshman year; not renewable. *Number:* 1. *Amount:* $10,000.

Eligibility Requirements: Applicant must be enrolled or expecting to enroll full-time at a four-year institution or university. Applicant must be learning disabled. Applicant must have 3.0 GPA or higher. Available to U.S. citizens.

Application Requirements: Application, essay, financial need analysis, references, test scores, transcript. *Deadline:* December 31.

Contact: Meaghan Carey, Coordinator
National Center for Learning Disabilities, Inc.
381 Park Avenue South, Suite 1401
New York, NY 10016-8806
Phone: 212-545-7510 Ext. 233
Fax: 212-545-9665
E-mail: mcarey@ncld.org

NATIONAL COUNCIL OF JEWISH WOMEN NEW YORK SECTION
http://www.ncjwny.org

JACKSON-STRICKS SCHOLARSHIP

Scholarship provides financial aid to a physically challenged person for academic study or vocational training that leads to independent living.

Award: Scholarship for use in freshman, sophomore, junior, or senior years. *Number:* 1.

Eligibility Requirements: Applicant must be enrolled or expecting to enroll full or part-time at a two-year or four-year institution or university and resident of New York. Applicant must be physically disabled. Available to U.S. citizens.

Application Requirements: Application, essay, references, transcript. *Deadline:* April 14.

Contact: Jackson-Stricks Scholarship
National Council of Jewish Women New York Section
820 2nd Avenue
New York, NY 10017
Phone: 212-687-5030
Fax: 212-687-5032

NATIONAL FEDERATION OF THE BLIND
http://www.nfb.org

E. U. PARKER SCHOLARSHIP
• See page 546

HERMIONE GRANT CALHOUN SCHOLARSHIP
• See page 546

JENNICA FERGUSON MEMORIAL SCHOLARSHIP
• See page 546

KENNETH JERNIGAN SCHOLARSHIP
• See page 546

KUCHLER-KILLIAN MEMORIAL SCHOLARSHIP
• See page 546

MELVA T. OWEN MEMORIAL SCHOLARSHIP
• See page 546

SALLY S. JACOBSEN SCHOLARSHIP
• See page 546

NATIONAL FEDERATION OF THE BLIND OF MISSOURI
http://www.nfbmo.org

NATIONAL FEDERATION OF THE BLIND OF MISSOURI SCHOLARSHIPS TO LEGALLY BLIND STUDENTS

Awards are based on achievement, commitment to community, and financial need. Recipients must be legally blind. Amount of money each year available for program will vary.

Award: Scholarship for use in freshman, sophomore, junior, senior, graduate, or postgraduate years; not renewable. *Number:* up to 2. *Amount:* $500–$1500.

Eligibility Requirements: Applicant must be enrolled or expecting to enroll full or part-time at a two-year or four-year or technical institution or university. Applicant must be visually impaired. Available to U.S. citizens.

Application Requirements: Application, autobiography, essay, financial need analysis, interview, references, transcript. *Deadline:* February 1.

Contact: Gary Wunder, President
National Federation of the Blind of Missouri
3910 Tropical Lane
Columbia, MO 65202
Phone: 573-874-1774
Fax: 573-442-5617
E-mail: president@nfbmo.org

NATIONAL KIDNEY FOUNDATION OF INDIANA, INC.
http://www.kidneyindiana.org

LARRY SMOCK SCHOLARSHIP

Financial assistance for kidney dialysis and transplant patients to pursue postsecondary education. Applicant must be resident of Indiana over the age of 17. Applicants must have a high school diploma or its equivalent.

Award: Scholarship for use in freshman, sophomore, junior, or senior years; not renewable. *Number:* 1. *Amount:* varies.

Eligibility Requirements: Applicant must be age 18; enrolled or expecting to enroll full or part-time at a two-year or four-year or technical institution or university and resident of Indiana. Applicant must be physically disabled. Available to U.S. citizens.

Application Requirements: Application, references, transcript. *Deadline:* varies.

Contact: Marilyn Winn, Program Director, National Kidney Foundation of Indiana
National Kidney Foundation of Indiana, Inc.
911 86th Street, Suite 100
Indianapolis, IN 46240-1840
Phone: 317-722-5640
Fax: 317-722-5650
E-mail: nkfi@myvine.com

NATIONAL PKU NEWS
http://www.pkunews.org

ROBERT GUTHRIE PKU SCHOLARSHIP AND AWARDS

Award program is open only to persons with phenylketonuria (PKU) who are on a special diet for PKU treatment. Award is for full- or part-time study at any accredited U.S. institution.

Award: Scholarship for use in freshman, sophomore, junior, senior, graduate, or postgraduate years; not renewable. *Number:* 6–12. *Amount:* $2000–$2500.

Eligibility Requirements: Applicant must be enrolled or expecting to enroll full or part-time at a two-year or four-year or technical institution or university. Applicant must be physically disabled. Available to U.S. and non-U.S. citizens.

Application Requirements: Application, autobiography, essay, photo, resume, references, test scores, transcript. *Deadline:* November 1.

Contact: Virginia Schuett, Director
National PKU News
6869 Woodlawn Avenue, NE
Suite 116
Seattle, WA 98115-5469
Phone: 206-525-8140
Fax: 206-525-5023
E-mail: schuett@pkunews.org

NATIONAL UNION OF PUBLIC AND GENERAL EMPLOYEES
http://www.nupge.ca

TERRY FOX MEMORIAL SCHOLARSHIP
• See page 507

NEW YORK STATE GRANGE
http://www.nysgrange.com/

CAROLINE KARK AWARD

This award is given to a Grange individual who is preparing for a career working with the deaf, or a deaf individual who is furthering his or her education beyond high school. The recipient must be a New York State resident.

Award: Scholarship for use in freshman year. *Number:* 1. *Amount:* up to $500.

Eligibility Requirements: Applicant must be enrolled or expecting to enroll full or part-time at a four-year institution or university and resident of New York. Applicant must be hearing impaired. Available to U.S. citizens.

Application Requirements: Application. *Deadline:* April 15.

Contact: Ann Hall, Program Manager
New York State Grange
100 Grange Place
Cortland, NY 13045
Phone: 607-756-7553
Fax: 607-756-7757
E-mail: nysgrange@nysgrange.com

NORTH CAROLINA DIVISION OF SERVICES FOR THE BLIND

NORTH CAROLINA DIVISION OF SERVICES FOR THE BLIND REHABILITATION SERVICES

Financial assistance is available for North Carolina residents who are blind or visually impaired and who require vocational rehabilitation to help find employment. Tuition and other assistance provided based on need. Open to U.S. citizens and legal residents of United States. Applicants goal must be to work after receiving vocational services. To apply, contact the local DSB office and apply for vocational rehabilitation services.

Award: Scholarship for use in freshman, sophomore, junior, or senior years; renewable. *Number:* 1. *Amount:* varies.

Eligibility Requirements: Applicant must be enrolled or expecting to enroll full or part-time at a two-year or four-year or technical institution or university and resident of North Carolina. Applicant must be visually impaired. Available to U.S. citizens.

Application Requirements: Application, financial need analysis, interview, proof of eligibility. *Deadline:* Continuous.

Contact: JoAnn Strader, Chief of Rehabilitation Field Services
North Carolina Division of Services for the Blind
2601 Mail Service Center
Raleigh, NC 27699-2601
Phone: 919-733-9700
Fax: 919-715-8771
E-mail: joann.strader@ncmail.net

NORTH CAROLINA DIVISION OF VOCATIONAL REHABILITATION SERVICES
http://www.dhhs.state.nc.us/

TRAINING SUPPORT FOR YOUTH WITH DISABILITIES

Public service program that helps persons with disabilities obtain jobs. To qualify, student must have a mental or physical disability that is an impediment to employment. Each program designed individually with the student. Assistance is based on need and type of program in which student enrolls.

Award: Grant for use in freshman, sophomore, junior, or senior years; renewable. *Number:* 1. *Amount:* varies.

Eligibility Requirements: Applicant must be enrolled or expecting to enroll full or part-time at a two-year or four-year or technical institution or university and resident of North Carolina. Applicant must be hearing impaired, learning disabled, physically disabled, or visually impaired. Available to U.S. citizens.

North Carolina Division of Vocational Rehabilitation Services (continued)

Application Requirements: Application, financial need analysis, interview, test scores, transcript. *Deadline:* Continuous.

Contact: Alma Taylor, Program Specialist for Transition
North Carolina Division of Vocational Rehabilitation Services
2801 Mail Service Center
Raleigh, NC 27699-2801
Phone: 919-855-3572
Fax: 919-715-0616
E-mail: alma.taylor@ncmail.net

OPTIMIST INTERNATIONAL FOUNDATION
http://www.optimist.org

COMMUNICATIONS CONTEST FOR THE DEAF AND HARD OF HEARING

College scholarship (district level) for young people through grade 12 in the U.S. and Canada, to CEGEP in Quebec and grade 13 in the Caribbean. Students interested in participating in the contest must submit the results of an audiogram conducted no longer than 24 months prior to the date of the contest from a qualified audiologist. Students must be certified to have a hearing loss of 40 decibels or more by a qualified audiologist and supported by the audiogram to be eligible to compete

Award: Scholarship for use in freshman, sophomore, junior, or senior years; not renewable. *Number:* 20–53. *Amount:* up to $1500.

Eligibility Requirements: Applicant must be enrolled or expecting to enroll full or part-time at a two-year or four-year or technical institution or university. Applicant must be hearing impaired. Available to U.S. and Canadian citizens.

Application Requirements: Application, applicant must enter a contest, self-addressed stamped envelope, speech/presentation. *Deadline:* varies.

Contact: Ms. Danielle Baugher, International Programs Coordinator
Optimist International Foundation
4494 Lindell Boulevard
St. Louis, MO 63108
Phone: 314-371-6000 Ext. 235
Fax: 314-371-6006
E-mail: baugherd@optimist.org

OREGON COMMUNITY FOUNDATION
http://www.ocf1.org/

HARRY LUDWIG SCHOLARSHIP FUND

Scholarship for visually impaired students, for use in the pursuit of a postsecondary education at a college or university.

Award: Scholarship for use in freshman, sophomore, junior, or senior years. *Number:* 1.

Eligibility Requirements: Applicant must be enrolled or expecting to enroll at a two-year or four-year institution or university; resident of Oregon and studying in Oregon. Applicant must be visually impaired. Available to U.S. citizens.

Application Requirements: *Deadline:* varies.

Contact: Dianne Causey, Program Associate for Scholarships/Grants
Oregon Community Foundation
1221 South West Yamhill, Suite 100
Portland, OR 97205
Phone: 503-227-6846

OREGON STUDENT ASSISTANCE COMMISSION
http://www.osac.state.or.us

AFSCME: AMERICAN FEDERATION OF STATE, COUNTY, AND MUNICIPAL EMPLOYEES LOCAL 75 SCHOLARSHIP
• See page 510

HARRY LUDWIG MEMORIAL SCHOLARSHIP

Award for visually-impaired Oregon residents planning to enroll full time in undergraduate or graduate studies. Must document visual impairment with a letter from a physician. Must enroll in an Oregon college.

Award: Scholarship for use in freshman, sophomore, junior, or senior or graduate years; renewable. *Number:* 7. *Amount:* $1643.

Eligibility Requirements: Applicant must be enrolled or expecting to enroll full-time at a two-year or four-year institution or university; resident of Oregon and studying in Oregon. Applicant must be visually impaired. Available to U.S. citizens.

Application Requirements: Application, essay, financial need analysis, references, transcript, documentation of visual impairment. *Deadline:* March 1.

Contact: Director of Grant Programs
Oregon Student Assistance Commission
1500 Valley River Drive, Suite 100
Eugene, OR 97401-7020
Phone: 800-452-8807 Ext. 7395

PATIENT ADVOCATE FOUNDATION
http://www.patientadvocate.org

CHERYL GRIMMEL AWARD

Scholarship for a survivor of a life threatening, chronic or debilitating disease. Applicant must maintain an overall 3.0 GPA.

Award: Scholarship for use in freshman, sophomore, junior, senior, or graduate years. *Amount:* up to $2000.

Eligibility Requirements: Applicant must be enrolled or expecting to enroll at a two-year or four-year institution or university. Applicant must be physically disabled. Applicant must have 3.0 GPA or higher. Available to U.S. citizens.

Application Requirements: Application, essay, financial need analysis, references, transcript. *Deadline:* varies.

Contact: Ruth Anne Reed, Executive Vice President of Admin. Operations
Patient Advocate Foundation
700 Thimble Shoals Boulevard, Suite 200
Newport News, VA 23606
Phone: 800-532-5274
Fax: 757-873-8999
E-mail: ruthar@patientadvocate.org

MONICA BAILES AWARD

Award for a survivor of a life threatening, chronic or debilitating disease. Applicant must maintain an overall 3.0 GPA.

Award: Scholarship for use in freshman, sophomore, junior, senior, or graduate years; not renewable. *Amount:* up to $2000.

Eligibility Requirements: Applicant must be enrolled or expecting to enroll at a two-year or four-year institution or university. Applicant must be physically disabled. Available to U.S. citizens.

Application Requirements: Application, essay, financial need analysis, references, transcript, written documentation from physician. *Deadline:* varies.

Contact: Ruth Anne Reed, Executive Vice President of Admin. Operations
Patient Advocate Foundation
700 Thimble Shoals Boulevard, Suite 200
Newport News, VA 23606
Phone: 800-532-5274
Fax: 757-873-8999
E-mail: ruthar@patientadvocate.org

PFIZER
http://www.epilepsy-scholarship.com

PFIZER EPILEPSY SCHOLARSHIP AWARD

Award for students with epilepsy who excel academically and in extracurricular activities. Must be pursuing an undergraduate degree or be a college senior entering first year of graduate school. Must be under the care of a physician for epilepsy to qualify.

Award: Scholarship for use in freshman, sophomore, junior, senior, or graduate years; not renewable. *Number:* 16. *Amount:* up to $3000.

Eligibility Requirements: Applicant must be enrolled or expecting to enroll full or part-time at a two-year or four-year or technical institution or university. Applicant must be physically disabled. Available to U.S. and non-U.S. citizens.

Application Requirements: Application, essay, references, test scores, transcript. *Deadline:* March 1.

Contact: Caren Zoppi
Pfizer
Eden Communications Group
515 Valley Street, Suite 200
Maplewood, NJ 07040
Phone: 973-275-6512
Fax: 973-275-9792
E-mail: czoppi@edencomgroup.com

RECORDING FOR THE BLIND & DYSLEXIC
http://www.rfbd.org

MARION HUBER LEARNING THROUGH LISTENING AWARDS
• See page 513

MARY P. OENSLAGER SCHOLASTIC ACHIEVEMENT AWARDS
• See page 513

SERTOMA INTERNATIONAL
http://www.sertoma.org

SERTOMA SCHOLARSHIP FOR DEAF OR HARD OF HEARING STUDENT

Applicants must have a minimum 40dB bilateral hearing loss as evidenced on audiogram by an SRT of 40dB or greater in both ears. Must have a minimum 3.2 on a 4.0 scale un-weighted GPA or be at least 85% in all courses.

Award: Scholarship for use in freshman, sophomore, junior, or senior years; not renewable. *Number:* 20–40. *Amount:* up to $1000.

Eligibility Requirements: Applicant must be enrolled or expecting to enroll full-time at a four-year institution or university. Applicant must be hearing impaired. Available to U.S. citizens.

Application Requirements: Application, essay, references, transcript, proof of hearing loss. *Deadline:* May 1.

Contact: Hearing Impaired Scholarship Program
Sertoma International
1912 East Meyer Boulevard
Kansas City, MO 64132
Phone: 816-333-8300
Fax: 816-333-4320
E-mail: infosertoma@sertoma.org

SICKLE CELL DISEASE ASSOCIATION OF AMERICA/ CONNECTICUT CHAPTER, INC.
http://www.sicklecellct.org

I. H. MCLENDON MEMORIAL SCHOLARSHIP

The I.H. McLendon Memorial Scholarship provides a one-time scholarship to graduating high school seniors with sickle cell disease in Connecticut who will enter college, university, or technical training. Minimum 3.0 GPA required.

Award: Scholarship for use in freshman year; not renewable. *Number:* 1. *Amount:* $1000.

Eligibility Requirements: Applicant must be high school student; planning to enroll or expecting to enroll full or part-time at a two-year or four-year or technical institution or university and resident of Connecticut. Applicant must be physically disabled. Applicant must have 3.0 GPA or higher. Available to U.S. citizens.

Application Requirements: Application, autobiography, interview, references, self-addressed stamped envelope, transcript, letter from applicant's physician attesting to existence of sickle cell disease. *Deadline:* April 30.

Contact: Samuel Byrd, Program Assistant
Sickle Cell Disease Association of America/Connecticut Chapter, Inc.
Gengras Ambulatory Center
114 Woodland Street, Suite 2101
Hartford, CT 06105-1299
Phone: 860-527-0119
Fax: 860-714-8007
E-mail: scdaa@iconn.net

SIR EDWARD YOUDE MEMORIAL FUND COUNCIL
http://www.sfaa.gov.hk

SIR EDWARD YOUDE MEMORIAL OVERSEAS SCHOLARSHIP FOR DISABLED STUDENTS

This program is for outstanding disabled students, of any citizenship, who are permanent residents of Hong Kong, for overseas undergraduate studies. Applicant's impairment may be visual, hearing, or physical in nature. The award is not restricted to any specific academic or career area, but cannot be used for medical studies. Upon return from overseas studies, students are expected to contribute significantly to the development of Hong Kong. For further details visit Web site: http://www.info.gov.hk/sfaa

Award: Scholarship for use in freshman, sophomore, junior, or senior years; renewable. *Number:* 1. *Amount:* up to $29,744.

Eligibility Requirements: Applicant must be enrolled or expecting to enroll full-time at a four-year institution or university. Applicant must be hearing impaired, physically disabled, or visually impaired. Available to U.S. citizens.

Application Requirements: Application, applicant must enter a contest, autobiography, essay, interview, photo, resume, references, test scores, transcript. *Deadline:* September 30.

Contact: Y. K. Wong, Council Secretariat
Sir Edward Youde Memorial Fund Council
Room 1217, 12/F., Cheung Sha Wan Government Offices
303 Cheung Sha Wan Road
Kowloon
Hong Kong
Phone: 852 2150 6103
Fax: 852 2511 2720
E-mail: sgl3@sfaa.gov.hk

SISTER KENNY REHABILITATION INSTITUTE
http://www.allina.com/

INTERNATIONAL ART SHOW FOR ARTISTS WITH DISABILITIES

One-time award for artwork submitted by artists of any age with visual, hearing, physical, or learning impairment. Contact Sister Kenny Rehabilitation Institute for show information. Application deadline is March 17. This is a one-time prize, not an academic scholarship.

Award: Prize for use in freshman, sophomore, junior, senior, or graduate years; not renewable. *Number:* 25–70. *Amount:* $25–$500.

Eligibility Requirements: Applicant must be enrolled or expecting to enroll at an institution or university and must have an interest in art. Applicant must be hearing impaired, learning disabled, physically disabled, or visually impaired. Available to U.S. and non-U.S. citizens.

Application Requirements: Application, applicant must enter a contest. *Deadline:* March 17.

Contact: Laura Swift, Administrative Assistant
Sister Kenny Rehabilitation Institute
800 East 28th Street
Minneapolis, MN 55407-3799
Phone: 612-863-4466
Fax: 612-863-8942
E-mail: laura.swift@allina.com

SPINA BIFIDA ASSOCIATION OF AMERICA
http://www.sbaa.org

LAZOF FAMILY FOUNDATION SCHOLARSHIP

Scholarship for a high school junior/senior with spina bifida. Must graduate from a four-year college or university within 4 years. Students will be granted $2500 in tuition every year for 4 years. A physician statement of disability is required, including the physician's address and phone number.

Award: Scholarship for use in freshman year. *Amount:* $2500–$10,000.

Eligibility Requirements: Applicant must be high school student and planning to enroll or expecting to enroll at a four-year institution or university. Applicant must be physically disabled. Applicant must have 3.0 GPA or higher. Available to U.S. citizens.

Spina Bifida Association of America (continued)

Application Requirements: Application, transcript, physician's statement of disability.

Contact: Maya House, Resource Center Coordinator
Spina Bifida Association of America
4590 MacArthur Boulevard, Suite 250
Washington, DC 20007-4226
Phone: 202-944-3285
Fax: 202-944-3295
E-mail: sbaa@sbaa.org

SBAA ONE-YEAR SCHOLARSHIP

Scholarship available for a student with spina bifida who is an applicant of, enrolled in, or accepted by a junior college, approved trade, vocational or business school.

Award: Scholarship for use in freshman or sophomore years. *Amount:* $2000.

Eligibility Requirements: Applicant must be enrolled or expecting to enroll at a four-year or technical institution or university. Applicant must be physically disabled. Available to U.S. citizens.

Application Requirements: Application, transcript, physician's statement of disability.

Contact: Maya House, Resource Center Coordinator
Spina Bifida Association of America
4590 MacArthur Boulevard, Suite 250
Washington, DC 20007-4226
Phone: 202-944-3285
Fax: 202-944-3295
E-mail: sbaa@sbaa.org

SPINA BIFIDA ASSOCIATION OF AMERICA FOUR-YEAR SCHOLARSHIP FUND

Renewable award for a young person born with spina bifida to achieve his/her potential through higher education, and attend a four-year college otherwise outside of his/her family's financial reach. Minimum 2.5 GPA required. Open to U.S. citizens. Application deadline is March 1.

Award: Scholarship for use in freshman year; renewable. *Number:* 1. *Amount:* $5000.

Eligibility Requirements: Applicant must be high school student and planning to enroll or expecting to enroll full-time at an institution or university. Applicant must be physically disabled. Applicant must have 2.5 GPA or higher. Available to U.S. citizens.

Application Requirements: Application, essay, financial need analysis, references, test scores, transcript, physician's statement of disability. *Deadline:* March 1.

Contact: Maya House, Resource Center Coordinator
Spina Bifida Association of America
4590 MacArthur Boulevard, Suite 250
Washington, DC 20007-4226
Phone: 202-944-3285
Fax: 202-944-3295
E-mail: sbaa@sbaa.org

THURGOOD MARSHALL SCHOLARSHIP FUND   http://www.thurgoodmarshallfund.org

NEW HORIZONS SCHOLARSHIP FUND

Undergraduate scholarships to African American and Hispanic students who have hepatitis C or are dependents of someone with hepatitis C. Students could qualify for up to $2500 per year for four years.

Award: Scholarship for use in freshman year. *Number:* up to 50. *Amount:* up to $2500.

Eligibility Requirements: Applicant must be Black (non-Hispanic) or Hispanic; high school student and planning to enroll or expecting to enroll at an institution or university. Applicant must be physically disabled. Applicant must have 2.5 GPA or higher. Available to U.S. citizens.

Application Requirements: Application, autobiography, financial need analysis, transcript.

Contact: Paul Allen, Director of National Programs
Thurgood Marshall Scholarship Fund
80 Maiden Lane, Suite 2204
New York, NY 10038
Phone: 212-573-8888
Fax: 212-573-8497
E-mail: pallen@tmsf.org

TRAVELERS PROTECTIVE ASSOCIATION OF AMERICA   http://www.tpahq.org

TRAVELERS PROTECTIVE ASSOCIATION SCHOLARSHIP TRUST FOR THE DEAF AND NEAR DEAF

Scholarships are awarded to deaf or hearing-impaired persons of any age, race, or religion for specialized education, mechanical devices, or medical or specialized treatment. Based on financial need. Deadline: March 1.

Award: Scholarship for use in freshman, sophomore, junior, senior, or graduate years; not renewable. *Number:* varies. *Amount:* $200–$1000.

Eligibility Requirements: Applicant must be enrolled or expecting to enroll at a two-year or four-year or technical institution or university. Applicant must be hearing impaired. Available to U.S. citizens.

Application Requirements: Application, financial need analysis, photo. *Deadline:* March 1.

Contact: B K. Schulte, Executive Secretary
Travelers Protective Association of America
3755 Lindell Boulevard
St. Louis, MO 63108
Phone: 314-371-0533
Fax: 314-371-0537

ULMAN CANCER FUND FOR YOUNG ADULTS   http://www.ulmanfund.org/

MATT STAUFFER MEMORIAL SCHOLARSHIP

To support the financial needs of college students who are battling or have overcome cancer who display financial need. The deadline is April 1.

Award: Scholarship for use in freshman, sophomore, junior, or senior years; not renewable. *Number:* 3–8. *Amount:* $1000.

Eligibility Requirements: Applicant must be age 16-39 and enrolled or expecting to enroll full or part-time at a two-year or four-year or technical institution or university. Applicant must be physically disabled. Available to U.S. and non-U.S. citizens.

Application Requirements: Application, autobiography, essay, financial need analysis, references, medical history. *Deadline:* April 1.

Contact: Fay Baker, Scholarship Coordinator
Ulman Cancer Fund for Young Adults
4725 Dorsey Hall Drive, Suite A
PO Box 505
Ellicott City, MD 21042
Phone: 410-964-0202
Fax: 410-964-0402
E-mail: scholarship@ulmanfund.org

UNITED STATES ASSOCIATION FOR BLIND ATHLETES   http://www.usaba.org

ARTHUR E. AND HELEN COPELAND SCHOLARSHIPS

Scholarship is awarded annually to a college student who is blind or visually impaired. All applicants must be current members of USABA. Grant to be awarded November 1st of each year.

Award: Scholarship for use in freshman, sophomore, junior, or senior years; not renewable. *Number:* 1–2. *Amount:* $500.

Eligibility Requirements: Applicant must be enrolled or expecting to enroll full-time at a two-year or four-year or technical institution or university. Applicant must be visually impaired. Available to U.S. citizens.

Application Requirements: Application, autobiography, references, transcript, proof of acceptance into program for which scholarship funds will be used. *Deadline:* October 1.

Contact: Mark Lucas, Executive Director
United States Association for Blind Athletes
33 North Institute Street
Colorado Springs, CO 80903
Phone: 719-630-0422 Ext. 13
Fax: 719-630-0616
E-mail: mlucas@usaba.org

WISCONSIN HIGHER EDUCATIONAL AIDS BOARD
http://www.heab.state.wi.us

HANDICAPPED STUDENT GRANT-WISCONSIN

One-time award available to residents of Wisconsin who have severe or profound hearing or visual impairment. Must be enrolled at least half-time at a nonprofit institution. If the handicap prevents the student from attending a Wisconsin school, the award may be used out-of-state in a specialized college. Please refer to Web site for further details: http://www.heab.state.wi.us

Award: Grant for use in freshman, sophomore, junior, or senior years; not renewable. *Number:* varies. *Amount:* $250–$1800.

Eligibility Requirements: Applicant must be enrolled or expecting to enroll full or part-time at a two-year or four-year or technical institution or university and resident of Wisconsin. Applicant must be hearing impaired or visually impaired. Available to U.S. citizens.

Application Requirements: Application, financial need analysis. *Deadline:* Continuous.

Contact: Sandy Thomas, Program Coordinator
Wisconsin Higher Educational Aids Board
PO Box 7885
Madison, WI 53707-7885
Phone: 608-266-0888
Fax: 608-267-2808
E-mail: sandy.thomas@heab.state.wi.us

YES I CAN! FOUNDATION
http://www.yesican.org

STANLEY E. JACKSON SCHOLARSHIP AWARDS

Four awards for full-time post secondary education for disabled students entering their first post secondary year for the first time, who provide evidence of financial need. Contact for specific award criteria. Past recipients are ineligible for current or future awards. Submit goals statement as well as statement verifying disability. Applicant must have a disability and also be a member of an ethnic minority group, such as African-American, Hispanic, Native American, or Asian.

Award: Scholarship for use in freshman year; not renewable. *Number:* 4–10. *Amount:* up to $500.

Eligibility Requirements: Applicant must be American Indian/Alaska Native, Asian/Pacific Islander, Black (non-Hispanic), or Hispanic; enrolled or expecting to enroll full-time at a two-year or four-year or technical institution or university and must have an interest in designated field specified by sponsor. Applicant must be hearing impaired, learning disabled, physically disabled, or visually impaired. Available to U.S. citizens.

Application Requirements: Application, essay, financial need analysis, references, transcript, verification of disability. *Deadline:* varies.

Contact: Jessa Foor, Program Development Specialist
Yes I Can! Foundation
1110 North Glebe Road, Suite 300
Arlington, VA 22201
Phone: 703-245-0607
Fax: 703-620-4334
E-mail: yesican@cec.sped.org

MILITARY SERVICE: AIR FORCE

AEROSPACE EDUCATION FOUNDATION
http://www.aef.org

AIR SPACE EDUCATION FOUNDATION SPOUSE SCHOLARSHIP

Awarded internationally to spouses of Air Force active duty, Air National Guard, or Air Force Reserve members during the spring semester. Spouses who are military members are not eligible. Minimum 3.5 GPA required.

Award: Scholarship for use in freshman, sophomore, junior, senior, or graduate years; not renewable. *Number:* 30. *Amount:* $1000.

Eligibility Requirements: Applicant must be enrolled or expecting to enroll full or part-time at a two-year or four-year or technical institution or university. Applicant must have 3.5 GPA or higher. Available to U.S. and non-U.S. citizens. Applicant or parent must meet one or more of the following requirements: Air Force or Air Force National Guard experience; retired from active duty; disabled or killed as a result of military service; prisoner of war; or missing in action.

Application Requirements: Application, essay, references, transcript, letter of college acceptance. *Deadline:* April 15.

Contact: Michelle Makinen, Program Assistance
Aerospace Education Foundation
1501 Lee Highway
Arlington, VA 22209
Phone: 800-291-8480
Fax: 703-247-5853
E-mail: mmakinen@aef.org

AIR FORCE AID SOCIETY
http://www.afas.org

GENERAL HENRY H. ARNOLD EDUCATION GRANT PROGRAM

$1500 grant provided to selected sons and daughters of active duty, Title 10 AGR/Reserve, Title 32 AGR performing full-time active duty, retired reserve and deceased Air Force members; spouses (stateside) of active members and Title 10 AGR/Reservist; and surviving spouses of deceased personnel for their undergraduate studies. Dependent children must be unmarried and under the age of 23. High school seniors may apply. Minimum 2.0 GPA is required. Applicant must reapply for subsequent years.

Award: Grant for use in freshman, sophomore, junior, or senior years; not renewable. *Number:* 3500–4000. *Amount:* $1500.

Eligibility Requirements: Applicant must be enrolled or expecting to enroll full-time at a two-year or four-year or technical institution or university. Available to U.S. citizens. Applicant or parent must meet one or more of the following requirements: Air Force or Air Force National Guard experience; retired from active duty; disabled or killed as a result of military service; prisoner of war; or missing in action.

Application Requirements: Application, financial need analysis, self-addressed stamped envelope, transcript, program's own financial forms, USAF military orders (member/parent). *Deadline:* March 10.

Contact: Education Assistance Department
Air Force Aid Society
1745 Jefferson Davis Highway, Suite 202
Arlington, VA 22202-3410
Phone: 800-429-9475
Fax: 703-607-3022
E-mail: ed@afas-hq.org

AIR FORCE RESERVE OFFICER TRAINING CORPS
http://www.afrotc.com

AIR FORCE ROTC COLLEGE SCHOLARSHIP

Air Force ROTC offers college scholarships in both technical and non-technical majors that cover tuition, books, fees and up to $400 spending cash per academic month. Air Force ROTC college scholarships can be used at over 1000 college and universities across the U.S. and Puerto Rico. Please use online application: http://www.afrotc.com

Award: Scholarship for use in freshman, sophomore, junior, or senior years; renewable. *Number:* 2000–4000. *Amount:* $9000–$15,000.

Eligibility Requirements: Applicant must be age 17-30 and enrolled or expecting to enroll full-time at a four-year institution or university. Applicant must have 3.0 GPA or higher. Available to U.S. citizens. Applicant must have served in the Air Force.

Application Requirements: Application, interview, test scores, transcript. *Deadline:* December 1.

Contact: Ty Christian, Chief Air Force ROTC Advertising Manager
Air Force Reserve Officer Training Corps
551 East Maxwell Boulevard
Maxwell Air Force Base, AL 36112-6106
Phone: 334-953-2278
Fax: 334-953-6167
E-mail: ty.christian@maxwell.af.mil

AIRMEN MEMORIAL FOUNDATION   http://www.amf.org

AIRMEN MEMORIAL FOUNDATION SCHOLARSHIP

Scholarship for full-time undergraduate studies of dependent children of Air Force, Air Force Reserve Command and Air National Guard members in active duty, retired or veteran status. Must be under age 23, have minimum combined score of 1650 on SAT 1 or 24 on ACT, and a minimum GPA of 3.5. See Web site for more information: http://www.afsahq.org/body_education02. htm. Deadline is March 31.

Award: Scholarship for use in freshman, sophomore, junior, or senior years; not renewable. *Number:* up to 17. *Amount:* $1000–$1500.

Eligibility Requirements: Applicant must be age 23 or under and enrolled or expecting to enroll full-time at a four-year institution or university. Applicant must have 3.5 GPA or higher. Available to U.S. citizens. Applicant must have served in the Air Force or Air Force National Guard.

Application Requirements: Application, essay, references, transcript. *Deadline:* March 31.

Contact: Airmen Memorial Foundation
PO Box 50
Temple Hills, MD 20748
Phone: 301-899-3500
Fax: 301-899-8136
E-mail: staff@afsahq.org.

THE AIR FORCE SERGEANTS ASSOCIATION SCHOLARSHIP

Scholarships awarded to dependent youth of Air Force Sergeants Association/ Auxiliary members. Must be under the age of 23, be enrolled or accepted as an undergraduate in an accredited college or university, have minimum combined score of 1650 on SAT 1 or 24 on ACT, and a minimum GPA of 3.5. See Web site for more information: http://www.afsahq.org/body_education02. htm. Deadline is March 31.

Award: Scholarship for use in freshman, sophomore, junior, or senior years; not renewable. *Number:* 12. *Amount:* $1500–$2500.

Eligibility Requirements: Applicant must be age 23 or under and enrolled or expecting to enroll full-time at a four-year institution or university. Applicant must have 3.5 GPA or higher. Available to U.S. citizens. Applicant must have served in the Air Force.

Application Requirements: Application, references, self-addressed stamped envelope, transcript. *Deadline:* March 31.

Contact: Airmen Memorial Foundation
PO Box 50
Temple Hills, MD 20748
Phone: 301-899-3500
Fax: 301-899-8136
E-mail: staff@afsahq.org.

THE CHIEF MASTER SERGEANTS OF THE AIR FORCE SCHOLARSHIP PROGRAM

Scholarship to financially assist the full-time undergraduate studies of dependent children of Air Force, Air Force Reserve Command and Air National Guard enlisted members in active duty, retired or veteran status. Must be under age 23 and participating in the Airmen Memorial Foundation Scholarship Program. Must have minimum combined score of 1650 on SAT 1 or 24 on ACT, and a minimum GPA of 3.5. See Web site for more information: http://www.afsahq.org/body_education02.htm

Award: Scholarship for use in freshman, sophomore, junior, or senior years; not renewable. *Amount:* $500–$3000.

Eligibility Requirements: Applicant must be age 23 or under and enrolled or expecting to enroll full-time at a four-year institution or university. Applicant must have 3.5 GPA or higher. Available to U.S. citizens. Applicant must have served in the Air Force or Air Force National Guard.

Application Requirements: Application, essay, references, self-addressed stamped envelope, transcript. *Deadline:* March 31.

Contact: Sam Parish, chairman
Phone: 800-638-0594

COMMANDER WILLIAM S. STUHR SCHOLARSHIP FUND FOR MILITARY SONS AND DAUGHTERS

COMMANDER WILLIAM S. STUHR SCHOLARSHIP FUND FOR MILITARY SONS AND DAUGHTERS

Must be a high school senior and a dependent of an active duty or retired career officer/enlisted person. Must include photo and copy of military ID card. Deadline: March 1. Must be in upper 10% of class. One award given for each branch of service, including the Reserves and the National Guard.

Award: Scholarship for use in freshman year; not renewable. *Number:* up to 6. *Amount:* up to $1125.

Eligibility Requirements: Applicant must be high school student and planning to enroll or expecting to enroll full-time at a four-year institution. Applicant must have 3.5 GPA or higher. Available to U.S. citizens. Applicant or parent must meet one or more of the following requirements: general military experience; retired from active duty; disabled or killed as a result of military service; prisoner of war; or missing in action.

Application Requirements: Application, autobiography, essay, financial need analysis, photo, references, self-addressed stamped envelope, test scores, transcript, military ID. *Deadline:* March 1.

Contact: Commander William S. Stuhr Scholarship Fund
Commander William S. Stuhr Scholarship Fund for Military Sons and Daughters
1200 Fifth Avenue, Suite 9-D
New York, NY 10029
Fax: 212-722-0139
E-mail: stuhrstudents@earthlink.net

DAUGHTERS OF THE CINCINNATI   http://www.fdncenter.org

DAUGHTERS OF THE CINCINNATI SCHOLARSHIP

Need and merit-based award available to graduating high school seniors. Minimum GPA of 3.0 required. Must be daughter of commissioned officer in regular Army, Navy, Coast Guard, Air Force, Marines (active, retired, or deceased). Must submit parent's rank and branch of service.

Award: Scholarship for use in freshman, sophomore, junior, or senior years; renewable. *Number:* up to 10. *Amount:* $1000–$3000.

Eligibility Requirements: Applicant must be high school student; planning to enroll or expecting to enroll full-time at a four-year institution and female. Applicant must have 3.0 GPA or higher. Available to U.S. citizens. Applicant or parent must meet one or more of the following requirements: Air Force, Army, Coast Guard, Marine Corps, or Navy experience; retired from active duty; disabled or killed as a result of military service; prisoner of war; or missing in action.

Application Requirements: Application, essay, financial need analysis, references, self-addressed stamped envelope, test scores, transcript. *Deadline:* March 15.

Contact: Robert Ducas, Scholarship Administrator
Daughters of the Cincinnati
122 East 58th Street
New York, NY 10022
Phone: 212-319-6915

OREGON STUDENT ASSISTANCE COMMISSION   http://www.osac.state.or.us

AFSCME: AMERICAN FEDERATION OF STATE, COUNTY, AND MUNICIPAL EMPLOYEES LOCAL 75 SCHOLARSHIP
• See page 510

SECOND BOMBARDMENT ASSOCIATION

SECOND BOMBARDMENT ASSOCIATION SCHOLARSHIP
• See page 514

SPECIAL OPERATIONS WARRIOR FOUNDATION   http://www.specialops.org

SCHOLARSHIP FOR CHILDREN OF SPECIAL OPERATIONS FORCES WHO ARE KILLED IN THE LINE OF DUTY

Scholarships for children of Special Operations Forces (Army, Navy, or Air Force) who have died as a result of an operational mission or training accident. The funds are used by the student for tuition, books, fees, room & board, transportation and personal costs.

Award: Scholarship for use in freshman, sophomore, junior, or senior years; renewable. *Number:* varies. *Amount:* varies.

Eligibility Requirements: Applicant must be age 14 and enrolled or expecting to enroll full or part-time at a two-year or four-year or technical institution. Available to U.S. citizens. Applicant or parent must meet one or more of the following requirements: Air Force, Army, or Navy experience; retired from active duty; disabled or killed as a result of military service; prisoner of war; or missing in action.

Application Requirements: Application, financial need analysis, photo, test scores, transcript, DD 1300. *Deadline:* June 15.

Contact: Carolyn Becker, Director of Education and Family Services
Special Operations Warrior Foundation
4409 El Prado Boulevard
PO Box 14385
Tampa, FL 33629
Phone: 813-805-9400
Fax: 813-805-0567
E-mail: warrior@specialops.org

MILITARY SERVICE: AIR FORCE NATIONAL GUARD

AEROSPACE EDUCATION FOUNDATION   http://www.aef.org

AIR SPACE EDUCATION FOUNDATION SPOUSE SCHOLARSHIP
• See page 567

AIR FORCE AID SOCIETY   http://www.afas.org

GENERAL HENRY H. ARNOLD EDUCATION GRANT PROGRAM
• See page 567

AIRMEN MEMORIAL FOUNDATION   http://www.amf.org

AIRMEN MEMORIAL FOUNDATION SCHOLARSHIP
• See page 568

THE CHIEF MASTER SERGEANTS OF THE AIR FORCE SCHOLARSHIP PROGRAM
• See page 568

ALABAMA COMMISSION ON HIGHER EDUCATION   http://www.ache.state.al.us

ALABAMA NATIONAL GUARD EDUCATIONAL ASSISTANCE PROGRAM

Renewable award aids Alabama residents who are members of the Alabama National Guard and are enrolled in an accredited college in Alabama. Forms must be signed by a representative of the Alabama Military Department and financial aid officer. Recipient must be in a degree-seeking program.

Award: Grant for use in freshman, sophomore, junior, senior, or graduate years; renewable. *Number:* varies. *Amount:* up to $1000.

Eligibility Requirements: Applicant must be enrolled or expecting to enroll full or part-time at a two-year or four-year or technical institution or university; resident of Alabama and studying in Alabama. Available to U.S. citizens. Applicant must have served in the Air Force National Guard or Army National Guard.

Application Requirements: Application. *Deadline:* Continuous.

Contact: William Wall, Associate Executive Director for Student Assistance
Alabama Commission on Higher Education
PO Box 302000
Montgomery, AL 36130-2000
Phone: 334-242-2271
Fax: 334-242-0268
E-mail: wwall@ache.state.al.us

COMMANDER WILLIAM S. STUHR SCHOLARSHIP FUND FOR MILITARY SONS AND DAUGHTERS

COMMANDER WILLIAM S. STUHR SCHOLARSHIP FUND FOR MILITARY SONS AND DAUGHTERS
• See page 568

DELAWARE NATIONAL GUARD   http://www.delawarenationalguard.com

STATE TUITION ASSISTANCE

Award providing tuition assistance for any member of the Air or Army National Guard attending a Delaware two-year or four-year college. Awards are renewable. Applicant's minimum GPA must be 2.0. For full- or part-time study. Amount of award varies.

Award: Scholarship for use in freshman, sophomore, junior, or senior years; renewable. *Number:* varies. *Amount:* varies.

Eligibility Requirements: Applicant must be enrolled or expecting to enroll full or part-time at a two-year or four-year institution or university and studying in Delaware. Applicant must have 2.5 GPA or higher. Available to U.S. citizens. Applicant must have served in the Air Force National Guard or Army National Guard.

Application Requirements: Application, transcript. *Deadline:* varies.

Contact: Robert Csizmadia, State Tuition Assistance Manager
Delaware National Guard
1st Regiment Road
Wilmington, DE 19808-2191
Phone: 302-326-7012
Fax: 302-326-7029
E-mail: robert.csizmadi@de.ngb.army.mil

DEPARTMENT OF VETERANS AFFAIRS (VA)   http://www.gibill.va.gov

MONTGOMERY GI BILL (SELECTED RESERVE)

This is an educational assistance program for members of the Selected Reserve of the Army, Navy, Air Force, Marine Corps and Coastal Guard, as well as the Army and Air National Guard. Available to all reservists and National Guard personnel who commit to a six-year obligation, and remain in the Reserve or Guard during the six years. Award is renewable. Monthly benefit is $297 for up to thirty-six months for full-time. For more information call 1-888-442-4551 or visit Web site: http://www.gibill.va.gov.

Award: Scholarship for use in freshman, sophomore, junior, senior, or postgraduate years; renewable. *Number:* varies. *Amount:* up to $10,692.

Eligibility Requirements: Applicant must be enrolled or expecting to enroll at a two-year or four-year or technical institution or university. Available to U.S. citizens. Applicant must have general military experience.

Application Requirements: Application, military service of 6 years in the reserve or guard. *Deadline:* Continuous.

Contact: Kieth M. Wilson, Director, Education Service
Department of Veterans Affairs (VA)
810 Vermont Avenue, NW
Washington, DC 20420
Phone: 888-442-4551

ENLISTED ASSOCIATION OF THE NATIONAL GUARD OF NEW JERSEY   http://www.eang-nj.org/scholarships.html

CSM VINCENT BALDASSARI MEMORIAL SCHOLARSHIP PROGRAM

Scholarships open to the legal children of New Jersey National Guard Members who are also members of the Enlisted Association. Also open to any drilling guardsperson who is a member of the Enlisted Association. Along with application, submit proof of parent's membership and a letter stating their reason for applying and future intents.

Award: Scholarship for use in freshman, sophomore, junior, senior, graduate, or postgraduate years; not renewable. *Number:* 6. *Amount:* $1000.

Eligibility Requirements: Applicant must be enrolled or expecting to enroll full-time at a two-year or four-year or technical institution or university. Available to U.S. citizens. Applicant or parent must meet one or more of the following requirements: Air Force National Guard

Enlisted Association of the National Guard of New Jersey (continued)

or Army National Guard experience; retired from active duty; disabled or killed as a result of military service; prisoner of war; or missing in action.

Application Requirements: Application, essay, photo, references, transcript. *Deadline:* April 15.

Contact: Scholarship Chairperson - EANG-NJ, Enlisted Association
National Guard of New Jersey
Enlisted Association of the National Guard of New Jersey
101 Eggert Crossing Road
Lawrenceville, NJ 08648

USAA SCHOLARSHIP

Scholarship open to any drilling guardsperson (need not be a member of the EANGNJ).

Award: Scholarship for use in freshman year; not renewable. *Amount:* $1000.

Eligibility Requirements: Applicant must be enrolled or expecting to enroll full-time at a technical institution. Available to U.S. citizens. Applicant or parent must meet one or more of the following requirements: Air Force National Guard or Army National Guard experience; retired from active duty; disabled or killed as a result of military service; prisoner of war; or missing in action.

Application Requirements: Application, essay, photo, transcript. *Deadline:* April 15.

Contact: SGM. Leonard Mayersohn, Scholarship Committee Chairman
Enlisted Association of the National Guard of New Jersey
Scholarship Committee
101 Eggerts Crossing Road
Lawrenceville, NJ 08648
Phone: 609-758-3446
E-mail: len.mayersohn@njdmava.state.nj.us

ILLINOIS STUDENT ASSISTANCE COMMISSION (ISAC)
http://www.collegezone.org

ILLINOIS NATIONAL GUARD GRANT PROGRAM

Award for qualified National Guard personnel which pays tuition and fees at Illinois public universities and community colleges. Must provide documentation of service. Applications are due October 1 of the academic year for full year, March 1 for second/third term, or June 15 for the summer term. Deadline dates are October 5, March 6, and June 15.

Award: Grant for use in freshman, sophomore, junior, senior, graduate, or postgraduate years; renewable. *Number:* 2000–3000. *Amount:* $1300–$1700.

Eligibility Requirements: Applicant must be enrolled or expecting to enroll full or part-time at a two-year or four-year institution or university and studying in Illinois. Available to U.S. citizens. Applicant must have served in the Air Force National Guard or Army National Guard.

Application Requirements: Application, documentation of service. *Deadline:* Continuous.

Contact: College Zone Counselor
Illinois Student Assistance Commission (ISAC)
1755 Lake Cook Road
Deerfield, IL 60015-5209
Phone: 800-899-4722
E-mail: collegezone@isac.org

IOWA COLLEGE STUDENT AID COMMISSION
http://www.iowacollegeaid.org

IOWA NATIONAL GUARD EDUCATION ASSISTANCE PROGRAM

Program provides postsecondary tuition assistance to members of Iowa National Guard Units. Must study at a postsecondary institution in Iowa. Contact for additional information.

Award: Grant for use in freshman, sophomore, junior, or senior years; not renewable. *Number:* varies. *Amount:* up to $1200.

Eligibility Requirements: Applicant must be enrolled or expecting to enroll full or part-time at a two-year or four-year or technical institution or university; resident of Iowa and studying in Iowa.

Available to U.S. citizens. Applicant must have served in the Air Force National Guard or Army National Guard.

Application Requirements: Application. *Deadline:* Continuous.

Contact: Julie Leeper, Director, State Student Aid Programs
Iowa College Student Aid Commission
200 10th Street, 4th Floor
Des Moines, IA 50309-3609
Phone: 515-242-3370
Fax: 515-242-3388
E-mail: icsac@max.state.ia.us

KANSAS NATIONAL GUARD EDUCATIONAL ASSISTANCE PROGRAM

KANSAS NATIONAL GUARD TUITION ASSISTANCE AWARD PROGRAM

Service scholarship for enlisted soldiers in the Kansas National Guard. Pays up to 100% of tuition and fees based on funding. Must attend a state-supported institution. Recipients will be required to serve in the KNG for three months for every semester of benefits after the last payment of state tuition assistance. Must not have over 15 years of service at time of application. Deadlines are February 1 and September 1. Contact KNG Education Services Specialist for further information. Must be Kansas resident.

Award: Scholarship for use in freshman, sophomore, junior, or senior years; renewable. *Number:* up to 400. *Amount:* $250–$3500.

Eligibility Requirements: Applicant must be enrolled or expecting to enroll full or part-time at a two-year or four-year or technical institution or university; resident of Kansas and studying in Kansas. Available to U.S. citizens. Applicant must have served in the Air Force National Guard or Army National Guard.

Application Requirements: Application. *Deadline:* varies.

Contact: Ray Bergman, Education Services Officer
Kansas National Guard Educational Assistance Program
2800 South West Topeka Boulevard
Topeka, KS 66611-1287
Phone: 785-274-1081
Fax: 785-274-1609
E-mail: ray.bergman@ng.army.mil

KENTUCKY NATIONAL GUARD
http://www.kyloui.ang.af.mil

KENTUCKY AIR NATIONAL GUARD EDUCATIONAL ASSISTANCE

Students receive up to $272 each month toward an undergraduate degree. May attend any college and receive up to 36 months of benefits and a maximum of $9792. Must have a high school diploma or GED and be a member of the Kentucky Air National Guard. For additional information see Web site: http://www.kyloui.ang.af.mil.

Award: Grant for use in freshman, sophomore, junior, or senior years; renewable. *Number:* varies. *Amount:* up to $3312.

Eligibility Requirements: Applicant must be enrolled or expecting to enroll at a two-year or four-year or technical institution or university. Available to U.S. citizens. Applicant must have served in the Air Force National Guard.

Application Requirements: Application. *Deadline:* Continuous.

Contact: MSGT. Scott Crimm, Relation Office Manager
Kentucky National Guard
1101 Grade Lane
Louisville, KY 40213-2616
Phone: 502-364-9604
E-mail: scott.crimm@kyloui.ang.af.mil

KENTUCKY NATIONAL GUARD TUITION AWARD PROGRAM

Tuition award available to all members of the Kentucky National Guard. Award is for study at state institutions. Members must be in good standing to be eligible for awards. Applications deadlines are April 1 and October 1. Completed AGO-18-7 required. Undergraduate study given priority.

Award: Scholarship for use in freshman, sophomore, junior, senior, or graduate years; not renewable. *Number:* varies. *Amount:* varies.

Eligibility Requirements: Applicant must be enrolled or expecting to enroll full or part-time at a two-year or four-year or technical

institution or university and studying in Kentucky. Available to U.S. citizens. Applicant must have served in the Air Force National Guard or Army National Guard.

Application Requirements: AGO-18-7. *Deadline:* varies.

Contact: Michelle Kelley, Administration Specialist
Kentucky National Guard
Education Office, 100 Minuteman Parkway
Frankfort, KY 40601
Phone: 502-607-1039
Fax: 502-607-1264
E-mail: kelleyam@bng.dma.state.ky.us

LOUISIANA NATIONAL GUARD - STATE OF LOUISIANA, JOINT TASK FORCE
LA   http://www.la.ngb.army.mil

LOUISIANA NATIONAL GUARD STATE TUITION EXEMPTION PROGRAM

Renewable award for college undergraduates to receive tuition exemption upon satisfactory performance in the Louisiana National Guard. Applicant must attend a state-funded institution in Louisiana, be a resident and registered voter in Louisiana, meet the academic and residency requirements of the university attended, and provide documentation of Louisiana National Guard enlistment. The exemption can be used for up to 15 semesters. Minimum 2.5 GPA required.

Award: Scholarship for use in freshman, sophomore, junior, or senior years; renewable. *Number:* 1. *Amount:* varies.

Eligibility Requirements: Applicant must be enrolled or expecting to enroll full or part-time at a two-year or four-year or technical institution or university; resident of Louisiana and studying in Louisiana. Applicant must have 2.5 GPA or higher. Available to U.S. citizens. Applicant must have served in the Air Force National Guard or Army National Guard.

Application Requirements: *Deadline:* Continuous.

Contact: Jona M. Hughes, Education Services Officers
Louisiana National Guard - State of Louisiana, Joint Task Force LA
Building 35, Jackson Barracks, JI-PD
New Orleans, LA 70146-0330
Phone: 504-278-8531 Ext. 8304
Fax: 504-278-8025
E-mail: hughesj@la-arng.ngb.army.mil

MINNESOTA DEPARTMENT OF MILITARY AFFAIRS
http://www.dma.state.mn.us

LEADERSHIP, EXCELLENCE AND DEDICATED SERVICE SCHOLARSHIP

Awarded to high school seniors who enlist in the Minnesota National Guard. The award recognizes demonstrated leadership, community services and potential for success in the Minnesota National Guard. For more information, applicant may contact any Minnesota army national guard recruiter at 1-800-go-guard or visit the Web site http://www.dma.state.mn.us.

Award: Scholarship for use in freshman year; not renewable. *Number:* 30. *Amount:* $1000.

Eligibility Requirements: Applicant must be high school student and planning to enroll or expecting to enroll full or part-time at a two-year or four-year or technical institution or university. Available to U.S. and non-U.S. citizens. Applicant must have served in the Air Force National Guard or Army National Guard.

Application Requirements: Essay, resume, references, transcript. *Deadline:* March 15.

Contact: Barbara O'Reilly, Education Services Officer
Minnesota Department of Military Affairs
Veterans Services Building
20 West 12th Street
St. Paul, MN 55155-2098
Phone: 651-282-4508
E-mail: barbara.oreilly@mn.ngb.army.mil

NATIONAL GUARD ASSOCIATION OF COLORADO EDUCATION FOUNDATION
http://www.ngaco.org

ENLISTED ASSOCIATION OF THE NATIONAL GUARD OF THE UNITED STATES CSM VIRGIL R. WILLIAMS SCHOLARSHIP

Scholarships for undergraduate students. Current members of EANGUS are eligible. Awarded in the amount of $2000. Awards will be sent directly to the recipient with each check made payable to the recipient's choice of school.

Award: Scholarship for use in freshman, sophomore, junior, or senior years. *Number:* 2. *Amount:* $2000.

Eligibility Requirements: Applicant must be enrolled or expecting to enroll full-time at a four-year institution or university. Available to U.S. citizens. Applicant must have served in the Air Force National Guard or Army National Guard.

Application Requirements: Financial need analysis, references, transcript. *Deadline:* July 1.

Contact: Col. Jay Gates, President NGACO Education Foundation
National Guard Association of Colorado Education Foundation
6848 South Revere Parkway
Suite 2-234
Centennial, CO 80112-6703
Phone: 720-847-7700
E-mail: Jay.Gates@cobuck.ang.af.mil

NATIONAL GUARD ASSOCIATION OF COLORADO (NGACO) EDUCATION FOUNDATION INC. SCHOLARSHIP

Scholarships for current members of the Colorado National Guard. Applicants must be enrolled as full or part-time at a college, university, trade or business school.

Award: Scholarship for use in freshman, sophomore, junior, senior, or postgraduate years. *Number:* 11. *Amount:* $500–$1000.

Eligibility Requirements: Applicant must be enrolled or expecting to enroll full or part-time at a four-year or technical institution or university. Available to U.S. citizens. Applicant must have served in the Air Force National Guard or Army National Guard.

Application Requirements: Essay, references, transcript. *Deadline:* varies.

Contact: Col. Jay C. Gates, President NGACO Education Foundation
Phone: 720-847-7700
E-mail: Jay.Gates@cobuck.ang.af.mil

NEBRASKA NATIONAL GUARD   http://www.neguard.com

NEBRASKA NATIONAL GUARD TUITION CREDIT

Renewable award for members of the Nebraska National Guard. Pays 75% of enlisted soldier's tuition until he or she has received a baccalaureate degree.

Award: Scholarship for use in freshman, sophomore, junior, or senior years; renewable. *Number:* up to 1200.

Eligibility Requirements: Applicant must be enrolled or expecting to enroll full or part-time at a four-year or technical institution or university; resident of Nebraska and studying in Nebraska. Available to U.S. citizens. Applicant must have served in the Air Force National Guard or Army National Guard.

Application Requirements: Application. *Deadline:* Continuous.

Contact: Cindy York, Administrative Assistant
Nebraska National Guard
1300 Military Road
Lincoln, NE 68508-1090
Phone: 402-309-7143
Fax: 402-309-7128

NORTH CAROLINA NATIONAL GUARD
http://www.nc.ngb.army.mil/education

NORTH CAROLINA NATIONAL GUARD TUITION ASSISTANCE PROGRAM

Scholarship for members of the North Carolina Air and Army National Guard who will remain in the service for two years following the period for which assistance is provided. Applicants must reapply for each academic period. For use at approved North Carolina institutions. Deadline: last day of late registration period set by the school. Applicant must currently be serving in

North Carolina National Guard (continued)

the Air National Guard or Army National Guard. Annual maximum (July 1 through June 30) of $2000. Career maximum of $8000.

Award: Grant for use in freshman, sophomore, junior, senior, or graduate years; not renewable. *Number:* varies. *Amount:* up to $2000.

Eligibility Requirements: Applicant must be enrolled or expecting to enroll full or part-time at a two-year or four-year or technical institution or university and studying in North Carolina. Available to U.S. citizens. Applicant must have served in the Air Force National Guard or Army National Guard.

Application Requirements: Application. *Deadline:* varies.

Contact: Capt. Miriam Gray, Education Services Officer
North Carolina National Guard
4105 Reedy Creek Road
Raleigh, NC 27607-6410
Phone: 800-621-4136 Ext. 6272
Fax: 919-664-6520
E-mail: miriam.gray@nc.ngb.army.mil

OHIO ADJUTANT GENERAL'S DEPARTMENT
http://www.ohionationalguard.com

OHIO NATIONAL GUARD SCHOLARSHIP PROGRAM

Scholarships are for undergraduate studies at an approved Ohio postsecondary institution. Applicants must enlist for six years of Selective Service Reserve Duty in the Ohio National Guard. Scholarship pays 100% instructional and general fees for public institutions and an average of cost of public schools is available for private schools. Must be 18 years of age or older. Award is renewable. Deadlines: July 1, November 1, February 1, April 1.

Award: Scholarship for use in freshman, sophomore, junior, or senior years; renewable. *Number:* 3500–8000. *Amount:* $3000.

Eligibility Requirements: Applicant must be age 18 and enrolled or expecting to enroll full or part-time at a four-year institution or university. Available to U.S. citizens. Applicant must have served in the Air Force National Guard or Army National Guard.

Application Requirements: Application. *Deadline:* varies.

Contact: Toni E. Davis, Grants Administrator
Phone: 614-336-7032
E-mail: davist@tagoh.org

OHIO NATIONAL GUARD
http://www.ongsp.org

OHIO NATIONAL GUARD SCHOLARSHIP PROGRAM

Scholarships are for undergraduate studies at an approved Ohio postsecondary institution. Applicants must enlist for six years of Selective Service Reserve Duty in the Ohio National Guard. Scholarship pays 100% instructional and general fees for public institutions and an average of cost of public schools is available for private schools. Must be 18 years of age or older. Award is renewable. Deadlines: July 1, November 1, February 1, April 1.

Award: Scholarship for use in freshman, sophomore, junior, or senior years; renewable. *Number:* 3500–8000. *Amount:* up to $3000.

Eligibility Requirements: Applicant must be age 18; enrolled or expecting to enroll full or part-time at a two-year or four-year or technical institution or university and studying in Ohio. Available to U.S. citizens. Applicant must have served in the Air Force National Guard or Army National Guard.

Application Requirements: Application. *Deadline:* varies.

Contact: Toni Davis, Grants Administrator
Ohio National Guard
2825 West Dublin Granville Road
Columbus, OH 43235-2789
Phone: 614-336-7032
Fax: 614-336-7318
E-mail: toni.davis@tagoh.org

OREGON STUDENT ASSISTANCE COMMISSION
http://www.osac.state.or.us

AFSCME: AMERICAN FEDERATION OF STATE, COUNTY, AND MUNICIPAL EMPLOYEES LOCAL 75 SCHOLARSHIP
• *See page 510*

STATE STUDENT ASSISTANCE COMMISSION OF INDIANA (SSACI)
http://www.in.gov/ssaci

INDIANA NATIONAL GUARD SUPPLEMENTAL GRANT

The award is a supplement to the Indiana Higher Education Grant program. Applicants must be members of the Indiana National Guard. All Guard paperwork must be completed prior to the start of each semester. The FAFSA must be received by March 10. Award covers certain tuition and fees at select public colleges.

Award: Grant for use in freshman, sophomore, junior, or senior years; not renewable. *Number:* 503–925. *Amount:* $200–$6516.

Eligibility Requirements: Applicant must be enrolled or expecting to enroll full or part-time at a two-year or four-year institution or university; resident of Indiana and studying in Indiana. Available to U.S. citizens. Applicant must have served in the Air Force National Guard or Army National Guard.

Application Requirements: Application. *Deadline:* March 10.

Contact: Grants Counselor
State Student Assistance Commission of Indiana (SSACI)
150 West Market Street, Suite 500
Indianapolis, IN 46204-2805
Phone: 317-232-2350
Fax: 317-232-2360
E-mail: grants@ssaci.state.in.us

TEXAS HIGHER EDUCATION COORDINATING BOARD
http://www.collegefortexans.com

TEXAS NATIONAL GUARD TUITION ASSISTANCE PROGRAM

Provides exemption from the payment of tuition to certain members of the Texas National Guard, Texas Air Guard or the State Guard. Must be Texas resident and attend school in Texas. Visit the TNG Web site at: http://www.agd.state.tx.us/education_office/state_tuition.htm.

Award: Scholarship for use in freshman, sophomore, junior, or senior years; renewable. *Number:* varies. *Amount:* varies.

Eligibility Requirements: Applicant must be enrolled or expecting to enroll at a four-year institution or university; resident of Texas and studying in Texas. Available to U.S. citizens. Applicant must have served in the Air Force National Guard or Army National Guard.

Application Requirements: Application. *Deadline:* varies.

Contact: State Adjutant General's Office
Texas Higher Education Coordinating Board
PO Box 5218
Austin, TX 78763-5218
Phone: 512-465-5515
E-mail: education.office@tx.ngb.army.mil

WASHINGTON NATIONAL GUARD
http://www.washingtonguard.com

WASHINGTON NATIONAL GUARD SCHOLARSHIP PROGRAM

A state funded retention incentive/loan program for both Washington Army and Air Guard members meeting all eligibility requirements. The loans are forgiven if the soldier/airman completes their service requirements. Failure to meet/complete service obligations incurs the requirement to repay the loan plus 8% interest. Minimum 2.5 GPA required. Deadline is April 30.

Award: Forgivable loan for use in freshman, sophomore, junior, or senior years; not renewable. *Number:* varies. *Amount:* $200–$4000.

Eligibility Requirements: Applicant must be enrolled or expecting to enroll full or part-time at a two-year or four-year or technical institution or university and resident of Washington. Applicant must have 2.5 GPA or higher. Available to U.S. and non-U.S. citizens. Applicant must have served in the Air Force National Guard or Army National Guard.

Application Requirements: Application, transcript, enlistment/extension documents. *Deadline:* April 30.

Contact: Mark Rhoden, Educational Services Officer
Washington National Guard
Building 15, Camp Murray
Tacoma, WA 98430-5073
Phone: 253-512-8899
Fax: 253-512-8936
E-mail: mark.rhoden@wa.ngb.army.mil

MILITARY SERVICE: ARMY

ARMY OFFICERS' WIVES CLUB OF GREATER WASHINGTON AREA   http://www.fmthriftshop.org

ARMY OFFICERS' WIVES' CLUB OF THE GREATER WASHINGTON AREA SCHOLARSHIP

Scholarship for high school seniors, college students or children or spouses of U.S. Army personnel. Scholarship awards are based on scholastic merit and community involvement.

Award: Scholarship for use in freshman, sophomore, junior, or senior years. *Number:* 1.

Eligibility Requirements: Applicant must be enrolled or expecting to enroll at a four-year institution or university. Available to U.S. citizens. Applicant or parent must meet one or more of the following requirements: Army experience; retired from active duty; disabled or killed as a result of military service; prisoner of war; or missing in action.

Application Requirements: Application, essay, references, self-addressed stamped envelope, transcript, military dependent ID card. *Deadline:* April 3.

Contact: Lynn Wilson, Scholarship Committee Chair
Army Officers' Wives Club of Greater Washington Area
7753 Jewelweed Court
PO Box 1112
Fort Myer, VA 22211
Phone: 703-527-0664
E-mail: scholar@fmthriftshop.org

COMMANDER WILLIAM S. STUHR SCHOLARSHIP FUND FOR MILITARY SONS AND DAUGHTERS

COMMANDER WILLIAM S. STUHR SCHOLARSHIP FUND FOR MILITARY SONS AND DAUGHTERS
• *See page 568*

DAUGHTERS OF THE CINCINNATI   http://www.fdncenter.org

DAUGHTERS OF THE CINCINNATI SCHOLARSHIP
• *See page 568*

DEPARTMENT OF THE ARMY   http://www.rotc.monroe.army.mil

ARMY ROTC HISTORICALLY BLACK COLLEGES AND UNIVERSITIES PROGRAM

One-time award for students attending college for the first time or freshmen in a documented five-year degree program. Must attend a historically black college or university and must join school's ROTC program. Must pass physical. Must have a qualifying SAT or ACT score. Applicant must be at least 17 by college enrollment and under thirty-one years of age in the year of graduation.

Award: Scholarship for use in freshman or sophomore years; not renewable. *Number:* 180–250. *Amount:* $5000–$16,000.

Eligibility Requirements: Applicant must be age 17-30 and enrolled or expecting to enroll full-time at a four-year institution or university. Applicant must have 2.5 GPA or higher. Available to U.S. citizens. Applicant must have served in the Army or Army National Guard.

Application Requirements: Application, essay, interview, test scores, transcript. *Deadline:* December 1.

Contact: Linda Morris, Scholarship System Analyst
Department of the Army
U.S. Army Cadet Command
Fort Monroe, VA 23651-5000
Phone: 757-788-4559
Fax: 757-727-2393
E-mail: linda.morris@usacc.army.mil

ARMY ROTC TWO-YEAR, THREE-YEAR AND FOUR-YEAR SCHOLARSHIPS FOR ACTIVE DUTY ARMY ENLISTED PERSONNEL

Award for freshman, sophomore, and junior year for use at a four-year institution for Army enlisted personnel. Merit considered. Must also be member of the school's ROTC program. Must pass physical and have completed two years of active duty. Applicant must be at least seventeen years of age by college enrollment and under thirty-one years of age in the year of graduation. Submit recommendations from Commanding Officer and Field Grade Commander. Include DODMERB Physical Forms and DA Form 2A.

Award: Scholarship for use in freshman, sophomore, or junior years; not renewable. *Number:* 150–350. *Amount:* $5000–$16,000.

Eligibility Requirements: Applicant must be age 17-30 and enrolled or expecting to enroll full-time at a four-year institution or university. Applicant must have 2.5 GPA or higher. Available to U.S. citizens. Applicant must have served in the Army or Army National Guard.

Application Requirements: Application, essay, photo, references, test scores, transcript, DA Form 2A, DODMERB physical, APFT, GT. *Deadline:* April 1.

Contact: Linda Morris, Scholarship System Analyst
Department of the Army
U.S. Army Cadet Command
Fort Monroe, VA 23651-5000
Phone: 757-788-4559
Fax: 757-727-2393
E-mail: linda.morris@usacc.army.mil

FOUR-YEAR AND THREE-YEAR ADVANCE DESIGNEES SCHOLARSHIP

One-time award for students entering college for the first time or freshmen in a documented five-year degree program. Must join school's ROTC program. Must pass physical and submit teacher evaluations. Must be a U.S. citizen and have a qualifying SAT or ACT score. Applicant must be at least seventeen years of age by college enrollment and under thirty-one years of age in the year of graduation. Online application available.

Award: Scholarship for use in freshman or sophomore years; not renewable. *Number:* 700–3000. *Amount:* $5000–$20,000.

Eligibility Requirements: Applicant must be age 17-30 and enrolled or expecting to enroll full-time at a four-year institution. Applicant must have 2.5 GPA or higher. Available to U.S. citizens. Applicant must have served in the Army or Army National Guard.

Application Requirements: Application, essay, interview, references, test scores, transcript. *Deadline:* December 1.

Contact: Linda Morris, Scholarship System Analyst
Department of the Army
U.S. Army Cadet Command
Fort Monroe, VA 23651-5000
Phone: 757-788-4559
Fax: 757-727-2393
E-mail: linda.morris@usacc.army.mil

TWO- AND THREE-YEAR CAMPUS-BASED SCHOLARSHIPS

One-time award for college sophomores or juniors or students with BA who need two years to obtain graduate degree. Must be a member of school's ROTC program. Must pass physical. Minimum 2.5 GPA required. Professor of military science must submit application. Applicant must be at least 17 when enrolled in college and under thirty-one years of age in the year of graduation. Deadline is December 1.

Award: Scholarship for use in sophomore, junior, or graduate years; not renewable. *Number:* 250–1500. *Amount:* $5000–$16,000.

Eligibility Requirements: Applicant must be age 17-30 and enrolled or expecting to enroll full-time at a four-year institution. Applicant must have 2.5 GPA or higher. Available to U.S. citizens. Applicant must have served in the Army or Army National Guard.

Department of the Army (continued)

Application Requirements: Application, test scores, transcript. *Deadline:* December 1.

Contact: Linda Morris, Scholarship System Analyst
Department of the Army
U.S. Army Cadet Command
Fort Monroe, VA 23651-5000
Phone: 757-788-4559
Fax: 757-727-2393
E-mail: linda.morris@usacc.army.mil

1ST CAVALRY DIVISION ASSOCIATION
http://www.1cda.org

1ST CAVALRY DIVISION ASSOCIATION SCHOLARSHIP

Scholarships of $1,000 per year for up to four years to the children of 1st Cavalry Division troopers who have died or become totally and permanently disabled while serving in the Division in combat.

Award: Scholarship for use in freshman, sophomore, junior, or senior years; renewable. *Amount:* $1000–$4000.

Eligibility Requirements: Applicant must be enrolled or expecting to enroll at an institution or university. Available to U.S. citizens. Applicant or parent must meet one or more of the following requirements: Army experience; retired from active duty; disabled or killed as a result of military service; prisoner of war; or missing in action.

Application Requirements: Application, self-addressed stamped envelope. *Deadline:* August 1.

Contact: 1st Cavalry Division Association Scholarship Foundation
1st Cavalry Division Association
302 North Main Street
Copperas Cove, TX 76522-1703
E-mail: firstcav@1cda.org

FIRST INFANTRY DIVISION FOUNDATION
http://www.bigredone.org

LIEUTENANT GENERAL CLARENCE R. HUEBNER SCHOLARSHIP PROGRAM

Renewable award for undergraduate study for children and grandchildren of veterans of the 1st Infantry Division, U.S. Army. Essay, letter of acceptance, proof of registration with Selective Service (if male), and proof of parent's or grandparent's service required. Must be high school senior to apply. Send self-addressed stamped envelope for essay topic and details. The award is for up to $4000 payable to the school in four annual installments of not more than $1000 per year.

Award: Scholarship for use in freshman, sophomore, junior, or senior years; renewable. *Number:* 3–6. *Amount:* $1000–$4000.

Eligibility Requirements: Applicant must be high school student and planning to enroll or expecting to enroll full-time at a four-year institution or university. Available to U.S. citizens. Applicant or parent must meet one or more of the following requirements: Army experience; retired from active duty; disabled or killed as a result of military service; prisoner of war; or missing in action.

Application Requirements: Application, essay, references, self-addressed stamped envelope, test scores, transcript, letter of acceptance, proof of parent's or grandparent's service with the First Infantry Division. *Deadline:* June 1.

Contact: Rosemary A. Wirs, Secretary-Treasurer
First Infantry Division Foundation
1933 Morris Road
Blue Bell, PA 19422-1422
Phone: 215-661-1969
Fax: 215-661-1934
E-mail: fdn1ld@aol.com

FISHER HOUSE FOUNDATION, INC.
http://www.fisherhouse.org

SCHOLARSHIPS FOR MILITARY CHILDREN PROGRAM

Scholarship for dependent, unmarried children under age 21 (23 if enrolled as a full time student) of active duty personnel, reserve/guard and retired military members, or survivors of deceased members. Applicants must be enrolled, or planning to enroll, in a full-time undergraduate degree program at an accredited college or university.

Award: Scholarship for use in freshman, sophomore, junior, or senior years. *Amount:* $1500.

Eligibility Requirements: Applicant must be enrolled or expecting to enroll full-time at a four-year institution or university. Available to U.S. citizens. Applicant or parent must meet one or more of the following requirements: Army experience; retired from active duty; disabled or killed as a result of military service; prisoner of war; or missing in action.

Application Requirements: Application, essay, references, transcript. *Deadline:* February 22.

Contact: Fisher House Foundation, Inc.
Fisher House Foundation, Inc, 1401 Rockville Pike, Suite 600
Rockville, MD 20852
Phone: 301-294-8560
Fax: 301-294-8562
E-mail: info@fisherhouse.org

FOUNDATION OF THE FIRST CAVALRY DIVISION ASSOCIATION
http://www.1cda.org

FOUNDATION OF THE FIRST CAVALRY DIVISION ASSOCIATION IA DRANG SCHOLARSHIP

Award for children and grandchildren of soldiers of First Cavalry Division, U.S. Air Force Forward Air Controllers and A1E pilots, and war correspondents who served in designated qualifying units which were involved in battles of the Drang Valley during the period of November 3-19, 1965. Include self-addressed stamped envelope. Total number of available awards vary each year depending on the number of applications received. More information on www.1cda.org

Award: Scholarship for use in freshman, sophomore, junior, senior, graduate, or postgraduate years; renewable. *Number:* varies. *Amount:* up to $1000.

Eligibility Requirements: Applicant must be enrolled or expecting to enroll full-time at a two-year or four-year institution or university. Available to U.S. citizens. Applicant or parent must meet one or more of the following requirements: Army experience; retired from active duty; disabled or killed as a result of military service; prisoner of war; or missing in action.

Application Requirements: Application, self-addressed stamped envelope, birth certificate(s), proof of father or grandfather's participation. *Deadline:* Continuous.

Contact: Lorinda Davison, Office Manager
Foundation of the First Cavalry Division Association
302 North Main Street
Copperas Cove, TX 76522-1799
Phone: 254-547-6537
Fax: 254-547-8853
E-mail: firstcav@1cda.org

MAINE BUREAU OF VETERANS SERVICES
http://www.state.me.us

VETERANS DEPENDENTS EDUCATIONAL BENEFITS-MAINE

Tuition waiver award for dependents or spouses of veterans who were prisoners of war, missing in action, or permanently disabled as a result of service. Veteran must have been Maine resident at service entry for five years preceding application. For use at Maine University system, technical colleges and Maine Maritime. Must be high school graduate. Must submit birth certificate and proof of VA disability of veteran. Award renewable for eight semesters for those under 22 years of age.

Award: Scholarship for use in freshman, sophomore, junior, or senior years; renewable. *Number:* varies. *Amount:* varies.

Eligibility Requirements: Applicant must be age 21-25; enrolled or expecting to enroll full or part-time at a technical institution or university; resident of Maine and studying in Maine. Available to U.S. citizens. Applicant or parent must meet one or more of the following requirements: general military experience; retired from active duty; disabled or killed as a result of military service; prisoner of war; or missing in action.

Application Requirements: Application. *Deadline:* Continuous.

Contact: Roland Lapointe, Director
Maine Bureau of Veterans Services
State House Station 117
Augusta, ME 04333-0117
Phone: 207-626-4464
Fax: 207-626-4471
E-mail: mvs@me.ngb.army.mil

MARYLAND HIGHER EDUCATION COMMISSION   http://www.mhec.state.md.us

EDWARD T. CONROY MEMORIAL SCHOLARSHIP PROGRAM

Scholarship for dependents of deceased or 100% disabled U.S. Armed Forces personnel; the son, daughter, or surviving spouse of a victim of the September 11, 2001, terrorist attacks who died as a result of the attacks on the World Trade Center in New York City, the attack on the Pentagon in Virginia, or the crash of United Airlines Flight 93 in Pennsylvania; a POW/MIA of the Vietnam Conflict or his/her son or daughter; the son, daughter or surviving spouse (who has not remarried), of a state or local public safety employee or volunteer who died in the line of duty; or a state or local public safety employee or volunteer who was 100% disabled in the line of duty. Must be Maryland resident at time of disability. Submit applicable VA certification. Must be at least 16 years of age and attend Maryland institution.

Award: Scholarship for use in freshman, sophomore, junior, senior, or graduate years; renewable. *Number:* up to 70. *Amount:* $7200–$8550.

Eligibility Requirements: Applicant must be age 16-24; enrolled or expecting to enroll full or part-time at a two-year or four-year institution or university; resident of Maryland and studying in Maryland. Available to U.S. citizens. Applicant or parent must meet one or more of the following requirements: Army experience; retired from active duty; disabled or killed as a result of military service; prisoner of war; or missing in action.

Application Requirements: Application, birth and death certificate, and disability papers. *Deadline:* July 30.

Contact: Margaret Crutchley, Office of Student Financial Assistance
Maryland Higher Education Commission
839 Bestgate Road, Suite 400
Annapolis, MD 21401-3013
Phone: 410-260-4545
Fax: 410-260-3203
E-mail: osfamail@mhec.state.md.us

101ST AIRBORNE DIVISION ASSOCIATION   http://www.screamingeagle.org

101ST AIRBORNE DIVISION ASSOCIATION CHAPPIE HALL SCHOLARSHIP PROGRAM

To provide financial assistance to students who have the potential to become assets to our nation. The major factors to be considered in the evaluation and rating of applicants are eligibility, career objectives, academic record, financial need, and insight gained from the letter requesting consideration, and letters of recommendation. Applicant's parents, grandparents, or spouse, living or deceased must have/had membership with 101st Airborne Division.

Award: Scholarship for use in freshman, sophomore, junior, senior, graduate, or postgraduate years; not renewable. *Number:* 4. *Amount:* $1000.

Eligibility Requirements: Applicant must be enrolled or expecting to enroll full-time at a two-year or four-year or technical institution or university. Available to U.S. and non-U.S. citizens. Applicant or parent must meet one or more of the following requirements: Army experience; retired from active duty; disabled or killed as a result of military service; prisoner of war; or missing in action.

Application Requirements: Application, autobiography, financial need analysis, photo, references, transcript. *Deadline:* Continuous.

Contact: Executive Secretary-Treasurer
101st Airborne Division Association
PO Box 929
Fort Campbell, KY 42223-0929
Phone: 270-439-0445
Fax: 270-439-6645
E-mail: assn101abn@aol.com

102ND INFANTRY DIVISION ASSOCIATION

102ND INFANTRY DIVISION ASSOCIATION MEMORIAL SCHOLARSHIP PROGRAM

Awards scholarships to descendants of association members. Awardees selected competitively by scholarship committee who are members of the association. To be eligible, the applicant must be a student whose father, grandfather or great-grandfather was an active member of the 102nd Infantry Division during August, 1942-March, 1946 and currently or at time of death was a life member or dues paying member. Write for application and further specifics.

Award: Scholarship for use in freshman, sophomore, or junior years; not renewable. *Number:* 20. *Amount:* $1000.

Eligibility Requirements: Applicant must be enrolled or expecting to enroll full or part-time at a two-year or four-year or technical institution or university. Available to U.S. and non-U.S. citizens. Applicant or parent must meet one or more of the following requirements: Army experience; retired from active duty; disabled or killed as a result of military service; prisoner of war; or missing in action.

Application Requirements: Application, essay, photo, references, test scores, transcript. *Deadline:* varies.

Contact: James A. Alspaugh, Committee Secretary
102nd Infantry Division Association
4311 East 55th Street
Tulsa, OK 74135-4830
Phone: 918-492-7304
E-mail: jaalsp@aol.com

OREGON STUDENT ASSISTANCE COMMISSION   http://www.osac.state.or.us

AFSCME: AMERICAN FEDERATION OF STATE, COUNTY, AND MUNICIPAL EMPLOYEES LOCAL 75 SCHOLARSHIP
• See page 510

SOCIETY OF DAUGHTERS OF THE UNITED STATES ARMY

SOCIETY OF DAUGHTERS OF THE UNITED STATES ARMY SCHOLARSHIPS

Applicants for Roberts, Wagner, Prickett, Simpson & DU.S.A scholarships must be daughter or granddaughter (step or adopted) of a career warrant (WO 1-5) or commissioned (2nd & 1st LT, CPT, MAJ, LTC, COL, and BG, MG, LT or full General) officer in the U.S. Army who: (1) is currently on active duty; (2) retired from active duty after at least 20 years of service; (3) was medically retired before 20 years of active service; (4) died while on active duty; (5) died after retiring from active duty with 20 or more years of service. U.S. Army must have been the primary occupation. Officer's name, rank, component (Active, Reserve, Retired), and inclusive dates of active duty must be included in request for application for these scholarships. Do not send birth certificates or original documents. Minimum GPA 3.0. Undergraduate students only. Must send self-addressed, stamped business envelope. Must be postmarked between November 1 and March 1.

Award: Scholarship for use in freshman, sophomore, junior, or senior years; renewable. *Number:* varies. *Amount:* $1000.

Eligibility Requirements: Applicant must be enrolled or expecting to enroll full-time at a two-year or four-year or technical institution or university; female and must have an interest in leadership. Applicant must have 3.0 GPA or higher. Available to U.S. citizens. Applicant or parent must meet one or more of the following requirements: Army experience; retired from active duty; disabled or killed as a result of military service; prisoner of war; or missing in action.

Application Requirements: Application, essay, resume, references, self-addressed stamped envelope, test scores, transcript, proof of service of qualifying service member (state relationship to member). *Deadline:* varies.

Contact: Mary P. Maroney, Chairperson, Memorial and Scholarship Funds
Society of Daughters of the United States Army
11804 Grey Birch Place
Reston, VA 20191

SPECIAL OPERATIONS WARRIOR FOUNDATION
http://www.specialops.org

SCHOLARSHIP FOR CHILDREN OF SPECIAL OPERATIONS FORCES WHO ARE KILLED IN THE LINE OF DUTY
* See page 568

WOMEN'S ARMY CORPS VETERANS ASSOCIATION
http://www.armywomen.org

WOMEN'S ARMY CORPS VETERANS ASSOCIATION SCHOLARSHIP

Scholarship available to child, grandchild, niece or nephew of an Army Service Woman. Applicant must submit documentation of sponsor's military service. Deadline is May 1. Please refer to Web site for further details: http://www.armywomen.org

Award: Scholarship for use in freshman, sophomore, junior, or senior years; renewable. *Number:* 1. *Amount:* $1500.

Eligibility Requirements: Applicant must be enrolled or expecting to enroll full-time at a four-year institution or university. Applicant must have 3.5 GPA or higher. Available to U.S. citizens. Applicant or parent must meet one or more of the following requirements: Army experience; retired from active duty; disabled or killed as a result of military service; prisoner of war; or missing in action.

Application Requirements: Application, autobiography, references, transcript, proof of relative's military service. *Deadline:* May 1.

Contact: Eldora Engebretson
Women's Army Corps Veterans Association
PO Box 5577
Fort McClellan, AL 36205-5577
Phone: 623-566-9299
E-mail: info@armywomen.org

MILITARY SERVICE: ARMY NATIONAL GUARD

ALABAMA COMMISSION ON HIGHER EDUCATION
http://www.ache.state.al.us

ALABAMA NATIONAL GUARD EDUCATIONAL ASSISTANCE PROGRAM
* See page 569

COMMANDER WILLIAM S. STUHR SCHOLARSHIP FUND FOR MILITARY SONS AND DAUGHTERS

COMMANDER WILLIAM S. STUHR SCHOLARSHIP FUND FOR MILITARY SONS AND DAUGHTERS
* See page 568

CONNECTICUT ARMY NATIONAL GUARD
http://www.ct.ngb.army.mil

CONNECTICUT ARMY NATIONAL GUARD 100% TUITION WAIVER

100% Tuition Waiver Program is for any active member of the Connecticut Army National Guard in good standing. Must be a resident of Connecticut attending any Connecticut state (public) university, community-technical college or regional vocational-technical school.

Award: Scholarship for use in freshman, sophomore, junior, or senior years; not renewable. *Number:* varies. *Amount:* varies.

Eligibility Requirements: Applicant must be age 17-65; enrolled or expecting to enroll full or part-time at a two-year or four-year or technical institution or university; resident of Connecticut and studying in Connecticut. Available to U.S. and non-U.S. citizens. Applicant must have served in the Army National Guard.

Application Requirements: Application. *Deadline:* July 1.

Contact: Capt. Jeremy Lingenfelser, Education Services Officer
Phone: 860-524-4816
Fax: 860-524-4904
E-mail: education@ct.ngb.army.mil

DELAWARE NATIONAL GUARD
http://www.delawarenationalguard.com

STATE TUITION ASSISTANCE
* See page 569

DEPARTMENT OF THE ARMY
http://www.rotc.monroe.army.mil

ARMY ROTC HISTORICALLY BLACK COLLEGES AND UNIVERSITIES PROGRAM
* See page 573

ARMY ROTC TWO-YEAR, THREE-YEAR AND FOUR-YEAR SCHOLARSHIPS FOR ACTIVE DUTY ARMY ENLISTED PERSONNEL
* See page 573

DEDICATED MILITARY JUNIOR COLLEGE PROGRAM

One-time award for high school graduates who wish to attend a two-year military junior college. Must serve simultaneously in the Army National Guard or Reserve and qualify for the ROTC Advanced Course. Must have a minimum GPA of 2.5. Must also be eighteen years of age by October 1 and under twenty-seven years of age on June 30 in the year of graduation. On-line application available. Deadline: August 25. Must be used at one of five military junior colleges.

Award: Scholarship for use in freshman year; not renewable. *Number:* 60. *Amount:* up to $20,000.

Eligibility Requirements: Applicant must be age 18-26 and enrolled or expecting to enroll full-time at a two-year institution. Applicant must have 2.5 GPA or higher. Available to U.S. citizens. Applicant must have served in the Army National Guard.

Application Requirements: Application, essay, interview, test scores, transcript. *Deadline:* August 25.

Contact: Linda Morris, Scholarship System Analyst
Department of the Army
U.S. Army Cadet Command
Fort Monroe, VA 23651-5000
Phone: 757-788-4559
Fax: 757-727-2393
E-mail: linda.morris@usacc.army.mil

FOUR-YEAR AND THREE-YEAR ADVANCE DESIGNEES SCHOLARSHIP
* See page 573

TWO- AND THREE-YEAR CAMPUS-BASED SCHOLARSHIPS
* See page 573

TWO-YEAR RESERVE FORCES DUTY SCHOLARSHIPS

One-time award for college juniors or two-year graduate degree students. Must be a member of school's ROTC program. Must pass physical. Minimum 2.5 GPA required. Applicant must be at least seventeen years of age when enrolled in college and under thirty-one years of age in the year of graduation.

Award: Scholarship for use in junior, or graduate years; not renewable. *Number:* 140–300. *Amount:* $5000–$16,000.

Eligibility Requirements: Applicant must be age 17-30 and enrolled or expecting to enroll full-time at a four-year institution or university. Applicant must have 2.5 GPA or higher. Available to U.S. citizens. Applicant must have served in the Army National Guard.

Application Requirements: Application, transcript. *Deadline:* April 16.

Contact: Linda Morris, Scholarship System Analyst
Department of the Army
U.S. Army Cadet Command
Fort Monroe, VA 23651-5000
Phone: 757-788-4559
Fax: 757-727-2393
E-mail: linda.morris@usacc.army.mil

DEPARTMENT OF VETERANS AFFAIRS (VA)
http://www.gibill.va.gov

MONTGOMERY GI BILL (SELECTED RESERVE)
* See page 569

ENLISTED ASSOCIATION OF THE NATIONAL GUARD OF NEW JERSEY
http://www.eang-nj.org/scholarships.html

CSM VINCENT BALDASSARI MEMORIAL SCHOLARSHIP PROGRAM
• See page 569

USAA SCHOLARSHIP
• See page 570

ILLINOIS STUDENT ASSISTANCE COMMISSION (ISAC)
http://www.collegezone.org

ILLINOIS NATIONAL GUARD GRANT PROGRAM
• See page 570

IOWA COLLEGE STUDENT AID COMMISSION
http://www.iowacollegeaid.org

IOWA NATIONAL GUARD EDUCATION ASSISTANCE PROGRAM
• See page 570

KANSAS NATIONAL GUARD EDUCATIONAL ASSISTANCE PROGRAM

KANSAS NATIONAL GUARD TUITION ASSISTANCE AWARD PROGRAM
• See page 570

KENTUCKY NATIONAL GUARD
http://www.kyloui.ang.af.mil

KENTUCKY ARMY NATIONAL GUARD FEDERAL TUITION ASSISTANCE

Awards available to a Guard member with satisfactory standing, who has completed basic and advanced individual training, and attends an approved accredited school to pursue a vocational, associate, bachelor, or graduate program.

Award: Scholarship for use in freshman, sophomore, junior, senior, or graduate years. *Amount:* $200.

Eligibility Requirements: Applicant must be enrolled or expecting to enroll full-time at a two-year or four-year institution or university. Available to U.S. citizens. Applicant or parent must meet one or more of the following requirements: Army National Guard experience; retired from active duty; disabled or killed as a result of military service; prisoner of war; or missing in action.

Application Requirements: Application.

Contact: Education Services Office
Kentucky National Guard
Boone National Guard Center, Vets Building, Room 124, 100
Minuteman Parkway
Frankfort, KY 40601
Phone: 502-607-1550

KENTUCKY NATIONAL GUARD TUITION AWARD PROGRAM
• See page 570

LOUISIANA NATIONAL GUARD - STATE OF LOUISIANA, JOINT TASK FORCE LA
http://www.la.ngb.army.mil

LOUISIANA NATIONAL GUARD STATE TUITION EXEMPTION PROGRAM
• See page 571

MAINE BUREAU OF VETERANS SERVICES
http://www.state.me.us

VETERANS DEPENDENTS EDUCATIONAL BENEFITS-MAINE
• See page 574

MINNESOTA DEPARTMENT OF MILITARY AFFAIRS
http://www.dma.state.mn.us

LEADERSHIP, EXCELLENCE AND DEDICATED SERVICE SCHOLARSHIP
• See page 571

NATIONAL GUARD ASSOCIATION OF COLORADO EDUCATION FOUNDATION
http://www.ngaco.org

ENLISTED ASSOCIATION OF THE NATIONAL GUARD OF THE UNITED STATES CSM VIRGIL R. WILLIAMS SCHOLARSHIP
• See page 571

NATIONAL GUARD ASSOCIATION OF COLORADO (NGACO) EDUCATION FOUNDATION INC. SCHOLARSHIP
• See page 571

NEBRASKA NATIONAL GUARD
http://www.neguard.com

NEBRASKA NATIONAL GUARD TUITION CREDIT
• See page 571

NORTH CAROLINA NATIONAL GUARD
http://www.nc.ngb.army.mil/education

NORTH CAROLINA NATIONAL GUARD TUITION ASSISTANCE PROGRAM
• See page 571

OHIO ADJUTANT GENERAL'S DEPARTMENT
http://www.ohionationalguard.com

OHIO NATIONAL GUARD SCHOLARSHIP PROGRAM
• See page 572

OHIO NATIONAL GUARD
http://www.ongsp.org

OHIO NATIONAL GUARD SCHOLARSHIP PROGRAM
• See page 572

OREGON STUDENT ASSISTANCE COMMISSION
http://www.osac.state.or.us

AFSCME: AMERICAN FEDERATION OF STATE, COUNTY, AND MUNICIPAL EMPLOYEES LOCAL 75 SCHOLARSHIP
• See page 510

STATE STUDENT ASSISTANCE COMMISSION OF INDIANA (SSACI)
http://www.in.gov/ssaci

INDIANA NATIONAL GUARD SUPPLEMENTAL GRANT
• See page 572

TEXAS HIGHER EDUCATION COORDINATING BOARD
http://www.collegefortexans.com

TEXAS NATIONAL GUARD TUITION ASSISTANCE PROGRAM
• See page 572

WASHINGTON NATIONAL GUARD
http://www.washingtonguard.com

WASHINGTON NATIONAL GUARD SCHOLARSHIP PROGRAM
• See page 572

MILITARY SERVICE: COAST GUARD

COMMANDER WILLIAM S. STUHR SCHOLARSHIP FUND FOR MILITARY SONS AND DAUGHTERS

COMMANDER WILLIAM S. STUHR SCHOLARSHIP FUND FOR MILITARY SONS AND DAUGHTERS
• See page 568

DAUGHTERS OF THE CINCINNATI
http://www.fdncenter.org

DAUGHTERS OF THE CINCINNATI SCHOLARSHIP
• See page 568

FLEET RESERVE ASSOCIATION   http://www.fra.org

COLONEL HAZEL ELIZABETH BENN U.S.M.C. SCHOLARSHIP

Scholarship available for freshman or sophomore undergraduate education for an unmarried dependent child of a Fleet Reserve Association member in good standing who served or is now serving in the U.S. Navy with an enlisted medical rating, serving with the United States Marine Corps.

Award: Scholarship for use in freshman or sophomore years; not renewable. *Amount:* up to $2000.

Eligibility Requirements: Applicant must be enrolled or expecting to enroll full-time at an institution or university and single. Available to U.S. citizens. Applicant or parent must meet one or more of the following requirements: Coast Guard, Marine Corps, or Navy experience; retired from active duty; disabled or killed as a result of military service; prisoner of war; or missing in action.

Application Requirements: Application, essay, financial need analysis, references, transcript. *Deadline:* April 15.

Contact: Vince Cuthie, Scholarship Administrator
Fleet Reserve Association
125 North West Street
Alexandria, VA 22314-2754
Phone: 703-683-1400
E-mail: fra@fra.org

FLEET RESERVE ASSOCIATION SCHOLARSHIP
• *See page 499*

SCHUYLER S. PYLE AWARD

Dependent children/grandchildren and spouses of members in good standing on the Fleet Reserve Association or a member in good standing at time of death, and members of FRA may be eligible for up to $5000. Selection is based on financial need, academic standing, character and leadership qualities. Deadline: April 15.

Award: Scholarship for use in freshman, sophomore, junior, or senior years; not renewable. *Number:* 1. *Amount:* up to $5000.

Eligibility Requirements: Applicant must be enrolled or expecting to enroll full-time at a two-year or four-year institution or university. Applicant must have 3.0 GPA or higher. Available to U.S. citizens. Applicant or parent must meet one or more of the following requirements: Coast Guard, Marine Corps, or Navy experience; retired from active duty; disabled or killed as a result of military service; prisoner of war; or missing in action.

Application Requirements: Application, essay, financial need analysis, references, test scores, transcript. *Deadline:* April 15.

Contact: Scholarship Administrator
Fleet Reserve Association
125 North West Street
Alexandria, VA 22314-2754
Phone: 703-683-1400

STANLEY A. DORAN MEMORIAL SCHOLARSHIP

Dependent children of members in good standing of the Fleet Reserve Association or of a member in good standing at time of death are eligible for this scholarship. Deadline: April 15.

Award: Scholarship for use in freshman, sophomore, junior, or senior years; not renewable. *Number:* 1. *Amount:* up to $3000.

Eligibility Requirements: Applicant must be enrolled or expecting to enroll full-time at a two-year or four-year institution or university. Applicant must have 3.0 GPA or higher. Available to U.S. citizens. Applicant or parent must meet one or more of the following requirements: Coast Guard, Marine Corps, or Navy experience; retired from active duty; disabled or killed as a result of military service; prisoner of war; or missing in action.

Application Requirements: Application, essay, financial need analysis, references, test scores, transcript. *Deadline:* April 15.

Contact: Scholarship Administrator
Fleet Reserve Association
125 North West Street
Alexandria, VA 22314-2754

LADIES AUXILIARY OF THE FLEET RESERVE ASSOCIATION   http://www.la-fra.org

ALLIE MAE ODEN MEMORIAL SCHOLARSHIP
• *See page 504*

NEW YORK COUNCIL NAVY LEAGUE   http://www.nynavyleague.org/

NEW YORK COUNCIL NAVY LEAGUE SCHOLARSHIP FUND

Renewable, merit-based award available for undergraduate study to dependents of active, retired, disabled or deceased (in line of duty or after retirement) members of regular or reserve Navy, Marine Corps, Coast Guard or Merchant Marine. Must be a Connecticut, New Jersey or New York resident. Minimum 3.0 GPA required.

Award: Scholarship for use in freshman, sophomore, junior, or senior years; renewable. *Number:* 15. *Amount:* $3000–$5000.

Eligibility Requirements: Applicant must be enrolled or expecting to enroll full-time at a two-year or four-year institution or university and resident of Connecticut, New Jersey, or New York. Applicant must have 3.0 GPA or higher. Available to U.S. citizens. Applicant or parent must meet one or more of the following requirements: Coast Guard, Marine Corps, or Navy experience; retired from active duty; disabled or killed as a result of military service; prisoner of war; or missing in action.

Application Requirements: Application, financial need analysis, references, self-addressed stamped envelope, test scores, transcript. *Deadline:* June 15.

Contact: Donald Sternberg, Executive Administrator
New York Council Navy League
c/o USCG Battery Park Building, 1 South Street, Room 314
New York, NY 10004
Phone: 212-825-7333
Fax: 212-668-2138
E-mail: chiefync@aol.com

OREGON STUDENT ASSISTANCE COMMISSION   http://www.osac.state.or.us

AFSCME: AMERICAN FEDERATION OF STATE, COUNTY, AND MUNICIPAL EMPLOYEES LOCAL 75 SCHOLARSHIP
• *See page 510*

TAILHOOK EDUCATIONAL FOUNDATION   http://www.tailhook.org

TAILHOOK EDUCATIONAL FOUNDATION SCHOLARSHIP
• *See page 551*

MILITARY SERVICE: GENERAL

ALABAMA DEPARTMENT OF VETERANS AFFAIRS   http://www.va.state.al.us

ALABAMA G.I. DEPENDENTS SCHOLARSHIP PROGRAM

Full scholarship for dependents of Alabama disabled, prisoner-of-war, or missing-in-action veterans. Child or stepchild must initiate training before 26th birthday; age 30 deadline may apply in certain situations. No age deadline for spouses or widows. Contact for application procedures and deadline.

Award: Scholarship for use in freshman, sophomore, junior, senior, or graduate years; renewable. *Number:* varies. *Amount:* varies.

Eligibility Requirements: Applicant must be enrolled or expecting to enroll full or part-time at a four-year or technical institution or university; resident of Alabama and studying in Alabama. Available to U.S. and non-U.S. citizens. Applicant or parent must meet one or more of the following requirements: general military experience; retired from active duty; disabled or killed as a result of military service; prisoner of war; or missing in action.

Application Requirements: Application. *Deadline:* varies.

Contact: Willie E. Moore, Scholarship Administrator
Alabama Department of Veterans Affairs
PO Box 1509
Montgomery, AL 36102-1509
Phone: 334-242-5077
Fax: 334-242-5102
E-mail: wmoore@va.state.al.us

AMERICAN LEGION AUXILIARY, DEPARTMENT OF ALABAMA

AMERICAN LEGION AUXILIARY DEPARTMENT OF ALABAMA SCHOLARSHIP PROGRAM

Merit-based scholarships for Alabama residents, preferably ages 17-25, who are children or grandchildren of veterans of World War I, World War II, Korea, Vietnam, Operation Desert Storm, Beirut, Grenada, or Panama. Submit proof of relationship and service record. Renewable awards of $850 each. Send self-addressed stamped envelope for application.

Award: Scholarship for use in freshman, sophomore, junior, or senior years; renewable. *Number:* 40. *Amount:* $850.

Eligibility Requirements: Applicant must be age 17-25; enrolled or expecting to enroll full or part-time at a four-year institution or university and resident of Alabama. Applicant must have 3.5 GPA or higher. Available to U.S. citizens. Applicant or parent must meet one or more of the following requirements: general military experience; retired from active duty; disabled or killed as a result of military service; prisoner of war; or missing in action.

Application Requirements: Application, financial need analysis, photo, references, self-addressed stamped envelope, test scores, transcript. *Deadline:* April 1.

Contact: Anita Barber, Education and Scholarship Chairperson
American Legion Auxiliary, Department of Alabama
120 North Jackson Street
Montgomery, AL 36104-3811
Phone: 334-262-1176
Fax: 334-262-1176
E-mail: americanlegionaux1@juno.com

AMERICAN LEGION AUXILIARY, DEPARTMENT OF ARKANSAS

AMERICAN LEGION AUXILIARY DEPARTMENT OF ARKANSAS ACADEMIC SCHOLARSHIP

One-time award for Arkansas residents who are the children of veterans who served during eligibility dates for membership. Must attend school in Arkansas. Open to high school seniors. Must complete 1,000-word essay entitled "What my country's flag means to me." Contact local American Legion Auxiliary.

Award: Scholarship for use in freshman or senior years; not renewable. *Number:* 1. *Amount:* $1000.

Eligibility Requirements: Applicant must be high school student; planning to enroll or expecting to enroll full-time at a two-year or four-year or technical institution or university; resident of Arkansas and studying in Arkansas. Available to U.S. citizens. Applicant or parent must meet one or more of the following requirements: general military experience; retired from active duty; disabled or killed as a result of military service; prisoner of war; or missing in action.

Application Requirements: Application, essay, financial need analysis, references, self-addressed stamped envelope, test scores, transcript, copy of veteran discharge papers, branch of service, dates of service, DD Form 214. *Deadline:* March 1.

Contact: Department Secretary
American Legion Auxiliary, Department of Arkansas
1415 West 7th Street
Little Rock, AR 72201
Phone: 501-374-5836

AMERICAN LEGION AUXILIARY, DEPARTMENT OF CONNECTICUT

AMERICAN LEGION AUXILIARY DEPARTMENT OF CONNECTICUT MEMORIAL EDUCATIONAL GRANT

• *See page 484*

AMERICAN LEGION AUXILIARY, DEPARTMENT OF FLORIDA
http://www.floridalegion.org

AMERICAN LEGION AUXILIARY DEPARTMENT OF FLORIDA DEPARTMENT SCHOLARSHIPS

Scholarship for children of veterans who were honorably discharged. Must be Florida resident attending an institution within Florida for full-time undergraduate study. Minimum 2.5 GPA. Must submit copy of parent's military discharge.

Award: Scholarship for use in freshman, sophomore, junior, or senior years; not renewable. *Number:* 16–22. *Amount:* $500–$1000.

Eligibility Requirements: Applicant must be enrolled or expecting to enroll full-time at a two-year or four-year or technical institution or university; resident of Florida and studying in Florida. Applicant must have 2.5 GPA or higher. Available to U.S. citizens. Applicant or parent must meet one or more of the following requirements: general military experience; retired from active duty; disabled or killed as a result of military service; prisoner of war; or missing in action.

Application Requirements: Application, financial need analysis, references, transcript, proof of discharge from branch of armed services. *Deadline:* January 1.

Contact: Marie Mahoney, Department Secretary and Treasurer
American Legion Auxiliary, Department of Florida
PO Box 547917
Orlando, FL 32854-7917
Phone: 407-293-7411
Fax: 407-299-6522
E-mail: alaflorida@aol.com

AMERICAN LEGION AUXILIARY, DEPARTMENT OF IDAHO

AMERICAN LEGION AUXILIARY, DEPARTMENT OF IDAHO NATIONAL PRESIDENT'S SCHOLARSHIP

Undergraduate scholarship for children of veterans who served in the Armed Forces during during WWI, WWII, Korean or Vietnam Wars, Grenada and Lebanon, Panama, Persian Gulf. Must be high school senior and Idaho resident. Must be entered by local American Legion Auxiliary Unit. One-time award of $2000-$2500.

Award: Scholarship for use in freshman year; not renewable. *Number:* up to 15. *Amount:* $2000–$2500.

Eligibility Requirements: Applicant must be high school student; planning to enroll or expecting to enroll full-time at a two-year or four-year or technical institution or university and resident of Idaho. Available to U.S. citizens. Applicant or parent must meet one or more of the following requirements: general military experience; retired from active duty; disabled or killed as a result of military service; prisoner of war; or missing in action.

Application Requirements: Application, essay, references, self-addressed stamped envelope, transcript. *Deadline:* March 1.

Contact: Mary Chase, Secretary
American Legion Auxiliary, Department of Idaho
905 South Warren Street
Boise, ID 83706-3825
Phone: 208-342-7066
Fax: 208-342-7066
E-mail: idalegionaux@msn.com

AMERICAN LEGION AUXILIARY, DEPARTMENT OF IOWA
http://www.ialegion.org/ala

AMERICAN LEGION AUXILIARY DEPARTMENT OF IOWA CHILDREN OF VETERANS SCHOLARSHIP

One-time award available to high school senior, who is the child of a veteran who served in the armed forces during eligibility dates for American Legion membership. Must be U.S. citizen and Iowa resident enrolled at an Iowa institution.

Award: Scholarship for use in freshman year; not renewable. *Number:* 10. *Amount:* $300.

Eligibility Requirements: Applicant must be high school student; planning to enroll or expecting to enroll full or part-time at a two-year or four-year or technical institution or university; resident of Iowa and studying in Iowa. Available to U.S. citizens. Applicant or parent must

American Legion Auxiliary, Department of Iowa (continued)

meet one or more of the following requirements: general military experience; retired from active duty; disabled or killed as a result of military service; prisoner of war; or missing in action.

Application Requirements: Application, autobiography, essay, financial need analysis, photo, references, self-addressed stamped envelope, test scores, transcript. *Deadline:* June 1.

Contact: Marlene Valentine, Secretary/Treasurer
American Legion Auxiliary, Department of Iowa
720 Lyon Street
Des Moines, IA 50309
Phone: 515-282-7987
Fax: 515-282-7583

AMERICAN LEGION AUXILIARY, DEPARTMENT OF MARYLAND

AMERICAN LEGION AUXILIARY GIRL SCOUT ACHIEVEMENT AWARD

Scholarship available to Girl Scout who has received the Girl Scout Gold Award. Must be senior in high school, an active member of her religious institution, and must have received the appropriate religious emblem, Cadette or Senior Scout level. For more information check Web site: www.legion-aux.org

Award: Prize for use in freshman year. *Number:* 1. *Amount:* $1000.

Eligibility Requirements: Applicant must be high school student; planning to enroll or expecting to enroll at a four-year institution or university and female. Available to U.S. citizens. Applicant or parent must meet one or more of the following requirements: general military experience; retired from active duty; disabled or killed as a result of military service; prisoner of war; or missing in action.

Application Requirements: Application, references, 4 letters of recommendation and testimony (1 letter required from each of the following group leaders: religious institution, school, community, and scouting), nomination application. *Deadline:* February 10.

Contact: Anna Thompson, Department Secretary
American Legion Auxiliary, Department of Maryland
1589 Sulphur Spring Road, Suite 105
Baltimore, MD 21227
Phone: 410-242-9519
Fax: 410-242-9553
E-mail: anna@alamd.org

AMERICAN LEGION AUXILIARY NATIONAL PRESIDENT'S SCHOLARSHIP

Daughters, step-daughters, sons or step-sons of veterans who served in the Armed Forces during eligibility dates for membership in the American Legion are eligible. Previous National President's Scholarship recipients are not eligible. Check Web site for more information: www.legion-aux.org.

Award: Scholarship for use in senior year. *Number:* up to 15. *Amount:* $5500.

Eligibility Requirements: Applicant must be enrolled or expecting to enroll at an institution or university. Available to U.S. citizens. Applicant or parent must meet one or more of the following requirements: general military experience; retired from active duty; disabled or killed as a result of military service; prisoner of war; or missing in action.

Application Requirements: Application, financial need analysis, references, transcript, 1 letter from either the principal or guidance counselor, clergyman/clergywoman, recipient organization verifying 50 hours of voluntary service, 2 letters from adult citizens, original article, applicant's high school grades, ACT or SAT scores. *Deadline:* March 1.

Contact: Anna Thompson, Department Secretary
American Legion Auxiliary, Department of Maryland
1589 Sulphur Spring Road, Suite 105
Baltimore, MD 21227
Phone: 410-242-9519
Fax: 410-242-9553
E-mail: anna@alamd.org

AMERICAN LEGION AUXILIARY SCHOLARSHIP FOR NON-TRADITIONAL STUDENTS

Scholarship available for a student who has had at least one year of college and is in need of financial assistance to pursue an undergraduate degree. Must

be a member of the American Legion Auxiliary or Sons of the American Legion and have paid dues for the previous two years and the year in which application is made. For more information check Web site: www.legion-aux.org

Award: Scholarship for use in freshman, sophomore, junior, senior, graduate, or postgraduate years. *Number:* up to 5. *Amount:* up to $1000.

Eligibility Requirements: Applicant must be enrolled or expecting to enroll at a two-year or four-year or technical institution or university. Available to U.S. citizens. Applicant or parent must meet one or more of the following requirements: general military experience; retired from active duty; disabled or killed as a result of military service; prisoner of war; or missing in action.

Application Requirements: Application, financial need analysis. *Deadline:* March 1.

Contact: Anna Thompson, Department Secretary
American Legion Auxiliary, Department of Maryland
1589 Sulphur Spring Road, Suite 105
Baltimore, MD 21227
Phone: 410-242-9519
Fax: 410-242-9553
E-mail: anna@alamd.org

AMERICAN LEGION AUXILIARY SPIRIT OF YOUTH SCHOLARSHIP FOR JUNIOR MEMBERS

One junior member in each division will receive a scholarship. The applicant must have held membership in the American Legion Auxiliary for the immediate past three years, currently hold a 2006 membership card, and continue to maintain her membership throughout the four-year scholarship period. For more information check Web site: www.legion-aux.org

Award: Prize for use in freshman, sophomore, junior, or senior years; renewable. *Amount:* $1000.

Eligibility Requirements: Applicant must be high school student and planning to enroll or expecting to enroll at an institution or university. Applicant must have 3.0 GPA or higher. Available to U.S. citizens. Applicant or parent must meet one or more of the following requirements: general military experience; retired from active duty; disabled or killed as a result of military service; prisoner of war; or missing in action.

Application Requirements: Application, financial need analysis, references, transcript, 1 letter from either the principal or guidance counselor, clergyman/clergywoman, recipient organization verifying 50 hours of voluntary service, 2 letters from adult citizens, original article, applicant's high school grades, ACT or SAT scores. *Deadline:* March 1.

Contact: Anna Thompson, Department Secretary
American Legion Auxiliary, Department of Maryland
1589 Sulphur Spring Road, Suite 105
Baltimore, MD 21227
Phone: 410-242-9519
Fax: 410-242-9553
E-mail: anna@alamd.org

AMERICAN LEGION AUXILIARY, DEPARTMENT OF MICHIGAN http://www.michalaux.org

AMERICAN LEGION AUXILIARY DEPARTMENT OF MICHIGAN MEMORIAL SCHOLARSHIP

For daughters, granddaughters, and great-granddaughters of any honorably discharged or deceased veteran of U.S. wars or conflicts. Must be Michigan resident for minimum of one year, females between 16 and 21, and attend college in Michigan. Include copy of discharge and copy of parent or guardian's IRS 1040 form.

Award: Scholarship for use in freshman, sophomore, junior, or senior years; not renewable. *Number:* 10–35. *Amount:* $500.

Eligibility Requirements: Applicant must be age 16-21; enrolled or expecting to enroll full or part-time at a two-year or four-year or technical institution or university; female; resident of Michigan and studying in Michigan. Available to U.S. citizens. Applicant or parent must meet one or more of the following requirements: general military experience; retired from active duty; disabled or killed as a result of military service; prisoner of war; or missing in action.

Application Requirements: Application, financial need analysis, references, transcript, discharge papers. *Deadline:* March 15.

Contact: Leisa Eldred, Scholarship Coordinator
American Legion Auxiliary, Department of Michigan
212 North Verlinden Avenue
Lansing, MI 48915
Phone: 517-371-4720 Ext. 19
Fax: 517-371-2401
E-mail: michalaux@voyager.net

AMERICAN LEGION AUXILIARY NATIONAL PRESIDENT'S SCHOLARSHIP

One-time scholarship for son or daughter of veterans who were in Armed Forces, during eligibility dates for American Legion membership. Must be high school senior in Michigan. Only one candidate per Unit. Applicant must complete 50 hours of volunteer service in the community. Submit essay of no more than 1000 words on a specified topic.

Award: Scholarship for use in freshman or senior years; not renewable. *Number:* up to 15. *Amount:* $1000–$2500.

Eligibility Requirements: Applicant must be high school student; planning to enroll or expecting to enroll full or part-time at a two-year or four-year institution or university and resident of Michigan. Available to U.S. citizens. Applicant or parent must meet one or more of the following requirements: general military experience; retired from active duty; disabled or killed as a result of military service; prisoner of war; or missing in action.

Application Requirements: Application, essay, financial need analysis, references, test scores, transcript, one letter from either the principal or guidance, a clergyman/clergywoman, recipient organization verifying fifty (50) hours of voluntary service, two letters from adult citizens, an original article consisting of no more than 1,000 words. *Deadline:* March 1.

Contact: Leisa Eldred, Scholarship Coordinator
American Legion Auxiliary, Department of Michigan
212 North Verlinden Avenue
Lansing, MI 48915
Phone: 517-371-4720 Ext. 19
Fax: 517-371-2401
E-mail: michalaux@voyager.net

SCHOLARSHIP FOR NON-TRADITIONAL STUDENT

Applicant must be a dependent of a veteran. Must be one of the following: nontraditional student returning to classroom after some period of time in which their education was interrupted, student over 22 attending college for the first time pursuing a degree, or student over the age of 22 attending a trade or vocational school. Michigan residents only; must attend Michigan institution. Judging based on: need-25 points, character/leadership-25 points, scholastic standing-25 points, initiative/goal-25 points.

Award: Scholarship for use in freshman, sophomore, junior, or senior years; not renewable. *Number:* 5. *Amount:* $1000.

Eligibility Requirements: Applicant must be age 23; enrolled or expecting to enroll full or part-time at a two-year or four-year or technical institution or university; resident of Michigan and studying in Michigan. Available to U.S. citizens. Applicant or parent must meet one or more of the following requirements: general military experience; retired from active duty; disabled or killed as a result of military service; prisoner of war; or missing in action.

Application Requirements: Application, financial need analysis, transcript. *Deadline:* March 1.

Contact: Leisa Eldred, Scholarship Coordinator
American Legion Auxiliary, Department of Michigan
212 North Verlinden Avenue
Lansing, MI 48915
Phone: 517-371-4720 Ext. 19
Fax: 517-371-2401
E-mail: michalaux@voyager.net

AMERICAN LEGION AUXILIARY, DEPARTMENT OF MINNESOTA

AMERICAN LEGION AUXILIARY DEPARTMENT OF MINNESOTA SCHOLARSHIPS

Seven $1000 awards for the sons, daughters, grandsons, or granddaughters of veterans who served in the Armed Forces during specific eligibility dates.

Must be a Minnesota resident, a high school senior or graduate, in need of financial assistance, of good character, having a good scholastic record and at least a C average. Must be planning to attend a Minnesota postsecondary institution.

Award: Scholarship for use in freshman, sophomore, junior, or senior years; not renewable. *Number:* 7. *Amount:* $1000.

Eligibility Requirements: Applicant must be enrolled or expecting to enroll at a two-year or four-year or technical institution or university; resident of Minnesota and studying in Minnesota. Available to U.S. citizens. Applicant or parent must meet one or more of the following requirements: general military experience; retired from active duty; disabled or killed as a result of military service; prisoner of war; or missing in action.

Application Requirements: Application, essay, financial need analysis, references, transcript. *Deadline:* March 15.

Contact: Eleanor Johnson, Executive Secretary
American Legion Auxiliary, Department of Minnesota
State Veterans Service Building, 20 West 12th Street, Room 314
St. Paul, MN 55155
Phone: 651-224-7634
Fax: 651-224-5243

AMERICAN LEGION AUXILIARY, DEPARTMENT OF MISSOURI

AMERICAN LEGION AUXILIARY MISSOURI STATE NATIONAL PRESIDENT'S SCHOLARSHIP
• See page 485

LELA MURPHY SCHOLARSHIP
• See page 485

AMERICAN LEGION AUXILIARY, DEPARTMENT OF NEBRASKA

AMERICAN LEGION AUXILIARY DEPARTMENT OF NEBRASKA PRESIDENT'S SCHOLARSHIPS

One-time award for Nebraska high school students who were entered into the national competition and did not win. Contact address below for more information. Must be child of a veteran. Must rank in the upper third of class or have minimum 3.0 GPA.

Award: Scholarship for use in freshman year; not renewable. *Number:* 1. *Amount:* $200.

Eligibility Requirements: Applicant must be high school student; planning to enroll or expecting to enroll full-time at a two-year or four-year or technical institution or university and resident of Nebraska. Applicant must have 3.0 GPA or higher. Available to U.S. citizens. Applicant or parent must meet one or more of the following requirements: general military experience; retired from active duty; disabled or killed as a result of military service; prisoner of war; or missing in action.

Application Requirements: Application, essay, references, test scores, transcript. *Deadline:* April 1.

Contact: Terry Walker, Department Secretary
American Legion Auxiliary, Department of Nebraska
PO Box 5227
Lincoln, NE 68505
Phone: 402-466-1808
Fax: 402-466-0182
E-mail: neaux@alltel.net

AMERICAN LEGION AUXILIARY DEPARTMENT OF NEBRASKA STUDENT AID GRANTS

One-time award for veteran or veteran's child in financial need. Must be a Nebraska resident of at least five years. Must be accepted or enrolled at an institution of higher learning. If in school, must rank in upper third of class or have a minimum 3.0 GPA.

Award: Grant for use in freshman, sophomore, junior, or senior years; not renewable. *Number:* 1–30. *Amount:* $200–$300.

Eligibility Requirements: Applicant must be enrolled or expecting to enroll full-time at a two-year or four-year or technical institution or university and resident of Nebraska. Applicant must have 3.0 GPA or higher. Available to U.S. citizens. Applicant or parent must meet one or more of the following requirements: general military experience;

American Legion Auxiliary, Department of Nebraska (continued)

retired from active duty; disabled or killed as a result of military service; prisoner of war; or missing in action.

Application Requirements: Application, financial need analysis, references, test scores, transcript. *Deadline:* April 1.

Contact: Terry Walker, Department Secretary
American Legion Auxiliary, Department of Nebraska
PO Box 5227
Lincoln, NE 68505
Phone: 402-466-1808
Fax: 402-466-0182
E-mail: neaux@alltel.net

RUBY PAUL CAMPAIGN FUND SCHOLARSHIP
• *See page 485*

AMERICAN LEGION AUXILIARY, DEPARTMENT OF NORTH DAKOTA
http://www.ndlegion.org

AMERICAN LEGION AUXILIARY, NATIONAL PRESIDENT'S SCHOLARSHIP
• *See page 538*

AMERICAN LEGION AUXILIARY, DEPARTMENT OF OHIO

AMERICAN LEGION AUXILIARY DEPARTMENT OF OHIO DEPARTMENT PRESIDENT'S SCHOLARSHIP

Scholarship for children or grandchildren of veterans who served in Armed Forces during eligibility dates for American Legion membership. Must be high school senior, ages 16 to 18, Ohio resident, and U.S. citizen. Award for full-time undergraduate study. One-time award of $1000-$2500. Deadline is March 1.

Award: Scholarship for use in freshman year; not renewable. *Number:* 2. *Amount:* $1000–$2500.

Eligibility Requirements: Applicant must be high school student; age 16-18; planning to enroll or expecting to enroll full-time at a two-year or four-year institution or university and resident of Ohio. Available to U.S. citizens. Applicant or parent must meet one or more of the following requirements: general military experience; retired from active duty; disabled or killed as a result of military service; prisoner of war; or missing in action.

Application Requirements: Application, essay, financial need analysis, references, transcript. *Deadline:* March 1.

Contact: Reva McClure, Department Scholarship Coordinator
American Legion Auxiliary, Department of Ohio
PO Box 2760
Zanesville, OH 43702-2760
Phone: 740-452-8245
Fax: 740-452-2620
E-mail: ala_pam@rrohio.com

AMERICAN LEGION AUXILIARY, DEPARTMENT OF OREGON

AMERICAN LEGION AUXILIARY, DEPARTMENT OF OREGON NATIONAL PRESIDENT'S SCHOLARSHIP

One-time award for children of veterans who served in the Armed Forces during eligibility dates for American Legion membership. Must be high school senior and Oregon resident. Must be entered by a local American Legion auxiliary unit. Two scholarships of varying amounts.

Award: Scholarship for use in freshman year; not renewable. *Number:* 2. *Amount:* $1000–$2500.

Eligibility Requirements: Applicant must be high school student; planning to enroll or expecting to enroll at an institution or university and resident of Oregon. Available to U.S. citizens. Applicant or parent must meet one or more of the following requirements: general military experience; retired from active duty; disabled or killed as a result of military service; prisoner of war; or missing in action.

Application Requirements: Application, essay, financial need analysis, interview, references, transcript. *Deadline:* March 10.

Contact: Pat Calhoun-Floren, Secretary
American Legion Auxiliary, Department of Oregon
PO Box 1730
Wilsonville, OR 97070
Phone: 503-682-3162
Fax: 503-685-5008

AMERICAN LEGION AUXILIARY, DEPARTMENT OF TENNESSEE

VARA GRAY SCHOLARSHIP-GENERAL

One-time award for high school senior who is the child of a veteran. Must be Tennessee resident and single. Award must be used within one year. Contact for more information.

Award: Scholarship for use in freshman year; not renewable. *Number:* 3. *Amount:* $500.

Eligibility Requirements: Applicant must be high school student; planning to enroll or expecting to enroll full-time at a two-year or four-year institution or university; single and resident of Tennessee. Available to U.S. citizens. Applicant or parent must meet one or more of the following requirements: general military experience; retired from active duty; disabled or killed as a result of military service; prisoner of war; or missing in action.

Application Requirements: Application, financial need analysis, references, test scores, transcript. *Deadline:* March 1.

Contact: Sue Milliken, Department Secretary and Treasurer
American Legion Auxiliary, Department of Tennessee
104 Point East Drive
Nashville, TN 37216
Phone: 615-226-8648
Fax: 615-226-8649
E-mail: alatn@bellsouth.net

AMERICAN LEGION AUXILIARY, DEPARTMENT OF TEXAS
http://www.alatexas.org

AMERICAN LEGION AUXILIARY, DEPARTMENT OF TEXAS GENERAL EDUCATION SCHOLARSHIP

Scholarships available for Texas residents. Must be a child of a veteran who served in the Armed Forces during eligibility dates. Some additional criteria used for selection are recommendations, academics, and finances. For specific information contact your local American Legion Auxiliary unit. Deadline is February 1. Number and value of awards varies.

Award: Scholarship for use in freshman, sophomore, junior, senior, graduate, or postgraduate years; not renewable. *Number:* varies. *Amount:* $500.

Eligibility Requirements: Applicant must be enrolled or expecting to enroll full-time at a two-year or four-year or technical institution or university and resident of Texas. Available to U.S. citizens. Applicant or parent must meet one or more of the following requirements: general military experience; retired from active duty; disabled or killed as a result of military service; prisoner of war; or missing in action.

Application Requirements: Application, financial need analysis, photo, resume, references, transcript, letter stating qualifications and intentions. *Deadline:* February 1.

Contact: Paula Raney, Department Secretary
American Legion Auxiliary, Department of Texas
3401 Ed Bluestein Boulevard, Suite 200
Austin, TX 78721-2902
Phone: 512-476-7278
Fax: 512-482-8391
E-mail: alatexas@txlegion.org

AMERICAN LEGION AUXILIARY, DEPARTMENT OF UTAH
http://www.legion-aux.org

AMERICAN LEGION AUXILIARY NATIONAL PRESIDENTS SCHOLARSHIP
• *See page 485*

AMERICAN LEGION AUXILIARY, DEPARTMENT OF WASHINGTON
http://www.walegion-aux.org

AMERICAN LEGION AUXILIARY, DEPARTMENT OF WASHINGTON GIFT SCHOLARSHIPS

For a child of an incapacitated or deceased veteran. Award is for high school seniors and should be used within twelve months of receipt. Submit statement of military service of veteran parent through which applicant is eligible. One-time award of $400 for residents of Washington.

Award: Scholarship for use in freshman year; not renewable. *Number:* 1. *Amount:* $400.

Eligibility Requirements: Applicant must be high school student; age 20 or under; planning to enroll or expecting to enroll full or part-time at a two-year or four-year or technical institution or university and resident of Washington. Available to U.S. citizens. Applicant or parent must meet one or more of the following requirements: general military experience; retired from active duty; disabled or killed as a result of military service; prisoner of war; or missing in action.

Application Requirements: Application, applicant must enter a contest, essay, references, transcript. *Deadline:* April 1.

Contact: Crystal Lawrence, Department Secretary
American Legion Auxiliary, Department of Washington
3600 Ruddell Road
Lacey, WA 98503
Phone: 360-456-5995
Fax: 360-491-7442
E-mail: alawash@qwest.net

DAYLE AND FRANCES PEIPER SCHOLARSHIP

One-time award for a dependent of a veteran and a resident of Washington state. Application deadline: April 1.

Award: Scholarship for use in freshman year; not renewable. *Number:* 1. *Amount:* $500.

Eligibility Requirements: Applicant must be high school student; age 20 or under; planning to enroll or expecting to enroll full or part-time at a two-year or four-year or technical institution or university and resident of Washington. Available to U.S. citizens. Applicant or parent must meet one or more of the following requirements: general military experience; retired from active duty; disabled or killed as a result of military service; prisoner of war; or missing in action.

Application Requirements: Application, applicant must enter a contest, essay, transcript. *Deadline:* April 1.

Contact: Crystal Lawrence, Department Secretary
American Legion Auxiliary, Department of Washington
3600 Ruddell Road
Lacey, WA 98503
Phone: 360-456-5995
Fax: 360-491-7442
E-mail: alawash@qwest.net

AMERICAN LEGION AUXILIARY, NATIONAL HEADQUARTERS
http://www.legion-aux.org

AMERICAN LEGION AUXILIARY NATIONAL PRESIDENT'S SCHOLARSHIPS

These scholarships are awarded to children of veterans who served in the Armed Forces during the eligibility dates for The American Legion. One $2500 scholarship, one $2000 scholarship, and one $1000 scholarship will be awarded in each Division. Ten outstanding students will be awarded a total of $27,500 to further their higher education.

Award: Scholarship for use in freshman year; not renewable. *Number:* up to 10. *Amount:* $2000–$2500.

Eligibility Requirements: Applicant must be high school student and planning to enroll or expecting to enroll full-time at a two-year or four-year institution or university. Available to U.S. citizens. Applicant or parent must meet one or more of the following requirements: general military experience; retired from active duty; disabled or killed as a result of military service; prisoner of war; or missing in action.

Application Requirements: Application, essay, references, self-addressed stamped envelope, test scores, transcript. *Deadline:* March 1.

Contact: Department Secretary
American Legion Auxiliary, National Headquarters
777 North Meridan Street, 3rd Floor
Indianapolis, IN 46204-1189
Phone: 317-955-3853
Fax: 317-955-3884
E-mail: aef@legion-aux.org

AMERICAN LEGION SAMSUNG SCHOLARSHIP

Scholarship for undergraduate study. Eligible candidates include high school juniors who participate in and complete either an American Legion Boys State or American Legion Auxiliary Girls State Program and are a direct descendant, i.e. child, grandchild, great grandchild, etc. or a legally adopted child, of a U.S. wartime veteran who served on active duty during one or more of the periods of war officially designated as eligibility dates for membership in The American Legion by the U.S. government.

Award: Scholarship for use in freshman, sophomore, junior, or senior years. *Number:* up to 98. *Amount:* $1000–$20,000.

Eligibility Requirements: Applicant must be high school student and planning to enroll or expecting to enroll full-time at a four-year institution or university. Available to U.S. citizens. Applicant or parent must meet one or more of the following requirements: general military experience; retired from active duty; disabled or killed as a result of military service; prisoner of war; or missing in action.

Application Requirements: Application, financial need analysis, references, test scores, transcript. *Deadline:* varies.

Contact: American Legion Auxiliary, National Headquarters
777 North Meridian Street, 3rd Floor
Indianapolis, IN 46204

AMERICAN LEGION, DEPARTMENT OF IDAHO
http://home.mindspring.com/~idlegion

AMERICAN LEGION, DEPARTMENT OF IDAHO SCHOLARSHIP
• *See page 487*

AMERICAN LEGION, DEPARTMENT OF KANSAS
http://www.ksamlegion.org

ALBERT M. LAPPIN SCHOLARSHIP
• *See page 488*

HUGH A. SMITH SCHOLARSHIP FUND
• *See page 488*

ROSEDALE POST 346 SCHOLARSHIP
• *See page 488*

TED AND NORA ANDERSON SCHOLARSHIPS
• *See page 488*

AMERICAN LEGION, DEPARTMENT OF MAINE

DANIEL E. LAMBERT MEMORIAL SCHOLARSHIP

One-time award for a senior at an accredited Maine high school. Parent must be a veteran. Award is based on financial need and good character. Must be U.S. citizen. Applicant must show evidence of being enrolled, or attending accredited college or vocational technical school.

Award: Scholarship for use in freshman year; not renewable. *Number:* 1–2. *Amount:* $500.

Eligibility Requirements: Applicant must be high school student; planning to enroll or expecting to enroll full-time at an institution or university and resident of Maine. Available to U.S. citizens. Applicant or parent must meet one or more of the following requirements: general military experience; retired from active duty; disabled or killed as a result of military service; prisoner of war; or missing in action.

Application Requirements: Application, financial need analysis, references. *Deadline:* May 1.

Contact: Jerry Greenwell
American Legion, Department of Maine
PO Box 4
Bethel, ME 04217
E-mail: legionme@wtvl.net

American Legion, Department of Maine (continued)

JAMES V. DAY SCHOLARSHIP
• See page 488

AMERICAN LEGION, DEPARTMENT OF MARYLAND
http://www.mdlegion.org

AMERICAN LEGION DEPARTMENT OF MARYLAND GENERAL SCHOLARSHIP FUND

Nonrenewable scholarship for veterans or children of veterans who served in the Armed Forces during dates of eligibility for American Legion membership. Merit-based award. Deadline is June 1. Application available on Web site: http://mdlegion.org.

Award: Scholarship for use in freshman, sophomore, junior, or senior years; not renewable. *Number:* 11. *Amount:* $500.

Eligibility Requirements: Applicant must be enrolled or expecting to enroll full-time at an institution or university and resident of Maryland. Available to U.S. citizens. Applicant or parent must meet one or more of the following requirements: general military experience; retired from active duty; disabled or killed as a result of military service; prisoner of war; or missing in action.

Application Requirements: Application, essay, financial need analysis, transcript. *Deadline:* June 1.

Contact: Thomas Davis, Department Adjutant
American Legion, Department of Maryland
101 North Gay, Room E
Baltimore, MD 21202
Phone: 410-752-1405
Fax: 410-752-3822
E-mail: tom@mdlegion.org

AMERICAN LEGION, DEPARTMENT OF MICHIGAN
http://www.michiganlegion.org

GUY M. WILSON SCHOLARSHIPS

One-time award of $500 each for undergraduate use at a Michigan college. Must be resident of Michigan and the son or daughter of a veteran, living or deceased. Must submit copy of veteran's honorable discharge. Must have minimum 2.5 GPA. Total number of awards given vary each year depending upon the number of applications received. Deadline: 1st week of January.

Award: Scholarship for use in freshman, sophomore, junior, or senior years; not renewable. *Number:* varies. *Amount:* $500.

Eligibility Requirements: Applicant must be high school student; planning to enroll or expecting to enroll full or part-time at a two-year or four-year institution or university; resident of Michigan and studying in Michigan. Applicant must have 2.5 GPA or higher. Available to U.S. citizens. Applicant or parent must meet one or more of the following requirements: general military experience; retired from active duty; disabled or killed as a result of military service; prisoner of war; or missing in action.

Application Requirements: Application, essay, financial need analysis, test scores, transcript. *Deadline:* January 1.

Contact: Deanna Clark, Programs Secretary
American Legion, Department of Michigan
212 North Verlinden Avenue
Lansing, MI 48915
Phone: 517-371-4720 Ext. 11
Fax: 517-371-2401
E-mail: programs@michiganlegion.org

WILLIAM D. AND JEWELL W. BREWER SCHOLARSHIP TRUSTS

One-time award for residents of Michigan who are the sons or daughters of veterans, living or deceased. Must submit copy of veteran's honorable discharge. Several scholarships of $500 each. Must have minimum 2.5 GPA. Scholarship can be applied to any college or university within the United States. Total number of awards given vary each year depending upon the number of applications received. Deadline: 1st week of January.

Award: Scholarship for use in freshman, sophomore, junior, or senior years; not renewable. *Number:* varies. *Amount:* $500.

Eligibility Requirements: Applicant must be enrolled or expecting to enroll full or part-time at a two-year or four-year institution or university and resident of Michigan. Applicant must have 2.5 GPA or

higher. Available to U.S. citizens. Applicant or parent must meet one or more of the following requirements: general military experience; retired from active duty; disabled or killed as a result of military service; prisoner of war; or missing in action.

Application Requirements: Application, essay, financial need analysis, test scores, transcript. *Deadline:* January 1.

Contact: Deanna Clark, Programs Secretary
American Legion, Department of Michigan
212 North Verlinden Avenue
Lansing, MI 48915
Phone: 517-371-4720 Ext. 11
Fax: 517-371-2401
E-mail: programs@michiganlegion.org

AMERICAN LEGION, DEPARTMENT OF MINNESOTA
http://www.mnlegion.org

AMERICAN LEGION DEPARTMENT OF MINNESOTA MEMORIAL SCHOLARSHIP
• See page 489

MINNESOTA LEGIONNAIRES INSURANCE TRUST SCHOLARSHIP
• See page 489

AMERICAN LEGION, DEPARTMENT OF MISSOURI
http://www.missourilegion.org

CHARLES L. BACON MEMORIAL SCHOLARSHIP
• See page 489

ERMAN W. TAYLOR MEMORIAL SCHOLARSHIP

One-time $500 award given to a descendant of honorably discharged veteran who served 90 or more days of active duty in the armed forces. Applicant must provide copy of discharge certificate. Applicant must be a full-time student at accredited college or university. Must also submit an essay of 500 words or less on the subject, "Which of the Presidents was the greatest and why?" Applicant must be Missouri resident.

Award: Scholarship for use in freshman year; not renewable. *Number:* 2. *Amount:* $500.

Eligibility Requirements: Applicant must be enrolled or expecting to enroll full-time at a four-year institution or university; single and resident of Missouri. Available to U.S. citizens. Applicant or parent must meet one or more of the following requirements: general military experience; retired from active duty; disabled or killed as a result of military service; prisoner of war; or missing in action.

Application Requirements: Application, applicant must enter a contest, essay, test scores, veteran discharge certificate. *Deadline:* April 20.

Contact: Mr. John Doane, Chairman
American Legion, Department of Missouri
PO Box 179
Jefferson City, MO 65102
Phone: 417-924-8186
Fax: 573-893-2980

LILLIE LOIS FORD SCHOLARSHIP FUND

One-time award of $1000 given out to a male and female that attended a full session of the American Legion Boys/Girls State of Missouri or a full session of the Department's Cadet Patrol Academy in Jefferson City. Applicant must be Missouri resident.

Award: Scholarship for use in freshman year; not renewable. *Number:* 2. *Amount:* $1000.

Eligibility Requirements: Applicant must be high school student; age 21 or under; planning to enroll or expecting to enroll full-time at a four-year institution or university; single and resident of Missouri. Available to U.S. citizens. Applicant or parent must meet one or more of the following requirements: general military experience; retired from active duty; disabled or killed as a result of military service; prisoner of war; or missing in action.

Application Requirements: Application, financial need analysis, test scores. *Deadline:* April 20.

Contact: Mr. John Doane, Chairman
American Legion, Department of Missouri
PO Box 179
Jefferson City, MO 65102
Phone: 417-924-8186
Fax: 573-893-2980

AMERICAN LEGION, DEPARTMENT OF NEBRASKA
http://www.legion.org

EDGAR J. BOSCHULT MEMORIAL SCHOLARSHIP

One-time award available to ROTC students or veterans attending a University of Nebraska system school. Must be a full-time student to qualify. Several awards ranging from $200 to $400. Minimum 2.5 GPA required.

Award: Scholarship for use in freshman, sophomore, junior, senior, or graduate years; not renewable. *Number:* 1–5. *Amount:* $200–$400.

Eligibility Requirements: Applicant must be enrolled or expecting to enroll full-time at a four-year institution or university and studying in Nebraska. Applicant must have 2.5 GPA or higher. Available to U.S. citizens. Applicant or parent must meet one or more of the following requirements: general military experience; retired from active duty; disabled or killed as a result of military service; prisoner of war; or missing in action.

Application Requirements: Application. *Deadline:* March 1.

Contact: Burdette Burkhart, Activities Director
American Legion, Department of Nebraska
PO Box 5205
Lincoln, NE 68505-0205
Phone: 402-464-6338
Fax: 402-464-6330
E-mail: actdirlegion@alltel.net

MAYNARD JENSEN AMERICAN LEGION MEMORIAL SCHOLARSHIP
• See page 489

AMERICAN LEGION, DEPARTMENT OF NORTH DAKOTA
http://www.ndlegion.org

HATTIE TEDROW MEMORIAL FUND SCHOLARSHIP

Applicants must be a legal resident of North Dakota, a high school senior, and a direct descendent of a veteran with honorable service in the U.S. military. The student will have two (2) years from the date of graduation from high school to use his/her award.

Award: Scholarship for use in freshman year; not renewable. *Number:* varies. *Amount:* up to $2000.

Eligibility Requirements: Applicant must be high school student; planning to enroll or expecting to enroll at an institution or university and resident of North Dakota. Available to U.S. citizens. Applicant or parent must meet one or more of the following requirements: general military experience; retired from active duty; disabled or killed as a result of military service; prisoner of war; or missing in action.

Application Requirements: Application, self-addressed stamped envelope, test scores. *Deadline:* April 15.

Contact: The National Finance Director
American Legion, Department of North Dakota
PO Box 1055
Indianapolis, IN 46206

AMERICAN LEGION, DEPARTMENT OF WASHINGTON
http://www.walegion.org

AMERICAN LEGION DEPARTMENT OF WASHINGTON CHILDREN AND YOUTH SCHOLARSHIPS
• See page 490

AMERICAN LEGION, DEPARTMENT OF WEST VIRGINIA

WILLIAM F. "BILL" JOHNSON MEMORIAL SCHOLARSHIP SPONSORED BY SONS OF THE AMERICAN LEGION
• See page 490

AMERICAN LEGION, NATIONAL HEADQUARTERS
http://www.legion.org

AMERICAN LEGACY SCHOLARSHIP

Scholarship for child/children, or legally adopted child/children, of active duty United States military and Guard, and Reserve personnel who were federalized and died on active duty on or after September 11, 2001. Must be a high school senior or high school graduate. For undergraduate study at a U.S. school of higher education.

Award: Scholarship for use in freshman, sophomore, junior, or senior years. *Amount:* $26,000.

Eligibility Requirements: Applicant must be enrolled or expecting to enroll full-time at a four-year institution or university. Available to U.S. citizens. Applicant or parent must meet one or more of the following requirements: general military experience; retired from active duty; disabled or killed as a result of military service; prisoner of war; or missing in action.

Application Requirements: Application, financial need analysis, test scores, transcript, photocopy of veteran's Certificate of Death. *Deadline:* April 15.

Contact: Michael Buss, Assistant Director
American Legion, National Headquarters
PO Box 1055
Indianapolis, IN 46206-1055
Phone: 317-630-1249
Fax: 317-630-1369
E-mail: acy@legion.org

SAMSUNG AMERICAN LEGION SCHOLARSHIP

Scholarship is for high school juniors for their undergraduate study at an accredited U.S. college or university. Recipients must be enrolled as a full-time student to request his/her scholarship funds. Must be direct descendants of U.S. wartime veterans who served during one or more of the periods of war officially designated as such by the United States government.

Award: Scholarship for use in freshman year; renewable. *Number:* 98. *Amount:* $5000–$20,000.

Eligibility Requirements: Applicant must be high school student and planning to enroll or expecting to enroll full-time at a four-year institution or university. Available to U.S. citizens. Applicant or parent must meet one or more of the following requirements: general military experience; retired from active duty; disabled or killed as a result of military service; prisoner of war; or missing in action.

Application Requirements: Application, essay, financial need analysis, references, test scores. *Deadline:* varies.

Contact: Michael Buss, Assistant Director
American Legion, National Headquarters
PO Box 1055
Indianapolis, IN 46206-1055
Phone: 317-630-1249
Fax: 317-630-1369
E-mail: acy@legion.org

AMERICAN MILITARY RETIREES ASSOCIATION
http://www.amra1973.org

SERGEANT MAJOR DOUGLAS R. DRUM MEMORIAL SCHOLARSHIP FUND

One-time award limited to dependents (spouse, child, grandchild) of members of the American Military Retirees' Association, founded by Douglas R. Drum. It is to be used only for tuition, books, room and board. Must be U.S. citizen. Scholarship awarded in August.

Award: Scholarship for use in freshman, sophomore, junior, or senior years; not renewable. *Number:* 1–15. *Amount:* $500–$2000.

Eligibility Requirements: Applicant must be enrolled or expecting to enroll full-time at a two-year or four-year or technical institution or university. Available to U.S. citizens. Applicant or parent must meet one or more of the following requirements: general military experience; retired from active duty; disabled or killed as a result of military service; prisoner of war; or missing in action.

American Military Retirees Association (continued)

Application Requirements: Application, autobiography, financial need analysis, photo, references, test scores, transcript. *Deadline:* May 1.

Contact: Kathy Dow, Committee Chairperson
American Military Retirees Association
5436 Peru Street, Suite 1
Plattsburgh, NY 12901
Phone: 518-563-9479
Fax: 518-324-5204
E-mail: info@amra1973.org

AMVETS DEPARTMENT OF ILLINOIS
http://www.ilamvets.org

ILLINOIS AMVETS LADIES AUXILIARY MEMORIAL SCHOLARSHIP

Applicant must be an Illinois high school senior and a child of an honorably discharged veteran who served after September 15, 1940. Must submit ACT scores and IRS 1040 form. Submit high school rank and grades.

Award: Scholarship for use in freshman, sophomore, junior, or senior years; not renewable. *Number:* 1–3. *Amount:* $500.

Eligibility Requirements: Applicant must be high school student; planning to enroll or expecting to enroll full-time at a two-year or four-year or technical institution or university and resident of Illinois. Available to U.S. citizens. Applicant or parent must meet one or more of the following requirements: general military experience; retired from active duty; disabled or killed as a result of military service; prisoner of war; or missing in action.

Application Requirements: Application, financial need analysis, test scores, transcript, IRS 1040 form. *Deadline:* March 1.

Contact: Sara Van Dyke, Scholarship Director
AMVETS Department of Illinois
2200 South Sixth Street
Springfield, IL 62703-3496
Phone: 217-528-4713
Fax: 217-528-9896

ILLINOIS AMVETS SERVICE FOUNDATION SCHOLARSHIP AWARD

Applicant must be an Illinois high school senior. Must submit ACT scores and IRS 1040 form. Must be the child or grandchild of an honorably discharged veteran who served after September 15, 1940, or is currently serving in the military. Renewable award of $1000.

Award: Scholarship for use in freshman, sophomore, junior, or senior years; renewable. *Number:* 30. *Amount:* $1000.

Eligibility Requirements: Applicant must be high school student; age 17-18; planning to enroll or expecting to enroll full-time at a two-year or four-year or technical institution or university and resident of Illinois. Available to U.S. citizens. Applicant or parent must meet one or more of the following requirements: general military experience; retired from active duty; disabled or killed as a result of military service; prisoner of war; or missing in action.

Application Requirements: Application, financial need analysis, test scores, transcript, IRS 1040 form. *Deadline:* March 1.

Contact: Sara Van Dyke, Scholarship Director
AMVETS Department of Illinois
2200 South Sixth Street
Springfield, IL 62703-3496
Phone: 217-528-4713
Fax: 217-528-9896
E-mail: scholarship@amvetsillinois.com

ILLINOIS AMVETS TRADE SCHOOL SCHOLARSHIP

Applicant must be an Illinois high school senior who has been accepted in a pre-approved trade school program (a copy of an acceptance letter must accompany the application) and must be a child or grandchild of a veteran who served after September 15th, 1940, and honorably discharged or is presently serving in the military. Scholarship renews for two years, paying annually $500.

Award: Scholarship for use in freshman or sophomore years; renewable. *Number:* 1–2. *Amount:* up to $1000.

Eligibility Requirements: Applicant must be high school student; age 17-18; planning to enroll or expecting to enroll full-time at a technical institution and resident of Illinois. Available to U.S. citizens. Applicant

or parent must meet one or more of the following requirements: general military experience; retired from active duty; disabled or killed as a result of military service; prisoner of war; or missing in action.

Application Requirements: Application, acceptance letter. *Deadline:* March 1.

Contact: Sara Van Dyke, Scholarship Director
AMVETS Department of Illinois
2200 South Sixth Street
Springfield, IL 62703-3496
Phone: 217-528-4713
Fax: 217-528-9896
E-mail: scholarship@amvetsillinois.com

ARKANSAS DEPARTMENT OF HIGHER EDUCATION
http://www.arkansashighered.com

MISSING IN ACTION/KILLED IN ACTION DEPENDENT'S SCHOLARSHIP-ARKANSAS

Available to Arkansas residents whose parent or spouse was classified either as missing in action, killed in action, or a prisoner-of-war. Must attend state-supported institution in Arkansas. Renewable waiver of tuition, fees, room and board. Submit proof of casualty.

Award: Scholarship for use in freshman, sophomore, junior, or senior years; renewable. *Amount:* up to $2500.

Eligibility Requirements: Applicant must be enrolled or expecting to enroll full-time at a two-year or four-year or technical institution or university; resident of Arkansas and studying in Arkansas. Available to U.S. citizens. Applicant or parent must meet one or more of the following requirements: general military experience; retired from active duty; disabled or killed as a result of military service; prisoner of war; or missing in action.

Application Requirements: Application, report of casualty. *Deadline:* Continuous.

Contact: Lillian K. Williams, Assistant Coordinator
Arkansas Department of Higher Education
114 East Capitol
Little Rock, AR 72201
Phone: 501-371-2050
Fax: 501-371-2001

BLINDED VETERANS ASSOCIATION
http://www.bva.org

KATHERN F. GRUBER SCHOLARSHIP

This award is available for undergraduate or graduate study to dependent children and spouses of legally blind veterans. The veteran's blindness may be either service or non-service connected. High school seniors may apply. Applicant must be enrolled or accepted for admission as a full-time student in an accredited institution of higher learning, business, secretarial, or vocational school. Award is for one year; however, recipient may reapply and receive scholarship a maximum of four times.

Award: Scholarship for use in freshman, sophomore, junior, senior, or graduate years; not renewable. *Number:* up to 16. *Amount:* $1000–$2000.

Eligibility Requirements: Applicant must be enrolled or expecting to enroll full-time at a two-year or four-year or technical institution or university. Available to U.S. citizens. Applicant or parent must meet one or more of the following requirements: general military experience; retired from active duty; disabled or killed as a result of military service; prisoner of war; or missing in action.

Application Requirements: Application, essay, references, transcript. *Deadline:* April 11.

Contact: Brigitte Jones, Administrative Assistant
Blinded Veterans Association
477 H Street, NW
Washington, DC 20001-2694
Phone: 202-371-8880
Fax: 202-371-8258
E-mail: bva@bva.org

COLLEGE FOUNDATION OF NORTH CAROLINA, INC
http://www.cfnc.org

NORTH CAROLINA VETERANS SCHOLARSHIPS

Scholarship assists children of certain deceased or disabled veterans, or children of veterans who were listed as POW/MIA. Veteran must have been a legal resident of North Carolina at time of entry into service, or child must have been born in North Carolina and resided there continuously.

Award: Scholarship for use in freshman, sophomore, junior, senior, or graduate years. *Amount:* $1500–$4500.

Eligibility Requirements: Applicant must be enrolled or expecting to enroll at a four-year institution or university and resident of North Carolina. Available to U.S. citizens. Applicant or parent must meet one or more of the following requirements: general military experience; retired from active duty; disabled or killed as a result of military service; prisoner of war; or missing in action.

Application Requirements: Application.

Contact: College Foundation of North Carolina, Inc
North Carolina Division of Veterans Affairs, 1315 Mail Service Center
Raleigh, NC 27699-1315
Phone: 919-733-3851

DATATEL, INC.
http://www.datatel.com/dsf

ANGELFIRE SCHOLARSHIP

For any student who is a 1964-1975 Vietnam Veteran, or spouse or child of same. Also available to refugees from Cambodia, Laos, or Vietnam. Applicant must attend a Datatel client institution. Completed on-line applications must be submitted by January 31.

Award: Scholarship for use in freshman, sophomore, junior, senior, or graduate years; not renewable. *Number:* 15. *Amount:* $1000–$2400.

Eligibility Requirements: Applicant must be enrolled or expecting to enroll full or part-time at a two-year or four-year or technical institution or university. Available to U.S. and non-U.S. citizens. Applicant or parent must meet one or more of the following requirements: general military experience; retired from active duty; disabled or killed as a result of military service; prisoner of war; or missing in action.

Application Requirements: Application, essay, references, transcript. *Deadline:* January 31.

Contact: Marissa Solis, Project Leader
Datatel, Inc.
4375 Fair Lakes Court
Fairfax, VA 22033
Phone: 800-486-4332
Fax: 703-968-4573
E-mail: scholars@datatel.com

DEFENSE COMMISSARY AGENCY
http://www.militaryscholar.org

SCHOLARSHIPS FOR MILITARY CHILDREN

One-time award to unmarried dependents of military personnel for full-time undergraduate study at a four-year institution. Must be 23 years of age. Minimum 3.0 GPA. Application deadline is February 22. Further information and applications available at Web site http://www.militaryscholar.org

Award: Scholarship for use in freshman, sophomore, junior, or senior years; not renewable. *Number:* 500. *Amount:* $1500.

Eligibility Requirements: Applicant must be age 23 or under; enrolled or expecting to enroll full-time at a four-year institution and single. Applicant must have 3.0 GPA or higher. Available to U.S. citizens. Applicant or parent must meet one or more of the following requirements: general military experience; retired from active duty; disabled or killed as a result of military service; prisoner of war; or missing in action.

Application Requirements: Application, essay, references, transcript, valid military dependent's identification card. *Deadline:* February 22.

Contact: Mr. Bernard Cote
Defense Commissary Agency
307 Provincetown Road
Cherry Hill, NJ 08134
Phone: 856-573-9400
E-mail: militaryscholar@scholarshipmanagers.com

DELAWARE DEPARTMENT OF EDUCATION
http://www.doe.k12.de.us

EDUCATIONAL BENEFITS FOR CHILDREN OF DECEASED VETERANS AND OTHERS

Award for legal residents of Delaware. Must be a child of deceased U.S. military veterans or state police officers whose cause of death was service related or of military veterans held prisoner of war or declared missing in action. Must be 16 to 24 years old. Must attain full- or part-time undergraduate student admission at a public institution in Delaware. Award must not exceed tuition and fees at a Delaware public institution adjusted for other colleges.

Award: Grant for use in freshman, sophomore, junior, or senior years; renewable. *Number:* 4.

Eligibility Requirements: Applicant must be age 16-24; enrolled or expecting to enroll full or part-time at a two-year or four-year institution or university and resident of Delaware. Available to U.S. citizens. Applicant or parent must meet one or more of the following requirements: general military experience; retired from active duty; disabled or killed as a result of military service; prisoner of war; or missing in action.

Application Requirements: Application, transcript. *Deadline:* varies.

Contact: Maureen Laffey, Director
Delaware Department of Education
Carvel State Office Building, 820 North French Street
Wilmington, DE 19801
Phone: 302-577-5240
Fax: 302-577-6765
E-mail: dedoe@doe.k12.de.us

DELAWARE HIGHER EDUCATION COMMISSION
http://www.doe.state.de.us

EDUCATIONAL BENEFITS FOR CHILDREN OF DECEASED MILITARY AND STATE POLICE
• See page 540

DEPARTMENT OF VETERANS AFFAIRS (VA)
http://www.gibill.va.gov

MONTGOMERY GI BILL (ACTIVE DUTY) CHAPTER 30

MGIB provides up to 36 months of education benefits to eligible veterans for college, business school, technical courses, vocational courses, correspondence courses, apprenticeships/job training, or flight training. Must be an eligible veteran with an Honorable Discharge and have high school diploma or GED before applying for benefits. For more details on specific requirements see Web site: http://www.gibill.va.gov or call 1-888-442-4551.

Award: Scholarship for use in freshman, sophomore, junior, senior, or postgraduate years; renewable. *Number:* varies. *Amount:* $37,224.

Eligibility Requirements: Applicant must be enrolled or expecting to enroll full or part-time at a two-year or four-year or technical institution or university. Available to U.S. citizens. Applicant must have general military experience.

Application Requirements: Application, active military service of at least 2 years. *Deadline:* Continuous.

Contact: Kieth M. Wilson, Director, Education Service
Department of Veterans Affairs (VA)
810 Vermont Avenue, NW
Washington, DC 20420
Phone: 888-442-4551
E-mail: co225a@vba.va.gov

Department of Veterans Affairs (VA) (continued)

MONTGOMERY GI BILL (SELECTED RESERVE)
• See page 569

SURVIVORS AND DEPENDENTS EDUCATIONAL ASSISTANCE (CHAPTER 35)-VA

Monthly $695 benefits for up to 45 months. Must be spouses or children under age 26 of current veterans missing in action or of deceased or totally and permanently disabled (service-related) service persons. For more information call 1-888-442-4551 or visit Web site: http://www.gibill.va.gov.

Award: Scholarship for use in freshman, sophomore, junior, or senior years; renewable. *Number:* 10,733. *Amount:* up to $31,275.

Eligibility Requirements: Applicant must be age 25 or under and enrolled or expecting to enroll full or part-time at a two-year or four-year or technical institution or university. Available to U.S. and non-U.S. citizens. Applicant or parent must meet one or more of the following requirements: general military experience; retired from active duty; disabled or killed as a result of military service; prisoner of war; or missing in action.

Application Requirements: Application, parent or spouse must have had qualifying service. *Deadline:* Continuous.

Contact: Kieth M. Wilson, Director, Education Service
Department of Veterans Affairs (VA)
810 Vermont Avenue, NW
Washington, DC 20420
Phone: 888-442-4551

DEVRY, INC.   http://www.devry.edu

DEVRY/KELLER MILITARY SERVICE GRANT

Grant is available to students called to active duty at a time which necessitates the interruption of studies during a term. The grant is available only to those students who resume their studies following their active duty service. Upon resuming their studies, students must provide written documentation of active duty service. The grant is to be used during the first term the student resumes.

Award: Grant for use in freshman, sophomore, junior, senior, or graduate years; not renewable. *Number:* varies. *Amount:* $7830.

Eligibility Requirements: Applicant must be enrolled or expecting to enroll full or part-time at an institution or university. Available to U.S. citizens. Applicant must have general military experience.

Application Requirements: Documentation of active duty service. *Deadline:* Continuous.

Contact: Kathy Facenda, Director of Student Finance Operations
DeVry, Inc.
One Tower Lane
Oakbrook Terrace, IL 60181-4624
Phone: 630-706-3141
Fax: 630-574-1963
E-mail: kfacenda@devry.com

EXPLOSIVE ORDNANCE DISPOSAL MEMORIAL COMMITTEE   http://www.eodmemorial.org

EXPLOSIVE ORDNANCE DISPOSAL MEMORIAL SCHOLARSHIP
• See page 541

FLORIDA DEPARTMENT OF EDUCATION   http://www.floridastudentfinancialaid.org

SCHOLARSHIPS FOR CHILDREN OF DECEASED OR DISABLED VETERANS OR CHILDREN OF SERVICEMEN CLASSIFIED AS POW OR MIA

Scholarship provides full tuition assistance for children of deceased or disabled veterans or of servicemen classified as POW or MIA who are in full-time attendance at eligible public or non-public Florida institutions. Service connection must be as specified under Florida statute. Amount of payment to non-public institutions is equal to cost at public institutions at the comparable level. Must be between 16 and 22. Qualified veteran and applicant must meet residency requirements.

Award: Scholarship for use in freshman, sophomore, junior, or senior years; renewable. *Number:* 160.

Eligibility Requirements: Applicant must be age 17-21; enrolled or expecting to enroll full or part-time at a two-year or four-year or technical institution or university; resident of Florida and studying in Florida. Available to U.S. citizens. Applicant or parent must meet one or more of the following requirements: general military experience; retired from active duty; disabled or killed as a result of military service; prisoner of war; or missing in action.

Application Requirements: Application. *Deadline:* April 1.

Contact: Barb Dombrowski, Education Director, Policy and Training
Florida Department of Education
Office of Student Financial Assistance
1940 North Monroe, Suite 70
Tallahassee, FL 32303-4759
Phone: 850-410-5191
Fax: 850-488-5966
E-mail: barb.dombrowski@fldoe.org

FOUNDATION OF THE FIRST CAVALRY DIVISION ASSOCIATION   http://www.1cda.org

FOUNDATION OF THE FIRST CAVALRY DIVISION ASSOCIATION UNDERGRADUATE SCHOLARSHIP

Several scholarships for children of the First Cavalry Division soldiers who died or have been declared permanently and 100% disabled during the Vietnam War or Desert Storm. Show proof of relationship, death or disability of parent, and acceptance at higher education institution. Include self-addressed stamped envelope.

Award: Scholarship for use in freshman, sophomore, junior, senior, graduate, or postgraduate years; renewable. *Number:* varies. *Amount:* up to $1000.

Eligibility Requirements: Applicant must be enrolled or expecting to enroll full or part-time at a two-year or four-year institution or university. Available to U.S. citizens. Applicant or parent must meet one or more of the following requirements: general military experience; retired from active duty; disabled or killed as a result of military service; prisoner of war; or missing in action.

Application Requirements: Application, self-addressed stamped envelope, transcript, birth certificate, proof of service with the division. *Deadline:* Continuous.

Contact: Lorinda Davison, Office Manager
Foundation of the First Cavalry Division Association
302 North Main Street
Copperas Cove, TX 76522-1799
Phone: 254-547-6537
Fax: 254-547-8853
E-mail: firstcav@1cda.org

IDAHO STATE BOARD OF EDUCATION   http://www.boardofed.idaho.gov

FREEDOM SCHOLARSHIP

Scholarship for children of Idaho citizens determined by the federal government to have been prisoners of war, missing in action, or killed in action or died of injuries or wounds sustained in action in southeast Asia, including Korea, or who shall become so hereafter, in any area of armed conflict in which the United States is a party. Applicant must attend an Idaho public college or university and meet all requirements for regular admission.

Award: Scholarship for use in freshman, sophomore, junior, senior, graduate, or postgraduate years; not renewable. *Amount:* $1000.

Eligibility Requirements: Applicant must be enrolled or expecting to enroll at a two-year or four-year or technical institution or university; resident of Idaho and studying in Idaho. Available to U.S. citizens. Applicant or parent must meet one or more of the following requirements: general military experience; retired from active duty; disabled or killed as a result of military service; prisoner of war; or missing in action.

Application Requirements: Application.

Contact: Dana Kelly, Program Manager
Idaho State Board of Education
PO Box 83720
Boise, ID 83720-0037
Phone: 208-332-1574
E-mail: dana.kelly@osbe.idaho.gov

ILLINOIS DEPARTMENT OF VETERANS AFFAIRS
http://www.state.il.us/agency/dva

VETERANS' CHILDREN EDUCATIONAL OPPORTUNITIES

Award is provided to each child age 18 or younger of a veteran who died or became totally disabled as a result of service during World War I, World War II, Korean, or Vietnam War. Must be studying in Illinois. Death must be service-connected. Disability must be rated 100% for two or more years.

Award: Grant for use in freshman year; not renewable. *Number:* varies. *Amount:* up to $250.

Eligibility Requirements: Applicant must be age 10-18; enrolled or expecting to enroll at an institution or university and resident of Illinois. Available to U.S. citizens. Applicant or parent must meet one or more of the following requirements: general military experience; retired from active duty; disabled or killed as a result of military service; prisoner of war; or missing in action.

Application Requirements: Application. *Deadline:* June 30.

Contact: Tracy Mahan, Grants Section
Illinois Department of Veterans' Affairs
833 South Spring Street
Springfield, IL 62794-9432
Phone: 217-782-3564
Fax: 217-782-4161

ILLINOIS STUDENT ASSISTANCE COMMISSION (ISAC)
http://www.collegezone.org

ILLINOIS VETERAN GRANT PROGRAM - IVG

Award for qualified veterans for tuition and fees at Illinois public universities and community colleges. Must provide documentation of service (DD214). Deadlines for submission of applications are January 15, September 15, and May 25.

Award: Grant for use in freshman, sophomore, junior, senior, or graduate years; renewable. *Number:* 11,000–13,000. *Amount:* $1400–$1600.

Eligibility Requirements: Applicant must be enrolled or expecting to enroll full or part-time at a two-year or four-year institution or university; resident of Illinois and studying in Illinois. Available to U.S. citizens. Applicant must have general military experience.

Application Requirements: Application, documentation of service. *Deadline:* Continuous.

Contact: College Zone Counselor
Illinois Student Assistance Commission (ISAC)
1755 Lake Cook Road
Deerfield, IL 60015-5209
Phone: 800-899-4722
E-mail: collegezone@isac.org

INDIANA DEPARTMENT OF VETERANS AFFAIRS
http://www.ai.org/veteran/index.html

CHILD OF DISABLED VETERAN GRANT OR PURPLE HEART RECIPIENT GRANT

Free tuition at Indiana state-supported colleges or universities for children of disabled veterans or Purple Heart recipients. Must submit Form DD214 or service record.

Award: Grant for use in freshman, sophomore, junior, senior, graduate, or postgraduate years; renewable. *Number:* varies. *Amount:* varies.

Eligibility Requirements: Applicant must be enrolled or expecting to enroll full or part-time at a two-year or four-year institution or university; resident of Indiana and studying in Indiana. Available to U.S. citizens. Applicant or parent must meet one or more of the following requirements: general military experience; retired from active duty; disabled or killed as a result of military service; prisoner of war; or missing in action.

Application Requirements: Application. *Deadline:* Continuous.

Contact: Jon Brinkley, State Service Officer
Indiana Department of Veterans' Affairs
302 West Washington Street, Room E-120
Indianapolis, IN 46204-2738
Phone: 317-232-3910
Fax: 317-232-7721
E-mail: jbrinkley@dva.state.in.us

DEPARTMENT OF VETERANS AFFAIRS FREE TUITION FOR CHILDREN OF POW/MIA'S IN VIETNAM

Renewable award for residents of Indiana who are the children of veterans declared missing in action or prisoner-of-war after January 1, 1960. Provides tuition at Indiana state-supported institutions for undergraduate study.

Award: Grant for use in freshman, sophomore, junior, senior, graduate, or postgraduate years; renewable. *Number:* varies. *Amount:* varies.

Eligibility Requirements: Applicant must be age 24 or under; enrolled or expecting to enroll at a two-year or four-year institution or university; resident of Indiana and studying in Indiana. Available to U.S. citizens. Applicant or parent must meet one or more of the following requirements: general military experience; retired from active duty; disabled or killed as a result of military service; prisoner of war; or missing in action.

Application Requirements: Application. *Deadline:* March 10.

Contact: Jon Brinkley, State Service Officer
Indiana Department of Veterans' Affairs
302 West Washington Street, Room E-120
Indianapolis, IN 46204-2738
Phone: 317-232-3910
Fax: 317-232-7721
E-mail: jbrinkley@dva.state.in.us

KANSAS COMMISSION ON VETERANS AFFAIRS
http://www.kcva.org

KANSAS EDUCATIONAL BENEFITS FOR CHILDREN OF MIA, POW, AND DECEASED VETERANS OF THE VIETNAM WAR

Full-tuition scholarship awarded to students who are children of veterans. Must show proof of parent's status as missing in action, prisoner-of-war, or killed in action in the Vietnam War. Kansas residence required of veteran at time of entry to service. Must attend a state-supported postsecondary school.

Award: Scholarship for use in freshman, sophomore, junior, or senior years; not renewable. *Number:* 1.

Eligibility Requirements: Applicant must be enrolled or expecting to enroll at a two-year or four-year or technical institution or university and studying in Kansas. Available to U.S. citizens. Applicant or parent must meet one or more of the following requirements: general military experience; retired from active duty; disabled or killed as a result of military service; prisoner of war; or missing in action.

Application Requirements: Application, report of casualty, birth certificate, school acceptance letter, Military discharge of veteran.. *Deadline:* Continuous.

Contact: Wayne Bollig, Program Director
Kansas Commission on Veterans Affairs
700 Southwest Jackson Street, Room 701
Topeka, KS 66603
Phone: 785-291-3422
Fax: 785-296-1462
E-mail: kcva004@ink.org

LOUISIANA DEPARTMENT OF VETERANS AFFAIRS
http://www.vetaffairs.com/VAMain.htm

LOUISIANA DEPARTMENT OF VETERANS AFFAIRS STATE AID PROGRAM

Tuition exemption at any state supported college, university, or technical institute for children (dependents between the ages of 18-25) of veterans that are rated 90% or above service connected disabled by the U.S. Department of Veterans Affairs. Tuition exemption also available for the surviving spouse and children (dependents between the ages of 18-25) of veterans who died on active duty, in line of duty, or where death was the result of a disability incurred in or aggravated by military service. For residents of Louisiana who are attending a Louisiana institution.

Louisiana Department of Veterans Affairs (continued)

Award: Grant for use in freshman, sophomore, junior, senior, graduate, or postgraduate years; renewable. *Number:* 1. *Amount:* varies.

Eligibility Requirements: Applicant must be age 16-25; enrolled or expecting to enroll full-time at a two-year or four-year or technical institution or university; resident of Louisiana and studying in Louisiana. Available to U.S. citizens. Applicant or parent must meet one or more of the following requirements: general military experience; retired from active duty; disabled or killed as a result of military service; prisoner of war; or missing in action.

Application Requirements: Application. *Deadline:* Continuous.

Contact: Richard Blackwell, Veterans Affairs Regional Manager
Louisiana Department of Veteran Affairs
PO Box 94095
Capitol Station
Baton Rouge, LA 70804-4095
Phone: 225-922-0500 Ext. 203
Fax: 225-922-0511
E-mail: rblackwell@vetaffairs.com

MAINE BUREAU OF VETERANS SERVICES
http://www.state.me.us

VETERANS DEPENDENTS EDUCATIONAL BENEFITS-MAINE
• See page 574

MICHIGAN VETERANS TRUST FUND
http://www.michigan.gov/dmva

MICHIGAN VETERANS TRUST FUND TUITION GRANT PROGRAM

Tuition grant of $2,800 for children of Michigan veterans who died on active duty or subsequently declared 100% disabled as the result of service-connected illness or injury. Must be 17 to 25 years old, be a Michigan resident, and attend a private or public institution in Michigan.

Award: Grant for use in freshman, sophomore, junior, or senior years; renewable. *Number:* varies. *Amount:* up to $2800.

Eligibility Requirements: Applicant must be age 17-25; enrolled or expecting to enroll full-time at a two-year or four-year or technical institution or university; resident of Michigan and studying in Michigan. Available to U.S. citizens. Applicant or parent must meet one or more of the following requirements: general military experience; retired from active duty; disabled or killed as a result of military service; prisoner of war; or missing in action.

Application Requirements: Application. *Deadline:* Continuous.

Contact: Phyllis Ochis, Department of Military and Veterans Affairs
Michigan Veterans Trust Fund
2500 South Washington Avenue
Lansing, MI 48913
Phone: 517-483-5469

MILITARY OFFICERS ASSOCIATION OF AMERICA (MOAA)
http://www.moaa.org

GENERAL JOHN RATAY EDUCATIONAL FUND GRANTS

Grants available to the children of the surviving spouse of retired officers. Must be under 24 years old and the child of a deceased retired officer who was a member of MOAA. For more details and an application go to Web site: http://www.moaa.org/education.

Award: Grant for use in freshman, sophomore, junior, or senior years; not renewable. *Number:* varies. *Amount:* $4000.

Eligibility Requirements: Applicant must be age 23 or under and enrolled or expecting to enroll full-time at a two-year or four-year or technical institution or university. Applicant must have 3.0 GPA or higher. Available to U.S. citizens. Applicant or parent must meet one or more of the following requirements: general military experience; retired from active duty; disabled or killed as a result of military service; prisoner of war; or missing in action.

Application Requirements: Application, financial need analysis, test scores, transcript. *Deadline:* March 1.

Contact: Cindy Amos
Military Officers Association of America (MOAA)
201 North Washington Street
Alexandria, VA 22314-2529
Phone: 800-234-6622
Fax: 703-838-5819
E-mail: edassist@moaa.org

MOAA AMERICAN PATRIOT SCHOLARSHIP

Scholarship available to a student under 24 years old who is the child of a member of the uniformed services of the United States who died in active duty. For more details and an application go to Web site: http://www.moaa.org/education.

Award: Scholarship for use in freshman, sophomore, junior, or senior years; not renewable. *Number:* varies. *Amount:* $2500.

Eligibility Requirements: Applicant must be age 23 or under and enrolled or expecting to enroll full-time at a two-year or four-year institution or university. Available to U.S. citizens. Applicant or parent must meet one or more of the following requirements: general military experience; retired from active duty; disabled or killed as a result of military service; prisoner of war; or missing in action.

Application Requirements: Application, test scores, transcript. *Deadline:* March 1.

Contact: Cindy Amos
Phone: 800-234-6622

MOAA BASE/POST SCHOLARSHIP

Recipients are randomly selected from dependent sons and daughters of active duty officers, members of the Drill and Reserve, National Guard, and enlisted military personnel. Eligible applicants will be under the age of 24. For more details and an application go to Web site: http://www.moaa.org/education

Award: Scholarship for use in freshman, sophomore, junior, or senior years; not renewable. *Number:* 25. *Amount:* $1000.

Eligibility Requirements: Applicant must be age 23 or under and enrolled or expecting to enroll full-time at a two-year or four-year institution or university. Available to U.S. citizens. Applicant or parent must meet one or more of the following requirements: general military experience; retired from active duty; disabled or killed as a result of military service; prisoner of war; or missing in action.

Application Requirements: Application, test scores, transcript, service parent's Leave and Earning Statement (LES). *Deadline:* March 1.

Contact: Cindy Amos
Military Officers Association of America (MOAA)
201 North Washington Street
Alexandria, VA 22314-2529
Phone: 800-234-6622
Fax: 703-838-5819
E-mail: edassist@moaa.org

MILITARY ORDER OF THE PURPLE HEART
http://www.purpleheart.org

MILITARY ORDER OF THE PURPLE HEART SCHOLARSHIP

Scholarship for children or grandchildren of Purple Heart recipients. Must submit essay, proof of full-time college registration, and proof of receipt of Purple Heart or membership in Order. Must be U.S. citizen and high school graduate with minimum GPA of 3.5. Contact for information.

Award: Scholarship for use in freshman, sophomore, junior, senior, graduate, or postgraduate years; not renewable. *Number:* 8. *Amount:* $2000.

Eligibility Requirements: Applicant must be enrolled or expecting to enroll full-time at a two-year or four-year or technical institution or university. Applicant must have 3.5 GPA or higher. Available to U.S. citizens. Applicant or parent must meet one or more of the following requirements: general military experience; retired from active duty; disabled or killed as a result of military service; prisoner of war; or missing in action.

Application Requirements: Application, essay, references, test scores, transcript, proof of receipt of Purple Heart or MOPH membership-copy of birth certificate. *Fee:* $5. *Deadline:* January 16.

Contact: Scholarship Coordinator
Military Order of the Purple Heart
5413-B Backlick Road
Springfield, VA 22151-3960
Phone: 703-642-5360
Fax: 703-642-2054
E-mail: info@purpleheart.org

MINNESOTA HIGHER EDUCATION SERVICES OFFICE   http://www.getreadyforcollege.org

MINNESOTA STATE VETERANS' DEPENDENTS ASSISTANCE PROGRAM

Tuition assistance to dependents of persons considered to be prisoner-of-war or missing in action after August 1, 1958. Must be Minnesota resident attending Minnesota two- or four-year school.

Award: Scholarship for use in freshman, sophomore, junior, or senior years; renewable. *Number:* 1. *Amount:* varies.

Eligibility Requirements: Applicant must be enrolled or expecting to enroll at a two-year or four-year institution; resident of Minnesota and studying in Minnesota. Available to U.S. citizens. Applicant or parent must meet one or more of the following requirements: general military experience; retired from active duty; disabled or killed as a result of military service; prisoner of war; or missing in action.

Application Requirements: Application. *Deadline:* Continuous.

Contact: Minnesota Higher Education Services Office
1450 Energy Park Drive, Suite 350
St. Paul, MN 55108-5227

NATIONAL MILITARY FAMILY ASSOCIATION   http://www.nmfa.org

NMFA JOANNE HOLBROOK PATTON MILITARY SPOUSE SCHOLARSHIPS

Scholarships awarded to spouses of Uniformed Services members (active duty, National Guard and Reserve, retirees, and survivors) to obtain professional certification or to attend post secondary or graduate school. Scholarships are normally in the amount of $1000 and the number awarded each year varies depending on funding. Scholarship funds may be used for tuition, fees, books, and school room and board. Applications are only accepted on-line. For more information see the Web site: http://www.nmfa.org

Award: Scholarship for use in freshman, sophomore, junior, or senior years. *Amount:* $1000.

Eligibility Requirements: Applicant must be enrolled or expecting to enroll full or part-time at a four-year institution or university and female. Available to U.S. citizens. Applicant or parent must meet one or more of the following requirements: general military experience; retired from active duty; disabled or killed as a result of military service; prisoner of war; or missing in action.

Application Requirements: Copy of current Uniformed Services ID Card/ DEERS card, proof of status as a military spouse or surviving spouse. *Deadline:* April 15.

Contact: National Military Family Association
2500 North Van Dorn Street, Suite 102
Alexandria, VA 22302-1601

NEW HAMPSHIRE POSTSECONDARY EDUCATION COMMISSION   http://www.state.nh.us/postsecondary

SCHOLARSHIPS FOR ORPHANS OF VETERANS-NEW HAMPSHIRE

Awards for New Hampshire residents whose parent died as a result of service in WWI, WWII, the Korean Conflict, or the Southeast Asian Conflict. Parent must have been a New Hampshire resident at time of death. Possible full tuition and $1000 per year with automatic renewal on reapplication. Contact department for application deadlines. Must be under 26. Must include proof of eligibility and proof of parent's death.

Award: Scholarship for use in freshman, sophomore, junior, or senior years; renewable. *Number:* 1–10. *Amount:* varies.

Eligibility Requirements: Applicant must be age 16-25; enrolled or expecting to enroll full-time at a two-year or four-year institution or university and resident of New Hampshire. Available to U.S. citizens. Applicant or parent must meet one or more of the following requirements: general military experience; retired from active duty; disabled or killed as a result of military service; prisoner of war; or missing in action.

Application Requirements: Application, VA approval. *Deadline:* varies.

Contact: Melanie K. Deshaies, Program Assistant
New Hampshire Postsecondary Education Commission
3 Barrell Court, Suite 300
Concord, NH 03301-8543
Phone: 603-271-2555 Ext. 356
Fax: 603-271-2696
E-mail: mdeshaies@pec.state.nh.us

NEW JERSEY DEPARTMENT OF MILITARY AND VETERANS AFFAIRS   http://www.state.nj.us/military

NEW JERSEY WAR ORPHANS TUITION ASSISTANCE

Renewable award for New Jersey residents who are high school seniors ages 16-21 and who are children of veterans killed or disabled in duty, missing in action, or prisoner-of-war. For use at a two- or four-year college or university. Write for more information. Deadlines: October 1 for Fall semester and March 1 for Spring semester.

Award: Scholarship for use in freshman, sophomore, junior, or senior years; renewable. *Number:* varies. *Amount:* $2000–$8000.

Eligibility Requirements: Applicant must be high school student; age 16-21; planning to enroll or expecting to enroll full-time at a two-year or four-year institution or university and resident of New Jersey. Available to U.S. citizens. Applicant or parent must meet one or more of the following requirements: general military experience; retired from active duty; disabled or killed as a result of military service; prisoner of war; or missing in action.

Application Requirements: Application, transcript. *Deadline:* varies.

Contact: Patricia Richter, Grants Manager
New Jersey Department of Military and Veterans Affairs
PO Box 340
Trenton, NJ 08625-0340
Phone: 609-530-6854
Fax: 609-530-6970
E-mail: patricia.richter@njdmava.state.nj.us

TUITION ASSISTANCE FOR CHILDREN OF POW/MIAS

Assists children of military service personnel declared missing in action or prisoner-of-war after January 1, 1960. Must be a resident of New Jersey. Renewable grants provide tuition for undergraduate study in New Jersey. Apply by October 1 for fall, March 1 for spring. Must be high school senior to apply.

Award: Scholarship for use in freshman, sophomore, or junior years; renewable. *Number:* varies. *Amount:* $500.

Eligibility Requirements: Applicant must be high school student; planning to enroll or expecting to enroll full-time at a two-year or four-year institution or university; resident of New Jersey and studying in New Jersey. Applicant must have 2.5 GPA or higher. Available to U.S. citizens. Applicant or parent must meet one or more of the following requirements: general military experience; retired from active duty; disabled or killed as a result of military service; prisoner of war; or missing in action.

Application Requirements: Application, transcript. *Deadline:* varies.

Contact: Patricia Richter, Grants Manager
New Jersey Department of Military and Veterans Affairs
PO Box 340
Trenton, NJ 08625-0340
Phone: 609-530-6854
Fax: 609-530-6970
E-mail: patricia.richter@njdmava.state.nj.us

VETERANS' TUITION CREDIT PROGRAM-NEW JERSEY

Award for veterans who served in the armed forces between December 31, 1960, and May 7, 1975. Must have been a New Jersey resident at time of induction or discharge or for one year prior to application. Apply by October 1 for fall, March 1 for spring. Renewable award of $200-$400.

Award: Scholarship for use in freshman, sophomore, junior, or senior years; renewable. *Number:* varies. *Amount:* $200–$400.

New Jersey Department of Military and Veterans Affairs (continued)

Eligibility Requirements: Applicant must be enrolled or expecting to enroll full or part-time at a two-year or four-year or technical institution or university. Available to U.S. citizens. Applicant must have general military experience.

Application Requirements: Application. *Deadline:* varies.

Contact: Patricia Richter, Grants Manager
New Jersey Department of Military and Veterans Affairs
PO Box 340
Trenton, NJ 08625-0340
Phone: 609-530-6854
Fax: 609-530-6970
E-mail: patricia.richter@njdmava.state.nj.us

NEW MEXICO COMMISSION ON HIGHER EDUCATION   http://www.hed.state.nm.us

VIETNAM VETERANS' SCHOLARSHIP PROGRAM

Award for New Mexico residents who are Vietnam veterans enrolled in undergraduate or master's-level course work at public or selected private New Mexico postsecondary institutions. Award may include tuition, required fees, and book allowance. Contact financial aid office of any public or eligible private New Mexico postsecondary institution for deadline.

Award: Scholarship for use in freshman, sophomore, junior, senior, or graduate years; not renewable. *Number:* 1.

Eligibility Requirements: Applicant must be enrolled or expecting to enroll full or part-time at a two-year or four-year institution; resident of New Mexico and studying in New Mexico. Available to U.S. citizens. Applicant must have general military experience.

Application Requirements: Application, certification by the NM Veteran's commission. *Deadline:* varies.

Contact: Ofelia Morales, Director of Financial Aid
New Mexico Commission on Higher Education
1068 Cerrillos Road, PO Box 15910
Santa Fe, NM 87505
Phone: 505-476-6506
E-mail: ofelia.morales@state.nm.us

NEW MEXICO VETERANS SERVICE COMMISSION   http://www.state.nm.us/veterans

CHILDREN OF DECEASED VETERANS SCHOLARSHIP-NEW MEXICO

Award for New Mexico residents who are children of veterans killed or disabled as a result of service, prisoner-of-war, or veterans missing-in-action. Must be between ages 16 to 26. For use at New Mexico schools for undergraduate study. Submit parent's death certificate and DD form 214.

Award: Scholarship for use in freshman, sophomore, junior, or senior years; renewable.

Eligibility Requirements: Applicant must be age 16-26; enrolled or expecting to enroll full or part-time at an institution or university; resident of New Mexico and studying in New Mexico. Available to U.S. citizens. Applicant or parent must meet one or more of the following requirements: general military experience; retired from active duty; disabled or killed as a result of military service; prisoner of war; or missing in action.

Application Requirements: Application, transcript, death certificate or notice of casualty. *Deadline:* Continuous.

Contact: Alan Martinez, Director, State Benefits Division
New Mexico Veterans' Service Commission
PO Box 2324
Sante Fe, NM 87504
Phone: 505-827-6300
Fax: 505-827-6372

NEW MEXICO VIETNAM VETERANS' SCHOLARSHIP

Renewable award for Vietnam veterans who are New Mexico residents attending state-sponsored schools. Must have been awarded the Vietnam Campaign medal. Submit DD214. Must include discharge papers.

Award: Scholarship for use in freshman, sophomore, junior, or senior years; renewable. *Amount:* up to $2020.

Eligibility Requirements: Applicant must be enrolled or expecting to enroll full or part-time at an institution or university; resident of New Mexico and studying in New Mexico. Available to U.S. citizens. Applicant must have general military experience.

Application Requirements: Application, copy of DD214. *Deadline:* Continuous.

Contact: Alan Martinez, Director, State Benefits Division
New Mexico Veterans' Service Commission
PO Box 2324
Sante Fe, NM 87504
Phone: 505-827-6300
Fax: 505-827-6372
E-mail: alan.martinez@state.nm.us

NORTH CAROLINA DIVISION OF VETERANS AFFAIRS

NORTH CAROLINA VETERANS SCHOLARSHIPS CLASS I-B

Renewable awards for children of veterans rated by U.S. DVA as 100% disabled due to wartime service as defined in the law, and currently or at time of death drawing compensation for such disability. Parent must have been a North Carolina resident at time of entry into service. Duration of the scholarship is four academic years (8 semesters) if used within 8 years. Free tuition and exemption from certain mandatory fees as set forth in the law in Public, Community & Technical Colleges/Institutions. No limit on number awarded each year.

Award: Scholarship for use in freshman, sophomore, junior, or senior years; renewable. *Number:* varies. *Amount:* $1500.

Eligibility Requirements: Applicant must be enrolled or expecting to enroll full or part-time at a two-year or four-year or technical institution or university and studying in North Carolina. Available to U.S. citizens. Applicant or parent must meet one or more of the following requirements: general military experience; retired from active duty; disabled or killed as a result of military service; prisoner of war; or missing in action.

Application Requirements: Application, financial need analysis, interview, transcript. *Deadline:* Continuous.

Contact: Charles Smith, Assistant Secretary
325 North Salisbury Street
Raleigh, NC 27603
Phone: 919-733-3851
Fax: 919-733-2834

NORTH CAROLINA VETERANS SCHOLARSHIPS CLASS II

Renewable awards for children of veterans rated by U.S. DVA as much as 20% but less than 100% disabled due to wartime service as defined in the law, or awarded Purple Heart Medal for wounds received. Parent must have been a North Carolina resident at time of entry into service. Duration of the scholarship is four academic years (8 semesters) if used within 8 years. Free tuition and exemption from certain mandatory fees as set forth in the law in Public, Community & Technical Colleges/Institutions. $4500 per nine month academic year in Private Colleges & Junior Colleges. Up to 100 awarded each year. Deadline is March 31.

Award: Scholarship for use in freshman, sophomore, junior, or senior years; renewable. *Number:* up to 100. *Amount:* up to $4500.

Eligibility Requirements: Applicant must be enrolled or expecting to enroll full or part-time at a two-year or four-year or technical institution or university and studying in North Carolina. Available to U.S. citizens. Applicant or parent must meet one or more of the following requirements: general military experience; retired from active duty; disabled or killed as a result of military service; prisoner of war; or missing in action.

Application Requirements: Application, financial need analysis, interview, transcript. *Deadline:* March 31.

Contact: Charles Smith, Assistant Secretary
325 North Salisbury Street
Raleigh, NC 27603
Phone: 919-733-3851
Fax: 919-733-2834

NORTH CAROLINA VETERANS SCHOLARSHIPS CLASS III

Renewable awards for children of a veteran who died or was, at time of death, drawing a pension for total and permanent disability as rated by U.S. DVA, was honorably discharged and does not qualify for Class I, II, or IV, scholarships, or served in a combat zone or waters adjacent to a combat zone and received a campaign badge or medal and does not qualify under Class I, II, IV, or V. Parent must have been a North Carolina resident at time of entry into service. Duration of the scholarship is four academic years (8 semesters) if used within eight years. Free tuition and exemption from certain mandatory fees as set forth in the law in Public, Community & Technical Colleges/Institutions. $4500 per nine month academic year in Private Colleges & Junior Colleges. See Web site for details and where to procure an application. Up to 100 awarded each year. Deadline is March 31.

Award: Scholarship for use in freshman, sophomore, junior, or senior years; renewable. *Number:* up to 100. *Amount:* up to $4500.

Eligibility Requirements: Applicant must be enrolled or expecting to enroll full or part-time at a two-year or four-year or technical institution or university and studying in North Carolina. Available to U.S. citizens. Applicant or parent must meet one or more of the following requirements: general military experience; retired from active duty; disabled or killed as a result of military service; prisoner of war; or missing in action.

Application Requirements: Application, financial need analysis, interview, transcript. *Deadline:* March 31.

Contact: Charles Smith, Assistant Secretary
325 North Salisbury Street
Raleigh, NC 27603
Phone: 919-733-3851
Fax: 919-733-2834

NORTH CAROLINA VETERANS SCHOLARSHIPS CLASS IV

Renewable awards for children of a veteran who was a POW or MIA. Parent must have been a North Carolina resident at time of entry into service. Duration of the scholarship is four academic years (8 semesters) if used within eight years. No limit on number awarded per year. The student receives free tuition, a room allowance, a board allowance, and exemption from certain mandatory fees as set forth in the law in public, community and technical colleges or institutions. The scholarship is $4500 per nine-month academic year in private colleges and junior colleges.

Award: Scholarship for use in freshman, sophomore, junior, or senior years; renewable. *Number:* varies. *Amount:* up to $4500.

Eligibility Requirements: Applicant must be enrolled or expecting to enroll full or part-time at a two-year or four-year or technical institution or university and studying in North Carolina. Available to U.S. citizens. Applicant or parent must meet one or more of the following requirements: general military experience; retired from active duty; disabled or killed as a result of military service; prisoner of war; or missing in action.

Application Requirements: Application, financial need analysis, interview, transcript. *Deadline:* March 31.

Contact: Charles Smith, Assistant Secretary
325 North Salisbury Street
Raleigh, NC 27603
Phone: 919-733-3851
Fax: 919-733-2834

NORTH CAROLINA VIETNAM VETERANS, INC.   http://www.ncneighbors.com

NORTH CAROLINA VIETNAM VETERANS, INC., SCHOLARSHIP PROGRAM

Award of $500 for residents of Wake, Durham, Harnett, Chatham, Nash, Franklin, Johnson, Lee, or Granville counties in North Carolina who were awarded the Vietnam service medal, or for the spouse, child, dependent, or grandchild of a Vietnam veteran. Must submit personal statement and document community or high school activities and awards. Must reapply to renew award. Must write 400-600 word essay. Topic changes each year.

Award: Scholarship for use in freshman, sophomore, junior, or senior years; not renewable. *Number:* 4–10. *Amount:* $500.

Eligibility Requirements: Applicant must be enrolled or expecting to enroll full or part-time at a two-year or four-year or technical institution or university and resident of North Carolina. Available to U.S. and non-U.S. citizens. Applicant or parent must meet one or more of the following requirements: general military experience; retired from active duty; disabled or killed as a result of military service; prisoner of war; or missing in action.

Application Requirements: Application, essay, personal statement, birth certificate and/or marriage license. *Deadline:* varies.

Contact: Bud Gross, Board of Director and Scholarship Administrator
North Carolina Vietnam Veterans, Inc.
PO Box 10333
Raleigh, NC 27605
Phone: 919-787-7228
Fax: 919-785-0354
E-mail: budgross@nc.rr.com

OHIO AMERICAN LEGION   http://ohioamericanlegion.org

OHIO AMERICAN LEGION SCHOLARSHIPS
• See page 510

OHIO BOARD OF REGENTS   http://www.regents.state.oh.us

OHIO MISSING IN ACTION AND PRISONERS OF WAR ORPHANS SCHOLARSHIP

Renewable award aids children of Vietnam conflict servicemen who have been classified as missing in action or prisoner of war. Must be an Ohio resident, be 16-21, and be enrolled full-time at an Ohio college. Full tuition awards.

Award: Scholarship for use in freshman, sophomore, junior, or senior years; renewable. *Number:* 1–5. *Amount:* varies.

Eligibility Requirements: Applicant must be age 16-21; enrolled or expecting to enroll full-time at a four-year institution or university; resident of Ohio and studying in Ohio. Available to U.S. citizens. Applicant or parent must meet one or more of the following requirements: general military experience; retired from active duty; disabled or killed as a result of military service; prisoner of war; or missing in action.

Application Requirements: Application. *Deadline:* July 1.

Contact: Sarina Wilks, Program Administrator
Ohio Board of Regents
30 East Broad Street, 36th Floor, PO Box 182452
Columbus, OH 43215-3414
Phone: 614-752-9528
Fax: 614-752-5903
E-mail: swilks@regents.state.oh.us

OHIO WAR ORPHANS SCHOLARSHIP

Aids Ohio residents attending an eligible college in Ohio. Must be between the ages of 16-21, the child of a disabled or deceased veteran, and enrolled full-time. Renewable up to five years. Amount of award varies. Must include Form DD214.

Award: Scholarship for use in freshman, sophomore, junior, or senior years; renewable. *Number:* 300–450. *Amount:* varies.

Eligibility Requirements: Applicant must be age 16-21; enrolled or expecting to enroll full-time at a two-year or four-year institution or university; resident of Ohio and studying in Ohio. Available to U.S. citizens. Applicant or parent must meet one or more of the following requirements: general military experience; retired from active duty; disabled or killed as a result of military service; prisoner of war; or missing in action.

Application Requirements: Application. *Deadline:* July 1.

Contact: Sarina Wilks, Program Administrator
Ohio Board of Regents
30 East Broad Street, 36th Floor
Columbus, OH 43215-3414
Phone: 614-752-9528
Fax: 614-752-5903
E-mail: swilks@regents.state.oh.us

OREGON DEPARTMENT OF VETERANS AFFAIRS   http://www.odva.state.or.us

OREGON VETERANS' EDUCATION AID

To be eligible, veteran must have served in U.S. armed forces 90 days and been discharged under honorable conditions; U.S. citizen and Oregon resident; Korean War veteran or received campaign or expeditionary medal or ribbon awarded by U.S. armed forces for services after June 30, 1958. Full-time students receive $50/month, part-time students receive $35/month.

Oregon Department of Veterans' Affairs (continued)

Award: Grant for use in freshman, sophomore, junior, senior, graduate, or postgraduate years; not renewable. *Number:* varies. *Amount:* varies.

Eligibility Requirements: Applicant must be enrolled or expecting to enroll full-time at a two-year or four-year or technical institution or university; resident of Oregon and studying in Oregon. Available to U.S. citizens. Applicant must have general military experience.

Application Requirements: Application, certified copy of DD Form 214. *Deadline:* Continuous.

Contact: Mary Kluver, Educational Aid Coordinator
Oregon Department of Veterans' Affairs
700 Summer Street, NE
Salem, OR 97301-1289
Phone: 503-373-2085
Fax: 503-373-2392

OREGON STUDENT ASSISTANCE COMMISSION
http://www.osac.state.or.us

AFSCME: AMERICAN FEDERATION OF STATE, COUNTY, AND MUNICIPAL EMPLOYEES LOCAL 75 SCHOLARSHIP
• *See page 510*

AMERICAN EX-PRISONER OF WAR SCHOLARSHIPS: PETER CONNACHER MEMORIAL SCHOLARSHIP

Renewable award for American prisoners-of-war and their descendants. Written proof of prisoner-of-war status and discharge papers from the U.S. Armed Forces must accompany application. Statement of relationship between applicant and former prisoner-of-war is required. See Web site at http://www.osac.state.or.us for details.

Award: Scholarship for use in freshman, sophomore, junior, or senior years; renewable. *Number:* 4. *Amount:* $1150.

Eligibility Requirements: Applicant must be enrolled or expecting to enroll at a two-year or four-year institution and resident of Oregon. Available to U.S. citizens. Applicant or parent must meet one or more of the following requirements: general military experience; retired from active duty; disabled or killed as a result of military service; prisoner of war; or missing in action.

Application Requirements: Application, essay, financial need analysis, transcript, activities chart. *Deadline:* March 1.

Contact: Director of Grant Programs
Oregon Student Assistance Commission
1500 Valley River Drive, Suite 100
Eugene, OR 97401-7020
Phone: 800-452-8807 Ext. 7395

MARIA JACKSON/GENERAL GEORGE A. WHITE SCHOLARSHIP

Available to Oregon residents who served or whose parents serve or have served in the U.S. Armed Forces and resided in Oregon at time of enlistment. Must have at least 3.75 GPA and submit documentation of service. For use at Oregon colleges only. U.S. Bancorp employees, their children or close relatives, not eligible.

Award: Scholarship for use in freshman, sophomore, junior, senior, or graduate years; not renewable. *Number:* 54. *Amount:* $622.

Eligibility Requirements: Applicant must be enrolled or expecting to enroll full-time at a four-year institution or university; resident of Oregon and studying in Oregon. Available to U.S. citizens. Applicant or parent must meet one or more of the following requirements: general military experience; retired from active duty; disabled or killed as a result of military service; prisoner of war; or missing in action.

Application Requirements: Application, essay, financial need analysis, test scores, transcript, documentation of service. *Deadline:* March 1.

Contact: Director of Grant Programs
Oregon Student Assistance Commission
1500 Valley River Drive, Suite 100
Eugene, OR 97401-7020
Phone: 800-452-8807 Ext. 7395

PENNSYLVANIA BUREAU FOR VETERANS AFFAIRS
EDUCATIONAL GRATUITY PROGRAM

This program is for eligible dependents of 100% disabled or deceased veterans whose disability was incurred during a period of war or armed conflict. Must be a Pennsylvania resident attending a Pennsylvania school. Up to $500 per semester may be awarded.

Award: Grant for use in freshman, sophomore, junior, or senior years; renewable. *Number:* varies. *Amount:* $500.

Eligibility Requirements: Applicant must be age 16-23; enrolled or expecting to enroll full-time at a two-year or four-year or technical institution or university; resident of Pennsylvania and studying in Pennsylvania. Available to U.S. citizens. Applicant or parent must meet one or more of the following requirements: general military experience; retired from active duty; disabled or killed as a result of military service; prisoner of war; or missing in action.

Application Requirements: Application, driver's license, financial need analysis, transcript, birth certificate. *Deadline:* Continuous.

Contact: Sophie Matukewicz, Program Manager
Pennsylvania Bureau for Veterans Affairs
Department of Military and Veterans Affairs, Building S-0-47, Ft. Indiantown Gap
Annville, PA 17003-5003
Phone: 717-861-8610
Fax: 717-861-8589
E-mail: smatukewic@state.pa.us

PENNSYLVANIA HIGHER EDUCATION ASSISTANCE AGENCY
http://www.pheaa.org

ARMED FORCES LOAN FORGIVENESS PROGRAM

Loan forgiveness for non residents of Pennsylvania who served in Armed Forces in an active duty status between September 11, 2001 and June 30, 2006. Student either left a PA approved institution of postsecondary education due to call to active duty, or was lilving in PA at time of enlistment, or enlisted in military immediately after attending a PA approved institution of postsecondary education. Must have an eligible, non-default loan.

Award: Forgivable loan for use in freshman, sophomore, junior, or senior years; not renewable. *Amount:* up to $2500.

Eligibility Requirements: Applicant must be enrolled or expecting to enroll at a two-year or four-year or technical institution or university and resident of Pennsylvania. Available to U.S. citizens. Applicant or parent must meet one or more of the following requirements: general military experience; retired from active duty; disabled or killed as a result of military service; prisoner of war; or missing in action.

Application Requirements: Application. *Deadline:* December 31.

Contact: Pennsylvania Higher Education Assistance Agency
AES Lender School Team, PO Box 2461
Harrisburg, PA 17105-2461

POSTSECONDARY EDUCATION GRATUITY PROGRAM

Waiver of tuition and fees for children of Pennsylvania police officers, firefighters, rescue or ambulance squad members, corrections facility employees, or National Guard members who died in line of duty after January 1, 1976. child by birth or adoption of a deceased sheriff, deputy sheriff, National Guard member or other individual who was on federal or state active military duty who died since September 11, 2001, as a direct result of performing official duties.

Award: Grant for use in freshman, sophomore, junior, or senior years; renewable. *Number:* 1. *Amount:* varies.

Eligibility Requirements: Applicant must be age 25 or under; enrolled or expecting to enroll full-time at a two-year or four-year institution or university; resident of Pennsylvania and studying in Pennsylvania. Available to U.S. citizens. Applicant or parent must meet one or more of the following requirements: general military experience; retired from active duty; disabled or killed as a result of military service; prisoner of war; or missing in action.

Application Requirements: Application. *Deadline:* March 31.

Contact: PHEAA State Grant and Special Programs Division
Pennsylvania Higher Education Assistance Agency
1200 North Seventh Street
Harrisburg, PA 17102-1444
Phone: 800-692-7392

RESERVE OFFICERS ASSOCIATION   http://www.roa.org

HENRY J. REILLY MEMORIAL SCHOLARSHIP-HIGH SCHOOL SENIORS AND FIRST YEAR FRESHMEN
- *See page 514*

HENRY J. REILLY MEMORIAL UNDERGRADUATE SCHOLARSHIP PROGRAM FOR COLLEGE ATTENDEES
- *See page 514*

RETIRED ENLISTED ASSOCIATION   http://www.trea.org

RETIRED ENLISTED ASSOCIATION SCHOLARSHIP

One-time award for dependent children or grandchildren of a TREA or TREA auxiliary member in good standing.

Award: Scholarship for use in freshman, sophomore, junior, or senior years; not renewable. *Number:* 42. *Amount:* $1000–$1500.

Eligibility Requirements: Applicant must be enrolled or expecting to enroll full-time at a two-year or four-year or technical institution or university. Available to U.S. and non-U.S. citizens. Applicant or parent must meet one or more of the following requirements: general military experience; retired from active duty; disabled or killed as a result of military service; prisoner of war; or missing in action.

Application Requirements: Application, essay, financial need analysis, photo, references, test scores, transcript, copy of IRS tax forms. *Deadline:* April 30.

Contact: Donnell Minnis, Executive Assistant
Retired Enlisted Association
Attention: National Scholarship Committee
1111 South Abilene Court
Aurora, CO 80012-4909
Phone: 303-752-0660
Fax: 303-752-0835
E-mail: execasst@trea.org

STATE OF WYOMING, ADMINISTERED BY UNIVERSITY OF WYOMING   http://www.uwyo.edu/scholarships

VIETNAM VETERANS AWARD/WYOMING

Available to Wyoming residents who served in the armed forces between August 5, 1964, and May 7, 1975, and received a Vietnam service medal. Award is free tuition at the University of Wyoming or a state (WY) community college.

Award: Scholarship for use in freshman, sophomore, junior, or senior years; renewable. *Number:* varies. *Amount:* varies.

Eligibility Requirements: Applicant must be enrolled or expecting to enroll full or part-time at a two-year or four-year institution or university; resident of Wyoming and studying in Wyoming. Available to U.S. citizens. Applicant must have general military experience.

Application Requirements: Application. *Deadline:* Continuous.

Contact: Joel Anne Berrigan, Assistant Director, Scholarships
State of Wyoming, administered by University of Wyoming
Student Financial Aid, Department 3335, 1000 East University Avenue
Laramie, WY 82071-3335
Phone: 307-766-2117
Fax: 307-766-3800
E-mail: finaid@uwyo.edu

TET '68 SCHOLARSHIP   http://www.tet68.org

CHILDREN OF VIETNAM VETERANS SCHOLARSHIP FUND

Scholarships are given to graduating high school seniors who are citizens of the U.S., Canada, and Australia who are dependents of a Vietnam Veteran. Applicants must submit an essay "What is Freedom?". Must submit DD Form 214 showing prior service in the military. More information can be found at http://www.tet68.org/TET68sch.html.

Award: Scholarship for use in freshman year; not renewable. *Number:* 3–5. *Amount:* up to $1000.

Eligibility Requirements: Applicant must be high school student and planning to enroll or expecting to enroll full or part-time at a two-year or four-year or technical institution or university. Available to U.S. and non-U.S. citizens. Applicant or parent must meet one or more of the

following requirements: general military experience; retired from active duty; disabled or killed as a result of military service; prisoner of war; or missing in action.

Application Requirements: Application, applicant must enter a contest, essay, DD Form 214. *Deadline:* March 31.

Contact: William Kirkland, President
Tet '68 Scholarship
PO Box 31885
Richmond, VA 23294
Phone: 804-550-3692
E-mail: tet68info@aol.com

V.E.T.S. - VICTORY ENSURED THROUGH SERVICE

V.E.T.S. ANNUAL SCHOLARSHIP

Scholarships for graduating high school seniors, junior college students, continuing university (college) students, graduate students and vocational school students. Applicants must be a veteran, or a spouse, child, grandchild of a veteran and be a U.S. citizen. Must have maintained a 3.0 grade point average with no failing grades in any subject. Amount awarded is usually $500, but Board of Directors can grant special scholarships up to $1500 based on need and qualifications. Must apply by April 1 of every year, open only to residents of California, Arizona, and Washington.

Award: Scholarship for use in freshman, sophomore, junior, senior, graduate, or postgraduate years; not renewable. *Number:* 6. *Amount:* $500–$1500.

Eligibility Requirements: Applicant must be enrolled or expecting to enroll full-time at a two-year or four-year or technical institution or university and resident of Arizona, California, or Washington. Applicant must have 3.0 GPA or higher. Available to U.S. citizens. Applicant or parent must meet one or more of the following requirements: general military experience; retired from active duty; disabled or killed as a result of military service; prisoner of war; or missing in action.

Application Requirements: Application, financial need analysis, photo, references, test scores, transcript, DD Form 214 or military discharge "Honorable". *Deadline:* April 1.

Contact: Gregory Filek, Scholarship Chair
V.E.T.S. - Victory Ensured Through Service
8698 Midview Drive
Palo Cedro, CA 96073
Phone: 530-547-3776

VETERANS OF FOREIGN WARS OF THE UNITED STATES   http://www.vfw.org

VETERAN'S TRIBUTE SCHOLARSHIP

Award available to children of all United States military veterans, active duty, Reserves, and National Guard. Further information and application can be found on Web site http://www.vfw.org

Award: Scholarship for use in freshman year; not renewable. *Number:* up to 3. *Amount:* $3000–$10,000.

Eligibility Requirements: Applicant must be age 16-18 and enrolled or expecting to enroll at an institution or university. Available to U.S. citizens. Applicant or parent must meet one or more of the following requirements: general military experience; retired from active duty; disabled or killed as a result of military service; prisoner of war; or missing in action.

Application Requirements: Application, transcript, DD Form 214, documentation of community service. *Deadline:* December 31.

Contact: Veterans' Tribute Scholarship/VFW National Headquarters
Veterans of Foreign Wars of the United States
406 West 34th Street, Suite 902
Kansas City, MO 64111
E-mail: swilson@vfw.org

VIRGINIA DEPARTMENT OF VETERANS SERVICES   http://www.vdva.vipnet.org/education_benefits.htm

VIRGINIA WAR ORPHANS EDUCATION PROGRAM

Scholarships for postsecondary students between ages 16 and 25 to attend Virginia state supported institutions. Must be child or surviving child of veteran who has either been permanently or totally disabled due to war or

Virginia Department of Veterans Services (continued)

other armed conflict; died as a result of war or other armed conflict; or been listed as a POW or MIA. Parent must also meet Virginia residency requirements. Contact for application procedures and deadline.

Award: Scholarship for use in freshman, sophomore, junior, senior, or graduate years; renewable. *Number:* varies. *Amount:* varies.

Eligibility Requirements: Applicant must be age 16-25; enrolled or expecting to enroll full-time at a two-year or four-year or technical institution or university; resident of Virginia and studying in Virginia. Available to U.S. citizens. Applicant or parent must meet one or more of the following requirements: general military experience; retired from active duty; disabled or killed as a result of military service; prisoner of war; or missing in action.

Application Requirements: Application. *Deadline:* varies.

Contact: Doris Marie Sullivan, Coordinator
Virginia Department of Veterans Services
Poff Federal Building, 270 Franklin Road SW, Room 503
Roanoke, VA 24011-2215
Phone: 540-857-7101 Ext. 213
Fax: 540-857-7573

WINSTON-SALEM FOUNDATION   http://www.wsfoundation.org

MARY ROWENA COOPER SCHOLARSHIP FUND

Purpose is to provide need-based financial aid for students seeking degrees, certificates, or diplomas at vocational schools, technical schools, community colleges, and universities and colleges. Preference for applicants is: orphaned children of Vietnam vets of any service unit designation and, next, children not orphaned whose parent(s) served in the military during the Vietnam conflict. The fund has particular interest in, though is not restricted to, assisting students going into medicine, law, engineering and teaching. Application fee is $20.

Award: Scholarship for use in freshman, sophomore, junior, senior, or graduate years; not renewable. *Number:* varies. *Amount:* up to $2500.

Eligibility Requirements: Applicant must be enrolled or expecting to enroll full-time at a two-year or four-year or technical institution or university. Available to U.S. citizens. Applicant or parent must meet one or more of the following requirements: general military experience; retired from active duty; disabled or killed as a result of military service; prisoner of war; or missing in action.

Application Requirements: Application, financial need analysis, interview, transcript. *Fee:* $20. *Deadline:* Continuous.

Contact: Kay Dillon, Student Aid Director
Winston-Salem Foundation
860 West Fifth Street
Winston-Salem, NC 27101
Phone: 336-725-2382
Fax: 336-727-0581
E-mail: kdillon@wsfoundation.org

WISCONSIN DEPARTMENT OF VETERANS AFFAIRS   http://www.dva.state.wi.us

WISCONSIN DEPARTMENT OF VETERANS AFFAIRS RETRAINING GRANTS

Renewable award for veterans, unmarried spouses of deceased veterans, or dependents of deceased veterans. Must be resident of Wisconsin and attend an institution in Wisconsin. Veteran must be recently unemployed and show financial need. Must enroll in a vocational or technical program that can reasonably be expected to lead to employment. Course work at four-year colleges or universities does not qualify as retraining.

Award: Grant for use in freshman or sophomore years; renewable. *Number:* varies. *Amount:* up to $3000.

Eligibility Requirements: Applicant must be enrolled or expecting to enroll full or part-time at a technical institution; resident of Wisconsin and studying in Wisconsin. Available to U.S. citizens. Applicant or parent must meet one or more of the following requirements: general military experience; retired from active duty; disabled or killed as a result of military service; prisoner of war; or missing in action.

Application Requirements: Application, financial need analysis. *Deadline:* varies.

Contact: Mike Keatley, Grants Coordinator
Wisconsin Department of Veterans Affairs
PO Box 7843
Madison, WI 53707-7843
Phone: 608-266-1311
E-mail: mike.keatley@dva.state.wi.us

WISCONSIN VETERANS PART-TIME STUDY REIMBURSEMENT GRANT

Open only to Wisconsin veterans. Renewable for continuing study. Contact office for more details. Application deadline is no later than sixty days after the course completion. Veterans may be reimbursed up to 100% of tuition and fees.

Award: Grant for use in freshman, sophomore, junior, or senior years; renewable. *Number:* varies. *Amount:* $300–$2000.

Eligibility Requirements: Applicant must be enrolled or expecting to enroll part-time at a four-year or technical institution or university; resident of Wisconsin and studying in Wisconsin. Available to U.S. citizens. Applicant or parent must meet one or more of the following requirements: general military experience; retired from active duty; disabled or killed as a result of military service; prisoner of war; or missing in action.

Application Requirements: Application. *Deadline:* varies.

Contact: Mike Keatley, Grants Coordinator
Wisconsin Department of Veterans Affairs
PO Box 7843
Madison, WI 53707-7843
Phone: 608-266-1311

MILITARY SERVICE: MARINES

COMMANDER WILLIAM S. STUHR SCHOLARSHIP FUND FOR MILITARY SONS AND DAUGHTERS

COMMANDER WILLIAM S. STUHR SCHOLARSHIP FUND FOR MILITARY SONS AND DAUGHTERS

• See page 568

DAUGHTERS OF THE CINCINNATI   http://www.fdncenter.org

DAUGHTERS OF THE CINCINNATI SCHOLARSHIP

• See page 568

FIRST MARINE DIVISION ASSOCIATION   http://www.1stmarinedivisionassociation.org

FIRST MARINE DIVISION ASSOCIATION SCHOLARSHIP FUND

Award for graduating high school seniors or undergraduate dependents of deceased or 100% totally and permanently disabled veterans who served with the 1st Marine Division. Applicant's birth certificate and proof of parent's death or disability and service with the Division required. Must attend college full-time. At the present time, students are receiving grants of $1500 per student. Contact for further instructions.

Award: Scholarship for use in freshman, sophomore, junior, or senior years; not renewable. *Number:* varies. *Amount:* $1500.

Eligibility Requirements: Applicant must be age 22 or under; enrolled or expecting to enroll full-time at a four-year institution or university and single. Available to U.S. citizens. Applicant or parent must meet one or more of the following requirements: Marine Corps experience; retired from active duty; disabled or killed as a result of military service; prisoner of war; or missing in action.

Application Requirements: Application, essay, photo, birth certificate, proof of parent's death or disability and service with the division, social security number. *Deadline:* Continuous.

Contact: Ed Stiteler, Scholarship Chairman
First Marine Division Association
210 Funston Place
San Antonio, TX 78209
Phone: 210-828-5773

FLEET RESERVE ASSOCIATION
http://www.fra.org

COLONEL HAZEL ELIZABETH BENN U.S.M.C. SCHOLARSHIP
• See page 578

FLEET RESERVE ASSOCIATION SCHOLARSHIP
• See page 499

SCHUYLER S. PYLE AWARD
• See page 578

STANLEY A. DORAN MEMORIAL SCHOLARSHIP
• See page 578

LADIES AUXILIARY OF THE FLEET RESERVE ASSOCIATION
http://www.la-fra.org

ALLIE MAE ODEN MEMORIAL SCHOLARSHIP
• See page 504

MARINE CORPS SCHOLARSHIP FOUNDATION, INC.
http://www.marine-scholars.org

MARINE CORPS SCHOLARSHIP FOUNDATION

Available to undergraduate dependent children of current or former Marine Corps members whose family income does not exceed $63,000. Must submit proof of parent's service. Send for applications in the winter.

Award: Scholarship for use in freshman, sophomore, junior, or senior years; not renewable. *Number:* 1000. *Amount:* $500–$2500.

Eligibility Requirements: Applicant must be enrolled or expecting to enroll full or part-time at a two-year or four-year or technical institution or university. Available to U.S. citizens. Applicant or parent must meet one or more of the following requirements: Marine Corps experience; retired from active duty; disabled or killed as a result of military service; prisoner of war; or missing in action.

Application Requirements: Application, essay, financial need analysis, photo, transcript. *Deadline:* April 15.

Contact: June Hering, Scholarship Program Director
Marine Corps Scholarship Foundation, Inc.
PO Box 3008
Princeton, NJ 08543-3008
Phone: 800-292-7777
Fax: 609-452-2259
E-mail: mcsf@marine-scholars.org

MARINE CORPS TANKERS ASSOCIATION, INC.

MARINE CORPS TANKERS ASSOCIATION, JOHN CORNELIUS/MAX ENGLISH SCHOLARSHIP

Award for Marine tankers or former Marine tankers, or dependents of Marines who served in a tank unit and are on active duty, retired, reserve or have been honorably discharged. Applicant must be a high school graduate or planning to graduate in June. May be enrolled in college, undergraduate or graduate or have previously attended college. Must be a member of MCTA or will join.

Award: Scholarship for use in freshman, sophomore, junior, senior, or graduate years; not renewable. *Number:* 10. *Amount:* $1500.

Eligibility Requirements: Applicant must be enrolled or expecting to enroll full-time at a two-year or four-year or technical institution or university. Available to U.S. citizens. Applicant or parent must meet one or more of the following requirements: Marine Corps experience; retired from active duty; disabled or killed as a result of military service; prisoner of war; or missing in action.

Application Requirements: Application, essay, photo, references, test scores, transcript. *Deadline:* March 15.

Contact: Phil Morell, Scholarship Chair
Marine Corps Tankers Association, Inc.
1112 Alpine Heights Road
Alpine, CA 91901-2814
Phone: 619-445-8423
Fax: 619-445-8423

NAVAL SERVICE TRAINING COMMAND/NROTC
http://www.nrotc.navy.mil

NROTC SCHOLARSHIP PROGRAM

NROTC scholarships are based on merit and are awarded through a highly competitive national selection process. NROTC scholarships pay for college tuition, fees, uniforms, a book stipend, a monthly allowance and other financial benefits. Room and board expenses are not covered. Scholarship nominees must be medically qualified for the NROTC Scholarship Program.

Award: Scholarship for use in freshman, sophomore, junior, or senior years; renewable. *Number:* varies. *Amount:* varies.

Eligibility Requirements: Applicant must be age 17-23 and enrolled or expecting to enroll full-time at a four-year institution or university. Available to U.S. citizens. Applicant must have served in the Marine Corps or Navy.

Application Requirements: Application, applicant must enter a contest, essay, interview, references, test scores, transcript. *Deadline:* January 7.

Contact: NROTC Scholarship Selection Office (OD2A)
Naval Service Training Command/NROTC
250 Dallas Street, Suite A
Pensacola, FL 32508-5220
Phone: 800-NAV-ROTC
Fax: 850-452-3779
E-mail: pnsc_nrotc.scholarship@navy.mil

NAVY-MARINE CORPS RELIEF SOCIETY
http://www.nmcrs.org/

ADMIRAL MIKE BOORDA SCHOLARSHIP PROGRAM

Grants of up to $2000 for active duty members of Navy or Marine Corps enrolled in NROTC, ECP, MECEP, and MECP programs. Based on financial need. Minimum 2.0 GPA required. Must verify GPA and show military ID of student. One-time award for undergraduate use. Deadline: May 1.

Award: Grant for use in freshman, sophomore, junior, or senior years; not renewable. *Number:* varies. *Amount:* up to $2000.

Eligibility Requirements: Applicant must be age 22 or under; enrolled or expecting to enroll full-time at a two-year or four-year or technical institution or university and single. Available to U.S. citizens. Applicant must have served in the Marine Corps or Navy.

Application Requirements: Application, financial need analysis, copy of military ID/orders. *Deadline:* May 1.

Contact: NMCRS, Education Division
Navy-Marine Corps Relief Society
875 North Randolph Street Suite 225
Arlington, VA 22203
Phone: 703-696-4960
Fax: 703-696-0144
E-mail: education@nmcrs.org

NAVY-MARINE CORPS RELIEF SOCIETY-CHILDREN OF DECEASED SERVICE MEMBER DIED AFTER RETIREMENT FROM ACTIVE DUTY.

For students under 23 whose service member parent died after retiring. Must have current, valid dependent's Uniform Service Identification or Privilege Card, proof of service and member's status in Navy or Marine Corps, and proof of parent's death. Minimum 2.0 GPA required. Must verify GPA. Deadline is March 1st.

Award: Grant for use in freshman, sophomore, junior, or senior years; not renewable. *Number:* varies. *Amount:* up to $3000.

Eligibility Requirements: Applicant must be age 22 or under; enrolled or expecting to enroll full-time at a two-year or four-year or technical institution or university and single. Applicant must have 2.5 GPA or higher. Available to U.S. citizens. Applicant or parent must meet one or more of the following requirements: Marine Corps or Navy experience; retired from active duty; disabled or killed as a result of military service; prisoner of war; or missing in action.

Application Requirements: Application, financial need analysis, copy of military ID card, DD 214, death certificate. *Deadline:* March 1.

Navy-Marine Corps Relief Society (continued)

Contact: NMCRS, Education Division
Navy-Marine Corps Relief Society
875 North Randolph Street, Suite 225
Arlington, VA 22203
Phone: 703-696-4960
Fax: 703-696-0144

NAVY-MARINE CORPS RELIEF SOCIETY-SURVIVING CHILDREN OF DECEASED WHILE ON ACTIVE DUTY

One-time grants for full-time undergraduates who are military dependents of deceased service members (retired or deceased service members, service members who died on active duty). One of the specific funds is the Pentagon Assistance Fund, which is limited to children and spouses of the terrorist attack on September 11, 2001. Minimum 2.0 GPA required. Deadline: March 1.

Award: Grant for use in freshman, sophomore, junior, or senior years; not renewable. *Number:* varies. *Amount:* up to $3000.

Eligibility Requirements: Applicant must be age 23 or under; enrolled or expecting to enroll full-time at a two-year or four-year or technical institution or university and single. Available to U.S. citizens. Applicant or parent must meet one or more of the following requirements: Marine Corps or Navy experience; retired from active duty; disabled or killed as a result of military service; prisoner of war; or missing in action.

Application Requirements: Application, financial need analysis, contact NMCRS Education Division. *Deadline:* March 1.

Contact: NMCRS, Education Division
Navy-Marine Corps Relief Society
875 North Randolph Street, Suite 225
Arlington, VA 22203
Phone: 703-696-4960
Fax: 703-696-0144
E-mail: education@hq.nmcrs.org

USS TENNESSEE SCHOLARSHIP FUND

Fund provides grants of up to $2,000 for an academic year to dependent children of service members who are serving or have served aboard the U.S.S. Tennessee. Applicant must be enrolled, or planning to enroll, as a full-time undergraduate at a postsecondary, technical, or vocational institution. Each December, Tennessee application forms are posted on Web site: http://www. nmcrs.org/education.html. Between December and February, applications are available from NMCRS offices in Bangor, Groton, Guam, Kings Bay, Norfolk, and Pearl Harbor. Minimum 2.0 GPA required.

Award: Grant for use in freshman, sophomore, junior, or senior years; not renewable. *Amount:* up to $2000.

Eligibility Requirements: Applicant must be age 22 or under; enrolled or expecting to enroll full-time at a two-year or four-year or technical institution or university and single. Available to U.S. citizens. Applicant or parent must meet one or more of the following requirements: Marine Corps or Navy experience; retired from active duty; disabled or killed as a result of military service; prisoner of war; or missing in action.

Application Requirements: Application, financial need analysis, copy of military ID, proof of service in Tennessee. *Deadline:* March 1.

Contact: NMCRS, Education Division
Navy-Marine Corps Relief Society
875 North Randolph Street Suite 225
Arlington, VA 22203
Phone: 703-696-4960
Fax: 703-696-0144
E-mail: education@hq.nmcrs.org

NEW YORK COUNCIL NAVY LEAGUE   http://www.nynavyleague.org/

NEW YORK COUNCIL NAVY LEAGUE SCHOLARSHIP FUND
• See page 578

OREGON STUDENT ASSISTANCE COMMISSION   http://www.osac.state.or.us

AFSCME: AMERICAN FEDERATION OF STATE, COUNTY, AND MUNICIPAL EMPLOYEES LOCAL 75 SCHOLARSHIP
• See page 510

SECOND MARINE DIVISION ASSOCIATION   http://www.2marine.com

SECOND MARINE DIVISION ASSOCIATION MEMORIAL SCHOLARSHIP FUND

Renewable award for students who are unmarried sons, daughters or grandchildren of former or current members of 2nd Marine Division or attached units. Must submit proof of parent's service. Family adjusted gross income must not exceed $42,000. Award is merit-based. Minimum 2.5 GPA required.

Award: Scholarship for use in freshman, sophomore, junior, or senior years; renewable. *Number:* 25–35. *Amount:* $1000.

Eligibility Requirements: Applicant must be enrolled or expecting to enroll full-time at a two-year or four-year or technical institution or university and single. Applicant must have 2.5 GPA or higher. Available to U.S. and non-U.S. citizens. Applicant or parent must meet one or more of the following requirements: Marine Corps experience; retired from active duty; disabled or killed as a result of military service; prisoner of war; or missing in action.

Application Requirements: Application, financial need analysis, references, self-addressed stamped envelope, transcript. *Deadline:* April 1.

Contact: C. W. Van Horne, Executive Secretary
Second Marine Division Association
PO Box 8180
Camp LeJeune, NC 28547-8180
Phone: 910-451-3167
Fax: 910-451-3167

TAILHOOK EDUCATIONAL FOUNDATION   http://www.tailhook.org

TAILHOOK EDUCATIONAL FOUNDATION SCHOLARSHIP
• See page 551

THIRD MARINE DIVISION ASSOCIATION, INC.   http://www.caltrap.com

THIRD MARINE DIVISION ASSOCIATION MEMORIAL SCHOLARSHIP FUND

For dependents of Third Marine Division personnel (Marine or Navy) deceased or 100% service-connected disabled veterans; and two-year members of the Association, living or dead. For further details visit Web site: http://www.caltrap.com

Award: Scholarship for use in freshman, sophomore, junior, or senior years; renewable. *Number:* varies. *Amount:* $250–$1500.

Eligibility Requirements: Applicant must be age 17-26; enrolled or expecting to enroll full or part-time at a two-year or four-year or technical institution or university and single. Available to U.S. citizens. Applicant or parent must meet one or more of the following requirements: Marine Corps or Navy experience; retired from active duty; disabled or killed as a result of military service; prisoner of war; or missing in action.

Application Requirements: Application, financial need analysis, photo, transcript, birth certificate/adoption order (if applicable). *Deadline:* April 15.

Contact: Royal Q. Zilliox, Secretary
Third Marine Division Association, Inc.
3111 Sundial Drive
Dallas, TX 75229-3757
Phone: 972-247-6549
E-mail: rqzilliox@aol.com

MILITARY SERVICE: NAVY

AMERICAN CHEMICAL SOCIETY
http://www.chemistry.org

UNITED STATES NAVAL ACADEMY CLASS OF 1963 FOUNDATION GRANT

Awards are available to undergraduate and graduate students who are dependent children or deceased members of the Naval Academy Class of 1963 and who are currently enrolled at an accredited two- or four-year college, university, or technical school.

Award: Grant for use in freshman, sophomore, junior, senior, or graduate years; renewable. *Amount:* $1000–$4000.

Eligibility Requirements: Applicant must be age 35 or under and enrolled or expecting to enroll full-time at a two-year or four-year or technical institution or university. Available to U.S. and non-U.S. citizens. Applicant or parent must meet one or more of the following requirements: Navy experience; retired from active duty; disabled or killed as a result of military service; prisoner of war; or missing in action.

Application Requirements: Application. *Deadline:* Continuous.

Contact: Capt. Frank Hilton, Scholarship Committee Chairman
American Chemical Society
104 Kingfarm Boulevard C-401
Rockville, MD 20850
Phone: 301-519-0706
E-mail: fhilton@erols.com

ANCHOR SCHOLARSHIP FOUNDATION
http://www.anchorscholarship.com/

SURFLANT SCHOLARSHIP

Applicant must be a dependent of a Navy service member who has served at least three years under the administrative control of Commander, Naval Surface Force, U.S. Atlantic or Pacific Fleet Support Activities for a minimum of 6 years after 1975. To obtain an application, submit military sponsor's full name and rank/rate, list of SURFLANT duty stations, homeports, ship hull numbers and dates on board, applicant's name, and a self-addressed, stamped envelope. Selection is based upon academics, extracurricular activities, character and financial report. Information is available on Web site: http://www.cnsl.spear.navy.mil/scholarship

Award: Scholarship for use in freshman, sophomore, junior, or senior years; not renewable. *Number:* varies. *Amount:* $500–$3000.

Eligibility Requirements: Applicant must be enrolled or expecting to enroll full-time at a four-year institution. Available to U.S. citizens. Applicant or parent must meet one or more of the following requirements: Navy experience; retired from active duty; disabled or killed as a result of military service; prisoner of war; or missing in action.

Application Requirements: Application, essay, financial need analysis, references, self-addressed stamped envelope, test scores, transcript. *Deadline:* March 15.

Contact: Sally Ingram, Administrator
Anchor Scholarship Foundation
PO Box 9535
Norfolk, VA 23505
Phone: 757-374-3769
E-mail: cnslschf@erols.com

COMMANDER WILLIAM S. STUHR SCHOLARSHIP FUND FOR MILITARY SONS AND DAUGHTERS

COMMANDER WILLIAM S. STUHR SCHOLARSHIP FUND FOR MILITARY SONS AND DAUGHTERS
• See page 568

DAUGHTERS OF THE CINCINNATI
http://www.fdncenter.org

DAUGHTERS OF THE CINCINNATI SCHOLARSHIP
• See page 568

DOLPHIN SCHOLARSHIP FOUNDATION
http://www.dolphinscholarship.org

DOLPHIN SCHOLARSHIPS

Renewable award for undergraduate students. Applicant's parent or stepparent must meet one of the following requirements: be current member of the U.S. Navy who qualified in submarines and served in the Submarine Force for at least 8 years; current or former member of the Navy who served in submarine support activities for at least 10 years; or Navy member who died while on active duty in the Submarine Force. Must be single, age 23 or under. Based on academic merit, need, and leadership.

Award: Scholarship for use in freshman, sophomore, junior, or senior years; renewable. *Number:* 25–30. *Amount:* up to $3000.

Eligibility Requirements: Applicant must be age 23 or under; enrolled or expecting to enroll full-time at a four-year institution or university and single. Available to U.S. citizens. Applicant or parent must meet one or more of the following requirements: Navy experience; retired from active duty; disabled or killed as a result of military service; prisoner of war; or missing in action.

Application Requirements: Application, essay, financial need analysis, references, self-addressed stamped envelope, test scores, transcript. *Deadline:* March 15.

Contact: Tomi Roeske, Scholarship Administrator
Dolphin Scholarship Foundation
5040 Virginia Beach Boulevard, Suite 104A
Virginia Beach, VA 23462
Phone: 757-671-3200
Fax: 757-671-3330

FLEET RESERVE ASSOCIATION
http://www.fra.org

COLONEL HAZEL ELIZABETH BENN U.S.M.C. SCHOLARSHIP
• See page 578

FLEET RESERVE ASSOCIATION SCHOLARSHIP
• See page 499

SCHUYLER S. PYLE AWARD
• See page 578

STANLEY A. DORAN MEMORIAL SCHOLARSHIP
• See page 578

GAMEWARDENS OF VIETNAM ASSOCIATION, INC.
http://www.tf116.org

GAMEWARDENS OF VIETNAM SCHOLARSHIP

Scholarship for entering freshman who is a descendant of a U.S. Navy man or woman who worked with TF-116 in Vietnam. One-time award but applicant may reapply.

Award: Scholarship for use in freshman year; not renewable. *Number:* up to 3. *Amount:* up to $500.

Eligibility Requirements: Applicant must be high school student; age 16–21 and planning to enroll or expecting to enroll full-time at a two-year or four-year or technical institution or university. Applicant must have 2.5 GPA or higher. Available to U.S. and non-U.S. citizens. Applicant or parent must meet one or more of the following requirements: Navy experience; retired from active duty; disabled or killed as a result of military service; prisoner of war; or missing in action.

Application Requirements: Application. *Deadline:* April 1.

Contact: David Ajax, Scholarship Coordinator
Gamewardens of Vietnam Association, Inc.
6630 Perry Court
Arvada, CO 80003
Phone: 303-426-6385
Fax: 303-426-6186
E-mail: dpajax@comcast.net

LADIES AUXILIARY OF THE FLEET RESERVE ASSOCIATION
http://www.la-fra.org

ALLIE MAE ODEN MEMORIAL SCHOLARSHIP
• See page 504

NAVAL SERVICE TRAINING COMMAND/NROTC
http://www.nrotc.navy.mil

NROTC SCHOLARSHIP PROGRAM
• See page 597

NAVAL SPECIAL WARFARE FOUNDATION
http://www.nswfoundation.org

AGRON SEAL SCHOLARSHIP

Scholarship for academic study at any accredited college or university for an associate or bachelors degree. The applicant can be either a current high school student or an existing college student. The recipient must maintain a GPA of 3.2 or higher in their college courses to continue to receive the grant. Only active duty SEALs, their current spouse, and immediate children are eligible.

Award: Scholarship for use in freshman, sophomore, junior, or senior years; renewable. *Number:* 1. *Amount:* up to $1000.

Eligibility Requirements: Applicant must be enrolled or expecting to enroll full or part-time at an institution or university. Applicant must have 3.0 GPA or higher. Available to U.S. citizens. Applicant or parent must meet one or more of the following requirements: Navy experience; retired from active duty; disabled or killed as a result of military service; prisoner of war; or missing in action.

Application Requirements: Application. *Deadline:* March 13.

Contact: Robert Rieve, Executive Director
Naval Special Warfare Foundation
PO Box 5965
Virginia Beach, VA 23471
Phone: 757-363-7490
Fax: 757-363-7491
E-mail: info@nswfoundation.org

HAD RICHARDS UDT-SEAL MEMORIAL SCHOLARSHIP

One-time award for dependent children of UDT-SEAL Association members. Freshmen given priority. Applicant may not be older than 22. Must be U.S. citizen.

Award: Scholarship for use in freshman, sophomore, junior, or senior years; not renewable. *Number:* varies. *Amount:* $1000.

Eligibility Requirements: Applicant must be age 22 or under; enrolled or expecting to enroll full-time at a two-year or four-year or technical institution or university and single. Available to U.S. citizens. Applicant or parent must meet one or more of the following requirements: Navy experience; retired from active duty; disabled or killed as a result of military service; prisoner of war; or missing in action.

Application Requirements: Application, essay, photo, test scores, transcript, member must have paid UDT-SEAL Association dues for the last four consecutive years. *Deadline:* April 21.

Contact: Robert Rieve, Executive Director
Naval Special Warfare Foundation
PO Box 5965
Virginia Beach, VA 23471
Phone: 757-363-7490
Fax: 757-363-7491
E-mail: info@nswfoundation.org

NAVAL SPECIAL WARFARE SCHOLARSHIP

Awards given to active duty SEAL's, SWCC's, and other active duty military serving in a Naval Special Warfare command or their spouses and dependents.

Award: Scholarship for use in freshman, sophomore, junior, or senior years; not renewable. *Number:* 1. *Amount:* varies.

Eligibility Requirements: Applicant must be enrolled or expecting to enroll full or part-time at a two-year or four-year institution or university. Available to U.S. citizens. Applicant or parent must meet one or more of the following requirements: Navy experience; retired from active duty; disabled or killed as a result of military service; prisoner of war; or missing in action.

Application Requirements: Application, financial need analysis, transcript, proof of active duty or parent/spouse's active duty. *Deadline:* March 21.

Contact: Robert Rieve, Executive Director
Naval Special Warfare Foundation
PO Box 5965
Virginia Beach, VA 23471
Phone: 757-363-7490
Fax: 757-363-7491
E-mail: info@nswfoundation.org

UDT-SEAL SCHOLARSHIP

One-time award for dependent children of UDT-SEAL Association members. Freshmen given priority. Applicant may not be older than 22. Must be U.S. citizen.

Award: Scholarship for use in freshman, sophomore, junior, or senior years; not renewable. *Number:* 4–12. *Amount:* $1000.

Eligibility Requirements: Applicant must be age 22 or under; enrolled or expecting to enroll full-time at a two-year or four-year or technical institution or university and single. Available to U.S. citizens. Applicant or parent must meet one or more of the following requirements: Navy experience; retired from active duty; disabled or killed as a result of military service; prisoner of war; or missing in action.

Application Requirements: Application, essay, photo, test scores, transcript. *Deadline:* April 21.

Contact: Robert Rieve, Executive Director
Naval Special Warfare Foundation
PO Box 5965
Virginia Beach, VA 23471
Phone: 757-363-7490
Fax: 757-363-7491
E-mail: info@nswfoundation.org

NAVY-MARINE CORPS RELIEF SOCIETY
http://www.nmcrs.org/

ADMIRAL MIKE BOORDA SCHOLARSHIP PROGRAM
• See page 597

NAVY-MARINE CORPS RELIEF SOCIETY-CHILDREN OF DECEASED SERVICE MEMBER DIED AFTER RETIREMENT FROM ACTIVE DUTY.
• See page 597

NAVY-MARINE CORPS RELIEF SOCIETY-SURVIVING CHILDREN OF DECEASED WHILE ON ACTIVE DUTY
• See page 598

USS TENNESSEE SCHOLARSHIP FUND
• See page 598

NEW YORK COUNCIL NAVY LEAGUE
http://www.nynavyleague.org/

NEW YORK COUNCIL NAVY LEAGUE SCHOLARSHIP FUND
• See page 578

OREGON STUDENT ASSISTANCE COMMISSION
http://www.osac.state.or.us

AFSCME: AMERICAN FEDERATION OF STATE, COUNTY, AND MUNICIPAL EMPLOYEES LOCAL 75 SCHOLARSHIP
• See page 510

SEABEE MEMORIAL SCHOLARSHIP ASSOCIATION, INC.
http://www.seabee.org

SEABEE MEMORIAL ASSOCIATION SCHOLARSHIP

Award available to children or grandchildren of current or former members of the Naval Construction Force (Seabees) or Naval Civil Engineer Corps. High school students may apply. Not available for graduate study or to great-grandchildren of Seabees.

Award: Scholarship for use in freshman, sophomore, junior, or senior years; renewable. *Number:* 90. *Amount:* $1300–$2000.

Eligibility Requirements: Applicant must be enrolled or expecting to enroll full-time at a four-year institution. Available to U.S. citizens. Applicant or parent must meet one or more of the following requirements: Navy experience; retired from active duty; disabled or killed as a result of military service; prisoner of war; or missing in action.

Application Requirements: Application, essay, financial need analysis, test scores, transcript. *Deadline:* April 15.

Contact: Sheryl Chiogioji, Administrative Assistant
Seabee Memorial Scholarship Association, Inc.
PO Box 6574
Silver Spring, MD 20916
Phone: 301-570-2850
Fax: 301-570-2873
E-mail: smsa@erols.com

SPECIAL OPERATIONS WARRIOR FOUNDATION
http://www.specialops.org

SCHOLARSHIP FOR CHILDREN OF SPECIAL OPERATIONS FORCES WHO ARE KILLED IN THE LINE OF DUTY
• See page 568

TAILHOOK EDUCATIONAL FOUNDATION
http://www.tailhook.org

TAILHOOK EDUCATIONAL FOUNDATION SCHOLARSHIP
• See page 551

THIRD MARINE DIVISION ASSOCIATION, INC.
http://www.caltrap.com

THIRD MARINE DIVISION ASSOCIATION MEMORIAL SCHOLARSHIP FUND
• See page 598

UNITED STATES SUBMARINE VETERANS, INC.
http://ussvcf.org/scolyrs.htm

UNITED STATES SUBMARINE VETERANS INC. NATIONAL SCHOLARSHIP PROGRAM
• See page 552

NATIONALITY OR ETHNIC HERITAGE

A K STEEL FOUNDATION
http://www.aksteel.com

LOUIE F. COX MEMORIAL AK STEEL AFRICAN- AMERICAN SCHOLARSHIPS

Scholarships for African-American high school seniors are renewable for three years and potentially worth a total of $16,000 each.

Award: Scholarship for use in freshman year; renewable. *Number:* 2. *Amount:* up to $16,000.

Eligibility Requirements: Applicant must be Black (non-Hispanic); enrolled or expecting to enroll at an institution or university and resident of Ohio. Available to U.S. citizens.

Application Requirements: Application. *Deadline:* varies.

Contact: Christopher Ross, Finance manager
A K Steel Foundation
703 Curtis Street
Middletown, OH 45043
Phone: 513-425-5595

ADMINISTRATIVE MANAGEMENT SERVICES (AMS)
http://home.cogeco.ca

DAIMLER CHRYSLER SCHOLARSHIP PROGRAM
• See page 524

SYNCRUDE HIGHER EDUCATION AWARDS PROGRAM
• See page 524

ALBERTA HERITAGE SCHOLARSHIP FUND/ ALBERTA SCHOLARSHIP PROGRAMS
http://www.alis.gov.ab.ca

ADULT HIGH SCHOOL EQUIVALENCY SCHOLARSHIPS

Designed to recognize outstanding achievement in the attainment of high school equivalency. Students are eligible if they have been out of high school for three years, have achieved a minimum average of 80 per cent as a full-time student in courses required for entry into a postsecondary program, and are nominated by their institution. Must study in and be a resident of Alberta, Canada. Nomination deadline: September 1.

Award: Scholarship for use in freshman year; not renewable. *Number:* 200. *Amount:* $434.

Eligibility Requirements: Applicant must be Canadian citizen; enrolled or expecting to enroll full-time at a two-year or four-year or technical institution or university; resident of Alberta and studying in Alberta. Applicant must have 3.0 GPA or higher.

Application Requirements: Application, The Institute must nominate the applicant. *Deadline:* September 1.

Contact: Stuart Dunn, Manager
Alberta Heritage Scholarship Fund/Alberta Scholarship Programs
9940 106th Street, 4th Floor, Box 28000 Station Main
Edmonton, AB T5J 4R4
Canada
Phone: 780-427-8640
Fax: 780-422-4516
E-mail: heritage@gov.ab.ca

ALBERTA BLUE CROSS 50TH ANNIVERSARY SCHOLARSHIPS FOR ABORIGINAL STUDENTS

Award of CAN$500 to CAN$1500 will be awarded to three outstanding aboriginal students to encourage further studies at the postsecondary level. Applicants must be Registered Indian, Inuit, be residents of Alberta, and entering their first year of postsecondary study at an accredited Alberta postsecondary institution. For more details see Web site: http://www.alis.gov. ab.ca or http://www.ab.bluecross.ca

Award: Scholarship for use in freshman year; not renewable. *Number:* 3. *Amount:* $430–$1291.

Eligibility Requirements: Applicant must be American Indian/Alaska Native; high school student; planning to enroll or expecting to enroll full-time at a two-year or four-year or technical institution or university; resident of Alberta and studying in Alberta. Available to Canadian citizens.

Application Requirements: Application. *Deadline:* June 1.

Contact: Stuart Dunn, Manager
Alberta Heritage Scholarship Fund/Alberta Scholarship Programs
4th Floor, 9940 106th Street, Box 28000 Station Main
Edmonton, AB T5J 4R4
Canada
Phone: 780-427-8640
Fax: 780-427-1288
E-mail: scholarships@gov.ab.ca

ALBERTA HERITAGE SCHOLARSHIP FUND ALBERTA PRESS COUNCIL SCHOLARSHIP

Award for Alberta high school student enrolling in postsecondary studies for CAN$ 1000. Up to three runners-up may be selected to share a $500 award. Based on ability to write essay on specified topic. Application deadline is January 15. Please refer to Web site for topic: http://www.alis.gov.ab.ca/scholarships/.

Award: Scholarship for use in freshman year; not renewable. *Number:* 1. *Amount:* $861.

Eligibility Requirements: Applicant must be Canadian citizen; high school student; planning to enroll or expecting to enroll full-time at a two-year or four-year or technical institution or university; resident of Alberta and must have an interest in writing.

Application Requirements: Application, applicant must enter a contest, essay. *Deadline:* January 15.

Alberta Heritage Scholarship Fund/Alberta Scholarship Programs (continued)

Contact: Stuart Dunn, Manager
Alberta Heritage Scholarship Fund/Alberta Scholarship Programs
4th Floor, 9940 106th Street, Box 28000 Station Main
Edmonton, AB T5J 4R4
Canada
Phone: 780-427-8640
Fax: 780-427-1288
E-mail: scholarships@gov.ab.ca

ALBERTA HERITAGE SCHOLARSHIP FUND CANA SCHOLARSHIPS
• See page 525

ALEXANDER RUTHERFORD SCHOLARSHIPS FOR HIGH SCHOOL ACHIEVEMENT

The scholarships are awarded to students earning a minimum of 80% in five designated subjects in grades 10, 11, and 12. Applicants must be Alberta residents who plan to enroll in a full-time postsecondary program. May 1 deadline for September entry; December 1 deadline for January entry.

Award: Scholarship for use in freshman year; not renewable. *Number:* 8400. *Amount:* $344–$2153.

Eligibility Requirements: Applicant must be Canadian citizen; high school student; planning to enroll or expecting to enroll full-time at a two-year or four-year or technical institution or university and resident of Alberta. Applicant must have 3.0 GPA or higher.

Application Requirements: Application, transcript. *Deadline:* varies.

Contact: Stuart Dunn, Manager
Alberta Heritage Scholarship Fund/Alberta Scholarship Programs
4th Floor, 9940 106th Street, Box 28000 Station Main
Edmonton, AB T5J 4R4
Canada
Phone: 780-427-8640
Fax: 780-427-1288
E-mail: scholarships@gov.ab.ca

CHARLES S. NOBLE JUNIOR "A" HOCKEY SCHOLARSHIPS

Scholarships are awarded to individuals who have participated in Junior A Hockey and who are currently enrolled in full-time postsecondary study in Alberta. Nominations are made by their respective teams manager or coach. The awards are co-sponsored by the Alberta Heritage Scholarship Fund and the Junior A Hockey League. Must be a resident of Alberta, Canada. Applicants must maintain a minimum average of 2.0 on a 4.0 scale in their previous semester. Application deadline is December 1.

Award: Scholarship for use in freshman, sophomore, junior, or senior years; not renewable. *Number:* 10. *Amount:* $861.

Eligibility Requirements: Applicant must be Canadian citizen; enrolled or expecting to enroll full-time at a two-year or four-year or technical institution or university; resident of Alberta; studying in Alberta and must have an interest in athletics/sports.

Application Requirements: Application, essay, transcript. *Deadline:* December 1.

Contact: Stuart Dunn, Manager
Alberta Heritage Scholarship Fund/Alberta Scholarship Programs
4th Floor, 9940 106th Street, Box 28000 Station Main
Edmonton, AB T5J 4R4
Canada
Phone: 780-427-8640
Fax: 780-427-1288
E-mail: scholarships@gov.ab.ca

CHARLES S. NOBLE JUNIOR FOOTBALL SCHOLARSHIPS

Scholarships are awarded to junior football players who are currently enrolled full-time in a postsecondary institution in Alberta and are nominated by their team. The awards are co-sponsored by the Alberta Heritage Scholarship Fund and the three Alberta teams in the Junior Football League. Must be a resident of Alberta, Canada. Must rank in upper half of class or have a minimum 2.5 GPA.

Award: Scholarship for use in freshman, sophomore, junior, or senior years; not renewable. *Number:* 30. *Amount:* up to $861.

Eligibility Requirements: Applicant must be Canadian citizen; enrolled or expecting to enroll full-time at a two-year or four-year or technical

institution or university; resident of Alberta; studying in Alberta and must have an interest in athletics/sports. Applicant must have 2.5 GPA or higher.

Application Requirements: Application, transcript. *Deadline:* October 1.

Contact: Stuart Dunn, Manager
Alberta Heritage Scholarship Fund/Alberta Scholarship Programs
4th Floor, 9940 106th Street, Box 28000 Station Main
Edmonton, AB T5J 4R4
Canada
Phone: 780-427-8640
Fax: 780-422-4516
E-mail: scholarships@gov.ab.ca

DR. ERNEST AND MINNIE MEHL SCHOLARSHIP

Award given to a student graduating from an Alberta high school and enrolling in a postsecondary degree program. Selection based on diploma examination marks, financial need and personal commitment. Application deadline is June 1.

Award: Scholarship for use in freshman, sophomore, junior, or senior years; not renewable. *Number:* 1. *Amount:* $3014.

Eligibility Requirements: Applicant must be Canadian citizen; high school student; planning to enroll or expecting to enroll full-time at a two-year or four-year or technical institution or university and resident of Alberta.

Application Requirements: Application, financial need analysis, transcript. *Deadline:* June 1.

Contact: Stuart Dunn, Manager
Alberta Heritage Scholarship Fund/Alberta Scholarship Programs
4th Floor, 9940 106th Street, Box 28000 Station Main
Edmonton, AB T5J 4R4
Canada
Phone: 780-427-8640
Fax: 780-427-1288
E-mail: scholarships@gov.ab.ca

FELLOWSHIPS FOR FULL-TIME STUDIES IN FRENCH-UNIVERSITY

One-time awards for Canadian citizens who are Alberta residents pursuing full-time postsecondary studies in French in any discipline at a Canadian university. Travel grant is available for studies outside of Alberta. Application deadline is November 15.

Award: Scholarship for use in freshman, sophomore, junior, or senior years; not renewable. *Number:* 300. *Amount:* $430–$861.

Eligibility Requirements: Applicant must be Canadian citizen; enrolled or expecting to enroll full-time at a four-year institution or university and resident of Alberta.

Application Requirements: Application, transcript. *Deadline:* November 15.

Contact: Stuart Dunn, Manager
Alberta Heritage Scholarship Fund/Alberta Scholarship Programs
4th Floor, 9940 106th Street, Box 28000 Station Main
Edmonton, AB T5J 4R4
Canada
Phone: 780-427-8640
Fax: 780-427-1288
E-mail: scholarships@gov.ab.ca

GRANT MACEWAN UNITED WORLD COLLEGE SCHOLARSHIPS

To reward Alberta's best Grade 11 students with a chance to complete their high school at one of the ten United World Colleges located throughout the world. These awards are based on academic ability, leadership capability, references, and an interview. Applicants must be Alberta residents in the process of completing Grade 11. Tuition, room and board, and one return trip home per year. The scholarship covers both years of the program. Application deadline is February 15.

Award: Scholarship for use in freshman year; renewable. *Number:* 8. *Amount:* varies.

Eligibility Requirements: Applicant must be Canadian citizen; high school student; age 16-17; planning to enroll or expecting to enroll at an institution or university and resident of Alberta. Applicant must have 3.5 GPA or higher.

Application Requirements: Application, essay, interview, references, transcript. *Deadline:* February 15.

Contact: Stuart Dunn, Manager
Alberta Heritage Scholarship Fund/Alberta Scholarship Programs
4th Floor, 9940 106th Street, Box 28000 Station Main
Edmonton, AB T5J 4R4
Canada
Phone: 780-427-8640
Fax: 780-427-1288
E-mail: scholarships@gov.ab.ca

JIMMIE CONDON ATHLETIC SCHOLARSHIPS

One-time award for Canadian citizens who are residents of Alberta and are full-time students in an undergraduate, professional or graduate program at a university, college or technical institute in Alberta and nominee must be a member of a designated sports team or a member of Provincial Disabled Athletic Team recognized by the Alberta Athlete Development Program. Must maintain at least a 65% average. Deadline: November 1.

Award: Scholarship for use in freshman, sophomore, junior, senior, or graduate years; not renewable. *Number:* up to 2000. *Amount:* $1550.

Eligibility Requirements: Applicant must be Canadian citizen; enrolled or expecting to enroll full-time at a two-year or four-year or technical institution or university; resident of Alberta; studying in Alberta and must have an interest in athletics/sports. Applicant must have 2.5 GPA or higher.

Application Requirements: Application, nominee must be a member of a designated sports team or a member of Provincial Disabled Athletic Team recognized by the Alberta Athlete Development Program. *Deadline:* November 1.

Contact: Stuart Dunn, Manager
Alberta Heritage Scholarship Fund/Alberta Scholarship Programs
4th Floor, 9940 106th Street, Box 28000 Station Main
Edmonton, AB T5J 4R4
Canada
Phone: 780-427-8640
Fax: 780-427-1288
E-mail: scholarships@gov.ab.ca

LAURENCE DECOR STUDENT LEADERSHIP AWARDS

A total of 100 awards are available to recognize outstanding leadership in the areas of student government, student societies, clubs or organizations at the postsecondary level. Students are nominated by their Alberta postsecondary institution. Must be a resident of Alberta, Canada.

Award: Scholarship for use in freshman, sophomore, junior, or senior years; not renewable. *Number:* 100. *Amount:* $430.

Eligibility Requirements: Applicant must be Canadian citizen; enrolled or expecting to enroll full-time at a two-year or four-year or technical institution or university; resident of Alberta; studying in Alberta and must have an interest in leadership.

Application Requirements: Application. *Deadline:* March 1.

Contact: Stuart Dunn, Manager
Alberta Heritage Scholarship Fund/Alberta Scholarship Programs
4th Floor, 9940 106th Street, Box 28000 Station Main
Edmonton, AB T5J 4R4
Canada
Phone: 780-427-8640
Fax: 780-422-4516
E-mail: scholarships@gov.ab.ca

LOUISE MCKINNEY POSTSECONDARY SCHOLARSHIPS

Students enrolled in programs within Alberta are nominated by the awards office of their institution. Albertans enrolled in programs outside the province because their program of study is not offered in Alberta should contact the Alberta Heritage Scholarship Fund office. Must be a resident of Alberta. Must be ranked in upper quarter of class or have a minimum 3.5 GPA.

Award: Scholarship for use in sophomore, junior, senior, or graduate years; renewable. *Number:* 950. *Amount:* $2152.

Eligibility Requirements: Applicant must be Canadian citizen; enrolled or expecting to enroll full-time at a two-year or four-year institution or university and resident of Alberta. Applicant must have 3.5 GPA or higher.

Application Requirements: Application, transcript. *Deadline:* June 1.

Contact: Stuart Dunn, Manager
Alberta Heritage Scholarship Fund/Alberta Scholarship Programs
4th Floor, 9940 106th Street, Box 28000 Station Main
Edmonton, AB T5J 4R4
Canada
Phone: 780-427-8640
Fax: 780-427-1288
E-mail: scholarships@gov.ab.ca

NORTHERN ALBERTA DEVELOPMENT COUNCIL BURSARY

Applicants must have been residents of Alberta for a minimum of two years prior to applying. Students should also be in their latter years of academic study. Recipients are required to live and work for one year within the Northern Alberta Development Council boundary upon graduation. Application deadline is May 15. Please refer to these Web sites for more information: http://www3.gov.ab.ca/nadc; http://www.opportunitynorth.ca/

Award: Scholarship for use in junior, senior, or graduate years; not renewable. *Number:* 125–250. *Amount:* $1291–$2583.

Eligibility Requirements: Applicant must be Canadian citizen; enrolled or expecting to enroll full-time at a two-year or four-year or technical institution or university and resident of Alberta.

Application Requirements: Application, essay, financial need analysis, transcript. *Deadline:* May 15.

Contact: Carol Vesak, Bursary Coordinator
Alberta Heritage Scholarship Fund/Alberta Scholarship Programs
2nd Floor, Provincial Building, 9621-96 Avenue, PO Box 900-14
Peace River, AB T8S 1T4
Canada
Phone: 780-624-6545
E-mail: nadc.bursary@gov.ab.ca

PERSONS CASE SCHOLARSHIPS

Awards recognize students whose studies will contribute to the advancement of women, or who are studying in fields where members of their sex are traditionally few in number. Selection is based on program of studies, academic achievement, and financial need. Must study in and be a resident of Alberta, Canada. Must be ranked in upper third of class or have a minimum 3.0 GPA.

Award: Scholarship for use in freshman, sophomore, junior, or senior years; not renewable. *Number:* 5–20. *Amount:* $861–$4306.

Eligibility Requirements: Applicant must be Canadian citizen; enrolled or expecting to enroll full-time at a two-year or four-year or technical institution or university; female; resident of Alberta and studying in Alberta. Applicant must have 3.0 GPA or higher.

Application Requirements: Application, essay, transcript. *Deadline:* September 30.

Contact: Stuart Dunn, Manager
Alberta Heritage Scholarship Fund/Alberta Scholarship Programs
9940 106th Street, 4th Floor, Box 28000 Station Main
Edmonton, AB T5J 4R4
Canada
Phone: 780-427-8640
Fax: 780-427-1288
E-mail: scholarships@gov.ab.ca

QUEEN ELIZABETH II GOLDEN JUBILEE CITIZENSHIP MEDAL

Awards to honor the most outstanding recipients of the Premier's Citizenship Award, which recognizes students graduating from high school who have supported and contributed to Alberta communities through public service and voluntary endeavors. Winners will receive the Medal, a letter of recommendation from the Lieutenant Governor, and CAN$5000. Must be winner of the Premiers Citizenship Award from their high school in Alberta.

Award: Prize for use in freshman year; not renewable. *Number:* 5. *Amount:* $4305.

Eligibility Requirements: Applicant must be Canadian citizen; high school student and planning to enroll or expecting to enroll full or part-time at a two-year or four-year or technical institution or university.

Application Requirements: Premier's Citizenship Award Winner. *Deadline:* June 15.

Alberta Heritage Scholarship Fund/Alberta Scholarship Programs (continued)

Contact: Stuart Dunn, Manager
Alberta Heritage Scholarship Fund/Alberta Scholarship Programs
4th Floor, 9940 106th Street, Box 28000 Station Main
Edmonton, AB T5J 4R4
Canada
Phone: 780-427-8640
Fax: 780-427-1288
E-mail: scholarships@gov.ab.ca

RUTHERFORD SCHOLARS

The top ten students graduating from grade 12, as determined solely on the basis of Diploma Examination results in English 30 or Francais 30, Social Studies 30, and three other subjects, averages normally are in the 97% to 98.8% range are recognized as "Rutherford Scholars" and receive a plaque and CAN$1500 in addition to their Alexander Rutherford scholarship. Only the first writing of any Diploma Exam will be considered. Must be a resident of Alberta, Canada.

Award: Scholarship for use in freshman year; not renewable. *Number:* 10. *Amount:* $1291.

Eligibility Requirements: Applicant must be Canadian citizen; high school student; planning to enroll or expecting to enroll full-time at a two-year or four-year or technical institution or university and resident of Alberta. Applicant must have 3.5 GPA or higher.

Application Requirements: Transcript. *Deadline:* August 1.

Contact: Stuart Dunn, Manager
Alberta Heritage Scholarship Fund/Alberta Scholarship Programs
4th Floor, 9940 106th Street, Box 28000 Station Main
Edmonton, AB T5J 4R4
Canada
Phone: 780-427-8640
Fax: 780-427-1288
E-mail: scholarships@gov.ab.ca

ALBUQUERQUE COMMUNITY FOUNDATION   http://www.albuquerquefoundation.org

ACF- NOTAH BEGAY III SCHOLARSHIP PROGRAM FOR NATIVE AMERICAN SCHOLAR ATHLETES

$500 per year will be awarded to graduating high school seniors who are residents of New Mexico, have at least 50% Indian Blood, played varsity level sports in high school, and maintain a 3.0 GPA. Must attend an accredited, not-for-profit educational institution in the United States.

Award: Scholarship for use in freshman, sophomore, junior, or senior years; not renewable. *Number:* 4–6. *Amount:* $500.

Eligibility Requirements: Applicant must be American Indian/Alaska Native; high school student; planning to enroll or expecting to enroll full-time at a two-year or four-year or technical institution or university and resident of New Mexico. Applicant must have 3.0 GPA or higher. Available to U.S. citizens.

Application Requirements: Application, essay, financial need analysis, resume, references, test scores, transcript, certificate of Indian blood. *Deadline:* March 16.

Contact: Nancy Johnson, Program Director
Albuquerque Community Foundation
PO Box 36960
Albuquerque, NM 87176-6960
Phone: 505-883-6240
E-mail: acf@albuquerquefoundation.org

AMERICAN ASSOCIATION OF COLLEGES OF OSTEOPATHIC MEDICINE   http://www.aacom.org

SHERRY R. ARNSTEIN MINORITY STUDENT SCHOLARSHIP

One award will be given to a current student and one award will be given to an incoming minority student pursuing research and/or a degree in osteopathic medicine. Must be a minority and a U.S. citizen.

Award: Scholarship for use in freshman, sophomore, junior, graduate, or postgraduate years; not renewable. *Number:* 2. *Amount:* $500–$1000.

Eligibility Requirements: Applicant must be American Indian/Alaska Native, Asian/Pacific Islander, Black (non-Hispanic), or Hispanic and enrolled or expecting to enroll full-time at a four-year institution or university. Available to U.S. citizens.

Application Requirements: Application, essay. *Deadline:* March 31.

Contact: Office of Government Relations
American Association of Colleges of Osteopathic Medicine
5550 Friendship Boulevard, Suite 310
Chevy Chase, MD 20815-7231

AMERICAN BAPTIST FINANCIAL AID PROGRAM   http://www.abc-usa.org

AMERICAN BAPTIST FINANCIAL AID PROGRAM NATIVE AMERICAN GRANTS

Renewable award of $1,000 to $2,000 for Native-American who are members of an American Baptist Church/U.S.A congregation. Must be a U.S. citizen and attending an accredited educational institution in the United States.

Award: Grant for use in freshman, sophomore, junior, senior, or graduate years; renewable. *Number:* varies. *Amount:* $1000–$2000.

Eligibility Requirements: Applicant must be Baptist; American Indian/Alaska Native and enrolled or expecting to enroll full-time at a four-year institution or university. Available to U.S. citizens.

Application Requirements: Application, financial need analysis, references. *Deadline:* May 31.

Contact: Lynne Eckman, Director of Financial Aid
American Baptist Financial Aid Program
PO Box 851
Valley Forge, PA 19482-0851
E-mail: lynne.eckman@abc-usa.org

AMERICAN FEDERATION OF STATE, COUNTY, AND MUNICIPAL EMPLOYEES   http://www.afscme.org

AFSCME/UNCF UNION SCHOLARS PROGRAM

One-time award for a second semester sophomore or junior majoring in ethnic studies, women's studies, labor studies, American studies, sociology, anthropology, history, political science, psychology, social work or economics. Must be African-American, Hispanic-American, Asian Pacific Islander, or American-Indian/Alaska Native. Minimum 3.0 GPA. Receipt of scholarship requires a ten-week internship. See Web site at http://www.afscme.org for further details.

Award: Scholarship for use in sophomore or junior years; not renewable. *Number:* varies. *Amount:* $4000–$5000.

Eligibility Requirements: Applicant must be American Indian/Alaska Native, Asian/Pacific Islander, Black (non-Hispanic), or Hispanic and enrolled or expecting to enroll at a four-year institution. Applicant must have 2.5 GPA or higher. Available to U.S. citizens.

Application Requirements: Application, essay, references, transcript. *Deadline:* February 27.

Contact: Genevieve Marcus, Scholarship Coordinator
American Federation of State, County, and Municipal Employees
1625 L Street, NW
Washington, DC 20036
Phone: 202-429-1250
Fax: 202-429-1272

AMERICAN GEOLOGICAL INSTITUTE   http://www.agiweb.org

AMERICAN GEOLOGICAL INSTITUTE MINORITY SCHOLARSHIP

One-time award for minority geosciences majors, including the sub-disciplines of geophysics, geochemistry, hydrology, meteorology, physical oceanography, planetary geology, or earth science education. The program does not support students in other natural sciences, mathematics, or engineering. May apply for renewal. Application available at Web site http://www.agiweb.org. Deadline is March 1.

Award: Scholarship for use in freshman, sophomore, junior, senior, or graduate years; renewable. *Number:* varies. *Amount:* $250–$1000.

Eligibility Requirements: Applicant must be American Indian/Alaska Native, Asian/Pacific Islander, Black (non-Hispanic), or Hispanic and enrolled or expecting to enroll full-time at a two-year or four-year institution or university. Available to U.S. citizens.

Application Requirements: Application, references, test scores, transcript. *Deadline:* March 1.

Contact: Geoscience Student Scholarship Coordinator
American Geological Institute
Attention: Government Affairs Program
4220 King Street
Alexandria, VA 22302-1507
Phone: 703-379-2480
Fax: 703-379-7563

AMERICAN INDIAN EDUCATION FOUNDATION
http://www.aiefprograms.org

AMERICAN INDIAN EDUCATION FOUNDATION SCHOLARSHIP

AIEF provides tuition and living expenses for American Indian students. Scholarships are awarded based on student's history of volunteerism, their commitment to return to their community, and an ACT score of at least 16.

Award: Scholarship for use in freshman, sophomore, junior, or senior years; not renewable. *Number:* 100–150. *Amount:* $1500–$3000.

Eligibility Requirements: Applicant must be American Indian/Alaska Native and enrolled or expecting to enroll full-time at a two-year or four-year or technical institution or university. Available to U.S. citizens.

Application Requirements: Application, essay, financial need analysis, test scores. *Deadline:* May 3.

Contact: Belle Cantor, Scholarship Coordinator
American Indian Education Foundation
10029 SW Nimbus Avenue
Suite 200
Beaverton, OR 97008
Phone: 866-866-8642
Fax: 503-641-0495
E-mail: scholarships@nrc1.org

AMERICAN INDIAN GRADUATE CENTER
http://www.aigcs.org

GATES MILLENNIUM SCHOLARS PROGRAM

Award enables American-Indian/Alaska Native students to complete an undergraduate and graduate education. Must be entering a U.S. accredited college or university as a full-time degree-seeking student. Minimum 3.3 GPA required. Must demonstrate leadership abilities. Must meet federal Pell Grant eligibility criteria. Visit Web site at http://www.gmsp.org

Award: Scholarship for use in freshman, sophomore, junior, senior, or graduate years; renewable. *Number:* 150. *Amount:* $500–$40,000.

Eligibility Requirements: Applicant must be American Indian/Alaska Native and enrolled or expecting to enroll full-time at a four-year institution or university. Available to U.S. citizens.

Application Requirements: Application, financial need analysis, nomination packet. *Deadline:* January 16.

Contact: Christa Moya, GMS Representative
American Indian Graduate Center
4520 Montgomery Boulevard, NE, Suite 1B
Albuquerque, NM 87109
Phone: 866-884-7007
Fax: 505-884-8683
E-mail: christa@aigc.org

AMERICAN INSTITUTE FOR FOREIGN STUDY
http://www.aifsabroad.com

AMERICAN INSTITUTE FOR FOREIGN STUDY MINORITY SCHOLARSHIPS

Applications will be accepted from African-American, Asian-American, Native-American, Hispanic-American and Pacific Islanders who are currently enrolled as undergraduates at a U.S. institution applying to an AIFS study abroad program. Applicants must demonstrate financial need, leadership ability, and academic accomplishment and meet program requirements. One full scholarship and three runners-up scholarships are awarded each semester. Submit application by April 15 for fall or October 15 for spring. Application fee is $95.

Award: Scholarship for use in freshman, sophomore, junior, or senior years; not renewable. *Number:* up to 2. *Amount:* $2000.

Eligibility Requirements: Applicant must be American Indian/Alaska Native, Asian/Pacific Islander, Black (non-Hispanic), or Hispanic; age 17; enrolled or expecting to enroll full-time at a two-year or four-year institution or university and must have an interest in leadership. Applicant must have 3.0 GPA or higher. Available to U.S. and non-U.S. citizens.

Application Requirements: Application, essay, financial need analysis, photo, references, transcript. *Fee:* $95. *Deadline:* October 1.

Contact: David Mauro, Admissions Counselor
American Institute for Foreign Study
River Plaza, 9 West Broad Street
Stamford, CT 06902-3788
Phone: 800-727-2437 Ext. 5163
Fax: 203-399-5597
E-mail: college.info@aifs.com

ARAB AMERICAN HERITAGE COUNCIL SCHOLARSHIP

ARAB AMERICAN HERITAGE COUNCIL SCHOLARSHIP

Award available for high school seniors who are of Arab-American heritage. Applicant's parent/guardian must be a member of the AAHC.

Award: Scholarship for use in freshman year. *Number:* 1.

Eligibility Requirements: Applicant must be of Arab heritage; high school student and planning to enroll or expecting to enroll at an institution or university. Available to U.S. citizens.

Application Requirements: Application. *Deadline:* varies.

Contact: Arab American Heritage Council Scholarship
Arab American Heritage Council Scholarship
1000 Beach Street
Flint, MI 48502
Phone: 810-235-2722

ARAB AMERICAN INSTITUTE FOUNDATION
http://www.aaiusa.org/aaif.htm

AMEEN RIHANI SCHOLARSHIP PROGRAM

Scholarship (ARS) provides Lebanese Americans and other Arab Americans with an opportunity to complete a college education, particularly those intending to study literature, philosophy or political science. Applicants must have a cumulative GPA of 3.25.

Award: Scholarship for use in freshman year; not renewable. *Amount:* up to $1500.

Eligibility Requirements: Applicant must be of Arab or Lebanese heritage and enrolled or expecting to enroll full-time at a four-year institution or university. Applicant must have 3.0 GPA or higher. Available to U.S. citizens.

Application Requirements: Application, essay, photo, transcript. *Deadline:* May 31.

Contact: Ameen Rihani Scholarship Program
Arab American Institute Foundation
The Ameen Rihani Organization, 1010 Wayne Avenue, Suite 420
Silver Spring, MD 20910

LEBANESE AMERICAN HERITAGE CLUB SCHOLARSHIP

Scholarships awards $1000 to qualiied high school senior or college student of Arab descent. Undergraduate student applicants must have at least a 3.0 GPA, graduate student applicants must have at least a 3.5 GPA. Financial need will be considered.Must be U.S. citizen or permanent resident, and a resident of Michigan.

Award: Scholarship for use in freshman, sophomore, junior, or senior years. *Amount:* up to $1000.

Eligibility Requirements: Applicant must be of Arab heritage; enrolled or expecting to enroll full-time at a four-year institution or university and resident of Michigan. Available to U.S. citizens.

Arab American Institute Foundation (continued)

Application Requirements: Application, essay, references, transcript, Student Aid Report (SAR). *Deadline:* varies.

Contact: Arab American Institute Foundation
Lebanese American Heritage Club, Arab American Scholarship Foundation, 4337 Maple Road
Dearborn, MI 48126
Phone: 313-846-8480
Fax: 313-846-2710
E-mail: lahc@lahc.org

ARAB AMERICAN SCHOLARSHIP FOUNDATION
http://www.lahc.org

LEBANESE AMERICAN HERITAGE CLUB'S SCHOLARSHIP FUND

Scholarship for high school, undergraduate, or graduate students who are of Arab descent. Undergraduate student applicants must have at least a 3.0 GPA, graduate student applicants must have at least a 3.5 GPA, and senior high school students must have at least a 3.0 GPA. Must be U.S. citizens.

Award: Scholarship for use in freshman, sophomore, junior, senior, or graduate years. *Amount:* up to $1000.

Eligibility Requirements: Applicant must be of Arab heritage and enrolled or expecting to enroll at a four-year institution or university. Applicant must have 3.0 GPA or higher. Available to U.S. citizens.

Application Requirements: Application, essay, financial need analysis, references, transcript, current Student Aid Report (SAR). *Deadline:* April 10.

Contact: Ali Berry, President
Arab American Scholarship Foundation
The Lebanese American Heritage Club
4337 Maple Road
Dearborn, MI 48126
Phone: 313-846-8480
Fax: 313-846-2710
E-mail: lahc@lahc.org

ARIZONA ASSOCIATION OF CHICANOS IN HIGHER EDUCATION (AACHE)
http://www.aache.org/

AACHE SCHOLARSHIP

Scholarship available to students of Chicano/Hispanic/Latino heritage and identity who are residents of Arizona and enrolled full-time in one of the 10 Maricopa County, Arizona Community Colleges or who are transferring from one of these community colleges to a 4 year college or university in Arizona. Application deadline is April 2.

Award: Scholarship for use in sophomore, junior, senior, or graduate years; not renewable. *Number:* 10–50. *Amount:* $100–$300.

Eligibility Requirements: Applicant must be Hispanic; enrolled or expecting to enroll full-time at a two-year or four-year institution or university; resident of Arizona and studying in Arizona. Applicant must have 2.5 GPA or higher. Available to U.S. citizens.

Application Requirements: Application, autobiography, essay, transcript. *Deadline:* April 2.

Contact: Luvia Rivera, Scholarship Chair
Arizona Association of Chicanos in Higher Education (AACHE)
3000 North Dysart Road
Avondale, AZ 85323
Phone: 623-935-8321
E-mail: luvia.rivera@emcmail.maricopa.edu

ARMENIAN RELIEF SOCIETY OF EASTERN USA, INC. -REGIONAL OFFICE
http://www.arseastus.org

ARMENIAN RELIEF SOCIETY UNDERGRADUATE SCHOLARSHIP

Applicant must be an undergraduate student attending an accredited four-year college or university in the U.S. Award for full-time Armenian students only. Must be U.S. or Canadian citizen. Scholarship for use at a four-year college or university. High school students may not apply.

Award: Scholarship for use in freshman, sophomore, junior, or senior years; not renewable. *Number:* varies. *Amount:* $13,000–$15,000.

Eligibility Requirements: Applicant must be of Armenian heritage and enrolled or expecting to enroll full-time at a four-year institution or university. Available to U.S. and Canadian citizens.

Application Requirements: Application, financial need analysis, references, self-addressed stamped envelope, transcript. *Deadline:* April 1.

Contact: Scholarship Undergraduate Committee
Armenian Relief Society of Eastern USA, Inc. -Regional Office
80 Bigelow Avenue, Suite 200
Watertown, MA 02472
Phone: 617-926-3801
Fax: 617-924-7238
E-mail: arseastus@aol.com

ARMENIAN STUDENTS ASSOCIATION OF AMERICA, INC.

ARMENIAN STUDENTS ASSOCIATION OF AMERICA, INC. SCHOLARSHIPS

One-time award for students of Armenian descent. Must be undergraduate in sophomore, junior, or senior years, or graduate student, attending accredited U.S. institution full-time. Award based on need, merit, and character. Show proof of tuition costs and enrollment. Application fee: $15.

Award: Scholarship for use in freshman, sophomore, junior, senior, or graduate years; not renewable. *Number:* 30. *Amount:* $1000–$3500.

Eligibility Requirements: Applicant must be of Armenian heritage and enrolled or expecting to enroll full-time at a four-year institution or university. Available to U.S. citizens.

Application Requirements: Application, essay, financial need analysis, references, transcript. *Fee:* $15. *Deadline:* March 15.

Contact: Nathalie Yaghoobian, Scholarship Administrator
Armenian Students Association of America, Inc.
333 Atlantic Avenue
Warwick, RI 02888
Phone: 401-461-6114
Fax: 401-461-6112
E-mail: headasa.com@aol.com

ASSOCIATED MEDICAL SERVICES, INC.
http://www.ams-inc.on.ca

ASSOCIATED MEDICAL SERVICES, INC. BIOETHICS STUDENTSHIP

Studentship available for Canadian citizens or permanent residents registered in a full-time undergraduate program at a Canadian university. Must pursue research in the field of bioethics. Project proposal required. Deadline is January 15. Additional information on Web site: http://www.ams-inc.on.ca

Award: Scholarship for use in freshman, sophomore, junior, or senior years. *Number:* 1–10. *Amount:* up to $4532.

Eligibility Requirements: Applicant must be Canadian citizen and enrolled or expecting to enroll full-time at a four-year institution or university.

Application Requirements: Application, references, transcript. *Deadline:* January 15.

Contact: Sheena Lee, Grants Consultant
Associated Medical Services, Inc.
162 Cumberland Street
Suite 228
Toronto M5R 3N5
Canada
Phone: 416-924-3368
Fax: 416-323-3338
E-mail: grantsof@ams-inc.on.ca

ASSOCIATION OF INTERNATIONAL EDUCATION, JAPAN (AIEJ)

SPONSOR-CROWNED INTERNATIONAL STUDENT SCHOLARSHIP

One-time award available to undergraduate or graduate Japanese students studying at a four-year college or university. Amounts and deadlines vary.

Award: Scholarship for use in freshman, sophomore, junior, senior, or graduate years; not renewable. *Number:* 82. *Amount:* $24,744–$41,232.

Eligibility Requirements: Applicant must be Asian/Pacific Islander and enrolled or expecting to enroll full-time at a four-year institution or university. Available to citizens of countries other than the U.S. or Canada.

Application Requirements: Applicant must enter a contest, to be decided by each funding source. *Deadline:* varies.

Contact: Fumihiko Adachihara, Student Affairs Division, AIEJ
Association of International Education, Japan (AIEJ)
4-5-29 Komaba, Meguro-ku
Tokyo 153-8503
Japan
Phone: 81-03-5454-5213
Fax: 81-03-5454-5233
E-mail: sa1@aiej.or.jp

ASSOCIATION ON AMERICAN INDIAN AFFAIRS (AAIA)   http://www.indian-affairs.org

ADOLPH VAN PELT SPECIAL FUND FOR INDIAN SCHOLARSHIPS

This scholarship is awarded to undergraduate students based upon need and merit. Grants are paid directly to the educational institute and are renewable up to four years for any one degree. Each year $100 is added to the scholarship amount to a maximum of $800.

Award: Scholarship for use in freshman, sophomore, junior, or senior years; renewable. *Number:* varies. *Amount:* $500–$800.

Eligibility Requirements: Applicant must be American Indian/Alaska Native and enrolled or expecting to enroll at an institution or university. Available to U.S. citizens.

Application Requirements: Application, essay, references, transcript, certificate of enrollment and blood quantum from applicant's tribe or BIA, class schedule, FA award letter. *Deadline:* July 20.

Contact: Scholarship Coordinator
Association on American Indian Affairs (AAIA)
PO Box 268
Sisseton, SD 57262
Phone: 605-698-3998
Fax: 605-698-3316
E-mail: aaia@sbtc.net

DISPLACED HOMEMAKER SCHOLARSHIP

This scholarship will augment the unmet needs associated with usual and expected expenses such as child care, transportation, and some basic living expenses, in addition to educational costs.

Award: Scholarship for use in freshman, sophomore, junior, senior, graduate, or postgraduate years; not renewable. *Number:* varies. *Amount:* $1500.

Eligibility Requirements: Applicant must be American Indian/Alaska Native and enrolled or expecting to enroll full-time at an institution or university. Available to U.S. citizens.

Application Requirements: Application, essay, references, transcript, certificate of enrollment and blood quantum from applicant's tribe, monthly budget, class schedule, FA award letter. *Deadline:* July 20.

Contact: Scholarship Coordinator
Association on American Indian Affairs (AAIA)
PO Box 268
Sisseton, SD 57262
Phone: 605-698-3998
Fax: 605-698-3316
E-mail: aaia@sbtc.net

EMERGENCY AID AND HEALTH PROFESSIONALS SCHOLARSHIP PROGRAM

This scholarship is awarded to full time undergraduate students based on financial need and is limited to availability of funds. Emergency Aid is available during both Fall and Spring semesters. Students may only receive one scholarship per academic year.

Award: Scholarship for use in freshman, sophomore, junior, or senior years; not renewable. *Number:* varies. *Amount:* $100–$400.

Eligibility Requirements: Applicant must be American Indian/Alaska Native and enrolled or expecting to enroll full-time at an institution or university. Available to U.S. citizens.

Application Requirements: Application, essay, transcript, certificate of enrollment and blood quantum from applicant's tribe or BIA, FA award letter, class schedule. *Deadline:* Continuous.

Contact: Scholarship Coordinator
Association on American Indian Affairs (AAIA)
PO Box 268
Sisseton, SD 57262
Phone: 605-698-3998
Fax: 605-698-3316
E-mail: aaia@sbtc.net

AUSTRALIAN FEDERATION OF UNIVERSITY WOMEN-SA

PADNENDADLU UNDERGRADUATE BURSARIES

Bursary open to Indigenous Australian women undergraduates in each of the South Australian universities. Applicants must be undertaking subjects for the final year of their Bachelor degree, or undertaking an Honours year.

Award: Scholarship for use in senior year.

Eligibility Requirements: Applicant must be of Australian heritage; enrolled or expecting to enroll full-time at an institution or university and female. Available to U.S. and non-U.S. citizens.

Application Requirements: Application, resume. *Deadline:* varies.

Contact: Rachel Spencer, Trustee
Australian Federation of University Women-SA
GPO Box 634
Adelaide, SA 5001
Australia
Phone: 61-08-8201-3986
E-mail: rachel.spencer@flinders.edu.au

BECA FOUNDATION, INC.   http://www.becafoundation.org

DANIEL GUTIERREZ MEMORIAL GENERAL SCHOLARSHIP FUND

Scholarships to full-time Latino students from San Diego County; high school graduate entering college in the fall of the same year. May pursue their education anywhere in the United States and pursue any profession. Financial need, scholastic determination and community/cultural awareness are considered.

Award: Scholarship for use in freshman year; not renewable. *Number:* varies. *Amount:* $500–$1000.

Eligibility Requirements: Applicant must be of Hispanic heritage; high school student; planning to enroll or expecting to enroll full-time at a four-year institution or university and resident of California. Applicant must have 2.5 GPA or higher. Available to U.S. citizens.

Application Requirements: Application, essay, financial need analysis, references, transcript. *Deadline:* March 1.

Contact: Ana Garcia, Operations Manager
BECA Foundation, Inc.
830 E Grand Avenue
Suite B
Escondido, CA 92025
Phone: 760-741-8246

GENERAL SCHOLARSHIP FUND

Scholarships to full-time Latino students from North San Diego County; high school graduate entering college in the fall of the same year. May pursue their education anywhere in the United States and pursue any profession. Financial need, scholastic determination and community/cultural awareness are considered.

Award: Scholarship for use in freshman year; not renewable. *Number:* varies. *Amount:* $500–$1000.

Eligibility Requirements: Applicant must be of Hispanic heritage; high school student; planning to enroll or expecting to enroll full-time at an institution or university and resident of California. Applicant must have 2.5 GPA or higher. Available to U.S. citizens.

BECA Foundation, Inc. (continued)

Application Requirements: Application, essay, financial need analysis, references, transcript. *Deadline:* March 1.

Contact: Ana Garcia, Operations Manager
BECA Foundation, Inc.
830 E Grand Avenue
Suite B
Escondido, CA 92025
Phone: 760-741-8246

BLACKFEET NATION HIGHER EDUCATION PROGRAM
http://www.blackfeetnation.com

BLACKFEET NATION HIGHER EDUCATION GRANT

Up to 140 grants of up to $3500 will be awarded to students who are enrolled members of the Blackfeet Tribe and actively pursuing an undergraduate degree. Must submit a certification of Blackfeet blood. The deadline is March 1.

Award: Grant for use in freshman, sophomore, junior, or senior years; renewable. *Number:* 140. *Amount:* $3500.

Eligibility Requirements: Applicant must be American Indian/Alaska Native and enrolled or expecting to enroll full-time at a two-year or four-year institution or university. Available to U.S. citizens.

Application Requirements: Application, essay, financial need analysis, transcript, certification of Blackfeet blood. *Deadline:* March 1.

Contact: Conrad LaFromboise, Director
Blackfeet Nation Higher Education Program
PO Box 850
Browning, MT 59417
Phone: 406-338-7539
Fax: 406-338-7530
E-mail: bhep@blackfeetnation.com

CABRILLO CIVIC CLUBS OF CALIFORNIA, INC.
http://www.cabrillocivicclubs.org

CABRILLO CIVIC CLUBS OF CALIFORNIA SCHOLARSHIP

Graduating California high school seniors of Portuguese heritage and American citizenship, with an overall 3.5 GPA can apply within a March 1 to April 1 deadline. Scholarship screening is conducted by club members (fourteen clubs) on point system for leadership, promise, grades, activities, and work.

Award: Scholarship for use in freshman year; not renewable. *Number:* 75–100. *Amount:* $500.

Eligibility Requirements: Applicant must be of Portuguese heritage; high school student; planning to enroll or expecting to enroll full-time at a technical institution and resident of California. Applicant must have 3.5 GPA or higher. Available to U.S. citizens.

Application Requirements: Application, autobiography, photo, resume, references, self-addressed stamped envelope, transcript. *Deadline:* April 1.

Contact: Breck Austin, State Scholarship Chairman
Cabrillo Civic Clubs of California, Inc.
PO Box 3005
Visalia, CA 93278
Phone: 760-967-2111
Fax: 760-967-2113
E-mail: scholarship@cabrillocivicclubs.org

CANADA MILLENNIUM SCHOLARSHIP FOUNDATION
http://www.millenniumscholarships.ca

CANADA MILLENNIUM EXCELLENCE AWARD PROGRAM

Entrance and in-course awards for postsecondary study in Canada recognizing community involvement, leadership, innovation, and academics.

Award: Scholarship for use in freshman or junior years; renewable. *Number:* up to 2300. *Amount:* $3267–$4084.

Eligibility Requirements: Applicant must be Canadian citizen and enrolled or expecting to enroll full-time at a two-year or four-year or technical institution or university. Applicant must have 3.0 GPA or higher.

Application Requirements: Application, references, transcript. *Deadline:* varies.

Contact: Maria Modafferi, Information Officer
Canada Millennium Scholarship Foundation
1000 Sherbrooke Street W
Suite 800
Montreal, QC H3A 3R2
Canada
Phone: 514-284-7230
Fax: 514-985-5987
E-mail: millennium.foundation@bm-ms.org

CAP FOUNDATION
http://www.ronbrown.org

RON BROWN SCHOLAR PROGRAM

Program seeks to identify African-American high school seniors who will make significant contributions to society. Applicants must excel academically, show exceptional leadership potential, participate in community service activities, and demonstrate financial need. Must be a U.S. citizen or hold permanent resident visa. Must plan to attend a four-year college or university. Deadlines: November 15 and January 9.

Award: Scholarship for use in freshman, sophomore, junior, or senior years; renewable. *Number:* 10–20. *Amount:* $10,000–$40,000.

Eligibility Requirements: Applicant must be Black (non-Hispanic); high school student; planning to enroll or expecting to enroll full-time at a four-year institution or university and must have an interest in leadership. Applicant must have 3.5 GPA or higher. Available to U.S. citizens.

Application Requirements: Application, essay, financial need analysis, interview, photo, references, test scores, transcript. *Deadline:* varies.

Contact: Ms. Fran Hardey, Executive Assistant, Ron Brown Scholar Program
CAP Foundation
1160 Pepsi Place, Suite 206
Charlottesville, VA 22901
Phone: 434-964-1588
Fax: 434-964-1589
E-mail: franh@ronbrown.org

CENTER FOR SCHOLARSHIP ADMINISTRATION
http://www.scholarshipprograms.org

HISPANIC LEAGUE OF THE PIEDMONT TRIAD SCHOLARSHIP

Non-renewable scholarships are available to students of Hispanic ethnicity who reside in one of the following counties in North Carolina: Forsyth, Guilford, Davidson, Surry, Stokes, or Yadkin. Must have taken English as a second language. Contact high school counselor for deadlines and more detailed information on additional criteria.

Award: Scholarship for use in freshman, sophomore, junior, or senior years; not renewable. *Number:* 4. *Amount:* $1500.

Eligibility Requirements: Applicant must be Hispanic; enrolled or expecting to enroll at a two-year or four-year or technical institution or university and resident of North Carolina. Available to U.S. citizens.

Application Requirements: Application. *Deadline:* varies.

Contact: Sandra Lee, President
Center for Scholarship Administration
PO Box 1465
Taylors, SC 29687-0031
Phone: 864-268-3363
Fax: 864-268-7160
E-mail: sandralee41@bellsouth.net

CENTRAL COUNCIL, TLINGIT AND HAIDA INDIAN TRIBES OF ALASKA
http://www.hied.org

ALUMNI STUDENT ASSISTANCE PROGRAM

The ASAP provides annual scholarship awards to all enrolled Tlingit or Haida tribal members regardless of service area, community affiliation, origination, residence, tribal compact, or signatory status.

Award: Scholarship for use in freshman, sophomore, junior, senior, graduate, or postgraduate years; not renewable. *Number:* varies. *Amount:* $200–$500.

Eligibility Requirements: Applicant must be American Indian/Alaska Native and enrolled or expecting to enroll full-time at a two-year or four-year institution or university. Applicant must have 2.5 GPA or higher. Available to U.S. citizens.

Application Requirements: Application, essay, financial need analysis, references, transcript, tribal enrollment certification form, letter of admission. *Deadline:* September 15.

Contact: Miss. Leslie Rae Isturis, Education Specialist
Central Council, Tlingit and Haida Indian Tribes of Alaska
3239 Hospital Drive
Juneau, AK 99801
Phone: 907-463-7375
Fax: 907-463-7173
E-mail: listuris@ccthita.org

COLLEGE STUDENT ASSISTANCE PROGRAM

A federally funded program which authorizes a program of assistance, by educational grants, to Indians seeking higher education. Awards available only to enrolled T&H members. Minimum 2.0 GPA required.

Award: Scholarship for use in freshman, sophomore, junior, senior, graduate, or postgraduate years; renewable. *Number:* varies. *Amount:* up to $2000.

Eligibility Requirements: Applicant must be American Indian/Alaska Native and enrolled or expecting to enroll full-time at a two-year or four-year institution or university. Available to U.S. citizens.

Application Requirements: Application, test scores, transcript, letter of admission. *Deadline:* May 15.

Contact: Miss. Leslie Rae Isturis, Education Specialist
Central Council, Tlingit and Haida Indian Tribes of Alaska
3239 Hospital Drive
Juneau, AK 99801
Phone: 907-463-7375
Fax: 907-463-7173
E-mail: listuris@ccthita.org

CHEROKEE NATION OF OKLAHOMA
http://www.cherokee.org

CHEROKEE NATION HIGHER EDUCATION SCHOLARSHIP

A supplementary program that provides financial assistance to Cherokee Nation Members only. It is a need-based program which provides assistance in seeking a bachelor's degree.

Award: Scholarship for use in freshman, sophomore, junior, or senior years; renewable. *Number:* 1200–1500. *Amount:* $500–$1000.

Eligibility Requirements: Applicant must be American Indian/Alaska Native and enrolled or expecting to enroll full-time at a two-year or four-year institution or university. Available to U.S. citizens.

Application Requirements: Application, financial need analysis, test scores, transcript, written request for the application. *Deadline:* June 17.

Contact: Dale Miller, Higher Education Specialist
Cherokee Nation of Oklahoma
PO Box 948
Tahlequah, OK 74465
Phone: 918-458-6195
E-mail: dmiller@cherokee.org

CHICANA/LATINA FOUNDATION
http://www.chicanalatina.org

SCHOLARSHIPS FOR LATINA STUDENTS

Scholarships are awarded to Latina students enrolled in two-year, four-year or graduate levels. Applicants must be from the nine counties of Northern California. Application deadline is March every year. Application online: http://www.chicanalatina.org.

Award: Scholarship for use in freshman, sophomore, junior, senior, or graduate years; not renewable. *Number:* 15–20. *Amount:* $1500.

Eligibility Requirements: Applicant must be of Hispanic heritage; enrolled or expecting to enroll full-time at a two-year or four-year institution or university; female and resident of California. Applicant must have 2.5 GPA or higher. Available to U.S. and non-U.S. citizens.

Application Requirements: Application, essay, interview, references, transcript. *Deadline:* March.

Contact: Olga Talamante, Executive Director
Chicana/Latina Foundation
1419 Burlingame Avenue
Suite N
Burlingame, CA 94044
Phone: 650-373-1083
Fax: 650-373-1090
E-mail: olgapacifica@yahoo.com

CHINESE PROFESSIONAL CLUB OF HOUSTON
http://www.cpchouston.com

T.P. WANG SCHOLARSHIP

Scholarship available toward tuition payment for undergraduate, graduate, leadership or community service development studies. Must be a current Chinese Professional Club of Houston member or the offspring of a current CPC member.

Award: Scholarship for use in freshman, sophomore, junior, senior, or graduate years; not renewable. *Number:* 1. *Amount:* $1000–$2000.

Eligibility Requirements: Applicant must be of Chinese heritage; Asian/Pacific Islander; enrolled or expecting to enroll full-time at a four-year institution or university and resident of Texas. Available to U.S. citizens.

Application Requirements: Application, essay, resume, references, transcript. *Deadline:* varies.

Contact: Anita Eng Dawson, CPC Scholarship Committee
Chinese Professional Club of Houston
5826 New Territory Boulevard
Sugar Land, TX 77479-5948
Phone: 281-565-5655

THE CHINESE PROFESSIONAL CLUB SCHOLARSHIP

Award to full time undergraduate students. Must be a student of Chinese descent and resident of Greater Houston Metropolitan Area.

Award: Scholarship for use in freshman, sophomore, junior, or senior years; not renewable. *Number:* up to 10. *Amount:* $1000–$2000.

Eligibility Requirements: Applicant must be of Chinese heritage; Asian/Pacific Islander; enrolled or expecting to enroll full-time at a four-year institution or university and resident of Texas. Available to U.S. citizens.

Application Requirements: Application, essay, references, transcript. *Deadline:* February.

Contact: Anita Eng Dawson, CPC Scholarship Committee
Chinese Professional Club of Houston
5826 New Territory Boulevard
Sugar Land, TX 77479-5948
Phone: 281-565-5655

CIRI FOUNDATION
http://www.thecirifoundation.org

TYONEK NATIVE CORPORATION SCHOLARSHIP AND GRANT FUND

To encourage Alaska Native student to prepare for professional career after high school. Applicant must be accepted or enrolled full time in an accredited or otherwise approved postsecondary college, university, or technical skills education program. Semester scholarship: $1000; Vocational Training/Career Upgrade Grant: up to $1500 received during a calendar year. See Web site for more details: http://www.ciri.com/tcf

Award: Scholarship for use in freshman, sophomore, junior, senior, or graduate years; not renewable. *Number:* varies. *Amount:* $1000–$1500.

Eligibility Requirements: Applicant must be American Indian/Alaska Native and enrolled or expecting to enroll full-time at a four-year or technical institution or university. Available to U.S. citizens.

CIRI Foundation (continued)

Application Requirements: Application, essay, references, transcript, proof of eligibility, birth certificate or adoption decree. *Deadline:* varies.

Contact: Susan Anderson, President/CEO
CIRI Foundation
3600 San Jeronimo Drive, Suite 256
Anchorage, AK 99508
Phone: 907-793-3575
Fax: 907-793-3585
E-mail: tcf@thecirifoundation.org

CITY COLLEGE OF SAN FRANCISCO LATINO EDUCATIONAL ASSOCIATION   http://www.ccsf.edu

LATINO EDUCATION ASSOCIATION SCHOLARSHIP

Latina or Latino students with at least 60 transferable credits who have been accepted at any college or university will be evaluated for the scholarship based on financial need, academic excellence, community service and student activism while at CCSF. Application deadline is first Friday in April.

Award: Scholarship for use in freshman, sophomore, junior, or senior years; not renewable. *Number:* 3. *Amount:* $500.

Eligibility Requirements: Applicant must be Hispanic; enrolled or expecting to enroll at a four-year institution or university and resident of California. Applicant must have 3.0 GPA or higher. Available to U.S. citizens.

Application Requirements: Application, autobiography, essay, references, transcript. *Deadline:* April.

Contact: Latino Educational Association Scholarships
City College of San Francisco Latino Educational Association
Scholarship Office
50 Phelan Avenue, Box L230, Batmale Hall, Room 366
San Francisco, CA 94112
Phone: 415-239-3339
E-mail: gsaucedo@ccsf.org

COLLEGE FOUNDATION OF NORTH CAROLINA, INC   http://www.cfnc.org

COUNCIL FOR EXCEPTIONAL CHILDREN

Scholarships include awards specifically for gifted and talented students with disabilities and can also be a member of an ethnic minority group, such as African-American, Hispanic, Native American or Asian. Applicants must be anticipating enrollment for the first time in full-time, postsecondary education or training, and be able to demonstrate financial need.

Award: Scholarship for use in freshman year. *Number:* 5–10. *Amount:* up to $500.

Eligibility Requirements: Applicant must be American Indian/Alaska Native, Asian/Pacific Islander, or Hispanic; high school student and planning to enroll or expecting to enroll full-time at a two-year or technical institution. Available to U.S. citizens.

Application Requirements: Application, financial need analysis, references, transcript, statement verifying disability. *Deadline:* February 1.

Contact: College Foundation of North Carolina, Inc
1110 North Glebe Road, Suite 300
Arlington, VA 22201

LATINO DIAMANTE SCHOLARSHIP FUND

Scholarship to high school seniors recognizing contributions to the community, leadership qualities, and the achievements of Hispanic youth in North Carolina. Graduating high school seniors who plan to enroll at North Carolina institutions of higher education can apply for this scholarship.

Award: Scholarship for use in freshman year. *Number:* up to 2. *Amount:* up to $500.

Eligibility Requirements: Applicant must be Hispanic; high school student; planning to enroll or expecting to enroll at a two-year or four-year institution or university and studying in North Carolina. Applicant must have 2.5 GPA or higher. Available to U.S. citizens.

Application Requirements: Application, essay, references, transcript. *Deadline:* August 15.

Contact: College Foundation of North Carolina, Inc
106 Lochwood East Drive
Cary, NC 27511
Phone: 919-852-0075
E-mail: scholarships@diamanteinc.org

NORTH CAROLINA HISPANIC COLLEGE FUND SCHOLARSHIP

Four-year renewable scholarship for Hispanic students who graduated from a North Carolina high school within the past 2 years, who have been accepted into a 2- or 4-year college or university. Must have a four-year cumulative GPA of 2.5 or better (3.5 on a 5.0 scale). Preference is given to full-time students but part-time students may apply. Preference will be given to foreign-born applicants or native-born children of foreign-born parents.

Award: Scholarship for use in freshman, sophomore, junior, senior, graduate, or postgraduate years; renewable. *Amount:* $500–$2500.

Eligibility Requirements: Applicant must be Hispanic and enrolled or expecting to enroll full or part-time at a two-year or four-year or technical institution or university. Available to U.S. and non-U.S. citizens.

Application Requirements: Application, transcript.

Contact: NC Society of Hispanic People
Phone: 919-654-4516
E-mail: mailbox@theNCHSP.org

COLLEGE WOMEN'S ASSOCIATION OF JAPAN   http://www.cwaj.org

SCHOLARSHIP FOR THE VISUALLY IMPAIRED TO STUDY ABROAD
• See page 556

SCHOLARSHIP FOR THE VISUALLY IMPAIRED TO STUDY IN JAPAN
• See page 556

COMMUNITY FOUNDATION FOR PALM BEACH AND MARTIN COUNTIES, INC.   http://www.yourcommunityfoundation.org

COLONIAL BANK SCHOLARSHIP

For minority student graduating from Palm Beach Lakes or Santaluces High Schools who has a 2.5 GPA or higher and demonstrates financial need.

Award: Scholarship for use in freshman year; not renewable. *Amount:* $750–$2500.

Eligibility Requirements: Applicant must be American Indian/Alaska Native, Asian/Pacific Islander, Black (non-Hispanic), or Hispanic; high school student; planning to enroll or expecting to enroll full-time at a two-year or four-year or technical institution or university and resident of Florida. Applicant must have 2.5 GPA or higher. Available to U.S. citizens.

Application Requirements: Application, financial need analysis, transcript. *Deadline:* February 1.

Contact: Carolyn Jenco, Grants Manager/Scholarship Coordinator
Community Foundation for Palm Beach and Martin Counties, Inc.
700 South Dixie Highway, Suite 200
West Palm Beach, FL 33401
Phone: 561-659-6800
Fax: 561-832-6542
E-mail: cjenco@cfpbmc.org

COMMUNITY FOUNDATION OF WESTERN MASSACHUSETTS   http://www.communityfoundation.org

AFRICAN-AMERICAN ACHIEVEMENT SCHOLARSHIP

Scholarship for African-American residents of Hampden, Hampshire, or Franklin counties who attend or plan to attend a four-year college. Advised by the Urban League of Springfield.

Award: Scholarship for use in freshman, sophomore, junior, or senior years; renewable. *Number:* up to 9. *Amount:* $2500–$3000.

Eligibility Requirements: Applicant must be of African heritage; Black (non-Hispanic); enrolled or expecting to enroll full-time at a four-year institution and resident of Massachusetts. Available to U.S. citizens.

Application Requirements: Application, essay, financial need analysis, transcript, parent and student federal income tax returns. *Deadline:* March 31.

Contact: Dorothy Theriaque, Education Associate
Community Foundation of Western Massachusetts
1500 Main Street, PO Box 15769
Springfield, MA 01115
Phone: 413-732-2858
Fax: 413-733-8565
E-mail: dtheriaque@communityfoundation.org

HERIBERTO FLORES SCHOLARSHIP

For students of Puerto Rican ancestry from Hampshire or Hampden counties who are graduates of Springfield Technical Community College or Holyoke Community College planning to attend a Massachusetts state college.

Award: Scholarship for use in senior year; renewable. *Number:* up to 2. *Amount:* up to $500.

Eligibility Requirements: Applicant must be of Hispanic heritage; enrolled or expecting to enroll full or part-time at a two-year or four-year institution; resident of Massachusetts and studying in Massachusetts. Available to U.S. citizens.

Application Requirements: Application, financial need analysis, transcript, parent and student federal income tax returns, GPA. *Deadline:* March 31.

Contact: Dorothy Theriaque, Education Associate
Community Foundation of Western Massachusetts
1500 Main Street, PO Box 15769
Springfield, MA 01115
Phone: 413-732-2858
Fax: 413-733-8565
E-mail: dtheriaque@communityfoundation.org

LATINO SCHOLARSHIP

For graduating Latino students in Hampden and Hampshire counties who are entering their first year of college and are family and/or community service oriented.

Award: Scholarship for use in freshman year; renewable. *Number:* up to 6. *Amount:* $1000.

Eligibility Requirements: Applicant must be of Latin American/Caribbean heritage; Hispanic; enrolled or expecting to enroll full or part-time at a two-year or four-year institution and resident of Massachusetts. Available to U.S. citizens.

Application Requirements: Application, financial need analysis, transcript, parent and student federal income tax returns, GPA. *Deadline:* March 31.

Contact: Dorothy Theriaque, Education Associate
Community Foundation of Western Massachusetts
1500 Main Street, PO Box 15769
Springfield, MA 01115
Phone: 413-732-2858
Fax: 413-733-8565
E-mail: dtheriaque@communityfoundation.org

PUTNAM SCHOLARSHIP FUND

Provides scholarships for African-American and Latino students who attend college.

Award: Scholarship for use in freshman, sophomore, junior, or senior years; renewable. *Number:* up to 7. *Amount:* $1000–$2000.

Eligibility Requirements: Applicant must be Black (non-Hispanic) or Hispanic; enrolled or expecting to enroll full or part-time at a two-year or four-year institution or university and resident of Connecticut or Massachusetts. Available to U.S. citizens.

Application Requirements: Application, financial need analysis, references, transcript, pastoral letter of reference from any denomination, parent and student federal income tax returns, GPA. *Deadline:* March 31.

Contact: Dorothy Theriaque, Education Associate
Community Foundation of Western Massachusetts
1500 Main Street, PO Box 15769
Springfield, MA 01115
Phone: 413-732-2858
Fax: 413-733-8565
E-mail: dtheriaque@communityfoundation.org

CONFEDERATED TRIBES OF GRAND RONDE
http://www.grandronde.org

ADULT VOCATIONAL TRAINING EDUCATION SCHOLARSHIPS

Available to any enrolled member of the Confederated Tribes of Grand Ronde. Two $6,000 full-time and one $3,000 part-time awards are given each year. Intended for programs of study two years or less in length.

Award: Scholarship for use in freshman or sophomore years; renewable. *Number:* 3. *Amount:* $3000–$6000.

Eligibility Requirements: Applicant must be American Indian/Alaska Native and enrolled or expecting to enroll full or part-time at a two-year or technical institution. Available to U.S. and non-U.S. citizens.

Application Requirements: Application, essay, references, test scores, transcript, verification of Tribal enrollment. *Deadline:* April 30.

Contact: Tribal Scholarship Coordinator
Confederated Tribes of Grand Ronde
9615 Grand Ronde Road
Grand Ronde, OR 97347
Phone: 800-422-0232 Ext. 2275
Fax: 503-879-2286
E-mail: education@grandronde.org

UNDERGRADUATE EDUCATION SCHOLARSHIPS

Available to any enrolled member of the Confederated Tribes of Grand Ronde. Five $3,000, two $4,500, and three $6,000 full-time awards, and two $3,000 part-time awards are given each year. Renewable for twelve terms/eight semesters of continuous study. Scholarship may be used at community colleges for transfer credits.

Award: Scholarship for use in freshman, sophomore, junior, or senior years; renewable. *Number:* 12. *Amount:* $3000–$6000.

Eligibility Requirements: Applicant must be American Indian/Alaska Native and enrolled or expecting to enroll full or part-time at a two-year or four-year institution or university. Available to U.S. and non-U.S. citizens.

Application Requirements: Application, essay, references, test scores, transcript, verification of Tribal enrollment. *Deadline:* April 30.

Contact: Tribal Scholarship Coordinator
Confederated Tribes of Grand Ronde
9615 Grand Ronde Road
Grand Ronde, OR 97347
Phone: 800-422-0232 Ext. 2275
Fax: 503-879-2286
E-mail: education@grandronde.org

CONGRESSIONAL HISPANIC CAUCUS INSTITUTE
http://www.chciyouth.org

CONGRESSIONAL HISPANIC CAUCUS INSTITUTE SCHOLARSHIP AWARDS

One-time award for Latino students who have a history of public service-oriented activities. $2500 to attend a four-year or graduate level institution, $1000 to attend a two-year community college. Must be enrolled full time. See Web site at http://www.chci.org for further information.

Award: Scholarship for use in freshman, sophomore, junior, senior, or graduate years; not renewable. *Number:* 111. *Amount:* $1000–$2500.

Eligibility Requirements: Applicant must be Hispanic and enrolled or expecting to enroll full-time at a two-year or four-year institution or university. Available to U.S. citizens.

Application Requirements: Application, essay, resume, references, transcript. *Deadline:* March 1.

Contact: Sylvia Hernandez, Programs Coordinator
Congressional Hispanic Caucus Institute
911 2nd Street, NE
Washington, DC 20002
Phone: 202-543-1771 Ext. 236
Fax: 202-546-2143
E-mail: sarez@chci.org

CONNECTICUT ASSOCIATION OF LATIN AMERICANS IN HIGHER EDUCATION (CALAHE)
http://www.calahe.org

CONNECTICUT ASSOCIATION OF LATIN AMERICANS IN HIGHER EDUCATION SCHOLARSHIPS

Must demonstrate involvement with, and commitment to, activities that promote Latino pursuit of education. Must have a 3.0 GPA, be a U.S. citizen or permanent resident, be a resident of Connecticut, and attend a Connecticut higher education institution. Application deadline is April 17.

Award: Scholarship for use in freshman, sophomore, junior, or senior years; not renewable. *Number:* 5–9. *Amount:* $1000.

Eligibility Requirements: Applicant must be Hispanic; enrolled or expecting to enroll full-time at a two-year or four-year or technical institution or university; resident of Connecticut and studying in Connecticut. Applicant must have 3.0 GPA or higher. Available to U.S. citizens.

Application Requirements: Application, essay, financial need analysis, transcript, copy of Student Aid Report (SAR). *Deadline:* April 17.

Contact: Dr. Wilson Luna, Gateway Community-Technical College
Connecticut Association of Latin Americans in Higher Education (CALAHE)
60 Sargent Drive
New Haven, CT 06511
Phone: 203-285-2210
Fax: 203-285-2211
E-mail: wluna@gwcc.commnet.edu

CONSTANTINOPLE ARMENIAN RELIEF SOCIETY

CONSTANTINOPLE ARMENIAN RELIEF SOCIETY SCHOLARSHIP

Scholarships are only available to Armenian students enrolled in an accredited college or university in the U.S., starting with sophomore year. Emphasis on both merit and financial need. Students are required to complete and return the applications by August 30 in order to be considered. Scholarships can be renewed, but will only be awarded for two consecutive years. Must have minimum 3.0 GPA.

Award: Scholarship for use in freshman, sophomore, or junior years; renewable. *Number:* varies. *Amount:* $300.

Eligibility Requirements: Applicant must be of Armenian heritage; enrolled or expecting to enroll full-time at a four-year institution or university and studying in Connecticut, New Jersey, New York, or Pennsylvania. Applicant must have 3.0 GPA or higher. Available to U.S. and non-U.S. citizens.

Application Requirements: Application, financial need analysis, references, self-addressed stamped envelope, transcript. *Deadline:* August 31.

Contact: Talin Sesrtyan, Co-Chairperson, Scholarship Committee
Constantinople Armenian Relief Society
187 Villanova Drive
Paramus, NJ 07652
Phone: 201-447-7048
E-mail: talins11@hotmail.com

CORPORATION FOR OHIO APPALACHIAN DEVELOPMENT (COAD)
http://www.coadinc.org

THE DAVID V. STIVISON APPALACHIAN SCHOLARSHIP FUND

Financial assistance to students who are residents of the 30 counties in The Corporation for Ohio Appalachian Development's (COAD) service area and want to attend college, but lack the required resources. Individual income must not exceed $19,600. See Web site for application information: http://www.coadinc.org

Award: Scholarship for use in freshman, sophomore, junior, or senior years; not renewable. *Number:* 12. *Amount:* $1000.

Eligibility Requirements: Applicant must be American Indian/Alaska Native and enrolled or expecting to enroll full-time at a two-year or four-year institution or university. Available to U.S. citizens.

Application Requirements: Application, financial need analysis, transcript. *Deadline:* varies.

Contact: Roger McCauley, Executive Director
Corporation for Ohio Appalachian Development (COAD)
1 Pinchot Lane, PO Box 787
Athens, OH 45701-0787
Phone: 740-594-8499
Fax: 740-592-5994
E-mail: rmccauley@coadinc.org

COUNCIL FOR INTERNATIONAL EDUCATIONAL EXCHANGE
http://www.ciee.org/study

ROBERT B. BAILEY III MINORITY SCHOLARSHIPS FOR EDUCATION ABROAD
• See page 556

COUNCIL OF ENERGY RESOURCE TRIBES (CERT) EDUCATION FUND, INC.
http://www.certredearth.com

COUNCIL OF ENERGY RESOURCES TRIBES EDUCATION FUND SCHOLARSHIP

Renewable scholarship for full-time Native-American students. Award applicable to any accredited two- or four-year institution including trade or technical school. Applicant must submit application, transcript, recommendations, and certificate proving Native-American heritage. Financial need will be taken into account. Must be accepted and have completed the 6 week T program at The University of New Mexico to be eligible for the CERT Scholarship.

Award: Scholarship for use in freshman, sophomore, junior, senior, or graduate years; renewable. *Number:* 30–40. *Amount:* up to $1000.

Eligibility Requirements: Applicant must be American Indian/Alaska Native and enrolled or expecting to enroll full-time at a two-year or four-year or technical institution or university. Applicant must have 2.5 GPA or higher. Available to U.S. and Canadian citizens.

Application Requirements: Application, financial need analysis, references, transcript, certificate of Indian blood. *Deadline:* August 23.

Contact: Mary Lopez, Program Assistant
Council of Energy Resource Tribes (CERT) Education Fund, Inc.
695 South Colorado Boulevard, Suite 10
Denver, CO 80246
Phone: 303-282-7576 Ext. 19
Fax: 303-282-7584
E-mail: redearth@certredearth.com

CROATIAN SCHOLARSHIP FUND
http://www.croatianscholarship.org

CROATIAN SCHOLARSHIP FUND SCHOLARSHIP PROGRAM

The scholarship is given to individuals with high grades ("A"), financial needs of family and appropriate degree selection. Scholarships are given depending on funds availability and number of applicants.

Award: Scholarship for use in freshman, sophomore, junior, or senior years; renewable. *Number:* varies. *Amount:* up to $1200.

Eligibility Requirements: Applicant must be of Croatian/Serbian heritage; age 18-25 and enrolled or expecting to enroll full-time at a four-year institution. Applicant must have 3.5 GPA or higher. Available to U.S. and non-U.S. citizens.

Application Requirements: Application, autobiography, financial need analysis, photo, references, test scores, transcript. *Deadline:* April 15.

Contact: Vesna Brekalo, Scholarship Liaison
Croatian Scholarship Fund
31 Mesa Vista Court
San Ramon, CA 94583
Phone: 925-556-6263
Fax: 925-556-6263
E-mail: vbrekalo@msn.com

DIVERSITY CITY MEDIA
http://www.blacknews.com

BLACKNEWS.COM SCHOLARSHIP ESSAY CONTEST

Scholarship will award $500 to an African-American student for the best essay submitted. Must be a U.S. citizen.

Award: Scholarship for use in freshman, sophomore, junior, or senior years. *Amount:* up to $500.

Eligibility Requirements: Applicant must be Black (non-Hispanic) and enrolled or expecting to enroll at an institution or university. Available to U.S. citizens.

Application Requirements: Application, essay. *Deadline:* April 1.

Contact: Dante Lee, President and CEO
Diversity City Media
750-Q Cross Pointe Road, 225 West 3rd Street
Suite 203
Columbus, OH 43230
Phone: 562-209-0616
E-mail: scholarship@blacknews.com

EDMONTON COMMUNITY FOUNDATION
http://www.DollarsForLearners.com

BELCOURT BROSSEAU METIS AWARDS

Scholarship for an Alberta resident in an academic or training program at a qualified postsecondary institution in Alberta. Priority will be given to students who are entering the first year of a postsecondary program for the first time. Students pursuing studies at the graduate level are not eligible.

Award: Prize for use in freshman, sophomore, junior, or senior years; renewable. *Number:* 80. *Amount:* $1000.

Eligibility Requirements: Applicant must be Canadian citizen; enrolled or expecting to enroll full or part-time at a four-year institution or university; resident of Alberta and studying in Alberta. Available to U.S. and Canadian citizens.

Application Requirements: Application, financial need analysis, interview, references, transcript, personal letter. *Deadline:* May 15.

Contact: Dollars for Learners
Phone: 780-426-0015
E-mail: info@dollarsforlearners.com

CHARMAINE LETOURNEAU FUND
• See page 557

YOUTH FORMERLY IN CARE BURSARY

Scholarship funds awarded to disadvantaged young people to support their postsecondary education and training. Supports students who are residents of Alberta and who have spent a minimum of two years in the care and/or guardianship of Alberta Children's Services. Students considering part-time studies may be considered for an award.

Award: Grant for use in freshman, sophomore, junior, or senior years; not renewable. *Number:* 1. *Amount:* $1000.

Eligibility Requirements: Applicant must be Canadian citizen; enrolled or expecting to enroll full-time at a four-year institution or university and resident of Alberta.

Application Requirements: Application, financial need analysis, interview, references, transcript, personal letter. *Deadline:* May 15.

Contact: Reg Basken, Scholarships Officer
Edmonton Community Foundation
710 Royal Bank Building, 9910-103 Street NW
10117 Jasper Avenue
Edmonton T5K 2V7
Canada
Phone: 780-426-0015
Fax: 780-425-0121
E-mail: info@dollarsforlearners.com

ESPERANZA, INC.
http://www.esperanzainc.com

ESPERANZA SCHOLARSHIPS

One-year award valid only for full-time tuition and/or books at an accredited college or university. Recipients are eligible to apply yearly until they have completed their curriculum. Award restricted to residents of Cuyahoga or Lorain counties in Ohio. GPA of at least 2.75.

Award: Scholarship for use in freshman, sophomore, junior, or senior years; renewable. *Number:* 50. *Amount:* $500–$1500.

Eligibility Requirements: Applicant must be of Hispanic heritage; enrolled or expecting to enroll full-time at a two-year or four-year institution or university and resident of Ohio. Available to U.S. and non-U.S. citizens.

Application Requirements: Application, essay, interview, references, test scores, transcript. *Deadline:* March 17.

Contact: Olga Ferrer, Office Assistant
Esperanza, Inc.
4115 Bridge Avenue
Room 108
Cleveland, OH 44113
Phone: 216-651-7178
Fax: 216-651-7183
E-mail: hope4ed@aol.com

FIRST CATHOLIC SLOVAK LADIES ASSOCIATION
http://www.fcsla.com

FIRST CATHOLIC SLOVAK LADIES ASSOCIATION FRATERNAL SCHOLARSHIP AWARD FOR COLLEGE AND GRADUATE STUDY

Must be FCSLA member in good standing for at least three years. Must attend accredited college in the U.S. or Canada in undergraduate or graduate degree program. Must submit certified copy of college acceptance. One-time tuition award; win once as undergraduate, up to $1250; once as graduate, up to $1750.

Award: Scholarship for use in freshman, sophomore, junior, senior, graduate, or postgraduate years; not renewable. *Number:* 125. *Amount:* $1250–$1750.

Eligibility Requirements: Applicant must be Roman Catholic; of Slavic/Czech heritage and enrolled or expecting to enroll full-time at a two-year or four-year institution or university. Available to U.S. and non-U.S. citizens.

Application Requirements: Application, autobiography, essay, photo, references, test scores, transcript. *Deadline:* March 1.

Contact: Dorothy Szumski, Director of Fraternal Scholarships
First Catholic Slovak Ladies Association
24950 Chagrin Boulevard
Beachwood, OH 44122
Phone: 216-464-8015 Ext. 134
Fax: 216-464-9260
E-mail: info@fcsla.com

FLORIDA DEPARTMENT OF EDUCATION
http://www.floridastudentfinancialaid.org

JOSE MARTI SCHOLARSHIP CHALLENGE GRANT FUND

Award available to Hispanic-American students who were born in, or whose parent was born in a Hispanic country. Must have lived in Florida for one year, be enrolled full-time in Florida at an eligible school, and have a GPA of 3.0 or above. Must be U.S. citizen or eligible non-citizen. Renewable award of $2000. Application must be postmarked by April 1. Free Application for Federal Student Aid must be processed by May 15.

Award: Scholarship for use in freshman, sophomore, junior, senior, or graduate years; renewable. *Number:* 63. *Amount:* $2000.

Eligibility Requirements: Applicant must be of Hispanic heritage; enrolled or expecting to enroll full-time at a two-year or four-year or technical institution or university; resident of Florida and studying in Florida. Applicant must have 3.0 GPA or higher. Available to U.S. citizens.

Application Requirements: Application, financial need analysis, FAFSA. *Deadline:* April 1.

Contact: Barb Dombrowski, Education Director, Policy and Training
Florida Department of Education
Office of Student Financial Assistance
1940 North Monroe, Suite 70
Tallahassee, FL 32303-4759
Phone: 850-410-5191
Fax: 850-488-5966
E-mail: barb.dombrowski@fldoe.org

ROSEWOOD FAMILY SCHOLARSHIP FUND

Renewable award for eligible minority students to attend a Florida public postsecondary institution on a full-time basis. Preference given to direct descendants of African-American Rosewood families affected by the incidents of January 1923. Must be Black, Hispanic, Asian, Pacific Islander,

Florida Department of Education (continued)

American-Indian, or Alaska Native. Free Application for Federal Student Aid (and Student Aid Report for nonresidents of Florida) must be processed by May 15.

Award: Scholarship for use in freshman, sophomore, junior, or senior years; renewable. *Number:* up to 25. *Amount:* up to $4000.

Eligibility Requirements: Applicant must be American Indian/Alaska Native, Asian/Pacific Islander, Black (non-Hispanic), or Hispanic; enrolled or expecting to enroll full-time at a two-year or four-year or technical institution or university and studying in Florida. Available to U.S. citizens.

Application Requirements: Application, financial need analysis. *Deadline:* April 1.

Contact: Barb Dombrowski, Education Director, Policy and Training
Florida Department of Education
Office of Student Financial Assistance
1940 North Monroe, Suite 70
Tallahassee, FL 32303-4759
Phone: 850-410-5191
Fax: 850-488-5966
E-mail: barb.dombrowski@fldoe.org

GENERAL BOARD OF GLOBAL MINISTRIES
http://www.gbgm-umc.org

NATIONAL LEADERSHIP DEVELOPMENT GRANTS

Award for racial and ethnic minority members of the United Methodist Church who are pursuing undergraduate study. Must be U.S. citizen, resident alien, or reside in U.S. as a refugee. Renewable award of $500 to $5000. Deadline: May 31.

Award: Grant for use in freshman, sophomore, junior, or senior years; renewable. *Number:* 75. *Amount:* $500–$5000.

Eligibility Requirements: Applicant must be Methodist; American Indian/Alaska Native, Asian/Pacific Islander, Black (non-Hispanic), or Hispanic and enrolled or expecting to enroll full-time at a two-year or four-year or technical institution or university. Available to U.S. and Canadian citizens.

Application Requirements: Application, essay, financial need analysis, photo, references, transcript. *Deadline:* May 31.

Contact: Lisa Katzenstein Gomez, Administrator
General Board of Global Ministries
475 Riverside Drive, Room 1351
New York, NY 10115
Phone: 212-870-3787
Fax: 212-870-3932
E-mail: scholars@gbgm-umc.org

GEORGE BIRD GRINNELL AMERICAN INDIAN FUND
http://www.grinnellfund.org/

SCHUYLER M. MEYER, JR. AWARD

Up to $1000 scholarship for American-Indian/Alaska Native students enrolled in either an undergraduate or graduate program. Applicants must demonstrate financial need, submit personal statement, proof of school enrollment or acceptance and proof of tribal enrollment. Award of scholarship is totally contingent upon raising the needed funds. Application deadline is June 1. Please include self-addressed stamped envelope.

Award: Scholarship for use in freshman, sophomore, junior, senior, graduate, or postgraduate years; renewable. *Number:* up to 20. *Amount:* up to $1000.

Eligibility Requirements: Applicant must be American Indian/Alaska Native and enrolled or expecting to enroll full or part-time at a two-year or four-year institution or university. Available to U.S. citizens.

Application Requirements: Application, essay, financial need analysis, references, self-addressed stamped envelope, transcript, proof of tribal enrollment. *Deadline:* June 1.

Contact: Paula Mintzies, President
George Bird Grinnell American Indian Fund
PO Box 59033
Potomac, MD 20859
Phone: 301-424-2440
Fax: 301-424-8281

GREEK WOMEN'S UNIVERSITY CLUB

GREEK WOMEN'S UNIVERSITY CLUB SCHOLARSHIPS

Award for female full-time college students with at least sophomore standing or full-time graduate students. Must be U.S. citizen with at least one parent of Greek descent and resident of Chicago metropolitan area. Must have minimum 3.0 GPA. Deadline: October 26.

Award: Scholarship for use in sophomore, junior, senior, graduate, or postgraduate years; not renewable. *Number:* 2. *Amount:* $500–$1000.

Eligibility Requirements: Applicant must be of Greek heritage; enrolled or expecting to enroll full-time at a four-year institution or university; female and resident of Illinois. Applicant must have 3.0 GPA or higher. Available to U.S. citizens.

Application Requirements: Application, autobiography, essay, financial need analysis, interview, references, transcript. *Deadline:* October 26.

Contact: Regina Kulidas, Scholarship Committee Chair
Greek Women's University Club
180 Birch
Park Forest, IL 60466
Phone: 708-283-0963
E-mail: John2greek@aol.com

HBCU-CENTRAL.COM
http://www.hbcu-central.com/

HBCU-CENTRAL.COM MINORITY SCHOLARSHIP PROGRAM

Targeted to minorities that choose to attend Historically Black Colleges and Universities. Recipients are selected based on essay submissions, grades and financial need.

Award: Scholarship for use in freshman, sophomore, junior, or senior years; not renewable. *Number:* 3–10. *Amount:* $1000.

Eligibility Requirements: Applicant must be American Indian/Alaska Native, Asian/Pacific Islander, Black (non-Hispanic), or Hispanic and enrolled or expecting to enroll full-time at a four-year institution or university. Available to U.S. citizens.

Application Requirements: Application, autobiography, essay, interview, transcript. *Deadline:* June 1.

Contact: William Moss, Scholarship Administrator
HBCU-Central.com
750-Q Cross Pointe Road
Columbus, OH 43230
Phone: 614-284-3007
Fax: 215-893-5398
E-mail: wrmoss@hbcu-central.com

HELLENIC TIMES SCHOLARSHIP FUND
http://www.htsfund.org

HELLENIC TIMES SCHOLARSHIP FUND

One-time award to students of Greek/Hellenic descent. Must be between the ages of 17-30. For use in any year of undergraduate education. Deadline is January 16.

Award: Scholarship for use in freshman, sophomore, junior, or senior years; not renewable. *Number:* 30–40. *Amount:* $500–$10,000.

Eligibility Requirements: Applicant must be of Greek heritage; age 17-30 and enrolled or expecting to enroll full or part-time at a two-year or four-year or technical institution or university. Available to U.S. and non-U.S. citizens.

Application Requirements: Application, financial need analysis, resume, references, transcript. *Deadline:* January 16.

Contact: Nick Katsoris
Hellenic Times Scholarship Fund
823 11th Avenue, 5th Floor
New York, NY 10019-3535
Phone: 212-986-6881
Fax: 212-977-3662
E-mail: htsfund@aol.com

HELLENIC UNIVERSITY CLUB OF PHILADELPHIA
http://www.hucphila.org

ANDREW G. CHRESSANTHIS MEMORIAL SCHOLARSHIP

Scholarship will be awarded to students with outstanding academic qualifications and financial need. Must be enrolled full time in a degree program at an accredited four-year college or university. High school seniors accepted for enrollment in such a degree program may also apply. Must be of Greek descent, U.S. citizen, and lawful permanent resident of Berks, Bucks, Chester, Delaware, Lancaster, Lehigh, Montgomery, or Philadelphia counties in Pennsylvania; Atlantic, Burlington, Camden, Cape May, Cumberland, Gloucester or Salem counties in New Jersey.

Award: Scholarship for use in freshman, sophomore, junior, or senior years. *Amount:* $2000.

Eligibility Requirements: Applicant must be of Greek heritage; enrolled or expecting to enroll full-time at a four-year institution or university and resident of New Jersey or Pennsylvania. Available to U.S. citizens.

Application Requirements: Application, financial need analysis. *Deadline:* April 20.

Contact: Zoe Tripolitis, Scholarship Chairman
Hellenic University Club of Philadelphia
PO Box 42199
Philadelphia, PA 19101
Phone: 215-483-7440
E-mail: zoe.tripolitis@arkemagroup.com

THE CHRISTOPHER DEMETRIS SCHOLARSHIP

Scholarship will be awarded to students with outstanding academic qualifications and financial need. Must be enrolled full time in a degree program at an accredited four-year college or university. High school seniors accepted for enrollment in such a degree program may also apply. Must be of Greek descent, U.S. citizen, and lawful permanent resident of Berks, Bucks, Chester, Delaware, Lancaster, Lehigh, Montgomery, or Philadelphia counties in Pennsylvania; Atlantic, Burlington, Camden, Cape May, Cumberland, Gloucester or Salem counties in New Jersey.

Award: Scholarship for use in freshman, sophomore, junior, or senior years. *Amount:* $1200.

Eligibility Requirements: Applicant must be of Greek heritage; enrolled or expecting to enroll full-time at a four-year institution or university and resident of New Jersey or Pennsylvania. Available to U.S. citizens.

Application Requirements: Application, financial need analysis. *Deadline:* April 20.

Contact: Zoe Tripolitis, Scholarship Chairman
Hellenic University Club of Philadelphia
PO Box 42199
Philadelphia, PA 19101
Phone: 215-483-7440
E-mail: zoe.tripolitis@arkemagroup.com

THE DORIZAS MEMORIAL SCHOLARSHIP

Scholarship will be awarded to students with outstanding academic qualifications and financial need. Must be enrolled full time in a degree program at an accredited four-year college or university. High school seniors accepted for enrollment in such a degree program may also apply. Must be of Greek descent, U.S. citizen, and lawful permanent resident of Berks, Bucks, Chester, Delaware, Lancaster, Lehigh, Montgomery, or Philadelphia counties in Pennsylvania; Atlantic, Burlington, Camden, Cape May, Cumberland, Gloucester or Salem counties in New Jersey.

Award: Scholarship for use in freshman, sophomore, junior, or senior years. *Amount:* $3000.

Eligibility Requirements: Applicant must be of Greek heritage; enrolled or expecting to enroll full-time at a four-year institution or university and resident of New Jersey or Pennsylvania. Available to U.S. citizens.

Application Requirements: Application, financial need analysis. *Deadline:* April 20.

Contact: Zoe Tripolitis, Scholarship Chairman
Hellenic University Club of Philadelphia
PO Box 42199
Philadelphia, PA 19101
Phone: 215-483-7440
E-mail: zoe.tripolitis@arkemagroup.com

THE DR. NICHOLAS PADIS MEMORIAL GRADUATE SCHOLARSHIP

Scholarship in the amount of $5000 will be awarded to a qualifying senior undergraduate or graduate student pursuing a graduate degree full time at an accredited university or professional school. Academic excellence is the primary consideration for this scholarship.

Award: Scholarship for use in senior, or graduate years. *Amount:* $5000.

Eligibility Requirements: Applicant must be of Greek heritage; enrolled or expecting to enroll full-time at a four-year institution or university and resident of New Jersey or Pennsylvania. Available to U.S. citizens.

Application Requirements: Application. *Deadline:* April 20.

Contact: Zoe Tripolitis, Scholarship Chairman
Hellenic University Club of Philadelphia
PO Box 42199
Philadelphia, PA 19101
Phone: 215-483-7440
E-mail: zoe.tripolitis@arkemagroup.com

THE FOUNDERS SCHOLARSHIP

Scholarship will be awarded to students with outstanding academic qualifications and financial need. Must be enrolled full time in a degree program at an accredited four-year college or university. High school seniors accepted for enrollment in such a degree program may also apply. Must be of Greek descent, U.S. citizen, and lawful permanent resident of Berks, Bucks, Chester, Delaware, Lancaster, Lehigh, Montgomery, or Philadelphia counties in Pennsylvania; Atlantic, Burlington, Camden, Cape May, Cumberland, Gloucester or Salem counties in New Jersey.

Award: Scholarship for use in freshman, sophomore, junior, or senior years. *Amount:* $3000.

Eligibility Requirements: Applicant must be of Greek heritage; enrolled or expecting to enroll full-time at a four-year institution or university and resident of New Jersey or Pennsylvania. Available to U.S. citizens.

Application Requirements: Application, financial need analysis. *Deadline:* April 20.

Contact: Zoe Tripolitis, Scholarship Chairman
Hellenic University Club of Philadelphia
PO Box 42199
Philadelphia, PA 19101
Phone: 215-483-7440
E-mail: zoe.tripolitis@arkemagroup.com

THE JAMES COSMOS MEMORIAL SCHOLARSHIP

Scholarship will be awarded to students with outstanding academic qualifications and financial need. Must be enrolled full time in a degree program at an accredited four-year college or university. High school seniors accepted for enrollment in such a degree program may also apply. Must be of Greek descent, U.S. citizen, and lawful permanent resident of Berks, Bucks, Chester, Delaware, Lancaster, Lehigh, Montgomery, or Philadelphia counties in Pennsylvania; Atlantic, Burlington, Camden, Cape May, Cumberland, Gloucester or Salem counties in New Jersey.

Award: Scholarship for use in freshman, sophomore, junior, or senior years. *Amount:* $1000.

Eligibility Requirements: Applicant must be of Greek heritage; enrolled or expecting to enroll full-time at a four-year institution or university and resident of New Jersey or Pennsylvania. Available to U.S. citizens.

Application Requirements: Application, financial need analysis. *Deadline:* April 20.

Hellenic University Club of Philadelphia (continued)

Contact: Zoe Tripolitis, Scholarship Chairman
Hellenic University Club of Philadelphia
PO Box 42199
Philadelphia, PA 19101
Phone: 215-483-7440
E-mail: zoe.tripolitis@arkemagroup.com

THE PAIDEIA SCHOLARSHIP

Scholarship available to students enrolled full-time in a degree program at an accredited four-year college or university. High school seniors accepted for enrollment in such a degree program may also apply. Academic excellence is the primary consideration; no financial information is required. The parent(s) must be current members in good standing of the Hellenic University Club of Philadelphia for at least three years. Must be of Greek descent, U.S. citizen, and lawful permanent resident of Berks, Bucks, Chester, Delaware, Lancaster, Lehigh, Montgomery, or Philadelphia counties in Pennsylvania; Atlantic, Burlington, Camden, Cape May, Cumberland, Gloucester or Salem counties in New Jersey.

Award: Scholarship for use in freshman, sophomore, junior, or senior years. *Amount:* $3000.

Eligibility Requirements: Applicant must be of Greek heritage; enrolled or expecting to enroll full-time at a four-year institution or university and resident of New Jersey or Pennsylvania. Available to U.S. citizens.

Application Requirements: Application. *Deadline:* April 20.

Contact: Zoe Tripolitis, Scholarship Chairman
Hellenic University Club of Philadelphia
PO Box 42199
Philadelphia, PA 19101
Phone: 215-483-7440
E-mail: zoe.tripolitis@arkemagroup.com

HISPANIC ASSOCIATION OF COLLEGES AND UNIVERSITIES (HACU) http://www.hacu.net

HISPANIC ASSOCIATION OF COLLEGES AND UNIVERSITIES SCHOLARSHIP PROGRAMS

The scholarship programs are sponsored by corporate and federal organizations. To be eligible, students must attend a HACU member college or university and meet all additional criteria.

Award: Scholarship for use in freshman, sophomore, junior, senior, or graduate years; not renewable. *Number:* up to 200. *Amount:* $500–$3000.

Eligibility Requirements: Applicant must be Hispanic and enrolled or expecting to enroll full or part-time at a two-year or four-year institution or university. Applicant must have 3.0 GPA or higher. Available to U.S. citizens.

Application Requirements: Application, essay, financial need analysis, resume, transcript, enrollment certification form. *Deadline:* May 19.

Contact: Anna Esquivel, Executive Director Student Services
Hispanic Association of Colleges and Universities (HACU)
High Point Tower, 8415 Data Point Drive, Suite 400
San Antonio, TX 78229
Phone: 210-692-3805
E-mail: scholarship@hacu.net

HISPANIC COLLEGE FUND, INC. http://www.hispanicfund.org

FIRST IN MY FAMILY SCHOLARSHIP PROGRAM

One-time scholarship open to full-time undergraduates of Hispanic descent who are the first in their family to attend college. Must be a U.S. citizen residing in the United States or Puerto Rico and have a minimum 3.0 GPA.

Award: Scholarship for use in freshman, sophomore, junior, or senior years; not renewable. *Number:* 100–200. *Amount:* $500–$5000.

Eligibility Requirements: Applicant must be Hispanic and enrolled or expecting to enroll full-time at a two-year or four-year or technical institution or university. Applicant must have 3.0 GPA or higher. Available to U.S. citizens.

Application Requirements: Application, essay, financial need analysis, resume, references, test scores, transcript, college acceptance letter, copy of taxes, copy of Student Aid Report (SAR). *Deadline:* April 15.

Contact: Stina Augustsson, Program Manager
Hispanic College Fund, Inc.
1717 Pennsylvania Avenue, NW, Suite 460
Washington, DC 20006
Phone: 202-296-5400
Fax: 202-296-3774
E-mail: hcf-info@hispanicfund.org

HISPANIC COLLEGE FUND SCHOLARSHIP PROGRAM

This program awards scholarships to full-time students of Hispanic origin who have demonstrated academic excellence, leadership skills and financial need to pursue an undergraduate degree. Must be a U.S. permanent resident or U.S. citizen and have a minimum of a 3.0 GPA.

Award: Scholarship for use in freshman, sophomore, junior, or senior years; renewable. *Number:* 600–750. *Amount:* $1000–$5000.

Eligibility Requirements: Applicant must be Hispanic and enrolled or expecting to enroll full-time at a two-year or four-year institution or university. Applicant must have 3.0 GPA or higher. Available to U.S. citizens.

Application Requirements: Application, essay, financial need analysis, resume, references, transcript, copy of tax return, copy of Student Aid Report (SAR). *Deadline:* April 15.

Contact: Stina Augustsson, Program Manager
Hispanic College Fund, Inc.
1717 Pennsylvania Avenue, NW, Suite 460
Washington, DC 20006
Phone: 202-296-5400
Fax: 202-296-3774
E-mail: hcf-info@hispanicfund.org

HISPANIC EDUCATION ENDOWMENT FUND http://www.heef.org/scholarships/index.htm

HISPANIC EDUCATION ENDOWMENT FUND SCHOLARSHIPS

Scholarships for Orange County, California, Hispanic students with financial need at all levels along the education continuum. Each fund or program has its own criteria. See Web site for specific scholarships and requirements: http://www.heef.org/scholarships/index.htm

Award: Scholarship for use in freshman, sophomore, junior, senior, or graduate years. *Number:* 1.

Eligibility Requirements: Applicant must be Hispanic and enrolled or expecting to enroll at a four-year institution or university. Available to U.S. citizens.

Application Requirements: Application, essay, transcript. *Deadline:* February 13.

Contact: Orange County HEEF Scholarship Program
Hispanic Education Endowment Fund
Orange County Community Foundation, 30 Corporate Park, Suite 410
Irvine, CA 92606

HISPANIC HERITAGE FOUNDATION AWARDS http://www.hispanicheritageawards.org

HHAF SPORTS YOUTH AWARD

Educational grants are awarded to two Hispanic students in each of twelve regions for demonstrated interest in sports and academic excellence in general. One student will receive $2000 and the other will receive $3000. One national winner will receive a $5000 educational grant from the pool of regional winners. For more details or an application see Web site: http://www.hispanicheritageawards.org.

Award: Grant for use in freshman year; not renewable. *Number:* 25. *Amount:* $2000–$5000.

Eligibility Requirements: Applicant must be of Hispanic heritage; high school student and planning to enroll or expecting to enroll at an institution or university. Available to U.S. citizens.

Application Requirements: Application, references, transcript.
Deadline: February 10.

Contact: Clarissa Sandoval, Coordinator
Hispanic Heritage Foundation Awards
2600 Virginia Avenue, NW, Suite 406
Washington, DC 20037-1905
Phone: 202-861-9797
Fax: 202-861-9799
E-mail: clarissa@hispanicheritage.org

HISPANIC METROPOLITAN CHAMBER SCHOLARSHIPS
http://www.hmccoregon.com/

HISPANIC METROPOLITAN CHAMBER SCHOLARSHIPS

Scholarships to encourage Hispanics to continue their higher education, applicant must have at least 2.75 GPA.

Award: Scholarship for use in freshman, sophomore, junior, or senior years. *Amount:* $2500.

Eligibility Requirements: Applicant must be Hispanic; enrolled or expecting to enroll full-time at a four-year institution or university and resident of Oregon. Available to U.S. citizens.

Application Requirements: Application, essay, transcript. *Deadline:* February 4.

Contact: Scholarship Committee
Hispanic Metropolitan Chamber Scholarships
PO Box 1837
Portland, OR 97207
Phone: 503-222-0280

HISPANIC PUBLIC RELATIONS ASSOCIATION
http://www.hpra-usa.org

SCHOLARSHIP PROGRAM FOR HISPANIC STUDENT

Scholarship open to South California junior and senior students of Hispanic descent with at least a 2.7 cumulative GPA and 3.0 GPA in their major subject. Preference is given to students majoring in public relations but students in communication studies, journalism, advertising and/or marketing will be considered. Students majoring in other disciplines who have a desire to work in public relations industry are invited to apply. For more details and application see Web site http://www.hprala.org

Award: Scholarship for use in junior or senior years; not renewable. *Number:* 10. *Amount:* $1000.

Eligibility Requirements: Applicant must be Hispanic; enrolled or expecting to enroll full-time at a four-year institution or university and studying in California. Available to U.S. and non-U.S. citizens.

Application Requirements: Application, essay, resume, references, transcript, writing sample. *Deadline:* June 30.

Contact: Norma Gonzalez, College Outreach Committee Director
Hispanic Public Relations Association
PO Box 86760
Los Angeles, CA 90086-0760
Phone: 714-748-6385
E-mail: njzalez-hpra@yahoo.com

HISPANIC SCHOLARSHIP FUND
http://www.hsf.net

COLLEGE SCHOLARSHIP PROGRAM

Awards available to full-time undergraduate or graduate students of Hispanic origin. Applicants must have 12 college units with a minimum 2.7 GPA before applying. Merit-based award for U.S. citizens or permanent residents. Must include financial aid award letter and SAR.

Award: Scholarship for use in sophomore, junior, senior, or graduate years; not renewable. *Number:* 2900–3500. *Amount:* $1000–$3000.

Eligibility Requirements: Applicant must be of Latin American/Caribbean, Mexican, or Spanish heritage; Hispanic and enrolled or expecting to enroll full-time at a two-year or four-year institution or university. Applicant must have 3.0 GPA or higher. Available to U.S. citizens.

Application Requirements: Application, essay, financial need analysis, references, transcript, copy of Student Aid Report (SAR). *Deadline:* October 15.

Contact: Carolina Martin, Director of Community and Scholar Relations
Hispanic Scholarship Fund
55 Second Street, Suite 1500
San Francisco, CA 94105
Phone: 877-473-4636
Fax: 415-808-2302
E-mail: cmartin@HSF.net

COMMUNITY COLLEGE TRANSFER PROGRAMS

Available to community college students in certain geographical areas transferring on a full-time basis to four-year institution in fall of following year. Must be of Hispanic descent, U.S. citizen or legal permanent resident with a minimum GPA of 3.0.

Award: Scholarship for use in freshman or sophomore years; not renewable. *Number:* varies. *Amount:* $1500–$2500.

Eligibility Requirements: Applicant must be of Hispanic heritage and enrolled or expecting to enroll full-time at a two-year institution. Applicant must have 3.0 GPA or higher. Available to U.S. and non-Canadian citizens.

Application Requirements: Application, essay, references, transcript, copy of Student Aid Report (SAR). *Deadline:* February 1.

Contact: Rita d'Escoto, Program Assistant
Hispanic Scholarship Fund
55 Second Street, Suite 1500
San Francisco, CA 94105
Phone: 415-808-2370
Fax: 415-808-2304
E-mail: rdescoto@hsf.net

GATES MILLENNIUM SCHOLARS PROGRAM

Award enables Hispanic-American students to complete an undergraduate or graduate education. Must be entering a U.S. accredited college or university as a full-time degree seeking student. Minimum 3.3 GPA required. Must demonstrate leadership abilities. Must meet federal Pell Grant eligibility criteria. Visit Web site at http://www.gmsp.org

Award: Scholarship for use in freshman, sophomore, junior, senior, or graduate years; renewable. *Number:* 1000. *Amount:* varies.

Eligibility Requirements: Applicant must be American Indian/Alaska Native, Asian/Pacific Islander, Black (non-Hispanic), or Hispanic and enrolled or expecting to enroll full-time at a four-year institution or university. Available to U.S. citizens.

Application Requirements: Application, financial need analysis, nomination packet. *Deadline:* January 13.

Contact: GMS Representative
Hispanic Scholarship Fund
55 Second Street, Suite 1500
San Francisco, CA 94105
Phone: 877-473-4636
Fax: 415-808-2302
E-mail: gmsinfo@hsf.net

HIGH SCHOOL SCHOLARSHIP PROGRAM

Designed to increase educational attainment of U.S. and Puerto Rico Hispanic high school students. Minimum 3.0 GPA required. Must be high school senior planning to attend accredited college or university the following fall semester after graduation.

Award: Scholarship for use in freshman year; not renewable. *Number:* varies. *Amount:* $1000–$2500.

Eligibility Requirements: Applicant must be of Hispanic heritage; high school student and planning to enroll or expecting to enroll full-time at a two-year or four-year institution or university. Applicant must have 3.0 GPA or higher. Available to U.S. and non-Canadian citizens.

Application Requirements: Application, essay, financial need analysis, references, transcript, copy of Student Aid Report (SAR). *Deadline:* December 15.

Hispanic Scholarship Fund (continued)

Contact: Sara Piredes, Program Office, High School Scholarship
Program
Hispanic Scholarship Fund
55 Second Street, Suite 1500
San Francisco, CA 94105
Phone: 877-473-4636 Ext. 2372
Fax: 415-808-2304
E-mail: highschool@hsf.net

HSF/CAMINO AL EXITO SCHOLARSHIP PROGRAM

Scholarship available on a competitive basis to Hispanic high school and
college students in the metropolitan areas of Los Angeles, New York, Miami,
and Chicago. Awards of $5000 for students attending private colleges or
universities and $2500 for students attending public colleges or universities.

Award: Scholarship for use in freshman, sophomore, junior, senior, or
graduate years. *Number:* varies. *Amount:* $2500–$5000.

Eligibility Requirements: Applicant must be Hispanic and enrolled or
expecting to enroll full-time at an institution or university. Available to
U.S. citizens.

Application Requirements: Application, financial need analysis,
transcript, copy of Student Aid Report (SAR), copy of application for
federal financial aid. *Deadline:* February 28.

Contact: Program Officer
Hispanic Scholarship Fund
55 Second Street, Suite 1500
San Francisco, CA 94105
Phone: 877-473-4636
Fax: 415-808-2302

HSF/CLUB MUSICA LATINA SCHOLARSHIP

Scholarships are available to Hispanic students entering their freshman or
sophomore year at an accredited U.S. four-year college. Must be a member of
Club Musica Latina. For more details, deadlines and an application see Web
site: http://www.hsf.net .

Award: Scholarship for use in freshman or sophomore years; not
renewable. *Number:* varies. *Amount:* up to $2500.

Eligibility Requirements: Applicant must be Hispanic and enrolled or
expecting to enroll full-time at a four-year institution or university.
Applicant must have 3.0 GPA or higher. Available to U.S. citizens.

Application Requirements: Application.

Contact: Program Officer
Hispanic Scholarship Fund
55 Second Street, Suite 1500
San Francisco, CA 94105
Phone: 877-473-4636
Fax: 415-808-2302

HSF/TOYOTA FOUNDATION SCHOLARSHIP PROGRAM-PUERTO RICO

Scholarships are available to graduating high school seniors who are residents
of Puerto Rico entering their freshman year at a Puerto Rican institution. For
more details, deadlines and an application see Web site: http://www.hsf.net .

Award: Scholarship for use in freshman year; not renewable. *Number:*
varies. *Amount:* up to $2500.

Eligibility Requirements: Applicant must be Hispanic; high school
student; planning to enroll or expecting to enroll full-time at a
two-year or four-year or technical institution or university; resident of
Puerto Rico and studying in Puerto Rico. Applicant must have 3.5 GPA
or higher. Available to U.S. citizens.

Application Requirements: Application, essay, financial need analysis,
references, transcript, copy of Student Aid Report (SAR). *Deadline:*
May 15.

Contact: Program Officer
Hispanic Scholarship Fund
55 Second Street, Suite 1500
San Francisco, CA 94105
Phone: 877-473-4636
Fax: 415-808-2302

NEW HORIZONS SCHOLARS PROGRAM

Renewable award available to Hispanic and African-American students who
are infected with Hepatitis C or who are the dependents of a person infected
with Hepatitis C. Students are eligible for $2500 per year for four years. Must
maintain academic standard of 2.5 GPA. For more details and an application
see Web site: http://www.hsf.net or http://www.thurgoodmarshallfund.org.
Application deadline is February 20. Program is funded by the Roche
Foundation.

Award: Scholarship for use in freshman year; renewable. *Number:* up
to 50. *Amount:* $2500.

Eligibility Requirements: Applicant must be Black (non-Hispanic) or
Hispanic; high school student and planning to enroll or expecting to
enroll full-time at a four-year institution or university. Applicant must
have 2.5 GPA or higher. Available to U.S. citizens.

Application Requirements: Application, driver's license, essay, financial
need analysis, references, transcript, verification by physician of
Hepatitis C infection, or must be dependent of someone with Hepatitis
C, Student Aid Report (SAR). *Deadline:* February.

Contact: New Horizons Scholars Program
Hispanic Scholarship Fund
55 Second Street, Suite 1500
San Francisco, CA 94105
Phone: 877-473-4636
Fax: 415-808-2302

HOPI TRIBE   http://www.hopi.nsn.us

BIA HIGHER EDUCATION GRANT

Grant provides financial support for eligible Hopi individuals pursuing
postsecondary education. Minimum 2.5 GPA required. Deadlines are July 31
for fall, and November 30 for spring.

Award: Grant for use in freshman, sophomore, junior, senior, or
graduate years; not renewable. *Number:* 1–130. *Amount:* $50–$2500.

Eligibility Requirements: Applicant must be American Indian/Alaska
Native and enrolled or expecting to enroll full or part-time at a
two-year or four-year institution or university. Applicant must have 2.5
GPA or higher. Available to U.S. citizens.

Application Requirements: Application, financial need analysis, test
scores, transcript, certificate of Indian blood. *Deadline:* varies.

Contact: Theresa Lomakema, Administrative Secretary
Hopi Tribe
PO Box 123
Kykotsmovi, AZ 86039-0123
Phone: 928-734-3533
Fax: 928-734-9575
E-mail: talomakema@hopi.nsn.us

HOPI SCHOLARSHIP

Scholarship awarded to eligible Hopi students on the basis of academic merit.
Entering Freshmen must be in the Top 10% of their graduating class or score
a minimum composite score of 930 on the SAT or a minimum of 21 on the
ACT. Undergraduates must maintain a minimum 3.0 GPA for all
undergraduate course work and other graduate, post graduate, and
professional degree students must maintain a minimum 3.2 GPA for all
graduate course work .

Award: Scholarship for use in freshman, sophomore, junior, senior, or
graduate years. *Number:* up to 5. *Amount:* varies.

Eligibility Requirements: Applicant must be American Indian/Alaska
Native and enrolled or expecting to enroll full-time at an institution or
university. Applicant must have 3.0 GPA or higher. Available to U.S.
citizens.

Application Requirements: Application, financial need analysis, test
scores, transcript. *Deadline:* July 1.

Contact: Theresa Lomakema, Administrative Secretary
Hopi Tribe
PO Box 123
Kykotsmovi, AZ 86039-0123
Phone: 928-734-3533
Fax: 928-734-3533
E-mail: talomakema@hopi.nsn.us

HOPI SUPPLEMENTAL GRANT

Grant provides financial support for eligible Hopi individuals pursuing
postsecondary education. Minimum 2.5 GPA required. Deadlines are April 30
for summer, July 31 for fall, and November 30 for spring.

Award: Grant for use in freshman, sophomore, junior, senior, or graduate years; not renewable. *Number:* 1–400. *Amount:* $50–$1500.

Eligibility Requirements: Applicant must be American Indian/Alaska Native and enrolled or expecting to enroll full or part-time at a two-year or four-year institution or university. Applicant must have 2.5 GPA or higher. Available to U.S. citizens.

Application Requirements: Application, financial need analysis, test scores, transcript, certificate of Indian blood. *Deadline:* varies.

Contact: Theresa Lomakema, Administrative Secretary
Hopi Tribe
PO Box 123
Kykotsmovi, AZ 86039-0123
Phone: 928-734-3533
Fax: 928-734-9575
E-mail: talomakema@hopi.nsn.us

HTGSP GRANT & TUITION/BOOK SCHOLARSHIP

Scholarship available to Hopi students pursuing postsecondary education for reasons of personal growth, career enhancement/change, continuing education, part time students or students who show no financial need.

Award: Scholarship for use in freshman, sophomore, junior, or senior years. *Number:* up to 150. *Amount:* up to $1500.

Eligibility Requirements: Applicant must be American Indian/Alaska Native and enrolled or expecting to enroll full or part-time at a four-year institution or university. Applicant must have 3.0 GPA or higher. Available to U.S. citizens.

Application Requirements: Application, financial need analysis, test scores, transcript. *Deadline:* July 1.

Contact: Theresa Lomakema, Administration Secretary
Hopi Tribe
PO Box 123
Kykotsmovi, AZ 86039-0123
Phone: 928-734-3533
Fax: 928-734-9575
E-mail: talomakema@hopi.nsn.us

PEABODY SCHOLARSHIP

Scholarship provides financial support for eligible Hopi individuals pursuing postsecondary education. Minimum 3.0 GPA required. Deadline is July 31.

Award: Scholarship for use in freshman, sophomore, junior, senior, graduate, or postgraduate years; not renewable. *Number:* 1–90. *Amount:* $50–$1000.

Eligibility Requirements: Applicant must be American Indian/Alaska Native and enrolled or expecting to enroll full-time at a two-year or four-year institution or university. Applicant must have 3.0 GPA or higher. Available to U.S. citizens.

Application Requirements: Application, financial need analysis, test scores, transcript, certificate of Indian blood. *Deadline:* July 31.

Contact: Theresa Lomakema, Administration Secretary
Hopi Tribe
PO Box 123
Kykotsmovi, AZ 86039-0123
Phone: 928-734-3533
Fax: 928-734-9575
E-mail: talomakema@hopi.nsn.us

HOUSTON COMMUNITY SERVICES
http://houston-com-services.tripod.com

AZTECA SCHOLARSHIP

Scholarships are awarded annually to a male and female high school senior planning to attend a university or a college as first-time, first-year students. Applicant must be a Chicano or Mexicano or of Raza descent. Must be a resident of the Houston metropolitan area.

Award: Scholarship for use in freshman year. *Number:* 2. *Amount:* $500.

Eligibility Requirements: Applicant must be of Mexican heritage; Hispanic; enrolled or expecting to enroll full-time at a two-year or four-year institution or university and resident of Texas. Available to U.S. citizens.

Application Requirements: Application, essay, photo, transcript, income tax report, letter of acceptance. *Deadline:* April 29.

Contact: HCS-Education Committee
Phone: 713-926-8771
E-mail: hcsaztlan@sbcglobal.net

IDAHO STATE BOARD OF EDUCATION
http://www.boardofed.idaho.gov

IDAHO MINORITY AND "AT RISK" STUDENT SCHOLARSHIP
• *See page 559*

INDIAN AMERICAN CULTURAL ASSOCIATION
http://www.iasf.org

INDIAN AMERICAN SCHOLARSHIP FUND

Scholarships for descendents of families who are from modern-day India and are graduating from public or private high schools in Georgia. They must be enrolled in four-year colleges or universities. There are both academic and need-based awards available through this program. See the Web site (http://www.iasf.org) for details and application forms. Deadline is May 3 for merit scholarships and May 24 for financial aid scholarships.

Award: Scholarship for use in freshman, sophomore, junior, or senior years; renewable. *Number:* up to 3. *Amount:* $500–$2500.

Eligibility Requirements: Applicant must be of Indian heritage; Asian/Pacific Islander; high school student; planning to enroll or expecting to enroll full-time at a four-year institution or university and resident of Georgia. Applicant must have 3.0 GPA or higher. Available to U.S. citizens.

Application Requirements: Application, essay, financial need analysis, resume, test scores, transcript, IRS 1040 form. *Deadline:* varies.

Contact: Dr. Anuj Manocha
Indian American Cultural Association
719 Vinings Estates Drive
Mableton, GA 30126
E-mail: manochaa@bellsouth.net

INTERNATIONAL ORDER OF THE KING'S DAUGHTERS AND SONS
http://www.iokds.org

INTERNATIONAL ORDER OF THE KING'S DAUGHTERS AND SONS NORTH AMERICAN INDIAN SCHOLARSHIP

For enrolled American-Indians. Proof of reservation registration, college acceptance letter, and financial aid office address required. Request application form by March 1 and return by April 15. Merit-based award. Send self-addressed stamped envelope.

Award: Scholarship for use in freshman, sophomore, junior, or senior years; renewable. *Number:* 45–60. *Amount:* $500–$650.

Eligibility Requirements: Applicant must be American Indian/Alaska Native and enrolled or expecting to enroll full-time at a two-year or four-year or technical institution or university. Applicant must have 2.5 GPA or higher. Available to U.S. and Canadian citizens.

Application Requirements: Application, essay, financial need analysis, references, self-addressed stamped envelope, transcript, written documentation of reservation registration. *Deadline:* April 15.

Contact: Director, North American Indian Department
International Order of the King's Daughters and Sons
PO Box 1017
Chautauqua, NY 14722-1040
Phone: 716-357-4951

INTER-TRIBAL COUNCIL OF MICHIGAN, INC.
http://www.itcmi.org

MICHIGAN INDIAN TUITION WAIVER

Renewable award provides free tuition for Native-American of one-quarter or more blood degree who attend a Michigan public college or university. Must be a Michigan resident for at least one year. The tuition waiver program covers part-time and summer school students, as well as Masters and Doctoral work. For more details and deadlines contact college financial aid office.

Award: Scholarship for use in freshman, sophomore, junior, senior, graduate, or postgraduate years; renewable. *Number:* 1. *Amount:* varies.

Inter-Tribal Council of Michigan, Inc. (continued)

Eligibility Requirements: Applicant must be American Indian/Alaska Native; enrolled or expecting to enroll full or part-time at a two-year or four-year institution or university; resident of Michigan and studying in Michigan. Available to U.S. and Canadian citizens.

Application Requirements: Application, driver's license, tribal certification. *Deadline:* Continuous.

Contact: Christin McKerchie, Executive Assistant to Programs
Inter-Tribal Council of Michigan, Inc.
2956 Ashmun Street
Sault Ste. Marie, MI 49783
Phone: 906-632-6896 Ext. 136
Fax: 906-632-6878

ITALIAN CATHOLIC FEDERATION, INC.   http://www.icf.org

ICF COLLEGE SCHOLARSHIPS TO HIGH SCHOOL SENIORS

Renewable awards for high school students who are residents of California, Illinois, Arizona and Nevada and plan to pursue postsecondary education. Must have minimum 3.2 GPA. Must be a U.S. citizen, Catholic, and of Italian descent or if non-Italian the student's parents or grandparents must be members of the Federation for the student to qualify. Applicants must submit the last two pages of parents' income tax return, along with other required materials as listed on the application.

Award: Scholarship for use in freshman, sophomore, junior, or senior years; renewable. *Number:* 170–200. *Amount:* $400–$1000.

Eligibility Requirements: Applicant must be Roman Catholic; of Italian heritage; high school student; planning to enroll or expecting to enroll full-time at a two-year or four-year institution or university and resident of Arizona, California, Illinois, or Nevada. Applicant must have 3.0 GPA or higher. Available to U.S. citizens.

Application Requirements: Application, essay, financial need analysis, references, test scores, transcript, copy of pages 1 and 2 of parent or guardian's most recently filed federal income tax return. *Deadline:* March 15.

Contact: Scholarship Director
Italian Catholic Federation, Inc.
675 Hegenberger Road, Suite 230
Oakland, CA 94621
Phone: 510-633-9058
Fax: 510-633-9758

ITALIAN-AMERICAN CHAMBER OF COMMERCE MIDWEST   http://www.italianchamber.us

ITALIAN-AMERICAN CHAMBER OF COMMERCE OF CHICAGO SCHOLARSHIP

One-time awards for Illinois residents of Italian descent. Available to high school seniors and college students for use at a four-year institution. Applicants must have a 3.5 GPA. Must reside in Cook, Du Page, Kane, Lake, McHenry, or Will counties in Illinois.

Award: Scholarship for use in freshman, sophomore, junior, or senior years; not renewable. *Number:* 1. *Amount:* up to $1000.

Eligibility Requirements: Applicant must be of Italian heritage; enrolled or expecting to enroll full-time at a four-year institution and resident of Illinois. Applicant must have 3.5 GPA or higher. Available to U.S. citizens.

Application Requirements: Application, autobiography, essay, photo, references, self-addressed stamped envelope, transcript. *Deadline:* May 31.

Contact: Frank Pugno, Scholarship Chairman
Italian-American Chamber of Commerce Midwest
30 South Michigan Avenue, Suite 504
Chicago, IL 60603
Phone: 312-553-9137 Ext. 13
Fax: 312-553-9142
E-mail: info.chicago@italchambers.net

JACKIE ROBINSON FOUNDATION   http://www.jackierobinson.org

JACKIE ROBINSON SCHOLARSHIP

Scholarship for graduating minority high school seniors who have been accepted to accredited four-year colleges or universities. Must be U.S. citizen and show financial need, leadership potential and a high level of academic achievement. Application deadline: March 31.

Award: Scholarship for use in freshman or sophomore years; renewable. *Number:* 50–60. *Amount:* up to $6000.

Eligibility Requirements: Applicant must be American Indian/Alaska Native, Asian/Pacific Islander, Black (non-Hispanic), or Hispanic; high school student and planning to enroll or expecting to enroll full-time at a four-year institution or university. Available to U.S. citizens.

Application Requirements: Application, essay, financial need analysis, references, test scores, transcript, application must be submitted online only. *Deadline:* March 31.

Contact: Scholarship Program
Jackie Robinson Foundation
3 West 35th Street, 11th Floor
New York, NY 10001-2204
Phone: 212-290-8600
Fax: 212-290-8081

JAMES C. CALDWELL SCHOLARSHIP

JAMES C. CALDWELL ASSISTING MEN AND WOMEN OF TOLEDO SCHOLARSHIP

Renewable scholarships for minority residents of the greater Toledo, Ohio area for use in undergraduate study in a college or university. Must maintain 3.0 GPA. Must be African-American, Asian-American, Hispanic-American or Native American. Write for application and enclose a self-addressed stamped envelope.

Award: Scholarship for use in freshman, sophomore, junior, or senior years; renewable. *Number:* up to 20. *Amount:* varies.

Eligibility Requirements: Applicant must be American Indian/Alaska Native, Asian/Pacific Islander, Black (non-Hispanic), or Hispanic; enrolled or expecting to enroll at a two-year or four-year institution or university and resident of Ohio. Applicant must have 3.0 GPA or higher. Available to U.S. citizens.

Application Requirements: Application, self-addressed stamped envelope, transcript. *Deadline:* Continuous.

Contact: James Caldwell, Executive Director
James C. Caldwell Scholarship
PO Box 80056
Toledo, OH 43608
Phone: 419-842-8440

KAISER PERMANENTE   http://financialaid.kp.org

KAISER PERMANENTE ASIAN PACIFIC AMERICAN NETWORK SCHOLARSHIP PROGRAM

Award for graduating high school senior planning to attend college, university, trade or technical school. Must be of Asian descent and have a minimum GPA of 3.0.

Award: Scholarship for use in freshman year. *Amount:* $500–$2000.

Eligibility Requirements: Applicant must be Asian/Pacific Islander and enrolled or expecting to enroll at a two-year or four-year or technical institution or university. Applicant must have 3.0 GPA or higher. Available to U.S. citizens.

Application Requirements: Application, essay, references, self-addressed stamped envelope, transcript. *Deadline:* April 15.

Contact: Pauline Tsai, Scholarship Committee
Kaiser Permanente
PO Box 950
Pasadena, CA 91102-0950
E-mail: pauline.b.tsai@kp.org

KIMBO FOUNDATION   http://www.kimbofoundation.org

KIMBO FOUNDATION SCHOLARSHIP

Scholarship available to Korean-American students only. It is for full time study only. Application deadline varies every year.

Award: Scholarship for use in freshman, sophomore, junior, senior, graduate, or postgraduate years; not renewable. *Number:* varies. *Amount:* varies.

Eligibility Requirements: Applicant must be of Korean heritage; Asian/Pacific Islander and enrolled or expecting to enroll full-time at a two-year or four-year or technical institution or university. Available to citizens of countries other than the U.S. or Canada.

Application Requirements: Application, essay, references, transcript, copy of household income tax return. *Deadline:* varies.

Contact: Jennifer Chung, Program Coordinator
Kimbo Foundation
430 Shotwell Street
San Francisco, CA 94110
Phone: 415-285-4100
Fax: 415-285-4103
E-mail: info@kimbofoundation.org

KNIGHTS OF COLUMBUS   http://www.kofc.org

FOURTH DEGREE PRO DEO AND PRO PATRIA (CANADA)
• *See page 503*

KNIGHTS OF LITHUANIA   http://www.knightsoflithuania.com

KNIGHTS OF LITHUANIA NATIONAL SCHOLARSHIPS
• *See page 503*

KONIAG EDUCATION
FOUNDATION   http://www.koniageducation.org

GLENN GODFREY MEMORIAL SCHOLARSHIP

Scholarship to help applicants pursue self-improvement and positive leadership qualities. Applicants must be Alaska Native shareholders or descendants (may be adopted) of the Koniag Region.

Award: Scholarship for use in sophomore, junior, or senior years; renewable. *Number:* 1. *Amount:* up to $5000.

Eligibility Requirements: Applicant must be American Indian/Alaska Native; enrolled or expecting to enroll full-time at an institution or university and resident of Alaska. Applicant must have 2.5 GPA or higher. Available to U.S. citizens.

Application Requirements: Application, essay, interview, photo, resume, references, transcript, birth certificate (for descendants only). *Deadline:* August 10.

Contact: Koniag Education Foundation
6927 Old Seward Highway, Suite 103
Anchorage, AK 99518

KONIAG EDUCATION CAREER DEVELOPMENT GRANT

Applicants must be Alaska Native shareholders or descendents (may be adopted) of the Koniag Region. Applicants must be accepted or enrolled in a career development course and able to demonstrate how the training will assist the student in gaining employment or job security and/or advancement. Applicants may apply for up to two Career Development grants per year.

Award: Grant for use in freshman year. *Number:* 1.

Eligibility Requirements: Applicant must be American Indian/Alaska Native and enrolled or expecting to enroll part-time at a technical institution. Available to U.S. citizens.

Application Requirements: Application, autobiography, resume.

Contact: Koniag Education Foundation
6927 Old Seward Highway, Suite 103
Anchorage, AK 99518
Fax: 907-562-9023

KONIAG EDUCATION FOUNDATION ACADEMIC/GRADUATE SCHOLARSHIP

Scholarships available to Koniag, Inc. shareholders and their descendants for education following high school. Must be Alaska Native. Deadlines are March 15 and June 1.

Award: Scholarship for use in freshman, sophomore, junior, senior, graduate, or postgraduate years; renewable. *Number:* 130–170. *Amount:* $500–$2500.

Eligibility Requirements: Applicant must be American Indian/Alaska Native and enrolled or expecting to enroll full or part-time at a two-year or four-year or technical institution or university. Available to U.S. and Canadian citizens.

Application Requirements: Application, autobiography, essay, financial need analysis, photo, references, transcript, proof of eligibility from Koniag, Inc.. *Deadline:* varies.

Contact: Tom Murphy, Executive Director
Koniag Education Foundation
6927 Old Seward Highway, Suite 103
Anchorage, AK 99518
Phone: 907-562-9093
Fax: 907-562-9023
E-mail: kef@alaska.com

KONIAG EDUCATION FOUNDATION COLLEGE/UNIVERSITY BASIC SCHOLARSHIP

Applicants must be Alaska Native shareholders or descendents (may be adopted) of the Koniag Region and must maintain a minimum cumulative GPA of 2.00 or equivalent scores.

Award: Scholarship for use in freshman, sophomore, junior, or senior years. *Amount:* up to $1000.

Eligibility Requirements: Applicant must be American Indian/Alaska Native and enrolled or expecting to enroll at an institution or university. Available to U.S. and Canadian citizens.

Application Requirements: Application, essay, references, transcript. *Deadline:* varies.

Contact: Koniag Education Foundation
6927 Old Seward Highway, Suite 103
Anchorage, AK 99518
Phone: 907-562-9093
Fax: 907-562-9023
E-mail: kef@alaska.com

KOREAN AMERICAN SCHOLARSHIP
FOUNDATION   http://www.kasf.org

KOREAN-AMERICAN SCHOLARSHIP FOUNDATION EASTERN REGION SCHOLARSHIPS

Scholarships available to Korean-American and Korean students enrolled in a full-time undergraduate or graduate program in the United States. Selection based on financial need, academic achievement, school activities, and community services. Each applicant must submit an application to the respective KASF region. For more details and an application see Web site: http://www.kasf.org

Award: Scholarship for use in freshman, sophomore, junior, senior, graduate, or postgraduate years; not renewable. *Number:* varies. *Amount:* $1000.

Eligibility Requirements: Applicant must be of Korean heritage; Asian/Pacific Islander; enrolled or expecting to enroll full-time at a two-year or four-year institution and studying in Delaware, District of Columbia, Kentucky, Maryland, North Carolina, Pennsylvania, Virginia, or West Virginia. Available to U.S. and non-U.S. citizens.

Application Requirements: Application, essay, financial need analysis, photo, references, self-addressed stamped envelope, transcript. *Deadline:* May 31.

Contact: Dr. Patrick Lee, KASF Scholarship Committee
Korean American Scholarship Foundation
1984 Isaac Newton Square West, Suite 106
Reston, VA 20190
Phone: 703-748-5935
Fax: 703-748-1874
E-mail: eastern@kasf.org

KOREAN-AMERICAN SCHOLARSHIP FOUNDATION NORTHEASTERN REGION SCHOLARSHIPS

Scholarships available to Korean-American and Korean students enrolled in a full-time undergraduate or graduate program in the United States. Selection based on financial need, academic achievement, school activities, and community services. Each applicant must submit an application to the respective KASF region. For more details and an application see Web site: http://www.kasf.org

Korean American Scholarship Foundation (continued)

Award: Scholarship for use in freshman, sophomore, junior, senior, graduate, or postgraduate years; not renewable. *Number:* up to 60. *Amount:* $1000–$2500.

Eligibility Requirements: Applicant must be of Korean heritage; Asian/Pacific Islander; enrolled or expecting to enroll full-time at a four-year institution or university and studying in Connecticut, Maine, Massachusetts, New Hampshire, New Jersey, New York, Rhode Island, or Vermont. Available to U.S. citizens.

Application Requirements: Application, essay, financial need analysis, photo, references, transcript. *Deadline:* June 23.

Contact: Mr. William Y. Kim, Scholarship Committee Chairman for the NE Regional Chapter
Korean American Scholarship Foundation
51 West Overlook
Port Washington, NY 11050
Phone: 516-883-1142
Fax: 516-883-1964
E-mail: kim.william@gmail.com

KOREAN-AMERICAN SCHOLARSHIP FOUNDATION WESTERN REGION SCHOLARSHIPS

Scholarships available to Korean-American and Korean students enrolled in a full-time undergraduate or graduate program in the United States. Selection based on financial need, academic achievement, school activities, and community services. Each applicant must submit an application to the respective KASF region. For more details and an application see Web site: http://www.kasf.org

Award: Scholarship for use in freshman, sophomore, junior, senior, graduate, or postgraduate years; not renewable. *Number:* varies. *Amount:* $1000.

Eligibility Requirements: Applicant must be of Korean heritage; Asian/Pacific Islander; enrolled or expecting to enroll full-time at an institution or university and studying in Alaska, Arizona, California, Colorado, Hawaii, Idaho, Montana, Nevada, New Mexico, Oregon, Utah, or Washington. Available to U.S. and non-U.S. citizens.

Application Requirements: Application, essay, financial need analysis, photo, references, transcript. *Deadline:* February 28.

Contact: KASF Western Regional Chapter
Korean American Scholarship Foundation
3435 Wilshire Boulevard, Suite 2450B
Los Angeles, CA 90010
Phone: 213-380-5273
Fax: 213-380-5273
E-mail: western@kasf.org

KOREAN UNIVERSITY CLUB

KOREAN UNIVERSITY CLUB SCHOLARSHIP

Scholarship for graduating high school seniors entering their freshman year in a Hawaiian college or university. Must be a Hawaiian resident, a U.S. citizen, and be of Korean ancestry. Must show academic progress. Write for details.

Award: Scholarship for use in freshman year; renewable. *Number:* 1. *Amount:* up to $1500.

Eligibility Requirements: Applicant must be of Korean heritage; Asian/Pacific Islander; high school student; planning to enroll or expecting to enroll full-time at a two-year or four-year institution or university; resident of Hawaii and studying in Hawaii. Available to U.S. citizens.

Application Requirements: Application, essay, financial need analysis, references, self-addressed stamped envelope, test scores, transcript. *Deadline:* March 15.

Contact: Young P. Kang, Jr.
Korean University Club
6871 Hawaii Kai Drive
Honolulu, HI 96825

KOSCIUSZKO FOUNDATION   http://www.kosciuszkofoundation.org

KOSCIUSZKO FOUNDATION TUITION SCHOLARSHIP

This scholarship is reserved for U.S. citizens of Polish descent, Poles who are permanent residents in the United States, and for Americans engaged in study of Polish subjects. Minimum 3.0 GPA required. Must submit a personal statement. Application fee: $25. Several one-time scholarships ranging from $1000 to $7000. Check http://www.KosciuzkoFoundation.org for complete details. Tuition scholarship application is available for download from September through December. Application deadline is January 15.

Award: Scholarship for use in freshman, sophomore, junior, senior, graduate, or postgraduate years; not renewable. *Number:* 100–140. *Amount:* $1000–$7000.

Eligibility Requirements: Applicant must be of Polish heritage; enrolled or expecting to enroll full-time at a four-year institution or university and must have an interest in Polish language. Applicant must have 3.0 GPA or higher. Available to U.S. citizens.

Application Requirements: Application, essay, financial need analysis, photo, references, transcript, personal statement. *Fee:* $25. *Deadline:* January 15.

Contact: Addy Tymczyszyn, Grants Department
Kosciuszko Foundation
15 East 65th Street
New York, NY 10021-6595
Phone: 212-734-2130 Ext. 210

MASSACHUSETTS FEDERATION OF POLISH WOMEN'S CLUBS SCHOLARSHIPS

Nonrenewable award for sophomores, juniors, and seniors attending an accredited four-year college or university. Preference given to MFPWC members and children or grandchildren of members. In the event that no members apply, the scholarship may be awarded to residents of Massachusetts or New England. Submit proof of Polish ancestry. Minimum 3.0 GPA required. Application fee $25. See Web site http://www.kosciuszkofoundation.org for complete details.

Award: Scholarship for use in sophomore, junior, or senior years; not renewable. *Number:* 3. *Amount:* $1250.

Eligibility Requirements: Applicant must be of Polish heritage; enrolled or expecting to enroll full-time at a four-year institution or university and resident of Connecticut, Maine, Massachusetts, New Hampshire, Rhode Island, or Vermont. Applicant must have 3.0 GPA or higher. Available to U.S. citizens.

Application Requirements: Application, essay, financial need analysis, photo, references, transcript, proof of Polish ancestry. *Fee:* $25. *Deadline:* January 15.

Contact: Addy Tymczyszyn, Grants Department
Kosciuszko Foundation
15 East 65th Street
New York, NY 10021-6595
Phone: 212-734-2130 Ext. 210

POLISH AMERICAN CLUB OF NORTH JERSEY SCHOLARSHIPS

Scholarships provide funding of $1,000 to qualified students for full-time undergraduate and graduate studies at accredited colleges and universities in the United States.

Award: Scholarship for use in freshman, sophomore, junior, senior, or graduate years; renewable. *Amount:* $1000.

Eligibility Requirements: Applicant must be of Polish heritage and enrolled or expecting to enroll full-time at a four-year institution or university. Applicant must have 3.0 GPA or higher. Available to U.S. citizens.

Application Requirements: Application, transcript. *Fee:* $25.

Contact: Addy Tymczyszyn, Director of Scholarships and Grants for Americans
Kosciuszko Foundation
15 East 65th Street
New York, NY 10021-6595
Phone: 212-734-2130
Fax: 212-628-4552
E-mail: thekfaddy@aol.com

POLISH NATIONAL ALLIANCE OF BROOKLYN, USA, INC. SCHOLARSHIPS

Scholarships provide funding of $2,000 to qualified undergraduate students for full-time studies at accredited colleges and universities in the United States.

Award: Scholarship for use in freshman, sophomore, junior, or senior years. *Amount:* $2000.

Eligibility Requirements: Applicant must be of Polish heritage and enrolled or expecting to enroll full-time at an institution or university. Applicant must have 3.0 GPA or higher. Available to U.S. citizens.

Application Requirements: Application, photo, transcript. *Fee:* $25.

Contact: Addy Tymczyszyn, Director of Scholarships and Grants for Americans
Kosciuszko Foundation
15 East 65th Street
New York, NY 10021-6595
Phone: 212-734-2130
Fax: 212-628-4552
E-mail: thekfaddy@aol.com

LANDMARK PUBLISHING GROUP
http://www.landmarkcommunications.com

LANDMARK SCHOLARS PROGRAM

Scholarship for a college sophomore. Must be a U.S. citizen or a registered permanent resident. Applicant must be a member of a minority group including: Asian, Hispanic, African-American, Native American. Must maintain a 2.5 grade point average.

Award: Scholarship for use in sophomore year. *Amount:* up to $5000.

Eligibility Requirements: Applicant must be American Indian/Alaska Native, Asian/Pacific Islander, Black (non-Hispanic), or Hispanic and enrolled or expecting to enroll full-time at a four-year institution or university. Applicant must have 2.5 GPA or higher. Available to U.S. citizens.

Application Requirements: Application, essay, financial need analysis, references, transcript. *Deadline:* January 1.

Contact: Ann Morris, Managing Editor, Greensboro News & Record
Landmark Publishing Group
200 East Market Street
Greensboro, NC 27401
E-mail: amorris@news-record.com

LEAGUE OF UNITED LATIN AMERICAN CITIZENS NATIONAL EDUCATIONAL SERVICE CENTERS, INC.
http://www.lnesc.org

LULAC NATIONAL SCHOLARSHIP FUND

LULAC Councils will award scholarships to qualified Hispanic students who are enrolled or are planning to enroll in accredited colleges or universities in the United States. Applicants must be U.S. citizens or legal residents. Scholarships may be used for the payment of tuition, academic fees, room, board and the purchase of required educational materials. For additional information applicants should check LULAC Web site at http://www.lnesc.org to see a list of participating councils or send a self-addressed stamped envelope.

Award: Scholarship for use in freshman, sophomore, junior, senior, or graduate years; not renewable. *Number:* 1000. *Amount:* $250–$2000.

Eligibility Requirements: Applicant must be Hispanic and enrolled or expecting to enroll full-time at a two-year or four-year institution or university. Available to U.S. citizens.

Application Requirements: Application, autobiography, essay, financial need analysis, interview, references, self-addressed stamped envelope, test scores, transcript. *Deadline:* March 31.

Contact: Lorena Maymi-Garrido, Scholarship Coordinator
League of United Latin American Citizens National Educational Service Centers, Inc.
2000 L Street, NW, Suite 610
Washington, DC 20036
Phone: 202-835-9646
Fax: 202-835-9685
E-mail: lnescaward@aol.com

LOS PADRES FOUNDATION
http://www.lospadresfoundation.org

GILBERT RIOS MEMORIAL AWARD

Award for one male and one female Puerto Rican/Latino college or university student who is interested in pursuing a graduate education. Must be first generation in the family to attend graduate school. The award is for a full-time accredited graduate or professional degree program that terminates in two to four years.

Award: Grant for use in freshman, sophomore, junior, or senior years. *Number:* 2. *Amount:* $5000.

Eligibility Requirements: Applicant must be of Hispanic or Latin American/Caribbean heritage and enrolled or expecting to enroll full-time at a two-year or four-year institution or university. Applicant must have 3.0 GPA or higher. Available to U.S. citizens.

Application Requirements: Resume, transcript, family must meet federal guidelines for low income. *Deadline:* February 1.

Contact: Scholarship Coordinator
Los Padres Foundation
658 Live Oak Drive
McLean, VA 22101
Phone: 703-790-9870
Fax: 703-790-9742
E-mail: lpfadmin@lospadresfoundation.com

MAGIC JOHNSON FOUNDATION, INC.
http://www.magicjohnson.org

TAYLOR MICHAELS SCHOLARSHIP FUND

Scholarship to provide support for deserving minority high school students who exemplify a strong potential for academic achievement but face social-economic conditions that hinder them from reaching their full potential. Must have strong community service involvement. Must be a resident of Atlanta, GA; Cleveland, OH; Detroit, MI; Houston, TX; Los Angeles, CA; or New York, NY.

Award: Scholarship for use in freshman year; renewable. *Amount:* $500–$1000.

Eligibility Requirements: Applicant must be American Indian/Alaska Native, Asian/Pacific Islander, Black (non-Hispanic), or Hispanic; high school student; planning to enroll or expecting to enroll full-time at a two-year or four-year or technical institution or university and resident of California, Georgia, Michigan, Ohio, or Texas. Applicant must have 2.5 GPA or higher. Available to U.S. citizens.

Application Requirements: Application, essay, references, transcript. *Deadline:* February 3.

Contact: Taylor Michaels Scholarship Fund
Magic Johnson Foundation, Inc.
9100 Wilshire Boulevard., Suite 700, East Tower
Beverly Hills, CA 90212

MENOMINEE INDIAN TRIBE OF WISCONSIN
http://www.menominee-nsn.gov

MENOMINEE INDIAN TRIBE ADULT VOCATIONAL TRAINING PROGRAM

Renewable award for enrolled Menominee tribal members to use at vocational or technical schools. Must be at least 1/4 Menominee and show proof of Indian blood. Must complete financial aid form. Deadlines: March 1 and November 1.

Award: Grant for use in freshman or sophomore years; renewable. *Number:* 50–70. *Amount:* $100–$2200.

Eligibility Requirements: Applicant must be American Indian/Alaska Native and enrolled or expecting to enroll full or part-time at a technical institution. Available to U.S. citizens.

Application Requirements: Application, financial need analysis. *Deadline:* varies.

Contact: Virginia Nuske, Education Director
Menominee Indian Tribe of Wisconsin
PO Box 910
Keshena, WI 54135
Phone: 715-799-5110
Fax: 715-799-5102
E-mail: vnuske@mitw.org

MENOMINEE INDIAN TRIBE OF WISCONSIN HIGHER EDUCATION GRANTS

Renewable award for enrolled Menominee tribal member to use at a two- or four-year college or university. Must be at least 1/4 Menominee and show proof of Indian blood. Must complete financial aid form. Contact for deadline information.

Menominee Indian Tribe of Wisconsin (continued)

Award: Grant for use in freshman, sophomore, junior, or senior years; renewable. *Number:* 136. *Amount:* $100–$1100.

Eligibility Requirements: Applicant must be American Indian/Alaska Native and enrolled or expecting to enroll full or part-time at a two-year or four-year institution or university. Available to U.S. citizens.

Application Requirements: Application, financial need analysis. *Deadline:* Continuous.

Contact: Virginia Nuske, Education Director
Menominee Indian Tribe of Wisconsin
PO Box 910
Keshena, WI 54135
Phone: 715-799-5110
Fax: 715-799-5102
E-mail: vnuske@mitw.org

MESCALERO TRIBAL EDUCATION

MESCALERO APACHE TRIBAL SCHOLARSHIP

Award available to Mescalero Apache tribal members as a supplement to other forms of financial aid. Reapplication is required each year. Freshmen and sophomores must meet with the Tribal Education Committee each year when applying or reapplying. Must have letter of acceptance from institution and signed grade release each semester. Deadline: June 1 for Fall, November 1 for Spring.

Award: Scholarship for use in freshman, sophomore, junior, senior, or graduate years; not renewable. *Number:* up to 180. *Amount:* up to $8000.

Eligibility Requirements: Applicant must be American Indian/Alaska Native and enrolled or expecting to enroll full or part-time at a two-year or four-year or technical institution or university. Available to U.S. citizens.

Application Requirements: Application, essay, financial need analysis, references, transcript, privacy statement. *Deadline:* varies.

Contact: Rutalee Bob, Assistant Director of Tribal Education
Mescalero Tribal Education
148 Cottonwood Drive, PO Box 176
Mescalero, NM 88340
Phone: 505-464-4500
Fax: 505-464-4508
E-mail: mesceduc@trailnet.com

MINNESOTA INDIAN SCHOLARSHIP OFFICE   http://www.mheso.state.mn.us

MINNESOTA INDIAN SCHOLARSHIP PROGRAM

One-time award for Minnesota Native-American. Applicant must be one quarter Native-American and a resident of Minnesota. Must re-apply for scholarship annually.

Award: Scholarship for use in freshman, sophomore, junior, or senior years; not renewable. *Number:* varies. *Amount:* $3300–$6600.

Eligibility Requirements: Applicant must be American Indian/Alaska Native; enrolled or expecting to enroll full or part-time at a two-year or four-year or technical institution or university; resident of Minnesota and studying in Minnesota. Available to U.S. citizens.

Application Requirements: Application, financial need analysis. *Deadline:* July 1.

Contact: Lea Perkins, Director
Minnesota Indian Scholarship Office
Minnesota Department of Education, 1500 Highway 36W
Roseville, MN 55113-4266
Phone: 800-657-3927
E-mail: cfl.indianeducation@state.mn.us

MONGOLIA SOCIETY, INC.   http://www.indiana.edu/~mongsoc

DR. GOMBOJAB HANGIN MEMORIAL SCHOLARSHIP

One-time award for students of Mongolian heritage only. Must have permanent residency in Mongolia, the People's Republic of China, or the former Soviet Union. Award is for tuition at U.S. institutions. Upon conclusion of award year, recipient must write a report of his or her activities. Application requests must be in English and the application must be filled out in English. Deadline is January 1. Write or e-mail for application.

Award: Scholarship for use in freshman, sophomore, junior, senior, or graduate years; not renewable. *Number:* 1. *Amount:* up to $2400.

Eligibility Requirements: Applicant must be of Mongolian heritage and Chinese or Russian citizen and enrolled or expecting to enroll at a four-year institution or university. Available to U.S. citizens.

Application Requirements: Application, resume, references, curriculum vitae, copy of ID card and passport. *Deadline:* January 1.

Contact: Susie Drost, Treasurer
Mongolia Society, Inc.
322 Goodbody Hall
Indiana University,1011 East 3rd Street
Bloomington, IN 47405-7005
Phone: 815-855-4078
Fax: 815-855-7500
E-mail: monsoc@indiana.edu

MONTANA GUARANTEED STUDENT LOAN PROGRAM, OFFICE OF COMMISSIONER OF HIGHER EDUCATION   http://www.mgslp.state.mt.us

INDIAN STUDENT FEE WAIVER

Fee waiver awarded by the Montana University System to undergraduate and graduate students meeting the criteria. Amount varies depending upon the tuition and registration fee at each participating college. Students must provide documentation of 1/4 Indian blood or more; must be a resident of Montana for at least one year prior to enrolling in school and must demonstrate financial need. Full-or part-time study qualifies. Complete and submit the FAFSA by March 1 and a Montana Indian Fee Waiver application form. Contact the financial aid office at the college of attendance to determine eligibility.

Award: Scholarship for use in freshman, sophomore, junior, senior, or graduate years; renewable. *Number:* 600. *Amount:* $2000.

Eligibility Requirements: Applicant must be American Indian/Alaska Native; enrolled or expecting to enroll full or part-time at a two-year or four-year institution or university; resident of Montana and studying in Montana. Available to U.S. citizens.

Application Requirements: Application, financial need analysis, FAFSA, documentation of Indian blood. *Deadline:* March 1.

Contact: Ellen Swaney, Scholarship Coordinator
Montana Guaranteed Student Loan Program, Office of Commissioner of Higher Education
PO Box 203101
Helena, MT 59620-3101
Phone: 406-444-0332

NAACP LEGAL DEFENSE AND EDUCATIONAL FUND, INC.   http://www.naacpldf.org/scholarships

HERBERT LEHMAN SCHOLARSHIP PROGRAM

Renewable award for successful African-American high school seniors to attend a four-year college on a full-time basis. Must be a U.S. citizen. Must request an application in writing by March 15. Application deadline is April 30.

Award: Scholarship for use in freshman, sophomore, junior, or senior years; renewable. *Number:* 25–30. *Amount:* $2000.

Eligibility Requirements: Applicant must be Black (non-Hispanic); high school student and planning to enroll or expecting to enroll full-time at a four-year institution or university. Available to U.S. citizens.

Application Requirements: Application, essay, photo, references, test scores, transcript. *Deadline:* April 30.

Contact: Micheal Bagley, Program Director
NAACP Legal Defense and Educational Fund, Inc.
99 Hudson Street, Suite 1600
New York, NY 10013
Phone: 212-965-2225
Fax: 212-219-1595

NATIONAL ASSOCIATION FOR CAMPUS ACTIVITIES
http://www.naca.org

MULTICULTURAL SCHOLARSHIP PROGRAM

Scholarships will be given to applicants identified as African-American, Latina/Latino, Native-American, Asian-American or Pacific Islander ethnic minorities. A letter of recommendation affirming his/her ethnic minority status, his/her financial need, and that he/she will be in the campus activity field at least one year following the program for which a scholarship is being sought, should accompany applications.

Award: Scholarship for use in sophomore, junior, senior, or graduate years; not renewable. *Number:* varies. *Amount:* $250–$300.

Eligibility Requirements: Applicant must be American Indian/Alaska Native, Asian/Pacific Islander, Black (non-Hispanic), or Hispanic; enrolled or expecting to enroll at a two-year or four-year institution or university and must have an interest in leadership. Available to U.S. citizens.

Application Requirements: Application, essay, financial need analysis, references. *Deadline:* May 1.

Contact: Dionne Ellison, Administrative Assistant
National Association for Campus Activities
13 Harbison Way
Columbia, SC 29212-3401
Phone: 803-732-6222
Fax: 803-749-1047
E-mail: dionnee@naca.org

NATIONAL ASSOCIATION FOR THE ADVANCEMENT OF COLORED PEOPLE
http://www.naacp.org

AGNES JONES JACKSON SCHOLARSHIP
• See page 505

ROY WILKINS SCHOLARSHIP
• See page 505

NATIONAL ASSOCIATION OF COLORED WOMEN'S CLUBS
http://www.nacwc.org

HALLIE Q. BROWN SCHOLARSHIP

Scholarships awarded biennially to students who are recommended by an active member of NACWC and endorsed by the member's club. Must be a high school graduate who has completed at least one semester in a postsecondary accredited institution with a minimum C average. Must demonstrate need for financial assistance. Application deadline is March 31.

Award: Scholarship for use in freshman, sophomore, junior, or senior years; not renewable. *Number:* 4–6. *Amount:* $1000–$2000.

Eligibility Requirements: Applicant must be Black (non-Hispanic) and enrolled or expecting to enroll full-time at an institution or university. Available to U.S. citizens.

Application Requirements: Application, references, transcript. *Deadline:* March 31.

Contact: Dr. Gerldine Jenkins, Program Coordinator
National Association of Colored Women's Clubs
1601 R Street, NW
Washington, DC 20009
Phone: 202-667-4080
Fax: 202-667-2574

NATIONAL ITALIAN AMERICAN FOUNDATION
http://www.niaf.org

EMANUELE AND EMILIA INGLESE MEMORIAL SCHOLARSHIP

Scholarship available to Italian American undergraduate students who trace their lineage to the Lombardy region, and who are the first generation of their family to attend college. Applicants must have a 3.0 or higher GPA and financial need. Applicants must be enrolled in an accredited institution of higher education and be a United States citizen or a permanent resident alien. For further information, deadlines, and application see Web site: http://www. niaf.org/scholarships/index.asp

Award: Scholarship for use in freshman, sophomore, junior, or senior years. *Number:* 1. *Amount:* $2500.

Eligibility Requirements: Applicant must be of Italian heritage and enrolled or expecting to enroll at a two-year or four-year or technical institution or university. Applicant must have 3.0 GPA or higher. Available to U.S. citizens.

Application Requirements: Application. *Deadline:* April 30.

Contact: Elissa Ruffino
Phone: 202-939-3106
E-mail: elissa@niaf.org

NATIONAL ITALIAN AMERICAN FOUNDATION CATEGORY I SCHOLARSHIP

Award available to Italian-American students who have outstanding potential and high academic achievements. Minimum 3.25 GPA required. Must be a U.S. citizen and be enrolled in an accredited institution of higher education. Application can only be submitted online. For further information, deadlines, and online application visit Web site: http://www.niaf.org/scholarships/index. asp.

Award: Scholarship for use in freshman, sophomore, junior, senior, or graduate years; not renewable. *Number:* varies. *Amount:* $2500–$10,000.

Eligibility Requirements: Applicant must be of Italian heritage and enrolled or expecting to enroll full or part-time at a four-year institution or university. Available to U.S. citizens.

Application Requirements: Application, essay, references, transcript. *Deadline:* March 1.

Contact: Michelle Arbeit, Assistant, Education and Culture
National Italian American Foundation
1860 19th Street, NW
Washington, DC 20009
Phone: 202-387-0600
Fax: 202-387-0800
E-mail: marbeit@niaf.org

NATIONAL MERIT SCHOLARSHIP CORPORATION

NATIONAL ACHIEVEMENT SCHOLARSHIP PROGRAM

Competition of African-American students for recognition and undergraduate scholarships. Students enter by taking the Preliminary SAT/National Merit Scholar Qualifying Test and by meeting other participation requirements. Most of the awards are one-time scholarships of $2,500; others are renewable for four years, and valued between $500 and $2,000 or more. Contact high school counselor by fall of junior year. Those qualifying for recognition are notified through their high school. Participation requirements are available in the PSAT/NMSQT Student Bulletin and on the NMSC Web site at http://www.nationalmerit.org

Award: Scholarship for use in freshman year; renewable. *Number:* 800. *Amount:* $500–$2500.

Eligibility Requirements: Applicant must be Black (non-Hispanic); high school student and planning to enroll or expecting to enroll full-time at a four-year institution or university. Available to U.S. citizens.

Application Requirements: Application, autobiography, essay, references, test scores, transcript. *Deadline:* Continuous.

Contact: student's high school counselor

NATIONAL MINORITY JUNIOR GOLF SCHOLARSHIP ASSOCIATION
http://www.nmjgsa.org

NATIONAL MINORITY JUNIOR GOLF SCHOLARSHIP

Awards for minority students based on academic achievement, financial need, evidence of community service, and golfing ability. Available to high school seniors who have entered information into the database located at http://www.nmjgsa.org, as well as to undergraduate students who previously received a scholarship as a freshman. Application deadline is May 15.

Award: Scholarship for use in freshman, sophomore, junior, or senior years; not renewable. *Number:* varies. *Amount:* $1000–$6000.

Eligibility Requirements: Applicant must be American Indian/Alaska Native, Asian/Pacific Islander, Black (non-Hispanic), or Hispanic; enrolled or expecting to enroll full-time at a two-year or four-year or technical institution or university and must have an interest in golf. Available to U.S. citizens.

National Minority Junior Golf Scholarship Association (continued)

Application Requirements: Application, essay, financial need analysis, photo, references, test scores, transcript. *Deadline:* May 15.

Contact: Scholarship Committee
National Minority Junior Golf Scholarship Association
4950 E Thomas Road
Phoenix, AZ 85018
Phone: 602-258-7851
Fax: 602-258-3412
E-mail: sdean@nmjgsa.org

NATIONAL SOCIETY DAUGHTERS OF THE AMERICAN REVOLUTION
http://www.dar.org

NATIONAL SOCIETY DAUGHTERS OF THE AMERICAN REVOLUTION AMERICAN INDIAN SCHOLARSHIP

Nonrenewable award for Native-American striving for a college or vocational education. Must be U.S. citizen with 2.75 GPA. Submit letter with family history, financial status, and goals. Based on need and academic achievement. Deadlines: July 1 for Fall term and November 1 for Spring term. Must submit self-addressed stamped envelope to be considered.

Award: Scholarship for use in freshman, sophomore, junior, senior, or graduate years; not renewable. *Number:* up to 50. *Amount:* $500.

Eligibility Requirements: Applicant must be American Indian/Alaska Native and enrolled or expecting to enroll at a two-year or four-year or technical institution or university. Available to U.S. citizens.

Application Requirements: Application, financial need analysis, references, self-addressed stamped envelope, transcript. *Deadline:* varies.

Contact: Committee Services Office, American Indian Scholarship
National Society Daughters of the American Revolution
1776 D Street, NW
Washington, DC 20006-5392

NATIONAL SOCIETY DAUGHTERS OF THE AMERICAN REVOLUTION FRANCES CRAWFORD MARVIN AMERICAN INDIAN SCHOLARSHIP

Nonrenewable award available for Native-American to attend any two- or four-year college. Must demonstrate financial need, academic achievement, and have a 3.0 GPA or higher. Must submit a self-addressed stamped envelope to be considered. Deadline is February 1.

Award: Scholarship for use in freshman, sophomore, junior, or senior years; not renewable. *Number:* 1. *Amount:* varies.

Eligibility Requirements: Applicant must be American Indian/Alaska Native and enrolled or expecting to enroll full-time at a two-year or four-year institution or university. Applicant must have 3.0 GPA or higher. Available to U.S. citizens.

Application Requirements: Application, financial need analysis, self-addressed stamped envelope, transcript. *Deadline:* February 1.

Contact: Committee Services Office, Scholarship
National Society Daughters of the American Revolution
1776 D Street, NW
Washington, DC 20006-5303

NATIONAL UNION OF PUBLIC AND GENERAL EMPLOYEES
http://www.nupge.ca

SCHOLARSHIP FOR ABORIGINAL CANADIANS
• See page 507

SCHOLARSHIP FOR VISIBLE MINORITIES
• See page 507

TERRY FOX MEMORIAL SCHOLARSHIP
• See page 507

TOMMY DOUGLAS SCHOLARSHIP
• See page 507

NATIONAL WELSH-AMERICAN FOUNDATION
http://www.wales-usa.org

EXCHANGE SCHOLARSHIP

Limited to colleges/universities in Wales only. Applicant must have a Welsh background through birth and be willing to promote Welsh-American relations both here and abroad. Requested to consider becoming a member of NWAF upon completion of study. Required to complete four-year college study in U.S.A. Applicant must be 21 years of age or older.

Award: Scholarship for use in freshman, sophomore, junior, senior, or graduate years; not renewable. *Number:* 1. *Amount:* $5000.

Eligibility Requirements: Applicant must be of Welsh heritage; age 21 and enrolled or expecting to enroll full-time at a four-year institution or university. Available to U.S. citizens.

Application Requirements: Application, autobiography, references, test scores. *Deadline:* March 1.

Contact: Phillip Davies, Chairman, Scholarship Committee
National Welsh-American Foundation
24 Essex Road
Scotch Plains, NJ 07076
Phone: 908-594-6827
Fax: 908-889-5888
E-mail: philip_davies@merck.com

NATIONAL WOMEN'S STUDIES ASSOCIATION
http://www.nwsa.org

ABAFAZI-AFRICANA WOMEN'S STUDIES ESSAY AWARD

Two $400 awards open to female, African-American, undergraduate and graduate students. Scholarly essays may cover any subject relevant to African-American female children, women's issues and/or experiences in the United States or throughout the diaspora. Preference given to NWSA members.

Award: Prize for use in freshman, sophomore, junior, senior, or graduate years; not renewable. *Number:* 2. *Amount:* $400.

Eligibility Requirements: Applicant must be Black (non-Hispanic); enrolled or expecting to enroll at an institution or university; female and must have an interest in writing. Available to U.S. and non-U.S. citizens.

Application Requirements: Application, essay. *Deadline:* February 15.

Contact: Pat Washington
Phone: 619-582-5383
Fax: 619-229-8226
E-mail: themorgangirl@aol.com

NEW YORK STATE HIGHER EDUCATION SERVICES CORPORATION
http://www.hesc.com/

NEW YORK STATE AID TO NATIVE AMERICANS

Award for enrolled members of a New York State tribe and their children who are attending or planning to attend a New York State college and who are New York State residents. Award for full-time-students up to $1550 annually; part-time awards approximately $85 per credit hour. Application deadline: July 15 for the Fall semester; December 31 for the Spring semester; and by May 20 for Summer session.

Award: Scholarship for use in freshman, sophomore, junior, or senior years; not renewable. *Number:* varies. *Amount:* up to $1550.

Eligibility Requirements: Applicant must be American Indian/Alaska Native; enrolled or expecting to enroll full or part-time at a two-year or four-year or technical institution or university; resident of New York and studying in New York. Available to U.S. citizens.

Application Requirements: Application.

Contact: Native American Education Unit, New York State Education Department
New York State Higher Education Services Corporation
EBA Room 374
Albany, NY 12234
Phone: 518-474-0537

NEXTGEN NETWORK, INC.
http://www.nextgennetwork.com

DONNA JAMISON LAGO MEMORIAL SCHOLARSHIP

Awards to assist with future educational expenses of African-American, U.S. citizens. The essay competition is open to those who would complete their studies in that current year. Applicants must be seeking acceptance to an accredited U.S. college or university. The essay competition encourages high school seniors to think critically about important issues that affect their lives.

Award: Scholarship for use in freshman year; not renewable. *Number:* 9. *Amount:* $500–$2500.

Eligibility Requirements: Applicant must be Black (non-Hispanic); high school student and planning to enroll or expecting to enroll at an institution or university. Available to U.S. citizens.

Application Requirements: Application, applicant must enter a contest, autobiography, essay, photo, references. *Deadline:* March 17.

Contact: Brookes Gore, Donna Jamison Lago Scholarship Coordinator
NextGen Network, Inc.
NextGen Network Inc., c/o Urbanomics Consulting Group,
1010 Wisconsin Avenue, NW, Suite 430
Washington, DC 20007
Phone: 202-686-9260
Fax: 202-944-3322
E-mail: ngn@urbanomics.com

NISEI STUDENT RELOCATION COMMEMORATIVE FUND
http://www.nsrcfund.org

NISEI STUDENT RELOCATION COMMEMORATIVE FUND

Scholarships are made available to graduating high school seniors who are SE Asian refugees or children of refugees. For more details see Web site: http://www.nsrcfund.org. Deadline varies.

Award: Scholarship for use in freshman year; not renewable. *Number:* up to 5. *Amount:* up to $1000.

Eligibility Requirements: Applicant must be Asian/Pacific Islander; high school student and planning to enroll or expecting to enroll full-time at a two-year or four-year or technical institution or university. Available to U.S. citizens.

Application Requirements: Application, autobiography, essay, financial need analysis, references, test scores, transcript. *Deadline:* varies.

Contact: Jean Hibino, Executive Secretary
Nisei Student Relocation Commemorative Fund
19 Scenic Drive
Portland, CT 06480
E-mail: jeanhibino@aol.com

NORTHERN CHEYENNE TRIBAL EDUCATION DEPARTMENT

HIGHER EDUCATION SCHOLARSHIP PROGRAM

Scholarships are only provided for enrolled Northern Cheyenne Tribal Members who meet the requirements listed in the higher education guidelines. Must be U.S. citizen enrolled in a postsecondary institution. Minimum 2.0 GPA required. Deadline is March 1.

Award: Grant for use in freshman, sophomore, junior, or senior years; renewable. *Number:* 72. *Amount:* $50–$6000.

Eligibility Requirements: Applicant must be American Indian/Alaska Native and enrolled or expecting to enroll full or part-time at a two-year or four-year institution or university. Available to U.S. citizens.

Application Requirements: Application, essay, financial need analysis, references, test scores, transcript. *Deadline:* March 1.

Contact: Norma Bixby, Director
Northern Cheyenne Tribal Education Department
Box 307
Lame Deer, MT 59043
Phone: 406-477-6602
Fax: 406-477-8150
E-mail: norma@rangeweb.net

NORTHERN VIRGINIA URBAN LEAGUE
http://www.nvul.org/

NORTHERN VIRGINIA URBAN LEAGUE SCHOLARSHIP PROGRAM

Program awards four $3750 scholarships to eligible African American students from the Northern Virginia region. Applicant must be a graduating high school senior. Application deadline is February.

Award: Scholarship for use in freshman year; not renewable. *Number:* 4. *Amount:* $3750.

Eligibility Requirements: Applicant must be Black (non-Hispanic); high school student; planning to enroll or expecting to enroll full-time at a two-year or four-year institution and resident of Virginia. Available to U.S. citizens.

Application Requirements: Application, autobiography, essay, interview, references, transcript. *Deadline:* February 24.

Contact: Tyrone Maceo Moorer, Director of Programs and Development
Phone: 703-836-2858
Fax: 703-836-8948
E-mail: tmoorer@nvul.org

NORWAY-AMERICA ASSOCIATION
http://www.noram.no

NORWAY-AMERICA UNDERGRADUATE SCHOLARSHIP PROGRAM

Scholarships are provided for Norwegian citizens interested in studying at the undergraduate level in the United States. Students should apply directly to the Norway-American Association for consideration for these awards totaling at least 30% reduction in tuition and room and board for one academic year. Applicant must be a member of the Norway-America Association.

Award: Scholarship for use in freshman, sophomore, junior, or senior years; not renewable. *Number:* up to 70.

Eligibility Requirements: Applicant must be Norwegian citizen and enrolled or expecting to enroll at a four-year institution or university. Available to citizens of countries other than the U.S. or Canada.

Application Requirements: Application, references, transcript, proof of NAA membership, teacher evaluations. *Deadline:* varies.

Contact: Johan H. Andresen
Norway-America Association
Radhusgaten 23 B
Oslo 0158
Norway
Phone: 47-23 35 71 60
Fax: 47-23 35 71 75

OFFICE OF NAVAJO NATION SCHOLARSHIP AND FINANCIAL ASSISTANCE
http://www.onnsfa.org

CHIEF MANUELITO SCHOLARSHIP PROGRAM

One-time, $7000 scholarship available to a high-achieving Navajo high school student. Minimum 3.0 GPA and 21 ACT score required. (SAT scores will be converted.) Deadline: April 1. Must submit letter of college acceptance and Certificate of Indian Blood (CIB). High school student must have completed one unit of Navajo language and one-half unit of Navajo government courses.

Award: Scholarship for use in freshman, sophomore, junior, or senior years; not renewable. *Number:* 1. *Amount:* $7000.

Eligibility Requirements: Applicant must be American Indian/Alaska Native and enrolled or expecting to enroll full-time at a two-year or four-year institution or university. Applicant must have 3.0 GPA or higher. Available to U.S. citizens.

Application Requirements: Application, financial need analysis, test scores, transcript. *Deadline:* April 1.

Contact: Roxanne Gorman, Program Manager
Office of Navajo Nation Scholarship and Financial Assistance
PO Box 1870
Window Rock, AZ 86515-1870
Phone: 928-871-7434
Fax: 928-871-6561

ONEIDA TRIBE OF INDIANS OF WISCONSIN
http://www.oneidanation.org

ONEIDA HIGHER EDUCATION GRANT PROGRAM

Renewable award available to enrolled members of the Oneida Tribe of Indians of Wisconsin who are accepted into an accredited postsecondary institution within the United States. Have a High School Diploma, HSED or GED.

Award: Grant for use in freshman, sophomore, junior, senior, or graduate years; renewable. *Number:* varies. *Amount:* up to $20,000.

Eligibility Requirements: Applicant must be American Indian/Alaska Native and enrolled or expecting to enroll full or part-time at a technical institution or university. Available to U.S. citizens.

Oneida Tribe of Indians of Wisconsin (continued)

Application Requirements: Application, financial need analysis, Oneida Tribal Enrollment. *Deadline:* varies.

Contact: Oneida Higher Education
Oneida Tribe of Indians of Wisconsin
PO Box 365
Oneida, WI 54155
Phone: 800-236-2214 Ext. 4033
Fax: 920-869-4039

OREGON NATIVE AMERICAN CHAMBER OF COMMERCE SCHOLARSHIP   http://www.onacc.org

OREGON NATIVE AMERICAN CHAMBER OF COMMERCE SCHOLARSHIP

Scholarships available to Native American students living in Oregon and enrolled in a program of undergraduate study at an Oregon college or university. Must verify Native American status and be actively involved in the Native American community.

Award: Scholarship for use in freshman, sophomore, junior, or senior years. *Amount:* $1000.

Eligibility Requirements: Applicant must be American Indian/Alaska Native; enrolled or expecting to enroll at a four-year institution or university and resident of Oregon. Available to U.S. citizens.

Application Requirements: Application, references, transcript. *Deadline:* September 16.

Contact: Kelly Anne Ilagan
Oregon Native American Chamber of Commerce Scholarship
PO Box 502
Clackamas, OR 97015

OREGON STUDENT ASSISTANCE COMMISSION   http://www.osac.state.or.us

AFSCME: AMERICAN FEDERATION OF STATE, COUNTY, AND MUNICIPAL EMPLOYEES LOCAL 75 SCHOLARSHIP
• See page 510

VERL AND DOROTHY MILLER NATIVE AMERICAN VOCATIONAL SCHOLARSHIP

Scholarship available to students of Native American ancestry who plan to enroll full time in an eligible trade or vocational school. Must provide proof of eligibility. Specific details found on Web site http://www.osac.state.or.us. Deadline is March 1.

Award: Scholarship for use in freshman or sophomore years; renewable. *Number:* varies. *Amount:* $500.

Eligibility Requirements: Applicant must be American Indian/Alaska Native; enrolled or expecting to enroll full-time at a technical institution and resident of Oregon. Available to U.S. citizens.

Application Requirements: Application, essay, financial need analysis, transcript, certification of Native American ancestry, Johnson O'Malley Student Eligibility Form. *Deadline:* March 1.

Contact: Director of Grant Programs
Oregon Student Assistance Commission
1500 Valley River Drive, Suite 100
Eugene, OR 97401-7020
Phone: 800-452-8807 Ext. 7395

ORGANIZATION OF CHINESE AMERICANS   http://www.ocanatl.org

GATES MILLENNIUM SCHOLARS

Award enables Asian Pacific Islander American students to complete an undergraduate and graduate education. Must be entering a U.S. accredited college or university as a full-time degree-seeking student. Minimum 3.3 GPA required. Must demonstrate leadership abilities. Must meet federal Pell Grant eligibility criteria. Visit Web site at http://www.gmsp.org.

Award: Scholarship for use in freshman, sophomore, junior, senior, or graduate years; renewable. *Number:* up to 1000. *Amount:* varies.

Eligibility Requirements: Applicant must be Asian/Pacific Islander and enrolled or expecting to enroll full-time at a four-year institution or university. Available to U.S. citizens.

Application Requirements: Application, essay, financial need analysis, resume, test scores, transcript, nomination packet. *Deadline:* January 16.

Contact: Catherine Claro Domaoan, GMS/APIA Representative
Organization of Chinese Americans
1001 Connecticut Avenue, NW, Suite 601
Washington, DC 20036
Phone: 866-274-4677
Fax: 202-530-0643
E-mail: gmspinfo@ocanatl.org

OCA AVON COLLEGE SCHOLARSHIP

Scholarships for Asian Pacific American women who will be entering first year of college in the upcoming fall.

Award: Scholarship for use in freshman year; not renewable. *Number:* 8–15. *Amount:* $1500–$2000.

Eligibility Requirements: Applicant must be Asian/Pacific Islander; high school student; planning to enroll or expecting to enroll full-time at a two-year or four-year institution or university and female. Applicant must have 3.0 GPA or higher. Available to U.S. citizens.

Application Requirements: Application, essay, financial need analysis, self-addressed stamped envelope, transcript, letter of acceptance, letter of intent to enroll. *Deadline:* April 18.

Contact: OCA-Avon Scholarship
Organization of Chinese Americans
1001 Connecticut Avenue, NW, Suite 601
Washington, DC 20036
Phone: 202-223-5500
Fax: 202-296-0540
E-mail: oca@ocanatl.org

OCA NATIONAL ESSAY CONTEST

Contest for Asian Pacific American students between grades 9 and 12. First place $1000, second place $500, third place $300. Submit five copies of essay.

Award: Prize for use in freshman year; not renewable. *Number:* 3. *Amount:* $300–$1000.

Eligibility Requirements: Applicant must be Asian/Pacific Islander; high school student and planning to enroll or expecting to enroll at a two-year or four-year institution. Available to U.S. citizens.

Application Requirements: Applicant must enter a contest, essay. *Deadline:* April 18.

Contact: Keith McCallister, Director of Communications
Phone: 202-223-5500
Fax: 202-296-0540
E-mail: oca@ocanatl.org

OCA/UPS FOUNDATION GOLD MOUNTAIN SCHOLARSHIP

Scholarships for Asian Pacific Americans who are the first person in their immediate family to attend college. Must be entering first year of college in the upcoming fall. Winners attend OCA National Convention.

Award: Scholarship for use in freshman year; not renewable. *Number:* 8–15. *Amount:* $2000.

Eligibility Requirements: Applicant must be Asian/Pacific Islander; high school student and planning to enroll or expecting to enroll full-time at a two-year or four-year institution or university. Applicant must have 3.0 GPA or higher. Available to U.S. citizens.

Application Requirements: Application, essay, financial need analysis, resume, self-addressed stamped envelope, transcript. *Deadline:* April 18.

Contact: OCA-NPS Scholarship
Organization of Chinese Americans
1001 Connecticut Avenue, NW, Suite 601
Washington, DC 20036
Phone: 202-223-5500
Fax: 202-296-0540
E-mail: oca@ocanatl.org

OCA-AXA ACHIEVEMENT SCHOLARSHIP

A college achievement scholarship for Asian Pacific Americans entering their first year of college.

Award: Scholarship for use in freshman year; not renewable. *Number:* 6. *Amount:* $2000.

Eligibility Requirements: Applicant must be Asian/Pacific Islander; high school student and planning to enroll or expecting to enroll full-time at a two-year or four-year institution or university. Applicant must have 3.0 GPA or higher. Available to U.S. citizens.

Application Requirements: Application, essay, financial need analysis, self-addressed stamped envelope, transcript. *Deadline:* May 1.

Contact: OCA AXA Scholarship
Organization of Chinese Americans
1001 Connecticut Avenue, NW, Suite 601
Washington, DC 20036
Fax: 202-296-0540
E-mail: oca@ocanatl.org

OCA-SYSCO SCHOLARSHIP

Scholarship for Asian Pacific Americans who are financially disadvantaged and will be entering their first year of college.

Award: Scholarship for use in freshman year; not renewable. *Number:* 6. *Amount:* $2000.

Eligibility Requirements: Applicant must be Asian/Pacific Islander; high school student and planning to enroll or expecting to enroll full-time at a two-year or four-year institution or university. Applicant must have 3.0 GPA or higher. Available to U.S. citizens.

Application Requirements: Application, essay, financial need analysis, self-addressed stamped envelope, transcript. *Deadline:* May 1.

Contact: OCA-SYSCO Scholarship
Organization of Chinese Americans
1001 Connecticut Avenue, NW, Suite 601
Washington, DC 20036
Phone: 202-223-5500
E-mail: oca@ocanatl.org

OCA-VERIZON SCHOLARSHIP

Scholarships for Asian Pacific Americans who are financially disadvantaged and will be entering their first year of college.

Award: Scholarship for use in freshman year; not renewable. *Number:* 20–25. *Amount:* $1500–$2000.

Eligibility Requirements: Applicant must be Asian/Pacific Islander; high school student and planning to enroll or expecting to enroll full-time at a two-year or four-year institution or university. Applicant must have 3.0 GPA or higher. Available to U.S. citizens.

Application Requirements: Application, essay, financial need analysis, self-addressed stamped envelope, transcript. *Deadline:* May 1.

Contact: OCA-Verizon Scholarship
Organization of Chinese Americans
1001 Connecticut Avenue, NW, Suite 601
Washington, DC 20036
Phone: 202-223-5500
E-mail: oca@ocanatl.org

OSAGE SCHOLARSHIP FUND

MAE LASSLEY OSAGE SCHOLARSHIP FUND

Renewable awards to Osage Indian Tribe members who are members of the Roman Catholic Church. Must attend an accredited college or university as an undergraduate or graduate student on a full-time basis. Minimum 2.5 GPA required. Application deadline is April 15.

Award: Scholarship for use in freshman, sophomore, junior, senior, or graduate years; renewable. *Number:* 12–20. *Amount:* $500–$1000.

Eligibility Requirements: Applicant must be Roman Catholic; American Indian/Alaska Native and enrolled or expecting to enroll full-time at a two-year or four-year institution or university. Applicant must have 2.5 GPA or higher. Available to U.S. citizens.

Application Requirements: Application, financial need analysis, references, transcript, CDIB card. *Deadline:* April 15.

Contact: Sarah Jameson, Administrative Assistant
Osage Scholarship Fund
PO Box 690240
Tulsa, OK 74169-0240
Phone: 918-294-1904 Ext. 128
Fax: 918-294-0920
E-mail: sarah.jameson@dioceseoftulsa.org

OSAGE TRIBAL EDUCATION COMMITTEE
http://www.osagetribaleducation.com/

OSAGE TRIBAL EDUCATION COMMITTEE SCHOLARSHIP

Available for Osage Tribal members only. 150 to 250 renewable scholarship awards. Spring deadline: December 31. Fall deadline: July 1. Summer deadline: May 1.

Award: Scholarship for use in freshman, sophomore, junior, or senior years; renewable. *Number:* 150–250. *Amount:* $200–$400.

Eligibility Requirements: Applicant must be American Indian/Alaska Native and enrolled or expecting to enroll full or part-time at a two-year or four-year or technical institution or university. Available to U.S. citizens.

Application Requirements: Photo, references. *Deadline:* varies.

Contact: Cheryl Lewis, Business Manager
Osage Tribal Education Committee
4149 Highline Boulevard, Suite 380
Oklahoma City, OK 73108
Phone: 405-605-6051 Ext. 304
Fax: 405-605-6057

OSAGE TRIBAL EDUCATION DEPARTMENT
http://www.osagetribaleducation.com

OSAGE HIGHER EDUCATION GRANT

Award available only to those who have proof of Osage Indian descent. Must submit proof of financial need. Deadlines are August 1 for the Fall, December 31 for the Spring, and May 1 for Summer.

Award: Grant for use in freshman, sophomore, junior, senior, graduate, or postgraduate years; not renewable. *Number:* varies. *Amount:* $300–$1200.

Eligibility Requirements: Applicant must be American Indian/Alaska Native and enrolled or expecting to enroll full or part-time at a two-year or four-year institution or university. Available to U.S. citizens.

Application Requirements: Application, financial need analysis, transcript, verification of enrollment, proof of Osage Indian descent, copy of CDIB card. *Deadline:* varies.

Contact: Jennifer Holding, Scholarship Coordinator
Osage Tribal Education Department
HC 66, PO Box 900
Hominy, OK 74035
Phone: 800-390-6724
Fax: 918-287-2416
E-mail: jholding@osagetribe.org

PETER AND ALICE KOOMRUIAN FUND

PETER AND ALICE KOOMRUIAN ARMENIAN EDUCATION FUND

One-time award for students of Armenian descent to pursue postsecondary studies in any field at any accredited college or university in the U.S. Submit student identification and letter of enrollment. Must rank in upper third of class or have minimum GPA of 3.0.

Award: Scholarship for use in freshman, sophomore, junior, senior, graduate, or postgraduate years; not renewable. *Number:* 5–20. *Amount:* $1000–$2250.

Eligibility Requirements: Applicant must be of Armenian heritage and enrolled or expecting to enroll full-time at a two-year or four-year institution or university. Applicant must have 3.0 GPA or higher. Available to U.S. and non-U.S. citizens.

Application Requirements: Application, photo, references, self-addressed stamped envelope, transcript, school ID and school enrollment letter. *Deadline:* varies.

Contact: Terenik Koujakian, Awards Committee Member
Peter and Alice Koomruian Fund
PO Box 0268
Moorpark, CA 93020-0268
Phone: 818-990-7454
E-mail: terenikkoujakian@hotmail.com

PETER DOCTOR MEMORIAL INDIAN SCHOLARSHIP FOUNDATION, INC.

PETER DOCTOR MEMORIAL IROQUOIS SCHOLARSHIP

One-time award available to enrolled N.Y. State Iroquois Indian students. Must be sophomore level or above attending full-time in a postsecondary institution.

Award: Scholarship for use in sophomore, junior, senior, or graduate years; not renewable. *Number:* varies. *Amount:* $700–$1500.

Eligibility Requirements: Applicant must be American Indian/Alaska Native; enrolled or expecting to enroll full-time at a two-year or four-year or technical institution or university and resident of New York. Available to U.S. citizens.

Application Requirements: Application, autobiography, financial need analysis, references, tribal certification. *Deadline:* May 31.

Contact: Clara Hill, Treasurer
Peter Doctor Memorial Indian Scholarship Foundation, Inc.
PO Box 431
Basom, NY 14013
Phone: 716-542-2025
E-mail: cehill@wnynet.net

PHILIPINO-AMERICAN ASSOCIATION OF NEW ENGLAND   http://www.pamas.org/members.htm

BLESSED LEON OF OUR LADY OF THE ROSARY AWARD

Scholarship for high school student. Must be of Filipino descent and a resident of New England. Minimum GPA of 3.3 required.

Award: Scholarship for use in freshman year. *Amount:* up to $250.

Eligibility Requirements: Applicant must be Asian/Pacific Islander; high school student; planning to enroll or expecting to enroll at a two-year or four-year or technical institution or university and resident of Connecticut, Maine, Massachusetts, New Hampshire, Rhode Island, or Vermont. Available to U.S. citizens.

Application Requirements: Application, essay, references, transcript. *Deadline:* June 30.

Contact: Scholarship Committee
Philipino-American Association of New England
Quincy Post Office, PO Box 690372
Quincy, MA 02269-0372

CAPARANGA AWARD

Scholarship for a Filipino-American high school student who is active in the Filipino community and a resident of New England. Minimum GPA of 3.3 required

Award: Scholarship for use in freshman year. *Amount:* up to $250.

Eligibility Requirements: Applicant must be Asian/Pacific Islander; high school student; planning to enroll or expecting to enroll at a two-year or four-year or technical institution or university and resident of Connecticut, Maine, Massachusetts, New Hampshire, Rhode Island, or Vermont. Available to U.S. citizens.

Application Requirements: Application, references, transcript. *Deadline:* June 30.

Contact: Scholarship Committee
Philipino-American Association of New England
Quincy Post Office, PO Box 690372
Quincy, MA 02269-0372

DR. ALFRED AND SUSAN CHAN AWARD

Scholarship for a Filipino-American high school student who is a resident of New England. Minimum GPA of 3.3 required.

Award: Scholarship for use in freshman year. *Amount:* up to $250.

Eligibility Requirements: Applicant must be Asian/Pacific Islander; high school student; planning to enroll or expecting to enroll at a two-year or four-year or technical institution or university and resident of Connecticut, Maine, Massachusetts, New Hampshire, Rhode Island, or Vermont. Available to U.S. citizens.

Application Requirements: Application, essay, references, transcript. *Deadline:* June 30.

Contact: Philipino-American Association of New England
Quincy Post Office
PO Box 690372
Quincy, MA 02269-0372

PAMAS RESTRICTED SCHOLARSHIP AWARD

Award for high school seniors. Any sons or daughters of PAMAS members who are currently active in PAMAS projects and activities. Must be of Filipino descent and a resident of New England. Must have a GPA of 3.3 or better.

Award: Scholarship for use in freshman year. *Amount:* up to $500.

Eligibility Requirements: Applicant must be Asian/Pacific Islander; enrolled or expecting to enroll at an institution or university and resident of Connecticut, Maine, Massachusetts, New Hampshire, Rhode Island, or Vermont. Available to U.S. citizens.

Application Requirements: Application, essay, references, transcript. *Deadline:* June 30.

Contact: Scholarship Committee
Philipino-American Association of New England
Quincy Post Office, PO Box 690372
Quincy, MA 02269-0372

RAVENSCROFT FAMILY AWARD

Award for high school student who is active in the Filipino community. Must be of Filipino descent and a resident of New England. Minimum GPA of 3.3 required.

Award: Scholarship for use in freshman year. *Amount:* up to $250.

Eligibility Requirements: Applicant must be Asian/Pacific Islander; high school student; planning to enroll or expecting to enroll at a two-year or four-year or technical institution or university and resident of Connecticut, Maine, Massachusetts, New Hampshire, Rhode Island, or Vermont. Available to U.S. citizens.

Application Requirements: Application, essay, references, transcript. *Deadline:* June 30.

Contact: Scholarship Committee
Philipino-American Association of New England
Quincy Post Office, PO Box 690372
Quincy, MA 02269-0372

POLISH HERITAGE ASSOCIATION OF MARYLAND

DR KENNETH AND NANCY WILLIAMS SCHOLARSHIP

Scholarship available for study towards a baccalaureate degree in a college or university in the U.S. Must be of Polish descent (at least two Polish grandparents), a resident of Maryland, and a U.S. citizen. Application deadline is March 31.

Award: Scholarship for use in freshman, sophomore, junior, or senior years; not renewable. *Number:* 1. *Amount:* up to $1000.

Eligibility Requirements: Applicant must be of Polish heritage and enrolled or expecting to enroll full-time at a two-year institution or university. Available to U.S. citizens.

Application Requirements: Application, financial need analysis, references, transcript, copy of family's tax returns. *Deadline:* March 31.

Contact: Thomas Hollowak, Scholarship Committee Chair
Phone: 410-837-4268
E-mail: thollowak@ubalt.edu

DR. JOSEPHINE WTULICH MEMORIAL SCHOLARSHIP

Scholarship will be awarded to a student whose major is in the humanities, sociology, or anthropology. Must be of Polish descent (at least two Polish grandparents), a resident of Maryland, and a U.S. citizen. Application deadline is March 31.

Award: Scholarship for use in freshman, sophomore, junior, or senior years; not renewable. *Number:* 1. *Amount:* up to $1500.

Eligibility Requirements: Applicant must be of Polish heritage and enrolled or expecting to enroll full-time at a two-year institution or university. Available to U.S. citizens.

Application Requirements: Application, essay, interview, photo, references, test scores, transcript. *Deadline:* March 31.

Contact: Thomas Hollowak
   Phone: 410-837-4268
   E-mail: thollowak@ubalt.edu

EARL L. CAREY, JR. MEMORIAL SCHOLARSHIP

Scholarship available for study towards a baccalaureate degree in a college or university in the U.S. Must be of Polish descent (at least two Polish grandparents), a legal resident of Maryland, attending an accredited high school as a senior or a college or university in the U.S. Deadline is March 31

Award: Scholarship for use in freshman, sophomore, junior, or senior years; not renewable. *Number:* 1. *Amount:* up to $1500.

Eligibility Requirements: Applicant must be of Polish heritage and enrolled or expecting to enroll full-time at a two-year institution or university. Available to U.S. citizens.

Application Requirements: Application, essay, resume, transcript, copy of family's tax returns. *Deadline:* March 31.

Contact: Thomas Hollowak
   Phone: 410-837-4268
   E-mail: thollowak@ubalt.edu

LAURA GORALSKI MEMORIAL SCHOLARSHIP

Scholarship for study towards a baccalaureate degree in a college or university in the U.S. Must be of Polish descent (at least two Polish grandparents), a resident of Maryland, and a U.S. citizen. Application deadline is March 31.

Award: Scholarship for use in freshman, sophomore, junior, or senior years; not renewable. *Number:* 1. *Amount:* up to $1500.

Eligibility Requirements: Applicant must be of Polish heritage and enrolled or expecting to enroll full-time at a two-year institution or university. Available to U.S. citizens.

Application Requirements: Application, essay, financial need analysis, resume, transcript.

Contact: Thomas Hollowak, Scholarship Committee Chair
   Phone: 410-837-4268

POLISH HERITAGE SCHOLARSHIP

Scholarships given to individual of Polish descent (at least two Polish grandparents) who demonstrates academic excellence, financial need, and promotes their Polish Heritage. Must be a legal Maryland resident. Deadline is March 31.

Award: Scholarship for use in freshman, sophomore, junior, or senior years; not renewable. *Number:* 1. *Amount:* up to $1500.

Eligibility Requirements: Applicant must be of Polish heritage; enrolled or expecting to enroll full-time at a two-year or four-year institution or university and resident of Maryland. Applicant must have 3.0 GPA or higher. Available to U.S. citizens.

Application Requirements: Application, essay, financial need analysis, interview, photo, references, transcript, copy of family's tax returns. *Deadline:* March 31.

Contact: Victoria Leshinskie
   Phone: 410-962-8611
   E-mail: vleshinskie@anes.umm.edu

POLISH NATIONAL ALLIANCE   http://www.pna-znp.org

POLISH NATIONAL ALLIANCE SCHOLARSHIP AWARD

This program is awarded to Polish National Alliance members only. Must be a member for at least three years. Must currently be enrolled full-time in an accredited college as an undergraduate sophomore, junior or senior. Applicants with 3.0 GPA or greater preferred, but not required.

Award: Scholarship for use in sophomore, junior, or senior years; renewable. *Number:* 250. *Amount:* $500.

Eligibility Requirements: Applicant must be of Polish heritage and enrolled or expecting to enroll full-time at a four-year institution. Applicant must have 3.0 GPA or higher. Available to U.S. citizens.

Application Requirements: Application, photo, test scores, transcript. *Deadline:* April 15.

Contact: Teresa Abick, Vice President and Chair of Scholarship Program
   Polish National Alliance
   Education Department
   6100 North Cicero Avenue
   Chicago, IL 60646
   Phone: 773-286-0500
   Fax: 773-286-0842

PORTUGUESE FOUNDATION, INC.   http://www.pfict.org

PORTUGUESE FOUNDATION SCHOLARSHIP PROGRAM

Scholarship funds available through Foundation. Award based on need and scholastic achievement. Applicants must be Connecticut resident and of Portuguese descendant. Minimum 2.5 GPA required. Must be U.S. citizen.

Award: Scholarship for use in freshman, sophomore, junior, senior, or graduate years; not renewable. *Number:* 8. *Amount:* $2000.

Eligibility Requirements: Applicant must be of Portuguese heritage; enrolled or expecting to enroll full or part-time at a two-year or four-year or technical institution or university and resident of Connecticut. Applicant must have 2.5 GPA or higher. Available to U.S. citizens.

Application Requirements: Application, autobiography, driver's license, essay, financial need analysis, interview, photo, portfolio, resume, references, self-addressed stamped envelope, test scores, transcript. *Deadline:* March 15.

Contact: Jose P. Bravado, Secretary
   Portuguese Foundation, Inc.
   PO Box 331441
   West Hartford, CT 06133-1441
   Phone: 860-236-5514
   Fax: 860-236-5514

PRESBYTERIAN CHURCH (USA)   http://www.pcusa.org/financialaid

NATIVE AMERICAN EDUCATION GRANTS

Grants available for Native American students enrolled in an accredited institution as a full-time student. Must show financial need and proof of tribal membership.

Award: Grant for use in freshman, sophomore, junior, senior, graduate, or postgraduate years; renewable. *Number:* 10–125. *Amount:* $1500–$2500.

Eligibility Requirements: Applicant must be American Indian/Alaska Native and enrolled or expecting to enroll full-time at a two-year or four-year or technical institution or university. Applicant must have 2.5 GPA or higher. Available to U.S. citizens.

Application Requirements: Application, essay, financial need analysis, test scores, transcript, tribal membership. *Deadline:* June 30.

Contact: Laura A. Bryan, Program Assistant for Graduate Grant Programs
   Presbyterian Church (USA)
   Financial Aid for Studies, 100 Witherspoon Street, MO65
   Louisville, KY 40202-1396
   Phone: 888-728-7228 Ext. 5735
   E-mail: lbryan@ctr.pcusa.org

PUEBLO OF ISLETA, DEPARTMENT OF EDUCATION   http://www.isletaeducation.org

HIGHER EDUCATION SUPPLEMENTAL SCHOLARSHIP

Applicants must be students seeking a post secondary degree. The degree granting institution must be a nationally accredited vocational or post secondary institution, offering a certificate, associate, bachelors, masters or doctorate degree. Enrolled tribal members of the Isleta Pueblo may apply for this scholarship if they also apply for additional scholarships from different sources. Deadlines: Summer, April 1; Spring, October 1; Fall, July 1.

Award: Scholarship for use in freshman, sophomore, junior, senior, graduate, or postgraduate years; not renewable. *Number:* up to 150. *Amount:* $500–$7000.

Eligibility Requirements: Applicant must be American Indian/Alaska Native and enrolled or expecting to enroll full or part-time at a

Pueblo of Isleta, Department of Education (continued)

two-year or four-year or technical institution or university. Applicant must have 2.5 GPA or higher. Available to U.S. citizens.

Application Requirements: Application, financial need analysis, transcript, certificate of Indian blood, class schedule. *Deadline:* varies.

Contact: Joanna Garcia, Higher Education Director
Pueblo of Isleta, Department of Education
PO Box 1270
Isleta, NM 87022
Phone: 505-869-2680
Fax: 505-869-7690
E-mail: isletahighered@yahoo.com

PUEBLO OF SAN JUAN, DEPARTMENT OF EDUCATION
http://www.sanjuaned.org/

OHKAY OWINGEH TRIBAL SCHOLARSHIP OF THE PUEBLO OF SAN JUAN

Scholarship for members of the Pueblo of San Juan tribe only. Applicant must have applied for other scholarships and use this scholarship for supplemental funds. Minimum GPA of 2.0 is required. Must complete required number of hours of community service in the San Juan Pueblo. Call the Education Coordinator for deadlines and other information.

Award: Scholarship for use in freshman, sophomore, junior, senior, or graduate years; renewable. *Number:* 1–30. *Amount:* $250–$1000.

Eligibility Requirements: Applicant must be American Indian/Alaska Native; enrolled or expecting to enroll full or part-time at a two-year or four-year or technical institution or university and resident of New Mexico. Available to U.S. citizens.

Application Requirements: Application, transcript. *Deadline:* varies.

Contact: Elvie Aquino, Education Coordinator
Pueblo of San Juan, Department of Education
PO Box 1529
San Juan Pueblo, NM 87566
Phone: 505-852-3477
Fax: 505-852-3030
E-mail: psj_deptofed_ema@yahoo.com

POP'AY SCHOLARSHIP

Scholarship for members of Pueblo of San Juan tribe who are pursuing their first associate or baccalaureate degree. Applicants must have applied for other scholarships and use this scholarship for supplemental funds. Must complete a minimum of 20 hours of community service within the San Juan Pueblo. Must maintain minimum GPA of 2.0. Deadlines are December 30 for Spring, April 30 for Summer, and June 30 for Fall. Contact Education Coordinator for more information.

Award: Scholarship for use in freshman, sophomore, junior, or senior years; renewable. *Number:* up to 17. *Amount:* up to $2500.

Eligibility Requirements: Applicant must be American Indian/Alaska Native; enrolled or expecting to enroll full-time at a two-year or four-year institution or university and resident of New Mexico. Available to U.S. citizens.

Application Requirements: Application, transcript, letter of acceptance. *Deadline:* varies.

Contact: Elvie Aquino, Education Coordinator
Pueblo of San Juan, Department of Education
PO Box 1529
San Juan Pueblo, NM 87566
Phone: 505-852-3477
Fax: 505-852-3030
E-mail: psj_deptofed_ema@yahoo.com

RHODE ISLAND FOUNDATION
http://www.rifoundation.org

RAYMOND H. TROTT SCHOLARSHIP

One-time scholarships of $1000 is awarded to a minority student, who is a Rhode Island resident entering his/her senior year at an accredited college. Must plan to pursue a career in banking.

Award: Scholarship for use in senior year; not renewable. *Number:* 1. *Amount:* $1000.

Eligibility Requirements: Applicant must be American Indian/Alaska Native, Asian/Pacific Islander, Black (non-Hispanic), or Hispanic; enrolled or expecting to enroll full-time at a four-year institution or university and resident of Rhode Island. Available to U.S. citizens.

Application Requirements: Application, essay, transcript. *Deadline:* June 10.

Contact: Libby Monahan, Scholarship Coordinator
Rhode Island Foundation
1 Union Station
Providence, RI 02903
Phone: 401-274-4564
Fax: 401-272-1359
E-mail: libbym@rifoundation.org

RONALD MCDONALD HOUSE CHARITIES
http://www.rmhc.org

RHMC ASIAN STUDENTS INCREASING ACHIEVEMENT SCHOLARSHIP PROGRAM

One-time award for graduating high school senior with at least one parent of Asian origin. Must attend a two-year or four-year college full time. Award is based on academic achievement, financial need, community involvement and personal qualities. Must be from a geographic area served by the program. See Web site at http://www.rmhc.org for list of geographic regions, further details and scholarship application.

Award: Scholarship for use in freshman year; not renewable. *Number:* varies. *Amount:* up to $1000.

Eligibility Requirements: Applicant must be Asian/Pacific Islander; high school student and planning to enroll or expecting to enroll full-time at a two-year or four-year institution or university. Available to U.S. citizens.

Application Requirements: Application, financial need analysis, references, transcript. *Deadline:* February 1.

Contact: Palmer Moody, Director, RMHC
Ronald McDonald House Charities
1 Kroc Drive
Department 014
Oak Brook, IL 60523
Phone: 630-623-7048
E-mail: palmer.moody@med.com

RMHC/AFRICAN AMERICAN FUTURE ACHIEVERS SCHOLARSHIP PROGRAM

One-time award for graduating high school senior with at least one parent of African-American origin. Must attend a two-year or four-year college full time. Award is based on academic achievement, financial need, community involvement and personal qualities. Must be from a geographic area served by the program. See Web site at http://www.rmhc.org for list of geographic regions, further details and scholarship application.

Award: Scholarship for use in freshman, sophomore, junior, or senior years; not renewable. *Number:* varies. *Amount:* up to $1000.

Eligibility Requirements: Applicant must be Black (non-Hispanic); high school student and planning to enroll or expecting to enroll full-time at a two-year or four-year institution or university. Available to U.S. citizens.

Application Requirements: Application, financial need analysis, references, transcript. *Deadline:* February 1.

Contact: Application available at Web site.

RYU FAMILY FOUNDATION, INC.

SEOL BONG SCHOLARSHIP

One-time award to support and advance education and research. Must be Korean residing in DE, PA, NJ, NY, CT, VT, RI, NH, MA or ME. Minimum 3.5 GPA required. Deadline is November 15.

Award: Scholarship for use in freshman, sophomore, junior, senior, or graduate years; not renewable. *Number:* 25. *Amount:* $1500–$2000.

Eligibility Requirements: Applicant must be of Korean heritage; enrolled or expecting to enroll full-time at a four-year institution or university; resident of Connecticut, Delaware, Maine, Massachusetts, New Hampshire, New Jersey, New York, Pennsylvania, Rhode Island, or Vermont and studying in Connecticut, Delaware, Maine, Massachusetts, New Hampshire, New Jersey, New York, Pennsylvania,

Rhode Island, or Vermont. Applicant must have 3.5 GPA or higher. Available to U.S. and non-Canadian citizens.

Application Requirements: Application, essay, photo, references, test scores, transcript. *Deadline:* November 15.

Contact: Jenny Kang
Ryu Family Foundation, Inc.
901 Murray Road
East Hanover, NJ 07936
Phone: 973-560-9696
Fax: 973-560-0661
E-mail: jennyk@toplineus.com

SAINT ANDREW'S SOCIETY OF THE STATE OF NEW YORK   http://www.standrewsny.org

ST. ANDREWS SCHOLARSHIP

Scholarship for senior undergraduate students who will obtain a bachelor's degree from an accredited college or university in the spring and can demonstrate the significance of studying in Scotland. Proof of application to their selected school will be required for finalists. Applicant must be of Scottish descent and preferably reside within 250-mile radius of New York.

Award: Scholarship for use in senior year. *Number:* 2. *Amount:* up to $15,000.

Eligibility Requirements: Applicant must be of Scottish heritage and enrolled or expecting to enroll full-time at an institution or university. Available to U.S. citizens.

Application Requirements: Application, applicant must enter a contest. *Deadline:* December 15.

Contact: Kimberly Howland, Office Manager
Saint Andrew's Society of the State of New York
150 East 55th Street
New York, NY 10022
Phone: 212-223-4248
Fax: 212-223-0748
E-mail: office@standrewsny.org

SALVADORAN AMERICAN LEADERSHIP AND EDUCATIONAL FUND   http://www.salef.org

FULFILLING OUR DREAMS SCHOLARSHIP FUND

Up to sixty scholarships ranging from $500-$2500 will be awarded to students who come from a Latino heritage. Must have a 2.5 GPA. See Web site for more details: http://www.salef.org

Award: Scholarship for use in freshman, sophomore, junior, senior, graduate, or postgraduate years; not renewable. *Number:* 50–60. *Amount:* $500–$2500.

Eligibility Requirements: Applicant must be of Hispanic or Latin American/Caribbean heritage; enrolled or expecting to enroll full-time at a two-year or four-year institution or university; resident of California and studying in California. Applicant must have 2.5 GPA or higher. Available to citizens of countries other than the U.S. or Canada.

Application Requirements: Application, essay, financial need analysis, interview, photo, resume, references, self-addressed stamped envelope, test scores, transcript. *Deadline:* June 30.

Contact: Mayra Soriano, Educational & Youth Programs Manager
Salvadoran American Leadership and Educational Fund
Salvadoran American Leadership and Educational Fund (SALEF),
ôFulfilling Our Dreamsö Scholarship Fund, 1625 West Olympic Boulevard, Suite 718
Los Angeles, CA 90015
Phone: 213-480-1052
Fax: 213-487-2530
E-mail: msoriano@salef.org

SANTO DOMINGO SCHOLARSHIP PROGRAM

SANTO DOMINGO SCHOLARSHIP

Fourth degree Santo Domingo-enrolled with tribe. Letter of acceptance from high school or college. For any tribal member to have the opportunity to get an undergraduate degree. 2.0 GPA required. If full time 12 credits or more must be completed each semester. Amount is need based. Supported by Bureau of Indian Affairs. Deadlines: March 1 for Fall; November 1 for Spring.

Award: Scholarship for use in freshman, sophomore, junior, or senior years; renewable. *Number:* up to 60. *Amount:* up to $1000.

Eligibility Requirements: Applicant must be American Indian/Alaska Native and enrolled or expecting to enroll full or part-time at a two-year or four-year or technical institution or university. Available to U.S. citizens.

Application Requirements: Application, essay, references, transcript, certificate of Indian blood. *Deadline:* varies.

Contact: Maria Crespin, Education
Santo Domingo Scholarship Program
PO Box 99
Santo Domingo, NM 87052
Phone: 505-465-2214
Fax: 505-465-2688
E-mail: kewaeduc@yahoo.com

SCOTTISH RITE CHARITABLE FOUNDATION OF CANADA   http://www.srcf.ca

SCOTTISH RITE CHARITABLE FOUNDATION COLLEGE BURSARIES
• See page 550

SEMINOLE TRIBE OF FLORIDA   http://www.seminoletribe.com

SEMINOLE TRIBE OF FLORIDA BILLY L. CYPRESS SCHOLARSHIP PROGRAM

The Seminole Tribe of Florida awards full scholarships to applicants who meet membership requirements (must have a membership number). Must maintain a 2.0 GPA with 12 semester credit hours earned each semester. Must be a member of the Seminole Tribe of Florida.

Award: Scholarship for use in freshman, sophomore, junior, senior, graduate, or postgraduate years; renewable. *Amount:* varies.

Eligibility Requirements: Applicant must be American Indian/Alaska Native and enrolled or expecting to enroll full or part-time at a two-year or four-year institution or university. Available to U.S. citizens.

Application Requirements: Application, transcript, acceptance letter from university. *Deadline:* varies.

Contact: Linda Iley, Higher Education Advisor
Seminole Tribe of Florida
3100 North 63rd Avenue
Hollywood, FL 33024-2153
Phone: 954-989-6840 Ext. 1311
E-mail: eiley@semtribe.com

SENECA NATION OF INDIANS   http://www.sni.org

SENECA NATION HIGHER EDUCATION PROGRAM

Renewable award for enrolled Senecas of the Cattaraugus and Allegany Indian reservations who are in need of financial assistance. Application deadlines: Fall deadline is July 1; Spring deadline is December 1; Summer deadline is May 1. Must be degree seeking and enrolled in a two-year college, four-year college or university.

Award: Scholarship for use in freshman, sophomore, junior, senior, graduate, or postgraduate years; renewable. *Number:* varies. *Amount:* $3000–$8000.

Eligibility Requirements: Applicant must be American Indian/Alaska Native and enrolled or expecting to enroll full or part-time at a two-year or four-year institution or university. Applicant must have 2.5 GPA or higher. Available to U.S. and non-U.S. citizens.

Application Requirements: Application, essay, financial need analysis, references, transcript, tribal certification. *Deadline:* varies.

Contact: Debra M. Hoag, Higher Education Coordinator
Seneca Nation of Indians
PO Box 231
Salamanca, NY 14779
Phone: 716-945-1790 Ext. 3103
Fax: 716-945-7170
E-mail: snieduc@localnet.com

SOCIETY OF MEXICAN AMERICAN ENGINEERS AND SCIENTISTS
http://www.maes-natl.org

PADRINO SCHOLARSHIPS

Scholarships to assist Hispanic students in completing their higher education goals.

Award: Scholarship for use in freshman, sophomore, junior, senior, or graduate years. *Amount:* up to $3000.

Eligibility Requirements: Applicant must be Hispanic and enrolled or expecting to enroll full-time at a four-year institution or university. Available to U.S. citizens.

Application Requirements: Application, applicant must enter a contest, financial need analysis, references, transcript. *Deadline:* varies.

Contact: Society of Mexican American Engineers and Scientists
711 West Bay Area Boulevard, Suite 206
Webster, TX 77598-4051

SONS OF ITALY FOUNDATION
http://www.osia.org

SONS OF ITALY NATIONAL LEADERSHIP GRANTS COMPETITION GENERAL SCHOLARSHIPS

Scholarships for undergraduate or graduate students who are U.S. citizens of Italian descent. Must demonstrate academic excellence. For more details see Web site http://www.osia.org

Award: Scholarship for use in freshman, sophomore, junior, senior, or graduate years; not renewable. *Number:* 10–13. *Amount:* $4000–$25,000.

Eligibility Requirements: Applicant must be of Italian heritage and enrolled or expecting to enroll full-time at a four-year institution or university. Available to U.S. citizens.

Application Requirements: Application, essay, resume, references, test scores, transcript. *Fee:* $30. *Deadline:* February 28.

Contact: National Leadership Grant Competition
Sons of Italy Foundation
219 East Street, NE
Washington, DC 20002

SONS OF ITALY NATIONAL LEADERSHIP GRANTS COMPETITION HENRY SALVATORI SCHOLARSHIPS

Scholarships for collegebound high school seniors who demonstrate exceptional leadership, distinguished scholarship, and a deep understanding and respect for the principles upon which our nation was founded: liberty, freedom, and equality. Must be a U.S. citizen of Italian descent. For more details see Web site: http://www.osia.org

Award: Scholarship for use in freshman year; not renewable. *Number:* 1. *Amount:* $5000.

Eligibility Requirements: Applicant must be of Italian heritage; high school student and planning to enroll or expecting to enroll full-time at a four-year institution or university. Available to U.S. citizens.

Application Requirements: Application, essay, resume, references, test scores, transcript. *Fee:* $30. *Deadline:* February 28.

Contact: National Leadership Grant Competition
Sons of Italy Foundation
219 East Street, NE
Washington, DC 20002

SONS OF ITALY NATIONAL LEADERSHIP GRANTS COMPETITION LANGUAGE SCHOLARSHIP

Scholarships for undergraduate students in their junior or senior year of study who are majoring in Italian language studies. Must be a U.S. citizen of Italian descent. For more details see Web site: http://www.osia.org

Award: Scholarship for use in junior or senior years; not renewable. *Number:* 1. *Amount:* $10,000.

Eligibility Requirements: Applicant must be of Italian heritage and enrolled or expecting to enroll full-time at a four-year institution or university. Available to U.S. citizens.

Application Requirements: Application, essay, resume, references, test scores, transcript. *Fee:* $30. *Deadline:* February 28.

Contact: National Leadership Grant Competition
Sons of Italy Foundation
219 East Street, NE
Washington, DC 20002

SONS OF NORWAY FOUNDATION
http://www.sofn.com

ASTRID G. CATES AND MYRTLE BEINHAUER SCHOLARSHIP FUNDS
• See page 515

SRP/NAVAJO GENERATING STATION
http://www.srpnet.com

NAVAJO GENERATING STATION NAVAJO SCHOLARSHIP

SRP at the Navajo Generating Station (NGS) is offering scholarships to Navajo college students. The competitively awarded scholarships may be used at any accredited college or university. Priority is given to math, engineering, and environmental studies. Must be an enrolled member of the Navajo Nation.

Award: Scholarship for use in freshman, sophomore, junior, or senior years; renewable. *Number:* 1–10. *Amount:* $1000.

Eligibility Requirements: Applicant must be American Indian/Alaska Native and enrolled or expecting to enroll full-time at a four-year institution or university. Applicant must have 3.0 GPA or higher. Available to U.S. citizens.

Application Requirements: Application, financial need analysis, resume, references, transcript, statement of goals. *Deadline:* April 30.

Contact: Linda Dawavendewa, HR Coordinator
SRP/Navajo Generating Station
PO Box 850
Page, AZ 86040
Phone: 928-645-6539
Fax: 928-645-7295
E-mail: ljdwave@srp.com

ST. ANDREW'S SOCIETY OF WASHINGTON, DC
http://www.saintandrewsociety.org

DONALD MALCOLM MACARTHUR SCHOLARSHIP

One-time award is available for U.S. students to study in Scotland or students from Scotland to study in the U.S. Special attention will be given to applicants whose work would demonstrably contribute to enhanced knowledge of Scottish history or culture. Must be a college junior, senior, or graduate student to apply. Need for financial assistance and academic record considered. Visit Web site for details and application: http://www.thecapitalscot.com/standrew/scholarships.html.

Award: Scholarship for use in junior, senior, or graduate years; not renewable. *Number:* 1. *Amount:* up to $2500.

Eligibility Requirements: Applicant must be of Scottish heritage; enrolled or expecting to enroll full-time at a four-year institution or university and resident of Delaware, District of Columbia, Maryland, New Jersey, North Carolina, Pennsylvania, Virginia, or Wisconsin. Available to U.S. and non-U.S. citizens.

Application Requirements: Application, essay, financial need analysis, references, self-addressed stamped envelope. *Deadline:* May 1.

Contact: T. J. Holland, Chairman, Scholarship Committee
St. Andrew's Society of Washington, DC
1443 Laurel Hill Road
Vienna, VA 22182-1711
E-mail: tjholland@wmalumni.com

STATE OF NORTH DAKOTA
http://www.ndus.nodak.edu

NORTH DAKOTA INDIAN SCHOLARSHIP PROGRAM

Assists Native-American North Dakota residents in obtaining a college education. Priority given to full-time undergraduate students and those having a 3.5 GPA or higher. Certification of tribal enrollment required. For use at North Dakota institution.

Award: Scholarship for use in freshman, sophomore, junior, senior, or graduate years; renewable. *Number:* 150–170. *Amount:* $500–$2000.

Eligibility Requirements: Applicant must be American Indian/Alaska Native; enrolled or expecting to enroll at a two-year or four-year institution or university; resident of North Dakota and studying in North Dakota. Applicant must have 3.5 GPA or higher. Available to U.S. citizens.

Application Requirements: Application, financial need analysis, transcript, proof of tribal enrollment, budget completed by a financial aid officer at the institution being attended. *Deadline:* July 15.

Contact: Rhonda Schauer, Coordinator of American Indian Higher Education
State of North Dakota
600 East Boulevard Avenue, Department 215
Bismarck, ND 58505-0230
Phone: 701-328-9661

STEVEN KNEZEVICH TRUST

STEVEN KNEZEVICH GRANT

One-time grant for students of Serbian descent. Award not restricted to citizens of the U.S. Amount of award varies. Applicants must be attending an accredited institution of higher learning. Grant will be applied toward student's spring semester. To receive additional information and the application itself, applicant must send SASE, along with proof of Serbian descent.

Award: Grant for use in freshman, sophomore, junior, senior, or graduate years; not renewable. *Number:* varies. *Amount:* $100–$800.

Eligibility Requirements: Applicant must be of Croatian/Serbian heritage and enrolled or expecting to enroll full or part-time at a two-year or four-year or technical institution or university. Available to U.S. and non-U.S. citizens.

Application Requirements: Application, self-addressed stamped envelope, transcript, proof of Serbian heritage. *Deadline:* November 30.

Contact: Stanley Hack, Trustee
Steven Knezevich Trust
9830 North Courtland Drive
Mequon, WI 53092-6052
Phone: 262-241-5663
Fax: 262-241-5645

SWEDISH INSTITUTE/SVENSKA INSTITUTET
http://www.sweden.se

VISBY PROGRAM: HIGHER EDUCATION AND RESEARCH

Scholarships to pursue studies in Sweden are available to citizens of Baltic countries, Belarus, and Ukraine. For more details see Web site: http://www.si.se

Award: Scholarship for use in freshman, sophomore, junior, senior, or graduate years; not renewable. *Number:* varies. *Amount:* $7500–$9000.

Eligibility Requirements: Applicant must be of Latvian, Lithuanian, Polish, Russian, or Ukrainian heritage and enrolled or expecting to enroll at a four-year institution or university. Available to citizens of countries other than the U.S. or Canada.

Application Requirements: Application. *Deadline:* varies.

Contact: Swedish Institute/Svenska Institutet
The Swedish Institute, Box 7434
Stockholm SE-103 91
Sweden
Fax: 46-8-207-248
E-mail: grant@si.se

SWISS BENEVOLENT SOCIETY

CLEMENT AND FRIEDA AMSTUTZ SCHOLARSHIP

Scholarships are available to students who are residents of the greater San Francisco Bay area and of Swiss descent. Education may be in any field of endeavor at any accredited university or college in the U.S.

Award: Scholarship for use in sophomore, junior, or senior years; not renewable. *Number:* 1.

Eligibility Requirements: Applicant must be of Swiss heritage and enrolled or expecting to enroll full-time at a four-year institution or university. Applicant must have 3.0 GPA or higher. Available to U.S. citizens.

Application Requirements: Application, references, test scores, transcript. *Deadline:* April 30.

Contact: Program Coordinator
Swiss Benevolent Society
456 Montgomery Street, Suite 1500
San Francisco, CA 94104-1233

GENERAL FUND SCHOLARSHIPS

Scholarships for students who are residents of the greater San Francisco Bay area and of Swiss descent. Education may be in any field of endeavor at any accredited university or college in the U.S. Minimum GPA of 3.2 for senior high school, 2.75 for undergraduate, 3.0 for graduate.

Award: Scholarship for use in freshman, sophomore, junior, senior, or graduate years; not renewable. *Number:* 1.

Eligibility Requirements: Applicant must be of Swiss heritage; enrolled or expecting to enroll at a four-year institution or university and resident of California. Available to U.S. citizens.

Application Requirements: Application, financial need analysis, references, transcript. *Deadline:* April 30.

Contact: Program Coordinator
Swiss Benevolent Society
456 Montgomery Street, Suite 1500
San Francisco, CA 94104-1233

SWISS BENEVOLENT SOCIETY OF CHICAGO
http://www.sbschicago.org/

SWISS BENEVOLENT SOCIETY OF CHICAGO SCHOLARSHIPS

Renewable scholarship for full-time students of documented Swiss descent. College students need a 3.5 GPA. High school students need a 26 on ACT or 1,050 on SAT. Must live in Illinois or southern Wisconsin. Applications may be requested after December 15.

Award: Scholarship for use in freshman, sophomore, junior, or senior years; renewable. *Number:* 30. *Amount:* $750–$2500.

Eligibility Requirements: Applicant must be of Swiss heritage; enrolled or expecting to enroll full-time at a four-year institution or university and resident of Illinois or Wisconsin. Applicant must have 3.5 GPA or higher. Available to U.S. citizens.

Application Requirements: Application, essay, self-addressed stamped envelope, test scores, transcript. *Deadline:* March 15.

Contact: Franziska Lys, Chair
Swiss Benevolent Society of Chicago
PO Box 2137
Chicago, IL 60690-2137
E-mail: education@sbschicago.org

SWISS BENEVOLENT SOCIETY OF NEW YORK
http://www.swissbenevolentny.com

MEDICUS STUDENT EXCHANGE

One-time award to students of Swiss nationality or parentage. U.S. residents study in Switzerland and Swiss residents study in the U.S. Awards to undergraduates are based on merit and need; those to graduates based only on merit. Open to all U.S. residents. Must be proficient in foreign language of instruction.

Award: Grant for use in freshman, sophomore, junior, senior, or graduate years; not renewable. *Number:* 1–5. *Amount:* $2000–$10,000.

Eligibility Requirements: Applicant must be of Swiss heritage; enrolled or expecting to enroll full-time at a four-year institution or university and must have an interest in foreign language. Applicant must have 3.5 GPA or higher. Available to U.S. and non-Canadian citizens.

Application Requirements: Application, financial need analysis, references, test scores, transcript. *Deadline:* March 31.

Swiss Benevolent Society of New York (continued)

Contact: Scholarship Committee
Swiss Benevolent Society of New York
500 Fifth Avenue, Room 1800
New York, NY 10110
Phone: 212-246-0655
Fax: 212-246-1366

PELLEGRINI SCHOLARSHIP GRANTS

Award to students who have a minimum 3.0 GPA, and show financial need. Must submit proof of Swiss nationality or descent. Must be a resident of Connecticut, Delaware, New Jersey, New York, or Pennsylvania. Fifty grants of up to $2500.

Award: Grant for use in freshman, sophomore, junior, senior, or graduate years; not renewable. *Number:* 50. *Amount:* $500–$2500.

Eligibility Requirements: Applicant must be of Swiss heritage; enrolled or expecting to enroll full or part-time at a two-year or four-year or technical institution or university and resident of Connecticut, Delaware, New Jersey, New York, or Pennsylvania. Applicant must have 3.0 GPA or higher. Available to U.S. and non-Canadian citizens.

Application Requirements: Application, financial need analysis, references, test scores, transcript. *Deadline:* March 31.

Contact: Scholarship Committee
Swiss Benevolent Society of New York
500 Fifth Avenue, Room 1800
New York, NY 10110
Phone: 212-246-0655
Fax: 212-246-1366

TERRY FOX HUMANITARIAN AWARD PROGRAM   http://www.terryfox.org

TERRY FOX HUMANITARIAN AWARD

Award granted to Canadian students entering postsecondary education. Criteria includes commitment to voluntary humanitarian work, courage in overcoming obstacles, excellence in academics, fitness and amateur sports. Must also show involvement in extracurricular activities. Value of award is CAN$7000 awarded annually for maximum of four years. Must be no older than 25.

Award: Scholarship for use in sophomore or junior years; renewable. *Number:* 20. *Amount:* $6282.

Eligibility Requirements: Applicant must be Canadian citizen; age 25 or under and enrolled or expecting to enroll full-time at a two-year or four-year or technical institution or university.

Application Requirements: Application, references, self-addressed stamped envelope, transcript. *Deadline:* February 1.

Contact: W. Lorne Davis, Executive Director
Terry Fox Humanitarian Award Program
Simon Fraser University
8888 University Drive
Burnaby V5A 1S6
Canada
Phone: 604-291-3057
Fax: 604-291-3311
E-mail: terryfox@sfu.ca

TEXAS BLACK BAPTIST SCHOLARSHIP COMMITTEE   http://www.bgct.org

TEXAS BLACK BAPTIST SCHOLARSHIP

Renewable award for Texas resident attending a Baptist educational institution in Texas. Must be of African-American descent with a minimum 2.0 GPA. Must be a member in good standing of a Baptist church.

Award: Scholarship for use in freshman, sophomore, junior, or senior years; renewable. *Number:* varies. *Amount:* $800.

Eligibility Requirements: Applicant must be Baptist; Black (non-Hispanic); age 18; enrolled or expecting to enroll full or part-time at a two-year or four-year institution or university; resident of Texas and studying in Texas. Available to U.S. citizens.

Application Requirements: Application, autobiography, financial need analysis, interview, photo, portfolio, resume, references, test scores, transcript. *Deadline:* Continuous.

Contact: Michael A. Evans, Sr., Director of African American Ministries
Texas Black Baptist Scholarship Committee
333 North Washington, Suite 340 N
Dallas, TX 75246-1798
Phone: 214-828-5130
Fax: 214-828-5284
E-mail: robinson@bgct.org

THE ASIAN REPORTER   http://www.arfoundation.net

ASIAN REPORTER SCHOLARSHIP

Scholarships available to students of Asian descent. Must be a resident of Washington or Oregon and attend school full-time in either state. Must have a minimum 3.0 GPA and demonstrate involvement in community or school related activities as well as financial need. Applicants must be a graduating high school student or current college student.

Award: Scholarship for use in freshman, sophomore, junior, or senior years. *Number:* 4. *Amount:* $500–$1000.

Eligibility Requirements: Applicant must be Asian/Pacific Islander; enrolled or expecting to enroll full-time at a four-year institution or university; resident of Oregon or Washington and studying in Oregon or Washington. Applicant must have 3.0 GPA or higher. Available to U.S. citizens.

Application Requirements: Application, driver's license, essay, financial need analysis, photo, references, transcript. *Deadline:* March 15.

Contact: Program Director
The Asian Reporter
922 North Killingsworth Street
Suite 1A
Portland, OR 97217
Phone: 503-283-4440
Fax: 503-283-4445
E-mail: arfoundation@asianreporter.com

THURGOOD MARSHALL SCHOLARSHIP FUND   http://www.thurgoodmarshallfund.org

NEW HORIZONS SCHOLARSHIP FUND
• See page 566

TRIANGLE NATIVE AMERICAN SOCIETY   http://www.tnasweb.org

TRIANGLE NATIVE AMERICAN SOCIETY SCHOLARSHIP FUND

The TNAS Scholarship is for any state or federally recognized U.S. Native-American rising sophomore, junior, or senior at any one of the 16 University of North Carolina system schools. Minimum GPA is 2.5. Must be a resident of North Carolina.

Award: Scholarship for use in sophomore, junior, or senior years; not renewable. *Number:* 1–3. *Amount:* $500–$1000.

Eligibility Requirements: Applicant must be American Indian/Alaska Native; enrolled or expecting to enroll full-time at a four-year institution or university; resident of North Carolina and studying in North Carolina. Applicant must have 2.5 GPA or higher. Available to U.S. citizens.

Application Requirements: Application, essay, references, transcript, proof of Native American ancestry. *Deadline:* June 10.

Contact: Alisa Hunt-Lowery, Scholarship Chair
Triangle Native American Society
PO Box 26841
Raleigh, NC 27611
Phone: 919-553-7449
E-mail: tnasscholarship@tnasweb.org

UKRAINIAN FRATERNAL ASSOCIATION
http://members.tripod.com/~ufa_home

UKRAINIAN FRATERNAL ASSOCIATION EUGENE R. AND ELINOR R. KOTUR SCHOLARSHIP TRUST FUND

Award for students of Ukrainian ancestry who are enrolled in selected colleges and universities at sophomore, junior, or senior level. Deadline is May 31.

Award: Scholarship for use in sophomore, junior, or senior years; renewable. *Number:* varies.

Eligibility Requirements: Applicant must be of Ukrainian heritage and enrolled or expecting to enroll full-time at a four-year institution or university. Available to U.S. citizens.

Application Requirements: Application, autobiography, photo, references, transcript. *Deadline:* May 31.

Contact: Christina Shablovsky, Supreme Secretary
Ukrainian Fraternal Association
371 North 9th Avenue
Scranton, PA 18504-2005
Phone: 570-342-0937

UKRAINIAN FRATERNAL ASSOCIATION IVAN FRANKO SCHOLARSHIP FUND

Award for senior in high school or student attending accredited university or college. Must have been member of Ukrainian Fraternal Association for at least two years. Must write essay on topic chosen by Scholarship Commission. Submit recommendation. Deadline is May 31.

Award: Scholarship for use in freshman, sophomore, junior, or senior years; not renewable. *Number:* 3. *Amount:* $500–$1000.

Eligibility Requirements: Applicant must be of Ukrainian heritage and enrolled or expecting to enroll full or part-time at a four-year institution or university. Available to U.S. and Canadian citizens.

Application Requirements: Application, autobiography, essay, financial need analysis, photo, references, transcript. *Deadline:* May 31.

Contact: Christine Shablovsky, Supreme Secretary
Ukrainian Fraternal Association
371 North 9th Avenue
Scranton, PA 18504-2005
Phone: 570-342-0937

UKRAINIAN FRATERNAL ASSOCIATION STUDENT AID

Award for students of Ukrainian ancestry who have been a member in good standing of the Ukrainian Fraternal Association for at least two years. Must have completed one year of college and have minimum GPA of 2.0. Aid is awarded over two years: $300 for the first year and $300 for the second year.

Award: Scholarship for use in sophomore, junior, or senior years; not renewable. *Number:* varies. *Amount:* up to $300.

Eligibility Requirements: Applicant must be of Ukrainian heritage and enrolled or expecting to enroll at a four-year institution. Available to U.S. citizens.

Application Requirements: Application, autobiography, photo, references, transcript. *Deadline:* May 31.

Contact: Christine Shablovsky, Supreme Secretary
Ukrainian Fraternal Association
371 North 9th Avenue
Scranton, PA 18504-2005
Phone: 570-342-0937

UNICO NATIONAL, INC
http://www.unico.org

MAJOR DON S. GENTILE SCHOLARSHIP

Scholarship available to graduating high school senior of Italian descent. Applicant must reside and attend high school within the corporate limits or adjoining suburbs of a city wherein an active chapter of UNICO National is located. Application must be signed by student's principal and properly certified by sponsoring Chapter President and Chapter Secretary. Must have letter of endorsement from President or Scholarship Chairperson of sponsoring Chapter.

Award: Scholarship for use in freshman, sophomore, junior, or senior years; renewable. *Number:* 1. *Amount:* up to $1500.

Eligibility Requirements: Applicant must be of Italian heritage; high school student and planning to enroll or expecting to enroll at a four-year institution. Available to U.S. citizens.

Application Requirements: Application, financial need analysis, references, transcript. *Deadline:* varies.

Contact: UNICO National, Inc
UNICO National, Inc
271 US Highway 46 West, Suite A-108
Fairfield, NJ 07004
Phone: 973-808-0035
Fax: 973-808-0043

WILLIAM C. DAVINI SCHOLARSHIP

Scholarship available to graduating high school senior of Italian descent. Applicant must reside and attend high school within the corporate limits or adjoining suburbs of a city wherein an active chapter of UNICO National is located. Application must be signed by student's principal and properly certified by sponsoring Chapter President and Chapter Secretary. Must have letter of endorsement from President or Scholarship Chairperson of sponsoring Chapter.

Award: Scholarship for use in freshman, sophomore, junior, or senior years; renewable. *Number:* 1. *Amount:* up to $1500.

Eligibility Requirements: Applicant must be of Italian heritage; high school student and planning to enroll or expecting to enroll at a four-year institution. Available to U.S. citizens.

Application Requirements: Application, financial need analysis, references, transcript. *Deadline:* varies.

Contact: UNICO National, Inc
UNICO National, Inc
271 US Highway 46 West, Suite A-108
Fairfield, NJ 07004
Phone: 973-808-0035
Fax: 973-808-0043

UNITED METHODIST CHURCH
http://www.umc.org

UNITED METHODIST CHURCH ETHNIC SCHOLARSHIP

Awards for minority students pursuing undergraduate degree. Must have been certified members of the United Methodist Church for one year. Proof of membership and pastor's statement required. One-time award but is renewable by application each year. Minimum 2.5 GPA required.

Award: Scholarship for use in freshman, sophomore, junior, or senior years; not renewable. *Number:* 430–500. *Amount:* $800–$1000.

Eligibility Requirements: Applicant must be Methodist; American Indian/Alaska Native, Asian/Pacific Islander, Black (non-Hispanic), or Hispanic and enrolled or expecting to enroll full-time at a two-year or four-year institution or university. Applicant must have 2.5 GPA or higher. Available to U.S. and non-Canadian citizens.

Application Requirements: Application, essay, references, transcript, membership proof, pastor's statement. *Deadline:* May 1.

Contact: Patti J. Zimmerman, Scholarships Administrator
United Methodist Church
PO Box 340007
Nashville, TN 37203-0007
Phone: 615-340-7344
E-mail: pzimmer@gbhem.org

UNITED METHODIST CHURCH HISPANIC, ASIAN, AND NATIVE AMERICAN SCHOLARSHIP

Award for members of United Methodist Church who are Hispanic, Asian, Native-American, or Pacific Islander college juniors, seniors, or graduate students. Need membership proof and pastor's letter. Minimum 2.8 GPA required.

Award: Scholarship for use in freshman, sophomore, junior, senior, or graduate years; not renewable. *Number:* 200–250. *Amount:* $1000–$3000.

Eligibility Requirements: Applicant must be Methodist; American Indian/Alaska Native, Asian/Pacific Islander, or Hispanic and enrolled or expecting to enroll full-time at a four-year institution or university. Available to U.S. citizens.

Application Requirements: Application, essay, references, transcript, membership proof, pastor's letter. *Deadline:* April 1.

United Methodist Church (continued)

Contact: Patti J. Zimmerman, Scholarships Administrator
United Methodist Church
PO Box 340007
Nashville, TN 37203-0007
Phone: 615-340-7344
E-mail: pzimmer@gbhem.org

UNITED METHODIST YOUTH ORGANIZATION
http://www.umyouth.org

RICHARD S. SMITH SCHOLARSHIP

Open to racial/ethnic minority youth only. Must be a United Methodist Youth who has been active in local church for at least one year prior to application. Must be a graduating senior in high school (who maintained at least a "C" average) entering the first year of undergraduate study and be pursuing a "church-related" career.

Award: Scholarship for use in freshman year; not renewable. *Number:* 1–2. *Amount:* up to $1000.

Eligibility Requirements: Applicant must be Methodist; American Indian/Alaska Native, Asian/Pacific Islander, Black (non-Hispanic), or Hispanic; high school student and planning to enroll or expecting to enroll full-time at an institution or university. Available to U.S. citizens.

Application Requirements: Application, essay, financial need analysis, transcript, certification of church membership. *Deadline:* June 1.

Contact: Grants Coordinator, Division on Ministries with Young People, General Board of Discipleship
United Methodist Youth Organization
PO Box 340003
Nashville, TN 37203-0003

UNITED NEGRO COLLEGE FUND
http://www.uncf.org

ABBINGTON, VALLANTEEN SCHOLARSHIP

Must enroll in UNCF Member College or University. Must have minimum 3.3 GPA after sophomore year and minimum 3.5 GPA after junior year. Please visit Web site for more information: http://www.uncf.org

Award: Scholarship for use in freshman year; renewable. *Number:* varies. *Amount:* $5000.

Eligibility Requirements: Applicant must be Black (non-Hispanic); enrolled or expecting to enroll at a four-year institution or university and resident of Missouri. Applicant must have 3.0 GPA or higher. Available to U.S. citizens.

Application Requirements: Application, financial need analysis, FAFSA, Student Aid Report (SAR). *Deadline:* varies.

Contact: Rebecca Bennett, Director, Program Services
United Negro College Fund
8260 Willow Oaks Corporate Drive
Fairfax, VA 22031-8044
Phone: 800-331-2244
E-mail: rbennett@uncf.org

BANK OF AMERICA SCHOLARSHIP

Scholarship supports freshman attending a UNCF member college or university located in any of the Bank of America core states. Minimum 2.5 GPA required. Prospective applicants should complete the Student Profile found at Web site: http://www.uncf.org

Award: Scholarship for use in freshman year; not renewable. *Amount:* $1000.

Eligibility Requirements: Applicant must be Black (non-Hispanic); enrolled or expecting to enroll full-time at a four-year institution or university and studying in Florida, Georgia, North Carolina, South Carolina, or Texas. Applicant must have 2.5 GPA or higher. Available to U.S. citizens.

Application Requirements: Application. *Deadline:* November 25.

Contact: Rebecca Bennett, Director, Program Services
United Negro College Fund
8260 Willow Oaks Corporate Drive
Fairfax, VA 22031-8044
Phone: 800-331-2244
E-mail: rbennett@uncf.org

BILDNER FAMILY SCHOLARSHIP

Scholarship open to New Jersey residents attending a UNCF member college or university. 2.5 GPA required. Prospective applicants should complete the Student Profile found at Web site: http://www.uncf.org.

Award: Scholarship for use in freshman, sophomore, junior, or senior years; not renewable. *Amount:* $1000–$2500.

Eligibility Requirements: Applicant must be Black (non-Hispanic); enrolled or expecting to enroll at a four-year institution or university and resident of New Jersey. Applicant must have 2.5 GPA or higher. Available to U.S. citizens.

Application Requirements: Application. *Deadline:* Continuous.

Contact: Rebecca Bennett, Director, Program Services
United Negro College Fund
8260 Willow Oaks Corporate Drive
Fairfax, VA 22031-8044
Phone: 800-331-2244
E-mail: rbennett@uncf.org

BUSHROD CAMPBELL AND ADAH HALL SCHOLARSHIP

Scholarships for students who are Boston, Massachusetts residents and are enrolled in a UNCF Member College or University. Please visit Web site for more information: http://www.uncf.org

Award: Scholarship for use in freshman, sophomore, junior, senior, or graduate years. *Number:* varies. *Amount:* $1000–$5000.

Eligibility Requirements: Applicant must be Black (non-Hispanic); enrolled or expecting to enroll at a four-year institution or university and resident of Massachusetts. Applicant must have 2.5 GPA or higher. Available to U.S. citizens.

Application Requirements: Application, financial need analysis, FAFSA, Student Aid Report (SAR). *Deadline:* varies.

Contact: Rebecca Bennett, Director, Program Services
United Negro College Fund
8260 Willow Oaks Corporate Drive
Fairfax, VA 22031-8044
Phone: 800-331-2244
E-mail: rbennett@uncf.org

CASIMIR, DOMINIQUE AND JAQUES SCHOLARSHIP

Four scholarships available for two males and two females who are residents of Texas. Must be undergraduate sophomore or junior at time of application. Please visit Web site for more information: http://www.uncf.org

Award: Scholarship for use in sophomore or junior years. *Number:* 4. *Amount:* $1500.

Eligibility Requirements: Applicant must be Black (non-Hispanic); enrolled or expecting to enroll at a four-year institution or university and resident of Texas. Applicant must have 2.5 GPA or higher. Available to U.S. citizens.

Application Requirements: Application, financial need analysis, FAFSA, Student Aid Report (SAR). *Deadline:* varies.

Contact: Rebecca Bennett, Director, Program Services
United Negro College Fund
8260 Willow Oaks Corporate Drive
Fairfax, VA 22031-8044
Phone: 800-331-2244
E-mail: rbennett@uncf.org

CHICAGO INTER-ALUMNI COUNCIL SCHOLARSHIP

Three winners of the annual Chicago Inter-Alumni Council pageant will receive scholarships to attend a UNCF member college or university. Must be a high school senior in Chicago. Please visit Web site for more information: http://www.uncf.org

Award: Scholarship for use in freshman year. *Number:* 3. *Amount:* varies.

Eligibility Requirements: Applicant must be Black (non-Hispanic); high school student; planning to enroll or expecting to enroll at a four-year institution or university and resident of Illinois. Applicant must have 2.5 GPA or higher. Available to U.S. citizens.

Application Requirements: Application, applicant must enter a contest, financial need analysis, FAFSA, Student Aid Report (SAR). *Deadline:* varies.

Contact: Rebecca Bennett, Director, Program Services
United Negro College Fund
8260 Willow Oaks Corporate Drive
Fairfax, VA 22031-8044
Phone: 800-331-2244
E-mail: rbennett@uncf.org

CHICAGO PUBLIC SCHOOLS UNCF CAMPAIGN

Scholarship awarded to students who have attended Chicago public schools. Award covers up to four years of tuition and fees. Please visit Web site for more information: http://www.uncf.org

Award: Scholarship for use in freshman, sophomore, junior, senior, or graduate years; renewable. *Number:* 1. *Amount:* varies.

Eligibility Requirements: Applicant must be Black (non-Hispanic) and enrolled or expecting to enroll at a four-year institution or university. Applicant must have 2.5 GPA or higher. Available to U.S. citizens.

Application Requirements: Application, financial need analysis, FAFSA, Student Aid Report (SAR). *Deadline:* varies.

Contact: Rebecca Bennett, Director, Program Services
United Negro College Fund
8260 Willow Oaks Corporate Drive
Fairfax, VA 22031-8044
Phone: 800-331-2244
E-mail: rbennett@uncf.org

CLEVELAND FOUNDATION SCHOLARSHIP

Up to $3000 available for Cleveland, Ohio students enrolled in a UNCF member college or university. Please visit Web site for more information: http://www.uncf.org

Award: Scholarship for use in freshman, sophomore, junior, senior, or graduate years. *Number:* varies. *Amount:* up to $3000.

Eligibility Requirements: Applicant must be Black (non-Hispanic); enrolled or expecting to enroll at a four-year institution or university and resident of Ohio. Applicant must have 2.5 GPA or higher. Available to U.S. citizens.

Application Requirements: Application, financial need analysis, FAFSA, Student Aid Report (SAR). *Deadline:* varies.

Contact: Rebecca Bennett, Director, Program Services
United Negro College Fund
8260 Willow Oaks Corporate Drive
Fairfax, VA 22031-8044
Phone: 800-331-2244
E-mail: rbennett@uncf.org

CLEVELAND MUNICIPAL SCHOOL SCHOLARSHIP

Scholarship awarded to graduating high school senior who attends a Cleveland district high school. Please visit Web site for more information: http://www.uncf.org

Award: Scholarship for use in freshman year. *Number:* 1. *Amount:* varies.

Eligibility Requirements: Applicant must be Black (non-Hispanic); high school student; planning to enroll or expecting to enroll at a four-year institution or university and resident of Ohio. Applicant must have 2.5 GPA or higher. Available to U.S. citizens.

Application Requirements: Application, financial need analysis, FAFSA, Student Aid Report (SAR). *Deadline:* varies.

Contact: Rebecca Bennett, Director, Program Services
United Negro College Fund
8260 Willow Oaks Corporate Drive
Fairfax, VA 22031-8044
Phone: 800-331-2244
E-mail: rbennett@uncf.org

CLOROX COMPANY FOUNDATION SCHOLARSHIP

Scholarship awarded to five students attending UNCF member colleges or universities. Must be resident of San Francisco Bay Area, California. Please visit Web site for more information: http://www.uncf.org

Award: Scholarship for use in freshman, sophomore, junior, senior, or graduate years. *Number:* 5. *Amount:* $2000.

Eligibility Requirements: Applicant must be Black (non-Hispanic); enrolled or expecting to enroll at a four-year institution or university and resident of California. Applicant must have 2.5 GPA or higher. Available to U.S. citizens.

Application Requirements: Application, financial need analysis, FAFSA, Student Aid Report (SAR). *Deadline:* varies.

Contact: Rebecca Bennett, Director, Program Services
United Negro College Fund
8260 Willow Oaks Corporate Drive
Fairfax, VA 22031-8044
Phone: 800-331-2244
E-mail: rbennett@uncf.org

COLUMBUS FOUNDATION SCHOLARSHIP

Scholarship of up to $3000 available for students attending a UNCF member college or university. Must be a resident of Columbus, Ohio. Please visit Web site for more information: http://www.uncf.org

Award: Scholarship for use in freshman, sophomore, junior, senior, or graduate years. *Number:* varies. *Amount:* up to $3000.

Eligibility Requirements: Applicant must be Black (non-Hispanic); enrolled or expecting to enroll at a four-year institution or university and resident of Ohio. Applicant must have 2.5 GPA or higher. Available to U.S. citizens.

Application Requirements: Application, financial need analysis, FAFSA, Student Aid Report (SAR). *Deadline:* varies.

Contact: Rebecca Bennett, Director, Program Services
United Negro College Fund
8260 Willow Oaks Corporate Drive
Fairfax, VA 22031-8044
Phone: 800-331-2244
E-mail: rbennett@uncf.org

COMMUNITY FOUNDATION OF GREATER BIRMINGHAM SCHOLARSHIP

Scholarship available to a student attending: Miles College, Oakwood College, Stillman College, Talladega College, or Tuskegee University. Please visit Web site for more information: http://www.uncf.org

Award: Scholarship for use in freshman, sophomore, junior, senior, or graduate years. *Number:* varies. *Amount:* $10,000.

Eligibility Requirements: Applicant must be Black (non-Hispanic) and enrolled or expecting to enroll at a four-year institution or university. Applicant must have 2.5 GPA or higher. Available to U.S. citizens.

Application Requirements: Application, financial need analysis, FAFSA, Student Aid Report (SAR). *Deadline:* varies.

Contact: Rebecca Bennett, Director, Program Services
United Negro College Fund
8260 Willow Oaks Corporate Drive
Fairfax, VA 22031-8044
Phone: 800-331-2244
E-mail: rbennett@uncf.org

COSTCO SCHOLARSHIP

Renewable scholarship for students from Washington and Oregon attending UNCF member colleges and universities. Minimum 2.5 GPA required. Prospective applicants should complete the student profile found at Web site: http://www.uncf.org

Award: Scholarship for use in freshman, sophomore, junior, or senior years; renewable. *Amount:* $5000.

Eligibility Requirements: Applicant must be Black (non-Hispanic); enrolled or expecting to enroll at a four-year institution or university and resident of Oregon or Washington. Applicant must have 2.5 GPA or higher. Available to U.S. citizens.

Application Requirements: Application. *Deadline:* Continuous.

United Negro College Fund (continued)

Contact: Rebecca Bennett, Director, Program Services
United Negro College Fund
8260 Willow Oaks Corporate Drive
Fairfax, VA 22031-8044
Phone: 800-331-2244
E-mail: rbennett@uncf.org

DALLAS INDEPENDENT SCHOOL DISTRICT SCHOLARSHIP

Applicant must be graduating high school senior from the Dallas Independent School District. Mandatory essay addressing: "Why it is important to attend a Historically Black College or University." Essay may be minimum 250 words to 500 words maximum. Please visit Web site for more information: http://www.uncf.org

Award: Scholarship for use in freshman year; renewable. *Number:* varies. *Amount:* $2500.

Eligibility Requirements: Applicant must be Black (non-Hispanic); high school student; planning to enroll or expecting to enroll at a four-year institution or university and resident of Texas. Applicant must have 2.5 GPA or higher. Available to U.S. citizens.

Application Requirements: Application, essay, financial need analysis, FAFSA, Student Aid Report (SAR). *Deadline:* varies.

Contact: Rebecca Bennett, Director, Program Services
United Negro College Fund
8260 Willow Oaks Corporate Drive
Fairfax, VA 22031-8044
Phone: 800-331-2244
E-mail: rbennett@uncf.org

DALLAS MAVERICKS

Scholarship awarded to student from greater Dallas/Ft. Worth, Texas, attending a UNCF member college or university. Amount of award varies, based on need. Minimum 2.5 GPA. Prospective applicants should complete the Student Profile found at Web site: http://www.uncf.org

Award: Scholarship for use in freshman, sophomore, junior, or senior years; not renewable. *Number:* 1. *Amount:* varies.

Eligibility Requirements: Applicant must be Black (non-Hispanic); enrolled or expecting to enroll full-time at a four-year institution or university and resident of Texas. Applicant must have 2.5 GPA or higher. Available to U.S. citizens.

Application Requirements: Application, financial need analysis. *Deadline:* Continuous.

Contact: Rebecca Bennett, Director, Program Services
United Negro College Fund
8260 Willow Oaks Corporate Drive
Fairfax, VA 22031-8044
Phone: 800-331-2244
E-mail: rbennett@uncf.org

DALLAS METROPLEX COUNCIL OF BLACK ALUMNI ASSOCIATION SCHOLARSHIP

Need-based scholarship offered by the Dallas Metroplex Council of Black Alumni Association. Please visit Web site for more information: http://www.uncf.org.

Award: Scholarship for use in freshman, sophomore, junior, senior, or graduate years. *Number:* 1. *Amount:* varies.

Eligibility Requirements: Applicant must be Black (non-Hispanic) and enrolled or expecting to enroll at a four-year institution or university. Applicant must have 2.5 GPA or higher. Available to U.S. citizens.

Application Requirements: Application, financial need analysis, FAFSA, Student Aid Report (SAR). *Deadline:* varies.

Contact: Rebecca Bennett, Director, Program Services
United Negro College Fund
8260 Willow Oaks Corporate Drive
Fairfax, VA 22031-8044
Phone: 800-331-2244
E-mail: rbennett@uncf.org

DAVENPORT FORTE PEDESTAL FUND

Scholarship awards a first semester undergraduate freshman who attends a UNCF member college or university. Applicant must have graduated from the Detroit Public Schools System. Must have minimum 2.7 GPA. Please visit Web site for more information: http://www.uncf.org.

Award: Scholarship for use in freshman year; renewable. *Number:* 1. *Amount:* $10,000.

Eligibility Requirements: Applicant must be Black (non-Hispanic) and enrolled or expecting to enroll at a four-year institution or university. Available to U.S. citizens.

Application Requirements: Application, financial need analysis, FAFSA, Student Aid Report (SAR). *Deadline:* varies.

Contact: Rebecca Bennett, Director, Program Services
United Negro College Fund
8260 Willow Oaks Corporate Drive
Fairfax, VA 22031-8044
Phone: 800-331-2244
E-mail: rbennett@uncf.org

DUPONT SCHOLARSHIP

Scholarship awarded to residents of Delaware. Applicant must either be Philadelphia Louis Stokes AMP student or attend a UNCF college or university. Please visit Web site for more information: http://www.uncf.org

Award: Scholarship for use in freshman, sophomore, junior, senior, or graduate years. *Number:* 1. *Amount:* varies.

Eligibility Requirements: Applicant must be Black (non-Hispanic); enrolled or expecting to enroll at a four-year institution or university and resident of Delaware. Applicant must have 2.5 GPA or higher. Available to U.S. citizens.

Application Requirements: Application, financial need analysis, FAFSA, Student Aid Report (SAR). *Deadline:* varies.

Contact: Rebecca Bennett, Director, Program Services
United Negro College Fund
8260 Willow Oaks Corporate Drive
Fairfax, VA 22031-8044
Phone: 800-331-2244
E-mail: rbennett@uncf.org

DUQUESNE LIGHT COMPANY SCHOLARSHIP

Need-based scholarship awarded to student who lives in Allegheny or Beaver County, Pennsylvania. Student must be nominated. Please visit Web site for more information: http://www.uncf.org

Award: Scholarship for use in freshman, sophomore, junior, senior, or graduate years; renewable. *Number:* 1. *Amount:* varies.

Eligibility Requirements: Applicant must be Black (non-Hispanic); enrolled or expecting to enroll at a four-year institution or university and resident of Pennsylvania. Applicant must have 2.5 GPA or higher. Available to U.S. citizens.

Application Requirements: Financial need analysis, references, FAFSA, Student Aid Report (SAR). *Deadline:* varies.

Contact: Rebecca Bennett, Director, Program Services
United Negro College Fund
8260 Willow Oaks Corporate Drive
Fairfax, VA 22031-8044
Phone: 800-331-2244
E-mail: rbennett@uncf.org

FIFTH/THIRD SCHOLARS PROGRAM

Scholarship awards students who are residents of Dayton, Columbus or Cincinnati, Ohio. Student must attend a UNCF member college or university. Please visit Web site for more information: http://www.uncf.org

Award: Scholarship for use in freshman, sophomore, junior, senior, or graduate years. *Number:* 1. *Amount:* varies.

Eligibility Requirements: Applicant must be Black (non-Hispanic); enrolled or expecting to enroll at a four-year institution or university and resident of Ohio. Applicant must have 2.5 GPA or higher. Available to U.S. citizens.

Application Requirements: Application, financial need analysis, FAFSA, Student Aid Report (SAR). *Deadline:* varies.

Contact: Rebecca Bennett, Director, Program Services
United Negro College Fund
8260 Willow Oaks Corporate Drive
Fairfax, VA 22031-8044
Phone: 800-331-2244
E-mail: rbennett@uncf.org

FORT WORTH INDEPENDENT SCHOOL DISTRICT SCHOLARSHIP

Scholarship awarded to graduating high school senior from the Fort Worth Independent School District. Applicant must submit 250-500 word essay addressing: "Why it is important to attend a Historically Black College or University." Please visit Web site for more information: http://www.uncf.org

Award: Scholarship for use in freshman year. *Number:* varies. *Amount:* up to $2500.

Eligibility Requirements: Applicant must be Black (non-Hispanic); high school student; planning to enroll or expecting to enroll at a four-year institution or university and resident of Texas. Applicant must have 2.5 GPA or higher. Available to U.S. citizens.

Application Requirements: Application, essay, financial need analysis, FAFSA, Student Aid Report (SAR). *Deadline:* varies.

Contact: Rebecca Bennett, Director, Program Services
United Negro College Fund
8260 Willow Oaks Corporate Drive
Fairfax, VA 22031-8044
Phone: 800-331-2244
E-mail: rbennett@uncf.org

FORTUNE BRANDS SCHOLARS PROGRAM

Program for students who are college juniors. Selected students will participate in an 8-10 week summer internship at Fortune Brands corporate headquarters and are eligible to receive a merit scholarship of up to $3500. Please visit Web site for more information: http://www.uncf.org

Award: Scholarship for use in junior, or graduate years. *Number:* varies. *Amount:* up to $3500.

Eligibility Requirements: Applicant must be American Indian/Alaska Native, Asian/Pacific Islander, Black (non-Hispanic), or Hispanic and enrolled or expecting to enroll at a four-year institution or university. Applicant must have 2.5 GPA or higher. Available to U.S. citizens.

Application Requirements: Application, financial need analysis, resume, references, transcript, FAFSA, Student Aid Report (SAR). *Deadline:* varies.

Contact: Fortune Brands/UNCF Corporate Scholars Program (CSP)
UNCF, Inc
United Negro College Fund
8260 Willow Oaks Corporate Drive, Suite 400
Fairfax, VA 22031

GATES MILLENNIUM SCHOLARS PROGRAM (GATES FOUNDATION)

Award enables African-American students to complete an undergraduate and graduate education. Must be entering a U.S. accredited college or university as a full-time degree-seeking student. Minimum 3.3 GPA required. Must demonstrate leadership abilities. Must meet federal Pell Grant eligibility criteria. Visit Web site at http://www.gmsp.org. Prospective applicants should complete the Student Profile found at Web site: http://www.uncf.org.

Award: Scholarship for use in freshman, sophomore, junior, senior, or graduate years; renewable. *Number:* up to 1000.

Eligibility Requirements: Applicant must be Black (non-Hispanic) and enrolled or expecting to enroll full-time at a four-year institution or university. Available to U.S. citizens.

Application Requirements: Application, financial need analysis, nomination packet. *Deadline:* varies.

Contact: Mary Williams, Gates Millennium Scholars
Phone: 703-205-2041
E-mail: mary.williams@gmsp.org

GHEENS FOUNDATION SCHOLARSHIP

This scholarship supports students from Louisville, Kentucky, who are enrolled in a HBCU participating school. Please visit Web site for more information: http://www.uncf.org

Award: Scholarship for use in freshman, sophomore, junior, senior, or graduate years. *Number:* varies. *Amount:* up to $2000.

Eligibility Requirements: Applicant must be Black (non-Hispanic); enrolled or expecting to enroll at a four-year institution or university and resident of Kentucky. Applicant must have 2.5 GPA or higher. Available to U.S. citizens.

Application Requirements: Application, financial need analysis, transcript. *Deadline:* varies.

Contact: Rebecca Bennett, Director, Program Services
United Negro College Fund
8260 Willow Oaks Corporate Drive
Fairfax, VA 22031-8044
Phone: 800-331-2244
E-mail: rbennett@uncf.org

HOUGHTON-MIFFLIN COMPANY FELLOWS PROGRAM

Scholarship is awarded to undergraduate junior after completion of paid internship to introduce selected students to careers in the publishing industry. Must attend a UNCF member college or university. Minimum 3.0 GPA required. Prospective applicants should complete the Student Profile found at Web site: http://www.uncf.org.

Award: Scholarship for use in junior year; not renewable. *Amount:* $3700.

Eligibility Requirements: Applicant must be Black (non-Hispanic) and enrolled or expecting to enroll at a four-year institution or university. Applicant must have 3.0 GPA or higher. Available to U.S. citizens.

Application Requirements: Application, financial need analysis. *Deadline:* varies.

Contact: Rebecca Bennett, Director, Program Services
United Negro College Fund
8260 Willow Oaks Corporate Drive
Fairfax, VA 22031-8044
Phone: 800-331-2244
E-mail: rbennett@uncf.org

JESSE JONES, JR. SCHOLARSHIP

Four $5000 awards to minority students pursuing a degree in automotive studies or other related areas. Financial need considered, but not necessary. Demonstrated academic achievement and career interest also considered.

Award: Scholarship for use in freshman, sophomore, junior, or senior years; not renewable. *Number:* 4. *Amount:* $2000–$5000.

Eligibility Requirements: Applicant must be Black (non-Hispanic) and enrolled or expecting to enroll at a four-year institution or university. Available to U.S. citizens.

Application Requirements: Application, financial need analysis. *Deadline:* Continuous.

Contact: Rebecca Bennett, Director, Program Services
United Negro College Fund
8260 Willow Oaks Corporate Drive
Fairfax, VA 22031-8044
Phone: 800-331-2244
E-mail: rbennett@uncf.org

JOHN W. ANDERSON FOUNDATION SCHOLARSHIP

Need-based scholarship for students from Indiana attending UNCF member colleges and universities. Prospective applicants should complete the Student Profile found at Web site: http://www.uncf.org.

Award: Scholarship for use in freshman, sophomore, junior, or senior years; not renewable. *Amount:* up to $3000.

Eligibility Requirements: Applicant must be Black (non-Hispanic); enrolled or expecting to enroll at a four-year institution or university and resident of Indiana. Applicant must have 2.5 GPA or higher. Available to U.S. citizens.

Application Requirements: Application, financial need analysis. *Deadline:* Continuous.

Contact: Scholarship Coordinator, 50 Men and Women of Toledo, Inc
United Negro College Fund
PO Box 80056
Toledo, OH 43608
Phone: 419-729-4654

JOSEPH A. TOWLES AFRICAN STUDY ABROAD SCHOLARSHIP

Award to students who have been accepted into a study abroad program in Africa. Must have 3.0 GPA. Please visit Web site for more information: http://www.uncf.org

United Negro College Fund (continued)

Award: Scholarship for use in freshman, sophomore, junior, or senior years; renewable. *Number:* varies. *Amount:* up to $15,000.

Eligibility Requirements: Applicant must be Black (non-Hispanic) and enrolled or expecting to enroll at an institution or university. Applicant must have 3.0 GPA or higher. Available to U.S. citizens.

Application Requirements: Application, financial need analysis, FAFSA, Student Aid Report (SAR). *Deadline:* varies.

Contact: Rebecca Bennett, Director, Program Services
United Negro College Fund
8260 Willow Oaks Corporate Drive
Fairfax, VA 22031-8044
Phone: 800-331-2244
E-mail: rbennett@uncf.org

KANSAS CITY INITIATIVE SCHOLARSHIP

Award for a minority student in the Kansas City Metropolitan area, who plans to attend a UNCF member college or university or the University of Missouri at Kansas City. Please visit Web site for more information: http://www.uncf.org

Award: Scholarship for use in freshman, sophomore, junior, or senior years; renewable. *Number:* varies. *Amount:* $2500–$5000.

Eligibility Requirements: Applicant must be Black (non-Hispanic); enrolled or expecting to enroll at a four-year institution or university and resident of Kansas or Missouri. Applicant must have 3.0 GPA or higher. Available to U.S. citizens.

Application Requirements: Application, financial need analysis, FAFSA, Student Aid Report (SAR). *Deadline:* varies.

Contact: Rebecca Bennett, Director, Program Services
United Negro College Fund
8260 Willow Oaks Corporate Drive
Fairfax, VA 22031-8044
Phone: 800-331-2244
E-mail: rbennett@uncf.org

KROGER SCHOLARSHIP

Award for students residing in targeted Kroger retail store locations (GA, AL, SC, TN) who will be attending a UNCF participating college or university.

Award: Scholarship for use in freshman, sophomore, junior, or senior years. *Amount:* up to $5000.

Eligibility Requirements: Applicant must be Black (non-Hispanic); enrolled or expecting to enroll at a four-year institution or university and resident of Alabama, Georgia, South Carolina, or Tennessee. Applicant must have 2.5 GPA or higher. Available to U.S. citizens.

Application Requirements: Application, financial need analysis, FAFSA, Student Aid Report (SAR). *Deadline:* April 30.

Contact: Rebecca Bennett, Director, Program Services
United Negro College Fund
8260 Willow Oaks Corporate Drive
Fairfax, VA 22031-8044
Phone: 800-331-2244
E-mail: rbennett@uncf.org

KROGER/PEPSI SCHOLARSHIP

Student must be a resident of the Kroger Great Lakes marketing area (lower peninsula of Michigan, central and northern Ohio and northern West Virginia). Must be a high school senior planning to attend a UNCF institution or a 4-year fully accredited institution of higher learning.

Award: Scholarship for use in freshman year. *Number:* varies. *Amount:* $5000.

Eligibility Requirements: Applicant must be Black (non-Hispanic); high school student; planning to enroll or expecting to enroll at a four-year institution or university and resident of Michigan, Ohio, or West Virginia. Applicant must have 2.5 GPA or higher. Available to U.S. citizens.

Application Requirements: Application, essay, financial need analysis, photo, references, transcript, FAFSA. *Deadline:* varies.

Contact: Rebecca Bennett, Director, Program Services
United Negro College Fund
8260 Willow Oaks Corporate Drive
Fairfax, VA 22031-8044
Phone: 800-331-2244
E-mail: rbennett@uncf.org

KUNTZ FOUNDATION SCHOLARSHIP

Need-based scholarship for students attending a UNCF member college or university. Minimum 2.5 GPA required. Prospective applicants should complete the Student Profile found at Web site: http://www.uncf.org.

Award: Scholarship for use in freshman, sophomore, junior, or senior years; not renewable. *Number:* 1. *Amount:* $500.

Eligibility Requirements: Applicant must be Black (non-Hispanic) and enrolled or expecting to enroll at a four-year institution or university. Applicant must have 2.5 GPA or higher. Available to U.S. citizens.

Application Requirements: Application, financial need analysis. *Deadline:* Continuous.

Contact: Rebecca Bennett, Director, Program Services
United Negro College Fund
8260 Willow Oaks Corporate Drive
Fairfax, VA 22031-8044
Phone: 800-331-2244
E-mail: rbennett@uncf.org

LEON JACKSON, JR. SCHOLARSHIP
• See page 536

LIMITED, INC. AND INTIMATE BRANDS, INC. SCHOLARSHIP

Scholarships awarded to students attending a UNCF member college or university. Minimum 2.5 GPA required. Prospective applicants should complete the Student Profile found at Web site: http://www.uncf.org.

Award: Scholarship for use in freshman, sophomore, junior, or senior years; not renewable. *Number:* 1. *Amount:* $500.

Eligibility Requirements: Applicant must be Black (non-Hispanic); enrolled or expecting to enroll at a four-year institution or university and resident of Ohio. Applicant must have 2.5 GPA or higher. Available to U.S. citizens.

Application Requirements: Application, financial need analysis. *Deadline:* Continuous.

Contact: Rebecca Bennett, Director, Program Services
United Negro College Fund
8260 Willow Oaks Corporate Drive
Fairfax, VA 22031-8044
Phone: 800-331-2244
E-mail: rbennett@uncf.org

MARTIN LUTHER KING JR. CHILDREN'S CHOIR SCHOLARSHIP

Scholarship for students who were part of a class action suit. This is a one-time award and may be used at any college or university. Please visit Web site for more information: http://www.uncf.org.

Award: Scholarship for use in freshman, sophomore, junior, or senior years; not renewable. *Amount:* $1000.

Eligibility Requirements: Applicant must be Black (non-Hispanic) and enrolled or expecting to enroll at a four-year institution or university. Applicant must have 2.5 GPA or higher. Available to U.S. citizens.

Application Requirements: Application, financial need analysis. *Deadline:* varies.

Contact: Rebecca Bennett, Director, Program Services
United Negro College Fund
8260 Willow Oaks Corporate Drive
Fairfax, VA 22031-8044
Phone: 800-331-2244
E-mail: rbennett@uncf.org

MEDTRONIC FOUNDATION INTERNSHIP/SCHOLARSHIP

Scholarship for undergraduate sophomores and juniors majoring in engineering or science and attending a UNCF member college or university. A paid summer internship is included in the award. Minimum 3.3 GPA required. Prospective applicants should complete the Student Profile found at Web site: http://www.uncf.org.

Award: Scholarship for use in sophomore or junior years; not renewable. *Amount:* $5000.

Eligibility Requirements: Applicant must be Black (non-Hispanic) and enrolled or expecting to enroll at a four-year institution or university. Available to U.S. citizens.

Application Requirements: Application, autobiography, financial need analysis, resume, references. *Deadline:* April 15.

Contact: Rebecca Bennett, Director, Program Services
United Negro College Fund
8260 Willow Oaks Corporate Drive
Fairfax, VA 22031-8044
Phone: 800-331-2244
E-mail: rbennett@uncf.org

NEW JERSEY MAYOR'S TASK FORCE SCHOLARSHIP

Awards available for African American students who live in one of the New Jersey Task Force participating cities. Must attend a historically black college or university, or a UNCF member institution. Requirements may vary for each city. Check Web site for details. http://www.uncf.org

Award: Scholarship for use in freshman, sophomore, junior, or senior years; renewable. *Number:* varies. *Amount:* $1350.

Eligibility Requirements: Applicant must be Black (non-Hispanic); enrolled or expecting to enroll at a four-year institution or university and resident of New Jersey. Applicant must have 2.5 GPA or higher. Available to U.S. citizens.

Application Requirements: Application, essay, financial need analysis, photo, references, transcript, FAFSA, Student Aid Report (SAR). *Deadline:* varies.

Contact: Rebecca Bennett, Director, Program Services
United Negro College Fund
8260 Willow Oaks Corporate Drive
Fairfax, VA 22031-8044
Phone: 800-331-2244
E-mail: rbennett@uncf.org

PAUL AND EDITH BABSON SCHOLARSHIP

Applicant must be from Boston, Massachusetts in order to be eligible. Please visit Web site for more information: http://www.uncf.org

Award: Scholarship for use in freshman, sophomore, junior, senior, or graduate years. *Number:* varies. *Amount:* $1000–$3500.

Eligibility Requirements: Applicant must be Black (non-Hispanic); enrolled or expecting to enroll at a four-year institution or university and resident of Massachusetts. Applicant must have 2.5 GPA or higher. Available to U.S. citizens.

Application Requirements: Application, financial need analysis, FAFSA, Student Aid Report (SAR). *Deadline:* varies.

Contact: Rebecca Bennett, Director, Program Services
United Negro College Fund
8260 Willow Oaks Corporate Drive
Fairfax, VA 22031-8044
Phone: 800-331-2244
E-mail: rbennett@uncf.org

RELIABLE LIFE INSURANCE COMPANY SCHOLARSHIP PROGRAM

Scholarships available to African American students residing in Missouri, Texas, Arkansas, or Oklahoma. Must attend a UNCF member college or university. Minimum 2.5 GPA. Information on Web site at http://www.uncf.org

Award: Scholarship for use in freshman, sophomore, junior, or senior years. *Number:* varies. *Amount:* $5000.

Eligibility Requirements: Applicant must be Black (non-Hispanic); enrolled or expecting to enroll at a four-year institution or university and resident of Arkansas, Missouri, Oklahoma, or Texas. Applicant must have 2.5 GPA or higher. Available to U.S. citizens.

Application Requirements: Application, financial need analysis, FAFSA, Student Aid Report (SAR). *Deadline:* July 1.

Contact: Rebecca Bennett, Director, Program Services
United Negro College Fund
8260 Willow Oaks Corporate Drive
Fairfax, VA 22031-8044
Phone: 800-331-2244
E-mail: rbennett@uncf.org

RICHMOND SCHOLARSHIP

Scholarships available to students who reside in Central Virginia. Minimum 2.5 GPA required. Must attend a UNCF member college or university. Details on Web site at http://www.uncf.org

Award: Scholarship for use in freshman, sophomore, junior, or senior years; renewable. *Number:* varies. *Amount:* up to $2000.

Eligibility Requirements: Applicant must be Black (non-Hispanic); enrolled or expecting to enroll at a four-year institution or university and resident of Virginia. Applicant must have 2.5 GPA or higher. Available to U.S. citizens.

Application Requirements: Application, financial need analysis, FAFSA, Student Aid Report (SAR). *Deadline:* varies.

Contact: Rebecca Bennett, Director, Program Services
United Negro College Fund
8260 Willow Oaks Corporate Drive
Fairfax, VA 22031-8044
Phone: 800-331-2244
E-mail: rbennett@uncf.org

RONALD MCDONALD'S CHICAGOLAND SCHOLARSHIP

Scholarships awarded to students attending a UNCF member college or university. Prospective applicants should complete the Student Profile found at Web site: http://www.uncf.org.

Award: Scholarship for use in freshman, sophomore, junior, or senior years; renewable. *Amount:* up to $3000.

Eligibility Requirements: Applicant must be Black (non-Hispanic) and enrolled or expecting to enroll full-time at a four-year institution or university. Applicant must have 2.5 GPA or higher. Available to U.S. citizens.

Application Requirements: Application, financial need analysis. *Deadline:* Continuous.

Contact: Rebecca Bennett, Program Services Department
United Negro College Fund
8260 Willow Oaks Corporate Drive, PO Box 10444
Fairfax, VA 22031
Phone: 703-205-3538

RONALD MCDONALD'S HOUSE CHARITIES SCHOLARSHIP-OHIO

Scholarships available for African American students residing in Ohio. Must attend a UNCF member college or university. Must have a minimum 2.5 GPA. Information on Web site at http://www.uncf.org

Award: Scholarship for use in freshman, sophomore, junior, or senior years; renewable. *Number:* 1. *Amount:* varies.

Eligibility Requirements: Applicant must be Black (non-Hispanic); enrolled or expecting to enroll at a four-year institution or university and resident of Ohio. Applicant must have 2.5 GPA or higher. Available to U.S. citizens.

Application Requirements: Application, financial need analysis, FAFSA, Student Aid Report (SAR). *Deadline:* varies.

Contact: Rebecca Bennett, Director, Program Services
United Negro College Fund
8260 Willow Oaks Corporate Drive
Fairfax, VA 22031-8044
Phone: 800-331-2244
E-mail: rbennett@uncf.org

SALLIE MAE FUND AMERICAN DREAM SCHOLARSHIP

Awards from $500 to $5000 to African-American students with financial need enrolled in a two or four year title IV accredited college or university. Open to incoming freshmen as well as current undergraduate students. Please visit Web site for more information: http://www.uncf.org

Award: Scholarship for use in freshman, sophomore, junior, or senior years; renewable. *Number:* varies. *Amount:* $500–$5000.

Eligibility Requirements: Applicant must be Black (non-Hispanic) and enrolled or expecting to enroll at a two-year or four-year institution or university. Applicant must have 2.5 GPA or higher. Available to U.S. citizens.

United Negro College Fund (continued)

Application Requirements: Application, essay, financial need analysis, references, transcript, FAFSA, Student Aid Report (SAR). *Deadline:* April 15.

Contact: Cynthia Nair, Senior Program Manager
United Negro College Fund
PO Box 10444
Fairfax, VA 22031

SAN JOSE MERCURY NEWS SCHOLARSHIP

Award established to benefit a student from Silicon Valley, CA. Must have 2.5 GPA. Please visit Web site for more information: http://www.uncf.org.

Award: Scholarship for use in freshman, sophomore, junior, or senior years; renewable. *Number:* 1. *Amount:* $2000.

Eligibility Requirements: Applicant must be Black (non-Hispanic); enrolled or expecting to enroll at an institution or university and resident of California. Applicant must have 2.5 GPA or higher. Available to U.S. citizens.

Application Requirements: Application, financial need analysis, FAFSA, Student Aid Report (SAR). *Deadline:* varies.

Contact: Rebecca Bennett, Director, Program Services
United Negro College Fund
8260 Willow Oaks Corporate Drive
Fairfax, VA 22031-8044
Phone: 800-331-2244
E-mail: rbennett@uncf.org

SCHRAFT CHARITABLE TRUST SCHOLARSHIP

Award available to Boston, MA residents who are enrolled in a historically black college or university. Please visit Web site for more information: http://www.uncf.org.

Award: Scholarship for use in freshman, sophomore, junior, or senior years; renewable. *Number:* varies. *Amount:* $3000.

Eligibility Requirements: Applicant must be Black (non-Hispanic); enrolled or expecting to enroll at an institution or university and resident of Massachusetts. Applicant must have 2.5 GPA or higher. Available to U.S. citizens.

Application Requirements: Application, financial need analysis, FAFSA, Student Aid Report (SAR). *Deadline:* varies.

Contact: Rebecca Bennett, Director, Program Services
United Negro College Fund
8260 Willow Oaks Corporate Drive
Fairfax, VA 22031-8044
Phone: 800-331-2244
E-mail: rbennett@uncf.org

SHELL/EQUILON UNCF CLEVELAND SCHOLARSHIP FUND

Award for Cuyahoga County, OH residents who are attending a UNCF member college or university. Please visit Web site for more information: http://www.uncf.org

Award: Scholarship for use in freshman, sophomore, junior, or senior years; renewable. *Number:* varies. *Amount:* $3000.

Eligibility Requirements: Applicant must be Black (non-Hispanic); enrolled or expecting to enroll at an institution or university and resident of Ohio. Applicant must have 2.5 GPA or higher. Available to U.S. citizens.

Application Requirements: Application, financial need analysis, FAFSA, Student Aid Report (SAR). *Deadline:* varies.

Contact: Rebecca Bennett, Director, Program Services
United Negro College Fund
8260 Willow Oaks Corporate Drive
Fairfax, VA 22031-8044
Phone: 800-331-2244
E-mail: rbennett@uncf.org

SHREVEPORT CAMPAIGN

Award is for students residing in the Shreveport, LA area. Please visit Web site for more information: http://www.uncf.org

Award: Scholarship for use in freshman, sophomore, junior, or senior years; renewable. *Number:* varies. *Amount:* $1500.

Eligibility Requirements: Applicant must be Black (non-Hispanic); enrolled or expecting to enroll at an institution or university and resident of Louisiana. Applicant must have 2.5 GPA or higher. Available to U.S. citizens.

Application Requirements: Application, financial need analysis, FAFSA, Student Aid Report (SAR). *Deadline:* varies.

Contact: Rebecca Bennett, Director, Program Services
United Negro College Fund
8260 Willow Oaks Corporate Drive
Fairfax, VA 22031-8044
Phone: 800-331-2244
E-mail: rbennett@uncf.org

SIRAGUSA FOUNDATION SCHOLARSHIP

Scholarships available to students attending a UNCF member college or university. Minimum 2.5 GPA required. Prospective applicants should complete the Student Profile found at Web site: http://www.uncf.org.

Award: Scholarship for use in freshman, sophomore, junior, or senior years; not renewable. *Amount:* $2000.

Eligibility Requirements: Applicant must be Black (non-Hispanic) and enrolled or expecting to enroll at a four-year institution or university. Applicant must have 2.5 GPA or higher. Available to U.S. citizens.

Application Requirements: Application, financial need analysis. *Deadline:* Continuous.

Contact: Rebecca Bennett, Director, Program Services
United Negro College Fund
8260 Willow Oaks Corporate Drive
Fairfax, VA 22031-8044
Phone: 800-331-2244
E-mail: rbennett@uncf.org

ST. PETERSBURG GOLF CLASSIC SCHOLARSHIP

Each year two men and two women students from the Tampa Bay, Florida area are chosen to receive this scholarship. Please visit Web site for more information: http://www.uncf.org

Award: Scholarship for use in freshman, sophomore, junior, or senior years; renewable. *Number:* 4. *Amount:* up to $5000.

Eligibility Requirements: Applicant must be Black (non-Hispanic); enrolled or expecting to enroll at an institution or university and resident of Florida. Applicant must have 2.5 GPA or higher. Available to U.S. citizens.

Application Requirements: Application, financial need analysis, FAFSA, Student Aid Report (SAR). *Deadline:* July 22.

Contact: Rebecca Bennett, Director, Program Services
United Negro College Fund
8260 Willow Oaks Corporate Drive
Fairfax, VA 22031-8044
Phone: 800-331-2244
E-mail: rbennett@uncf.org

STERLING BANK SCHOLARSHIP

Scholarship available to students attending UNCF member colleges or universities. Minimum 2.5 GPA required. Prospective applicants should complete the Student Profile found at Web site: http://www.uncf.org.

Award: Scholarship for use in freshman, sophomore, junior, or senior years; not renewable. *Amount:* up to $1000.

Eligibility Requirements: Applicant must be Black (non-Hispanic) and enrolled or expecting to enroll at a four-year institution or university. Applicant must have 2.5 GPA or higher. Available to U.S. citizens.

Application Requirements: Application, financial need analysis. *Deadline:* Continuous.

Contact: Rebecca Bennett, Director, Program Services
United Negro College Fund
8260 Willow Oaks Corporate Drive
Fairfax, VA 22031-8044
Phone: 800-331-2244
E-mail: rbennett@uncf.org

TEXAS HEALTH RESOURCES SCHOLARSHIP

Award for students from the Dallas/Ft. Worth, TX area. Must have 2.5 GPA. Amount varies, based on need. Please visit Web site for more information: http://www.uncf.org.

Award: Scholarship for use in freshman, sophomore, junior, or senior years; renewable. *Number:* 1. *Amount:* varies.

Eligibility Requirements: Applicant must be Black (non-Hispanic); enrolled or expecting to enroll at an institution or university and resident of Texas. Applicant must have 2.5 GPA or higher. Available to U.S. citizens.

Application Requirements: Application, financial need analysis, FAFSA, Student Aid Report (SAR). *Deadline:* varies.

Contact: Rebecca Bennett, Director, Program Services
United Negro College Fund
8260 Willow Oaks Corporate Drive
Fairfax, VA 22031-8044
Phone: 800-331-2244
E-mail: rbennett@uncf.org

TEXTRON FELLOWS PROGRAM

Award for students in their junior year residing in Providence, RI. Must have 3.0 GPA. Amount varies, based on need. Please visit Web site for more information: http://www.uncf.org

Award: Scholarship for use in junior year; renewable. *Number:* 1. *Amount:* varies.

Eligibility Requirements: Applicant must be Black (non-Hispanic); enrolled or expecting to enroll at an institution or university and resident of Rhode Island. Applicant must have 3.0 GPA or higher. Available to U.S. citizens.

Application Requirements: Application, financial need analysis, FAFSA, Student Aid Report (SAR). *Deadline:* varies.

Contact: Rebecca Bennett, Director, Program Services
United Negro College Fund
8260 Willow Oaks Corporate Drive
Fairfax, VA 22031-8044
Phone: 800-331-2244
E-mail: rbennett@uncf.org

TJX FOUNDATION SCHOLARSHIP

Award available to Massachusetts residents who live near TJ Maxx stores. Must have 2.5 GPA. Please visit Web site for more information: http://www.uncf.org

Award: Scholarship for use in freshman, sophomore, junior, or senior years; renewable. *Number:* varies. *Amount:* $1000.

Eligibility Requirements: Applicant must be Black (non-Hispanic); enrolled or expecting to enroll at an institution or university and resident of Massachusetts. Applicant must have 2.5 GPA or higher. Available to U.S. citizens.

Application Requirements: Application, financial need analysis, FAFSA, Student Aid Report (SAR). *Deadline:* varies.

Contact: Rebecca Bennett, Director, Program Services
United Negro College Fund
8260 Willow Oaks Corporate Drive
Fairfax, VA 22031-8044
Phone: 800-331-2244
E-mail: rbennett@uncf.org

TRULL FOUNDATION SCHOLARSHIP

Need-based scholarship to students attending a UNCF member college or university. Minimum 2.5 GPA required. Prospective applicants should complete the Student Profile found at Web site: http://www.uncf.org

Award: Scholarship for use in freshman, sophomore, junior, or senior years; not renewable. *Amount:* up to $5000.

Eligibility Requirements: Applicant must be Black (non-Hispanic) and enrolled or expecting to enroll at a four-year institution or university. Applicant must have 2.5 GPA or higher. Available to U.S. citizens.

Application Requirements: Application, financial need analysis. *Deadline:* Continuous.

Contact: Rebecca Bennett, Director, Program Services
United Negro College Fund
8260 Willow Oaks Corporate Drive
Fairfax, VA 22031-8044
Phone: 800-331-2244
E-mail: rbennett@uncf.org

UNION BANK OF CALIFORNIA

Scholarship available to all California students who attend a UNCF member college or university. Minimum 2.5 GPA required. Prospective applicants should complete the Student Profile found at Web site: http://www.uncf.org.

Award: Scholarship for use in freshman, sophomore, junior, or senior years; not renewable. *Number:* 1.

Eligibility Requirements: Applicant must be Black (non-Hispanic); enrolled or expecting to enroll at a four-year institution or university and resident of California. Applicant must have 2.5 GPA or higher. Available to U.S. citizens.

Application Requirements: Application, financial need analysis. *Deadline:* Continuous.

Contact: Rebecca Bennett, Director, Program Services
United Negro College Fund
8260 Willow Oaks Corporate Drive
Fairfax, VA 22031-8044
Phone: 800-331-2244
E-mail: rbennett@uncf.org

UNITED INSURANCE SCHOLARSHIP

Students or the parents of students applying for this award must have a policy with United Insurance Company. Please visit Web site for more information: http://www.uncf.org

Award: Scholarship for use in freshman, sophomore, junior, or senior years; renewable. *Number:* varies. *Amount:* $5000.

Eligibility Requirements: Applicant must be Black (non-Hispanic) and enrolled or expecting to enroll at an institution or university. Applicant must have 2.5 GPA or higher. Available to U.S. citizens.

Application Requirements: Application, financial need analysis, FAFSA, Student Aid Report (SAR). *Deadline:* August 31.

Contact: Rebecca Bennett, Director, Program Services
United Negro College Fund
8260 Willow Oaks Corporate Drive
Fairfax, VA 22031-8044
Phone: 800-331-2244
E-mail: rbennett@uncf.org

UNITED PARCEL SERVICE FOUNDATION SCHOLARSHIP

This award provides students with financial support for tuition and other education costs. Based on need amount varies. Please visit Web site for more information: http://www.uncf.org

Award: Scholarship for use in freshman, sophomore, junior, or senior years; renewable. *Number:* varies. *Amount:* varies.

Eligibility Requirements: Applicant must be Black (non-Hispanic) and enrolled or expecting to enroll at an institution or university. Applicant must have 2.5 GPA or higher. Available to U.S. citizens.

Application Requirements: Application, financial need analysis, FAFSA, Student Aid Report (SAR). *Deadline:* varies.

Contact: Rebecca Bennett, Director, Program Services
United Negro College Fund
8260 Willow Oaks Corporate Drive
Fairfax, VA 22031-8044
Phone: 800-331-2244
E-mail: rbennett@uncf.org

UNITED WAY OF NEW ORLEANS EMERGENCY ASSISTANCE FUND

Award providing emergency assistance for students at Dillard University and Xavier University in Louisiana.

Award: Scholarship for use in freshman, sophomore, junior, or senior years; renewable. *Number:* varies. *Amount:* up to $2500.

Eligibility Requirements: Applicant must be Black (non-Hispanic); enrolled or expecting to enroll at an institution or university and studying in Louisiana. Applicant must have 2.5 GPA or higher. Available to U.S. citizens.

United Negro College Fund (continued)

Application Requirements: Application, financial need analysis, FAFSA, Student Aid Report (SAR). *Deadline:* varies.

Contact: Rebecca Bennett, Director, Program Services
United Negro College Fund
8260 Willow Oaks Corporate Drive
Fairfax, VA 22031-8044
Phone: 800-331-2244
E-mail: rbennett@uncf.org

UNITED WAY OF WESTCHESTER AND PUTNAM, INC./ UNCF EMERGENCY ASSISTANCE FUND

Award providing emergency assistance for students from the Westchester/Putnam, NY area. A 2.5 GPA is required if attending a UNCF school, or 2.0 if attending Mercy College or Westchester Community College. Students are only eligible to receive emergency assistance for two consecutive semesters. Please visit Web site for more information: http://www.uncf.org.

Award: Scholarship for use in freshman, sophomore, junior, or senior years; not renewable. *Number:* varies. *Amount:* up to $5000.

Eligibility Requirements: Applicant must be Black (non-Hispanic) or Hispanic; enrolled or expecting to enroll full or part-time at an institution or university; resident of New York and studying in New York. Available to U.S. citizens.

Application Requirements: Application, financial need analysis, FAFSA, Student Aid Report (SAR). *Deadline:* August 31.

Contact: Rebecca Bennett, Director, Program Services
United Negro College Fund
8260 Willow Oaks Corporate Drive
Fairfax, VA 22031-8044
Phone: 800-331-2244
E-mail: rbennett@uncf.org

V103/UNCF EMERGENCY ASSISTANCE SCHOLARSHIP FUND

Scholarship available to students attending one of the following UNCF member colleges or universities: Clark Atlanta, Interdenominational Center, Morehouse, Morris Brown, or Spelman. Minimum 2.5 GPA required. Prospective applicants should complete the Student Profile found at Web site: http://www.uncf.org

Award: Scholarship for use in senior year; not renewable. *Number:* 1.

Eligibility Requirements: Applicant must be Black (non-Hispanic) and enrolled or expecting to enroll at a four-year institution or university. Applicant must have 2.5 GPA or higher. Available to U.S. citizens.

Application Requirements: Application, financial need analysis. *Deadline:* varies.

Contact: Rebecca Bennett, Director, Program Services
United Negro College Fund
8260 Willow Oaks Corporate Drive
Fairfax, VA 22031-8044
Phone: 800-331-2244
E-mail: rbennett@uncf.org

VERIZON FOUNDATION SCHOLARSHIP

Scholarship for residents of the Verizon service area (Northeastern states) attending a UNCF member college or university, or Ohio State University. Minimum 2.5 GPA required. Prospective applicants should complete the Student Profile found at Web site: http://www.uncf.org

Award: Scholarship for use in freshman, sophomore, junior, or senior years; not renewable. *Amount:* $2000–$4000.

Eligibility Requirements: Applicant must be Black (non-Hispanic); enrolled or expecting to enroll at a four-year institution or university and resident of New Jersey, New York, or Pennsylvania. Applicant must have 2.5 GPA or higher. Available to U.S. citizens.

Application Requirements: Application, financial need analysis. *Deadline:* varies.

Contact: Rebecca Bennett, Director, Program Services
United Negro College Fund
8260 Willow Oaks Corporate Drive
Fairfax, VA 22031-8044
Phone: 800-331-2244
E-mail: rbennett@uncf.org

WENDELL SCOTT, SR./NASCAR SCHOLARSHIP

Award for full-time junior or senior undergraduates or part-time graduate students. Undergraduates must have a 3.0 GPA and graduate students must have a 3.2 GPA. Undergraduates receive an award of $1500. Graduate recipients receive $2000. Please visit Web site for more information: http://www.uncf.org.

Award: Scholarship for use in junior, senior, or graduate years; renewable. *Amount:* $1500–$2000.

Eligibility Requirements: Applicant must be Black (non-Hispanic) and enrolled or expecting to enroll full or part-time at a two-year or four-year institution or university. Applicant must have 3.0 GPA or higher. Available to U.S. citizens.

Application Requirements: Application, financial need analysis, photo, resume, references, transcript, FAFSA, Student Aid Report (SAR). *Deadline:* April 22.

Contact: William Dunham, Wendell Scott Sr./NASCAR Scholarship
United Negro College Fund
8260 Willow Oaks Corporate Drive, PO Box 10444
Fairfax, VA 22031

WESTERN ASSOCIATION OF LADIES SCHOLARSHIP

Award for a student from Philadelphia County, PA. Must have 2.5 GPA. Please visit Web site for more information: http://www.uncf.org.

Award: Scholarship for use in freshman, sophomore, junior, or senior years; renewable. *Number:* 1. *Amount:* up to $5000.

Eligibility Requirements: Applicant must be Black (non-Hispanic); enrolled or expecting to enroll at an institution or university and resident of Pennsylvania. Applicant must have 2.5 GPA or higher. Available to U.S. citizens.

Application Requirements: Application, financial need analysis, FAFSA, Student Aid Report (SAR). *Deadline:* varies.

Contact: Rebecca Bennett, Director, Program Services
United Negro College Fund
8260 Willow Oaks Corporate Drive
Fairfax, VA 22031-8044
Phone: 800-331-2244
E-mail: rbennett@uncf.org

WHIRLPOOL FOUNDATION SCHOLARSHIP

Renewable award for students participating in Whirlpool's INROADS program in LaPorte, IN; Benton Harbor, MI; and LaVerne, TN. Must have 3.0 GPA. Please visit Web site for more information: http://www.uncf.org.

Award: Scholarship for use in freshman, sophomore, junior, or senior years; renewable. *Number:* varies. *Amount:* $2500.

Eligibility Requirements: Applicant must be Black (non-Hispanic); enrolled or expecting to enroll at an institution or university and resident of Indiana, Michigan, or Tennessee. Applicant must have 3.0 GPA or higher. Available to U.S. citizens.

Application Requirements: Application, financial need analysis, FAFSA, Student Aid Report (SAR). *Deadline:* varies.

Contact: Rebecca Bennett, Director, Program Services
United Negro College Fund
8260 Willow Oaks Corporate Drive
Fairfax, VA 22031-8044
Phone: 800-331-2244
E-mail: rbennett@uncf.org

WISCONSIN STUDENT AID

Award for African-American Wisconsin residents. Must have 2.5 GPA. Please visit Web site for more information: http://www.uncf.org.

Award: Scholarship for use in freshman, sophomore, junior, or senior years; renewable. *Number:* varies. *Amount:* up to $2500.

Eligibility Requirements: Applicant must be Black (non-Hispanic); enrolled or expecting to enroll at an institution or university and resident of Wisconsin. Applicant must have 2.5 GPA or higher. Available to U.S. citizens.

Application Requirements: Application, financial need analysis, FAFSA, Student Aid Report (SAR). *Deadline:* varies.

Contact: Rebecca Bennett, Director, Program Services
United Negro College Fund
8260 Willow Oaks Corporate Drive
Fairfax, VA 22031-8044
Phone: 800-331-2244
E-mail: rbennett@uncf.org

UNITED SOUTH AND EASTERN TRIBES, INC.
http://www.usetinc.org

UNITED SOUTH AND EASTERN TRIBES SCHOLARSHIP FUND

One-time award for American-Indian students who are members of a United South and Eastern Tribes member tribe. Submit college acceptance letter per proof of enrollment, certificate of tribal affiliation, letter stating intended use of award, application, transcript if available, financial need analysis, and essay.

Award: Scholarship for use in freshman, sophomore, junior, senior, graduate, or postgraduate years; not renewable. *Number:* 4–8. *Amount:* up to $500.

Eligibility Requirements: Applicant must be American Indian/Alaska Native and enrolled or expecting to enroll full or part-time at a two-year or four-year or technical institution or university. Available to U.S. and Canadian citizens.

Application Requirements: Application, essay, financial need analysis, transcript, proof of tribal enrollment. *Deadline:* April 30.

Contact: Theresa Embry, Executive Assistant to Director
United South and Eastern Tribes, Inc.
711 Stewarts Ferry Pike, Suite 100
Nashville, TN 37214-2634
Phone: 615-872-7900
Fax: 615-872-7417

UNITED STATES HISPANIC LEADERSHIP INSTITUTE
http://www.ushli.com

DR. JUAN ANDRADE, JR. SCHOLARSHIP

Scholarship for young Hispanic leaders. Applicants must be enrolled or accepted for enrollment as a full-time student in a four-year institution in the U.S. or U.S. territories, and demonstrate a verifiable need for financial support. At least one parent must be of Hispanic ancestry.

Award: Scholarship for use in freshman, sophomore, junior, or senior years. *Amount:* $500–$1000.

Eligibility Requirements: Applicant must be Hispanic and enrolled or expecting to enroll full-time at a two-year or four-year institution. Available to U.S. citizens.

Application Requirements: Application, autobiography, essay, photo, resume, references, transcript. *Deadline:* January 13.

Contact: Scholarship Coordinator
United States Hispanic Leadership Institute
431 South Dearborn, Suite 1203
Chicago, IL 60505
Phone: 312-427-8683
Fax: 312-427-5183
E-mail: ushli@aol.com

WASHINGTON HIGHER EDUCATION COORDINATING BOARD
http://www.hecb.wa.gov

AMERICAN INDIAN ENDOWED SCHOLARSHIP

Awarded to financially needy undergraduate and graduate students with close social and cultural ties to a Native-American community. Must be Washington resident, enrolled full time at Washington School. Deadline is May 15.

Award: Scholarship for use in freshman, sophomore, junior, senior, or graduate years; renewable. *Number:* up to 15. *Amount:* $500–$2000.

Eligibility Requirements: Applicant must be American Indian/Alaska Native; enrolled or expecting to enroll full-time at a two-year or four-year or technical institution or university; resident of Washington and studying in Washington. Available to U.S. citizens.

Application Requirements: Application, financial need analysis. *Deadline:* May 15.

Contact: Ann Lee
Washington Higher Education Coordinating Board
917 Lakeridge Way, SW, PO Box 43430
Olympia, WA 98504-3430
Phone: 360-755-7843
Fax: 360-753-7808
E-mail: annl@hecb.wa.gov

WELSH SOCIETY OF PHILADELPHIA

CYMDEITHAS GYMREIG/PHILADELPHIA SCHOLARSHIP

Awards for undergraduate students of Welsh descent. Must participate in or be members of Welsh organizations or events, which should be evident in applicant's essay. Proof of Welsh heritage required. Must live or attend college within 150 miles of Philadelphia. Minimum 3.0 GPA required. Mandatory meeting held in November.

Award: Scholarship for use in freshman, sophomore, junior, or senior years; renewable. *Number:* 5–7. *Amount:* $1000.

Eligibility Requirements: Applicant must be Protestant; of Welsh heritage; enrolled or expecting to enroll full-time at a two-year or four-year institution or university and must have an interest in designated field specified by sponsor. Applicant must have 3.0 GPA or higher. Available to U.S. citizens.

Application Requirements: Application, autobiography, essay, references, self-addressed stamped envelope, test scores, transcript. *Deadline:* March 1.

Contact: Chairman, Scholarship Committee
Welsh Society of Philadelphia
Hen Dy Hapus, 367 South River Street
Wilkes-Barre, PA 18702-3813
E-mail: cymro_w18702@juno.com

WHITE EARTH TRIBAL COUNCIL

WHITE EARTH SCHOLARSHIP PROGRAM

Renewable scholarship of at least $3000 awarded to Native-American Indian students. Must be enrolled member of the White Earth Band of Ojibwa. Financial need is considered. To be used for any undergraduate or graduate year of a trade/technical institution, two- or four-year college or university. Minimum 2.5 GPA required. Deadline is May 31.

Award: Scholarship for use in freshman, sophomore, junior, senior, graduate, or postgraduate years; renewable. *Number:* 200. *Amount:* $3000.

Eligibility Requirements: Applicant must be American Indian/Alaska Native and enrolled or expecting to enroll full or part-time at a two-year or four-year or technical institution or university. Applicant must have 2.5 GPA or higher. Available to U.S. citizens.

Application Requirements: Application, financial need analysis, transcript. *Deadline:* May 31.

Contact: Leslie Nessman, Scholarship Manager
White Earth Tribal Council
PO Box 418
White Earth, MN 56591-0418
Phone: 218-983-3285 Ext. 1227
Fax: 218-983-4299

WISCONSIN HIGHER EDUCATIONAL AIDS BOARD
http://www.heab.state.wi.us

MINORITY UNDERGRADUATE RETENTION GRANT-WISCONSIN

Provides financial assistance to African-American, Native-American, Hispanic, and former citizens of Laos, Vietnam, and Cambodia, for study in Wisconsin. Must be Wisconsin resident, enrolled at least half-time in a two-year or four-year nonprofit college, and must show financial need. Please refer to Web site for further details: http://www.heab.state.wi.us

Award: Grant for use in freshman, sophomore, junior, senior, or graduate years; not renewable. *Number:* varies. *Amount:* $250–$2500.

Eligibility Requirements: Applicant must be American Indian/Alaska Native, Asian/Pacific Islander, Black (non-Hispanic), or Hispanic; enrolled or expecting to enroll full or part-time at a two-year or

Wisconsin Higher Educational Aids Board (continued)

four-year or technical institution or university; resident of Wisconsin and studying in Wisconsin. Available to U.S. and non-U.S. citizens.

Application Requirements: Application, financial need analysis. *Deadline:* Continuous.

Contact: Mary Lou Kuzdas, Program Coordinator
Wisconsin Higher Educational Aids Board
PO Box 7885
Madison, WI 53707-7885
Phone: 608-267-2212
Fax: 608-267-2808
E-mail: mary.kuzdas@heab.state.wi.us

WISCONSIN NATIVE AMERICAN/ INDIAN STUDENT ASSISTANCE GRANT

Grants for Wisconsin residents who are at least one-quarter American-Indian. Must be attending a college or university within the state. Please refer to Web site for further details: http://www.heab.state.wi.us

Award: Grant for use in freshman, sophomore, junior, senior, graduate, or postgraduate years; not renewable. *Number:* varies. *Amount:* $250–$1100.

Eligibility Requirements: Applicant must be American Indian/Alaska Native; enrolled or expecting to enroll full or part-time at a two-year or four-year or technical institution or university; resident of Wisconsin and studying in Wisconsin. Available to U.S. citizens.

Application Requirements: Application, financial need analysis. *Deadline:* Continuous.

Contact: Sandra Thomas, Program Coordinator
Wisconsin Higher Educational Aids Board
PO Box 7885
Madison, WI 53707-7885
Phone: 608-266-0888
Fax: 608-267-2808
E-mail: sandy.thomas@heab.state.wi.us

WOMEN OF THE EVANGELICAL LUTHERAN CHURCH IN AMERICA http://www.womenoftheelca.org

AMELIA KEMP SCHOLARSHIP

Scholarships provided for ELCA women who are of an ethnic minority in undergraduate, graduate, professional or vocational courses of study. Must be at least 21 years old and hold membership in the ELCA. Must have experienced an interruption in education of two or more years since the completion of high school. For more details see Web site: http://www.elca.org/wo.

Award: Scholarship for use in freshman, sophomore, junior, senior, or graduate years; not renewable. *Number:* 1. *Amount:* up to $1200.

Eligibility Requirements: Applicant must be Lutheran; American Indian/Alaska Native, Asian/Pacific Islander, Black (non-Hispanic), or Hispanic; age 21; enrolled or expecting to enroll full or part-time at a two-year or four-year or technical institution or university and female. Available to U.S. citizens.

Application Requirements: *Deadline:* February 1.

Contact: Application available at Web site.

WORLDSTUDIO FOUNDATION http://www.worldstudio.org

SPECIAL ANIMATION AND ILLUSTRATION SCHOLARSHIP

Scholarships are for minority and economically disadvantaged students who are studying illustration, cartooning, and animation in American colleges and universities. Scholarship recipients are selected not only for their ability and their need, but also for their demonstrated commitment to giving back to the larger community through their work.

Award: Scholarship for use in freshman, sophomore, junior, senior, or graduate years; not renewable. *Number:* 25. *Amount:* $1500.

Eligibility Requirements: Applicant must be American Indian/Alaska Native, Asian/Pacific Islander, Black (non-Hispanic), or Hispanic and enrolled or expecting to enroll full-time at a two-year or four-year or technical institution or university. Applicant must have 2.5 GPA or higher. Available to U.S. and non-U.S. citizens.

Application Requirements: Application, essay, financial need analysis, photo, portfolio, references, self-addressed stamped envelope, transcript. *Deadline:* March 19.

Contact: Scholarship Coordinator
Worldstudio Foundation
200 Varick Street, 5th Floor
New York, NY 10014
Phone: 212-366-1317 Ext. 18
Fax: 212-807-0024
E-mail: scholarships@worldstudio.org

YEMENI AMERICAN ASSOCIATION

YEMENI AMERICAN ASSOCIATION SCHOLARSHIPS

One-time scholarships of $1000 for high school seniors of Yemeni heritage.

Award: Scholarship for use in freshman year; not renewable. *Number:* up to 10. *Amount:* up to $1000.

Eligibility Requirements: Applicant must be of Yemeni heritage; high school student and planning to enroll or expecting to enroll at an institution or university. Available to U.S. citizens.

Application Requirements: Application. *Deadline:* varies.

Contact: Yemeni American Association
2770 Salina Street
Dearborn, MI 48120

YES I CAN! FOUNDATION http://www.yesican.org

STANLEY E. JACKSON SCHOLARSHIP AWARDS

• See page 567

YMCA BLACK ACHIEVERS SCHOLARSHIP http://www.ymcaofcentralky.org/

YMCA BLACK ACHIEVERS SCHOLARSHIP

Need-based scholarships awarded to deserving African-American students.

Award: Scholarship for use in freshman, sophomore, junior, or senior years. *Amount:* $1000–$1500.

Eligibility Requirements: Applicant must be Black (non-Hispanic) and enrolled or expecting to enroll at a two-year or four-year or technical institution or university. Available to U.S. citizens.

Application Requirements: Application, financial need analysis. *Deadline:* varies.

Contact: Freddie Brown, Director, Black Achievers
YMCA Black Achievers Scholarship
Central Kentucky YMCA
239 East High Street
Lexington, KY 40507
Phone: 859-258-9622 Ext. 15
Fax: 859-233-3561
E-mail: fbrown@ymcaofcentralky.org

YOUTH OPPORTUNITIES FOUNDATION http://www.yoflatinoscholars.com

YOUTH OPPORTUNITIES FOUNDATION SCHOLARSHIPS

Scholarships for Hispanic/Latino high school students that rank in the top 10% of their class and score at least 1000 on the SATs. AP classes, leadership skills and community activities will be weighed toward consideration. Must be California resident. At least one parent must be of Hispanic descent. Students must write foundation for an application.

Award: Scholarship for use in freshman year; not renewable. *Number:* 100. *Amount:* $100–$500.

Eligibility Requirements: Applicant must be Hispanic; high school student; planning to enroll or expecting to enroll full-time at a two-year or four-year institution or university; resident of California and must have an interest in leadership. Available to U.S. citizens.

Application Requirements: Application, photo, references, test scores, transcript. *Deadline:* March 31.

Contact: Felix Castro, Executive Director
Youth Opportunities Foundation
8616 La Tijera Boulevard, Suite 3030, PO Box 45762
Los Angeles, CA 90045
Phone: 310-670-7664
Fax: 310-670-5238

RELIGIOUS AFFILIATION

AMERICAN BAPTIST FINANCIAL AID PROGRAM   http://www.abc-usa.org

AMERICAN BAPTIST FINANCIAL AID PROGRAM NATIVE AMERICAN GRANTS
• See page 604

AMERICAN BAPTIST SCHOLARSHIPS

One-time award for undergraduates who are members of American Baptist Church. Must be attending an accredited college or university in the United States or Puerto Rico. If attending an ABC-related school, the scholarship amount is $2000 for the year. If not ABC-related, the amount is $1000. Deadline: May 31. Minimum GPA of 2.75 required.

Award: Scholarship for use in freshman, sophomore, junior, or senior years; not renewable. *Number:* varies. *Amount:* $1000–$2000.

Eligibility Requirements: Applicant must be Baptist and enrolled or expecting to enroll full-time at a four-year institution or university. Available to U.S. citizens.

Application Requirements: Application, financial need analysis, references. *Deadline:* May 31.

Contact: Lynne Eckman, Director of Financial Aid
American Baptist Financial Aid Program
PO Box 851
Valley Forge, PA 19482-0851
Phone: 610-768-2067
Fax: 610-768-2056
E-mail: lynne.eckman@abc-usa.org

AMERICAN SEPHARDI FOUNDATION   http://www.asfonline.org

BROOME AND ALLEN BOYS CAMP AND SCHOLARSHIP FUND

The Broome and Allen Scholarship is awarded to students of Sephardic origin or those working in Sephardic studies. Both graduate and undergraduate degree candidates as well as those doing research projects will be considered. It is awarded for one year and must be renewed for successive years. Enclose copy of tax returns with application. Deadline is May 15.

Award: Scholarship for use in freshman, sophomore, junior, senior, graduate, or postgraduate years; not renewable. *Number:* 25–60. *Amount:* $500–$2000.

Eligibility Requirements: Applicant must be Jewish and enrolled or expecting to enroll full or part-time at a two-year or four-year or technical institution or university. Available to U.S. and non-U.S. citizens.

Application Requirements: Application, essay, financial need analysis, references, transcript, copy of tax returns. *Deadline:* May 15.

Contact: Esme Berg, Director
American Sephardi Foundation
15 West 16th Street
New York, NY 10011
Phone: 212-294-8350
Fax: 212-294-8348
E-mail: eberg@asf.cjh.org

BANK OF AMERICA

WILLIAM HEATH EDUCATION SCHOLARSHIP FOR MINISTERS, PRIESTS AND MISSIONARIES
• See page 453

CATHOLIC AID ASSOCIATION   http://www.catholicaid.com

CATHOLIC AID ASSOCIATION COLLEGE TUITION SCHOLARSHIP

Applicants must have been a Catholic Aid Association member for at least two years. $300 scholarships for state and non-Catholic institutions, $500 for Catholic Colleges and Universities. Must be a member of the Catholic Aid Association. Application deadline is in February.

Award: Scholarship for use in freshman or sophomore years; not renewable. *Number:* 200. *Amount:* $300–$500.

Eligibility Requirements: Applicant must be Roman Catholic and enrolled or expecting to enroll full-time at a two-year or four-year or technical institution or university. Available to U.S. citizens.

Application Requirements: Application, essay, references, transcript. *Deadline:* February 15.

Contact: Jessica Schadt, Administrative Assistant
Catholic Aid Association
3499 North Lexington Avenue
St. Paul, MN 55126-8089
Phone: 651-490-0170
Fax: 651-490-0746
E-mail: jschadt@catholicaid.com

CATHOLIC KOLPING SOCIETY OF AMERICA   http://www.kolping.org

FATHER KREWITT SCHOLARSHIP
• See page 495

CENTRAL SCHOLARSHIP BUREAU   http://www.centralsb.org

THE LESSANS FAMILY SCHOLARSHIP

Scholarship available for Jewish students who attend accredited undergraduate colleges, universities or vocational schools. Awards are based on need and merit. The scholarship committee determines award amounts. Deadline is May 31.

Award: Scholarship for use in freshman, sophomore, junior, or senior years; renewable. *Number:* 1.

Eligibility Requirements: Applicant must be Jewish and enrolled or expecting to enroll at a four-year institution or university. Applicant must have 3.0 GPA or higher. Available to U.S. citizens.

Application Requirements: Application, essay. *Deadline:* May 31.

Contact: Roberta Goldman, Program Director
Central Scholarship Bureau
1700 Reisterstown Road
Suite 220
Baltimore, MD 21208-2903
Phone: 410-415-5558
Fax: 410-415-5501
E-mail: roberta@centralsb.org

COMMUNITY FOUNDATION OF WESTERN MASSACHUSETTS   http://www.communityfoundation.org

KIMBER RICHTER FAMILY SCHOLARSHIP

Scholarship is given to a student of the Bahai faith who attends or plans to attend college. For more information or application visit http://www.communityfoundation.org.

Award: Scholarship for use in freshman, sophomore, junior, or senior years; renewable. *Number:* 1. *Amount:* up to $500.

Eligibility Requirements: Applicant must be Baha'i faith; enrolled or expecting to enroll full or part-time at a four-year institution and resident of Massachusetts. Available to U.S. citizens.

Application Requirements: Application, financial need analysis, transcript. *Deadline:* March 31.

Contact: Dorothy Theriaque, Education Associate
Community Foundation of Western Massachusetts
1500 Main Street, PO Box 15769
Springfield, MA 01115
Phone: 413-732-2858
Fax: 413-733-8565
E-mail: dtheriaque@communityfoundation.org

EASTERN ORTHODOX COMMITTEE ON SCOUTING
http://www.eocs.org

EASTERN ORTHODOX COMMITTEE ON SCOUTING SCHOLARSHIPS
• See page 498

FADEL EDUCATIONAL FOUNDATION, INC.
http://www.fadelfoundation.org

ANNUAL AWARD PROGRAM

Grants awarded on the basis of merit, financial need, and the potential of an applicant to positively impact Muslims' lives in the U.S

Award: Grant for use in freshman, sophomore, junior, senior, graduate, or postgraduate years; not renewable. *Number:* 20–45. *Amount:* $400–$2000.

Eligibility Requirements: Applicant must be Muslim faith and enrolled or expecting to enroll full or part-time at a two-year or four-year or technical institution or university. Available to U.S. citizens.

Application Requirements: Application, essay, financial need analysis, references, test scores, transcript. *Deadline:* varies.

Contact: Ayman Hossam Fadel, Secretary
Fadel Educational Foundation, Inc.
PO Box 212135
Augusta, GA 30917-2135
Fax: 866-705-9495
E-mail: afadel@bww.com

FIRST CATHOLIC SLOVAK LADIES ASSOCIATION
http://www.fcsla.com

FIRST CATHOLIC SLOVAK LADIES ASSOCIATION FRATERNAL SCHOLARSHIP AWARD FOR COLLEGE AND GRADUATE STUDY
• See page 613

FIRST PRESBYTERIAN CHURCH
http://www.firstchurchtulsa.org

CLARENCE WARREN SCHOLARSHIP FUND

Scholarship for undergraduate study for student in financial need. Must be member of the Presbyterian Church; preference given to members of the First Presbyterian Church, Tulsa, OK.

Award: Scholarship for use in freshman, sophomore, junior, or senior years; not renewable. *Amount:* $500–$2000.

Eligibility Requirements: Applicant must be Presbyterian and enrolled or expecting to enroll full-time at a four-year institution or university. Available to U.S. citizens.

Application Requirements: Application, financial need analysis, interview, references, transcript. *Deadline:* April 15.

Contact: Tonye Briscoe, Administrative Assistant
First Presbyterian Church
706 South Boston Avenue
Tulsa, OK 74119-1629
Phone: 918-584-4701
Fax: 918-584-5233
E-mail: tbriscoe@firstchurchtulsa.org

CYDNA ANN HUFFSTETLER MEMORIAL TRUST FUND

Award for First Presbyterian Church member to attend an accredited university, college or vocational school.

Award: Scholarship for use in freshman, sophomore, junior, senior, graduate, or postgraduate years; not renewable. *Amount:* $500–$1000.

Eligibility Requirements: Applicant must be Presbyterian and enrolled or expecting to enroll at a two-year or four-year or technical institution or university. Available to U.S. citizens.

Application Requirements: Application, financial need analysis, interview, references, transcript. *Deadline:* April 15.

Contact: Tonye Briscoe, Administrative Assistant
First Presbyterian Church
706 South Boston Avenue
Tulsa, OK 74119-1629
Phone: 918-584-4701
Fax: 918-584-5233
E-mail: tbriscoe@firstchurchtulsa.org

ETHEL FRANCIS CRATE SCHOLARSHIP FUND

Scholarships for students who are members of the Presbyterian Church and who are in their junior or senior year of college. Must demonstrate financial need. Preference given to members of the First Presbyterian Church, Tulsa, OK.

Award: Scholarship for use in junior or senior years; not renewable. *Amount:* $500–$2000.

Eligibility Requirements: Applicant must be Presbyterian and enrolled or expecting to enroll full-time at a four-year institution or university. Available to U.S. citizens.

Application Requirements: Application, financial need analysis, interview, references, transcript. *Deadline:* April 15.

Contact: Tonye Briscoe, Administrative Assistant
First Presbyterian Church
706 South Boston Avenue
Tulsa, OK 74119-1629
Phone: 918-584-4701
Fax: 918-584-5233
E-mail: tbriscoe@firstchurchtulsa.org

HARRY ALLEN MEMORIAL TRUST FUND

Need-based scholarships for members of First Presbyterian Church to pursue postsecondary education.

Award: Scholarship for use in freshman, sophomore, junior, senior, graduate, or postgraduate years; not renewable. *Amount:* $500–$2000.

Eligibility Requirements: Applicant must be Presbyterian and enrolled or expecting to enroll at a two-year or four-year or technical institution or university. Available to U.S. citizens.

Application Requirements: Application, financial need analysis, interview, references, transcript. *Deadline:* April 15.

Contact: Tonye Briscoe, Administrative Assistant
First Presbyterian Church
706 South Boston Avenue
Tulsa, OK 74119-1629
Phone: 918-584-4701
Fax: 918-584-5233
E-mail: tbriscoe@firstchurchtulsa.org

GENERAL BOARD OF GLOBAL MINISTRIES
http://www.gbgm-umc.org

NATIONAL LEADERSHIP DEVELOPMENT GRANTS
• See page 614

HERMAN OSCAR SCHUMACHER SCHOLARSHIP FUND

HERMAN OSCAR SCHUMACHER SCHOLARSHIP FUND FOR MEN

Up to 70 $500 scholarships will be awarded to male residents of Spokane County, WA. Preference will be given to orphans and the financially needy. Must provide proof of enrollment in a trade/technical school or college and that at least one year has been completed. Scholarship amount may vary.

Award: Scholarship for use in sophomore, junior, senior, or graduate years; renewable. *Number:* 40–70. *Amount:* $500.

Eligibility Requirements: Applicant must be Christian; enrolled or expecting to enroll full-time at a two-year or four-year or technical institution or university; male and resident of Washington. Available to U.S. citizens.

Application Requirements: Application, transcript, proof of enrollment. *Deadline:* October 1.

Contact: Chad Legate, Assistant Vice President and Relationship Manager
Herman Oscar Schumacher Scholarship Fund
Washington Trust Bank, Trust Department
PO Box 2127
Spokane, WA 99210
Phone: 509-353-3881
Fax: 509-353-2278
E-mail: clegate@watrust.com

ITALIAN CATHOLIC FEDERATION, INC.
http://www.icf.org

ICF COLLEGE SCHOLARSHIPS TO HIGH SCHOOL SENIORS
• See page 620

JEWISH FAMILY AND CHILDREN'S SERVICES
http://www.jfcs.org

ANNA AND CHARLES STOCKWITZ CHILDREN AND YOUTH FUND

Must be Jewish resident of San Francisco, San Mateo, northern Santa Clara, Marin, or Sonoma county. Award to assist children and teens with education, social, or psychological experience, or to assist them in attending undergraduate school. For more details and an application see Web site: http://www.jfcs.org.

Award: Grant for use in freshman, sophomore, junior, or senior years; not renewable. *Number:* varies. *Amount:* up to $6000.

Eligibility Requirements: Applicant must be Jewish; enrolled or expecting to enroll at a two-year or four-year or technical institution or university and resident of California. Available to U.S. citizens.

Application Requirements: Application, financial need analysis, transcript. *Deadline:* September 1.

Contact: Eric Singer, Director, Financial Aid Center
Jewish Family and Children's Services
2150 Post Street
San Francisco, CA 94115
Phone: 415-449-1226
E-mail: erics@jfcs.org

BUTRIMOVITZ FAMILY ENDOWMENT FUND FOR JEWISH EDUCATION

Must be Jewish resident of San Francisco, San Mateo, Marin, or Sonoma county. Scholarships for individuals in need who wish to pursue traditional Jewish education in context of a Jewish day school, undergraduate, or graduate school setting. For more details and an application see Web site: http://www.jfcs.org.

Award: Scholarship for use in freshman, sophomore, junior, senior, or graduate years; not renewable. *Number:* 2–4. *Amount:* up to $500.

Eligibility Requirements: Applicant must be Jewish; age 13-17; enrolled or expecting to enroll at a four-year institution or university and resident of California. Available to U.S. citizens.

Application Requirements: Application, financial need analysis, transcript. *Deadline:* Continuous.

Contact: Eric Singer, Director, Financial Aid Center
Jewish Family and Children's Services
2150 Post Street
San Francisco, CA 94115
Phone: 415-449-1226
E-mail: erics@jfcs.org

DAVID, NANCY, AND LIZA CHERNEY SCHOLARSHIP FUND

Annual scholarships of $100 towards a young woman's college education.

Award: Grant for use in freshman year. *Number:* 1.

Eligibility Requirements: Applicant must be Jewish; enrolled or expecting to enroll at a two-year or four-year institution or university and studying in California. Available to U.S. citizens.

Application Requirements: Application, financial need analysis.

Contact: Eric Singer, Director, Financial Aid Center
Jewish Family and Children's Services
2150 Post Street
San Francisco, CA 94115
Phone: 415-449-1226
E-mail: erics@jfcs.org

MIRIAM S. GRUNFIELD SCHOLARSHIP FUND

Must be Jewish resident of San Francisco, San Mateo, northern Santa Clara, Marin, or Sonoma county. Annual grants to educate young people who otherwise would not be able to fulfill their educational aspirations. For more information and an application see Web site: http://www.jfcs.org.

Award: Scholarship for use in freshman, sophomore, junior, or senior years; not renewable. *Number:* 4–6. *Amount:* up to $950.

Eligibility Requirements: Applicant must be Jewish; age 26 or under; enrolled or expecting to enroll at an institution or university and resident of California. Available to U.S. citizens.

Application Requirements: Application, financial need analysis, transcript. *Deadline:* Continuous.

Contact: Eric Singer, Director, Financial Aid Center
Jewish Family and Children's Services
2150 Post Street
San Francisco, CA 94115
Phone: 415-449-1226
E-mail: erics@jfcs.org

STANLEY OLSON YOUTH SCHOLARSHIP

Annual college or vocational school scholarships is provided to two young Jewish men and two young Jewish women attending an institution in California who demonstrate academic achievement, promise, and financial need.

Award: Scholarship for use in freshman, sophomore, junior, or senior years; not renewable. *Number:* 2. *Amount:* up to $2500.

Eligibility Requirements: Applicant must be Jewish; age 26 or under; enrolled or expecting to enroll at a technical institution and studying in California. Available to U.S. citizens.

Application Requirements: Application, financial need analysis.

Contact: Eric Singer, Director, Financial Aid Center
Jewish Family and Children's Services
2150 Post Street
San Francisco, CA 94115
Phone: 415-449-1226
E-mail: erics@jfcs.org

JEWISH FOUNDATION FOR EDUCATION OF WOMEN
http://www.jfew.org

BILLER/JEWISH FOUNDATION FOR EDUCATION OF WOMEN

This program provides scholarships to female Jewish permanent residents in the NY metropolitan area for undergraduate and graduate study. Financial need and reasonableness of course of study are the primary criteria. Must study full-time in NY. Check Web site for further details: http://www.jfew.org. Deadline is June 15.

Award: Scholarship for use in freshman, sophomore, junior, senior, or graduate years; not renewable. *Number:* varies. *Amount:* $2000–$5000.

Eligibility Requirements: Applicant must be Jewish; enrolled or expecting to enroll full-time at a two-year or four-year or technical institution or university; female; resident of New York and studying in New York. Available to U.S. and non-Canadian citizens.

Application Requirements: Application, essay, financial need analysis. *Deadline:* June 15.

Contact: Marge Goldwater, Executive Director
Jewish Foundation for Education of Women
135 East 64th Street
New York, NY 10021
Phone: 212-288-3931
Fax: 212-288-5798
E-mail: fdnscholar@aol.com

JEWISH SOCIAL SERVICE AGENCY OF METROPOLITAN WASHINGTON   http://www.jssa.org

DAVID KORN SCHOLARSHIP FUND

One-time award available to full-time undergraduate or graduate student accepted into an accredited program. Must be Jewish, under the age of 30, and a resident of the Washington metropolitan area. Must be a U.S. citizen or working towards citizenship. Decision is based primarily on financial need.

Award: Scholarship for use in freshman, sophomore, junior, senior, or graduate years; not renewable. *Number:* 2–3. *Amount:* $1000–$2000.

Eligibility Requirements: Applicant must be Jewish; age 29 or under; enrolled or expecting to enroll full-time at a two-year or four-year institution or university; resident of District of Columbia and studying in Washington. Available to U.S. citizens.

Application Requirements: Application, financial need analysis, college admission letter. *Deadline:* March 10.

Contact: Lynn Ponton, Scholarship and Loan Coordinator
    Jewish Social Service Agency of Metropolitan Washington
    6123 Montrose Road
    Rockville, MD 20852
    Phone: 301-881-3700 Ext. 611

HERBERT F. SACKS MEMORIAL SCHOLARSHIP

Award based primarily on financial need and academic merit. Available for the 2007-2008 school year.

Award: Scholarship for use in freshman, sophomore, junior, or senior years. *Amount:* up to $6500.

Eligibility Requirements: Applicant must be Jewish; enrolled or expecting to enroll full-time at a four-year institution and resident of District of Columbia. Available to U.S. citizens.

Application Requirements: Application, financial need analysis, transcript. *Deadline:* March 10.

Contact: Lynn Ponton, Scholarship and Loan Coordinator
    Jewish Social Service Agency of Metropolitan Washington
    6123 Montrose Road
    Rockville, MD 20852
    Phone: 301-881-3700 Ext. 611

HYMAN P. MOLDOVER SCHOLARSHIP

Scholarship based primarily on financial need, high academic leadership, and potential.

Award: Scholarship for use in freshman, sophomore, junior, or senior years. *Amount:* up to $5000.

Eligibility Requirements: Applicant must be Jewish; enrolled or expecting to enroll part-time at an institution or university and resident of District of Columbia. Available to U.S. citizens.

Application Requirements: Application, financial need analysis. *Deadline:* March 10.

Contact: Lynn Ponton, Scholarship and Loan Coordinator
    Jewish Social Service Agency of Metropolitan Washington
    6123 Montrose Road
    Rockville, MD 20852
    Phone: 301-881-3700 Ext. 611

JEWISH SOCIAL SERVICE AGENCY OF METROPOLITAN WASHINGTON MAX AND EMMY DREYFUSS UNDERGRADUATE SCHOLARSHIP FUND

One-time award given to a full-time Jewish student, no older than 30, from the metropolitan Washington, D.C. area. Primarily based on financial need. Student must be entering or already enrolled in an accredited four-year undergraduate degree program. Special consideration given to refugees. Recipients are required to complete a questionnaire describing their educational experience. Student must be a U.S. citizen or working towards citizenship.

Award: Scholarship for use in freshman, sophomore, junior, or senior years; not renewable. *Number:* 8–10. *Amount:* $1500–$2000.

Eligibility Requirements: Applicant must be Jewish; age 30 or under; enrolled or expecting to enroll full-time at a four-year institution or university and resident of District of Columbia. Available to U.S. citizens.

Application Requirements: Application, financial need analysis, references, transcript. *Deadline:* March 10.

Contact: Donna Becker
    Jewish Social Service Agency of Metropolitan Washington
    6123 Montrose Road
    Rockville, MD 20852
    Phone: 301-816-2630

MELVIN MANDELL MEMORIAL SCHOLARSHIP

Award based primarily on financial need and academic merit. (available for the 2006-07 school year)

Award: Scholarship for use in freshman year. *Amount:* $1000–$4000.

Eligibility Requirements: Applicant must be Jewish; enrolled or expecting to enroll full-time at a four-year institution and resident of District of Columbia. Available to U.S. citizens.

Application Requirements: Application, financial need analysis, transcript. *Deadline:* March 10.

Contact: Lynn Ponton, Scholarship and Loan Coordinator
    Jewish Social Service Agency of Metropolitan Washington
    6123 Montrose Road
    Rockville, MD 20852
    Phone: 301-881-3700 Ext. 611

MORTON A. GIBSON MEMORIAL SCHOLARSHIP

Awarded to high school seniors who have completed significant volunteer services within the local Jewish community. Must be a Jewish resident of the greater Washington metropolitan area. Must be a U.S. citizen or working towards citizenship. Must be accepted into an accredited four-year undergraduate program on a full-time basis.

Award: Scholarship for use in freshman year; not renewable. *Number:* 2. *Amount:* $2500.

Eligibility Requirements: Applicant must be Jewish; high school student; planning to enroll or expecting to enroll full-time at a four-year institution and resident of District of Columbia. Available to U.S. citizens.

Application Requirements: Application, essay, financial need analysis, references, college admission letter. *Deadline:* March 10.

Contact: Lynn Ponton, Scholarship and Loan Coordinator
    Jewish Social Service Agency of Metropolitan Washington
    6123 Montrose Road
    Rockville, MD 20852
    Phone: 301-881-3700 Ext. 611

JEWISH VOCATIONAL SERVICE - LOS ANGELES   http://www.jvsla.org/scholarship_fund.html

JEWISH VOCATIONAL SERVICE SCHOLARSHIP PROGRAM

Scholarship to support financially needy Jewish students from Los Angeles County in their pursuit of college, graduate, and vocational education. Applicants must be a Jew and must maintain a minimum 2.7 GPA.

Award: Scholarship for use in freshman, sophomore, junior, senior, or postgraduate years; renewable. *Amount:* $500–$5000.

Eligibility Requirements: Applicant must be Jewish and enrolled or expecting to enroll full-time at a four-year institution or university. Available to U.S. citizens.

Application Requirements: Application, essay, references, test scores, transcript, FAFSA, Student Aid Report (SAR), proof of permanent U.S. residency. *Deadline:* April 15.

Contact: Hilary Mandel, Scholarship Fund and Program Manager
    Phone: 323-761-8888 Ext. 8868
    Fax: 323-761-8575
    E-mail: scholarship@jvsla.org

JVS JEWISH COMMUNITY SCHOLARSHIP FUND   http://www.jvsla.org

JVS JEWISH COMMUNITY SCHOLARSHIP

Educational support award for Jewish. Must be a permanent and legal resident of Los Angeles County. Must be planning to attend full-time (12 units minimum per term) at an approved college or vocational school in the United States. Must have a minimum 2.7 GPA.

Award: Scholarship for use in freshman, sophomore, junior, senior, graduate, or postgraduate years; renewable. *Number:* varies. *Amount:* $500–$6000.

Eligibility Requirements: Applicant must be Jewish; enrolled or expecting to enroll full-time at a two-year or four-year or technical institution or university and resident of California. Available to U.S. citizens.

Application Requirements: Application, essay, financial need analysis, interview, references, transcript, Student Aid Report (SAR). *Deadline:* April 15.

Contact: Arlene Hisaker, Scholarship Administrator
JVS Jewish Community Scholarship Fund
6505 Wilshire Boulevard, Suite 200
Los Angeles, CA 90048
Phone: 323-761-8888
Fax: 323-761-8575
E-mail: jgaynor@jvsla.org

KNIGHTS OF COLUMBUS   http://www.kofc.org

FOURTH DEGREE PRO DEO AND PRO PATRIA (CANADA)
• *See page 503*

FRANCIS P. MATTHEWS AND JOHN E. SWIFT EDUCATIONAL TRUST SCHOLARSHIPS
• *See page 503*

JOHN W. MC DEVITT (FOURTH DEGREE) SCHOLARSHIPS
• *See page 503*

KNIGHTS OF LITHUANIA   http://www.knightsoflithuania.com

KNIGHTS OF LITHUANIA NATIONAL SCHOLARSHIPS
• *See page 503*

MORRIS J. AND BETTY KAPLUN FOUNDATION   http://www.kaplunfoundation.org/kaplun

MORRIS J. AND BETTY KAPLUN FOUNDATION ANNUAL ESSAY CONTEST

Essay contest awards winning written work from applicants in grades 7 through 12. Essays address specific questions related to Jewish faith. Please refer to Web site for further details: http://www.kaplun.org

Award: Prize for use in freshman year; not renewable. *Number:* 12–18. *Amount:* $750–$1800.

Eligibility Requirements: Applicant must be Jewish; high school student and planning to enroll or expecting to enroll at an institution or university. Available to U.S. and non-U.S. citizens.

Application Requirements: Applicant must enter a contest, essay. *Deadline:* March 20.

Contact: Eve Seligson, Essay Contest Committee
Morris J. and Betty Kaplun Foundation
PO Box 234428
Great Neck, NY 11023
Phone: 212-966-5020
Fax: 212-966-6205

MUSLIM SCHOLARSHIP FUND - AL-AMEEN

AL-AMEEN SCHOLARSHIP

Available each year to one male and one female undergraduate. Preference given to U.S. resident Muslims. Will award each term up to two years.

Award: Scholarship for use in freshman, sophomore, junior, or senior years; renewable. *Number:* 1–2. *Amount:* up to $3000.

Eligibility Requirements: Applicant must be Muslim faith; high school student and planning to enroll or expecting to enroll full-time at a four-year institution or university. Applicant must have 3.0 GPA or higher. Available to U.S. citizens.

Application Requirements: Application, essay, financial need analysis, test scores, transcript. *Deadline:* July 1.

Contact: Ali Din
Muslim Scholarship Fund - AL-AMEEN
14252 Culver Boulevard, Suite A714
Irvine, CA 92604
Phone: 310-871-8229
E-mail: alameenscholarship@yahoo.com

OSAGE SCHOLARSHIP FUND

MAE LASSLEY OSAGE SCHOLARSHIP FUND
• *See page 629*

TEXAS BLACK BAPTIST SCHOLARSHIP COMMITTEE   http://www.bgct.org

TEXAS BLACK BAPTIST SCHOLARSHIP
• *See page 636*

UNITED METHODIST CHURCH   http://www.umc.org

J. A. KNOWLES MEMORIAL SCHOLARSHIP

One-time award for Texas residents attending a United Methodist institution in Texas. Must have been United Methodist Church member for at least one year. Must be U.S. citizens or permanent residents. Minimum 2.5 GPA required.

Award: Scholarship for use in freshman, sophomore, junior, senior, or graduate years; not renewable. *Number:* 70–80. *Amount:* $800–$1200.

Eligibility Requirements: Applicant must be Methodist; enrolled or expecting to enroll full-time at a two-year or four-year institution or university; resident of Texas and studying in Texas. Applicant must have 2.5 GPA or higher. Available to U.S. citizens.

Application Requirements: Application, essay, references, transcript. *Deadline:* June 1.

Contact: Patti J. Zimmerman, Scholarships Administrator
United Methodist Church
PO Box 340007
Nashville, TN 37203-0007
Phone: 615-340-7344
E-mail: pzimmer@gbhem.org

PRISCILLA R. MORTON SCHOLARSHIP

One-time award for undergraduate study. Preference given to students at United Methodist-related schools. Must verify United Methodist membership. Must have at least a 3.5 GPA. Must be U.S. citizen or permanent resident. Must have completed one semester of study.

Award: Scholarship for use in freshman, sophomore, junior, or senior years; not renewable. *Number:* 30–35. *Amount:* $800–$1000.

Eligibility Requirements: Applicant must be Methodist and enrolled or expecting to enroll full-time at a two-year or four-year institution or university. Applicant must have 3.5 GPA or higher. Available to U.S. citizens.

Application Requirements: Application, essay, references, transcript, membership proof. *Deadline:* June 1.

Contact: Patti J. Zimmerman, Scholarships Administrator
United Methodist Church
PO Box 340007
Nashville, TN 37203-0007
Phone: 615-340-7344
E-mail: pzimmer@gbhem.org

UNITED METHODIST CHURCH ETHNIC SCHOLARSHIP
• *See page 637*

UNITED METHODIST CHURCH HISPANIC, ASIAN, AND NATIVE AMERICAN SCHOLARSHIP
• *See page 637*

UNITED METHODIST YOUTH ORGANIZATION   http://www.umyouth.org

DAVID W. SELF SCHOLARSHIP

Must be a United Methodist Youth who has been active in local church for at least one year prior to application. Must be a graduating senior in high school (who maintained at least a "C" average) entering the first year of undergraduate study. Must be pursuing a "church-related" career.

Award: Scholarship for use in freshman year; not renewable. *Number:* up to 2. *Amount:* up to $1000.

Eligibility Requirements: Applicant must be Methodist; high school student and planning to enroll or expecting to enroll full-time at an institution or university. Available to U.S. citizens.

United Methodist Youth Organization (continued)

Application Requirements: Application, essay, financial need analysis, transcript, certification of church membership. *Deadline:* June 1.

Contact: Grants Coordinator, Division on Ministries with Young
People, General Board of Discipleship
United Methodist Youth Organization
PO Box 340003
Nashville, TN 37203-0003

RICHARD S. SMITH SCHOLARSHIP
• *See page 638*

WELSH SOCIETY OF PHILADELPHIA

CYMDEITHAS GYMREIG/PHILADELPHIA SCHOLARSHIP
• *See page 647*

WOMAN'S MISSIONARY UNION
FOUNDATION   http://www.wmufoundation.com

WOMAN'S MISSIONARY UNION SCHOLARSHIP PROGRAM

Primarily for Baptist young women with high scholastic accomplishments and service through Baptist organizations. Must have an interest in Christian women's leadership development or missionary service. Preference is given for WMU/Acteen membership in a Baptist church. Application deadline is October 1.

Award: Scholarship for use in freshman, sophomore, junior, senior, graduate, or postgraduate years; not renewable. *Number:* 5–10. *Amount:* $500–$1500.

Eligibility Requirements: Applicant must be Baptist and enrolled or expecting to enroll full-time at a two-year or four-year institution or university. Available to U.S. and non-U.S. citizens.

Application Requirements: Application, references, transcript, WMU endorsements. *Deadline:* October 1.

Contact: Linda Lucas
Woman's Missionary Union Foundation
PO Box 11346
Birmingham, AL 35202-1346
Phone: 205-408-5525
E-mail: llucas@wmu.org

WOMEN OF THE EVANGELICAL LUTHERAN
CHURCH IN AMERICA   http://www.womenoftheelca.org

AMELIA KEMP SCHOLARSHIP
• *See page 648*

RESIDENCE/LOCATION OF STUDY

A K STEEL FOUNDATION   http://www.aksteel.com

LOUIE F. COX MEMORIAL AK STEEL AFRICAN- AMERICAN SCHOLARSHIPS
• *See page 601*

A.W. BODINE-SUNKIST GROWERS,
INC.   http://www.sunkist.com

A.W. BODINE-SUNKIST MEMORIAL SCHOLARSHIP
• *See page 537*

ABBIE SARGENT MEMORIAL SCHOLARSHIP,
INC.   http://www.nhfarmbureau.org

ABBIE SARGENT MEMORIAL SCHOLARSHIP

Up to three awards between $400 and $500 will be provided to deserving New Hampshire residents who plan to attend an institute of higher learning. Must be a U.S. citizen. Application deadline is March 15.

Award: Scholarship for use in freshman, sophomore, junior, senior, graduate, or postgraduate years; not renewable. *Number:* 1–3. *Amount:* $400–$500.

Eligibility Requirements: Applicant must be enrolled or expecting to enroll full or part-time at a two-year or four-year or technical institution or university and resident of New Hampshire. Available to U.S. citizens.

Application Requirements: Application, autobiography, financial need analysis, photo, references, transcript. *Deadline:* March 15.

Contact: Melanie Phelps, Treasurer
Abbie Sargent Memorial Scholarship, Inc.
295 Sheep Davis Road
Concord, NH 03301

AKRON URBAN LEAGUE

AKRON URBAN LEAGUE SCHOLARSHIP PROGRAM

Scholarship is designated for 17-19 year-old high school students who are planning on furthering their education. Awards range from $250 to full tuition. Applications available in January. Restricted to applicants who are residents of Ohio.

Award: Scholarship for use in freshman year; renewable. *Number:* 40–45.

Eligibility Requirements: Applicant must be high school student; age 17-19; planning to enroll or expecting to enroll full-time at a two-year or four-year or technical institution or university and resident of Ohio. Applicant must have 2.5 GPA or higher. Available to U.S. citizens.

Application Requirements: Application, essay, financial need analysis, interview, photo, references, test scores, transcript.

Contact: Anthony Burwell, Scholarship manager
Akron Urban League
250 East Market Street
Akron, OH 44308
Phone: 303-434-3101
Fax: 303-434-2716
E-mail: aul250@aol.com

ALABAMA COMMISSION ON HIGHER
EDUCATION   http://www.ache.state.al.us

ALABAMA NATIONAL GUARD EDUCATIONAL ASSISTANCE PROGRAM
• *See page 569*

ALABAMA STUDENT GRANT PROGRAM

Renewable awards available to Alabama residents for undergraduate study at certain independent colleges within the state. Both full and half-time students are eligible. Deadlines: September 15, January 15, and February 15.

Award: Grant for use in freshman, sophomore, junior, or senior years; renewable. *Number:* varies. *Amount:* up to $1200.

Eligibility Requirements: Applicant must be enrolled or expecting to enroll full or part-time at a four-year institution or university; resident of Alabama and studying in Alabama. Available to U.S. citizens.

Application Requirements: Application. *Deadline:* varies.

Contact: William Wall, Associate Executive Director for Student
Assistance, ACHE
Alabama Commission on Higher Education
PO Box 302000
Montgomery, AL 36130-2000
Phone: 334-242-2271
Fax: 334-242-0268
E-mail: wwall@ache.state.al.us

POLICE OFFICERS AND FIREFIGHTERS SURVIVORS EDUCATION ASSISTANCE PROGRAM-ALABAMA
• *See page 537*

ROBERT C. BYRD HONORS SCHOLARSHIP-ALABAMA

Approximately a hundred and five awards. Must be Alabama resident and a high school senior. Minimum 3.5 GPA. Contact school guidance counselor for an application and deadlines.

Award: Scholarship for use in freshman, sophomore, junior, or senior years; renewable. *Number:* 105. *Amount:* $1500.

Eligibility Requirements: Applicant must be high school student; planning to enroll or expecting to enroll full-time at a two-year or four-year institution or university and resident of Alabama. Applicant must have 3.5 GPA or higher. Available to U.S. citizens.

Application Requirements: Application, test scores, transcript. *Deadline:* varies.

Contact: Freda Thrower, Education Specialist
Alabama Commission on Higher Education
PO Box 302101
Montgomery, AL 36130-2101
Phone: 334-242-8059
Fax: 334-242-0482

ALABAMA DEPARTMENT OF VETERANS AFFAIRS
http://www.va.state.al.us

ALABAMA G.I. DEPENDENTS SCHOLARSHIP PROGRAM
• *See page 578*

ALASKA SEA SERVICES SCHOLARSHIP FUND

ALASKA SEA SERVICES SCHOLARSHIP

Scholarship for dependent child or spouse of a legal resident of Alaska who is (or was at the time of death or missing-in-action status) a regular or reserve Navy, Marine Corps or Coast Guard member. Applicant must be enrolled in an accredited four-year college or university pursuing a full-time undergraduate degree.

Award: Scholarship for use in freshman, sophomore, junior, or senior years. *Amount:* up to $1000.

Eligibility Requirements: Applicant must be enrolled or expecting to enroll full-time at a four-year institution or university and resident of Alaska. Available to U.S. citizens.

Application Requirements: Application, references, transcript, FAFSA. *Deadline:* March 1.

Contact: Caroline Jarvis, Alaska Sea Services Scholarship
Alaska Sea Services Scholarship Fund
c/o US Navy League Council 55-151
2300 Wilson Boulevard
Arlington, VA 22201

ALASKA STATE DEPARTMENT OF EDUCATION
http://www.eed.state.ak.us

GEAR UP ALASKA SCHOLARSHIP

Scholarship provides up to $7000 each year for up to four years of undergraduate study (up to $3,500 each year for half-time study). The federal government funds the scholarships. Alaska GEAR UP scholarships are available to students who have participated in GEAR UP Programs in 6th, 7th, and 8th grade and have met the academic milestones established by their district.

Award: Scholarship for use in freshman, sophomore, junior, or senior years. *Amount:* $3500–$7000.

Eligibility Requirements: Applicant must be age 21 or under; enrolled or expecting to enroll full or part-time at a four-year institution or university and resident of Alaska. Available to U.S. citizens.

Application Requirements: Application, references, transcript. *Deadline:* May 31.

Contact: Alaska State Department of Education
801 West 10th Street, Suite 200
Goldbelt Place, PO Box 110500
Juneau, AK 99811-0500
Phone: 907-465-2800
Fax: 907-465-4156

ALBERTA AGRICULTURE FOOD AND RURAL DEVELOPMENT 4-H BRANCH
http://www.4h.ab.ca

ALBERTA AGRICULTURE FOOD AND RURAL DEVELOPMENT 4-H SCHOLARSHIP PROGRAM

Awards will be given to current and incoming students attending any institute of higher learning. Must have been a member of the Alberta 4-H Program and be a Canadian citizen. Must be a resident of Alberta. Application deadline is May 5.

Award: Scholarship for use in freshman, sophomore, junior, senior, or graduate years; not renewable. *Number:* 115–120. *Amount:* $200–$1500.

Eligibility Requirements: Applicant must be enrolled or expecting to enroll full-time at a two-year or four-year or technical institution or university and resident of Alberta. Available to Canadian citizens.

Application Requirements: Application, essay, references, transcript. *Deadline:* May 5.

Contact: Susann McGowan
Alberta Agriculture Food and Rural Development 4-H Branch
RRI West Rose
Edmonton, AB T0C 2V0
Canada
Phone: 780-682-2153
E-mail: foundation@4hav.com

ALBERTA HERITAGE SCHOLARSHIP FUND/ ALBERTA SCHOLARSHIP PROGRAMS
http://www.alis.gov.ab.ca

ADULT HIGH SCHOOL EQUIVALENCY SCHOLARSHIPS
• *See page 601*

ALBERTA BLUE CROSS 50TH ANNIVERSARY SCHOLARSHIPS FOR ABORIGINAL STUDENTS
• *See page 601*

ALBERTA HERITAGE SCHOLARSHIP FUND ALBERTA PRESS COUNCIL SCHOLARSHIP
• *See page 601*

ALBERTA HERITAGE SCHOLARSHIP FUND CANA SCHOLARSHIPS
• *See page 525*

ALBERTA OPPORTUNITIES BURSARY

Award to offset the rising costs of postsecondary education and related student debt loads. An assistance of CAN$500 to CAN $1500. Must be enrolled in your first or second year of full-time postsecondary studies at a participating institution; and qualify for an Alberta student loan of at least $4,000. Students are automatically considered for Alberta Opportunities Bursaries when they apply for a student loan at a participating institution.

Award: Scholarship for use in freshman, sophomore, junior, or senior years; not renewable. *Number:* varies. *Amount:* $430–$1291.

Eligibility Requirements: Applicant must be enrolled or expecting to enroll full-time at a four-year institution or university; resident of Alberta and studying in Alberta. Available to U.S. and Canadian citizens.

Application Requirements: Application. *Deadline:* Continuous.

Contact: Stuart Dunn
Alberta Heritage Scholarship Fund/Alberta Scholarship Programs
9940 106th Street, 4th Floor
Box 28000, Station Main
Edmonton T5J 4R4
Canada
Phone: 780-427-8640
Fax: 780-427-1288
E-mail: scholarships@gov.ab.ca

ALEXANDER RUTHERFORD SCHOLARSHIPS FOR HIGH SCHOOL ACHIEVEMENT
• *See page 602*

BOYS AND GIRLS CLUB OF ALBERTA SCHOLARSHIPS
• *See page 483*

CANADA MILLENNIUM BURSARY

Award to help Alberta's highest financial need students. The program provides non-repayable assistance from CAN$2,250 to CAN$3,000. Must be enrolled full-time at a Canadian postsecondary institution attending their second or subsequent year of undergraduate study or any year of a professional program. Students are automatically considered for Canada Millennium Bursaries when they apply for a student loan. For more information see the Web site: http://www.millenniumscholarships.ca/

Award: Scholarship for use in freshman, sophomore, junior, or senior years; not renewable. *Number:* varies. *Amount:* $1937–$2583.

Eligibility Requirements: Applicant must be enrolled or expecting to enroll full-time at a four-year institution or university and resident of Alberta.

Alberta Heritage Scholarship Fund/Alberta Scholarship Programs (continued)

Application Requirements: Financial need analysis. *Deadline:* Continuous.

Contact: Stuart Dunn, Manager
Alberta Heritage Scholarship Fund/Alberta Scholarship Programs
4th Floor, 9940 106 Street, Box 28000 Station Main
Edmonton, AB T5J 4R4
Canada
Phone: 780-427-8640
Fax: 780-427-1288
E-mail: scholarships@gov.ab.ca

CENTRAL ALBERTA RURAL ELECTRIFICATION ASSOCIATION SCHOLARSHIP

A CAN$1000 scholarship will be awarded to the top male and the top female to recognize the academic accomplishment of children of members of the Central Alberta Rural Electrification Association and to assist and encourage higher education. Must be a Canadian citizen and Alberta resident. For more details see Web site: http://www.alis.gov.ab.ca

Award: Scholarship for use in freshman year; not renewable. *Number:* 2. *Amount:* $861.

Eligibility Requirements: Applicant must be high school student; planning to enroll or expecting to enroll full-time at a two-year institution and resident of Alberta. Available to Canadian citizens.

Application Requirements: Application. *Deadline:* July 1.

Contact: Stuart Dunn, Manager
Alberta Heritage Scholarship Fund/Alberta Scholarship Programs
4th Floor, 9940 106th Street, Box 28000 Station Main
Edmonton, AB T5J 4R4
Canada
Phone: 780-427-8640
Fax: 780-427-1288
E-mail: scholarships@gov.ab.ca

CHARLES S. NOBLE JUNIOR "A" HOCKEY SCHOLARSHIPS
• See page 602

CHARLES S. NOBLE JUNIOR FOOTBALL SCHOLARSHIPS
• See page 602

DR. ERNEST AND MINNIE MEHL SCHOLARSHIP
• See page 602

EARL AND COUNTESS OF WESSEX-WORLD CHAMPIONSHIPS IN ATHLETICS SCHOLARSHIPS

Two CAN$3000 scholarships are available to recognize the top male and female Alberta students who have excelled in track and field, have a strong academic record, and plan to continue their studies at the postsecondary level in Alberta. Must be a Canadian citizen and Alberta resident. Application deadline is October 1. For more details see Web site: http://www.alis.gov.ab.ca

Award: Scholarship for use in freshman year; not renewable. *Number:* 2. *Amount:* $2583.

Eligibility Requirements: Applicant must be high school student; planning to enroll or expecting to enroll full-time at a two-year or four-year or technical institution or university; resident of Alberta; studying in Alberta and must have an interest in athletics/sports. Available to Canadian citizens.

Application Requirements: Application, transcript. *Deadline:* October 1.

Contact: Stuart Dunn, Manager
Alberta Heritage Scholarship Fund/Alberta Scholarship Programs
4th Floor, 9940 106th Street, Box 28000 Station Main
Edmonton, AB T5J 4R4
Canada
Phone: 780-427-8640
Fax: 780-427-1288
E-mail: scholarships@gov.ab.ca

FELLOWSHIPS FOR FULL-TIME STUDIES IN FRENCH-UNIVERSITY
• See page 602

GRANT MACEWAN UNITED WORLD COLLEGE SCHOLARSHIPS
• See page 602

JASON LANG SCHOLARSHIP

A CAN$1000 scholarship will be awarded for the outstanding academic achievement of Alberta postsecondary students who are continuing full-time into their second, third or fourth year of an undergraduate program. Must be a Canadian citizen and Alberta resident. Application deadline is October 15 and February 15. Must have minimum GPA of 3.2 on a 4.0 scale. For more details and deadlines see Web site: http://www.alis.gov.ab.ca

Award: Scholarship for use in sophomore, junior, or senior years; not renewable. *Number:* 8500. *Amount:* $861.

Eligibility Requirements: Applicant must be enrolled or expecting to enroll full-time at a four-year institution or university; resident of Alberta and studying in Alberta. Applicant must have 3.5 GPA or higher. Available to Canadian citizens.

Application Requirements: Application, transcript. *Deadline:* varies.

Contact: Stuart Dunn, Manager
Alberta Heritage Scholarship Fund/Alberta Scholarship Programs
4th Floor, 9940 106th Street, Box 28000 Station Main
Edmonton, AB T5J 4R4
Canada
Phone: 780-427-8640
Fax: 780-427-1288
E-mail: scholarships@gov.ab.ca

JIMMIE CONDON ATHLETIC SCHOLARSHIPS
• See page 603

LAURENCE DECOR STUDENT LEADERSHIP AWARDS
• See page 603

LOUISE MCKINNEY POSTSECONDARY SCHOLARSHIPS
• See page 603

MICHAEL LUCHKOVICH SCHOLARSHIPS FOR CAREER DEVELOPMENT

Award of up to CAN$ 2000 for residents of Alberta who have been working full-time in Alberta for a minimum of three years. Application deadline is August 1 for start date between September-December; December 1 for start date between January-April; April 1 for start date between May-August.

Award: Scholarship for use in freshman, sophomore, junior, or senior years; not renewable. *Number:* varies. *Amount:* up to $2000.

Eligibility Requirements: Applicant must be enrolled or expecting to enroll full or part-time at a four-year institution or university and resident of Alberta. Available to U.S. and Canadian citizens.

Application Requirements: Application, essay. *Deadline:* varies.

Contact: Stuart Dunn, Manager
Alberta Heritage Scholarship Fund/Alberta Scholarship Programs
4th Floor, 9940 106 Street, Box 28000 Station Main
Edmonton, AB T5J 4R4
Canada
Phone: 780-427-8640
Fax: 780-427-1288
E-mail: scholarships@gov.ab.ca

NEW APPRENTICESHIP SCHOLARSHIPS

A CAN$1000 scholarship is available for apprentices in a trade and trainees in a designated occupation to encourage recipients to complete their apprenticeship or occupational training programs. Must be a Canadian citizen or landed immigrant and Alberta resident. For more details see Web site: http://www.alis.gov.ab.ca.

Award: Scholarship for use in freshman year; not renewable. *Number:* 170. *Amount:* $861.

Eligibility Requirements: Applicant must be enrolled or expecting to enroll full-time at a technical institution and resident of Alberta. Available to Canadian citizens.

Application Requirements: Application. *Deadline:* July 31.

Contact: Stuart Dunn, Manager
Alberta Heritage Scholarship Fund/Alberta Scholarship Programs
4th Floor, 9940 106 Street, Box 28000, Station Main
Edmonton, AB T5J 4R4
Canada
Phone: 780-427-8640
Fax: 780-427-1288
E-mail: scholarships@gov.ab.ca

NORTHERN ALBERTA DEVELOPMENT COUNCIL BURSARY
• See page 603

NORTHERN ALBERTA DEVELOPMENT COUNCIL BURSARY PARTNERSHIP PROGRAM

Bursary of CAN$ 1500 for one year of study to assist students in pursuing a postsecondary education. Must be residents of Alberta and plan to enroll full-time in a postsecondary program. In addition, applicants must demonstrate a financial need and be willing to live and work in northern Alberta after completion of the program.

Award: Scholarship for use in freshman, sophomore, junior, or senior years; not renewable. *Amount:* $1291.

Eligibility Requirements: Applicant must be enrolled or expecting to enroll full-time at a four-year institution or university; resident of Alberta and studying in Alberta.

Application Requirements: Application. *Deadline:* February 1.

Contact: Carol Vesak, Bursary Coordinator
Alberta Heritage Scholarship Fund/Alberta Scholarship Programs
2nd Floor, Provincial Building, 9621-96 Avenue, PO Box 900-14
Peace River, AB T8S 1T4
Canada
Phone: 780-624-6545
E-mail: nadc.bursary@gov.ab.ca

NORTHERN STUDENT SUPPLEMENT

An award of CAN$ 500 to CAN$ 1500 depending on financial need for northern Alberta students to enter postsecondary programs. If applicants receive the Northern Student Supplement, the student loan will be reduced by an equivalent amount. Must be northern Alberta resident if you have lived in the Northern Alberta Development Council (NADC) area for two consecutive years

Award: Scholarship for use in freshman, sophomore, junior, or senior years; not renewable. *Number:* varies. *Amount:* $430–$1291.

Eligibility Requirements: Applicant must be enrolled or expecting to enroll full-time at a four-year institution or university; resident of Alberta and studying in Alberta. Available to U.S. and Canadian citizens.

Application Requirements: Application, financial need analysis. *Deadline:* Continuous.

Contact: Stuart Dunn, Manager
Alberta Heritage Scholarship Fund/Alberta Scholarship Programs
4th Floor, 9940 106 Street, Box 28000 Station Main
Edmonton, AB T5J 4R4
Canada
Phone: 780-427-8640
Fax: 780-427-1228
E-mail: scholarships@gov.ab.ca

PERSONS CASE SCHOLARSHIPS
• See page 603

PRAIRIE BASEBALL ACADEMY SCHOLARSHIPS

Up to CAN$40,000 in scholarships of between CAN$500 and CAN$2500 Scholarships awarded to postsecondary students in Alberta who are participants in the Prairie Baseball Academy. Must have earned a minimum GPA of 2.0 on a 4.0 scale in their previous semester. Recipients are chosen based on academic standing, community involvement, and baseball achievements. Application deadline is October 15.

Award: Scholarship for use in freshman, sophomore, junior, or senior years. *Number:* 16–80. *Amount:* $430–$2152.

Eligibility Requirements: Applicant must be enrolled or expecting to enroll full-time at a four-year institution or university; studying in Alberta and must have an interest in athletics/sports. Available to U.S. and Canadian citizens.

Application Requirements: Application, references, transcript, membership in Prairie Baseball Academy. *Deadline:* October 15.

Contact: Stuart Dunn, Manager
Alberta Heritage Scholarship Fund/Alberta Scholarship Programs
4th Floor, 9940 106th Street, Box 28000 Station Main
Edmonton, AB T5J 4R4
Canada
Phone: 780-427-8640
Fax: 780-427-1288
E-mail: scholarships@gov.ab.ca

REGISTERED APPRENTICESHIP PROGRAM SCHOLARSHIP

A CAN $1000 scholarship is available to recognize the accomplishments of Alberta high school students enrolled in the Registered Apprenticeship Program (RAP); and to encourage them to enter into a regular apprenticeship program after graduation. Funds are distributed CAN $700 in the first year and CAN $300 in the second year. Must be a Canadian citizen or landed immigrant, and Alberta resident. Deadline: June 30. For more details see Web site: http://www.alis.gov.ab.ca

Award: Scholarship for use in freshman year; not renewable. *Number:* up to 50. *Amount:* $861.

Eligibility Requirements: Applicant must be enrolled or expecting to enroll full-time at a two-year or four-year or technical institution or university and resident of Alberta. Available to Canadian citizens.

Application Requirements: Application. *Deadline:* June 30.

Contact: Stuart Dunn, Manager
Alberta Heritage Scholarship Fund/Alberta Scholarship Programs
4th Floor, 9940 106th Street, Box 28000 Station Main
Edmonton, AB T5J 4R4
Canada
Phone: 780-427-8640
Fax: 780-427-1288
E-mail: scholarships@gov.ab.ca

RUTHERFORD SCHOLARS
• See page 604

STREAM-FLO/MASTER FLO SCHOLARSHIPS
• See page 525

ALBUQUERQUE COMMUNITY FOUNDATION
http://www.albuquerquefoundation.org

ACF- NOTAH BEGAY III SCHOLARSHIP PROGRAM FOR NATIVE AMERICAN SCHOLAR ATHLETES
• See page 604

ALBUQUERQUE COMMUNITY FOUNDATION NEW MEXICO MANUFACTURED HOUSING SCHOLARSHIP PROGRAM

One $1000 award will be made to one New Mexico high school senior graduating with a 3.0 GPA and living in a mobile/manufactured home. Award is to be used for study in a two-year, four-year, or vocational institution. Annual application deadline is in March. Refer to Web site for details and application: http://www.albuquerquefoundation.org

Award: Scholarship for use in freshman, sophomore, junior, or senior years; not renewable. *Number:* 1. *Amount:* $1000.

Eligibility Requirements: Applicant must be high school student; planning to enroll or expecting to enroll full-time at a two-year or four-year or technical institution or university; resident of New Mexico and studying in New Mexico. Applicant must have 3.0 GPA or higher. Available to U.S. citizens.

Application Requirements: Application, financial need analysis, resume, references, test scores, transcript. *Deadline:* varies.

Contact: Nancy Johnson, Program Director
Albuquerque Community Foundation
PO Box 36960
Albuquerque, NM 87176-6960
Phone: 505-883-6240
E-mail: acf@albuquerquefoundation.org

SUSSMAN-MILLER EDUCATIONAL ASSISTANCE FUND

Program to provide financial aid to enable students to continue with an undergraduate program. This is a "gap" program based on financial need. Must be resident of New Mexico. Do not write or call for information. Please visit Web site: http://www.albuquerquefoundation.org for complete information. Minimum 3.0 GPA required. Deadline varies.

Albuquerque Community Foundation (continued)

Award: Grant for use in freshman, sophomore, junior, or senior years; not renewable. *Number:* 30–40. *Amount:* $500–$3000.

Eligibility Requirements: Applicant must be enrolled or expecting to enroll full-time at a four-year institution or university and resident of New Mexico. Applicant must have 3.0 GPA or higher. Available to U.S. citizens.

Application Requirements: Application, autobiography, essay, financial need analysis, resume, references, test scores, transcript. *Deadline:* June 29.

Contact: Nancy Johnson, Program Director
Albuquerque Community Foundation
PO Box 36960
Albuquerque, NM 87176-6960
Phone: 505-883-6240
E-mail: acf@albuquerquefoundation.org

ALERT SCHOLARSHIP

ALERT SCHOLARSHIP

We offer a $500 scholarship for the best essay on drug and alcohol abuse. Applicant must be high school student between the ages of 16 and 19 living in Washington, Idaho, Montana, Wyoming, Colorado, North Dakota, or South Dakota. Minimum 2.5 GPA required.

Award: Scholarship for use in freshman year; not renewable. *Number:* 16. *Amount:* $500.

Eligibility Requirements: Applicant must be high school student; age 16-19; planning to enroll or expecting to enroll full or part-time at a two-year or four-year or technical institution or university and resident of Colorado, Idaho, Montana, North Dakota, South Dakota, Washington, or Wyoming. Applicant must have 2.5 GPA or higher. Available to U.S. citizens.

Application Requirements: Essay, photo, transcript. *Deadline:* Continuous.

Contact: Jolene Smith, Coordinator
Alert Scholarship
PO Box 4833
Boise, ID 83711
Phone: 208-375-7911
Fax: 208-376-0770

ALEXANDER GRAHAM BELL ASSOCIATION FOR THE DEAF AND HARD OF HEARING
http://www.agbell.org

ELSIE M. BELL GROSVENOR SCHOLARSHIP
• See page 553

AMERICAN ASSOCIATION OF UNIVERSITY WOMEN - HARRISBURG BRANCH
http://www.aauwharrisburg.org/

BEVERLY J. SMITH MEMORIAL SCHOLARSHIP

Award for a female student attending an accredited college or university located in Pennsylvania and a permanent resident of Dauphin, Cumberland or Perry County. Candidates must demonstrate academic achievement and financial need, and have completed at least 60 credits. At least a 3.4 GPA required. Application date varies.

Award: Scholarship for use in freshman, sophomore, junior, or senior years; not renewable. *Number:* 2. *Amount:* $2500.

Eligibility Requirements: Applicant must be enrolled or expecting to enroll full-time at a four-year institution or university; female; resident of Pennsylvania and studying in Pennsylvania. Available to U.S. and non-U.S. citizens.

Application Requirements: Application, essay, financial need analysis, interview, references, transcript, proof of enrollment. *Deadline:* May 13.

Contact: Colleen Willard-Holt, Scholarship Chair
American Association of University Women - Harrisburg Branch
PO Box 1625
Harrisburg, PA 17105-1625
Phone: 717-948-6208
Fax: 717-948-6064
E-mail: Scholarship@aauwharrisburg.org

MARTHA M. DOHNER MEMORIAL SCHOLARSHIP

Award for a female student who is a resident of, and attends college in, Dauphin or Cumberland counties, Pennsylvania. Applicants must have earned at least 15 credits, and demonstrate academic achievement and financial need. At least 3.25 GPA required.

Award: Scholarship for use in freshman, sophomore, junior, or senior years; not renewable. *Number:* 1. *Amount:* $1000.

Eligibility Requirements: Applicant must be enrolled or expecting to enroll full-time at a four-year institution or university; female; resident of Pennsylvania and studying in Pennsylvania. Available to U.S. and non-U.S. citizens.

Application Requirements: Application, essay, financial need analysis, interview, references, transcript, proof of enrollment. *Deadline:* May 13.

Contact: Colleen Willard-Holt, Scholarship Chair
American Association of University Women - Harrisburg Branch
PO Box 1625
Harrisburg, PA 17105-1625
Phone: 717-948-6208
Fax: 717-948-6064
E-mail: Scholarship@aauwharrisburg.org

AMERICAN CANCER SOCIETY, FLORIDA DIVISION, INC.
http://www.cancer.org

AMERICAN CANCER SOCIETY, FLORIDA DIVISION R O C K COLLEGE SCHOLARSHIP PROGRAM

To be eligible for an American Cancer Society Florida Division Scholarship, Reaching Out to Cancer Kids Program, applicants must have had a personal diagnosis of cancer, be a Florida resident between the ages of 18 and 21, and plan to attend college in Florida. Must have Minimum 2.0 GPA score. Awards will be based on financial need, scholarship, leadership, and community service. Application deadline is April 10.

Award: Grant for use in freshman, sophomore, junior, or senior years; renewable. *Number:* 150–175. *Amount:* $1850–$2300.

Eligibility Requirements: Applicant must be age 18-21; enrolled or expecting to enroll full or part-time at a two-year or four-year or technical institution or university; resident of Florida and studying in Florida. Applicant must have 2.5 GPA or higher. Available to U.S. citizens.

Application Requirements: Application, essay, financial need analysis, interview, resume, references, test scores, transcript, SAT and/or ACT scores. *Deadline:* April 10.

Contact: Marilyn Westley, Director of Childhood Cancer
American Cancer Society, Florida Division, Inc.
3709 West Jetton Avenue
Tampa, FL 33629
Phone: 813-253-0541
Fax: 813-254-5857
E-mail: mwestley@cancer.org

AMERICAN CANCER SOCIETY, INC.-GREAT LAKES DIVISION
http://www.cancer.org

COLLEGE SCHOLARSHIPS FOR CANCER SURVIVORS

Scholarships for Michigan and Indiana residents who have had a diagnosis of cancer before the age of 21. Applicant must be under 21 at time of application. To be used for undergraduate degrees at any accredited Michigan or Indiana college or university. Deadline: mid-April. Open to U.S. citizens only.

Award: Scholarship for use in freshman, sophomore, junior, or senior years; renewable. *Number:* up to 72. *Amount:* $1000–$2250.

Eligibility Requirements: Applicant must be age 17-20; enrolled or expecting to enroll full-time at a two-year or four-year or technical institution or university; resident of Indiana or Michigan and studying in Indiana or Michigan. Available to U.S. citizens.

Application Requirements: Application, essay, financial need analysis, references, test scores, transcript. *Deadline:* April 18.

Contact: Deb Dillingham, Director of Quality of Life
American Cancer Society, Inc.-Great Lakes Division
1755 Abbey Road
East Lansing, MI 48823
Phone: 800-723-0360
Fax: 517-664-1497
E-mail: deb.dillingham@cancer.org

AMERICAN LEGION AUXILIARY, DEPARTMENT OF ALABAMA

AMERICAN LEGION AUXILIARY DEPARTMENT OF ALABAMA SCHOLARSHIP PROGRAM
• *See page 579*

AMERICAN LEGION AUXILIARY, DEPARTMENT OF ARKANSAS

AMERICAN LEGION AUXILIARY DEPARTMENT OF ARKANSAS ACADEMIC SCHOLARSHIP
• *See page 579*

AMERICAN LEGION AUXILIARY, DEPARTMENT OF FLORIDA   http://www.floridalegion.org

AMERICAN LEGION AUXILIARY DEPARTMENT OF FLORIDA DEPARTMENT SCHOLARSHIPS
• *See page 579*

AMERICAN LEGION AUXILIARY DEPARTMENT OF FLORIDA MEMORIAL SCHOLARSHIP
• *See page 484*

AMERICAN LEGION AUXILIARY, DEPARTMENT OF IDAHO

AMERICAN LEGION AUXILIARY, DEPARTMENT OF IDAHO NATIONAL PRESIDENT'S SCHOLARSHIP
• *See page 579*

AMERICAN LEGION AUXILIARY, DEPARTMENT OF IOWA   http://www.ialegion.org/ala

AMERICAN LEGION AUXILIARY DEPARTMENT OF IOWA CHILDREN OF VETERANS SCHOLARSHIP
• *See page 579*

AMERICAN LEGION AUXILIARY, DEPARTMENT OF MICHIGAN   http://www.michalaux.org

AMERICAN LEGION AUXILIARY DEPARTMENT OF MICHIGAN MEMORIAL SCHOLARSHIP
• *See page 580*

AMERICAN LEGION AUXILIARY NATIONAL PRESIDENT'S SCHOLARSHIP
• *See page 581*

SCHOLARSHIP FOR NON-TRADITIONAL STUDENT
• *See page 581*

AMERICAN LEGION AUXILIARY, DEPARTMENT OF MINNESOTA

AMERICAN LEGION AUXILIARY DEPARTMENT OF MINNESOTA SCHOLARSHIPS
• *See page 581*

AMERICAN LEGION AUXILIARY, DEPARTMENT OF MISSOURI

AMERICAN LEGION AUXILIARY MISSOURI STATE NATIONAL PRESIDENT'S SCHOLARSHIP
• *See page 485*

LELA MURPHY SCHOLARSHIP
• *See page 485*

AMERICAN LEGION AUXILIARY, DEPARTMENT OF NEBRASKA

AMERICAN LEGION AUXILIARY DEPARTMENT OF NEBRASKA PRESIDENT'S SCHOLARSHIP FOR JUNIOR MEMBERS
• *See page 485*

AMERICAN LEGION AUXILIARY DEPARTMENT OF NEBRASKA PRESIDENT'S SCHOLARSHIPS
• *See page 581*

AMERICAN LEGION AUXILIARY DEPARTMENT OF NEBRASKA STUDENT AID GRANTS
• *See page 581*

RUBY PAUL CAMPAIGN FUND SCHOLARSHIP
• *See page 485*

AMERICAN LEGION AUXILIARY, DEPARTMENT OF NORTH DAKOTA   http://www.ndlegion.org

AMERICAN LEGION AUXILIARY DEPARTMENT OF NORTH DAKOTA SCHOLARSHIPS

One-time award for North Dakota residents who are already attending a North Dakota institution of higher learning. Contact local or nearest American Legion Auxiliary Unit for more information. Must be a U.S. citizen.

Award: Scholarship for use in sophomore, junior, senior, or graduate years; not renewable. *Number:* 3. *Amount:* $400.

Eligibility Requirements: Applicant must be enrolled or expecting to enroll full-time at a two-year or four-year or technical institution or university; resident of North Dakota and studying in North Dakota. Available to U.S. citizens.

Application Requirements: Application, autobiography, essay, financial need analysis, references, self-addressed stamped envelope, test scores, transcript. *Deadline:* January 15.

Contact: Myrna Runholm, Department Secretary
American Legion Auxiliary, Department of North Dakota
PO Box 1060
Jamestown, ND 58402-1060
Phone: 701-253-5992

AMERICAN LEGION AUXILIARY, NATIONAL PRESIDENT'S SCHOLARSHIP
• *See page 538*

AMERICAN LEGION AUXILIARY, DEPARTMENT OF OHIO

AMERICAN LEGION AUXILIARY DEPARTMENT OF OHIO DEPARTMENT PRESIDENT'S SCHOLARSHIP
• *See page 582*

AMERICAN LEGION AUXILIARY, DEPARTMENT OF OREGON

AMERICAN LEGION AUXILIARY, DEPARTMENT OF OREGON NATIONAL PRESIDENT'S SCHOLARSHIP
• *See page 582*

AMERICAN LEGION AUXILIARY, DEPARTMENT OF TENNESSEE

VARA GRAY SCHOLARSHIP-GENERAL
• *See page 582*

AMERICAN LEGION AUXILIARY, DEPARTMENT OF TEXAS   http://www.alatexas.org

AMERICAN LEGION AUXILIARY, DEPARTMENT OF TEXAS GENERAL EDUCATION SCHOLARSHIP
• *See page 582*

AMERICAN LEGION AUXILIARY, DEPARTMENT OF UTAH
http://www.legion-aux.org

AMERICAN LEGION AUXILIARY NATIONAL PRESIDENTS SCHOLARSHIP
• See page 485

AMERICAN LEGION AUXILIARY, DEPARTMENT OF WASHINGTON
http://www.walegion-aux.org

AMERICAN LEGION AUXILIARY DEPARTMENT OF WASHINGTON SUSAN BURDETT SCHOLARSHIP

Applicant must be a former citizen of Evergreen Girls State. Applications must be obtained and processed through a Washington State American Legion Auxiliary Unit. One-time award of $300.

Award: Scholarship for use in freshman, sophomore, junior, or senior years; not renewable. *Number:* 1. *Amount:* $300.

Eligibility Requirements: Applicant must be enrolled or expecting to enroll at an institution or university; female and resident of Washington. Available to U.S. citizens.

Application Requirements: Application, applicant must enter a contest, essay, references, transcript. *Deadline:* April 1.

Contact: Crystal Lawrence, Department Secretary
American Legion Auxiliary, Department of Washington
3600 Ruddell Road
Lacey, WA 98503
Phone: 360-456-5995
Fax: 360-491-7442
E-mail: alawash@qwest.net

AMERICAN LEGION AUXILIARY, DEPARTMENT OF WASHINGTON GIFT SCHOLARSHIPS
• See page 583

DAYLE AND FRANCES PEIPER SCHOLARSHIP
• See page 583

AMERICAN LEGION AUXILIARY, DEPARTMENT OF WISCONSIN
http://www.amlegionauxwi.org

DELLA VAN DEUREN MEMORIAL SCHOLARSHIP
• See page 485

H.S. AND ANGELINA LEWIS SCHOLARSHIPS
• See page 486

MERIT AND MEMORIAL SCHOLARSHIPS
• See page 486

PAST PRESIDENTS PARLEY HEALTH CAREER SCHOLARSHIPS
• See page 486

STATE PRESIDENT'S SCHOLARSHIPS
• See page 486

AMERICAN LEGION, DEPARTMENT OF ALASKA

AMERICAN LEGION WESTERN DISTRICT POSTSECONDARY SCHOLARSHIP

One-time award to graduating high school senior for use in postsecondary schooling. Minimum 2.5 GPA required. Must be resident of Western District of Alaska. Submit community service activities. Deadline is February 15.

Award: Scholarship for use in freshman year; not renewable. *Number:* 3–5. *Amount:* $500–$750.

Eligibility Requirements: Applicant must be high school student; planning to enroll or expecting to enroll full-time at a two-year or four-year or technical institution or university and resident of Alaska. Applicant must have 2.5 GPA or higher. Available to U.S. citizens.

Application Requirements: Application, essay, transcript. *Deadline:* February 15.

Contact: Bill Caswell, Western District Scholarship Chairman
American Legion, Department of Alaska
1550 Charter Circle
Anchorage, AK 99508
Phone: 907-351-1043
E-mail: sbcas@mtaonline.net

AMERICAN LEGION, DEPARTMENT OF ARIZONA
http://www.azlegion.org

AMERICAN LEGION, DEPARTMENT OF ARIZONA HIGH SCHOOL ORATORICAL CONTEST

Each student must present an 8-10 minute prepared oration on any part of the U.S. Constitution. This is done before an audience. No notes, podiums or coaching. It is done from memory. Then the student does a 3-5 minute oration on one of the four assigned topics. The student doesn't know which assigned topic will be picked so they must prepare for all.

Award: Prize for use in freshman, sophomore, junior, or senior years; not renewable. *Number:* 10–50. *Amount:* $50–$1500.

Eligibility Requirements: Applicant must be high school student; age 18 or under; planning to enroll or expecting to enroll full-time at a two-year or four-year institution or university and resident of Arizona. Available to U.S. citizens.

Application Requirements: Application, applicant must enter a contest. *Deadline:* January 15.

Contact: Jim Burke, Department Oratorical Chairman
American Legion, Department of Arizona
4701 North 19th Avenue
Phoenix, AZ 85015-3799
Phone: 602-264-7706
Fax: 602-264-0029

AMERICAN LEGION, DEPARTMENT OF ARKANSAS
http://www.arklegion.homestead.com

AMERICAN LEGION DEPARTMENT OF ARKANSAS ORATORICAL CONTEST

Oratorical contest open to students in 9th-12th grades of any accredited Arkansas high school. Begins with finalists at the post level and proceeds through area and district levels to national contest.

Award: Scholarship for use in freshman year; not renewable. *Number:* 4. *Amount:* $1250–$3500.

Eligibility Requirements: Applicant must be high school student; age 19 or under; planning to enroll or expecting to enroll full or part-time at a two-year or four-year or technical institution or university and resident of Arkansas. Applicant must have 2.5 GPA or higher. Available to U.S. citizens.

Application Requirements: Application, applicant must enter a contest, photo, references. *Deadline:* December 15.

Contact: William Winchell, Department Adjutant
American Legion, Department of Arkansas
PO Box 3280
Little Rock, AR 72203-3280
Phone: 501-375-1104
Fax: 501-375-4236
E-mail: alegion@swbell.net

AMERICAN LEGION, DEPARTMENT OF HAWAII
http://www.legion.org

AMERICAN LEGION DEPARTMENT OF HAWAII STATE ORATORICAL CONTEST

Oratorical contest open to students in 9th-12th grades of any accredited Hawaii high school. Speech contests begin in January at post level and continue on to national competition. Contact local American Legion post or department for deadlines and application details.

Award: Prize for use in freshman, sophomore, junior, or senior years; not renewable. *Number:* varies. *Amount:* up to $1500.

Eligibility Requirements: Applicant must be high school student; age 20 or under; planning to enroll or expecting to enroll full-time at a four-year institution or university and resident of Hawaii. Available to U.S. citizens.

Application Requirements: Application, applicant must enter a contest. *Deadline:* varies.

Contact: Bernard K. Y. Lee, Department Adjutant/Oratorical Contest Chairman
American Legion, Department of Hawaii
612 McCully Street
Honolulu, HI 96826-3935
Phone: 808-946-6383
Fax: 808-947-3957
E-mail: aldepthi@hawaii.rr.com

AMERICAN LEGION, DEPARTMENT OF IDAHO
http://home.mindspring.com/~idlegion

AMERICAN LEGION, DEPARTMENT OF IDAHO SCHOLARSHIP
• See page 487

AMERICAN LEGION, DEPARTMENT OF ILLINOIS
http://www.illegion.org

AMERICAN ESSAY CONTEST SCHOLARSHIP
• See page 487

AMERICAN LEGION ORATORICAL CONTEST-ILLINOIS

Multi-level oratorical contest with winners advancing to next level. Open to students in 9th-12th grades of any accredited high school in Illinois. Seniors must be in attendance as of January 1. Fifteen prizes in the form of tuition scholarships from $75-$1600 will be awarded. Contact local American Legion Post or Department Headquarters for complete information and applications, which will be available in the fall.

Award: Prize for use in freshman year; not renewable. *Number:* 15. *Amount:* $75-$1600.

Eligibility Requirements: Applicant must be high school student; age 20 or under; planning to enroll or expecting to enroll full or part-time at a two-year or four-year or technical institution or university and resident of Illinois. Available to U.S. citizens.

Application Requirements: Application, applicant must enter a contest, transcript. *Deadline:* January 15.

Contact: Bill Bechtel, Assistant Adjutant
American Legion, Department of Illinois
PO Box 2910
Bloomington, IL 61702
Phone: 309-663-0361
Fax: 309-663-5783

AMERICAN LEGION, DEPARTMENT OF ILLINOIS SCHOLARSHIPS
• See page 487

AMERICAN LEGION, DEPARTMENT OF ILLINOIS, BOY SCOUT/EXPLORER SCHOLARSHIP
• See page 487

AMERICAN LEGION, DEPARTMENT OF INDIANA
http://www.indlegion.org

AMERICAN LEGION, DEPARTMENT OF INDIANA STATE ORATORICAL CONTEST

Oratorical contest open to students in grades 9-12 of any accredited Indiana high school. Speech contests begin in November at post level and continue on to national competition. Contact local American Legion post for deadline and application details.

Award: Prize for use in freshman year; not renewable. *Number:* 4-8. *Amount:* $500-$1200.

Eligibility Requirements: Applicant must be high school student; age 19 or under; planning to enroll or expecting to enroll full or part-time at a two-year or four-year or technical institution or university; resident of Indiana and must have an interest in public speaking. Available to U.S. citizens.

Application Requirements: Application, applicant must enter a contest. *Deadline:* varies.

Contact: B.J. McWilliams, Program Coordinator
American Legion, Department of Indiana
777 North Meridan Street, Room 104
Indianapolis, IN 46204
Phone: 317-630-1264
Fax: 317-237-9891
E-mail: bjmcwilliams@indlegion.org

FRANK W. MCHALE MEMORIAL SCHOLARSHIPS

One-time award for Indiana high school juniors who recently participated in the Boys State Program. Must be nominated by Boys State official. Write for more information and deadline.

Award: Scholarship for use in freshman, sophomore, junior, or senior years; not renewable. *Number:* 3. *Amount:* $1500-$2000.

Eligibility Requirements: Applicant must be high school student; planning to enroll or expecting to enroll full or part-time at a two-year or four-year or technical institution or university; male; resident of Indiana and must have an interest in leadership. Available to U.S. citizens.

Application Requirements: Application, participation in the Boys State Program, must be nominated by a Boys State official. *Deadline:* June 13.

Contact: Susan Long, Program Coordinator
American Legion, Department of Indiana
777 North Meridan Street, Room 104
Indianapolis, IN 46204
Phone: 317-630-1264
Fax: 317-237-9891
E-mail: slong@indlegion.org

AMERICAN LEGION, DEPARTMENT OF IOWA
http://www.ialegion.org

AMERICAN LEGION DEPARTMENT OF IOWA EAGLE SCOUT OF THE YEAR SCHOLARSHIP
• See page 488

ORATORICAL CONTEST SCHOLARSHIP-IOWA

All contestants in the Department of Iowa American Legion High School Oratorical Contest shall be citizens or lawful permanent residents of the United States. The Department of Iowa American Legion High School Oratorical Contest shall consist of one contestant from each of the three Area Contests (an Area consisting of three Districts). The Area Contest shall consist of one contestant from each District in the designated Area.

Award: Prize for use in freshman, sophomore, junior, or senior years; not renewable. *Number:* 3. *Amount:* $1000-$2000.

Eligibility Requirements: Applicant must be enrolled or expecting to enroll full-time at a two-year or four-year institution or university; resident of Iowa and must have an interest in public speaking. Available to U.S. citizens.

Application Requirements: Applicant must enter a contest. *Deadline:* varies.

Contact: Program Director
American Legion, Department of Iowa
720 Lyon Street
Des Moines, IA 50309

AMERICAN LEGION, DEPARTMENT OF KANSAS
http://www.ksamlegion.org

ALBERT M. LAPPIN SCHOLARSHIP
• See page 488

DR. CLICK COWGER BASEBALL SCHOLARSHIP

Scholarship available to a high school senior or college freshman or sophomore who plays or has played Kansas American Legion baseball. Scholarships must be used at an approved Kansas institution. Must be Kansas resident.

Award: Scholarship for use in freshman or sophomore years; not renewable. *Number:* 1. *Amount:* $500.

Eligibility Requirements: Applicant must be enrolled or expecting to enroll at a two-year or four-year or technical institution or university;

American Legion, Department of Kansas (continued)

resident of Kansas; studying in Kansas and must have an interest in athletics/sports. Available to U.S. citizens.

Application Requirements: Application, photo. *Deadline:* July 15.

Contact: Scholarship Administrator
American Legion, Department of Kansas
1314 Southwest Topeka Boulevard
Topeka, KS 66612-1886

HUGH A. SMITH SCHOLARSHIP FUND
• *See page 488*

PAUL FLAHERTY ATHLETIC SCHOLARSHIP

Scholarship available to student who has participated in any form of Kansas high school athletics. Award must be used at an approved Kansas college, university, or trade school. Must be a Kansas resident.

Award: Scholarship for use in freshman or sophomore years; not renewable. *Number:* 1. *Amount:* $250.

Eligibility Requirements: Applicant must be enrolled or expecting to enroll at a two-year or four-year or technical institution or university; resident of Kansas; studying in Kansas and must have an interest in athletics/sports. Available to U.S. citizens.

Application Requirements: Application, financial need analysis, photo, transcript. *Deadline:* July 15.

Contact: Scholarship Administrator
American Legion, Department of Kansas
1314 Southwest Topeka Boulevard
Topeka, KS 66612-1886

ROSEDALE POST 346 SCHOLARSHIP
• *See page 488*

TED AND NORA ANDERSON SCHOLARSHIPS
• *See page 488*

AMERICAN LEGION, DEPARTMENT OF MAINE

AMERICAN LEGION DEPARTMENT OF MAINE CHILDREN AND YOUTH SCHOLARSHIP

Scholarships available to high school seniors, college students, and veterans who are residents of Maine. Based on financial need and character. Must be in upper half of high school class. One-time award of $500.

Award: Scholarship for use in freshman, sophomore, junior, or senior years; not renewable. *Number:* 7. *Amount:* $500.

Eligibility Requirements: Applicant must be enrolled or expecting to enroll full-time at a two-year or four-year or technical institution or university and resident of Maine. Applicant must have 2.5 GPA or higher. Available to U.S. citizens.

Application Requirements: Application, essay, financial need analysis, references, transcript. *Deadline:* April 10.

Contact: Steve Page
American Legion, Department of Maine
54 South Upper Narrows Lane
Winthrop, ME 04364
Phone: 207-873-3229
Fax: 207-872-0501
E-mail: legionme@wtvl.net

DANIEL E. LAMBERT MEMORIAL SCHOLARSHIP
• *See page 583*

JAMES V. DAY SCHOLARSHIP
• *See page 488*

AMERICAN LEGION, DEPARTMENT OF MARYLAND
http://www.mdlegion.org

AMERICAN LEGION DEPARTMENT OF MARYLAND GENERAL SCHOLARSHIP

Scholarship of $500 for Maryland high school students. Must plan on attending a two-year or four-year college or university in the state of Maryland. Nonrenewable award. Based on financial need and citizenship. Applications available on Web site: http://mdlegion.org. Deadline is March 31.

Award: Scholarship for use in freshman year; not renewable. *Number:* 4. *Amount:* $500.

Eligibility Requirements: Applicant must be high school student; age 19 or under; planning to enroll or expecting to enroll full-time at a two-year or four-year institution or university; resident of Maryland and studying in Maryland. Available to U.S. citizens.

Application Requirements: Application, essay, financial need analysis, transcript. *Deadline:* March 31.

Contact: Thomas Davis, Department Adjutant
American Legion, Department of Maryland
101 North Gay, Room E
Baltimore, MD 21202
Phone: 410-752-1405
Fax: 410-752-3822
E-mail: tom@mdlegion.org

AMERICAN LEGION DEPARTMENT OF MARYLAND GENERAL SCHOLARSHIP FUND
• *See page 584*

AMERICAN LEGION, DEPARTMENT OF MICHIGAN
http://www.michiganlegion.org

AMERICAN LEGION DEPARTMENT OF MICHIGAN ORATORICAL CONTEST

Oratorical contest open to students in 9th-12th grades of any accredited Michigan high school or state accredited home school. Five one-time awards of varying amounts. Speech contests begin in January at zone level and continue on to national competition. Contact for deadlines and application details.

Award: Prize for use in freshman year; not renewable. *Number:* 5. *Amount:* $600–$1000.

Eligibility Requirements: Applicant must be high school student; age 20 or under; planning to enroll or expecting to enroll full or part-time at a two-year or four-year or technical institution or university; resident of Michigan and must have an interest in public speaking. Available to U.S. citizens.

Application Requirements: Application, applicant must enter a contest. *Deadline:* January 31.

Contact: Deanna Clark, Program Secretary
American Legion, Department of Michigan
212 North Verlinden Avenue
Lansing, MI 48915
Phone: 517-371-4720 Ext. 11
Fax: 517-371-2401
E-mail: programs@michiganlegion.org

GUY M. WILSON SCHOLARSHIPS
• *See page 584*

WILLIAM D. AND JEWELL W. BREWER SCHOLARSHIP TRUSTS
• *See page 584*

AMERICAN LEGION, DEPARTMENT OF MINNESOTA
http://www.mnlegion.org

AMERICAN LEGION DEPARTMENT OF MINNESOTA MEMORIAL SCHOLARSHIP
• *See page 489*

AMERICAN LEGION DEPARTMENT OF MINNESOTA STATE ORATORICAL CONTEST

Oratorical contest open to students in 9th-12th grades of any accredited Minnesota high school. Speech contests begin in January at post level and continue to the national competition. Contact local American Legion Post for deadlines and application details. Four one-time awards of varying amounts.

Award: Scholarship for use in freshman year; not renewable. *Number:* 4. *Amount:* $500–$1200.

Eligibility Requirements: Applicant must be high school student; planning to enroll or expecting to enroll full or part-time at a two-year or four-year or technical institution or university; resident of Minnesota and must have an interest in public speaking. Available to U.S. citizens.

Application Requirements: Application, applicant must enter a contest. *Deadline:* January 31.

Contact: Jennifer Kelley, Program Coordinator
American Legion, Department of Minnesota
20 West 12th Street, Room 300-A
St. Paul, MN 55155
Phone: 651-291-1800
Fax: 651-291-1057
E-mail: department@mnlegion.org

MINNESOTA LEGIONNAIRES INSURANCE TRUST SCHOLARSHIP
• *See page 489*

AMERICAN LEGION, DEPARTMENT OF MISSOURI
http://www.missourilegion.org

CHARLES L. BACON MEMORIAL SCHOLARSHIP
• *See page 489*

ERMAN W. TAYLOR MEMORIAL SCHOLARSHIP
• *See page 584*

LILLIE LOIS FORD SCHOLARSHIP FUND
• *See page 584*

AMERICAN LEGION, DEPARTMENT OF MONTANA
http://www.mtlegion.org

ORATORICAL CONTEST

Applicants participate in a statewide memorized oratorical contest on the U.S. Constitution. Four places are awarded. Must be a Montana high school student. Contact state adjutant American Legion Department of Montana for further details. Each state winner who competes in the first round of the national contest will receive a $1000 scholarship. Participants in the second round who do not advance to the National Final round will receive an additional $1,000 scholarship

Award: Scholarship for use in freshman year; not renewable. *Number:* 1–4. *Amount:* $300–$2000.

Eligibility Requirements: Applicant must be high school student; planning to enroll or expecting to enroll full-time at a two-year or four-year or technical institution or university; resident of Montana and must have an interest in public speaking. Available to U.S. citizens.

Application Requirements: Application, applicant must enter a contest, memorized speech. *Deadline:* Continuous.

Contact: Gary White, State Adjutant
American Legion, Department of Montana
PO Box 6075
Helena, MT 59604
Phone: 406-324-3989
Fax: 406-324-3990
E-mail: amlegmt@in-tch.com

AMERICAN LEGION, DEPARTMENT OF NEBRASKA
http://www.legion.org

EDGAR J. BOSCHULT MEMORIAL SCHOLARSHIP
• *See page 585*

MAYNARD JENSEN AMERICAN LEGION MEMORIAL SCHOLARSHIP
• *See page 489*

AMERICAN LEGION, DEPARTMENT OF NEW YORK
http://www.ny.legion.org

AMERICAN LEGION DEPARTMENT OF NEW YORK STATE HIGH SCHOOL ORATORICAL CONTEST

Oratorical contest open to students under 20 years in 9th-12th grades of any accredited New York high school. Speech contests begin in November at post levels and continue to national competition. Contact local American Legion post for deadlines. Must be U.S. citizen or lawful permanent resident. Payments are made directly to college and are awarded over a four-year period.

Award: Scholarship for use in freshman year; not renewable. *Number:* 65. *Amount:* $1000–$6000.

Eligibility Requirements: Applicant must be high school student; age 19 or under; planning to enroll or expecting to enroll at an institution or university; resident of New York and must have an interest in public speaking. Available to U.S. citizens.

Application Requirements: Application, applicant must enter a contest. *Deadline:* varies.

Contact: Richard Pedro, Department Adjutant
American Legion, Department of New York
112 State Street, Suite 400
Albany, NY 12207
Phone: 518-463-2215
Fax: 518-427-8443
E-mail: newyork@legion.org

AMERICAN LEGION, DEPARTMENT OF NORTH CAROLINA
http://nclegion.org

AMERICAN LEGION DEPARTMENT OF NORTH CAROLINA HIGH SCHOOL ORATORICAL CONTEST

Objective is to develop a deeper knowledge and appreciation of the U.S. Constitution, develop leadership qualities, think and speak clearly and intelligently, and prepare for acceptance of duties, responsibilities, rights, and privileges of American citizenship. Open to North Carolina high school students. Must be U.S. citizen or lawful permanent resident.

Award: Prize for use in freshman year; renewable. *Number:* 5. *Amount:* $500–$2000.

Eligibility Requirements: Applicant must be high school student; age 20 or under; planning to enroll or expecting to enroll full or part-time at a two-year or four-year or technical institution or university and resident of North Carolina. Available to U.S. citizens.

Application Requirements: Application, applicant must enter a contest, applications are available in the respective schools. *Deadline:* January 1.

Contact: Debra Rose, Department Executive Secretary
American Legion, Department of North Carolina
4 North Blount Street, PO Box 26657
Raleigh, NC 27611-6657
Phone: 919-832-7506
Fax: 919-832-6428
E-mail: drose-nclegion@nc.rr.com

AMERICAN LEGION, DEPARTMENT OF NORTH DAKOTA
http://www.ndlegion.org

AMERICAN LEGION DEPARTMENT OF NORTH DAKOTA NATIONAL HIGH SCHOOL ORATORICAL CONTEST

Oratorical contest for high school students in grades 9-12. Contestants must prepare to speak on the topic of the U.S. Constitution. Must graduate from an accredited North Dakota high school. Contest begins at the local level and continues to the national level. Several one-time awards of $100-$2000.

Award: Prize for use in freshman year; not renewable. *Number:* 38. *Amount:* $100–$2000.

Eligibility Requirements: Applicant must be high school student; planning to enroll or expecting to enroll at an institution or university; resident of North Dakota and must have an interest in public speaking. Available to U.S. citizens.

Application Requirements: Application, applicant must enter a contest, speech contest. *Deadline:* November 30.

Contact: Vern Fetch, Chairman, Department Oratorical Contest Committee
American Legion, Department of North Dakota
1626 North 26th Street, Box 2666
Bismarck, ND 58501-2666
Phone: 701-222-1384

HATTIE TEDROW MEMORIAL FUND SCHOLARSHIP
• *See page 585*

AMERICAN LEGION, DEPARTMENT OF OREGON

NATIONAL ORATORICAL SCHOLARSHIP CONTEST

Students give two orations, one prepared and one extemporaneous on an assigned topic pertaining to the Constitution of the United States of America. Awards are given at Post, District, and State level with the state winner

American Legion, Department of Oregon (continued)

advancing to the National level contest. This is open to students enrolled in high schools within the state of Oregon.

Award: Scholarship for use in freshman, sophomore, junior, or senior years; not renewable. *Number:* 4. *Amount:* $200–$500.

Eligibility Requirements: Applicant must be high school student; planning to enroll or expecting to enroll full-time at a two-year or four-year or technical institution or university and resident of Oregon. Available to U.S. citizens.

Application Requirements: Application, applicant must enter a contest. *Deadline:* December 1.

Contact: Barry Snyder
American Legion, Department of Oregon
PO Box 1730
Wilsonville, OR 97070-1730
Phone: 503-685-5006
Fax: 503-685-5008
E-mail: orelegion@aol.com

AMERICAN LEGION, DEPARTMENT OF PENNSYLVANIA   http://www.pa-legion.com

AMERICAN LEGION DEPARTMENT OF PENNSYLVANIA STATE ORATORICAL CONTEST

Oratorical contest open to students in 9th-12th grades of any accredited Pennsylvania high school. Speech contests begin in January at post level and continue on to national competition. Contact local American Legion post for deadlines and application details. Three one-time awards ranging from $7500 for first place, Second place $5000 and third place $4000.

Award: Prize for use in freshman year; not renewable. *Number:* 3. *Amount:* $4000–$7500.

Eligibility Requirements: Applicant must be high school student; planning to enroll or expecting to enroll at an institution or university; resident of Pennsylvania and must have an interest in public speaking. Available to U.S. citizens.

Application Requirements: Application, applicant must enter a contest. *Deadline:* varies.

Contact: James H. Hales, Jr., Department Commander
American Legion, Department of Pennsylvania
PO Box 2324
Harrisburg, PA 17105-2324
Phone: 717-730-9100
Fax: 717-975-2836
E-mail: hq@pa-legion.com

JOSEPH P. GAVENONIS COLLEGE SCHOLARSHIP (PLAN I)
• *See page 490*

AMERICAN LEGION, DEPARTMENT OF SOUTH DAKOTA   http://www.sdlegion.org

SOUTH DAKOTA HIGH SCHOOL ORATORICAL CONTEST

Provide a 8-10 minute oration on some phase of the U.S. Constitution. Be prepared to speak extemporaneously for 3.5 minutes on specified articles or amendments. Compete at Local, District, and State levels. State winner goes on to National Contest and opportunity to win $18,000 in scholarships. Contact local American Legion post for contest dates.

Award: Prize for use in freshman, sophomore, junior or senior years; not renewable. *Number:* 1–4. *Amount:* $200–$1000.

Eligibility Requirements: Applicant must be high school student; age 19 or under; planning to enroll or expecting to enroll at a two-year or four-year or technical institution or university and resident of South Dakota. Available to U.S. citizens.

Application Requirements: Applicant must enter a contest, oration. *Deadline:* varies.

Contact: Ronald Boyd, Department Adjutant
American Legion, Department of South Dakota
PO Box 67
Watertown, SD 57201-0067
Phone: 605-886-3604
Fax: 605-886-2870
E-mail: sdlegion@dailypost.com

AMERICAN LEGION, DEPARTMENT OF TEXAS   http://www.txlegion.org

AMERICAN LEGION HIGH SCHOOL ORATORICAL CONTEST

Scholarships will be given to the winners of oratorical contests. Contestants must be in high school with plans to further their education in a postsecondary institution. Success on a local level may allow the student to compete on a national level for more money.

Award: Prize for use in freshman year; renewable. *Number:* up to 20. *Amount:* $500–$2000.

Eligibility Requirements: Applicant must be high school student; age 19 or under; planning to enroll or expecting to enroll full or part-time at a two-year or four-year or technical institution or university and resident of Texas. Available to U.S. citizens.

Application Requirements: Application, applicant must enter a contest, essay, interview. *Deadline:* February 1.

Contact: Robert Squyres, Director of Internal Affairs
American Legion, Department of Texas
3401 Ed Bluestein Boulevard
Austin, TX 78721-2902
Phone: 512-472-4138
Fax: 512-472-0603
E-mail: programs@txlegion.org

AMERICAN LEGION, DEPARTMENT OF VERMONT   http://www.legionvthq.com/

AMERICAN LEGION DEPARTMENT OF VERMONT DEPARTMENT SCHOLARSHIPS

Award for high school seniors who attend a Vermont high school or similar school in an adjoining state whose parents are legal residents of Vermont, or reside in an adjoining state and attend a Vermont secondary school.

Award: Scholarship for use in freshman, sophomore, junior, or senior years; not renewable. *Number:* 12. *Amount:* $500–$2000.

Eligibility Requirements: Applicant must be high school student; planning to enroll or expecting to enroll full-time at a two-year or four-year or technical institution or university and resident of Vermont. Available to U.S. citizens.

Application Requirements: Application, financial need analysis, references, test scores, transcript. *Deadline:* April 1.

Contact: Huzon Stewart, Chairman
American Legion, Department of Vermont
PO Box 396
Montpelier, VT 05601-0396
Phone: 802-223-7131
Fax: 802-223-0318
E-mail: alvt@sover.net

AMERICAN LEGION EAGLE SCOUT OF THE YEAR
• *See page 490*

AMERICAN LEGION, DEPARTMENT OF VIRGINIA   http://www.valegion.org

AMERICAN LEGION DEPARTMENT OF VIRGINIA HIGH SCHOOL ORATORICAL CONTEST AWARD

Oratorical contest open to applicants who are winners of the Virginia Department oratorical contest and who attend high school in Virginia. Competitors must demonstrate their knowledge of the U.S. Constitution. Must be student in 9th-12th grades at accredited Virginia high school. Three one-time awards of up to $1100.

Award: Prize for use in freshman year; not renewable. *Number:* 3. *Amount:* $600–$1100.

Eligibility Requirements: Applicant must be high school student; age 20 or under; planning to enroll or expecting to enroll full-time at a two-year or four-year or technical institution or university and resident of Virginia. Available to U.S. citizens.

Application Requirements: Application, applicant must enter a contest, references, transcript. *Deadline:* December 1.

Contact: Dale Chapman, Adjutant
American Legion, Department of Virginia
1708 Commonwealth Avenue
Richmond, VA 23230
Phone: 804-353-6606
Fax: 804-358-1940
E-mail: eeccleston@valegion.org

AMERICAN LEGION, DEPARTMENT OF WASHINGTON
http://www.walegion.org

AMERICAN LEGION DEPARTMENT OF WASHINGTON CHILDREN AND YOUTH SCHOLARSHIPS
• See page 490

AMERICAN LEGION, DEPARTMENT OF WEST VIRGINIA

AMERICAN LEGION DEPARTMENT OF WEST VIRGINIA STATE ORATORICAL CONTEST

Oratorical contest open to student in 9th-12th grades of any accredited West Virginia high school. Speech contests begin in January at post level and continue on to national competition. Contact local American Legion Post for deadlines and application details. Deadline is January 1.

Award: Scholarship for use in freshman year; not renewable. *Number:* up to 39. *Amount:* $25–$100.

Eligibility Requirements: Applicant must be high school student; planning to enroll or expecting to enroll full-time at a four-year institution; resident of West Virginia and must have an interest in public speaking. Available to U.S. citizens.

Application Requirements: Application, applicant must enter a contest. *Deadline:* January 1.

Contact: Miles Epling, State Adjutant
American Legion, Department of West Virginia
2016 Kanawha Boulevard, East, PO Box 3191
Charleston, WV 25332-3191
Phone: 304-343-7591
Fax: 304-343-7592
E-mail: wvlegion@aol.com

AMERICAN LEGION, DEPARTMENT OF WEST VIRGINIA BOARD OF REGENTS SCHOLARSHIP

One-time prize awarded annually to the winner of the West Virginia American Legion State Oratorical Contest. Must be in 9th-12th grades of accredited West Virginia high school to compete. For use at West Virginia institution. Deadline is January 1.

Award: Scholarship for use in freshman year; not renewable. *Number:* 1. *Amount:* up to $1500.

Eligibility Requirements: Applicant must be high school student; planning to enroll or expecting to enroll full-time at a four-year institution; resident of West Virginia; studying in West Virginia and must have an interest in public speaking. Available to U.S. citizens.

Application Requirements: Application, applicant must enter a contest. *Deadline:* January 1.

Contact: Miles Epling, State Adjutant
American Legion, Department of West Virginia
2016 Kanawha Boulevard, East, PO Box 3191
Charleston, WV 25332-3191
Phone: 304-343-7591
Fax: 304-343-7592
E-mail: wvlegion@aol.com

WILLIAM F. "BILL" JOHNSON MEMORIAL SCHOLARSHIP SPONSORED BY SONS OF THE AMERICAN LEGION
• See page 490

AMERICAN QUARTER HORSE FOUNDATION (AQHF)
http://www.aqha.org/aqhya

ARIZONA QUARTER HORSE YOUTH RACING SCHOLARSHIP
• See page 491

DR. GERALD O'CONNOR MICHIGAN SCHOLARSHIP
• See page 491

INDIANA QUARTER HORSE YOUTH SCHOLARSHIP
• See page 492

JOAN CAIN FLORIDA QUARTER HORSE YOUTH SCHOLARSHIP
• See page 492

NEBRASKA QUARTER HORSE YOUTH SCHOLARSHIP
• See page 492

RAY MELTON MEMORIAL VIRGINIA QUARTER HORSE YOUTH SCHOLARSHIP
• See page 492

SWAYZE WOODRUFF SCHOLARSHIP
• See page 492

AMERICAN SOCIETY FOR CLINICAL LABORATORY SCIENCE
http://www.ascls.org

ASCLS REGION VI MISSOURI ORGANIZATION FOR CLINICAL LABORATORY SCIENCE STUDENT SCHOLARSHIP

Scholarship provides financial assistance to clinical laboratory science or medical laboratory technology students who are beginning or continuing their formal education, or conducting research that directly relates to laboratory science. Applicant must submit proof of acceptance or enrollment in the educational program. Please refer to Web site for further information and application: http://www.mocls.org

Award: Scholarship for use in freshman, sophomore, junior, senior, or graduate years; not renewable. *Number:* varies. *Amount:* $200.

Eligibility Requirements: Applicant must be enrolled or expecting to enroll full or part-time at a two-year or four-year or technical institution or university and resident of Missouri. Available to U.S. citizens.

Application Requirements: Application, references, personal letter, research proposal. *Deadline:* varies.

Contact: Tom Reddig, Missouri Scholarship Fund Chair
American Society for Clinical Laboratory Science
31 West 59th Street
Kansas City, MO 64113
Phone: 816-931-8686

AMERICAN SOCIETY OF TRAVEL AGENTS (ASTA) FOUNDATION
http://www.astanet.com

ARIZONA CHAPTER DEPENDENT/EMPLOYEE MEMBERSHIP SCHOLARSHIP
• See page 493

AMVETS DEPARTMENT OF ILLINOIS
http://www.ilamvets.org

ILLINOIS AMVETS LADIES AUXILIARY MEMORIAL SCHOLARSHIP
• See page 586

ILLINOIS AMVETS SERVICE FOUNDATION SCHOLARSHIP AWARD
• See page 586

ILLINOIS AMVETS TRADE SCHOOL SCHOLARSHIP
• See page 586

ARAB AMERICAN INSTITUTE FOUNDATION
http://www.aaiusa.org/aaif.htm

LEBANESE AMERICAN HERITAGE CLUB SCHOLARSHIP
• See page 605

ARIZONA ASSOCIATION OF CHICANOS IN HIGHER EDUCATION (AACHE)
http://www.aache.org/

AACHE SCHOLARSHIP
• See page 606

ARIZONA COMMISSION FOR POSTSECONDARY EDUCATION
http://www.azhighered.org/

ARIZONA PRIVATE POSTSECONDARY EDUCATION STUDENT FINANCIAL ASSISTANCE PROGRAM

Provides grants to financially needy Arizona Community College graduates, to attend a private postsecondary baccalaureate degree-granting institution.

Award: Forgivable loan for use in freshman, sophomore, junior, or senior years; renewable. *Number:* varies. *Amount:* up to $1000.

Eligibility Requirements: Applicant must be enrolled or expecting to enroll full-time at a four-year institution or university; resident of Arizona and studying in Arizona. Available to U.S. citizens.

Application Requirements: Financial need analysis, transcript, promissory note. *Deadline:* June 30.

Contact: Danny Lee, PFAP Program Manager
Arizona Commission for Postsecondary Education
2020 North Central Avenue, Suite 550
Phoenix, AZ 85004-4503
Phone: 602-258-2435 Ext. 103
Fax: 602-258-2483
E-mail: dan_lee@azhighered.org

LEVERAGING EDUCATIONAL ASSISTANCE PARTNERSHIP

LEAP provides grants to financially needy students, who enroll in and attend postsecondary education or training in Arizona schools. LEAP Program was formerly known as the State Student Incentive Grant or SSIG Program.

Award: Grant for use in freshman, sophomore, junior, senior, or graduate years; not renewable. *Number:* varies. *Amount:* $100–$2500.

Eligibility Requirements: Applicant must be enrolled or expecting to enroll full or part-time at a two-year or four-year or technical institution or university; resident of Arizona and studying in Arizona. Available to U.S. citizens.

Application Requirements: Financial need analysis. *Deadline:* April 30.

Contact: Mila A. Zaporteza, Business Manager/LEAP Financial Aid Manager
Arizona Commission for Postsecondary Education
2020 North Central Avenue, Suite 550
Phoenix, AZ 85004-4503
Phone: 602-258-2435 Ext. 102
Fax: 602-258-2483
E-mail: mila@azhighered.org

ARIZONA PRIVATE SCHOOL ASSOCIATION
http://www.arizonapsa.org

ARIZONA PRIVATE SCHOOL ASSOCIATION SCHOLARSHIP

Scholarships are for graduating students from Arizona and the High School determines the recipients of the Awards. Each Spring the Arizona Private School Association awards two $1000 Scholarships to every High School in Arizona. Application deadline is April 30.

Award: Scholarship for use in freshman year; not renewable. *Number:* 600. *Amount:* $1000.

Eligibility Requirements: Applicant must be high school student; planning to enroll or expecting to enroll full-time at a technical institution; resident of Arizona and studying in Arizona. Available to U.S. citizens.

Application Requirements: Application, essay. *Deadline:* April 30.

Contact: Fred Lockhart, Executive Director
Arizona Private School Association
202 East McDowell Road, Suite 273
Phoenix, AZ 85004
Phone: 602-254-5199
Fax: 602-254-5073
E-mail: apsa@eschelon.com

ARKANSAS DEPARTMENT OF HIGHER EDUCATION
http://www.arkansashighered.com

ARKANSAS ACADEMIC CHALLENGE SCHOLARSHIP PROGRAM

Awards for Arkansas residents who are graduating high school seniors to study at an Arkansas institution. Must have at least a 2.75 GPA, meet minimum ACT composite score standards, and have financial need. Renewable up to three additional years.

Award: Scholarship for use in freshman, sophomore, junior, or senior years; renewable. *Amount:* $2000–$3000.

Eligibility Requirements: Applicant must be high school student; planning to enroll or expecting to enroll full-time at a two-year or four-year institution or university; resident of Arkansas and studying in Arkansas. Available to U.S. citizens.

Application Requirements: Application, financial need analysis, test scores, transcript. *Deadline:* June 1.

Contact: Elyse Price, Assistant Coordinator
Arkansas Department of Higher Education
114 East Capitol
Little Rock, AR 72201
Phone: 501-371-2050
Fax: 501-371-2001

ARKANSAS STUDENT ASSISTANCE GRANT PROGRAM

Award for Arkansas residents attending a college within the state. Must be enrolled full-time, have financial need, and maintain satisfactory progress. One-time award for undergraduate use only. Application is the FAFSA that each student submits as soon as possible after January 1 of each year.

Award: Grant for use in freshman, sophomore, junior, or senior years; not renewable. *Number:* 600–5500. *Amount:* $600.

Eligibility Requirements: Applicant must be enrolled or expecting to enroll full-time at a two-year or four-year or technical institution or university; resident of Arkansas and studying in Arkansas. Available to U.S. citizens.

Application Requirements: Application, financial need analysis, FAFSA. *Deadline:* April 1.

Contact: Philip Axelroth, Assistant Coordinator
Arkansas Department of Higher Education
114 East Capitol
Little Rock, AR 72201
Phone: 501-371-2050
Fax: 501-371-2001

GOVERNOR'S SCHOLARS-ARKANSAS

Awards for outstanding Arkansas high school seniors. Must be an Arkansas resident and have a high school GPA of at least 3.5 or have scored at least 27 on the ACT. Award is $4000 per year for four years of full-time undergraduate study. Applicants who attain 32 or above on ACT, 1410 or above on SAT and have an academic 3.50 GPA, or are selected as National Merit or National Achievement finalists may receive an award equal to tuition, mandatory fees, room, and board up to $10,000 per year at any Arkansas institution.

Award: Scholarship for use in freshman, sophomore, junior, or senior years; renewable. *Number:* 75–250. *Amount:* $4000–$10,000.

Eligibility Requirements: Applicant must be high school student; planning to enroll or expecting to enroll full-time at a two-year or four-year institution or university; resident of Arkansas and studying in Arkansas. Applicant must have 3.5 GPA or higher. Available to U.S. citizens.

Application Requirements: Application, test scores, transcript. *Deadline:* February 1.

Contact: Philip Axelroth, Assistant Coordinator of Financial Aid
Arkansas Department of Higher Education
114 East Capitol
Little Rock, AR 72201
Phone: 501-371-2050
Fax: 501-371-2001
E-mail: phila@adhe.arknet.edu

LAW ENFORCEMENT OFFICERS' DEPENDENTS SCHOLARSHIP-ARKANSAS
• See page 539

MISSING IN ACTION/KILLED IN ACTION DEPENDENT'S SCHOLARSHIP-ARKANSAS
• See page 586

SECOND EFFORT SCHOLARSHIP

Awarded to those scholars who achieved one of the 10 highest scores on the Arkansas High School Diploma Test (GED). Must be at least age 18 and not have graduated from high school. Students do not apply for this award, they are contacted by the Arkansas Department of Higher Education.

Award: Scholarship for use in freshman, sophomore, junior, or senior years; renewable. *Number:* 10. *Amount:* up to $1000.

Eligibility Requirements: Applicant must be age 18; enrolled or expecting to enroll full or part-time at a two-year or four-year institution or university; resident of Arkansas and studying in Arkansas. Applicant must have 2.5 GPA or higher. Available to U.S. citizens.

Application Requirements: Application.

Contact:
>   *Phone:* 501-371-2050
>   *Fax:* 501-371-2001

ARKANSAS SINGLE PARENT SCHOLARSHIP FUND   http://www.aspsf.org/default.htm

ARKANSAS SINGLE PARENT SCHOLARSHIP

Scholarships for single parents who reside in Arkansas to pursue higher education. Eligible applicants are single parents living in Arkansas who are considered economically disadvantaged and who have custodial care of one or more children under the age of eighteen and those who have not previously earned a diploma or degree from a four-year institution of higher learning. Award value varies.

Award: Scholarship for use in freshman, sophomore, junior, senior, or graduate years; renewable. *Number:* 1.

Eligibility Requirements: Applicant must be enrolled or expecting to enroll full or part-time at a two-year or four-year institution or university; single and resident of Arkansas. Available to U.S. citizens.

Application Requirements: Application, essay, financial need analysis, transcript. *Deadline:* varies.

Contact: Ralph H. Nesson, Executive Director
>   Arkansas Single Parent Scholarship Fund
>   614 East Emma Avenue, Suite 119
>   Springdale, AR 72764
>   *Phone:* 479-927-1402
>   *Fax:* 479-751-1110
>   *E-mail:* rnesson@jtlshop.jonesnet.org

ARRL FOUNDATION, INC.   http://www.arrl.org/arrlf/scholgen.html

IRARC MEMORIAL/JOSEPH P. RUBINO, WA4MMD, SCHOLARSHIP
• See page 494

NORMAN E. STROHMEIER, W2VRS MEMORIAL SCHOLARSHIP

One-time award available to students who are residents of Western New York and are amateur radio operators with a technician license. Preference is given to graduating high school students. Must have a 3.2 GPA or better. Deadline is February 1.

Award: Scholarship for use in freshman, sophomore, junior, or senior years; not renewable. *Number:* 1. *Amount:* $500.

Eligibility Requirements: Applicant must be enrolled or expecting to enroll full-time at an institution or university; resident of New York and must have an interest in amateur radio. Applicant must have 3.5 GPA or higher. Available to U.S. citizens.

Application Requirements: Application, transcript. *Deadline:* February 1.

Contact: Mary Hobart, Secretary Foundation
>   ARRL Foundation, Inc.
>   225 Main Street
>   Newington, CT 06111-1494
>   *Phone:* 860-594-0397
>   *E-mail:* k1mmh@arrl.org

SIX METER CLUB OF CHICAGO SCHOLARSHIP

For licensed amateur radio operators who are Illinois residents pursuing an undergraduate degree. Applicants from Indiana and Wisconsin will be considered if none from Illinois selected. Deadline is February 1.

Award: Scholarship for use in freshman, sophomore, junior, or senior years; not renewable. *Number:* 1. *Amount:* $500.

Eligibility Requirements: Applicant must be enrolled or expecting to enroll full-time at a two-year or four-year or technical institution or university; studying in Illinois and must have an interest in amateur radio. Available to U.S. citizens.

Application Requirements: Application, transcript. *Deadline:* February 1.

Contact: Mary Hobart, Secretary Foundation
>   ARRL Foundation, Inc.
>   225 Main Street
>   Newington, CT 06111-1494
>   *Phone:* 860-594-0397
>   *E-mail:* k1mmh@arrl.org

ASAP/UNION BANK & TRUST COMPANY - LINCOLN JOURNAL STAR'S NEWSPAPERS IN EDUCATION   http://www.ubt.com

WE HAVE MONEY TO LEARN SCHOLARSHIPS

Scholarships for Nebraska high school seniors who will be attending a Nebraska postsecondary institution on a full-time basis. Applications are considered for selection based on several criteria including ACT, GPA, essay, class rank, and school and community involvement.

Award: Scholarship for use in freshman year; not renewable. *Number:* up to 24. *Amount:* up to $500.

Eligibility Requirements: Applicant must be high school student; planning to enroll or expecting to enroll full-time at a two-year or four-year institution or university; resident of Nebraska and studying in Nebraska. Applicant must have 3.0 GPA or higher. Available to U.S. citizens.

Application Requirements: Application, essay, photo, resume, test scores, parental/guardian signature. *Deadline:* March 15.

Contact: Franny Madsen, Marketing Representative
>   ASAP/Union Bank & Trust Company - Lincoln Journal Star's
>   Newspapers in Education
>   18 West 23rd Street
>   Kearney, NE 68847
>   *Phone:* 308-237-7593
>   *Fax:* 308-237-5729
>   *E-mail:* franny.madsen@ubt.com

ASHLEY FOUNDATION   http://www.theashleyfoundation.org

ASHLEY TAMBURRI SCHOLARSHIP

Scholarship for a cancer survivor or individual currently diagnosed with cancer. An active cancer patient does not have to be receiving treatment to qualify. The cancer may be in remission or deemed cured. Applicant must be a senior, attending a high school in a county served by the Foundation as of the beginning of that current academic year. Students attending a high school in Carroll, Frederick, Howard, Montgomery, or Washington County, Maryland are eligible to apply.

Award: Scholarship for use in freshman year; renewable. *Amount:* up to $1000.

Eligibility Requirements: Applicant must be high school student; planning to enroll or expecting to enroll at an institution or university and studying in Maryland. Available to U.S. citizens.

Application Requirements: Application, references, letter from the applicant's physician supporting the cancer diagnosis, acceptance letter from the college or university of the student's choice.

Contact: Ashley Foundation
>   22 South Market Street, Suite 17
>   Frederick, MD 21701

ASTHMA AND ALLERGY FOUNDATION OF AMERICA (AAFA) GREATER KANSAS CITY CHAPTER   http://www.aafakc.org

BERRI MITCHEL MEMORIAL SCHOLARSHIP
• See page 555

BARKING FOUNDATION http://www.barkingfoundation.org

BARKING FOUNDATION GRANTS

One-time award of $3000 available to Maine residents. Minimum GPA of 3.5 is desirable. Only first 300 completed applications will be accepted. Essay, financial information, and transcripts required. Available to full- and part-time students. Scholarships vary in number from year to year.

Award: Scholarship for use in freshman, sophomore, junior, senior, graduate, or postgraduate years; not renewable. *Number:* up to 25. *Amount:* $3000.

Eligibility Requirements: Applicant must be enrolled or expecting to enroll full or part-time at a four-year institution or university and resident of Maine. Applicant must have 3.5 GPA or higher. Available to U.S. citizens.

Application Requirements: Application, essay, financial need analysis, references, transcript, copy of Student Aid Report (SAR). *Deadline:* February 15.

Contact: Stephanie Leonard, Administrator
Barking Foundation
PO Box 855
Bangor, ME 04402
Phone: 207-990-2910
Fax: 207-990-2975
E-mail: info@barkingfoundation.org

BECA FOUNDATION, INC. http://www.becafoundation.org

DANIEL GUTIERREZ MEMORIAL GENERAL SCHOLARSHIP FUND
• See page 607

GENERAL SCHOLARSHIP FUND
• See page 607

BIG 33 SCHOLARSHIP FOUNDATION, INC. http://www.big33.org

BIG 33 SCHOLARSHIP FOUNDATION, INC. SCHOLARSHIPS

Open to all high school seniors in Pennsylvania and Ohio. Quantity of scholarships awarded, dollar amount of each, and type of scholarships varies each year. One-time award only. Minimum 2.0 GPA required. Applications are available at Web site: http://www.big33.org

Award: Scholarship for use in freshman year; not renewable. *Number:* 150–200. *Amount:* $500–$4500.

Eligibility Requirements: Applicant must be high school student; planning to enroll or expecting to enroll full-time at a two-year or four-year or technical institution or university and resident of Ohio or Pennsylvania. Available to U.S. citizens.

Application Requirements: Application, essay, transcript. *Deadline:* February 6.

Contact: Mickey Minnich, Executive Director
Big 33 Scholarship Foundation, Inc.
511 Bridge Street
PO Box 213
New Cumberland, PA 17070
Phone: 717-774-3303
Fax: 717-774-1749
E-mail: info@big33.org

BIG Y FOODS, INC. http://www.bigy.com

BIG Y SCHOLARSHIPS

Awards for customers or dependents of customers of Big Y Foods. Big Y trade area covers Norfolk county, western and central Massachusetts, and Connecticut. Also awards for Big Y employees and dependents of employees. Awards are based on academic excellence. Grades, board scores and two letters of recommendation required.

Award: Scholarship for use in freshman, sophomore, junior, senior, or graduate years; not renewable. *Number:* 200–300. *Amount:* $500–$2000.

Eligibility Requirements: Applicant must be enrolled or expecting to enroll full or part-time at a two-year or four-year or technical institution or university; resident of Connecticut or Massachusetts and studying in Connecticut or Massachusetts. Available to U.S. and non-U.S. citizens.

Application Requirements: Application, resume, references, test scores, transcript. *Deadline:* February 1.

Contact: Missy Lajoie, Scholarship Committee
Big Y Foods, Inc.
PO Box 7840
Springfield, MA 01102-7840
Phone: 413-504-4047
Fax: 413-504-6509
E-mail: wecare@bigy.com

BLUE GRASS ENERGY http://www.bgenergy.com/

BLUE GRASS ENERGY ACADEMIC SCHOLARSHIP

Scholarships for Kentucky high school seniors whose parents or guardians are members of Blue Grass Energy residing in the service area. Must have minimum GPA of 3.0 and have demonstrated academic achievement. Must demonstrate financial need and submit biographical sketch, photo, account of personal involvement in school and community affairs, and justification for financial aid. For application and information, visit Web site: http://www.bgenergy.com

Award: Scholarship for use in freshman year; not renewable. *Number:* 10. *Amount:* $1000.

Eligibility Requirements: Applicant must be high school student; planning to enroll or expecting to enroll full-time at a two-year or four-year or technical institution or university and resident of Kentucky. Applicant must have 3.0 GPA or higher. Available to U.S. citizens.

Application Requirements: Application, financial need analysis, transcript, handwritten request for scholarship. *Deadline:* March 1.

Contact: Blue Grass Energy
PO Box 990
Nicholasville, KY 40340-0990
Phone: 888-546-4243
E-mail: tonyw@bgenergy.com

BLUEGRASS CELLULAR, INC. http://www.myblueworks.com

BLUEGRASS CELLULAR, INC. SCHOLARSHIP

One-time award available to Kentucky high school seniors who live and attend school within Bluegrass Cellular's 34-county home coverage area. Parents/guardian must be current customer who has received service for a minimum of 12 months, in good payment standing. Must be enrolling as freshman in a postsecondary institution for fall semester. Minimum GPA of 2.5 required. Student or family member may not be employed by Bluegrass Cellular. Application available at Web site: http://www.bluegrasscellular.com.

Award: Scholarship for use in freshman year; not renewable. *Number:* 15. *Amount:* up to $1000.

Eligibility Requirements: Applicant must be enrolled or expecting to enroll full-time at a two-year or four-year or technical institution or university and resident of Kentucky. Applicant must have 2.5 GPA or higher. Available to U.S. citizens.

Application Requirements: Application, essay, references, transcript. *Deadline:* April 3.

Contact: Marketing Manager
Bluegrass Cellular, Inc.
2902 Ring Road
Elizabethtown, KY 42701
Phone: 270-352-7422

BOYS AND GIRLS CLUBS OF CHICAGO http://www.bgcc.org

BOYS AND GIRLS CLUBS OF CHICAGO SCHOLARSHIPS
• See page 495

BROWN FOUNDATION FOR EDUCATIONAL EQUITY, EXCELLENCE, AND RESEARCH   http://www.brownvboard.org/foundatn/sclrbroc.htm

BROWN FOUNDATION GOODYEAR TIRE AND RUBBER COMPANY SCHOLARSHIP FOR COLLEGE STUDENTS

Scholarship for college student who must be enrolled at least half-time as defined by the higher education institution of attendance. Applicant must be a resident of Kansas and enrolled at an accredited institution of higher education within the state of Kansas.

Award: Scholarship for use in freshman or sophomore years. *Number:* 1. *Amount:* up to $500.

Eligibility Requirements: Applicant must be enrolled or expecting to enroll full-time at a four-year institution or university; resident of Kansas and studying in Kansas. Applicant must have 3.0 GPA or higher. Available to U.S. citizens.

Application Requirements: Application, essay, references, test scores, transcript. *Deadline:* March 30.

Contact: Chelsey Smith, Staff/Administrative Assistant
Brown Foundation for Educational Equity, Excellence, and Research
PO Box 4862
Topeka, KS 66604
Phone: 785-235-3939
Fax: 785-235-1001
E-mail: brownfound@juno.com

BROWN FOUNDATION GOODYEAR TIRE AND RUBBER COMPANY SCHOLARSHIPS FOR HIGH SCHOOL SENIORS

One-time, non-renewable scholarship available to high school seniors across the state of Kansas who plan to attend accredited Kansas colleges. Award is $300 to be used for the freshman year.

Award: Scholarship for use in freshman year; not renewable. *Number:* 1. *Amount:* up to $300.

Eligibility Requirements: Applicant must be high school student; planning to enroll or expecting to enroll full-time at an institution or university and resident of Kansas. Available to U.S. citizens.

Application Requirements: Application, references, test scores, transcript. *Deadline:* March 30.

Contact: Scholarship Committee
Brown Foundation for Educational Equity, Excellence, and Research
PO Box 4862
Topeka, KS 66604
Phone: 785-235-3939
Fax: 785-235-1001
E-mail: brownfound@juno.com

BUFFALO AFL-CIO COUNCIL

AFL-CIO COUNCIL OF BUFFALO SCHOLARSHIP
• See page 495

CABRILLO CIVIC CLUBS OF CALIFORNIA, INC.   http://www.cabrillocivicclubs.org

CABRILLO CIVIC CLUBS OF CALIFORNIA SCHOLARSHIP
• See page 608

CALIFORNIA ASSOCIATION OF PRIVATE POSTSECONDARY SCHOOLS   http://www.cappsonline.org

CAPPS SCHOLARSHIP PROGRAM

Schools participating in the CAPPS Scholarship Program offer both full- and partial-tuition scholarships to graduating high school students and adults wishing to pursue their education at a private career school. Scholarships are for tuition only. Applications are sent to the school of the applicant's choice; that school selects scholarship recipients using their own criteria. Among other qualifications listed on the application, recipients must meet that school's admissions requirements and be a California resident and a U.S. legal citizen to qualify. Written inquiries must include a self-addressed stamped envelope for reply.

Award: Scholarship for use in freshman year; not renewable. *Number:* 200–250. *Amount:* $1000–$25,000.

Eligibility Requirements: Applicant must be enrolled or expecting to enroll full or part-time at a technical institution or university; resident of California and studying in California. Available to U.S. citizens.

Application Requirements: Application. *Deadline:* June 10.

Contact: Jamie Strong, Scholarship Coordinator
California Association of Private Postsecondary Schools
400 Capitol Mall, Suite 1560
Sacramento, CA 95814
Phone: 916-447-5500
Fax: 916-440-8970
E-mail: info@cappsoline.org

CALIFORNIA COMMUNITY COLLEGES   http://www.cccco.edu/

COOPERATIVE AGENCIES RESOURCES FOR EDUCATION PROGRAM

Renewable award available to California resident attending a two-year California community college. Must have no more than 70 degree-applicable units, currently receive CALWORKS/TANF, and have at least one child under fourteen years of age. Must be in EOPS, single head of household, and 18 or older. Contact local college EOPS-CARE office.

Award: Grant for use in freshman or sophomore years; renewable. *Number:* up to 10,000.

Eligibility Requirements: Applicant must be age 18; enrolled or expecting to enroll full-time at a two-year institution; single; resident of California and studying in California. Available to U.S. citizens.

Application Requirements: Application, financial need analysis, test scores, transcript. *Deadline:* Continuous.

Contact: Cheryl Fong, CARE Coordinator
California Community Colleges
1102 Q Street
Sacramento, CA 95814-6511
Phone: 916-323-5954
Fax: 916-327-8232
E-mail: cfong@cccco.edu

CALIFORNIA CONGRESS OF PARENTS AND TEACHERS, INC.   http://www.capta.org

CALIFORNIA CONGRESS OF PARENTS AND TEACHERS, INC. SCHOLARSHIP

Scholarships awarded to California State PTA members for education and continuing education. Eligible applicants will be California residents. Deadlines are November 30 and March 15.

Award: Scholarship for use in freshman, sophomore, junior, senior, or graduate years; not renewable. *Number:* varies. *Amount:* $500–$5000.

Eligibility Requirements: Applicant must be enrolled or expecting to enroll full or part-time at a two-year or four-year or technical institution or university and resident of California. Available to U.S. and non-U.S. citizens.

Application Requirements: Application, references, transcript. *Deadline:* varies.

Contact: Becky Reece, Scholarship Coordinator
California Congress of Parents and Teachers, Inc.
930 Georgia Street
Los Angeles, CA 90015
Phone: 213-620-1100 Ext. 316
Fax: 213-620-1411
E-mail: grants@capta.org

CALIFORNIA CORRECTIONAL PEACE OFFICERS ASSOCIATION   http://www.ccpoa.org

CALIFORNIA CORRECTIONAL PEACE OFFICERS ASSOCIATION JOE HARPER SCHOLARSHIP
• See page 539

CALIFORNIA COUNCIL OF THE BLIND
http://www.ccbnet.org

CALIFORNIA COUNCIL OF THE BLIND SCHOLARSHIPS
• See page 555

CALIFORNIA GRANGE FOUNDATION
http://www.grangeonline.org

CALIFORNIA GRANGE FOUNDATION SCHOLARSHIP
• See page 495

CALIFORNIA JUNIOR MISS SCHOLARSHIP PROGRAM
http://www.ajm.org/california

CALIFORNIA JUNIOR MISS SCHOLARSHIP PROGRAM

Scholarship program to recognize and reward outstanding high school junior females in the areas of academics, leadership, athletics, public speaking, and the performing arts. Must be single, female, a U.S. citizen, and resident of California. Minimum 3.0 GPA required.

Award: Scholarship for use in freshman, sophomore, junior, or senior years; not renewable. *Number:* 25. *Amount:* $500–$11,500.

Eligibility Requirements: Applicant must be high school student; age 15-17; planning to enroll or expecting to enroll full-time at a two-year or four-year or technical institution or university; single female; resident of California and must have an interest in leadership. Applicant must have 3.0 GPA or higher. Available to U.S. citizens.

Application Requirements: Application, applicant must enter a contest, essay, interview, test scores, transcript. *Deadline:* varies.

Contact: Joan McDonald, State Contact
California Junior Miss Scholarship Program
3523 Glenbrook Lane
Napa, CA 94558
Phone: 760-420-4177

CALIFORNIA MASONIC FOUNDATION
http://www.freemason.org/index.php

CALIFORNIA MASONIC FOUNDATION SCHOLARSHIP AWARDS

Scholarships range from $1,000 to $12,000; most are renewable annually. An interview may or may not be part of the selection process. Must be a U.S. citizen and a resident of California for at least one year. Must be a high school senior. Must have a minimum 3.0 GPA and plan to attend an accredited two- or four-year institution of higher learning as a full-time undergraduate freshman in the fall following high school graduation.

Award: Scholarship for use in freshman year; renewable. *Amount:* $1000–$12,000.

Eligibility Requirements: Applicant must be high school student; planning to enroll or expecting to enroll full-time at a two-year or four-year institution or university and resident of California. Applicant must have 3.0 GPA or higher. Available to U.S. citizens.

Application Requirements: Application, essay, financial need analysis, interview, references, self-addressed stamped envelope, test scores, transcript. *Deadline:* February 15.

Contact: Doug Ismail, Director Scholarships
California Masonic Foundation
1111 California Street
San Francisco, CA 94108-2284
Phone: 415-776-7000
E-mail: dismail@freemason.org

CALIFORNIA STATE PARENT-TEACHER ASSOCIATION
http://www.capta.org

CONTINUING EDUCATION - PTA VOLUNTEERS SCHOLARSHIP

Available annually from the California State PTA to be used for continuing education at accredited colleges, universities, trade or technical schools. Scholarships recognize volunteer service in PTA and enable PTA volunteers to continue their education, may be utilized during the period January 1 to December 31. Must have given three year's volunteer service to PTA/PTSA and must hold current membership in a PTA/PTSA unit in good standing. Deadline Nov 15.

Award: Scholarship for use in freshman, sophomore, junior, senior, or graduate years. *Amount:* up to $500.

Eligibility Requirements: Applicant must be enrolled or expecting to enroll full or part-time at a two-year or four-year or technical institution or university and resident of California. Available to U.S. citizens.

Application Requirements: Application, essay, references, copy of membership card. *Deadline:* November 15.

Contact: Becky Reece, Scholarship and Award Chairman
California State Parent-Teacher Association
930 Georgia Street
Los Angeles, CA 90015-1322
Phone: 213-620-1100
Fax: 213-620-1141

CALIFORNIA STUDENT AID COMMISSION
http://www.csac.ca.gov

CAL GRANT C

Award for California residents who are enrolled in a short-term vocational training program. Program must lead to a recognized degree or certificate. Course length must be a minimum of 4 months and no longer than 24 months. Students must be attending an approved California institution and show financial need.

Award: Grant for use in freshman, sophomore, junior, or senior years; renewable. *Number:* up to 7761. *Amount:* $576–$3168.

Eligibility Requirements: Applicant must be enrolled or expecting to enroll full or part-time at a two-year or technical institution; resident of California and studying in California. Available to U.S. citizens.

Application Requirements: Application, financial need analysis, GPA verification. *Deadline:* March 2.

Contact: Student Support Services Branch
California Student Aid Commission
PO Box 419027
Rancho Cordova, CA 95741-9027
Phone: 916-526-7590
Fax: 916-526-8002
E-mail: custsvcs@csac.ca.gov

CHILD DEVELOPMENT TEACHER AND SUPERVISOR GRANT PROGRAM

Award is for those students pursuing an approved course of study leading to a Child Development Permit issued by the California Commission on Teacher Credentialing. In exchange for each year funding is received, recipients agree to provide one year of service in a licensed childcare center.

Award: Grant for use in freshman, sophomore, junior, or senior years; renewable. *Number:* up to 300. *Amount:* $1000–$2000.

Eligibility Requirements: Applicant must be enrolled or expecting to enroll full or part-time at a two-year or four-year or technical institution or university; resident of California and studying in California. Available to U.S. citizens.

Application Requirements: Application, financial need analysis, references, FAFSA. *Deadline:* June 1.

Contact: California Student Aid Commission
PO Box 419027
Rancho Cordova, CA 95741-9027
Phone: 916-526-7590
Fax: 916-526-8002
E-mail: custsvcs@csac.ca.gov

COMPETITIVE CAL GRANT A

Award for California residents who are not recent high school graduates attending an approved college or university within the state. Must show financial need and meet minimum 3.0 GPA requirement.

Award: Grant for use in freshman, sophomore, junior, or senior years; renewable. *Number:* up to 22,500. *Amount:* $2046–$9708.

Eligibility Requirements: Applicant must be enrolled or expecting to enroll full or part-time at a two-year or four-year or technical institution or university; resident of California and studying in California. Applicant must have 3.0 GPA or higher. Available to U.S. citizens.

Application Requirements: Application, financial need analysis, GPA verification. *Deadline:* March 2.

Contact: Student Support Services Branch
California Student Aid Commission
PO Box 419027
Rancho Cordova, CA 95741-9027
Phone: 916-526-7590
Fax: 916-526-8002
E-mail: custsvcs@csac.ca.gov

COMPETITIVE CAL GRANT B

Award is for California residents who are not recent high school graduates attending an approved college or university within the state. Must show financial need and meet the minimum 2.0 GPA requirement.

Award: Grant for use in freshman, sophomore, or junior years; renewable. *Number:* up to 22,500. *Amount:* $700–$11,259.

Eligibility Requirements: Applicant must be age 23 or under; enrolled or expecting to enroll full or part-time at a two-year or four-year or technical institution or university; resident of California and studying in California. Available to U.S. citizens.

Application Requirements: Application, financial need analysis, GPA verification. *Deadline:* March 2.

Contact: Student Support Services Branch
California Student Aid Commission
PO Box 419027
Rancho Cordova, CA 95741-9027
Phone: 916-526-7590
Fax: 916-526-8002
E-mail: custsvcs@csac.ca.gov

ENTITLEMENT CAL GRANT A

Award is for California residents who are recent high school graduates attending an approved college or university within the state. Must show financial need and meet the minimum 3.0 GPA requirement.

Award: Grant for use in freshman, sophomore, junior, or senior years; renewable. *Number:* varies. *Amount:* $2046–$9708.

Eligibility Requirements: Applicant must be enrolled or expecting to enroll full or part-time at a two-year or four-year or technical institution or university; resident of California and studying in California. Applicant must have 3.0 GPA or higher. Available to U.S. citizens.

Application Requirements: Application, financial need analysis, GPA verification. *Deadline:* March 2.

Contact: Student Support Services Branch
California Student Aid Commission
PO Box 419027
Rancho Cordova, CA 95741-9027
Phone: 916-526-7590
Fax: 916-526-8002
E-mail: custsvcs@csac.ca.gov

ENTITLEMENT CAL GRANT B

Award for California residents who are high school graduates attending an approved college or university within the state. Must show financial need and meet the minimum 2.0 GPA requirement.

Award: Grant for use in freshman, sophomore, junior, or senior years; renewable. *Number:* varies. *Amount:* $700–$11,259.

Eligibility Requirements: Applicant must be age 23 or under; enrolled or expecting to enroll full or part-time at a two-year or four-year or technical institution or university; resident of California and studying in California. Available to U.S. citizens.

Application Requirements: Application, financial need analysis. *Deadline:* March 2.

Contact: Student Support Services Branch
California Student Aid Commission
PO Box 419027
Rancho Cordova, CA 95741-9027
Phone: 916-526-7590
Fax: 916-526-8002
E-mail: custsvcs@csac.ca.gov

ROBERT C. BYRD HONORS SCHOLARSHIP-CALIFORNIA

Federally funded award is available to California high school seniors. Students are awarded based on outstanding academic merit. Students must be nominated by their high school. Recipients must maintain satisfactory academic progress.

Award: Scholarship for use in freshman, sophomore, junior, or senior years; renewable. *Number:* 700–800. *Amount:* $1500.

Eligibility Requirements: Applicant must be high school student; planning to enroll or expecting to enroll full-time at a four-year institution or university and resident of California. Applicant must have 3.5 GPA or higher. Available to U.S. citizens.

Application Requirements: Application, financial need analysis, test scores. *Deadline:* April 15.

Contact: California Student Aid Commission
PO Box 419029
Rancho Cordova, CA 95741-9027
Phone: 916-526-7590
Fax: 916-526-8002
E-mail: custsvcs@csac.ca.gov

CALIFORNIA TABLE GRAPE COMMISSION   http://www.freshcaliforniagrapes.com

CALIFORNIA TABLE GRAPE FARM WORKERS SCHOLARSHIP PROGRAM
• *See page 539*

CALIFORNIA WINE GRAPE GROWERS FOUNDATION   http://www.cawg.org/cwggf

CALIFORNIA WINE GRAPE GROWERS FOUNDATION SCHOLARSHIP

Scholarship for high school seniors whose parents or legal guardians are vineyard employees of wine grape growers. Recipients may study the subject of their choice at any campus of the University of California system, the California State University system, or the California Community College system.

Award: Scholarship for use in freshman, sophomore, junior, or senior years; not renewable. *Number:* 2. *Amount:* $1000–$4000.

Eligibility Requirements: Applicant must be high school student; planning to enroll or expecting to enroll full-time at a two-year or four-year institution or university; resident of California and studying in California. Applicant must have 2.5 GPA or higher. Available to U.S. citizens.

Application Requirements: Application, essay, references, test scores, transcript. *Deadline:* April 1.

Contact:
Phone: 916-924-5370
E-mail: info@cawg.org

CANADA ICELAND FOUNDATION, INC. SCHOLARSHIPS

CANADA ICELAND FOUNDATION SCHOLARSHIP PROGRAM

One scholarship of $500, to be awarded annually. To be offered to a university student studying towards a degree in any Canadian university.

Award: Scholarship for use in freshman, sophomore, junior, or senior years. *Number:* 1. *Amount:* $500.

Eligibility Requirements: Applicant must be enrolled or expecting to enroll full-time at a four-year institution or university and studying in Alberta, British Columbia, Manitoba, New Brunswick, Nova Scotia, Ontario, or Quebec. Available to U.S. and Canadian citizens.

Canada Iceland Foundation, Inc. Scholarships (continued)

Application Requirements: *Deadline:* varies.

Contact: Canada Iceland Foundation, Inc. Scholarships
Box 27012
C-360 Main Street
Winnipeg R3C 4T3
Canada

CAREER COLLEGES AND SCHOOLS OF TEXAS
http://www.colleges-schools.org

CAREER COLLEGES AND SCHOOLS OF TEXAS SCHOLARSHIP PROGRAM

One-time award available to graduating high school seniors who plan to attend a Texas trade or technical institution. Must be a Texas resident. Criteria selection, which is determined independently by each school's guidance counselors, may be based on academic excellence, financial need, or student leadership. Must be U.S. citizen.

Award: Scholarship for use in freshman year; not renewable. *Number:* up to 6000. *Amount:* up to $1000.

Eligibility Requirements: Applicant must be high school student; planning to enroll or expecting to enroll full or part-time at a technical institution; resident of Texas and studying in Texas. Available to U.S. citizens.

Application Requirements: *Deadline:* Continuous.

Contact: Jerry Foster, Scholarship Chairman
Career Colleges and Schools of Texas
6460 Hiller, Suite D
El Paso, TX 79925
Phone: 915-779-0900
Fax: 915-779-1145
E-mail: jdfoster@ibcelpaso.edu

CASDA-LOT (CAPITAL AREA SCHOOL DEVELOPMENT ASSOCIATION)
http://www.nylottery.org/lot

NEW YORK LOTTERY LEADERS OF TOMORROW (LOT) SCHOLARSHIP

The goal of this program is to reinforce the lottery's education mission by awarding four-year scholarships, $1000 per year for up to four years. One scholarship is available to every New York high school, public or private, that awards a high school diploma.

Award: Scholarship for use in freshman, sophomore, junior, or senior years; renewable. *Number:* varies. *Amount:* $1000.

Eligibility Requirements: Applicant must be high school student; planning to enroll or expecting to enroll full-time at a two-year or four-year or technical institution or university; resident of New York and studying in New York. Applicant must have 3.0 GPA or higher. Available to U.S. citizens.

Application Requirements: Application, essay, transcript. *Deadline:* March 19.

Contact: Betsey Morgan, Program Coordinator
CASDA-LOT (Capital Area School Development Association)
The University at Albany East Campus
1 University Place A-409
Rensselaer, NY 12144-3456
Phone: 518-525-2788
Fax: 518-525-2797
E-mail: casdalot@uamail.albany.edu

CENTER FOR SCHOLARSHIP ADMINISTRATION
http://www.scholarshipprograms.org

BAPRM SCHOLARSHIP PROGRAM

Non-renewable award available to seniors attending high schools in one of the following six Bay Area counties in California: Alameda, Contra Costa, Marin, San Francisco, San Mateo, or Santa Clara. For more details and an application, see Web site.

Award: Scholarship for use in freshman, sophomore, junior, or senior years; not renewable. *Number:* 2. *Amount:* $1000.

Eligibility Requirements: Applicant must be high school student; planning to enroll or expecting to enroll full-time at a two-year or four-year or technical institution or university and resident of California. Applicant must have 2.5 GPA or higher. Available to U.S. citizens.

Application Requirements: Application, essay, financial need analysis, references, transcript. *Deadline:* February 15.

Contact: Sandra Lee, President
Center for Scholarship Administration
PO Box 1465
Taylors, SC 29687-0031
Phone: 864-268-3363
Fax: 864-268-7160
E-mail: sandralee41@bellsouth.net

HISPANIC LEAGUE OF THE PIEDMONT TRIAD SCHOLARSHIP
• See page 608

KITTIE M. FAIREY EDUCATIONAL FUND SCHOLARSHIPS

Renewable scholarships are for graduating high school seniors residing in South Carolina. Scholarships provide funding for half tuition and room and board (for boarding students). For more details and an application see Web site: http://www.scholarshipprograms.org

Award: Scholarship for use in freshman, sophomore, or junior years; renewable. *Number:* 1. *Amount:* varies.

Eligibility Requirements: Applicant must be enrolled or expecting to enroll full-time at a two-year or four-year institution or university and resident of South Carolina. Applicant must have 3.0 GPA or higher. Available to U.S. citizens.

Application Requirements: Application. *Deadline:* January 31.

Contact: Sandra Lee, President
Center for Scholarship Administration
PO Box 1465
Taylors, SC 29687-0031
Phone: 864-268-3363
Fax: 864-268-7160
E-mail: sandralee41@bellsouth.net

MILLIKEN & COMPANY SCHOLARSHIP
• See page 527

SOUTH CAROLINA JUNIOR GOLF FOUNDATION SCHOLARSHIP

Scholarships are available to student residents of South Carolina who have a competitive or recreational interest in golf. Must have and maintain a 2.75 cumulative GPA. For more details and an application see Web site: http://www.scholarshipprograms.org

Award: Scholarship for use in freshman, sophomore, junior, or senior years; renewable. *Number:* varies. *Amount:* $2500.

Eligibility Requirements: Applicant must be enrolled or expecting to enroll full or part-time at a four-year institution or university; resident of South Carolina; studying in South Carolina and must have an interest in golf. Available to U.S. citizens.

Application Requirements: Application, essay, financial need analysis, references, transcript. *Deadline:* February 15.

Contact: Sandra Lee, President
Center for Scholarship Administration
PO Box 1465
Taylors, SC 29687-0031
Phone: 864-268-3363
Fax: 864-268-7160
E-mail: sandralee41@bellsouth.net

SOUTHERN CALIFORNIA RELOCATION COUNCIL SCHOLARSHIP PROGRAM

One-time award to a senior attending public high school in one of the following Southern California counties: Orange, Los Angeles, San Diego, Riverside, Kern, and Ventura. Applicants must have relocated a minimum of 50 miles into one of these counties within the past two years. The award is also open to students who have moved into the U.S. from a foreign country during the same time frame. Must be a U.S. citizen and must have at least 2.75 GPA.

Award: Scholarship for use in freshman, sophomore, junior, or senior years; not renewable. *Number:* 1. *Amount:* $1000–$2000.

Eligibility Requirements: Applicant must be high school student; planning to enroll or expecting to enroll full-time at a two-year or four-year or technical institution and resident of California. Available to U.S. citizens.

Application Requirements: Application, essay, references, transcript. *Deadline:* February 15.

Contact: Sandra Lee, President
Center for Scholarship Administration
PO Box 1465
Taylors, SC 29687-0031
Phone: 864-268-3363
Fax: 864-268-7160
E-mail: sandralee41@bellsouth.net

CENTRAL NATIONAL BANK & TRUST COMPANY OF ENID, TRUSTEE http://www.onecentralsource.us/trust_services.html

MAY T. HENRY SCHOLARSHIP FOUNDATION

A $1000 scholarship renewed annually for four years. Awarded to any student enrolled in a state of Oklahoma supported college, university or tech school. Based on need, scholastic performance and personal traits valued by May T. Henry. Minimum 3.0 GPA required.

Award: Scholarship for use in freshman, sophomore, junior, senior, or postgraduate years; renewable. *Number:* up to 15. *Amount:* $1000.

Eligibility Requirements: Applicant must be enrolled or expecting to enroll full or part-time at a two-year or four-year or technical institution or university and studying in Oklahoma. Applicant must have 3.0 GPA or higher. Available to U.S. citizens.

Application Requirements: Application, essay, financial need analysis, references, test scores, transcript. *Deadline:* April 1.

Contact: Wayne Aholt, Trust Department
Central National Bank & Trust Company of Enid, Trustee
Central National Bank & Trust Co, PO Box 3448
Enid, OK 73702-3448
Phone: 580-213-1612
Fax: 580-249-5926
E-mail: waholt@cnb-enid.com

CENTRAL SCHOLARSHIP BUREAU http://www.centralsb.org

MARY RUBIN AND BENJAMIN M. RUBIN SCHOLARSHIP FUND

Renewable scholarship for tuition only to women who are attending a college, university, or other institution of higher learning. Must be a resident of Maryland. Have a GPA of 3.0 or better and meet the financial requirements. Contact for application or download from Web site: http://www.centralsb.org

Award: Scholarship for use in freshman, sophomore, junior, senior, graduate, or postgraduate years; renewable. *Number:* 30–35. *Amount:* $500–$2500.

Eligibility Requirements: Applicant must be enrolled or expecting to enroll full or part-time at a two-year or four-year or technical institution or university; female and resident of Maryland. Applicant must have 3.0 GPA or higher. Available to U.S. citizens.

Application Requirements: Application, essay, financial need analysis, references, transcript. *Deadline:* March 1.

Contact: Roberta Goldman, Program Director
Central Scholarship Bureau
1700 Reisterstown Road
Suite 220
Baltimore, MD 21208-2903
Phone: 410-415-5558
Fax: 410-415-5501
E-mail: roberta@centralsb.org

SHOE CITY-WB54/WB50 SCHOLARSHIP

Scholarship for high school seniors who are permanent residents of Maryland or Washington D.C. Deadline is April 1.

Award: Scholarship for use in freshman year; not renewable. *Number:* 4. *Amount:* $1500.

Eligibility Requirements: Applicant must be high school student; planning to enroll or expecting to enroll at a four-year institution or university and resident of District of Columbia or Maryland. Available to U.S. citizens.

Application Requirements: Application, essay, financial need analysis, references, transcript. *Deadline:* April 1.

Contact: Roberta Goldman, Program Director
Central Scholarship Bureau
1700 Reisterstown Road
Suite 220
Baltimore, MD 21208-2903
Phone: 410-415-5558
Fax: 410-415-5501
E-mail: roberta@centralsb.org

CHICANA/LATINA FOUNDATION http://www.chicanalatina.org

SCHOLARSHIPS FOR LATINA STUDENTS
• *See page 609*

CHINESE PROFESSIONAL CLUB OF HOUSTON http://www.cpchouston.com

T.P. WANG SCHOLARSHIP
• *See page 609*

THE CHINESE PROFESSIONAL CLUB SCHOLARSHIP
• *See page 609*

CIRI FOUNDATION http://www.thecirifoundation.org

HOWARD ROCK FOUNDATION SCHOLARSHIP PROGRAM

Award for Alaska Native Student from an Alaska Village Initiative member organization. Must be enrolled full time in a four-year undergraduate program or in a graduate program. Must have a GPA of 2.5 or better and be in a field that promotes economic development in rural Alaska. Deadline: March 31.

Award: Scholarship for use in freshman, sophomore, junior, senior, or graduate years; not renewable. *Number:* 3. *Amount:* $2500–$5000.

Eligibility Requirements: Applicant must be enrolled or expecting to enroll full-time at a four-year institution or university and resident of Alaska. Applicant must have 2.5 GPA or higher. Available to U.S. citizens.

Application Requirements: Application, essay, financial need analysis, references, transcript. *Deadline:* varies.

Contact: CIRI Foundation
2600 Cordova Street, Suite 206
Anchorage, AK 99503
Phone: 907-263-5582
Fax: 907-263-5588
E-mail: tcf@ciri.com

CITY COLLEGE OF SAN FRANCISCO LATINO EDUCATIONAL ASSOCIATION http://www.ccsf.edu

LATINO EDUCATION ASSOCIATION SCHOLARSHIP
• *See page 610*

CIVIL SERVICE EMPLOYEES INSURANCE COMPANY http://www.cseinsurance.com

YOUTH AUTOMOBILE SAFETY SCHOLARSHIP ESSAY COMPETITION FOR CHILDREN OF PUBLIC EMPLOYEES
• *See page 539*

COLEMAN A. YOUNG FOUNDATION http://www.cayf.org

COLEMAN A. YOUNG FOUNDATION SCHOLARSHIP

Renewable award to Detroit area high school seniors who demonstrate leadership qualities. Minimum 2.5 GPA required. Must be single and U.S. citizen. Deadline is April 1. Aimed at students who would not ordinarily qualify for traditional scholarships. Must be enrolled full-time in a four year college in Michigan or attend an accredited, historically black institution.

Award: Scholarship for use in freshman, sophomore, junior, or senior years; renewable. *Number:* 5–10. *Amount:* up to $20,000.

Eligibility Requirements: Applicant must be high school student; planning to enroll or expecting to enroll full-time at a four-year

Coleman A. Young Foundation (continued)

institution or university; single and resident of Michigan. Applicant must have 2.5 GPA or higher. Available to U.S. citizens.

Application Requirements: Application, essay, financial need analysis, interview, resume, references, test scores, transcript. *Deadline:* April 1.

Contact: Thelma Bush, Program Manager
Coleman A. Young Foundation
2111 Woodward Avenue, Suite 600
Detroit, MI 48201
Phone: 313-962-2200
Fax: 313-962-2208
E-mail: thelmabush@cayf.org

COLLEGE FOUNDATION OF NORTH CAROLINA, INC
http://www.cfnc.org

ASSISTANCE LEAGUE OF THE TRIANGLE SCHOLARSHIP PROGRAM

Scholarship assists individuals in the Research Triangle area of North Carolina through service, resources and financial support. Award is available to graduating high school seniors who live in the Research Triangle area and plan to enroll as freshmen at any of North Carolina's postsecondary institutions.

Award: Scholarship for use in freshman year; renewable. *Amount:* up to $1000.

Eligibility Requirements: Applicant must be high school student; planning to enroll or expecting to enroll at an institution or university and resident of North Carolina. Applicant must have 2.5 GPA or higher. Available to U.S. citizens.

Application Requirements: Application. *Deadline:* March 10.

Contact: College Foundation of North Carolina, Inc
Assistance League of the Triangle Area Scholarship Committee, PO Box 98477
Raleigh, NC 27624
Phone: 919-235-4554

AUBREY LEE BROOKS SCHOLARSHIPS

Awards are made annually to 17 graduating high school seniors who plan to enroll as full-time students in a degree-granting program at North Carolina State University, the University of North Carolina at Chapel Hill, or the University of North Carolina at Greensboro. Recipients must permanently reside in one of the counties listed on Web site. Must maintain a 2.75 cumulative GPA.

Award: Scholarship for use in freshman year; renewable. *Number:* up to 17. *Amount:* up to $7300.

Eligibility Requirements: Applicant must be high school student; planning to enroll or expecting to enroll full-time at an institution or university and resident of North Carolina. Available to U.S. citizens.

Application Requirements: Application, essay, transcript. *Deadline:* February 1.

Contact: College Foundation of North Carolina, Inc
Brooks Foundation, NCSEAA, PO Box 13663
Research Triangle Park, NC 27709-3663

CRUMLEY AND ASSOCIATES - CRIB TO COLLEGE SCHOLARSHIP

Scholarship will provide financial assistance and laptop computers to five outstanding North Carolina high school seniors. Applicants must be a graduating senior at a North Carolina high school and enroll at an accredited 4 year college or university or an accredited two-year technical school or community college

Award: Scholarship for use in freshman year. *Number:* up to 5. *Amount:* up to $1000.

Eligibility Requirements: Applicant must be high school student; planning to enroll or expecting to enroll at a two-year or four-year or technical institution or university and studying in North Carolina. Applicant must have 3.0 GPA or higher. Available to U.S. citizens.

Application Requirements: Application. *Deadline:* March 15.

Contact: Crumley and Associates - Crib to College Scholarship
Phone: 336-333-0044
E-mail: smkeaney@crumleyandassociates.com

GLAXOSMITHKLINE OPPORTUNITY SCHOLARSHIPS

Scholarships for students who have been a permanent resident of Chatham, Durham, Orange, or Wake County in North Carolina for the past six months. GlaxoSmithKline Inc. and Triangle Community Foundation employees or their family members are not eligible.

Award: Scholarship for use in freshman year. *Number:* 4–6. *Amount:* up to $5000.

Eligibility Requirements: Applicant must be enrolled or expecting to enroll at a four-year institution or university and resident of North Carolina. Available to U.S. citizens.

Application Requirements: Application. *Deadline:* March 15.

Contact: Linda Depo
College Foundation of North Carolina, Inc
Triangle Community Foundation Scholarship Program, PO Box 12834
Research Triangle Park, NC 27709
Phone: 919-474-8370
Fax: 919-941-9208
E-mail: linda@trianglecf.org

GOLDEN LEAF SCHOLARSHIP - FOUR YEAR UNIVERSITY PROGRAM

Renewable scholarship for current high school seniors and current community college students planning to enter North Carolina public four-year university.Must be a permanent resident of a rural NC county that is economically distressed and/or tobacco crop-dependent. Deadline is May 31.

Award: Scholarship for use in freshman, sophomore, junior, or senior years; renewable. *Number:* 500. *Amount:* $3000.

Eligibility Requirements: Applicant must be enrolled or expecting to enroll at a four-year institution or university and studying in North Carolina. Available to U.S. citizens.

Application Requirements: Application. *Deadline:* May 31.

Contact: College Foundation of North Carolina, Inc
PO Box 41966
Raleigh, NC 27629-1966
Phone: 888-234-6400
E-mail: programinformation@CFNC.org

LATINO DIAMANTE SCHOLARSHIP FUND
• *See page 610*

NORTH CAROLINA 4-H DEVELOPMENT FUND SCHOLARSHIPS

Scholarship for a resident of North Carolina, enrolling as an undergraduate in a four-year accredited North Carolina college or university or a junior or community college in the state, provided the program of study selected is transferable to a four-year college.

Award: Scholarship for use in freshman, sophomore, junior, or senior years. *Amount:* $500–$2500.

Eligibility Requirements: Applicant must be enrolled or expecting to enroll at a two-year or four-year institution or university and resident of North Carolina. Available to U.S. citizens.

Application Requirements: Application.

Contact: College Foundation of North Carolina, Inc
PO Box 41966
Raleigh, NC 27629-1966
Phone: 919-515-2801
E-mail: programinformation@CFNC.org

NORTH CAROLINA BAR ASSOCIATION SCHOLARSHIP

Award is available to natural or adopted children of a North Carolina law enforcement officer who was killed or permanently disabled in the line of duty. Recipient must be enrolled or accepted for admission in a college, vocational training school or other educational institution approved by the scholarship committee of the Young Lawyers Division of the North Carolina Bar Association.

Award: Scholarship for use in freshman, sophomore, junior, senior, or graduate years. *Amount:* up to $2000.

Eligibility Requirements: Applicant must be enrolled or expecting to enroll at a two-year or four-year or technical institution or university and resident of North Carolina. Available to U.S. citizens.

Application Requirements: Application. *Deadline:* April 1.

Contact: College Foundation of North Carolina, Inc
North Carolina Bar Association Scholarship, PO Box 3688
Cary, NC 27519
Phone: 800-662-7407
E-mail: jtfount@mail.ncbar.org

NORTH CAROLINA STUDENT INCENTIVE GRANT

Award available to a student who is a U.S. citizen and a North Carolina resident, who is not enrolled in a program designed primarily for career preparation in a religious vocation.

Award: Grant for use in freshman, sophomore, junior, or senior years. *Amount:* up to $700.

Eligibility Requirements: Applicant must be enrolled or expecting to enroll full-time at a four-year institution or university and resident of North Carolina. Available to U.S. citizens.

Application Requirements: Application. *Deadline:* March 15.

Contact: College Foundation of North Carolina, Inc
PO Box 41966
Raleigh, NC 27629-1966
Phone: 888-234-6400
E-mail: programinformation@CFNC.org

NORTH CAROLINA VETERANS SCHOLARSHIPS

• *See page 587*

UNIVERSITY OF NORTH CAROLINA NEED BASED GRANT

Grants available for eligible students attending one of the 16 campuses of the University of North Carolina. Students must be enrolled in at least 6 credit hours at one of the 16 constituent institutions of The University of North Carolina. Award amounts vary, based on legislative appropriations. No formal deadline has been established.

Award: Grant for use in freshman, sophomore, junior, or senior years. *Number:* 1.

Eligibility Requirements: Applicant must be enrolled or expecting to enroll at a four-year institution or university and studying in North Carolina. Available to U.S. citizens.

Application Requirements: Application. *Deadline:* Continuous.

Contact: College Foundation of North Carolina, Inc
PO Box 41966
Raleigh, NC 27629-1966
Phone: 888-234-6400

COLLEGEBOUND FOUNDATION
http://www.collegeboundfoundation.org

BALTIMORE JUNIOR ASSOCIATION OF COMMERCE (BJAC) SCHOLARSHIP

Award for Baltimore City public high school graduates. Please see Web site: http://www.collegeboundfoundation.org for complete information on application process. Must have participated in verifiable community service activities and submit a one-page typed essay describing in detail the community service in which you have been involved and the importance of these activities to you. Minimum GPA of 3.0. Must submit CollegeBound Competitive Scholarship/Last-Dollar Grant Application.

Award: Scholarship for use in freshman year; not renewable. *Number:* 2. *Amount:* $500.

Eligibility Requirements: Applicant must be enrolled or expecting to enroll full-time at a two-year or four-year institution or university and resident of Maryland. Applicant must have 3.0 GPA or higher. Available to U.S. citizens.

Application Requirements: Application, essay, financial need analysis, transcript, financial aid award letters, Student Aid Report (SAR). *Deadline:* March 19.

Contact: April Bell, Associate Program Director
CollegeBound Foundation
300 Water Street, Suite 300
Baltimore, MD 21202
Phone: 410-783-2905 Ext. 208
Fax: 410-727-5786
E-mail: abell@collegeboundfoundation.org

BALTIMORE ROTARY SERVICE ABOVE SELF AWARD PROGRAM

Award for Baltimore City public high school graduates. Please see Web site: http://www.collegeboundfoundation.org for complete information on application process. Must submit CollegeBound Competitive Scholarship/Last-Dollar Grant Application. Two non-renewable scholarships for female students and two for male students. Must have verifiable community service, submit a one-page essay describing the community service in detail and the importance of this activity to you. Provide list of references for community involvement.

Award: Scholarship for use in freshman year; not renewable. *Number:* 4. *Amount:* $1000–$1500.

Eligibility Requirements: Applicant must be enrolled or expecting to enroll full-time at a two-year or four-year institution or university and resident of Maryland. Applicant must have 2.5 GPA or higher. Available to U.S. citizens.

Application Requirements: Application, essay, financial need analysis, references, transcript, financial aid award letters, Student Aid Report (SAR). *Deadline:* March 19.

Contact: April Bell, Associate Program Director
CollegeBound Foundation
300 Water Street, Suite 300
Baltimore, MD 21202
Phone: 410-783-2905 Ext. 208
Fax: 410-727-5786
E-mail: abell@collegeboundfoundation.org

CARMEN V. D'ANNA MEMORIAL SCHOLARSHIP OF THE MARS SUPERMARKET EDUCATIONAL FUND

Scholarship for a senior at a Baltimore City public high school entering a Maryland state college or university. Must demonstrate financial need; exhibit a strong desire to achieve; and submit a typed one-page essay describing a hardship that you had to overcome.

Award: Scholarship for use in freshman year; renewable. *Number:* 1. *Amount:* $10,000.

Eligibility Requirements: Applicant must be enrolled or expecting to enroll at an institution or university and resident of Maryland. Available to U.S. citizens.

Application Requirements: Application, essay, financial need analysis. *Deadline:* March 19.

Contact: April Bell, Associate Program Director
CollegeBound Foundation
300 Water Street, Suite 300
Baltimore, MD 21202
Phone: 410-783-2905 Ext. 208
Fax: 410-727-5786
E-mail: abell@collegeboundfoundation.org

COLLEGE BOUND LAST-DOLLAR GRANT

Need-based grants for Baltimore City public high school graduates whose family contribution and financial aid package total less than the cost to attend college. Awardees are eligible to receive up to $3000 per year, renewable for up to five years.

Award: Grant for use in freshman, sophomore, junior, or senior years; renewable. *Number:* 90–250. *Amount:* $400–$3000.

Eligibility Requirements: Applicant must be enrolled or expecting to enroll full-time at a two-year or four-year institution or university and resident of Maryland. Available to U.S. citizens.

Application Requirements: Application, financial need analysis. *Deadline:* March 19.

CollegeBound Foundation (continued)

Contact: April Bell, Associate Program Director
CollegeBound Foundation
300 Water Street, Suite 300
Baltimore, MD 21202
Phone: 410-783-2905 Ext. 208
Fax: 410-727-5786
E-mail: abell@collegeboundfoundation.org

COMMERCIAL REAL ESTATE WOMEN (CREW)-BALTIMORE SCHOLARSHIP

Award for female Baltimore City public high school graduates. Please see Web site: http://www.collegeboundfoundation.org for complete information on application process. Minimum GPA of 3.0, combined SAT of 1000. Two letters of recommendation and 500-1000-word essay describing your college expectations. Must submit CollegeBound Competitive Scholarship/Last-Dollar Grant Application.

Award: Scholarship for use in freshman year; not renewable. *Number:* 2. *Amount:* $1000.

Eligibility Requirements: Applicant must be enrolled or expecting to enroll full-time at a four-year institution or university; female and resident of Maryland. Applicant must have 3.0 GPA or higher. Available to U.S. citizens.

Application Requirements: Application, essay, financial need analysis, references, transcript, financial aid award letters, Student Aid Report (SAR). *Deadline:* March 19.

Contact: April Bell, Associate Program Director
CollegeBound Foundation
300 Water Street, Suite 300
Baltimore, MD 21202
Phone: 410-783-2905 Ext. 208
Fax: 410-727-5786
E-mail: abell@collegeboundfoundation.org

COX EDUCATION FUND SCHOLARSHIP

Award for Baltimore City public high school graduates. Please see Web site: http://www.collegeboundfoundation.org for complete information on application process. You must be Valedictorian of your high school graduating class; be ranked in the top ten of your class at the time you apply for the award. Must apply for the CollegeBound Last-Dollar Grant.

Award: Scholarship for use in freshman year; not renewable. *Number:* 4. *Amount:* $300.

Eligibility Requirements: Applicant must be high school student; planning to enroll or expecting to enroll full-time at a two-year or four-year institution or university and resident of Maryland. Available to U.S. citizens.

Application Requirements: Application, financial need analysis, references, transcript, financial aid award letters, Student Aid Report (SAR). *Deadline:* March 19.

Contact: April Bell, Associate Program Director
CollegeBound Foundation
300 Water Street, Suite 300
Baltimore, MD 21202
Phone: 410-783-2905 Ext. 208
Fax: 410-727-5786
E-mail: abell@collegeboundfoundation.org

ERICA LYNNE E. DURANT MEMORIAL SCHOLARSHIP

• See page 556

EXCHANGE CLUB OF BALTIMORE SCHOLARSHIP

Award for Baltimore City public high school graduates. Please see Web site: http://www.collegeboundfoundation.org for complete information on application process. Must submit CollegeBound Competitive Scholarship/Last-Dollar Grant Application. Must have verifiable community service during high school. Minimum GPA of 3.0, SAT score of 1000 required. Submit one-page essay describing personal and professional goals. Must attend a Maryland college or university.

Award: Scholarship for use in freshman year; not renewable. *Number:* 5. *Amount:* $1000–$2000.

Eligibility Requirements: Applicant must be enrolled or expecting to enroll full-time at a two-year or four-year institution or university; resident of Maryland and studying in Maryland. Available to U.S. citizens.

Application Requirements: Application, essay, financial need analysis, references, transcript, financial aid award letters, Student Aid Report (SAR). *Deadline:* March 19.

Contact: April Bell, Associate Program Director
CollegeBound Foundation
300 Water Street, Suite 300
Baltimore, MD 21202
Phone: 410-783-2905 Ext. 208
Fax: 410-727-5786
E-mail: abell@collegeboundfoundation.org

GREEN FAMILY BOOK AWARD

Award for Baltimore City public high school graduates. Please see Web site: http://www.collegeboundfoundation.org for complete information on application process. Minimum GPA of 3.0, verifiable community service. Must have financial need. Must submit essay (250-500 words) describing a significant experience, achievement, or risk that you have taken and its impact on you. Must submit CollegeBound Competitive Scholarship/Last-Dollar Grant Application.

Award: Scholarship for use in freshman year; not renewable. *Number:* 1. *Amount:* $400.

Eligibility Requirements: Applicant must be enrolled or expecting to enroll full-time at a two-year or four-year institution or university and resident of Maryland. Applicant must have 3.0 GPA or higher. Available to U.S. citizens.

Application Requirements: Application, essay, financial need analysis, transcript, financial aid award letters, Student Aid Report (SAR). *Deadline:* March 19.

Contact: April Bell, Associate Program Director
CollegeBound Foundation
300 Water Street, Suite 300
Baltimore, MD 21202
Phone: 410-783-2905 Ext. 208
Fax: 410-727-5786
E-mail: abell@collegeboundfoundation.org

HY ZOLET STUDENT ATHLETE SCHOLARSHIP

Scholarship available to high school athlete with a minimum GPA of 2.5. Must furnish at least two letters verifying participation in high school athletics, evidence you possess a good work ethic, fairness and courage in addition to outstanding leadership and athletic skills. Must submit a one-page essay indicating why you should receive this award; submit a letter of acceptance to a four year school, and recent transcripts.

Award: Scholarship for use in freshman year; not renewable. *Number:* 4. *Amount:* $1000.

Eligibility Requirements: Applicant must be high school student; planning to enroll or expecting to enroll at an institution or university; resident of Maryland and must have an interest in athletics/sports. Applicant must have 2.5 GPA or higher. Available to U.S. citizens.

Application Requirements: Application, essay, references, test scores. *Deadline:* March 19.

Contact: April Bell, Associate Program Director
CollegeBound Foundation
300 Water Street, Suite 300
Baltimore, MD 21202
Phone: 410-783-2905 Ext. 208
Fax: 410-727-5786
E-mail: abell@collegeboundfoundation.org

KENNETH HOFFMAN SCHOLARSHIP

Award for Baltimore City public high school graduates. Please see Web site: http://www.collegeboundfoundation.org for complete information on application process. Minimum GPA of 3.0 required and verifiable community service. Must submit CollegeBound Competitive Scholarship/Last-Dollar Grant Application.

Award: Scholarship for use in freshman year; not renewable. *Number:* 1. *Amount:* $500.

Eligibility Requirements: Applicant must be enrolled or expecting to enroll full-time at a two-year or four-year institution or university and resident of Maryland. Applicant must have 3.0 GPA or higher. Available to U.S. citizens.

Application Requirements: Application, financial need analysis, references, transcript, financial aid award letters, Student Aid Report (SAR). *Deadline:* March 19.

Contact: April Bell, Associate Program Director
CollegeBound Foundation
300 Water Street, Suite 300
Baltimore, MD 21202
Phone: 410-783-2905 Ext. 208
Fax: 410-727-5786
E-mail: abell@collegeboundfoundation.org

LESLIE MOORE FOUNDATION SCHOLARSHIP

Three awards for Baltimore City public high school graduates, two from other Baltimore county schools. Please see Web site: http://www.collegeboundfoundation.org for complete information on application process. Must submit CollegeBound Competitive Scholarship/Last-Dollar Grant Application. Must have GPA of at least 2.0, verifiable community service. Submit essay (500-1000 words) describing the importance of a college education and community service activities you have completed. Must be available for interview with selection committee.

Award: Scholarship for use in freshman, sophomore, junior, or senior years; renewable. *Number:* 5. *Amount:* $2500.

Eligibility Requirements: Applicant must be enrolled or expecting to enroll full-time at a two-year or four-year or technical institution or university; resident of Maryland and studying in Maryland. Available to U.S. citizens.

Application Requirements: Application, essay, financial need analysis, interview, references, transcript, financial aid award letters, Student Aid Report (SAR). *Deadline:* March 19.

Contact: April Bell, Associate Program Director
CollegeBound Foundation
300 Water Street, Suite 300
Baltimore, MD 21202
Phone: 410-783-2905 Ext. 208
Fax: 410-727-5786
E-mail: abell@collegeboundfoundation.org

MARYLAND HOTEL AND LODGING ASSOCIATION SCHOLARSHIP

Award for Baltimore City public high school graduates. Please see Web site: http://www.collegeboundfoundation.org for complete information on application process. Priority will be given to children of employees of the hotels and motels in Maryland and/or students who plan to study hospitality, tourism, or business. Must complete CollegeBound Competitive Scholarship/Last-Dollar Grant Application.

Award: Scholarship for use in freshman, sophomore, junior, or senior years; renewable. *Number:* 1. *Amount:* $500–$2000.

Eligibility Requirements: Applicant must be enrolled or expecting to enroll full-time at a two-year or four-year institution or university and resident of Maryland. Available to U.S. citizens.

Application Requirements: Application, financial need analysis, references, transcript, financial aid award letters, Student Aid Report (SAR). *Deadline:* March 19.

Contact: April Bell, Associate Program Director
CollegeBound Foundation
300 Water Street, Suite 300
Baltimore, MD 21202
Phone: 410-783-2905 Ext. 208
Fax: 410-727-5786
E-mail: abell@collegeboundfoundation.org

RICHARD E. DUNNE, III SCHOLARSHIP

Award for Baltimore City public high school graduates. Please see Web site: http://www.collegeboundfoundation.org for complete information on application process. Must have GPA of 3.0 or better, verifiable community service. Must submit CollegeBound Competitive Scholarship/Last-Dollar Grant Application.

Award: Scholarship for use in freshman year; not renewable. *Number:* 1. *Amount:* $500.

Eligibility Requirements: Applicant must be enrolled or expecting to enroll full-time at a two-year or four-year institution or university and resident of Maryland. Applicant must have 3.0 GPA or higher. Available to U.S. citizens.

Application Requirements: Application, financial need analysis, references, transcript, financial aid award letters, Student Aid Report (SAR). *Deadline:* March 19.

Contact: April Bell, Associate Program Director
CollegeBound Foundation
300 Water Street, Suite 300
Baltimore, MD 21202
Phone: 410-783-2905 Ext. 208
Fax: 410-727-5786
E-mail: abell@collegeboundfoundation.org

SCARBOROUGH-SCHEELER SCHOLARSHIP

Scholarship available to a resident of greater Baltimore and graduate of a Baltimore City Public High School. Must have high school GPA of at least 2.5, demonstrate financial need, submit an essay (500-1,000 words) describing your college expectations. Must attend Goucher College, McDaniel College, or University of Maryland, College Park.

Award: Scholarship for use in freshman year; not renewable. *Number:* 1. *Amount:* $1000.

Eligibility Requirements: Applicant must be enrolled or expecting to enroll at an institution or university and resident of Maryland. Applicant must have 2.5 GPA or higher. Available to U.S. citizens.

Application Requirements: Application, essay, financial need analysis. *Deadline:* March 19.

Contact: April Bell, Associate Program Director
CollegeBound Foundation
300 Water Street, Suite 300
Baltimore, MD 21202
Phone: 410-783-2905 Ext. 208
Fax: 410-727-5786
E-mail: abell@collegeboundfoundation.org

THE ANDERSON-BELL FAMILY COLLEGE CARE PACKAGE AWARD

Award available for first-generation college student, graduated from a Baltimore City Public School who has a cumulative GPA of at least a 2.0. Must submit an essay (500-1,000 words) describing/honoring a family member who had a positive influence in your life and be accepted at a two or four- year college/university.Must have applied for the CollegeBound Last Dollar Grant. Award includes dorm room furnishings and supplies, suitcase, footlocker, bedding. Finalist must be available for an interview with the selection committee.

Award: Prize for use in freshman, sophomore, junior, or senior years. *Number:* 1.

Eligibility Requirements: Applicant must be enrolled or expecting to enroll at a two-year or four-year institution and resident of Maryland. Available to U.S. citizens.

Application Requirements: Application, essay. *Deadline:* March 19.

Contact: April Bell, Associate Program Director
CollegeBound Foundation
300 Water Street, Suite 300
Baltimore, MD 21202
Phone: 410-783-2905 Ext. 208
Fax: 410-727-5786
E-mail: abell@collegeboundfoundation.org

THE JANE AND CLARENCE SPILMAN SCHOLARSHIP

You must: have a cumulative high school GPA of at least 3.0; verifiable community service; be a resident of Baltimore City and graduate from a Baltimore City Public High School.

Award: Scholarship for use in freshman year; not renewable. *Number:* 1. *Amount:* $1000.

Eligibility Requirements: Applicant must be high school student; planning to enroll or expecting to enroll at a four-year institution or university and resident of Maryland. Applicant must have 3.0 GPA or higher. Available to U.S. citizens.

Application Requirements: Application. *Deadline:* March 19.

Contact: April Bell, Associate Program Director
CollegeBound Foundation
300 Water Street, Suite 300
Baltimore, MD 21202
Phone: 410-783-2905 Ext. 208
Fax: 410-727-5786
E-mail: abell@collegeboundfoundation.org

WALTER G. AMPREY SCHOLARSHIP

Award for Baltimore City public high school graduates. Please see Web site: http://www.collegeboundfoundation.org for complete information on appli-

CollegeBound Foundation (continued)

cation process. Minimum GPA of 3.0. Must demonstrate financial need. Must submit CollegeBound Competitive Scholarship/Last-Dollar Grant Application.

Award: Scholarship for use in freshman year; not renewable. *Number:* 1. *Amount:* $1000.

Eligibility Requirements: Applicant must be enrolled or expecting to enroll full-time at a two-year or four-year institution or university and resident of Maryland. Applicant must have 3.0 GPA or higher. Available to U.S. citizens.

Application Requirements: Application, financial need analysis, references, transcript, financial aid award letters, Student Aid Report (SAR). *Deadline:* March 19.

Contact: April Bell, Associate Program Director
CollegeBound Foundation
300 Water Street, Suite 300
Baltimore, MD 21202
Phone: 410-783-2905 Ext. 208
Fax: 410-727-5786
E-mail: abell@collegeboundfoundation.org

COLORADO COMMISSION ON HIGHER EDUCATION
http://www.state.co.us/cche

COLORADO LEVERAGING EDUCATIONAL ASSISTANCE PARTNERSHIP (CLEAP) AND SLEAP

Renewable awards for Colorado residents who are attending Colorado state-supported postsecondary institutions at the undergraduate level. Must document financial need. Contact colleges for complete information and deadlines.

Award: Grant for use in freshman, sophomore, junior, or senior years; not renewable. *Number:* 5000. *Amount:* $50–$900.

Eligibility Requirements: Applicant must be enrolled or expecting to enroll full or part-time at a two-year or four-year or technical institution or university; resident of Colorado and studying in Colorado. Available to U.S. citizens.

Application Requirements: Application, financial need analysis. *Deadline:* varies.

Contact: Financial Aid Office at college/institution
Colorado Commission on Higher Education
1380 Lawrence Street, Suite 1200
Denver, CO 80204-2059
Phone: 303-866-2723
E-mail: cche@state.co.us

COLORADO STUDENT GRANT

Assists Colorado residents attending eligible public, private, or vocational institutions within the state. Application deadlines vary by institution. Renewable award for undergraduates. Contact the financial aid office at the college/institution for more information and an application.

Award: Grant for use in freshman, sophomore, junior, or senior years; renewable. *Number:* varies. *Amount:* $1500–$3000.

Eligibility Requirements: Applicant must be enrolled or expecting to enroll full or part-time at a two-year or four-year or technical institution or university; resident of Colorado and studying in Colorado. Available to U.S. citizens.

Application Requirements: Application, financial need analysis. *Deadline:* varies.

Contact: Financial Aid Office at college/institution
Colorado Commission on Higher Education
1380 Lawrence Street, Suite 1200
Denver, CO 80204-2059
Phone: 303-866-2723
E-mail: cche@state.co.us

COLORADO UNDERGRADUATE MERIT SCHOLARSHIPS

Renewable awards for students attending Colorado state-supported institutions at the undergraduate level. Must demonstrate superior scholarship or talent. Contact college financial aid office for complete information and deadlines.

Award: Scholarship for use in freshman, sophomore, junior, or senior years; renewable. *Number:* 10,823. *Amount:* $1230.

Eligibility Requirements: Applicant must be enrolled or expecting to enroll full or part-time at a two-year or four-year or technical institution or university; resident of Colorado and studying in Colorado. Applicant must have 3.0 GPA or higher. Available to U.S. citizens.

Application Requirements: Application, test scores, transcript. *Deadline:* varies.

Contact: Financial Aid Office at college/institution
Colorado Commission on Higher Education
1380 Lawrence Street, Suite 1200
Denver, CO 80204-2059
Phone: 303-866-2723
E-mail: cche@state.co.us

GOVERNOR'S OPPORTUNITY SCHOLARSHIP

Scholarship available for the most needy first-time freshmen whose parents' adjusted gross income is less than $26,000. Must be U.S. citizen or permanent legal resident. Work-study is part of the program.

Award: Scholarship for use in freshman year; renewable. *Number:* 250. *Amount:* up to $10,700.

Eligibility Requirements: Applicant must be high school student; planning to enroll or expecting to enroll full-time at a two-year or four-year or technical institution or university; resident of Colorado and studying in Colorado. Available to U.S. citizens.

Application Requirements: Application, financial need analysis, test scores, transcript. *Deadline:* Continuous.

Contact: Governor's Opportunity Scholarship Program
Phone: 303-866-2723
Fax: 303-866-4266
E-mail: gos@cche.state.co.us

COLORADO MASONS BENEVOLENT FUND ASSOCIATION
http://www.coloradomasons.org

COLORADO MASONS BENEVOLENT FUND SCHOLARSHIPS

Applicants must be graduating seniors from a Colorado public high school accepted at a Colorado postsecondary institution. The maximum grant is $7000 renewable over four years. Obtain scholarship materials and specific requirements from high school counselor.

Award: Scholarship for use in freshman, sophomore, junior, or senior years; renewable. *Number:* 10–14. *Amount:* up to $7000.

Eligibility Requirements: Applicant must be high school student; planning to enroll or expecting to enroll full-time at a two-year or four-year or technical institution or university; resident of Colorado and studying in Colorado. Available to U.S. citizens.

Application Requirements: Application, essay, financial need analysis, interview, references, transcript. *Deadline:* March 7.

Contact: Ron Kadera, Scholarship Administrator
Colorado Masons Benevolent Fund Association
1130 Panorama Drive
Colorado Springs, CO 80904
Phone: 800-482-4441 Ext. 29
Fax: 800-440-3520
E-mail: scholarships@coloradomasons.org

COMMON KNOWLEDGE SCHOLARSHIP FOUNDATION
http://www.cksf.org

THE FLORIDA AUTISM COMMON KNOWLEDGE CHALLENGE

Quiz contest developed by faculty and staff at the UM-NSU Center for Autism and Related Disabilities (CARD) and the Clinics in Speech, Language, and Communication. The scholarship focus is what participants know about autism and associated speech, language, and communication disorders. For more information and online registration check Web site: www.cksf.org

Award: Prize for use in freshman, sophomore, junior, or senior years. *Number:* 2. *Amount:* $250.

Eligibility Requirements: Applicant must be enrolled or expecting to enroll at a technical institution and resident of Florida. Available to U.S. citizens.

Application Requirements: Applicant must enter a contest. *Deadline:* varies.

Contact: Daryl Hulce, President
Common Knowledge Scholarship Foundation
PO Box 290361
Davie, FL 33329-0361
Phone: 954-262-8553
Fax: 954-262-3940
E-mail: hulce@cksf.org

COMMUNITY BANKER ASSOCIATION OF ILLINOIS

COMMUNITY BANKER ASSOCIATION OF ILLINOIS ANNUAL SCHOLARSHIP PROGRAM

Essay competition open to Illinois high school seniors who are sponsored by a CBAI member bank. Student bank employees, plus immediate families of bank employees, board members, stockholders, CBAI employees, and judges are ineligible. For more details see Web site: http://www.cbai.com

Award: Scholarship for use in freshman year; not renewable. *Number:* up to 13. *Amount:* $1000–$4000.

Eligibility Requirements: Applicant must be high school student; planning to enroll or expecting to enroll full-time at a two-year or four-year or technical institution or university and resident of Illinois. Available to U.S. citizens.

Application Requirements: Applicant must enter a contest, essay. *Deadline:* February 13.

Contact:

COMMUNITY BANKER ASSOCIATION OF ILLINOIS CHILDREN OF COMMUNITY BANKING SCHOLARSHIP
• See page 496

COMMUNITY FOUNDATION FOR GREATER BUFFALO   http://www.cfgb.org

COMMUNITY FOUNDATION FOR GREATER BUFFALO SCHOLARSHIPS

Scholarships restricted to current residents of western New York (several only to Erie County), who have been accepted for admission to any nonprofit school in the U.S. for full-time study at the undergraduate level. Must maintain a "C" average. Must submit estimated family contribution as indicated on Student Aid Report, FAFSA form.

Award: Scholarship for use in freshman, sophomore, junior, or senior years; not renewable. *Number:* 600–900. *Amount:* $200–$4500.

Eligibility Requirements: Applicant must be enrolled or expecting to enroll full-time at a two-year or four-year institution or university and resident of New York. Available to U.S. and non-U.S. citizens.

Application Requirements: Application, essay, financial need analysis, references, self-addressed stamped envelope, transcript. *Deadline:* June 1.

Contact: Johnna Mauro, Scholarship Officer
Community Foundation for Greater Buffalo
712 Main Street
Buffalo, NY 14202
Phone: 716-852-2857
Fax: 716-852-2861
E-mail: johnnam@cfgb.org

COMMUNITY FOUNDATION FOR PALM BEACH AND MARTIN COUNTIES, INC.   http://www.yourcommunityfoundation.org

ARTHUR C. TILLEY MEMORIAL SCHOLARSHIP

Scholarship awarded to Palm Beach or Martin County graduating high school senior, public or private schooled, plans to pursue a 2-4 year degree in a traditional or non-traditional technical institution. Applicant must maintain C average or better. Deadline is February 1. Applications are available online http://www.yourcommunityfoundation.org

Award: Scholarship for use in freshman year; not renewable. *Number:* varies. *Amount:* $750–$2500.

Eligibility Requirements: Applicant must be high school student; planning to enroll or expecting to enroll at a two-year or four-year or technical institution or university and resident of Florida. Available to U.S. citizens.

Application Requirements: Application, financial need analysis. *Deadline:* February 1.

Contact: Carolyn Jenco, Grants Manager/Scholarship Coordinator
Community Foundation for Palm Beach and Martin Counties, Inc.
700 South Dixie Highway, Suite 200
West Palm Beach, FL 33401
Phone: 561-659-6800
Fax: 561-832-6542
E-mail: cjenco@cfpbmc.org

CLAIRE B. SCHULTZ MEMORIAL SCHOLARSHIP

Graduating seniors from a Palm Beach County High School. Based on financial need. Special preference to handicapped or minority students.

Award: Scholarship for use in freshman, sophomore, junior, or senior years; not renewable. *Number:* 1–3. *Amount:* $750–$2500.

Eligibility Requirements: Applicant must be high school student; planning to enroll or expecting to enroll full-time at a two-year or four-year or technical institution or university and resident of Florida. Available to U.S. citizens.

Application Requirements: Application, financial need analysis. *Deadline:* February 1.

Contact: Carolyn Jenco, Grants Manager/Scholarship Coordinator
Community Foundation for Palm Beach and Martin Counties, Inc.
700 South Dixie Highway, Suite 200
West Palm Beach, FL 33401
Phone: 561-659-6800
Fax: 561-832-6542
E-mail: cjenco@cfpbmc.org

COLONIAL BANK SCHOLARSHIP
• See page 610

COMMUNITY FOUNDATION FOR PALM BEACH AND MARTIN COUNTIES GENERAL SCHOLARSHIP

Applicant must be resident of Palm Beach or Martin County and maintain a 2.0 GPA. Deadline is February 1. Applications are available online: http://www.yourcommunityfoundation.org

Award: Scholarship for use in freshman year; not renewable. *Number:* varies. *Amount:* $750–$2500.

Eligibility Requirements: Applicant must be enrolled or expecting to enroll at a four-year institution or university and resident of Florida. Available to U.S. citizens.

Application Requirements: Application, financial need analysis. *Deadline:* February 1.

Contact: Carolyn Jenco, Grants Manager/Scholarship Coordinator
Community Foundation for Palm Beach and Martin Counties, Inc.
700 South Dixie Highway, Suite 200
West Palm Beach, FL 33401
Phone: 561-659-6800
Fax: 561-832-6542
E-mail: cjenco@cfpbmc.org

COURTLANDT AND GINA MILER SCHOLARSHIP

Scholarship awarded to high school seniors demonstrating financial need; preference given to minority applicants. Applications available online http://www.yourcommunityfoundation.org. Deadline is February 1.

Award: Scholarship for use in freshman year; not renewable. *Number:* 1–3. *Amount:* $750–$2500.

Eligibility Requirements: Applicant must be high school student; planning to enroll or expecting to enroll full-time at an institution or university and resident of Florida. Available to U.S. citizens.

Application Requirements: Application, financial need analysis. *Deadline:* February 1.

Community Foundation for Palm Beach and Martin Counties, Inc.
(continued)

Contact: Carolyn Jenco, Grants Manager/Scholarship Coordinator
Community Foundation for Palm Beach and Martin Counties, Inc.
700 South Dixie Highway, Suite 200
West Palm Beach, FL 33401
Phone: 561-659-6800
Fax: 561-832-6542
E-mail: cjenco@cfpbmc.org

DAVE YANIS SCHOLARSHIP FUND

Scholarship awarded to graduating high school seniors from Palm Beach, Martin, or Broward counties. Preference is given to students of Jewish faith, Russian immigrants, or direct descendents of Russian immigrants. Deadline is February 1. Applications are available online http://www. yourcommunityfoundation.org

Award: Scholarship for use in freshman year; not renewable. *Number:* varies. *Amount:* $750–$2500.

Eligibility Requirements: Applicant must be high school student; planning to enroll or expecting to enroll at a four-year institution or university and resident of Florida. Available to U.S. citizens.

Application Requirements: Application. *Deadline:* February 1.

Contact: Carolyn Jenco, Grants Manager/Scholarship Coordinator
Community Foundation for Palm Beach and Martin Counties, Inc.
700 South Dixie Highway, Suite 200
West Palm Beach, FL 33401
Phone: 561-659-6800
Fax: 561-832-6542
E-mail: cjenco@cfpbmc.org

DENISE LYNN PADGETT SCHOLARSHIP FUND

Female graduating senior from Palm Beach or Martin Counties. Minimum of two years participation on high school/women's softball team; demonstrates financial aid.

Award: Scholarship for use in freshman year; not renewable. *Number:* 1. *Amount:* $750–$2500.

Eligibility Requirements: Applicant must be high school student; planning to enroll or expecting to enroll full-time at a two-year or four-year or technical institution or university; female and resident of Florida. Available to U.S. citizens.

Application Requirements: Application, financial need analysis. *Deadline:* February 1.

Contact: Carolyn Jenco, Grants Manager/Scholarship Coordinator
Community Foundation for Palm Beach and Martin Counties, Inc.
700 South Dixie Highway, Suite 200
West Palm Beach, FL 33401
Phone: 561-659-6800
Fax: 561-832-6542
E-mail: cjenco@cfpbmc.org

ERNEST FRANK SCHOLARSHIP FUND

Scholarship awarded to Palm Beach or Martin County resident graduating from a public or private high school in those counties. Student must demonstrate academic excellence, extracurricular activities, community service, and financial need. Deadline is February 1. Applications are available online http://www.yourcommunityfoundation.org

Award: Scholarship for use in freshman year; not renewable. *Number:* varies. *Amount:* $750–$2500.

Eligibility Requirements: Applicant must be high school student; planning to enroll or expecting to enroll full-time at a four-year institution or university and resident of Florida. Available to U.S. citizens.

Application Requirements: Application, financial need analysis. *Deadline:* February 1.

Contact: Carolyn Jenco, Grants Manager/Scholarship Coordinator
Community Foundation for Palm Beach and Martin Counties, Inc.
700 South Dixie Highway, Suite 200
West Palm Beach, FL 33401
Phone: 561-659-6800
Fax: 561-832-6542
E-mail: cjenco@cfpbmc.org

GUBELMANN FAMILY FOUNDATION SCHOLARSHIP FUND

For Palm Beach County and Martin County, Florida graduating high school seniors demonstrating financial need. Preference given to minority applicants. May be from public or private institutions.

Award: Scholarship for use in freshman year; not renewable. *Amount:* $750–$2500.

Eligibility Requirements: Applicant must be high school student; planning to enroll or expecting to enroll full-time at a two-year or four-year or technical institution or university and resident of Florida. Available to U.S. citizens.

Application Requirements: Application, financial need analysis. *Deadline:* February 1.

Contact: Carolyn Jenco, Grants Manager/Scholarship Coordinator
Community Foundation for Palm Beach and Martin Counties, Inc.
700 South Dixie Highway, Suite 200
West Palm Beach, FL 33401
Phone: 561-659-6800
Fax: 561-832-6542
E-mail: cjenco@cfpbmc.org

H. DAVID FAUST MEMORIAL SCHOLARSHIP

Scholarship awarded to high school seniors from Palm Beach and Martin counties demonstrating academic excellence. Applications available online http://www.yourcommunityfoundation.org. Deadline is February 1.

Award: Scholarship for use in freshman year; not renewable. *Number:* 1–3. *Amount:* $750–$2500.

Eligibility Requirements: Applicant must be high school student; planning to enroll or expecting to enroll full-time at an institution or university and resident of Florida. Available to U.S. citizens.

Application Requirements: Application, financial need analysis. *Deadline:* February 1.

Contact: Carolyn Jenco, Grants Manager/Scholarship Coordinator
Community Foundation for Palm Beach and Martin Counties, Inc.
700 South Dixie Highway, Suite 200
West Palm Beach, FL 33401
Phone: 561-659-6800
Fax: 561-832-6542
E-mail: cjenco@cfpbmc.org

HARRY AND BERTHA BRONSTEIN MEMORIAL SCHOLARSHIP

For graduating high school seniors who are residents of Palm Beach and Martin Counties demonstrating financial need with special preference given to students who are either members of a minority group or handicapped. These may be two or four year scholarships but are restricted to undergraduate support.

Award: Scholarship for use in freshman, sophomore, junior, or senior years; renewable. *Amount:* $750–$2500.

Eligibility Requirements: Applicant must be high school student; planning to enroll or expecting to enroll full-time at a two-year or four-year institution or university and resident of Florida. Available to U.S. citizens.

Application Requirements: Application, financial need analysis. *Deadline:* February 1.

Contact: Carolyn Jenco, Grants Manager/Scholarship Coordinator
Community Foundation for Palm Beach and Martin Counties, Inc.
700 South Dixie Highway, Suite 200
West Palm Beach, FL 33401
Phone: 561-659-6800
Fax: 561-832-6542
E-mail: cjenco@cfpbmc.org

JULIAN AND EUNICE COHEN SCHOLARSHIP

Scholarship awarded to Palm Beach or Martin County graduating high school student. Applicant must be involved in extracurricular activities as well as achieve academic excellence. Deadline is February 1. Applications are available online http://www.yourcommunityfoundation.org

Award: Scholarship for use in freshman year; not renewable. *Number:* varies. *Amount:* $750–$2500.

Eligibility Requirements: Applicant must be high school student; planning to enroll or expecting to enroll at a four-year institution or university and resident of Florida. Available to U.S. citizens.

Application Requirements: Application, financial need analysis. *Deadline:* February 1.

Contact: Carolyn Jenco, Grants Manager/Scholarship Coordinator
Community Foundation for Palm Beach and Martin Counties, Inc.
700 South Dixie Highway, Suite 200
West Palm Beach, FL 33401
Phone: 561-659-6800
Fax: 561-832-6542
E-mail: cjenco@cfpbmc.org

LOBLOLLY SCHOLARSHIP FUND

Available to any student who demonstrates financial need and is in the top 25% of the graduating class in Palm Beach and Martin counties, Florida. Students in the second quartile of the class are also eligible if they possess an outstanding extracurricular record or if they were required to work during high school to help support their families. Participation in school athletics and meaningful community service is a plus.

Award: Scholarship for use in freshman year; not renewable. *Amount:* $750–$2500.

Eligibility Requirements: Applicant must be high school student; planning to enroll or expecting to enroll full-time at a two-year or four-year or technical institution or university and resident of Florida. Applicant must have 3.5 GPA or higher. Available to U.S. citizens.

Application Requirements: Application, financial need analysis, transcript. *Deadline:* February 1.

Contact: Carolyn Jenco, Grants Manager/Scholarship Coordinator
Community Foundation for Palm Beach and Martin Counties, Inc.
700 South Dixie Highway, Suite 200
West Palm Beach, FL 33401
Phone: 561-659-6800
Fax: 561-832-6542
E-mail: cjenco@cfpbmc.org

MATTHEW "BUMP" MITCHELL /SUN-SENTINEL SCHOLARSHIP

Graduating student from South Palm Beach County, Florida who excels in scholastics, demonstrates community service and has financial need. Preference given to minority students.

Award: Scholarship for use in freshman year; not renewable. *Number:* 1. *Amount:* $750–$2500.

Eligibility Requirements: Applicant must be high school student; planning to enroll or expecting to enroll full-time at a two-year or four-year or technical institution or university and resident of Florida. Available to U.S. citizens.

Application Requirements: Application, financial need analysis. *Deadline:* February 1.

Contact: Carolyn Jenco, Grants Manager/Scholarship Coordinator
Community Foundation for Palm Beach and Martin Counties, Inc.
700 South Dixie Highway, Suite 200
West Palm Beach, FL 33401
Phone: 561-659-6800
Fax: 561-832-6542
E-mail: cjenco@cfpbmc.org

MAURA AND WILLIAM BENJAMIN SCHOLARSHIP

Scholarship awarded to applicant with an excellent scholastic record, as well as representing qualities of leadership. Applicant should have experience in community service. Deadline is February 1. Restricted to residents of Palm Beach or Martin County. Applications are available online: http://www.yourcommunityfoundation.org

Award: Scholarship for use in freshman year; not renewable. *Number:* varies. *Amount:* $750–$2500.

Eligibility Requirements: Applicant must be enrolled or expecting to enroll at a four-year institution or university and resident of Florida. Available to U.S. citizens.

Application Requirements: Application. *Deadline:* February 1.

Contact: Carolyn Jenco, Grants Manager/Scholarship Coordinator
Community Foundation for Palm Beach and Martin Counties, Inc.
700 South Dixie Highway, Suite 200
West Palm Beach, FL 33401
Phone: 561-659-6800
Fax: 561-832-6542
E-mail: cjenco@cfpbmc.org

RALPH O. WOOD SCHOLARSHIP

Scholarship awarded to Palm Beach or Martin County graduating senior in a public or private high school. Must be involved in extracurricular activities. Deadline is February 1. Applications are available online: http://www.yourcommunityfoundation.org

Award: Scholarship for use in freshman year; not renewable. *Number:* varies. *Amount:* $750–$2500.

Eligibility Requirements: Applicant must be high school student; planning to enroll or expecting to enroll at a four-year institution and resident of Florida. Applicant must have 3.0 GPA or higher. Available to U.S. citizens.

Application Requirements: Application, financial need analysis. *Deadline:* February 1.

Contact: Carolyn Jenco, Grants Manager/Scholarship Coordinator
Community Foundation for Palm Beach and Martin Counties, Inc.
700 South Dixie Highway, Suite 200
West Palm Beach, FL 33401
Phone: 561-659-6800
Fax: 561-832-6542
E-mail: cjenco@cfpbmc.org

ROBERTA AND STEPHEN R. WEINER SCHOLARSHIP

Scholarship awarded to Palm Beach or Martin County graduating high school senior who wishes to continue their education with traditional or non-traditional technical training. Deadline is February 1. Applications are available online: http://www.yourcommunityfoundation.org

Award: Scholarship for use in freshman year; not renewable. *Number:* varies. *Amount:* $750–$2500.

Eligibility Requirements: Applicant must be high school student; planning to enroll or expecting to enroll at a two-year or four-year or technical institution and resident of Florida. Available to U.S. citizens.

Application Requirements: Application. *Deadline:* February 1.

Community Foundation for Palm Beach and Martin Counties, Inc. (continued)

Contact: Carolyn Jenco, Grants Manager/Scholarship Coordinator
Community Foundation for Palm Beach and Martin Counties, Inc.
700 South Dixie Highway, Suite 200
West Palm Beach, FL 33401
Phone: 561-659-6800
Fax: 561-832-6542
E-mail: cjenco@cfpbmc.org

TERRY DARBY MEMORIAL SCHOLARSHIP

Scholarship awarded to Palm Beach or Martin County graduating high school senior that has been actively involved with soccer throughout his or her high school career. Deadline is February 1. Applications available online http://www.yourcommunityfoundation.org

Award: Scholarship for use in freshman year; not renewable. *Number:* varies. *Amount:* $750–$2500.

Eligibility Requirements: Applicant must be high school student; planning to enroll or expecting to enroll at a four-year institution or university; resident of Florida and must have an interest in athletics/sports. Available to U.S. citizens.

Application Requirements: Application. *Deadline:* February 1.

Contact: Carolyn Jenco, Grants Manager/Scholarship Coordinator
Community Foundation for Palm Beach and Martin Counties, Inc.
700 South Dixie Highway, Suite 200
West Palm Beach, FL 33401
Phone: 561-659-6800
Fax: 561-832-6542
E-mail: cjenco@cfpbmc.org

WALTER AND ADI BLUM SCHOLARSHIP

Scholarship rewarded to high school senior attending public or private school in Palm Beach or Martin County. Must attend approved school in United States. Preference given to applicants that have immigrated to United States. Deadline is February 1. Applications are available online http://www.yourcommunityfoundation.org

Award: Scholarship for use in freshman year; not renewable. *Number:* varies. *Amount:* $750–$2500.

Eligibility Requirements: Applicant must be high school student; planning to enroll or expecting to enroll full-time at a two-year or four-year or technical institution or university and resident of Florida. Applicant must have 2.5 GPA or higher. Available to U.S. citizens.

Application Requirements: Application, financial need analysis. *Deadline:* February 1.

Contact: Carolyn Jenco, Grants Manager/Scholarship Coordinator
Community Foundation for Palm Beach and Martin Counties, Inc.
700 South Dixie Highway, Suite 200
West Palm Beach, FL 33401
Phone: 561-659-6800
Fax: 561-832-6542
E-mail: cjenco@cfpbmc.org

COMMUNITY FOUNDATION OF CAPE COD
http://www.capecodfoundation.org

ANNIE S. CROWELL SCHOLARSHIP FUND

Award to graduating high school senior or continuing college student who is a relative of an alumnus from the Hyannis Normal School, or the Hyannis State Teacher's College. For more details see Web site: http://www.capecodfoundation.org.

Award: Scholarship for use in freshman, sophomore, junior, senior, or graduate years; not renewable. *Number:* 1–4. *Amount:* up to $1000.

Eligibility Requirements: Applicant must be enrolled or expecting to enroll full-time at a two-year or four-year or technical institution or university and resident of Massachusetts. Available to U.S. citizens.

Application Requirements: Application, essay, resume, references, test scores, transcript. *Deadline:* April 1.

Contact: Kristin O'Malley, Program Officer/Scholarship Associate
Community Foundation of Cape Cod
259 Willow Street
Yarmouthport, MA 02675
Phone: 508-790-3040
Fax: 508-790-4069
E-mail: komalley@capecodfoundation.org

FRANK X. AND MARY E. WENY SCHOLARSHIP FUND
• See page 556

HYANNIS NORMAL SCHOOL ALUMNI SCHOLARSHIP

Hyannis Normal School Alumni Scholarship provides awards to students who have graduated from high school in Barnstable County. For more details see Web site: http://www.capecodfoundation.org.

Award: Scholarship for use in freshman, sophomore, junior, or senior years; not renewable. *Number:* 1–7. *Amount:* up to $2000.

Eligibility Requirements: Applicant must be enrolled or expecting to enroll full-time at a two-year or four-year or technical institution or university and resident of Massachusetts. Available to U.S. citizens.

Application Requirements: Application, essay, resume, references, test scores, transcript. *Deadline:* April 1.

Contact: Pauline Greenberg, Scholarship Associate
Community Foundation of Cape Cod
259 Willow Street
Yarmouthport, MA 02675
Phone: 508-790-3040
Fax: 508-790-4069
E-mail: pgreenberg@capecodfoundation.org

COMMUNITY FOUNDATION OF WESTERN MASSACHUSETTS
http://www.communityfoundation.org

AFRICAN-AMERICAN ACHIEVEMENT SCHOLARSHIP
• See page 610

CALEB L. BUTLER SCHOLARSHIP

For former or current residents of Hillcrest Educational Centers who are graduating seniors pursuing postsecondary education, or for graduating high school seniors from Franklin, Berkshire, Hampden, or Hampshire counties who are in the custody of Department of Social Services.

Award: Scholarship for use in freshman year; renewable. *Number:* up to 2. *Amount:* up to $1000.

Eligibility Requirements: Applicant must be enrolled or expecting to enroll full or part-time at a two-year or four-year institution and resident of Massachusetts. Available to U.S. citizens.

Application Requirements: Application, financial need analysis, transcript, copy of family's tax returns, Student Aid Report (SAR). *Deadline:* March 31.

Contact: Dorothy Theriaque, Education Associate
Community Foundation of Western Massachusetts
1500 Main Street, PO Box 15769
Springfield, MA 01115
Phone: 413-732-2858
Fax: 413-733-8565
E-mail: dtheriaque@communityfoundation.org

DEERFIELD PLASTICS/BARKER FAMILY SCHOLARSHIP
• See page 529

FIRST NATIONAL BANK OF AMHERST CENTENNIAL EDUCATIONAL SCHOLARSHIP

For students from Northampton High School, Hopkins Academy, Amherst-Pelham Regional High School, UMass, Amherst College, and Hampshire College. Visit http://www.communityfoundation.org for more information.

Award: Scholarship for use in freshman, or graduate years; renewable. *Number:* up to 4. *Amount:* up to $350.

Eligibility Requirements: Applicant must be enrolled or expecting to enroll full or part-time at a two-year or four-year or technical institution or university; resident of Massachusetts and studying in Massachusetts. Available to U.S. citizens.

Application Requirements: Application, financial need analysis, transcript, parent and student federal income tax returns. *Deadline:* March 31.

Contact: Dorothy Theriaque, Education Associate
Community Foundation of Western Massachusetts
1500 Main Street, PO Box 15769
Springfield, MA 01115
Phone: 413-732-2858
Fax: 413-733-8565
E-mail: dtheriaque@communityfoundation.org

FRANK W. JENDRYSIK, JR. MEMORIAL SCHOLARSHIP

One award for undergraduate study for residents of Chicopee, Holyoke, or Springfield.

Award: Scholarship for use in freshman, sophomore, junior, or senior years; renewable. *Number:* 1. *Amount:* up to $800.

Eligibility Requirements: Applicant must be enrolled or expecting to enroll full or part-time at a two-year or four-year institution or university and resident of Massachusetts. Available to U.S. citizens.

Application Requirements: Application, financial need analysis, transcript, parent and student federal income tax returns, GPA. *Deadline:* March 31.

Contact: Dorothy Theriaque, Education Associate
Community Foundation of Western Massachusetts
1500 Main Street, PO Box 15769
Springfield, MA 01115
Phone: 413-732-2858
Fax: 413-733-8565
E-mail: dtheriaque@communityfoundation.org

FRED K. LANE SCHOLARSHIP

Available for graduating high school seniors who are past or current members (individual or family) or employees of the Orchards Golf Club, South Hadley, MA.

Award: Scholarship for use in freshman year; not renewable. *Number:* 1. *Amount:* up to $1000.

Eligibility Requirements: Applicant must be high school student; planning to enroll or expecting to enroll full-time at an institution or university and resident of Massachusetts. Available to U.S. citizens.

Application Requirements: Application, financial need analysis, transcript, parent's and student's federal income tax returns, Student Aid Report (SAR). *Deadline:* March 31.

Contact: Dorothy Theriaque, Education Associate
Community Foundation of Western Massachusetts
1500 Main Street, PO Box 15769
Springfield, MA 01115
Phone: 413-732-2858
Fax: 413-733-8565
E-mail: dtheriaque@communityfoundation.org

HERIBERTO FLORES SCHOLARSHIP
• *See page 611*

JAMES L. SHRIVER SCHOLARSHIP

For Western Massachusetts residents pursuing technical careers through college, trade, or technical school. Visit http://www.communityfoundation.org for more information.

Award: Scholarship for use in freshman, sophomore, junior, or senior years; renewable. *Number:* 1. *Amount:* up to $800.

Eligibility Requirements: Applicant must be enrolled or expecting to enroll full or part-time at a two-year or four-year or technical institution or university and resident of Massachusetts. Available to U.S. citizens.

Application Requirements: Application, financial need analysis, transcript, parent and student federal income tax returns. *Deadline:* March 31.

Contact: Dorothy Theriaque, Education Associate
Community Foundation of Western Massachusetts
1500 Main Street, PO Box 15769
Springfield, MA 01115
Phone: 413-732-2858
Fax: 413-733-8565
E-mail: dtheriaque@communityfoundation.org

JAMES Z. NAURISON SCHOLARSHIP

For undergraduate and graduate students who are residents of Hampden, Hampshire, Franklin, and Berkshire counties in Massachusetts and Enfield and Suffield counties in Connecticut. May be awarded up to four years based upon discretion of the scholarship committee. Applicants need to reapply every year. Visit http://www.communityfoundation.org.

Award: Scholarship for use in freshman, sophomore, junior, senior, or graduate years; renewable. *Amount:* up to $1000.

Eligibility Requirements: Applicant must be enrolled or expecting to enroll full or part-time at a two-year or four-year institution or university and resident of Connecticut or Massachusetts. Available to U.S. citizens.

Application Requirements: Application, financial need analysis, transcript, personal statement. *Deadline:* March 31.

Contact: Dawn Lapierre, Education Assistant
Community Foundation of Western Massachusetts
1500 Main Street, PO Box 15769
Springfield, MA 01115
Phone: 413-732-2858
Fax: 413-733-8565
E-mail: scholar@communityfoundation.org

KIMBER RICHTER FAMILY SCHOLARSHIP
• *See page 649*

LATINO SCHOLARSHIP
• *See page 611*

MASSMUTUAL SCHOLARS PROGRAM

For graduating high school seniors who reside in Hampden County, MA or Hartford County, CT who maintain a B average or better for four consecutive marking periods.

Award: Scholarship for use in freshman, sophomore, junior, or senior years; renewable. *Number:* 50. *Amount:* $7000.

Eligibility Requirements: Applicant must be enrolled or expecting to enroll full or part-time at a two-year or four-year institution or university and resident of Connecticut or Massachusetts. Applicant must have 3.0 GPA or higher. Available to U.S. citizens.

Application Requirements: Application, essay, financial need analysis, transcript, parent and student federal income tax returns, GPA. *Deadline:* March 31.

Contact: Dorothy Theriaque, Education Associate
Community Foundation of Western Massachusetts
1500 Main Street, PO Box 15769
Springfield, MA 01115
Phone: 413-732-2858
Fax: 413-733-8565
E-mail: dtheriaque@communityfoundation.org

NATIONAL ASSOCIATION OF INSURANCE AND FINANCIAL ADVISORS SCHOLARSHIP

For graduating high school seniors, residing in Berkshire, Hampden, Hampshire, and Franklin counties, who have lost a parent through death or have a parent receiving social security disability benefits.

Award: Scholarship for use in freshman year; renewable. *Number:* 6. *Amount:* up to $2500.

Eligibility Requirements: Applicant must be high school student; planning to enroll or expecting to enroll full or part-time at a two-year or four-year or technical institution or university and resident of Massachusetts. Available to U.S. citizens.

Application Requirements: Application, financial need analysis, transcript, student's federal income tax return. *Deadline:* March 31.

Community Foundation of Western Massachusetts (continued)

Contact: Dorothy Theriaque, Education Associate
Community Foundation of Western Massachusetts
1500 Main Street, PO Box 15769
Springfield, MA 01115
Phone: 413-732-2858
Fax: 413-733-8565
E-mail: dtheriaque@communityfoundation.org

PERMELIA A. BUTTERFIELD SCHOLARSHIP

Support and education of orphan children (students with one or no living parents or those deprived of parental care) who are residents of Athol, Erving, New Salem, Wendell, Orange, Shutesbury, and Franklin County, or for other students from these areas. Visit http://www.communityfoundation.org.

Award: Scholarship for use in freshman, sophomore, junior, senior, or graduate years; renewable. *Number:* up to 2. *Amount:* up to $1700.

Eligibility Requirements: Applicant must be enrolled or expecting to enroll full or part-time at a two-year or four-year institution or university and resident of Massachusetts. Available to U.S. citizens.

Application Requirements: Application, financial need analysis, transcript, parent and student federal income tax returns. *Deadline:* March 31.

Contact: Dorothy Theriaque, Education Associate
Community Foundation of Western Massachusetts
1500 Main Street, PO Box 15769
Springfield, MA 01115
Phone: 413-732-2858
Fax: 413-733-8565
E-mail: dtheriaque@communityfoundation.org

PUTNAM SCHOLARSHIP FUND
• See page 611

STANLEY CIEJEK SR. SCHOLARSHIP

Scholarships given to residents of Hampden, Hampshire, and Franklin counties who will be attending Massachusetts institutions of higher education. For more information or application visit http://www.communityfoundation. org.

Award: Scholarship for use in freshman, sophomore, junior, or senior years; renewable. *Number:* up to 8. *Amount:* $1000.

Eligibility Requirements: Applicant must be enrolled or expecting to enroll full or part-time at a two-year or four-year or technical institution or university; resident of Massachusetts and studying in Massachusetts. Available to U.S. citizens.

Application Requirements: Application, financial need analysis, transcript, parent and student federal income tax returns. *Deadline:* March 31.

Contact: Dorothy Theriaque, Education Associate
Community Foundation of Western Massachusetts
1500 Main Street, PO Box 15769
Springfield, MA 01115
Phone: 413-732-2858
Fax: 413-733-8565
E-mail: dtheriaque@communityfoundation.org

UNITED WAY/YWCA SCHOLARSHIP FUND FOR WOMEN

For women with financial need who are residents of Holyoke, South Hadley, or Granby. Applicants must be age 18 or older and currently enrolled in college or have plans to enter college. The award is paid over a two-year period and comes from a fund established from proceeds of the dissolution of the former Holyoke YWCA.

Award: Scholarship for use in freshman, sophomore, junior, or senior years; renewable. *Number:* 1. *Amount:* up to $2500.

Eligibility Requirements: Applicant must be age 18; enrolled or expecting to enroll full or part-time at a two-year or four-year institution or university; female and resident of Massachusetts. Available to U.S. citizens.

Application Requirements: Application, financial need analysis, transcript, parent and student federal income tax returns, GPA. *Deadline:* March 31.

Contact: Dorothy Theriaque, Education Associate
Community Foundation of Western Massachusetts
1500 Main Street, PO Box 15769
Springfield, MA 01115
Phone: 413-732-2858
Fax: 413-733-8565
E-mail: dtheriaque@communityfoundation.org

CONNECTICUT ARMY NATIONAL GUARD   http://www.ct.ngb.army.mil

CONNECTICUT ARMY NATIONAL GUARD 100% TUITION WAIVER
• See page 576

CONNECTICUT ASSOCIATION OF LATIN AMERICANS IN HIGHER EDUCATION (CALAHE)   http://www.calahe.org

CONNECTICUT ASSOCIATION OF LATIN AMERICANS IN HIGHER EDUCATION SCHOLARSHIPS
• See page 612

CONNECTICUT DEPARTMENT OF HIGHER EDUCATION   http://www.ctdhe.org

CAPITOL SCHOLARSHIP PROGRAM

Award for Connecticut residents attending eligible institutions in Connecticut or in a state with reciprocity with Connecticut (Delaware, Maine, Massachusetts, New Hampshire, Pennsylvania, Rhode Island, Vermont, or Washington, D.C). Must be U.S. citizen or permanent resident alien who is a high school senior or graduate. Must rank in top 20% of class or score at least 1200 on SAT. Must show financial need.

Award: Scholarship for use in freshman, sophomore, junior, or senior years; renewable. *Number:* varies. *Amount:* $500–$3000.

Eligibility Requirements: Applicant must be enrolled or expecting to enroll at a two-year institution; resident of Connecticut and studying in Connecticut, Delaware, District of Columbia, Maine, Massachusetts, New Hampshire, Pennsylvania, Rhode Island, or Vermont. Applicant must have 3.5 GPA or higher. Available to U.S. citizens.

Application Requirements: Application, financial need analysis, test scores. *Deadline:* February 15.

Contact: John Siegrist, Financial Aid Office
Connecticut Department of Higher Education
61 Woodland Street
Hartford, CT 06105-2326
Phone: 860-947-1855
Fax: 860-947-1311

CONNECTICUT INDEPENDENT COLLEGE STUDENT GRANTS

Award for Connecticut residents attending an independent college or university within the state on at least a half-time basis. Renewable awards based on financial need. Application deadline varies by institution. Apply at college financial aid office.

Award: Grant for use in freshman, sophomore, junior, or senior years; renewable. *Number:* varies. *Amount:* $7700–$8500.

Eligibility Requirements: Applicant must be enrolled or expecting to enroll full or part-time at a two-year or four-year institution or university; resident of Connecticut and studying in Connecticut. Available to U.S. citizens.

Application Requirements: Application, financial need analysis, transcript. *Deadline:* varies.

Contact: John Siegrist, Financial Aid Office
Connecticut Department of Higher Education
61 Woodland Street
Hartford, CT 06105-2326
Phone: 860-947-1855
Fax: 860-947-1311

CONNECTICUT FOREST AND PARK ASSOCIATION   http://www.ctwoodlands.org

JAMES L. AND GENEVIEVE H. GOODWIN MEMORIAL SCHOLARSHIP

To support Connecticut residents enrolled in a curriculum of silviculture or forest resource management.

Award: Scholarship for use in freshman, sophomore, junior, senior, or graduate years; not renewable. *Number:* up to 10. *Amount:* $1000–$5000.

Eligibility Requirements: Applicant must be enrolled or expecting to enroll full-time at a two-year or four-year institution or university and resident of Connecticut. Available to U.S. citizens.

Application Requirements: Application, essay, financial need analysis, transcript. *Deadline:* April 1.

Contact: Adam R. Moore, Executive Director
Connecticut Forest and Park Association
16 Meriden Road
Rockfall, CT 06481-2961
Phone: 860-346-2372
Fax: 860-347-7463
E-mail: info@ctwoodlands.org

CONNECTICUT STUDENT LOAN FOUNDATION http://www.cslf.com

VINCENT J. MAIOCCO SCHOLARSHIP

One-time award of $1000 to $3000, given to full-time students who have received a Federal Stafford Loan guaranteed by Connecticut Student Loan Foundation. Must be a U.S. citizen and a resident of Connecticut. Award will be paid directly to the recipient's Stafford Loan lender and will be applied to the loan balance.

Award: Scholarship for use in sophomore, junior, or senior years; not renewable. *Number:* 1–4. *Amount:* $1000–$3000.

Eligibility Requirements: Applicant must be enrolled or expecting to enroll full-time at a four-year institution or university and resident of Connecticut. Available to U.S. citizens.

Application Requirements: Application, essay, transcript, financial aid award letter. *Deadline:* Continuous.

Contact: Melissa Trombley, Executive Manager
Connecticut Student Loan Foundation
525 Brook Street, PO Box 1009
Rocky Hill, CT 06067
Phone: 800-237-9721 Ext. 204
E-mail: mtrombl@mail.cslf.org

CONSTANTINOPLE ARMENIAN RELIEF SOCIETY

CONSTANTINOPLE ARMENIAN RELIEF SOCIETY SCHOLARSHIP
• See page 612

CORE PHILLY http://www.corephilly.org/

CORE PHILLY SCHOLARSHIP PROGRAM

Scholarships of up to $3,000 to high school seniors to help pay first-year college expenses. Applicant should be a resident of the City of Philadelphia and a graduate of a school district of Philadelphia public, charter, archdiocese, or private high school planning to pursue an associate or bachelor's degree at a participating college or university.

Award: Scholarship for use in freshman year; not renewable. *Amount:* up to $3000.

Eligibility Requirements: Applicant must be high school student; planning to enroll or expecting to enroll at an institution or university and resident of Pennsylvania. Available to U.S. citizens.

Application Requirements: Application, FAFSA, proof of residency for private or parochial school students. *Deadline:* June 1.

Contact: Thomas Butler, Executive Director
CORE Philly
1601 Market Street, Suite 2500
Philadelphia, PA 19103-2301
Phone: 215-246-3513
E-mail: scholarship@corephilly.org

COUNTY PROSECUTORS ASSOCIATION OF NEW JERSEY FOUNDATION

JOHN S. STAMLER MEMORIAL SCHOLARSHIP
• See page 540

COURAGE CENTER, VOCATIONAL SERVICES DEPARTMENT http://www.courage.org

SCHOLARSHIP FOR PEOPLE WITH DISABILITIES
• See page 557

DALLAS MORNING NEWS http://www.dallasnews.com

DALLAS MORNING NEWS ANNUAL TEENAGE CITIZENSHIP TRIBUTE
• See page 540

DAVIS-ROBERTS SCHOLARSHIP FUND, INC.

DAVIS-ROBERTS SCHOLARSHIPS
• See page 497

DAYTON FOUNDATION http://www.daytonfoundation.org

BRIGHTWELL FAMILY MEMORIAL SCHOLARSHIP FUND

Scholarship awarded to a high-school senior who is a child of current or retired full-time Dayton firefighter.

Award: Scholarship for use in freshman year; not renewable. *Amount:* up to $1000.

Eligibility Requirements: Applicant must be high school student; planning to enroll or expecting to enroll full-time at an institution or university and resident of Ohio. Available to U.S. citizens.

Application Requirements: Application, financial need analysis, transcript. *Deadline:* varies.

Contact: Diane Timmons, Director Grants and Programs
Dayton Foundation
2300 Kettering Tower
Dayton, OH 45423
Phone: 937-225-9966
E-mail: dtimmons@daytonfoundation.org

DAYTON SUPERIOR CORPORATION SCHOLARSHIP FUND

Scholarship to assist the children of full-time, regular employees of Dayton Superior Corporation, its affiliates and subsidiaries, to further their studies at an accredited institution of higher learning.

Award: Scholarship for use in freshman year; not renewable. *Amount:* up to $2500.

Eligibility Requirements: Applicant must be enrolled or expecting to enroll full-time at a four-year institution or university and resident of Ohio. Available to U.S. citizens.

Application Requirements: Application, financial need analysis, transcript. *Deadline:* varies.

Contact: Douglas Good, Scholarship Coordinator
Dayton Foundation
721 Richard Street
Miamisburg, OH 45342
Phone: 937-866-0711 Ext. 260
E-mail: douggood@daytonsuperior.com

DELAWARE DEPARTMENT OF EDUCATION http://www.doe.k12.de.us

DIAMOND STATE SCHOLARSHIP

Award of $1250 per year and renewable for up to three additional years. Must be a legal residents of Delaware. The deadline is March 31.

Award: Scholarship for use in freshman, sophomore, junior, or senior years; renewable. *Number:* 50. *Amount:* $1250–$5000.

Eligibility Requirements: Applicant must be high school student; planning to enroll or expecting to enroll full-time at a two-year or four-year or technical institution or university and resident of Delaware. Available to U.S. citizens.

Application Requirements: Application, transcript. *Deadline:* March 31.

Contact: Maureen Laffey, Director
Delaware Department of Education
Carvel State Office Building, 820 North French Street
Wilmington, DE 19801
Phone: 302-577-5240
Fax: 302-577-6765
E-mail: dedoe@doe.k12.de.us

Delaware Department of Education (continued)

EDUCATIONAL BENEFITS FOR CHILDREN OF DECEASED VETERANS AND OTHERS
• See page 587

GOVERNOR'S WORKFORCE DEVELOPMENT GRANT

Award for residents of Delaware and a U.S. citizen. Must be employed by a company in Delaware that contributes to the Blue Collar Training Fund Program. Must attend a participating college in Delaware on a part-time basis. Individual income must not exceed $32,417 annually. Full-time students are not eligible. The maximum Governor's Workforce Development Grant for one academic year is $2000 for part-time undergraduate study. Applications are due by the end of the free drop/add period each term.

Award: Grant for use in freshman, sophomore, junior, or senior years; not renewable. *Number:* 1. *Amount:* $2000.

Eligibility Requirements: Applicant must be age 18; enrolled or expecting to enroll part-time at a two-year or four-year institution or university; resident of Delaware and studying in Delaware. Available to U.S. citizens.

Application Requirements: Application, transcript. *Deadline:* varies.

Contact: Maureen Laffey, Director
Delaware Department of Education
Carvel State Office Building, 820 North French Street
Wilmington, DE 19801
Phone: 302-577-5240
Fax: 302-577-6765
E-mail: dedoe@doe.k12.de.us

LEGISLATIVE ESSAY SCHOLARSHIP

Award for high school seniors from Delaware in public or private schools or in home school programs, who plan to enroll full-time at a nonprofit, regionally accredited college. Must submit an essay of between 500-2000 words. See Web site for essay topic and more information: http://www.doe.k12.de.us/ Deadline is December 1. Three statewide, nonrenewable awards of $7500, $3750, and $2250.

Award: Scholarship for use in freshman year; not renewable. *Number:* 3. *Amount:* $2250–$7500.

Eligibility Requirements: Applicant must be high school student; planning to enroll or expecting to enroll full-time at an institution or university and resident of Delaware. Available to U.S. citizens.

Application Requirements: Application, essay. *Deadline:* December 1.

Contact: Maureen Laffey, Director
Delaware Department of Education
Carvel State Office Building, 820 North French Street
Wilmington, DE 19801
Phone: 302-577-5240
Fax: 302-577-6765
E-mail: dedoe@doe.k12.de.us

MICHAEL C. FERGUSON ACHIEVEMENT AWARD

Merit-based awards for eighth and tenth grade students who demonstrate superior performance on the Delaware Student Testing Program (DSPT) in reading, writing, and mathematics. Annual award of $1,000.

Award: Scholarship for use in freshman year; not renewable. *Amount:* $1000.

Eligibility Requirements: Applicant must be enrolled or expecting to enroll at an institution or university and resident of Delaware. Available to U.S. citizens.

Application Requirements: Application, transcript. *Deadline:* varies.

Contact: Tony J. Marchio, Superintendent
Delaware Department of Education
118 South Sixth Street, PO Box 4010
Odessa, DE 19730-4010

SCHOLARSHIP INCENTIVE PROGRAM (SCIP)

Award for legal residents of Delaware who plan to enroll full-time in an undergraduate degree program at a non-profit regionally accredited institution college in Delaware or Pennsylvania. Must have a minimum cumulative, unweighted GPA of 2.5. Graduate students attending the University of Delaware or Delaware State University are not eligible. Awards for undergraduate is $700 to $2200, depending on GPA and for graduate is $1000. Deadline is April 15.

Award: Grant for use in freshman, sophomore, junior, or senior years; not renewable. *Number:* up to 2. *Amount:* $700–$2250.

Eligibility Requirements: Applicant must be enrolled or expecting to enroll full-time at a two-year or four-year institution or university; resident of Delaware and studying in Delaware or Pennsylvania. Applicant must have 2.5 GPA or higher. Available to U.S. citizens.

Application Requirements: Application, transcript. *Deadline:* April 15.

Contact: Maureen Laffey, Director
Delaware Department of Education
Carvel State Office Building, 820 North French Street
Wilmington, DE 19801
Phone: 302-577-5240
Fax: 302-577-6765
E-mail: dedoe@doe.k12.de.us

DELAWARE HIGHER EDUCATION COMMISSION
http://www.doe.k12.de.us

AGENDA FOR DELAWARE WOMEN TRAILBLAZER SCHOLARSHIP

Scholarships given to women residing in Delaware and enrolling in a public or private non-profit college in Delaware as an undergraduate student. Must have a 2.5 GPA. Deadline: April 13.

Award: Scholarship for use in freshman, sophomore, junior, or senior years; renewable. *Number:* 1. *Amount:* $2500.

Eligibility Requirements: Applicant must be enrolled or expecting to enroll at a two-year or four-year institution or university; female; resident of Delaware and studying in Delaware. Applicant must have 2.5 GPA or higher. Available to U.S. citizens.

Application Requirements: Application, financial need analysis. *Deadline:* April 13.

Contact: Donna Myers, Field Agent/Program Administrator
Delaware Higher Education Commission
820 North French Street, 5th Floor
Wilmington, DE 19711-3509
Phone: 302-577-3240
Fax: 302-577-6765
E-mail: dmyers@doe.k12.de.us

DIAMOND STATE SCHOLARSHIP

Renewable award for Delaware high school seniors enrolling full-time at an accredited college or university. Must be ranked in upper quarter of class and score 1200 on SAT or 27 on the ACT.

Award: Scholarship for use in freshman year; renewable. *Number:* 50–200. *Amount:* $1250.

Eligibility Requirements: Applicant must be high school student; planning to enroll or expecting to enroll full-time at a four-year institution or university and resident of Delaware. Applicant must have 3.5 GPA or higher. Available to U.S. citizens.

Application Requirements: Application, essay, test scores, transcript. *Deadline:* March 31.

Contact: Donna Myers, Field Agent/Program Administrator
Delaware Higher Education Commission
820 North French Street, 5th Floor
Wilmington, DE 19711-3509
Phone: 302-577-3240
Fax: 302-577-6765
E-mail: dmyers@doe.k12.de.us

EDUCATIONAL BENEFITS FOR CHILDREN OF DECEASED MILITARY AND STATE POLICE
• See page 540

FIRST STATE MANUFACTURED HOUSING ASSOCIATION SCHOLARSHIP

Scholarship given to Delaware residents living in a manufactured home. May be used for any type of accredited training, licensing, or certification program or for any accredited degree program.

Award: Scholarship for use in freshman, sophomore, junior, or senior years; renewable. *Number:* up to 2. *Amount:* $2000–$4000.

Eligibility Requirements: Applicant must be enrolled or expecting to enroll at a two-year or four-year or technical institution or university and resident of Delaware. Available to U.S. citizens.

Application Requirements: Essay, financial need analysis, references, transcript. *Deadline:* March 10.

Contact: Donna Myers, Field Agent/Program Administrator
Delaware Higher Education Commission
820 North French Street, 5th Floor
Wilmington, DE 19711-3509
Phone: 302-577-3240
Fax: 302-577-6765
E-mail: dmyers@doe.k12.de.us

LEGISLATIVE ESSAY SCHOLARSHIP

Must be a senior in high school and Delaware resident. Submit an essay of 500 to 2000 words on a designated historical topic (changes annually). For more information visit: http://www.doe.state.de.us/high-ed

Award: Scholarship for use in freshman year; not renewable. *Number:* 62–65. *Amount:* $750–$7500.

Eligibility Requirements: Applicant must be high school student; planning to enroll or expecting to enroll full or part-time at a two-year or four-year or technical institution or university and resident of Delaware. Available to U.S. citizens.

Application Requirements: Application, applicant must enter a contest, essay. *Deadline:* varies.

Contact: Donna Myers, Field Agent/Program Administrator
Delaware Higher Education Commission
820 North French Street, 5th Floor
Wilmington, DE 19711-3509
Phone: 302-577-3240
Fax: 302-577-6765
E-mail: dmyers@doe.k12.de.us

ROBERT C. BYRD HONORS SCHOLARSHIP-DELAWARE

Available to Delaware residents who are graduating high school seniors. Based on outstanding academic merit. Awards are renewable up to four years. Must be ranked in upper quarter of class and have a score of 1200 on SAT or 27 on ACT.

Award: Scholarship for use in freshman year; renewable. *Number:* 16–80. *Amount:* $1500.

Eligibility Requirements: Applicant must be high school student; planning to enroll or expecting to enroll full-time at a two-year or four-year institution or university and resident of Delaware. Applicant must have 3.5 GPA or higher. Available to U.S. citizens.

Application Requirements: Application, essay, test scores, transcript. *Deadline:* March 31.

Contact: Donna Myers, Field Agent/Program Administrator
Delaware Higher Education Commission
820 North French Street, 5th Floor
Wilmington, DE 19711-3509
Phone: 302-577-3240
Fax: 302-577-6765
E-mail: dmyers@doe.k12.de.us

SCHOLARSHIP INCENTIVE PROGRAM-DELAWARE

One-time award for Delaware residents with financial need. May be used at an institution in Delaware or Pennsylvania, or at another out-of-state institution if a program is not available at a publicly-supported school in Delaware. Must have minimum 2.5 GPA.

Award: Grant for use in freshman, sophomore, junior, senior, or graduate years; not renewable. *Number:* 1000–1300. *Amount:* $700–$2200.

Eligibility Requirements: Applicant must be enrolled or expecting to enroll full-time at a two-year or four-year institution or university; resident of Delaware and studying in Delaware or Pennsylvania. Applicant must have 2.5 GPA or higher. Available to U.S. citizens.

Application Requirements: Application, financial need analysis, transcript. *Deadline:* April 15.

Contact: Donna Myers, Field Agent/Program Administrator
Delaware Higher Education Commission
820 North French Street, 5th Floor
Wilmington, DE 19711-3509
Phone: 302-577-3240
Fax: 302-577-6765
E-mail: dmyers@doe.k12.de.us

DELAWARE NATIONAL GUARD   http://www.delawarenationalguard.com

STATE TUITION ASSISTANCE
• *See page 569*

DEVRY, INC.   http://www.devry.edu

ALBERTA CENTENNIAL SCHOLARSHIP

Award of $1000 per semester. Valued at up to $9000. Must be a high school graduate from Alberta; each high school in Alberta is allotted one scholarship. Must be in top 50% of class or have a GPA of 2.7. Must have completed one full year of Algebra 1 or higher math with a grade of B or better. Deadline: July 1.

Award: Scholarship for use in freshman year; not renewable. *Amount:* $1000–$9000.

Eligibility Requirements: Applicant must be enrolled or expecting to enroll full-time at an institution or university and resident of Alberta. Available to Canadian citizens.

Application Requirements: Application. *Deadline:* July 1.

Contact: Thonie Simpson, National HS Program Manager
DeVry, Inc.
1 Tower Lane
Oakbrook Terrace, IL 60181
Phone: 630-706-3122
Fax: 630-574-1696
E-mail: outreach@devry.edu

DEVRY COMMUNITY COLLEGE SCHOLAR AWARD

Scholarship designed for students who have earned a career-oriented associate degree. Two students in each community college in Colorado, Illinois, and Texas are awarded $1,000 per semester scholarships for up to 4 semesters toward the DeVry's bachelor degree program of their choice.

Award: Scholarship for use in junior or senior years; renewable. *Number:* 266. *Amount:* $4000.

Eligibility Requirements: Applicant must be enrolled or expecting to enroll full-time at an institution or university and studying in Colorado, Illinois, or Texas. Applicant must have 2.5 GPA or higher. Available to U.S. citizens.

Application Requirements: Application, interview, references, test scores, transcript. *Deadline:* varies.

Contact: Thonie Simpson, National HS Program Manager
DeVry, Inc.
1 Tower Lane
Oak Brook Terrace, IL 60181-4624
Phone: 630-706-3122
Fax: 630-574-1696
E-mail: tsimpson@devry.com

DEVRY DEAN'S SCHOLARSHIPS

Awards to high school seniors who apply to DeVry University who have SAT scores of 1100 or higher or ACT scores of 24 or higher. Canada 'Composite CPT of 430 or higher. There is no separate scholarship application, any application for admittance to DeVry University will be reviewed for qualifying scores. Deadline: One year from high school graduation to apply and start at DeVry. Applications must be received by July 1.

Award: Scholarship for use in freshman, sophomore, junior, or senior years; renewable. *Number:* varies. *Amount:* $1500–$13,500.

Eligibility Requirements: Applicant must be high school student; planning to enroll or expecting to enroll full-time at an institution or university and studying in Alberta, Arizona, California, Colorado, Florida, Georgia, Illinois, Missouri, New Jersey, New York, Ohio, or Pennsylvania. Applicant must have 3.0 GPA or higher. Available to U.S. and Canadian citizens.

Application Requirements: Application, interview, test scores, transcript. *Deadline:* July 1.

DeVry, Inc. (continued)

Contact: Thonie Simpson, National HS Program Manager
DeVry, Inc.
1 Tower Lane
Oakbrook Terrace, IL 60181-4624
Phone: 630-706-3122
Fax: 630-574-1696
E-mail: outreach@devry.edu

DEVRY HIGH SCHOOL COMMUNITY SCHOLARS AWARD

Scholarships to approximately 4700 graduates from public high schools in the 24 metropolitan areas served by DeVry's campuses. Recipients of this award must demonstrate proficiency in mathematics and rank in the top fifty percent of their class. Deadline: July 1.

Award: Scholarship for use in freshman, sophomore, junior, or senior years; renewable. *Number:* 4753. *Amount:* $1000–$9000.

Eligibility Requirements: Applicant must be high school student; planning to enroll or expecting to enroll full-time at an institution or university and studying in Alberta, Arizona, California, Colorado, Florida, Georgia, Illinois, Missouri, New Jersey, New York, Ohio, or Pennsylvania. Applicant must have 2.5 GPA or higher. Available to U.S. and Canadian citizens.

Application Requirements: Application, interview, references, test scores, transcript. *Deadline:* July 1.

Contact: Thonie Simpson, National HS Program Manager
DeVry, Inc.
1 Tower Lane
Oakbrook Terrace, IL 60181
Phone: 630-706-3122
Fax: 630-574-1696
E-mail: outreach@devry.edu

DEVRY PRESIDENTIAL SCHOLARSHIPS

Two full-tuition scholarships are awarded by each of the 24 DeVry University campuses each year. Contenders are chosen from those who receive a Dean's Scholarship. Winners are determined by committees at each campus on the basis of their academic records, SAT or ACT scores, and an essay on a topic chosen by the committee. Deadline: March 10.

Award: Scholarship for use in freshman, sophomore, junior, or senior years; renewable. *Number:* 48. *Amount:* up to $64,000.

Eligibility Requirements: Applicant must be high school student; planning to enroll or expecting to enroll full-time at an institution or university and studying in Alberta, Arizona, California, Colorado, Florida, Georgia, Illinois, Missouri, New Jersey, New York, Ohio, or Pennsylvania. Applicant must have 3.0 GPA or higher. Available to U.S. and Canadian citizens.

Application Requirements: Application, essay, interview, test scores, transcript. *Deadline:* March 10.

Contact: Thonie Simpson, National HS Program Manager
DeVry, Inc.
1 Tower Lane
Oakbrook Terrace, IL 60181-4624
Phone: 630-706-3122
Fax: 630-574-1696
E-mail: outreach@devry.edu

DEVRY UNIVERSITY REGIONAL FIRST SCHOLAR AWARDS

One full-tuition scholarship in each of ten regions to high school seniors who participate in the FIRST Regional Robotics competition. Students must enroll at DeVry University within one calendar year of receipt of the award.

Award: Scholarship for use in freshman, sophomore, junior, or senior years; renewable. *Number:* 10. *Amount:* $21,280–$53,370.

Eligibility Requirements: Applicant must be high school student; planning to enroll or expecting to enroll full-time at an institution or university and studying in Arizona, California, Colorado, Florida, Georgia, Illinois, New York, Pennsylvania, or Texas. Available to U.S. and non-U.S. citizens.

Application Requirements: Application, applicant must enter a contest, essay, references, test scores, transcript. *Deadline:* March 1.

Contact: Marisa Russo, National Outreach Services Manager
DeVry, Inc.
1 Tower Lane
Oakbrook Terrace, IL 60181-4624
Phone: 630-928-6478
Fax: 630-574-1991
E-mail: mrusso@devry.com

LITTLE BROTHERS LITTLE SISTERS OF NEW YORK CITY SCHOLARSHIP

Award of full-tuition plus $700 book stipend per semester for high school graduates in one of the 5 boroughs of NYC (Manhattan, Brooklyn, Queens, Bronx, Staten Island). Must have completed the Big Brothers and Big Sisters (BBBS) of NYC's workplace mentoring program. Must apply within one year from high school graduation to a DeVry institution.

Award: Scholarship for use in freshman year; not renewable. *Amount:* $700.

Eligibility Requirements: Applicant must be enrolled or expecting to enroll full-time at an institution or university and resident of New York. Available to U.S. citizens.

Application Requirements: Application. *Deadline:* Continuous.

Contact: Thonie Simpson, National HS Program Manager
DeVry, Inc.
1 Tower Lane
Oakbrook Terrace, IL 60181
Phone: 630-706-3122
Fax: 630-574-1696
E-mail: outreach@devry.edu

DISTRICT OF COLUMBIA PUBLIC SCHOOLS

ROBERT C. BYRD HONORS SCHOLARSHIP-DISTRICT OF COLUMBIA

Federally-funded, state-administered program to recognize exceptionally able high school seniors who show promise of continued excellence in postsecondary education. Must be a U.S. citizen and permanent resident of District of Columbia.

Award: Scholarship for use in freshman year; renewable. *Number:* 28. *Amount:* $1500–$6000.

Eligibility Requirements: Applicant must be enrolled or expecting to enroll full-time at a two-year or four-year or technical institution or university and resident of District of Columbia. Available to U.S. citizens.

Application Requirements: Application, transcript. *Deadline:* varies.

Contact: Michon Peck, Scholarship Coordinator
District of Columbia Public Schools
825 North Capitol Street, NE, 6th Floor, Room 6077
Washington, DC 20002
Phone: 202-442-5110
Fax: 202-442-5303
E-mail: michon.peck@k12.dc.us

DISTRICT OF COLUMBIA STATE EDUCATION OFFICE
http://www.seo.dc.gov

DC LEVERAGING EDUCATIONAL ASSISTANCE PARTNERSHIP PROGRAM (LEAP)

Available to Washington, D.C. residents who have financial need. Must also apply for the Federal Pell Grant. Must attend an eligible college at least half time. Contact financial aid office or local library for more information. Proof of residency may be required. Deadline is last Friday in June.

Award: Grant for use in freshman, sophomore, junior, or senior years; renewable. *Number:* 2274–2300. *Amount:* $250–$1500.

Eligibility Requirements: Applicant must be enrolled or expecting to enroll full or part-time at a two-year or four-year or technical institution or university and resident of District of Columbia. Available to U.S. citizens.

Application Requirements: Application, financial need analysis, transcript, Student Aid Report (SAR), FASFA. *Deadline:* June 28.

Contact: Miss. Carol Talley
District of Columbia State Education Office
441 4th Street, NW, 350 North
Washington, DC 20001
Phone: 202-724-7784

DC TUITION ASSISTANCE GRANT PROGRAM

The D.C. Tuition Assistance Grant Program pays the difference between in-state and out-of-state tuition and fees at any public college or university in the United States up to $10,000 per year. It also pays up to $2500 per year of tuition and fees at private colleges and universities in the Washington metropolitan area, and at historically black colleges and universities throughout the United States. Students must be enrolled in a degree-granting program at an eligible institution, and be domiciled in the District of Columbia.

Award: Grant for use in freshman, sophomore, junior, or senior years; renewable. *Number:* up to 7000. *Amount:* $2500–$10,000.

Eligibility Requirements: Applicant must be age 24 or under; enrolled or expecting to enroll full or part-time at a two-year or four-year institution or university and resident of District of Columbia. Available to U.S. citizens.

Application Requirements: Application, supporting documents. *Deadline:* June 30.

Contact: Emilia Del Arroyo, Program/Disbursement Analyst Bilingual
District of Columbia State Education Office
441 4th Street, NW, Suite 350 N
Washington, DC 20001
Phone: 202-727-8193
Fax: 202-727-2834
E-mail: emiliadelarroyo@dc.gov

DISTRICT OF COLUMBIA ADOPTION SCHOLARSHIP

Scholarship program designed for adopted individuals who are wards of the District. Applicants must show proof of adoption, current postsecondary enrollment status, and social security number.

Award: Grant for use in freshman, sophomore, junior, or senior years; not renewable. *Number:* varies. *Amount:* up to $10,000.

Eligibility Requirements: Applicant must be age 24 or under; enrolled or expecting to enroll full-time at a two-year or four-year or technical institution or university and resident of District of Columbia. Available to U.S. citizens.

Application Requirements: Application, proof of adoption, enrollment verification. *Deadline:* Continuous.

Contact: Roslyn Stewart Christian, Senior Policy Advisor
District of Columbia State Education Office
441 4th Street, NW, Suite 350 North
Washington, DC 20001
Phone: 202-724-7869
Fax: 202-724-2019
E-mail: roslyn.christian@dc.gov

DIXIE BOYS BASEBALL   http://www.dixie.org

DIXIE BOYS BASEBALL SCHOLARSHIP PROGRAM

Eleven scholarships are presented annually to deserving high school seniors who have participated in the Dixie Boys Baseball Program. Citizenship, scholarship, residency in a state with Dixie Baseball Programs and financial need are considered in determining the awards.

Award: Scholarship for use in freshman year; not renewable. *Number:* 11. *Amount:* $1500.

Eligibility Requirements: Applicant must be high school student; planning to enroll or expecting to enroll full-time at a two-year or four-year institution or university and resident of Alabama, Arkansas, Florida, Georgia, Louisiana, Mississippi, North Carolina, South Carolina, Tennessee, Texas, or Virginia. Available to U.S. citizens.

Application Requirements: Application, financial need analysis, photo, references. *Deadline:* March 15.

Contact: Bernie H. Varnadore, Scholarship Chairman
Dixie Boys Baseball
2684 Orchid Avenue
North Charleston, SC 29405
Phone: 843-744-7612
Fax: 843-747-7612
E-mail: hbvrmvpfl@aol.com

DIXIE YOUTH SCHOLARSHIP PROGRAM

Thirty scholarships are presented annually to deserving high school seniors who participated in the Dixie Youth Baseball program while age 12 and under. Financial need is considered. Parents must submit a copy of 1040 tax return.

Award: Scholarship for use in freshman year; not renewable. *Number:* 30. *Amount:* $2000.

Eligibility Requirements: Applicant must be high school student; planning to enroll or expecting to enroll full-time at a two-year or four-year or technical institution or university and resident of Alabama, Arkansas, Florida, Georgia, Louisiana, Mississippi, North Carolina, South Carolina, Tennessee, Texas, or Virginia. Available to U.S. citizens.

Application Requirements: Application, essay, financial need analysis, photo, references, transcript, 1040 form. *Deadline:* March 1.

Contact: P. L. Corley, Scholarship Chairman
Dixie Boys Baseball
PO Box 877
Marshall, TX 75671-0877
Phone: 903-927-2255
Fax: 903-927-1846
E-mail: dyb@dixie.org

DOGRIB TREATY 11 SCHOLARSHIP COMMITTEE   http://www.dt11sc.ca

DIAVIK DIAMONDS, INC. UNIVERSITY SCHOLARSHIPS

Award for students of Dogrib ancestry who are permanent residents of one of four Dogrib communities (Wekweti, Wha Ti, Gamet, or Rae-Edzo). Applicants must be enrolled full time in a Canadian University degree program and interested and active in community affairs.

Award: Scholarship for use in freshman, sophomore, junior, senior, or graduate years. *Number:* 4. *Amount:* $5000.

Eligibility Requirements: Applicant must be enrolled or expecting to enroll full-time at an institution or university and resident of North West Territories. Available to U.S. and Canadian citizens.

Application Requirements: Application, references, transcript. *Deadline:* July 15.

Contact: Morven MacPherson, Post Secondary Student Support Coordinator
Dogrib Treaty 11 Scholarship Committee
c/o CJBRHS
PO Box 1
Rae-Edzo X0E 0Y0
Canada
Phone: 867-371-3815
Fax: 867-371-3813
E-mail: morvenm@dogrib.net

EAST LOS ANGELES COMMUNITY UNION (TELACU) EDUCATION FOUNDATION   http://www.telacu.com

LINC TELACU SCHOLARSHIP PROGRAM

Scholarships available to low-income applicants from the Greater East Side of Los Angeles. Must be U.S. citizen or permanent resident. Must be a resident of one of the following communities: East Los Angeles, Bell Gardens, Commerce, Huntington Park, Montebello, Monterey Park, Pico Rivera, Santa Ana, South Gate, and the City of Los Angeles. Must be the first generation in their family to achieve a college degree. Must have a record of community service. Further restriction see Web site.

Award: Scholarship for use in freshman, sophomore, junior, or senior years; not renewable. *Number:* 100–150. *Amount:* $500–$5000.

Eligibility Requirements: Applicant must be enrolled or expecting to enroll full-time at a two-year or four-year institution or university;

East Los Angeles Community Union (TELACU) Education Foundation
(continued)

resident of California and studying in California. Applicant must have 2.5 GPA or higher. Available to U.S. citizens.

Application Requirements: Application, essay, financial need analysis, interview, references, transcript. *Deadline:* April 1.

Contact: Blanca Anchondo, Scholarship Director
East Los Angeles Community Union (TELACU) Education Foundation
5400 East Olympic Boulevard, Suite 300
Los Angeles, CA 90022
Phone: 323-721-1655
Fax: 323-724-3372
E-mail: info@telacu.com

EDMONTON COMMUNITY
FOUNDATION   http://www.DollarsForLearners.com

BELCOURT BROSSEAU METIS AWARDS
• *See page 613*

YOUTH FORMERLY IN CARE BURSARY
• *See page 613*

EDMUND F. MAXWELL
FOUNDATION   http://www.maxwell.org

EDMUND F. MAXWELL FOUNDATION SCHOLARSHIP

Scholarships awarded to residents of western Washington to attend accredited independent colleges or universities. Awards of up to $5000 per year based on need, merit, citizenship, and activities. Renewable for up to four years if academic progress is suitable and financial need is unchanged.

Award: Scholarship for use in freshman year; renewable. *Number:* 110. *Amount:* up to $5000.

Eligibility Requirements: Applicant must be enrolled or expecting to enroll full-time at a four-year institution or university and resident of Washington. Available to U.S. citizens.

Application Requirements: Application, essay, financial need analysis, test scores, transcript, employment history. *Deadline:* April 30.

Contact: Administrator
Edmund F. Maxwell Foundation
PO Box 22537
Seattle, WA 98122
E-mail: admin@maxwell.org

EDWARDS SCHOLARSHIP FUND

EDWARDS SCHOLARSHIP

College scholarships for students under 25 years of age whose permanent address is in the city of Boston, Massachusetts. Must have lived in Boston since the beginning of junior year in high school. Must maintain a "C" or GPA of 2.0.

Award: Scholarship for use in freshman, sophomore, junior, senior, graduate, or postgraduate years; not renewable. *Number:* varies. *Amount:* $250–$5000.

Eligibility Requirements: Applicant must be age 24 or under; enrolled or expecting to enroll full-time at a two-year or four-year or technical institution or university and resident of Massachusetts. Available to U.S. and non-U.S. citizens.

Application Requirements: Application, financial need analysis, interview, references, test scores, transcript, Student Aid Report (SAR). *Deadline:* March 1.

Contact: Brenda McCarthy, Executive Secretary
Edwards Scholarship Fund
10 Post Office Square
Boston, MA 02109
Phone: 617-654-8628

ELMER O. AND IDA PRESTON EDUCATIONAL
TRUST

ELMER O. AND IDA PRESTON EDUCATIONAL TRUST GRANTS AND LOANS

Provides financial assistance to students attending Iowa colleges or universities and who are preparing for a life of Christian service. Portion of loan must be repaid. Must be an Iowa resident.

Award: Grant for use in freshman, sophomore, junior, or senior years; renewable. *Number:* varies. *Amount:* $250–$5000.

Eligibility Requirements: Applicant must be enrolled or expecting to enroll full-time at an institution or university; resident of Iowa and studying in Iowa. Available to U.S. citizens.

Application Requirements: Application, driver's license, interview, transcript. *Deadline:* June 1.

Contact: Elmer O. and Ida Preston Educational Trust
801 Grand Avenue, Suite 3700
Des Moines, IA 50309

EPILEPSY FOUNDATION OF
IDAHO   http://www.epilepsyidaho.org

GREGORY W. GILE MEMORIAL SCHOLARSHIP PROGRAM
• *See page 558*

MARK MUSIC MEMORIAL SCHOLARSHIP
• *See page 558*

ESPERANZA, INC.   http://www.esperanzainc.com

ESPERANZA SCHOLARSHIPS
• *See page 613*

EVERLY SCHOLARSHIP FUND, INC.

EVERLY SCHOLARSHIP

Renewable award for New Jersey residents attending an accredited institution full-time. Must be undergraduate. Minimum 3.0 GPA required and minimum SAT score of 1100. Total Number of awards varies each year.

Award: Scholarship for use in freshman, sophomore, junior, or senior years; renewable. *Number:* 5. *Amount:* $2500.

Eligibility Requirements: Applicant must be high school student; planning to enroll or expecting to enroll full-time at a four-year institution or university and resident of New Jersey. Applicant must have 3.0 GPA or higher. Available to U.S. citizens.

Application Requirements: Application, autobiography, essay, financial need analysis, interview, references, test scores, transcript. *Deadline:* May 1.

Contact: John R. Lolio, Jr., President
Everly Scholarship Fund, Inc.
4300 Haddonfield Road, Suite 311
Pennsauken, NJ 08109
Phone: 856-661-2094
Fax: 856-662-0165
E-mail: jlolio@sskrplaw.com

FINANCE AUTHORITY OF
MAINE   http://www.famemaine.com

NEXTGEN ACCESS SCHOLARSHIP PROGRAM

Students attending Maine institutions are eligible for up to $1000 with a minimum award of $250. Students attending out-of-state-institutions are eligible for up to $500 with a minimum award of $250. The financial aid officer at each institution selects recipients. Applicant must be first year attendees.

Award: Scholarship for use in freshman, sophomore, junior, senior, graduate, or postgraduate years. *Amount:* $250–$1000.

Eligibility Requirements: Applicant must be enrolled or expecting to enroll at a two-year or four-year or technical institution or university and resident of Maine. Available to U.S. citizens.

Application Requirements: Application.

Contact: Cathy Kimball, Manager of Education Finance Programs
Finance Authority of Maine
5 Community Drive
PO Box 949
Augusta, ME 04332-0949
Phone: 800-228-3734
Fax: 207-623-0095
E-mail: cathy@famemaine.com

NEXTGEN STUDENT GRANT PROGRAM

Need-based grant program available to undergraduate students who are Maine residents. Students can apply for this grant by filing the (FAFSA) by May 1st each year.

Award: Grant for use in freshman, sophomore, junior, or senior years. *Amount:* $400–$1000.

Eligibility Requirements: Applicant must be enrolled or expecting to enroll full-time at a four-year institution or university and resident of Maine. Available to U.S. citizens.

Application Requirements: Application.

Contact: Cathy Kimball, Manager of Education Finance Programs
Finance Authority of Maine
5 Community Drive
PO Box 949
Augusta, ME 04332-0949
Phone: 800-228-3734
Fax: 207-623-0095
E-mail: cathy@famemaine.com

TUITION WAIVER PROGRAMS
• *See page 541*

FLEMING-MASON ENERGY   http://www.fmenergy.net

FLEMING-MASON ENERGY ANNUAL MEETING SCHOLARSHIP

Awards for graduating Kentucky high school senior in good standing who is a child of a member of Fleming-Mason Energy, whose primary residence is on co-op lines. Application and information may be obtained from high school guidance counselor or by calling Director of Member Services. Deadline for application is in mid-April.

Award: Scholarship for use in freshman year; not renewable. *Number:* 10. *Amount:* up to $1000.

Eligibility Requirements: Applicant must be high school student; planning to enroll or expecting to enroll at a two-year or four-year or technical institution or university and resident of Kentucky. Available to U.S. citizens.

Application Requirements: Application.

Contact: Mary Nance, Director of Member Services
Fleming-Mason Energy
PO Box 328
Flemingsburg, KY 41041
Phone: 800-464-3144
Fax: 606-845-1008
E-mail: mbnance@fmenergy.net

FLORIDA ASSOCIATION OF POSTSECONDARY SCHOOLS AND COLLEGES   http://www.fapsc.org

FLORIDA ASSOCIATION OF POSTSECONDARY SCHOOLS AND COLLEGES SCHOLARSHIP PROGRAM

Full and partial scholarship to private career schools in Florida are awarded to students either graduating from high school or receiving GED in the current school year. Must be a resident of Florida. Minimum 2.5 GPA required. The Dollar value for the award varies.

Award: Scholarship for use in freshman year; not renewable. *Number:* up to 225. *Amount:* up to $3500.

Eligibility Requirements: Applicant must be high school student; planning to enroll or expecting to enroll full-time at a technical institution; resident of Florida and studying in Florida. Applicant must have 2.5 GPA or higher. Available to U.S. citizens.

Application Requirements: Application, essay, references, transcript. *Deadline:* March 1.

Contact: Wanda Taylor, Deputy Executive Director Membership Services
Florida Association of Postsecondary Schools and Colleges
150 South Monroe Street, Suite 303
Tallahassee, FL 32301
Phone: 850-577-3139
Fax: 850-577-3133
E-mail: scholarship@fapsc.org

FLORIDA DEPARTMENT OF EDUCATION   http://www.floridastudentfinancialaid.org

ACCESS TO BETTER LEARNING AND EDUCATION GRANT

Provides tuition assistance to Florida undergraduates enrolled full-time in degree programs at eligible independent postsecondary institutions in Florida. Students must be US citizens or eligible non-citizens and must meet Florida residency requirements. Contact the financial aid administrator for application deadlines and student eligibility requirements.

Award: Grant for use in freshman, sophomore, junior, or senior years.

Eligibility Requirements: Applicant must be enrolled or expecting to enroll full-time at a four-year institution or university; resident of Florida and studying in Florida. Available to U.S. citizens.

Application Requirements: Application. *Deadline:* varies.

Contact: Barb Dombrowski, Education Director, Policy and Training
Florida Department of Education
Office of Student Financial Assistance
1940 North Monroe, Suite 70
Tallahassee, FL 32303-4759
Phone: 850-410-5191
Fax: 850-488-5966
E-mail: barb.dombrowski@fldoe.org

CRITICAL TEACHER SHORTAGE STUDENT LOAN FORGIVENESS PROGRAM-FLORIDA
• *See page 541*

ETHICS IN BUSINESS SCHOLARSHIP

Provides assistance to undergraduate college students who enroll at community colleges and eligible Florida colleges or universities. Scholarships are funded by private and state contributions. Awards are dependent on private matching funds. For more information contact the financial aid office at participating institutions, which are listed on the Florida Department of Education Web site at http://www.firn.edu/doe/ofsa

Award: Scholarship for use in freshman, sophomore, junior, or senior years; not renewable. *Number:* varies.

Eligibility Requirements: Applicant must be enrolled or expecting to enroll at a two-year or four-year institution or university and studying in Florida. Available to U.S. citizens.

Application Requirements: Application. *Deadline:* varies.

Contact: Barb Dombrowski, Education Director, Policy and Training
Florida Department of Education
Office of Student Financial Assistance
1940 North Monroe, Suite 70
Tallahassee, FL 32303-4759
Phone: 850-410-5191
Fax: 850-488-5966
E-mail: barb.dombrowski@fldoe.org

FLORIDA PRIVATE STUDENT ASSISTANCE GRANT

Grants for Florida residents who are U.S. citizens or eligible non-citizens attending eligible independent nonprofit colleges or universities in Florida. Must be full-time student and demonstrate substantial financial need. Renewable for up to nine semesters, fourteen quarters, or until receipt of bachelor's degree. Deadline to be determined by individual eligible institutions.

Award: Grant for use in freshman, sophomore, junior, or senior years; renewable. *Number:* varies. *Amount:* $200–$1672.

Eligibility Requirements: Applicant must be enrolled or expecting to enroll full-time at a two-year or four-year institution or university; resident of Florida and studying in Florida. Available to U.S. citizens.

Florida Department of Education (continued)

Application Requirements: Application, financial need analysis, FAFSA. *Deadline:* varies.

Contact: Barb Dombrowski, Education Director, Policy and Training
Florida Department of Education
Office of Student Financial Assistance
1940 North Monroe, Suite 70
Tallahassee, FL 32303-4759
Phone: 850-410-5191
Fax: 850-488-5966
E-mail: barb.dombrowski@fldoe.org

FLORIDA PUBLIC STUDENT ASSISTANCE GRANT

Grants for Florida residents, U.S. citizens, or eligible non-citizens attending a Florida public college or university full-time. Based on financial need. Renewable up to 9 semesters, 14 quarters, or until receipt of bachelor's degree. Deadline set by eligible participating institutions.

Award: Grant for use in freshman, sophomore, junior, or senior years; renewable. *Number:* varies. *Amount:* $200–$1672.

Eligibility Requirements: Applicant must be enrolled or expecting to enroll full or part-time at a two-year or four-year institution or university; resident of Florida and studying in Florida. Available to U.S. citizens.

Application Requirements: Application, financial need analysis, FAFSA. *Deadline:* varies.

Contact: Barb Dombrowski, Education Director, Policy and Training
Florida Department of Education
Office of Student Financial Assistance
1940 North Monroe, Suite 70
Tallahassee, FL 32303-4759
Phone: 850-410-5191
Fax: 850-488-5966
E-mail: barb.dombrowski@fldoe.org

JOSE MARTI SCHOLARSHIP CHALLENGE GRANT FUND

• See page 613

MARY MCLEOD BETHUNE SCHOLARSHIP

Available to Florida students with a GPA of 3.0 or above who will attend Florida Agricultural and Mechanical University, Edward Waters College, Bethune-Cookman College, or Florida Memorial College. Based on need and merit. Further information, deadlines, and applications available at the financial aid office at the school.

Award: Scholarship for use in freshman, sophomore, junior, or senior years; renewable. *Amount:* $3000.

Eligibility Requirements: Applicant must be enrolled or expecting to enroll full-time at a two-year or four-year institution or university; resident of Florida and studying in Florida. Applicant must have 3.0 GPA or higher. Available to U.S. citizens.

Application Requirements: Application, financial need analysis. *Deadline:* varies.

Contact: Barb Dombrowski, Education Director, Policy and Training
Florida Department of Education
Office of Student Financial Assistance
1940 North Monroe, Suite 70
Tallahassee, FL 32303-4759
Phone: 850-410-5191
Fax: 850-488-5966
E-mail: barb.dombrowski@fldoe.org

ROBERT C. BYRD HONORS SCHOLARSHIP-FLORIDA

One applicant per high school may be nominated. Must be Florida resident. Must be U.S. citizen or eligible non-citizen. Application must be submitted in the same year as graduation. Must meet Selective Service System registration requirements. May attend any postsecondary accredited institution.

Award: Scholarship for use in freshman year; renewable. *Number:* 1400. *Amount:* up to $1500.

Eligibility Requirements: Applicant must be high school student; planning to enroll or expecting to enroll full-time at a technical institution and resident of Florida. Available to U.S. citizens.

Application Requirements: Application, references, test scores, transcript. *Deadline:* April 15.

Contact: Barb Dombrowski, Education Director, Policy and Training
Florida Department of Education
Office of Student Financial Assistance
1940 North Monroe, Suite 70
Tallahassee, FL 32303-4759
Phone: 850-410-5191
Fax: 850-488-5966
E-mail: barb.dombrowski@fldoe.org

ROSEWOOD FAMILY SCHOLARSHIP FUND

• See page 613

SCHOLARSHIPS FOR CHILDREN OF DECEASED OR DISABLED VETERANS OR CHILDREN OF SERVICEMEN CLASSIFIED AS POW OR MIA

• See page 588

WILLIAM L. BOYD IV FLORIDA RESIDENT ACCESS GRANT

Awards given to Florida residents attending an independent non-profit college or university in Florida for undergraduate study. Cannot have previously received bachelor's degree. Must enroll minimum 12 credit hours. Deadline set by eligible postsecondary financial aid offices. Contact financial aid administrator for application information. Reapply for renewal.

Award: Grant for use in freshman, sophomore, junior, or senior years; not renewable. *Number:* varies. *Amount:* up to $2850.

Eligibility Requirements: Applicant must be enrolled or expecting to enroll full-time at a four-year institution or university; resident of Florida and studying in Florida. Available to U.S. citizens.

Application Requirements: Application. *Deadline:* April 1.

Contact: Barb Dombrowski, Education Director, Policy and Training
Florida Department of Education
Office of Student Financial Assistance
1940 North Monroe, Suite 70
Tallahassee, FL 32303-4759
Phone: 850-410-5191
Fax: 850-488-5966
E-mail: barb.dombrowski@fldoe.org

FLORIDA WOMEN'S STATE GOLF ASSOCIATION
http://www.fwsga.org

FLORIDA WOMEN'S STATE GOLF ASSOCIATION JUNIOR GIRLS' SCHOLARSHIP FUND

The FWSGA Scholarship Fund is designed to assist young women to whom golf is meaningful with their education. Applicants must be Florida residents, play golf, maintain a 3.0 GPA, attend a Florida college or university, and have a need for financial assistance.

Award: Scholarship for use in freshman, sophomore, junior, or senior years; renewable. *Number:* 1–4. *Amount:* $2500–$5000.

Eligibility Requirements: Applicant must be enrolled or expecting to enroll full-time at a two-year or four-year institution or university; female; resident of Florida; studying in Florida and must have an interest in golf. Applicant must have 3.0 GPA or higher. Available to U.S. citizens.

Application Requirements: Application, financial need analysis, interview, references, test scores, transcript. *Deadline:* April 1.

Contact: Kelly Tarala, Executive Director
Florida Women's State Golf Association
8875 Hidden River Parkway, Suite 110
Tampa, FL 33637
Phone: 813-864-2130
Fax: 813-864-2129
E-mail: info@fwsga.org

FRESH START SCHOLARSHIP FOUNDATION, INC.
http://www.wwb.org/freshstart.html

FRESH START SCHOLARSHIP

Scholarship offering a "fresh start" to women who are returning to school after a hiatus of two years to better their life and opportunities. Must be entering an undergraduate program in Delaware.

Award: Scholarship for use in freshman, sophomore, junior, or senior years; not renewable. *Number:* up to 10. *Amount:* $750–$2000.

Eligibility Requirements: Applicant must be age 20; enrolled or expecting to enroll full or part-time at a two-year or four-year institution or university; female and studying in Delaware. Available to U.S. and non-U.S. citizens.

Application Requirements: Application, essay, financial need analysis, references, transcript. *Deadline:* May 31.

Contact: Cindy Cheyney, Secretary
Fresh Start Scholarship Foundation, Inc.
PO Box 7784
Wilmington, DE 19803
Phone: 302-656-4411
Fax: 610-347-0438
E-mail: ccheyney@delanet.com

GALLUP ORGANIZATION/CORNHUSKER STATE GAMES   http://www.cornhuskerstategames.com

GALLUP CSG SCHOLARSHIP PROGRAM

One-time award for Nebraska students who are participants in the Cornhusker State Games. For use at a Nebraska postsecondary institution. Deadline is June 20. See Web site at http://www.cornhuskerstategames.com for further details.

Award: Scholarship for use in freshman, sophomore, junior, senior, graduate, or postgraduate years; not renewable. *Number:* 5. *Amount:* $1000.

Eligibility Requirements: Applicant must be enrolled or expecting to enroll full or part-time at a two-year or four-year or technical institution or university; resident of Nebraska and studying in Nebraska. Available to U.S. citizens.

Application Requirements: Application, applicant must enter a contest, essay, transcript. *Deadline:* June 20.

Contact: Jon Bohaty, Director of Marketing
Gallup Organization/Cornhusker State Games
PO Box 29366
4903 North 57th Street
Lincoln, NE 68529
Phone: 402-471-2544
Fax: 402-471-9712
E-mail: jbohaty@nebraskasportscouncil.com

GENERAL FEDERATION OF WOMEN'S CLUBS OF MASSACHUSETTS   http://www.gfwcma.org/

GENERAL FEDERATION OF WOMEN'S CLUBS OF MASSACHUSETTS STUDY ABROAD SCHOLARSHIP

Scholarship for undergraduate or graduate study abroad. Applicant must submit personal statement and letter of endorsement from the president of the sponsoring General Federation of Women's Clubs of Massachusetts. Must be resident of Massachusetts.

Award: Scholarship for use in freshman, sophomore, junior, senior, or graduate years; not renewable. *Number:* 1. *Amount:* $800.

Eligibility Requirements: Applicant must be enrolled or expecting to enroll full-time at a two-year or four-year institution or university and resident of Massachusetts. Available to U.S. citizens.

Application Requirements: Application, essay, interview, references, self-addressed stamped envelope, transcript. *Deadline:* March 1.

Contact: Jane Howard, Scholarship Chairperson
General Federation of Women's Clubs of Massachusetts
PO Box 679
Sudbury, MA 01776-0679
Phone: 978-444-9105

GENERAL FEDERATION OF WOMEN'S CLUBS OF VERMONT

BARBARA JEAN BARKER MEMORIAL SCHOLARSHIP FOR A DISPLACED HOMEMAKER

A non-traditional scholarship designed for a woman who has been primarily a homemaker for fourteen to twenty years and has lost her main means of support through divorce, separation or death of a spouse, and needs retraining for re-entry to the world of work. Must be a Vermont resident.

Award: Grant for use in freshman, sophomore, junior, senior, or graduate years; not renewable. *Number:* 1–3. *Amount:* $500–$1500.

Eligibility Requirements: Applicant must be age 35; enrolled or expecting to enroll full or part-time at a two-year or four-year or technical institution or university; female and resident of Vermont. Available to U.S. citizens.

Application Requirements: Application, autobiography, financial need analysis, interview, references. *Deadline:* March 15.

Contact: Joyce Lindamood, State President
General Federation of Women's Clubs of Vermont
PO Box 92
Springfield, VT 05156
Phone: 802-885-4690

GEORGE AND MARY JOSEPHINE HAMMAN FOUNDATION   http://www.hammanfoundation.org/

GEORGE AND MARY JOSEPHINE HAMMAN FOUNDATION SCHOLARSHIP PROGRAM

Scholarship available to high school seniors in the following Texas counties only: Brazoria, Chambers, Ft. Bend, Galveston, Harris, Liberty, Montgomery, and Waller. Please refer to Web site for specific details http://www.hammanfoundation.org/

Award: Scholarship for use in freshman, sophomore, junior, or senior years; not renewable. *Number:* 60. *Amount:* $12,000.

Eligibility Requirements: Applicant must be high school student; planning to enroll or expecting to enroll full-time at a four-year institution or university and resident of Texas. Available to U.S. and non-U.S. citizens.

Application Requirements: Application, financial need analysis, interview, photo, test scores, transcript. *Deadline:* February 28.

Contact: George and Mary Josephine Hamman Foundation
George and Mary Josephine Hamman Foundation
3336 Richmond, Suite 310
Houston, TX 77098

GEORGIA STUDENT FINANCE COMMISSION   http://www.gsfc.org

GEORGIA LEVERAGING EDUCATIONAL ASSISTANCE PARTNERSHIP GRANT PROGRAM

Based on financial need. Recipients must be eligible for the Federal Pell Grant. Renewable award for Georgia residents enrolled in a state postsecondary institution. Must be U.S. citizen.

Award: Grant for use in freshman, sophomore, junior, or senior years; renewable. *Number:* 3000–3500. *Amount:* up to $2000.

Eligibility Requirements: Applicant must be enrolled or expecting to enroll full or part-time at a two-year or four-year or technical institution or university; resident of Georgia and studying in Georgia. Available to U.S. citizens.

Application Requirements: Application, financial need analysis. *Deadline:* Continuous.

Contact: William Flook, Director of Scholarships and Grants
Georgia Student Finance Commission
2082 East Exchange Place, Suite 100
Tucker, GA 30084
Phone: 770-724-9052
Fax: 770-724-9031
E-mail: billf@gsfc.org

GEORGIA PUBLIC SAFETY MEMORIAL GRANT/LAW ENFORCEMENT PERSONNEL DEPARTMENT GRANT
• See page 542

GEORGIA TUITION EQUALIZATION GRANT (GTEG)

Award for Georgia residents pursuing undergraduate study at an accredited two- or four-year Georgia private institution. Complete the Georgia Student Grant Application. Available to residents of Georgia who live near the State borders to attend certain four-year public colleges out-of-state, so that a four-year public college. Award is $909 per academic year

Award: Grant for use in freshman, sophomore, junior, or senior years; renewable.

Eligibility Requirements: Applicant must be enrolled or expecting to enroll full-time at a two-year or four-year institution or university;

Georgia Student Finance Commission (continued)

resident of Georgia and studying in Alabama, Florida, Georgia, or Tennessee. Available to U.S. citizens.

Application Requirements: Application, Social Security number. *Deadline:* Continuous.

Contact: William Flook, Grants Director
Georgia Student Finance Commission
2082 East Exchange Place, Suite 100
Tucker, GA 30084
Phone: 770-724-9052
Fax: 770-724-9031
E-mail: billf@gsfc.org

GOVERNOR'S SCHOLARSHIP-GEORGIA

Award to assist students selected as Georgia scholars, STAR students, valedictorians, and salutatorians. For use at two- and four-year colleges and universities in Georgia. Recipients are selected as entering freshmen. Renewable award of up to $1000. Minimum 3.0 GPA required.

Award: Scholarship for use in freshman, sophomore, junior, or senior years; renewable. *Number:* 900–3000. *Amount:* up to $1000.

Eligibility Requirements: Applicant must be high school student; planning to enroll or expecting to enroll full-time at a two-year or four-year institution or university; resident of Georgia and studying in Georgia. Applicant must have 3.0 GPA or higher. Available to U.S. citizens.

Application Requirements: Application, transcript. *Deadline:* Continuous.

Contact: William Flook, Director of Scholarships and Grants Division
Georgia Student Finance Commission
2082 East Exchange Place, Suite 100
Tucker, GA 30084
Phone: 770-724-9052
Fax: 770-724-9031
E-mail: billf@gsfc.org

HOPE—HELPING OUTSTANDING PUPILS EDUCATIONALLY

Grant program for Georgia residents who are college undergraduates to attend an accredited two or four-year Georgia institution. Tuition and fees may be covered by the grant. Minimum 3.0 GPA required. Renewable if student maintains grades and reapplies. Write for deadlines.

Award: Scholarship for use in freshman, sophomore, junior, or senior years; renewable. *Number:* 140,000–170,000. *Amount:* $300–$3900.

Eligibility Requirements: Applicant must be enrolled or expecting to enroll full or part-time at a two-year or four-year institution or university; resident of Georgia and studying in Georgia. Applicant must have 3.0 GPA or higher. Available to U.S. citizens.

Application Requirements: Application. *Deadline:* Continuous.

Contact: William Flook, Director of Scholarships and Grants Division
Georgia Student Finance Commission
2082 East Exchange Place, Suite 100
Tucker, GA 30084
Phone: 770-724-9052
Fax: 770-724-9031
E-mail: billf@gsfc.org

GRAND LODGE OF IOWA, AF AND AM
http://www.gl-iowa.org

GRAND LODGE OF IOWA MASONIC SCHOLARSHIP PROGRAM

Scholarships are awarded based on scholastics, school and community activity, and leadership. Applicants are selected to be interviewed based on their written application. Recipients are selected based on those interviews. Application deadline is February 1.

Award: Scholarship for use in freshman year; not renewable. *Number:* 60–70. *Amount:* up to $2000.

Eligibility Requirements: Applicant must be high school student; planning to enroll or expecting to enroll full-time at a two-year or four-year or technical institution or university and resident of Iowa. Available to U.S. and non-U.S. citizens.

Application Requirements: Application, autobiography, interview, references, transcript. *Deadline:* February 1.

Contact: Scholarship Selection Committee
Grand Lodge of Iowa, AF and AM
PO Box 279
Cedar Rapids, IA 52406-0279
Phone: 319-365-1438
Fax: 319-365-1439
E-mail: scholarships@gl-iowa.org

GRAND RAPIDS COMMUNITY FOUNDATION
http://www.grfoundation.org

GERALD M. CRANE MEMORIAL MUSIC SCHOLARSHIP FUND

For high school students (9th-12th grade) who are residents of Kent or Ottawa counties in Michigan to further pursue their musical endeavors. This may include, but is not limited to formal music training, seminars, workshops, music lessons, music concerts, musical instruments, music books, or summer enrichment programs. Refer to Web site for details and application: http://www.grfoundation.org

Award: Scholarship for use in freshman year. *Number:* varies. *Amount:* $250–$1000.

Eligibility Requirements: Applicant must be high school student; planning to enroll or expecting to enroll at a two-year or four-year institution or university; resident of Michigan and must have an interest in music. Available to U.S. citizens.

Application Requirements: Application, essay, interview, references. *Deadline:* April 1.

Contact: See Web site.

GRAND RAPIDS COMBINED THEATRE SCHOLARSHIP

For students with experience in any Grand Rapids area community theatre venue to pursue study in theatre arts. For more details and an application refer to Web site: http://www.grfoundation.org

Award: Scholarship for use in freshman, sophomore, junior, or senior years; not renewable. *Number:* varies. *Amount:* $1000–$3000.

Eligibility Requirements: Applicant must be enrolled or expecting to enroll full-time at a four-year institution or university and resident of Michigan. Available to U.S. citizens.

Application Requirements: Application, essay, financial need analysis, references. *Deadline:* April 1.

Contact: See Web site.

GRANGE INSURANCE ASSOCIATION
http://www.grange.com

GRANGE INSURANCE GROUP SCHOLARSHIP

One-time award for Grange Insurance Association policyholders and their children or grandchildren. Must be a U.S. citizen. See Web site at http://www.grange.com for further details. Application deadline is April 15.

Award: Scholarship for use in freshman, sophomore, junior, senior, graduate, or postgraduate years; not renewable. *Number:* 25–28. *Amount:* $750–$1000.

Eligibility Requirements: Applicant must be enrolled or expecting to enroll full or part-time at a two-year or four-year or technical institution or university and resident of California, Colorado, Idaho, Montana, Oregon, Washington, or Wyoming. Available to U.S. citizens.

Application Requirements: Application, autobiography, essay, financial need analysis, references, transcript. *Deadline:* April 15.

Contact: Application available at Web site.

GRAYSON RURAL ELECTRIC COOPERATIVE CORPORATION (RECC)
http://www.graysonrecc.com

GRAYSON RURAL ELECTRIC COOPERATIVE CORPORATION SCHOLARSHIP

Scholarships available to Kentucky high school graduating seniors who are planning to enroll full-time in a 2- or 4-year college, university, or trade/technical institution. Must reside in Grayson RECC service area, or primary residence of parent/guardian must be in Grayson RECC service area.

Scholarship funds will be paid to institution. Must submit 200-word personal narrative. Application and information on Web site: http://www.graysonrecc.coop.

Award: Scholarship for use in freshman year; not renewable. *Number:* 7. *Amount:* $1000.

Eligibility Requirements: Applicant must be high school student; planning to enroll or expecting to enroll full-time at a two-year or four-year or technical institution or university and resident of Kentucky. Available to U.S. citizens.

Application Requirements: Application, essay, test scores, transcript. *Deadline:* April 15.

Contact: Julie Lewis, Communications Specialist
Grayson Rural Electric Cooperative Corporation (RECC)
109 Bagby Park
Grayson, KY 41143
Phone: 606-475-2191
Fax: 606-474-5862
E-mail: julie.lewis@graysonrecc.coop

GREAT LAKES HEMOPHILIA FOUNDATION
http://www.glhf.org/scholar.htm

EDUCATION AND TRAINING ASSISTANCE PROGRAM
• *See page 558*

GREATER BRIDGEPORT AREA FOUNDATION
http://www.gbafoundation.org

GREATER BRIDGEPORT AREA FOUNDATION'S SCHOLARSHIP AWARD PROGRAM

The Greater Bridgeport Area Foundation Scholarship Award program primarily supports high school seniors entering their freshman year in college. Scholarships average $1100 for one year. Awards given to students from towns in GBAF service area: Bridgeport, Easton, Fairfield, Milford, Monroe, Shelton, Stratford, Trumbull, and Westport with minimum GPA of 2.7

Award: Scholarship for use in freshman year; not renewable. *Number:* 100–150. *Amount:* $1100.

Eligibility Requirements: Applicant must be enrolled or expecting to enroll full-time at a four-year institution or university and resident of Connecticut. Available to U.S. citizens.

Application Requirements: Application, essay, references, transcript. *Deadline:* varies.

Contact: Bernadette Deamico, Education Associate
Greater Bridgeport Area Foundation
211 State Street, 3rd Floor
Bridgeport, CT 06604
Phone: 203-334-7511
Fax: 203-333-4652
E-mail: bdeamico@gbafoundation.org

GREATER KANAWHA VALLEY FOUNDATION
http://www.tgkvf.org

KID'S CHANCE OF WEST VIRGINIA SCHOLARSHIP

Awarded to children (between the ages of 16-25) of a parent(s) injured in a WV work-related accident. Preference shall be given to students with financial need, academic performance, leadership abilities, demonstrated and potential contributions to school and community who are pursuing any field of study in any accredited trade, vocational school, college, or university. May apply for two Foundation scholarships but will only be chosen for one.

Award: Scholarship for use in freshman, sophomore, junior, or senior years; renewable. *Number:* up to 13. *Amount:* $1000.

Eligibility Requirements: Applicant must be age 16-25; enrolled or expecting to enroll full-time at a two-year or four-year or technical institution; resident of West Virginia and must have an interest in leadership. Applicant must have 2.5 GPA or higher. Available to U.S. citizens.

Application Requirements: Application, essay, financial need analysis, references, transcript, IRS 1040 form, worker's compensation number. *Deadline:* February 15.

Contact: Susan Hoover, Scholarship Coordinator
Greater Kanawha Valley Foundation
PO Box 3041
Charleston, WV 25331
Phone: 304-346-3620
Fax: 304-346-3640

NORMAN S. AND BETTY M. FITZHUGH FUND

Awarded to students who demonstrate academic excellence and financial need to attend any accredited college or university. Scholarships are awarded for one or more years. May apply for two Foundation scholarships but will only be chosen for one. Must be a resident of West Virginia.

Award: Scholarship for use in freshman, sophomore, junior, or senior years; renewable. *Number:* 1. *Amount:* $500.

Eligibility Requirements: Applicant must be enrolled or expecting to enroll full-time at a four-year institution or university and resident of West Virginia. Applicant must have 2.5 GPA or higher. Available to U.S. citizens.

Application Requirements: Application, essay, financial need analysis, references, transcript, IRS 1040 form. *Deadline:* February 15.

Contact: Susan Hoover, Scholarship Coordinator
Greater Kanawha Valley Foundation
PO Box 3041
Charleston, WV 25331
Phone: 304-346-3620
Fax: 304-346-3640

R. RAY SINGLETON FUND

Renewable award based on academic excellence and financial need. May apply for two Foundation scholarships, but will be chosen only for one. Must be a resident of West Virginia and attend a school in West Virginia. Be a resident in one of the following counties: Kanawha, Boone, Clay, Putnam, Lincoln or Fayette Counties.

Award: Grant for use in freshman, sophomore, junior, senior, or graduate years; renewable. *Number:* 5. *Amount:* $1000.

Eligibility Requirements: Applicant must be enrolled or expecting to enroll full-time at a four-year institution or university; resident of West Virginia and studying in West Virginia. Applicant must have 2.5 GPA or higher. Available to U.S. citizens.

Application Requirements: Application, essay, financial need analysis, references, self-addressed stamped envelope, test scores, transcript. *Deadline:* February 15.

Contact: Susan Hoover, Scholarship Coordinator
Greater Kanawha Valley Foundation
PO Box 3041
Charleston, WV 25331
Phone: 304-346-3620
Fax: 304-346-3640
E-mail: shoover@tgkvf.org

RUTH ANN JOHNSON SCHOLARSHIP

Awarded to students who demonstrate academic excellence and financial need to attend any accredited college or university in any state or county. Scholarships are awarded for one or more years. May apply for two Foundation scholarships but will only be chosen for one. Must be a resident of West Virginia.

Award: Scholarship for use in freshman, sophomore, junior, or senior years; renewable. *Number:* up to 50. *Amount:* $1000.

Eligibility Requirements: Applicant must be enrolled or expecting to enroll full-time at a four-year institution or university and resident of West Virginia. Applicant must have 2.5 GPA or higher. Available to U.S. citizens.

Application Requirements: Application, essay, financial need analysis, references, transcript, IRS 1040 form. *Deadline:* February 15.

Contact: Susan Hoover, Scholarship Coordinator
Greater Kanawha Valley Foundation
PO Box 3041
Charleston, WV 25331
Phone: 304-346-3620
Fax: 304-346-3640

Greater Kanawha Valley Foundation (continued)

SCPA SCHOLARSHIP FUND
• See page 542

W. P. BLACK SCHOLARSHIP FUND

Renewable award for West Virginia residents who demonstrate academic excellence and financial need and who are enrolled in an undergraduate program in any accredited college or university. May apply for two Foundation scholarships but will only be chosen for one.

Award: Scholarship for use in freshman, sophomore, junior, or senior years; renewable. *Number:* 98–106. *Amount:* $1000.

Eligibility Requirements: Applicant must be enrolled or expecting to enroll at a two-year or four-year institution or university and resident of West Virginia. Applicant must have 2.5 GPA or higher. Available to U.S. citizens.

Application Requirements: Application, essay, financial need analysis, references, self-addressed stamped envelope, test scores, transcript. *Deadline:* February 15.

Contact: Susan Hoover, Scholarship Coordinator
Greater Kanawha Valley Foundation
PO Box 3041
Charleston, WV 25331
Phone: 304-346-3620
Fax: 304-346-3640

WEST VIRGINIA GOLF ASSOCIATION FUND
• See page 542

WESTMORELAND COAL COMPANY FUND FOR MEDICAL STUDENTS

Applicant must be studying medicine at an accredited medical college. Preference is given to residents of Boone County. Scholarships are awarded and conditional on a promise that the recipient will practice medicine in Boone County, West Virginia. Contact the Greater Kanawha Valley Foundation for application, or download from Web site: http://www.tgkvf.org

Award: Scholarship for use in freshman, sophomore, junior, senior, or graduate years; renewable. *Number:* up to 2. *Amount:* up to $5000.

Eligibility Requirements: Applicant must be enrolled or expecting to enroll full-time at an institution or university and resident of West Virginia. Applicant must have 2.5 GPA or higher. Available to U.S. citizens.

Application Requirements: Application, essay, references, test scores, transcript, activities form, IRS 1040 form. *Deadline:* February 15.

Contact: Susan Hoover, Scholarship Coordinator
Greater Kanawha Valley Foundation
PO Box 3041
Charleston, WV 25331
Phone: 304-346-3620
Fax: 304-346-3640
E-mail: shoover@tgkvf.org

GREATER LAFAYETTE COMMUNITY FOUNDATION http://www.glcfonline.org

LILLY ENDOWMENT COMMUNITY SCHOLARSHIP, TIPPECANOE COUNTY

Scholarship is for four years of full tuition and fees at the accredited Indiana college or university of the recipient's choice, plus $800 per year for required books and equipment. Must be a resident of Tippecanoe County, Indiana. Minimum 2.75 GPA required. Visit the Web site: http://www.glcfonline.org for more information.

Award: Scholarship for use in sophomore, junior, or senior years; not renewable. *Number:* 6. *Amount:* $6250–$25,000.

Eligibility Requirements: Applicant must be enrolled or expecting to enroll full-time at a four-year institution or university; resident of Indiana and studying in Indiana. Available to U.S. citizens.

Application Requirements: Application, essay, financial need analysis, interview, references, test scores, transcript. *Deadline:* January 27.

Contact: Carol Crochet, Program Director
Greater Lafayette Community Foundation
1114 State Street
PO Box 225
Lafayette, IN 47902-0225
Phone: 765-742-9078 Ext. 225
Fax: 765-742-2428
E-mail: carol@glcfonline.org

GREATER WASHINGTON URBAN LEAGUE http://gwulparentcenter.org/rtc

ANHEUSER-BUSCH URBAN SCHOLARSHIP

Renewable award to graduating high school students who reside in the service area of the League. Applicants must complete an essay on a subject selected by the sponsors and must have completed 90% of their school district's community service requirement. Must have GPA of 3.0 or better.

Award: Scholarship for use in freshman year; renewable. *Number:* 4. *Amount:* $2500.

Eligibility Requirements: Applicant must be high school student; planning to enroll or expecting to enroll at an institution or university and resident of District of Columbia. Applicant must have 3.0 GPA or higher. Available to U.S. citizens.

Application Requirements: Application, essay. *Deadline:* February 15.

Contact: Audrey Epperson, Director of Education
Greater Washington Urban League
2901 14th Street, NW
Washington, DC 20009
Phone: 202-265-8200
Fax: 202-387-7019
E-mail: epperson@gwulpartencenter.org

SAFEWAY/GREATER WASHINGTON URBAN LEAGUE SCHOLARSHIP

Award to graduating high school students who reside in the service area of the League. Applicants must complete an essay on a subject selected by the sponsors and must have completed 90% of their school district's community service requirement. Must have GPA of 3.0 or better.

Award: Scholarship for use in freshman year. *Number:* 6. *Amount:* $3000.

Eligibility Requirements: Applicant must be high school student; planning to enroll or expecting to enroll at an institution or university and resident of District of Columbia. Applicant must have 3.0 GPA or higher. Available to U.S. citizens.

Application Requirements: Application, essay. *Deadline:* February 15.

Contact: Audrey Epperson, Director of Education
Greater Washington Urban League
2901 14th Street, NW
Washington, DC 20009
Phone: 202-265-8200
Fax: 202-387-7019
E-mail: epperson@gwulpartencenter.org

GREEK WOMEN'S UNIVERSITY CLUB

GREEK WOMEN'S UNIVERSITY CLUB SCHOLARSHIPS
• See page 614

HAWAII COMMUNITY FOUNDATION http://www.hawaiicommunityfoundation.org

HAWAII COMMUNITY FOUNDATION SCHOLARSHIPS

The Hawaii Community Foundation offers postsecondary scholarships to residents of the state of Hawaii. The average amount is $1400. Please visit our Web site at http://www.communityfoundation.org for more information.

Award: Scholarship for use in freshman, sophomore, junior, or senior years. *Number:* 2200. *Amount:* $1400.

Eligibility Requirements: Applicant must be enrolled or expecting to enroll full-time at a two-year or four-year or technical institution or university and resident of Hawaii. Applicant must have 2.5 GPA or higher. Available to U.S. citizens.

Application Requirements: Application, financial need analysis. *Deadline:* March 1.

Contact: Kalei Stern, Scholarship Officer
Hawaii Community Foundation
1164 Bishop Street Suite 800
Honolulu, HI 96813
Phone: 808-566-5505
E-mail: scholarships@hcf-hawaii.org

HAWAII EDUCATION ASSOCIATION
http://www.heaed.com/

HAWAII EDUCATION ASSOCIATION HIGH SCHOOL STUDENT SCHOLARSHIP
• See page 500

HAWAII HOTEL AND LODGING ASSOCIATION
http://www.hawaiihotels.org

CLEM JUDD, JR., MEMORIAL SCHOLARSHIP

Scholarship for a Hawaii resident who must be able to prove Hawaiian ancestry. Applicant must be enrolled full-time at a U.S. accredited university/college majoring in hotel management. Applicant must have a minimum 3.0 GPA.

Award: Scholarship for use in freshman, sophomore, junior, or senior years. *Amount:* $1000–$2500.

Eligibility Requirements: Applicant must be enrolled or expecting to enroll full-time at a four-year institution and resident of Hawaii. Applicant must have 3.0 GPA or higher. Available to U.S. citizens.

Application Requirements: Application. *Deadline:* July 1.

Contact: HHLA
Hawaii Hotel and Lodging Association
2250 Kalakaua Avenue, Suite 404-4
Honolulu, HI 96815
Phone: 808-923-0407
Fax: 808-924-3843
E-mail: hhla@hawaiihotels.org

HAWAII STATE POSTSECONDARY EDUCATION COMMISSION

HAWAII STATE STUDENT INCENTIVE GRANT

Grants are given to residents of Hawaii who are enrolled in a participating Hawaiian state school. Funds are for undergraduate tuition only. Applicants must submit a financial need analysis.

Award: Grant for use in freshman, sophomore, junior, or senior years; renewable. *Number:* up to 470. *Amount:* $200–$2000.

Eligibility Requirements: Applicant must be enrolled or expecting to enroll full or part-time at a two-year or four-year or technical institution or university; resident of Hawaii and studying in Hawaii. Available to U.S. citizens.

Application Requirements: Financial need analysis. *Deadline:* Continuous.

Contact: Janine Oyama, Financial Aid Specialist
Hawaii State Postsecondary Education Commission
University of Hawaii
Honolulu, HI 96822
Phone: 808-956-6066

HELLENIC UNIVERSITY CLUB OF PHILADELPHIA
http://www.hucphila.org

ANDREW G. CHRESSANTHIS MEMORIAL SCHOLARSHIP
• See page 615

THE CHRISTOPHER DEMETRIS SCHOLARSHIP
• See page 615

THE DORIZAS MEMORIAL SCHOLARSHIP
• See page 615

THE DR. NICHOLAS PADIS MEMORIAL GRADUATE SCHOLARSHIP
• See page 615

THE FOUNDERS SCHOLARSHIP
• See page 615

THE JAMES COSMOS MEMORIAL SCHOLARSHIP
• See page 615

THE PAIDEIA SCHOLARSHIP
• See page 616

HERBERT HOOVER PRESIDENTIAL LIBRARY ASSOCIATION
http://www.hooverassociation.org

HERBERT HOOVER UNCOMMON STUDENT AWARD

Only juniors in an Iowa high school or home school program may apply. Grades and test scores are not evaluated. Applicants are chosen on the basis of project proposals they submit. Those chosen complete their project and make a presentation. All receive $750. Three are chosen for $5000 award.

Award: Scholarship for use in freshman or sophomore years; not renewable. *Number:* 15. *Amount:* $750–$5000.

Eligibility Requirements: Applicant must be high school student; planning to enroll or expecting to enroll full-time at a two-year or four-year institution; resident of Iowa and studying in Iowa. Available to U.S. citizens.

Application Requirements: Application, references, project proposal. *Deadline:* March 31.

Contact: Patricia Hand, Manager of Academic Programs
Herbert Hoover Presidential Library Association
302 Parkside Drive, PO Box 696
West Branch, IA 52358
Phone: 800-828-0475
Fax: 319-643-2391
E-mail: scholarship@hooverassociation.org

HERMAN OSCAR SCHUMACHER SCHOLARSHIP FUND

HERMAN OSCAR SCHUMACHER SCHOLARSHIP FUND FOR MEN
• See page 650

HERSCHEL C. PRICE EDUCATIONAL FOUNDATION

HERSCHEL C. PRICE EDUCATIONAL FOUNDATION SCHOLARSHIPS

Open to undergraduates, graduates, and high school seniors. Must be a U.S. citizen, and either a resident of West Virginia, or attend a West Virginia college. Based on academic achievement and financial need. Deadlines are April 1 for Fall and October 1 for Spring. Undergraduates are shown preference.

Award: Scholarship for use in freshman, sophomore, junior, senior, or graduate years; not renewable. *Number:* 200–300. *Amount:* $500–$5000.

Eligibility Requirements: Applicant must be enrolled or expecting to enroll full or part-time at a two-year or four-year institution or university and resident of West Virginia. Available to U.S. citizens.

Application Requirements: Application, financial need analysis, interview, test scores, transcript. *Deadline:* varies.

Contact: Jonna Hughes, Trustee/Director
Herschel C. Price Educational Foundation
PO Box 412
Huntington, WV 25708-0412
Phone: 304-529-3852

HISPANIC METROPOLITAN CHAMBER SCHOLARSHIPS
http://www.hmccoregon.com/

HISPANIC METROPOLITAN CHAMBER SCHOLARSHIPS
• See page 617

HISPANIC PUBLIC RELATIONS ASSOCIATION
http://www.hpra-usa.org

SCHOLARSHIP PROGRAM FOR HISPANIC STUDENT
• See page 617

HISPANIC SCHOLARSHIP FUND
http://www.hsf.net

HSF/TOYOTA FOUNDATION SCHOLARSHIP PROGRAM-PUERTO RICO
• See page 618

HOUSTON COMMUNITY SERVICES
http://houston-com-services.tripod.com

AZTECA SCHOLARSHIP
• See page 619

HUMANE SOCIETY OF THE UNITED STATES
http://www.hsus.org

SHAW-WORTH MEMORIAL SCHOLARSHIP

Scholarship for a New England high school senior who has made a meaningful contribution to animal protection over a significant amount of time. A passive liking of animals or the desire to enter an animal care field does not justify the award. Application deadline: March 15.

Award: Scholarship for use in freshman year; not renewable. *Number:* 1. *Amount:* $1500.

Eligibility Requirements: Applicant must be high school student; planning to enroll or expecting to enroll full-time at a two-year or four-year or technical institution or university and resident of Connecticut, Maine, Massachusetts, New Hampshire, Rhode Island, or Vermont. Available to U.S. citizens.

Application Requirements: Essay, references. *Deadline:* March 15.

Contact: Hillary Twining, Program Coordinator
Humane Society of the United States
PO Box 619
Jacksonville, VT 05342-0619
Phone: 802-368-2790
Fax: 802-368-2756
E-mail: htwining@hsus.org

IDAHO STATE BOARD OF EDUCATION
http://www.boardofed.idaho.gov

FREEDOM SCHOLARSHIP
• See page 588

IDAHO GOVERNOR'S CHALLENGE SCHOLARSHIP

Renewable scholarship available to Idaho residents enrolled full-time in an undergraduate academic or vocational-technical program at an eligible Idaho public or private college or university. Minimum GPA: 2.8. Merit-based award. Must be a high school senior and U.S. citizen to apply. Number of awards is conditional on the availability of funds. Must have a demonstrated commitment to public service.

Award: Scholarship for use in freshman, sophomore, junior, or senior years; renewable. *Number:* 10–25. *Amount:* $3000.

Eligibility Requirements: Applicant must be high school student; planning to enroll or expecting to enroll full-time at a two-year or four-year or technical institution or university; resident of Idaho and studying in Idaho. Available to U.S. citizens.

Application Requirements: Application, essay, portfolio, references, test scores, transcript. *Deadline:* January 15.

Contact: Lynn Humphrey, Manager, Student Aid Programs
Idaho State Board of Education
PO Box 83720
Boise, ID 83720-0037
Phone: 208-334-2270
Fax: 208-334-2632
E-mail: lhumphre@osbe.state.id.us

IDAHO MINORITY AND "AT RISK" STUDENT SCHOLARSHIP
• See page 559

IDAHO PROMISE CATEGORY A SCHOLARSHIP PROGRAM

Renewable award available to Idaho residents who are graduating high school seniors. Must attend an approved Idaho institute of higher education full-time. Based on class rank (must be verified by school official), GPA, and ACT scores. Professional-technical student applicants must take COMPASS.

Award: Scholarship for use in freshman, sophomore, junior, or senior years; renewable. *Number:* 25–30. *Amount:* $3000.

Eligibility Requirements: Applicant must be high school student; planning to enroll or expecting to enroll full-time at a two-year or four-year or technical institution or university; resident of Idaho and studying in Idaho. Applicant must have 3.5 GPA or higher. Available to U.S. citizens.

Application Requirements: Application, test scores. *Deadline:* December 15.

Contact: Lynn Humphrey, Manager, Student Aid Programs
Idaho State Board of Education
PO Box 83720
Boise, ID 83720-0037
Phone: 208-334-2270
Fax: 208-334-2632
E-mail: lhumphre@osbe.state.id.us

IDAHO PROMISE CATEGORY B SCHOLARSHIP PROGRAM

Available to Idaho residents entering college for the first time prior to the age of 22. Must have completed high school or its equivalent in Idaho and have a minimum GPA of 3.0 or an ACT score of 20 or higher. Scholarship limited to two years or 4 semesters.

Award: Scholarship for use in freshman or sophomore years; renewable. *Number:* varies. *Amount:* $500.

Eligibility Requirements: Applicant must be age 21 or under; enrolled or expecting to enroll full-time at a two-year or four-year or technical institution or university; resident of Idaho and studying in Idaho. Applicant must have 3.0 GPA or higher. Available to U.S. citizens.

Application Requirements: Application, transcript. *Deadline:* Continuous.

Contact: Lynn Humphrey, Manager, Student Aid Programs
Idaho State Board of Education
PO Box 83720
Boise, ID 83720-0037
Phone: 208-334-2270
Fax: 208-334-2632

LEVERAGING EDUCATIONAL ASSISTANCE STATE PARTNERSHIP PROGRAM (LEAP)

One-time award assists students attending participating Idaho trade schools, colleges, and universities majoring in any field except theology or divinity. Must be U.S. citizen or permanent resident, and show financial need. Application deadlines vary by institution.

Award: Grant for use in freshman, sophomore, junior, senior, or graduate years; not renewable. *Number:* varies. *Amount:* $400–$5000.

Eligibility Requirements: Applicant must be enrolled or expecting to enroll full or part-time at a two-year or four-year or technical institution or university; resident of Idaho and studying in Idaho. Available to U.S. citizens.

Application Requirements: Application, financial need analysis, self-addressed stamped envelope. *Deadline:* varies.

Contact: Lynn Humphrey, Manager, Student Aid Programs
Idaho State Board of Education
PO Box 83720
Boise, ID 83720-0037
Phone: 208-334-2270
Fax: 208-334-2632

PUBLIC SAFETY OFFICER DEPENDENT SCHOLARSHIP
• See page 543

ROBERT C. BYRD HONORS SCHOLARSHIP-IDAHO

Renewable scholarships available to Idaho residents based on outstanding academic achievement. Students must apply as high school seniors.

Award: Scholarship for use in freshman, sophomore, junior, or senior years; renewable. *Number:* 90. *Amount:* $1500.

Eligibility Requirements: Applicant must be high school student; planning to enroll or expecting to enroll full-time at a two-year or four-year or technical institution or university and resident of Idaho. Applicant must have 3.5 GPA or higher. Available to U.S. citizens.

Application Requirements: Application, references, test scores, transcript. *Deadline:* February 14.

Contact: Lynn Humphrey, Manager, Student Aid Programs
Idaho State Board of Education
PO Box 83720
Boise, ID 83720-0037
Phone: 208-334-2270
Fax: 208-334-2632
E-mail: lhumphre@osbe.state.id.us

ILLINOIS COUNCIL OF THE BLIND
http://www.icbonline.org

FLOYD CARGILL SCHOLARSHIP
• See page 559

ILLINOIS DEPARTMENT OF VETERANS' AFFAIRS
http://www.state.il.us/agency/dva

VETERANS' CHILDREN EDUCATIONAL OPPORTUNITIES
• See page 589

ILLINOIS STUDENT ASSISTANCE COMMISSION (ISAC)
http://www.collegezone.org

GRANT PROGRAM FOR DEPENDENTS OF POLICE, FIRE, OR CORRECTIONAL OFFICERS
• See page 543

HIGHER EDUCATION LICENSE PLATE PROGRAM — HELP

Need-based grants for students at Illinois institutions participating in program whose funds are raised by sale of special license plates commemorating the institutions. Must be Illinois resident. May be eligible to receive the grant for the equivalent of 10 semesters of full-time enrollment.

Award: Grant for use in freshman, sophomore, junior, or senior years; not renewable. *Number:* 175–200. *Amount:* $1000–$2000.

Eligibility Requirements: Applicant must be enrolled or expecting to enroll full or part-time at a two-year or four-year institution or university; resident of Illinois and studying in Illinois. Available to U.S. citizens.

Application Requirements: Financial need analysis, FAFSA. *Deadline:* June 30.

Contact: College Zone Counselor
Illinois Student Assistance Commission (ISAC)
1755 Lake Cook Road
Deerfield, IL 60015-5209
Phone: 800-899-4722
E-mail: collegezone@isac.org

ILLINOIS COLLEGE SAVINGS BOND BONUS INCENTIVE GRANT PROGRAM

Program offers holders of Illinois College Savings Bonds a $20 grant for each year of bond maturity payable upon bond redemption if at least 70% of proceeds are used to attend college in Illinois. May not be used by students attending religious or divinity schools.

Award: Grant for use in freshman, sophomore, junior, senior, graduate, or postgraduate years; not renewable. *Number:* 1200–1400. *Amount:* $40–$440.

Eligibility Requirements: Applicant must be enrolled or expecting to enroll full or part-time at a two-year or four-year or technical institution or university and studying in Illinois. Available to U.S. citizens.

Application Requirements: Application. *Deadline:* May 30.

Contact: College Zone Counselor
Illinois Student Assistance Commission (ISAC)
1755 Lake Cook Road
Deerfield, IL 60015-5209
Phone: 800-899-4722
E-mail: collegezone@isac.org

ILLINOIS GENERAL ASSEMBLY SCHOLARSHIP

Scholarships available for Illinois students enrolled at an Illinois four-year state-supported college. Must contact the General Assembly member from your district for eligibility criteria.

Award: Scholarship for use in freshman, sophomore, junior, or senior years. *Number:* 1. *Amount:* varies.

Eligibility Requirements: Applicant must be enrolled or expecting to enroll at a four-year institution or university; resident of Illinois and studying in Illinois. Available to U.S. citizens.

Application Requirements: Application. *Deadline:* Continuous.

Contact: College Zone Counselor
Illinois Student Assistance Commission (ISAC)
1755 Lake Cook Road
Deerfield, IL 60015-5209
Phone: 800-899-4722
E-mail: collegezone@isac.org

ILLINOIS MONETARY AWARD PROGRAM

Award for eligible students attending Illinois public universities, private colleges and universities, community colleges, and some proprietary institutions. Applicable only to tuition and fees. Based on financial need. Deadline dates are August 15 for renewal and September 30 for new applications.

Award: Grant for use in freshman, sophomore, junior, or senior years; renewable. *Number:* 135,000–145,000. *Amount:* up to $4968.

Eligibility Requirements: Applicant must be enrolled or expecting to enroll full-time at a two-year or four-year or technical institution or university; resident of Illinois and studying in Illinois. Available to U.S. citizens.

Application Requirements: Financial need analysis, FAFSA online. *Deadline:* September 30.

Contact: College Zone Counselor
Illinois Student Assistance Commission (ISAC)
1755 Lake Cook Road
Deerfield, IL 60015-5209
Phone: 800-899-4722
E-mail: collegezone@isac.org

ILLINOIS NATIONAL GUARD GRANT PROGRAM
• See page 570

ILLINOIS STUDENT-TO-STUDENT PROGRAM OF MATCHING GRANTS

Award provides matching funds for need-based grants at participating Illinois public universities and community colleges. Contact financial aid office at the institution in which you are enrolled for eligibility. Deadline dates are October 15, February 15, April 15, and June 15.

Award: Grant for use in freshman, sophomore, junior, or senior years; not renewable. *Number:* 2000–4000. *Amount:* $300–$1000.

Eligibility Requirements: Applicant must be enrolled or expecting to enroll full or part-time at a two-year or four-year institution or university; resident of Illinois and studying in Illinois. Available to U.S. citizens.

Application Requirements: Application, financial need analysis. *Deadline:* Continuous.

Contact: College Zone Counselor
Illinois Student Assistance Commission (ISAC)
1755 Lake Cook Road
Deerfield, IL 60015-5209
Phone: 800-899-4722
E-mail: collegezone@isac.org

ILLINOIS VETERAN GRANT PROGRAM - IVG
• See page 589

MERIT RECOGNITION SCHOLARSHIP (MRS) PROGRAM

Award for Illinois high school seniors graduating in the top 4% of their class and attending Illinois post secondary institution or one of the nation's four approved Military Service Academies. Students scoring in the top 4% in one of the college entrance tests among Illinois residents are also eligible. Contact for application procedures.

Award: Scholarship for use in freshman year; not renewable. *Number:* 5000–6000. *Amount:* up to $1000.

Eligibility Requirements: Applicant must be high school student; planning to enroll or expecting to enroll full or part-time at a two-year or four-year institution or university; resident of Illinois and studying in Illinois. Applicant must have 3.5 GPA or higher. Available to U.S. citizens.

Application Requirements: Application. *Deadline:* August 1.

Illinois Student Assistance Commission (ISAC) (continued)

Contact: College Zone Counselor
Illinois Student Assistance Commission (ISAC)
1755 Lake Cook Road
Deerfield, IL 60015-5209
Phone: 800-899-4722
E-mail: collegezone@isac.org

ROBERT C. BYRD HONORS SCHOLARSHIP-ILLINOIS

Available to Illinois residents who are graduating high school seniors. Based on outstanding academic merit. Awards are renewable up to four years. Must be accepted on a full-time basis as an undergraduate student.

Award: Scholarship for use in freshman, sophomore, junior, or senior years; renewable. *Number:* 1100–1200. *Amount:* up to $1500.

Eligibility Requirements: Applicant must be high school student; planning to enroll or expecting to enroll full-time at a two-year or four-year institution or university and resident of Illinois. Applicant must have 3.5 GPA or higher. Available to U.S. citizens.

Application Requirements: Application, test scores, transcript. *Deadline:* March 1.

Contact: College Zone Counselor
Illinois Student Assistance Commission (ISAC)
1755 Lake Cook Road
Deerfield, IL 60015-5209
Phone: 800-899-4722
E-mail: collegezone@isac.org

SILAS PURNELL ILLINOIS INCENTIVE FOR ACCESS PROGRAM

Award for eligible first-time freshmen enrolling in approved Illinois institutions. One-time grant of up to $500 may be used for any educational expense. Using the FAFSA, applicants are encouraged to apply as quickly as possible after January 1st preceding the academic year.

Award: Grant for use in freshman year; not renewable. *Number:* 19,000–22,000. *Amount:* $500.

Eligibility Requirements: Applicant must be enrolled or expecting to enroll full or part-time at a two-year or four-year or technical institution or university; resident of Illinois and studying in Illinois. Available to U.S. citizens.

Application Requirements: Financial need analysis, FAFSA online. *Deadline:* Continuous.

Contact: College Zone Counselor
Illinois Student Assistance Commission (ISAC)
1755 Lake Cook Road
Deerfield, IL 60015-5209
Phone: 800-899-4722
E-mail: collegezone@isac.org

INDEPENDENT COLLEGES OF WASHINGTON
http://www.ICWashington.org

CORPORATE SPONSORED SCHOLARSHIP PROGRAM

All scholarships restricted to students attending one of ten independent colleges located in Washington State. Colleges include Gonzaga University, Heritage College, Pacific Lutheran University, Saint Martin's College, Seattle Pacific University, Seattle University, University of Puget Sound, Walla Walla College, Whitman College, Whitworth College. For more details see Web site: http://www.icwashington.org.

Award: Scholarship for use in freshman, sophomore, junior, or senior years; not renewable. *Number:* 20–70. *Amount:* $400–$3500.

Eligibility Requirements: Applicant must be enrolled or expecting to enroll full-time at a four-year institution and studying in Washington. Available to U.S. and non-U.S. citizens.

Application Requirements: Application, essay, resume, references, transcript. *Deadline:* April 15.

Contact: Samantha Waoker, Administrative Assistant
Independent Colleges of Washington
600 Stewart Street, Suite 600
Seattle, WA 98101
Phone: 206-623-4494
Fax: 206-625-9621
E-mail: info@ICWashington.org

INDIAN AMERICAN CULTURAL ASSOCIATION
http://www.iasf.org

INDIAN AMERICAN SCHOLARSHIP FUND
• *See page 619*

INDIANA DEPARTMENT OF VETERANS' AFFAIRS
http://www.ai.org/veteran/index.html

CHILD OF DISABLED VETERAN GRANT OR PURPLE HEART RECIPIENT GRANT
• *See page 589*

DEPARTMENT OF VETERANS AFFAIRS FREE TUITION FOR CHILDREN OF POW/MIA'S IN VIETNAM
• *See page 589*

INDIANA FARM BUREAU INSURANCE
http://www.infarmbureau.com

EXCEL AWARDS

All Indiana high school students are eligible to participate in eXceL Awards, including private school and home-schooled students. A first, second and third place winner will be named in each of the six eXceL Awards competition categories. Deadline is January 23-27.

Award: Prize for use in freshman, sophomore, junior, or senior years; not renewable. *Number:* up to 6. *Amount:* $2000–$3000.

Eligibility Requirements: Applicant must be high school student; planning to enroll or expecting to enroll full-time at an institution or university and resident of Indiana. Available to U.S. citizens.

Application Requirements: Application, applicant must enter a contest, presentation on the topic. *Deadline:* January 23.

Contact: Pam Walker, Program Contact
Indiana Farm Bureau Insurance
PO Box 1250
Indianapolis, IN 46202-1250
Phone: 800-723-3276

INTER-COUNTY ENERGY
http://www.intercountyenergy.net

INTER-COUNTY ENERGY SCHOLARSHIP

Scholarship available for Kentucky high school senior who is a child of a resident of the Inter-County Energy service area and an active member of the cooperative. Student must plan to enroll in a postsecondary institution: two- or four-year college, university, or trade/technical institution. Must submit a brief biography. Write or call for application.

Award: Scholarship for use in freshman, sophomore, junior, or senior years; not renewable. *Number:* 6. *Amount:* up to $1000.

Eligibility Requirements: Applicant must be high school student; planning to enroll or expecting to enroll at a two-year or four-year or technical institution or university and resident of Kentucky. Available to U.S. citizens.

Application Requirements: Application, autobiography, financial need analysis, references, transcript. *Deadline:* April 3.

Contact: Hank Smith
Inter-County Energy
1009 Hustonville Road
Danville, KY 40422
Phone: 859-236-4561
E-mail: hank@intercountyenergy.net

INTER-TRIBAL COUNCIL OF MICHIGAN, INC.
http://www.itcmi.org

MICHIGAN INDIAN TUITION WAIVER
• *See page 619*

IOWA COLLEGE STUDENT AID COMMISSION
http://www.iowacollegeaid.org

GOVERNOR TERRY E. BRANSTAD IOWA STATE FAIR SCHOLARSHIP

Up to four scholarships ranging from $500 to $1000 will be awarded to students graduating from an Iowa high school. Must actively participate at the Iowa State Fair. For more details see Web site: http://www.iowacollegeaid.org.

Award: Scholarship for use in freshman year; not renewable. *Number:* up to 4. *Amount:* $500–$1000.

Eligibility Requirements: Applicant must be high school student; planning to enroll or expecting to enroll at an institution or university; resident of Iowa and studying in Iowa. Available to U.S. citizens.

Application Requirements: Application, essay, financial need analysis, references, transcript. *Deadline:* May 1.

Contact: Brenda Easter, Director, Special Programs
Iowa College Student Aid Commission
200 10th Street, 4th Floor
Des Moines, IA 50309-3609
Phone: 515-242-3380
Fax: 515-242-3388

IOWA FOSTER CHILD GRANTS

Grants renewable up to four years will be awarded to students graduating from an Iowa high school who are in Iowa foster care under the care and custody of the Iowa Department of Human Service. Must have a minimum GPA of 2.25 and have applied to an accredited Iowa college or university. For more details see Web site: http://www.iowacollegeaid.org.

Award: Grant for use in freshman year; renewable. *Number:* varies. *Amount:* $2000–$4200.

Eligibility Requirements: Applicant must be high school student; planning to enroll or expecting to enroll at a two-year or four-year institution or university; resident of Iowa and studying in Iowa. Available to U.S. citizens.

Application Requirements: Application. *Deadline:* April 15.

Contact: Brenda Easter, Director, Special Programs
Iowa College Student Aid Commission
200 10th Street, 4th Floor
Des Moines, IA 50309-3609
Phone: 515-242-3380
Fax: 515-242-3388

IOWA GRANTS

Statewide need-based program to assist high-need Iowa residents. Recipients must demonstrate a high level of financial need to receive awards ranging from $100 to $1,000. Awards are prorated for students enrolled for less than full-time. Awards must be used at Iowa postsecondary institutions.

Award: Grant for use in freshman, sophomore, junior, or senior years; not renewable. *Number:* varies. *Amount:* $100–$1000.

Eligibility Requirements: Applicant must be enrolled or expecting to enroll full or part-time at a two-year or four-year or technical institution or university; resident of Iowa and studying in Iowa. Available to U.S. citizens.

Application Requirements: Application, financial need analysis. *Deadline:* Continuous.

Contact: Julie Leeper, Director, State Student Aid Programs
Iowa College Student Aid Commission
200 10th Street, 4th Floor
Des Moines, IA 50309-3609
Phone: 515-242-3370
Fax: 515-242-3388
E-mail: icsac@max.state.ia.us

IOWA NATIONAL GUARD EDUCATION ASSISTANCE PROGRAM
• See page 570

IOWA TUITION GRANT PROGRAM

Program assists students who attend independent postsecondary institutions in Iowa. Iowa residents currently enrolled, or planning to enroll, for at least three semester hours at one of the eligible Iowa postsecondary institutions may apply. Awards currently range from $100 to $4000. Grants may not exceed the difference between independent college and university tuition and fees and the average tuition and fees at the three public Regent universities.

Award: Grant for use in freshman, sophomore, junior, or senior years; not renewable. *Number:* varies. *Amount:* $100–$4000.

Eligibility Requirements: Applicant must be enrolled or expecting to enroll full or part-time at a two-year or four-year institution or university; resident of Iowa and studying in Iowa. Available to U.S. citizens.

Application Requirements: Application, financial need analysis. *Deadline:* July 1.

Contact: Julie Leeper, Director, State Student Aid Programs
Iowa College Student Aid Commission
200 10th Street, 4th Floor
Des Moines, IA 50309-3609
Phone: 515-242-3370
Fax: 515-242-3388
E-mail: icsac@max.state.ia.us

IOWA VOCATIONAL-TECHNICAL TUITION GRANT PROGRAM

Program provides need-based financial assistance to Iowa residents enrolled in career education (vocational-technical), and career option programs at Iowa area community colleges. Grants range from $150 to $650, depending on the length of program, financial need, and available funds.

Award: Grant for use in freshman or sophomore years; not renewable. *Number:* varies. *Amount:* $150–$650.

Eligibility Requirements: Applicant must be enrolled or expecting to enroll full or part-time at a technical institution; resident of Iowa and studying in Iowa. Available to U.S. citizens.

Application Requirements: Application, financial need analysis. *Deadline:* July 1.

Contact: Julie Leeper, Director, State Student Aid Programs
Iowa College Student Aid Commission
200 10th Street, 4th Floor
Des Moines, IA 50309-3609
Phone: 515-242-3370
Fax: 515-242-3388
E-mail: icsac@max.state.ia.us

ROBERT C. BYRD HONORS SCHOLARSHIP-IOWA

Scholarships up to $1500 are awarded to exceptionally able Iowa high school seniors who show promise of continued academic excellence. Must have a minimum of a 28 ACT or 1240 SAT, a 3.5 GPA and rank in the top 10% of the student's high school graduating class. For more details see Web site: http://www.iowacollegeaid.org.

Award: Scholarship for use in freshman year; renewable. *Number:* up to 70. *Amount:* up to $1500.

Eligibility Requirements: Applicant must be high school student; planning to enroll or expecting to enroll at an institution or university and resident of Iowa. Applicant must have 3.5 GPA or higher. Available to U.S. citizens.

Application Requirements: Application, test scores, transcript. *Deadline:* February 1.

Contact: Brenda Easter, Director, Special Programs
Iowa College Student Aid Commission
200 10th Street, 4th Floor
Des Moines, IA 50309-3609
Phone: 515-242-3380
Fax: 515-242-3388

STATE OF IOWA SCHOLARSHIP PROGRAM

Program provides recognition and financial honorarium to Iowa's academically talented high school seniors. Honorary scholarships are presented to all qualified candidates. Approximately 1700 top-ranking candidates are designated State of Iowa Scholars every March, from an applicant pool of nearly 5000 high school seniors. Must be used at an Iowa post secondary institution. Minimum 3.5 GPA required.

Award: Scholarship for use in freshman year; not renewable. *Number:* up to 1700. *Amount:* up to $400.

Eligibility Requirements: Applicant must be high school student; planning to enroll or expecting to enroll full-time at a two-year or four-year or technical institution or university; resident of Iowa and studying in Iowa. Applicant must have 3.5 GPA or higher. Available to U.S. citizens.

Application Requirements: Application, test scores. *Deadline:* November 1.

Contact: Julie Leeper, Director, State Student Aid Programs
Iowa College Student Aid Commission
200 10th Street, 4th Floor
Des Moines, IA 50309-3609
Phone: 515-242-3370
Fax: 515-242-3388
E-mail: icsac@max.state.ia.us

IOWA DIVISION OF VOCATIONAL REHABILITATION SERVICES   http://www.ivrs.iowa.gov

IOWA VOCATIONAL REHABILITATION
• See page 559

ITALIAN CATHOLIC FEDERATION, INC.   http://www.icf.org

ICF COLLEGE SCHOLARSHIPS TO HIGH SCHOOL SENIORS
• See page 620

ITALIAN-AMERICAN CHAMBER OF COMMERCE MIDWEST   http://www.italianchamber.us

ITALIAN-AMERICAN CHAMBER OF COMMERCE OF CHICAGO SCHOLARSHIP
• See page 620

J. CRAIG AND PAGE T. SMITH SCHOLARSHIP FOUNDATION   http://jcraigsmithfoundation.org

FIRST IN FAMILY SCHOLARSHIP

Scholarships available for graduating Alabama high school seniors. Must be planning to enroll in an Alabama institution in fall and pursue a 4-year degree. Students who apply must want to give back to their community by volunteer and civic work. Special consideration will be given to applicants who would be the first in either their mother's or father's family (or both) to attend college.

Award: Scholarship for use in freshman year; renewable. *Number:* 10. *Amount:* $12,500–$15,000.

Eligibility Requirements: Applicant must be high school student; planning to enroll or expecting to enroll full-time at a four-year institution or university; resident of Alabama and studying in Alabama. Applicant must have 2.5 GPA or higher. Available to U.S. citizens.

Application Requirements: Application, essay, financial need analysis, references, test scores, transcript. *Deadline:* January 15.

Contact: Ahrian Tyler, Foundation Administrator
J. Craig and Page T. Smith Scholarship Foundation
505 North 20th Street, Suite 1800
Birmingham, AL 35203
Phone: 205-250-6669
Fax: 205-328-7234
E-mail: scholarships@jcraigsmithfoundation.org

JACKSON ENERGY COOPERATIVE   http://www.jacksonenergy.com

JACKSON ENERGY SCHOLARSHIP

Scholarships awarded to winners in an essay contest. Must be at least a senior in a Kentucky high school and no more than age 21. Parents or legal guardian must be Jackson Energy Cooperative member, but not an employee of Jackson Energy. Essay must be on a subject related to rural electrification and is due by March 1. Call or e-mail for application.

Award: Scholarship for use in freshman, sophomore, junior, or senior years; not renewable. *Number:* 16. *Amount:* $1000.

Eligibility Requirements: Applicant must be age 21 or under; enrolled or expecting to enroll at a two-year or four-year or technical institution or university and resident of Kentucky. Available to U.S. citizens.

Application Requirements: Application, applicant must enter a contest, essay. *Deadline:* March 1.

Contact: Karen Combs, Director of Public Relations
Jackson Energy Cooperative
PO Box 307
McKee, KY 40447
Phone: 800-262-7480
E-mail: jec@prtcnet.org

JACKSON PURCHASE ENERGY CORPORATION   http://www.jpenergy.com

JACKSON PURCHASE ENERGY CORPORATION SCHOLARSHIP

Scholarships available to Kentucky high school seniors residing in Jackson Purchase Energy's service area. Must be enrolled or planning to enroll in a Kentucky two- or four-year college, or university. Must have GPA of 3.0 or higher and a comprehensive score of 18 or better on the ACT. Applications are available from high school guidance counselors or online at http://www.jpenergy.com. Deadline date is noted on application, usually mid-April.

Award: Scholarship for use in freshman year. *Number:* 6. *Amount:* $1000.

Eligibility Requirements: Applicant must be high school student; planning to enroll or expecting to enroll full-time at a two-year or four-year institution or university; resident of Kentucky and studying in Kentucky. Applicant must have 3.0 GPA or higher. Available to U.S. citizens.

Application Requirements: Application, test scores, transcript. *Deadline:* varies.

Contact: Jackson Purchase Energy Corporation
2900 Irvin Cobb Drive
PO Box 4030
Paducah, KY 42002-4030
Phone: 800-633-4044
E-mail: electricity@jpenergy.com

JAMES C. CALDWELL SCHOLARSHIP

JAMES C. CALDWELL ASSISTING MEN AND WOMEN OF TOLEDO SCHOLARSHIP
• See page 620

JAMES F. BYRNES FOUNDATION   http://www.byrnesscholars.org

JAMES F. BYRNES SCHOLARSHIP

Renewable award for residents of South Carolina ages 17-22 with one or both parents deceased. Must show financial need; a satisfactory scholastic record; and qualities of character, ability, and enterprise. Award is for undergraduate study. Results of SAT must be provided. Information available on Web site: http://www.byrnesscholars.org.

Award: Scholarship for use in freshman, sophomore, junior, or senior years; renewable. *Number:* 10–20. *Amount:* up to $2750.

Eligibility Requirements: Applicant must be age 17-22; enrolled or expecting to enroll full-time at a four-year institution and resident of South Carolina. Available to U.S. citizens.

Application Requirements: Application, autobiography, financial need analysis, interview, photo, references, test scores, transcript. *Deadline:* February 15.

Contact: Genny White, Executive Secretary
James F. Byrnes Foundation
PO Box 6781
Columbia, SC 29260-6781
Phone: 803-254-9325
Fax: 803-254-9354
E-mail: info@byrnesscholars.org

JEWISH FAMILY AND CHILDREN'S SERVICES   http://www.jfcs.org

ANNA AND CHARLES STOCKWITZ CHILDREN AND YOUTH FUND
• See page 651

BUTRIMOVITZ FAMILY ENDOWMENT FUND FOR JEWISH EDUCATION
• See page 651

DAVID, NANCY, AND LIZA CHERNEY SCHOLARSHIP FUND
• See page 651

MIRIAM S. GRUNFIELD SCHOLARSHIP FUND
• See page 651

STANLEY OLSON YOUTH SCHOLARSHIP
• See page 651

JEWISH FOUNDATION FOR EDUCATION OF WOMEN   http://www.jfew.org

BILLER/JEWISH FOUNDATION FOR EDUCATION OF WOMEN
• See page 651

JEWISH SOCIAL SERVICE AGENCY OF METROPOLITAN WASHINGTON   http://www.jssa.org

DAVID KORN SCHOLARSHIP FUND
• See page 652

HERBERT F. SACKS MEMORIAL SCHOLARSHIP
• See page 652

HYMAN P. MOLDOVER SCHOLARSHIP
• See page 652

JEWISH SOCIAL SERVICE AGENCY EDUCATIONAL SCHOLARSHIP

One-time award available to full-time undergraduate student. Must be a resident of the Washington Metropolitan area. Must be a U.S. citizen or working towards citizenship.

Award: Scholarship for use in freshman year; not renewable. *Number:* 1. *Amount:* up to $6000.

Eligibility Requirements: Applicant must be high school student; planning to enroll or expecting to enroll full-time at a four-year or technical institution or university and resident of District of Columbia. Available to U.S. citizens.

Application Requirements: Application. *Deadline:* March 10.

Contact: Lynn Ponton, Scholarship and Loan Coordinator
Jewish Social Service Agency of Metropolitan Washington
6123 Montrose Road
Rockville, MD 20852
Phone: 301-881-3700 Ext. 611

JEWISH SOCIAL SERVICE AGENCY OF METROPOLITAN WASHINGTON MAX AND EMMY DREYFUSS UNDERGRADUATE SCHOLARSHIP FUND
• See page 652

MELVIN MANDELL MEMORIAL SCHOLARSHIP
• See page 652

MORTON A. GIBSON MEMORIAL SCHOLARSHIP
• See page 652

JVS JEWISH COMMUNITY SCHOLARSHIP FUND   http://www.jvsla.org

JVS JEWISH COMMUNITY SCHOLARSHIP
• See page 652

KANSAS COMMISSION ON VETERANS AFFAIRS   http://www.kcva.org

KANSAS EDUCATIONAL BENEFITS FOR CHILDREN OF MIA, POW, AND DECEASED VETERANS OF THE VIETNAM WAR
• See page 589

KANSAS NATIONAL GUARD EDUCATIONAL ASSISTANCE PROGRAM

KANSAS NATIONAL GUARD TUITION ASSISTANCE AWARD PROGRAM
• See page 570

KENTUCKY DEPARTMENT OF EDUCATION   http://www.kde.state.ky.us

ROBERT C. BYRD HONORS SCHOLARSHIP–KENTUCKY

Scholarship available to high school seniors who show past high achievement and potential for continued academic success. Must have applied for admission or have been accepted for enrollment at a public or private nonprofit postsecondary school. Must be a Kentucky resident. Deadline for applications is the second Friday in March.

Award: Scholarship for use in freshman, sophomore, junior, or senior years; renewable. *Number:* varies. *Amount:* up to $1500.

Eligibility Requirements: Applicant must be high school student; planning to enroll or expecting to enroll full-time at a two-year or four-year institution or university and resident of Kentucky. Applicant must have 3.5 GPA or higher. Available to U.S. citizens.

Application Requirements: Application, test scores. *Deadline:* varies.

Contact: Donna Melton
Kentucky Department of Education
500 Mero Street, 19th Floor
Frankfort, KY 40601
Phone: 502-564-1479
E-mail: dmelton@kde.state.ky.us

KENTUCKY HIGHER EDUCATION ASSISTANCE AUTHORITY (KHEAA)   http://www.kheaa.com

COLLEGE ACCESS PROGRAM (CAP) GRANT

Award for U.S. citizen and Kentucky resident with no previous college degree. Applicants seeking degrees in religion are not eligible. Applicants seeking degrees in religion are not eligible. Must demonstrate financial need and submit Free Application for Federal Student Aid. Priority deadline is March 15.

Award: Grant for use in freshman, sophomore, junior, or senior years; not renewable. *Number:* 35,000–40,000. *Amount:* up to $1700.

Eligibility Requirements: Applicant must be enrolled or expecting to enroll full or part-time at a two-year or four-year or technical institution or university; resident of Kentucky and studying in Kentucky. Available to U.S. citizens.

Application Requirements: Financial need analysis.

Contact: Michael D. Morgan, Program Coordinator
Kentucky Higher Education Assistance Authority (KHEAA)
PO Box 798
Frankfort, KY 40602-0798
Phone: 502-696-7394
Fax: 502-696-7373
E-mail: mmorgan@kheaa.com

KENTUCKY TUITION GRANT (KTG)

Available to Kentucky residents who are full-time undergraduates at an independent college within the state. Must not be enrolled in a religion program. Based on financial need. Submit Free Application for Federal Student Aid. Priority deadline is March 15.

Award: Grant for use in freshman, sophomore, junior, or senior years; not renewable. *Number:* 10,000–12,000. *Amount:* $200–$2800.

Eligibility Requirements: Applicant must be enrolled or expecting to enroll full-time at a two-year or four-year institution or university; resident of Kentucky and studying in Kentucky. Available to U.S. citizens.

Application Requirements: Application, financial need analysis, FAFSA. *Deadline:* Continuous.

Contact: Tim Phelps, Student Aid Branch Manager
Kentucky Higher Education Assistance Authority (KHEAA)
PO Box 798
Frankfort, KY 40602-0798
Phone: 502-696-7393
Fax: 502-696-7496
E-mail: tphelps@kheaa.com

KENTUCKY NATIONAL GUARD   http://www.kyloui.ang.af.mil

KENTUCKY NATIONAL GUARD TUITION AWARD PROGRAM
• See page 570

KENTUCKY TOUCHSTONE ENERGY COOPERATIVES

TOUCHSTONE ENERGY ALL "A" CLASSIC SCHOLARSHIP

Award of $1000 for senior student in good standing at a Kentucky high school. Applicant must plan to attend a postsecondary institution in Kentucky in the upcoming year as a full-time student and be drug free. Deadline is December 2.

Award: Scholarship for use in freshman year; not renewable. *Number:* 12. *Amount:* $1000.

Eligibility Requirements: Applicant must be high school student; planning to enroll or expecting to enroll full-time at a two-year or four-year institution or university; resident of Kentucky and studying in Kentucky. Available to U.S. citizens.

Kentucky Touchstone Energy Cooperatives (continued)

Application Requirements: Application, essay, photo, references, transcript. *Deadline:* December 2.

Contact: H.D. Cowden, Coordinator
Kentucky Touchstone Energy Cooperatives
Hancock County High School, 80 State Route 271 South
Lewisport, KY 42351
Phone: 859-744-4812

KONIAG EDUCATION FOUNDATION   http://www.koniageducation.org

GLENN GODFREY MEMORIAL SCHOLARSHIP
• *See page 621*

KOREAN AMERICAN SCHOLARSHIP FOUNDATION   http://www.kasf.org

KOREAN-AMERICAN SCHOLARSHIP FOUNDATION EASTERN REGION SCHOLARSHIPS
• *See page 621*

KOREAN-AMERICAN SCHOLARSHIP FOUNDATION NORTHEASTERN REGION SCHOLARSHIPS
• *See page 621*

KOREAN-AMERICAN SCHOLARSHIP FOUNDATION WESTERN REGION SCHOLARSHIPS
• *See page 622*

KOREAN UNIVERSITY CLUB

KOREAN UNIVERSITY CLUB SCHOLARSHIP
• *See page 622*

KOSCIUSZKO FOUNDATION   http://www.kosciuszkofoundation.org

MASSACHUSETTS FEDERATION OF POLISH WOMEN'S CLUBS SCHOLARSHIPS
• *See page 622*

LA KELLEY COMMUNICATIONS   http://www.kelleycom.com

CALVIN DAWSON MEMORIAL SCHOLARSHIP
• *See page 560*

HEMOPHILIA FOUNDATION OF MICHIGAN ACADEMIC SCHOLARSHIP
• *See page 560*

LEE-JACKSON EDUCATIONAL FOUNDATION   http://www.lee-jackson.org

LEE-JACKSON EDUCATIONAL FOUNDATION SCHOLARSHIP COMPETITION

Essay contest for junior and senior Virginia high school students. Must demonstrate appreciation for the exemplary character and soldierly virtues of Generals Robert E. Lee and Thomas J. "Stonewall" Jackson. Three one-time awards of $1000 in each of Virginia's eight regions. A bonus scholarship of $1000 will be awarded to the author of the best essay in each of the eight regions. An additional award of $8000 will go to the essay judged the best in the state.

Award: Scholarship for use in freshman, junior, or senior years; not renewable. *Number:* 27. *Amount:* $1000–$10,000.

Eligibility Requirements: Applicant must be high school student; planning to enroll or expecting to enroll at a four-year institution or university; resident of Virginia and must have an interest in writing. Available to U.S. citizens.

Application Requirements: Application, applicant must enter a contest, essay, transcript. *Deadline:* December 21.

Contact: Stephanie Leech, Administrator
Lee-Jackson Educational Foundation
PO Box 8121
Charlottesville, VA 22906
Phone: 434-977-1861
E-mail: salp_leech@yahoo.com

LIBERTY GRAPHICS, INC.   http://www.lgtees.com

ANNUAL LIBERTY GRAPHICS ART CONTEST

One-time scholarship goes to the successful student who submits the winning design for depicting human powered outdoor activities, not wind or motor powered. Liberty Graphics reserves the right not to award. Applicants must be residents of Maine and be high school student.

Award: Scholarship for use in freshman year; not renewable. *Number:* 1. *Amount:* $1000.

Eligibility Requirements: Applicant must be high school student; planning to enroll or expecting to enroll full or part-time at a two-year or four-year institution or university and resident of Maine. Available to U.S. citizens.

Application Requirements: Application, applicant must enter a contest, self-addressed stamped envelope, artwork in keeping with the contest theme. *Deadline:* May 3.

Contact: Scholarship Coordinator
Liberty Graphics, Inc.
Liberty Graphics, Main Street, PO Box 5
Liberty, ME 04949
Phone: 207-589-4596
Fax: 207-589-4415
E-mail: jay@lgtees.com

LIGHTHOUSE INTERNATIONAL   http://www.lighthouse.org

SCHOLARSHIP AWARDS
• *See page 561*

LINCOLN COMMUNITY FOUNDATION   http://www.lcf.org

ANONYMOUS SCHOLARSHIP BENEFITING GRADUATES OF THAYER COUNTY IN NEBRASKA

Scholarship for graduating seniors from Thayer County high schools in Nebraska; namely Hebron, Deshler, Chester, Bruning, and Davenport. Need not excel academically. Must demonstrate financial need. Scholarship may be renewed for no more than five years for any one recipient.

Award: Scholarship for use in freshman year; renewable. *Number:* 3. *Amount:* $5000.

Eligibility Requirements: Applicant must be high school student; planning to enroll or expecting to enroll full-time at a two-year or four-year or technical institution or university and resident of Nebraska. Available to U.S. citizens.

Application Requirements: Application, financial need analysis, test scores, transcript. *Deadline:* April 30.

Contact: Debra Shoemaker, Director of Program and Distribution
Lincoln Community Foundation
215 Centennial Mall South, Suite 200
Lincoln, NE 68508
Phone: 402-474-2345
Fax: 402-476-8535
E-mail: debs@lcf.org

BRYAN/LGH MEDICAL CENTER WEST AUXILIARY JUNIOR VOLUNTEER SCHOLARSHIP

Scholarship for graduating seniors from high school who have volunteered at least 150 hours at Bryan/LGH Medical Center West in Lincoln, NE.

Award: Scholarship for use in freshman year; not renewable. *Number:* 1. *Amount:* $500–$2000.

Eligibility Requirements: Applicant must be high school student; planning to enroll or expecting to enroll full-time at a two-year or

four-year or technical institution or university and resident of
Nebraska. Applicant must have 2.5 GPA or higher. Available to U.S.
citizens.

Application Requirements: Application, essay, test scores, transcript,
verification of volunteer hours. *Deadline:* April 15.

Contact: Debra Shoemaker, Director of Program and Distribution
Lincoln Community Foundation
215 Centennial Mall South, Suite 200
Lincoln, NE 68508
Phone: 402-474-2345
Fax: 402-476-8532
E-mail: debs@lcf.org

COLLEEN FARRELL GERLEMAN SCHOLARSHIP

Scholarship for current graduating high school seniors from public or private
high schools in the greater Lincoln, Nebraska area or must have received a
Gerleman Scholarship previously. Must attend a two- or four-year college in
Nebraska.

Award: Scholarship for use in freshman, sophomore, junior, or senior
years; not renewable. *Number:* 5–10. *Amount:* $500–$750.

Eligibility Requirements: Applicant must be enrolled or expecting to
enroll full-time at a two-year or four-year or technical institution or
university; resident of Nebraska and studying in Nebraska. Applicant
must have 2.5 GPA or higher. Available to U.S. citizens.

Application Requirements: Application, essay, financial need analysis,
interview, references, test scores, transcript. *Deadline:* April 15.

Contact: Debra Shoemaker, Director of Program and Distribution
Lincoln Community Foundation
215 Centennial Mall South, Suite 200
Lincoln, NE 68508
Phone: 402-474-2345
Fax: 402-476-8532
E-mail: debs@lcf.org

DUNCAN E. AND LILLIAN M. MCGREGOR SCHOLARSHIP

Scholarship for graduating seniors or former graduates of the high schools in
Ansley, Arcadia, Gibbon, Ord, Shelton, or Sargent high schools in Nebraska.
Must have resided in a community served by the Nebraska Central Telephone
Company during his/her high school education.

Award: Scholarship for use in freshman, sophomore, junior, or senior
years; not renewable. *Number:* 80–100. *Amount:* $500–$1000.

Eligibility Requirements: Applicant must be enrolled or expecting to
enroll full-time at a two-year or four-year or technical institution or
university and resident of Nebraska. Applicant must have 2.5 GPA or
higher. Available to U.S. citizens.

Application Requirements: Application, financial need analysis, test
scores, transcript. *Deadline:* April 15.

Contact: Debra Shoemaker, Director of Program and Distribution
Lincoln Community Foundation
215 Centennial Mall South, Suite 200
Lincoln, NE 68508
Phone: 402-474-2345
Fax: 402-476-8532
E-mail: debs@lcf.org

GEORGE WATTERS-NEBRASKA PETROLEUM MARKETERS ASSOCIATION SCHOLARSHIP
• See page 544

HARRY AND LENORA RICHARDSON-NATIONAL ASSOCIATION OF POSTMASTERS OF THE UNITED STATES SCHOLARSHIP
• See page 544

HARRY AND LENORA RICHARDSON-NEBRASKA BRANCH OF THE NATIONAL LEAGUE OF POSTMASTERS SCHOLARSHIP
• See page 544

JENNINGS AND BEULAH HAGGERTY SCHOLARSHIP

Scholarship for graduating seniors from public or private high schools in
Lincoln, NE area. Must be in the top third of graduating class, and enroll in
a two- or four-year institution in Nebraska. Must demonstrate financial need
and academic achievement. Applications must be received between April 1
and July 1.

Award: Scholarship for use in freshman year; not renewable. *Number:*
10–20. *Amount:* $500–$1000.

Eligibility Requirements: Applicant must be high school student;
planning to enroll or expecting to enroll full-time at a two-year or
four-year or technical institution or university; resident of Nebraska
and studying in Nebraska. Applicant must have 3.0 GPA or higher.
Available to U.S. citizens.

Application Requirements: Application, essay, financial need analysis,
interview, references, test scores, transcript. *Deadline:* July 1.

Contact: Debra Shoemaker, Director of Program and Distribution
Lincoln Community Foundation
215 Centennial Mall South, Suite 200
Lincoln, NE 68508
Phone: 402-474-2345
Fax: 402-476-8532
E-mail: debs@lcf.org

LOUIS C. AND AMY E. NUERNBERGER MEMORIAL SCHOLARSHIP
• See page 545

MAX AND MARGARET PUMPHREY SCHOLARSHIP

Scholarship for graduating seniors or former graduates of public or private
high schools in Lancaster County, NE. Preference given to those attending
Nebraska colleges/universities. Must demonstrate financial need and academic
success. Applications must be received between April 1 and July 1.

Award: Scholarship for use in freshman, sophomore, junior, or senior
years; not renewable. *Number:* 35–40. *Amount:* $500–$1000.

Eligibility Requirements: Applicant must be enrolled or expecting to
enroll full-time at a two-year or four-year or technical institution or
university and resident of Nebraska. Applicant must have 2.5 GPA or
higher. Available to U.S. citizens.

Application Requirements: Application, essay, financial need analysis,
interview, references, test scores, transcript. *Deadline:* July 1.

Contact: Debra Shoemaker, Director of Program and Distribution
Lincoln Community Foundation
215 Centennial Mall South, Suite 200
Lincoln, NE 68508
Phone: 402-474-2345
Fax: 402-476-8532
E-mail: debs@lcf.org

MIRIAM CROFT MOELLER CITIZENSHIP AWARD

Scholarship for current graduating seniors from public or private high schools
in the greater Lincoln, NE area who uphold a keen interest in citizenship and
participate in, and demonstrate enthusiasm for, community betterment and
leadership. Need not excel academically.

Award: Scholarship for use in freshman year; not renewable. *Number:*
4. *Amount:* $500–$2000.

Eligibility Requirements: Applicant must be high school student;
planning to enroll or expecting to enroll full-time at a two-year or
four-year or technical institution or university; resident of Nebraska
and must have an interest in designated field specified by sponsor or
leadership. Applicant must have 2.5 GPA or higher. Available to U.S.
citizens.

Application Requirements: Application, essay, references, test scores,
transcript. *Deadline:* April 15.

Contact: Debra Shoemaker, Director of Program and Distribution
Lincoln Community Foundation
215 Centennial Mall South, Suite 200
Lincoln, NE 68508
Phone: 402-474-2345
Fax: 402-476-8532
E-mail: debs@lcf.org

NEBRASKA RURAL SCHOOLS SCHOLARSHIP

Scholarships for graduating seniors or former graduates of rural high schools
in Nebraska (by "rural" it is to be understood as a community with a
population of less than 10,000). Must attend a college, university, or
community college in Nebraska. Applicants must have graduated in the top
10% of his/her high school graduating class or must currently maintain a 3.5
GPA or better on a 4.0 scale at the college or university he/she is attending.
Must be a Nebraska resident. Applications due between June 1 and August 1.

Lincoln Community Foundation (continued)

Award: Scholarship for use in freshman, sophomore, junior, or senior years; not renewable. *Number:* 4. *Amount:* $500–$2000.

Eligibility Requirements: Applicant must be enrolled or expecting to enroll full-time at a two-year or four-year or technical institution or university; resident of Nebraska and studying in Nebraska. Applicant must have 3.5 GPA or higher. Available to U.S. citizens.

Application Requirements: Application, essay, financial need analysis, test scores, transcript. *Deadline:* August 1.

Contact: Debra Shoemaker, Director of Program and Distribution
Lincoln Community Foundation
215 Centennial Mall South, Suite 200
Lincoln, NE 68508
Phone: 402-474-2345
Fax: 402-476-8532
E-mail: debs@lcf.org

NORMAN AND RUTH GOOD EDUCATIONAL ENDOWMENT

Scholarship for a degree-seeking junior or senior at a private college in Nebraska. Must have GPA of 3.5 or above. Application deadline: April 15.

Award: Scholarship for use in junior or senior years; not renewable. *Number:* 10–15. *Amount:* $500–$2000.

Eligibility Requirements: Applicant must be enrolled or expecting to enroll full-time at a four-year institution or university and studying in Nebraska. Applicant must have 3.5 GPA or higher. Available to U.S. citizens.

Application Requirements: Application, test scores, transcript. *Deadline:* April 15.

Contact: Debra Shoemaker, Director of Program and Distribution
Lincoln Community Foundation
215 Centennial Mall South, Suite 200
Lincoln, NE 68508
Phone: 402-474-2345
Fax: 402-476-8532
E-mail: debs@lcf.org

P.G. RICHARDSON MASONIC MEMORIAL SCHOLARSHIP

Scholarship for graduating high school seniors who have a family member belonging to Custer Lodge Number 148 A.F. & A.M. The deadline for applications is March 6. Must be Nebraska resident.

Award: Scholarship for use in freshman year; not renewable. *Number:* 1. *Amount:* $500–$2000.

Eligibility Requirements: Applicant must be high school student; planning to enroll or expecting to enroll full-time at a two-year or four-year or technical institution or university and resident of Nebraska. Applicant must have 2.5 GPA or higher. Available to U.S. citizens.

Application Requirements: Application, references, test scores, transcript. *Deadline:* March 6.

Contact: Doug Sadler, Masonic Scholarship Chairman
Lincoln Community Foundation
611 South North Street
Broken Bow, NE 68822

RALPH AND JEAN CUCA SCHOLARSHIP

Scholarship for graduating high school seniors from a public high school in the greater Lincoln, NE area who demonstrate financial need and academic success.

Award: Scholarship for use in freshman year; not renewable. *Number:* 1. *Amount:* $500–$1000.

Eligibility Requirements: Applicant must be high school student; planning to enroll or expecting to enroll full-time at a two-year or four-year or technical institution or university and resident of Nebraska. Applicant must have 2.5 GPA or higher. Available to U.S. citizens.

Application Requirements: Application, financial need analysis, references, test scores, transcript. *Deadline:* April 1.

Contact: Debra Shoemaker, Director of Program and Distribution
Lincoln Community Foundation
215 Centennial Mall South, Suite 200
Lincoln, NE 68508
Phone: 402-474-2345
Fax: 402-476-8532
E-mail: debs@lcf.org

THOMAS C. WOODS, JR. MEMORIAL SCHOLARSHIP
• See page 545

LONG & FOSTER REAL ESTATE, INC.   http://www.longandfoster.com

LONG & FOSTER SCHOLARSHIP PROGRAM

One-time award for residents of MD, PA, DC, VA, DE, NJ, and NC. Students may pursue any academic major they desire. The Scholarship Committee will be seeking academically strong high school seniors who are well rounded and demonstrate leadership and involvement in a variety of school activities. Must be U.S. citizen. Minimum 3.0 GPA required. More information at http://www.longandfoster.com/about_us/Scholarship_Program.aspx

Award: Scholarship for use in freshman year; not renewable. *Number:* 150–200. *Amount:* $1000.

Eligibility Requirements: Applicant must be high school student; planning to enroll or expecting to enroll full-time at a four-year institution or university and resident of Delaware, District of Columbia, Maryland, New Jersey, North Carolina, Pennsylvania, or Virginia. Applicant must have 3.0 GPA or higher. Available to U.S. citizens.

Application Requirements: Application, essay, financial need analysis, references, test scores, transcript. *Deadline:* March 1.

Contact: Erin L. Wendel, Public Relations Specialist
Long & Foster Real Estate, Inc.
11351 Random Hills Road
Fairfax, VA 22030
Phone: 703-359-1757
Fax: 703-591-5493
E-mail: erin.wendel@longandfoster.com

LOS ANGELES PHILHARMONIC   http://www.laphil.org

BRONISLAW KAPER AWARDS FOR YOUNG ARTISTS

Competition for young musicians under the age of 18, or a senior in high school. Offers cash prizes. The instrumental category alternates annually between piano and strings. This award is not for postsecondary students. Must be a California resident. Call or visit Web site for deadlines. http://www.laphil.com/

Award: Prize for use in freshman year; not renewable. *Number:* 4. *Amount:* $500–$2500.

Eligibility Requirements: Applicant must be age 9-17; enrolled or expecting to enroll at an institution or university; resident of California and must have an interest in music. Available to U.S. citizens.

Application Requirements: Application, applicant must enter a contest, audition. *Deadline:* varies.

Contact: Education Department
Los Angeles Philharmonic
151 South Grand Avenue
Los Angeles, CA 90012
Phone: 213-972-0704
Fax: 213-972-7650
E-mail: education@laphil.org

LOS PADRES FOUNDATION   http://www.lospadresfoundation.org

COLLEGE TUITION ASSISTANCE PROGRAM

Program for eligible high school students who are the first family member to attend college. Must be a legal resident or citizen of the U.S. and a resident of New York or New Jersey. Must have a 3.0 GPA. For further information, refer to Web site http://www.lospadresfoundation.org.

Award: Scholarship for use in freshman, sophomore, junior, or senior years; renewable. *Number:* varies. *Amount:* $1000–$2000.

Eligibility Requirements: Applicant must be enrolled or expecting to enroll full-time at a two-year or four-year or technical institution or university and resident of New Jersey or New York. Applicant must have 3.0 GPA or higher. Available to U.S. citizens.

Application Requirements: Application, essay, financial need analysis, references, transcript. *Deadline:* January 16.

Contact: Los Padres Foundation
658 Live Oak Drive
McLean, VA 22101
Phone: 703-790-9870
Fax: 703-790-9742
E-mail: cta@lospadresfoundation.com

SECOND CHANCE SCHOLARSHIPS

Scholarships granted to Puerto Rican/Latinos students who wish to return to college, trade school or apprenticeship program. Must be a resident of New York or New Jersey. Must demonstrate financial need. For further information, refer to Web site http://www.lospadresfoundation.org.

Award: Scholarship for use in freshman, sophomore, junior, or senior years; not renewable. *Number:* up to 5. *Amount:* up to $2000.

Eligibility Requirements: Applicant must be enrolled or expecting to enroll full-time at a two-year or four-year or technical institution or university and resident of New Jersey or New York. Available to U.S. citizens.

Application Requirements: Application, financial need analysis, transcript. *Deadline:* January 16.

Contact: Los Padres Foundation
658 Live Oak Drive
McLean, VA 22101
Phone: 703-790-9870
Fax: 703-790-9742
E-mail: cta@lospadresfoundation.com

LOUISE C. NACCA MEMORIAL FOR EDUCATIONAL AID FOR THE HANDICAPPED TRUST

LOUISE NACCA MEMORIAL TRUST
• See page 562

LOUISIANA DEPARTMENT OF VETERAN AFFAIRS   http://www.vetaffairs.com/VAMain.htm

LOUISIANA DEPARTMENT OF VETERANS AFFAIRS STATE AID PROGRAM
• See page 589

LOUISIANA NATIONAL GUARD - STATE OF LOUISIANA, JOINT TASK FORCE LA   http://www.la.ngb.army.mil

LOUISIANA NATIONAL GUARD STATE TUITION EXEMPTION PROGRAM
• See page 571

LOUISIANA OFFICE OF STUDENT FINANCIAL ASSISTANCE   http://www.osfa.state.la.us

LEVERAGING EDUCATIONAL ASSISTANCE PROGRAM (LEAP)

LEAP program provides federal and state funds to provide need-based grants to academically qualified students. Individual award determined by Financial Aid Office and governed by number of applicants and availability of funds. File FAFSA by school deadline to apply each year. For Louisiana students attending Louisiana postsecondary institutions. Required GPA is 2.0 and above.

Award: Grant for use in freshman, sophomore, junior, or senior years; not renewable. *Number:* 3000–4000. *Amount:* $200–$2000.

Eligibility Requirements: Applicant must be enrolled or expecting to enroll full or part-time at a two-year or four-year or technical institution or university; resident of Louisiana and studying in Louisiana. Available to U.S. citizens.

Application Requirements: Application, financial need analysis. *Deadline:* varies.

Contact: Public Information
Louisiana Office of Student Financial Assistance
PO Box 91202
Baton Rouge, LA 70821-9202
Phone: 800-259-5626 Ext. 1012
Fax: 225-922-0790
E-mail: custserv@osfa.state.la.us

TOPS ALTERNATE PERFORMANCE AWARD

Program awards an amount equal to tuition plus a $400 annual stipend to students attending a Louisiana public institution, or an amount equal to the weighted average public tuition plus a $400 annual stipend to students attending a LAICU private institution. Must have a minimum high school GPA of 3.0 based on TOPS core curriculum, ACT score of 24, completion of 10 honors courses, and completion of a 16.5 unit core curriculum. Must be a resident of Louisiana.

Award: Scholarship for use in freshman, sophomore, junior, or senior years; renewable. *Number:* varies. *Amount:* varies.

Eligibility Requirements: Applicant must be enrolled or expecting to enroll full-time at a two-year or four-year or technical institution or university; resident of Louisiana and studying in Louisiana. Applicant must have 3.0 GPA or higher. Available to U.S. citizens.

Application Requirements: Application, test scores. *Deadline:* July 1.

Contact: Public Information Representative
Louisiana Office of Student Financial Assistance
PO Box 91202
Baton Rouge, LA 70821-9202
Phone: 800-259-5626 Ext. 1012
Fax: 225-922-0790
E-mail: custserv@osfa.state.la.us

TOPS HONORS AWARD

Program awards an amount equal to tuition plus an $800 per year stipend to students attending a Louisiana public institution, or an amount equal to the weighted average public tuition plus an $800 per year stipend to students attending a LAICU private institution. Must have a minimum high school GPA of 3.5 based on TOPS core curriculum, ACT score of 27, and complete a 16.5 unit core curriculum. Must be resident of Louisiana.

Award: Scholarship for use in freshman, sophomore, junior, or senior years; renewable. *Number:* varies. *Amount:* varies.

Eligibility Requirements: Applicant must be high school student; planning to enroll or expecting to enroll full-time at a two-year or four-year or technical institution or university; resident of Louisiana and studying in Louisiana. Applicant must have 3.5 GPA or higher. Available to U.S. citizens.

Application Requirements: Application, test scores. *Deadline:* July 1.

Contact: Public Information
Louisiana Office of Student Financial Assistance
PO Box 91202
Baton Rouge, LA 70821-9202
Phone: 800-259-5626 Ext. 1012
Fax: 225-922-0790
E-mail: custserv@osfa.state.la.us

TOPS OPPORTUNITY AWARD

Program awards an amount equal to tuition to students attending a Louisiana public institution, or an amount equal to the weighted average public tuition to students attending a LAICU private institution. Must have a minimum high school GPA of 2.5 based on the TOPS core curriculum, the prior year's state average ACT score, and complete a 16.5 unit core curriculum. Must be a Louisiana resident.

Award: Scholarship for use in freshman, sophomore, junior, or senior years; renewable. *Number:* varies. *Amount:* $741–$3094.

Eligibility Requirements: Applicant must be enrolled or expecting to enroll full-time at a two-year or four-year or technical institution or university; resident of Louisiana and studying in Louisiana. Applicant must have 2.5 GPA or higher. Available to U.S. citizens.

Application Requirements: Application, test scores. *Deadline:* July 1.

Louisiana Office of Student Financial Assistance (continued)

Contact: Public Information
Louisiana Office of Student Financial Assistance
PO Box 91202
Baton Rouge, LA 70821-9202
Phone: 800-259-5626 Ext. 1012
Fax: 225-922-0790
E-mail: custserv@osfa.state.la.us

TOPS PERFORMANCE AWARD

Program awards an amount equal to tuition plus a $400 annual stipend to students attending a Louisiana public institution, or an amount equal to the weighted average public tuition plus a $400 annual stipend to students attending a LAICU private institution. Must have a minimum high school GPA of 3.5 based on the TOPS core curriculum, an ACT score of 23 and completion of a 16.5 unit core curriculum. Must be a Louisiana resident.

Award: Scholarship for use in freshman, sophomore, junior, or senior years; renewable. *Number:* varies. *Amount:* varies.

Eligibility Requirements: Applicant must be high school student; planning to enroll or expecting to enroll full-time at a two-year or four-year or technical institution or university; resident of Louisiana and studying in Louisiana. Applicant must have 3.5 GPA or higher. Available to U.S. citizens.

Application Requirements: Application, test scores. *Deadline:* July 1.

Contact: Public Information
Louisiana Office of Student Financial Assistance
PO Box 91202
Baton Rouge, LA 70821-9202
Phone: 800-259-5626 Ext. 1012
Fax: 225-922-0790
E-mail: custserv@osfa.state.la.us

TOPS TECH AWARD

Program awards an amount equal to tuition for up to two years of technical training at a Louisiana postsecondary institution that offers a vocational or technical education certificate or diploma program, or a non-academic degree program. Must have a 2.5 high school GPA based on TOPS Tech core curriculum, an ACT score of 17, and complete the TOPS-Tech core curriculum. Must be a Louisiana resident.

Award: Scholarship for use in freshman or sophomore years; renewable. *Number:* varies. *Amount:* $741–$1592.

Eligibility Requirements: Applicant must be enrolled or expecting to enroll full-time at a technical institution; resident of Louisiana and studying in Louisiana. Applicant must have 2.5 GPA or higher. Available to U.S. citizens.

Application Requirements: Application, test scores, FAFSA. *Deadline:* July 1.

Contact: Public Information
Louisiana Office of Student Financial Assistance
PO Box 91202
Baton Rouge, LA 70821-9202
Phone: 800-259-5626 Ext. 1012
Fax: 225-922-0790
E-mail: custserv@osfa.state.la.us

LOUISIANA STATE DEPARTMENT OF EDUCATION   http://www.doe.state.la.us

ROBERT C. BYRD HONORS SCHOLARSHIP-LOUISIANA

Applicant must have earned a diploma from a public or private secondary school or received the recognized equivalent of a high school diploma (GED) in the State of Louisiana in the same academic year in which the scholarship is to be awarded. Must have a GPA of 3.5. Must be a U.S. citizen and legal resident of Louisiana. Total number of awards vary each year. Deadline is March 10.

Award: Scholarship for use in senior year; not renewable. *Amount:* up to $6000.

Eligibility Requirements: Applicant must be enrolled or expecting to enroll full-time at an institution or university and resident of Louisiana. Applicant must have 3.5 GPA or higher. Available to U.S. citizens.

Application Requirements: Application, essay, test scores, transcript, selective service form. *Deadline:* March 10.

Contact: Melissa Hollins, Scholarship Coordinator
Louisiana State Department of Education
PO Box 94064
Baton Rouge, LA 70804
Phone: 225-342-2098
E-mail: melissa.hollins@la.gov

LYNDON BAINES JOHNSON FOUNDATION   http://www.lbjlib.utexas.edu

LYNDON BAINES JOHNSON FOUNDATION GRANTS-IN-AID RESEARCH

A limited number of grants in aid of research are available for the periods October 1 through March 31 and April 1 through September 30. October through March deadline is August 31. April through September deadline is February 28. Funds are to help defray cost while doing research at the LBJ Library. Contact the archives division of the library prior to submitting proposal concerning material availability for the proposed topic. Candidates for assistance should have thoughtful and well-written proposals that state clearly and precisely how the holdings of the Lyndon Baines Johnson Library will contribute to historical research.

Award: Grant for use in freshman, sophomore, junior, senior, graduate, or postgraduate years; not renewable. *Number:* varies. *Amount:* $500–$2000.

Eligibility Requirements: Applicant must be enrolled or expecting to enroll at a two-year or four-year or technical institution or university and studying in Texas. Available to U.S. and Canadian citizens.

Application Requirements: Application, references, research proposal. *Deadline:* varies.

Contact: Executive Director
Lyndon Baines Johnson Foundation
2313 Red River Street
Austin, TX 78705
Phone: 512-478-7829
Fax: 512-478-9104
E-mail: library@johnson.nara.gov

M E COMPANIES, INC.   http://www.mecompanies.com

M E COMPANIES INC SCHOLARSHIP FUND

Annual scholarships to foster college participation in students from southern and southeastern Ohio. Students entering all career fields are eligible, but emphasis is given to those applicants interested in pursuing full-time study in the field of civil engineering at an accredited university. Must be a resident of Adams, Athens, Fairfield, Guernsey, Hocking, Meigs, Morgan, Muskingum, Noble, Perry, Scioto, Vinton, or Washington county. Deadline is April 1.

Award: Scholarship for use in senior year; not renewable. *Number:* up to 2. *Amount:* up to $2000.

Eligibility Requirements: Applicant must be enrolled or expecting to enroll full-time at a four-year institution or university; resident of Ohio and studying in Ohio. Applicant must have 2.5 GPA or higher. Available to U.S. citizens.

Application Requirements: Application, essay, references, transcript. *Deadline:* April 1.

Contact: Crystal Smith, Human Resources Manager
M E Companies, Inc.
635 Brooksedge Boulevard
Westerville, OH 43081
Phone: 614-818-4900
Fax: 614-818-4902
E-mail: mailbox@mecompanies.com

MAGIC JOHNSON FOUNDATION, INC.   http://www.magicjohnson.org

TAYLOR MICHAELS SCHOLARSHIP FUND
• See page 623

MAINE BUREAU OF VETERANS SERVICES   http://www.state.me.us

VETERANS DEPENDENTS EDUCATIONAL BENEFITS-MAINE
• See page 574

MAINE COMMUNITY COLLEGE SYSTEM
http://www.mccs.me.edu

DIRIGO MACHINE TOOL SCHOLARSHIP

For students interested in a career in precision manufacturing. Scholarship covers one year tuition in exchange for a one year commitment to work for a sponsoring Maine Metal Products Association member company. Refer to Web site: http://www.mccs.me.edu/scholarships.html.

Award: Scholarship for use in freshman or sophomore years. *Number:* varies. *Amount:* up to $2400.

Eligibility Requirements: Applicant must be enrolled or expecting to enroll full-time at a two-year or technical institution; resident of Maine and studying in Maine. Available to U.S. citizens.

Application Requirements: Application. *Deadline:* varies.

Contact: Scholarship Coordinator
Maine Community College System
323 State Street
Augusta, ME 04330
Phone: 207-629-4000
Fax: 207-629-4048

EARLY COLLEGE PROGRAM

For high school students who have not made plans for college but are academically capable of success in college. Recipients are selected by their school principal or director. Refer to Web site: http://www.mccs.me.edu/scholarships.html. Students must be entering a Maine Community College.

Award: Scholarship for use in freshman year; not renewable. *Number:* up to 200. *Amount:* up to $2000.

Eligibility Requirements: Applicant must be high school student; planning to enroll or expecting to enroll full-time at a two-year institution; resident of Maine and studying in Maine. Available to U.S. citizens.

Application Requirements: Application. *Deadline:* varies.

Contact: Scholarship Coordinator
Maine Community College System
323 State Street
Augusta, ME 04330
Phone: 207-629-4000
Fax: 207-629-4048

GEORGE J. MITCHELL PEACE SCHOLARSHIP

An annual exchange and scholarship to Ireland for students from the Maine Community College System and the University of Maine System. Scholarship will provide opportunity for student to study at a university or institute of technology in Ireland. Refer to Web site for details: http://www.mccs.me.edu

Award: Scholarship for use in freshman, sophomore, junior, or senior years. *Number:* 1. *Amount:* varies.

Eligibility Requirements: Applicant must be age 18; enrolled or expecting to enroll full-time at a two-year institution or university and resident of Maine. Applicant must have 3.0 GPA or higher. Available to U.S. citizens.

Application Requirements: *Deadline:* February 15.

Contact: Center for Career Development-Peace Exchange
Maine Community College System
Center for Career Development-Peace Exchange, 2 Fort Road
South Portland, ME 04106
Phone: 207-767-5210 Ext. 4117

MAINE COMMUNITY COLLEGE SCHOLARSHIP

Participating high schools and technical centers/regions identify students to apply for the scholarship during their junior year. Students must be both nominated by their school and accepted into a Maine community college program of study. Award is $500 per semester, $1000 per year for a one-year program and a maximum of $2000 for a two-year program, so long as student meets program requirements. For details see Web site: http://www.ccd.me.edu/scholarship

Award: Scholarship for use in freshman or sophomore years; renewable. *Number:* varies. *Amount:* $200–$2000.

Eligibility Requirements: Applicant must be high school student; planning to enroll or expecting to enroll at a two-year or technical institution; resident of Maine and studying in Maine. Available to U.S. citizens.

Application Requirements: *Deadline:* varies.

Contact: Dorry French, Career Assistant
Maine Community College System
2 Fort Road
South Portland, ME 04106
Phone: 207-767-5210 Ext. 4117
E-mail: dfrench@ccd.me.edu

MAINE HOSPITALS ENGINEERS SOCIETY SCHOLARSHIP

Scholarship for Maine Community College student majoring in engineering or related areas. Refer to Web site for more details: http://www.mccs.me.edu/scholarships.html

Award: Scholarship for use in freshman or sophomore years; not renewable. *Number:* 1. *Amount:* up to $2000.

Eligibility Requirements: Applicant must be enrolled or expecting to enroll full-time at a two-year institution; resident of Maine and studying in Maine. Available to U.S. citizens.

Application Requirements: *Deadline:* varies.

Contact: Scholarship Coordinator
Maine Community College System
323 State Street
Augusta, ME 04330
Phone: 207-629-4000
Fax: 207-629-4048

OSHER SCHOLARSHIP

For Maine residents who are not currently enrolled at any college or university and have accumulated no more than 24 college credits. Applicant must be accepted into an AA in liberal/general studies program. Eligible applicant will receive two core courses tuition free. See Web site for more details: http://www.mccs.me.edu/osher.html

Award: Scholarship for use in freshman year. *Number:* varies. *Amount:* up to $444.

Eligibility Requirements: Applicant must be enrolled or expecting to enroll at a two-year institution; resident of Maine and studying in Maine. Available to U.S. citizens.

Application Requirements: *Deadline:* varies.

Contact: Maine Community College Financial Aid Department
Maine Community College System
323 State Street
Augusta, ME 04330
Phone: 207-629-4000
Fax: 207-629-4048
E-mail: info@mccs.me.edu

MAINE COMMUNITY FOUNDATION, INC.
http://www.mainecf.org

CHALLENGER MEMORIAL SCHOLARSHIP FUND

Renewable scholarship, granted on the basis of established Maine residency, academic or artistic talents, aspirations, leadership skills, and financial need. Scholarships will range in size up to ten percent of the receiving scholar's stated tuition. Deadline April 1. Total number of available awards and the dollar value depends on the applications received. See Web site for more information: http://www.mainecf.org/pdfs/7/challenger.pdf

Award: Scholarship for use in freshman year; renewable. *Number:* 1.

Eligibility Requirements: Applicant must be high school student; planning to enroll or expecting to enroll full-time at an institution or university and resident of Maine. Available to U.S. citizens.

Application Requirements: Application, essay, transcript. *Deadline:* April 1.

Contact: Amy Pollien, Program Administrator
Maine Community Foundation, Inc.
245 Main Street
Ellsworth, ME 04605
Phone: 207-667-9735
Fax: 207-667-9735
E-mail: apollien@mainecf.org

CMP GROUP SCHOLARSHIP FUND

Nonrenewable scholarship available to dependents of CMP Group and CMP Group affiliate employees or retirees, and reside within Central Maine Power

Maine Community Foundation, Inc. (continued)

Company's service area.. Must be high school senior graduating from a Maine secondary school. Three or more awards will be made annually and will range from $1000 to $5000. Deadline is May 1. For more information, see Web site: http://www.mainecf.org/pdfs/7/cmpgroup.pdf

Award: Scholarship for use in freshman year; not renewable. *Number:* 3. *Amount:* $1000–$10,000.

Eligibility Requirements: Applicant must be high school student; planning to enroll or expecting to enroll full-time at a two-year or four-year or technical institution or university and resident of Maine. Available to U.S. citizens.

Application Requirements: Application, essay, financial need analysis, references, transcript. *Deadline:* May 1.

Contact: Jean Warren, Scholarship Coordinator
Maine Community Foundation, Inc.
245 Main Street
Ellsworth, ME 04605-1613
Phone: 207-667-9735
Fax: 207-667-0447
E-mail: jwarren@mainecf.org

JOSEPH W. MAYO ALS SCHOLARSHIP FUND

Program that assists men and women who are children, step-children, grandchildren, spouses, domestic partners or the primary care givers of ALS patients. Must have graduated from a high school in Maine. Deadline is May 1. For more information see Web site: http://www.mainecf.org/pdfs/7/mayo.pdf

Award: Scholarship for use in freshman year; not renewable. *Amount:* $500–$1500.

Eligibility Requirements: Applicant must be enrolled or expecting to enroll full-time at an institution or university and resident of Maine. Available to U.S. citizens.

Application Requirements: Application, essay. *Deadline:* May 1.

Contact: Joseph Pietroski, President
Maine Community Foundation, Inc.
132 State Street, PO Box 735
Augusta, ME 04332-0735
Phone: 207-622-6131
Fax: 207-622-0314

LEST WE FORGET POW/MIA/KIA SCHOLARSHIP

Scholarship supports Maine veterans of the United States Armed Services who served in the Vietnam theater and their descendants. A second priority for scholarships is given to children of veterans of the United States Armed Services. "Descendants" include natural and legally adopted children and their descendants.

Award: Scholarship for use in freshman, sophomore, junior, or senior years; not renewable. *Number:* 3–6. *Amount:* up to $1000.

Eligibility Requirements: Applicant must be enrolled or expecting to enroll full-time at a four-year institution or university and resident of Maine. Available to U.S. citizens.

Application Requirements: Application, essay, financial need analysis, references, transcript. *Deadline:* May 1.

Contact: Amy Pollien, Program Administrator
Maine Community Foundation, Inc.
The Maine Vietnam Veterans/Lest We Forget Scholarship Fund, c/o Maine Community Foundation, 245 Main Street
Ellsworth, ME 04605-1613
Phone: 207-667-9735
Fax: 207-667-0447
E-mail: info@mainecf.org

RICE SCHOLARSHIP FUND

Scholarship support for students who have resided a substantial part of their formative years on one of the off-shore islands of Maine in the area from Seguin to Eastport, and who are attending accredited degree-granting colleges or vocational training schools. Recipients will be selected based on financial need and community service. Deadline is May 1. Refer http://www.mainecf.org/pdfs/7/rice.pdf for details.

Award: Scholarship for use in freshman year; renewable. *Number:* 1.

Eligibility Requirements: Applicant must be high school student; planning to enroll or expecting to enroll full-time at a two-year or four-year or technical institution and resident of Maine. Available to U.S. citizens.

Application Requirements: Application, essay, financial need analysis, references, transcript. *Deadline:* May 1.

Contact: Amy Pollien, Program Administrator
Maine Community Foundation, Inc.
Rice Scholarship Fund, c/o Maine Community Foundation, 245 Main Street
Ellsworth, ME 04605
Phone: 207-667-9735
Fax: 207-667-0447
E-mail: info@mainecf.org

SENATOR GEORGE J. MITCHELL SCHOLARSHIP FUND

Scholarship granted to a graduating senior from every public high school in Maine. $5000 for students who are pursuing a four-year degree and $2500 for students pursuing a two-year degree (i.e., $1250 for each year of school). For more information see Web site: http://www.mitchellinstitute.org/scholarships.html

Award: Scholarship for use in senior year; not renewable. *Amount:* $2500–$5000.

Eligibility Requirements: Applicant must be enrolled or expecting to enroll full-time at an institution or university and resident of Maine. Available to U.S. citizens.

Application Requirements: Application, essay, financial need analysis, references, transcript. *Deadline:* May 1.

Contact: Patty Higgins, Director of Scholarship Programs
Maine Community Foundation, Inc.
Mitchell Institute, 22 Monument Square, Suite 200
Portland, ME 04101
Phone: 207-773-7700 Ext. 102
Fax: 207-773-1133
E-mail: info@mitchellinstitute.org

MAINE EDUCATION SERVICES   http://www.mesfoundation.com/

MAINE MASONIC AID FOR CONTINUING EDUCATION

Scholarships are available for 12 adults pursuing higher education. May be full or part-time students. Students must meet federal criteria for an independent student. In addition, they must have exceptional financial need, have a serious educational plan, and contribute to the community

Award: Scholarship for use in freshman, sophomore, junior, senior, graduate, or postgraduate years; renewable. *Number:* 12. *Amount:* $1000.

Eligibility Requirements: Applicant must be age 23; enrolled or expecting to enroll full or part-time at a two-year or four-year or technical institution or university and resident of Maine. Available to U.S. citizens.

Application Requirements: Application, essay, financial need analysis, references, transcript. *Deadline:* April 14.

Contact: Kim Benjamin, Vice President of Operations
Maine Education Services
One City Center
11th Floor
Portland, ME 04101
Phone: 207-791-3600
Fax: 207-791-3616
E-mail: kbenjamin@mesfoundation.com

MAINE STATE CHAMBER OF COMMERCE SCHOLARSHIP - ADULT LEARNER

Scholarship available for an adult learner planning to pursue an education at a two-year degree-granting college. Preference may be given to a student attending a Maine college and seeking a degree in a business- or education-related field. Must be 23 years or older and have legal dependents other than a spouse.

Award: Scholarship for use in freshman, sophomore, junior, or senior years; renewable. *Number:* 1. *Amount:* $1500.

Eligibility Requirements: Applicant must be age 23; enrolled or expecting to enroll full or part-time at a two-year or four-year or technical institution or university and resident of Maine. Available to U.S. citizens.

Application Requirements: Application, essay, financial need analysis, references, transcript. *Deadline:* April 14.

Contact: Kim Benjamin, Vice President of Operations
Maine Education Services
One City Center
11th Floor
Portland, ME 04101
Phone: 207-791-3600
Fax: 207-791-3616
E-mail: kbenjamin@mesfoundation.com

MAINE STATE CHAMBER OF COMMERCE SCHOLARSHIP - HIGH SCHOOL SENIOR

Two scholarships available to graduating high school seniors: one who is planning to pursue an associate's degree in a technical program and one who is planning to pursue a bachelor's degree in a business-related area. Preference may be given to students attending Maine colleges. Awards are based on academic excellence, student activities, financial need, letters of recommendation, and a required essay.

Award: Scholarship for use in freshman year; renewable. *Number:* 2. *Amount:* $1500.

Eligibility Requirements: Applicant must be high school student; planning to enroll or expecting to enroll full-time at a two-year or four-year or technical institution or university and resident of Maine. Available to U.S. citizens.

Application Requirements: Application, financial need analysis, references, transcript. *Deadline:* April 14.

Contact: Kim Benjamin, Vice President of Operations
Maine Education Services
One City Center
11th Floor
Portland, ME 04101
Phone: 207-791-3600
Fax: 207-791-3616
E-mail: kbenjamin@mesfoundation.com

TD BANKNORTH PROMISE SCHOLARSHIP

Ten scholarships for graduating high school seniors who will enroll in a postsecondary institution. The recipients are offered a three-month paid internship position with the bank after their first year of postsecondary education. This program is intended for students from low to moderate-income households in Maine. Awards are based on financial need, academic achievement, involvement in school activities, community volunteer activity, work experience, and a required essay

Award: Scholarship for use in freshman year; renewable. *Number:* 10. *Amount:* $2500.

Eligibility Requirements: Applicant must be high school student; planning to enroll or expecting to enroll full-time at a two-year or four-year institution or university and resident of Maine. Available to U.S. citizens.

Application Requirements: Application, essay, financial need analysis, references, transcript. *Deadline:* April 14.

Contact: Kim Benjamin, Vice President of Operations
Maine Education Services
One City Center
11th Floor
Portland, ME 04101
Phone: 207-791-3600
Fax: 207-791-3616
E-mail: kbenjamin@mesfoundation.com

MAINE STATE SOCIETY FOUNDATION OF WASHINGTON, D.C., INC. http://www.mainestatesociety.org

MAINE STATE SOCIETY FOUNDATION SCHOLARSHIP

Each scholarship will be awarded to full-time students enrolled in undergraduate courses at a four-year degree-granting, nonprofit institution in Maine. Must be Maine resident. All inquiries must be accompanied by a self-addressed stamped envelope. Applicant must be 25 or younger. Minimum 3.0 GPA.

Award: Scholarship for use in sophomore, junior, or senior years; not renewable. *Number:* 5–10. *Amount:* $1000–$2500.

Eligibility Requirements: Applicant must be age 25 or under; enrolled or expecting to enroll full-time at a four-year institution or university; resident of Maine and studying in Maine. Applicant must have 3.0 GPA or higher. Available to U.S. citizens.

Application Requirements: Application, autobiography, essay, self-addressed stamped envelope, transcript. *Deadline:* April 15.

Contact: Hugh L. Dwelley, Director
Maine State Society Foundation of Washington, D.C., Inc.
3508 Wilson Street
Fairfax, VA 22030-2936
Phone: 703-352-0846
E-mail: hldwelley@aol.com

MARYLAND HIGHER EDUCATION COMMISSION   http://www.mhec.state.md.us

DELEGATE SCHOLARSHIP PROGRAM-MARYLAND

Delegate scholarships help Maryland residents attending Maryland degree-granting institutions, certain career schools, or nursing diploma schools. May attend out-of-state institution if Maryland Higher Education Commission deems major to be unique and not offered at a Maryland institution. Free Application for Federal Student Aid may be required. Students interested in this program should apply by contacting their legislative district delegate.

Award: Scholarship for use in freshman, sophomore, junior, senior, or graduate years; not renewable. *Number:* up to 3500. *Amount:* $200–$7950.

Eligibility Requirements: Applicant must be enrolled or expecting to enroll full or part-time at a two-year or four-year or technical institution or university; resident of Maryland and studying in Maryland. Available to U.S. citizens.

Application Requirements: Application, financial need analysis. *Deadline:* Continuous.

Contact: Barbara Fantom, Office of Student Financial Assistance
Maryland Higher Education Commission
839 Bestgate Road, Suite 400
Annapolis, MD 21401-3013
Phone: 410-260-4547
Fax: 410-260-3200
E-mail: osfamail@mhec.state.md.us

DISTINGUISHED SCHOLAR AWARD-MARYLAND

Renewable award for Maryland students enrolled full-time at Maryland institutions. National Merit Scholar Finalists automatically offered award. Others may qualify for the award in satisfying criteria of a minimum 3.7 GPA or in combination with high test scores, or for Talent in Arts competition in categories of music, drama, dance, or visual arts. Must maintain annual 3.0 GPA in college for award to be renewed. Contact for further details.

Award: Scholarship for use in freshman, sophomore, junior, or senior years; renewable. *Number:* up to 2000. *Amount:* up to $3000.

Eligibility Requirements: Applicant must be high school student; planning to enroll or expecting to enroll full-time at a two-year or four-year institution or university; resident of Maryland and studying in Maryland. Available to U.S. citizens.

Application Requirements: Application, test scores, transcript. *Deadline:* varies.

Contact: Monica Tipton, Office of Student Financial Assistance
Maryland Higher Education Commission
839 Bestgate Road, Suite 400
Annapolis, MD 21401-3013
Phone: 410-260-4568
Fax: 410-260-3200
E-mail: ofsamail@mhec.state.md.us

EDUCATIONAL ASSISTANCE GRANTS-MARYLAND

Award for Maryland residents accepted or enrolled in a full-time undergraduate degree or certificate program at a Maryland institution or hospital nursing school. Must submit financial aid form by March 1. Must earn 2.0 GPA in college to maintain award.

Maryland Higher Education Commission (continued)

Award: Grant for use in freshman, sophomore, junior, or senior years; renewable. *Number:* 11,000–20,000. *Amount:* $400–$2700.

Eligibility Requirements: Applicant must be enrolled or expecting to enroll full-time at a two-year or four-year institution or university; resident of Maryland and studying in Maryland. Available to U.S. citizens.

Application Requirements: Application, financial need analysis. *Deadline:* March 1.

Contact: Barbara Fantom, Office of Student Financial Assistance
Maryland Higher Education Commission
839 Bestgate Road, Suite 400
Annapolis, MD 21401-3013
Phone: 410-260-4547
Fax: 410-260-3200
E-mail: osfamail@mhec.state.md.us

EDWARD T. CONROY MEMORIAL SCHOLARSHIP PROGRAM
• See page 575

GUARANTEED ACCESS GRANT-MARYLAND

Award for Maryland resident enrolling full-time in an undergraduate program at a Maryland institution. Must be under 22 at time of first award and begin college within one year of completing high school in Maryland with a minimum 2.5 GPA. Must have an annual family income less than 130% of the federal poverty level guideline.

Award: Grant for use in freshman, sophomore, junior, senior, or graduate years; renewable. *Number:* up to 1000. *Amount:* $400–$13,800.

Eligibility Requirements: Applicant must be age 21 or under; enrolled or expecting to enroll full-time at a two-year or four-year institution or university; resident of Maryland and studying in Maryland. Applicant must have 2.5 GPA or higher. Available to U.S. citizens.

Application Requirements: Application, financial need analysis, transcript. *Deadline:* Continuous.

Contact: Theresa Lowe, Office of Student Financial Assistance
Maryland Higher Education Commission
839 Bestgate Road, Suite 400
Annapolis, MD 21401-3013
Phone: 410-260-4555
Fax: 410-260-3200
E-mail: osfamail@mhec.state.md.us

J.F. TOLBERT MEMORIAL STUDENT GRANT PROGRAM

Available to Maryland residents attending a private career school in Maryland with at least 18 clock hours per week.

Award: Grant for use in freshman or sophomore years; not renewable. *Number:* 400. *Amount:* up to $400.

Eligibility Requirements: Applicant must be enrolled or expecting to enroll at a technical institution; resident of Maryland and studying in Maryland. Available to U.S. citizens.

Application Requirements: Application, financial need analysis. *Deadline:* Continuous.

Contact: Carla Rich, Office of Student Financial Assistance
Maryland Higher Education Commission
839 Bestgate Road, Suite 400
Annapolis, MD 21401-3013
Phone: 410-260-4513
Fax: 410-260-3200
E-mail: osfamail@mhec.state.md.us

PART-TIME GRANT PROGRAM-MARYLAND

Funds provided to Maryland colleges and universities. Eligible students must be enrolled on a part-time basis (6-11 credits) in an undergraduate degree program. Must demonstrate financial need and also be Maryland resident. Contact financial aid office at institution for more information.

Award: Grant for use in freshman, sophomore, junior, or senior years; renewable. *Number:* 1800–9000. *Amount:* $200–$1000.

Eligibility Requirements: Applicant must be enrolled or expecting to enroll part-time at a two-year or four-year institution or university; resident of Maryland and studying in Maryland. Available to U.S. citizens.

Application Requirements: Application, financial need analysis. *Deadline:* March 1.

Contact: Andrea Hunt, Director
Maryland Higher Education Commission
839 Bestgate Road, Suite 400
Annapolis, MD 21401-3013
Phone: 410-260-4558
Fax: 410-260-3202
E-mail: ahunt@mhec.state.md.us

SENATORIAL SCHOLARSHIPS-MARYLAND

Renewable award for Maryland residents attending a Maryland degree-granting institution, nursing diploma school, or certain private career schools. May be used out-of-state only if Maryland Higher Education Commission deems major to be unique and not offered at Maryland institution.

Award: Scholarship for use in freshman, sophomore, junior, senior, or graduate years; renewable. *Number:* up to 7000. *Amount:* $200–$2000.

Eligibility Requirements: Applicant must be enrolled or expecting to enroll full or part-time at a two-year or four-year or technical institution or university; resident of Maryland and studying in Maryland. Available to U.S. citizens.

Application Requirements: Application, financial need analysis, test scores, application to Legislative District Senator. *Deadline:* March 1.

Contact: Barbara Fantom, Office of Student Financial Assistance
Maryland Higher Education Commission
839 Bestgate Road, Suite 400
Annapolis, MD 21401-3013
Phone: 410-260-4547
Fax: 410-260-3200
E-mail: osfamail@mhec.state.md.us

TUITION WAIVER FOR FOSTER CARE RECIPIENTS

Applicant must be a high school graduate or recipient of a GED under the age of 21. Applicant must either have resided in a foster care home in Maryland at time of high school graduation or GED reception, or until 14th birthday and had been adopted after 14th birthday. Applicant, if status approved, will be exempt from paying tuition and mandatory fees at a public college in Maryland.

Award: Scholarship for use in freshman, sophomore, junior, senior, or graduate years; renewable. *Number:* 1. *Amount:* varies.

Eligibility Requirements: Applicant must be age 20 or under; enrolled or expecting to enroll full or part-time at a two-year or four-year institution or university and studying in Maryland. Available to U.S. citizens.

Application Requirements: Application, financial need analysis. *Deadline:* March 1.

Contact: Inquire at financial aid office of your school.

MASSACHUSETTS OFFICE OF STUDENT FINANCIAL ASSISTANCE   http://www.osfa.mass.edu

CHRISTIAN A. HERTER MEMORIAL SCHOLARSHIP

Renewable award for Massachusetts residents who are in the tenth-eleventh grades and whose socio-economic backgrounds and environment may inhibit their ability to attain educational goals. Must exhibit severe personal or family-related difficulties, medical problems, or have overcome a personal obstacle. Provides up to 50% of the student's calculated need, as determined by Federal methodology, at the college of their choice within the continental U.S.

Award: Scholarship for use in freshman, sophomore, junior, or senior years; renewable. *Number:* 25. *Amount:* up to $15,000.

Eligibility Requirements: Applicant must be high school student; planning to enroll or expecting to enroll full-time at a two-year or four-year or technical institution or university and resident of Massachusetts. Applicant must have 2.5 GPA or higher. Available to U.S. citizens.

Application Requirements: Application, autobiography, financial need analysis, interview, references. *Deadline:* March 31.

Contact: Ken Smith
Massachusetts Office of Student Financial Assistance
454 Broadway, Suite 200
Revere, MA 02151
Phone: 617-727-9420
Fax: 617-727-0667
E-mail: osfa@osfa.mass.edu

MASSACHUSETTS ASSISTANCE FOR STUDENT SUCCESS PROGRAM

Provides need-based financial assistance to Massachusetts residents to attend undergraduate postsecondary institutions in Connecticut, Maine, Massachusetts, New Hampshire, Pennsylvania, Rhode Island, Vermont, and District of Columbia. High school seniors may apply. Timely filing of FAFSA required.

Award: Grant for use in freshman, sophomore, junior, or senior years; not renewable. *Number:* 25,000–30,000. *Amount:* $300–$2300.

Eligibility Requirements: Applicant must be enrolled or expecting to enroll full-time at a two-year or four-year or technical institution or university; resident of Massachusetts and studying in Connecticut, District of Columbia, Maine, Massachusetts, New Hampshire, Pennsylvania, Rhode Island, or Vermont. Available to U.S. citizens.

Application Requirements: Financial need analysis, FAFSA. *Deadline:* May 1.

Contact: Robert Brun, Director of Scholarships and Grants
Massachusetts Office of Student Financial Assistance
454 Broadway
Suite 200
Revere, MA 02151
Phone: 617-727-9420
Fax: 617-727-0667

MASSACHUSETTS CASH GRANT PROGRAM

A need-based grant to assist with mandatory fees and non-state supported tuition, this supplemental award is available to Massachusetts residents who are undergraduates at public two-year colleges, four-year colleges and universities in Massachusetts. Must file FAFSA before May 1. Contact college financial aid office for information.

Award: Grant for use in freshman, sophomore, junior, or senior years; not renewable. *Number:* varies. *Amount:* $150–$1900.

Eligibility Requirements: Applicant must be enrolled or expecting to enroll full-time at a two-year or four-year institution or university; resident of Massachusetts and studying in Massachusetts. Available to U.S. citizens.

Application Requirements: Financial need analysis, FAFSA. *Deadline:* Continuous.

Contact: College Financial Aid Office

MASSACHUSETTS PART-TIME GRANT PROGRAM

Award for permanent Massachusetts resident for at least one year enrolled part-time in a state-approved postsecondary school. Recipient must not have first bachelor's degree. FAFSA must be filed before May 1. Contact college financial aid office for further information.

Award: Grant for use in freshman, sophomore, junior, or senior years; not renewable. *Number:* 200. *Amount:* $200–$1150.

Eligibility Requirements: Applicant must be enrolled or expecting to enroll part-time at a two-year or four-year or technical institution or university; resident of Massachusetts and studying in Massachusetts. Available to U.S. citizens.

Application Requirements: Financial need analysis, FAFSA. *Deadline:* May 1.

Contact: College Financial Aid Office

MASSACHUSETTS PUBLIC SERVICE GRANT PROGRAM
• *See page 545*

PERFORMANCE BONUS GRANT PROGRAM

One-time award to residents of Massachusetts enrolled in a Massachusetts postsecondary institution. Minimum 3.0 GPA required. Timely filing of FAFSA required. Must be sophomore-, junior-, or senior-level undergraduate.

Award: Grant for use in sophomore, junior, or senior years; not renewable. *Number:* varies. *Amount:* $350–$500.

Eligibility Requirements: Applicant must be enrolled or expecting to enroll full-time at a two-year or four-year institution or university;

resident of Massachusetts and studying in Massachusetts. Applicant must have 3.0 GPA or higher. Available to U.S. citizens.

Application Requirements: Financial need analysis, FAFSA. *Deadline:* May 1.

Contact: Scholarship Information
Massachusetts Office of Student Financial Assistance
454 Broadway, Suite 200
Revere, MA 02151
Phone: 617-727-9420
Fax: 617-727-0667

MELLINGER EDUCATIONAL FOUNDATION   http://www.mellinger.org

MELLINGER SCHOLARSHIPS

Renewable scholarship grants provided annually for the balance of the additional years of a four-year college educational program, so long as the recipient is maintaining satisfactory process toward obtaining his or her degree or diploma. Foundation considers only applicants who reside in six western Illinois counties Fulton, Henderson, Knox, Mc Donough, Mercer, Warren.

Award: Scholarship for use in junior or senior years; renewable. *Number:* 300–350. *Amount:* $300–$1200.

Eligibility Requirements: Applicant must be enrolled or expecting to enroll full or part-time at a two-year or four-year or technical institution or university and resident of Illinois. Available to U.S. citizens.

Application Requirements: Application, financial need analysis, test scores, transcript. *Deadline:* May 1.

Contact: David Fleming, President
Mellinger Educational Foundation
1025 East Broadway, Box 770
Monmouth, IL 61462
Phone: 309-734-2419
Fax: 309-734-4435

MELLON NEW ENGLAND

CHARLES C. ELY EDUCATIONAL FUND

Award for men who are residents of Massachusetts. Academic performance, character and financial need will be considered. Application deadline is April 15.

Award: Scholarship for use in freshman, sophomore, junior, or senior years; not renewable. *Number:* varies. *Amount:* $1000–$3000.

Eligibility Requirements: Applicant must be enrolled or expecting to enroll full-time at a two-year or four-year or technical institution or university; male and resident of Massachusetts. Available to U.S. citizens.

Application Requirements: *Deadline:* April 15.

Contact: Sandra Brown-McMullen, Vice President
Mellon New England
One Boston Place, 024-0084
Boston, MA 02108
Phone: 617-722-3891
E-mail: brown-McMullen.s@mellon.com

MIAMI-DADE AND BROWARD COUNTY FORD AND LINCOLN-MERCURY DEALERS   http://www.stescholarships.org

SALUTE TO EDUCATION, INC.

Scholarships of $1000 for college-bound public and private high school seniors in Miami-Dade and Broward counties. Minimum GPA of 3.0.

Award: Scholarship for use in freshman year; not renewable. *Number:* 200–240. *Amount:* $1000.

Eligibility Requirements: Applicant must be high school student; planning to enroll or expecting to enroll at a two-year or four-year institution or university and resident of Florida. Applicant must have 3.0 GPA or higher. Available to U.S. citizens.

Miami-Dade and Broward County Ford and Lincoln-Mercury Dealers (continued)

Application Requirements: Application, essay. *Deadline:* January 5.

Contact: Nicole Rodriguez, Program Coordinator
Miami-Dade and Broward County Ford and Lincoln-Mercury Dealers
2600 Douglas Boulevard., Suite 610
Coral Gables, FL 33134
Phone: 305-476-7709
Fax: 305-476-7710
E-mail: nrodriguez@stescholarships.org

MICHIGAN BUREAU OF STUDENT FINANCIAL ASSISTANCE
http://www.michigan.gov/studentaid

MICHIGAN ADULT PART-TIME GRANT

Grant for part-time, needy, independent undergraduates at an approved, degree-granting Michigan college or university. Eligibility is limited to two years. Must be Michigan resident. Deadlines determined by college.

Award: Grant for use in freshman, sophomore, junior, or senior years; not renewable. *Number:* varies. *Amount:* up to $600.

Eligibility Requirements: Applicant must be enrolled or expecting to enroll part-time at a two-year or four-year institution or university; resident of Michigan and studying in Michigan. Available to U.S. citizens.

Application Requirements: Financial need analysis. *Deadline:* varies.

Contact: Program Director
Michigan Bureau of Student Financial Assistance
PO Box 30462
Lansing, MI 48909-7962
Phone: 888-447-2687
E-mail: osg@michigan.gov

MICHIGAN COMPETITIVE SCHOLARSHIP

Awards limited to tuition. Must maintain a C average and meet the college's academic progress requirements. Must file Free Application for Federal Student Aid. Deadline: March 1. Must be Michigan resident. Renewable award of $1300 for undergraduate study at a Michigan institution.

Award: Scholarship for use in freshman, sophomore, junior, or senior years; renewable. *Number:* varies. *Amount:* $100–$1300.

Eligibility Requirements: Applicant must be enrolled or expecting to enroll at a two-year or four-year institution or university; resident of Michigan and studying in Michigan. Available to U.S. citizens.

Application Requirements: Application, financial need analysis, test scores, FAFSA. *Deadline:* March 1.

Contact: Scholarship and Grant Director
Michigan Bureau of Student Financial Assistance
PO Box 30466
Lansing, MI 48909

MICHIGAN EDUCATIONAL OPPORTUNITY GRANT

Need-based program for Michigan residents who are at least half-time undergraduates attending public Michigan colleges. Must maintain good academic standing. Deadline determined by college. Award of up to $1000.

Award: Grant for use in freshman, sophomore, junior, or senior years; not renewable. *Number:* varies. *Amount:* up to $1000.

Eligibility Requirements: Applicant must be enrolled or expecting to enroll full or part-time at a two-year or four-year institution or university; resident of Michigan and studying in Michigan. Available to U.S. citizens.

Application Requirements: Financial need analysis. *Deadline:* varies.

Contact: Program Director
Michigan Bureau of Student Financial Assistance
PO Box 30462
Lansing, MI 48909-7962
Phone: 888-447-2687
E-mail: osg@michigan.gov

MICHIGAN MERIT AWARD

Scholarship for students scoring well on state's standardized assessment tests. Students will have four years from high school graduation to use the award.

Award: Scholarship for use in freshman, sophomore, junior, or senior years; not renewable. *Number:* varies. *Amount:* $1000–$2500.

Eligibility Requirements: Applicant must be high school student; planning to enroll or expecting to enroll full or part-time at a two-year or four-year or technical institution or university and resident of Michigan. Available to U.S. citizens.

Application Requirements: Test scores.

Contact: Program Director
Michigan Bureau of Student Financial Assistance
PO Box 30466
Lansing, MI 48909-7962
Phone: 888-447-2687
E-mail: osg@michigan.gov

MICHIGAN TUITION GRANT

Need-based program. Students must attend a Michigan private, nonprofit, degree-granting college. Must file the Free Application for Federal Student Aid and meet the college's academic progress requirements. Deadline: March 1. Must be Michigan resident. Renewable award of $2000.

Award: Grant for use in freshman, sophomore, junior, senior, or graduate years; renewable. *Number:* varies. *Amount:* $100–$2000.

Eligibility Requirements: Applicant must be enrolled or expecting to enroll full or part-time at a two-year or four-year institution or university; resident of Michigan and studying in Michigan. Available to U.S. citizens.

Application Requirements: Financial need analysis. *Deadline:* March 1.

Contact: Scholarship and Grant Director
Michigan Bureau of Student Financial Assistance
PO Box 30462
Lansing, MI 48909-7962

TUITION INCENTIVE PROGRAM (TIP)

Award for Michigan residents who receive or have received Medicaid for required period of time through the Family Independence Agency. Scholarship provides two years tuition towards an associate's degree at a Michigan college or university. Apply before graduating from high school or earning General Education Development diploma.

Award: Grant for use in freshman, sophomore, junior, or senior years; renewable. *Number:* varies.

Eligibility Requirements: Applicant must be high school student; planning to enroll or expecting to enroll full or part-time at a two-year or four-year institution or university; resident of Michigan and studying in Michigan. Available to U.S. citizens.

Application Requirements: Application, Medicaid eligibility for specified period of time. *Deadline:* Continuous.

Contact: Program Director
Michigan Bureau of Student Financial Assistance
PO Box 30462
Lansing, MI 48909-7962
Phone: 888-447-2687
E-mail: osg@michigan.gov

MICHIGAN VETERANS TRUST FUND
http://www.michigan.gov/dmva

MICHIGAN VETERANS TRUST FUND TUITION GRANT PROGRAM
• See page 590

MIDWESTERN HIGHER EDUCATION COMPACT
http://msep.mhec.org

MIDWEST STUDENT EXCHANGE PROGRAM (MSEP)

Over 125 colleges and universities in Kansas, Michigan, Minnesota, Missouri, Nebraska, North Dakota and Wisconsin participate in MSEP. The MSEP is not a scholarship but rather a means of tuition reduction. To apply for admission as a MSEP student, you should contact the MSEP Campus Administrator at the participating MSEP institution directly. Special restrictions on enrollment may apply. All of the enrollment and eligibility decisions for the program are made by the institution. MSEP status can be renewed. For more details, please search the MSEP Access Navigator (http://msep.mhec.org) by your home state of residence to find participating institutions and Campus Administrator contact information.

Award: Grant for use in freshman, sophomore, junior, senior, graduate, or postgraduate years; renewable. *Number:* varies. *Amount:* varies.

Eligibility Requirements: Applicant must be enrolled or expecting to enroll full or part-time at a two-year or four-year or technical institution or university; resident of Kansas, Michigan, Minnesota, Missouri, Nebraska, North Dakota, or Wisconsin and studying in Kansas, Michigan, Minnesota, Missouri, Nebraska, North Dakota, or Wisconsin. Available to U.S. citizens.

Application Requirements: Application, varies by institution. *Deadline:* varies.

Contact: Ms. Jennifer Dahlquist, Director of Student Initiatives
Midwestern Higher Education Compact
1300 South Second Street, Suite 130
Minneapolis, MN 55454-1079
Phone: 612-626-1602
Fax: 612-626-8290
E-mail: jenniferd@mhec.org

MINNESOTA AFL-CIO   http://www.mnaflcio.org

BILL PETERSON SCHOLARSHIP
• *See page 504*

MARTIN DUFFY ADULT LEARNER SCHOLARSHIP AWARD
• *See page 504*

MINNESOTA AFL-CIO SCHOLARSHIPS
• *See page 504*

MINNESOTA HIGHER EDUCATION SERVICES OFFICE   http://www.getreadyforcollege.org

MINNESOTA ACADEMIC EXCELLENCE SCHOLARSHIP

Students must demonstrate outstanding ability, achievement, and potential in one of the following subjects: English or creative writing, fine arts, foreign language, math, science, or social science. Implementation depends on the availability of funds, which are to come from the sale of special collegiate license plates. Apply directly to college. Must be a Minnesota resident and study in Minnesota. At public institutions, the scholarship may cover up to the full price of tuition and fees for one academic year. At private institutions, the scholarship may cover either the actual tuition and fees charged by that school, or the tuition and fees in comparable public institutions.

Award: Scholarship for use in freshman, sophomore, junior, or senior years; renewable. *Number:* varies. *Amount:* $6500.

Eligibility Requirements: Applicant must be enrolled or expecting to enroll full-time at a four-year institution or university; resident of Minnesota; studying in Minnesota and must have an interest in English language or foreign language. Available to U.S. citizens.

Application Requirements: Application, transcript. *Deadline:* varies.

Contact: Minnesota Higher Education Services Office
1450 Energy Park Drive, Suite 350
St. Paul, MN 55108-5227
Phone: 651-642-0567 Ext. 1

MINNESOTA RECIPROCAL AGREEMENT

Renewable tuition waiver for Minnesota residents. Waives all or part of non-resident tuition surcharge at public institutions in Iowa, Kansas, Michigan, Missouri, Nebraska, North Dakota, South Dakota, and Wisconsin. Deadline is last day of academic term.

Award: Scholarship for use in freshman, sophomore, junior, senior, graduate, or postgraduate years; renewable. *Number:* 1. *Amount:* varies.

Eligibility Requirements: Applicant must be enrolled or expecting to enroll full or part-time at a two-year or four-year or technical institution or university; resident of Minnesota and studying in Iowa, Kansas, Michigan, Missouri, Nebraska, North Dakota, South Dakota, or Wisconsin. Available to U.S. citizens.

Application Requirements: Application. *Deadline:* varies.

Contact: Minnesota Higher Education Services Office
1450 Energy Park Drive, Suite 350
St. Paul, MN 55108-5227
Phone: 651-642-0567 Ext. 1

MINNESOTA STATE GRANT PROGRAM

Need-based grant program available for Minnesota residents attending Minnesota colleges. Student covers 46% of cost with remainder covered by Pell Grant, parent contribution and state grant. Students apply with FAFSA and college administers the program on campus.

Award: Grant for use in freshman, sophomore, junior, or senior years; not renewable. *Number:* 71,000–75,000. *Amount:* $100–$7861.

Eligibility Requirements: Applicant must be age 17; enrolled or expecting to enroll full or part-time at a two-year or four-year or technical institution or university; resident of Minnesota and studying in Minnesota. Available to U.S. citizens.

Application Requirements: Application, financial need analysis. *Deadline:* varies.

Contact: Minnesota Higher Education Services Office
1450 Energy Park Drive, Suite 350
St. Paul, MN 55108
Phone: 651-642-0567 Ext. 1

MINNESOTA STATE VETERANS' DEPENDENTS ASSISTANCE PROGRAM
• *See page 591*

POSTSECONDARY CHILD CARE GRANT PROGRAM-MINNESOTA

One-time grant available for students not receiving MFIP. Based on financial need. Cannot exceed actual child care costs or maximum award chart (based on income). Must be Minnesota resident. For use at Minnesota two- or four-year school, including public technical colleges.

Award: Grant for use in freshman, sophomore, junior, or senior years; not renewable. *Number:* varies. *Amount:* $100–$2300.

Eligibility Requirements: Applicant must be enrolled or expecting to enroll full or part-time at a two-year or four-year or technical institution or university; resident of Minnesota and studying in Minnesota. Available to U.S. citizens.

Application Requirements: Application, financial need analysis. *Deadline:* Continuous.

Contact: Minnesota Higher Education Services Office
1450 Energy Park Drive, Suite 350
St. Paul, MN 55108-5227
Phone: 651-642-0567 Ext. 1

SAFETY OFFICERS' SURVIVOR GRANT PROGRAM
• *See page 545*

MINNESOTA INDIAN SCHOLARSHIP OFFICE   http://www.mheso.state.mn.us

MINNESOTA INDIAN SCHOLARSHIP PROGRAM
• *See page 624*

MISSISSIPPI STATE STUDENT FINANCIAL AID   http://www.mississippiuniversities.com

HIGHER EDUCATION LEGISLATIVE PLAN (HELP)

Eligible applicant must be resident of Mississippi and be freshmen and/or sophomore student who graduated from high school within the immediate past two years. Must demonstrate need as determined by the results of the Free Application for Federal Student Aid, documenting an average family adjusted gross income of $36,500 or less over the prior two years. Must be enrolled full-time at a Mississippi college or university, have a cumulative grade point average of 2.5 and have scored 20 on the ACT.

Award: Scholarship for use in freshman or sophomore years; renewable. *Number:* 1.

Eligibility Requirements: Applicant must be enrolled or expecting to enroll full-time at a four-year institution or university; resident of Mississippi and studying in Mississippi. Applicant must have 2.5 GPA or higher. Available to U.S. citizens.

Mississippi State Student Financial Aid (continued)

Application Requirements: Application, financial need analysis, test scores, transcript, FAFSA. *Deadline:* March 31.

Contact: Mississippi Student Financial Aid
Mississippi State Student Financial Aid
3825 Ridgewood Road
Jackson, MS 39211-6453
Phone: 800-327-2980
E-mail: sfa@ihl.state.ms.us

MISSISSIPPI EMINENT SCHOLARS GRANT

Award for high-school seniors who are residents of Mississippi. Applicants must achieve a grade point average of 3.5 after a minimum of seven semesters in high school and must have scored 29 on the ACT. Must enroll full-time at an eligible Mississippi college or university.

Award: Grant for use in freshman, sophomore, junior, or senior years; renewable. *Number:* varies. *Amount:* up to $2500.

Eligibility Requirements: Applicant must be enrolled or expecting to enroll full-time at a two-year or four-year institution or university; resident of Mississippi and studying in Mississippi. Applicant must have 3.5 GPA or higher. Available to U.S. citizens.

Application Requirements: Application, test scores, transcript. *Deadline:* September 15.

Contact: Mississippi Student Financial Aid
Mississippi State Student Financial Aid
3825 Ridgewood Road
Jackson, MS 39211-6453
Phone: 800-327-2980
E-mail: sfa@ihl.state.ms.us

MISSISSIPPI RESIDENT TUITION ASSISTANCE GRANT

Must be a resident of Mississippi enrolled full-time at an eligible Mississippi college or university. Must maintain a minimum 2.5 GPA each semester. MTAG awards may be up to $500 per academic year for freshmen and sophomores and $1,000 per academic year for juniors and seniors. Funds will be made available to eligible participants for eight semesters or the normal time required to complete the degree program, whichever comes first. Refer to Web site for application information http://www.mississippiuniversities.com

Award: Grant for use in freshman, sophomore, junior, or senior years; renewable. *Amount:* $500–$1000.

Eligibility Requirements: Applicant must be enrolled or expecting to enroll full-time at a two-year or four-year institution or university; resident of Mississippi and studying in Mississippi. Applicant must have 2.5 GPA or higher. Available to U.S. citizens.

Application Requirements: Application, test scores, transcript. *Deadline:* September 15.

Contact: Mississippi Student Financial Aid
Mississippi State Student Financial Aid
3825 Ridgewood Road
Jackson, MS 39211-6453
Phone: 800-327-2980
E-mail: sfa@ihl.state.ms.us

NISSAN SCHOLARSHIP

Renewable award for Mississippi residents attending a Mississippi institution. The scholarship will pay full tuition and a book allowance. Minimum GPA of 2.0 as well as an ACT composite of at least 20 or combined SAT scores of 940 or better. Must demonstrate financial need and leadership abilities. Application deadline is March 1.

Award: Scholarship for use in freshman, sophomore, junior or senior years; renewable. *Number:* 1.

Eligibility Requirements: Applicant must be high school student; planning to enroll or expecting to enroll full-time at a two-year or four-year institution or university; resident of Mississippi and studying in Mississippi. Available to U.S. citizens.

Application Requirements: Application, essay, financial need analysis, references, test scores, transcript. *Deadline:* March 1.

Contact: Mississippi Student Financial Aid
Mississippi State Student Financial Aid
3825 Ridgewood Road
Jackson, MS 39211-6453
Phone: 800-327-2980
E-mail: sfa@ihl.state.ms.us

MISSOURI BAR FOUNDATION   http://www.mobar.org

HENRY C. MCDOUGAL SCHOLARSHIP

One-time award for students attending an accredited law school in Missouri. Must be a resident of northwest Missouri. Scholarship and financial need are the factors that will be weighed the most in making the award. See Web site at http://www.mobar.org for further details.

Award: Scholarship for use in freshman, or graduate years; not renewable. *Number:* 2–3. *Amount:* $1200–$2800.

Eligibility Requirements: Applicant must be enrolled or expecting to enroll full-time at an institution or university; resident of Missouri and studying in Missouri. Available to U.S. citizens.

Application Requirements: Application, financial need analysis. *Deadline:* July 1.

Contact: Stephen Murrell, Governmental Relations Consultant
Missouri Bar Foundation
PO Box 119
Jefferson City, MO 65101
Phone: 573-635-4128
Fax: 573-635-2811

MISSOURI DEPARTMENT OF ELEMENTARY AND SECONDARY EDUCATION   http://www.dese.mo.gov

ROBERT C. BYRD HONORS SCHOLARSHIP-MISSOURI

Award for Missouri high school seniors who are residents of Missouri. The amount of the award per student each year depends on the amount the state is allotted by the U.S. Department of Education. The highest amount of award per student is $1500. Students must rank in top 10% of high school class and score in top 10% of ACT test.

Award: Scholarship for use in freshman year; renewable. *Number:* 100–150. *Amount:* $1100–$1500.

Eligibility Requirements: Applicant must be high school student; planning to enroll or expecting to enroll full-time at a two-year or four-year or technical institution or university and resident of Missouri. Applicant must have 3.5 GPA or higher. Available to U.S. citizens.

Application Requirements: Application, test scores, transcript, 7th semester transcripts. *Deadline:* April 15.

Contact: Laura Harrison, Administrative Assistant II
Missouri Department of Elementary and Secondary Education
PO Box 480
Jefferson City, MO 65102-0480
Phone: 573-751-1668
Fax: 573-526-3580
E-mail: laura.harrison@dese.mo.gov

MISSOURI DEPARTMENT OF HIGHER EDUCATION   http://www.dhe.mo.gov

CHARLES GALLAGHER STUDENT ASSISTANCE PROGRAM

Available to Missouri residents attending Missouri colleges or universities full-time. Must be undergraduates with financial need. Free Application for Federal Student Aid (FAFSA) or a renewal must be received by the federal processor by April 1 to be considered.

Award: Grant for use in freshman, sophomore, junior, or senior years; not renewable. *Number:* varies. *Amount:* $100–$1500.

Eligibility Requirements: Applicant must be enrolled or expecting to enroll full-time at a two-year or four-year or technical institution or university; resident of Missouri and studying in Missouri. Available to U.S. citizens.

Application Requirements: Financial need analysis, FAFSA. *Deadline:* April 1.

Contact: MDHE Information Center
Missouri Department of Higher Education
3515 Amazonas Drive
Jefferson City, MO 65109
Phone: 800-473-6757
Fax: 573-751-6635
E-mail: icweb@dhe.mo.gov

MARGUERITE ROSS BARNETT MEMORIAL SCHOLARSHIP

Applicant must be employed (at least 20 hours per week) and attending school part-time. Must be Missouri resident and enrolled at a participating Missouri post secondary school. Awards not available during summer term. Minimum age is 18. Scholarships can be renewed annually.

Award: Scholarship for use in freshman, sophomore, junior, or senior years; renewable. *Number:* varies. *Amount:* $900–$1700.

Eligibility Requirements: Applicant must be age 18; enrolled or expecting to enroll part-time at a two-year or four-year institution or university; resident of Missouri and studying in Missouri. Available to U.S. citizens.

Application Requirements: Application, financial need analysis, FAFSA. *Deadline:* April 1.

Contact: MDHE Information Center
Missouri Department of Higher Education
3515 Amazonas Drive
Jefferson City, MO 65109
Phone: 800-473-6757 Ext. 1
Fax: 573-751-6635
E-mail: icweb@dhe.mo.gov

MISSOURI COLLEGE GUARANTEE PROGRAM

Available to Missouri residents attending Missouri colleges full-time. Minimum 2.5 GPA required. Must have participated in high school extracurricular activities.

Award: Scholarship for use in freshman, sophomore, junior, or senior years; not renewable. *Number:* varies. *Amount:* $100–$4900.

Eligibility Requirements: Applicant must be enrolled or expecting to enroll full-time at a two-year or four-year institution or university; resident of Missouri and studying in Missouri. Applicant must have 2.5 GPA or higher. Available to U.S. citizens.

Application Requirements: Financial need analysis, test scores, FAFSA. *Deadline:* April 1.

Contact: MDHE Information Center
Missouri Department of Higher Education
3515 Amazonas Drive
Jefferson City, MO 65109
Phone: 800-473-6757 Ext. 1
Fax: 573-751-6635
E-mail: icweb@dhe.mo.gov

MISSOURI HIGHER EDUCATION ACADEMIC SCHOLARSHIP (BRIGHT FLIGHT)

Awards of $2000 for Missouri high school seniors. Must be in top 3% of Missouri SAT or ACT scorers. Must attend Missouri institution as full-time undergraduate. Must be Missouri resident and U.S. citizen.

Award: Scholarship for use in freshman, sophomore, junior, or senior years; not renewable. *Number:* varies. *Amount:* $2000.

Eligibility Requirements: Applicant must be high school student; planning to enroll or expecting to enroll full-time at a two-year or four-year or technical institution or university; resident of Missouri and studying in Missouri. Available to U.S. citizens.

Application Requirements: Test scores. *Deadline:* July 31.

Contact: MDHE Information Center
Missouri Department of Higher Education
3515 Amazonas Drive
Jefferson City, MO 65109
Phone: 800-473-6757 Ext. 1
Fax: 573-751-6635
E-mail: icweb@dhe.mo.gov

MITCHELL INSTITUTE   http://www.mitchellinstitute.org

SENATOR GEORGE J. MITCHELL SCHOLARSHIP RESEARCH INSTITUTE SCHOLARSHIPS

The Mitchell Institute awards a scholarship to a graduating senior from every public high school in Maine. The scholarship award is in the amount of up to $5000 for students who are pursuing a four-year degree and $2500 for students pursuing a two-year degree. One scholarship per county in the amount of $6000 ($1500 per year) is awarded with a preference to a first-generation college student.

Award: Scholarship for use in freshman year; renewable. *Number:* up to 130. *Amount:* $2500–$6000.

Eligibility Requirements: Applicant must be high school student; planning to enroll or expecting to enroll full or part-time at an institution or university and resident of Maine. Available to U.S. citizens.

Application Requirements: Application, essay, financial need analysis, photo, references, transcript. *Deadline:* April 1.

Contact: Patricia Higgins, Director of Scholarship Programs
Mitchell Institute
22 Monument Square, Suite 200
Portland, ME 04101
Phone: 207-773-7700
Fax: 207-773-1133
E-mail: phiggins@mitchellinstitute.org

MLGPA FOUNDATION   http://www.mlgpa.org

JOEL ABROMSON MEMORIAL FOUNDATION

One-time award, for full-time post secondary study, available to winner of essay contest. Open to Maine residents only. Contact for essay topic and complete information. SASE. Deadline is April 15.

Award: Scholarship for use in freshman year; not renewable. *Number:* up to 2. *Amount:* $500–$1000.

Eligibility Requirements: Applicant must be high school student; planning to enroll or expecting to enroll full-time at a two-year or four-year or technical institution or university and resident of Maine. Available to U.S. citizens.

Application Requirements: Application, applicant must enter a contest, essay, references, self-addressed stamped envelope, copy of acceptance letter to institution of higher learning. *Deadline:* April 15.

Contact: Betsy Smith, Scholarship Coordinator
MLGPA Foundation
PO Box 1951
Portland, ME 04104
Phone: 207-761-3732
Fax: 207-761-8484
E-mail: mlgpa@mlgpa.org

MONTANA GUARANTEED STUDENT LOAN PROGRAM, OFFICE OF COMMISSIONER OF HIGHER EDUCATION   http://www.mgslp.state.mt.us

INDIAN STUDENT FEE WAIVER
• See page 624

MONTANA HIGHER EDUCATION OPPORTUNITY GRANT

This grant is awarded based on need to undergraduate students attending either part-time or full-time who are residents of Montana and attending participating Montana schools. Awards are limited to the most needy students. A specific major or program of study is not required. This grant does not need to be repaid, and students may apply each year. Apply by filing a free application for Federal Student Aid by March 1 and contacting the financial aid office at the admitting college.

Award: Grant for use in freshman, sophomore, junior, or senior years; not renewable. *Number:* up to 800. *Amount:* $400–$600.

Eligibility Requirements: Applicant must be enrolled or expecting to enroll full or part-time at a two-year or four-year institution or university; resident of Montana and studying in Montana. Available to U.S. citizens.

Montana Guaranteed Student Loan Program, Office of Commissioner of Higher Education (continued)

Application Requirements: Application, financial need analysis, FAFSA. *Deadline:* March 1.

Contact: Jamie Bushin, Scholarship Coordinator
Montana Guaranteed Student Loan Program, Office of Commissioner of Higher Education
PO Box 203101
Helena, MT 59620-3101
Phone: 406-444-0364
Fax: 406-444-1869
E-mail: jbushin@mgslp.state.mt.us

MONTANA TUITION ASSISTANCE PROGRAM-BAKER GRANT

Need-based grant for Montana residents attending participating Montana schools who have earned at least $2575 during the previous calendar year. Must be enrolled full time. Grant does not need to be repaid. Award covers the first undergraduate degree or certificate. Apply by filing a free application for Federal Student Aid by March 1 and contacting the financial aid office at the admitting college.

Award: Grant for use in freshman, sophomore, junior, or senior years; not renewable. *Number:* 1000–3000. *Amount:* $100–$1000.

Eligibility Requirements: Applicant must be enrolled or expecting to enroll full-time at a two-year or four-year institution or university; resident of Montana and studying in Montana. Available to U.S. citizens.

Application Requirements: Application, financial need analysis, FAFSA. *Deadline:* March 1.

Contact: Jamie Bushin, Scholarship Coordinator
Montana Guaranteed Student Loan Program, Office of Commissioner of Higher Education
PO Box 203101
Helena, MT 59620-3101
Phone: 406-444-0364
Fax: 406-444-1869
E-mail: jbushin@mgslp.state.mt.us

MONTANA UNIVERSITY SYSTEM HONOR SCHOLARSHIP

Scholarship provides a four-year renewable fee waiver of tuition and registration and is awarded to graduating high school seniors from accredited high schools in Montana. 300-400 scholarships are awarded each year averaging $2000-$3000 per recipient. The value of the award varies, depending on the tuition and registration fee at each participating Montana university or college. Must have a minimum 3.5 GPA, meet all college preparatory requirements, and be enrolled in an accredited high school for at least three years prior to graduation. Awarded to highest-ranking student in class attending a participating school. Contact high school counselor to apply. Deadline: January 31.

Award: Scholarship for use in freshman, sophomore, junior, or senior years; renewable. *Number:* 300–400. *Amount:* $2000–$3000.

Eligibility Requirements: Applicant must be high school student; planning to enroll or expecting to enroll full or part-time at a two-year or four-year institution or university; resident of Montana and studying in Montana. Applicant must have 3.5 GPA or higher. Available to U.S. citizens.

Application Requirements: Application, transcript. *Deadline:* January 31.

Contact: Janice Kirkpatrick, Grant and Scholarship Coordinator
Montana Guaranteed Student Loan Program, Office of Commissioner of Higher Education
PO Box 203101
Helena, MT 59620-3101
Phone: 406-444-0638
Fax: 406-444-1869
E-mail: jkirkpatrick@mgslp.state.mt.us

MONTANA STATE OFFICE OF PUBLIC INSTRUCTION
http://www.opi.mt.gov

ROBERT C. BYRD HONORS SCHOLARSHIP-MONTANA

Aim of this program is "to promote student excellence and achievement and to recognize exceptionally able students who show promise of continued

excellence." The scholarship is available to graduating seniors and graduates of GED programs who will be entering college as freshmen. Minimum 3.6 GPA required. Award restricted to Montana residents.

Award: Scholarship for use in freshman, sophomore, junior, or senior years; renewable. *Number:* 22–23. *Amount:* $1500.

Eligibility Requirements: Applicant must be high school student; planning to enroll or expecting to enroll full or part-time at a two-year or four-year or technical institution or university and resident of Montana. Available to U.S. citizens.

Application Requirements: Application, essay, test scores, transcript. *Deadline:* March 3.

Contact: Judy Birch, Program Director
Montana State Office of Public Instruction
PO Box 202501
Helena, MT 59620-2501
Phone: 406-444-5663
Fax: 406-444-1373
E-mail: jbirch@state.mt.us

UNITED STATES SENATE YOUTH PROGRAM-THE WILLIAM RANDOLPH HEARST FOUNDATION

Two high school juniors or seniors from Montana have a weeklong orientation in Washington, D.C. on the operation of the United States Senate and other components of the federal government. Potential awardees compete for the scholarship by taking a 50-point test, then the top ten applicants answer 5-7 questions in a video presentation. Scholarship money is given directly to school each student attends. Must be currently serving in a high school government office. See Web site for specific details: http://www.opi.state.mt.us

Award: Scholarship for use in freshman year; not renewable. *Number:* 2. *Amount:* $5000.

Eligibility Requirements: Applicant must be high school student; planning to enroll or expecting to enroll at a four-year institution or university and resident of Montana. Available to U.S. citizens.

Application Requirements: Application, interview, test scores, video presentation. *Deadline:* October 12.

Contact: Judy Birch, Program Director
Montana State Office of Public Instruction
PO Box 202501
Helena, MT 59620-2501
Phone: 406-444-5663
Fax: 406-444-1373
E-mail: jbirch@state.mt.us

MOUNT VERNON URBAN RENEWAL AGENCY
http://www.ci.mount-vernon.ny.us

THOMAS E. SHARPE MEMORIAL SCHOLARSHIP

Award offered only to residents of the city of Mount Vernon of low and moderate income for the purpose of pursuing higher education at a vocational/technical school or college. Students can receive from $300 to $1200 per academic year.

Award: Grant for use in freshman, sophomore, junior, or senior years; renewable. *Number:* 150. *Amount:* $400–$1200.

Eligibility Requirements: Applicant must be enrolled or expecting to enroll full-time at a two-year or four-year or technical institution or university and resident of New York. Applicant must have 2.5 GPA or higher. Available to U.S. citizens.

Application Requirements: Application, driver's license, essay, financial need analysis, transcript. *Deadline:* varies.

Contact: Mary E. Fleming, Director, Scholarship Programs
Mount Vernon Urban Renewal Agency
City Hall, Roosevelt Square, Department of Planning
Mount Vernon, NY 10550
Phone: 914-699-7230 Ext. 110
Fax: 914-699-1435
E-mail: mfleming@ci.mount-vernon.ny.us

NASA FLORIDA SPACE GRANT CONSORTIUM
http://fsgc.engr.ucf.edu

FLORIDA/NASA MATCHING GRANT PROGRAM

One-time award for aerospace and technology research. Grant is for research in Florida only. Submit research proposal with budget. Applicants must be from a university, college, or industry in Florida. Deadline varies.

Award: Grant for use in freshman, sophomore, junior, senior, graduate, or postgraduate years; not renewable. *Number:* 9–12.

Eligibility Requirements: Applicant must be enrolled or expecting to enroll full or part-time at a two-year or four-year or technical institution or university and studying in Florida. Available to U.S. citizens.

Application Requirements: Proposal with budget. *Deadline:* March 5.

Contact: Dr. Jaydeep Mukherjee, FSGC Administrator
NASA Florida Space Grant Consortium
Mail Code: FSGC
Kennedy Space Center, FL 32899
Phone: 321-452-4301
Fax: 321-449-0739
E-mail: fsgc@mail.ucf.edu

NASA RHODE ISLAND SPACE GRANT CONSORTIUM
http://www.planetary.brown.edu/RI_Space_Grant

NASA RHODE ISLAND SPACE GRANT CONSORTIUM UNDERGRADUATE SCHOLARSHIP

Scholarship for undergraduate students for study and/or outreach related to NASA and Space Sciences, Engineering and/or technology. Must attend a Rhode Island Space Grant Consortium participating school. Recipients are expected to devote a maximum of four hours per week in science education for K-12 children and teachers. See Web site for additional information: http://www.spacegrant.brown.edu

Award: Scholarship for use in sophomore, junior, or senior years; not renewable. *Number:* up to 2. *Amount:* up to $4000.

Eligibility Requirements: Applicant must be enrolled or expecting to enroll full-time at a four-year institution or university and studying in Rhode Island. Applicant must have 3.0 GPA or higher. Available to U.S. citizens.

Application Requirements: Application, essay, resume, references, transcript. *Deadline:* February 27.

Contact: Dorcas Metcalf, Program Manager
NASA Rhode Island Space Grant Consortium
Brown University, PO Box 1846
Providence, RI 02912
Phone: 401-863-1151
Fax: 401-863-1242
E-mail: dorcas_metcalf@brown.edu

NASA RISGC SCIENCE EN ESPA±OL SCHOLARSHIP FOR UNDERGRADUATE STUDENTS

Award for undergraduate students at a Rhode Island Space Grant Consortium participating school who is studying in any space-related field of science, math, engineering, or other field with applications in space study. Recipients are expected to devote a maximum of 8 hours per week in outreach activities, supporting ESL teachers with science instruction. See Web site for additional information: http://www.spacegrant.brown.edu.

Award: Scholarship for use in sophomore, junior, or senior years; not renewable. *Number:* up to 2. *Amount:* up to $4000.

Eligibility Requirements: Applicant must be enrolled or expecting to enroll full-time at a four-year institution or university and studying in Rhode Island. Applicant must have 3.0 GPA or higher. Available to U.S. citizens.

Application Requirements: Application, essay, resume, transcript. *Deadline:* February 27.

Contact: Dorcas Metcalf, Program Manager
NASA Rhode Island Space Grant Consortium
Brown University, Box 1846
Providence, RI 02912
Phone: 401-863-1151
Fax: 401-863-1242
E-mail: dorcas_metcalf@brown.edu

NASA RISGC SUMMER SCHOLARSHIP FOR UNDERGRADUATE STUDENTS

Scholarship for full-time summer study. Students are expected to devote 75% of their time to a research project with a faculty advisor and 25% to outreach activities in science education for K-12 students and teachers. Must attend a Rhode Island Space Grant Consortium participating school. See Web site for additional information: http://www.spacegrant.brown.edu

Award: Scholarship for use in sophomore, junior, or senior years. *Number:* up to 2. *Amount:* up to $4000.

Eligibility Requirements: Applicant must be enrolled or expecting to enroll full-time at a four-year institution or university and studying in Rhode Island. Applicant must have 3.0 GPA or higher. Available to U.S. citizens.

Application Requirements: Application, resume, references, letter of interest. *Deadline:* February 27.

Contact: Dorcas Metcalf, Program Manager
NASA Rhode Island Space Grant Consortium
Brown University, PO Box 1846
Providence, RI 02912
Phone: 401-863-1151
Fax: 401-863-1242
E-mail: dorcas_metcalf@brown.edu

NASA SOUTH CAROLINA SPACE GRANT CONSORTIUM
http://www.cofc.edu/~scsgrant

UNDERGRADUATE RESEARCH PROGRAM

Applicant must be enrolled full-time at SCSG member institutions. Applicants can be focused on any field that can be related to NASA, specifically math, science and engineering. Deadline varies, usually in January or into early spring. Must be U.S. citizen. See Web site for additional information: http://www.cofc.edu/~scsgrant

Award: Grant for use in freshman, sophomore, junior, or senior years; renewable. *Number:* 10. *Amount:* $500–$3000.

Eligibility Requirements: Applicant must be enrolled or expecting to enroll full-time at a four-year institution or university and studying in South Carolina. Available to U.S. citizens.

Application Requirements: Application, essay, references, transcript, research proposal.

Contact: Tara B. Scozzaro, Program Manager
NASA South Carolina Space Grant Consortium
66 George Street, College of Charleston
Charleston, SC 29424
Phone: 843-953-5463
Fax: 843-953-5446
E-mail: scozzarot@cofc.edu

NASA SOUTH DAKOTA SPACE GRANT CONSORTIUM
http://www.sdsmt.edu/space/

SOUTH DAKOTA SPACE GRANT CONSORTIUM UNDERGRADUATE SCHOLARSHIPS

Up to $1000 per semester available for undergraduate students pursuing studies in science, engineering, aviation, and aerospace, or related fields. Women and minorities are encouraged to apply. For more information, see Web site: http://www.sdsmt.edu/space/.

Award: Scholarship for use in freshman, sophomore, junior, or senior years; renewable. *Number:* varies. *Amount:* $2000.

Eligibility Requirements: Applicant must be enrolled or expecting to enroll full or part-time at a four-year institution or university and studying in South Dakota. Applicant must have 3.0 GPA or higher. Available to U.S. citizens.

NASA South Dakota Space Grant Consortium (continued)

Application Requirements: Application, transcript. *Deadline:* varies.

Contact: Tom Durkin, Deputy Director and Coordinator
NASA South Dakota Space Grant Consortium
501 East Saint Joseph Street
Rapid City, SD 57701-3995
Phone: 605-394-1975
Fax: 605-394-5360
E-mail: jeanette.nilson@sdsmt.edu

NATIONAL ASSOCIATION FOR CAMPUS ACTIVITIES
http://www.naca.org

LORI RHETT MEMORIAL SCHOLARSHIP

Scholarships will be given to undergraduate or graduate students with a cumulative GPA of 2.5 or better at the time of the application and during the academic term in which the scholarship is awarded. Must demonstrate significant leadership skill and ability while holding a significant leadership position on campus. Applicants must have made contributions via volunteer involvement, either on or off campus. Must be enrolled in college/university in the NACA Pacific Northwest Region.

Award: Scholarship for use in freshman, sophomore, junior, senior, or graduate years; not renewable. *Number:* 1. *Amount:* $250–$300.

Eligibility Requirements: Applicant must be enrolled or expecting to enroll at a two-year or four-year institution or university; studying in Alaska, Idaho, Montana, Oregon, or Washington and must have an interest in leadership. Applicant must have 2.5 GPA or higher. Available to U.S. citizens.

Application Requirements: Application, resume, references, transcript. *Deadline:* June 30.

Contact: Dionne Ellison, Administrative Assistant
National Association for Campus Activities
13 Harbison Way
Columbia, SC 29212-3401
Phone: 803-732-6222
Fax: 803-749-1047
E-mail: dionnee@naca.org

MARKLEY SCHOLARSHIP

Scholarship is to recognize and honor involved students who have made significant contributions to the Central region. Must be classified as a junior, senior or graduate student at a four-year school located in the former NACA South Central region, or a sophomore in the former NACA South Central region. Must have minimum 2.5 GPA.

Award: Scholarship for use in sophomore, junior, senior, or graduate years; not renewable. *Number:* varies. *Amount:* $250–$300.

Eligibility Requirements: Applicant must be enrolled or expecting to enroll at a two-year or four-year institution or university and studying in Arkansas, Louisiana, New Mexico, Oklahoma, or Texas. Applicant must have 2.5 GPA or higher. Available to U.S. citizens.

Application Requirements: Application, resume. *Deadline:* September 1.

Contact: Dionne Ellison, Administrative Assistant
National Association for Campus Activities
13 Harbison Way
Columbia, SC 29212-3401
Phone: 803-732-6222
Fax: 803-749-1047
E-mail: dionnee@naca.org

NATIONAL ASSOCIATION FOR CAMPUS ACTIVITIES EAST COAST HIGHER EDUCATION RESEARCH SCHOLARSHIP

Scholarships will be given to students showing that their research will add to the college student personnel knowledge base, particularly campus activities, or address issues challenging student affairs practitioners or higher education as they relate to campus activities. A statement of the problem, purpose of project, plan, timeline to address the question, anticipated results, and statement of the project's anticipated contribution to the profession must accompany the application. Must be enrolled in a college/university in the NACA East Coast Region.

Award: Scholarship for use in freshman, sophomore, junior, senior, or graduate years; not renewable. *Number:* varies. *Amount:* $250–$300.

Eligibility Requirements: Applicant must be enrolled or expecting to enroll at an institution or university and studying in Delaware, Maryland, New Jersey, New York, or Pennsylvania. Available to U.S. citizens.

Application Requirements: Application, essay, references, research proposal. *Deadline:* June 15.

Contact: Dionne Ellison, Administrative Assistant
National Association for Campus Activities
13 Harbison Way
Columbia, SC 29212-3401
Phone: 803-732-6222
Fax: 803-749-1047
E-mail: dionnee@naca.org

NATIONAL ASSOCIATION FOR CAMPUS ACTIVITIES EAST COAST UNDERGRADUATE SCHOLARSHIP FOR STUDENT LEADERS

Scholarships will be awarded to undergraduate students who are in good standing at the time of the application and during the academic term in which the scholarship is awarded. Applicants must maintain a 2.5 GPA, demonstrate leadership skills and abilities while holding a significant leadership position on campus or in community, and have made significant contributions via volunteer involvement. Eligible students must be attending a college or university within the NACA East Coast Region.

Award: Scholarship for use in freshman, sophomore, junior, or senior years; not renewable. *Number:* up to 2. *Amount:* $250–$300.

Eligibility Requirements: Applicant must be enrolled or expecting to enroll at a two-year or four-year institution or university; studying in Delaware, District of Columbia, Maryland, New Jersey, New York, or Pennsylvania and must have an interest in leadership. Applicant must have 2.5 GPA or higher. Available to U.S. citizens.

Application Requirements: Application, essay, resume, references, transcript. *Deadline:* March 31.

Contact: Dionne Ellison, Administrative Assistant
National Association for Campus Activities
13 Harbison Way
Columbia, SC 29212-3401
Phone: 803-732-6222
Fax: 803-749-1047
E-mail: dionnee@naca.org

NATIONAL ASSOCIATION FOR CAMPUS ACTIVITIES SOUTHEAST REGION STUDENT LEADERSHIP SCHOLARSHIP

Scholarships will be given to full-time undergraduate students in good standing at the time of the application and during the academic term in which the scholarship is awarded. Must demonstrate significant leadership skill and ability while holding a significant leadership position on campus. Applicants must have made contributions via volunteer involvement, either on or off campus. Must be enrolled in a college/university in the NACA Southeast Region.

Award: Scholarship for use in freshman, sophomore, junior, or senior years; not renewable. *Number:* up to 3. *Amount:* $250–$300.

Eligibility Requirements: Applicant must be enrolled or expecting to enroll full-time at a two-year or four-year institution or university; studying in Alabama, Florida, Georgia, Mississippi, North Carolina, Puerto Rico, South Carolina, Tennessee, or Virginia and must have an interest in leadership. Available to U.S. citizens.

Application Requirements: Application, essay, resume, references, transcript. *Deadline:* March 31.

Contact: Dionne Ellison, Administrative Assistant
National Association for Campus Activities
13 Harbison Way
Columbia, SC 29212-3401
Phone: 803-732-6222
Fax: 803-749-1047
E-mail: dionnee@naca.org

NATIONAL ASSOCIATION FOR CAMPUS ACTIVITIES WI REGION STUDENT LEADERSHIP SCHOLARSHIP

Scholarships will be awarded to undergraduate or graduate students in good standing and enrolled in the equivalent of at least six academic credits at the time of the application and during the academic term in which the scholarship is awarded. Must be currently enrolled in or received a degree from a college or university within the NACA Wisconsin Region or Michigan (area code 906) and demonstrated leadership skill and significant service to their campus community.

Award: Scholarship for use in freshman, sophomore, junior, senior, or graduate years; not renewable. *Number:* 1. *Amount:* $250–$300.

Eligibility Requirements: Applicant must be enrolled or expecting to enroll full or part-time at a two-year or four-year institution or university; studying in Michigan or Wisconsin and must have an interest in leadership. Available to U.S. citizens.

Application Requirements: Application, essay, resume, references, transcript. *Deadline:* January 15.

Contact: Dionne Ellison, Administrative Assistant
National Association for Campus Activities
13 Harbison Way
Columbia, SC 29212-3401
Phone: 803-732-6222
Fax: 803-749-1047
E-mail: dionnee@naca.org

TESS CALDARELLI MEMORIAL SCHOLARSHIP

Scholarship available to undergraduate or graduate students with a minimum 3.0 GPA. Must demonstrate significant leadership skills and hold a significant position on campus. Must attend school in the NACA Great Lakes Region.

Award: Scholarship for use in freshman, sophomore, junior, senior, or graduate years. *Number:* varies. *Amount:* $250–$300.

Eligibility Requirements: Applicant must be enrolled or expecting to enroll at a two-year or four-year institution or university; studying in Kentucky, Michigan, Ohio, Pennsylvania, or West Virginia and must have an interest in leadership. Applicant must have 3.0 GPA or higher. Available to U.S. citizens.

Application Requirements: Application, resume, references, transcript. *Deadline:* November 1.

Contact: Dionne Ellison, Administrative Assistant
National Association for Campus Activities
13 Harbison Way
Columbia, SC 29212-3401
Phone: 803-732-6222
Fax: 803-749-1047
E-mail: dionnee@naca.org

ZAGUNAS STUDENT LEADERS SCHOLARSHIP

Scholarships will be awarded to undergraduate or graduate students maintaining a cumulative GPA of 3.0 or better at the time of the application and during the academic term in which the scholarship is awarded. Applicants should demonstrate leadership skills and abilities while holding a significant leadership position on campus. Applicants must submit two letters of recommendation and a description of the applicant's leadership activities, skills, abilities and accomplishments. Must be enrolled in a college/university in the NACA Great Lakes Region.

Award: Scholarship for use in freshman, sophomore, junior, senior, or graduate years; not renewable. *Number:* 1. *Amount:* $300.

Eligibility Requirements: Applicant must be enrolled or expecting to enroll at a two-year or four-year institution or university; studying in Kentucky, Michigan, Ohio, Pennsylvania, or West Virginia and must have an interest in leadership. Applicant must have 3.0 GPA or higher. Available to U.S. citizens.

Application Requirements: Application, resume, references, transcript. *Deadline:* November 1.

Contact: Dionne Ellison, Administrative Assistant
National Association for Campus Activities
13 Harbison Way
Columbia, SC 29212-3401
Phone: 803-732-6222
Fax: 803-749-1047
E-mail: dionnee@naca.org

NATIONAL ASSOCIATION TO ADVANCE FAT ACCEPTANCE (NEW ENGLAND CHAPTER)　http://www.necnaafa.com

NEW ENGLAND CHAPTER-NATIONAL ASSOCIATION TO ADVANCE FAT ACCEPTANCE SCHOLARSHIP

Nonrenewable scholarship for single New England high school seniors who are overweight. Essay required with application. Must have a minimum GPA

of 2.5. Must be single. Must study in Connecticut, Maine, Massachusetts, New Hampshire, Rhode Island, or Vermont.

Award: Scholarship for use in freshman year; not renewable. *Number:* 2. *Amount:* $500.

Eligibility Requirements: Applicant must be high school student; planning to enroll or expecting to enroll full-time at a two-year or four-year or technical institution or university; single; resident of Connecticut, Maine, Massachusetts, New Hampshire, Rhode Island, or Vermont and studying in Connecticut, Maine, Massachusetts, New Hampshire, Rhode Island, or Vermont. Applicant must have 2.5 GPA or higher. Available to U.S. citizens.

Application Requirements: Application, autobiography, essay, photo, references, self-addressed stamped envelope, transcript. *Deadline:* May 1.

Contact: Roni Krinsky, Chairperson, Scholarship Committee
National Association to Advance Fat Acceptance (New England Chapter)
PO Box 51820
Boston, MA 02205-1820
Phone: 781-986-2232
Fax: 617-782-8460
E-mail: ronikrink@aol.com

NATIONAL BURGLAR AND FIRE ALARM ASSOCIATION　http://www.alarm.org

NBFAA/SECURITY DEALER YOUTH SCHOLARSHIP PROGRAM
• See page 545

NATIONAL COUNCIL OF JEWISH WOMEN NEW YORK SECTION　http://www.ncjwny.org

JACKSON-STRICKS SCHOLARSHIP
• See page 562

NATIONAL DEFENSE TRANSPORTATION ASSOCIATION-SCOTT ST. LOUIS CHAPTER　http://www.ndtascottstlouis.org

NATIONAL DEFENSE TRANSPORTATION ASSOCIATION, SCOTT AIR FORCE BASE- ST. LOUIS AREA CHAPTER SCHOLARSHIP

Three scholarships of $2000 each are open to any high school students that meet the eligibility criteria. One scholarship of $2000 is available for eligible college students enrolled in a degree program. An additional $2000 scholarship is set aside for immediate family members of active NDTA Scott/St. Louis Chapter members. Minimum 3.0 GPA required. Must be full-time student in CO, IA, IL, IN, KS, MI, MN, MO, MT, ND, NE, SD, WI, WY.

Award: Scholarship for use in freshman, sophomore, junior, or senior years; not renewable. *Number:* 5. *Amount:* $2000.

Eligibility Requirements: Applicant must be enrolled or expecting to enroll full-time at a two-year or four-year institution or university and studying in Colorado, Illinois, Indiana, Iowa, Kansas, Michigan, Minnesota, Missouri, Montana, Nebraska, North Dakota, or South Dakota. Applicant must have 3.0 GPA or higher. Available to U.S. citizens.

Application Requirements: Application, essay, references, test scores, transcript. *Deadline:* March 1.

Contact: Mr. Michael Carnes, Chairman, Professional Development Committee
National Defense Transportation Association-Scott St. Louis Chapter
926 Thornbury Place, PO Box 25486
Scott Air Force Base, IL 62225
Phone: 618-628-4208 Ext. 273
Fax: 618-628-4790
E-mail: mcarnes@csc.com

NATIONAL ESSAY COMPETITION http://www.rotman.utoronto.ca/essaycompetition

OSLER, HOSKIN AND HARCOURT NATIONAL ESSAY COMPETITION

Open to full-time undergraduate students enrolled in a non-professional faculty of a Canadian university or Cegep. Submit a maximum 1500 word essay in English in answer to the competition's annual question. Must submit your essay via email.

Award: Prize for use in freshman, sophomore, junior, or senior years; not renewable. *Number:* 3. *Amount:* $743–$3714.

Eligibility Requirements: Applicant must be enrolled or expecting to enroll full-time at a four-year institution or university and studying in Alberta, British Columbia, Manitoba, New Brunswick, Newfoundland, North West Territories, Nova Scotia, Ontario, Prince Edward Island, Quebec, Saskatchewan, or Yukon. Available to U.S. and non-U.S. citizens.

Application Requirements: Application, applicant must enter a contest, essay. *Deadline:* April 5.

Contact: Request information via e-mail
E-mail: essaycompetition@rotman.utoronto.ca

NATIONAL KIDNEY FOUNDATION OF INDIANA, INC. http://www.kidneyindiana.org

LARRY SMOCK SCHOLARSHIP
• See page 563

NATIONAL SYMPHONY ORCHESTRA EDUCATION PROGRAM http://www.kennedy-center.org

NATIONAL SYMPHONY ORCHESTRA YOUNG SOLOISTS' COMPETITION- BILL CERRI SCHOLARSHIP/HIGH SCHOOL DIVISION

Prize for the best soloist in competition. Winner will perform with the National Symphony Orchestra in Washington, D.C. Must be a high school student residing in Washington, D.C., Maryland, or Virginia. Visit Web site for guidelines and deadline. One-time award of $1000. Application fee: $15.

Award: Prize for use in freshman year; not renewable. *Number:* 1. *Amount:* $1000.

Eligibility Requirements: Applicant must be high school student; planning to enroll or expecting to enroll at an institution or university; resident of District of Columbia, Maryland, or Virginia and must have an interest in music/singing. Available to U.S. citizens.

Application Requirements: Application, applicant must enter a contest. *Fee:* $15. *Deadline:* February 17.

Contact: Sharyn L. Byer, Competition Administrator
National Symphony Orchestra Education Program
115 Gresham Place
Falls Church, VA 22046

NATIONAL UNION OF PUBLIC AND GENERAL EMPLOYEES http://www.nupge.ca

SCHOLARSHIP FOR ABORIGINAL CANADIANS
• See page 507

SCHOLARSHIP FOR VISIBLE MINORITIES
• See page 507

TERRY FOX MEMORIAL SCHOLARSHIP
• See page 507

TOMMY DOUGLAS SCHOLARSHIP
• See page 507

NEBRASKA DECA http://www.nedeca.org

NEBRASKA DECA LEADERSHIP SCHOLARSHIP
• See page 508

NEBRASKA DEPARTMENT OF EDUCATION http://www.nde.state.ne.us/byrd

ROBERT C. BYRD HONORS SCHOLARSHIP-NEBRASKA

Up to $1500 each year for up to four years. Must be U.S. citizen and Nebraska resident. Awards designed to promote student excellence and achievement and to recognize able students who show promise of continued excellence. Funded scholars must submit Renewal Application each year. Renewal based on continuing eligibility requirements. Must have minimum ACT score of 30. Please refer to Web site for application and further details: http://www.nde.state.ne.us/byrd.

Award: Scholarship for use in freshman, sophomore, junior, or senior years; renewable. *Number:* 40–45. *Amount:* $1500.

Eligibility Requirements: Applicant must be high school student; planning to enroll or expecting to enroll full-time at a two-year or four-year or technical institution or university and resident of Nebraska. Available to U.S. citizens.

Application Requirements: Application, test scores, transcript. *Deadline:* March 15.

Contact: Mardi North, Robert C. Byrd Scholarship Information
Nebraska Department of Education
301 Centennial Mall South, PO Box 94987
Lincoln, NE 68509-4987
Phone: 402-471-3962
Fax: 402-471-8850
E-mail: mardi.north@nde.ne.gov

NEBRASKA NATIONAL GUARD http://www.neguard.com

NEBRASKA NATIONAL GUARD TUITION CREDIT
• See page 571

NELNET COLLEGE PLANNING http://www.collegeplanning.nelnet.net

COLORADO SCHOLARSHIP

Award for Colorado high school seniors. Applicants must be 13 years or older and a registered member of Nelnet College Planning.

Award: Scholarship for use in freshman year. *Amount:* up to $1000.

Eligibility Requirements: Applicant must be high school student; age 13; planning to enroll or expecting to enroll at an institution or university; resident of Colorado and studying in Colorado. Available to U.S. citizens.

Application Requirements: Application. *Deadline:* March 31.

Contact: Teffenie Davies, Senior Vice President and Director
Nelnet College Planning
3015 South Parker Road, Suite 400
Aurora, CO 80014
Phone: 866-426-6765
E-mail: nelnetconsolidations@nelnet.net

FLORIDA SCHOLARSHIP

Applicant must be a high school senior and a legal resident of Florida. Must be 13 years or older and a registered member of Nelnet College Planning.

Award: Scholarship for use in freshman year. *Amount:* up to $1000.

Eligibility Requirements: Applicant must be high school student; age 13; planning to enroll or expecting to enroll at an institution or university; resident of Florida and studying in Florida. Available to U.S. citizens.

Application Requirements: Application. *Deadline:* varies.

Contact: Teffenie Davies, Senior Vice President and Director
Nelnet College Planning
3015 South Parker Road, Suite 400
Aurora, CO 80014
Phone: 866-426-6765
E-mail: nelnetconsolidations@nelnet.net

INDIANA SCHOLARSHIP

Applicant must be a high school senior and legal resident of Indiana. Must be 13 years or older and a registered member of Nelnet College Planning.

Award: Scholarship for use in freshman year. *Amount:* up to $1000.

Eligibility Requirements: Applicant must be high school student; age 13; planning to enroll or expecting to enroll at an institution or university; resident of Indiana and studying in Indiana. Available to U.S. citizens.

Application Requirements: Application. *Deadline:* March 31.

Contact: Teffenie Davies, Senior Vice President and Director
Nelnet College Planning
3015 South Parker Road, Suite 400
Aurora, CO 80014
Phone: 866-426-6765
E-mail: nelnetconsolidations@nelnet.net

LOUISIANA SCHOLARSHIP

Applicant must be a high school senior and a legal resident of Louisiana. Must be 13 years or older and a registered member of Nelnet College Planning..

Award: Scholarship for use in freshman year. *Amount:* up to $1000.

Eligibility Requirements: Applicant must be high school student; age 13; planning to enroll or expecting to enroll at an institution or university; resident of Louisiana and studying in Louisiana. Available to U.S. citizens.

Application Requirements: Application. *Deadline:* March 31.

Contact: Teffenie Davies, Senior Vice President and Director
Nelnet College Planning
3015 South Parker Road, Suite 400
Aurora, CO 80014
Phone: 866-426-6765
E-mail: nelnetconsolidations@nelnet.net

MAINE SCHOLARSHIP

Scholarship for high school senior or newly admitted non-traditional student planning on attending college. Must be legal resident of Maine and 13 years or older.

Award: Scholarship for use in freshman year. *Amount:* up to $10,000.

Eligibility Requirements: Applicant must be high school student; age 13; planning to enroll or expecting to enroll at an institution or university; resident of Maine and studying in Maine. Available to U.S. citizens.

Application Requirements: Application. *Deadline:* May 31.

Contact: Teffenie Davies, Senior Vice President and Director
Nelnet College Planning
3015 South Parker Road, Suite 400
Aurora, CO 80014
Phone: 866-426-6765
E-mail: nelnetconsolidations@nelnet.net

NEW MEXICO SCHOLARSHIP

Scholarship for a high school senior who is a legal resident of New Mexico. Must be 13 years or older and a registered member of Nelnet College Planning.

Award: Scholarship for use in freshman year. *Amount:* up to $1000.

Eligibility Requirements: Applicant must be high school student; age 13; planning to enroll or expecting to enroll at an institution or university; resident of New Mexico and studying in New Mexico. Available to U.S. citizens.

Application Requirements: Application. *Deadline:* March 31.

Contact: Teffenie Davies, Senior Vice President and Director
Nelnet College Planning
3015 South Parker Road, Suite 400
Aurora, CO 80014
Phone: 866-426-6765
E-mail: nelnetconsolidations@nelnet.net

NEW YORK EXCELLENCE SCHOLARSHIP

Scholarship for high school student who is a legal resident of New York. Applicant must be a registered member of Nelnet College Planning.

Award: Scholarship for use in freshman year. *Amount:* up to $5000.

Eligibility Requirements: Applicant must be high school student; planning to enroll or expecting to enroll full-time at an institution or university; resident of New York and studying in New York. Available to U.S. citizens.

Application Requirements: Application, financial need analysis, test scores. *Deadline:* March 31.

Contact: Teffenie Davies, Senior Vice President and Director
Nelnet College Planning
3015 South Parker Road, Suite 400
Aurora, CO 80014
Phone: 866-426-6765
E-mail: nelnetconsolidations@nelnet.net

NEW YORK SCHOLARSHIP

Scholarship for a high school student who is a legal resident of New York. Must be 13 years or older and a registered member of Nelnet College Planning.

Award: Scholarship for use in freshman year. *Amount:* up to $1000.

Eligibility Requirements: Applicant must be high school student; age 13; planning to enroll or expecting to enroll at an institution or university; resident of New York and studying in New York. Available to U.S. citizens.

Application Requirements: Application. *Deadline:* March 31.

Contact: Teffenie Davies, Senior Vice President and Director
Nelnet College Planning
3015 South Parker Road, Suite 400
Aurora, CO 80014
Phone: 866-426-6765
E-mail: nelnetconsolidations@nelnet.net

TEXAS SCHOLARSHIP

Scholarship for high school senior who is a legal resident of Texas. Must be 13 years or older and a registered member of Nelnet College Planning.

Award: Scholarship for use in freshman year. *Amount:* up to $1000.

Eligibility Requirements: Applicant must be high school student; age 13; planning to enroll or expecting to enroll at an institution or university; resident of Texas and studying in Texas. Available to U.S. citizens.

Application Requirements: Application. *Deadline:* March 31.

Contact: Teffenie Davies, Senior Vice President and Director
Nelnet College Planning
3015 South Parker Road, Suite 400
Aurora, CO 80014
Phone: 866-426-6765
E-mail: nelnetconsolidations@nelnet.net

NEVADA DEPARTMENT OF EDUCATION   http://www.doe.nv.gov/index.html

NEVADA STUDENT INCENTIVE GRANT

Award available to Nevada residents for use at an accredited Nevada college or university. Must show financial need. Any field of study eligible. High school students may not apply. One-time award of up to $5000. Contact financial aid office at local college.

Award: Grant for use in freshman, sophomore, junior, or senior years; not renewable. *Number:* 400–800. *Amount:* $100–$5000.

Eligibility Requirements: Applicant must be enrolled or expecting to enroll full or part-time at a two-year or four-year or technical institution or university; resident of Nevada and studying in Nevada. Available to U.S. citizens.

Application Requirements: Application, financial need analysis. *Deadline:* Continuous.

Contact: Wendi Skibinski, Program Coordinator
Nevada Department of Education
700 East 5th Street
Carson City, NV 89701
Phone: 775-687-9228
Fax: 775-687-9101
E-mail: wendi@nsn.k12.nv.us

ROBERT C. BYRD HONORS SCHOLARSHIP-NEVADA

Award for senior graduating from public or private Nevada high school. Must be Nevada resident and Nevada High School Scholars Program recipient. Renewable award of $1500. No application necessary. Nevada scholars are chosen from a database supplied by ACT and SAT. Please request SAT score be mailed to 2707 on your registration form. SAT scores of 1100 and above qualify as initial application. ACT score is automatically submitted for a score of 25 or greater. GPA (unweighted) must be 3.5 or higher.

Nevada Department of Education (continued)

Award: Scholarship for use in freshman, sophomore, junior, or senior years; renewable. *Number:* 40–60. *Amount:* $1500.

Eligibility Requirements: Applicant must be high school student; planning to enroll or expecting to enroll full-time at a two-year or four-year or technical institution or university and resident of Nevada. Applicant must have 3.5 GPA or higher. Available to U.S. citizens.

Application Requirements: Test scores, transcript. *Deadline:* Continuous.

Contact: Wendi Skibinski, Program Coordinator
Nevada Department of Education
700 East 5th Street
Carson City, NV 89701
Phone: 775-687-9228
Fax: 775-687-9101
E-mail: wendi@nsn.k12.nv.us

NEVADA OFFICE OF THE STATE TREASURER
http://nevadatreasurer.gov/millennium/programinfo.asp

GOVERNOR GUINN MILLENNIUM SCHOLARSHIP

Scholarship for high school graduates with a diploma from a Nevada public or private high school in the graduating class of the year 2000 or later. Must complete high school with at least a 3.10 GPA for 2005 and 2006. 3.25 GPA for 2007 and later. A student attending a university who is enrolled in 12 semester credit hours would be eligible to receive $960 or a student attending a community college who is enrolled in 9 semester credit hours would be eligible to receive $360.

Award: Scholarship for use in freshman, sophomore, junior, or senior years. *Number:* 1.

Eligibility Requirements: Applicant must be enrolled or expecting to enroll full-time at a two-year or four-year institution and resident of Nevada. Available to U.S. citizens.

Application Requirements: Application, financial need analysis, references, test scores. *Deadline:* varies.

Contact: Susan K. Moore, Director
Phone: 702-486-3383
Fax: 702-486-3246
E-mail: millennium@NevadaTreasurer.gov

NEVADA WOMEN'S FUND
http://www.nevadawomensfund.org/

NEVADA WOMEN'S FUND SCHOLARSHIPS

Awards for women for a variety of academic and vocational training scholarships. Must be a resident of Nevada. Preference given to applicants from northern Nevada. Renewable award of $500 to $5000. Application deadline is the last Friday in February. Application can be downloaded from Web site: http://www.nevadawomensfund.org

Award: Scholarship for use in freshman, sophomore, junior, senior, graduate, or postgraduate years; renewable. *Number:* 50–80. *Amount:* $500–$5000.

Eligibility Requirements: Applicant must be enrolled or expecting to enroll full or part-time at a two-year or four-year or technical institution or university; female and resident of Nevada. Available to U.S. citizens.

Application Requirements: Application, financial need analysis, references, transcript. *Deadline:* varies.

Contact: Fritsi Ericson, President and CEO
Nevada Women's Fund
770 Smithridge Drive, Suite 300
Reno, NV 89502
Phone: 775-786-2335
Fax: 775-786-8152
E-mail: fritsi@nevadawomensfund.org

NEW ENGLAND BOARD OF HIGHER EDUCATION
http://www.nebhe.org

NEW ENGLAND REGIONAL STUDENT PROGRAM (NEW ENGLAND BOARD OF HIGHER EDUCATION)

For residents of Connecticut, Maine, Massachusetts, New Hampshire, Rhode Island, and Vermont. Through Regional Student Program, students pay reduced out-of-state tuition at public colleges or universities in other New England states when enrolling in certain majors not offered at public institutions in home state. Deadline: College application deadline.

Award: Scholarship for use in freshman, sophomore, junior, senior, or graduate years; renewable. *Number:* 1. *Amount:* varies.

Eligibility Requirements: Applicant must be enrolled or expecting to enroll full or part-time at a two-year or four-year institution or university; resident of Connecticut, Maine, Massachusetts, New Hampshire, Rhode Island, or Vermont and studying in Connecticut, Maine, Massachusetts, New Hampshire, Rhode Island, or Vermont. Available to U.S. citizens.

Application Requirements: College application. *Deadline:* Continuous.

Contact: Wendy Lindsay, Director of Regional Student Program
New England Board of Higher Education
45 Temple Place
Boston, MA 02111-1305
Phone: 617-357-9620 Ext. 111
Fax: 617-338-1577
E-mail: tuitionbreak@nebhe.org

NEW HAMPSHIRE CHARITABLE FOUNDATION
http://www.nhcf.org

ADULT STUDENT AID PROGRAM

Award for New Hampshire residents who are at least 24 years old, or who have served in the military, are wards of the court, have not been claimed by their parents for two consecutive years, are married, or who have dependent children. Application deadlines are August 15, December 15, and May 15. Application fee is $15. Further information and application available at Web site http://www.nhcf.org

Award: Grant for use in freshman, sophomore, junior, or senior years; not renewable. *Number:* 100–200. *Amount:* $100–$1500.

Eligibility Requirements: Applicant must be age 24; enrolled or expecting to enroll full or part-time at a two-year or four-year or technical institution or university and resident of New Hampshire. Available to U.S. citizens.

Application Requirements: Application, financial need analysis, resume, references. *Fee:* $15. *Deadline:* varies.

Contact: Norma Daviault, Program Assistant
New Hampshire Charitable Foundation
37 Pleasant Street
Concord, NH 03301-4005
Phone: 603-225-6641 Ext. 226
E-mail: nd@nhcf.org

NEW HAMPSHIRE DEPARTMENT OF EDUCATION
http://www.state.nh.us/doe/

ROBERT C. BYRD HONORS SCHOLARSHIP-NEW HAMPSHIRE

Scholarships awarded to graduates of approved New Hampshire secondary schools based on academic achievement. Contact department for application deadlines. May be funded through four years of college if recipient maintains high academic achievement. Must be high school senior to apply and must submit letters of recommendation. Award is offered in senior year of high school. Minimum 3.0 GPA required.

Award: Scholarship for use in freshman, sophomore, junior, or senior years; renewable. *Number:* 26–30. *Amount:* $1500.

Eligibility Requirements: Applicant must be high school student; planning to enroll or expecting to enroll full or part-time at a two-year or four-year institution or university and resident of New Hampshire. Applicant must have 3.0 GPA or higher. Available to U.S. citizens.

Application Requirements: Application, essay, references, test scores, transcript. *Deadline:* varies.

Contact: Marie Gage, Program Specialist II
New Hampshire Department of Education
101 Pleasant Street
Concord, NH 03301
Phone: 603-271-6051
Fax: 603-271-2632
E-mail: mgage@ed.state.nh.us

NEW HAMPSHIRE POSTSECONDARY EDUCATION COMMISSION
http://www.state.nh.us/postsecondary

LEVERAGED INCENTIVE GRANT PROGRAM

Award open to New Hampshire residents attending school in New Hampshire. Must be in sophomore, junior, or senior year. Award based on financial need and merit. Contact financial aid office for more information and deadline.

Award: Grant for use in sophomore, junior, or senior years; not renewable. *Number:* varies. *Amount:* $200–$7500.

Eligibility Requirements: Applicant must be enrolled or expecting to enroll full-time at a two-year or four-year or technical institution or university; resident of New Hampshire and studying in New Hampshire. Available to U.S. citizens.

Application Requirements: Application, financial need analysis. *Deadline:* varies.

Contact: Judith A Knapp, Scholarship Coordinator
New Hampshire Postsecondary Education Commission
3 Barrell Court, Suite 300
Concord, NH 03301-8543
Phone: 603-271-2555
Fax: 603-271-2696
E-mail: jknapp@pec.state.nh.us

MARY MILLIKEN SCHOLARSHIP

Grant available to New Hampshire residents enrolled at a New Hampshire institution of higher education. Must demonstrate financial need. Contact financial aid office for more information.

Award: Grant for use in freshman, sophomore, junior, or senior years; renewable. *Number:* varies. *Amount:* $1000.

Eligibility Requirements: Applicant must be enrolled or expecting to enroll full-time at a two-year or four-year or technical institution or university; resident of New Hampshire and studying in New Hampshire. Available to U.S. citizens.

Application Requirements: Application, financial need analysis. *Deadline:* May 1.

Contact: Judith A Knapp, Scholarship Coordinator
New Hampshire Postsecondary Education Commission
3 Barrell Court, Suite 300
Concord, NH 03301-8543
Phone: 603-271-2555
Fax: 603-271-2696
E-mail: jknapp@pec.state.nh.us

NEW HAMPSHIRE INCENTIVE PROGRAM (NHIP)

One-time grants for New Hampshire residents attending school in New England. Must have financial need. Deadline is May 1. Complete Free Application for Federal Student Aid. Grant is not automatically renewable. Applicant must reapply.

Award: Grant for use in freshman, sophomore, junior, or senior years; renewable. *Number:* 3000–4300. *Amount:* $125–$1000.

Eligibility Requirements: Applicant must be enrolled or expecting to enroll full or part-time at a two-year or four-year or technical institution or university; resident of New Hampshire and studying in Connecticut, Maine, Massachusetts, New Hampshire, Rhode Island, or Vermont. Available to U.S. citizens.

Application Requirements: Application, financial need analysis, FAFSA. *Deadline:* May 1.

Contact: Sherrie Tucker, Program Assistant
New Hampshire Postsecondary Education Commission
3 Barrell Court, Suite 300
Concord, NH 03301-8512
Phone: 603-271-2555 Ext. 355
Fax: 603-271-2696
E-mail: stucker@pec.state.nh.us

SCHOLARSHIPS FOR ORPHANS OF VETERANS-NEW HAMPSHIRE
• See page 591

NEW JERSEY DEPARTMENT OF MILITARY AND VETERANS AFFAIRS
http://www.state.nj.us/military

NEW JERSEY WAR ORPHANS TUITION ASSISTANCE
• See page 591

TUITION ASSISTANCE FOR CHILDREN OF POW/MIAS
• See page 591

NEW JERSEY HIGHER EDUCATION STUDENT ASSISTANCE AUTHORITY
http://www.hesaa.org

DANA CHRISTMAS SCHOLARSHIP FOR HEROISM

Honors young New Jersey residents for acts of heroism. Scholarship is a non-renewable award of up to $10,000 for up to five recipients. This scholarship may be used for undergraduate or graduate study. Deadline: October 1 for Fall and March 1 for Spring.

Award: Scholarship for use in freshman, sophomore, junior, senior, or graduate years; not renewable. *Number:* up to 5. *Amount:* up to $10,000.

Eligibility Requirements: Applicant must be age 21 or under; enrolled or expecting to enroll full or part-time at a four-year institution or university and resident of New Jersey. Available to U.S. citizens.

Application Requirements: Application. *Deadline:* varies.

Contact: Gisele Joachim, Director of Financial Aid Services
New Jersey Higher Education Student Assistance Authority
PO Box 540
Trenton, NJ 08625
Phone: 800-792-8670
Fax: 609-588-7389

EDWARD J. BLOUSTEIN DISTINGUISHED SCHOLARS

Renewable scholarship for students who place in top 10% of their classes and have a minimum combined SAT score of 1260, or are ranked first, second or third in their class as of end of junior year. Must be New Jersey resident. Must attend a New Jersey two-year college, four-year college or university, or approved programs at proprietary institutions. Secondary schools forward to HESAA, names and class standings for all nominees. Deadline: October 1 for Fall and March 1 for Spring.

Award: Scholarship for use in freshman, sophomore, junior, senior, or graduate years; renewable. *Number:* varies. *Amount:* $1000.

Eligibility Requirements: Applicant must be high school student; planning to enroll or expecting to enroll full-time at a two-year or four-year institution or university; resident of New Jersey and studying in New Jersey. Available to U.S. citizens.

Application Requirements: Test scores, nominated by high school. *Deadline:* varies.

Contact: Carol Muka, Assistant Director of Grants and Scholarships
New Jersey Higher Education Student Assistance Authority
PO Box 540
Trenton, NJ 08625
Phone: 800-792-8670
Fax: 609-588-2228

LAW ENFORCEMENT OFFICER MEMORIAL SCHOLARSHIP
• See page 547

NEW JERSEY WORLD TRADE CENTER SCHOLARSHIP

Established by the legislature to aid the dependent children and surviving spouses of NJ residents who were killed in the terrorist attacks, or who are missing and officially presumed dead as a direct result of the attacks; applies to in-state and out-of-state institutions for students seeking undergraduate degrees. Deadline varies: March 1 for Fall, October 1 for Spring.

New Jersey Higher Education Student Assistance Authority (continued)

Award: Scholarship for use in freshman, sophomore, junior, or senior years; renewable. *Number:* varies. *Amount:* up to $6500.

Eligibility Requirements: Applicant must be enrolled or expecting to enroll full-time at a four-year institution or university and resident of New Jersey. Available to U.S. citizens.

Application Requirements: Application. *Deadline:* varies.

Contact: Giselle Joachim, Director of Financial Aid Services
New Jersey Higher Education Student Assistance Authority
PO Box 540
Trenton, NJ 08625
Phone: 800-792-8670
Fax: 609-588-7389

NJ STUDENT TUITION ASSISTANCE REWARD SCHOLARSHIP

Scholarship for students who graduate in the top 20% of their high school class. Recipients may be awarded up to 5 semesters of tuition (up to 15 credits per term) and approved fees at one of New Jersey's 19 county colleges.

Award: Scholarship for use in freshman or sophomore years; renewable. *Number:* 1.

Eligibility Requirements: Applicant must be high school student; planning to enroll or expecting to enroll full-time at a two-year institution; resident of New Jersey and studying in New Jersey. Applicant must have 3.0 GPA or higher. Available to U.S. citizens.

Application Requirements: Application, transcript. *Deadline:* varies.

Contact: Carol Muka, Assistant Director of Grants and Scholarships
New Jersey Higher Education Student Assistance Authority
PO Box 540
Trenton, NJ 08625
Phone: 800-792-8670
Fax: 609-588-2228
E-mail: cmuka@hessa.org

OUTSTANDING SCHOLAR RECRUITMENT PROGRAM

Students who meet the eligibility criteria and enrolled as first-time freshmen at participating New Jersey institutions receive annual scholarship awards of $2500 to $7500. The award amounts vary on a sliding scale depending on class rank and combined SAT scores. Must maintain a B average for renewal. Deadline: October 1 for Fall and March 1 for Spring.

Award: Scholarship for use in freshman, sophomore, junior, or senior years; renewable. *Number:* varies. *Amount:* $2500–$7500.

Eligibility Requirements: Applicant must be enrolled or expecting to enroll at a four-year institution or university; resident of New Jersey and studying in New Jersey. Available to U.S. citizens.

Application Requirements: Test scores. *Deadline:* varies.

Contact: Carol Muka, Assistant Director of Grants and Scholarships
New Jersey Higher Education Student Assistance Authority
PO Box 540
Trenton, NJ 08625
Phone: 800-792-8670
Fax: 609-588-2228

PART-TIME TUITION AID GRANT (TAG) FOR COUNTY COLLEGES

Provides financial aid to eligible part-time undergraduate students enrolled for 6-11 credits at participating NJ community colleges. Deadline varies: March 1 for Fall, October 1 for Spring.

Award: Grant for use in freshman, sophomore, junior, or senior years; renewable. *Number:* varies. *Amount:* $116–$375.

Eligibility Requirements: Applicant must be enrolled or expecting to enroll part-time at a two-year or four-year institution or university; resident of New Jersey and studying in New Jersey. Available to U.S. citizens.

Application Requirements: Application, financial need analysis. *Deadline:* varies.

Contact: Sherri Fox, Acting Director of Grants and Scholarships
New Jersey Higher Education Student Assistance Authority
PO Box 540
Trenton, NJ 08625
Phone: 800-792-8670
Fax: 609-588-2228

SURVIVOR TUITION BENEFITS PROGRAM
• *See page 547*

TUITION AID GRANT

The Tuition Aid Grant (TAG) program provides financial aid to eligible undergraduate students attending participating in-state institutions. Deadline varies: March 1 for Fall, October 1 for Spring.

Award: Grant for use in freshman, sophomore, junior, or senior years; renewable. *Number:* varies. *Amount:* $868–$7272.

Eligibility Requirements: Applicant must be enrolled or expecting to enroll full-time at a two-year or four-year institution or university; resident of New Jersey and studying in New Jersey. Available to U.S. citizens.

Application Requirements: Application, financial need analysis. *Deadline:* varies.

Contact: Sherri Fox, Acting Director of Grants and Scholarships
New Jersey Higher Education Student Assistance Authority
PO Box 540
Trenton, NJ 08625
Phone: 800-792-8670
Fax: 609-588-2228

URBAN SCHOLARS

Renewable scholarship to high achieving students attending public secondary schools in the State's urban and economically distressed areas of New Jersey. Students must rank in the top 10% of their class and have a GPA of at least 3.0 at the end of their junior year. Must be New Jersey resident. Must attend a New Jersey two-year college, four-year college or university, or approved programs at proprietary institutions. Students do not apply directly for scholarship consideration. Secondary schools forward to HESAA the names and class standing for all nominees.

Award: Scholarship for use in freshman, sophomore, junior, or senior years; renewable. *Number:* varies. *Amount:* $1000.

Eligibility Requirements: Applicant must be high school student; planning to enroll or expecting to enroll full-time at a two-year or four-year institution or university; resident of New Jersey and studying in New Jersey. Applicant must have 3.0 GPA or higher. Available to U.S. citizens.

Application Requirements: Test scores, nominated by school. *Deadline:* varies.

Contact: Carol Muka, Assistant Director of Grants and Scholarships
New Jersey Higher Education Student Assistance Authority
PO Box 540
Trenton, NJ 08625
Phone: 800-792-8670
Fax: 609-588-2228

NEW JERSEY PRESS FOUNDATION   http://www.njpa.org/foundation/

COLLEGE STUDENT CORRESPONDENT SCHOLARSHIP PROGRAM

Available to New Jersey residents who work as interns or student correspondents/stringers for New Jersey weekly or daily newspapers. Student is awarded a scholarship based on the quality of work performed. Recipients must have at least one term of college remaining following the announcement of scholarships.

Award: Scholarship for use in freshman, sophomore, junior, or senior years; not renewable. *Number:* 5–12. *Amount:* $1000.

Eligibility Requirements: Applicant must be enrolled or expecting to enroll full-time at a two-year or four-year institution or university and resident of New Jersey. Available to U.S. citizens.

Application Requirements: Application, essay, portfolio, resume, references. *Deadline:* varies.

Contact: Thomas Engleman, Director
New Jersey Press Foundation
840 Bear Tavern Road, Suite 305
West Trenton, NJ 08628-1019
Phone: 609-406-0600 Ext. 19
Fax: 609-406-0300
E-mail: foundation@njpa.org

INTERNSHIP/SCHOLARSHIP PROGRAM

For New Jersey residents. Students selected will be assigned paid internships at New Jersey newspapers (minimum $300/week for ten weeks). Scholarship awarded after successful completion of internship. Recipients must have at least one term of college left following the internship.

Award: Scholarship for use in freshman, sophomore, junior, or senior years; not renewable. *Number:* 5–6. *Amount:* $3000.

Eligibility Requirements: Applicant must be enrolled or expecting to enroll full-time at a two-year or four-year institution or university and resident of New Jersey. Available to U.S. citizens.

Application Requirements: Application, essay, portfolio, resume, references, transcript. *Deadline:* November 15.

Contact: Thomas Engleman, Director
New Jersey Press Foundation
840 Bear Tavern Road, Suite 305
West Trenton, NJ 08628-1019
Phone: 609-406-0600 Ext. 19
Fax: 609-406-0300
E-mail: foundation@njpa.org

NEW JERSEY STATE GOLF ASSOCIATION   http://www.njsga.org

NEW JERSEY STATE GOLF ASSOCIATION CADDIE SCHOLARSHIP
• *See page 547*

NEW JERSEY VIETNAM VETERANS' MEMORIAL FOUNDATION   http://www.njvvmf.org

NEW JERSEY VIETNAM VETERANS' MEMORIAL FOUNDATION SCHOLARSHIP

Applicants must be New Jersey residents who are graduating high school seniors. Eligible applicants will have visited the New Jersey Vietnam Veterans' Memorial and write an essay about the visit. The deadline is April 7.

Award: Scholarship for use in freshman year; not renewable. *Number:* 2. *Amount:* up to $2500.

Eligibility Requirements: Applicant must be high school student; age 17-19; planning to enroll or expecting to enroll full or part-time at a two-year institution; single and resident of New Jersey. Available to U.S. and non-U.S. citizens.

Application Requirements: Application, essay, acceptance letter. *Deadline:* April 7.

Contact: Kelly Watts, Executive Director
New Jersey Vietnam Veterans' Memorial Foundation
1 Memorial Lane, PO Box 648
Holmdel, NJ 07733
Phone: 732-335-0033
Fax: 732-335-1107
E-mail: klwatts@njvvmf.org

NEW MEXICO COMMISSION ON HIGHER EDUCATION   http://www.hed.state.nm.us

LEGISLATIVE ENDOWMENT SCHOLARSHIPS

Awards for undergraduate students with substantial financial need who are attending public postsecondary institutions in New Mexico. Preference given to returning adult students at two-year and four-year institutions and students transferring from two-year to four-year institutions. Deadline set by each institution. Must be resident of New Mexico. Contact financial aid office of any New Mexico public postsecondary institution to apply.

Award: Scholarship for use in freshman, sophomore, junior, or senior years; not renewable. *Amount:* $1000–$2500.

Eligibility Requirements: Applicant must be enrolled or expecting to enroll full or part-time at a two-year or four-year or technical institution or university; resident of New Mexico and studying in New Mexico. Available to U.S. citizens.

Application Requirements: Application, financial need analysis, FAFSA. *Deadline:* varies.

Contact: Ofelia Morales, Director of Financial Aid
New Mexico Commission on Higher Education
1068 Cerrillos Road, PO Box 15910
Santa Fe, NM 87505
Phone: 505-476-6506
E-mail: ofelia.morales@state.nm.us

LOTTERY SUCCESS SCHOLARSHIPS

Awards equal to 100% of tuition at New Mexico public postsecondary institution. Must have New Mexico high school degree and be enrolled at New Mexico public college or university in first regular semester following high school graduation. Must obtain 2.5 GPA during this semester. May be eligible for up to eight consecutive semesters of support. Deadlines vary by institution. Apply through financial aid office of any New Mexico public postsecondary institution.

Award: Scholarship for use in freshman, sophomore, junior, or senior years; renewable. *Number:* 1.

Eligibility Requirements: Applicant must be enrolled or expecting to enroll full-time at a two-year or four-year institution; resident of New Mexico and studying in New Mexico. Applicant must have 2.5 GPA or higher. Available to U.S. citizens.

Application Requirements: Application. *Deadline:* varies.

Contact: Ofelia Morales, Director of Financial Aid
New Mexico Commission on Higher Education
1068 Cerrillos Road, PO Box 15910
Santa Fe, NM 87505
Phone: 505-476-6506
E-mail: ofelia.morales@state.nm.us

NEW MEXICO COMPETITIVE SCHOLARSHIP

Scholarship available to encourage out-of-state students who have demonstrated high academic achievement to enroll in public institutions of higher education in New Mexico. One-time award for undergraduate students. Deadlines set by each institution. Contact financial aid office of any New Mexico public postsecondary institution to apply.

Award: Scholarship for use in freshman, sophomore, junior, or senior years; not renewable. *Amount:* $100.

Eligibility Requirements: Applicant must be enrolled or expecting to enroll full or part-time at a two-year or four-year institution or university and studying in New Mexico. Applicant must have 3.0 GPA or higher. Available to U.S. citizens.

Application Requirements: Application, essay, references, test scores. *Deadline:* varies.

Contact: Ofelia Morales, Director of Financial Aid
New Mexico Commission on Higher Education
1068 Cerrillos Road
Santa Fe, NM 87505
Phone: 505-476-6506
Fax: 505-827-7392
E-mail: ofelia.morales@state.nm.us

NEW MEXICO SCHOLARS' PROGRAM

Several scholarships to encourage New Mexico high school graduates to enroll in college at a public or selected private nonprofit postsecondary institution in New Mexico before their 22nd birthday. Selected private colleges are College of Santa Fe, St. John's College in Santa Fe, and College of the Southwest. Must have graduated in top 5% of their class or obtained an ACT score of 25 or SAT score of 1140. One-time scholarship for tuition, books, and fees. Contact financial aid office at college to apply.

Award: Scholarship for use in freshman, sophomore, junior, or senior years; not renewable. *Number:* 1.

Eligibility Requirements: Applicant must be age 22 or under; enrolled or expecting to enroll full or part-time at a two-year or four-year institution; resident of New Mexico and studying in New Mexico. Available to U.S. citizens.

Application Requirements: Application, financial need analysis, test scores, FAFSA. *Deadline:* varies.

New Mexico Commission on Higher Education (continued)

Contact: Ofelia Morales, Director of Financial Aid
New Mexico Commission on Higher Education
1068 Cerrillos Road, PO Box 15910
Santa Fe, NM 87505
Phone: 505-476-6506
E-mail: ofelia.morales@state.nm.us

NEW MEXICO STUDENT INCENTIVE GRANT

Several grants available for resident undergraduate students attending public and selected private nonprofit institutions in New Mexico. Must demonstrate financial need. To apply contact financial aid office at any public or private nonprofit postsecondary institution in New Mexico.

Award: Grant for use in freshman, sophomore, junior, or senior years; not renewable. *Amount:* $200–$2500.

Eligibility Requirements: Applicant must be enrolled or expecting to enroll full or part-time at a two-year or four-year or technical institution or university; resident of New Mexico and studying in New Mexico. Available to U.S. citizens.

Application Requirements: Application, financial need analysis, FAFSA. *Deadline:* varies.

Contact: Ofelia Morales, Director of Financial Aid
New Mexico Commission on Higher Education
1068 Cerrillos Road, PO Box 15910
Santa Fe, NM 87505
Phone: 505-476-6506
E-mail: ofelia.morales@state.nm.us

3% SCHOLARSHIP PROGRAM

Award equal to tuition and required fees for New Mexico residents who are undergraduate students attending public postsecondary institutions in New Mexico. Contact financial aid office of any public postsecondary institution in New Mexico for deadline.

Award: Scholarship for use in freshman, sophomore, junior, senior, or graduate years; not renewable. *Number:* 1.

Eligibility Requirements: Applicant must be enrolled or expecting to enroll full or part-time at a two-year or four-year institution or university; resident of New Mexico and studying in New Mexico. Available to U.S. citizens.

Application Requirements: Application. *Deadline:* varies.

Contact: Ofelia Morales, Director of Financial Aid
New Mexico Commission on Higher Education
1068 Cerrillos Road, PO Box 15910
Santa Fe, NM 87505
Phone: 505-476-6506
E-mail: ofelia.morales@state.nm.us

VIETNAM VETERANS' SCHOLARSHIP PROGRAM
• *See page 592*

NEW MEXICO VETERANS' SERVICE COMMISSION
http://www.state.nm.us/veterans

CHILDREN OF DECEASED VETERANS SCHOLARSHIP-NEW MEXICO
• *See page 592*

NEW MEXICO VIETNAM VETERANS' SCHOLARSHIP
• *See page 592*

NEW YORK COUNCIL NAVY LEAGUE
http://www.nynavyleague.org/

NEW YORK COUNCIL NAVY LEAGUE SCHOLARSHIP FUND
• *See page 578*

NEW YORK STATE AFL-CIO
http://www.nysaflcio.org

NEW YORK STATE AFL-CIO SCHOLARSHIP
• *See page 508*

NEW YORK STATE EDUCATION DEPARTMENT
http://www.highered.nysed.gov

ROBERT C. BYRD HONORS SCHOLARSHIP-NEW YORK

Award for outstanding high school seniors accepted to U.S. college or university. Based on SAT score and high school average. Minimum 3.5 GPA required; minimum 1250 combined SAT score from one sitting. Must be legal resident of New York and a U.S. citizen. Renewable for up to four years. General Education Degree holders eligible.

Award: Scholarship for use in freshman, sophomore, junior, or senior years; renewable. *Number:* 400. *Amount:* $1500.

Eligibility Requirements: Applicant must be high school student; planning to enroll or expecting to enroll full-time at a two-year or four-year institution or university and resident of New York. Applicant must have 3.5 GPA or higher. Available to U.S. citizens.

Application Requirements: Application, test scores, transcript. *Deadline:* March 1.

Contact: Lewis J. Hall, Coordinator
New York State Education Department
Room 1078 EBA
Albany, NY 12234
Phone: 518-486-1319
Fax: 518-486-5346

SCHOLARSHIP FOR ACADEMIC EXCELLENCE

Renewable award for New York residents. Scholarship winners must attend a college or university in New York. 2000 scholarships are for $1500 and 6000 are for $500. The selection criteria used are based on Regents test scores and rank in class. Must be U.S. citizen or permanent resident.

Award: Scholarship for use in freshman, sophomore, junior, or senior years; renewable. *Number:* up to 8000. *Amount:* $500–$1500.

Eligibility Requirements: Applicant must be high school student; planning to enroll or expecting to enroll full-time at a two-year or four-year institution or university; resident of New York and studying in New York. Applicant must have 3.5 GPA or higher. Available to U.S. citizens.

Application Requirements: Application. *Deadline:* December 19.

Contact: Lewis J. Hall, Coordinator
New York State Education Department
Room 1078 EBA
Albany, NY 12234
Phone: 518-486-1319
Fax: 518-486-5346

NEW YORK STATE GRANGE
http://www.nysgrange.com/

CAROLINE KARK AWARD
• *See page 563*

SUSAN W. FREESTONE EDUCATION AWARD
• *See page 508*

NEW YORK STATE HIGHER EDUCATION SERVICES CORPORATION
http://www.hesc.com/

NEW YORK AID FOR PART-TIME STUDY (APTS)

Renewable scholarship provides tuition assistance to part-time undergraduate students who are New York residents attending New York accredited institutions. Deadline varies. Must be U.S. citizen.

Award: Grant for use in freshman, sophomore, junior, or senior years; renewable. *Number:* varies. *Amount:* up to $2000.

Eligibility Requirements: Applicant must be enrolled or expecting to enroll part-time at a two-year or four-year institution or university; resident of New York and studying in New York. Available to U.S. citizens.

Application Requirements: Application. *Deadline:* varies.

Contact: Student Information
New York State Higher Education Services Corporation
99 Washington Avenue, Room 1320
Albany, NY 12255
Phone: 518-473-3887
Fax: 518-474-2839

NEW YORK MEMORIAL SCHOLARSHIPS FOR FAMILIES OF DECEASED POLICE OFFICERS, FIRE FIGHTERS AND PEACE OFFICERS
• See page 547

NEW YORK STATE AID TO NATIVE AMERICANS
• See page 626

NEW YORK STATE TUITION ASSISTANCE PROGRAM

Award for New York state residents attending a New York postsecondary institution. Must be full-time student in approved program with tuition over $200 per year. Must show financial need and not be in default in any other state program. Renewable award of $500-$5000.

Award: Grant for use in freshman, sophomore, junior, or senior years; renewable. *Number:* 350,000–360,000. *Amount:* $500–$5000.

Eligibility Requirements: Applicant must be enrolled or expecting to enroll full-time at a two-year or four-year institution or university; resident of New York and studying in New York. Available to U.S. citizens.

Application Requirements: Application, financial need analysis. *Deadline:* May 1.

Contact: Student Information
New York State Higher Education Services Corporation
99 Washington Avenue, Room 1320
Albany, NY 12255

REGENTS PROFESSIONAL OPPORTUNITY SCHOLARSHIPS

Award for New York State residents pursuing career in certain licensed professions. Must attend New York State college. Priority given to economically disadvantaged members of minority group underrepresented in chosen profession and graduates of SEEK, College Discovery, EOP, and HEOP. Must work in New York State in chosen profession one year for each annual payment. Scholarships are awarded to undergraduate or graduate students, depending on the program.

Award: Scholarship for use in freshman, sophomore, junior, senior, or graduate years; not renewable. *Number:* 220. *Amount:* $1000–$5000.

Eligibility Requirements: Applicant must be enrolled or expecting to enroll full-time at a two-year or four-year institution or university; resident of New York and studying in New York. Available to U.S. citizens.

Application Requirements: Application. *Deadline:* May 3.

Contact: New York State Education Department, Bureau of HEOP/VATEA/Scholarships
New York State Higher Education Services Corporation
Education Building Addition Room 1071
Albany, NY 12234
Phone: 518-486-1319

WORLD TRADE CENTER MEMORIAL SCHOLARSHIP

Renewable awards of up to the average cost of attendance at a State University of New York four-year college. Available to the families and financial dependents of victims who died or were severely and permanently disabled as a result of the September 11, 2001 terrorist attacks on the U.S. and the rescue and recovery efforts.

Award: Scholarship for use in freshman, sophomore, junior, or senior years; renewable. *Number:* 1. *Amount:* varies.

Eligibility Requirements: Applicant must be enrolled or expecting to enroll full-time at a two-year or four-year institution or university; resident of New York and studying in New York. Available to U.S. citizens.

Application Requirements: Application. *Deadline:* May 1.

Contact: HESC Scholarship Unit
New York State Higher Education Services Corporation
99 Washington Avenue, Room 1320
Albany, NY 12255
Phone: 518-402-6494

NORTH CAROLINA ASSOCIATION OF EDUCATORS   http://www.ncae.org

NORTH CAROLINA ASSOCIATION OF EDUCATORS MARTIN LUTHER KING, JR. SCHOLARSHIP

One-time award for high school seniors who are North Carolina residents to attend a postsecondary institution. Must be a U.S. citizen. Based upon financial need, GPA, and essay. Must have a GPA of at least 4.0 on a 5.0 scale and a 3.0 on a 4.0 scale.

Award: Scholarship for use in freshman year; not renewable. *Number:* 3–4. *Amount:* $500–$1000.

Eligibility Requirements: Applicant must be high school student; planning to enroll or expecting to enroll full-time at an institution or university and resident of North Carolina. Available to U.S. citizens.

Application Requirements: Application, essay, financial need analysis, references, transcript. *Deadline:* February 1.

Contact: Jackie Vaughn, Scholarship Coordinator
North Carolina Association of Educators
PO Box 27347
Raleigh, NC 27611
Phone: 919-832-3000
Fax: 919-839-8229
E-mail: Jvaughn@nea.org

NORTH CAROLINA BAR ASSOCIATION   http://www.ncbar.org

NORTH CAROLINA BAR ASSOCIATION YOUNG LAWYERS DIVISION SCHOLARSHIP
• See page 547

NORTH CAROLINA DIVISION OF SERVICES FOR THE BLIND

NORTH CAROLINA DIVISION OF SERVICES FOR THE BLIND REHABILITATION SERVICES
• See page 563

NORTH CAROLINA DIVISION OF VETERANS' AFFAIRS

NORTH CAROLINA VETERANS SCHOLARSHIPS CLASS I-B
• See page 592

NORTH CAROLINA VETERANS SCHOLARSHIPS CLASS II
• See page 592

NORTH CAROLINA VETERANS SCHOLARSHIPS CLASS III
• See page 592

NORTH CAROLINA VETERANS SCHOLARSHIPS CLASS IV
• See page 593

NORTH CAROLINA DIVISION OF VOCATIONAL REHABILITATION SERVICES   http://www.dhhs.state.nc.us/

TRAINING SUPPORT FOR YOUTH WITH DISABILITIES
• See page 563

NORTH CAROLINA NATIONAL GUARD   http://www.nc.ngb.army.mil/education

NORTH CAROLINA NATIONAL GUARD TUITION ASSISTANCE PROGRAM
• See page 571

NORTH CAROLINA STATE EDUCATION ASSISTANCE AUTHORITY   http://www.ncseaa.edu

AUBREY LEE BROOKS SCHOLARSHIPS

Renewable award for high school seniors who are residents of designated North Carolina counties and are planning to attend North Carolina State University, the University of North Carolina at Chapel Hill or the University of North Carolina at Greensboro. Award provides approximately half of the cost of an undergraduate education. Write for further details and deadlines, or visit Web site: http://www.cfnc.org.

Award: Scholarship for use in freshman, sophomore, junior, or senior years; renewable. *Number:* 17–19. *Amount:* up to $7300.

Eligibility Requirements: Applicant must be high school student; planning to enroll or expecting to enroll full-time at an institution or university; resident of North Carolina and studying in North Carolina. Applicant must have 3.0 GPA or higher. Available to U.S. and non-Canadian citizens.

North Carolina State Education Assistance Authority (continued)

Application Requirements: Application, essay, financial need analysis, interview, photo, references, test scores, transcript. *Deadline:* February 1.

Contact: Bill Carswell, Manager of Scholarship and Grant Division
North Carolina State Education Assistance Authority
PO Box 14103
Research Triangle Park, NC 27709
Phone: 919-549-8614
Fax: 919-549-4687
E-mail: carswellb@ncseaa.edu

JAGANNATHAN SCHOLARSHIP

Available to graduating high school seniors who plan to enroll as college freshmen in a full-time degree program at one of the constituent institutions of The University of North Carolina. Applicant must be resident of North Carolina. Applicant must document financial need.

Award: Scholarship for use in freshman year. *Number:* varies. *Amount:* up to $3500.

Eligibility Requirements: Applicant must be high school student; planning to enroll or expecting to enroll full-time at a four-year institution or university; resident of North Carolina and studying in North Carolina. Applicant must have 3.0 GPA or higher. Available to U.S. citizens.

Application Requirements: Application, financial need analysis, must be nominated. *Deadline:* February 14.

Contact: Bill Carswell, Manager of Scholarship and Grant Division
North Carolina State Education Assistance Authority
PO Box 14103
Research Triangle Park, NC 27709
Phone: 919-549-8614
Fax: 919-248-4687
E-mail: carswellb@ncseaa.edu

NORTH CAROLINA COMMUNITY COLLEGE GRANT PROGRAM

Annual award for North Carolina residents enrolled at least part-time in a North Carolina community college curriculum program. Priority given to those enrolled in college transferable curriculum programs, persons seeking new job skills, women in non-traditional curricula, and those participating in an ABE, GED, or high school diploma program. Contact financial aid office of institution the student attends for information and deadline. Must complete Free Application for Federal Student Aid.

Award: Grant for use in freshman or sophomore years; renewable. *Number:* up to 13,000. *Amount:* $683.

Eligibility Requirements: Applicant must be enrolled or expecting to enroll full or part-time at a two-year or technical institution; resident of North Carolina and studying in North Carolina. Available to U.S. citizens.

Application Requirements: Application, financial need analysis, FAFSA. *Deadline:* varies.

Contact: Bill Carswell, Manager, Scholarship and Grants Division
North Carolina State Education Assistance Authority
PO Box 14103
Research Triangle Park, NC 27709
Phone: 919-549-8614
Fax: 919-248-4687
E-mail: carswellb@ncseaa.edu

NORTH CAROLINA LEGISLATIVE TUITION GRANT PROGRAM (NCLTG)

Renewable aid for North Carolina residents attending approved private colleges or universities within the state. Must be enrolled full-time in an undergraduate program not leading to a religious vocation. Contact college financial aid office for deadlines.

Award: Grant for use in freshman, sophomore, junior, or senior years; renewable. *Number:* varies. *Amount:* $1500–$1800.

Eligibility Requirements: Applicant must be enrolled or expecting to enroll full-time at a two-year or four-year institution or university; resident of North Carolina and studying in North Carolina. Available to U.S. citizens.

Application Requirements: Application. *Deadline:* varies.

Contact: Bill Carswell, Manager of Scholarship and Grant Division
North Carolina State Education Assistance Authority
PO Box 14103
Research Triangle Park, NC 27709
Phone: 919-549-8614
Fax: 919-248-4687
E-mail: carswellb@ncseaa.edu

STATE CONTRACTUAL SCHOLARSHIP FUND PROGRAM-NORTH CAROLINA

Renewable award for North Carolina residents already attending an approved private college or university in the state in pursuit of an undergraduate degree. Must have financial need. Contact college financial aid office for deadline and information. May not be enrolled in a program leading to a religious vocation.

Award: Scholarship for use in freshman, sophomore, junior, or senior years; renewable. *Number:* varies. *Amount:* up to $1100.

Eligibility Requirements: Applicant must be enrolled or expecting to enroll full or part-time at a two-year or four-year institution or university; resident of North Carolina and studying in North Carolina. Available to U.S. citizens.

Application Requirements: Application, financial need analysis. *Deadline:* varies.

Contact: Bill Carswell, Manager of Scholarship and Grant Division
North Carolina State Education Assistance Authority
PO Box 14103
Research Triangle Park, NC 27709
Phone: 919-549-8614
Fax: 919-248-4687
E-mail: carswellb@ncseaa.edu

UNIVERSITY OF NORTH CAROLINA NEED-BASED GRANT

Must be enrolled in at least 6 credit hours at one of 16 UNC system universities. Eligibility based on need; applicant must have submitted Free Application for Federal Student Aid. Award varies, consideration for grant automatic when FAFSA is filed. Late applications may be denied due to insufficient funds.

Award: Grant for use in freshman, sophomore, junior, or senior years; renewable. *Number:* varies. *Amount:* varies.

Eligibility Requirements: Applicant must be enrolled or expecting to enroll full or part-time at an institution or university and studying in North Carolina. Available to U.S. citizens.

Application Requirements: Application, financial need analysis, FAFSA. *Deadline:* varies.

Contact: Bill Carswell, Manager of Scholarship and Grant Division
North Carolina State Education Assistance Authority
PO Box 14103
Research Triangle Park, NC 27709
Phone: 919-549-8614
Fax: 919-248-4687
E-mail: carswellb@ncseaa.edu

NORTH CAROLINA VIETNAM VETERANS, INC.   http://www.ncneighbors.com

NORTH CAROLINA VIETNAM VETERANS, INC., SCHOLARSHIP PROGRAM
• *See page 593*

NORTH DAKOTA DEPARTMENT OF PUBLIC INSTRUCTION   http://www.dpi.state.nd.us

ROBERT C. BYRD HONORS SCHOLARSHIP-NORTH DAKOTA

Renewable award to exceptionally able high school seniors who show promise of continued excellence in postsecondary education. Must be resident of North Dakota and a U.S. citizen. Deadline second week in April.

Award: Scholarship for use in freshman, sophomore, junior, or senior years; renewable. *Number:* 10–12. *Amount:* $1500.

Eligibility Requirements: Applicant must be high school student; planning to enroll or expecting to enroll full-time at a two-year or four-year or technical institution or university and resident of North Dakota. Available to U.S. citizens.

Application Requirements: Application, essay, references, test scores, transcript, college acceptance letter. *Deadline:* April.

Contact: Pauline Bjornson, Scholarship Contact
North Dakota Department of Public Instruction
600 East Boulevard Avenue
Bismarck, ND 58505-0440
Phone: 701-328-4518
E-mail: pbjornson@state.nd.us

NORTHERN VIRGINIA URBAN LEAGUE   http://www.nvul.org/

NORTHERN VIRGINIA URBAN LEAGUE SCHOLARSHIP PROGRAM
• See page 627

OHIO 4-H   http://www.ohio4h.org

CHARLES & GWYENNA LIFER 4-H SCHOLARSHIP
• See page 509

MR. & MRS. G. DEMING SEYMOUR 4-H SCHOLARSHIP
• See page 509

OHIO ASSOCIATION FOR ADULT AND CONTINUING EDUCATION   http://oaace.org/

LIFELONG LEARNING SCHOLARSHIP

Scholarship available for a Ohio resident student with Ohio High School Equivalence Diploma (GED) or high school diploma who is currently enrolled in any adult education program or has been enrolled within the last twelve months. Musr enroll in post secondary education or training within six months of receiving scholarship.

Award: Scholarship for use in freshman year. *Amount:* $1500.

Eligibility Requirements: Applicant must be enrolled or expecting to enroll at a four-year institution or university and resident of Ohio. Available to U.S. citizens.

Application Requirements: Application, references. *Deadline:* March 1.

Contact: Brian McCoy, Administrative Assistant
Ohio Association for Adult and Continuing Education
PMB 103, 1601 West Fifth Avenue
Columbus, OH 43212-2310
Phone: 866-996-2223
Fax: 740-435-212
E-mail: bmccoy@oaace.org

LINDA LUCA MEMORIAL GED SCHOLARSHIP

Award for Ohio resident student who scored in the top 100 of GED scores for the year. Eligible students will be mailed application. Must enroll in post secondary education or training within six months of receiving scholarship.

Award: Scholarship for use in freshman year. *Amount:* $1500.

Eligibility Requirements: Applicant must be enrolled or expecting to enroll at a four-year institution or university and resident of Ohio. Available to U.S. citizens.

Application Requirements: Application, references. *Deadline:* varies.

Contact: Brian McCoy, Administrative Assistant
Ohio Association for Adult and Continuing Education
PMB 103, 1601 West Fifth Avenue
Columbus, OH 43212-2310
Phone: 866-996-2223
Fax: 740-435-212
E-mail: bmccoy@oaace.org

MAX WAY SCHOLARSHIP

Scholarship for a student with a Ohio High School Equivalence Diploma (GED) or high school diploma who will enroll in post secondary education or training within six months of receiving scholarship. Must be Ohio resident.

Award: Scholarship for use in freshman year. *Amount:* $1000.

Eligibility Requirements: Applicant must be enrolled or expecting to enroll at a four-year institution or university and resident of Ohio. Available to U.S. citizens.

Application Requirements: Application, references. *Deadline:* March 1.

Contact: Brian McCoy, Administrative Assistant
Ohio Association for Adult and Continuing Education
PMB 103, 1601 West Fifth Avenue
Columbus, OH 43212-2310
Phone: 866-996-2223
Fax: 740-435-212
E-mail: bmccoy@oaace.org

OAACE MEMBER SCHOLARSHIP

Scholarship for Ohio resident and member of OAACE for at least one year prior to applying for the scholarship. Will enroll in post secondary education or professional development training within six months of receiving scholarship.

Award: Scholarship for use in freshman year. *Amount:* $2000.

Eligibility Requirements: Applicant must be enrolled or expecting to enroll at a four-year institution or university and resident of Ohio. Available to U.S. citizens.

Application Requirements: Application, references. *Deadline:* March 15.

Contact: Brian McCoy, Administrative Assistant
Ohio Association for Adult and Continuing Education
PMB 103, 1601 West Fifth Avenue
Columbus, OH 43212-2310
Phone: 866-996-2223
Fax: 740-435-212
E-mail: bmccoy@oaace.org

OHIO ASSOCIATION OF COLLEGIATE REGISTRARS AND ADMISSIONS OFFICERS   http://www.oacrao.ohiou.edu

OHIO ASSOCIATION OF COLLEGIATE REGISTRARS AND ADMISSION OFFICERS SCHOLARSHIP

Nonrenewable scholarship available to a student currently enrolled in an accredited/chartered high school or joint vocational school in the State of Ohio. Must have a minimum cumulative GPA of 2.75 at the end of the junior year.

Award: Scholarship for use in freshman year; not renewable. *Amount:* $500.

Eligibility Requirements: Applicant must be high school student; planning to enroll or expecting to enroll full or part-time at a four-year institution or university and resident of Ohio. Applicant must have 2.5 GPA or higher. Available to U.S. citizens.

Application Requirements: Application, references, personal statement. *Deadline:* February 21.

Contact: Daniel Wilson, Scholarship Committee Chair
Ohio Association of Collegiate Registrars and Admissions Officers
The Ohio State University
730 Lincoln Tower, 1800 Cannon Drive
Columbus, OH 43210-1288
Phone: 740-826-8211
E-mail: dwilson@muskingum.edu

OHIO BOARD OF REGENTS   http://www.regents.state.oh.us

OHIO ACADEMIC SCHOLARSHIP PROGRAM

Award for academically outstanding Ohio residents planning to attend an approved Ohio college. Must be a high school senior intending to enroll full-time. Award is renewable for up to four years. Must rank in upper quarter of class or have a minimum GPA of 3.5.

Award: Scholarship for use in freshman, sophomore, junior, or senior years; renewable. *Number:* 1000. *Amount:* $2205.

Eligibility Requirements: Applicant must be high school student; planning to enroll or expecting to enroll full-time at a two-year or four-year institution; resident of Ohio and studying in Ohio. Applicant must have 3.5 GPA or higher. Available to U.S. citizens.

Ohio Board of Regents (continued)

Application Requirements: Application, test scores, transcript.
Deadline: February 23.

Contact: Sarina Wilks, Program Administrator
Ohio Board of Regents
30 East Broad Street, 36th Floor, PO Box 182452
Columbus, OH 43215-3414
Phone: 614-752-9528
Fax: 614-752-5903
E-mail: swilks@regents.state.oh.us

OHIO INSTRUCTIONAL GRANT

Award for low- and middle-income Ohio residents attending an approved college or school in Ohio or Pennsylvania. Must be enrolled full-time and have financial need. Average award is $630. May be used for any course of study except theology.

Award: Grant for use in freshman, sophomore, junior, or senior years; renewable. *Number:* varies. *Amount:* $78–$5466.

Eligibility Requirements: Applicant must be enrolled or expecting to enroll full-time at a two-year or four-year institution or university; resident of Ohio and studying in Ohio or Pennsylvania. Available to U.S. citizens.

Application Requirements: Application, financial need analysis.
Deadline: October 1.

Contact: Lamar Burch, Program Administrator
Ohio Board of Regents
30 East Broad Street, 36th Floor, PO Box 182452
Columbus, OH 43215-3414
Phone: 614-752-9489
Fax: 614-752-5903
E-mail: lburch@regents.state.oh.us

OHIO MISSING IN ACTION AND PRISONERS OF WAR ORPHANS SCHOLARSHIP
• *See page 593*

OHIO SAFETY OFFICERS COLLEGE MEMORIAL FUND
• *See page 548*

OHIO STUDENT CHOICE GRANT PROGRAM

Renewable award available to Ohio residents attending private colleges within the state. Must be enrolled full-time in a bachelor's degree program. Do not apply to state. Check with financial aid office of college.

Award: Grant for use in freshman, sophomore, junior, or senior years; renewable. *Number:* varies. *Amount:* up to $900.

Eligibility Requirements: Applicant must be enrolled or expecting to enroll full-time at a four-year institution or university; resident of Ohio and studying in Ohio. Available to U.S. citizens.

Application Requirements: *Deadline:* Continuous.

Contact: Barbara Metheney, Program Administrator
Ohio Board of Regents
30 East Broad Street, 36th Floor, PO Box 182452
Columbus, OH 43215-3414
Phone: 614-752-9535
Fax: 614-752-5903
E-mail: bmethene@regents.state.oh.us

OHIO WAR ORPHANS SCHOLARSHIP
• *See page 593*

PART-TIME STUDENT INSTRUCTIONAL GRANT

Renewable grants for part-time undergraduates who are Ohio residents. Award amounts vary. Must attend an Ohio institution.

Award: Grant for use in freshman, sophomore, junior, or senior years; renewable. *Number:* varies. *Amount:* varies.

Eligibility Requirements: Applicant must be enrolled or expecting to enroll part-time at a two-year or four-year institution or university; resident of Ohio and studying in Ohio. Available to U.S. citizens.

Application Requirements: Application, financial need analysis.
Deadline: Continuous.

Contact: Barbara Metheney, Program Administrator
Ohio Board of Regents
30 East Broad Street, 36th Floor
Columbus, OH 43215-3414
Phone: 614-752-9535
Fax: 614-752-5903
E-mail: bmethene@regents.state.oh.us

STUDENT WORKFORCE DEVELOPMENT GRANT PROGRAM

Provides tuition assistance to Ohio students. Students must be pursuing an associate or bachelor's degree and must not have been enrolled full-time in a private career school prior to July 1, 2000.

Award: Grant for use in freshman, sophomore, junior, or senior years. *Amount:* $300.

Eligibility Requirements: Applicant must be enrolled or expecting to enroll full-time at a four-year institution or university; resident of Ohio and studying in Ohio. Available to U.S. citizens.

Contact: Barbara Metheney, Program Administrator
Phone: 614-752-9535
Fax: 614-752-5903
E-mail: bmethene@regents.state.oh.us

OHIO CIVIL SERVICE EMPLOYEES ASSOCIATION   http://www.ocsea.org

LES BEST SCHOLARSHIP
• *See page 510*

OHIO DEPARTMENT OF EDUCATION   http://www.ode.state.oh.us

ROBERT C. BYRD HONORS SCHOLARSHIP-OHIO

Renewable award for graduating high school seniors who demonstrate outstanding academic achievement. Each Ohio high school receives applications by January of each year. School can submit one application for every 200 students in the senior class. Application deadline is the second Friday in March.

Award: Scholarship for use in freshman, sophomore, junior, or senior years; renewable. *Number:* varies. *Amount:* up to $1500.

Eligibility Requirements: Applicant must be high school student; planning to enroll or expecting to enroll at a two-year or four-year institution or university and resident of Ohio. Applicant must have 3.5 GPA or higher. Available to U.S. citizens.

Application Requirements: Application, test scores. *Deadline:* varies.

Contact: Ohio Department of Education
Ohio Department of Education
25 South Front Street, Second Floor
Columbus, OH 43215
Phone: 614-466-4590

OHIO EDUCATIONAL CREDIT UNION   http://www.ohioedcu.com

OHIO EDUCATIONAL CREDIT UNION SCHOLARSHIP

Scholarship for an OECU member in good standing who is a high school senior or recent high school graduate enrolled or planning to enroll full-time in a college or postsecondary technical school or currently attending a college or certified, postsecondary school on a full-time basis. Applicant's most recent cumulative GPA must be at least 2.5. Deadline is April 28.

Award: Scholarship for use in freshman year; not renewable. *Number:* up to 8. *Amount:* $500–$1000.

Eligibility Requirements: Applicant must be enrolled or expecting to enroll full-time at a two-year or four-year or technical institution or university and studying in Ohio. Applicant must have 2.5 GPA or higher. Available to U.S. citizens.

Application Requirements: Application, references, transcript.
Deadline: April 28.

Contact: Barb Miller, OECU Scholarship coordinator
Ohio Educational Credit Union
1075 Linden Avenue, PO Box 606
Zanesville, OH 43702-0606
Phone: 740-453-1009
Fax: 740-453-9063

OHIO FORESTRY ASSOCIATION
http://www.ohioforest.org

OHIO FORESTRY ASSOCIATION MEMORIAL SCHOLARSHIP

Minimum of one scholarship will be awarded to provide assistance toward forest resource education to quality college students. Preference given to students attending Ohio colleges and universities. Scholarship awards vary.

Award: Scholarship for use in freshman, sophomore, junior, or senior years; not renewable. *Number:* 1. *Amount:* up to $1000.

Eligibility Requirements: Applicant must be enrolled or expecting to enroll at a two-year or four-year or technical institution or university and resident of Ohio. Available to U.S. citizens.

Application Requirements: Application, essay, test scores. *Deadline:* April 15.

Contact: Bob Romig, Executive Director
Ohio Forestry Association
PO Box 970
4080 South High Street
Columbus, OH 43207
Phone: 614-497-9580
Fax: 614-497-9581
E-mail: bobr@ohioforest.org

OHIO NATIONAL GUARD
http://www.ongsp.org

OHIO NATIONAL GUARD SCHOLARSHIP PROGRAM
• *See page 572*

OHIO PARTNERS IN CHARACTER EDUCATION
http://www.charactereducationohio.org

LAWS OF LIFE CONTEST:

All Ohio schools that hold Laws of Life, Foundations for Life or other character-related essay contests, or contest awards ceremonies during the school year are eligible to participate. Both middle and high school students are eligible. All submissions must be submitted no later than May 19.

Award: Prize for use in freshman year. *Number:* up to 18. *Amount:* $75–$500.

Eligibility Requirements: Applicant must be enrolled or expecting to enroll at an institution or university; resident of Ohio and must have an interest in writing. Available to U.S. citizens.

Application Requirements: Application, essay. *Deadline:* May 19.

Contact: Dr. Lucy Frontera, OPCE Director
Ohio Partners in Character Education
c/o Council for Ethics in Economics
191 West Nationwide Boulevard, Suite 300B
Columbus, OH 43215
Phone: 614-221-8661
Fax: 614-221-8707
E-mail: frontera@pipeline.com

OHIO POLICE CORPS
http://www.hhs.utoledo.edu/ohiopolicecorps/default.htm

OHIO POLICE CORPS SCHOLARSHIP

Scholarships available for students with a Bachelor's degree or a full-time college senior. Must be a U.S. citizen with a minimum 2.75 GPA. Must agree to work for a municipal police department, Sheriff's Department, or Ohio State Patrol for a minimum of 4 years. See Web site for details at http://www.ohiopolicecorps.utoledo.edu

Award: Scholarship for use in senior, or graduate years; renewable. *Number:* 10. *Amount:* $3750.

Eligibility Requirements: Applicant must be enrolled or expecting to enroll full-time at a four-year institution or university and resident of Ohio. Available to U.S. citizens.

Application Requirements: Application, driver's license, essay, photo, references, transcript, DD Form 214 if applicable. *Deadline:* Continuous.

Contact: D. Michael Collins, Director
Ohio Police Corps
University of Toledo
MS 400, 2801 W. Bancroft Street
Toledo, OH 43606-3390
Phone: 419-530-6246
Fax: 419-530-6244

OKLAHOMA ALUMNI & ASSOCIATES OF FHA, HERO AND FCCLA, INC.
http://www.okfccla.org

OKLAHOMA ALUMNI & ASSOCIATES OF FHA, HERO AND FCCLA, INC. SCHOLARSHIP
• *See page 510*

OKLAHOMA STATE DEPARTMENT OF EDUCATION
http://www.sde.state.ok.us

ROBERT C. BYRD HONORS SCHOLARSHIP-OKLAHOMA

Scholarships available to high school seniors. Applicants must be a U.S. citizen or national, or be a permanent resident of the United States. Must be a legal resident of Oklahoma. Must have a minimum ACT composite score of 32 and/or a minimum SAT combined score of 1420 and/or 2130 or a minimum GED score of 700.

Award: Scholarship for use in freshman year. *Amount:* $1500.

Eligibility Requirements: Applicant must be high school student; planning to enroll or expecting to enroll at a four-year institution and resident of Oklahoma. Available to U.S. citizens.

Application Requirements: Application, essay, references, transcript. *Deadline:* March 16.

Contact: Paul Simon, Director, Professional Services
Oklahoma State Department of Education
Oliver Hodge Memorial Education Building
2500 North Lincoln Boulevard, Suite 212
Oklahoma City, OK 73105-4599
Phone: 405-521-2808

OKLAHOMA STATE REGENTS FOR HIGHER EDUCATION
http://www.okhighered.org

ACADEMIC SCHOLARS PROGRAM

Encourages students of high academic ability to attend institutions in Oklahoma. Renewable up to four years. ACT or SAT scores must fall between 99.5 and 100th percentiles, or applicant must be designated as a National Merit scholar or finalist.

Award: Scholarship for use in freshman, sophomore, junior, or senior years; renewable. *Number:* varies. *Amount:* $1800–$2800.

Eligibility Requirements: Applicant must be high school student; planning to enroll or expecting to enroll full-time at a two-year or four-year institution or university and studying in Oklahoma. Available to U.S. citizens.

Application Requirements: Application, test scores, transcript. *Deadline:* Continuous.

Contact: Scholarship Programs Coordinator
Oklahoma State Regents for Higher Education
PO Box 108850
Oklahoma City, OK 73101-8850
Phone: 800-858-1840
Fax: 405-225-9230
E-mail: studentinfo@osrhe.edu

OKLAHOMA TUITION AID GRANT

Award for Oklahoma residents enrolled at an Oklahoma institution at least part time each semester in a degree program. May be enrolled in two or four-year or approved vocational-technical institution. Award of up to $1000 per year. Application is made through FAFSA.

Award: Grant for use in freshman, sophomore, junior, senior, or graduate years; renewable. *Number:* 23,000. *Amount:* $200–$1000.

Eligibility Requirements: Applicant must be enrolled or expecting to enroll full or part-time at a two-year or four-year or technical

Oklahoma State Regents for Higher Education (continued)

institution or university; resident of Oklahoma and studying in Oklahoma. Available to U.S. citizens.

Application Requirements: Application, financial need analysis, FAFSA. *Deadline:* April 30.

Contact: Oklahoma State Regents for Higher Education
PO Box 3020
Oklahoma City, OK 73101-3020
Phone: 405-225-9456
Fax: 405-225-9392
E-mail: otaginfo@otag.org

REGIONAL UNIVERSITY BACCALAUREATE SCHOLARSHIP

Renewable award for Oklahoma residents attending one of 11 participating Oklahoma public universities. Must have an ACT composite score of at least 30 or be a National Merit semifinalist or commended student. In addition to the award amount, each recipient will receive a resident tuition waiver from the institution. Must maintain a 3.25 GPA. Deadlines vary depending upon the institution attended.

Award: Scholarship for use in freshman, sophomore, junior, or senior years; renewable. *Number:* up to 165. *Amount:* $3000.

Eligibility Requirements: Applicant must be enrolled or expecting to enroll full-time at an institution or university; resident of Oklahoma and studying in Oklahoma. Available to U.S. citizens.

Application Requirements: Application. *Deadline:* varies.

Contact: Alicia Harris, Scholarship Programs Coordinator
Oklahoma State Regents for Higher Education
PO Box 108850
Oklahoma City, OK 73101-8850
Phone: 405-225-9131
Fax: 405-225-9230
E-mail: aharris@osrhe.edu

WILLIAM P. WILLIS SCHOLARSHIP

Renewable award for Oklahoma residents attending an Oklahoma institution. Must be a full-time undergraduate. Contact institution financial aid office for application deadline.

Award: Scholarship for use in freshman, sophomore, junior, or senior years; renewable. *Number:* 32. *Amount:* $2000–$3000.

Eligibility Requirements: Applicant must be enrolled or expecting to enroll full-time at a two-year or four-year institution or university; resident of Oklahoma and studying in Oklahoma. Available to U.S. citizens.

Application Requirements: Application. *Deadline:* varies.

Contact: Alicia Harris, Scholarship Programs Coordinator
Oklahoma State Regents for Higher Education
PO Box 108850
Oklahoma City, OK 73101-8850
Phone: 405-225-9131
Fax: 405-225-9230
E-mail: aharris@osrhe.edu

OREGON COLLECTORS ASSOCIATION (ORCA) SCHOLARSHIP FUND   http://www.orcascholarshipfund.com

OREGON COLLECTORS ASSOCIATION BOB HASSON MEMORIAL SCHOLARSHIP FUND

Scholarship available to Oregon high school seniors for use as full-time students at an Oregon accredited public or private 2- or 4-year college, university, or trade school. Must start attendance within 12 months of the award. Must submit fictional essay on "the proper use of credit in the 21st century." Applicants may not be children/grandchildren of owners or officers of collection agencies in Oregon. For application see Web site: http://www.orcascholarshipfund.com.

Award: Scholarship for use in freshman year; not renewable. *Number:* 3. *Amount:* $1500–$3000.

Eligibility Requirements: Applicant must be high school student; planning to enroll or expecting to enroll full-time at a two-year or four-year or technical institution or university; resident of Oregon and studying in Oregon. Available to U.S. citizens.

Application Requirements: Application, essay. *Deadline:* March 1.

Contact: Doug Jones, Director
Oregon Collectors Association (ORCA) Scholarship Fund
PO Box 42409
Portland, OR 97242
Phone: 888-622-3588
E-mail: dcj@pandhbilling.com

OREGON COMMUNITY FOUNDATION   http://www.ocf1.org/

ERNEST ALAN AND BARBARA PARK MEYER SCHOLARSHIP FUND

Scholarship for Oregon high school graduates for use in the pursuit of a postsecondary education (undergraduate and graduate) at a nonprofit two or four year college or university.

Award: Scholarship for use in freshman, sophomore, junior, senior, or graduate years. *Number:* 1.

Eligibility Requirements: Applicant must be enrolled or expecting to enroll at a two-year or four-year institution or university and resident of Oregon. Available to U.S. citizens.

Application Requirements: *Deadline:* varies.

Contact: Dianne Causey, Program Associate for Scholarships/Grants
Oregon Community Foundation
1221 South West Yamhill, Suite 100
Portland, OR 97205

FRIENDS OF BILL RUTHERFORD EDUCATION FUND

Scholarship for Oregon high school graduates or GED recipients who are dependent children of individuals holding statewide elected office or currently serving in the Oregon State Legislature. Students must be enrolled full-time in a two- or four-year college or university.

Award: Scholarship for use in sophomore, junior, or senior years.

Eligibility Requirements: Applicant must be enrolled or expecting to enroll at a two-year or four-year institution or university and resident of Oregon. Available to U.S. citizens.

Application Requirements: *Deadline:* varies.

Contact: Dianne Causey, Program Associate for Scholarships/Grants
Oregon Community Foundation
1221 South West Yamhill, Suite 100
Portland, OR 97205
Phone: 503-227-6846
Fax: 503-274-7771
E-mail: info@ocf1.org

HARRY LUDWIG SCHOLARSHIP FUND
• See page 564

MARY E. HORSTKOTTE SCHOLARSHIP FUND

Award available for academically talented and financially needy students, for use in the pursuit of a postsecondary education.

Award: Scholarship for use in freshman, sophomore, junior, or senior years. *Number:* 1.

Eligibility Requirements: Applicant must be enrolled or expecting to enroll at a two-year or four-year or technical institution or university and resident of Oregon. Available to U.S. citizens.

Application Requirements: *Deadline:* varies.

Contact: Dianne Causey, Program Associate for Scholarships/Grants
Oregon Community Foundation
1221 South West Yamhill, Suite 100
Portland, OR 97205
Phone: 503-227-6846
Fax: 503-274-7771
E-mail: info@ocf1.org

RUBE AND MINAH LESLIE EDUCATIONAL FUND

Scholarship for Oregon residents, for the pursuit of a postsecondary education. Selection is based on financial need.

Award: Scholarship for use in freshman, sophomore, junior, or senior years. *Number:* 1.

Eligibility Requirements: Applicant must be enrolled or expecting to enroll at a two-year or four-year or technical institution or university; resident of Oregon and studying in Oregon. Available to U.S. citizens.

Application Requirements: Application, financial need analysis. *Deadline:* varies.

Contact: Dianne Causey, Program Associate for Scholarships/Grants
Oregon Community Foundation
1221 South West Yamhill, Suite 100
Portland, OR 97205
Phone: 503-227-6846

WILLIAM L. AND DELLA WAGGONER SCHOLARSHIP FUND

Scholarship for graduates of any Oregon high school who show academic potential and financial need, for use in the pursuit of a postsecondary education.

Award: Scholarship for use in freshman, sophomore, junior, or senior years. *Number:* 1.

Eligibility Requirements: Applicant must be enrolled or expecting to enroll at a two-year or four-year or technical institution or university; resident of Oregon and studying in Oregon. Available to U.S. citizens.

Application Requirements: *Deadline:* varies.

Contact: Dianne Causey, Program Associate for Scholarships/Grants
Oregon Community Foundation
1221 South West Yamhill, Suite 100
Portland, OR 97205
Phone: 503-227-6846
Fax: 503-274-7771
E-mail: info@ocf1.org

OREGON DEPARTMENT OF VETERANS' AFFAIRS
http://www.odva.state.or.us

OREGON VETERANS' EDUCATION AID
• *See page 593*

OREGON NATIVE AMERICAN CHAMBER OF COMMERCE SCHOLARSHIP
http://www.onacc.org

OREGON NATIVE AMERICAN CHAMBER OF COMMERCE SCHOLARSHIP
• *See page 628*

OREGON STUDENT ASSISTANCE COMMISSION
http://www.osac.state.or.us

A. VICTOR ROSENFELD SCHOLARSHIP
• *See page 532*

AFSCME: AMERICAN FEDERATION OF STATE, COUNTY, AND MUNICIPAL EMPLOYEES LOCAL 1724 SCHOLARSHIP
• *See page 510*

AFSCME: AMERICAN FEDERATION OF STATE, COUNTY, AND MUNICIPAL EMPLOYEES LOCAL 75 SCHOLARSHIP
• *See page 510*

ALBINA FUEL COMPANY SCHOLARSHIP
• *See page 532*

AMERICAN EX-PRISONER OF WAR SCHOLARSHIPS: PETER CONNACHER MEMORIAL SCHOLARSHIP
• *See page 594*

ANGELINA AND PETE COSTANZO VOCATIONAL SCHOLARSHIP

Award open to high school grads or GED recipients seeking job skills but not a baccalaureate degree. Must be enrolled at least part-time at a vocational school or two-year college. Must be a resident of Clackamas, Columbia, Multnomah, or Washington counties. Renewable for one additional year.

Award: Scholarship for use in freshman or sophomore years; renewable. *Number:* 9. *Amount:* $2333.

Eligibility Requirements: Applicant must be enrolled or expecting to enroll full or part-time at a two-year or technical institution and resident of Oregon. Available to U.S. citizens.

Application Requirements: Application, essay, financial need analysis, transcript, activity chart. *Deadline:* March 1.

Contact: Director of Grant Programs
Oregon Student Assistance Commission
1500 Valley River Drive, Suite 100
Eugene, OR 97401-7020
Phone: 800-452-8807 Ext. 7395

BANDON SUBMARINE CABLE COUNCIL SCHOLARSHIP

Renewable award for Oregon residents and high school graduates who have not matriculated as postsecondary students. Additional preferences, in this order, are for members or dependent children of members of the Bandon Submarine Council; any commercial fisherman or family members who reside in Coos County; any commercial fisherman or family member anywhere in Oregon; any postsecondary student residing in Clatsop, Tillamook, Lincoln, Lane, Coos or Curry County; any postsecondary student in Oregon.

Award: Scholarship for use in freshman, sophomore, junior, or senior years; renewable. *Number:* varies. *Amount:* $500.

Eligibility Requirements: Applicant must be enrolled or expecting to enroll at an institution or university and resident of Oregon. Available to U.S. citizens.

Application Requirements: Application, essay, financial need analysis, transcript, activities chart. *Deadline:* March 1.

Contact: Director of Grant Programs
Oregon Student Assistance Commission
1500 Valley River Drive, Suite 100
Eugene, OR 97401-7020
Phone: 800-452-8807 Ext. 7395

BANK OF THE CASCADES SCHOLARSHIP
• *See page 532*

BEN SELLING SCHOLARSHIP

Award for Oregon residents enrolling as sophomores or higher in college. College GPA 3.50 or higher required. Apply/compete annually. Must be U.S. citizen or permanent resident. Wells Fargo employees, their children or near relatives must provide complete disclosure of employment status to receive this award.

Award: Scholarship for use in sophomore, junior, or senior years; not renewable. *Number:* 25. *Amount:* $1000.

Eligibility Requirements: Applicant must be enrolled or expecting to enroll full-time at a two-year or four-year or technical institution or university and resident of Oregon. Applicant must have 3.5 GPA or higher. Available to U.S. citizens.

Application Requirements: Application, essay, financial need analysis, references, transcript, activity chart. *Deadline:* March 1.

Contact: Director of Grant Programs
Oregon Student Assistance Commission
1500 Valley River Drive, Suite 100
Eugene, OR 97401-7020
Phone: 800-452-8807 Ext. 7395

BENJAMIN FRANKLIN/EDITH GREEN SCHOLARSHIP

One-time award open to graduating Oregon high school seniors. Must attend a four-year public Oregon college. See Web site at http://www.osac.state.or.us for more information.

Award: Scholarship for use in freshman year; not renewable. *Number:* 14. *Amount:* $1000.

Eligibility Requirements: Applicant must be high school student; planning to enroll or expecting to enroll full-time at a four-year institution or university; resident of Oregon and studying in Oregon. Available to U.S. citizens.

Application Requirements: Application, essay, financial need analysis, transcript, activity chart. *Deadline:* March 1.

Contact: Director of Grant Programs
Oregon Student Assistance Commission
1500 Valley River Drive, Suite 100
Eugene, OR 97401-7020
Phone: 800-452-8807 Ext. 7395

BLUE HERON PAPER EMPLOYEE DEPENDENTS SCHOLARSHIP
• *See page 533*

Oregon Student Assistance Commission (continued)

CARPENTERS AND JOINERS LOCAL 2130 SCHOLARSHIP
• See page 548

CHANDLER SCHOLARS PROGRAM SCHOLARSHIP

One-time award open to current residents and graduates of a high school in Del Norte County, California, or one of the following Oregon counties: Baker, Curry, Deschutes, Harney, Jefferson, Umatilla, or Union. Must have a minimum cumulative 2.5 high school GPA. Additional essay required. See Web site for details. (http://www.osac.state.or.us).

Award: Scholarship for use in freshman, sophomore, junior, or senior years; renewable. *Number:* 14. *Amount:* $1000.

Eligibility Requirements: Applicant must be enrolled or expecting to enroll full-time at an institution or university and resident of California or Oregon. Applicant must have 2.5 GPA or higher. Available to U.S. citizens.

Application Requirements: Application, essay, financial need analysis, transcript, activity chart. *Deadline:* March 1.

Contact: Director of Grant Programs
Oregon Student Assistance Commission
1500 Valley River Drive, Suite 100
Eugene, OR 97401-7020
Phone: 800-452-8807 Ext. 7395

CHILDREN, ADULT, AND FAMILY SERVICES SCHOLARSHIP

One-time award for graduating high school seniors, GED recipients, and college students currently or formerly in foster care or an Independent Living Program (ILP) financially supported through the Oregon State Office for Services to Children and Families. Must attend an Oregon public college. Visit Web site for more details (http://www.osac.state.or.us). Award varies between $500-$5000.

Award: Scholarship for use in freshman, sophomore, junior, senior, or graduate years; renewable. *Number:* varies. *Amount:* $500–$5000.

Eligibility Requirements: Applicant must be enrolled or expecting to enroll full-time at a two-year or four-year institution; resident of Oregon and studying in Oregon. Available to U.S. citizens.

Application Requirements: Application, essay, financial need analysis, references, transcript, activity chart. *Deadline:* March 1.

Contact: Director of Grant Programs
Oregon Student Assistance Commission
1500 Valley River Drive, Suite 100
Eugene, OR 97401-7020
Phone: 800-452-8807 Ext. 7395

DAN KONNIE MEMORIAL DEPENDENTS SCHOLARSHIP
• See page 533

DAVID FAMILY SCHOLARSHIP

Award for residents of Clackamas, Lane, Multnomah, and Washington counties. First preference to applicants enrolling at least half-time in upper-division or graduate programs at four-year colleges. College sophomores and above. Students with 2.50-3.50 GPA.

Award: Scholarship for use in freshman, sophomore, junior, or graduate years; renewable. *Number:* 15. *Amount:* $2530.

Eligibility Requirements: Applicant must be enrolled or expecting to enroll full or part-time at a four-year institution or university and resident of Oregon. Applicant must have 2.5 GPA or higher. Available to U.S. citizens.

Application Requirements: Application, essay, financial need analysis, transcript, activity chart. *Deadline:* March 1.

Contact: Director of Grant Programs
Oregon Student Assistance Commission
1500 Valley River Drive, Suite 100
Eugene, OR 97401-7020
Phone: 800-452-8807 Ext. 7395

DOROTHY CAMPBELL MEMORIAL SCHOLARSHIP

Renewable award for female Oregon high school graduates with a minimum 2.75 GPA. Must submit essay describing strong, continuing interest in golf and the contribution that sport has made to applicant's development.

Award: Scholarship for use in freshman, sophomore, junior, or senior years; renewable. *Number:* 2. *Amount:* $1500.

Eligibility Requirements: Applicant must be high school student; planning to enroll or expecting to enroll full-time at a four-year institution or university; female; resident of Oregon; studying in Oregon and must have an interest in golf. Available to U.S. citizens.

Application Requirements: Application, essay, financial need analysis, transcript, activity chart. *Deadline:* March 1.

Contact: Director of Grant Programs
Oregon Student Assistance Commission
1500 Valley River Drive, Suite 100
Eugene, OR 97401-7020
Phone: 800-452-8807 Ext. 7395

ESSEX SCHOLARSHIP
• See page 533

FORD OPPORTUNITY PROGRAM

Award for Oregon residents who are single heads of household with custody of a dependent child or children. Must plan to work toward a four-year degree. Only for use at Oregon colleges. Minimum 3.0 GPA. If minimum requirements not met, Special Recommendation Form (see high school counselor or contact OSAC) must be submitted. May apply for this program or Ford Scholars or Ford Restart.

Award: Scholarship for use in freshman, sophomore, junior, or senior years; renewable. *Number:* 52. *Amount:* $11,261.

Eligibility Requirements: Applicant must be enrolled or expecting to enroll full or part-time at a two-year or four-year institution; single; resident of Oregon and studying in Oregon. Applicant must have 3.0 GPA or higher. Available to U.S. citizens.

Application Requirements: Application, essay, financial need analysis, interview, transcript, activity chart. *Deadline:* March 1.

Contact: Director of Grant Programs
Oregon Student Assistance Commission
1500 Valley River Drive, Suite 100
Eugene, OR 97401-7020
Phone: 800-452-8807 Ext. 7395

FORD RESTART PROGRAM SCHOLARSHIP

Award for Oregon residents 26 years of age or older as of March 1 who have a high school degree or GED and wish to pursue technical, community college, or four-year degrees at an Oregon college. Preference given to those with limited college experience. Must complete ReStart Reference Form. Contact OSAC. Apply for this program, or Ford Opportunity, or Ford Scholars.

Award: Scholarship for use in freshman, sophomore, junior, or senior years; renewable. *Number:* 30. *Amount:* $7781.

Eligibility Requirements: Applicant must be age 26; enrolled or expecting to enroll at a two-year or four-year or technical institution or university; resident of Oregon and studying in Oregon. Available to U.S. citizens.

Application Requirements: Application, essay, financial need analysis, interview, transcript, activity chart. *Deadline:* March 1.

Contact: Director of Grant Programs
Oregon Student Assistance Commission
1500 Valley River Drive, Suite 100
Eugene, OR 97401-7020
Phone: 800-452-8807 Ext. 7395

FORD SCHOLARS

Award for Oregon graduating seniors, Oregon high school graduates not yet full-time undergraduates, or those who have completed two years of undergraduate study at an Oregon community college and will enter junior year at a four-year Oregon college. Minimum cumulative 3.0 GPA. If minimum requirements not met, Special Recommendation Form (see high school counselor or contact OSAC) must be submitted. May apply for this program, or Ford Opportunity, or Ford Restart. Must plan to work toward a four-year degree.

Award: Scholarship for use in freshman, sophomore, junior, or senior years; renewable. *Number:* 136. *Amount:* $5836.

Eligibility Requirements: Applicant must be enrolled or expecting to enroll at a two-year or four-year institution or university; resident of Oregon and studying in Oregon. Applicant must have 3.0 GPA or higher. Available to U.S. citizens.

Application Requirements: Application, essay, financial need analysis, interview, test scores, transcript, activity chart. *Deadline:* March 1.

Contact: Director of Grant Programs
Oregon Student Assistance Commission
1500 Valley River Drive, Suite 100
Eugene, OR 97401-7020
Phone: 800-452-8807 Ext. 7395

FORD SONS AND DAUGHTERS OF EMPLOYEES OF ROSEBURG FOREST PRODUCTS COMPANY SCHOLARSHIP
• *See page 533*

GLENN JACKSON SCHOLARS SCHOLARSHIPS (OCF)
• *See page 533*

HARRY LUDWIG MEMORIAL SCHOLARSHIP
• *See page 564*

IDA M. CRAWFORD SCHOLARSHIP

One-time scholarship awarded to Oregon high school seniors with a cumulative GPA of 3.5. Not available to applicants majoring in law, medicine, theology, teaching, or music. U.S. Bancorp employees, their children or near relatives, are not eligible. Must supply proof of birth in the continental U.S.

Award: Scholarship for use in freshman year; not renewable. *Number:* 63. *Amount:* $577.

Eligibility Requirements: Applicant must be high school student; planning to enroll or expecting to enroll at an institution or university and resident of Oregon. Applicant must have 3.5 GPA or higher. Available to U.S. citizens.

Application Requirements: Application, essay, financial need analysis, transcript, activities chart. *Deadline:* March 1.

Contact: Director of Grant Programs
Oregon Student Assistance Commission
1500 Valley River Drive, Suite 100
Eugene, OR 97401-7020
Phone: 800-452-8807 Ext. 7395

INTERNATIONAL BROTHERHOOD OF ELECTRICAL WORKERS LOCAL 280 SCHOLARSHIP
• *See page 511*

INTERNATIONAL UNION OF OPERATING ENGINEERS LOCAL 701 SCHOLARSHIP
• *See page 511*

IRMGARD SCHULZ SCHOLARSHIP

Award for graduating seniors of a U.S. public high school with first preference going to applicants from high schools in Josephine County, Oregon. Second preference is for applicants who are orphans or from foster or single-parent homes. Prior-year recipients may reapply annually. Application deadline is March 1.

Award: Scholarship for use in freshman, sophomore, junior, senior, or graduate years; renewable. *Number:* 30. *Amount:* $308.

Eligibility Requirements: Applicant must be high school student; planning to enroll or expecting to enroll at an institution or university and resident of Oregon. Available to U.S. citizens.

Application Requirements: Application, essay, financial need analysis, transcript, activities chart. *Deadline:* March 1.

Contact: Director of Grant Programs
Oregon Student Assistance Commission
1500 Valley River Drive, Suite 100
Eugene, OR 97401-7020
Phone: 800-452-8807 Ext. 7395

JEROME B. STEINBACH SCHOLARSHIP

Award for Oregon residents enrolled in Oregon institution as sophomore or above with minimum 3.5 GPA. Award for undergraduate study. U.S. Bancorp employees, their children or close relatives, not eligible. Must submit proof of U.S. birth.

Award: Scholarship for use in sophomore, junior, or senior years; renewable. *Number:* 93. *Amount:* $685.

Eligibility Requirements: Applicant must be enrolled or expecting to enroll full-time at a four-year institution or university; resident of Oregon and studying in Oregon. Applicant must have 3.5 GPA or higher. Available to U.S. citizens.

Application Requirements: Application, essay, financial need analysis, transcript. *Deadline:* March 1.

Contact: Director of Grant Programs
Oregon Student Assistance Commission
1500 Valley River Drive, Suite 100
Eugene, OR 97401-7020
Phone: 800-452-8807 Ext. 7395

JOSE D. GARCIA MIGRANT EDUCATION SCHOLARSHIP

One-time award for U.S. citizens or permanent residents in Oregon Migrant Education program, who are also high school graduates or GED recipients enrolling at least half-time in freshman year undergraduate study. Must enter parent names in membership section of application.

Award: Scholarship for use in freshman year; not renewable. *Number:* 1. *Amount:* $500.

Eligibility Requirements: Applicant must be enrolled or expecting to enroll full or part-time at an institution or university; resident of Oregon and must have an interest in designated field specified by sponsor. Available to U.S. citizens.

Application Requirements: Application, essay, financial need analysis, transcript, activity chart. *Deadline:* March 1.

Contact: Director of Grant Programs
Oregon Student Assistance Commission
1500 Valley River Drive, Suite 100
Eugene, OR 97401-7020
Phone: 800-452-8807 Ext. 7395

MARIA JACKSON/GENERAL GEORGE A. WHITE SCHOLARSHIP
• *See page 594*

MC GARRY MACHINE INC. SCHOLARSHIP
• *See page 533*

OREGON AFL-CIO SCHOLARSHIP
• *See page 548*

OREGON COLLECTORS ASSOCIATION BOB HASSON MEMORIAL SCHOLARSHIP

One-time award for graduating Oregon high school seniors and recent Oregon high school graduates, enrolling in an Oregon college within one year of graduation. Children and grandchildren of owners and officers of collection agencies registered in Oregon are not eligible. Award is based on a 3-4 page essay titled "The Proper Use of Credit." See Web site (http://www.osac.state.or.us) for important application information.

Award: Scholarship for use in freshman year; not renewable. *Number:* 3. *Amount:* $1500–$3000.

Eligibility Requirements: Applicant must be enrolled or expecting to enroll at a two-year or four-year or technical institution; resident of Oregon and studying in Oregon. Available to U.S. citizens.

Application Requirements: Application, applicant must enter a contest, essay, financial need analysis, test scores, transcript, activity chart. *Deadline:* March 1.

Contact: Director of Grant Programs
Oregon Student Assistance Commission
1500 Valley River Drive, Suite 100
Eugene, OR 97401-7020
Phone: 800-452-8807 Ext. 7395

OREGON DUNGENESS CRAB COMMISSION SCHOLARSHIP
• *See page 548*

OREGON METRO FEDERAL CREDIT UNION SCHOLARSHIP

One scholarship available to an Oregon high school graduate who is a Oregon Metro Federal Credit Union member. Preference given to graduating high school senior and applicant who plans to attend an Oregon college. One-time award.

Award: Scholarship for use in freshman year; renewable. *Number:* 5. *Amount:* $500.

Eligibility Requirements: Applicant must be enrolled or expecting to enroll full-time at an institution or university; resident of Oregon and studying in Oregon. Available to U.S. citizens.

Application Requirements: Application, essay, financial need analysis, references, transcript, activity chart. *Deadline:* March 1.

Oregon Student Assistance Commission (continued)

Contact: Director of Grant Programs
Oregon Student Assistance Commission
1500 Valley River Drive, Suite 100
Eugene, OR 97401-7020
Phone: 800-452-8807 Ext. 7395

OREGON OCCUPATIONAL SAFETY AND HEALTH DIVISION WORKERS MEMORIAL SCHOLARSHIP
• *See page 548*

OREGON PUBLISHING COMPANY/HILLIARD SCHOLARSHIP
• *See page 511*

OREGON SALMON COMMISSION SCHOLARSHIP
• *See page 549*

OREGON SCHOLARSHIP FUND COMMUNITY COLLEGE STUDENT AWARD

Scholarship open to Oregon residents enrolled or planning to enroll in Oregon community college programs. May apply for one additional year.

Award: Scholarship for use in freshman or sophomore years; renewable. *Number:* varies. *Amount:* $500.

Eligibility Requirements: Applicant must be enrolled or expecting to enroll full-time at a two-year institution; resident of Oregon and studying in Oregon. Available to U.S. citizens.

Application Requirements: Application, essay, financial need analysis, transcript, activity chart. *Deadline:* March 1.

Contact: Director of Grant Programs
Oregon Student Assistance Commission
1500 Valley River Drive, Suite 100
Eugene, OR 97401-7020
Phone: 800-452-8807 Ext. 7395

OREGON SCHOLARSHIP FUND TRANSFER STUDENT AWARD

Award open to Oregon residents who are currently enrolled in their second year at a community college and are planning to transfer to a four-year college in Oregon. Prior recipients may apply for one additional year.

Award: Scholarship for use in junior or senior years; renewable. *Number:* varies. *Amount:* $500.

Eligibility Requirements: Applicant must be enrolled or expecting to enroll full-time at a four-year institution or university; resident of Oregon and studying in Oregon. Available to U.S. citizens.

Application Requirements: Application, essay, financial need analysis, transcript, activity chart. *Deadline:* March 1.

Contact: Director of Grant Programs
Oregon Student Assistance Commission
1500 Valley River Drive, Suite 100
Eugene, OR 97401-7020
Phone: 800-452-8807 Ext. 7395

OREGON STATE FISCAL ASSOCIATION SCHOLARSHIP
• *See page 511*

OREGON STUDENT ASSISTANCE COMMISSION EMPLOYEE AND DEPENDENT SCHOLARSHIP

One-time award for current permanent employee of the Oregon Student Assistance Commission or legally dependent children of employee. Also available to dependent children of an employee who retires, is permanently disabled, or deceased directly from employment at OSAC. Dependent must enroll full time. Employee may enroll part time.

Award: Scholarship for use in freshman, sophomore, junior, or senior years; renewable. *Number:* 7. *Amount:* $500.

Eligibility Requirements: Applicant must be enrolled or expecting to enroll full or part-time at an institution or university and resident of Oregon. Available to U.S. citizens.

Application Requirements: Application, essay, transcript, activities chart. *Deadline:* March 1.

Contact: Director of Grant Programs
Oregon Student Assistance Commission
1500 Valley River Drive, Suite 100
Eugene, OR 97401-7020
Phone: 800-452-8807 Ext. 7395

OREGON TRAWL COMMISSION SCHOLARSHIP
• *See page 549*

OREGON TRUCKING ASSOCIATION SCHOLARSHIP
• *See page 534*

PACIFIC NW FEDERAL CREDIT UNION SCHOLARSHIP

One scholarship available to graduating high school senior who is a member of Pacific North West Federal Credit Union. A special essay is required employing the theme, "Why is My Credit Union an Important Consumer Choice?" Employers and officials of the Credit Union and their dependents are not eligible. One-time award.

Award: Scholarship for use in freshman year; not renewable. *Number:* up to 2. *Amount:* $750.

Eligibility Requirements: Applicant must be high school student; planning to enroll or expecting to enroll full-time at a four-year institution and resident of Oregon. Available to U.S. citizens.

Application Requirements: Application, essay, references, transcript. *Deadline:* March 1.

Contact: Director of Grant Programs
Oregon Student Assistance Commission
1500 Valley River Drive, Suite 100
Eugene, OR 97401-7020
Phone: 800-452-8807 Ext. 7395

PACIFICSOURCE SCHOLARSHIP
• *See page 534*

PENDLETON POSTAL WORKERS SCHOLARSHIP
• *See page 549*

PETER CROSSLEY MEMORIAL SCHOLARSHIP

Open to graduating seniors of an Oregon public alternative high school. Must submit essay on "How I Faced Challenges and Overcame Obstacles to Graduate from High School." See Web site at http://www.osac.state.or.us for more information.

Award: Scholarship for use in freshman, sophomore, junior, or senior years; renewable. *Number:* 1. *Amount:* $500.

Eligibility Requirements: Applicant must be high school student; planning to enroll or expecting to enroll full or part-time at a four-year institution and resident of Oregon. Available to U.S. citizens.

Application Requirements: Application, essay, financial need analysis, transcript, activity chart. *Deadline:* March 1.

Contact: Director of Grant Programs
Oregon Student Assistance Commission
1500 Valley River Drive, Suite 100
Eugene, OR 97401-7020
Phone: 800-452-8807 Ext. 7395

PORTLAND WOMEN'S CLUB SCHOLARSHIP

Renewable award open to graduates of any Oregon high school. Must have a minimum 3.0 cumulative GPA. Preference for female students.

Award: Scholarship for use in freshman, sophomore, junior, or senior years; renewable. *Number:* 5. *Amount:* $1500.

Eligibility Requirements: Applicant must be enrolled or expecting to enroll at an institution or university and resident of Oregon. Applicant must have 3.0 GPA or higher. Available to U.S. citizens.

Application Requirements: Application, essay, financial need analysis, transcript, activity chart. *Deadline:* March 1.

Contact: Director of Grant Programs
Oregon Student Assistance Commission
1500 Valley River Drive, Suite 100
Eugene, OR 97401-7020
Phone: 800-452-8807 Ext. 7395

REED'S FUEL AND TRUCKING COMPANY SCHOLARSHIP
• *See page 534*

RICHARD F. BRENTANO MEMORIAL SCHOLARSHIP
• *See page 534*

ROBERT C. BYRD HONORS SCHOLARSHIP-OREGON

Renewable award available to Oregon high school seniors with a GPA of at least 3.85 and combined SAT scores of at least 1300 or ACT scores of at least

29. Fifteen awards per federal congressional district. See Web site at http://www.osac.state.or.us for more information.

Award: Scholarship for use in freshman, sophomore, junior, or senior years; renewable. *Number:* 15. *Amount:* $1500.

Eligibility Requirements: Applicant must be high school student; planning to enroll or expecting to enroll at a two-year or four-year institution and resident of Oregon. Available to U.S. citizens.

Application Requirements: Application, essay, financial need analysis, test scores, transcript, activity chart. *Deadline:* March 1.

Contact: Grants & Scholarships Division
Oregon Student Assistance Commission
1500 Valley River Drive, Suite 100
Eugene, OR 97401-7020
Phone: 541-687-7395

ROBERT D. FORSTER SCHOLARSHIP
• *See page 534*

ROGER W. EMMONS MEMORIAL SCHOLARSHIP
• *See page 534*

SP NEWSPRINT COMPANY, NEWBERG MILL, EMPLOYEE DEPENDENTS SCHOLARSHIP
• *See page 534*

STIMSON LUMBER COMPANY SCHOLARSHIP
• *See page 535*

TAYLOR MADE LABELS SCHOLARSHIP
• *See page 535*

TEAMSTERS CLYDE C. CROSBY/JOSEPH M. EDGAR MEMORIAL SCHOLARSHIP
• *See page 511*

TEAMSTERS COUNCIL 37 FEDERAL CREDIT UNION SCHOLARSHIP
• *See page 511*

TEAMSTERS LOCAL 305 SCHOLARSHIP
• *See page 511*

TYKESON FAMILY SCHOLARSHIP
• *See page 549*

UMATILLA ELECTRIC COOPERATIVE SCHOLARSHIP

Applicant may be either high school graduate (including home-school graduate) or GED recipient. Applicant or applicant's parents/legal guardians must be active members of the Umatilla Electric Cooperative (UEC) and be receiving service from UEC at their primary residence. Married applicants with UEC membership in a spouse's name are eligible.

Award: Scholarship for use in freshman, sophomore, junior, or senior years; renewable. *Number:* 7. *Amount:* $1000.

Eligibility Requirements: Applicant must be enrolled or expecting to enroll full-time at a four-year institution and resident of Oregon. Available to U.S. citizens.

Application Requirements: Application, essay, financial need analysis, references, transcript, activity chart. *Deadline:* March 1.

Contact: Director of Grant Programs
Oregon Student Assistance Commission
1500 Valley River Drive, Suite 100
Eugene, OR 97401-7020
Phone: 800-452-8807 Ext. 7395

VERL AND DOROTHY MILLER NATIVE AMERICAN VOCATIONAL SCHOLARSHIP
• *See page 628*

WALTER DAVIES SCHOLARSHIP
• *See page 535*

WILLETT AND MARGUERITE LAKE SCHOLARSHIP
• *See page 549*

WILLIAM D. AND RUTH D. ROY SCHOLARSHIP

Scholarships available for Oregon high school graduates, home schoolers, and GED recipients. Preference given to Engineering majors attending Portland State University of Oregon State University. Deadline is March 1.

Award: Scholarship for use in freshman, sophomore, junior, or senior years; renewable. *Number:* varies. *Amount:* $500.

Eligibility Requirements: Applicant must be enrolled or expecting to enroll at a four-year institution or university and resident of Oregon. Available to U.S. citizens.

Application Requirements: Application, essay, financial need analysis, transcript, activities chart. *Deadline:* March 1.

Contact: Director of Grant Programs
Oregon Student Assistance Commission
1500 Valley River Drive, Suite 100
Eugene, OR 97401-7020
Phone: 800-452-8807 Ext. 7395

WOODARD FAMILY SCHOLARSHIP
• *See page 535*

OWEN ELECTRIC COOPERATIVE
http://www.owenelectric.com

OWEN ELECTRIC COOPERATIVE SCHOLARSHIP PROGRAM

Scholarships available to college juniors and seniors who are enrolled full-time at a four-year college or university. Parents of applicant must have an active Owen Electric account in good standing. If applicant has not earned 60 hours at time of application, must provide additional transcript upon completion of 60 hours. Must submit 400-700-word essay. Essay topics, application, and additional information on Web site: http://www.owenelectric.com.

Award: Scholarship for use in junior or senior years; not renewable. *Number:* 12. *Amount:* $2000.

Eligibility Requirements: Applicant must be enrolled or expecting to enroll full-time at a four-year institution or university and resident of Kentucky. Applicant must have 3.0 GPA or higher. Available to U.S. citizens.

Application Requirements: Application, essay, references, transcript. *Deadline:* February 1.

Contact: Brian Linder, Manager of Key Accounts, Owen Electric Cooperative
Owen Electric Cooperative
8205 Highway 127 N
PO Box 400
Owenton, KY 40359-0400
Phone: 800-372-7612 Ext. 3542
E-mail: blinder@owenelectric.com

PENNSYLVANIA AFL-CIO
http://www.paaflcio.org

PA AFL-CIO UNIONISM IN AMERICA ESSAY CONTEST
• *See page 512*

PENNSYLVANIA BUREAU FOR VETERANS AFFAIRS

EDUCATIONAL GRATUITY PROGRAM
• *See page 594*

PENNSYLVANIA BURGLAR AND FIRE ALARM ASSOCIATION
http://www.pbfaa.com

PENNSYLVANIA BURGLAR AND FIRE ALARM ASSOCIATION YOUTH SCHOLARSHIP PROGRAM
• *See page 549*

PENNSYLVANIA FEDERATION OF DEMOCRATIC WOMEN, INC.
http://www.pfdw.org

PENNSYLVANIA FEDERATION OF DEMOCRATIC WOMEN, INC. ANNUAL SCHOLARSHIP AWARDS
• *See page 512*

PENNSYLVANIA HIGHER EDUCATION ASSISTANCE AGENCY
http://www.pheaa.org

ARMED FORCES LOAN FORGIVENESS PROGRAM
• *See page 594*

PENNSYLVANIA STATE GRANTS

Award for Pennsylvania residents attending an approved postsecondary institution as undergraduates in a program of at least two years duration. Renewable for up to eight semesters if applicants show continued need and

Pennsylvania Higher Education Assistance Agency (continued)

academic progress. Submit Free Application for Federal Student Aid. Deadline is May 1 for renewal applicants and new applicants who plan to enroll in an undergraduate baccalaureate degree and August 1 for new applicants in specific school given in research URL

Award: Grant for use in freshman, sophomore, junior, or senior years; renewable. *Number:* up to 151,000. *Amount:* $300–$3300.

Eligibility Requirements: Applicant must be enrolled or expecting to enroll full or part-time at a two-year or four-year or technical institution or university and resident of Pennsylvania. Available to U.S. and Canadian citizens.

Application Requirements: Application, financial need analysis. *Deadline:* varies.

Contact: Keith New, Director of Communications and Press Office
Pennsylvania Higher Education Assistance Agency
1200 North Seventh Street
Harrisburg, PA 17102-1444
Phone: 717-720-2509
Fax: 717-720-3903

POSTSECONDARY EDUCATION GRATUITY PROGRAM
• See page 594

ROBERT C. BYRD HONORS SCHOLARSHIP-PENNSYLVANIA

Available to Pennsylvania residents who are graduating high school seniors. Must rank in the top 5% of graduating class, have at least a 3.5 GPA and score 1150 or above on the SAT, 25 or above on the ACT, or 355 or above on the GED. Renewable award of $1500. Applicants are expected to be a full-time freshman student enrolled at an eligible institution of higher education, in continental United States, following high school graduation.

Award: Scholarship for use in freshman, sophomore, junior, or senior years; renewable. *Number:* varies. *Amount:* $1500.

Eligibility Requirements: Applicant must be high school student; planning to enroll or expecting to enroll full-time at an institution or university and resident of Pennsylvania. Applicant must have 3.5 GPA or higher. Available to U.S. citizens.

Application Requirements: Application, test scores, transcript. *Deadline:* May 1.

Contact: Keith R. New, Director of Communications and Press Office
Pennsylvania Higher Education Assistance Agency
1200 North Seventh Street
Harrisburg, PA 17102
Phone: 717-720-2509
Fax: 717-720-3903

PENNSYLVANIA RIGHT TO WORK DEFENSE AND EDUCATION FOUNDATION   http://www.parighttowork.org

PENNSYLVANIA RIGHT TO WORK DEFENSE AND EDUCATION FOUNDATION JAMES SCOTT II ESSAY CONTEST

Prizes are awarded for 1st, 2nd, 3rd place in essay contest. May not necessarily be awarded if judges do not find essays worthy.

Award: Prize for use in freshman, sophomore, junior, senior, graduate, or postgraduate years; not renewable. *Number:* up to 3. *Amount:* $100–$500.

Eligibility Requirements: Applicant must be high school student; planning to enroll or expecting to enroll at an institution or university and resident of Pennsylvania. Available to U.S. citizens.

Application Requirements: Application, applicant must enter a contest, essay. *Deadline:* April 7.

Contact: Pennsylvania Right to Work Defense and Education
Foundation
225 State Street, Suite 300
Harrisburg, PA 17101
Phone: 717-233-1227
Fax: 717-234-5588
E-mail: info@parighttowork.org

PENNSYLVANIA YOUTH FOUNDATION   http://www.pagrandlodge.org/pmyf

PENNSYLVANIA MASONIC YOUTH FOUNDATION SCHOLARSHIP
• See page 512

PETER DOCTOR MEMORIAL INDIAN SCHOLARSHIP FOUNDATION, INC.

PETER DOCTOR MEMORIAL IROQUOIS SCHOLARSHIP
• See page 630

PHILIPINO-AMERICAN ASSOCIATION OF NEW ENGLAND   http://www.pamas.org/members.htm

BLESSED LEON OF OUR LADY OF THE ROSARY AWARD
• See page 630

CAPARANGA AWARD
• See page 630

DR. ALFRED AND SUSAN CHAN AWARD
• See page 630

PAMAS RESTRICTED SCHOLARSHIP AWARD
• See page 630

RAVENSCROFT FAMILY AWARD
• See page 630

PINE TREE STATE 4-H CLUB FOUNDATION/4-H POSTSECONDARY SCHOLARSHIP   http://www.umaine.edu/4hfoundation

PARKER-LOVEJOY SCHOLARSHIP

Scholarship is awarded to an outstanding Maine 4-H member for postsecondary study.

Award: Scholarship for use in freshman, sophomore, junior, or senior years; not renewable. *Amount:* up to $1000.

Eligibility Requirements: Applicant must be enrolled or expecting to enroll at a four-year institution or university and resident of Maine. Available to U.S. citizens.

Application Requirements: Application. *Deadline:* varies.

Contact: Annie Brown, Assistant
Pine Tree State 4-H Club Foundation/4-H Postsecondary
Scholarship
c/o University of Maine
5717 Corbett Hall
Orono, ME 04469-5717
Phone: 207-581-3739
Fax: 207-581-1387
E-mail: brendaz@umext.maine.edu

WAYNE S. RICH SCHOLARSHIP

Scholarship for an outstanding Maine or New Hampshire 4-H member for postsecondary study. It is available to a Maine student on odd numbered years and goes to a New Hampshire student on even numbered years.

Award: Scholarship for use in freshman, sophomore, junior, or senior years; not renewable. *Amount:* up to $1000.

Eligibility Requirements: Applicant must be enrolled or expecting to enroll at a four-year institution or university and resident of Maine or New Hampshire. Available to U.S. citizens.

Application Requirements: Application. *Deadline:* varies.

Contact: Angela Martin, Pine Tree State 4-H Foundation Office
Pine Tree State 4-H Club Foundation/4-H Postsecondary
Scholarship
5741 Libby Hall
Orono, ME 04469-5741
Phone: 207-581-3739
Fax: 207-581-1387
E-mail: brendaz@umext.maine.edu

POLISH HERITAGE ASSOCIATION OF MARYLAND

POLISH HERITAGE SCHOLARSHIP
• See page 631

PORTUGUESE FOUNDATION, INC.   http://www.pfict.org

PORTUGUESE FOUNDATION SCHOLARSHIP PROGRAM
• See page 631

POTLATCH FOUNDATION FOR HIGHER EDUCATION SCHOLARSHIP   http://www.potlatchcorp.com

POTLATCH FOUNDATION FOR HIGHER EDUCATION SCHOLARSHIP

Granted to students living within 30 miles of a major Potlatch facility and based on financial need. Deadline is February 15.

Award: Scholarship for use in freshman, sophomore, junior, or senior years; renewable. *Number:* 50–80. *Amount:* $1400.

Eligibility Requirements: Applicant must be enrolled or expecting to enroll full-time at a two-year or four-year or technical institution or university and resident of Arkansas, Idaho, Minnesota, or Washington. Available to U.S. citizens.

Application Requirements: Application, transcript. *Deadline:* February 15.

Contact: Sharon Pegau, Corporate Programs and Board Administrator
Potlatch Foundation For Higher Education Scholarship
601 West Riverside Avenue, Suite 1100
Spokane, WA 99201
Phone: 509-835-1515
Fax: 509-835-1566
E-mail: foundation@potlatchcorp.com

PRIDE FOUNDATION   http://www.pridefoundation.org

PRIDE FOUNDATION/GREATER SEATTLE BUSINESS ASSOCIATION SCHOLARSHIP

Scholarships available for gay, lesbian, bisexual, transgendered, and allied students. Must be a resident of Washington, Alaska, Montana, Idaho, or Oregon. Foundation administers various scholarships with varying requirements. Submit one application to be considered for all available awards. Deadline varies. Check Web site for more information. http://www.pridefoundation.org

Award: Scholarship for use in freshman, sophomore, junior, senior, graduate, or postgraduate years; not renewable. *Number:* 90–100. *Amount:* $500–$10,000.

Eligibility Requirements: Applicant must be enrolled or expecting to enroll full or part-time at a two-year or four-year or technical institution or university and resident of Alaska, Idaho, Montana, Oregon, or Washington. Available to U.S. citizens.

Application Requirements: Application, essay, financial need analysis, interview, references, transcript. *Deadline:* varies.

Contact: Randy Brians, Scholarship Manager
Pride Foundation
1122 East Pike, Suite 1001
Seattle, WA 98122-3934
Phone: 206-323-3318
Fax: 206-323-1017
E-mail: randy@pridefoundation.org

PROJECT BEST SCHOLARSHIP FUND   http://www.projectbest.com

PROJECT BEST SCHOLARSHIP
• See page 513

PUEBLO OF SAN JUAN, DEPARTMENT OF EDUCATION   http://www.sanjuaned.org/

OHKAY OWINGEH TRIBAL SCHOLARSHIP OF THE PUEBLO OF SAN JUAN
• See page 632

POP'AY SCHOLARSHIP
• See page 632

RHODE ISLAND FOUNDATION   http://www.rifoundation.org

A.T. CROSS SCHOLARSHIP
• See page 535

ALDO FREDA LEGISLATIVE PAGES SCHOLARSHIP

One-time scholarships of $1000 are awarded to support Rhode Island Legislative Pages enrolled in a college or university. The deadline is April 7.

Award: Scholarship for use in freshman, sophomore, junior, or senior years; not renewable. *Number:* 2–3. *Amount:* $1000.

Eligibility Requirements: Applicant must be enrolled or expecting to enroll full or part-time at a two-year or four-year institution or university and resident of Rhode Island. Available to U.S. citizens.

Application Requirements: Application. *Deadline:* April 7.

Contact: Libby Monahan, Scholarship Coordinator
Rhode Island Foundation
1 Union Station
Providence, RI 02903
Phone: 401-274-4564
Fax: 401-272-1359
E-mail: libbym@rifoundation.org

BRUCE AND MARJORIE SUNDLUN SCHOLARSHIP

Scholarships for low-income single parents seeking to upgrade their career skills. Preference given to single parents previously receiving state support. Also for those previously incarcerated. Must be a Rhode Island resident and attend school in Rhode Island.

Award: Scholarship for use in freshman, sophomore, junior, or senior years; not renewable. *Number:* 3–5. *Amount:* $250–$1000.

Eligibility Requirements: Applicant must be enrolled or expecting to enroll full or part-time at a two-year or four-year or technical institution or university; single; resident of Rhode Island and studying in Rhode Island. Available to U.S. citizens.

Application Requirements: Application, essay, financial need analysis, references, self-addressed stamped envelope. *Deadline:* June 14.

Contact: Libby Monahan, Scholarship Coordinator
Rhode Island Foundation
1 Union Station
Providence, RI 02903
Phone: 401-274-4564
Fax: 401-272-1359

LILY AND CATELLO SORRENTINO MEMORIAL SCHOLARSHIP

Scholarships for Rhode Island residents 45 years or older wishing to attend college or university in Rhode Island (only students attending non-parochial schools). Must demonstrate financial need. Preference to first-time applicants.

Award: Scholarship for use in freshman, sophomore, junior, or senior years; not renewable. *Number:* varies. *Amount:* $350–$1000.

Eligibility Requirements: Applicant must be age 45; enrolled or expecting to enroll full or part-time at a four-year institution or university; resident of Rhode Island and studying in Rhode Island. Available to U.S. citizens.

Application Requirements: Application, financial need analysis, self-addressed stamped envelope, transcript. *Deadline:* May 14.

Contact: Scholarship Coordinator
Rhode Island Foundation
1 Union Station
Providence, RI 02903
Phone: 401-274-4564
Fax: 401-272-1359

MICHAEL P. METCALF MEMORIAL SCHOLARSHIP

One-time awards between $2000 and $5000 are awarded to encourage personal growth through travel, study, and public service programs for college sophomores and juniors. Must be a Rhode Island resident. Award is for educational enrichment outside of the classroom: therefore, the awards are not to be used for school tuition.

Award: Scholarship for use in freshman, sophomore, or junior years; not renewable. *Number:* 2–4. *Amount:* $2000–$5000.

Eligibility Requirements: Applicant must be enrolled or expecting to enroll full-time at an institution or university and resident of Rhode Island. Available to U.S. citizens.

Rhode Island Foundation (continued)

Application Requirements: Application. *Deadline:* varies.

Contact: Libby Monahan, Scholarship Coordinator
Rhode Island Foundation
1 Union Station
Providence, RI 02903
Phone: 401-274-4564
Fax: 401-272-1359
E-mail: libbym@rifoundation.org

PATTY AND MELVIN ALPERIN FIRST GENERATION SCHOLARSHIP/ DAVID M. GOLDEN MEMORIAL SCHOLARSHIP

To benefit college-bound Rhode Island high school graduates whose parents did not have the benefit of attending college. Must be enrolled in an accredited nonprofit postsecondary institution offering either a two-year or a four-year college degree.

Award: Scholarship for use in freshman, sophomore, junior, or senior years; renewable. *Number:* 2–3. *Amount:* $1000.

Eligibility Requirements: Applicant must be enrolled or expecting to enroll full-time at a two-year or four-year institution or university and resident of Rhode Island. Available to U.S. citizens.

Application Requirements: Application, self-addressed stamped envelope. *Deadline:* May 8.

Contact: Libby Monahan, Scholarship Coordinator
Rhode Island Foundation
1 Union Station
Providence, RI 02903
Phone: 401-274-4564
Fax: 401-272-1359
E-mail: libbym@rifoundation.org

RAYMOND H. TROTT SCHOLARSHIP
• *See page 632*

RHODE ISLAND COMMISSION ON WOMEN/FREDA GOLDMAN EDUCATION AWARD

Renewable award to provide financial support for Rhode Island women to pursue their education or job training beyond high school. Can be used for transportation, child-care, tutoring, educational materials, and/or other support services. Preference given to highly motivated, self-supported, and low-income women.

Award: Scholarship for use in freshman, sophomore, junior, or senior years; renewable. *Number:* 2. *Amount:* $300–$600.

Eligibility Requirements: Applicant must be enrolled or expecting to enroll at an institution or university; female and resident of Rhode Island. Available to U.S. citizens.

Application Requirements: Application, essay, self-addressed stamped envelope, transcript. *Deadline:* June 12.

Contact: Libby Monahan, Scholarship Coordinator
Rhode Island Foundation
1 Union Station
Providence, RI 02903
Phone: 401-274-4564
Fax: 401-272-1359
E-mail: libbym@rifoundation.org

RHODE ISLAND FOUNDATION ASSOCIATION OF FORMER LEGISLATORS SCHOLARSHIP

One-time award for graduating high school seniors who are Rhode Island residents. Must have outstanding public service record, excellent grades, and demonstrate financial need. Must be a U.S. citizen.

Award: Scholarship for use in freshman year; not renewable. *Number:* 5. *Amount:* $1500.

Eligibility Requirements: Applicant must be high school student; planning to enroll or expecting to enroll full-time at a four-year institution and resident of Rhode Island. Available to U.S. citizens.

Application Requirements: Application, essay, financial need analysis, references, self-addressed stamped envelope, test scores, transcript. *Deadline:* June 1.

Contact: Libby Monahan, Scholarship Coordinator
Rhode Island Foundation
1 Union Station
Providence, RI 02903
Phone: 401-274-4564
Fax: 401-272-1359

RHODE ISLAND HIGHER EDUCATION ASSISTANCE AUTHORITY
http://www.riheaa.org

COLLEGE BOUND FUND ACADEMIC PROMISE SCHOLARSHIP

Award to graduating high school seniors. Eligibility based on financial need and SAT/ACT scores. Must maintain specified grade point averages each year for renewal. Must be Rhode Island resident and attend college full time. Must complete the Free Application for Federal Student Aid (FAFSA). FAFSA deadline is March 1. GPA : First Year - 2.50; Second Year - 2.62; Third Year - 2.75.

Award: Scholarship for use in freshman year; renewable. *Number:* 100. *Amount:* $2500.

Eligibility Requirements: Applicant must be high school student; planning to enroll or expecting to enroll full-time at an institution or university and resident of Rhode Island. Available to U.S. citizens.

Application Requirements: Application, financial need analysis, test scores. *Deadline:* March 1.

Contact: Ms. Mary Ann Welch, Director of Program Administration
Rhode Island Higher Education Assistance Authority
560 Jefferson Boulevard
Warwick, RI 02886
Phone: 401-736-1171
Fax: 401-736-1178
E-mail: mawelch@riheaa.org

RHODE ISLAND HIGHER EDUCATION GRANT PROGRAM

Grants for residents of Rhode Island attending an approved school in the U.S., Canada, or Mexico. Based on need. Renewable for up to four years if in good academic standing. Applications accepted January 1 through March 1. Several awards of variable amounts. Must be U.S. citizen or registered alien.

Award: Grant for use in freshman, sophomore, junior, or senior years; renewable. *Number:* 10,000–12,900. *Amount:* $300–$1400.

Eligibility Requirements: Applicant must be enrolled or expecting to enroll full or part-time at an institution or university and resident of Rhode Island. Available to U.S. citizens.

Application Requirements: Application, financial need analysis. *Deadline:* March 1.

Contact: Ms. Mary Ann Welch, Director of Program Administration
Rhode Island Higher Education Assistance Authority
560 Jefferson Boulevard
Warwick, RI 02886
Phone: 401-736-1171
Fax: 401-736-1178
E-mail: mawelch@riheaa.org

RYU FAMILY FOUNDATION, INC.

SEOL BONG SCHOLARSHIP
• *See page 632*

SACRAMENTO BEE
http://www.sacbee.com

SACRAMENTO BEE SCHOLAR ATHLETE SCHOLARSHIP

This scholarship recognizes college-bound high school seniors who are outstanding students as well as sports competitors. Applicants should have a minimum cumulative grade point average of 3.4 and have received two varsity letters by the end of the current academic year. Applicants must reside in the Sacramento metropolitan area. For further information view Web site: http://www.sacbee.com/scholarships

Award: Scholarship for use in freshman year. *Number:* 1–6. *Amount:* $1000–$2500.

Eligibility Requirements: Applicant must be high school student; planning to enroll or expecting to enroll at an institution or university and resident of California. Available to U.S. citizens.

Application Requirements: Application, essay, resume, references, transcript. *Deadline:* January 30.

Contact: Cathy Rodriguez, Public Affairs Representative
Sacramento Bee
PO Box 15779
Sacramento, CA 95852
Phone: 916-321-1880
Fax: 916-321-1783
E-mail: crodriguez@sacbee.com

SACRAMENTO BEE WILLIAM GLACKIN SCHOLARSHIP PROGRAM

Scholarship for a student pursuing a degree in Dance, Theatre, Music or Arts Management. Applicants must be graduating high school seniors who are accepted at an accredited school of higher education or college students attending an accredited school. College students must have completed at least one term and have one remaining. High school applicants must have minimum GPA of 3.0 and college students a GPA of 2.5. Applicants must reside in Sacramento metropolitan area. Visit Web site: http://www.sacbee.com/scholarships

Award: Scholarship for use in freshman, sophomore, junior, or senior years. *Number:* 1. *Amount:* $2500.

Eligibility Requirements: Applicant must be enrolled or expecting to enroll at a two-year or four-year institution or university and resident of California. Available to U.S. citizens.

Application Requirements: Application, essay, resume, references, transcript, portfolio of samples. *Deadline:* January 30.

Contact: Cathy Rodriguez, Public Affairs Representative
Sacramento Bee
PO Box 15779
Sacramento, CA 95852
Phone: 916-321-1880
Fax: 916-321-1783
E-mail: crodriguez@sacbee.com

SALT RIVER ELECTRIC COOPERATIVE CORPORATION   http://www.srelectric.com

SALT RIVER ELECTRIC SCHOLARSHIP PROGRAM

Scholarships available to Kentucky high school seniors who reside in Salt River Electric Service area or the primary residence of their parents/guardian is in the service area. Must be enrolled or plan to enroll in a postsecondary institution. Minimum GPA of 2.5 required. Must demonstrate financial need. Must submit a 500-word essay on a topic chosen from the list on the Web site. Application and additional information available on Web site: http://www.srelectric.com

Award: Scholarship for use in freshman year; not renewable. *Number:* 4. *Amount:* $1000.

Eligibility Requirements: Applicant must be high school student; planning to enroll or expecting to enroll at a two-year or four-year or technical institution or university and resident of Kentucky. Applicant must have 2.5 GPA or higher. Available to U.S. citizens.

Application Requirements: Application, essay, financial need analysis, photo, transcript. *Deadline:* April 8.

Contact: Nicky Rapier, Scholarship Coordinator
Salt River Electric Cooperative Corporation
111 West Brashear Avenue
Bardstown, KY 40004
Phone: 502-348-3931
E-mail: nickyr@srelectric.com

SALVADORAN AMERICAN LEADERSHIP AND EDUCATIONAL FUND   http://www.salef.org

FULFILLING OUR DREAMS SCHOLARSHIP FUND
• *See page 633*

SALVATORE TADDONIO FAMILY FOUNDATION

TADDONIO SCHOLARSHIP
• *See page 550*

SAN FRANCISCO FOUNDATION   http://www.sff.org

JOSEPH HENRY JACKSON LITERARY AWARD

Award presented annually to an author of an unpublished work in progress: fiction, nonfiction, prose, or poetry. Must be California or Nevada resident for three consecutive years and be between 20-35 years of age. Submit manuscript. One-time award of $2000 is not a scholarship. Applications accepted from November 15 to January 31.

Award: Prize for use in freshman, sophomore, junior, senior, graduate, or postgraduate years; not renewable. *Number:* 1. *Amount:* $2000.

Eligibility Requirements: Applicant must be age 20-35; enrolled or expecting to enroll at an institution or university; resident of California or Nevada and must have an interest in writing. Available to U.S. and non-U.S. citizens.

Application Requirements: Application, applicant must enter a contest, self-addressed stamped envelope, manuscript. *Deadline:* January 31.

Contact: Awards Coordinator-Literary Awards
San Francisco Foundation
225 Bush Street, Suite 500
San Francisco, CA 94104-4224
E-mail: rec@sff.org

SCHOLARSHIPS FOUNDATION, INC.   http://www.fdncenter.org/grantmaker/scholarships

FOUNDATION SCHOLARSHIPS

Grants to graduate and undergraduate students enrolled in academic programs either full- or part-time. Priority is given to students studying in NY state or residents of NY state studying elsewhere. Grants are based on merit and need.

Award: Scholarship for use in freshman, sophomore, junior, senior, or graduate years; not renewable. *Number:* 20–30. *Amount:* $1500–$3500.

Eligibility Requirements: Applicant must be enrolled or expecting to enroll full or part-time at a two-year or four-year institution or university and resident of New York. Available to U.S. and non-U.S. citizens.

Application Requirements: Application, financial need analysis, references, self-addressed stamped envelope, transcript. *Deadline:* Continuous.

Contact: Susan Benedict, Director
Scholarships Foundation, Inc.
PO Box 286020
New York, NY 10128
Phone: 212-427-4125
E-mail: sfi1921@aol.com

SCOTTISH RITE CHARITABLE FOUNDATION OF CANADA   http://www.srcf.ca

SCOTTISH RITE CHARITABLE FOUNDATION COLLEGE BURSARIES
• *See page 550*

SERVICE EMPLOYEES INTERNATIONAL UNION - CALIFORNIA STATE COUNCIL OF SERVICE EMPLOYEES   http://www.seiuca.org

CHARLES HARDY MEMORIAL SCHOLARSHIP AWARDS
• *See page 514*

SHOPKO STORES, INC.   http://www.shopko.com

SHOPKO SCHOLARS PROGRAM

Must live within 100 miles of a ShopKo store. Scholars selected on the basis of academic record, potential to succeed, leadership, and participation in school and community activities, honors, work, experience, a statement of educational and career goals, and an outside appraisal. Financial need is not considered.

Award: Scholarship for use in freshman, sophomore, junior, or senior years; not renewable. *Number:* 100–110. *Amount:* up to $1000.

Eligibility Requirements: Applicant must be enrolled or expecting to enroll full-time at a two-year or four-year or technical institution or university and resident of California, Colorado, Idaho, Illinois, Iowa, Michigan, Minnesota, Montana, Nebraska, Nevada, Oregon, South

ShopKo Stores, Inc. (continued)

Dakota, Utah, Washington, or Wisconsin. Applicant must have 2.5 GPA or higher. Available to U.S. citizens.

Application Requirements: Application, essay, photo, references, self-addressed stamped envelope, transcript. *Deadline:* varies.

Contact: Customer Service
ShopKo Stores, Inc.
PO Box 19060
Green Bay, WI 54307-9060
Phone: 920-429-2211

SICKLE CELL DISEASE ASSOCIATION OF AMERICA/ CONNECTICUT CHAPTER, INC. http://www.sicklecellct.org

I. H. MCLENDON MEMORIAL SCHOLARSHIP
• *See page 565*

SYBIL FONG SAM SCHOLARSHIP ESSAY CONTEST

The Sybil Fong Sam Scholarship Essay Contest provides three scholarships to graduating high school seniors based upon submission of an essay on a pre-selected topic. 3.0 minimum GPA required. Must be a Connecticut resident.

Award: Scholarship for use in freshman year; not renewable. *Number:* 3. *Amount:* $200–$500.

Eligibility Requirements: Applicant must be high school student; planning to enroll or expecting to enroll full or part-time at a two-year or four-year or technical institution or university and resident of Connecticut. Applicant must have 3.0 GPA or higher. Available to U.S. citizens.

Application Requirements: Application, applicant must enter a contest, essay, references, transcript. *Deadline:* April 30.

Contact: Samuel Byrd, Program Assistant
Sickle Cell Disease Association of America/Connecticut Chapter, Inc.
Gengras Ambulatory Center
114 Woodland Street, Suite 2101
Hartford, CT 06105-1299
Phone: 860-527-0119
Fax: 860-714-8007
E-mail: scdaa@iconn.net

SIGMA DELTA CHI FOUNDATION OF WASHINGTON, D.C. http://www.spj.org/washdcpro

SIGMA DELTA CHI SCHOLARSHIPS

One-time award to help pay tuition for full-time students in their junior or senior year demonstrating a clear intention to become journalists. Must demonstrate financial need; grades and skills are also considered. Must be enrolled in a college or university in the Washington, D.C., metropolitan area. Sponsored by the Society of Professional Journalists.

Award: Scholarship for use in junior or senior years; not renewable. *Number:* 4–5. *Amount:* $3000–$4000.

Eligibility Requirements: Applicant must be enrolled or expecting to enroll full-time at a four-year institution or university; studying in District of Columbia, Maryland, or Virginia and must have an interest in designated field specified by sponsor, leadership, or writing. Available to U.S. and non-U.S. citizens.

Application Requirements: Application, essay, financial need analysis, interview, portfolio, references, transcript. *Deadline:* February 24.

Contact: Lee Thornton, Scholarship Committee Chair
Sigma Delta Chi Foundation of Washington, D.C.
PO Box 19555
Washington, DC 20036-0555
Phone: 301-405-5292
Fax: 301-314-9166
E-mail: lthornton@jmail.umd.edu

SOCIETY OF WOMEN ENGINEERS http://www.swe.org

SWE SOUTH OHIO SCIENCE FAIR SCHOLARSHIP

Two $300 scholarships awarded to graduating high school senior females for outstanding achievement in engineering or the related sciences.

Award: Scholarship for use in freshman year; not renewable. *Number:* 2. *Amount:* $300.

Eligibility Requirements: Applicant must be high school student; planning to enroll or expecting to enroll at a four-year institution; female and resident of Ohio. Available to U.S. citizens.

Application Requirements: Science fair project. *Deadline:* varies.

Contact: Alison Haskins
Society of Women Engineers
PO Box 284
Oxford, OH 45056-0284
Phone: 513-785-7277
E-mail: alison.haskins@swe.org

SOUTH CAROLINA COMMISSION ON HIGHER EDUCATION http://www.che.sc.gov

LEGISLATIVE INCENTIVES FOR FUTURE EXCELLENCE PROGRAM

Scholarship for students from South Carolina to attend an institution of higher education in South Carolina. For students attending a four-year institution, two of the following three criteria must be met: 1) minimum 3.0 GPA, 2) 1100 SAT or 24 ACT, or 3) graduate in the top 30% of class. Students attending a two-year or technical college must have a 3.0 GPA (SAT and class rank requirements are waived).

Award: Scholarship for use in freshman, sophomore, junior, senior, or graduate years; renewable. *Number:* varies. *Amount:* $2000–$5000.

Eligibility Requirements: Applicant must be enrolled or expecting to enroll full-time at a two-year or four-year or technical institution or university; resident of South Carolina and studying in South Carolina. Applicant must have 3.0 GPA or higher. Available to U.S. citizens.

Application Requirements: Test scores, transcript. *Deadline:* Continuous.

Contact: Bichevia Green, LIFE Scholarship Coordinator
South Carolina Commission on Higher Education
1333 Main Street, Suite 200
Columbia, SC 29201
Phone: 803-737-2280
Fax: 803-737-2297
E-mail: bgreen@che.sc.gov

SOUTH CAROLINA NEED-BASED GRANTS PROGRAM

Award based on results of Free Application for Federal Student Aid. A student may receive up to $2500 annually for full-time and up to $1250 annually for part-time study. The grant must be applied toward the cost of attendance at a South Carolina college for up to eight full-time equivalent terms. Student must be degree-seeking.

Award: Grant for use in freshman, sophomore, junior, senior, or graduate years; renewable. *Number:* 1–23,485. *Amount:* $1250–$2500.

Eligibility Requirements: Applicant must be enrolled or expecting to enroll full or part-time at a two-year or four-year or technical institution or university; resident of South Carolina and studying in South Carolina. Available to U.S. citizens.

Application Requirements: Application, financial need analysis. *Deadline:* Continuous.

Contact: Sherry Hubbard, Coordinator
South Carolina Commission on Higher Education
1333 Main Street, Suite 200
Columbia, SC 29201
Phone: 803-737-2260
Fax: 803-737-2297
E-mail: shubbard@che.sc.gov

SOUTH CAROLINA DEPARTMENT OF EDUCATION

ROBERT C. BYRD HONORS SCHOLARSHIP-SOUTH CAROLINA

Renewable award of $1500 for graduating high school seniors from South Carolina who will be attending a two- or four-year institution. Applicants should be superior students who demonstrate academic achievement and show promise of continued success at a postsecondary institution. Interested applicants should contact their high school counselors after the first week in December for an application.

Award: Scholarship for use in freshman, sophomore, junior, or senior years; renewable. *Number:* 96. *Amount:* $1500.

Eligibility Requirements: Applicant must be high school student; planning to enroll or expecting to enroll full-time at a two-year or four-year institution and resident of South Carolina. Applicant must have 3.5 GPA or higher. Available to U.S. citizens.

Application Requirements: Application, references, test scores, transcript, extracurricular activities. *Deadline:* February 2.

Contact: Beth Cope, Program Coordinator
South Carolina Department of Education
1424 Senate Street
Columbia, SC 29201
Phone: 803-734-8116
Fax: 803-734-4387
E-mail: bcope@sde.state.sc.us

SOUTH CAROLINA STATE EMPLOYEES ASSOCIATION   http://www.SCSEA.com

RICHLAND/LEXINGTON SCSEA SCHOLARSHIP
• See page 515

SOUTH CAROLINA TUITION GRANTS COMMISSION   http://www.sctuitiongrants.com

SOUTH CAROLINA TUITION GRANTS PROGRAM

Assists South Carolina residents attending one of twenty approved South Carolina independent colleges. Freshmen must be in upper 3/4 of high school class or have SAT score of at least 900. Upper-class students must complete 24 semester hours per year to be eligible.

Award: Grant for use in freshman, sophomore, junior, or senior years; renewable. *Number:* up to 11,000. *Amount:* $100–$3240.

Eligibility Requirements: Applicant must be enrolled or expecting to enroll full-time at a two-year or four-year institution or university; resident of South Carolina and studying in South Carolina. Available to U.S. citizens.

Application Requirements: Application, financial need analysis, test scores, transcript, FAFSA. *Deadline:* June 30.

Contact: Toni Cave, Financial Aid Counselor
South Carolina Tuition Grants Commission
101 Business Park Boulevard, Suite 2100
Columbia, SC 29203-9498
Phone: 803-896-1120
Fax: 803-896-1126
E-mail: toni@sctuitiongrants.org

SOUTH DAKOTA BOARD OF REGENTS   http://www.sdbor.edu

SOUTH DAKOTA BOARD OF REGENTS MARLIN R. SCARBOROUGH MEMORIAL SCHOLARSHIP

One-time award for a student who is a junior at a South Dakota public university. Must be nominated by the university. Merit-based. Must have community service and leadership experience. Minimum 3.5 GPA required. Contact University Financial Aid Office for application deadline.

Award: Scholarship for use in junior year; not renewable. *Number:* 1. *Amount:* $1500.

Eligibility Requirements: Applicant must be enrolled or expecting to enroll at an institution or university; resident of South Dakota; studying in South Dakota and must have an interest in leadership. Applicant must have 3.5 GPA or higher. Available to U.S. citizens.

Application Requirements: Application, essay. *Deadline:* varies.

Contact: Scholarship Committee
South Dakota Board of Regents
306 East Capitol Avenue, Suite 200
Pierre, SD 57501-3159

SOUTH DAKOTA DEPARTMENT OF EDUCATION   http://www.doe.sd.gov/

ROBERT C. BYRD HONORS SCHOLARSHIP-SOUTH DAKOTA

For South Dakota residents in their senior year of high school. Must have a minimum 3.5 GPA and a minimum ACT score of 30 or above. Awards are renewable up to four years. Contact high school guidance office for more details.

Award: Scholarship for use in freshman year; renewable. *Number:* up to 20. *Amount:* $1500.

Eligibility Requirements: Applicant must be high school student; planning to enroll or expecting to enroll full-time at a two-year or technical institution and resident of South Dakota. Applicant must have 3.5 GPA or higher. Available to U.S. citizens.

Application Requirements: Application, test scores, transcript. *Deadline:* May 2.

Contact: Mr. Mark Gageby, Management Analyst
South Dakota Department of Education
700 Governors Drive
Pierre, SD 57501-2291
Phone: 605-773-3248
Fax: 605-773-6139
E-mail: mark.gageby@state.sd.us

SOUTH KENTUCKY RURAL ELECTRIC COOPERATIVE CORPORATION   http://www.skrecc.com

SENIOR SCHOLARSHIPS

Twelve $1000 scholarships to be awarded to Kentucky high school seniors in counties where more than 500 people are served by the South Kentucky Rural Electric Cooperative. Students from Adair, Casey, Clinton, Lincoln, McCreary, Pulaski, Russell, and Wayne County High Schools and Monticello, Somerset, and Southwestern high schools are eligible to apply. In addition, one scholarship will be given to a senior attending a private school or being home-schooled in one of these counties.

Award: Scholarship for use in freshman year. *Number:* up to 12. *Amount:* $1000.

Eligibility Requirements: Applicant must be high school student; planning to enroll or expecting to enroll at a four-year institution and resident of Kentucky. Available to U.S. citizens.

Application Requirements: Application, essay. *Deadline:* April 20.

Contact: Scholarship Coordinator
South Kentucky Rural Electric Cooperative Corporation
Senior Scholarships, PO Box 910
Somerset, KY 42501
Phone: 800-264-5112
Fax: 606-679-8279

SOUTHERN TEXAS PGA   http://www.stpga.com

HARDY LAUDERMILK SCHOLARSHIP

One-Time award of $1500 in honor of PGA professional Hardy Laudermilk, will be awarded to a resident of Bexar County or one of the five counties contiguous to Bexar County.

Award: Scholarship for use in freshman, sophomore, junior, or senior years; not renewable. *Number:* 1. *Amount:* up to $1500.

Eligibility Requirements: Applicant must be enrolled or expecting to enroll full-time at a two-year or four-year institution or university; resident of Texas and must have an interest in golf. Applicant must have 2.5 GPA or higher. Available to U.S. citizens.

Application Requirements: Application, financial need analysis, test scores, transcript, extracurricular activities. *Deadline:* April 5.

Contact: Louisa Bergsma
Southern Texas PGA
1830 South Millbend Drive
Spring, TX 77380
Phone: 281-419-7421 Ext. 206
E-mail: stexas@pgahq.com

SOUTHWEST STUDENT SERVICES CORPORATION   http://www.sssc.com/

ARIZONA COMMUNITY COLLEGE SCHOLARSHIP

Four renewable $500 scholarships are awarded annually to Arizona high school students with strong service/activities and academic backgrounds, who are planning to attend a two-year community college in Arizona.

Award: Scholarship for use in freshman year; renewable. *Number:* 4. *Amount:* $500.

Eligibility Requirements: Applicant must be high school student; planning to enroll or expecting to enroll full-time at a two-year

Southwest Student Services Corporation (continued)

institution; resident of Arizona and studying in Arizona. Applicant must have 2.5 GPA or higher. Available to U.S. citizens.

Application Requirements: Application, essay, transcript. *Deadline:* April 30.

Contact: Linda Walker, Community Outreach Representative
Southwest Student Services Corporation
PO Box 41150
Mesa, AZ 85274
Phone: 480-461-6566
Fax: 480-461-6595
E-mail: scholarships@sssc.com

ARIZONA COUNSELOR OF THE YEAR SCHOLARSHIP

One-time $500 award to the graduating high school senior for nominating the high school counselor who wins the Arizona Counselor of the Year Scholarship.

Award: Scholarship for use in freshman year; not renewable. *Number:* 1. *Amount:* $500.

Eligibility Requirements: Applicant must be high school student; planning to enroll or expecting to enroll full-time at a two-year or four-year or technical institution or university and resident of Arizona. Available to U.S. citizens.

Application Requirements: Application, essay. *Deadline:* varies.

Contact: Linda Walker, Community Outreach Representative
Southwest Student Services Corporation
PO Box 41150
Mesa, AZ 85274
Phone: 480-461-6566
Fax: 480-461-6595
E-mail: scholarships@sssc.com

ST. ANDREW'S SOCIETY OF WASHINGTON, DC
http://www.saintandrewsociety.org

DONALD MALCOLM MACARTHUR SCHOLARSHIP
• See page 634

STATE COUNCIL OF HIGHER EDUCATION FOR VIRGINIA
http://www.schev.edu

COLLEGE SCHOLARSHIP ASSISTANCE PROGRAM

Need-based scholarship for undergraduate study by a Virginia resident at a participating Virginia two- or four-year college, or university. Contact financial aid office at the participating institution.

Award: Grant for use in freshman, sophomore, junior, or senior years; renewable. *Number:* varies. *Amount:* $400–$5000.

Eligibility Requirements: Applicant must be enrolled or expecting to enroll full or part-time at a two-year or four-year institution or university; resident of Virginia and studying in Virginia. Available to U.S. citizens.

Application Requirements: Application, financial need analysis, FAFSA.

Contact: Lee Andes, Assistant Director for Financial Aid
State Council of Higher Education for Virginia
James Monroe Building, 10th Floor
101 North 14th Street
Richmond, VA 23219
Phone: 804-225-2614
Fax: 804-225-2604
E-mail: leeandes@schev.edu

VIRGINIA COMMONWEALTH AWARD

Need-based award for undergraduate or graduate study at a Virginia public two- or four-year college, or university. Undergraduates must be Virginia residents. The application and awards process are administered by the financial aid office at the Virginia public institution where student is enrolled. Contact financial aid office for application and deadlines.

Award: Grant for use in freshman, sophomore, junior, senior, or graduate years; renewable. *Number:* varies. *Amount:* varies.

Eligibility Requirements: Applicant must be enrolled or expecting to enroll full or part-time at a two-year or four-year institution or university; resident of Virginia and studying in Virginia. Available to U.S. citizens.

Application Requirements: Application, financial need analysis, FAFSA.

Contact: Lee Andes, Assistant Director for Financial Aid
State Council of Higher Education for Virginia
James Monroe Building, 10th Floor
101 North 14th Street
Richmond, VA 23219
Phone: 804-225-2614
Fax: 804-225-2604
E-mail: leeandes@schev.edu

VIRGINIA GUARANTEED ASSISTANCE PROGRAM

Awards to undergraduate students proportional to their need, up to full tuition, fees and book allowance. Must be a graduate of a Virginia high school, not home-schooled. High school GPA of 2.5 required. Must be enrolled full-time in a Virginia 2- or 4-year institution and demonstrate financial need. Contact financial aid office of your institution for application process and deadlines. Must maintain minimum college GPA of 2.0 for renewal awards.

Award: Scholarship for use in freshman, sophomore, junior, or senior years; renewable. *Number:* varies. *Amount:* varies.

Eligibility Requirements: Applicant must be enrolled or expecting to enroll full-time at a two-year or four-year institution or university; resident of Virginia and studying in Virginia. Applicant must have 2.5 GPA or higher. Available to U.S. citizens.

Application Requirements: Application, financial need analysis, transcript, FAFSA.

Contact: Lee Andes, Assistant Director for Financial Aid
State Council of Higher Education for Virginia
James Monroe Building, 10th Floor
101 North 14th Street
Richmond, VA 23219
Phone: 804-225-2614
Fax: 804-225-2604
E-mail: leeandes@schev.edu

VIRGINIA TUITION ASSISTANCE GRANT PROGRAM (PRIVATE INSTITUTIONS)

Renewable awards of approximately $1900-$2500 each for undergraduate, graduate, and first professional degree students attending an approved private, non-profit college within Virginia. Must be a Virginia resident and be enrolled full-time. Not to be used for religious study. Preferred deadline July 31. Others are wait-listed. Information and application available from participating Virginia colleges' financial aid office.

Award: Grant for use in freshman, sophomore, junior, senior, or graduate years; renewable. *Number:* 18,600. *Amount:* $1900–$2500.

Eligibility Requirements: Applicant must be enrolled or expecting to enroll full-time at a four-year institution or university; resident of Virginia and studying in Virginia. Available to U.S. citizens.

Application Requirements: Application. *Deadline:* July 31.

Contact: Lee Andes, Financial Aid Manager
State Council of Higher Education for Virginia
James Monroe Building, 10th Floor, 101 North 14th Street
Richmond, VA 23219
Phone: 804-225-2614
E-mail: fainfo@schev.edu

STATE OF NEBRASKA COORDINATING COMMISSION FOR POSTSECONDARY EDUCATION
http://www.ccpe.state.ne.us

NEBRASKA STATE GRANT

Available to undergraduates attending a participating postsecondary institution in Nebraska. Available to Pell Grant recipients only. Nebraska residency required. Awards determined by each participating institution. Contact financial aid office at institution for application and additional information.

Award: Grant for use in freshman, sophomore, junior, or senior years; not renewable. *Number:* varies. *Amount:* $100–$1032.

Eligibility Requirements: Applicant must be enrolled or expecting to enroll full or part-time at a two-year or four-year or technical institution or university; resident of Nebraska and studying in Nebraska. Available to U.S. citizens.

Application Requirements: Application, financial need analysis. *Deadline:* Continuous.

Contact: J. Ritchie Morrow, Financial Aid Coordinator
State of Nebraska Coordinating Commission for Postsecondary Education
140 North 8th Street, Suite 300, PO Box 95005
Lincoln, NE 68509-5005
Phone: 402-471-0032
Fax: 402-471-2886
E-mail: rmorrow@ccpe.st.ne.us

STATE OF NORTH DAKOTA   http://www.ndus.nodak.edu

NORTH DAKOTA INDIAN SCHOLARSHIP PROGRAM
• See page 634

NORTH DAKOTA SCHOLARS PROGRAM

Provides scholarships equal to cost of tuition at the public colleges in North Dakota for North Dakota residents. Must score at or above the 95th percentile on ACT and rank in top twenty percent of high school graduation class. Must take ACT in fall. For high school seniors with a minimum 3.5 GPA. Application deadline is the October or June ACT test date.

Award: Scholarship for use in freshman year; renewable. *Number:* 15–20. *Amount:* varies.

Eligibility Requirements: Applicant must be high school student; planning to enroll or expecting to enroll full-time at a two-year or four-year institution or university; resident of North Dakota and studying in North Dakota. Applicant must have 3.5 GPA or higher. Available to U.S. citizens.

Application Requirements: Test scores. *Deadline:* varies.

Contact: Peggy Wipf, Director of Financial Aid
State of North Dakota
600 East Boulevard Avenue, Department 215
Bismarck, ND 58505-0230
Phone: 701-328-4114

NORTH DAKOTA STATE STUDENT INCENTIVE GRANT PROGRAM

Grants to North Dakota residents pursuing their undergraduate degree who attend North Dakota's public, private (not-for-profit), and tribal colleges.

Award: Grant for use in freshman, sophomore, junior, or senior years. *Number:* 2500. *Amount:* $600–$1000.

Eligibility Requirements: Applicant must be enrolled or expecting to enroll full-time at a four-year institution or university and resident of North Dakota. Available to U.S. citizens.

Application Requirements: Application. *Deadline:* March 15.

Contact:
Phone: 701-328-4114
E-mail: peggy.wipf@ndus.nodak.edu

NORTH DAKOTA STATE STUDENT INCENTIVE GRANT PROGRAM

Aids North Dakota residents attending an approved college or university in North Dakota. Must be enrolled in a program of at least nine months in length.

Award: Grant for use in freshman, sophomore, junior, or senior years; not renewable. *Number:* 2500–2600. *Amount:* up to $600.

Eligibility Requirements: Applicant must be enrolled or expecting to enroll full-time at a two-year or four-year institution or university; resident of North Dakota and studying in North Dakota. Available to U.S. and non-U.S. citizens.

Application Requirements: Financial need analysis, FAFSA. *Deadline:* March 15.

Contact: Peggy Wipf, Director of Financial Aid
State of North Dakota
600 East Boulevard Avenue, Department 215
Bismarck, ND 58505-0230
Phone: 701-328-4114

STATE OF WYOMING, ADMINISTERED BY UNIVERSITY OF WYOMING   http://www.uwyo.edu/scholarships

VIETNAM VETERANS AWARD/WYOMING
• See page 595

STATE STUDENT ASSISTANCE COMMISSION OF INDIANA (SSACI)   http://www.in.gov/ssaci

FRANK O'BANNON GRANT PROGRAM

The Higher Education Award is a need-based, tuition-restricted program for students attending Indiana public, private, or proprietary institutions seeking a first undergraduate degree. Students (and parents of dependent students) who are U.S. citizens and Indiana residents must file the FAFSA yearly by the March 10 deadline.

Award: Grant for use in freshman, sophomore, junior, or senior years; not renewable. *Number:* 38,000–43,660. *Amount:* $200–$4700.

Eligibility Requirements: Applicant must be enrolled or expecting to enroll full-time at a two-year or four-year or technical institution or university; resident of Indiana and studying in Indiana. Available to U.S. citizens.

Application Requirements: Application, financial need analysis, FAFSA. *Deadline:* March 10.

Contact: Grants Counselor
State Student Assistance Commission of Indiana (SSACI)
150 West Market Street, Suite 500
Indianapolis, IN 46204-2805
Phone: 317-232-2350
Fax: 317-232-3260
E-mail: grants@ssaci.state.in.us

HOOSIER SCHOLAR AWARD

The Hoosier Scholar Award is a $500 nonrenewable award. Based on the size of the senior class, one to three scholars are selected by the guidance counselor(s) of each accredited high school in Indiana. The award is based on academic merit and may be used for any educational expense at an eligible Indiana institution of higher education.

Award: Scholarship for use in freshman year; not renewable. *Number:* 790–840. *Amount:* $500.

Eligibility Requirements: Applicant must be high school student; planning to enroll or expecting to enroll full-time at a two-year or four-year institution or university; resident of Indiana and studying in Indiana. Applicant must have 3.5 GPA or higher. Available to U.S. citizens.

Application Requirements: Application, references. *Deadline:* March 10.

Contact: Ada Sparkman, Program Coordinator
State Student Assistance Commission of Indiana (SSACI)
150 West Market Street, Suite 500
Indianapolis, IN 46204-2805
Phone: 317-232-2350
Fax: 317-232-3260

INDIANA NATIONAL GUARD SUPPLEMENTAL GRANT
• See page 572

PART-TIME GRANT PROGRAM

Program is designed to encourage part-time undergraduates to start and complete their associate or baccalaureate degrees or certificates by subsidizing part-time tuition costs. It is a term-based award that is based on need. State residency requirements must be met and a FAFSA must be filed. Eligibility is determined at the institutional level subject to approval by SSACI.

Award: Grant for use in freshman, sophomore, junior, or senior years; not renewable. *Number:* 4680–6700. *Amount:* $50–$4000.

Eligibility Requirements: Applicant must be enrolled or expecting to enroll part-time at a two-year or four-year or technical institution or university; resident of Indiana and studying in Indiana. Available to U.S. citizens.

State Student Assistance Commission of Indiana (SSACI) (continued)

Application Requirements: Application, financial need analysis. *Deadline:* Continuous.

Contact: Grants Counselor
State Student Assistance Commission of Indiana (SSACI)
150 West Market Street, Suite 500
Indianapolis, IN 46204-2805
Phone: 317-232-2350
Fax: 317-232-3260
E-mail: grants@ssaci.state.in.us

ROBERT C. BYRD HONORS SCHOLARSHIP-INDIANA

Scholarship is designed to recognize academic achievement and requires a minimum SAT score of 1300 or ACT score of 31, or recent GED score of 65. The scholarship is awarded equally among Indiana's congressional districts. The amount of the scholarship varies depending upon federal funding and is automatically renewed if the institution's satisfactory academic progress requirements are met.

Award: Scholarship for use in freshman, sophomore, junior, or senior years; renewable. *Number:* 550–570. *Amount:* $1500.

Eligibility Requirements: Applicant must be enrolled or expecting to enroll full-time at a two-year or four-year institution or university and resident of Indiana. Applicant must have 3.5 GPA or higher. Available to U.S. citizens.

Application Requirements: Application, test scores, transcript. *Deadline:* April 24.

Contact: Yvonne Heflin, Director, Special Programs
State Student Assistance Commission of Indiana (SSACI)
150 West Market Street, Suite 500
Indianapolis, IN 46204-2805
Phone: 317-232-2350
Fax: 317-232-3260

TWENTY-FIRST CENTURY SCHOLARS GEAR UP SUMMER SCHOLARSHIP

Grant of up to $1500 that pays for summer school tuition and regularly assessed course fees (but it does not cover other costs such as text books or room and board).

Award: Scholarship for use in freshman, sophomore, junior, or senior years. *Amount:* up to $1500.

Eligibility Requirements: Applicant must be enrolled or expecting to enroll full-time at a two-year or four-year institution or university; resident of Indiana and studying in Indiana. Available to U.S. citizens.

Application Requirements: Application. *Deadline:* varies.

Contact: GEAR UP Coordinator, Office of Twenty-first Century Scholars
State Student Assistance Commission of Indiana (SSACI)
150 West Market Street, Suite 500
Indianapolis, IN 46204
Phone: 317-234-1394
E-mail: 21stscholars@ssaci.in.gov

STEPHEN T. MARCHELLO SCHOLARSHIP FOUNDATION   http://www.stmfoundation.org

A LEGACY OF HOPE SCHOLARSHIPS FOR SURVIVORS OF CHILDHOOD CANCER

A scholarship of up to $10,000 per year for four years of postsecondary undergraduate education. Applicant must be a survivor of childhood cancer. Submit letter from doctor, clinic or hospital where applicant was treated for cancer. Residents of Colorado, Arizona, California, and Montana are eligible. Must be U.S. citizen. Minimum 2.5 GPA required.

Award: Scholarship for use in freshman, sophomore, junior, or senior years; renewable. *Number:* 1–6. *Amount:* $1000–$10,000.

Eligibility Requirements: Applicant must be high school student; planning to enroll or expecting to enroll full or part-time at a two-year or four-year or technical institution or university and resident of Arizona, California, Colorado, or Montana. Applicant must have 2.5 GPA or higher. Available to U.S. citizens.

Application Requirements: Application, essay, references, self-addressed stamped envelope, test scores, transcript. *Deadline:* March 15.

Contact: Franci Marchello, President
Stephen T. Marchello Scholarship Foundation
1170 East Long Place
Centennial, CO 80122
Phone: 303-886-5018
E-mail: fmarchello@earthlink.net

SWISS BENEVOLENT SOCIETY

GENERAL FUND SCHOLARSHIPS
• See page 635

SWISS BENEVOLENT SOCIETY OF CHICAGO   http://www.sbschicago.org/

SWISS BENEVOLENT SOCIETY OF CHICAGO SCHOLARSHIPS
• See page 635

SWISS BENEVOLENT SOCIETY OF NEW YORK   http://www.swissbenevolentny.com

PELLEGRINI SCHOLARSHIP GRANTS
• See page 636

TENNESSEE EDUCATION ASSOCIATION   http://www.teateachers.org

TEA DON SAHLI-KATHY WOODALL SONS AND DAUGHTERS SCHOLARSHIP
• See page 515

TENNESSEE STUDENT ASSISTANCE CORPORATION   http://www.state.tn.us/tsac

DEPENDENT CHILDREN SCHOLARSHIP PROGRAM
• See page 551

TENNESSEE EDUCATION LOTTERY SCHOLARSHIP PROGRAM TENNESSEE HOPE ACCESS GRANT

Non-renewable award of $2000 for students at Four-year colleges or $1250 for students at Two-year colleges. Entering freshmen must have a minimum GPA of 2.75 and parents income must be $36,000 or less. Recipients will be eligible for Tennessee HOPE Scholarship by meeting HOPE Scholarship renewal criteria.

Award: Grant for use in freshman, sophomore, junior, or senior years; not renewable. *Number:* varies. *Amount:* $1575–$2400.

Eligibility Requirements: Applicant must be enrolled or expecting to enroll full or part-time at a two-year or four-year or technical institution or university; resident of Tennessee and studying in Tennessee. Available to U.S. citizens.

Application Requirements: Application, financial need analysis. *Deadline:* May 1.

Contact: Robert Biggers, Lottery Scholarship Program Administrator
Tennessee Student Assistance Corporation
404 James Robertson Parkway, Suite 1950
Nashville, TN 37243-0820
Phone: 800-342-1663
Fax: 615-253-3867
E-mail: tsac.aidinfo@state.tn.us

TENNESSEE EDUCATION LOTTERY SCHOLARSHIP PROGRAM TENNESSEE HOPE SCHOLARSHIP

Award of $3000 per year for students at Four-year colleges or $1500 per year for students at Two-year colleges.

Award: Scholarship for use in freshman, sophomore, junior, or senior years; renewable. *Number:* varies. *Amount:* $1650–$3300.

Eligibility Requirements: Applicant must be enrolled or expecting to enroll full or part-time at a two-year or four-year or technical institution or university; resident of Tennessee and studying in Tennessee. Applicant must have 3.0 GPA or higher. Available to U.S. citizens.

Application Requirements: Application, financial need analysis. *Deadline:* May 1.

Contact: Robert Biggers, Lottery Scholarship Program Administrator
Tennessee Student Assistance Corporation
404 James Robertson Parkway, Suite 1950
Nashville, TN 37243-0820
Phone: 800-342-1663
Fax: 615-253-3867
E-mail: tsac.aidinfo@state.tn.us

TENNESSEE EDUCATION LOTTERY SCHOLARSHIP PROGRAM WILDER-NAIFEH TECHNICAL SKILLS GRANT

Award of $1300 for students enrolled in Tennessee Technology Centers. Cannot be prior recipient of Tennessee HOPE Scholarship.

Award: Grant for use in freshman, sophomore, junior, or senior years. *Number:* varies. *Amount:* $1300.

Eligibility Requirements: Applicant must be enrolled or expecting to enroll full or part-time at a technical institution; resident of Tennessee and studying in Tennessee. Available to U.S. citizens.

Application Requirements: Application, financial need analysis. *Deadline:* May 1.

Contact: Robert Biggers, Lottery Scholarship Program Administrator
Tennessee Student Assistance Corporation
404 James Robertson Parkway, Suite 1950
Nashville, TN 37243-0820
Phone: 800-342-1663
Fax: 615-253-3867
E-mail: tsac.aidinfo@state.tn.us

TENNESSEE STUDENT ASSISTANCE AWARD PROGRAM

Assists Tennessee residents attending an approved college or university within the state. Complete a Free Application for Federal Student Aid form. Apply by January 1. FAFSA must be processed by May 1 for priority consideration.

Award: Grant for use in freshman, sophomore, junior, or senior years; renewable. *Number:* 26,000. *Amount:* $100–$2130.

Eligibility Requirements: Applicant must be enrolled or expecting to enroll full or part-time at a two-year or four-year or technical institution or university; resident of Tennessee and studying in Tennessee. Available to U.S. citizens.

Application Requirements: Application, financial need analysis. *Deadline:* May 1.

Contact: Naomi Derryberry, Grant and Scholarship Administrator
Tennessee Student Assistance Corporation
404 James Robertson Parkway, Suite 1950, Parkway Towers
Nashville, TN 37243-0820
Phone: 615-741-1346
Fax: 615-741-6101
E-mail: naomi.derryberry@state.tn.us

TEXAS 4-H YOUTH DEVELOPMENT FOUNDATION
http://texas4-h.tamu.edu

TEXAS 4-H OPPORTUNITY SCHOLARSHIP

Renewable award for Texas 4-H members to attend a Texas college or university. Minimum GPA of 2.5 required. Must attend full-time. Deadline is February 17.

Award: Scholarship for use in freshman, sophomore, junior, or senior years; renewable. *Number:* 150. *Amount:* $1500–$15,000.

Eligibility Requirements: Applicant must be enrolled or expecting to enroll full-time at a two-year or four-year or technical institution or university; resident of Texas and studying in Texas. Applicant must have 2.5 GPA or higher. Available to U.S. citizens.

Application Requirements: Application, essay, financial need analysis, interview, references, test scores, transcript. *Deadline:* February 17.

Contact: Philip Pearce, Executive Director
Texas 4-H Youth Development Foundation
Texas A&M University
7606 Eastmark Drive, Suite 101
College Station, TX 77843-2473
Phone: 979-845-1213
Fax: 979-845-6495
E-mail: p-pearce@tamu.edu

TEXAS AFL-CIO
http://www.aflcio.org

TEXAS AFL-CIO SCHOLARSHIP PROGRAM
• See page 516

TEXAS BLACK BAPTIST SCHOLARSHIP COMMITTEE
http://www.bgct.org

TEXAS BLACK BAPTIST SCHOLARSHIP
• See page 636

TEXAS CHRISTIAN UNIVERSITY NEELY SCHOOL OF BUSINESS ENTREPRENEURSHIP PROGRAM
http://www.neeley.tcu.edu/

TCU TEXAS YOUTH ENTREPRENEUR OF THE YEAR

Award available to currently enrolled Texas high school students who started and managed a business for at least one year. Must submit description of currently-operating business they founded, must be resident of Texas. Finalists must attend TCU Young Entrepreneurs Days and individually participate in interviews. Award may be applied to any college; award is doubled if the student attends TCU. Information and application is on Web site: http://www.nep.tcu.edu

Award: Scholarship for use in freshman year; not renewable. *Number:* 6. *Amount:* $1000–$5000.

Eligibility Requirements: Applicant must be high school student; age 14-19; planning to enroll or expecting to enroll full or part-time at a two-year or four-year or technical institution or university and resident of Texas. Available to U.S. citizens.

Application Requirements: Application, interview, references, description of business started and managed by applicant. *Deadline:* varies.

Contact: Sheryl Doll, Program Director
Texas Christian University Neely School of Business Entrepreneurship Program
PO Box 298530
Ft. Worth, TX 76109
Phone: 817-257-5078
Fax: 817-257-5775
E-mail: s.doll@tcu.edu

TEXAS HIGHER EDUCATION COORDINATING BOARD
http://www.collegefortexans.com

ACADEMIC COMMON MARKET WAIVER

For Texas residents who are students pursuing a degree in a field of study not offered in Texas. May qualify for special tuition rates. Deadlines vary by institution. Must be studying in the South.

Award: Scholarship for use in freshman, sophomore, junior, senior, or graduate years; renewable. *Number:* 1. *Amount:* varies.

Eligibility Requirements: Applicant must be enrolled or expecting to enroll full or part-time at a four-year institution or university; resident of Texas and studying in Alabama, Arkansas, Florida, Georgia, Kentucky, Louisiana, Mississippi, Missouri, Oklahoma, South Carolina, Tennessee, or Virginia. Available to U.S. citizens.

Application Requirements: Application. *Deadline:* varies.

Contact: Linda McDonough, ACM Coordinator
Texas Higher Education Coordinating Board
PO Box 12788
Austin, TX 78711-2788
Phone: 512-427-6525

TEXAS NATIONAL GUARD TUITION ASSISTANCE PROGRAM
• See page 572

TOWARD EXCELLENCE, ACCESS AND SUCCESS (TEXAS GRANT)

Renewable aid for students enrolled in a public or private non-profit, college or university in Texas. Based on need. Amount of award is determined by the financial aid office of each school. Deadlines vary. Contact the college/university financial aid office for application information.

Award: Grant for use in freshman, sophomore, junior, or senior years; renewable. *Number:* varies. *Amount:* $1552–$4392.

Eligibility Requirements: Applicant must be enrolled or expecting to enroll full or part-time at a two-year or four-year or technical

Texas Higher Education Coordinating Board (continued)

institution or university; resident of Texas and studying in Texas. Applicant must have 2.5 GPA or higher. Available to U.S. citizens.

Application Requirements: Application, financial need analysis, transcript. *Deadline:* varies.

Contact: Financial Aid Office
Texas Higher Education Coordinating Board
PO Box 12788
Austin, TX 78711-2788
Phone: 512-427-6101
Fax: 512-427-6127
E-mail: grantinfo@thecb.state.tx.us

TUITION EQUALIZATION GRANT (TEG) PROGRAM

Renewable award for Texas residents enrolled at least half-time at an independent college or university within the state. Based on financial need. Maintain an overall college GPA of at least 2.5 on a 4.0 scale. Deadlines vary by institution. Must not be receiving athletic scholarship. Contact college/university financial aid office for application information.

Award: Grant for use in freshman, sophomore, junior, or senior years; renewable. *Number:* varies. *Amount:* up to $3444.

Eligibility Requirements: Applicant must be enrolled or expecting to enroll full or part-time at a two-year or four-year institution or university; resident of Texas and studying in Texas. Available to U.S. citizens.

Application Requirements: Financial need analysis, FAFSA. *Deadline:* varies.

Contact: Financial Aid Office
Texas Higher Education Coordinating Board
PO Box 12788
Austin, TX 78711-2788
Phone: 512-427-6101
Fax: 512-427-6127
E-mail: grantinfo@thecb.state.tx.us

TEXAS TENNIS FOUNDATION
http://texastennisfoundation.com

TEXAS TENNIS FOUNDATION SCHOLARSHIPS AND ENDOWMENTS

College scholarships for highly recommended students residing in Texas, with an interest in tennis. Financial need is considered. Must be between the ages of 17 and 19.

Award: Scholarship for use in freshman, sophomore, junior, or senior years; not renewable. *Number:* 10–15. *Amount:* $1000.

Eligibility Requirements: Applicant must be age 17-19; enrolled or expecting to enroll full-time at a two-year or four-year or technical institution or university; resident of Texas and must have an interest in athletics/sports. Available to U.S. citizens.

Application Requirements: Application, essay, financial need analysis, photo, references, test scores, transcript, copy of parent or guardian's federal tax return, SAT or ACT scores, list of extracurricular activities (including tennis). *Deadline:* April 1.

Contact: Katie Cox, Awards Coordinator
Texas Tennis Foundation
2111 Dickson, Suite 33
Austin, TX 78704-4788
Phone: 512-443-1334 Ext. 218
Fax: 512-443-4748
E-mail: pjaeger@texas.usta.com

THE ASIAN REPORTER
http://www.arfoundation.net

ASIAN REPORTER SCHOLARSHIP
• See page 636

THE EDUCATION PARTNERSHIP
http://www.edpartnership.org

CHARLES A. MORVILLO MEMORIAL SCHOLARSHIPS

For students who demonstrate financial need, integrity, leadership, a determination to gain a higher education and make a positive impact on the community. $10,000 is paid to the college or university over four years, and

$2500 is paid directly to the scholar upon graduation. Must be a senior from a Providence or North Providence high school. Application deadline is May 30.

Award: Scholarship for use in freshman, sophomore, junior, or senior years; renewable. *Number:* 2. *Amount:* $12,500.

Eligibility Requirements: Applicant must be high school student; age 18 or under; planning to enroll or expecting to enroll full-time at a two-year or four-year institution or university and resident of Rhode Island. Applicant must have 2.5 GPA or higher. Available to U.S. citizens.

Application Requirements: Application, essay, financial need analysis, references, test scores, transcript. *Deadline:* May 30.

Contact: Keturah Johnson, Scholarships and Communications Coordinator
The Education Partnership
345 South Main Street
Providence, RI 02903
Phone: 401-331-5222 Ext. 112
Fax: 401-331-1659
E-mail: kjohnson@edpartnership.org

THE HEART OF A MARINE FOUNDATION
http://www.heartofamarine.org

LANCE CORPORAL PHILLIP E. FRANK MEMORIAL SCHOLARSHIP

Scholarships available to residents of New Jersey and Illinois in an effort to encourage youth who exemplify the spirit of "the Heart of a Marine" ideal which is honor, patriotism, loyalty, respect and concern for others. See Web site for application and additional information: http://www.heartofamarine. org

Award: Scholarship for use in freshman year; not renewable. *Number:* 2. *Amount:* $500.

Eligibility Requirements: Applicant must be enrolled or expecting to enroll full or part-time at a two-year or four-year or technical institution or university and resident of Illinois or New Jersey. Available to U.S. citizens.

Application Requirements: Application, driver's license, essay, photo, references. *Deadline:* March 31.

Contact: Georgette Frank, Executive Director
The Heart of a Marine Foundation
PO Box 1732
Elk Grove Village, IL 60007
E-mail: theheartofamarine@comcast.net

TIDEWATER SCHOLARSHIP FOUNDATION
http://www.access-tsf.org

ACCESS SCHOLARSHIP/LAST DOLLAR AWARD

The Tidewater Scholarship Foundation's ACCESS Program helps participating students in Norfolk, Portsmouth, and Virginia Beach, Virginia secure scholarships and financial aid for college. ACCESS also offers a "Last Dollar Scholarship" that is awarded based on unmet financial need for students who enrolled in the ACCESS program in 9th grade.

Award: Scholarship for use in freshman, sophomore, junior, or senior years; renewable. *Number:* varies. *Amount:* $500–$1000.

Eligibility Requirements: Applicant must be high school student; planning to enroll or expecting to enroll full-time at a two-year or four-year institution or university and resident of Virginia. Applicant must have 2.5 GPA or higher. Available to U.S. citizens.

Application Requirements: Financial need analysis, ACCESS Challenge agreement. *Deadline:* August 15.

Contact: Bonnie Sutton, President and CEO
Tidewater Scholarship Foundation
800 E City Hall Avenue
PO Box 1357
Norfolk, VA 23501-1357
Phone: 757-628-3942
Fax: 757-628-3842
E-mail: bsutton@access-tsf.org

TIGER WOODS FOUNDATION
http://www.tigerwoodsfoundation.org

ALFRED "TUP" HOLMES MEMORIAL SCHOLARSHIP

Given yearly to one worthy Atlanta metropolitan area graduating high school senior who has displayed high moral character while demonstrating leadership potential and academic excellence. Must be U.S. citizen. Minimum 3.0 GPA required. Application deadline is April 1.

Award: Scholarship for use in freshman or senior years; not renewable. *Number:* 1. *Amount:* $2500.

Eligibility Requirements: Applicant must be enrolled or expecting to enroll full-time at a two-year or four-year institution or university and resident of Georgia. Applicant must have 3.0 GPA or higher. Available to U.S. citizens.

Application Requirements: Application, essay, references, test scores, transcript. *Deadline:* April 1.

Contact: Michelle Bernis, Director, Events
Tiger Woods Foundation
4281 Katella Avenue, Suite 111
Los Alamitos, CA 90720
Phone: 714-816-1806
Fax: 714-816-1869

TKE EDUCATIONAL FOUNDATION
http://www.tkefoundation.org

ELMER AND DORIS SCHMITZ SR. MEMORIAL SCHOLARSHIP
• See page 517

TOWNSHIP OFFICIALS OF ILLINOIS
http://www.toi.org

TOWNSHIP OFFICIALS OF ILLINOIS SCHOLARSHIP FUND

The TOI scholarships are awarded to graduating Illinois high school seniors who have a B average or above, have demonstrated an active interest in school activities, who have submitted an essay on "The Importance of Township Government," high school transcript, and letters of recommendation. Students must attend Illinois institutions, either four-year or junior colleges. Must be full-time student.

Award: Scholarship for use in freshman year; not renewable. *Number:* 10. *Amount:* up to $1000.

Eligibility Requirements: Applicant must be high school student; planning to enroll or expecting to enroll full-time at a two-year or four-year institution or university; resident of Illinois and studying in Illinois. Applicant must have 3.0 GPA or higher. Available to U.S. citizens.

Application Requirements: Application, essay, references, test scores, transcript. *Deadline:* March 1.

Contact: Bryan Smith, Editor and Executive Director
Township Officials of Illinois
408 South 5th Street
Springfield, IL 62701-1804
Phone: 217-744-2212
Fax: 217-744-7419
E-mail: bryantoi@toi.org

TREACY COMPANY

TREACY COMPANY SCHOLARSHIPS

Renewable award for college freshmen and sophomores. Must be a resident of Montana, Idaho, North Dakota, or South Dakota. Write to Treacy Company for application and more information.

Award: Scholarship for use in freshman or sophomore years; renewable. *Number:* 25–35. *Amount:* $400.

Eligibility Requirements: Applicant must be enrolled or expecting to enroll full or part-time at a two-year or four-year or technical institution or university and resident of Idaho, Montana, North Dakota, or South Dakota. Available to U.S. citizens.

Application Requirements: Application, photo, transcript. *Deadline:* June 15.

Contact: James O'Connell, Trustee
Treacy Company
PO Box 1479
Helena, MT 59624-1700

TRIANGLE COMMUNITY FOUNDATION
http://www.trianglecf.org

GLAXO SMITH KLINE OPPORTUNITIES SCHOLARSHIP

Renewable award for any type of education or training program. Must be a legal resident of the United States with a permanent residence in Durham, Orange, Wake, or Chatham counties. No income limitations. Application deadline is March 15. For further information see Web site at http://www.tranglecf.org.

Award: Scholarship for use in freshman, sophomore, junior, senior, or graduate years; renewable. *Number:* 1–5. *Amount:* $5000–$20,000.

Eligibility Requirements: Applicant must be enrolled or expecting to enroll full-time at a two-year or four-year institution or university; resident of North Carolina and studying in North Carolina. Available to U.S. citizens.

Application Requirements: Application, autobiography, essay, financial need analysis, references, test scores, transcript, proof of U.S. citizenship. *Deadline:* March 15.

Contact: Linda Depo, Philanthropic Services Associate
Triangle Community Foundation
4813 Emperor Boulevard
Cambridge Hall
Durham, NC 27703
Phone: 919-474-8370
Fax: 919-949-9208
E-mail: linda@trianglecf.org

TRIANGLE NATIVE AMERICAN SOCIETY
http://www.tnasweb.org

TRIANGLE NATIVE AMERICAN SOCIETY SCHOLARSHIP FUND
• See page 636

UNITED COMMUNITY SERVICES FOR WORKING FAMILIES

RONALD LORAH MEMORIAL SCHOLARSHIP
• See page 518

UNITED DAUGHTERS OF THE CONFEDERACY
http://www.hqudc.org

GERTRUDE BOTTS-SAUCIER SCHOLARSHIP
• See page 520

LOLA B. CURRY SCHOLARSHIP
• See page 521

UNITED FEDERATION OF TEACHERS
http://www.uft.org/

ALBERT SHANKER COLLEGE SCHOLARSHIP FUND OF THE UNITED FEDERATION OF TEACHERS

Renewable award for eligible students graduating from New York City public high schools to pursue undergraduate studies. Scholarship is $1250 a year for four years. Submit transcript, autobiography, essay, references, and financial need analysis with application. Deadline is third week of December. There are nine graduate awards including a renewable medical and a renewable law award. Applicants must be current undergraduate award winners.

Award: Scholarship for use in freshman, sophomore, junior, senior, or graduate years; renewable. *Number:* 200. *Amount:* $1250.

Eligibility Requirements: Applicant must be enrolled or expecting to enroll full-time at a two-year or four-year institution or university and resident of New York. Available to U.S. citizens.

Application Requirements: Application, autobiography, essay, financial need analysis, references, transcript. *Deadline:* varies.

Contact: Jeffrey A. Huart, Director
United Federation of Teachers
52 Broadway, 11th Floor
New York, NY 10004-1603
Phone: 212-529-2110
Fax: 212-510-6429
E-mail: shankerfund@worldnet.att.com

UNITED METHODIST CHURCH   http://www.umc.org

J. A. KNOWLES MEMORIAL SCHOLARSHIP
• See page 653

UNITED NEGRO COLLEGE FUND   http://www.uncf.org

ABBINGTON, VALLANTEEN SCHOLARSHIP
• See page 638

BANK OF AMERICA SCHOLARSHIP
• See page 638

BILDNER FAMILY SCHOLARSHIP
• See page 638

BRITTON FUND SCHOLARSHIP PROGRAM

Scholarships available to students from Northern Ohio enrolled in a UNCF member college or university. Please visit Web site for more information: http://www.uncf.org

Award: Scholarship for use in freshman, sophomore, junior, senior, or graduate years. *Number:* 1. *Amount:* varies.

Eligibility Requirements: Applicant must be enrolled or expecting to enroll at a four-year institution or university and resident of Ohio. Applicant must have 2.5 GPA or higher. Available to U.S. citizens.

Application Requirements: Application, financial need analysis, FAFSA, Student Aid Report (SAR). *Deadline:* varies.

Contact: Rebecca Bennett, Director, Program Services
United Negro College Fund
8260 Willow Oaks Corporate Drive
Fairfax, VA 22031-8044
Phone: 800-331-2244
E-mail: rbennett@uncf.org

BUSHROD CAMPBELL AND ADAH HALL SCHOLARSHIP
• See page 638

CASIMIR, DOMINIQUE AND JAQUES SCHOLARSHIP
• See page 638

CHICAGO INTER-ALUMNI COUNCIL SCHOLARSHIP
• See page 638

CLEVELAND FOUNDATION SCHOLARSHIP
• See page 639

CLEVELAND MUNICIPAL SCHOOL SCHOLARSHIP
• See page 639

CLOROX COMPANY FOUNDATION SCHOLARSHIP
• See page 639

COLUMBUS FOUNDATION SCHOLARSHIP
• See page 639

COSTCO SCHOLARSHIP
• See page 639

DALLAS INDEPENDENT SCHOOL DISTRICT SCHOLARSHIP
• See page 640

DALLAS MAVERICKS
• See page 640

DUPONT SCHOLARSHIP
• See page 640

DUQUESNE LIGHT COMPANY SCHOLARSHIP
• See page 640

FIFTH/THIRD SCHOLARS PROGRAM
• See page 640

FORT WORTH INDEPENDENT SCHOOL DISTRICT SCHOLARSHIP
• See page 641

GHEENS FOUNDATION SCHOLARSHIP
• See page 641

JOHN W. ANDERSON FOUNDATION SCHOLARSHIP
• See page 641

KANSAS CITY INITIATIVE SCHOLARSHIP
• See page 642

KROGER SCHOLARSHIP
• See page 642

KROGER/PEPSI SCHOLARSHIP
• See page 642

LIMITED, INC. AND INTIMATE BRANDS, INC. SCHOLARSHIP
• See page 642

NEW JERSEY MAYOR'S TASK FORCE SCHOLARSHIP
• See page 643

PAUL AND EDITH BABSON SCHOLARSHIP
• See page 643

RELIABLE LIFE INSURANCE COMPANY SCHOLARSHIP PROGRAM
• See page 643

RICHMOND SCHOLARSHIP
• See page 643

RONALD MCDONALD'S HOUSE CHARITIES SCHOLARSHIP-OHIO
• See page 643

SAN JOSE MERCURY NEWS SCHOLARSHIP
• See page 644

SCHRAFT CHARITABLE TRUST SCHOLARSHIP
• See page 644

SHELL/EQUILON UNCF CLEVELAND SCHOLARSHIP FUND
• See page 644

SHREVEPORT CAMPAIGN
• See page 644

ST. PETERSBURG GOLF CLASSIC SCHOLARSHIP
• See page 644

TEXAS HEALTH RESOURCES SCHOLARSHIP
• See page 644

TEXTRON FELLOWS PROGRAM
• See page 645

TJX FOUNDATION SCHOLARSHIP
• See page 645

UNION BANK OF CALIFORNIA
• See page 645

UNITED WAY OF NEW ORLEANS EMERGENCY ASSISTANCE FUND
• See page 645

UNITED WAY OF WESTCHESTER AND PUTNAM, INC./ UNCF EMERGENCY ASSISTANCE FUND
• See page 646

VERIZON FOUNDATION SCHOLARSHIP
• See page 646

WESTERN ASSOCIATION OF LADIES SCHOLARSHIP
• See page 646

WHIRLPOOL FOUNDATION SCHOLARSHIP
• See page 646

WISCONSIN STUDENT AID
• See page 646

UNIVERSITY AVIATION ASSOCIATION   http://www.aviation.siu.edu

CHICAGO AREA BUSINESS AVIATION ASSOCIATION SCHOLARSHIP

One-time awards worth $2500 each. Must be a U.S. citizen. Minimum GPA of 2.5. Priority given to Chicagoland residents followed by Illinois residents. Deadline is April 29.

Award: Scholarship for use in freshman, sophomore, junior, senior, graduate, or postgraduate years; not renewable. *Number:* up to 6. *Amount:* up to $2500.

Eligibility Requirements: Applicant must be enrolled or expecting to enroll full-time at a two-year or four-year or technical institution or university and resident of Illinois. Applicant must have 2.5 GPA or higher. Available to U.S. citizens.

Application Requirements: Application, essay, references. *Deadline:* April 29.

Contact: David A. NewMyer, Department Chair, Aviation Management and Flight
University Aviation Association
Southern Illinois University at Carbondale, College of Applied Sciences and Arts, 1365 Douglas Drive
Carbondale, IL 62901-6623
Phone: 618-453-8898
Fax: 618-453-7286
E-mail: newmyer@siu.edu

UTAH HIGHER EDUCATION ASSISTANCE AUTHORITY   http://www.uheaa.org

LEVERAGING EDUCATIONAL ASSISTANCE PARTNERSHIP (LEAP)

Available to students with substantial financial need for use at participating Utah schools. Contact Financial Aid Office of specific school for application requirements and deadlines. Must be Utah resident.

Award: Grant for use in freshman, sophomore, junior, or senior years; not renewable. *Number:* up to 4008. *Amount:* $300–$2500.

Eligibility Requirements: Applicant must be enrolled or expecting to enroll full or part-time at a two-year or four-year or technical institution or university; resident of Utah and studying in Utah. Available to U.S. citizens.

Application Requirements: Application, financial need analysis. *Deadline:* Continuous.

Contact: Financial Aid Office
Phone: 801-321-7207
Fax: 801-366-8470

UTAH CENTENNIAL OPPORTUNITY PROGRAM FOR EDUCATION

Renewable awards for undergraduate college student in Utah institution. Must be a Utah resident. Contact financial aid office at participating institutions for more information.

Award: Grant for use in freshman, sophomore, junior, or senior years; not renewable. *Number:* up to 2807. *Amount:* $300–$5000.

Eligibility Requirements: Applicant must be enrolled or expecting to enroll full or part-time at a two-year or four-year or technical institution or university; resident of Utah and studying in Utah. Available to U.S. citizens.

Application Requirements: Application, financial need analysis. *Deadline:* Continuous.

Contact: Financial Aid Office
Phone: 801-321-7207
Fax: 801-366-8470

UTAH LEAGUE OF CREDIT UNIONS   http://www.ulcu.com

UTAH CREDIT UNION SCHOLARSHIP CONTEST

Entrants, who must be Utah credit union members, or whose parents are members, write an essay for the contest. Must be a graduating high school senior and a U.S. citizen. For additional information visit Web site at http://www.ulcu.com

Award: Prize for use in freshman year; not renewable. *Number:* 3. *Amount:* $500–$1500.

Eligibility Requirements: Applicant must be high school student; planning to enroll or expecting to enroll full or part-time at a two-year or four-year or technical institution or university and resident of Utah. Available to U.S. citizens.

Application Requirements: Application, applicant must enter a contest, essay. *Deadline:* April 23.

Contact: Stephen Nelson, Director of Communication
Utah League of Credit Unions
1805 South Redwood Road
Salt Lake City, UT 84104
Phone: 800-662-8684 Ext. 343
E-mail: stephen@ulcu.com

UTAH STATE BOARD OF REGENTS   http://www.utahsbr.edu/

NEW CENTURY SCHOLARSHIP

Scholarship for qualified high school graduates of Utah. Must attend Utah state-operated college. Award depends on number of hours student enrolled. Please contact for further eligibility requirements. Eligible recipients receive an award equal to 75% of tuition for 60 credit hours toward the completion of a bachelor's degree. For more details see Web site: http://www.utahsbr.edu.

Award: Scholarship for use in freshman, sophomore, junior, or senior years; renewable. *Number:* 145. *Amount:* $1060–$3400.

Eligibility Requirements: Applicant must be enrolled or expecting to enroll full or part-time at a four-year institution or university; resident of Utah and studying in Utah. Available to U.S. citizens.

Application Requirements: Application, transcript, GPA/copy of enrollment verification from an eligible Utah 4-year institution, verification from Registrar of completion of requirements for associate's degree. *Deadline:* Continuous.

Contact: Charles Downer, Compliance Officer
Utah State Board of Regents
Board of Regents Building, the Gateway
60 South 400 West
Salt Lake City, UT 84101-1284
Phone: 801-321-7221
Fax: 801-366-8470
E-mail: cdowner@utahsbr.edu

V.E.T.S. - VICTORY ENSURED THROUGH SERVICE

V.E.T.S. ANNUAL SCHOLARSHIP
• See page 595

VERMONT STUDENT ASSISTANCE CORPORATION   http://services.vsac.org/ilwwcm/connect/VSAC

VERMONT INCENTIVE GRANTS

Renewable grants for Vermont residents based on financial need. Must meet needs test. Must be college undergraduate or graduate student enrolled full-time at an approved post secondary institution. Only available to U.S. citizens or permanent residents.

Award: Grant for use in freshman, sophomore, junior, senior, or graduate years; renewable. *Number:* varies. *Amount:* $500–$9800.

Eligibility Requirements: Applicant must be enrolled or expecting to enroll full-time at a two-year or four-year or technical institution or university and resident of Vermont. Available to U.S. citizens.

Application Requirements: Application, financial need analysis, FAFSA. *Deadline:* Continuous.

Contact: Grant Program
Vermont Student Assistance Corporation
PO Box 2000
Winooski, VT 05404-2000
Phone: 802-655-9602
Fax: 802-654-3765

VERMONT PART-TIME STUDENT GRANTS

For undergraduates carrying less than twelve credits per semester who have not received a bachelor's degree. Must be Vermont resident. Based on financial need. Complete Vermont Financial Aid Packet to apply. May be used at any approved post secondary institution.

Award: Grant for use in freshman, sophomore, junior, or senior years; renewable. *Number:* varies. *Amount:* $250–$7350.

Eligibility Requirements: Applicant must be enrolled or expecting to enroll part-time at a four-year institution or university and resident of Vermont. Available to U.S. citizens.

Vermont Student Assistance Corporation (continued)

Application Requirements: Application, financial need analysis. *Deadline:* Continuous.

Contact: Grant Program
Vermont Student Assistance Corporation
PO Box 2000
Winooski, VT 05404-2000
Phone: 802-655-9602
Fax: 802-654-3765

VINCENT L. HAWKINSON FOUNDATION FOR PEACE AND JUSTICE   http://www.graceattheu.org

VINCENT L. HAWKINSON SCHOLARSHIP FOR PEACE AND JUSTICE

The scholarship is awarded to students who have demonstrated a commitment to peace and justice. This generally involves participation in a peace and justice project, leadership and participation in a peace organization, or serving as a role model. The scholarship selection committee of the foundation uses essays and letters of reference to screen candidates and a personal interview in Minneapolis to select a winner. Applicant must either reside or study in Iowa, Minnesota, North Dakota, South Dakota, or Wisconsin.

Award: Scholarship for use in freshman, sophomore, junior, senior, or graduate years; not renewable. *Number:* 1–6. *Amount:* $500–$1500.

Eligibility Requirements: Applicant must be enrolled or expecting to enroll full-time at a two-year or four-year institution or university; resident of Iowa, Minnesota, North Dakota, South Dakota, or Wisconsin and studying in Iowa, Minnesota, North Dakota, South Dakota, or Wisconsin. Available to U.S. and non-U.S. citizens.

Application Requirements: Application, essay, interview, references, transcript. *Deadline:* April 1.

Contact: Vincent L. Hawkinson Foundation for Peace and Justice
Grace University Lutheran Church
324 Harvard Street SE
Minneapolis, MN 55414
Phone: 612-331-8125
E-mail: info@graceattheu.org

VIRGINIA BUSINESS AND PROFESSIONAL WOMEN'S FOUNDATION   http://www.bpwva.org

BUENA M. CHESSHIR MEMORIAL WOMEN'S EDUCATIONAL SCHOLARSHIP

One-time award assists mature women seeking to complete or enhance their education. Its purposes are helping women who are employed or seeking employment, increasing the number of women qualified for promotion, and helping women achieve economic self-sufficiency. Award may be used for tuition, fees, books, transportation, living expenses, or dependent care. Must be a Virginia resident and studying in Virginia.

Award: Scholarship for use in freshman, sophomore, junior, senior, or graduate years; not renewable. *Number:* 1–10. *Amount:* $100–$1000.

Eligibility Requirements: Applicant must be age 25; enrolled or expecting to enroll at a two-year or four-year institution or university; female; resident of Virginia and studying in Virginia. Available to U.S. citizens.

Application Requirements: Application, essay, financial need analysis, references, transcript. *Deadline:* April 1.

Contact: Sheila Barry-Oliver, Senior Trustee
Virginia Business and Professional Women's Foundation
PO Box 4842
McLean, VA 22103-4842
Phone: 703-759-2081
Fax: 703-759-2053
E-mail: bpwva@advocate.net

KAREN B. LEWIS CAREER EDUCATION SCHOLARSHIP

This scholarship is offered to women pursuing postsecondary job-oriented career education, offering training in business, trade and industrial occupations (not to be used for education leading to a bachelor's or higher degree). This award may be used for tuition, fees, books, transportation, living expenses, or dependent care. Must be a Virginia resident studying in Virginia.

Award: Scholarship for use in freshman or sophomore years; not renewable. *Number:* 1–10. *Amount:* $100–$1000.

Eligibility Requirements: Applicant must be enrolled or expecting to enroll full or part-time at a two-year or technical institution; female; resident of Virginia and studying in Virginia. Available to U.S. citizens.

Application Requirements: Application, essay, financial need analysis, references, transcript. *Deadline:* April 1.

Contact: Sheila Barry-Oliver, Senior Trustee
Virginia Business and Professional Women's Foundation
PO Box 4842
McLean, VA 22103-4842
Phone: 703-759-2081
Fax: 703-759-2053
E-mail: bpwva@advocate.net

NETTIE TUCKER YOWELL SCHOLARSHIP

One-time award offered to Virginia high school seniors who have been accepted for enrollment as freshmen in a Virginia college or university for the fall semester following graduation. Scholarship recipients must attend a Virginia college or university to receive funds, which are disbursed directly to the college or university. Minimum 3.0 GPA required.

Award: Scholarship for use in freshman, sophomore, junior, or senior years; not renewable. *Number:* 1–10. *Amount:* $250–$1000.

Eligibility Requirements: Applicant must be high school student; planning to enroll or expecting to enroll full or part-time at a four-year institution or university; resident of Virginia and studying in Virginia. Applicant must have 3.0 GPA or higher. Available to U.S. citizens.

Application Requirements: Application, essay, financial need analysis, references, test scores, transcript. *Deadline:* April 1.

Contact: Sheila Barry-Oliver, Senior Trustee
Virginia Business and Professional Women's Foundation
PO Box 4842
McLean, VA 22103-4842
Phone: 703-759-2081
Fax: 703-759-2053
E-mail: bpwva@advocate.net

VIRGINIA DEPARTMENT OF EDUCATION   http://www.pen.k12.va.us

GRANVILLE P. MEADE SCHOLARSHIP

High school seniors only are eligible to apply for this scholarship. Students are selected based upon grade point average, standardized test scores, letters of recommendations, extra curricular activities, and financial need.

Award: Scholarship for use in freshman, sophomore, junior, or senior years; renewable. *Number:* 5. *Amount:* $2000.

Eligibility Requirements: Applicant must be high school student; planning to enroll or expecting to enroll full-time at a two-year or four-year or technical institution or university and resident of Virginia. Available to U.S. citizens.

Application Requirements: Application, essay, financial need analysis, references, test scores, transcript. *Deadline:* March 15.

Contact: Sylinda Gilchrist, School Counseling Specialist
Virginia Department of Education
PO Box 2120
Richmond, VA 23218-2120
Phone: 804-786-9377
Fax: 804-786-5466
E-mail: sgilchri@mail.vak12ed.edu

ROBERT C. BYRD HONORS SCHOLARSHIP-VIRGINIA

High school seniors are the only students eligible to apply for the scholarships. Students are selected based upon grade point average, standardized test scores, letters of recommendation, extracurricular activities, and community involvement. Deadline: April 7.

Award: Scholarship for use in freshman, sophomore, junior, or senior years; renewable. *Number:* 100–150. *Amount:* $750–$1500.

Eligibility Requirements: Applicant must be high school student; planning to enroll or expecting to enroll full-time at a two-year or four-year or technical institution or university and resident of Virginia. Available to U.S. citizens.

Application Requirements: Application, references, test scores, transcript. *Deadline:* April 7.

Contact: Sylinda Gilchrist, School Counseling Specialist
Virginia Department of Education
PO Box 2120
Richmond, VA 23218-2120
Phone: 804-786-9377
Fax: 804-786-5466
E-mail: sgilchri@mail.vak12ed.edu

WACHOVIA CITIZENSHIP SCHOLARSHIP

Scholarships available for students graduating from a Virginia High School League (Group A, AA & AAA) member schools to further their education at a college, university, or trade school. Must have demonstrated outstanding traits of citizenship throughout their high school career.

Award: Scholarship for use in freshman year. *Number:* up to 6. *Amount:* $1000–$6000.

Eligibility Requirements: Applicant must be high school student; planning to enroll or expecting to enroll at a two-year or four-year or technical institution or university and resident of Virginia. Available to U.S. citizens.

Application Requirements: Application, essay. *Deadline:* March 15.

Contact: Bob Button
Phone: 434-977-8475

VIRGINIA DEPARTMENT OF VETERANS SERVICES   http://www.vdva.vipnet.org/education_benefits.htm

VIRGINIA WAR ORPHANS EDUCATION PROGRAM
• See page 595

WASHINGTON HIGHER EDUCATION COORDINATING BOARD   http://www.hecb.wa.gov

AMERICAN INDIAN ENDOWED SCHOLARSHIP
• See page 647

EDUCATIONAL OPPORTUNITY GRANT

Annual grants of $2500 to encourage financially needy, place bound students to complete bachelor's degree. Must be unable to continue education due to family or work commitments, health concerns, financial needs or similar. Must be Washington residents, live in one of 13 designated counties, and have completed two years of college. Grant only used at eligible four-year colleges in Washington. Applications accepted beginning in April and following months until funds are depleted.

Award: Grant for use in freshman, sophomore, junior, or senior years; renewable. *Number:* 1350. *Amount:* $2500.

Eligibility Requirements: Applicant must be enrolled or expecting to enroll full-time at a four-year institution or university; resident of Washington and studying in Washington. Available to U.S. citizens.

Application Requirements: Application, financial need analysis. *Deadline:* Continuous.

Contact: Dawn Cypriano-McAferty, Program Manager
Washington Higher Education Coordinating Board
917 Lakeridge Way, SW, PO Box 43430
Olympia, WA 98504-3430
Phone: 360-753-7800
Fax: 360-753-7808
E-mail: eog@hecb.wa.gov

STATE NEED GRANT

Grants for undergraduate students with significant financial need. Must be Washington resident and attend school in Washington. Must have family income equal or less than 55% of state median. The financial aid office at each school makes awards to eligible students.

Award: Grant for use in freshman, sophomore, junior, or senior years; renewable. *Number:* 55,000. *Amount:* $2200–$4300.

Eligibility Requirements: Applicant must be enrolled or expecting to enroll full or part-time at a two-year or four-year or technical institution or university; resident of Washington and studying in Washington. Available to U.S. citizens.

Application Requirements: Application, financial need analysis, FAFSA. *Deadline:* Continuous.

Contact: Financial Aid Director of school to which you are applying

WASHINGTON AWARD FOR VOCATIONAL EXCELLENCE (WAVE)

Award to honor three vocational students from each of the state's 49 legislative districts. Grants for up to two years of undergraduate resident tuition. Must be enrolled in Washington high school, skills center, or technical college at time of application. Complete 360 hours in single vocational program in high school or one year at technical college. Contact principal or guidance counselor for more information.

Award: Grant for use in freshman, sophomore, junior, or senior years; renewable. *Number:* up to 147. *Amount:* varies.

Eligibility Requirements: Applicant must be enrolled or expecting to enroll full-time at a two-year or four-year or technical institution or university; resident of Washington and studying in Washington. Available to U.S. citizens.

Application Requirements: *Deadline:* Continuous.

Contact: Ann Lee, Program Manager
Washington Higher Education Coordinating Board
917 Lakeridge Way, SW, PO Box 43430
Olympia, WA 98504-3430
Phone: 360-753-7843
Fax: 360-753-7808
E-mail: annl@hecb.wa.gov

WASHINGTON PROMISE SCHOLARSHIP

College scholarships to low- and middle-income students in high school. Must either rank in top 15 percent of senior class or score a combined 1200 on SAT or 27 on ACT on first attempt. Family income cannot exceed 135% of state median family income. Must be Washington resident, attend a Washington school. School must identify applicants. Contact principal or guidance counselor for more information.

Award: Scholarship for use in freshman or sophomore years; renewable. *Number:* varies. *Amount:* up to $1000.

Eligibility Requirements: Applicant must be high school student; planning to enroll or expecting to enroll full or part-time at a two-year or four-year or technical institution or university; resident of Washington and studying in Washington. Available to U.S. citizens.

Application Requirements: Financial need analysis. *Deadline:* Continuous.

Contact: John Klacik
Washington Higher Education Coordinating Board
917 Lakeridge Way, SW, PO Box 43430
Olympia, WA 98504-3430
Phone: 360-753-7851
Fax: 360-753-7808
E-mail: johnk@hecb.wa.gov

WASHINGTON SCHOLARS PROGRAM

Awarded to three high school students from each of the 49 state legislative districts. Must be Washington resident and enroll in college or university in Washington. Scholarships equal up to four years of full-time resident undergraduate tuition and fees. Contact principal or guidance counselor for more information.

Award: Grant for use in freshman, sophomore, junior, or senior years; renewable. *Number:* varies. *Amount:* varies.

Eligibility Requirements: Applicant must be high school student; planning to enroll or expecting to enroll full-time at a four-year institution or university; resident of Washington and studying in Washington. Available to U.S. citizens.

Application Requirements: *Deadline:* Continuous.

Contact: Ann Lee, Program Manager
Washington Higher Education Coordinating Board
917 Lakeridge Way, SW, PO Box 43430
Olympia, WA 98504-3430
Phone: 360-753-7843
Fax: 360-753-7808
E-mail: annl@hecb.wa.gov

WASHINGTON NATIONAL GUARD
http://www.washingtonguard.com

WASHINGTON NATIONAL GUARD SCHOLARSHIP PROGRAM
• *See page 572*

WASHINGTON STATE PARENT TEACHER ASSOCIATION SCHOLARSHIPS FOUNDATION
http://www.wastatepta.org

WASHINGTON STATE PARENT TEACHER ASSOCIATION SCHOLARSHIPS FOUNDATION

One-time scholarships for students who have graduated from a public high school in state of Washington, and who greatly need financial help to begin full-time postsecondary education. For entering freshmen only.

Award: Scholarship for use in freshman year; not renewable. *Number:* 60–80. *Amount:* $1000–$2000.

Eligibility Requirements: Applicant must be enrolled or expecting to enroll full-time at a two-year or four-year or technical institution or university and resident of Washington. Available to U.S. and non-U.S. citizens.

Application Requirements: Application, essay, financial need analysis, references, transcript. *Deadline:* March 31.

Contact: Jean Carpenter, Executive Director
Washington State Parent Teacher Association Scholarships Foundation
2003 65th Avenue West
Tacoma, WA 98466-6215
Phone: 253-565-2153

WASHINGTON STATE TRIAL LAWYERS ASSOCIATION
http://www.wstla.org

WASHINGTON STATE TRIAL LAWYERS ASSOCIATION PRESIDENTS' SCHOLARSHIP

Recipients are selected based on demonstrated academic achievement and planned advancement toward a higher degree; a documented need for financial assistance; a history of achievement despite having been a victim of injury or overcoming a disability, handicap, or similar challenge; a record of commitment to helping people in need; a plan to apply higher education to helping others; and Washington State residency. May visit Web site: http://www.wstla.org.

Award: Scholarship for use in freshman, sophomore, or junior years; not renewable. *Number:* 1. *Amount:* $2000–$2500.

Eligibility Requirements: Applicant must be enrolled or expecting to enroll full-time at a two-year or four-year institution or university and resident of Washington. Available to U.S. citizens.

Application Requirements: Autobiography, essay, financial need analysis, resume, references, transcript. *Deadline:* March 15.

Contact: Gregg L. Tinker, Chairman
Washington State Trial Lawyers Association
400 Winslow Way East, Suite 230
Bainbridge Island, WA 98110-2402

WSTLA AMERICAN JUSTICE ESSAY SCHOLARSHIP CONTEST

WSTLA is committed to foster an awareness and understanding of the American justice system. The essay contest deals with advocacy in the American justice system and related topics. Three scholarships are available, at the law student, college and high school levels. Topics are selected annually and will be available in September of each school year. May visit Web site at http://www.wstla.org.

Award: Prize for use in freshman, sophomore, junior, senior, or graduate years; not renewable. *Number:* 3. *Amount:* $1000–$3000.

Eligibility Requirements: Applicant must be enrolled or expecting to enroll full or part-time at a two-year or four-year or technical institution or university and studying in Washington. Available to U.S. and non-U.S. citizens.

Application Requirements: Applicant must enter a contest, essay. *Deadline:* March 15.

Contact: Rebecca Parker, Director of Membership and Community Outreach
Washington State Trial Lawyers Association
1809 Seventh Avenue, Suite 1500
Seattle, WA 98101-1328
Phone: 206-464-1011
Fax: 206-464-0703
E-mail: rebecca@wstla.org

WASHINGTON STATE WORKFORCE TRAINING AND EDUCATION COORDINATING BOARD
http://www.wtb.wa.gov/

WASHINGTON AWARD FOR VOCATIONAL EXCELLENCE

Tuition-only award for those completing a vocational education program as graduating seniors or community/technical college students who have completed first year of a two-year program. The scholarship is for 6 quarters or 4 semesters. Three are awarded in each of 49 legislative districts in the state. Must be a Washington State resident attending a postsecondary institution in Washington State.

Award: Grant for use in freshman, sophomore, junior, or senior years; renewable. *Number:* 147. *Amount:* $2445–$5506.

Eligibility Requirements: Applicant must be enrolled or expecting to enroll full or part-time at a two-year or four-year or technical institution or university; resident of Washington and studying in Washington. Available to U.S. and non-U.S. citizens.

Application Requirements: Application, essay, references. *Deadline:* March 1.

Contact: Lee Williams, Program Administrator
Washington State Workforce Training and Education Coordinating Board
128 10th Avenue SW
PO Box 43105
Olympia, WA 98504-3105
Phone: 360-586-3321
Fax: 360-586-5862
E-mail: lwilliams@wtb.wa.gov

WATERBURY FOUNDATION
http://www.conncf.org/

FERRIS ELLIS LITERARY AWARDS

Award for high school students who excel in writing. Deadline is April 1.

Award: Scholarship for use in freshman year. *Amount:* $100–$450.

Eligibility Requirements: Applicant must be high school student; planning to enroll or expecting to enroll at an institution or university; resident of Connecticut; studying in Connecticut and must have an interest in writing. Available to U.S. citizens.

Application Requirements: Application. *Deadline:* April 1.

Contact: Josh Carey, Program Officer
Waterbury Foundation
43 Field Street
Waterbury, CT 06702-1216
Phone: 203-753-1315
Fax: 203-756-3054
E-mail: jcarey@conncf.org

REGIONAL AND RESTRICTED SCHOLARSHIP AWARD PROGRAM

Supports accredited college or university study for residents of the Connecticut Community twenty-one town service area. Regional awards are restricted to Connecticut colleges/universities only. Twenty-five restricted award programs are based on specific fund criteria (residency, ethnicity or course of study).

Award: Scholarship for use in freshman, sophomore, junior, or senior years; renewable. *Number:* 200–250. *Amount:* $250–$5000.

Eligibility Requirements: Applicant must be enrolled or expecting to enroll full or part-time at a two-year or four-year institution or university and resident of Connecticut. Applicant must have 2.5 GPA or higher. Available to U.S. citizens.

Application Requirements: Application, essay, financial need analysis, references, transcript. *Deadline:* March 1.

Contact: Josh Carey, Program Officer
Waterbury Foundation
43 Field Street
Waterbury, CT 06702
Phone: 203-753-1315
Fax: 203-756-3054
E-mail: jcarey@conncf.org

WESTERN GOLF ASSOCIATION-EVANS SCHOLARS FOUNDATION   http://www.evansscholarsfoundation.com

CHICK EVANS CADDIE SCHOLARSHIP
• *See page 552*

WESTERN INTERSTATE COMMISSION FOR HIGHER EDUCATION   http://www.wiche.edu/

WESTERN UNDERGRADUATE EXCHANGE PROGRAM

Residents of Alaska, Arizona, Colorado, Hawaii, Idaho, Montana, Nevada, New Mexico, North Dakota, Oregon, South Dakota, Utah, Washington and Wyoming can enroll in designated two- and four-year undergraduate programs at public institutions in participating states at reduced tuition level (resident tuition plus half). Contact Western Interstate Commission for Higher Education for list and deadlines.

Award: Scholarship for use in freshman, sophomore, junior, or senior years; renewable.

Eligibility Requirements: Applicant must be enrolled or expecting to enroll full or part-time at a two-year or four-year institution; resident of Alaska, Arizona, Colorado, Hawaii, Idaho, Montana, Nevada, New Mexico, North Dakota, Oregon, South Dakota, Utah, Washington, or Wyoming and studying in Alaska, Arizona, Colorado, Hawaii, Idaho, Montana, Nevada, New Mexico, North Dakota, Oregon, South Dakota, or Utah. Available to U.S. citizens.

Application Requirements: Application.

Contact: Sandy Jackson, Program Coordinator
Western Interstate Commission for Higher Education
PO Box 9752
Boulder, CO 80301-9752
Phone: 303-541-0214
Fax: 303-541-0291
E-mail: info-sep@wiche.edu

WILLA CATHER FOUNDATION   http://www.willacather.org

COTTEY/CATHER WRITING PRIZE

Prize awarded for winning entries in one or two categories: poetry, drama, short fiction, or non-fiction. Must be a high school junior or senior, a female, and a resident of Nebraska, Iowa, Missouri, South Dakota, Wyoming or Kansas.

Award: Prize for use in freshman year; not renewable. *Amount:* $200–$3000.

Eligibility Requirements: Applicant must be high school student; planning to enroll or expecting to enroll at an institution or university; female; resident of Iowa, Kansas, Missouri, Nebraska, or Wyoming and must have an interest in writing. Available to U.S. citizens.

Application Requirements: Application. *Deadline:* varies.

Contact: Writing Contest, Cottey College
Willa Cather Foundation
1000 West Austin
Nevada, MO 64772

WILLIAM D. SQUIRES EDUCATIONAL FOUNDATION, INC.   http://www.wmd-squires-foundation.org

WILLIAM D. SQUIRES SCHOLARSHIP

Scholarship award is $3000 per calendar year and is renewable for three additional years under specified conditions. Available to students planning to pursue a degree, certificate or diploma full-time at an accredited college, university, technical or business school. A minimum 3.2 GPA is required.

Award: Scholarship for use in freshman, sophomore, junior, or senior years; renewable. *Amount:* $3000.

Eligibility Requirements: Applicant must be enrolled or expecting to enroll full-time at an institution or university; resident of Ohio and studying in Ohio. Available to U.S. citizens.

Application Requirements: Application, essay, references, transcript. *Deadline:* April 5.

Contact: William D. Squires Educational Foundation, Inc.
PO Box 2940
Jupiter, FL 33468-2940
E-mail: wmdsquires@adelphia.net

WILLIAM F. COOPER SCHOLARSHIP TRUST

WILLIAM F. COOPER SCHOLARSHIP

Scholarship trust to provide financial assistance to women living within the state of Georgia for undergraduate studies. Cannot be used for law, theology or medicine fields of study. Nursing is an approved area of study.

Award: Scholarship for use in freshman, sophomore, junior, or senior years; renewable. *Number:* varies. *Amount:* $1000.

Eligibility Requirements: Applicant must be enrolled or expecting to enroll full or part-time at a four-year institution or university; female and resident of Georgia. Available to U.S. citizens.

Application Requirements: Application, financial need analysis, test scores, transcript, tax info/W-2. *Deadline:* April 1.

Contact: Judge William F. Cooper Scholarship Fund
William F. Cooper Scholarship Trust
4320-G Wade Hampton Boulevard
Taylors, SC 29687
Phone: 866-608-0001
E-mail: sallyking@bellsouth.net

WILLIAM G. AND MARIE SELBY FOUNDATION   http://www.selbyfdn.org

SELBY SCHOLAR PROGRAM

Scholarships awarded up to $5000 annually, not to exceed 1/3 of individual's financial need. Renewable for four years if student is full-time undergraduate at accredited college or university. Must demonstrate values of leadership and service to the community. Must reside in Sarasota, Manatee, Charlotte, or DeSoto counties in Florida.

Award: Scholarship for use in freshman, sophomore, junior, or senior years; renewable. *Number:* 30. *Amount:* up to $5000.

Eligibility Requirements: Applicant must be enrolled or expecting to enroll full-time at a four-year institution or university and resident of Florida. Applicant must have 3.0 GPA or higher. Available to U.S. citizens.

Application Requirements: Application, essay, financial need analysis, interview, references, test scores, transcript. *Deadline:* April 1.

Contact: Jan Noah, Grants Manager
William G. and Marie Selby Foundation
1800 Second Street, Suite 750
Sarasota, FL 34236
Phone: 941-957-0442
Fax: 941-957-3135
E-mail: jnoah@selbyfdn.org

WILLIAM P. WILLIS SCHOLARSHIP

WILLIAM P. WILLIS SCHOLARSHIP

Scholarship for a full-time undergraduate. Must have an annual income of $20,000 or less. Must be an Oklahoma resident.

Award: Scholarship for use in freshman, sophomore, junior, or senior years. *Amount:* up to $2400.

Eligibility Requirements: Applicant must be enrolled or expecting to enroll full-time at a four-year institution or university and resident of Oklahoma. Available to U.S. citizens.

Application Requirements: Application. *Deadline:* April 15.

Contact: Dawn Scott
William P. Willis Scholarship
500 Education Building
State Capitol Complex
Oklahoma City, OK 73105
Phone: 405-524-9153

WILLIS AND MILDRED PELLERIN FOUNDATION

WILLIS AND MILDRED PELLERIN SCHOLARSHIPS

Scholarship is awarded for Louisiana residents to attend an approved Louisiana institution as a full-time undergraduate.

Award: Scholarship for use in freshman, sophomore, junior, or senior years. *Amount:* $300–$650.

Eligibility Requirements: Applicant must be enrolled or expecting to enroll full-time at a four-year institution or university; resident of Louisiana and studying in Louisiana. Available to U.S. citizens.

Application Requirements: Application. *Deadline:* February 1.

Contact: Lynne Hotfelter, Administrative Assistant
Willis and Mildred Pellerin Foundation
PO Box 400
Kenner, LA 70063-0400

WISCONSIN DEPARTMENT OF VETERANS AFFAIRS
http://www.dva.state.wi.us

WISCONSIN DEPARTMENT OF VETERANS AFFAIRS RETRAINING GRANTS
• See page 596

WISCONSIN VETERANS PART-TIME STUDY REIMBURSEMENT GRANT
• See page 596

WISCONSIN HIGHER EDUCATIONAL AIDS BOARD
http://www.heab.state.wi.us

HANDICAPPED STUDENT GRANT-WISCONSIN
• See page 567

MINORITY UNDERGRADUATE RETENTION GRANT-WISCONSIN
• See page 647

TALENT INCENTIVE PROGRAM GRANT

Assists residents of Wisconsin who are attending a nonprofit institution in Wisconsin and have substantial financial need. Must meet income criteria, be considered economically and educationally disadvantaged and be enrolled at least half-time. Please refer to Web site for further details: http://www.heab.state.wi.us

Award: Grant for use in freshman, sophomore, junior, or senior years; renewable. *Number:* varies. *Amount:* $250–$1800.

Eligibility Requirements: Applicant must be enrolled or expecting to enroll full or part-time at a two-year or four-year or technical institution or university; resident of Wisconsin and studying in Wisconsin. Available to U.S. citizens.

Application Requirements: Financial need analysis, nomination. *Deadline:* Continuous.

Contact: John Whitt, Program Coordinator
Wisconsin Higher Educational Aids Board
PO Box 7885
Madison, WI 53707-7885
Phone: 608-266-1665
Fax: 608-267-2808
E-mail: john.whitt@heab.state.wi.us

WISCONSIN ACADEMIC EXCELLENCE SCHOLARSHIP

Renewable award for high school seniors with the highest GPA in graduating class. Must be a Wisconsin resident. Award covers tuition for up to four years. Must maintain 3.0 GPA for renewal. Scholarships of up to $2250 each. Must attend a nonprofit Wisconsin institution full-time. Please refer to Web site for further details: http://www.heab.state.wi.us

Award: Scholarship for use in freshman, sophomore, junior, or senior years; renewable. *Number:* 3445. *Amount:* up to $2250.

Eligibility Requirements: Applicant must be enrolled or expecting to enroll full-time at a two-year or four-year or technical institution or university; resident of Wisconsin and studying in Wisconsin. Applicant must have 3.5 GPA or higher. Available to U.S. citizens.

Application Requirements: Transcript. *Deadline:* Continuous.

Contact: Alice Winters, Program Coordinator
Wisconsin Higher Educational Aids Board
PO Box 7885
Madison, WI 53707-7885
Phone: 608-267-2213
Fax: 608-267-2808
E-mail: alice.winters@heab.state.wi.us

WISCONSIN HIGHER EDUCATION GRANTS (WHEG)

Grants for residents of Wisconsin attending a campus of the University of Wisconsin or Wisconsin Technical College. Must be enrolled at least half-time and show financial need. Please refer to Web site for further details: http://www.heab.state.wi.us

Award: Grant for use in freshman, sophomore, junior, or senior years; not renewable. *Number:* varies. *Amount:* $250–$2500.

Eligibility Requirements: Applicant must be enrolled or expecting to enroll full or part-time at a two-year or four-year or technical institution or university; resident of Wisconsin and studying in Wisconsin. Available to U.S. citizens.

Application Requirements: Application, financial need analysis. *Deadline:* Continuous.

Contact: Sandra Thomas, Program Coordinator
Wisconsin Higher Educational Aids Board
PO Box 7885
Madison, WI 53707-7885
Phone: 608-266-0888
Fax: 608-267-2808
E-mail: sandy.thomas@heab.state.wi.us

WISCONSIN NATIVE AMERICAN/ INDIAN STUDENT ASSISTANCE GRANT
• See page 648

WISCONSIN SCHOOL COUNSELORS ASSOCIATION
http://www.wscaweb.com/

MSCA/TCF BANK SCHOLARSHIP PROGRAM

Award offered for students who are residing in Minnesota and plan to attend a postsecondary institution.

Award: Scholarship for use in freshman year. *Number:* 11. *Amount:* $500.

Eligibility Requirements: Applicant must be high school student; planning to enroll or expecting to enroll full-time at a two-year or four-year or technical institution or university and resident of Minnesota. Available to U.S. and non-U.S. citizens.

Application Requirements: Application, essay. *Deadline:* May.

Contact: Education Financing Center
Wisconsin School Counselors Association
801 Marquette Avenue South
Minneapolis, MN 55402
Phone: 800-247-1092 Ext. 8100

WSCA/TCF BANK SCHOLARSHIP PROGRAM

Scholarship available to high school seniors who are currently attending public or private high school in Wisconsin and plan to attend a postsecondary institution in the fall.

Award: Scholarship for use in freshman year; not renewable. *Amount:* $1000.

Eligibility Requirements: Applicant must be high school student; planning to enroll or expecting to enroll at a two-year or four-year institution or university and resident of Wisconsin. Available to U.S. citizens.

Application Requirements: Application, essay. *Deadline:* February.

Contact: Wisconsin School Counselors Association
300 12th Avenue
PO Box 252
Neenah, WI 54953

WOMEN IN RURAL ELECTIRFICATION (KENTUCKY WIRE)

WOMEN IN RURAL ELECTRIFICATION SCHOLARSHIP

Scholarships available to a junior or senior in a Kentucky college or university whose immediate family is served by one of the state's 24 rural electric distribution cooperatives. Must have at least 60 credit hours by the beginning of the fall semester. Deadline is June 15. See Web site for application: http://www.kaec.org/info/archive06/wire06scholar.htm

Award: Scholarship for use in junior or senior years. *Number:* up to 3. *Amount:* $1000.

Eligibility Requirements: Applicant must be enrolled or expecting to enroll at a four-year institution or university and resident of Kentucky. Available to U.S. citizens.

Application Requirements: Application, financial need analysis, references, transcript. *Deadline:* June 15.

Contact: Ellie Hobgood
Women in Rural Electirfication (Kentucky WIRE)
PO Box 32170
Louisville, KY 40232
Phone: 502-451-2430
Fax: 502-459-3209

WYOMING DEPARTMENT OF EDUCATION

DOUVAS MEMORIAL SCHOLARSHIP

Available to Wyoming residents who are first-generation Americans. Must be between 18-22 years old. Must be used at any Wyoming public institution of higher education for study in freshman year.

Award: Scholarship for use in freshman year; not renewable. *Number:* 1. *Amount:* up to $500.

Eligibility Requirements: Applicant must be age 18-22; enrolled or expecting to enroll at a two-year or four-year institution; resident of Wyoming and studying in Wyoming. Available to U.S. citizens.

Application Requirements: Application. *Deadline:* March 24.

Contact: Bruce Hayes, Consultant
Wyoming Department of Education
2300 Capitol Avenue, Hathaway Building, 2nd Floor
Cheyenne, WY 82002-0050
Phone: 307-777-7690
Fax: 307-777-6234

HATHAWAY SCHOLARSHIP

Scholarship for Wyoming students to pursue postsecondary education within the state.

Award: Scholarship for use in freshman, sophomore, junior, or senior years. *Number:* 1.

Eligibility Requirements: Applicant must be enrolled or expecting to enroll full-time at an institution or university and resident of Wyoming. Available to U.S. citizens.

Application Requirements: Application.

Contact: Gerry Mass
Phone: 307-777-6282

ROBERT C. BYRD HONORS SCHOLARSHIP-WYOMING

Available to Wyoming residents who show outstanding academic ability. Must attend an accredited postsecondary institution, have a minimum 3.8 GPA, and be a high school senior. Renewable award of $1500. Applications are mailed to all high school counselors in the spring.

Award: Scholarship for use in freshman year; renewable. *Number:* 11. *Amount:* $1500.

Eligibility Requirements: Applicant must be high school student; planning to enroll or expecting to enroll full-time at a two-year or four-year institution or university and resident of Wyoming. Available to U.S. citizens.

Application Requirements: Application, essay, test scores, transcript, nomination. *Deadline:* March 24.

Contact: Bruce Hayes, Consultant
Wyoming Department of Education
2300 Capitol Avenue, 2nd Floor
Cheyenne, WY 82002-0050
Phone: 307-777-7690
Fax: 307-777-6234
E-mail: bhayes1@state.wy.us

WYOMING FARM BUREAU FEDERATION　　http://www.wyfb.org

KING-LIVINGSTON SCHOLARSHIP
• See page 523

WYOMING FARM BUREAU CONTINUING EDUCATION SCHOLARSHIPS
• See page 523

WYOMING FARM BUREAU FEDERATION SCHOLARSHIPS
• See page 524

YOUTH OPPORTUNITIES FOUNDATION　　http://www.yoflatinoscholars.com

YOUTH OPPORTUNITIES FOUNDATION SCHOLARSHIPS
• See page 648

TALENT

ALBERTA HERITAGE SCHOLARSHIP FUND/ ALBERTA SCHOLARSHIP PROGRAMS　　http://www.alis.gov.ab.ca

ALBERTA HERITAGE SCHOLARSHIP FUND ALBERTA PRESS COUNCIL SCHOLARSHIP
• See page 601

CHARLES S. NOBLE JUNIOR "A" HOCKEY SCHOLARSHIPS
• See page 602

CHARLES S. NOBLE JUNIOR FOOTBALL SCHOLARSHIPS
• See page 602

EARL AND COUNTESS OF WESSEX-WORLD CHAMPIONSHIPS IN ATHLETICS SCHOLARSHIPS
• See page 656

JIMMIE CONDON ATHLETIC SCHOLARSHIPS
• See page 603

LAURENCE DECOR STUDENT LEADERSHIP AWARDS
• See page 603

PRAIRIE BASEBALL ACADEMY SCHOLARSHIPS
• See page 657

AMERICAN ALLIANCE FOR HEALTH, PHYSICAL EDUCATION, RECREATION AND DANCE　　http://www.aahperd.org

THE RUTH ABERNATHY PRESIDENTIAL SCHOLARSHIP

One graduate and two undergraduate awards given in pursuit of a degree in health, physical education, recreation, or dance disciplines. Applicant must be a current member of AAHPERD.

Award: Scholarship for use in junior, senior, or graduate years; not renewable. *Number:* 2–3. *Amount:* $1000–$1500.

Eligibility Requirements: Applicant must be enrolled or expecting to enroll full-time at a four-year institution or university and must have an interest in leadership. Applicant must have 3.5 GPA or higher. Available to U.S. and non-U.S. citizens.

American Alliance for Health, Physical Education, Recreation and Dance (continued)

Application Requirements: Application, references, transcript. *Deadline:* October 15.

Contact: Debbie Callis, Secretary to Chief Executive Officer
American Alliance for Health, Physical Education, Recreation and Dance
1900 Association Drive
Reston, VA 20191
Phone: 703-476-3405
Fax: 703-476-9537
E-mail: dcallis@aahperd.org

AMERICAN BOWLING CONGRESS   http://www.bowl.com

CHUCK HALL STAR OF TOMORROW SCHOLARSHIP
• *See page 483*

AMERICAN INSTITUTE FOR FOREIGN STUDY   http://www.aifsabroad.com

AMERICAN INSTITUTE FOR FOREIGN STUDY INTERNATIONAL SCHOLARSHIPS

Awards are available to undergraduates on an AIFS study abroad program. Applicants must demonstrate leadership potential, have a minimum 3.0 cumulative GPA and meet program requirements. Submit application by March 15 for summer, April 15 for fall or October 15 for spring. The application fee is $75.

Award: Scholarship for use in freshman, sophomore, junior, or senior years; not renewable. *Number:* up to 150. *Amount:* $1000–$2000.

Eligibility Requirements: Applicant must be age 17; enrolled or expecting to enroll full-time at a two-year or four-year institution or university and must have an interest in leadership. Applicant must have 3.0 GPA or higher. Available to U.S. and non-U.S. citizens.

Application Requirements: Application, essay, photo, references, transcript. *Fee:* $75. *Deadline:* varies.

Contact: David Mauro, Admissions Counselor
American Institute for Foreign Study
River Plaza, 9 West Broad Street
Stamford, CT 06902-3788
Phone: 800-727-2437 Ext. 5163
Fax: 203-399-5598
E-mail: college.info@aifs.com

AMERICAN INSTITUTE FOR FOREIGN STUDY MINORITY SCHOLARSHIPS
• *See page 605*

AMERICAN LEGION, DEPARTMENT OF INDIANA   http://www.indlegion.org

AMERICAN LEGION, DEPARTMENT OF INDIANA STATE ORATORICAL CONTEST
• *See page 661*

FRANK W. MCHALE MEMORIAL SCHOLARSHIPS
• *See page 661*

AMERICAN LEGION, DEPARTMENT OF IOWA   http://www.ialegion.org

ORATORICAL CONTEST SCHOLARSHIP-IOWA
• *See page 661*

AMERICAN LEGION, DEPARTMENT OF KANSAS   http://www.ksamlegion.org

DR. CLICK COWGER BASEBALL SCHOLARSHIP
• *See page 661*

PAUL FLAHERTY ATHLETIC SCHOLARSHIP
• *See page 662*

AMERICAN LEGION, DEPARTMENT OF MICHIGAN   http://www.michiganlegion.org

AMERICAN LEGION DEPARTMENT OF MICHIGAN ORATORICAL CONTEST
• *See page 662*

AMERICAN LEGION, DEPARTMENT OF MINNESOTA   http://www.mnlegion.org

AMERICAN LEGION DEPARTMENT OF MINNESOTA STATE ORATORICAL CONTEST
• *See page 662*

AMERICAN LEGION, DEPARTMENT OF MONTANA   http://www.mtlegion.org

ORATORICAL CONTEST
• *See page 663*

AMERICAN LEGION, DEPARTMENT OF NEW YORK   http://www.ny.legion.org

AMERICAN LEGION DEPARTMENT OF NEW YORK STATE HIGH SCHOOL ORATORICAL CONTEST
• *See page 663*

AMERICAN LEGION, DEPARTMENT OF NORTH DAKOTA   http://www.ndlegion.org

AMERICAN LEGION DEPARTMENT OF NORTH DAKOTA NATIONAL HIGH SCHOOL ORATORICAL CONTEST
• *See page 663*

AMERICAN LEGION, DEPARTMENT OF PENNSYLVANIA   http://www.pa-legion.com

AMERICAN LEGION DEPARTMENT OF PENNSYLVANIA STATE ORATORICAL CONTEST
• *See page 664*

AMERICAN LEGION, DEPARTMENT OF WEST VIRGINIA

AMERICAN LEGION DEPARTMENT OF WEST VIRGINIA STATE ORATORICAL CONTEST
• *See page 665*

AMERICAN LEGION, DEPARTMENT OF WEST VIRGINIA BOARD OF REGENTS SCHOLARSHIP
• *See page 665*

AMERICAN LEGION, NATIONAL HEADQUARTERS   http://www.legion.org

AMERICAN LEGION NATIONAL HEADQUARTERS NATIONAL HIGH SCHOOL ORATORICAL CONTEST

Several prizes awarded to high school students (freshmen through seniors) who give a speech lasting eight to ten minutes on the U.S. Constitution and an assigned topic speech of three to five minutes. Winners advance to higher level. Contact local chapter for entry information. One-time award of $1500-$18,000.

Award: Scholarship for use in freshman, sophomore, junior, senior, or graduate years; not renewable. *Number:* 54. *Amount:* $1500–$18,000.

Eligibility Requirements: Applicant must be high school student; planning to enroll or expecting to enroll full-time at a two-year or four-year institution or university and must have an interest in public speaking. Available to U.S. citizens.

Application Requirements: Application. *Deadline:* December 1.

Contact: Michael Buss, Assistant Director
American Legion, National Headquarters
PO Box 1055
Indianapolis, IN 46206-1055
Phone: 317-630-1249
Fax: 317-630-1369
E-mail: acy@legion.org

AMERICAN MORGAN HORSE INSTITUTE
http://www.morganhorse.com

AMERICAN MORGAN HORSE INSTITUTE EDUCATIONAL SCHOLARSHIPS

Selection is based on the ability and aptitude for serious study, community service, leadership, and financial need. Must be actively involved with registered Morgan horses association. Application deadline varies every year. For information and application go to http://www.morganhorse.com.

Award: Scholarship for use in freshman year; not renewable. *Number:* 5. *Amount:* $3000.

Eligibility Requirements: Applicant must be enrolled or expecting to enroll full or part-time at a two-year or four-year or technical institution or university and must have an interest in designated field specified by sponsor. Available to U.S. and non-U.S. citizens.

Application Requirements: Application, essay, photo, references, transcript. *Deadline:* March 1.

Contact: Application available at Web site.

AMERICAN MORGAN HORSE INSTITUTE GRAND PRIX DRESSAGE AWARD

Award available to riders of registered Morgan horses who reach a certain proficiency at the Grand Prix dressage level. For information and application go to http://www.morganhorse.com. The application deadline varies every year.

Award: Scholarship for use in freshman, sophomore, junior, senior, graduate, or postgraduate years; not renewable. *Number:* 1. *Amount:* $2500.

Eligibility Requirements: Applicant must be enrolled or expecting to enroll full or part-time at a two-year or four-year or technical institution or university and must have an interest in designated field specified by sponsor. Available to U.S. and non-U.S. citizens.

Application Requirements: Application, essay, photo, references, transcript, copy of Horse USDF report. *Deadline:* varies.

Contact: Application available at Web site.

AMERICAN MORGAN HORSE INSTITUTE GRAYWOOD YOUTH HORSEMANSHIP GRANT

Provides a youth who is an active member of the American Morgan Horse Association (AMHA) or an AMHA youth group with the opportunity to further his/her practical study of Morgan horses. For information and application go to http://www.morganhorse.com

Award: Grant for use in freshman year; not renewable. *Number:* 1–2. *Amount:* $300–$500.

Eligibility Requirements: Applicant must be age 13-21; enrolled or expecting to enroll full or part-time at a two-year or four-year or technical institution or university and must have an interest in designated field specified by sponsor. Available to U.S. and non-U.S. citizens.

Application Requirements: Application, essay, photo, references, transcript. *Deadline:* March 1.

Contact: Application available at Web site.

AMERICAN MORGAN HORSE INSTITUTE VAN SCHAIK DRESSAGE SCHOLARSHIP

Awarded to an individual wishing to further their proficiency in classically ridden dressage on a registered Morgan horse. For information and application go to http://www.morganhorse.com. Application deadline varies every year.

Award: Scholarship for use in freshman, sophomore, junior, senior, graduate, or postgraduate years; not renewable. *Number:* 1. *Amount:* $1000.

Eligibility Requirements: Applicant must be enrolled or expecting to enroll full or part-time at a two-year or four-year or technical institution or university and must have an interest in designated field specified by sponsor. Available to U.S. and non-U.S. citizens.

Application Requirements: Application, essay, photo, references, narrative. *Deadline:* November 30.

Contact: Application available at Web site.

AMERICAN SHEEP INDUSTRY ASSOCIATION/ NATIONAL MAKE IT YOURSELF WITH WOOL
http://www.sheepusa.org

NATIONAL "MAKE IT YOURSELF WITH WOOL" COMPETITION

Awards are available for entrants ages 13-24 years. Must enter at state level with home-constructed garment of at least 60% wool. Applicant must model garment. Applications are accepted August through December. $10 fee at time of entry. See Web site at http://www.sheepusa.org for more information.

Award: Prize for use in freshman, sophomore, junior, or senior years; not renewable. *Number:* 2–4. *Amount:* up to $2000.

Eligibility Requirements: Applicant must be age 13-24; enrolled or expecting to enroll full or part-time at a two-year or four-year or technical institution or university and must have an interest in sewing. Available to U.S. citizens.

Application Requirements: Application, applicant must enter a contest, self-addressed stamped envelope, 5 x 5 sample of fabric. *Fee:* $10.

Contact: Marie Lehfeldt, Coordinator
American Sheep Industry Association/National Make It Yourself With Wool
PO Box 175
Lavina, MT 59046
Phone: 406-636-2731
Fax: 406-636-2731

AMERICAN STRING TEACHERS ASSOCIATION
http://www.astaweb.com

NATIONAL SOLO COMPETITION

Twenty-six individual awards totaling $30,000 will be awarded. Instrument categories are violin, viola, cello, double bass, classical guitar, and harp. Applicants competing in Junior Division must be under age 19. Senior Division competitors must be ages 19-25. Application fee is $60. Visit Web site for application forms. Applicant must be a member of ASTA.

Award: Prize for use in freshman, sophomore, junior, senior, or graduate years; not renewable. *Number:* 26. *Amount:* $500–$7000.

Eligibility Requirements: Applicant must be age 25 or under; enrolled or expecting to enroll full-time at an institution or university and must have an interest in music. Available to U.S. and Canadian citizens.

Application Requirements: Application, applicant must enter a contest, proof of age, proof of membership. *Fee:* $60. *Deadline:* varies.

Contact: Michael Carrera, ASTA National Solo Competition, Committee Chair
American String Teachers Association
4153 Chain Bridge Road
Fairfax, VA 22030
Phone: 703-279-2113
Fax: 703-279-2114
E-mail: carrera@ohio.edu

AMERICAN SWEDISH INSTITUTE
http://www.americanswedishinst.org/

LILLY LORENZEN SCHOLARSHIP

One-time award for a Minnesota resident, or student attending a school in Minnesota. Must have a working knowledge of Swedish and present a creditable plan for study in Sweden. Must be a U.S. citizen.

Award: Scholarship for use in freshman, sophomore, junior, senior, graduate, or postgraduate years; not renewable. *Number:* 1. *Amount:* $1500–$2500.

Eligibility Requirements: Applicant must be enrolled or expecting to enroll full or part-time at a two-year or four-year or technical institution or university and must have an interest in Scandinavian language. Available to U.S. citizens.

American Swedish Institute (continued)

Application Requirements: Application, interview, transcript. *Deadline:* May 1.

Contact: Nina Clark, Education Programs Coordinator
American Swedish Institute
2600 Park Avenue
Minneapolis, MN 55407-1090
Phone: 612-870-3374
Fax: 612-871-8682
E-mail: ninac@americanswedishinst.org

MALMBERG SCHOLARSHIP FOR STUDY IN SWEDEN

Award for a U.S. resident interested in Sweden and Swedish-America, who is either a student enrolled in a degree-granting program at an accredited college or university, or a qualified scholar engaged in study or research whose work can be enhanced by study in Sweden. Scholarships are usually granted for a full academic year term (nine months), but can be for study periods of shorter duration.

Award: Scholarship for use in senior, graduate, or postgraduate years; renewable. *Amount:* up to $10,000.

Eligibility Requirements: Applicant must be age 18; enrolled or expecting to enroll full-time at a four-year institution or university and must have an interest in Scandinavian language. Available to U.S. citizens.

Application Requirements: Application, essay, resume, references, letter of invitation from host institution. *Deadline:* November 15.

Contact: Nina Clark, Education Programs Coordinator
American Swedish Institute
2600 Park Avenue
Minneapolis, MN 55407
Phone: 612-871-3374
Fax: 612-871-8682
E-mail: ninac@americanswedishinst.org

AMERICAN THEATRE ORGAN SOCIETY, INC.   http://www.atos.org

AMERICAN THEATRE ORGAN SOCIETY ORGAN PERFORMANCE SCHOLARSHIP

Renewable awards available to students between the ages of 13-27. Must have a talent in music and have an interest in theater organ performance studies (not for general music studies). There are two categories for this scholarship Category A: Organ students studying with professional theatre organ instructors. Category B: Theatre organ students furthering their musical education by working toward a college organ performance degree. Application deadline is April 15.

Award: Scholarship for use in freshman, sophomore, junior, or senior years; renewable. *Number:* 11. *Amount:* $500–$1000.

Eligibility Requirements: Applicant must be age 13-27; enrolled or expecting to enroll full or part-time at a two-year or four-year institution or university and must have an interest in music. Available to U.S. and non-U.S. citizens.

Application Requirements: Application, essay, references. *Deadline:* April 15.

Contact: Carlton B. Smith, Chairperson, Scholarship Program
American Theatre Organ Society, Inc.
2175 North Irwin Street
Indianapolis, IN 46219-2220
Phone: 317-356-1270
Fax: 317-322-9379
E-mail: smith@atos.org

AMERICAN WATER SKI EDUCATIONAL FOUNDATION   http://www.waterskihalloffame.com

AMERICAN WATER SKI EDUCATIONAL FOUNDATION SCHOLARSHIP
• See page 493

AMERICAN-SCANDINAVIAN FOUNDATION   http://www.amscan.org

AMERICAN-SCANDINAVIAN FOUNDATION TRANSLATION PRIZE

Two prizes are awarded for outstanding English translations of poetry, fiction, drama or literary prose originally written in Danish, Finnish, Icelandic, Norwegian or Swedish. One-time award of $2000.

Award: Prize for use in freshman, sophomore, junior, senior, graduate, or postgraduate years; not renewable. *Number:* 2. *Amount:* $2000.

Eligibility Requirements: Applicant must be enrolled or expecting to enroll at an institution or university and must have an interest in Scandinavian language. Available to U.S. citizens.

Application Requirements: Application, applicant must enter a contest, resume. *Deadline:* June 1.

Contact: Ellen McKey, Director of Fellowships and Grants
American-Scandinavian Foundation
58 Park Avenue
New York, NY 10016
Phone: 212-879-9779
Fax: 212-686-2115
E-mail: info@amscan.org

ANGELUS AWARDS STUDENT FILM FESTIVAL   http://www.angelus.org

ANGELUS AWARDS STUDENT FILM FESTIVAL

Student Film Festival grants awards for student films, documentaries and animation that reflect the complexity of the human condition. $10,000 grand prize; all work screened at the Directors Guild of America, Hollywood. Festival entries are open to all undergraduate and graduate students in film schools or universities. No high school entries. All films/videos submitted must be in English, subtitled in English or dubbed in English.

Award: Prize for use in freshman, sophomore, junior, senior, or graduate years; not renewable. *Number:* 5–7. *Amount:* $1500–$10,000.

Eligibility Requirements: Applicant must be enrolled or expecting to enroll full or part-time at a two-year or four-year or technical institution or university and must have an interest in photography/photogrammetry/filmmaking. Available to U.S. and non-U.S. citizens.

Application Requirements: Application, applicant must enter a contest, autobiography, photo, resume, VHS or DVD copy of film, written description of film, proof of college attendance. *Fee:* $25. *Deadline:* July 1.

Contact: Monika Moreno, Director, Angelus Awards
Angelus Awards Student Film Festival
7201 Sunset Boulevard
Los Angeles, CA 90046
Phone: 323-874-6633 Ext. 24
Fax: 323-874-1168
E-mail: monika@angelus.org

APPALACHIAN CENTER AND APPALACHIAN STUDIES ASSOCIATION   http://www.appalachianstudies.org

WEATHERFORD AWARD

One-time award given to the best work of fiction, non-fiction, book, poetry, or short piece about the Appalachian South published in the most recent calendar year. Two awards will be given: one for non-fiction; one for fiction and poetry. Nominations must be received by December 31. Seven copies of the nominated work must be sent to the chair of the award committee.

Award: Prize for use in freshman, sophomore, junior, or senior years; not renewable. *Number:* 2. *Amount:* up to $500.

Eligibility Requirements: Applicant must be enrolled or expecting to enroll at an institution or university and must have an interest in designated field specified by sponsor. Available to U.S. and non-U.S. citizens.

Application Requirements: Application, applicant must enter a contest, nomination, 7 copies of the book. *Deadline:* December 31.

Contact: Gordon McKinney, Chair, Weatherford Award Committee
Appalachian Center and Appalachian Studies Association
College Box 2166
Berea, KY 40404
Phone: 859-985-3000
E-mail: gordon_mckinney@berea.edu

APPALOOSA HORSE CLUB-APPALOOSA YOUTH PROGRAM   http://www.appaloosa.com

APPALOOSA YOUTH EDUCATIONAL SCHOLARSHIPS
• See page 493

ARRL FOUNDATION, INC.   http://www.arrl.org/arrlf/scholgen.html

ALBERT H. HIX, W8AH, MEMORIAL SCHOLARSHIP

One-time award available to students who are licensed as general class or higher amateur radio operators and who live in the West Virginia section or the Roanoke Division or attend postsecondary school in West Virginia section. Minimum GPA of 3.0. Deadline is February 1.

Award: Scholarship for use in freshman, sophomore, junior, or senior years; not renewable. *Number:* 1. *Amount:* $500.

Eligibility Requirements: Applicant must be enrolled or expecting to enroll full-time at a two-year or four-year or technical institution or university and must have an interest in amateur radio. Applicant must have 3.0 GPA or higher. Available to U.S. citizens.

Application Requirements: Application, transcript. *Deadline:* February 1.

Contact: Mary Hobart, Secretary Foundation
ARRL Foundation, Inc.
225 Main Street
Newington, CT 06111-1494
Phone: 860-594-0397
E-mail: k1mmh@arrl.org

ARRL FOUNDATION GENERAL FUND SCHOLARSHIPS

Available to students who are amateur radio operators. Students can be licensed in any class of operators. Nonrenewable award for use in undergraduate years. Multiple awards per year. Contact Amateur Radio Relay League for more information. Deadline is February 1.

Award: Scholarship for use in freshman, sophomore, junior, or senior years; not renewable. *Amount:* $1000.

Eligibility Requirements: Applicant must be enrolled or expecting to enroll full-time at an institution or university and must have an interest in amateur radio. Available to U.S. citizens.

Application Requirements: Application, transcript. *Deadline:* February 1.

Contact: Mary Hobart, Secretary Foundation
ARRL Foundation, Inc.
225 Main Street
Newington, CT 06111-1494
Phone: 860-594-0397
E-mail: k1mmh@arrl.org

ARRL SENATOR BARRY GOLDWATER (K7UGA) SCHOLARSHIP

Scholarship for students who are licensed amateur radio operators, novice minimum. Applicants must be enrolled in a regionally accredited institution. Preference is given to baccalaureate or higher degree candidates. One-time award of $5000.

Award: Scholarship for use in freshman, sophomore, junior, senior, or graduate years; not renewable. *Number:* 1. *Amount:* $5000.

Eligibility Requirements: Applicant must be enrolled or expecting to enroll full-time at a four-year institution or university and must have an interest in amateur radio. Available to U.S. citizens.

Application Requirements: Application, transcript. *Deadline:* February 1.

Contact: Mary Hobart, Secretary Foundation
ARRL Foundation, Inc.
225 Main Street
Newington, CT 06111-4845
Phone: 860-594-0397
E-mail: k1mmh@arrl.org

CENTRAL ARIZONA DX ASSOCIATION SCHOLARSHIP

Award available to students who are licensed amateur radio operators with a technician license. Preference given to residents of Arizona. Graduating high school students will be considered before current college students. Must have 3.2 GPA or above. Deadline is February 1.

Award: Scholarship for use in freshman year; not renewable. *Number:* 1. *Amount:* $500.

Eligibility Requirements: Applicant must be enrolled or expecting to enroll full-time at an institution or university and must have an interest in amateur radio. Applicant must have 3.5 GPA or higher.

Application Requirements: Application, transcript. *Deadline:* February 1.

Contact: Mary Hobart, Secretary Foundation
ARRL Foundation, Inc.
225 Main Street
Newington, CT 06111-1494
Phone: 860-594-0397
E-mail: k1mmh@arrl.org

CHARLES CLARKE CORDLE MEMORIAL SCHOLARSHIP

One-time award for students who are licensed amateur radio operators. Preference given to residents of Georgia and Alabama and students attending school in that region. Must have minimum GPA of 2.5. Deadline is February 1.

Award: Scholarship for use in freshman, sophomore, junior, or senior years; not renewable. *Number:* 1. *Amount:* $1000.

Eligibility Requirements: Applicant must be enrolled or expecting to enroll full-time at an institution or university and must have an interest in amateur radio. Applicant must have 2.5 GPA or higher. Available to U.S. citizens.

Application Requirements: Application, transcript. *Deadline:* February 1.

Contact: Mary Lau, Secretary Foundation
ARRL Foundation, Inc.
225 Main Street
Newington, CT 06111-1494
Phone: 860-594-0397
E-mail: k1mmh@arrl.org

CHICAGO FM CLUB SCHOLARSHIPS

Multiple awards available to students who are licensed amateur radio operators with technician license. Preference given to residents of FCC Ninth Call District (Indiana, Illinois, Wisconsin) who are high school seniors or graduates. Must be U.S. citizen or within 3 months of citizenship. Deadline is February 1.

Award: Scholarship for use in freshman, sophomore, junior, or senior years; not renewable. *Amount:* $500.

Eligibility Requirements: Applicant must be enrolled or expecting to enroll full-time at a two-year or four-year or technical institution and must have an interest in amateur radio. Available to U.S. citizens.

Application Requirements: Application, transcript. *Deadline:* February 1.

Contact: Mary Hobart, Secretary Foundation
ARRL Foundation, Inc.
225 Main Street
Newington, CT 06111-1494
Phone: 860-594-0397
E-mail: k1mmh@arrl.org

EUGENE "GENE" SALLEE, W4YFR MEMORIAL SCHOLARSHIP

Available to students licensed as amateur radio operator technicians. Preference given to residents of Georgia who have a 3.0 GPA or higher. Deadline is February 1.

ARRL Foundation, Inc. (continued)

Award: Scholarship for use in freshman, sophomore, junior, or senior years; not renewable. *Number:* 1. *Amount:* $500.

Eligibility Requirements: Applicant must be enrolled or expecting to enroll full-time at an institution or university and must have an interest in amateur radio. Applicant must have 3.0 GPA or higher. Available to U.S. citizens.

Application Requirements: Application, transcript. *Deadline:* February 1.

Contact: Mary Hobart, Secretary Foundation
ARRL Foundation, Inc.
225 Main Street
Newington, CT 06111-1494
Phone: 860-594-0397
E-mail: k1mmh@arrl.org

FRANCIS WALTON MEMORIAL SCHOLARSHIP

One or more $500 scholarships available to student radio operators with 5 WPM certification. Prefer Illinois resident or resident of ARRL Central Division (IL, IN, WI). Must be pursuing a baccalaureate or higher degree at a regionally accredited institution. Deadline is February 1.

Award: Scholarship for use in freshman, sophomore, junior, senior, or graduate years; not renewable. *Amount:* $500.

Eligibility Requirements: Applicant must be enrolled or expecting to enroll full-time at a four-year institution or university and must have an interest in amateur radio. Available to U.S. citizens.

Application Requirements: Application, transcript. *Deadline:* February 1.

Contact: Mary Hobart, Secretary Foundation
ARRL Foundation, Inc.
225 Main Street
Newington, CT 06111-1494
Phone: 860-594-0397
E-mail: k1mmh@arrl.org

IRARC MEMORIAL/JOSEPH P. RUBINO, WA4MMD, SCHOLARSHIP
• See page 494

K2TEO MARTIN J. GREEN SR. MEMORIAL SCHOLARSHIP

Available to students with a general amateur license for radio operation. Preference given to students from a "ham" operator family. Nonrenewable award for use in undergraduate years. Contact Amateur Radio Relay League for more information.

Award: Scholarship for use in freshman, sophomore, junior, or senior years; not renewable. *Number:* 1. *Amount:* $1000.

Eligibility Requirements: Applicant must be enrolled or expecting to enroll full-time at an institution or university and must have an interest in amateur radio. Available to U.S. citizens.

Application Requirements: Application, transcript. *Deadline:* February 1.

Contact: Mary Hobart, Secretary Foundation
ARRL Foundation, Inc.
225 Main Street
Newington, CT 06111-1494
Phone: 860-594-0397
E-mail: k1mmh@arrl.org

MARY LOU BROWN SCHOLARSHIP

Multiple awards available to students who are general licensed amateur radio operators. Preference given to residents of Alaska, Idaho, Montana, Oregon, and Washington pursuing baccalaureate or higher course of study. GPA of 3.0 or higher. Must demonstrate interest in promoting Amateur Radio Service. Deadline is February 1.

Award: Scholarship for use in freshman, sophomore, junior, senior, or graduate years; not renewable. *Amount:* $2500.

Eligibility Requirements: Applicant must be enrolled or expecting to enroll full-time at a four-year institution or university and must have an interest in amateur radio. Applicant must have 3.0 GPA or higher. Available to U.S. citizens.

Application Requirements: Application, transcript. *Deadline:* February 1.

Contact: Mary Hobart, Secretary Foundation
ARRL Foundation, Inc.
225 Main Street
Newington, CT 06111-1494
Phone: 860-594-0397
E-mail: k1mmh@arrl.org

NEW ENGLAND FEMARA SCHOLARSHIPS

One-time award available to students licensed as amateur radio operator technicians. Applicants must reside in Vermont, Maine, New Hampshire, Rhode Island, Massachusetts, or Connecticut. Contact Amateur Radio Relay League for more information.

Award: Scholarship for use in freshman, sophomore, junior, or senior years; not renewable. *Amount:* $1000.

Eligibility Requirements: Applicant must be enrolled or expecting to enroll full-time at an institution or university and must have an interest in amateur radio. Available to U.S. citizens.

Application Requirements: Application, transcript. *Deadline:* February 1.

Contact: Mary Hobart, Secretary Foundation
ARRL Foundation, Inc.
225 Main Street
Newington, CT 06111-4845
Phone: 860-594-0397
E-mail: k1mmh@arrl.org

NORMAN E. STROHMEIER, W2VRS MEMORIAL SCHOLARSHIP
• See page 667

SIX METER CLUB OF CHICAGO SCHOLARSHIP
• See page 667

TOM AND JUDITH COMSTOCK SCHOLARSHIP

One-time award for high school seniors who are members of the American Radio Relay League. Preference given to residents of Texas and Oklahoma. Must be licensed amateur radio operator. Must be accepted at a two- or four-year institution. Deadline is February 1.

Award: Scholarship for use in freshman year; not renewable. *Number:* 1. *Amount:* $1000.

Eligibility Requirements: Applicant must be high school student; planning to enroll or expecting to enroll full-time at a two-year or four-year institution or university and must have an interest in amateur radio. Available to U.S. citizens.

Application Requirements: Application, transcript. *Deadline:* February 1.

Contact: Mary Hobart, Secretary Foundation
ARRL Foundation, Inc.
225 Main Street
Newington, CT 06111-1494
Phone: 860-594-0397
E-mail: k1mmh@arrl.org

YANKEE CLIPPER CONTEST CLUB, INC. YOUTH SCHOLARSHIP
• See page 494

YOU'VE GOT A FRIEND IN PENNSYLVANIA SCHOLARSHIP
• See page 494

ARTIST'S MAGAZINE   http://www.artistsmagazine.com

ARTIST'S MAGAZINE'S ANNUAL ART COMPETITION

One-time award for any artist winning annual art competition. Five separate categories. Send self-addressed stamped envelope for rules and entry form. Deadline is May 1. Must submit slides of work. Application fee: $12 per slide.

Award: Prize for use in freshman, sophomore, junior, senior, graduate, or postgraduate years; not renewable. *Number:* up to 30. *Amount:* $100–$2500.

Eligibility Requirements: Applicant must be enrolled or expecting to enroll full or part-time at a two-year or four-year or technical institution or university and must have an interest in art. Available to U.S. and non-U.S. citizens.

Application Requirements: Application, applicant must enter a contest, self-addressed stamped envelope. *Fee:* $12. *Deadline:* May 1.

Contact: Terri Boes, Customer Service Representative
Artist's Magazine
4700 East Galbraith Road
Cincinnati, OH 45236
Phone: 513-531-2690 Ext. 1328
Fax: 513-531-0798
E-mail: arts-competition@fwpubs.com

ASSOCIATION FOR WOMEN IN SPORTS MEDIA
http://www.awsmonline.org/

WOMEN IN SPORTS MEDIA SCHOLARSHIP/INTERNSHIP PROGRAM

The top entrant is selected in four categories: writing, copy editing, broadcast, and public relations, who receive a $1000 scholarship, a $500 stipend for housing during their internship, and $250 for travel expenses. Runners-up receive an internship, $500 for housing, and $250 for travel.

Award: Scholarship for use in freshman, sophomore, junior, senior, or graduate years; not renewable. *Number:* 5–10. *Amount:* $1000.

Eligibility Requirements: Applicant must be enrolled or expecting to enroll full-time at a four-year institution or university; female and must have an interest in athletics/sports or writing. Available to U.S. and non-U.S. citizens.

Application Requirements: Application, applicant must enter a contest, essay, interview, portfolio, resume, references. *Fee:* $5. *Deadline:* November 1.

Contact: Jean Tenuta, AWSM Scholarship Chair
Association for Women in Sports Media
9110 32nd Avenue
Kenosha, WI 53142
Phone: 262-697-4043
Fax: 262-697-4043

AUTHOR SERVICES, INC. http://www.writersofthefuture.com

L. RON HUBBARD'S ILLUSTRATORS OF THE FUTURE CONTEST

An ongoing competition for new and amateur artists judged by professional artists. Eligible submissions consist of three science fiction or fantasy illustrations in a black-and-white medium. Quarterly deadlines are December 31, March 30, June 30 and September 30. All entrants retain rights to artwork.

Award: Prize for use in freshman, sophomore, junior, senior, graduate, or postgraduate years; not renewable. *Number:* up to 12. *Amount:* $500–$5000.

Eligibility Requirements: Applicant must be enrolled or expecting to enroll at an institution or university and must have an interest in art. Available to U.S. and non-U.S. citizens.

Application Requirements: Applicant must enter a contest, self-addressed stamped envelope, 3 illustrations. *Deadline:* varies.

Contact: Judy Young, Contest Administrator
Author Services, Inc.
PO Box 3190
Los Angeles, CA 90078
Phone: 323-466-3310
Fax: 323-466-6474
E-mail: contests@authorservicesinc.com

L. RON HUBBARD'S WRITERS OF THE FUTURE CONTEST

An ongoing competition for new and amateur writers judged by professional writers. Eligible submissions are short stories and novelettes of science fiction or fantasy. Quarterly deadlines are December 31, March 31, June 30 and September 30. Visit Web site: http://www.writersofthefuture.com, for contest rules. Inside All entrants retain rights to manuscripts.

Award: Prize for use in freshman, sophomore, junior, senior, graduate, or postgraduate years; not renewable. *Number:* up to 12. *Amount:* $500–$5000.

Eligibility Requirements: Applicant must be enrolled or expecting to enroll full or part-time at an institution or university and must have an interest in writing. Available to U.S. and non-U.S. citizens.

Application Requirements: Applicant must enter a contest, self-addressed stamped envelope, copy of the manuscript. *Deadline:* varies.

Contact: Judy Young, Contest Administrator
Author Services, Inc.
PO Box 1630
Los Angeles, CA 90078
Phone: 323-466-3310
Fax: 323-466-6474
E-mail: contests@authorservicesinc.com

AYN RAND INSTITUTE http://www.aynrand.org

FOUNTAINHEAD COLLEGE SCHOLARSHIP ESSAY CONTEST

Prizes totaling $43,500 awarded to 11th and 12th grades for essays on Ayn Rand's "Fountainhead". Essay should be between 800 and 1600 words. Names of winners will be announced on June 4. Semifinalist and finalist prizes also awarded. All information necessary to enter the contest is available at http://www.aynrand.org/contests.

Award: Prize for use in freshman year; not renewable. *Number:* 251. *Amount:* $50–$10,000.

Eligibility Requirements: Applicant must be high school student; planning to enroll or expecting to enroll at an institution or university and must have an interest in writing. Available to U.S. and non-U.S. citizens.

Application Requirements: Applicant must enter a contest, essay. *Deadline:* April 15.

Contact: Ayn Rand Institute
PO Box 57044
Irvine, CA 92619-7044
E-mail: essay@aynrand.org

BALANCE BAR COMPANY http://www.balance.com/grants/

INDIVIDUALS/TEAMS BALANCE BAR GRANTS

Grants available for athletic activities/course of study that an individual wishes to pursue for heath and fitness goals or for a career. Must submit statement of purpose as to how the grant will be used. Applicant must be 18 years of age or older and U.S. citizens.

Award: Grant for use in freshman, sophomore, junior, senior, graduate, or postgraduate years; not renewable. *Number:* 4. *Amount:* $500–$10,000.

Eligibility Requirements: Applicant must be age 18; enrolled or expecting to enroll at a two-year or four-year or technical institution or university and must have an interest in athletics/sports. Available to U.S. citizens.

Application Requirements: Application, essay. *Deadline:* August 30.

Contact: BALANCE BAR Grants
Balance Bar Company
41 Madison Ave, 5th Floor
New York, NY 10010

BILLIE JEAN KING WTT CHARITIES, INC. http://www.wtt.com

WORLD TEAM TENNIS DONNELLY AWARDS

Awards available for education, tennis development, and/or medical care. One given to student living within 100 miles of one of the World Team Tennis cities, and one given nationally. Updated information, application, and list of current cities is available on Web site. Student must have Type 1 diabetes, be a high school, college, or tournament tennis competitor, show strong character, values, sportsmanship, and community involvement. Demonstrate financial need. Available to males and females in good academic standing. http://www.wtt.com.

Award: Scholarship for use in freshman, sophomore, junior, senior, or graduate years; not renewable. *Number:* varies. *Amount:* $5000.

Eligibility Requirements: Applicant must be age 14-21; enrolled or expecting to enroll full or part-time at a two-year or four-year or technical institution or university and must have an interest in athletics/sports. Available to U.S. citizens.

Billie Jean King WTT Charities, Inc. (continued)

Application Requirements: Application, essay, financial need analysis, references, transcript, proof of competitive tennis play, physician's statement verifying applicant has diabetes. *Deadline:* May 1.

Contact: Diane Stone, c/o Billie Jean King WTT Charities, Donnelly Awards
Billie Jean King WTT Charities, Inc.
1776 Broadway, Suite 600
New York, NY 10019
Phone: 212-586-3422 Ext. 20
E-mail: dstone@wtt.com

BOYS & GIRLS CLUBS OF AMERICA
http://www.bgca.org

BOYS & GIRLS CLUBS OF AMERICA NATIONAL YOUTH OF THE YEAR AWARD
• See page 494

C.O.L.A.G.E.
http://www.colage.org

LEE DUBIN SCHOLARSHIP FUND

This scholarship is available to the sons and daughters of LGBT parents attending college who have a demonstrated ability in and commitment to affecting change in the LGBT community, including working against homophobia, and increasing positive awareness of LGBT families. Maintain a minimum GPA of 2.0.

Award: Scholarship for use in freshman, sophomore, junior, or senior years; not renewable. *Number:* 3–5. *Amount:* $500–$1000.

Eligibility Requirements: Applicant must be enrolled or expecting to enroll full-time at a two-year or four-year or technical institution or university and must have an interest in designated field specified by sponsor or leadership. Available to U.S. citizens.

Application Requirements: Application, essay, financial need analysis, transcript, proof of enrollment. *Deadline:* varies.

Contact: Scholarship Committee
C.O.L.A.G.E.
3543 18th Street, Suite 1
San Francisco, CA 94110
Phone: 415-861-5437
E-mail: colage@colage.org

CALIFORNIA JUNIOR MISS SCHOLARSHIP PROGRAM
http://www.ajm.org/california

CALIFORNIA JUNIOR MISS SCHOLARSHIP PROGRAM
• See page 670

CAP FOUNDATION
http://www.ronbrown.org

RON BROWN SCHOLAR PROGRAM
• See page 608

CENTER FOR SCHOLARSHIP ADMINISTRATION
http://www.scholarshipprograms.org

SOUTH CAROLINA JUNIOR GOLF FOUNDATION SCHOLARSHIP
• See page 672

CHICK AND SOPHIE MAJOR MEMORIAL DUCK CALLING CONTEST
http://stuttgartarkansas.com/contest/future.shtml

CHICK AND SOPHIE MAJOR DUCK CALLING CONTEST

Scholarship awarded to the high school senior who wins the duck calling contest held Thanksgiving Weekend in Stuttgart, Arkansas. $1500 to winner, $500 first runner-up, $300 to second runner-up, $200 to third runner-up. Must be senior in high school and be sponsored by a Ducks Unlimited Chapter or wildlife association chapter. Write for more information, and see Web site: http://www.stuttgartarkansas.com

Award: Scholarship for use in freshman year; not renewable. *Number:* 4. *Amount:* $200–$1500.

Eligibility Requirements: Applicant must be high school student; planning to enroll or expecting to enroll full-time at a two-year or

four-year or technical institution or university and must have an interest in animal/agricultural competition or athletics/sports. Available to U.S. citizens.

Application Requirements: Application, applicant must enter a contest, references. *Deadline:* Continuous.

Contact: Charlie Holt, Committee Chair
Chick and Sophie Major Memorial Duck Calling Contest
9018 Trulock Bay Road
Sherrill, AR 72152
Phone: 870-673-6911
Fax: 870-672-4282

COCA-COLA SCHOLARS FOUNDATION, INC.
http://www.coca-colascholars.org

COCA-COLA SCHOLARS PROGRAM

Awards based on leadership, academic performance, extracurricular activities, employment, and community involvement. Finalists represent every state in the U.S. 40% of the recipients are minorities. Must apply in senior year of high school. Deadline is October 31. Recipient has six years in which to use award. Two hundred $4000 awards and fifty $20,000 awards granted annually. Must apply through Web site: http://www.coca-colascholars.org. Paper applications not offered.

Award: Scholarship for use in freshman, sophomore, junior, or senior years; renewable. *Number:* 250. *Amount:* $4000–$20,000.

Eligibility Requirements: Applicant must be high school student; planning to enroll or expecting to enroll full or part-time at a two-year or four-year or technical institution or university and must have an interest in leadership. Applicant must have 3.0 GPA or higher. Available to U.S. citizens.

Application Requirements: Application, essay, interview, references, test scores, transcript. *Deadline:* October 31.

Contact: Mark Davis, President
Coca-Cola Scholars Foundation, Inc.
PO Box 442
Atlanta, GA 30301-0442
Phone: 800-306-2653
Fax: 404-733-5439
E-mail: scholars@na.ko.com

COLLEGEBOUND FOUNDATION
http://www.collegeboundfoundation.org

HY ZOLET STUDENT ATHLETE SCHOLARSHIP
• See page 676

COLUMBIA 300
http://columbia300.com

COLUMBIA 300 JOHN JOWDY SCHOLARSHIP

Renewable award given to a graduating high school senior who is actively involved in the sport of bowling. Selection based on academic performance and bowling accomplishments. Application deadline is April 1. For further details and an application visit Web site: http://www.columbia300.com/jjowdy.pdf.

Award: Scholarship for use in freshman, sophomore, junior, or senior years; renewable. *Number:* 1. *Amount:* $500.

Eligibility Requirements: Applicant must be high school student; planning to enroll or expecting to enroll full or part-time at a four-year institution and must have an interest in bowling. Applicant must have 3.0 GPA or higher. Available to U.S. citizens.

Application Requirements: Application. *Deadline:* April 1.

Contact: Dale Garner
Columbia 300
Columbia 300, Inc., PO Box 13430
San Antonio, TX 78213
Phone: 800-531-5920

COLUMBIA UNIVERSITY, DEPARTMENT OF MUSIC
http://www.music.columbia.edu

JOSEPH H. BEARNS PRIZE IN MUSIC

The Joseph H. Bearns Prize is open to U.S. citizens between 18 and 25 years of age on January 1st of the competition year, and offers prizes for both short form and long form works of music in order to encourage talented young composers in the U.S.

Award: Prize for use in freshman, sophomore, junior, or senior years; renewable. *Number:* 2. *Amount:* $2000–$3000.

Eligibility Requirements: Applicant must be age 18-25; enrolled or expecting to enroll full or part-time at a two-year or four-year or technical institution or university and must have an interest in music. Available to U.S. citizens.

Application Requirements: Applicant must enter a contest, self-addressed stamped envelope, music score, information regarding prior studies, social security number. *Deadline:* March 15.

Contact: Bearns Prize Committee
Columbia University, Department of Music
2960 Broadway, 621 Dodge Hall, MC# 1813
New York, NY 10027
Phone: 212-854-3825
Fax: 212-854-8191

COMMUNITY FOUNDATION FOR PALM BEACH AND MARTIN COUNTIES, INC.
http://www.yourcommunityfoundation.org

TERRY DARBY MEMORIAL SCHOLARSHIP
• See page 682

CONCERT ARTISTS GUILD
http://www.concertartists.org

CONCERT ARTISTS GUILD COMPETITION

Award for young professional-level classical musicians. Suggested age for instrumentalists and ensembles is under 30, and for singers, under 35. Concert Artists Guild presents and manages prize-winning artists. Winner receives $5000 and a management contract. Runners-up receive management contracts. Submit two tapes. Application fee is $75. Visit Web site for deadline information.

Award: Prize for use in freshman, sophomore, junior, senior, or graduate years; not renewable. *Number:* varies. *Amount:* $5000.

Eligibility Requirements: Applicant must be enrolled or expecting to enroll at an institution or university and must have an interest in music. Available to U.S. and non-U.S. citizens.

Application Requirements: Application, applicant must enter a contest, two tapes. *Fee:* $75. *Deadline:* October 31.

Contact: Amy Frawley, Competition Manager
Concert Artists Guild
850 7th Avenue, Suite 1205
New York, NY 10019-5230
Phone: 212-333-5200 Ext. 14
Fax: 212-977-7149
E-mail: caguild@concertartists.org

CONCORD REVIEW
http://www.tcr.org

RALPH WALDO EMERSON PRIZE

Prize awarded to high school students who have submitted an essay to the Concord Review. Essay must be from 4,000 to 6,000 words with Turabian endnotes and bibliography. Pages must be unformatted. Essay may focus on any historical topic. Please refer to Web site for further details: http://www.tcr.org

Award: Prize for use in freshman year; not renewable. *Number:* varies. *Amount:* up to $3000.

Eligibility Requirements: Applicant must be high school student; planning to enroll or expecting to enroll at an institution or university and must have an interest in writing. Available to U.S. and non-U.S. citizens.

Application Requirements: Application, applicant must enter a contest, essay, self-addressed stamped envelope. *Fee:* $40. *Deadline:* Continuous.

Contact: Will Fitzhugh, Editor
Concord Review
730 Boston Road, Suite 24
Sudbury, MA 01776
Phone: 978-443-0022
E-mail: fitzhugh@tcr.org

CONTEMPORARY RECORD SOCIETY
http://www.crsnews.org

CONTEMPORARY RECORD SOCIETY NATIONAL FESTIVAL FOR THE PERFORMING ARTS SCHOLARSHIP

Renewable award for composers or performing artists who demonstrate a high level of artistic skill. Must submit a copy of work that has not been previously recorded in the United States. $50 application fee required. Submit self-addressed stamped envelope for application.

Award: Scholarship for use in freshman, sophomore, junior, senior, or graduate years; renewable. *Number:* 1. *Amount:* $1900–$5500.

Eligibility Requirements: Applicant must be enrolled or expecting to enroll at an institution or university and must have an interest in music/singing. Available to U.S. citizens.

Application Requirements: References, self-addressed stamped envelope. *Fee:* $95. *Deadline:* May 15.

Contact: Administrative Assistant
Contemporary Record Society
724 Winchester Road
Broomall, PA 19008
Phone: 610-544-5920
Fax: 610-544-5921
E-mail: crsnews@verizon.net

NATIONAL COMPETITION FOR COMPOSERS' RECORDINGS

Work must be non-published and not commercially recorded. First prize is a recording grant. Limit of nine performers and twenty-five minutes. One work may be submitted. Send self-addressed stamped envelope with $3 postage if applicant wants work returned. Application fee is $50. Applicants must send a self-addressed stamped envelope for application. Deadline: March 10.

Award: Prize for use in freshman, sophomore, junior, senior, or graduate years; not renewable. *Number:* 1. *Amount:* $1500–$5000.

Eligibility Requirements: Applicant must be enrolled or expecting to enroll at an institution or university and must have an interest in music/singing. Available to U.S. citizens.

Application Requirements: Application, applicant must enter a contest, autobiography, resume, references, self-addressed stamped envelope. *Fee:* $50. *Deadline:* March 10.

Contact: Administrative Assistant
Contemporary Record Society
724 Winchester Road
Broomall, PA 19008
Phone: 610-544-5920
Fax: 610-544-5921
E-mail: crsnews@verizon.net

CULTURAL SERVICES OF THE FRENCH EMBASSY
http://www.frenchculture.org

TEACHING ASSISTANTSHIP IN FRANCE

Grants support American students as they teach English in the French school system. Must be US Citizen or a Permanent Resident. Must Have working knowledge of French. Have not received a similar grant from the French Government for the last 3 years. For more details, deadlines and applications go to Web site: http://www.frenchculture.org/education/teaching/spcd/index.html

Award: Grant for use in freshman, sophomore, junior, senior, graduate, or postgraduate years; renewable. *Number:* 1000–1500. *Amount:* up to $6750.

Eligibility Requirements: Applicant must be age 20-30; enrolled or expecting to enroll full or part-time at a two-year or four-year or technical institution or university; single and must have an interest in French language. Available to U.S. and Canadian citizens.

Cultural Services of the French Embassy (continued)

Application Requirements: Application, photo, references, self-addressed stamped envelope, transcript. *Deadline:* January 26.

Contact: Meg Merwin, Assistantship Coordinator
Cultural Services of the French Embassy
4101 Reservoir Road
Washington, DC 20007
Phone: 202-944-6294
Fax: 202-944-6268
E-mail: meghan.merwin@diplomatie.fr

DALLAS MORNING NEWS   http://www.dallasnews.com

DALLAS MORNING NEWS ANNUAL TEENAGE CITIZENSHIP TRIBUTE
• See page 540

DIET - LIVE POETS SOCIETY   http://www.geocities.com/diet-lps

NATIONAL HIGH SCHOOL POETRY CONTEST/EASTERDAY POETRY AWARD

Nonrenewable scholarship for high school student interested in writing. Must submit a poem of 20 lines or less. Application deadline varies. For more information visit Web site: http://geocities.com/diet-lps

Award: Scholarship for use in freshman year; not renewable. *Number:* 1. *Amount:* $100–$1000.

Eligibility Requirements: Applicant must be high school student; planning to enroll or expecting to enroll full-time at a two-year or four-year institution or university and must have an interest in English language or writing. Available to U.S. citizens.

Application Requirements: Applicant must enter a contest, self-addressed stamped envelope, poem 20 lines or less. *Deadline:* varies.

Contact: D. Edwards, Editor
DIET - Live Poets Society
PO Box 8841
Turnersville, NJ 08012
Phone: 856-584-1868
E-mail: diet@voicenet.com

DOMENIC TROIANO GUITAR SCHOLARSHIP   http://www.domenictroiano.com/

DOMENIC TROIANO GUITAR SCHOLARSHIP

Scholarship of $1500 is presented annually to a Canadian guitarist who will be pursuing postsecondary guitar education in Canada or elsewhere. Any university, college or private institution guitar program will be funded. The scholarship funds will be forwarded directly to the chosen institution of the winner.

Award: Scholarship for use in freshman, sophomore, junior, or senior years. *Amount:* $1500.

Eligibility Requirements: Applicant must be enrolled or expecting to enroll at a four-year institution or university and must have an interest in music.

Application Requirements: Resume, references, 1-page letter outlining background and reasons why applicant should be considered for the scholarship, 2-song demo of the applicant playing guitar unaccompanied. *Deadline:* October 31.

Contact: Clinton Somerton
Domenic Troiano Guitar Scholarship
c/o Metronome Canada Culture Heritage Foundation
118 Sherbourne Street
Toronto
Canada
Phone: 416-367-0162
Fax: 416-367-1569
E-mail: clinton@domenictroiano.com

DUPONT IN COOPERATION WITH GENERAL LEARNING COMMUNICATIONS   http://www.glcomm.com/dupont

DUPONT CHALLENGE SCIENCE ESSAY AWARDS PROGRAM

Science essay competition. Students must submit an essay of 700 to 1,000 words discussing a scientific or technological development, event, or theory that has captured their interest. For students in grades 7-12. For more details go to Web site: http://www.glcomm.com/dupont

Award: Prize for use in freshman year; not renewable. *Number:* 70. *Amount:* $50–$1500.

Eligibility Requirements: Applicant must be age 12-17; enrolled or expecting to enroll full-time at an institution or university and must have an interest in designated field specified by sponsor or writing. Available to U.S. and Canadian citizens.

Application Requirements: Applicant must enter a contest, essay, official entry form. *Deadline:* January 25.

Contact: Du Pont Challenge Science Essay Awards Program
DuPont in Cooperation with General Learning Communications
900 Skokie Boulevard, Suite 200
Northbrook, IL 60062-4028
Phone: 847-205-3000
Fax: 847-564-8197

ELIE WIESEL FOUNDATION FOR HUMANITY   http://www.eliewieselfoundation.org

ELIE WIESEL PRIZE IN ETHICS ESSAY CONTEST

Applicant must be registered as a full-time junior or senior at a four-year accredited college or university in the United States. Submit student entry form, faculty sponsor form and three copies of essay. Visit Web site (http://www.eliewieselfoundation.org) for application and guidelines. Deadline is early December.

Award: Prize for use in junior or senior years; not renewable. *Number:* up to 5. *Amount:* $500–$5000.

Eligibility Requirements: Applicant must be enrolled or expecting to enroll full-time at a four-year institution or university and must have an interest in writing. Available to U.S. citizens.

Application Requirements: Application, applicant must enter a contest, essay, self-addressed stamped envelope, student entry form, faculty sponsor form.. *Deadline:* December.

Contact: Alex Zolan, Essay Contest Coordinator
Elie Wiesel Foundation for Humanity
529 Fifth Avenue, Suite 1802
New York, NY 10022
Phone: 212-490-7788
Fax: 212-490-6006
E-mail: azolan@eliewieselfoundation.org

EXECUTIVE WOMEN INTERNATIONAL   http://www.executivewomen.org

EXECUTIVE WOMEN INTERNATIONAL SCHOLARSHIP PROGRAM

Competitive award to high school juniors planning careers in any business or professional field of study which requires a four-year college degree. Award is renewable based on continuing eligibility. All awards are given through local chapters of the EWI. Applicant must apply through nearest chapter and live within 100 miles of it. Student must have a sponsoring teacher and school to be considered. For more details visit Web site: http://www.executivewomen.org

Award: Scholarship for use in freshman, sophomore, junior, or senior years; renewable. *Number:* 75–100. *Amount:* $1000–$10,000.

Eligibility Requirements: Applicant must be high school student; planning to enroll or expecting to enroll full-time at a four-year institution or university and must have an interest in designated field specified by sponsor. Applicant must have 2.5 GPA or higher. Available to U.S. and non-U.S. citizens.

Application Requirements: Application, autobiography, interview, references, transcript. *Deadline:* March 1.

Contact: Suzette Smith, Education Manager
Executive Women International
515 South 700 East, Suite 2A
Salt Lake City, UT 84102
Phone: 801-355-2800
Fax: 801-355-2852
E-mail: suzette@executivewomen.org

FINANCIAL SERVICE CENTERS OF AMERICA, INC. http://www.fisca.org

FINANCIAL SERVICE CENTERS OF AMERICA SCHOLARSHIP FUND

The FiSCA Scholarship Program awards cash grants of at least $2000 to two students from each of the 5 geographic regions across the country. Criteria is based on academic achievement, financial need, leadership skills in schools and the community, and an essay written expressly for the competition. Applicant must be single. See Web site for information on the 5 geographic regions and names and addresses of the Regional Chairmen. Applications should be mailed to the appropriate Regional Chairman.

Award: Grant for use in freshman year; not renewable. *Number:* 10–22. *Amount:* $2000.

Eligibility Requirements: Applicant must be high school student; planning to enroll or expecting to enroll full-time at a two-year or four-year institution or university; single and must have an interest in leadership. Available to U.S. citizens.

Application Requirements: Application, essay, financial need analysis, photo, references, transcript. *Deadline:* May 1.

Contact: Regional Chairman

FLEET RESERVE ASSOCIATION http://www.fra.org

FLEET RESERVE ASSOCIATION SCHOLARSHIP
• *See page 499*

FLORIDA WOMEN'S STATE GOLF ASSOCIATION http://www.fwsga.org

FLORIDA WOMEN'S STATE GOLF ASSOCIATION JUNIOR GIRLS' SCHOLARSHIP FUND
• *See page 692*

FORT COLLINS SYMPHONY ASSOCIATION http://www.fcsymphony.org

ADELINE ROSENBERG MEMORIAL PRIZE

Senior Division (25 years or under). Instrumental competitions held in odd numbered years. Piano competitions held in even numbered years. Auditions required. Applicant must submit proof of age and perform a standard concerto. Must be recommended by music teacher. Send self-addressed stamped envelope for application. Fee of $50. 1st place winner receives $6000, 2nd place receives $4000. The two finalists will perform with the Fort Collins Symphony Orchestra.

Award: Prize for use in freshman, sophomore, junior, senior, graduate, or postgraduate years; not renewable. *Number:* 2. *Amount:* $4000–$6000.

Eligibility Requirements: Applicant must be age 25 or under; enrolled or expecting to enroll full or part-time at an institution or university and must have an interest in music/singing. Available to U.S. and non-U.S. citizens.

Application Requirements: Application, applicant must enter a contest, autobiography, references, self-addressed stamped envelope, proof of age. *Fee:* $50. *Deadline:* January 15.

Contact: Sidney Thompson, Chairman of the competition
Fort Collins Symphony Association
PO Box 1963
Fort Collins, CO 80522
Phone: 970-482-4823
Fax: 970-482-4858
E-mail: note@fcsymphony.org

FORT COLLINS SYMPHONY ASSOCIATION YOUNG ARTIST COMPETITION, JUNIOR DIVISION

Junior division (between 12 and 18 years of age on day of competition); piano and instrumental competition held every year. Auditions required. Limited to the first twenty applicants and two alternates per division. Must submit verification of age. Applicant must perform one movement of a standard concerto and be recommended by music teacher. Send self-addressed stamped envelope for application. Fee of $35. Deadline varies.

Award: Prize for use in freshman, sophomore, junior, senior, graduate, or postgraduate years; not renewable. *Number:* 4. *Amount:* $300–$500.

Eligibility Requirements: Applicant must be age 12-18; enrolled or expecting to enroll full or part-time at an institution or university and must have an interest in music/singing. Available to U.S. and non-U.S. citizens.

Application Requirements: Application, applicant must enter a contest, autobiography, references, self-addressed stamped envelope, proof of age. *Fee:* $35.

Contact: Sidney Thompson, Chairman of the competition
Fort Collins Symphony Association
PO Box 1963
Fort Collins, CO 80522
Phone: 970-482-4823
Fax: 970-482-4858
E-mail: note@fcsymphony.org

GAMMA THETA UPSILON-INTERNATIONAL GEOGRAPHIC HONOR SOCIETY http://gtuhonors.org/

GAMMA THETA UPSILON SCHOLARSHIPS

Five scholarships awarded each year to graduate/undergraduate students who have completed at least 3 geography classes. Must rank in upper third of class or have a minimum 3.0 GPA. Must belong to Gamma Theta Upsilon. High school students not eligible.

Award: Scholarship for use in freshman, sophomore, junior, senior, or graduate years; not renewable. *Number:* 7. *Amount:* $500.

Eligibility Requirements: Applicant must be enrolled or expecting to enroll full-time at a two-year or four-year institution or university and must have an interest in designated field specified by sponsor. Applicant must have 3.0 GPA or higher. Available to U.S. and non-U.S. citizens.

Application Requirements: Application. *Deadline:* varies.

Contact: Carol Rosen, GTU President
Gamma Theta Upsilon-International Geographic Honor Society
800 West Main Street
Whitewater, WI 53190
Phone: 262-472-5119
Fax: 262-472-5633
E-mail: rosenc@post.uww.edu

GLENN MILLER BIRTHPLACE SOCIETY http://www.glennmiller.org

GLENN MILLER INSTRUMENTAL SCHOLARSHIP

One-time awards for high school seniors and college freshmen, awarded as competition prizes, to be used for any education-related expense. Must submit ten minute, high-quality audiotape of pieces selected for competition or those of similar style. Applicant is responsible for travel to and lodging at competition.

Award: Scholarship for use in freshman or sophomore years; not renewable. *Number:* 2. *Amount:* $1200–$2400.

Glenn Miller Birthplace Society (continued)

Eligibility Requirements: Applicant must be enrolled or expecting to enroll full-time at a four-year institution or university and must have an interest in music/singing. Available to U.S. and non-U.S. citizens.

Application Requirements: Application, applicant must enter a contest, essay, self-addressed stamped envelope, performance tape/CD. *Deadline:* March 15.

Contact: Arlene Leonard, Secretary
Glenn Miller Birthplace Society
107 East Main Street, PO Box 61
Clarinda, IA 51632-0061
Phone: 712-542-2461
Fax: 712-542-2461
E-mail: gmbs@heartland.net

JACK PULLAN MEMORIAL SCHOLARSHIP

One scholarship for male or female vocalist, awarded as competition prize, to be used for any education-related expense. Must submit ten minute, high-quality audiotape of pieces selected for competition or those of similar style. Applicant is responsible for travel to and lodging at competition. One-time award for high school seniors and college freshmen. More information on http://www.glennmiller.org/scholar.htm

Award: Scholarship for use in freshman or sophomore years; not renewable. *Number:* 1. *Amount:* $1000.

Eligibility Requirements: Applicant must be enrolled or expecting to enroll full-time at a four-year institution or university and must have an interest in music/singing. Available to U.S. and non-U.S. citizens.

Application Requirements: Application, applicant must enter a contest, essay, self-addressed stamped envelope, performance tape. *Deadline:* March 15.

Contact: Arlene Leonard, Secretary
Glenn Miller Birthplace Society
107 East Main Street, PO Box 61
Clarinda, IA 51632-0061
Phone: 712-542-2461
Fax: 712-542-2461
E-mail: gmbs@heartland.net

RALPH BREWSTER VOCAL SCHOLARSHIP

One scholarship for male or female vocalist, awarded as competition prize, to be used for any education-related expense. Must submit ten minute, high-quality audiotape of pieces selected for competition or those of similar style. Applicant is responsible for travel to and lodging at competition. One-time award for high school seniors and college freshmen.

Award: Scholarship for use in freshman or sophomore years; not renewable. *Number:* 1. *Amount:* $2000.

Eligibility Requirements: Applicant must be enrolled or expecting to enroll full-time at a four-year institution or university and must have an interest in music/singing. Available to U.S. and non-U.S. citizens.

Application Requirements: Application, applicant must enter a contest, essay, self-addressed stamped envelope, performance tape of competition or concert quality of up to five minutes duration.. *Deadline:* March 15.

Contact: Arlene Leonard, Secretary
Glenn Miller Birthplace Society
107 East Main Street, PO Box 61
Clarinda, IA 51632-0061
Phone: 712-542-2461
Fax: 712-542-2461
E-mail: gmbs@heartland.net

GOLDEN KEY INTERNATIONAL HONOUR SOCIETY   http://www.goldenkey.org

INTERNATIONAL STUDENT LEADERS AWARD
• See page 500

LITERARY ACHIEVEMENT AWARDS

$1000 will be awarded to winners in each of the following four categories: fiction, non-fiction, poetry, feature writing. Winners may be published in CONCEPTS Magazine. See Web site for more information: http://goldenkey.gsu.edu.

Award: Prize for use in junior, senior, graduate, or postgraduate years; not renewable. *Number:* 4. *Amount:* $1000.

Eligibility Requirements: Applicant must be enrolled or expecting to enroll at an institution or university and must have an interest in writing. Available to U.S. citizens.

Application Requirements: Application, applicant must enter a contest, original composition. *Deadline:* April 1.

Contact: Scholarship Program Administrators
Golden Key International Honour Society
PO Box 23737
Nashville, TN 37202-3737
Phone: 800-377-2401
E-mail: scholarships@goldenkey.org

GRAND RAPIDS COMMUNITY FOUNDATION   http://www.grfoundation.org

GERALD M. CRANE MEMORIAL MUSIC SCHOLARSHIP FUND
• See page 694

GREATER KANAWHA VALLEY FOUNDATION   http://www.tgkvf.org

KID'S CHANCE OF WEST VIRGINIA SCHOLARSHIP
• See page 695

HAPCO MUSIC FOUNDATION, INC.   http://www.hapcopromo.org

TRADITIONAL MARCHING BAND EXTRAVAGANZA SCHOLARSHIP AWARD

Scholarship is offered to deserving students that will continue their participation in any college music program.

Award: Scholarship for use in freshman, sophomore, junior, or senior years. *Amount:* $250–$1000.

Eligibility Requirements: Applicant must be enrolled or expecting to enroll full-time at a four-year institution or university and must have an interest in music. Applicant must have 3.0 GPA or higher. Available to U.S. citizens.

Application Requirements: Application, essay, photo, references, test scores, transcript. *Deadline:* December 31.

Contact: HapCo Music Foundation, Inc.
PO Box 784581
Winter Garden, FL 34778
Phone: 407-877-2262
E-mail: hapcopromo@aol.com

HARNESS HORSE YOUTH FOUNDATION   http://www.hhyf.org

CURT GREENE MEMORIAL SCHOLARSHIP

One-time award with preference given to those under age 24 who have a passion for harness racing. Based on merit, need, and horsemanship or racing experience. Minimum 2.5 GPA required. For study in any field. May reapply.

Award: Scholarship for use in freshman, sophomore, junior, or senior years; not renewable. *Number:* 1–2. *Amount:* $2500.

Eligibility Requirements: Applicant must be age 23 or under; enrolled or expecting to enroll full-time at a two-year or four-year or technical institution or university and must have an interest in animal/agricultural competition. Applicant must have 2.5 GPA or higher. Available to U.S. citizens.

Application Requirements: Application, essay, references, transcript, page 1 of parents' IRS form. *Deadline:* April 30.

Contact: Ellen Taylor, Executive Director
Harness Horse Youth Foundation
16575 Carey Road
Westfield, IN 46074
Phone: 317-867-5877
Fax: 317-867-5896
E-mail: ellen@hhyf.org

HOSTESS COMMITTEE SCHOLARSHIPS/MISS AMERICA PAGEANT
http://www.missamerica.org

MISS AMERICA ORGANIZATION COMPETITION SCHOLARSHIPS

Scholarship competition open to 51 contestants, each serving as state representative. Women will be judged in Private Interview, Swimsuit, Evening Wear and Talent competition. Other awards may be based on points assessed by judges during competitions. Upon reaching the National level, award values range from $5000 to $50,000. Additional awards not affecting the competition can be won with values from $1000 to $10,000. Awards designed to provide contestants with the opportunity to enhance professional and educational goals.

Award: Scholarship for use in freshman, sophomore, junior, senior, or graduate years; not renewable. *Number:* up to 69. *Amount:* $1000–$50,000.

Eligibility Requirements: Applicant must be enrolled or expecting to enroll at a two-year or four-year or technical institution or university; female and must have an interest in beauty pageant. Available to U.S. citizens.

Application Requirements: Applicant must enter a contest.

Contact: See Web site.

HOUSTON SYMPHONY
http://www.houstonsymphony.org

HOUSTON SYMPHONY IMA HOGG YOUNG ARTIST COMPETITION

Competition for musicians 19-29 who play standard instruments of the symphony orchestra. Goal is to offer a review by panel of music professionals and further career of advanced student or professional musician. Participants must be U.S. citizens or studying in the U.S. Application fee is $25.

Award: Prize for use in freshman, sophomore, junior, senior, graduate, or postgraduate years; not renewable. *Number:* 3. *Amount:* $300–$5000.

Eligibility Requirements: Applicant must be age 19-29; enrolled or expecting to enroll full or part-time at a two-year or four-year or technical institution or university and must have an interest in music. Available to U.S. and non-U.S. citizens.

Application Requirements: Application, applicant must enter a contest, cassette/CD with required repertoire. *Fee:* $25. *Deadline:* February 18.

Contact: Carol Wilson, Education Coordinator
Houston Symphony
615 Louisiana
Houston, TX 77002
Phone: 713-238-1447
Fax: 713-224-0453
E-mail: e&o@houstonsymphony.org

INSTITUTE FOR HUMANE STUDIES
http://www.theihs.org

FELIX MORLEY JOURNALISM COMPETITION

Competitors in the Morley Competition are judged on demonstrated writing ability, potential for development as a writer, and appreciation of classical liberal ideas as evidenced in submitted publications. Competition open to young writers and students (25 years and younger).

Award: Prize for use in freshman, sophomore, junior, senior, or graduate years; not renewable. *Number:* 6. *Amount:* $250–$2500.

Eligibility Requirements: Applicant must be age 25 or under; enrolled or expecting to enroll full-time at a two-year or four-year or technical institution or university and must have an interest in writing. Available to U.S. and non-U.S. citizens.

Application Requirements: Application, 3-5 published articles. *Deadline:* December 1.

Contact: Dan Alban, Morley Competition
Institute for Humane Studies
3301 North Fairfax Drive, Suite 440
Arlington, VA 22201-4432
Phone: 703-993-4880
Fax: 703-993-4890
E-mail: ihs@gmu.edu

J. WOOD PLATT CADDIE SCHOLARSHIP TRUST
http://www.gapgolf.org

J. WOOD PLATT CADDIE SCHOLARSHIP TRUST
• See page 544

JANE AUSTEN SOCIETY OF NORTH AMERICA
http://www.jasna.org

JANE AUSTEN SOCIETY OF NORTH AMERICA ESSAY CONTEST

Essay contest with three divisions: high school, college undergraduate, and graduate student. First prize in each division is free trip to conference, or cash equivalent ($750-$1000). Essay topic is posted each winter on the Web site: http://www.jasna.org. Essay must be 1200-2000 words and should contain personal, original insight into Jane Austen's artistry, ideas, and values; not primarily a research paper. Must also include a brief statement of less than 100 words about the teacher or professor who most influenced you to enter the contest. Application and essay deadline is May 1.

Award: Prize for use in freshman, sophomore, junior, senior, graduate, or postgraduate years; not renewable. *Number:* 9. *Amount:* up to $1000.

Eligibility Requirements: Applicant must be enrolled or expecting to enroll full or part-time at a two-year or four-year institution or university and must have an interest in English language or writing. Available to U.S. and non-U.S. citizens.

Application Requirements: Application, applicant must enter a contest, essay, references. *Deadline:* May 1.

Contact: Petrina Morgan, University of Colorado at Denver, Health Sciences Center, Downtown Denver, Campus Box 112
Jane Austen Society of North America
PO Box 173364
Denver, CO 80217-3364
E-mail: janebrs@starband.net

JUNIOR ACHIEVEMENT
http://www.ja.org

HUGH B. SWEENY SCHOLARSHIP

Award recognizes graduating seniors who demonstrate extraordinary results in impacting a community through entrepreneurship and similar initiatives. Must have completed Junior Achievement Company Program or JA Economics.

Award: Scholarship for use in freshman year; not renewable. *Number:* 1. *Amount:* up to $5000.

Eligibility Requirements: Applicant must be high school student; planning to enroll or expecting to enroll full-time at a four-year institution or university and must have an interest in leadership. Applicant must have 3.0 GPA or higher. Available to U.S. citizens.

Application Requirements: Application, essay, financial need analysis, references. *Deadline:* February 1.

Contact: Scholarship Coordinator
Junior Achievement
1 Education Way
Colorado Springs, CO 80906
Phone: 719-540-8000
Fax: 719-540-6299
E-mail: scholarships@ja.org

JUNIOR ACHIEVEMENT JOE FRANCOMANO SCHOLARSHIP
• See page 502

JUNIOR ACHIEVEMENT OFFICE DEPOT SCHOLARSHIP
• See page 502

KINGSBURY CORPORATION
http://www.kingsburycorp.com/

KINGSBURY FUND SCHOLARSHIPS
• See page 531

KOSCIUSZKO FOUNDATION
http://www.kosciuszkofoundation.org

KOSCIUSZKO FOUNDATION TUITION SCHOLARSHIP
• See page 622

KUMU KAHUA THEATRE

KUMU KAHUA THEATER/UHM THEATER DEPARTMENT PLAYWRITING CONTEST, PACIFIC RIM PRIZE

Contest for residents and non-residents of Hawaii. Play must be set in or deal with the Pacific Islands, the Pacific Rim, or the Pacific/Asian-American experience. Restricted to full-length plays of a minimum of 50 pages in standard form. Write for details.

Award: Prize for use in freshman, sophomore, junior, senior, graduate, or postgraduate years; not renewable. *Number:* 1. *Amount:* $450.

Eligibility Requirements: Applicant must be enrolled or expecting to enroll at an institution or university and must have an interest in writing. Available to U.S. and non-U.S. citizens.

Application Requirements: Applicant must enter a contest, 3 copies of manuscript. *Deadline:* January 2.

Contact: Kuma Kahua Playwriting Contest
Kumu Kahua Theatre
46 Merchant Street
Honolulu, HI 96813
E-mail: info@kumukahua.com

LA KELLEY COMMUNICATIONS   http://www.kelleycom.com

ARTISTIC ENDEAVORS SCHOLARSHIP
• See page 560

LADIES AUXILIARY TO THE VETERANS OF FOREIGN WARS   http://www.ladiesauxvfw.com

JUNIOR GIRLS SCHOLARSHIP PROGRAM
• See page 504

YOUNG AMERICAN CREATIVE PATRIOTIC ART AWARDS PROGRAM

One-time awards for high school students in grades 9 through 12. Must submit an original work of art expressing their patriotism. First-place state-level winners go on to national competition. Three awards of varying amounts. Must reside in same state as sponsoring organization.

Award: Scholarship for use in freshman, sophomore, junior, or senior years; not renewable. *Number:* up to 3. *Amount:* $2500–$10,000.

Eligibility Requirements: Applicant must be high school student; planning to enroll or expecting to enroll full-time at a two-year or four-year or technical institution; single and must have an interest in designated field specified by sponsor. Available to U.S. citizens.

Application Requirements: Application, applicant must enter a contest, references, student must be sponsored by a Ladies Auxiliary VFW which is located in the same state as the student attends school. *Deadline:* March 29.

Contact: Judith Millick, Administrator of Programs
Ladies Auxiliary to the Veterans of Foreign Wars
406 West 34th Street
Kansas City, MO 64111
Phone: 816-561-8655
Fax: 816-931-4753
E-mail: info@ladiesauxvfw.com

LEE-JACKSON EDUCATIONAL FOUNDATION   http://www.lee-jackson.org

LEE-JACKSON EDUCATIONAL FOUNDATION SCHOLARSHIP COMPETITION
• See page 704

LIEDERKRANZ FOUNDATION   http://www.liederkranznycity.org

LIEDERKRANZ FOUNDATION SCHOLARSHIP AWARD FOR VOICE

Non-renewable awards for voice for both full- and part-time study. Those studying general voice must be between ages 20 to 35 years old while those studying Wagnerian voice must be between ages 25 to 45 years old. Application fee: $40. Applications not available before August/September. Deadline: November 15.

Award: Scholarship for use in freshman, sophomore, junior, senior, or graduate years; not renewable. *Number:* 14–18. *Amount:* $1000–$5000.

Eligibility Requirements: Applicant must be age 20-45; enrolled or expecting to enroll full or part-time at an institution or university and must have an interest in music/singing. Available to U.S. and non-U.S. citizens.

Application Requirements: Application, applicant must enter a contest, driver's license, self-addressed stamped envelope, proof of age. *Fee:* $35. *Deadline:* November 15.

Contact: Cynthia M. Kessel, Administrative Assistant
Liederkranz Foundation
6 East 87th Street
New York, NY 10128
Phone: 212-534-0880
Fax: 212-828-5372

LINCOLN COMMUNITY FOUNDATION   http://www.lcf.org

GEORGE WATTERS-NEBRASKA PETROLEUM MARKETERS ASSOCIATION SCHOLARSHIP
• See page 544

MIRIAM CROFT MOELLER CITIZENSHIP AWARD
• See page 705

LOS ANGELES PHILHARMONIC   http://www.laphil.org

BRONISLAW KAPER AWARDS FOR YOUNG ARTISTS
• See page 706

MARTIN D. ANDREWS SCHOLARSHIP   http://mdascholarship.tripod.com

MARTIN D. ANDREWS MEMORIAL SCHOLARSHIP FUND

One-time award for student seeking undergraduate or graduate degree. Recipient must have been in a Drum Corp for at least three years. Must submit essay and two recommendations. Must be U.S. citizen.

Award: Scholarship for use in freshman, sophomore, junior, senior, graduate, or postgraduate years; not renewable. *Number:* 2–5. *Amount:* $300–$1000.

Eligibility Requirements: Applicant must be enrolled or expecting to enroll full or part-time at a two-year or four-year institution or university and must have an interest in drum corps. Available to U.S. citizens.

Application Requirements: Application, essay, references. *Deadline:* April 1.

Contact: Peter D. Andrews
Martin D. Andrews Scholarship
2069 Perkins Street
Bristol, CT 06010
Phone: 860-673-2929
E-mail: mdandrewsscholarship@address.com

MARY ROBERTS RINEHART FUND   http://www.creativewriting.gmu.edu

MARY ROBERTS RINEHART AWARDS

One-time award available to individuals with excellent writing ability. Applicants do not have to be enrolled in an educational institution but must be nominated by a writing teacher, a recognized writer, an editor, or a publisher. Please send self-addressed stamped envelope for guidelines or visit Web site at http://www.gmu.edu/departments/writing. Grants are only for unpublished works in fiction, nonfiction or poetry. Entries must be postmarked by November 30.

Award: Prize for use in freshman, sophomore, junior, senior, graduate, or postgraduate years; not renewable. *Number:* 3. *Amount:* up to $2000.

Eligibility Requirements: Applicant must be enrolled or expecting to enroll full or part-time at an institution or university and must have an interest in writing. Available to U.S. and non-U.S. citizens.

Application Requirements: Applicant must enter a contest, autobiography, references, self-addressed stamped envelope, nomination, manuscript. *Deadline:* November 30.

Contact: William Miller, Director
Mary Roberts Rinehart Fund
4400 University Drive, MSN 3E4, George Mason University
Fairfax, VA 22030-4444
Phone: 703-993-1180
E-mail: writing@gmu.edu

MCCURRY FOUNDATION, INC.
http://www.mccurryfoundation.org

MCCURRY FOUNDATION SCHOLARSHIP

Scholarship open to all public high school seniors, with preference given to applicants from Clay, Duval, Nassau, and St. Johns Counties, Florida and from Glynn County, Georgia. Scholarship emphasizes leadership, work ethic, and academic excellence. A minimum GPA of 3.0 is required and family income cannot exceed a maximum of $75,000 (AGI).

Award: Scholarship for use in freshman year; not renewable. *Number:* 1. *Amount:* varies.

Eligibility Requirements: Applicant must be high school student; planning to enroll or expecting to enroll full-time at a two-year or four-year or technical institution or university and must have an interest in leadership. Applicant must have 3.0 GPA or higher. Available to U.S. citizens.

Application Requirements: Application, essay, financial need analysis, interview, resume, references, transcript, report card, tax return. *Deadline:* March 31.

Contact: Scholarship Selection Committee
McCurry Foundation, Inc.
11645 Beach Boulevard, Suite 200
Jacksonville, FL 32246
Phone: 904-645-6555

MINNESOTA HIGHER EDUCATION SERVICES OFFICE
http://www.getreadyforcollege.org

MINNESOTA ACADEMIC EXCELLENCE SCHOLARSHIP
• *See page 715*

MISS AMERICAN COED PAGEANTS, INC.

MISS AMERICAN COED PAGEANT

Awards available for girls ages 3-22. Must be single and maintain a 3.0 GPA where applicable. Prizes are awarded by age groups. Winners of state competitions may compete at the national level. Application fee would vary for each state between $25 to $35 and will be refunded if not accepted into competition. Deadline varies each year.

Award: Prize for use in freshman year; not renewable. *Number:* varies. *Amount:* varies.

Eligibility Requirements: Applicant must be age 3-22; enrolled or expecting to enroll full or part-time at a two-year or four-year institution or university; single female and must have an interest in beauty pageant. Applicant must have 3.0 GPA or higher. Available to U.S. citizens.

Application Requirements: Application, applicant must enter a contest, transcript. *Fee:* $35. *Deadline:* varies.

Contact: George Scarborough, National Director
Miss American Coed Pageants, Inc.
3695 Wimbledon Drive
Pensacola, FL 32504-4555
Phone: 850-432-0069
Fax: 850-469-8841
E-mail: amerteen@aol.com

NATIONAL ASSOCIATION FOR CAMPUS ACTIVITIES
http://www.naca.org

LORI RHETT MEMORIAL SCHOLARSHIP
• *See page 720*

MULTICULTURAL SCHOLARSHIP PROGRAM
• *See page 625*

NATIONAL ASSOCIATION FOR CAMPUS ACTIVITIES EAST COAST UNDERGRADUATE SCHOLARSHIP FOR STUDENT LEADERS
• *See page 720*

NATIONAL ASSOCIATION FOR CAMPUS ACTIVITIES REGIONAL COUNCIL STUDENT LEADER SCHOLARSHIPS

Scholarships will be given to undergraduate students in good standing at the time of the application and during the academic term in which the scholarship is awarded. Must demonstrate significant leadership skill and ability while holding a significant leadership position on campus.

Award: Scholarship for use in freshman, sophomore, junior, or senior years; not renewable. *Number:* up to 7. *Amount:* $250–$300.

Eligibility Requirements: Applicant must be enrolled or expecting to enroll at a four-year institution or university and must have an interest in leadership. Available to U.S. citizens.

Application Requirements: Application, essay, resume, references, transcript. *Deadline:* May 1.

Contact: Dionne Ellison, Administrative Assistant
National Association for Campus Activities
13 Harbison Way
Columbia, SC 29212-3401
Phone: 803-732-6222
Fax: 803-749-1047
E-mail: dionnee@naca.org

NATIONAL ASSOCIATION FOR CAMPUS ACTIVITIES SOUTHEAST REGION STUDENT LEADERSHIP SCHOLARSHIP
• *See page 720*

NATIONAL ASSOCIATION FOR CAMPUS ACTIVITIES WI REGION STUDENT LEADERSHIP SCHOLARSHIP
• *See page 720*

SCHOLARSHIPS FOR STUDENT LEADERS

Scholarships will be awarded to undergraduate students in good standing at the time of the application and who, during the academic term in which the scholarship is awarded, hold a significant leadership position on their campus. Must make significant contributions to their campus communities and demonstrate leadership skills and abilities. Applicants must submit two letters of recommendation and a description of the applicant's leadership activities, skills, and abilities.

Award: Scholarship for use in freshman, sophomore, junior, or senior years; not renewable. *Number:* up to 6. *Amount:* $250–$300.

Eligibility Requirements: Applicant must be enrolled or expecting to enroll at a two-year or four-year institution or university and must have an interest in leadership. Available to U.S. citizens.

Application Requirements: Application, resume, references, transcript. *Deadline:* November 1.

Contact: Dionne Ellison, Administrative Assistant
National Association for Campus Activities
13 Harbison Way
Columbia, SC 29212-3401
Phone: 803-732-6222
Fax: 803-749-1047
E-mail: dionnee@naca.org

TESS CALDARELLI MEMORIAL SCHOLARSHIP
• *See page 721*

ZAGUNAS STUDENT LEADERS SCHOLARSHIP
• *See page 721*

NATIONAL ASSOCIATION OF SECONDARY SCHOOL PRINCIPALS
http://www.principals.org

PRINCIPAL'S LEADERSHIP AWARD

One-time award available to high school seniors only, for use at an accredited two- or four-year college or university. Based on leadership and school or community involvement. Application fee: $6. Deadline is December 2. Contact school counselor or principal. Citizens of countries other than the U.S. may only apply if they are attending a United States overseas institution. Minimum GPA 3.0.

Award: Scholarship for use in freshman year; not renewable. *Number:* 100. *Amount:* $1000.

National Association of Secondary School Principals (continued)

Eligibility Requirements: Applicant must be high school student; planning to enroll or expecting to enroll full-time at a two-year or four-year institution or university and must have an interest in leadership. Applicant must have 3.0 GPA or higher. Available to U.S. citizens.

Application Requirements: Application, essay, references, test scores, transcript. *Fee:* $6. *Deadline:* December 2.

Contact: local school principal or guidance counselor

NATIONAL FEDERATION OF STATE POETRY SOCIETIES (NFSPS)   http://www.nfsps.com

NATIONAL FEDERATION OF STATE POETRY SOCIETIES SCHOLARSHIP AWARDS- COLLEGE/UNIVERSITY LEVEL POETRY COMPETITION

Must submit application and ten original poems, forty-line per-poem limit. Manuscript must be titled. For more information, visit the Web site.

Award: Scholarship for use in freshman, sophomore, junior, or senior years; not renewable. *Number:* 2. *Amount:* $500.

Eligibility Requirements: Applicant must be enrolled or expecting to enroll at a two-year or four-year institution or university and must have an interest in writing. Available to U.S. citizens.

Application Requirements: Application, applicant must enter a contest, must be notarized. *Deadline:* February 1.

Contact: Colwell Snell, Chairman
National Federation of State Poetry Societies (NFSPS)
3444 South Dover Terrace, PO Box 520698
Salt Lake City, UT 84152-0698
Phone: 801-484-3113
E-mail: sbsenior@juno.com

NATIONAL MINORITY JUNIOR GOLF SCHOLARSHIP ASSOCIATION   http://www.nmjgsa.org

NATIONAL MINORITY JUNIOR GOLF SCHOLARSHIP
• See page 625

NATIONAL SYMPHONY ORCHESTRA EDUCATION PROGRAM   http://www.kennedy-center.org

NATIONAL SYMPHONY ORCHESTRA YOUNG SOLOISTS' COMPETITION- BILL CERRI SCHOLARSHIP/COLLEGE DIVISION

Prize for the best soloist in competition. Winner will perform with the National Symphony Orchestra in Washington, D.C. Must be a college student attending school or residing in D.C. metropolitan area. $15 application fee. Visit Web site for guidelines and deadlines. Pianists and instrumentalists must be no older than 23, singers must be no older than 26.

Award: Prize for use in freshman, sophomore, junior, or senior years; not renewable. *Number:* 1. *Amount:* $1000.

Eligibility Requirements: Applicant must be enrolled or expecting to enroll at an institution or university and must have an interest in music/singing. Available to U.S. and non-U.S. citizens.

Application Requirements: Application, applicant must enter a contest. *Fee:* $15. *Deadline:* February 3.

Contact: Sharyn L. Byer, Competition Administrator
National Symphony Orchestra Education Program
115 Gresham Place
Falls Church, VA 22046

NATIONAL SYMPHONY ORCHESTRA YOUNG SOLOISTS' COMPETITION- BILL CERRI SCHOLARSHIP/HIGH SCHOOL DIVISION
• See page 722

NATIONAL WOMEN'S STUDIES ASSOCIATION   http://www.nwsa.org

ABAFAZI-AFRICANA WOMEN'S STUDIES ESSAY AWARD
• See page 626

NORTHEASTERN LOGGERS' ASSOCIATION, INC.   http://www.loggertraining.com

NORTHEASTERN LOGGERS' ASSOCIATION SCHOLARSHIPS
• See page 509

OHIO PARTNERS IN CHARACTER EDUCATION   http://www.charactereducationohio.org

LAWS OF LIFE CONTEST:
• See page 733

OMAHA SYMPHONY GUILD   http://www.omahasymphony.org

OMAHA SYMPHONY GUILD INTERNATIONAL NEW MUSIC COMPETITION

One-time award for those 25 and over for the best composition of symphony music. Prize also includes possible performance of winning composition by the Omaha Symphony Chamber Orchestra. Submit two copies of score with application. Application fee $30.

Award: Prize for use in junior, senior, graduate, or postgraduate years; not renewable. *Number:* 1. *Amount:* up to $3000.

Eligibility Requirements: Applicant must be age 25; enrolled or expecting to enroll full or part-time at a two-year or four-year or technical institution or university and must have an interest in music/singing. Available to U.S. and non-U.S. citizens.

Application Requirements: Application, applicant must enter a contest. *Fee:* $30. *Deadline:* April 15.

Contact: Tim Dickmeyer, Touring and Education Coordinator
Omaha Symphony Guild
1605 Howard Street
Omaha, NE 68102-2705
Phone: 402-342-3836 Ext. 107
Fax: 402-342-3819
E-mail: tdickmeyer@omahasymphony.org

ORANGE COUNTY COMMUNITY FOUNDATION   http://www.heef.org

FUTURE LEADERS OF AMERICA SCHOLARSHIP

Scholarships awarded to graduating high school seniors who have demonstrated community leadership by volunteering at least 30 hours at a community-based non-profit organization. Deadline is February 13.

Award: Scholarship for use in freshman year; not renewable. *Number:* 1–2. *Amount:* up to $1000.

Eligibility Requirements: Applicant must be high school student; planning to enroll or expecting to enroll at an institution or university and must have an interest in leadership. Available to U.S. citizens.

Application Requirements: Application, essay, self-addressed stamped envelope, transcript. *Deadline:* February 13.

Contact: Rose Garris, Hispanic Education Endowment Fund
Orange County Community Foundation
30 Corporate Park, Suite 410
Irvine, CA 92606
Phone: 949-543-4202 Ext. 23
Fax: 949-553-4211

OREGON COMMUNITY FOUNDATION   http://www.ocf1.org/

DOROTHY S. CAMPBELL MEMORIAL SCHOLARSHIP FUND

Scholarship for female graduates of Oregon high schools with a strong and continuing interest in the game of golf. For use in the pursuit of a postsecondary education at a four-year college or university in Oregon.

Award: Scholarship for use in freshman, sophomore, junior, or senior years. *Number:* 1.

Eligibility Requirements: Applicant must be enrolled or expecting to enroll at a four-year institution or university; female and must have an interest in golf. Available to U.S. citizens.

Application Requirements: *Deadline:* varies.

Contact: Dianne Causey, Program Associate for Scholarships/Grants
Oregon Community Foundation
1221 South West Yamhill, Suite 100
Portland, OR 97205
Phone: 503-227-6846
Fax: 503-274-7771
E-mail: info@ocf1.org

OREGON STUDENT ASSISTANCE COMMISSION · http://www.osac.state.or.us

DOROTHY CAMPBELL MEMORIAL SCHOLARSHIP
• *See page 736*

JOSE D. GARCIA MIGRANT EDUCATION SCHOLARSHIP
• *See page 737*

OUR WORLD UNDERWATER SCHOLARSHIP SOCIETY · http://www.owuscholarship.org/

OUR WORLD UNDERWATER SCHOLARSHIPS

Annual award for individual planning to pursue a career in a water-related discipline through practical exposure to various fields and leaders of underwater endeavors. Scuba experience required. Must be at least 21 but not yet 25 by March 1. Application fee is $25.

Award: Scholarship for use in freshman, sophomore, junior, senior, or graduate years; not renewable. *Number:* 1. *Amount:* up to $20,000.

Eligibility Requirements: Applicant must be age 21-24; enrolled or expecting to enroll full-time at a two-year or four-year or technical institution or university and must have an interest in scuba diving. Available to U.S. and non-U.S. citizens.

Application Requirements: Application, autobiography, essay, interview, resume, references, transcript, diver certification. *Fee:* $25. *Deadline:* November 30.

Contact: Scholarship Application Coordinator
Our World Underwater Scholarship Society
PO Box 4428
Chicago, IL 60680-4428
Phone: 800-969-6690
Fax: 630-969-6690
E-mail: info@owuscholarship.org

PI LAMBDA THETA, INC. · http://www.pilambda.org

NADEEN BURKEHOLDER WILLIAMS MUSIC SCHOLARSHIP
• *See page 550*

PIRATE'S ALLEY FAULKNER SOCIETY · http://www.wordsandmusic.org/

WILLIAM FAULKNER-WILLIAM WISDOM CREATIVE WRITING COMPETITION

Talent search for unpublished manuscripts written in English. One prize awarded in each category: $7500, novel; $2500, novella; $2000 novel-in-progress; $1500, short story; $1000, essay; $750, poem; $750 high school short story-student author, $250 sponsoring teacher. Manuscripts will not be returned, must be mailed, not emailed or faxed, and accompanied by entry fee ranging from $10 for high school category to $35 for novel. Must get entry form from Web site: http://www.wordsandmusic.org or request by mail. Deadline for submission of entry form, manuscript, and entry fee is April 1.

Award: Prize for use in freshman, sophomore, junior, senior, graduate, or postgraduate years; not renewable. *Number:* 7. *Amount:* $250–$7500.

Eligibility Requirements: Applicant must be enrolled or expecting to enroll at a two-year or four-year institution or university and must have an interest in English language or writing. Available to U.S. and non-U.S. citizens.

Application Requirements: Application, applicant must enter a contest, manuscript, entry fee. *Deadline:* April 1.

Contact: Rosemary James, Writing Competition Coordinator
Pirate's Alley Faulkner Society
632 Pirate's Alley
New Orleans, LA 70116-3254
Phone: 504-586-1612
Fax: 504-522-9725
E-mail: faulkhouse@aol.com

PONY OF THE AMERICAS CLUB · http://www.poac.org

PONY OF THE AMERICAS SCHOLARSHIP
• *See page 513*

PRO BOWLERS ASSOCIATION · http://www.pba.com

BILLY WELU BOWLING SCHOLARSHIP

Scholarship awarded annually, recognizing exemplary qualities in male and female college students who compete in the sport of bowling.

Award: Scholarship for use in freshman, sophomore, junior, or senior years; not renewable. *Number:* 1. *Amount:* $1000.

Eligibility Requirements: Applicant must be enrolled or expecting to enroll full-time at a two-year or four-year institution or university and must have an interest in bowling. Applicant must have 2.5 GPA or higher. Available to U.S. citizens.

Application Requirements: Application, essay, references, transcript. *Deadline:* May 31.

Contact: Karen Day, Controller
Pro Bowlers Association
719 Second Avenue, Suite 701
Seattle, WA 98104
Phone: 206-654-6002
Fax: 206-654-6030
E-mail: karen.day@pba.com

PROFESSIONAL BOWLERS ASSOCIATION · http://www.pba.com

PROFESSIONAL BOWLERS ASSOCIATION BILLY WELU MEMORIAL SCHOLARSHIP
• *See page 513*

QUEEN ELISABETH INTERNATIONAL MUSIC COMPETITION OF BELGIUM · http://www.qeimc.be

QUEEN ELISABETH COMPETITION

Various prizes and awards available. Competitions, which vary from year to year, are in the following: piano, singing, violin, and composition. Award for 1st place in piano 20,000 Euros, in singing 20,000 Euros, and composition 7500 Euros. Age limits vary for each competition. Application fee is 55 Euros. Available to U.S. and Canadian citizens. Visit Web site for complete information, requirements and applications. Deadline January 15. Composition competition will be held in 2006, piano competition will be held in 2007.

Award: Prize for use in freshman, sophomore, junior, senior, graduate, or postgraduate years; not renewable. *Number:* varies. *Amount:* $1206–$24,125.

Eligibility Requirements: Applicant must be enrolled or expecting to enroll at a four-year institution or university and must have an interest in music or music/singing. Available to U.S. and non-U.S. citizens.

Application Requirements: Application, applicant must enter a contest, photo. *Fee:* $55. *Deadline:* January 15.

Contact: Michel-Etienne Van Neste, Secretary General
Queen Elisabeth International Music Competition of Belgium
Rue Aux Lanes 20
Brussels 1000
Belgium
Phone: 32-2-2134050
Fax: 32-2-5143297
E-mail: info@qeimc.be

QUILL AND SCROLL FOUNDATION
http://www.uiowa.edu/~quill-sc

QUILL AND SCROLL INTERNATIONAL WRITING/PHOTO CONTEST

One-time contest for best journalistic writing/reporting and photographs in several categories. Only high school students may enter. Winners receive gold key in addition to being eligible to apply for journalism scholarships. Contact Quill and Scroll for more details and application. Application fee: $2 per entry.

Award: Prize for use in freshman year; not renewable. *Number:* up to 12. *Amount:* $500.

Eligibility Requirements: Applicant must be high school student; planning to enroll or expecting to enroll at an institution or university and must have an interest in photography/photogrammetry/filmmaking or writing. Available to U.S. and non-U.S. citizens.

Application Requirements: Application, applicant must enter a contest, essay, photo. *Fee:* $2. *Deadline:* February 5.

Contact: Richard Johns, Executive Director
Quill and Scroll Foundation
312 WSSH, School of Journalism
Iowa City, IA 52242-1528
Phone: 319-335-3321
Fax: 319-335-5210
E-mail: quill-scroll@uiowa.edu

RECORDING FOR THE BLIND & DYSLEXIC
http://www.rfbd.org

MARION HUBER LEARNING THROUGH LISTENING AWARDS
• See page 513

MARY P. OENSLAGER SCHOLASTIC ACHIEVEMENT AWARDS
• See page 513

RESERVE OFFICERS ASSOCIATION OF THE US
http://www.roa.org

HENRY J. REILLY MEMORIAL SCHOLARSHIP-HIGH SCHOOL SENIORS AND FIRST YEAR FRESHMEN
• See page 514

RHODE ISLAND FOUNDATION
http://www.rifoundation.org

EDWARD LEON DUHAMEL FREEMASONS SCHOLARSHIP

Scholarship provides tuition support to descendants of members of the Franklin Lodge of Freemasons in Westerly, Rhode Island. Applicants must be descendants of a member of Franklin Lodge or descendants of other freemasons in Rhode Island.

Award: Scholarship for use in freshman, sophomore, junior, or senior years; renewable. *Number:* 2–4. *Amount:* $500–$1000.

Eligibility Requirements: Applicant must be enrolled or expecting to enroll full-time at a four-year institution or university and must have an interest in designated field specified by sponsor. Available to U.S. citizens.

Application Requirements: Application, essay, financial need analysis, self-addressed stamped envelope, transcript. *Deadline:* May 19.

Contact: Libby Monahan, Scholarship Coordinator
Rhode Island Foundation
1 Union Station
Providence, RI 02903
Phone: 401-274-4564
Fax: 401-272-1359
E-mail: libbym@rifoundation.org

MJSA EDUCATION FOUNDATION JEWELRY SCHOLARSHIP

Scholarships are available for undergraduate or graduate students enrolled in tool making, design, metals fabrication or other jewelry related courses of study at accredited colleges, universities or nonprofit technical schools on the postsecondary level in the U.S.

Award: Scholarship for use in freshman, sophomore, junior, senior, or graduate years; renewable. *Number:* varies. *Amount:* $500–$2000.

Eligibility Requirements: Applicant must be enrolled or expecting to enroll full-time at a four-year or technical institution or university and must have an interest in designated field specified by sponsor. Available to U.S. citizens.

Application Requirements: Application, essay, financial need analysis, self-addressed stamped envelope, transcript. *Deadline:* June 1.

Contact: Scholarship Coordinator
Rhode Island Foundation
1 Union Station
Providence, RI 02903
Phone: 401-274-4564
Fax: 401-272-1359

ROTARY FOUNDATION OF ROTARY INTERNATIONAL
http://www.rotary.org

ROTARY FOUNDATION ACADEMIC-YEAR AMBASSADORIAL SCHOLARSHIPS

One-time award funds travel, tuition, room and board for one academic year of study in foreign country. Applicant must have completed at least two years of university course work and be proficient in language of host country. Application through local Rotary club; appearances before clubs required during award period. Deadlines vary (March-August). See Web site at http://www.rotary.org for updated information.

Award: Scholarship for use in freshman, sophomore, junior, senior, graduate, or postgraduate years; not renewable. *Number:* 750–1000. *Amount:* up to $26,000.

Eligibility Requirements: Applicant must be enrolled or expecting to enroll full or part-time at a four-year institution or university and must have an interest in foreign language. Available to U.S. and non-U.S. citizens.

Application Requirements: Application, autobiography, essay, interview, resume, references, transcript. *Deadline:* varies.

Contact: Scholarship Program
Rotary Foundation of Rotary International
1560 Sherman Avenue
Evanston, IL 60201
Phone: 847-866-4459
E-mail: scholarshipinquiries@rotary.org

ROTARY MULTI-YEAR AMBASSADORIAL SCHOLARSHIPS

Awarded for two years (depending on availability through sponsoring Rotary district) of degree-oriented study in another country. Applicant must have completed at least two years of university course work and be proficient in language of host country. Application through local Rotary club. Appearances before clubs required during award period. Application deadlines vary between March and August. See Web site at http://www.rotary.org for updated information.

Award: Scholarship for use in junior, senior, or graduate years; not renewable. *Number:* 100–150. *Amount:* $26,000.

Eligibility Requirements: Applicant must be enrolled or expecting to enroll full-time at a four-year institution or university and must have an interest in foreign language. Available to U.S. and Canadian citizens.

Application Requirements: Application, autobiography, essay, interview, resume, references, transcript. *Deadline:* varies.

Contact: Scholarship Program
Rotary Foundation of Rotary International
1560 Sherman Avenue
Evanston, IL 60201
Phone: 847-866-4459

SAN FRANCISCO FOUNDATION
http://www.sff.org

JOSEPH HENRY JACKSON LITERARY AWARD
• See page 743

SCIENCE SERVICE, INC.
http://www.sciserv.org/

DISCOVERY CHANNEL YOUNG SCIENTIST CHALLENGE

Scholarship for students in the fifth through eighth grade to be used for future college enrollment. Must participate in a science fair. For additional information, visit Web site at http://www.discovery.com/dysc

Award: Scholarship for use in freshman year; not renewable. *Number:* up to 40. *Amount:* $500–$20,000.

Eligibility Requirements: Applicant must be enrolled or expecting to enroll full-time at a four-year institution or university and must have an interest in designated field specified by sponsor. Available to U.S. citizens.

Application Requirements: Application, applicant must enter a contest, essay, references. *Deadline:* varies.

Contact: Michele Glidden, DCYSC Program Manager
Science Service, Inc.
1719 N Street, NW
Washington, DC 20036
Phone: 202-785-2255
Fax: 202-785-1243
E-mail: mglidden@sciserv.org

INTEL INTERNATIONAL SCIENCE AND ENGINEERING FAIR

Culminating event in a series of local, regional, and state science fairs. Students in ninth through twelfth grades must compete at local fairs in order to be nominated for international competition. Awards include scholarships. Visit Web site for more information: http://www.sciserv.org.

Award: Scholarship for use in freshman, sophomore, junior, or senior years. *Amount:* $500–$50,000.

Eligibility Requirements: Applicant must be high school student; planning to enroll or expecting to enroll full-time at a four-year institution or university and must have an interest in designated field specified by sponsor. Available to U.S. and non-U.S. citizens.

Application Requirements: Application, applicant must enter a contest, essay, interview. *Deadline:* varies.

Contact: Intel ISEF Program Manager
Science Service, Inc.
1719 N Street, NW
Washington, DC 20036
Phone: 202-785-2255
Fax: 202-785-1243

INTEL SCIENCE TALENT SEARCH

Science competition for high school seniors. Students must submit an individually researched project. Forty finalists will be chosen to attend Science Talent Institute in Washington, DC to exhibit their project and compete for $100,000 four-year scholarship. For more information, visit Web site: http://www.sciserv.org

Award: Scholarship for use in freshman, sophomore, junior, or senior years; renewable. *Number:* 40. *Amount:* $1000–$100,000.

Eligibility Requirements: Applicant must be high school student; planning to enroll or expecting to enroll full-time at a four-year institution or university and must have an interest in designated field specified by sponsor. Available to U.S. citizens.

Application Requirements: Application, applicant must enter a contest, essay, references, test scores, transcript. *Deadline:* varies.

Contact: Intel STS Program Manager
Science Service, Inc.
1719 N Street, NW
Washington, DC 20036
Phone: 202-785-2255
Fax: 202-785-1243
E-mail: kstafford@sciserv.org

SEVENTEEN MAGAZINE http://www.seventeen.com

SEVENTEEN MAGAZINE FICTION CONTEST

Applicants must submit original fiction stories of no more than 2000 words typed, double-spaced, single side of paper. Name, address, birth date in upper right corner. One-time award. Applicant must be between 13 and 21 years old, as of July 30. Applicant must apply by mail.

Award: Prize for use in freshman, sophomore, junior, senior, or graduate years; not renewable. *Number:* 8. *Amount:* $50–$1000.

Eligibility Requirements: Applicant must be age 13-21; enrolled or expecting to enroll at an institution or university and must have an interest in writing. Available to U.S. citizens.

Application Requirements: Applicant must enter a contest, copy of story. *Deadline:* December 31.

Contact: Seventeen, 2006 Fiction Contest
Seventeen Magazine
1440 Broadway, 13th Floor
New York, NY 10018
Phone: 917-934-6500

SIGMA DELTA CHI FOUNDATION OF WASHINGTON, D.C. http://www.spj.org/washdcpro

SIGMA DELTA CHI SCHOLARSHIPS
• See page 744

SINFONIA FOUNDATION http://www.sinfonia.org

SINFONIA FOUNDATION SCHOLARSHIP

Award to assist the collegiate members and chapters of Sinfonia in their endeavors. Must be a collegiate member at least two years. Submit a short essay (250 words or less) on "Sinfonia." Minimum 3.3 cumulative GPA required.

Award: Scholarship for use in freshman, sophomore, junior, senior, or graduate years; not renewable. *Number:* up to 4. *Amount:* up to $500.

Eligibility Requirements: Applicant must be enrolled or expecting to enroll full-time at a four-year institution or university and must have an interest in music. Available to U.S. citizens.

Application Requirements: Application, essay, references, transcript. *Deadline:* May 1.

Contact: Cheri Faith Spicer, Administrative Coordinator
Sinfonia Foundation
10600 Old State Road
Evansville, IN 47711-1399
Phone: 812-867-2433
E-mail: lyrecrest@sinfonia.org

SISTER KENNY REHABILITATION INSTITUTE http://www.allina.com/

INTERNATIONAL ART SHOW FOR ARTISTS WITH DISABILITIES
• See page 565

SOCIETY OF DAUGHTERS OF THE UNITED STATES ARMY

SOCIETY OF DAUGHTERS OF THE UNITED STATES ARMY SCHOLARSHIPS
• See page 575

SOUTH DAKOTA BOARD OF REGENTS http://www.sdbor.edu

SOUTH DAKOTA BOARD OF REGENTS MARLIN R. SCARBOROUGH MEMORIAL SCHOLARSHIP
• See page 745

SOUTHERN TEXAS PGA http://www.stpga.com

BYRON NELSON SCHOLARSHIP

One-time award of $1000 will be made on an annual basis to encourage and promote higher education goals for youth who have demonstrated a high level of achievement during high school or college, have financial need, and have shown an interest in the game of golf.

Award: Scholarship for use in freshman, sophomore, junior, senior, graduate, or postgraduate years; renewable. *Number:* 1. *Amount:* $1000.

Eligibility Requirements: Applicant must be enrolled or expecting to enroll at a two-year or four-year institution or university and must have an interest in golf. Available to U.S. citizens.

Southern Texas PGA (continued)

Application Requirements: Application, financial need analysis, test scores, transcript.

Contact: Eddie Dey, STPGA Foundation Scholarship Program Administrator
Southern Texas PGA
1830 South Millbend Drive, Suite A
The Woodlands, TX 77380-0967
Phone: 281-419-7421
Fax: 281-419-1842
E-mail: stexas@pgahq.com

DICK FORESTER COLLEGE SCHOLARSHIP

One-time award of $4,000 to encourage and promote the attainment of higher education goals for youth who have demonstrated a high level of achievement during high school or college, have financial need, and have shown an interest in the game of golf.

Award: Scholarship for use in freshman, sophomore, junior, senior, graduate, or postgraduate years; not renewable. *Number:* 1. *Amount:* $4000.

Eligibility Requirements: Applicant must be enrolled or expecting to enroll at a two-year or four-year institution or university and must have an interest in golf. Available to U.S. citizens.

Application Requirements: Application, financial need analysis, test scores, transcript. *Deadline:* April 4.

Contact: Eddie Dey, STPGA Foundation Scholarship Program Administrator
Southern Texas PGA
1830 South Millbend Drive, Suite A
The Woodlands, TX 77380-0967
Phone: 281-419-7421
Fax: 281-419-1842
E-mail: stexas@pgahq.com

HARDY LAUDERMILK SCHOLARSHIP
• See page 745

JOE FINGER SCHOLARSHIP

One-time award of $1000 will be made on an annual basis to encourage and promote higher education goals for youth who have demonstrated a high level of achievement during high school or college, have financial need, and have shown an interest in the game of golf.

Award: Scholarship for use in freshman, sophomore, junior, senior, graduate, or postgraduate years. *Number:* 1. *Amount:* $1000.

Eligibility Requirements: Applicant must be enrolled or expecting to enroll at a two-year or four-year institution or university and must have an interest in golf. Available to U.S. citizens.

Application Requirements: Application, financial need analysis, test scores, transcript.

Contact: Eddie Dey, STPGA Foundation Scholarship Program Administrator
Southern Texas PGA
1830 South Millbend Drive, Suite A
The Woodlands, TX 77380-0967
Phone: 281-419-7421
Fax: 281-419-1842
E-mail: stexas@pgahq.com

JOE MOORE SCHOLARSHIP

One-time award of $1000 will be made to applicants on a annual basis to encourage and promote higher education goals for youth who have demonstrated a high level of achievement during high school or college, have financial need, and have shown an interest in the game of golf.

Award: Scholarship for use in freshman, sophomore, junior, senior, graduate, or postgraduate years. *Number:* 1. *Amount:* $1000.

Eligibility Requirements: Applicant must be enrolled or expecting to enroll at a two-year or four-year institution or university and must have an interest in golf. Available to U.S. citizens.

Contact: Eddie Dey, STPGA Foundation Scholarship Program Administrator
Southern Texas PGA
1830 South Millbend Drive, Suite A
The Woodlands, TX 77380-0967
Phone: 281-419-7421
Fax: 281-419-1842
E-mail: stexas@pgahq.com

STONEHOUSE PUBLISHING COMPANY
http://www.stonehousegolf.com

STONEHOUSE GOLF YOUTH SCHOLARSHIP

Twenty scholarships will be awarded based on the criteria of: academics, golf accomplishments, and community service participation. Seniors who have played at least two years on their high school golf team and have earned a GPA of at least 3.5 are eligible to apply. Applicants must participate in the Stonehouse Calendar Fundraiser to be eligible.

Award: Scholarship for use in freshman year; not renewable. *Number:* 20. *Amount:* $500–$10,000.

Eligibility Requirements: Applicant must be high school student; planning to enroll or expecting to enroll full-time at a two-year or four-year institution or university and must have an interest in golf. Applicant must have 3.5 GPA or higher. Available to U.S. citizens.

Application Requirements: Application, references, self-addressed stamped envelope, test scores, transcript. *Deadline:* May 1.

Contact: Patrick Drickey, Program Director
Stonehouse Publishing Company
1508 Leavenworth Street
Omaha, NE 68102
Phone: 402-341-7273
Fax: 402-344-3563
E-mail: pdrickey@stonehousegolf.com

SWISS BENEVOLENT SOCIETY OF NEW YORK
http://www.swissbenevolentny.com

MEDICUS STUDENT EXCHANGE
• See page 635

TEXAS TENNIS FOUNDATION
http://texastennisfoundation.com

TEXAS TENNIS FOUNDATION SCHOLARSHIPS AND ENDOWMENTS
• See page 750

TKE EDUCATIONAL FOUNDATION
http://www.tkefoundation.org

ALL-TKE ACADEMIC TEAM RECOGNITION AND JOHN A. COURSON TOP SCHOLAR AWARD
• See page 516

CANADIAN TKE SCHOLARSHIP
• See page 516

CHARLES WALGREEN, JR. SCHOLARSHIP
• See page 516

DONALD A. FISHER MEMORIAL SCHOLARSHIP
• See page 516

DWAYNE R. WOERPEL MEMORIAL LEADERSHIP AWARD
• See page 516

ELMER AND DORIS SCHMITZ SR. MEMORIAL SCHOLARSHIP
• See page 517

EUGENE C. BEACH MEMORIAL SCHOLARSHIP
• See page 517

J. RUSSEL SALSBURY MEMORIAL SCHOLARSHIP
• See page 517

MICHAEL J. MORIN MEMORIAL SCHOLARSHIP
• See page 517

MILES GRAY MEMORIAL SCHOLARSHIP
• See page 517

RONALD REAGAN LEADERSHIP AWARD
• *See page 517*

T.J. SCHMITZ SCHOLARSHIP
• *See page 518*

WALLACE MCCAULEY MEMORIAL SCHOLARSHIP
• *See page 518*

WILLIAM V. MUSE SCHOLARSHIP
• *See page 518*

WILLIAM WILSON MEMORIAL SCHOLARSHIP
• *See page 518*

TOURO SYNAGOGUE FOUNDATION
http://www.tourosynagogue.org/

AARON AND RITA SLOM SCHOLARSHIP FUND FOR FREEDOM AND DIVERSITY

Scholarship available for high school seniors who plan to enroll in an institute of higher learning for a minimum of 6 credits. Entries should consist of a completed application and an interpretative work focusing on the Historic George Washington Letter to the congregation in context with the present time. Text of the letter is available on our Web site. Submissions may be written: essays, stories, poems; or audio-visual: films, videos, or computer presentations. Applications, guidelines, resource materials are available on Web site: http://www.tourosynagogue.org

Award: Scholarship for use in freshman year; not renewable. *Number:* 2. *Amount:* $500.

Eligibility Requirements: Applicant must be high school student; planning to enroll or expecting to enroll full or part-time at a two-year or four-year or technical institution or university and must have an interest in writing. Available to U.S. citizens.

Application Requirements: Application, interpretative work based on Historic George Washington Letter. *Deadline:* April 1.

Contact: Michael Balaban, Executive Director/CEO
Touro Synagogue Foundation
85 Touro Street
Newport, RI 02840
Phone: 401-847-4794 Ext. 31
Fax: 401-845-6790
E-mail: michael@tourosynagogue.org

ULMAN CANCER FUND FOR YOUNG ADULTS
http://www.ulmanfund.org/

MESSAGE OF HOPE AWARD

Essay contest for the Message of Hope Award. Submissions can be made through our Message of Hope application on our Web site.

Award: Scholarship for use in freshman, sophomore, junior, or senior years.

Eligibility Requirements: Applicant must be enrolled or expecting to enroll full or part-time at an institution or university and must have an interest in writing. Available to U.S. citizens.

Application Requirements: Application. *Deadline:* April 1.

Contact: Fay Baker, Scholarship Coordinator
Ulman Cancer Fund for Young Adults
4725 Dorsey Hall Drive, Suite A
PO Box 505
Ellicott City, MD 21042
Phone: 410-964-0202
Fax: 410-964-0402
E-mail: scholarship@ulmanfund.org

USA BADMINTON REGION 1
http://www.northeastbadminton.net

BADMINTON SCHOLARSHIP PROGRAM

Award to a collegiate varsity badminton player exhibiting outstanding achievement, participation, and performance during the badminton playing season.

Award: Scholarship for use in freshman, sophomore, junior, or senior years; not renewable. *Number:* 1. *Amount:* $1000.

Eligibility Requirements: Applicant must be enrolled or expecting to enroll at an institution or university and must have an interest in athletics/sports. Available to U.S. citizens.

Application Requirements: Application, references. *Deadline:* varies.

Contact: Eric Miller, USA Badminton Program
USA Badminton Region 1
125 Prospect Street
Phoenixville, PA 19460
E-mail: scholarship@northeastbadminton.net

USA TODAY/GOT MILK?
http://www.whymilk.com

SCHOLAR ATHLETE MILK MUSTACHE OF THE YEAR

One-time award for senior high school athletes who also achieve in academics, community service, and leadership. Open to legal residents of the 48 contiguous United States and District of Columbia. Residents of Hawaii, Alaska, and Puerto Rico are not eligible. Must submit essay of 75 words, or less on how drinking milk has been a part of their life and training regimen. Application only through Web site: http://www.whymilk.com

Award: Scholarship for use in freshman year; not renewable. *Number:* 25. *Amount:* $7500.

Eligibility Requirements: Applicant must be high school student; planning to enroll or expecting to enroll full-time at a four-year institution or university and must have an interest in athletics/sports or leadership. Available to U.S. citizens.

Application Requirements: Application, applicant must enter a contest, essay, references, transcript. *Deadline:* March 3.

Contact: Debbie McGovern
USA Today/Got Milk?
6701 Democracy Boulevard, Suite 300
Bethesda, MD 20817
Phone: 800-828-4414

VETERANS OF FOREIGN WARS OF THE UNITED STATES
http://www.vfw.org

PATRIOT'S PEN

Nationwide essay contest that gives students in grades six, seven and eight the opportunity to write essays expressing their views on democracy.

Award: Prize for use in freshman year. *Amount:* $1000–$10,000.

Eligibility Requirements: Applicant must be high school student; planning to enroll or expecting to enroll at an institution or university and must have an interest in writing. Available to U.S. citizens.

Application Requirements: Application, essay.

Contact: Kris Harmer, Secretary
Veterans of Foreign Wars of the United States
VFW Building
406 West 34th Street
Kansas City, MO 64111
Phone: 816-968-1117
Fax: 816-968-1149
E-mail: kharmer@vfw.org

VSA ARTS
http://www.vsarts.org

VSA ARTS PLAYWRIGHT DISCOVERY AWARD

One-time award for students in grades 6-12 with and without disabilities. One-act script must explore the experience of living with a disability. One script is selected for production and one is selected for a staged reading at the

VSA arts (continued)

John F. Kennedy Center for the Performing Arts. A jury of theater professionals selects the winning scripts, and award recipients receive monetary awards and a trip to Washington, D.C. to view the reading or production.

Award: Scholarship for use in freshman year; not renewable. *Number:* 2. *Amount:* $1000.

Eligibility Requirements: Applicant must be enrolled or expecting to enroll at an institution or university and must have an interest in writing. Available to U.S. citizens.

Application Requirements: Application, applicant must enter a contest, autobiography, two copies of typed script. *Deadline:* April 14.

Contact: Elena Widder, Director of Performing Arts
VSA arts
818 Connecticut Avenue, NW, Suite 600
Washington, DC 20006
Phone: 800-933-8721
Fax: 202-737-0725
E-mail: info@vsarts.org

W. EUGENE SMITH MEMORIAL FUND, INC. http://www.smithfund.org

W. EUGENE SMITH GRANT IN HUMANISTIC PHOTOGRAPHY

One-time award for a photojournalist whose past work and proposed project follows the humanistic tradition of W. Eugene Smith. Financed by Nikon, Inc.

Award: Grant for use in junior, senior, graduate, or postgraduate years; not renewable. *Number:* varies. *Amount:* $2500–$30,000.

Eligibility Requirements: Applicant must be enrolled or expecting to enroll at an institution or university and must have an interest in photography/photogrammetry/filmmaking. Available to U.S. and non-U.S. citizens.

Application Requirements: Application, essay, portfolio, resume, self-addressed stamped envelope. *Deadline:* July 15.

Contact: Suzanne Nicholas, c/o ICP
W. Eugene Smith Memorial Fund, Inc.
1133 Avenue of Americas
New York, NY 10036
Phone: 212-857-9720

WASHINGTON CROSSING FOUNDATION http://www.gwcf.org

WASHINGTON CROSSING FOUNDATION SCHOLARSHIP

Renewable, merit-based awards available to high school seniors who are planning a career in government service. Must write an essay stating reason for deciding on a career in public service. Minimum 3.0 GPA required. Write for details.

Award: Scholarship for use in freshman, sophomore, junior, or senior years; renewable. *Number:* 5–10. *Amount:* $1000–$20,000.

Eligibility Requirements: Applicant must be high school student; planning to enroll or expecting to enroll full-time at a four-year institution and must have an interest in designated field specified by sponsor. Applicant must have 3.0 GPA or higher. Available to U.S. citizens.

Application Requirements: Application, essay, references, test scores, transcript. *Deadline:* January 15.

Contact: Eugene Fish, Vice Chairman
Washington Crossing Foundation
PO Box 503
Levittown, PA 19058-0503
Phone: 215-949-8841

WATERBURY FOUNDATION http://www.conncf.org/

FERRIS ELLIS LITERARY AWARDS
• See page 756

WELSH SOCIETY OF PHILADELPHIA

CYMDEITHAS GYMREIG/PHILADELPHIA SCHOLARSHIP
• See page 647

WHOMENTORS.COM, INC. http://www.whomentors.com/

GENERATION "E" GRANTS AND SCHOLARSHIPS

Five awards of $1000 to encourage both full-time and part-time students of at least 21 years of age to obtain formal mentor education and competency certification and to seek designation as an appointed mentor. Applicants should have a specific interest in mentoring. Contact for further information.

Award: Grant for use in freshman, sophomore, junior, senior, or graduate years; not renewable. *Number:* 5. *Amount:* $1000.

Eligibility Requirements: Applicant must be age 17-21; enrolled or expecting to enroll full or part-time at a four-year institution or university and must have an interest in designated field specified by sponsor. Available to U.S. citizens.

Application Requirements: Application, autobiography, interview, photo, self-addressed stamped envelope, test scores, transcript. *Deadline:* May 31.

Contact: Rauhmel Fox Robinson, President and CEO
WHOmentors.com, Inc.
110 Pacific Avenue, Suite 250
San Francisco, CA 94111
Phone: 888-946-6368
E-mail: rauhmel@whomentors.com

WILLA CATHER FOUNDATION http://www.willacather.org

COTTEY/CATHER WRITING PRIZE
• See page 757

WILLIAM RANDOLPH HEARST FOUNDATION http://www.hearstfdn.org/

UNITED STATES SENATE YOUTH PROGRAM

For high school juniors and seniors holding elected student offices. Must attend high school in state of parents' or guardians' legal residence. Two students selected from each state and the selection process will vary by state. Contact school principal or state department of education for information. Application deadline is in the early fall of each year for most states but the actual date will vary by state. Program is open to citizens and permanent residents of the United States Department of Defense schools overseas and the District of Columbia (not the territories). More information at Web site: http://www.ussenateyouth.org.

Award: Scholarship for use in freshman year; not renewable. *Number:* 104. *Amount:* $5000.

Eligibility Requirements: Applicant must be high school student; planning to enroll or expecting to enroll full or part-time at a two-year or four-year or technical institution or university and must have an interest in leadership. Available to U.S. citizens.

Application Requirements: Application procedures will vary by state. *Deadline:* varies.

Contact: Rita Almon, Program Director
William Randolph Hearst Foundation
90 New Montgomery Street, Suite 1212
San Francisco, CA 94105-4504
Phone: 800-841-7048
Fax: 415-243-0760
E-mail: ussyp@hearstfdn.org

WOMEN'S BASKETBALL COACHES ASSOCIATION http://www.wbca.org

WBCA SCHOLARSHIP AWARD

One-time award for two women's basketball players who have demonstrated outstanding commitment to the sport of women's basketball and to academic excellence. Minimum 3.5 GPA required. Must be nominated by the head coach of women's basketball who is a member of the WBCA.

Award: Scholarship for use in freshman, sophomore, junior, senior, or graduate years; not renewable. *Number:* 2. *Amount:* $1000.

Eligibility Requirements: Applicant must be enrolled or expecting to enroll full or part-time at a four-year or technical institution or university; female and must have an interest in athletics/sports. Applicant must have 3.5 GPA or higher. Available to U.S. and non-U.S. citizens.

Application Requirements: Application, references, statistics. *Deadline:* February 7.

Contact: Kristen Miller, Manager of Office Administration and Awards
Women's Basketball Coaches Association
4646 Lawrenceville Highway
Lilburn, GA 30247-3620
Phone: 770-279-8027 Ext. 102
Fax: 770-279-6290
E-mail: kmiller@wbca.org

WOMEN'S INTERNATIONAL BOWLING CONGRESS http://www.bowl.com

ALBERTA E. CROWE STAR OF TOMORROW AWARD
• *See page 523*

WOMEN'S SPORTS FOUNDATION http://www.womenssportsfoundation.org

TRAVEL AND TRAINING FUND

Award to provide financial assistance to aspiring female athletes with successful competitive regional or national records who have the potential to achieve even higher performance levels and rankings. Must be a U.S. citizen or legal resident.

Award: Grant for use in freshman, sophomore, junior, or senior years; not renewable. *Number:* 25–100. *Amount:* $500–$4000.

Eligibility Requirements: Applicant must be enrolled or expecting to enroll full or part-time at an institution or university; female and must have an interest in athletics/sports. Available to U.S. citizens.

Application Requirements: Application, references. *Deadline:* December 31.

Contact: Women's Sports Foundation
Eisenhower Park
East Meadow, NY 11554
Phone: 800-227-3988
E-mail: wosport@aol.com

WOMEN'S WESTERN GOLF FOUNDATION

WOMEN'S WESTERN GOLF FOUNDATION SCHOLARSHIP

Scholarships for female high school seniors for use at a four-year college or university. Based on academic record, financial need, character, and involvement in golf. (Golf skill not a criterion.) Twenty awards annually for incoming freshmen; approximately 60 scholarships renewed. Must maintain 2.5 GPA as freshman; 3.0 upperclassman GPA. Must continue to have financial need. Award is $2000 per student per year. Applicant must be 17-18 years of age.

Award: Scholarship for use in freshman, sophomore, junior, or senior years; renewable. *Number:* up to 80. *Amount:* $2000.

Eligibility Requirements: Applicant must be high school student; age 17-18; planning to enroll or expecting to enroll full-time at a four-year institution or university; female and must have an interest in golf. Applicant must have 3.5 GPA or higher. Available to U.S. citizens.

Application Requirements: Application, essay, financial need analysis, self-addressed stamped envelope, test scores, transcript. *Deadline:* April 5.

Contact: Richard Willis, Scholarship Chairman
Women's Western Golf Foundation
393 Ramsay Road
Deerfield, IL 60015

WRITER'S DIGEST http://www.writersdigest.com

WRITER'S DIGEST ANNUAL WRITING COMPETITION

Annual writing competition. Only original, unpublished entries in any of the ten categories. Send self-addressed stamped envelope for guidelines and entry form. Deadline is May 15. Application fee: $15.

Award: Prize for use in freshman, sophomore, junior, senior, or graduate years; not renewable. *Number:* 100. *Amount:* $25–$1000.

Eligibility Requirements: Applicant must be enrolled or expecting to enroll full or part-time at a two-year or four-year or technical institution or university and must have an interest in writing. Available to U.S. and non-U.S. citizens.

Application Requirements: Application, applicant must enter a contest, self-addressed stamped envelope. *Fee:* $15. *Deadline:* May 15.

Contact: Terri Boes, Customer Service Representative
Writer's Digest
4700 East Galbraith Road
Cincinnati, OH 45236
Phone: 513-531-2690 Ext. 1328
Fax: 513-531-0798
E-mail: competitions@fwpubs.com

WRITER'S DIGEST POPULAR FICTION AWARDS

Writing contest: enter as many manuscripts as you like in each of the following categories: Romance, Mystery/Crime Fiction, Sci-fi/Fantasy, Thriller/Suspense and Horror. Manuscripts must not be more than 4,000 words.

Award: Prize for use in freshman, sophomore, junior, senior, graduate, or postgraduate years. *Number:* 6. *Amount:* up to $500.

Eligibility Requirements: Applicant must be enrolled or expecting to enroll full or part-time at a technical institution and must have an interest in writing. Available to U.S. and non-U.S. citizens.

Application Requirements: Application, self-addressed stamped envelope. *Fee:* $12. *Deadline:* November 1.

Contact: Terri Boes, Customer Service Representative
Writer's Digest
4700 East Galbraith Road
Cincinnati, OH 45236
Phone: 513-531-2690 Ext. 1328
Fax: 513-531-0798
E-mail: competitions@fwpubs.com

WRITER'S DIGEST SELF-PUBLISHED BOOK AWARDS

Awards open to self-published books for which the author has paid full cost. Send self-addressed stamped envelope for guidelines and entry form. Deadline is June 1. Application fee: $100.

Award: Prize for use in freshman, sophomore, junior, senior, graduate, or postgraduate years; not renewable. *Number:* 10. *Amount:* $500–$3000.

Eligibility Requirements: Applicant must be enrolled or expecting to enroll full or part-time at a two-year or four-year or technical institution or university and must have an interest in writing. Available to U.S. and non-U.S. citizens.

Application Requirements: Application, applicant must enter a contest, self-addressed stamped envelope. *Fee:* $100. *Deadline:* June 1.

Contact: Terri Boes, Customer Service Representative
Writer's Digest
4700 East Galbraith Road
Cincinnati, OH 45236
Phone: 513-531-2690 Ext. 1328
Fax: 513-531-0798
E-mail: competitions@fwpubs.com

YES I CAN! FOUNDATION http://www.yesican.org

STANLEY E. JACKSON SCHOLARSHIP AWARDS
• *See page 567*

YOUNG AMERICAN BOWLING ALLIANCE (YABA) http://www.bowl.com

GIFT FOR LIFE SCHOLARSHIP
• *See page 524*

Young American Bowling Alliance (YABA) (continued)

PEPSI-COLA YOUTH BOWLING CHAMPIONSHIPS
• *See page 524*

USBC ALBERTA E. CROWE STAR OF TOMORROW AWARD

Award given to recognize star qualities in a female high school or college student who competes in the sport of bowling. Applicants must be current USBC Youth or USBC members in good standing and currently competing in certified events. Deadline is October 1.

Award: Prize for use in freshman, sophomore, junior, or senior years; renewable. *Amount:* $1500.

Eligibility Requirements: Applicant must be age 22 or under; enrolled or expecting to enroll full-time at a four-year institution or university; female and must have an interest in bowling. Applicant must have 2.5 GPA or higher. Available to U.S. citizens.

Application Requirements: Application, financial need analysis, references, transcript. *Deadline:* October 1.

Contact: Karen Richter, Smart Accounts Administrator
Young American Bowling Alliance (YABA)
5301 South 76th Street
Greendale, WI 53129-1192
Phone: 800-514-2695 Ext. 3318
Fax: 414-423-3014
E-mail: kricht@bowlinginc.com

USBC ANNUAL ZEB SCHOLARSHIP

Scholarship awarded to a USBC Youth member who achieves academic success and gives back to the community through service. Candidates must have a current GPA of 2.0 or better. Deadline is April 1.

Award: Scholarship for use in freshman year. *Number:* 1. *Amount:* $2500.

Eligibility Requirements: Applicant must be high school student; planning to enroll or expecting to enroll at an institution or university and must have an interest in bowling. Available to U.S. citizens.

Application Requirements: Application, financial need analysis, references, transcript. *Deadline:* April 1.

Contact: Karen Richter, Smart Accounts Administrator
Young American Bowling Alliance (YABA)
5301 South 76th Street
Greendale, WI 53129-1192
Phone: 800-514-2695 Ext. 3318
Fax: 414-423-3014
E-mail: kricht@bowlinginc.com

USBC CHUCK HALL STAR OF TOMORROW SCHOLARSHIP

Scholarship is given to recognize star qualities in a male high school senior or college student who competes in the sport of bowling. Applicant must be a current USBC Youth or USBC member in good standing and currently compete in certified events. Deadline is October 1.

Award: Scholarship for use in freshman, sophomore, junior, or senior years; renewable. *Amount:* $1500.

Eligibility Requirements: Applicant must be age 22 or under; enrolled or expecting to enroll full-time at a four-year institution or university; male and must have an interest in bowling. Applicant must have 2.5 GPA or higher. Available to U.S. citizens.

Application Requirements: Application, essay, financial need analysis, references. *Deadline:* October 1.

Contact: Karen Richter, Smart Accounts Administrator
Young American Bowling Alliance (YABA)
5301 South 76th Street
Greendale, WI 53129-1192
Phone: 800-514-2695 Ext. 3318
Fax: 414-423-3014
E-mail: kricht@bowlinginc.com

USBC EARL ANTHONY MEMORIAL SCHOLARSHIPS

Scholarship given to recognize male and/or female bowlers for their community involvement and academic achievements, both in high school and

college. Candidates must be enrolled in their senior year of high school or presently attending college and be current members of USBC in good standing. Deadline is May 1.

Award: Scholarship for use in freshman, sophomore, junior, or senior years; not renewable. *Number:* 5. *Amount:* $5000.

Eligibility Requirements: Applicant must be enrolled or expecting to enroll at a four-year institution or university and must have an interest in bowling. Applicant must have 2.5 GPA or higher. Available to U.S. citizens.

Application Requirements: Application, financial need analysis, references, transcript. *Deadline:* May 1.

Contact: Karen Richter, Smart Accounts Administrator
Young American Bowling Alliance (YABA)
5301 South 76th Street
Greendale, WI 53129-1192
Phone: 800-514-2695 Ext. 3318
Fax: 414-423-3014
E-mail: kricht@bowlinginc.com

USBC MALE AND FEMALE YOUTH LEADERS OF THE YEAR SCHOLARSHIP

Scholarship presented to one male and one female Youth Leader who has demonstrated outstanding skills in organizing, administering and promoting youth bowling at the local and/or state level. Nomination deadline is January 15.

Award: Scholarship for use in freshman year; not renewable. *Number:* 2.

Eligibility Requirements: Applicant must be age 18; enrolled or expecting to enroll at an institution or university and must have an interest in bowling. Available to U.S. citizens.

Application Requirements: Application. *Deadline:* January 15.

Contact: Karen Richter, Smart Accounts Administrator
Young American Bowling Alliance (YABA)
5301 South 76th Street
Greendale, WI 53129-1192
Phone: 800-514-2695 Ext. 3318
Fax: 414-423-3014
E-mail: kricht@bowlinginc.com

WHO'S WHO SPORTS EDITION ALL-ACADEMIC BOWLING TEAM SCHOLARSHIP

Award for students who are listed in ECI's Who's Who Sports Edition. Candidates must be current USBC Youth members. Deadline is April 1.

Award: Scholarship for use in freshman, sophomore, or junior years; not renewable. *Number:* 20. *Amount:* $1000.

Eligibility Requirements: Applicant must be high school student; planning to enroll or expecting to enroll at a four-year institution and must have an interest in bowling. Applicant must have 2.5 GPA or higher. Available to U.S. citizens.

Application Requirements: Application, references, transcript. *Deadline:* April 1.

Contact: Karen Richter, Smart Accounts Administrator
Young American Bowling Alliance (YABA)
5301 South 76th Street
Greendale, WI 53129-1192
Phone: 800-514-2695 Ext. 3318
Fax: 414-423-3014
E-mail: kricht@bowlinginc.com

YOUTH OPPORTUNITIES FOUNDATION   http://www.yoflatinoscholars.com

YOUTH OPPORTUNITIES FOUNDATION SCHOLARSHIPS
• *See page 648*

Y'S MEN INTERNATIONAL   http://www.ysmenusa.com

ALEXANDER SCHOLARSHIP LOAN FUND

The purpose of the Alexander Scholarship Loan Fund is to promote the training of staff of the YMCA and/or those seeking to become members of staff of the YMCA. Must include $1 for postage and handling. Loan is forgiven if recipient enters YMCA employment after graduation. Application deadline for the Fall semester must be postmarked by May 30, and for the Spring semester postmarked by October 30.

Award: Forgivable loan for use in freshman, junior, or senior years; renewable. *Number:* varies. *Amount:* $500–$2500.

Eligibility Requirements: Applicant must be enrolled or expecting to enroll full or part-time at a two-year institution and must have an interest in designated field specified by sponsor. Available to U.S. citizens.

Application Requirements: Application. *Fee:* $1. *Deadline:* varies.

Contact: Dean Currie, U.S. Area Service Director
Y's Men International
629 Lantana Lane
Imperial, CA 92251
Fax: 602-935-6322

Miscellaneous Criteria

AAA

http://www.aaa.com/travelchallenge

AAA HIGH SCHOOL TRAVEL CHALLENGE

Students have the opportunity to compete for more than $100,000 in scholarship money, including $25,000 scholarships to the top three finishers and $10,000 scholarships to three runners-up. Each will receive an expense-paid trip to Universal Orlando, with chaperone, to participate in the national contest.

Award: Scholarship for use in freshman year; not renewable. *Number:* 8. *Amount:* $500–$25,000.

Eligibility Requirements: Applicant must be high school student; age 13-18 and planning to enroll or expecting to enroll full or part-time at a two-year or four-year or technical institution or university. Available to U.S. citizens.

Application Requirements: Application, applicant must enter a contest, online application/test. *Deadline:* January 19.

Contact: AAA
c/o Curley and Pynn
801 N Magnolia Avenue, Suite 210
Orlando, FL 32803
E-mail: aaatravelchallenge@national.aaa.com

AAA OHIO

http://www.aaaohio.com

ANNUAL SENIOR HIGH COMMUNICATION CONTEST

State and national award contest for best public service announcement in poster or A/V format on this year's auto safety subject. Students must reside within the AAA Ohio service area; winners of state awards progress to national level.

Award: Prize for use in freshman year. *Amount:* $150–$5000.

Eligibility Requirements: Applicant must be high school student and planning to enroll or expecting to enroll at an institution or university. Available to U.S. citizens.

Application Requirements: Audio or video public service announcements 30 seconds or less, posters (hand drawn or computer generated). *Deadline:* January 17.

Contact: Deborah Troyan, AAA Ohio Traffic Safety Department
AAA Ohio
90 East Wilson Bridge Road
Worthington, OH 43085
Phone: 614-431-7882
E-mail: dtroyan@aaaohio.com

THE SCHOOL SAFETY PATROL $1000 GRANT AWARD FOR HIGH SCHOOL SENIORS

Grant awards are not limited to students planning to attend a university or college. The grant money can be used for an apprenticeship program, enrollment in a trade school or participation in any other program that will help students expand their education following graduation from high school.

Award: Grant for use in freshman year. *Number:* 10. *Amount:* $1000.

Eligibility Requirements: Applicant must be high school student and planning to enroll or expecting to enroll full or part-time at a four-year institution or university. Available to U.S. citizens.

Application Requirements: Application, essay, references, transcript. *Deadline:* March 10.

Contact: Deborah Troyan, AAA Ohio Traffic Safety Department
AAA Ohio
90 East Wilson Bridge Road
Worthington, OH 43085
Phone: 614-431-7882
E-mail: dtroyan@aaaohio.com

ADMINISTRATIVE MANAGEMENT SERVICES (AMS)

http://home.cogeco.ca

DAIMLER CHRYSLER SERVICES CANADA INC. SCHOLARSHIP PROGRAM

Scholarship for student graduating from high school and enrolling in first year of a three- to four-year degree program. Twelve students are chosen based on academic performance, extracurricular activities, and community service. Once in the program they could be eligible for four awards as long as a "B" average is maintained on a full workload. Open to Canadian citizens who are dependents of employees of Daimler Chrysler Canada, Inc.

Award: Scholarship for use in freshman year; renewable. *Amount:* up to $1000.

Eligibility Requirements: Applicant must be high school student and planning to enroll or expecting to enroll full-time at an institution or university.

Application Requirements: Application. *Deadline:* April 30.

Contact: Scholarship Coordinator
Administrative Management Services (AMS)
Suite 412, 829 Norwest Road
Kingston, ON K7P 2N3
Canada
Phone: 613-634-4350
Fax: 613-634-4209
E-mail: chrisb7@cogeco.ca

AIA NEW JERSEY SCHOLARSHIP FOUNDATION, INC.

NJSA SCHOLARSHIP PROGRAM

Award: Scholarship for use in sophomore, junior, senior, or graduate years.

Eligibility Requirements: Applicant must be enrolled or expecting to enroll at an institution or university.

Contact:

AIFS COLLEGE DIVISION

http://www.aifsabroad.com

INTERNATIONAL SCHOLARSHIPS

To promote international understanding through study abroad. Applicants for summer programs must apply by March 15, fall semester by April 15 and spring semester by October 1.

Award: Scholarship for use in freshman, sophomore, junior, or senior years. *Number:* up to 50. *Amount:* up to $1000.

Eligibility Requirements: Applicant must be enrolled or expecting to enroll at a four-year institution or university. Applicant must have 3.0 GPA or higher. Available to U.S. citizens.

Application Requirements: Application, essay, scholarship application. *Fee:* $395. *Deadline:* varies.

Contact: AIFS College Division
AIFS College Division, River Plaza, 9 West Broad Street
Stamford, CT 06902-3788

STUDY AGAIN WITH AIFS SCHOLARSHIP

Scholarships for AIFS Alumni. Applicants who have already studied abroad with AIFS can apply for scholarships toward another study abroad trip. Scholarship cannot be used towards the cost of an AIFS Partnership program. Amount and deadline date varies. See Web site for details: http://www.aifsabroad.com/css/scholarships.htm#alumni

Award: Scholarship for use in sophomore, junior, or senior years. *Number:* up to 50. *Amount:* $500–$1500.

Eligibility Requirements: Applicant must be enrolled or expecting to enroll at an institution or university. Available to U.S. citizens.

Application Requirements: Application. *Deadline:* varies.

Contact: AIFS College Division
AIFS College Division, River Plaza, 9 West Broad Street
Stamford, CT 06902-3788
Phone: 800-727-2437

AIKEN ELECTRIC COOPERATIVE, INC.
http://www.aikenco-op.org

TRUSTEE SCHOLARSHIP

Scholarship is awarded to high school graduating senior in the cooperative service area. Application must be postmarked by March 10. The primary residence of the applicant must have an account with either: Aiken Electric Cooperative, Inc or Aikenelectric.net.

Award: Scholarship for use in freshman year; not renewable. *Number:* 1. *Amount:* up to $1000.

Eligibility Requirements: Applicant must be high school student and planning to enroll or expecting to enroll full-time at an institution or university. Available to U.S. citizens.

Application Requirements: Application, essay, financial need analysis. *Deadline:* March 10.

Contact: Marilyn Gerrity, Manager, Marketing & Strategic Services
Aiken Electric Cooperative, Inc.
PO Box 417
Aiken, SC 29802
Phone: 803-649-6245
Fax: 803-641-8310
E-mail: aec@aikenco-op.org

AKADEMOS, INC.
http://www.textbookx.com

TEXTBOOKX.COM SPRING SCHOLARSHIP

Students must write an essay and reference one book on the assigned topic. The current essay question is "How has the technology of the past 20 years affected the relationship between the individual and society?" Essay must be between 250 and 750 words. One grand prize winner is selected and two runners-up.

Award: Scholarship for use in freshman, sophomore, junior, or senior years; not renewable. *Number:* up to 3. *Amount:* $250–$2000.

Eligibility Requirements: Applicant must be high school student and planning to enroll or expecting to enroll full or part-time at a four-year institution or university. Available to U.S. citizens.

Application Requirements: Application, applicant must enter a contest, essay. *Deadline:* April 30.

Contact: Akademos, Inc.
25 Van Zant Street
Norwalk, CT 06855-1727
Phone: 800-221-8480
Fax: 203-866-0199

ALABAMA DEPARTMENT OF REHABILITATION SERVICES
http://www.rehab.state.al.us

ALABAMA SCHOLARSHIP FOR DEPENDENTS OF BLIND PARENTS

Award: Scholarship for use in freshman, sophomore, junior, or senior years.

Eligibility Requirements: Applicant must be enrolled or expecting to enroll at an institution or university.

Contact: Deborah Culver, Coordinator of Blind Services
Alabama Department of Rehabilitation Services
Alabama Scholarship for Dependents of Blind Parents
2129 E South Boulevard
Montgomery, AL 36111
Phone: 800-441-7607

ALASKA POLICE CORPS
http://www.uaf.edu/akcorps

ALASKA POLICE CORPS SCHOLARSHIP

College seniors or graduates are eligible for reimbursement of educational expenses. Must complete training academy and agree to four-year work commitment at a participating Alaska law enforcement agency. Check Web site for specific details: http://www.uaf.edu/akcorps

Award: Scholarship for use in senior year. *Number:* 10. *Amount:* up to $23,000.

Eligibility Requirements: Applicant must be enrolled or expecting to enroll at a four-year institution or university. Applicant must have 2.5 GPA or higher. Available to U.S. citizens.

Application Requirements: Application, driver's license, essay, references, transcript. *Deadline:* Continuous.

Contact: Dan Hoffman
Alaska Police Corps
800 Cushman Street
Fairbanks, AK 99701
Phone: 800-221-0083
Fax: 907-459-6767
E-mail: dphoffman@ci.fairbanks.ak.us

ALBERTA HERITAGE SCHOLARSHIP FUND/ ALBERTA SCHOLARSHIP PROGRAMS
http://www.alis.gov.ab.ca

ALBERTA CENTENNIAL PREMIER'S SCHOLARSHIPS - ALBERTA

Twenty-five awards for each province and territory in Canada of CAN$ 2005. Must be Canadian citizens or permanent residents of Canada

Award: Scholarship for use in freshman year. *Number:* 25. *Amount:* up to $1726.

Eligibility Requirements: Applicant must be enrolled or expecting to enroll full-time at a technical institution.

Application Requirements: Application.

Contact: Stuart Dunn, Manager
Alberta Heritage Scholarship Fund/Alberta Scholarship Programs
4th Floor, 9940 106th Street, Box 28000 Station Main
Edmonton, AB T5J 4R4
Canada
Phone: 780-427-8640
Fax: 780-427-1288
E-mail: scholarships@gov.ab.ca

ALBERTA CENTENNIAL PREMIER'S SCHOLARSHIPS - CANADA

Twenty-five awards for each province and territory in Canada for CAN$ 2005.

Award: Scholarship for use in freshman, sophomore, junior, or senior years. *Number:* 25. *Amount:* $1726.

Eligibility Requirements: Applicant must be enrolled or expecting to enroll full-time at a technical institution.

Application Requirements: Application, financial need analysis.

Contact: Stuart Dunn, Manager
Alberta Heritage Scholarship Fund/Alberta Scholarship Programs
4th Floor, 9940 106th Street, Box 28000 Station Main
Edmonton, AB T5J 4R4
Canada
Phone: 780-427-8640
Fax: 780-427-1288
E-mail: scholarships@gov.ab.ca

INTERNATIONAL EDUCATION AWARDS–UKRAINE

Awards of $5000 CAN are available for students taking a practicum, internship, co-op, or apprenticeship program. Students must be from Ukraine and studying in Alberta or from Alberta and studying in Ukraine. One-term research projects may also be considered. Application deadline is January 1.

Award: Scholarship for use in freshman, sophomore, junior, or senior years. *Number:* 5. *Amount:* $4305.

Eligibility Requirements: Applicant must be enrolled or expecting to enroll full-time at a four-year institution or university. Available to U.S. and non-U.S. citizens.

Application Requirements: Application. *Deadline:* January 1.

Contact: Stuart Dunn, Manager
Alberta Heritage Scholarship Fund/Alberta Scholarship Programs
4th Floor, 9940 106th Street, Box 28000 Station Main
Edmonton, AB T5J 4R4
Canada
Phone: 780-427-8640
Fax: 780-427-1288
E-mail: scholarships@gov.ab.ca

...e Scholarship Fund/Alberta Scholarship Programs (continued)

QUEEN ELIZABETH II GOLDEN JUBILEE CITIZENSHIP MEDAL

• *See page* 603

ALEXANDER GRAHAM BELL ASSOCIATION FOR THE DEAF AND HARD OF HEARING
http://www.agbell.org

HERBERT P. FEIBELMAN, JR. SCHOLARSHIP

Scholarship for the child of a parent who is a member in good standing of AG Bell

Award: Scholarship for use in freshman, sophomore, junior, or senior years; not renewable. *Number:* 1. *Amount:* $2500.

Eligibility Requirements: Applicant must be enrolled or expecting to enroll full-time at a four-year institution or university. Available to U.S. citizens.

Application Requirements: Application, references, transcript. *Deadline:* April 15.

Contact: Financial Aid Coordinator
Alexander Graham Bell Association for the Deaf and Hard of Hearing
3417 Volta Place, NW
Washington, DC 20007-2778
E-mail: financialaid@agbell.org

ALFRED G. AND ELMA M. MILOTTE SCHOLARSHIP FUND
http://www.milotte.org

ALFRED G. AND ELMA M. MILOTTE SCHOLARSHIP

Grant of $4000 to high school graduate or to students holding the GED. Applicants should have been acceptance at a trade school, art school, two-year or four-year college or university for either undergraduate or graduate studies. Applicant should be a nature lover.

Award: Scholarship for use in freshman, sophomore, junior, senior, or graduate years; not renewable. *Amount:* up to $4000.

Eligibility Requirements: Applicant must be enrolled or expecting to enroll at a two-year or four-year or technical institution or university. Applicant must have 3.0 GPA or higher. Available to U.S. citizens.

Application Requirements: Application, references, samples of work expressing applicant's observations of the natural world. *Deadline:* March 31.

Contact: The Alfred G. & Elma M. Milotte Scholarship Fund
Alfred G. and Elma M. Milotte Scholarship Fund
715 Peachtree Street, 8th Floor
Atlanta, GA 30308

ALL-INK.COM PRINTER SUPPLIES ONLINE
http://www.all-ink.com

ALL-INK.COM COLLEGE SCHOLARSHIP PROGRAM

One-time award for any level of post secondary education. Minimum 2.5 GPA. Must apply online only at Web site http://www.all-ink.com. Recipients selected annually. Application deadline is December 31.

Award: Scholarship for use in freshman, sophomore, junior, senior, graduate, or postgraduate years; not renewable. *Number:* 5–10. *Amount:* $1000–$2500.

Eligibility Requirements: Applicant must be enrolled or expecting to enroll full-time at a two-year or four-year or technical institution or university. Applicant must have 2.5 GPA or higher. Available to U.S. citizens.

Application Requirements: Application, essay. *Deadline:* December 31.

Contact: All-Ink.com Printer Supplies Online
1460 North Main Street, Suite 2
PO Box 50868
Spanish Fork, UT 84660-0868
E-mail: scholarship@all-ink.com

ALPHA KAPPA ALPHA
http://www.akaeaf.org

AKA EDUCATIONAL ADVANCEMENT FOUNDATION UNMET FINANCIAL NEED SCHOLARSHIP

Scholarship for stusents who have completed a minimum of one year in a degree granting institution and need financial aid to continue their studies in such an institution. May also be a student in a non-institutional based program that may or may not grant degrees, and must submit a course of study outline. Must have a minimum GPA of 2.5.

Award: Scholarship for use in sophomore, junior, or senior years. *Amount:* up to $1500.

Eligibility Requirements: Applicant must be enrolled or expecting to enroll at a four-year institution or university. Applicant must have 2.5 GPA or higher. Available to U.S. citizens.

Application Requirements: Application. *Deadline:* January 15.

Contact: Linda M. White, President
Alpha Kappa Alpha
5656 South Stony Island Avenue
Chicago, IL 60637
Phone: 773-947-0026
E-mail: akaeaf@aol.com

AKA EDUCATIONAL ADVANCEMENT FOUNDATION YOUTH PARTNERS ACCESSING CAPITAL SCHOLARSHIP

Scholarship for a member of Alpha Kappa Alpha Sorority. Must be an undergraduate of at least sophomore status. Must have a minimum GPA of 3.0 and participate in leadership, volunteer, civic, or campus activities. Must demonstrate academic achievement or financial need.

Award: Scholarship for use in sophomore, junior, or senior years. *Number:* 1.

Eligibility Requirements: Applicant must be enrolled or expecting to enroll at a four-year institution or university. Applicant must have 3.0 GPA or higher. Available to U.S. citizens.

Application Requirements: Application. *Deadline:* January 15.

Contact: Linda M. White, President
Alpha Kappa Alpha
5656 South Stony Island Avenue
Chicago, IL 60637
Phone: 773-947-0026
E-mail: akaeaf@aol.com

ALPHA KAPPA ALPHA EDUCATIONAL ADVANCEMENT FOUNDATION, INC.
http://www.akaeaf.org

ALPHA KAPPA ALPHA SORORITY, INC. FINANCIAL ASSISTANCE SCHOLARSHIPS

Scholarships available to undergraduate students, sophomore or beyond, who are currently enrolled in an accredited institution. May be a degree granting institution or a non-institutional based program that may or may not grant degrees. Additional information and all inquiries must be obtained via Web site only: http://www.akaeaf.org.

Award: Scholarship for use in sophomore, junior, senior, or graduate years; not renewable. *Number:* varies. *Amount:* $750–$1500.

Eligibility Requirements: Applicant must be enrolled or expecting to enroll at a two-year or four-year or technical institution or university. Applicant must have 2.5 GPA or higher. Available to U.S. citizens.

Application Requirements: Application, financial need analysis, references, transcript. *Deadline:* January 15.

Contact: AKA-EAF
Alpha Kappa Alpha Educational Advancement Foundation, Inc.
5656 South Stony Island Avenue
Chicago, IL 60637

ALPHA KAPPA ALPHA SORORITY, INC. MERIT SCHOLARSHIP

Scholarships available for students currently enrolled with sophomore through graduate school standing at an accredited institution. Must have a minimum 3.0 GPA and have demonstrated community service and involvement. Additional information and all inquiries must be obtained via Web site only. http://www.akaeaf.org.

Award: Scholarship for use in sophomore, junior, senior, or graduate years; not renewable. *Number:* varies. *Amount:* $1000.

Eligibility Requirements: Applicant must be enrolled or expecting to enroll at a four-year institution or university. Applicant must have 3.0 GPA or higher. Available to U.S. citizens.

Application Requirements: Application, financial need analysis, references, transcript. *Deadline:* January 15.

Contact: AKA-EAF
Alpha Kappa Alpha Educational Advancement Foundation, Inc.
5656 South Stony Island Avenue
Chicago, IL 60637

ALPHA LAMBDA DELTA   http://www.nationalald.org

JO ANNE J. TROW SCHOLARSHIPS

One-time award for initiated members of Alpha Lambda Delta. Minimum 3.5 GPA required. Must be nominated by chapter.

Award: Scholarship for use in junior year; not renewable. *Number:* up to 35. *Amount:* $1000.

Eligibility Requirements: Applicant must be enrolled or expecting to enroll full-time at a four-year institution. Applicant must have 3.5 GPA or higher. Available to U.S. and non-U.S. citizens.

Application Requirements: Application, essay, references, transcript. *Deadline:* May 1.

Contact: Dr. Glenda Earwood, Executive Director
Alpha Lambda Delta
PO Box 4403
Macon, GA 31208-4403
Phone: 478-744-9595
Fax: 478-744-9929

AMERICAN ANGUS AUXILIARY   http://www.angus.org

AMERICAN ANGUS AUXILIARY SCHOLARSHIP

Award for a graduating high school senior. Any unmarried girl or unmarried boy recommended by a state or regional auxiliary is eligible. Must be a member of National Junior Angus Association and have demonstrated interest and involvement in Angus projects.

Award: Scholarship for use in freshman year; not renewable. *Number:* 10. *Amount:* $850–$1200.

Eligibility Requirements: Applicant must be high school student; planning to enroll or expecting to enroll full or part-time at an institution or university and single. Available to U.S. citizens.

Application Requirements: Application. *Deadline:* May 10.

Contact: American Angus Auxiliary
3201 Frederick Avenue
St. Joseph, MO 64506
Phone: 816-383-5100
Fax: 816-233-9703

AMERICAN ASSOCIATION OF SCHOOL ADMINISTRATORS/DISCOVER CARD TRIBUTE AWARD PROGRAM   http://www.aasa.org

DISCOVER CARD TRIBUTE AWARD SCHOLARSHIP PROGRAM

Applicants should be current high school juniors with minimum 2.75 GPA. Nine scholarships available in each state and Washington, D.C. Nine $25,000 awards at the national level in three categories. Must plan to further education beyond high school in any accredited certification, licensing or training program or institution of higher education. Must demonstrate outstanding accomplishments in three areas: special talents, leadership, and community service and have faced a significant roadblock(s) or challenge(s). Visit Web site for application and more information: http://www.aasa.org/discover.htm

Award: Scholarship for use in freshman year; not renewable. *Number:* 310. *Amount:* $2500–$25,000.

Eligibility Requirements: Applicant must be high school student and planning to enroll or expecting to enroll full or part-time at a two-year or four-year or technical institution or university. Available to U.S. and non-U.S. citizens.

Application Requirements: Application, essay, references, transcript. *Deadline:* January 31.

Contact: Program Director
American Association of School Administrators/Discover Card Tribute Award Program
PO Box 9338
Arlington, VA 22219
Phone: 703-875-0708
E-mail: tributeaward@aasa.org

AMERICAN ASSOCIATION OF STATE TROOPERS, INC.   http://www.statetroopers.org

AMERICAN ASSOCIATION OF STATE TROOPERS SCHOLARSHIP

The American Association of State Troopers Scholarship Foundation (AASTSF) provides scholarships to AAST member's children by natural birth, legally adopted, step child, or legal guardian raised as their own child. For a dependent to be eligible, the parent must have been a member of AAST for one year prior to the scholarship application deadline.

Award: Scholarship for use in freshman, sophomore, junior, or senior years; not renewable. *Number:* 4. *Amount:* $500–$1500.

Eligibility Requirements: Applicant must be high school student and planning to enroll or expecting to enroll full or part-time at a two-year or four-year institution or university. Applicant must have 2.5 GPA or higher. Available to U.S. citizens.

Application Requirements: Application, essay, photo, transcript. *Deadline:* varies.

Contact: American Association of State Troopers, Inc.
1949 Raymond Diehl Road
Tallahassee, FL 32308
Phone: 850-385-7904
Fax: 850-385-8697

AMERICAN FEDERATION OF TEACHERS   http://www.aft.org

ROBERT G. PORTER SCHOLARS PROGRAM-AFT DEPENDENTS

$8000 scholarship ($2000 per year) for high school seniors who are dependents of AFT members. Submit transcript, test scores, essay, and recommendations with application. Deadline: March 31. Must be U.S. citizen. Applicant should preferably be pursuing a career in labor, education, healthcare, or government service.

Award: Scholarship for use in freshman year; renewable. *Number:* 4. *Amount:* $8000.

Eligibility Requirements: Applicant must be high school student and planning to enroll or expecting to enroll full or part-time at a four-year institution or university. Available to U.S. citizens.

Application Requirements: Application, essay, references, test scores, transcript. *Deadline:* March 31.

Contact: Bernadette Bailey, Scholarship Coordinator
American Federation of Teachers
555 New Jersey Avenue, NW
Washington, DC 20001
Phone: 202-879-4481
Fax: 202-879-4406
E-mail: bbailey@aft.org

AMERICAN FIRE SPRINKLER ASSOCIATION   http://www.afsascholarship.org

NATIONAL SCHOLARSHIP CONTEST

One-time award; applicants must be high school seniors. Must submit essay, application and recommendation and must take a online test. Not based on financial need or GPA. Please visit Web site for essay topic and to apply: http://www.afsascholarship.org.

Award: Scholarship for use in freshman year; not renewable. *Number:* 4. *Amount:* up to $5000.

Eligibility Requirements: Applicant must be high school student and planning to enroll or expecting to enroll full-time at a two-year or four-year or technical institution or university. Available to U.S. citizens.

American Fire Sprinkler Association (continued)

Application Requirements: Application, applicant must enter a contest, essay, references, online test. *Deadline:* varies.

Contact: D'Arcy Montalvo, Public Relations Manager
American Fire Sprinkler Association
9696 Skillman Street, Suite 300
Dallas, TX 75243
Phone: 214-349-5965
Fax: 214-343-8898

AMERICAN FOUNDATION FOR TRANSLATION AND INTERPRETATION
http://www.afti.org

AFTI SCHOLARSHIPS IN SCIENTIFIC AND TECHNICAL TRANSLATION, LITERARY TRANSLATION, AND INTERPRETATION

AFTI annually offers academic year scholarships for full-time students enrolled or planning to enroll in a degree program in scientific and technical translation, literary translation, or interpreter training. Must have a 3.0 GPA. Application deadline is June 1.

Award: Scholarship for use in freshman, sophomore, junior, senior, or graduate years; not renewable. *Number:* 1–2. *Amount:* up to $2500.

Eligibility Requirements: Applicant must be enrolled or expecting to enroll full-time at a four-year institution or university. Applicant must have 3.0 GPA or higher. Available to U.S. citizens.

Application Requirements: Application, essay, references, transcript, admission to T/I program. *Deadline:* June 1.

Contact: Eleanor Krawutschke, Executive Director, AFTI
American Foundation for Translation and Interpretation
Columbia Plaza-Suite 101, 350 East Michigan Avenue
Kalamazoo, MI 49007
Phone: 269-383-6893
E-mail: aftiorg@aol.com

AMERICAN INSTITUTE FOR FOREIGN STUDY
http://www.aifsabroad.com

STUDY AGAIN SCHOLARSHIPS

AIFS summer program students will receive a $1,500 scholarship to study abroad on an AIFS semester or academic year program. AIFS semester or academic year program students will receive a $500 scholarship towards a four or five week summer program, or a $750 scholarship towards a summer program of six weeks or more.

Award: Scholarship for use in freshman, sophomore, junior, or senior years; not renewable. *Number:* varies. *Amount:* $500–$1500.

Eligibility Requirements: Applicant must be enrolled or expecting to enroll full-time at a two-year or four-year institution or university. Applicant must have 2.5 GPA or higher. Available to U.S. and non-U.S. citizens.

Application Requirements: Application, essay, photo, references, transcript, previously studied abroad with AIFS. *Fee:* $75. *Deadline:* varies.

Contact: David Mauro, Admissions Counselor
American Institute for Foreign Study
9 West Broad Street, River Plaza
Stamford, CT 06902-3788
Phone: 203-399-5163
Fax: 203-399-5598
E-mail: college.info@aifs.com

AMERICAN JEWISH LEAGUE FOR ISRAEL
http://www.americanjewishleague.org

AMERICAN JEWISH LEAGUE FOR ISRAEL SCHOLARSHIP PROGRAM

The AJLI Scholarship Program provides support with tuition for a full year of study (September-May) at one of seven universities in Israel; Bar Ilan, Ben Gurion, Haifa, Hebrew, Tel Aviv, Technion, and Weizmann, Interdisciplinary Center at Herzliya. Deadline is May 1. Additional information is available on Web site: http://www.americanjewishleague.org

Award: Scholarship for use in freshman, sophomore, junior, senior, graduate, or postgraduate years; not renewable. *Number:* 3–10. *Amount:* up to $2000.

Eligibility Requirements: Applicant must be enrolled or expecting to enroll full-time at an institution or university. Available to U.S. citizens.

Application Requirements: Application, transcript. *Deadline:* May 1.

Contact: Dr. Martin Kalmanson, University Scholarship Fund
American Jewish League for Israel
400 North Flagler Drive PH4D
West Palm Beach, FL 33401
Phone: 561-659-0402

AMERICAN LEGION AUXILIARY, DEPARTMENT OF COLORADO

AMERICAN LEGION AUXILIARY DEPARTMENT OF COLORADO DEPARTMENT PRESIDENT'S SCHOLARSHIP FOR JUNIOR MEMBER

Award: Scholarship for use in freshman year.

Eligibility Requirements: Applicant must be enrolled or expecting to enroll at an institution or university.

Contact:

AMERICAN LEGION AUXILIARY DEPARTMENT OF COLORADO PAST PRESIDENT PARLEY NURSES SCHOLARSHIP

Award: Scholarship for use in freshman, sophomore, junior, or senior years.

Eligibility Requirements: Applicant must be enrolled or expecting to enroll at an institution or university.

Contact:

AMERICAN LEGION AUXILIARY, DEPARTMENT OF FLORIDA
http://www.floridalegion.org

AMERICAN LEGION AUXILIARY DEPARTMENT OF FLORIDA NATIONAL PRESIDENT'S SCHOLARSHIP

Award: Scholarship for use in freshman year.

Eligibility Requirements: Applicant must be enrolled or expecting to enroll at an institution or university.

Contact: Marie Mahoney, Department Secretary and Treasurer
American Legion Auxiliary, Department of Florida
PO Box 547917
Orlando, FL 32854-7917
Phone: 407-293-7411
Fax: 407-299-6522
E-mail: alaflorida@aol.com

AMERICAN LEGION AUXILIARY, DEPARTMENT OF INDIANA
http://www.amlegauxin.org

EDNA M. BURCUS MEMORIAL SCHOLARSHIP

Award: Scholarship for use in freshman year.

Eligibility Requirements: Applicant must be enrolled or expecting to enroll at an institution or university.

Contact: Judy Otey, Department Secretary and Treasurer
American Legion Auxiliary, Department of Indiana
777 North Meridian, Room 107
Indianapolis, IN 46204
Phone: 317-630-1390
Fax: 317-630-1277
E-mail: ala777@sbc.com

HOOSIER SCHOOLHOUSE SCHOLARSHIP

Award: Scholarship for use in freshman year.

Eligibility Requirements: Applicant must be enrolled or expecting to enroll at an institution or university.

Contact: Judy Otey, Department Secretary and Treasurer
American Legion Auxiliary, Department of Indiana
777 North Meridian, Room 107
Indianapolis, IN 46204
Phone: 317-630-1390
Fax: 317-630-1277
E-mail: ala777@sbc.com

AMERICAN LEGION AUXILIARY, DEPARTMENT OF KENTUCKY

LAURA BLACKBURN MEMORIAL SCHOLARSHIP

Award: Scholarship for use in freshman year.

Eligibility Requirements: Applicant must be enrolled or expecting to enroll at an institution or university.

Contact:

MARY BARRETT MARSHALL SCHOLARSHIP

Award: Scholarship for use in freshman, sophomore, junior, or senior years.

Eligibility Requirements: Applicant must be enrolled or expecting to enroll at an institution or university.

Contact:

AMERICAN LEGION AUXILIARY, DEPARTMENT OF MAINE
http://www.mainelegion.org

AMERICAN LEGION AUXILIARY DEPARTMENT OF MAINE SCHOLARSHIP

Award: Scholarship for use in freshman year.

Eligibility Requirements: Applicant must be enrolled or expecting to enroll at an institution or university.

Contact: Madeline Sweet, Secretary
American Legion Auxiliary, Department of Maine
21 College Avenue
PO Box 887
Waterville, ME 04901
Phone: 207-596-5866
Fax: 207-469-0598

AMERICAN LEGION AUXILIARY, DEPARTMENT OF MAINE NATIONAL PRESIDENT'S SCHOLARSHIP

Award: Scholarship for use in freshman year.

Eligibility Requirements: Applicant must be enrolled or expecting to enroll at an institution or university.

Contact: Madeline Sweet, Secretary
American Legion Auxiliary, Department of Maine
21 College Avenue
PO Box 887
Waterville, ME 04901
Phone: 207-596-5866
Fax: 207-469-0598

AMERICAN LEGION AUXILIARY, DEPARTMENT OF MARYLAND

AMERICAN LEGION AUXILIARY DEPARTMENT OF MARYLAND CHILDREN AND YOUTH SCHOLARSHIPS

Award: Scholarship for use in freshman, sophomore, junior, or senior years.

Eligibility Requirements: Applicant must be enrolled or expecting to enroll at an institution or university.

Contact: Anna Thompson, Department Secretary
American Legion Auxiliary, Department of Maryland
1589 Sulphur Spring Road, Suite 105
Baltimore, MD 21227
Phone: 410-242-9519
Fax: 410-242-9553
E-mail: anna@alamd.org

AMERICAN LEGION AUXILIARY DEPARTMENT OF MARYLAND PAST PRESIDENT'S PARLEY NURSING SCHOLARSHIP

Award: Scholarship for use in freshman, sophomore, junior, or senior years.

Eligibility Requirements: Applicant must be enrolled or expecting to enroll at an institution or university.

Contact: Anna Thompson, Department Secretary
American Legion Auxiliary, Department of Maryland
1589 Sulphur Spring Road, Suite 105
Baltimore, MD 21227
Phone: 410-242-9519
Fax: 410-242-9553
E-mail: anna@alamd.org

AMERICAN LEGION AUXILIARY, DEPARTMENT OF MASSACHUSETTS

AMERICAN LEGION AUXILIARY DEPARTMENT OF MASSACHUSETTS PAST PRESIDENT'S PARLEY SCHOLARSHIP

Award: Scholarship for use in freshman, sophomore, junior, or senior years.

Eligibility Requirements: Applicant must be enrolled or expecting to enroll at an institution or university.

Contact: Beverly Monaco, Secretary and Treasurer
American Legion Auxiliary, Department of Massachusetts
546-2 State House
Boston, MA 02133-1044
Phone: 617-727-2958

AMERICAN LEGION AUXILIARY, DEPARTMENT OF MASSACHUSETTS DEPARTMENT PRESIDENT'S SCHOLARSHIP

Award: Scholarship for use in freshman, sophomore, junior, or senior years.

Eligibility Requirements: Applicant must be enrolled or expecting to enroll at an institution or university.

Contact: Beverly Monaco, Secretary and Treasurer
American Legion Auxiliary, Department of Massachusetts
546-2 State House
Boston, MA 02133-1044
Phone: 617-727-2958

AMERICAN LEGION AUXILIARY, DEPARTMENT OF MICHIGAN
http://www.michalaux.org

GIRL SCOUT ACHIEVEMENT AWARD

Scholarship available valued at $1000, and trip to national convention to receive award after graduation from high school. Must have received the Girl Scout Gold Award, be an active member of her religious institution and must have received the appropriate religious emblem, Cadette or Senior Scout level.

Award: Prize for use in freshman year. *Amount:* $1000.

Eligibility Requirements: Applicant must be enrolled or expecting to enroll at an institution or university. Available to U.S. citizens.

Application Requirements: Application, references, 4 letters of recommendation and testimony (1 letter required from each of the following group leaders: religious institution, school, community, and scouting), nomination application. *Deadline:* February 10.

Contact: Leisa Eldred, Scholarship Coordinator
American Legion Auxiliary, Department of Michigan
212 North Verlinden Avenue
Lansing, MI 48915
Phone: 517-371-4720
Fax: 517-371-2401
E-mail: michalaux@voyager.net

SPIRIT OF YOUTH SCHOLARSHIP

Scholarship valued at $1000 per year for four years is available to one junior member in each division.. The applicant must have held membership in the American Legion Auxiliary for the immediate past three years, currently hold a 2006 membership card and continue to maintain her membership throughout the four-year scholarship period.

Award: Scholarship for use in freshman, sophomore, junior, or senior years. *Amount:* $1000.

Eligibility Requirements: Applicant must be high school student and planning to enroll or expecting to enroll at an institution or university. Applicant must have 3.0 GPA or higher. Available to U.S. citizens.

Application Requirements: Application, references, letter from principal or guidance counselor, a clergyman/clergywoman, recipient

American Legion Auxiliary, Department of Michigan (continued)

organization, verification of 50 hours of voluntary service, 2 letters from adult citizens, original article consisting of no more than 1,000 words (typed, double-spaced). *Deadline:* March 1.

Contact: Leisa Eldred, Scholarship Coordinator
American Legion Auxiliary, Department of Michigan
212 North Verlinden Avenue
Lansing, MI 48915
Phone: 517-371-4720
Fax: 517-371-2401
E-mail: michalaux@voyager.net

AMERICAN LEGION AUXILIARY, DEPARTMENT OF PENNSYLVANIA

AMERICAN LEGION AUXILIARY DEPARTMENT OF PENNSYLVANIA PAST DEPARTMENT PRESIDENT'S MEMORIAL SCHOLARSHIP

Award: Scholarship for use in freshman, sophomore, or junior years.

Eligibility Requirements: Applicant must be enrolled or expecting to enroll at an institution or university.

Contact: Colleen Watson, Executive Secretary and Treasurer
American Legion Auxiliary, Department of Pennsylvania
PO Box 2643
Harrisburg, PA 17105-2643
Phone: 717-763-7545
Fax: 717-763-0617

AMERICAN LEGION AUXILIARY DEPARTMENT OF PENNSYLVANIA SCHOLARSHIP FOR DEPENDENTS OF DISABLED OR DECEASED VETERANS

Award: Scholarship for use in freshman, sophomore, junior, or senior years.

Eligibility Requirements: Applicant must be enrolled or expecting to enroll at an institution or university.

Contact: Colleen Watson, Executive Secretary and Treasurer
American Legion Auxiliary, Department of Pennsylvania
PO Box 2643
Harrisburg, PA 17105-2643
Phone: 717-763-7545
Fax: 717-763-0617

AMERICAN LEGION AUXILIARY DEPARTMENT OF PENNSYLVANIA SCHOLARSHIP FOR DEPENDENTS OF LIVING VETERANS

Award: Scholarship for use in freshman, sophomore, junior, or senior years.

Eligibility Requirements: Applicant must be enrolled or expecting to enroll at an institution or university.

Contact: Colleen Watson, Executive Secretary and Treasurer
American Legion Auxiliary, Department of Pennsylvania
PO Box 2643
Harrisburg, PA 17105-2643
Phone: 717-763-7545
Fax: 717-763-0617

AMERICAN LEGION, DEPARTMENT OF INDIANA
http://www.indlegion.org

AMERICAN LEGION DEPARTMENT OF INDIANA, AMERICANISM AND GOVERNMENT TEST

Award: Scholarship for use in freshman year.

Eligibility Requirements: Applicant must be enrolled or expecting to enroll at an institution or university.

Contact: Susan Long, Program Coordinator
American Legion, Department of Indiana
777 North Meridan Street, Room 104
Indianapolis, IN 46204
Phone: 317-630-1264
Fax: 317-237-9891
E-mail: slong@indlegion.org

AMERICAN LEGION, DEPARTMENT OF KANSAS
http://www.ksamlegion.org

CHARLES W. AND ANNETTE HILL SCHOLARSHIP

Award: Scholarship for use in freshman or sophomore years.

Eligibility Requirements: Applicant must be enrolled or expecting to enroll at an institution or university.

Contact: Scholarship Administrator
American Legion, Department of Kansas
1314 Southwest Topeka Boulevard
Topeka, KS 66612-1886

NATIONAL HIGH SCHOOL ORATORICAL CONTEST

Award: Prize for use in freshman year.

Eligibility Requirements: Applicant must be enrolled or expecting to enroll at an institution or university.

Contact: Scholarship Administrator
American Legion, Department of Kansas
1314 Southwest Topeka Boulevard
Topeka, KS 66612-1886

AMERICAN LEGION, DEPARTMENT OF NEBRASKA
http://www.legion.org

AMERICAN LEGION DEPARTMENT OF NEBRASKA ORATORICAL AWARDS

Award: Prize for use in freshman year.

Eligibility Requirements: Applicant must be enrolled or expecting to enroll at an institution or university.

Contact: Burdette Burkhart, Activities Director
American Legion, Department of Nebraska
200 North 56th Street
PO Box 5205
Lincoln, NE 68505-0205
Phone: 402-464-6338
Fax: 402-464-6330
E-mail: nebraska@legion.org or actdirlegion@alltel.net

AMERICAN LEGION, DEPARTMENT OF TENNESSEE

AMERICAN LEGION DEPARTMENT OF TENNESSEE EAGLE SCOUT OF THE YEAR

Award: Scholarship for use in freshman year.

Eligibility Requirements: Applicant must be enrolled or expecting to enroll at an institution or university.

Contact: Darlene Burgess, Executive Assistant
American Legion, Department of Tennessee
215 Eighth Avenue North
Nashville, TN 37203
Phone: 615-254-0568
Fax: 615-255-1551

AMERICAN LEGION DEPARTMENT OF TENNESSEE ORATORICAL CONTEST

Award: Prize for use in freshman year.

Eligibility Requirements: Applicant must be enrolled or expecting to enroll at an institution or university.

Contact: Darlene Burgess, Executive Assistant
American Legion, Department of Tennessee
215 Eighth Avenue North
Nashville, TN 37203
Phone: 615-254-0568
Fax: 615-255-1551

AMERICAN NATIONAL CATTLEWOMEN, INC.
http://www.ancw.org

NATIONAL BEEF AMBASSADOR PROGRAM

Award's purpose is to train young spokespersons in the beef industry. Applicant must be fully prepared to answer questions and debate focusing on topic related to beef consumption and distribution, as well as social factors related to the industry. Details and tools for preparation are available on the Web site: http://www.ancw.org

Award: Prize for use in freshman year; not renewable. *Number:* 1–3. *Amount:* $500–$2500.

Eligibility Requirements: Applicant must be high school student; age 16-19 and planning to enroll or expecting to enroll at an institution or university. Available to U.S. citizens.

Application Requirements: Applicant must enter a contest. *Deadline:* August 13.

Contact: Carol Abrahamzon, Project Manager
American National CattleWomen, Inc.
PO Box 3881
Englewood, CO 80155
E-mail: cabrahamzon@beef.org

AMERICAN NEPHROLOGY NURSES' ASSOCIATION   http://www.annanurse.org

AMERICAN NEPHROLOGY NURSES' ASSOCIATION BIOETHICS GRANT

Award: Grant for use in junior, senior, or graduate years.

Eligibility Requirements: Applicant must be enrolled or expecting to enroll at an institution or university.

Contact: Charlotte Thomas-Hawkins, American Nephrology Nurses'
Association
American Nephrology Nurses' Association
East Holly Avenue
Box 56
Pitman, NJ 08071-0056
Phone: 856-256-2320
Fax: 856-589-7463
E-mail: anna@ajj.com

AMERICAN PHYSIOLOGICAL SOCIETY   http://www.the-aps.org

DAVID S. BRUCE AWARDS FOR EXCELLENCE IN UNDERGRADUATE RESEARCH

Award available for research in physiology. The student must be enrolled as an undergraduate student at the time of the application and at the time of the EB meeting. The applicant must be the first author on a submitted abstract for the EB meeting and must be working with an APS member who attests that the student is deserving of the first authorship.

Award: Prize for use in freshman, sophomore, junior, or senior years. *Amount:* up to $500.

Eligibility Requirements: Applicant must be enrolled or expecting to enroll full-time at a four-year institution or university. Available to U.S. citizens.

Application Requirements: Application. *Deadline:* varies.

Contact: Melinda Lowy, Education Office
American Physiological Society
9650 Rockville Pike
Bethesda, MD 20814
Phone: 301-634-7098
E-mail: mlowy@the-aps.org

AMERICAN PUBLIC POWER ASSOCIATION

DEMONSTRATION OF ENERGY EFFICIENT DEVELOPMENTS SCHOLARSHIP

Award: Scholarship for use in sophomore, junior, or senior years.

Eligibility Requirements: Applicant must be enrolled or expecting to enroll at an institution or university.

Contact:

AMERICAN ROAD & TRANSPORTATION BUILDERS ASSOCIATION-TRANSPORTATION DEVELOPMENT FOUNDATION (ARTBA-TDF   http://www.artba.org

ARTBA-TDF HIGHWAY WORKERS MEMORIAL SCHOLARSHIP PROGRAM

The ARTBA-TDF Highway Worker Memorial Scholarship Program provides financial assistance to help the sons, daughters or legally adopted children of highway workers killed or permanently disabled in the line of duty pursue post-high school education. Minimum 2.5 GPA required.

Award: Scholarship for use in freshman, sophomore, junior, senior, or graduate years; not renewable. *Number:* varies. *Amount:* $1000–$2000.

Eligibility Requirements: Applicant must be enrolled or expecting to enroll full or part-time at a two-year or four-year or technical institution or university. Applicant must have 2.5 GPA or higher. Available to U.S. citizens.

Application Requirements: Application, essay, financial need analysis, photo, references, transcript, copy of current year's federal tax return, copy of parents' current year federal tax return. *Deadline:* March 1.

Contact: Rhonda Britton, Scholarship and Awards Manager
American Road & Transportation Builders Association-
Transportation Development Foundation (ARTBA-TDF
1219 28th Street, NW
Washington, DC 20007
Phone: 202-289-4434
E-mail: rbritton@artba.org

AMERICAN SAVINGS FOUNDATION SCHOLARSHIP   http://www.americansavingsfoundation.org/

AMERICAN SAVINGS FOUNDATION SCHOLARSHIP

Scholarship for students entering any year of a 2- or 4-year undergraduate program or technical/ vocational program at an accredited institution. Current college students and nontraditional adult students working on no higher than a first bachelor's degree can also apply. Applicants must be a resident of one of the 64 Connecticut towns served by American Savings Foundation.

Award: Scholarship for use in freshman, sophomore, junior, or senior years; renewable. *Amount:* $500–$3000.

Eligibility Requirements: Applicant must be enrolled or expecting to enroll at a two-year or four-year institution or university. Applicant must have 2.5 GPA or higher. Available to U.S. citizens.

Application Requirements: Application, references, transcript, Student Aid Report (SAR). *Deadline:* March 31.

Contact: Maria Falvo, Senior Program Officer
American Savings Foundation Scholarship
American Savings Foundation, 185 Main Street
New Britain, CT 06051
Phone: 860-827-2556
E-mail: info@asfdn.org

AMERICAN SCHOOL OF CLASSICAL STUDIES AT ATHENS   http://www.ascsa.edu.gr

THE CHARLES M. EDWARDS SCHOLARSHIP

Scholarship is awarded to an exceptional undergraduate.

Award: Scholarship for use in freshman, sophomore, junior, or senior years. *Amount:* up to $500.

Eligibility Requirements: Applicant must be enrolled or expecting to enroll at a four-year institution or university. Available to U.S. citizens.

Application Requirements: Application. *Deadline:* varies.

Contact: Timothy F. Winters, Chair, Committee on the Summer
Sessions
American School of Classical Studies at Athens
6-8 Charlton Street
Princeton, NJ 08540-5232
Phone: 609-683-0800
Fax: 609-924-0578
E-mail: ascsa@ascsa.org

AMERICAN SOCIETY OF MECHANICAL ENGINEERS (ASME INTERNATIONAL)   http://www.asme.org

AMERICAN SOCIETY OF MECHANICAL ENGINEERS STEPHEN T. KUGLE SCHOLARSHIP

Scholarship available to an ASME member attending a public college in ASME Region 10. Must be a U.S. citizen and have a 3.0 minimum GPA. For study in the junior and senior year. Application deadline is March 15.

Award: Scholarship for use in junior or senior years; not renewable. *Number:* 1. *Amount:* $2000.

Eligibility Requirements: Applicant must be enrolled or expecting to enroll full-time at a two-year or four-year institution or university. Applicant must have 3.0 GPA or higher. Available to U.S. citizens.

American Society of Mechanical Engineers (ASME International)
(continued)

Application Requirements: Application, transcript. *Deadline:* March 15.

Contact: Maisha Phillips, Coordinator, Student Development ASME
American Society of Mechanical Engineers (ASME International)
3 Park Avenue
New York, NY 10016-5990
Phone: 212-591-8131
Fax: 212-591-7143
E-mail: phillipsm@asme.org

AMERICAN WELDING SOCIETY   http://www.aws.org

JERRY ROBINSON-INWELD CORPORATION SCHOLARSHIP

Awarded to a student with significant financial need interested in pursuing a career in welding. Applicant must have a 2.5 overall grade point average. Applicant must be 18 years of age by October 1 of the year the scholarship is awarded. Must be U.S. citizen.

Award: Scholarship for use in freshman, sophomore, junior, or senior years; renewable. *Number:* 1. *Amount:* $2500.

Eligibility Requirements: Applicant must be age 18 and enrolled or expecting to enroll full-time at a four-year institution. Applicant must have 2.5 GPA or higher. Available to U.S. citizens.

Application Requirements: Application, autobiography, essay, financial need analysis, photo, references, transcript, copies of student's and parents'/guardians' previous year's tax returns. *Deadline:* January 15.

Contact: Vicki Pinsky, Manager Foundation
American Welding Society
550 Northwest Le Jeune Road
Miami, FL 33126
Phone: 800-443-9353 Ext. 212
Fax: 305-443-7559
E-mail: vpinsky@aws.org

AMERICAN WOMAN'S SOCIETY OF CERTIFIED PUBLIC ACCOUNTANTS–SAN FRANCISCO AFFILIATE   http://www.awscpa.org

NATIONAL SCHOLARSHIP

Scholarship for an entering senior, 5th year student, or graduate student. Applicant must have a 3.0 GPA in accounting and a 3.0 GPA overall. Applicant must be a U.S. citizen.

Award: Scholarship for use in senior, or graduate years. *Amount:* up to $2200.

Eligibility Requirements: Applicant must be enrolled or expecting to enroll at a four-year institution or university. Applicant must have 3.0 GPA or higher. Available to U.S. citizens.

Application Requirements: Application, essay, transcript. *Deadline:* varies.

Contact: Irma Cayanan, Scholarship Chairperson
American Woman's Society of Certified Public Accountants–
San Francisco Affiliate
PO Box 193213
San Francisco, CA 94119
Phone: 415-974-6000
E-mail: icayanan@hlwcpa.com

AMERICA'S JUNIOR MISS SCHOLARSHIP PROGRAM   http://www.ajm.org

AMERICA'S JUNIOR MISS SCHOLARSHIP PROGRAM

Awards are given to contestants in local, regional and national levels of competition. Contestants must be female, high school juniors or seniors, U.S. citizens and legal residents of the county and state of competition. Contestants are evaluated on scholastics, interview, talent, fitness and poise. The number of awards and their amount vary from year to year. For more information visit http://www.ajm.org

Award: Scholarship for use in freshman, sophomore, junior, or senior years; not renewable. *Number:* varies. *Amount:* varies.

Eligibility Requirements: Applicant must be high school student; age 16-18; planning to enroll or expecting to enroll full-time at a two-year or four-year institution or university and single female. Available to U.S. citizens.

Application Requirements: Application, applicant must enter a contest, test scores, transcript, birth certificate, certificate of health. *Deadline:* Continuous.

Contact: Becky Jo Peterson, Executive Director
America's Junior Miss Scholarship Program
751 Government Street
Mobile, AL 36652-2786
Phone: 251-438-3621
Fax: 251-431-0063
E-mail: beckyjo@ajm.org

AMVETS DEPARTMENT OF ILLINOIS   http://www.ilamvets.org

ILLINOIS AMVETS JUNIOR ROTC SCHOLARSHIPS

Four-year scholarship of $1,000 per year for students who have taken the ACT or SAT tests. Preference will be given to children or grandchildren of a veteran.

Award: Scholarship for use in freshman, sophomore, junior, or senior years; renewable. *Amount:* up to $1000.

Eligibility Requirements: Applicant must be high school student and planning to enroll or expecting to enroll at a four-year institution or university. Available to U.S. citizens.

Application Requirements: Application, test scores. *Deadline:* March 1.

Contact: Sara Van Dyke, Scholarship Director
AMVETS Department of Illinois
State Headquarters
2200 South Sixth Street
Springfield, IL 62703
Phone: 217-528-4713
Fax: 217-528-9896
E-mail: scholarship@amvetsillinois.com

ANCIENT ACCEPTED SCOTTISH RITE OF FREEMASONRY, NORTHERN JURISDICTION SUPREME COUNCIL, 33   http://www.supremecouncil.org

LEON M. ABBOTT SCHOLARSHIPS

Awards for the continuing education of young men and women from Scottish Rite families and Masonic-related youth groups. May be the child or grandchild of a Scottish Rite Mason in the Northern Masonic Jurisdiction, or a graduate of one of the 32nd degree Masonic Learning Centers for Children in the Northern Masonic Jurisdiction.

Award: Scholarship for use in freshman, sophomore, junior, or senior years.

Eligibility Requirements: Applicant must be enrolled or expecting to enroll at a two-year or four-year or technical institution or university. Applicant must have 2.5 GPA or higher. Available to U.S. citizens.

Application Requirements: Application, financial need analysis, transcript, FAFSA. *Deadline:* varies.

Contact: David Olmstead, Public Relations
Ancient Accepted Scottish Rite of Freemasonry, Northern Jurisdiction Supreme Council, 33
PO Box 519
Lexington, MA 02420-0519
Phone: 781-862-4410
Fax: 781-862-1833
E-mail: dolmstead@supremecouncil.org

ARIZONA POLICE CORPS   http://www.azpolicecorps.com

ARIZONA POLICE CORPS SCHOLARSHIP

Scholarships available for full-time undergraduate students and part-time graduate students. Must complete police training academy and agree to a four year employment commitment as an officer in a state or local police force. See Web site for details and an application. http://www.azpolicecorps.com

Award: Scholarship for use in freshman, sophomore, junior, senior, or graduate years. *Number:* 10. *Amount:* up to $23,000.

Eligibility Requirements: Applicant must be enrolled or expecting to enroll full or part-time at a four-year institution or university. Applicant must have 2.5 GPA or higher. Available to U.S. citizens.

Application Requirements: Application, driver's license, references, transcript, DD Form 214. *Deadline:* Continuous.

Contact: Jon Heiden
Arizona Police Corps
8470 N Overfield Road
Coolidge, AZ 85228
Phone: 800-460-1395
E-mail: info@azpolicecorps.com

ARIZONA STATE DEPARTMENT OF EDUCATION
http://www.ade.state.az.us

ROBERT C. BYRD HONORS SCHOLARSHIP-ARIZONA

Federally funded program for high school graduates who show academic excellence and the promise of continued postsecondary education. A Byrd Scholar receives $1500 for each academic year for a maximum of four years to be applied toward undergraduate study at any accredited college or university in the United States. The number of scholarships awarded each year is subject to change due to funding. Deadline is March 27.

Award: Scholarship for use in freshman, sophomore, junior, or senior years; renewable. *Number:* 50–100. *Amount:* $3000–$6000.

Eligibility Requirements: Applicant must be high school student and planning to enroll or expecting to enroll full or part-time at a two-year or four-year or technical institution or university. Available to U.S. citizens.

Application Requirements: Application, transcript. *Deadline:* March 27.

Contact: Jessica Enders, Robert C. Byrd Scholarship Coordinator
Arizona State Department of Education
1535 West Jefferson
Phoenix, AZ 85007
Phone: 602-542-3710
Fax: 602-364-1532
E-mail: jenders@ade.az.gov

ARKANSAS STATE DEPARTMENT OF EDUCATION
http://arkedu.state.ar.us

ROBERT C. BYRD HONORS SCHOLARSHIP-ARKANSAS

Federally funded program for high school graduates who show academic excellence and the promise of continued postsecondary education. Award is $1500 for each academic year for a maximum of four years to be applied toward undergraduate study at any accredited college or university in the United States. The number of scholarships awarded each year is subject to change due to funding. Deadline is February 17.

Award: Scholarship for use in freshman, sophomore, junior, or senior years; renewable. *Number:* 62–100. *Amount:* $3000–$6000.

Eligibility Requirements: Applicant must be enrolled or expecting to enroll full or part-time at a two-year or four-year or technical institution or university. Available to U.S. and non-Canadian citizens.

Application Requirements: Application, transcript. *Deadline:* February 17.

Contact: Margaret Amps, Program Coordinator
Arkansas State Department of Education
4 State Capitol Mall, Room 107A
Little Rock, AR 72201
Phone: 501-682-4396
E-mail: mcrank@arkedu.k12.ar.us

ART INSTITUTES
http://www.artinstitutes.edu

EVELYN KEEDY MEMORIAL SCHOLARSHIP

A $30,000 tuition scholarship awarded to a worthy high school senior who has enrolled at one of the eligible Art Institute locations. Recipients must begin program of study in the summer or fall quarter following high school graduation, and be accepted in order to validate the scholarship.

Award: Scholarship for use in freshman, sophomore, junior, or senior years; renewable. *Number:* 1. *Amount:* up to $30,000.

Eligibility Requirements: Applicant must be high school student and planning to enroll or expecting to enroll full-time at a technical institution. Applicant must have 2.5 GPA or higher. Available to U.S. citizens.

Application Requirements: Application, essay, resume, references, transcript. *Deadline:* May 1.

Contact: Art Institutes
3601 West Sunflower Avenue
Santa Ana, CA 92704-9888
Phone: 888-549-3055

ASSOCIATED MEDICAL SERVICES, INC.
http://www.ams-inc.on.ca

ASSOCIATED MEDICAL SERVICES, INC. BIOETHICS STUDENTSHIP
• *See page 606*

ASSOCIATION FOR IRON AND STEEL TECHNOLOGY
http://www.aist.org

ASSOCIATION FOR IRON AND STEEL TECHNOLOGY MIDWEST CHAPTER NON-ENGINEERING SCHOLARSHIP

Scholarship will be awarded to a graduating high school senior, or undergraduate freshman, sophomore, or junior enrolled in a fully AIST accredited college or university. Applicant must be in good academic standing. Applicant must be a dependent of an AIST Midwest Chapter member.

Award: Scholarship for use in freshman, sophomore, or junior years; not renewable. *Number:* 2. *Amount:* $1000.

Eligibility Requirements: Applicant must be enrolled or expecting to enroll full-time at a four-year institution or university. Available to U.S. citizens.

Application Requirements: Application, essay, references, transcript. *Deadline:* May 15.

Contact: Michael Heaney, Division Manager Maintenance and Engineering, ISG Indiana Harbor
Association for Iron and Steel Technology
3001 Dickey Road
East Chicago, IN 46312

ASSOCIATION FOR IRON AND STEEL TECHNOLOGY MIDWEST CHAPTER WESTERN STATES SCHOLARSHIP

Scholarship will be awarded to a graduating high school senior, or undergraduate freshman, sophomore, or junior enrolled in a fully AIST accredited college or university. Applicant must be in good academic standing. Applicant must be a dependent of an AIST Midwest Chapter member.

Award: Scholarship for use in freshman, sophomore, or junior years; not renewable. *Number:* 1. *Amount:* $2500.

Eligibility Requirements: Applicant must be enrolled or expecting to enroll full-time at a four-year institution or university. Available to U.S. citizens.

Application Requirements: Application, essay, references, transcript. *Deadline:* May 15.

Contact: Michael Heaney, Division Manager Maintenance and Engineering, ISG Indiana Harbor
Association for Iron and Steel Technology
3001 Dickey Road
East Chicago, IN 46312

ASSOCIATION OF INTERNATIONAL EDUCATION, JAPAN (AIEJ)

SHORT-TERM STUDENT EXCHANGE PROMOTION PROGRAM SCHOLARSHIP

Scholarship available for qualified students accepted by Japanese universities under the student exchange agreement on a short-term basis from three months to one year. Scholarship includes a $645 monthly stipend, a $200 settling-in allowance, and round-trip, economy-class airfare. Application should be filed by Japanese host institution. Inquiries should be addressed to the international office of the home institution. Deadline decided by host institution.

Association of International Education, Japan (AIEJ) (continued)

Award: Scholarship for use in freshman, sophomore, junior, senior, or graduate years; not renewable. *Number:* 1950. *Amount:* $5650–$8244.

Eligibility Requirements: Applicant must be enrolled or expecting to enroll full-time at a two-year or four-year institution or university. Available to U.S. and non-U.S. citizens.

Application Requirements: Applicant must enter a contest, to be decided by home and host institutions. *Deadline:* varies.

Contact: Chika Hotta, Program Coordinator, Office for Cooperation
with Extrabudgetary Funding Sources, AIEJ
Association of International Education, Japan (AIEJ)
4-5-29 Komaba, Meguro-ku
Tokyo 153-8503
Japan
Phone: 81-03-5454-5290
Fax: 81-03-5454-5299
E-mail: efs@aiej.or.jp

ASSOCIATION OF NEW JERSEY ENVIRONMENTAL COMMISSIONS   http://www.anjec.org

LECHNER SCHOLARSHIP

Award of $1000 scholarship for a student entering his/her junior or senior year at an accredited New Jersey college or university. Must be a New Jersey resident and have a GPA of 3.0. Application deadline is April 14.

Award: Scholarship for use in junior or senior years; not renewable. *Number:* 1. *Amount:* up to $1000.

Eligibility Requirements: Applicant must be enrolled or expecting to enroll full-time at a four-year institution or university. Applicant must have 3.0 GPA or higher. Available to U.S. citizens.

Application Requirements: Application, essay, references, transcript. *Deadline:* April 14.

Contact: Abigali Fair, Water Resources Director
Association of New Jersey Environmental Commissions
PO Box 157
Mendham, NJ 07945
Phone: 973-539-7547
Fax: 973-539-7713
E-mail: afair@anjec.org

ASSOCIATION ON AMERICAN INDIAN AFFAIRS (AAIA)   http://www.indian-affairs.org

EMILIE HESSMEYER MEMORIAL SCHOLARSHIP

Award: Scholarship for use in freshman, sophomore, junior or senior years.

Eligibility Requirements: Applicant must be enrolled or expecting to enroll at an institution or university.

Contact: Scholarship Coordinator
Association on American Indian Affairs (AAIA)
966 Hungerford Drive
Suite 12-B
Rockville, MD 20850
Phone: 605-698-3998
Fax: 605-698-3316
E-mail: aaia@sbtc.net

AUTOMATION ALLEY SCHOLARSHIP   http://www.automationalley.com

AUTOMATION ALLEY SCHOLARSHIP PROGRAM

Scholarships for an employee or immediate family member of an employee of an Automation Alley member company.

Award: Scholarship for use in freshman, sophomore, junior, or senior years. *Number:* 1.

Eligibility Requirements: Applicant must be enrolled or expecting to enroll full or part-time at a two-year or four-year institution or university. Available to U.S. citizens.

Application Requirements: Application.

Contact: Automation Alley Resource Center
Phone: 800-427-5100
E-mail: info@automationalley.com

AUTOMOTIVE RECYCLERS ASSOCIATION SCHOLARSHIP FOUNDATION   http://www.autorecyc.org

AUTOMOTIVE RECYCLERS ASSOCIATION SCHOLARSHIP FOUNDATION SCHOLARSHIP

Scholarships are available for the post-high school educational pursuits for the children of employees of direct ARA member companies. The deadline for completed scholarship applications is March 15 of each year.

Award: Scholarship for use in freshman, sophomore, junior, or senior years; not renewable. *Number:* 35–45. *Amount:* $500–$1000.

Eligibility Requirements: Applicant must be high school student and planning to enroll or expecting to enroll full-time at a two-year or four-year or technical institution or university. Applicant must have 3.0 GPA or higher. Available to U.S. and non-U.S. citizens.

Application Requirements: Application, transcript. *Deadline:* March 15.

Contact: Kelly Badillo, Director Member Services
Automotive Recyclers Association Scholarship Foundation
3975 Fair Ridge Drive, Suite 20-North
Fairfax, VA 22033
Phone: 703-385-1001 Ext. 26
Fax: 703-385-1494
E-mail: kelly@a-r-a.org

BANK OF AMERICA STUDENT BANKING GROUP   http://www.bankofamerica.com/studentbanking

BANK OF AMERICA FINANCIAL AID SWEEPSTAKES

Sweepstakes award to students. Five awards of $1000. Online application available at http://www.bankofamerica.com. Must be legal resident of U.S., including the District of Columbia, 13 years of age or older and high school seniors or college students attending a high school or college or university within the U.S. Eligible minors must have their parent's or legal guardian's permission to enter.

Award: Scholarship for use in freshman, sophomore, junior, or senior years; not renewable. *Number:* up to 5. *Amount:* up to $1000.

Eligibility Requirements: Applicant must be age 13 and enrolled or expecting to enroll full-time at a two-year or four-year institution or university. Available to U.S. and non-U.S. citizens.

Application Requirements: Application. *Deadline:* August 1.

Contact: Program Manager
Bank of America Student Banking Group
PO Box 515210
Los Angeles, CA 90051-6510
Phone: 213-345-2244

BEST BUY CHILDREN FOUNDATION   http://communications.bestbuy.com

BEST BUY SCHOLARSHIPS

Scholarships available to students based on outstanding community service and high academic achievement. Must be entering an accredited U.S. university, college or technical school in the fall immediately following their high school graduation.

Award: Scholarship for use in freshman, graduate, or postgraduate years. *Number:* 60. *Amount:* $1000–$25,000.

Eligibility Requirements: Applicant must be enrolled or expecting to enroll full or part-time at a two-year or four-year or technical institution or university. Available to U.S. citizens.

Application Requirements: *Deadline:* February 15.

Contact: Brad Anderson, CEO
Best Buy Children Foundation
PO Box 9421
Minneapolis, MN 55440
E-mail: CommunityRelations@BestBuy.com

BOY SCOUTS OF AMERICA - MUSKINGUM VALLEY COUNCIL
http://www.learning-for-life.org

YOUNG AMERICAN AWARD

Award given to young adults between the ages of 15 and 25 who have achieved excellence in the fields of art, athletics, business, education, government, humanities, literature, music, religion, science or service and have been involved in service to their community, state or country that adds to the quality of life. Each council selects and submits their top nominee for consideration for the five national awards.

Award: Prize for use in freshman, sophomore, or junior years. *Number:* 5. *Amount:* $5000.

Eligibility Requirements: Applicant must be age 15-25 and enrolled or expecting to enroll at a four-year institution. Available to U.S. citizens.

Application Requirements: Application, references, transcript. *Deadline:* January 2.

Contact: Boy Scouts of America - Muskingum Valley Council
1325 West Walnut Hill Lane, PO Box 152079
Irving, TX 75015-2079
Fax: 972-580-2137

BOYS AND GIRLS CLUBS OF GREATER SAN DIEGO
http://www.sdyouth.org

BOYS AND GIRLS CLUBS FOUNDATION SCHOLARSHIP

Renewable scholarship for graduating high school seniors from a qualified high school in the Club's service area. Must have been a member of the Boys and Girls Clubs of Greater San Diego for one or more years. Application deadline is April 15.

Award: Scholarship for use in freshman, sophomore, junior, or senior years; renewable. *Number:* varies. *Amount:* $1000.

Eligibility Requirements: Applicant must be high school student and planning to enroll or expecting to enroll full-time at a four-year institution or university. Applicant must have 3.0 GPA or higher. Available to U.S. citizens.

Application Requirements: Application, financial need analysis. *Deadline:* April 15.

Contact: Danny Sherlock, President and Chief Executive Officer
Boys and Girls Clubs of Greater San Diego
115 West Woodward Avenue
Escondido, CA 92025
Phone: 760-746-3315

BREAD AND ROSES COMMUNITY FUND
http://www.breadrosesfund.org

JONATHAN R. LAX SCHOLARSHIP FUND

Scholarship to encourage gay men to obtain additional education, aspire to positions in which they contribute to society, be open about their sexual preference and act as role models for other gay men with similar potential. Several awards available, at least one graduate and one undergraduate award of $20,000. Award restricted to those from Philadelphia studying elsewhere or students from anywhere studying in Philadelphia.

Award: Scholarship for use in freshman, sophomore, junior, senior, or graduate years; not renewable. *Number:* 8–10. *Amount:* $5000–$20,000.

Eligibility Requirements: Applicant must be enrolled or expecting to enroll full or part-time at a two-year or four-year institution or university and male. Available to U.S. citizens.

Application Requirements: Application, essay, financial need analysis, interview, references, transcript. *Deadline:* January 16.

Contact: Salih Watts, Lax Outreach Coordinator
Bread and Roses Community Fund
1500 Walnut Street, Suite 1305
Philadelphia, PA 19102
Phone: 215-731-1107 Ext. 205
Fax: 215-731-0453
E-mail: info@breadrosesfund.org

BRITISH COLUMBIA MINISTRY OF ADVANCED EDUCATION
http://www.aved.gov.bc.ca/

IRVING K. BARBER BRITISH COLUMBIA SCHOLARSHIP PROGRAM

Scholarship open to students who, after completing two years at a B.C. public community college, university college or institute, must transfer to another public post secondary institution in B.C. to complete their degree. Students must demonstrate merit as well as exceptional involvement in their institution and community. Must have a GPA of at least 3.5 or 87.5 per cent for the 54 credits completed.

Award: Scholarship for use in junior or senior years. *Number:* up to 150. *Amount:* up to $5000.

Eligibility Requirements: Applicant must be enrolled or expecting to enroll full-time at a four-year institution or university. Applicant must have 3.5 GPA or higher.

Application Requirements: Application, essay, references, test scores, transcript. *Deadline:* March 31.

Contact: Loan Remission and Management Unit
British Columbia Ministry of Advanced Education
PO Box 9173
Stn Prov Govt
Victoria V8W 9H7
Canada
Phone: 800-561-1818

BUREAU OF INDIAN AFFAIRS OFFICE OF INDIAN EDUCATION PROGRAMS
http://www.oiep.bia.edu

BUREAU OF INDIAN AFFAIRS HIGHER EDUCATION GRANT PROGRAM

Award: Grant for use in freshman, sophomore, junior, or senior years.

Eligibility Requirements: Applicant must be enrolled or expecting to enroll at an institution or university.

Contact: Garry Martin, Special Assistant
Bureau of Indian Affairs Office of Indian Education Programs
1849 C Street, NW
MS 3512-MIB
Washington, DC 20240
Phone: 202-208-3478
Fax: 202-219-9583
E-mail: gary_martin@bia.gov

CALIFORNIA STATE PARENT-TEACHER ASSOCIATION
http://www.capta.org/sections/programs/scholarships.cfm

GRADUATING HIGH SCHOOL SENIOR SCHOLARSHIP

Scholarships are available annually from the California State PTA to high school seniors graduating between January and June of each calendar year. Applicant must have volunteered in the school and community and must be graduating from a California public high school that has a PTA unit in good standing. Applicant must be a member of the PTA/PTSA unit at his/her high school. Deadline February 1.

Award: Scholarship for use in freshman year; renewable. *Number:* 500.

Eligibility Requirements: Applicant must be high school student and planning to enroll or expecting to enroll full-time at an institution or university. Available to U.S. citizens.

Application Requirements: Application, essay, references, copy of membership card. *Deadline:* February 1.

Contact: Becky Reece, Scholarship and Award Chairman
California State Parent-Teacher Association
930 Georgia Street
Los Angeles, CA 90015-1322
Phone: 213-620-1100
Fax: 213-620-1411

CANADA MILLENNIUM SCHOLARSHIP FOUNDATION
http://www.millenniumscholarships.ca

CANADA MILLENNIUM EXCELLENCE AWARD PROGRAM
• *See page 608*

CANTOR FITZGERALD RELIEF FUND
(SEPT. 11)
http://www.cantorrelief.org

CANTOR FITZGERALD RELIEF FUND

Part of relief fund will provide assistance with college tuition. Help will go to the families of any victims of the World Trade Center disaster who were employed by Cantor Fitzgerald.

Award: Scholarship for use in freshman, sophomore, junior, or senior years; not renewable. *Number:* 1. *Amount:* varies.

Eligibility Requirements: Applicant must be enrolled or expecting to enroll at an institution or university. Available to U.S. citizens.

Application Requirements: *Deadline:* varies.

Contact: Cantor Fitzgerald Relief Fund (Sept. 11)
110 East 59th Street, 5th Floor
New York, NY 10022
Phone: 212-829-4770
Fax: 212-829-4895

CAREER COLLEGE FOUNDATION
http://www.careercollegefoundation.com

IMAGINE AMERICA SCHOLARSHIP

One-time award available to graduating high school seniors. Must attend an accredited private postsecondary institution. Must be nominated by school counselor or principal. Must enroll by October 31. See Web site: http://www.careercollegefoundation.com. Contact the guidance counselor at high school.

Award: Scholarship for use in freshman year; not renewable. *Number:* up to 8500. *Amount:* $1000.

Eligibility Requirements: Applicant must be high school student; age 17-18 and planning to enroll or expecting to enroll full-time at a two-year or four-year or technical institution. Applicant must have 2.5 GPA or higher. Available to U.S. citizens.

Application Requirements: Applicant must enter a contest, financial need analysis, nomination. *Deadline:* December 31.

Contact: Robert Martin, Executive Director/Vice President
Career College Foundation
10 G Street, NE, Suite 750
Washington, DC 20002-4213
Phone: 202-336-6800
Fax: 202-408-8102
E-mail: bobm@career.org

CAREERFITTER.COM
http://www.careerfitter.net

CAREERFITTER.COM SCHOLARSHIP

Scholarship available to qualified student enrolled, or planning to enroll, in a technical school, college, or university program for the next school term. Must be a U.S. citizen or permanent resident. Must submit an original essay with application. All applications and essays must be submitted online. Deadline dates are posted next to each scholarship at Web site: http://www.careerfitter.com

Award: Scholarship for use in freshman, sophomore, junior, senior, graduate, or postgraduate years; not renewable. *Number:* 4–5. *Amount:* $500–$1000.

Eligibility Requirements: Applicant must be enrolled or expecting to enroll full or part-time at a two-year or four-year or technical institution or university. Applicant must have 2.5 GPA or higher. Available to U.S. and non-U.S. citizens.

Application Requirements: Application, applicant must enter a contest, essay. *Deadline:* varies.

Contact: Troy Norton
CareerFitter.com
269 South Beverly Drive, Suite 224
Beverly Hills, CA 90212
Phone: 310-990-8769
E-mail: admin3@CareerFitter.com

CARGILL
http://www.cargill.com

CARGILL COMMUNITY SCHOLARSHIP PROGRAM

One-time scholarships administered by the National FFA Organization. Each award is valued at $1000, and also enables the recipient's high school to become eligible for a $200 library grant. Award is designed for students pursuing a two- or four-year degree in the U.S. Applicants must be U.S. high school students who live in or near Cargill communities. Students are required to obtain a signature on their applications from a manager at a local Cargill facility or subsidiary.

Award: Scholarship for use in freshman year; not renewable. *Number:* 350. *Amount:* $1000.

Eligibility Requirements: Applicant must be high school student and planning to enroll or expecting to enroll full-time at a two-year or four-year or technical institution or university. Available to U.S. citizens.

Application Requirements: Application. *Deadline:* February 15.

Contact: Bonnie Blue, Cargill Community Relations
Cargill
PO Box 9300
Minneapolis, MN 55440-9300
Phone: 952-742-6247
Fax: 952-742-7224
E-mail: bonnie_l_blue@cargill.com

CARGILL NATIONAL MERIT SCHOLARSHIP PROGRAM FOR SONS AND DAUGHTERS

10 renewable scholarships of $1000 for children of Cargill and Cargill joint-venture employees in the United States. Students apply as juniors.

Award: Scholarship for use in freshman year; renewable. *Number:* 10. *Amount:* $1000.

Eligibility Requirements: Applicant must be high school student and planning to enroll or expecting to enroll at a four-year institution or university. Available to U.S. citizens.

Application Requirements: Application.

Contact: Bonnie Blue, Cargill Community Relations
Cargill
PO Box 9300
Minneapolis, MN 55440-9300
Phone: 952-742-6247
Fax: 952-742-7224
E-mail: bonnie_l_blue@cargill.com

CARGILL SCHOLARSHIP PROGRAM FOR SONS AND DAUGHTERS

Awards 40 one-time scholarships of $3000 to high-school seniors who are the children of Cargill and Cargill joint-venture employees in the United States.

Award: Scholarship for use in freshman year; not renewable. *Number:* 40. *Amount:* $3000.

Eligibility Requirements: Applicant must be high school student and planning to enroll or expecting to enroll full-time at an institution or university. Available to U.S. citizens.

Application Requirements: Application.

Contact: Bonnie Blue, Cargill Community Relations
Cargill
PO Box 9300
Minneapolis, MN 55440-9300
Phone: 952-742-6247
Fax: 952-742-7224
E-mail: bonnie_l_blue@cargill.com

CARPE DIEM FOUNDATION OF ILLINOIS
http://www.carpediemfoundation.org

CARPE DIEM FOUNDATION OF ILLINOIS SCHOLARSHIP COMPETITION

Renewable awards for U.S. citizens studying full time at accredited U.S. educational institutions, including colleges, universities, music conservatories, schools of design, and academies of the arts. For undergraduate study only. Merit based. The award is open to all, but priority is given to students whose parents are or have been employed in education: local, state, or federal government, social service or public health; the administration of justice; the fine arts. Must maintain a B average. Must demonstrate commitment to public service. Application deadline is first week of May. See Web site: http://www.carpediemfoundation.org to download application.

Award: Scholarship for use in freshman, sophomore, junior, or senior years; renewable. *Number:* 10–15. *Amount:* $2500–$5000.

Eligibility Requirements: Applicant must be enrolled or expecting to enroll full-time at a four-year institution or university. Applicant must have 3.0 GPA or higher. Available to U.S. citizens.

Application Requirements: Application, essay, references, self-addressed stamped envelope, test scores, transcript, portfolio, CD, tape (if arts or music candidate). *Fee:* $14. *Deadline:* May.

Contact: Gordon V. Levine, Executive Director
Carpe Diem Foundation of Illinois
PO Box 3194
Chicago, IL 60690-3194
Phone: 312-263-3416
E-mail: glevine@carpediemfoundation.org

CATHOLIC WORKMAN   http://www.fcsla.com

THERESA SAJAN SCHOLARSHIP FOR GRADUATE STUDENTS

Scholarship available to a member in good standing of the First Catholic Slovak Ladies Association.Must be member of the Association for at least three years prior to date of application. For more information check the Web site: www.fcsla.com

Award: Scholarship for use in freshman, sophomore, junior, or senior years; renewable. *Number:* 15–55. *Amount:* $1250–$1750.

Eligibility Requirements: Applicant must be enrolled or expecting to enroll full-time at a four-year institution. Available to U.S. and non-U.S. citizens.

Application Requirements: Application, autobiography, test scores, transcript, document of acceptance.

Contact: Lenore Krava, Executive Secretary
Catholic Workman
24950 Chagrin Boulevard
Beachwood, OH 44122-5634
Phone: 216-464-8015
Fax: 216-464-9260
E-mail: info@fcsla.com

CENTER FOR SCHOLARSHIP
ADMINISTRATION   http://www.scholarshipprograms.org

AFL/FUJIKURA SCHOLARSHIP PROGRAM

Scholarship available for dependent children (defined as natural, adopted and resident step-children) of eligible employees of AFL Telecommunications. Deadline is March 10.

Award: Scholarship for use in freshman year; renewable. *Amount:* $2000.

Eligibility Requirements: Applicant must be high school student and planning to enroll or expecting to enroll at an institution or university. Applicant must have 3.0 GPA or higher. Available to U.S. citizens.

Application Requirements: Application, essay, references, transcript. *Deadline:* March 10.

Contact: Sandra Lee, President
Center for Scholarship Administration
PO Box 1465
Taylors, SC 29687-0031
Phone: 864-268-3363
Fax: 864-268-7160
E-mail: sandralee41@bellsouth.net

ANDERSON AREA SOCIETY FOR HUMAN RESOURCE MANAGEMENT NON-MEMBER SCHOLARSHIP PROGRAM

Award: Scholarship for use in freshman year.

Eligibility Requirements: Applicant must be enrolled or expecting to enroll at an institution or university.

Contact: Sandra Lee, President
Center for Scholarship Administration
PO Box 1465
Taylors, SC 29687-0031
Phone: 864-268-3363
Fax: 864-268-7160
E-mail: sandralee41@bellsouth.net

ANDERSON AREA SOCIETY FOR HUMAN RESOURCE MANAGEMENT SCHOLARSHIP PROGRAM

Award: Scholarship for use in freshman, sophomore, junior, or senior years.

Eligibility Requirements: Applicant must be enrolled or expecting to enroll at an institution or university.

Contact: Sandra Lee, President
Center for Scholarship Administration
PO Box 1465
Taylors, SC 29687-0031
Phone: 864-268-3363
Fax: 864-268-7160
E-mail: sandralee41@bellsouth.net

ETHEL W. CROWLEY MEMORIAL EDUCATION FUND

Award: Scholarship for use in freshman, sophomore, junior, or senior years.

Eligibility Requirements: Applicant must be enrolled or expecting to enroll at an institution or university.

Contact: Sandra Lee, President
Center for Scholarship Administration
PO Box 1465
Taylors, SC 29687-0031
Phone: 864-268-3363
Fax: 864-268-7160
E-mail: sandralee41@bellsouth.net

MAYER SCHOLARSHIP FUND (LIBERTY HARDWARE MANUFACTURING COMPANY)

Award: Scholarship for use in freshman, sophomore, junior, or senior years.

Eligibility Requirements: Applicant must be enrolled or expecting to enroll at an institution or university.

Contact: Sandra Lee, President
Center for Scholarship Administration
PO Box 1465
Taylors, SC 29687-0031
Phone: 864-268-3363
Fax: 864-268-7160
E-mail: sandralee41@bellsouth.net

MICHELIN NORTH AMERICA DEPENDENT SCHOLARSHIP PROGRAM

Scholarship available for natural or legally adopted child or resident stepchild who is a dependent of an eligible Michelin North America, Inc., U.S.A. employee. Deadline is March 1.

Award: Scholarship for use in freshman, sophomore, junior, or senior years; renewable. *Number:* 15. *Amount:* $1000–$2000.

Eligibility Requirements: Applicant must be high school student; age 23; planning to enroll or expecting to enroll at a four-year institution or university and single. Applicant must have 3.0 GPA or higher. Available to U.S. citizens.

Application Requirements: Application. *Deadline:* March 1.

Contact: Sandra Lee, President
Center for Scholarship Administration
PO Box 1465
Taylors, SC 29687-0031
Phone: 864-268-3363
Fax: 864-268-7160
E-mail: sandralee41@bellsouth.net

SOFTBASE MANAGEMENT CORPORATION SCHOLARSHIP

Competitive scholarship available for high shool seniors who are dependent children of employees of Softbase Management Corporation.Award amounts

Center for Scholarship Administration (continued)

will be determined by the financial information submitted by the parents. Minimum GPA of 2.5. Deadline is April 15.

Award: Scholarship for use in freshman, sophomore, junior, or senior years; renewable. *Number:* 1.

Eligibility Requirements: Applicant must be high school student and planning to enroll or expecting to enroll at an institution or university. Applicant must have 2.5 GPA or higher. Available to U.S. citizens.

Application Requirements: Application, essay, references, transcript, copies of parents' federal tax form 1040 (page 1 only) and W-2 forms. *Deadline:* April 15.

Contact: Sandra Lee, President
Center for Scholarship Administration
PO Box 1465
Taylors, SC 29687-0031
Phone: 864-268-3363
Fax: 864-268-7160
E-mail: sandralee41@bellsouth.net

STANDARD GYPSUM SCHOLARSHIP

Scholarship available for dependent children of active employees of Standard Gypsum LP. Recipients will be selected on the basis of academic achievement and potential to succeed in the student's chosen educational field. Deadline is March 15.

Award: Scholarship for use in freshman, sophomore, junior, or senior years; renewable. *Number:* 2. *Amount:* $2000.

Eligibility Requirements: Applicant must be high school student and planning to enroll or expecting to enroll at an institution or university. Applicant must have 2.5 GPA or higher. Available to U.S. citizens.

Application Requirements: Application, essay, references, transcript, copies of parents' federal tax form 1040 (page 1 only) and W-2 forms. *Deadline:* March 15.

Contact: Sandra Lee, President
Center for Scholarship Administration
PO Box 1465
Taylors, SC 29687-0031
Phone: 864-268-3363
Fax: 864-268-7160
E-mail: sandralee41@bellsouth.net

THYSSENKRUPP BUDD-UAW LOCAL 2383 VENDING MACHINE REVENUE COMMITTEE SCHOLARSHIP PROGRAM

Award: Scholarship for use in freshman, sophomore, junior, or senior years.

Eligibility Requirements: Applicant must be enrolled or expecting to enroll at an institution or university.

Contact: Sandra Lee, President
Center for Scholarship Administration
PO Box 1465
Taylors, SC 29687-0031
Phone: 864-268-3363
Fax: 864-268-7160
E-mail: sandralee41@bellsouth.net

UNIVERSAL AMERICAN FINANCIAL CORPORATION SCHOLARSHIP PROGRAM

Award: Scholarship for use in freshman, sophomore, junior, or senior years.

Eligibility Requirements: Applicant must be enrolled or expecting to enroll at an institution or university.

Contact: Sandra Lee, President
Center for Scholarship Administration
PO Box 1465
Taylors, SC 29687-0031
Phone: 864-268-3363
Fax: 864-268-7160
E-mail: sandralee41@bellsouth.net

WACHOVIA INROADS INTERNSHIP SCHOLARSHIP PROGRAM

One-time award to returning interns who have completed at least one summer in the Wachovia INROADS Internship Program.

Award: Scholarship for use in freshman, sophomore, junior, or senior years; not renewable. *Number:* up to 2. *Amount:* $1000.

Eligibility Requirements: Applicant must be enrolled or expecting to enroll at an institution or university. Applicant must have 3.0 GPA or higher. Available to U.S. citizens.

Application Requirements: Application, essay, references, transcript. *Deadline:* February 15.

Contact: Sandra Lee, President
Center for Scholarship Administration
PO Box 1465
Taylors, SC 29687-0031
Phone: 864-268-3363
Fax: 864-268-7160
E-mail: sandralee41@bellsouth.net

CENTRAL SCHOLARSHIP BUREAU   http://www.centralsb.org

CENTRAL SCHOLARSHIP BUREAU GRANTS

A limited number of grants are available each year on a competitive basis. Applicant must be a CSB loan recipient for at least one year prior to applying for this grant.

Award: Grant for use in sophomore, junior, or senior years; not renewable. *Number:* 1.

Eligibility Requirements: Applicant must be enrolled or expecting to enroll at a four-year institution or university. Applicant must have 3.0 GPA or higher. Available to U.S. citizens.

Application Requirements: Application, essay.

Contact: Roberta Goldman, Program Director
Central Scholarship Bureau
1700 Reisterstown Road
Suite 220
Baltimore, MD 21208-2903
Phone: 410-415-5558
Fax: 410-415-5501
E-mail: roberta@centralsb.org

CHATTANOOGA ADVERTISING FEDERATION   http://www.chattadfed.com/students.htm

CHATTANOOGA ADVERTISING FEDERATION SCHOLARSHIP

Scholarship available to a college student in good academic standing who has completed at least two semesters or three quarters. Consideration will be given first to students preparing for careers in advertising. Deadline is March 1.

Award: Scholarship for use in sophomore, junior, or senior years; not renewable. *Number:* up to 3. *Amount:* $1000–$1500.

Eligibility Requirements: Applicant must be enrolled or expecting to enroll at a four-year institution or university. Available to U.S. citizens.

Application Requirements: Application, interview. *Deadline:* March 1.

Contact: Kenny Hammontree
Chattanooga Advertising Federation
The Krystal Company, One Union Square
Chattanooga, TN 37402
Phone: 423-757-1591
E-mail: khammontree@krystalco.com

CHELA EDUCATION FINANCING   http://www.loans4students.org

MONEY MATTERS SCHOLARSHIP

Twenty $5000 scholarships will be awarded to college students who will be enrolled at least halftime. The application requires an essay with a maximum of 300 words in response to the following statement : "How am I financing my college education". Students should focus on responsible borrowing and money management. A 2.0 GPA is required. Application available on Web site: http://www.loans4students.org

Award: Scholarship for use in freshman, sophomore, junior, senior, or graduate years; not renewable. *Number:* 20. *Amount:* $5000.

Eligibility Requirements: Applicant must be enrolled or expecting to enroll full or part-time at a two-year or four-year institution or university. Available to U.S. citizens.

Application Requirements: Application, essay. *Deadline:* varies.

Contact: Jennifer Cox, Scholarship and Outreach Specialist
Chela Education Financing
388 Market Street
12th Floor
San Francisco, CA 94111
Phone: 415-283-2874
Fax: 415-283-2874
E-mail: scholarships@chelafin.org

CHEMICAL INSTITUTE OF CANADA
http://www.cheminst.ca

SNC LAVALIN PLANT DESIGN COMPETITION

Award: Prize for use in freshman, sophomore, junior, or senior years.

Eligibility Requirements: Applicant must be enrolled or expecting to enroll at an institution or university.

Contact: Gale Thirlwall-Wilbee, Manager of Outreach and Career Services
Chemical Institute of Canada
130 Slater Street, Suite 550
Ottawa K1P 6E2
Canada
Phone: 613-232-6252 Ext. 223
Fax: 613-232-5862
E-mail: gwilbee@cheminst.ca

CIRI FOUNDATION
http://www.thecirifoundation.org

CAREER UPGRADE GRANTS

Applicant must be accepted or enrolled part time in a course of study that directly contributes toward potential employment or employment upgrade. May reapply each quarter until grant cap is reached. Must be Alaska Native Student only, CIRI original enrollee or descendant. Minimum 2.5 GPA required. Application deadlines are March 31, June 30, September 30, December 1.

Award: Grant for use in freshman, sophomore, junior, senior, graduate, or postgraduate years; not renewable. *Number:* varies. *Amount:* up to $3000.

Eligibility Requirements: Applicant must be enrolled or expecting to enroll part-time at a two-year or four-year institution or university. Applicant must have 2.5 GPA or higher. Available to U.S. citizens.

Application Requirements: Application, essay, references, transcript, proof of eligibility, birth certificate or adoption decree. *Deadline:* varies.

Contact: Susan Anderson, President/CEO
CIRI Foundation
2600 Cordova Street, Suite 206
Anchorage, AK 99503
Phone: 907-263-5582
Fax: 907-263-5588
E-mail: tcf@ciri.com

CIRI FOUNDATION ACHIEVEMENT ANNUAL SCHOLARSHIPS

Merit scholarships for applicants with exceptional academic promise. Annual award includes two academic semesters. Must be Alaska Native student. Minimum 3.0 GPA required.

Award: Scholarship for use in freshman, sophomore, junior, senior, or graduate years; not renewable. *Number:* varies. *Amount:* $7000–$8000.

Eligibility Requirements: Applicant must be enrolled or expecting to enroll full-time at a two-year or four-year institution or university. Applicant must have 3.0 GPA or higher. Available to U.S. citizens.

Application Requirements: Application, essay, references, transcript, proof of eligibility, birth certificate or adoption decree. *Deadline:* June 1.

Contact: Susan Anderson, President/CFO
CIRI Foundation
2600 Cordova Street, Suite 206
Anchorage, AK 99503
Phone: 907-263-5582
Fax: 907-263-5588
E-mail: tcf@ciri.com

CIRI FOUNDATION EXCELLENCE ANNUAL SCHOLARSHIPS

Merit scholarships for outstanding academic and community services experience. Annual award includes two academic semesters. Minimum 3.5 GPA required. Must be Alaska Native student.

Award: Scholarship for use in freshman, sophomore, junior, senior, or graduate years; not renewable. *Number:* varies. *Amount:* $9000–$10,000.

Eligibility Requirements: Applicant must be enrolled or expecting to enroll full-time at a four-year institution or university. Applicant must have 3.5 GPA or higher. Available to U.S. citizens.

Application Requirements: Application, essay, references, transcript, proof of eligibility, birth certificate or adoption decree. *Deadline:* June 1.

Contact: Susan Anderson, President/CEO
CIRI Foundation
2600 Cordova Street, Suite 206
Anchorage, AK 99503
Phone: 907-263-5582
Fax: 907-263-5588
E-mail: tcf@ciri.com

CIRI FOUNDATION GENERAL FELLOWSHIP GRANTS

Applicant must be accepted or enrolled in a seminar or conference that is accredited, authorized, or approved by the CIRI Foundation. For special employment-related non-credit workshops or seminars. Must be Alaska Native Student, CIRI original enrollee, or descendant at least 18 years of age. Application deadlines are March 31, June 30, September 30, and December 1.

Award: Grant for use in freshman, sophomore, junior, senior, graduate, or postgraduate years; not renewable. *Number:* varies. *Amount:* up to $500.

Eligibility Requirements: Applicant must be age 18 and enrolled or expecting to enroll full or part-time at a two-year or four-year or technical institution or university. Applicant must have 2.5 GPA or higher. Available to U.S. citizens.

Application Requirements: Application, essay, references, transcript, proof of eligibility, birth certificate or adoption decree. *Deadline:* varies.

Contact: Susan Anderson, President/CEO
CIRI Foundation
2600 Cordova Street, Suite 206
Anchorage, AK 99503
Phone: 907-263-5582
Fax: 907-263-5588
E-mail: tcf@ciri.com

CIRI FOUNDATION GENERAL SEMESTER SCHOLARSHIP

Merit scholarships for applicants with academic promise. $2000 per semester award. Minimum 2.5 GPA. Must be Alaska Native student. Deadlines are June 1 and December 1.

Award: Scholarship for use in sophomore, junior, senior, or graduate years; not renewable. *Number:* varies. *Amount:* $2000.

Eligibility Requirements: Applicant must be enrolled or expecting to enroll full-time at a two-year or four-year institution or university. Applicant must have 2.5 GPA or higher. Available to U.S. citizens.

Application Requirements: Application, essay, references, transcript, proof of eligibility, birth certificate or adoption decree. *Deadline:* varies.

Contact: Susan Anderson, President/CEO
CIRI Foundation
2600 Cordova Street, Suite 206
Anchorage, AK 99503
Phone: 907-263-5582
Fax: 907-263-5588
E-mail: tcf@ciri.com

CIRI FOUNDATION SPECIAL EXCELLENCE SCHOLARSHIP

Merit scholarships for exceptional academic and community service experience, offered as encouragement to students to attend outstanding

CIRI Foundation (continued)

colleges and universities in the United States. Must be Alaska Native Student original enrollees/descendants of Cook Inlet Region, Inc. Must have a cumulative GPA of 3.7 or better. Preference given to study in fields of business, education, math, sciences, health services, and engineering.

Award: Scholarship for use in freshman, sophomore, junior, senior, or graduate years; not renewable. *Number:* varies. *Amount:* $18,000–$20,000.

Eligibility Requirements: Applicant must be enrolled or expecting to enroll full-time at a four-year institution or university. Available to U.S. citizens.

Application Requirements: Application, essay, references, transcript, proof of eligibility, birth certificate or adoption decree. *Deadline:* June 1.

Contact: Susan Anderson, President/CEO
CIRI Foundation
2600 Cordova Street, Suite 206
Anchorage, AK 99503
Phone: 907-263-5582

JOHN N. COLBERG ENDOWMENT SCHOLARSHIP FUND

Award: Scholarship for use in freshman, sophomore, junior, senior, or graduate years.

Eligibility Requirements: Applicant must be enrolled or expecting to enroll at an institution or university.

Contact: Susan Anderson, President/CEO
CIRI Foundation
3600 San Jeronimo Drive, Suite 256
Anchorage, AK 99508
Phone: 907-793-3575
Fax: 907-793-3585
E-mail: tcf@thecirifoundation.org

KENAI NATIVES ASSOCIATION (KNA) SCHOLARSHIP AND GRANT FUND

Award: Scholarship for use in freshman, sophomore, junior, senior, or graduate years.

Eligibility Requirements: Applicant must be enrolled or expecting to enroll at an institution or university.

Contact: Susan Anderson, President/CEO
CIRI Foundation
3600 San Jeronimo Drive, Suite 256
Anchorage, AK 99508
Phone: 907-793-3575
Fax: 907-793-3585
E-mail: tcf@thecirifoundation.org

KIRBY MCDONALD EDUCATION ENDOWMENT SCHOLARSHIP FUND

Award: Scholarship for use in freshman, sophomore, junior, senior, or graduate years.

Eligibility Requirements: Applicant must be enrolled or expecting to enroll at an institution or university.

Contact: Susan Anderson, President/CEO
CIRI Foundation
3600 San Jeronimo Drive, Suite 256
Anchorage, AK 99508
Phone: 907-793-3575
Fax: 907-793-3585
E-mail: tcf@thecirifoundation.org

LAWRENCE MATSON MEMORIAL ENDOWMENT SCHOLARSHIP FUND

Award: Scholarship for use in freshman, sophomore, junior, senior, or graduate years.

Eligibility Requirements: Applicant must be enrolled or expecting to enroll at an institution or university.

Contact: Susan Anderson, President/CEO
CIRI Foundation
3600 San Jeronimo Drive, Suite 256
Anchorage, AK 99508
Phone: 907-793-3575
Fax: 907-793-3585
E-mail: tcf@thecirifoundation.org

NINILCHIK NATIVE ASSOCIATION INC. SCHOLARSHIP AND GRANT PROGRAM

Award: Scholarship for use in freshman, sophomore, junior, senior, or graduate years.

Eligibility Requirements: Applicant must be enrolled or expecting to enroll at an institution or university.

Contact: Susan Anderson, President/CEO
CIRI Foundation
3600 San Jeronimo Drive, Suite 256
Anchorage, AK 99508
Phone: 907-793-3575
Fax: 907-793-3585
E-mail: tcf@thecirifoundation.org

PETER KALIFORNSKY MEMORIAL ENDOWMENT SCHOLARSHIP FUND

Award: Scholarship for use in freshman, sophomore, junior, senior, or graduate years.

Eligibility Requirements: Applicant must be enrolled or expecting to enroll at an institution or university.

Contact: Susan Anderson, President/CEO
CIRI Foundation
3600 San Jeronimo Drive, Suite 256
Anchorage, AK 99508
Phone: 907-793-3575
Fax: 907-793-3585
E-mail: tcf@thecirifoundation.org

ROY M. HUHNDORF HEALTH SCIENCES ENDOWMENT SCHOLARSHIP FUND

Award: Scholarship for use in freshman, sophomore, junior, senior, or graduate years.

Eligibility Requirements: Applicant must be enrolled or expecting to enroll at an institution or university.

Contact: Susan Anderson, President/CEO
CIRI Foundation
3600 San Jeronimo Drive, Suite 256
Anchorage, AK 99508
Phone: 907-793-3575
Fax: 907-793-3585
E-mail: tcf@thecirifoundation.org

SALAMATOF NATIVE ASSOCIATION, INC. (SNAI) SCHOLARSHIP PROGRAM

Award: Scholarship for use in freshman, sophomore, junior, senior, or graduate years.

Eligibility Requirements: Applicant must be enrolled or expecting to enroll at an institution or university.

Contact: Susan Anderson, President/CEO
CIRI Foundation
3600 San Jeronimo Drive, Suite 256
Anchorage, AK 99508
Phone: 907-793-3575
Fax: 907-793-3585
E-mail: tcf@thecirifoundation.org

VOCATIONAL TRAINING GRANTS

Award: Grant for use in freshman, sophomore, junior, senior, or graduate years.

Eligibility Requirements: Applicant must be enrolled or expecting to enroll at an institution or university.

Contact: Susan Anderson, President/CEO
CIRI Foundation
3600 San Jeronimo Drive, Suite 256
Anchorage, AK 99508
Phone: 907-793-3575
Fax: 907-793-3585
E-mail: tcf@thecirifoundation.org

CITIZENS FOR GLOBAL SOLUTIONS
http://www.globalsolutions.org

HARLAN M. SMITH "BUILDERS OF A BETTER WORLD" SCHOLARSHIP COMPETITION

Essay competition for students whose goals have the potential to most closely contribute to the World Federalist Association's vision for a better world. Applicants must be between the ages of 18 and 25 and be members of Citizens for Global Solutions or children of members. Visit Web site at http://www.globalsolutions.org for further information.

Award: Scholarship for use in freshman, sophomore, junior, senior, or graduate years.

Eligibility Requirements: Applicant must be enrolled or expecting to enroll at an institution or university.

Contact: Citizens for Global Solutions
418 Seventh Street, SE
Washington, DC 20003

COCA-COLA SCHOLARS FOUNDATION, INC.
http://www.coca-colascholars.org

COCA-COLA TWO-YEAR COLLEGES SCHOLARSHIP

Non-renewable awards based on community involvement, leadership, and academic performance. Essay is required. Finalists represent every state in the U.S. Must pursue a two-year degree. Each institution may nominate up to two applicants. Minimum 2.5 GPA is required. See Web site: http://www.coca-colascholars.org for additional information.

Award: Scholarship for use in freshman or sophomore years; not renewable. *Number:* 400. *Amount:* $1000.

Eligibility Requirements: Applicant must be enrolled or expecting to enroll full or part-time at a two-year institution. Applicant must have 2.5 GPA or higher. Available to U.S. citizens.

Application Requirements: Application, essay, nomination from institution. *Deadline:* May 31.

Contact: Ryan Rodriguez, Program Facilitator
Coca-Cola Scholars Foundation, Inc.
PO Box 442
Atlanta, GA 30301-0442
Phone: 800-306-2653
Fax: 404-733-5439
E-mail: scholars@na.ko.com

CODA INTERNATIONAL
http://www.coda-international.org

MILLIE BROTHER ANNUAL SCHOLARSHIP FOR CHILDREN OF DEAF ADULTS

Scholarship awarded to any higher education student who is the hearing child of deaf parents. One-time award based on transcripts, letters of reference, and essay. Deadline is the first Friday in May.

Award: Scholarship for use in freshman, sophomore, junior, or senior years; not renewable. *Number:* up to 2. *Amount:* up to $3000.

Eligibility Requirements: Applicant must be enrolled or expecting to enroll full-time at a two-year or four-year or technical institution or university. Available to U.S. and non-U.S. citizens.

Application Requirements: Application, essay, references, self-addressed stamped envelope, transcript. *Deadline:* varies.

Contact: Dr. Robert J. Hoffmeister, Chair Millie Brother CODA Scholarship
CODA International
605 Commonwealth Avenue, Boston University
Boston, MA 02215
Phone: 617-353-3205
E-mail: rhoff@bu.edu

COLLEGE FOUNDATION OF NORTH CAROLINA, INC
http://www.cfnc.org

FEDERAL SUPPLEMENTAL EDUCATIONAL OPPORTUNITY GRANT PROGRAM

Federal program providing funds for students with exceptional financial need. The amount of financial need is determined by the educational institution the student attends. The award is available only to undergraduate students. Recipient must be a citizen or permanent resident of the United States. Priority is given to students who receive Federal Pell Grants.

Award: Grant for use in freshman, sophomore, junior, or senior years. *Amount:* $100–$4000.

Eligibility Requirements: Applicant must be enrolled or expecting to enroll at a four-year institution or university. Available to U.S. citizens.

Application Requirements: Application.

Contact: College Foundation of North Carolina, Inc
Federal Student Aid Information Center, PO Box 84
Washington, DC 20044
Phone: 800-433-3243

GOLDEN LEAF SCHOLARS PROGRAM - TWO-YEAR COLLEGES

Need- and merit-based scholarships of up to $750 per semester, including summer session, for curriculum students and up to $250 per semester for occupational education students. Student must be a permanent resident of one of the 84 eligible counties and be enrolled at one of the 58 member institutions of the North Carolina Community College System. Must demonstrate a need under federal TRIO formula.

Award: Scholarship for use in freshman, sophomore, junior, or senior years. *Amount:* up to $1500.

Eligibility Requirements: Applicant must be enrolled or expecting to enroll at a two-year or four-year or technical institution or university. Available to U.S. citizens.

Application Requirements: Application, applicant must enter a contest, transcript.

Contact:
Phone: 888-234-6400
E-mail: programinformation@CFNC.org

NORTH CAROLINA EDUCATION AND TRAINING VOUCHER PROGRAM

Four-year scholarship for foster youth and former foster youth. Applicants must have aged out of the foster care system at age 18 or were adopted from foster care with adoption finalization after their 16th birthday. Must be under 21 years of age at time of application, accepted into or enrolled in a degree, certificate, or other accredited program at a college or vocational program and show progress towards that degree or certificate. Applicant must not have personal assets greater than $10,000.

Award: Scholarship for use in freshman, sophomore, junior, or senior years. *Amount:* up to $5000.

Eligibility Requirements: Applicant must be age 21 or under and enrolled or expecting to enroll at a four-year institution or university. Available to U.S. and non-U.S. citizens.

Application Requirements: Application, essay.

Contact: College Foundation of North Carolina, Inc
PO Box 41966
Raleigh, NC 27629-1966
Phone: 888-234-6400
E-mail: etv@statevoucher.org

STATE EMPLOYEES ASSOCIATION OF NORTH CAROLINA (SEANC) SCHOLARSHIPS

Scholarships available to SEANC members, their spouses and dependents seeking full- or part-time postsecondary education. Three categories of awards: based on academic merit only; financial need only; and awards for SEANC members only. Deadline is April 15.

Award: Scholarship for use in freshman, sophomore, junior, or senior years. *Amount:* $500–$1000.

Eligibility Requirements: Applicant must be enrolled or expecting to enroll full-time at a four-year institution or university. Available to U.S. citizens.

Application Requirements: Application. *Deadline:* April 15.

Contact: College Foundation of North Carolina, Inc
PO Box 41966
Raleigh, NC 27629-1966
Phone: 888-234-6400
E-mail: programinformation@CFNC.org

COLLEGE PHOTOGRAPHER OF THE YEAR
http://www.cpoy.org

COLLEGE PHOTOGRAPHER OF THE YEAR COMPETITION

Awards are made based on the juried contest of individual photographs, picture stories and photographic essay and multimedia presentations. Judges are from the working media. Visit Web site: http://www.cpoy.org for more information.

Award: Scholarship for use in freshman, sophomore, junior, senior, or graduate years; not renewable. *Number:* 42–60. *Amount:* up to $3000.

Eligibility Requirements: Applicant must be enrolled or expecting to enroll full or part-time at a two-year or four-year or technical institution or university. Available to U.S. and non-U.S. citizens.

Application Requirements: Application, applicant must enter a contest, photo. *Fee:* $25. *Deadline:* varies.

Contact: Rita Ann Reed, Director, College Photographer of the Year
College Photographer of the Year
107 Lee Hills Hall, University of Missouri, School of Journalism
Columbia, MO 65211
Phone: 573-882-2198
Fax: 573-884-4999
E-mail: info@cpoy.org

COLLEGEFINANCIALAIDINFORMATION.COM

FRANK O'NEILL MEMORIAL SCHOLARSHIP

One-time award available to anyone who is attending or aspiring to attend a postsecondary education program. Must submit essay explaining educational goals and financial need. Application deadline is August 31.

Award: Scholarship for use in freshman, sophomore, junior, senior, or graduate years; not renewable. *Number:* 2. *Amount:* $1000.

Eligibility Requirements: Applicant must be enrolled or expecting to enroll full or part-time at a two-year or four-year or technical institution or university. Available to U.S. and non-U.S. citizens.

Application Requirements: Essay. *Deadline:* August 31.

Contact: CollegeFinancialAidInformation.com
PO Box 124
Youngtown, AZ 85363

COLLEGENET
http://www.collegenet.com

COLLEGENET SCHOLARSHIP

Award for student who completes and sends an application for college admission through CollegeNET. Must have enrolled in classes by fall term. A complete program description is available at the Web site (http://www.collegenet.com). Student must have applied to a member school to make the first level of qualification. Schools nominate from this pool of students based on their own criteria.

Award: Scholarship for use in freshman, sophomore, junior, senior, graduate, or postgraduate years; not renewable. *Number:* 1–3. *Amount:* $1000–$10,000.

Eligibility Requirements: Applicant must be enrolled or expecting to enroll full-time at a two-year or four-year or technical institution or university. Available to U.S. and non-U.S. citizens.

Application Requirements: Applicant must enter a contest, essay, nomination. *Deadline:* varies.

Contact: Heidi Peterson, Scholarship Coordinator
CollegeNET
805 SW Broadway, Suite 1600
Portland, OR 97205
Phone: 503-973-5200
Fax: 503-973-5252
E-mail: heidip@unival.com

COMMON KNOWLEDGE SCHOLARSHIP FOUNDATION
http://www.cksf.org

AMERICAN HEROES - U.S. MILITARY CHALLENGE

Quiz challenge available to high school and college students in the United States questions are based on what you know about the brave men and women that make up the U.S. Military. It is an overview of all branches of the military, training, education, weapons, and history. For more information and online registration check Web site: www.cksf.org

Award: Prize for use in freshman, sophomore, junior, or senior years; not renewable. *Number:* 1. *Amount:* $250.

Eligibility Requirements: Applicant must be enrolled or expecting to enroll at a two-year or four-year institution. Available to U.S. citizens.

Application Requirements: Applicant must enter a contest. *Deadline:* varies.

Contact: Daryl Hulce, President
Common Knowledge Scholarship Foundation
PO Box 290361
Davie, FL 33329-0361
Phone: 954-262-8553
Fax: 954-262-3940
E-mail: hulce@cksf.org

COMMON KNOWLEDGE SCHOLARSHIP

Students register at the CKSF Web site, and then take a series of multiple-choice quizzes. Each question is worth 500 points, and 1 point is deducted for every second it takes to complete each question. The person with the most points at the end of the competition is the scholarship winner.

Award: Scholarship for use in freshman, sophomore, junior, senior, or graduate years; not renewable. *Number:* 5–30. *Amount:* $250–$5000.

Eligibility Requirements: Applicant must be age 13 or under and enrolled or expecting to enroll full or part-time at a two-year or four-year or technical institution or university. Available to U.S. citizens.

Application Requirements: Applicant must enter a contest, test scores, Internet registration. *Deadline:* varies.

Contact: Daryl Hulce, President
Common Knowledge Scholarship Foundation
PO Box 290361
Davie, FL 33329-0361
Phone: 954-262-8553
Fax: 954-262-3940
E-mail: hulce@cksf.org

HIGH SCHOOL INTERNET CHALLENGE

The program tests a students' knowledge on both academic and common knowledge topics. Open to students in grades 9-12. For more information and online registration check Web site: www.cksf.org

Award: Prize for use in freshman year; not renewable. *Number:* 1.

Eligibility Requirements: Applicant must be high school student and planning to enroll or expecting to enroll at an institution or university. Available to U.S. citizens.

Application Requirements: Applicant must enter a contest. *Deadline:* varies.

Contact: Daryl Hulce, President
Common Knowledge Scholarship Foundation
PO Box 290361
Davie, FL 33329-0361
Phone: 954-262-8553
Fax: 954-262-3940
E-mail: hulce@cksf.org

THE BIBLICAL COMMON KNOWLEDGE CHALLENGE

Quiz tests one's knowledge of the Holy Bible. Quiz answers are not based on interpretation of the Old and New Testament, but rather on facts as outlined in the scripture or passage. This program is available to parents, high school and college students in the United States. For more information and online registration check Web site: www.cksf.org

Award: Prize for use in freshman, sophomore, junior, or senior years; not renewable. *Amount:* $150.

Eligibility Requirements: Applicant must be high school student and planning to enroll or expecting to enroll at a two-year or four-year institution. Available to U.S. citizens.

Application Requirements: Applicant must enter a contest.

Contact: Daryl Hulce, President
Common Knowledge Scholarship Foundation
PO Box 290361
Davie, FL 33329-0361
Phone: 954-262-8553
Fax: 954-262-3940
E-mail: hulce@cksf.org

THE BLACK HISTORY COMMON KNOWLEDGE CHALLENGE

Quiz tests the knowledge of Black cultural, education, and milestones of the African-American experience. This program is available to all students enrolled at a high school within the United States and its territories. For more information and online registration check Web site: www.cksf.org

Award: Prize for use in freshman year; not renewable. *Number:* 2. *Amount:* $1000.

Eligibility Requirements: Applicant must be high school student and planning to enroll or expecting to enroll at an institution or university. Available to U.S. citizens.

Application Requirements: Applicant must enter a contest.

Contact: Daryl Hulce, President
Common Knowledge Scholarship Foundation
PO Box 290361
Davie, FL 33329-0361
Phone: 954-262-8553
Fax: 954-262-3940
E-mail: hulce@cksf.org

THE FBI COMMON KNOWLEDGE CHALLENGE

Quiz contest developed to educate participants about the mission, goals, history, and inner workings of the Federal Bureau of Investigation. Contests are open to any 9-12 grade students. For more information and online registration check the Web site: www.cksf.org

Award: Prize for use in freshman year. *Number:* 2. *Amount:* $250.

Eligibility Requirements: Applicant must be high school student and planning to enroll or expecting to enroll at an institution or university. Available to U.S. citizens.

Application Requirements: Applicant must enter a contest. *Deadline:* varies.

Contact: Daryl Hulce, President
Common Knowledge Scholarship Foundation
PO Box 290361
Davie, FL 33329-0361
Phone: 954-262-8553
Fax: 954-262-3940
E-mail: hulce@cksf.org

THE NASCAR COMMON KNOWLEDGE CHALLENGE

National scholarship quiz open to parents, high school and college students in the United States. It tests one's history, drivers, teams and general knowledge of NASCAR. For more information and online registration check Web site: www.cksf.org

Award: Prize for use in freshman, sophomore, junior, or senior years. *Number:* 1. *Amount:* $250.

Eligibility Requirements: Applicant must be enrolled or expecting to enroll at a two-year or four-year institution. Available to U.S. citizens.

Application Requirements: Applicant must enter a contest. *Deadline:* varies.

Contact: Daryl Hulce, President
Common Knowledge Scholarship Foundation
PO Box 290361
Davie, FL 33329-0361
Phone: 954-262-8553
Fax: 954-262-3940
E-mail: hulce@cksf.org

COMMUNITY FOUNDATION FOR PALM BEACH AND MARTIN COUNTIES, INC.　　　　http://www.yourcommunityfoundation.org

WEITZ COMPANY SCHOLARSHIP

Scholarship awarded to Palm Beach or Martin County graduating high school senior, or child of a Weitz employee, regardless of residence. Student must prove acceptance into college or vocational school with a major emphasis in a construction related field. Deadline is February 1. Applications are available online http://www.yourcommunityfoundation.org

Award: Scholarship for use in freshman year; not renewable. *Number:* varies. *Amount:* $750–$2500.

Eligibility Requirements: Applicant must be high school student and planning to enroll or expecting to enroll at a two-year or four-year or technical institution. Applicant must have 2.5 GPA or higher. Available to U.S. citizens.

Application Requirements: Application, financial need analysis. *Deadline:* February 1.

Contact: Carolyn Jenco, Grants Manager/Scholarship Coordinator
Community Foundation for Palm Beach and Martin Counties, Inc.
700 South Dixie Highway, Suite 200
West Palm Beach, FL 33401
Phone: 561-659-6800
Fax: 561-832-6542
E-mail: cjenco@cfpbmc.org

COMMUNITY FOUNDATION OF CAPE COD　　　　http://www.capecodfoundation.org

CAPE COD RESTAURANTS, INC. SCHOLARSHIP

Scholarship for an employee or children of employees of Cape Cod Restaurants, Inc. and subsidiary companies, which include The Flying Bridge, The Coonamesset Inn, and Pine Hills. Scholarship amount varies.

Award: Scholarship for use in freshman, sophomore, junior, senior, graduate, or postgraduate years. *Number:* 1.

Eligibility Requirements: Applicant must be enrolled or expecting to enroll at a two-year or four-year or technical institution or university. Available to U.S. citizens.

Application Requirements: Application, essay, transcript. *Deadline:* April 1.

Contact: Kristin O'Malley, Program Officer/Scholarship Associate
Community Foundation of Cape Cod
259 Willow Street
Yarmouthport, MA 02675
Phone: 508-790-3040
Fax: 508-790-4069
E-mail: komalley@capecodfoundation.org

THE CAPE COD FOUNDATION SCHOLARSHIP

Scholarship for a graduating senior or a returning non-traditional student from Cape Cod or the Islands who has significant financial need and displays perseverance and a strong work ethic.

Award: Scholarship for use in freshman, sophomore, junior, or senior years. *Number:* 1.

Eligibility Requirements: Applicant must be high school student and planning to enroll or expecting to enroll full-time at a four-year institution or university. Available to U.S. citizens.

Application Requirements: Application, essay, financial need analysis, transcript. *Deadline:* April 1.

Contact: Kristin O'Malley, Program Officer/Scholarship Associate
Community Foundation of Cape Cod
259 Willow Street
Yarmouthport, MA 02675
Phone: 508-790-3040
Fax: 508-790-4069
E-mail: komalley@capecodfoundation.org

COMMUNITY FOUNDATION OF WESTERN MASSACHUSETTS　　　　http://www.communityfoundation.org

CHRISTINE MITUS ROSE MEMORIAL SCHOLARSHIP

Scholarship available to students who have had a parent die; preference to those who have had a parent die of cancer.

Award: Scholarship for use in freshman, sophomore, junior, or senior years; not renewable. *Number:* 1. *Amount:* up to $500.

Eligibility Requirements: Applicant must be high school student and planning to enroll or expecting to enroll full-time at a four-year institution or university. Available to U.S. citizens.

y Foundation of Western Massachusetts (continued)

Application Requirements: Application, financial need analysis, transcript, parent's and student's federal income tax returns, Student Aid Report (SAR). *Deadline:* March 31.

Contact: Dorothy Theriaque, Education Associate
Community Foundation of Western Massachusetts
1500 Main Street, PO Box 15769
Springfield, MA 01115
Phone: 413-732-2858
Fax: 413-733-8565
E-mail: dtheriaque@communityfoundation.org

SEPTEMBER 11TH REMEMBRANCE SCHOLARSHIP

Scholarship for high school seniors who are residents of Hampden, Hampshire, Franklin, and Berkshire counties. Established by the Diocese of Springfield Catholic Charities and the families of victims in memory of the tragedies of September 11th.

Award: Scholarship for use in freshman year; not renewable. *Number:* up to 2. *Amount:* up to $900.

Eligibility Requirements: Applicant must be high school student and planning to enroll or expecting to enroll full-time at an institution or university. Available to U.S. citizens.

Application Requirements: Application, financial need analysis, transcript, parent's and student's federal income tax returns, Student Aid Report (SAR). *Deadline:* March 31.

Contact: Dorothy Theriaque, Education Associate
Community Foundation of Western Massachusetts
1500 Main Street, PO Box 15769
Springfield, MA 01115
Phone: 413-732-2858
Fax: 413-733-8565
E-mail: dtheriaque@communityfoundation.org

COMTO-BOSTON CHAPTER   http://www.bostoncomto.org

COMTO BOSTON/GARRETT A. MORGAN SCHOLARSHIP

Award: Scholarship for use in freshman or sophomore years.

Eligibility Requirements: Applicant must be enrolled or expecting to enroll at an institution or university.

Contact: Virginia Turner, Scholarship Chairperson
COMTO-Boston Chapter
Scholarship Program
PO Box 1272
Boston, MA 02117-1173
Phone: 617-248-2878
Fax: 617-248-2904
E-mail: virginia.turner@state.ma.us

CONGRESSIONAL BLACK CAUCUS SPOUSES PROGRAM   http://www.cbcfinc.org

CONGRESSIONAL BLACK CAUCUS SPOUSES EDUCATION SCHOLARSHIP FUND

Award made to students who reside or attend school in a Congressional district represented by an African-American member of Congress. Awards scholarships to academically talented and highly motivated students who intend to pursue full-time undergraduate, graduate or doctoral degrees. Minimum 2.5 GPA required. Contact the Congressional office in the appropriate district for information and applications. Visit http://www.cbcfinc.org for a list of district offices. Any correspondence sent to the CBC Foundation Office at Pennsylvania Avenue will be discarded and may disqualify applicant for the award.

Award: Scholarship for use in freshman, sophomore, junior, senior, or graduate years; renewable. *Number:* 200. *Amount:* $500–$4000.

Eligibility Requirements: Applicant must be enrolled or expecting to enroll full-time at a two-year or four-year or technical institution or university. Applicant must have 2.5 GPA or higher. Available to U.S. citizens.

Application Requirements: Application, essay, financial need analysis, interview, photo, references, transcript. *Deadline:* May 1.

Contact: Appropriate Congressional District Office
Phone: 202-263-2836

SAILING FOR SCHOLARS SCHOLARSHIP

Award: Scholarship for use in freshman, sophomore, junior, or senior years.

Eligibility Requirements: Applicant must be enrolled or expecting to enroll at an institution or university.

Contact: Nakia Kelly, Scholarship Coordinator
Congressional Black Caucus Spouses Program
1720 Massachusetts Ave NW
Washington, DC 20036
Phone: 202-263-2840
Fax: 202-263-0848
E-mail: cbcspouces@cbcfinc.org

CONNECTICUT STUDENT LOAN FOUNDATION   http://www.cslf.com

CONNECTICUT INNOVATIONS TECHNOLOGY SCHOLAR PROGRAM

An earned scholarship program available to Connecticut high school seniors who plan on studying within the fields of science or technology at an accredited Connecticut college or university. Must work within the State of Connecticut for two years following graduation.

Award: Scholarship for use in freshman, sophomore, junior, or senior years.

Eligibility Requirements: Applicant must be enrolled or expecting to enroll at an institution or university.

Contact: Connecticut Student Loan Foundation
525 Brook Street
PO Box 1009
Rocky Hill, CT 06067

COUNCIL FOR INTERNATIONAL EDUCATIONAL EXCHANGE   http://www.ciee.org/study

BOWMAN TRAVEL GRANT

The Bowman Travel Grant is awarded only to eligible students participating in a life study or volunteer programs in less traditional destinations. Recipients must be attending a CIEE member or academic consortium member institution. Recipients receive awards to be used as partial reimbursement for travel costs to program destination. Application deadlines are April 1 and November 1. For more information see Web site:http://www.ciee.org/study/scholarships.aspx#bowman

Award: Grant for use in freshman, sophomore, junior, or senior years; not renewable. *Number:* 20–30. *Amount:* $500–$1000.

Eligibility Requirements: Applicant must be enrolled or expecting to enroll full-time at a two-year or four-year or technical institution or university. Applicant must have 3.5 GPA or higher. Available to U.S. citizens.

Application Requirements: Application, essay, financial need analysis, references, transcript. *Deadline:* varies.

Contact: Kate Dunkerley, Senior Program Coordinator-Grants Program
Council for International Educational Exchange
3 Copley Place, 2nd Floor
Boston, MA 02116
Phone: 800-448-9944 Ext. 368
Fax: 617-247-2911
E-mail: kdunkerley@ciee.org

COUNCIL ON INTERNATIONAL EDUCATIONAL EXCHANGE SCHOLARSHIP

Scholarships offered to students who demonstrate both academic excellence and financial need. Available to CIEE Study Center (CSC) applicants from Academic Consortium (AC) member institutions only. Application deadlines are April 1 and November 1. For more information see Web site: http://www.ciee.org/study/scholarships.aspx#isp

Award: Scholarship for use in freshman, sophomore, junior, or senior years; not renewable. *Number:* 60–70. *Amount:* $500–$1000.

Eligibility Requirements: Applicant must be enrolled or expecting to enroll full-time at a two-year or four-year or technical institution or university. Applicant must have 3.5 GPA or higher. Available to U.S. and non-U.S. citizens.

Application Requirements: Application, essay, financial need analysis, references, transcript. *Deadline:* varies.

Contact: Kate Dunkerley, Senior Program Coordinator-Grants
Program
Council for International Educational Exchange
3 Copley Place, 2nd Floor
Boston, MA 02116
Phone: 800-448-9944 Ext. 368
Fax: 617-247-2911
E-mail: kdunkerley@ciee.org

CUBAN AMERICAN SCHOLARSHIP FUND

CUBAN AMERICAN SCHOLARSHIP FUND

Award: Scholarship for use in freshman, sophomore, junior, senior, or graduate years.

Eligibility Requirements: Applicant must be enrolled or expecting to enroll at an institution or university.

Contact: Victor Cueto, President CASF
Cuban American Scholarship Fund
PO Box 6422
Santa Ana, CA 92706
Phone: 714-835-7676
Fax: 714-835-7776

D.W. SIMPSON & COMPANY   http://www.dwsimpson.com

D.W. SIMPSON ACTUARIAL SCIENCE SCHOLARSHIP

One-time award for full-time actuarial science students. Must be entering senior year of undergraduate study in actuarial science. GPA of 3.2 or better in actuarial science and an overall GPA of 3.0 or better required. Must have passed at least one Actuarial Exam and be eligible to work in the U.S. Application deadline is April 30 for Fall and October 31 for Spring.

Award: Scholarship for use in freshman, sophomore, junior, or senior years; not renewable. *Number:* 2. *Amount:* up to $1000.

Eligibility Requirements: Applicant must be enrolled or expecting to enroll full-time at a four-year institution. Applicant must have 3.0 GPA or higher. Available to U.S. citizens.

Application Requirements: Application, essay, resume, test scores. *Deadline:* varies.

Contact: David Simpson
D.W. Simpson & Company
1800 West Larchmont Avenue
Chicago, IL 60613
Phone: 312-867-2300
Fax: 312-951-8386
E-mail: scholarship@dwsimpson.com

DATATEL, INC.   http://www.datatel.com/dsf

DATATEL SCHOLARS FOUNDATION SCHOLARSHIP

One-time award for students attending institutions which use Datatel administrative software. Available for part-time and full-time students. Completed on-line applications must be submitted by January 31.

Award: Scholarship for use in freshman, sophomore, junior, senior, graduate, or postgraduate years; not renewable. *Number:* varies. *Amount:* $1000–$2400.

Eligibility Requirements: Applicant must be enrolled or expecting to enroll full or part-time at a two-year or four-year or technical institution or university. Available to U.S. and non-U.S. citizens.

Application Requirements: Application, essay, references, transcript. *Deadline:* January 31.

Contact: Marissa Solis, Project Leader
Datatel, Inc.
4375 Fair Lakes Court
Fairfax, VA 22033
Phone: 800-486-4332
Fax: 703-968-4573
E-mail: scholars@datatel.com

RETURNING STUDENT SCHOLARSHIP

For any student who has returned to higher education within the previous academic year, after a five-year or more absence. Applicant must attend a Datatel client institution. Completed on-line applications must be submitted by January 31.

Award: Scholarship for use in freshman, sophomore, junior, senior, graduate, or postgraduate years; not renewable. *Number:* 25–50. *Amount:* $1500.

Eligibility Requirements: Applicant must be enrolled or expecting to enroll full or part-time at a two-year or four-year or technical institution or university. Available to U.S. and non-U.S. citizens.

Application Requirements: Application, essay, references, transcript. *Deadline:* January 31.

Contact: Marissa Solis, Project Leader
Datatel, Inc.
4375 Fair Lakes Court
Fairfax, VA 22033
Phone: 800-486-4332
Fax: 703-968-4573
E-mail: scholars@datatel.com

DAVID AND DOVETTA WILSON SCHOLARSHIP FUND, INC.   http://www.wilsonfund.org

DAVID AND DOVETTA WILSON SCHOLARSHIP FUND

Award for use in freshman year of college. Applicants selected on basis of academic achievement and involvement in community or religious activities. Minimum 3.0 GPA required. Nine awards ranging from $250 to $1000. Application fee: $20. Deadline: March 31. Send self-addressed stamped envelope for application requests or visit Web site at: http://www.wilsonfund.org.

Award: Scholarship for use in freshman year; not renewable. *Number:* 9. *Amount:* $250–$1000.

Eligibility Requirements: Applicant must be high school student and planning to enroll or expecting to enroll full-time at a two-year or four-year institution or university. Applicant must have 3.0 GPA or higher. Available to U.S. citizens.

Application Requirements: Application, essay, financial need analysis, photo, references, self-addressed stamped envelope, transcript. *Fee:* $20. *Deadline:* March 31.

Contact: Timothy Wilson, Treasurer
David and Dovetta Wilson Scholarship Fund, Inc.
115-67 237th Street
Elmont, NY 11003-3926
Phone: 516-285-4573
E-mail: ddwsf4@aol.com

DAVIS-PUTTER SCHOLARSHIP FUND   http://www.davisputter.org

DAVIS-PUTTER SCHOLARSHIP FUND

Provides need-based grants to student activists who are able to do academic work at the college level and are actively involved in building the movement for social and economic justice. For details regarding eligibility and instructions for receiving an application, contact: http://www.davisputter.org

Award: Scholarship for use in freshman, sophomore, junior, senior, graduate, or postgraduate years; renewable. *Number:* 25–30. *Amount:* $1000–$6000.

Eligibility Requirements: Applicant must be enrolled or expecting to enroll full or part-time at a two-year or four-year institution or university. Available to U.S. and non-U.S. citizens.

Davis-Putter Scholarship Fund (continued)

Application Requirements: Application, essay, financial need analysis, photo, references, self-addressed stamped envelope, transcript. *Deadline:* April 1.

Contact: Jan Phillips, Secretary
Davis-Putter Scholarship Fund
PO Box 7307
New York, NY 10116-7307
E-mail: information@davisputter.com

DAYTON ADVERTISING CLUB   http://www.daytonadclub.org/scholarship.php

THOMAS J. DORAN JR. MEMORIAL SCHOLARSHIP

Scholarship available to members of Dayton Advertising Club, their children and legal dependents or an employee of a DAC company member. Deadline is March 31.

Award: Scholarship for use in freshman, sophomore, junior, senior, graduate, or postgraduate years; not renewable. *Amount:* $750.

Eligibility Requirements: Applicant must be enrolled or expecting to enroll at a four-year institution or university. Available to U.S. citizens.

Application Requirements: Application, essay. *Deadline:* May 31.

Contact: Mike Fariello, Thomas J. Doran Jr. Memorial Scholarship
Dayton Advertising Club
PO Box 225
Dayton, OH 45401
Phone: 937-879-3212

DELTA SIGMA PI   http://www.dspnet.org

THOMAS M. MOCELLA SCHOLARSHIP

Scholarship for collegiate members of Delta Sigma Pi who are in good standing and from chapters within 75 miles of downtown Chicago and located within the same region as the Chicago Alumni Chapter.

Award: Scholarship for use in freshman, sophomore, junior, or senior years; not renewable. *Amount:* $500–$600.

Eligibility Requirements: Applicant must be enrolled or expecting to enroll full-time at an institution or university. Applicant must have 3.0 GPA or higher. Available to U.S. citizens.

Application Requirements: Application, essay, references. *Deadline:* June 30.

Contact: Bill Schilling, Executive Director
Delta Sigma Pi
330 South Campus Avenue
Oxford, OH 45056-0230
Phone: 513-523-1907
Fax: 513-523-7292
E-mail: bill@dspnet.org

DEMOLAY FOUNDATION OF CALIFORNIA SCHOLARSHIP   http://www.norcaldemolay.com

DEMOLAY FOUNDATION OF CALIFORNIA, INC SCHOLARSHIP PROGRAM

Renewable scholarships available to DeMornay members in chapters within the Northern California Jurisdiction. Awards of $2000 for those who attend a four-year college or university and $750 for those who attend a community college or accredited vocational school. Must not have reached the age of 21.

Award: Scholarship for use in freshman, sophomore, junior, senior, or graduate years. *Amount:* $750–$2000.

Eligibility Requirements: Applicant must be age 21 or under and enrolled or expecting to enroll at a two-year or four-year institution or university. Available to U.S. citizens.

Application Requirements: Application, financial need analysis, photo, references, transcript. *Deadline:* April 1.

Contact: Redentor M. Manuto, Scholarship Committee Chairman
DeMolay Foundation of California Scholarship
4631 Nevin Avenue
Richmond, CA 94805
Phone: 408-528-0529
E-mail: dmanuto@pacbell.net

DEVRY, INC.   http://www.devry.edu

DEVRY COMMUNITY COLLEGE SCHOLARSHIPS

Scholarships in the amount of $1500 per semester to students who have earned an associate's degree with a minimum of a 3.30 grade point average in the past year, and who wish to pursue a bachelor's degree on a full-time basis at DeVry either onsite or online. Deadline: One year from community college graduation to apply and start at DeVry.

Award: Scholarship for use in junior or senior years; renewable. *Number:* varies. *Amount:* $1500–$9000.

Eligibility Requirements: Applicant must be enrolled or expecting to enroll full-time at an institution or university. Applicant must have 3.0 GPA or higher. Available to U.S. and Canadian citizens.

Application Requirements: Application, interview, transcript. *Deadline:* Continuous.

Contact: Thonie Simpson, National HS Program Manager
DeVry, Inc.
1 Tower Lane
Oakbrook Terrace, IL 60181-4624
Phone: 630-706-3122
Fax: 630-574-1696
E-mail: outreach@devry.edu

DEVRY SKILLS USA SCHOLARSHIPS

Half-tuition per semester valued at up to $32,000 and $1,500 per semester scholarships to second and $1000 third place winners in the Internetworking, Electronics Applications, and Electronics Technology categories for both the secondary and postsecondary divisions, at the National SkillsUSA competition. Deadline: One year from high school graduation to apply and start at DeVry.

Award: Scholarship for use in freshman, sophomore, junior, or senior years; renewable. *Number:* 18. *Amount:* $9000–$32,000.

Eligibility Requirements: Applicant must be enrolled or expecting to enroll full-time at an institution or university. Available to U.S. citizens.

Application Requirements: Application, applicant must enter a contest. *Deadline:* Continuous.

Contact: Thonie Simpson, National HS Program Manager
DeVry, Inc.
1 Tower Lane
Oakbrook Terrace, IL 60181-4624
Phone: 630-706-3122
Fax: 630-574-1696
E-mail: outreach@devry.edu

DEVRY UNIVERSITY FIRST SCHOLAR AWARD

Full and half-tuition awards valued at up to $64,000 and $32,000. Must be a registered participant in any regional First Robotics Competition. Must have an ACT composite score of 19 or SAT combined math and verbal/critical reading score of at least 900. Student must enroll at DeVry University within one calendar year of receipt of the award.

Award: Scholarship for use in freshman, sophomore, junior, or senior years; renewable. *Number:* 1. *Amount:* $32,000–$64,000.

Eligibility Requirements: Applicant must be high school student and planning to enroll or expecting to enroll full-time at an institution or university. Available to U.S. citizens.

Application Requirements: Application, applicant must enter a contest, essay, references, test scores, transcript. *Deadline:* Continuous.

Contact: Thonie Simpson, National HS Program Manager
DeVry, Inc.
1 Tower Lane
Oakbrook Terrace, IL 60181-4624
Phone: 630-706-3122
Fax: 630-574-1696
E-mail: outreach@devry.edu

GIRL SCOUT GOLD AWARD SCHOLARSHIP- HIGH SCHOOL GRADUATE

Award of $2000 per semester for high school graduates or GED recipients. Must have earned a Girl Scout Gold Award and apply one year from high school graduation to a DeVry institution.

Award: Scholarship for use in freshman year. *Amount:* $2000–$18,000.

Eligibility Requirements: Applicant must be enrolled or expecting to enroll at an institution or university and female. Available to U.S. and Canadian citizens.

Application Requirements: Application. *Deadline:* Continuous.

Contact: Thonie Simpson, National HS Program Manager
DeVry, Inc.
1 Tower Lane
Oakbrook Terrace, IL 60181
Phone: 630-706-3122
Fax: 630-574-1696
E-mail: outreach@devry.edu

DOGRIB TREATY 11 SCHOLARSHIP COMMITTEE
http://www.dt11sc.ca

BHP BILLITON UNIVERSITY SCHOLARSHIPS

Award for students of Dogrib ancestry. Must be enrolled full time in a Canadian university degree program and be interested and active in community affairs. Available to undergraduate, masters or Ph. D degree students.

Award: Scholarship for use in freshman, sophomore, junior, senior, graduate, or postgraduate years; not renewable. *Number:* 4. *Amount:* up to $5000.

Eligibility Requirements: Applicant must be enrolled or expecting to enroll full-time at an institution or university. Available to U.S. and Canadian citizens.

Application Requirements: Application, references, transcript. *Deadline:* July 15.

Contact: Post Secondary Student Support Coordinator, Dogrib Treaty 11 Scholarship Committee, c/o Chief Jimmy Bruneau Regional High School
Dogrib Treaty 11 Scholarship Committee
Bag 1
Rae-Edzo, NT X0E 0Y0
Canada

DIAVIK DIAMONDS, INC. SCHOLARSHIPS FOR COLLEGE STUDENTS

Award: Scholarship for use in freshman, sophomore, junior, or senior years.

Eligibility Requirements: Applicant must be enrolled or expecting to enroll at an institution or university.

Contact: Morven MacPherson, Post Secondary Student Support Coordinator
Dogrib Treaty 11 Scholarship Committee
c/o CJBRHS
PO Box 1
Rae-Edzo X0E 0Y0
Canada
Phone: 867-371-3815
Fax: 867-371-3813
E-mail: morvenm@dogrib.net

FIRST YEAR ACADEMIC ACHIEVEMENT AWARDS

Award for students of Dogrib ancestry who have completed the first year of a full-time program in a technical school, college, or university. Eight of the ten awards will be allocated for students whose permanent homes are in one of the four Dogrib Treaty 11 communities.

Award: Scholarship for use in sophomore year; not renewable. *Number:* 10. *Amount:* $1000.

Eligibility Requirements: Applicant must be enrolled or expecting to enroll full-time at a two-year or four-year or technical institution or university. Available to U.S. and Canadian citizens.

Application Requirements: Application, transcript. *Deadline:* July 15.

Contact: Morven MacPherson, Post Secondary Student St
Coordinator
Dogrib Treaty 11 Scholarship Committee
c/o CJBRHS
PO Box 1
Rae-Edzo X0E 0Y0
Canada
Phone: 867-371-3815
Fax: 867-371-3813
E-mail: morvenm@dogrib.net

SECOND YEAR ACADEMIC ACHIEVEMENT AWARDS

Award for students of Dogrib ancestry who have completed the second year of a full-time program in a technical school, college, or university. Eight of the ten awards will be allocated for students whose permanent homes are in one of the four Dogrib Treaty 11 communities.

Award: Scholarship for use in junior year; not renewable. *Number:* 10. *Amount:* $1000.

Eligibility Requirements: Applicant must be enrolled or expecting to enroll full-time at a four-year or technical institution or university. Available to U.S. and Canadian citizens.

Application Requirements: Application, transcript. *Deadline:* July 15.

Contact: Morven MacPherson, Post Secondary Student Support Coordinator
Dogrib Treaty 11 Scholarship Committee
c/o CJBRHS
PO Box 1
Rae-Edzo X0E 0Y0
Canada
Phone: 867-371-3815
Fax: 867-371-3813
E-mail: morvenm@dogrib.net

THIRD YEAR ACADEMIC ACHIEVEMENT AWARDS

Award for students of Dogrib ancestry who have completed the third year of a full-time program in a technical school, college, or university. Eight of the ten awards will be allocated for students whose permanent homes are in one of the four Dogrib Treaty 11 communities.

Award: Scholarship for use in senior year. *Number:* 10. *Amount:* $1000.

Eligibility Requirements: Applicant must be enrolled or expecting to enroll at a four-year or technical institution or university. Available to U.S. and Canadian citizens.

Application Requirements: Application, transcript. *Deadline:* July 15.

Contact: Morven MacPherson, Post Secondary Student Support Coordinator
Dogrib Treaty 11 Scholarship Committee
c/o CJBRHS
PO Box 1
Rae-Edzo X0E 0Y0
Canada
Phone: 867-371-3815
Fax: 867-371-3813
E-mail: morvenm@dogrib.net

DOLLARSHIP

DOLLARSHIP

Dollarship grants unlimited $500 scholarships every three months to students worldwide. Applicants dollar fee will contribute fifty cents to another $500 scholarship. Refer to Web site for further details: http://www.dollarship.com

Award: Scholarship for use in freshman, sophomore, junior, senior, graduate, or postgraduate years. *Number:* varies. *Amount:* $500.

Eligibility Requirements: Applicant must be enrolled or expecting to enroll full or part-time at a two-year or four-year or technical institution or university. Available to U.S. and non-U.S. citizens.

Application Requirements: Essay. *Fee:* $1. *Deadline:* Continuous.

Contact: Christina Barsch, Vice President of Operations
Dollarship
11200 West Wisconsin, Suite 10
Youngtown, AZ 85363
Phone: 623-215-2898
Fax: 623-215-2899
E-mail: cbarsch@dollarship.com

DOW JONES NEWSPAPER FUND
http://djnewspaperfund.dowjones.com

BUSINESS REPORTING INTERNSHIP PROGRAM FOR MINORITY COLLEGE SOPHOMORES AND JUNIORS

One-time paid business reporting internship and $1000 scholarship for minority college sophomores and juniors returning to undergraduate studies. Must submit application, essay, transcript, clips, and resume; must take a test. Deadline is November 1.

Award: Scholarship for use in sophomore or junior years; not renewable. *Number:* 12–15. *Amount:* $1000.

Eligibility Requirements: Applicant must be enrolled or expecting to enroll full-time at a two-year or four-year institution or university. Available to U.S. and non-U.S. citizens.

Application Requirements: Application, essay, portfolio, resume, references, transcript, one-hour reporting test. *Deadline:* November 1.

Contact: Linda Waller Shockley, Deputy Director
Dow Jones Newspaper Fund
PO Box 300
Princeton, NJ 08543-0300
Phone: 609-452-2820
Fax: 609-520-5804
E-mail: newsfund@wsj.dowjones.com

EARTH ISLAND INSTITUTE
http://www.earthisland.org

BROWER YOUTH AWARDS

An annual national award that recognizes 6 young people for their outstanding activism and achievements in the fields of environmental and social justice advocacy. The winners of the award receive $3000 in cash, a trip to California for the award ceremony and Yosemite camping trip, and ongoing access to resources and opportunities to further their work at Earth Island Institute. More details at : http://www.broweryouthawards.org

Award: Prize for use in freshman, sophomore, junior, or senior years; not renewable. *Number:* 6. *Amount:* $3000.

Eligibility Requirements: Applicant must be age 13-22 and enrolled or expecting to enroll full or part-time at a two-year or four-year or technical institution or university. Available to U.S. and non-U.S. citizens.

Application Requirements: Application, essay, photo, references. *Deadline:* June 1.

Contact: Earth Island Institute
300 Broadway, Suite 28
San Francisco, CA 94133
E-mail: bya@earthisland.org

EAST BAY FOOTBALL OFFICIALS ASSOCIATION
http://www.ebfoa.org

EAST BAY FOOTBALL OFFICIALS ASSOCIATION COLLEGE SCHOLARSHIP

Scholarship for a East Bay area high school senior who currently participates in one of the football programs served by the East Bay Football Officials Association. Must be a resident of California, achieve at least a 3.0 GPA and have plans to attend any accredited two or four-year institution in the fall. Must not be a family member of any EBFOA member.

Award: Scholarship for use in freshman year. *Number:* 1.

Eligibility Requirements: Applicant must be high school student and planning to enroll or expecting to enroll at a two-year or four-year institution or university. Applicant must have 3.0 GPA or higher. Available to U.S. citizens.

Application Requirements: Application, essay, references, transcript. *Deadline:* October 15.

Contact: Sam Moriana, EBFOA Scholarship Program
East Bay Football Officials Association
21 Chatham Pointe
Alameda, CA 94502
Phone: 510-521-4121
E-mail: smoriana@comcast.net

EASTERN AMPUTEE GOLF ASSOCIATION
http://www.eaga.org/

EASTERN AMPUTEE GOLF ASSOCIATION SCHOLARSHIP FUND

Renewable scholarship available for $1000 per year based on continuing eligibility. Applicant must maintain a minimum 2.0 GPA each semester, and prove continuing evidence of financial need. Applicant must be an amputee or a dependent of an amputee, as well as member in good standing of the EAGA. Please refer to Web site for further details: http://www.eaga.org

Award: Scholarship for use in freshman, sophomore, junior, or senior years; renewable. *Number:* 1–8. *Amount:* $1000.

Eligibility Requirements: Applicant must be enrolled or expecting to enroll full or part-time at a two-year or four-year or technical institution or university. Available to U.S. and Canadian citizens.

Application Requirements: Application, autobiography, essay, financial need analysis, resume, transcript, Student Aid Report (SAR). *Deadline:* June 30.

Contact: Linda Buck, EAGA Secretary
Eastern Amputee Golf Association
2015 Amherst Drive
Bethlehem, PA 18015-5606
Phone: 888-868-0992
Fax: 610-867-9295
E-mail: info@eaga.org

E-COLLEGEDEGREE.COM
http://e-collegedegree.com

E-COLLEGEDEGREE.COM ONLINE EDUCATION SCHOLARSHIP AWARD

This award is to be used for online education. Application must be submitted online. Deadline is December 15. Please visit Web site for more information and application: http://www.e-collegedegree.com

Award: Scholarship for use in freshman, sophomore, junior, senior, graduate, or postgraduate years; not renewable. *Number:* 1. *Amount:* $1000.

Eligibility Requirements: Applicant must be age 19 and enrolled or expecting to enroll full or part-time at a two-year or four-year or technical institution or university. Available to U.S. citizens.

Application Requirements: Application, essay. *Deadline:* December 15.

Contact: Chris Lee, Site Manager
e-CollegeDegree.com
9109 West 101st Terrace
Overland Park, KS 66212
Phone: 913-341-6949
E-mail: scholarship@e-collegedegree.com

EDDIE ROBINSON FOUNDATION
http://www.eddierobinson.com

EDDIE ROBINSON FOUNDATION EIGHTH GRADE SCHOLARSHIP

Open to all eighth-grade students who have distinguished themselves as leaders among peers in school, community, and athletics and who display a can-do attitude despite obstacles. Awards overall candidate, not strictly students with high GPA. Must be a U.S. citizen. Essay required. For additional information visit Web site: http://www.eddierobinson.com.

Award: Scholarship for use in freshman, sophomore, junior, or senior years; renewable. *Number:* 2–4. *Amount:* $20,000.

Eligibility Requirements: Applicant must be enrolled or expecting to enroll full-time at a four-year institution or university. Applicant must have 2.5 GPA or higher. Available to U.S. citizens.

Application Requirements: Application, essay, references, transcript. *Deadline:* February 16.

Contact: Cherie Kirkland, Vice President
Eddie Robinson Foundation
3391 Piedmont Road
Suite 105
Atlanta, GA 30305
Phone: 404-475-8408
Fax: 404-475-4408
E-mail: info@eddierobinson.com

EDDIE ROBINSON FOUNDATION HIGH SCHOOL SENIOR SCHOLARSHIP

Open to all high school seniors. Selection process based on a system using scholastic achievements, athletic accomplishments, leadership skills, and community involvement. Essay also required. Awards overall candidate, not strictly students with high GPA. Must be U.S. citizen. For additional information visit Web site http://www.eddierobinson.com

Award: Scholarship for use in freshman, sophomore, junior, or senior years; renewable. *Number:* 2–4. *Amount:* $20,000.

Eligibility Requirements: Applicant must be high school student and planning to enroll or expecting to enroll full-time at a four-year institution or university. Applicant must have 2.5 GPA or higher. Available to U.S. citizens.

Application Requirements: Application, essay, references, test scores, transcript. *Deadline:* February 16.

Contact: Cherie Kirkland, Vice President
Eddie Robinson Foundation
3391 Piedmont Road
Suite 105
Atlanta, GA 30305
Phone: 404-475-8408
Fax: 404-475-4408
E-mail: info@eddierobinson.com

EDFINANCIAL SERVICES   http://www.edfinancial.com

EDSCHOLAR SCHOLARSHIP

Renewable scholarships to qualified students in their freshman year. Minimum 3.25 high school GPA for 7 semesters, or ACT composite of 23 or SAT of 1070. Deadline varies.

Award: Scholarship for use in freshman year. *Amount:* $1000.

Eligibility Requirements: Applicant must be high school student and planning to enroll or expecting to enroll full-time at a four-year institution or university. Applicant must have 3.0 GPA or higher. Available to U.S. and non-U.S. citizens.

Application Requirements: Application, essay, financial need analysis, references, test scores, transcript. *Deadline:* varies.

Contact: Program Manager
Edfinancial Services
PO Box 36014
Knoxville, TN 37930-6014
Phone: 865-342-5500
Fax: 877-337-8439

EDUCAID, WACHOVIA CORPORATION   http://www.educaid.com

EDUCAID GIMME FIVE SCHOLARSHIP SWEEPSTAKES

Each year, Educaid will award twelve high school seniors $5000 for their first year at an accredited college or trade school. The scholarships are not based on grades or financial need, so every eligible high school senior who enters has an equal chance of winning. Apply online at: http://www.educaid.com.

Award: Prize for use in freshman year; not renewable. *Number:* 12. *Amount:* up to $5000.

Eligibility Requirements: Applicant must be high school student and planning to enroll or expecting to enroll full-time at a two-year or four-year or technical institution or university. Available to U.S. citizens.

Application Requirements: Application. *Deadline:* varies.

Contact: Educaid, Wachovia Corporation
PO Box 13667
Sacramento, CA 95853-3667
Phone: 877-689-0763

EDUCATION IS FREEDOM FOUNDATION   http://www.educationisfreedom.com/default.asp

EDUCATION IS FREEDOM NATIONAL SCHOLARSHIP

Applicants for this renewable scholarship must be high school seniors planning full-time undergraduate study at a 2 or 4-year college or university. Selection criteria is based on financial need, leadership and activities, work history, and candidate appraisal. Application available online at: http://www.educationisfreedom.com

Award: Scholarship for use in freshman, sophomore, junior, or senior years; renewable. *Number:* up to 225. *Amount:* $2000.

Eligibility Requirements: Applicant must be high school student and planning to enroll or expecting to enroll full-time at a two-year or four-year institution or university. Applicant must have 3.5 GPA or higher. Available to U.S. citizens.

Application Requirements: Application, financial need analysis, references, transcript. *Deadline:* January 15.

Contact: Barb Weber, Director of Operations
Education is Freedom Foundation
Scholarship America
Saint Peter, MN 56082

EDUCATIONAL COMMUNICATIONS SCHOLARSHIP FOUNDATION   http://www.ecisf.org

CHAIRMAN'S SCHOLARSHIP AWARD

Five awards of $5000 each are available to all high school students who are legal residents of the U.S., and have taken the SAT or ACT examination. Students who are listed in ECI's publications will automatically be sent an application. Deadline is May 15.

Award: Scholarship for use in freshman year; not renewable. *Number:* 5. *Amount:* $5000.

Eligibility Requirements: Applicant must be high school student and planning to enroll or expecting to enroll full-time at an institution or university. Applicant must have 3.0 GPA or higher. Available to U.S. citizens.

Application Requirements: Application, essay, financial need analysis. *Fee:* $4. *Deadline:* May 15.

Contact: Shanan Durda, Scholarship Coordinator
Educational Communications Scholarship Foundation
7211 Circle South Road
Austin, TX 78714-9319
Phone: 512-440-2705
Fax: 512-447-1687

ECI ACADEMIC AWARD SCHOLARSHIP

Scholarships of $1000 each are available to all high school students who are listed in ECI's Who's Who publications, are legal residents of the U.S., and have taken the SAT or ACT examination. Deadline is May 15.

Award: Scholarship for use in freshman year; not renewable. *Number:* 45. *Amount:* $1000.

Eligibility Requirements: Applicant must be high school student and planning to enroll or expecting to enroll full-time at an institution or university. Applicant must have 3.0 GPA or higher. Available to U.S. citizens.

Application Requirements: Application, essay, financial need analysis. *Fee:* $4. *Deadline:* May 15.

Contact: Shanan Durda, Scholarship Coordinator
Educational Communications Scholarship Foundation
7211 Circle South Road
Austin, TX 78714-9319
Phone: 512-440-2705
Fax: 512-447-1687

ECI CHANCELLOR'S SCHOLARSHIP

Award of $1000 for ten students who are legal residents of the U.S. Students who have been listed in ECI's publication, The Chancellor's List, are automatically eligible to compete. Scholarship awards are for graduate or doctoral study at any accredited, postsecondary institution in the field of study of their choice. Deadline is May 15.

Award: Scholarship for use in freshman, sophomore, junior, or senior years; not renewable. *Number:* 10. *Amount:* $1000.

Eligibility Requirements: Applicant must be enrolled or expecting to enroll full-time at a four-year institution or university. Applicant must have 3.0 GPA or higher. Available to U.S. citizens.

Application Requirements: Application, essay, financial need analysis. *Fee:* $4. *Deadline:* May 15.

Educational Communications Scholarship Foundation (continued)

Contact: Shanan Durda, Scholarship Coordinator
Educational Communications Scholarship Foundation
7211 Circle South Road
Austin, TX 78714-9319
Phone: 512-440-2705
Fax: 512-447-1687

ECI SPORTS SCHOLARSHIP

Award of $1000 available to all students who are legal residents of the U.S. and have taken the SAT or ACT examination. Students who are listed in ECI's publication, Who's Who Among America's High School Students-Sports Edition, are automatically eligible to compete. Deadline is May 15.

Award: Scholarship for use in freshman year; not renewable. *Number:* 10. *Amount:* $1000.

Eligibility Requirements: Applicant must be enrolled or expecting to enroll full-time at an institution or university. Applicant must have 3.0 GPA or higher. Available to U.S. citizens.

Application Requirements: Application, essay, financial need analysis. *Fee:* $4. *Deadline:* May 15.

Contact: Shanan Durda, Scholarship Coordinator
Educational Communications Scholarship Foundation
7211 Circle South Road
Austin, TX 78714-9319
Phone: 512-440-2705
Fax: 512-447-1687

FOUNDERS SCHOLARSHIP

Award of $6000 available to students who are legal residents of the U.S. and have taken the SAT or ACT examination. Students who have a listing in one of the publications of ECI (Who's Who Among American High School Students, etc.) will automatically be sent an application. Minimum GPA of 3.0. Application Deadline: May 15.

Award: Scholarship for use in freshman year; not renewable. *Number:* 1. *Amount:* $6000.

Eligibility Requirements: Applicant must be high school student and planning to enroll or expecting to enroll full-time at an institution or university. Applicant must have 3.0 GPA or higher. Available to U.S. citizens.

Application Requirements: Application. *Fee:* $4. *Deadline:* May 15.

Contact: Shanan Durda, Program Coordinator
Educational Communications Scholarship Foundation
7211 Circle South Road
Austin, TX 78714-9319
Phone: 512-440-2705
Fax: 512-447-1687

OUTSTANDING ACHIEVEMENT SCHOLARSHIPS

Ten awards of $2500 each are available to all high school students who are legal residents of the U.S. and have taken the SAT or ACT examination. Students who are listed in ECI's publications will automatically be sent an application. Deadline is May 15.

Award: Scholarship for use in freshman year; not renewable. *Number:* 10. *Amount:* $2500.

Eligibility Requirements: Applicant must be high school student and planning to enroll or expecting to enroll full-time at an institution or university. Applicant must have 3.0 GPA or higher. Available to U.S. citizens.

Application Requirements: Application, essay, financial need analysis. *Fee:* $4. *Deadline:* May 15.

Contact: Shanan Durda, Scholarship Coordinator
Educational Communications Scholarship Foundation
7211 Circle South Road
Austin, TX 78714-9319
Phone: 512-440-2705
Fax: 512-447-1687

ELKS NATIONAL FOUNDATION   http://www.elks.org/enf

ELKS GOLD AWARDS

Scholarship for young women who have achieved the highest ranking in Girl Scouting û the Gold Award. Eight annual scholarships to Gold Award winners selected by the Girl Scouts of the United States of America. One girl from each Girl Scout Service Area will receive a $6,000 scholarship ($1,500 per year). Gold Award scholarships are based on academics, activities, community involvement, leadership, and pursuit of individual interests. Applicants must be Gold Award winners and graduating high school seniors.

Award: Prize for use in freshman year. *Amount:* up to $1500.

Eligibility Requirements: Applicant must be enrolled or expecting to enroll at an institution or university and female. Available to U.S. citizens.

Application Requirements: Application. *Deadline:* January.

Contact: College Scholarships Program, Membership, and Research
Girl Scouts of the USA
Elks National Foundation
420 Fifth Avenue
New York, NY 10018-2798
Phone: 800-478-7248

ELKS MOST VALUABLE STUDENT CONTEST

Five hundred four-year awards are allocated for graduating high school seniors nationally by state quota. Based on scholarship, leadership, and financial need. Renewable awards with two first place awards at $60,000, two second place awards at $40,000 and two third place awards at $20,000. The awards will be distributed over four years. The remainder of the 494 awards will continue to be worth $4000 over four years. Applications available at local Elks Lodge, at the Web site: http://www.elks.org (keyword: scholarship), or by sending a SASE to the Foundation.

Award: Scholarship for use in freshman, sophomore, junior, or senior years; renewable. *Number:* 500. *Amount:* $4000–$60,000.

Eligibility Requirements: Applicant must be high school student and planning to enroll or expecting to enroll full-time at a two-year or four-year institution or university. Available to U.S. citizens.

Application Requirements: Application, applicant must enter a contest, essay, financial need analysis, references, self-addressed stamped envelope, test scores, transcript. *Deadline:* January 13.

Contact: Robin Edison, Scholarship Coordinator
Elks National Foundation
2750 North Lakeview Avenue
Chicago, IL 60614-1889
Phone: 773-755-4732
Fax: 773-755-4733
E-mail: scholarship@elks.org

EPSILON SIGMA ALPHA FOUNDATION   http://www.esaintl.com/esaf

EPSILON SIGMA ALPHA SCHOLARSHIPS

Awards for various fields of study. Some scholarships are restricted by gender, residency, grade point average or location of school. Applications must be sent to the Epsilon Sigma Alpha designated state counselor. See Web site at http://www.esaintl.com/esaf for further information, application forms and a list of state counselors. Application deadline is February 1.

Award: Scholarship for use in freshman, sophomore, junior, senior, or graduate years; not renewable. *Number:* 100–125. *Amount:* $500–$1500.

Eligibility Requirements: Applicant must be enrolled or expecting to enroll full or part-time at an institution or university. Available to U.S. citizens.

Application Requirements: Application, essay, references. *Deadline:* February 1.

Contact: Lynn Hughes, Scholarship Chairman
Epsilon Sigma Alpha Foundation
PO Box 270517
Fort Collins, CO 80527
Phone: 970-223-2824
Fax: 970-223-4456
E-mail: orcycler@vsisp.net

EXECUTIVE WOMEN INTERNATIONAL   http://www.executivewomen.org

ADULT STUDENTS IN SCHOLASTIC TRANSITION

A scholarship for adult students at transitional points in their lives. Applicants may be single parents, individuals just entering the workforce, or displaced homemakers. Chapter awards vary in amount; the Corporate level awards 12 scholarships valued at $1000 each. Application deadline is April 1. Applications are available on the organization's Web site.

Award: Scholarship for use in junior, senior, graduate, or postgraduate years; renewable. *Number:* 100–150. *Amount:* $1000–$2000.

Eligibility Requirements: Applicant must be enrolled or expecting to enroll full-time at a two-year or four-year or technical institution. Available to U.S. and non-U.S. citizens.

Application Requirements: Application. *Deadline:* April 1.

Contact: Suzette Smith, Education Manager
Executive Women International
515 South 700 East, Suite 2A
Salt Lake City, UT 84102
Phone: 801-355-2800
Fax: 801-362-3212
E-mail: suzette@executivewomen.org

FEDERATION OF AMERICAN CONSUMERS AND TRAVELERS   http://www.fact-org.org

FEDERATION OF AMERICAN CONSUMERS AND TRAVELERS CURRENT STUDENT SCHOLARSHIP

Award: Scholarship for use in freshman, sophomore, junior, or senior years.

Eligibility Requirements: Applicant must be enrolled or expecting to enroll at an institution or university.

Contact: Vicki Rolens, Managing Director
Federation of American Consumers and Travelers
PO Box 104
Edwardsville, IL 62025
Phone: 800-872-3228
Fax: 618-656-5369
E-mail: vrolens@fact-org.org

FEDERATION OF AMERICAN CONSUMERS AND TRAVELERS RETURNING STUDENT SCHOLARSHIP

Award: Scholarship for use in freshman, sophomore, junior, or senior years.

Eligibility Requirements: Applicant must be enrolled or expecting to enroll at an institution or university.

Contact: Vicki Rolens, Managing Director
Federation of American Consumers and Travelers
PO Box 104
Edwardsville, IL 62025
Phone: 800-872-3228
Fax: 618-656-5369
E-mail: vrolens@fact-org.org

FEDERATION OF AMERICAN CONSUMERS AND TRAVELERS TRADE SCHOOL SCHOLARSHIP

Award: Scholarship for use in freshman, sophomore, junior, or senior years.

Eligibility Requirements: Applicant must be enrolled or expecting to enroll at an institution or university.

Contact: Vicki Rolens, Managing Director
Federation of American Consumers and Travelers
PO Box 104
Edwardsville, IL 62025
Phone: 800-872-3228
Fax: 618-656-5369
E-mail: vrolens@fact-org.org

FIRST CATHOLIC SLOVAK LADIES ASSOCIATION   http://www.fcsla.com

FIRST CATHOLIC SLOVAK LADIES ASSOCIATION HIGH SCHOOL SCHOLARSHIPS

Scholarship for high school students. A written report of approximately 250 words on "What This High School Scholarship Will Do for Me" must be submitted with this application. Candidate must have been a beneficial member of the Association for at least three years prior to date of application.

Award: Scholarship for use in freshman year; renewable. *Number:* up to 28. *Amount:* $1000.

Eligibility Requirements: Applicant must be high school student and planning to enroll or expecting to enroll full-time at an institution or university. Available to U.S. and Canadian citizens.

Application Requirements: Application, essay, photo, transcript. *Deadline:* March 1.

Contact: Director of Fraternal Scholarship Aid
First Catholic Slovak Ladies Association
24950 Chagrin Boulevard
Beachwood, OH 44122
Phone: 800-464-4642
E-mail: info@fcsla.com

FIRST DATA WESTERN UNION FOUNDATION   http://www.firstdatawesternunion.org

FIRST DATA WESTERN UNION FOUNDATION SCHOLARSHIP

Scholarship to provide an opportunity for low-income, non-traditional students to realize their educational dreams. Must be resident of U.S. or Puerto Rico who has overcome personal challenges, has initiative and a commitment to learning and hard work. Must demonstrate financial need.

Award: Scholarship for use in freshman or sophomore years; renewable. *Amount:* $500–$3000.

Eligibility Requirements: Applicant must be enrolled or expecting to enroll full-time at a four-year institution or university. Applicant must have 2.5 GPA or higher. Available to U.S. citizens.

Application Requirements: Application. *Deadline:* April 1.

Contact: Progaram Associate
First Data Western Union Foundation
6200 South Quebec Street, Suite 370AU
Greenwood Village, CO 80111
Phone: 303-967-6305

FLORIDA DEPARTMENT OF EDUCATION   http://www.floridastudentfinancialaid.org

FLORIDA WORK EXPERIENCE PROGRAM

Program is offered at participating state public universities and community colleges and eligible private, non-profit postsecondary institutions. Contact the financial aid administrator for application deadlines and student eligibility requirements.

Award: Grant for use in freshman, sophomore, junior, or senior years.

Eligibility Requirements: Applicant must be enrolled or expecting to enroll full or part-time at a two-year or four-year institution or university. Available to U.S. citizens.

Application Requirements: Application, financial need analysis, FAFSA. *Deadline:* varies.

Contact: Barb Dombrowski, Education Director, Policy and Training
Florida Department of Education
Office of Student Financial Assistance
1940 North Monroe, Suite 70
Tallahassee, FL 32303-4759
Phone: 850-410-5191
Fax: 850-488-5966
E-mail: barb.dombrowski@fldoe.org

FOND DU LAC RESERVATION   http://www.fdlrez.com

FOND DU LAC SCHOLARSHIP PROGRAM

Must be enrolled tribal member of the Fond du lac reservation and have high school diploma or GED. Must be accepted for admission at accredited college, university or technical school. Must complete FAFSA and all other required applications. All recipients must submit grades at the end of each term, must maintain 2.0 GPA for continued funding. Deadline is July 1.

Award: Scholarship for use in freshman, sophomore, junior, senior, graduate, or postgraduate years; renewable. *Number:* 75–100. *Amount:* $500–$12,000.

Eligibility Requirements: Applicant must be enrolled or expecting to enroll full or part-time at a two-year or four-year or technical institution or university. Available to U.S. citizens.

Fond Du Lac Reservation (continued)

Application Requirements: Application, financial need analysis, transcript. *Deadline:* July 1.

Contact: Bonnie Wallace, Scholarship Director
Fond Du Lac Reservation
1720 Big Lake Road, Federal Tribal Center
Cloquet, MN 55720
Phone: 218-879-4593 Ext. 2681
Fax: 218-878-7529
E-mail: scholarships@fdlrez.com

FOUNDATION FOR INDEPENDENT HIGHER EDUCATION   http://www.fihe.org

LIBERTY MUTUAL SCHOLARSHIP PROGRAM

Funded by Liberty Mutual and administered by the Foundation for Independent Higher Education. $5000 combined with an opportunity for a summer internship. Renewable for senior year. Students should have an interest in a career in a business environment. Must be a resident of or studying in one of the following states: CA, IL, NH, NY, TX, GA, MA, NJ, PA, or WI. Deadline changes every year, usually in the month of November.

Award: Scholarship for use in junior or senior years; renewable. *Number:* 17. *Amount:* $5000.

Eligibility Requirements: Applicant must be enrolled or expecting to enroll full-time at a four-year institution or university. Applicant must have 3.5 GPA or higher. Available to U.S. and non-U.S. citizens.

Application Requirements: Application, resume, transcript, questionnaire. *Deadline:* varies.

Contact: Jose Palacios, Director of Finance and Operations
Foundation for Independent Higher Education
1920 N Street, NW, Suite 210
Washington, DC 20036
Phone: 202-367-0333
Fax: 202-367-0334
E-mail: fihe@fihe.org

FOUNDATION FOR OUTDOOR ADVERTISING RESEARCH AND EDUCATION (FOARE)   http://www.oaaa.org

FOARE SCHOLARSHIP PROGRAM

Assistance to students enrolled in undergraduate and graduate college and university programs. Must be high school seniors accepted to an undergraduate program at an accredited institution.

Award: Scholarship for use in freshman, sophomore, junior, senior, or graduate years. *Amount:* up to $2000.

Eligibility Requirements: Applicant must be enrolled or expecting to enroll full-time at a four-year institution or university. Available to U.S. citizens.

Application Requirements: Application, essay, financial need analysis, transcript. *Deadline:* June 15.

Contact: Geeta Razack, Coordinator, Membership & Administration
Foundation for Outdoor Advertising Research and Education (FOARE)
c/o Thomas M. Smith and Associates
4601 Tilden Street, NW
Washington, DC 20036
Phone: 202-833-5566
Fax: 202-833-1522
E-mail: grazack@oaaa.org

FOUNDATION OF THE WALL AND CEILING INDUSTRY   http://www.awci.org/thefoundation.shtml

FOUNDATION OF THE WALL AND CEILING INDUSTRY SCHOLARSHIP PROGRAM

Award: Scholarship for use in freshman, sophomore, junior, senior, or graduate years.

Eligibility Requirements: Applicant must be enrolled or expecting to enroll at an institution or university.

Contact: Jane Northern, Director of Membership Marketing and Programs
Foundation of the Wall and Ceiling Industry
803 West Broad Street, Suite 600
Falls Church, VA 22046
Phone: 703-538-1615
Fax: 703-534-8307
E-mail: northern@awci.org

FRANK H. AND EVA B. BUCK FOUNDATION   http://www.buckfoundation.org

FRANK H. BUCK SCHOLARSHIPS

Award: Scholarship for use in freshman, sophomore, junior, senior, or graduate years. *Number:* 8–16.

Eligibility Requirements: Applicant must be enrolled or expecting to enroll at an institution or university.

Contact: Gloria Brown, Scholarship Director
Frank H. and Eva B. Buck Foundation
PO Box 5610
Vacaville, CA 95696-5610
Phone: 707-446-7700
Fax: 707-446-7766
E-mail: gbrown@buckfoundation.org

FRATERNAL ORDER OF POLICE ASSOCIATES OF OHIO, INC.   http://www.fopaohio.org

FRATERNAL ORDER OF POLICE ASSOCIATES SCHOLARSHIP

Scholarship available to a graduating high school senior whose parent or guardian is a member in good standing of FOPA. Total amount will be $4000 payable over a four-year period. $500 paid in August and December of each year to the recipient with proof of enrollment from an accredited college or university. A one-time award of $500 will be given to the first runner-up. Visit http://www.fopaohio.org/scholarship.htm for more information. Deadline is May 1.

Award: Scholarship for use in freshman year; not renewable. *Number:* 1–2. *Amount:* $500–$4000.

Eligibility Requirements: Applicant must be high school student and planning to enroll or expecting to enroll full-time at an institution or university. Applicant must have 2.5 GPA or higher. Available to U.S. citizens.

Application Requirements: Application, financial need analysis, photo, references, transcript, proof of guardianship. *Deadline:* May 1.

Contact: Michael J. Esposito, FOPA State Secretary
Fraternal Order of Police Associates of Ohio, Inc.
PO Box 14564
Cincinnati, OH 45250-0564
Phone: 513-684-4755
E-mail: mje@fopaohio.org

FREEDOM FROM RELIGION FOUNDATION   http://www.ffrf.org

FREEDOM FROM RELIGION FOUNDATION COLLEGE ESSAY CONTEST

Any currently enrolled college student may submit college essays. Essays should be typed, double-spaced pages with standard margins. Contestants must choose an original title for essay. Each contestant must include a paragraph biography giving campus and permanent addresses, phone numbers, and email(s). Please identify the college or university the contestant is attending, year in school, major, and interests. The essay topic and specific guidelines are posted in February. For more information visit: http://www.ffrf.org/

Award: Prize for use in freshman, sophomore, junior, or senior years; not renewable. *Number:* 3. *Amount:* $500–$2000.

Eligibility Requirements: Applicant must be enrolled or expecting to enroll at a two-year or four-year or technical institution or university. Available to U.S. citizens.

Application Requirements: Applicant must enter a contest, essay. *Deadline:* July 1.

Contact: College Essay Competition, FFRF, Inc.
Freedom From Religion Foundation
PO Box 750
Madison, WI 53701

FREEDOM FROM RELIGION FOUNDATION HIGH SCHOOL ESSAY CONTEST

High-school essays should be typed, double-spaced pages with standard margins. Contestants must choose an original title for essay. Each entrant must include a paragraph biography giving campus and permanent addresses, phone numbers and emails. Identify the high school from which the student will have graduated and the college/university the student will be attending. The essay topic and specific guidelines are posted in February. For more information visit: http://www.ffrf.org/.

Award: Prize for use in freshman year; not renewable. *Number:* 3. *Amount:* $500–$2000.

Eligibility Requirements: Applicant must be high school student and planning to enroll or expecting to enroll full-time at a two-year or four-year or technical institution or university. Available to U.S. and Canadian citizens.

Application Requirements: Applicant must enter a contest, essay. *Deadline:* June 1.

Contact: High School Essay Competition, FFRF, Inc.
Freedom From Religion Foundation
PO Box 750
Madison, WI 53701

GARDEN CLUB OF AMERICA   http://www.gcamerica.org

CAROLINE THORN KISSEL SUMMER ENVIRONMENTAL STUDIES SCHOLARSHIP

For college students, graduate students, or non-degree seeking applicants above the high school level. Applicants must be U.S. citizens and either residents of New Jersey studying in New Jersey or elsewhere, or non residents pursuing a study in New Jersey or its surrounding waters.

Award: Scholarship for use in freshman, sophomore, junior, senior, graduate, or postgraduate years. *Amount:* $1500.

Eligibility Requirements: Applicant must be enrolled or expecting to enroll at an institution or university. Available to U.S. citizens.

Application Requirements: Application, essay, references. *Deadline:* February 10.

Contact: Ms. Judy Smith
Garden Club of America
14 East 60th Street
New York, NY 10022-1002
Phone: 212-753-8287
Fax: 212-753-0134

ZELLER SUMMER SCHOLARSHIP IN MEDICINAL BOTANY

For field work or research in Medicinal Botany. Work may award academic credit. Applicants may apply following their freshman, sophomore, junior and senior years. A report is required at the end of the summer study. See Web site for further details.

Award: Scholarship for use in freshman, sophomore, junior, senior, or postgraduate years. *Number:* 1. *Amount:* $1500.

Eligibility Requirements: Applicant must be enrolled or expecting to enroll at a two-year or four-year institution or university. Available to U.S. citizens.

Application Requirements: Application, essay, references, transcript. *Deadline:* February 1.

Contact: Ms. Judy Smith
Garden Club of America
14 East 60th Street
New York, NY 10022-1002
Phone: 212-753-8287
Fax: 212-753-0134

GENERAL FEDERATION OF WOMEN'S CLUBS IN WYOMING

MARY N. BROOKS DAUGHTER/GRANDDAUGHTER SCHOLARSHIP

Award: Scholarship for use in freshman, sophomore, junior, or senior years.

Eligibility Requirements: Applicant must be enrolled or expecting to enroll at an institution or university.

Contact:

MARY N. BROOKS WYOMING GIRL SCHOLARSHIP

Award: Scholarship for use in freshman, sophomore, junior, or senior years.

Eligibility Requirements: Applicant must be enrolled or expecting to enroll at an institution or university.

Contact:

GEORGIA POLICE CORPS

GEORGIA POLICE CORPS SCHOLARSHIP

Awards available for reimbursement of educational expenses for undergraduate and graduate study. Obligation to commit to four years of service at a participating law enforcement agency. Check Web site for application and updated information.

Award: Scholarship for use in freshman, sophomore, junior, senior, or graduate years. *Number:* 10. *Amount:* up to $30,000.

Eligibility Requirements: Applicant must be enrolled or expecting to enroll at a four-year institution or university. Available to U.S. citizens.

Application Requirements: Application, essay, references, transcript. *Deadline:* February 1.

Contact: Bob Gaylor, Program Director
Georgia Police Corps
1000 Indian Springs Drive
Forsyth, GA 31029
Phone: 877-267-4630
Fax: 478-993-4560
E-mail: bgaylor@gpstc.state.ga.us

GEORGIA STUDENT FINANCE COMMISSION   http://www.gsfc.org

ROBERT C. BYRD HONORS SCHOLARSHIP-GEORGIA

Complete the application provided by the Georgia Department of Education. Renewable awards for outstanding graduating Georgia high school seniors to be used for full-time undergraduate study at eligible U.S. institution. Must a legal resident of Georgia and a U.S. citizen.

Award: Scholarship for use in freshman, sophomore, junior, or senior years; renewable. *Number:* 600–720. *Amount:* up to $1500.

Eligibility Requirements: Applicant must be high school student and planning to enroll or expecting to enroll full-time at a two-year or four-year institution or university. Available to U.S. citizens.

Application Requirements: Application, transcript. *Deadline:* February 1.

Contact: William Flook, Director of Scholarships and Grants Division
Georgia Student Finance Commission
2082 East Exchange Place, Suite 100
Tucker, GA 30084
Phone: 770-724-9052
Fax: 770-724-9031
E-mail: billf@gsfc.org

GERMAN ACADEMIC EXCHANGE SERVICE (DAAD)   http://www.daad.org

GERMAN ACADEMIC EXCHANGE SERVICE (DAAD) EDU DE UNDERGRADUATE AWARDS

Award: Scholarship for use in junior or senior years. *Number:* 1.

German Academic Exchange Service (DAAD) (continued)

Eligibility Requirements: Applicant must be enrolled or expecting to enroll at an institution or university.

Contact: German Academic Exchange Service (DAAD)
871 United Nations Plaza
New York, NY 10017
Phone: 212-758-3223
Fax: 212-755-5780
E-mail: daadny@daad.org

GERMAN STUDIES RESEARCH GRANTS

Award: Grant for use in junior, senior, or graduate years. *Amount:* $1500–$2500.

Eligibility Requirements: Applicant must be enrolled or expecting to enroll at an institution or university.

Contact: German Academic Exchange Service (DAAD)
871 United Nations Plaza
New York, NY 10017
Phone: 212-758-3223
Fax: 212-755-5780
E-mail: daadny@daad.org

HOCHSCHULSOMMERKURSE AT GERMAN UNIVERSITIES

Award: Scholarship for use in junior, senior, or graduate years.

Eligibility Requirements: Applicant must be enrolled or expecting to enroll at an institution or university.

Contact: German Academic Exchange Service (DAAD)
871 United Nations Plaza
New York, NY 10017
Phone: 212-758-3223
Fax: 212-755-5780
E-mail: daadny@daad.org

GIRL SCOUTS OF GULFCOAST FLORIDA, INC.   http://www.girlscoutsgulfcoastfl.org

GULFCOAST COLLEGE SCHOLARSHIP AWARD

Award: Scholarship for use in freshman or sophomore years.

Eligibility Requirements: Applicant must be enrolled or expecting to enroll at an institution or university.

Contact: Sue Zimmerman, Director of Administrative Services
Girl Scouts of Gulfcoast Florida, Inc.
4780 Cattlemen Road
Sarasota, FL 34233
Phone: 941-921-5358
Fax: 941-923-5241
E-mail: suez@girlscoutsgulfcoastfl.org

GLAMOUR   http://www.glamour.com

TOP TEN COLLEGE WOMEN COMPETITION

Glamour is looking for female students with leadership experience on and off campus, excellence in field of study, and inspiring goals. Award is $2000 and a trip to New York City. Must be a junior studying full-time with a minimum GPA of 3.0. Non-U.S. citizens may apply if attending U.S. postsecondary institutions.

Award: Prize for use in junior year; not renewable. *Number:* 10. *Amount:* $2000.

Eligibility Requirements: Applicant must be enrolled or expecting to enroll full-time at a four-year institution or university and female. Applicant must have 3.0 GPA or higher. Available to U.S. and non-U.S. citizens.

Application Requirements: Application, essay, photo, references, transcript, list of activities. *Deadline:* March 31.

Contact: Lynda Laux-Bachand, Reader Services Editor
Glamour
4 Times Square, 16th Floor
New York, NY 10036-6593
Phone: 212-286-6667
Fax: 212-286-6922

GLORIA BARRON PRIZE FOR YOUNG HEROES   http://www.barronprize.org

GLORIA BARRON PRIZE FOR YOUNG HEROES

Award honors young people ages 8 to 18 who have shown leadership and courage in public service to people or to the planet. Must be nominated by a responsible adult who is not a relative. Award is to be applied to higher education or a service project. For further information and nomination forms, see Web site at http://www.barronprize.org.

Award: Prize for use in freshman year; not renewable. *Number:* 10–20. *Amount:* up to $2000.

Eligibility Requirements: Applicant must be age 8-18 and enrolled or expecting to enroll at an institution or university. Available to U.S. and Canadian citizens.

Application Requirements: Application, autobiography, driver's license, essay, financial need analysis, interview, photo, portfolio, resume, references, self-addressed stamped envelope, test scores, transcript, nomination. *Deadline:* April 30.

Contact: Barbara Ann Richman, Executive Director
Gloria Barron Prize for Young Heroes
545 Pearl Street
Boulder, CO 80302
E-mail: ba_richman@barronprize.org

GOVERNOR'S OFFICE

GOVERNOR'S OPPORTUNITY SCHOLARSHIP

Award: Scholarship for use in junior, senior, or graduate years.

Eligibility Requirements: Applicant must be enrolled or expecting to enroll at an institution or university.

Contact: Trish Fontana, Administrative Assistant
Governor's Office
State Capitol Building
Sacramento, CA 95814
Phone: 916-445-7097

GRAND RAPIDS COMMUNITY FOUNDATION   http://www.grfoundation.org

ALTRUSA INTERNATIONAL OF GRAND RAPIDS SCHOLARSHIP

Award: Scholarship for use in freshman, sophomore, junior, or senior years. *Number:* 1.

Eligibility Requirements: Applicant must be enrolled or expecting to enroll at an institution or university.

Contact: Ruth Bishop, Education Program Officer
Grand Rapids Community Foundation
161 Ottawa Avenue, NW, 209 C
Grand Rapids, MI 49503-2757
Phone: 616-454-1751
Fax: 616-454-6455
E-mail: rbishop@grfoundation.org

DONALD J. DEYOUNG SCHOLARSHIP

Award: Scholarship for use in freshman year. *Number:* 1.

Eligibility Requirements: Applicant must be enrolled or expecting to enroll at an institution or university.

Contact: Ruth Bishop, Education Program Officer
Grand Rapids Community Foundation
161 Ottawa Avenue, NW, 209 C
Grand Rapids, MI 49503-2757
Phone: 616-454-1751
Fax: 616-454-6455
E-mail: rbishop@grfoundation.org

JOSHUA ESCH MITCHELL AVIATION SCHOLARSHIP

Award: Scholarship for use in sophomore, junior, or senior years. *Number:* 1.

Eligibility Requirements: Applicant must be enrolled or expecting to enroll at an institution or university.

Contact: Ruth Bishop, Education Program Officer
Grand Rapids Community Foundation
161 Ottawa Avenue, NW, 209 C
Grand Rapids, MI 49503-2757
Phone: 616-454-1751
Fax: 616-454-6455
E-mail: rbishop@grfoundation.org

LLEWELLYN L. CAYVAN STRING INSTRUMENT SCHOLARSHIP

Award: Scholarship for use in freshman, sophomore, junior, or senior years. *Number:* 1.

Eligibility Requirements: Applicant must be enrolled or expecting to enroll at an institution or university.

Contact: Ruth Bishop, Education Program Officer
Grand Rapids Community Foundation
161 Ottawa Avenue, NW, 209 C
Grand Rapids, MI 49503-2757
Phone: 616-454-1751
Fax: 616-454-6455
E-mail: rbishop@grfoundation.org

GUARDIAN LIFE INSURANCE COMPANY OF AMERICA http://www.girlsgoingplaces.com

GIRLS GOING PLACES SCHOLARSHIP PROGRAM

Rewards enterprising girls students between ages 12 and 16 who demonstrate budding entrepreneurship, are taking the first steps toward financial independence, and make a difference in their school and community.

Award: Prize for use in freshman year; not renewable. *Number:* 15. *Amount:* $1000–$10,000.

Eligibility Requirements: Applicant must be high school student; age 12-16; planning to enroll or expecting to enroll full-time at a two-year or four-year or technical institution or university and single female. Available to U.S. citizens.

Application Requirements: Application, essay. *Deadline:* February 24.

Contact: Diana Acevedo, Project Manager
Guardian Life Insurance Company of America
7 Hanover Square 26-C
New York, NY 10004
Phone: 212-598-7881
Fax: 212-919-2586
E-mail: diana_acevedo@glic.com

GUERNSEY-MUSKINGUM ELECTRIC COOPERATIVE, INC. http://www.gmenergy.com

HIGH SCHOOL SENIOR SCHOLARSHIP

Two $1000 scholarships, two $500 scholarships, two $300 scholarships, and two $200 scholarships are available to a boy or girl graduating from high school whose parents or legal guardian receives electric service from Guernsey-Muskingum Electric Cooperative. Deadline is February 1.

Award: Scholarship for use in freshman year; not renewable. *Number:* up to 10. *Amount:* $200–$1000.

Eligibility Requirements: Applicant must be high school student and planning to enroll or expecting to enroll full-time at an institution or university. Applicant must have 2.5 GPA or higher. Available to U.S. citizens.

Application Requirements: Application, references, transcript. *Deadline:* February 1.

Contact: Darrell Cubbison, Manager, Member Services
Guernsey-Muskingum Electric Cooperative, Inc.
17 South Liberty Street
New Concord, OH 43762
Phone: 740-826-7661
Fax: 740-826-7171
E-mail: mailbox@gmenergy.com

HAROLD B. & DOROTHY A. SNYDER FOUNDATION, INC.

HAROLD B. AND DOROTHY A. SNYDER FOUNDATION, INC., PROGRAM

Award: Scholarship for use in freshman, sophomore, junior, senior, or graduate years.

Eligibility Requirements: Applicant must be enrolled or expecting to enroll at an institution or university.

Contact: Audrey Snyder, Executive Director
Harold B. & Dorothy A. Snyder Foundation, Inc.
525 Eaglebrook Drive
Moorestown, NJ 08057

HAWAII DEPARTMENT OF EDUCATION http://doe.k12.hi.us

ROBERT C. BYRD HONORS SCHOLARSHIP-HAWAII

The Robert C. Byrd Honors Scholarship is available to students planning to attend college. The scholarship is federally funded, state-administered and recognizes exceptional high school seniors who show promise of continued excellence in the postsecondary educational system. Award of $1500 renewable for four years. Must have a minimum GPA of 3.2 and 1270 SAT. Deadline is March 17.

Award: Scholarship for use in freshman year; renewable. *Number:* 28. *Amount:* $1500–$6000.

Eligibility Requirements: Applicant must be enrolled or expecting to enroll full-time at an institution or university. Applicant must have 3.0 GPA or higher. Available to U.S. citizens.

Application Requirements: Application, transcript, community service. *Deadline:* March 17.

Contact: Deanna Helber, Education Specialist
Hawaii Department of Education
641 18th Avenue, Building V, Room 201
Honolulu, HI 96816-4444
Phone: 808-735-6222
Fax: 808-733-9890
E-mail: dee_helber@notes.k12.hi.us

HAWAII EDUCATION ASSOCIATION http://www.heaed.com/

HAWAII EDUCATION ASSOCIATION UNDERGRADUATE COLLEGE STUDENT SCHOLARSHIP

Award: Scholarship for use in freshman, sophomore, junior, or senior years.

Eligibility Requirements: Applicant must be enrolled or expecting to enroll at an institution or university.

Contact: Carol Yoneshige, Executive Director
Hawaii Education Association
1649 Kalakaua Avenue
Honolulu, HI 96826
Phone: 808-949-6657
Fax: 808-944-2032
E-mail: hea.office@heaed.com

HAWAII SCHOOLS FEDERAL CREDIT UNION http://www.hawaiischoolsfcu.org/

EDWIN KUNIYUKI MEMORIAL SCHOLARSHIP

Annual scholarship for an incoming college freshman in recognition of academic excellence. Applicant must be Hawaii Schools Federal Credit Union member for one year prior to scholarship application.

Award: Scholarship for use in freshman year; not renewable. *Number:* 1. *Amount:* $1000.

Eligibility Requirements: Applicant must be high school student and planning to enroll or expecting to enroll full-time at a two-year or four-year or technical institution or university. Applicant must have 3.0 GPA or higher. Available to U.S. citizens.

Hawaii Schools Federal Credit Union (continued)

Application Requirements: Application, essay, references, transcript. *Deadline:* varies.

Contact: Stephanie Lachance, Administrative Assistant
Hawaii Schools Federal Credit Union
233 South Vineyard Street
Honolulu, HI 96813
Phone: 808-521-0302
Fax: 808-538-3231
E-mail: slachance@hawaiischoolsfcu.org

HCR MANOR CARE, INC.

HCR MANOR CARE NURSING SCHOLARSHIP PROGRAM

Award: Scholarship for use in freshman, sophomore, junior, or senior years.

Eligibility Requirements: Applicant must be enrolled or expecting to enroll at an institution or university.

Contact:

HELEN GOUGH SCHOLARSHIP FOUNDATION

HELEN GOUGH SCHOLARSHIP

Award: Scholarship for use in freshman, sophomore, junior, senior, or graduate years.

Eligibility Requirements: Applicant must be enrolled or expecting to enroll at an institution or university.

Contact:

HELPING HANDS FOUNDATION   http://www.helpinghandsbookscholarship.com

HELPING HANDS BOOK SCHOLARSHIP PROGRAM

The HHBSP was created to assist students with the high cost of textbooks and study materials. Awards are open to individuals ages 16 and up who are planning to attend or are currently attending a two- or four-year college or university or a technical/vocational institution. Application fee is $5.

Award: Grant for use in freshman, sophomore, junior, senior, graduate, or postgraduate years; not renewable. *Number:* 20–30. *Amount:* $100–$1000.

Eligibility Requirements: Applicant must be age 16 and enrolled or expecting to enroll full or part-time at a two-year or four-year or technical institution or university. Available to U.S. and non-U.S. citizens.

Application Requirements: Application, essay, self-addressed stamped envelope, transcript. *Fee:* $5. *Deadline:* July 15.

Contact: Scholarship Director
Helping Hands Foundation
4480-H South Cobb Drive, PO Box 435
Smyrna, GA 30080

HENKEL CONSUMER ADHESIVES, INC.   http://www.ducktapeclub.com

DUCK BRAND DUCT TAPE "STUCK AT PROM" SCHOLARSHIP CONTEST

Contest is open to residents of the United States and Canada. Must be 14 years or older. First place winners now receiving a $3000 college scholarship each a total of $6000 for the couple and $3000 for the high school hosting the winning couple prom. The second place winners will each receive a $2000 college scholarship, with the high school receiving $2000. The third place couple will each win a $1000 college scholarship, and the high school will receive $1000.

Award: Prize for use in freshman, sophomore, junior, or senior years; not renewable. *Number:* 3. *Amount:* $1000–$3000.

Eligibility Requirements: Applicant must be age 14 and enrolled or expecting to enroll full or part-time at a two-year or four-year or technical institution or university. Available to U.S. and Canadian citizens.

Application Requirements: Application, applicant must enter a contest, photo, entry form, release form. *Deadline:* June 9.

Contact: Michelle Heffner, Digital Marketing Communications Manager
Henkel Consumer Adhesives, Inc.
32150 Just Imagine Drive
Avon, OH 44011-1355
Phone: 440-937-7000

HENRY SACHS FOUNDATION   http://www.sachsfoundation.org

SACHS FOUNDATION SCHOLARSHIPS

Award: Scholarship for use in freshman year.

Eligibility Requirements: Applicant must be enrolled or expecting to enroll at an institution or university.

Contact: Lisa Harris, Secretary and Treasurer
Henry Sachs Foundation
90 S Cascade Avenue, Suite 1410
Colorado Springs, CO 80903
Phone: 719-633-2353
E-mail: info@sachsfoundation.org

HERMAN O. WEST FOUNDATION

HERMAN O. WEST FOUNDATION SCHOLARSHIP PROGRAM

Award: Scholarship for use in freshman, sophomore, junior, or senior years.

Eligibility Requirements: Applicant must be enrolled or expecting to enroll at an institution or university.

Contact:

HONOR SOCIETY OF PHI KAPPA PHI   http://www.phikappaphi.org

STUDY ABROAD GRANT COMPETITION

Grants up to $1000 will be awarded to undergraduate Phi Kappa Phi members as support in seeking knowledge and experience by studying abroad. For more details see Web site: http://www.phikappaphi.org/Web/Scholarships/studyabroad/studyabroad_instructions.html

Award: Grant for use in freshman, sophomore, junior, or senior years; not renewable. *Number:* 38. *Amount:* $1000.

Eligibility Requirements: Applicant must be enrolled or expecting to enroll full-time at a four-year institution or university. Applicant must have 3.5 GPA or higher. Available to U.S. and non-U.S. citizens.

Application Requirements: Application, references, transcript, letter of acceptance into a study abroad program. *Deadline:* February 15.

Contact: Theresa Bard, Programs Coordinator
Honor Society of Phi Kappa Phi
305 French House, Highland Road, Louisiana State University
Baton Rouge, LA 70893-6000
Phone: 225-388-4917 Ext. 13
Fax: 225-388-4900
E-mail: awards@phikappaphi.org

HORATIO ALGER ASSOCIATION OF DISTINGUISHED AMERICANS   http://www.horatioalger.org

HORATIO ALGER ASSOCIATION SCHOLARSHIP PROGRAM

The Horatio Alger Association provides financial assistance to students in the United States who have exhibited integrity and perseverance in overcoming personal adversity and who aspire to pursue higher education. Scholarship award for full-time students seeking undergraduate degree. Minimum 2.0 GPA required.

Award: Scholarship for use in freshman, sophomore, junior, or senior years; renewable. *Number:* 100. *Amount:* $10,000.

Eligibility Requirements: Applicant must be high school student and planning to enroll or expecting to enroll full-time at a two-year or four-year institution or university. Available to U.S. citizens.

Application Requirements: Application, essay, financial need analysis, references, transcript. *Deadline:* March 20.

Contact: Scholarship Coordinator
Horatio Alger Association of Distinguished Americans
99 Canal Center Plaza, Suite 320
Alexandria, VA 22314
E-mail: programs@horatioalger.com

HOSPITAL CENTRAL SERVICES, INC.
http://www.giveapint.org

HOSPITAL CENTRAL SERVICES STUDENT VOLUNTEER SCHOLARSHIP

Award to a graduating high school senior who has completed a minimum of 135 hours of volunteer service to the Hospital Central Services Blood Center in the Lehigh Valley region of Pennsylvania and northwestern New Jersey, in no less than a cumulative two calendar year period. Must have maintained an overall 2.5 GPA.

Award: Scholarship for use in freshman year. *Amount:* up to $1000.

Eligibility Requirements: Applicant must be high school student and planning to enroll or expecting to enroll at an institution or university. Applicant must have 2.5 GPA or higher. Available to U.S. citizens.

Application Requirements: Application, references. *Deadline:* March 31.

Contact: Marie Clemens, Director, Community Relations
Hospital Central Services, Inc.
Miller-Keystone Memorial Blood Center Volunteer Scholarship
1465 Valley Center Parkway
Bethlehem, PA 18017
Phone: 610-791-2222 Ext. 2293

HOSTESS COMMITTEE SCHOLARSHIPS/MISS AMERICA PAGEANT
http://www.missamerica.org

MARCHING BAND SCHOLARSHIPS

Scholarships initiated as part of the Miss America Organization's effort to extend scholarship to students who participated in the Miss America Parade as part of high school marching bands.

Award: Scholarship for use in senior year. *Number:* up to 4. *Amount:* $1000–$5000.

Eligibility Requirements: Applicant must be enrolled or expecting to enroll at a two-year institution. Available to U.S. citizens.

Contact: Hostess Committee Scholarships/Miss America Pageant
Two Miss America Way, Suite 1000
Atlantic City, NJ 08401

HUGH FULTON BYAS MEMORIAL FUNDS, INC.

HUGH FULTON BYAS MEMORIAL GRANT

Award: Grant for use in sophomore, junior, senior, or graduate years.

Eligibility Requirements: Applicant must be enrolled or expecting to enroll at an institution or university.

Contact: Linda Maffei, Administrator
Hugh Fulton Byas Memorial Funds, Inc.
261 Bradley Street
New Haven, CT 06511
Phone: 203-777-8356
Fax: 203-562-6288

INDEPENDENT COLLEGES OF SOUTHERN CALIFORNIA

MACERICH COMPANY SCHOLARSHIP

Award: Scholarship for use in freshman year.

Eligibility Requirements: Applicant must be enrolled or expecting to enroll at an institution or university.

Contact:

INDEPENDENT INSTITUTE
http://www.independent.org

OLIVE W. GARVEY FELLOWSHIP COMPETITION

An international essay contest held every other year. College or university students, part-time or full-time, undergraduate or graduate, from all nations and academic disciplines are eligible. The specific topic changes with each contest. Applicants must be no older than 35. See Web site for more information: http://www.independent.org/students/garvey.

Award: Prize for use in freshman, sophomore, junior, senior, graduate, or postgraduate years; not renewable. *Number:* 6. *Amount:* $1000–$10,000.

Eligibility Requirements: Applicant must be age 35 or under and enrolled or expecting to enroll full or part-time at a two-year or four-year institution or university. Available to U.S. and non-U.S. citizens.

Application Requirements: Application, applicant must enter a contest, essay, references. *Deadline:* May 1.

Contact: Mr. Carl Close, Academic Affairs Director, The Independent Institute
Independent Institute
100 Swan Way
Oakland, CA 94621-1428
Phone: 510-632-1366
Fax: 510-568-6040
E-mail: cclose@independent.org

INDIANA POLICE CORPS
http://www.in.gov/cji/policecorps

POLICE CORPS INCENTIVE SCHOLARSHIP

Scholarships are available to highly qualified men and women entering the Police Corps. Up to $15,000 a year for four years can be used to cover the expenses of study toward a baccalaureate or graduate degree. Must agree to serve four years in community policing in Indiana. For more details and an application see Web site: http://www.in.gov/cji.policecorps

Award: Scholarship for use in freshman, sophomore, junior, senior, or graduate years; renewable. *Number:* up to 20. *Amount:* $3750–$15,000.

Eligibility Requirements: Applicant must be enrolled or expecting to enroll full-time at a two-year or four-year institution or university. Available to U.S. citizens.

Application Requirements: Application, driver's license, references, transcript. *Deadline:* Continuous.

Contact: Application available at Web site.

INSTITUTE FOR OPERATIONS RESEARCH AND THE MANAGEMENT SCIENCES
http://www.informs.org

GEORGE NICHOLSON STUDENT PAPER COMPETITION

To honor outstanding papers in the field of operations research and the management sciences. Entrant must be student on or after the year of application. Research papers present original results and be written by student. Electronic submission of paper required. Refer to Web site for details.

Award: Prize for use in junior, senior, graduate, or postgraduate years. *Number:* up to 6. *Amount:* $100–$600.

Eligibility Requirements: Applicant must be enrolled or expecting to enroll at an institution or university. Available to U.S. citizens.

Application Requirements: *Deadline:* June 30.

Contact: See Web site.

INSTITUTE OF INTERNATIONAL EDUCATION
http://www.iie.org

NATIONAL SECURITY EDUCATION PROGRAM DAVID L. BOREN UNDERGRADUATE SCHOLARSHIPS

The National Security Education Program (NSEP) awards scholarships to American undergraduate students for study abroad in regions critical to U.S. national interest. Emphasized world areas include Africa, Asia, Central and Eastern Europe, the NIS, Latin America and the Caribbean, and the Middle East. NSEP scholarship recipients incur a service agreement. Must be a U.S. citizen.

Award: Scholarship for use in freshman, sophomore, junior, or senior years; not renewable. *Number:* 150–200. *Amount:* $2500–$20,000.

Eligibility Requirements: Applicant must be enrolled or expecting to enroll full or part-time at a two-year or four-year institution or university. Available to U.S. citizens.

Institute of International Education (continued)

Application Requirements: Application, essay, financial need analysis, references, transcript, campus review. *Deadline:* February 10.

Contact: Nicki Creatore, Specialist, Research and Education
Institute of International Education
1400 K Street, NW, Suite 650
Washington, DC 20005-2403
Phone: 800-618-6737
Fax: 202-326-7697
E-mail: nsep@iie.org

INTER-COUNTY ENERGY   http://www.intercountyenergy.net

KENTUCKY WOMEN IN RURAL ELECTRIFICATION SCHOLARSHIP

Scholarship for Kentucky student whose family is served by a Kentucky rural electric cooperative. The student must have at least 60 credit hours at the beginning of the 2006 fall college term. The student must attend a Kentucky college or university.

Award: Scholarship for use in junior or senior years. *Amount:* up to $1000.

Eligibility Requirements: Applicant must be enrolled or expecting to enroll at a four-year institution. Available to U.S. citizens.

Application Requirements: Application, financial need analysis, references. *Deadline:* June 15.

Contact: Ellie Hobgood
Inter-County Energy
PO Box 32170
Louisville, KY 40232
Phone: 502-451-2430
Fax: 502-459-3209

INTERNATIONAL BROTHERHOOD OF TEAMSTERS SCHOLARSHIP FUND   http://www.teamster.org

JAMES R. HOFFA MEMORIAL SCHOLARSHIP FUND

Scholarships available to the children and dependents of members of the International Brotherhood of Teamsters. Scholarships will be renewed on an annual basis. The recipients must maintain a B average (3.0)

Award: Scholarship for use in freshman, sophomore, junior, senior, graduate, or postgraduate years; renewable. *Number:* up to 100. *Amount:* $1000–$10,000.

Eligibility Requirements: Applicant must be high school student and planning to enroll or expecting to enroll at a two-year or four-year or technical institution or university. Applicant must have 3.0 GPA or higher. Available to U.S. and Canadian citizens.

Application Requirements: Application, references, transcript, ACT or SAT scores. *Deadline:* March 31.

Contact: James R. Hoffa Memorial Scholarship Fund
Phone: 202-624-8735
E-mail: scholarship@teamster.org

INTERNATIONAL ORGANIZATION OF MASTERS, MATES AND PILOTS HEALTH AND BENEFIT PLAN   http://www.bridgedeck.org

M.M. & P. HEALTH AND BENEFIT PLAN SCHOLARSHIP PROGRAM

Scholarships available to dependent children (under 23 years of age) of parents who meet the eligibility requirements set forth by the MM&P Health and Benefit Plan. Selection of winners will be based on test scores, high school record, extracurricular activities, leadership qualities, recommendations, and students' own statements. High school students who apply must take the SAT and indicate code for MM&P to receive scores. Applications with complete guidelines may be obtained from any port office or from the plan office in Maryland. Deadline November 30.

Award: Scholarship for use in freshman, sophomore, junior, or senior years; renewable. *Number:* 6. *Amount:* up to $5000.

Eligibility Requirements: Applicant must be age 22 or under; enrolled or expecting to enroll full-time at an institution or university and single. Available to U.S. citizens.

Application Requirements: Application, test scores. *Deadline:* November 30.

Contact: Mary Ellen Beach, Scholarship Program
International Organization of Masters, Mates and Pilots Health and Benefit Plan
700 Maritime Boulevard
Linthicum Heights, MD 21090-1941
Phone: 410-850-8624
Fax: 410-850-8655

INTERNATIONAL SOCIETY FOR OPTICAL ENGINEERING-SPIE   http://www.spie.org/info/scholarships

D.J. LOVELL SCHOLARSHIP

Scholarship for full-time student in the optical engineering field who is not also a full-time employee in industry, government or academia. Applicants must be presenting an accepted paper at an SPIE-sponsored meeting.

Award: Scholarship for use in freshman, sophomore, junior, or senior years. *Amount:* up to $5000.

Eligibility Requirements: Applicant must be enrolled or expecting to enroll full-time at a four-year institution or university. Available to U.S. citizens.

Application Requirements: Application, references, written support from a Chair (letter or email) of the conference in which the paper will be presented.

Contact: SPIE Scholarship Committee
International Society for Optical Engineering-SPIE
PO Box 10
Bellingham, WA 98227-0010
Phone: 360-685-5452
Fax: 360-647-1445
E-mail: scholarships@spie.org

INTERNATIONAL SOCIETY OF LOGISTICS, TENNESSEE VALLEY CHAPTER   http://www.hats.org

LOGISTICS SCHOLARSHIP

Scholarship for a graduating high school senior. Must be planning to enter an accredited university in pursuit of a technical degree that could reasonably lead to a career in logistics. A logistics program of study, however, is not required. Eligible seniors should apply to the Tennessee Valley Chapter Scholarship Committee. Award is for one year only, but the recipient can re-apply for additional scholarship awards upon successfully progress toward a degree. See Web site for application form: http://www.hats.org/sole/news.htm

Award: Scholarship for use in freshman year. *Amount:* up to $1000.

Eligibility Requirements: Applicant must be high school student and planning to enroll or expecting to enroll full-time at an institution or university. Available to U.S. citizens.

Application Requirements: Application, essay, references, transcript. *Deadline:* April 15.

Contact: Robert Hardison, Vice Chairman, Technical
International Society of Logistics, Tennessee Valley Chapter
PO Box 1104
Huntsville, AL 35807
Phone: 256-655-4832
E-mail: robert.hardison@amrdec.army.mil

INTERNATIONAL UNION OF BRICKLAYERS AND ALLIED CRAFTWORKERS   http://www.bacweb.org

HARRY C. BATES SCHOLARSHIP

Renewable award program designated to financially assist the children of the members of the Bricklayers and Allied Craftworkers International Union. Qualified applicants must be National Merit Scholarship semi-finalist. Minimum 3.0 GPA required.

Award: Scholarship for use in freshman year; renewable. *Number:* 2–3. *Amount:* $1027–$1284.

Eligibility Requirements: Applicant must be enrolled or expecting to enroll full-time at a two-year or four-year or technical institution or university. Applicant must have 3.0 GPA or higher. Available to U.S. and Canadian citizens.

Application Requirements: Application, references, test scores, transcript. *Deadline:* June 1.

Contact: Connie Lambert, Director of Education
International Union of Bricklayers and Allied Craftworkers
1776 Eye Street, NW
Washington, DC 20005
Phone: 202-783-3788
Fax: 202-772-3800
E-mail: askbac@bacweb.org

JACK KENT COOKE FOUNDATION
http://www.jackkentcookefoundation.org/

JACK KENT COOKE FOUNDATION UNDERGRADUATE TRANSFER SCHOLARSHIP PROGRAM

The Jack Kent Cooke Foundation Undergraduate Transfer Scholarship Program provides scholarships to students and recent alumni from community college to complete their bachelor's degrees at accredited four-year colleges or universities in the United States or abroad. Candidates must be nominated by a faculty representative from their community college.

Award: Scholarship for use in freshman, sophomore, junior, or senior years; renewable. *Number:* 30. *Amount:* up to $30,000.

Eligibility Requirements: Applicant must be enrolled or expecting to enroll full-time at a two-year or four-year institution or university. Applicant must have 3.5 GPA or higher. Available to U.S. and non-U.S. citizens.

Application Requirements: Application, essay, financial need analysis, references, transcript. *Deadline:* February 1.

Contact: Jack Kent Cooke Foundation Faculty Representative
Phone: 800-498-6478
E-mail: jkc-u@act.org.

JAMES F. LINCOLN ARC WELDING FOUNDATION
http://www.jflf.org

JAMES F. LINCOLN ARC WELDING FOUNDATION AWARDS PROGRAM

Applicants may apply for prize money, which will be awarded to the winners of a contest that requires the submission of a photo or drawing of a welding project that they have built. Must have minimum 2.5 GPA. Application deadline is June 1. Must include self-addressed stamped envelope.

Award: Prize for use in freshman, sophomore, junior, senior, graduate, or postgraduate years; not renewable. *Number:* 200–400. *Amount:* $50–$2000.

Eligibility Requirements: Applicant must be age 15-80 and enrolled or expecting to enroll full or part-time at a two-year or four-year or technical institution or university. Applicant must have 2.5 GPA or higher. Available to U.S. and non-U.S. citizens.

Application Requirements: Application, applicant must enter a contest, photo, self-addressed stamped envelope, transcript. *Deadline:* June 1.

Contact: Secretary, The James F. Lincoln Arc Welding Foundation
James F. Lincoln Arc Welding Foundation
PO Box 17188
Cleveland, OH 44117-9949

JAYCEE WAR MEMORIAL FUND
http://www.usjaycees.org/

JAYCEE WAR MEMORIAL FUND SCHOLARSHIP

Twenty-five (25) scholarships awarded annually. Applicants must be citizens of the U.S., possess academic potential and leadership qualities, and show financial need. The scholarship is an award of $1000 sent directly to the recipient's college or university of choice. Minimum 2.5 GPA required.

Award: Scholarship for use in freshman, junior, or senior years; not renewable. *Number:* up to 25. *Amount:* $1000.

Eligibility Requirements: Applicant must be enrolled or expecting to enroll full or part-time at a two-year or four-year or technical institution or university. Applicant must have 2.5 GPA or higher. Available to U.S. citizens.

Application Requirements: Application, financial need, self-addressed stamped envelope, transcript. *Fee:* $5. *De*

Contact: War Memorial Fund Scholarship
Jaycee War Memorial Fund
PO Box 7
Tulsa, OK 74114-1116
Phone: 918-584-2481
Fax: 918-584-4422

JEANNETTE RANKIN FOUNDATION, INC.
http://www.rankinfoundation.org

JEANNETTE RANKIN FOUNDATION AWARDS

Applicants must be low-income women, age 35 or older, who are pursuing a technical/vocational education, an associate's degree, or a first-time bachelor's degree. Applications are available November-February. Download materials from the Web site: http://www.rankinfoundation.org or send a self-addressed stamped envelope to request an application by mail.

Award: Grant for use in freshman, sophomore, junior, or senior years; renewable. *Number:* 65. *Amount:* $2000.

Eligibility Requirements: Applicant must be age 35; enrolled or expecting to enroll full or part-time at a two-year or four-year or technical institution or university and female. Available to U.S. citizens.

Application Requirements: Application, essay, financial need analysis, references, self-addressed stamped envelope, transcript. *Deadline:* March 1.

Contact: Andrea Anderson, Program Coordinator
Jeannette Rankin Foundation, Inc.
PO Box 6653
Athens, GA 30604-6653
Phone: 706-208-1211
Fax: 706-548-0202
E-mail: info@rankinfoundation.org

JOHN F. KENNEDY LIBRARY FOUNDATION
http://www.jfklibrary.org

PROFILE IN COURAGE ESSAY CONTEST

Essay contest open to all high school students, grades 9-12. Students in U.S. territories and U.S. citizens attending schools overseas may also apply. Essay must be original work; attach bibliography. Essay must be no longer than 1000 words. All essays will be judged on the overall originality of topic and the clear communication of ideas through language. Essayist must have an English or History teacher as nominating teacher. Winner and their nominating teacher are invited to Kennedy Library to accept award. Winner receives $3000, nomination teacher receives grant of $500; second place receives $1000 and five finalists receive $500. For further information about essay topic go to Web site: http://www.jfkcontest.org

Award: Prize for use in freshman year; not renewable. *Number:* 7. *Amount:* $500–$3000.

Eligibility Requirements: Applicant must be high school student; age 19 or under and planning to enroll or expecting to enroll at an institution or university. Available to U.S. citizens.

Application Requirements: Applicant must enter a contest, essay. *Deadline:* January 7.

Contact: Esther Kohn, Profile in Courage Essay Contest Coordinator
John F. Kennedy Library Foundation
Columbia Point
Boston, MA 02125
Phone: 617-514-1649
Fax: 617-514-1641
E-mail: profiles@nara.gov

JOHN GYLES EDUCATION AWARDS
http://www.johngyleseducationcenter.com

JOHN GYLES EDUCATION AWARDS

Financial assistance available to full-time students in the U.S. and Canada. Full Canadian or U.S. citizenship is required. Available to both male and female students for all areas of postsecondary study. Minimum GPA of 2.7 required. Filing dates for mailing applications are June 1 and November 15. Students may send a stamped, self-addressed standard letter sized envelope in order to receive an application or go to Web site: http://www.

John Gyles Education Awards (continued)

johngyleseducationcenter.com. High school students are eligible but may only apply during the last half of their senior year.

Award: Scholarship for use in freshman, sophomore, junior, or senior years; not renewable. *Amount:* up to $3000.

Eligibility Requirements: Applicant must be enrolled or expecting to enroll full-time at a two-year or four-year institution or university. Available to U.S. and Canadian citizens.

Application Requirements: Application, financial need analysis, test scores. *Fee:* $8. *Deadline:* June 1.

Contact: R. James Cougle, Administrator
John Gyles Education Awards
259-103 Brunswick Street, PO Box 4808
Fredericton, NB E3B 5G4
Canada

JUST WITHIN REACH FOUNDATION

ENVIRONMENTAL SCIENCES AND MARINE STUDIES SCHOLARSHIP

Three $2000 awards are given to environmental science scholars and three $2000 awards are given to marine studies scholars. Must be U.S. citizens and must be either undergraduate students currently enrolled in a postsecondary institution or high school seniors accepted as full-time students of an accredited, public or private four-year college or university in the U.S. Minimum 3.0 GPA required.

Award: Scholarship for use in freshman, sophomore, junior, or senior years; not renewable. *Number:* 6. *Amount:* $2000.

Eligibility Requirements: Applicant must be enrolled or expecting to enroll full-time at a four-year institution or university. Applicant must have 3.0 GPA or higher. Available to U.S. citizens.

Application Requirements: Application, essay, financial need analysis, resume, references, transcript. *Deadline:* March 12.

Contact: Vicki Hanna, Scholarship Committee
Just Within Reach Foundation
3940 Laurel Canyon Boulevard
PMB 256
Studio City, CA 91604

KAPLAN/NEWSWEEK   http://www.kaptest.com

MY TURN ESSAY COMPETITION

Essay contest open to high school students entering college or university. Can win up to $5000. Must be U.S. citizen. To enter, student must submit 500-1000 word essay expressing their opinion, experience, or personal feelings on a topic of their own choice. 1st prize, $5000; 2nd prize, $2000; 8 finalists awarded $1000. For more information visit Web site or call 1-800-KAPTEST.

Award: Prize for use in freshman year; not renewable. *Number:* up to 10. *Amount:* $1000–$5000.

Eligibility Requirements: Applicant must be high school student and planning to enroll or expecting to enroll at a four-year institution or university. Available to U.S. citizens.

Application Requirements: Application, applicant must enter a contest, essay. *Deadline:* March 1.

Contact: Kaplan/Newsweek
888 Seventh Avenue
New York, NY 10106
Phone: 800-527-8378

KAPPA SIGMA ENDOWMENT FUND   http://www.ksendowmentfund.org/

SCHOLARSHIP-LEADERSHIP AWARDS PROGRAM

Award: Scholarship for use in freshman, sophomore, junior, or senior years.

Eligibility Requirements: Applicant must be enrolled or expecting to enroll at an institution or university.

Contact: James Eldridge, Director of Annual Giving
Kappa Sigma Endowment Fund
PO Box 5643
Charlottesville, VA 22905
Phone: 434-979-5733 Ext. 125
Fax: 434-296-5733
E-mail: jamese@imh.kappasigma.org

KARMEL SCHOLARSHIP   http://www.karenandmelody.com

KARMEL SCHOLARSHIP

Scholarship to encourage students to write or create something that will express their views on the gay/lesbian/bi/transgender topic. Must be GLBT related. Deadline is March 31.

Award: Scholarship for use in freshman, sophomore, junior, senior, graduate, or postgraduate years; not renewable. *Number:* 2. *Amount:* $300–$400.

Eligibility Requirements: Applicant must be enrolled or expecting to enroll full or part-time at a two-year or four-year or technical institution or university. Available to U.S. and non-U.S. citizens.

Application Requirements: Application, applicant must enter a contest. *Deadline:* March 31.

Contact: KarMel Scholarship Committee
KarMel Scholarship
PO Box 70382
Sunnyvale, CA 94086
E-mail: KarMel2006@KarenandMelody.com

KCNC-TV CHANNEL 4 NEWS   http://www.news4colorado.com

NEWS 4 PETER ROGOT MEDIA SCHOLARSHIP

Award: Scholarship for use in freshman year.

Eligibility Requirements: Applicant must be enrolled or expecting to enroll at an institution or university.

Contact: Elaine Torres, Community Affairs Director
KCNC-TV Channel 4 News
1044 Lincoln Street
Denver, CO 80203
Phone: 303-861-4444
Fax: 303-830-6537
E-mail: edtorres@cbs.com

KENERGY CORPORATION   http://www.kenergycorp.com

KENERGY SCHOLARSHIP

Award: Scholarship for use in freshman, sophomore, junior, senior, or graduate years.

Eligibility Requirements: Applicant must be enrolled or expecting to enroll at an institution or university.

Contact: Beverly Hooper, Scholarship Coordinator
Kenergy Corporation
PO Box 18
Henderson, KY 42419-0018
Phone: 800-844-4832 Ext. 6
Fax: 270-826-3999
E-mail: scholarships@kenergycorp.com

KENNEDY FOUNDATION

KENNEDY FOUNDATION SCHOLARSHIPS

Renewable scholarship for current high school students for up to four years of undergraduate study. Renewal contingent upon academic performance. Must maintain a GPA of 2.0. Send self-addressed stamped envelope for application.

Award: Scholarship for use in freshman, sophomore, junior, or senior years; renewable. *Number:* 8–14. *Amount:* $2000.

Eligibility Requirements: Applicant must be enrolled or expecting to enroll full-time at a two-year or four-year or technical institution or university. Applicant must have 2.5 GPA or higher. Available to U.S. citizens.

Application Requirements: Application, self-addressed stamped envelope, test scores, transcript. *Deadline:* June 30.

Contact: Jonathan Kennedy, Vice President
Kennedy Foundation
PO Box 27296
Denver, CO 80227
Phone: 303-933-2435
Fax: 303-933-0199
E-mail: jonathan@columbinecorp.com

KENTUCKY DEPARTMENT OF VETERANS AFFAIRS

DEPARTMENT OF VA TUITION WAIVER-KY KRS 164-515

Award: Scholarship for use in freshman, sophomore, junior, or senior years.

Eligibility Requirements: Applicant must be enrolled or expecting to enroll at an institution or university.

Contact: Jennifer Waddell, Administrative Specialist
Kentucky Department of Veterans Affairs
545 South Third Street
Room 123
Louisville, KY 40202-9095
Phone: 502-595-4447
Fax: 502-595-4448
E-mail: jennifer.waddell@ky.gov

DEPARTMENT OF VETERANS AFFAIRS TUITION WAIVER-KENTUCKY KRS 164-505

Award: Scholarship for use in freshman, sophomore, junior, senior, or graduate years.

Eligibility Requirements: Applicant must be enrolled or expecting to enroll at an institution or university.

Contact: Jennifer Waddell, Administrative Specialist
Kentucky Department of Veterans Affairs
545 South Third Street
Room 123
Louisville, KY 40202-9095
Phone: 502-595-4447
Fax: 502-595-4448
E-mail: jennifer.waddell@ky.gov

DEPARTMENT OF VETERANS AFFAIRS TUITION WAIVER-KY 164-512

Award: Scholarship for use in freshman, sophomore, junior, or senior years.

Eligibility Requirements: Applicant must be enrolled or expecting to enroll at an institution or university.

Contact: Jennifer Waddell, Administrative Specialist
Kentucky Department of Veterans Affairs
545 South Third Street
Room 123
Louisville, KY 40202-9095
Phone: 502-595-4447
Fax: 502-595-4448
E-mail: jennifer.waddell@ky.gov

DEPARTMENT OF VETERANS AFFAIRS TUITION WAIVER-KY KRS 164-507

Award: Scholarship for use in freshman, sophomore, junior, or senior years.

Eligibility Requirements: Applicant must be enrolled or expecting to enroll at an institution or university.

Contact: Jennifer Waddell, Administrative Specialist
Kentucky Department of Veterans Affairs
545 South Third Street
Room 123
Louisville, KY 40202-9095
Phone: 502-595-4447
Fax: 502-595-4448
E-mail: jennifer.waddell@ky.gov

KENTUCKY POLICE CORPS
http://docjt.jus.state.ky.us/pcorps/

KENTUCKY POLICE CORPS SCHOLARSHIP

Scholarships available for students who are attending, or who have graduated, from a four-year college or university. May be reimbursed for prior educational expenses. Must complete four years of service at a participating Kentucky law enforcement agency. See Web site for details: http://www.docjt.jus.state.ky.us/pcorps.

Award: Scholarship for use in junior or senior years; renewable. *Number:* 10. *Amount:* $7500–$30,000.

Eligibility Requirements: Applicant must be enrolled or expecting to enroll full-time at a four-year institution or university. Available to U.S. citizens.

Application Requirements: Application, references, test scores, transcript. *Deadline:* Continuous.

Contact: Bill Stewart, Scholarship Committee
Kentucky Police Corps
Department of Criminal Justice Training, Funderburk Building
521 Lancaster Avenue
Richmond, KY 40475
Phone: 866-592-6777
Fax: 859-622-5027
E-mail: william.stewart@mail.state.ky.us

KENTUCKY RESTAURANT ASSOCIATION EDUCATIONAL FOUNDATION

KENTUCKY RESTAURANT ASSOCIATION EDUCATIONAL FOUNDATION SCHOLARSHIP

Award: Scholarship for use in freshman, sophomore, junior, senior, or graduate years.

Eligibility Requirements: Applicant must be enrolled or expecting to enroll at an institution or university.

Contact: Betsy Byrd, Director of Member Relations
Kentucky Restaurant Association Educational Foundation
133 Evergreen Road, Suite 201
Louisville, KY 40243
Phone: 502-896-0464
Fax: 502-896-0465
E-mail: info@kyra.org

KNIGHT RIDDER

KNIGHT RIDDER MERIT SCHOLARSHIP PROGRAM

Award: Scholarship for use in freshman, sophomore, junior, or senior years.

Eligibility Requirements: Applicant must be enrolled or expecting to enroll at an institution or university.

Contact:

KNIGHT RIDDER MINORITY SCHOLARSHIP PROGRAM

Award: Scholarship for use in freshman, sophomore, junior, or senior years.

Eligibility Requirements: Applicant must be enrolled or expecting to enroll at an institution or university.

Contact:

KNIGHTS OF PYTHIAS
http://www.pythias.org

KNIGHTS OF PYTHIAS POSTER CONTEST

Poster contest open to all high school students in the U.S. and Canada. Contestants must submit an original drawing. Eight awards are given out. The winners are not required to attend higher institution.

Award: Prize for use in freshman year; not renewable. *Number:* 8. *Amount:* $100–$1000.

Eligibility Requirements: Applicant must be high school student and planning to enroll or expecting to enroll at an institution or university. Available to U.S. and Canadian citizens.

Knights of Pythias (continued)

Application Requirements: Applicant must enter a contest. *Deadline:* April 30.

Contact: Alfred Saltzman, Supreme Secretary
Knights of Pythias
Office of Supreme Lodge
59 Coddington Street, Suite 202
Quincy, MA 02169-4150
Phone: 617-472-8800
Fax: 617-376-0363
E-mail: kop@earthlink.net

KOREAN AMERICAN SCHOLARSHIP FOUNDATION

http://www.kasf.org

KOREAN-AMERICAN SCHOLARSHIP FOUNDATION MIDEASTERN REGION SCHOLARSHIPS

Award: Scholarship for use in freshman, sophomore, junior, senior, or graduate years.

Eligibility Requirements: Applicant must be enrolled or expecting to enroll at an institution or university.

Contact: George Hong, President
Korean American Scholarship Foundation
National Office
1952 Gallows Road, Suite 340 B
Vienna, VA 22182
Phone: 703-748-5935
Fax: 703-467-8167
E-mail: eastern@kasf.org

KOREAN-AMERICAN SCHOLARSHIP FOUNDATION MIDWESTERN REGION SCHOLARSHIPS

Award: Scholarship for use in freshman, sophomore, junior, senior, or graduate years.

Eligibility Requirements: Applicant must be enrolled or expecting to enroll at an institution or university.

Contact: George Hong, President
Korean American Scholarship Foundation
National Office
1952 Gallows Road, Suite 340 B
Vienna, VA 22182
Phone: 703-748-5935
Fax: 703-467-8167
E-mail: eastern@kasf.org

KUMU KAHUA THEATRE

KUMU KAHUA THEATER/UHM THEATER DEPARTMENT PLAYWRITING CONTEST, HAWAII PRIZE

Award: Prize for use in freshman, sophomore, junior, senior, or graduate years.

Eligibility Requirements: Applicant must be enrolled or expecting to enroll at an institution or university.

Contact:

KUMU KAHUA THEATER/UHM THEATER DEPARTMENT PLAYWRITING CONTEST, RESIDENT PRIZE

Award: Prize for use in freshman, sophomore, junior, senior, or graduate years.

Eligibility Requirements: Applicant must be enrolled or expecting to enroll at an institution or university.

Contact:

LA KELLEY COMMUNICATIONS

http://www.kelleycom.com

BILL MCADAM SCHOLARSHIP FUND

Person with hemophilia, VWD or other bleeding disorder; or spouse, partner, child or sibling planning to attend an accredited college, university or certified training program.

Award: Scholarship for use in freshman, sophomore, junior, senior, or graduate years. *Amount:* $2000.

Eligibility Requirements: Applicant must be enrolled or expecting to enroll full or part-time at a two-year or four-year or technical institution or university. Available to U.S. citizens.

Application Requirements: Application. *Deadline:* May 15.

Contact: LA Kelley Communications
22226 Doxtator
Dearbourn, MI 48128
Phone: 313-563-1412

CHRISTOPHER MARK PITKIN MEMORIAL SCHOLARSHIP

Award available to all members of the hemophilia community, including spouses and siblings. Applicants must be pursuing a post high school college or technical/trade school education. People with HIV and hemophilia and their families are encouraged to apply. Southern CA residents given preference.

Award: Scholarship for use in freshman, sophomore, junior, or senior years. *Number:* 2. *Amount:* $1200.

Eligibility Requirements: Applicant must be enrolled or expecting to enroll full or part-time at an institution or university. Available to U.S. citizens.

Application Requirements: Application. *Deadline:* August 26.

Contact: Hemophilia Foundation of Southern California
LA Kelley Communications
33 South Catalina Avenue, Suite 102
Pasedena, CA 91106
Phone: 626-793-6192
Fax: 626-796-5605
E-mail: hfsc@earthlink.net

PARENT CONTINUING EDUCATION SCHOLARSHIP

Scholarship for parent of a school-age child with a blood clotting disorder. For use in furthering the parent's own education.

Award: Scholarship for use in freshman year. *Amount:* $1500.

Eligibility Requirements: Applicant must be enrolled or expecting to enroll at a technical institution. Available to U.S. citizens.

Application Requirements: Application. *Deadline:* April 1.

Contact: Sandy Aultman
LA Kelley Communications
1045 West Pinhook Road, Suite 101
Lafayette, LA 70503
Phone: 337-261-9787
Fax: 337-261-1787

LATIN AMERICAN EDUCATIONAL FOUNDATION

http://www.laef.org

LATIN AMERICAN EDUCATIONAL FOUNDATION SCHOLARSHIPS

Award: Scholarship for use in freshman, sophomore, junior, or senior years.

Eligibility Requirements: Applicant must be enrolled or expecting to enroll at an institution or university.

Contact: Scholarship Selection Committee
Latin American Educational Foundation
924 West Colfax Avenue, Suite 103
Denver, CO 80204-4417
Phone: 303-446-0541
Fax: 303-446-0526
E-mail: laef@uswest.net

LEOPOLD SCHEPP FOUNDATION

http://www.scheppfoundation.org

LEOPOLD SCHEPP SCHOLARSHIP

Awards are given to those under 30 pursuing a bachelor's degree and those under 40 pursuing a graduate degree. Applicants must be U.S citizens. Must have a minimum GPA of 3.0.

Award: Scholarship for use in freshman, sophomore, junior, senior, or graduate years; renewable. *Amount:* up to $8000.

Eligibility Requirements: Applicant must be enrolled or expecting to enroll full-time at a four-year institution or university. Applicant must have 3.0 GPA or higher. Available to U.S. citizens.

Application Requirements: Application, financial need analysis, references, transcript. *Deadline:* varies.

Contact: Leopold Schepp Scholarship
Leopold Schepp Foundation
551 5th Avenue
New York, NY 10176-2597
Phone: 212-986-3078

LESBIAN, BISEXUAL, GAY AND TRANSGENDERED UNITED EMPLOYEES (LEAGUE) AT AT&T FOUNDATION
http://www.league-att.org

LEAGUE AT AT&T FOUNDATION ACADEMIC SCHOLARSHIP

Scholarship awarded to graduating high school seniors who are gay, lesbian, bisexual, or transgender. Must have a 3.0 GPA. Deadline: April 21. Visit http://www.league-att.org/foundation/fscholarships.html for more information.

Award: Scholarship for use in freshman year; not renewable. *Number:* 3–4. *Amount:* $500–$1500.

Eligibility Requirements: Applicant must be high school student and planning to enroll or expecting to enroll full-time at a two-year or four-year or technical institution or university. Applicant must have 3.0 GPA or higher. Available to U.S. citizens.

Application Requirements: Application, essay, references, test scores, transcript, support from 3 sponsors, copy of college or university acceptance letter. *Deadline:* April 21.

Contact: Charles Eader, President
Lesbian, Bisexual, Gay and Transgendered United Employees (LEAGUE) at AT&T Foundation
LEAGUE, AT&T Foundation, One AT&T Way, Room 4B214J
Bedminster, NJ 07921
Phone: 703-691-5734
E-mail: attleague@aol.com

LIQUITEX ARTIST MATERIALS PURCHASE AWARD PROGRAM
http://www.liquitex.com

LIQUITEX EXCELLENCE IN ART PURCHASE AWARD PROGRAM-SECONDARY CATEGORY

Prizes up to $500 in cash plus $250 in Liquitex products will be awarded to the best art submissions. Submissions should be made in 35mm slides. Void in Quebec or where prohibited by law. For more details see Web site: http://www.liquitex.com

Award: Prize for use in freshman, sophomore, junior, senior, graduate, or postgraduate years; not renewable. *Number:* 3. *Amount:* $350–$750.

Eligibility Requirements: Applicant must be enrolled or expecting to enroll full or part-time at a two-year or four-year or technical institution or university. Available to U.S. and Canadian citizens.

Application Requirements: Application, applicant must enter a contest. *Deadline:* January 15.

Contact: Renée LaMontagne, Senior Product Manager
Liquitex Artist Materials Purchase Award Program
11 Constitution Avenue
PO Box 1396
Piscataway, NJ 08855-1396
Phone: 732-562-0770
Fax: 732-562-0941
E-mail: renee@liquitex.com

LOGAN TELEPHONE CO-OP
http://www.logantele.com

LOGAN TELEPHONE COOPERATIVE EDUCATIONAL SCHOLARSHIP

Scholarship for high school seniors. To qualify, the student's phone number must begin with 539, 542, 657, 728, 755, or 934 which are the exchanges the Cooperative serves. Only students whose parents or guardians have membership in good standing with Logan Telephone Cooperative qualify for these scholarships.

Award: Scholarship for use in freshman year. *Number:* up to 3. *Amount:* up to $1000.

Eligibility Requirements: Applicant must be enrolled or expecting to enroll at an institution or university. Applicant must have 2.5 GPA or higher. Available to U.S. citizens.

Application Requirements: Application, essay, financial need analysis, photo, references, test scores, transcript. *Deadline:* April 13.

Contact: Scholarships
Logan Telephone Co-op
PO Box 97
Auburn, KY 42206

LOWE'S COMPANIES, INC.
http://www.lowes.com

LOWE'S EDUCATIONAL SCHOLARSHIP

Financial support available to students enrolled at one of Lowe's targeted community colleges and technical schools. Must have satisfactorily completed at least one semester with a GPA of 2.0 or higher.

Award: Scholarship for use in freshman, sophomore, junior, or senior years. *Number:* 1.

Eligibility Requirements: Applicant must be age 18 and enrolled or expecting to enroll at a technical institution. Available to U.S. citizens.

Application Requirements: Application, resume. *Deadline:* varies.

Contact: Scholarship Committee
Lowe's Companies, Inc.
PO Box 1111
North Wilkesboro, NC 28659
Phone: 800-445-6937

MAINE COMMUNITY FOUNDATION, INC.
http://www.mainecf.org

ISLAND INSTITUTE SCHOLARSHIP FUND

Financial aid to available to Maine's year-round island residents for educational purposes. For information see Web site: http://www.mainecf.org/pdfs/7/islandinstitute.pdf for more information or Contact Island Institute Education Outreach Officer, Ruth Kermish-Allen at (207) 594-9209, ext. 117. Deadline is April 15.

Award: Scholarship for use in freshman, sophomore, junior, or senior years; renewable. *Number:* 1.

Eligibility Requirements: Applicant must be enrolled or expecting to enroll full-time at a two-year or four-year institution. Available to U.S. citizens.

Application Requirements: Application, essay, financial need analysis, photo, references, transcript. *Deadline:* April 15.

Contact: Amy Pollien, Program Administrator
Maine Community Foundation, Inc.
Island Institute Scholarship Fund, c/o Maine Community Foundation, 245 Main Street
Ellsworth, ME 04605-1613
Phone: 207-667-9735
Fax: 207-667-0447
E-mail: info@mainecf.org

MAINE EDUCATION SERVICES
http://www.mesfoundation.com/

MAINE LEGISLATIVE MEMORIAL SCHOLARSHIP

Sixteen awards (one per county) are made annually to students going to a two- or four-year degree granting Maine school. Scholarships are available to graduating high school seniors or full/part-time postsecondary students accepted or enrolled in a Maine college. Graduate students are also eligible. Awards are based on academic excellence, school and community contributions, financial need, letters of recommendation, and a required essay

Award: Scholarship for use in freshman, sophomore, junior, senior, graduate, or postgraduate years; renewable. *Number:* 16. *Amount:* $1000.

Eligibility Requirements: Applicant must be enrolled or expecting to enroll full or part-time at a two-year or four-year or technical institution or university. Available to U.S. citizens.

on Services (continued)

Requirements: Application, essay, financial need analysis, references, transcript. *Deadline:* April 14.

Contact: Kim Benjamin, Vice President of Operations
Maine Education Services
One City Center
11th Floor
Portland, ME 04101
Phone: 207-791-3600
Fax: 207-791-3616
E-mail: kbenjamin@mesfoundation.com

MARGARET MCNAMARA MEMORIAL FUND
http://www.wbfn.org

MARGARET MCNAMARA MEMORIAL FUND FELLOWSHIPS

One-time award for female students from developing countries enrolled in accredited graduate programs relating to women and children. Must be attending an accredited institution in the U.S. Candidates must plan to return to their countries within two years. Must be over 25 years of age. U.S. citizens are not eligible. Please refer to Web site for application and further details: http://www.worldbank.org/yournet

Award: Grant for use in freshman, sophomore, junior, senior, graduate, or postgraduate years; not renewable. *Number:* 5–6. *Amount:* $11,000.

Eligibility Requirements: Applicant must be age 25; enrolled or expecting to enroll full-time at a four-year institution or university and female. Available to citizens of countries other than the U.S. or Canada.

Application Requirements: Application, essay, financial need analysis, photo, references, transcript. *Deadline:* February 10.

Contact: Chairman, M.M.M.F. Selection Committee
Margaret McNamara Memorial Fund
1818 H Street, NW, MSN-H2-204
Washington, DC 20433
Phone: 202-473-8751
Fax: 202-522-3142
E-mail: mmmf@worldbank.org

MARY T. PATTERSON SCHOLARSHIP

MARY T. PATTERSON SCHOLARSHIP

One nonrenewable scholarship worth $500 awarded to Ohio resident of 18 years of age as of June. Must submit proof of attending the head start program. Deadline is April 30.

Award: Scholarship for use in freshman year; not renewable. *Number:* 1. *Amount:* up to $500.

Eligibility Requirements: Applicant must be age 18 or under and enrolled or expecting to enroll full-time at an institution or university. Available to U.S. citizens.

Application Requirements: Application, essay, proof of attending the head start program. *Deadline:* April 30.

Contact: Linda Primrose-Barker, Scholarship Coordinator
Mary T. Patterson Scholarship
Council on Rural Service Programs Inc., 201 R.M. Davis
Parkway, PO Box 601
Piqua, OH 45356

MARYLAND POLICE CORPS

MARYLAND POLICE CORPS SCHOLARSHIP

Award: Scholarship for use in junior or senior years.

Eligibility Requirements: Applicant must be enrolled or expecting to enroll at an institution or university.

Contact:

MARYLAND STATE DEPARTMENT OF EDUCATION
http://www.msde.state.md.us/

AIMMS EXCELLENCE SCHOLARSHIP

Scholarships to recognize high school students who have demonstrated academic success as well as made significant contributions to better understanding and appreciation among diverse groups. The awards, which are provided by corporate sponsors, consist of $500 scholarships to be given to 10 students selected from local school systems in Maryland.

Award: Scholarship for use in freshman year. *Number:* 10. *Amount:* $500.

Eligibility Requirements: Applicant must be high school student and planning to enroll or expecting to enroll at an institution or university. Applicant must have 3.0 GPA or higher. Available to U.S. citizens.

Application Requirements: Application, essay, references, transcript, nomination form. *Deadline:* January 10.

Contact: Mr. Woodrow Grant
Maryland State Department of Education
200 West Baltimore Street
Baltimore, MD 21201
Phone: 410-767-0425

NICK RIZZI SCHOLARSHIP

Scholarship available to an External Diploma Program (EDP) graduate who is going on to higher education. This scholarship fund is supported by donations to the National External Diploma Program Council. The scholarship is awarded annually as funds permit.

Award: Scholarship for use in freshman year. *Number:* 1.

Eligibility Requirements: Applicant must be enrolled or expecting to enroll at a two-year or technical institution. Available to U.S. citizens.

Application Requirements: Application. *Deadline:* varies.

Contact: Bette Huckabee
Maryland State Department of Education
944 Laurel Avenue
Bridgeport, CT 06604
Phone: 203-338-0503
E-mail: betthuck@aol.com

REGINA MILIO SCHOLARSHIP

Maryland Association for Adult Community and Continuing Education (MAACCE) provides funds for the scholarship which awards a minimum of $500 to qualified GED graduates and is awarded annually as the fund permits.

Award: Scholarship for use in freshman year. *Amount:* $500.

Eligibility Requirements: Applicant must be enrolled or expecting to enroll at a two-year or four-year or technical institution. Available to U.S. citizens.

Application Requirements: Application. *Deadline:* varies.

Contact: Michelle Frazier
Maryland State Department of Education
200 West Baltimore Street
Baltimore, MD 21201
E-mail: mfrazier@msde.state.md.us

ROBERT C. BYRD HONORS SCHOLARSHIP-MARYLAND

Scholarship amount changes each year, however, it has ranged from $1000-1500. Amount received by the students is based on the total cost of attendance at each institution of higher education, awarded on merit basis.

Award: Scholarship for use in freshman, sophomore, junior, or senior years. *Amount:* $1000–$1500.

Eligibility Requirements: Applicant must be enrolled or expecting to enroll full-time at a two-year or four-year or technical institution or university. Available to U.S. citizens.

Application Requirements: Application. *Deadline:* varies.

Contact: William Cappe
Maryland State Department of Education
200 West Baltimore Street
Baltimore, MD 21201
Phone: 888-246-0016
E-mail: wcappe@msde.state.md.us

MELLON NEW ENGLAND

JOHN L. BATES SCHOLARSHIP

Award: Scholarship for use in freshman, sophomore, junior, or senior years.

Eligibility Requirements: Applicant must be enrolled or expecting to enroll at an institution or university.

Contact:

MERCEDES-BENZ USA　　　　http://www.mbusa.com

DRIVE YOUR FUTURE: THE MERCEDES-BENZ USA SCHOLARSHIP PROGRAM

Award: Scholarship for use in freshman year.

Eligibility Requirements: Applicant must be enrolled or expecting to enroll at an institution or university.

Contact: Scholarship America
Mercedes-Benz USA
Corporate Communications Department
One Mercedes Drive
Montvale, NJ 07645

METAVUE CORPORATION　　　http://www.metavue.com

THE CHARLES SHAFAE' SCHOLARSHIP FUND

The Papercheck.com Essay Contest is available to undergraduate students enrolled at an accredited college or university in the U.S. with a minimum 3.2 GPA. Applicant must write a minimum 1000 word essay answering the questions listed on the Web site.

Award: Scholarship for use in freshman, sophomore, junior, or senior years. *Amount:* $500.

Eligibility Requirements: Applicant must be enrolled or expecting to enroll at a four-year institution or university. Applicant must have 3.0 GPA or higher. Available to U.S. citizens.

Application Requirements: Essay. *Deadline:* January 1.

Contact: Michael Rufflo
Metavue Corporation
1110 Surrey Drive
Sun Prairie, WI 53590
Phone: 608-577-0642
Fax: 512-685-4074
E-mail: rufflo@metavue.com

MICROSOFT CORPORATION

YOU CAN MAKE A DIFFERENCE SCHOLARSHIP

Award: Scholarship for use in freshman year.

Eligibility Requirements: Applicant must be enrolled or expecting to enroll at an institution or university.

Contact:

MINNESOTA GAY/LESBIAN/BISEXUAL/ TRANSGENDER EDUCATIONAL FUND　　http://www.philanthrofund.org

MINNESOTA GAY/LESBIAN/BISEXUAL/TRANSGENDER SCHOLARSHIP FUND

The Minnesota Gay/Lesbian, Bisexual, Transgender (GLBT) scholarship fund, administered by (GLBT) Philanthrofund Foundation, annually awards students who are gay/lesbian, bisexual, transgender identified, from a GLBT family, and/or pursuing a GLBT course of study. Applicants must either be a Minnesota resident or be planning to study in Minnesota.

Award: Scholarship for use in freshman, sophomore, junior, senior, graduate, or postgraduate years; not renewable. *Number:* 20–30. *Amount:* $1000–$3500.

Eligibility Requirements: Applicant must be enrolled or expecting to enroll full or part-time at a two-year or four-year or technical institution or university. Available to U.S. and non-U.S. citizens.

Application Requirements: Application, essay, photo, references, transcript, confidentiality statement, press release. *Deadline:* February 1.

Contact: Kit Briem, Executive Director
Minnesota Gay/Lesbian/Bisexual/Transgender Educational Fund
1409 Willow Street
Suite 305
Minneapolis, MN 55403
Phone: 612-870-1806
Fax: 612-871-6587
E-mail: philanth@scc.net

MINNESOTA POLICE CORPS

MINNESOTA POLICE CORPS SCHOLARSHIP

Scholarships available for full-time undergraduate students, full- or part-time graduate students, and recent college graduates. Must commit to four years of employment in a participating Minnesota law enforcement agency after field training program. Minimum 2.5 GPA required. Check Web site for details: http://www.dps.state.mn.us/patrol/policecorps/.

Award: Scholarship for use in freshman, sophomore, junior, senior, graduate, or postgraduate years. *Number:* 10. *Amount:* $7500–$30,000.

Eligibility Requirements: Applicant must be enrolled or expecting to enroll full or part-time at a four-year institution or university. Applicant must have 2.5 GPA or higher. Available to U.S. citizens.

Application Requirements: Application, driver's license, essay, interview, references, transcript. *Deadline:* February 28.

Contact: Minnesota Police Corps
Minnesota Police Corps
1900 West County Road 1
Shoreview, MN 55126
Phone: 651-628-6722
Fax: 651-628-6797
E-mail: tammy.sachs@state.mn.us

MISSISSIPPI STATE STUDENT FINANCIAL AID　　http://www.mississippiuniversities.com

WILLIAM WINTER TEACHER SCHOLAR LOAN

Scholarship available to a junior or senior student at a four year Mississippi college or university. Applicants must enroll in a program of study leading to a Class "A" teacher educator license.

Award: Scholarship for use in junior or senior years; renewable. *Amount:* up to $4000.

Eligibility Requirements: Applicant must be enrolled or expecting to enroll full-time at a four-year institution or university. Applicant must have 2.5 GPA or higher. Available to U.S. citizens.

Application Requirements: Application. *Deadline:* March 31.

Contact: Mississippi Student Financial Aid
Mississippi State Student Financial Aid
3825 Ridgewood Road
Jackson, MS 39211-6453
Phone: 800-327-2980
E-mail: sfa@ihl.state.ms.us

MISSOURI POLICE CORPS

MISSOURI POLICE CORPS FUND

Award: Scholarship for use in sophomore, junior, or senior years.

Eligibility Requirements: Applicant must be enrolled or expecting to enroll at an institution or university.

Contact:

NAAS-USA FUND　　　　http://www.naas.org

NAAS II NATIONAL SCHOLARSHIP AWARDS

One renewable scholarship available for tuition, room, board, books, and academic supplies. Applicant must be college freshman or sophomore attending an American college/university. U.S. citizenship is not required. Download applications at: http://www.naas.org/college.htm. Applicants that request an application by mail must enclose a $3 handling fee and a self-addressed stamped envelope.

Award: Scholarship for use in freshman or sophomore years; renewable. *Number:* 1. *Amount:* $500–$3000.

Eligibility Requirements: Applicant must be age 24 or under and enrolled or expecting to enroll full-time at a four-year institution or university. Available to U.S. and non-U.S. citizens.

NAAS-USA Fund (continued)

Application Requirements: Application, self-addressed stamped envelope, SAT/ACT test scores. *Fee:* $3. *Deadline:* May 1.

Contact: NAAS-USA FUND
NAAS-USA Fund
PO Box 337380
North Las Vegas, NV 89031-7380
E-mail: staff@naas.org

NAAS-USA AWARDS

A series of pure, merit-based scholarships available for tuition, room, board, books, and academically-related supplies. Applicants must be high school seniors or equivalent home-school seniors and be U.S. citizen or permanent resident. Application periods are September 15 to May 1. Required GPA 2.0.

Award: Scholarship for use in freshman year; renewable. *Number:* 10–14. *Amount:* $200–$10,000.

Eligibility Requirements: Applicant must be high school student and planning to enroll or expecting to enroll full-time at a four-year institution or university. Available to U.S. citizens.

Application Requirements: Application, self-addressed stamped envelope. *Fee:* $3. *Deadline:* May 1.

Contact: NAAS-USA FUND
NAAS-USA Fund
PO Box 337380
North Las Vegas, NV 89031-7380
E-mail: staff@naas.org

NATIONAL ALLIANCE OF POSTAL AND FEDERAL EMPLOYEES (NAPFE) http://www.napfe.com

ASHBY B. CARTER MEMORIAL SCHOLARSHIP FUND FOUNDERS AWARD

Award: Scholarship for use in freshman year.

Eligibility Requirements: Applicant must be enrolled or expecting to enroll at an institution or university.

Contact: Melissa Jeffries-Stewart, Director
National Alliance of Postal and Federal Employees (NAPFE)
1628 11th Street, NW
Washington, DC 20001
Phone: 202-939-6325 Ext. 239
Fax: 202-939-6389
E-mail: headquarters@napfe.org

NATIONAL ASSOCIATION OF RAILWAY BUSINESS WOMEN http://www.narbw.org

NARBW SCHOLARSHIP

Scholarship is awarded only to the members of National Association of Railway Business Women and their relatives.

Award: Scholarship for use in freshman, sophomore, junior, or senior years. *Amount:* $500–$1000.

Eligibility Requirements: Applicant must be enrolled or expecting to enroll at a two-year or four-year or technical institution or university and female. Available to U.S. citizens.

Application Requirements: Application, financial need analysis. *Deadline:* varies.

Contact: Scholarship chairman
National Association of Railway Business Women
2631 Daleton Boulevard, NE
Roanoke, VA 24012
E-mail: narbwinfo@narbw.org

NATIONAL BUSINESS AVIATION ASSOCIATION, INC. http://www.nbaa.org/scholarships

AVFUEL MICHIGAN BUSINESS AVIATION SCHOLARSHIP

Award for $500 for students pursuing an aviation degree at one of the following eligible schools: Andrews University, Eastern Michigan University, Lansing Community College, Northwestern Michigan College, or Western Michigan University. Must be a U.S. citizen, have a 3.0 minimum GPA. Include with application: 250 word essay describing the applicant's interest in aviation and goals for a career in the business aviation industry and a letter of recommendation from the aviation department faculty at the institution at which the applicant is enrolled. For further information, visit Web site: http://www.nbaa.org

Award: Scholarship for use in freshman, sophomore, junior, senior, or graduate years. *Number:* 1. *Amount:* $500.

Eligibility Requirements: Applicant must be enrolled or expecting to enroll at a four-year institution or university. Applicant must have 3.0 GPA or higher. Available to U.S. citizens.

Application Requirements: Application, essay, resume, references, transcript. *Deadline:* August 1.

Contact: Jay Evans, Director, Operations
National Business Aviation Association, Inc.
1200 18th Street, NW, Suite 400
Washington, DC 20036-2527
Phone: 202-783-9353
Fax: 202-331-8364
E-mail: info@nbaa.org

CANADIAN SCHEDULERS AND DISPATCHERS SCHOLARSHIP

Scholarship for further college education or industry training in aviation scheduling and dispatching. Applicant must be a Canadian citizen. Scholarship recipients must complete all professional/educational training by Feb 1, 2008.

Award: Scholarship for use in freshman, sophomore, junior, senior, or graduate years. *Number:* 1. *Amount:* $5000.

Eligibility Requirements: Applicant must be enrolled or expecting to enroll at a technical institution. Available to U.S. and Canadian citizens.

Application Requirements: Application, essay, references. *Deadline:* November 14.

Contact: Jay Evans, Director, Operations
National Business Aviation Association, Inc.
1200 18th Street, NW, Suite 400
Washington, DC 20036-2527
Phone: 202-783-9353
Fax: 202-331-8364
E-mail: info@nbaa.org

NATIONAL CHAMBER OF COMMERCE FOR WOMEN http://www.businessfinance.com

MILLIE BELAFONTE WRIGHT SCHOLARSHIP AND GRANT EVALUATION

Award: Scholarship for use in freshman, sophomore, junior, senior, or graduate years.

Eligibility Requirements: Applicant must be enrolled or expecting to enroll at an institution or university.

Contact: Caroline Westbrook, Coordinator
National Chamber of Commerce for Women
10 Waterside Plaza
Suite 6H
New York, NY 10010
Phone: 212-685-3454
Fax: 212-685-4547
E-mail: commerce-for-women@juno.com

NATIONAL CHRISTMAS TREE ASSOCIATION http://www.realchristmastrees.org

NCTA HELP SANTA FIND THE PERFECT REAL CHRISTMAS TREE

Participants submit an essay of 300 words or less on why their real Christmas tree is perfect. A photograph of the tree must accompany the essay. Ages 6-16 are eligible to win a $5000 - $10,000 scholarship or theme-park trip for 4. Essay deadline is December 31.

Award: Prize for use in freshman year; not renewable. *Number:* 3. *Amount:* $5000–$10,000.

Eligibility Requirements: Applicant must be age 6-16 and enrolled or expecting to enroll full or part-time at a two-year or four-year or technical institution or university. Available to U.S. citizens.

Application Requirements: Application, applicant must enter a contest, essay, photo. *Deadline:* December 31.

Contact: Pheniece Jones, Marketing Assistant
National Christmas Tree Association
99 Canal Center Plaza, Suite 410
Alexandria, VA 22314
Phone: 703-740-1755
Fax: 703-740-1775
E-mail: pjones@smithharroff.com

NATIONAL COMMISSION FOR COOPERATIVE EDUCATION http://www.co-op.edu

NATIONAL COMMISSION FOR COOPERATIVE EDUCATION CO-OP SCHOLARSHIP

The award designed to assist and encourage talented high school and transfer students of a college, as well as their selection of a cooperative education program from among "The Best of Co-op." Minimum 3.5 GPA required.

Award: Scholarship for use in freshman year; renewable. *Number:* 113. *Amount:* $5000.

Eligibility Requirements: Applicant must be high school student and planning to enroll or expecting to enroll full-time at a two-year or four-year institution or university. Applicant must have 3.5 GPA or higher. Available to U.S. and non-U.S. citizens.

Application Requirements: Application, essay, extracurricular activities, work experience. *Deadline:* February 15.

Contact: Frank T. Schettino, Director
Phone: 617-373-3406
Fax: 617-373-3463
E-mail: f.schettino@neu.edu

NATIONAL COURT REPORTERS ASSOCIATION http://www.ncraonline.org

COUNCIL ON APPROVED STUDENT EDUCATION'S SCHOLARSHIP FUND

Student must be writing between 140-180 wpm, and must be in an NCRA-approved court reporting program. Student must write a two-page essay on topic chosen for the year. Deadline: April 1. Student enters a competition, first place is $1500, second place is $1000, and third place is $500.

Award: Scholarship for use in sophomore year; not renewable. *Number:* 3. *Amount:* $500–$1500.

Eligibility Requirements: Applicant must be enrolled or expecting to enroll full or part-time at a two-year or four-year or technical institution or university. Applicant must have 3.0 GPA or higher. Available to U.S. and Canadian citizens.

Application Requirements: Application, applicant must enter a contest, essay, references, transcript. *Deadline:* April 1.

Contact: Donna M. Gaede, Approval Program Manager
National Court Reporters Association
8224 Old Courthouse Road
Vienna, VA 22182
Phone: 703-556-6272
Fax: 703-556-6291
E-mail: dgaede@ncrahq.org

FRANK SARLI MEMORIAL SCHOLARSHIP

One-time award to a student who is nearing graduation from a trade/technical school or four-year college. Must be enrolled in a court reporting program. Minimum 3.5 GPA required.

Award: Scholarship for use in freshman, sophomore, junior, or senior years; not renewable. *Number:* 1. *Amount:* $500.

Eligibility Requirements: Applicant must be enrolled or expecting to enroll full or part-time at a four-year or technical institution or university. Applicant must have 3.5 GPA or higher. Available to U.S. citizens.

Application Requirements: Application. *Deadline:* February 28.

Contact: B J. Shorak, Deputy Executive Director, National Court Reporters Foundation
National Court Reporters Association
8224 Old Courthouse Road
Vienna, VA 22182-3808
Phone: 703-556-6272 Ext. 126
Fax: 703-556-6291
E-mail: bjshorak@ncrahq.org

STUDENT MEMBER TUITION GRANT

Four $500 awards for students in good academic standing at school. Students required to write 120-200 wpm. Deadline is May 31.

Award: Grant for use in freshman or sophomore years. *Number:* 4. *Amount:* $500.

Eligibility Requirements: Applicant must be enrolled or expecting to enroll at an institution or university. Available to U.S. citizens.

Application Requirements: Application. *Deadline:* May 31.

Contact: Amy Davidson
E-mail: adavidson@ncrahq.org

WILLIAM E. WEBER SCHOLARSHIP

One scholarship available for NCRA student members that are currently enrolled at NCRA-approved programs. The nominee must have passed at least one of the court reporting program's Q & A tests at a minimum of 200 wpm. Applicants are required to have a minimum 3.5 overall GPA and demonstrated need for financial assistance. Contact for further information and deadlines.

Award: Scholarship for use in sophomore, junior, or senior years; not renewable. *Number:* 1. *Amount:* $500.

Eligibility Requirements: Applicant must be enrolled or expecting to enroll full or part-time at a four-year or technical institution or university. Applicant must have 3.5 GPA or higher. Available to U.S. citizens.

Application Requirements: Application, financial need analysis. *Deadline:* varies.

Contact: B J. Shorak, Deputy Executive Director, National Court Reporters Foundation
National Court Reporters Association
8224 Old Courthouse Road
Vienna, VA 22182-3808
Phone: 703-556-6272 Ext. 126
Fax: 703-556-6291
E-mail: bjshorak@ncrahq.org

NATIONAL FEDERATION OF THE BLIND OF CALIFORNIA http://www.nfbcal.org

GERALD DRAKE MEMORIAL SCHOLARSHIP

Award: Scholarship for use in freshman, sophomore, junior, senior, or graduate years.

Eligibility Requirements: Applicant must be enrolled or expecting to enroll at an institution or university.

JULIE LANDUCCI SCHOLARSHIP

Award: Scholarship for use in freshman, sophomore, junior, senior, or graduate years.

Eligibility Requirements: Applicant must be enrolled or expecting to enroll at an institution or university.

LA VYRL "PINKY" JOHNSON MEMORIAL SCHOLARSHIP

Award: Scholarship for use in freshman, sophomore, junior, senior, or graduate years.

Eligibility Requirements: Applicant must be enrolled or expecting to enroll at an institution or university.

LAWRENCE "MUZZY" MARCELINO MEMORIAL SCHOLARSHIP

Award: Scholarship for use in freshman, sophomore, junior, senior, or graduate years.

National Federation of the Blind of California (continued)

Eligibility Requirements: Applicant must be enrolled or expecting to enroll at an institution or university.

NATIONAL FEDERATION OF THE BLIND OF CALIFORNIA MERIT SCHOLARSHIPS

Award: Scholarship for use in freshman, sophomore, junior, senior, or graduate years.

Eligibility Requirements: Applicant must be enrolled or expecting to enroll at an institution or university.

NATIONAL FFA ORGANIZATION   http://www.ffa.org

NATIONAL FFA COLLEGE AND VOCATIONAL/TECHNICAL SCHOOL SCHOLARSHIP PROGRAM

Nearly $2,000,000 awarded to high school seniors planning to enroll in a full-time course of study at an accredited vocational/technical school, college or university. A smaller number of awards are available to currently enrolled undergraduates. Most of the awards require that the applicant be an FFA member. However some awards are available to high school seniors who are not FFA members. Some awards require an agricultural major, while others are for any major. See the Web site for more details.

Award: Scholarship for use in freshman, sophomore, junior, or senior years; not renewable. *Number:* up to 1700. *Amount:* $1000–$15,000.

Eligibility Requirements: Applicant must be enrolled or expecting to enroll full-time at a two-year or four-year or technical institution or university. Available to U.S. citizens.

Application Requirements: Application. *Deadline:* February 15.

Contact: Carrie Powers, Scholarship Program Coordinator
National FFA Organization
6060 FFA Drive, PO Box 68960
Indianapolis, IN 46268-0960
Phone: 317-802-4321
Fax: 317-802-5321
E-mail: scholarships@ffa.org

NATIONAL FUNERAL DIRECTORS AND MORTICIANS ASSOCIATION   http://www.nfdma.com

NATIONAL FUNERAL DIRECTORS AND MORTICIANS ASSOCIATION SCHOLARSHIP

Awards for high school graduates who have preferably worked in or had one year of apprenticeship in the funeral home business. Scholarship amount varies.

Award: Scholarship for use in freshman year; not renewable. *Number:* 1.

Eligibility Requirements: Applicant must be enrolled or expecting to enroll at an institution or university. Available to U.S. citizens.

Application Requirements: Application, resume, references, test scores. *Deadline:* April 1.

Contact: Scholarship Committee
National Funeral Directors and Morticians Association
3951 Snapfinger Parkway, Suite 570
Decatur, GA 30035
Phone: 404-286-6680
E-mail: nfdma@mindspring.com

NATIONAL GROUND WATER ASSOCIATION   http://www.ngwa.org

NATIONAL GROUND WATER EDUCATION FOUNDATION LEN ASSANTE SCHOLARSHIP FUND

The scholarship is available to high school graduates and students in college (four-year programs or well drilling two-year Associate Degree programs). A 2.5 GPA is mandatory for all applicants. Previous recipients are ineligible. For more information see Web site: http://www.ngwa.org

Award: Scholarship for use in freshman, sophomore, junior, or senior years; not renewable. *Number:* up to 7. *Amount:* $1000–$2000.

Eligibility Requirements: Applicant must be enrolled or expecting to enroll full-time at a two-year or four-year institution or university. Applicant must have 2.5 GPA or higher. Available to U.S. and non-U.S. citizens.

Application Requirements: Application, autobiography, essay, transcript. *Deadline:* April 1.

Contact: Michelle Islam, NGWA Scholarship Coordinator
National Ground Water Association
601 Dempsey Road
Westerville, OH 43081
Phone: 800-551-7379 Ext. 530
Fax: 614-898-7786
E-mail: mislam@ngwa.org

NATIONAL HOT ROD ASSOCIATION   http://www.nhra.com

SEARS CRAFTSMAN SCHOLARSHIP

Scholarship awarded to graduating high school seniors to continue their education. Applicant must possess a minimum 2.0 GPA and planning to attend an accredited college, university, or technical/vocational program. Deadline is May 1.

Award: Scholarship for use in freshman year; not renewable. *Number:* 21. *Amount:* $1000.

Eligibility Requirements: Applicant must be high school student and planning to enroll or expecting to enroll at a two-year or four-year or technical institution or university. Available to U.S. and non-U.S. citizens.

Application Requirements: Application, essay, financial need analysis, references. *Deadline:* May 1.

Contact: Youth and Education Services
National Hot Rod Association
2035 Financial Way
Glendora, CA 91741-4602
Phone: 626-914-4761
Fax: 626-963-5360
E-mail: yes@nhra.com

NATIONAL ITALIAN AMERICAN FOUNDATION   http://www.niaf.org

THE JOHN R. MOTT FOUNDATION SCHOLARSHIPS

Scholarship for outstanding students who have demonstrated academic achievement, good citizenship, and good moral character. Deadline is April 1.

Award: Scholarship for use in freshman, sophomore, junior, or senior years. *Amount:* up to $10,000.

Eligibility Requirements: Applicant must be enrolled or expecting to enroll at a four-year institution or university. Available to U.S. citizens.

Application Requirements: Application, transcript. *Deadline:* April 1.

Contact: S. Cantoni, Mott Scholarship
National Italian American Foundation
1860 19th Street, NW
Washington, DC 20009
Fax: 202-387-0800

NATIONAL JUNIOR ANGUS ASSOCIATION   http://www.njaa.info

AMERICAN ANGUS AUXILIARY SCHOLARSHIP

Scholarship available to graduating high school senior. May only apply in one state. Any unmarried girl or unmarried boy recommended by a state or regional Auxiliary is eligible.

Award: Scholarship for use in freshman year. *Amount:* $850–$1200.

Eligibility Requirements: Applicant must be high school student; planning to enroll or expecting to enroll full-time at an institution or university and single. Available to U.S. citizens.

Application Requirements: Application, autobiography, photo, references. *Deadline:* September 1.

Contact: Richard Wilson
National Junior Angus Association
3201 Frederick Avenue
St. Joseph, MO 64506
Phone: 816-383-5100
Fax: 816-233-9703
E-mail: info@njaa.info

NATIONAL MERIT SCHOLARSHIP CORPORATION   http://www.nationalmerit.org

NATIONAL MERIT SCHOLARSHIP PROGRAM

Award: Scholarship for use in freshman year.

Eligibility Requirements: Applicant must be enrolled or expecting to enroll at an institution or university.

NATIONAL SCIENCE TEACHERS ASSOCIATION   http://www.nsta.org

TOSHIBA/NSTA EXPLORAVISION AWARDS PROGRAM

A competition for all students in grades K-12 attending a public, private or home school in the U.S., Canada, or U.S. Territories. It is designed to encourage students to combine their imagination with their knowledge of science and technology to explore visions of the future.

Award: Prize for use in freshman, sophomore, junior, senior, graduate, or postgraduate years; not renewable. *Number:* 16–32. *Amount:* $5000–$10,000.

Eligibility Requirements: Applicant must be age 21 or under and enrolled or expecting to enroll full-time at a two-year or four-year or technical institution or university. Available to U.S. and Canadian citizens.

Application Requirements: Application, applicant must enter a contest, essay, Web pages. *Deadline:* February 3.

Contact: National Science Teachers Association
National Science Teachers Association
1840 Wilson Boulevard
Arlington, VA 22201
Phone: 800-EXP-LOR9
Fax: 703-243-7177
E-mail: exploravision@nsta.org

NATIONAL SOCIETY DAUGHTERS OF THE AMERICAN REVOLUTION   http://www.dar.org

NATIONAL SOCIETY DAUGHTERS OF THE AMERICAN REVOLUTION MARGARET HOWARD HAMILTON SCHOLARSHIP

Awarded to a graduating high school seniors. This award is $1,000 annually for up to four years with annual transcript review by the National Chairman required for renewal. Deadline is April 15.

Award: Scholarship for use in freshman year. *Amount:* $1000.

Eligibility Requirements: Applicant must be enrolled or expecting to enroll full-time at an institution or university. Available to U.S. citizens.

Application Requirements: Application. *Deadline:* April 15.

Contact: Committee Services Office, Scholarship
National Society Daughters of the American Revolution
1776 D Street, NW
Washington, DC 20006-5303

NATIONAL TEEN-AGER SCHOLARSHIP FOUNDATION   http://www.nationalteen.com

AMERICA'S NATIONAL TEENAGER SCHOLARSHIP PROGRAM

One-time award for young women of leadership and intellect. Award based on school and community leadership, communication skills, academics and personal presentation. 3-5 awards per state. Awards come in the form of savings bonds from $500-1000 and in cash from $5000-10,000. Must be between the ages of 12-18 and be a U.S. citizen. Minimum 3.0 GPA required. $20 application fee. Deadline varies by state. For more details see Web site: http://www.nationalteen.com

Award: Scholarship for use in freshman year; not renewable. *Number:* 250–1510. *Amount:* $500–$10,000.

Eligibility Requirements: Applicant must be age 12-18; enrolled or expecting to enroll full-time at a two-year or four-year institution or university and single female. Applicant must have 3.0 GPA or higher. Available to U.S. citizens.

Application Requirements: Application, applicant must enter a contest, interview, photo, self-addressed stamped envelope, transcript. *Fee:* $20. *Deadline:* varies.

Contact: Jenny Telwar, National Director
National Teen-Ager Scholarship Foundation
808 Deer Crossing Court
Nashville, TN 37220
Phone: 615-370-4338
Fax: 615-377-0223
E-mail: telwar@comcast.net

NATIONAL WOMAN'S RELIEF CORPS   http://suvcw.org/wrc.htm

NATIONAL WOMAN'S RELIEF CORPS SCHOLARSHIP

Award: Scholarship for use in freshman, sophomore, junior, or senior years.

Eligibility Requirements: Applicant must be enrolled or expecting to enroll at an institution or university.

Contact: Lurene Wentworth, National Secretary
National Woman's Relief Corps
PO Box 165
New Durham, NH 03855-0165
Phone: 603-859-2861
E-mail: liwntwrth@aol.com

NEEDHAM AND COMPANY WTC SCHOLARSHIP FUND   http://www.needhamco.com/

NEEDHAM AND COMPANY SEPTEMBER 11TH SCHOLARSHIP FUND

Scholarship going to those individuals who had a pre-September 11th gross income of less than $125,000. To be eligible applicants must be currently accepted or attending an accredited university or college. Recipients decided on a case-by-case basis. Fund designed to benefit the children of the victims who lost their lives at the World Trade Center. Visit Web site for additional information.

Award: Scholarship for use in freshman, sophomore, junior, or senior years; not renewable. *Number:* varies. *Amount:* varies.

Eligibility Requirements: Applicant must be enrolled or expecting to enroll at an institution or university. Available to U.S. citizens.

Application Requirements: Application, financial need analysis. *Deadline:* Continuous.

Contact: Needham and Company WTC Scholarship Fund
445 Park Avenue
New York, NY 10022
Phone: 212-705-0314
E-mail: jturano@needhamco.com

NELNET COLLEGE PLANNING   http://www.collegeplanning.nelnet.net

NATIONAL SCHOLARSHIP

Sweepstakes award for high school seniors. Applicant must be a registered member of Nelnet College Planning.

Award: Scholarship for use in freshman year. *Amount:* up to $1000.

Eligibility Requirements: Applicant must be high school student; age 13 and planning to enroll or expecting to enroll at an institution or university. Available to U.S. citizens.

Application Requirements: Application. *Deadline:* March 31.

Contact: Teffenie Davies, Senior Vice President and Director
Nelnet College Planning
3015 South Parker Road, Suite 400
Aurora, CO 80014
Phone: 866-426-6765
E-mail: nelnetconsolidations@nelnet.net

NETHERLANDS ORGANIZATION FOR INTERNATIONAL COOPERATION IN HIGHER EDUCATION
http://www.nuffic.nl

DUTCH EDUCATION: LEARNING AT TOP LEVEL ABROAD SCHOLARSHIP

Scholarships available to students under age 35 who wish to study in the Netherlands. Must be a citizen of Indonesia, Taiwan, South Africa, or the People's Republic of China. Must study for a period of between three and twelve months at a participating university. See Web site for specific information and requirements: http://www.nufflc.nl

Award: Scholarship for use in freshman, sophomore, junior, senior, or graduate years. *Number:* 300. *Amount:* $2764–$13,603.

Eligibility Requirements: Applicant must be age 34 or under and enrolled or expecting to enroll at a four-year institution or university. Available to citizens of countries other than the U.S. or Canada.

Application Requirements: Application. *Deadline:* varies.

Contact: Rita van de Wetering, General Affairs
Netherlands Organization for International Cooperation in Higher Education
Kortenaerkade 11, Postbus 29777
PO Box 29777
LT The Hague 2502
Netherlands
Phone: 310-70-426-0260
E-mail: nuffic@nuffic.nl

HUYGENS SCHOLARSHIP

Scholarships available to students who wish to pursue their graduate degree at a Dutch institute of higher education. Must be accepted at institution, prove ability to speak Dutch, and be a citizen of an eligible country. Check Web site for more details. http://www.nuffic.nl

Award: Scholarship for use in senior, or graduate years. *Number:* up to 175. *Amount:* $1733.

Eligibility Requirements: Applicant must be age 35 or under and enrolled or expecting to enroll at a four-year institution or university. Available to citizens of countries other than the U.S. or Canada.

Application Requirements: Application, resume, references, test scores, transcript, TOEFL, Cambridge certificate. *Deadline:* March 1.

Contact: Department for International Academic Relations
Netherlands Organization for International Cooperation in Higher Education
Kortenaerkade 11, PO Box 29777
LT The Hague 2502
Netherlands
Phone: 310-704-260-260
E-mail: huygens@nuffic.nl

NEVADA POLICE CORPS
http://www.nevadapolicecorps.state.nv.us

NEVADA POLICE CORPS PROGRAM

Renewable award available to upper level, full-time undergraduates or graduate students. Must complete four year degree, complete required training and agree to serve a Nevada law enforcement agency for four years. Must be a U.S. citizen. Minimum 2.5 GPA required.

Award: Scholarship for use in freshman, sophomore, junior, senior, or graduate years; renewable. *Number:* 8–10. *Amount:* up to $15,000.

Eligibility Requirements: Applicant must be enrolled or expecting to enroll full-time at a four-year institution or university. Applicant must have 2.5 GPA or higher. Available to U.S. citizens.

Application Requirements: Application, driver's license, essay, interview, references, transcript, peace officer selection process. *Deadline:* Continuous.

Contact: Greg Befort, Director
Nevada Police Corps
WNCC, Cedar Building Room 309-312
2201 West College Parkway
Carson City, NV 89703
Phone: 775-684-8720
Fax: 775-684-8775
E-mail: gbefort@post.state.nv.us

NEW JERSEY DEPARTMENT OF EDUCATION
http://www.state.nj.us

ROBERT C. BYRD HONORS SCHOLARSHIP-NEW JERSEY

Federally-funded award for outstanding graduating high school seniors from either a public or private high school who have been accepted for full-time study at a U.S. college or university. Must have a minimum of 3.5 grade point average, and be nominated by high school. Award renewable for up to four years. Must be legal resident of New Jersey and a U.S. citizen. Contact guidance counselor for information.

Award: Scholarship for use in freshman year; renewable. *Amount:* up to $1500.

Eligibility Requirements: Applicant must be enrolled or expecting to enroll full-time at an institution or university. Available to U.S. citizens.

Application Requirements: Application. *Deadline:* varies.

Contact: Richard Vespucci, Robert Byrd Scholarship
New Jersey Department of Education
PO Box 500
Trenton, NJ 08625-0500
Phone: 609-292-1126

NEW MEXICO STATE DEPARTMENT OF EDUCATION
http://www.ped.state.nm.us

ROBERT C. BYRD HONORS SCHOLARSHIP-NEW MEXICO

Federally-funded award for outstanding graduating high school seniors from either a public or private high school who have been accepted for full-time study at a U.S. college or university. Must have a minimum of 3.5 grade point average, and be nominated by high school. Must be legal resident of New Mexico and a U.S. citizen. Contact guidance counselor for information.

Award: Scholarship for use in freshman year; renewable. *Amount:* up to $1500.

Eligibility Requirements: Applicant must be high school student and planning to enroll or expecting to enroll full-time at an institution or university. Applicant must have 3.5 GPA or higher. Available to U.S. citizens.

Application Requirements: Application. *Deadline:* varies.

Contact: Ruth Williams, Public Outreach Director
New Mexico State Department of Education
300 Don Gaspar
Santa Fe, NM 87501-2786
Phone: 505-827-5800

NIMROD INTERNATIONAL JOURNAL OF PROSE AND POETRY
http://www.utulsa.edu/nimrod

KATHERINE ANNE PORTER PRIZE FOR FICTION

A first place prize of $2000 and a second place prize of $1000 will be awarded for fiction. The award includes publication in Nimrod. $20 entry fee includes one year subscription to Nimrod. For more details see Web site: http://www.utulsa.edu/nimrod.

Award: Prize for use in freshman, sophomore, junior, senior, graduate, or postgraduate years; not renewable. *Number:* 2. *Amount:* $1000–$2000.

Eligibility Requirements: Applicant must be enrolled or expecting to enroll full or part-time at a two-year or four-year or technical institution or university. Available to U.S. citizens.

Application Requirements: Applicant must enter a contest. *Fee:* $20. *Deadline:* April 30.

Contact: Eilis O'Neal, Managing Editor
Nimrod International Journal of Prose and Poetry
NIMROD International Journal of Poetry & Prose, University of Tulsa, 600 South College Avenue
Tulsa, OK 74104-3189
Phone: 918-631-3080
Fax: 918-631-3033
E-mail: nimrod@utulsa.edu

PABLO NERUDA PRIZE FOR POETRY

A first place prize of $2000 and a second place prize of $1000 will be awarded for poetry. The award includes publication in Nimrod. $20 entry fee includes one year subscription to Nimrod. For more details see Web site: http://www.utulsa.edu/nimrod

Award: Prize for use in freshman, sophomore, junior, senior, graduate, or postgraduate years; not renewable. *Number:* 2. *Amount:* $1000–$2000.

Eligibility Requirements: Applicant must be enrolled or expecting to enroll full or part-time at a two-year or four-year or technical institution or university. Available to U.S. citizens.

Application Requirements: Application, applicant must enter a contest, essay, manuscript. *Fee:* $20. *Deadline:* April 30.

Contact: Eilis O'Neal, Managing Editor
Nimrod International Journal of Prose and Poetry
600 South College Avenue
Tulsa, OK 74104
Phone: 918-631-3080
Fax: 918-631-3033
E-mail: nimrod@utulsa.edu

NO-ADDICTION SCHOLARSHIP ESSAY CAMPAIGN
http://www.solarcosmetics.com

NO-AD CAMPAIGN ESSAY CONTEST

This essay contest is open to students in middle school and high school. Only one entry per student. Middle school students can receive savings bonds and high school students college scholarship. For essay topics or any other questions contact noad@aol.com or ediaz@no-ad.com, or visit Web site: http://www.NO-ADdiction.org

Award: Scholarship for use in freshman, sophomore, junior, or senior years; not renewable. *Number:* 10–20. *Amount:* $200–$500.

Eligibility Requirements: Applicant must be high school student and planning to enroll or expecting to enroll full-time at a two-year or four-year institution. Available to U.S. citizens.

Application Requirements: Application, applicant must enter a contest, essay, photo. *Deadline:* varies.

Contact: Elizabeth Calabrese, Coordinator
NO-ADdiction Scholarship Essay Campaign
4920 NW 165th Street
Miami Lakes, FL 33014
Phone: 800-662-3342
Fax: 305-621-0536
E-mail: noad@aol.com

NON COMMISSIONED OFFICERS ASSOCIATION (NCOA)
http://www.ncoausa.org

BETSY ROSS EDUCATIONAL FUND

Awards to assist in defraying the cost of taking a course at a local business or technical school. Must be NCOA Auxiliary Division members who wish to prepare themselves for employment or improve on employable skills. Deadline is March 1.

Award: Grant for use in freshman year; not renewable. *Number:* 6. *Amount:* $250.

Eligibility Requirements: Applicant must be enrolled or expecting to enroll at a technical institution. Available to U.S. citizens.

Application Requirements: Application. *Deadline:* March 1.

Contact: Hilda Atkinson, Scholarship Department
Non Commissioned Officers Association (NCOA)
10635 IH 35 North
PO Box 33610
San Antonio, TX 78233
Phone: 210-653-6161 Ext. 231
Fax: 210-637-3337
E-mail: hatkinso@ncoausa.org

NORTH CAROLINA DIVISION OF VETERANS AFFAIRS

NORTH CAROLINA VETERANS SCHOLARSHIPS CLASS I-A

Award: Scholarship for use in freshman, sophomore, junior, or senior years.

Eligibility Requirements: Applicant must be enrolled or expecting to enroll at an institution or university.

Contact: Charles Smith, Assistant Secretary
325 North Salisbury Street
Raleigh, NC 27603
Phone: 919-733-3851
Fax: 919-733-2834

NORWAY-AMERICA ASSOCIATION
http://www.noram.no

NORWAY-AMERICA UNDERGRADUATE SCHOLARSHIP PROGRAM
• See page 627

ODD FELLOWS AND REBEKAHS
http://ioofme.org/

ODD FELLOWS AND REBEKAHS ELLEN F. WASHBURN NURSES TRAINING AWARD

Award: Scholarship for use in freshman, sophomore, junior, or senior years.

Eligibility Requirements: Applicant must be enrolled or expecting to enroll at an institution or university.

Contact: Joyce Young, Chairman
Odd Fellows and Rebekahs
131 Queen Street Extension
Gorham, ME 04038
Phone: 207-839-4723

OFFICE OF PERSONNEL MANAGEMENT
http://www.sfs.opm.gov

SCHOLARSHIP FOR SERVICE (SFS) PROGRAM

Scholarships for undergraduate and graduate students.Fully funds the typical costs that students pay for books, tuition, and room and board while attending an approved institution of higher learning. Additionally, participants receive stipends of up to $8000 for undergraduate and $12,000 for graduate students.

Award: Scholarship for use in junior, senior, or graduate years; renewable. *Amount:* $8000.

Eligibility Requirements: Applicant must be enrolled or expecting to enroll full-time at a four-year institution or university. Available to U.S. citizens.

Application Requirements: *Deadline:* varies.

Contact: Scholarship For Service Program Office
Office of Personnel Management
8610 Broadway, Suite 305
San Antonio, TX 78217-6352

OHIO 4-H
http://www.ohio4h.org

KATHRYN BEICH 4-H SCHOLARSHIP

One $500 scholarship to be awarded. Applicants must be high school seniors and current 4-H members planning to enroll in the fall at any accredited post secondary institution in any course of study. Applicants must also reside in a county that participated in a Nestle-Beich candy fundraising program.

Award: Scholarship for use in freshman year. *Number:* 1. *Amount:* $500.

Eligibility Requirements: Applicant must be enrolled or expecting to enroll at an institution or university. Available to U.S. citizens.

Application Requirements: Application, essay, resume, references, transcript. *Deadline:* January 27.

Contact: Jeff King, Assistant Director
Ohio 4-H
State 4-H Office, Room 25 Agriculture Administration Building
2120 Fyffe Road
Columbus, OH 43210-1084
Phone: 614-292-4444
Fax: 614-292-5937
E-mail: 4hweb@ag.osu.edu

OHIO ASSOCIATION OF CAREER COLLEGES AND SCHOOLS

LEGISLATIVE SCHOLARSHIP

Award: Scholarship for use in freshman or sophomore years.

Ohio Association of Career Colleges and Schools (continued)

Eligibility Requirements: Applicant must be enrolled or expecting to enroll at an institution or university.

Contact: Max Lerner, Executive Director
Ohio Association of Career Colleges and Schools
1857 Northwest Boulevard
Columbus, OH 43212
Phone: 614-487-8180
Fax: 614-487-8190

OKLAHOMA STATE REGENTS FOR HIGHER EDUCATION   http://www.okhighered.org

HEARTLAND SCHOLARSHIP FUND

Renewable award for dependent children of individuals killed as a result of the 1995 Oklahoma City bombing, or a surviving dependent child who was injured in the Alfred P. Murrah Federal Building day care center as a result of the bombing. The awards are applicable to the cost of tuition, fees, special fees, books and room and board. The award is for undergraduate study anywhere in the United States, and for graduate study at an Oklahoma institution.

Award: Scholarship for use in freshman, sophomore, junior, senior, or graduate years; renewable. *Number:* varies. *Amount:* $3500–$5500.

Eligibility Requirements: Applicant must be enrolled or expecting to enroll full-time at a two-year or four-year institution or university. Available to U.S. citizens.

Application Requirements: Application. *Deadline:* Continuous.

Contact: Alicia Harris, Scholarship Programs Coordinator
Oklahoma State Regents for Higher Education
PO Box 108850
Oklahoma City, OK 73101-8850
Phone: 405-225-9131
Fax: 405-225-9230
E-mail: aharris@osrhe.edu

OP LOFTBED COMPANY   http://www.oploftbed.com/scholarship/index.php

OP LOFTBED $500 SCHOLARSHIP AWARD

Scholarship is awarded to the student whose answers to the application questions on the OP Loftbed Web site were the most creative and amusing. Must be a U.S. citizen who is enrolled in a college or university in the U.S. Submit entry on Web site: http://www.oploftbed.com

Award: Scholarship for use in freshman year. *Number:* 1. *Amount:* $500.

Eligibility Requirements: Applicant must be enrolled or expecting to enroll full or part-time at a four-year institution or university. Available to U.S. citizens.

Application Requirements: Application, applicant must enter a contest, essay. *Deadline:* July 31.

Contact: Program Coordinator
OP Loftbed Company
PO Box 573
Thomasville, NC 27361-0573
Phone: 866-567-5638

OPTIMIST INTERNATIONAL FOUNDATION   http://www.optimist.org

OPTIMIST INTERNATIONAL ESSAY CONTEST

The guidelines require that contestants be under age 19 as of December 31 of the current school year. Club winners advance to the District contest to compete for a $650 college scholarship. Each District winner is automatically entered into the International Essay contest where a panel of judges select the top three essays. Scholarships are awarded as follows: first place-$5000; second place-$3000; and third place-$2000.

Award: Scholarship for use in freshman, sophomore, junior, or senior years; not renewable. *Number:* 53–56. *Amount:* $650–$5000.

Eligibility Requirements: Applicant must be age 19 or under and enrolled or expecting to enroll at a two-year or four-year or technical institution or university. Available to U.S. and Canadian citizens.

Application Requirements: Application, applicant must enter a contest, essay, self-addressed stamped envelope, birth certificate. *Deadline:* varies.

Contact: Ms. Danielle Baugher, International Programs Coordinator
Optimist International Foundation
4494 Lindell Boulevard
St. Louis, MO 63108
Phone: 314-371-6000 Ext. 235
Fax: 314-371-6006
E-mail: baugherd@optimist.org

OPTIMIST INTERNATIONAL ORATORICAL CONTEST

The Optimist Oratorical Contest gives youngsters the chance to speak to the world. Districts have the opportunity to provide two $1,500 scholarships or a first place scholarship of $1,500, a second place scholarship of $1000, and a third place scholarship of $500.

Award: Scholarship for use in freshman or sophomore years; not renewable. *Number:* up to 106. *Amount:* $500–$1500.

Eligibility Requirements: Applicant must be high school student; age 16 or under and planning to enroll or expecting to enroll at a two-year or four-year or technical institution or university. Available to U.S. and non-U.S. citizens.

Application Requirements: Application, applicant must enter a contest, self-addressed stamped envelope, birth certificate, speech. *Deadline:* varies.

Contact: Ms. Danielle Baugher, International Programs Coordinator
Optimist International Foundation
4494 Lindell Boulevard
St. Louis, MO 63108
Phone: 314-371-6000 Ext. 235
Fax: 314-371-6006
E-mail: baugherd@optimist.org

ORANGE COUNTY COMMUNITY FOUNDATION   http://www.heef.org

COMMUNITY COLLEGE TRANSFER SCHOLARSHIP PROGRAM

Scholarships to provide support for Orange County, CA college students who are currently enrolled at a community college and plan to transfer to a four-year institution. Awards may be applied to any accredited college or university.

Award: Scholarship for use in freshman, sophomore, junior, or senior years; not renewable. *Number:* up to 20. *Amount:* up to $1000.

Eligibility Requirements: Applicant must be enrolled or expecting to enroll at a four-year institution or university. Available to U.S. citizens.

Application Requirements: Application, essay, self-addressed stamped envelope, transcript. *Deadline:* February 13.

Contact: Rose Garris, Hispanic Education Endowment Fund
Orange County Community Foundation
30 Corporate Park, Suite 410
Irvine, CA 92606
Phone: 949-543-4202 Ext. 23
Fax: 949-553-4211

THE EISNER FOUNDATION FUND SCHOLARSHIP

Fund provides support for youth that are active participants in the non-profit organization, Disney GOALS. The awards may be used for tutoring costs or scholarships at all levels along the education continuum. Deadline is February 13.

Award: Scholarship for use in freshman, sophomore, junior, senior, graduate, or postgraduate years; not renewable. *Number:* 5. *Amount:* $500–$1000.

Eligibility Requirements: Applicant must be enrolled or expecting to enroll at a two-year or four-year or technical institution or university. Available to U.S. citizens.

Application Requirements: Application, essay, transcript. *Deadline:* February 13.

Contact: Rose Garris, Hispanic Education Endowment Fund
Orange County Community Foundation
30 Corporate Park, Suite 410
Irvine, CA 92606
Phone: 949-543-4202 Ext. 23
Fax: 949-553-4211

OREGON POLICE CORPS   http://www.portlandonline.com

OREGON POLICE CORPS

Scholarships available for undergraduate juniors and seniors and graduate students, or for reimbursement of educational expenses for college graduates. Must agree to commit to four years of employment at a participating law enforcement agency. Check Web site for details: http://www.oregonpolicecorps.com

Award: Scholarship for use in junior, senior, or graduate years. *Number:* 10. *Amount:* up to $30,000.

Eligibility Requirements: Applicant must be enrolled or expecting to enroll full-time at a four-year institution or university. Available to U.S. citizens.

Application Requirements: Application, driver's license, essay, interview, resume, references. *Deadline:* Continuous.

Contact: Tim Evans
Oregon Police Corps
1120 SW 5th Avenue, Room 404
Portland, OR 97204
Phone: 888-735-4259
E-mail: tevans@police.ci.portland.or.us

ORPHAN FOUNDATION OF AMERICA   http://www.orphan.org

OFA NATIONAL SCHOLARSHIP/CASEY FAMILY SCHOLARS

Scholarships are given to young people who were in foster care for at least one year at the time of their 18th birthday. Must be under 25 years old. Must have been accepted into an accredited postsecondary school or program. Must not currently be a Casey Family Program CEJT participant.

Award: Scholarship for use in freshman, sophomore, junior, or senior years; renewable. *Number:* 350. *Amount:* $2000–$6000.

Eligibility Requirements: Applicant must be age 24 or under and enrolled or expecting to enroll full or part-time at a two-year or four-year or technical institution or university. Available to U.S. and non-U.S. citizens.

Application Requirements: Application, essay, financial need analysis, references, transcript, foster care verification/parents' death certificates. *Deadline:* March 31.

Contact: Tina Raheem, Scholarship Coordinator
Orphan Foundation of America
21351 Gentry Drive, Suite 130
Sterling, VA 20166
Phone: 571-203-0270
Fax: 571-203-0273
E-mail: scholarship@orphan.org

OUTSTANDING STUDENTS OF AMERICA   http://www.outstandingstudentsofamerica.com

OUTSTANDING STUDENTS OF AMERICA SCHOLARSHIP

Scholarships available for $1000 each and are payable to the college of the student's choice. The focus of the scholarship committee will be the student with record of community/school involvement who maintains a GPA of 3.0 or above.

Award: Scholarship for use in freshman year. *Amount:* $1000.

Eligibility Requirements: Applicant must be enrolled or expecting to enroll at a four-year institution or university. Applicant must have 3.0 GPA or higher. Available to U.S. citizens.

Application Requirements: Application, self-addressed stamped envelope. *Deadline:* October 15.

Contact: Scholarship Committee
Outstanding Students of America
3047 Sagefield Road
Tuscaloosa, AL 35405
Phone: 205-344-6322
E-mail: info@outstandingstudentsofamerica.com

PADGETT BUSINESS SERVICES FOUNDATION   http://smallbizpros.com

PADGETT BUSINESS SERVICES FOUNDATION SCHOLARSHIP PROGRAM

Scholarships are awarded to the dependents of small business owners in the U.S. and Canada. Must be a high school senior. Recipients of the scholarships qualify for a $4,000 International Scholarship. See Web site for details, http://www.smallbizpros.com

Award: Scholarship for use in freshman year; not renewable. *Number:* 65–75. *Amount:* $500–$50,000.

Eligibility Requirements: Applicant must be high school student and planning to enroll or expecting to enroll full-time at a two-year or four-year institution or university. Available to U.S. and Canadian citizens.

Application Requirements: Application, essay, test scores, transcript, school activities. *Deadline:* March 1.

Contact: Heather Stokley, Administrator, Padgett Foundation Scholarship Program
Padgett Business Services Foundation
160 Hawthorne Park
Athens, GA 30606
Phone: 800-723-4388
Fax: 800-548-1040
E-mail: hstokley@smallbizpros.com

PAPER, ALLIED-INDUSTRIAL, CHEMICAL AND ENERGY WORKERS INTERNATIONAL UNION

NICHOLAS C. VRATARIC SCHOLARSHIP FUND

Award: Scholarship for use in freshman, sophomore, junior, or senior years.

Eligibility Requirements: Applicant must be enrolled or expecting to enroll at an institution or university.

Contact:

PACE SCHOLARSHIP AWARDS

Award: Scholarship for use in freshman year.

Eligibility Requirements: Applicant must be enrolled or expecting to enroll at an institution or university.

Contact:

PAPERCHECK.COM   http://www.papercheck.com/scholarship.asp

PAPERCHECK.COM CHARLES SHAFAE' SCHOLARSHIP FUND

Two $500 scholarships each year (one per long semester) to winners of the Papercheck Essay Contest. Must be enrolled at an accredited four-year college or university. Must maintain a cumulative GPA of at least 3.2. Scholarship guidelines available at: http://www.papercheck.com

Award: Scholarship for use in freshman, sophomore, junior, or senior years; not renewable. *Number:* 2. *Amount:* $500.

Eligibility Requirements: Applicant must be enrolled or expecting to enroll at a four-year institution or university. Applicant must have 3.0 GPA or higher. Available to U.S. citizens.

Application Requirements: Essay. *Deadline:* September 1.

Contact: Papercheck.com
The Charles Shafae' Scholarship Fund
PO Box 642
Half Moon Bay, CA 94019
Phone: 650-712-9440
E-mail: info@papercheck.com

PARALYZED VETERANS OF AMERICA - SPINAL CORD RESEARCH FOUNDATION   http://www.pva.org/

PARALYZED VETERANS OF AMERICA EDUCATIONAL SCHOLARSHIP PROGRAM

Open to PVA members, their spouses and unmarried children, under 24 years of age, to obtain a postsecondary education. Applicant must be U.S. citizen accepted or enrolled as full-time student in degree program. For details and application visit Web site: http://www.pva.org

Paralyzed Veterans of America - Spinal Cord Research Foundation (continued)

Award: Scholarship for use in freshman, sophomore, junior, or senior years. *Number:* 10–20. *Amount:* $500–$1000.

Eligibility Requirements: Applicant must be age 24 or under and enrolled or expecting to enroll full or part-time at an institution or university. Available to U.S. citizens.

Application Requirements: Application, references, transcript, personal statement, verification of enrollment. *Deadline:* June 15.

Contact: Trish Hoover
Paralyzed Veterans of America - Spinal Cord Research Foundation
801 Eighteenth Street, NW
Washington, DC 20006-3517
Phone: 800-424-8200 Ext. 619
E-mail: trishh@pva.org

PARENT RELOCATION COUNCIL   http://www.parentrelocationcouncil.com

PARENT RELOCATION COUNCIL SCHOLARSHIP

Scholarship available to high school seniors planning to attend a four-year university, community college, or trade school. One $2000 scholarship and three $1000 scholarships will be awarded.

Award: Scholarship for use in freshman year. *Number:* 3. *Amount:* $1000–$2000.

Eligibility Requirements: Applicant must be high school student and planning to enroll or expecting to enroll full or part-time at a two-year or four-year or technical institution or university. Available to U.S. citizens.

Application Requirements: Application, essay. *Deadline:* May 15.

Contact: Barbara Casserly, National Program Director
Phone: 949-637-4687
E-mail: barbara@parentrelocationcouncil.com

PARENTS, FAMILIES, AND FRIENDS OF LESBIANS AND GAYS-ATLANTA   http://www.pflagatl.org

PFLAG SCHOLARSHIP AWARDS PROGRAM

Must be Georgia resident or enrolled in a postsecondary institution in Georgia. Applicant must have turned 16 by April 1 in order to be eligible. Must be openly gay, lesbian, bisexual or transexuals or advocates of the same. Application must be postmarked by March 31.

Award: Scholarship for use in freshman, sophomore, junior, senior, or graduate years; not renewable. *Number:* 5–10. *Amount:* $500–$3000.

Eligibility Requirements: Applicant must be age 16 and enrolled or expecting to enroll full or part-time at a two-year or four-year or technical institution or university. Available to U.S. and non-U.S. citizens.

Application Requirements: Application, autobiography, essay, financial need analysis, references, test scores, transcript. *Deadline:* March 31.

Contact: PFLAG Scholarship Program
Parents, Families, and Friends of Lesbians and Gays-Atlanta
PO Box 450393
Atlanta, GA 31145-0393

PATIENT ADVOCATE FOUNDATION   http://www.patientadvocate.org

SCHOLARSHIPS FOR SURVIVORS

The purpose of these scholarships is to provide support to patients seeking to initiate or complete a course of study that has been interrupted or delayed by a diagnosis of cancer or another critical or life threatening illness. Eight awards of $2000 available to U.S. citizens. Minimum 3.0 GPA required.

Award: Scholarship for use in freshman, sophomore, junior, senior, graduate, or postgraduate years; renewable. *Number:* 8. *Amount:* $2000.

Eligibility Requirements: Applicant must be enrolled or expecting to enroll full-time at a two-year or four-year institution or university. Applicant must have 3.0 GPA or higher. Available to U.S. citizens.

Application Requirements: Application, essay, financial need analysis, references, transcript, physician letter. *Deadline:* May 1.

Contact: Ruth Anne Reed, Executive Vice President of Administrative Operations
Patient Advocate Foundation
700 Thimble Shoals Boulevard, Suite 200
Newport News, VA 23606
Phone: 800-532-5274
Fax: 757-873-8999
E-mail: info@patientadvocate.org

PENGUIN PUTNAM, INC.   http://www.penguinputnam.com

SIGNET CLASSIC SCHOLARSHIP ESSAY CONTEST

Contest is open to high school juniors and seniors. Students should submit a two- to three-page double-spaced essay answering one of three possible questions on a designated novel. Entries must be submitted by a high school English teacher. For more information visit http://www.penguinputnam.com/scessay or call 212-366-2377.

Award: Scholarship for use in freshman year; not renewable. *Number:* 5. *Amount:* $1000.

Eligibility Requirements: Applicant must be high school student and planning to enroll or expecting to enroll at an institution or university. Available to U.S. citizens.

Application Requirements: Applicant must enter a contest, essay, references. *Deadline:* April 15.

Contact: Academic Marketing Department
Penguin Putnam, Inc.
375 Hudson Street
New York, NY 10014

PHILLIPS FOUNDATION   http://www.thephillipsfoundation.org

PHILLIPS FOUNDATION RONALD REAGAN FUTURE LEADERS SCHOLARSHIP PROGRAM

The program offers renewable scholarships to college juniors and seniors who demonstrate leadership on behalf of freedom, American values, and constitutional principles. Winners will receive a scholarship for their junior year and may apply for renewal before their senior year.

Award: Scholarship for use in junior or senior years; not renewable. *Number:* 10–20. *Amount:* $2500–$10,000.

Eligibility Requirements: Applicant must be enrolled or expecting to enroll full-time at a two-year or four-year institution or university. Available to U.S. citizens.

Application Requirements: Application, essay, resume, references, transcript. *Deadline:* January 15.

Contact: Jeff Hollingsworth, Assistant Secretary
Phillips Foundation
7811 Montrose Road, Suite 100
Potomac, MD 20854
Phone: 301-340-2100
E-mail: jhollingsworth@phillips.com

POLANKI, POLISH WOMEN'S CULTURAL CLUB   http://www.polanki.org

ARTHUR B. GURDA MEMORIAL AWARD

Award to students of Polish heritage and to non-Polish students studying Polish language, history, society, or culture. Applicants must be college juniors, seniors, or graduate students and must be Wisconsin residents or attend college in Wisconsin. Successful applicants will should have a 3.0 GPA.

Award: Scholarship for use in junior, senior, or graduate years. *Number:* varies. *Amount:* $500–$1000.

Eligibility Requirements: Applicant must be enrolled or expecting to enroll at a four-year institution or university. Available to U.S. citizens.

Application Requirements: Application, transcript. *Deadline:* February 25.

Contact: Susan Mikos
Polanki, Polish Women's Cultural Club
of Milwaukee, Wisconsin, U.S.A.
4160 South 1st Street
PO Box 341458
Milwaukee, WI 53234
Phone: 414-332-1728
E-mail: polanki@polanki.org

EVELYN APPLEYARD MEMORIAL AWARD

Award for students of Polish heritage and to non-Polish students studying Polish language, history, society, or culture. Applicants must be college juniors, seniors, or graduate students and must be Wisconsin residents or attend college in Wisconsin. Successful applicants will usually have a 3.0 GPA.

Award: Scholarship for use in junior, senior, or graduate years. *Number:* varies. *Amount:* $500–$1000.

Eligibility Requirements: Applicant must be enrolled or expecting to enroll at a four-year institution or university. Available to U.S. citizens.

Application Requirements: Application, transcript. *Deadline:* March 1.

Contact: Susan Mikos
Polanki, Polish Women's Cultural Club
of Milwaukee, Wisconsin, U.S.A.
4160 South 1st Street
PO Box 341458
Milwaukee, WI 53234
Phone: 414-332-1728
E-mail: polanki@polanki.org

HARRIET GOSTOMSKI MEMORIAL AWARD

Award to students of Polish heritage and to non-Polish students studying Polish language, history, society, or culture. Applicants must be college juniors, seniors, or graduate students and must be Wisconsin residents or attend college in Wisconsin. Successful applicants will usually have a 3.0 GPA.

Award: Scholarship for use in junior, senior, or graduate years. *Number:* varies. *Amount:* $500–$1000.

Eligibility Requirements: Applicant must be enrolled or expecting to enroll at a four-year institution or university. Available to U.S. citizens.

Application Requirements: Application, transcript. *Deadline:* March 1.

Contact: Susan Mikos
Polanki, Polish Women's Cultural Club
of Milwaukee, Wisconsin, U.S.A.
4160 South 1st Street
PO Box 341458
Milwaukee, WI 53234
Phone: 414-332-1728
E-mail: polanki@polanki.org

JANET DZIADULEWICZ BRANDEN MEMORIAL AWARD

Award to an outstanding student in Polish studies. Applicants must be college juniors, seniors, or graduate students and must be Wisconsin residents or attend college in Wisconsin. Successful applicants will usually have a 3.0 GPA.

Award: Scholarship for use in junior, senior, or graduate years. *Number:* 1. *Amount:* $500–$1000.

Eligibility Requirements: Applicant must be enrolled or expecting to enroll at a four-year institution or university. Available to U.S. citizens.

Application Requirements: Application, transcript. *Deadline:* March 1.

Contact: Susan Mikos
Polanki, Polish Women's Cultural Club
of Milwaukee, Wisconsin, U.S.A.
4160 South 1st Street
PO Box 341458
Milwaukee, WI 53234
Phone: 414-332-1728
E-mail: polanki@polanki.org

MONSIGNOR ALPHONSE S. POPEK MEMORIAL AWARD

Award to students of Polish heritage and to non-Polish students studying Polish language, history, society, or culture. Applicants must be college juniors, seniors, or graduate students and must be Wisconsin residents or attend college in Wisconsin. Successful applicants will usually have a 3.0 GPA.

Award: Scholarship for use in junior, senior, or graduate years. *Number:* varies. *Amount:* $500–$1000.

Eligibility Requirements: Applicant must be enrolled or expecting to enroll at a four-year institution or university. Available to U.S. citizens.

Application Requirements: Application, transcript. *Deadline:* March 1.

Contact: Susan Mikos
Polanki, Polish Women's Cultural Club
of Milwaukee, Wisconsin, U.S.A.
4160 South 1st Street
PO Box 341458
Milwaukee, WI 53234
Phone: 414-332-1728
E-mail: polanki@polanki.org

POLANKI COLLEGE ACHIEVEMENT AWARDS AND MEMORIALS

Award to students of Polish heritage and to non-Polish students studying Polish language, history, society, or culture. Applicants must be college juniors, seniors, or graduate students and must be Wisconsin residents or attend college in Wisconsin. Successful applicants will usually have a 3.0 GPA.

Award: Scholarship for use in junior, senior, or graduate years. *Number:* varies. *Amount:* $500–$1000.

Eligibility Requirements: Applicant must be enrolled or expecting to enroll at a four-year institution or university. Available to U.S. citizens.

Application Requirements: Application, transcript. *Deadline:* March 1.

Contact: Susan Mikos
Polanki, Polish Women's Cultural Club
of Milwaukee, Wisconsin, U.S.A.
4160 South 1st Street
PO Box 341458
Milwaukee, WI 53234
Phone: 414-332-1728
E-mail: polanki@polanki.org

STANLEY F. AND HELEN BALCERZAK AWARD

Award to a student of Polish heritage who is an outstanding student in any field or to a non-Polish student studying Polish language, history, society, or culture. Applicants must be college juniors, seniors, or graduate students and must be Wisconsin residents or attend college in Wisconsin. Successful applicants will usually have a GPA of 3.0.

Award: Scholarship for use in junior, senior, or graduate years. *Number:* 1. *Amount:* $500–$1000.

Eligibility Requirements: Applicant must be enrolled or expecting to enroll at a four-year institution or university. Available to U.S. citizens.

Application Requirements: Application, transcript. *Deadline:* March 1.

Contact: Susan Mikos
Polanki, Polish Women's Cultural Club
of Milwaukee, Wisconsin, U.S.A.
4160 South 1st Street
PO Box 341458
Milwaukee, WI 53234
Phone: 414-332-1728
E-mail: polanki@polanki.org

POLISH WOMEN'S ALLIANCE   http://www.pwaa.org

POLISH WOMEN'S ALLIANCE SCHOLARSHIP

Scholarships are given to members of the Polish Women's Alliance of America who have been in good standing for five years. Recipients of the awards must remain members of the PWA of A for at least seven years after school. The deadline is March 15. Full-time students may apply beginning with the second year of undergraduate study.

Award: Scholarship for use in sophomore, junior, or senior years; renewable. *Number:* 5. *Amount:* $1000.

Eligibility Requirements: Applicant must be enrolled or expecting to enroll full-time at a two-year or four-year or technical institution or university. Available to U.S. citizens.

Application Requirements: Application, essay, photo, transcript. *Deadline:* March 15.

MISCELLANEOUS CRITERIA

Polish Women's Alliance (continued)

Contact: Ms. Sharon Zago, Vice President and Scholarship Chairman
Polish Women's Alliance
205 South Northwest Highway
Park Ridge, IL 60068
Phone: 847-384-1208
E-mail: vpres@pwaa.org

PRESIDENTIAL FREEDOM SCHOLARSHIP   http://www.nationalservice.org

PRESIDENTIAL FREEDOM SCHOLARSHIP

The Presidential Freedom Scholarship program is designed to highlight and promote service and citizenship by students and to recognize students for their leadership in those areas. Each high school in the county may select up to 2 students to receive a $1000 scholarship. With funds appropriated by Congress, the Corporation for National and Community Service provides $500, which must be matched with $500 secured by the school from the community.

Award: Scholarship for use in freshman year; not renewable. *Number:* 500–1000. *Amount:* $500.

Eligibility Requirements: Applicant must be high school student and planning to enroll or expecting to enroll full or part-time at a two-year or four-year or technical institution or university. Available to U.S. citizens.

Application Requirements: Application, essay. *Deadline:* May 12.

Contact: Scholarship Staff
Presidential Freedom Scholarship
1150 Connecticut Avenue, NW, Suite 1100
Washington, DC 20036
Phone: 866-291-7700
E-mail: info@studentservicescholarship.org

PUERTO RICO DEPARTMENT OF EDUCATION

ROBERT C. BYRD HONORS SCHOLARSHIP-PUERTO RICO

This grant is sponsored by the Puerto Rico Department of Education and is granted to gifted students. These are students chosen from public and private schools who graduate from high school and are admitted to an accredited university in Puerto Rico or in the United States and who show promise to complete a college career. It is granted for a period of four years if the student maintains a satisfactory academic progress. Must be a U.S. citizen and rank in the upper quarter of class or have a minimum 3.5 GPA.

Award: Scholarship for use in freshman, sophomore, junior, or senior years; renewable. *Number:* 74–85. *Amount:* up to $1500.

Eligibility Requirements: Applicant must be high school student and planning to enroll or expecting to enroll full-time at a four-year institution or university. Applicant must have 3.5 GPA or higher. Available to U.S. citizens.

Application Requirements: Application, financial need analysis, interview, portfolio, references, test scores, transcript. *Deadline:* May 30.

Contact: Marta Colon-Rivera, Coordinator
Puerto Rico Department of Education
PO Box 19900
San Juan, PR 00910-1900
Phone: 787-759-8313
Fax: 787-758-2281
E-mail: hernandez_eli@de.gobierno.pr

PUSH FOR EXCELLENCE   http://www.pushexcel.org

ORA LEE SANDERS SCHOLARSHIP

Renewable awards for undergraduate or trade/technical study. Full time or part time, minimum 2.5 GPA. Write to Push for Excellence for further information and application forms. Deadline is April.

Award: Scholarship for use in freshman, sophomore, junior, or senior years; renewable. *Number:* varies. *Amount:* up to $1000.

Eligibility Requirements: Applicant must be enrolled or expecting to enroll full or part-time at a two-year or four-year or technical institution or university. Applicant must have 2.5 GPA or higher. Available to U.S. citizens.

Application Requirements: Application, essay, references, self-addressed stamped envelope, transcript. *Deadline:* April.

Contact: Renee Thomas
Push for Excellence
930 E 50th Street
Chicago, IL 60615
Phone: 773-373-3366
Fax: 773-373-4105

QUAKER CHEMICAL FOUNDATION (THE)   http://www.quakerchem.com

QUAKER CHEMICAL FOUNDATION SCHOLARSHIPS

Award: Scholarship for use in freshman, sophomore, junior, or senior years.

Eligibility Requirements: Applicant must be enrolled or expecting to enroll at an institution or university.

Contact: Katherine Coughenour, Chair
Quaker Chemical Foundation (The)
901 Hector Street
Conshohocken, PA 19428-0809
Phone: 610-832-4301
Fax: 610-832-4494

R.O.S.E. FUND   http://www.rosefund.org

R.O.S.E. FUND SCHOLARSHIP PROGRAM

The ROSE scholarship program acknowledges women who are survivors of violence or abuse. Primarily awarded to women who have successfully completed one year of undergraduate studies. Scholarships are for tuition and expenses at any accredited college or university in New England. Must be U.S. resident. Deadlines are June 17 for the fall semester, December 3 for the spring semester.

Award: Scholarship for use in freshman, sophomore, junior, or senior years; renewable. *Number:* 10–15. *Amount:* $1000–$10,000.

Eligibility Requirements: Applicant must be age 18; enrolled or expecting to enroll full or part-time at a two-year or four-year institution or university and female. Applicant must have 2.5 GPA or higher. Available to U.S. citizens.

Application Requirements: Application, autobiography, essay, financial need analysis, interview, references, test scores, transcript. *Deadline:* varies.

Contact: Alison Justus, Director of Programs
R.O.S.E. Fund
175 Federal Street, Suite 455
Boston, MA 02110
Phone: 617-482-5400 Ext. 11
Fax: 617-482-3443
E-mail: ajustus@rosefund.org

RAILWAY SUPPLY INSTITUTE   http://www.rsiweb.org

RSI UNDERGRADUATE SCHOLARSHIP PROGRAM

Scholarship available to a full-time student enrolled in a four- or five-year program leading to a bachelor's degree. Applicants must be age 22 or under and be the dependent son, daughter, grandson or granddaughter of a railroad employee who is a member of one of the Mechanical Associations listed in the Web site. For application and association list go to: http://www.rsiweb.org/scholarship/

Award: Scholarship for use in freshman, sophomore, junior, or senior years. *Amount:* up to $3000.

Eligibility Requirements: Applicant must be age 22 or under and enrolled or expecting to enroll at a four-year institution or university. Available to U.S. and non-U.S. citizens.

Application Requirements: Application, essay, resume, references, transcript. *Deadline:* March 17.

Contact: RSI Scholarship
Railway Supply Institute
29W 140 Butterfield Road
Suite 103-A
Warrenville, IL 60555
Phone: 630-393-0106
Fax: 630-393-0108
E-mail: rsupplya@aol.com

RESOURCE CENTER   http://www.resourcecenterscholarshipinfo.com

HEATHER JOY MEMORIAL SCHOLARSHIP

One-time award of up to $1000 given to students in honor of Heather Joy, who lost her young life due to financial needs. Available to part- or full-time students, enrolled in technical school, college or university. Deadlines are May 1 and November 1. Recipient selection will be based on a 250-word original essay and referral letters. Applications are available via the Web site only: http://www.resourcecenterscholarshipinfo.com.

Award: Scholarship for use in freshman, sophomore, junior, senior, graduate, or postgraduate years; not renewable. *Number:* 1–10. *Amount:* $50–$1000.

Eligibility Requirements: Applicant must be enrolled or expecting to enroll full or part-time at a two-year or four-year or technical institution or university. Available to U.S. and non-U.S. citizens.

Application Requirements: Application, essay, references, self-addressed stamped envelope, transcript. *Fee:* $5. *Deadline:* varies.

Contact: Heather Joy Memorial Scholarship
Resource Center
16362 Wilson Boulevard
Masaryktown, FL 34604-7335
E-mail: info@resourcecentershholarshipinfo.com

RHODE ISLAND FOUNDATION   http://www.rifoundation.org

JAMES J. BURNS AND C.A. HAYNES SCHOLARSHIP

Award for students enrolled in a textile program at the following schools: Dartmouth, Philadelphia University, North Carolina State, Clemson, Georgia Tech, Auburn. Preference given to children of members of National Association of Textile Supervisors.

Award: Scholarship for use in sophomore, junior, or senior years; not renewable. *Number:* 1–2. *Amount:* up to $1000.

Eligibility Requirements: Applicant must be enrolled or expecting to enroll full-time at a two-year or four-year institution or university. Available to U.S. citizens.

Application Requirements: Application. *Deadline:* varies.

Contact: Libby Monahan, Scholarship Coordinator
Rhode Island Foundation
1 Union Station
Providence, RI 02903
Phone: 401-274-4564
Fax: 401-272-1359
E-mail: libbym@rifoundation.org

RONALD MCDONALD HOUSE CHARITIES   http://www.rmhc.org

RMHC/HISPANIC AMERICAN COMMITMENT TO EDUCATIONAL RESOURCES SCHOLARSHIP PROGRAM

Award: Scholarship for use in freshman year.

Eligibility Requirements: Applicant must be enrolled or expecting to enroll at an institution or university.

Contact: Palmer Moody, Director, RMHC
Ronald McDonald House Charities
1 Kroc Drive
Department 014
Oak Brook, IL 60523
Phone: 630-623-7048
E-mail: palmer.moody@med.com

ROOTHBERT FUND, INC.   http://www.roothbertfund.org

ROOTHBERT FUND, INC. SCHOLARSHIP

Award for those pursuing undergraduate degree or higher in U.S. institution and satisfying academic standards. Non-U.S. citizens must be living in U.S. must travel at own expense to interview in Philadelphia, New Haven, or Washington, D.C. Deadline: February 1. Provide SASE when requesting an application.

Award: Scholarship for use in freshman, sophomore, junior, senior, or graduate years; renewable. *Number:* 20. *Amount:* $2000–$3000.

Eligibility Requirements: Applicant must be enrolled or expecting to enroll full-time at a two-year or four-year or technical institution or university. Available to U.S. citizens.

Application Requirements: Application, autobiography, essay, financial need analysis, interview, photo, references, self-addressed stamped envelope, test scores, transcript. *Deadline:* February 1.

Contact: Roothbert Fund, Inc.
475 Riverside Drive, Room 252
New York, NY 10115
Phone: 212-870-3116

ROPAGE GROUP LLC   http://www.ropage-group.com

PATRICIA M. MCNAMARA MEMORIAL SCHOLARSHIP

Scholarship open to students who are already attending college or will be attending college within a year of the deadline. Students must utilize the online form to submit the scholarship application and essay: http://www.patricias-scholarship.org. Deadline is May 31.

Award: Scholarship for use in freshman, sophomore, junior, senior, graduate, or postgraduate years; not renewable. *Number:* 1. *Amount:* $5000.

Eligibility Requirements: Applicant must be enrolled or expecting to enroll full or part-time at a two-year or four-year or technical institution or university. Available to U.S. and non-U.S. citizens.

Application Requirements: Application, essay. *Deadline:* May 31.

Contact: Ms. Paula Hart
Ropage Group LLC
8877 North 107th Avenue, Suite 302, PO Box 287
Peoria, AZ 85345
E-mail: paula@patricias-scholarship.org

SACRAMENTO BEE   http://www.sacbee.com

SCHOLARSHIP FOR DEPENDENT CHILDREN OF BEE EMPLOYEES

Scholarship for graduating high school senior accepted at an accredited school of higher education who is a dependent child of a Bee's employee.

Award: Scholarship for use in freshman year. *Amount:* $1000.

Eligibility Requirements: Applicant must be high school student and planning to enroll or expecting to enroll at a four-year institution or university. Available to U.S. citizens.

Application Requirements: Application, essay, resume, transcript. *Deadline:* January 31.

Contact: Cathy Rodriguez, Public Affairs Representative
Sacramento Bee
PO Box 15779
Sacramento, CA 95852
Phone: 916-321-1880
Fax: 916-321-1783
E-mail: crodriguez@sacbee.com

SALLIE MAE FUND   http://www.thesalliemaefund.org

SALLIE MAE 911 EDUCATION FUND LOAN RELIEF

Enables spouses, same-sex partners and co-borrowers of those killed or totally disabled in the September 11, 2001 terrorist attacks on the United States to pay off their student loans that meet the eligibility requirements that can be found on the web at http://www.thesalliemaefund.org, and are owned or serviced by Sallie Mae. Also available to those who were permanently disabled by the September 11 terrorist attacks and hold a private education student loan owned or serviced by Sallie Mae.

Award: Forgivable loan for use in sophomore, junior, or senior years; not renewable. *Amount:* up to $5000.

Sallie Mae Fund (continued)

Eligibility Requirements: Applicant must be enrolled or expecting to enroll at a two-year or four-year or technical institution or university. Available to U.S. citizens.

Application Requirements: Application, supporting documents. *Deadline:* Continuous.

Contact: Kenny Emson, Sallie Mae 911 Education Fund Scholarship Program, c/o The Community Foundation For the National Capital Region
Sallie Mae Fund
1201 15th Street, NW, Suite 420
Washington, DC 20005

SALLIE MAE 911 EDUCATION FUND SCHOLARSHIP PROGRAM

Provides scholarships to children of those lost or permanently disabled as a result of the terrorist attacks on America, including children of those police, fire safety or medical personnel who were killed or suffered debilitating casualties in their attempt to rescue those who were victims of the attacks. Eligible children would be able to pursue postsecondary education where they reside. Applicant must already be enrolled full time in an approved postsecondary education program. Applications available at http://www. thesalliemaefund.org, http://www.wiredscholar.com or at the financial aid office of their school.

Award: Scholarship for use in freshman year; renewable. *Amount:* up to $2500.

Eligibility Requirements: Applicant must be enrolled or expecting to enroll full-time at a two-year or four-year institution or university. Available to U.S. citizens.

Application Requirements: Application, financial need analysis, proof of death or disability of parent.

Contact: Sallie Mae 911 Education Fund Scholarship Program, c/o The Community Foundation For the National Capital Region
Sallie Mae Fund
1201 15th Street, NW, Suite 420
Washington, DC 20005

SALLIE MAE FUND SCHOLARSHIPS

Scholarship renewals available for students with a combined family income of $35,000 or less. Must be a prior scholarship recipient enrolled as full-time undergraduate or graduate student at an approved, accredited institution.

Award: Scholarship for use in freshman, sophomore, junior, senior, or graduate years; renewable. *Number:* varies. *Amount:* $500–$2000.

Eligibility Requirements: Applicant must be enrolled or expecting to enroll full-time at a two-year or four-year institution or university. Available to U.S. citizens.

Application Requirements: Application, financial need analysis, transcript.

Contact: c/o Scholarship America
Sallie Mae Fund
One Scholarship Way, PO Box 297
Saint Peter, MN 56082
Phone: 507-931-1682

SALLIE MAE FUND UNMET NEED SCHOLARSHIP PROGRAM

Award: Scholarship for use in freshman, sophomore, junior, or senior years.

Eligibility Requirements: Applicant must be enrolled or expecting to enroll at an institution or university.

Contact: Sallie Mae Fund
12061 Bluemont Way
Reston, VA 20190
Phone: 888-272-5543
Fax: 800-848-1949

SAMUEL HUNTINGTON FUND

SAMUEL HUNTINGTON PUBLIC SERVICE AWARD

Award provides a $10,000 stipend to a graduating college senior to perform a one-year public service project anywhere in the world immediately following graduation. Proposals are requested with application. Proposal must be written in 1000 words or less. It may deal with any activity that furthers the public good. Awards will be based on quality of proposal, academic record, and other personal achievements. Semi-finalists will be interviewed.

Award: Grant for use in senior, or graduate years; not renewable. *Number:* 1–3. *Amount:* $10,000.

Eligibility Requirements: Applicant must be enrolled or expecting to enroll at a four-year institution or university. Available to U.S. and non-U.S. citizens.

Application Requirements: Application, essay, financial need analysis, resume, references, transcript. *Deadline:* February 15.

Contact: Amy F. Stacy, Legal Assistant
Samuel Huntington Fund
25 Research Drive
Westborough, MA 01582
Phone: 508-389-3390
Fax: 508-389-2463
E-mail: amy.stacy@us.ngrid.com

SAN DIEGO COUNTY FORD DEALERS AND FORD MOTOR COMPANY   http://www.salutetoeducation.com/

SALUTE TO EDUCATION SCHOLARSHIP

Numerous scholarships are given to graduating high school seniors in San Diego County, CA. Any student from an accredited public or private high school in the county may apply through their high school guidance office, regardless of their GPA. Students apply under various academic categories, arts, and athletics and are judged on personal achievement and school/ community service.

Award: Scholarship for use in freshman year. *Amount:* $1000.

Eligibility Requirements: Applicant must be high school student and planning to enroll or expecting to enroll full-time at an institution or university. Available to U.S. citizens.

Application Requirements: Application, essay. *Deadline:* varies.

Contact: LeAnn Eldridge
San Diego County Ford Dealers and Ford Motor Company
4300 El Cajon Boulevard
San Diego, CA 92105
Phone: 619-521-2404
Fax: 619-283-1327
E-mail: salute2education@aol.com

SARA LAZARUS MEMORIAL SCHOLARSHIP   http://www.saralazarus.org

SARA LAZARUS MEMORIAL SCHOLARSHIP

Annual, non-renewable scholarship of $500 to recognize individuals who share a bond with a role model/mentor outside of their family, and best describe this person and the impact he/she has had on their life in a one-page essay. Application form available on the organization's Web site.

Award: Scholarship for use in freshman, sophomore, junior, senior, or graduate years; not renewable. *Amount:* $500.

Eligibility Requirements: Applicant must be enrolled or expecting to enroll full or part-time at a two-year or four-year institution or university. Available to U.S. citizens.

Application Requirements: Application, essay. *Deadline:* March 31.

Contact: Lia Kettenis
E-mail: sara_lararus@yahoo.com

SCHOLARSHIP WORKSHOP LLC   http://www.scholarshipworkshop.com

LEADING THE FUTURE SCHOLARSHIP

The "Leading the Future" Scholarship is designed to elevate students' consciousness about their future and their role in helping others once they receive a college degree and become established in a community. It is open to U.S. residents only who are high school seniors or college undergraduates at any level. Students must visit http://www.scholarshipworkshop.com for application information. Application fee is $3. Fee should be sent with completed applications, not to request an application. Send SASE for application requests.

Award: Scholarship for use in freshman, sophomore, junior, or senior years; not renewable. *Number:* 1–3.

Eligibility Requirements: Applicant must be enrolled or expecting to enroll full-time at a four-year institution or university. Available to U.S. citizens.

Application Requirements: Application, essay, self-addressed stamped envelope. *Fee:* $3. *Deadline:* March 1.

Contact: Scholarship Coordinator
Scholarship Workshop LLC
PO Box 176
Centreville, VA 20122
Phone: 703-579-4245
Fax: 703-579-4245
E-mail: scholars@scholarshipworkshop.com

RAGINS/BRASWELL NATIONAL SCHOLARSHIP

The scholarship is available to high school seniors, undergraduate, and graduate students who attend The Scholarship Workshop presentation or an online class given by Marianne Ragins. Award is based on use of techniques taught in the workshop or class, application, essay, leadership, extracurricular activities, achievements, and community responsibility. Interested students should visit http://www.scholarshipworkshop.com for more details. Scholarship amounts vary.

Award: Scholarship for use in freshman, sophomore, junior, senior, or graduate years; not renewable. *Number:* 1–3.

Eligibility Requirements: Applicant must be enrolled or expecting to enroll full-time at a four-year institution or university. Available to U.S. citizens.

Application Requirements: Application, essay. *Deadline:* April 30.

Contact: Scholarship Coordinator
Scholarship Workshop LLC
PO Box 176
Centreville, VA 20122
Phone: 703-579-4245
Fax: 703-579-4245
E-mail: scholars@scholarshipworkshop.com

SECOND MARINE DIVISION ASSOCIATION   http://www.2marine.com

BEIRUT RELIEF FUND SCHOLARSHIPS

Award: Scholarship for use in freshman, sophomore, junior, or senior years.

Eligibility Requirements: Applicant must be enrolled or expecting to enroll at an institution or university.

Contact: C. Van Horne, Executive Secretary
Second Marine Division Association
PO Box 8180
Camp LeJeune, NC 28547-8180
Phone: 910-451-3167
Fax: 910-451-3167

SICKLE CELL DISEASE ASSOCIATION OF AMERICA, INC.   http://www.sicklecelldisease.org

KERMIT B. NASH, JR. ACADEMIC SCHOLARSHIP

Scholarship is only for individuals with sickle cell disease. Must be a graduating senior intending to attend an accredited four-year college or university. Must be U.S. citizen or a permanent resident of the U.S. Awarded in four yearly increments of $5000.

Award: Scholarship for use in freshman year; renewable. *Number:* 1. *Amount:* $5000–$20,000.

Eligibility Requirements: Applicant must be high school student and planning to enroll or expecting to enroll full-time at a four-year institution or university. Applicant must have 3.0 GPA or higher. Available to U.S. citizens.

Application Requirements: Application, essay, interview, photo, references, self-addressed stamped envelope, test scores, transcript. *Deadline:* May 31.

Contact: SCDAA Scholarship Selection Committee
Sickle Cell Disease Association of America, Inc.
200 Corporate Pointe, Suite 495
Culver City, CA 90230-8727
Phone: 310-216-6363
Fax: 310-215-3722
E-mail: scdaa@sicklecelldisease.org

SIGMA CHI FOUNDATION   http://www.sigmachi.org

GENERAL SCHOLARSHIP GRANTS

Award: Scholarship for use in sophomore, junior, or senior years.

Eligibility Requirements: Applicant must be enrolled or expecting to enroll at an institution or university.

Contact: Chris Mashio, Associate Director of Education
Sigma Chi Foundation
PO Box 469
1714 Hinman Avenue
Evanston, IL 60201-0469
Phone: 847-869-3655
Fax: 847-869-4906
E-mail: chris.mashio@sigmachi.org

SIMON YOUTH FOUNDATION   http://simonyouth.scholarshipamerica.org

SIMON YOUTH FOUNDATION COMMUNITY SCHOLARSHIP PROGRAM

Scholarship available to any high school senior, living in a community that hosts a Simon property, who plans to enroll in a full-time undergraduate course of study at an accredited two- or four-year college, university, or vocational/technical school.

Award: Scholarship for use in freshman year. *Amount:* up to $1200.

Eligibility Requirements: Applicant must be enrolled or expecting to enroll at a two-year or four-year or technical institution or university. Available to U.S. citizens.

Application Requirements: Application, financial need analysis, test scores, transcript. *Deadline:* January 3.

Contact: Scholarship America, C/o SYF Scholarship Programs
Simon Youth Foundation
PO Box 297
Saint Peter, MN 56082
Phone: 800-537-4180

SIMON YOUTH FOUNDATION ERC SCHOLARSHIP PROGRAM

Scholarship for Education Resource Center students. Applicants must be graduating ERC students who plan to enroll in a full-time undergraduate course of study at an accredited two- or four-year college, university, or vocational/technical school.

Award: Scholarship for use in freshman year. *Amount:* $1000–$2000.

Eligibility Requirements: Applicant must be enrolled or expecting to enroll at a two-year or four-year or technical institution or university. Available to U.S. citizens.

Application Requirements: Application, test scores, transcript. *Deadline:* January 3.

Contact: Simon Youth Foundation
c/o Scholarship Management Services, Scholarship America
One Scholarship Way, PO Box 297
St. Peter, MN 56082

SINFONIA FOUNDATION   http://www.sinfonia.org

DELTA IOTA ALUMNI SCHOLARSHIP

Scholarship for the collegiate members and chapters of Sinfonia. Minimum 3.3 Cumulative GPA required. Must have been a collegiate member in good standing for at least 2 semesters. Must submit the names and phone numbers of at least 3 references.

Award: Scholarship for use in freshman, sophomore, junior, senior, or graduate years. *Amount:* up to $500.

Sinfonia Foundation (continued)

Eligibility Requirements: Applicant must be enrolled or expecting to enroll full-time at a four-year institution or university. Available to U.S. citizens.

Application Requirements: Application, essay. *Deadline:* May 1.

Contact: Cheri Faith Spicer, Administrative Coordinator
Sinfonia Foundation
10600 Old State Road
Evansville, IN 47711-1399
Phone: 812-867-2433
E-mail: lyrecrest@sinfonia.org

SIR EDWARD YOUDE MEMORIAL FUND COUNCIL
http://www.sfaa.gov.hk

SIR EDWARD YOUDE MEMORIAL SCHOLARSHIPS FOR OVERSEAS STUDIES

This program is for outstanding students, of any citizenship, who are permanent residents of Hong Kong, for overseas undergraduate studies. The award is not restricted to any specific academic or career area, but cannot be used for medical studies. Upon return from overseas studies, students are expected to contribute significantly to the development of Hong Kong. For further details visit Web site: http://www.info.gov.hk/sfaa

Award: Scholarship for use in freshman, sophomore, junior, or senior years; renewable. *Number:* varies. *Amount:* up to $29,744.

Eligibility Requirements: Applicant must be enrolled or expecting to enroll full-time at an institution or university. Available to U.S. citizens.

Application Requirements: Application, applicant must enter a contest, autobiography, essay, interview, photo, resume, references, test scores, transcript. *Deadline:* September 30.

Contact: Y. K. Wong, Council Secretariat
Sir Edward Youde Memorial Fund Council
Room 1217, 12/F., Cheung Sha Wan Government Offices
303 Cheung Sha Wan Road
Kowloon
Hong Kong
Phone: 852 2150 6103
Fax: 852 2511 2720
E-mail: sgl3@sfaa.gov.hk

SKILLSUSA
http://www.skillsusa.org

INTERNATIONAL SKILLSUSA DEGREE SCHOLARSHIP

Scholarship for students who successfully receive their degree. To qualify, all candidates must submit a letter of application for the scholarship within 45 days of receipt of the degree. The scholarship candidate must include with the application copies of receipts for lodging, meals, travel, and preparation of the presentation.

Award: Scholarship for use in senior year. *Amount:* up to $1000.

Eligibility Requirements: Applicant must be enrolled or expecting to enroll full-time at a four-year institution or university. Available to U.S. citizens.

Application Requirements: Application, references. *Deadline:* May 1.

Contact: Karen Perrino
SkillsUSA
PO Box 3000
Leesburg, VA 20177-0300
Phone: 703-737-0610
E-mail: kperrino@skillsusa.org

NTHS SKILLSUSA SCHOLARSHIP

NTHS will award two $1,000 scholarships to SkillsUSA members at the 2006 SkillsUSA National Leadership Conference. One scholarship will be awarded to a high school member, and one scholarship will be awarded to a college/postsecondary member. Students must be active, dues-paying members of both SkillsUSA and NTHS.

Award: Scholarship for use in freshman, sophomore, junior, or senior years. *Number:* 2. *Amount:* $1000.

Eligibility Requirements: Applicant must be enrolled or expecting to enroll full-time at an institution or university. Available to U.S. citizens.

Application Requirements: Application, references. *Deadline:* March 1.

Contact: NTHS Scholarship Program
SkillsUSA
PO Box 3000
Leesburg, VA 20176

SKILLSUSA ALUMNI & FRIENDS MERIT SCHOLARSHIP

Scholarship of $1000 recognizes qualities of leadership, commitment to community service, improving the image of career and technical education, and improving the image of his/her chosen occupation.

Award: Scholarship for use in freshman year. *Amount:* up to $1000.

Eligibility Requirements: Applicant must be enrolled or expecting to enroll full-time at an institution or university. Available to U.S. citizens.

Application Requirements: Application, references. *Deadline:* June 15.

Contact: Chris Powell
SkillsUSA
PO Box 3000
Leesburg, VA 20177-0300
Phone: 703-737-0621
E-mail: cpowell@skillsusa.org

SLOVENIAN WOMEN'S UNION OF AMERICA
http://www.swua.org/

CONTINUING EDUCATION AWARD

$500 will be awarded to four applicants to continue or update their education. Applicant must be an active participant of the Slovenian Women's Union for the past three years prior to applying for an award. Deadline is March 1.

Award: Scholarship for use in freshman, sophomore, junior, senior, or graduate years; not renewable. *Number:* 4. *Amount:* $500.

Eligibility Requirements: Applicant must be enrolled or expecting to enroll full or part-time at a two-year or four-year or technical institution or university and female. Available to U.S. and non-U.S. citizens.

Application Requirements: Application, autobiography, essay, financial need analysis, photo, resume, references, test scores, transcript. *Deadline:* March 1.

Contact: Mary H. Turvey, Director
Slovenian Women's Union of America
52 Oakridge Drive
Marquette, MI 49855
Phone: 906-249-4288
E-mail: mturvey@aol.com

SLOVENIAN WOMEN'S UNION OF AMERICA SCHOLARSHIP PROGRAM

One-time award for full-time study only. Deadline is March 1. Applicant must have been an active participant or member of Slovenian Women's Union for past three years. Essay, transcripts of grades, letters of recommendation from principal/teacher and SWU branch officer required. Financial need form, photo, civic, church activities information required. Open to high school seniors.

Award: Scholarship for use in sophomore, junior, or senior years; not renewable. *Number:* 5. *Amount:* $1000–$2000.

Eligibility Requirements: Applicant must be enrolled or expecting to enroll full-time at a two-year or four-year institution or university and female. Available to U.S. and non-U.S. citizens.

Application Requirements: Application, autobiography, essay, financial need analysis, photo, resume, references, test scores, transcript. *Deadline:* March 1.

Contact: Mary Turvey, Director
Slovenian Women's Union of America
52 Oakridge Drive
Marquette, MI 49855
Phone: 906-249-4288
E-mail: mturvey@aol.com

SOCIETY FOR ADVANCEMENT OF CHICANOS AND NATIVE AMERICANS IN SCIENCE (SACNAS)
http://www.sacnas.org

SACNAS FINANCIAL AID: LODGING AND TRAVEL AWARD

Undergraduate and graduate students are encouraged to apply for lodging and travel to attend the SACNAS National Conference. The conference offers students the opportunity to be mentored, to present their research, attend scientific symposiums in all science disciplines, and professional development sessions to enhance their educational careers. Please refer to Web site for more information and application: http://www.sacnas.org

Award: Scholarship for use in freshman, sophomore, junior, senior, or graduate years; not renewable. *Number:* 400–550. *Amount:* $800–$1000.

Eligibility Requirements: Applicant must be enrolled or expecting to enroll full or part-time at a two-year or four-year or technical institution or university. Available to U.S. citizens.

Application Requirements: Application, essay, references, current enrollment verification. *Deadline:* November 18.

Contact: Rosalina Aranda, Student Program Manager
Society for Advancement of Chicanos and Native Americans in Science (SACNAS)
333 Front Street
Suite 104
Santa Cruz, CA 95060
Phone: 831-459-0170 Ext. 224
Fax: 831-459-0194
E-mail: rosalina@sacnas.org

SOCIETY FOR THE PRESERVATION OF ENGLISH LANGUAGE AND LITERATURE (SPELL)
http://www.spellorg.com

STEPHEN J. MANHARD SCHOLARSHIP-ESSAY CONTEST

Applicant must submit 500 word essay related to the proposition that standards of good English usage are still important in today's cultural environment. Applicant must be high school senior. First prize receives $1000, second place receives $300, and third place will receive $200. Applicant must submit very brief biographical information with his or her essay. Please see Web site for further details: http://www.mindspring.com/~spellorg

Award: Prize for use in freshman year; not renewable. *Number:* 3. *Amount:* $200–$1000.

Eligibility Requirements: Applicant must be high school student and planning to enroll or expecting to enroll full or part-time at an institution or university. Available to U.S. and non-U.S. citizens.

Application Requirements: Application, applicant must enter a contest, autobiography, essay. *Deadline:* March 1.

Contact: James Wallace, President
Society for the Preservation of English Language and Literature (SPELL)
PO Box 321
Braselton, GA 30517
Fax: 770-868-0578
E-mail: spellgang@juno.com

SOROPTIMIST INTERNATIONAL OF THE AMERICAS
http://www.soroptimist.org

SOROPTIMIST WOMEN'S OPPORTUNITY AWARD

Applicant must be a woman who is head of household and working toward vocational or undergraduate degree. Recipients are chosen on the basis of financial need as well as a statement of clear career goals. One-time award of $10,000. Send a self-addressed stamped business-size envelope with 60 cents postage for information, or download the application from the Web site. Must be a resident of SIA's member countries and territories.

Award: Prize for use in freshman, sophomore, junior, or senior years; not renewable. *Number:* 3. *Amount:* $10,000.

Eligibility Requirements: Applicant must be enrolled or expecting to enroll full or part-time at a two-year or four-year or technical institution or university and female. Available to U.S. and non-U.S. citizens.

Application Requirements: Application, essay, financial need analysis, references, self-addressed stamped envelope. *Deadline:* December 1.

Contact: Award Chairperson
Soroptimist International of the Americas
1709 Spruce Street
Philadelphia, PA 19103-6103
E-mail: siahq@soroptimist.org

SOUTH CAROLINA DIVISION OF VETERANS AFFAIRS
http://www.govoepp.state.sc.us/vetaff.htm

EDUCATIONAL ASSISTANCE FOR CERTAIN WAR VETERAN'S DEPENDENTS-SOUTH CAROLINA

Award: Scholarship for use in freshman, sophomore, junior, or senior years.

Eligibility Requirements: Applicant must be enrolled or expecting to enroll at an institution or university.

Contact: Lauren Hugg, Free Tuition Assistant
South Carolina Division of Veterans Affairs
1205 Pendleton Street, Suite 369
South Carolina Governor's Office
Columbia, SC 29201
Phone: 803-255-4317
Fax: 803-255-4257
E-mail: va@oepp.sc.gov

SOUTH CAROLINA POLICE CORPS
http://www.citadel.edu

SOUTH CAROLINA POLICE CORPS SCHOLARSHIP

Tuition reimbursement scholarship available to a full time student of an U.S. accredited college. Must agree to serve for four years on community patrol with a participating South Carolina police or sheriff's department. Up to $7500 per academic year with a limit of $30,000 per student.

Award: Scholarship for use in freshman, sophomore, junior, senior, or graduate years; renewable. *Number:* 20. *Amount:* $7500–$30,000.

Eligibility Requirements: Applicant must be enrolled or expecting to enroll full-time at a four-year institution or university. Available to U.S. citizens.

Application Requirements: Application, autobiography, driver's license, essay, interview, references, test scores, transcript. *Deadline:* varies.

Contact: Bryan C. Jones, Community Action Team
South Carolina Police Corps
5623 Two Notch Road
Columbia, SC 29223
Phone: 803-865-4486
E-mail: Bryan.jones@hcahealthcare.com

SOUTH CAROLINA STATE EMPLOYEES ASSOCIATION
http://www.SCSEA.com

ANNE A. AGNEW SCHOLARSHIP

Nonrenewable scholarship for full-time study only. Must be a sophomore, junior, senior, graduate or postgraduate student. Application forms are available after January 1 of each year; completed applications must be received by April 1. Please do not submit applications between April 1 and January 1, as they will not be accepted.

Award: Scholarship for use in sophomore, junior, senior, graduate, or postgraduate years; not renewable. *Number:* 3. *Amount:* $1000.

Eligibility Requirements: Applicant must be enrolled or expecting to enroll full-time at a four-year institution or university. Available to U.S. and non-U.S. citizens.

Application Requirements: Application, essay, financial need analysis, transcript. *Deadline:* April 1.

Contact: Broadus Jamerson, Executive Director
South Carolina State Employees Association
PO Box 8447
Columbia, SC 29202
Phone: 803-765-0680
Fax: 803-779-6558
E-mail: scsea@scsea.com

SOUTH DAKOTA INVESTMENT COUNCIL
http://www.southdakota529.com/scholarship.html

SOUTH DAKOTA SCHOLARSHIP PROGRAM

One-time $2000 awards to high school seniors. Recipients will be chosen on the basis of their ACT score (minimum of 27) with their GPA used as a tiebreaker and the date the application is received as final tiebreaker, if needed. Qualifying applicants must be on track to complete the Regent Scholar curriculum by graduation. To maintain renewal eligibility if renewal is

South Dakota Investment Council (continued)

offered, a student shall maintain a full course load each consecutive semester starting in the fall of 2006 and maintain a minimum cumulative GPA of 3.0 at each year end.

Award: Scholarship for use in freshman, sophomore, junior, or senior years; renewable. *Amount:* $2000.

Eligibility Requirements: Applicant must be high school student and planning to enroll or expecting to enroll full-time at an institution or university. Applicant must have 3.0 GPA or higher. Available to U.S. citizens.

Application Requirements: Application, test scores. *Deadline:* March 15.

Contact: Program Coordinator
South Dakota Investment Council
2187 Atlantic Street
Stamford, CT 06902
Phone: 866-529-7462

SOUTH KENTUCKY RURAL ELECTRIC COOPERATIVE CORPORATION   http://www.skrecc.com

WOMEN IN RURAL ELECTRIFICATION (WIRE) SCHOLARSHIPS

Scholarship available to Kentucky students who are juniors or seniors in a Kentucky college or university and have 60 credit hours by fall semester. Immediate family of student must be served by one of the state's 24 rural electric distribution cooperatives. Awards based on academic achievement, extracurricular activities, career goals, recommendations.

Award: Scholarship for use in freshman, sophomore, junior, senior, graduate, or postgraduate years. *Number:* 3. *Amount:* $1000.

Eligibility Requirements: Applicant must be enrolled or expecting to enroll full or part-time at a two-year or four-year or technical institution or university. Available to U.S. citizens.

Application Requirements: Application. *Deadline:* June 15.

Contact: Ellie Hobgood, W.I.R.E. Scholarships
South Kentucky Rural Electric Cooperative Corporation
PO Box 32170
Louisville, KY 40232
Phone: 800-264-5112

ST. CLAIRE REGIONAL MEDICAL CENTER   http://www.st-claire.org/

SR. MARY JEANNETTE WESS, S.N.D. SCHOLARSHIP

Scholarships available for an undergraduate or graduate student, junior level or above, in any field of study, who demonstrates academic achievement, leadership, service, and financial need. Must have graduated from an eastern Kentucky high school in one of the following counties: Bath, Carter, Elliott, Fleming, Lewis, Magoffin, Menifee, Montgomery, Morgan, Rowan, or Wolfe. Call for information.

Award: Scholarship for use in freshman, sophomore, junior, senior, or graduate years; not renewable. *Number:* 1–2. *Amount:* $750.

Eligibility Requirements: Applicant must be enrolled or expecting to enroll full-time at a four-year institution or university. Available to U.S. citizens.

Application Requirements: Application, financial need analysis. *Deadline:* April 15.

Contact: Shirley Caudill, St. Claire Regional Medical Center
St. Claire Regional Medical Center
222 Medical Circle
Morehead, KY 40351
Phone: 606-783-6512
E-mail: sacaudill@st-claire.org

STATE DEPARTMENT FEDERAL CREDIT UNION ANNUAL SCHOLARSHIP PROGRAM   http://www.sdfcu.org/youth/scholar.html

STATE DEPARTMENT FEDERAL CREDIT UNION ANNUAL SCHOLARSHIP PROGRAM

Scholarships available to members who are currently enrolled in a degree program and have completed 12 credit hours of coursework at an accredited college or university. Must have an account in good standing in their name with SDFCU, have a minimum 2.5 GPA, submit official cumulative transcripts, and describe need for financial assistance to continue their education.

Award: Scholarship for use in freshman, sophomore, junior, or senior years; renewable.

Eligibility Requirements: Applicant must be enrolled or expecting to enroll at a four-year institution or university. Applicant must have 2.5 GPA or higher. Available to U.S. citizens.

Application Requirements: Application, financial need analysis, transcript. *Deadline:* April 14.

Contact: Scholarship Coordinator
State Department Federal Credit Union Annual Scholarship Program
SDFCU, 1630 King Street
Alexandria, VA 22314
Phone: 703-706-5019
E-mail: marketing@sdfcu.org

STATE OF SOUTH DAKOTA/COLLEGEACCESS 529   http://www.southdakota529.com

ALLIANZ SOUTH DAKOTA SCHOLARSHIP PROGRAM

Scholarship for high school seniors who have achieved a high academic standard and plan to attend a two- or four-year accredited higher education institution located in South Dakota. Must have minimum cumulative GPA of 3.0.

Award: Scholarship for use in freshman year; renewable. *Amount:* up to $2000.

Eligibility Requirements: Applicant must be enrolled or expecting to enroll at a two-year or four-year institution. Applicant must have 3.0 GPA or higher. Available to U.S. citizens.

Application Requirements: Application. *Deadline:* March 15.

Contact: Coordinator
State of South Dakota/CollegeAccess 529
4009 West 49th Street, Suite 300
Sioux Falls, SD 57106
Phone: 866-529-7462
E-mail: info@ris.sdbor.edu

STEPHEN PHILLIPS MEMORIAL SCHOLARSHIP FUND   http://www.phillips-scholarship.org

STEPHEN PHILLIPS MEMORIAL SCHOLARSHIP FUND

Award open to full-time undergraduate students with financial need who display academic excellence, strong citizenship and character, and a desire to make a meaningful contribution to society. For more details see Web site: http://www.phillips-scholarship.org

Award: Scholarship for use in freshman, sophomore, junior, or senior years; renewable. *Number:* 150–200. *Amount:* $3000–$10,000.

Eligibility Requirements: Applicant must be enrolled or expecting to enroll full-time at a four-year institution or university. Applicant must have 3.0 GPA or higher. Available to U.S. citizens.

Application Requirements: Application, essay, financial need analysis, references, test scores, transcript. *Deadline:* May 1.

Contact: Karen Emery, Scholarship Coordinator
Stephen Phillips Memorial Scholarship Fund
PO Box 870
Salem, MA 01970
Phone: 978-744-2111
Fax: 978-744-0456
E-mail: kemery@spscholars.org

STRAIGHT FORWARD MEDIA   http://www.straightforwardmedia.com

DALE E. FRIDELL MEMORIAL SCHOLARSHIP

Non-renewable scholarship. Award based on essay of fewer than 1000 words which must be submitted via email. For further information and email address go to Web site: http://www.straightforwardmedia.com.

Award: Scholarship for use in freshman, sophomore, junior, senior, graduate, or postgraduate years; not renewable. *Number:* 1. *Amount:* $500–$1000.

Eligibility Requirements: Applicant must be enrolled or expecting to enroll full or part-time at a two-year or four-year or technical institution or university. Available to U.S. and non-U.S. citizens.

Application Requirements: Applicant must enter a contest, essay. *Deadline:* Continuous.

Contact: Christina Barsch, Vice President of Operations
Straight Forward Media
11200 West Wisconsin, Suite 10
Youngtown, AZ 85363
Phone: 623-215-2898
Fax: 623-215-2899
E-mail: cbarsch@dollarship.com

GET OUT OF DEBT SCHOLARSHIP

One-time award available to anyone attending or aspiring to attend a postsecondary education program. Application deadline is January 31. Applications must be submitted via Web site: http://www.straightforwardmedia.com

Award: Scholarship for use in freshman, sophomore, junior, senior, graduate, or postgraduate years. *Number:* 1. *Amount:* $500.

Eligibility Requirements: Applicant must be enrolled or expecting to enroll full or part-time at a two-year or four-year or technical institution or university. Available to U.S. and non-U.S. citizens.

Application Requirements: *Deadline:* Continuous.

Contact: Christina Barsch, Vice President of Operations
Straight Forward Media
8088 North 110th Drive
PO Box 2560
Peoria, AZ 85345
Phone: 623-215-2898
Fax: 623-215-2899
E-mail: cbarsch@dollarship.com

MESOTHELIOMA MEMORIAL SCHOLARSHIP

One-time award available to anyone attending or aspiring to attend a postsecondary education program. Applications must be submitted via Web site: http://www.straightforwardmedia.com. One scholarship is awarded every 3 months.

Award: Scholarship for use in freshman, sophomore, junior, senior, graduate, or postgraduate years. *Number:* 1. *Amount:* $500.

Eligibility Requirements: Applicant must be enrolled or expecting to enroll at a two-year or four-year or technical institution or university. Available to U.S. and non-U.S. citizens.

Application Requirements: *Deadline:* Continuous.

Contact: Christina Barsch, Vice President of Operations
Straight Forward Media
8088 North 110th Drive
PO Box 2560
Peoria, AZ 85345
Phone: 623-215-2898
Fax: 623-215-2899
E-mail: cbarsch@dollarship.com

STUDENT INSIGHTS   http://www.student-view.com

STUDENT-VIEW SCHOLARSHIP PROGRAM

Scholarship available by random drawing from the pool of entrants who responded to an online survey from Student Insights marketing organization.. The applicant must be below the age of 18, and must have parent's permission to participate.

Award: Scholarship for use in freshman year. *Number:* 1. *Amount:* $500–$3000.

Eligibility Requirements: Applicant must be high school student; age 17 or under and planning to enroll or expecting to enroll full-time at an institution or university. Available to U.S. citizens.

Application Requirements: Application. *Deadline:* April 15.

Contact: Program Coordinator
Student Insights
136 Justice Drive
Valencia, PA 16059

SUNTRUST BANK   http://www.suntrusteducation.com

OFF TO COLLEGE SCHOLARSHIP SWEEPSTAKES

Registration begins on Sept. 15, 2006. First drawing will be held on Oct. 31, 2006. A $1,000 scholarship and a $250 gift card given away every two weeks until May 2006. Entrants must be a high school senior planning to attend college in the fall of 2007. Winner's school of attendance will also receive a $1,000 scholarship for their general scholarship fund.

Award: Scholarship for use in freshman year; not renewable. *Number:* 15. *Amount:* up to $1000.

Eligibility Requirements: Applicant must be age 13 and enrolled or expecting to enroll at a two-year or four-year or technical institution or university. Available to U.S. citizens.

Application Requirements: Application. *Deadline:* varies.

Contact: James M. (Jim) Wells III, President and COO
SunTrust Bank
PO Box 27172
1001 Semmes Avenue, 5th Floor
Richmond, VA 23261-7172
Phone: 404-588-7711
Fax: 404-332-3875

SUPERCOLLEGE.COM   http://www.supercollege.com

SUPERCOLLEGE.COM SCHOLARSHIP

An award for outstanding high school students or college undergraduates. Based on academic and extracurricular achievement, leadership, and integrity. May study any major and attend or plan to attend any accredited college or university in the United States. No paper applications accepted. Applications are only available online at http://www.supercollege.com

Award: Scholarship for use in freshman, sophomore, junior, or senior years; not renewable. *Number:* 1–2. *Amount:* $500–$2500.

Eligibility Requirements: Applicant must be enrolled or expecting to enroll full-time at a four-year institution or university. Available to U.S. citizens.

Application Requirements: Application, essay, self-addressed stamped envelope. *Deadline:* July 31.

Contact: Kelly Tanabe, Chief Operating Officer
SuperCollege.com
4546 B10 El Camino Real, Suite 281
Los Altos, CA 94022
Phone: 650-493-2219
E-mail: supercollege@supercollege.com

SUPREME COUNCIL OF SES   http://www.seslife.org/

SUPREME COUNCIL OF SOCIEDADE DO ESPIRITO SANTO SCHOLARSHIP PROGRAM

Applicant must be a member of the SES for a minimum of two years prior to filling date of scholarship and have insurance premiums paid to date. Applicants must be graduating seniors or have graduated during the year and maintained a GPA of 3.0 in their sophomore, junior, and first semester senior years.

Award: Scholarship for use in freshman or sophomore years. *Number:* 35. *Amount:* $500–$1200.

Eligibility Requirements: Applicant must be enrolled or expecting to enroll full-time at a four-year institution or university. Applicant must have 3.0 GPA or higher. Available to U.S. citizens.

Application Requirements: Application, essay, resume, transcript. *Deadline:* March 15.

Contact: SES Scholarship Committee
Supreme Council of SES
PO Box 247
Santa Clara, CA 95052-0247

SURFACE NAVY ASSOCIATION   http://www.navysna.org

VICE ADMIRAL ROBERT L. WALTERS SCHOLARSHIP

Scholarship for a child, stepchild, ward, or spouse of a Surface Navy Association member. The member must be in their second or subsequent consecutive year of membership.

Award: Scholarship for use in freshman, sophomore, junior, or senior years; renewable. *Amount:* $2000.

Eligibility Requirements: Applicant must be enrolled or expecting to enroll at a four-year institution or university. Applicant must have 3.0 GPA or higher. Available to U.S. citizens.

Application Requirements: Application, essay, references, transcript. *Deadline:* March 15.

Contact: Surface Navy Association
2550 Huntington Avenue, Suite 202
Alexandria, VA 22303

SWISS BENEVOLENT SOCIETY

SILVIO CANONICA SCHOLARSHIP

Scholarships are available for students in the greater San Francisco Bay area who are of Swiss descent. Education may be in any field of endeavor at any accredited university or college in the U.S.

Award: Scholarship for use in junior, senior, or graduate years; not renewable. *Number:* up to 1.

Eligibility Requirements: Applicant must be enrolled or expecting to enroll full-time at a four-year institution or university. Applicant must have 3.0 GPA or higher. Available to U.S. citizens.

Application Requirements: Application, references, test scores, transcript. *Deadline:* April 30.

Contact: Program Coordinator
Swiss Benevolent Society
456 Montgomery Street, Suite 1500
San Francisco, CA 94104-1233

TAKE ME AWAY TO COLLEGE SCHOLARSHIP COMPETITION   http://www.takemeaway.com

CALGON, TAKE ME AWAY TO COLLEGE SCHOLARSHIP COMPETITION

One-time award designed for students pursuing a degree at a 4-year accredited college or university. The award recognizes originality and expression as well as academic excellence, community involvement, and overall achievement. Award designated for female applicants. Must be U.S. citizen or legal resident studying at an institution in the United States. Applications accepted only through Web site: http://www.takemeaway.com

Award: Scholarship for use in freshman, sophomore, junior, or senior years; not renewable. *Number:* 9. *Amount:* $500–$5000.

Eligibility Requirements: Applicant must be age 18; enrolled or expecting to enroll full-time at a four-year institution or university and female. Available to U.S. citizens.

Application Requirements: Application, essay, transcript. *Deadline:* February 28.

Contact: Application available at Web site.
E-mail: quickspritz@takemeaway.com

CALGON, TAKE ME AWAY TO COLLEGE SCHOLARSWEEPS

Contest format. Award is open to anyone pursuing education at any two- or four-year accredited college, university or trade/technical school. Must be U.S. citizen or legal resident studying at an institution in the U.S. Applications accepted only through Web site: http://www.takemeaway.com

Award: Scholarship for use in freshman, sophomore, junior, or senior years; not renewable. *Number:* 3. *Amount:* $500–$1500.

Eligibility Requirements: Applicant must be enrolled or expecting to enroll full or part-time at a two-year or four-year or technical institution or university. Available to U.S. citizens.

Application Requirements: Application, applicant must enter a contest. *Deadline:* June 30.

Contact: Application available at Web site.
E-mail: quickspritz@takemeaway.com

TALBOTS CHARITABLE FOUNDATION   http://www1.talbots.com/

TALBOTS WOMEN'S SCHOLARSHIP FUND

One-time scholarship for women who earned their high school diploma or GED at least 10 years ago, and who are now seeking an undergraduate college degree.

Award: Scholarship for use in freshman, sophomore, junior, or senior years; not renewable. *Number:* 5–50. *Amount:* $1000–$10,000.

Eligibility Requirements: Applicant must be enrolled or expecting to enroll full or part-time at a two-year or four-year or technical institution or university and female. Available to U.S. citizens.

Application Requirements: Application, essay, financial need analysis, references, transcript. *Deadline:* January 3.

Contact: Deb Johnson, Scholarship America
Talbots Charitable Foundation
1 Scholarship Way, PO Box 297
Saint Peter, MN 56082
Phone: 507-931-0452
Fax: 507-931-9278
E-mail: debj@scholarshipamerica.org

TALL CLUBS INTERNATIONAL FOUNDATION, INC, AND TALL CLUBS INTERNATIONAL, INC.   http://www.tall.org

KAE SUMNER EINFELDT SCHOLARSHIP

Females 5'10" or males 6'2" (minimum heights) are eligible to apply for the TCI International Foundation Inc., scholarships. Interested individuals should contact their local Tall Clubs Chapter. Canadian and U.S. winners are selected from finalists submitted by each local chapter.

Award: Scholarship for use in freshman year; not renewable. *Number:* 2–4. *Amount:* $1000.

Eligibility Requirements: Applicant must be age 17-21 and enrolled or expecting to enroll full-time at a two-year or four-year or technical institution or university. Available to U.S. and Canadian citizens.

Application Requirements: Application, essay, photo, references, transcript, verification of height. *Deadline:* April 1.

Contact: Barry Umbs, Director
Tall Clubs International Foundation, Inc, and Tall Clubs International, Inc.
6770 River Terrace Drive
Franklin, WI 53132
Phone: 414-529-9887
Fax: 414-382-4444
E-mail: baumbs@ra.rockwell.com

TARGET CORPORATION   http://www.target.com

TARGET ALL-AROUND SCHOLARSHIP PROGRAM

Organization awards over six hundred $1,000 All-Around Scholarships each year, including one $25,000 scholarship, to high school seniors and college students age 24 or younger.

Award: Scholarship for use in freshman, sophomore, junior, or senior years; not renewable. *Number:* up to 650. *Amount:* $1000–$25,000.

Eligibility Requirements: Applicant must be age 24 or under and enrolled or expecting to enroll full-time at a two-year or four-year or technical institution or university. Available to U.S. citizens.

Application Requirements: Application, essay, transcript. *Deadline:* November 1.

Contact: Target Corporation
c/o Scholarship America
One Scholarship Way, PO Box 480
St. Peter, MN 56082-0480
Phone: 800-316-6142
E-mail: smsinfo@scholarshipamerica.org

TECHNICAL ASSOCIATION OF THE PULP & PAPER INDUSTRY (TAPPI)
http://www.tappi.org

COATING AND GRAPHIC ARTS DIVISION SCHOLARSHIP

Up to four $1000 scholarships will be made available to undergraduate juniors and seniors and graduate students who have a demonstrated interest in a career in the coating and graphic arts industry. Must be a TAPPI student member or a member of a TAPPI Student Chapter. Must have minimum cumulative grade point average of 3.0 out of 4.0. Application deadline is January 31.

Award: Scholarship for use in junior, senior, or graduate years; not renewable. *Number:* 1–4. *Amount:* $1000.

Eligibility Requirements: Applicant must be enrolled or expecting to enroll full-time at a four-year institution or university. Applicant must have 3.0 GPA or higher. Available to U.S. and non-U.S. citizens.

Application Requirements: Application, references, transcript. *Deadline:* January 31.

Contact: Veranda Edmondson, Member Group Specialist-TAPPI
Technical Association of the Pulp & Paper Industry (TAPPI)
15 Technology Parkway South
Norcross, GA 30092
Phone: 770-209-7536
Fax: 770-446-6947
E-mail: vedmondson@tappi.org

CORRUGATED PACKAGING DIVISION SCHOLARSHIPS

Several $1000 and $2000 scholarships are available to juniors and seniors who demonstrate an interest in the pulp and paper industry or, especially, the corrugated container industry. Must maintain a 3.0 GPA. Deadline is February 28 or July 31 of each year. Must pursue a career in the corrugated packaging industry.

Award: Scholarship for use in junior, senior, or graduate years; not renewable. *Number:* 8. *Amount:* $1000–$2000.

Eligibility Requirements: Applicant must be enrolled or expecting to enroll full or part-time at a four-year institution or university. Applicant must have 3.0 GPA or higher. Available to U.S. and non-U.S. citizens.

Application Requirements: Application, references, transcript. *Deadline:* February 28.

Contact: Veranda Edmondson, Member Group Specialist-TAPPI
Technical Association of the Pulp & Paper Industry (TAPPI)
15 Technology Parkway South
Norcross, GA 30092
Phone: 770-209-7536
Fax: 770-446-6947
E-mail: vedmondson@tappi.org

ENGINEERING DIVISION SCHOLARSHIP

Two $1500 scholarships will be awarded to juniors or rising seniors who are enrolled in an engineering or science program. Must demonstrate a significant interest in the pulp and paper industry, be a member of a TAPPI Student Chapter, and have a minimum GPA of 3.0. Deadline is January 31.

Award: Scholarship for use in junior or senior years; not renewable. *Number:* 1–2. *Amount:* up to $1500.

Eligibility Requirements: Applicant must be enrolled or expecting to enroll full-time at a four-year institution or university. Applicant must have 3.0 GPA or higher. Available to U.S. and non-U.S. citizens.

Application Requirements: Application, essay, references, transcript. *Deadline:* January 31.

Contact: Veranda Edmondson, TAPPI-Member Group Specialist
Technical Association of the Pulp & Paper Industry (TAPPI)
15 Technology Parkway South
Norcross, GA 30092
Phone: 770-209-7536
Fax: 770-446-6947
E-mail: vedmondson@tappi.org

ENVIRONMENTAL DIVISION SCHOLARSHIP

One $2500 scholarship is available to a full-time student who is at or above the level of sophomore and has a strong desire to pursue a career in environmental control as it relates to the pulp, paper and related industries. Must have a 3.0 GPA. An interview may be required. Application deadline is January 31. Must have an attendance at an ABET (Accreditation Board for Engineering & Technology, Inc.) accredited or equivalent college.

Award: Scholarship for use in sophomore, junior, or senior years; not renewable. *Number:* 1. *Amount:* up to $2500.

Eligibility Requirements: Applicant must be enrolled or expecting to enroll full-time at a four-year institution. Applicant must have 3.0 GPA or higher. Available to U.S. and non-U.S. citizens.

Application Requirements: Application, essay, interview, references, transcript. *Deadline:* January 31.

Contact: Veranda Edmondson, TAPPI-Member Group Specialist
Technical Association of the Pulp & Paper Industry (TAPPI)
15 Technology Parkway South
Norcross, GA 30092
Phone: 770-209-7536
Fax: 770-446-6947
E-mail: vedmondson@tappi.org

NONWOVENS DIVISION SCHOLARSHIP

One $1000 scholarship is available to full-time students enrolled in a state-accredited undergraduate program. Must be in a program that will prepare the student in a career in the nonwovens industry or demonstrate an interest in the areas covered by TAPPI's Nonwovens Division. Application deadline is January 31.

Award: Scholarship for use in freshman, sophomore, junior, or senior years; not renewable. *Number:* 1. *Amount:* $1000.

Eligibility Requirements: Applicant must be enrolled or expecting to enroll full-time at a four-year institution. Applicant must have 3.0 GPA or higher. Available to U.S. and non-U.S. citizens.

Application Requirements: Application, references, transcript. *Deadline:* January 31.

Contact: Veranda Edmondson, TAPPI-Member Group Specialist
Technical Association of the Pulp & Paper Industry (TAPPI)
15 Technology Parkway South
Norcross, GA 30092
Phone: 770-209-7536
Fax: 770-446-6947
E-mail: vedmondson@tappi.org

PAPER AND BOARD DIVISION SCHOLARSHIPS

Several $1000 scholarships are available to TAPPI student members or an undergraduate member of a TAPPI Student Chapter who are enrolled as a college or university undergraduate in an engineering or science program. Must be a sophomore, junior, or senior with a significant interest in the paper industry. Deadline is January 31.

Award: Scholarship for use in sophomore, junior, or senior years; not renewable. *Number:* 4. *Amount:* $1000.

Eligibility Requirements: Applicant must be enrolled or expecting to enroll full-time at a four-year institution. Available to U.S. and non-U.S. citizens.

Application Requirements: Application, references, transcript. *Deadline:* January 31.

Contact: Veranda Edmondson, TAPPI-Member Group Specialist
Technical Association of the Pulp & Paper Industry (TAPPI)
15 Technology Parkway South
Norcross, GA 30092
Phone: 770-209-7536
Fax: 770-446-6947
E-mail: vedmondson@tappi.org

PULP MANUFACTURE DIVISION SCHOLARSHIPS

Up to five scholarships ranging from $500 to $2000 will be provided for students who are at least rising sophomores in a southern school of forest resources.

Award: Scholarship for use in sophomore, junior, or senior years; not renewable. *Number:* up to 5. *Amount:* $500–$2000.

Eligibility Requirements: Applicant must be enrolled or expecting to enroll full-time at a four-year institution. Available to U.S. and non-U.S. citizens.

Application Requirements: Application, essay, references, transcript. *Deadline:* May 15.

Technical Association of the Pulp & Paper Industry (TAPPI) (continued)

Contact: Veranda Edmondson, TAPPI-Member Group Specialist
Technical Association of the Pulp & Paper Industry (TAPPI)
15 Technology Parkway South
Norcross, GA 30092
Phone: 770-209-7536
Fax: 770-446-6947
E-mail: vedmondson@tappi.org

RALPH A. KLUCKEN SCHOLARSHIP AWARD

One $1000 scholarship is available to a high school senior or college freshman, sophomore or junior for the study of a field of activity covered by the Polymers, Laminations and Coatings Division. Applicants must provide a demonstration of responsibility and maturity through a history of part-time and summer employment. Deadline is May 31.

Award: Scholarship for use in freshman, sophomore, or junior years; not renewable. *Number:* 1. *Amount:* $1000.

Eligibility Requirements: Applicant must be enrolled or expecting to enroll full-time at a four-year institution. Applicant must have 2.5 GPA or higher. Available to U.S. and non-U.S. citizens.

Application Requirements: Application, references, transcript. *Deadline:* May 31.

Contact: Veranda Edmondson, TAPPI-Member Group Specialist
Technical Association of the Pulp & Paper Industry (TAPPI)
15 Technology Parkway South
Norcross, GA 30092
Phone: 770-209-7536
Fax: 770-446-6947
E-mail: vedmondson@tappi.org

WILLIAM L. CALLISON SCHOLARSHIP

One $8000 scholarship is available to junior and senior undergraduates who have demonstrated outstanding leadership abilities and demonstrated a significant interest in the pulp and paper industry. Award is given in two yearly $4000 increments. Must attend a college or university that offers pulp and paper programs or have a TAPPI Student Chapter. Deadline is May 1.

Award: Scholarship for use in junior or senior years; renewable. *Number:* 1. *Amount:* $8000.

Eligibility Requirements: Applicant must be enrolled or expecting to enroll full-time at a four-year institution or university. Applicant must have 3.5 GPA or higher. Available to U.S. and non-U.S. citizens.

Application Requirements: Application, essay, references, transcript. *Deadline:* May 1.

Contact: Veranda Edmondson, TAPPI-Member Group Specialist
Technical Association of the Pulp & Paper Industry (TAPPI)
15 Technology Parkway South
Norcross, GA 30092
Phone: 770-209-7536
Fax: 770-446-6947
E-mail: vedmondson@tappi.org

TERRY FOX HUMANITARIAN AWARD PROGRAM   http://www.terryfox.org

TERRY FOX HUMANITARIAN AWARD
• See page 636

TEXAS MUTUAL INSURANCE COMPANY   http://www.texasmutual.com/

TEXAS MUTUAL INSURANCE COMPANY SCHOLARSHIP PROGRAM

A scholarship program open to qualified family members of policyholder employees who died from on-the-job injuries or accidents, policyholder employees who qualify for lifetime income benefits pursuant to the Texas Workers' Compensation Act, and family members of injured employees who qualify for lifetime income benefits. Award up to $4000 per semester.

Award: Scholarship for use in freshman, sophomore, junior, or senior years; renewable. *Number:* varies. *Amount:* up to $4000.

Eligibility Requirements: Applicant must be age 17 and enrolled or expecting to enroll full or part-time at a two-year or four-year or technical institution or university. Applicant must have 2.5 GPA or higher. Available to U.S. and non-U.S. citizens.

Application Requirements: Application, financial need analysis, test scores, transcript, fee bill, death certificate. *Deadline:* varies.

Contact: Temetria McVea, Administrative Assistant
Texas Mutual Insurance Company
221 West 6th Street, Suite 300
Austin, TX 78701
Phone: 800-859-5995 Ext. 3907
Fax: 512-404-3999
E-mail: tmcvea@texasmutual.com

THE CHRISTOPHERS   http://www.christophers.org

POSTER CONTEST FOR HIGH SCHOOL STUDENTS

Students in grades 9 through 12 are invited to interpret the theme: "You can make a difference." Posters must include this statement and illustrate the idea that one person can change the world for the better. Judging is based on overall impact, content, originality and artistic merit. More information can be found at http://www.christophers.org.

Award: Prize for use in freshman year; not renewable. *Number:* up to 8. *Amount:* $100–$1000.

Eligibility Requirements: Applicant must be high school student and planning to enroll or expecting to enroll full or part-time at an institution or university. Available to U.S. citizens.

Application Requirements: Application, applicant must enter a contest, poster. *Deadline:* January 9.

Contact: Nick Monteoeone, Youth Coordinator
The Christophers
12 East 48th Street
New York, NY 10017
Phone: 212-759-4050
Fax: 212-838-5073
E-mail: youth@christophers.org

VIDEO CONTEST FOR COLLEGE STUDENTS

Using any style or format, college students are invited to express the following theme: "One person can make a difference." Entries can be up to five minutes in length and must be submitted in standard, full-sized VHS format. Entries will be judged on content, artistic and technical proficiency, and adherence to contest rules. Deadline: June 9. More information is available at http://www.christophers.org

Award: Prize for use in freshman, sophomore, junior, senior, or graduate years; not renewable. *Number:* 8. *Amount:* $100–$3000.

Eligibility Requirements: Applicant must be enrolled or expecting to enroll full or part-time at a two-year or four-year or technical institution or university. Available to U.S. and non-U.S. citizens.

Application Requirements: Application, applicant must enter a contest, VHS tape or DVD. *Deadline:* June 9.

Contact: Nick Monteoeone, Youth Coordinator
The Christophers
12 East 48th Street
New York, NY 10017
Phone: 212-759-4050
Fax: 212-838-5073
E-mail: youth@christophers.org

THE FREEMAN FOUNDATION/INSTITUTE OF INTERNATIONAL EDUCATION   http://www.iie.org/Freeman-ASIA

FREEMAN AWARDS FOR STUDY IN ASIA

Need-based Awards for study in East/Southeast Asia.

Award: Grant for use in freshman, sophomore, junior, or senior years; not renewable. *Number:* varies. *Amount:* $3000–$7000.

Eligibility Requirements: Applicant must be enrolled or expecting to enroll full-time at a two-year or four-year institution or university. Applicant must have 2.5 GPA or higher. Available to U.S. citizens.

Application Requirements: Application, applicant must enter a contest, essay, financial need analysis, study abroad adviser approval and endorsement. *Deadline:* varies.

Contact:

 Phone: 212-984-5542
 Fax: 212-984-5325
 E-mail: freeman-asia@iie.org

THETA DELTA CHI EDUCATIONAL FOUNDATION, INC.   http://www.tdx.org

THETA DELTA CHI EDUCATIONAL FOUNDATION INC. SCHOLARSHIP

Scholarships for undergraduate or graduate students enrolled in an accredited institution. Awards are based on candidate's history of service to the fraternity, scholastic achievement, and need. See Web site for application and additional information: http://www.tdx.org/scholarship/scholarship.html

Award: Scholarship for use in freshman, sophomore, junior, senior, or graduate years. *Amount:* $1000–$5000.

Eligibility Requirements: Applicant must be enrolled or expecting to enroll at a four-year institution or university. Available to U.S. citizens.

Application Requirements: Application, financial need analysis, references, transcript. *Deadline:* May 15.

Contact: William McClung, Executive Director
 Theta Delta Chi Educational Foundation, Inc.
 214 Lewis Wharf
 Boston, MA 02110-3927
 Phone: 617-742-8886
 E-mail: execdir@tdx.org

THIRD WAVE FOUNDATION   http://www.thirdwavefoundation.org

SCHOLARSHIP FOR YOUNG WOMEN

Our scholarship program is available to all full-time or part-time female students aged 17-30 who are enrolled in, or have been accepted to, an accredited university, college, or community college in the United States. The primary criterion for funding is financial need. Students should also be involved as activists, artists, or cultural workers working on issues such as racism, homophobia, sexism, or other forms of inequality. Application deadlines are April 1 and October 1. Application available at Web site http://www.thirdwavefoundation.org

Award: Scholarship for use in freshman, sophomore, junior, senior, or graduate years; not renewable. *Number:* 15. *Amount:* $500–$3000.

Eligibility Requirements: Applicant must be age 30 or under; enrolled or expecting to enroll full or part-time at a two-year or four-year or technical institution or university and female. Applicant must have 2.5 GPA or higher. Available to U.S. and non-U.S. citizens.

Application Requirements: Application, essay, financial need analysis, resume, references, self-addressed stamped envelope, transcript. *Deadline:* varies.

Contact: Mia Herndon, Network Coordinator
 Third Wave Foundation
 511 West 25th Street, Suite 301
 New York, NY 10001
 Phone: 212-675-0700
 Fax: 212-255-6653
 E-mail: info@thirdwavefoundation.org

37TH DIVISION VETERANS ASSOCIATION

37TH DIVISION VETERANS ASSOCIATION SCHOLARSHIP

Award: Scholarship for use in freshman, sophomore, junior, senior, or graduate years.

Eligibility Requirements: Applicant must be enrolled or expecting to enroll at an institution or university.

Contact: Executive Secretary
 37th Division Veterans Association
 35 East Chestnut
 Room 425
 Columbus, OH 43215

THURGOOD MARSHALL SCHOLARSHIP FUND   http://www.thurgoodmarshallfund.org

THURGOOD MARSHALL SCHOLARSHIP

Merit scholarships for students attending 1 of 45 member HBCU's (historically black colleges, universities) including 5 member law schools. Must maintain an average of 3.0 and have a financial need. Must be a U.S. citizen. 3.0 GPA required to renew. No applications accepted at TMSF. Must apply through the HBCUs, through a campus scholarship coordinator. Please refer to Web site for further details: http://www.thurgoodmarshallfund.org.

Award: Scholarship for use in freshman, sophomore, junior, senior, or graduate years; renewable. *Number:* varies. *Amount:* up to $4400.

Eligibility Requirements: Applicant must be enrolled or expecting to enroll full-time at a four-year institution or university. Applicant must have 3.0 GPA or higher. Available to U.S. citizens.

Application Requirements: Application, essay, financial need analysis, interview, photo, resume, references, test scores, transcript. *Deadline:* varies.

Contact: Programs Officer
 Thurgood Marshall Scholarship Fund
 100 Park Avenue, 10th Floor
 New York, NY 10017

TRIANGLE COMMUNITY FOUNDATION   http://www.trianglecf.org

GEORGE AND MARY NEWTON SCHOLARSHIP

One scholarship per year is granted to a child of a Newton Instrument Company employee. Applications available at Newton Instruments. Should be returned to the Triangle Community Foundation by March 15.

Award: Scholarship for use in freshman, sophomore, junior, or senior years; renewable. *Number:* 5. *Amount:* $500–$20,000.

Eligibility Requirements: Applicant must be enrolled or expecting to enroll full or part-time at a four-year institution or university. Available to U.S. and non-U.S. citizens.

Application Requirements: Application, transcript. *Deadline:* March 15.

Contact: Linda Depo, Philanthropic Services Associate
 Triangle Community Foundation
 4813 Emperor Boulevard, Suite 130
 Durham, NC 27703
 Phone: 919-474-8370
 Fax: 919-941-9208
 E-mail: linda@trianglecf.org

TRIANGLE EDUCATION FOUNDATION   http://www.triangle.org

MORTIN SCHOLARSHIP

One-time award for an active member of the Triangle Fraternity. Must be full-time male student who has completed at least two full academic years of school. Minimum 3.0 GPA. Application must be postmarked by Feb 15. Further information available at Web site http://www.triangle.org

Award: Scholarship for use in freshman, sophomore, junior, or senior years; not renewable. *Number:* 1. *Amount:* up to $2500.

Eligibility Requirements: Applicant must be enrolled or expecting to enroll full-time at a four-year institution or university and male. Applicant must have 3.0 GPA or higher. Available to U.S. citizens.

Application Requirements: Application, essay, financial need analysis, references, self-addressed stamped envelope, transcript. *Deadline:* February 15.

Contact: Scott Bova, President
 Triangle Education Foundation
 120 South Center Street
 Plainfield, IN 46168-1214
 Phone: 317-705-9803
 Fax: 317-837-9642
 E-mail: sbova@triangle.org

PETER AND BARBARA BYE SCHOLARSHIP

Scholarship for a Triangle Fraternity member for undergraduate study. Preference given to applicants from Cornell University Triangle chapter.

Triangle Education Foundation (continued)

Applicant must have a minimum GPA of 2.7/4.0. Deadline is February 15. Additional information on Web site http://www.triangle.org

Award: Scholarship for use in freshman, sophomore, junior, or senior years; not renewable. *Number:* 1. *Amount:* up to $1500.

Eligibility Requirements: Applicant must be enrolled or expecting to enroll at a four-year institution or university and male. Applicant must have 3.0 GPA or higher. Available to U.S. citizens.

Application Requirements: Application, financial need analysis, references, transcript. *Deadline:* February 15.

Contact: Scott Bova, President
Triangle Education Foundation
120 South Center Street
Plainfield, IN 46168-1214
Phone: 317-705-9803
Fax: 317-837-9642
E-mail: sbova@triangle.org

RUST SCHOLARSHIP

One-time award for active member of the Triangle Fraternity. Must be full-time male student who has completed at least two full academic years of school. Minimum 3.0 GPA. Application must be postmarked by April 30. Further information available at Web site http://www.triangle.org

Award: Scholarship for use in freshman, sophomore, junior, or senior years; not renewable. *Number:* 1. *Amount:* up to $4000.

Eligibility Requirements: Applicant must be enrolled or expecting to enroll full-time at a four-year institution or university and male. Applicant must have 3.0 GPA or higher. Available to U.S. citizens.

Application Requirements: Application, essay, financial need analysis, references, self-addressed stamped envelope, transcript. *Deadline:* February 15.

Contact: Scott Bova, President
Triangle Education Foundation
120 South Center Street
Plainfield, IN 46168-1214
Phone: 317-705-9803
Fax: 317-837-9642
E-mail: sbova@triangle.org

TWIN TOWERS ORPHAN FUND   http://www.ttof.org

TWIN TOWERS ORPHAN FUND

Fund offers assistance to children who lost one or both parents in the terrorist attacks on September 11, 2001. Long-term education program established to provide higher education needs to children until they complete their uninterrupted studies, or reach age of majority. Visit Web site for additional information.

Award: Scholarship for use in freshman, sophomore, junior, senior, or graduate years; renewable. *Number:* varies. *Amount:* $5000–$7000.

Eligibility Requirements: Applicant must be enrolled or expecting to enroll full or part-time at a two-year or four-year or technical institution or university. Available to U.S. and non-U.S. citizens.

Application Requirements: Application, financial need analysis, references, verification documentation, birth certificate, parent's death certificate, marriage license. *Deadline:* varies.

Contact: Twin Towers Orphan Fund
4800 Easton Drive, Suite 109
Bakersfield, CA 93309
Phone: 661-633-9076
E-mail: info@ttof.org

TWO TEN FOOTWEAR FOUNDATION   http://www.twoten.org

CLASSIC SCHOLARSHIPS

Two- to four-year awards available to students affiliated with the footwear or allied industries. Scholarship awards are based on academic record, personal promise, character and financial need. Awards of up to $3,000 are renewable for four years of undergraduate study.

Award: Scholarship for use in freshman, sophomore, junior, or senior years; renewable. *Amount:* up to $3000.

Eligibility Requirements: Applicant must be enrolled or expecting to enroll full-time at a four-year institution. Available to U.S. citizens.

Application Requirements: Application, essay, financial need analysis, references, transcript. *Deadline:* varies.

Contact: Catherine Nelson, Scholarship Director
Two Ten Footwear Foundation
1466 Main Street
Waltham, MA 02451-1623
Phone: 781-736-1503
E-mail: scholarship@twoten.org

TWO TEN SUPER SCHOLARSHIPS

Scholarship available for the candidates who meet the Two Ten scholarship criteria and exhibit extraordinary financial need. Super scholarship worth up to $15,000 per year and renewable for four years of undergraduate study.

Award: Scholarship for use in freshman, sophomore, junior, or senior years; renewable. *Amount:* up to $15,000.

Eligibility Requirements: Applicant must be enrolled or expecting to enroll full-time at a four-year institution. Available to U.S. citizens.

Application Requirements: Application, essay, references, transcript. *Deadline:* varies.

Contact: Catherine Nelson, Scholarship Director
Two Ten Footwear Foundation
1466 Main Street
Waltham, MA 02451
Phone: 781-736-1503
E-mail: scholarship@twoten.org

U.S. BANK INTERNET SCHOLARSHIP PROGRAM   http://www.usbank.com

U.S. BANK INTERNET SCHOLARSHIP PROGRAM

One-time award for high school seniors who are planning to enroll full-time in an accredited two- or four-year college or university. Must apply online at Web site: http://www.usbank.com/studentbanking. Application available October to February. Please do not send any requests for application to address.

Award: Scholarship for use in freshman year; not renewable. *Number:* up to 30. *Amount:* up to $1000.

Eligibility Requirements: Applicant must be high school student and planning to enroll or expecting to enroll full-time at a two-year or four-year institution or university. Available to U.S. citizens.

Application Requirements: Application. *Deadline:* February 28.

Contact: Mary Ennis, Scholarship Coordinator
U.S. Bank Internet Scholarship Program
2322 East Sprague Avenue
Spokane, WA 99202
Phone: 800-242-1200
Fax: 888-329-8775
E-mail: mary.ennis@usbank.com

U.S. DEPARTMENT OF EDUCATION   http://www.ed.gov

HOPE SCHOLARSHIP

$1500 scholarship is available for students in the first two years of college (or other eligible postsecondary training). For more information see Web site: http://www.ed.gov.

Award: Scholarship for use in freshman or sophomore years. *Amount:* up to $1500.

Eligibility Requirements: Applicant must be enrolled or expecting to enroll at a four-year institution or university. Available to U.S. citizens.

Application Requirements: Application. *Deadline:* varies.

Contact: Darryl Davis, Robert Byrd Scholarships
U.S. Department of Education
1990 K Street, North West, 6th floor
Washington, DC 20006-8512
Phone: 202-502-7657
Fax: 202-502-7861
E-mail: darryl.davis@ed.gov

ULMAN CANCER FUND FOR YOUNG ADULTS
http://www.ulmanfund.org/

CANCER TEACHES US SURVIVORSHIP AWARD

Scholarship for adult cancer survivor/patient/caregiver and/or survivor of childhood cancer. Must be between the ages of 15-40 and seeking or receiving higher education or professional training.

Award: Scholarship for use in freshman, sophomore, junior, or senior years. *Amount:* up to $1000.

Eligibility Requirements: Applicant must be enrolled or expecting to enroll full or part-time at a four-year institution or university. Available to U.S. citizens.

Application Requirements: Application. *Deadline:* April 1.

Contact: Fay Baker, Scholarship Coordinator
Ulman Cancer Fund for Young Adults
4725 Dorsey Hall Drive, Suite A
PO Box 505
Ellicott City, MD 21042
Phone: 410-964-0202
Fax: 410-964-0402
E-mail: scholarship@ulmanfund.org

MARILYN YETSO MEMORIAL SCHOLARSHIP

To support the financial needs of college students who have a parent with cancer or who have lost a parent to cancer. The deadline is April 1.

Award: Scholarship for use in freshman, sophomore, junior, senior, graduate, or postgraduate years; not renewable. *Number:* 2. *Amount:* $1000.

Eligibility Requirements: Applicant must be age 16-39 and enrolled or expecting to enroll full or part-time at a two-year or four-year or technical institution or university. Available to U.S. and non-U.S. citizens.

Application Requirements: Application, autobiography, essay, financial need analysis, references, self-addressed stamped envelope, parent's medical history. *Deadline:* April 1.

Contact: Fay Baker, Scholarship Coordinator
Ulman Cancer Fund for Young Adults
4725 Dorsey Hall Drive, Suite A
PO Box 505
Ellicott City, MD 21042
Phone: 410-964-0202
Fax: 410-964-0402
E-mail: scholarship@ulmanfund.org

UNICO NATIONAL, INC
http://www.unico.org

ALPHONSE A. MIELE SCHOLARSHIP

Scholarship available to graduating high school senior. Must reside and attend high school within the corporate limits or adjoining suburbs of a city wherein an active chapter of UNICO National is located. Application must be signed by student's principal and properly certified by sponsoring Chapter President and Chapter Secretary. Must have letter of endorsement from President or Scholarship Chairperson of sponsoring Chapter.

Award: Scholarship for use in freshman, sophomore, junior, or senior years; renewable. *Number:* 1. *Amount:* up to $1500.

Eligibility Requirements: Applicant must be high school student and planning to enroll or expecting to enroll at a four-year institution. Available to U.S. citizens.

Application Requirements: Application, financial need analysis, references, transcript. *Deadline:* varies.

Contact: UNICO National, Inc
UNICO National, Inc
271 US Highway 46 West, Suite A-108
Fairfield, NJ 07004
Phone: 973-808-0035
Fax: 973-808-0043

UNITED NEGRO COLLEGE FUND
http://www.uncf.org

KECK FOUNDATION SCHOLARSHIP

Scholarship is available to any students attending UNCF colleges and universities whose families have suffered a financial hardship as a result of the September 11 tragedy.

Award: Scholarship for use in freshman, sophomore, junior, or senior years; renewable. *Number:* varies. *Amount:* $2000-$5000.

Eligibility Requirements: Applicant must be enrolled or expecting to enroll at a four-year institution or university. Applicant must have 2.5 GPA or higher. Available to U.S. citizens.

Application Requirements: Application. *Deadline:* varies.

Contact: Rebecca Bennett, Director, Program Services
United Negro College Fund
8260 Willow Oaks Corporate Drive
Fairfax, VA 22031-8044
Phone: 800-331-2244
E-mail: rbennett@uncf.org

UNCF LIBERTY SCHOLARSHIP

Scholarship for children of victims of the September 11th terrorist attacks. Candidates, regardless of race, creed, age, or color will be provided full scholarship for enrollment in any of the 39 UNCF member colleges and universities. Must maintain satisfactory academic standards. Prospective applicants should complete the Student Profile found at Web site: http://www.uncf.org.

Award: Scholarship for use in freshman, sophomore, junior, or senior years; renewable. *Number:* 1.

Eligibility Requirements: Applicant must be enrolled or expecting to enroll full-time at an institution or university. Available to U.S. citizens.

Application Requirements: Application. *Deadline:* Continuous.

Contact: Rebecca Bennett, Director, Program Services
United Negro College Fund
8260 Willow Oaks Corporate Drive
Fairfax, VA 22031-8044
Phone: 800-331-2244
E-mail: rbennett@uncf.org

WELLS FARGO SCHOLARSHIP

Renewable award for freshmen. Must have 2.5 GPA. Please visit Web site for more information: http://www.uncf.org.

Award: Scholarship for use in freshman, sophomore, junior, or senior years; renewable. *Number:* varies. *Amount:* up to $5000.

Eligibility Requirements: Applicant must be enrolled or expecting to enroll at an institution or university. Applicant must have 2.5 GPA or higher. Available to U.S. citizens.

Application Requirements: Application, financial need analysis, FAFSA, Student Aid Report (SAR). *Deadline:* varies.

Contact: Rebecca Bennett, Director, Program Services
United Negro College Fund
8260 Willow Oaks Corporate Drive
Fairfax, VA 22031-8044
Phone: 800-331-2244
E-mail: rbennett@uncf.org

UNITED STATES JUNIOR CHAMBER OF COMMERCE
http://www.usjaycees.org

JAYCEE WAR MEMORIAL FUND SCHOLARSHIP

Students who are U.S. citizens, possess academic potential and leadership qualities, and show financial need are eligible to apply. To receive an application, send $5 application fee and stamped, self-addressed envelope between July 1 and February 1. Application deadline is March 1.

Award: Scholarship for use in freshman, sophomore, junior, or senior years; not renewable. *Number:* 25-30. *Amount:* $1000-$5000.

Eligibility Requirements: Applicant must be enrolled or expecting to enroll full-time at a two-year or four-year or technical institution or university. Available to U.S. citizens.

Application Requirements: Application, financial need analysis, self-addressed stamped envelope, transcript. *Fee:* $5. *Deadline:* March 1.

Contact: Karen Fitzgerald, Customer Service/Data Processing
United States Junior Chamber of Commerce
PO Box 7
Tulsa, OK 74102-0007
Phone: 918-584-2484
Fax: 918-584-4422
E-mail: customerservice@usjaycees.org

UNITED STATES NAVAL SEA CADET CORPS
http://www.seacadets.org

HARRY AND ROSE HOWELL SCHOLARSHIP

Renewable award for sea cadets only. Two Howell Scholarships of $2500 each and one scholarship of $2000. Applicants must be U.S. citizens with a minimum 3.0 GPA. Application deadline is May 1.

Award: Scholarship for use in freshman, sophomore, junior, or senior years; renewable. *Number:* 1. *Amount:* $2000–$2500.

Eligibility Requirements: Applicant must be enrolled or expecting to enroll full-time at a two-year or four-year institution or university. Applicant must have 3.0 GPA or higher. Available to U.S. citizens.

Application Requirements: Application, references, test scores, transcript. *Deadline:* May 1.

Contact: M. Ford, Executive Director
United States Naval Sea Cadet Corps
2300 Wilson Boulevard
Arlington, VA 22201-3308
Phone: 703-243-1546
Fax: 703-243-3985
E-mail: mford@navyleague.org

KINGSLEY FOUNDATION AWARDS

One-time award to assist cadets in continuing their education at an accredited four-year college or university. Must be a member of NSCC for at least two years. Minimum 3.0 GPA required. Application deadline is May 1.

Award: Scholarship for use in freshman, sophomore, junior, or senior years; not renewable. *Number:* 5. *Amount:* $1000.

Eligibility Requirements: Applicant must be enrolled or expecting to enroll full-time at a four-year institution or university. Applicant must have 3.0 GPA or higher. Available to U.S. citizens.

Application Requirements: Application, financial need analysis, references, test scores, transcript. *Deadline:* May 1.

Contact: M. Ford, Executive Director
United States Naval Sea Cadet Corps
2300 Wilson Boulevard
Arlington, VA 22201-3308
Phone: 703-243-1546
Fax: 703-243-3985
E-mail: mford@navyleague.org

NSCC SCHOLARSHIP PROGRAM

One-time award to assist cadets in continuing their education at an accredited four-year college or university. Must be a member of NSCC for at least two years. Minimum 3.0 GPA required. Deadline is May 1.

Award: Scholarship for use in freshman, sophomore, junior, or senior years; not renewable. *Number:* 4. *Amount:* $1000.

Eligibility Requirements: Applicant must be enrolled or expecting to enroll full-time at a four-year institution or university. Applicant must have 3.0 GPA or higher. Available to U.S. citizens.

Application Requirements: Application, financial need analysis, references, test scores, transcript. *Deadline:* May 1.

Contact: M. Ford, Executive Director
United States Naval Sea Cadet Corps
2300 Wilson Boulevard
Arlington, VA 22201-3308
Phone: 703-243-1546
Fax: 703-243-3985
E-mail: mford@navyleague.org

ROBERT AND HELEN HUTTON SCHOLARSHIP

Renewable award for sea cadets only. Applicant must be a U.S. citizen with a minimum 3.0 GPA. Application deadline is May 1.

Award: Scholarship for use in freshman, sophomore, junior, or senior years; renewable. *Number:* 1. *Amount:* $1000.

Eligibility Requirements: Applicant must be enrolled or expecting to enroll full-time at a two-year or four-year institution or university. Applicant must have 3.0 GPA or higher. Available to U.S. citizens.

Application Requirements: Application, financial need analysis, references, test scores, transcript. *Deadline:* May 1.

Contact: M. Ford, Executive Director
United States Naval Sea Cadet Corps
2300 Wilson Boulevard
Arlington, VA 22201-3308
Phone: 703-243-1546
Fax: 703-243-3985
E-mail: mford@navyleague.org

STOCKHOLM SCHOLARSHIP PROGRAM

Renewable award for a selected cadet, to be designated a "Stockholm Scholar." Must be a member of NSCC for at least two years. Assistance provided for no more than four consecutive years at an accredited college or university. Minimum 3.0 GPA required. Deadline is May 1.

Award: Scholarship for use in freshman, sophomore, junior, or senior years; renewable. *Number:* 1. *Amount:* $2000–$2500.

Eligibility Requirements: Applicant must be enrolled or expecting to enroll full-time at a four-year institution or university. Applicant must have 3.0 GPA or higher. Available to U.S. citizens.

Application Requirements: Application, financial need analysis, references, test scores, transcript. *Deadline:* May 1.

Contact: M. Ford, Executive Director
United States Naval Sea Cadet Corps
2300 Wilson Boulevard
Arlington, VA 22201-3308
Phone: 703-243-1546
Fax: 703-243-3985
E-mail: mford@navyleague.org

UNITED STATES SUBMARINE VETERANS OF WWII

U.S. SUBMARINE VETERANS OF WWII SCHOLARSHIP PROGRAM

Award: Scholarship for use in freshman, sophomore, junior, or senior years.

Eligibility Requirements: Applicant must be enrolled or expecting to enroll at an institution or university.

Contact: Tomi Roeske, Scholarship Administrator
United States Submarine Veterans of WWII
5040 Virginia Beach Boulevard, Suite 104-A
Virginia Beach, VA 23462
Phone: 757-671-3200
Fax: 757-671-3330
E-mail: dsfscholars@exis.net

UNITED STATES-INDONESIA SOCIETY
http://www.usindo.org

UNITED STATES-INDONESIA SOCIETY TRAVEL GRANTS

These grants are provided to help fund travel to Indonesia for students and professors to conduct research, language training or other independent study/research.

Award: Grant for use in freshman, sophomore, junior, senior, or graduate years; not renewable. *Number:* 1–15. *Amount:* $1500–$2000.

Eligibility Requirements: Applicant must be enrolled or expecting to enroll full-time at a four-year institution or university. Applicant must have 3.0 GPA or higher. Available to U.S. citizens.

Application Requirements: Resume, references, transcript. *Deadline:* Continuous.

Contact: Dan Getz
United States-Indonesia Society
1625 Massachusetts Avenue NW, Suite 550
Washington, DC 20036-2260
Phone: 202-232-1400
Fax: 202-232-7300
E-mail: usindo@usindo.org

URBAN FINANCIAL SERVICES COALITION-DELAWARE

URBAN BANKERS OF DELAWARE SCHOLARSHIP

Award: Scholarship for use in freshman year.

Eligibility Requirements: Applicant must be enrolled or expecting to enroll at an institution or university.

Contact:

USA TODAY   http://www.allstars.usatoday.com

ALL-U.S.A. COLLEGE ACADEMIC TEAM

A $2500 prize for four-year college or university sophomores, juniors, and seniors who excel in leadership roles both on and off campus. U.S. citizenship is not required but students must be enrolled at an U.S. institution and studying full time. Students must be nominated by their schools. For more information go to: http://allstars.usatoday.com

Award: Prize for use in sophomore, junior, or senior years; not renewable. *Number:* 20. *Amount:* $2500.

Eligibility Requirements: Applicant must be enrolled or expecting to enroll full-time at a four-year institution or university. Available to U.S. and non-U.S. citizens.

Application Requirements: Application, applicant must enter a contest, essay, references, transcript. *Deadline:* varies.

Contact: Carol Skalsk, Senior Administrator
USA Today
7950 Jones Branch Drive
McLean, VA 22108
Phone: 703-854-5890
E-mail: cskalski@usatoday.com

ALL-U.S.A. COMMUNITY AND JR. COLLEGE ACADEMIC TEAM

A $2500 prize for community and junior college students. May be full-time or part-time students. Must be nominated by school. Application deadline: December 5. Must be studying in the U.S. or its territories. Must maintain a 3.25 GPA. For more information, go to: http://allstars.usatoday.com or http://www.ptk.org/schol/aaat/announce.htm

Award: Prize for use in junior year; not renewable. *Number:* 20. *Amount:* $2500.

Eligibility Requirements: Applicant must be enrolled or expecting to enroll full or part-time at a two-year institution. Available to U.S. and non-U.S. citizens.

Application Requirements: Application, applicant must enter a contest, essay, references, transcript. *Deadline:* December 5.

Contact: Heather Johnson, Scholarship Coordinator, Phi Theta Kappa
USA Today
1625 Eastover Drive
Jackson, MS 39211
Phone: 601-984-3560
E-mail: heather.johnson@pti.org

ALL-U.S.A. HIGH SCHOOL ACADEMIC TEAM

$2500 prize given to high school students based on outstanding original academic, artistic, or leadership endeavors. Students must be nominated by their schools. For more information, go to http://allstars.usatoday.com. Deadline is usually the third Friday in February.

Award: Prize for use in freshman year; not renewable. *Number:* 20. *Amount:* $2500.

Eligibility Requirements: Applicant must be high school student and planning to enroll or expecting to enroll full-time at an institution or university. Available to U.S. and non-U.S. citizens.

Application Requirements: Application, applicant must enter a contest, essay, references, test scores, transcript. *Deadline:* February 28.

Contact: Carol Skalski, Senior Administrator
USA Today
7950 Jones Branch Drive
McLean, VA 22108
Phone: 703-854-5890
E-mail: cskalski@usatoday.com

VETERANS OF FOREIGN WARS OF THE UNITED STATES   http://www.vfw.org

VOICE OF DEMOCRACY PROGRAM

Student must be sponsored by a local VFW Post. Student submits a three to five minute audio essay on a contest theme (changes each year). Open to high school students (9th-12th grade). Award available for all levels of postsecondary study in an American institution. Open to permanent U.S.

residents only. Competition starts at local level. No entries are to be submitted to the National Headquarters. Visit Web site (http://www.vfw.org) for more information.

Award: Prize for use in freshman, sophomore, junior, senior, graduate, or postgraduate years; not renewable. *Number:* 59. *Amount:* $1000–$30,000.

Eligibility Requirements: Applicant must be high school student; age 19 or under and planning to enroll or expecting to enroll full or part-time at a two-year or four-year or technical institution or university. Available to U.S. and non-Canadian citizens.

Application Requirements: Applicant must enter a contest, essay, audio cassette tape. *Deadline:* November 1.

Contact: Kris Harmer, Secretary
Veterans of Foreign Wars of the United States
VFW Building
406 West 34th Street
Kansas City, MO 64111
Phone: 816-968-1117
Fax: 816-968-1149
E-mail: kharmer@vfw.org

VIETNOW NATIONAL HEADQUARTERS   http://www.vietnow.com

VIETNOW NATIONAL SCHOLARSHIP

One-time award available to dependents of members of Vietnow only. Applicants' academic achievements, abilities and extracurricular activities will be reviewed. Must be U.S. citizen and under age 35.

Award: Scholarship for use in freshman, sophomore, junior, senior, or graduate years; not renewable. *Number:* 1–5. *Amount:* $500–$1000.

Eligibility Requirements: Applicant must be age 35 or under and enrolled or expecting to enroll full or part-time at a two-year or four-year or technical institution or university. Available to U.S. citizens.

Application Requirements: Application, autobiography, essay, test scores, transcript. *Deadline:* April 1.

Contact: Eileen Shoemaker
VietNow National Headquarters
1835 Broadway
Rockford, IL 61104
Phone: 815-227-5100
Fax: 815-227-5127
E-mail: vnnatl@inwave.com

VIRGINIA DEPARTMENT OF EDUCATION   http://www.pen.k12.va.us

ANNUAL JAMES MONROE SCHOLARSHIP AWARD

Writing contest for students who are juniors or seniors in a public, private, or home-school high school program. See Web site for topics: http://www.jamesmonroe.org/monroeflyer.PDF.

Award: Scholarship for use in freshman year. *Number:* up to 3. *Amount:* $500–$2500.

Eligibility Requirements: Applicant must be enrolled or expecting to enroll at an institution or university. Available to U.S. citizens.

Application Requirements: Application. *Deadline:* March 12.

Contact: Sylinda Gilchrist, School Counseling Specialist
Virginia Department of Education
James Monroe Building
101 North 14th Street
Richmond, VA 23218-2120
Phone: 804-786-9377
Fax: 804-786-5466
E-mail: sgilchri@mail.vak12ed.edu

NATIONAL BETA SCHOLARSHIP

Selection of National Beta Club Scholars is based on a number of factors with special emphasis placed upon academic excellence, demonstrated leadership, character, and school/community service. Applicants must submit test scores from SAT or ACT.

Award: Scholarship for use in freshman year. *Number:* up to 210. *Amount:* $1000–$15,000.

Virginia Department of Education (continued)

Eligibility Requirements: Applicant must be enrolled or expecting to enroll at an institution or university. Available to U.S. citizens.

Application Requirements: Application, essay, test scores. *Deadline:* December 10.

Contact: Kenneth Dinkins, Superintendent
Virginia Department of Education
151 Beta Club Way
Spartanburg, SC 29306-3012
Phone: 800-845-8281
Fax: 864-542-9300

VIRGINIA SOCIETY OF CERTIFIED PUBLIC ACCOUNTANTS EDUCATION FOUNDATION   http://www.vscpa.com

GOODMAN & COMPANY ANNUAL SCHOLARSHIP

Scholarship for student currently enrolled in an accredited Virginia college or university who has demonstrated academic excellence and financial need.

Award: Scholarship for use in junior or senior years. *Amount:* $2500.

Eligibility Requirements: Applicant must be enrolled or expecting to enroll full-time at a four-year institution or university. Applicant must have 3.0 GPA or higher. Available to U.S. citizens.

Application Requirements: Application, resume, references, transcript. *Deadline:* April 15.

Contact: Tracey Zink, Public Relations Coordinator
Virginia Society of Certified Public Accountants Education Foundation
PO Box 4620
Glen Allen, VA 23058-4620
Phone: 800-733-8272
Fax: 804-273-1741
E-mail: tzink@vscpa.com

WAL-MART FOUNDATION   http://www.walmartfoundation.org

SAM WALTON COMMUNITY SCHOLARSHIP

Award for high school seniors not affiliated with Wal-Mart stores. Based on academic merit, financial need, and school or work activities. Each store awards one nonrenewable scholarship. For use at an accredited two- or four-year U.S. institution. Must have 2.5 GPA. Applications available only through local Wal-Mart or Sam's Club stores starting in December. Applications are not available from the corporate office.

Award: Scholarship for use in freshman year; not renewable. *Number:* 2900–3400. *Amount:* $1000.

Eligibility Requirements: Applicant must be high school student and planning to enroll or expecting to enroll full-time at a two-year or four-year institution or university. Applicant must have 2.5 GPA or higher. Available to U.S. citizens.

Application Requirements: Application, essay, financial need analysis, test scores, transcript. *Deadline:* February 1.

Contact: Jenny Harral
Wal-Mart Foundation
702 Southwest 8th Street
Bentonville, AR 72716-0150
Phone: 800-530-9925
Fax: 501-273-6850

WASHINGTON HIGHER EDUCATION COORDINATING BOARD   http://www.hecb.wa.gov

HEALTH PROFESSIONAL LOAN REPAYMENT AND SCHOLARSHIP PROGRAMS

Award: Scholarship for use in junior, senior, or graduate years.

Eligibility Requirements: Applicant must be enrolled or expecting to enroll at an institution or university.

Contact: Karola Longoria, Administrative Assistant, Student Financial Assist
Washington Higher Education Coordinating Board
917 Lakeridge Way, SW
PO Box 43430
Olympia, WA 98504-3430
Phone: 360-753-7850
Fax: 360-753-7808
E-mail: karolal@hecb.wa.gov

WASHINGTON HOSPITAL HEALTHCARE SYSTEM   http://www.whhs.com

WASHINGTON HOSPITAL EMPLOYEE ASSOCIATION SCHOLARSHIP

Scholarship for a dependent of a Washington Hospital Employee. Must be a graduating senior, community college student, transferring community college student, or a student attending a four-year institution. Deadline is March 1.

Award: Scholarship for use in freshman, sophomore, junior, or senior years; not renewable. *Amount:* up to $2000.

Eligibility Requirements: Applicant must be high school student and planning to enroll or expecting to enroll full or part-time at a four-year institution or university. Available to U.S. citizens.

Application Requirements: Application, essay, references, transcript. *Deadline:* March 1.

Contact: Mary Kinnear, WHEA Scholarship Chair, c/o Personnel Department
Washington Hospital Healthcare System
2500 Mowry Avenue
Fremont, CA 94538

WINSTON-SALEM FOUNDATION   http://www.wsfoundation.org

FLOW AUTOMOTIVE COMPANIES SCHOLARSHIP

College scholarships available for dependent children of Flow Companies employees.

Award: Scholarship for use in freshman, sophomore, junior, or senior years. *Number:* 1.

Eligibility Requirements: Applicant must be enrolled or expecting to enroll full-time at a four-year institution or university. Available to U.S. citizens.

Application Requirements: Application, references, test scores, transcript. *Deadline:* varies.

Contact: Kay Dillon, Student Aid Director
Winston-Salem Foundation
860 West Fifth Street
Winston-Salem, NC 27101-2506
Phone: 336-725-2382
Fax: 336-727-0581
E-mail: kdillon@wsfoundation.org

WISCONSIN ASSOCIATION FOR FOOD PROTECTION   http://www.wafp-wi.org

WAFP MEMORIAL SCHOLARSHIP

Scholarship for a child or dependent of a current or deceased Wisconsin Association of Food Protection (WAFP) member, or applicant may be a WAFP student member. Must have been accepted in an accredited post-high school degree program in a university, college, or technical institute.

Award: Scholarship for use in freshman year. *Amount:* $750.

Eligibility Requirements: Applicant must be enrolled or expecting to enroll at a four-year institution or university. Available to U.S. citizens.

Application Requirements: Application. *Deadline:* varies.

Contact: Wisconsin Association for Food Protection
c/o George Nelson, 1207 Main Street East
Menomie, WI 54751

WISCONSIN FOUNDATION FOR INDEPENDENT COLLEGES, INC.   http://www.wficweb.org

AMERICAN FAMILY INSURANCE COMMUNITY INVOLVEMENT SCHOLARSHIP

Award: Scholarship for use in freshman, sophomore, junior, or senior years.

Eligibility Requirements: Applicant must be enrolled or expecting to enroll at an institution or university.

Contact: Christy Miller, Marketing Program Manager
Wisconsin Foundation for Independent Colleges, Inc.
735 North Water Street, Suite 600
Milwaukee, WI 53202
Phone: 414-273-5980
Fax: 414-273-5995
E-mail: wfic@execpc.com

LAND'S END SCHOLARSHIP

Award: Scholarship for use in freshman, sophomore, junior, or senior years.

Eligibility Requirements: Applicant must be enrolled or expecting to enroll at an institution or university.

Contact: Christy Miller, Marketing Program Manager
Wisconsin Foundation for Independent Colleges, Inc.
735 North Water Street, Suite 600
Milwaukee, WI 53202
Phone: 414-273-5980
Fax: 414-273-5995
E-mail: wfic@execpc.com

RATH DISTINGUISHED SCHOLARSHIP

Award: Scholarship for use in freshman, sophomore, junior, or senior years.

Eligibility Requirements: Applicant must be enrolled or expecting to enroll at an institution or university.

Contact: Christy Miller, Marketing Program Manager
Wisconsin Foundation for Independent Colleges, Inc.
735 North Water Street, Suite 600
Milwaukee, WI 53202
Phone: 414-273-5980
Fax: 414-273-5995
E-mail: wfic@execpc.com

SENTRY 21 CLUB SCHOLARSHIP

Award: Scholarship for use in freshman, sophomore, junior, or senior years.

Eligibility Requirements: Applicant must be enrolled or expecting to enroll at an institution or university.

Contact: Christy Miller, Marketing Program Manager
Wisconsin Foundation for Independent Colleges, Inc.
735 North Water Street, Suite 600
Milwaukee, WI 53202
Phone: 414-273-5980
Fax: 414-273-5995
E-mail: wfic@execpc.com

THRIVENT FINANCIAL FOR LUTHERANS COMMUNITY LEADERS SCHOLARSHIP PROGRAM

Award: Scholarship for use in freshman, sophomore, junior, or senior years.

Eligibility Requirements: Applicant must be enrolled or expecting to enroll at an institution or university.

Contact: Christy Miller, Marketing Program Manager
Wisconsin Foundation for Independent Colleges, Inc.
735 North Water Street, Suite 600
Milwaukee, WI 53202
Phone: 414-273-5980
Fax: 414-273-5995
E-mail: wfic@execpc.com

UPS SCHOLARSHIP

Award: Scholarship for use in freshman, sophomore, junior, or senior years.

Eligibility Requirements: Applicant must be enrolled or expecting to enroll at an institution or university.

Contact: Christy Miller, Marketing Program Manager
Wisconsin Foundation for Independent Colleges, Inc.
735 North Water Street, Suite 600
Milwaukee, WI 53202
Phone: 414-273-5980
Fax: 414-273-5995
E-mail: wfic@execpc.com

WE ENERGIES SCHOLARSHIP

Award: Scholarship for use in freshman, sophomore, junior, or senior years.

Eligibility Requirements: Applicant must be enrolled or expecting to enroll at an institution or university.

Contact: Christy Miller, Marketing Program Manager
Wisconsin Foundation for Independent Colleges, Inc.
735 North Water Street, Suite 600
Milwaukee, WI 53202
Phone: 414-273-5980
Fax: 414-273-5995
E-mail: wfic@execpc.com

WISCONSIN FIRST SCHOLARSHIP PROGRAM

Award: Scholarship for use in freshman, sophomore, junior, or senior years.

Eligibility Requirements: Applicant must be enrolled or expecting to enroll at an institution or university.

Contact: Christy Miller, Marketing Program Manager
Wisconsin Foundation for Independent Colleges, Inc.
735 North Water Street, Suite 600
Milwaukee, WI 53202
Phone: 414-273-5980
Fax: 414-273-5995
E-mail: wfic@execpc.com

WOMEN ECONOMIC DEVELOPERS OF LONG ISLAND   http://www.wedli.org

MADELYN ORSINI SCHOLARSHIPS

Scholarships of up to $1000 will be awarded to college students in either freshman, sophmore or junior year of college located on Long Island, NY. No specific limit on the number of the awards but maximum amount is $1000. Application available at Web site: http://www.wedli.org/orsini_application1.html

Award: Scholarship for use in freshman, sophomore, or junior years; renewable. *Amount:* up to $1000.

Eligibility Requirements: Applicant must be enrolled or expecting to enroll full or part-time at a two-year or four-year institution or university and female. Available to U.S. citizens.

Application Requirements: Application, autobiography, essay, financial need analysis, references, transcript. *Deadline:* May 2.

Contact: Michele A. Pincus, Esq., President & WEDLI Scholarship Coordinator
Women Economic Developers of Long Island
c/o Lazer, Aptheker, Rosella & Yedid, P.C., 225 Old Country Road
Melville, NY 11747
Phone: 631-761-0800
Fax: 631-761-0013
E-mail: pincus@larypc.com

WOMEN IN DEFENSE (WID), A NATIONAL SECURITY ORGANIZATION   http://wid.ndia.org

HORIZONS FOUNDATION SCHOLARSHIP

Scholarships are awarded to provide financial assistance to further educational objectives of women either employed or planning careers in defense or national security arenas (not law enforcement or criminal justice). Must be U.S. citizen. Minimum 3.5 GPA required. Deadline is July 1.

Award: Scholarship for use in junior, senior, graduate, or postgraduate years; renewable. *Number:* 5–10. *Amount:* $500–$1000.

Women in Defense (WID), A National Security Organization (continued)

Eligibility Requirements: Applicant must be enrolled or expecting to enroll full or part-time at a four-year institution or university and female. Applicant must have 3.5 GPA or higher. Available to U.S. citizens.

Application Requirements: Application, essay, financial need analysis, references, self-addressed stamped envelope, transcript. *Deadline:* July 1.

Contact: Jane Patrick Casey, Program contact, Application available at Web site.
Women in Defense (WID), A National Security Organization
2111 Wilson Boulevard, Suite 400
Arlington, VA 22201-3061
Phone: 703-247-2564
Fax: 703-522-1885
E-mail: wid@ndia.org

WOMEN'S JEWELRY ASSOCIATION   http://www.womensjewelry.org

WJA MEMBER GRANT

Member Grants are generally up to $500 in value and can be used by members to pay for any aspect of further education during the year. For more information please visit Web site: http://www.womensjewelry.org/

Award: Grant for use in freshman, sophomore, junior, senior, or graduate years. *Amount:* up to $500.

Eligibility Requirements: Applicant must be enrolled or expecting to enroll at a two-year or four-year institution or university. Available to U.S. citizens.

Application Requirements: Application. *Deadline:* varies.

Contact: Scholarship Committee
Women's Jewelry Association
333 B Route 46 West, Suite B 201
Fairfield, NJ 07004
Phone: 973-575-7190
Fax: 973-575-1445

WOODMEN OF THE WORLD   http://www.denverwoodmen.com

WOODMEN OF THE WORLD SCHOLARSHIP PROGRAM

One-time award for full-time study at a trade/technical school, two-year college, four-year college or university. Applicant must be a member or child of a member by a family rider of Woodman of the World of Denver, Colorado. Applicant must have minimum 2.5 GPA.

Award: Scholarship for use in freshman, sophomore, junior, senior, or graduate years; not renewable. *Number:* 45. *Amount:* $500–$1500.

Eligibility Requirements: Applicant must be enrolled or expecting to enroll full-time at a two-year or four-year or technical institution or university. Applicant must have 2.5 GPA or higher. Available to U.S. citizens.

Application Requirements: Application, essay, photo, transcript. *Deadline:* March 15.

Contact: Scholarship Committee
Woodmen of the World
PO Box 266000
Highlands Ranch, CO 80163-6000
Phone: 303-792-9777
Fax: 303-792-9793

ZETA PHI BETA SORORITY, INC. NATIONAL EDUCATIONAL FOUNDATION   http://www.zphib1920.org

GENERAL UNDERGRADUATE SCHOLARSHIP

Scholarships available for undergraduate students. Awarded for full-time study for one academic year. Check Web site for information and application: http://www.zphib1920.org

Award: Scholarship for use in freshman, sophomore, junior, or senior years; not renewable. *Number:* varies. *Amount:* $500–$1000.

Eligibility Requirements: Applicant must be enrolled or expecting to enroll full-time at a four-year institution or university. Available to U.S. citizens.

Application Requirements: Application, essay, references, transcript, proof of enrollment. *Deadline:* February 1.

Contact: Cheryl Williams, National Second Vice President
Zeta Phi Beta Sorority, Inc. National Educational Foundation
1734 New Hampshire Avenue, NW
Washington, DC 20009-2595
Fax: 318-631-4028
E-mail: 2ndanti@zphib1920.org

LULLELIA W. HARRISON SCHOLARSHIP IN COUNSELING

Scholarships available for students enrolled in a graduate or undergraduate degree program in counseling. Awarded for full-time study for one academic year. See Web site for additional information and application. http://www.zphibl920.org

Award: Scholarship for use in freshman, sophomore, junior, senior, or graduate years; not renewable. *Number:* varies. *Amount:* $500–$1000.

Eligibility Requirements: Applicant must be enrolled or expecting to enroll full-time at a four-year institution or university. Available to U.S. citizens.

Application Requirements: Application, essay, references, transcript, proof of enrollment. *Deadline:* February 1.

Contact: Cheryl Williams, National Second Vice President
Zeta Phi Beta Sorority, Inc. National Educational Foundation
1734 New Hampshire Avenue, NW
Washington, DC 20009-2595
Fax: 318-631-4028
E-mail: 2ndanti@zphib1920.org

Indexes

Award Name

American Baptist Financial Aid Program Native
American Grants 604
American Baptist Scholarships 649
American Board of Funeral Service Education
Scholarships 313
American Cancer Society, Florida Division R O C K
College Scholarship Program 658
American Chemical Society, Rubber Division
Undergraduate Scholarship 158
American College of Musicians/National Guild of Piano
Teachers 200-Dollar Scholarships 401
American Council of Engineering Companies of Oregon
Scholarship 167
American Council of the Blind Scholarships 554
American Criminal Justice Association-Lambda Alpha
Epsilon National Scholarship 198
American Dental Association Foundation Dental
Assisting Scholarship Program 204
American Dental Association Foundation Dental
Hygiene Scholarship Program 204
American Dental Association Foundation Dental Lab
Technology Scholarship 204
American Dental Association Foundation Dental
Student Scholarship Program 204
American Dental Association Foundation Minority
Dental Student Scholarship Program 204
American Dental Hygienists' Association Institute
Minority Scholarship 205
American Dental Hygienists' Association Institute
Research Grant 205
American Dental Hygienists' Association Part-Time
Scholarship 205
American Dietetic Association Foundation Scholarship
Program 300
American Electroplaters and Surface Finishers
Scholarships 158
American Essay Contest Scholarship 487
American Express Scholarship Program 350
American Express Travel Scholarship 472
American Ex-Prisoner of War Scholarships: Peter
Connacher Memorial Scholarship 594
American Family Insurance Community Involvement
Scholarship 853
American Federation of State, County, and Municipal
Employees Scholarship Program 483
American Foreign Service Association (AFSA) Financial
Aid Award Program 484
American Foreign Service Association (AFSA)/AAFSW
Merit Award Program 484
American Geological Institute Minority Scholarship 604
American Ground Water Trust-AMTROL, Inc.
Scholarship 170
American Ground Water Trust-Claude Laval
Corporation The Ben Everson Scholarship 170
American Heroes - U.S. Military Challenge 802
American Indian Education Foundation Scholarship 605
American Indian Endowed Scholarship 647
American Indian Nurse Scholarship Awards 429
American Institute for Foreign Study International
Scholarships 760
American Institute for Foreign Study Minority
Scholarships 605
American Institute of Architects Minority/Disadvantaged
Scholarship 97
American Institute of Architects/American Architectural
Foundation Minority/Disadvantaged Scholarships 98
American Institute of Architecture (AIA) Dayton
Architectural Scholarship Fund 99
American Jewish League for Israel Scholarship
Program 788
American Legacy Scholarship 585
American Legion Auxiliary Department of Alabama
Scholarship Program 579
American Legion Auxiliary Department of Arizona
Health Care Occupation Scholarships 319
American Legion Auxiliary Department of Arizona
Nurses' Scholarships 415
American Legion Auxiliary Department of Arizona
Wilma Hoyal-Maxine Chilton Memorial
Scholarship 449
American Legion Auxiliary Department of Arkansas
Academic Scholarship 579
American Legion Auxiliary Department of Arkansas
Nurse Scholarship 415
American Legion Auxiliary Department of Colorado
Department President's Scholarship for Junior
Member 788
American Legion Auxiliary Department of Colorado
Past President Parley Nurses Scholarship 788
American Legion Auxiliary Department of Connecticut
Memorial Educational Grant 484
American Legion Auxiliary Department of Florida
Department Scholarships 579

American Legion Auxiliary Department of Florida
Memorial Scholarship 484
American Legion Auxiliary Department of Florida
National President's Scholarship 788
American Legion Auxiliary Department of Iowa
Children of Veterans Scholarship 579
American Legion Auxiliary Department of Maine
Scholarship 789
American Legion Auxiliary Department of Maryland
Children and Youth Scholarships 789
American Legion Auxiliary Department of Maryland
Past President's Parley Nursing Scholarship 789
American Legion Auxiliary Department of Massachusetts
Past President's Parley Scholarship 789
American Legion Auxiliary Department of Michigan
Memorial Scholarship 580
American Legion Auxiliary Department of Minnesota
Past President Parley Health Care Scholarship 320
American Legion Auxiliary Department of Minnesota
Scholarships 581
American Legion Auxiliary Department of Nebraska
Nurse's Gift Tuition Scholarship 416
American Legion Auxiliary Department of Nebraska
Practical Nurse Scholarship 416
American Legion Auxiliary Department of Nebraska
President's Scholarship for Junior Members 485
American Legion Auxiliary Department of Nebraska
President's Scholarships 581
American Legion Auxiliary Department of Nebraska
Student Aid Grants 581
American Legion Auxiliary Department of New Mexico
Past President Parley Nurses Scholarship 416
American Legion Auxiliary Department of North Dakota
Past President's Parley Nurses' Scholarship 417
American Legion Auxiliary Department of North Dakota
Scholarships 659
American Legion Auxiliary Department of Ohio
Department President's Scholarship 582
American Legion Auxiliary Department of Ohio Past
President's Parley Nurses' Scholarship 417
American Legion Auxiliary Department of Oregon
Nurses Scholarship 417
American Legion Auxiliary Department of Pennsylvania
Past Department President's Memorial
Scholarship 790
American Legion Auxiliary Department of Pennsylvania
Scholarship for Dependents of Disabled or Deceased
Veterans 790
American Legion Auxiliary Department of Pennsylvania
Scholarship for Dependents of Living Veterans 790
American Legion Auxiliary Department of Washington
Susan Burdett Scholarship 660
American Legion Auxiliary Girl Scout Achievement
Award 486
American Legion Auxiliary Girl Scout Achievement
Award 580
American Legion Auxiliary Missouri State National
President's Scholarship 485
American Legion Auxiliary National Presidents
Scholarship 485
American Legion Auxiliary National President's
Scholarship 581
American Legion Auxiliary National President's
Scholarship 580
American Legion Auxiliary National President's
Scholarships 583
American Legion Auxiliary Non-Traditional Students
Scholarships 487
American Legion Auxiliary Scholarship For Non-
Traditional Students 580
American Legion Auxiliary Spirit Of Youth Scholarship
For Junior Members 580
American Legion Auxiliary Spirit of Youth Scholarships
for Junior Members 487
American Legion Auxiliary, Department of Idaho
National President's Scholarship 579
American Legion Auxiliary, Department of Idaho
Nursing Scholarship 415
American Legion Auxiliary, Department of Maine
National President's Scholarship 789
American Legion Auxiliary, Department of
Massachusetts Department President's
Scholarship 789
American Legion Auxiliary, Department of Oregon
National President's Scholarship 582
American Legion Auxiliary, Department of Texas
General Education Scholarship 582
American Legion Auxiliary, Department of Texas Past
President's Parley Medical Scholarship 320
American Legion Auxiliary, Department of Washington
Gift Scholarships 583
American Legion Auxiliary, National President's
Scholarship 538

American Legion Department of Arkansas Oratorical
Contest 660
American Legion Department of Hawaii State Oratorical
Contest 660
American Legion Department of Indiana, Americanism
and Government Test 790
American Legion Department of Iowa Eagle Scout of
the Year Scholarship 488
American Legion Department of Maine Children and
Youth Scholarship 662
American Legion Department of Maryland General
Scholarship 662
American Legion Department of Maryland General
Scholarship Fund 584
American Legion Department of Maryland Math-Science
Scholarship 444
American Legion Department of Michigan Oratorical
Contest 662
American Legion Department of Minnesota Memorial
Scholarship 489
American Legion Department of Minnesota State
Oratorical Contest 662
American Legion Department of Nebraska Oratorical
Awards 790
American Legion Department of New York State High
School Oratorical Contest 663
American Legion Department of North Carolina High
School Oratorical Contest 663
American Legion Department of North Dakota National
High School Oratorical Contest 663
American Legion Department of Pennsylvania State
Oratorical Contest 664
American Legion Department of Tennessee Eagle Scout
of the Year 790
American Legion Department of Tennessee Oratorical
Contest 790
American Legion Department of Vermont Department
Scholarships 664
American Legion Department of Virginia High School
Oratorical Contest Award 664
American Legion Department of Washington Children
and Youth Scholarships 490
American Legion Department of West Virginia State
Oratorical Contest 665
American Legion Eagle Scout of the Year 490
American Legion High School Oratorical Contest 664
American Legion National Headquarters Eagle Scout of
the Year 490
American Legion National Headquarters National High
School Oratorical Contest 760
American Legion Oratorical Contest-Illinois 661
American Legion Press Club of New Jersey and Post 170
Arthur Dehardt Memorial Scholarship 178
American Legion Samsung Scholarship 583
American Legion Scholarship—Ohio 489
American Legion Western District Postsecondary
Scholarship 660
American Legion, Department of Arizona High School
Oratorical Contest 660
American Legion, Department of Idaho Scholarship 487
American Legion, Department of Illinois
Scholarships 487
American Legion, Department of Illinois, Boy Scout/
Explorer Scholarship 487
American Legion, Department of Indiana State
Oratorical Contest 661
American Legion, Department of West Virginia Board
of Regents Scholarship 665
American Medical Technologists Student
Scholarship 207
American Meteorological Society 75th Anniversary
Scholarship 397
American Meteorological Society Dr. Pedro Grau
Undergraduate Scholarship 397
American Meteorological Society Howard H. Hanks, Jr.
Meteorological Scholarship 397
American Meteorological Society Howard T. Orville
Meteorology Scholarship 398
American Meteorological Society Industry
Undergraduate Scholarships 89
American Meteorological Society Mark J. Schroeder
Scholarship in Meteorology 398
American Meteorological Society Richard and Helen
Hagemeyer Scholarship 398
American Meteorological Society Werner A. Baum
Undergraduate Scholarship 398
American Meteorological Society/Industry Minority
Scholarships 398
American Montessori Society Teacher Education
Scholarship Fund 220
American Morgan Horse Institute Educational
Scholarships 761

American Morgan Horse Institute Grand Prix Dressage Award *761*
American Morgan Horse Institute Graywood Youth Horsemanship Grant *761*
American Morgan Horse Institute van Schaik Dressage Scholarship *761*
American Nephrology Nurses' Association American Regent Career Mobility Scholarship *418*
American Nephrology Nurses' Association AMGEN Career Mobility Scholarship *419*
American Nephrology Nurses' Association Anthony J. Janetti, Inc. Career Mobility Scholarship *419*
American Nephrology Nurses' Association Bioethics Grant *791*
American Nephrology Nurses' Association Career Mobility Scholarship *419*
American Nephrology Nurses' Association NNCC Career Mobility Scholarship *419*
American Nephrology Nurses' Association Watson Pharma, Inc. Career Mobility Scholarship *419*
American Nuclear Society James R. Vogt Scholarship *248*
American Nuclear Society Operations and Power Scholarship *248*
American Nuclear Society Undergraduate Scholarships *249*
American Occupational Therapy Foundation State Association Scholarships *321*
American Orff-Schulwerk Association Research Grant *220*
American Pharmacy Services Corporation Scholarship/ Loan *442*
American Physical Society Corporate-Sponsored Scholarship for Minority Undergraduate Students Who Major in Physics *447*
American Physical Society Scholarship for Minority Undergraduate Physics Majors *444*
American Press Institute Scholarship *361*
American Quarter Horse Foundation Youth Scholarships *491*
American Restaurant Scholarship *201*
American Savings Foundation Scholarship *791*
American Society for Enology and Viticulture Scholarships *78*
American Society of Agricultural and Biological Engineers Foundation Scholarship *78*
American Society of Agricultural and Biological Engineers Student Engineer of the Year Scholarship *251*
American Society of Certified Engineering Technicians Small Cash Grant *251*
American Society of Civil Engineers-Maine High School Scholarship *172*
American Society of Criminology Gene Carte Student Paper Competition *199*
American Society of Heating, Refrigeration, and Air Conditioning Engineering Technology Scholarship *90*
American Society of Mechanical Engineers Foundation Scholarship *252*
American Society of Mechanical Engineers Solid Waste Processing Division Undergraduate Scholarship *391*
American Society of Mechanical Engineers Stephen T. Kugle Scholarship *791*
American Society of Mechanical Engineers/First Robotics Competition Scholarship *392*
American Society of Mechanical Engineers-American Society of Mechanical Engineers Auxiliary First Clarke Scholarship *393*
American Society of Naval Engineers Scholarship *90*
American Society of Women Accountants Scholarship *54*
American Society of Women Accountants Two Year College Scholarship *54*
American Theatre Organ Society Organ Performance Scholarship *762*
American Water Ski Educational Foundation Scholarship *493*
American Welding Society District Scholarship Program *285*
American Welding Society International Scholarship *253*
American Woman's Society of Certified Public Accountants- Georgia Affiliate Scholarship *54*
American-Scandinavian Foundation Translation Prize *762*
America's Intercultural Magazine (AIM) Short Story Contest *382*
America's Junior Miss Scholarship Program *792*
America's National Teenager Scholarship Program *829*
AMVETS National Ladies Auxiliary Scholarship *493*
Amy Lowell Poetry Traveling Scholarship *383*

Anderson Area Society for Human Resource Management Non-Member Scholarship Program *797*
Anderson Area Society for Human Resource Management Scholarship Program *797*
Andrew G. Chressanthis Memorial Scholarship *615*
Andrew K. Ruotolo, Jr. Memorial Scholarship *376*
Angelfire Scholarship *587*
Angelina and Pete Costanzo Vocational Scholarship *735*
Angelus Awards Student Film Festival *762*
Angus Foundation Scholarships *506*
Anheuser-Busch Urban Scholarship *696*
ANLA National Scholarship Endowment-Usrey Family Scholarship *341*
Ann Lane Home Economics Scholarship *305*
Anna and Charles Stockwitz Children and Youth Fund *651*
Anna and John Kolesar Memorial Scholarships *218*
Anne A. Agnew Scholarship *841*
Anne Ford Scholarship *562*
Anne Lindeman Memorial Scholarship *142*
Anne Maureen Whitney Barrow Memorial Scholarship *277*
Anne Seaman Professional Grounds Management Society Memorial Scholarship *84*
Anne U. White Fund *494*
Annie S. Crowell Scholarship Fund *682*
Annual Award Program *650*
Annual James Monroe Scholarship Award *851*
Annual Liberty Graphics Art Contest *704*
Annual Scholarship Grant Program *306*
Annual Senior High Communication Contest *784*
Anonymous Scholarship Benefiting Graduates of Thayer County in Nebraska *704*
ANS Incoming Freshman Scholarship *413*
AOPA Air Safety Foundation/Donald Burnside Memorial Scholarship *119*
AOPA Air Safety Foundation/Koch Corporation Scholarship *119*
AOPA Air Safety Foundation/McAllister Memorial Scholarship *119*
Apha Delta Kappa Foundation Fine Arts Grants *108*
Appaloosa Youth Educational Scholarships *493*
Applegate/Jackson/Parks Future Teacher Scholarship *232*
Appraisal Institute Educational Scholarship Program *451*
APTRA-Clete Roberts Memorial Journalism Scholarship Award *358*
APTRA-Kathyrn Dettman Memorial Scholarship *359*
AQHF Education or Nursing Scholarship *220*
AQHF Journalism or Communications Scholarship *178*
AQHF Racing Scholarships *86*
AQHF Telephony Scholarship for Senior Veterinary Students *86*
AQHF Working Student Scholarship *491*
Arab American Heritage Council Scholarship *605*
Arby's-Big Brothers Big Sisters Scholarship Award *493*
ARC of Washington Trust Fund Stipend Program *461*
Archbold Scholarship Program *327*
Architecture and Engineering Scholarship Program *102*
Architecture, Construction, and Engineering Mentor Program Scholarships *101*
AREMA Michael R. Garcia Scholarship *250*
AREMA Undergraduate Scholarships *250*
Arizona Chapter Dependent/Employee Membership Scholarship *493*
Arizona Chapter Gold Scholarship *473*
Arizona Community College Scholarship *745*
Arizona Counselor of the Year Scholarship *746*
Arizona Hydrological Survey Student Scholarship *212*
Arizona Nursery Association Foundation Scholarship *342*
Arizona Police Corps Scholarship *792*
Arizona Private Postsecondary Education Student Financial Assistance Program *666*
Arizona Private School Association Scholarship *666*
Arizona Quarter Horse Youth Racing Scholarship *491*
Arizona Section Scholarship *277*
Arkansas Academic Challenge Scholarship Program *666*
Arkansas Health Education Grant Program (ARHEG) *86*
Arkansas Minority Teacher Scholars Program *221*
Arkansas Single Parent Scholarship *667*
Arkansas Student Assistance Grant Program *666*
Armed Forces Communications and Electronics Association Educational Foundation Distance-Learning Scholarship *191*
Armed Forces Communications and Electronics Association General Emmett Paige Scholarship *191*
Armed Forces Communications and Electronics Association General John A. Wickham Scholarship *192*
Armed Forces Communications and Electronics Association ROTC Scholarship Program *120*
Armed Forces Loan Forgiveness Program *594*

Armenian Relief Society Undergraduate Scholarship *606*
Armenian Students Association of America, Inc. Scholarships *606*
Army Officers' Wives' Club of the Greater Washington Area Scholarship *573*
Army ROTC Historically Black Colleges and Universities Program *573*
Army ROTC Two-Year, Three-Year and Four-Year Scholarships for Active Duty Army Enlisted Personnel *573*
Arne Engebretsen Wisconsin Mathematics Council Scholarship *240*
ARRL Foundation General Fund Scholarships *763*
ARRL Senator Barry Goldwater (K7UGA) Scholarship *763*
Arsham Amirikian Engineering Scholarship *172*
ARTBA-TDF Highway Workers Memorial Scholarship Program *791*
Arthur and Gladys Cervenka Scholarship Award *272*
Arthur B. Gurda Memorial Award *834*
Arthur C. Tilley Memorial Scholarship *679*
Arthur E. and Helen Copeland Scholarships *566*
Artie Cutler Memorial Scholarship *303*
Artistic Endeavors Scholarship *560*
Artist's- Blacksmith's Association of North America, Inc. Scholarship Program *109*
Artist's Magazine's Annual Art Competition *764*
Artist's-Blacksmith's Association of North America, Inc. Affiliate Visiting Artist Grant Program *109*
Arts Recognition and Talent Search (ARTS) *113*
Arts Scholarship Program *114*
ASCLS Region II Virginia Society for Clinical Laboratory Science Scholarships *323*
ASCLS Region IV Ohio Society for Clinical Laboratory Science Geraldine Diebler/Stella Griffin Award *323*
ASCLS Region IV Ohio Society for Clinical Laboratory Science Stella Griffin Memorial Scholarship *323*
ASCLS Region IX Clinical Laboratory Scientists of Alaska Sharon O'Meara Continuing Education Scholarship Fund *161*
ASCLS Region VI Missouri Organization for Clinical Laboratory Science Education Scholarship *162*
ASCLS Region VI Missouri Organization for Clinical Laboratory Science Student Scholarship *665*
ASCPA Educational Foundation Scholarship *53*
ASCPA High School Scholarships *54*
ASCPA University Scholarships *55*
ASCSA Summer Sessions Open Scholarships *88*
Ashby B. Carter Memorial Scholarship Fund Founders Award *826*
Ashby B. Carter Memorial Scholarship Program *505*
Ashley Tamburri Scholarship *667*
ASHRAE Memorial Scholarship *251*
ASHRAE Region IV Benny Bootle Scholarship *252*
ASHRAE Region VIII Scholarship *252*
ASHRAE Scholarships *252*
Asian Reporter Scholarship *636*
Asian-American Journalists Association Scholarship *179*
ASID Educational Foundation/Irene Winifred Eno Grant *355*
ASID Educational Foundation/Joel Polsky Academic Achievement Award *355*
ASID Educational Foundation/Yale R. Burge Competition *355*
ASLA Council of Fellows Scholarship *371*
ASM Materials Education Foundation Scholarships *255*
ASM Outstanding Scholars Awards *255*
ASSE-Edwin P. Granberry, Jr. Distinguished Service Award Scholarship *435*
ASSE-Gulf Coast Past Presidents Scholarship *435*
ASSE-Marsh Risk Consulting Scholarship *435*
ASSE-Region IV/Edwin P. Granberry Scholarship *435*
ASSE-United Parcel Service Scholarship *435*
Assistance League of the Triangle Scholarship Program *674*
Associate Degree Nursing Scholarship Program *424*
Associated General Contractors of America-New York State Chapter Scholarship Program *173*
Associated Medical Services, Inc. Bioethics Studentship *606*
Associated Medical Services, Inc. Hannah Studentship *324*
Associated Press Television/Radio Association-Clete Roberts Journalism Scholarship Awards *358*
Association for Facilities Engineering Cedar Valley Chapter # 132 Scholarship *19*
Association for Food and Drug Officials Scholarship Fund *301*
Association for Iron and Steel Technology Baltimore Chapter Scholarship *387*
Association for Iron and Steel Technology Benjamin F. Fairless Scholarship *388*

Association for Iron and Steel Technology David H. Samson Scholarship *162*

Association for Iron and Steel Technology Ferrous Metallurgy Education Today (FeMET) *388*

Association for Iron and Steel Technology Midwest Chapter Betty McKern Scholarship *257*

Association for Iron and Steel Technology Midwest Chapter Don Nelson Scholarship *257*

Association for Iron and Steel Technology Midwest Chapter Engineering Scholarship *257*

Association for Iron and Steel Technology Midwest Chapter Jack Gill Scholarship *257*

Association for Iron and Steel Technology Midwest Chapter Mel Nickel Scholarship *258*

Association for Iron and Steel Technology Midwest Chapter Non-Engineering Scholarship *793*

Association for Iron and Steel Technology Midwest Chapter Western States Scholarship *793*

Association for Iron and Steel Technology National Merit Scholarship *258*

Association for Iron and Steel Technology Northwest Member Chapter Scholarship *258*

Association for Iron and Steel Technology Ohio Valley Chapter Scholarship *135*

Association for Iron and Steel Technology Pittsburgh Chapter Scholarship *258*

Association for Iron and Steel Technology Ronald E. Lincoln Scholarship *388*

Association for Iron and Steel Technology Southeast Member Chapter Scholarship *258*

Association for Iron and Steel Technology Willy Korf Memorial Scholarship *388*

Association for Women in Architecture Scholarship *98*

Association for Women in Science College Scholarship *86*

Association of California Water Agencies Scholarships *91*

Association of Energy Service Companies Scholarship Program *505*

Association of Hispanic Professionals for Education Scholarship *152*

Association of Peri-Operative Registered Nurses *420*

Astral Career Grant *406*

Astrid G. Cates and Myrtle Beinhauer Scholarship Funds *515*

Astronaut Scholarship Foundation *92*

ATFAR Scholarship *372*

Atlanta Press Club Journalism Scholarship Program *179*

Aubrey Lee Brooks Scholarships *729*

Aubrey Lee Brooks Scholarships *674*

Audiology Foundation of America's Outstanding AUD Student Scholarship *116*

Automation Alley Scholarship Program *794*

Automotive Hall of Fame Educational Funds *162*

Automotive Recyclers Association Scholarship Foundation Scholarship *794*

Avfuel Michigan Business Aviation Scholarship *826*

Aviation Council of Pennsylvania Scholarship Program *120*

Award of Excellence Asthma Scholarship Program *554*

AWIS Kirsten R. Lorentzen Award in Physics *213*

AWSCPA and Boston Affiliate scholarship *54*

AXA Foundation Fund Achievement Scholarship *154*

Aylesworth and Old Salt Scholarships *385*

Azteca Scholarship *619*

B.J. Harrod Scholarship *277*

B.K. Krenzer Memorial Reentry Scholarship *277*

Bach Organ and Keyboard Scholarship Fund *406*

BACUS Scholarship *287*

Badminton Scholarship Program *779*

Ball Horticultural Company Scholarship *342*

Baltimore Junior Association of Commerce (BJAC) Scholarship *675*

Baltimore Rotary Service Above Self Award Program *675*

Bandon Submarine Cable Council Scholarship *735*

Bank of America ADA Abilities Scholarship *56*

Bank of America Financial Aid Sweepstakes *794*

Bank of America Minority Scholarship *146*

Bank of America Scholarship *638*

Bank of the Cascades Scholarship *532*

BAPRM Scholarship Program *672*

Barbara Carlson Scholarship *343*

Barbara Jackson Sichel Memorial Scholarship *519*

Barbara Jean Barker Memorial Scholarship for a Displaced Homemaker *693*

Barbara Palo Foster Memorial Scholarship *433*

Barbara S. Miller Memorial Scholarship *146*

Barking Foundation Grants *668*

Barry K. Wendt Memorial Scholarship *269*

Barry M. Goldwater Scholarship and Excellence in Education Program *92*

Battelle Scholars Program *283*

Bea Cleveland 4-H Scholarship *170*

Bechtel Corporation Scholarship *176*

Becoming a Chef Scholarship *303*

BEEM Foundation Scholarship *401*

Beinecke Scholarship for Graduate Study *109*

Beirut Relief Fund Scholarships *839*

Belcourt Brosseau Metis Awards *613*

Belo Texas Broadcast Education Foundation Scholarship *187*

Ben Selling Scholarship *735*

Ben W. Brannon Memorial Scholarship Fund *60*

Bendix/King Avionics Scholarship *116*

Benjamin C. Blackburn Scholarship *293*

Benjamin Franklin/Edith Green Scholarship *735*

Bennion Family Scholarship *553*

Berna Lou Cartwright Scholarship *394*

Bernice Pickins Parsons Fund *377*

Berntsen International Scholarship in Surveying *464*

Berntsen International Scholarship in Surveying Technology *464*

Berri Mitchel Memorial Scholarship *555*

Bertha Lamme Memorial Scholarship *246*

Bertha P. Singer Nurses Scholarship *432*

BESLA Scholarship Legal Writing Competition *375*

Best Buy Enterprise Employee Scholarship *70*

Best Buy Scholarships *794*

Best Teen Chef Culinary Scholarship Competition *200*

Betsy Ross Educational Fund *831*

Betty Hansen Continuing Education Grant *497*

Beulah Frey Environmental Scholarship *293*

Beverly J. Smith Memorial Scholarship *658*

BHP Billiton University Scholarships *807*

BIA Higher Education Grant *618*

Big 33 Scholarship Foundation, Inc. Scholarships *668*

Big Y Scholarships *668*

Bildner Family Scholarship *638*

Bill Farr Scholarship *369*

Bill Mason Memorial Scholarship Fund *80*

Bill McAdam Scholarship Fund *822*

Bill Moon Scholarship *507*

Bill Peterson Scholarship *504*

Biller/Jewish Foundation for Education of Women *651*

Billy Welu Bowling Scholarship *775*

Bi-Lo John Rohaley Scholarship *525*

Binkley-Stephenson Award *85*

BioQuip Undergraduate Scholarship *290*

BioQuip Undergraduate Scholarship *290*

Black Broadcasters Alliance Scholarship *179*

Black Executive Exchange Program Jerry Bartow Scholarship Fund *151*

Blackfeet Nation Higher Education Grant *608*

BlackNews.com Scholarship Essay Contest *612*

Blessed Leon of Our Lady of the Rosary Award *630*

Blue Grass Energy Academic Scholarship *668*

Blue Heron Paper Employee Dependents Scholarship *533*

Bluegrass Cellular, Inc. Scholarship *668*

BMI Student Composer Awards *110*

BMW/SAE Engineering Scholarship *129*

Bob East Scholarship *443*

Bob Elliot- WMTW-TV 8 Journalism Scholarship *190*

Bobbi McCallum Memorial Scholarship *368*

Bonitz (Bill Rogers) Scholarship *525*

Bonner McLane Texas Broadcast Education Foundation Scholarship *187*

Booz, Allen & Hamilton/William F. Stasior Internship *154*

Bowman Travel Grant *804*

Boys & Girls Clubs of America National Youth of the Year Award *494*

Boys and Girls Club of Alberta Scholarships *483*

Boys and Girls Clubs Foundation Scholarship *795*

Boys and Girls Clubs of Chicago Scholarships *495*

BP/IEE Faraday Lecture Scholarship *244*

BPW Career Advancement Scholarship Program for Women *136*

Bradford White Corporation Scholarship *102*

Breakthrough to Nursing Scholarships for Racial/Ethnic Minorities *422*

Brian L. Moody Memorial Aviation Scholarship *128*

Bridging Scholarships *311*

Brightwell Family Memorial Scholarship Fund *685*

Britton Fund Scholarship Program *752*

Broadcast Scholarship Program *478*

Brodart/Pennsylvania Library Association Undergraduate Scholarship Grant *381*

Bronislaw Kaper Awards for Young Artists *706*

Brookmire-Hastings Scholarships *240*

Broome and Allen Boys Camp and Scholarship Fund *649*

Brower Youth Awards *808*

Brown Foundation Goodyear Tire and Rubber Company Scholarship for College Students *669*

Brown Foundation Goodyear Tire and Rubber Company Scholarships for High School Seniors *669*

Brown Scholar *221*

Bruce and Marjorie Sundlun Scholarship *741*

Bruce B. Melchert Scholarship *450*

Bryan Close Polo Grill Scholarship *303*

Bryan/LGH Medical Center West Auxiliary Junior Volunteer Scholarship *704*

Buckingham Memorial Scholarship *537*

Bud Glover Memorial Scholarship *116*

Bud Ohlman Scholarship *343*

Budweiser Conservation Scholarship Program *140*

Buena M. Chesshir Memorial Women's Educational Scholarship *754*

Bullivant Houser Bailey-African American Chamber of Commerce Community College Scholarship Fund *152*

Bureau of Alcohol, Tobacco, Firearms and Explosives Scholarship-Law Enforcement *373*

Bureau of Indian Affairs Higher Education Grant Program *795*

Burlington Northern Santa Fe Foundation Scholarship *89*

Bushrod Campbell and Adah Hall Scholarship *638*

Business Achievement Award *147*

Business Reporting Internship Program for Minority College Sophomores and Juniors *808*

Butler Manufacturing Company Foundation Scholarship Program *525*

Butrimovitz Family Endowment Fund for Jewish Education *651*

Buzzard- Maxfield- Richason and Rechlin Scholarship *314*

Byron Nelson Scholarship *777*

C. Merrill Barber, P.E., Memorial Scholarship *260*

C.B. Gambrell Undergraduate Scholarship *263*

C.J. Davidson Scholarship for FCCLA *340*

C.R. Bard Scholarship and Internship Program *154*

Cabrillo Civic Clubs of California Scholarship *608*

Cady McDonnell Memorial Scholarship *464*

Cal Grant C *670*

Caleb L. Butler Scholarship *682*

Calgon, Take Me Away to College Scholarship Competition *844*

Calgon, Take Me Away to College Scholarsweeps *844*

California Broadcasters Foundation Intern Scholarship *476*

California Citrus Mutual Scholarship *79*

California Congress of Parents and Teachers, Inc. Scholarship *669*

California Correctional Peace Officers Association Joe Harper Scholarship *539*

California Council of the Blind Scholarships *555*

California Farm Bureau Scholarship *73*

California Grange Foundation Scholarship *495*

California Groundwater Association Scholarship *213*

California Junior Miss Scholarship Program *670*

California Masonic Foundation Scholarship Awards *670*

California Mathematics Council - South Secondary Education Scholarships *390*

California Table Grape Farm Workers Scholarship Program *539*

California Teachers Association Scholarship for Dependent Children *495*

California Teachers Association Scholarship for Members *495*

California Water Awareness Campaign Water Scholar *79*

California Wine Grape Growers Foundation Scholarship *671*

Calvin Dawson Memorial Scholarship *560*

Campus Safety, Health and Environmental Management Association Scholarship Award Program *295*

Canada Iceland Foundation Scholarship Program *671*

Canada Millennium Bursary *655*

Canada Millennium Excellence Award Program *608*

Canadian Direct Marketing Scholarship for Business Students *150*

Canadian Institute of Ukrainian Studies Research Grants *104*

Canadian Schedulers And Dispatchers Scholarship *826*

Canadian TKE Scholarship *516*

Cancer Teaches Us Survivorship Award *849*

Cantor Fitzgerald Relief Fund *796*

Cap Lathrop Scholarship Program *477*

Caparanga Award *630*

Cape Cod Restaurants, Inc. Scholarship *803*

Capitol Scholarship Program *684*

CAPPS Scholarship Program *669*

Captain James J. Regan Scholarship *373*

Cardinal Health Scholarship *70*

Cardinal Logistics Management, Inc. Scholarships *525*

Career Colleges and Schools of Texas Scholarship Program *672*

Constantinople Armenian Relief Society Scholarship *612*
Contemporary Record Society National Competition for Performing Artists *439*
Contemporary Record Society National Festival for the Performing Arts Scholarship *767*
Continental Society, Daughters of Indian Wars Scholarship *224*
Continuing Education - Credential Teachers and Counselors Scholarship *221*
Continuing Education - PTA Volunteers Scholarship *670*
Continuing Education Award *840*
Continuing Education for School Nurses Scholarship *420*
Continuing Education Scholarship Program *477*
Cooperative Agencies Resources for Education Program *669*
Cooperative Studies Scholarships *74*
Copernicus Award *413*
Cora Bell Wesley Memorial Scholarship *519*
CORE Philly Scholarship Program *685*
Cornelia Branch Stone Scholarship *519*
Corporate Sponsored Scholarship Program *700*
Corrugated Packaging Division Scholarships *845*
Costco Scholarship *639*
Cottey/Cather Writing Prize *757*
Council for Exceptional Children *610*
Council of Energy Resources Tribes Education Fund Scholarship *612*
Council on Approved Student Education's Scholarship Fund *827*
Council on International Educational Exchange Scholarship *804*
Counselor, Advocate, and Support Staff Scholarship Program *69*
Courtland Paul Scholarship *371*
Courtlandt and Gina Miler Scholarship *679*
Cox Education Fund Scholarship *676*
CPA Review Course Scholarship *64*
Critical Needs Teacher Loan/Scholarship *231*
Critical Teacher Shortage Student Loan Forgiveness Program-Florida *541*
Critical Teacher Shortage Tuition Reimbursement-Florida *225*
Croatian Scholarship Fund Scholarship Program *612*
Cross-Cultural Experience Program *78*
Crumley and Associates - Crib to College Scholarship *674*
CSCPA Candidate's Award *58*
CSCPA Junior Award *58*
CSM Vincent Baldassari Memorial Scholarship Program *569*
C-SPAN Scholarship Program *189*
Cuban American Scholarship Fund *805*
Culinary Trust Scholarship Program for Culinary Study and Research *302*
Culinary, Vinifera, and Hospitality Scholarship *301*
Cultural Fellowship Grants *383*
Culture Connection Foundation Scholarship *73*
Curt Greene Memorial Scholarship *770*
CVS/Pharmacy Scholarship *442*
CWA Joe Beirne Foundation Scholarship Program *501*
Cydna Ann Huffstetler Memorial Trust Fund *650*
Cymdeithas Gymreig/Philadelphia Scholarship *647*
Cyprus American Archaeological Research Institute Helena Wylde and Stuart Swiny Fellowship *96*
Cyril W. Neff, P.E., P.S., Memorial Scholarship *260*
Cystic Fibrosis Scholarship *557*
D.J. Lovell Scholarship *818*
D.W. Simpson Actuarial Science Scholarship *805*
Daedalean Foundation Matching Scholarship Program *121*
Daimler Chrysler Corporation Scholarship *246*
Daimler Chrysler Scholarship Program *524*
Daimler Chrysler Services Canada Inc. Scholarship Program *784*
Dale E. Fridell Memorial Scholarship *842*
Dale E. Siefkes Scholarship *229*
Dallas Architectural Foundation - Harrell and Hamilton Scholarship Fund *99*
Dallas Independent School District Scholarship *640*
Dallas Mavericks *640*
Dallas Metroplex Council of Black Alumni Association Scholarship *640*
Dallas Morning News Annual Teenage Citizenship Tribute *540*
Dan Konnie Memorial Dependents Scholarship *533*
Dan L. Meisinger, Sr. Memorial Learn to Fly Scholarship *126*
Dan Reichard Jr. Scholarship *144*
Dan River Foundation Scholarship *526*
Dan Schutte Scholarship *403*
Dana Campbell Memorial Scholarship *303*
Dana Christmas Scholarship for Heroism *725*

Daniel Cubicciotti Student Award of the San Francisco Section of the Electrochemical Society, Sponsored by Structural Integrity Associates *137*
Daniel E. Lambert Memorial Scholarship *583*
Daniel Gutierrez Memorial General Scholarship Fund *607*
Dassault Falcon Jet Corporation Scholarship *132*
Datatel Scholars Foundation Scholarship *805*
Daughters of the Cincinnati Scholarship *568*
Dave Yanis Scholarship Fund *680*
Davenport Forte Pedestal Fund *640*
David A. Koch Scholarship *530*
David Alan Quick Scholarship *121*
David and Dovetta Wilson Scholarship Fund *805*
David Arver Memorial Scholarship *117*
David Birenbaum Scholarship Fund *483*
David Edgcumbe Scholarship *304*
David Family Scholarship *736*
David J. Fitzmaurice Engineering Scholarship *265*
David Korn Scholarship Fund *652*
David S. Barr Award *365*
David S. Bruce Awards for Excellence in Undergraduate Research *791*
David Stephen Wylie Scholarship *520*
David Tamotsu Kagiwada Memorial Scholarship *453*
David W. Miller Award for Student Journalists *370*
David W. Self Scholarship *653*
David, Nancy, and Liza Cherney Scholarship Fund *651*
Davis-Putter Scholarship Fund *805*
Davis-Roberts Scholarships *497*
Dayle and Frances Peiper Scholarship *583*
Dayton Superior Corporation Scholarship Fund *685*
DC Leveraging Educational Assistance Partnership Program (LEAP) *688*
DC Tuition Assistance Grant Program *689*
DEA Drug Abuse Prevention Service Awards *373*
Deaf and Hard of Hearing Section Scholarship Fund *553*
Decatur H. Miller Scholarship *338*
Decommissioning, Decontamination, and Reutilization Scholarship *249*
Dedicated Military Junior College Program *576*
Deerfield Plastics/Barker Family Scholarship *529*
Del Jones Memorial Travel Award *459*
Delaware Solid Waste Authority John P. "Pat" Healy Scholarship *291*
Delayed Education for Women Scholarships *249*
Delegate Scholarship Program-Maryland *711*
Dell Computer Corporation Scholarships *194*
Dell/UNCF Corporate Scholars Program *155*
Della Van Deuren Memorial Scholarship *485*
Deloras Jones RN Scholarship Program *425*
Delta Air Lines Aircraft Maintenance Technology Scholarship *132*
Delta Air Lines Engineering Scholarship *132*
Delta Air Lines Maintenance Management/Aviation Business Management Scholarship *133*
Delta Apparel, Inc. Scholarship *526*
Delta Delta Delta Graduate Scholarship *497*
Delta Delta Delta Undergraduate Scholarship *497*
Delta Faucet Company Scholarship Program *102*
Delta Gamma Foundation Florence Margaret Harvey Memorial Scholarship *219*
Delta Gamma Foundation Scholarships *498*
Delta Iota Alumni Scholarship *839*
Delta Phi Epsilon Educational Foundation Grant *498*
Democratic Nursing Organization of South Africa Study Fund *421*
DeMolay Foundation of California, Inc Scholarship Program *806*
Demonstration of Energy Efficient Developments Scholarship *791*
Denise Lynn Padgett Scholarship Fund *680*
Denny Lydic Scholarship *130*
Denny's/Hispanic College Fund Scholarship *62*
Dental Assisting Scholarships *208*
Dental Hygiene Scholarships *208*
Department of Education Scholarship for Programs in China *225*
Department of Energy Scholarship Program *148*
Department of VA Tuition Waiver-KY KRS 164-515 *821*
Department of Veterans Affairs Free Tuition for Children of POW/MIA's in Vietnam *589*
Department of Veterans Affairs Tuition Waiver-Kentucky KRS 164-505 *821*
Department of Veterans Affairs Tuition Waiver-KY 164-512 *821*
Department of Veterans Affairs Tuition Waiver-KY KRS 164-507 *821*
Dependent Children Scholarship Program *551*
Deseo at the Westin Scholarship *202*
Desk and Derrick Educational Trust *92*
Detroit Chapter One-Founding Chapter Scholarship *273*
Detroit Section SAE Technical Scholarship *270*

Developmental Disabilities Awareness Awards for Lutheran High School Students *460*
Developmental Disabilities Scholastic Achievement Scholarship for Lutheran College Students *208*
DeVry Community College Scholar Award *687*
DeVry Community College Scholarships *806*
DeVry Dean's Scholarships *687*
DeVry High School Community Scholars Award *688*
DeVry Presidential Scholarships *688*
DeVry Skills USA Scholarships *806*
DeVry University First Scholar Award *806*
DeVry University Regional First Scholar Awards *688*
DeVry/Keller Military Service Grant *588*
Diamond State Scholarship *686*
Diamond State Scholarship *685*
Diana Donald Scholarship *481*
Diavik Diamonds, Inc. Scholarships for College Students *807*
Diavik Diamonds, Inc. University Scholarships *689*
Dick Forester College Scholarship *778*
Dick Larsen Scholarship Program *189*
Director's Scholarship Award *273*
Dirigo Machine Tool Scholarship *709*
disABLEDperson Inc. College Scholarship Award *557*
Disciple Chaplains' Scholarship *454*
Discover Card Tribute Award Scholarship Program *787*
Discovery Channel Young Scientist Challenge *776*
Displaced Homemaker Scholarship *607*
Distinguished Scholar Award-Maryland *711*
Distinguished Scholar-Teacher Education Awards *230*
Distinguished Student Scholar Award *235*
District of Columbia Adoption Scholarship *689*
Dixie Boys Baseball Scholarship Program *689*
Dixie Youth Scholarship Program *689*
Dollarship *807*
Dolphin Scholarships *599*
Domenic Troiano Guitar Scholarship *768*
Dominick Sarci Memorial Scholarship *268*
Donald A. Fisher Memorial Scholarship *516*
Donald A. Williams Scholarship Soil Conservation Scholarship *216*
Donald and Jean Cleveland-Willamette Valley Section Scholarship *172*
Donald and Shirley Hastings Scholarship *253*
Donald C. Hyde Essay Program *171*
Donald Estey Scholarship Fund-Rocky Mountain Chapter *473*
Donald F. and Mildred Topp Othmer Foundation-National Scholarship Awards *159*
Donald F. Hastings Scholarship *253*
Donald J. DeYoung Scholarship *814*
Donald Malcolm MacArthur Scholarship *634*
Donald Riebhoff Memorial Scholarship *356*
Donald W. Fogarty International Student Paper Competition *144*
Donaldson Company, Inc. Scholarship Program *529*
Donna Jamison Lago Memorial Scholarship *626*
Donna Reed Performing Arts Scholarships *439*
Dorchester Women's Club Scholarship *402*
Dorothy Campbell Memorial Scholarship *736*
Dorothy Lemke Howarth Scholarships *278*
Dorothy M. and Earl S. Hoffman Scholarship *278*
Dorothy Morris Scholarship *278*
Dorothy S. Campbell Memorial Scholarship Fund *774*
Dorothy Williams Scholarship *520*
Dosatron International, Inc., Scholarship *343*
Dottie Martin Teachers Scholarship *222*
Doug Brown Scholarship *542*
Douvas Memorial Scholarship *759*
Dow Jones-Sports Editing Program *360*
Downriver Detroit Chapter 198 Scholarship *273*
Dr Kenneth and Nancy Williams Scholarship *630*
Dr. Alan Beaven Forestry Scholarship *294*
Dr. Alfred and Susan Chan Award *630*
Dr. Alfred C. Fones Scholarship *206*
Dr. Click Cowger Baseball Scholarship *661*
Dr. Ernest and Minnie Mehl Scholarship *602*
Dr. Franz and Kathryn Stenzel Fund *330*
Dr. Freeman A. Hrabowski, III Scholarship *259*
Dr. George M. Smerk Scholarship *471*
Dr. Gerald O'Connor Michigan Scholarship *491*
Dr. Gombojab Hangin Memorial Scholarship *624*
Dr. Harold Hillenbrand Scholarship *206*
Dr. Hilda Richards Scholarship *427*
Dr. James L. Lawson Memorial Scholarship *178*
Dr. Josephine Wtulich Memorial Scholarship *630*
Dr. Juan Andrade, Jr. Scholarship *647*
Dr. Juan D. Villarreal/ Hispanic Dental Association Foundation *209*
Dr. Lauranne Sams Scholarship *427*
Dr. Manny Horowitz Scholarship *133*
Dr. Richard W. Kimbrough Memorial Scholarship *326*
Dr. William J. Steger Scholarship Awards *333*

Florence Wood/Arkansas Occupational Therapy Association Scholarship *321*

Florida Association of Postsecondary Schools and Colleges Scholarship Program *691*

Florida Bankers Educational Foundation Scholarship/ Loan *147*

Florida Environmental Health Association Scholarship *291*

Florida Private Student Assistance Grant *691*

Florida Public Student Assistance Grant *692*

Florida Scholarship *722*

Florida Women's State Golf Association Junior Girls' Scholarship Fund *692*

Florida Work Experience Program *811*

Florida/NASA Matching Grant Program *719*

Flow Automotive Companies Scholarship *852*

Flowers Industries Scholarship *155*

Floyd Boring Award *374*

Floyd Cargill Scholarship *559*

FOARE Scholarship Program *812*

Foley & Lardner Minority Scholarship Program *377*

Fond du Lac Scholarship Program *811*

Ford Motor Company Engineering and Leadership Scholarship *262*

Ford Motor Company Scholarship *279*

Ford Motor Company Scholarship-Undergraduate *435*

Ford Opportunity Program *736*

Ford Restart Program Scholarship *736*

Ford Scholars *736*

Ford Sons and Daughters of Employees of Roseburg Forest Products Company Scholarship *533*

Ford/UNCF Corporate Scholars Program *71*

Fort Collins Symphony Association Young Artist Competition, Junior Division *769*

Fort Wayne Chapter 56 Scholarship *274*

Fort Worth Independent School District Scholarship *641*

Fortune Brands Scholars Program *641*

Foundation for Accounting Education Scholarship *67*

Foundation for Surgical Technology Scholarship Fund *325*

Foundation of Research and Education Undergraduate Merit Scholarships *335*

Foundation of the First Cavalry Division Association Ia Drang Scholarship *574*

Foundation of The First Cavalry Division Association Undergraduate Scholarship *588*

Foundation of the National Student Nurses' Association Career Mobility Scholarship *422*

Foundation of the National Student Nurses' Association General Scholarships *423*

Foundation of the National Student Nurses' Association Specialty Scholarship *423*

Foundation of the Wall and Ceiling Industry Scholarship Program *812*

Foundation Scholarships *743*

Founders Scholarship *810*

Fountainhead College Scholarship Essay Contest *765*

Fourth Degree Pro Deo and Pro Patria (Canada) *503*

Four-Year and Three-Year Advance Designees Scholarship *573*

Fran Johnson Scholarship for Non-Traditional Students *344*

Frances M. Peacock Scholarship for Native Bird Habitat *408*

Francis and Evelyn Clark Soil Biology Scholarship *78*

Francis Blackduck Memorial "Strong Like Two People" Awards *293*

Francis D. Lyon Scholarships *298*

Francis J. Flynn Memorial Scholarship *239*

Francis L. Booth Medical Scholarship sponsored by LAVFW Department of Maine *327*

Francis P. Matthews and John E. Swift Educational Trust Scholarships *503*

Francis Sylvia Zverina Scholarship *348*

Francis Walton Memorial Scholarship *764*

Frank H. Buck Scholarships *812*

Frank L. Greathouse Government Accounting Scholarship *148*

Frank O'Bannon Grant Program *747*

Frank O'Neill Memorial Scholarship *802*

Frank S. Land Scholarship *529*

Frank Sarli Memorial Scholarship *827*

Frank W. Jendrysik, Jr. Memorial Scholarship *683*

Frank W. McHale Memorial Scholarships *661*

Frank William and Dorothy Given Miller Scholarship *392*

Frank X. and Mary E. Weny Scholarship Fund *556*

Franks Foundation Scholarship *432*

Fraternal Order of Police Associates Scholarship *812*

Fred K. Lane Scholarship *683*

Fred M. Young Sr./SAE Engineering Scholarship *270*

Fred R. McDaniel Memorial Scholarship *178*

Fred Scheigert Scholarship Program *557*

Frederic Fairfield Memorial Fund Award *141*

Freedom From Religion Foundation College Essay Contest *812*

Freedom From Religion Foundation High School Essay Contest *813*

Freedom Scholarship *588*

Freeman Awards for Study in Asia *846*

Fresh Start Scholarship *692*

Freshman Engineering Scholarship for Dallas Women *282*

Friends of Bill Rutherford Education Fund *734*

Friends of Oregon Students Scholarship *234*

Fukunaga Scholarship Foundation *147*

Fulbright Program *222*

Fulfilling Our Dreams Scholarship Fund *633*

Funk Family Memorial Scholarship *403*

Future Culinarian of America Scholarship *201*

Future Journalists Scholarship Program *180*

Future Leaders of America Scholarship *774*

Future Teacher of America Scholarship *223*

Future Teacher Scholarship-Oklahoma *234*

Future Teachers Conditional Scholarship and Loan Repayment Program *240*

G. Brooks Earnest-Ohio Society of Professional Engineers, Cleveland Chapter Memorial Scholarship *260*

G. Layton Grier Scholarship *208*

GAE GFIE Scholarship for Aspiring Teachers *226*

Gallup CSG Scholarship Program *693*

Gamewardens of Vietnam Scholarship *599*

Gamma Theta Upsilon Scholarships *769*

Gannett Foundation/Madelyn P. Jennings Scholarship Award *530*

Garden Club of America Awards for Summer Environmental Studies *80*

Garden Club of America Summer Scholarship in Field Botany *347*

Garland Duncan Scholarship *392*

GARMIN Scholarship *117*

Garth Reeves, Jr. Memorial Scholarships *187*

GAT Wings to the Future Management Scholarship *133*

Gates Millennium Scholars *628*

Gates Millennium Scholars Program *605*

Gates Millennium Scholars Program *617*

Gates Millennium Scholars Program (Gates Foundation) *641*

Gateway Press Scholarship *530*

Gayle and Harvey Rubin Scholarship Fund *330*

GCSAA Scholars Competition *348*

GE/LULAC Scholarship *150*

GEAR UP Alaska Scholarship *655*

GEICO Life Scholarship *499*

Gene Hovis Memorial Scholarship *202*

General Electric Foundation Scholarship *279*

General Electric Women's Network Scholarship *279*

General Federation of Women's Clubs of Massachusetts Music Scholarship *225*

General Federation of Women's Clubs of Massachusetts Pennies For Art *111*

General Federation of Women's Clubs of Massachusetts Study Abroad Scholarship *693*

General Fund Scholarships *635*

General Henry H. Arnold Education Grant Program *567*

General John Ratay Educational Fund Grants *590*

General Motors Engineering Scholarship *284*

General Motors Foundation Undergraduate Scholarships *168*

General Scholarship Fund *607*

General Scholarship Grants *839*

General Undergraduate Scholarship *854*

Generation "E" Grants and Scholarships *780*

George A. Hall / Harold F. Mayfield Award *87*

George A. Nielsen Public Investor Scholarship *148*

George A. Roberts Scholarship *256*

George and Mary Josephine Hamman Foundation Scholarship Program *693*

George and Mary Newton Scholarship *847*

George E. Parmenter Aeronautical Scholarship Fund *121*

George J. Mitchell Peace Scholarship *709*

George M. Brooker Collegiate Scholarship for Minorities *452*

George Nicholson Student Paper Competition *817*

George R. Crafton Scholarship *81*

George Reinke Scholarships *473*

George S. Benton Scholarship *399*

George V. McGowan Scholarship *259*

George W. Woolery Memorial Scholarship *188*

George Watters-Nebraska Petroleum Marketers Association Scholarship *544*

Georgia Chapter of ASSE Annual Scholarship *436*

Georgia Leveraging Educational Assistance Partnership Grant Program *693*

Georgia Police Corps Scholarship *813*

Georgia Press Educational Foundation Scholarships *361*

Georgia PROMISE Teacher Scholarship Program *226*

Georgia Public Safety Memorial Grant/Law Enforcement Personnel Department Grant *542*

Georgia Trust for Historic Preservation Scholarship *337*

Georgia Tuition Equalization Grant (GTEG) *693*

Gerald Boyd/Robin Stone Non-Sustaining Scholarship *364*

Gerald Drake Memorial Scholarship *827*

Gerald M. Crane Memorial Music Scholarship Fund *694*

Gerald O. Mott Scholarship *79*

German Academic Exchange Information Visits *296*

German Academic Exchange Service (DAAD) edu de Undergraduate Awards *813*

German Studies Research Grants *814*

Gertrude B. Elion Mentored Medical Student Research Awards *333*

Gertrude Botts-Saucier Scholarship *520*

Gertrude M. Gigliotti Memorial Scholarship *61*

Get Out of Debt Scholarship *843*

Gheens Foundation Scholarship *641*

GIA Publication Pastoral Musician Scholarship *404*

Gift for Life Scholarship *524*

Gil Purcell Memorial Journalism Scholarship for Native Canadians *359*

Gilbane Scholarship/Internship *283*

Gilbert Rios Memorial Award *623*

Giles Sutherland Rich Memorial Scholarship *376*

Gina Bachauer International Artists Piano Competition Award *439*

Gino Cofacci Memorial Scholarship *304*

Girl Scout Achievement Award *789*

Girl Scout Gold Award Scholarship- High School Graduate *806*

Girls Going Places Scholarship Program *815*

Gladys Stone Wright Scholarship *240*

Glaxo Smith Kline Opportunities Scholarship *751*

GlaxoSmithKline Opportunity Scholarships *674*

Glenn Godfrey Memorial Scholarship *621*

Glenn Jackson Scholars Scholarships (OCF) *533*

Glenn Miller Instrumental Scholarship *769*

Glenn R. and Juanita B. Struble Scholarship II *102*

GLHF Individual Class Scholarship *558*

Gloria Barron Prize for Young Heroes *814*

GM/LULAC Scholarship *265*

GMP Memorial Scholarship Program *499*

GNC Nutrition Research Grant *335*

Gold Country Section and Region II Scholarship *436*

Golden Apple Scholars of Illinois *226*

Golden Gate Restaurant Association Scholarship Foundation *307*

Golden Key Study Abroad Scholarships *499*

Golden LEAF Scholars Program - Two-Year Colleges *801*

Golden LEAF Scholarship - Four Year University Program *674*

Goldman Family Fund, New Leader Scholarship *210*

Golf Course Superintendents Association of America Legacy Award *500*

Golf Course Superintendents Association of America Student Essay Contest *75*

Goodman & Company Annual Scholarship *852*

Gordon Scheer Scholarship *57*

Governor Guinn Millennium Scholarship *724*

Governor Terry E. Branstad Iowa State Fair Scholarship *700*

Governor's Opportunity Scholarship *814*

Governor's Opportunity Scholarship *678*

Governor's Scholars-Arkansas *666*

Governor's Scholarship-Georgia *694*

Governor's Workforce Development Grant *686*

Graco Inc. Scholarship Program *530*

Graduate and Professional Scholarship Program- Maryland *210*

Graduate Student Scholar Award *236*

Graduate Study in Cancer Research or Nurse Practitioner *423*

Graduating High School Senior Scholarship *795*

Grand Lodge of Iowa Masonic Scholarship Program *694*

Grand Rapids Combined Theatre Scholarship *694*

Grange Insurance Group Scholarship *694*

Grant MacEwan United World College Scholarships *602*

Grant Program for Dependents of Police, Fire, or Correctional Officers *543*

Granville P. Meade Scholarship *754*

Grayson Rural Electric Cooperative Corporation Scholarship *694*

GRE and Graduate Applications Waiver *95*

Great Falls Broadcasters Association Scholarship *479*

Greater Bridgeport Area Foundation's Scholarship Award Program *695*

Greater Springfield Accountants Scholarship *57*

Greater Washington Society of CPAs Scholarship *62*

Illinois Society of Professional Engineers/Peppy
  Moldovan Memorial Award *263*
Illinois Special Education Teacher Tuition Waiver *462*
Illinois State Treasurer's Office Excellence in Agriculture
  Scholarship Program *80*
Illinois Student-to-Student Program of Matching
  Grants *699*
Illinois Tool Works Welding Companies Scholarship *254*
Illinois Veteran Grant Program - IVG *589*
Imagine America Scholarship *796*
Immune Deficiency Foundation Scholarship *559*
Independent Laboratories Institute Scholarship
  Alliance *93*
Indian American Scholarship Fund *619*
Indian Health Service Health Professions Pre-graduate
  Scholarships *209*
Indian Health Service Health Professions Pre-
  professional Scholarship *318*
Indian Student Fee Waiver *624*
Indiana Broadcasters Foundation Scholarship *362*
Indiana Engineering Scholarship *263*
Indiana Health Care Foundation Nursing
  Scholarship *425*
Indiana National Guard Supplemental Grant *572*
Indiana Nursing Scholarship Fund *433*
Indiana Quarter Horse Youth Scholarship *492*
Indiana Retired Teachers Association Foundation
  Scholarship *228*
Indiana Scholarship *722*
Indiana Sheriffs' Association Scholarship Program *199*
Individuals/Teams Balance Bar Grants *765*
Industrial Designers Society of America Undergraduate
  Scholarship *353*
Inez Peppers Lovett Scholarship Fund *223*
Institute of Food Technologists Food Engineering
  Division Junior/Senior Scholarship *302*
Institute of Food Technologists Freshman
  Scholarships *302*
Institute of Food Technologists Quality Assurance
  Division Junior/Senior Scholarships *302*
Institute of Food Technologists Sophomore
  Scholarships *302*
Institute of Food Technologists/Master Foods USA
  Undergraduate Mentored Scholarship *303*
Institute of Management Accountants Memorial
  Education Fund Diversity Scholarships *63*
Institute of Management Accountants Memorial
  Education Fund Scholarships *63*
Instrumentation, Systems, and Automation Society (ISA)
  Scholarship Program *123*
Intel International Science and Engineering Fair *777*
Intel Science Talent Search *777*
Inter-County Energy Scholarship *700*
International Airlines Travel Agent Network Ronald A.
  Santana Memorial Scholarship *350*
International Art Show for Artists with Disabilities *565*
International Association of Fire Chiefs Foundation
  Scholarship *299*
International Association of Fire Chiefs Foundation
  Scholarship Award *543*
International Associations of Fire Chiefs Foundation
  Scholarship *300*
International Brotherhood of Electrical Workers Local
  280 Scholarship *511*
International Cake Exploration Societe Scholarship *201*
International Communications Industries Foundation
  AV Scholarship *182*
International Education Awards–Ukraine *785*
International Executive Housekeepers Association
  Educational Foundation Spartan Scholarship *351*
International Executive Housekeepers Educational
  Foundation *307*
International Federation of Professional and Technical
  Engineers Annual Scholarship *501*
International Foodservice Editorial Council
  Communications Scholarship *182*
International Music Competition of the ARD
  Munich *403*
International Order Of The Golden Rule Award of
  Excellence *313*
International Order of the King's Daughters and Sons
  North American Indian Scholarship *619*
International Order of the King's Daughters and Sons
  Student Ministry Scholarship *455*
International Scholarships *784*
International SkillsUSA Degree Scholarship *840*
International Society of Women Airline Pilots Airline
  Scholarships *123*
International Society of Women Airline Pilots Financial
  Scholarship *123*
International Society of Women Airline Pilots Fiorenza
  de Bernardi Merit Scholarship *123*

International Society of Women Airline Pilots Grace
  McAdams Harris Scholarship *124*
International Society of Women Airline Pilots Holly
  Mullens Memorial Scholarship *124*
International Society of Women Airline Pilots North
  Carolina Financial Scholarship *124*
International Student Leaders Award *500*
International Teacher Education Scholarship *218*
International Technology Education Association
  Undergraduate Scholarship *228*
International Technology Education Association
  Undergraduate Scholarship in Technology
  Education *265*
International Union of Operating Engineers Local 701
  Scholarship *511*
Internship/Scholarship Program *726*
Iowa Foster Child Grants *701*
Iowa Grants *701*
Iowa National Guard Education Assistance Program *570*
Iowa Teacher Forgivable Loan Program *229*
Iowa Tuition Grant Program *701*
Iowa Vocational Rehabilitation *559*
Iowa Vocational-Technical Tuition Grant Program *701*
IRARC Memorial/Joseph P. Rubino, WA4MMD,
  Scholarship *494*
Irene E. Newman Scholarship *206*
Irish Research Funds *105*
Irmgard Schulz Scholarship *737*
Irving K. Barber British Columbia Scholarship
  Program *795*
Irving W. Cook, WA0CGS, Scholarship *90*
Isabel M. Herson Scholarship in Education *241*
Island Institute Scholarship Fund *823*
Italian-American Chamber of Commerce of Chicago
  Scholarship *620*
IUE-CWA International Bruce Van Ess Scholarship *501*
Ivy Parker Memorial Scholarship *279*
J .J. Barr Scholarship *139*
J. A. Knowles Memorial Scholarship *653*
J. Fielding Reed Scholarship *79*
J. Russel Salsbury Memorial Scholarship *517*
J. Wilmar Mirandon Scholarship *153*
J. Wood Platt Caddie Scholarship Trust *544*
J.F. Tolbert Memorial Student Grant Program *712*
Jack Gilstrap Scholarship *171*
Jack J. Isgur Foundation Scholarship *111*
Jack Kent Cooke Foundation Undergraduate Transfer
  Scholarship Program *819*
Jack Pullan Memorial Scholarship *770*
Jack Shaheen Mass Communications Scholarship
  Award *177*
Jackie Robinson Scholarship *620*
Jackson Energy Scholarship *702*
Jackson Foundation Journalism Scholarship *367*
Jackson Foundation Journalism Scholarship Fund *366*
Jackson Purchase Energy Corporation Scholarship *702*
Jackson-Stricks Scholarship *562*
Jacob Van Namen/Vans Marketing Scholarship *74*
Jagannathan Scholarship *730*
James A. Suffridge United Food and Commercial
  Workers Scholarship Program *522*
James A. Turner, Jr. Memorial Scholarship *144*
James Beard Foundation General Scholarships *304*
James Bridenbaugh Memorial Scholarship *344*
James C. Caldwell Assisting Men and Women of Toledo
  Scholarship *620*
James Carlson Memorial Scholarship *234*
James F. Byrnes Scholarship *702*
James F. Lincoln Arc Welding Foundation Awards
  Program *819*
James J. Burns and C.A. Haynes Scholarship *837*
James J. Wychor Scholarship *479*
James L. and Genevieve H. Goodwin Memorial
  Scholarship *684*
James L. Shriver Scholarship *683*
James R. Hoffa Memorial Scholarship Fund *818*
James Rathmell, Jr. Memorial Scholarship *344*
James V. Day Scholarship *488*
James Z. Naurison Scholarship *683*
Jane Austen Society of North America Essay Contest *771*
Jane M. Klausman Women in Business Scholarships *158*
Janet B. Seippel Scholarship *521*
Janet B. Sondheim Scholarship *110*
Janet Dziadulewicz Branden Memorial Award *835*
Janet Ishikawa-Daniel Fullmer Scholarship in
  Counseling *450*
Janet L. Hoffmann Loan Assistance Repayment
  Program *230*
Japan Studies Scholarship *312*
Japanese Studies Scholarship *105*
Japan-U.S. Friendship Commission Prize for the
  Translation of Japanese Literature *311*
Jason Lang Scholarship *656*

Jaycee Charles R. Ford Scholarship *522*
Jaycee Thomas Wood Baldridge Scholarship *523*
Jaycee War Memorial Fund Scholarship *849*
Jaycee War Memorial Fund Scholarship *819*
Jeanette C. and Isadore N. Stern Scholarship *317*
Jeanette R. Wolman Scholarship *375*
Jeanne E. Bray Memorial Scholarship Program *506*
Jeannette Mowery Scholarship *211*
Jeannette Rankin Foundation Awards *819*
Jennica Ferguson Memorial Scholarship *546*
Jennifer Curtis Byler Scholarship for the Study of Public
  Affairs *184*
Jennings and Beulah Haggerty Scholarship *705*
Jere W. Thompson, Jr., Scholarship Fund *173*
Jerman-Cahoon Student Scholarship *323*
Jerome B. Steinbach Scholarship *737*
Jerry Clark Memorial Scholarship *449*
Jerry L. Pettis Memorial Scholarship *320*
Jerry Robinson-Inweld Corporation Scholarship *792*
Jesse Brown Memorial Youth Scholarship Program *541*
Jesse Jones, Jr. Scholarship *641*
Jewish Social Service Agency Educational
  Scholarship *703*
Jewish Social Service Agency of Metropolitan
  Washington Max and Emmy Dreyfuss
  Undergraduate Scholarship Fund *652*
Jewish Vocational Service Scholarship Program *652*
Jim Allard Broadcast Journalism Scholarship *359*
Jim Bourque Scholarship *220*
Jim Perry/Holden L. Bettinger Scholarship *345*
Jimmie Condon Athletic Scholarships *603*
Jimmy A. Young Memorial Education Recognition
  Award *322*
Jo Anne J. Trow Scholarships *787*
Joan Cain Florida Quarter Horse Youth Scholarship *492*
Joan K. Hunt and Rachel M. Hunt Summer Scholarship
  in Field Botany *347*
Joe Finger Scholarship *778*
Joe Francis Haircare Scholarship Program *198*
Joe Lipper Memorial Scholarship *368*
Joe Moore Scholarship *778*
Joel Abromson Memorial Foundation *717*
Joel Garcia Memorial Scholarship *180*
John and Elsa Gracik Scholarships *392*
John and Muriel Landis Scholarship Awards *249*
John Bayliss Broadcast Radio Scholarship *182*
John C. Bajus Scholarship *386*
John C. Lincoln Memorial Scholarship *254*
John C. Santistevan Memorial Scholarship *111*
John Charles Wilson Scholarship *300*
John Dennis Scholarship *199*
John E. Godwin, Jr. Memorial Scholarship Award *126*
John Edgar Thomson Foundation Grants *544*
John F. and Anna Lee Stacey Scholarship Fund *112*
John Gyles Education Awards *819*
John Hjorth Scholarship Fund-San Diego Chapter *473*
John Holden Memorial Vocational Scholarship *345*
John J. McKetta Undergraduate Scholarship *159*
John Kimball, Jr. Memorial Trust Scholarship Program
  for the Study of History *339*
John L. and Sarah G. Merriam Scholarship *78*
John L. Bates Scholarship *824*
John L. Tomasovic, Sr., Scholarship *345*
John Lennon Scholarship Program *401*
John M. Azarian Memorial Armenian Youth Scholarship
  Fund *149*
John M. Haniak Scholarship *256*
John M. Will Journalism Scholarship *362*
John Mabry Forestry Scholarship *410*
John N. Colberg Endowment Scholarship Fund *800*
John R. Hope Scholarship *399*
John R. Lamarsh Scholarship *249*
John S. Stamler Memorial Scholarship *540*
John W. Anderson Foundation Scholarship *641*
John W. Mc Devitt (Fourth Degree) Scholarships *503*
John Wiley & Sons Best JASIST Paper Award *191*
Johnny Davis Memorial Scholarship *117*
Johnson Controls Foundation Scholarship Program *531*
Johnson F. Hammond, MD Memorial Scholarship *320*
Jonathan R. Lax Scholarship Fund *795*
Jose D. Garcia Migrant Education Scholarship *737*
Jose Marti Scholarship Challenge Grant Fund *613*
Joseph A. Towles African Study Abroad Scholarship *641*
Joseph B. Shafferman, Sr. Memorial Scholarship
  Fund *536*
Joseph C. Basile, II, Memorial Scholarship Fund *226*
Joseph C. Johnson Memorial Grant *251*
Joseph F. Taricani Memorial Scholarship *68*
Joseph Fitcher Scholarship Contest *83*
Joseph Frasca Excellence in Aviation Scholarship *131*
Joseph H. Bearns Prize in Music *767*
Joseph Henry Jackson Literary Award *743*
Joseph M. Parish Memorial Grant *251*

Millie Brother Annual Scholarship for Children of Deaf Adults *801*
Millie Gonzalez Memorial Scholarship *561*
Milliken & Company Scholarship *527*
Milton J. Boone Horticultural Scholarship *342*
Mineralogical Society of America-Grant for Student Research in Mineralogy and Petrology *214*
Mineralogy Society of America-Grant for Research in Crystallography *215*
Minnesota Academic Excellence Scholarship *715*
Minnesota AFL-CIO Scholarships *504*
Minnesota Gay/Lesbian/Bisexual/Transgender Scholarship Fund *825*
Minnesota Indian Scholarship Program *624*
Minnesota Legionnaires Insurance Trust Scholarship *489*
Minnesota Nurses Loan Forgiveness Program *328*
Minnesota Police Corps Scholarship *825*
Minnesota Reciprocal Agreement *715*
Minnesota Soybean Research and Promotion Council Youth Soybean Scholarship *75*
Minnesota Space Grant Consortium *124*
Minnesota State Grant Program *715*
Minnesota State Veterans' Dependents Assistance Program *591*
Minnesota SWE Section Scholarship *280*
Minnie Pearl Scholarship Program *557*
Minorities in Government Finance Scholarship *62*
Minority Affairs Committee Award for Outstanding Scholastic Achievement *160*
Minority Nurse Magazine Scholarship Program *426*
Minority Scholarship Award for Academic Excellence in Physical Therapy *321*
Minority Scholarship Award for Academic Excellence-Physical Therapist Assistant *322*
Minority Scholarship Awards for College Students *160*
Minority Scholarship Awards for Incoming College Freshmen *160*
Minority Student Summer Scholarship *109*
Minority Teacher Incentive Grant Program *224*
Minority Teachers of Illinois Scholarship Program *228*
Minority Travel Fund Award *401*
Minority Undergraduate Retention Grant-Wisconsin *647*
Minority Undergraduate Student Awards *142*
Minoru Yasui Memorial Scholarship Award *358*
Miriam Croft Moeller Citizenship Award *705*
Miriam S. Grunfield Scholarship Fund *651*
Miss America Organization Competition Scholarships *771*
Miss American Coed Pageant *773*
Missing in Action/Killed in Action Dependent's Scholarship-Arkansas *586*
Mississippi Association of Broadcasters Scholarship *479*
Mississippi Eminent Scholars Grant *716*
Mississippi Health Care Professions Loan/Scholarship Program *328*
Mississippi Press Association Education Foundation Scholarship *363*
Mississippi Resident Tuition Assistance Grant *716*
Mississippi Scholarship *90*
Missouri Broadcasters Association Scholarship *479*
Missouri College Guarantee Program *717*
Missouri Funeral Directors Association Scholarships *313*
Missouri Higher Education Academic Scholarship (Bright Flight) *717*
Missouri Insurance Education Foundation Scholarship *354*
Missouri Minority Teaching Scholarship *231*
Missouri Police Corps Fund *825*
Missouri Teacher Education Scholarship (General) *232*
Missouri Travel Council Tourism Scholarship *307*
MJSA Education Foundation Jewelry Scholarship *776*
MOAA American Patriot Scholarship *590*
MOAA Base/Post Scholarship *590*
Money Matters Scholarship *798*
Monica Bailes Award *564*
Monsanto Agri-business Scholarship *81*
Monsignor Alphonse S. Popek Memorial Award *835*
Monster Non-RN Undergraduate Scholarship *422*
Montana Higher Education Opportunity Grant *717*
Montana Society of Certified Public Accountants Scholarship *65*
Montana Space Grant Scholarship Program *125*
Montana Tuition Assistance Program-Baker Grant *718*
Montana University System Honor Scholarship *718*
Monte Mitchell Global Scholarship *118*
Montgomery GI Bill (Active Duty) Chapter 30 *587*
Montgomery GI Bill (Selected Reserve) *569*
Morris J. and Betty Kaplun Foundation Annual Essay Contest *653*
Morris K. Udall Undergraduate Scholarships *294*
Morris Newspaper Corporation Scholarship *361*
Mortin Scholarship *847*
Morton A. Gibson Memorial Scholarship *652*

Morton B. Duggan, Jr. Memorial Education Recognition Award *322*
Mosmiller Scholar Program *143*
Mr. & Mrs. G. Deming Seymour 4-H Scholarship *509*
MRA Institute of Management Endowment Fund Scholarship *151*
MRCA Foundation Scholarship Program *94*
Mrs. Ella M. Franklin Scholarship *521*
Mrs. L. H. Raines Memorial Scholarship *522*
MSCA/TCF Bank Scholarship Program *758*
MSPE Auxiliary Grant for Undergraduate Study *174*
Mu Phi Epsilon Scholarship Fund *402*
Multicultural Scholarship Program *625*
Music Committee Scholarship *401*
Music Technology Scholarship *241*
MuSonics Scholarship *404*
My Turn Essay Competition *820*
Myra Levick Scholarship Fund *466*
Myrtle and Earl Walker Scholarship Fund *275*
NAACP Lillian and Samuel Sutton Education Scholarship *232*
NAAS II National Scholarship Awards *825*
NAAS-USA Awards *826*
NABJ Scholarship *183*
NACME Scholars Program *268*
NACME/NASA Space Station Engineering Scholars Program *268*
Nadeen Burkeholder Williams Music Scholarship *550*
NAIW College Scholarship *354*
NAIW Education Foundation Professional Scholarship *151*
Nancy Curry Scholarship *301*
Nancy Goodhue Lynch Scholarship *470*
Nancy Stewart Scholarship Fund-Allegheny Chapter *474*
NARBW Scholarship *826*
NASA Delaware Space Grant Undergraduate Tuition Scholarship *94*
NASA Idaho Space Grant Consortium Scholarship Program *94*
NASA Maryland Space Grant Consortium Undergraduate Scholarships *139*
NASA Nebraska Space Grant *125*
NASA Rhode Island Space Grant Consortium Outreach Scholarship for Undergraduate Students *288*
NASA Rhode Island Space Grant Consortium Undergraduate Scholarship *719*
NASA RISGC Science En Espa±ol Scholarship for Undergraduate Students *719*
NASA RISGC Summer Scholarship for Undergraduate Students *719*
NATA Business Scholarship *127*
National "Make It Yourself With Wool" Competition *761*
National Academy of Television Arts and Sciences John Cannon Memorial Scholarship *183*
National Achievement Scholarship Program *625*
National Alpha Mu Gamma Scholarships *310*
National Aquarium in Baltimore Henry Hall Scholarship *136*
National Art Honor Society Scholarship *109*
National Art Materials Trade Association Academic Scholarship *532*
National Art Materials Trade Association Art Major Scholarship *113*
National Asian-American Journalists Association Mosmiller Scholarship *358*
National Asphalt Pavement Association Scholarship Program *175*
National Association for Campus Activities East Coast Higher Education Research Scholarship *720*
National Association for Campus Activities East Coast Undergraduate Scholarship for Student Leaders *720*
National Association for Campus Activities Regional Council Student Leader Scholarships *773*
National Association for Campus Activities Southeast Region Student Leadership Scholarship *720*
National Association for Campus Activities WI Region Student Leadership Scholarship *720*
National Association of Black Journalists and Newhouse Foundation Scholarship *364*
National Association of Black Journalists Non-Sustaining Scholarship Awards *364*
National Association of Broadcasters Grants for Research in Broadcasting *183*
National Association of Directors of Nursing Administration in Long Term Care-Upward Bound Scholarship *427*
National Association of Food Equipment Dealers, Inc. Scholarship *496*
National Association of Geoscience Teachers - Far Western Section scholarship *215*
National Association of Insurance and Financial Advisors Scholarship *683*

National Association of Insurance Women/Junior Achievement of Maine Scholarship *217*
National Association of Pastoral Musicians Members' Scholarship *404*
National Association of Water Companies-New Jersey Chapter Scholarship *139*
National Athletic Trainer's Association Research and Education Foundation Scholarship Program *329*
National Aviation Explorer Scholarships *121*
National Beef Ambassador Program *790*
National Beta Club Scholarship *505*
National Beta Scholarship *851*
National Commission for Cooperative Education Co-Op Scholarship *827*
National Community Pharmacist Association Foundation Presidential Scholarship *329*
National Competition for Composers' Recordings *767*
National Conference of CPA Practitioners, Inc. Scholarship *65*
National Council of State Garden Clubs, Inc. Scholarship *82*
National Customs Brokers and Forwarders Association of America Scholarship Award *472*
National Dairy Shrine Lager Dairy Scholarship *82*
National Dairy Shrine/Dairy Marketing, Inc. Milk Marketing Scholarships *82*
National Dairy Shrine/Klussendorf Scholarship *82*
National Defense Transportation Association, Scott Air Force Base- St. Louis Area Chapter Scholarship *721*
National Environmental Health Association/American Academy of Sanitarians Scholarship *437*
National Federation of Paralegal Associates, Inc. West Scholarship *378*
National Federation of State Poetry Societies Scholarship Awards- College/University Level Poetry Competition *774*
National Federation of the Blind Computer Science Scholarship *193*
National Federation of the Blind Educator of Tomorrow Award *232*
National Federation of the Blind Humanities Scholarship *353*
National Federation of the Blind of California Merit Scholarships *828*
National Federation of the Blind of Missouri Scholarships to Legally Blind Students *563*
National FFA College and Vocational/Technical School Scholarship Program *828*
National Foster Parent Association Scholarship *506*
National Fraternal Society of the Deaf Scholarships *506*
National Funeral Directors and Morticians Association Scholarship *828*
National Garden Clubs Scholarship *349*
National Garden Clubs, Inc. Scholarship Program *83*
National Gay and Lesbian Task Force Messenger-Anderson Journalism Scholarship *183*
National Greenhouse Manufacturers Association Scholarship *346*
National Ground Water Education Foundation Len Assante Scholarship Fund *828*
National Guard Association of Colorado (NGACO) Education Foundation Inc. Scholarship *571*
National Health Service Corps Scholarship Program *325*
National High School Journalist of the Year/Sister Rita Jeanne Scholarships *182*
National High School Oratorical Contest *790*
National High School Poetry Contest/Easterday Poetry Award *768*
National Hispanic Explorers Scholarship Program *93*
National Honor Society Scholarships *505*
National Institute for Labor Relations Research William B. Ruggles Journalism Scholarship *184*
National Italian American Foundation Category I Scholarship *625*
National Italian American Foundation Category II Scholarship *106*
National Junior Classical League Scholarship *311*
National Latin Exam Scholarship *310*
National Leadership Development Grants *614*
National Merit Scholarship Program *829*
National Merit Scholarships Funded by Omnova Solutions Foundation *532*
National Military Intelligence Association Scholarship *506*
National Minority Junior Golf Scholarship *625*
National Network for Environmental Management Studies Fellowship *411*
National Oceanic and Atmospheric Administration Educational Partnership Program with Minority Serving Institutions Undergraduate Scholarship *268*
National Oratorical Scholarship Contest *663*
National Peace Essay Contest *438*
National Poster Design Contest *315*

North Dakota State Student Incentive Grant Program 747

North Dakota Teacher Shortage Loan Forgiveness Program 233

North East Roofing Educational Foundation Scholarship 508

Northeast Fresh Foods Alliance Scholarship Awards Program 509

Northeast Utilities System Scholarship Program 156

Northeastern Illinois Chapter Scholarship 436

Northeastern Loggers' Association Scholarships 509

Northern Alberta Development Council Bursary 603

Northern Alberta Development Council Bursary for Pharmacy Students 441

Northern Alberta Development Council Bursary Partnership Program 657

Northern California Chapter Richard Epping Scholarship 474

Northern Ontario Aboriginal Nurses Award 414

Northern Student Supplement 657

Northern Virginia Urban League Scholarship Program 627

Northrop Grumman Corporation Scholarships 130

Northwest Automatic Vending Association Scholarship 533

Northwest Journalists of Color Scholarship 365

Norway-America Undergraduate Scholarship Program 627

Notre Dame Law School Feminist Jurisprudence Writing Competition 376

NPM Board of Directors Scholarship 404

NPM Composers and Authors Scholarship 404

NPM Koinonia/Board of Directors Scholarship 404

NPM Miami Valley Catholic Church Musicians Scholarship 405

NPM Perrot Scholarship 405

NROTC Scholarship Program 597

NSA Louis and Fannie Sager Memorial Scholarship Award 65

NSCA Minority Scholarship 336

NSCC Scholarship Program 850

NSPA Journalism Honor Roll Scholarship 365

NTHS SkillsUSA Scholarship 840

Nurse Education Scholarship Loan Program (NESLP) 430

Nurse Scholars Program—Undergraduate (North Carolina) 430

Nursing Education Loan/Scholarship-BSN 426

Nursing Loan Forgiveness for Healthier Futures Program 432

Nursing Scholarship for High School Seniors 434

Nursing Scholastic Achievement Scholarship for Lutheran College Students 420

Nursing Spectrum Scholarship 428

Nursing Student Loan Program 434

Nursing Student Loan-For-Service Program 429

Nursing Student Scholarship 426

NYSSPE-Past Officers' Scholarship 508

OAACE Member Scholarship 731

OAB Broadcast Scholarship 185

OCA Avon College Scholarship 628

OCA National Essay Contest 628

OCA/UPS Foundation Gold Mountain Scholarship 628

OCA-AXA Achievement Scholarship 628

OCA-SYSCO Scholarship 629

OCA-Verizon Scholarship 629

Odd Fellows and Rebekahs Ellen F. Washburn Nurses Training Award 831

OFA National Scholarship/Casey Family Scholarship 833

Off To College Scholarship Sweepstakes 843

Ohio Academic Scholarship Program 731

Ohio American Legion Scholarships 510

Ohio Association of Collegiate Registrars and Admission Officers Scholarship 731

Ohio Educational Credit Union Scholarship 732

Ohio Environmental Science & Engineering Scholarships 295

Ohio Forestry Association Memorial Scholarship 733

Ohio Instructional Grant 732

Ohio Missing in Action and Prisoners of War Orphans Scholarship 593

Ohio National Guard Scholarship Program 572

Ohio National Guard Scholarship Program 572

Ohio Newspaper Women's Scholarship 366

Ohio Newspapers Foundation Minority Scholarship 366

Ohio Newspapers Foundation University Journalism Scholarship 366

Ohio Police Corps Scholarship 733

Ohio Safety Officers College Memorial Fund 548

Ohio Student Choice Grant Program 732

Ohio War Orphans Scholarship 593

Ohkay Owingeh Tribal Scholarship of the Pueblo of San Juan 632

Oklahoma Alumni & Associates of FHA, HERO and FCCLA, Inc. Scholarship 510

Oklahoma Educational Foundation for Osteopathic Medicine Endowed Student Scholarship Program 329

Oklahoma Tuition Aid Grant 733

Olive Lynn Salembier Scholarship 280

Olive W. Garvey Fellowship Competition 817

Om and Saraswati Bahethi Scholarship 399

Omaha Symphony Guild International New Music Competition 774

101st Airborne Division Association Chappie Hall Scholarship Program 575

102nd Infantry Division Association Memorial Scholarship Program 575

Oneida Higher Education Grant Program 627

ONF-Smith Education Scholarship 432

ONS Foundation Ethnic Minority Bachelor's Scholarship 430

ONS Foundation Josh Gottheil Memorial Bone Marrow Transplant Career Development Awards 431

ONS Foundation Nursing Outcomes Research Grant 330

ONS Foundation Oncology Nursing Society Research Grant 330

ONS Foundation Roberta Pierce Scofield Bachelor's Scholarships 431

ONS Foundation/Oncology Nursing Certification Corporation Bachelor's Scholarships 431

ONS Foundation/Pearl Moore Career Development Awards 431

OP Loftbed $500 Scholarship Award 832

Opportunities Scholarship Program 421

Optimist International Essay Contest 832

Optimist International Oratorical Contest 832

Ora Lee Sanders Scholarship 836

Oral-B Laboratories Dental Hygiene Scholarship 206

Orange County Chapter/Harry Jackson Scholarship Fund 474

Oratorical Contest 663

Oratorical Contest Scholarship-Iowa 661

Ordean Scholarship Program 67

Oregon AFL-CIO Scholarship 548

Oregon Catholic Press Scholarship 405

Oregon Collectors Association Bob Hasson Memorial Scholarship 737

Oregon Collectors Association Bob Hasson Memorial Scholarship Fund 734

Oregon Dungeness Crab Commission Scholarship 548

Oregon Education Association Scholarship 235

Oregon Foundation for Blacktail Deer Outdoor and Wildlife Scholarship 140

Oregon Metro Federal Credit Union Scholarship 737

Oregon Native American Chamber of Commerce Scholarship 628

Oregon Occupational Safety and Health Division Workers Memorial Scholarship 548

Oregon Police Corps 833

Oregon Publishing Company/Hilliard Scholarship 511

Oregon Salmon Commission Scholarship 549

Oregon Scholarship Fund Community College Student Award 738

Oregon Scholarship Fund Transfer Student Award 738

Oregon Sheep Growers Association Memorial Scholarship 84

Oregon State Fiscal Association Scholarship 511

Oregon Student Assistance Commission Employee and Dependent Scholarship 738

Oregon Trawl Commission Scholarship 549

Oregon Trucking Association Scholarship 534

Oregon Veterans' Education Aid 593

Oregon Wine Brotherhood Scholarship 203

Osage Higher Education Grant 629

Osage Tribal Education Committee Scholarship 629

Oscar W. Rittenhouse Memorial Scholarship 376

OSCPA Educational Foundation Scholarship Program 68

Osher Scholarship 709

Osler, Hoskin and Harcourt National Essay Competition 722

Our World Underwater Scholarships 775

Outdoor Writers Association of America Bodie McDowell Scholarship Award 185

Outstanding Achievement Scholarships 810

Outstanding Community College Accounting Student Award 58

Outstanding Rural Scholar Program 333

Outstanding Scholar Recruitment Program 726

Outstanding Student Chapter Advisor Award 160

Outstanding Students of America Scholarship 833

Overseas Press Club Foundation Scholarships 367

Owen Electric Cooperative Scholarship Program 739

P.G. Richardson Masonic Memorial Scholarship 706

PA AFL-CIO Unionism in America Essay Contest 512

PAAC Scholarship 357

Pablo Neruda Prize for Poetry 830

PACD Auxiliary Scholarships 76

PACE Scholarship Awards 833

Pacific Northwest Chapter-William Hunt Scholarship Fund 474

Pacific NW Federal Credit Union Scholarship 738

PacificSource Scholarship 534

Padgett Business Services Foundation Scholarship Program 833

Padnendadlu Undergraduate Bursaries 607

Padrino Scholarships 634

Pagel Graphic Arts Scholarship Fund 185

Paluch Family Foundation/World Library Publications Scholarship 405

Palwaukee Airport Pilots Association Scholarship Program 128

PAMAS Restricted Scholarship Award 630

Paper and Board Division Scholarships 845

PaperCheck.com Charles Shafae' Scholarship Fund 833

Paralyzed Veterans of America Educational Scholarship Program 833

Paraprofessional Teacher Preparation Grant 231

Parent Continuing Education Scholarship 822

Parent Relocation Council Scholarship 834

Parents Without Partners International Scholarship Program 512

Paris Fracasso Production Floriculture Scholarship 346

Park Espenschade Memorial Scholarship 294

Parker-Lovejoy Scholarship 740

Parsons Brinckerhoff-Jim Lammie Scholarship 171

Part-time Grant Program 747

Part-time Grant Program-Maryland 712

Part-time Student Instructional Grant 732

Part-time Tuition Aid Grant (TAG) for County Colleges 726

Past Presidents Parley Health Care Scholarship 207

Past Presidents Parley Health Career Scholarships 486

Past Presidents Parley Registered Nurse Scholarship 417

Past Presidents Parley Scholarship-Missouri 416

Past Presidents Scholarships 281

Pat and Jim Host Scholarship 309

Patricia M. McNamara Memorial Scholarship 837

Patriot's Pen 779

Patty and Melvin Alperin First Generation Scholarship/ David M. Golden Memorial Scholarship 742

Paul A. & Ethel I. Smith 4-H Scholarship 83

Paul A. Stewart Awards 88

Paul A. Whelan Aviation Scholarship 131

Paul and Edith Babson Scholarship 643

Paul and Helen L. Grauer Scholarship 91

Paul and Helen Trussel Science and Technology Scholarship 93

Paul Cole Scholarship 332

Paul Douglas Teacher Scholarship (PDTS) Program 228

Paul Flaherty Athletic Scholarship 662

Paul H. Robbins Honorary Scholarship 166

Paul Hagelbarger Memorial Fund Scholarship 53

Paul Jennings Scholarship Award 501

Paul W. Rodgers Scholarship 214

Paul W. Ruckes Scholarship 190

Paychex Entrepreneur Scholarship 61

Paychex, Inc. Entrepreneur Scholarship 59

Payzer Scholarship 122

Peabody Scholarship 619

Peermusic Latin Scholarship 401

Pellegrini Scholarship Grants 636

Pendleton Postal Workers Scholarship 549

Pennsylvania Burglar and Fire Alarm Association Youth Scholarship Program 549

Pennsylvania Federation of Democratic Women, Inc. Annual Scholarship Awards 512

Pennsylvania Institute of Certified Public Accountants Sophomore Scholarship 68

Pennsylvania Masonic Youth Foundation Scholarship 512

Pennsylvania Right to Work Defense and Education Foundation James Scott II Essay Contest 740

Pennsylvania State Grants 739

Pepsi-Cola Youth Bowling Championships 524

Performance Bonus Grant Program 713

Permelia A. Butterfield Scholarship 684

Perry F. Hadlock Memorial Scholarship 243

Persina Scholarship for Minorities in Journalism 360

Persons Case Scholarships 603

Peter and Alice Koomruian Armenian Education Fund 629

Peter and Barbara Bye Scholarship 847

Peter Crossley Memorial Scholarship 738

Peter D. Courtois Concrete Construction Scholarship 97

Peter Doctor Memorial Iroquois Scholarship 630

Peter Kalifornsky Memorial Endowment Scholarship Fund 800

Peter Kong-Ming New Student Prize 332

Ron Brown Scholar Program *608*
Ronald E. McNair Scholarship in Space and Optical
  Physics *448*
Ronald Lorah Memorial Scholarship *518*
Ronald McDonald's Chicagoland Scholarship *643*
Ronald McDonald's House Charities Scholarship-
  Ohio *643*
Ronald P. Guerrette Future Farmers of America
  Scholarship Fund *81*
Ronald Reagan Leadership Award *517*
Roothbert Fund, Inc. Scholarship *837*
Roscoe Hogan Environmental Law Essay Contest *379*
Rosedale Post 346 Scholarship *488*
Rosewood Family Scholarship Fund *613*
Rotary Foundation Academic-Year Ambassadorial
  Scholarships *776*
Rotary Foundation Cultural Ambassadorial
  Scholarship *312*
Rotary Multi-Year Ambassadorial Scholarships *776*
ROV Scholarship *386*
Rowley/Ministerial Education Scholarship *454*
Rowntree Lewis Price and Wycoff Scholarship *314*
Roy M. Huhndorf Health Sciences Endowment
  Scholarship Fund *800*
Roy Wilkins Scholarship *505*
Royal Bank Aboriginal Student Awards *153*
Royce Osborn Minority Student Scholarship *323*
Royden M. Bodley Scholarship *87*
RSI Undergraduate Scholarship Program *836*
Rube and Minah Leslie Educational Fund *734*
Ruby Paul Campaign Fund Scholarship *485*
Rudolph Dillman Memorial Scholarship *219*
Rural Health Student Loan Program *210*
Russell A. Cookingham Scholarship *140*
Rust Scholarship *848*
Ruth Ann Johnson Scholarship *695*
Ruth Clark Scholarship *111*
Ruth Hancock Memorial Scholarship *180*
Rutherford Scholars *604*
S. Evelyn Lewis Memorial Scholarship in Medical Health
  Sciences *334*
S. Truett Cathy Scholar Awards *529*
S.A. Cunningham Scholarship *522*
Sachs Foundation Scholarships *816*
SACNAS Financial Aid: Lodging and Travel Award *840*
Sacramento Bee Journalism Scholarship Program *368*
Sacramento Bee Scholar Athlete Scholarship *742*
Sacramento Bee William Glackin Scholarship
  Program *743*
SAE Baltimore Section Bill Brubaker Scholarship *270*
SAE Long Term Member Sponsored Scholarship *271*
SAE William G. Belfrey Memorial Grant *271*
Safety and Chemical Engineering Education (SACHE)
  Student Essay Award For Safety *161*
Safety and Health National Student Design Competition
  Award for Safety *161*
Safety Officers' Survivor Grant Program *545*
Safeway/Greater Washington Urban League
  Scholarship *696*
Sailing for Scholars Scholarship *804*
SAJA Journalism Scholarship *369*
Salamatof Native Association, Inc. (SNAI) Scholarship
  Program *800*
Sales Professionals- USA Scholarship *153*
Sallie Mae 911 Education Fund Loan Relief *837*
Sallie Mae 911 Education Fund Scholarship
  Program *838*
Sallie Mae Fund American Dream Scholarship *643*
Sallie Mae Fund Scholarships *838*
Sallie Mae Fund Unmet Need Scholarship Program *838*
Sally S. Jacobsen Scholarship *546*
Salt River Electric Scholarship Program *743*
Salute to Education Scholarship *838*
Salute to Education, Inc. *713*
Sam Walton Community Scholarship *852*
Samsung American Legion Scholarship *585*
Samuel Huntington Public Service Award *838*
Samuel M. and Gertrude G. Levy Scholarship Fund *554*
San Fernando Valley Chapter of the Ninety-Nines
  Career Scholarship *128*
San Jose Mercury News Scholarship *644*
Sandy Brown Memorial Scholarship *378*
Sanford D'Amato Scholarship *202*
Santa Clara University School of Law Computer and
  High Technology Law Journal Comment
  Contest *368*
Santo Domingo Scholarship *633*
Sara Conlon Memorial Scholarship Award *241*
Sara Lazarus Memorial Scholarship *838*
Sara Lee Branded Apparel Scholarships *527*
SARA Student Design Competition *103*
Sarah Klenke Memorial Teaching Scholarship
  Program *236*

Sarnia Chemical Engineering Community
  Scholarship *163*
SBAA One-Year Scholarship *566*
SBC Foundation Scholarship *156*
SBC Pacific Bell Foundation Scholarship *156*
Scarborough-Scheeler Scholarship *677*
Scholar Athlete Milk Mustache of the Year *779*
Scholarship Awards *561*
Scholarship for Aboriginal Canadians *507*
Scholarship for Academic Excellence *728*
Scholarship for Children of Special Operations Forces
  Who are Killed in the Line of Duty *568*
Scholarship for Dependent Children of Bee
  Employees *837*
Scholarship for Minority College Students *224*
Scholarship for Minority High School Students *224*
Scholarship for Non-Traditional Student *581*
Scholarship for People with Disabilities *557*
Scholarship For Service (SFS) Program *831*
Scholarship For The Visually Impaired To Study
  Abroad *556*
Scholarship For The Visually Impaired To Study In
  Japan *556*
Scholarship for Visible Minorities *507*
Scholarship for Young Women *847*
Scholarship Incentive Program (ScIP) *686*
Scholarship Incentive Program-Delaware *687*
Scholarship of the Maine School Food Service
  Association *305*
Scholarship Program for Former Soviet Union Emigres
  Training in the Health Sciences *209*
Scholarship Program For Hispanic Student *617*
Scholarship Program for the Blind and Visually
  Impaired *555*
Scholarship-Leadership Awards Program *820*
Scholarships for Children of Deceased or Disabled
  Veterans or Children of Servicemen Classified as
  POW or MIA *588*
Scholarships for Dependents of Fallen Officers *543*
Scholarships for Education, Business and Religion *148*
Scholarships for Latina Students *609*
Scholarships for Military Children *587*
Scholarships for Military Children Program *574*
Scholarships for Minority Accounting Students *54*
Scholarships for Minority Accounting Students *55*
Scholarships for Orphans of Veterans-New
  Hampshire *591*
Scholarships for Student Leaders *773*
Scholarships for Survivors *834*
Scholastic Art and Writing Awards-Art Section *108*
Schonstedt Scholarship in Surveying *465*
Schraft Charitable Trust Scholarship *644*
Schuyler M. Meyer, Jr. Award *614*
Schuyler S. Pyle Award *578*
Schwan's Food Service Scholarship *301*
Scott Dominguez-Craters of the Moon Scholarship *436*
Scott Tarbell Scholarship *558*
Scottish Rite Charitable Foundation College
  Bursaries *550*
Scotts Company Scholars Program *348*
SCPA Scholarship Fund *542*
Screen Actors Guild Foundation/John L. Dales
  Scholarship (Transitional) *514*
Seabee Memorial Association Scholarship *600*
Sears Craftsman Scholarship *828*
Seaspace Scholarship Program *458*
Second Bombardment Association Scholarship *514*
Second Chance Scholarships *707*
Second Effort Scholarship *666*
Second Marine Division Association Memorial
  Scholarship Fund *598*
Second Year Academic Achievement Awards *807*
Seed Companies Scholarship *346*
Sehar Saleha Ahmad and Abrahim Ekramullah Zafar
  Foundation Scholarship *384*
Selby Scholar Program *757*
Seminole Tribe of Florida Billy L. Cypress Scholarship
  Program *633*
Senator George J. Mitchell Scholarship Fund *710*
Senator George J. Mitchell Scholarship Research
  Institute Scholarships *717*
Senatorial Scholarships-Maryland *712*
Seneca Nation Higher Education Program *633*
Senior Scholarships *745*
Sentry 21 Club Scholarship *853*
Seol Bong Scholarship *632*
Sepracor Achievement Award for Excellence in
  Pulmonary Disease State Management *323*
September 11th Remembrance Scholarship *804*
Sergeant Major Douglas R. Drum Memorial Scholarship
  Fund *585*
Sertoma Communicative Disorders Scholarship
  Program *116*

Sertoma Scholarship for Deaf or Hard of Hearing
  Student *565*
Service League Volunteer Scholarship *336*
Sevcik Scholarship *283*
SevenSECURE Scholarship *561*
Seventeen Magazine Fiction Contest *777*
Sharon Christa McAuliffe Teacher Education-Critical
  Shortage Grant Program *230*
Shaw-Worth Memorial Scholarship *698*
Shearman and Sterling Scholarship Program *378*
Sheila Z. Kolman Memorial Scholarships *222*
Shelby Energy Cooperative Scholarships *536*
Shell/Equilon UNCF Cleveland Scholarship Fund *644*
Sherry R. Arnstein Minority Student Scholarship *604*
Sheryl A. Horak Memorial Scholarship *374*
Sheryl A. Horak Memorial Scholarship *373*
Shoe City-WB54/WB50 Scholarship *673*
ShopKo Scholars Program *743*
Short-term Student Exchange Promotion Program
  Scholarship *793*
Shreveport Campaign *644*
SIA's Scholarship *304*
Sibling Continuing Education Scholarship *561*
Sid Richardson Memorial Fund *550*
Siemens Scholar Award *317*
Sigma Alpha Iota Graduate Performance Awards *406*
Sigma Alpha Iota Jazz Performance Awards *406*
Sigma Alpha Iota Jazz Studies Scholarship *406*
Sigma Alpha Iota Music Business/Technology
  Scholarship *407*
Sigma Alpha Iota Music Therapy Scholarship *407*
Sigma Alpha Iota Philanthropies Undergraduate
  Performance Scholarships *407*
Sigma Alpha Iota Philanthropies Undergraduate
  Scholarships *236*
Sigma Alpha Iota Summer Music Scholarships in the
  U.S. or abroad *407*
Sigma Alpha Iota Visually Impaired Scholarship *236*
Sigma Delta Chi Scholarships *744*
Sigma Phi Alpha Undergraduate Scholarship *207*
Sigma Xi Grants-In-Aid of Research *84*
Signet Classic Scholarship Essay Contest *834*
Silas Purnell Illinois Incentive for Access Program *700*
Silvio Canonica Scholarship *844*
Simon Youth Foundation Community Scholarship
  Program *839*
Simon Youth Foundation ERC Scholarship Program *839*
Sinfonia Foundation Scholarship *777*
Sir Edward Youde Memorial Overseas Scholarship for
  Disabled Students *565*
Sir Edward Youde Memorial Scholarships for Overseas
  Studies *840*
Siragusa Foundation Scholarship *644*
Sister Mary Petronia Van Straten Wisconsin
  Mathematics Council Scholarship *240*
Six Meter Club of Chicago Scholarship *667*
SkillsUSA Alumni & Friends Merit Scholarship *840*
Skoch Scholarship *385*
Slovak Gymnastic Union SOKOL, USA/Milan Getting
  Scholarship *515*
Slovenian Women's Union of America Scholarship
  Program *840*
SME Corporate Scholars *275*
SME Family Scholarship *275*
SNC LAVALIN Plant Design Competition *799*
Societie des Casinos du Quebec Scholarship *309*
Society for Foodservice Management Scholarship *310*
Society for Technical Communication Scholarship
  Program *186*
Society of Daughters of the United States Army
  Scholarships *575*
Society of Hispanic Professional Engineers
  Foundation *168*
Society of Louisiana CPAs Scholarships *69*
Society of Naval Architects and Marine Engineers
  Undergraduate Scholarships *276*
Society of Physics Students Outstanding Student in
  Research *515*
Society of Physics Students Peggy Dixon 2-Year College
  Scholarship *515*
Society of Physics Students Scholarships *448*
Society of Plastics Engineers Scholarship Program *168*
Society of Women Engineers - Twin Tiers Section
  Scholarship *196*
Society of Women Engineers-Rocky Mountain Section
  Scholarship Program *196*
Sodexho Scholarship *333*
Softbase Management Corporation Scholarship *797*
Sonne Scholarship *424*
Sonoco Scholarship *527*
Sons of Italy National Leadership Grants Competition
  General Scholarships *634*

The FW Rausch Arts and Humanities Paper Contest *112*
The International Congress on Insect Neurochemistry and Neurophysiology (ICINN) Student Recognition Award in Insect Physiology, Biochemistry, Toxicology, and Molecular Biology *290*
The James Cosmos Memorial Scholarship *615*
The Jane and Clarence Spilman Scholarship *677*
The John R. Mott Foundation Scholarships *828*
The Lessans Family Scholarship *649*
The MNCPA Scholarship Program *64*
The MTS Student Scholarship *386*
The NASCAR Common Knowledge Challenge *803*
The National Nursing Scholarship *421*
The Nicholas S. Hetos, DDS, Memorial Graduate Scholarship *208*
The Paideia Scholarship *616*
The Palace Restaurant in the Cincinnatian Hotel Culinary Scholarship *203*
The Park People $2000 Scholarship *102*
The Park People $4000 Scholarship *410*
The Paros-Digiquartz Scholarship *386*
The Peter Cameron Scholarship *203*
The Ron Vellekamp Environmental Scholarship *457*
The Ruth Abernathy Presidential Scholarship *759*
The School Safety Patrol $1000 Grant Award for High School Seniors *784*
The Sidney B. Williams, Jr. Intellectual Property Law School Scholarship *379*
The Virginia Peninsula Post of the Society of American Military Engineers (S.A.M.E.) Scholarship *103*
Theodore Mazza Scholarship *103*
Theresa Sajan Scholarship for Graduate Students *797*
Theta Delta Chi Educational Foundation Inc. Scholarship *847*
Third Marine Division Association Memorial Scholarship Fund *598*
Third Year Academic Achievement Awards *807*
37th Division Veterans Association Scholarship *847*
Thomas C. Woods, Jr. Memorial Scholarship *545*
Thomas Conrete of Georgia Scholarship *61*
Thomas E. Sharpe Memorial Scholarship *718*
Thomas F. Seay Scholarship *452*
Thomas J. Doran Jr. Memorial Scholarship *806*
Thomas M. Mocella Scholarship *806*
Thomas R. Dargan Minority Scholarship *182*
Thomas William Bennett Memorial Scholarship *223*
Thomas Wood Baldridge Scholarship *502*
Thomson Delmar Learning Surgical Technology Scholarship *324*
Thoroughbred Horse Racing's United Scholarship Trust *370*
3% Scholarship Program *728*
Thrivent Financial for Lutherans Community Leaders Scholarship Program *853*
Thurgood Marshall Scholarship *847*
Thurgood Marshall Scholarship Fund *232*
ThyssenKrupp Budd-UAW Local 2383 Vending Machine Revenue Committee Scholarship Program *798*
Tietex International Scholarship *528*
Tilford Fund *213*
Timothy L. Taschwer Scholarship *216*
TJX Foundation Scholarship *645*
TLMI 4 Year Colleges/Full-Time Students Scholarship *290*
TLMI SCHOLARSHIP GRANT for Students of 2 Year Colleges *300*
TMC/SAE Donald D. Dawson Technical Scholarship *129*
TMS J. Keith Brimacombe Presidential Scholarship *266*
TMS Outstanding Student Paper Contest-Undergraduate *266*
TMS/EMPMD Gilbert Chin Scholarship *266*
TMS/EPD Scholarship *267*
TMS/International Symposium on Superalloys Scholarship Program *267*
TMS/LMD Scholarship Program *267*
TMS/Structural Materials Division Scholarship *267*
Tobin Sorenson Physical Education Scholarship *463*
Tom and Judith Comstock Scholarship *764*
Tom Reiff Texas Broadcast Education Foundation Scholarship *187*
Tommy Douglas Scholarship *507*
Tomorrow's Teachers Scholarship Program *231*
Top Ten College Women Competition *814*
TOPS Alternate Performance Award *707*
TOPS Honors Award *707*
TOPS Opportunity Award *707*
TOPS Performance Award *708*
TOPS Tech Award *708*
Toshiba/NSTA ExploraVision Awards Program *829*
Touchstone Energy All "A" Classic Scholarship *703*
Toward Excellence, Access and Success (TEXAS Grant) *749*

Townsend and Townsend and Crew LLP Diversity Scholarship Program *379*
Township Officials of Illinois Scholarship Fund *751*
Toyota Scholarship *157*
Traditional Marching Band Extravaganza Scholarship Award *770*
Training Support for Youth with Disabilities *563*
Transit Hall of Fame Scholarship Award Program *171*
Transportation Clubs International Charlotte Woods Scholarship *130*
Transportation Clubs International Fred A. Hooper Memorial Scholarship *131*
Transportation Clubs International Ginger and Fred Deines Canada Scholarship *131*
Transportation Clubs International Ginger and Fred Deines Mexico Scholarship *131*
Travel and Training Fund *781*
Travel Grants *312*
Travelers Protective Association Scholarship Trust for the Deaf and Near Deaf *566*
Treacy Company Scholarships *751*
Triangle Native American Society Scholarship Fund *636*
Tribal Business Management Program (TBM) *55*
Trimmer Education Foundation Scholarships for Construction Management *172*
Tri-State Surveying and Photogrammetry Kris M. Kunze Memorial Scholarship *143*
Truckload Carriers Association Scholarship Fund *154*
Trull Foundation Scholarship *645*
Truman D. Picard Scholarship *75*
Trustee Scholarship *785*
Trustee Scholarship Program *183*
TRW Information Technology Minority Scholarship *197*
TSA Sponsored ITEA Scholarship *229*
Tuition Aid Grant *726*
Tuition Assistance for Children of POW/MIAs *591*
Tuition Equalization Grant (TEG) Program *750*
Tuition Exchange Scholarships *551*
Tuition Incentive Program (TIP) *714*
Tuition Reduction for Non-Resident Nursing Students *426*
Tuition Waiver for Foster Care Recipients *712*
Tuition Waiver Programs *541*
Tulsa Scholarship Awards *309*
Tupperware U.S., Inc. Scholarship *528*
Turf and Ornamental Communicators Association Scholarship Program *142*
Twenty-first Century Scholars Gear Up Summer Scholarship *748*
Twin Cities Chapter Undergraduate Scholarship *65*
Twin Cities Graduate MBA Scholarship *65*
Twin Towers Orphan Fund *848*
Two- and Three-Year Campus-Based Scholarships *573*
Two Ten Super Scholarships *848*
Two/Ten International Footwear Foundation Scholarship *552*
Two-Year Reserve Forces Duty Scholarships *576*
Tykeson Family Scholarship *549*
Tyonek Native Corporation Scholarship and Grant Fund *609*
Type I: Library Degree for Law School Graduates *375*
Type III: Library Degree for Non-Law School Graduates *380*
U.S. Aircraft Insurance Group PDP Scholarship *128*
U.S. Bank Internet Scholarship Program *848*
U.S. Marine Corps Historical Center Grants *340*
U.S. Submarine Veterans of WWII Scholarship Program *850*
UDT-SEAL Scholarship *600*
Ukrainian Fraternal Association Eugene R. and Elinor R. Kotur Scholarship Trust Fund *637*
Ukrainian Fraternal Association Ivan Franko Scholarship Fund *637*
Ukranian Fraternal Association Student Aid *637*
Ullery Charitable Trust Fund *455*
Umatilla Electric Cooperative Scholarship *739*
UNCF Liberty Scholarship *849*
Undergraduate Education Scholarships *611*
Undergraduate Research Program *719*
Undergraduate Scholarship *498*
Undergraduate Scholarship Award *300*
Undergraduate Texas Broadcast Education Foundation Scholarship *188*
Union Bank of California *645*
Union Bank of California Scholarship *152*
Union Plus Credit Card Scholarship Program *484*
Union Plus Scholarship Program *518*
United Agribusiness League Scholarship Program *77*
United Agricultural Benefit Trust Scholarship *77*
United Insurance Scholarship *645*
United Methodist Church Ethnic Scholarship *637*
United Methodist Church Hispanic, Asian, and Native American Scholarship *637*

United Parcel Service Diversity Scholarship Program *292*
United Parcel Service Foundation Scholarship *645*
United Parcel Service Scholarship for Female Students *264*
United South and Eastern Tribes Scholarship Fund *647*
United States Naval Academy Class of 1963 Foundation Grant *599*
United States Senate Youth Program *780*
United States Senate Youth Program-The William Randolph Hearst Foundation *718*
United States Submarine Veterans Inc. National Scholarship Program *552*
United States-Indonesia Society Travel Grants *850*
United Way of New Orleans Emergency Assistance Fund *645*
United Way of Westchester and Putnam, Inc./ UNCF Emergency Assistance Fund *646*
United Way/YWCA Scholarship Fund for Women *684*
Universal American Financial Corporation Scholarship Program *798*
Universities Space Research Association Scholarship Program *96*
University and Community College System of Nevada NASA Space Grant and Fellowship Program *125*
University Film and Video Association Carole Fielding Student Grants *299*
University of North Carolina Need Based Grant *675*
University of North Carolina Need-Based Grant *730*
UPS Corporate Scholars Program/Internship *157*
UPS Scholarship *853*
UPS Scholarship for Minority Students *264*
Urban Bankers of Delaware Scholarship *850*
Urban Scholars *726*
USAA Scholarship *570*
USBC Alberta E. Crowe Star of Tomorrow Award *782*
USBC Annual Zeb Scholarship *782*
USBC Chuck Hall Star of Tomorrow Scholarship *782*
USBC Earl Anthony Memorial Scholarships *782*
USBC Male and Female Youth Leaders of the Year Scholarship *782*
USENIX Association Scholarship *197*
USS Tennessee Scholarship Fund *598*
Utah Centennial Opportunity Program for Education *753*
Utah Credit Union Scholarship Contest *753*
Utah Police Corps Scholarship Program *374*
Utah Society of Professional Engineers Scholarship *169*
Utility Workers Union of America Scholarship Awards Program *523*
V. Mohan Malhotra Scholarship *97*
V.E.T.S. Annual Scholarship *595*
V103/UNCF Emergency Assistance Scholarship Fund *646*
Valley Press Club Scholarships, The Republican Scholarship; Photojournalism Scholarship, Channel 22 Scholarship *189*
Vann Kennedy Texas Broadcast Education Foundation Scholarship *188*
Vara Gray Scholarship-General *582*
Varian Radiation Therapy Student Scholarship *324*
VASWCD Educational Foundation, Inc. Scholarship Awards Program *296*
Verizon Foundation Scholarship *646*
Verl and Dorothy Miller Native American Vocational Scholarship *628*
Vermont Incentive Grants *753*
Vermont Part-time Student Grants *753*
Vermont Space Grant Consortium Scholarship Program *94*
Vermont Teacher Diversity Scholarship Program *239*
Vertical Flight Foundation Scholarship *132*
Veterans' Children Educational Opportunities *589*
Veterans Dependents Educational Benefits-Maine *574*
Veteran's Tribute Scholarship *595*
Veterans' Tuition Credit Program-New Jersey *591*
Veterinary Technician Student Scholarships *87*
Vice Admiral Jerry O. Tuttle, USN (Ret.) and Mrs. Barbara A. Tuttle Science and Technology Scholarship *255*
Vice Admiral Robert L. Walters Scholarship *844*
Victor and Margaret Ball Program *144*
Video Contest for College Students *846*
Vietnam Veterans Award/Wyoming *595*
Vietnam Veterans' Scholarship Program *592*
VietNow National Scholarship *851*
Vincent Abate Memorial Scholarship *543*
Vincent Chin Memorial Scholarship *358*
Vincent J. Maiocco Scholarship *685*
Vincent L. Hawkinson Scholarship for Peace and Justice *754*
Virchow, Krause and Company Scholarship *71*
Virgil Thompson Memorial Scholarship Contest *76*

Virginia Association of Broadcasters Scholarship Award *189*
Virginia Commonwealth Award *746*
Virginia Guaranteed Assistance Program *746*
Virginia Henry Memorial Scholarship *167*
Virginia Society for Healthcare Human Resources Administration Scholarship *318*
Virginia Society of CPAs Educational Foundation Minority Undergraduate Scholarship *71*
Virginia Society of CPAs Educational Foundation Undergraduate Scholarship *72*
Virginia Space Grant Consortium Community College Scholarships *125*
Virginia Space Grant Consortium Teacher Education Scholarships *125*
Virginia Tuition Assistance Grant Program (Private Institutions) *746*
Virginia War Orphans Education Program *595*
Visby Program: Higher Education and Research *635*
Vistakon Award of Excellence in Contact Lens Patient Care *321*
Visual and Performing Arts Achievement Awards *111*
Visual Task Force Scholarship *443*
Vocational Scholarship Program *453*
Vocational Scholarship Program *491*
Vocational School Scholarship Program *477*
Vocational Training Grants *800*
Voice of Democracy Program *851*
Volkwein Memorial Scholarship *241*
Volta Scholarship Fund *554*
VSA arts Playwright Discovery Award *779*
VSA arts-Panasonic Young Soloist Award *440*
VSA arts-Rosemary Kennedy International Young Soloist Award *441*
W. Allan Herzog Scholarship *70*
W. David Smith, Jr. Graduate Student Paper Award *161*
W. Eugene Smith Grant in Humanistic Photography *780*
W. P. Black Scholarship Fund *696*
W.H. "Howie" McClennan Scholarship *544*
W.R. Grace Scholarship Award *97*
Wachovia Citizenship Scholarship *755*
Wachovia Dependent Scholarships *528*
Wachovia INROADS Internship Scholarship Program *798*
Wachovia Technical Scholarship Program *469*
WAFP Memorial Scholarship *852*
Wallace McCauley Memorial Scholarship *518*
Wallace S. and Wilma K. Laughlin Scholarship *313*
Wally Joe Scholarship *305*
Wal-Mart Associate Scholarships *536*
Wal-Mart Higher Reach Scholarship *536*
Walt Bartram Memorial Education Award *276*
Walt Disney Company Foundation Scholarship *112*
Walter and Adi Blum Scholarship *682*
Walter and Marie Schmidt Scholarship *432*
Walter Davies Scholarship *535*
Walter G. Amprey Scholarship *677*
Walter L. Mitchell Memorial Awards *501*
Walter Reed Smith Scholarship *154*
Walter Samuel McAfee Scholarship in Space Physics *448*
Walter W. and Thelma C. Hissey College Scholarship Fund *554*
Walton Family Foundation Scholarship *536*
Walton Family Foundation Scholarship *537*
Warner Norcross and Judd LLP Scholarship for Minority Students *377*
Warren, Sanders, McNaughton Oceanographic Scholarship *437*
Washington Award for Vocational Excellence *756*
Washington Award for Vocational Excellence (WAVE) *755*
Washington Crossing Foundation Scholarship *780*
Washington Hospital Employee Association Scholarship *852*
Washington National Guard Scholarship Program *572*
Washington Press Club Foundation Scholarships *370*
Washington Promise Scholarship *755*
Washington Scholars Program *755*
Washington State Parent Teacher Association Scholarships Foundation *756*
Washington State Trial Lawyers Association Presidents' Scholarship *756*
Wayne C. Cornils Memorial Scholarship *478*
Wayne Kay High School Scholarship *276*
Wayne S. Rich Scholarship *740*
WBCA Scholarship Award *780*
We Energies Scholarship *853*
We Have Money to Learn Scholarships *667*
Weatherford Award *762*
Weitz Company Scholarship *803*
Wellness Works Scholarship *331*

Wells Fargo Scholarship *849*
Wendell Scott, Sr./NASCAR Scholarship *646*
Wesley-Logan Prize *73*
West Virginia Broadcasters Association Fund *181*
West Virginia Golf Association Fund *542*
West Virginia Society of Architects/AIA Scholarship *104*
West Virginia Space Grant Consortium Undergraduate Scholarship Program *126*
Western Association of Ladies Scholarship *646*
Western Fraternal Life Association National Scholarship *523*
Western Michigan Greenhouse Association Scholarship *347*
Western Reserve Herb Society Scholarship *348*
Western Undergraduate Exchange Program *757*
Westmoreland Coal Company Fund for Medical Students *696*
Westvaco/Wickliffe Scholarship *165*
Weyerhaeuser Company Foundation Scholarships *537*
Weyerhaeuser/UNCF Corporate Scholars *157*
Whirlpool Foundation Scholarship *646*
White Earth Scholarship Program *647*
Who's Who Sports Edition All-Academic Bowling Team Scholarship *782*
Wichita Chapter 52 Scholarship *276*
WIF Foundation Scholarship *299*
Wildlife Leadership Awards *141*
Wiley Manuel Law Foundation Scholarship *380*
Willamette Valley Section Martina Testa Memorial Scholarship *282*
Willard H. Erwin, Jr. Memorial Scholarship Fund *148*
Willett and Marguerite Lake Scholarship *549*
William A. and Ann M. Brothers Scholarship *286*
William and Dorothy Ferrel Scholarship *555*
William B. Howell Memorial Scholarship *255*
William C. Davini Scholarship *637*
William C. Rogers Scholarship *362*
William D. and Jewell W. Brewer Scholarship Trusts *584*
William D. and Ruth D. Roy Scholarship *739*
William D. Squires Scholarship *757*
William Donald Schaefer Scholarship *451*
William E. Weber Scholarship *827*
William E. Weisel Scholarship Fund *246*
William F. "Bill" Johnson Memorial Scholarship sponsored by Sons of the American Legion *490*
William F. Cooper Scholarship *757*
William Faulkner-William Wisdom Creative Writing Competition *775*
William H. Bailey Jr. Memorial Scholarship *269*
William H. Price Scholarship *288*
William Heath Education Scholarship for Ministers, Priests and Missionaries *453*
William J. & Marijane E. Adams, Jr. Scholarship *393*
William J. and Marijane E. Adams, Jr. Scholarship *78*
William Kapell International Piano Competition and Festival *438*
William L. and Della Waggoner Scholarship Fund *735*
William L. Boyd IV Florida Resident Access Grant *692*
William L. Callison Scholarship *846*
William P. Willis Scholarship *734*
William P. Willis Scholarship *757*
William P. Woodside Founder's Scholarship *256*
William Pew Religious Freedom Scholarship Competition *374*
William R. Goldfarb Memorial Scholarship *145*
William S. Bullinger Scholarship *376*
William V. Muse Scholarship *518*
William Wilson Memorial Scholarship *518*
William Winter Teacher Scholar Loan *825*
William Winter Teacher Scholar Loan Program *231*
Willie Hobbs Moore, Harry L. Morrison, and Arthur B.C. Walker Physics Scholarships *448*
Willie Rudd Scholarship *502*
Willis and Mildred Pellerin Scholarships *758*
Willits Foundation Scholarship Program *537*
Wilma Motley California Merit Scholarship *207*
Windstar Environmental Studies Scholarships *284*
Winnie Davis-Children of the Confederacy Scholarship *522*
Winston-Salem/Forsyth County Public Schools Scholarship *239*
Wisconsin Academic Excellence Scholarship *758*
Wisconsin Department of Veterans Affairs Retraining Grants *596*
Wisconsin First Scholarship Program *853*
Wisconsin Higher Education Grants (WHEG) *758*
Wisconsin League for Nursing Inc., Scholarship *434*
Wisconsin Native American/ Indian Student Assistance Grant *648*
Wisconsin Society of Professional Engineers Scholarships *284*

Wisconsin Space Grant Consortium Undergraduate Research Program *126*
Wisconsin Space Grant Consortium Undergraduate Scholarship Program *126*
Wisconsin Student Aid *646*
Wisconsin Veterans Part-time Study Reimbursement Grant *596*
Wiss Edward W. O'Connell Memorial Scholarship *73*
WJA Member Grant *854*
Wm. Wrigley, Jr. Company Scholars Program *157*
WNGGA Scholarship Program *107*
Woman's Missionary Union Scholarship Program *654*
Women in Aviation, International Achievement Awards *134*
Women in Aviation, International Management Scholarships *134*
Women in Corporate Aviation Career Scholarships *134*
Women in Logistics Scholarship *157*
Women in Rural Electrification (WIRE) Scholarships *842*
Women in Rural Electrification Scholarship *759*
Women in Science and Technology Scholarship *143*
Women in Sports Media Scholarship/Internship Program *765*
Women Military Aviators, Inc. Memorial Scholarship *134*
Women's Architectural Auxiliary Eleanor Allwork Scholarship Grants *98*
Women's Army Corps Veterans Association Scholarship *576*
Women's Jewelry Association Scholarship Program *471*
Women's Western Golf Foundation Scholarship *781*
Woodard Family Scholarship *535*
Woodmen of the World Scholarship Program *854*
Workforce Incentive Program *233*
World Team Tennis Donnelly Awards *765*
World Trade Center Memorial Scholarship *729*
Worldfest Student Film Award *299*
Worldstudio AIGA Scholarships *115*
Worldstudio Foundation Scholarship Program *104*
Worthy Goal Scholarship Fund *307*
WOWT-TV Broadcasting Scholarship Program *481*
WRI College Scholarship Program *177*
Writer's Digest Annual Writing Competition *781*
Writer's Digest Popular Fiction Awards *781*
Writer's Digest Self-Published Book Awards *781*
WSCA/TCF Bank Scholarship Program *758*
WSCPA Accounting Scholarships *72*
WSCPA Scholarships for Accounting Majors *72*
WSCPA Scholarships for Minority Accounting Majors *72*
WSTLA American Justice Essay Scholarship Contest *756*
WXYZ-TV Broadcasting Scholarship *479*
Wyeth Scholarship *142*
Wyoming Farm Bureau Continuing Education Scholarships *523*
Wyoming Farm Bureau Federation Scholarships *524*
Wyoming Society of Certified Public Accountants Memorial Scholarships *73*
Wyoming Trucking Association Trust Fund Scholarship *158*
Yankee Clipper Contest Club, Inc. Youth Scholarship *494*
Yanmar/SAE Scholarship *271*
Year Abroad Program in Poland *105*
Yellow Ribbon Scholarship *310*
Yemeni American Association Scholarships *648*
YMCA Black Achievers Scholarship *648*
Yoshiyama Award for Exemplary Service to the Community *551*
You Can Make a Difference Scholarship *825*
Young American Award *795*
Young American Broadcasters Scholarship *481*
Young American Creative Patriotic Art Awards Program *772*
Young Artist Competition *441*
Young Composers Awards *406*
Young Epidemiology Scholars Competition *291*
Young Epidemiology Scholars Competition *332*
Young Women in Public Affairs Award *552*
Youth Activity Fund *412*
Youth Automobile Safety Scholarship Essay Competition for Children of Public Employees *539*
Youth Formerly In Care Bursary *613*
Youth Opportunities Foundation Scholarships *648*
Youth Scholarship *480*
YouthForce 2020 Scholarship Program *103*
You've Got a Friend in Pennsylvania Scholarship *494*
Z/I Imaging Scholarship *91*
Zagunas Student Leaders Scholarship *721*
Zeller Summer Scholarship in Medicinal Botany *813*

Sponsor

Brown Foundation for Educational Equity, Excellence, and Research *221, 669*
Buffalo AFL-CIO Council *495*
Bureau of Health Professions *325*
Bureau of Indian Affairs Office of Indian Education Programs *795*
Business and Professional Women's Foundation *136*
Butler Manufacturing Company *525*
C.O.L.A.G.E. *766*
Cabrillo Civic Clubs of California, Inc. *608*
California Alliance for Arts Education (CAAE) *110*
California Association of Private Postsecondary Schools *669*
California Broadcasters Foundation *476*
California Chicano News Media Association (CCNMA) *180*
California Citrus Mutual Scholarship Foundation *79*
California Community Colleges *669*
California Congress of Parents and Teachers, Inc. *669*
California Correctional Peace Officers Association *539*
California Council of the Blind *555*
California Farm Bureau Scholarship Foundation *73*
California Grange Foundation *495*
California Groundwater Association *213*
California Junior Miss Scholarship Program *670*
California Library Association *380*
California Masonic Foundation *670*
California Mathematics Council - South *390*
California Restaurant Association Educational Foundation *306*
California School Library Association *381*
California Society of Certified Public Accountants *55*
California State Parent-Teacher Association *221, 420, 670, 795*
California Student Aid Commission *670, 671*
California Table Grape Commission *539*
California Teachers Association (CTA) *222, 495*
California Water Awareness Campaign *79*
California Wine Grape Growers Foundation *671*
Canada Iceland Foundation, Inc. Scholarships *671*
Canada Millennium Scholarship Foundation *608*
Canadian Association of Broadcasters *180, 359*
Canadian Institute of Ukrainian Studies *104*
Canadian Press *359*
Canadian Recreational Canoeing Association *80*
Canadian Society for Medical Laboratory Science *317*
Cantor Fitzgerald Relief Fund (Sept. 11) *796*
CAP Foundation *608*
Career College Foundation *796*
Career Colleges and Schools of Texas *672*
CareerFitter.com *796*
Careers Through Culinary Arts Program, Inc. *200*
Cargill *796*
Carol Welch Memorial Scholarship Fund *325*
Carpe Diem Foundation of Illinois *796*
CASDA-LOT (Capital Area School Development Association) *672*
Case Western Reserve University *438*
Casualty Actuarial Society/Society of Actuaries Joint Committee on Minority Recruiting *145*
Casualty Actuaries of the Southeast *354*
Catching the Dream *55, 145*
Catholic Aid Association *649*
Catholic Knights of America *453*
Catholic Kolping Society of America *495*
Catholic Workman *453, 797*
Center for Lesbian and Gay Studies (C.L.A.G.S.) *383*
Center for Scholarship Administration *56, 496, 525, 526, 527, 528, 608, 672, 797, 798*
Central Council, Tlingit and Haida Indian Tribes of Alaska *608, 609*
Central Intelligence Agency *56*
Central National Bank & Trust Company of Enid, Trustee *673*
Central Scholarship Bureau *649, 673, 798*
Chairscholars Foundation, Inc. *539*
Charles & Lucille King Family Foundation, Inc. *180*
Charlie Trotter's Culinary Education Foundation *200*
Charlotte Observer *146*
Chattanooga Advertising Federation *798*
Chef2Chef Scholarship Fund *201*
Chela Education Financing *798*
Chemical Institute of Canada *92, 162, 163, 799*
Cherokee Nation of Oklahoma *609*
Chesapeake Corporation Foundation *528*
Chicago Chapter of Recording Academy *375*
Chicana/Latina Foundation *609*

Chick and Sophie Major Memorial Duck Calling Contest *766*
Chick-fil-A, Inc. *529*
Child Nutrition Foundation *301*
Children's Hospital of Atlanta *420, 421*
Chinese Historical Society of Southern California *352*
Chinese Professional Club of Houston *609*
Chips Quinn Scholars *359*
Chopin Foundation of the United States *402*
Christian Record Services, Inc. *556*
CHS Foundation *74*
CIRI Foundation *56, 110, 383, 477, 609, 673, 799, 800*
Citizens for Global Solutions *801*
City College of San Francisco Latino Educational Association *610*
Civil Air Patrol, USAF Auxiliary *121, 496*
Civil Service Employees Insurance Company *539*
Clan MacBean Foundation *104*
Clara Abbott Foundation *529*
Clarice Smith Performing Arts Center at Maryland *438*
Club Foundation *350*
Coca-Cola Scholars Foundation, Inc. *766, 801*
CODA International *801*
Cohen & Company CPAs *56*
Coleman A. Young Foundation *673*
College Assistance Migrant Program *540*
College Board/Robert Wood Johnson Foundation YES Program *291*
College Foundation of North Carolina, Inc *222, 469, 587, 610, 674, 675, 801*
College Photographer of the Year *802*
College Women's Association of Japan *556*
CollegeBound Foundation *110, 136, 222, 259, 338, 375, 556, 675, 676, 677*
CollegeFinancialAidInformation.com *802*
CollegeNET *802*
Colorado Broadcasters Association *477*
Colorado Commission on Higher Education *678*
Colorado Masons Benevolent Fund Association *678*
Colorado Society of Certified Public Accountants Educational Foundation *56, 57*
Columbia 300 *766*
Columbia University, Department of Music *767*
Comcast Leaders and Achievers Scholarship Program *496*
Commander William S. Stuhr Scholarship Fund for Military Sons and Daughters *568*
Commission Franco-Americaine d'Echanges Universitaires et Culturels *222*
Common Knowledge Scholarship Foundation *223, 421, 456, 678, 802, 803*
Community Banker Association of Illinois *496, 679*
Community Foundation for Greater Buffalo *679*
Community Foundation for Palm Beach and Martin Counties, Inc. *57, 146, 223, 311, 342, 610, 679, 680, 681, 682, 803*
Community Foundation of Cape Cod *121, 402, 556, 682, 803*
Community Foundation of Western Massachusetts *57, 223, 421, 497, 529, 610, 611, 649, 682, 683, 684, 803, 804*
COMTO-Boston Chapter *804*
Concert Artists Guild *767*
Concord Review *767*
Confederated Tribes of Grand Ronde *223, 611*
Congressional Black Caucus Spouses Program *318, 438, 804*
Congressional Hispanic Caucus Institute *611*
Connecticut Army National Guard *576*
Connecticut Association for Health, Physical Education, Recreation and Dance *224*
Connecticut Association of Latin Americans in Higher Education (CALAHE) *612*
Connecticut Association of Women Police *199*
Connecticut Chapter of Society of Professional Journalists *359*
Connecticut Chapter of the American Planning Association *481*
Connecticut Department of Higher Education *224, 462, 684*
Connecticut Education Foundation, Inc. *224*
Connecticut Forest and Park Association *684*
Connecticut Nurserymen's Foundation, Inc. *342*
Connecticut Police Corps *540*
Connecticut Society of Certified Public Accountants *58*
Connecticut Student Loan Foundation *685, 804*
Conservation Federation of Missouri *136*

Constantinople Armenian Relief Society *612*
Contemporary Record Society *439, 767*
Continental Society, Daughters of Indian Wars *224*
CORE Philly *685*
Corporation for Ohio Appalachian Development (COAD) *612*
Costume Society of America *105*
Council for International Educational Exchange *225, 556, 804*
Council of Citizens with Low Vision International c/o American Council of the Blind *557*
Council of Energy Resource Tribes (CERT) Education Fund, Inc. *612*
County Prosecutors Association of New Jersey Foundation *376, 540*
Courage Center, Vocational Services Department *557*
Croatian Scholarship Fund *612*
Cuban American National Foundation *146*
Cuban American Scholarship Fund *805*
Culinary Trust *302*
Cultural Services of the French Embassy *767*
Culture Connection *73*
Cystic Fibrosis Scholarship Foundation *557*
D.W. Simpson & Company *805*
Daedalian Foundation *121*
Dallas Architectural Foundation-HKS/John Humphries Minority Scholarship *99, 173*
Dallas Morning News *540*
Dallas-Fort Worth Association of Black Communicators *180*
Danish Sisterhood of America *421, 497*
Datatel, Inc. *470, 587, 805*
Daughters of the Cincinnati *568*
David and Dovetta Wilson Scholarship Fund, Inc. *805*
Davis-Putter Scholarship Fund *805*
Davis-Roberts Scholarship Fund, Inc. *497*
Dayton Advertising Club *146, 806*
Dayton Foundation *99, 259, 402, 442, 685*
DECA (Distributive Education Clubs of America) *146*
Defense Commissary Agency *587*
Delaware Department of Education *352, 587, 685, 686*
Delaware Higher Education Commission *225, 291, 540, 686, 687*
Delaware National Guard *569*
Delaware State Dental Society *208*
Delta Delta Delta Foundation *497*
Delta Gamma Foundation *498*
Delta Omicron International Music Fraternity/Delta Omicron Foundation, Inc. *402*
Delta Phi Epsilon Educational Foundation *498*
Delta Sigma Pi *498, 806*
Democratic Nursing Organization of South Africa *421*
DeMolay Foundation Incorporated *529*
DeMolay Foundation of California Scholarship *806*
Department of the Army *573, 576*
Department of Veterans Affairs (VA) *569, 587, 588*
Desk and Derrick Educational Trust *92*
DeVry, Inc. *260, 588, 687, 688, 806*
DIET - Live Poets Society *768*
Disabled American Veterans *541*
disABLEDperson Inc. College Scholarship *557*
Disciples of Christ Homeland Ministries *453, 454*
District of Columbia Public Schools *688*
District of Columbia State Education Office *688, 689*
Diversity City Media *612*
Dixie Boys Baseball *689*
Dogrib Treaty 11 Scholarship Committee *293, 689, 807*
Dollarship *807*
Dolphin Scholarship Foundation *599*
Domenic Troiano Guitar Scholarship *768*
Donald Keene Center of Japanese Culture *311*
Donaldson Company *529*
Donna Reed Foundation for the Performing Arts *439*
Dow Jones Newspaper Fund *360, 808*
Duke Energy Corporation *530*
DuPont in Cooperation with General Learning Communications *768*
EAA Aviation Foundation, Inc. *121, 122*
Ear Foundation Minnie Pearl Scholarship Program *557*
Earth Island Institute *808*
East Bay Football Officials Association *808*
East Los Angeles Community Union (TELACU) Education Foundation *163, 689*
Eastern Amputee Golf Association *808*
Eastern Orthodox Committee on Scouting *498*
Eaton Corporation *530*
e-CollegeDegree.com *808*

Media Action Network for Asian Americans *112*
Mellinger Educational Foundation *713*
Mellon New England *713, 824*
Memorial Foundation for Jewish Culture *106*
Mennonite Education Agency *437*
Menominee Indian Tribe of Wisconsin *623*
Mental Health Association in New York State, Inc. *328*
Mercedes-Benz USA *825*
Mescalero Tribal Education *624*
Metavue Corporation *94, 112, 825*
Miami-Dade and Broward County Ford and Lincoln-Mercury Dealers *713*
Michigan Association of Broadcasters Foundation *479*
Michigan Association of CPAs *64*
Michigan Bureau of Student Financial Assistance *426, 714*
Michigan League for Nursing *426*
Michigan Society of Professional Engineers *165, 174*
Michigan Veterans Trust Fund *590*
Micron Technology Foundation, Inc. *165*
Microsoft Corporation *825*
Midland Community Theater *440*
Midwest Roofing Contractors Association *94*
Midwestern Higher Education Compact *714*
Military Benefit Association *504*
Military Officers Association of America (MOAA) *590*
Military Order of the Purple Heart *590*
Mineralogical Society of America *214, 215*
Minerals, Metals, and Materials Society (TMS) *266, 267*
Minnesota AFL-CIO *504*
Minnesota Broadcasters Association *479*
Minnesota Department of Health *328*
Minnesota Department of Military Affairs *571*
Minnesota Gay/Lesbian/Bisexual/Transgender Educational Fund *825*
Minnesota Higher Education Services Office *545, 591, 715*
Minnesota Indian Scholarship Office *624*
Minnesota Police Corps *825*
Minnesota Society of Certified Public Accountants *64*
Minnesota Soybean Research and Promotion Council *75*
Minority Nurse Magazine *426*
Miss American Coed Pageants, Inc. *773*
Mississippi Association of Broadcasters *479*
Mississippi Press Association Education Foundation *363*
Mississippi State Student Financial Aid *231, 294, 328, 426, 715, 716, 825*
Missouri Bar Foundation *716*
Missouri Broadcasters Association Scholarship Program *479*
Missouri Department of Elementary and Secondary Education *231, 232, 716*
Missouri Department of Health and Senior Services *210, 328*
Missouri Department of Higher Education *716, 717*
Missouri Funeral Director's Association *313*
Missouri Insurance Education Foundation *354*
Missouri Police Corps *825*
Missouri Sheriffs' Association *199*
Missouri Travel Council *307*
Mitchell Institute *717*
MLGPA Foundation *717*
Mongolia Society, Inc. *624*
Monsanto Agribusiness Scholarship *81*
Montana Broadcasters Association *479*
Montana Federation of Garden Clubs *138, 349*
Montana Guaranteed Student Loan Program, Office of Commissioner of Higher Education *624, 717, 718*
Montana Society of Certified Public Accountants *65*
Montana State Office of Public Instruction *718*
Morris J. and Betty Kaplun Foundation *653*
Morris K. Udall Foundation *294*
Mount Vernon Urban Renewal Agency *718*
MRA-The Management Association *151*
Muslim Scholarship Fund - AL-AMEEN *653*
NAACP Legal Defense and Educational Fund, Inc. *377, 378, 624*
NAAS-USA Fund *825, 826*
NASA Delaware Space Grant Consortium *94*
NASA Florida Space Grant Consortium *719*
NASA Idaho Space Grant Consortium *94*
NASA Minnesota Space Grant Consortium *124*
NASA Montana Space Grant Consortium *125*
NASA Nebraska Space Grant Consortium *125*
NASA Nevada Space Grant Consortium *125*
NASA Rhode Island Space Grant Consortium *288, 719*
NASA South Carolina Space Grant Consortium *719*

NASA South Dakota Space Grant Consortium *719*
NASA Vermont Space Grant Consortium *94*
NASA Virginia Space Grant Consortium *125*
NASA West Virginia Space Grant Consortium *126*
NASA Wisconsin Space Grant Consortium *126*
NASA/Maryland Space Grant Consortium *139*
National Academy of Television Arts and Sciences *183*
National Academy of Television Arts and Sciences-National Capital/Chesapeake Bay Chapter *363*
National Action Council for Minorities in Engineering-NACME, Inc. *268*
National Air Transportation Association Foundation *126, 127*
National Alliance of Postal and Federal Employees (NAPFE) *505, 826*
National AMBUCS, Inc. *328*
National Art Materials Trade Association *113, 532*
National Asphalt Pavement Association *175*
National Association for Campus Activities *625, 720, 721, 773*
National Association for the Advancement of Colored People *139, 151, 166, 232, 505*
National Association of Black Journalists *183, 364, 443*
National Association of Broadcasters *183*
National Association of Colored Women's Clubs *625*
National Association of Directors of Nursing Administration in Long Term Care *427*
National Association of Energy Service Companies *505*
National Association of Geoscience Teachers–Far Western Section *215*
National Association of Insurance Women Education Foundation *151, 354*
National Association of Pastoral Musicians *403, 404, 405*
National Association of Railway Business Women *826*
National Association of Secondary School Principals *505, 773*
National Association of Water Companies *139*
National Association of Water Companies-New Jersey Chapter *139*
National Association of Women in Construction *100, 470*
National Association to Advance Fat Acceptance (New England Chapter) *721*
National Athletic Trainers' Association Research and Education Foundation *329*
National Beta Club *505*
National Black Law Students Association *378*
National Black MBA Association-Twin Cities Chapter *65*
National Black Nurses Association, Inc. *427, 428*
National Black Police Association *199*
National Burglar and Fire Alarm Association *545*
National Business Aviation Association, Inc. *127, 128, 826*
National Center for Learning Disabilities, Inc. *562*
National Chamber of Commerce for Women *826*
National Christmas Tree Association *826*
National Commission for Cooperative Education *827*
National Community Pharmacist Association (NCPA) Foundation *329*
National Conference of CPA Practitioners, Inc. *65*
National Council of Jewish Women New York Section *562*
National Council of State Garden Clubs, Inc. Scholarship *82*
National Court Reporters Association *827*
National Customs Brokers and Forwarders Association of America *472*
National Dairy Shrine *75, 82, 83*
National Defense Transportation Association-Scott St. Louis Chapter *721*
National Environmental Health Association/American Academy of Sanitarians *437*
National Essay Competition *722*
National Federation of Paralegal Associations, Inc. (NFPA) *378*
National Federation of State Poetry Societies (NFSPS) *774*
National Federation of the Blind *101, 193, 232, 312, 353, 546*
National Federation of the Blind of California *827, 828*
National Federation of the Blind of Missouri *563*
National FFA Organization *828*
National Fish and Wildlife Foundation *140*
National Foster Parent Association *506*
National Foundation for Advancement in the Arts *113, 406*
National Fraternal Society of the Deaf *506*

National Funeral Directors and Morticians Association *828*
National Garden Clubs, Inc. *83*
National Gay and Lesbian Task Force *183*
National Ground Water Association *828*
National Guard Association of Colorado Education Foundation *571*
National Guild of Community Schools of the Arts *406*
National Hot Rod Association *828*
National Institute for Labor Relations Research *184, 232*
National Institute of Building Sciences, Multihazard Mitigation Council *101*
National Institute of General Medical Sciences, National Institute of Health *140*
National Institutes of Health *140*
National Inventors Hall of Fame *95*
National Italian American Foundation *106, 625, 828*
National Junior Angus Association *506, 828*
National Kidney Foundation of Indiana, Inc. *563*
National League of American Pen Women, Inc. *113*
National Merit Scholarship Corporation *625, 829*
National Military Family Association *591*
National Military Intelligence Association *506*
National Minority Junior Golf Scholarship Association *625*
National Oceanic and Atmospheric Administration *268*
National Opera Association *113*
National PKU News *563*
National Potato Council Women's Auxiliary *76*
National Poultry and Food Distributors Association *76*
National Press Foundation *364*
National Press Photographers Foundation, Inc. *443, 443, 443, 443*
National Restaurant Association Educational Foundation *308*
National Rifle Association *506*
National Safety Council *295*
National Scholastic Press Association *365*
National Science Teachers Association *829*
National Sculpture Society *113*
National Security Agency *194*
National Society Daughters of the American Revolution *217, 329, 338, 428, 429, 506, 626, 829*
National Society of Accountants *65, 66*
National Society of Black Physicists *447, 448*
National Society of Newspaper Columnists *365*
National Society of Professional Engineers *166, 167, 268, 269*
National Society of The Colonial Dames of America *429*
National Speakers Association *184*
National Stone, Sand and Gravel Association (NSSGA) *184, 269*
National Strength and Conditioning Association *335, 336*
National Symphony Orchestra Education Program *722, 774*
National Teen-Ager Scholarship Foundation *829*
National Tourism Foundation *308, 309, 310, 351*
National Union of Public and General Employees *507*
National Urban League *151*
National Welsh-American Foundation *626*
National Woman's Relief Corps *829*
National Women's Studies Association *626*
National Writers Association Foundation *184*
Native American Journalists Association *365*
NATSO Foundation *507*
Naval Service Training Command/NROTC *597*
Naval Special Warfare Foundation *600*
Navy-Marine Corps Relief Society *597, 598*
Nebraska DECA *508*
Nebraska Department of Education *722*
Nebraska Health and Human Services System, Office of Rural Health *210*
Nebraska National Guard *571*
Nebraska Press Association *365*
Nebraska Society of Certified Public Accountants *66*
Needham and Company WTC Scholarship Fund *829*
Nelnet College Planning *722, 723, 829*
Netherlands Organization for International Cooperation in Higher Education *830*
Network of Executive Women in Hospitality *101*
Nevada Department of Education *723*
Nevada Office of the State Treasurer *724*
Nevada Police Corps *547, 830*
Nevada Society of Certified Public Accountants *66*
Nevada Women's Fund *724*
New England Board of Higher Education *724*

New England Employee Benefits Council *151*
New England Film and Video Festival *297*
New England Printing and Publishing Council *315*
New England Water Works Association *175*
New Hampshire Charitable Foundation *724*
New Hampshire Department of Education *724*
New Hampshire Food Industries Education Foundation *532*
New Hampshire Postsecondary Education Commission *233, 591, 725*
New Hampshire Society of Certified Public Accountants *66*
New Jersey Association of Realtors *452*
New Jersey Broadcasters Association *184*
New Jersey Department of Education *830*
New Jersey Department of Military and Veterans Affairs *591*
New Jersey Division of Fish and Wildlife/NJ Chapter of the Wildlife Society *140*
New Jersey Higher Education Student Assistance Authority *547, 725, 726*
New Jersey Historical Commission *339*
New Jersey Press Foundation *726*
New Jersey Society of Architects/AIA New Jersey Scholarship Foundation *101*
New Jersey Society of Certified Public Accountants *66, 67*
New Jersey State Golf Association *547*
New Jersey Vietnam Veterans Memorial Foundation *727*
New Mexico Commission on Higher Education *210, 429, 592, 727, 728*
New Mexico State Department of Education *830*
New Mexico Veterans Service Commission *592*
New York Council Navy League *578*
New York State AFL-CIO *508*
New York State Education Department *67, 728*
New York State Grange *83, 429, 508, 563*
New York State Higher Education Services Corporation *547, 626, 728, 729*
New York State Society of Certified Public Accountants Foundation for Accounting Education *67*
New York State Society of Professional Engineers *508*
Newspaper Guild-CWA *365*
Newton Nurse Scholars Rhode Island Foundation *429*
NextGen Network, Inc. *626*
Nightingale Awards of Pennsylvania *430*
Nimrod International Journal of Prose and Poetry *830*
Ninety-Nines, Inc. *128*
Ninety-Nines, San Fernando Valley Chapter/Van Nuys Airport *128*
Nisei Student Relocation Commemorative Fund *627*
NO-ADdiction Scholarship Essay Campaign *831*
Non Commissioned Officers Association (NCOA) *508, 831*
North Carolina Association of Broadcasters *480*
North Carolina Association of Educators *233, 729*
North Carolina Bar Association *547*
North Carolina Division of Services for the Blind *563*
North Carolina Division of Veterans Affairs *592, 593, 831*
North Carolina Division of Vocational Rehabilitation Services *563*
North Carolina National Guard *571*
North Carolina Police Corps *200*
North Carolina State Education Assistance Authority *200, 211, 233, 430, 729, 730*
North Carolina Teaching Fellows Commission *233*
North Carolina Vietnam Veterans, Inc. *593*
North Dakota Board of Nursing *430*
North Dakota Department of Public Instruction *730*
North Dakota Society of Certified Public Accountants *67*
North Dakota University System *233*
North East Roofing Educational Foundation *508*
Northeast Fresh Foods Alliance *509*
Northeastern Loggers' Association, Inc. *509*
Northern Cheyenne Tribal Education Department *627*
Northern Virginia Urban League *627*
Northwest Journalists of Color *365*
Norway-America Association *627*
Norwich Jubilee Esperanto Foundation *312*
Odd Fellows and Rebekahs *831*
Office of Navajo Nation Scholarship and Financial Assistance *627*
Office of Personnel Management *831*
Ohio 4-H *83, 170, 509, 831*
Ohio Academy of Science/Ohio Environmental Education Fund *295*

Ohio Adjutant General's Department *572*
Ohio American Legion *510*
Ohio Association for Adult and Continuing Education *731*
Ohio Association of Career Colleges and Schools *831*
Ohio Association of Collegiate Registrars and Admissions Officers *731*
Ohio Board of Regents *548, 593, 731*
Ohio Civil Service Employees Association *510*
Ohio Department of Education *732*
Ohio Educational Credit Union *732*
Ohio Farmers Union *76, 83*
Ohio Forestry Association *733*
Ohio National Guard *572*
Ohio Newspapers Foundation *366*
Ohio Partners in Character Education *733*
Ohio Police Corps *733*
Oklahoma Alumni & Associates of FHA, HERO and FCCLA, Inc. *510*
Oklahoma Educational Foundation for Osteopathic Medicine *329*
Oklahoma State Department of Education *733*
Oklahoma State Regents for Higher Education *234, 733, 734, 832*
Omaha Symphony Guild *774*
Omnova Solutions Foundation *532*
101st Airborne Division Association *575*
102nd Infantry Division Association *575*
Oneida Tribe of Indians of Wisconsin *627*
ONS Foundation *330, 430, 431*
OP Loftbed Company *832*
Optimist International Foundation *564, 832*
Orange County Community Foundation *102, 114, 152, 330, 774, 832*
Ordean Foundation *67*
Oregon Association of Broadcasters *185*
Oregon Collectors Association (ORCA) Scholarship Fund *734*
Oregon Community Foundation *152, 330, 366, 431, 564, 734, 735, 774*
Oregon Department of Veterans Affairs *593*
Oregon Native American Chamber of Commerce Scholarship *628*
Oregon Nurses Association *432*
Oregon Police Corps *833*
Oregon PTA *234*
Oregon Sheep Growers Association *84*
Oregon Student Assistance Commission *68, 84, 87, 102, 128, 140, 167, 194, 203, 211, 234, 235, 296, 330, 331, 367, 384, 432, 465, 510, 511, 532, 533, 534, 535, 548, 549, 564, 594, 628, 735, 736, 737, 738, 739*
Organization of American Historians *85*
Organization of Chinese Americans *628, 629*
Orgone Biophysical Research Laboratory *459*
Orphan Foundation of America *833*
Osage Scholarship Fund *629*
Osage Tribal Education Committee *629*
Osage Tribal Education Department *629*
OSCPA Educational Foundation *68*
OUM Chiropractor Program *331*
Our World Underwater Scholarship Society *775*
Outdoor Writers Association of America *185*
Outstanding Students of America *833*
Overseas Press Club Foundation *367*
Owen Electric Cooperative *739*
Ozarka Natural Spring Water *215*
Pacers Foundation, Inc. *331*
Pacific and Asian Affairs Council *357*
Padgett Business Services Foundation *833*
PAGE Foundation, Inc. *235*
Palwaukee Airport Pilots Association *128*
Paper, Allied-Industrial, Chemical and Energy Workers International Union *833*
Papercheck.com *833*
Paralyzed Veterans of America - Spinal Cord Research Foundation *833*
Parapsychology Foundation *459*
Parent Relocation Council *834*
Parents Without Partners International Scholarship Program *512*
Parents, Families, and Friends of Lesbians and Gays-Atlanta *834*
Park People *102, 410*
Patient Advocate Foundation *564, 834*
Penguin Putnam, Inc. *834*
Pennsylvania AFL-CIO *512*

Pennsylvania Association of Conservation Districts Auxiliary *76*
Pennsylvania Bureau for Veterans Affairs *594*
Pennsylvania Burglar and Fire Alarm Association *549*
Pennsylvania Federation of Democratic Women, Inc. *512*
Pennsylvania Fish and Boat Commission *295*
Pennsylvania Higher Education Assistance Agency *235, 432, 457, 594, 739, 740*
Pennsylvania Institute of Certified Public Accountants *68*
Pennsylvania Library Association *381*
Pennsylvania Right to Work Defense and Education Foundation *740*
Pennsylvania Youth Foundation *512*
Peter and Alice Koomruian Fund *629*
Peter Doctor Memorial Indian Scholarship Foundation, Inc. *630*
Pfizer *564*
Phi Alpha Theta History Honor Society, Inc. *339*
Phi Delta Theta Educational Foundation *298*
Phi Kappa Tau Foundation *512*
Phi Sigma Pi National Honor Fraternity *512*
Philadelphia Association of Black Journalists *367*
Philipino-American Association of New England *630*
Phillips Foundation *834*
Phoenix Suns Charities/Sun Students Scholarship *463*
Physician Assistant Foundation *331*
Pi Lambda Theta, Inc. *235, 236, 450, 463, 550*
Pilot International Foundation *331, 332*
Pine Tree State 4-H Club Foundation/4-H Postsecondary Scholarship *740*
Pirate's Alley Faulkner Society *775*
Pittsburgh Intellectual Property Law Association *378*
Plastics Institute of America *269*
Playwrights' Center *384*
Plumbing-Heating-Cooling Contractors Association Education Foundation *102, 103*
PNC Bank Trust Department *211*
Polanki, Polish Women's Cultural Club of Milwaukee, Wisconsin, U.S.A. *413, 834, 835*
Polish Arts Club of Buffalo Scholarship Foundation *108*
Polish Heritage Association of Maryland *353, 630, 631*
Polish National Alliance *631*
Polish Women's Alliance *835*
Pony of the Americas Club *513*
Portuguese Foundation, Inc. *631*
Potlatch Foundation For Higher Education Scholarship *741*
Presbyterian Church (USA) *631*
Presidential Freedom Scholarship *836*
Pride Foundation *741*
Print and Graphic Scholarship Foundation *315*
Printing and Imaging Association of MidAmerica *316*
Printing Industries of Michigan, Inc. Scholarship *316*
Printing Industries of Wisconsin Education Foundation Scholarships *185, 316*
Printing Industry of Minnesota Education Foundation *316*
Pro Bowlers Association *775*
Procter & Gamble Fund *535*
Professional Aviation Maintenance Foundation *129*
Professional Bowlers Association *513*
Professional Construction Estimators Association *212*
Professional Grounds Management Society *84*
Professional Horsemen's Scholarship Fund, Inc. *513*
Project BEST Scholarship Fund *513*
Project Cambio Scholarship Awards *152*
Public Relations Student Society of America *185*
Pueblo of Isleta, Department of Education *631*
Pueblo of San Juan, Department of Education *632*
Puerto Rican Legal Defense and Education Fund *379*
Puerto Rico Department of Education *836*
Push for Excellence *836*
Quaker Chemical Foundation (The) *836*
Queen Elisabeth International Music Competition of Belgium *775*
Quill and Scroll Foundation *368, 776*
R.O.S.E. Fund *836*
Radio-Television News Directors Association and Foundation *185, 186*
Railway Supply Institute *836*
Railway Tie Association *410*
Recording for the Blind & Dyslexic *513*
Recreational Boating Industries Educational Foundation *141*
Reserve Officers Association *514*

Academic Fields/ Career Goals

Accounting

Accountancy Board of Ohio Educational Assistance Program 53
Accountemps/American Institute of Certified Public Accountants Student Scholarship 53
AICPA/Accountemps Student Scholarship 55
Alliant Techsystems Internship/Scholarship 70
Amarillo Area Foundation Scholarships 53
American Society of Women Accountants Scholarship 54
American Society of Women Accountants Two Year College Scholarship 54
American Woman's Society of Certified Public Accountants- Georgia Affiliate Scholarship 54
ASCPA Educational Foundation Scholarship 53
ASCPA High School Scholarships 54
ASCPA University Scholarships 55
AWSCPA and Boston Affiliate scholarship 54
Bank of America ADA Abilities Scholarship 56
Ben W. Brannon Memorial Scholarship Fund 60
Best Buy Enterprise Employee Scholarship 70
Cardinal Health Scholarship 70
Cargill Scholarship Program 70
Carl H. Marrs Scholarship Fund 56
Carl W. Christiansen Scholarship 68
Central Intelligence Agency Undergraduate Scholarship Program 56
Chapter Awarded Scholarships 60
Charleston Chapter of CPA's Accounting Scholarship Fund 72
Cherry, Bekaert and Holland, LLP Accounting Scholarship 60
Children of CSCPA Members Scholarship Program 58
Cohen and Company CPAs Scholarship 56
Collins/Moody - Company Scholarship 60
Colorado College and University Scholarships 56
Colorado High School Scholarships 57
Con Edison Scholarship 70
Counselor, Advocate, and Support Staff Scholarship Program 69
CPA Review Course Scholarship 64
CSCPA Candidate's Award 58
CSCPA Junior Award 58
Denny's/Hispanic College Fund Scholarship 62
Economic Club of Grand Rapids Business Study Abroad Scholarship 62
Educational Foundation Direct Scholarships 60
Educational Foundation Scholarships 59
Emerson Electric Company Scholarship 71
Ethnic Diversity College and University Scholarships 57
Ethnic Diversity High School Scholarships 57
Excellence in Accounting Scholarship 69
F. Grant Waite, CPA, Memorial Scholarship 58
FICPA Educational Foundation Scholarships 59
Fifth/Graduate Year Student Scholarship 64
Financial Services Institution Scholarship 71
Ford/UNCF Corporate Scholars Program 71
Foundation for Accounting Education Scholarship 67
Gertrude M. Gigliotti Memorial Scholarship 61
Gordon Scheer Scholarship 57
Greater Springfield Accountants Scholarship 57
Greater Washington Society of CPAs Scholarship 62
Harry J. Donnelly Memorial Scholarship 69
Herman J. Neal Scholarship 63
Herman, Silver and Associates Scholarship 61
Homestead Capital Housing Scholarship 68
HSCPA Scholarship Program for Accounting Students 62
HSF-ALPFA Scholarships 55
ICI Educational Foundation Scholarship Program 62
Institute of Management Accountants Memorial Education Fund Diversity Scholarships 63
Institute of Management Accountants Memorial Education Fund Scholarships 63
Joseph F. Taricani Memorial Scholarship 68

Julius M. Johnson Memorial Scholarship 61
Kathleen M. Peabody, CPA, Memorial Scholarship 58
Kentucky Society of Certified Public Accountants College Scholarship 63
Kentucky Society of Certified Public Accountants High School Scholarships 64
Kim Love Satory Scholarship 57
Lawrence P. Doss Scholarship Foundation 64
M & T Bank/ Hispanic College Fund Scholarship Program 63
Minorities in Government Finance Scholarship 62
Montana Society of Certified Public Accountants Scholarship 65
National Conference of CPA Practitioners, Inc. Scholarship 65
National Society of Accountants Scholarship 65
Nebraska Society of CPAs Scholarship 66
Nevada Society of CPAs Scholarship 66
New Hampshire Society of Certified Public Accountants Scholarship Fund 66
New Jersey Society of Certified Public Accountants College Scholarship Program 66
New Jersey Society of Certified Public Accountants High School Scholarship Program 67
North Dakota Society of Certified Public Accountants scholarship 67
NSA Louis and Fannie Sager Memorial Scholarship Award 65
Ordean Scholarship Program 67
OSCPA Educational Foundation Scholarship Program 68
Outstanding Community College Accounting Student Award 58
Paul Hagelbarger Memorial Fund Scholarship 53
Paychex Entrepreneur Scholarship 61
Paychex, Inc. Entrepreneur Scholarship 59
Pennsylvania Institute of Certified Public Accountants Sophomore Scholarship 68
Regents Professional Opportunity Scholarship 67
Rhode Island Society of Certified Public Accountants Scholarship 68
Ritchie-Jennings Memorial Scholarship 55
Robert H. Lange Memorial Scholarship 61
Scholarships for Minority Accounting Students 54
Scholarships for Minority Accounting Students 55
Society of Louisiana CPAs Scholarships 69
South Dakota Retailers Association Scholarship Program 69
Sprint Scholarship/Internship 71
Stanley H. Stearman Scholarship 66
Stuart Cameron and Margaret McLeod Memorial Scholarship 63
Student Essay Competition 59
Student Scholarship in Accounting MD Association of CPAs 64
1040 K Race Scholarships 59
1040K Race Scholarships 59
Tennessee Society of CPA Scholarship 69
The Charles Earp Memorial Scholarship 66
The MNCPA Scholarship Program 64
Thomas Conrete of Georgia Scholarship 61
Tribal Business Management Program (TBM) 55
Twin Cities Chapter Undergraduate Scholarship 65
Twin Cities Graduate MBA Scholarship 65
Virchow, Krause and Company Scholarship 71
Virginia Society of CPAs Educational Foundation Minority Undergraduate Scholarship 71
Virginia Society of CPAs Educational Foundation Undergraduate Scholarship 72
W. Allan Herzog Scholarship 70
Wiss Edward W. O'Connell Memorial Scholarship 73
WSCPA Accounting Scholarships 72
WSCPA Scholarships for Accounting Majors 72
WSCPA Scholarships for Minority Accounting Majors 72
Wyoming Society of Certified Public Accountants Memorial Scholarships 73

African Studies

Culture Connection Foundation Scholarship 73
Wesley-Logan Prize 73

Agribusiness

Agriculture Scholarships 74
California Farm Bureau Scholarship 73
Cooperative Studies Scholarships 74
Edward R. Hall Scholarship 76
Golf Course Superintendents Association of America Student Essay Contest 75
Harold Bettinger Memorial Scholarship 74
Jacob Van Namen/Vans Marketing Scholarship 74
Karl "Pete" Fuhrmann IV Memorial Scholarship 74
Maine Rural Rehabilitation Fund Scholarship Program 75
Masonic Range Science Scholarship 76
Minnesota Soybean Research and Promotion Council Youth Soybean Scholarship 75
National Poultry and Food Distributors Association Scholarship Foundation 76
NDS Student Recognition Contest 75
PACD Auxiliary Scholarships 76
Potato Industry Scholarship 76
South Dakota Board of Regents Bjugstad Scholarship 77
Truman D. Picard Scholarship 75
United Agribusiness League Scholarship Program 77
United Agricultural Benefit Trust Scholarship 77
Virgil Thompson Memorial Scholarship Contest 76

Agriculture

Agricultural-Women-In-Network Scholarship 84
Agriculture Scholarships 74
Alberta Barley Commission Eugene Boyko Memorial Scholarship 77
Amarillo Area Foundation Scholarships 53
American Society for Enology and Viticulture Scholarships 78
American Society of Agricultural and Biological Engineers Foundation Scholarship 78
Anne Seaman Professional Grounds Management Society Memorial Scholarship 84
Bill Mason Memorial Scholarship Fund 80
California Citrus Mutual Scholarship 79
California Farm Bureau Scholarship 73
California Water Awareness Campaign Water Scholar 79
Careers in Agriculture Scholarship Program 77
Cargill Scholarship Program 70
Conservation of Natural Resources Scholarship 81
Conservation of Natural Resources Scholarship for Nontraditional Students 81
Cooperative Studies Scholarships 74
Cross-Cultural Experience Program 78
Edward R. Hall Scholarship 76
Francis and Evelyn Clark Soil Biology Scholarship 78
Garden Club of America Awards for Summer Environmental Studies 80
George R. Crafton Scholarship 81
Gerald O. Mott Scholarship 79
Hank Beachell Future Leader Scholarship 79
Harold Bettinger Memorial Scholarship 74
Harry J. Larsen/Yara Memorial Scholarship 79
Heart of America Restaurants and Inns/Machine Shed Agriculture Scholarship 80
Howard F. DeNise Scholarship 83
Illinois State Treasurer's Office Excellence in Agriculture Scholarship Program 80
J. Fielding Reed Scholarship 79
John L. and Sarah G. Merriam Scholarship 78
Joseph Fitcher Scholarship Contest 83
Key Technology Scholarship 84
Kildee Scholarships 82
Maine Rural Rehabilitation Fund Scholarship Program 75

Marshall E. McCullough- National Dairy Shrine
Scholarships *82*
Mary Macey Scholarship *85*
Masonic Range Science Scholarship *76*
Master Brewers Association of the Americas *81*
Minnesota Soybean Research and Promotion Council
Youth Soybean Scholarship *75*
Monsanto Agri-business Scholarship *81*
National Council of State Garden Clubs, Inc.
Scholarship *82*
National Dairy Shrine Lager Dairy Scholarship *82*
National Dairy Shrine/Dairy Marketing, Inc. Milk
Marketing Scholarships *82*
National Dairy Shrine/Klussendorf Scholarship *82*
National Garden Clubs, Inc. Scholarship Program *83*
National Poultry and Food Distributors Association
Scholarship Foundation *76*
NDS Student Recognition Contest *75*
Oregon Sheep Growers Association Memorial
Scholarship *84*
PACD Auxiliary Scholarships *76*
Paul A. & Ethel I. Smith 4-H Scholarship *83*
Potato Industry Scholarship *76*
Progressive Dairy Producer Award *83*
Ronald P. Guerrette Future Farmers of America
Scholarship Fund *81*
Sigma Xi Grants-In-Aid of Research *84*
South Dakota Board of Regents Bjugstad Scholarship *77*
SWCS Melville H. Cohee Student Leader Conservation
Scholarship *85*
Truman D. Picard Scholarship *75*
United Agribusiness League Scholarship Program *77*
United Agricultural Benefit Trust Scholarship *77*
Virgil Thompson Memorial Scholarship Contest *76*
William J. and Marijane E. Adams, Jr. Scholarship *78*

American Studies

Binkley-Stephenson Award *85*
Platt Family Scholarship Prize Essay Contest *85*
Texas History Essay Contest *85*

Animal/Veterinary Sciences

AQHF Racing Scholarships *86*
AQHF Telephony Scholarship for Senior Veterinary
Students *86*
Arkansas Health Education Grant Program (ARHEG) *86*
Association for Women in Science College
Scholarship *86*
Cargill Scholarship Program *70*
Edward R. Hall Scholarship *76*
George A. Hall / Harold F. Mayfield Award *87*
Illinois State Treasurer's Office Excellence in Agriculture
Scholarship Program *80*
Lew and JoAnn Eklund Educational Scholarship *86*
Maine Rural Rehabilitation Fund Scholarship
Program *75*
Marshall E. McCullough- National Dairy Shrine
Scholarships *82*
Masonic Range Science Scholarship *76*
National Dairy Shrine/Dairy Marketing, Inc. Milk
Marketing Scholarships *82*
National Poultry and Food Distributors Association
Scholarship Foundation *76*
NDS Student Recognition Contest *75*
Oregon Sheep Growers Association Memorial
Scholarship *84*
Paul A. Stewart Awards *88*
Rockefeller State Wildlife Scholarship *87*
Royden M. Bodley Scholarship *87*
Sigma Xi Grants-In-Aid of Research *84*
United Agribusiness League Scholarship Program *77*
United Agricultural Benefit Trust Scholarship *77*
Veterinary Technician Student Scholarships *87*

Anthropology

ASCSA Summer Sessions Open Scholarships *88*
Bill Mason Memorial Scholarship Fund *80*
Culture Connection Foundation Scholarship *73*
Exploration Fund Grants *88*
Lambda Alpha National Collegiate Honor Society for
Anthropology National Dean's List Award *88*

Applied Sciences

A.T. Anderson Memorial Scholarship *89*
AeA- Oregon Council Technology Scholarship
Program *88*
AIAA Undergraduate Scholarship *89*
Alfred Bader Scholarship *92*
American Meteorological Society Industry
Undergraduate Scholarships *89*

American Society of Heating, Refrigeration, and Air
Conditioning Engineering Technology
Scholarship *90*
American Society of Naval Engineers Scholarship *90*
Association of California Water Agencies
Scholarships *91*
Astronaut Scholarship Foundation *92*
Barry M. Goldwater Scholarship and Excellence in
Education Program *92*
Burlington Northern Santa Fe Foundation
Scholarship *89*
Carrol C. Hall Memorial Scholarship *95*
Charles N. Fisher Memorial Scholarship *90*
Clair A. Hill Scholarship *91*
Coates, Wolff, Russell Mining Industry Scholarship *95*
Collegiate Inventors Competition - Grand Prize *95*
Collegiate Inventors Competition for Undergraduate
Students *95*
Desk and Derrick Educational Trust *92*
GRE and Graduate Applications Waiver *95*
Henry Broughton, K2AE Memorial Scholarship *90*
Herb Society Research Grants *92*
Independent Laboratories Institute Scholarship
Alliance *93*
Irving W. Cook, WA0CGS, Scholarship *90*
Mississippi Scholarship *90*
MRCA Foundation Scholarship Program *94*
NASA Delaware Space Grant Undergraduate Tuition
Scholarship *94*
NASA Idaho Space Grant Consortium Scholarship
Program *94*
National Hispanic Explorers Scholarship Program *93*
Paul and Helen L. Grauer Scholarship *91*
Paul and Helen Trussel Science and Technology
Scholarship *93*
Robert E. Altenhofen Memorial Scholarship *91*
Rockefeller State Wildlife Scholarship *87*
Space Imaging Award for Application of High
Resolution Digital Satellite Imagery *91*
SPIE Educational Scholarships in Optical Science and
Engineering *93*
The Dr. Robert Rufflo Sciences Paper Contest *94*
Universities Space Research Association Scholarship
Program *96*
Vermont Space Grant Consortium Scholarship
Program *94*
Z/I Imaging Scholarship *91*

Archaeology

ASCSA Summer Sessions Open Scholarships *88*
Cyprus American Archaeological Research Institute
Helena Wylde and Stuart Swiny Fellowship *96*
Exploration Fund Grants *88*
Harvard Travellers Club Grants *96*

Architecture

AACE International Competitive Scholarship *96*
AIA West Virginia Scholarship Program *98*
Alan Lucas Memorial Educational Scholarship *100*
American Institute of Architects Minority/Disadvantaged
Scholarship *97*
American Institute of Architects/American Architectural
Foundation Minority/Disadvantaged Scholarships *98*
American Institute of Architecture (AIA) Dayton
Architectural Scholarship Fund *99*
Architecture and Engineering Scholarship Program *102*
Architecture, Construction, and Engineering Mentor
Program Scholarships *101*
ASCSA Summer Sessions Open Scholarships *88*
Association for Women in Architecture Scholarship *98*
Bradford White Corporation Scholarship *102*
Dallas Architectural Foundation - Harrell and Hamilton
Scholarship Fund *99*
Delta Faucet Company Scholarship Program *102*
Denny's/Hispanic College Fund Scholarship *62*
El Nuevo Constructor Scholarship Program *99*
F. Lammot Belin Arts Scholarship *103*
FEFPA Assistantship *99*
Glenn R. and Juanita B. Struble Scholarship II *102*
Hawaiian Lodge Scholarships *99*
Homestead Capital Housing Scholarship *68*
Howard Brown Rickard Scholarship *101*
IFMA Foundation Scholarships *100*
Kumar Mehta Scholarship *97*
MRCA Foundation Scholarship Program *94*
NAWIC Undergraduate Scholarships *100*
Network of Executive Women in Hospitality, Inc.
Scholarship *101*
New Jersey Society of Architects Scholarship *101*
Peter D. Courtois Concrete Construction Scholarship *97*
PHCC Educational Foundation Need-Based
Scholarship *102*

PHCC Educational Foundation Scholarship
Program *103*
Regents Professional Opportunity Scholarship *67*
Robert W. Thunen Memorial Scholarships *100*
Robert W. Thunen Memorial Scholarships *100*
SARA Student Design Competition *103*
The Dimitri J. Ververelli Memorial Scholarship for
Architecture and/or Engineering *99*
The Douglas Haskell Award for Student Journalism *98*
The Park People $2000 Scholarship *102*
The Virginia Peninsula Post of the Society of American
Military Engineers (S.A.M.E.) Scholarship *103*
Theodore Mazza Scholarship *103*
V. Mohan Malhotra Scholarship *97*
W.R. Grace Scholarship Award *97*
West Virginia Society of Architects/AIA Scholarship *104*
Women's Architectural Auxiliary Eleanor Allwork
Scholarship Grants *98*
Worldstudio Foundation Scholarship Program *104*
YouthForce 2020 Scholarship Program *103*

Area/Ethnic Studies

Adele Filene Travel Award *105*
Canadian Institute of Ukrainian Studies Research
Grants *104*
Clan MacBean Foundation Grant Program *104*
Culture Connection Foundation Scholarship *73*
Exploration Fund Grants *88*
Harvard Travellers Club Grants *96*
Henri Cardinaux Memorial Scholarship *106*
Irish Research Funds *105*
Japanese Studies Scholarship *105*
King Olav V Norwegian-American Heritage Fund *106*
Leo J. Krysa Undergraduate Scholarship *104*
Memorial Foundation for Jewish Culture International
Scholarship Program for Community Service *106*
National Italian American Foundation Category II
Scholarship *106*
Stella Blum Research Grant *105*
Tadeusz Sendzimir Scholarships-Academic Year
Scholarships *106*
Tadeusz Sendzimir Scholarships-Summer School
Programs *107*
Wesley-Logan Prize *73*
WNGGA Scholarship Program *107*
Year Abroad Program in Poland *105*

Art History

Adele Filene Travel Award *105*
ASCSA Summer Sessions Open Scholarships *88*
Culture Connection Foundation Scholarship *73*
Florence Lemcke Memorial Scholarship in Fine Arts *107*
Herb Society Research Grants *92*
Library Research Grants *107*
Mary Olive Eddy Jones Art Scholarship *108*
Polish Arts Club of Buffalo Scholarship Foundation
Trust *108*
Stella Blum Research Grant *105*
The Douglas Haskell Award for Student Journalism *98*
Theodore Mazza Scholarship *103*

Arts

Academy of Television Arts and Sciences College
Television Awards *108*
Adele Filene Travel Award *105*
Apha Delta Kappa Foundation Fine Arts Grants *108*
Artist's- Blacksmith's Association of North America, Inc.
Scholarship Program *109*
Artist's-Blacksmith's Association of North America, Inc.
Affiliate Visiting Artist Grant Program *109*
Arts Recognition and Talent Search (ARTS) *113*
Arts Scholarship Program *114*
ASCSA Summer Sessions Open Scholarships *88*
Beinecke Scholarship for Graduate Study *109*
BMI Student Composer Awards *110*
CIRI Foundation Susie Qimmiqsak Bevins Endowment
Scholarship Fund *110*
Constant Memorial Scholarship for Aquidneck Island
Residents *114*
Elizabeth Greenshields Award/Grant *110*
Emerging Texas Artist Scholarship *114*
Emerging Young Artist Awards *110*
F. Lammot Belin Arts Scholarship *103*
Federal Junior Duck Stamp Conservation and Design
Competition *115*
Film and Fiction Scholarship *111*
Florence Lemcke Memorial Scholarship in Fine Arts *107*
General Federation of Women's Clubs of Massachusetts
Pennies For Art *111*
Glenn R. and Juanita B. Struble Scholarship II *102*
Haymarket Gallery Emerging Artists Scholarship *112*
Herb Society Research Grants *92*

Houston Symphony/ Top Ladies Scholarship *115*
Jack J. Isgur Foundation Scholarship *111*
Janet B. Sondheim Scholarship *110*
John C. Santistevan Memorial Scholarship *111*
John F. and Anna Lee Stacey Scholarship Fund *112*
Learning Scholarship *115*
Library Research Grants *107*
Liquitex Excellence in Art Purchase Award Program *112*
Lois McMillen Memorial Scholarship Fund *115*
MANAA Media Scholarships for Asian American Students *112*
Mary Olive Eddy Jones Art Scholarship *108*
Minority Student Summer Scholarship *109*
National Art Honor Society Scholarship *109*
National Art Materials Trade Association Art Major Scholarship *113*
National Sculpture Competition for Young Sculptors *113*
National Sculpture Society Scholarships *113*
NLAPW Virginia Liebeler Biennial Grants for Mature Women (Arts) *113*
NOA Vocal Competition/ Legacy Award Program *113*
Polish Arts Club of Buffalo Scholarship Foundation Trust *108*
Ruth Clark Scholarship *111*
Scholastic Art and Writing Awards-Art Section *108*
Stella Blum Research Grant *105*
Teleteon Animation Scholarship Award Competition *114*
The FW Rausch Arts and Humanities Paper Contest *112*
Theodore Mazza Scholarship *103*
Visual and Performing Arts Achievement Awards *111*
Walt Disney Company Foundation Scholarship *112*
Worldstudio AIGA Scholarships *115*
Worldstudio Foundation Scholarship Program *104*

Asian Studies
Culture Connection Foundation Scholarship *73*

Audiology
Audiology Foundation of America's Outstanding AUD Student Scholarship *116*
Sertoma Communicative Disorders Scholarship Program *116*

Aviation/Aerospace
AACE International Competitive Scholarship *96*
ADMA Scholarship *120*
Aerospace Undergraduate Research Scholarships *125*
AFCEA Scholarship for Working Professionals *120*
AIAA Undergraduate Scholarship *89*
Air Traffic Control Association Scholarship *116*
Airbus Leadership Grant *132*
Alaskan Aviation Safety Foundation Memorial Scholarship Fund *119*
Alice Glaisyer Warfield Memorial Scholarship *130*
Amelia Earhart Memorial Career Scholarship Fund *128*
American Association of Airport Executives Foundation Scholarship *119*
American Association of Airport Executives Foundation Scholarship-Native American *119*
American Society of Naval Engineers Scholarship *90*
AOPA Air Safety Foundation/Donald Burnside Memorial Scholarship *119*
AOPA Air Safety Foundation/Koch Corporation Scholarship *119*
AOPA Air Safety Foundation/McAllister Memorial Scholarship *119*
Armed Forces Communications and Electronics Association ROTC Scholarship Program *120*
Association for Facilities Engineering Cedar Valley Chapter # 132 Scholarship *120*
Astronaut Scholarship Foundation *92*
Aviation Council of Pennsylvania Scholarship Program *120*
Bendix/King Avionics Scholarship *116*
BMW/SAE Engineering Scholarship *129*
Brian L. Moody Memorial Aviation Scholarship *128*
Bud Glover Memorial Scholarship *116*
Chuck Peacock Memorial Scholarship *116*
Cincinnati Heart of it All Chapter Women in Aviation, International Elisha Hall Memorial Scholarship *132*
Daedaliean Foundation Matching Scholarship Program *121*
Dan L. Meisinger, Sr. Memorial Learn to Fly Scholarship *126*
Dassault Falcon Jet Corporation Scholarship *132*
David Alan Quick Scholarship *121*
David Arver Memorial Scholarship *117*
Delta Air Lines Aircraft Maintenance Technology Scholarship *132*
Delta Air Lines Engineering Scholarship *132*

Delta Air Lines Maintenance Management/Aviation Business Management Scholarship *133*
Denny Lydic Scholarship *130*
Dr. Manny Horowitz Scholarship *133*
Dutch and Ginger Arver Scholarship *117*
EAA Aviation Achievement Scholarships *121*
Edward D. Hendrickson/SAE Engineering Scholarship *129*
Edward W. Stimpson "Aviation Excellence" Award *122*
Field Aviation Co., Inc., Scholarship *117*
GARMIN Scholarship *117*
GAT Wings to the Future Management Scholarship *133*
George E. Parmenter Aeronautical Scholarship Fund *121*
GRE and Graduate Applications Waiver *95*
H. P. "Bud" Milligan Aviation Scholarship *122*
Hansen Scholarship *122*
Harold S. Wood Award for Excellence *122*
Herbert L. Cox Memorial Scholarship *122*
Hispanic Engineer National Achievement Awards Corporation Scholarship Program *122*
Illinois Pilots Association Memorial Scholarship *123*
Instrumentation, Systems, and Automation Society (ISA) Scholarship Program *123*
International Society of Women Airline Pilots Airline Scholarships *123*
International Society of Women Airline Pilots Financial Scholarship *123*
International Society of Women Airline Pilots Fiorenza de Bernardi Merit Scholarship *123*
International Society of Women Airline Pilots Grace McAdams Harris Scholarship *124*
International Society of Women Airline Pilots Holly Mullens Memorial Scholarship *124*
International Society of Women Airline Pilots North Carolina Financial Scholarship *124*
John E. Godwin, Jr. Memorial Scholarship Award *126*
Johnny Davis Memorial Scholarship *117*
Joseph Frasca Excellence in Aviation Scholarship *131*
Judith Resnik Memorial Scholarship *130*
Keep Flying Scholarship *133*
L-3 Avionics Systems Scholarship *117*
Lawrence "Larry" Frazier Memorial Scholarship *124*
Lee Tarbox Memorial Scholarship *118*
Lowell Gaylor Memorial Scholarship *118*
Major General Lucas V. Beau Flight Scholarships Sponsored by the Order of Daedalians *121*
Mid-Continent Instrument Scholarship *118*
Minnesota Space Grant Consortium *124*
Montana Space Grant Scholarship Program *125*
Monte Mitchell Global Scholarship *118*
NASA Delaware Space Grant Undergraduate Tuition Scholarship *94*
NASA Idaho Space Grant Consortium Scholarship Program *94*
NASA Nebraska Space Grant *125*
NATA Business Scholarship *127*
National Aviation Explorer Scholarships *121*
National Hispanic Explorers Scholarship Program *93*
NBAA International Operators Scholarship *127*
NBAA Janice K. Barden Scholarship *127*
NBAA Lawrence Ginocchio Aviation Scholarship *127*
NBAA William M. Fanning Maintenance Scholarship *127*
Northrop Grumman Corporation Scholarships *130*
Palwaukee Airport Pilots Association Scholarship Program *128*
Paul A. Whelan Aviation Scholarship *131*
Payzer Scholarship *122*
Pioneers of Flight Scholarship Program *127*
Pratt and Whitney Maintenance Scholarships *133*
Private Pilot Magazine Scholarship *118*
Professional Aviation Maintenance Foundation Student Scholarship Program *129*
Professional Publications Services, Inc. Corporate Aviation Scholarship *133*
Rhode Island Pilots Association Scholarship *129*
Rockwell Collins Engineering/Technical Scholarship *134*
San Fernando Valley Chapter of the Ninety-Nines Career Scholarship *128*
SPIE Educational Scholarships in Optical Science and Engineering *93*
Sporty's Pilot Shop/Cincinnati Avionics *118*
Student Pilot Network-Flight Dream Award *130*
Texas Transportation Scholarship *130*
The Boeing Career Enhancement Scholarship *134*
TMC/SAE Donald D. Dawson Technical Scholarship *129*
Transportation Clubs International Charlotte Woods Scholarship *130*
Transportation Clubs International Fred A. Hooper Memorial Scholarship *131*
Transportation Clubs International Ginger and Fred Deines Canada Scholarship *131*

Transportation Clubs International Ginger and Fred Deines Mexico Scholarship *131*
U.S. Aircraft Insurance Group PDP Scholarship *128*
Universities Space Research Association Scholarship Program *96*
University and Community College System of Nevada NASA Space Grant and Fellowship Program *125*
Vermont Space Grant Consortium Scholarship Program *94*
Vertical Flight Foundation Scholarship *132*
Virginia Space Grant Consortium Community College Scholarships *125*
Virginia Space Grant Consortium Teacher Education Scholarships *125*
West Virginia Space Grant Consortium Undergraduate Scholarship Program *126*
Wisconsin Space Grant Consortium Undergraduate Research Program *126*
Wisconsin Space Grant Consortium Undergraduate Scholarship Program *126*
Women in Aviation, International Achievement Awards *134*
Women in Aviation, International Management Scholarships *134*
Women in Corporate Aviation Career Scholarships *134*
Women Military Aviators, Inc. Memorial Scholarship *134*

Biology
A.T. Anderson Memorial Scholarship *89*
Alberta Heritage Scholarship Fund Aboriginal Health Careers Bursary *135*
Anne Lindeman Memorial Scholarship *142*
Association for Iron and Steel Technology Ohio Valley Chapter Scholarship *135*
Association for Women in Science College Scholarship *86*
Association of California Water Agencies Scholarships *91*
Astronaut Scholarship Foundation *92*
Barry M. Goldwater Scholarship and Excellence in Education Program *92*
BPW Career Advancement Scholarship Program for Women *136*
Budweiser Conservation Scholarship Program *140*
Burlington Northern Santa Fe Foundation Scholarship *89*
Cargill Scholarship Program *70*
Carol A. Ratza Memorial Scholarship *138*
Carrol C. Hall Memorial Scholarship *95*
Charles P. Bell Conservation Scholarship *136*
Clair A. Hill Scholarship *91*
Collegiate Inventors Competition - Grand Prize *95*
Collegiate Inventors Competition for Undergraduate Students *95*
Daniel Cubicciotti Student Award of the San Francisco Section of the Electrochemical Society, Sponsored by Structural Integrity Associates *137*
Edward R. Hall Scholarship *76*
Emergency Secondary Education Loan Program *135*
Environmental Protection Agency Tribal Lands Environmental Science Scholarship *135*
Federated Garden Clubs of Connecticut, Inc. *137*
Frederic Fairfield Memorial Fund Award *141*
George A. Hall / Harold F. Mayfield Award *87*
GRE and Graduate Applications Waiver *95*
H.H. Dow Memorial Student Achievement Award of the Industrial Electrolysis and Electrochemical Engineering Division of the Electrochemical Society, Inc. *137*
Hawaiian Lodge Scholarships *99*
Heinz Environmental Fellows Program *142*
Herb Society Research Grants *92*
High Technology Scholars Program *141*
Hispanic Engineer National Achievement Awards Corporation Scholarship Program *122*
Howard Brown Rickard Scholarship *101*
Independent Laboratories Institute Scholarship Alliance *93*
J .J. Barr Scholarship *139*
Libbie H. Hyman Memorial Scholarship *141*
Life Member Montana Federation of Garden Clubs Scholarship *138*
Louis Stokes Science and Technology Award *139*
Loy McCandless Marks Scholarship in Tropical Ornamental Horticulture *138*
MARC Undergraduate Student Training in Academic Research U*Star Awards *140*
Master Brewers Association of the Americas *81*
Math and Science Scholarship Program for Alabama Teachers *135*
Minority Undergraduate Student Awards *142*
Montana Space Grant Scholarship Program *125*

NASA Idaho Space Grant Consortium Scholarship
Program 94
NASA Maryland Space Grant Consortium
Undergraduate Scholarships 139
NASA Nebraska Space Grant 125
National Aquarium in Baltimore Henry Hall
Scholarship 136
National Association of Water Companies-New Jersey
Chapter Scholarship 139
National Council of State Garden Clubs, Inc.
Scholarship 82
National Garden Clubs, Inc. Scholarship Program 83
National Hispanic Explorers Scholarship Program 93
NIH Undergraduate Scholarship Program for Students
from Disadvantaged Backgrounds 140
Oregon Foundation for Blacktail Deer Outdoor and
Wildlife Scholarship 140
PACD Auxiliary Scholarships 76
Paul A. Stewart Awards 88
Paul and Helen Trussel Science and Technology
Scholarship 93
Payzer Scholarship 122
Recreational Boating Industries Educational Foundation
Scholarships 141
Russell A. Cookingham Scholarship 140
Sigma Xi Grants-In-Aid of Research 84
Student Achievement Awards of the Industrial
Electrolysis and Electrochemical Engineering
Division of the Electrochemical Society, Inc. 137
Student Research Awards of the Battery Division of the
Electrochemical Society, Inc. 137
Turf and Ornamental Communicators Association
Scholarship Program 142
Vermont Space Grant Consortium Scholarship
Program 94
Wildlife Leadership Awards 141
William J. and Marijane E. Adams, Jr. Scholarship 78
Women in Science and Technology Scholarship 143
Wyeth Scholarship 142

Business/Consumer Services

A.T. Anderson Memorial Scholarship 89
Actuarial Scholarships for Minority Students 145
AICPA/Accountemps Student Scholarship 55
ALLStudentLoan.org College Scholarship Program 143
Association of Hispanic Professionals for Education
Scholarship 152
AXA Foundation Fund Achievement Scholarship 154
Bank of America ADA Abilities Scholarship 56
Bank of America Minority Scholarship 146
Barbara S. Miller Memorial Scholarship 146
Ben W. Brannon Memorial Scholarship Fund 60
Best Buy Enterprise Employee Scholarship 70
Black Executive Exchange Program Jerry Bartow
Scholarship Fund 151
Booz, Allen & Hamilton/William F. Stasior
Internship 154
Bradford White Corporation Scholarship 102
Bullivant Houser Bailey-African American Chamber of
Commerce Community College Scholarship
Fund 152
Burlington Northern Santa Fe Foundation
Scholarship 89
Business Achievement Award 147
C.R. Bard Scholarship and Internship Program 154
Canadian Direct Marketing Scholarship for Business
Students 150
Cardinal Health Scholarship 70
Carl H. Marrs Scholarship Fund 56
Castle Rock Foundation Scholarship 154
Central Intelligence Agency Undergraduate Scholarship
Program 56
Charlotte Observer Minority Scholarships 146
Counselor, Advocate, and Support Staff Scholarship
Program 69
Dan Reichard Jr. Scholarship 144
Dell/UNCF Corporate Scholars Program 155
Delta Faucet Company Scholarship Program 102
Denny's/Hispanic College Fund Scholarship 62
Department of Energy Scholarship Program 148
Donald W. Fogarty International Student Paper
Competition 144
Earl G. Graves NAACP Scholarship 151
Economic Club of Grand Rapids Business Study Abroad
Scholarship 62
FCCLA Regional Scholarships 147
FCCLA Texas Farm Bureau Scholarship 147
Financial Services Institution Scholarship 71
Florida Bankers Educational Foundation Scholarship/
Loan 147
Flowers Industries Scholarship 155
Frank L. Greathouse Government Accounting
Scholarship 148

Fukunaga Scholarship Foundation 147
GE/LULAC Scholarship 150
George A. Nielsen Public Investor Scholarship 148
Glenn R. and Juanita B. Struble Scholarship II 102
Greater Springfield Accountants Scholarship 57
Harold Bettinger Memorial Scholarship 74
Harold F. Wilkins Scholarship Program 143
Harry A. Applegate Scholarship 146
Homestead Capital Housing Scholarship 68
HSF/General Motors Scholarship 149
HSF/Little Village Chamber of Commerce Ambassadors
Scholarship Program 149
HSF/Toyota Scholarship Program 149
HSF-ALPFA Scholarships 55
ICI Educational Foundation Scholarship Program 62
J .J. Barr Scholarship 139
J. Wilmar Mirandon Scholarship 153
James A. Turner, Jr. Memorial Scholarship 144
Jane M. Klausman Women in Business Scholarships 158
John M. Azarian Memorial Armenian Youth Scholarship
Fund 149
KeyCorp Scholars Program/Internship 155
Lagrant Foundation Scholarship for Undergraduates 150
Lawrence "Larry" Frazier Memorial Scholarship 124
Lawrence P. Doss Scholarship Foundation 64
M & T Bank/ Hispanic College Fund Scholarship
Program 63
Malcolm Baldrige Scholarship 157
Mary Macey Scholarship 85
Maryland Association of Private Colleges and Career
Schools Scholarship 150
Mas Family Scholarship Award 149
Mas Family Scholarships 146
MasterCard Scholars Program 155
Math, Engineering, Science, Business, Education,
Computers Scholarships 145
Maytag Company Scholarship 155
MBIA/William O. Bailey Scholars Program 155
Minorities in Government Finance Scholarship 62
Monsanto Agri-business Scholarship 81
Mosmiller Scholar Program 143
MRA Institute of Management Endowment Fund
Scholarship 151
MRCA Foundation Scholarship Program 94
NAIW Education Foundation Professional
Scholarship 151
National Association of Water Companies-New Jersey
Chapter Scholarship 139
Native American Leadership in Education (NALE) 145
New England Employee Benefits Council Scholarship
Program 151
North Dakota Society of Certified Public Accountants
scholarship 67
Northeast Utilities System Scholarship Program 156
PHCC Educational Foundation Need-Based
Scholarship 102
PHCC Educational Foundation Scholarship
Program 103
Principal Financial Group Scholarships 156
Project Cambio Scholarship Awards 152
Ray Foley Memorial Youth Education Foundation
Scholarship 144
Rockwell/UNCF Corporate Scholars Program 156
Royal Bank Aboriginal Student Awards 153
Sales Professionals- USA Scholarship 153
SBC Foundation Scholarship 156
SBC Pacific Bell Foundation Scholarship 156
Scholarships for Education, Business and Religion 148
South Dakota Retailers Association Scholarship
Program 69
SouthTrust Scholarship 156
Sprint Scholarship/Internship 71
Stuart Cameron and Margaret McLeod Memorial
Scholarship 63
Teaming to Win Business Scholarship 153
Texas Family Business Association Scholarship 153
Toyota Scholarship 157
Tribal Business Management Program (TBM) 55
Tri-State Surveying and Photogrammetry Kris M. Kunze
Memorial Scholarship 143
Truckload Carriers Association Scholarship Fund 154
Twin Cities Chapter Undergraduate Scholarship 65
Twin Cities Graduate MBA Scholarship 65
Union Bank of California Scholarship 152
UPS Corporate Scholars Program/Internship 157
Victor and Margaret Ball Program 144
Virginia Society of CPAs Educational Foundation
Minority Undergraduate Scholarship 71
Virginia Society of CPAs Educational Foundation
Undergraduate Scholarship 72
W. Allan Herzog Scholarship 70
Walt Disney Company Foundation Scholarship 112
Walter Reed Smith Scholarship 154

Weyerhaeuser/UNCF Corporate Scholars 157
Willard H. Erwin, Jr. Memorial Scholarship Fund 148
William R. Goldfarb Memorial Scholarship 145
Wm. Wrigley, Jr. Company Scholars Program 157
Women in Logistics Scholarship 157
Wyeth Scholarship 142
Wyoming Trucking Association Trust Fund
Scholarship 158

Canadian Studies

Canadian Institute of Ukrainian Studies Research
Grants 104

Chemical Engineering

AACE International Competitive Scholarship 96
AeA- Oregon Council Technology Scholarship
Program 88
Al Qoyawayma Award 163
Al-Ben Scholarship for Academic Incentive 164
Al-Ben Scholarship for Professional Merit 165
Al-Ben Scholarship for Scholastic Achievement 165
American Chemical Society, Rubber Division
Undergraduate Scholarship 158
American Council of Engineering Companies of Oregon
Scholarship 167
American Electroplaters and Surface Finishers
Scholarships 158
American Society for Enology and Viticulture
Scholarships 78
ASCLS Region IX Clinical Laboratory Scientists of
Alaska Sharon O'Meara Continuing Education
Scholarship Fund 161
ASCLS Region VI Missouri Organization for Clinical
Laboratory Science Education Scholarship 162
Association for Facilities Engineering Cedar Valley
Chapter # 132 Scholarship 120
Association for Iron and Steel Technology David H.
Samson Scholarship 162
Association for Women in Science College
Scholarship 86
Astronaut Scholarship Foundation 92
Automotive Hall of Fame Educational Funds 162
Barry M. Goldwater Scholarship and Excellence in
Education Program 92
BMW/SAE Engineering Scholarship 129
Cargill Scholarship Program 70
ChemE-Car National Level Competition 159
Chevron Texaco Corporation Scholarships 168
Coates, Wolff, Russell Mining Industry Scholarship 95
Collegiate Inventors Competition - Grand Prize 95
Collegiate Inventors Competition for Undergraduate
Students 95
Daniel Cubicciotti Student Award of the San Francisco
Section of the Electrochemical Society, Sponsored
by Structural Integrity Associates 137
Denny's/Hispanic College Fund Scholarship 62
Department of Energy Scholarship Program 148
Desk and Derrick Educational Trust 92
Donald F. and Mildred Topp Othmer Foundation-
National Scholarship Awards 159
Dupont Company Scholarships 168
Edmonton Chemical Engineering Scholarship 162
Edward D. Hendrickson/SAE Engineering
Scholarship 129
Engineering Scholarship 158
Environmental Division Graduate Student Paper
Award 159
Environmental Division Undergraduate Student Paper
Award 159
Environmental Protection Agency Tribal Lands
Environmental Science Scholarship 135
Environmental Protection Scholarships 164
General Motors Foundation Undergraduate
Scholarships 168
GRE and Graduate Applications Waiver 95
Gulf Coast Hurricane Scholarship 168
H.H. Dow Memorial Student Achievement Award of the
Industrial Electrolysis and Electrochemical
Engineering Division of the Electrochemical Society,
Inc. 137
Hawaiian Lodge Scholarships 99
High Technology Scholars Program 141
Hispanic Engineer National Achievement Awards
Corporation Scholarship Program 122
HSF/General Motors Scholarship 149
Hubertus W.V. Willems Scholarship for Male
Students 166
Independent Laboratories Institute Scholarship
Alliance 93
Instrumentation, Systems, and Automation Society (ISA)
Scholarship Program 123
John J. McKetta Undergraduate Scholarship 159
LINC TELACU Engineering Award 163

President's $2500 Scholarship *186*
Public Relations Society of America Multicultural Affairs Scholarship *185*
RDW Group, Inc. Minority Scholarship for Communications *186*
Reader's Digest Scholarship *189*
Robin Roberts/WBCA Sports Communications Scholarship Award *190*
Russell A. Cookingham Scholarship *140*
Ruth Hancock Memorial Scholarship *180*
Society for Technical Communication Scholarship Program *186*
Student Texas Broadcast Education Foundation Scholarship *187*
Texas Gridiron Club Scholarships *188*
Texas Outdoor Writers Association Scholarship *188*
Thomas R. Dargan Minority Scholarship *182*
Tom Reiff Texas Broadcast Education Foundation Scholarship *187*
Toyota Scholarship *157*
Trustee Scholarship Program *183*
Undergraduate Texas Broadcast Education Foundation Scholarship *188*
Valley Press Club Scholarships, The Republican Scholarship; Photojournalism Scholarship, Channel 22 Scholarship *189*
Vann Kennedy Texas Broadcast Education Foundation Scholarship *188*
Virginia Association of Broadcasters Scholarship Award *189*
West Virginia Broadcasters Association Fund *181*
Wyoming Trucking Association Trust Fund Scholarship *158*

Computer Science/Data Processing

AACE International Competitive Scholarship *96*
Accenture Scholarship *197*
AeA- Oregon Council Technology Scholarship Program *88*
AFCEA Scholarship for Working Professionals *120*
AFCEA Sgt. Jeannette L. Winters, USMC Memorial Scholarship *191*
AFCEA/Lockheed Martin Orincon IT Scholarship *191*
Agilent Mentoring Scholarship *194*
Al-Ben Scholarship for Academic Incentive *164*
Al-Ben Scholarship for Professional Merit *165*
Al-Ben Scholarship for Scholastic Achievement *165*
Alice L. Haltom Educational Fund Scholarship *190*
American Meteorological Society Industry Undergraduate Scholarships *89*
Armed Forces Communications and Electronics Association Educational Foundation Distance-Learning Scholarship *191*
Armed Forces Communications and Electronics Association General Emmett Paige Scholarship *191*
Armed Forces Communications and Electronics Association General John A. Wickham Scholarship *192*
Armed Forces Communications and Electronics Association ROTC Scholarship Program *120*
Association for Iron and Steel Technology Ohio Valley Chapter Scholarship *135*
Association for Women in Science College Scholarship *86*
Astronaut Scholarship Foundation *92*
Bank of America ADA Abilities Scholarship *56*
Barry M. Goldwater Scholarship and Excellence in Education Program *92*
Booz, Allen & Hamilton/William F. Stasior Internship *154*
BPW Career Advancement Scholarship Program for Women *136*
Cardinal Health Scholarship *70*
Cargill Scholarship Program *70*
Carol A. Ratza Memorial Scholarship *138*
Central Intelligence Agency Undergraduate Scholarship Program *56*
Cisco/UNCF Scholars Program *197*
Collegiate Inventors Competition - Grand Prize *95*
Collegiate Inventors Competition for Undergraduate Students *95*
Con Edison Scholarship *70*
Conditional Grant Program *176*
Dell Computer Corporation Scholarships *194*
Dell/UNCF Corporate Scholars Program *155*
Denny's/Hispanic College Fund Scholarship *62*
Economic Club of Grand Rapids Business Study Abroad Scholarship *62*
Electronic Document Systems Foundation Scholarship Awards *180*
Emerson Electric Company Scholarship *71*
Flowers Industries Scholarship *155*
Ford/UNCF Corporate Scholars Program *71*

Guidant Corporation Scholarship *195*
Hawaiian Lodge Scholarships *99*
High Technology Scholars Program *141*
Hispanic Engineer National Achievement Awards Corporation Scholarship Program *122*
Howard Vollum American Indian Scholarship *194*
HSF/Society of Hispanic Professional Engineers, Inc. Scholarship Program *174*
HSF/Toyota Scholarship Program *149*
ICI Educational Foundation Scholarship Program *62*
ICIF Scholarship for Dependents of Member Organizations *181*
International Communications Industries Foundation AV Scholarship *182*
John Wiley & Sons Best JASIST Paper Award *191*
Kathi Bowles Scholarship for Women in Computing *192*
Kodak Engineering Excellence Program Scholarship *197*
LINC TELACU Engineering Award *163*
Lockheed Martin Scholarship Program *164*
Louis Stokes Science and Technology Award *139*
Lydia I. Pickup Memorial Scholarship *195*
M & T Bank/ Hispanic College Fund Scholarship Program *63*
Malcolm Pirnie, Inc. Scholars Program *169*
MARC Undergraduate Student Training in Academic Research U*Star Awards *140*
Maryland Association of Private Colleges and Career Schools Scholarship *150*
Math, Engineering, Science, Business, Education, Computers Scholarships *145*
Maytag Company Scholarship *155*
Mentor Graphics Scholarship *194*
Micron Science and Technology Scholars Program *165*
Microsoft Corporation Scholarships *195*
Minnesota Space Grant Consortium *124*
Montana Space Grant Scholarship Program *125*
NASA Idaho Space Grant Consortium Scholarship Program *94*
NASA Maryland Space Grant Consortium Undergraduate Scholarship *139*
NASA Nebraska Space Grant *125*
National Association of Water Companies-New Jersey Chapter Scholarship *139*
National Federation of the Blind Computer Science Scholarship *193*
National Hispanic Explorers Scholarship Program *93*
National Security Agency Stokes Educational Scholarship Program *194*
National Society of Women Engineers Scholarships *196*
Northeast Utilities System Scholarship Program *156*
Northrop Grumman Corporation Scholarships *130*
Paul and Helen Trussel Science and Technology Scholarship *93*
Paul W. Ruckes Scholarship *190*
PHD ARA Scholarship *179*
Principal Financial Group Scholarships *156*
Royal Bank Aboriginal Student Awards *153*
SBC Foundation Scholarship *156*
SBC Pacific Bell Foundation Scholarship *156*
Society of Women Engineers - Twin Tiers Section Scholarship *196*
Society of Women Engineers-Rocky Mountain Section Scholarship Program *196*
South Dakota Retailers Association Scholarship Program *69*
Sprint Scholarship/Internship *71*
SWE Baltimore-Washington Section Scholarships *195*
SWE Baton Rouge Section Scholarships *195*
SWE California Golden Gate Section Scholarships *195*
SWE Connecticut Section Jean R. Beers Scholarship *196*
SWE Greater New Orleans Section Scholarship *196*
Technical Minority Scholarship *169*
Tribal Business Management Program (TBM) *55*
TRW Information Technology Minority Scholarship *197*
University and Community College System of Nevada NASA Space Grant and Fellowship Program *125*
UPS Corporate Scholars Program/Internship *157*
USENIX Association Scholarship *197*
Walter Reed Smith Scholarship *154*
West Virginia Space Grant Consortium Undergraduate Scholarship Program *126*
William R. Goldfarb Memorial Scholarship *145*
Women in Science and Technology Scholarship *143*
Wyoming Trucking Association Trust Fund Scholarship *158*

Construction Engineering/Management

Architecture, Construction, and Engineering Mentor Program Scholarships *101*
Daniel Cubicciotti Student Award of the San Francisco Section of the Electrochemical Society, Sponsored by Structural Integrity Associates *137*

H.H. Dow Memorial Student Achievement Award of the Industrial Electrolysis and Electrochemical Engineering Division of the Electrochemical Society, Inc. *137*
Student Achievement Awards of the Industrial Electrolysis and Electrochemical Engineering Division of the Electrochemical Society, Inc. *137*
Student Research Awards of the Battery Division of the Electrochemical Society, Inc. *137*

Cosmetology

Joe Francis Haircare Scholarship Program *198*

Criminal Justice/Criminology

Alphonso Deal Scholarship Award *199*
American Criminal Justice Association-Lambda Alpha Epsilon National Scholarship *198*
American Society of Criminology Gene Carte Student Paper Competition *199*
Connecticut Association of Women Police Scholarship *199*
Indiana Sheriffs' Association Scholarship Program *199*
John Dennis Scholarship *199*
North Carolina Police Corps Scholarship *200*
North Carolina Sheriffs' Association Undergraduate Criminal Justice Scholarships *200*
Ritchie-Jennings Memorial Scholarship *55*
Robert C. Carson Memorial Bursary *198*

Culinary Arts

Allen Susser Scholarship *201*
American Restaurant Scholarship *201*
Best Teen Chef Culinary Scholarship Competition *200*
Careers Through Culinary Arts Program Cooking Competition for Scholarships *200*
Chaine des Rotisseurs Scholarships *200*
Charlie Trotter Scholarship *201*
Charlie Trotter's Culinary Education Scholarship *200*
Ciroc Grape Chefs of America Culinary Scholarships *202*
Clay Triplette Scholarship *202*
Deseo at the Westin Scholarship *202*
Future Culinarian of America Scholarship *201*
Gene Hovis Memorial Scholarship *202*
International Cake Exploration Societe Scholarship *201*
Les Dames d'Escoffier Scholarship *203*
Oregon Wine Brotherhood Scholarship *203*
Sanford D'Amato Scholarship *202*
St. Regis Houston Scholarship *202*
The Chef2Chef Culinary Student Grant *201*
The Palace Restaurant in the Cincinnatian Hotel Culinary Scholarship *203*
The Peter Cameron Scholarship *203*

Dental Health/Services

Academy of LDS Dentists scholarship *203*
ADEA/Oral-B Laboratories Scholarship *205*
ADEA/Sigma Phi Alpha Linda DeVore Scholarship *205*
ADHA Institute General Scholarships *205*
Alberta Heritage Scholarship Fund Aboriginal Health Careers Bursary *135*
Alice Newell Joslyn Medical Fund *207*
Allied Health Student Loan Program-New Mexico *210*
American Dental Association Foundation Dental Assisting Scholarship Program *204*
American Dental Association Foundation Dental Hygiene Scholarship Program *204*
American Dental Association Foundation Dental Lab Technology Scholarship *204*
American Dental Association Foundation Dental Student Scholarship Program *204*
American Dental Association Foundation Minority Dental Student Scholarship Program *204*
American Dental Hygienists' Association Institute Minority Scholarship *205*
American Dental Hygienists' Association Institute Research Grant *205*
American Dental Hygienists' Association Part-Time Scholarship *205*
American Medical Technologists Student Scholarship *207*
Anne Lindeman Memorial Scholarship *142*
Arkansas Health Education Grant Program (ARHEG) *86*
BPW Career Advancement Scholarship Program for Women *136*
Charles R. Morris Student Research Award *203*
Colgate "Bright Smiles, Bright Futures" Minority Scholarship *206*
Dental Assisting Scholarships *208*
Dental Hygiene Scholarships *208*
Developmental Disabilities Scholastic Achievement Scholarship for Lutheran College Students *208*
Dr. Alfred C. Fones Scholarship *206*

Electrical Engineering/Electronics

Energy and Power Engineering

General Motors Foundation Undergraduate
Scholarships 168
GRE and Graduate Applications Waiver 95
Guidant Corporation Scholarship 195
H.H. Dow Memorial Student Achievement Award of the
Industrial Electrolysis and Electrochemical
Engineering Division of the Electrochemical Society,
Inc. 137
Hawaiian Lodge Scholarships 99
HENAAC Scholars Program 290
Henry Adams Scholarship 252
Henry Broughton, K2AE Memorial Scholarship 90
Henry Rodriguez Reclamation College Scholarship and
Internship 285
High Technology Scholars Program 141
Howard E. Adkins Memorial Scholarship 253
HSF/General Motors Scholarship 149
HSF/Society of Hispanic Professional Engineers, Inc.
Scholarship Program 174
Hubertus W.V. Willems Scholarship for Male
Students 166
IEE Engineering Degree Scholarships for Women 287
IEE Funding Undergraduates to Study Engineering
(FUSE) Scholarship 287
IFMA Foundation Scholarships 100
Illinois Tool Works Welding Companies Scholarship 254
Independent Laboratories Institute Scholarship
Alliance 93
Instrumentation, Systems, and Automation Society (ISA)
Scholarship Program 123
J .J. Barr Scholarship 139
Jack Gilstrap Scholarship 171
John C. Lincoln Memorial Scholarship 254
KSEA Scholarships 245
Laser Technology, Engineering and Applications
Scholarship 288
LINC TELACU Engineering Award 163
Lockheed Martin Scholarship Program 164
Logistics Education Foundation Scholarship 290
Louis Stokes Science and Technology Award 139
Louis T. Klauder Scholarship 171
M & T Bank/ Hispanic College Fund Scholarship
Program 63
Maine Society of Professional Engineers Vernon T.
Swaine- Robert E. Chute Scholarship 266
Marliave Fund 213
Mas Family Scholarship Award 149
Mas Family Scholarships 146
Matsuo Bridge Company, Ltd., of Japan Scholarship 172
Maureen L. and Howard N. Blitman, PE Scholarship to
Promote Diversity in Engineering 166
Micron Science and Technology Scholars Program 165
NASA Delaware Space Grant Undergraduate Tuition
Scholarship 94
NASA Nebraska Space Grant 125
NASA Rhode Island Space Grant Consortium Outreach
Scholarship for Undergraduate Students 288
National Hispanic Explorers Scholarship Program 93
National Society of Professional Engineers/Auxiliary
Scholarship 166
NAWIC Undergraduate Scholarships 100
Northeast Utilities System Scholarship Program 156
Parsons Brinckerhoff-Jim Lammie Scholarship 171
Paul H. Robbins Honorary Scholarship 166
PHCC Educational Foundation Need-Based
Scholarship 102
PHCC Educational Foundation Scholarship
Program 103
Plastics Pioneers Scholarships 269
Praxair International Scholarship 254
Professional Engineers in Industry Scholarship 167
Ralph K. Hillquist Honorary SAE Scholarship 270
Robert Greenberg/Harold E. Ennes Scholarship Fund
and Ennes Educational Foundation Broadcast
Technology Scholarship 271
Robert W. Thunen Memorial Scholarships 100
SAE William G. Belfrey Memorial Grant 271
Society for Technical Communication Scholarship
Program 186
Society of Hispanic Professional Engineers
Foundation 168
SPIE Educational Scholarships in Optical Science and
Engineering 93
Student Achievement Awards of the Industrial
Electrolysis and Electrochemical Engineering
Division of the Electrochemical Society, Inc. 137
Student Research Awards of the Battery Division of the
Electrochemical Society, Inc. 137
Technical Minority Scholarship 169
TLMI 4 Year Colleges/Full-Time Students
Scholarship 290
TMC/SAE Donald D. Dawson Technical Scholarship 129
TMS J. Keith Brimacombe Presidential Scholarship 266

TMS Outstanding Student Paper Contest-
Undergraduate 266
TMS/EMPMD Gilbert Chin Scholarship 266
TMS/EPD Scholarship 267
TMS/International Symposium on Superalloys
Scholarship Program 267
TMS/LMD Scholarship Program 267
TMS/Structural Materials Division Scholarship 267
Transit Hall of Fame Scholarship Award Program 171
Tribal Business Management Program (TBM) 55
Trimmer Education Foundation Scholarships for
Construction Management 172
Vermont Space Grant Consortium Scholarship
Program 94
Vice Admiral Jerry O. Tuttle, USN (Ret.) and Mrs.
Barbara A. Tuttle Science and Technology
Scholarship 255
Virginia Henry Memorial Scholarship 167
West Virginia Space Grant Consortium Undergraduate
Scholarship Program 126
William A. and Ann M. Brothers Scholarship 286
William B. Howell Memorial Scholarship 255
William H. Price Scholarship 288
Yanmar/SAE Scholarship 271

Entomology

BioQuip Undergraduate Scholarship 290
BioQuip Undergraduate Scholarship 290
The International Congress on Insect Neurochemistry
and Neurophysiology (ICINN) Student Recognition
Award in Insect Physiology, Biochemistry,
Toxicology, and Molecular Biology 290

Environmental Health

Delaware Solid Waste Authority John P. "Pat" Healy
Scholarship 291
E.H. Marth Food and Environmental Scholarship 291
Environmental Scholarships 291
Florida Environmental Health Association
Scholarship 291
Windstar Environmental Studies Scholarships 284
Young Epidemiology Scholars Competition 291

Environmental Science

Allegheny Mountain Section Air & Waste Management
Association Scholarship 292
Association for Iron and Steel Technology Ohio Valley
Chapter Scholarship 135
Association of California Water Agencies
Scholarships 91
Benjamin C. Blackburn Scholarship 293
Beulah Frey Environmental Scholarship 293
Bill Mason Memorial Scholarship Fund 80
California Water Awareness Campaign Water Scholar 79
Campus Safety, Health and Environmental Management
Association Scholarship Award Program 295
Carl W. Kreitzberg Endowed Scholarship 292
Clair A. Hill Scholarship 91
Coastal Plains Chapter of the Air and Waste
Management Association Environmental Steward
Scholarship 292
Collegiate Inventors Competition - Grand Prize 95
Collegiate Inventors Competition for Undergraduate
Students 95
Conservation of Natural Resources Scholarship 81
Conservation of Natural Resources Scholarship for
Nontraditional Students 81
Department of Energy Scholarship Program 148
Dr. Alan Beaven Forestry Scholarship 294
EPOC Environmental Scholarship Fund 293
Eugene Borson Scholarship 293
Exploration Fund Grants 88
Francis Blackduck Memorial "Strong Like Two People"
Awards 293
George R. Crafton Scholarship 81
GRE and Graduate Applications Waiver 95
Gulf Coast Research Laboratory Minority Summer
Grant 294
Henry Rodriguez Reclamation College Scholarship and
Internship 285
Morris K. Udall Undergraduate Scholarships 294
National Aquarium in Baltimore Henry Hall
Scholarship 136
National Council of State Garden Clubs, Inc.
Scholarship 82
National Garden Clubs, Inc. Scholarship Program 83
National Oceanic and Atmospheric Administration
Educational Partnership Program with Minority
Serving Institutions Undergraduate Scholarship 268
Ohio Environmental Science & Engineering
Scholarships 295
PACD Auxiliary Scholarships 76

Park Espenschade Memorial Scholarship 294
Paul W. Rodgers Scholarship 214
R.V. "Gadabout" Gaddis Charitable Fund 294
Ralph W. Abele Conservation Scholarship 295
Royden M. Bodley Scholarship 87
Russell A. Cookingham Scholarship 140
Statewide Scholarships 215
Texas Outdoor Writers Association Scholarship 188
The Park People $2000 Scholarship 102
United Parcel Service Diversity Scholarship Program 292
VASWCD Educational Foundation, Inc. Scholarship
Awards Program 296
Virginia Space Grant Consortium Teacher Education
Scholarships 125
West Virginia Space Grant Consortium Undergraduate
Scholarship Program 126
Weyerhaeuser/UNCF Corporate Scholars 157

European Studies

Canadian Institute of Ukrainian Studies Research
Grants 104
Culture Connection Foundation Scholarship 73
Cyprus American Archaeological Research Institute
Helena Wylde and Stuart Swiny Fellowship 96
German Academic Exchange Information Visits 296
Mayme and Herbert Frank Educational Fund 216

Fashion Design

Fashion Group International of Portland
Scholarship 296
Worldstudio Foundation Scholarship Program 104

Filmmaking/Video

Academy of Motion Picture Student Academy Award-
Honorary Foreign Film 297
Academy of Motion Pictures Student Academy
Awards 297
Academy of Television Arts and Sciences College
Television Awards 108
Advertising Federation of Fort Wayne, Inc.,
Scholarship 178
Alan Lucas Memorial Educational Scholarship 100
Arts Recognition and Talent Search (ARTS) 113
Charles and Lucille King Family Foundation
Scholarships 180
Film and Fiction Scholarship 111
Francis D. Lyon Scholarships 298
ICIF Scholarship for Dependents of Member
Organizations 181
International Communications Industries Foundation
AV Scholarship 182
Jack Shaheen Mass Communications Scholarship
Award 177
Lou Wolf Memorial Scholarship 298
MANAA Media Scholarships for Asian American
Students 112
National Writers Association Foundation
Scholarships 184
New England Film and Video Festival Awards 297
Outdoor Writers Association of America Bodie
McDowell Scholarship Award 185
Phelan Art Award in Filmmaking 298
Phelan Art Award in Video 298
Polish Arts Club of Buffalo Scholarship Foundation
Trust 108
Rhode Island Edsal Advertising Scholarship 298
Robert W. Thunen Memorial Scholarships 100
Student Paper Award 299
Teletoon Animation Scholarship Award
Competition 114
University Film and Video Association Carole Fielding
Student Grants 299
WIF Foundation Scholarship 299
Worldfest Student Film Award 299
Worldstudio Foundation Scholarship Program 104

Fire Sciences

Firefighter, Ambulance, and Rescue Squad Member
Tuition Reimbursement Program-Maryland 300
Independent Laboratories Institute Scholarship
Alliance 93
International Association of Fire Chiefs Foundation
Scholarship 299
International Associations of Fire Chiefs Foundation
Scholarship 300
John Charles Wilson Scholarship 300

Flexography

TLMI 4 Year Colleges/Full-Time Students
Scholarship 290
TLMI SCHOLARSHIP GRANT for Students of 2 Year
Colleges 300

Food Science/Nutrition

AAA Five Diamond Scholarship *303*
American Dietetic Association Foundation Scholarship
Program *300*
American Society for Enology and Viticulture
Scholarships *78*
Ann Lane Home Economics Scholarship *305*
Anne Lindeman Memorial Scholarship *142*
Artie Cutler Memorial Scholarship *303*
Association for Food and Drug Officials Scholarship
Fund *301*
Bea Cleveland 4-H Scholarship *170*
Becoming a Chef Scholarship *303*
Bryan Close Polo Grill Scholarship *303*
Cargill Scholarship Program *70*
Culinary Trust Scholarship Program for Culinary Study
and Research *302*
Culinary, Vinifera, and Hospitality Scholarship *301*
Dana Campbell Memorial Scholarship *303*
David Edgcumbe Scholarship *304*
Gino Cofacci Memorial Scholarship *304*
Goldman Family Fund, New Leader Scholarship *210*
Herb Society Research Grants *92*
Institute of Food Technologists Food Engineering
Division Junior/Senior Scholarship *302*
Institute of Food Technologists Freshman
Scholarships *302*
Institute of Food Technologists Quality Assurance
Division Junior/Senior Scholarships *302*
Institute of Food Technologists Sophomore
Scholarships *302*
Institute of Food Technologists/Master Foods USA
Undergraduate Mentored Scholarship *303*
International Foodservice Editorial Council
Communications Scholarship *182*
James Beard Foundation General Scholarships *304*
La Toque Scholarship *304*
Les Dames d'Escoffier Scholarship *203*
Mabel Sarbaugh 4-H Scholarship *170*
Marion A. and Eva S. Peeples Scholarships *230*
Maryland Association of Private Colleges and Career
Schools Scholarship *150*
Master Brewers Association of the Americas *81*
Minnesota Soybean Research and Promotion Council
Youth Soybean Scholarship *75*
Nancy Curry Scholarship *301*
National Dairy Shrine/Dairy Marketing, Inc. Milk
Marketing Scholarships *82*
National Hispanic Explorers Scholarship Program *93*
National Poultry and Food Distributors Association
Scholarship Foundation *76*
NDS Student Recognition Contest *75*
Oregon Wine Brotherhood Scholarship *203*
Peter Kump Memorial Scholarship *304*
Potato Industry Scholarship *76*
Professional Growth Scholarship *301*
Scholarship of the Maine School Food Service
Association *305*
Schwan's Food Service Scholarship *301*
SIA's Scholarship *304*
Undergraduate Scholarship Award *300*
United Agribusiness League Scholarship Program *77*
United Agricultural Benefit Trust Scholarship *77*
Wally Joe Scholarship *305*
Walter Reed Smith Scholarship *154*

Food Service/Hospitality

Academic Scholarship for High School Seniors *306*
Academic Scholarship for Undergraduate Students *306*
American Academy of Chefs Chaine des Rotisseurs
Scholarship *306*
Ann Lane Home Economics Scholarship *305*
Annual Scholarship Grant Program *306*
Cleveland Legacy I and II Scholarship Awards *308*
Coca-Cola Salute to Excellence Scholarship Award *308*
Culinary Trust Scholarship Program for Culinary Study
and Research *302*
Culinary, Vinifera, and Hospitality Scholarship *301*
Flowers Industries Scholarship *155*
Golden Gate Restaurant Association Scholarship
Foundation *307*
Harry A. Applegate Scholarship *146*
International Executive Housekeepers Educational
Foundation *307*
International Foodservice Editorial Council
Communications Scholarship *182*
Mary Macey Scholarship *85*
Missouri Travel Council Tourism Scholarship *307*
Nancy Curry Scholarship *301*
National Poultry and Food Distributors Association
Scholarship Foundation *76*

National Restaurant Association Educational Foundation
Professional Development Scholarship for
Educators *308*
National Restaurant Association Educational Foundation
Undergraduate Scholarships for College
Students *308*
National Restaurant Association Educational Foundation
Undergraduate Scholarships for High School
Seniors *308*
Network of Executive Women in Hospitality, Inc.
Scholarship *101*
New Horizons Kathy Le Tarte Scholarship *309*
Pat and Jim Host Scholarship *309*
Professional Growth Scholarship *301*
ProStart® National Certificate of Achievement
Scholarship *308*
Scholarship of the Maine School Food Service
Association *305*
Schwan's Food Service Scholarship *301*
Societie des Casinos du Quebec Scholarship *309*
Society for Foodservice Management Scholarship *310*
South Dakota Retailers Association Scholarship
Program *69*
Tampa, Hillsborough Legacy Scholarship *309*
Tauck Scholars Scholarships *309*
Tulsa Scholarship Awards *309*
Worthy Goal Scholarship Fund *307*
Yellow Ribbon Scholarship *310*

Foreign Language

Bridging Scholarships *311*
Carol A. Ratza Memorial Scholarship *138*
Central Intelligence Agency Undergraduate Scholarship
Program *56*
Culture Connection Foundation Scholarship *73*
Emergency Secondary Education Loan Program *135*
Henri Cardinaux Memorial Scholarship *106*
Japan Studies Scholarship *312*
Japan-U.S. Friendship Commission Prize for the
Translation of Japanese Literature *311*
Kor Memorial Scholarship *312*
Languages in Teacher Education Scholarships *218*
Michael and Marie Marucci Scholarship *312*
Minority Student Summer Scholarship *109*
National Alpha Mu Gamma Scholarships *310*
National Junior Classical League Scholarship *311*
National Latin Exam Scholarship *310*
National Security Agency Stokes Educational Scholarship
Program *194*
Rotary Foundation Cultural Ambassadorial
Scholarship *312*
Stephen Madry Peck, Jr. Memorial Scholarship *311*
Travel Grants *312*
West Virginia Broadcasters Association Fund *181*
Workforce Incentive Program *233*
Year Abroad Program in Poland *105*

Funeral Services/Mortuary Science

American Board of Funeral Service Education
Scholarships *313*
Illinois Funeral Directors Association Scholarships *313*
International Order Of The Golden Rule Award of
Excellence *313*
Missouri Funeral Directors Association Scholarships *313*
Wallace S. and Wilma K. Laughlin Scholarship *313*

Gemology

Mineralogical Society of America-Grant for Student
Research in Mineralogy and Petrology *214*
Mineralogy Society of America-Grant for Research in
Crystallography *215*

Geography

Association for Iron and Steel Technology Ohio Valley
Chapter Scholarship *135*
Bill Mason Memorial Scholarship Fund *80*
Budweiser Conservation Scholarship Program *140*
Buzzard- Maxfield- Richason and Rechlin
Scholarship *314*
Central Intelligence Agency Undergraduate Scholarship
Program *56*
Christopherson Geosystems Scholarship *314*
GTU John Wiley-Strahler Physical Geography
Scholarship *314*
Harvard Travellers Club Grants *96*
National Oceanic and Atmospheric Administration
Educational Partnership Program with Minority
Serving Institutions Undergraduate Scholarship *268*
Paul and Helen Trussel Science and Technology
Scholarship *93*
Rowntree Lewis Price and Wycoff Scholarship *314*

German Studies

German Academic Exchange Information Visits *296*

Graphics/Graphic Arts/Printing

Advertising Federation of Fort Wayne, Inc.,
Scholarship *178*
Carol A. Ratza Memorial Scholarship *138*
Central Intelligence Agency Undergraduate Scholarship
Program *56*
Clampitt Paper/Henry Phillips Memorial
Scholarship *316*
Denny's/Hispanic College Fund Scholarship *62*
Electronic Document Systems Foundation Scholarship
Awards *180*
Future Journalists Scholarship Program *180*
Hallmark Graphic Arts Scholarship *315*
International Foodservice Editorial Council
Communications Scholarship *182*
Madison Area Club of Printing House Craftsmen
Scholarship *316*
Maine Graphics Art Association *315*
Mary Olive Eddy Jones Art Scholarship *108*
National Poster Design Contest *315*
New England Graphic Arts Scholarship *315*
Print and Graphics Scholarships *315*
Printing Industries of Michigan Scholarship Fund *316*
Printing Industry of Minnesota Education Foundation
Scholarship Fund *316*
Rhode Island Edsal Advertising Scholarship *298*
South Dakota Retailers Association Scholarship
Program *69*
Texas Graphic Arts Educational Foundation
Scholarships *317*
TLMI 4 Year Colleges/Full-Time Students
Scholarship *290*
Visual and Performing Arts Achievement Awards *111*
Worldstudio Foundation Scholarship Program *104*

Health Administration

Alberta Heritage Scholarship Fund Aboriginal Health
Careers Bursary *135*
Burlington Northern Santa Fe Foundation
Scholarship *89*
Congressional Black Caucus Spouses Health
Initiatives *318*
Developmental Disabilities Scholastic Achievement
Scholarship for Lutheran College Students *208*
E.V. Booth Scholarship Award *317*
Elaine Osborne Jacobson Award for Women Working in
Health Care Law *318*
Goldman Family Fund, New Leader Scholarship *210*
HIMSS Foundation Scholarship Program *318*
Indian Health Service Health Professions Pre-
professional Scholarship *318*
Jeanette C. and Isadore N. Stern Scholarship *317*
North Carolina Student Loan Program for Health,
Science, and Mathematics *211*
Siemens Scholar Award *317*
Virginia Society for Healthcare Human Resources
Administration Scholarship *318*
Willard H. Erwin, Jr. Memorial Scholarship Fund *148*

Health and Medical Sciences

A.T. Anderson Memorial Scholarship *89*
ACES/PRIMO Program *328*
Alberta Heritage Scholarship Fund Aboriginal Health
Careers Bursary *135*
Alice Newell Joslyn Medical Fund *207*
Allied Health Student Loan Program-New Mexico *210*
AMA Foundation National Scholarship *320*
AMBUCS Scholars-Scholarships for Therapists *328*
American Association for Health Education William M.
Kane Scholarship *219*
American Association of Pharmaceutical Scientists
Gateway Scholarship Program *319*
American Legion Auxiliary Department of Arizona
Health Care Occupation Scholarships *319*
American Legion Auxiliary Department of Minnesota
Past President Parley Health Care Scholarship *320*
American Legion Auxiliary, Department of Texas Past
President's Parley Medical Scholarship *320*
American Medical Technologists Student
Scholarship *207*
American Occupational Therapy Foundation State
Association Scholarships *321*
Anne Lindeman Memorial Scholarship *142*
Archbold Scholarship Program *327*
Arkansas Health Education Grant Program (ARHEG) *86*
ASCLS Region II Virginia Society for Clinical
Laboratory Science Scholarships *323*
ASCLS Region IV Ohio Society for Clinical Laboratory
Science Geraldine Diebler/Stella Griffin Award *323*

Health Information Management/ Technology

Heating, Air-Conditioning, and Refrigeration Mechanics

Historic Preservation and Conservation

History

Home Economics

FCCLA Houston Livestock Show and Rodeo
Scholarship *340*
FCCLA Regional Scholarships *147*
FCCLA Texas Farm Bureau Scholarship *147*
International Executive Housekeepers Educational
Foundation *307*
Mabel Sarbaugh 4-H Scholarship *170*
Maryland Association of Private Colleges and Career
Schools Scholarship *150*
National Poultry and Food Distributors Association
Scholarship Foundation *76*
Scholarship of the Maine School Food Service
Association *305*
Stella Blum Research Grant *105*
Walter Reed Smith Scholarship *154*

Horticulture/Floriculture

Alabama Golf Course Superintendent's Association's
Donnie Arthur Memorial Scholarship *341*
American Society for Enology and Viticulture
Scholarships *78*
ANLA National Scholarship Endowment-Usrey Family
Scholarship *341*
Anne Seaman Professional Grounds Management
Society Memorial Scholarship *84*
Arizona Nursery Association Foundation
Scholarship *342*
Ball Horticultural Company Scholarship *342*
Barbara Carlson Scholarship *343*
Benjamin C. Blackburn Scholarship *293*
Bud Ohlman Scholarship *343*
Carl F. Deitz Memorial Scholarship *343*
Carville M. Akehurst Memorial Scholarship *341*
Connecticut Nurserymen's Foundation, Inc.
Scholarships *342*
Dosatron International, Inc., Scholarship *343*
Earl Dedman Memorial Scholarship *343*
Ecke Family Scholarship *344*
Ed Markham International Scholarship *344*
Edward R. Hall Scholarship *76*
Federated Garden Clubs of Connecticut, Inc. *137*
Fran Johnson Scholarship for Non-Traditional
Students *344*
Francis Sylvia Zverina Scholarship *348*
Garden Club of America Summer Scholarship in Field
Botany *347*
GCSAA Scholars Competition *348*
Golf Course Superintendents Association of America
Student Essay Contest *75*
Harold Bettinger Memorial Scholarship *74*
Harold F. Wilkins Scholarship Program *143*
Herb Society Research Grants *92*
Horticulture Research Institute Timothy Bigelow and
Palmer W. Bigelow, Jr. Scholarship *341*
Horticulture Scholarships *348*
International Executive Housekeepers Educational
Foundation *307*
Jacob Van Namen/Vans Marketing Scholarship *74*
James Bridenbaugh Memorial Scholarship *344*
James Rathmell, Jr. Memorial Scholarship *344*
Jim Perry/Holden L. Bettinger Scholarship *345*
Joan K. Hunt and Rachel M. Hunt Summer Scholarship
in Field Botany *347*
John Holden Memorial Vocational Scholarship *345*
John L. Tomasovic, Sr., Scholarship *345*
Joseph Shinoda Memorial Scholarship *349*
Karl "Pete" Fuhrmann IV Memorial Scholarship *74*
Katharine M. Grosscup Scholarship *347*
LAF/CLASS Fund Ornamental Horticulture
Program *349*
Landscape Architecture Foundation/California
Landscape Architecture Student Fund University
Scholarship Program *349*
Leonard Bettinger Scholarship *345*
Life Member Montana Federation of Garden Clubs
Scholarship *138*
Long Island Flower Growers Scholarship *345*
Loy McCandless Marks Scholarship in Tropical
Ornamental Horticulture *138*
Milton J. Boone Horticultural Scholarship *342*
Mosmiller Scholar Program *143*
National Council of State Garden Clubs, Inc.
Scholarship *82*
National Garden Clubs Scholarship *349*
National Garden Clubs, Inc. Scholarship Program *83*
National Greenhouse Manufacturers Association
Scholarship *346*
Norm Moll Scholarship *346*
PACD Auxiliary Scholarships *76*
Paris Fracasso Production Floriculture Scholarship *346*
Potato Industry Scholarship *76*
Richard E. Barrett Scholarship *346*
Scotts Company Scholars Program *348*

Seed Companies Scholarship *346*
Southeast Greenhouse Conference Scholarship *347*
Spring Meadow Nursery Scholarship *342*
The Park People $2000 Scholarship *102*
Turf and Ornamental Communicators Association
Scholarship Program *142*
United Agribusiness League Scholarship Program *77*
United Agricultural Benefit Trust Scholarship *77*
Victor and Margaret Ball Program *144*
Western Michigan Greenhouse Association
Scholarship *347*
Western Reserve Herb Society Scholarship *348*

Hospitality Management

Academy of Travel and Tourism Scholarships *351*
American Express Scholarship Program *350*
Annual Scholarship Grant Program *306*
Cleveland Legacy I and II Scholarship Awards *308*
Culinary, Vinifera, and Hospitality Scholarship *301*
Denny's/Hispanic College Fund Scholarship *62*
Emerson Electric Company Scholarship *71*
Golden Gate Restaurant Association Scholarship
Foundation *307*
International Airlines Travel Agent Network Ronald A.
Santana Memorial Foundation *350*
International Executive Housekeepers Association
Educational Foundation Spartan Scholarship *351*
International Foodservice Editorial Council
Communications Scholarship *182*
Lodging Management Program Scholarships *350*
Missouri Travel Council Tourism Scholarship *307*
Network of Executive Women in Hospitality, Inc.
Scholarship *101*
New Horizons Kathy Le Tarte Scholarship *309*
Pat and Jim Host Scholarship *309*
R.W. Bob Holden Scholarship *350*
Scholarship of the Maine School Food Service
Association *305*
Societie des Casinos du Quebec Scholarship *309*
South Dakota Retailers Association Scholarship
Program *69*
Student Scholarship Program *350*
Tampa, Hillsborough Legacy Scholarship *309*
Tauck Scholars Scholarships *309*
Tulsa Scholarship Awards *309*
Yellow Ribbon Scholarship *310*

Humanities

ASCSA Summer Sessions Open Scholarships *88*
Beinecke Scholarship for Graduate Study *109*
BPW Career Advancement Scholarship Program for
Women *136*
Charles L. Hebner Memorial Scholarship *352*
CHSSC Scholarship Award *352*
Developmental Disabilities Scholastic Achievement
Scholarship for Lutheran College Students *208*
Florence Lemcke Memorial Scholarship in Fine Arts *107*
Francis L. Booth Medical Scholarship sponsored by
LAVFW Department of Maine *327*
Harvard Travellers Club Grants *96*
Irish Research Funds *105*
Jack J. Isgur Foundation Scholarship *111*
Leo J. Krysa Undergraduate Scholarship *104*
Lois Hole Humanities and Social Sciences
Scholarship *351*
Math, Engineering, Science, Business, Education,
Computers Scholarships *145*
McClare Family Trust Scholarship *353*
Minority Student Summer Scholarship *109*
NASA Maryland Space Grant Consortium
Undergraduate Scholarships *139*
National Federation of the Blind Humanities
Scholarship *353*
National Junior Classical League Scholarship *311*
Native American Leadership in Education (NALE) *145*
Polish Arts Club of Buffalo Scholarship Foundation
Trust *108*
Research Development Initiative *237*
Robert P. Pula Memorial Scholarship *353*
The FW Rausch Arts and Humanities Paper Contest *112*
Wesley-Logan Prize *73*

Hydrology

Association of California Water Agencies
Scholarships *91*
California Water Awareness Campaign Water Scholar *79*
Clair A. Hill Scholarship *91*
Hydro Power Contest *247*
Paul W. Rodgers Scholarship *214*

Industrial Design

Downriver Detroit Chapter 198 Scholarship *273*
El Nuevo Constructor Scholarship Program *99*
Fort Wayne Chapter 56 Scholarship *274*
Industrial Designers Society of America Undergraduate
Scholarship *353*
North Central Region 9 Scholarship *275*
Phoenix Chapter 67 Scholarship *275*
Ruth Clark Scholarship *111*
Society of Plastics Engineers Scholarship Program *168*
Student Design Competition *354*
Wichita Chapter 52 Scholarship *276*
Worldstudio Foundation Scholarship Program *104*

Insurance and Actuarial Science

Actuarial Scholarships for Minority Students *355*
Casualty Actuaries of the Southeast Scholarship
Program *354*
Missouri Insurance Education Foundation
Scholarship *354*
NAIW College Scholarship *354*
NAIW Education Foundation Professional
Scholarship *151*
Spencer Risk Management and Insurance
Scholarship *355*
Spencer Scholarship *355*

Interior Design

Alan Lucas Memorial Educational Scholarship *100*
ASID Educational Foundation/Irene Winifred Eno
Grant *355*
ASID Educational Foundation/Joel Polsky Academic
Achievement Award *355*
ASID Educational Foundation/Yale R. Burge
Competition *355*
Association for Women in Architecture Scholarship *98*
Charles D. Mayo Scholarship *356*
IFDA Student Scholarship *356*
NAWIC Undergraduate Scholarships *100*
Network of Executive Women in Hospitality, Inc.
Scholarship *101*
Regents Professional Opportunity Scholarship *67*
Robert W. Thunen Memorial Scholarships *100*
Robert W. Thunen Memorial Scholarships *100*
South Dakota Retailers Association Scholarship
Program *69*
Worldstudio Foundation Scholarship Program *104*

International Studies

Central Intelligence Agency Undergraduate Scholarship
Program *56*
Culture Connection Foundation Scholarship *73*
Donald Riebhoff Memorial Scholarship *356*
Japan Studies Scholarship *312*
Malcolm Baldrige Scholarship *157*
Mayme and Herbert Frank Educational Fund *216*
Michael and Marie Marucci Scholarship *312*
PAAC Scholarship *357*

Journalism

AAJA/Cox Foundation Scholarship *357*
Abe Schecter Graduate Scholarship *185*
Academy of Television Arts and Sciences College
Television Awards *108*
Al Neuharth Free Spirit Scholarship *360*
Allison Fisher Scholarship *364*
American Legion Press Club of New Jersey and Post 170
Arthur Dehardt Memorial Scholarship *178*
American Press Institute Scholarship *361*
APTRA-Clete Roberts Memorial Journalism Scholarship
Award *358*
APTRA-Kathyrn Dettman Memorial Scholarship *359*
AQHF Journalism or Communications Scholarship *178*
Asian-American Journalists Association Scholarship *179*
Associated Press Television/Radio Association-Clete
Roberts Journalism Scholarship Awards *358*
Atlanta Press Club Journalism Scholarship Program *179*
Best Buy Enterprise Employee Scholarship *70*
Bill Farr Scholarship *369*
Bob Elliot- WMTW-TV 8 Journalism Scholarship *190*
Bobbi McCallum Memorial Scholarship *368*
Carl Greenberg Scholarship *369*
Carol A. Ratza Memorial Scholarship *138*
Carole Simpson Scholarship *185*
Charlotte Observer Minority Scholarships *146*
Chips Quinn Scholars Program *360*
Chips Quinn Scholarship *359*
Columnist Scholarship Contest *365*
Connecticut SPJ Bob Eddy Scholarship Program *359*
C-SPAN Scholarship Program *189*
David S. Barr Award *365*
David W. Miller Award for Student Journalists *370*

Dick Larsen Scholarship Program *189*
Dow Jones-Sports Editing Program *360*
Durwood McAlister Scholarship *361*
Economic Journalism Award *217*
Edward J. Nell Memorial Scholarship in Journalism *368*
Edward R. Hall Scholarship *76*
Entercom Portland Radio Scholarship Fund *367*
Ernest Hemingway Writing Awards *363*
Fisher Broadcasting, Inc., Scholarship for Minorities *181*
Future Journalists Scholarship Program *180*
Garth Reeves, Jr. Memorial Scholarships *187*
Georgia Press Educational Foundation Scholarships *361*
Gerald Boyd/Robin Stone Non-Sustaining Scholarship *364*
Gil Purcell Memorial Journalism Scholarship for Native Canadians *359*
Guy P. Gannett Scholarship Fund *363*
Harold K. Douthit Scholarship *366*
Harriet Irsay Scholarship Grant *178*
Hearin-Chandler Journalism Scholarship *362*
Helen Johnson Scholarship *369*
Herb Robinson Scholarship Program *190*
High School Journalism Workshops for Minorities *360*
Indiana Broadcasters Foundation Scholarship *362*
International Foodservice Editorial Council Communications Scholarship *182*
Jack Shaheen Mass Communications Scholarship Award *177*
Jackson Foundation Journalism Scholarship *367*
Jackson Foundation Journalism Scholarship Fund *366*
Jennifer Curtis Byler Scholarship for the Study of Public Affairs *184*
Jim Allard Broadcast Journalism Scholarship *359*
Joe Lipper Memorial Scholarship *368*
Joel Garcia Memorial Scholarship *180*
John Bayliss Broadcast Radio Scholarship *182*
John M. Will Journalism Scholarship *362*
Journalism and Broadcasting Scholarships *362*
Kathryn Dettman Memorial Journalism Scholarship *358*
Ken Inouye Scholarship *369*
Ken Kashiwahara Scholarship *186*
Kirk Sutlive Scholarship *361*
Lagrant Foundation Scholarship for Undergraduates *150*
Landmark Scholars Program *363*
Leonard M. Perryman Communications Scholarship for Ethnic Minority Students *189*
Lou and Carole Prato Sports Reporting Scholarship *186*
Lynn Dean Ford IABJ Scholarship Awards *181*
Mark Hass Journalism Award *367*
Mary Moy Quan Ing Memorial Scholarship Award *357*
Maryland SPJ Pro Chapter College Scholarship *369*
Mas Family Scholarship Award *149*
Mas Family Scholarships *146*
Michael S. Libretti Scholarship *184*
Mike Reynolds $1,000 Scholarship *186*
Minoru Yasui Memorial Scholarship Award *358*
Mississippi Press Association Education Foundation Scholarship *363*
Morris Newspaper Corporation Scholarship *361*
NABJ Scholarship *183*
National Asian-American Journalists Association Newhouse Scholarship *358*
National Association of Black Journalists and Newhouse Foundation Scholarship *364*
National Association of Black Journalists Non-Sustaining Scholarship Awards *364*
National Association of Broadcasters Grants for Research in Broadcasting *183*
National Gay and Lesbian Task Force Messenger-Anderson Journalism Scholarship *183*
National High School Journalist of the Year/Sister Rita Jeanne Scholarships *182*
National Institute for Labor Relations Research William B. Ruggles Journalism Scholarship *184*
National Writers Association Foundation Scholarships *184*
Native American Journalists Association Scholarships *365*
Nebraska Press Association Foundation, Inc., Scholarship *365*
Northwest Journalists of Color Scholarship *365*
NSPA Journalism Honor Roll Scholarship *365*
OAB Broadcast Scholarship *185*
Ohio Newspaper Women's Scholarship *366*
Ohio Newspapers Foundation Minority Scholarship *366*
Ohio Newspapers Foundation University Journalism Scholarship *366*
Outdoor Writers Association of America Bodie McDowell Scholarship Award *185*
Overseas Press Club Foundation Scholarships *367*
Pagel Graphic Arts Scholarship Fund *185*
Persina Scholarship for Minorities in Journalism *360*
PHD ARA Scholarship *179*

Philadelphia Association of Black Journalists Scholarship *367*
Philadelphia Tribune Scholarship *367*
Polish Arts Club of Buffalo Scholarship Foundation Trust *108*
President's $2500 Scholarship *186*
Reader's Digest Scholarship *189*
Robin Roberts/WBCA Sports Communications Scholarship Award *190*
Sacramento Bee Journalism Scholarship Program *368*
SAJA Journalism Scholarship *369*
Santa Clara University School of Law Computer and High Technology Law Journal Comment Contest *368*
South Carolina Press Association Foundation Newspaper Scholarships *370*
Texas Gridiron Club Scholarships *188*
The Betty Endicott/NTA-NCCB Student Scholarship *363*
The Carlos M. Castaneda Journalism Scholarship *361*
The Evert Clark/Seth Payne Award *364*
Thoroughbred Horse Racing's United Scholarship Trust *370*
Valley Press Club Scholarships, The Republican Scholarship; Photojournalism Scholarship, Channel 22 Scholarship *189*
Vincent Chin Memorial Scholarship *358*
Washington Press Club Foundation Scholarships *370*
William C. Rogers Scholarship *362*

Landscape Architecture

ANLA National Scholarship Endowment-Usrey Family Scholarship *341*
Anne Seaman Professional Grounds Management Society Memorial Scholarship *84*
ASLA Council of Fellows Scholarship *371*
Association for Women in Architecture Scholarship *98*
Benjamin C. Blackburn Scholarship *293*
California Water Awareness Campaign Water Scholar *79*
Carville M. Akehurst Memorial Scholarship *341*
Connecticut Nurserymen's Foundation, Inc. Scholarships *342*
Courtland Paul Scholarship *371*
Federated Garden Clubs of Connecticut, Inc. *137*
FEFPA Assistantship *99*
Francis Sylvia Zverina Scholarship *348*
Hawaii Chapter/David T. Woolsey Scholarship *371*
Herb Society Research Grants *92*
Horticulture Research Institute Timothy Bigelow and Palmer W. Bigelow, Jr. Scholarship *341*
Landscape Architecture Foundation/California Landscape Architectural Student Fund Scholarships Program *371*
Landscape Architecture Foundation/California Landscape Architecture Student Fund University Scholarship Program *349*
Life Member Montana Federation of Garden Clubs Scholarship *138*
National Garden Clubs, Inc. Scholarship Program *83*
NAWIC Undergraduate Scholarships *100*
Network of Executive Women in Hospitality, Inc. Scholarship *101*
Rain Bird Company Scholarship *372*
Regents Professional Opportunity Scholarship *67*
Spring Meadow Nursery Scholarship *342*
Ted Wilson Memorial Scholarship Foundation *212*
The Douglas Haskell Award for Student Journalism *98*
The EDSA Minority Scholarship *372*
United Agribusiness League Scholarship Program *77*
United Agricultural Benefit Trust Scholarship *77*
Western Reserve Herb Society Scholarship *348*
Worldstudio Foundation Scholarship Program *104*

Law Enforcement/Police Administration

Alphonso Deal Scholarship Award *199*
American Society of Criminology Gene Carte Student Paper Competition *199*
ATFAR Scholarship *372*
Bureau of Alcohol, Tobacco, Firearms and Explosives Scholarship-Law Enforcement *373*
Captain James J. Regan Scholarship *373*
Connecticut Association of Women Police Scholarship *199*
DEA Drug Abuse Prevention Service Awards *373*
Federal Criminal Investigators' Service Award *374*
Federal Criminal Investigators' Service Award *373*
Floyd Boring Award *374*
Illinois Police Corps Scholarship *373*
Indiana Sheriffs' Association Scholarship Program *199*
John Charles Wilson Scholarship *300*
North Carolina Police Corps Scholarship *200*
North Carolina Sheriffs' Association Undergraduate Criminal Justice Scholarship *200*
Robert C. Carson Memorial Bursary *198*

Sheryl A. Horak Memorial Scholarship *374*
Sheryl A. Horak Memorial Scholarship *373*
South Dakota Retailers Association Scholarship Program *69*
Utah Police Corps Scholarship Program *374*

Law/Legal Services

Alphonso Deal Scholarship Award *199*
American Criminal Justice Association-Lambda Alpha Epsilon National Scholarship *198*
American Society of Criminology Gene Carte Student Paper Competition *199*
Andrew K. Ruotolo, Jr. Memorial Scholarship *376*
Bernice Pickins Parsons Fund *377*
BESLA Scholarship Legal Writing Competition *375*
BPW Career Advancement Scholarship Program for Women *136*
Bullivant Houser Bailey-African American Chamber of Commerce Community College Scholarship Fund *152*
Culture Connection Foundation Scholarship *73*
Decatur H. Miller Scholarship *338*
Earl Warren Legal Training General Scholarship *377*
Elaine Osborne Jacobson Award for Women Working in Health Care Law *318*
Entertainment Law Initiative Legal Writing Contest *375*
Foley & Lardner Minority Scholarship Program *377*
Gayle and Harvey Rubin Scholarship Fund *330*
Giles Sutherland Rich Memorial Scholarship *376*
Graduate and Professional Scholarship Program-Maryland *210*
H. Fletcher Brown Scholarship *211*
Harry J. Donnelly Memorial Scholarship *69*
Harry Y. Cotton Memorial Scholarship *376*
Howard Brown Rickard Scholarship *101*
J.J. Barr Scholarship *139*
Janet L. Hoffmann Loan Assistance Repayment Program *230*
Jeanette R. Wolman Scholarship *375*
Jeannette Mowery Scholarship *211*
Law Student Essay Competition *375*
Law Student's Best Paper Award *377*
Lawrence "Larry" Frazier Memorial Scholarship *124*
National Association of Water Companies-New Jersey Chapter Scholarship *139*
National Federation of Paralegal Associates, Inc. West Scholarship *378*
NBLS Nelson Mandela Scholarship *378*
Notre Dame Law School Feminist Jurisprudence Writing Competition *376*
Oscar W. Rittenhouse Memorial Scholarship *376*
PIPLA Intellectual Property Law Student Leadership Scholarship *378*
Puerto Rican Bar Association Scholarship Award *379*
Raymond W. Cannon Memorial Scholarship Program *333*
Regents Professional Opportunity Scholarship *67*
Robert C. Carson Memorial Bursary *198*
Roscoe Hogan Environmental Law Essay Contest *379*
Sandy Brown Memorial Scholarship *378*
Santa Clara University School of Law Computer and High Technology Law Journal Comment Contest *368*
Shearman and Sterling Scholarship Program *378*
Spence Reese Scholarship Fund *259*
The Sidney B. Williams, Jr. Intellectual Property Law School Scholarship *379*
Townsend and Townsend and Crew LLP Diversity Scholarship Program *379*
Type I: Library Degree for Law School Graduates *375*
Warner Norcross and Judd LLP Scholarship for Minority Students *377*
Wiley Manuel Law Foundation Scholarship *380*
William Pew Religious Freedom Scholarship Competition *374*
William S. Bullinger Scholarship *376*

Library and Information Sciences

AIME Scholarship Fund *381*
Alice L. Haltom Educational Fund Scholarship *190*
Bernice Pickins Parsons Fund *377*
Brodart/Pennsylvania Library Association Undergraduate Scholarship Grant *381*
C-SPAN Scholarship Program *189*
E.J. Josey Scholarship Award *380*
Idaho Library Association Gardner Hanks Scholarship *381*
Idaho Library Association Library Science Scholarships *381*
John Wiley & Sons Best JASIST Paper Award *191*
Law Librarians in Continuing Education Courses *380*
Library Media Teacher Scholarship in Honor of Gene White and the Martha Dean Children *381*

Special Libraries Association Affirmative Action
Scholarship 381
Special Libraries Association Scholarship 382
The Begun Scholarship 380
Type I: Library Degree for Law School Graduates 375
Type III: Library Degree for Non-Law School
Graduates 380

Literature/English/Writing

ACES Copy Editing Scholarship 382
America's Intercultural Magazine (AIM) Short Story
Contest 382
Amy Lowell Poetry Traveling Scholarship 383
Arts Recognition and Talent Search (ARTS) 113
Atlanta Press Club Journalism Scholarship Program 179
Center for Gay and Lesbian Studies Undergraduate
Paper Awards 383
CIRI Foundation Susie Qimmiqsak Bevins Endowment
Scholarship Fund 110
Cultural Fellowship Grants 383
F. Lammot Belin Arts Scholarship 103
Film and Fiction Scholarship 111
Florence Lemcke Memorial Scholarship in Fine Arts 107
GUIDEPOSTS Young Writer's Contest 384
Helen James Brewer Scholarship 340
Herb Society Research Grants 92
International Foodservice Editorial Council
Communications Scholarship 182
Jack J. Isgur Foundation Scholarship 111
Justin G. Schiller Prize for Bibliographical Work in
Pre-20th-Century Children's Books 383
Lambda Iota Tau Literature Scholarship 384
Many Voices Residency Program 384
Michael and Marie Marucci Scholarship 312
National Ten Minute Play Contest 382
National Writers Association Foundation
Scholarships 184
Norma Ross Walter Scholarship 385
Outdoor Writers Association of America Bodie
McDowell Scholarship Award 185
R.L. Gillette Scholarship 382
Reader's Digest Scholarship 189
Robert P. Pula Memorial Scholarship 353
Scholastic Art and Writing Awards-Art Section 108
Sehar Saleha Ahmad and Abrahim Ekramullah Zafar
Foundation Scholarship 384
The Evert Clark/Seth Payne Award 364
Toyota Scholarship 157

Marine Biology

Aylesworth and Old Salt Scholarships 385
Bill Mason Memorial Scholarship Fund 80
Charles H. Bussman Undergraduate Scholarship 385
Frederic Fairfield Memorial Fund Award 141
John C. Bajus Scholarship 386
National Oceanic and Atmospheric Administration
Educational Partnership Program with Minority
Serving Institutions Undergraduate Scholarship 268
Paul W. Rodgers Scholarship 214
Rockefeller State Wildlife Scholarship 87
Skoch Scholarship 385
The MTS Student Scholarship 386

Marine/Ocean Engineering

American Society of Naval Engineers Scholarship 90
Association for Iron and Steel Technology David H.
Samson Scholarship 162
Charles H. Bussman Undergraduate Scholarship 385
Daniel Cubicciotti Student Award of the San Francisco
Section of the Electrochemical Society, Sponsored
by Structural Integrity Associates 137
H.H. Dow Memorial Student Achievement Award of the
Industrial Electrolysis and Electrochemical
Engineering Division of the Electrochemical Society,
Inc. 137
John C. Bajus Scholarship 386
ROV Scholarship 386
Society of Naval Architects and Marine Engineers
Undergraduate Scholarships 276
Student Achievement Awards of the Industrial
Electrolysis and Electrochemical Engineering
Division of the Electrochemical Society, Inc. 137
Student Research Awards of the Battery Division of the
Electrochemical Society, Inc. 137
The MTS Student Scholarship 386
The Paros-Digiquartz Scholarship 386

Materials Science, Engineering, and Metallurgy

AeA- Oregon Council Technology Scholarship
Program 88
AIAA Undergraduate Scholarship 89

AIST Alfred B. Glossbrenner and John Klusch
Scholarships 257
AIST William E. Schwabe Memorial Scholarship 257
Al Qoyawayma Award 163
Al-Ben Scholarship for Academic Incentive 164
Al-Ben Scholarship for Professional Merit 165
Al-Ben Scholarship for Scholastic Achievement 165
American Chemical Society, Rubber Division
Undergraduate Scholarship 158
American Electroplaters and Surface Finishers
Scholarships 158
American Society of Naval Engineers Scholarship 90
Arsham Amirikian Engineering Scholarship 172
ASM Materials Education Foundation Scholarships 255
ASM Outstanding Scholars Awards 255
Association for Facilities Engineering Cedar Valley
Chapter # 132 Scholarship 120
Association for Iron and Steel Technology Baltimore
Chapter Scholarship 387
Association for Iron and Steel Technology Benjamin F.
Fairless Scholarship 388
Association for Iron and Steel Technology David H.
Samson Scholarship 162
Association for Iron and Steel Technology Ferrous
Metallurgy Education Today (FeMET) 388
Association for Iron and Steel Technology National
Merit Scholarship 258
Association for Iron and Steel Technology Northwest
Member Chapter Scholarship 258
Association for Iron and Steel Technology Ohio Valley
Chapter Scholarship 135
Association for Iron and Steel Technology Pittsburgh
Chapter Scholarship 258
Association for Iron and Steel Technology Ronald E.
Lincoln Scholarship 388
Association for Iron and Steel Technology Southeast
Member Chapter Scholarship 258
Association for Iron and Steel Technology Willy Korf
Memorial Scholarship 388
Association for Women in Science College
Scholarship 86
Astronaut Scholarship Foundation 92
Barry M. Goldwater Scholarship and Excellence in
Education Program 92
BMW/SAE Engineering Scholarship 129
Coates, Wolff, Russell Mining Industry Scholarship 95
Collegiate Inventors Competition - Grand Prize 95
Collegiate Inventors Competition for Undergraduate
Students 95
Daniel Cubicciotti Student Award of the San Francisco
Section of the Electrochemical Society, Sponsored
by Structural Integrity Associates 137
Department of Energy Scholarship Program 148
Donald and Jean Cleveland-Willamette Valley Section
Scholarship 172
Donald and Shirley Hastings Scholarship 253
Edward D. Hendrickson/SAE Engineering
Scholarship 129
Edward J. Dulis Scholarship 256
Edward R. Hall Scholarship 76
Engineering Scholarship 158
Environmental Protection Scholarships 164
George A. Roberts Scholarship 256
Guidant Corporation Scholarship 195
H.H. Dow Memorial Student Achievement Award of the
Industrial Electrolysis and Electrochemical
Engineering Division of the Electrochemical Society,
Inc. 137
H.H. Harris Foundation Annual Scholarship 389
HENAAC Scholars Program 290
Hispanic Engineer National Achievement Awards
Corporation Scholarship Program 122
Independent Laboratories Institute Scholarship
Alliance 93
John M. Haniak Scholarship 256
Kumar Mehta Scholarship 97
Lockheed Martin Scholarship Program 164
Maine Metal Products Association Scholarship
Program 389
Mas Family Scholarship Award 149
Maureen L. and Howard N. Blitman, PE Scholarship to
Promote Diversity in Engineering 166
Micron Science and Technology Scholars Program 165
Mineralogy Society of America-Grant for Research in
Crystallography 215
MRCA Foundation Scholarship Program 94
National Society of Professional Engineers/Auxiliary
Scholarship 166
Nicholas J. Grant Scholarship 256
Northrop Grumman Corporation Scholarships 130
Paul H. Robbins Honorary Scholarship 166
Peter D. Courtois Concrete Construction Scholarship 97
Plastics Pioneers Scholarships 269

Professional Engineers in Industry Scholarship 167
Resistance Welder Manufacturers' Association
Scholarship 254
Robert L. Peaslee Detroit Brazing and Soldering Division
Scholarship 254
Society of Hispanic Professional Engineers
Foundation 168
Society of Plastics Engineers Scholarship Program 168
SPIE Educational Scholarships in Optical Science and
Engineering 93
Student Achievement Awards of the Industrial
Electrolysis and Electrochemical Engineering
Division of the Electrochemical Society, Inc. 137
Student Research Awards of the Battery Division of the
Electrochemical Society, Inc. 137
Technical Minority Scholarship 169
TMC/SAE Donald D. Dawson Technical Scholarship 129
TMS J. Keith Brimacombe Presidential Scholarship 266
TMS Outstanding Student Paper Contest-
Undergraduate 266
TMS/EPMD Gilbert Chin Scholarship 266
TMS/EPD Scholarship 267
TMS/International Symposium on Superalloys
Scholarship Program 267
TMS/LMD Scholarship Program 267
TMS/Structural Materials Division Scholarship 267
Universities Space Research Association Scholarship
Program 96
V. Mohan Malhotra Scholarship 97
Vermont Space Grant Consortium Scholarship
Program 94
Virginia Henry Memorial Scholarship 167
W.R. Grace Scholarship Award 97
William P. Woodside Founder's Scholarship 256
Yanmar/SAE Scholarship 271

Mathematics

Actuarial Scholarships for Minority Students 145
Arne Engebretsen Wisconsin Mathematics Council
Scholarship 240
California Mathematics Council - South Secondary
Education Scholarships 390
Dr. Freeman A. Hrabowski, III Scholarship 259
Ethel A. Neijahr Wisconsin Mathematics Council
Scholarship 240
HENAAC Scholars Program 290
Montana Space Grant Scholarship Program 125
NASA Rhode Island Space Grant Consortium Outreach
Scholarship for Undergraduate Students 288
National Oceanic and Atmospheric Administration
Educational Partnership Program with Minority
Serving Institutions Undergraduate Scholarship 268
Sister Mary Petronia Van Straten Wisconsin
Mathematics Council Scholarship 240

Mechanical Engineering

AACE International Competitive Scholarship 96
AeA- Oregon Council Technology Scholarship
Program 88
Agilent Mentoring Scholarship 194
Agnes Malakate Kezios Scholarship 393
AIAA Undergraduate Scholarship 89
Al Qoyawayma Award 163
Al-Ben Scholarship for Academic Incentive 164
Al-Ben Scholarship for Professional Merit 165
Al-Ben Scholarship for Scholastic Achievement 165
Allen J. Baldwin Scholarship 393
Alwin B. Newton Scholarship Fund 242
American Chemical Society, Rubber Division
Undergraduate Scholarship 158
American Council of Engineering Companies of Oregon
Scholarship 167
American Society of Mechanical Engineers Foundation
Scholarship 252
American Society of Mechanical Engineers Solid Waste
Processing Division Undergraduate Scholarship 391
American Society of Mechanical Engineers/First
Robotics Competition Scholarship 392
American Society of Mechanical Engineers-American
Society of Mechanical Engineers Auxiliary First
Clarke Scholarship 393
American Society of Naval Engineers Scholarship 90
Association for Facilities Engineering Cedar Valley
Chapter # 132 Scholarship 120
Association for Women in Science College
Scholarship 86
Astronaut Scholarship Foundation 92
Automotive Hall of Fame Educational Funds 162
Barry M. Goldwater Scholarship and Excellence in
Education Program 92
Bechtel Corporation Scholarship 176
Berna Lou Cartwright Scholarship 394
BMW/SAE Engineering Scholarship 129

Bradford White Corporation Scholarship *102*
Cargill Scholarship Program *70*
Chevron Texaco Corporation Scholarships *168*
Chevron/Texaco Scholars Program *177*
Coates, Wolff, Russell Mining Industry Scholarship *95*
Con Edison Scholarship *70*
Daimler Chrysler Corporation Scholarship *246*
Daniel Cubicciotti Student Award of the San Francisco
    Section of the Electrochemical Society, Sponsored
    by Structural Integrity Associates *137*
Dell Computer Corporation Scholarships *194*
Delta Air Lines Engineering Scholarship *132*
Delta Faucet Company Scholarship Program *102*
Department of Energy Scholarship Program *148*
Donald C. Hyde Essay Program *171*
Downriver Detroit Chapter 198 Scholarship *273*
Dupont Company Scholarships *168*
Edward D. Hendrickson/SAE Engineering
    Scholarship *129*
Engineering Scholarship *158*
F.W. "Beich" Beichley Scholarship *392*
FEFPA Assistantship *99*
Fort Wayne Chapter 56 Scholarship *274*
Frank William and Dorothy Given Miller
    Scholarship *392*
Garland Duncan Scholarship *392*
General Motors Foundation Undergraduate
    Scholarships *168*
Guidant Corporation Scholarship *195*
H.H. Dow Memorial Student Achievement Award of the
    Industrial Electrolysis and Electrochemical
    Engineering Division of the Electrochemical Society,
    Inc. *137*
High Technology Scholars Program *141*
Hispanic Engineer National Achievement Awards
    Corporation Scholarship Program *122*
HSF/General Motors Scholarship *149*
HSF/Society of Hispanic Professional Engineers, Inc.
    Scholarship Program *174*
HSF/Toyota Scholarship Program *149*
Independent Laboratories Institute Scholarship
    Alliance *93*
Instrumentation, Systems, and Automation Society (ISA)
    Scholarship Program *123*
Jack Gilstrap Scholarship *171*
John and Elsa Gracik Scholarships *392*
Kenneth Andrew Roe Scholarship *392*
Key Technology Scholarship *84*
LINC TELACU Engineering Award *163*
Lockheed Aeronautics Company Scholarships *246*
Louis T. Klauder Scholarship *171*
Maine Metal Products Association Scholarship *395*
Maine Metal Products Association Scholarship
    Program *389*
Mas Family Scholarship Award *149*
Mas Family Scholarships *146*
Maureen L. and Howard N. Blitman, PE Scholarship to
    Promote Diversity in Engineering *166*
Melvin R. Green Scholarship *393*
Michigan Society of Professional Engineers
    Undesignated Grant *165*
Micron Science and Technology Scholars Program *165*
Montana Space Grant Scholarship Program *125*
MRCA Foundation Scholarship Program *94*
NASA Delaware Space Grant Undergraduate Tuition
    Scholarship *94*
National Society of Professional Engineers/Auxiliary
    Scholarship *166*
NAWIC Undergraduate Scholarships *100*
North Central Region 9 Scholarship *275*
Northrop Grumman Corporation Scholarships *130*
Parsons Brinckerhoff-Jim Lammie Scholarship *171*
Paul H. Robbins Honorary Scholarship *166*
PHCC Educational Foundation Need-Based
    Scholarship *102*
PHCC Educational Foundation Scholarship
    Program *103*
Phoenix Chapter 67 Scholarship *275*
Professional Engineers in Industry Scholarship *167*
Ralph K. Hillquist Honorary SAE Scholarship *270*
Reuben Trane Scholarship *242*
Robert F. Sammataro Pressure Vessels and Piping
    Division Memorial Scholarship *393*
Rocky Mountain Coal Mining Institute Scholarship *167*
SBC Foundation Scholarship *156*
Sigma Xi Grants-In-Aid of Research *84*
Society of Hispanic Professional Engineers
    Foundation *168*
Society of Plastics Engineers Scholarship Program *168*
SPIE Educational Scholarships in Optical Science and
    Engineering *93*

Student Achievement Awards of the Industrial
    Electrolysis and Electrochemical Engineering
    Division of the Electrochemical Society, Inc. *137*
Student Research Awards of the Battery Division of the
    Electrochemical Society, Inc. *137*
Sylvia W. Farny Scholarship *394*
Technical Minority Scholarship *169*
Ted Wilson Memorial Scholarship Foundation *212*
Texas Society of Professional Engineers (TSPE) Regional
    Scholarships *169*
TMC/SAE Donald D. Dawson Technical Scholarship *129*
Transit Hall of Fame Scholarship Award Program *171*
Trimmer Education Foundation Scholarships for
    Construction Management *172*
Universities Space Research Association Scholarship
    Program *96*
UPS Corporate Scholars Program/Internship *157*
Utah Society of Professional Engineers Scholarship *169*
Vertical Flight Foundation Scholarship *132*
Virginia Henry Memorial Scholarship *167*
Westvaco/Wickliffe Scholarship *165*
Wichita Chapter 52 Scholarship *276*
William E. Weisel Scholarship Fund *246*
William J. & Marijane E. Adams, Jr. Scholarship *393*
Wyoming Trucking Association Trust Fund
    Scholarship *158*
Yanmar/SAE Scholarship *271*
YouthForce 2020 Scholarship Program *103*

Meteorology/Atmospheric Science

A.T. Anderson Memorial Scholarship *89*
Alabama Funeral Directors Association Scholarship *397*
American Meteorological Society 75th Anniversary
    Scholarship *397*
American Meteorological Society Dr. Pedro Grau
    Undergraduate Scholarship *397*
American Meteorological Society Howard H. Hanks, Jr.
    Meteorological Scholarship *397*
American Meteorological Society Howard T. Orville
    Meteorology Scholarship *398*
American Meteorological Society Industry
    Undergraduate Scholarships *89*
American Meteorological Society Mark J. Schroeder
    Scholarship in Meteorology *398*
American Meteorological Society Richard and Helen
    Hagemeyer Scholarship *398*
American Meteorological Society Werner A. Baum
    Undergraduate Scholarship *398*
American Meteorological Society/Industry Minority
    Scholarships *398*
Association for Women in Science College
    Scholarship *86*
Astronaut Scholarship Foundation *92*
Burlington Northern Santa Fe Foundation
    Scholarship *89*
Carl W. Kreitzberg Endowed Scholarship *292*
Carrol C. Hall Memorial Scholarship *95*
Daniel Cubicciotti Student Award of the San Francisco
    Section of the Electrochemical Society, Sponsored
    by Structural Integrity Associates *137*
Environmental Protection Agency Tribal Lands
    Environmental Science Scholarship *135*
Ethan and Allan Murphy Memorial Scholarship *398*
Father James B. MacElwane Annual Awards *399*
Garden Club of America Awards for Summer
    Environmental Studies *80*
George S. Benton Scholarship *399*
Guillermo Salazar Rodrigues Scholarship *399*
H.H. Dow Memorial Student Achievement Award of the
    Industrial Electrolysis and Electrochemical
    Engineering Division of the Electrochemical Society,
    Inc. *137*
John R. Hope Scholarship *399*
Loren W. Crow Scholarship *399*
Math and Science Scholarship Program for Alabama
    Teachers *135*
NASA Delaware Space Grant Undergraduate Tuition
    Scholarship *94*
National Oceanic and Atmospheric Administration
    Educational Partnership Program with Minority
    Serving Institutions Undergraduate Scholarship *268*
National Oceanic and Atmospheric Administration
    Educational Partnership Program with Minority
    Serving Institutions Undergraduate Scholarship *268*
Om and Saraswati Bahethi Scholarship *399*
Paul and Helen Trussel Science and Technology
    Scholarship *93*
Sigma Xi Grants-In-Aid of Research *84*
Student Achievement Awards of the Industrial
    Electrolysis and Electrochemical Engineering
    Division of the Electrochemical Society, Inc. *137*
Student Research Awards of the Battery Division of the
    Electrochemical Society, Inc. *137*

University and Community College System of Nevada
    NASA Space Grant and Fellowship Program *125*
Vermont Space Grant Consortium Scholarship
    Program *94*
West Virginia Space Grant Consortium Undergraduate
    Scholarship Program *126*

Military and Defense Studies

Lockheed Martin Scholarship Program *164*

Museum Studies

Adele Filene Travel Award *105*
ASCSA Summer Sessions Open Scholarships *88*
Mineralogical Society of America-Grant for Student
    Research in Mineralogy and Petrology *214*
Mineralogy Society of America-Grant for Research in
    Crystallography *215*
Stella Blum Research Grant *105*
U.S. Marine Corps Historical Center Grants *340*

Music

American College of Musicians/National Guild of Piano
    Teachers 200-Dollar Scholarships *401*
American Orff-Schulwerk Association Research
    Grant *220*
Apha Delta Kappa Foundation Fine Arts Grants *108*
Astral Career Grant *406*
Bach Organ and Keyboard Scholarship Fund *406*
BEEM Foundation Scholarship *401*
Charlotte Plummer Owen Memorial Scholarship *407*
Chopin Foundation of the United States Scholarship *402*
Constant Memorial Scholarship for Aquidneck Island
    Residents *114*
Dan Schutte Scholarship *403*
Dorchester Women's Club Scholarship *402*
Elaine Rendler-Rene Dosogne-Georgetown Chorale
    Scholarship *403*
Emerging Young Artist Awards *110*
F. Lammot Belin Arts Scholarship *103*
Funk Family Memorial Scholarship *403*
General Federation of Women's Clubs of Massachusetts
    Music Scholarship *225*
GIA Publication Pastoral Musician Scholarship *404*
Gladys Stone Wright Scholarship *240*
Helen May Bulter Memorial Scholarship *241*
Houston Symphony League Concerto Competition *403*
International Music Competition of the ARD
    Munich *403*
Jack J. Isgur Foundation Scholarship *111*
Janet B. Sondheim Scholarship *110*
John Lennon Scholarship Program *401*
Martha Ann Stark Memorial Scholarship *241*
Minority Travel Fund Award *401*
Mu Phi Epsilon Scholarship Fund *402*
Music Committee Scholarship *401*
Music Technology Scholarship *241*
MuSonics Scholarship *404*
National Association of Pastoral Musicians Members'
    Scholarship *404*
NPM Board of Directors Scholarship *404*
NPM Composers and Authors Scholarship *404*
NPM Koinonia/Board of Directors Scholarship *404*
NPM Miami Valley Catholic Church Musicians
    Scholarship *405*
NPM Perrot Scholarship *405*
Oregon Catholic Press Scholarship *405*
Paluch Family Foundation/World Library Publications
    Scholarship *405*
Peermusic Latin Scholarship *401*
R.L. Gillette Scholarship *382*
Richard and Ethel Koff Memorial Scholarship Fund *402*
Sigma Alpha Iota Graduate Performance Awards *406*
Sigma Alpha Iota Jazz Performance Awards *406*
Sigma Alpha Iota Jazz Studies Scholarship *406*
Sigma Alpha Iota Music Business/Technology
    Scholarship *407*
Sigma Alpha Iota Music Therapy Scholarship *407*
Sigma Alpha Iota Philanthropies Undergraduate
    Performance Scholarships *407*
Sigma Alpha Iota Summer Music Scholarships in the
    U.S. or abroad *407*
Sigma Alpha Iota Visually Impaired Scholarship *236*
Steven C. Warner Scholarship *405*
Summer Music Scholarships *402*
Theodore Mazza Scholarship *103*
Volkwein Memorial Scholarship *241*
Young Composers Awards *406*

Natural Resources

A.T. Anderson Memorial Scholarship *89*
American Ground Water Trust-AMTROL, Inc.
    Scholarship *170*

American Ground Water Trust-Claude Laval
Corporation The Ben Everson Scholarship *170*
Arizona Hydrological Survey Student Scholarship *212*
Association of California Water Agencies
Scholarships *91*
Benjamin C. Blackburn Scholarship *293*
Bill Mason Memorial Scholarship Fund *80*
Budweiser Conservation Scholarship Program *140*
California Groundwater Association Scholarship *213*
California Water Awareness Campaign Water Scholar *79*
Carol A. Ratza Memorial Scholarship *138*
Charles A. Holt Indiana Wildlife Federation Endowment
Scholarship *409*
Charles P. Bell Conservation Scholarship *136*
Clair A. Hill Scholarship *91*
Coates, Wolff, Russell Mining Industry Scholarship *95*
Conservation of Natural Resources Scholarship *81*
Conservation of Natural Resources Scholarship for
Nontraditional Students *81*
Department of Energy Scholarship Program *148*
Desk and Derrick Educational Trust *92*
Donald A. Williams Scholarship Soil Conservation
Scholarship *216*
Donald W. Fogarty International Student Paper
Competition *144*
Dr. Alan Beaven Forestry Scholarship *294*
Edward R. Hall Scholarship *76*
Frances M. Peacock Scholarship for Native Bird
Habitat *408*
Francis Blackduck Memorial "Strong Like Two People"
Awards *293*
Garden Club of America Awards for Summer
Environmental Studies *80*
George A. Hall / Harold F. Mayfield Award *87*
George R. Crafton Scholarship *81*
Henry Rodriguez Reclamation College Scholarship and
Internship *285*
Howard Brown Rickard Scholarship *101*
J .J. Barr Scholarship *139*
Jim Bourque Scholarship *220*
John Mabry Forestry Scholarship *410*
Maine Campground Owners Association
Scholarship *409*
Malcolm Pirnie, Inc. Scholars Program *169*
Masonic Range Science Scholarship *76*
Mellon Ecology Program (S.E.E.D.S) *411*
Melville H. Cohee Student Leader Conservation
Scholarship *410*
Mineralogical Society of America-Grant for Student
Research in Mineralogy and Petrology *214*
Mineralogy Society of America-Grant for Research in
Crystallography *215*
National Association of Water Companies-New Jersey
Chapter Scholarship *139*
National Network for Environmental Management
Studies Fellowship *411*
New England Water Works George E. Watters Memorial
Scholarship. *175*
Oregon Foundation for Blacktail Deer Outdoor and
Wildlife Scholarship *140*
PACD Auxiliary Scholarships *76*
Paul A. Stewart Awards *88*
Paul and Helen Trussel Science and Technology
Scholarship *93*
Paul W. Rodgers Scholarship *214*
Ralph W. Abele Conservation Scholarship *295*
Recreational Boating Industries Educational Foundation
Scholarships *141*
Richard A. Herbert Memorial Scholarship *408*
Rockefeller State Wildlife Scholarship *87*
Royden M. Bodley Scholarship *87*
Russell A. Cookingham Scholarship *140*
South Dakota Board of Regents Bjugstad Scholarship *77*
SWCS Melville H. Cohee Student Leader Conservation
Scholarship *85*
SWCS/Betty Broemmelsiek Scholarship *410*
Texas Outdoor Writers Association Scholarship *188*
The Park People $4000 Scholarship *410*
Timothy L. Taschwer Scholarship *216*
Truman D. Picard Scholarship *75*
VASWCD Educational Foundation, Inc. Scholarship
Awards Program *296*
Weyerhaeuser/UNCF Corporate Scholars *157*
Wildlife Leadership Awards *141*

Natural Sciences

A.T. Anderson Memorial Scholarship *89*
Association for Women in Science College
Scholarship *86*
Association of California Water Agencies
Scholarships *91*
Barry M. Goldwater Scholarship and Excellence in
Education Program *92*

Beulah Frey Environmental Scholarship *293*
Bill Mason Memorial Scholarship Fund *80*
Budweiser Conservation Scholarship Program *140*
Burlington Northern Santa Fe Foundation
Scholarship *89*
Carol A. Ratza Memorial Scholarship *138*
Clair A. Hill Scholarship *91*
Coates, Wolff, Russell Mining Industry Scholarship *95*
Copernicus Award *413*
Department of Energy Scholarship Program *148*
Desk and Derrick Educational Trust *92*
Donald A. Williams Scholarship Soil Conservation
Scholarship *216*
Edward R. Hall Scholarship *76*
Environmental Protection Agency Tribal Lands
Environmental Science Scholarship *135*
Exploration Fund Grants *88*
Harvard Travellers Club Grants *96*
Henry Rodriguez Reclamation College Scholarship and
Internship *285*
Jim Bourque Scholarship *220*
MARC Undergraduate Student Training in Academic
Research U*Star Awards *140*
Math and Science Scholarship Program for Alabama
Teachers *135*
Mineralogical Society of America-Grant for Student
Research in Mineralogy and Petrology *214*
Mineralogy Society of America-Grant for Research in
Crystallography *215*
MRCA Foundation Scholarship Program *94*
NASA Nebraska Space Grant *125*
Oregon Foundation for Blacktail Deer Outdoor and
Wildlife Scholarship *140*
Paul and Helen Trussel Science and Technology
Scholarship *93*
Paul W. Rodgers Scholarship *214*
Paul W. Ruckes Scholarship *190*
Royden M. Bodley Scholarship *87*
Society of Hispanic Professional Engineers
Foundation *168*
SWCS Melville H. Cohee Student Leader Conservation
Scholarship *85*
Vermont Space Grant Consortium Scholarship
Program *94*
West Virginia Space Grant Consortium Undergraduate
Scholarship Program *126*
William R. Goldfarb Memorial Scholarship *145*
Youth Activity Fund *412*

Near and Middle East Studies

ASCSA Summer Sessions Open Scholarships *88*
Cyprus American Archaeological Research Institute
Helena Wylde and Stuart Swiny Fellowship *96*
Paul W. Ruckes Scholarship *190*

Nuclear Science

A.T. Anderson Memorial Scholarship *89*
American Nuclear Society James R. Vogt
Scholarship *248*
American Nuclear Society Operations and Power
Scholarship *248*
American Nuclear Society Undergraduate
Scholarships *249*
American Society of Naval Engineers Scholarship *90*
ANS Incoming Freshman Scholarship *413*
Arizona Hydrological Survey Student Scholarship *212*
Association for Women in Science College
Scholarship *86*
Barry M. Goldwater Scholarship and Excellence in
Education Program *92*
Burlington Northern Santa Fe Foundation
Scholarship *89*
Charles (Tommy) Thomas Memorial Scholarship
Division Scholarship *249*
Decommissioning, Decontamination, and Reutilization
Scholarship *249*
Delayed Education for Women Scholarships *249*
Department of Energy Scholarship Program *148*
Desk and Derrick Educational Trust *92*
Hispanic Engineer National Achievement Awards
Corporation Scholarship Program *122*
John and Muriel Landis Scholarship Awards *249*
John R. Lamarsh Scholarship *249*
Joseph R. Dietrich Scholarship *250*
Paul and Helen Trussel Science and Technology
Scholarship *93*
Paul Cole Scholarship *332*
Raymond DiSalvo Scholarship *413*
Robert G. Lacy Scholarship *250*
Robert T. (Bob) Liner Scholarship *250*
Society of Hispanic Professional Engineers
Foundation *168*

Universities Space Research Association Scholarship
Program *96*
West Virginia Space Grant Consortium Undergraduate
Scholarship Program *126*

Nursing

AACN Educational Advancement Scholarships-BSN
Completion *415*
Abbott/Pamela Balzer Career Mobility Scholarship *418*
Additional ENA Foundation Undergraduate
Scholarships *421*
AETNA Scholarship *427*
Albert and Florence Newton Nurse Scholarship Newton
Fund *429*
Albert E. and Florence W. Newton Nurse
Scholarship *433*
Alberta Heritage Scholarship Fund Aboriginal Health
Careers Bursary *135*
Alice Newell Joslyn Medical Fund *207*
Allied Health Student Loan Program-New Mexico *210*
Amarillo Area Foundation Scholarships *53*
American Indian Nurse Scholarship Awards *429*
American Legion Auxiliary Department of Arizona
Nurses' Scholarships *415*
American Legion Auxiliary Department of Arkansas
Nurse Scholarship *415*
American Legion Auxiliary Department of Nebraska
Nurse's Gift Tuition Scholarship *416*
American Legion Auxiliary Department of Nebraska
Practical Nurse Scholarship *416*
American Legion Auxiliary Department of New Mexico
Past President Parley Nurses Scholarship *416*
American Legion Auxiliary Department of North Dakota
Past President's Parley Nurses' Scholarship *417*
American Legion Auxiliary Department of Ohio Past
President's Parley Nurses' Scholarship *417*
American Legion Auxiliary Department of Oregon
Nurses Scholarship *417*
American Legion Auxiliary, Department of Idaho
Nursing Scholarship *415*
American Nephrology Nurses' Association American
Regent Career Mobility Scholarship *418*
American Nephrology Nurses' Association AMGEN
Career Mobility Scholarship *419*
American Nephrology Nurses' Association Anthony J.
Janetti, Inc. Career Mobility Scholarship *419*
American Nephrology Nurses' Association Career
Mobility Scholarship *419*
American Nephrology Nurses' Association NNCC
Career Mobility Scholarship *419*
American Nephrology Nurses' Association Watson
Pharma, Inc. Career Mobility Scholarship *419*
Anne Lindeman Memorial Scholarship *142*
AQHF Education or Nursing Scholarship *220*
Archbold Scholarship Program *327*
Associate Degree Nursing Scholarship Program *424*
Association of Peri-Operative Registered Nurses *420*
Barbara Palo Foster Memorial Scholarship *433*
Bernice Pickins Parsons Fund *377*
Bertha P. Singer Nurses Scholarship *432*
Breakthrough to Nursing Scholarships for Racial/Ethnic
Minorities *422*
Central Valley Nursing Scholarship *424*
CHANCES Scholarship Program *420*
Charles Kunz Memorial Undergraduate Scholarship *422*
Continuing Education for School Nurses
Scholarship *420*
Deloras Jones RN Scholarship Program *425*
Democratic Nursing Organization of South Africa Study
Fund *421*
Dr. Franz and Kathryn Stenzel Fund *330*
Dr. Hilda Richards Scholarship *427*
Dr. Lauranne Sams Scholarship *427*
Education Incentive Loan Forgiveness Contract-
Idaho *227*
Eight & Forty Lung and Respiratory Disease Nursing
Scholarship Fund *418*
Eleanor M. Morrissey Scholarship *421*
Eleanora G. Wylie Scholarship Fund for Nursing *423*
Elizabeth Garde Nursing Scholarship *421*
ENA Foundation CEN Undergraduate Scholarship *422*
Foundation of the National Student Nurses' Association
Career Mobility Scholarship *422*
Foundation of the National Student Nurses' Association
General Scholarships *423*
Foundation of the National Student Nurses' Association
Specialty Scholarship *423*
Francis L. Booth Medical Scholarship sponsored by
LAVFW Department of Maine *327*
Franks Foundation Scholarship *432*
Goldman Family Fund, New Leader Scholarship *210*
Graduate and Professional Scholarship Program-
Maryland *210*

Graduate Study in Cancer Research or Nurse Practitioner *423*
Gustavus B. Capito Fund *423*
Health Careers Scholarship *209*
Health Professions Education Scholarship Program *208*
Health Professions Preparatory Scholarship Program *425*
Health Resources and Services Administration-Bureau of Health Professions Scholarships for Disadvantaged Students *211*
Hobble (LPN) Nursing Scholarship *418*
Illinois Department of Public Health Center for Rural Health Nursing Education Scholarship Program *327*
Indian Health Service Health Professions Pre-professional Scholarship *318*
Indiana Health Care Foundation Nursing Scholarship *425*
Indiana Nursing Scholarship Fund *433*
Janet L. Hoffmann Loan Assistance Repayment Program *230*
June Gill Nursing Scholarship *429*
Kaiser Permanente School of Anesthesia Scholarship *427*
Loan Forgiveness Program for Nurses, Doctors, Midwives, and Pharmacists *325*
Loan Forgiveness Program for State Veterans Homes Nurses *432*
M.D. "Jack" Murphy Memorial Scholarship *418*
M.V. McCrae Memorial Nurses Scholarship *416*
Margaret Miller Memorial Undergraduate Scholarship *422*
Margarite McAlpin Nurse's Scholarship *417*
Marion A. and Eva S. Peeples Scholarships *230*
Marion A. Lindeman Scholarship *331*
Martha R. Dudley LVN/LPN Scholarship *428*
Mary Marshall Practical Nursing Scholarships *434*
Mary Marshall Registered Nursing Program Scholarships *434*
Maryland State Nursing Scholarship and Living Expenses Grant *425*
Massachusetts Gilbert Matching Student Grant Program *426*
Mayo Foundations Scholarship *428*
McFarland Charitable Nursing Scholarship *423*
Medical Career Scholarship *319*
Michigan Nursing Scholarship *426*
Minnesota Nurses Loan Forgiveness Program *328*
Minority Nurse Magazine Scholarship Program *426*
Monster Non-RN Undergraduate Scholarship *422*
National Association of Directors of Nursing Administration in Long Term Care-Upward Bound Scholarship *427*
National Health Service Corps Scholarship Program *325*
National Society Daughters of the American Revolution Caroline E. Holt Nursing Scholarships *428*
National Society Daughters of the American Revolution Irene and Daisy MacGregor Memorial Scholarship *329*
National Society Daughters of the American Revolution Madeline Pickett (Halbert) Cogswell Nursing Scholarship *329*
National Society Daughters of the American Revolution Mildred Nutting Nursing Scholarship *429*
NBNA Board of Directors Scholarship *428*
Neuroscience Nursing Foundation Scholarship *415*
Nightingale Awards of Pennsylvania Nursing Scholarship *430*
NLN Ella McKinney Scholarship Fund *431*
North Carolina Student Loan Program for Health, Science, and Mathematics *211*
North Dakota Board of Nursing Education Loan Program *430*
Northern Ontario Aboriginal Nurses Award *414*
Nurse Education Scholarship Loan Program (NESLP) *430*
Nurse Scholars Program—Undergraduate (North Carolina) *430*
Nursing Education Loan/Scholarship-BSN *426*
Nursing Loan Forgiveness for Healthier Futures Program *432*
Nursing Scholarship for High School Seniors *434*
Nursing Scholastic Achievement Scholarship for Lutheran College Students *420*
Nursing Spectrum Scholarship *428*
Nursing Student Loan Program *434*
Nursing Student Loan-For-Service Program *429*
Nursing Student Scholarship *426*
ONF-Smith Education Scholarship *432*
ONS Foundation Ethnic Minority Bachelor's Scholarship *430*
ONS Foundation Josh Gottheil Memorial Bone Marrow Transplant Career Development Awards *431*
ONS Foundation Nursing Outcomes Research Grant *330*
ONS Foundation Oncology Nursing Society Research Grant *330*

ONS Foundation Roberta Pierce Scofield Bachelor's Scholarships *431*
ONS Foundation/Oncology Nursing Certification Corporation Bachelor's Scholarships *431*
ONS Foundation/Pearl Moore Career Development Awards *431*
Opportunities Scholarship Program *421*
Ordean Scholarship Program *67*
Past Presidents Parley Health Care Scholarship *207*
Past Presidents Parley Registered Nurse Scholarship *417*
Past Presidents Parley Scholarship-Missouri *416*
Phoebe Pember Memorial Scholarship *433*
Pilot International Foundation Ruby Newhall Memorial Scholarship *331*
Pilot International Foundation Scholarship Program *331*
Pilot International Foundation/Lifeline Scholarship Program *332*
Primary Care Resource Initiative for Missouri Loan Program *210*
Promise of Nursing Scholarship *423*
Regents Professional Opportunity Scholarship *67*
Registered Nurse Education Loan Repayment Program *424*
RN Education Scholarship Program *424*
Scholarship Program for Former Soviet Union Emigres Training in the Health Sciences *209*
Sodexho Scholarship *333*
Sonne Scholarship *424*
Suburban Hospital Healthcare System Scholarship *333*
The National Nursing Scholarship *421*
Tuition Reduction for Non-Resident Nursing Students *426*
Walter and Marie Schmidt Scholarship *432*
Walter Reed Smith Scholarship *154*
William R. Goldfarb Memorial Scholarship *145*
Wisconsin League for Nursing Inc., Scholarship *434*
Workforce Incentive Program *233*

Occupational Safety and Health

America Responds Memorial Scholarship *434*
ASSE-Edwin P. Granberry, Jr. Distinguished Service Award Scholarship *435*
ASSE-Gulf Coast Past Presidents Scholarship *435*
ASSE-Marsh Risk Consulting Scholarship *435*
ASSE-Region IV/Edwin P. Granberry Scholarship *435*
ASSE-United Parcel Service Scholarship *435*
Campus Safety, Health and Environmental Management Association Scholarship Award Program *295*
Ford Motor Company Scholarship-Undergraduate *435*
Georgia Chapter of ASSE Annual Scholarship *436*
Gold Country Section and Region II Scholarship *436*
Harold F. Polston Scholarship *436*
Harry Taback 9/11 Memorial Scholarship *436*
John C. Bajus Scholarship *386*
Liberty Mutual Scholarship *436*
National Environmental Health Association/American Academy of Sanitarians Scholarship *437*
Northeastern Illinois Chapter Scholarship *436*
Scott Dominguez-Craters of the Moon Scholarship *436*
The MTS Student Scholarship *386*
United Parcel Service Diversity Scholarship Program *292*

Oceanography

Bill Mason Memorial Scholarship Fund *80*
Charles H. Bussman Undergraduate Scholarship *385*
National Oceanic and Atmospheric Administration Educational Partnership Program with Minority Serving Institutions Undergraduate Scholarship *268*
Warren, Sanders, McNaughton Oceanographic Scholarship *437*

Peace and Conflict Studies

Mayme and Herbert Frank Educational Fund *216*
National Peace Essay Contest *438*
Racial/Ethnic Leadership Education (RELE) *437*

Performing Arts

Academy of Television Arts and Sciences College Television Awards *108*
Adele Filene Travel Award *105*
American Orff-Schulwerk Association Research Grant *220*
Arts Recognition and Talent Search (ARTS) *113*
Arts Scholarship Program *114*
Astral Career Grant *406*
Charlotte Plummer Owen Memorial Scholarship *407*
Chopin Foundation of the United States Scholarship *402*
CIRI Foundation Susie Qimmiqsak Bevins Endowment Scholarship Fund *110*
Congressional Black Caucus Spouses Performing Arts Scholarship *438*

Contemporary Record Society National Competition for Performing Artists *439*
Cultural Fellowship Grants *383*
Donna Reed Performing Arts Scholarships *439*
Dorchester Women's Club Scholarship *402*
Emerging Young Artist Awards *110*
F. Lammot Belin Arts Scholarship *103*
General Federation of Women's Clubs of Massachusetts Music Scholarship *225*
Gina Bachauer International Artists Piano Competition Award *439*
Gladys Stone Wright Scholarship *240*
Gunild Keetman Assistance Fund *220*
Helen May Butler Memorial Scholarship *241*
Jack J. Isgur Foundation Scholarship *111*
Kosciuszko Foundation Chopin Piano Competition *439*
Lotte Lenya Competition for Singers *440*
Madeira Shaner Scholarship *440*
Marc A. Klein Playwright Award *438*
Martha Ann Stark Memorial Scholarship *241*
Music Committee Scholarship *401*
Music Technology Scholarship *241*
NOA Vocal Competition/ Legacy Award Program *113*
Polish Arts Club of Buffalo Scholarship Foundation Trust *108*
Robert W. Thunen Memorial Scholarships *100*
Sigma Alpha Iota Graduate Performance Awards *406*
Sigma Alpha Iota Philanthropies Undergraduate Performance Scholarships *407*
Sigma Alpha Iota Philanthropies Undergraduate Scholarships *236*
Sigma Alpha Iota Summer Music Scholarships in the U.S. or abroad *407*
Sigma Alpha Iota Visually Impaired Scholarship *236*
Sorantin Young Artist Award *440*
Stella Blum Research Grant *105*
Volkwein Memorial Scholarship *241*
VSA arts-Panasonic Young Soloist Award *440*
VSA arts-Rosemary Kennedy International Young Soloist Award *441*
William Kapell International Piano Competition and Festival *438*
Young Artist Competition *441*
Young Composers Awards *406*

Pharmacy

American Pharmacy Services Corporation Scholarship/ Loan *442*
Cardinal Health Scholarship *70*
CVS/Pharmacy Scholarship *442*
Edna Aimes Scholarship *328*
Health Professions Preparatory Scholarship Program *425*
Loan Forgiveness Program for Nurses, Doctors, Midwives, and Pharmacists *325*
Northern Alberta Development Council Bursary for Pharmacy Students *441*
Phi Lambda Sigma-Glaxo Wellcome-AFPE First Year Graduate Scholarship *441*
Regents Professional Opportunity Scholarship *67*
Wyeth Scholarship *142*

Philosophy

ASCSA Summer Sessions Open Scholarships *88*

Photojournalism/Photography

Academy of Television Arts and Sciences College Television Awards *108*
American Legion Press Club of New Jersey and Post 170 Arthur Dehardt Memorial Scholarship *178*
Arts Recognition and Talent Search (ARTS) *113*
Asian-American Journalists Association Scholarship *179*
Bob East Scholarship *443*
Carol A. Ratza Memorial Scholarship *138*
Connecticut SPJ Bob Eddy Scholarship Program *359*
Fisher Broadcasting, Inc., Scholarship for Minorities *181*
Future Journalists Scholarship Program *180*
International Foodservice Editorial Council Communications Scholarship *182*
Janet B. Sondheim Scholarship *110*
Joel Garcia Memorial Scholarship *180*
Larry Fullerton Photojournalism Scholarship *442*
Leonard M. Perryman Communications Scholarship for Ethnic Minority Students *189*
Lynn Dean Ford IABJ Scholarship Awards *181*
National Association of Black Journalists Non-Sustaining Scholarship Awards *364*
National Press Photographers Foundation Still Photographer Scholarship *443*
National Press Photographers Foundation Television News Scholarship *443*
National Writers Association Foundation Scholarships *184*

Nebraska Press Association Foundation, Inc., Scholarship *365*
Outdoor Writers Association of America Bodie McDowell Scholarship Award *185*
Reid Blackburn Scholarship *443*
Texas Gridiron Club Scholarships *188*
Valley Press Club Scholarships, The Republican Scholarship; Photojournalism Scholarship, Channel 22 Scholarship *189*
Visual Task Force Scholarship *443*

Physical Sciences and Math

A.T. Anderson Memorial Scholarship *89*
AFCEA Scholarship for Working Professionals *120*
AFCEA Sgt. Jeannette L. Winters, USMC Memorial Scholarship *191*
AFCEA/Lockheed Martin Orincon IT Scholarship *191*
AIAA Undergraduate Scholarship *89*
Al-Ben Scholarship for Academic Incentive *164*
Al-Ben Scholarship for Professional Merit *165*
Al-Ben Scholarship for Scholastic Achievement *165*
Alice T. Schafer Mathematics Prize for Excellence in Mathematics by an Undergraduate Woman *445*
American Legion Department of Maryland Math-Science Scholarship *444*
American Meteorological Society Industry Undergraduate Scholarships *89*
American Physical Society Corporate-Sponsored Scholarship for Minority Undergraduate Students Who Major in Physics *447*
American Physical Society Scholarship for Minority Undergraduate Physics Majors *444*
American Society of Naval Engineers Scholarship *90*
Arizona Hydrological Survey Student Scholarship *212*
Armed Forces Communications and Electronics Association General Emmett Paige Scholarship *191*
Armed Forces Communications and Electronics Association General John A. Wickham Scholarship *192*
Armed Forces Communications and Electronics Association ROTC Scholarship Program *120*
Association for Iron and Steel Technology Ohio Valley Chapter Scholarship *135*
Association for Women in Science College Scholarship *86*
AWIS Kirsten R. Lorentzen Award in Physics *213*
Barry M. Goldwater Scholarship and Excellence in Education Program *92*
Booz, Allen & Hamilton/William F. Stasior Internship *154*
BPW Career Advancement Scholarship Program for Women *136*
Burlington Northern Santa Fe Foundation Scholarship *89*
Carrol C. Hall Memorial Scholarship *95*
Coastal Plains Chapter of the Air and Waste Management Association Environmental Steward Scholarship *292*
Collegiate Inventors Competition - Grand Prize *95*
Collegiate Inventors Competition for Undergraduate Students *95*
Copernicus Award *413*
Economic Club of Grand Rapids Business Study Abroad Scholarship *62*
Elmer S. Imes Scholarship in Physics *447*
Emergency Secondary Education Loan Program *135*
Environmental Protection Agency Tribal Lands Environmental Science Scholarship *135*
Francis J. Flynn Memorial Scholarship *239*
Garden Club of America Awards for Summer Environmental Studies *80*
H. Fletcher Brown Scholarship *211*
Hach Scientific Foundation Scholarships *446*
Harvey Washington Banks Scholarship in Astronomy *447*
Heinz Environmental Fellows Program *142*
High Technology Scholars Program *141*
Howard Brown Rickard Scholarship *101*
Howard Vollum American Indian Scholarship *194*
HSF/Society of Hispanic Professional Engineers, Inc. Scholarship Program *174*
Hubertus W.V. Willems Scholarship for Male Students *166*
Independent Laboratories Institute Scholarship Alliance *93*
Lockheed Martin Scholarship Program *164*
Louis Stokes Science and Technology Award *139*
Math and Science Scholarship *262*
Math and Science Scholarship Program for Alabama Teachers *135*
Math, Engineering, Science, Business, Education, Computers Scholarships *145*
Michael P. Anderson Scholarship in Space Science *447*

Micron Science and Technology Scholars Program *165*
Mineralogical Society of America-Grant for Student Research in Mineralogy and Petrology *214*
Mineralogy Society of America-Grant for Research in Crystallography *215*
Minnesota Space Grant Consortium *124*
NASA Delaware Space Grant Undergraduate Tuition Scholarship *94*
NASA Idaho Space Grant Consortium Scholarship Program *94*
NASA Maryland Space Grant Consortium Undergraduate Scholarships *139*
NASA Nebraska Space Grant *125*
National Association of Water Companies-New Jersey Chapter Scholarship *139*
National Oceanic and Atmospheric Administration Educational Partnership Program with Minority Serving Institutions Undergraduate Scholarship *268*
National Security Agency Stokes Educational Scholarship Program *194*
National Society of Black Physicists and Lawrence Livermore National Library Undergraduate Scholarship *447*
Native American Leadership in Education (NALE) *145*
North Carolina Student Loan Program for Health, Science, and Mathematics *211*
Paul and Helen Trussel Science and Technology Scholarship *93*
Paul W. Ruckes Scholarship *190*
Payzer Scholarship *122*
Puget Sound Chapter Scholarship *213*
Raymond Davis Scholarship *270*
Ronald E. McNair Scholarship in Space and Optical Physics *448*
Sigma Xi Grants-In-Aid of Research *84*
Society of Physics Students Scholarships *448*
Space Imaging Award for Application of High Resolution Digital Satellite Imagery *91*
Sprint Scholarship/Internship *71*
SWE California Golden Gate Section Scholarships *195*
SWE Connecticut Section Jean R. Beers Scholarship *196*
Technical Minority Scholarship *169*
Universities Space Research Association Scholarship Program *96*
University and Community College System of Nevada NASA Space Grant and Fellowship Program *125*
Vermont Space Grant Consortium Scholarship Program *94*
Virginia Space Grant Consortium Teacher Education Scholarships *125*
Walter Samuel McAfee Scholarship in Space Physics *448*
West Virginia Space Grant Consortium Undergraduate Scholarship Program *126*
Willie Hobbs Moore, Harry L. Morrison, and Arthur B.C. Walker Physics Scholarships *448*
Women in Science and Technology Scholarship *143*
Wyeth Scholarship *142*
Z/I Imaging Scholarship *91*

Political Science

Academy of Travel and Tourism Scholarships *351*
American Legion Auxiliary Department of Arizona Wilma Hoyal-Maxine Chilton Memorial Scholarship *449*
Bruce B. Melchert Scholarship *450*
Budweiser Conservation Scholarship Program *140*
Central Intelligence Agency Undergraduate Scholarship Program *56*
C-SPAN Scholarship Program *189*
Decatur H. Miller Scholarship *338*
Dick Larsen Scholarship Program *189*
Harry S. Truman Library Institute Undergraduate Student Grant *217*
Herb Robinson Scholarship Program *190*
Jennifer Curtis Byler Scholarship for the Study of Public Affairs *184*
Jerry Clark Memorial Scholarship *449*
Mas Family Scholarships *146*
Mayme and Herbert Frank Educational Fund *216*
Michael and Marie Marucci Scholarship *312*
Minorities in Government Finance Scholarship *62*
National Society Daughters of the American Revolution Enid Hall Griswold Memorial Scholarship *217*
Sodexho Scholarship *333*
Spence Reese Scholarship Fund *259*

Psychology

Counselor, Advocate, and Support Staff Scholarship Program *69*
Critical Needs Teacher Loan/Scholarship *231*
Edna Aimes Scholarship *328*
Janet Ishikawa-Daniel Fullmer Scholarship in Counseling *450*

Mississippi Health Care Professions Loan/Scholarship Program *328*
Pilot International Foundation Ruby Newhall Memorial Scholarship *331*
Pilot International Foundation Scholarship Program *331*
Pilot International Foundation/Lifeline Scholarship Program *332*
Regents Professional Opportunity Scholarship *67*
Rockwell/UNCF Corporate Scholars Program *156*

Public Health

Edna Aimes Scholarship *328*
National Environmental Health Association/American Academy of Sanitarians Scholarship *437*
Young Epidemiology Scholars Competition *291*

Public Policy and Administration

American Legion Auxiliary Department of Arizona Wilma Hoyal-Maxine Chilton Memorial Scholarship *449*
Frank L. Greathouse Government Accounting Scholarship *148*
George A. Nielsen Public Investor Scholarship *148*
Minorities in Government Finance Scholarship *62*
Morris K. Udall Undergraduate Scholarships *294*
William Donald Schaefer Scholarship *451*

Radiology

Jerman-Cahoon Student Scholarship *323*
Royce Osborn Minority Student Scholarship *323*
Siemens Scholar Award *317*
Varian Radiation Therapy Student Scholarship *324*

Real Estate

Appraisal Institute Educational Scholarship Program *451*
Educational Scholarship Program *451*
George M. Brooker Collegiate Scholarship for Minorities *452*
Homestead Capital Housing Scholarship *68*
ICSC John. T Riordan Professional Education Scholarship *452*
Illinois Real Estate Educational Foundation Academic Scholarships *452*
New Jersey Association of Realtors Educational Foundation Scholarship Program *452*
Thomas F. Seay Scholarship *452*

Recreation, Parks, Leisure Studies

Bill Mason Memorial Scholarship Fund *80*
Maine Campground Owners Association Scholarship *409*
Robert W. Crawford Student Literary Award *452*

Religion/Theology

ASCSA Summer Sessions Open Scholarships *88*
Dan Schutte Scholarship *403*
David Tamotsu Kagiwada Memorial Scholarship *453*
Disciple Chaplains' Scholarship *454*
Ed E. and Gladys Hurley Foundation Scholarship *454*
Edwin G. and Lauretta M. Michael Scholarship *454*
Elaine Rendler-Rene Dosogne-Georgetown Chorale Scholarship *403*
Elsa Everett Memorial Trust Fund *455*
Ernest and Eurice Miller Bass Scholarship Fund *456*
First Catholic Slovak Ladies Association Seminarian (College) Scholarship *453*
First Presbyterian Church Scholarship Program *455*
Franks Foundation Scholarship *432*
Funk Family Memorial Scholarship *403*
GIA Publication Pastoral Musician Scholarship *404*
International Order of the King's Daughters and Sons Student Ministry Scholarship *455*
Katherine J. Shutze Memorial Scholarship *454*
Leonard M. Perryman Communications Scholarship for Ethnic Minority Students *189*
Lynn E. May, Jr. Study Grant *339*
Mary E. Bivins Religious Scholarship *455*
Memorial Foundation for Jewish Culture International Scholarship Program for Community Service *106*
MuSonics Scholarship *404*
National Association of Pastoral Musicians Members' Scholarship *404*
NPM Board of Directors Scholarship *404*
NPM Composers and Authors Scholarship *404*
NPM Koinonia/Board of Directors Scholarship *404*
NPM Miami Valley Catholic Church Musicians Scholarship *405*
NPM Perrot Scholarship *405*
Oregon Catholic Press Scholarship *405*
Paluch Family Foundation/World Library Publications Scholarship *405*
Racial/Ethnic Leadership Education (RELE) *437*

Rowley/Ministerial Education Scholarship 454
Scholarships for Education, Business and Religion 148
Star Supporter Scholarship/Loan 454
Steven C. Warner Scholarship 405
Ullery Charitable Trust Fund 455
Vocational Scholarship Program 453
William Heath Education Scholarship for Ministers, Priests and Missionaries 453

Science, Technology, and Society

AIAA Undergraduate Scholarship 89
Al Qoyawayma Award 163
American Chemical Society, Rubber Division Undergraduate Scholarship 158
Arizona Hydrological Survey Student Scholarship 212
Carol A. Ratza Memorial Scholarship 138
Detroit Section SAE Technical Scholarship 270
GRE and Graduate Applications Waiver 95
HIMSS Foundation Scholarship Program 318
HSF/Society of Hispanic Professional Engineers, Inc. Scholarship Program 174
KSEA Scholarships 245
Math and Science Scholarship 262
Math, Engineering, Science, Business, Education, Computers Scholarships 145
Micron Science and Technology Scholars Program 165
Montana Space Grant Scholarship Program 125
MRCA Foundation Scholarship Program 94
NASA Delaware Space Grant Undergraduate Tuition Scholarship 94
NASA Idaho Space Grant Consortium Scholarship Program 94
NASA Nebraska Space Grant 125
NASA Rhode Island Space Grant Consortium Outreach Scholarship for Undergraduate Students 288
Native American Leadership in Education (NALE) 145
New Economy Technology Scholarship (NETS)-SciTech Scholarships 457
New Economy Technology Scholarship-Technology Scholarships 457
Paul and Helen Trussel Science and Technology Scholarship 93
Seaspace Scholarship Program 458
Sigma Xi Grants-In-Aid of Research 84
Society of Hispanic Professional Engineers Foundation 168
The Chemistry Common Knowledge Challenge 456
The Ron Vellekamp Environmental Scholarship 457
Universities Space Research Association Scholarship Program 96
Vice Admiral Jerry O. Tuttle, USN (Ret.) and Mrs. Barbara A. Tuttle Science and Technology Scholarship 255
Women in Science and Technology Scholarship 143
Youth Activity Fund 412

Social Sciences

Allied Health Student Loan Program-New Mexico 210
Alphonso Deal Scholarship Award 199
American Criminal Justice Association-Lambda Alpha Epsilon National Scholarship 198
American Society of Criminology Gene Carte Student Paper Competition 199
Anne Lindeman Memorial Scholarship 142
Beinecke Scholarship for Graduate Study 109
BPW Career Advancement Scholarship Program for Women 136
Center for Gay and Lesbian Studies Undergraduate Paper Awards 383
Charles L. Hebner Memorial Scholarship 352
Charles T. and Judith A. Tart Student Incentive 459
CHSSC Scholarship Award 352
Counselor, Advocate, and Support Staff Scholarship Program 69
Del Jones Memorial Travel Award 459
Edward H. and Rosamund B. Spicer Travel Award 460
Eileen J. Garrett Scholarship for Parapsychological Research 459
Exploration Fund Grants 88
Goldman Family Fund, New Leader Scholarship 210
Irish Research Funds 105
Japan Studies Scholarship 312
Jeanette R. Wolman Scholarship 375
Leo J. Krysa Undergraduate Scholarship 104
Lois Hole Humanities and Social Sciences Scholarship 351
Lou Hochberg Awards 459
Math, Engineering, Science, Business, Education, Computers Scholarships 145
NIH Undergraduate Scholarship Program for Students from Disadvantaged Backgrounds 140
Peter Kong-Ming New Student Prize 332
Research Development Initiative 237

Robert P. Pula Memorial Scholarship 353
Sigma Xi Grants-In-Aid of Research 84

Social Services

Alphonso Deal Scholarship Award 199
American Legion Auxiliary Department of Arizona Wilma Hoyal-Maxine Chilton Memorial Scholarship 449
Anne Lindeman Memorial Scholarship 142
Continental Society, Daughters of Indian Wars Scholarship 224
Counselor, Advocate, and Support Staff Scholarship Program 69
Developmental Disabilities Awareness Awards for Lutheran High School Students 460
Developmental Disabilities Scholastic Achievement Scholarship for Lutheran College Students 208
Fannie Mae Foundation Scholarship 461
Friends of Oregon Students Scholarship 234
Goldman Family Fund, New Leader Scholarship 210
Graduate and Professional Scholarship Program-Maryland 210
Health Professions Preparatory Scholarship Program 425
Janet L. Hoffmann Loan Assistance Repayment Program 230
Kaiser Permanente Allied Healthcare Scholarship 326
Memorial Foundation for Jewish Culture International Scholarship Program for Community Service 106
Morris K. Udall Undergraduate Scholarships 294
Ordean Scholarship Program 67
Regents Professional Opportunity Scholarship 67
Sodexho Scholarship 333
Ted Bricker Scholarship 461
Vocational Scholarship Program 453
William Heath Education Scholarship for Ministers, Priests and Missionaries 453

Special Education

American Legion Auxiliary Department of Arizona Wilma Hoyal-Maxine Chilton Memorial Scholarship 449
Anna and John Kolesar Memorial Scholarships 218
Anne Lindeman Memorial Scholarship 142
Applegate/Jackson/Parks Future Teacher Scholarship 232
ARC of Washington Trust Fund Stipend Program 461
Brookmire-Hastings Scholarships 240
Connecticut Special Education Teacher Incentive Grant 462
Developmental Disabilities Awareness Awards for Lutheran High School Students 460
Developmental Disabilities Scholastic Achievement Scholarship for Lutheran College Students 208
Emergency Secondary Education Loan Program 135
Higher Education Teacher Assistance Program 237
Illinois Special Education Teacher Tuition Waiver 462
James Carlson Memorial Scholarship 234
Minority Teachers of Illinois Scholarship Program 228
Pilot International Foundation Ruby Newhall Memorial Scholarship 331
Pilot International Foundation Scholarship Program 331
Pilot International Foundation/Lifeline Scholarship Program 332
Robert G. Porter Scholars Program-AFT Members 219
South Carolina Teacher Loan Program 237
Workforce Incentive Program 233

Sports-Related

GNC Nutrition Research Grant 335
Linda Craig Memorial Scholarship presented by St. Vincent Sports Medicine 331
Linda Riddle/SGMA Scholarship 463
Mary Benevento CAHPERD Scholarship 224
National Athletic Trainer's Association Research and Education Foundation Scholarship Program 329
National Strength and Conditioning Association Challenge Scholarship 335
National Strength and Conditioning Association High School Scholarship 336
National Strength and Conditioning Association Undergraduate Research Grant 336
National Strength and Conditioning Association Women's Scholarship 336
NSCA Minority Scholarship 336
Power Systems Professional Scholarship 336
Qwest Leadership Challenge 463
Ray and Rosalee Weiss Research Endowment 319
Tobin Sorenson Physical Education Scholarship 463

Surveying; Surveying Technology, Cartography, or Geographic Information Science

ACSM Fellows Scholarship 463
American Association for Geodetic Surveying Joseph F. Dracup Scholarship Award 463
Arizona Hydrological Survey Student Scholarship 212
Associated General Contractors of America-New York State Chapter Scholarship Program 173
Association of California Water Agencies Scholarships 91
Berntsen International Scholarship in Surveying 464
Berntsen International Scholarship in Surveying Technology 464
Budweiser Conservation Scholarship Program 140
Cady McDonnell Memorial Scholarship 464
Cartography and Geographic Information Society Scholarship 464
Central Intelligence Agency Undergraduate Scholarship Program 56
Clair A. Hill Scholarship 91
Edward R. Hall Scholarship 76
MRCA Foundation Scholarship Program 94
National Society of Professional Surveyors Board of Governors Scholarship 464
National Society of Professional Surveyors for Equal Opportunity/Mary Feindt Scholarship 464
National Society of Professional Surveyors Scholarships 465
Nettie Dracup Memorial Scholarship 465
Professional Land Surveyors of Oregon Scholarships 465
Schonstedt Scholarship in Surveying 465
Ted Wilson Memorial Scholarship Foundation 212

Therapy/Rehabilitation

Alberta Heritage Scholarship Fund Aboriginal Health Careers Bursary 135
Alice Newell Joslyn Medical Fund 207
Allied Health Student Loan Program-New Mexico 210
AMBUCS Scholars-Scholarships for Therapists 328
American Occupational Therapy Foundation State Association Scholarships 321
Anne Lindeman Memorial Scholarship 142
Carlotta Welles Scholarship 321
Counselor, Advocate, and Support Staff Scholarship Program 69
Critical Needs Teacher Loan/Scholarship 231
Delta Gamma Foundation Florence Margaret Harvey Memorial Scholarship 219
Developmental Disabilities Scholastic Achievement Scholarship for Lutheran College Students 208
Dr. William J. Steger Scholarship Awards 333
Florence Wood/Arkansas Occupational Therapy Association Scholarship 321
Francis L. Booth Medical Scholarship sponsored by LAVFW Department of Maine 327
General Federation of Women's Clubs of Massachusetts Music Scholarship 225
GNC Nutrition Research Grant 335
Goldman Family Fund, New Leader Scholarship 210
Health Careers Scholarship 209
Health Resources and Services Administration-Bureau of Health Professions Scholarships for Disadvantaged Students 211
Indian Health Service Health Professions Pre-professional Scholarship 318
Janet L. Hoffmann Loan Assistance Repayment Program 230
Jimmy A. Young Memorial Education Recognition Award 322
Kaiser Permanente Allied Healthcare Scholarship 326
Linda Craig Memorial Scholarship presented by St. Vincent Sports Medicine 331
Marion A. Lindeman Scholarship 331
Medical Career Scholarship 319
Mississippi Health Care Professions Loan/Scholarship Program 328
Morton B. Duggan, Jr. Memorial Education Recognition Award 322
Myra Levick Scholarship Fund 466
National Athletic Trainer's Association Research and Education Foundation Scholarship Program 329
National Society Daughters of the American Revolution Medical Occupational Therapy Scholarships 467
National Strength and Conditioning Association Challenge Scholarship 335
National Strength and Conditioning Association High School Scholarship 336
National Strength and Conditioning Association Undergraduate Research Grant 336
National Strength and Conditioning Association Women's Scholarship 336

NBRC/AMP Robert M. Lawrence, MD, Education Recognition Award *322*
NBRC/AMP William W. Burgin, MD Education Recognition Award *322*
North Carolina Student Loan Program for Health, Science, and Mathematics *211*
NSCA Minority Scholarship *336*
Past Presidents Parley Health Care Scholarship *207*
Physical and Occupational Therapists and Assistants Grant Program *467*
Pilot International Foundation Ruby Newhall Memorial Scholarship *331*
Pilot International Foundation Scholarship Program *331*
Pilot International Foundation/Lifeline Scholarship Program *332*
Power Systems Professional Scholarship *336*
Rehabilitation Training Program Scholarship *468*
Rudolph Dillman Memorial Scholarship *219*
Scholarship Program for Former Soviet Union Emigres Training in the Health Sciences *209*
Sepracor Achievement Award for Excellence in Pulmonary Disease State Management *323*
Sigma Alpha Iota Music Therapy Scholarship *407*
Suburban Hospital Healthcare System Scholarship *333*
Tobin Sorenson Physical Education Scholarship *463*

Trade/Technical Specialties

AFL-CIO Skill Trades Scholarship *469*
AFL-CIO Skilled Trades Exploring Scholarships *470*
AGC Education and Research Foundation Undergraduate Scholarships *173*
Airgas Jerry Baker Scholarship *285*
Airgas-Terry Jarvis Memorial Scholarship *253*
Alberta Apprenticeship and Industry Training Scholarships *468*
Alwin B. Newton Scholarship Fund *242*
American Society of Heating, Refrigeration, and Air Conditioning Engineering Technology Scholarship *90*
American Welding Society District Scholarship Program *285*
American Welding Society International Scholarship *253*
Arsham Amirikian Engineering Scholarship *172*
ASHRAE Memorial Scholarship *251*
ASHRAE Scholarships *252*
Association for Facilities Engineering Cedar Valley Chapter # 132 Scholarship *120*
Automotive Hall of Fame Educational Funds *162*
Bradford White Corporation Scholarship *102*
Bud Glover Memorial Scholarship *116*
Charles D. Mayo Scholarship *356*
Charles N. Fisher Memorial Scholarship *90*
Clinton J. Helton Manufacturing Scholarship Award Fund *272*
Delta Faucet Company Scholarship Program *102*
Donald and Jean Cleveland-Willamette Valley Section Scholarship *172*
Donald F. Hastings Scholarship *253*
Downriver Detroit Chapter 198 Scholarship *273*
Duane Hanson Scholarship *285*
E. Wayne Kay Community College Scholarship Award *273*
E. Wayne Kay Scholarship *273*
Edward J. Brady Memorial Scholarship *253*
Field Aviation Co., Inc., Scholarship *117*
Firefighter, Ambulance, and Rescue Squad Member Tuition Reimbursement Program-Maryland *300*
Fort Wayne Chapter 56 Scholarship *274*
Henry Adams Scholarship *252*
Howard E. Adkins Memorial Scholarship *253*
IFDA Student Scholarship *356*
Illinois Tool Works Welding Companies Scholarship *254*
International Executive Housekeepers Educational Foundation *307*
Irving W. Cook, WA0CGS, Scholarship *90*
John C. Lincoln Memorial Scholarship *254*
Lowell Gaylor Memorial Scholarship *118*
Maine Metal Products Association Scholarship *395*
Maine Metal Products Association Scholarship Program *389*
Marion A. and Eva S. Peeples Scholarships *230*
Maryland Association of Private Colleges and Career Schools Scholarship *150*
Matsuo Bridge Company, Ltd., of Japan Scholarship *172*
Miller Electric International World Skills Competition Scholarship *254*
Mississippi Scholarship *90*
Monte Mitchell Global Scholarship *118*
MRCA Foundation Scholarship Program *94*
Myrtle and Earl Walker Scholarship Fund *275*
Nancy Goodhue Lynch Scholarship *470*
National Association of Water Companies-New Jersey Chapter Scholarship *139*

NAWIC Construction Trades Scholarship *470*
NAWIC Undergraduate Scholarships *100*
North Central Region 9 Scholarship *275*
Paul and Helen L. Grauer Scholarship *91*
PHCC Educational Foundation Need-Based Scholarship *102*
PHCC Educational Foundation Scholarship Program *103*
Phoenix Chapter 67 Scholarship *275*
Plastics Pioneers Scholarships *269*
Praxair International Scholarship *254*
Professional Aviation Maintenance Foundation Student Scholarship Program *129*
Progress Energy Scholarship Program *469*
Reuben Trane Scholarship *242*
Robert W. Valimont Endowment Fund Scholarship (Part II) *468*
Scholarship of the Maine School Food Service Association *305*
SME Corporate Scholars *275*
Society of Plastics Engineers Scholarship Program *168*
South Dakota Retailers Association Scholarship Program *69*
Specialty Equipment Market Association Memorial Scholarship Fund *282*
Wachovia Technical Scholarship Program *469*
West Virginia Broadcasters Association Fund *181*
Wichita Chapter 52 Scholarship *276*
William A. and Ann M. Brothers Scholarship *286*
William B. Howell Memorial Scholarship *255*
William E. Weisel Scholarship Fund *246*
Women in Logistics Scholarship *157*
Women's Jewelry Association Scholarship Program *471*
Wyoming Trucking Association Trust Fund Scholarship *158*

Transportation

Alice Glaisyer Warfield Memorial Scholarship *130*
Associated General Contractors of America-New York State Chapter Scholarship Program *173*
Dan Reichard Jr. Scholarship *144*
Denny Lydic Scholarship *130*
Donald C. Hyde Essay Program *171*
Dr. George M. Smerk Scholarship *471*
Jack Gilstrap Scholarship *171*
Louis T. Klauder Scholarship *171*
NASA Nebraska Space Grant *125*
National Customs Brokers and Forwarders Association of America Scholarship Award *472*
Parsons Brinckerhoff-Jim Lammie Scholarship *171*
San Fernando Valley Chapter of the Ninety-Nines Career Scholarship *128*
Texas Transportation Scholarship *130*
Transit Hall of Fame Scholarship Award Program *171*
Transportation Clubs International Charlotte Woods Scholarship *130*
Transportation Clubs International Fred A. Hooper Memorial Scholarship *131*
Transportation Clubs International Ginger and Fred Deines Canada Scholarship *131*
Transportation Clubs International Ginger and Fred Deines Mexico Scholarship *131*
Truckload Carriers Association Scholarship Fund *154*
Vermont Space Grant Consortium Scholarship Program *94*
Women in Logistics Scholarship *157*
Wyoming Trucking Association Trust Fund Scholarship *158*

Travel/Tourism

Academy of Travel and Tourism Scholarships *351*
American Express Travel Scholarship *472*
Arizona Chapter Gold Scholarship *473*
Bill Mason Memorial Scholarship Fund *80*
Cleveland Legacy I and II Scholarship Awards *308*
Donald Estey Scholarship Fund-Rocky Mountain Chapter *473*
George Reinke Scholarships *473*
Healy Scholarship *473*
Holland-America Line Westours Scholarships *473*
International Airlines Travel Agent Network Ronald A. Santana Memorial Foundation *350*
International Foodservice Editorial Council Communications Scholarship *182*
John Hjorth Scholarship Fund-San Diego Chapter *473*
Joseph R. Stone Scholarships *474*
Missouri Travel Council Tourism Scholarship *307*
Nancy Stewart Scholarship Fund-Allegheny Chapter *474*
Network of Executive Women in Hospitality, Inc. Scholarship *101*
New Horizons Kathy Le Tarte Scholarship *309*
Northern California Chapter Richard Epping Scholarship *474*

Orange County Chapter/Harry Jackson Scholarship Fund *474*
Pacific Northwest Chapter-William Hunt Scholarship Fund *474*
Pat and Jim Host Scholarship *309*
Princess Cruises and Princess Tours Scholarship *475*
R.W. Bob Holden Scholarship *350*
Recreational Boating Industries Educational Foundation Scholarships *141*
Societie des Casinos du Quebec Scholarship *309*
South Dakota Retailers Association Scholarship Program *69*
Southeast American Society of Travel Agents Chapter Scholarship *475*
Southern California Chapter/Pleasant Hawaiian Holidays Scholarship *475*
Stan and Leone Pollard Scholarships *475*
Tampa, Hillsborough Legacy Scholarship *309*
Tauck Scholars Scholarships *309*
Tribal Business Management Program (TBM) *55*
Tulsa Scholarship Awards *309*
Yellow Ribbon Scholarship *310*

TV/Radio Broadcasting

AAJA/Cox Foundation Scholarship *357*
Abe Schecter Graduate Scholarship *185*
Academy of Television Arts and Sciences College Television Awards *108*
Advertising Federation of Fort Wayne, Inc., Scholarship *178*
Alabama Broadcasters Association Scholarship *476*
American Legion Press Club of New Jersey and Post 170 Arthur Dehardt Memorial Scholarship *178*
APTRA-Clete Roberts Memorial Journalism Scholarship Award *358*
APTRA-Kathryn Dettman Memorial Scholarship *359*
Asian-American Journalists Association Scholarship *179*
Associated Press Television/Radio Association-Clete Roberts Journalism Scholarship Awards *358*
Atlanta Press Club Journalism Scholarship Program *179*
Belo Texas Broadcast Education Foundation Scholarship *187*
Bob Elliot- WMTW-TV 8 Journalism Scholarship *190*
Bonner McLane Texas Broadcast Education Foundation Scholarship *187*
Broadcast Scholarship Program *478*
California Broadcasters Foundation Intern Scholarship *476*
Cap Lathrop Scholarship Program *477*
Carol A. Ratza Memorial Scholarship *138*
Carole Simpson Scholarship *185*
Charles and Lucille King Family Foundation Scholarships *180*
Continuing Education Scholarship Program *477*
C-SPAN Scholarship Program *189*
Elks Eagle Scout Awards *477*
Entercom Portland Radio Scholarship Fund *367*
Fisher Broadcasting, Inc., Scholarship for Minorities *181*
Future Journalists Scholarship Program *180*
Great Falls Broadcasters Association Scholarship *479*
Hawaii Association of Broadcasters Scholarship *478*
Helen Johnson Scholarship *369*
Indiana Broadcasters Foundation Scholarship *362*
Jack Shaheen Mass Communications Scholarship Award *177*
James J. Wychor Scholarship *479*
Jim Allard Broadcast Journalism Scholarship *359*
Joel Garcia Memorial Scholarship *180*
John Bayliss Broadcast Radio Scholarship *182*
Journalism and Broadcasting Scholarships *362*
Kathryn Dettman Memorial Journalism Scholarship *358*
Ken Kashiwahara Scholarship *186*
Leonard M. Perryman Communications Scholarship for Ethnic Minority Students *189*
LinTV Minority Scholarship *478*
Lou and Carole Prato Sports Reporting Scholarship *186*
Lynn Dean Ford IABJ Scholarship Awards *181*
MANAA Media Scholarships for Asian American Students *112*
Maryland Association of Private Colleges and Career Schools Scholarship *150*
MBA Student Broadcaster Scholarship *479*
Michael S. Libretti Scholarship *184*
Mike Reynolds $1,000 Scholarship *186*
Minoru Yasui Memorial Scholarship Award *358*
Mississippi Association of Broadcasters Scholarship *479*
Missouri Broadcasters Association Scholarship *479*
NABJ Scholarship *183*
National Academy of Television Arts and Sciences John Cannon Memorial Scholarship *183*
National Association of Black Journalists Non-Sustaining Scholarship Awards *364*

Civic, Professional, Social, or Union Affiliation

AFL-CIO
AFL-CIO Council of Buffalo Scholarship 495
Bill Peterson Scholarship 504
CWA Joe Beirne Foundation Scholarship Program 501
Martin Duffy Adult Learner Scholarship Award 504
Minnesota AFL-CIO Scholarships 504
New York State AFL-CIO Scholarship 508
PA AFL-CIO Unionism in America Essay Contest 512
Project BEST Scholarship 513
Ronald Lorah Memorial Scholarship 518
Ted Bricker Scholarship 461
Texas AFL-CIO Scholarship Program 516
Union Plus Scholarship Program 518

Airline Pilots Association
Air Line Pilots Association Scholarship Program 483

Alpha Mu Gamma
National Alpha Mu Gamma Scholarships 310

American Academy of Physicians Assistants
Physician Assistant Foundation Annual Scholarship 331

American Angus Association
Angus Foundation Scholarships 506

American Association of Bioanalysts
David Birenbaum Scholarship Fund 483

American Association of Critical Care Nurses
AACN Educational Advancement Scholarships-BSN Completion 415

American Association of Law Librarians
Law Librarians in Continuing Education Courses 380
Type III: Library Degree for Non-Law School Graduates 380

American College of Musicians
American College of Musicians/National Guild of Piano Teachers 200-Dollar Scholarships 401

American College of Sports Medicine
Ray and Rosalee Weiss Research Endowment 319

American Congress on Surveying and Mapping
ACSM Fellows Scholarship 463
American Association for Geodetic Surveying Joseph F. Dracup Scholarship Award 463
Berntsen International Scholarship in Surveying 464
Berntsen International Scholarship in Surveying Technology 464
Cady McDonnell Memorial Scholarship 464
Cartography and Geographic Information Society Scholarship 464
National Society of Professional Surveyors Board of Governors Scholarship 464
National Society of Professional Surveyors for Equal Opportunity/Mary Feindt Scholarship 464
National Society of Professional Surveyors Scholarships 465
Nettie Dracup Memorial Scholarship 465
Schonstedt Scholarship in Surveying 465
Tri-State Surveying and Photogrammetry Kris M. Kunze Memorial Scholarship 143

American Criminal Justice Association
American Criminal Justice Association-Lambda Alpha Epsilon National Scholarship 198

American Dental Assistants Association
Juliette A. Southard/Oral B Laboratories Scholarship 204

American Dental Education Association
ADEA/Oral-B Laboratories Scholarship 205
ADEA/Sigma Phi Alpha Linda DeVore Scholarship 205

American Dental Hygienist's Association
ADHA Institute General Scholarships 205
American Dental Hygienists' Association Institute Minority Scholarship 205
American Dental Hygienists' Association Institute Research Grant 205
American Dental Hygienists' Association Part-Time Scholarship 205
Colgate "Bright Smiles, Bright Futures" Minority Scholarship 206
Dr. Alfred C. Fones Scholarship 206
Dr. Harold Hillenbrand Scholarship 206
Irene E. Newman Scholarship 206
Margaret E. Swanson Scholarship 206
Marsh Affinity Group Services Scholarship 206
Oral-B Laboratories Dental Hygiene Scholarship 206
Sigma Phi Alpha Undergraduate Scholarship 207
Wilma Motley California Merit Scholarship 207

American Dietetic Association
American Dietetic Association Foundation Scholarship Program 300

American Federation of State, County, and Municipal Employees
AFSCME: American Federation of State, County, and Municipal Employees Local 1724 Scholarship 510
AFSCME: American Federation of State, County, and Municipal Employees Local 75 Scholarship 510
American Federation of State, County, and Municipal Employees Scholarship Program 483
American Press Institute Scholarship 361
Jerry Clark Memorial Scholarship 449
Union Plus Credit Card Scholarship Program 484

American Foreign Service Association
American Foreign Service Association (AFSA) Financial Aid Award Program 484
American Foreign Service Association (AFSA)/AAFSW Merit Award Program 484

American Health Information Management Association
Foundation of Research and Education Undergraduate Merit Scholarships 335

American Legion or Auxiliary
Albert M. Lappin Scholarship 488
American Essay Contest Scholarship 487
American Legion Auxiliary Department of Connecticut Memorial Educational Grant 484
American Legion Auxiliary Department of Florida Memorial Scholarship 484
American Legion Auxiliary Department of Minnesota Past President Parley Health Care Scholarship 320
American Legion Auxiliary Department of Nebraska President's Scholarship for Junior Members 485
American Legion Auxiliary Department of North Dakota Past President's Parley Nurses' Scholarship 417
American Legion Auxiliary Missouri State National President's Scholarship 485
American Legion Auxiliary National Presidents Scholarship 485
American Legion Auxiliary Non-Traditional Students Scholarships 487
American Legion Auxiliary Spirit of Youth Scholarships for Junior Members 487

American Legion Department of Minnesota Memorial Scholarship 489
American Legion Department of Washington Children and Youth Scholarships 490
American Legion National Headquarters Eagle Scout of the Year 490
American Legion Scholarship—Ohio 489
American Legion, Department of Idaho Scholarship 487
American Legion, Department of Illinois Scholarships 487
Charles L. Bacon Memorial Scholarship 489
Della Van Deuren Memorial Scholarship 485
H.S. and Angelina Lewis Scholarships 486
Hugh A. Smith Scholarship Fund 488
James V. Day Scholarship 488
Joseph P. Gavenonis College Scholarship (Plan I) 490
Lela Murphy Scholarship 485
M.V. McCrae Memorial Nurses Scholarship 416
Maynard Jensen American Legion Memorial Scholarship 489
Merit and Memorial Scholarships 486
Minnesota Legionnaires Insurance Trust Scholarship 489
Ohio American Legion Scholarships 510
Past Presidents Parley Health Career Scholarships 486
Past Presidents Parley Registered Nurse Scholarship 417
Past Presidents Parley Scholarship-Missouri 416
Rosedale Post 346 Scholarship 488
Ruby Paul Campaign Fund Scholarship 485
State President's Scholarships 486
Ted and Nora Anderson Scholarships 488
William F. "Bill" Johnson Memorial Scholarship sponsored by Sons of the American Legion 490

American Nephrology Nurses' Association
Abbott/Pamela Balzer Career Mobility Scholarship 418
American Nephrology Nurses' Association American Regent Career Mobility Scholarship 418
American Nephrology Nurses' Association AMGEN Career Mobility Scholarship 419
American Nephrology Nurses' Association Anthony J. Janetti, Inc. Career Mobility Scholarship 419
American Nephrology Nurses' Association Career Mobility Scholarship 419
American Nephrology Nurses' Association NNCC Career Mobility Scholarship 419
American Nephrology Nurses' Association Watson Pharma, Inc. Career Mobility Scholarship 419

American Occupational Therapy Association
American Occupational Therapy Foundation State Association Scholarships 321
Carlotta Welles Scholarship 321

American Orff-Schulwerk Association
American Orff-Schulwerk Association Research Grant 220
Gunild Keetman Assistance Fund 220

American Postal Workers Union
Vocational Scholarship Program 491

American Quarter Horse Association
American Quarter Horse Foundation Youth Scholarships 491
AQHF Education or Nursing Scholarship 220
AQHF Journalism or Communications Scholarship 178
AQHF Racing Scholarships 86
AQHF Telephony Scholarship for Senior Veterinary Students 86
AQHF Working Student Scholarship 491
Arizona Quarter Horse Youth Racing Scholarship 491
Dr. Gerald O'Connor Michigan Scholarship 491
Excellence in Equine/Agricultural Involvement Scholarship 491

Farm and Ranch Heritage Scholarship *492*
Guy Stoops Memorial Professional Horsemen's Family Scholarship *492*
Indiana Quarter Horse Youth Scholarship *492*
Joan Cain Florida Quarter Horse Youth Scholarship *492*
Nebraska Quarter Horse Youth Scholarship *492*
Ray Melton Memorial Virginia Quarter Horse Youth Scholarship *492*
Swayze Woodruff Scholarship *492*

American Radio Relay League
Donald Riebhoff Memorial Scholarship *356*
Earl I. Anderson Scholarship *243*
Edmond A. Metzger Scholarship *243*
IRARC Memorial/Joseph P. Rubino, WA4MMD, Scholarship *494*
Yankee Clipper Contest Club, Inc. Youth Scholarship *494*
You've Got a Friend in Pennsylvania Scholarship *494*

American School Food Service Association
Nancy Curry Scholarship *301*
Professional Growth Scholarship *301*
Schwan's Food Service Scholarship *301*

American Society for Clinical Laboratory Science
ASCLS Region IX Clinical Laboratory Scientists of Alaska Sharon O'Meara Continuing Education Scholarship Fund *161*
ASCLS Region VI Missouri Organization for Clinical Laboratory Science Education Scholarship *162*

American Society for Photogrammetry and Remote Sensing
Robert E. Altenhofen Memorial Scholarship *91*
Space Imaging Award for Application of High Resolution Digital Satellite Imagery *91*

American Society of Safety Engineers
America Responds Memorial Scholarship *434*
ASSE-Edwin P. Granberry, Jr. Distinguished Service Award Scholarship *435*
ASSE-Gulf Coast Past Presidents Scholarship *435*
ASSE-Marsh Risk Consulting Scholarship *435*
ASSE-Region IV/Edwin P. Granberry Scholarship *435*
ASSE-United Parcel Service Scholarship *435*
Ford Motor Company Scholarship-Undergraduate *435*
Georgia Chapter of ASSE Annual Scholarship *436*
Gold Country Section and Region II Scholarship *436*
Liberty Mutual Scholarship *436*
Northeastern Illinois Chapter Scholarship *436*
Scott Dominguez-Craters of the Moon Scholarship *436*
United Parcel Service Diversity Scholarship Program *292*

American Society of Travel Agents
Arizona Chapter Dependent/Employee Membership Scholarship *493*
Donald Estey Scholarship Fund-Rocky Mountain Chapter *473*
John Hjorth Scholarship Fund-San Diego Chapter *473*
Joseph R. Stone Scholarships *474*
Nancy Stewart Scholarship Fund-Allegheny Chapter *474*
Orange County Chapter/Harry Jackson Scholarship Fund *474*
Pacific Northwest Chapter-William Hunt Scholarship Fund *474*
Southeast American Society of Travel Agents Chapter Scholarship *475*

AMVETS Auxiliary
AMVETS National Ladies Auxiliary Scholarship *493*

Appaloosa Horse Club/Appaloosa Youth Association
Appaloosa Youth Educational Scholarships *493*
Lew and JoAnn Eklund Educational Scholarship *86*

ASM International
ASM Materials Education Foundation Scholarships *255*
ASM Outstanding Scholars Awards *255*
Edward J. Dulis Scholarship *256*
George A. Roberts Scholarship *256*
John M. Haniak Scholarship *256*
Nicholas J. Grant Scholarship *256*
William P. Woodside Founder's Scholarship *256*

Association of American Geographers
Anne U. White Fund *494*

Association of Energy Service Companies
Association of Energy Service Companies Scholarship Program *505*

Association of Engineering Geologists
Tilford Fund *213*

Association of Operating Room Nurses
Association of Peri-Operative Registered Nurses *420*

Big Brothers/Big Sisters
Arby's-Big Brothers Big Sisters Scholarship Award *493*

Boy Scouts
American Legion Department of Iowa Eagle Scout of the Year Scholarship *488*
American Legion Eagle Scout of the Year *490*
American Legion National Headquarters Eagle Scout of the Year *490*
American Legion, Department of Illinois, Boy Scout/Explorer Scholarship *487*
E. Urner Goodman Scholarship *494*
Eastern Orthodox Committee on Scouting Scholarships *498*
Elks Eagle Scout Awards *477*
Royden M. Bodley Scholarship *87*

Boys or Girls Club
Boys & Girls Clubs of America National Youth of the Year Award *494*
Boys and Girls Club of Alberta Scholarships *483*
Boys and Girls Clubs of Chicago Scholarships *495*

California Teachers Association
California Teachers Association Scholarship for Dependent Children *495*
California Teachers Association Scholarship for Members *495*
CSCPA Candidate's Award *58*
Martin Luther King, Jr. Memorial Scholarship *222*

Canadian Society for Chemical Engineering
Edmonton Chemical Engineering Scholarship *162*
Sarnia Chemical Engineering Community Scholarship *163*

Canadian Society for Chemistry
Alfred Bader Scholarship *92*

Canadian Society for Medical Laboratory Science
E.V. Booth Scholarship Award *317*

Catholic Kolping Society of America
Father Krewitt Scholarship *495*

Civil Air Patrol
Civil Air Patrol Academic Scholarships *496*
Major General Lucas V. Beau Flight Scholarships Sponsored by the Order of Daedalians *121*

Community Banker Association of Illinois
Comcast Leaders and Achievers Scholarship *496*
Community Banker Association of Illinois Children of Community Banking Scholarship *496*

Costume Society of America
Adele Filene Travel Award *105*
Stella Blum Research Grant *105*

Danish Sisterhood of America
Betty Hansen Continuing Education Grant *497*
Elizabeth Garde Nursing Scholarship *421*
National Scholarship, Mildred Sorensen, Olga Christensen and Betty Hansen Scholarships *497*

Daughters of the American Revolution
National Society Daughters of the American Revolution American History Scholarship *338*
National Society Daughters of the American Revolution Lillian and Arthur Dunn Scholarship *506*
National Society Daughters of the American Revolution Madeline Pickett (Halbert) Cogswell Nursing Scholarship *429*

Democratic Party
Pennsylvania Federation of Democratic Women, Inc. Annual Scholarship Awards *512*

Demolay
Davis-Roberts Scholarships *497*

Distribution Ed Club or Future Business Leaders of America
Harry A. Applegate Scholarship *146*
Nebraska DECA Leadership Scholarship *508*

Elks Club
Elks Emergency Educational Grants *498*
Elks National Foundation Legacy Awards *499*

Emergency Nurses Association
Additional ENA Foundation Undergraduate Scholarships *421*
Charles Kunz Memorial Undergraduate Scholarship *422*
ENA Foundation CEN Undergraduate Scholarship *422*
Margaret Miller Memorial Undergraduate Scholarship *422*

Entomological Society of America
The International Congress on Insect Neurochemistry and Neurophysiology (ICINN) Student Recognition Award in Insect Physiology, Biochemistry, Toxicology, and Molecular Biology *290*

Experimental Aircraft Association
David Alan Quick Scholarship *121*
EAA Aviation Achievement Scholarships *121*
H. P. "Bud" Milligan Aviation Scholarship *122*
Hansen Scholarship *122*
Herbert L. Cox Memorial Scholarship *122*
Payzer Scholarship *122*

Family, Career and Community Leaders of America
Ann Lane Home Economics Scholarship *305*
C.J. Davidson Scholarship for FCCLA *340*
FCCLA Houston Livestock Show and Rodeo Scholarship *340*
FCCLA Regional Scholarships *147*
FCCLA Texas Farm Bureau Scholarship *147*
Oklahoma Alumni & Associates of FHA, HERO and FCCLA, Inc. Scholarship *510*

Federation of American Consumers and Travelers
Federation of American Consumers and Travelers Graduating High School Senior Scholarship *499*

Fleet Reserve Association/Auxiliary
Allie Mae Oden Memorial Scholarship *504*
Fleet Reserve Association Scholarship *499*

Freemasons
Pennsylvania Masonic Youth Foundation Scholarship *512*

Girl Scouts
American Legion Auxiliary Girl Scout Achievement Award *486*
Eastern Orthodox Committee on Scouting Scholarships *498*
Elks National Foundation Gold Award Scholarships *498*

Glass, Molders, Pottery, Plastics and Allied Workers International Union
GMP Memorial Scholarship Program *499*

Golden Key National Honor Society
Ford Motor Company Engineering and Leadership Scholarship *262*
GEICO Life Scholarship *499*
Golden Key Study Abroad Scholarships *499*
International Student Leaders Award *500*

Golf Course Superintendents Association of America
GCSAA Scholars Competition *348*
Golf Course Superintendents Association of America Legacy Award *500*
Golf Course Superintendents Association of America Student Essay Contest *75*
Joseph S. Garshe Collegiate Grant Program *500*

Grange Association
California Grange Foundation Scholarship *495*
June Gill Nursing Scholarship *429*
Susan W. Freestone Education Award *508*

Graphic Communication International Union
A.J. DeAndrade Scholarship Program *500*

Greek Organization

All-TKE Academic Team Recognition and John A. Courson Top Scholar Award 516
Bruce B. Melchert Scholarship 450
Canadian TKE Scholarship 516
Carrol C. Hall Memorial Scholarship 95
Charles Walgreen, Jr. Scholarship 516
Delta Delta Delta Graduate Scholarship 497
Delta Delta Delta Undergraduate Scholarship 497
Delta Gamma Foundation Scholarships 498
Delta Phi Epsilon Educational Foundation Grant 498
Donald A. Fisher Memorial Scholarship 516
Dwayne R. Woerpel Memorial Leadership Award 516
Elena Lucrezia Cornaro Piscopia Scholarship For Graduate Studies 503
Elmer and Doris Schmitz Sr. Memorial Scholarship 517
Eugene C. Beach Memorial Scholarship 517
Francis J. Flynn Memorial Scholarship 239
George W. Woolery Memorial Scholarship 188
Harry J. Donnelly Memorial Scholarship 69
J. Russel Salsbury Memorial Scholarship 517
Kappa Alpha Theta Foundation Merit Based Scholarship Program 502
Kappa Alpha Theta Foundation Named Endowment Grant Program 503
Lambda Iota Tau Literature Scholarship 384
Michael J. Morin Memorial Scholarship 517
Miles Gray Memorial Scholarship 517
Phi Kappa Tau Foundation Scholarships 512
Richard Cecil Todd and Clauda Pennock Todd Tripod Scholarship 512
Ronald Reagan Leadership Award 517
Student Support Scholarship 236
T.J. Schmitz Scholarship 518
Undergraduate Scholarship 498
W. Allan Herzog Scholarship 70
Wallace McCauley Memorial Scholarship 518
William V. Muse Scholarship 518
William Wilson Memorial Scholarship 518

Greenville Area Personnel Association

Greenville Area Personnel Association Walter L. Martin Memorial Scholarship Program 496

Hawaii Education Association

Hawaii Education Association High School Student Scholarship 500
Hawaii Education Association Student Teacher Scholarship 227

Healthcare Information and Management Systems Society

HIMSS Foundation Scholarship Program 318

Hebrew Immigrant Aid Society

Hebrew Immigrant Aid Society Scholarship Awards Competition 500

Idaho Library Association

Idaho Library Association Gardner Hanks Scholarship 381
Idaho Library Association Library Science Scholarships 381

Indiana Sheriffs' Association

Indiana Sheriffs' Association Scholarship Program 199

Indiana State Teachers Association

Indiana Retired Teachers Association Foundation Scholarship 228

Institute of Industrial Engineers

A.O. Putnam Memorial Scholarship 263
C.B. Gambrell Undergraduate Scholarship 263
Dwight D. Gardner Scholarship 263
IIE Council of Fellows Undergraduate Scholarship 264
Lisa Zaken Award For Excellence 264
Marvin Mundel Memorial Scholarship 264
United Parcel Service Scholarship for Female Students 264
UPS Scholarship for Minority Students 264

International Brotherhood of Electrical Workers

International Brotherhood of Electrical Workers Local 280 Scholarship 511

International Chemical Workers Union

Walter L. Mitchell Memorial Awards 501

International Executive Housekeepers Association

International Executive Housekeepers Association Educational Foundation Spartan Scholarship 351
International Executive Housekeepers Educational Foundation 307

International Federation of Professional and Technical Engineers

International Federation of Professional and Technical Engineers Annual Scholarship 501

International Society for Optical Engineering (SPIE)

SPIE Educational Scholarships in Optical Science and Engineering 93

International Technology Education Association

International Technology Education Association Undergraduate Scholarship in Technology Education 265
Maley/Foundation for Technology Education Scholarship 265

International Union of Electronic, Electrical, Salaries, Machine and Furniture Workers

David J. Fitzmaurice Engineering Scholarship 265
IUE-CWA International Bruce Van Ess Scholarship 501
Paul Jennings Scholarship Award 501
Willie Rudd Scholarship 502

International Union of Operating Engineers

International Union of Operating Engineers Local 701 Scholarship 511

Jaycees

Charles Ford Scholarship 502
Jaycee Charles R. Ford Scholarship 522
Jaycee Thomas Wood Baldrige Scholarship 523
Thomas Wood Baldrige Scholarship 502

Jobs Daughters

Davis-Roberts Scholarships 497

Junior Achievement

Junior Achievement Joe Francomano Scholarship 502
Junior Achievement Office Depot Scholarship 502
National Association of Insurance Women/Junior Achievement of Maine Scholarship 217
Walt Disney Company Foundation Scholarship 112

Junior Classical League

National Junior Classical League Scholarship 311

Knights of Columbus

Fourth Degree Pro Deo and Pro Patria (Canada) 503
Francis P. Matthews and John E. Swift Educational Trust Scholarships 503
John W. Mc Devitt (Fourth Degree) Scholarships 503

Knights of Lithuania

Knights of Lithuania National Scholarships 503

Korean-American Scientists and Engineers Association

KSEA Scholarships 245

Lambda Alpha National Collegiate Honor Society for Anthropology

ASLA Council of Fellows Scholarship 371
Lambda Alpha National Collegiate Honor Society for Anthropology National Dean's List Award 88

Michigan Society of Professional Engineers

Michigan Society of Professional Engineers Undesignated Grant 165

Minnesota Medical Association

Military Benefit Association scholarship 504

Mutual Benefit Society

Astrid G. Cates and Myrtle Beinhauer Scholarship Funds 515

National 4-H

All American Youth Horse Show Foundation 4-H Scholarship 509
Charles & Gwenna Lifer 4-H Scholarship 509
Mary E. Border Ohio Scholarship 509
Mr. & Mrs. G. Deming Seymour 4-H Scholarship 509
Paul A. & Ethel I. Smith 4-H Scholarship 83

National Alliance of Postal and Federal Employees

Ashby B. Carter Memorial Scholarship Program 505

National Association for the Advancement of Colored People

Agnes Jones Jackson Scholarship 505
Hubertus W.V. Willems Scholarship for Male Students 166
Louis Stokes Science and Technology Award 139
NAACP Lillian and Samuel Sutton Education Scholarship 232
Roy Wilkins Scholarship 505

National Association of Food Equipment Dealers

National Association of Food Equipment Dealers, Inc. Scholarship 496

National Beta Club

National Beta Club Scholarship 505

National Black Nurses' Association

AETNA Scholarship 427
Dr. Hilda Richards Scholarship 427
Dr. Lauranne Sams Scholarship 427
Kaiser Permanente School of Anesthesia Scholarship 427
Martha R. Dudley LVN/LPN Scholarship 428
Mayo Foundations Scholarship 428
NBNA Board of Directors Scholarship 428
Nursing Spectrum Scholarship 428

National Foster Parent Association

National Foster Parent Association Scholarship 506

National Fraternal Society of the Deaf

National Fraternal Society of the Deaf Scholarships 506

National Honor Society

National Honor Society Scholarships 505

National Military Intelligence Association

National Military Intelligence Association Scholarship 506

National Rifle Association

Jeanne E. Bray Memorial Scholarship Program 506

National Roofing Contractors Association

North East Roofing Educational Foundation Scholarship 508

National Society of Accountants

Stanley H. Stearman Scholarship 66

National Society of Professional Engineers

Paul H. Robbins Honorary Scholarship 166

National Strength and Conditioning Association

GNC Nutrition Research Grant 335
National Strength and Conditioning Association Challenge Scholarship 335
National Strength and Conditioning Association High School Scholarship 336
National Strength and Conditioning Association Undergraduate Research Grant 336
National Strength and Conditioning Association Women's Scholarship 336
NSCA Minority Scholarship 336
Power Systems Professional Scholarship 336

National Union of Public and General Employees

Scholarship for Aboriginal Canadians 507
Scholarship for Visible Minorities 507
Terry Fox Memorial Scholarship 507
Tommy Douglas Scholarship 507

NATSO Foundation

Bill Moon Scholarship 507

New York State Society of Professional Engineers
NYSSPE-Past Officers' Scholarship 508

Non Commissioned Officers Association
Non-Commissioned Officers Association Scholarships 508

Northeast Fresh Foods Alliance
Northeast Fresh Foods Alliance Scholarship Awards Program 509

Northeastern Loggers Association
Northeastern Loggers' Association Scholarships 509

Ohio Civil Service Employee Association
Les Best Scholarship 510

Ohio Farmers Union
Joseph Fitcher Scholarship Contest 83
Virgil Thompson Memorial Scholarship Contest 76

Order of the Arrow
E. Urner Goodman Scholarship 494

Oregon State Fiscal Association
Oregon State Fiscal Association Scholarship 511

Other Student Academic Clubs
American Society of Agricultural and Biological Engineers Foundation Scholarship 78
American Society of Agricultural and Biological Engineers Student Engineer of the Year Scholarship 251
Berna Lou Cartwright Scholarship 394
John L. and Sarah G. Merriam Scholarship 78
Mary Morrow-Edna Richards Scholarship 233
Oregon Publishing Company/Hilliard Scholarship 511
Phi Alpha Theta Paper Prizes 339
Phi Alpha Theta World History Association Paper Prize 339
Phi Alpha Theta/Western Front Association Paper Prize 339
Sylvia W. Farny Scholarship 394
William J. and Marijane E. Adams, Jr. Scholarship 78

Parents Without Partners
Parents Without Partners International Scholarship Program 512

Phi Kappa Phi
Literacy Initiative Grant Competition 501
Promotion of Excellence Grants Program 227

Pony of the Americas Club
Pony of the Americas Scholarship 513

Professional Horsemen Association
Guy Stoops Memorial Professional Horsemen's Family Scholarship 492
Professional Horsemen's Scholarship Fund 513

Recording for the Blind and Dyslexic
Marion Huber Learning Through Listening Awards 513
Mary P. Oenslager Scholastic Achievement Awards 513

Reserve Officers Association
Henry J. Reilly Memorial Scholarship-High School Seniors and First Year Freshmen 514
Henry J. Reilly Memorial Undergraduate Scholarship Program for College Attendees 514

Screen Actors' Guild
Monster Non-RN Undergraduate Scholarship 422
Screen Actors Guild Foundation/John L. Dales Scholarship (Transitional) 514

Second Bombardment Association
Second Bombardment Association Scholarship 514

Service Employees International Union
Charles Hardy Memorial Scholarship Awards 514

Society of Architectural Historians
Richland/Lexington SCSEA Scholarship 515

Society of Automotive Engineers
Detroit Section SAE Technical Scholarship 270
SAE Baltimore Section Bill Brubaker Scholarship 270
SAE Long Term Member Sponsored Scholarship 271

Society of Motion Picture and Television Engineers
Lou Wolf Memorial Scholarship 298
Student Paper Award 299

Society of Physics Students
Society of Physics Students Outstanding Student in Research 515
Society of Physics Students Peggy Dixon 2-Year College Scholarship 515
Society of Physics Students Scholarships 448

Society of Women Engineers
Bechtel Corporation Scholarship 176
Chevron Texaco Corporation Scholarships 168
Daimler Chrysler Corporation Scholarship 246
Judith Resnik Memorial Scholarship 130
SWE St. Louis Scholarship 282

Soil and Water Conservation Society
Donald A. Williams Scholarship Soil Conservation Scholarship 216
Melville H. Cohee Student Leader Conservation Scholarship 410

SOKOL, USA
Slovak Gymnastic Union SOKOL, USA/Milan Getting Scholarship 515

Springfield Newspaper 25-Year Club
Horace Hill Scholarship 497

Tau Beta Pi Association
Tau Beta Pi Scholarship Program 282

Teamsters
Teamsters Clyde C. Crosby/Joseph M. Edgar Memorial Scholarship 511
Teamsters Council 37 Federal Credit Union Scholarship 511
Teamsters Local 305 Scholarship 511

Tennessee Education Association
TEA Don Sahli-Kathy Woodall Sons and Daughters Scholarship 515
TEA Don Sahli-Kathy Woodall Undergraduate Scholarship 238

Tire Industry Association
Michelin/TIA Scholarships 496

Transportation Club International
Transportation Clubs International Charlotte Woods Scholarship 130

United Agribusiness League
United Agricultural Benefit Trust Scholarship 77

United Daughters of the Confederacy
Admiral Raphael Semmes Scholarship 519
Barbara Jackson Sichel Memorial Scholarship 519
Charlotte M. F. Bentley / New York Chapter 103 Scholarship 519
Cody Bachman Scholarship 519
Cora Bell Wesley Memorial Scholarship 519
Cornelia Branch Stone Scholarship 519
David Stephen Wylie Scholarship 520
Dorothy Williams Scholarship 520
Elizabeth and Wallace Kingsbury Scholarship 520

Gertrude Botts-Saucier Scholarship 520
Hector W. Church Scholarship 520
Helen James Brewer Scholarship 340
Henry Clay Darsey Scholarship 520
Janet B. Seippel Scholarship 521
Lola B. Curry Scholarship 521
M. B. Poppenheim Memorial Scholarship 521
Major Madison Bell Scholarship 521
Matthew Fontaine Maury Scholarship 521
Mrs. Ella M. Franklin Scholarship 521
Mrs. L. H. Raines Memorial Scholarship 522
Phoebe Pember Memorial Scholarship 433
S.A. Cunningham Scholarship 522
Stonewall Jackson Scholarship 522
Walter Reed Smith Scholarship 154
Winnie Davis-Children of the Confederacy Scholarship 522

United Food and Commercial Workers
James A. Suffridge United Food and Commercial Workers Scholarship Program 522

USA Water Ski
American Water Ski Educational Foundation Scholarship 493

Utility Workers Union of America
Utility Workers Union of America Scholarship Awards Program 523

Veterans of Foreign Wars or Auxiliary
Francis L. Booth Medical Scholarship sponsored by LAVFW Department of Maine 327
Junior Girls Scholarship Program 504

West Virginia Broadcasters Association
West Virginia Broadcasters Association Fund 181

Western Fraternal Life Association
Western Fraternal Life Association National Scholarship 523

Women in Aviation, International
Airbus Leadership Grant 132
Cincinnati Heart of it All Chapter Women in Aviation, International Elisha Hall Memorial Scholarship 132
Dassault Falcon Jet Corporation Scholarship 132
Delta Air Lines Aircraft Maintenance Technology Scholarship 132
Delta Air Lines Engineering Scholarship 132
Delta Air Lines Maintenance Management/Aviation Business Management Scholarship 133
Dr. Manny Horowitz Scholarship 133
GAT Wings to the Future Management Scholarship 133
Keep Flying Scholarship 133
Pratt and Whitney Maintenance Scholarships 133
Professional Publications Services, Inc. Corporate Aviation Scholarship 133
Rockwell Collins Engineering/Technical Scholarship 134
The Boeing Career Enhancement Scholarship 134
Women in Aviation, International Achievement Awards 134
Women in Aviation, International Management Scholarships 134
Women in Corporate Aviation Career Scholarships 134
Women Military Aviators, Inc. Memorial Scholarship 134

Women in Logistics
Women in Logistics Scholarship 157

Wyoming Farm Bureau
King-Livingston Scholarship 523
Wyoming Farm Bureau Continuing Education Scholarships 523
Wyoming Farm Bureau Federation Scholarships 524

Young American Bowling Alliance
Alberta E. Crowe Star of Tomorrow Award 523
Chuck Hall Star of Tomorrow Scholarship 483
Gift for Life Scholarship 524
Pepsi-Cola Youth Bowling Championships 524
Professional Bowlers Association Billy Welu Memorial Scholarship 513

Corporate Affiliation

Employment Experience

Agriculture

A.W. Bodine-Sunkist Memorial Scholarship *537*
College Assistance Migrant Program at St. Edward's
University *540*
Minnesota Soybean Research and Promotion Council
Youth Soybean Scholarship *75*

Air Traffic Controller Field

Air Traffic Control Association Scholarship *116*
Buckingham Memorial Scholarship *537*
San Fernando Valley Chapter of the Ninety-Nines
Career Scholarship *128*

Aviation Maintenance

San Fernando Valley Chapter of the Ninety-Nines
Career Scholarship *128*

Banking

Community Banker Association of Illinois Children of
Community Banking Scholarship *496*
Florida Bankers Educational Foundation Scholarship/
Loan *147*

Brewing Industry

Master Brewers Association of the Americas *81*

Coal Industry

SCPA Scholarship Fund *542*

Community Service

AETNA Scholarship *427*
American Legion Auxiliary Girl Scout Achievement
Award *486*
American Legion Auxiliary Missouri State National
President's Scholarship *485*
American Legion Auxiliary, National President's
Scholarship *538*
American Legion Eagle Scout of the Year *490*
American Legion National Headquarters Eagle Scout of
the Year *490*
Arby's-Big Brothers Big Sisters Scholarship Award *493*
Chairscholars Foundation, Inc. Scholarships *539*
Dallas Morning News Annual Teenage Citizenship
Tribute *540*
Delta Delta Delta Graduate Scholarship *497*
Delta Delta Delta Undergraduate Scholarship *497*
Distinguished Student Scholar Award *235*
Dr. Hilda Richards Scholarship *427*
Dr. Lauranne Sams Scholarship *427*
E. U. Parker Scholarship *546*
Foundation of the National Student Nurses' Association
Career Mobility Scholarship *422*
Foundation of the National Student Nurses' Association
Specialty Scholarship *423*
Graduate Student Scholar Award *236*
Harris Wofford Awards *551*
Hermione Grant Calhoun Scholarship *546*
Howard Brown Rickard Scholarship *101*
Jennica Ferguson Memorial Scholarship *546*
Kaiser Permanente School of Anesthesia Scholarship *427*
Kenneth Jernigan Scholarship *546*
King Olav V Norwegian-American Heritage Fund *106*
Kuchler-Killian Memorial Scholarship *546*
Marion Huber Learning Through Listening Awards *513*
Martha R. Dudley LVN/LPN Scholarship *428*
Mary P. Oenslager Scholastic Achievement Awards *513*
Mayo Foundations Scholarship *428*
Melva T. Owen Memorial Scholarship *546*
National Association of Insurance Women/Junior
Achievement of Maine Scholarship *217*
National Federation of the Blind Computer Science
Scholarship *193*
National Federation of the Blind Educator of Tomorrow
Award *232*
National Federation of the Blind Humanities
Scholarship *353*
NBNA Board of Directors Scholarship *428*
Nursing Spectrum Scholarship *428*
Project Higher *538*
Sally S. Jacobsen Scholarship *546*

Taddonio Scholarship *550*
Ted Bricker Scholarship *461*
The Virginia Peninsula Post of the Society of American
Military Engineers (S.A.M.E.) Scholarship *103*
Yoshiyama Award for Exemplary Service to the
Community *551*
Young Women in Public Affairs Award *552*

Construction

Project BEST Scholarship *513*

Customs Broker

National Customs Brokers and Forwarders Association
of America Scholarship Award *472*

Designated Career Field

A. Victor Rosenfeld Scholarship *532*
AACN Educational Advancement Scholarships-BSN
Completion *415*
Abbott/Pamela Balzer Career Mobility Scholarship *418*
Albert E. and Florence W. Newton Nurse
Scholarship *433*
Albina Fuel Company Scholarship *532*
American Nephrology Nurses' Association American
Regent Career Mobility Scholarship *418*
American Nephrology Nurses' Association AMGEN
Career Mobility Scholarship *419*
American Nephrology Nurses' Association Anthony J.
Janetti, Inc. Career Mobility Scholarship *419*
American Nephrology Nurses' Association Career
Mobility Scholarship *419*
American Nephrology Nurses' Association NNCC
Career Mobility Scholarship *419*
American Nephrology Nurses' Association Watson
Pharma, Inc. Career Mobility Scholarship *419*
American Orff-Schulwerk Association Research
Grant *220*
Arizona Chapter Dependent/Employee Membership
Scholarship *493*
Arizona Chapter Gold Scholarship *473*
Barbara Carlson Scholarship *343*
Bill Moon Scholarship *507*
California Correctional Peace Officers Association Joe
Harper Scholarship *539*
California Table Grape Farm Workers Scholarship
Program *539*
Carpenters and Joiners Local 2130 Scholarship *548*
Charles Hardy Memorial Scholarship Awards *514*
Chesapeake Corporation Foundation Scholarship
Program for Chesapeake Employees' Children *528*
Clara Abbott Scholarship Program *529*
David A. Koch Scholarship *530*
Deerfield Plastics/Barker Family Scholarship *529*
Donald A. Williams Scholarship Soil Conservation
Scholarship *216*
Donald Estey Scholarship Fund-Rocky Mountain
Chapter *473*
Ford Sons and Daughters of Employees of Roseburg
Forest Products Company Scholarship *533*
Foundation of the National Student Nurses' Association
Career Mobility Scholarship *422*
Friends of Oregon Students Scholarship *234*
George A. Nielsen Public Investor Scholarship *148*
George Reinke Scholarships *473*
George Watters-Nebraska Petroleum Marketers
Association Scholarship *544*
Glenn Jackson Scholars Scholarships (OCF) *533*
Graco Inc. Scholarship Program *530*
Gunild Keetman Assistance Fund *220*
Guy Stoops Memorial Professional Horsemen's Family
Scholarship *492*
Holland-America Line Westours Scholarships *473*
Jennifer Curtis Byler Scholarship for the Study of Public
Affairs *184*
John Hjorth Scholarship Fund-San Diego Chapter *473*
Joseph R. Stone Scholarships *474*
King Olav V Norwegian-American Heritage Fund *106*
Kingsbury Fund Scholarships *531*
Law Librarians in Continuing Education Courses *380*
Louis C. and Amy E. Nuernberger Memorial
Scholarship *545*

Marion A. Lindeman Scholarship *331*
Mc Garry Machine Inc. Scholarship *533*
Nancy Stewart Scholarship Fund-Allegheny Chapter *474*
North East Roofing Educational Foundation
Scholarship *508*
ONS Foundation Ethnic Minority Bachelor's
Scholarship *430*
ONS Foundation Josh Gottheil Memorial Bone Marrow
Transplant Career Development Awards *431*
ONS Foundation Nursing Outcomes Research Grant *330*
ONS Foundation Oncology Nursing Society Research
Grant *330*
ONS Foundation Roberta Pierce Scofield Bachelor's
Scholarships *431*
ONS Foundation/Oncology Nursing Certification
Corporation Bachelor's Scholarships *431*
ONS Foundation/Pearl Moore Career Development
Awards *431*
Orange County Chapter/Harry Jackson Scholarship
Fund *474*
Oregon AFL-CIO Scholarship *548*
Oregon Dungeness Crab Commission Scholarship *548*
Oregon Occupational Safety and Health Division
Workers Memorial Scholarship *548*
Oregon Salmon Commission Scholarship *549*
Oregon Trawl Commission Scholarship *549*
Oregon Trucking Association Scholarship *534*
Pacific Northwest Chapter-William Hunt Scholarship
Fund *474*
Pendleton Postal Workers Scholarship *549*
Procter & Gamble Fund Scholarship Competition for
Employees' Children *535*
Reed's Fuel and Trucking Company Scholarship *534*
Robert D. Forster Scholarship *534*
Roger W. Emmons Memorial Scholarship *534*
Rural Health Student Loan Program *210*
Screen Actors Guild Foundation/John L. Dales
Scholarship (Transitional) *514*
Sepracor Achievement Award for Excellence in
Pulmonary Disease State Management *323*
Sid Richardson Memorial Fund *550*
Southeast American Society of Travel Agents Chapter
Scholarship *475*
SP Newsprint Company, Newberg Mill, Employee
Dependents Scholarship *534*
Stimson Lumber Company Scholarship *535*
Tailhook Educational Foundation Scholarship *551*
Taylor Made Labels Scholarship *535*
Teamsters Clyde C. Crosby/Joseph M. Edgar Memorial
Scholarship *511*
Teamsters Council 37 Federal Credit Union
Scholarship *511*
Thomas C. Woods, Jr. Memorial Scholarship *545*
Truckload Carriers Association Scholarship Fund *154*
Tuition Exchange Scholarships *551*
Tuition Waiver Programs *541*
Tykeson Family Scholarship *549*
Wal-Mart Associate Scholarships *536*
Wal-Mart Higher Reach Scholarship *536*
West Virginia Broadcasters Association Fund *181*
Willett and Marguerite Lake Scholarship *549*
WNGGA Scholarship Program *107*
Woodard Family Scholarship *535*
Youth Automobile Safety Scholarship Essay Competition
for Children of Public Employees *539*

Explosive Ordnance Disposal

Explosive Ordnance Disposal Memorial Scholarship *541*

Farming

Excellence in Equine/Agricultural Involvement
Scholarship *491*
Farm and Ranch Heritage Scholarship *492*
Minnesota Soybean Research and Promotion Council
Youth Soybean Scholarship *75*

Federal/Postal Service

FEEA Scholarships *541*
Harry and Lenora Richardson-National Association of
Postmasters of the United States Scholarship *544*

Harry and Lenora Richardson-Nebraska Branch of the National League of Postmasters Scholarship *544*

Vocational Scholarship Program *491*

Fire Service

International Association of Fire Chiefs Foundation Scholarship Award *543*

NBFAA/Security Dealer Youth Scholarship Program *545*

Food Service

Chick-fil-A Leadership Scholarship *529*

Coca-Cola Salute to Excellence Scholarship Award *308*

Culinary Trust Scholarship Program for Culinary Study and Research *302*

Nancy Curry Scholarship *301*

National Restaurant Association Educational Foundation Professional Development Scholarship for Educators *308*

National Restaurant Association Educational Foundation Undergraduate Scholarships for College Students *308*

National Restaurant Association Educational Foundation Undergraduate Scholarships for High School Seniors *308*

Northeast Fresh Foods Alliance Scholarship Awards Program *509*

Professional Growth Scholarship *301*

Schwan's Food Service Scholarship *301*

Harness Racing

Charles Bradley Memorial Scholarship *542*

Doug Brown Scholarship *542*

Harness Tracks of America Scholarship *543*

Vincent Abate Memorial Scholarship *543*

Helping Handicapped

Foundation of the National Student Nurses' Association Career Mobility Scholarship *422*

Foundation of the National Student Nurses' Association Specialty Scholarship *423*

Jesse Brown Memorial Youth Scholarship Program *541*

Scottish Rite Charitable Foundation College Bursaries *550*

Hospitality/Hotel Administration/Operations

American Express Scholarship Program *350*

Holland-America Line Westours Scholarships *473*

Human Services

Counselor, Advocate, and Support Staff Scholarship Program *69*

Journalism

Asian-American Journalists Association Scholarship *179*

Horace Hill Scholarship *497*

Leather/Footwear

Two/Ten International Footwear Foundation Scholarship *552*

Migrant Worker

Military Benefit Association scholarship *504*

Police/Firefighting

Connecticut Police Corps Program *540*

Dependent Children Scholarship Program *551*

Educational Benefits for Children of Deceased Military and State Police *540*

Firefighter, Ambulance, and Rescue Squad Member Tuition Reimbursement Program-Maryland *300*

Georgia Public Safety Memorial Grant/Law Enforcement Personnel Department Grant *542*

Grant Program for Dependents of Police, Fire, or Correctional Officers *543*

John S. Stamler Memorial Scholarship *540*

Law Enforcement Officer Memorial Scholarship *547*

Law Enforcement Officers' Dependents Scholarship-Arkansas *539*

Massachusetts Public Service Grant Program *545*

NBFAA/Security Dealer Youth Scholarship Program *545*

Nevada Police Corps Scholarship for Dependent Children of Officers Slain in the Line of Duty *547*

New York Memorial Scholarships for Families of Deceased Police Officers, Fire Fighters and Peace Officers *547*

North Carolina Bar Association Young Lawyers Division Scholarship *547*

North Carolina Sheriffs' Association Undergraduate Criminal Justice Scholarships *200*

Ohio Safety Officers College Memorial Fund *548*

Pennsylvania Burglar and Fire Alarm Association Youth Scholarship Program *549*

Police Officers and Firefighters Survivors Education Assistance Program-Alabama *537*

Public Safety Officer Dependent Scholarship *543*

Safety Officers' Survivor Grant Program *545*

Scholarships for Dependents of Fallen Officers *543*

Survivor Tuition Benefits Program *547*

Tuition Waiver Programs *541*

W.H. "Howie" McClennan Scholarship *544*

Private Club/Caddying

Chick Evans Caddie Scholarship *552*

J. Wood Platt Caddie Scholarship Trust *544*

New Jersey State Golf Association Caddie Scholarship *547*

West Virginia Golf Association Fund *542*

Railroad Industry

John Edgar Thomson Foundation Grants *544*

Roadway Worker

Roadway Worker Memorial Scholarship Program *538*

Seafaring

United States Submarine Veterans Inc. National Scholarship Program *552*

Teaching

Critical Teacher Shortage Student Loan Forgiveness Program-Florida *541*

Critical Teacher Shortage Tuition Reimbursement-Florida *225*

Fulbright Program *222*

Indiana Retired Teachers Association Foundation Scholarship *228*

Iowa Teacher Forgivable Loan Program *229*

Maley/Foundation for Technology Education Scholarship *265*

Nadeen Burkeholder Williams Music Scholarship *550*

North Dakota Teacher Shortage Loan Forgiveness Program *233*

U.S. Government Foreign Service

American Foreign Service Association (AFSA) Financial Aid Award Program *484*

American Foreign Service Association (AFSA)/AAFSW Merit Award Program *484*

Impairment

Hearing Impaired

AFSCME: American Federation of State, County, and Municipal Employees Local 75 Scholarship *510*
Allie Raney Hunt Scholarship *552*
Bank of America ADA Abilities Scholarship *56*
Bennion Family Scholarship *553*
Caroline Kark Award *563*
Chairscholars Foundation, Inc. Scholarships *539*
Charmaine Letourneau Fund *557*
Communications Contest for the Deaf and Hard of Hearing *564*
Deaf and Hard of Hearing Section Scholarship Fund *553*
disABLEDperson Inc. College Scholarship Award *557*
Elsie M. Bell Grosvenor Scholarship *553*
Federation of Jewish Women's Organization Scholarship *553*
Handicapped Student Grant-Wisconsin *567*
Idaho Minority and "At Risk" Student Scholarship *559*
International Art Show for Artists with Disabilities *565*
Iowa Vocational Rehabilitation *559*
Ladies Auxiliary National Rural Letter Carriers Scholarship *553*
Louise Nacca Memorial Trust *562*
Lucille B. Abt Scholarship *553*
Minnie Pearl Scholarship Program *557*
Robert B. Bailey III Minority Scholarships for Education Abroad *556*
Robert H. Weitbrecht Scholarship *553*
Samuel M. and Gertrude G. Levy Scholarship Fund *554*
Sara Conlon Memorial Scholarship Award *241*
Scholarship for People with Disabilities *557*
Sertoma Scholarship for Deaf or Hard of Hearing Student *565*
Sir Edward Youde Memorial Overseas Scholarship for Disabled Students *565*
Stanley E. Jackson Scholarship Awards *567*
Terry Fox Memorial Scholarship *507*
Training Support for Youth with Disabilities *563*
Travelers Protective Association Scholarship Trust for the Deaf and Near Deaf *566*
Volta Scholarship Fund *554*
VSA arts-Panasonic Young Soloist Award *440*
VSA arts-Rosemary Kennedy International Young Soloist Award *441*
Walter W. and Thelma C. Hissey College Scholarship Fund *554*
Yellow Ribbon Scholarship *310*

Learning Disabled

AFSCME: American Federation of State, County, and Municipal Employees Local 75 Scholarship *510*
Anne Ford Scholarship *562*
Annual Scholarship Grant Program *306*
disABLEDperson Inc. College Scholarship Award *557*
Erica Lynne E. Durant Memorial Scholarship *556*
International Art Show for Artists with Disabilities *565*
Iowa Vocational Rehabilitation *559*
Kentucky Department of Vocational Rehabilitation *559*
Marion Huber Learning Through Listening Awards *513*
Robert B. Bailey III Minority Scholarships for Education Abroad *556*
Sara Conlon Memorial Scholarship Award *241*
Stanley E. Jackson Scholarship Awards *567*
Terry Fox Memorial Scholarship *507*
Training Support for Youth with Disabilities *563*
VSA arts-Panasonic Young Soloist Award *440*
VSA arts-Rosemary Kennedy International Young Soloist Award *441*

Physically Disabled

AFSCME: American Federation of State, County, and Municipal Employees Local 75 Scholarship *510*
Artistic Endeavors Scholarship *560*
Award of Excellence Asthma Scholarship Program *554*
Bank of America ADA Abilities Scholarship *56*
Berri Mitchel Memorial Scholarship *555*
Calvin Dawson Memorial Scholarship *560*
Chairscholars Foundation, Inc. Scholarships *539*
Cheryl Grimmel Award *564*
Cystic Fibrosis Scholarship *557*
disABLEDperson Inc. College Scholarship Award *557*
Education and Training Assistance Program *558*
Eric Dostie Memorial College Scholarship *560*
Erica Lynne E. Durant Memorial Scholarship *556*
Frank X. and Mary E. Weny Scholarship Fund *556*
GLHF Individual Class Scholarship *558*
Gregory W. Gile Memorial Scholarship Program *558*
Hemophilia Federation of America *560*
Hemophilia Foundation of Michigan Academic Scholarship *560*
Hemophilia Health Services Memorial Scholarship *558*
Hemophilia Health Services Memorial Scholarship Fund *560*
I. H. McLendon Memorial Scholarship *565*
Idaho Minority and "At Risk" Student Scholarship *559*
Immune Deficiency Foundation Scholarship *559*
Institute of Management Accountants Memorial Education Fund Diversity Scholarships *63*
International Art Show for Artists with Disabilities *565*
Iowa Vocational Rehabilitation *559*
Jackson-Stricks Scholarship *562*
Kentucky Department of Vocational Rehabilitation *559*
Kevin Child Scholarship *560*
Larry Smock Scholarship *563*
Lawrence Madeiros Memorial Scholarship *561*
Lazof Family Foundation Scholarship *565*
Lilly Reintegration Scholarship *562*
Louise Nacca Memorial Trust *562*
Mark Music Memorial Scholarship *558*
Matt Stauffer Memorial Scholarship *566*
Michael Bendix Sutton Foundation *561*
Mike Hylton and Ron Niederman Memorial Scholarships *561*
Millie Gonzalez Memorial Scholarship *561*
Monica Bailes Award *564*
New Horizons Scholarship Fund *566*
Pfizer Epilepsy Scholarship Award *564*
Rachel Warner Scholarship *561*
Robert B. Bailey III Minority Scholarships for Education Abroad *556*
Robert Guthrie PKU Scholarship and Awards *563*
Sara Conlon Memorial Scholarship Award *241*
SBAA One-Year Scholarship *566*
Scholarship for People with Disabilities *557*
Scott Tarbell Scholarship *558*
SevenSECURE Scholarship *561*
Sibling Continuing Education Scholarship *561*
Sir Edward Youde Memorial Overseas Scholarship for Disabled Students *565*
Soozie Courter Hemophilia Scholarship Program *561*
Spina Bifida Association of America Four-Year Scholarship Fund *566*
Stanley E. Jackson Scholarship Awards *567*
Terry Fox Memorial Scholarship *507*
Training Support for Youth with Disabilities *563*
VSA arts-Panasonic Young Soloist Award *440*
VSA arts-Rosemary Kennedy International Young Soloist Award *441*
Yellow Ribbon Scholarship *310*

Visually Impaired

AFSCME: American Federation of State, County, and Municipal Employees Local 75 Scholarship *510*
American Council of the Blind Scholarships *554*
Arthur E. and Helen Copeland Scholarships *566*
Bank of America ADA Abilities Scholarship *56*
California Council of the Blind Scholarships *555*
Chairscholars Foundation, Inc. Scholarships *539*
Christian Record Services Inc. Scholarships *556*
Delta Gamma Foundation Florence Margaret Harvey Memorial Scholarship *219*
disABLEDperson Inc. College Scholarship Award *557*
E. U. Parker Scholarship *546*
Ferdinand Torres Scholarship *554*
Floyd Cargill Scholarship *559*
Fred Scheigert Scholarship Program *557*
GuildScholar Award *559*
Handicapped Student Grant-Wisconsin *567*
Harry Ludwig Memorial Scholarship *564*
Harry Ludwig Scholarship Fund *564*
Hermione Grant Calhoun Scholarship *546*
Howard Brown Rickard Scholarship *101*
Idaho Minority and "At Risk" Student Scholarship *559*
International Art Show for Artists with Disabilities *565*
Iowa Vocational Rehabilitation *559*
Jennica Ferguson Memorial Scholarship *546*
Kenneth Jernigan Scholarship *546*
Kuchler-Killian Memorial Scholarship *546*
Louise Nacca Memorial Trust *562*
Mary P. Oenslager Scholastic Achievement Awards *513*
Melva T. Owen Memorial Scholarship *546*
Michael and Marie Marucci Scholarship *312*
National Federation of the Blind Computer Science Scholarship *193*
National Federation of the Blind Educator of Tomorrow Award *232*
National Federation of the Blind Humanities Scholarship *353*
National Federation of the Blind of Missouri Scholarships to Legally Blind Students *563*
North Carolina Division of Services for the Blind Rehabilitation Services *563*
Paul W. Ruckes Scholarship *190*
R.L. Gillette Scholarship *382*
Reggie Johnson Memorial Scholarship *555*
Robert B. Bailey III Minority Scholarships for Education Abroad *556*
Rudolph Dillman Memorial Scholarship *219*
Sally S. Jacobsen Scholarship *546*
Sara Conlon Memorial Scholarship Award *241*
Scholarship Awards *561*
Scholarship for People with Disabilities *557*
Scholarship For The Visually Impaired To Study Abroad *556*
Scholarship For The Visually Impaired To Study In Japan *556*
Scholarship Program for the Blind and Visually Impaired *555*
Sigma Alpha Iota Visually Impaired Scholarship *236*
Sir Edward Youde Memorial Overseas Scholarship for Disabled Students *565*
Stanley E. Jackson Scholarship Awards *567*
Terry Fox Memorial Scholarship *507*
Training Support for Youth with Disabilities *563*
VSA arts-Panasonic Young Soloist Award *440*
VSA arts-Rosemary Kennedy International Young Soloist Award *441*
William and Dorothy Ferrel Scholarship *555*
Yellow Ribbon Scholarship *310*

Military Service

Air Force

AFSCME: American Federation of State, County, and
  Municipal Employees Local 75 Scholarship *510*
Air Force ROTC College Scholarship *567*
Air Space Education Foundation Spouse Scholarship *567*
Airmen Memorial Foundation Scholarship *568*
Commander William S. Stuhr Scholarship Fund for
  Military Sons and Daughters *568*
Daughters of the Cincinnati Scholarship *568*
General Henry H. Arnold Education Grant Program *567*
Scholarship for Children of Special Operations Forces
  Who are Killed in the Line of Duty *568*
Second Bombardment Association Scholarship *514*
The Air Force Sergeants Association Scholarship *568*
The Chief Master Sergeants of the Air Force Scholarship
  Program *568*

Air Force National Guard

AFSCME: American Federation of State, County, and
  Municipal Employees Local 75 Scholarship *510*
Air Space Education Foundation Spouse Scholarship *567*
Airmen Memorial Foundation Scholarship *568*
Alabama National Guard Educational Assistance
  Program *569*
Commander William S. Stuhr Scholarship Fund for
  Military Sons and Daughters *568*
CSM Vincent Baldassari Memorial Scholarship
  Program *569*
Enlisted Association of the National Guard of the
  United States CSM Virgil R. Williams
  Scholarship *571*
General Henry H. Arnold Education Grant Program *567*
Illinois National Guard Grant Program *570*
Indiana National Guard Supplemental Grant *572*
Iowa National Guard Education Assistance Program *570*
Kansas National Guard Tuition Assistance Award
  Program *570*
Kentucky Air National Guard Educational
  Assistance *570*
Kentucky National Guard Tuition Award Program *570*
Leadership, Excellence and Dedicated Service
  Scholarship *571*
Louisiana National Guard State Tuition Exemption
  Program *571*
Montgomery GI Bill (Selected Reserve) *569*
National Guard Association of Colorado (NGACO)
  Education Foundation Inc. Scholarship *571*
Nebraska National Guard Tuition Credit *571*
North Carolina National Guard Tuition Assistance
  Program *571*
Ohio National Guard Scholarship Program *572*
Ohio National Guard Scholarship Program *572*
State Tuition Assistance *569*
Texas National Guard Tuition Assistance Program *572*
The Chief Master Sergeants of the Air Force Scholarship
  Program *568*
USAA Scholarship *570*
Washington National Guard Scholarship Program *572*

Army

AFSCME: American Federation of State, County, and
  Municipal Employees Local 75 Scholarship *510*
American Legion Auxiliary, Department of Texas Past
  President's Parley Medical Scholarship *320*
Army Officers' Wives' Club of the Greater Washington
  Area Scholarship *573*
Army ROTC Historically Black Colleges and Universities
  Program *573*
Army ROTC Two-Year, Three-Year and Four-Year
  Scholarships for Active Duty Army Enlisted
  Personnel *573*
Commander William S. Stuhr Scholarship Fund for
  Military Sons and Daughters *568*
Daughters of the Cincinnati Scholarship *568*
Edward T. Conroy Memorial Scholarship Program *575*
1st Cavalry Division Association Scholarship *574*
Foundation of the First Cavalry Division Association Ia
  Drang Scholarship *574*
Four-Year and Three-Year Advance Designees
  Scholarship *573*

Lieutenant General Clarence R. Huebner Scholarship
  Program *574*
101st Airborne Division Association Chappie Hall
  Scholarship Program *575*
102nd Infantry Division Association Memorial
  Scholarship Program *575*
Scholarship for Children of Special Operations Forces
  Who are Killed in the Line of Duty *568*
Scholarships for Military Children Program *574*
Society of Daughters of the United States Army
  Scholarships *575*
Two- and Three-Year Campus-Based Scholarships *573*
Veterans Dependents Educational Benefits-Maine *574*
Women's Army Corps Veterans Association
  Scholarship *576*

Army National Guard

AFSCME: American Federation of State, County, and
  Municipal Employees Local 75 Scholarship *510*
Alabama National Guard Educational Assistance
  Program *569*
Army ROTC Historically Black Colleges and Universities
  Program *573*
Army ROTC Two-Year, Three-Year and Four-Year
  Scholarships for Active Duty Army Enlisted
  Personnel *573*
Commander William S. Stuhr Scholarship Fund for
  Military Sons and Daughters *568*
Connecticut Army National Guard 100% Tuition
  Waiver *576*
CSM Vincent Baldassari Memorial Scholarship
  Program *569*
Dedicated Military Junior College Program *576*
Enlisted Association of the National Guard of the
  United States CSM Virgil R. Williams
  Scholarship *571*
Four-Year and Three-Year Advance Designees
  Scholarship *573*
Illinois National Guard Grant Program *570*
Indiana National Guard Supplemental Grant *572*
Iowa National Guard Education Assistance Program *570*
Kansas National Guard Tuition Assistance Award
  Program *570*
Kentucky Army National Guard Federal Tuition
  Assistance *577*
Kentucky National Guard Tuition Award Program *570*
Leadership, Excellence and Dedicated Service
  Scholarship *571*
Louisiana National Guard State Tuition Exemption
  Program *571*
Montgomery GI Bill (Selected Reserve) *569*
National Guard Association of Colorado (NGACO)
  Education Foundation Inc. Scholarship *571*
Nebraska National Guard Tuition Credit *571*
North Carolina National Guard Tuition Assistance
  Program *571*
Ohio National Guard Scholarship Program *572*
Ohio National Guard Scholarship Program *572*
State Tuition Assistance *569*
Texas National Guard Tuition Assistance Program *572*
Two- and Three-Year Campus-Based Scholarships *573*
Two-Year Reserve Forces Duty Scholarships *576*
USAA Scholarship *570*
Veterans Dependents Educational Benefits-Maine *574*
Washington National Guard Scholarship Program *572*

Coast Guard

AFSCME: American Federation of State, County, and
  Municipal Employees Local 75 Scholarship *510*
Allie Mae Oden Memorial Scholarship *504*
Colonel Hazel Elizabeth Benn U.S.M.C. Scholarship *578*
Commander William S. Stuhr Scholarship Fund for
  Military Sons and Daughters *568*
Daughters of the Cincinnati Scholarship *568*
Fleet Reserve Association Scholarship *499*
New York Council Navy League Scholarship Fund *578*
Schuyler S. Pyle Award *578*
Stanley A. Doran Memorial Scholarship *578*
Tailhook Educational Foundation Scholarship *551*

General

AFCEA/Lockheed Martin Orincon IT Scholarship *191*
AFSCME: American Federation of State, County, and
  Municipal Employees Local 75 Scholarship *510*
Alabama G.I. Dependents Scholarship Program *578*
Albert M. Lappin Scholarship *488*
American Ex-Prisoner of War Scholarships: Peter
  Connacher Memorial Scholarship *594*
American Legacy Scholarship *585*
American Legion Auxiliary Department of Alabama
  Scholarship Program *579*
American Legion Auxiliary Department of Arkansas
  Academic Scholarship *579*
American Legion Auxiliary Department of Arkansas
  Nurse Scholarship *415*
American Legion Auxiliary Department of Connecticut
  Memorial Educational Grant *484*
American Legion Auxiliary Department of Florida
  Department Scholarships *579*
American Legion Auxiliary Department of Iowa
  Children of Veterans Scholarship *579*
American Legion Auxiliary Department of Michigan
  Memorial Scholarship *580*
American Legion Auxiliary Department of Minnesota
  Scholarships *581*
American Legion Auxiliary Department of Nebraska
  Nurse's Gift Tuition Scholarship *416*
American Legion Auxiliary Department of Nebraska
  Practical Nurse Scholarship *416*
American Legion Auxiliary Department of Nebraska
  President's Scholarships *581*
American Legion Auxiliary Department of Nebraska
  Student Aid Grants *581*
American Legion Auxiliary Department of New Mexico
  Past President Parley Nurses Scholarship *416*
American Legion Auxiliary Department of North Dakota
  Past President's Parley Nurses' Scholarship *417*
American Legion Auxiliary Department of Ohio
  Department President's Scholarship *582*
American Legion Auxiliary Department of Ohio Past
  President's Parley Nurses' Scholarship *417*
American Legion Auxiliary Department of Oregon
  Nurses Scholarship *417*
American Legion Auxiliary Girl Scout Achievement
  Award *580*
American Legion Auxiliary Missouri State National
  President's Scholarship *485*
American Legion Auxiliary National Presidents
  Scholarship *485*
American Legion Auxiliary National President's
  Scholarship *581*
American Legion Auxiliary National President's
  Scholarship *580*
American Legion Auxiliary National President's
  Scholarships *583*
American Legion Auxiliary Scholarship For Non-
  Traditional Students *580*
American Legion Auxiliary Spirit Of Youth Scholarship
  For Junior Members *580*
American Legion Auxiliary, Department of Idaho
  National President's Scholarship *579*
American Legion Auxiliary, Department of Idaho
  Nursing Scholarship *415*
American Legion Auxiliary, Department of Oregon
  National President's Scholarship *582*
American Legion Auxiliary, Department of Texas
  General Education Scholarship *582*
American Legion Auxiliary, Department of Washington
  Gift Scholarships *583*
American Legion Auxiliary, National President's
  Scholarship *538*
American Legion Department of Maryland General
  Scholarship Fund *584*
American Legion Department of Maryland Math-Science
  Scholarship *444*
American Legion Department of Minnesota Memorial
  Scholarship *489*
American Legion Department of Washington Children
  and Youth Scholarships *490*
American Legion Press Club of New Jersey and Post 170
  Arthur Dehardt Memorial Scholarship *178*
American Legion Samsung Scholarship *583*

Nationality or Ethnic Heritage

American Indian/Alaska Native

A.T. Anderson Memorial Scholarship 89
ACF- Notah Begay III Scholarship Program for Native American Scholar Athletes 604
Actuarial Scholarships for Minority Students 145
Actuarial Scholarships for Minority Students 355
Adolph Van Pelt Special Fund for Indian Scholarships 607
Adult Vocational Training Education Scholarships 611
AFSCME/UNCF Union Scholars Program 604
Agnes Jones Jackson Scholarship 505
Al Qoyawayma Award 163
Al-Ben Scholarship for Academic Incentive 164
Al-Ben Scholarship for Professional Merit 165
Al-Ben Scholarship for Scholastic Achievement 165
Alberta Blue Cross 50th Anniversary Scholarships for Aboriginal Students 601
Alberta Heritage Scholarship Fund Aboriginal Health Careers Bursary 135
Alumni Student Assistance Program 608
Amelia Kemp Scholarship 648
American Association of Airport Executives Foundation Scholarship-Native American 119
American Baptist Financial Aid Program Native American Grants 604
American Dental Association Foundation Minority Dental Student Scholarship Program 204
American Dental Hygienists' Association Institute Minority Scholarship 205
American Geological Institute Minority Scholarship 604
American Indian Education Foundation Scholarship 605
American Indian Endowed Scholarship 647
American Indian Nurse Scholarship Awards 429
American Institute for Foreign Study Minority Scholarships 605
American Meteorological Society/Industry Minority Scholarships 398
American Physical Society Corporate-Sponsored Scholarship for Minority Undergraduate Students Who Major in Physics 447
American Physical Society Scholarship for Minority Undergraduate Physics Majors 444
Arkansas Minority Teacher Scholars Program 221
Bank of America Minority Scholarship 146
BIA Higher Education Grant 618
Blackfeet Nation Higher Education Grant 608
Breakthrough to Nursing Scholarships for Racial/Ethnic Minorities 422
Brown Scholar 221
Burlington Northern Santa Fe Foundation Scholarship 89
Cap Lathrop Scholarship Program 477
Carole Simpson Scholarship 185
Charlotte Observer Minority Scholarships 146
Cherokee Nation Higher Education Scholarship 609
Chief Manuelito Scholarship Program 627
Chips Quinn Scholars Program 360
Colgate "Bright Smiles, Bright Futures" Minority Scholarship 206
College Student Assistance Program 609
Colonial Bank Scholarship 610
Conditional Grant Program 176
Continental Society, Daughters of Indian Wars Scholarship 224
Council for Exceptional Children 610
Council of Energy Resources Tribes Education Fund Scholarship 612
Displaced Homemaker Scholarship 607
Earl G. Graves NAACP Scholarship 151
Educational Assistance Program 451
Emergency Aid and Health Professionals Scholarship Program 607
Environmental Protection Agency Tribal Lands Environmental Science Scholarship 135
Ethnic Diversity College and University Scholarships 57

Ethnic Diversity High School Scholarships 57
Eula Petite Memorial Education Scholarships 223
Fisher Broadcasting, Inc., Scholarship for Minorities 181
Foley & Lardner Minority Scholarship Program 377
Fortune Brands Scholars Program 641
Future Journalists Scholarship Program 180
Garth Reeves, Jr. Memorial Scholarships 187
Gates Millennium Scholars Program 605
Gates Millennium Scholars Program 617
General Motors Engineering Scholarship 284
George M. Brooker Collegiate Scholarship for Minorities 452
Gil Purcell Memorial Journalism Scholarship for Native Canadians 359
Glenn Godfrey Memorial Scholarship 621
Gulf Coast Research Laboratory Minority Summer Grant 294
HBCU-Central.com Minority Scholarship Program 614
Health Professions Preparatory Scholarship Program 425
High School Journalism Workshops for Minorities 360
Higher Education Scholarship Program 627
Higher Education Supplemental Scholarship 631
Hopi Scholarship 618
Hopi Supplemental Grant 618
Howard Vollum American Indian Scholarship 194
HTGSP Grant & Tuition/Book Scholarship 619
Hubertus W.V. Willems Scholarship for Male Students 166
Idaho Minority and "At Risk" Student Scholarship 559
Indian Health Service Health Professions Pre-graduate Scholarships 209
Indian Health Service Health Professions Pre-professional Scholarship 318
Indian Student Fee Waiver 624
Institute of Food Technologists/Master Foods USA Undergraduate Mentored Scholarship 303
International Order of the King's Daughters and Sons North American Indian Scholarship 619
Jackie Robinson Scholarship 620
James C. Caldwell Assisting Men and Women of Toledo Scholarship 620
Jimmy A. Young Memorial Education Recognition Award 322
John C. Santistevan Memorial Scholarship 111
Judith McManus Price Scholarship 481
Ken Inouye Scholarship 369
Ken Kashiwahara Scholarship 186
Kentucky Minority Educator Recruitment and Retention (KMERR) Scholarship 229
Koniag Education Career Development Grant 621
Koniag Education Foundation Academic/Graduate Scholarship 621
Koniag Education Foundation College/University Basic Scholarship 621
Lagrant Foundation Scholarship for Undergraduates 150
Landmark Scholars Program 363
Landmark Scholars Program 623
Leonard M. Perryman Communications Scholarship for Ethnic Minority Students 189
LinTV Minority Scholarship 478
Louis Stokes Science and Technology Award 139
Lucinda Todd Book Scholarship 221
Mae Lassley Osage Scholarship Fund 629
Many Voices Residency Program 384
MARC Undergraduate Student Training in Academic Research U*Star Awards 140
Martin Luther King, Jr. Memorial Scholarship 222
Math, Engineering, Science, Business, Education, Computers Scholarships 145
Maureen L. and Howard N. Blitman, PE Scholarship to Promote Diversity in Engineering 166
Menominee Indian Tribe Adult Vocational Training Program 623
Menominee Indian Tribe of Wisconsin Higher Education Grants 623
Mescalero Apache Tribal Scholarship 624

Michigan Indian Tuition Waiver 619
Mike Reynolds $1,000 Scholarship 186
Minnesota Indian Scholarship Program 624
Minorities in Government Finance Scholarship 62
Minority Affairs Committee Award for Outstanding Scholastic Achievement 160
Minority Nurse Magazine Scholarship Program 426
Minority Scholarship Award for Academic Excellence in Physical Therapy 321
Minority Scholarship Award for Academic Excellence-Physical Therapist Assistant 322
Minority Scholarship Awards for College Students 160
Minority Scholarship Awards for Incoming College Freshmen 160
Minority Student Summer Scholarship 109
Minority Teacher Incentive Grant Program 224
Minority Teachers of Illinois Scholarship Program 228
Minority Travel Fund Award 401
Minority Undergraduate Retention Grant-Wisconsin 647
Minority Undergraduate Student Awards 142
Missouri Minority Teaching Scholarship 231
Morris K. Udall Undergraduate Scholarships 294
Multicultural Scholarship Program 625
NAACP Lillian and Samuel Sutton Education Scholarship 232
NACME Scholars Program 268
National Leadership Development Grants 614
National Minority Junior Golf Scholarship 625
National Society Daughters of the American Revolution American Indian Scholarship 626
National Society Daughters of the American Revolution Frances Crawford Marvin American Indian Scholarship 626
Native American Education Grants 631
Native American Journalists Association Scholarships 365
Native American Leadership in Education (NALE) 145
Navajo Generating Station Navajo Scholarship 634
New York State Aid to Native Americans 626
North Dakota Indian Scholarship Program 634
Northwest Journalists of Color Scholarship 365
NSCA Minority Scholarship 336
Ohio Newspapers Foundation Minority Scholarship 366
Ohkay Owingeh Tribal Scholarship of the Pueblo of San Juan 632
Oneida Higher Education Grant Program 627
ONS Foundation Ethnic Minority Bachelor's Scholarship 430
Oregon Native American Chamber of Commerce Scholarship 628
Osage Higher Education Grant 629
Osage Tribal Education Committee Scholarship 629
Peabody Scholarship 619
Persina Scholarship for Minorities in Journalism 360
Peter Doctor Memorial Iroquois Scholarship 630
PoP'ay Scholarship 632
Public Relations Society of America Multicultural Affairs Scholarship 185
Racial/Ethnic Leadership Education (RELE) 437
Raymond H. Trott Scholarship 632
RDW Group, Inc. Minority Scholarship for Communications 186
Richard S. Smith Scholarship 638
Robert B. Bailey III Minority Scholarships for Education Abroad 556
Rosewood Family Scholarship Fund 613
Roy Wilkins Scholarship 505
Royal Bank Aboriginal Student Awards 153
Royce Osborn Minority Student Scholarship 323
Santo Domingo Scholarship 633
Sara Conlon Memorial Scholarship Award 241
Scholarship for Minority College Students 224
Scholarship for Minority High School Students 224
Scholarship for Visible Minorities 507
Scholarships for Minority Accounting Students 54
Scholarships for Minority Accounting Students 55

Cardinal Health Scholarship 70
Cargill Scholarship Program 70
Carole Simpson Scholarship 185
Carter and Burgess Scholarship 283
Casimir, Dominique and Jaques Scholarship 638
Castle Rock Foundation Scholarship 154
CDM Scholarship/Internship 177
Charlotte Observer Minority Scholarships 146
Chevron/Texaco Scholars Program 177
Chicago Inter-Alumni Council Scholarship 638
Chicago Public Schools UNCF Campaign 639
Chips Quinn Scholars Program 360
Cisco/UNCF Scholars Program 197
Cleveland Foundation Scholarship 639
Cleveland Municipal School Scholarship 639
Clorox Company Foundation Scholarship 639
Colgate "Bright Smiles, Bright Futures" Minority
    Scholarship 206
Colonial Bank Scholarship 610
Columbus Foundation Scholarship 639
Community Foundation of Greater Birmingham
    Scholarship 639
Con Edison Scholarship 70
Conditional Grant Program 176
Costco Scholarship 639
C-SPAN Scholarship Program 189
CVS/Pharmacy Scholarship 442
Dallas Independent School District Scholarship 640
Dallas Mavericks 640
Dallas Metroplex Council of Black Alumni Association
    Scholarship 640
Davenport Forte Pedestal Fund 640
Del Jones Memorial Travel Award 459
Dell/UNCF Corporate Scholars Program 155
Donna Jamison Lago Memorial Scholarship 626
DuPont Scholarship 640
Duquesne Light Company Scholarship 640
E.J. Josey Scholarship Award 380
Earl G. Graves NAACP Scholarship 151
Earl Warren Legal Training General Scholarship 377
Educational Assistance Program 451
Emerson Electric Company Scholarship 71
Ethnic Diversity College and University Scholarships 57
Ethnic Diversity High School Scholarships 57
Fannie Mae Foundation Scholarship 461
Fifth/Third Scholars Program 640
Financial Services Institution Scholarship 71
Fisher Broadcasting, Inc., Scholarship for Minorities 181
Flowers Industries Scholarship 155
Foley & Lardner Minority Scholarship Program 377
Ford/UNCF Corporate Scholars Program 71
Fort Worth Independent School District Scholarship 641
Fortune Brands Scholars Program 641
Future Journalists Scholarship Program 180
Garth Reeves, Jr. Memorial Scholarships 187
Gates Millennium Scholars Program 617
Gates Millennium Scholars Program (Gates
    Foundation) 641
Gene Hovis Memorial Scholarship 202
George M. Brooker Collegiate Scholarship for
    Minorities 452
Gerald Boyd/Robin Stone Non-Sustaining
    Scholarship 364
Gheens Foundation Scholarship 641
Gilbane Scholarship/Internship 283
Gulf Coast Research Laboratory Minority Summer
    Grant 294
Hallie Q. Brown Scholarship 625
HBCU-Central.com Minority Scholarship Program 614
Heinz Environmental Fellows Program 142
Herbert Lehman Scholarship Program 624
Herman J. Neal Scholarship 63
High School Journalism Workshops for Minorities 360
Houghton-Mifflin Company Fellows Program 641
Houston Symphony/ Top Ladies Scholarship 115
Hubertus W.V. Willems Scholarship for Male
    Students 166
Idaho Minority and "At Risk" Student Scholarship 559
Inez Peppers Lovett Scholarship Fund 223
Institute of Food Technologists/Master Foods USA
    Undergraduate Mentored Scholarship 303
Jackie Robinson Scholarship 620
James C. Caldwell Assisting Men and Women of Toledo
    Scholarship 620
Jesse Jones, Jr. Scholarship 641
Jimmy A. Young Memorial Education Recognition
    Award 322
John C. Santistevan Memorial Scholarship 111
John W. Anderson Foundation Scholarship 641
Joseph A. Towles African Study Abroad Scholarship 641
Judith McManus Price Scholarship 481
Kansas City Initiative Scholarship 642
Ken Inouye Scholarship 369

Ken Kashiwahara Scholarship 186
Kentucky Minority Educator Recruitment and Retention
    (KMERR) Scholarship 229
KeyCorp Scholars Program/Internship 155
Kodak Engineering Excellence Program Scholarship 197
Kroger Scholarship 642
Kroger/Pepsi Scholarship 642
Kuntz Foundation Scholarship 642
Lagrant Foundation Scholarship for Undergraduates 150
Landmark Scholars Program 363
Landmark Scholars Program 623
Leon Jackson, Jr. Scholarship 536
Leonard M. Perryman Communications Scholarship for
    Ethnic Minority Students 189
Limited, Inc. and Intimate Brands, Inc. Scholarship 642
LinTV Minority Scholarship 478
Louie F. Cox Memorial AK Steel African- American
    Scholarships 601
Louis Stokes Science and Technology Award 139
Lucinda Todd Book Scholarship 221
Lynn Dean Ford IABJ Scholarship Awards 181
Malcolm Pirnie, Inc. Scholars Program 169
Many Voices Residency Program 384
MARC Undergraduate Student Training in Academic
    Research U*Star Awards 140
Martha R. Dudley LVN/LPN Scholarship 428
Martin Luther King Jr. Children's Choir Scholarship 642
Martin Luther King, Jr. Memorial Scholarship 222
MasterCard Scholars Program 155
Maureen L. and Howard N. Blitman, PE Scholarship to
    Promote Diversity in Engineering 166
Maytag Company Scholarship 155
MBIA/William O. Bailey Scholars Program 155
McClare Family Trust Scholarship 353
Medtronic Foundation Internship/Scholarship 642
Mellon Ecology Program (S.E.E.D.S) 411
Mike Reynolds $1,000 Scholarship 186
Minorities in Government Finance Scholarship 62
Minority Affairs Committee Award for Outstanding
    Scholastic Achievement 160
Minority Nurse Magazine Scholarship Program 426
Minority Scholarship Award for Academic Excellence in
    Physical Therapy 321
Minority Scholarship Award for Academic Excellence-
    Physical Therapist Assistant 322
Minority Scholarship Awards for College Students 160
Minority Scholarship Awards for Incoming College
    Freshmen 160
Minority Student Summer Scholarship 109
Minority Teacher Incentive Grant Program 224
Minority Teachers of Illinois Scholarship Program 228
Minority Travel Fund Award 401
Minority Undergraduate Retention Grant-Wisconsin 647
Minority Undergraduate Student Awards 142
Missouri Minority Teaching Scholarship 231
Multicultural Scholarship Program 625
NAACP Lillian and Samuel Sutton Education
    Scholarship 232
NABJ Scholarship 183
NACME Scholars Program 268
National Achievement Scholarship Program 625
National Association of Black Journalists and Newhouse
    Foundation Scholarship 364
National Association of Black Journalists Non-Sustaining
    Scholarship Awards 364
National Leadership Development Grants 614
National Minority Junior Golf Scholarship 625
National Oceanic and Atmospheric Administration
    Educational Partnership Program with Minority
    Serving Institutions Undergraduate Scholarship 268
NBLS Nelson Mandela Scholarship 378
New Horizons Scholars Program 618
New Horizons Scholarship Fund 566
New Jersey Mayor's Task Force Scholarship 643
Northeast Utilities System Scholarship Program 156
Northern Virginia Urban League Scholarship
    Program 627
Northwest Journalists of Color Scholarship 365
NSCA Minority Scholarship 336
Ohio Newspapers Foundation Minority Scholarship 366
ONS Foundation Ethnic Minority Bachelor's
    Scholarship 430
Paul and Edith Babson Scholarship 643
Persina Scholarship for Minorities in Journalism 360
Philadelphia Association of Black Journalists
    Scholarship 367
Philadelphia Tribune Scholarship 367
Principal Financial Group Scholarships 156
Public Relations Society of America Multicultural Affairs
    Scholarship 185
Putnam Scholarship Fund 611
Racial/Ethnic Leadership Education (RELE) 437
Raymond H. Trott Scholarship 632

Raymond W. Cannon Memorial Scholarship
    Program 333
RDW Group, Inc. Minority Scholarship for
    Communications 186
Reader's Digest Scholarship 189
Reliable Life Insurance Company Scholarship
    Program 643
Richard S. Smith Scholarship 638
Richmond Scholarship 643
RMHC/African American Future Achievers Scholarship
    Program 632
Robert B. Bailey III Minority Scholarships for Education
    Abroad 556
Rockwell/UNCF Corporate Scholars Program 156
Ron Brown Scholar Program 608
Ronald McDonald's Chicagoland Scholarship 643
Ronald McDonald's House Charities Scholarship-
    Ohio 643
Rosewood Family Scholarship Fund 613
Roy Wilkins Scholarship 505
Royce Osborn Minority Student Scholarship 323
Sallie Mae Fund American Dream Scholarship 643
San Jose Mercury News Scholarship 644
Sandy Brown Memorial Scholarship 378
Sara Conlon Memorial Scholarship Award 241
SBC Foundation Scholarship 156
SBC Pacific Bell Foundation Scholarship 156
Scholarship for Minority College Students 224
Scholarship for Minority High School Students 224
Scholarship for Visible Minorities 507
Scholarships for Minority Accounting Students 54
Scholarships for Minority Accounting Students 55
Schraft Charitable Trust Scholarship 644
Sevcik Scholarship 283
Shearman and Sterling Scholarship Program 378
Shell/Equilon UNCF Cleveland Scholarship Fund 644
Sherry R. Arnstein Minority Student Scholarship 604
Shreveport Campaign 644
Siragusa Foundation Scholarship 644
Sodexho Scholarship 333
SouthTrust Scholarship 156
Special Animation and Illustration Scholarship 648
Special Libraries Association Affirmative Action
    Scholarship 381
Sprint Scholarship/Internship 71
St. Petersburg Golf Classic Scholarship 644
Stanley E. Jackson Scholarship Awards 567
Star Supporter Scholarship/Loan 454
Stephen Madry Peck, Jr. Memorial Scholarship 311
Sterling Bank Scholarship 644
Taylor Michaels Scholarship Fund 623
TEA Don Sahli-Kathy Woodall Minority
    Scholarship 238
Technical Minority Scholarship 169
1040 K Race Scholarships 59
1040K Race Scholarships 59
Texas Black Baptist Scholarship 636
Texas Health Resources Scholarship 644
Textron Fellows Program 645
The EDSA Minority Scholarship 372
The Sidney B. Williams, Jr. Intellectual Property Law
    School Scholarship 379
Thomas R. Dargan Minority Scholarship 182
Thurgood Marshall Scholarship Fund 232
TJX Foundation Scholarship 645
Townsend and Townsend and Crew LLP Diversity
    Scholarship Program 379
Toyota Scholarship 157
Trull Foundation Scholarship 645
TRW Information Technology Minority Scholarship 197
Twin Cities Chapter Undergraduate Scholarship 65
Twin Cities Graduate MBA Scholarship 65
Union Bank of California 645
United Insurance Scholarship 645
United Methodist Church Ethnic Scholarship 637
United Parcel Service Diversity Scholarship Program 292
United Parcel Service Foundation Scholarship 645
United Way of New Orleans Emergency Assistance
    Fund 645
United Way of Westchester and Putnam, Inc./ UNCF
    Emergency Assistance Fund 646
UPS Corporate Scholars Program/Internship 157
UPS Scholarship for Minority Students 264
USENIX Association Scholarship 197
V103/UNCF Emergency Assistance Scholarship
    Fund 646
Verizon Foundation Scholarship 646
Vermont Teacher Diversity Scholarship Program 239
Virginia Society of CPAs Educational Foundation
    Minority Undergraduate Scholarship 71
Visual Task Force Scholarship 443
Warner Norcross and Judd LLP Scholarship for
    Minority Students 377

Religious Affiliation

Baha'i Faith
Kimber Richter Family Scholarship *649*

Baptist
American Baptist Financial Aid Program Native
    American Grants *604*
American Baptist Scholarships *649*
Texas Black Baptist Scholarship *636*
Woman's Missionary Union Scholarship Program *654*

Christian
Herman Oscar Schumacher Scholarship Fund for
    Men *650*
International Order of the King's Daughters and Sons
    Student Ministry Scholarship *455*
Mary E. Bivins Religious Scholarship *455*

Disciple of Christ
David Tamotsu Kagiwada Memorial Scholarship *453*
Disciple Chaplains' Scholarship *454*
Edwin G. and Lauretta M. Michael Scholarship *454*
Katherine J. Shutze Memorial Scholarship *454*
Rowley/Ministerial Education Scholarship *454*
Star Supporter Scholarship/Loan *454*

Eastern Orthodox
Eastern Orthodox Committee on Scouting
    Scholarships *498*

Episcopalian
William Heath Education Scholarship for Ministers,
    Priests and Missionaries *453*

Jewish
Anna and Charles Stockwitz Children and Youth
    Fund *651*
Biller/Jewish Foundation for Education of Women *651*

Broome and Allen Boys Camp and Scholarship
    Fund *649*
Butrimovitz Family Endowment Fund for Jewish
    Education *651*
David Korn Scholarship Fund *652*
David, Nancy, and Liza Cherney Scholarship Fund *651*
Herbert F. Sacks Memorial Scholarship *652*
Hyman P. Moldover Scholarship *652*
Jewish Social Service Agency of Metropolitan
    Washington Max and Emmy Dreyfuss
    Undergraduate Scholarship Fund *652*
Jewish Vocational Service Scholarship Program *652*
JVS Jewish Community Scholarship *652*
Melvin Mandell Memorial Scholarship *652*
Memorial Foundation for Jewish Culture International
    Scholarship Program for Community Service *106*
Miriam S. Grunfield Scholarship Fund *651*
Morris J. and Betty Kaplun Foundation Annual Essay
    Contest *653*
Morton A. Gibson Memorial Scholarship *652*
Stanley Olson Youth Scholarship *651*
The Lessans Family Scholarship *649*

Lutheran
Amelia Kemp Scholarship *648*
Developmental Disabilities Scholastic Achievement
    Scholarship for Lutheran College Students *208*
Nursing Scholastic Achievement Scholarship for
    Lutheran College Students *420*

Methodist
David W. Self Scholarship *653*
Ernest and Eurice Miller Bass Scholarship Fund *456*
J. A. Knowles Memorial Scholarship *653*
Leonard M. Perryman Communications Scholarship for
    Ethnic Minority Students *189*
National Leadership Development Grants *614*
Priscilla R. Morton Scholarship *653*
Richard S. Smith Scholarship *638*

United Methodist Church Ethnic Scholarship *637*
United Methodist Church Hispanic, Asian, and Native
    American Scholarship *637*
William Heath Education Scholarship for Ministers,
    Priests and Missionaries *453*

Muslim Faith
Al-Ameen Scholarship *653*
Annual Award Program *650*

Presbyterian
Clarence Warren Scholarship Fund *650*
Cydna Ann Huffstetler Memorial Trust Fund *650*
Elsa Everett Memorial Trust Fund *455*
Ethel Francis Crate Scholarship Fund *650*
First Presbyterian Church Scholarship Program *455*
Harry Allen Memorial Trust Fund *650*
Ullery Charitable Trust Fund *455*

Protestant
Cymdeithas Gymreig/Philadelphia Scholarship *647*
Ed E. and Gladys Hurley Foundation Scholarship *454*

Roman Catholic
Catholic Aid Association College Tuition
    Scholarship *649*
Father Krewitt Scholarship *495*
First Catholic Slovak Ladies Association Fraternal
    Scholarship Award for College and Graduate
    Study *613*
Fourth Degree Pro Deo and Pro Patria (Canada) *503*
Francis P. Matthews and John E. Swift Educational
    Trust Scholarships *503*
ICF College Scholarships to High School Seniors *620*
John W. Mc Devitt (Fourth Degree) Scholarships *503*
Knights of Lithuania National Scholarships *503*
Mae Lassley Osage Scholarship Fund *629*
Vocational Scholarship Program *453*

Residence

Alabama

Alabama Broadcasters Association Scholarship 476
Alabama Funeral Directors Association Scholarship 397
Alabama G.I. Dependents Scholarship Program 578
Alabama National Guard Educational Assistance
    Program 569
Alabama Student Grant Program 654
American Legion Auxiliary Department of Alabama
    Scholarship Program 579
Dana Campbell Memorial Scholarship 303
Dixie Boys Baseball Scholarship Program 689
Dixie Youth Scholarship Program 689
First in Family Scholarship 702
Gulf Coast Hurricane Scholarship 168
Hearin-Chandler Journalism Scholarship 362
Helen James Brewer Scholarship 340
John M. Will Journalism Scholarship 362
Kroger Scholarship 642
Lola B. Curry Scholarship 521
Police Officers and Firefighters Survivors Education
    Assistance Program-Alabama 537
Robert C. Byrd Honors Scholarship-Alabama 654
Southeast American Society of Travel Agents Chapter
    Scholarship 475
Swayze Woodruff Scholarship 492
William Heath Education Scholarship for Ministers,
    Priests and Missionaries 453

Alaska

Alaska Sea Services Scholarship 655
Alaskan Aviation Safety Foundation Memorial
    Scholarship Fund 119
American Legion Western District Postsecondary
    Scholarship 660
Cady McDonnell Memorial Scholarship 464
GEAR UP Alaska Scholarship 655
Glenn Godfrey Memorial Scholarship 621
Howard Rock Foundation Scholarship Program 673
Pacific Northwest Chapter-William Hunt Scholarship
    Fund 474
Pride Foundation/Greater Seattle Business Association
    Scholarship 741
Wally Joe Scholarship 305
Western Undergraduate Exchange Program 757

Alberta

Adult High School Equivalency Scholarships 601
Alberta Agriculture Food and Rural Development 4-H
    Scholarship Program 655
Alberta Barley Commission Eugene Boyko Memorial
    Scholarship 77
Alberta Blue Cross 50th Anniversary Scholarships for
    Aboriginal Students 601
Alberta Centennial Scholarship 687
Alberta Heritage Scholarship Fund Aboriginal Health
    Careers Bursary 135
Alberta Heritage Scholarship Fund Alberta Press Council
    Scholarship 601
Alberta Heritage Scholarship Fund CANA
    Scholarships 525
Alberta Opportunities Bursary 655
Alexander Rutherford Scholarships for High School
    Achievement 602
Anna and John Kolesar Memorial Scholarships 218
Belcourt Brosseau Metis Awards 613
Bill Mason Memorial Scholarship Fund 80
Boys and Girls Club of Alberta Scholarships 483
Canada Millennium Bursary 655
Central Alberta Rural Electrification Association
    Scholarship 656
Charles S. Noble Junior "A" Hockey Scholarships 602
Charles S. Noble Junior Football Scholarships 602
Dr. Ernest and Minnie Mehl Scholarship 602
Earl and Countess of Wessex-World Championships in
    Athletics Scholarships 602
Fellowships for Full-time Studies in French-
    University 602
Grant MacEwan United World College Scholarships 602
Jason Lang Scholarship 656
Jimmie Condon Athletic Scholarships 603
Laurence Decor Student Leadership Awards 603
Leo J. Krysa Undergraduate Scholarship 104

Lois Hole Humanities and Social Sciences
    Scholarship 351
Louise McKinney Postsecondary Scholarships 603
Michael Luchkovich Scholarships for Career
    Development 656
New Apprenticeship Scholarships 656
Northern Alberta Development Council Bursary 603
Northern Alberta Development Council Bursary for
    Pharmacy Students 441
Northern Alberta Development Council Bursary
    Partnership Program 657
Northern Student Supplement 657
Persons Case Scholarships 603
Registered Apprenticeship Program Scholarship 657
Robert C. Carson Memorial Bursary 198
Rutherford Scholars 604
Scottish Rite Charitable Foundation College
    Bursaries 550
Teletoon Animation Scholarship Award
    Competition 114
Youth Formerly In Care Bursary 613

Arizona

A Legacy of Hope Scholarships for Survivors of
    Childhood Cancer 748
A.W. Bodine-Sunkist Memorial Scholarship 537
AACHE Scholarship 606
American Legion Auxiliary Department of Arizona
    Health Care Occupation Scholarships 319
American Legion Auxiliary Department of Arizona
    Nurses' Scholarships 415
American Legion Auxiliary Department of Arizona
    Wilma Hoyal-Maxine Chilton Memorial
    Scholarship 449
American Legion, Department of Arizona High School
    Oratorical Contest 660
Arizona Chapter Dependent/Employee Membership
    Scholarship 493
Arizona Chapter Gold Scholarship 473
Arizona Community College Scholarship 745
Arizona Counselor of the Year Scholarship 746
Arizona Hydrological Survey Student Scholarship 212
Arizona Private Postsecondary Education Student
    Financial Assistance Program 666
Arizona Private School Association Scholarship 666
Arizona Quarter Horse Youth Racing Scholarship 491
Burlington Northern Santa Fe Foundation
    Scholarship 89
Cady McDonnell Memorial Scholarship 464
Careers Through Culinary Arts Program Cooking
    Competition for Scholarships 200
ICF College Scholarships to High School Seniors 620
J. Wilmar Mirandon Scholarship 153
Leveraging Educational Assistance Partnership 666
Qwest Leadership Challenge 463
Rocky Mountain Coal Mining Institute Scholarship 167
V.E.T.S. Annual Scholarship 595
Walt Bartram Memorial Education Award 276
Western Undergraduate Exchange Program 757
Youth Automobile Safety Scholarship Essay Competition
    for Children of Public Employees 539

Arkansas

American Legion Auxiliary Department of Arkansas
    Academic Scholarship 579
American Legion Auxiliary Department of Arkansas
    Nurse Scholarship 415
American Legion Department of Arkansas Oratorical
    Contest 660
Arkansas Academic Challenge Scholarship Program 666
Arkansas Health Education Grant Program (ARHEG) 86
Arkansas Minority Teacher Scholars Program 221
Arkansas Single Parent Scholarship 667
Arkansas Student Assistance Grant Program 666
Bryan Close Polo Grill Scholarship 303
Dana Campbell Memorial Scholarship 303
Dixie Boys Baseball Scholarship Program 689
Dixie Youth Scholarship Program 689
Ed E. and Gladys Hurley Foundation Scholarship 454
Emergency Secondary Education Loan Program 135
Florence Wood/Arkansas Occupational Therapy
    Association Scholarship 321

Governor's Scholars-Arkansas 666
Law Enforcement Officers' Dependents Scholarship-
    Arkansas 539
Missing in Action/Killed in Action Dependent's
    Scholarship-Arkansas 586
Potlatch Foundation for Higher Education
    Scholarship 741
Reliable Life Insurance Company Scholarship
    Program 643
Second Effort Scholarship 666
Swayze Woodruff Scholarship 492
Vocational Scholarship Program 453

British Columbia

Bill Mason Memorial Scholarship Fund 80
Leo J. Krysa Undergraduate Scholarship 104
Paul and Helen Trussel Science and Technology
    Scholarship 93
Scottish Rite Charitable Foundation College
    Bursaries 550
Teletoon Animation Scholarship Award
    Competition 114

California

A Legacy of Hope Scholarships for Survivors of
    Childhood Cancer 748
A.W. Bodine-Sunkist Memorial Scholarship 537
Anna and Charles Stockwitz Children and Youth
    Fund 651
APTRA-Clete Roberts Memorial Journalism Scholarship
    Award 358
APTRA-Kathryn Dettman Memorial Scholarship 359
Associate Degree Nursing Scholarship Program 424
Association of California Water Agencies
    Scholarships 91
BAPRM Scholarship Program 672
BEEM Foundation Scholarship 401
Bill Farr Scholarship 369
Bronislaw Kaper Awards for Young Artists 706
Burlington Northern Santa Fe Foundation
    Scholarship 89
Butrimovitz Family Endowment Fund for Jewish
    Education 651
Cabrillo Civic Clubs of California Scholarship 608
Cady McDonnell Memorial Scholarship 464
Cal Grant C 670
California Broadcasters Foundation Intern
    Scholarship 476
California Citrus Mutual Scholarship 79
California Congress of Parents and Teachers, Inc.
    Scholarship 669
California Correctional Peace Officers Association Joe
    Harper Scholarship 539
California Council of the Blind Scholarships 555
California Farm Bureau Scholarship 73
California Grange Foundation Scholarship 495
California Groundwater Association Scholarship 213
California Junior Miss Scholarship Program 670
California Masonic Foundation Scholarship Awards 670
California Water Awareness Campaign Water Scholar 79
California Wine Grape Growers Foundation
    Scholarship 671
CAPPS Scholarship Program 669
Careers Through Culinary Arts Program Cooking
    Competition for Scholarships 200
Carl Greenberg Scholarship 369
Central Valley Nursing Scholarship 424
Chandler Scholars Program Scholarship 736
Charles Hardy Memorial Scholarship Awards 514
Child Development Teacher and Supervisor Grant
    Program 670
CHSSC Scholarship Award 352
Clair A. Hill Scholarship 91
Clorox Company Foundation Scholarship 639
Competitive Cal Grant A 670
Competitive Cal Grant B 671
Continuing Education - Credential Teachers and
    Counselors Scholarship 221
Continuing Education - PTA Volunteers Scholarship 670
Continuing Education for School Nurses
    Scholarship 420

American Legion Auxiliary Department of Iowa
Children of Veterans Scholarship *579*
American Legion Department of Iowa Eagle Scout of
the Year Scholarship *488*
Association for Facilities Engineering Cedar Valley
Chapter # 132 Scholarship *120*
Cooperative Studies Scholarships *74*
Cottey/Cather Writing Prize *757*
Elmer O. and Ida Preston Educational Trust Grants and
Loans *690*
Governor Terry E. Branstad Iowa State Fair
Scholarship *700*
Grand Lodge of Iowa Masonic Scholarship Program *694*
Harriet Hoffman Memorial Scholarship for Teacher
Training *219*
Herbert Hoover Uncommon Student Award *697*
Houston Symphony/ Top Ladies Scholarship *115*
Iowa Foster Child Grants *701*
Iowa Grants *701*
Iowa National Guard Education Assistance Program *570*
Iowa Teacher Forgivable Loan Program *229*
Iowa Tuition Grant Program *701*
Iowa Vocational Rehabilitation *559*
Iowa Vocational-Technical Tuition Grant Program *701*
M.V. McCrae Memorial Nurses Scholarship *416*
MRA Institute of Management Endowment Fund
Scholarship *151*
Oratorical Contest Scholarship-Iowa *661*
Robert C. Byrd Honors Scholarship-Iowa *701*
ShopKo Scholars Program *743*
State of Iowa Scholarship Program *701*
Vincent L. Hawkinson Scholarship for Peace and
Justice *754*
Vocational Scholarship Program *453*
Young Artist Competition *441*

Kansas

Agriculture Scholarships *74*
Berri Mitchel Memorial Scholarship *555*
Brown Foundation Goodyear Tire and Rubber
Company Scholarship for College Students *669*
Brown Foundation Goodyear Tire and Rubber
Company Scholarships for High School Seniors *669*
Bryan Close Polo Grill Scholarship *303*
Burlington Northern Santa Fe Foundation
Scholarship *89*
Cooperative Studies Scholarships *74*
Cottey/Cather Writing Prize *757*
Dan L. Meisinger, Sr. Memorial Learn to Fly
Scholarship *126*
Dr. Click Cowger Baseball Scholarship *661*
Hobble (LPN) Nursing Scholarship *418*
Kansas City Initiative Scholarship *642*
Kansas National Guard Tuition Assistance Award
Program *570*
Midwest Student Exchange Program (MSEP) *714*
Paul Flaherty Athletic Scholarship *662*
Sales Professionals- USA Scholarship *153*
Ted and Nora Anderson Scholarships *488*
Young Artist Competition *441*

Kentucky

Blue Grass Energy Academic Scholarship *668*
Bluegrass Cellular, Inc. Scholarship *668*
College Access Program (CAP) Grant *703*
Conservation of Natural Resources Scholarship *81*
Conservation of Natural Resources Scholarship for
Nontraditional Students *81*
Dana Campbell Memorial Scholarship *303*
Deerfield Plastics/Barker Family Scholarship *529*
Early Childhood Development Scholarship *170*
Fleming-Mason Energy Annual Meeting Scholarship *691*
George R. Crafton Scholarship *81*
Gheens Foundation Scholarship *641*
Grayson Rural Electric Cooperative Corporation
Scholarship *694*
Inter-County Energy Scholarship *700*
Jackson Energy Scholarship *702*
Jackson Purchase Energy Corporation Scholarship *702*
Kentucky Minority Educator Recruitment and Retention
(KMERR) Scholarship *229*
Kentucky Society of Certified Public Accountants
College Scholarship *63*
Kentucky Society of Certified Public Accountants High
School Scholarships *64*
Kentucky Teacher Scholarship Program *229*
Kentucky Transportation Cabinet Civil Engineering
Scholarship Program *174*
Kentucky Tuition Grant (KTG) *703*
NBFAA/Security Dealer Youth Scholarship Program *545*
Owen Electric Cooperative Scholarship Program *739*
Robert C. Byrd Honors Scholarship–Kentucky *703*
Salt River Electric Scholarship Program *743*

Senior Scholarships *745*
Southeast American Society of Travel Agents Chapter
Scholarship *475*
Touchstone Energy All "A" Classic Scholarship *703*
William Heath Education Scholarship for Ministers,
Priests and Missionaries *453*
Women in Rural Electrification Scholarship *759*

Louisiana

Broadcast Scholarship Program *478*
Bryan Close Polo Grill Scholarship *303*
Dana Campbell Memorial Scholarship *303*
Dixie Boys Baseball Scholarship Program *689*
Dixie Youth Scholarship Program *689*
Ed E. and Gladys Hurley Foundation Scholarship *454*
Gertrude Botts-Saucier Scholarship *520*
Gulf Coast Hurricane Scholarship *168*
Leveraging Educational Assistance Program (LEAP) *707*
Louisiana Department of Veterans Affairs State Aid
Program *589*
Louisiana National Guard State Tuition Exemption
Program *571*
Louisiana Scholarship *723*
NBFAA/Security Dealer Youth Scholarship Program *545*
Robert C. Byrd Honors Scholarship-Louisiana *708*
Rockefeller State Wildlife Scholarship *87*
Shreveport Campaign *644*
SIA's Scholarship *304*
Society of Louisiana CPAs Scholarships *69*
Southeast American Society of Travel Agents Chapter
Scholarship *475*
Swayze Woodruff Scholarship *492*
SWE Baton Rouge Section Scholarships *195*
SWE Greater New Orleans Section Scholarship *196*
TOPS Alternate Performance Award *707*
TOPS Honors Award *707*
TOPS Opportunity Award *707*
TOPS Performance Award *708*
TOPS Tech Award *708*
Vocational Scholarship Program *453*
Wally Joe Scholarship *305*
William Heath Education Scholarship for Ministers,
Priests and Missionaries *453*
Willis and Mildred Pellerin Scholarships *758*

Maine

American Legion Department of Maine Children and
Youth Scholarship *662*
American Society of Civil Engineers-Maine High School
Scholarship *172*
Annual Liberty Graphics Art Contest *704*
Barking Foundation Grants *668*
Blessed Leon of Our Lady of the Rosary Award *630*
Bob Elliot- WMTW-TV 8 Journalism Scholarship *190*
Caparanga Award *630*
Challenger Memorial Scholarship Fund *709*
CMP Group Scholarship Fund *709*
Daniel E. Lambert Memorial Scholarship *583*
Dirigo Machine Tool Scholarship *709*
Dr. Alfred and Susan Chan Award *630*
Early College Program *709*
George J. Mitchell Peace Scholarship *709*
Guy P. Gannett Scholarship Fund *363*
Horticulture Research Institute Timothy Bigelow and
Palmer W. Bigelow, Jr. Scholarship *341*
James V. Day Scholarship *488*
Joel Abromson Memorial Foundation *717*
Joseph W. Mayo ALS Scholarship Fund *710*
Lest We Forget POW/MIA/KIA Scholarship *710*
Maine Campground Owners Association
Scholarship *409*
Maine Community College Scholarship *709*
Maine Graphics Art Association *315*
Maine Hospitals Engineers Society Scholarship *709*
Maine Masonic Aid for Continuing Education *710*
Maine Metal Products Association Scholarship *395*
Maine Metal Products Association Scholarship
Program *389*
Maine Rural Rehabilitation Fund Scholarship
Program *75*
Maine Scholarship *723*
Maine Society of Professional Engineers Vernon T.
Swaine- Robert E. Chute Scholarship *266*
Maine State Chamber of Commerce Scholarship - Adult
Learner *710*
Maine State Chamber of Commerce Scholarship - High
School Senior *711*
Maine State Society Foundation Scholarship *711*
Massachusetts Federation of Polish Women's Clubs
Scholarships *622*
National Association of Insurance Women/Junior
Achievement of Maine Scholarship *217*

New England Chapter-National Association to Advance
Fat Acceptance Scholarship *721*
New England Employee Benefits Council Scholarship
Program *151*
New England Film and Video Festival Awards *297*
New England Graphic Arts Scholarship *315*
New England Regional Student Program (New England
Board of Higher Education) *724*
NextGen Access Scholarship Program *690*
NextGen Student Grant Program *691*
Osher Scholarship *709*
PAMAS Restricted Scholarship Award *630*
Parker-Lovejoy Scholarship *740*
R.V. "Gadabout" Gaddis Charitable Fund *294*
Ravenscroft Family Award *630*
Rice Scholarship Fund *710*
Ronald P. Guerrette Future Farmers of America
Scholarship Fund *81*
Scholarship Awards *561*
Scholarship of the Maine School Food Service
Association *305*
Senator George J. Mitchell Scholarship Fund *710*
Senator George J. Mitchell Scholarship Research
Institute Scholarships *717*
Seol Bong Scholarship *632*
Shaw-Worth Memorial Scholarship *698*
TD Banknorth Promise Scholarship *711*
Tuition Waiver Programs *541*
Veterans Dependents Educational Benefits-Maine *574*
Wayne S. Rich Scholarship *740*

Manitoba

Bill Mason Memorial Scholarship Fund *80*
Dr. Alan Beaven Forestry Scholarship *294*
Leo J. Krysa Undergraduate Scholarship *104*
Scottish Rite Charitable Foundation College
Bursaries *550*
Teletoon Animation Scholarship Award
Competition *114*
Young Artist Competition *441*

Maryland

Alice G. Pinderhughes Scholarship *222*
American Legion Department of Maryland General
Scholarship *662*
American Legion Department of Maryland General
Scholarship Fund *584*
American Legion Department of Maryland Math-Science
Scholarship *444*
Baltimore Junior Association of Commerce (BJAC)
Scholarship *675*
Baltimore Rotary Service Above Self Award Program *675*
Carmen V. D'Anna Memorial Scholarship of the Mars
Supermarket Educational Fund *675*
Carville M. Akehurst Memorial Scholarship *341*
Child Care Provider Program-Maryland *230*
College Bound Last-Dollar Grant *675*
Commercial Real Estate Women (CREW)-Baltimore
Scholarship *676*
Cox Education Fund Scholarship *676*
Dana Campbell Memorial Scholarship *303*
Decatur H. Miller Scholarship *338*
Delegate Scholarship Program-Maryland *711*
Distinguished Scholar Award-Maryland *711*
Distinguished Scholar-Teacher Education Awards *230*
Donald Malcolm MacArthur Scholarship *634*
Dr. Freeman A. Hrabowski, III Scholarship *259*
Educational Assistance Grants-Maryland *711*
Edward T. Conroy Memorial Scholarship Program *575*
Erica Lynne E. Durant Memorial Scholarship *556*
Exchange Club of Baltimore Scholarship *676*
Firefighter, Ambulance, and Rescue Squad Member
Tuition Reimbursement Program-Maryland *300*
George V. McGowan Scholarship *259*
Graduate and Professional Scholarship Program-
Maryland *210*
Green Family Book Award *676*
Guaranteed Access Grant-Maryland *712*
Hy Zolet Student Athlete Scholarship *676*
J.F. Tolbert Memorial Student Grant Program *712*
Janet B. Sondheim Scholarship *110*
Janet L. Hoffmann Loan Assistance Repayment
Program *230*
Jeanette R. Wolman Scholarship *375*
Kenneth Hoffman Scholarship *676*
Leslie Moore Foundation Scholarship *677*
Long & Foster Scholarship Program *706*
M & T Bank/ Hispanic College Fund Scholarship
Program *63*
Mary Rubin and Benjamin M. Rubin Scholarship
Fund *673*
Maryland Association of Private Colleges and Career
Schools Scholarship *150*

Maryland Hotel and Lodging Association
Scholarship 677
Maryland SPJ Pro Chapter College Scholarship 369
Maryland State Nursing Scholarship and Living
Expenses Grant 425
NASA Maryland Space Grant Consortium
Undergraduate Scholarships 139
National Aquarium in Baltimore Henry Hall
Scholarship 136
National Symphony Orchestra Young Soloists'
Competition- Bill Cerri Scholarship/High School
Division 722
NBFAA/Security Dealer Youth Scholarship Program 545
Part-time Grant Program-Maryland 712
Physical and Occupational Therapists and Assistants
Grant Program 467
Polish Heritage Scholarship 631
Richard E. Dunne, III Scholarship 677
Scarborough-Scheeler Scholarship 677
Scholarship Awards 561
Senatorial Scholarships-Maryland 712
Sharon Christa McAuliffe Teacher Education-Critical
Shortage Grant Program 230
Sheila Z. Kolman Memorial Scholarship 222
Shoe City-WB54/WB50 Scholarship 673
Student Scholarship in Accounting MD Association of
CPAs 64
Suburban Hospital Healthcare System Scholarship 333
The Anderson-Bell Family College Care Package
Award 677
The Jane and Clarence Spilman Scholarship 677
Walter G. Amprey Scholarship 677
William Donald Schaefer Scholarship 451
William Heath Education Scholarship for Ministers,
Priests and Missionaries 453

Massachusetts

African-American Achievement Scholarship 610
Annie S. Crowell Scholarship Fund 682
Big Y Scholarships 668
Blessed Leon of Our Lady of the Rosary Award 630
Bushrod Campbell and Adah Hall Scholarship 638
Caleb L. Butler Scholarship 682
Caparanga Award 630
Careers Through Culinary Arts Program Cooking
Competition for Scholarships 200
Catherine E. Philbin Scholarship 326
Charles C. Ely Educational Fund 713
Christian A. Herter Memorial Scholarship 712
Deerfield Plastics/Barker Family Scholarship 529
Dorchester Women's Club Scholarship 402
Dr. Alfred and Susan Chan Award 630
Edwards Scholarship 690
First National Bank of Amherst Centennial Educational
Scholarship 682
Frank W. Jendrysik, Jr. Memorial Scholarship 683
Frank X. and Mary E. Weny Scholarship Fund 556
Fred K. Lane Scholarship 683
General Federation of Women's Clubs of Massachusetts
Music Scholarship 225
General Federation of Women's Clubs of Massachusetts
Pennies For Art 111
General Federation of Women's Clubs of Massachusetts
Study Abroad Scholarship 693
George E. Parmenter Aeronautical Scholarship Fund 121
Graduate Study in Cancer Research or Nurse
Practitioner 423
Greater Springfield Accountants Scholarship 57
Henry Broughton, K2AE Memorial Scholarship 90
Heriberto Flores Scholarship 611
Horticulture Research Institute Timothy Bigelow and
Palmer W. Bigelow, Jr. Scholarship 341
Hyannis Normal School Alumni Scholarship 682
James L. Shriver Scholarship 683
James Z. Naurison Scholarship 683
Kathleen M. Peabody, CPA, Memorial Scholarship 58
Kimber Richter Family Scholarship 649
Latino Scholarship 611
Margaret E. and Agnes K. O'Donnell Scholarship
Fund 223
Massachusetts Assistance for Student Success
Program 713
Massachusetts Cash Grant Program 713
Massachusetts Federation of Polish Women's Clubs
Scholarships 622
Massachusetts Gilbert Matching Student Grant
Program 426
Massachusetts Part-time Grant Program 713
Massachusetts Public Service Grant Program 545
MassMutual Scholars Program 683
National Association of Insurance and Financial
Advisors Scholarship 683

New England Chapter-National Association to Advance
Fat Acceptance Scholarship 721
New England Employee Benefits Council Scholarship
Program 151
New England Film and Video Festival Awards 297
New England Graphic Arts Scholarship 315
New England Regional Student Program (New England
Board of Higher Education) 724
Newtonville Woman's Club Scholarships 225
Northeast Utilities System Scholarship Program 156
PAMAS Restricted Scholarship Award 630
Paraprofessional Teacher Preparation Grant 231
Paul and Edith Babson Scholarship 643
Paychex, Inc. Entrepreneur Scholarship 59
Performance Bonus Grant Program 713
Permelia A. Butterfield Scholarship 684
Putnam Scholarship Fund 611
Ravenscroft Family Award 630
Richard and Ethel Koff Memorial Scholarship Fund 402
Scholarship Awards 561
Schraft Charitable Trust Scholarship 644
Seol Bong Scholarship 632
Shaw-Worth Memorial Scholarship 698
Stanley Ciejek Sr. Scholarship 684
TJX Foundation Scholarship 645
Tomorrow's Teachers Scholarship Program 231
United Way/YWCA Scholarship Fund for Women 684
Valley Press Club Scholarships, The Republican
Scholarship; Photojournalism Scholarship, Channel
22 Scholarship 189

Michigan

American Legion Auxiliary Department of Michigan
Memorial Scholarship 580
American Legion Auxiliary National President's
Scholarship 581
American Legion Department of Michigan Oratorical
Contest 662
Carol A. Ratza Memorial Scholarship 138
Coleman A. Young Foundation Scholarship 673
College Scholarships for Cancer Survivors 658
Dr. Gerald O'Connor Michigan Scholarship 491
Economic Club of Grand Rapids Business Study Abroad
Scholarship 62
Ford/UNCF Corporate Scholars Program 71
Gerald M. Crane Memorial Music Scholarship Fund 694
Grand Rapids Combined Theatre Scholarship 694
Guy M. Wilson Scholarships 584
Hemophilia Foundation of Michigan Academic
Scholarship 560
Kroger/Pepsi Scholarship 642
Lawrence P. Doss Scholarship Foundation 64
Lebanese American Heritage Club Scholarship 605
Medical Career Scholarship 319
Michigan Adult Part-Time Grant 714
Michigan Competitive Scholarship 714
Michigan Educational Opportunity Grant 714
Michigan Indian Tuition Waiver 619
Michigan Merit Award 714
Michigan Nursing Scholarship 426
Michigan Society of Professional Engineers
Undesignated Grant 165
Michigan Tuition Grant 714
Michigan Veterans Trust Fund Tuition Grant
Program 590
Midwest Student Exchange Program (MSEP) 714
MSPE Auxiliary Grant for Undergraduate Study 174
New Horizons Kathy Le Tarte Scholarship 309
Nursing Student Scholarship 426
Printing Industries of Michigan Scholarship Fund 316
Recreational Boating Industries Educational Foundation
Scholarships 141
SBC Foundation Scholarship 156
Scholarship for Non-Traditional Student 581
ShopKo Scholars Program 743
Taylor Michaels Scholarship Fund 623
Tuition Incentive Program (TIP) 714
Western Michigan Greenhouse Association
Scholarship 347
Whirlpool Foundation Scholarship 646
William D. and Jewell W. Brewer Scholarship Trusts 584
WXYZ-TV Broadcasting Scholarship 479
Young Artist Competition 441

Minnesota

Agriculture Scholarships 74
American Legion Auxiliary Department of Minnesota
Past President Parley Health Care Scholarship 320
American Legion Auxiliary Department of Minnesota
Scholarships 581
American Legion Department of Minnesota Memorial
Scholarship 489

American Legion Department of Minnesota State
Oratorical Contest 662
Bill Peterson Scholarship 504
Burlington Northern Santa Fe Foundation
Scholarship 89
Carol A. Ratza Memorial Scholarship 138
Cooperative Studies Scholarships 74
James J. Wychor Scholarship 479
Many Voices Residency Program 384
Martin Duffy Adult Learner Scholarship Award 504
Midwest Student Exchange Program (MSEP) 714
Minnesota Academic Excellence Scholarship 715
Minnesota Indian Scholarship Program 624
Minnesota Legionnaires Insurance Trust Scholarship 489
Minnesota Reciprocal Agreement 715
Minnesota Soybean Research and Promotion Council
Youth Soybean Scholarship 75
Minnesota State Grant Program 715
Minnesota State Veterans' Dependents Assistance
Program 591
MSCA/TCF Bank Scholarship Program 758
NBFAA/Security Dealer Youth Scholarship Program 545
Ordean Scholarship Program 67
Postsecondary Child Care Grant Program-
Minnesota 715
Potlatch Foundation for Higher Education
Scholarship 741
Printing Industry of Minnesota Education Foundation
Scholarship Fund 316
Safety Officers' Survivor Grant Program 545
Scholarship for People with Disabilities 557
ShopKo Scholars Program 743
The MNCPA Scholarship Program 64
Twin Cities Graduate MBA Scholarship 65
Vincent L. Hawkinson Scholarship for Peace and
Justice 754
Young Artist Competition 441

Mississippi

Bryan Close Polo Grill Scholarship 303
Dana Campbell Memorial Scholarship 303
Dixie Boys Baseball Scholarship Program 689
Dixie Youth Scholarship Program 689
Gertrude Botts-Saucier Scholarship 520
Gulf Coast Hurricane Scholarship 168
Gulf Coast Research Laboratory Minority Summer
Grant 294
Hearin-Chandler Journalism Scholarship 362
Higher Education Legislative Plan (HELP) 715
John M. Will Journalism Scholarship 362
Mississippi Association of Broadcasters Scholarship 479
Mississippi Eminent Scholars Grant 716
Mississippi Health Care Professions Loan/Scholarship
Program 328
Mississippi Press Association Education Foundation
Scholarship 363
Mississippi Resident Tuition Assistance Grant 716
Mississippi Scholarship 90
Nissan Scholarship 716
Nursing Education Loan/Scholarship-BSN 426
Southeast American Society of Travel Agents Chapter
Scholarship 475
Swayze Woodruff Scholarship 492
Wally Joe Scholarship 305
William Heath Education Scholarship for Ministers,
Priests and Missionaries 453
William Winter Teacher Scholar Loan Program 231

Missouri

Abbington, Vallanteen Scholarship 638
American Legion Auxiliary Missouri State National
President's Scholarship 485
ASCLS Region VI Missouri Organization for Clinical
Laboratory Science Student Scholarship 665
Berri Mitchel Memorial Scholarship 555
Charles Gallagher Student Assistance Program 716
Charles L. Bacon Memorial Scholarship 489
Charles P. Bell Conservation Scholarship 136
Cottey/Cather Writing Prize 757
Dan L. Meisinger, Sr. Memorial Learn to Fly
Scholarship 126
Dana Campbell Memorial Scholarship 303
Emerson Electric Company Scholarship 71
Erman W. Taylor Memorial Scholarship 584
Henry C. McDougal Scholarship 716
John Dennis Scholarship 199
Kansas City Initiative Scholarship 642
Lela Murphy Scholarship 485
Lillie Lois Ford Scholarship Fund 584
M.D. "Jack" Murphy Memorial Scholarship 418
Marguerite Ross Barnett Memorial Scholarship 717
Midwest Student Exchange Program (MSEP) 714
Missouri Broadcasters Association Scholarship 479

The Dr. Peter A. Theodos Memorial Graduate
 Scholarship 326
The Founders Scholarship 615
The James Cosmos Memorial Scholarship 615
The Nicholas S. Hetos, DDS, Memorial Graduate
 Scholarship 208
The Paideia Scholarship 616
Verizon Foundation Scholarship 646
Vocational Scholarship Program 453
Western Association of Ladies Scholarship 646

Prince Edward Island

Bill Mason Memorial Scholarship Fund 80
Leo J. Krysa Undergraduate Scholarship 104
Scottish Rite Charitable Foundation College
 Bursaries 550
Teletoon Animation Scholarship Award
 Competition 114

Puerto Rico

HSF/Toyota Foundation Scholarship Program-Puerto
 Rico 618
Young Epidemiology Scholars Competition 291

Quebec

Bill Mason Memorial Scholarship Fund 80
Carol A. Ratza Memorial Scholarship 138
Leo J. Krysa Undergraduate Scholarship 104
Scottish Rite Charitable Foundation College
 Bursaries 550
Societie des Casinos du Quebec Scholarship 309
Teletoon Animation Scholarship Award
 Competition 114

Rhode Island

A.T. Cross Scholarship 535
Albert E. and Florence W. Newton Nurse
 Scholarship 433
Aldo Freda Legislative Pages Scholarship 741
Bach Organ and Keyboard Scholarship Fund 406
Blessed Leon of Our Lady of the Rosary Award 630
Bruce and Marjorie Sundlun Scholarship 741
Caparanga Award 630
Carl W. Christiansen Scholarship 68
Charles A. Morvillo Memorial Scholarships 750
College Bound Fund Academic Promise Scholarship 742
Constant Memorial Scholarship for Aquidneck Island
 Residents 114
Dr. Alfred and Susan Chan Award 630
Horticulture Research Institute Timothy Bigelow and
 Palmer W. Bigelow, Jr. Scholarship 341
Lily and Catello Sorrentino Memorial Scholarship 741
Massachusetts Federation of Polish Women's Clubs
 Scholarships 622
Michael P. Metcalf Memorial Scholarship 741
New England Chapter-National Association to Advance
 Fat Acceptance Scholarship 721
New England Employee Benefits Council Scholarship
 Program 151
New England Film and Video Festival Awards 297
New England Graphic Arts Scholarship 315
New England Regional Student Program (New England
 Board of Higher Education) 724
PAMAS Restricted Scholarship Award 630
Patty and Melvin Alperin First Generation Scholarship/
 David M. Golden Memorial Scholarship 742
Ravenscroft Family Award 630
Raymond H. Trott Scholarship 632
RDW Group, Inc. Minority Scholarship for
 Communications 186
Rhode Island Commission on Women/Freda Goldman
 Education Award 742
Rhode Island Edsal Advertising Scholarship 298
Rhode Island Foundation Association of Former
 Legislators Scholarship 742
Rhode Island Higher Education Grant Program 742
Rhode Island Pilots Association Scholarship 129
Scholarship Awards 561
Seol Bong Scholarship 632
Shaw-Worth Memorial Scholarship 698
Textron Fellows Program 645

Saskatchewan

Bill Mason Memorial Scholarship Fund 80
Leo J. Krysa Undergraduate Scholarship 104
Scottish Rite Charitable Foundation College
 Bursaries 550
Teletoon Animation Scholarship Award
 Competition 114

South Carolina

Charlotte Observer Minority Scholarships 146
Dana Campbell Memorial Scholarship 303

Dixie Boys Baseball Scholarship Program 689
Dixie Youth Scholarship Program 689
Helen James Brewer Scholarship 340
James F. Byrnes Scholarship 702
Kittie M. Fairey Educational Fund Scholarships 672
Kroger Scholarship 642
Legislative Incentives for Future Excellence Program 744
Richland/Lexington SCSEA Scholarship 515
Robert C. Byrd Honors Scholarship-South Carolina 744
South Carolina Junior Golf Foundation Scholarship 672
South Carolina Need-Based Grants Program 744
South Carolina Teacher Loan Program 237
South Carolina Tuition Grants Program 745
Southeast American Society of Travel Agents Chapter
 Scholarship 475
William Heath Education Scholarship for Ministers,
 Priests and Missionaries 453

South Dakota

Agriculture Scholarships 74
Alert Scholarship 658
Burlington Northern Santa Fe Foundation
 Scholarship 89
Cooperative Studies Scholarships 74
Haines Memorial Scholarship 237
Robert C. Byrd Honors Scholarship-South Dakota 745
ShopKo Scholars Program 743
South Dakota Board of Regents Annis I. Fowler/Kaden
 Scholarship 237
South Dakota Board of Regents Bjugstad Scholarship 77
South Dakota Board of Regents Marlin R. Scarborough
 Memorial Scholarship 745
South Dakota High School Oratorical Contest 664
Treacy Company Scholarships 751
Vincent L. Hawkinson Scholarship for Peace and
 Justice 754
Western Undergraduate Exchange Program 757
Young Artist Competition 441

Tennessee

Dependent Children Scholarship Program 551
Dixie Boys Baseball Scholarship Program 689
Dixie Youth Scholarship Program 689
Helen James Brewer Scholarship 340
Kroger Scholarship 642
NBFAA/Security Dealer Youth Scholarship Program 545
Southeast American Society of Travel Agents Chapter
 Scholarship 475
Swayze Woodruff Scholarship 492
TEA Don Sahli-Kathy Woodall Future Teachers of
 America Scholarship 238
TEA Don Sahli-Kathy Woodall Minority
 Scholarship 238
TEA Don Sahli-Kathy Woodall Sons and Daughters
 Scholarship 515
TEA Don Sahli-Kathy Woodall Undergraduate
 Scholarship 238
Tennessee Education Lottery Scholarship Program
 Tennessee HOPE Access Grant 748
Tennessee Education Lottery Scholarship Program
 Tennessee HOPE Scholarship 748
Tennessee Education Lottery Scholarship Program
 Wilder-Naifeh Technical Skills Grant 749
Tennessee Society of CPA Scholarship 69
Tennessee Student Assistance Award Program 749
Tennessee Teaching Scholars Program 238
Vara Gray Scholarship-General 582
Vocational Scholarship Program 453
Wally Joe Scholarship 305
Whirlpool Foundation Scholarship 646
William Heath Education Scholarship for Ministers,
 Priests and Missionaries 453

Texas

Academic Common Market Waiver 749
Amarillo Area Foundation Scholarships 53
American Legion Auxiliary, Department of Texas
 General Education Scholarship 582
American Legion Auxiliary, Department of Texas Past
 President's Parley Medical Scholarship 320
American Legion High School Oratorical Contest 664
Ann Lane Home Economics Scholarship 305
Azteca Scholarship 619
Bryan Close Polo Grill Scholarship 303
C.J. Davidson Scholarship for FCCLA 340
Career Colleges and Schools of Texas Scholarship
 Program 672
Carter and Burgess Scholarship 283
Casimir, Dominique and Jaques Scholarship 638
Conditional Grant Program 176
Dallas Architectural Foundation - Harrell and Hamilton
 Scholarship Fund 99
Dallas Independent School District Scholarship 640

Dallas Mavericks 640
Dallas Morning News Annual Teenage Citizenship
 Tribute 540
Dana Campbell Memorial Scholarship 303
Dell/UNCF Corporate Scholars Program 155
Dixie Boys Baseball Scholarship Program 689
Dixie Youth Scholarship Program 689
Dr. Juan D. Villarreal/ Hispanic Dental Association
 Foundation 209
Ed E. and Gladys Hurley Foundation Scholarship 454
FCCLA Houston Livestock Show and Rodeo
 Scholarship 340
FCCLA Regional Scholarships 147
FCCLA Texas Farm Bureau Scholarship 147
Fort Worth Independent School District Scholarship 641
Freshman Engineering Scholarship for Dallas
 Women 282
Future Journalists Scholarship Program 180
George and Mary Josephine Hamman Foundation
 Scholarship Program 693
Gertrude Botts-Saucier Scholarship 520
Gulf Coast Hurricane Scholarship 168
Hardy Laudermilk Scholarship 745
J. A. Knowles Memorial Scholarship 653
Jere W. Thompson, Jr., Scholarship Fund 173
Madeira Shaner Scholarship 440
Mary E. Bivins Religious Scholarship 455
Micron Science and Technology Scholars Program 165
Outstanding Rural Scholar Program 333
Reliable Life Insurance Company Scholarship
 Program 643
Rocky Mountain Coal Mining Institute Scholarship 167
SIA's Scholarship 304
St. Regis Houston Scholarship 202
Statewide Scholarships 215
T.P. Wang Scholarship 609
Taylor Michaels Scholarship Fund 623
TCU Texas Youth Entrepreneur of the Year 749
Texas 4-H Opportunity Scholarship 749
Texas AFL-CIO Scholarship Program 516
Texas Black Baptist Scholarship 636
Texas Family Business Association Scholarship 153
Texas Health Resources Scholarship 644
Texas National Guard Tuition Assistance Program 572
Texas Outdoor Writers Association Scholarship 188
Texas Scholarship 723
Texas Society of Professional Engineers (TSPE) Regional
 Scholarships 169
Texas Tennis Foundation Scholarships and
 Endowments 750
The Chinese Professional Club Scholarship 609
Toward Excellence, Access and Success (TEXAS
 Grant) 749
Tuition Equalization Grant (TEG) Program 750
Vocational Scholarship Program 453

Utah

Agriculture Scholarships 74
American Legion Auxiliary National Presidents
 Scholarship 485
Cady McDonnell Memorial Scholarship 464
Cooperative Studies Scholarships 74
Donald Estey Scholarship Fund-Rocky Mountain
 Chapter 473
Leveraging Educational Assistance Partnership
 (LEAP) 753
Micron Science and Technology Scholars Program 165
New Century Scholarship 753
Rocky Mountain Coal Mining Institute Scholarship 167
ShopKo Scholars Program 743
Terrill H. Bell Teaching Incentive Loan 239
Utah Centennial Opportunity Program for
 Education 753
Utah Credit Union Scholarship Contest 753
Utah Society of Professional Engineers Scholarship 169
Western Undergraduate Exchange Program 757
Youth Automobile Safety Scholarship Essay Competition
 for Children of Public Employees 539

Vermont

American Legion Department of Vermont Department
 Scholarships 664
American Legion Eagle Scout of the Year 490
Barbara Jean Barker Memorial Scholarship for a
 Displaced Homemaker 693
Blessed Leon of Our Lady of the Rosary Award 630
Caparanga Award 630
Dr. Alfred and Susan Chan Award 630
Henry Broughton, K2AE Memorial Scholarship 90
Horticulture Research Institute Timothy Bigelow and
 Palmer W. Bigelow, Jr. Scholarship 341
Massachusetts Federation of Polish Women's Clubs
 Scholarships 622

Location of Study

Wilma Motley California Merit Scholarship *207*
Women in Logistics Scholarship *157*

Colorado

Agriculture Scholarships *74*
Chick Evans Caddie Scholarship *552*
Clinton J. Helton Manufacturing Scholarship Award
    Fund *272*
Colorado College and University Scholarships *56*
Colorado High School Scholarships *57*
Colorado Leveraging Educational Assistance Partnership
    (CLEAP) and SLEAP *678*
Colorado Masons Benevolent Fund Scholarships *678*
Colorado Scholarship *722*
Colorado Student Grant *678*
Colorado Undergraduate Merit Scholarships *678*
Cooperative Studies Scholarships *74*
DeVry Community College Scholar Award *687*
DeVry Dean's Scholarships *687*
DeVry High School Community Scholars Award *688*
DeVry Presidential Scholarships *688*
DeVry University Regional First Scholar Awards *688*
Donald Estey Scholarship Fund-Rocky Mountain
    Chapter *473*
Ethnic Diversity College and University Scholarships *57*
Ethnic Diversity High School Scholarships *57*
Gordon Scheer Scholarship *57*
Governor's Opportunity Scholarship *678*
Korean-American Scholarship Foundation Western
    Region Scholarships *622*
MARC Undergraduate Student Training in Academic
    Research U*Star Awards *140*
National Defense Transportation Association, Scott Air
    Force Base- St. Louis Area Chapter Scholarship *721*
Sales Professionals- USA Scholarship *153*
Society of Women Engineers-Rocky Mountain Section
    Scholarship Program *196*
Taddonio Scholarship *550*
Western Undergraduate Exchange Program *757*

Connecticut

American Institute of Architecture (AIA) Dayton
    Architectural Scholarship Fund *99*
Big Y Scholarships *668*
Capitol Scholarship Program *684*
Children of CSCPA Members Scholarship Program *58*
Connecticut Army National Guard 100% Tuition
    Waiver *576*
Connecticut Association of Latin Americans in Higher
    Education Scholarships *612*
Connecticut Association of Women Police
    Scholarship *199*
Connecticut Independent College Student Grants *684*
Connecticut Special Education Teacher Incentive
    Grant *462*
Constantinople Armenian Relief Society Scholarship *612*
CSCPA Candidate's Award *58*
CSCPA Junior Award *58*
Diana Donald Scholarship *481*
Ferris Ellis Literary Awards *756*
Korean-American Scholarship Foundation Northeastern
    Region Scholarships *621*
Malcolm Baldrige Scholarship *157*
Mary Benevento CAHPERD Scholarship *224*
Massachusetts Assistance for Student Success
    Program *713*
New England Chapter-National Association to Advance
    Fat Acceptance Scholarship *721*
New England Employee Benefits Council Scholarship
    Program *151*
New England Regional Student Program (New England
    Board of Higher Education) *724*
New Hampshire Incentive Program (NHIP) *725*
Outstanding Community College Accounting Student
    Award *58*
Scholarship Awards *561*
Scholarship for Minority College Students *224*
Scholarship for Minority High School Students *224*
Seol Bong Scholarship *632*

Delaware

Agenda For Delaware Women Trailblazer
    Scholarship *686*
Capitol Scholarship Program *684*
Charles L. Hebner Memorial Scholarship *352*
Christa McAuliffe Teacher Scholarship Loan-
    Delaware *225*
Delaware Solid Waste Authority John P. "Pat" Healy
    Scholarship *291*
Fresh Start Scholarship *692*
Governor's Workforce Development Grant *686*

Korean-American Scholarship Foundation Eastern
    Region Scholarships *621*
MARC Undergraduate Student Training in Academic
    Research U*Star Awards *140*
NASA Delaware Space Grant Undergraduate Tuition
    Scholarship *94*
National Association for Campus Activities East Coast
    Higher Education Research Scholarship *720*
National Association for Campus Activities East Coast
    Undergraduate Scholarship for Student Leaders *720*
Scholarship Awards *561*
Scholarship Incentive Program (ScIP) *686*
Scholarship Incentive Program-Delaware *687*
Seol Bong Scholarship *632*
State Tuition Assistance *569*

District of Columbia

Capitol Scholarship Program *684*
CVS/Pharmacy Scholarship *442*
Foley & Lardner Minority Scholarship Program *377*
Greater Washington Society of CPAs Scholarship *62*
Korean-American Scholarship Foundation Eastern
    Region Scholarships *621*
Massachusetts Assistance for Student Success
    Program *713*
National Association for Campus Activities East Coast
    Undergraduate Scholarship for Student Leaders *720*
Scholarship Awards *561*
Sigma Delta Chi Scholarships *744*
Suburban Hospital Healthcare System Scholarship *333*
SWE Baltimore-Washington Section Scholarships *195*
The Betty Endicott/NTA-NCCB Student Scholarship *363*

Florida

Academic Common Market Waiver *749*
Access to Better Learning and Education Grant *691*
American Cancer Society, Florida Division R O C K
    College Scholarship Program *658*
American Institute of Architecture (AIA) Dayton
    Architectural Scholarship Fund *99*
American Legion Auxiliary Department of Florida
    Department Scholarships *579*
American Legion Auxiliary Department of Florida
    Memorial Scholarship *484*
American Restaurant Scholarship *201*
Aylesworth and Old Salt Scholarships *385*
Bank of America Scholarship *638*
Casualty Actuaries of the Southeast Scholarship
    Program *354*
Critical Teacher Shortage Student Loan Forgiveness
    Program-Florida *541*
Critical Teacher Shortage Tuition Reimbursement-
    Florida *225*
Dental Assisting Scholarships *208*
Dental Hygiene Scholarships *208*
DeVry Dean's Scholarships *687*
DeVry High School Community Scholars Award *688*
DeVry Presidential Scholarships *688*
DeVry University Regional First Scholar Awards *688*
Educational Foundation Scholarships *59*
Edward S. Roth Manufacturing Engineering
    Scholarship *274*
Ethics in Business Scholarship *691*
FEFPA Assistantship *99*
FICPA Educational Foundation Scholarships *59*
Florida Association of Postsecondary Schools and
    Colleges Scholarship Program *691*
Florida Bankers Educational Foundation Scholarship/
    Loan *147*
Florida Private Student Assistance Grant *691*
Florida Public Student Assistance Grant *692*
Florida Scholarship *722*
Florida Women's State Golf Association Junior Girls'
    Scholarship Fund *692*
Florida/NASA Matching Grant Program *719*
Foley & Lardner Minority Scholarship Program *377*
Georgia Tuition Equalization Grant (GTEG) *693*
Jose Marti Scholarship Challenge Grant Fund *613*
MARC Undergraduate Student Training in Academic
    Research U*Star Awards *140*
Mary McLeod Bethune Scholarship *692*
National Association for Campus Activities Southeast
    Region Student Leadership Scholarship *720*
Promise of Nursing Scholarship *423*
Rosewood Family Scholarship Fund *613*
Scholarship Awards *561*
Scholarships for Children of Deceased or Disabled
    Veterans or Children of Servicemen Classified as
    POW or MIA *588*
Skoch Scholarship *385*
Southeast Greenhouse Conference Scholarship *347*
SWE Florida Space Coast Section Scholarship *281*
Tampa, Hillsborough Legacy Scholarship *309*

Ted Wilson Memorial Scholarship Foundation *212*
1040 K Race Scholarships *59*
1040K Race Scholarships *59*
U.S. Aircraft Insurance Group PDP Scholarship *128*
William L. Boyd IV Florida Resident Access Grant *692*

Georgia

Academic Common Market Waiver *749*
American Woman's Society of Certified Public
    Accountants- Georgia Affiliate Scholarship *54*
ASHRAE Region IV Benny Bootle Scholarship *252*
Atlanta Press Club Journalism Scholarship Program *179*
Bank of America Scholarship *638*
Casualty Actuaries of the Southeast Scholarship
    Program *354*
Connie and Robert T. Gunter Scholarship *272*
DeVry Dean's Scholarships *687*
DeVry High School Community Scholars Award *688*
DeVry Presidential Scholarships *688*
DeVry University Regional First Scholar Awards *688*
GAE GFIE Scholarship for Aspiring Teachers *226*
Georgia Leveraging Educational Assistance Partnership
    Grant Program *693*
Georgia Press Educational Foundation Scholarships *361*
Georgia PROMISE Teacher Scholarship Program *226*
Georgia Public Safety Memorial Grant/Law Enforcement
    Personnel Department Grant *542*
Georgia Trust for Historic Preservation Scholarship *337*
Georgia Tuition Equalization Grant (GTEG) *693*
Governor's Scholarship-Georgia *694*
HOPE—Helping Outstanding Pupils Educationally *694*
MARC Undergraduate Student Training in Academic
    Research U*Star Awards *140*
Milliken & Company Scholarship *527*
National Association for Campus Activities Southeast
    Region Student Leadership Scholarship *720*
Promise of Nursing Scholarship *423*
Southeast American Society of Travel Agents Chapter
    Scholarship *475*
Southeast Greenhouse Conference Scholarship *347*
Ted Wilson Memorial Scholarship Foundation *212*

Hawaii

Hawaii State Student Incentive Grant *697*
Korean University Club Scholarship *622*
Korean-American Scholarship Foundation Western
    Region Scholarships *622*
MARC Undergraduate Student Training in Academic
    Research U*Star Awards *140*
May and Hubert Everly HEA Scholarship *227*
National Association of Geoscience Teachers - Far
    Western Section scholarship *215*
R.W. Bob Holden Scholarship *350*
Western Undergraduate Exchange Program *757*
William J. & Marijane E. Adams, Jr. Scholarship *393*

Idaho

Agricultural-Women-In-Network Scholarship *84*
Agriculture Scholarships *74*
American Legion, Department of Idaho Scholarship *487*
ARC of Washington Trust Fund Stipend Program *461*
Cooperative Studies Scholarships *74*
Education Incentive Loan Forgiveness Contract-
    Idaho *227*
Fashion Group International of Portland
    Scholarship *296*
Freedom Scholarship *588*
Idaho Governor's Challenge Scholarship *698*
Idaho Minority and "At Risk" Student Scholarship *559*
Idaho Promise Category A Scholarship Program *698*
Idaho Promise Category B Scholarship Program *698*
Korean-American Scholarship Foundation Western
    Region Scholarships *622*
Leveraging Educational Assistance State Partnership
    Program (LEAP) *698*
Lori Rhett Memorial Scholarship *720*
NASA Idaho Space Grant Consortium Scholarship
    Program *94*
Public Safety Officer Dependent Scholarship *543*
Wayne C. Cornils Memorial Scholarship *478*
Western Undergraduate Exchange Program *757*

Illinois

American Legion, Department of Illinois
    Scholarships *487*
Carol A. Ratza Memorial Scholarship *138*
Chick Evans Caddie Scholarship *552*
David Arver Memorial Scholarship *117*
DeVry Community College Scholar Award *687*
DeVry Dean's Scholarships *687*
DeVry High School Community Scholars Award *688*
DeVry Presidential Scholarships *688*

DeVry University Regional First Scholar Awards *688*
Edmond A. Metzger Scholarship *243*
Edward S. Roth Manufacturing Engineering
    Scholarship *274*
Floyd Cargill Scholarship *559*
Foley & Lardner Minority Scholarship Program *377*
Golden Apple Scholars of Illinois *226*
Grant Program for Dependents of Police, Fire, or
    Correctional Officers *543*
Heart of America Restaurants and Inns/Machine Shed
    Agriculture Scholarship *80*
Herman J. Neal Scholarship *63*
Higher Education License Plate Program — HELP *699*
Illinois College Savings Bond Bonus Incentive Grant
    Program *699*
Illinois Funeral Directors Association Scholarships *313*
Illinois Future Teachers Corps Program *228*
Illinois General Assembly Scholarship *699*
Illinois Monetary Award Program *699*
Illinois National Guard Grant Program *570*
Illinois Pilots Association Memorial Scholarship *123*
Illinois Real Estate Educational Foundation Academic
    Scholarships *452*
Illinois Society of Professional Engineers Advantage
    Award/Foundation Scholarship *262*
Illinois Society of Professional Engineers/Melvin E.
    Amstutz Memorial Award *263*
Illinois Society of Professional Engineers/Peppy
    Moldovan Memorial Award *263*
Illinois Special Education Teacher Tuition Waiver *462*
Illinois State Treasurer's Office Excellence in Agriculture
    Scholarship Program *80*
Illinois Student-to-Student Program of Matching
    Grants *699*
Illinois Veteran Grant Program - IVG *589*
Indiana Health Care Foundation Nursing
    Scholarship *425*
Merit Recognition Scholarship (MRS) Program *699*
Minority Teachers of Illinois Scholarship Program *228*
MRA Institute of Management Endowment Fund
    Scholarship *151*
National Defense Transportation Association, Scott Air
    Force Base- St. Louis Area Chapter Scholarship *721*
Palwaukee Airport Pilots Association Scholarship
    Program *128*
Promise of Nursing Scholarship *423*
Silas Purnell Illinois Incentive for Access Program *700*
Six Meter Club of Chicago Scholarship *667*
Sonne Scholarship *424*
St. Louis Chapter No. 17 Scholarship Fund *275*
SWE St. Louis Scholarship *282*
Township Officials of Illinois Scholarship Fund *751*

Indiana

Carol A. Ratza Memorial Scholarship *138*
Charles A. Holt Indiana Wildlife Federation Endowment
    Scholarship *409*
Chick Evans Caddie Scholarship *552*
Child of Disabled Veteran Grant or Purple Heart
    Recipient Grant *589*
College Scholarships for Cancer Survivors *658*
David Arver Memorial Scholarship *117*
Department of Veterans Affairs Free Tuition for
    Children of POW/MIA's in Vietnam *589*
Edmond A. Metzger Scholarship *243*
Fort Wayne Chapter 56 Scholarship *274*
Frank O'Bannon Grant Program *747*
Hoosier Scholar Award *747*
Indiana Broadcasters Foundation Scholarship *362*
Indiana Engineering Scholarship *263*
Indiana Health Care Foundation Nursing
    Scholarship *425*
Indiana National Guard Supplemental Grant *572*
Indiana Nursing Scholarship Fund *433*
Indiana Retired Teachers Association Foundation
    Scholarship *228*
Indiana Scholarship *722*
Indiana Sheriffs' Association Scholarship Program *199*
Lilly Endowment Community Scholarship, Tippecanoe
    County *696*
Marion A. and Eva S. Peeples Scholarships *230*
National Defense Transportation Association, Scott Air
    Force Base- St. Louis Area Chapter Scholarship *721*
Part-time Grant Program *747*
Twenty-first Century Scholars Gear Up Summer
    Scholarship *748*
U.S. Aircraft Insurance Group PDP Scholarship *128*

Iowa

Agriculture Scholarships *74*
American Legion Auxiliary Department of Iowa
    Children of Veterans Scholarship *579*

American Legion Department of Minnesota Memorial
    Scholarship *489*
Association for Facilities Engineering Cedar Valley
    Chapter # 132 Scholarship *120*
Cooperative Studies Scholarships *74*
David Arver Memorial Scholarship *117*
Elmer O. and Ida Preston Educational Trust Grants and
    Loans *690*
Governor Terry E. Branstad Iowa State Fair
    Scholarship *700*
Harriet Hoffman Memorial Scholarship for Teacher
    Training *219*
Heart of America Restaurants and Inns/Machine Shed
    Agriculture Scholarship *80*
Herbert Hoover Uncommon Student Award *697*
Iowa Foster Child Grants *701*
Iowa Grants *701*
Iowa National Guard Education Assistance Program *570*
Iowa Teacher Forgivable Loan Program *229*
Iowa Tuition Grant Program *701*
Iowa Vocational-Technical Tuition Grant Program *701*
M.V. McCrae Memorial Nurses Scholarship *416*
Minnesota Legionnaires Insurance Trust Scholarship *489*
Minnesota Reciprocal Agreement *715*
MRA Institute of Management Endowment Fund
    Scholarship *151*
National Defense Transportation Association, Scott Air
    Force Base- St. Louis Area Chapter Scholarship *721*
North Central Region 9 Scholarship *275*
Paul and Helen L. Grauer Scholarship *91*
State of Iowa Scholarship Program *701*
Vincent L. Hawkinson Scholarship for Peace and
    Justice *754*

Kansas

Agriculture Scholarships *74*
Albert M. Lappin Scholarship *488*
American Restaurant Scholarship *201*
Brown Foundation Goodyear Tire and Rubber
    Company Scholarship for College Students *669*
Chick Evans Caddie Scholarship *552*
Cooperative Studies Scholarships *74*
David Arver Memorial Scholarship *117*
Dr. Click Cowger Baseball Scholarship *661*
Heart of America Restaurants and Inns/Machine Shed
    Agriculture Scholarship *80*
Hobble (LPN) Nursing Scholarship *418*
Hugh A. Smith Scholarship Fund *488*
Kansas Educational Benefits for Children of MIA, POW,
    and Deceased Veterans of the Vietnam War *589*
Kansas National Guard Tuition Assistance Award
    Program *570*
Midwest Student Exchange Program (MSEP) *714*
Minnesota Reciprocal Agreement *715*
Music Committee Scholarship *401*
National Defense Transportation Association, Scott Air
    Force Base- St. Louis Area Chapter Scholarship *721*
Paul and Helen L. Grauer Scholarship *91*
Paul Flaherty Athletic Scholarship *662*
Rosedale Post 346 Scholarship *488*
Sales Professionals- USA Scholarship *153*
Ted and Nora Anderson Scholarships *488*
Wichita Chapter 52 Scholarship *276*

Kentucky

Academic Common Market Waiver *749*
Casualty Actuaries of the Southeast Scholarship
    Program *354*
College Access Program (CAP) Grant *703*
Conservation of Natural Resources Scholarship *81*
Conservation of Natural Resources Scholarship for
    Nontraditional Students *81*
Early Childhood Development Scholarship *170*
Environmental Protection Scholarships *164*
George R. Crafton Scholarship *81*
Indiana Health Care Foundation Nursing
    Scholarship *425*
Jackson Purchase Energy Corporation Scholarship *702*
Kentucky Minority Educator Recruitment and Retention
    (KMERR) Scholarship *229*
Kentucky National Guard Tuition Award Program *570*
Kentucky Society of Certified Public Accountants
    College Scholarship *63*
Kentucky Society of Certified Public Accountants High
    School Scholarships *64*
Kentucky Teacher Scholarship Program *229*
Kentucky Transportation Cabinet Civil Engineering
    Scholarship Program *174*
Kentucky Tuition Grant (KTG) *703*
Korean-American Scholarship Foundation Eastern
    Region Scholarships *621*
Pat and Jim Host Scholarship *309*

Southeast American Society of Travel Agents Chapter
    Scholarship *475*
Tess Caldarelli Memorial Scholarship *721*
Touchstone Energy All "A" Classic Scholarship *703*
Zagunas Student Leaders Scholarship *721*

Louisiana

Academic Common Market Waiver *749*
ASHRAE Region VIII Scholarship *252*
Broadcast Scholarship Program *478*
Casualty Actuaries of the Southeast Scholarship
    Program *354*
Leveraging Educational Assistance Program (LEAP) *707*
Louisiana Department of Veterans Affairs State Aid
    Program *589*
Louisiana National Guard State Tuition Exemption
    Program *571*
Louisiana Scholarship *723*
MARC Undergraduate Student Training in Academic
    Research U*Star Awards *140*
Markley Scholarship *720*
Rockefeller State Wildlife Scholarship *87*
Society of Louisiana CPAs Scholarships *69*
Southeast American Society of Travel Agents Chapter
    Scholarship *475*
TOPS Alternate Performance Award *707*
TOPS Honors Award *707*
TOPS Opportunity Award *707*
TOPS Performance Award *708*
TOPS Tech Award *708*
United Way of New Orleans Emergency Assistance
    Fund *645*
Willis and Mildred Pellerin Scholarships *758*

Maine

Capitol Scholarship Program *684*
Dirigo Machine Tool Scholarship *709*
Early College Program *709*
Korean-American Scholarship Foundation Northeastern
    Region Scholarships *621*
Maine Community College Scholarship *709*
Maine Hospitals Engineers Society Scholarship *709*
Maine Metal Products Association Scholarship
    Program *389*
Maine Scholarship *723*
Maine Society of Professional Engineers Vernon T.
    Swaine- Robert E. Chute Scholarship *266*
Maine State Society Foundation Scholarship *711*
Massachusetts Assistance for Student Success
    Program *713*
New England Chapter-National Association to Advance
    Fat Acceptance Scholarship *721*
New England Employee Benefits Council Scholarship
    Program *151*
New England Regional Student Program (New England
    Board of Higher Education) *724*
New Hampshire Incentive Program (NHIP) *725*
Osher Scholarship *709*
Scholarship Awards *561*
Scholarship of the Maine School Food Service
    Association *305*
Seol Bong Scholarship *632*
Tuition Waiver Programs *541*
Veterans Dependents Educational Benefits-Maine *574*

Manitoba

Associated Medical Services, Inc. Hannah
    Studentship *324*
Bill Mason Memorial Scholarship Fund *80*
Canada Iceland Foundation Scholarship Program *671*
Field Aviation Co., Inc., Scholarship *117*
Jim Allard Broadcast Journalism Scholarship *359*
Leo J. Krysa Undergraduate Scholarship *104*
Osler, Hoskin and Harcourt National Essay
    Competition *722*
Ruth Hancock Memorial Scholarship *180*
Scholarship for Aboriginal Canadians *507*
Scholarship for Visible Minorities *507*
Scottish Rite Charitable Foundation College
    Bursaries *550*
Terry Fox Memorial Scholarship *507*
Tommy Douglas Scholarship *507*

Maryland

American Legion Department of Maryland General
    Scholarship *662*
Ashley Tamburri Scholarship *667*
Child Care Provider Program-Maryland *230*
Delegate Scholarship Program-Maryland *711*
Distinguished Scholar Award-Maryland *711*
Distinguished Scholar-Teacher Education Awards *230*
Educational Assistance Grants-Maryland *711*

Edward T. Conroy Memorial Scholarship Program 575
Erica Lynne E. Durant Memorial Scholarship 556
Exchange Club of Baltimore Scholarship 676
Firefighter, Ambulance, and Rescue Squad Member
    Tuition Reimbursement Program-Maryland 300
Graduate and Professional Scholarship Program-
    Maryland 210
Guaranteed Access Grant-Maryland 712
J.F. Tolbert Memorial Student Grant Program 712
Janet L. Hoffmann Loan Assistance Repayment
    Program 230
Korean-American Scholarship Foundation Eastern
    Region Scholarships 621
Leslie Moore Foundation Scholarship 677
MARC Undergraduate Student Training in Academic
    Research U*Star Awards 140
Maryland Association of Private Colleges and Career
    Schools Scholarship 150
Maryland State Nursing Scholarship and Living
    Expenses Grant 425
NASA Maryland Space Grant Consortium
    Undergraduate Scholarships 139
National Association for Campus Activities East Coast
    Higher Education Research Scholarship 720
National Association for Campus Activities East Coast
    Undergraduate Scholarship for Student Leaders 720
Part-time Grant Program-Maryland 712
Physical and Occupational Therapists and Assistants
    Grant Program 467
Scholarship Awards 561
Senatorial Scholarships-Maryland 712
Sharon Christa McAuliffe Teacher Education-Critical
    Shortage Grant Program 230
Sigma Delta Chi Scholarships 744
Student Scholarship in Accounting MD Association of
    CPAs 64
Suburban Hospital Healthcare System Scholarship 333
SWE Baltimore-Washington Section Scholarships 195
The Betty Endicott/NTA-NCCB Student Scholarship 363
Tuition Reduction for Non-Resident Nursing
    Students 426
Tuition Waiver for Foster Care Recipients 712
William Donald Schaefer Scholarship 451

Massachusetts

Big Y Scholarships 668
Capitol Scholarship Program 684
Edward S. Roth Manufacturing Engineering
    Scholarship 274
First National Bank of Amherst Centennial Educational
    Scholarship 682
Heriberto Flores Scholarship 611
Korean-American Scholarship Foundation Northeastern
    Region Scholarships 621
Massachusetts Assistance for Student Success
    Program 713
Massachusetts Cash Grant Program 713
Massachusetts Gilbert Matching Student Grant
    Program 426
Massachusetts Part-time Grant Program 713
Massachusetts Public Service Grant Program 545
New England Chapter-National Association to Advance
    Fat Acceptance Scholarship 721
New England Employee Benefits Council Scholarship
    Program 151
New England Regional Student Program (New England
    Board of Higher Education) 724
New Hampshire Incentive Program (NHIP) 725
Paychex, Inc. Entrepreneur Scholarship 59
Performance Bonus Grant Program 713
Promise of Nursing Scholarship 423
Scholarship Awards 561
Seol Bong Scholarship 632
Stanley Ciejek Sr. Scholarship 684
Student Essay Competition 59
Tomorrow's Teachers Scholarship Program 231

Michigan

American Legion Auxiliary Department of Michigan
    Memorial Scholarship 580
Carol A. Ratza Memorial Scholarship 138
Casualty Actuaries of the Southeast Scholarship
    Program 354
Chick Evans Caddie Scholarship 552
College Scholarships for Cancer Survivors 658
CVS/Pharmacy Scholarship 442
David Arver Memorial Scholarship 117
Detroit Chapter One-Founding Chapter Scholarship 273
Downriver Detroit Chapter 198 Scholarship 273
Foley & Lardner Minority Scholarship Program 377
Guy M. Wilson Scholarships 584
Indiana Health Care Foundation Nursing
    Scholarship 425

Kalamazoo Chapter 116-Roscoe Douglas Memorial
    Scholarship Award 274
Medical Career Scholarship 319
Michigan Adult Part-Time Grant 714
Michigan Competitive Scholarship 714
Michigan Educational Opportunity Grant 714
Michigan Indian Tuition Waiver 619
Michigan Nursing Scholarship 426
Michigan Society of Professional Engineers
    Undesignated Grant 165
Michigan Tuition Grant 714
Michigan Veterans Trust Fund Tuition Grant
    Program 590
Midwest Student Exchange Program (MSEP) 714
Minnesota Reciprocal Agreement 715
MSPE Auxiliary Grant for Undergraduate Study 174
National Association for Campus Activities WI Region
    Student Leadership Scholarship 720
National Defense Transportation Association, Scott Air
    Force Base- St. Louis Area Chapter Scholarship 721
North Central Region 9 Scholarship 275
Nursing Student Scholarship 426
Promise of Nursing Scholarship 423
Scholarship for Non-Traditional Student 581
Tess Caldarelli Memorial Scholarship 721
Tuition Incentive Program (TIP) 714
U.S. Aircraft Insurance Group PDP Scholarship 128
WXYZ-TV Broadcasting Scholarship 479
Zagunas Student Leaders Scholarship 721

Minnesota

Agriculture Scholarships 74
American Legion Auxiliary Department of Minnesota
    Past President Parley Health Care Scholarship 320
American Legion Auxiliary Department of Minnesota
    Scholarships 581
American Legion Department of Minnesota Memorial
    Scholarship 489
Bill Peterson Scholarship 504
Carol A. Ratza Memorial Scholarship 138
Chick Evans Caddie Scholarship 552
Cooperative Studies Scholarships 74
David Arver Memorial Scholarship 117
Edward S. Roth Manufacturing Engineering
    Scholarship 274
Heart of America Restaurants and Inns/Machine Shed
    Agriculture Scholarship 80
Many Voices Residency Program 384
MARC Undergraduate Student Training in Academic
    Research U*Star Awards 140
Martin Duffy Adult Learner Scholarship Award 504
Midwest Student Exchange Program (MSEP) 714
Minnesota Academic Excellence Scholarship 715
Minnesota AFL-CIO Scholarships 504
Minnesota Indian Scholarship Program 624
Minnesota Legionnaires Insurance Trust Scholarship 489
Minnesota Space Grant Consortium 124
Minnesota State Grant Program 715
Minnesota State Veterans' Dependents Assistance
    Program 591
Minnesota SWE Section Scholarship 280
National Defense Transportation Association, Scott Air
    Force Base- St. Louis Area Chapter Scholarship 721
North Central Region 9 Scholarship 275
Ordean Scholarship Program 67
Postsecondary Child Care Grant Program-
    Minnesota 715
Printing Industry of Minnesota Education Foundation
    Scholarship Fund 316
Safety Officers' Survivor Grant Program 545
The MNCPA Scholarship Program 64
Twin Cities Graduate MBA Scholarship 65
Vincent L. Hawkinson Scholarship for Peace and
    Justice 754

Mississippi

Academic Common Market Waiver 749
Critical Needs Teacher Loan/Scholarship 231
Gulf Coast Research Laboratory Minority Summer
    Grant 294
Higher Education Legislative Plan (HELP) 715
MARC Undergraduate Student Training in Academic
    Research U*Star Awards 140
Mississippi Association of Broadcasters Scholarship 479
Mississippi Eminent Scholars Grant 716
Mississippi Health Care Professions Loan/Scholarship
    Program 328
Mississippi Press Association Education Foundation
    Scholarship 363
Mississippi Resident Tuition Assistance Grant 716
Mississippi Scholarship 90
National Association for Campus Activities Southeast
    Region Student Leadership Scholarship 720

Nissan Scholarship 716
Nursing Education Loan/Scholarship-BSN 426
Southeast American Society of Travel Agents Chapter
    Scholarship 475
William Winter Teacher Scholar Loan Program 231

Missouri

Academic Common Market Waiver 749
American Restaurant Scholarship 201
Charles Gallagher Student Assistance Program 716
Charles P. Bell Conservation Scholarship 136
Chick Evans Caddie Scholarship 552
David Arver Memorial Scholarship 117
DeVry Dean's Scholarships 687
DeVry High School Community Scholars Award 688
DeVry Presidential Scholarships 688
Harry S. Truman Library Institute Undergraduate
    Student Grant 217
Henry C. McDougal Scholarship 716
John Dennis Scholarship 199
Marguerite Ross Barnett Memorial Scholarship 717
Midwest Student Exchange Program (MSEP) 714
Minnesota Reciprocal Agreement 715
Missouri Broadcasters Association Scholarship 479
Missouri College Guarantee Program 717
Missouri Higher Education Academic Scholarship
    (Bright Flight) 717
Missouri Insurance Education Foundation
    Scholarship 354
Missouri Minority Teaching Scholarship 231
Missouri Teacher Education Scholarship (General) 232
Missouri Travel Council Tourism Scholarship 307
National Defense Transportation Association, Scott Air
    Force Base- St. Louis Area Chapter Scholarship 721
Paul and Helen L. Grauer Scholarship 91
Primary Care Resource Initiative for Missouri Loan
    Program 210
Sales Professionals- USA Scholarship 153
St. Louis Chapter No. 17 Scholarship Fund 275
SWCS/Betty Broemmelsiek Scholarship 410
SWE St. Louis Scholarship 282
U.S. Aircraft Insurance Group PDP Scholarship 128

Montana

Agriculture Scholarships 74
Cooperative Studies Scholarships 74
Great Falls Broadcasters Association Scholarship 479
Indian Student Fee Waiver 624
Korean-American Scholarship Foundation Western
    Region Scholarships 622
Life Member Montana Federation of Garden Clubs
    Scholarship 138
Lori Rhett Memorial Scholarship 720
Montana Higher Education Opportunity Grant 717
Montana Society of Certified Public Accountants
    Scholarship 65
Montana Space Grant Scholarship Program 125
Montana Tuition Assistance Program-Baker Grant 718
Montana University System Honor Scholarship 718
National Defense Transportation Association, Scott Air
    Force Base- St. Louis Area Chapter Scholarship 721
Western Undergraduate Exchange Program 757

Nebraska

Agriculture Scholarships 74
Colleen Farrell Gerleman Scholarship 705
Cooperative Studies Scholarships 74
Dale E. Siefkes Scholarship 229
David Arver Memorial Scholarship 117
Edgar J. Boschult Memorial Scholarship 585
Gallup CSG Scholarship Program 693
George Watters-Nebraska Petroleum Marketers
    Association Scholarship 544
Harry and Lenora Richardson-National Association of
    Postmasters of the United States Scholarship 544
Harry and Lenora Richardson-Nebraska Branch of the
    National League of Postmasters Scholarship 544
Haymarket Gallery Emerging Artists Scholarship 112
Jennings and Beulah Haggerty Scholarship 705
Lawrence "Larry" Frazier Memorial Scholarship 124
MARC Undergraduate Student Training in Academic
    Research U*Star Awards 140
Maynard Jensen American Legion Memorial
    Scholarship 489
Midwest Student Exchange Program (MSEP) 714
Minnesota Reciprocal Agreement 715
NASA Nebraska Space Grant 125
National Defense Transportation Association, Scott Air
    Force Base- St. Louis Area Chapter Scholarship 721
Nebraska National Guard Tuition Credit 571
Nebraska Press Association Foundation, Inc.,
    Scholarship 365

Nebraska Rural Community Schools Association
Scholarship *230*
Nebraska Rural Schools Scholarship *705*
Nebraska State Grant *746*
Norman and Ruth Good Educational Endowment *706*
North Central Region 9 Scholarship *275*
Paul and Helen L. Grauer Scholarship *91*
Rural Health Student Loan Program *210*
Thomas C. Woods, Jr. Memorial Scholarship *545*
We Have Money to Learn Scholarships *667*

Nevada

APTRA-Clete Roberts Memorial Journalism Scholarship
Award *358*
APTRA-Kathryn Dettman Memorial Scholarship *359*
Associated Press Television/Radio Association-Clete
Roberts Journalism Scholarship Awards *358*
Kathryn Dettman Memorial Journalism Scholarship *358*
Korean-American Scholarship Foundation Western
Region Scholarships *622*
National Association of Geoscience Teachers - Far
Western Section scholarship *215*
Nevada Student Incentive Grant *723*
Northern California Chapter Richard Epping
Scholarship *474*
Robert W. Thunen Memorial Scholarships *100*
Robert W. Thunen Memorial Scholarships *100*
University and Community College System of Nevada
NASA Space Grant and Fellowship Program *125*
Western Undergraduate Exchange Program *757*
William J. & Marijane E. Adams, Jr. Scholarship *393*

New Brunswick

Associated Medical Services, Inc. Hannah
Studentship *324*
Bill Mason Memorial Scholarship Fund *80*
Canada Iceland Foundation Scholarship Program *671*
Field Aviation Co., Inc., Scholarship *117*
Jim Allard Broadcast Journalism Scholarship *359*
Leo J. Krysa Undergraduate Scholarship *104*
Osler, Hoskin and Harcourt National Essay
Competition *722*
Ruth Hancock Memorial Scholarship *180*
Scholarship for Aboriginal Canadians *507*
Scholarship for Visible Minorities *507*
Scottish Rite Charitable Foundation College
Bursaries *550*
Terry Fox Memorial Scholarship *507*
Tommy Douglas Scholarship *507*

New Hampshire

Capitol Scholarship Program *684*
Korean-American Scholarship Foundation Northeastern
Region Scholarships *621*
Leveraged Incentive Grant Program *725*
Mary Milliken Scholarship *725*
Massachusetts Assistance for Student Success
Program *713*
New England Chapter-National Association to Advance
Fat Acceptance Scholarship *721*
New England Employee Benefits Council Scholarship
Program *151*
New England Regional Student Program (New England
Board of Higher Education) *724*
New Hampshire Incentive Program (NHIP) *725*
Scholarship Awards *561*
Seol Bong Scholarship *632*
Workforce Incentive Program *233*

New Jersey

Andrew K. Ruotolo, Jr. Memorial Scholarship *376*
Constantinople Armenian Relief Society Scholarship *612*
DeVry Dean's Scholarships *687*
DeVry High School Community Scholars Award *688*
DeVry Presidential Scholarships *688*
Edward J. Bloustein Distinguished Scholars *725*
Harry Y. Cotton Memorial Scholarship *376*
John S. Stamler Memorial Scholarship *540*
Korean-American Scholarship Foundation Northeastern
Region Scholarships *621*
Law Enforcement Officer Memorial Scholarship *547*
Martin Luther King Physician/Dentist Scholarships *211*
National Association for Campus Activities East Coast
Higher Education Research Scholarship *720*
National Association for Campus Activities East Coast
Undergraduate Scholarship for Student Leaders *720*
National Association of Water Companies-New Jersey
Chapter Scholarship *139*
New Jersey Educational Opportunity Fund Grants *212*
New Jersey Society of Certified Public Accountants
College Scholarship Program *66*
NJ Student Tuition Assistance Reward Scholarship *726*

Oscar W. Rittenhouse Memorial Scholarship *376*
Outstanding Scholar Recruitment Program *726*
Part-time Tuition Aid Grant (TAG) for County
Colleges *726*
Promise of Nursing Scholarship *423*
Scholarship Awards *561*
Seol Bong Scholarship *632*
Survivor Tuition Benefits Program *547*
The Ron Vellekamp Environmental Scholarship *457*
Tuition Aid Grant *726*
Tuition Assistance for Children of POW/MIAs *591*
U.S. Aircraft Insurance Group PDP Scholarship *128*
Urban Scholars *726*

New Mexico

Albuquerque Community Foundation New Mexico
Manufactured Housing Scholarship Program *657*
Allied Health Student Loan Program-New Mexico *210*
Children of Deceased Veterans Scholarship-New
Mexico *592*
Korean-American Scholarship Foundation Western
Region Scholarships *622*
Legislative Endowment Scholarships *727*
Lottery Success Scholarships *727*
MARC Undergraduate Student Training in Academic
Research U*Star Awards *140*
Markley Scholarship *720*
New Mexico Competitive Scholarship *727*
New Mexico Scholars' Program *727*
New Mexico Scholarship *723*
New Mexico Student Incentive Grant *728*
New Mexico Vietnam Veterans' Scholarship *592*
Nursing Student Loan-For-Service Program *429*
3% Scholarship Program *728*
Vietnam Veterans' Scholarship Program *592*
Western Undergraduate Exchange Program *757*

New York

AFL-CIO Council of Buffalo Scholarship *495*
Albert E. Wischmeyer Memorial Scholarship Award *271*
Biller/Jewish Foundation for Education of Women *651*
Carol A. Ratza Memorial Scholarship *138*
Center for Gay and Lesbian Studies Undergraduate
Paper Awards *383*
Constantinople Armenian Relief Society Scholarship *612*
DeVry Dean's Scholarships *687*
DeVry High School Community Scholars Award *688*
DeVry Presidential Scholarships *688*
DeVry University Regional First Scholar Awards *688*
Edna Aimes Scholarship *328*
Foundation for Accounting Education Scholarship *67*
Korean-American Scholarship Foundation Northeastern
Region Scholarships *621*
MARC Undergraduate Student Training in Academic
Research U*Star Awards *140*
Milliken & Company Scholarship *527*
National Association for Campus Activities East Coast
Higher Education Research Scholarship *720*
National Association for Campus Activities East Coast
Undergraduate Scholarship for Student Leaders *720*
New York Aid for Part-time Study (APTS) *728*
New York Excellence Scholarship *723*
New York Lottery Leaders of Tomorrow (Lot)
Scholarship *672*
New York Memorial Scholarships for Families of
Deceased Police Officers, Fire Fighters and Peace
Officers *547*
New York Scholarship *723*
New York State AFL-CIO Scholarship *508*
New York State Aid to Native Americans *626*
New York State Tuition Assistance Program *729*
Polish Arts Club of Buffalo Scholarship Foundation
Trust *108*
Printing Industry of Minnesota Education Foundation
Scholarship Fund *316*
Regents Professional Opportunity Scholarship *67*
Regents Professional Opportunity Scholarships *729*
Scholarship Awards *561*
Scholarship for Academic Excellence *728*
Seol Bong Scholarship *632*
Susan W. Freestone Education Award *508*
United Way of Westchester and Putnam, Inc./ UNCF
Emergency Assistance Fund *646*
Women's Architectural Auxiliary Eleanor Allwork
Scholarship Grants *98*
World Trade Center Memorial Scholarship *729*

Newfoundland

Associated Medical Services, Inc. Hannah
Studentship *324*
Bill Mason Memorial Scholarship Fund *80*
Field Aviation Co., Inc., Scholarship *117*

Jim Allard Broadcast Journalism Scholarship *359*
Leo J. Krysa Undergraduate Scholarship *104*
Osler, Hoskin and Harcourt National Essay
Competition *722*
Ruth Hancock Memorial Scholarship *180*
Scholarship for Aboriginal Canadians *507*
Scholarship for Visible Minorities *507*
Scottish Rite Charitable Foundation College
Bursaries *550*
Terry Fox Memorial Scholarship *507*
Tommy Douglas Scholarship *507*

North Carolina

ASHRAE Region IV Benny Bootle Scholarship *252*
Aubrey Lee Brooks Scholarships *729*
Bank of America Scholarship *638*
Casualty Actuaries of the Southeast Scholarship
Program *354*
Crumley and Associates - Crib to College
Scholarship *674*
Foley & Lardner Minority Scholarship Program *377*
Glaxo Smith Kline Opportunities Scholarship *751*
Golden LEAF Scholarship - Four Year University
Program *674*
Jagannathan Scholarship *730*
Korean-American Scholarship Foundation Eastern
Region Scholarships *621*
L. Phil Wicker Scholarship *179*
Latino Diamante Scholarship Fund *610*
Mary Morrow-Edna Richards Scholarship *233*
Milliken & Company Scholarship *527*
National Association for Campus Activities Southeast
Region Student Leadership Scholarship *720*
North Carolina Community College Grant Program *730*
North Carolina Legislative Tuition Grant Program
(NCLTG) *730*
North Carolina National Guard Tuition Assistance
Program *571*
North Carolina Sheriffs' Association Undergraduate
Criminal Justice Scholarships *200*
North Carolina Teaching Fellows Scholarship
Program *233*
North Carolina Veterans Scholarships Class I-B *592*
North Carolina Veterans Scholarships Class II *592*
North Carolina Veterans Scholarships Class III *592*
North Carolina Veterans Scholarships Class IV *593*
Nurse Education Scholarship Loan Program
(NESLP) *430*
Nurse Scholars Program—Undergraduate (North
Carolina) *430*
Scholarship Awards *561*
Southeast American Society of Travel Agents Chapter
Scholarship *475*
Southeast Greenhouse Conference Scholarship *347*
State Contractual Scholarship Fund Program-North
Carolina *730*
Teacher Assistant Scholarship Program *233*
Ted Wilson Memorial Scholarship Foundation *212*
Triangle Native American Society Scholarship Fund *636*
University of North Carolina Need Based Grant *675*
University of North Carolina Need-Based Grant *730*
Wachovia Technical Scholarship Program *469*

North Dakota

Agriculture Scholarships *74*
American Legion Auxiliary Department of North Dakota
Past President's Parley Nurses' Scholarship *417*
American Legion Auxiliary Department of North Dakota
Scholarships *659*
American Legion Auxiliary, National President's
Scholarship *538*
American Legion Department of Minnesota Memorial
Scholarship *489*
Cooperative Studies Scholarships *74*
David Arver Memorial Scholarship *117*
Midwest Student Exchange Program (MSEP) *714*
Minnesota Legionnaires Insurance Trust Scholarship *489*
Minnesota Reciprocal Agreement *715*
Minnesota SWE Section Scholarship *280*
National Defense Transportation Association, Scott Air
Force Base- St. Louis Area Chapter Scholarship *721*
North Central Region 9 Scholarship *275*
North Dakota Indian Scholarship Program *634*
North Dakota Scholars Program *747*
North Dakota State Student Incentive Grant
Program *747*
North Dakota Teacher Shortage Loan Forgiveness
Program *233*
U.S. Aircraft Insurance Group PDP Scholarship *128*
Vincent L. Hawkinson Scholarship for Peace and
Justice *754*
Western Undergraduate Exchange Program *757*

Northwest Territories

Associated Medical Services, Inc. Hannah
  Studentship *324*
Bill Mason Memorial Scholarship Fund *80*
Field Aviation Co., Inc., Scholarship *117*
Jim Allard Broadcast Journalism Scholarship *359*
Osler, Hoskin and Harcourt National Essay
  Competition *722*
Ruth Hancock Memorial Scholarship *180*
Scholarship for Aboriginal Canadians *507*
Scholarship for Visible Minorities *507*
Scottish Rite Charitable Foundation College
  Bursaries *550*
Terry Fox Memorial Scholarship *507*
Tommy Douglas Scholarship *507*

Nova Scotia

Associated Medical Services, Inc. Hannah
  Studentship *324*
Bill Mason Memorial Scholarship Fund *80*
Canada Iceland Foundation Scholarship Program *671*
Field Aviation Co., Inc., Scholarship *117*
Jim Allard Broadcast Journalism Scholarship *359*
Leo J. Krysa Undergraduate Scholarship *104*
Osler, Hoskin and Harcourt National Essay
  Competition *722*
Ruth Hancock Memorial Scholarship *180*
Scholarship for Aboriginal Canadians *507*
Scholarship for Visible Minorities *507*
Scottish Rite Charitable Foundation College
  Bursaries *550*
Terry Fox Memorial Scholarship *507*
Tommy Douglas Scholarship *507*

Ohio

Accountancy Board of Ohio Educational Assistance
  Program *53*
American Institute of Architecture (AIA) Dayton
  Architectural Scholarship Fund *99*
Bea Cleveland 4-H Scholarship *170*
C. Merrill Barber, P.E., Memorial Scholarship *260*
Carol A. Ratza Memorial Scholarship *138*
Charles & Gwyenna Lifer 4-H Scholarship *509*
Chick Evans Caddie Scholarship *552*
Cohen and Company CPAs Scholarship *56*
Cyril W. Neff, P.E., P.S., Memorial Scholarship *260*
DeVry Dean's Scholarships *687*
DeVry High School Community Scholars Award *688*
DeVry Presidential Scholarships *688*
Edward S. Roth Manufacturing Engineering
  Scholarship *274*
Engineers Foundation of Ohio General Fund
  Scholarship *260*
G. Brooks Earnest-Ohio Society of Professional
  Engineers, Cleveland Chapter Memorial
  Scholarship *260*
Harold K. Douthit Scholarship *366*
Homer T. Borton, P.E., Scholarship *261*
Indiana Health Care Foundation Nursing
  Scholarship *425*
Larry Fullerton Photojournalism Scholarship *442*
M E Companies Inc Scholarship Fund *708*
Mabel Sarbaugh 4-H Scholarship *170*
Melvin Bauer, P.E., P.S.-Ohio Society of Professional
  Engineers North Central -Memorial Scholarship *261*
Mr. & Mrs. G. Deming Seymour 4-H Scholarship *509*
Norm Moll Scholarship *346*
Ohio Academic Scholarship Program *731*
Ohio Educational Credit Union Scholarship *732*
Ohio Environmental Science & Engineering
  Scholarships *295*
Ohio Instructional Grant *732*
Ohio Missing in Action and Prisoners of War Orphans
  Scholarship *593*
Ohio National Guard Scholarship Program *572*
Ohio Newspapers Foundation Minority Scholarship *366*
Ohio Newspapers Foundation University Journalism
  Scholarship *366*
Ohio Safety Officers College Memorial Fund *548*
Ohio Student Choice Grant Program *732*
Ohio War Orphans Scholarship *593*
Part-time Student Instructional Grant *732*
Paul A. & Ethel I. Smith 4-H Scholarship *83*
Project BEST Scholarship *513*
Raymond H. Fuller, P.E., Memorial Scholarship *261*
Student Workforce Development Grant Program *732*
Tess Caldarelli Memorial Scholarship *721*
William D. Squires Scholarship *757*
Zagunas Student Leaders Scholarship *721*

Oklahoma

Academic Common Market Waiver *749*
Academic Scholars Program *733*
Agriculture Scholarships *74*
ASHRAE Region VIII Scholarship *252*
Cooperative Studies Scholarships *74*
Future Teacher Scholarship-Oklahoma *234*
Markley Scholarship *720*
May T. Henry Scholarship Foundation *673*
Oklahoma Tuition Aid Grant *733*
Regional University Baccalaureate Scholarship *734*
Tulsa Scholarship Awards *309*
U.S. Aircraft Insurance Group PDP Scholarship *128*
William P. Willis Scholarship *734*

Ontario

Bill Mason Memorial Scholarship Fund *80*
Canada Iceland Foundation Scholarship Program *671*
Carol A. Ratza Memorial Scholarship *138*
Field Aviation Co., Inc., Scholarship *117*
Jim Allard Broadcast Journalism Scholarship *359*
Leo J. Krysa Undergraduate Scholarship *104*
Osler, Hoskin and Harcourt National Essay
  Competition *722*
Ruth Hancock Memorial Scholarship *180*
Scholarship for Aboriginal Canadians *507*
Scholarship for Visible Minorities *507*
Scottish Rite Charitable Foundation College
  Bursaries *550*
Terry Fox Memorial Scholarship *507*
Tommy Douglas Scholarship *507*

Oregon

AeA- Oregon Council Technology Scholarship
  Program *88*
Agricultural-Women-In-Network Scholarship *84*
Agriculture Scholarships *74*
American Council of Engineering Companies of Oregon
  Scholarship *167*
ARC of Washington Trust Fund Stipend Program *461*
Asian Reporter Scholarship *636*
Bank of the Cascades Scholarship *532*
Benjamin Franklin/Edith Green Scholarship *735*
Bertha P. Singer Nurses Scholarship *432*
Bullivant Houser Bailey-African American Chamber of
  Commerce Community College Scholarship
  Fund *152*
Chick Evans Caddie Scholarship *552*
Children, Adult, and Family Services Scholarship *736*
Columbia River Section Scholarships *278*
Cooperative Studies Scholarships *74*
Dorothy Campbell Memorial Scholarship *736*
Dr. Franz and Kathryn Stenzel Fund *330*
Fashion Group International of Portland
  Scholarship *296*
Ford Opportunity Program *736*
Ford Restart Program Scholarship *736*
Ford Scholars *736*
Harry Ludwig Memorial Scholarship *564*
Harry Ludwig Scholarship Fund *564*
Homestead Capital Housing Scholarship *68*
Jackson Foundation Journalism Scholarship *367*
Jackson Foundation Journalism Scholarship Fund *366*
Jeannette Mowery Scholarship *211*
Jerome B. Steinbach Scholarship *737*
Korean-American Scholarship Foundation Western
  Region Scholarships *622*
Lori Rhett Memorial Scholarship *720*
Maria Jackson/General George A. White Scholarship *594*
Marian Du Puy Memorial Scholarship *235*
NLN Ella McKinney Scholarship Fund *431*
OAB Broadcast Scholarship *185*
ONF-Smith Education Scholarship *432*
Oregon Collectors Association Bob Hasson Memorial
  Scholarship *737*
Oregon Collectors Association Bob Hasson Memorial
  Scholarship Fund *737*
Oregon Education Association Scholarship *235*
Oregon Foundation for Blacktail Deer Outdoor and
  Wildlife Scholarship *140*
Oregon Metro Federal Credit Union Scholarship *737*
Oregon Scholarship Fund Community College Student
  Award *738*
Oregon Scholarship Fund Transfer Student Award *738*
Oregon State Fiscal Association Scholarship *511*
Oregon Veterans' Education Aid *593*
Oregon Wine Brotherhood Scholarship *203*
OSCPA Educational Foundation Scholarship Program *738*
Professional Land Surveyors of Oregon Scholarships *465*
Reed's Fuel and Trucking Company Scholarship *534*
Robert W. Thunen Memorial Scholarships *100*
Robert W. Thunen Memorial Scholarships *100*

Royden M. Bodley Scholarship *87*
Rube and Minah Leslie Educational Fund *734*
Teacher Education Scholarship *234*
Tykeson Family Scholarship *549*
Western Undergraduate Exchange Program *757*
William L. and Della Waggoner Scholarship Fund *735*
Woodard Family Scholarship *535*

Pennsylvania

Allegheny Mountain Section Air & Waste Management
  Association Scholarship *292*
American Restaurant Scholarship *201*
Aviation Council of Pennsylvania Scholarship
  Program *120*
Beverly J. Smith Memorial Scholarship *658*
Brodart/Pennsylvania Library Association Undergraduate
  Scholarship Grant *381*
Capitol Scholarship Program *684*
Carol A. Ratza Memorial Scholarship *138*
Chick Evans Caddie Scholarship *552*
Constantinople Armenian Relief Society Scholarship *612*
DeVry Dean's Scholarships *687*
DeVry High School Community Scholars Award *688*
DeVry Presidential Scholarships *688*
DeVry University Regional First Scholar Awards *688*
Educational Gratuity Program *594*
Joseph F. Taricani Memorial Scholarship *68*
Joseph P. Gavenonis College Scholarship (Plan I) *490*
Korean-American Scholarship Foundation Eastern
  Region Scholarships *621*
Martha M. Dohner Memorial Scholarship *658*
Massachusetts Assistance for Student Success
  Program *713*
NASA Delaware Space Grant Undergraduate Tuition
  Scholarship *94*
National Association for Campus Activities East Coast
  Higher Education Research Scholarship *720*
National Association for Campus Activities East Coast
  Undergraduate Scholarship for Student Leaders *720*
New Economy Technology Scholarship (NETS)-SciTech
  Scholarships *457*
New Economy Technology Scholarship-Technology
  Scholarships *457*
Ohio Instructional Grant *732*
PACD Auxiliary Scholarships *76*
Pennsylvania Institute of Certified Public Accountants
  Sophomore Scholarship *68*
Postsecondary Education Gratuity Program *594*
Robert W. Valimont Endowment Fund Scholarship
  (Part II) *468*
Scholarship Awards *561*
Scholarship Incentive Program (ScIP) *686*
Scholarship Incentive Program-Delaware *687*
Seol Bong Scholarship *632*
Tess Caldarelli Memorial Scholarship *721*
Zagunas Student Leaders Scholarship *721*

Prince Edward Island

Associated Medical Services, Inc. Hannah
  Studentship *324*
Bill Mason Memorial Scholarship Fund *80*
Field Aviation Co., Inc., Scholarship *117*
Jim Allard Broadcast Journalism Scholarship *359*
Leo J. Krysa Undergraduate Scholarship *104*
Osler, Hoskin and Harcourt National Essay
  Competition *722*
Ruth Hancock Memorial Scholarship *180*
Scholarship for Aboriginal Canadians *507*
Scholarship for Visible Minorities *507*
Scottish Rite Charitable Foundation College
  Bursaries *550*
Terry Fox Memorial Scholarship *507*
Tommy Douglas Scholarship *507*

Puerto Rico

HSF/Toyota Foundation Scholarship Program-Puerto
  Rico *618*
National Association for Campus Activities Southeast
  Region Student Leadership Scholarship *720*

Quebec

Associated Medical Services, Inc. Hannah
  Studentship *324*
Bill Mason Memorial Scholarship Fund *80*
Canada Iceland Foundation Scholarship Program *671*
Carol A. Ratza Memorial Scholarship *138*
Field Aviation Co., Inc., Scholarship *117*
Jim Allard Broadcast Journalism Scholarship *359*
Leo J. Krysa Undergraduate Scholarship *104*
Osler, Hoskin and Harcourt National Essay
  Competition *722*
Ruth Hancock Memorial Scholarship *180*

Women in Science and Technology Scholarship *143*

Washington

Agricultural-Women-In-Network Scholarship *84*
Agriculture Scholarships *74*
American Indian Endowed Scholarship *647*
American Institute of Architecture (AIA) Dayton Architectural Scholarship Fund *99*
American Legion Department of Washington Children and Youth Scholarships *490*
ARC of Washington Trust Fund Stipend Program *461*
Ashley Tamburri Scholarship *667*
Asian Reporter Scholarship *636*
Bobbi McCallum Memorial Scholarship *368*
Bullivant Houser Bailey-African American Chamber of Commerce Community College Scholarship Fund *152*
Chick Evans Caddie Scholarship *552*
Columbia River Section Scholarships *278*
Cooperative Studies Scholarships *74*
Corporate Sponsored Scholarship Program *700*
Culinary, Vinifera, and Hospitality Scholarship *301*
David Korn Scholarship Fund *652*
DeVry Dean's Scholarships *687*
DeVry High School Community Scholars Award *688*
DeVry Presidential Scholarships *688*
Dick Larsen Scholarship Program *189*
Educational Opportunity Grant *755*
Fashion Group International of Portland Scholarship *296*
Future Teachers Conditional Scholarship and Loan Repayment Program *240*
Herb Robinson Scholarship Program *190*
Homestead Capital Housing Scholarship *68*
Korean-American Scholarship Foundation Western Region Scholarships *622*
Lori Rhett Memorial Scholarship *720*
Puget Sound Chapter Scholarship *213*
Robert W. Thunen Memorial Scholarships *100*
Robert W. Thunen Memorial Scholarships *100*
State Need Grant *755*
The Betty Endicott/NTA-NCCB Student Scholarship *363*
Washington Award for Vocational Excellence *756*
Washington Award for Vocational Excellence (WAVE) *755*
Washington Promise Scholarship *755*
Washington Scholars Program *755*
Western Undergraduate Exchange Program *757*
WSCPA Accounting Scholarships *72*
WSCPA Scholarships for Accounting Majors *72*
WSCPA Scholarships for Minority Accounting Majors *72*
WSTLA American Justice Essay Scholarship Contest *756*

West Virginia

Academic Common Market Waiver *749*
Allegheny Mountain Section Air & Waste Management Association Scholarship *292*

American Legion, Department of West Virginia Board of Regents Scholarship *665*
Charleston Chapter of CPA's Accounting Scholarship Fund *72*
Dr. William J. Steger Scholarship Awards *333*
Gustavus B. Capito Fund *423*
Joseph C. Basile, II, Memorial Scholarship Fund *226*
Korean-American Scholarship Foundation Eastern Region Scholarships *621*
L. Phil Wicker Scholarship *179*
Mary Olive Eddy Jones Art Scholarship *108*
Project BEST Scholarship *513*
R. Ray Singleton Fund *695*
Scholarship Awards *561*
Teaming to Win Business Scholarship *153*
Tess Caldarelli Memorial Scholarship *721*
West Virginia Golf Association Fund *542*
West Virginia Space Grant Consortium Undergraduate Scholarship Program *126*
Willard H. Erwin, Jr. Memorial Scholarship Fund *148*
Zagunas Student Leaders Scholarship *721*

Wisconsin

Agriculture Scholarships *74*
American Legion Department of Minnesota Memorial Scholarship *489*
Carol A. Ratza Memorial Scholarship *138*
Chapter 4 Lawrence A. Wacker Memorial Scholarship *272*
Chick Evans Caddie Scholarship *552*
Cooperative Studies Scholarships *74*
David Arver Memorial Scholarship *117*
E.H. Marth Food and Environmental Scholarship *291*
Edmond A. Metzger Scholarship *243*
Ethel A. Neijahr Wisconsin Mathematics Council Scholarship *240*
Foley & Lardner Minority Scholarship Program *377*
Heart of America Restaurants and Inns/Machine Shed Agriculture Scholarship *80*
Midwest Student Exchange Program (MSEP) *714*
Minnesota Legionnaires Insurance Trust Scholarship *489*
Minnesota Reciprocal Agreement *715*
Minority Undergraduate Retention Grant-Wisconsin *647*
MRA Institute of Management Endowment Fund Scholarship *151*
National Association for Campus Activities WI Region Student Leadership Scholarship *720*
National Defense Transportation Association, Scott Air Force Base- St. Louis Area Chapter Scholarship *721*
North Central Region 9 Scholarship *275*
Nursing Scholarship for High School Seniors *434*
Nursing Student Loan Program *434*
Pagel Graphic Arts Scholarship Fund *185*
Printing Industry of Minnesota Education Foundation Scholarship Fund *316*
Sister Mary Petronia Van Straten Wisconsin Mathematics Council Scholarship *240*
Talent Incentive Program Grant *758*

Vincent L. Hawkinson Scholarship for Peace and Justice *754*
Virchow, Krause and Company Scholarship *71*
Wisconsin Academic Excellence Scholarship *758*
Wisconsin Department of Veterans Affairs Retraining Grants *596*
Wisconsin Higher Education Grants (WHEG) *758*
Wisconsin League for Nursing Inc., Scholarship *434*
Wisconsin Native American/ Indian Student Assistance Grant *648*
Wisconsin Space Grant Consortium Undergraduate Research Program *126*
Wisconsin Space Grant Consortium Undergraduate Scholarship Program *126*
Wisconsin Veterans Part-time Study Reimbursement Grant *596*

Wyoming

Agriculture Scholarships *74*
Cooperative Studies Scholarships *74*
Donald Estey Scholarship Fund-Rocky Mountain Chapter *473*
Douvas Memorial Scholarship *759*
King-Livingston Scholarship *523*
Korean-American Scholarship Foundation Western Region Scholarships *622*
National Defense Transportation Association, Scott Air Force Base- St. Louis Area Chapter Scholarship *721*
Past Presidents Parley Health Care Scholarship *207*
Society of Women Engineers-Rocky Mountain Section Scholarship Program *196*
Superior Student in Education Scholarship-Wyoming *238*
Vietnam Veterans Award/Wyoming *595*
Western Undergraduate Exchange Program *757*
Wyoming Farm Bureau Continuing Education Scholarships *523*
Wyoming Farm Bureau Federation Scholarships *524*
Wyoming Society of Certified Public Accountants Memorial Scholarships *73*
Wyoming Trucking Association Trust Fund Scholarship *158*

Yukon

Associated Medical Services, Inc. Hannah Studentship *324*
Bill Mason Memorial Scholarship Fund *80*
Field Aviation Co., Inc., Scholarship *117*
Jim Allard Broadcast Journalism Scholarship *359*
Osler, Hoskin and Harcourt National Essay Competition *722*
Ruth Hancock Memorial Scholarship *180*
Scholarship for Aboriginal Canadians *507*
Scholarship for Visible Minorities *507*
Scottish Rite Charitable Foundation College Bursaries *550*
Terry Fox Memorial Scholarship *507*
Tommy Douglas Scholarship *507*

Talent

Amateur Radio

Albert H. Hix, W8AH, Memorial Scholarship 763
ARRL Foundation General Fund Scholarships 763
ARRL Senator Barry Goldwater (K7UGA)
   Scholarship 763
Central Arizona DX Association Scholarship 763
Charles Clarke Cordle Memorial Scholarship 763
Charles N. Fisher Memorial Scholarship 90
Chicago FM Club Scholarships 763
Donald Riebhoff Memorial Scholarship 356
Dr. James L. Lawson Memorial Scholarship 178
Earl I. Anderson Scholarship 243
Edmond A. Metzger Scholarship 243
Eugene "Gene" Sallee, W4YFR Memorial
   Scholarship 763
Francis Walton Memorial Scholarship 764
Fred R. McDaniel Memorial Scholarship 178
Henry Broughton, K2AE Memorial Scholarship 90
IRARC Memorial/Joseph P. Rubino, WA4MMD,
   Scholarship 494
Irving W. Cook, WA0CGS, Scholarship 90
K2TEO Martin J. Green Sr. Memorial Scholarship 764
L. Phil Wicker Scholarship 179
Mary Lou Brown Scholarship 764
Mississippi Scholarship 90
New England FEMARA Scholarships 764
Norman E. Strohmeier, W2VRS Memorial
   Scholarship 667
Outdoor Writers Association of America Bodie
   McDowell Scholarship Award 185
Paul and Helen L. Grauer Scholarship 91
Perry F. Hadlock Memorial Scholarship 243
PHD ARA Scholarship 179
Six Meter Club of Chicago Scholarship 667
Tom and Judith Comstock Scholarship 764
William R. Goldfarb Memorial Scholarship 145
Yankee Clipper Contest Club, Inc. Youth
   Scholarship 494
You've Got a Friend in Pennsylvania Scholarship 494

Animal/Agricultural Competition

Appaloosa Youth Educational Scholarships 493
Chick and Sophie Major Duck Calling Contest 766
Curt Greene Memorial Scholarship 770
Pony of the Americas Scholarship 513

Art

Al Qoyawayma Award 163
Apha Delta Kappa Foundation Fine Arts Grants 108
Artistic Endeavors Scholarship 560
Artist's Magazine's Annual Art Competition 764
Constant Memorial Scholarship for Aquidneck Island
   Residents 114
Elizabeth Greenshields Award/Grant 110
Florence Lemcke Memorial Scholarship in Fine Arts 107
General Federation of Women's Clubs of Massachusetts
   Pennies For Art 111
Haymarket Gallery Emerging Artists Scholarship 112
International Art Show for Artists with Disabilities 565
John F. and Anna Lee Stacey Scholarship Fund 112
L. Ron Hubbard's Illustrators of the Future Contest 765
Library Research Grants 107
National Sculpture Competition for Young
   Sculptors 113
National Sculpture Society Scholarships 113
NLAPW Virginia Liebeler Biennial Grants for Mature
   Women (Arts) 113
Outdoor Writers Association of America Bodie
   McDowell Scholarship Award 185
Scholastic Art and Writing Awards-Art Section 108
Visual and Performing Arts Achievement Awards 111

Athletics/Sports

Badminton Scholarship Program 779
Charles S. Noble Junior "A" Hockey Scholarships 602
Charles S. Noble Junior Football Scholarships 602
Chick and Sophie Major Duck Calling Contest 766
Dr. Click Cowger Baseball Scholarship 661
Earl and Countess of Wessex-World Championships in
   Athletics Scholarships 656
Hy Zolet Student Athlete Scholarship 676

Individuals/Teams Balance Bar Grants 765
Jimmie Condon Athletic Scholarships 603
Linda Riddle/SGMA Scholarship 463
Paul Flaherty Athletic Scholarship 662
Prairie Baseball Academy Scholarships 657
Qwest Leadership Challenge 463
Robin Roberts/WBCA Sports Communications
   Scholarship Award 190
Scholar Athlete Milk Mustache of the Year 779
Terry Darby Memorial Scholarship 682
Texas Tennis Foundation Scholarships and
   Endowments 750
Travel and Training Fund 781
WBCA Scholarship Award 780
Women in Sports Media Scholarship/Internship
   Program 765
World Team Tennis Donnelly Awards 765

Automotive

Automotive Hall of Fame Educational Funds 162
Specialty Equipment Market Association Memorial
   Scholarship Fund 282

Beauty Pageant

Miss America Organization Competition
   Scholarships 771
Miss American Coed Pageant 773

Bowling

Alberta E. Crowe Star of Tomorrow Award 523
Billy Welu Bowling Scholarship 775
Chuck Hall Star of Tomorrow Scholarship 483
Columbia 300 John Jowdy Scholarship 766
Gift for Life Scholarship 524
Pepsi-Cola Youth Bowling Championships 524
Professional Bowlers Association Billy Welu Memorial
   Scholarship 513
USBC Alberta E. Crowe Star of Tomorrow Award 782
USBC Annual Zeb Scholarship 782
USBC Chuck Hall Star of Tomorrow Scholarship 782
USBC Earl Anthony Memorial Scholarships 782
USBC Male and Female Youth Leaders of the Year
   Scholarship 782
Who's Who Sports Edition All-Academic Bowling Team
   Scholarship 782

Designated Field Specified by Sponsor

Alexander Scholarship Loan Fund 782
American Morgan Horse Institute Educational
   Scholarships 761
American Morgan Horse Institute Grand Prix Dressage
   Award 761
American Morgan Horse Institute Graywood Youth
   Horsemanship Grant 761
American Morgan Horse Institute van Schaik Dressage
   Scholarship 761
Arts Scholarship Program 114
ASCSA Summer Sessions Open Scholarships 88
Carl W. Kreitzberg Endowed Scholarship 292
Connecticut Association of Women Police
   Scholarship 199
Cymdeithas Gymreig/Philadelphia Scholarship 647
DEA Drug Abuse Prevention Service Awards 373
Decommissioning, Decontamination, and Reutilization
   Scholarship 249
Discovery Channel Young Scientist Challenge 776
DuPont Challenge Science Essay Awards Program 768
Edward Leon Duhamel Freemasons Scholarship 776
Executive Women International Scholarship
   Program 768
Frank L. Greathouse Government Accounting
   Scholarship 148
Gamma Theta Upsilon Scholarships 769
Garth Reeves, Jr. Memorial Scholarships 187
Generation "E" Grants and Scholarships 780
Intel International Science and Engineering Fair 777
Intel Science Talent Search 777
International Executive Housekeepers Educational
   Foundation 307
James J. Wychor Scholarship 479
Jose D. Garcia Migrant Education Scholarship 737

Joseph Frasca Excellence in Aviation Scholarship 131
Joseph Shinoda Memorial Scholarship 349
Lee Dubin Scholarship Fund 766
Miriam Croft Moeller Citizenship Award 705
MJSA Education Foundation Jewelry Scholarship 776
Northeastern Loggers' Association Scholarships 509
Print and Graphics Scholarships 315
Sigma Delta Chi Scholarships 744
Stanley E. Jackson Scholarship Awards 567
Washington Crossing Foundation Scholarship 780
Weatherford Award 762
Wildlife Leadership Awards 141
Women in Logistics Scholarship 157
Women's Jewelry Association Scholarship Program 471
Young American Creative Patriotic Art Awards
   Program 772

Drum Corps

Martin D. Andrews Memorial Scholarship Fund 772

English Language

Jane Austen Society of North America Essay Contest 771
Kim Love Satory Scholarship 57
Minnesota Academic Excellence Scholarship 715
National High School Poetry Contest/Easterday Poetry
   Award 768
National Writers Association Foundation
   Scholarships 184
William Faulkner-William Wisdom Creative Writing
   Competition 775

Foreign Language

Department of Education Scholarship for Programs in
   China 225
Kor Memorial Scholarship 312
Medicus Student Exchange 635
Minnesota Academic Excellence Scholarship 715
National Junior Classical League Scholarship 311
Rotary Foundation Academic-Year Ambassadorial
   Scholarships 776
Rotary Multi-Year Ambassadorial Scholarships 776

French Language

Teaching Assistantship in France 767

German Language

High-Tech in Old Munich 261

Golf

Byron Nelson Scholarship 777
Dick Forester College Scholarship 778
Dorothy Campbell Memorial Scholarship 736
Dorothy S. Campbell Memorial Scholarship Fund 774
Florida Women's State Golf Association Junior Girls'
   Scholarship Fund 692
Hardy Laudermilk Scholarship 745
J. Wood Platt Caddie Scholarship Trust 544
Joe Finger Scholarship 778
Joe Moore Scholarship 778
National Minority Junior Golf Scholarship 625
South Carolina Junior Golf Foundation Scholarship 672
Stonehouse Golf Youth Scholarship 778
Women's Western Golf Foundation Scholarship 781

Greek Language

National Latin Exam Scholarship 310

Italian Language

National Italian American Foundation Category II
   Scholarship 106

Japanese Language

Japanese Studies Scholarship 105

Latin Language

National Latin Exam Scholarship 310

Leadership

Airbus Leadership Grant 132

AIST Alfred B. Glossbrenner and John Klusch Scholarships 257
All-TKE Academic Team Recognition and John A. Courson Top Scholar Award 516
Alwin B. Newton Scholarship Fund 242
American Institute for Foreign Study International Scholarships 760
American Institute for Foreign Study Minority Scholarships 605
American Society of Heating, Refrigeration, and Air Conditioning Engineering Technology Scholarship 90
American Water Ski Educational Foundation Scholarship 493
Appaloosa Youth Educational Scholarships 493
ASHRAE Scholarships 252
Association for Iron and Steel Technology Benjamin F. Fairless Scholarship 388
Association for Iron and Steel Technology Ohio Valley Chapter Scholarship 135
Association for Iron and Steel Technology Ronald E. Lincoln Scholarship 388
Association for Iron and Steel Technology Willy Korf Memorial Scholarship 388
AXA Foundation Fund Achievement Scholarship 154
Berna Lou Cartwright Scholarship 394
Boys & Girls Clubs of America National Youth of the Year Award 494
Bruce B. Melchert Scholarship 450
California Junior Miss Scholarship Program 670
Canadian TKE Scholarship 516
Cardinal Health Scholarship 70
Carrol C. Hall Memorial Scholarship 95
Charles Walgreen, Jr. Scholarship 516
Coca-Cola Scholars Program 766
Dallas Morning News Annual Teenage Citizenship Tribute 540
Director's Scholarship Award 273
Distinguished Student Scholar Award 235
Donald A. Fisher Memorial Scholarship 516
Dwayne R. Woerpel Memorial Leadership Award 516
Eight & Forty Lung and Respiratory Disease Nursing Scholarship Fund 418
Elmer and Doris Schmitz Sr. Memorial Scholarship 517
Eugene C. Beach Memorial Scholarship 517
Financial Service Centers of America Scholarship Fund 769
Fleet Reserve Association Scholarship 499
Florida Bankers Educational Foundation Scholarship/Loan 147
Ford Motor Company Scholarship 279
Francis J. Flynn Memorial Scholarship 239
Frank W. McHale Memorial Scholarships 661
Future Leaders of America Scholarship 774
General Motors Foundation Undergraduate Scholarships 168
George W. Woolery Memorial Scholarship 188
George Watters-Nebraska Petroleum Marketers Association Scholarship 544
Graduate Student Scholar Award 236
Harry A. Applegate Scholarship 146
Harry J. Donnelly Memorial Scholarship 69
Henry Adams Scholarship 252
Henry L. Reilly Memorial Scholarship-High School Seniors and First Year Freshmen 514
Hugh B. Sweeny Scholarship 771
International Student Leaders Award 500
J. Russel Salsbury Memorial Scholarship 517
Jim Allard Broadcast Journalism Scholarship 359
Juliette A. Southard/Oral B Laboratories Scholarship 204
Junior Achievement Joe Francomano Scholarship 502
Junior Achievement Office Depot Scholarship 502
Junior Girls Scholarship Program 504
Kid's Chance of West Virginia Scholarship 695
Kim Love Satory Scholarship 57
Kingsbury Fund Scholarships 531
Laurence Decor Student Leadership Awards 603
Lee Dubin Scholarship Fund 766
Lori Rhett Memorial Scholarship 720
Margaret E. Swanson Scholarship 206
Marion Huber Learning Through Listening Awards 513
Mary P. Oenslager Scholastic Achievement Awards 513
Mas Family Scholarships 146
McCurry Foundation Scholarship 773
Michael J. Morin Memorial Scholarship 517
Micron Science and Technology Scholars Program 165
Miles Gray Memorial Scholarship 517
Miriam Croft Moeller Citizenship Award 705
Multicultural Scholarship Program 625
National Association for Campus Activities East Coast Undergraduate Scholarship for Student Leaders 720
National Association for Campus Activities Regional Council Student Leader Scholarships 773

National Association for Campus Activities Southeast Region Student Leadership Scholarship 720
National Association for Campus Activities WI Region Student Leadership Scholarship 720
Principal's Leadership Award 773
Rockwell Automation Scholarship 281
Rockwell/UNCF Corporate Scholars Program 156
Ron Brown Scholar Program 608
Ronald Reagan Leadership Award 517
Rotary Foundation Cultural Ambassadorial Scholarship 312
Ruth Hancock Memorial Scholarship 180
Scholar Athlete Milk Mustache of the Year 779
Scholarships for Student Leaders 773
Sigma Delta Chi Scholarships 744
Society of Daughters of the United States Army Scholarships 575
South Dakota Board of Regents Bjugstad Scholarship 77
South Dakota Board of Regents Marlin R. Scarborough Memorial Scholarship 745
SWE Lehigh Valley Section Scholarship 281
T.J. Schmitz Scholarship 518
Tess Caldarelli Memorial Scholarship 721
The Ruth Abernathy Presidential Scholarship 759
United States Senate Youth Program 780
W. Allan Herzog Scholarship 70
Wallace McCauley Memorial Scholarship 518
William V. Muse Scholarship 518
William Wilson Memorial Scholarship 518
Women in Aviation, International Management Scholarships 134
Youth Opportunities Foundation Scholarships 648
Zagunas Student Leaders Scholarship 721

Music

Al Qoyawayma Award 163
American Theatre Organ Society Organ Performance Scholarship 762
Apha Delta Kappa Foundation Fine Arts Grants 108
Arts Scholarship Program 114
Bronislaw Kaper Awards for Young Artists 706
Chopin Foundation of the United States Scholarship 402
Concert Artists Guild Competition 767
Constant Memorial Scholarship for Aquidneck Island Residents 114
Domenic Troiano Guitar Scholarship 768
Gerald M. Crane Memorial Music Scholarship Fund 694
Houston Symphony Ima Hogg Young Artist Competition 771
Joseph H. Bearns Prize in Music 767
Nadeen Burkeholder Williams Music Scholarship 550
National Solo Competition 761
NOA Vocal Competition/ Legacy Award Program 113
Queen Elisabeth Competition 775
Sinfonia Foundation Scholarship 777
Summer Music Scholarships 402
Traditional Marching Band Extravaganza Scholarship Award 770
William Kapell International Piano Competition and Festival 438
Young Artist Competition 441

Music/Singing

Adeline Rosenberg Memorial Prize 769
Al Qoyawayma Award 163
American Orff-Schulwerk Association Research Grant 220
Bach Organ and Keyboard Scholarship Fund 406
BMI Student Composer Awards 110
Contemporary Record Society National Competition for Performing Artists 439
Contemporary Record Society National Festival for the Performing Arts Scholarship 767
Dan Schutte Scholarship 403
Dorchester Women's Club Scholarship 402
Elaine Rendler-Rene Dosogne-Georgetown Chorale Scholarship 403
Fort Collins Symphony Association Young Artist Competition, Junior Division 769
Funk Family Memorial Scholarship 403
General Federation of Women's Clubs of Massachusetts Music Scholarship 225
GIA Publication Pastoral Musician Scholarship 404
Gina Bachauer International Artists Piano Competition Award 439
Gladys Stone Wright Scholarship 240
Glenn Miller Instrumental Scholarship 769
Gunild Keetman Assistance Fund 220
Helen May Butler Memorial Scholarship 241
Jack Pullan Memorial Scholarship 770
Kosciuszko Foundation Chopin Piano Competition 439
Liederkranz Foundation Scholarship Award for Voice 772

Lotte Lenya Competition for Singers 440
Martha Ann Stark Memorial Scholarship 241
Music Committee Scholarship 401
Music Technology Scholarship 241
MuSonics Scholarship 404
National Association of Pastoral Musicians Members' Scholarship 404
National Competition for Composers' Recordings 767
National Symphony Orchestra Young Soloists' Competition- Bill Cerri Scholarship/College Division 774
National Symphony Orchestra Young Soloists' Competition- Bill Cerri Scholarship/High School Division 722
NOA Vocal Competition/ Legacy Award Program 113
NPM Board of Directors Scholarship 404
NPM Composers and Authors Scholarship 404
NPM Koinonia/Board of Directors Scholarship 404
NPM Miami Valley Catholic Church Musicians Scholarship 405
Omaha Symphony Guild International New Music Competition 774
Oregon Catholic Press Scholarship 405
Paluch Family Foundation/World Library Publications Scholarship 405
Queen Elisabeth Competition 775
Ralph Brewster Vocal Scholarship 770
Sigma Alpha Iota Graduate Performance Awards 406
Sigma Alpha Iota Jazz Performance Awards 406
Sigma Alpha Iota Jazz Studies Scholarship 406
Sigma Alpha Iota Music Business/Technology Scholarship 407
Sigma Alpha Iota Music Therapy Scholarship 407
Sigma Alpha Iota Philanthropies Undergraduate Performance Scholarships 407
Sigma Alpha Iota Philanthropies Undergraduate Scholarships 236
Sigma Alpha Iota Summer Music Scholarships in the U.S. or abroad 407
Sigma Alpha Iota Visually Impaired Scholarship 236
Sorantin Young Artist Award 440
Steven C. Warner Scholarship 405
Summer Music Scholarships 402
Volkwein Memorial Scholarship 241
VSA arts-Panasonic Young Soloist Award 440
VSA arts-Rosemary Kennedy International Young Soloist Award 441
Young Composers Awards 406

Photography/Photogrammetry/Filmmaking

Angelus Awards Student Film Festival 762
Asian-American Journalists Association Scholarship 179
Carole Simpson Scholarship 185
Edward J. Nell Memorial Scholarship in Journalism 368
International Foodservice Editorial Council Communications Scholarship 182
Larry Fullerton Photojournalism Scholarship 442
National Writers Association Foundation Scholarships 184
NLAPW Virginia Liebeler Biennial Grants for Mature Women (Arts) 113
Outdoor Writers Association of America Bodie McDowell Scholarship Award 185
Quill and Scroll International Writing/Photo Contest 776
Robert E. Altenhofen Memorial Scholarship 91
Space Imaging Award for Application of High Resolution Digital Satellite Imagery 91
Valley Press Club Scholarships, The Republican Scholarship; Photojournalism Scholarship, Channel 22 Scholarship 189
W. Eugene Smith Grant in Humanistic Photography 780

Polish Language

Kosciuszko Foundation Tuition Scholarship 622
Year Abroad Program in Poland 105

Public Speaking

American Legion Department of Michigan Oratorical Contest 662
American Legion Department of Minnesota State Oratorical Contest 662
American Legion Department of New York State High School Oratorical Contest 663
American Legion Department of North Dakota National High School Oratorical Contest 663
American Legion Department of Pennsylvania State Oratorical Contest 664
American Legion Department of West Virginia State Oratorical Contest 665

TALENT
PUBLIC SPEAKING

NOTES

NOTES

Thomson Peterson's
Book Satisfaction Survey

Give Us Your Feedback

Thank you for choosing Thomson Peterson's as your source for personalized solutions for your education and career achievement. Please take a few minutes to answer the following questions. Your answers will go a long way in helping us to produce the most user-friendly and comprehensive resources to meet your individual needs.

When completed, please tear out this page and mail it to us at:

> Publishing Department
> Thomson Peterson's
> 2000 Lenox Drive
> Lawrenceville, NJ 08648

You can also complete this survey online at **www.petersons.com/booksurvey.**

1. **What is the ISBN of the book you have purchased? (The ISBN can be found on the book's back cover in the lower right-hand corner.)** _____

2. **Where did you purchase this book?**
   - ❏ Retailer, such as Barnes & Noble
   - ❏ Online reseller, such as Amazon.com
   - ❏ Petersons.com or Thomson Learning Bookstore
   - ❏ Other (please specify) _____

3. **If you purchased this book on Petersons.com or through the Thomson Learning Bookstore, please rate the following aspects of your online purchasing experience on a scale of 4 to 1 (4 = Excellent and 1 = Poor).**

	4	3	2	1
Comprehensiveness of Peterson's Online Bookstore page	❏	❏	❏	❏
Overall online customer experience	❏	❏	❏	❏

4. **Which category best describes you?**
   - ❏ High school student
   - ❏ Parent of high school student
   - ❏ College student
   - ❏ Graduate/professional student
   - ❏ Returning adult student
   - ❏ Teacher
   - ❏ Counselor
   - ❏ Working professional/military
   - ❏ Other (please specify) _____

5. **Rate your overall satisfaction with this book.**

Extremely Satisfied	Satisfied	Not Satisfied
❏	❏	❏

6. **Rate each of the following aspects of this book on a scale of 4 to 1 (4 = Excellent and 1 = Poor).**

	4	3	2	1
Comprehensiveness of the information	❑	❑	❑	❑
Accuracy of the information	❑	❑	❑	❑
Usability	❑	❑	❑	❑
Cover design	❑	❑	❑	❑
Book layout	❑	❑	❑	❑
Special features (e.g., CD, flashcards, charts, etc.)	❑	❑	❑	❑
Value for the money	❑	❑	❑	❑

7. **This book was recommended by:**
   ❑ Guidance counselor
   ❑ Parent/guardian
   ❑ Family member/relative
   ❑ Friend
   ❑ Teacher
   ❑ Not recommended by anyone—I found the book on my own
   ❑ Other (please specify) _____

8. **Would you recommend this book to others?**

   Yes   Not Sure   No
   ❑   ❑   ❑

9. **Please provide any additional comments.**

   _____

   _____

   _____

   _____

   _____

Remember, you can tear out this page and mail it to us at:

Publishing Department
Thomson Peterson's
2000 Lenox Drive
Lawrenceville, NJ 08648

or you can complete the survey online at **www.petersons.com/booksurvey**.

Your feedback is important to us at Thomson Peterson's, and we thank you for your time!

If you would like us to keep in touch with you about new products and services, please include your e-mail here: _____